The New College SPANISH & ENGLISH Dictionary

SECOND EDITION

EDWIN B. WILLIAMS
Professor of Romance Languages
University of Pennsylvania

AMSCO SCHOOL PUBLICATIONS, INC.
315 Hudson Street / New York, N.Y. 10013

THE NEW COLLEGE SPANISH & ENGLISH DICTIONARY, SECOND EDITION

When ordering this book, please specify:
either **R 471P** or SPANISH DICTIONARY

ISBN 0-87720-538-8

Published by Amsco School Publications, Inc., by arrangement with the copyright owners.

The cover shows the Palacio Episcopal, Astorga, by Antonio Gaudí. Courtesy of Ediciones Polígrafa, S.A., Barcelona.

Printed in the United States of America

13 14 15 02 01

CONTENTS

PREFACE TO THE FIRST EDITION

This book is based on primary spoken and written sources. It is designed for speakers of either language who wish to find words or the meanings of words in the foreign language. Its purpose is, therefore, fourfold. It gives to the English-speaking users (1) the Spanish words they need to express their thoughts in Spanish and (2) the English meanings of Spanish words they need to understand Spanish, and to the Spanish-speaking users (3) the English words they need to express their thoughts in English and (4) the Spanish meanings of English words they need to understand English.

To accomplish the purpose of (1) and (3), discriminations are provided in the source language except that, because of the special facility with which the subject of the verb can be shown in Spanish and because of the convenience of showing the object with personal **a,** discriminations in the form of subject and/or object are given in Spanish on the English-Spanish side as well as on the Spanish-English side. For the purpose of (2) and (4) discriminations are not needed and are not given because the user will always have the context of what he hears or reads to guide him. However, some glosses whose purpose is not to show discrimination but rather to elaborate on the meaning of what may be judged to be an unfamiliar or obscure word or expression in the user's native language are provided in that language.

All words are treated in a fixed order according to the parts of speech and the functions of verbs; and meanings with subject, usage, and regional labels come after more general meanings.

In order to facilitate the finding of the meaning and use sought for, changes within a vocabulary entry in part of speech and function of verb, in irregular inflection, in the gender of Spanish nouns, and in the pronunciation of English words are marked with parallels instead of the usual semicolons.

Periods are omitted after labels and grammatical abbreviations and at the end of vocabulary entries.

The feminine form of a Spanish adjective used as a noun (or a Spanish feminine noun having identical spelling with the feminine form of an adjective) that falls alphabetically in a separate position from the adjective is treated in that position and is listed again as a cross reference under the adjective.

The gender of Spanish nouns is shown on both sides of the Dictionary except that the gender of masculine nouns ending in **-o,** feminine nouns ending in **-a, -dad, -tad, -tud, -ión,** and **-umbre,** masculine nouns modified by an adjective ending in **-o,** and feminine nouns modified by an adjective ending in **-a** is not shown on the English-Spanish side.

Numbers referring to the conjugations of irregular Spanish verbs are placed before the abbreviations indicating the part of speech. The list at the end of the Spanish-English part of the Dictionary includes models of all verbs that show a combination of two types of irregularity, e.g., **esforzar, seguir, teñir.**

Proper nouns and abbreviations are listed in their alphabetical position in the main body of the Dictionary. Thus **España** and **español** do not have to be looked up in two different parts of the book. And all subentries are listed in strictly alphabetical order.

The centered period is used in vocabulary entries of irregularly inflected words to mark off the final syllable that has to be detached before the syllable showing the inflection is added, e.g., **lá•piz** *m* (*pl* **-pices**) and **falsi•fy** [ˈfɔlsɪ,faɪ] *v* (*pret & pp* **-fied**).

The pronunciation of all English simple words is shown in a new adaptation of the symbols of the International Phonetic Alphabet and in brackets. The pronunciation of English compound words is not shown provided the pronunciation of the components is shown where they appear as independent vocabulary entries.

Since vocabulary entries are not determined on the basis of etymology, homographs are included in a single entry. When the pronunciation of an English homograph changes, this is shown in the proper place after parallels.

PRÓLOGO DE LA PRIMERA EDICIÓN

Hemos basado este libro en fuentes originales del lenguaje hablado y escrito. Está destinado a los hablantes de uno u otro idioma que buscan palabras o significados de palabras en el idioma extranjero. Tiene, por lo tanto, los cuatro siguientes propósitos: al usuario de habla inglesa le suministra (1) las palabras españolas que necesita para expresar su pensamiento en español y (2) los significados ingleses de las palabras españolas que necesita para comprender el español; y al usuario de habla española le suministra (3) las palabras inglesas que necesita para expresar su pensamiento en inglés y (4) los significados españoles de las palabras inglesas que necesita para comprender el inglés.

Para lograr los propósitos indicados bajo los números (1) y (3), se suministran diferenciaciones (es decir, distinciones entre dos o más significados de una palabra) en la lengua-fuente; pero, dada la facilidad con que el sujeto del verbo puede indicarse en español y dada la conveniencia de destacar el objeto del verbo con la preposición **a**, las diferenciaciones consistentes en el sujeto o el objeto, o ambos, se dan en español tanto en la parte de inglés-español como en la parte de español-inglés. Para los propósitos indicados bajo los números (2) y (4) no se necesitan diferenciaciones y no se dan, porque el usuario siempre tendrá como guía el contexto de lo que oye o lee. Con todo, algunas glosas que no tienen por objeto indicar diferenciaciones sino más bien dilucidar el sentido de lo que parece ser una palabra o expresión raras u obscuras en la lengua nativa del usuario, se indican en esta lengua.

Los vocablos se tratan consecutivamente de acuerdo con las partes de la oración y las funciones verbales; y los significados marcados con calificativos de tema, uso y país van después de los significados más generales.

Para facilitar la búsqueda del significado y el uso deseados, los cambios en la parte de la oración y función verbal, en la flexión, en el género de los nombres españoles y en la pronunciación de las palabras inglesas van señalados con doble raya vertical, en vez del punto y coma de costumbre.

Se han omitido los puntos después de los calificativos y abreviaturas gramaticales y al fin de los artículos.

La forma femenina de un adjetivo español usado como sustantivo (o de un sustantivo femenino que se escribe lo mismo que la forma femenina de un adjetivo), que cae alfabéticamente en lugar apartado del adjetivo, se trata en este lugar y se consigna otra vez bajo el adjetivo con una referencia a la palabra traducida anteriormente.

El género de los nombres españoles aparece en ambas partes del Diccionario; pero no aparece en la parte de inglés-español el género de los nombres masculinos que terminan en **-o,** los nombres femeninos que terminan en **-a, -dad, -tad, -tud, -ión,** y **-umbre,** los nombres masculinos modificados por un adjetivo que termina en **-o** ni los nombres femeninos modificados por un adjetivo que termina en **-a.**

Los números que se refieren a los modelos de conjugación de los verbos españoles van antes de las abreviaturas que indican la parte de la oración. La lista completa de los modelos de conjugación incluye muchos que muestran una combinación de dos irregularidades, p.ej., **esforzar, seguir, teñir.**

Los nombres propios y las abreviaturas se consignan en su propio lugar alfabético en el texto del Diccionario. No hay, pues, que buscar **España** y **español** en dos partes distintas del libro. Y todos los artículos secundarios van colocados en riguroso orden alfabético.

Se usa el punto divisorio en los artículos de palabras de flexión irregular para señalar la sílaba final que debe separarse antes de agregar la sílaba que denota la flexión, p.ej., **lá•piz** (*pl* **-pices**) y **falsi•fy** [ˈfɔlsɪ,faɪ] *v* (*pret & pp* **-fied**).

La pronunciación de todas las palabras inglesas simples se muestra por medio de una nueva adaptación de los símbolos del Alfabeto fonético internacional y entre corchetes. No se muestra la pronunciación de las palabras inglesas compuestas cuando la pronunciación de los componentes consta en los lugares donde aparecen como artículos independientes.

The author wishes to express his gratitude to many persons who have worked with him in lexicographical research and development and who helped him directly in the compilation of this book and particularly to the following: Paul Aguilar, William Beigel, Henry H. Carter, Eugenio Chang-Rodríguez, R. Thomas Douglass, David Louis Gold, Allison Gronberg, James E. Iannucci, Christopher Stavrou, Roger J. Steiner, John C. Traupman, and José Vidal.

EDWIN B. WILLIAMS

PREFACE TO THE REVISED EDITION

The main objective of this revision has been to add about 3,200 recent words and meanings, primarily from the fields of science and technology (especially computers, medicine, and genetics), communication, environment, and economics and from colloquial speech. To accommodate the new text, we have omitted (1) the repetition of the infinitive particle **(to)** and (2) many alternative pronunciations, especially of British English.

The label (Am) has been deleted in most instances because this Dictionary focuses, in its entirety, on the Spanish of the Americas. The 22 regional labels have been retained.

Credit for work on this revision is due Mario Bernal, Gerald J. Mac Donald, Liliana Montano, Roger J. Steiner, Sol Steinmetz, Carlos Vega, Lawrence Weisburg, and Diane S. Aronson.

WALTER D. GLANZE

Como la constitución de los artículos no se ha determinado a base de su etimología, se incluyen bajo un mismo artículo todos los homógrafos de una palabra. Cuando varía la pronunciación de un homógrafo inglés, se indica en su propio lugar después de la doble raya vertical.

EDWIN B. WILLIAMS

PRÓLOGO DE LA EDICIÓN AUMENTADA

El objectivo mayor de esta revisión ha sido agregar aproximadamente 3,200 palabras y significados recientes, principalmente de las áreas de ciencia y tecnología (especialmente computadores, medicina y genética), comunicaciones, medio ambiente y economía, y del idioma de uso común. Para adaptar el texto nuevo, hemos omitido (1) la repetición del signo de infinitivo **(to)** y (2) muchas pronunciaciones alternativas, especialmente del inglés británico.

El calificativo (Am) ha sido omitido generalmente, porque este Diccionario se concentra en el español de las Américas. Los 22 calificativos regionales han sido retenidos.

Por el trabajo rendido en esta revisión, crédito es debido a Mario Bernal, Gerald J. Mac Donald, Liliana Montano, Roger J. Steiner, Sol Steinmetz, Carlos Vega, Lawrence Weisburg y Diane S. Aronson.

WALTER D. GLÁNZE

LABELS AND GRAMMATICAL ABBREVIATIONS

abbr abbreviation—abreviatura
(acronym) acrónimo—a word formed from the initial letters or syllables of a series of words—palabra formada de las letras o sílabas iniciales de una serie de palabras
adj adjective—adjetivo
adv adverb—adverbio
(aer) aeronautics—aeronáutica
(agr) agriculture—agricultura
(alg) algebra—álgebra
(Am) Spanish American—hispano-americano
(anat) anatomy—anatomía
(archaic) arcaico
(archeol) archeology—arqueología
(archit) architecture—arquitectura
(Arg) Argentine—argentino
(arith) arithmetic—aritmética
art article—artículo
(arti) artillery—artillería
(astr) astronomy—astronomía
(aut) automobiles—automóviles
(bact) bacteriology—bacteriología
(baseball) beisbol
(bb) bookbinding—encuadernación
(Bib) Biblical—bíblico
(billiards) billar
(biochem) biochemistry—bioquímica
(biol) biology—biología
(Bol) Bolivian—boliviano
(bowling) bolos
(bot) botany—botánica
(box) boxing—boxeo
(Brit) British—británico
(CAm) Central American—centroamericano
(cards) naipes
(carp) carpentry—carpintería
(chem) chemistry—química
(chess) ajedrez
(Chile) Chilean—chileno
(Col) Colombian—colombiano
(coll) colloquial—familiar
(com) commercial—comercial
comp comparative—comparativo
cond conditional—condicional
conj conjunction—conjunción
(C-R) Costa Rican—costarriqueño
(Cuba) Cuban—cubano
(culin) cooking—cocina
def definite—definido
dem demonstrative—demostrativo
(dent) dentistry—odontología
(dial) dialectal—dialectal
(eccl) ecclesiastical—eclesiástico
(econ) economics—economía
(Ecuad) Ecuadorian—ecuatoriano
(educ) education—educación
(elec) electricity—electricidad
(electron) electronics—electrónica
(El Salv) El Salvador
(ent) entomology—entomología
f feminine noun—nombre femenino
(fa) fine arts—bellas artes
fem feminine—femenino
(fencing) esgrima
(feud) feudalism—feudalismo
(fig) figurative—figurado
fpl feminine noun plural—nombre femenino plural
fsg feminine noun singular—nombre femenino singular
fut future—futuro
(geog) geography—geografía
(geol) geology—geología
(geom) geometry—geometría
ger gerund—gerundio
(gram) grammar—gramática
(Guat) Guatemalan—guatemalteco
(heral) heraldry—heráldica
(hist) history—historia
(Hond) Honduran—hondureño
(hort) horticulture—horticultura
(hum) humorous—jocoso
(hunt) hunting—caza
(ichth) ichthyology—ictiología
imperf imperfect—imperfecto
impers impersonal—impersonal
impv imperative—imperativo
ind indicative—indicativo
indecl indeclinable—indeclinable
indef indefinite—indefinido
inf infinitive—infinitivo
(ins) insurance—seguros
interj interjection—interjección
interr interrogative—interrogativo
intr intransitive verb—verbo intransitivo
invar invariable—invariable
(iron) ironical—irónico
(Lat) Latin—latín
(law) derecho
(letterword) a word in the form of an abbreviation which is pronounced by sounding the names of its letters in succession and which functions as a part of speech—palabra en forma de abreviatura la cual se pronuncia haciendo sonar el nombre de cada letra consecutivamente y que funciona como parte del discurso
(log) logic—lógica
m masculine noun—nombre masculino
(mach) machinery—maquinaria
(mas) masonry—albañilería
masc masculine—masculino
(math) mathematics—matemática
(mech) mechanics—mecánica
(med) medicine—medicina
(metal) metallurgy—metalurgia
(meteor) meteorology—meteorología
(Mex) Mexican—mejicano
mf masculine or feminine noun according

to sex—nombre masculino o nombre femenino según el sexo
(mil) military—militar
(min) mining—minería
(mineral) mineralogy—mineralogía
(mountaineering) alpinismo
(mov) moving pictures—cine
mpl masculine noun plural—nombre masculino plural
msg masculine noun singular—nombre masculino singular
(mus) music—música
(myth) mythology—mitología
m & f masculine and feminine noun without regard to sex—nombre masculino y femenino sin tener en cuenta el sexo
(naut) nautical—náutico
(nav) naval—naval militar
neut neuter—neutro
(obs) obsolete—desusado
(obstet) obstetrics—obstetricia
(opt) optics—óptica
(orn) ornithology—ornitología
(paint) painting—pintura
(Pan) Panamanian—panameño
(Para) Paraguayan—paraguayo
(pathol) pathology—patología
pers personal—personal
(Peru) Peruvian—peruano
(pharm) pharmacy—farmacia
(philol) philology—filología
(philos) philosophy—filosofía
(phonet) phonetics—fonética
(phot) photography—fotografía
(phys) physics—física
(physiol) physiology—fisiología
pl plural—plural
(poet) poetical—poético
(pol) politics—política
poss possessive—posesivo
pp past participle—participio pasado
(P-R) Puerto Rican—puertorriqueño
prep preposition—preposición
pres present—presente
pret preterit—pretérito
pron pronoun—pronombre
(psychoanalysis) sicoanálisis
(psychol) psychology—sicología
(rad) radio—radio
ref reflexive verb—verbo reflexivo
reflex reflexive—reflexivo
rel relative—relativo
(rhet) rhetoric—retórica
(rr) railway—ferrocarril
s substantive—substantivo
(SAm) South American—sudamericano
(scornful) despreciativo
(sculp) sculpture—escultura
(S-D) Santo Domingo—República Dominicana
(sew) sewing—costura
sg singular—singular
(slang) jerga
spl substantive plural—substantivo plural
(sport) deporte
ssg substantive singular—substantivo singular
subj subjunctive—subjuntivo
super superlative—superlativo
(surg) surgery—cirugía
(surv) surveying—agrimensura
(taur) bullfighting—tauromaquia
(telg) telegraphy—telegrafía
(telp) telephony—telefonía
(telv) television—televisión
(tennis) tenis
(theat) theater—teatro
(theol) theology—teología
tr transitive verb—verbo transitivo
(typ) printing—imprenta
(Urug) Uruguayan—uruguayo
v verb—verbo
var variant—variante
v aux auxiliary verb—verbo auxiliar
(Ven) Venezuelan—venezolano
(vet) veterinary medicine—veterinaria
(vulg) vulgar—grosero
(W-I) West Indian—antillano
(zool) zoology—zoología

SPANISH PRONUNCIATION

The Spanish alphabet has twenty-eight letters. Note that **ch, ll,** and **ñ** are considered to be separate single letters and are so treated in the alphabetization of Spanish words. While **rr** is considered to be a distinct sign for a particular sound, it is not included in the alphabet and, except in syllabification—notably for the division of words at the end of a line— is not treated as a separate letter, perhaps because words never begin with it.

LETTER	NAME	SOUND
a	a	Like **a** in English **father,** e.g., **casa, fácil.**
b	be	When initial or preceded by **m,** like **b** in English **book,** e.g., **boca, combate.** When standing between two vowels and when preceded by a vowel and followed by **l** or **r,** like **v** in English **voodoo** except that it is formed with both lips, e.g., **saber, hablar, sobre.** It is generally silent before **s** plus a consonant and often dropped in spelling, e.g., **oscuro** for **obscuro.**
c	ce	When followed by **e** or **i,** like **th** in English **think** in Castilian, and like **c** in English **cent** in American Spanish, e.g., **acento, cinco.** When followed by **a, o, u,** or a consonant, like **c** in English **come,** e.g., **cantar, como, cubo, acto, creer.**
ch	che	Like **ch** in English **much,** e.g., **escuchar.**
d	de	Generally, like **d** in **dog,** e.g., **diente, rendir.** When standing between two vowels, when preceded by a vowel and followed by **r,** and when final, like **th** in English **this,** e.g., **miedo, piedra, libertad.**
e	e	At the end of a syllable, like **a** in English **fate,** but without the glide the English sound sometimes has, e.g., **beso, menos.** When followed by a consonant in the same syllable, like **e** in English **met,** e.g., **perla, selva.**
f	efe	Like **f** in English **five,** e.g., **flor, efecto.**
g	ge	When followed by **e** or **i,** like **h** in English **home,** e.g., **gente, giro.** When followed by **a, o, u,** or a consonant, like **g** in English **go,** e.g., **gato, gota, agudo, grande.**
h	hache	Always silent, e.g., **hombre, alcohol.**
i	i	Like **i** in English **machine,** e.g., **camino, ida.** When preceded or followed by another vowel, it has the sound of English **y,** e.g., **tierra, reina.**
j	jota	Like **h** in English **home,** e.g., **jardín, junto.**
k	ka	Like English **k,** e.g., **kilociclo.**
l	ele	Like **l** in English **laugh,** e.g., **lado, ala.**
ll	elle	Somewhat like **lli** in **William** in Castilian and like **y** in English **yes** in American Spanish, e.g., **silla, llamar.**
m	eme	Like **m** in English **man,** e.g., **mesa, amar.**
n	ene	Generally, like **n** in English **name,** e.g., **andar, nube.** Before **v,** like **m** in English **man,** e.g., **invierno, enviar.** Before **c** [k] and **g** [g], like **n** in English **drink,** e.g., **finca, manga.**

ñ	eñe	Somewhat like **ni** in English **onion,** e.g., **año, enseñar.**
o	o	At the end of a syllable, like **o** in English **note,** but without the glide the English sound sometimes has, e.g, **boca, como.** When followed by a consonant in the same syllable, like **o** in English **organ,** e.g., **poste, norte.**
p	pe	Like **p** in English **pen,** e.g., **poco, aplicar.** It is often silent in **septiembre** and **séptimo.**
q	cu	Like **c** in English **come.** It is always followed by **ue** or **ui,** in which the **u** is silent, e.g., **querer, quitar.** The sound of English **qu** is represented in Spanish by **cu,** e.g., **frecuente.**
r	ere	Strongly trilled, when initial and when preceded by **l, n,** or **s,** e.g., **rico, alrededor, honra, israelí.** Pronounced with a single tap of the tongue in all other positions, e.g, **caro, grande, amar.**
rr	erre	Strongly trilled, e.g., **carro, tierra.**
s	ese	Generally, like **s** in English **say,** e.g., **servir, casa, este.** Before a voiced consonant **(b, d, g** [g], **l, r, m, n),** like **z** in English **zero,** e.g., **esbelto, desde, rasgar, eslabón, mismo, asno.**
t	te	Like **t** in English **stamp,** e.g., **tiempo, matar.**
u	u	Like **u** in English **rude,** e.g., **mudo, puño.** It is silent in **gue, gui, que,** and **qui,** but not in **güe** and **güi,** e.g., **guerra, guisa, querer, quitar,** but **agüero, lingüístico.** When preceded or followed by another vowel, it has the sound of English **w,** e.g., **fuego, deuda.**
v	ve or uve	Like Spanish **b** in all positions, e.g, **vengo, invierno, uva, huevo.**
x	equis	When followed by a consonant, like **s** in English **say,** e.g., **expresar, sexto.** Between two vowels, like **gs,** e.g., **examen, existencia, exótico;** and in some words, like **s** in **say,** e.g., **auxilio, exacto.** In **México** (for **Méjico**), like Spanish **j.**
y	ye or i griega	In the conjunction **y,** like **i** in English **machine.** When standing next to a vowel or between two vowels, like **y** in English **yes,** e.g., **yo, hoy, vaya.**
z	zeda or zeta	Like **th** in English **think** in Castilian, and like **c** in English **cent** in American Spanish, e.g., **zapato, zona.**

DIPHTHONG	SOUND
ai, ay	Like **i** in English **might,** e.g., **baile, hay**
au	Like **ou** in English **pound,** e.g., **causa**
ei, ey	Like **ey** in English **they,** e.g., **reina, ley**
eu	Like **ayw** in English **hayward,** e.g., **deuda**
oi, oy	Like **oy** in English **boy,** e.g., **estoy**

Spanish-English

A

A, a (a) *f* first letter of the Spanish alphabet
a *prep* at; for, to; on, upon; in, into; by; from; **a decir verdad** to tell the truth; **a la española** in the Spanish manner; **a lo que parece** as it seems; **a no ser por** if it weren't for; **a saberlo yo** if I had known it; **oler a** to smell of
abacería *f* grocery store
abace•ro -ra *mf* grocer
abad *m* abbot
abadejo *m* codfish; (orn) kinglet; (ent) Spanish fly
abadesa *f* abbess
abadía *f* abbacy; abbey
abajar *ref* to lower oneself
abaje•ño -ña *adj* (Mex) coastal, lowland || *mf* (Mex) lowlander
abaje•ro -ra *adj* (Arg) lower, under || *f* (Arg) bellyband, bellystrap; (Arg) saddlecloth
abaji•no -na *adj* (Col, Chile) northern || *mf* (Col, Chile) northerner
abajo *adv* down, underneath; downwards; downstairs; **abajo de** down; **más abajo** lower down; **río abajo** downstream || *interj* down with. . . !
abalanzar §60 *tr* to hurl || *ref* to rush; venture; (*un caballo*) rear
abalear *tr* (SAm) to shoot
abalizar §60 *tr* to mark with buoys || *ref* (naut) to take bearings
abalorio *m* glass bead
abaluartar *tr* to bulwark
abanar *tr* to fan
abanderado *m* colorbearer
abanderar *tr* (*un buque*) to register
abanderizar §60 *tr* to organize into bands || *ref* to band together; (Chile, Peru) to join up
abandona•do -da *adj* deserted; neglected; slovenly
abandonar *tr* to abandon, forsake || *intr* to give up || *ref* to abandon oneself; give up
abandonismo *m* defeatism
abandonista *adj & mf* defeatist
abandono *m* abandon, abandonment; neglect; forlornness; yielding
abanicar §73 *tr* to fan
abanico *m* fan; fanlight; sword; **abanico de chimenea** fire screen
abaniquear *tr* to fan
abaniqueo *m* fanning; gesticulations
abanto *adj* skittish (*bull*)
abaratamiento *m* cheapening
abaratar *tr* to cheapen; (*precios*) lower || *intr & ref* to get cheap
abarca *f* sandal
abarcar §73 *tr* to embrace; encompass; surround; corner, monopolize
abarloar *tr* (naut) to bring alongside || *ref* to snuggle up
abarquillar *tr & ref* to curl up
abarraganamiento *m* illicit cohabitation
abarrancar *ref* to get into a difficult situation
abarrota•do -da *adj* overcrowded
abarrotar *tr* to bar; bind, fasten; jam, pack, stuff; overstock || *ref* to become a glut on the market
abarrote *m* (naut) packing; **abarrotes** groceries; hardware
abarrotería *f* (Guat) grocery store; (CAm) hardware store
abarrote•ro -ra *mf* grocer
abastecer §22 *tr* to supply, provide
abastecimiento *m* supplying; supplies, provisions
abasto *m* supply; abundance; **dar abasto** to be sufficient
abatanar *tr* to full
abatí *m* (Arg, Para) corn; corn whiskey
abatible *adj* collapsible, folding
abati•do -da *adj* downcast; abject, contemptible || *f* abatis
abatimiento *m* discouragement; descent
abatir *tr* to lower; knock down; shoot down; take apart; humble; discourage || *intr* (aer) to drift; (naut) to have leeway || *ref* to be discouraged; be humbled; drop, fall; swoop down
abdicar §73 *tr & intr* to abdicate
abdomen *m* abdomen
abecé *m* **A B C**
abecedario *m* **A B C's**
abedul *m* birch
abeja *f* bee; **abeja maestra** or **abeja reina** queen bee
abejar *m* apiary, beehive
abejarrón *m* bumblebee
abeje•ro -ra *mf* beekeeper
abejorro *m* bumblebee
aberración *f* aberration; deviation
abertura *f* aperture; opening; crack, slit; cove; openness, frankness
abeto *m* fir tree; hemlock; **abeto del Norte, abeto falso** spruce tree
abier•to -ta *adj* open; frank
abigarra•do -da *adj* motley, variegated

abigeo *m* horse thief, cattle thief
abijar *tr* (Col) to sic
abiselar *tr* to bevel
abisma•do -da *adj* absorbed, lost in thought; mysterious
abismar *tr* to cast down; humble; spoil, ruin || *ref* to sink; cave in; be humbled; give in; lose oneself; be surprised
abismo *m* abyss, chasm
abjurar *tr* to abjure; renounce
ablandabre•vas *m* (*pl* **-vas**) or **ablandahi•gos** *m* (*pl* **-gos**) good-for-nothing
ablandar *tr* to soften; soften up; soothe; loosen || *intr* (*el tiempo*) to moderate || *ref* to soften; relent; (*el tiempo*) moderate
ablativo *m* ablative
abnegación *f* abnegation; self-denial
abnega•do -da *adj* self-denying
abnegar *ref* to deny oneself; sacrifice oneself
aboba•do -da *adj* stupid, stupid-looking
abobar *tr* to make stupid || *ref* to grow stupid
aboca•do -da *adj* (*vino*) mild, smooth; vulnerable; **abocado a** verging on
abocar §73 *tr* to bite; pour; bring near || *intr* to enter || *ref* to approach; have an interview
abocinar *tr* to give a flare to || *intr* to fall on the face || *ref* to flare
abochornar *tr* to overheat; make blush || *ref* to blush; wilt
abofa•do -da *adj* (Cuba, Mex) swollen
abofetear *tr* to slap in the face
abogacía *f* law, legal profession
abogaderas *fpl* (CAm) specious arguments
abogado *m* lawyer; **abogado criminalista** criminal lawyer; **abogado de secano** quack lawyer; **abogado firmón** lawyer who will sign anything; **abogado trampista** shyster
abogar §44 *intr* to plead; **abogar por** to advocate, back
abolengo *m* ancestry, descent; inheritance
abolición *f* abolition
abolir §1 *tr* to revoke, repeal
abolorio *m* ancestry
abolladura *f* dent; bump, bruise; embossing
abollar *tr* to bump, bruise; dent; stun; emboss || *ref* to get bumped, get bruised; dent, be dented
abollonar *tr* to emboss
abombar *tr* to make convex; stun, confound || *ref* to rot, decompose
abominable *adj* abominable, very bad
abominación *f* abomination
abominar *tr* to detest, abominate || *intr* — **abominar de** to abominate
abona•do -da *adj* trustworthy; apt, likely || *mf* subscriber; (*al gas, electricidad, etc.*) consumer; (*a una localidad en el teatro*) season-ticket holder; (*al ferrocarril*) commuter
abonanzar §60 *intr* (*el tiempo*) to clear up; (*el viento*) abate
abonar *tr* to vouch for; certify; improve; fertilize; **abonar en cuenta a** to credit to the account of || *intr* (*el tiempo*) to clear up || *ref* to subscribe
abonaré *m* promissory note
abono *m* subscription; credit; installment; voucher; fertilizer, manure
abordar *tr* to approach; accost; undertake, plan; (naut) to board; (naut) to run afoul of; (naut) to dock || *intr* to run afoul; (naut) to put into port
aborigen *adj invar* aboriginal, native; **aborígenes** *mpl* aborigines, natives
aborrascar §73 *ref* to get stormy
aborrecer §22 *tr* to abhor, detest, hate; bore || *ref* to get bored
aborrecible *adj* abhorrent, hateful
aborrega•do -da *adj* (*nubes*) fleecy; (*cielo*) mackerel
aborregar *ref* (SAm) to become stupid
abortar *tr & intr* to abort
abortista *mf* abortionist
aborto *m* abortion; miscarriage; **aborto despenalizado** legalized abortion
abotagar §44 *ref* to become bloated, swell up
abotonador *m* buttonhook
abotonar *tr* to button || *intr* to bud
abovedar *tr* to arch, vault
abozalar *tr* to muzzle
abra *f* cove; vale; fissure; (Mex) clearing
abrasa•dor -dora *adj* burning, hot
abrasar *tr* to set fire to, burn; parch; nip; squander; shame || *intr* to burn || *ref* to burn; become parched; (fig) to be burning up
abrasi•vo -va *adj & m* abrasive
abrazadera *f* clasp, clip, clamp; (typ) bracket
abrazar §60 *tr* to embrace, clasp; include; take in || *ref* (*dos personas*) to embrace
abrazo *m* embrace, hug
abrebo•cas *m* (*pl* **-cas**) mouth prop, mouth gag
abrebote•llas *m* (*pl* **-llas**) bottle opener
abrecar•tas *m* (*pl* **-tas**) knife, letter opener
abreco•ches *m* (*pl* **-ches**) doorman
abrela•tas *m* (*pl* **-tas**) can opener
abreos•tras *m* (*pl* **-tras**) oyster knife
abrevadero *m* watering place, drinking trough
abrevar *tr* to water; wet, soak; irrigate; size || *ref* to drink
abreviación *f* abridgment, abbreviation, shortening; hastening
abreviar *tr* to abridge; abbreviate; shorten; hasten || *intr* to be quick; **abreviar con** to make short work of
abreviatura *f* abbreviation; **en abreviatura** in a hurry
abridero *m* (Mex, P-R) dive, joint
abridor *m* opener; grafting knife; **abridor de guantes** glove stretcher
abridura *f* (act of) opening
abrigadero *m* windbreak
abrigar §44 *tr* to shelter; protect; (*esperanzas, sospechas*) harbor || *ref* to take shelter; wrap oneself up
abrigo *m* shelter; aid, support; cover, wrap; overcoat; (naut) harbor; **abrigo antiaéreo** air-raid shelter; **abrigo de entretiempo** topcoat, spring-and-fall coat; **al abrigo de** sheltered from, protected from; sheltered

by, protected by; (*ropa*) **de mucho abrigo** heavy
abril *m* April
abrillantar *tr* to polish; glaze
abrir *m* opening; **en un abrir y cerrar de ojos** in the twinkling of an eye || §83 *tr* to open; unlock, unfasten; (*el apetito*) whet; (*el bosque*) clear || *intr* to open || *ref* to open; **abrirse a** or **con** to unbosom oneself to
abrochador *m* buttonhook
abrochar *tr* to button, hook, fasten
abrogación *f* repeal; abrogation
abrogar *tr* to repeal; abrogate; annul
abrojo *m* thistle, thorn; **abrojos** reef, hidden rocks
abrótano *m* southernwood
abruma•do -da *adj* hazy; foggy
abruma•dor -dora *adj* crushing, oppressing; overwhelming
abrumar *tr* to crush, oppress; overwhelm; annoy || *ref* to become foggy
abrup•to -ta *adj* abrupt, steep; rough, rugged
absceso *m* abscess
absenta *f* absinth
ábsida *f* or **ábside** *m* apse
absolución *f* absolution; acquittal
absoluta *f* dogmatic statement; (mil) discharge
absolutamente *adv* absolutely; by no means
absolu•to -ta *adj* absolute; arbitrary || *m* absolute; **en absoluto** absolutely not || *f* see **absoluta**
absolvederas *fpl* — **tener buenas absolvederas** to be an indulgent confessor
absolver §47 & §83 *tr* to absolve; to solve, to answer
absorbente *adj* absorbent; (*interesante*) absorbing
absorber *tr* to absorb; use up; attract
absorción *f* absorption
absor•to -ta *adj* absorbed; entranced
abste•mio -mia *adj* abstemious
abstener §71 *ref* to abstain
abstensionismo *m* nonparticipation
abstinente *adj* abstinent
abstracción *f* abstraction; absorption, deep thought; **hacer abstracción de** to leave out, disregard
abstrac•to -ta *adj* abstract
abstraer §75 *tr* to abstract || *intr* — **abstraer de** to do without, leave aside || *ref* to be abstracted or absorbed; **abstraerse de** to do without, leave aside
abstraí•do -da *adj* absorbed in thought; withdrawn
abstru•so -sa *adj* abstruse
absurdidad *f* absurdity
absur•do -da *adj* absurd || *m* absurdity
abuchear *tr* & *intr* to boo, hoot
abuela *f* grandmother; **cuénteselo a su abuela** tell that to the marines
abuelo *m* grandparent; grandfather; **abuelos** grandparents; ancestors
abulta•do -da *adj* bulky, massive
abultar *tr* to enlarge; exaggerate || *intr* to be bulky
abundamiento *m* abundance; **a mayor abundamiento** with greater reason
abundancia *f* abundance, plenty
abundante *adj* abundant
abundar *intr* to abound
abur *interj* good-bye!, so long!
aburguesa•do -da *adj* middle-class, bourgeois
aburguesar *ref* to become middle-class, become bourgeois
aburri•do -da *adj* bored; tiresome
aburrimiento *m* weariness, fatigue; dullness
aburrir *tr* to bore, tire || *ref* to become bored
abusar *intr* to go too far; **abusar de** to abuse; impose on; overindulge in
abusión *f* superstition
abusi•vo -va *adj* abusive
abuso *m* abuse; imposition
abyec•to -ta *adj* abject
A.C. *abbr* **año de Cristo**
acá *adv* here, around here; **acá y allá** here and there; **de ayer acá** since yesterday; **¿de cuándo acá?** since when?; **desde entonces acá** since then; **más acá** here closer; **muy acá** right here
acaba•do -da *adj* complete, perfect; worn-out, exhausted || *m* finish
acabamiento *m* end; completion; death; decline
acabar *tr* to end, finish, complete || *intr* to end; die; **acabar con** to put an end to; end in; **acabar de** to finish; have just, e.g., **acaba de salir** he has just left; **acababa de salir** he had just left; **acabar por** to end in; end by; **no acabar de decidirse** to be unable to make up one's mind || *ref* to end; be exhausted; be all over; run out of, e.g., **se me acabó el café** I have run out of coffee
acabóse *m* limit, last straw
acacia *f* acacia; **acacia falsa** locust tree
academia *f* academy
académi•co -ca *adj* academic || *mf* academician
acaecer §22 *intr* to happen, occur
acaecimiento *m* happening, occurrence
acalenturar *ref* to get a fever
acalora•do -da *adj* heated; warm; fiery, excited
acaloramiento *m* ardor; passion
acalorar *tr* to heat, warm; incite, encourage; stir up || *ref* to become heated; warm up
acallar *tr* to quiet, silence; pacify
acampada *f* camp
acamar *tr* (*las mieses la lluvia o el viento*) to beat down, blow over
acampamento *m* camp, encampment
acampana•do -da *adj* bell-shaped
acampar *tr, intr* & *ref* to encamp
acanalar *tr* to groove; flute; channel; corrugate
acantila•do -da *adj* rocky; steep, precipitous || *m* cliff, bluff
acantonamiento *m* cantonment
acantonar *tr* to canton, quarter || *ref* to be quartered; **acantonarse en** to limit one's activities to

acaparar *tr* to corner; monopolize; hoard
acaramela•do -da *adj* candied; smooth, honey-tongued
acarar *tr* to bring face to face
acarear *tr* to bring face to face; face, brave
acariciar *tr* to caress; (*una ilusión*) cherish
acarraladura *f* (Chile, Peru) run (*in stockings*)
acarreadi•zo -za *adj* transportable
acarrear *tr* to cart, transport, carry along; cause, occasion || *ref* to incur, bring upon oneself
acarreo *m* cartage, drayage; conveyance
acartonar *ref* to shrivel up, become wizened
acasera•do -da *adj* (Chile, Peru) home-loving; (*parroquiano*) (Chile, Peru) regular || *mf* (Chile, Peru) stay-at-home, homebody; (Chile, Peru) regular customer
acaso *m* chance, accident; **al acaso** at random || *adv* maybe, perhaps; **por si acaso** in case of need, just in case
acatamiento *m* homage; respect
acatar *tr* to respect, hold in awe; observe
acatarrar *tr* to chill, give a cold to; (Chile, Mex) to bother, annoy || *ref* to catch cold; get tipsy
acaudala•do -da *adj* rich, well-to-do
acaudalar *tr* to acquire, accumulate
acaudillar *tr* to lead, command; direct
acceder *intr* to accede; agree
accesible *adj* accessible
accesión *f* accession; acquiescence; access, entry
accésit *m* second prize, honorable mention
acceso *m* access, approach; attack, fit, spell; **acceso prohibido** no admittance
acceso•rio -ria *adj* accessory || *m* accessory, fixture, attachment; **accesorios** (theat) properties
accidenta•do -da *adj* agitated; restless; rough, uneven || *mf* victim, casualty
accidental *adj* accidental; acting, protempore, temporary
accidentar *tr* to injure, hurt || *ref* to faint
accidente *m* accident; (*del terreno*) roughness, unevenness; fainting spell
acción *f* action; gesture; (*parte del capital de una sociedad*) share; stock certificate; **acción crecedera** growth stock; **acción de gracias** thanksgiving; **acción liberada** stock dividend; **poner en acción** to set in motion
accionar *tr* to drive || *intr* to gesticulate
accionista *mf* shareholder, stockholder
acebo *m* holly tree
acebuche *m* wild olive
acecinar *tr* to dry-cure, dry-salt; (*el salmón o el arenque*) kipper || *ref* to shrivel up
acechar *tr* to watch, to spy on
acecho *m* watching, spying; **al acecho** or **en acecho** on the watch, spying
acedar *tr* to turn sour; embitter || *ref* to turn sour; wither
acedía *f* sourness; crabbedness; heartburn
ace•do -da *adj* sour, tart; crabbed
aceitar *tr* to oil; grease
aceite *m* oil; olive oil; **aceite de hígado de bacalao** cod-liver oil; **aceite de linaza** linseed oil; **aceite de pie de buey** neat's-foot oil; **aceite de ricino** castor oil; **aceite mineral** coal oil
aceite•ro -ra *adj* oil || *mf* oiler; oil dealer || *f* oilcan; oil cup; **aceiteras** cruet stand
aceito•so -sa *adj* oily, greasy
aceituna *f* olive
aceituno *m* olive tree
aceleración *f* acceleration
acelerador *m* accelerator
acelerar *tr & ref* to accelerate; hasten, hurry
acelga *f* Swiss chard
acémila *f* beast of burden, pack animal; dolt; drudge
acendra•do -da *adj* refined; stainless, spotless
acendrar *tr* to refine; purify, make stainless
acento *m* accent; **acento de altura** pitch accent; **acento ortográfico** written accent, accent mark; **acento prosódico** stress accent, tonic accent
acentuar **§21** *tr* to accent; accentuate, emphasize
aceña *f* water-driven flour mill
acepción *f* meaning
acepillar *tr* to plane; brush; smooth
aceptable *adj* acceptable
aceptación *f* acceptance; **aceptación de personas** discrimination; partiality
aceptar *tr* to accept
acequia *f* irrigation ditch; (Bol, Col, Peru) stream, rivulet
acera *f* sidewalk
acera•do -da *adj* steel, steely; (fig) cutting, biting, sharp
acerar *tr* to steel, harden; line with a sidewalk || *ref* to harden; steel oneself
acer•bo -ba *adj* sour, bitter; harsh
acerca *adv* — **acerca de** about, with regard to
acercamiento *m* approach, rapprochement
acercar **§73** *tr* to bring near or nearer || *ref* to approach, come near or nearer
acería *f* steel mill
acerico *m* small cushion; pincushion
acero *m* steel; sword; courage, spirit
acérri•mo -ma *adj* all-out; (*enemigo*) bitter
acerrojar *tr* to bolt
acerta•do -da *adj* fit, right; skillful, sure; well-aimed
acertante *mf* winner
acertar **§2** *tr* to hit; hit upon; figure out correctly; find; do right || *intr* to be right; succeed; guess right; **acertar a** to happen to; succeed in; **acertar con** to come upon; find
acertijo *m* conundrum, riddle
acervo *m* heap; assets, estate; shoal; store, fund, hoard
acetato *m* acetate
acéti•co -ca *adj* acetic
acetificar **§73** *tr & ref* to acetify
acetileno *m* acetylene
acetona *f* acetone
acia•go -ga *adj* unlucky, ill-fated, evil
acial *m* (CAm, Ecuad) whip

acíbar *m* aloes; bitterness, sorrow
acicalar *tr* to polish, burnish; dress, dress up || *ref* to get all dressed up
acicate *m* long-pointed spur; incentive, stimulus
acicatear *tr* to spur, urge
acidez *f* acidity
acidificar **§73** *tr & ref* to acidify
áci•do -da *adj* acid, tart, sour || *m* acid
acierto *m* lucky hit, good shot; good guess; tact, prudence; ability, skill; accuracy; success
aci•mut *m* (*pl* **-muts**) azimut
aclamación *f* acclaim, applause
aclamar *tr & intr* to acclaim, to hail, to cheer
aclarar *tr* to brighten, clear; rinse; explain || *intr* to get bright; clear up; dawn
aclarato•rio -ria *adj* explanatory
aclimatar *tr & ref* to acclimate
acne *f* acne
acobardar *tr* to cow, intimidate || *ref* to be frightened
acocear *tr* to kick; trample upon, ill-treat
acocil *m* Mexican crayfish; **estar como un acocil** (Mex) to blush, be abashed
acoda•do -da *adj* elbow-shaped
acodar *tr* (*el brazo*) to lean; prop; (hort) to layer || *ref* to lean
acodillar *tr* to bend at an angle || *ref* to double up; to bend, to crumple
acogencia *f* (CAm) acceptance; reception
acoger **§17** *tr* to receive, welcome; accept || *ref* to take refuge; resort
acogida *f* reception, welcome; meeting place, confluence; refuge, shelter; **dar acogida a** (com) to honor
acolada *f* accolade
acolchar *tr* to quilt, pad
acolchí *m* (Mex) red-winged blackbird
acólito *m* acolyte; altar boy
acollador *m* (naut) lanyard
acomedi•do -da *adj* obliging
acometer *tr* to attack; undertake; (*el sueño, la enfermedad, el deseo a una persona*) overcome
acometida *f* attack; (*p.ej., de una línea eléctrica*) house connection
acomodación *f* accommodation
acomodadi•zo -za *adj* accommodating, obliging
acomoda•do -da *adj* convenient, suitable; comfort-loving; well-to-do
acomoda•dor -dora *adj* accommodating, obliging || *mf* usher
acomodar *tr* to accommodate; usher; reconcile; suit; furnish, supply || *intr* to be suitable, be convenient || *ref* to comply; come to terms; hire out; make oneself comfortable
acomodo *m* arrangement, adjustment; lodgings; job, position; (Chile) neatness, tidiness
acompañador *m* companion; accompanist
acompañamiento *m* accompaniment; escort, retinue; (theat) extras, supernumeraries
acompañanta *f* female companion or escort; accompanist
acompañante *m* companion; accompanist
acompañar *tr* to accompany; escort; enclose; sympathize with
acompaño *m* (CAm) meeting; encounter
acompasa•do -da *adj* rhythmic; slow; easy-going; cautious
acompleja•do -da *adj* full of complexes
aconchar *tr* to push to safety; (naut) to beach, run aground || *ref* to take shelter; (naut) to run aground; (Chile) to form a deposit
acondiciona•do -da *adj* conditioned; **bien acondicionado** well-disposed; in good condition; **mal acondicionado** ill-disposed; in bad condition
acondicionador *m* conditioner; **acondicionador de aire** air conditioner
acondicionamiento *m* conditioning; **acondicionamiento del aire** air conditioning
acondicionar *tr* to condition; put in condition; repair; season || *ref* to qualify; find a job
acongojar *tr* to grieve, afflict || *ref* to grieve
aconsejable *adj* advisable
aconsejar *tr* to advise, counsel, warn || *ref* to seek advice, get advice
acontecer **§22** *intr* to happen, occur
acontecimiento *m* happening, event
acopiar *tr* to gather together
acopio *m* gathering; stock; abundance
acoplado *m* (Arg, Chile, Urug) trailer trolley car
acoplamiento *m* coupling; joint; connection; linkup (in space)
acoplar *tr* to couple; join; connect; hitch; reconcile || *ref* to be reconciled; mate; be intimate
acoquinar *tr* to intimidate
acoraza•do -da *adj* armored, armor-plated; contrary || *m* battleship
acorazar **§60** *tr* to armor-plate
acorchar *tr* to line with cork; turn into cork || *ref* to get spongy; wither, shrivel; become corky or pithy; get numb
acorchetar *tr* to bracket
acordar **§61** *tr* to agree upon; authorize; reconcile; make level or flush; remind of; tune || *intr* to agree; blend || *ref* to be agreed, come to an agreement; remember; **acordarse de** to remember
acorde *adj* agreed, in accord; in tune || *m* accord; (mus) chord
acordeón *m* accordion
acordonar *tr* to cord, lace; (*monedas*) knurl, mill; rope off
acornar **§61** *tr* gore; butt
acornear *tr* to gore; butt
acorralar *tr* to corral, corner; intimidate
acortar *tr* to shorten; reduce; slow down; check, stop || *ref* to become shorter; hold back; be timid; slow down; shrink
acosar *tr* to harass; pester
acosijar *tr* (Mex) to pursue, press, track down
acostar **§61** *tr* to lay down; put to bed; (naut) to bring alongside || *ref* to lie down; go to bed; (CAm, Mex) to give birth

acostumbra•do -da *adj* accustomed; customary, usual
acostumbrar *tr* to accustom || *intr* to be accustomed || *ref* to accustom oneself; become accustomed
acotación *f* boundary mark; marginal note; elevation mark
acotamiento *m* boundary mark; marginal note; elevation mark; stage direction
acotar *tr* to mark off, map; annotate; admit, accept; check; vouch for; select; mark elevations on
acotillo *m* sledge hammer
acre *adj* acrid; austere; biting, mordant
acrecentamiento *m* increase, growth; promotion
acrecentar §2 *tr* to increase; promote || *ref* to increase; bud, blossom
acreditar *tr* to accredit; credit; get a reputation for || *ref* to get a reputation, prove oneself
acree•dor -dora *adj* accrediting; deserving || *mf* creditor; **acreedor hipotecario** mortgagee
acribar *tr* to sift; riddle
acribillar *tr* to riddle; harass, plague, pester
acriminar *tr* to incriminate; exaggerate
acrimonio•so -sa *adj* acrid; acrimonious
acriollar *ref* to acquire Spanish American ways
acrisolar *tr* to purify, refine; reveal, bring out
acrobacia *f* acrobatics
acróbata *mf* acrobat
acrobatismo *m* acrobatics
acrónimo *m* acronym
acrópo•lis *adj* (*pl* **-lis**) acropolis
acróstico *m* acrostic
acta *f* minutes; certificate; **acta notarial** affidavit; **actas** proceedings, transactions; **levantar acta** to write up the minutes
actitud *f* attitude; **en actitud de** getting ready to
activar *tr* to activate; hasten, expedite
actividad *f* activity
activista *mf* activist
acti•vo -va *adj* active || *m* (com) assets; (com) credit side
acto *m* act; ceremony, function; commencement; thesis; **acto carnal** sexual intercourse; **acto continuo** right afterward; **acto seguido** right afterward; **acto seguido de** right after; **en acto de servicio** in the line of duty; **hacer acto de presencia** to honor with one's presence
actor *m* actor; agent; **primer actor** leading man
ac•triz *f* (*pl* **-trices**) actress; **primera actriz** leading lady
actuación *f* acting, performance; action; operation; behavior; **actuación en directo** live performance; **actuaciones** legal proceedings
actual *adj* present, present-day; up-to-date || *m* current month
actualidad *f* present time; timeliness; **actualidades** current events; newsreel; **actualidad escénica** theater news; **actualidad gráfica** news in pictures
actualizar §60 *tr* to bring up to date
actualmente *adv* at present, at the present time
actuante *mf* participant
actuar §21 *tr* to actuate || *intr* to act; perform
actua•rio -ria *mf* actuary
acuaplano *m* aquaplane
acuarela *f* water color
acuario *m* aquarium; **Acuario** *m* (astr) Aquarius
acuartelar *tr* to billet, quarter
acuáti•co -ca *adj* aquatic
acuatizaje *m* (aer) alighting on water; (*de nave espacial)* splashdown
acuatizar §60 *intr* (aer) to alight on water
acucia *f* zeal, diligence; yearning
acuciar *tr* to goad, prod; harass; yearn for
acuclillar *ref* to squat, crouch
acuchilla•do -da *adj* knife-shaped; schooled by experience; (*vestido*) slashed
acuchillar *tr* to stab; stab to death; slash
acudir *intr* to come up, respond; apply; hang around; come to the rescue; **acudir a las urnas** to vote
acueducto *m* aqueduct
acuerdo *m* accord; agreement; memory; **de acuerdo con** in accord with; **de común acuerdo** with one accord; **estar en su acuerdo** to be in one's right mind; **ponerse de acuerdo** to come to an agreement; **recobrar su acuerdo** to come to; **tomar un acuerdo** to make a decision; **volver en su acuerdo** to come to; to change one's mind
acuitar *tr & ref* to grieve
acullá *adv* yonder, over there
acumulador *m* storage battery
acumular *tr* to accumulate, gather; store up || *intr & ref* to accumulate, gather
acunar *tr* to rock; cradle
acuñación *f* coining, minting; wedging
acuñar *tr* to coin, mint; wedge; key, lock; (typ) to quoin
acuo•so -sa *adj* watery; juicy
acupuntura *f* acupuncture
acurrucar §73 *ref* to squat, crouch; huddle
acusación *f* accusation
acusa•do -da marked || *mf* accused
acusar *tr* to accuse; show; (*recibo de una carta*) acknowledge || *ref* to confess
acusati•vo -va *adj & m* accusative
acuse *m* acknowledgment
acústi•co -ca *adj* acoustic || *f* acoustics
achacar §73 *tr* to impute, attribute
achaco•so -sa *adj* ailing, sickly
achaparra•do -da *adj* stocky; stubby; chubby
achaparrar *ref* to become stunted
achaque *m* sickliness, indisposition; excuse, pretext; matter, subject; weakness; (coll) monthlies
achatar *tr* to flatten || *ref* (Mex) to become frightened, afraid
achica•do -da *adj* childish; abashed, disconcerted
achicador *m* scoop

achicar §73 *tr* to make smaller; humble; bail, to bail out
achicoria *f* chicory
achicharrar *tr* to scorch; bedevil || *ref* to get scorched
achicharronar *tr* to squash
achín *m* (CAm) peddler; door-to-door salesman
achiquitar *ref* to lose heart, cower
achispa•do -da *adj* tipsy
achispar *tr* to make tipsy || *ref* to get tipsy
achuchar *tr* to incite; crumple, crush; jostle || *ref* (Arg, Urug) to shiver, have a chill
adagio *m* adage
adalid *m* chief; guide, leader; champion
adama•do -da *adj* womanish; chic, stylish
adamar *ref* to become effeminate
adán *m* dirty, ragged fellow; lazy, careless fellow || **Adán** *m* Adam
adaptación *f* adaptation
adaptar *tr* to adapt
adarga *f* oval or heart-shaped leather shield
adarvar *tr* to bewilder, stun
A. de C. *abbr* **año de Cristo**
adecentar *tr* to clean up, tidy up || *ref* to put on a clean shirt, dress up
adecua•do -da *adj* fitting, suitable
adecuar *tr* to fit, adapt
adefesio *m* nonsense; outlandish outfit; queer-looking fellow
adehala *f* gratuity, extra
adehesar *tr* to convert into pasture
adelanta•do -da *adj* precocious; bold, forward; (*reloj*) fast; **por adelantado** in advance || *m* provincial governor
adelantamiento *m* anticipation; advancement, promotion, progress
adelantar *tr* to move forward; outstrip, get ahead of; advance; promote; improve || *intr* to advance; improve; be fast || *ref* to move forward; gain, be fast
adelante *adv* ahead; forward; **más adelante** farther on; later || *interj* go ahead!; come in!
adelanto *m* advance, progress, improvement; advancement; payment in advance
adelfa *f* oleander
adelgazar §60 *tr* to make thin; taper; purify; argue subtly about; weaken, lessen || *intr* & *ref* to get thin; taper
ademán *m* attitude; gesture; **ademanes** manners; **en ademán de** getting ready to; **hacer ademán de** to make a move to
además *adv* moreover, besides; **además de** in addition to, besides
adentellar *tr* to sink one's teeth into
adentrar *intr* & *ref* to go in; **adentrarse en el mar** to go farther out to sea
adentro *adv* inside; **mar adentro** out at sea; **ser muy de adentro** to be like a member of the family; **tierra adentro** inland || **adentros** *mpl* inmost being, inmost thoughts; **en** or **para sus adentros** to oneself, to himself, etc.
adep•to -ta *adj* initiated || *mf* follower
aderezar §60 *tr* to dress, adorn; cook; (*una tela*) starch; season; repair; lead; (*bebidas*) mix; (*vinos*) blend || *ref* to dress, get ready
aderezo *m* dressing; seasoning, condiment; starch; finery; equipment; set of jewelry
adestrar §2 *tr* & *ref* var of **adiestrar**
adeuda•do -da *adj* indebted, in debt
adeudar *tr* to owe; to be liable for; charge || *intr* to become related by marriage || *ref* to run into debt
adeudo *m* debt, indebtedness; customs duty; charge, debit
adherencia *f* adhesion; **tener adherencias** to have connections
adherente *adj* adherent || *m* adherent; **adherentes** accessories
adherir §68 *intr* & *ref* to adhere; stick
adhesión *f* adherence, adhesion
adhesi•vo -va *adj* adhesive
adición *f* addition; (*en un café o restaurante*) check
adicionar *tr* to add; add to
adic•to -ta *adj* devoted; supporting || *mf* supporter, follower
adiestramiento *m* training; breaking in
adiestrar *tr* to train; teach; lead, guide || *ref* to train, practice
adietar *tr* to put on a diet
adinera•do -da *adj* wealthy, well-to-do
adiós *m* adieu, good-bye || *interj* adieu!, good-bye!
aditamento *m* addition; accessory
aditi•vo -va *adj* & *m* additive
adivinación *f* prophecy; guessing, divination; **adivinación del pensamiento** mind reading
adivina•dor -dora *mf* guesser; good guesser; **adivinador del pensamiento** mind reader
adivinaja *f* riddle, puzzle
adivinanza *f* riddle; guess
adivinar *tr* to prophesy; guess, divine; (*un enigma*) solve; (*el pensamiento ajeno*) read
adivi•no -na *mf* fortuneteller; guesser
adjetivo *m* adjective
adjudicar §73 *tr* to adjudge, award || *ref* to appropriate
adjuntar *tr* to join, connect; add; enclose
adjun•to -ta *adj* added, attached; enclosed || *mf* associate || *m* adjunct; adjective
adminículo *m* aid, auxiliary; gadget; meddler; **adminículos** emergency equipment
administración *f* administration, management; headquarters
administra•dor -dora *mf* administrator, manager; **administrador de correos** postmaster
administrar *tr* to administer, manage
admiración *f* admiration; wonder; exclamation mark
admira•dor -dora *mf* admirer
admirar *tr* to admire; surprise || *ref* to wonder; **admirarse de** to wonder at
admisible *adj* admissible
admisión *f* admission; (mach) intake
admitir *tr* to admit; allow; accept, recognize; agree to
adobar *tr* to repair, restore; dress, prepare; cook, stew; (*carne, pescado*) pickle; (*pieles*) tan

adobe *m* adobe
adobera *f* (SAm) brick-shaped cheese; mold for brick-shaped cheese
adobo *m* repairing; dressing; cooking; pickling; tanning; pickled meat or fish
adocena•do -da common, ordinary
adoctrinar *tr* to indoctrinate, teach, instruct
adolecer §22 *intr* to fall sick; **adolecer de** to suffer from || *ref* — **adolecerse de** (archaic) to sympathize with, feel sorry for
adolescencia *f* adolescence
adolescente *adj & mf* adolescent
adonde *conj* where, whither
adónde *adv* where, whither
adopción *f* adoption
adoptar *tr* to adopt
adoquín *m* paving stone, paving block; (coll) blockhead
adoquina•do -da *adj* paved with cobblestones || *m* cobblestone paving
adorable *adj* adorable
adoración *f* adoration, worship; **Adoración de los Reyes** Epiphany
adora•dor -dora *mf* adorer, worshiper || *m* suitor
adorar *tr & intr* to adore, worship
adormecer §22 *tr* to put to sleep || *ref* to go to sleep; get sleepy
adormeci•do -da *adj* sleepy, drowsy; numb; calm
adormidera *f* opium poppy
adormilar *ref* to doze, drowse
adornar *tr* to adorn; (*un cuento*) embroider
adornista *mf* decorator
adorno *m* adornment, decoration; **adorno de escaparate** window dressing
adosar *tr* to lean; push close
adquirir §40 *tr* to acquire; **adquirir en propiedad** to buy, purchase
adquisición *f* acquisition
adrede *adv* on purpose
Adriáti•co -ca *adj & m* Adriatic
adscribir §83 *tr* to attribute; assign
adscripción *f* attribution; assignment
aduana *f* customhouse; **aduana seca** inland customhouse; **exento de aduana** duty-free; **sujeto de aduana** dutiable
aduane•ro -ra *adj* customhouse; customs || *m* customhouse officer, customs inspector
aduar *m* Arab settlement; gipsy camp; Indian ranch
adueñar *ref* to take possession
adujar *tr* (naut) to coil || *ref* (naut) to curl up
adular *tr* to flatter, fawn on
adu•lón -lona *adj* fawning, groveling || *mf* fawner
adúltera *f* adulteress
adulterar *tr* to adulterate || *intr* to commit adultery || *ref* to become adulterated, to spoil
adulterio *m* adultery
adúlte•ro -ra *adj* adulterous || *m* adulterer || *f* see **adúltera**
adultez *f* adulthood
adul•to -ta *adj & mf* adult
adulzar §60 *tr* to sweeten; (*metales*) soften
adunar *tr* to join, bring together
adundar *ref* (CAm) to become stupid
adus•to -ta *adj* grim, stern, gloomy; scorching hot
advenedi•zo -za *adj* strange; foreign || *mf* stranger; foreigner; outsider; parvenu, upstart; nouveau riche
advenimiento *m* advent, coming; accession; **esperar el santo advenimiento** to wait in vain
advenir §79 *intr* to come, arrive; happen
adverbio *m* adverb
adversa•rio -ria *mf* adversary
adversidad *f* adversity
advertencia *f* observation; notice, remark; warning; preface
adverti•do -da *adj* capable, clever, wide-awake
advertir §68 *tr* to notice, observe; notify, warn; point out || *ref* to become aware
Adviento *m* (eccl) Advent
adyacente *adj* adjacent
aeración *f* aeration; ventilation; air conditioning
aére•o -a *adj* air, aerial; overhead, elevated; airy, light, fanciful
aerodinámi•co -ca *adj* aerodynamic || *f* aerodynamics
aeródromo *m* aerodrome, airdrome; **aeródromo de urgencia** emergency-landing field
aerofluyente *adj* streamlined
aeroespacial *adj* aerospace
aerofumigación *f* crop dusting
aeromedicina *f* aviation medicine
aeromodelismo *m* model-airplane building
aeromodelista *mf* model-airplane builder
aeromodelo *m* model airplane
aeromotor *m* windmill; airplane motor
aeromoza *f* air hostess, stewardess
aeronáuti•co -ca *adj* aeronautic || *f* aeronautics
aeronave *f* airship; **aeronave cohete** rocket ship
aeropista *f* landing strip
aeroplano *m* aeroplane
aeroposta *f* air mail
aeropostal *adj* air-mail
aeropropulsor *m* airplane engine; **aeropropulsor por reacción** jet engine
aeropuerto *m* airport
aeroscala *f* transit point
aerosol *m* aerosol
aeroste•ro -ra *adj* aviation || *m* flyer; airman
aerotaxi *m* air taxi
aeroterrestre *adj* air-ground
aerovía *f* airway
afable *adj* affable, friendly, agreeable
afama•do -da *adj* noted, famous
afamar *tr* to make famous || *ref* to become famous
afán *m* hard work; eagerness, zeal; task; worry
afanar *tr* to press, hurry || *intr* to strive, toil || *ref* to strive, toil; busy oneself
afano•so -sa *adj* hard, laborious; hard-working
afarolar *ref* to make a fuss, get excited

afear *tr* to deface, disfigure; blame
afeblecer §22 *intr* to grow feeble, get thin
afección *f* affection, fondness; (med) affection
afectación *f* affectation
afecta•do -da *adj* affected; **estar afectado de** (*p.ej., los riñones*) to have (*e.g., kidney*) trouble
afectar *tr* to affect; hurt, injure || *ref* to be moved, be stirred
afecti•vo -va *adj* emotional
afec•to -ta *adj* fond; kind; affected; **afecto a** fond of; (*un empleo, un servicio, etc.*) attached to; **afecto de** suffering from || *m* affection, fondness; emotion
afectuo•so -sa *adj* affectionate; kind
afeitado *m* shave; **afeitado a ras** close shave
afeitar *tr* to shave; adorn; || *ref* to shave; paint
afeite *m* cosmetics, rouge, make-up
afeminación *f* effeminacy
afemina•do -da *adj* effeminate
afeminar *tr* to effeminate || *ref* to become effeminate
aferra•do -da *adj* stubborn, obstinate
aferrar *tr* to seize; catch; hook; (naut) to moor; (naut) to furl || *ref* to interlock, hook together; cling; insist
Afganistán, el Afghanistan
afga•no -na *adj & mf* Afghan
afianzar §60 *tr* to guarantee, vouch for; bail; fasten; prop up; grasp; support || *ref* to hold fast, steady oneself
afición *f* fondness, liking, taste; ardor, zeal; fans, public
aficiona•do -da *adj* fond; amateur; **aficionado a** fond of || *mf* amateur; fan, follower
aficionar *tr* to win, win the attachment of || *ref* — **aficionarse a** or **de** to become fond of; become a follower of, become a fan of
afiebra•do -da *adj* feverish
afiebrar *ref* (SAm) to get a fever
afi•jo -ja *adj* affixed || *m* affix
afila•do -da *adj* sharp; tapering; pointed; peaked
afilador *m* grinder, sharpener; razor strop
afilalápi•ces *m* (*pl* **-ces**) pencil sharpener
afilar *tr* to grind, sharpen; (*una navaja de afeitar*) strop; (Arg & Urug) to flirt with || *ref* to sharpen, get sharp; taper, get thin
afiliar §77 **& regular** *tr* to affiliate, take in || *ref* — **afiliarse a** to join
afiligranar *tr* to filigree; adorn, embellish
afilón *m* knife sharpener; razor strop
afín *adj* near, bordering; like, similar; related || *mf* relative by marriage
afinador *m* tuner; tuning hammer, tuning key
afinar *tr* to purify, refine, perfect; trim; tune
afincar §73 *intr & ref* to buy up real estate
afinidad *f* affinity; **por afinidad** by marriage
afirmar *tr* to strengthen, secure, fasten; assert || *ref* to hold fast; steady oneself
afirmati•vo -va *adj & f* affirmative
aflicción *f* affliction; sorrow, grief
afligir §27 *tr* to afflict, grieve; (Mex) to beat, whip || *ref* to grieve
aflojar *tr* to slacken, let go; loosen || *intr* to slacken, slow up; abate, lessen || *ref* to come loose; slacken
aflora•do -da *adj* flour; fine, elegant
aflorar *tr* to sift || *intr* to crop out
afluencia *f* flowing; affluence, abundance; crowd, jam, rush; fluency; **horas de afluencia** rush hour
afluente *adj* flowing; abundant; fluent || *m* tributary
afluir §20 *intr* to flow; pour, flock
afmo. *abbr.* **afectísimo**
afofar *tr* to make fluffy, make spongy
afonizar §60 *tr & ref* to unvoice
aforar *tr* to gauge, measure; appraise
aforismo *m* aphorism
afortuna•do -da *adj* fortunate; happy
afrancesa•do -da *adj & mf* Francophile
afrecho *m* bran
afrenta *f* affront
afrentar *tr* to affront || *ref* to be ashamed
afrento•so -sa *adj* outrageous, disgraceful
Africa *f* Africa
africa•no -na *adj & mf* African
afrodisía•co -ca *adj & m* aphrodisiac
afrontamiento *m* confrontation
afrontar *tr* to bring face to face; defy || *ref* — **afrontarse con** to confront, meet face to face
afuera *adv* outside || *interj* clear the way!, look out! || **afueras** *fpl* outskirts, environs
afuetada *f* or **afuetadura** *f* (SAm) beating
agachadiza *f* snipe; **hacer la agachadiza** to duck
agachar *tr* to lower, bend down || *ref* to crouch, squat; cower; (SAm) to give in, yield
agalla *f* gallnut; (*de pez*) gill; (*de ave*) ear lobe; **agallas** courage, guts
ágape *m* banquet, love feast
agarradera *f* hold, grip; handle; **tener agarraderas** to have connections
agarrada *f* brawl, fight, scrap
agarra•do -da *adj* stingy, tight || *f* see **agarrada**
agarrar *tr* to grab, grasp; take hold of; get, obtain || *intr* to take hold; take root; stick || *ref* to grapple; have a good hold; worry; **agarrarse a** to take hold of, cling to
agarro *m* clench, clutch, grip
agarrochar *tr* to jab with a goad
agarrón *m* brawl, fight; grip, tug
agarrotar *tr* to garrote; bind, tie up || *ref* to become numb
agasajar *tr* to regale, lionize, make a fuss over
agasajo *m* kindness, attention; lionization; favor, gift; treat; party
agavillar *tr* to bind or tie in sheaves || *ref* to band together
agazapar *tr* to grab, to nab || *ref* to crouch; to hide
agencia *f* agency; bureau; (Chile) pawn shop; **agencia de noticias** news agency; **agencia matrimonial** marriage broker
agenciar *tr* to manage to bring about; promote || *ref* to manage
agenda *f* notebook

agente *m* agent; policeman; **agente de policía** policeman; **agente viajero** traveling salesman, commercial traveler

agigantar *tr* to make huge || *ref* to become huge

ágil *adj* agile; flexible, light

agilitar *tr & ref* to limber up

agita•do -da *adj* agitated, excited, exalted; (*mar*) rough

agitar *tr* to agitate; shake; wave; stir || *intr* to agitate || *ref* to be agitated; shake; wave; get excited; (*el mar*) get rough

aglomeración *f* agglomeration; crowd; built-up area

aglomerado *m* briquet, coal briquet

aglutinar *tr* to stick together || *ref* to cake

agnósti•co -ca *adj & mf* agnostic

agobiar *tr* to overburden; exhaust, oppress

agolpar *ref* to flock, throng

agonía *f* agony, throes of death; agony, anguish; yearning; craving

agonizar **§60** *tr* (*al moribundo*) to assist, attend; harass || *intr* to be in the throes of death

agorar **§3** *tr* to augur, foretell

agore•ro -ra *adj* fortunetelling; ill-omened; superstitious || *mf* fortuneteller

agostar *tr* to burn up, to parch || *ref* to dry up; (*la esperanza, la felicidad*) fade away

agostero *m* harvest helper

agosto *m* August; harvest; harvest time; **hacer su agosto** to make hay while the sun shines

agota•do -da *adj* exhausted; sold out; out of print

agotar *tr* to exhaust, wear out, use up || *ref* to become exhausted, be used up; go out of print; run out

agracia•do -da *adj* charming, graceful; nice, pretty || *mf* winner

agradable *adj* agreeable; pleasant

agradar *tr* to please || *intr* to be pleasing || *ref* to be pleased

agradecer **§22** *tr* to thank; **agradecerle a uno una cosa** to thank someone for something

agradeci•do -da *adj* thankful, grateful; rewarding

agradecimiento *m* thanks, gratitude

agrado *m* agreeableness, graciousness; pleasure, liking

agrandar *tr* to enlarge || *ref* to grow larger

agranelar *tr* (*cuero*) to grain, pebble

agrapar *tr* to clamp

agrariense *adj & mf* agrarian

agra•rio -ria *adj* agrarian

agravar *tr* to weigh down; aggravate; exaggerate; oppress || *ref* to get worse

agraviar *tr* to wrong, offend || *ref* to take offense

agravio *m* wrong, offense; **agravios de hecho** assault and battery

agravio•so -sa *adj* offensive, insulting

agraz *m* (*pl* **agraces**) sour grape; sour-grape juice; bitterness, displeasure; **en agraz** prematurely

agredir **§1** *tr* to attack, assault

agregado *m* aggregate; concrete block; attaché; (Arg) tenant farmer

agregar **§44** *tr* to add; attach; appoint || *ref* to join

agremiado *m* union member

agremiar *tr* to unionize

agresión *f* aggression

agresi•vo -va *adj* aggressive

agre•sor -sora *adj* aggressive || *mf* aggressor

agreste *adj* country, rustic; wild, rough; uncouth

agriar **§77 & regular** *tr* to make sour; exasperate || *ref* to turn sour; become exasperated

agrícola *adj* agricultural || *mf* farmer

agricultura *f* agriculture

agridulce *adj* bittersweet

agriera *f* (Chile) heartburn; **agrieras** (Col) cruet stand

agrietar *tr & ref* to crack

agrimensor *m* surveyor

agrimensura *f* surveying

agringar **§44** *ref* to act like a gringo

a•grio -gria *adj* sour, acrid; uneven, rough; brittle || **agrios** *mpl* citrus fruit

agronomía *f* agronomy

agropecua•rio -ria *adj* land-and-cattle, farm

agrumar *tr & ref* to curd, clot

agrupar *tr & ref* to group, cluster

agrura *f* sourness; unpleasantness; **agruras** citrus fruit

agua *f* water; (*de un tejado*) slope; **agua abajo** downstream; **agua arriba** upstream; **agua bendita** holy water; **agua corriente** running water; **agua de Colonia** eau de Cologne; **agua de marea** tidewater; **agua gaseosa** carbonated water; **agua oxigenada** hydrogen peroxide; **aguas** mineral springs; (*de sedas; de piedras preciosas*) water, sparkle; **aguas mayores** equinoctial tide; feces; **aguas menores** ordinary tide; urination; **cubrir aguas** to have under roof; **entre dos aguas** under water, under the surface of the water; (coll) undecided

aguacate *m* avocado, alligator pear; pear-shaped emerald

aguacero *m* shower

aguada *f* source of water; water color; watering station

aguade•ro -ra *adj* water || *m* watering place

agua•do -da *adj* watery; thin, watered; weak, washed out, limp; dull, insipid || *f* see **aguada**

agua•dor -dora *mf* water carrier || *m* paddle, bucket

aguafies•tas *mf* (*pl* **-tas**) kill-joy, wet blanket, crapehanger

aguafortista *mf* etcher

aguafuerte *f* etching; **grabar al aguafuerte** to etch

aguaitar *intr* to spy, watch || *tr* to watch, wait for

aguaje *m* watering place; tidal wave; strong current; (*de buque*) wake

aguamala *f* jellyfish

aguamanil *m* ewer, wash pitcher; washstand

aguama•nos *m* (*pl* **-nos**) water for washing hands; washstand
aguamarina *f* aquamarine
aguanie•ves *f* (*pl* **-ves**) wagtail
aguano•so -sa *adj* watery, soaked
aguantada *f* patience, forbearance
aguantar *tr* to hold up, sustain; bear, endure, tolerate; hold back, control || *intr* to last, hold out || *ref* to restrain oneself; keep quiet; **aguantarse las lágrimas** to swallow one's tears
aguante *m* patience, endurance; strength, vigor
aguar §**10** *tr* to water; spoil, mar || *ref* to become watery; fill up with water; be spoiled
aguardar *tr* to await, wait for; grant time to || *intr* to wait; **aguardar a que** to wait until
aguardentera *f* liquor bottle, brandy flask
aguardentería *f* liquor store
aguardento•so -sa *adj* brandy; (*voz*) whiskey
aguardiente *m* brandy; spirituous liquor; **aguardiente de caña** rum; **aguardiente de manzana** applejack
aguardo *m* hunter's blind
aguarrás *m* turpentine, oil of turpentine
aguasar *ref* (Arg & Chile) to become countrified
aguazal *m* swamp, pool
agudeza *f* acuteness, acuity; sharpness; witticism; **agudeza visual** visual acuity
agu•do -da *adj* acute; sharp; keen; witty
agüero *m* augury; omen; forecast
aguerri•do -da *adj* inured, hardened
aguijada *f* goad, spur; prod
aguijar *tr* to goad, spur, prod || *intr* to hurry along
aguijón *m* goad, spur; sting; thorn; stimulus; **dar coces contra el aguijón** to kick against the pricks
aguijonear to goad, incite; sting
águila *f* eagle; **¿águila o sol?** (Mex) heads or tails?; **ser un águila** to be wide-awake, be a wizard
aguile•ño -ña *adj* aquiline; sharp-featured
aguilón *m* (*de grúa*) boom, jib; (*del tejado*) gable
aguinaldo *m* Christmas gift, Epiphany gift; Christmas carol
aguja *f* needle; hatpin; steeple, spire; (*del reloj*) hand; **aguja de gancho** crochet needle; **aguja de hacer media** knitting needle; **aguja de zurcir** darning needle; **agujas** (rr) switch; **buscar una aguja en un pajar** to look for a needle in a haystack
agujerear *tr* to make a hole in, pierce, perforate
agujero *m* hole; pincushion; **agujero negro** black hole
agujeta *f* (*de la jeringa*) needle; shoestring; **agujetas** stitches, twinges
agusanar *ref* to get wormy; become worm-eaten
aguzanie•ves *f* (*pl* **-ves**) wagtail
aguzar §**60** *tr* to sharpen; incite, stir up; stare at; (*las orejas*) prick up
ah-chís *interj* kerchoo!
aherrojar *tr* to fetter, shackle; oppress
aherrumbrar *tr & ref* to rust
ahí *adv* there; **de ahí que** hence; **por ahí** that way
ahija•do -da *mf* godchild; protégé || *m* godson || *f* goddaughter
ahilar *ref* to faint from hunger; waste away; grow poorly; turn sour
ahincar §**73** *tr* to urge, press; importune || *ref* to hasten
ahinco *m* earnestness, zeal, eagerness
ahitar *tr* to cloy, surfeit, stuff
ahi•to -ta *adj* surfeited, stuffed; fed up, disgusted || *m* surfeit; indigestion
ahoga•do -da *adj* drowned; smothered; sunk; close, unventilated; **mate ahogado** stalemate; **perecer ahogado** to drown; **verse ahogado** to be swamped
ahogar §**44** *tr* to drown; suffocate, smother; (*cal*) slake; (*plantas*) soak; oppress; extinguish; stalemate || *ref* to drown; suffocate; drown oneself
ahogo *m* shortness of breath; great sorrow; stringency
ahondar *tr* to make deeper; go deep into || *intr* to go deep, go deeper
ahora *adv* now; presently; **ahora bien** now then, so then; **ahora mismo** right now; **por ahora** for the present
ahorcajar *ref* to sit astride
ahorcar §**73** *tr* to hang || *ref* to hang, be hanged; hang oneself
ahorra•do -da *adj* saving, thrifty
ahorrar *tr* to save; spare || *ref* to save or spare oneself
ahorrati•vo -va *adj* saving, thrifty; stingy || *f* economy
ahorro *m* economy; **ahorros** savings
ahuchar *tr* to hoard
ahuecar §**73** *tr* to hollow, hollow out; loosen, fluff up; **ahuecar la voz** to speak in deep and solemn tones || *ref* to be puffed up
ahula•do -da *adj* waterproof, impermeable *m* overshoe
ahumar *tr* to smoke || *intr* to be smoky || *ref* to get smoked up; look or taste smoky; get drunk
ahusar *tr & ref* to taper
ahuyentar *tr* to put to flight; scare away || *ref* to flee, run away
aira•do -da *adj* angry; wild; depraved
airar §**4** *tr* to anger || *ref* to get angry
aire *m* air; **al aire libre** in the open air; **darse aires** to put on airs
airear *tr* to air, aerate, ventilate || *ref* to get aired; catch cold
airón *m* aigrette, panache; gray heron
airo•so -sa *adj* airy; drafty; graceful, light; resplendent; successful
aislación *f* insulation
aislacionista *adj & mf* isolationist
aislador *m* insulator
aislamiento *m* isolation; (elec) insulation
aislar §**4** *tr* to isolate; detach, separate; (elec) to insulate || *ref* to live in seclusion

ajar *m* garlic field || *tr* to crumple, muss; (*marchitar*) wither; tamper with; abuse, ill-treat || *ref* to get mussed; wither
ajedrea *f* (bot) savory
ajedrecista *mf* chess player
ajedrez *m* chess; chess set
ajenjo *m* (*Artemisia*) wormwood; (*licor*) absinthe; (*sinsabores y penas*) (fig) wormwood, bitterness; **ajenjo del campo** or **ajenjo mayor** (*Artemisia absinthium*) wormwood
aje•no -na *adj* another's; extraneous, foreign; different; contrary; free; insane; uninformed; **lo ajeno** what belongs to someone else
ajetrear *tr* to drive, harass || *ref* to bustle about; fidget
ajetreo *m* bustle, fuss
ají *m* (*pl* **ajíes**) chili; chili sauce; **ponerse como un ají** (Chile) to turn red as a tomato
aji•mez *m* (*pl* **-meces**) mullioned window
ajo *m* garlic; garlic clove; garlic sauce
ajorca *f* bracelet, anklet
ajornalar *tr* to hire by the day || *ref* to hire out by the day
ajuar *m* housefurnishings; trousseau
ajuiciar *tr* to bring to one's senses || *ref* to come to one's senses
ajustable *adj* adjustable
ajusta•do -da *adj* just, right; tight, close-fitting
ajustar *tr* to adapt, fit, adjust; hire; arrange; reconcile; fasten; settle || *intr* to fit || *ref* to fit; hire out; be hired; come to an agreement
ajuste *m* fit; fitting, adjustment; hiring; arrangement; reconciliation; settlement; agreement
ajusticiar *tr* to execute, put to death
ala *f* wing; (*del sombrero*) brim; (*de puerta, mesa, etc.*) leaf; (*de pez*) fin; (*de hélice*) blade; (football) end; **ahuecar el ala** to beat it; **ala en flecha** (aer) sweptback wing; **alas** boldness, courage; **volar con sus propias alas** to stand on one's own feet
Alá *m* Allah
alabanza *f* praise
alabar *tr* to praise || *ref* to boast
alabarda *f* halberd
alabardero *m* halberdier; hired applauder, claqueur
alabastro *m* alabaster
álabe *m* drooping branch; bucket, paddle; cog
alabear *tr & ref* to warp
alacena *f* cupboard, wall closet; (naut) locker; (Mex) booth, stall
alacrán *m* scorpion
ala•do -da *adj* winged
alamar *m* frog (*button and loop on a garment*)
alambica•do -da *adj* precious, oversubtle, fine-spun; begrudged
alambicar §73 *tr* to distill; refine to excess
alambique *m* still, alembic; (*de laboratorio*) retort; **por alambique** sparingly
alambrada *f* chicken wire; wire mesh; (mil) barbed wire; (elec) wiring
alambrado *m* chicken wire; wire mesh; wire fence; (elec) wiring; (mil) wire entanglement
alambraje *m* (elec) wiring
alambrar *tr* to fence with wire; string with wire; wire
alambre *m* wire; **alambre cargado** live wire; **alambre de púas** barbed wire; **alambre sin aislar** bare wire
alambrera *f* wire screen; wire cover
alameda *f* poplar grove; mall, shaded walk
álamo *m* poplar; **álamo de Italia** Lombardy poplar; **álamo negro** black poplar; **álamo temblón** aspen
alampar *ref* to have a craving
alancear *tr* to lance, spear
alano *m* mastiff, great Dane
alarde *m* display, ostentation; (mil) review; **hacer alarde de** to make a show of; boast of
alardear *intr* to boast, brag, show off
alardo•so -sa *adj* showy, ostentatious
alargar §44 *tr* to extend, lengthen, stretch; hand; to increase; let out || *ref* to go away, withdraw; grow longer; be long-winded
alarido *m* howl, shout, yell, whoop
alarma *f* alarm; (aer) alert; **alarma aérea** air-raid warning; **alarma de incendios** fire alarm; **alarma de ladrones** burglar alarm
alarmar *tr* to alarm; alert || *ref* to become alarmed
alarmista *mf* alarmist
alastrar *tr* (*las orejas*) to throw back; (naut) to ballast || *ref* to lie flat, cower
ala•zán -zana *adj* sorrel, reddish-brown || *mf* sorrel horse
alba *f* dawn, daybreak
albacea *m* executor || *f* executrix
albahaquero *m* flowerpot
alba•nés -nesa *adj & mf* Albanian
albañal *m* sewer, drain
albañil *m* mason, bricklayer
albañilería *f* masonry
albarán *m* rent sign; bulletin; (com) check list
albarca *f* sandal
albarda *f* packsaddle
albardilla *f* (*tejadillo sobre los muros*) coping; shoulder pad
albaricoque *m* apricot
albaricoquero *m* apricot tree
alba•tros *m* (*pl* **-tros**) albatross
albayalde *m* white lead
albear *intr* to turn white; (Arg) to get up at dawn
albedrío *m* free will; fancy, caprice, pleasure; **libre albedrío** free will
albéitar *m* veterinarian
alberca *f* pond, pool; tank, reservoir; **en alberca** roofless
albérchigo *m* clingstone peach
albergar §44 *tr* to shelter, harbor; house || *intr & ref* to take shelter; take lodgings
albergue *m* shelter, refuge; lodging; den, lair
albero *m* dishcloth, dishrag; white earth

al•bo -ba *adj* (poet) white || *f* see **alba**
albóndiga *f* meat ball, fish ball
albor *m* whiteness; dawn
alborada *f* dawn; morning serenade; reveille
alborear *intr* to dawn
albor•noz *m* (*pl* **-noces**) terry cloth; burnoose; cardigan; beach robe
alborota•do -da *adj* hasty, rash; noisy; rough
alborota•dor -dora *mf* agitator, rioter
alborotapue•blos *mf* (*pl* **-blos**) (coll) rabble rouser
alborotar *tr* to agitate, arouse, stir up || *intr* to make a racket || *ref* to get excited; riot; (*la mar*) get rough
alboroto *m* agitation, disturbance; noise, riot; **alborotos** (CAm) candied popcorn; **armar un alboroto** to raise a racket
alborozar **§60** *tr* to gladden, cheer, overjoy, elate
alborozo *m* joy, merriment, elation
albricias *fpl* reward for good news; reward given on the occasion of some happy event; **en albricias de** as a token of || *interj* good news!, congratulations!
albufera *f* saltwater lagoon
ál•bum *m* (*pl* **-bumes**) album; **álbum de recortes** scrapbook
albumen *m* albumen
albúmina *f* albumin
albuminar *tr* (phot) to emulsify
albur *m* risk, chance
alcachofa *f* artichoke
alcahue•te -ta *mf* bawd, procurer, go-between; screen, fence; schemer; gossip
alcahuetear *tr* to procure; harbor || *intr* to pander
alcaide *m* governor, warden, jailer
alcalde *m* mayor, chief burgess; **alcalde de monterilla** small-town mayor; **tener el padre alcalde** to have a friend at court
alcaldesa *f* mayoress
álcali *m* alkali
alcali•no -na *adj* alkaline
alcallería *f* pottery
alcana *f* henna
alcance *m* reach, scope, extent; range; pursuit; capacity; late news; import; coverage; brains, intelligence; **al alcance de** within reach of, within range of; **alcance de la vista** eyesight, eyeshot; **alcance del oído** earshot; **dar alcance a** to catch up with
alcancía *f* child's bank; bin, hopper
alcanfor *m* camphor
alcantarilla *f* sewer; culvert
alcantarillar *tr* to sewer
alcanza•do -da *adj* needy, hard up
alcanzar **§60** *tr* to reach; overtake, catch up to; grasp; obtain; understand; live through || *intr* to succeed; (*un arma de fuego*) carry; manage; suffice
alcaparrosa *f* vitriol
alcaravea *f* caraway
alcatraz *m* gannet, pelican
alcázar *m* fortress; castle, royal palace; quarterdeck
alce *m* elk, moose
alcista *adj* bullish || *mf* (fig) bull
alcoba *f* bedroom; **alcoba de respeto** master bedroom
alcohol *m* alcohol
alcohóli•co -ca *adj & mf* alcoholic
alconafta *f* gasohol
alcor *m* hill, elevation, eminence
alcornoque *m* cork oak; blockhead
alcorque *m* cork-soled shoe; trench for water around a tree
alcorza *f* sugar paste, sugar icing; **ser una alcorza** (Arg) to be highly emotional
alcurnia *f* ancestry, lineage
alcuza *f* olive-oil can
aldaba *f* knocker, door knocker; bolt, crossbar; latch; hitching ring; **aldaba dormida** deadlatch; **tener buenas aldabas** to have pull
aldabonazo *m* knock on the door
aldea *f* village, hamlet
aldea•no -na *adj* village; rustic || *mf* villager
aleación *f* alloy
alear *tr* to alloy || *intr* to flap the wings; to flap one's arms; to convalesce
aleccionar *tr* to teach, instruct; to train, to coach
aleda•ño -ña *adj* bordering || *m* border, boundary
alega•dor -dora *adj* quarrelsome; litigious
alegar **§44** *tr* to allege; to declare, assert || *intr* (Col, Hond) to quarrel
alegoría *f* allegory
alegóri•co -ca *adj* allegoric(al)
alegrar *tr* to cheer, gladden; (*un fuego*) to stir || *ref* to be glad, to rejoice; to get tipsy
alegre *adj* glad; bright; cheerful, lighthearted; careless; fast, spicy; **alegre de cascos** scatterbrained
alegría *f* cheer, joy, gladness; brightness, gaiety
aleja•do -da *adj* distant, remote
alejandri•no -na *adj & mf* Alexandrine
alejar *tr & ref* to move aside, move away
alelar *tr* to make stupid || *ref* to grow stupid
aleluya *m & f* hallelujah || *m* Easter time || *f* doggerel; daub; **aleluya navideña** Christmas card || *interj* hallelujah!
ale•mán -mana *adj & mf* German
Alemania *f* Germany
alenta•do -da *adj* brave, spirited; proud, haughty; well, healthy || *f* deep breath
alentar **§2** *tr* to encourage, cheer up || *intr* to breathe || *ref* to take heart; get well, recover
alerce *m* larch
alergia *f* allergy
alero *m* eaves
alerón *m* aileron
alerta *adv* on the alert || *interj* watch out!, look out! || *m* (mil) alert; (mil) watchword
alertar *tr* to alert
aler•to -ta *adj* alert, watchful, vigilant
alesaje *m* bore
alesna *f* awl
aleta *f* small wing; (*de pez*) fin; (*de hélice*) blade; **aletas** (*natación*) flippers
aletargar **§44** *tr* to benumb; put to sleep || *ref* to get drowsy, fall asleep

aletear *intr* to flap the wings; flap, flip, flutter
aleve *adj* treacherous, perfidious
alevosía *f* treachery, perfidy
alevo•so -sa *adj* treacherous, perfidious
alfabetizar **§60** *tr* to alphabetize; teach reading and writing to
alfabeto *m* alphabet
alfaneque *m* buzzard
alfanje *m* cutlass
alfarería *f* pottery
alfarero *m* potter
alféizar *m* splay; embrasure
alfeñicar **§73** *tr* to candy, ice || *ref* to grow thin; be affected, finical
alfeñique *m* almond-flavored sugar paste; affectation, prudery; thin, delicate person; weakling
alfé•rez *m* (*pl* **-reces**) (mil) second lieutenant; (mil) subaltern (Brit); **alférez de fragata** (nav) ensign; **alférez de navío** (nav) lieutenant (j.g.)
alfil *m* bishop
alfiler *m* pin; **alfiler de corbata** stickpin, scarfpin; **alfiler de madera** clothespin; **alfiler de seguridad** safety pin; **alfileres** pin money
alfilerar *tr* to pin, pin up
alfiletero *m* pincase, needlecase
alfombra *f* carpet; rug
alfombrar *tr* to carpet
alforfón *m* buckwheat
alforja *f* shoulder bag; traveling supplies; **pasarse a la otra alforja** to go too far, take too much liberty
alforza *f* pleat, tuck
al•foz *m* (*pl* **-foces**) outskirts; dependence; mountain pass
alga *f* alga; **alga marina** seaweed; **algas** algae
algaida *f* brush, thicket; sandbank
algalia *f* civet; catheter
algarabía *f* Arabic; (coll) gibberish, jabber; (coll) hubbub, uproar
algarada *f* outcry; uproar
algarroba *f* carob bean
algarrobo *m* carob
algazara *f* Moorish battle cry; din, uproar
álgebra *f* algebra
algebrai•co -ca *adj* algebraic
álgi•do -da *adj* cold, icy, frigid
algo *pron indef* something; anything; **algo por el estilo** something of the sort || *adv* somewhat, a little, rather
algodón *m* cotton; **algodón pólvora** guncotton; **estar criado entre algodones** to be brought up in comfort
algodoncillo *m* milkweed
algodono•so -sa *adj* cottony
alguacil *m* bailiff; mounted police officer at the head of the processional entrance of the bullfighters
alguien *pron indef* somebody, someone
algún *adj indef* apocopated form of **alguno,** used only before masculine singular nouns and adjectives
algu•no -na *adj indef* some, any; not any; **alguna vez** sometimes; ever || *pron indef* someone; **algunos** some
alhaja *f* jewel, gem; **buena alhaja** a bad egg, a sly fellow
alhajera *f* or **alhajero** *m* jewelry box
alharaca *f* fuss, ado, ballyhoo; **hacer alharacas** to make a fuss
alharaquien•to -ta *adj* fussy, noisy
alhe•lí *m* (*pl* **-líes**) gillyflower (*Matthiola incana*); wallflower (*Cheiranthus*)
alheña *f* henna; blight, mildew
alheñar *tr* to henna; blight, mildew || *ref* (*el pelo*) to henna
alhucema *f* lavender
alhumajo *m* pine needles
alia•do -da *adj* allied || *mf* ally
aliaga *f* furze, gorse
alianza *f* alliance; wedding ring; (Bib) covenant
aliar **§77** *tr* to ally || *ref* to ally, become allied; form an alliance
alias *adj & m* alias
alicaí•do -da *adj* failing, weak; crestfallen, discouraged
alicates *mpl* pliers
aliciente *m* inducement, incentive
alienar *tr* to alienate; enrapture
aliento *m* breath, breathing; courage, spirit; **dar aliento a** to encourage; **de mucho aliento** arduous, difficult, endless; **nuevo aliento** second wind; **sin aliento** out of breath
alifafe *m* complaint, indisposition
aligerar *tr* to lighten; alleviate, ease; hasten; shorten
aligustre *m* privet
alijador *m* lighter; lighterman; sander
alijar *tr* to unload, lighten; sandpaper
aligeramiento *m* easing; alleviation; **aligeramiento de impuestos** tax relief
alimaña *f* varmint, small predacious animal
alimentante *mf* person obliged to provide child support
alimentar *tr* to feed, nourish; (*p.ej., esperanzas*) to cherish, foster || *ref* to feed, nourish oneself
alimenti•cio -cia *adj* alimentary, nourishing
alimento *m* food, nourishment; encouragement; **alimentos** foodstuffs; allowance; alimony
alindar *tr* to mark off; embellish, prettify || *intr* to border, be contiguous
alinea•do -da *adj* lined up, aligned; **no alineado** nonaligned, Third World
alinear *tr & ref* to align, line up
aliñar *tr* to dress, season
aliño *m* dressing, seasoning
aliquebra•do -da *adj* crestfallen
alisar *tr* to smooth; polish, sleek; iron lightly
aliso *m* alder tree
alistar *tr* to list; enlist, enroll; stripe || *ref* to enlist, enroll; get ready
aliteración *f* alliteration
aliviar *tr* to alleviate, relieve, soothe; remedy; lighten; hasten || *ref* to get better, recover

alivio *m* alleviation, relief; remedy
aljaba *f* quiver
aljama *f* mosque; synagogue; Moorish quarter; ghetto
aljamía *f* Spanish of Moors and Jews; Spanish written in Arabic characters
aljez *m* gypsum
aljibe *m* water tender, tank barge; oil tanker; cistern
aljófar *m* imperfect pearl; (fig) dewdrops
aljofifa *f* floor mop
aljofifar *tr* to mop
alma *f* soul, heart, spirit; (*persona*) living soul; crux, heart; sweetheart; (*de carril*) web; (*de cañón*) bore; (*de escalera*) newel; **dar el alma, entregar el alma, rendir el alma** to give up the ghost
almacén *m* warehouse; store, department store; storehouse; (phot) magazine
almacenaje *m* storage; **almacenaje de datos** (*ordenador*) data storage, memory
almacenamiento *m* storage; (*ordenador*) data storage, memory
almacenar *tr* to store; store up, hoard; to store (electronic) data
almacenista *mf* storekeeper || *m* warehouseman
almáciga *f* seedbed, tree nursery
almádana *f* spalling hammer
almagre *m* red ocher
almajara *f* (hort) hotbed
almanaque *m* almanac; calendar
almeja *f* clam
almena *f* merlon
almenaje *m* battlement
almendra *f* almond; (*de cualquier fruto drupáceo*) kernel; **almendra amarga** bitter almond; **almendra de Málaga** Jordan almond; **almendra tostada** burnt almond
almendrado *m* macaroon
almendro *m* almond tree
almiar *m* haystack, hayrick
almíbar *m* simple syrup; fruit juice; **estar hecho un almíbar** to be as sweet as pie
almibarar *tr* to preserve in syrup; (*sus palabras*) honey || *intr* to candy
almidón *m* starch; paste; **almidón de maíz** cornstarch
almidona•do -da *adj* starched; spruce, dapper; stiff, prim
almidonar *tr* to starch
alminar *m* minaret
almiranta *f* admiral's wife; flagship
almirante *m* admiral
almi•rez *m* (*pl* **-reces**) brass mortar
almizcle *m* musk
almizclera *f* muskrat
almizclero *m* musk deer
almohada *f* pillow; **consultar con la almohada** to sleep it over
almohadilla *f* cushion; pad; (Chile) pincushion
almohaza *f* currycomb
almohazar **§60** *tr* to currycomb
almoneda *f* auction; clearance sale
almonedar *tr* to auction
almorranas *fpl* piles, hemorrhoids
almorta *f* grass pea
almorzada *f* double handful, heavy breakfast
almorzar **§35** *tr* to lunch on || *intr* to lunch, have lunch
almuecín *m* or **almuédano** *m* muezzin
almuerzo *m* lunch
alna•do -da *mf* stepchild
aloca•do -da *adj* mad, wild, reckless || *mf* madcap
alocar **§73** *tr* to drive crazy
alocución *f* address, speech
áloe *m* or **aloe** *m* aloe; aloes
alojar *tr* to lodge; quarter, billet || *intr & ref* to lodge; be quartered or billeted
alojo *m* accommodations, lodging
alondra *f* lark
aloquecer **§22** *ref* to go crazy, lose one's mind
alosa *f* shad
alpaca *f* alpaca; alpaca wool; alpaca cloth; German silver
alpargata *f* hemp sandal, espadrille
alpende *m* tool shed; lean-to, penthouse
Alpes *mpl* Alps
alpestre *adj* alpine
alpinismo *m* mountain climbing
alpi•no -na *adj* alpine
alpiste *m* canary seed, birdseed; **quedarse alpiste** to be disappointed
alquería *f* farmhouse
alquibla *f* kiblah
alquiladi•zo -za *adj & mf* hireling
alquilar *tr* to rent, let, hire || *ref* to hire out; be for rent
alquiler *m* rent, rental, hire; **alquiler de coches** car-rental service; **alquiler sin chófer** drive-yourself service; **de alquiler** for rent, for hire
alquilona *f* cleaning woman, charwoman
alquimia *f* alchemy
alquitarar *tr* to distill
alquitrán *m* tar; **alquitrán de hulla** coal tar
alquitranado *m* tarpaulin
alquitranar *tr* to tar
alrededor *adv* around; **alrededor de** around; about, approximately || **alrededores** *mpl* environs, surroundings, outskirts
Alsacia *f* Alsace
alsacia•no -na *adj & mf* Alsatian
alta *f* discharge from hospital; (mil) certificate of induction into active service; **dar de alta** to discharge from the hospital; **darse de alta** to join, be admitted; (mil) to report for duty
altane•ro -ra *adj* towering; arrogant, haughty
altar *m* altar; **altar mayor** high altar; **conducir al altar** to lead to the altar
alta•voz *m* (*pl* **-voces**) loudspeaker
altea *f* (bot) marshmallow
alteración *f* alteration; disturbance; uneven pulse; altercation, quarrel
alterar *tr* to alter; disturb; agitate, upset; falsify; lessen || *ref* to alter; be disturbed; be agitated; lessen; (*el pulso*) flutter
altercación *f* or **altercado** *m* argument, wrangle, bickering
altercar **§73** *intr* to argue, bicker, wrangle

alternar *tr & intr* to alternate; **alternar con** to go around with

alternati•vo -va *adj* alternating, alternative; *f* choice, option; admission as a matador; **no tener alternativa** to have no choice

alter•no -na *adj* alternate

alteza *f* sublimity ‖ **Alteza** *f* (*tratamiento*) Highness

altibajo *m* downward thrust; **altibajos** uneven ground; ups and downs

altillo *m* hillock; (*oficina en una tienda o taller*) balcony; (Arg, Ecuad) attic, garret

altimetría *f* altimetry

altiplanicie *f* tableland

altitud *f* altitude; height

altivez *f* or **altiveza** *f* arrogance, haughtiness, pride

alti•vo -va *adj* haughty, proud; high, lofty

al•to -ta *adj* high; upper; top; loud; (*horas*) late; **ponerse tan alto** to take offense, be hoity-toity ‖ *m* height, altitude; story, floor; stop, halt; **de alto a bajo** from top to bottom; **hacer alto** to stop; **pasar por alto** to overlook, disregard ‖ *f* see **alta** ‖ **alto** *adv* high up; loud; aloud ‖ **alto** *interj* halt!

altoparlante *m* loudspeaker

altozanero *m* (Col) public errand boy

altozano *m* hill, knoll; upper part of town; (CAm, Col, Ven) parvis

altruísta *adj* altruistic ‖ *mf* altruist

altura *f* height, altitude; high seas; juncture, point, stage; (mus) pitch; (naut) latitude; **a estas alturas** at this juncture; **a la altura de** (naut) off; **estar a la altura de** to be up to, be equal to; be abreast of; **por estas alturas** around here

alucinación *f* hallucination

alucinante *adj* hallucinogenic

alud *m* avalanche

aludi•do -da *adj* above-mentioned

aludir *intr* to allude

alumbra•do -da *adj* lighted; enlightened; tipsy ‖ *m* lighting; lighting system

alumbramiento *m* lighting; childbirth, accouchement

alumbrar *tr* to light, illuminate; (*a los ciegos*) give sight to; enlighten; (*aguas subterráneas*) discover and bring to the surface ‖ *intr* to have a child ‖ *ref* to get tipsy

alumbre *m* alum

aluminio *m* aluminum

alumnado *m* student body

alum•no -na *mf* (*niño criado como si fuera hijo*) foster child; (*discípulo*) pupil, student; **alumno mimado** teacher's pet

alunizaje *m* lunar landing

alunizar §60 *intr* to land on the moon

alusión *f* allusion

álveo *m* bed of a stream, river bed

alvéolo *m* alveolus; (*de diente*) socket; (*de rueda de agua*) bucket

alza *f* rise, advance, increase; **jugar al alza** to bull the market

alzada *f* height (*e.g., of a horse*)

alza•do -da *adj* (SAm) insolent; rebellious; *m* lump sum, cash settlement; front elevation; (bb) quire, gathering

alzapaño *m* curtain holder; tieback

alzapié *m* snare, trap

alzaprima *f* crowbar, lever; (*de instrumento de arco*) (mus) bridge

alzaprimar *tr* to pry, pry up; arouse, stir up

alzapuer•tas *m* (*pl* **-tas**) (archaic) dumb player, supernumerary

alzar §60 *tr* to raise, lift, hoist; pick up; (*la hostia*) elevate; hide, lock up; (*naipes*) cut; (bb) to gather ‖ *ref* to rise, get up; revolt; **alzarse con** to abscond with

alzaválvu•las *m* (*pl* **-las**) tappet

alzo *m* (CAm) theft

allá *adv* there, over there; back there; **allá en** over in; back in; **el más allá** the beyond; **más allá** farther on, farther away; **más allá de** beyond; **por allá** thereabouts; that way

allanar *tr* to level, smooth, flatten; (*una dificultad*) iron out, overcome, get around; (*una casa*) break into; to subdue ‖ *intr* to level off ‖ *ref* to tumble down; yield, submit; humble oneself

allega•do -da *adj* near, close; related; partisan ‖ *mf* relative; partisan

allegar §44 *tr* to collect, gather; reap ‖ *intr* to approach ‖ *ref* to approach; be attached, be a follower, agree

allende *adv* beyond; **allende de** besides, in addition to ‖ *prep* beyond

allí *adv* there; **allí dentro** in there; **por allí** that way; around there

ama *f* housekeeper; housewife, lady of the house; landlady, proprietress; **ama de casa** housewife; **ama de cría** or **de leche** wet nurse; **ama de llaves** housekeeper; **ama seca** dry nurse

amable *adj* amiable, kind, obliging; (*digno de ser amado*) lovable

amachinar *ref* to cohabit; get intimate

ama•do -da *adj & mf* beloved

ama•dor -dora *adj* fond, loving ‖ *mf* lover

amadrigar §44 *tr* to welcome, receive with open arms ‖ *ref* to burrow; go into seclusion

amaestrar *tr* to teach, coach; (*a los animales*) train

amagar §44 *tr* to show signs of, threaten; feint ‖ *intr* to look threatening

amago *m* threat, menace; sign, indication; feint

amainar *tr* to lessen; (naut) to lower, shorten ‖ *intr* to subside, die down; lessen; yield ‖ *ref* to lessen; yield

amalgama *f* amalgam

amalgamar *tr & ref* to amalgamate

amamantar *tr* to nurse, to suckle

amancebamiento *m* cohabitation, concubinage, liaison

amancebar *ref* to cohabit, live in concubinage

amancillar *tr* to stain, spot; sully, tarnish

amanecer *m* dawn, daybreak ‖ *v* §22 *intr* to dawn, begin to get light; begin to appear; get awake, start the day

amanecida *f* dawn, daybreak
amanera•do -da *adj* mannered, affected
amansar *tr* (*animal*) to tame; (*caballo*) break; soothe, appease
amante *adj* fond, loving || *mf* lover
amaño *m* skill, cleverness, dexterity; trick; **amaños** tools, implements
amapola *f* poppy
amar *tr* to love
amaraje *m* alighting on water
amarar *intr* to alight on water
amargar §44 *tr* to make bitter; embitter; (*una tertulia, una velada*) spoil || *intr & ref* to become bitter; become embittered
amar•go -ga *adj* bitter; sour; distressing || **amargos** *mpl* bitters
amargura *f* bitterness; sorrow, grief
amarillear *intr* to turn yellow, show yellow
amarillecer §22 *intr* to become yellow
amarillen•to -ta *adj* yellowish
amarillez *f* yellowness
amari•llo -lla *adj & m* yellow
amarra *f* mooring cable; **amarras** support, protection; **soltar las amarras** (naut) to cast off
amarrar *tr* to moor; lash, tie up; (*las cartas*) stack
amartelar *tr* to make love to; make jealous || *ref* to fall in love; become jealous
amartillar *tr* to hammer; (*un arma de fuego*) to cock
amasar *tr* to knead; mix; massage; (*dinero*) amass; concoct
amatista *f* amethyst
Amazonas *m* Amazon
ambages *mpl* ambiguity, quibbling; **sin ambages** straight to the point
ámbar *m* amber
Amberes *f* Antwerp
ambición *f* ambition
ambicionar *tr* to strive for, be eager for
ambicio•so -sa *adj* ambitious; eager; **ambicioso de figurar** social climber
ambiental *adj* environmental
ambiente *m* atmosphere; **medio ambiente** environment; situation
ambi•gú *m* (*pl* **-gúes**) buffet supper; bar, refreshment bar
ambigüedad *f* ambiguity
ambi•guo -gua *adj* ambiguous; (*género*) (gram) common
ámbito *m* boundary, limit; compass, scope
ambladura *f* amble
amblar *intr* to amble
am•bos -bas *adj & pron indef* both; **ambos a dos** both, both together
ambrosía *f* ragweed
ambulancia *f* ambulance; **ambulancia de correos** mail car, railway post office
ambulante *adj* itinerant, traveling || *m* railway mail clerk
ambulato•rio -ria *adj* ambulatory || *m* welfare center, public clinic; ambulance
amedrentar *tr* to frighten, scare
amelona•do -da *adj* melon-shaped; mentally retarded; lovesick
amén *interj* amen! || *m* amen || *adv* — **amén de** aside from; in addition to
amenaza *f* threat, menace
amenazar §60 *tr* to threaten, menace
amenguar §10 *tr* to lessen, diminish; belittle; dishonor
amenidad *f* amenity
amenizar §60 *tr* to make pleasant, brighten, cheer
ame•no -na *adj* agreeable, pleasant
amento *m* catkin
América *f* America; **la América Central** Central America; **la América del Norte** North America; **la América del Sur** South America; **la América Latina** Latin America
americana *f* sack coat, jacket
americanizar §60 *tr* to Americanize
america•no -na *adj & mf* American; Spanish American || *f* see **americana**
amerizar §60 *intr* to alight on water
ametralladora *f* machine gun
ametrallar *tr* to machine-gun
amiba *f* amoeba
amiga *f* friend; mistress; schoolmistress; girls' school
amigable *adj* amicable, friendly
amigacho *m* chum, crony, pal
amígdala *f* tonsil
amigdalitis *f* tonsillitis
ami•go -ga *adj* friendly; fond || *mf* friend; sweetheart; **amigo del alma** bosom friend || *f* see **amiga**
amigote *m* chum, crony, pal
amilanar *tr* to terrify, intimidate
aminorar *tr* to lessen, diminish
amistad *f* friendship; liaison; **hacer las amistades** to make up; **romper las amistades** to fall out, become enemies
amistar *tr* to bring together || *ref* to become friends
amisto•so -sa *adj* friendly
amniocentesis *f* amniocentesis
amnistía *f* amnesty
amnistiar §77 *tr* to amnesty, grant amnesty to
amo *m* head of family; landlord, proprietor; boss; **ser el amo del cotarro** to rule the roost
amoblar §61 *tr* to furnish
amodorrar *ref* to get drowsy; fall asleep; grow numb
amohinar *tr* to annoy, irritate, vex
amojonar *tr* to mark off with landmarks
amoladera *f* grindstone, whetstone
amolar §61 *tr* to grind, sharpen; bore, annoy
amoldar *tr* to mold; model, pattern, fashion; adjust, adapt
amonestación *f* admonition; marriage banns
amonestar *tr* to admonish, warn; publish the banns of
amoníaco *m* ammonia
amontonar *tr* to heap, pile; accumulate; hoard || *ref* to collect, gather; crowd; get angry; (Mex) to gang up
amor *m* love; **al amor del agua** with the current; obligingly; **al amor de la lumbre**

by the fire, in the warmth of the fire; **amores** love affair; **amor propio** amour-propre; conceit; **por amor de** for the sake of
amorata•do -da *adj* livid, black-and-blue
amordazar §**60** *tr* to muzzle; gag
amorío *m* love-making; love affair
amoro•so -sa *adj* loving, affectionate, amorous
amortajar *tr* to shroud; (carp) to mortise
amortecer §**22** *tr* to deaden, muffle ‖ *ref* to die away, become faint
amortiguador *m* shock absorber; door check; (*de automóvil*) bumper; **amortiguador de luz** dimmer; **amortiguador de ruido** muffler
amortiguar §**10** *tr* to deaden, muffle; soften, tone down; dim; damp; (*un golpe*) cushion; (*ondas electromagnéticas*) damp
amortizar §**60** *tr* to amortize; (*una deuda*) pay off
amoscar §**73** *ref* to get peeved; (Mex) to blush, be embarrassed
amotina•do -da *adj* mutinous, rebellious ‖ *mf* mutineer, rebel, rioter
amotinar *tr* to stir up; incite to mutiny ‖ *ref* to rise up, mutiny, rebel
amover §**47** *tr* to discharge, dismiss
amovible *adj* removable, detachable
amparar *tr* to shelter, protect ‖ *ref* to seek shelter; protect oneself
amparo *m* shelter, protection, refuge; stall; aid, favor
amperio *m* ampere
amperio-hora *m* (*pl* **amperios-hora**) ampere-hour
ampliación *f* amplification; (phot) enlargement
ampliar §**77** *tr* to amplify, enlarge; widen; (phot) to enlarge
amplificador *m* amplifier
amplificar §**73** *tr* to amplify; expand, enlarge; magnify
am•plio -plia *adj* ample; spacious, roomy
amplitud *f* amplitude; roominess
ampo *m* dazzling white; snowflake
ampolla *f* blister; bubble; cruet; bulb, light bulb
ampollar *tr* & *ref* to blister
ampolleta *f* vial; sandglass, hourglass; bulb, light bulb; cruet
ampulosidad *f* bombast, pomposity
ampulo•so -sa *adj* bombastic, pompous
amputar *tr* to amputate
amueblar *tr* to furnish
amujera•do -da *adj* effeminate
amuleto *m* amulet, charm
amurallar *tr* to wall, wall in
amurcar §**73** *tr* to gore
amusgar §**44** *tr* (*las orejas el toro, el caballo*) to throw back
anacardo *m* cashew; cashew nut
anacróni•co -ca *adj* anachronistic
anacronismo *m* anachronism
ánade *mf* duck
anadear *intr* to waddle
anadeo *m* waddle, waddling
anales *mpl* annals
analfabetismo *m* illiteracy
analfabe•to -ta *adj* & *mf* illiterate
analgési•co -ca *adj* analgesic ‖ *m* painkiller, analgesic
análi•sis *m* & *f* (*pl* **-sis**) analysis; **análisis costobeneficio** cost-benefit analysis; **análisis de sistemas** systems analysis; **análisis gramatical** parsing; **análisis ocupacional** job analysis
analista *mf* analyst; annalist
analíti•co -ca *adj* analytic(al)
analizar §**60** *tr* to analyze; **analizar gramaticalmente** to parse
analogía *f* analogy; similarity
análo•go -ga *adj* analogous; similar
ana•ná *m* (*pl* **-naes**) pineapple
ananás *m* pineapple
anaquel *m* shelf
anaranja•do -da *adj* & *m* (*color*) orange
anarquía *f* anarchy
anárqui•co -ca *adj* anarchic(al)
anarquista *mf* anarch, anarchist
anatema *m* & *f* anathema; curse
anatomía *f* anatomy
anatómi•co -ca *adj* anatomic(al) ‖ *mf* anatomist
anatomista *mf* anatomist
anca *f* croup, haunch; buttock, rump; **a ancas** or **a las ancas** mounted behind another person; **anca de rana** frog's leg; **dar ancas vueltas** (Mex) to give odds
ancianidad *f* old age
ancia•no -na *adj* old, aged ‖ *m* old man; (eccl) elder ‖ *f* old woman
ancla *f* anchor; **echar anclas** to cast anchor; **levar anclas** to weigh anchor
anclar *intr* to anchor
anclote *m* kedge, kedge anchor
ancón *m* bay, cove
áncora *f* anchor
ancorar *intr* to anchor
ancheta *f* (Arg) foolishness; ridiculous act
an•cho -cha *adj* wide, broad; full, ample; loose, loose-fitting ‖ *m* width, breadth
anchoa *f* anchovy
anchura *f* width, breadth; fullness, ampleness; looseness; comfort, ease
anchuro•so -sa *adj* wide, broad; spacious, roomy
andada *f* thin, hard-baked cracker; **andadas** (*de conejos y otros animales*) tracks; **volver a las andadas** to revert to one's old tricks
andaderas *fpl* gocart, walker
anda•do -da *adj* gone by, elapsed; frequented, trodden; worn, used; ordinary ‖ *m* gait ‖ *f* see **andada**
andadores *mpl* leading strings
andadura *f* pace, gait; amble; (Mex) mount
Andalucía *f* Andalusia
anda•luz -luza *adj* & *mf* Andalusian
andaluzada *f* tall story, exaggeration, fish story
andamiaje *m* scaffolding
andamio *m* scaffold; platform

andanada *f* (naut) broadside; (taur) covered upper section; (coll) scolding; (fig) fusillade
andante *adj* walking; errant, wandering
andanza *f* wandering, rambling; fate, fortune
andar *m* gait, pace, walk || §5 *tr* (*p.ej., dos millas*) to go; (*un camino*) go down or up || *intr* to go, walk; run; travel; act, behave; (*p.ej., un reloj*) go, run, work; be, feel; go by, pass, elapse; go (*to bear up, to last*), e.g., **anduve diez horas sin comer** I went ten hours without eating || *ref* to go by, to pass, to elapse; to go away; **andarse sin** to go without
andarie•go -ga *adj* wandering, roving; swift, fleet
andas *fpl* litter; stretcher; bier
andén *m* railway platform; quay; footpath
Andes *mpl* Andes
andinismo *m* mountain climbing in the Andes
andi•no -na *adj* Andean
andraje•ro -ra *mf* ragpicker
andrajo *m* rag, tatter; ragamuffin, scalawag
andrajo•so -sa *adj* ragged, raggedy, in tatters
andurriales *mpl* byways, out-of-the-way place
anea *f* cattail, bulrush
aneblar §2 *tr* to cloud; becloud || *ref* to become clouded; get dark
anécdota *f* anecdote
anegar §44 *tr* to flood; drown || *ref* to become flooded; drown
ane•jo -ja *adj* annexed; accessory || *m* annex; dependency; supplement
anemia *f* anaemia
anémi•co -ca *adj* anaemic
anestesia *f* anaesthesia
anestesiar *tr* anaesthetize
anestési•co -ca *adj & m* anaesthetic
aneurisma *m & f* aneurysm
anexar *tr* to annex
ane•xo -xa *adj* annexed; accessory || *m* annex; dependency
anfi•bio -bia *adj* amphibious
anfiteatro *m* amphitheater
anfitrión *m* host
anfitriona *f* hostess
ánfora *f* voting urn, ballot box
anfractuo•so -sa *adj* winding, tortuous
angarillas *fpl* handbarrow; panniers; cruet stand
ángel *m* angel; **ángel custodio** or **de la guarda** guardian angel; **ángel patudo** wolf in sheep's clothing; **tener ángel** to have great charm
angelical or **angéli•co -ca** *adj* angelic(al)
angina *f* angina; **angina de pecho** angina pectoris
angloparlante *adj* English-speaking || *mf* speaker of English
anglosa•jón -jona *adj & mf* Anglo-Saxon
angos•to -ta *adj* narrow
anguila *f* eel; **anguilas** (*para botar un barco al agua*) ways; **escurrirse como una anguila** to be as slippery as an eel
angular *adj* angular
ángulo *m* angle; corner
angulo•so -sa *adj* (*facciones*) angular
angurria *f* (SAm) raging hunger; greed
angustia *f* anguish, distress, grief
angustia•do -da *adj* distressed, grieved
angustiar *tr* to distress, afflict, grieve
angustio•so -sa *adj* distressed, grieved; worrisome
anhelar *tr* to crave, want badly || *intr* to pant; yearn; **anhelar por** to long for
anhélito *m* hard breathing
anhelo *m* craving; yearning, longing
anhelo•so -sa *adj* eager, yearning; breathless, panting
anhi•dro -dra *adj* anhydrous
Aníbal *m* Hannibal
anidar *tr* to harbor, shelter || *intr & ref* to nestle, make a nest; live
anilina *f* aniline
anilla *f* curtain ring; (*en la gimnasia*) ring; hoop
anillo *m* ring; cigar band; **anillo de compromiso** or **de pedida** engagement ring; **anillo sigilar** signet ring
ánima *f* soul; (*de arma de fuego*) bore
animación *f* animation; liveliness; bustle, movement
anima•do -da *adj* animated, lively
animador *m* (*de un café-cantante*) master of ceremonies
animal *adj & m* animal
animar *tr* to enliven; encourage; strengthen; drive || *ref* to take heart, feel encouraged
ánimo *m* mind, spirit; courage, valor, energy; attention, thought
animosidad *f* animosity, ill will
animo•so -sa *adj* brave, courageous; spirited; ready, disposed
aniña•do -da *adj* babyish, childish
anión *m* anion
aniquilar *tr* to annihilate, destroy || *ref* to be annihilated; decline, waste away; be humbled
anís *m* anise; anise-flavored brandy
aniversa•rio -ria *adj & m* anniversary
anoche *adv* last night
anochecer *m* nightfall, dusk || *v* §22 *intr* to grow dark; arrive or happen at nightfall; end the day; go to sleep || *ref* to get dark; get cloudy; slip away
anochecida *f* nightfall, dusk
anodi•no -na *adj* innocuous, ineffective, harmless
ánodo *m* anode
anomalía *f* anomaly
anóma•lo -la *adj* anomalous
anonadar *tr* to annihilate, destroy; overwhelm; humble
anóni•mo -ma *adj* anonymous || *m* anonymity; **guardar** or **conservar el anónimo** to preserve one's anonymity
anorexia *f* anorexia
anormal *adj* abnormal
anotar *tr* to annotate; note, jot down; point out
anquilosa•do -da *adj* stiff-jointed; old-fashioned
ánsar *m* goose; wild goose

ansia *f* anxiety, anguish; eagerness; **ansias** (Ven) nausea
ansiar §77 & **regular** *tr* to long for, yearn for || *intr* to be madly in love
ansiedad *f* anxiety, worry; pain
ansio•so -sa *adj* anxious; anguished; longing; covetous
ant. *abbr* **anticuado**
anta *f* elk
antagonismo *m* antagonism
antaño *adv* last year; of yore, long ago
antárti•co -ca *adj* antarctic
ante *prep* before, in the presence of; in front of; at, with || *m* elk; buff
antea•do -da *adj* buff; (Mex) damaged, shopworn
anteanoche *adv* the night before last
anteayer *adv* the day before yesterday
antebrazo *m* forearm
antecámara *f* antechamber, anteroom
antecedente *adj* antecedent || *m* antecedent; **antecedentes** antecedents
anteceder *tr* to precede, go before
antece•sor -sora *mf* predecessor; ancestor
antedatar *tr* to antedate
antedi•cho -cha *adj* aforesaid, abovementioned
antelación *f* previousness, anticipation
antemano — **de antemano** in advance, beforehand
antena *f* (ent) antenna; (rad) antenna, aerial; **antena de conejo** rabbit ears; **en antena** on the air; **antena interior incorporada** built-in antenna; **llevar a las antenas** to put on the air
antenombre *m* title, honorific
anteojera *f* spectacle case; blinker, blinder
anteojo *m* eyeglass; spyglass; **anteojos** eyeglasses, spectacles; binoculars; blinkers
antepasa•do -da *adj* before last || **antepasados** *mpl* ancestors
antepecho *m* railing, guardrail; parapet; window sill
antepenúltima *f* antepenult
anteponer §54 *tr* to place in front; prefer
anteportada *f* half title, bastard title
anteportal *m* porch, vestibule
antepuerta *f* portière
antepuerto *m* entrance to a mountain pass; (naut) outer harbor
anterior *adj* front; previous; earlier
antes *adv* before; sooner, soonest; rather; previously; **antes bien** rather; on the contrary; **antes de** before; **antes (de) que** before; **cuanto antes** as soon as possible
antesala *f* antechamber; (*p.ej., de médico*) waiting room; **hacer antesala** to dance attendance
antiaére•o -a *adj* antiaircraft
antiartísti•co -ca *adj* inartistic
antibéli•co -ca *adj* antiwar
anticartel *adj* antitrust
anticientífi•co -ca *adj* unscientific
anticipación *f* preparation, anticipation; **con anticipación** in advance
anticipa•do -da *adj* future; advance; **por anticipado** in advance
anticipar *tr* to anticipate, hasten; to move ahead || *ref* to happen early; **anticiparse a** to anticipate, to get ahead of
anticipo *m* anticipation; advance payment, down payment; retaining fee
anticoncepti•vo -va *adj & m* contraceptive
anticongelante *m* antifreeze
anticonstitucional *adj* unconstitutional
anticua•do -da *adj* antiquated; old-fashioned; obsolete
anticua•rio -ria *adj* antiquarian || *mf* antiquarian, antiquary; antique dealer
anticuerpo *m* antibody
antideporti•vo -va *adj* unsportsmanlike
antiderrapante or **antideslizante** *adj* nonskid
antideslumbrante *adj* antiglare
antidetonante *adj & m* antiknock
antídoto *m* antidote
antieconómi•co -ca *adj* uneconomic(al)
antier *adv* the day before yesterday
antiesclavista *adj* antislavery || *mf* abolitionist
anti•faz *m* (*pl* **-faces**) veil, mask
antífona *f* anthem
antigás *adj invar* gas (*e.g., mask, shelter*)
antigramatical *adj* ungrammatical
antigravedad *f* weightlessness
antigualla *f* antique; relic, antique; has-been
antiguar §10 *intr & ref* to attain seniority
antigüedad *f* antiquity; seniority; (*mueble u otro objeto de arte antiguos*) antique; **antigüedades** antiquities; antiques
anti•guo -gua *adj* old; ancient; antique; former || *mf* veteran; senior
antihigiéni•co -ca *adj* unsanitary
antílope *m* antelope
antilla•no -na *adj & mf* West Indian
Antillas *fpl* Antilles
antimateria *f* antimatter
antimonio *m* antimony
antiobre•ro -ra *adj* antilabor
antiparras *spl* spectacles
antipatía *f* dislike, antipathy
antipáti•co -ca *adj* disagreeable, uncongenial
antipatrióti•co -ca *adj* unpatriotic
antiproyectil *adj* antimissile
antirreflejo *adj invar* nonreflecting
antirresbaladi•zo -za *adj* nonskid
antirrobo *adj invar* theft-proof, burglar-proof
antisemíti•co -ca *adj* anti-Semitic
antisépti•co -ca *adj & m* antiseptic
antisono•ro -ra *adj* soundproof
antisoviéti•co -ca *adj* anti-Soviet
antitanque *adj* antitank
antiterrorista *adj invar & mf* antiterrorist
antíte•sis *f* (*pl* **-sis**) antithesis
antitóxi•co -ca *adj* antitoxic
antitoxina *f* antitoxin
antojadi•zo -za *adj* capricious, whimsical
antojar *ref* to seem; fancy; seem likely; have a notion to + *inf;* take a fancy to + *inf*
antojo *m* caprice, fancy, whim; snap judgment; birthmark; **antojos** moles, warts; **a su antojo** as one pleases
antología *f* anthology
antónimo *m* antonym

antorcha *f* torch; **antorcha a soplete** blowtorch
antracita *f* anthracite
ántrax *m* anthrax
antro *m* cave, cavern; (fig) den
antropología *f* anthropology
antruejo *m* carnival
anual *adj* annual
anualidad *f* annuity; year's pay; annual occurrence
anuario *m* yearbook; directory; bulletin, catalogue; **anuario telefónico** telephone directory
anublar *tr* to cloud; dim, darken; blight, wither || *ref* to become cloudy; be withered; (*las esperanzas de uno*) fade away
anudar *tr* to tie, fasten, knot; unite; resume || *ref* to get knotted; be united; fade away, wilt, fail
anuente *adj* consenting
anular *tr* to annul; nullify; remove, discharge || *ref* to be passed over
anunciar *tr* to announce; advertise || *intr* to advertise
anunciante *mf* advertiser
anuncio *m* announcement; advertisement
anverso *m* obverse
anzuelo *m* fishhook; **picar en el anzuelo** or **tragar el anzuelo** to swallow the bait, swallow the hook
añadi•do -da *adj* additional || *m* false hair, switch
añadidura *f* addition; extra weight, extra measure; **de añadidura** extra, in the bargain; **por añadidura** besides
añadir *tr* to add; increase
añafil *m* straight Moorish trumpet
añagaza *f* bird call; decoy, lure; trap, trick
añe•jo -ja *adj* aged; stale; musty, rancid
añicos *mpl* bits, pieces; **hacer añicos** to tear to pieces, break to pieces; **hacerse añicos** to wear oneself out
añil *m* indigo; bluing
añilar *tr* to dye with indigo; (*la ropa blanca*) to blue
año *m* year; **año bisiesto** leap year; **año económico** fiscal year; **año lectivo** school year; **año luz** (*pl* **años luz**) light-year; **años** birthday; **cumplir . . . años** to be . . . years old
añoranza *f* longing, sorrow
añorar *tr* to long for, sorrow for; grieve over || *intr* to yearn; sorrow, grieve
año•so -sa *adj* aged, old
aojada *f* (Col) skylight; (Col) transom
aojar *tr* to cast the evil eye on, jinx
aojo *m* evil eye, jinx
aovar *intr* to lay eggs
ap. *abbr* **aparte, apóstol**
apabilar *tr* to trim
apabullar *tr* to mash, crush; squelch
apacentar §2 *tr & ref* to pasture, graze; feed
apacible *adj* gentle, mild; calm
apaciguamiento *m* pacification, appeasement
apaciguar §10 *tr* to pacify, appease || *ref* to calm down
apachurrar *tr* to crush, squash, mash
apadrinar *tr* to sponsor; act as godfather for; back, support; second
apagabron•cas *m* (*pl* **-cas**) bouncer
apagador *m* extinguisher; (*de piano*) damper
apagaincen•dios *m* (*pl* **-dios**) fire extinguisher
apagar §44 *tr* to extinguish, put out; (*la luz, la radio*) turn off; (*la cal*) slake; (*el sonido*) damp, muffle; (*el fuego del enemigo*) silence; (*la sed*) quench; (*el dolor*) deaden || *ref* to go out; subside, calm down, fade away
apagón *m* blackout
apalabrar *tr* to bespeak; consider || *ref* to agree
apalabrear *intr* (SAm) to make an appointment
apalancar §73 *tr* to raise with a lever or crowbar
apalear *tr* to shovel; beat; pile up
apandar *tr* to steal
apantallar *tr* to dazzle, amaze; (elec) to shield, screen
apañar *tr* to grasp; pick up; steal; repair, mend; wrap up || *ref* to be handy
apañuscar §73 *tr* to crumple, rumple; steal; (CAm, Col, Ven) to jam, crowd
aparador *m* sideboard, buffet; showcase; workshop; (Mex) show window, store window
aparar *tr* to prepare; adorn; block; (*las manos, la falda, el pañuelo, la capa*) hold out
aparato *m* apparatus; ostentation, show; exaggeration; radio set; television set; telephone; airplane; camera; bandage, application; (theat) scenery, properties; **aparato auditivo** hearing aid; **aparato de relojería** clockwork; **aparatos sanitarios** bathroom fixtures; **ponerse al aparato** to go or to come to the phone
aparato•so -sa *adj* showy, pompous, ostentatious
aparcamiento *m* parking; parking space; **aparcamiento subterraneo** underground garage
aparcar §44 *tr & intr* to park
aparcería *f* partnership, sharecropping
aparce•ro -ra *mf* partner, sharecropper; (Arg) customer
aparear *tr* to pair, match; mate || *ref* to pair; mate
aparecer §22 *intr & ref* to appear; show up
aparecido *m* ghost, specter
aparejador *m* builder
aparejar *tr* to prepare; prime, size; harness
aparejo *m* preparation; harness; set, kit; priming, sizing; (mas) bond; **aparejos** tools, implements, equipment
aparentar *tr* to feign, pretend; look, look to be
aparente *adj* apparent, seeming; evident; right, proper
aparición *f* apparition
apariencia *f* appearance, aspect; sign, indication; **salvar las apariencias** to save face
aparqueamiento *m* parking

aparquear *tr & intr* to park
aparqueo *m* parking
aparragar §44 *ref* to crouch, squat; (CAm) to loll, sprawl
apartadero *m* siding, side track; turnout
aparta•do -da *adj* distant, remote; aloof; (*camino*) side, back; different || *m* side room; post-office box; vocabulary entry; section
apartamento *m* apartment, apartment house
apartar *tr* to take aside; separate; push away; shunt; (*el ganado*) sort || *ref* to separate; move away, keep away, stand aside; withdraw; get divorced; give up
aparte *adv* apart, aside; **aparte de** apart from || *prep* apart from || *m* (theat) aside
apasiona•do -da *adj* passionate; devoted, tender, loving; sore
apasionar *tr* to impassion, appeal deeply to; afflict || *ref* to become impassioned; be stirred up; fall madly in love
apatía *f* apathy
apáti•co -ca *adj* apathetic
apatusco *m* ornament, finery
apdo. *abbr* **apartado**
apeadero *m* horse block; flag stop, wayside station; platform; temporary quarters
apear *tr* to help dismount, help down; bring down; remove; overcome; prop up || *ref* to dismount, get off; back down; stop, put up
apechugar §44 *intr* to push with the chest; **apechugar con** to make the best of
apedazar §60 *tr* to mend, patch; cut or tear to pieces
apedrear *tr* to stone; stone to death; pit; speckle || *intr* to hail || *ref* to be damaged by hail; be pitted
apegar §44 *ref* to become attached, grow fond
apego *m* attachment, fondness
apelación *f* medical consultation; remedy, help; (law) appeal
apelante *adj* appellate
apelar *intr* to appeal, make an appeal; have recourse; refer
apelativo *m* (CAm) surname, family name
apeldar *tr* — **apeldarlas** (coll) to flee, run away
apelmazar §60 *tr* to squeeze, compress || *ref* to cake
apelotonar *tr* to form into a ball || *ref* to form a ball; curl up
apellidar *tr* to call, name; proclaim
apellido *m* name; surname, last name, family name; **apellido de soltera** maiden name
apenar *tr & ref* to grieve
apenas *adv* hardly, scarcely; **apenas si** hardly, scarcely || *conj* no sooner, as soon as
apéndice *m* appendage; (anat) appendix
apendicitis *f* appendicitis
apercancar §73 *ref* (Chile) to get moldy, mildew
apercibir *tr* to prepare; provide; warn; perceive; collect || *ref* to get ready; be provided; **apercibirse de** to notice
apergaminar *ref* to dry up, become yellow and wrinkled
aperitivo *m* appetizer
aperla•do -da *adj* pearly
apero *m* tools, equipment, outfit; riding gear
aperrear *tr* to set the dogs on; harass, plague, pester
apersogar §44 *tr* to tether
apersona•do -da *adj* — **bien apersonado** presentable; **mal apersonado** unpresentable
apersonar *ref* to appear in person; have an interview
apertura *f* opening
apesadumbrar or **apesarar** *tr & ref* to grieve
apestar *tr* to infect with the plague; corrupt; sicken, nauseate; infest || *intr* to stink || *ref* to be infected with the plague
apesto•so -sa *adj* stinking, foul-smelling; pestilent; sickening
apetecer §22 *tr* to hunger for, thirst for, crave
apetecible *adj* desirable, tempting
apetencia *f* hunger, appetite, craving
apetito *m* appetite
apetito•so -sa *adj* tasty; tempting; gourmand
ápex *m* apex
apiadar *tr* to move to pity; take pity on || *ref* to have pity
ápice *m* apex; bit, whit; crux; **estar en los ápices de** to be up in
apilar *tr & ref* to pile, pile up
apimpollar *ref* to sprout, put forth shoots
apiñar *tr & ref* to crowd, jam
apio *m* celery
apisonadora *f* road roller
apisonar *tr* to tamp; roll
aplacar §73 *tr* to placate, appease, pacify; (*la sed*) to quench
aplanacalles *m* (SAm) idler; lazy person
aplanar *tr* to smooth, make even; to astonish; **aplanar las calles** to loaf, bum around || *ref* to collapse; become discouraged
aplanchar *tr* to iron
aplanetizar §60 *intr* to land on another planet
aplastar *tr* to flatten, crush, smash; dumbfound
aplaudida *f* applause
aplaudir *tr & intr* to applaud
aplauso *m* applause; **aplausos** applause
aplazada *f* or **aplazamiento** *m* delay; procrastination
aplazar §60 *tr* to postpone; convene; summon
aplicación *f* appliance, application; diligence
aplica•do -da *adj* industrious, studious; applied
aplicar §73 *tr* to apply; attribute || *ref* to apply; apply oneself
aplomar *tr* to plumb; make straight or vertical || *intr* to be vertical || *ref* to collapse; (Chile) to be embarrassed; (Mex) to be slow, be backward
aplomo *m* aplomb, poise, self-possession; gravity
apoca•do -da *adj* diffident, timid, irresolute; humble, lowly
apocar §73 *tr* to cramp, contract; narrow; humble, belittle

apodar *tr* to nickname; make fun of
apodera•do -da *adj* empowered, authorized || *m* proxy; attorney
apoderamiento *m* authorization; power of attorney
apoderar *tr* to empower, authorize || *ref*— **apoderarse de** to seize, grasp; take possession of
apodo *m* nickname
apofanía *f* ablaut
apogeo *m* apogee; (fig) height, apogee
apolilla•do -da *adj* moth-eaten, mothy
apolilladura *f* moth hole
apolillar *tr* (*la polilla, p.ej., las ropas*) to eat || *ref* to become moth-eaten
apoliti•co -ca *adj* apolitical, nonpolitical
apología *f* eulogy
apoltronar *ref* to loaf around; loll, sprawl
apontizaje *m* deck-landing
apontizar §60 *intr* to deck-land
apoplejía *f* apoplexy
apopléti•co -ca *adj & mf* apoplectic
aporcar §73 *tr* (*las hortalizas*) to hill
aporrear *tr* to beat, club, cudgel; annoy || *ref* to drudge, slave
aportación *f* contribution; dowry
aportar *tr* to contribute; bring; lead; (*como dote*) bring || *intr* to show up; reach port
aporte *m* contribution
aposentar *tr* to put up, lodge || *ref* to take lodging
aposento *m* lodging; room; inn
apostadero *m* stand, post; naval station
apostar *tr* to post, station || §61 *tr* to bet, wager || *intr* to bet; compete
apostilla *f* note, comment
apóstol *m* apostle
apóstrofe *m & f* apostrophe (*words addressed to absent person*)
apóstrofo *m* apostrophe (*written sign*)
apostura *f* neatness, spruceness; bearing, carriage
apoyabra•zos *m* (*pl* **-zos**) armrest
apoyali•bros *m* (*pl* **-bros**) book end
apoyar *tr* to support, hold up; lean, rest; abet, back || *intr & ref* to lean, rest, be supported
apoyatura *f* (mus) grace note
apoyo *m* support, prop; backing, approval
apreciable *adj* appreciable; estimable
apreciación *f* appraisal
apreciar *tr* to appreciate; appraise; esteem
aprecio *m* appreciation, esteem
aprehender *tr* to apprehend, catch; think, conceive
aprehensión *f* apprehension
aprehensi•vo -va *adj* apprehensive
aprehensor *m* captor
apremiar *tr* to press, urge; compel, force; hurry; harass; (*a un deudor*) dun || *intr* to be urgent
apremio *m* pressure; urgency; compulsion; oppression; surtax for late payment; (*demanda de pago*) dun
aprender *tr & intr* to learn; **aprender haciendo** to learn by doing
apren•diz -diza *mf* apprentice; **aprendiz de imprenta** printer's devil
aprendizaje *m* apprenticeship; **pagar el aprendizaje** to pay for one's inexperience
aprensar *tr* to press; oppress
aprensión *f* apprehension; misgiving, prejudice
aprensi•vo -va *adj* apprehensive
apresar *tr* to grasp, seize; capture
aprestador *m* primer
aprestar *tr* to prepare; (*tejidos*) process; prime; size || *ref* to get ready
apresto *m* preparation; equipment; priming; sizing
apresurar *tr & ref* to hurry, hasten
apretadera *f* strap, rope; **apretaderas** pressure
apreta•do -da *adj* compact, tight; close, intimate; dense, thick; difficult, dangerous; mean, stingy; **estar muy apretado** to be in a bad way
apretar §2 *tr* to tighten; squeeze; pinch; hug; harass, importune; afflict, beset; (*un botón*) press; (*los puños*) clench; (*los dientes*) grit; (*la mano*) shake || *intr* to pinch; insist; get worse; push hard, press forward; **apretar a correr** to start running; **apretar con** to close in on || *ref* to grieve, be distressed; crowd
apretón *m* pressure, squeeze; struggle; dash, run; **apretón de manos** handshake
apretura *f* crush, jam; tightness; fix, trouble; need, want
aprietarropa *m* clothespin
¡aprieta! *interj* (coll) baloney!
aprieto *m* crush, jam; fix
aprisa *adv* fast, quickly
aprisco *m* sheepfold
aprisionar *tr* to imprison; bind, tie; shackle
aprobación *f* approbation, approval; pass, passing grade
aproba•do -da *adj* excellent || *m* pass
aprobar §61 *tr & intr* to approve; pass
aprontar *tr* to hand over without delay; expedite
apropia•do -da *adj* appropriate, fitting, proper
apropiar *tr* to hand over; fit, adapt || *ref* to appropriate; preëmpt
aprovechable *adj* available, usable
aprovecha•do -da *adj* thrifty; stingy; diligent; well-spent || *mf* opportunist
aprovechar *tr* to make good use of, take advantage of; (*una caída de agua*) harness || *intr* to be useful; progress, improve || *ref*— **aprovecharse de** to avail oneself of, take advantage of
aprovisionar *tr* to provision, supply, furnish
aproxima•do -da *adj* approximate, rough
aproximar *tr* to bring near; approximate || *ref* to come near; approximate
aptitud *f* aptitude; suitability
ap•to -ta *adj* apt; suitable
apuesta *f* bet, wager
apues•to -ta *adj* neat, spruce, elegant || *f* see **apuesta**
apulgarar *ref* to become mildewed

apuntador *m* (theat) prompter
apuntalar *tr* to prop up, underpin
apuntar *tr* to point; point at; aim; aim at; take note of; sharpen; stitch, darn, patch; correct; prompt; stake, to put up; (theat) to prompt || *intr* to begin to appear; dawn || *ref* (*el vino*) to begin to turn sour; register; get tipsy
apunte *m* note; rough sketch; stake; rogue, rascal; (theat) cue
apuñalar *tr & intr* to stab
apuñear *tr* to punch
apura•do -da *adj* needy, hard up; difficult, dangerous; hurried, rushed
apurar *tr* to purify, refine; clear up, verify; finish; drain, use up, exhaust; hurry, press; annoy || *ref* to worry, grieve; exert oneself, strive
apuro *m* need, want; grief, sorrow; haste, urgency; **apuros** financial embarrassment
aquejar *tr* to grieve, afflict
aquel, aquella *adj dem* (*pl* **aquellos, aquellas**) that, that . . . yonder
aquél, aquélla *pron dem* (*pl* **aquéllos, aquéllas**) that; that one, that one yonder; the one; the former || *m* charm, appeal
aquelarre *m* witches' Sabbath
aquello *pron dem* that; that thing, that matter
aquende *adv* on this side || *prep* on this side of
aquerenciar *ref* to become fond or attached
aquí *adv* here; **aquí dentro** in here; **de aquí en adelante** from now on; **por aquí** this way
aquiescencia *f* acquiescence
aquietar *tr* to quiet, calm
aquilatar *tr* to assay; check; refine
Aquiles *m* Achilles
aquilón *m* north wind
ara *f* altar; altar slab; **en aras de** for the sake of
árabe *adj* Arab, Arabian; (archit) Moresque || *mf* Arab, Arabian || *m* (*idioma*) Arabic
Arabia, la Arabia
arábi•go -ga *adj* Arabian, Arabic || *m* (*idioma*) Arabic; **estar en arábigo** (coll) to be Greek
arabismo *m* (*estudio, voz, rasgo*) Arabism
aracanga *f* macaw
arado *m* plow
Aragón *m* Aragon
arago•nés -nesa *adj & mf* Aragonese
arancel *m* tariff
arancelar *tr* (CAm) to pay
arancela•rio -ria *adj* tariff, customs
arándano *m* whortleberry; **arándano agrio** cranberry
arandela *f* bobèche; (mach) washer
araña *f* spider; chandelier
arañar *tr* to scratch; scrape; scrape together
arañazo *m* scratch
araño *m* scratching
aráquida *f* peanut
arar *tr* to plow
arbitraje *m* arbitration
arbitrar *tr & intr* to arbitrate; referee; umpire
arbitra•rio -ria *adj* arbitrary
arbitrio *m* free will; means, ways; **arbitrios** excise taxes
arbitrista *mf* wild-eyed dreamer
árbi•tro -tra *mf* arbiter; referee || *m* umpire
árbol *m* tree; axle, shaft; **árbol del caucho** rubber plant; **árbol de levas** camshaft; **árbol de mando** drive shaft; **árbol de Navidad** Christmas tree; **árbol motor** drive shaft
arbola•do -da *adj* wooded; (*mar*) high || *m* woodland
arboleda *f* grove
arbollón *m* sewer, drain
arbotante *m* flying buttress
arbusto *m* shrub
arca *f* chest, coffer; tank; ark; **arca de agua** water tower; **arca de la alianza** ark of the covenant; **arca de Noé** ark, Noah's ark
arcada *f* arcade; archway; stroke of bow; **arcadas** retching
arcai•co -ca *adj* archaic
arcaísmo *m* archaism
arcaizante *adj* obsolescent
arcángel *m* archangel
arca•no -na *adj & m* secret
arcar **§73** *tr* to arch
arce *m* maple tree
arcilla *f* clay; **arcilla figulina** potter's clay
arco *m* arch; (*de cuna o mecedor*) rocker; (elec, geom) arc; (mus) bow; **arco iris** rainbow; **arco triunfal** triumphal arch; memorial arch
arcón *m* large chest; bin, bunker
archiduque *m* archduke
archienemigo *m* archenemy
archipiélago *m* archipelago; (coll) maze, entanglement || **Archipiélago** *m* Aegean Sea
archiva•dor -dora *mf* file clerk || *m* filing cabinet; letter file
archivar *tr* to file; file away; hide away
archivero *m* city clerk
archivo *m* archives; files; filing; (Col) office
ardentía *f* heartburn; (*en las olas de la mar*) phosphorescence
arder *tr* to burn || *intr* to burn; blaze; **estar que arde** to be coming to a head || *ref* to burn up
ardid *m* artifice, trick, wile
ardi•do -da *adj* burnt-up; bold, intrepid; angry
ardiendo *adj invar* burning
ardiente *adj* ardent; fiery, passionate; burning, hot
ardilla *f* squirrel; **ardilla de tierra** gopher; **ardilla ladradora** prairie dog; **ardilla listada** chipmunk
ardillón *m* gopher
ardite *m* old Spanish coin of little value; **no me importa un ardite** (coll) I don't care a hang; **no valer un ardite** to be not worth a straw
ardor *m* ardor; eagerness, fervor, zeal; vehemence; courage, dash
ardoro•so -sa *adj* fiery, enthusiastic; balky, restive
ar•duo -dua *adj* arduous, difficult

área *f* area; small plot; **área de descansar** rest area; **área de servicio** service area
arena *f* sand; grit; arena; **arena movediza** quicksand; **arenas** arena; (pathol) stones
arenal *m* sandy place; quicksand
arenga *f* harangue
arengar *tr & intr* to harangue
arenis•co -ca *adj* sandy, gritty; sand || *f* sandstone
areno•so -sa *adj* sandy
arenque *m* herring
areómetro *m* hydrometer
arepa *f* corn griddle cake
arete *m* eardrop, earring
arfada *f* (naut) pitching
arfar *intr* (naut) to pitch
argadijo *m* or **argadillo** *m* bobbin, reel; restless fellow
argado *m* prank, trick, artifice
argamasa *f* mortar
argamasar *tr* to mortar, plaster; (*los materiales de construcción*) mix
árgana *f* (mach) crane; **árganas** panniers
Argel *f* Algiers
Argelia *f* Algeria
argeli•no -na *adj & mf* Algerian
argentar *tr* to silver
argenti•no -na *adj & mf* Argentine, Argentinean || **la Argentina** Argentina, the Argentine
argolla *f* large iron ring; (*que se pone en la nariz a un animal*) ring; engagement ring
argonauta *m* Argonaut
argucia *f* subtlety; trick
argüir **§6** *tr* to argue, argue for; prove; accuse || *ref* to argue, dispute
argumenta•dor -dora *adj* argumentative || *mf* arguer
argumentar *tr* to argue for; prove || *intr & ref* to argue, dispute
argumento *m* argument
aria *f* (mus) aria
aridez *f* aridity, dryness
ári•do -da *adj* arid; (*aburrido, falto de interés*) dry
Aries *m* Aries
ariete *m* battering ram; **ariete hidráulico** hydraulic ram
arimez *m* projection
a•rio -ria *adj & mf* Aryan || *f* see **aria**
aris•co -ca *adj* churlish, surly, evasive; (*caballo*) vicious
arista *f* edge; (*intersección de dos planos*) ridge; (*del grano de trigo*) beard; **arista de encuentro** (archit) groin
aristocracia *f* aristocracy
aristócrata *mf* aristocrat
aristocráti•co -ca *adj* aristocratic
Aristóteles *m* Aristotle
aristotéli•co -ca *adj & mf* Aristotelian
aritméti•co -ca *adj* arithmetical || *mf* arithmetician || *f* arithmetic
arlequín *m* harlequin
arma *f* arm, weapon; **alzarse en armas** to rise up, rebel; **arma blanca** steel blade; **arma corta** pistol; **arma de fuego** firearm; **jugar a las armas** to fence; **sobre las armas** under arms
armada *f* fleet, armada; navy
armadía *f* raft, float
armadijo *m* trap, snare
arma•do -da *adj* armed; (*hormigón*) reinforced || *f* see **armada**
arma•dor -dora *mf* assembler || *m* recruiter of fishermen and whalers
armadura *f* armor; framework; skeleton; (elec) armature; (*de imán*) keeper
armamentismo *m* military preparedness
armamentis•to -ta *adj* militarist, arms || *mf* arms dealer
armamento *m* armament
armar *tr* to arm; (*un arma*) load; (*una bayoneta*) fix; mount, assemble; build; equip; (*el hormigón*) reinforce; (*una nave*) fit out; (*caballero*) dub; start, stir up; **armarla** to start a row || *ref* to arm oneself; get ready; balk
armario *m* closet, wardrobe; **armario botiquín** medicine cabinet; **armario de luna** wardrobe with mirror; **armario frigorífico** refrigerator
armatoste *m* hulk
armazón *f* frame; assemblage; skeleton
armella *f* screw eye, eyebolt
arme•nio -nia *adj & mf* Armenian || **Armenia** *f* Armenia
armería *f* arms shop; arms museum; arms
armero *m* gunsmith; (*para las armas*) rack
armiño *m* ermine
armisticio *m* armistice
armonía *f* harmony
armóni•co -ca *adj & m* harmonic || *f* harmonica; **armónica de boca** mouth organ
armonio•so -sa *adj* harmonious
armonizar **§60** *tr & intr* to harmonize
arnés *m* armor, coat of mail; harness; **arneses** harness, trappings; outfit, equipment; accessories
aro *m* hoop; rim; **aro de émbolo** piston ring
aroma *m* aroma, fragrance
aromáti•co -ca *adj* aromatic
arpa *f* harp
arpar *tr* to claw, scratch; tear, rend
arpegio *m* arpeggio
arpeo *m* grappling iron
arpía *f* harpy; shrew, jade
arpillera *f* burlap, sackcloth
arpista *mf* harpist
arpón *m* harpoon
arponear *tr & intr* to harpoon
arqueada *f* (mus) bow
arquear *tr* to arch; (*la lana*) beat; (*una nave*) gauge; to audit || *intr* to retch || *ref* to bow
arqueología *f* archeology
arquería *f* arcade
arquero *m* archer, bowman; goalkeeper, goalie
arquitecto *m* architect
arquitectóni•co -ca *adj* architectural
arquitectura *f* architecture
arrabal *m* suburb; **arrabales** outskirts
arracada *f* earring with pendant
arracimar *ref* to cluster, bunch

arraiga•do -da *adj* deep-rooted; property-owning, landed
arraigar §**44** *tr* to establish, strengthen || *intr* to take root || *ref* to take root; become settled
arraigo *m* taking root; stability; property, real estate
arramblar *tr* to cover with sand or gravel; sweep away
arrancadero *m* starting point
arrancar §**73** *tr* to root up, pull out, pull up; snatch, wrest; (*lágrimas*) draw forth || *intr* to start; set sail; leave; originate
arranque *m* pull; fit, impulse; jerk, sudden start; sally, outburst; (aut) start, starter; **arranque a mano** (aut) hand cranking; **arranque automático** (aut) self-starter
arrapiezo *m* rag, tatter; whippersnapper
arras *fpl* earnest money, pledge; dowry
arrasar *tr* to level; wreck, demolish; fill to the brim || *intr* to clear up || *ref* to clear up; fill up
arrastra•do -da *adj* mean, crooked || *mf* wretch, crook
arrastrar *tr* to drag, drag along; drag down; impel || *intr* to drag, trail; crawl, creep || *ref* to drag, trail; crawl, creep; drag on; cringe
arrastre *m* drag; crawl; washout; influence; haulage; (*influencia política y social*) (Cuba, Mex) drag
arrayán *m* myrtle
arre *interj* gee!, get up!
arreador *m* muleteer; (SAm) whip
arrear *tr* to drive || *intr* to hurry || *ref* to lose all one's money
arrebata•do -da *adj* rash, reckless; (*color del rostro*) flushed, ruddy
arrebatar *tr* to snatch; carry away; attract; move, stir || *ref* to be carried away, be overcome
arrebatiña *f* scuffle, scramble; **andar a la arrebatiña** to scramble
arrebato *m* rage, fury; ecstasy, rapture
arrebol *m* (*de las nubes*) red; (*de las mejillas*) rosiness; (*afeite*) rouge; **arreboles** red clouds
arrebozar §**60** *tr* to muffle || *ref* to muffle one's face
arrebujar *tr* to jumble together; wrap || *ref* to wrap oneself up
arreciar *intr & ref* to grow worse; become more violent; grow stronger
arrecife *m* stone-paved road; dike; reef; **arrecife de coral** coral reef
arredrar *tr* to drive back; frighten || *ref* to draw back; shrink; be frightened
arregazar §**60** *tr* to tuck up
arreglar *tr* to adjust, regulate, settle; arrange; fix, repair || *ref* to adjust, settle; arrange; conform; **arreglárselas** to manage, make out
arreglo *m* adjustment, regulation; settlement; arrangement; order, rule; agreement; **con arreglo a** in accordance with
arregostar *ref* to take a liking
arregosto *m* liking, taste
arrellanar *ref* to loll, sprawl; like one's work
arremangar §**44** *tr* (*las mangas*) to turn up; (*la ropa*) to tuck up || *ref* to turn up one's sleeves; tuck up one's dress; take a firm stand
arremeter *tr* to attack, assail; (*un caballo*) to spur || *intr* to attack; be offensive to look at; **arremeter contra** to light into, sail into
arremetida *f* attack; (*de un caballo*) sudden start; push; short, wild run
arremolinar *ref* to crowd, mill around; whirl
arrendajo *m* (orn) jay; mimic
arrendar §**2** *tr* to rent; (*una caballería*) tie || *ref* to rent, be rented
arreo *m* adornment; (SAm) drove; **arreos** harness, trappings
arrepenti•do -da *adj* repentant || *mf* penitent
arrepentimiento *m* repentance
arrepentir §**68** *ref* to repent, be repentant; **arrepentirse de** (*p.ej., un pecado*) to repent
arrequives *mpl* finery; attendant circumstances
arresta•do -da *adj* bold, daring
arrestar *tr* to arrest || *ref* to rush boldly
arresto *m* arrest; boldness, daring; **bajo arresto** under arrest
arrezagar §**44** *tr* to tuck up
arriada *f* flood
arriar §**77** *tr* to flood; (naut) to lower, strike; slacken || *ref* to be flooded
arriba *adv* up, upward; above; upstairs; uptown; on top; **arriba de** up; **de arriba abajo** from top to bottom; from beginning to end; superciliously; **más arriba** farther up; **río arriba** upstream || *interj* up with . . . !
arribada *f* arrival (*by sea*); **de arribada** (naut) emergency
arribar *intr* to put into port; arrive; to recover, make a comeback; (naut) to fall off to leeward
arribista *adj & mf* parvenu, upstart
arribo *m* arrival
arricete *m* shoal, bar
arriendo *m* rent, rental; lease
arriero *m* muleteer
arriesga•do -da *adj* dangerous, risky; bold, daring
arriesgar §**44** *tr* to risk, jeopardize || *ref* to take a risk
arriesgo *m* (SAm) risk; hazard
arrimadillo *m* wainscot
arrimar *tr* to bring close, move up; (*un golpe*) give; abandon, neglect; give up; get rid of || *ref* to come close, move up; snuggle up; lean; depend
arrinconar *tr* to corner; put aside; abandon, neglect; get rid of || *ref* to live in seclusion
arrisca•do -da *adj* enterprising; brisk, spirited; craggy
arriscar §**73** *tr* to risk || *ref* to take a risk; (*las reses*) plunge over a cliff
arrisco *m* risk
arritmia *f* arrhythmia
arrivista *adj & mf* parvenu, upstart
arrizar §**60** *tr* to reef

arroba *f* Spanish weight of about 25 pounds
arrobar *tr* to entrance, enrapture || *ref* to be enraptured
arrobo *m* ecstasy, rapture
arroce•ro -ra *adj* rice || *mf* rice grower; rice merchant
arrocinar *tr* to bestialize || *ref* to become bestialized; fall madly in love
arrodajar *ref* (CAm) to squat down with one's legs crossed
arrodillar *ref* to kneel, kneel down
arrogancia *f* arrogance
arrogante *adj* arrogant
arrogar §44 *tr* to adopt || *ref* to arrogate to oneself
arrojadi•zo -za *adj* for throwing, projectile
arroja•do -da *adj* bold, fearless, rash
arrojalla•mas *m* (*pl* **-mas**) flame thrower
arrojar *tr* to throw, hurl; emit; bring forth; yield || *ref* to rush, rush forward
arrojo *m* boldness, fearlessness, rashness
arrollado *m* (elec) coil
arrolla•dor -dora *adj* sweeping, devastating
arrollamiento *m* winding
arrollar *tr* to roll; roll up; wind, coil; (*al enemigo*) rout; dumbfound; knock down, run over
arropar *tr* to wrap, wrap up || *ref* to bundle up
arrope *m* grape syrup; honey syrup
arropía *f* taffy
arrostrar *tr* to face; to like || *intr*—**arrostrar con** or **por** to face, resist || *ref* to rush into the fight
arroyada *f* gully; flood, freshet
arroyo *m* stream, brook; gutter; street; (*de lágrimas, sangre, etc.*) stream
arroz *m* rice
arrufar *tr* to sic, incite
arruga *f* wrinkle; crease, rumple
arrugar §44 *tr* to wrinkle; crease, rumple; (*la frente*) to knit; (Cuba, Mex) to bother, annoy || *ref* to wrinkle; crease, rumple; shrink, shrivel; (Cuba, Mex) to lose courage, lose heart
arruinar *tr* to ruin || *ref* to go to ruin
arrullar *tr* to sing to sleep, lull to sleep; to court, woo || *intr* to coo || *ref* to coo; (*las palomas*) to bill
arrullo *m* billing and cooing; lullaby
arrumaje *m* stowage; ballast
arrumar *tr* to stow || *ref* to become overcast
arrumbar *tr* to cast aside, neglect; silence; (*una costa*) determine the lay of || *intr* (naut) to take bearings || *ref* to get seasick; (naut) to take bearings
arsenal *m* arsenal, armory; dockyard, shipyard
arsénico *m* arsenic
art. *abbr* **artículo**
arte *m* & *f* art; trick; knack; fishing gear; **artes y oficios** arts and crafts; **bellas artes** fine arts; **no tener arte ni parte en** to have nothing to do with
artefacto *m* artifact; appliance, device, contrivance; **artefactos de alumbrado** lighting fixtures; **artefactos sanitarios** bathroom fixtures
artemisa *f* sagebrush
arteria *f* artery
artería *f* craftiness, cunning
arte•ro -ra *adj* crafty, cunning, sly
artesa *f* trough; Indian canoe
artesanía *f* craftsmanship
artesa•no -na *mf* artisan, craftsman || *f* craftswoman
artesón *m* kitchen tub; coffer, caisson (*in ceiling*)
árti•co -ca *adj* arctic
articulación *f* articulation; (*de huesos*) joint; **articulación universal** universal joint
articular *tr* to articulate
articulista *mf* feature writer
artículo *m* article; item; joint; (*en un diccionario*) entry; **artículo de fondo** leader, editorial; **artículos de consumo** consumers' goods; **artículos de deporte** sporting goods; **artículos de primera necesidad** basic commodities; **artículos para caballeros** men's furnishings
artífice *mf* artificer; craftsman
artificial *adj* artificial
artificio *m* artifice; workmanship; appliance, device; cunning; trick, ruse
artificio•so -sa *adj* ingenious, skillful; cunning, scheming, deceptive
artilugio *m* contraption, jigger
artillería *f* artillery
artillero *m* artilleryman, gunner
artimaña *f* trap; trick, cunning
artista *mf* artist
artísti•co -ca *adj* artistic
artolas *fpl* mule chair, cacolet
artríti•co -ca *adj* & *mf* arthritic
artritis *f* arthritis
arúspice *m* diviner, soothsayer
arveja *f* vetch, tare; (Chile) pea
arzobispo *m* archbishop
arzón *m* saddletree; **arzón delantero** saddlebow; **arzón trasero** cantle
as *m* ace; **as de fútbol** football star; **as de la pantalla** movie star; **as del volante** speed king
asa *f* handle; juice; **en asas** with arms akimbo
asa•do -da *adj* roasted; **bien asado** well done; **poco asado** rare || *m* roast
asador *m* spit
asadura *f* entrails
asalaria•do -da *mf* wage earner
asaltar *tr* to assail, assault, storm; overtake, overcome
asalto *m* assault, attack; (box) round; (mil) storm; **tomar por asalto** to take by storm
asamblea *f* assembly
asar *tr* to roast || *ref* to be burning up
asbesto *m* asbestos
ascendencia *f* ancestry
ascendente *adj* ascending; up
ascender §51 *tr* to promote || *intr* to ascend, go up; be promoted; **ascender a** to amount to
ascendiente *adj* ascending; up || *mf* ancestor || *m* ascendancy, upper hand

ascensión *f* ascension, ascent
ascenso *m* ascent; promotion
ascensor *m* elevator; freight elevator
ascensorista *mf* elevator operator
asceta *mf* ascetic
ascéti•co -ca *adj* ascetic
asco *m* disgust, nausea, loathing; **dar asco** to turn the stomach; **estar hecho un asco** to be filthy; **hacer ascos de** to turn one's nose up at; **ser un asco** to be contemptible; be worthless
ascua *f* ember, live coal; **estar sobre ascuas** to be on needles and pins || **ascuas** *interj* ouch!
asea•do -da *adj* clean, neat, tidy
asear *tr & ref* to clean up, tidy up; make one's toilet
asechamiento *m* or **asechanza** *f* snare, trap
asechar *tr* to set a trap for
asediar *tr* to besiege; harass
asedio *m* siege
asegundar *tr* to repeat right away
asegurable *adj* insurable
aseguración *f* insurance policy
asegura•dor -dora *mf* insurer, underwriter
asegurar *tr* to fasten, secure; assure; assert; seize; imprison; (*garantizar por un precio contra determinado accidente o pérdida*) insure || *ref* to make sure; take out insurance
asemejar *tr* to make like; compare; resemble || *ref* to be similar
asenso *m* assent; **dar asenso a** to believe
asentada *f* sitting; **de una asentada** at one sitting
asentaderas *fpl* (coll) buttocks
asentadillas — **a asentadillas** sidesaddle
asenta•do -da *adj* sedate; stable || *f* see **asentada**
asentador *m* strap, razor strop
asentar **§2** *tr* to seat; place; establish; tamp down, level; hone, sharpen; note down; (*un golpe*) impart; (*en la mente de uno*) impress; affirm; suppose || *intr* to be becoming || *ref* to sit down; be established, establish oneself; settle
asentimiento *m* assent
asentir **§68** *intr* to assent
aseo *m* cleanliness, neatness, tidiness; care; toilet
asépti•co -ca *adj* aseptic
aseptizar **§60** *tr* to purify, make aseptic
asequible *adj* accessible, obtainable
aserción *f* assertion
aserradero *m* sawmill
aserra•dor -dora *mf* sawyer; (coll) fiddler || *f* power saw
aserraduras *fpl* sawdust
aserrar **§2** *tr* to saw
aserrín *m* sawdust
aserruchar *tr* (SAm) to saw
aserto *m* assertion
asesinar *tr* to assassinate, murder
asesinato *m* assassination, murder
asesi•no -na *adj* murderous || *mf* assassin, murderer
asesorar *tr* to advise || *ref* to seek advice; get advice
asestar *tr* to aim; shoot; (*un golpe*) deal
aseveración *f* assertion, declaration
aseverar *tr* to assert, declare
asfaltar *tr* to asphalt
asfalto *m* asphalt
asfixia *f* asphyxiation
asfixiar *tr* to asphyxiate
así *adv* so, thus; **así . . . como** both . . . and; **así como** as soon as; as well as; **así que** as soon as; with the result that; **así y todo** even so, anyhow; **por decirlo así** so to speak; **y así sucesivamente** and so on
Asia *f* Asia; **el Asia Menor** Asia Minor
asiáti•co -ca *adj & mf* Asian, Asiatic
asidero *m* handle; occasion, pretext
asi•duo -dua *adj* assiduous; frequent, persistent
asiento *m* seat; site; (*de un edificio*) settling; (*de una botella, una silla, etc.*) bottom; sediment; list, roll; wisdom, maturity; **asiento abatible** reclining seat; **asiento de rejilla** cane seat; **asiento lanzable** (aer) ejection seat; **asientos** buttocks; **planchar el asiento** to be a wallflower; **tome Vd. asiento** have a seat
asignación *f* assignment; salary; allowance
asignar *tr* to assign
asignatorio *m* heir, inheritor
asignatura *f* course, subject
asila•do -da *mf* inmate
asilar *tr* to shelter; place in an asylum; silo || *ref* to take refuge; be placed in an asylum
asilo *m* asylum; shelter, refuge; (*para menesterosos*) home; **asilo de huérfanos** orphan asylum; **asilo de locos** insane asylum; **asilo de pobres** poorhouse
asilla *f* fastener; collarbone; **asillas** shoulder pole
asimetría *f* asymmetry
asimilar *tr* to compare; take in || *intr* to be alike || *ref* to assimilate; **asimilarse a** to resemble
asimismo *adv* also, likewise
asir **§7** *tr* to grasp, seize || *intr* to take root || *ref* to take hold; fight, grapple; **asirse a** or **de** to cling to
Asiria *f* Assyria
asi•rio -ria *adj & mf* Assyrian
asistencia *f* attendance; assistance; reward; audience, persons present; welfare, social work; (Mex) sitting room, parlor; **asistencias** allowance, support
asistenta *f* charwoman, cleaning woman
asistente *adj* attendant; present || *m* assistant, helper; bystander, spectator, person present; (mil) orderly
asistir *tr* to assist, help; attend; serve, wait on || *intr* to be present; **asistir a** to be present at, attend
asma *f* asthma
asna *f* she-ass, jenny ass; **asnas** rafters
asnal *adj* donkey; brutish
asno *m* ass, donkey, jackass
asociación *f* association

asocia•do -da *adj* associated; associate || *mf* associate, partner
asociar *tr* to associate; take as partner || *ref* to become associated; become a partner; become partners
asolamiento *m* razing, destruction
asolar *tr* to parch, burn || *ref* to become parched || §61 *tr* to raze, destroy
asoleada *f* or **asoleadura** *f* (SAm) sunstroke
asolear *tr* to sun || *ref* to bask; get sunburned
asomar *tr* (*p.ej., la cabeza*) to show, stick out || *intr* to begin to show or appear; show || *ref* to show, appear; stick out; get tipsy
asombradi•zo -za *adj* timid, shy
asombrar *tr* to shade; (*un color*) darken; frighten; astonish, amaze || *ref* to be frightened; be astonished, amazed
asombro *m* fright; astonishment
asombro•so -sa *adj* astonishing, amazing
asomo *m* mark, token, sign; appearance; **ni por asomo** nothing of the kind, not by a long shot
asordar *tr* to deafen
aspa *f* X-shaped figure; reel; (*de molino de viento*) wheel, vane; propeller blade
aspar *tr* to reel; crucify; annoy, harass || *ref* to writhe; take great pains
aspaviento *m* fuss, excitement
aspecto *m* aspect
aspereza *f* harshness; roughness; bitterness, sourness; gruffness
asperjar *tr* to sprinkle; sprinkle with holy water
áspe•ro -ra *adj* harsh; rough; bitter; gruff
áspid *m* asp
aspirador *m* vacuum cleaner; **aspirador de gasolina** (aut) vacuum tank
aspirante *m* applicant, candidate; **aspirante a cabo** private first class; **aspirante de marina** midshipman
aspirar *tr* to suck in, draw in; inhale || *intr* to aspire; inhale, breathe in
aspirina *f* aspirin
asquear *tr* to loathe || *ref* to be nauseated
asquero•so -sa *adj* disgusting, loathsome; nauseating; squeamish
asta *f* spear; shaft; flagpole, staff, mast; antler; (*de toro*) horn; **a media asta** at half-mast; **dejar en las astas del toro** to leave high and dry
asta•do -da *adj* horned || *m* bull
ástato *m* astatine
aster *m* aster
asterisco *m* asterisk
astil *m* handle; shaft
astilla *f* chip, splinter
astillar *tr & ref* to chip, splinter
Astillejos *mpl* (astr) Castor and Pollux
astillero *m* dockyard, shipyard
astro *m* star, heavenly body; (fig) star, leading light
astrofísica *f* astrophysics
astrología *f* astrology
astronauta *m* astronaut
astronáuti•co -ca *adj* astronautic || *f* astronautics
astronave *f* spaceship; **astronave tripulada** manned spaceship
astronavegación *f* space travel
astronomía *f* astronomy
astronómi•co -ca *adj* astronomic(al)
astróno•mo -ma *mf* astronomer
astro•so -sa *adj* ill-fated; vile, contemptible; ragged, shabby
astucia *f* cunning, craftiness; trick
asturia•no -na *adj & mf* Asturian
astu•to -ta *adj* astute, cunning; tricky
asueto *m* day off; leisure
asumir *tr* to assume, take on
asunción *f* assumption
asunto *m* subject, matter; affair, business; theme; **asuntos internacionales** world affairs
asurar *tr* to burn; parch; harass, worry
asurcar §73 *tr* to furrow, plow
asustadi•zo -za *adj* scary, skittish
asustar *tr* to scare, frighten
atabal *m* kettledrum; timbrel
ataca•do -da *adj* irresolute, undecided; mean, stingy
atacar §73 *tr* to attack; attach, fasten; pack, jam; (*un barreno*) tamp; corner, contradict || *intr* to attack
ata•do -da *adj* timid, shy; weak, irresolute; insignificant; cramped || *m* pack, bundle, roll
ataguía *f* cofferdam
atajar *tr* to stop, intercept, interrupt; to partition off || *intr* to take a short cut || *ref* to be abashed
atajo *m* short cut; (*en un escrito*) cut
atalaya *m* guard, lookout || *f* watchtower; elevation
atalayar *tr* to watch from a watchtower; spy on
atanquía *f* depilatory ointment
atañer §70 *tr* to concern
ataque *m* attack; **ataque por sorpresa** surprise attack
atar *tr* to tie, fasten
ataracea *f* marquetry, inlaid work
atarantar *tr* to stun, daze
atardecer *m* late afternoon || *v* §22 *intr* to draw toward evening; happen in the late afternoon
atarea•do -da *adj* busy
atarear *tr* to give an assignment to; overload with work || *ref* to toil, work hard, keep busy
atarjea *f* sewer
atarugar §44 *tr* to peg, wedge; plug; stuff, fill; silence, shut up || *ref* to become confused
atasajar *tr* to slash, hack; (*carne*) jerk
atascadero *m* mudhole; (fig) pitfall
atascar §73 *tr* to stop, stop up, clog, obstruct || *ref* to get stuck; stuff oneself; clog, get clogged
atasco *m* sticking, clogging; obstruction
ataúd *m* casket, coffin
ataujía *f* damascene work
ataujiar §77 *tr* to damascene
ataviar §77 *tr* to dress, adorn, deck out

atávi•co -ca *adj* atavistic
atavío *m* dress, adornment; **atavíos** finery, frippery, chiffons
atediar *tr* to tire, bore
ateísmo *m* atheism
ateísta *mf* atheist
atelaje *m* harness
atemorizar §60 *tr* to frighten
atemperar *tr* to soften, moderate, temper; adjust, adapt
Atenas *f* Athens
atención *f* attention; **en atención a** in view of
atender §51 *tr* to attend to; heed, pay attention to; take care of; (*a los parroquianos*) wait on
atener §71 *ref*—**atenerse a** to abide by, rely on
ateniense *adj & mf* Athenian
atenta•do -da *adj* moderate, prudent; cautious || *m* attempt, assault
atentar *tr* to attempt, try to commit || *intr*—**atentar a** or **contra** (*p.ej., la vida de una persona*) to attempt || §2 *ref* to grope
aten•to -ta *adj* attentive; courteous, polite || *f* favor (*letter*)
atenuar §21 *tr* to extenuate
ate•o -a *adj & mf* atheist
aterciopela•do -da *adj* velvety
ateri•do -da *adj* stiff, numb with cold
aterrada *f* landfall
aterrajar *tr* to thread, tap
aterraje *m* landing
aterrar *tr* to terrify || §2 *tr* to destroy, demolish; cover with earth || *intr* to land || *ref* to stand inshore
aterrizaje *m* landing; **aterrizaje a ciegas** blind landing; **aterrizaje aplastado** or **en desplome** pancake landing; **aterrizaje forzoso** emergency landing; **aterrizaje sin choque** soft landing
aterrizar §60 *intr* to land
aterronar *tr* to make lumpy || *ref* to cake, lump
aterrorizar §60 *tr* to terrify
atesorar *tr* to treasure; hoard; (*virtudes, perfecciones*) possess
atesta•do -da *adj* stuffed, jammed; obstinate, stubborn || *m* certificate
atestar *tr* (law) to attest || §2 & **regular** *tr* to jam, pack, stuff, cram; stuff
atestiguar §10 *tr* to attest, testify, depose
atezar §60 *tr* to tan; blacken || *ref* to become tanned, become sunburned
atiborrar *tr* to stuff || *ref* to stuff, stuff oneself
atiesar *tr* to stiffen; tighten || *ref* to become stiff; become tight
atildar *tr* to mark with a tilde, dash, or accent mark; point out; find fault with; tidy up, trim, adorn
atina•do -da *adj* careful, keen, wise
atinar *tr* to find, come upon || *intr* to guess, guess right; be right; manage
atirantar *tr* (Mex) to make taut; brace || *ref* (Mex) to die, pass away
atisbadero *m* peephole
atisbar *tr* to watch, spy on
atisbo *m* glimpse, look, peek
atizar §60 *tr* to stir, poke; snuff; rouse; (*p.ej., un puntapié*) let go
Atlánti•co -ca *adj & m* Atlantic
at•las *m* (*pl* **-las**) atlas
atleta *mf* athlete
atleticismo *m* athletics
atléti•co -ca *adj* athletic || *f* athletics
atmósfera *f* atmosphere
atmosféri•co -ca *adj* atmospheric
atoar *tr* (naut) to tow
atocinar *tr* (*un cerdo*) to cut up; make into bacon; (coll) to murder || *ref* to get angry; fall madly in love
atocha *f* esparto
atolondra•do -da *adj* confused; scatterbrained
atolondrar *tr* to confuse, bewilder
atolladero *m* mudhole; obstacle, difficulty
atollar *intr & ref* to get stuck, get stuck in the mud
atómi•co -ca *adj* atomic
átomo *m* atom
atóni•to -ta *adj* astounded, aghast
atontar *tr* to stun; to confuse, bewilder
atorar *tr* to clog, obstruct || *intr & ref* to stick, get stuck; choke
atormentar *tr* to torment; torture
atornillar *tr* to screw, screw on
atortillar *tr* (SAm) to squash, flatten
atortolar *tr* to rattle, scare, intimidate
atosigar §44 *tr* to poison; harass || *ref* to be in a hurry
atrabanca•do -da *adj* overworked; (Mex) hasty, rash; (Ven) deep in debt
atrabancar §73 *tr & intr* to rush through
atrabilia•rio -ria *adj* irascible, grouchy
atracada *f* quarrel, row
atracador *m* hold-up man
atracar §73 *tr* to hold up; bring up; stuff; (naut) to bring alongside, dock || *intr* (naut) to come alongside, dock || *ref* to stuff; quarrel
atracción *f* attraction; amusement
atraco *m* holdup
atracón *m* stuffing, gluttony; fight; push, shove
atracti•vo -va *adj* attractive || *m* attraction; attractiveness
atraer §75 *tr* to attract
atragantar *tr* to choke down || *ref* to choke; **atragantarse con** to choke on
atraillar §4 *tr* to leash; master, subdue
atrampar *ref* to fall into a trap; be stopped up; stick; get stuck
atrancar §73 *tr* to bar; obstruct || *intr* to stride; read falteringly || *ref* to get stuck; (*una ventana*) stick; (Mex) to stick to one's opinion
atrapamos•cas *m* (*pl* **-cas**) flytrap; (bot) Venus's-flytrap
atrapar *tr* to trap, catch; get, land, net
atrás *adv* back, backward; behind; before; previously; **atrás de** back of, behind; **hacerse atrás** to back up, move back; **hacia atrás** backwards; the other way

atrasa•do -da *adj* late; (*reloj*) slow; needy; back; retarded; in arrears; **atrasado de medios** short of funds; **atrasado de noticias** behind the times
atrasar *tr* to slow down; retard; set back, turn back; delay; leave behind; postdate || *intr* to be slow || *ref* to be slow; lose time; lag, stay behind; be late; be in debt
atraso *m* delay, slowness; backwardness; lag; **atrasos** arrears, delinquency
atravesada *f* (SAm) crossing
atravesar §2 *tr* to cross, go across; pierce; pass through, go through; put crosswise; stake, wager || *ref* to butt in; fight, wrangle; get stuck
atrayente *adj* attractive
atreguar §10 *tr* to give a truce to; grant an extension to || *ref* to agree to a truce
atrever *ref* to dare; **atreverse con** or **contra** to be impudent toward
atrevi•do -da *adj* bold, daring; impudent
atrevimiento *m* boldness, daring; impudence
atribuir §20 *tr* to attribute, ascribe || *ref* to assume
atribular *tr & ref* to grieve
atributo *m* attribute
atril *m* lectern; music stand
atrincherar *tr* to entrench || *ref* to dig in
atrio *m* hall, vestibule; court, courtyard; parvis
atri•to -ta *adj* contrite
atrocidad *f* atrocity; enormity
atrofia *f* atrophy
atrofiar *tr & ref* to atrophy
atrojar *tr* (*granos*) to garner; (Mex) to befuddle
atrona•do -da *adj* reckless, thoughtless
atronar §61 *tr* to deafen; stun || *intr* to thunder
atropella•do -da *adj* brusk, violent; hasty; tumultuous
atropellar *tr* to trample; knock down; run over; disregard; do hurriedly || *intr & ref* to act hastily or recklessly
atropello *m* trampling; knocking down; running over; abuse, insult; outrage
a•troz *adj* (*pl* **-troces**) atrocious; huge, enormous
atto. *abbr* **atento**
atufar *tr* to anger, irritate || *ref* to get angry; (*el vino*) turn sour
atún *m* tuna
aturdi•do -da *adj* reckless, harebrained
aturdir *tr* to stun; perplex, bewilder
atusar *tr* to trim; smooth || *ref* to dress fancily; (*el bigote*) twist
audacia *f* audacity
au•daz *adj* (*pl* **-daces**) audacious
audición *f* audition; hearing; concert; listening
audiencia *f* audience, hearing; audience chamber; royal tribunal; provincial high court
audífono *m* hearing aid; earphone
audiofrecuencia *f* audio frequency
audiómetro *m* audiometer
auditor *m* judge advocate; **auditor de guerra** judge advocate (*in army*); **auditor de marina** judge advocate (*in navy*)
auditorio *m* (*concurso de oyentes*) audience; (*local*) auditorium
auge *m* height, acme; boom; vogue; **estar en auge** to be booming
augur *m* augur
augurar *tr* to augur; wish || *intr* to augur
augurio *m* augury; wish
augus•to -ta *adj* august
aula *f* classroom, lecture room; **aula magna** assembly hall
aulaga *f* gorse, furze
aullar §8 *intr* to howl
aullido *m* howl, howling
aúllo *m* howl
aumentar *tr* to augment, increase, enlarge; promote; exaggerate || *intr & ref* to augment, increase
aumento *m* augmentation, increase, enlargement; promotion; (Guat, Mex) postscript, addition; **ir en aumento** to be on the increase
aun *adv* even; **aun cuando** although
aún *adv* still, yet
aunar §8 *tr & ref* to join, unite; combine, mix
aunque *conj* although, though
aúpa *interj* up!; **de aúpa** swanky; **los de aúpa** (taur) the picadors
aupar §8 *tr* to help up; extol
aura *f* gentle breeze; breath; popularity; turkey vulture
áure•o -a *adj* gold, golden
aureola *f* halo, aureole
auricular *m* earpiece, receiver; **auricular de casco** headpiece
auriga *m* (poet) coachman, charioteer
aurora *f* aurora, dawn; roseate hue
ausencia *f* absence
ausentar *tr* to send away || *ref* to absent oneself
ausente *adj* absent; absent-minded || *mf* absentee
auspiciar *tr* to sponsor, foster, back
auspicio *m* auspice; **bajo los auspicios de** under the auspices of
auste•ro -ra *adj* austere; harsh; honest; penitent
Australia *f* Australia
australia•no -na *adj & mf* Australian
Austria *f* Austria
austría•co -ca *adj & mf* Austrian
austro *m* south wind
auténtica *f* certificate; certification
autenticar §73 *tr* to authenticate
auténti•co -ca *adj* authentic; real || *f* see **auténtica**
autillo *m* tawny owl
autísti•co -ca *adj* autistic
auto *m* edict; short Biblical play; miracle play; auto; **auto de prisión** commitment, warrant for arrest; **auto sacramental** play in honor of the Sacrament
autoabastecimiento *m* self-sufficiency
autoadhesi•vo -va *adj* self-adhesive

autoamortizable *adj* self-liquidating
autobanco *m* drive-in bank
autobiografía *f* autobiography
autobombo *m* self-glorification
autobús *m* autobus, bus
autocamión *m* motor truck
autocasa *f* motor home; mobile home; trailer
autocine *m* (Chile, Cuba) drive-in theater
autocinema *f* (Mex) drive-in theater
autocráti•co -ca *adj* autocratic(al)
autócto•no -na *adj* native, indigenous
autodefensa *f* self-defense
autodestrucción *f* self-destruction
autodeterminación *f* self-determination
autodidac•to -ta *adj* self-taught
autodisciplina *f* self-discipline
autodominio *m* self-control
autódromo *m* automobile race track
auto-escuela *f* driving school
autógena *f* welding
autogestión *f* self-administration; independence
autogobierno *m* self-government
autografiar §77 *tr* to autograph
autógra•fo -fa *adj & m* autograph
autoguia•do -da *adj* self-guided, homing
autolimpiador or **autolimpiante** *adj invar* self-cleaning
automación *f* automation
autómata *m* automaton
automáti•co -ca *adj* automatic
automatización *f* automation
automóvil *m* automobile
automovilista *mf* motorist
autonomía *f* autonomy; cruising radius
autóno•mo -ma *adj* autonomous, independent
autopega•do -da *adj* self-sealing
autopiano *m* player piano
autopista *f* turnpike, automobile road
autopsia *f* autopsy
au•tor -tora *mf* author; (*de un crimen*) perpetrator || *f* authoress
autoreactor *m* ramjet (engine)
autoridad *f* authority; pomp, display
autorita•rio -ria *adj & mf* authoritarian
autoriza•do -da *adj* authoritative
autorizar §60 *tr* to authorize; legalize; exalt
autorretrato *m* self-portrait
autoservicio *m* self-service
autostop *m* hitchhiking; **viajar en autostop** to hitchhike
autostopista *mf* hitchhiker
auto-teatro *m* drive-in movie theater
autovía *m* railway motor coach || *f* turnpike, automobile road
auxiliar *adj* auxiliary || *mf* auxiliary; aid, helper; substitute teacher || *v* §77 **& regular** *tr* to aid, help, assist; (*a un moribundo*) attend
auxilio *m* aid, help, assistance; **acudir en auxilio a** or **de** to come to the aid of; **auxilio en carretera** road service; **primeros auxilios** first aid
avahar *tr* to steam; breathe warmth on || *intr* to steam, give off vapor || *ref* to steam, give off vapor; warm one's hands with one's breath
aval *m* indorsement; countersignature
avalancha *f* avalanche
avalorar *tr* to estimate; encourage
avaluación *f* appraisal, valuation
avaluar §21 *tr* to appraise, estimate
avalúo *m* appraisal, valuation
avance *m* advance; advance payment; (com) balance; (com) estimate; (mov) preview; **avance rápido** (mach, mov) fast forward
avante *adv* (naut) fore
avanza•do -da *adj* advanced; **avanzado de edad** advanced in years || *f* outpost, advance guard
avanzar §60 *tr* to advance, extend; propose || *intr & ref* to advance; approach
avanzo *m* balance sheet; estimate
avaricia *f* avarice
avaricio•so -sa *adj* avaricious
avarien•to -ta *adj* avaricious || *mf* miser
ava•ro -ra *adj* miserly || *mf* miser
avasallar *tr* to subject, subjugate, enslave || *ref* to submit
ave *f* bird; fowl; **ave canora** songbird; **ave de corral** barnyard fowl; **ave de mal agüero** Jonah, jinx; **ave de paso** bird of passage; **ave de rapiña** bird of prey; **ave fría** lapwing; **ave zancuda** wading bird
avecinar *tr* to bring near || *ref* to approach; take up residence
avecindar *tr* to domicile || *ref* to become a resident
avejentar *tr & ref* to age prematurely
avejigar §44 *tr, intr & ref* to blister
avellana *f* hazelnut
avellanar *tr* to countersink || *ref* to shrivel, shrivel up
avellano *m* hazel, hazel tree
avemaría *f* Hail Mary, Ave Maria; **al avemaría** at sunset; **en un avemaría** in a jiffy; **saber como el avemaría** to have a thorough knowledge of
avena *f* oats
avenar *tr* to drain
avenate *m* gruel, oatmeal gruel
avenencia *f* agreement; deal, bargain
avenida *f* avenue; allée; flood, freshet; gathering, assemblage
aveni•do -da *adj* — **bien avenido** in agreement; **mal avenido** in disagreement || *f* see **avenida**
avenimiento *m* agreement; reconciliation
avenir §79 *tr* to reconcile, bring together || *ref* to be reconciled, agree; compromise; correspond
aventa•dor -dora *mf* winnower || *m* fan
aventaja•do -da *adj* excellent, outstanding; advantageous
aventajar *tr* to advance; put ahead; excel || *ref* to advance, win an advantage; excel
aventar §2 *tr* to fan; winnow; scatter to the winds; blow; drive away || *ref* to swell up; flee, run away
aventón *m* (Guat, Mex, Peru) push, shove; (*llevada gratuita*) (Mex) free ride; **pedir aventón** (Mex) to hitchhike

aventura *f* adventure; danger, risk
aventura•do -da *adj* hazardous, venturesome
aventurar *tr* to adventure, venture, hazard || *ref* to adventure, take a risk; venture, to risk
aventure•ro -ra *adj* adventuresome, adventurous || *m* adventurer, soldier of fortune || *f* adventuress
avergonzar §9 *tr* to shame; embarrass || *ref* to be ashamed; be embarrassed
avería *f* aviary; breakdown, failure; (com) damage; (naut) average
averiar §77 *tr* to damage || *ref* to suffer damage; break down
averiguable *adj* ascertainable
averiguar §10 *tr* to ascertain, find out
aversión *f* aversion, dislike; **cobrar aversión a** to take a dislike for
aves•truz *m* (*pl* **-truces**) ostrich
avezar §60 *tr* to accustom || *ref* to become accustomed
aviación *f* aviation
avia•dor -dora *mf* aviator, flyer || *m* aviator, airman; (mil) airman; **aviador postal** airmail pilot || *f* aviatrix, airwoman
aviar §77 *tr* to make ready, prepare; equip, provide; **estar, encontrarse** or **quedar aviado** to be in a mess, be in a jam || *ref* to hurry; (aer) to take off
avia•triz (*pl* **-trices**) aviatrix
avidez *f* avidity, greediness
ávi•do -da *adj* avid, greedy, eager
aviejar *tr & ref* to age prematurely
aviento *m* winnowing fork, pitchfork
avie•so -sa *adj* crooked, distorted; evil-minded, perverse
avilantar *ref* to be insolent
avilantez *f* insolence; meanness
avillana•do -da *adj* rustic, boorish
avillanar *tr* to debase, make boorish || *ref* to become boorish
avinagra•do -da *adj* vinegarish, sour, crabbed
avinagrar *tr* to sour || *ref* to become sour; turn into vinegar
avío *m* provision; arrangement; load; **¡al avío!** let's go!; **avíos** equipment, tools, outfit; **avíos de pescar** fishing tackle
avión *m* airplane; (orn) martin; **avión birreactor** twin-jet plane; **avión de caza** pursuit plane; **avión a chorro, avión de propulsión a chorro** or **a reacción** jet plane; **avión de travesía** airliner; **avión supersónico** supersonic aircraft
avión-correo *m* mailplane
avioneta *f* small plane; **avioneta de alquiler** taxiplane
avisaco•ches *m* (*pl* **-ches**) car caller
avisa•do -da *adj* prudent, wise; **mal avisado** rash, thoughtless
avisa•dor -dora *adj* warning || *mf* informer; adviser || *m* electric bell; **avisador de incendio** fire alarm
avisar *tr* to advise, inform; warn; report on
aviso *m* advice, information; warning; care, prudence; dispatch boat; advertisement; **sobre aviso** on the lookout
avispa *f* wasp
avispa•do -da *adj* brisk, wide-awake; (SAm) startled, scared
avispar *tr* to spur; to stir up || *ref* to fret, worry
avispón *m* hornet
avistar *tr* to descry || *ref* to meet, have an interview
avitaminosis *f* vitamin deficiency
avituallar *tr* to supply, provision || *ref* to take in supplies
avivar *tr* to brighten, enlive, revive || *intr & ref* to brighten, revive
avizor *adj* watchful, alert || *m* watcher; **avizores** (slang) eyes
avizorar *tr* to watch, spy on || *ref* to hide and watch, spy
ax *interj* ouch!, ow!
axioma *m* axiom
axiomáti•co -ca *adj* axiomatic
ay *interj* ay!, alas! **¡ay de mí!** woe is me! || *m* sigh
aya *f* nurse, governess
ayer *adj & m* yesterday
ayo *m* tutor
ayuda *m* valet; **ayuda de cámera** valet de chambre || *f* help, aid; enema
ayudanta *f* assistant; **ayudanta de cocina** kitchenmaid
ayudante *m* aid, assistant; adjutant; **ayudante de campo** aide-de-camp
ayudantía *f* (*universidad*) assistantship
ayudar *tr* to aid, help, assist
ayunar *intr* to fast
ayu•no -na *adj* fasting; uninformed; **en ayunas** or **en ayuno** fasting; before breakfast; uninformed; missing the point || *m* fast, fasting
ayuntamiento *m* town or city council; town or city hall; sexual intercourse
azabacha•do -da *adj* jet, jet-black
azabache *m* jet; **azabaches** jet trinkets
aza•cán -cana *adj* menial || *mf* drudge || *m* water carrier
azada *f* hoe
azadón *m* hoe; grub hoe; **azadón de peto** or **de pico** mattock
azadonar *tr* to hoe
azafata *f* air hostess, stewardess; lady of the queen's wardrobe
azafate *m* wicker tray
azafrán *m* saffron
azafrana•do -da *adj* saffron
azafranar *tr* to saffron
azahar *m* orange or lemon blossom
azar *m* chance, hazard; accident, misfortune; fate, destiny; losing card; losing throw; (*persona o cosa que traen mala suerte*) Jonah
azarar *ref* to go awry; get rattled
azaro•so -sa *adj* hazardous, risky; unlucky
ázi•mo -ma *adj* unleavened
azófar *m* brass
azoga•do da *adj* fidgety, restless || *m* quicksilver foil; **temblar como un azogado** to shake like a leaf

azogar §44 *tr* (*un espejo*) to silver || *ref* to have mercury poisoning; shake, become agitated
azogue *m* quicksilver; market place; (coll) mirror
azonza•do -da *adj* stupid, dumb
azor *m* goshawk
azorar *tr* to abash; excite, stir up
Azores *fpl* Azores
azotar *tr* to whip, scourge; beat; flail; beat down upon
azote *m* whip; lash; (fig) scourge; **azotes y galeras** tiresome fare
azotea *f* flat roof, roof terrace
azteca *adj & mf* Aztec
azúcar *m* sugar; **azúcar de caña** cane sugar; **azúcar de remolacha** beet sugar
azucarar *tr* to sugar, sugarcoat; sugar over
azucare•ro -ra *adj* sugar || *m* sugar bowl
azucena *f* Madonna lily, white lily
azufrar *tr* to sulfur
azufre *m* sulfur; brimstone
azul *adj & m* blue; **azul marino** navy blue
azular *tr* to color blue, dye blue
azulear *intr* to turn blue
azulejar *tr* to tile, cover with tiles
azulejo *m* glazed colored tile (orn) roller; (orn) indigo bunting; (orn) bee eater
azulones *mpl* blue jeans
azuzar §60 *tr* to sic; tease, incite

B

B, b (be) *f* second letter of the Spanish alphabet
B. *abbr* **Beato, Bueno**
baba *f* drivel, spittle, slobber; (*de culebras, peces, etc.*) slime
babear *intr* to slobber; froth
babel *m & f* (coll) bedlam, confusion; **estar en babel** to be daydreaming
babero *m* bib
Babia *f* — **estar en Babia** to be daydreaming
babieca *adj* silly, simple || *mf* simpleton
Babilonia *f* (*imperio*) Babylonia; (*ciudad*) Babylon
babilóni•co -ca *adj* Babylonian
babilo•nio -nia *adj & mf* Babylonian || *f* see **Babilonia**
bable *m* Asturian dialect; patois
babor *m* (naut) port
babosa *f* slug
babosada *f* (CAm, Mex) stupidity; foolish act
babosear *tr* to slobber over || *intr* to slobber
babo•so -sa *adj* slobbery; (*con las damas*) (coll) mushy || *m* (CAm) scoundrel || *f* see **babosa**
babucha *f* slipper, mule
babuino *m* baboon
bacalao or **bacallao** *m* codfish
baceta *f* (cards) widow
bacía *f* basin, vessel; shaving dish
bacilo *m* bacillus
bacín *m* chamber pot
Baco *m* Bacchus
bacteria *f* bacterium
bacteria•no -na *adj* bacterial
bacteriología *f* bacteriology
bacteriólo•go -ga *mf* bacteriologist
báculo *m* staff; crook; (fig) staff, comfort; **báculo pastoral** crozier
bacha *f* (Mex) (cigarette) butt
bache *m* hole, rut; blip; **bache aéreo** air pocket
bachi•ller -llera *adj* garrulous || *mf* garrulous person || **bachiller** *mf* bachelor
bachillerar *tr* to confer the bachelor's degree on || *ref* to receive the bachelor's degree
bachillerato *m* baccalaureate, bachelor's degree
bachillerear *intr* to babble, prattle
bachillería *f* babble, prattle; gossip
badajo *m* clapper
badana *f* (dressed) sheepskin; **zurrarle a uno la badana** to tan someone's hide
badén *m* gully, gutter
badil *m* fire shovel
badulaque *m* nincompoop
bagaje *m* beast of burden; (mil) baggage
bagatela *f* trinket; triviality; (Chile, Peru) pinball
bagazo *m* waste pulp, bagasse
bagre *adj* (Bol, Col) showy, gaudy; (CAm) sly, slick; (SAm) coarse, ill-bred; (Mex) stupid || *m* catfish
bahareque *m* (CAm, Col, Ven) small hut
bahía *f* bay
bahorrina *f* slop; riffraff
bailable *adj* for dancing || *m* ballet
bailadero *m* dance floor, dance hall
baila•dor -dora *mf* dancer
bailar *tr* (*p.ej., un vals*) to dance; (*un trompo*) spin || *intr* to dance; spin; wobble
baila•rín -rina *mf* dancer || *f* ballerina; **bailarina ombliguista** belly dancer
baile *m* dance; ball; ballet; **baile de etiqueta** dress ball, formal dance; **baile de los globos** bubble dance; **baile de máscaras** masked ball, masquerade ball; **baile de San Vito** (pathol) Saint Vitus's dance; **baile de trajes** costume ball, fancy-dress ball
baja *f* (*de los precios*) fall, drop; (*en la guerra*) casualty; **dar baja** to go down, decline; **dar de baja** to drop; (mil) to mark absent; **darse de baja** to drop out; **jugar a la baja** to bear the market

bajaca *f* (Ecuad) hair ribbon
bajada *f* descent; slope; downspout; (rad) lead-in wire
bajagua *f* (Mex) cheap tobacco
bajamar *f* low tide
bajar *tr* to lower, take down; bring down; (*la escalera*) go down, descend; humble || *intr* to come down, go down; get off || *ref* to bend down; get off; humble oneself
bajel *m* ship, vessel
bajeza *f* humbleness, lowliness; meanness, baseness
bajío *m* shoal, sandbank; pitfall; lowland
bajista *adj* bearish || *mf* (fig) bear
ba•jo -ja *adj* low, under, lower; short; mean, base; lowly, humble; (mus) bass || *m* shoal, sandbank; (mus) bass || *f* see **baja** || **bajo** *adv* down; low, in a low voice || **bajo** *prep* under
bajón *m* bassoon; (*en el caudal, la salud, etc.*) decline, loss
bajonista *mf* bassoon player
bajorrelieve *m* bas-relief
bala *f* bullet; bale; **bala fría** spent bullet; **bala perdida** stray bullet; **ni a bala** (SAm) under no circumstances
balaca *f* boasting, show
balaceo *m* or **balacera** *f* (SAm) shooting; shootout
balada *f* ballad; (mus) ballade
bala•dí *adj* (*pl* **-díes**) trivial, paltry, cheap
baladro *m* scream, shout, outcry
baladronada *f* boast, boasting
baladronear *intr* to boast, brag
bálago *m* chaff
balance *m* balance, balance sheet; rocking, swinging; hesitation, doubt; (*de una nave*) rolling
balancear *tr* to balance || *intr & ref* to rock, swing; hesitate, waver; (*la nave*) roll
balancín *m* balance beam; singletree; rocker arm; seesaw
balandra *f* sloop
balandrán *m* cassock
balanza *f* scales, balance; comparison, judgment; **balanza de pagos** balance of payments
balar *intr* to bleat; (coll) to pine
balastar *tr* to ballast
balasto *m* ballast
balaustre *m* baluster, banister
balay *m* wicker basket
balazo *m* shot; bullet wound
balbucear *tr* to stammer || *intr* to stammer, stutter; to babble, to prattle
balbucir **§1** *tr & intr* var of **balbucear**
Balcanes, los the Balkans
balcarrotas *fpl* (SAm) sideburns; (Mex) locks falling over sides of face
balcón *m* balcony
baldar *tr* to cripple; incapacitate; inconvenience; trump
balde *m* bucket, pail; **de balde** free, gratis; over, in excess; **en balde** in vain
baldear *tr* to wash with pails of water; (*una excavación*) bail out
baldí•o -a *adj* uncultivated; idle, lazy; careless; useless, vain; unfounded || *m* untilled land
baldón *m* insult; blot, disgrace
baldonar *tr* to insult; stain, disgrace
baldosa *f* floor tile, paving tile; flagstone
baldra•gas *m* (*pl* **-gas**) jellyfish
balduque *s* red tape, wrapping tape
balear *tr* to shoot at, shoot, shoot to death
baleo *m* (SAm) shooting
balido *m* bleat, bleating
balísti•co -ca *adj* ballistic
baliza *f* buoy, beacon; danger signal
balizaje *m* (aer) airway lighting; (naut) buoys
balizar **§60** *tr* to mark with buoys; mark off
balnea•rio -ria *adj* bathing || *m* watering place, spa
balompié *m* football, soccer
balón *m* football; bale; balloon
baloncesto *m* basketball
balota *f* ballot
balotar *intr* to ballot
balsa *f* pool, puddle; raft; float; corkwood; **balsa salvavidas** life float
bálsamo *m* balsam, balm
balsear *tr* to cross by raft; ferry across
balsero *m* ferryman
bálti•co -ca *adj* Baltic
baluarte *m* bulwark
balumba *f* confusion; row
ballena *f* whale; whalebone; (*de corsé*) stay
ballesta *f* crossbow; spring, auto spring
ba•llet *m* (*pl* **-llets**) ballet
bambalinas *fpl* (theat) flies, borders
bambolear *intr* to sway, reel, wobble
bambolla *f* hulk; show, sham; show-off
bam•bú *m* (*pl* **-búes**) bamboo
banana *f* banana; (rad) plug
banane•ro -ra *adj* banana || *m* banana tree
banano *m* banana tree
banas *fpl* (Mex) banns
banasta *f* hamper, large basket
banca *f* bench; banking; stand, fruit stand; (*en el juego*) bank; **banca de hielo** iceberg; **hacer saltar la banca** to break the bank
banca•rio -ria *adj* banking, bank
bancarrota *f* bankruptcy; **hacer bancarrota** to go bankrupt
bancarrote•ro -ra *adj & mf* bankrupt
banco *m* bench; bank; (*de peces*) school; **banco de ahorros** savings bank; **banco de datos** (*ordenador*) data bank; memory; **banco de hielo** iceberg; **banco de liquidación** clearing house
banda *f* band; ribbon; faction, party; flock; border, edge; bank, shore; (*de la mesa de billar*) cushion; **banda ciudadana** citizens band, CB; **banda de rodamiento** (aut) tread; **banda de tambores** drum corps; **irse a la banda** (naut) to list
bandada *f* flock, covey; (*de gente*) (coll) flock
bandaje *m* tire
bandazo *m* swerving; (naut) lurch
bandear *tr* to go through, pierce; to pursue; to make love to || *ref* to manage
bandeja *f* tray; dish, platter

bandera *f* flag, banner; **con banderas desplegadas** with flying colors
banderilla *f* (taur) banderilla; **poner una banderilla a** to taunt; hit for a loan
banderín *m* (mil) color corporal; recruiting post
banderola *f* streamer, pennant; transom
bandido *m* bandit
bando *m* proclamation; faction, side
bandolera *f* bandoleer; female bandit; **en bandolera** across the shoulders
bandolero *m* highwayman, brigand
bandurria *f* Spanish lute
banquero *m* banker
banqueta stool, footstool; (Guat, Mex) sidewalk
banquete *m* banquet
banquetear *tr*, *intr* & *ref* to banquet
banquisa *f* floe, iceberg
bañadera *f* bathtub
bañado *m* chamber pot; marshland
baña•dor -dora *adj* bathing ‖ *mf* bather ‖ *m* bathing suit
bañar *tr* to bathe; dip; coat by dipping ‖ *ref* to bathe
bañera *f* bathtub
bañista *mf* bather; frequenter of a spa or seaside resort
baño *m* bath; bathing; bathroom; bathtub; **baño de asiento** sitz bath; **baño de ducha** shower bath; **baños** bathing place; spa
bao *m* (naut) beam
baptista *adj* & *mf* Baptist
baptisterio *m* baptistery
baque *m* thud, thump; bump, bruise
baquelita *f* bakelite
ba•quet *m* (*pl* **-quets**) bucket seat
baqueta *f* ramrod; drumstick; **correr baquetas** or **pasar por baquetas** to run the gauntlet
baquía *f* knowledge of the road, paths, rivers, etc. of a region; manual skill
baquia•no -na *adj* skillful, expert ‖ *mf* scout, pathfinder, guide
báqui•co -ca *adj* Bacchic
bar *m* bar; cocktail bar
barahunda *f* uproar, tumult
baraja *f* (*de naipes*) deck, pack; gang, mob; confusion, mix-up
barajadura *f* shuffling; dispute, quarrel
barajar *tr* (*naipes*) to shuffle; jumble, to mix ‖ *intr* to shuffle; fight, quarrel ‖ *ref* to get jumbled or mixed
baranda *f* railing; (*de la mesa de billar*) cushion
barandilla *f* balustrade, railing
barata *f* cheapness; barter; (Mex) bargain sale; (Chile, Peru) cockroach; (Col, Mex) junk store
baratero *m* shopkeeper
baratía *f* (SAm) cheapness
baratija *f* trinket
baratillo *m* second-hand goods; second-hand shop; bargain counter
baratío *m* (CAm) junk store
bara•to -ta *adj* cheap ‖ *m* bargain sale; **dar de barato** to admit for the sake of argument; **de barato** gratis, free ‖ *f* see **barata** ‖ **barato** *adv* cheap
báratro *m* (poet) hell
baratura *f* cheapness
baraúnda *f* uproar, tumult
barba *f* (*parte de la cara*) chin; (*pelo en ella*) beard; (*del papel*) deckle edge; (*de ave*) gill, wattle; **barba española** Spanish moss; **barbas** whiskers; **hacer la barba a** to shave; to bore, annoy; (Mex) to fawn on; **llevar por la barba** to lead by the nose; **mentir por la barba** (coll) to tell fish stories ‖ *m* (theat) old man
barbacoa *f* barbecue; (Col) kitchen cupboard; (Peru) attic
barbada *f* lower jaw of horse; bridle curb ‖ **la Barbada** Barbados
barbar *intr* to grow a beard; strike root
barbaridad *f* barbarism; outrage; piece of folly; large amount; **¡qué barbaridad!** how awful!, what nonsense!
barbarie *f* barbarity, barbarism
barbarismo *m* illiteracy; outrage; (gram) barbarism
bárba•ro -ra *adj* barbaric; barbarous ‖ *mf* barbarian
barbear *tr* to reach with the chin; be as high as ‖ *intr* to reach the same height; **barbear con** to be as high as
barbechar *tr* to plow for seeding; fallow
barbecho *m* fallow; **firmar como en un barbecho** to sign with one's eyes closed
barbería *f* barber shop
barberil *adj* barber
barbe•ro -ra *mf* barber; (Mex) flatterer
barbilampi•ño -ña *adj* smooth-faced, beardless; beginning, green
barbilla *f* tip of chin; (*de pluma*) barb; (*de pez*) wattle
bar•bón -bona *adj* bearded ‖ *m* graybeard; solemn old fellow; billy goat
barboquejo *m* chin strap
barbotar *tr* & *intr* to mutter, mumble
barbuchas *adj* beardless
barbu•do -da *adj* bearded, long-bearded, heavy-bearded ‖ *m* shoot, sucker
barbullar *tr* & *intr* to blabber
barca *f* small boat; bark; **barca perforador** offshore (oil) rig
barcia *f* chaff
barco *m* boat, ship; **barco cisternas** or **barco tanque** tanker; **barco de carga** cargo boat; **barco náufrago** shipwreck
barchi•lón -lona *mf* (Ecuad, Peru) nurse, orderly; (Arg, Bol, Peru) quack
barda *f* thatch; bard, horse armor
bardana *f* burdock
bardar *tr* to thatch; (*caballo*) bard
bardo *m* bard
baremo *m* (*escala*) scale; rate table
bargueño *m* carved inlaid secretary
bario *m* barium
barjuleta *f* haversack
barloventear *intr* to wander around; turn to windward
barlovento *m* windward
barman *m* bartender

bar•niz *m* (*pl* **-nices**) varnish; (*de la loza, la porcelana, etc.*) glaze; gloss, polish; (*conocimientos superficiales*) smattering; (aer) dope
barnizar §**60** *tr* to varnish
barómetro *m* barometer; **barómetro aneroide** aneroid barometer
barón *m* baron
baronesa *f* baroness
barquero *m* boatman
barquilla *f* (naut) log; (naut) log chip; (aer) nacelle
barquillero *m* waffle iron; harbor boatman
barquillo *m* cone; waffle
barquín *m* bellows
barra *f* bar; (*de dinamita*) stick; (*en el tribunal*) bar, railing; **barra colectora** (elec) bus bar; **barra de labios** or **para los labios** lipstick; **barra imantada** bar magnet; **barras paralelas** (sport) parallel bars
barrabasada *f* fiendish prank, mean trick
barraca *f* cabin, hut; cottage; storage shed
barracón *m* barracks; fair booth
barragana *f* concubine
barranca *f* gorge, ravine, gully
barranco *m* gorge, ravine, gully; difficulty, obstruction; cliff, precipice
barrar *tr* to daub, smear
barrear *tr* to barricade; bar shut
barredera *f* street sweeper
barre•dor -dora *mf* sweeper; **barredora de alfombras** carpet sweeper; **barredora de nieve** snowplow
barredura *f* sweeping; **barreduras** sweepings
barremi•nas *m* (*pl* **-nas**) mine sweeper
barrena *f* auger, drill, gimlet; (*espiga para taladrar*) bit; (aer) spin; **barrena picada** (aer) tail spin; **entrar en barrena** (aer) to go into a spin
barrenar *tr* to drill; (*un buque*) to scuttle; blast; upset, frustrate; violate
barrende•ro -ra *mf* sweeper
barreno *m* large drill; drill hole; blast hole; pride, vanity; (Chile) mania, pet idea; **dar barreno a** (*un buque*) to scuttle
barreño *m* earthen dishpan
barrer *tr* to sweep, sweep away; graze || *intr* to sweep; **barrer hacia dentro** to look out for oneself
barrera *f* barrier; barricade; (mil) barrage; crockery cupboard; tollgate; (rr) crossing gate; (taur) fence around inside of ring; (taur) first row of seats; **barrera de arrecifes** barrier reef; **barrera de paso a nivel** (rr) crossing gate; **barrera de sonido** or **barrera sónica** sound barrier
barriada *f* district, quarter
barrial *m* (SAm) mudhole; muddy ground
barrica *f* cask, barrel
barriga *f* belly; (*de una vasija, una pared, etc.*) bulge
barri•gón -gona or **barrigu•do -da** *adj* big-bellied
barril *m* barrel
barrilero *m* cooper, barrel maker
barrio *m* ward, quarter; suburb; **barrio bajo** slums; **barrio comercial** shopping district, business district; **el otro barrio** the other world; **estar vestido de barrio** to be dressed in house clothes
barro *m* mud; clay; earthenware; pimple; (coll) money; (Arg, Urug) blunder
barro•co -ca *adj & m* baroque
barro•so -sa *adj* muddy; pimply
barrote *m* heavy bar; bolt; cross brace
barruntar *tr* to guess; to sense
barrunto *m* guess, conjecture; sign, token, foreboding
bartola *f* belly; **a la bartola** lazily
bartolina *f* (CAm, W-I) jail, dungeon
bártulos *mpl* household tools; **liar los bártulos** to pack up one's belongings
barullo *m* confusion, tumult
basar *tr* to base; build || *ref* — **basarse en** to base one's judgment on, rely on
basca *f* nausea, squeamishness; fit of temper, tantrum
basco•so -sa *adj* nauseated, squeamish
báscula *f* scales; platform scale
base *f* base; basis; **a base de** on the basis of
bási•co -ca *adj* basic
Basilea *f* Basle, Basel
basílica *f* basilica
basilisco *m* basilisk; **estar hecho un basilisco** to be in a rage
basquear *intr* to be nauseated
basquetbol *m* basketball
bastante *adj* enough || *adv* enough; fairly, rather || *m* enough
bastar *intr* to be enough, suffice; abound, be more than enough || *ref* to be self-sufficient
bastardilla *f* italics
bastar•do -da *adj & mf* bastard
bastedad *f* coarseness; roughness; (CAm) abundance; excess
bastidor *m* frame; stretcher; (theat) wing; **entre bastidores** behind the scenes
bastilla *f* hem
bastillar *tr* to hem
bas•to -ta *adj* coarse, rough; uncouth || *m* packsaddle; (*naipe*) club; **el basto** the ace of clubs
bastón *m* stick, staff; cane, walking stick; baton; **bastón de esquiar** ski pole or stick
bastoncillo *m* small stick; (*de la retina*) rod
bastonear *tr* to cane, beat
basura *f* sweepings; rubbish, litter, refuse; horse manure
basural *m* (SAm) dump; trash pile
basurero *m* trash can; rubbish dump; rubbish collector
basurita *f* trifle
bata *f* smock; dressing gown, wrapper; **bata de baño** bathrobe
batacazo *m* thud, bump
bataclán *m* (Cuba) burlesque show
bataclana *f* (Cuba) showgirl, stripteaser
batahola *f* racket, hubbub
batalla *f* battle; (*de un vehículo*) wheel base; (*de la silla de montar*) seat; (paint) battle piece; **batalla campal** pitched battle; **librar batalla** to do battle
batallar *intr* to battle, fight; hesitate, waver

bata•llón -llona *adj* (*cuestión*) controversial, moot || *m* battalion
batata *f* sweet potato; (Arg) timidity
bate *m* baseball bat
batea *f* tray; flat-bottomed boat; (rr) flatcar
bateador *m* batter
batear *tr & intr* to bat
batel *m* small boat
batelero *m* boatman
batería *f* battery; footlights; **batería de cocina** kitchen utensils
baterista *mf* drummer
batiboleo *m* (Cuba, Mex) noise; confusion
bati•do -da *adj* (*camino*) beaten; (*tejido*) moiré || *m* batter; milk shake; (rad) beat || *f* battue; combing, search
batidor *m* beater; scout, ranger; **batidor de huevos** egg beater; **batidor de oro** goldbeater
batidora • beater, mixer
batiente *m* jamb; (*hoja de puerta*) leaf, door; (*de piano*) damper; wash, place where surf breaks
batihoja *m* goldbeater; sheet-metal worker
batimiento *m* beating; (phys) beat
batín *m* smoking jacket
batintín *m* Chinese gong
batir *tr* to beat; batter, beat down; (*las alas*) flap; (*manos*) clap; (*las olas*) ply; **batir tiendas** (mil) to strike camp
batiscafo *m* bathyscaphe
bato *m* simpleton, rustic
batuque *m* (Arg) uproar, rumpus, jamboree; **armar un batuque** (Arg) to raise a rumpus
baturrillo *m* hodgepodge
batuta *f* (mus) baton; **llevar la batuta** to boss the show
baúl *m* trunk; **baúl mundo** large trunk; **baúl ropero** wardrobe trunk
bauprés *m* bowsprit
bautismo *m* baptism; **bautismo de aire** first flight
bautista *adj* Baptist || *mf* Baptist; baptizer; **el Bautista** John the Baptist
bautisterio *m* baptistery
bautizar **§60** *tr* to baptize; (*el vino*) water
bautizo *m* baptism; christening party
báva•ro -ra *adj & mf* Bavarian
Baviera *f* Bavaria
baya *f* berry
bayeta *f* baize
ba•yo -ya *adj* bay || *m* bay horse || *f* see **baya**
bayoneta *f* bayonet
bayonetear *tr* to bayonet
bayunca *f* or **bayuna** *f* (CAm) bar; tavern
baza *f* trick; **meter baza en** to butt into
bazar *m* bazaar
ba•zo -za *adj* yellowish-brown || *m* yellowish brown; spleen || *f* see **baza**
bazofia *f* refuse, offal, garbage
bazuca *f* bazooka
bazucar **§73** *tr* to stir, shake; tamper with
be *m* baa
beata *f* lay sister
beatería *f* cant, hypocrisy
beatificar **§73** *tr* to beatify
beatísi•mo -ma *adj* most holy
bea•to -ta *adj* blessed; pious, devout; bigoted, prudish || *mf* beatified person; devout person; bigot; churchgoer || *f* see **beata**
bebé *m* baby; doll
bebede•ro -ra *adj* (archaic) drinkable || *m* watering place; (Col, Ecuad, Mex) watering trough
bebedi•zo -za *adj* drinkable || *m* potion, philter
bebe•dor -dora *adj* drinking || *mf* drinker; hard drinker
beber *m* drink, drinking || *tr & intr* to drink; **beber de** or **en** to drink out of || *ref* to drink, drink up; (*p.ej., un libro*) to drink in
bebestible *adj* drinkable || *m* drink
bebezón *f* (Col) drunk, spree
bebible *adj* drinkable
bebi•do -da *adj* tipsy, unsteady || *f* drink
bebistrajo *m* dose, mixture
beborrotear *intr* to tipple
beca *f* scholarship, fellowship; (*de los colegiales*) sash
becacín *m* snipe, whole snipe
becacina *f* snipe, great snipe
becada *f* woodcock
beca•rio -ria *mf* scholar, fellow
becerra *f* snapdragon
becerrillo *m* calfskin
bece•rro -rra *mf* yearling calf || *m* calfskin || *f* see **becerra**
becuadro *m* (mus) natural sign
bedel *m* beadle
befa *f* jeer, flout, scoff
befar *tr* to jeer at, to scoff at || *intr* (*un caballo*) to move the lips
be•fo -fa *adj* blobber-lipped; knock-kneed || *m* (*de animal*) lip || *f* see **befa**
beisbol *m* baseball
beisbolero *m* or **beisbolista** *m* baseball player
bejuco *m* cane, liana
beldad *f* beauty
beldar **§2** *tr* to winnow
belén *m* crèche; bedlam, confusion; madhouse; gossip || **Belén** Bethlehem
bel•fo -fa *adj* (*labio*) blobber; blobber-lipped || *m* (*de animal*) lip; blobber lip
belga *adj & mf* Belgian
Bélgica *f* Belgium
bélgi•co -ca *adj* Belgian || *f* see **Bélgica**
belicista *mf* warmonger
béli•co -ca *adj* warlike
belico•so -sa *adj* bellicose
beligerante *adj & mf* belligerent
belitre *adj* low, mean || *m* scoundrel
bella•co -ca *adj* cunning, sly; wicked || *mf* scoundrel
bellaquear *intr* to cheat, be crooked; (SAm) to be stubborn; rear
bellaquería *f* cunning, slyness; wickedness
belleza *f* beauty; **belleza exótica** glamour girl
be•llo -lla *adj* beautiful, fair
bellota *f* acorn; carnation bud
bem•bo -ba *adj* thick-lipped; (Mex) simple, silly || *mf* (*persona*) thicklips
bemol *adj & m* (mus) flat; **tener bemoles** to be a tough job

bencedrina *f* benzedrine
bencina *f* benzine
bendecir §**11** *tr* to bless; consecrate; **bendecir la mesa** to say grace
bendición *f* benediction, blessing; godsend; (*en la mesa*) grace; **bendiciones** wedding ceremony; **echar la bendicióna** to have nothing more to do with
bendi•to -ta *adj* blessed, saintly; simple, silly; happy; (*agua*) holy; **como el pan bendito** as easy as pie || *m* simple-minded soul
benedícite *m* grace; **rezar el benedícite** to say grace
benedicti•no -na *adj & mf* Benedictine || *m* benedictine
beneficencia *f* beneficience; charity, welfare; social service
beneficia•do -da *mf* person or charity receiving the proceeds of a benefit performance
beneficiar *tr* to benefit; (*la tierra*) cultivate; (*una mina*) work, exploit; (*minerales*) process, reduce; (*una región del país*) serve; season; slaughter || *ref* — **beneficiarse de** to take advantage of
beneficia•rio -ria *mf* beneficiary
beneficio *m* benefit; profit, gain, yield; (*de una mina*) exploitation; smelting, ore reduction; benefit performance; **a beneficio de** for the benefit of; on the strength of; **beneficios sociales** fringe benefits
beneficio•so -sa *adj* beneficial, profitable
benéfi•co -ca *adj* charitable, benevolent
beneméri•to -ta *adj & mf* worthy; **benemérito de la patria** national hero
beneplácito *m* approval, consent
benevolencia *f* benevolence
benévo•lo -la *adj* benevolent, kind-hearted
bengala *f* Bengal light; (aer) flare
benignidad *f* benignity, mildness, kindness; (*del tiempo*) mildness
benig•no -na *adj* benign, mild, kind; (*tiempo*) clement, mild
benjamín *m* baby (*the youngest child*)
beodez *f* drunkenness
beo•do -da *adj & mf* drunk
bequista *mf* (CAm, Cuba) scholarship holder; grant winner
berbi•quí *m* (*pl* **-quíes**) brace; **berbiquí y barrena** brace and bit
berenjena *f* eggplant
berenjenal *m* eggplant patch; (coll) predicament, jam, fix
bergante *m* scoundrel, rascal
bergantín *m* (naut) brig; **bergantín goleta** (naut) brigantine
berilio *m* beryllium
berkelio *m* berkelium
berli•nés -nesa *adj* Berlin || *mf* Berliner
bermejear *intr* to turn bright red; look bright red
berme•jo -ja *adj* vermilion, bright-red
berme•jón -jona *adj* red, reddish
bermellón *m* vermilion
berrear *intr* to bellow, low; bawl, yowl
berrenchín *m* rage, tantrum
berrido *m* bellow; scream, yowl
berrín *m* touchy person, cross child
berrinche *m* tantrum, conniption
berro *m* water cress
berza *f* cabbage
berzal *m* cabbage patch
berzas *m* or **berzotas** *m* dunderhead, flop
besalamano *m* (obs) announcement, written in the third person and marked B.L.M. (*kisses your hand*)
besamanos *m* levee, reception at court; throwing kisses
besar *tr* to kiss; to graze || *ref* to bump heads together
beso *m* kiss; **beso sonado** buss
bestia *adj* stupid || *mf* dunce || *f* beast; **bestia de carga** beast of burden
bestial *adj* beastly; (coll) terrific
besucar §**73** *tr & intr* to keep on kissing
besu•cón -cona *adj* kissing || *mf* kisser
besuquear *tr & intr* to keep on kissing
betabel *m* (Mex) beet
betún *m* bitumen, pitch; shoe polish
bezo *m* blubber lip; proud flesh
bezu•do -da *adj* thick-lipped
biberón *m* nursing bottle
Biblia *f* Bible
bíbli•co -ca *adj* Biblical
bibliófi•lo -la *mf* bibliophile
bibliografía *f* bibliography
bibliógra•fo -fa *mf* bibliographer
biblioteca *f* library; **biblioteca de consulta** reference library; **biblioteca de préstamo** lending library
biblioteca•rio -ria *mf* librarian
bibliotecnia *f* bookmaking; library science
biblioteconomía *f* library science
bicameral *adj* bicameral
bicarbonato *m* bicarbonate
bicicleta *f* bicycle
bicherío *m* (SAm) vermin
bichero *m* boat hook
bicho *m* bug, insect; vermin; animal; fighting bull; simpleton; brat; **bicho viviente** living soul; **mal bicho** scoundrel; ferocious bull
bidón *m* (*bote, lata*) can; (*tonel de metal*) drum
biela *f* connecting rod
bielda *f* winnowing rack; winnowing
bieldar *tr* to winnow
bieldo *m* winnowing pitch rake
bien *adv* well; readily; very; indeed; **ahora bien** now then; **bien como** just as; **bien que** although; **más bien** rather; somewhat; **no bien** as soon as; scarcely || *s* welfare; property; darling; **bienes** wealth, riches, possessions; **bienes de fortuna** worldly possessions; **bienes dotales** dower; **bienes inmuebles** real estate; **bienes muebles** personal property; **bienes raíces** real estate; **bienes relictos** estate; **bienes semovientes** livestock; **bien público** commonweal; **en bien de** for the sake of
bienal *adj* biennial
bienama•do -da *adj* dearly beloved
bienandanza *f* happiness, prosperity
bienaventura•do -da *adj* happy, blissful; blessed; simple

bienaventuranza *f* happiness, bliss; blessedness
bienestar *m* well-being, welfare
bienhabla•do -da *adj* well-spoken
bienhada•do -da *adj* fortunate, lucky
bienhe•chor -chora *adj* beneficent || *m* benefactor || *f* benefactress
bienintenciona•do -da *adj* well-meaning
bienio *m* biennium
bienquerencia *f* affection, fondness
bienquistar *tr* to bring together, reconcile
bienvenida *f* safe arrival; welcome; **dar la bienvenida a** to welcome
bienveni•do -da *adj* welcome || *f* see **bienvenida**
bienvivir *intr* to live in comfort; live decently, properly
bif•tec *m* (*pl* **-tecs**) beefsteak
bifurcar §73 *ref* to branch, fork
bigamia *f* bigamy
bíga•mo -ma *adj* bigamous || *mf* bigamist
bigornia *f* two-horn anvil
bigote *m* mustache; **bigotes** (*del gato*) whiskers; **tener bigotes** to have a mind of one's own
bigudí *m* hair curler
bikini *m* bikini (swimsuit)
bilingüe *adj* bilingual
bilis *f* bile; **descargar la bilis** to vent one's spleen
bilma *f* (med) compress
billar *m* billiards; billiard table; billiard room; **billar romano** pinball
billete *m* ticket; note, bill; **billete de abono** season ticket; commutation ticket; **billete de banco** bank note; **billete de ida y vuelta** round-trip ticket; **billete kilométrico** mileage ticket; **medio billete** half fare
billetero *m* billfold; ticket agent
billón *m* (U.S.A.) trillion; (Brit) billion
bimba *f* top hat; (Mex) drinking spree
bimotor *adj* twin-motor || *m* twin-motor plane
biodegradable *adj* biodegradable
biofísi•co -ca *adj* biophysical || *f* biophysics
biografía *f* biography
biógra•fo -fa *mf* biographer
biología *f* biology
biólo•go -ga *mf* biologist
biombo *m* folding screen
bioplasma *f* bioplasm
biopsia *f* biopsy
bióxido *m* dioxide
bioquími•co -ca *adj* biochemical || *mf* biochemist || *f* biochemistry
bipartición *f* fission, splitting
bípe•do -da *adj* & *mf* biped; human
biplano *m* biplane
biplaza *m* (aer) two-seater
birimbao *m* jews'-harp
birlar *tr* to knock down, shoot down; outwit; **birlar algo a alguien** to snitch something from someone
birlocha *f* kite
Birmania *f* Burma
birma•no -na *adj* & *mf* Burmese
biro *m* or **birome** *f* (Arg) ball-point pen
birreta *f* biretta, red biretta
birrete *m* mortarboard, academic cap
bis *interj* encore! || *m* encore
bisabue•lo -la *mf* great-grandparent || *m* great-grandfather || *f* great-grandmother
bisagra *f* hinge
bisar *tr* to repeat
bisbisar *tr* to mutter, mumble
bisecar §73 *tr* to bisect
bisel *m* bevel edge
biselar *tr* to bevel
bisies•to -ta *adj* leap
bismuto *m* bismuth
bisnie•to -ta *mf* great-grandchild || *m* great-grandson || *f* great-granddaughter
biso•jo -ja *adj* squint-eyed, cross-eyed
bisonte *m* bison; buffalo
biso•ño -ña *adj* green, inexperienced || *mf* greenhorn, rookie
bisté *m* or **bistec** *m* beefsteak
bisun•to -ta *adj* dirty, greasy
bisutería *f* costume jewelry
bitácora *f* binnacle
bitoque *m* bung; (CAm) sewer; (Mex) spigot
Bizancio Byzantium
bizanti•no -na *adj* & *mf* Byzantine
bizarría *f* gallantry, bravery; magnanimity
biza•rro -rra *adj* gallant, brave; magnanimous
bizcar §73 *tr* to wink || *intr* to squint
biz•co -ca *adj* squint-eyed, cross-eyed
bizcocho *m* biscuit; cake, sponge cake; hardtack; bisque
bizma *f* poultice
bizmar *tr* to poultice
biznie•to -ta *mf* var of **bisnieto**
bizquear *intr* to squint
bizquera *f* squint
blanca *f* steel blade; **sin blanca** penniless
blanca•zo -za *adj* whitish
blan•co -ca *adj* white; (*tez*) fair; (*fuerza*) water; (*arma*) steel; (*cobarde*) yellow; blank || *mf* (*persona*) white; coward || *m* (*color*) white; blank; target; aim, object; interval; white heat; blank form; **dar en el blanco** to hit the mark; **en blanco** (*hoja*) blank; **hacer blanco** to hit the mark; **quedarse en blanco** to not get the point; to be disappointed || *f* see **blanca**
blancor *m* whiteness
blancura *f* whiteness; purity
blancuz•co -ca *adj* whitish; dirty-white
blandear *tr* to persuade; brandish || *intr* & *ref* to yield, give in
blandengue *adj* soft, colorless
blandir §1 *tr*, *intr* & *ref* to brandish
blan•do -da *adj* bland, soft; indulgent; flabby; sensual; cowardly; (*ojos*) tender
blandón *m* wax candle; candlestick
blandura *f* blandness, softness; tolerance; flabbiness; sensuality; flattery; mild weather; cowardice
blanqueadura *f* whitening; bleaching; whitewash
blanquear *tr* to whiten, bleach; blanch; whitewash; tin || *intr* to turn white
blanqueci•no -na *adj* whitish

blanqui•llo -lla *adj* white, whitish || *m* (Guat, Mex) egg; (Chile, Peru) white peach
blasfemar *tr* to blaspheme, curse
blasfemia *f* blasphemy
blasfe•mo -ma *adj* blasphemous || *mf* blasphemer
blasón *m* (*ciencia de los escudos de armas; escudo de armas*) heraldry; (heral) charge; (fig) glory, honor
blasonar *tr* to emblazon; (fig) to emblazon, extol || *intr* to boast; **blasonar de** to boast of being
bledo *m* straw; **no me importa un bledo** or **no se me da un bledo de ello** that doesn't matter a rap to me
blindaje *m* armor; (elec) shield
blindar *tr* to armor, armor-plate; (elec) to shield
B.L.M. *abbr* **besalamano**
bloc *m* (*pl* **bloques**) pad
blof *m* bluff
blofear *intr* to bluff
blon•do -da *adj* blond, fair, flaxen, light; (Arg) curly || *f* blond lace
bloque *m* block; (*de papel*) pad; **bloque de hormigón** concrete block
bloquear *tr* to blockade; (*un coche, un tren*) brake; (*créditos*) freeze
bloqueo *m* blockade; (*de crédito*) freezing; **bloqueo vertical** (telv) vertical hold
b.l.p. *abbr* **besa los pies**
blujins *mpl* blue jeans
blusa *f* blouse, smock; (*de mujer*) shirtwaist; (Col) jacket
boardilla *f* dormer window; garret
boato *m* show, pomp
bobada *f* folly, piece of folly
bobalías *mf* simpleton, dunce
bobali•cón -cona *adj* simple, silly || *mf* simpleton, nitwit
bobear *intr* to talk nonsense; to dawdle, loiter around
bobería *f* folly, nonsense
bóbilis—de bóbilis free, for nothing; without effort
bobina *f* bobbin; (elec) coil; **bobina de chispas** spark coil; **bobina de encendido** ignition coil, spark coil; **bobina de sintonía** tuning coil
bobinar *tr* to wind
bo•bo -ba *adj* simple, foolish, stupid || *mf* simpleton, fool || *m* (archaic) clown, jester
boca *f* mouth; speech; taste, flavor; (*del estómago*) pit; **a boca de jarro** immoderately; at close range; **boca de agua** hydrant; **boca de dragón** (bot) snapdragon; **boca de riego** hydrant; **buscarle a uno la boca** to draw someone out; **decir con la boca chica** to offer as a mere formality; **no decir esta boca es mía** to not say a word
bocacalle *f* street entrance; intersection
boca•caz *m* (*pl* **-caces**) spillway
bocadillo *m* tape, ribbon; snack, bite; farmer's snack in the field; sandwich
bocadito *m* little bit; (Cuba) cigarillo (*cigaret wrapped in tobacco*)
bocado *m* bite, morsel; bit; **bocado de Adán** Adam's apple; **no tener para un bocado** to not have a cent
bocal *m* narrow-mouthed pitcher; (*de un puerto*) narrows
bocallave *f* keyhole
bocamanga *f* cuff, wristband
bocanada *f* (*de líquido*) swallow; (*de humo*) puff; (*de viento*) gust; boasting
bocartear *tr* to crush, stamp
bocaza *f* loudmouth; gossip
bocera *f* smear on lips
boceto *m* sketch, outline; wax model, clay model
bocina *f* horn, trumpet; auto horn; phonograph horn; ear trumpet
bocio *m* goiter
bocoy *m* large barrel
bocha *f* bowling ball
bochar *tr* (Mex, Ven) to turn down; (Mex, Ven) insult
boche *m* small hole in ground for boys' game; (Ven) slight, snub
bochinche *m* uproar, tumult, row
bochorno *m* sultry weather; blush, embarrassment, shame
bochorno•so -sa *adj* sultry, stuffy; embarrassing, shameful
boda *f* marriage, wedding; **bodas de Camacho** banquet, lavish feast
bodega *f* wine cellar; dock warehouse; granary; grocery store; (*de nave*) hold; cellar; (*hombre que bebe mucho*) tank
bodegón *m* hash house, beanery; saloon; still life
bodegue•ro -ra *mf* cellarer; grocer
bodijo *m* unequal match; simple wedding
bodoque *m* lump; dunce, dolt; (Mex) bump, lump
bodoquera *f* peashooter
bóer *mf* Boer
bofe *adj invar* (CAm) unpleasant, disgusting || *m* (coll) lung; (P-R) cinch, snap; **echar el bofe** or **los bofes** to drudge, to grind; **bofes** lights (*of sheep, etc.*)
bofetada *f* slap in the face
boga *mf* rower || *f* vogue, fashion; rowing
bogar **§44** *intr* to row
bogavante *m* lobster
bohardilla *f* dormer window; garret
bohe•mio -mia *adj & mf* Bohemian
bohío *m* hut, shack
boicotear *tr* to boycott
boicoteo *m* boycott, boycotting
boina *f* beret
boj *m* boxwood
boja *f* southernwood
bojar *tr* to measure the perimeter of; (*el cuero*) scrape clean || *intr* to measure
bola *f* ball; marble; bowling; shoe polish; shoeshine; (cards) slam; lie, deceit; (Mex) brawl, riot; **bola de alcanfor** moth ball; **bola de cristal** crystal ball; **bola de nieve** snowball; **bola rompedora** wrecking ball; **bolas** Gaucho lasso tipped with balls; **dejar que ruede la bola** to let things take

their course; **raspar la bola** (Chile) to clear out, beat it

bolada *f* (*de una bola*) throw; luck, opportunity; (Arg) billiard stroke; (Chile) dainty, tidbit; (Guat, Mex) lie, fib

bolado *m* (CAm) rumor

bolazo *m* hit with a ball; **de bolazo** (coll) hurriedly, right away; (Mex) at random

bolchevique *adj & mf* Bolshevik

bolchevismo *m* Bolshevism

boleada *f* (Arg) hunting with bolas; (Mex) shoeshine; (Peru) flunking

bolear *tr* to throw; (Arg) to catch with bolas; (*zapatos*) (Mex) to shine; (SAm) to kick out, flunk || *intr* to play for fun; lie; boast || *ref* (Arg, Urug) to rear and fall backwards; upset; blush

bole•ro -ra *mf* bolero dancer || *m* bolero (*dance; music; jacket*); (Mex) bootblack || *f* bowling alley; **bolera encespada** bowling green

boleta *f* pass, permit, admission ticket; (mil) billet; ballot

boletería *f* ticket office

boletín *m* bulletin; ticket; form; press release

boleto *m* ticket

boliche *m* bowling; bowling alley; (SAm) hash house

bólido *m* fireball, bolide

bolígrafo *m* ball-point pen

bolilápiz *m* (Mex) ball-point pen

bolillo *m* bobbin for making lace; frame for stiffening lace cuffs

Bolivia *f* Bolivia

bolivia•no -na *adj & mf* Bolivian

bo•lo -la *adj* (CAm, Mex) drunk; *m* ninepin, tenpin; dunce, blockhead; (*de escalera*) newel; (cards) slam; **bolos** bowling, ninepins, tenpins; **jugar a los bolos** to bowl

Bolonia *f* Bologna

bolsa *f* purse, pocketbook; pouch; stock exchange, stock market; (*en el vestido*) bag, pucker; grant, award; **bolsa de agua caliente** hotwater bottle; **bolsa de aire** (aut) air bag; **bolsa de hielo** ice bag; **bolsa de trabajo** employment bureau; **bolsa isotérmica** Thermos bottle; **hacer bolsa** (*un vestido*) to bag; **jugar a la bolsa** to play the market

bolsear *tr* to pick the pocket of; (Arg, Bol, Urug) to jilt; (Chile) to sponge on

bolsero *m* (SAm) sponger; (Mex) pickpocket

bolsicalculadora *f* pocket calculator

bolsillo *m* pocket; purse, pocketbook

bolsista *m* broker, stockbroker; (CAm, Mex) pickpocket

bolso *m* purse, pocketbook; **bolso de mano** handbag

bollo *m* bun, roll; bump, lump; dent; (*en un vestido*) puff; (*en adorno de tapicería*) tuft; **bollo de crema** cream puff

bomba *f* pump; bomb; fire engine; lamp globe; high hat; firecracker; soap bubble; bombshell; **a prueba de bombas** bombproof; **bomba atómica** atomic bomb; **bomba coche** car bomb; **bomba cohete** rocket bomb; **bomba de engrase** grease gun; **bomba de hidrógeno** hydrogen bomb; **bomba de incendios** fire engine; **bomba de profundidad** depth bomb; **bomba de sentina** bilge pump; **bomba estomacal** stomach pump; **bomba neutrónica** neutron bomb; **bomba rompedora** blockbuster; **bomba volante** buzz bomb; **caer como una bomba** to fall like a bombshell; to burst in unexpectedly

bombachas *fpl* loose-fitting baggy trousers

bombardear *tr & intr* to bomb; bombard; **bombardear en picado** to dive-bomb

bombardeo *m* bombing; bombarding; **bombardeo en picado** dive bombing

bombardero *m* bomber; bombardier

bomba-reloj *f* time bomb

bombazo *m* bomb explosion; bomb hit; bomb damage

bombear *tr* to bomb; ballyhoo, puff up; pump; (SAm) to reconnoiter; (Col) to fire, dismiss || *ref* to camber, bulge

bombero *m* fireman; pumpman

bombilla *f* bulb, light bulb; lamp chimney; tube for sucking up maté; **bombilla de destello** flash bulb

bombillo *m* trap, stench trap; (naut) pump

bombista *m* lamp maker; (*el que da bombos*) booster

bom•bo -ba *adj* astounded, stunned; (W-I) lukewarm || *m* bass drum; ballyhoo; (naut) barge, lighter; **dar bombo a** to ballyhoo, puff up; **irse al bombo** (Arg) to fail || *f* see **bomba**

bombón *m* bonbon, candy

bombona *f* carboy

bombonera *f* candy box

bona•chón -chona *adj* goodnatured, kind, simple

bonancible *adj* (*tiempo*) fair; (*mar*) calm; (*viento*) moderate

bonanza *f* fair weather, calm seas; prosperity, boom; rich ore pocket

bona•zo -za *adj* kind-hearted

bondad *f* kindness; favor; **tener la bondad de** to have the kindness to

bondado•so -sa *adj* kind, generous

bonete *m* cap, hat; candy bowl

bonetería *f* hat shop; notion store

bongo *m* (SAm) barge; canoe

boniato *m* sweet potato

bonificar **§73** *tr* to improve; give a discount on

boni•to -ta *adj* pretty, nice; pretty good

bono *m* bond; food voucher

boñiga *f* manure, cow dung

boom *m* (*mercado, bolsa*) boom

boqueada *f* gasp of death

boquear *tr* to pronounce, utter || *intr* to gasp

boquerel *m* nozzle

boquete *m* gap, breach, opening

boquiabier•to -ta *adj* open-mouthed

boquian•cho -cha *adj* wide-mouthed

boquiangos•to -ta *adj* narrow-mouthed

boquihundi•do -da *adj* hollow-mouthed

boquilla *f* (*de instrumento de viento*) mouthpiece; (*de pipa*) stem; (*de cigarro*) tip; (*de aparato de alumbrado*) burner; cigar

holder, cigarette holder; (*de manguera*) nozzle; opening in irrigation canal; opening at bottom of trouser leg
boquirro•to -ta *adj* garrulous
boquiverde *adj* obscene, smutty
bórax *m* borax
borbollar or **borbollear** *intr* to bubble up
borbollón *m* bubbling; **a borbollones** impetuously
borborigmos *mpl* rumbling of the bowels
borbotar *intr* to bubble up, bubble over
borce•guí *m* (*pl* **-guíes**) high shoe
borda *f* hut; (naut) gunwale; **arrojar, echar** or **tirar por la borda** to throw overboard
bordada *f* (naut) tack; **dar bordadas** (naut) to tack; pace to and fro
bordado *m* embroidery
bordadura *f* embroidery
bordar *tr* to embroider
borde *m* border, edge; fringe; rim; **borde de la acera** curb; **borde del mar** seaside
bordear *tr* to border ‖ *intr* to go on the edge; (naut) to tack
bordo *m* (naut) board; (naut) side; (naut) tack; (Guat, Mex) dam, dike; **a bordo** (naut) on board; **al bordo** (naut) alongside; **de alto bordo** seagoing; distinguished, important
bordón *m* (*de tambor*) snare; pilgrim's staff; pet word; burden, refrain
bordonear *intr* to grope along with a stick; to go around begging
borgoña *m* Burgundy (*wine*) ‖ **la Borgoña** Burgundy
borgo•ñón -ñona *adj & mf* Burgundian
boricua or **borinque•ño -ña** *adj & mf* Puerto Rican
borla *f* tassel; powder puff; **tomar la borla** to take a higher degree, take the doctor's degree
borne *m* binding post; (*de la lanza*) tip
bornear *tr* to bend, twist; (*sillares pesados*) set in place ‖ *intr* to swing at anchor ‖ *ref* to warp
borra *f* fuzz, nap, lint
borrachera *f* drunkenness; spree, binge; great exaltation; (coll) piece of folly; **pegarse una borrachera** to go on a binge
borrachería *f* (Mex) bar, tavern
borrachín *m* drunkard
borra•cho -cha *adj* drunk; (*habitualmente*) drinking ‖ *mf* drunkard
borrador *m* blotter, day book; rough draft; eraser
borradura *f* striking out, scratching out
borraj *m* borax
borrajear *tr & intr* to scribble; doodle
borrar *tr* to scratch out, cross out; erase, rub out; darken, obscure; blot, smear
borrasca *f* storm, tempest; upset, setback
borrasco•so -sa *adj* stormy
borregos *mpl* fleecy clouds
borrica *f* she-ass; stupid woman
borrico *m* ass, donkey; sawhorse; stupid fellow, ass
borricón *m* or **borricote** *m* drudge
borrón *m* blot; rough draft; blemish; (fig) blot, stain
borronear *tr* to scribble
borro•so -sa *adj* blurred, smudgy, fuzzy; muddy, thick
boruca *f* noise, clamor, uproar
borujo *m* lump, clump
boscaje *m* woodland; (paint) woodland scene
bosque *m* forest, woodland; **bosque maderable** timberland
bosquejar *tr* to sketch, outline; make a rough model of
bosquejo *m* sketch, outline; rough model
bostezar **§60** *intr* to yawn, gape
bostezo *m* yawn, yawning
bota *f* shoe, boot; leather wine bag; liquid measure (*125 gallons or 516 liters*); **bota de agua** gum boot; **bota de montar** riding boot; **ponerse las botas** (coll) to hit the jack pot, come out on top
botador *m* boat pole; punch, nailset
botadura *f* launching
botafuego *m* hothead, firebrand
botalón *m* (naut) boom; **botalón de foque** (naut) jib boom
botáni•co -ca *adj* botanical ‖ *mf* botanist ‖ *f* botany
botanista *mf* botanist
botar *tr* to throw, hurl; throw away, throw out; (*un buque*) launch; (*el timón*) shift; fire, dismiss; squander ‖ *intr* to jump; bounce ‖ *ref* (*un caballo*) to buck
botarate *m* madcap, wild man; spendthrift
bote *m* boat, small boat; can, jar, pot; bounce; blow, thrust; (Mex) jug, jail; **bote de paso** ferryboat; **bote de porcelana** apothecary's jar; **bote de remos** rowboat; **bote de salvamento** or **bote salvavidas** lifeboat; **de bote en bote** crowded, jammed; **de bote y voleo** thoughtlessly
botella *f* bottle
botica *f* drug store; medicine
botica•rio -ria *mf* druggist, apothecary
botija *f* earthenware jug with short narrow neck; (CAm, Ven) hidden treasure; (SAm) belly; **decirle a uno botija verde** (Cuba) to let someone have it, tell someone off; **estar hecho una botija** (*un niño*) to be cross and scream; (*una persona*) be fat, be pudgy
botijo *m* earthenware jar with spout and handle
botín *m* booty, plunder, spoils; spat, legging; (Chile) sock
botina *f* shoe, high shoe
botiquín *m* medicine kit, first-aid kit; medicine chest; first-aid station; (Ven) saloon
bo•to -ta *adj* (*sin filo o punta*) blunt, dull; (fig) dull, slow ‖ *m* leather bag ‖ *f* see **bota**
botón *m* button; (*de mueble o puerta*) knob; (*de reloj de bolsillo*) stem; (bot) bud; (elec) push button; **botón de oro** buttercup; **botón de puerta** doorknob; **botones** *msg* bellboy, bellhop
bou *m* fishing with a dragnet between two boats

bóveda *f* dome, vault; crypt; (aut) cowl; **bóveda celeste** canopy of heaven
boxeador *m* boxer; (Mex) brass knuckles
boxear *intr* to box
boxeo *m* boxing
bóxer *m* brass knuckles
boxibalón *m* punching bag
boya *f* buoy; **boya salvavidas** life buoy
boyante *adj* buoyant; lucky, successful; (*que no cala lo que debe calar*) (naut) light
boyera *f* or **boyeriza** *f* ox stable
boyerizo *m* or **boyero** *m* ox driver
bozal *adj* simple, stupid ‖ *m* muzzle; head-harness bells; headstall
bozo *m* down on upper lip; lips, mouth; headstall
B.p. *abbr* **Bendición papal**
Br. *abbr* **bachiller**
bracear *intr* to swing the arms; swim with overhead strokes; struggle
brace•ro -ra *adj* arm, hand; thrown with the hand ‖ *m* man who offers his arm to a lady; day laborer; migrant worker; **de bracero** arm in arm
bra•co -ca *adj* pug-nosed
braga *f* diaper, clout; hoisting rope; **bragas** panties, step-ins; breeches; **calzarse las bragas** to wear the pants
bragadura *f* crotch
braga•zas *m* (*pl* **-zas**) easy mark, henpecked fellow
braguero *m* (*para hernias*) truss; (*entrepiernas*) crotch
bragueta *f* fly
bragui•llas *m (pl* **-llas**) brat
brama *f* rut, mating, mating time
bramante *adj* bellowing, roaring ‖ *m* packthread, twine
bramar *intr* to bellow, roar; (*el viento*) howl; rage, storm
bramido *m* bellow, roar; howling; raging
brasa *f* live coal, red-hot coal
brasero *m* brazier; (Col) bonfire; (Mex) hearth, fireplace
Brasil, el Brazil
brasile•ño -ña *adj & mf* Brazilian
bravata *f* bravado, bragging; **echar bravatas** to talk big
bravatear *intr* to brag, boast
bravear *intr* to talk big, four-flush
braveza *f* bravery; ferocity; (*de los elementos*) fury, violence
braví•o -a *adj* ferocious; wild, untamed, uncultivated; crude, unpolished; (*mar*) rough, wild; (*terreno*) rough, rugged
bra•vo -va *adj* (*valiente*) brave; fine, excellent; fierce, savage, wild; (*mar*) rough; magnificent; angry, mad; (*perro*) vicious; (*toro*) game; boasting; (*chili*) strong ‖ *interj* bravo!
bravu•cón -cona *adj* four-flushing ‖ *mf* four-flusher
bravura *f* bravery; fierceness; gameness; bravado, boasting
braza *f* fathom
brazada *f* stroke, pull (*with the arm*); **brazada de pecho** breast stroke
brazado *m* armful, armload
brazal *m* arm band; **brazal de luto** mourning band
brazalete *m* bracelet
brazo *m* arm; (*de animal*) foreleg; **a brazo partido** hand to hand (*i.e., without weapons*); **asidos del brazo** arm in arm; **brazo derecho** right-hand man; **brazos** hands, workmen; backers; **hecho un brazo de mar** dressed to kill
brea *f* tar, wood tar; calking substance; packing canvas; **brea seca** rosin
brear *tr* to annoy, mistreat, beat; tar
brebaje *m* beverage, drink
brécol *m* or **brécoles** *mpl* broccoli
brecha *f* opening; (*en un muro*) breach; breakthrough
brega *f* fight, struggle, quarrel; trickery; drudgery
bregar §**44** *intr* to strive, struggle, toil
breña *f* or **breñal** *m* or **breñar** *m* rocky thicket
breque *m* brake
brequear *tr & intr* to brake
bresca *f* honeycomb
Bretaña *f* Brittany; **la Gran Bretaña** Great Britain
brete *m* fetters, shackles; tight squeeze, fix
bretones *mpl* Brussels sprouts
breva *f* early fig; cinch, snap
breval *m* early-fig tree
breve *adj* brief, short; **en breve** shortly, soon
brevedad *f* brevity, shortness; **a la mayor brevedad** as soon as possible
brevete *m* note, mark
brezal *m* heath, moor
brezo *m* heath, heather
briba *f* loafing; **andar a la briba** to loaf around
bri•bón -bona *adj* loafing, crooked ‖ *mf* loafer, crook
bribonada *f* loafing, crookedness
bribonear *intr* to loaf around, be crooked
brida *f* bridle
brigada *f* brigade; gang, squad; warrant officer
brillante *adj* bright, brilliant, shining ‖ *m* diamond, gem
brillantez *f* brilliance
brillantina *f* brilliantine; metal polish
brillar *intr* to shine; sparkle
brillazón *f* (Arg, Bol, Urug) pampa mirage
brillo *m* brightness, brilliance; sparkle; **sacar brillo a** to shine
brillo•so -sa *adj* (*que brilla por el mucho uso*) shiny; shining, brilliant
brin *m* canvas
brincar §**73** *tr* to bounce up and down; skip, skip over ‖ *intr* to jump, leap; be touchy, get angry easily
brinco *m* bounce; jump, leap; **en dos brincos** or **en un brinco** in an instant
brindador *m* toaster
brindar *tr* to invite; offer; **brindar a uno con una cosa** to offer someone something ‖ *intr* — **brindar a** or **por** to drink to, toast ‖ *ref* — **brindarse a** to offer to

brin•dis *m* (*pl* **-dis**) invitation, treat; toast
brío *m* spirit, enterprise; elegance; **cortar los bríos a** to cut the wings of
brio•so -sa *adj* spirited, lively, enterprising; elegant
brisa *f* breeze; residue of pressed grapes
brisera *f* or **brisero** *m* glass lamp shade (*for candles*)
británi•co -ca *adj* British, Britannic
brita•no -na *adj* British || *mf* Briton, Britisher
brizna *f* chip, particle; (Ven) drizzle
brl. *abbr* **barril**
broca *f* reel, spindle; drill, bit
brocado *m* brocade
brocal *m* (*de pozo*) curbstone; (*de bota*) mouthpiece; (*de banqueta*) (Mex) curb
brocamantón *m* diamond brooch
bróculi *m* broccoli
brocha *f* brush; loaded dice; **de brocha gorda** house (*painter*); (coll) crude, heavy-handed
brochada *f* stroke with a brush; rough sketch
brochazo *m* stroke with a brush
broche *m* clasp, clip, fastener; (*conjunto de dos piezas*) hook and eye; (Chile) paper clip; **broche de oro** punch line; **broche de presión** snap, catch; **broches** (Ecuad) cuff buttons
brocheta *f* skewer
broma *f* joke, jest; fun; shipworm; **bromas aparte** joking aside; **en broma** in fun, jokingly; **gastar una broma a** to play a joke on
bromear *intr & ref* to joke, jest; have a good time
bromhídri•co -ca *adj* hydrobromic
bromista *adj* joking || *mf* joker
bromo *m* bromine
bromuro *m* bromide
bronca *f* row, quarrel; rough joke, poor joke; **armar una bronca** to start a row
bronce *m* bronze; **bronce de cañón** gun metal
broncea•do -da *adj* bronze; tanned, sunburned || *m* bronzing; bronze finish; tan, sunburn
bronceador *m* suntan lotion
broncear *tr, intr & ref* to bronze; tan, sunburn
bron•co -ca *adj* coarse, rough; gruff, crude; (*voz*) harsh, hoarse || *f* see **bronca**
bronquitis *f* bronchitis
broquel *m* buckler, shield; (fig) shield
broqueta *f* skewer
brota *f* bud, shoot
brotadura *f* budding, sprouting; gushing; (*de la piel*) eruption, rash
brotar *tr* to bring forth, produce || *intr* to bud, sprout; gush; (*la piel*) break out
brote *m* bud, shoot; outbreak; (*de petróleo*) gush, spurt
broza *f* (*maleza*) underbrush; (*hojas, ramas, cortezas*) brushwood; (*desperdicio*) trash, rubbish; printer's brush
bruces — **dar** or **caer de bruces** to fall on one's face
bruja *f* witch, sorceress; barn owl; (*mujer fea*) hag; (*mujer de mala vida*) prostitute; (W-I) spook
brujear *tr* (*bestias salvajes*) (Ven) to hunt || *intr* to practice witchcraft
brujería *f* witchcraft, sorcery, magic
brujo *m* sorcerer, wizard
brújula *f* (*flechilla*) magnetic needle; (*instrumento*) compass; (*agujero para la puntería*) sight; **perder la brújula** to lose one's touch
brujulear *tr* (*las cartas*) to uncover gradually; suspect
brulote *m* fire ship; (Arg, Chile, Bol) vulgarity, insult
bruma *f* fog, mist
brumo•so -sa *adj* foggy, misty
bruñido *m* burnish, polish; burnishing
bruñir §12 *tr* to burnish, polish; put rouge on; (CAm) to annoy
brus•co -ca *adj* brusque, gruff; sudden; (*curva*) sharp
bruselas *fpl* tweezers || **Bruselas** Brussels
brusquedad *f* brusqueness, gruffness; suddenness; (*de una curva*) sharpness
brutal *adj* brutal; sudden; huge, terrific; stunning
brutalidad *f* brutality; stupidity; tremendous amount
bruteza *f* brutality; (archaic) roughness
bru•to -ta *adj* brute; rough, coarse; stupid; gross || *mf* (*persona*) brute; blockhead || *m* (*animal*) brute
bu *m* (*pl* **búes**) bugaboo; **hacer el bu a** to scare, frighten
buceador *m* or **buceadora** *f* diver
bucear *intr* to dive, be a diver; delve, search
buceo *m* diving
bucle *m* curl, lock
buche *m* (*de ave*) craw, crop, maw; (*de líquido*) mouthful; (*del vestido*) bag, pucker; (*para secretos*) bosom; belly; (Ecuad) high hat; (Guat, Mex) goiter; **sacar el buche a** to make (*someone*) open up
budín *m* pudding
buen *adj* var of **bueno,** used before masculine singular nouns
buenamente *adv* with ease; gladly, willingly; conveniently
buenaventura *f* fortune, good luck; (*adivinación*) fortune; **decirle a uno la buenaventura** to tell someone his fortune
bue•no -na *adj* good; kind; (*sano*) well; (*tiempo*) good, fine; **a buenas** willingly; **¡buena es ésa** (or **ésta**)! that's a good one; **de buenas a primeras** all of a sudden; from the start; **¿de dónde bueno?** where have you been?, what's new?
buey *m* ox, bullock, steer
búfa•lo -la *mf* buffalo
bufanda *f* muffler, scarf
bufar *intr* to snort
bufete *m* writing desk; law office; (*de un abogado*) clients; law practice; refreshment; (Col) bedpan; **abrir bufete** to open a law office
bufido *m* snort

bu•fo -fa *adj* comic; (Ven) spongy ‖ *mf* buffoon
bu•fón -fona *adj* clownish ‖ *m* clown, buffoon; jester; peddler
bufonada *f* buffoonery; sarcasm
bufonería *f* buffoonery; peddling
bufones•co -ca *adj* clownish; coarse, crude
bugui-bugui *m* boogie-woogie
buharda *f* dormer; dormer window; garret
buhardilla *f* dormer window; garret
buho *m* eagle owl; shy fellow
buhonería *f* peddler's kit; peddler's wares
buhonero *m* peddler, hawker
buitre *m* vulture
buje *m* axle box, bushing
bujería *f* gewgaw, trinket
bujía *f* candle; candlestick; candle power; (*de motor de explosión*) spark plug
bulbo *m* bulb
bulevar *m* boulevard
bulevardero *m* boulevardier, man about town
Bulgaria *f* Bulgaria
búlga•ro -ra *adj & mf* Bulgarian
bulimia *f* bulimia
bulto *m* bulk, volume; bust, statue; parcel, piece of baggage; bump, swelling; pillowcase; form, mass; **a bulto** broadly, by guess; **buscar el bulto a** to keep after; **de bulto** evident; **escurrir** or **huir el bulto** to duck
bulla *f* noise; crowd; loud argument
bullaje *m* crush, mob (*of people*)
bullanga *f* racket, disturbance
bullebulle *mf* busybody, bustler
bulle•ro -ra *adj* noisy; inflammatory
bullicio *m* brawl, riot, uprising; (*rumor que hace mucha gente*) rumble
bullicio•so -sa *adj* brawling, riotous; rumbling ‖ *mf* rioter
bullir §13 *tr* to move ‖ *intr* to boil; abound; bustle, hustle; swarm; move, stir; be restless ‖ *ref* to move, stir
buniato *m* sweet potato
buñuelo *m* cruller, fritter, bun; botch, bungle
buque *m* ship, vessel; (*de una nave*) hull; (*de cualquier cosa*) capacity; (C-R) doorframe; **buque almirante** admiral; **buque cisterna** tanker; **buque de guerra** warship; **buque de vapor** steamer, steamship; **buque de vela** sailboat; **buque escucha** vedette; **buque escuela** training ship; **buque fanal** or **buque faro** lightship; **buque mercante** merchantman, merchant vessel; **buque portaminas** mine layer; **buque tanque** tanker; **buque velero** sailing vessel
burbuja *f* bubble
burbujear *intr* to bubble
burdégano *m* hinny
burdel *m* brothel, disorderly house
Burdeos Bordeaux
bur•do -da *adj* coarse, rough
burear *tr* (Col) to fool ‖ *intr* to have fun
burga *f* hot springs
bur•gués -guesa *adj* middle-class, bourgeois; (*antiartístico*) bourgeois ‖ *m* middle-class man ‖ *f* middle-class woman
burguesía *f* middle class, bourgeoisie; **alta burguesía** upper middle class; **pequeña burguesía** lower middle class
burla *f* hoax, trick; joke; ridicule; **burlas aparte** joking aside; **de burlas** in fun, for fun
burladero *m* safety island, safety zone; (*en las plazas de toros*) covert; (*en los túneles*) safety niche; hiding place
burla•dor -dora *adj* joking; deceptive ‖ *mf* wag, prankster, practical joker ‖ *m* seducer, libertine
burlar *tr* to make fun of; deceive; disappoint; outwit, frustrate; (*a una mujer*) seduce ‖ *intr* to scoff ‖ *ref* to joke; **burlarse de** to make fun of
burlería *f* derision, mockery; deception, trick; scorn, derision; fish story
burles•co -ca *adj* funny, comic, burlesque
burlete *m* weather stripping
bur•lón -lona *adj* joking ‖ *mf* joker ‖ *m* mockingbird
bu•ró *m* (*pl* **-rós**) writing desk; (Mex) night table
burócrata *mf* jobholder, bureaucrat
burra *f* she-ass; stupid woman; drudge (*woman*)
burrajear *tr & intr* to scribble; doodle
burra•jo -ja *adj* (Mex) coarse, stupid ‖ *m* dung (*used as fuel*)
bu•rro -rra *adj* stupid, asinine ‖ *m* donkey, jackass; sawbuck, sawhorse; (Mex) stepladder; **burro cargado de letras** learned jackass; **burro de carga** drudge ‖ *f* see **burra**
bursátil *adj* stock-market
busca *f* search; **en busca de** in search of
buscani•guas *m* (*pl* **-guas**) (Col) snake
buscapié *m* (*para dar a entender algo*) hint; (*para averiguar algo*) feeler ‖ **busca•piés** *m* (*pl* **-piés**) snake
buscaplei•tos *mf* (*pl* **-tos**) troublemaker
buscar §73 *tr* to seek, hunt, look for; (Mex) to provoke; **buscar tres pies al gato** to be looking for trouble ‖ *ref* to take care of oneself; **buscársela** to manage to get along; to ask for it
buscareta *f* wren
buscarrui•dos *mf* (*pl* **-dos**) troublemaker
buscavi•das *mf* (*pl* **-das**) snoop, busybody; go-getter
bus•cón -cona *adj* searching; cheating ‖ *mf* seeker; thief, cheat; (min) prospector ‖ *f* loose woman
busi•lis *m* (*pl* **-lis**) trouble; **ahí está el busilis** that's the trouble; **dar en el busilis** to hit the nail on the head
búsqueda *f* search, hunt
busto *m* bust
butaca *f* armchair, easy chair; orchestra seat
butifarra *f* Catalonian sausage; loose sock, loose stocking; (Peru) ham and salad sandwich
butión•do -da *adj* lewd, lustful
buz *m* (*pl* **buces**) kiss of gratitude and reverence; lip; **hacer el buz** (archaic) to bow and scrape

buzo *m* diver

buzón *m* plug, stopper; mailbox, letter box; (*agujero para echar las cartas*) slot, letter drop; **buzón de alcance** special-delivery box; late-collection slot

C

C, c (ce) *f* third letter of the Spanish alphabet

c. *abbr* **capítulo, compañía, corriente, cuenta**

c *abbr* **caja, cargo, contra, corriente**

cabal *adj* exact; full, complete, perfect; **no estar en sus cabales** to be not in one's right mind || *adv* exactly; completely || *interj* right!

cábala *f* intrigue; divination

cabalgada *f* raid on horseback; gathering of riders

cabalgador *m* rider, horseman

cabalgadura *f* mount, horse; beast of burden

cabalgar §44 *intr* to go horseback riding

cabalgata *f* cavalcade

caballa *f* mackerel

caballada *f* drove of horses; nonsense, stupidity

caballaje *m* stud service

caballazo *m* collision of two horses, trampling by a horse; (Chile, Peru) bitter attack

caballerango *m* (Mex) stableman

caballeres•co -ca *adj* chivalric, knightly; gentlemanly

caballerete *m* (coll) dude

caballería *f* mount, horse, mule; cavalry; chivalry, knighthood; **andarse en caballerías** to fall all over oneself in compliments; **caballería andante** knight-errantry; **caballería mayor** horse, mule; **cabellería menor** ass, donkey

caballeriza *f* stable; stable hands

caballerizo *m* groom, stableman

caballe•ro -ra *adj* riding, mounted; stubborn || *m* knight, nobleman; gentleman; mister; horseman, cavalier, rider; **armar caballero** to knight; **caballero andante** knight errant; **caballero de industria** crook, adventurer, sharper; **Caballero de la triste figura** Knight of the Rueful Countenance (*Don Quijote*); **ir caballero en** to ride

caballerosidad *f* chivalry, gentlemanliness

caballerote *m* boorish fellow, cad

caballete *m* (*bastidor para sostener un cuadro o pizarra*) easel; (*de tejado*) ridge, hip; (*lomo de tierra*) ridge; (*artificio usado como soporte*) trestle, sawbuck, horse; (*de la nariz*) bridge; chimney cap; (*del ave*) breastbone; little horse

caballista *m* horseman; mounted smuggler || *f* horsewoman

caballito *m* little horse; merry-go-round; **caballito del diablo** dragonfly

caballo *m* horse; (*en ajedrez*) knight; playing card (*figure on horseback equivalent to queen*); (slang) heroin; **a caballo** on horseback; **a caballo de** astride; **a caballo regalado no se le mira el diente** never look a gift horse in the mouth; **caballo blanco** (*persona que da dinero para una empresa dudosa*) angel; **caballo de batalla** battle horse; (*de una controversia*) gist, main point; (*aquello en que uno sobresale*) forte, strong point; **caballo de carreras** race horse; **caballo de fuerza** French horsepower, metric horsepower; **caballo de tiro** draft horse; **caballo de Troya** Trojan horse; **caballo de vapor** French horsepower, metric horsepower; **caballo de vapor inglés** horsepower; **caballo mecedor** rocking horse, hobbyhorse; **caballo padre** stallion; **caballo semental** stallion

caballu•no -na *adj* horse, horselike

cabaña *f* cabin, hut; drove, flock; livestock; pastoral scene; (Arg) cattlebreeding ranch

cabañuelas *fpl* (Arg, Bol) first summer rains; (Mex) winter rains

caba•ret *m* (*pl* **-rets**) cabaret

cabecear *tr* (*un libro*) to put a headband on; (*el vino*) head; (*una media*) put a new foot on || *intr* to nod; bob the head; (*en señal de negación*) shake the head; (*los caballos*) toss the head; (*la caja de un carruaje*) lurch; (*un buque*) pitch

cabeceo *m* (*de la cabeza*) nod, bob, shake; (*de la caja del carruaje*) lurching; (*del buque*) pitch, pitching

cabecera *f* (*de cama, mesa, etc.*) head; bedside; headboard; headwaters; (*de una casa, un campo*) end; (*del capítulo de un libro*) heading; (*de periódico*) headline; capital, county seat; bolster, pillow; (typ) headpiece, vignette; **cabecera de cartel** top billing; **cabecera de puente** (mil) bridgehead

cabecilla *mf* scalawag || *m* ringleader || *f* **cabecilla de alfiler** pinhead

cabellar *intr* to grow hair; to put on false hair || *ref* to put on false hair

cabellera *f* head of hair; foliage; (*del cometa*) coma; (bot) mistletoe

cabello *m* hair; **cabello de Venus** maidenhair; **cabellos de ángel** cotton candy; **en cabello** with the hair down; **en cabellos** bareheaded; **traído por los cabellos** far-fetched

cabellu•do -da *adj* hairy

caber §14 *intr* to fit, go; have enough room; be possible; happen, befall; **no cabe duda** there is no doubt; **no cabe más** that's the limit; **no caber de** to be bursting with; **no caber en sí** to be beside oneself; be puffed up with pride; **todo cabe en** anything can be expected of

cabestrar *tr* to put a halter on

cabestrillo *m* sling

cabestro *m* halter; **llevar** or **traer del cabestro** to lead by the halter; (fig) to lead by the nose

cabeza *f* head; chief city, capital; **cabeza de chorlito** scatterbrains; (Arg) forgetful person; **cabeza de motín** ringleader; **cabeza de playa** beachhead; **cabeza de puente** bridgehead; **cabeza de turco** butt, scapegoat; **cabeza mayor** head of cattle; **cabeza menor** head of sheep, goats, etc.; **de cabeza** headfirst; on end; on one's own; by heart; **ir cabeza abajo** to go downhill; **irse de la cabeza** to go out of one's mind; **mala cabeza** headstrong person; **por su cabeza** on one's own; **romperse la cabeza** to rack one's brains

cabezada *f* butt with the head; blow on the head; (*de buque*) pitch, pitching; (*de bota*) instep; (*de libro*) headband; **dar cabezadas** to nod; (*un buque*) to pitch

cabezal *m* pillow, cushion; bolster

cabezo *m* hillock; summit, peak; reef

cabe•zón -zona *adj* big-headed; stubborn; (*licor*) (Chile) strong || *m* (*en la ropa*) hole for the head; tax register

cabezonada *f* stubbornness

cabezu•do -da *adj* big-headed; headstrong; (*vino*) heady

cabezuela *f* little head; (*harina gruesa del trigo*) middling; cornflower

cabida *f* room, space, capacity; influence, pull; **tener cabida en** to be included in

cabildear *intr* to lobby

cabildeo *m* lobbying

cabildero *m* lobbyist

cabildo *m* chapter (*of a cathedral*); chapter meeting; town hall

cabina *f* cabin; (*locutorio del teléfono*) booth; bathhouse, dressing room

cabio *m* rafter; joist

cabizba•jo -ja *adj* crestfallen, downcast

cable *m* cable; rope, hawser; **cable de remolque** towline; **cable de retén** guy wire

cablegrafiar §77 *tr & intr* to cable

cablegráfi•co -ca *adj* cable

cablegrama *m* cablegram

cabo *m* end, tip; (*punta de tierra que penetra en el mar*) cape; (*mango*) handle; small bundle; small piece; boss, foreman; cord, rope, cable; (mil) corporal; **al cabo** finally, at last; **al cabo de** at the end of; **atar cabos** (coll) to put two and two together; **Cabo de Buena Esperanza** Cape of Good Hope; **Cabo de Hornos** Cape Horn; **cabos** (*de caballo*) paws, nose, and mane; eyes, eyebrows, and hair; clothing; **cabo suelto** loose end; **estar al cabo de** to be well informed about; **llevar a cabo** to carry out, to accomplish

cabotaje *m* coasting trade

cabra *f* goat; nanny goat; (Chile) light two-wheel carriage; (Chile) sawbuck; (Col, Cuba, Ven) trick, gyp, loaded dice; **cabras** light clouds

cabrahigo wild fig

cabrería *f* goat stable; goat-milk dairy

cabre•ro -ra *mf* goatherd

cabrestante *m* capstan

cabrilla *f* sawbuck, sawhorse; (ichth) grouper; **cabrillas** skipping stones; (*olas blancas en el mar*) whitecaps

cabrillear *intr* (*el mar*) to be covered with whitecaps; shimmer

cabrio *m* rafter; joist

cabrí•o -a *adj* goat; goatish || *m* herd of goats

cabriola *f* caper; somersault; **dar cabriolas** to cut capers

cabriolear *intr* to caper, frisk, prance

cabritilla *f* kid, kidskin

cabrito *m* kid; **cabritos** (Chile) popcorn

cabrón *m* buck, billy goat; complaisant cuckold; (Chile) pimp

cabronada *f* shamelessness; shameless forbearance

cabru•no -na *adj* goat

cacahuate *adj* (Mex) pocked || *m* peanut

cacahuete *m* peanut

cacahuete•ro -ra *mf* peanut vendor

cacalote *m* (Mex) raven; (CAm, Mex) candied popcorn; (Cuba) break, blunder

cacao *m* chocolate tree; cocoa, chocolate; **pedir cacao** to call quits; **tener mucho cacao** (Guat) to have a lot of pep

cacaraña *f* pit, pock

cacarear *tr* to crow over, boast of || *intr* (*la gallina*) to cackle; (*el gallo*) crow

cacareo *m* (*de la gallina*) cackling; (*del gallo*) crowing; (*de una persona*) (coll) crowing, boasting

cacatúa *f* cockatoo

cacea *f* trolling; **pescar a la cacea** to troll

cacear *tr* to stir with a dipper or ladle || *intr* to troll

cacería *f* hunting; hunting party; (*animales cobrados en la caza*) bag; hunting scene

cacerola *f* casserole, saucepan

cacique *m* Indian chief; bossy fellow; (*en asuntos políticos*) (coll) boss; (Chile) lazy lummox; **cacique veranero** Baltimore oriole, hangbird

caciquismo *m* bossism

cacle *m* (Mex) sandal

caco *m* thief, pickpocket; coward

cacto *m* cactus

cacumen *m* summit; acumen, keen insight

cacha•co -ca *adj* (SAm) sporty || *m* (SAm) sport, dude

cachada *f* thrust or wound made with the horns

cachalote *m* sperm whale

cachar *tr* to break to pieces; (*la madera*) slit, split; to butt with the horns; (Arg, Ecuad, Urug) to make fun of; (Chile) to grasp, understand

cacharpari *m* (Arg, Bol, Peru) send-off party

cacharro *m* crock, earthen pot; piece of crockery; piece of junk; (CAm, W-I) jail; (Col) trinket
cachaza *f* sloth, phlegm; rum; first froth on cane juice when boiled
cachazu•do -da *adj* slothful, phlegmatic || *mf* sluggard
cachear *tr* to frisk
cacheo *m* frisking
cachetada *f* box on the ear
cachete *m* slap in the face; cheek, swollen cheek; dagger
cachetear *tr* to box on the ear
cachetero *m* dagger; dagger man
cachetina *f* brawl, fistfight
cachicuer•no -na *adj* horn-handled
cachillada *f* brood, litter
cachimba *f* (*para fumar*) pipe; (Arg, Urug) well, spring; (Chile) revolver
cachimbo *m* (*para fumar*) pipe; (Cuba) sugar mill; **chupar cachimbo** (Ven) to smoke a pipe; (*un niño*) (Ven) to suck its finger
cachiporra *f* billy, bludgeon
cachivache *m* good-for-nothing; **cachivaches** broken pottery; pots and pans; junk, trash
cacho *m* slice, piece; (*mercadería que no se vende*) (Chile) drug on the market
cachón *m* (*ola de agua*) breaker; splash of water; **cachones** surf
cachon•do -da *adj* (*perra*) in rut; sexy
cacho•rro -rra *mf* cub, whelp, pup || *m* little pistol
cachucha *f* rowboat; cap; Andalusian dance
cachuela *f* gizzard; fricassee of pork
cachu•pín -pina *mf* (CAm, Mex) Spanish settler in Latin America
cada *adj* each; every; **cada vez más** more and more; **cada vez que** whenever
cadalso *m* stand, platform; (*para la ejecución de un reo*) scaffold
cadarzo *m* floss, floss silk
cadáver *m* corpse, cadaver
cadavéri•co -ca *adj* cadaverous
cadena *f* chain; (telv) network; **cadena antirresbaladiza** (aut) skid chain; **cadena de presidiarios** chain gang; **cadena perpetua** life imprisonment
cadencia *f* cadence, rhythm
cadencio•so -sa *adj* rhythmical
cadenero *m* (surv) lineman
cadera *f* hip
cadete *m* (mil) cadet; (Arg, Bol) apprentice (*without pay*), errand boy
cadillo *m* burdock
cadmio *m* cadmium
caducar §73 *intr* to be in one's dotage; be worn out; lapse, expire
caducidad *f* feebleness; expiration
caedi•zo -za *adj* tottery, ready to fall over || *m* lean-to
caer §15 *intr* to fall; droop; fall due; be, be found; fade; (*el sol, el día, el viento*) decline; happen; **caer a** to face, overlook; **caer bien** to fit; be becoming; make a hit; **caer de plano** to fall flat; **caer en** (*cierto día*) to come on, fall on, happen on; (*cierta página*) be found on; **caer en cama** to fall ill; **caer en favor** to be in favor; **caer en la cuenta** to catch on, get the point; **caer en que** to realize that; **caer mal** to fit badly; be unbecoming; fall flat; **no caigo** (coll) I don't get it || *ref* to fall, fall down; be, be found; **caerse de su peso, caerse de suyo** to be self-evident; **caerse muerto de** (*p.ej., alegría, miedo, risa*) to be overcome with
café *adj* tan || *m* coffee; coffee tree; coffee house; café; (Arg) reprimand; (Mex) tantrum; **café cantante** night club; **café de maquinilla** drip coffee; **café solo** black coffee
cafetal *m* coffee plantation
cafetalero *m* (SAm) coffee planter; coffee dealer
cafetear *intr* to drink coffee
cafetera *f* coffee pot; (Arg) jalopy; **cafetera eléctrica** electric percolator
cafetería *f* cafeteria
cafete•ro -ra *adj* coffee || *mf* coffee dealer; coffee-bean picker || *f* see **cafetera**
cafeto *m* coffee tree
cagar §44 *tr* to spot, stain, spoil || *intr* to defecate || *ref* to defecate; be scared
cagatin•ta *m* or **cagatin•tas** *m* (*pl* **-tas**) office drudge, penpusher
ca•gón -gona *adj* cowardly || *mf* coward
caída *f* fall; spill, tumble; drop; failure; blunder, slip; (*de una cortina*) hang; **a la caída de la noche** at nightfall; **a la caída del sol** at sunset; **caída de agua** waterfall; **caída radiactiva** fallout; **caídas** coarse wool; witticisms
caí•do -da *adj* fallen; (*cuello*) turndown; (*párpado, hombro*) drooping; dejected, crestfallen; **caído en desuso** obsolete || **caídos** *mpl* interest due; **los caídos** (*en la guerra*) the fallen || *f* see **caída**
caimán *m* alligator; schemer
Caín *m* Cain; **pasar las de Caín** (coll) to have a frightful time
Cairo, El Cairo
caja *f* box; case, chest, coffer; (*de caudales*) safe, strongbox; (*para dinero contante*) cashbox; (*dinero contante*) cash; (*ataúd*) casket, coffin; (*de reloj de bolsillo*) case; (*donde se pagan las cuentas en los hoteles*) desk; cashier's desk; (*del aparato de radio o televisión*) cabinet; (*de coche*) body; (*tambor*) drum; (*de fusil*) stock; (*de ascensor, de escalera*) shaft, well; (mach) housing; (typ) case; **caja alta** upper case; **caja baja** lower case; **caja clara** snare drum; **caja de ahorros** savings bank; **caja de cambio de marchas** transmission-gear box; **caja de caudales** safe; **caja de cigüeñal** crankcase; **caja de colores** paintbox; **caja de embalaje** packing box or case; **caja de enchufe** (elec) outlet; **caja de engranajes** gear case; **caja de fuego** firebox; **caja de fusibles** fuse box; **caja de ingletes** miter box; **caja de menores** petty cash; **caja de registro** manhole; **caja de reloj** watchcase; **caja de seguridad** safe; safe-deposit box; **caja de sorpresa** jack-in-the-box; **caja de velocidades** transmission-

gear box; **caja fuerte** safe, bank vault; **caja postal de ahorros** postal savings bank; **caja registradora** cash register; **despedir** or **echar con cajas destempladas** to send packing, give the gate

caje•ro -ra *mf* boxmaker; (*en un banco*) cashier, teller; (*en un hotel*) desk clerk

cajeta *f* little box; tobacco box; **de cajeta** (CAm, Mex) fine

cajetilla *f* pack (*of cigarettes*)

cajetín *m* rubber stamp; (typ) box

cajista *mf* compositor

cajón *m* large box, bin; (*caja movible de un mueble*) drawer; (*que se cierra con llave*) locker; (*que sirve de tienda*) booth, stall; (Chile) long gully; (Mex) dry-goods store; (SAm) coffin; **cajón de aire comprimido** caisson; **cajón de sastre** (coll) odds and ends; muddlehead; **ser de cajón** to be in vogue, be the thing

cal *f* lime; **cal apagada** slaked lime; **cal viva** quicklime; **de cal y canto** strong, tough

cala *f* calla lily; cove, inlet; (*de fruta*) sample slice; (*de buque*) hold; suppository

calabacear *tr* (*a un alumno*) to flunk; (*una mujer a un pretendiente*) to jilt

calabacera *f* calabash, pumpkin, squash

calabaza *f* calabash, gourd, pumpkin, squash; dolt; **dar calabaza** a (*un alumno*) to flunk; (*un pretendiente*) to jilt

calabo•bos *m* (*pl* **-bos**) steady drizzle

calabocero *m* jailer, warden

calabozo *m* dungeon; cell, prison cell

calada *f* soaking; (*del ave de rapiña*) swoop; scolding

calado *m* openwork, drawn work; fretwork; (*del agua*) depth; (naut) draught

calafatear *tr* to calk

calafateo *m* calking

calamar *m* squid

calambre *m* cramp

calamidad *f* calamity

calamita *f* magnetic needle

calamito•so -sa *adj* calamitous

cálamo *m* reed, stalk; (poet) pen; (poet) flute, reed

calamoca•no -na *adj* (*algo embriagado*) tipsy; (*chocho*) doddering

calaña *f* nature, kind; pattern; fan

calar *tr* to pierce; soak; wedge; cut open work in; (*un melón*) cut a plug in; (*la bayoneta*) fix; (*un puente levadizo*) lower; (*las redes de pesca*) lower in the water; (*un buque cierta profundidad*) draw; (*a una persona o las intenciones de una persona*) size up, see through; (Arg) to stare at ‖ *ref* to get soaked, get drenched; (*introducirse*) slip in; (*el ave de rapiña*) swoop down; miss fire; (*el sombrero*) pull down tight; (*las gafas*) stick on; **calarse hasta los huesos** to get soaked to the skin

cala•to -ta *adj* (Peru) naked; (Peru) penniless

calavera *m* daredevil; libertine ‖ *f* skull; (*imitación de la calavera*) death's-head; (Mex) tail light

calaverada *f* recklessness, daredeviltry; escapade

calaverear *tr* to spoil, make ugly ‖ *intr* to act recklessly; go on a spree

calcado *m* tracing

calcañal *m* or **calcañar** *m* heel

calcar §73 *tr* to trace; copy, imitate; tread on

calce *m* wedge; iron tire; iron tip; (*de un documento*) (CAm, Mex, P-R) bottom, foot

calceta *f* stocking; fetter, shackle; **hacer calceta** to knit

calcetería *f* hosiery; hosiery shop

calcete•ro -ra *mf* hosier; stocking mender

calcetín *m* sock

calcificar §73 *tr & ref* to calcify

calcio *m* calcium

calco *m* tracing; copy, imitation

calcula•dor -dora *adj* calculating; (*egoísta, interesado*) (fig) calculating ‖ *mf* calculator ‖ *f* calculating machine; **calculadora de bolsillo** pocket calculator

calcular *tr & intr* to calculate; (*suponer*) (fig) calculate

cálculo *m* calculation; (math, pathol) calculus; **cálculo biliar** gallstone; **cálculo renal** kidney stone

calchona *f* (Chile) goblin, bogey; (Chile) witch, old hag

calda *f* heating, warming; **caldas** hot springs

caldeamiento *m* heating

caldear *tr* to heat; weld ‖ *ref* to get hot; get overheated

caldeo *m* heating; welding

caldera *f* boiler; pot, kettle; (Arg) coffee pot, teapot

calderero *m* boilermaker

calderilla *f* holy-water vessel; copper coin; small change; mountain currant

caldero *m* kettle, pot; (*reloj de bolsillo*) (Arg) turnip

calderón *m* caldron; (*signo*) (mus) pause, hold

caldillo *m* light broth; sauce for fricassee; (Mex) meat bits in broth

caldo *m* broth; sauce, gravy, dressing; salad dressing; (Mex) syrup; (Mex) sugar-cane juice; **caldo de la reina** eggnog; **caldos** wet goods

calefacción *f* heating; **calefacción por agua caliente** hot-water heat; **calefacción por aire caliente** hot-air heat

calefactor *m* heater man; (electron) heater, heater element

calefón *m* (Arg) hot-water heater

calendar *tr* to date

calendario *m* calendar; **hacer calendarios** to meditate; to make wild predictions

calenta•dor -dora *adj* heating ‖ *m* heater; warming pan; (*reloj de bolsillo*) turnip; **calentador a gas** gas heater; **calentador de agua** water heater

calentamiento *m* heating

calentar §2 *tr* to heat; warm; beat; (Chile) to bore, annoy; **calentar la silla** (*detenerse demasiado*) to warm a chair ‖ *ref* to heat up, run hot; warm oneself; warm up; (*estar en celo las bestias*) be in heat; (Chile, Ven) to become annoyed, get angry

calentón *m* warm-up; **darse un calentón** to stop and warm up
calentura *f* fever, temperature
calenturien•to -ta *adj* feverish; exalted; (Chile) consumptive
calenturón *m* high fever
calenturo•so -sa *adj* feverish
calera *f* limekiln; limestone quarry
calesa *f* chaise
caleta *f* cove, inlet
caletre *m* judgment, acumen
calibrador *m* calipers; **calibrador de alambre** wire gauge
calibrar *tr* to calibrate; to gauge
calibre *m* caliber; gauge; bore, diameter
calicanto *m* rubble masonry
cali•có *m* (*pl* **-cós**) calico
calidad *f* quality; condition, term; rank, nobility; importance; **a calidad de que** provided that; **calidad de vida** quality of life; **en calidad de** in the capacity of
cáli•do -da *adj* warm, hot
calidoscopio *m* kaleidoscope
calientaca•mas *m* (*pl* **-mas**) bed warmer
calienta•piés *m* (*pl* **-piés**) foot warmer
caliente *adj* hot; fiery, vehement; (*en celo*) hot; **caliente de cascos** hotheaded; **en caliente** while hot; at once
califa *m* caliph
califato *m* caliphate
calificación *f* qualification; (*nota en un examen*) grade, mark; rating, standing
calificar **§73** *tr* to qualify; certify; ennoble; (*un examen*) mark; (*en los registros electorales*) (Chile) to register ‖ *ref* (archaic) to prove one's noble birth; (*en los registros electorales*) (Chile) to register
calificati•vo -va *adj* qualifying ‖ *m* (*nota en la escuela*) grade, mark; (*en un diccionario*) usage label
California *f* California; **la Baja California** Lower California
caligrafía *f* penmanship
calina *f* haze
calino•so -sa *adj* hazy
Calíope *f* Calliope
calipso *m* calypso ‖ **Calipso** *f* Calypso
calistenia *f* calisthenics
calisténi•co -ca *adj* calisthenic
cá•liz *m* (*pl* **-lices**) chalice; **cáliz de dolor** cup of sorrow
cali•zo -za *adj* lime, limestone ‖ *f* limestone
calma *f* calm; calm weather; quiet, tranquillity; slowness; (*cesación*) letup, suspension; **calma chicha** dead calm; **calmas ecuatoriales** doldrums; **en calma** in suspension; (*mercado*) steady; (*mar*) calm, smooth
calmante *adj* soothing; pain-relieving ‖ *m* sedative
calmar *tr* to calm, soothe ‖ *intr* to grow calm; abate ‖ *ref* to calm down
calmazo *m* dead calm
cal•mo -ma *adj* barren, treeless; fallow, uncultivated ‖ *f* see **calma**
calmo•so -sa *adj* calm; slow, lazy
calmu•do -da *adj* calm; (*viento*) (naut) light; (*tiempo*) (naut) mild
caló *m* gypsy slang, underworld slang
calofriar **§77** *ref* to become chilled
calofrío *m* chill
calor *m* heat; warmth; (fig) warmth, enthusiasm; **hace calor** it is hot, it is warm; **tener calor** (*una persona*) to be hot, be warm
calorífe•ro -ra *adj* heat ‖ *m* heater, furnace; heating system; foot warmer
calorífu•go -ga *adj* heatproof; fireproof
caloro•so -sa *adj* warm, hot; (fig) warm, enthusiastic, hearty
calotear *tr* (Arg) to gyp, cheat
calpul *m* (Guat) gathering, meeting; (Hond) Indian mound
caluma *f* (Peru) gorge in the Andes; (Peru) Indian hamlet
calumnia *f* calumny, slander
calumniar *tr* to slander
calumnio•so -sa *adj* slanderous
caluro•so -sa *adj* warm, hot; (fig) warm, enthusiastic, hearty
calva *f* bald spot; bare spot, clearing; (*en un tejido*) worn spot
calvario *m* (*sufrimiento moral*) cross; series of misfortunes; string of debts ‖ **Calvario** *m* Calvary; Stations of the Cross
calvero *m* clearing; clay pit
calvez *f* or **calvicie** *f* baldness
cal•vo -va *adj* bald; barren, bare ‖ *f* see **calva**
calza *f* wedge; stocking; **calzas** hose, breeches, tights; **en calzas prietas** in a tight fix
calzada *f* highway, causeway; (S-D) sidewalk
calzado *m* footwear, shoes
calzador *m* shoehorn
calzar **§60** *tr* to shoe, put shoes on; provide with shoes; (*cierto tamaño de zapatos, guantes, etc.*) wear, take; (*un zapato a una persona*) fit; wedge; (*una rueda*) block, scotch; (*la pata de una mesa*) block up; tip or trim with iron; (*plantas*) (hort) to hill ‖ *intr* (Arg) to get the place sought; **calzar bien** to wear good footwear; **calzar mal** to wear poor footwear ‖ *ref* to get; (*zapatos, guantes*) put on, wear; put one's shoes on; (*a una persona*) dominate, manage
calzo *m* wedge; chock, skid
calzón *m* trousers, pants; **calzones** trousers, breeches; **calzarse los calzones** to wear the pants
calzonarias *fpl* (Col) suspenders
calzona•zos *m* (*pl* **-zos**) jellyfish; henpecked husband
calzoncillos *mpl* underdrawers
callada *f* (naut) abatement, lull; **a las calladas** or **de callada** on the quiet; **dar la callada por respuesta** to give no answer
calla•do -da *adj* silent; mysterious, secret ‖ *f* see **callada**
callampa *f* (Chile) felt hat; (Chile) large ear; (Chile) mushroom
callana *f* (SAm) Indian baking bowl; (*reloj de bolsillo*) (Chile) turnip; (Chile) behind; (Chile, Peru) flowerpot
callao *m* pebble

callar *tr* to silence; not mention; (*un secreto*) keep; calm, quiet || *intr & ref* to become silent, keep silent; keep quiet, keep still; **callarse la boca** (coll) to shut up, clam up
calle *f* street; **calle de travesía** cross street; **calle mayor** main street; **dejar en la calle** to deprive of one's livelihood
calleja *f* side street, alley; subterfuge, pretext
callejear *intr* to walk around the streets, to ramble around
calleje•ro -ra *adj* street; gadabout || *m* street guide; list of addresses of newspaper subscribers
callejón *m* alley, lane; **callejón sin salida** blind alley
callejuela *f* side street, alley; subterfuge, pretext
callicida *m* corn cure
callo *m* callus; (*en el pie*) corn; **callos** tripe
callo•so -sa *adj* callous
cama *f* bed; (*para las bestias*) bedding, litter; **cama imperial** four-poster; **cama turca** day bed; **guardar cama** to be sick in bed
camachuelo *m* (orn) bullfinch
camada *f* brood, litter; layer, stratum; (*de ladrones*) den
camafeo *m* cameo
camaleón *m* chameleon
cámara *f* chamber; hall; (*cuerpo legislador*) house, chamber; (*aparato fotográfico*) camera; (*tubo de goma del neumático*) inner tube; (*del arma de fuego*) chamber, breech; (*para cartuchos*) magazine; board, council; (*mueble donde se conservan los alimentos*) icebox; (*evacuación*) bowels; (aer) cockpit; **cámara agrícola** grange; **cámara ardiente** funeral chamber; **cámara cinematografica** movie camera; **cámara de combustión** (aut) combustion chamber; **cámara de compensación** clearing house; **cámara de fuelle** folding camera; **cámara de las máquinas** (naut) engine room; **Cámara de los Comunes** House of Commons; **Cámara de los Lores** House of Lords; **cámara de oxígeno** oxygen tent; **Cámara de Representantes** House of Representatives; **cámara frigorífica** cold-storage room; **cámara indiscreta** candid camera; **cámaras** loose bowels
camarada *m* comrade
camarera *f* waitress; chambermaid, maid; (*en los barcos*) stewardess; (*que sirve a una reina o princesa*) lady in waiting
camarero *m* waiter; valet; (*en un barco o avión*) steward
camarilla *f* clique, coterie, cabal; palace coterie
camarín *m* boudoir; (theat) dressing room
cámaro *m* var of **camarón**
camarógrafo *m* cameraman
camarón *m* shrimp, prawn; (CAm, Col) tip, gratuity; (Ven) nap; **ponerse como un camarón** to blush
camarote *m* stateroom, cabin
camasquin•ce *mf* (*pl* **-ce**) meddlesome person, kibitzer
cambalachar *tr & intr* var of **cambalachear**
cambalache *m* exchange, swap; (Arg) second-hand shop
cambalachear *tr* to swap, exchange, trade off || *intr* to swap, exchange
cambiadis•cos *m* (*pl* **-cos**) record changer
cambiante *adj* changing; fickle; iridescent || **cambiantes** *mpl* iridescence
cambiar *tr* to change; exchange || *intr* to change; **cambiar de** (*p.ej., sombreros, ropa, trenes*) change; **cambiar de marcha** to shift gears || *ref* to change
cambiavía *m* switch; switchman
cambio *m* change; exchange; rate of exchange; (aut) shift; (rr) switch; **cambio de marchas, cambio de velocidades** gearshift; **en cambio** on the other hand
cambista *mf* moneychanger; banker || *m* (Arg) switchman
cambullón *m* (Mex, Col, Ven) barter, exchange; (Chile) subversion; (Peru) scheming, trickery
camelar *tr* to flirt with; cajole, tease
camelo *m* flirtation; joke; false rumor
camellero *m* camel driver
camello *m* camel
camellón *m* drinking trough; flower bed
came•ro -ra *adj* bed || *mf* maker of bedding || *m* (Col) highway
camilla *f* stretcher; couch; round table with heater underneath; (Mex) clothing store
camillero *m* stretcher-bearer
caminante *mf* walker; traveler on foot || *m* groom attending his master's horse
caminar *tr* (*cierta distancia*) to walk || *intr* to walk; go; travel, journey; behave
caminata *f* long walk, hike; outing, jaunt
camine•ro -ra *adj* road, highway
camino *m* road, way; (*viaje*) journey; (*tira larga que se pone en mesas o pisos*) (SAm) runner; **a medio camino (entre)** halfway (between); **camino de** on the way to; **camino de herradura** bridle path; **camino de hierro** railway; **camino de ruedas** wagon road; **Camino de Santiago** Way of St. James (*Milky Way*); **camino de sirga** towpath; **camino de tierra** dirt road; **camino real** highroad; **camino trillado** beaten path; **echar camino adelante** to strike out
camión *m* truck, motor truck; (Mex) bus; **camión volquete** dump truck
camionaje *m* trucking
camione•ro -ra *adj* truck || *m* trucker, teamster
camioneta *f* light truck; station wagon
camionetilla *f* (Guat) station wagon
camión-grua *m* tow truck
camionista *m* trucker, teamster
camisa *f* (*de hombre*) shirt; (*de mujer*) chemise; (*de la culebra*) slough; (*de un libro*) jacket; (*para papeles*) folder; (*de una pieza mecánica*) jacket, casing; (*de un horno de fundición*) lining; **camisa de agua** water jacket; **camisa de dormir** nightshirt; **camisa de fuerza** strait jacket; **cambiarse la camisa** to become a turncoat
camisería *f* haberdashery; shirt factory

camise•ro -ra *mf* haberdasher; shirt maker
camiseta *f* undershirt; (*de traje de baño*) top
camisola *f* stiff shirt
camisolín *m* dickey, shirt front
camón *m* bay window; **camón de vidrios** glass partition
camorra *f* quarrel, row; **armar camorra** to raise Cain, raise a row; **buscar camorra** to be looking for trouble
camorrista *adj* quarrelsome || *mf* quarrelsome person
camote *m* onion; (Mex) sweet potato; (Chile) lie, fib; (Chile, Peru) sweetheart; (Arg, Ecuad) blockhead; (Mex) churl; (El Salv) black-and-blue mark; **tomar un camote** to become infatuated
camotear *tr* (Arg) to filch, snitch; (Guat) to bother || *intr* (Mex) to wander around aimlessly
campal *adj* pitched (*battle*)
campamento *m* camp; encampment
campana *f* bell; (*para la protección de plantas*) bell glass, bell jar; (*de las guarniciones de alumbrado eléctrico*) canopy; **campana de buzo** diving bell; **por campana de vacante** (Mex) rarely, seldom
campanada *f* stroke of a bell, ring of a bell; scandal
campanario *m* belfry, steeple
campanear *tr* (*las campanas*) to ring || *intr* to ring the bells || *ref* to strut
campanero *m* bell ringer; bell founder
campanil *adj* bell || *m* belfry, bell tower
campanilla *f* hand bell; door bell; bubble; (anat) uvula; **de (muchas) campanillas** of great importance
campano *m* cowbell
campante *adj* proud, satisfied; outstanding
campanu•do -da *adj* bell-shaped; pompous, high-sounding
campaña *f* campaign; cruise; countryside
campar *intr* to camp; to excel, stand out
campear *intr* to go to pasture; (*las sementeras*) turn green; stand out, excel; reconnoiter; ride through the fields to check the cattle
campecha•no -na *adj* frank, good-natured, cheerful || *f* (Mex) mixed drink; (Ven) hammock
campeche *m* logwood
campeón *m* champion; **campeón de venta** best seller
campeona *f* championess
campeonato *m* championship
campe•ro -ra *adj* unsheltered, in the open
campesi•no -na *adj* country, rural, peasant || *mf* peasant, farmer || *m* countryman || *f* countrywoman
campestre *adj* country, rural
campiña *f* countryside, open country
campo *m* (*terreno sembradío; sitio o foco de varias actividades*) field; (*en oposición a la ciudad*) country; ground, background; (*campamento*) (mil) camp; **a campo traviesa** across country; **campo de batalla** battlefield; **campo de ensayos** proving ground; **campo de juego** playground; **campo de pruebas** testing ground; **campo de tiro** range, shooting range; **campo magnético** magnetic field; **campo santo** cemetery; **levantar el campo** (mil) to break camp; **quedar en el campo** to fall in battle
camposanto *m* cemetery
camuesa *f* pippin (*apple*)
camueso *m* pippin (*tree*)
camuflaje *m* camouflage
camuflar *tr* to camouflage
can *m* dog; (*de arma de fuego*) trigger
cana *f* gray hair; **echar una cana al aire** to cut loose, step out; **peinar canas** to be getting old
Canadá, el Canada
canadiense *adj & mf* Canadian
canal *m* (*cauce artificial*) canal; (*estrecho en el mar*) channel; (anat) duct, canal; (telv) channel; **Canal de la Mancha** English Channel; **Canal de Panamá** Panama Canal; **Canal de Suez** Suez Canal; **canal alimenticio** alimentary canal || *f* channel; (*conducto del tejado*) gutter; (*estría*) flute, groove; pipe; (*de un libro*) fore edge
canalización *f* (*de agua o gas*) mains, pipes; ductwork; (elec) wiring; **canalización de consumo** (elec) house current
canalizar §60 to channel; pipe; (elec) to wire
canalizo *m* (naut) waterway, fairway
canalón *m* rain-water spout; shovel hat; **canalones** ravioli
canalla *m* churl, scoundrel || *f* riffraff, canaille
canallada *f* dirty trick, meanness
canana *f* cartridge belt
canapé *m* sofa, couch
Canarias *fpl* Canaries
cana•rio -ria *adj & mf* Canarian || *m* canary, canary bird || *fpl* see **Canarias**
canasta *f* basket, hamper
canastilla *f* basket; (*ropa para el niño que ha de nacer*) layette; (*equipo de novia*) (dial) trousseau
canastillo *m* basket-weave tray
canasto *m* hamper || **canastos** *interj* confound it!
cáncamo *m* eyebolt; **cáncamo de argolla** ringbolt
cancanear *intr* to loaf around; stammer
cancel *m* storm door; folding screen
cancela *f* door of ironwork
cancelar *tr* to cancel; (*una deuda*) pay off
cáncer *m* cancer; **Cáncer** (astr) Cancer; **cáncer pulmonar** lung cancer
cancerología *f* cancer research; oncology
cancero•so -sa *adj* cancerous
cancilla *f* lattice gate
canciller *m* chancellor
cancillería *f* chancellery
canción *f* song; poem, lyric poem; **canción de amor** love song; **canción de cuna** cradlesong, lullaby; **canción típica** folk song; **volver a la misma canción** to sing the same old song
cancionero *m* songbook; anthology
cancionista *mf* popular singer

canco *m* (Chile) flowerpot; (Chile) earthen jug; (Chile) chamber pot; (Bol) buttock; **cancos** (Chile) woman's broad hips
cancón *m* bugaboo; **hacer un cancón a** (Mex) to try to bluff
cancha *f* field, ground; race track; golf links; tennis court; cockpit; (Urug) path, way; **estar en su cancha** (Arg, Chile, Urug) to be in one's element; **tener cancha** (Arg) to have pull || *interj* gangway!
canche *adj* (Col) tasteless, poorly seasoned; (CAm) blond
candado *m* padlock
candar *tr* to lock, padlock
candela *f* candle; candlestick; fire, light; **con la candela en la mano** at death's door
candelabro *m* candelabrum
candelecho *m* elevated hut for watching the vineyard
candelero *m* candlestick; brass olive-oil lamp; fishing torch
candelilla *f* catkin; (Arg, Chile) will-o'-the-wisp; glowworm
candida•to -ta *mf* candidate
candidatura *f* candidacy; list of candidates; voting paper
candidez *f* whiteness; innocence
cándi•do -da white; simple, innocent
candil *m* open olive-oil lamp
candilejas *fpl* footlights
candon•go -ga *adj* fawning, slick; loafing, shirking || *mf* fawner, flatterer; loafer, shirker || *f* fawning; teasing
candonguear *tr* to kid, tease || *intr* to scheme to get out of work
candor *m* innocence, ingenuousness
caneca *f* glazed earthen bottle
cane•co -ca *adj* (Arg, Bol) tipsy || *f* see **caneca**
canela *f* cinnamon; (*cosa fina*) (coll) peach
canela•do -da *adj* cinnamon-colored
cane•lo -la *adj* cinnamon || *m* (*árbol*) cinnamon || *f* see **canela**
canelón *m* rain-water spout; large icicle; cinnamon candy
cane•sú *m* (*pl* **-súes**) (*prenda*) guimpe; (*pieza de una prenda*) yoke
cangilón *m* jug, jar, bucket; (*de draga*) bucket, scoop; rut, track
cangrejo *m* crab
cangrena *f* gangrene
cangrenar *ref* to have gangrene
canguro *m* kangaroo
caníbal *adj & mf* cannibal
canica *f* (*bolita*) marble; (*juego*) marbles
canicie *f* whiteness (*of hair*)
canícula *f* dog days || **Canícula** *f* Dog Star
caniculares *mpl* dog days
cani•jo -ja *adj* (coll) weak, sickly || *mf* (coll) weakling
canilla *f* shank (*of leg*); (*espita, grifo*) tap; bobbin, spool; (Mex) strength
cani•no -na *adj* canine || *m* canine, canine tooth || *f* excrement of dogs
canje *m* exchange
canjear *tr* to exchange
ca•no -na *adj* gray; gray-haired; hoary, old || *f* see **cana**
canoa *f* canoe; launch
canoe•ro -ra *mf* canoeist
canon *m* canon
canóni•co -ca *adj* canonical || *f* rules of canonical life
canóniga *f* nap before eating; drunk
canónigo *m* canon
canonizar **§60** *tr* to canonize; approve
canonjía *f* sinecure
cano•ro -ra *adj* (*voz*) melodious; (*ave*) song, sweet-singing
cano•so -sa *adj* gray-haired
canotié *m* straw hat, skimmer
cansa•do -da *adj* tired, weary; exhausted, worn-out; tiresome
cansancio *m* tiredness, fatigue
cansar *tr* to tire, weary; bore || *intr* be tiresome || *ref* to tire, get tired
cantable *adj* tuneful, singable || *m* (*del libreto de una zarzuela*) lyric; (*de una zarzuela*) musical passage
canta•dor -dora *mf* singer of popular songs
cantaletear *tr* to say over and over again; make fun of
cantalupo *m* cantaloupe
cantante *adj* singing || *mf* singer
cantar *m* song, singing; chant; **Cantar de los Cantares** Song of Songs || *tr* to sing; chant; sing of; **cantarlas claras** to speak out || *intr* to sing; chant; creak, squeak; squeal, peach; **cantar de plano** to make a full confession
cántara *f* jug, pitcher
cantárida *f* Spanish fly
canta•rín -rina *adj* (*voz*) melodious; fond of singing || *mf* singer || *m* professional singer
cántaro *m* jug, pitcher; jugful; ballot box; **llover a cántaros** to rain pitchforks
canta•triz *f* (*pl* **-trices**) singer
cantautor *m* song writer
cantera *f* quarry; talent, genius
cántico *m* canticle
cantidad *f* quantity; amount; sum; **cantidad de movimiento** (mech) momentum
cantiga *f* poem of the troubadours
cantilena *f* ballad, song; **salir con la misma cantilena** to sing the same old song
cantimplora *f* siphon; carafe, decanter; (*frasco para llevar bebida*) canteen; (Col) powder flask; (Guat) mumps
cantina *f* cantine; lunchroom, station restaurant; barroom
cantinera *f* camp follower
cantinero *m* bartender
canto *m* song; singing; (*división del poema épico*) canto; (*de notas iguales y uniformes*) chant; (*extremidad*) edge; (*esquina*) corner; (*de cuchillo*) back; (*de pan*) crust; stone, pebble; **canto de corte** cutting edge; **canto del cisne** swan song
cantonera *f* corner reinforcement; corner table, corner shelf; streetwalker
cantonero *m* corner loafer
can•tor -tora *adj* singing; (*pájaro*) song || *mf* singer || *m* chanter; minstrel; poet, bard

canto•so -sa *adj* rocky, stony
canturrear *tr & intr* to hum
canturreo *m* hum, humming
canzonetista *mf* popular singer
caña *f* cane; reed; stalk, stem; (*del brazo o la pierna*) long bone; (*de bota o media*) leg; wineglass; **caña de azúcar** sugar cane; **caña de pescar** fishing rod
cañada *f* glen, ravine, gully; cattle path; brook
cañamazo *m* canvas, burlap; embroidered canvas
cañamiel *f* sugar cane
cáñamo *m* hemp
cañamones *mpl* birdseed
cañaveral *m* canebrake; sugar-cane plantation
cañería *f* pipe; pipe line; piping; **cañería maestra** gas main, water main
cañero *m* pipe fitter, plumber; sugar-cane dealer; (SAm) cheat; (SAm) bluffer
cañista *m* pipe fitter, plumber
caño *m* pipe, tube; gutter, sewer; ditch; (*chorro*) spurt, jet; (*canal angosto*) channel; organ pipe; (*río pequeño*) (Col) stream
cañón *m* (*pieza de artillería*) cannon; (*valle estrecho*) canyon; (*de arma de fuego; de pluma*) barrel; (*pluma de ave*) quill; (*de escalera*) well; (*de columna; de ascensor*) shaft; organ pipe; (Col) trunk of tree; **cañón de campaña** fieldpiece; **cañón de chimenea** flue, chimney flue; **cañón obús** howitzer
cañonear *tr* to cannonade, to shell
cañutazo *m* gossip
caoba *f* mahogany
caos *m* chaos
caóti•co -ca *adj* chaotic
cap. *abbr* **capitán, capítulo**
capa *f* cloak, cape, mantle; (*de pintura*) coat; (*lo que cubre*) bed, layer; (*apariencia, pretexto*) (fig) cloak, mask; **capa del cielo** canopy of heaven; **capa de ozono** ozone layer; **andar de capa caída** to be on the decline, be in a bad way; (*comedia*) **de capa y espada** cloak-and-sword; (*intriga, espionaje*) **de capa y espada** cloak-and-dagger; **so capa de** under the guise of
capacidad *f* capacity; **capacidad competitiva** competitiveness
capacitar *tr* to enable, qualify; to empower ‖ *ref* to become qualified
capacha *f* fruit basket; (SAm) jail
capacho *m* fruit basket; hamper; (*de albañil*) hod
capar *tr* to geld, castrate; curtail
caparazón *m* caparison; horse blanket; nose bag; (*de crustáceo*) shell
caparrosa *f* vitriol
capa•taz *m* (*pl* **-taces**) overseer, foreman, boss
ca•paz *adj* (*pl* **-paces**) (*grande*) capacious, spacious; (*que tiene cierta aptitud; diestro, instruído*) capable; **capaz de** capable of; with a capacity of; **capaz para** competent in; qualified for; with room for
capcio•so -sa *adj* crafty, deceptive
capea *f* amateur free-for-all bullfight
capear *tr* (*al toro*) to challenge; (*el mal tiempo*) weather; deceive, take in ‖ *intr* (naut) to lay to; (Guat) to play hooky
capellán *m* chaplain
capeo *m* capework (*of bullfighter*)
caperucita *f* little pointed hood; **Caperucita Roja** Little Red Ridinghood
caperuza *f* pointed hood; chimney cap
capilla *f* (*parte de una iglesia con altar*) chapel; (*de los reos de muerte*) death house; (*pliego suelto*) proof sheet; cowl, hood, cape; **estar en capilla** to be in the death house; to be on pins and needles; **estar expuesto en capilla ardiente** to be on view, to lie in state
capiller *m* churchwarden, sexton
capillo *m* baby cap; baptismal cap; hood; cocoon; (*del cigarro*) filler
capirotazo *m* fillip
capirote *m* hood; doctor's cap and hood; cardboard or paper cone (*worn on head*); fillip
capitación *f* poll tax
capital *adj* capital; main, principal; paramount; (*enemigo*) mortal ‖ *m* (*dinero que produce renta*) capital; (*dinero que se presta para producir renta*) principal; **capital de inversión** investment capital ‖ *f* capital
capitalismo *m* capitalism
capitalista *adj* capitalistic ‖ *mf* capitalist; shareholder, investor
capitalizar §60 *tr* to capitalize; (*los intereses devengados*) compound
capitán *m* captain; leader; **capitán de bandera** flag captain; **capitán de corbeta** (nav) lieutenant commander; **capitán del puerto** harbor master
capitana *f* flagship
capitanear *tr* to captain; lead, command
capitanía *f* captaincy; (mil) company
capitel *m* (*de una iglesia*) spire; (*de una columna*) capital
capitolio *m* capitol
capitoste *m* big shot
capítula *f* chapter (*of Scriptures*)
capitular *tr* to accuse; agree on ‖ *intr* to capitulate
capitulear *intr* (Arg, Chile, Peru) to lobby
capituleo *m* (Arg, Chile, Peru) lobbying
capitulero *m* (Arg, Chile, Peru) political henchman, lobbyist
capítulo *m* chapter; chapter house; subject, matter; errand; main point; **ganar capítulo** (coll) to win one's point; **llamar a capítulo** to take to task, call to account; **perder capítulo** to lose one's point
ca•pó *m* (*pl* **-pós**) hood (*of auto*)
capolar *tr* to cut to pieces, chop up
ca•pón -pona *adj* castrated ‖ *m* eunuch; (*pollo*) capon; bundle of firewood; (*golpe*) fillip ‖ *f* shoulder strap
caponera *f* coop for fattening capons; place of welcome; (*cárcel*) coop, jail
caporal *m* chief, leader; foreman (*on cattle ranch*)

capota *f* bonnet; (aer) cowling; (aut) top
capotaje *m* (aer) nosing over
capotar *intr* to upset; (aer) to nose over
capote *m* cape, cloak; (coll) frown, scowl; (Chile, Mex) beating; **capote de monte** poncho; **de capote** (Mex) on the sly; **dar capote a** to flabbergast; (*un rezagado*) to leave hungry; **decir para su capote** to say to oneself; **echar un capote** to turn the conversation
capotear *tr* (*al toro*) to challenge; (*dificultades*) evade, duck; beguile, take in; (*una obra teatral*) cut, make cuts in
Capricornio *m* Capricorn
capricho *m* caprice, whim, fancy
capricho•so -sa *adj* capricious, whimsical; willful
caprichu•do -da *adj* capricious, whimsical
cápsula *f* capsule; (*de botella*) cap
capsular *tr* to cap
captación *f* capture; (*de las aguas de un río*) harnessing; (rad) tuning in, picking up
captar *tr* to catch; (*la confianza de una persona*) win; (*las aguas de un río*) harness; (*las ondas radiofónicas*) tune in, pick up; (*lo que uno dice*) get, grasp || *ref* to attract, win
captura *f* capture, catch
capturar *tr* to capture, catch
capucha *f* cowl, hood; circumflex accent
capuchina *f* garden nasturtium, Indian cress; Capuchin nun; confection of egg yolks
capucho *m* cowl, hood
capuchón *m* lady's cloak and hood; (*de una plumafuente*) cap; (aut) valve cap
capullo *m* cocoon; coarse spun silk; bud; **capullo de rosa** rosebud
capuzar §60 *tr* to throw in headfirst; (*un buque*) overload at the bow
caqui *adj* khaki || *m* khaki; Japanese persimmon
caquinos *mpl* (Mex) guffaw, outburst of laughter
cara *f* face; look, countenance; façade, front; (*de disco de fonógrafo*) side; **a cara descubierta** openly; **a cara o cruz** heads or tails; **cara a** facing; **cara al público** with an audience; **cara de acelga** sallow face; **cara de ajo** vinegar face; **cara de hereje** (*persona de feo aspecto*) fright, baboon; **cara de vinagre** vinegar face; **dar la cara** to take the consequences; **de cara** in the face; facing; **echar a cara o cruz** to flip a coin; **hacer cara a** to stand up to; **tener buena cara** to look well, to look good; **tener mala cara** to look ill, to look bad
cárabe *m* amber
carabina *f* carbine; chaperon
caracol *m* snail; snail shell; (*de pelo*) curl; (*trazado en espiral*) spiral; (*del oído*) cochlea
carácter *m* (*pl* **caracteres**) character; (*marca que se pone a las reses*) brand
característi•co -ca *adj* characteristic || *m* (theat) old man || *f* characteristic; (theat) old woman
caracteriza•do -da *adj* distinguished
caracterizar §60 *tr* to characterize; to confer a distinction on; (*un personaje en la escena*) to interpret || *ref* to dress and make up for a role
caradu•ro -ra *adj* brazen; shameless || *f* scoundrel
caramba *interj* confound it!; upon my word!
carámbano *m* icicle
carambola *f* carom; double shot; trick, cheating
carambolear *intr* to carom || *ref* to get tipsy
caramelo *m* caramel; drop, lozenge
carantamaula *f* ugly false face; (*persona*) ugly mug
carantoña *f* ugly false face; **carantoñas** adulation, fawning
carátula *f* mask; (*profesión de actor*) stage, theater; title page; (*de reloj*) (Mex, Guat) face
caravana *f* caravan; (*casa rodante*) trailer
caravanera *f* caravansary
caray *m* var of **carey**
carbohielo *m* dry ice
carbóli•co -ca *adj* carbolic
carbón *m* (*de leña*) charcoal; (*de piedra*) coal; (*electrodo de carbono de la lámpara de arco o la pila*) carbon; black crayon; (*honguillo parásito*) smut; **carbón de bujía** cannel coal, jet coal; **carbón tal como sale** run-of-mine coal
carboncillo *m* charcoal, charcoal pencil
carbonera *f* bunker, coal bunker; coalbin; (Col) coal mine
carbonería *f* coalyard
carbone•ro -ra *adj* coal, charcoal; coaling || *mf* coaldealer; charcoal burner || *f* see **carbonera**
carbonilla *f* fine coal; (*en los cilindros*) carbon
carbonizar §60 *tr* to char
carbono *m* carbon
carbunclo *m* (*piedra*) carbuncle; (pathol) carbuncle
carbunco *m* (pathol) carbuncle
carbúnculo *m* (*piedra*) carbuncle
carburador *m* carburetor
carburo *m* carbide
carcacha *f* (Mex) jalopy
carcaj *m* quiver
carcajada *f* outburst of laughter
cárcel *f* jail, prison; (*para oprimir dos piezas de madera encoladas*) clamp
carcele•ro -ra *adj* jail || *m* jailer, warden
carcinóge•no -na *adj* carcinogenic; cancer-causing || *m* carcinogen
carcinoma *f* carcinoma
carcoma *f* woodworm, borer; anxiety, worry; spendthrift
carcomer *tr* to bore, gnaw away at; undermine, harass || *ref* to become worm-eaten
cardán *m* universal joint
cardenal *m* cardinal; cardinal bird; black-and-blue mark
cardenillo *m* verdigris
cárde•no -na *adj* purple; dapple-gray; (*agua*) opaline

cardía•co -ca *adj* cardiac || *mf* (*persona que padece del corazón*) cardiac || *m* (*remedio*) cardiac
cardinal *adj* cardinal
cardo *m* thistle
cardume *m* school (*of fish*)
carear *tr* to bring face to face; compare || *intr* — **carear a** to overlook || *ref* to meet face to face
carecer §22 *intr* — **carecer de** to lack, need, be in want of
carecimiento *m* lack, need, want
carencia *f* lack, need, want
carente *adj* — **carente de** lacking
careo *m* meeting; confrontation
care•ro -ra *adj* dear, expensive
carestía *f* scarcity, want, dearth; high prices; **carestía de la vida** high cost of living
careta *f* mask; **careta antigás** gas mask
carey *m* hawksbill turtle; tortoise shell
carga *f* load, loading; (*mercancías que se transportan*) freight, cargo; (*peso u obligación que pesan sobre una persona*) burden; (*de substancia explosiva, de electricidad, de soldados contra el enemigo*) charge; charge, responsibility, obligation; **carga de familia** dependent; **carga de punta** (elec) peak load; **carga por eje** axle load; **carga útil** pay load; **echar la carga a** to put the blame on; **volver a la carga** to keep at it
cargaderas *fpl* (Col) suspenders
cargadero *m* loading platform; freight station
carga•do -da *adj* loaded; (*cielo*) overcast, cloudy; (*atmósfera, tiempo*) close, sultry; (*alambre eléctrico*) hot, charged; (*café, té*) strong; (*rato, hora*) busy; **cargado de años** along in years; **cargado de espaldas** round-shouldered, stoop-shouldered
cargador *m* loader, stevedore; carrier, porter; (*de acumulador*) charger
cargamento *m* load; (naut) loading; (naut) cargo, shipment
cargante *adj* boring, annoying, tiresome
cargar §44 *tr* (*un peso, mercancías; un carro, un mulo, un barco; un horno; un arma de fuego; a una persona*) to load; (*a una persona con un peso u obligación*) burden; (*un acumulador; al enemigo*) charge; (*a una persona*) charge with; entrust with; annoy, bore, weary; **cargar en cuenta a** (*una persona*) to charge to the account of; **cargar** (*a una persona*) **de** to charge with; burden with || *intr* to load; (*el viento*) turn; crowd; incline, tip; (*el acento*) fall; eat too much, drink too much; **cargar con** to pick up; walk away with; (*un fusil*) shoulder; take on; **cargar sobre** to rest on; bother, pester; devolve on || *ref* (*el cielo*) to become overcast; (*el viento*) turn; become annoyed, be bored; **cargarse de** to have a lot of; (*lágrimas*) be bathed in
cargaréme *m* receipt, voucher
cargazón *f* loading; (*en el estómago, la cabeza, etc.*) heaviness; mass of heavy clouds; (Arg) clumsy job; (Chile) good crop; **cargazón alta** (coll) high office; high official
cargo *m* job, position; duty, responsibility; burden, weight; management; (*falta que se atribuye a uno; cantidad que uno debe y la acción de anotarla*) charge; **a cargo de** in charge of; **cargo de conciencia** sense of guilt; **girar a cargo de** to draw on; **hacerse cargo de** to take charge of; to realize, become aware of; to look into; **librar a cargo de** to draw on; **vestir el cargo** to look the part
cargosear *tr* (Arg, Chile) to pester
cargo•so -sa *adj* annoying, bothersome; onerous, costly
carguero *m* (naut) freighter; (Arg, Urug) beast of burden
cariaconteci•do -da *adj* downcast, woebegone
cariar §77 *tr & intr* to decay
cariátide *f* caryatid
Caribdis *f* Charybdis
caribe *adj* Caribbean || *m* savage, brute
caricatura *f* (*descripción o figura grotescas; retrato festivo*) caricature; (*retrato festivo*) cartoon
caricaturista *mf* caricaturist; cartoonist
caricaturizar §60 *tr* to caricature; cartoon
caricia *f* caress; endearment
caridad *f* charity; **la caridad bien ordenada empieza por uno mismo** charity begins at home
caries *f* decay, tooth decay; caries
carilla *f* (*de colmenero*) mask; (*de libro*) page
carille•no -na *adj* full-faced
carillón *m* carillon
carine•gro -gra *adj* swarthy
cariño *m* love, affection; loved one; (Chile) gift, present; **cariños** caresses, endearments; (Arg) greetings
cariño•so -sa *adj* loving, affectionate
caripare•jo -ja *adj* stone-faced, impassive
carirraí•do -da *adj* brazen-faced, shameless
carisma *f* charisma
carismáti•co -ca *adj* charismatic
carita *f* little face; **dar** or **hacer carita** (*una mujer coqueta*) (Mex) to smile back
caritati•vo -va *adj* charitable
cariz *m* (*de la atmósfera, el tiempo*) appearance, look; (*de un asunto*) look, outlook; (*de la cara de uno*) look; **mal cariz** angry look, scowl
carlinga *f* (aer) cockpit
Carlomagno *m* Charlemagne
Carlos *m* Charles
carlota *f* pudding; **carlota rusa** charlotte russe || **Carlota** *f* Charlotte
carmelita *f* (Hond) station wagon
carmen *m* song, poem; house and garden (*in Granada*)
carmesí (*pl* **-síes**) *adj & m* crimson
carnada *f* bait; (coll) bait, trap
carnal; *adj* carnal; (*hermano*) full; (*primo*) first
carnaval *m* carnival
carne *f* (*parte blanda del cuerpo humano y del animal*) flesh; (*la comestible del ani-*

mal) meat; **carne de cañón** cannon fodder; **carne de cerdo asada** roast pork; **carne de cordero** lamb; **carne de gallina** goose flesh; **carne de horca** gallows bird; **carne de res** beef; **carne de ternera** veal; **carne de vaca asada** roast of beef; **carne de venado** venison; **carne fiambre** cold meat; **carne sin hueso** cinch, snap; **carne y sangre** flesh and blood; **cobrar carnes** to put on flesh; **echar carnes** (Mex) to swear, curse; **en carnes** naked; **en vivas carnes** stark-naked

carnear *tr* (Arg, Chile, Urug) to butcher, slaughter; (Arg, Urug) to stab; (Chile) to take in, swindle

carnero *m* sheep; (*carne de este animal*) mutton; (*osario*) charnel house; family vault; (*persona que no tiene voluntad propia*) (Arg, Chile) sheep; **cantar para el carnero** (Arg, Bol, Urug) to die; **no hay tales carneros** there's no truth to it

car•net *m* (*pl* **-nets**) notebook; membership card; (Arg) dance card; **carnet de chófer** driver's license; **carnet de identidad** identification card

carnicería *f* butcher shop, meat market; (fig) carnage, massacre

carnice•ro -ra *adj* carnivorous; bloodthirsty || *mf* butcher

carnosidad *f* fleshiness, corpulence; (*excrecencia carnosa anormal*) proud flesh

carno•so -sa *adj* fleshy; meaty, fat

ca•ro -ra *adj* (*de subido precio; amado, querido*) dear || *f* see **cara** || **caro** *adv* dear

carpa *f* carp; awning, tent; stand at a fair; **carpa dorada** goldfish

carpanta *f* raging hunger

carpeta *f* (*cubierta para mesas*) table cover; (*par de cubiertas para documentos*) letter file, portfolio; (*factura*) invoice; (Col) accounting department; (Peru) writing desk

carpintería *f* carpentry; carpenter shop; **carpintería de taller** millwork

carpintero *m* carpenter; woodpecker; **carpintero de carreta** wheelwright

carra•co -ca *adj* old, decrepit || *f* (*barco viejo*) tub, hulk; (*instrumento de madera para producir un ruido desapacible*) rattle; (*berbiquí*) ratchet drill || **la Carraca** Cádiz navy yard

carraspear *intr* to be hoarse

carraspera *f* hoarseness

carrera *f* (*paso del que corre*) run; (*lucha de velocidad*) race; (*sitio para correr*) race track; (*espacio recorrido corriendo*) course, stretch; (*curso de la vida, profesión*) career; (*calle*) avenue, boulevard; (*raya, crencha*) part (*in hair*); (*en las medias*) run; (*hilera*) row, line; (*viga*) rafter, girder; (*movimiento del émbolo del motor*) stroke; **a carrera abierta** at full speed; **carrera a pie** foot race; **carrera armamentista** or **de armamentos** arms race; **carrera ascendente** upstroke; **carrera de baquetas** gauntlet; **carrera de caballos** horse race; **carrera de campanario** steeplechase; **carrera de obstáculos** obstacle race; steeplechase; **carrera de relevos** relay race; **carrera descendente** downstroke; **carrera de vallas** hurdle race; **carreras** horse racing, turf

carrerista *adj* horsy || *mf* racegoer; auto racer; bicycle racer || *m* outrider || *f* (slang) streetwalker

carreta *f* cart; **carreta de bueyes** oxcart

carrete *m* reel, spool; fishing reel; (elec) coil

carretear *tr* to cart, haul; (*un carro, una carreta*) drive; (aer) to taxi || *intr* (aer) to taxi

carretera *f* highway, road; **carretera de peaje** turnpike; **carretera de vía libre** expressway, limited-access highway

carretería *f* carts; wagon work; carting business; wagon shop

carrete•ro -ra *adj* wagon, carriage || *m* wheelwright; teamster; charioteer; **jurar como un carretero** to swear like a trooper || *f* see **carretera**

carretilla *f* wheelbarrow; baggage truck; (*para enseñar a los niños a andar*) gocart; (*buscapiés*) snake, serpent; (Arg, Chile, Urug) jaw; **carretilla de mano** handcart; **carretilla elevadora** lift truck; **de carretilla** offhand

carretón *m* cart, wagon, dray; gocart; (rr) truck; covered wagon

carricoche *m* covered wagon

carricuba *f* street sprinkler

carril *m* (*barra de acero en el ferrocarril*) rail, track; (*huella*) track, rut; (*hecho por el arado*) furrow; lane, path; (Chile) train; (Chile, P-R) railroad; **carril de toma** third rail

carrilera *f* track, rut

carrilero *m* (Peru) railroader

carrillera *f* jaw; chin strap

carrillo *m* cheek, jowl; pulley; **comer a dos carrillos** to eat like a glutton; have two sources of income; play both sides

carrizo *m* ditch reed

carro *m* cart, wagon; car, auto; (mach) carriage; **carro alegórico** float; **carro blindado** armored car; **carro correo** mail car; **carro de asalto** tank; **carro de combate** combat car, tank; **carro de equipajes** baggage car; **carro de mudanza** moving van; **carro de riego** street sprinkler; **carro frigorífero** refrigerator car; **carro fúnebre** hearse; **Carro mayor** Big Dipper; **Carro menor** Little Dipper; **carro romano** chariot; **pare Vd. el carro** hold your horses

ca•rró *m* (*pl* **-rrós**) diamond

carrocería *f* (*de automóvil*) body

carrocha *f* eggs (*of insect*)

carromato *m* covered wagon

carro•ño -ña *adj* & *f* carrion

carro-patrulla *f* (SAm) patrol car; police car

carroza *f* coach, carriage; **carroza alegórica** float; **carroza fúnebre** hearse

carruaje *m* carriage

carta *f* (*comunicación escrita*) letter; (*constitución escrita de un país*) charter; (*naipe*) card, playing card; map; **carta aérea** airmail letter; **carta blanca** carte blanche;

carta calumniosa poison-pen letter; **carta certificada** registered letter; **carta de marear** (naut) chart; **carta de naturaleza** naturalization papers; **carta general** form letter; **carta por avión** air-mail letter; **poner las cartas boca arriba** to put one's cards on the table

cartabón *m* carpenter's square

cartagi•nés -nesa *adj & mf* Carthaginian

Cartago *f* Carthage

cartapacio *m* notebook; schoolboy's satchel; writing book; (*papeles contenidos en una carpeta*) file, dossier

cartear *intr* to play low cards (*in order to see how the game stands*) || *ref* to write to each other

cartel *m* show bill, poster, placard; cartel, trust; (*pasquín*) lampoon; (*de toreros*) bill, line-up; (*del torero*) fame, reputation; **cartel de teatro** bill, show bill; **dar cartel a** to headline; **se prohibe fijar carteles** post no bills; **tener cartel** to be the rage

cartela *f* card; bracket

cartelera *f* billboard; (*en los periódicos*) amusement page, theater section

cartelero *m* billposter

cartelón *m* show bill

carteo *m* finessing; exchange of letters

cárter *m* (mach) housing; **cárter de engranajes** gearcase; **cárter del cigüeñal** crankcase

cartera *f* portfolio; pocket flap; **cartera de bolsillo** billfold, wallet

cartería *f* sorting room

carterista *m* pickpocket, purse snatcher

cartero *m* letter carrier, postman

cartilagino•so -sa *adj* gristly

cartílago *m* gristle

cartilla *f* primer, speller, reader; notebook; (*de la caja de ahorros*) deposit book; **cartilla de racionamiento** ration book

cartivana *f* (bb) hinge, joint

cartón *m* cardboard, pasteboard; cardboard box; **cartón de yeso y fieltro** plasterboard; **cartón picado** stencil; **cartón tabla** wallboard

cartoné — **en cartoné** (bb) in boards, bound in boards

cartucho *m* cartridge

cartulina *f* fine cardboard

casa *f* (*edificio para habitar*) house; (*hogar, domicilio*) home; (*establecimiento comercial o industrial*) firm, concern; (*familia*) household; (*escaque*) square; **a casa** home, homeward; **casa consistorial** town hall, city hall; **casa de azotea** penthouse; **casa de campo** country house; **casa de caridad** poorhouse; **casa de citas** house of assignation; **casa de correos** post office; **casa de empeños** pawnshop; **casa de expósitos** foundling home; **casa de fieras** menagerie; **casa de huéspedes** boarding house; **casa de juego** gambling house; **casa de locos** madhouse; **casa de modas** dress shop; **casa de moneda** mint; **casa de préstamos** pawnshop; **casa de salud** private hospital; **casa de socorro** first-aid station; **casa de vecindad** or **de vecinos** apartment house, tenement house; **casa editorial** publishing house; **casa matriz** main office; **casa pública** brothel; **casa real** royal palace; royal family; **casas baratas** low-cost housing; **casa solar** or **solariega** ancestral mansion, manor house; **casa y comida** board and lodging; **¡convida la casa!** the drinks are on the house!; **en casa** home, at home; **ir a buscar casa** to go house hunting; **poner casa** to set up housekeeping

casabe *m* var of **cazabe**

casaca *f* dress coat; marriage contract; (Guat, Hond) lively whispered conversation; **volver la casaca** to become a turncoat

casade•ro -ra *adj* marriageable

casa•do -da *adj* married || *mf* married person; **(los) no casados** (coll) singles

casal *m* country place; (Arg) pair, couple

casamente•ro -ra *adj* matchmaking || *mf* matchmaker

casamiento *m* marriage; wedding

casapuerta *f* entrance hall, vestibule

casaquilla *f* jacket

casar *tr* to marry; marry off; match; harmonize; (law) to annul, repeal || *intr* to marry, get married || *ref* to marry, get married; **no casarse con nadie** to get tied up with nobody

casatienda *f* store and home combined

cascabel *m* sleigh bell, jingle bell; rattlesnake; **ponerle cascabel al gato** to bell the cat

cascabelear *intr* to jingle; to act tactlessly

cascabeleo *m* jingle

cascabele•ro -ra *adj* tactless, thoughtless || *mf* featherbrain || *m* baby's rattle

cascabillo *m* jingle bell; chaff, husk; cup of acorn

cascada *f* cascade, waterfall

cascajo *m* pebble; gravel, rubble; broken jar; piece of junk; **estar hecho un cascajo** to be old and worn-out, be a wreck

cascanue•ces *m* (*pl* **-ces**) nutcracker

cascar §73 *tr* to crack, break, split; beat, strike, hit || *ref* to crack, break, split

cáscara *f* hull, peel, rind, shell; bark, crust; **cáscara rueda** (Arg) ring-around-a-rosy; **ser de la cáscara amarga** to be wild and flighty; hold advanced views; (Mex) to be determined

cascarón *m* eggshell

cascarra•bias *mf* (*pl* **-bias**) crab, grouch

casco *m* (*pieza que sirve para proteger la cabeza del soldado, el bombero, etc.*) helmet; (*uña de las caballerías*) hoof; (*pedazo de vasija rota*) potsherd; (*capa de la cebolla*) coat, shell; (*del sombrero*) crown; (*cuerpo de la nave*) hull; (*de un barco inservible*) hulk; (*barril, pipa*) barrel, tank, cask, vat; (*pieza del teléfono*) headset, headpiece; bottle; (mach) shell, casing; (*gajo de la naranja*) (Arg, Col, Chile) slice; (Peru) chest, breast; **casco de población** or **casco urbano** city limits; **romperse los cascos** to rack one's brain

casera *f* landlady; housekeeper

casería *f* country place; customers

caserío *m* country house; small settlement, hamlet
case•ro -ra *adj* homemade; homeloving; (*remedio*) household; house, home; (*sencillo*) homely ‖ *mf* owner, proprietor; renter; caretaker; janitor; huckster; vendor ‖ *m* landlord ‖ *f* see **casera**
caseta *f* (*casa sin piso alto*) cottage; (*de una feria*) stall, booth; bathhouse
casete *m* cassette
casi *adv* almost, nearly; **casi nada** next to nothing; **casi nunca** hardly ever
casilla *f* hut, shack, shed; cabin, lodge; stall, booth; (*escaque*) square; (*compartimiento en un mueble*) pigeonhole; (*división del papel rayado*) column, square; (*taquilla*) ticket office; (*de locomotora o camión*) cab; (Bol, Chile, Peru, Urug) post-office box; (Ecuad) water closet; (Cuba) bird trap; **sacarle a uno de sus casillas** to jolt someone out of his old habits; drive someone crazy
casille•ro -ra *mf* (rr) crossing guard ‖ *m* filing cabinet, set of pigeonholes
casino *m* casino; club; clubhouse
caso *m* case; chance; event; **caso de conformidad** in case you agree; **caso que** in case; **de caso pensado** deliberately, on purpose; **en todo caso** at all events; **hacer al caso** to be to the purpose; **hacer caso de** to take into account, pay attention to; **hacer caso omiso de** to pass over in silence, not mention; **no venir al caso** to be beside the point; **poner por caso** to take as an example; **venir al caso** to be just the thing
casorio *m* hasty marriage, unwise marriage
caspa *f* dandruff, scurf
cáspita *interj* well well!, upon my word!
caspo•so -sa *adj* full of dandruff
casquete *m* (*cubierta que se ajusta al casco de la cabeza*) skullcap; skull, cranium; (*pieza de la armadura que cubre el casco de la cabeza*) helmet; (*pieza del teléfono*) headset
casquillo *m* butt, cap, tip; bushing, sleeve; ferrule; horseshoe
casquiva•no -na *adj* scatterbrained
casta *f* caste; kind, quality; breed, race
castaña *f* chestnut; (*moño*) knot, chignon; demijohn; **castaña de Indias** horse chestnut; **castaña de Pará** Brazil nut
castañeta *f* castanet; snapping of the fingers
castañetear *tr* (*los dedos*) to snap, click; (*p.ej., una seguidilla*) click off with the castanets ‖ *intr* to click; (*los dientes*) chatter
casta•ño -ña *adj* chestnut, chestnut-colored; (*p.ej., pelo*) brown; (*p.ej., ojos*) hazel ‖ *m* chestnut tree; **castaño de Indias** horse chestnut ‖ *f* see **castaña**
castañuela *f* castanet; **estar como unas castañuelas** to be bubbling over with joy
castella•no -na *adj & mf* Castilian ‖ *m* Castilian, Spanish (*language*) ‖ *f* chatelaine
casticidad *f* purity, correctness (*in language*)
casticismo *m* purism
castidad *f* chastity
castiga•dor -dora *mf* punisher ‖ *m* seducer, Don Juan
castigar §44 *tr* to punish, chastise; (*la carne*) mortify; (*los gastos*) cut down, curtail; (*obras, escritos*) correct, emend; (*un tornillo*) (Mex) tighten
castigo *m* punishment, chastisement
Castilla *f* Castile; **Castilla la Nueva** New Castile; **Castilla la Vieja** Old Castile
castillete *m* (min) derrick; tower
castillo *m* castle; (*montura sobre un elefante*) howdah; **castillo en el aire** castle in Spain, castle in the air; **castillo de naipes** house of cards; **castillo de proa** forecastle
casti•zo -za *adj* chaste, pure, correct; pure-blooded; real, regular
cas•to -ta *adj* chaste, pure ‖ *f* see **casta**
castor *m* beaver
castrar *tr* to castrate; (*una planta*) prune, cut back; weaken
casual *adj* casual, accidental, chance
casualidad *f* accident, chance; chance event; **por casualidad** by chance
casuca or **casucha** *f* shack, shanty
casulla *f* chasuble
cata *f* tasting; taste, sample
catacal•dos *mf* (*pl* **-dos**) rolling stone; busybody
catacumba *f* catacomb
catafoto *m* (rear) reflector
cata•lán -lana *adj & mf* Catalan, Catalonian
catalejo *m* spyglass
catalogar §44 *tr* to catalogue
catálogo *m* catalogue
Cataluña *f* Catalonia
cataplasma *f* poultice; **cataplasma de mostaza** mustard plaster
catapulta *f* catapult
catapultar *tr* to catapult
catar *tr* to taste, sample; check, examine; be on the lookout for
catarata *f* cataract, waterfall; (pathol) cataract
catarro *m* (*inflamación de las membranas mucosas*) catarrh; (*resfriado*) head cold
catástrofe *f* catastrophe
catavino *m* cup for tasting wine
catavi•nos *m* (*pl* **-nos**) winetaster; (*borracho*) rounder
catear *tr* to hunt, look for; (*a un alumno*) to flunk; to explore; (*una casa*) to search
catecismo *m* catechism
cátedra *f* chair, professorship; academic subject; teacher's desk; classroom; **poner cátedra** to hold forth
catedral *f* cathedral
catedrático *m* university professor
categoría *f* category; status, standing; class, kind; condition, quality; **de categoría** prominent
caterva *f* throng, crowd
catéter *m* catheter
cateterizar §60 *tr* to catheterize
cátodo *m* cathode
católi•co -ca *adj* catholic; Catholic; **no estar muy católico** to be under the weather ‖ *mf*

Catholic; **católico romano** Roman Catholic
catorce *adj & pron* fourteen || *m* fourteen; (*en las fechas*) fourteenth
catorcea•vo -va *adj & m* fourteenth
catorza•vo -va *adj & m* fourteenth
catre *m* cot; **catre de tijera** folding cot
catrecillo *m* campstool, folding canvas chair
ca•trín -trina *adj* (CAm, Mex) sporty, swell || *mf* (CAm, Mex) sport, dude
caucasia•no -na or **caucási•co -ca** *adj & mf* Caucasian
Cáucaso *m* Caucasus
cauce *m* river bed; channel, ditch, trench
caución *f* precaution; (law) bail, security
caucionar *tr* to guard against; (law) to give bail for
cauchal *m* rubber plantation
caucho *m* rubber; rubber plant; (Col) rubber raincoat; **caucho esponjoso** foam rubber; **cauchos** (*chanclos*) rubbers
caudal *adj* of great volume || *m* (*de agua*) volume; abundance; wealth
caudalo•so -sa *adj* of great volume; abundant; rich, wealthy
caudillo *m* chief, leader; military leader; caudillo, head of state
causa *f* cause; (law) suit, trial; (Chile) bite, snack; (Peru) potato salad; **a** or **por causa de** on account of, because of
causa•dor -dora *adj* causing || *mf* (*persona*) cause
causante *mf* (*persona*) cause; (law) principal, constituent; (Mex) taxpayer
causar *tr* to cause
causear *tr* (Chile) to get the best of || *intr* (Chile) to have a bite
causeo *m* (Chile) bite, snack
cáusti•co -ca *adj* caustic
cautela *f* caution
cautelo•so -sa *adj* cautious, guarded
cauterizar §60 *tr* to cauterize
cautín *m* soldering iron
cautivar *tr* to take prisoner; attract, win over; (*encantar*) captivate
cautiverio *m* or **cautividad** *f* captivity
cauti•vo -va *adj & mf* captive
cau•to -ta *adj* cautious
cavar *tr* to dig, dig up || *intr* (*una herida*) to go deep; (*el caballo*) to paw; **cavar en** to study thoroughly, to delve into
caverna *f* cavern, cave
cavidad *f* cavity
cavilar *tr* to brood over || *intr* to worry, fret
cavilo•so -sa *adj* suspicious, mistrustful; (CAm) gossipy; (Col) touchy
cayado *m* (*de pastor*) crook; (*de obispo*) crozier
cayo *m* key, reef; **Cayo Hueso** Key West; **Cayos de la Florida** Florida Keys
caz *m* (*pl* **caces**) flume, millrace
caza *m* pursuit plane, fighter; **caza de reacción** jet fighter || *f* chase, hunt; hunting; (*animales que se cazan*) game; **a caza de** on the hunt for; **caza al hombre** man hunt; **caza de grillos** fool's errand, wild-goose chase; **ir de caza** to go hunting
cazaautógra•fos *mf* (*pl* **-fos**) autograph seeker
cazabe *m* cassava, manioc; cassava bread
caza•dor -dora *adj* hunting || *m* hunter; huntsman; **cazador de alforja** trapper; **cazador de cabezas** head-hunter; **cazador de dotes** fortune hunter; **cazador furtivo** poacher || *f* huntress; hunting jacket; jacket
cazanoti•cias (*pl* **-cias**) *m* newshawk || *f* newshen
cazasubmarinos *m* sub(marine) chaser
cazar §60 *tr* to chase; hunt; catch; (*en un descuido o error*) catch up; (*un descuido o error*) catch; (*adquirir con maña*) wangle; (*con halagos o engaños*) take in || *intr* to hunt
cazarreactor *m* jet fighter
cazcalear *intr* to buzz around
cazo *m* dipper, ladle; glue pot; (*de cuchillo*) back
cazuela *f* earthen casserole; stew; (archaic) gallery for women; (SAm) chicken stew
cazu•rro -rra *adj* sullen, surly
cazuz *m* ivy
C. de J. *abbr* **Compañía de Jesús**
cebada *f* barley
cebadera *f* nose bag
cebador *m* (mach) primer
cebar *tr* (*a un animal*) to fatten; (*un horno*) feed; (*un arma de fuego, una bomba, un carburador*) prime; (*una pasión, la esperanza*) nourish; (*atraer*) lure; (*un clavo, un tornillo*) make catch, make take hold; (*un anzuelo*) bait || *intr* (*un clavo, un tornillo*) to catch, take hold || *ref* (*una enfermedad, una epidemia*) to rage; **cebarse en** to be absorbed in; vent one's fury on
cebo *m* fattening; feed; bait; lure; (*carga de un arma de fuego*) primer; priming
cebolla *f* onion; bulb; (*del velón*) oil receptacle
cebra *f* zebra
ce•bú *m* (*pl* **-búes**) zebu
ceca *f* mint; **de Ceca en Meca** or **de la Ceca a la Meca** hither and thither, from pillar to post
cecear *intr* to lisp
ceceo *m* lisp, lisping
cecina *f* dried beef
cedazo *m* sieve
ceder *tr* to yield, cede, give up || *intr* to yield, give way, give in; slacken, relax; go down, decline
cedro *m* cedar; **cedro de Virginia** juniper, red cedar
cédula *f* (*de papel*) slip; form, blank; rent sign; certificate, document; **cédula de vecindad** or **cédula personal** identification papers
cedulón *m* proclamation, public notice; (*pasquín*) lampoon
céfiro *m* zephyr
cegar §66 *tr* to blind; (*un agujero*) plug, stop up; (*una puerta, una ventana*) wall up || *intr* to go blind; be blinded || *ref* to be blinded
cega•to -ta *adj* dim-sighted, weak-eyed
ceguedad *f* blindness

ceguera *f* blindness; blackout
Ceilán Ceylon
ceila•nés -nesa *adj & mf* Ceylonese
ceja *f* (*pelo sobre la cuenca del ojo*) eyebrow; edge, rim; cloud cap; clearing for a road; **arquear las cejas** to raise one's eyebrows; **fruncir las cejas** to knit one's brow; **quemarse las cejas** to burn the midnight oil
cejar *intr* to back up; turn back; slacken
cejijun•to -ta or **ceju•do -da** *adj* beetle-browed; scowling
celada *f* ambush; trap, trick
celador *m* guard (*e.g., in a museum*); (elec) lineman; (Urug) policeman
celaje *m* cloud effect; skylight, transom; ghost
celar *tr* to see to; watch over, keep an eye on; hide; carve
celda *f* cell; **celda de castigo** solitary confinement
celdilla *f* cell; niche
celebración *f* celebration; applause; (*de una reunión*) holding
celebrante *m* (*sacerdote*) celebrant
celebrar *tr* to celebrate; (*una reunión*) hold; (*aprobar*) welcome; (*un matrimonio*) perform; (*misa*) say || *intr* (*decir misa*) to celebrate; be glad || *ref* to take place, be held; be celebrated
célebre *adj* celebrated, famous; funny, witty; pretty
celebridad *f* (*fama; persona*) celebrity
celeridad *f* speed, swiftness
celeste *adj* celestial; sky-blue
celestial *adj* celestial, heavenly; stupid, silly
celestina *f* procuress, bawd
celestinaje *m* procuring, pandering
celibato *m* celibacy; bachelor
célibe *adj* celibate, single, unmarried || *mf* celibate, single person || *m* bachelor || *f* unmarried woman
celinda *f* mock orange
celo *m* zeal; envy; (*impulso reproductivo en las bestias*) heat, rut; **celos** jealousy
celofán *m* or **celofana** *f* cellophane
celosía *f* (*celotipia*) jealousy; (*enrejado de listoncillos*) lattice window, jalousie
celo•so -sa *adj* (*que tiene celo*) zealous; (*que tiene celos*) jealous; fearful, distrustful; (naut) unsteady
celotipia *f* jealousy
celta *adj* Celtic || *mf* Celt || *m* (*idioma*) Celtic
célti•co -ca *adj* Celtic
célula *f* cell
celuloide *m* celluloid; **llevar al celuloide** to put on the screen
cellisca *f* sleet, sleet storm
cellisquear *intr* to sleet
cementerio *m* cemetery
cemento *m* cement; concrete; **cemento armado** reinforced concrete
cena *f* supper; dinner || **la Cena** the Last Supper
cena•dor -dora *mf* diner-out || *m* arbor, bower, summerhouse
cenaduría *f* (Mex) supper club
cenagal *m* quagmire
cenago•so -sa *adj* muddy, miry
cenaoscu•ras *mf* (*pl* **-ras**) recluse; skinflint
cenar *tr* to have for supper, have for dinner || *intr* to have supper, have dinner
cencerrada *f* tin-pan serenade
cencerrear *intr* to keep jingling; rattle, jangle; play out of tune
cencerro *m* cowbell; **a cencerros tapados** cautiously
cendal *m* gauze, sendal
cenefa *f* edging, trimming, border
cenicero *m* ash tray
cenicien•to -ta *adj* ashen, ash-gray || **la Cenicienta** Cinderella
cenit *m* zenith
ceniza *f* ash; ashes; **cenizas** ashes; **huir de las cenizas y caer en las brasas** to jump from the frying pan into the fire
ceni•zo -za *adj* ashen, ash-gray || *f* see **ceniza**
cenojil *m* garter
cenote *m* (Mex) deep underground water reservoir
censo *m* census; **levantar el censo** to take the census
censor *m* censor; **censor jurado de cuentas** certified public accountant
censura *f* censure; censoring; gossip; **censura de cuentas** auditing
censurar *tr* (*criticar, reprobar*) to censure; (*formar juicio de*) censor
centauro *m* centaur
centa•vo -va *adj* hundredth || *m* hundredth; cent
centella *f* flash of lightning; flash of light; spark; (*de ingenio, de ira*) (fig) spark, flash
centellar or **centellear** *intr* to flash, spark; glimmer, gleam, twinkle
centenar *m* hundred; **a centenares** by the hundreds
centena•rio -ria *adj* centennial || *mf* centenarian || *m* centennial
cente•no -na *adj* hundredth || *m* rye
centési•mo -ma *adj & m* hundredth
centígra•do -da *adj* centigrade
centímetro *m* centimeter
cénti•mo -ma *adj* hundredth || *m* hundredth; centime
centinela *mf* (*persona*) watch, guard || *m & f* (*soldado*) sentinel, sentry; **hacer de centinela** to stand sentinel
centípedo *m* centipede
central *adj* central || *m* sugar mill, sugar refinery || *f* headquarters, main office; powerhouse; (telp) exchange, central; **central de correos** main post office; **central de teléfonos** telephone exchange
centralista *mf* telephone operator
centralizar **§60** *tr & ref* to centralize
centrar *tr* to center; hit the center || *ref* to concentrate; stress
céntri•co -ca *adj* center, central; (*próximo al centro de la ciudad*) downtown
centrifugadora *f* centrifuge; spin-dryer
centro *m* center; middle; business district, downtown; club; object, goal, purpose; **centro de mesa** centerpiece; **centro docente** educational institution; **pegar centro** (CAm) to hit the bull's-eye

Centro América *f* Central America
centroamerica•no -na *adj & mf* Central American
cénts. *abbr* **céntimos**
ceñi•do -da *adj* tight, tight-fitting; lithe, svelte; thrifty
ceñidor *m* belt, girdle, sash
ceñir **§72** *tr* to gird; girdle; fasten around the waist; fasten, tie; abridge, shorten; surround; (*la espada*) gird on; (mil) to besiege || *ref* (*reducirse en los gastos*) to tighten one's belt; (*a pocas palabras*) restrict oneself; adapt oneself; **ceñirse a** (*p.ej., un muro*) to hug, keep close to
ceño *m* frown; (*del cielo, las nubes, el mar*) threatening look; (*cerco, aro*) hoop, ring, band; **arrugar el ceño** to knit one's brow; **mirar con ceño** to frown at
ceño•so -sa or **ceñu•do -da** *adj* beetlebrowed; frowning, grim, gruff
cepa *f* (*de árbol*) stump; (*de la cola del animal*) stub; (*de la vid*) vinestalk; (*de una famila o linaje*) strain; **de buena cepa** of well-known quality
cepillar *tr* to plane; brush; smooth; (SAm) to flatter
cepillo *m* (*instrumento para alisar la madera*) plane; (*utensilio para limpieza*) brush; (*cepo para limosnas*) charity box, poor box; (CAm, Mex) flatterer; **cepillo de cabeza** hairbrush; **cepillo de dientes** toothbrush; **cepillo de ropa** clothesbrush; **cepillo de uñas** nail brush
cepo *m* (*de limosnas*) poor box; (*rama de árbol*) bough, branch; (*trampa*) snare, trap; (*del yunque*) stock; (*para devanar la seda*) reel; clamp, vise; (*para asegurar a un reo*) stocks, pillory; **¡cepos quedos!** quiet!, stop it!
cera *f* wax; **cera de abejas** beeswax; **cera de los oídos** earwax; **cera de lustrar** polishing wax; **cera de pisos** floor wax; **ceras** honeycomb; **ser como una cera** to be wax in one's hands
cerámi•co -ca *adj* ceramic
cerbatana *f* peashooter; ear trumpet; spokesperson, go-between
cerca *m* close-up; **tener buen cerca** to look good at close quarters || *f* fence, wall; **cerca viva** hedge || *adv* near; **cerca de** near, close to; about; to, at the court of; **de cerca** closely; at close range
cercado *m* fence, wall; walled-in garden or field
cercanía *f* nearness, proximity; **cercanías** neighborhood, vicinity
cerca•no -na *adj* close, near; adjoining, neighboring; (*que debe acontecer en breve*) early
cercar **§73** *tr* to fence in, wall in; encircle, surround; crowd around; (mil) to besiege
cercenar *tr* to clip, trim; curtail; cut out
cerciorar *tr* to inform, assure || *ref* to find out; **cerciorarse de** to ascertain, find out about
cerco *m* (*aro, anillo*) hoop, ring; (*marco de puerta o ventana*) casing, frame; (*círculo que aparece alrededor del sol o la luna*) halo; (*reunión de personas*) circle, group; fence, wall; (mil) siege; **poner cerco a** (mil) to lay siege to
cerda *f* bristle, horsehair; (*hembra del cerdo*) sow
cerdear *intr* to be weak in the forelegs; (*las cuerdas de un instrumento*) rasp, grate; hold back, look for excuses
Cerdeña *f* Sardinia
cerdo *m* hog; (*persona sucia*) pig, swine; (*hombre sin cortesía*) cad, ill-bred fellow; **cerdo de muerte** pig to be slaughtered; **cerdo de vida** pig not old enough to be slaughtered; **cerdo marino** porpoise
cerdo•so -sa *adj* bristly
cereal *adj & m* cereal
cerebro *m* brain; (*seso, inteligencia*) brain, brains
ceremonia *f* ceremony; formality; **de ceremonia** formal; **hacer ceremonias** to stand on ceremony; **por ceremonia** as a matter of form
ceremonio•so -sa *adj* ceremonious, punctilious; (*que gusta de ceremonias*) formal
cereza *f* cherry
cerezo *m* cherry tree
cerilla *f* wax taper; wax match
cerillera *f* or **cerillero** *m* match box
cerneja *f* fetlock
cerner **§51** *tr* to sift; (*el horizonte*) scan || *intr* to bud, blossom; drizzle || *ref* to waddle; (*el ave*) soar, hover; (*un mal*) threaten; **cernerse sobre** (*amenazar*) to hang over
cernícalo *m* (orn) sparrow hawk; ignoramus; jag, drunk
cernir **§28** *tr* to sift
cero *m* zero; **empezar de cero** to start from scratch; **ser un cero a la izquierda** to not count, be a nobody
cerote *m* shoemaker's wax; fear
cerotear *tr* (*el hilo*) to wax || *intr* (Chile) to drip
cerra•do -da *adj* closed; close; incomprehensible; (*cielo*) cloudy, overcast; (*barba*) thick; (*curva*) sharp; quiet, reserved, secretive; dense, stupid
cerradura *f* lock; closing, locking; **cerradura embutida** mortise lock
cerrajería *f* locksmith business; hardware; hardware store
cerrajero *m* locksmith; hardware dealer; (*el que trabaja el hierro frío*) ironworker
cerrar **§2** *tr* to close, shut; lock; bolt; (*el puño*) clench; enclose; (*la radio*) turn off; **cerrar con llave** to lock || *intr* to close, shut; (*la noche*) fall; **cerrar con** (*el enemigo*) to close in on; **cerrar en falso** (*una puerta, cerradura, etc.*) to not catch || *ref* to close, to shut; lock; **cerrarse en falso** to not heal right
cerrazón *f* gathering storm clouds; (Arg) heavy fog
cerre•ro -ra *adj* free, loose; untamed; haughty; (Mex) rough, unpolished; (*café*) (Ven) bitter

cerril *adj* rough, uneven; wild, untamed; boorish, rough
cerrillar *tr* to knurl, mill
cerro *m* hill, hillock; (*entre dos surcos*) ridge; (*espinazo*) backbone; (*del animal*) neck; **en cerro** bareback; **echar por los cerros de Úbeda** to talk nonsense; **por los cerros de Úbeda** off the beaten path
cerrojo *m* bolt; **cerrojo dormido** dead bolt
certamen *m* literary competition; contest, match
certe•ro -ra *adj* certain, sure, accurate; well-informed; (*tiro*) well-aimed; (*tirador*) good, crack
certeza *f* certainty
certidumbre *f* certainty; sureness
certificación *f* certification; certificate
certifica•do -da *adj* registered || *m* registered letter, registered package; certificate; **certificado de estudios** transcript
certificar **§73** *tr* to certify; (*una carta*) register
certitud *f* certainty
cerval *adj* deer; (*miedo*) intense
cervato *m* fawn
cervecería *f* brewery; beer saloon
cervece•ro -ra *adj* beer || *mf* brewer
cerveza *f* beer; **cerveza a presión** draught beer; **cerveza de marzo** bock beer
cer•viz *f* (*pl* **-vices**) cervix; nape of the neck; **bajar** or **doblar la cerviz** to humble oneself; **levantar la cerviz** to raise one's head, become proud; **ser de dura cerviz** to be ungovernable
cesación *f* cessation, suspension
cesante *adj* retired, out of office || *mf* pensioner
cesantía *f* retirement; dismissal (*of a public official*)
cesar *intr* to stop, cease
César *m* Caesar
cese *m* ceasing; notice of retirement; **cese de alarma** all-clear; **cese de fuego** ceasefire
césped *m* lawn, sward; sod, turf
cesta *f* basket; (*para jugar a la pelota*) wicker scoop; **cesta de costura** sewing basket; **cesta para compras** market basket
cesto *m* basket; washbasket; **cesto de la colada** clothesbasket, washbasket; **estar hecho un cesto** to be overcome with sleep; **ser un cesto** to be crude and ignorant
cetrería *f* falconry
cetrero *m* falconer
cetri•no -na *adj* (*tez*) sallow; jaundiced, melancholy
cetro *m* scepter; (*para aves*) perch, roost; (eccl) verge; **cetro de bufón** bauble; **cetro de locura** fool's scepter; **empuñar el cetro** to ascend the throne
cf. *abbr* **confesor**
cg. *abbr* **centigramo**
C.I. *abbr* **cociente intelectual**
cía. *abbr* **compañia**
cía *f* hipbone
cianamida *f* cyanamide
cianuro *m* cyanide
ciar **§77** *intr* to back up; back water; ease up
cibernética *f* cybernetics
ciborio *m* ciborium
cicatear *intr* to be stingy
cicate•ro -ra *adj* stingy || *mf* miser, niggard
cica•triz *f* (*pl* **-trices**) scar
cicatrizar **§60** *tr* to heal; (*una impresión dolorosa*) (Arg) to heal || *ref* to heal; to scar
Cicerón *m* Cicero
ciclamor *m* Judas tree; **ciclamor del Canadá** redbud
cícli•co -ca *adj* cyclic(al)
ciclismo *m* bicycle racing
ciclista *mf* bicyclist; bicycle racer
ciclo *m* cycle; series (of lectures); (*en las escuelas*) (Arg, Urug) term
ciclón *m* cyclone
cicuta *f* hemlock
cidra *f* citron (*fruit*)
cidrada *f* citron (*candied rind*)
cidro *m* citron (*tree or shrub*)
cie•go -ga *adj* blind; blocked, stopped up; **más ciego que un topo** blind as a bat || *mf* blind person || *m* blind man || *f* blind woman; **a ciegas** blindly; thoughtlessly; without looking
cielo *m* sky, heavens; (*clima, tiempo*) skies, climate, weather; (*de una cama*) canopy; (*mansión de los bienaventurados*) Heaven; **a cielo abierto** in the open air, outdoors; **a cielo descubierto** openly; **a cielo raso** in the open air, outdoors; in the country; **cielo de la boca** roof of the mouth; **cielo máximo** (aer) ceiling; **cielo raso** ceiling; **llovido del cielo** heaven-sent, manna from heaven
cielorraso *m* ceiling
ciem•piés *m* (*pl* **-piés**) centipede
cien *adj* hundred, a hundred, one hundred
ciénaga *f* swamp, marsh, mudhole
ciencia *f* science; knowledge; learning; **a ciencia cierta** with certainty
ciencia-ficción *f* science fiction
cieno *m* mud, mire, silt
cieno•so -sa *adj* muddy, miry, silty
ciento *adj & m* hundred, a hundred, one hundred; **por ciento** per cent
cierne *m* budding, blossoming; **en cierne** in blossom; only beginning
cierrarrenglón *m* marginal stop
cierre *m* closing; shutting; snap, clasp, fastener; latch, lock; (*de una tienda, de la Bolsa*) close; (*paro de trabajo*) shutdown; **cierre cremallera** zipper; **cierre de portada** metal shutter (*of store front*); **cierre de puerta** door check; **cierre hermético** weather stripping; **cierre relámpago** zipper
cierro *m* closing; shutting; (Chile) fence, wall; (Chile) envelope
cier•to -ta *adj* certain; a certain; (*acertado, verdadero*) true; (*seguro*) sure; **por cierto** for sure || **cierto** *adv* surely, certainly
cierva *f* hind
ciervo *m* deer, stag, hart
cierzo *m* cold north wind

cifra *f* (*número*) cipher; (*escritura secreta*) code; (*enlace de dos o más letras empleado en sellos*) device, monogram, emblem; abbreviation; amount, sum; **en cifra** in code; in brief; mysteriously
cifrar *tr* to cipher, code; abridge; calculate; **cifrar la dicha en** to base one's happiness in; **cifrar la esperanza en** to place one's hope in || *ref* to be abridged; **cifrarse en** to be based on
cifrario *m* (com) code
cigarra *f* harvest fly, locust
cigarrera *f* cigar case; cigar girl
cigarrería *f* cigar store, tobacco store
cigarre•ro -ra *mf* cigar maker; cigar dealer || *f* see **cigarrera**
cigarrillo *m* cigarette; **cigarrillo con filtro** filter cigarette
cigarro *m* cigar; **cigarro de papel** cigarette; **cigarro puro** cigar
cigoñal *m* well sweep; (*del motor de explosión*) crankshaft
cigüeña *f* stork; crank, winch
cigüeñal *m* var of **cigoñal**
cilampa *f* (CAm) drizzle
cilicio *m* haircloth, hair shirt
cilindrada *f* piston displacement
cilindrar *tr* to roll
cilíndri•co -ca *adj* cylindrical
cilindro *m* cylinder; roll, roller; (Mex) barrel organ, hand organ
cima *f* (*de árbol*) top; (*de montaña*) top, summit; **dar cima a** to complete, to carry out; **por cima** (coll) at the very top
cimarra *f* — **hacer cimarra** (Arg, Chile) to play hooky
cima•rrón -rrona *adj* (*animal*) wild, untamed; (*planta*) wild; (*esclavo*) fugitive; (*marinero*) lazy; (*maté*) (Arg, Urug) black, bitter
cimarronear *intr* (Arg, Urug) to drink black maté || *ref* (*el esclavo*) to flee, run away
címbalo *m* cymbal
cimbel *m* decoy pigeon, stool pigeon
cimborio or **cimborrio** *m* dome
cimbrar or **cimbrear** *tr* to brandish; swing, sway; bend; thrash, beat || *ref* to swing, sway; shake
cimbre•ño -ña *adj* flexible, pliant; lithe, willowy
cimentar §2 *tr* to found, establish; lay the foundations of
cime•ro -ra *adj* top, uppermost
cimiento *m* foundation, groundwork; basis, source
cimitarra *f* scimitar
cinabrio *m* cinnabar
cinanquia *f* quinsy
cinc *m* (*pl* **cinces**) zinc
cincel *m* chisel, graver
cincelar *tr* to chisel, engrave
cinco *adj & pron* five; **las cinco** five o'clock || *m* five; (*en las fechas*) fifth; **¡choque Vd. esos cinco!** or **¡vengan esos cinco!** put it here!, shake!; **decirle a uno cuántas son cinco** to tell someone what's what
cincograbado *m* zinc etching
cincuenta *adj, pron & m* fifty
cincuenta•vo -va *adj & m* fiftieth
cincha *f* cinch; **a revienta cinchas** at breakneck speed; reluctantly
cinchar *tr* to cinch; band, hoop
cincho *m* girdle, sash; iron hoop; iron tire
cine *m* movie; **cine en colores** color movies; **cine hablado** talkie; **cine mudo** silent movie; **cine parlante** talkie; **cine sonoro** sound movie
cineasta *mf* motion-picture producer; movie fan || *m* movie actor || *f* movie actress
cinedrama *m* screenplay
cinelandia *f* (coll) movieland
cinema *m* var of **cine**
cinemateca *f* film library
cinematografiar §77 *tr & intr* to cinematograph, film
cinematógrafo *m* cinematograph; motion picture; motion-picture projector; motion-picture theater
cinematurgo *m* scriptwriter
cinescopio (telv) *m* kinescope
cineteatro *m* movie house
cinéti•co -ca *adj* kinetic || *f* kinetics
cínga•ro -ra *adj & mf* gypsy
cíni•co -ca *adj* cynical; impudent; slovenly, untidy || *mf* cynic || *m* Cynic
cinismo *m* cynicism; impudence
cinta *f* ribbon; (*tira de papel, celuloide, etc.*) tape; film; measuring tape; (*borde de la acera*) curb; fillet, scroll; **cinta aislante** electric tape, friction tape; **cinta de medir** tape measure; **cinta de teleimpresor** ticker tape; **cinta grabada de televisión** video tape; **cinta perforada** punched tape
cintillo *m* hatband; fancy hat cord; ring set with a gem; (*borde de la acera*) (P-R) curb; hair ribbon
cinto *m* belt, girdle; waist
cintura *f* (*parte estrecha del cuerpo humano sobre las caderas*) waist; waistline; (*de una chimenea*) throat; **meter en cintura** to bring to reason
cinturón *m* belt, sash; sword belt; **cinturón de asiento** seat belt; **cinturón de seguridad** safety belt; **cinturón retráctil** retractable safety belt; **cinturón salvavidas** safety belt
cíper *m* (Mex) zipper
cipo *m* milestone; signpost; memorial pillar
cipote *adj* (Col, Ven) stupid; (Guat) chubby || *mf* (Hond, El Salv, Ven) brat
ciprés *m* cypress
circo *m* circus
circón *m* zircon
circonio *m* zirconium
circuito *m* circuit; (*de carreteras, ferrocarriles, etc.*) network; race track; **corto circuito** (elec) short circuit
circulación *f* circulation; traffic; **circulación rodada** vehicular traffic
circular *adj* circular || *f* circular, circular letter; **circular noticiera** newsletter || *tr & intr* to circulate
círculo *m* circle; club; clubhouse
circuncidar *tr* to circumcise; clip, curtail

circundante *adj* surrounding
circundar *tr* to surround, go around
circunferencia *f* circumference
circunfle•jo -ja *adj* circumflex
circunlocución *f* or **circunloquio** *m* circumlocution
circunnavegación *f* circumnavigation
circunnavegar §44 *tr* to circumnavigate
circunscribir §83 *tr* to circumscribe ‖ *ref* to hold oneself down; be held down
circunscripción *f* circumscription; district, subdivision
circunspec•to -ta *adj* circumspect
circunstancia *f* circumstance
circunstancia•do -da *adj* circumstantial, detailed
circunstancial *adj* circumstantial
circunstanciar *tr* to circumstantiate, to describe in detail
circunstante *adj* surrounding; present ‖ *mf* bystander, onlooker
circunveci•no -na *adj* neighboring
circunvolar §61 *tr* to fly around
cirial *m* (eccl) processional candlestick
ciriga•llo -lla *mf* gadabout
ciríli•co -ca *adj* Cyrillic
cirio *m* wax candle
Ciro *m* Cyrus
ciruela *f* plum; **ciruela claudia** greengage; **ciruela pasa** prune
ciruelo *m* plum, plum tree; stupid fellow
cirugía *f* surgery; **cirugía cosmética, decorativa** or **estética** face lifting
ciruja•no -na *mf* surgeon
ciscar §73 *tr* to soil, dirty; (Cuba, Mex) to shame; annoy ‖ *ref* to soil one's clothes, have an accident
cisco *m* culm; row, disturbance
cisma *m* schism; discord, disagreement; (Arg) worry, concern; (Col) gossip; (Col) fastidiousness
cismáti•co -ca *adj* schismatic; dissident; (Col) gossipy; (Col) fastidious ‖ *mf* schismatic; dissident
cisne *m* swan; (Arg) powder puff
cisterna *f* cistern; reservoir; toilet tank
cita *f* date, appointment, engagement; (*mención, pasaje textual*) citation, quotation; **cita a ciegas** blind date; **cita previa** by appointment; **darse cita** to make a date
citación *f* citation, quotation; (*ante un juez*) citation, summons
citar *tr* to make a date with, have an appointment with; cite, quote; (*ante un juez*) cite, summon; (*al toro*) incite, provoke ‖ *ref* to make a date, have an appointment
cítara *f* (mus) zither
ciudad *f* city; city council; **la ciudad Condal** Barcelona; **la ciudad del Apóstol** Santiago de Compostela; **la ciudad del Betis** Seville; **la ciudad del Cabo** Capetown or Cape Town; **la ciudad de los Califas** Cordova; **la ciudad de los Reyes** Lima, Peru; **la ciudad de María Santísima** Seville; **la ciudad Imperial** or **Imperial ciudad** Toledo
ciudadanía *f* citizenship
ciudada•no -na *adj* city; citizen; civic ‖ *mf* citizen; urbanite
ciudadela *f* citadel; (Cuba) tenement house
cívi•co -ca *adj* civic; city; domestic; public-spirited
civil *adj* civil; civilian ‖ *mf* civilian ‖ *m* guard, policeman
civilidad *f* civility
civilista *adj* civil-law ‖ *mf* authority on civil law; (Chile) antimilitarist
civilización *f* civilization
civilizar §60 *tr* to civilize
civismo *m* good citizenship
cizalla *f* shears; metal shaving, metal clipping; **cizalla de guillotina** gate shears, guillotine shears; **cizallas** shears
cizallar *tr* to shear
cizaña *f* darnel; contamination, corruption; discord; **sembrar cizaña** to sow discord
clac *m* (*pl* **claques**) opera hat, claque, crush hat; (*sombrero de tres picos*) cocked hat
clamar *tr* to cry out for ‖ *intr* to cry out; **clamar contra** to cry out against; **clamar por** to cry out for
clamor *m* clamor, outcry; (*toque de difuntos*) knell, toll; fame
clamorear *tr* to clamor for ‖ *intr* to clamor; (*tocar a muerto*) toll
clamoreo *m* clamoring; tolling
clamoro•so -sa *adj* clamorous; loud, noisy
clan *m* clan
clandestinista *mf* (Guat) bootlegger
clandesti•no -na *adj* clandestine
claque *f* claque, hired clappers
clara *f* white of egg; bald spot; (*de un trozo de tela*) thin spot; (*en el tiempo lluvioso*) break, let-up
claraboya *f* (*ventana en el techo*) skylight; (*en la parte alta de la pared*) transom; (*esp. en las iglesias la parte superior de la nave que tiene una serie de ventanas*) clerestory
clarear *tr* to brighten, light up ‖ *intr* (*empezar a amanecer*) to get light, dawn; (*el mal tiempo*) clear up ‖ *ref* (*una tela*) to show through; show one's hand
clarecer §22 *ref* to dawn
clarete *m* claret
claridad *f* clarity; clearness; brightness; fame, glory; blunt remark; **claridades** plain language
clarido•so -sa *adj* (CAm, Mex) blunt, rude, plain-spoken
clarificar §73 *tr* to clarify; brighten, light up; (*lo que estaba turbio*) clear
clarín *m* clarion; fine cambric; (Chile) sweet pea
clarinada *f* clarion call; uncalled-for remark
clarinete *m* clarinet
clarión *m* chalk
clarividencia *f* clairvoyance; clear-sightedness
clarividente *adj* clairvoyant; clear-sighted ‖ *mf* clairvoyant

cla•ro -ra *adj* clear; (*de color*) light; (*pelo*) thin, sparse; (*té*) weak; famous, illustrious; (*cerveza*) light; **a las claras** publicly, openly, frankly || *m* gap; (*en el bosque*) glade, clearing; space, interval; (*ventana u otra abertura*) light; (*claraboya*) skylight; (*en las nubes*) break; **claro de luna** brief moonlight; **de claro en claro** evidently; from one end to the other; **pasar la noche de claro en claro** to not sleep all night; **poner** or **sacar en claro** to explain, clear up; (*un borrador*) to copy || *f* see **clara** || **claro** *adv* clearly || **claro** *interj* sure!, of course!; **¡claro está!, ¡claro que sí!** sure!, of course!

claror *m* brightness; **claror de luna** moonlight, moonglow

claru•cho -cha *adj* watery, thin

clase *f* class; classroom; **clase alta** upper class; **clase baja** lower class; **clase media** middle class; **clase obrera** working class; **clases** noncommissioned officers, warrant officers; **clases pasivas** pensioners

clasicista *mf* classicist

clási•co -ca *adj* classical || *mf* classicist || *m* classic

clasificador *m* filing cabinet

clasificar **§73** *tr* to classify; class; sort; file || *ref* to class

clasismo *m* segregation

clasista *mf* segregationist

claudicar **§73** *intr* (*cojear*) to limp; (*obrar defectuosamente*) bungle; back down

claustral *adj* cloistral

claustro *m* cloister; (*junta de la universidad*) faculty

cláusula *f* (*de un contrato u otro documento*) clause; (gram) sentence

clausula•do -da *adj* (*estilo*) choppy || *m* series of clauses

clausular *tr* to close, finish, conclude

clausura *f* confinement; seclusion; enclosure; adjournment

clausurar *tr* (*una asamblea, un tribunal, etc.*) to close, adjourn; (*un comercio por orden gubernativa*) suspend, close up

clava *f* club

clavadista *mf* (Mex) diver

clava•do -da *adj* studded with nails; exact, precise; (*reloj*) stopped; sharp, e.g., **a las siete clavadas** at seven o'clock sharp || *m* (Mex) dive

clavar *tr* to nail; (*un clavo*) drive; (*una daga, un punzón*) stick; (*una piedra preciosa*) set; (*los ojos, la atención*) fix; (*a un caballo al herrarlo*) prick; cheat || *ref* to prick oneself; get cheated; (Mex) to dive; **clavárselas** (CAm) to get drunk

clave *m* harpsichord || *f* (*de un enigma, código, etc.*) key; (*piedra con que se cierra el arco*) (archit) keystone; (mus) clef

clavel *m* carnation, pink; **clavel de ramillete** sweet william; **clavel reventón** double-flowered carnation

clavelón *m* marigold

clavellina *f* carnation, pink

clave•ro -ra *mf* keeper of the keys || *m* clove tree || *f* nail hole

claveta *f* peg, wooden peg

clavetear *tr* to stud; tip, put a tip on; wind up, settle

clavicordio *m* clavichord

clavícula *f* clavicle, collarbone

clavija *f* pin, peg, dowel; (elec) plug; (mus) peg; **apretarle a uno las clavijas** to put the screws on someone

clavillo *m* or **clavito** *m* brad, tack; (*que sujeta las hojas de unas tijeras*) pin, rivet; clove

clavo *m* nail; (*capullo seco de la flor del clavero*) clove; migraine; keen sorrow; (*artículo que no se vende*) (Arg, Bol, Chile) drug on the market; (Col) bad deal; (Hond, Mex) rich vein of ore; (Ven) heartburn; **clavo de alambre** wire nail; **clavo de especia** (*flor*) clove; **clavo de herrar** horseshoe nail; **dar en el clavo** to hit the nail on the head

clemátide *f* clematis

clemencia *f* clemency

clemente *adj* clement, merciful

cleptóma•no -na *mf* kleptomaniac

clerecía *f* clergy

clerical *adj & m* clerical

clericato *m* or **clericatura** *f* priesthood

clerigalla *f* (contemptuous) priests

clérigo *m* cleric, priest; **clérigo de misa y olla** priestlet

clerizonte *m* shabby-looking priest; fake priest

clero *m* clergy

clerófo•bo -ba *adj* priest-hating || *mf* priest hater

cliché *m* (*lugar común*) cliché

cliente *mf* (*parroquiano de una tienda*) customer; (*de un abogado*) client; (*de un médico*) patient; (*de un hotel*) guest

clientela *f* customers; clientele; patronage, protection; practice

clima *m* climate; country, region; **clima artificial** air conditioning

climatización *f* air conditioning

climatizar **§60** *tr* to air-condition

clíni•co -ca *adj* clinical || *mf* clinician || *f* clinic; private hospital; **clínica de reposo** nursing home, convalescent home

clip *m* paper clip

cliqueteo *m* clicking

clisar *tr* (typ) to plate

clisé *m* (*plancha clisada*) cliché, plate; (phot) plate; (*lugar común*) cliché

clo *m* cluck; **decir clo** (Chile) to kick the bucket; **hacer clo clo** (*la gallina clueca*) to cluck

cloaca *f* sewer

clocar **§81** *intr* to cluck

cloquear *intr* to cluck

cloqueo *m* cluck, clucking

clorhídri•co -ca *adj* hydrochloric

cloro *m* chlorine

clorofila *f* chlorophyll

cloroformizar **§60** *tr* to chloroform

cloroformo *m* chloroform

cloruro *m* chloride

clóset *m* (SAm) (wall) closet
club *m* (*pl* **clubs**) club; **club náutico** yacht club
clubista *mf* club member
clue•co -ca *adj* broody; decrepit
c.m.b., C.M.B. *abbr* **cuyas manos beso**
coa *f* (Mex) hoe; (Chile) thieves' jargon
coacción *f* coercion, compulsion
coaccionar *tr* to coerce, compel
coacervar *tr* to pile up
coactar *tr* to coerce, compel
coadunar *tr & ref* to mix together
coadyuvar *tr & intr* to help, aid, assist
coagular *tr & ref* (*la sangre*) to coagulate; (*la leche*) curdle
coágulo *m* clot
coalición *f* coalition
coalla *f* woodcock
coartada *f* alibi
coartar *tr* to limit, restrict
coba *f* hoax; flattery
cobalto *m* cobalt
cobarde *adj* cowardly; timid; (*vista*) dim, weak || *mf* coward
cobardear *intr* to act cowardly; be timid
cobardía *f* cowardice; timidity
cobayo *m* guinea pig
cobertera *f* lid; bawd, procuress
cobertizo *m* shed; (*tejado saledizo*) covered balcony, penthouse
cobertor *m* bedcover, bedspread; lid
cobertura *f* cover; covering; (*garantía metálica*) coverage
cobija *f* curved tile; top, lid; short mantilla; (W-I) guano roof; **cobijas** bedclothes
cobijar *tr* to cover; shelter, protect
cobijo *m* covering; shelter, protection; (*hospedaje sin manutención*) lodging
cobra *f* team of mares used in threshing; (hunt) retrieval
cobra•dor -dora *adj* (*perro*) retrieving || *mf* collector; trolley conductor
cobranza *f* collecting; (hunt) retrieval
cobrar *tr* (*lo perdido*) to recover; (*lo que otro le debe*) collect; (*un cheque*) cash; (*cierto precio*) charge; acquire, get; (*una cuerda*) pull in; (*pedir, reclamar*) dun; (hunt) to retrieve; **cobrar afición a** to take a liking for; **cobrar al número llamado** (telp) to reverse the charges; **cobrar ánimo** to take courage; **cobrar carnes** to put on flesh; **cobrar fuerzas** to gain strength || *intr* to get hit || *ref* to recover, come to
cobre *m* copper; copper or brass kitchen utensils; **batir el cobre** to hustle, work with a will; **cobres** (mus) brasses
cobre•ño -ña *adj* copper
cobrero *m* coppersmith
cobri•zo -za *adj* coppery
cobro *m* collection; recovery; **cobro contra entrega** collect on delivery; **en cobro** in a safe place
coca *f* (*en una cuerda*) kink; (coll) head; (slang) cocaine; **de coca** (Mex) free; (Mex) in vain
cocaína *f* cocaine
cocción *f* cooking, baking; (*de objetos cerámicos*) baking, burning
cocear *intr* to kick; (*resistir*) balk, rebel
cocer **§16** *tr* to cook; boil; (*pan; ladrillos*) bake; digest || *intr* to cook; boil; ferment || *ref* to suffer a long time
coci•do -da *adj* cooked || *m* Spanish stew
cociente *m* quotient; **cociente intelectual** intelligence quotient
cocina *f* (*pieza*) kitchen; (*arte*) cooking, cuisine; (*aparato*) stove; **cocina de presión** pressure cooker; **cocina económica** kitchen range
cocinar *tr* to cook || *intr* to meddle
cocine•ro -ra *mf* cook
cocinilla *m* meddler || *f* kitchenette; chafing dish; **cocinilla sin fuego** fireless cooker
coco *m* cocoanut; (*moño*) topknot, chignon; (*duende*) bogeyman; (*gesto, mueca*) face, grimace; (*sombrero hongo*) (Col, Ecuad) derby hat; **hacer cocos** to make a face; (*los enamorados*) to make eyes
cocodrilo *m* crocodile
cócora *adj* boring, tiresome || *mf* bore, pest
coco•so -sa *adj* worm-eaten
cocotero *m* cocoanut palm or tree
coctel *m* or **cóctel** *m* cocktail; cocktail party
coctelera *f* cocktail shaker
cocuma *f* (Peru) roast corn on the cob
cochambre *m* dirty, stinking thing, pigsty
cochambro•so -sa *adj* dirty, stinking
coche *m* carriage; coach; car; taxi; (*puerco*) hog; **caminar en el coche de San Francisco** to go or to ride on shank's mare; **coche bar** (rr) club car; **coche bomba** fire engine; (coll) car bomb; **coche celular** Black Maria, prison van; **coche de alquiler** cab, hack; **coche de carreras** racing car; **coche de correos** mail car; **coche de plaza** or **de punto** cab, hack; **coche de reparto** (delivery) van; **coche de serie** (aut) stock car; **coche fúnebre** hearse; **coche rural** station wagon
coche-cama *m* (*pl* **coches-camas**) sleeping car
cochecillo *m* baby carriage; **cochecillo para inválidos** wheelchair; **cochecillo para niños** baby carriage
coche-comedor *m* (*pl* **coches-comedores**) (rr) diner, dining car
coche-correo *m* (*pl* **coches-correo**) (rr) mail car
coche-fumador *m* (*pl* **coches-fumadores**) (rr) smoker, smoking car
coche-habitación *m* (*pl* **coches-habitación**) trailer
cochera *f* coach house; livery stable; carbarn; garage
cochería *f* (Arg, Chile) livery stable
coche•ro -ra *adj* easy to cook || *m* coachman, driver; **cochero de punto** cabby, hackman || *f* see **cochera**
cocherón *m* coach house; (*depósito de locomotoras*) roundhouse
coche-salón *m* (*pl* **coches-salón**) (rr) parlor car
cochevira *f* lard

cochina *f* sow; (*mujer sucia y desaliñada*) trollop
cochinada *f* piggishness, filthiness; dirty trick
cochinillo *m* sucking pig
cochi•no -na *adj* piggish, filthy; (*tacaño*) stingy; (Ven) cowardly || *mf* hog; (*persona muy sucia*) (coll) pig, dirty person || *f* see **cochina**
cochite hervite *adj, adv & m* helter-skelter
cochitril *m* pigsty; den, hovel
cochura *f* batch of dough
codadura *f* (hort) layer
codal *adj* elbow || *m* prop, shoring
codazo *m* poke, nudge; **dar codazo a** (Mex) to tip off
codear *tr* (SAm) to sponge on || *intr* to elbow, elbow one's way || *ref* to hobnob, rub elbows
codelincuencia *f* complicity
codelincuente *mf* accomplice
codera *f* elbow patch; elbow itch
códice *m* codex
codicia *f* covetousness, greed, cupidity
codiciar *tr* to covet
codicilo *m* codicil
codicio•so -sa *adj* covetous, greedy; (*laborioso*) hard-working
codificar §73 *tr* to codify
código *m* code; **código penal** criminal code; **código universal de producto** universal product code (UPC)
codillo *m* (*de animal*) knee; (*estribo*) stirrup; (*de un tubo*) elbow; (*de la rama cortada*) stump
codo *m* elbow; (Guat, Mex) miser, tightwad; **dar de codo a** to nudge; to spurn; **empinar el codo** to crook the elbow; **hablar por los codos** to talk too much
codor•niz *f* (*pl* **-nices**) quail
coeducación *f* coeducation
coeficiente *adj & m* coefficient
coetáne•o -a *adj & mf* contemporary
coexistencia *f* coexistence
coexistir *intr* to coexist
cofa *f* (naut) top; **cofa de vigía** (naut) crow's-nest
cofrade *mf* member, fellow member || *m* brother || *f* sister
cofradía *f* brotherhood, sisterhood; association, fraternity
cofre *m* coffer, chest, trunk
cogedor *m* dustpan; coal shovel, ash shovel
coger §17 *tr* to catch, seize, take hold of: collect, gather, pick; overtake; surprise; hold || *intr* to be, be located; fit || *ref* to get caught; cling; get involved
cogida *f* collecting, gathering, picking; (taur) hook
cogollo *m* (*de la lechuga*) heart; (*de la berza*) head; (*de una planta*) shoot; (*del árbol*) top; (*lo mejor*) cream, pick
cogote *m* back of the neck
cogotera *f* havelock
cogotu•do -da *adj* thick-necked; (coll) proud, stiff-necked; (SAm) moneyed
cogulla *f* cowl, frock; **cogulla de fraile** (bot) monkshood
cohabitar *intr* to live together; (*el hombre y la mujer*) cohabit
cohechar *tr* to bribe; plow just before sowing || *intr* to take a bribe
cohecho *m* bribe
coherede•ro -ra *mf* coheir || *f* coheiress
coherente *adj* coherent
cohesión *f* cohesion
cohete *m* (*fuego artificial*) rocket, skyrocket; (*motor a reacción*) rocket; (coll) fidgety person; **cohete de señales** (aer) flare; **cohete intermedio** or **cohete de alcance medio** intermediate-range missile; **cohete lanzador** booster rocket
cohetería *f* missilery
cohibente *adj* (elec) nonconducting
cohibi•do -da *adj* timid, self-conscious
cohibir *tr* to check, restrain, inhibit; (Mex) to oblige
cohombro *m* cucumber
cohonestar *tr* to gloss over, rationalize
coima *f* rake-off paid to operator of a gambling table; concubine; (SAm) bribe
coincidencia *f* coincidence
coincidir *intr* to coincide; happen at the same time; be at the same time (*at a given place*); agree
coito *m* coition, coitus
coja *f* lame woman; lewd woman
cojear *intr* to limp; (*una mesa, una silla*) wobble; (*adolecer de algún vicio*) slip, lapse, have a weakness
cojera *f* (*anormalidad del que cojea*) lameness; (*movimiento del que cojea*) limp
cojijo *m* bug, insect; peeve
cojijo•so -sa *adj* peevish
cojín *m* cushion
cojincillo *m* pad
cojinete *m* cushion; sewing cushion; (mach) bearing; **cojinete de bolas** ball bearing; **cojinete de rodillos** roller bearing
co•jo -ja *adj* lame, crippled; (*mesa, silla*) wobbly; (*pierna*) game || *mf* lame person, cripple || *f* see **coja**
cojón *m* testicle
cok *m* var of **coque**
col. *abbr* **colonia, columna**
col *f* cabbage; **col de Bruselas** Brussels sprouts
cola *f* (*de animal, de ave, de cometa*) tail; (*de un vestido*) train, trail; (*de personas que esperan turno*) queue; (*extremidad posterior*) tail end, rear end; (*de una clase de alumnos*) bottom; (*pasta fuerte*) glue; **cola del pan** bread line; **cola de milano** or **de pato** dovetail; **cola de pescado** isinglass; **cola de retazo** size, sizing; **hacer cola** to queue, to stand in line
colaboración *f* collaboration; (*en un periódico, coloquio, etc.*) contribution
colaboracionista *mf* collaborationist
colabora•dor -dora *adj* collaborating || *mf* collaborator; contributor
colaborar *intr* to collaborate; (*en un periódico, coloquio, etc.*) contribute
colación *f* (*cotejo; refacción ligera*) collation; (*de un grado de universidad*) conferring;

parish land; **sacar a colación** to mention, bring up; **traer a colación** to bring up; adduce as proof; bring up irrelevantly
colacionar *tr* to collate; compare; (*un beneficio*) confer
colactánea *f* foster sister
colactáneo *m* foster brother
colada *f* washing powder; wash; (*garganta entre montañas*) gulch; cattle run; **todo saldrá en la colada** it will all come out in the wash; the day of reckoning will come
coladera *f* strainer; (Mex) sewer
coladero *m* strainer; cattle run; narrow pass
colador *m* strainer, colander
colapez *f* or **colapiscis** *f* isinglass
colapso *m* breakdown, collapse; **colapso nervioso** nervous breakdown
colar *tr* (*un grado universitario*) to confer || §**61** *tr* (*un líquido*) to strain; bleach in hot lye, buck; (*metales*) cast; (*una moneda falsa*) pass off; **colar el hueso por** (coll) to squeeze through || *intr* to run, ooze; squeeze through; come in, slip in; drink wine; **colar a fondo** to sink; **no colar** (*una cosa*) to not be believed || *ref* to seep, seep through; slip in, slip through; make a slip; lie; **colarse de gorra** to crash the gate
colateral *adj* collateral || *mf* (*pariente*) collateral || *m* (com) collateral
colcrén *m* cold cream
colcha *f* quilt, counterpane, bedspread
colchón *m* mattress; **colchón de aire** air mattress; **colchón de muelles** bedspring, spring mattress; **colchón de plumas** feather bed
coleada *f* wag (*of the tail*); (Mex, Ven) throwing the bull by twisting its tail
colear *tr* (taur) to grab by the tail; (*la res*) (Mex, Ven) to throw by twisting the tail; (Col, Ven) to nag, harass; (Guat) to trail after; (*reprobar en un examen*) (Chile) to flunk || *intr* to wag the tail; stay alive, keep going; (*los últimos vagones de un tren*) sway; (aer) to fishtail; **colear en** (*cierta edad*) (CAm, W-I) to border on, be close to; **todavía colea** it's not over yet
colección *f* collection
coleccionar *tr* to collect
coleccionista *mf* collector
colecta *f* collection for charity; (eccl) collect
colectar *tr* to collect; (*obras antes sueltas*) collect in one volume
colecti•cio -cia *adj* new, untrained, green; (*tomo*) omnibus
colecti•vo -va *adj* collective
colector *m* collector; catch basin; (elec) commutator; (aut) manifold
colega *mf* colleague || *m* confrere
colegial *m* schoolboy; (Mex) greenhorn, beginner
colegiala *f* schoolgirl
colegiatura *f* scholarship; (Mex) tuition
colegio *m* school, academy; (*sociedad de hombres de una misma profesión*) college (*e.g., of cardinals, electors*)
colegir §**57** *tr* to gather, collect; conclude, infer
cólera *m* cholera|| *f* anger, wrath; (*bilis*) bile; **montar en cólera** to fly into a rage
colérico -ca *adj* choleric, irascible
colesterol *m* cholesterol
coleta *f* pigtail; (*del torero*) cue, queue; (coll) postscript; **cortarse la coleta** to quit the bull ring; to quit, retire; **tener** or **traer coleta** to have serious consequences
coletero *m* wren
coleto *m* buff jacket; (coll) body, one's body, oneself; **decir para su coleto** (coll) to say to oneself; **echarse al coleto** to eat up, drink up; read from cover to cover
colgadero *m* hanger, hook; clothes rack
colgadizo *m* lean-to, penthouse; projection over a door, canopy
colga•do -da *adj* pending, unsettled; **dejar colgado** to disappoint, frustrate; **quedarse colgado** to be disappointed, frustrated
colgador *m* clothes hanger, coat hanger
colgajo *m* rag, tatter
colgante *adj* hanging, dangling; (*puente*) suspension || *m* drop, pendant; (archit) festoon; (P-R) watch fob
colgar §**63** *tr* to hang; impute, attribute; (*a un alumno*) flunk; (*a un reo*) hang || *intr* to hang, hang down, dangle; droop; (telp) to hang up; **colgar de** to hang from, hang on; depend on
coli•brí *m* (*pl* **-bríes**) humming bird
cóli•co -ca *adj & m* colic || *f* upset stomach
coliche *m* (coll) at-home, open house
coliflor *f* cauliflower
coligar §**44** *ref* to join forces, make common cause
colilla *f* butt, stump, stub
co•lín -lina *adj* (*caballo o yegua*) bobtailed || *m* bobwhite; **colín de Virginia** bobwhite || *f* see **colina**
colina *f* hill, knoll
colindante *adj* adjacent, contiguous
colindar *intr* to be adjacent
colino•so -sa *adj* hilly
colirio *m* eyewash
coliseo *m* coliseum
colisión *f* collision; bruise, bump
colista *mf* person standing in line
colitis *f* colitis
colma•do -da *adj* abundant, plentiful || *m* food store, grocery store; seafood restaurant
colmar *tr* to fill up; (*las esperanzas de uno*) fulfill; overwhelm; **colmar de** to shower with, overwhelm with
colmena *f* beehive
colmenar *m* apiary
colmene•ro -ra *mf* beekeeper
colmillo *m* eyetooth, canine tooth; (*del elefante*) tusk; **tener el colmillo retorcido** to cut one's eyeteeth
col•mo -ma *adj* brimful, overflowing || *m* overflow; thatch, thatch roof; (*de un sorbete*) topping; **eso es el colmo** (coll) that's the limit; **para colmo de** to top off
colocación *f* (*acción de poner una persona o cosa en un lugar*) location; (*disposición de una cosa respecto del lugar que ocupa*)

placement; (*inversión de dinero*) investment; (*empleo*) position, employment, job
colocar §73 *tr* to place, put; (*una trampa*) set || *ref* to get placed, find a job; (*venderse*) sell
colodra *f* milk bucket; drinking horn; (*bebedor de vino*) (coll) toper
colofón *m* colophon
colofonia *f* rosin
coloide *adj* & *m* coloid
colon *m* colon; (gram) main clause
Colón *m* Columbus
colonia *f* colony; cologne; silk ribbon; housing development; (W-I) sugar plantation || **Colonia** *f* Cologne; **la Colonia del Cabo** Cape Colony
colonial *adj* colonial; overseas || **coloniales** *mpl* imported foods
colonizar §60 *tr* & *intr* to colonize
colono *m* colonist, settler; tenant farmer; (W-I) owner of sugar plantation
coloquial *adj* colloquial
coloquialismo *m* colloquialism
coloquio *m* colloquy, talk, conference
color *m* color; (*substancia para pintar*) paint; (*para pintarse el rostro*) rouge; **colores** (*bandera*) colors; (*persona*) **de color** of color, colored; (*zapatos*) tan; **sacar los colores a** to make blush; **so color de** under color of, under pretext of; **verlo todo de color de rosa** to see everything through rose-colored glasses
colora•do -da *adj* red, reddish; (*libre, obsceno*) off-color; (*aparentemente justo y razonable*) specious; **ponerse colorado** to blush
colorado•te -ta *adj* ruddy, sanguine
colorante *adj* & *m* coloring
colorar *tr* to color; dye; stain
colorear *tr* to color; (fig) to color, excuse, palliate || *ref* (*la cereza, el tomate, etc.*) to redden, turn red
colorete *m* rouge; **ponerse colorete** to put on rouge
colorir §1 *tr* to color; (fig) to color, palliate || *intr* to take on color
colosal *adj* colossal
coloso *m* colossus
columbrar *tr* to discern, descry, glimpse; to guess
columna *f* column; **columna de dirección** steering column; **quinta columna** fifth column
columnata *f* colonnade
columnista *mf* columnist
columpiar *tr* to swing || *ref* to swing; to seesaw; (coll) to swing, swagger
columpio *m* swing; **columpio de tabla** seesaw
colusión *f* collusion
collada *f* mountain pass; (naut) steady blow
collado *m* hill, height
collar *m* necklace; dog collar, horse collar; (*aro de hierro asegurado al cuello del malhechor*) collar, band; (*plumas del cuello de ciertas aves*) frill, ring; (*cadena que rodea el cuello como insignia*) cord, chain; (mach) collar
collera *f* horse collar; chain gang; **colleras** (Arg, Chile) cuff links
co•llón -llona *adj* cowardly || *mf* coward
coma *m* (pathol) coma || *f* comma; (*en inglés se emplea el punto en aritmética para separar los enteros de las fracciones decimales*) decimal point
comadre *f* mother or godmother (*with respect to each other*); gossip (*woman*); friend, neighbor (*woman*)
comadrear *intr* to gossip, go around gossiping
comadreja *f* weasel
comadrería *f* gossip, idle gossip
comadre•ro -ra *adj* gossipy || *mf* gossip
comadrón *m* accoucheur
comadrona *f* midwife
comandancia *f* command; commander's headquarters; (mil) majority
comandante *m* commander, commandant; (mil) major
comandar *tr* (mil, nav) to command
comando *m* (mil) command; **comando a distancia** remote control
comarca *f* district, region, country
comarcar §73 *tr* to plant in a line at regular intervals || *intr* to border, be contiguous
comato•so -sa *adj* comatose
comba *f* bend, curve; warp, bulge; skipping rope; **saltar a la comba** to jump rope, skip rope
combar *tr* to bend, curve || *ref* to bend, curve; warp, bulge; sag
combate *m* combat, fight; **combate revancha** (box) return bout; **fuera de combate** hors de combat; (box) knockout
combatiente *adj* & *m* combatant
combatir *tr* to combat, fight; beat, beat upon || *intr* & *ref* to combat, fight, struggle
combinación *f* combination; (*de trenes*) connection
combinar *tr* & *ref* to combine
com•bo -ba *adj* bent, curved, crooked; warped || *m* trunk or rock to stand wine casks on || *f* see **comba**
combustible *adj* combustible || *m* (*substancia que arde con facilidad*) combustible; (*substancia que sirve para calentar, cocinar, etc.*) fuel; **combustible alternativo** alternate fuel
combustión *f* combustion
comede•ro -ra *adj* eatable || *m* manger, feed trough; (Mex) haunt, hangout; **limpiarle a uno el comedero** to deprive someone of his bread and butter
comedia *f* drama, play; theater; comedy; (fig) farce; **comedia cómica** (*drama de desenlace festivo*) comedy; **hacer la comedia** to pretend, make believe
comedian•te -ta *mf* hypocrite || *m* actor, comedian || *f* actress, comedienne
comedi•do -da *adj* courteous, polite; moderate; obliging, accommodating
comedimiento *m* courtesy, politeness; moderation

comediógra•fo -fa *mf* playwright
comedir §50 *ref* to be courteous; restrain oneself, be moderate; be obliging; **comedirse a** to offer to, volunteer to
comedón *m* blackhead
come•dor -dora *adj* heavy-eating ‖ *m* dining room; restaurant, eating place; dining-room suite; **comedor de beneficencia** soup kitchen
comején *m* termite
comendador *m* prelate, prior; knight commander; (*de una orden militar*) commander
comensal *mf* dependent, servant; table companion
comentar *tr* to comment on ‖ *intr* to comment; to gossip
comentario *m* comment, commentary; **commentarios** talk, gossip
comentarista *mf* commentator
comento *m* comment, commentary; deceit, falsehood
comenzar §18 *tr & intr* to commence, begin, start
comer *m* eating, food ‖ *tr* to eat; to feed on; to gnaw away; to consume; (*alguna renta*) to enjoy; to itch; (*una pieza en el juego de damas*) to take; **comer vivo** to have it in for; **sin comerlo ni beberlo** (coll) without having anything to do with it; **tener qué comer** to have enough to live on ‖ *intr* to eat; to dine, to have dinner; to itch ‖ *ref* to eat up; (*las uñas*) to bite; (*el dinero*) (coll) to consume, eat up; (*omitir*) to skip, skip over; **comerse unos a otros** to be at loggerheads
comerciable *adj* marketable; sociable
comercial *adj* commercial, business
comerciante *mf* merchant, trader, dealer; **comerciante al por mayor** wholesaler; **comerciante al por menor** retailer
comerciar *intr* to trade, deal
comercio *m* commerce, trade, business; store, shop; business center; commerce, intercourse; **comercio de artículos de regalo** gift shop; **comercio exterior** foreign trade
comestible *adj* eatable ‖ *m* food, foodstuff
cometa *m* comet ‖ *f* kite
cometer *tr* (*un crimen, una falta*) to commit; (*un negocio a una persona*) commit, entrust; (*figuras retóricas*) employ
cometido *m* assignment, duty; commitment
comezón *f* itch
comicastro *m* ham, ham actor
comicios *mpl* polls; **acudir a los comicios** to go to the polls
cómi•co -ca *adj* comic, comical; dramatic ‖ *mf* actor; comedian; **cómico de la legua** strolling player, barnstormer ‖ *f* actress; comedienne
comida *f* (*alimento*) food; (*el que se toma a horas señaladas*) meal; (*el principal de cada día*) dinner; **comida corrida** (Mex) table d'hôte
comidilla *f* hobby; **la comidilla del pueblo** the talk of the town
comienzo *m* beginning, start; **a comienzos de** around the beginning of
comilitona *f* spread, feast
comi•lón -lona *adj* heavy-eating ‖ *mf* hearty eater ‖ *f* hearty meal, spread
comillas *fpl* quotation marks
comineàr *intr* (*el hombre*) to fuss around like a woman
comiquear *intr* to put on amateur plays
comiquillo *m* ham, ham actor
comisar *tr* to seize, confiscate
comisario *m* commissary; commissioner; **comisario de a bordo** purser
comisión *f* commission; committee; (*recado*) errand
comisiona•do -da *mf* commissioner ‖ *m* committeeman
comisionar *tr* to commission
comiso *m* seizure, confiscation; confiscated goods
comisura *f* corner (*e.g., of lips*)
comité *m* committee; **comité planeador** steering committee
comitente *mf* constituent
comitiva *f* retinue, suite; procession
como *adv* as, like; so to speak, as it were ‖ *conj* as; when; if; so that; as soon as; as long as; inasmuch as; **así como** as well as; **como no** unless; **como que** because, inasmuch as; **como quien dice** so to speak; **tan luego como** as soon as
cómo *adv* how; why; what; **¿a cómo es. . . ?** how much is. . . ?; **¿cómo no?** why not?
cómoda *f* bureau, commode, chest
comodidad *f* comfort; convenience; advantage, interest
comodín *m* joker, wild card; gadget, jigger; excuse, alibi
cómo•do -da *adj* handy, convenient; comfortable ‖ *f* see **cómoda**
como•dón -dona *adj* comfort-loving, self-indulgent, easy-going
compac•to -ta *adj* compact
compadecer §22 *tr* to pity, feel sorry for ‖ *ref* to harmonize; **compadecerse con** to harmonize with; **compadecerse de** to pity, feel sorry for
compadraje *m* clique, cabal
compadrar *intr* to become a godfather; become friends
compadre *m* father or godfather (*with respect to each other*); friend, companion
compadrear *intr* to be close friends; (Arg, Urug) to brag, show off
compadrería *f* close companionship
compadrito *m* (Arg) bully
compaginar *tr* to arrange, put in order ‖ *ref* to fit, agree; blend
companage *m* snacks, cold cuts
compañerismo *m* companionship
compañe•ro -ra *mf* companion; partner; mate; **compañero de cama** bedfellow; **compañero de candidatura** (pol) running mate; **compañero de cuarto** roommate; **compañero de juego** playmate; **compañero de viaje** fellow traveler ‖ *f* (*esposa*) helpmeet

compañía *f* company; society; **compañía de desembarco** (nav) landing force; **compañía matriz** parent company; **hacerle compañía a una persona** to keep someone company
compañón *m* testicle; **compañón de perro** orchid
comparación *f* comparison
comparar *tr* to compare
comparati•vo -va *adj* comparative
comparecencia *f* (law) appearance
comparecer §22 *intr* (law) to appear
comparendo *m* (law) summons
comparsa *mf* (theat) supernumerary, extra || *f* supernumeraries, extras
compartimiento *m* distribution, division; compartment; **compartimiento estanco** watertight compartment
compartir *tr* to distribute, divide; share
compás *m* (*brújula*) compass; (*instrumento para trazar curvas*) compass or compasses; rule, measure; (mus) time, measure; (mus) bar, measure; (mus) beat; **a compás** (mus) in time; **compás de calibres** calipers; **compás de división** dividers; **llevar el compás** (mus) to keep time
compasible *adj* compassionate; pitiful
compasión *f* compassion; **¡por compasión!** for pity's sake!
compasi•vo -va *adj* compassionate
compatri•cio -cia *mf* or **compatriota** *mf* fellow countryman, compatriot
compeler *tr* to compel
compendiar *tr* to condense, summarize
compendio *m* compendium; **en compendio** in a word
compendio•so -sa *adj* compendious
compensación *f* compensation; (com) clearing, clearance
compensar *tr* to compensate; compensate for || *intr* to compensate || *ref* to be compensated for
competencia *f* (*aptitud*) competence; (*rivalidad*) competition; dispute; area, field; **de la competencia de** in the domain of; **sin competencia** unmatched (*prices*)
competente *adj* competent; reliable
competer *intr* to be incumbent
competición *f* competition
competi•dor -dora *adj* competing || *mf* competitor
competir §50 *intr* to compete; **poder competir** to be competitive
compilación *f* compilation
compilar *tr* to compile
compinche *mf* chum, crony, pal
complacencia *f* complacency
complacer §22 *tr* to please, humor || *ref* to be pleased, take pleasure
complaciente *adj* obliging; indulgent
comple•jo -ja *adj & m* complex; **complejo de inferioridad** inferiority complex
complementar *tr* to complement
complemento *m* complement; completion; perfection; accessory; **complemento directo** (gram) direct object
completar *tr* to complete; perfect
comple•to -ta *adj* complete; (*autobús, tranvía*) full
complexión *f* constitution
complexiona•do -da *adj* — **bien complexionado** strong, robust; **mal complexionado** weak, frail
comple•xo -xa *adj* complex
complica•do -da *adj* complicated, complex
complicar §73 *tr* to complicate; involve || *ref* to become complicated; become involved
cómplice *mf* accomplice, accessory
complicidad *f* complicity
com•plot *m* (*pl* **-plots**) plot, intrigue
compone•dor -dora *mf* composer, compositor; typesetter; arbitrator; repairer || *m* stick, composing stick; **amigable componedor** mediator, umpire
componenda *f* compromise, settlement, reconciliation
componente *adj* component, constituent || *m* component, constituent; member || *f* (mech) component
componer §54 *tr* to compose; compound; mend, repair; pacify, reconcile; arrange, put in order; restore, strengthen; (*huesos dislocados*) (Am) to set; (Col) to bewitch || *ref* to compose oneself; get dressed; make up, become friends again; (*pintarse el rostro*) make up; **componérselas** to make out, manage
comportable *adj* bearable, tolerable
comportamentismo *m* behaviorism
comportamiento *m* behavior, conduct
comportar *tr* to support; bring about, entail || *ref* to act, behave
comporte *m* behavior; carriage, bearing
composición *f* composition; agreement; (*circunspección*) composure, restraint; **hacer una composición de lugar** to lay one's plans carefully
compositi•vo -va *adj* (gram) combining
composi•tor -tora *mf* composer || *m* (Arg, Urug) horse trainer, trainer of fighting cocks
compostura *f* composition; agreement; (*circunspección*) composure, restraint; repair, repairing, mending; (*aseo*) neatness; adulteration; (Arg, Urug) training
compota *f* compote, preserves; **compota de frutas** stewed fruit; **compota de manzanas** applesauce
compotera *f* (*vasija*) compote
compra *f* purchase, buy; shopping; **compra al contado** cash purchase; **compra a plazos** installment buying; **hacer compras, ir de compras** to go shopping
compra•dor -dora *mf* purchaser, buyer; shopper
comprar *tr* to purchase, buy; (*sobornar*) buy off || *intr* to shop
compraventa *f* dealing, business, bargain, trading; resale
comprender *tr* (*entender*) to understand; (*entender; abrazar*) comprehend; (*contener, incluir*) comprise
comprensible *adj* comprehensible, understandable

comprensión *f* understanding, comprehension; inclusion

comprensi•vo -va *adj* understanding; comprehensive; **comprensivo de** inclusive of

compresa *f* (med) compress; **compresa higiénica** sanitary napkin

compresión *f* compression

comprimido *m* tablet

comprimir *tr* to compress; restrain, repress; flatten

comprobación *f* checking, verification; proof

comprobante *adj* proving || *m* certificate, voucher, warrant; proof; claim check

comprobar **§61** *tr* to check, verify; prove

comprometer *tr* to compromise, endanger, jeopardize; force, oblige; (*un negocio a un tercero*) entrust || *ref* to promise; commit oneself; become engaged

comprometi•do -da *adj* awkward, embarrassing; engaged to be married

comprometimiento *m* commitment, promise; predicament, awkward situation; compromise

compromiso *m* commitment, promise; appointment, engagement; predicament, awkward situation; betrothal

compuerta *f* hatch, half door; floodgate, sluice

compues•to -ta *adj* & *m* composite, compound

compulsar *tr* to collate; make an authentic copy of

compungi•do -da *adj* remorseful

compungir **§27** *tr* to make remorseful || *ref* to feel remorse

compurgar **§44** *tr* (*el reo la pena*) (Mex) to finish serving

computar *tr* & *intr* to compute

cómputo *m* computation, calculation

comulgante *mf* (eccl) communicant

comulgar **§44** *tr* to administer communion to || *intr* to take communion

comulgatorio *m* communion rail, altar rail

común *adj* common || *m* community; water closet; toilet; **el común de las gentes** the general run of people; **por lo común** commonly

comunal *adj* common; community || *m* community

comune•ro -ra *adj* popular || *m* shareholder

comunicación *f* communication; connection

comunicado *m* communiqué; letter to the editor, official announcement

comunica•dor -dora *adj* communicating

comunicante *mf* communicant, informant

comunicar **§73** *tr* to communicate; notify, inform; connect, put into communication || *intr* to communicate || *ref* to communicate; communicate with each other

comunicati•vo -va *adj* communicative

comunidad *f* community

comunión *f* communion; political party; sect

comunismo *m* communism

comunista *mf* communist

comunistizar **§60** *tr* to convert to communism || *ref* to become communistic

comunizar **§60** *tr* to communize

con *prep* with; to, towards; in spite of; **con que** and so; whereupon; **con tal (de) que** provided that; **con todo** however, nevertheless

conato *m* effort, endeavor; (*delito que no llegó a consumarse*) attempt

cónca•vo -va *adj* concave

concebible *adj* conceivable

concebir **§50** *tr* & *intr* to conceive

conceder *tr* to concede, admit; grant

concejal *m* alderman, councilman; **concejales** city fathers

concejo *m* town council; town hall; council meeting; (*expósito*) foundling

concentrar *tr* & *ref* to concentrate

concéntri•co -ca *adj* concentric

concepción *f* conception

concepto *m* concept; opinion, judgment; (*dicho ingenioso*) conceit, witticism; point of view; **en concepto de** under the head of; **tener buen concepto de** or **tener en buen concepto** to have a high opinion of, to hold in high esteem

conceptuar **§21** *tr* to deem, judge, regard

conceptuo•so -sa *adj* witty, epigrammatic

concerniente *adj* relative

concernir **§28** *tr* to concern

concertar **§2** *tr* to concert; mend, repair; (*un casamiento; la paz*) arrange; (*huesos dislocados*) set; (*poner de acuerdo*) reconcile; (*un pacto*) conclude; harmonize || *intr* to concert; agree || *ref* to come to terms, become reconciled; agree

concertino *m* concertmaster

concertista *mf* (mus) manager; (mus) performer, soloist

concesión *f* concession, admission; grant

concesionario *m* licensee; (*comerciante*) dealer

concesi•vo -va *adj* concessive

conciencia *f* (*conocimiento que uno tiene de su propia existencia*) consciousness; (*sentimiento del bien y del mal*) conscience; (*conocimiento*) awareness; **cobrar conciencia de** to become aware of; **en conciencia** in all conscience

concienciación *f* consciousness raising

concienzu•do -da *adj* conscientious; thorough

concierto *m* concert, harmony; (*función de música*) concert; (*composición de música*) concerto

concilia•dor -dora *adj* conciliatory

conciliar *tr* to conciliate, reconcile || *ref* (*el respeto, la estima, etc.*) to conciliate, win

concilio *m* (eccl) council

conci•so -sa *adj* concise

concitar *tr* to stir up, incite, agitate

conciudada•no -na *mf* fellow citizen

concluir **§20** *tr* to conclude; convince || *intr* & *ref* to conclude, end

conclusión *f* conclusion

concluyente *adj* conclusive, convincing

concomitar *tr* to accompany, go with

concordancia *f* concordance; (gram, mus) concord

concordar §61 *tr* to harmonize; reconcile; make agree || *intr* to agree
concordia *f* concord; **de concordia** by common consent
concre•to -ta *adj* concrete
concubina *f* concubine
concubio *m* (archaic) bedtime
concuñada *f* sister-in-law
concuñado *m* brother-in-law
concurrencia *f* (*acaecimiento de varios sucesos en un mismo tiempo*) concurrence; (*competencia comercial*) competition; (*ayuda*) assistance, crowd, gathering, attendance
concurrente *adj* concurrent; competing || *mf* competitor, contender, entrant
concurri•do -da *adj* crowded, full of people; well-attended
concurrir *intr* to concur; gather, meet, come together; compete, contend; coincide; **concurrir con** (*p.ej., dinero*) to contribute
concursante *mf* contender
concursar *tr* to declare insolvent || *intr* to contend, compete
concurso *m* contest, competition; (*de gente*) concourse, crowd, throng; backing, coöperation; show, exhibition; **concurso de acreedores** meeting of creditors; **concurso de belleza** beauty contest; **concurso hípico** horse show
concusión *f* concussion; extortion, shakedown
concha *f* (*de molusco o crustáceo*) shell; (*cada una de las dos partes del caparazón de los moluscos bivalvos*) half shell; (*en que se sirve el pescado*) scallop; (*carey*) tortoise shell; oyster; shellfish; horseshoe bay; (theat) prompter's box; **concha de peregrino** scallop shell; (zool) scallop; (*ostras*) **en su concha** on the half shell; **tener muchas conchas** to be sly, cunning
conchabanza *f* comfort; collusion, cabal
conchabar *tr* to join, unite; hire || *ref* to gang up; hire out
conchabero *m* (Col) pieceworker
condado *m* county; earldom
conde *m* count, earl; gypsy chief
condecoración *f* decoration
condecorar *tr* to decorate
condena *f* sentence; penalty, jail term; **condena judicial** conviction
condenación *f* condemnation; (*la eterna*) damnation
condena•do -da *adj* condemned; damned; (Chile) shrewd, clever || *mf* sentenced person; **los condenados** the damned
condenar *tr* to condemn; convict; (*a la pena eterna*) damn; (*p.ej., una ventana*) shut off, block up; (*una habitación*) padlock || *ref* to condemn oneself, confess one's guilt; (*a la pena eterna*) be damned
condensar *tr* to condense || *ref* to condense, be condensed
condesa *f* countess
condescendencia *f* acquiescence, compliance
condescender §51 *intr* to acquiesce, comply; **condescender a** to accede to
condescendiente *adj* acquiescent, obliging
condición *f* condition, state; position, situation; standing; nature, character, temperament; **a condición (de) que** on condition that; **en buenas condiciones** in good condition, in good shape; **tener condición** to have a bad temper
condicional *adj* conditional
condimentar *tr* to season
condimento *m* condiment, seasoning
condiscípulo *m* fellow student
condolencia *f* condolence
condoler §47 *ref* to condole; **condolerse de** to sympathize with, feel sorry for, commiserate with
condominio *m* condominium
condonar *tr* to condone, overlook
cóndor *m* condor; (Chile, Ecuad) gold coin
conducción *f* conveyance, transportation; guiding, leading; (aut) drive, driving; **conducción a la derecha** right-hand drive; **conducción a la izquierda** left-hand drive; **conducción interior** closed car
conducente *adj* conducive
conducir §19 *tr* to conduct; manage, direct; guide, lead; convey, transport; drive; employ, hire || *intr* to lead; conduce || *ref* to conduct oneself, behave
conducta *f* conduct; management, direction; guidance; conveyance; conduct, behavior
conducto *m* pipe; conduit; (anat) duct, canal; agency, intermediary, channel; **por conducto de** through
conduc•tor -tora *adj* conducting || *mf* driver, motorist; (*cobrador en un vehículo público*) conductor || *m & f* (elec & phys) conductor; **buen conductor, buena conductora** good conductor; **mal conductor, mala conductora** bad or poor conductor || *m* (rr) engineman, engine driver
conectar *tr* to connect
conecti•vo -va *adj* connective
conejera *f* burrow, warren; (coll) joint, dive
conejillo *m* young rabbit; **conejillo de Indias** guinea pig
conejo *m* rabbit
conexión *f* connection
conexionar *tr* to connect; put in touch || *ref* to connect; make contacts
confabulación *f* collusion, connivance
confabular *ref* to connive, scheme, plot
confección *f* making, preparation, confection; tailoring; ready-made suit; **confección a medida** suit made to order; **de confección** ready-made
confeccionar *tr* (*ropa*) to make; (*una receta*) make up, concoct
confeccionista *mf* ready-made clothier
confederación *f* confederacy; alliance
confedera•do -da *adj & mf* confederate
confederar *tr & ref* to confederate
conferencia *f* (*reunión para tratar asuntos internacionales, etc.*) conference; (*plática para tratar de algún negocio*) interview; (*disertación en público o en la universidad*) lecture; **conferencia telefónica** (telp) long-distance call

conferenciante *mf* conferee; lecturer
conferenciar *intr* to confer, hold an interview
conferencista *mf* (Arg) lecturer
conferir §68 *tr* to confer, award, bestow; discuss; compare || *intr* to confer
confesante *mf* confessor
confesar §2 *tr*, *intr* & *ref* to confess
confesión *f* confession; denomination, faith, religion
confe•so -sa *adj* confessed; (*judío*) converted || *mf* converted Jew || *m* lay brother
confesonario *m* confessional
confesor *m* confessor
confiable *adj* reliable, dependable
confia•do -da *adj* unsuspecting; haughty, self-confident
confianza *f* confidence; self-confidence, self-assurance; familiarity; secret deal; **de confianza** reliable
confianzu•do -da *adj* overconfident; overfamiliar
confiar §77 *tr* to confide, entrust; strengthen the confidence of || *intr* & *ref* to confide, trust; **confiar** or **confiarse de** or **en** to confide in, trust in; rely on
confidencia *f* confidence; secret; **de mayor confidencia** top secret
confidencial *adj* confidential
confiden•te -ta *adj* trustworthy, faithful || *mf* confident || *m* spy; informer; secret agent; love seat
configurar *tr* to shape, form
confín *m* confine, border, boundary; **los confines** the confines
confina•do -da *adj* exiled || *m* prisoner
confinamiento *m* confinement; abutment
confinar *tr* to exile; confine || *intr* to border
confirmar *tr* to confirm
confiscar §73 *tr* to confiscate
confita•do -da *adj* hopeful, confident; (*bañado de azúcar*) candied
confitar *tr* (*frutas*) to candy; (*en almíbar*) preserve; (*endulzar*) sweeten
confite *m* candy, bonbon, confection; **confites** confectionery
confitera *f* candy box; candy jar
confitería *f* confectionery; confectionery store
confite•ro -ra *mf* confectioner || *f* see **confitera**
confitura *f* preserves, confiture; **confituras** confectionery
conflagración *f* conflagration
conflagrar *tr* to set fire to
conflicti•vo -va *adj* conflicting; anguished
conflicto *m* conflict; (*apuro*) fix, jam
confluencia *f* confluence
confluir §20 *intr* to flow together; crowd, gather
conformador *m* hat block
conformar *tr* to shape; (*un sombrero*) to block || *intr* & *ref* to conform, comply, yield, agree
conforme *adj* in agreement || *adv* depending on circumstances; fine, O.K.; **conforme a** according to || *conj* as, in proportion as; as soon as || *m* approval
conformidad *f* conformance, conformity; resignation
confort *m* comfort
confortable *adj* comfortable; comforting
confortante *adj* comforting; tonic || *mf* comforter || *m* tonic
confr. *abbr* **confesor**
confricar §73 *tr* to rub
confrontar *tr* (*poner en presencia; cotejar*) to confront || *intr* to border; to agree || *ref* to get along, agree; **confrontarse con** (*hacer frente a*) to confront
confundir *tr* to confuse; (*turbar, dejar desarmado*) confound || *ref* to become confused; (*en la muchedumbre*) get lost
confusión *f* confusion
confutar *tr* to confute
congal *m* (Mex) brothel, whorehouse
congelador *m* freezer
congelar *tr* to congeal, freeze; (*créditos*) (fig) to freeze || *ref* to congeal, freeze
congenial *adj* congenial (*having the same nature*)
congeniar *intr* to be congenial, get along well
congéni•to -ta *adj* congenital
congestión *f* congestion
congestionar *tr* to congest || *ref* to congest, become congested
conglobar *tr* to lump together
congoja *f* anguish, grief
congojo•so -sa *adj* distressing; distressed
congosto *m* narrow mountain pass
congraciar *tr* to win over || *ref* to ingratiate oneself; **congraciarse con** to get into the good graces of
congratulación *f* congratulation
congratular *tr* to congratulate || *ref* to congratulate oneself, rejoice
congregación *f* congregation; **la Congregación de los fieles** the Roman Catholic Church
congregar §44 *tr* to bring together || *ref* to congregate, come together
congresal *m* (Arg, Chile) congressman
congresista *mf* delegate; member of congress || *m* congressman || *f* congresswoman
congreso *m* (*asamblea legislativa*) congress; (*reunión para deliberar sobre intereses comunes*) meeting, convention
congrio *m* conger eel
cóni•co -ca *adj* conical
conjetura *f* conjecture, guess
conjeturar *tr* & *intr* to conjecture, guess
conjugación *f* conjugation
conjugar §44 *tr* to conjugate; combine
conjunción *f* conjunction; combination
conjuntamente *adv* together
conjuntista *m* chorus man || *f* chorus girl
conjunti•vo -va *adj* conjunctive; subjunctive
conjun•to -ta *adj* joined, combined, united || *m* whole, entirety, ensemble; unit; group; (theat) chorus; **de conjunto** general; **en conjunto** as a whole; **en su conjunto** in its entirety
conjura or **conjuración** *f* conspiracy, plot

conjuramentar *tr* to swear in || *ref* to take an oath
conjurar *tr* to swear in; conjure, entreat; conjure away, exorcise || *intr* to conspire, plot || *ref* to conspire, join in a conspiracy
conjuro *m* (*invocación supersticiosa*) conjuration; adjuration, entreaty
conllevar *tr* (*los trabajos*) to share in bearing; (*a una persona*) tolerate, stand for; (*las adversidades*) suffer
conmemorar *tr* to commemorate, memorialize
conmigo *pron* with me, with myself
conmilitón *m* fellow soldier
conminar *tr* to threaten
conmoción *f* commotion; concussion, shock
conmove•dor -dora *adj* touching, moving, stirring
conmover §**47** *tr* to touch, move, affect; stir, stir up; shake, upset || *ref* to be touched, be moved
conmutación *f* commutation
conmutador *m* (elec) change-over switch; (SAm) telephone exchange
conmutar *tr* to commute
connivencia *f* connivance; **estar en connivencia** to connive
cono *m* cone; **cono de proa** nose cone; **cono de viento** (aer) wind cone, wind sock
conoce•dor -dora *adj* knowledgeable || *mf* expert, connoisseur
conocer §**22** *tr* to know; meet, get to know; tell, distinguish; (law) to try || *intr* to know; **conocer de** or **en** to know, have knowledge of || *ref* to know oneself; know each other; meet, meet each other
conoci•do -da *adj* known, well-known, familiar; distinguished, prominent || *mf* acquaintance
conocimiento *m* knowledge; understanding; acquaintance; consciousness; (com) bill of lading; **con conocimiento de causa** knowingly, with full knowledge; **conocimiento de embarque** (com) bill of lading; **conocimientos** knowledge; **hablar con pleno conocimiento de causa** to know what one is talking about; **perder el conocimiento** to lose consciousness; **por su real conocimiento** (Arg) for real money; **recobrar el conocimiento** to regain consciousness; **venir en conocimiento de** to come to know
conque *adv* and so || *m* condition, terms
conquista *f* conquest
conquista•dor -dora *adj* conquering || *m* conqueror; (*ladrón de corazones*) ladykiller
conquistar *tr* to conquer; (*ganar la voluntad de*) win over
consabi•do -da *adj* well-known; abovementioned
consagrar *tr* to consecrate; devote; dedicate; (*una nueva palabra*) authorize || *ref* to devote oneself; make a name for oneself
consciente *adj* conscious
conscripción *f* conscription
conscripto *m* conscript, draftee
consecución *f* obtaining, getting
consecuencia *f* (*correspondencia lógica entre sus elementos*) consistency; (*acontecimiento que resulta necesariamente de otro*) consequence; **en consecuencia** accordingly; **guardar consecuencia** to remain consistent; **traer a consecuencia** to bring in
consecuente *adj* (*que tiene proporción consigo mismo*) consistent; (*que sigue en orden a otra cosa*) consecutive
consecuti•vo -va *adj* consecutive
conseguir §**67** *tr* to get, obtain; **conseguir** + *inf* to succeed in + *ger*
conseja *f* story, fairy tale; cabal
conseje•ro -ra *adj* advisory || *mf* advisor, counselor; councilor
consejo *m* advice, counsel; board; council; **consejos** advice; **un consejo** a piece of advice
consenso *m* consensus
consenti•do -da *adj* spoiled, pampered; (*marido*) indulgent
consenti•dor -dora *adj* acquiescent; pampering || *mf* acquiescent person; (*de niños*) pamperer || *m* cuckold
consentimiento *m* consent
consentir §**68** *tr* to allow; admit; pamper, spoil || *intr* to consent; come loose; **consentir** + *inf* to think that + *ind*; **consentir con** to be indulgent toward; **consentir en** to consent to || *ref* to begin to crack up; (Arg) to be proud
conserje *m* janitor, concierge
conserva *f* preserves; preserved food; pickles; (naut) convoy; **conservas alimenticias** canned goods; **llevar en su conserva** (naut) to convoy; **navegar en (la) conserva** (naut) to sail in a convoy
conservación *f* conservation; preservation; self-preservation; maintenance, upkeep
conserva•dor -dora *adj* preservative; (pol) conservative || *mf* conservative || *m* curator
conservar *tr* to conserve, keep, maintain; preserve || *ref* to take good care of oneself; keep
conservati•vo -va *adj* conservative, preservative
conservatorio *m* (*p.ej., de música*) conservatory; (Arg) private school; (Chile) hothouse, greenhouse
conservera *f* cannery; (Mex) preserve dish
conservería *f* canning
conserve•ro -ra *adj* canning || *mf* canner || *f* see **conservera**
considerable *adj* considerable; large, great, important
consideración *f* consideration; **ser de consideración** to be of importance, be of concern; **someter a consideración** to take under advisement
considera•do -da *adj* (*que guarda consideración a los demás*) considerate; (*digno de respeto*) respected, esteemed; (*que obra con reflexión*) cautious, prudent
considerando *conj* & *m* whereas
considerar *tr* to consider; treat with consideration

consigna *f* slogan; watchword; (mil) orders; (rr) checkroom
consignación *f* consignment
consignar *tr* to consign; assign; state in writing, set forth
consignatario *m* consignee
consigo *pron* with him, with her, with them, with you; with himself, with herself, with themselves, with yourself or yourselves
consiguiente *adj* consequential; **ir** or **proceder consiguiente** to act consistently ‖ *m* consequence; **por consiguiente** consequently, therefore
consilia•rio -ria *mf* advisor, counselor
consistencia *f* consistence, consistency
consistente *adj* consistent
consistir *intr* to consist; **consistir en** (*estar compuesto de*) to consist of; (*residir en*) consist in
consistorio *m* consistory; town council; town hall
conso•cio -cia *mf* copartner; companion, fellow member
consola *f* console, console table; bracket
consolación *f* consolation
consolar **§61** *tr* to console
consolidar *tr* to fund, refund; strengthen; repair
consommé *m* consommé
consonancia *f* consonance; rhyme
consonante *adj* consonantal; rhyming ‖ *m* rhyme ‖ *f* consonant
consonar **§61** *intr* to be in harmony; rhyme
cónsone *adj* harmonious ‖ *m* (mus) chord
consorcio *m* consortium; partnership; fellowship
consorte *mf* consort, mate, spouse; partner, companion; **consortes** (law) colitigants; (law) accomplices
conspi•cuo -cua *adj* outstanding, prominent
conspiración *f* conspiracy
conspirar *intr* to conspire
constancia *f* constancy; certainty, proof
constante *adj* constant; steady, regular; sure, certain ‖ *f* constant
constar *intr* to be clear, be certain; be on record; have the right rhythm; **constar de** to consist of; **hacer constar** to state, make known; **y para que conste** in witness whereof
constatación *f* proof
constatar *tr* to prove, establish, show
constelación *f* constellation; climate, weather; epidemic
consternar *tr* to depress, dismay
constipación *f* or **constipado** *m* cold, cold in the head
constipar *tr* (*los poros*) to stop up ‖ *ref* to catch cold
constitución *f* constitution
constituir **§20** *tr* to constitute; establish, found; **constituir en** to force into ‖ *ref*— **constituirse en** to set oneself up as
constituti•vo -va *adj & m* constituent
constituyente *adj* (*para dictar o reformar la constitución*) constituent
constreñir **§72** *tr* to constrain, force, compel; constrict, compress
construcción *f* construction; building, structure; **construcción de buques** shipbuilding
construc•tor -tora *adj* construction ‖ *mf* builder, constructor; **constructor de buques** shipbuilder
construir **§20** *tr* to build, construct
consuegro *m* fellow father-in-law (*with respect to the father of one's son-in-law or daughter-in-law*), father-in-law of one's child
consuelda *f* comfrey; **consuelda real** field larkspur; **consuelda sarracena** goldenrod
consuelo *m* consolation; joy, delight; **sin consuelo** inconsolably; to excess
consueta *m* (theat) prompter
consuetudina•rio -ria *adj* customary, usual
cónsul *m* consul
consulado *m* consulate, consulship; (*casa u oficina*) consulate
consular *adj* consular
consulta *f* consultation; opinion; reference
consultación *f* consultation
consultar *tr* to consult; take up, discuss; advise ‖ *intr* to consult, confer
consulti•vo -va *adj* advisory
consul•tor -tora *mf* consultant
consultorio *m* dispensary
consuma•do -da *adj* consummate ‖ *m* consommé
consumar *tr* to consummate; fulfill, carry out
consumerismo *m* consumerism
consumición *f* consumption; drink (*in bar or restaurant*)
consumi•do -da *adj* thin, weak, emaciated; fretful
consumi•dor -dora *mf* consumer; customer (*in bar or restaurant*)
consumir *tr* to consume; exhaust; harass, wear down ‖ *ref* to consume, waste away; long, yearn
consumo *m* consumption; drink (*in bar or restaurant*); customers; **consumos** octroi
consunción *f* consumption; (pathol) consumption
consuno *adv* — **de consuno** together, in accord
consunti•vo -va *adj* consumptive; (*crédito*) consumer
contabilidad *f* accounting, bookkeeping
contabilista *mf* accountant, bookkeeper
contabilizadora *f* computer
contabilizar **§60** *tr* to enter in the ledger
contable *adj* countable ‖ *mf* accountant, bookkeeper
contactar *intr* to contact, be in contact
contacto *m* contact; **ponerse en contacto con** to get in touch with
conta•do -da *adj* scarce, rare; **al contado** cash, for cash; **contados** a few; **de contado** right away; **por de contado** of course
contador *m* counter; accountant; (*que mide el agua, gas, electricidad*) meter; (law) receiver; **contador de abonado** house meter; **contador de Geiger** Geiger counter; **contador kilométrico** speedometer; **contador**

público titulado certified public accountant
contaduría *f* accountancy; accountant's office; box office for advanced sales
contagiar *tr* to infect; corrupt
contagio *m* contagion
contagio•so -sa *adj* contagious
contaminación *f* contamination; **contaminación ambiental** environmental pollution
contaminante *m* pollutant
contaminar *tr* to contaminate; (*un texto*) corrupt; (*la ley de Dios*) break
contante *adj* (*dinero*) ready
contar **§61** *tr* to count; regard, consider; tell, relate; **contar . . . años** to be . . . years old; **dejarse contar diez** (box) to take the count; **tiene sus horas contadas** his days are numbered || *intr* to count; **a contar desde** beginning with; **contar con** to count on, rely on; reckon with; expect to
contemplación *f* contemplation; leniency, condescension
contemplar *tr* to contemplate; be lenient to || *intr* to contemplate
contemporáne•o -a *adj* contemporaneous, contemporary || *mf* contemporary
contemporizar **§60** *intr* to temporize
contención *f* containment; contention, strife; (law) suit, litigation
contencio•so -sa *adj* contentious
contender **§51** *intr* to contend
contendiente *mf* contender, contestant
contenedor *m* container
contener **§71** *tr* to contain || *ref* to contain oneself
conteni•do -da *adj* moderate, restrained || *m* content, contents
contenta *f* gift or treat; indorsement; (mil) certificate of good conduct; (law) release
contentadi•zo -za *adj* easy to please
contentamiento *m* contentment
contentar *tr* to content; reconcile; (com) to indorse
conten•to -ta *adj* content, contented, glad || *m* content, contentment; **a contento** to one's satisfaction; **no caber de contento** (coll) to be beside oneself with joy || *f* see **contenta**
conteo *m* calculation, estimate, count
contera *f* tip, metal tip
contesta *f* answer; (Mex) chat
contestación *f* answer; argument, debate; **mala contestación** back talk
contestar *tr* to answer || *intr* to answer; agree
contesto *m* (Mex) reply
contexto *m* interweaving; context
conticinio *m* dead of night
contienda *f* contest, dispute, fight
contigo *pron* with thee, with you
conti•guo -gua *adj* contiguous, adjoining
continencia *f* continence
continental *adj* continental
continente *adj* continent || *m* (*cosa que contiene en sí a otra*) container; (*aire del semblante, compostura del cuerpo*) mien, bearing; (*gran extensión de tierra rodeada por los océanos*) continent
contingencia *f* contingency
contingente *adj* contingent || *m* contingent; share, quota
continuar **§21** *tr & intr* to continue; **continuará** to be continued
continuidad *f* continuity
conti•nuo -nua *adj* continuous, continual; (mach) endless || **continuo** *adv* continuously
contonear *ref* to strut, swagger
contoneo *m* strut, swagger
contorcer **§74** *ref* to writhe
contorno *m* contour, outline; **contornos** environs, neighborhood
contorsión *f* contortion
contra *prep* against; toward, facing || *m* (*concepto opuesto*) con || *f* trouble, inconvenience; (*al comprador*) (Cuba) gift, extra; (Chile) antidote; **llevar la contra a** to disagree with
contraalmirante *m* rear admiral
contraatacar **§73** *tr & intr* to counterattack
contraataque *m* counterattack
contrabajo *m* contrabass, double bass
contrabajón *m* double bassoon
contrabalancear *tr* to counterbalance
contrabalanza *f* counterbalance
contrabandear *intr* to smuggle
contrabandista *adj* smuggling; contraband || *mf* smuggler, contrabandist
contrabando *m* smuggling, contraband; **meter de contrabando** to smuggle, smuggle in
contrabarrera *f* second row of seats (*in bull ring*)
contracalle *f* parallel side street
contracarril *m* (rr) guardrail
contracción *f* contraction; (*reducción del ritmo normal de los negocios*) recession; (*al estudio*) (Chile, Peru) concentration
contracepti•vo -va *adj & m* contraceptive
contracorriente *f* countercurrent, crosscurrent; (*entre aguas*) undertow
contracultura *f* counterculture
contrachapado *m* plywood
contradecir **§24** (*impv sg* **-dice**) *tr* to contradict
contradicción *f* contradiction
contradic•tor -tora *adj* contradictory || *mf* contradicter
contradicto•rio -ria *adj* contradictory
contraer **§75** *tr* to contract; (*deudas*) incur; (*el discurso o idea*) condense || *ref* to contract; shrink; (Chile, Peru) to concentrate, apply oneself
contraescalón *m* riser (*of stairway*)
contraespía *mf* counterspy
contraespionaje *m* counterespionage
contrafallar *tr & intr* to overtrump
contrafallo *m* overtrump
contrafigura *f* counterpart
contrafuero *m* infringement, violation
contrafuerte *m* abutment, buttress
contragolpe *m* counterstroke; kickback; (box) counter
contrahace•dor -dora *adj* counterfeiting; fake || *mf* counterfeiter; fake; impersonator

contrahacer §39 *tr* to counterfeit, copy, imitate; fake; impersonate; (*un libro*) pirate ‖ *ref* to pretend to be
contra•haz *f* (*pl* **-haces**) wrong side
contrahe•cho -cha *adj* counterfeit, fake; deformed
contrahechura *f* counterfeit, fake
contrahuella *f* riser (*of stairway*)
contralor *m* comptroller
contralto *mf* contralto (*person*) ‖ *m* contralto (*voice*)
contraluz *f* view against the light; **a contraluz** against the light
contramaestre *m* foreman; (naut) boatswain; **segundo contramaestre** boatswain's mate
contramandar *tr* to countermand
contramandato *m* countermand
contramano *adv* — **a contramano** in the wrong direction, the wrong way
contramarcha *f* countermarch; reverse
contramarchar *intr* to countermarch; to go in reverse
contraofensiva *f* counteroffensive
contraorden *f* cancellation
contraparte *f* counterpart
contrapasar *intr* to go over to the other side
contrapelo *adv* — **a contrapelo** against the hair, against the grain; the wrong way; **a contrapelo de** against, counter to
contrapesar *tr* to offset, counterbalance
contrapeso *m* counterweight; counterbalance; (*para completar el peso de carne, etc.*) makeweight
contraponer §54 *tr* to set opposite; oppose; compare
contraportada *f* (*del disco*) flip side
contraprestación *f* return favor
contraproducente *adj* self-defeating, unproductive
contraprueba *f* second proof
contrapuerta *f* storm door; vestibule door
contrapuntear *tr* to sing in counterpoint; taunt, be sarcastic to ‖ *ref* to taunt each other
contrapunto *m* counterpoint
contrapunzón *m* nailset, punch
contrariar §77 *tr* to counteract, oppose; annoy, provoke
contrariedad *f* opposition; interference; annoyance, bother
contra•rio -ria *adj* opposite, contrary; harmful ‖ *mf* enemy, opponent, rival ‖ *m* opposite, contrary; **al contrario** on the contrary; **de lo contrario** otherwise
contrarreferencia *f* cross reference
Contrarreforma *f* Counter Reformation
contrarregistro *m* (*para comprobar si algún género ha pasado por la frontera*) double check; (*de una experiencia científica*) control
contrarréplica *f* (law) rejoinder
contrarrestar *tr* to resist, counteract; (*la pelota*) return
contrarrevolución *f* counterrevolution
contrasentido *m* misinterpretation; mistranslation; nonsense
contraseña *f* countersign; baggage check; **contraseña de salida** (mov, theat) check
contrastar *tr* to resist; (*las pesas y medidas*) check ‖ *intr* to resist; contrast
contraste *m* resistance; contrast; assayer; assayer's office; (naut) sudden shift in the wind
contratar *tr* to contract for; hire, engage
contratiempo *m* misfortune, disappointment, setback
contratista *mf* contractor
contrato *m* contract
contratreta *f* counterplot
contratuerca *f* lock nut, jam nut
contravalidación *f* (*documento*) validation
contravalidar *tr* to validate; confirm
contraveneno *m* counterpoison, antidote
contravenir §79 *intr* to act contrary; **contravenir a** to contravene, act counter to
contraventana *f* window shutter
contravidriera *f* storm sash
contrayente *mf* contracting party (*to a marriage*)
contribución *f* contribution; tax; **contribución de sangre** military service; **contribución industrial** excise tax; **contribución territorial** land tax
contribui•dor -dora *mf* contributor; taxpayer
contribuir §20 *tr* & *intr* to contribute
contribuyente *mf* contributor; taxpayer
contrición *f* contrition
contrincante *m* competitor, rival; fellow candidate
contristar *tr* to sadden
contri•to -ta *adj* contrite
control *m* control, check; **control de la natalidad** or **de los nacimientos** birth control; **control remoto** remote control
controlador *m* controller; **controlador aéreo** air-traffic controller
controlar *tr* to control, check
controversia *f* controversy
controvertible *adj* controversial, controvertible
controvertir §68 *tr* to controvert
contubernio *m* cohabitation; evil alliance
contumacia *f* contumacy; (law) contempt
contu•maz *adj* (*pl* **-maces**) contumacious; germ-bearing; (law) guilty of contempt of court
contumelia *f* contumely
contundente *adj* bruising; impressive, convincing
contundir *tr* to bruise
conturbar *tr* to trouble, worry, upset
contusión *f* contusion
contusionar *tr* (Chile) to bruise
convalecencia *f* convalescence
convalecer §22 *intr* to convalesce, recover
convaleciente *adj* & *mf* convalescent
convalidar *tr* to confirm
conveci•no -na *adj* neighboring ‖ *mf* neighbor
convencer §78 *tr* to convince
convencimiento *m* conviction
convención *f* (*acuerdo; conformidad; asamblea*) convention; political convention
convencional *adj* conventional

convenible *adj* docile, compliant; (*precio*) fair, reasonable
conveniencia *f* (*comodidad*) convenience; (*acuerdo, convenio*) agreement; fitness, suitability; (*formas sociales*) propriety; domestic employment; **conveniencias** income, property
conveniencie•ro -ra *adj* comfort-loving
conveniente *adj* (*cómodo*) convenient; fit, suitable; advantageous; proper
convenio *m* pact, covenant, treaty
convenir §79 *intr* to agree; (*concurrir, juntarse*) convene; be suitable, be becoming; be important, be necessary; **conviene a saber** to wit, namely || *ref* to agree, come to an agreement
conventillo *m* (SAm) tenement house
convento *m* convent, monastery; **convento de religiosas** convent
converger §17 or **convergir** §27 *intr* to converge; concur
conversa *f* chat, conversation
conversación *f* conversation
conversacional *adj* conversational
conversar *intr* to converse; live, dwell
conversión *f* conversion
conver•so -sa *adj* converted || *mf* convert || *m* lay brother || *f* see **conversa**
convertible *adj* convertible || *m* (aut) convertible
convertir §68 *tr* to convert; turn || *ref* to convert; be converted; **convertirse en** to turn into, become
conve•xo -xa *adj* convex
convic•to -ta *adj* convicted, found guilty
convida•do -da *mf* guest || *f* treat
convidar *tr* to invite; treat; move, incite; **convidarle a uno con alguna cosa** to treat someone to something || *ref* to offer one's services
convincente *adj* convincing
convite *m* invitation; treat, banquet, party; **convite a escote** Dutch treat
convivir *intr* to live together
convocar §73 *tr* to convoke, call together; (*p.ej., una huelga*) call; acclaim
convoy *m* convoy; escort; cruet stand; (rr) train
convoyar *tr* to convoy
convulsionar *tr* to convulse
conyugal *adj* conjugal
cónyuge *mf* spouse, consort || **cónyuges** *mpl* couple, husband and wife
co•ñac *m* (*pl* **-ñacs** or **-ñaques**) cognac
cooperación *f* coöperation
cooperar *intr* to coöperate
cooperati•vo -va *adj* coöperative
cooptar *tr* to coöpt
coordena•do -da *adj* coördinate || *f* (math) coördinate
coordinante *adj* (gram) coördinating
coordinar *tr & intr* to coördinate
copa *f* goblet, wineglass; (*del sombrero*) crown; brazier; vase; drink; sundae; playing card, representing a bowl, equivalent to heart; (*del dolor*) (fig) cup; (sport) cup
copar *tr* (*la puesta equivalente a todo el dinero de la banca*) to cover; (*todos los puestos en una elección*) sweep; (mil) to cut off and capture
copartícipe *mf* copartner, joint partner
copear *intr* to sell wine or liquor by the glass; (coll) to tipple
copero *m* cabinet for wineglasses
copete *m* (*cabello levantado sobre la frente*) pompadour; (*de plumas; de una montaña*) crest; (*de un caballo*) forelock; (*de lana, cabello, plumas, etc.*) tuft; (*de un mueble*) top, finial; (*de un sorbete*) topping; **de alto copete** aristocratic, important; **tener mucho copete** to be high-hat
copetu•do -da *adj* tufted; high, lofty; high-hat
copia *f* plenty, abundance; copy; **copia al carbón** carbon copy; **copia fiel** true copy
copiador *m* or **copiadora** *f* copy(ing) machine; duplicator
copiante *mf* copier, copyist
copiar *tr* to copy, copy down
copiloto *m* copilot
copio•so -sa *adj* copious, abundant
copista *mf* copier, copyist
copla *f* couplet; ballad, popular song; **coplas** verse, poetry; **coplas de ciego** doggerel
cople•ro -ra *mf* vendor of ballads; poetaster
coplista *mf* poetaster
copo *m* bundle of cotton, flax, hemp, etc. to be spun; **copo de nieve** snowflake; **copos de jabón** soap flakes
copón *m* ciborium, pyx
copo•so -sa *adj* bushy; flaky, woolly
copu•do -da *adj* bushy, thick
copular *ref* to copulate
coque *m* coke
coqueluche *f* whooping cough
coqueta *adj* coquettish || *f* coquette, flirt; (W-I) dressing table
coquetear *intr* to coquette, flirt; try to please everybody
coquetería *f* coquetry, flirting; affectation
coque•tón -tona *adj* coquettish, kittenish || *m* flirt, lady-killer
coracha *f* leather bag
coraje *m* anger; mettle, spirit
coraju•do -da *adj* ill-tempered; (Arg) brave, courageous
coral *adj* (mus) choral || *m* (mus) chorale; (*zoófito; esqueleto calizo del zoófito; color*) coral; **corales** coral beads
corambre *f* hides, skins
Corán *m* Koran
coranvo•bis *m* (*pl* **-bis**) fat solemn look
coraza *f* armor; cuirass; (sport) guard
corazón *m* heart; (*centro de una cosa*) core; **de corazón** heartily; **hacer de tripas corazón** to pluck up courage
corazonada *f* impulsiveness; hunch, presentiment; entrails
corbata *f* necktie, cravat; scarf; **corbata de mariposa, corbata de lazo** bow tie; **corbata de nudo corredizo** four-in-hand tie
corbatín *m* bow tie
corbeta *f* corvette

Córcega *f* Corsica
corcel *m* steed, charger
corcova *f* hump, hunch
corcova•do -da *adj* humpbacked, hunchbacked || *mf* humpback, hunchback
corcovar *tr* to bend
corcovear *intr* to buck; grumble; (Mex) to be afraid
corcha *f* cork bark; cork bucket (*for cooling wine*)
corchea *f* (mus) quaver, eighth note
corche•ro -ra *adj* cork || *f* cork bucket (*for cooling wine*)
corcheta *f* eye (*of hook and eye*)
corchete *m* snap; hook and eye; hook (*of hook and eye*); (*signo*) bracket; **corchete de presión** snap fastener
corcho *m* cork; cork, cork stopper; cork wine cooler; cork box; cork mat; **corcho bornizo, corcho virgen** virgin cork
cordada *f* (mountaineering) party of two or three men roped together
cordaje *m* cordage; (naut) rigging
cordal *adj* wisdom (*tooth*) || *m* (mus) tailpiece
cordel *m* cord, string; (distance of) five steps; cattle run; **a cordel** in a straight line
cordelejo *m* string; **dar cordelejo a** to make fun of; (Mex) to keep putting off
cordera *f* ewe lamb; (*mujer dócil y humilde*) (fig) lamb
cordería *f* cordage
corderillo *m* lambskin
corderi•no -na *adj* lamb || *f* lambskin
cordero *m* lamb; lambskin; (*hombre dócil y humilde*) (fig) lamb
corderuna *f* lambskin
cordial *adj* cordial; (*dedo*) middle || *m* cordial
cordialidad *f* cordiality
cordillera *f* chain of mountains
cordobana *f* — **andar a la cordobana** to go naked
cordón *m* lace; (*de cuerda o alambre*) strand; cordon; milled edge of coin; (*de monje*) rope belt; **cordón umbilical** umbilical cord
cordoncillo *m* rib, ridge; braid; (*de monedas*) milling
cordura *f* prudence, wisdom
Corea *f* Korea; **la Corea del Norte** North Korea; **la Corea del Sur** South Korea
corea•no -na *adj & mf* Korean
corear *tr* to compose for a chorus; accompany with a chorus; join in singing; agree obsequiously with
coreografía *f* choreography
coriáce•o -a *adj* leathery
Corinto *f* Corinth
corista *m* choir priest; (theat) chorus man || *f* chorus girl, chorine
cori•to -ta *adj* naked; bashful, timid
cormorán *m* cormorant
cor•nac *m* (*pl* **-nacs**) or **cornaca** *m* mahout
cornada *f* hook with horns; goring; (*en la esgrima*) upward thrust
cornadura *f* or **cornamenta** *f* (*del toro, la vaca, etc.*) horns; (*del ciervo*) antlers
cornamusa *f* bagpipe
córnea *f* cornea
cornear *tr* to butt; to gore
corneja *f* daw, crow
cornejo *m* dogwood
córne•o -a *adj* horn, horny || *f* see **córnea**
corneta *f* bugle; swineherd's horn; **corneta acústica** ear trumpet; **corneta de llaves** cornet, cornet-à-pistons; **corneta de monte** hunting-horn
cornisa *f* cornice
cornisamento *m* (archit) entablature
corno *m* horn; dogwood; **corno inglés** (mus) English horn
Cornualles Cornwall
cornucopia *f* cornucopia; sconce with mirror
cornu•do -da *adj* horned, antlered; cuckold || *m* cuckold
coro *m* chorus; choir; choir loft; **a coros** alternately; **de coro** by heart; **hacer coro a** to echo
corolario *m* corollary
corona *f* (*cerco de metal; moneda; dignidad real; parte visible de una muela*) crown; (*cerco de flores*) garland, wreath; (*aureola*) halo; (*de eclesiástico*) tonsure; (*la que corresponde a un título nobiliario*) coronet; **corona nupcial** bridal wreath
coronación *f* coronation
coronamento *m* or **coronamiento** *m* coronation; completion, termination; (archit) coping; (naut) taffrail
coronar *tr* to crown; complete, finish; top, surmount; (checkers) to crown
coronel *m* colonel
coronelía *f* colonelcy
coronilla *f* (*de la cabeza*) crown; **andar** or **bailar de coronilla** to be hard at it; **estar hasta la coronilla** to be fed up
corotos *mpl* belongings; utensils
corpiño *m* bodice, waist; (Arg) brassiere
corporación *f* corporation
corporal *adj* corporal, bodily
corpu•do -da *adj* corpulent
corpulen•to -ta *adj* corpulent
corpúsculo *m* corpuscle; particle
corral *m* corral, stockyard; barnyard; fishpond; theater; **corral de madera** lumberyard; **corral de vacas** pigpen; **hacer corrales** to play hooky
correa *f* strap, thong; (aer, mach) belt; **besar la correa** to eat humble pie; **correa de seguridad** (aer, aut) safety belt
corrección *f* (*acción de corregir; reprensión*) correction; (*calidad de correcto*) correctness
correcti•vo -va *adj & m* corrective
correc•to -ta *adj* correct
correc•tor -tora *mf* corrector; **corrector de pruebas** proofreader
corredera *f* track, slide; slide valve; (*del trombón*) slide; (naut) log; (naut) log line; (*puerta*) **de corredera** sliding
corredi•zo -za *adj* slide; sliding; (*nudo*) slip
corre•dor -dora *adj* running || *mf* runner || *m* corridor; porch, gallery; (*el que interviene en compras y ventas de efectos comer-*

ciales, etc.) broker; (mil) scout; **corredor de apuestas** bookmaker
corregidor *m* Spanish magistrate; chief magistrate of Spanish town
corregir §57 *tr* to correct; temper, moderate || *intr* (W-I) to have a bowel movement || *ref* to mend one's ways
correlación *f* correlation
correlacionar *tr & intr* to correlate
correlati•vo -va *adj & m* correlative
corre•lón -lona *adj* (SAm) fast, swift; (Col, Mex) cowardly
correncia *f* bashfulness; looseness of the bowels
correntí•o -a *adj* running; free, easy || *f* looseness of the bowels
corren•tón -tona *adj* jolly, full of fun
corrento•so -sa *adj* swift, rapid
correo *m* mail; post office; mail train; postman; courier; **correo aéreo** air mail; **correo urgente** special delivery; **echar al correo** to mail, to post
correo•so -sa *adj* leathery, tough
correr *tr* (*un caballo*) to run, race; (*un riesgo*) run; travel over; overrun; (*una cortina*) draw; (*un toro*) fight; chase, pursue; auction; confuse; throw out; **correrla** to run around all night || *intr* to run; race; pass, elapse; circulate, be common talk; be current; **a todo correr** at full speed; **correr a** to sell for; **correr a cargo de** or **por cuenta de** to be the business of; **correr con** to be on good terms with; be in charge of; (*mes*) **que corre** current || *ref* (*a derecha o a izquierda*) to turn; be confused; be embarrassed, be ashamed; slide, glide; (*una bujía, un color*) run; go too far
correría *f* short trip, excursion; foray, raid
correspondencia *f* correspondence; contact, communication; agreement, harmony; (*en el metro*) connection; (*en una carretera*) interchange
corresponder *intr* to correspond; (*dos habitaciones*) communicate; **corresponder a** (*un beneficio, el afecto de una persona*) to return, reciprocate; concern; be up to || *ref* (*comunicarse por escrito*) to correspond; (*dos cosas*) correspond with each other; be in agreement; be attached to each other
correspondiente *adj* corresponding; correspondent; respective || *mf* correspondent
corresponsal *mf* correspondent
corretaje *m* brokerage
corretear *tr* to harass, pursue; (CAm) to drive away; (Chile) to speed up || *intr* to race around
correveidi•le *mf* (*pl* **-le**) gossip; go-between
corrida *f* run; bullfight; (*carrera de entrenamiento de un caballo*) trial run; **corrida de banco** run on the bank; **corrida de toros** bullfight
corri•do -da *adj* (*peso, medida*) in excess; (*letra*) cursive; continued, unbroken; abashed, ashamed; wordly-wise, sophisticated || *m* overhang; street ballad || *f* see **corrida**
corriente *adj* (*agua*) running; (*actual*) current; common, ordinary; regular; well-known; fluent || *adv* all right, O.K. || *m* current month; **al corriente** on time; informed, aware, posted || *f* current, stream; (elec) current; **corriente de aire** draft; **Corriente del Golfo** Gulf Stream; **ir contra la corriente** to go against the tide
corrillo *m* circle, clique
corrimiento *m* running; sliding; watery discharge; embarrassment, shyness; landslide; rheumatism
corro *m* (*cerco de gente; espacio circular*) ring; (*juego de niñas*) ring-around-a-rosy; **corro de brujas** fairy ring; **hacer corro** to make room
corroborar *tr* to corroborate; strengthen
corroer §62 *tr & ref* to corrode
corromper *tr* to corrupt; spoil; rot; seduce; bribe; annoy || *intr* to smell bad || *ref* to become corrupted; spoil; rot
corrosión *f* corrosion
corrosi•vo -va *adj & m* corrosive
corrugar §44 *tr* to shrink; wrinkle
corrupción *f* corruption; seduction; bribery; stench
corruptela *f* corruption
corruptible *adj* corruptible; (*p.ej., frutas*) perishable
corrusco *m* crust of bread
corsa *f* (naut) day's run
corsario *m* corsair
corsé *m* corset
cor•so -sa *adj & mf* Corsican || *m* (naut) privateering; (SAm) drive, promenade || *f* see **corsa**
corta *f* clearing, cutting, felling
cortaalam•bres *m* (*pl* **-bres**) wire cutter
cortabol•sas *m* (*pl* **-sas**) pick-pocket
cortacésped *m* lawn mower
cortaciga•rros *m* (*pl* **-rros**) cigar cutter
cortacircui•tos *m* (*pl* **-tos**) (elec) fuse
cortacorriente *m* (elec) change-over switch
cortada *f* cut, cutting
cortadillo *m* drinking cup
corta•do -da *adj* (*estilo*) choppy; (SAm) hard up || *f* see **cortada**
corta•dor -dora *adj* cutting || *mf* cutter || *m* butcher || *f* cutting machine
cortafrío *m* cold chisel
cortafuego *s* fire wall
cortahie•los *m* (*pl* **-los**) icebreaker
cortalápi•ces *m* (*pl* **-ces**) pencil sharpener
cortante *adj* cutting, sharp || *m* butcher; butcher knife
cortapape•les *m* (*pl* **-les**) paper cutter
cortapi•cos *m* (*pl* **-cos**) (ent) earwig; **cortapicos y callares** little children should be seen and not heard
cortaplu•mas *m* (*pl* **-mas**) penknife
cortapu•ros *m* (*pl* **-ros**) cigar cutter
cortar *tr* to cut; trim; chop; cut off; cut out, omit; cut short; cut up; carve; (*la corriente; la ignición*) cut off || *intr* to cut; (*el viento, el frío*) be cutting; **cortar de vestir** to cut cloth; gossip || *ref* to become speechless;

(*la leche*) curdle, turn sour; (*la piel*) chap, crack

cortarrenglón *m* marginal stop

cortaú•ñas *m* (*pl* **-ñas**) nail clipper

cortavi•drios *m* (*pl* **-drios**) glass cutter

cortaviento *m* windshield

corte *m* cut; cutting; (*filo de un arma, cuchillo, etc.; borde de un libro*) edge; cross section; (*de un vestido*) cut, fit; piece of material; harvest; **corte de pelo** haircut; **corte de pelo a cepillo** crew cut; **corte de traje** suiting || *f* (*de un rey*) court; (*corral*) yard; stable, fold; (*tribunal de justicia*) court; **Cortes** Parliament; **darse cortes** (SAm) to put on airs; **hacer la corte a** to pay court to; **la Corte** the Capital (*Madrid*)

cortedad *f* shortness; smallness; lack; bashfulness

cortejar *tr* to escort, attend, court; court, woo

cortejo *m* courting; courtship; (*séquito*) cortege; gift, treat; (coll) beau

cortera *f* (Chile) streetwalker

cortero *m* (Chile) day laborer

cortés *adj* courteous, polite, courtly

cortesana *f* courtesan

cortesana•zo -za *adj* overpolite, obsequious

cortesanía *f* courtliness

cortesa•no -na *adj* courtly, courteous || *m* courtier || *f* see **cortesana**

cortesía *f* courtesy, politeness, courtliness; gift, favor; (*inclinación de la cabeza o el cuerpo en señal de respeto*) curtsy; (*de una carta*) conclusion; **hecer una cortesía** to make a bow; curtsy

corteza *f* bark; peel, rind, skin; (*de pan*) crust; coarseness; (*envoltura exterior de un órgano*) cortex; **corteza cerebral** cortex

cortijo *m* farm, farmhouse

cortil *m* barnyard

cortina *f* curtain; **correr la cortina** to pull the curtain aside; **cortina de hierro** iron curtain; **cortina de humo** smoke screen

cortinal *m* fenced-in field

cortinilla *f* shade, window shade

cortisona *f* cortisone

cor•to -ta *adj* short; dull; bashful, shy; speechless; **a la corta o a la larga** sooner or later; **desde muy corta edad** from earliest childhood || *f* see **corta**

cortocircuitar *tr & ref* (elec) to short-circuit

cortocircuito *m* (elec) short circuit

cortometraje *m* (mov) short

corva *f* ham, back of knee; (vet) curb

corvejón *m* gambrel, hock; (orn) cormorant

cor•vo -va *adj* arched, bent, curved || *m* hook || *f* see **corva**

cor•zo -za *mf* roe deer

cosa *f* thing; **cosa de** a matter of; **cosa de cajón** a matter of course; **cosa de mieles** something fine; **cosa de nunca acabar** endless bore; **cosa de oír** something worth hearing; **cosa de risa** something to laugh at; **cosa de ver** something worth seeing; **cosa nunca vista** something unheard-of; **cosa que** so that; **cosa rara** strange to say; **como si tal cosa** as if nothing had happened; **en cosa de** in a matter of; **no . . . gran cosa** not much; **no haber tal cosa** to be not so; **otra cosa** something else; **¿qué cosa?** what's new?

cosa•co -ca *adj & mf* Cossack || *m* Cossack (*horseman*)

coscolina *f* (Mex) loose woman

cos•cón -cona *adj* sly, crafty

cosecha *f* crop, harvest; harvest time; **cosecha de vino** vintage; **de su cosecha** (coll) out of one's own head

cosechar *tr* to harvest, reap || *intr* to harvest

coseche•ro -ra *mf* harvester, reaper; vintner

cose-pape•les *m* (*pl* **-les**) stapler

coser *tr* to sew; join, unite closely; **coser a preguntas** to riddle with questions; **coser a puñaladas** to cut to pieces || *intr* to sew; **ser coser y cantar** to be a cinch || *ref*—**coserse con** or **contra** to be closely attached to

cosméti•co -ca *adj & m* cosmetic

cósmi•co -ca *adj* cosmic

cosmonauta *mf* cosmonaut

cosmonave *f* spacecraft

cosmonavegación *f* space travel

cosmopolita *adj & mf* cosmopolitan

cosmos *m* cosmos; (bot) cosmos

coso *m* enclosure for bullfighting

cosquillas *fpl* tickling, ticklishness; **buscarle a uno las cosquillas** to try to irritate a person; **no sufrir cosquillas** or **tener malas cosquillas** to be touchy

cosquillear *tr* to tickle; tease, taunt; stir up the curiosity of; scare || *intr* to tickle || *ref* to be curious; enjoy oneself

cosquilleo *m* tickling, tickling sensation

cosquillo•so -sa *adj* ticklish; (*que se ofende fácilmente*) touchy

costa *f* coast, shore; cost, price; **a toda costa** at all costs; **Costa Brava** Mediterranean coast in province of Gerona, Spain; **Costa Firme** Spanish Main; **costa marítima** seacoast; **costas** (law) costs

costado *m* side; (*del ejército*) flank; (Mex) station platform; **costados** ancestors, stock

costal *m* bag, sack; **costal de los pecados** human body (*full of sin*); **estar hecho un costal de huesos** to be nothing but skin and bones

costanera *f* slope; **costaneras** rafters

costane•ro -ra *adj* sloping; coastal || *f* see **costanera**

costanilla *f* short steep street

costar §61 *intr* to cost; **cueste lo que cueste** cost what it may

costarricense or **costarrique•ño -ña** *adj & mf* Costa Rican

coste *m* cost; **a coste y costas** at cost

costear *tr* to pay for, defray the cost of; sail along the coast of || *intr* to sail along the coast || *ref* to pay; pay one's way

coste•ño -ña *adj* sloping; coastal

coste•ro -ra *adj* coastal

costilla *f* rib; wealth; **costillas** back, shoulders

costillu•do -da *adj* heavy-set, broad-shouldered

costo *m* cost; **costo de la vida** cost of living; **costo, seguro y flete** cost, insurance, and freight
costo•so -sa *adj* costly, expensive; grievous
costra *f* scab, scale; (*moco de una vela*) snuff
costro•so -sa *adj* scabby, scaly
costumbre *f* custom, habit; **de costumbre** usual; usually; **tener por costumbre** to be in the habit of
costumbrista *mf* critic of manners and customs
costura *f* sewing, needlework; dressmaking; (*unión de dos piezas cosidas*) seam; **alta costura** fashion designing, haute couture
costurar or **costurear** *tr* (CAm, Mex) to sew
costurera *f* seamstress, dressmaker
costurero *m* sewing table
cota *f* coat of arms; coat of mail
cotarrera *f* gossipy woman
cotarro *m* night shelter (*for beggars and tramps*); **alborotar el cotarro** to raise a row
cotejar *tr* to compare, collate
cotejo *m* comparison, collation
cotidia•no -na *adj* daily, everyday
cotilla *f* gossip, tattletale
cotín *m* (sport) backstroke
cotización *f* quotation; dues
cotizante *adj* dues-paying
cotizar **§60** *tr* to quote; prorate || *intr* to collect dues; pay dues
coto *m* price; fixed price; term, limit
cotón *m* printed cotton
cotona *f* work shirt
cotonía *f* dimity
cotorra *f* parrot; parakeet; magpie; chatterbox; (Mex) night shelter
cotorrear *intr* to gossip, gabble
cotufa *f* Jerusalem artichoke; delicacy, tidbit; **hacer cotufas** (Bol) to be fastidious; **pedir cotufas en el golfo** to ask for the moon
coturno *m* buskin
covacha *f* cave; cubbyhole; shanty; doghouse
covachuelista *m* clerk, government clerk
coxcojita *f* hopscotch; **a coxcojita** hippety-hop
coy *m* (naut) hammock
coyunda *f* strap for yoking oxen; sandal string; marriage; tyranny
coyuntura *f* joint, articulation; (*sazón, oportunidad*) juncture
coz *f* (*pl* **coces**) kick; big end; ebb; (coll) insult; **dar coces contra el aguijón** to kick against the pricks
c.p.b., C.P.B. *abbr* **cuyos pies beso**
cps. *abbr* **compañeros**
crabrón *m* hornet
crac *m* (*ruido seco*) crack; crash; **hacer crac** to crash, fail
cráneo *m* cranium, skull
crápula *f* drunkenness, debauchery; riffraff
crapulo•so -sa *adj* drunken; vicious, evil
crascitar *intr* to crow, croak
cra•so -sa *adj* fat, greasy, thick; (*ignorancia*) crass, gross
cráter *m* crater
creación *f* creation
crea•dor -dora *adj* creative || *mf* creator
crear *tr* to create; appoint; found || *ref* to make for oneself, build up; trump up
creati•vo -va *adj* creative
crecede•ro -ra *adj* growth; large enough to allow for growth
crecepelo *m* hair restorer
crecer **§22** *intr* to grow; increase; (*el río*) rise, swell; (*la luna*) wax || *ref* to grow; take on more authority; get bolder
creces *fpl* growth, increase; excess, extra; **con creces** amply, in abundance
crecida *f* freshet, flood
creciente *adj* growing, increasing || *f*—**creciente de la luna** waxing of the moon, crescent; **creciente del mar** high tide, flood tide
crecimiento *m* growth, increase; **crecimiento cero** zero growth
credenciales *fpl* credentials
crédito *m* credit
credo *m* creed; credo; **con el credo en la boca** with one's heart in one's mouth; **en un credo** in a trice
crédu•lo -la *adj* credulous
creederas *fpl* — **tener buenas creederas** to be gullible
creencia *f* belief; (*crédito que se presta a un hecho*) credence; (*secta*) creed
creer **§43** *tr & intr* to believe; **¡ya lo creo!** I should say so! || *ref* to believe; believe oneself to be
creíble *adj* believable, credible
creí•do -da *adj* credulous; gullible
crema *f* cream; cold cream; shoe polish; (gram) diaeresis; **crema de menta** creme de menthe; **crema dental** or **crema dentífrica** toothpaste; **crema desvanecedora** vanishing cream
cremación *f* cremation
cremallera *f* rack; zipper
cremato•rio -ria *adj & m* crematory
crémor *m* cream of tartar
cremo•so -sa *adj* creamy
crencha *f* part (*in hair*); hair on each side of part
crepitar *intr* to crackle
crepuscular *adj* twilight
crepúsculo *m* twilight
cresa *f* maggot
crespar *tr & ref* to curl
cres•po -pa *adj* curly; curled; angry, irritated; stylish, conceited; (*estilo*) turgid || *m* curl
crespón *m* crape; **crespón fúnebre** crape; mourning band
cresta *f* crest; **cresta de gallo** cockscomb; (bot) cockscomb
creta *f* chalk || **Creta** *f* Crete
cretense *adj & mf* Cretan
cretona *f* cretonne
creyente *adj* believing || *mf* believer
creyón *m* crayon
cría *f* brood, litter; breeding; raising, rearing; nursing
criada *f* female servant, maid; **criada de casa, criada de servir** housemaid

criadero *m* nursery, tree nursery; fish hatchery; oyster bed
criadilla *f* testicle; potato
cria•do -da *adj* — **bien criado** well-bred; **mal criado** ill-bred ‖ *mf* servant ‖ *f* see **criada**
cria•dor -dora *mf* breeder ‖ *f* wet nurse
criamiento *m* care, upkeep
crianza *f* raising, rearing; nursing; (*urbanidad*) breeding, manners; **buena crianza** good breeding; **mala crianza** bad breeding
criar §77 *tr* to raise, rear, bring up; breed; grow; nurse, nourish; fatten; create; foster
criatura *f* (*toda cosa creada; persona que debe su cargo o situación a otra*) creature; little child, little creature
criba *f* screen, sieve
cribar *tr* to screen, sieve
cribo *m* screen, sieve
cric *m* (*pl* **crics**) jack
crimen *m* crime; **crimen de lesa majestad** lese majesty; **crímenes de oficinistas** white-collar crime
criminal *adj & mf* criminal
criminar *tr* to accuse, incriminate
criminología *f* criminology
crimino•so -sa *adj & mf* criminal
crines *fpl* mane
crío *m* (coll) baby, infant
crio•llo -lla *adj & mf* Creole
cripta *f* crypt
crisálida *f* chrysalis
crisantemo *m* chrysanthemum
cri•sis *f* (*pl* **-sis**) crisis; (*pánico económico*) depression, slump; mature judgment; **crisis del servicio doméstico** servant problem; **crisis de llanto** crying fit; **crisis de vivienda** housing shortage; **crisis energética** energy crisis; **crisis ministerial** cabinet crisis; **crisis nerviosa** fit of nerves
crisma *f* (coll) head, bean
crisol *m* crucible
crispar *tr* to cause to twitch ‖ *ref* to twitch
crispatura *f* twitch, twitching
crispir *tr* to grain, to marble
cristal *m* crystal; glass; pane of glass; mirror, looking glass; **cristal cilindrado** plate glass; **cristal de reloj** watch crystal; **cristal de roca** rock crystal; **cristal hilado** glass wool, spun glass; **cristal laminado** laminated glass, safety glass; **cristal tallado** cut glass
cristalera *f* China closet; sideboard; glass door
cristalería *f* glassworks, glass store; glassware; glass cabinet
cristali•no -na *adj* crystalline ‖ *m* lens, crystalline lens
cristalizar §60 *tr & ref* to crystallize
cristianar *tr* to baptize, christen
cristiandad *f* Christendom
cristianismo *m* Christianity
cristianizar §60 *tr* to Christianize
cristia•no -na *adj & mf* Christian ‖ *m* soul, person; Spanish; watered wine
Cristo *m* Christ; crucifix; **donde Cristo dió las tres voces** in the middle of nowhere
Cristóbal *m* Christopher
criterio *m* criterion
crítica *f* (*jucio sobre una obra literaria, etc.; censura de la conducta de alguno*) criticism; (*arte de juzgar una obra literaria, etc.*) critique; gossip
criticar §73 *tr & intr* to criticize
críti•co -ca *adj* critical; (*criticón*) critical (*faultfinding*) ‖ *mf* critic ‖ *f* see **crítica**
criti•cón -cona *adj* critical, faultfinding ‖ *mf* critic, faultfinder
critiquizar §60 *tr* to overcriticize
crizneja *f* braid of hair
croar *intr* to croak
croata *adj & mf* Croatian
crocante *m* almond brittle, peanut brittle
crocitar *intr* to crow, croak
croco *m* crocus
croché *m* crochet
crochet *m* (box) hook
croma•do -da *adj* chrome ‖ *m* chromium plating
cromar *tr* to chrome
cromo *m* chromium
cromosoma *m* chromosome
crónica *f* chronicle; news chronicle, feature story
cróni•co -ca *adj* chronic; longstanding; (*vicio*) inveterate ‖ *f* see **crónica**
cronista *mf* chronicler; reporter, feature writer; **cronista de radio** newscaster
cronología *f* chronology
cronometra•dor -dora *mf* (sport) timekeeper
cronometraje *m* (sport) clocking, timing
cronómetro *m* chronometer; stop watch
croqueta *f* croquette
cro•quis *m* (*pl* **-quis**) sketch
croscitar *intr* to crow, croak
crótalo *m* rattlesnake; castanet
cruce *m* crossing; crossroads, intersection; exchange (*e.g., of letters*); (*avería*) (elec) crossed wires, short circuit; **cruce a nivel** grade crossing; **cruce en trébol** cloverleaf intersection
crucero *m* crossroads; railroad crossing; (archit) transept; (aer, naut) cruise, cruising; (nav) cruiser; **crucero a nivel** grade crossing
crucial *adj* crucial
crucificar §73 *tr* to crucify
crucifijo *m* crucifix
crucifixión *f* crucifixion
crucigrama *m* crossword puzzle
cruda *f* (Mex) hangover
crudeza *f* crudeness, rawness; (*del agua*) hardness; harshness, roughness; blustering; **crudezas** undigested food
cru•do -da *adj* crude, raw; (*agua*) hard; harsh, rough; (*tiempo*) raw; (*lienzo*) unbleached; **estar crudo** (P-R) to be rusty; (Mex) to have a hangover ‖ *f* see **cruda**
cruel *adj* cruel
crueldad *f* cruelty
cruen•to -ta *adj* bloody
crujía *f* corridor, hall; hospital ward; block of houses; (naut) midship gangway; **crujía de**

piezas suite of rooms; **sufrir una crujía** (coll) to have a hard time of it

crujido *m* creak; crackle; clatter; chatter; rustle

crujir *intr* to creak; crackle; clatter; chatter; rustle; crunch

crup *m* croup

crustáce•o -a *adj* crustaceous || *m* crustacean

cruz *f* (*pl* **cruces**) cross; (*de una moneda*) tails; (typ) dagger; **Cruz del Sur** Southern Cross; **¡cruz y raya!** (coll) that's enough!; **de la cruz a la fecha** from beginning to end

cruza *f* (SAm) intersection; crossbreeding

cruzada *f* (*expedición contra los infieles; propaganda contra un vicio*) crusade; crossroads, intersection

cruza•do -da *adj* crossed; (*de raza mixta*) cross; double-breasted || *m* (*el que toma parte en una cruzada*) crusader; (*caballero de una orden militar*) knight; twill || *f* see **cruzada**

cruzar **§60** *tr* to cross; (*la tela*) twill; (*cartas*) exchange; crossbreed; (naut) to cruise, cruise over || *intr* to cross; cruise || *ref* to cross each other, cross one another's path; (*alistarse para una cruzada*) take the cross; **cruzarse con** (*otro automóvil*) to pass; **cruzarse de brazos** (*estar ocioso*) to cross one's arms

cs. *abbr* **céntimos, cuartos**

cte. *abbr* **corriente**

c/u *abbr* **cada uno**

cuad. *abbr* **cuadrado**

cuaderna *f* (naut) frame

cuaderno *m* notebook; folder; **cuaderno de bitácora** (naut) logbook; **cuaderno de hojas cambiables** or **sueltas** loose-leaf notebook

cuadra *f* hall, large room; stable; dormitory, ward; croup, rump; block

cuadra•do -da *adj* square; square-shouldered; perfect || *m* square; (*regla*) ruler; (*en las medias*) clock; **de cuadrado** perfectly; (*que se mira frente a frente*) full-faced

cuadragési•mo -ma *adj & m* fortieth

cuadrangular *adj* quadrangular || *m* home run

cuadrángu•lo -la *adj* quadrangular || *m* quadrangle

cuadrante *m* quadrant; (*de reloj*) face, dial; **cuadrante solar** sundial

cuadrar *tr* to square; please; (*al toro*) (taur) to square off, line up || *ref* to square; stand at attention; take on a serious air

cuadrilla *f* group, party; crew, gang

cuadrillazo *m* (SAm) surprise attack

cuadrillo *m* (*saeta*) bolt (*arrow*)

cuadrimotor *m* four-motor plane

cua•dro -dra *adj* square || *m* square; (*lienzo, pintura*) painting, picture; (*marco de pintura, ventana, etc.*) frame; (*de jardín*) patch, flower bed; staff, personnel; (mil) cadre; (sport) team; (theat) scene; (coll) sight, mess; **a cuadros** checked; **cuadro de costumbres** sketch of manners and customs; **cuadro de distribución** switchboard; **cuadro de mando** instrument panel; (aut) dashboard; **cuadro indicador** score board; **cuadro vivo** tableau; **en cuadro** square, e.g., **ocho pulgadas en cuadro** eight inches square; topsy-turvy; **quedarse en cuadro** to be all alone in the world; (mil) to be skeletonized || *f* see **cuadra**

cuadrúpe•do -da *adj & m* quadruped

cuádruple *adj & m* quadruple

cuadruplicar **§73** *tr & ref* to quadruple

cuajada *f* curd

cuajado *m* mincemeat

cuajar *tr* to curd, curdle, thicken, jelly; please, suit || *intr* to take hold, catch on, jell, take shape; (Mex) to chatter, prattle || *ref* to curd, curdle, thicken, jelly; sleep sound; become crowded

cuajo *m* curd; (Mex) chatter, prattle; (*en la escuela*) (Mex) recess

cual *adj rel & pron rel* such as; **el cual** which; who; **lo cual** which; **por lo cual** for which reason || *adv* as || *prep* like

cuál *adj interr & pron interr* which, what; which one

cualidad *f* quality, characteristic, trait

cualquier *adj indef* (*pl* **cualesquier**) apocopated form of **cualquiera,** used only before masculine nouns and adjectives

cualquiera (*pl* **cualesquiera**) *pron indef* anyone; **cualquiera que** whichever; whoever || *adj indef* any || *adj rel* whichever || *m* (*persona poco importante*) nobody

cuan *adv* as

cuán *adv* how, how much

cuando *conj* when; although; in case; since; **aun cuando** even if, even though; **cuando más** at most; **cuando menos** at least; **cuando mucho** at most; **cuando quiera** whenever; **de cuando en cuando** from time to time || *prep* (coll) at the time of

cuándo *adv* when; **cuándo . . . cuándo** sometimes . . . sometimes; **¿de cuándo acá?** since when?; how come?

cuantía *f* quantity; importance; **delito de mayor cuantía** felony; **delito de menor cuantía** misdemeanor; **de mayor cuantía** first-rate; **de menor cuantía** second-rate, of little importance

cuantiar **§77** *tr* to estimate, appraise

cuánti•co -ca *adj* quantum

cuantio•so -sa *adj* large, substantial

cuan•to -ta *adj rel & pron rel* as much as, whatever, all that which; **cuantos** as many as, all those who, everybody who; **unos cuantos** some few || **cuanto** *adv* as soon as; as long as; **cuanto antes** as soon as possible; **cuanto más . . . tanto más** the more . . . the more; **cuanto más que** all the more because; **en cuanto** as soon as; while; insofar as; **en cuanto a** as to, as for; **por cuanto** inasmuch as; **por cuanto . . . por tanto** inasmuch as . . . therefore || **cuan•to** *m* (*pl* **-ta**) quantum

cuán•to -ta *adj interr & pron interr* how much; **cuántos** how many || **cuánto** *adv* how, how much; how long; how long ago; **cada cuánto** how often

cuáque•ro -ra *adj & mf* Quaker
cuarenta *adj, pron & m* forty
cuarenta•vo -va *adj & m* fortieth
cuarentena *f* forty; quarantine; forty days, forty months, forty years; **poner en cuarentena** to quarantine; withhold one's credence in
cuaresma *f* Lent
cuaresmal *adj* Lenten
cuarta *f* fourth, fourth part; (*de la mano*) span; (CAm, W-I) horse whip
cuartago *m* nag, pony
cuartear *tr* to divide in four parts; divide; (*la aguja*) (naut) to box; (CAm, W-I) to whip ‖ *ref* to crack, split; (taur) to step aside, dodge
cuartel *m* quarter; (*de una ciudad*) section, ward; (*terreno*) lot; flower bed; (mil) barracks; (*buen trato*) (mil) quarter; (*armazón de tablas para cerrar la escotilla*) (naut) hatch; (coll) house, home; **cuartel de bomberos** engine house, firehouse; **cuarteles** (mil) quarters; **cuartel general** (mil) headquarters
cuartelada *f* mutiny, military uprising
cuartelazo *m* (mil) coup, putsch; (mil) takeover
cuarte•rón -rona *mf* quadroon ‖ *m* quarter; (*de puerta*) panel; (*de ventana*) shutter
cuarteto *m* quartet
cuartilla *f* sheet of paper
cuar•to -ta *adj* fourth; quarter ‖ *m* fourth; quarter; room, bedroom; quarter-hour; **cuarto creciente** (*de la luna*) first quarter; **cuarto de aseo** lavatory; **cuarto de baño** bathroom; **cuarto de dormir** bedroom; **cuarto de estar** living room; **cuarto delantero** (*de la res*) forequarter; **cuarto de los niños** nursery; **cuarto de luna** quarter; **cuarto menguante** (*de la luna*) last quarter; **cuarto obscuro** (phot) darkroom; **cuartos** money, cash; **cuarto trasero** (*p.ej., de vaca*) rump ‖ *f see* **cuarta**
cuarzo *m* quartz
cuate *adj* (Mex) twin; (Mex) like ‖ *mf* (Mex) twin; (Mex) pal
cuatrilli•zo -za *mf* quadruplet
cuatrinca *f* foursome
cuatro *adj & pron* four; (Mex) deceit, swindle; **las cuatro** four o'clock ‖ *m* four; (*en las fechas*) fourth; (*de voces*) quartet; **más de cuatro** (coll) quite a number
cuatrocien•tos -tas *adj & pron* four hundred ‖ **cuatrocientos** *m* four hundred
cuba *f* cask, barrel; tub, vat; (*persona de mucho vientre*) (coll) tub; (*persona que bebe mucho*) (coll) toper; **cuba de riego** street sprinkler
cuba•no -na *adj & mf* Cuban
cubertería *f* silverware, cutlery
cubeta *f* keg, cask; pail; bowl, toilet bowl; (*del termómetro*) cup; (chem, phot) tray; (Mex) high hat
cubicaje *m* piston displacement, cylinder capacity
cubicar *tr* (*elevar al cubo*) to cube; measure the volume of; have a piston displacement of
cúbi•co -ca *adj* cubic; (*raíz*) cube
cubierta *f* cover; envelope; roof; (*de un libro*) paper cover; (*de un neumático*) casing, shoe; (*del motor de un coche*) hood; (naut) deck; **bajo cubierta separada** under separate cover; **cubierta de aterrizaje** (nav) flight deck; **cubierta de cama** bedcover; **cubierta de mesa** table cover; **cubierta de paseo** (naut) promenade deck; **cubierta de vuelo** (nav) flight deck; **cubierta principal** (naut) main deck; **entre cubiertas** (naut) between decks
cubiertamente *adv* secretly
cubier•to -ta *adj* covered; (*cielo*) overcast ‖ *m* cover, roof, shelter; (*servicio de mesa para una persona*) cover; knife, fork, and spoon; table d'hôte, prix fixe; **a cubierto de** under cover of; protected from; **bajo cubierto** under cover, indoors ‖ *f* see **cubierta**
cubil *m* (*de fieras*) lair, den; (*de arroyo*) bed
cubilete *m* (*de cocinero*) copper mold; dicebox; mince pie; high hat; (SAm) scheming, wirepulling
cubo *m* bucket; (*de rueda*) hub; (*de un candelero; de una llave de caja*) socket; cube; (mach) barrel, drum; (math) cube; (Arg) finger bowl
cubreasiento *m* seat cover
cubrecama *f* counterpane, bedcover
cubrecorsé *m* corset cover
cubrefuego *m* curfew
cubrelibro *m* jacket
cubrenuca *f* havelock
cubrerrueda *f* mudguard
cubresexo *m* G-string
cubretablero *m* (aut) cowl
cubretetera *f* cozy, tea cozy
cubrir **§83** *tr* to cover, cover over, cover up ‖ *ref* to cover oneself; be covered; put one's hat on; (*el cielo*) become overcast; (*satisfacer una deuda*) cover
cucaña *f* greased pole to be climbed as a game; (coll) cinch
cucañe•ro -ra *mf* loafer, parasite
cucar §73 *tr* to wink; to make fun of; (*la caza*) to sight; to incite, stir up ‖ *intr* (*el ganado*) to go off on a run (*when bitten by flies*)
cucaracha *f* roach, cockroach
cucarache•ro -ra *adj* (W-I) sly, tricky; (W-I) amorous, lecherous
cucarda *f* cockade
cuclillas — **en cuclillas** squatting, crouching
cuclillo *m* cuckoo; (coll) cuckold
cu•co -ca *adj* sly, tricky; cute ‖ *mf* sly person ‖ *m* bogeyman; cuckoo; **hacer cuco a** to poke fun at
cu•cú *m* (*pl* **-cúes**) cuckoo (*call*)
cuculla *f* cowl, hood
cucurucho *m* paper cone, ice-cream cone; **hacer cucurucho a** (Chile) to deceive, take in

cuchara *f* spoon; (*cazo*) dipper, ladle; (*para áridos; para achicar el agua en los botes*) scoop; (*de albañil*) trowel; (Mex) pickpocket; **cuchara de sopa** tablespoon; **media cuchara** (Mex) mason's helper; ordinary fellow; fellow with heavy accent; **meter su cuchara** to butt in

cucharada *f* spoonful; ladleful; scoop

cucharear *tr* to spoon, ladle out

cucharetear *intr* to stir the pot, stir with a spoon; to meddle

cucharilla *f* teaspoon; (*de soldador*) ladle

cucharón *m* large spoon; soup ladle, dipper; scoop; **despacharse con el cucharón** to look out for number one

cuchichear *intr* to whisper

cuchilla *f* knife; (*hoja de arma blanca de corte*) blade; (*de patín de hielo*) runner; (*cerro escarpado*) hogback; (*de interruptor*) (elec) blade; (poet) sword; **cuchilla de carnicero** butcher knife, cleaver

cuchillada *f* slash, gash, hack; **cuchilladas** fight, quarrel; **dar cuchillada** (*un actor o un teatro*) to be the hit of the town

cuchillería *f* cutlery; cutler's shop

cuchillero *m* cutler

cuchillo *m* knife; (*en un vestido*) gore; (naut) triangular sail; **cuchillo de trinchar** carving knife; **cuchillo de vidriero** putty knife; **pasar a cuchillo** to put to the sword

cuchitril *m* hovel, den

cuchufleta *f* joke, fun, wisecrack

cuchufletear *intr* to joke, make fun, wisecrack

cuelga *f* fruit hung up for keeping; birthday present

cuelgaca•pas *m* (*pl* **-pas**) cloak hanger

cuello *m* (*del cuerpo*) neck; (*de una prenda*) collar; shirt collar; **cuello almidonado** stiff collar; **cuello de camisa** shirtband; **cuello de cisne** gooseneck; **cuello de pajarita** or **doblado** wing collar; **levantar el cuello** to get back on one's feet again

cuenca *f* wooden bowl; (*del ojo*) socket; basin, river basin; **cuenca de polvo** dust bowl

cuenco *m* earthen bowl; hollow

cuenta *f* count, calculation; account; (*factura*) bill; (*en un restaurante*) check; (*del rosario*) bead; **abonar en cuenta a** to credit to the account of; **a cuenta** or **a buena cuenta** on account; **adeudar en cuenta a** to charge to the account of; **a fin de cuentas** after all; **caer en la cuenta** to get the point; **cargar en cuenta a** to charge to the account of; **correr por cuenta de** to be the responsibility of, to be under the administration of; **cuenta atrás** countdown; **cuenta corriente** current account; **cuenta de gastos** expense account; **cuenta de la vieja** counting on one's fingers; **cuentas del gran capitán** overdrawn account; **cuentas galanas** illusions; **darse cuenta de** to realize, become aware of; **de cuenta** of importance; **más de la cuenta** too long; too much; **pedir cuentas a** to bring to account; **por la cuenta** apparently; **por mi cuenta** to my way of thinking; **tomar por su cuenta** to take upon oneself; **vamos a cuentas** (coll) let's settle this

cuentacorrentista *mf* depositor

cuentago•tas *m* (*pl* **-tas**) dropper, medicine dropper

cuentakilóme•tros *m* (*pl* **-tros**) odometer

cuente•ro -ra *adj* (coll) gossipy || *mf* (coll) gossip

cuentista *adj* (coll) gossipy || *mf* story teller; short-story writer; (coll) gossip

cuento *m* story, tale; short story; prop, support; tip, point; (*cómputo*) count; (coll) gossip, evil talk; (coll) disagreement; **cuento de hadas** fairty tale; **cuento del tío** (SAm) gyp, swindle; **cuento de nunca acabar** (coll) endless affair; **cuento de penas** (coll) hard-luck story; **cuento de viejas** old wives' tale; **Cuentos de Calleja** collection of nursery stories; **dejarse de cuentos** (coll) to come to the point; **estar en el cuento** to be well-informed; **¡puro cuento!** pure fiction!; **sin cuento** countless; **traer a cuento** to bring up; **venir a cuento** (coll) to be opportune; **vivir del cuento** to live by one's wits

cuerda *f* cord, rope; watch spring; winding a watch or clock; (*acción de ahorcar*) hanging; fishing line; (aer, anat, geom) chord; (mus) string; **acabarse la cuerda** to run down, e.g., **se acabó la cuerda** the watch ran down; **bajo cuerda** secretly, underhandedly; **cuerda de presos** chain gang; **cuerda de remolcar** tow rope; **cuerda de tripa** (mus) catgut; **cuerda tirante** tight rope; **dar cuerda a** to give free rein to; (*un reloj*) to wind; **estar en su cuerda** to be in one's element; **sin cuerda** unwound, rundown

cuer•do -da *adj* wise, prudent; sane || *f* see **cuerda**

cuerna *f* antler; horns

cuerno *m* horn; (mus) horn; **cuerno de caza** huntinghorn; **cuerno inglés** (mus) English horn

cuero *m* (*pellejo de buey*) hide; (*después de curtido*) leather; wineskin; **cuero cabelludo** scalp; **cuero en verde** rawhide; **en cueros** stark-naked

cuerpear *intr* (Arg) to duck, dodge

cuerpo *m* body; (*parte del vestido hasta la cintura*) waist; (*talle, aspecto*) build; (*de escritos, leyes, etc.*) corpus; corps, staff; (mil) corps; **cuerpo a cuerpo** hand to hand; **cuerpo celeste** heavenly body; **cuerpo compuesto** (chem) compound; **cuerpo de aviación** air corps; **cuerpo de baile** corps de ballet; **cuerpo de bomberos** fire brigade, fire company; **cuerpo de ejército** army corps; **Cuerpo de Paz** Peace Corps; **cuerpo de redacción** editorial staff, **cuerpo simple** (chem) simple substance; **dar con el cuerpo en tierra** (coll) to fall flat on the ground; **de cuerpo entero** full-length; **de medio cuerpo** half-length; **descubrir el cuerpo** to drop one's guard; **en cuerpo** or **en cuerpo de camisa** in shirt

sleeves; **estar de cuerpo presente** to be on view, to lie in state; **hacer del cuerpo** (coll) to have a movement of the bowels
cueru•do -da *adj* thick-skinned; annoying, boring; bold, shameless
cuervo *m* raven; **cuervo marino** cormorant; **cuervo merendero** rook
cuesco *m* (*de la fruta*) stone; (*del molino de aceite*) millstone; windiness
cuesta *f* hill, slope, grade; charity drive; **cuesta abajo** downhill; **cuesta arriba** uphill; **llevar a cuestas** to be burdened with
cuestión *f* question; dispute, quarrel; matter; **cuestión batallona** much-debated question; **cuestión palpitante** burning question; **en cuestión de** in a matter of
cuestionable *adj* questionable
cuestionar *tr* to question ‖ *intr* (Arg) to argue
cuestionario *m* questionnaire
cuestua•rio -ria or **cuestuo•so -sa** *adj* profitable, lucrative
cuetear *ref* (Col) to blow up, explode; (Col) to die, kick the bucket; (Mex) to get drunk
cueva *f* cave; cellar; (*de ladrones, fieras, etc.*) den
cufi•fo -fa *adj* (Chile) tipsy
cugulla *f* cowl
cui•co -ca *adj* foreign, outside ‖ *m* (Mex) cop, policeman
cuidado *m* care, concern, worry; **¡cuidado con . . .!** beware of . . .!, look out for!; **de cuidado** dangerously; **estar de cuidado** to be dangerously ill; **pierda Vd. cuidado** don't worry; **salir de su cuidado** (*una mujer*) to be delivered; **tener cuidado** to beware, be careful
cuidadora *f* (Mex) governess, chaperon
cuidado•so -sa *adj* careful, concerned, worried; watchful
cuidar *tr* to take care of, watch over ‖ *intr* — **cuidar de** to take care of, care for; care to ‖ *ref* to take care of oneself; **cuidarse de** to care about; be careful to
cuita *f* trouble, worry; longing, yearning
cuja *f* bedstead
culata *f* buttock, haunch; (*de la escopeta*) butt; (*de imán*) keeper, yoke; **culata de cilindro** cylinder head
culatazo *m* kick, recoil
culebra *f* snake; (*del alambique*) coil; **culebra de anteojos** cobra; **culebra de cascabel** rattlesnake; **saber más que las culebras** to be crafty
culebrear *intr* to wriggle; wind, meander; zigzag
culebrón *m* foxy fellow; (Mex) poor farce
cule•co -ca *adj* self-satisfied; madly in love
cu•lí *m* (*pl* **-líes**) coolie
culina•rio -ria *adj* culinary
culipandear *intr & ref* (CAm, W-I) to welsh, be evasive
culminar *intr* to culminate
culo *m* seat, behind, backside; (*de animal*) buttocks; (*de un vaso*) bottom; **culo de mal asiento** fidgety person; **volver el culo** to run away
culote *m* base
culpa *f* blame, guilt, fault; **echar la culpa a** to put the blame on; **tener la culpa** to be wrong, be to blame
culpable *adj* blamable, guilty, culpable
culpa•do -da *adj* guilty ‖ *mf* culprit
culpar *tr* to blame, censure, accuse ‖ *ref* to take the blame
cultedad *f* fustian, affectation
culteranismo *m* euphuism, Gongorism
cultiparlar *intr* to speak in a euphuistic manner
cultismo *m* learned word; cultism, Gongorism
cultivar *tr* to cultivate; till
cultivo *m* cultivation; **cultivo de secano** dry farming
cul•to -ta *adj* cultivated, cultured; (*vocablo*) learned ‖ *m* worship; cult; **culto a la personalidad** personality cult
cultura *f* culture, cultivation
culturar *tr* to cultivate, till
cumbre *adj* top, greatest ‖ *f* summit; acme, pinnacle; **conferencia en la cumbre** summit meeting
cúmel *m* kümmel
cumiche *m* (CAm) baby (*youngest member of family*)
cumpa *m* (SAm) pal, buddy; comrade
cúmplase *m* approval, O.K.
cumplea•ños *m* (*pl* **-ños**) birthday
cumpli•do -da *adj* full; perfect; (*en muestras de urbanidad*) correct ‖ *m* correctness; courtesy; present
cumplimentar *tr* to compliment; to pay a complimentary visit to; to carry out, execute; (*un cuestionario*) to fill out
cumplimente•ro -ra *adj* effusive, obsequious
cumplimiento *m* (*muestra de urbanidad*) compliment; (*conducta decorosa*) correctness; fulfillment; perfection; **por cumplimiento** as a matter of pure formality
cumplir *tr* to fulfill, perform, execute; **cumplir años** to have a birthday; **cumplir . . . años** to be . . . years old ‖ *intr* to fall due; to expire; to keep one's promise; to finish one's service in the army; **cumplir con** to fulfill; to fulfill one's obligation to; **cumplir por** to act on behalf of; to pay the respects of ‖ *ref* to be fulfilled, to come true; to fall due; **cúmplase** approved
cumquibus *m* wherewithal
cúmulo *m* heap, pile, lot
cuna *f* cradle
cundido *m* olive, vinegar, and salt for shepherds; olive oil, cheese, and honey to make children eat
cundir *intr* to spread; swell, puff up; increase
cunear *tr* to cradle, rock in a cradle ‖ *intr* to rock, swing, sway
cune•co -ca *mf* (Ven) baby (*youngest member of family*)
cuneta *f* gutter, ditch
cuña *f* wedge; (typ) quoin; **ser buena cuña** to take up a lot of room
cuñada *f* sister-in-law
cuñado *m* brother-in-law
cuñete *m* keg

cuño *m* die; stamp; mark
cuota *f* quota, share; fee, dues; tuition fee
cupé *m* coupé
cupo *m* quota, share; (Mex) capacity
cupón *m* coupon; **cupón de racionamiento** ration coupon
cúpula *f* cupola; dome
cuquillo *m* cuckoo
cura *m* curate; (coll) priest; **este cura** (*yo*) (coll) yours truly (*I*) || *f* cure; care, treatment; **cura de aguas** water cure; **cura de almas** care of souls; **cura de hambre** starvation diet; **cura de reposo** rest cure; **cura de urgencia** first aid; **no tener cura** to be hopeless, be incorrigible
curaca *m* (SAm) boss, chief || *f* (Bol, Peru) priest's housekeeper
curación *f* cure, treatment
curade•ro -ra *mf* caretaker || *m* (law) guardian
curande•ro -ra *mf* quack, healer
curar *tr* (*a un enfermo*) to treat; (*sanar*) cure, heal; (*curtir*) cure; (*la madera*) season; (*una herida*) dress || *intr* to cure; recover; **curar de** to take care of; recover from; mind, pay attention to || *ref* to cure; cure oneself; get well, recover; get drunk; **curarse de** to recover from, get over; **curarse en salud** to be forewarned
curati•vo -va *adj & f* curative
curda *f* jag, drunk
cureña *f* gun carriage
curia *f* (hist) curia; (*de rey*) court; (*conjunto de abogados*) bar
curiales•co -ca *adj* hairsplitting, legalistic
curiosear *tr* to pry into || *intr* to snoop; browse around
curiosidad *f* curiosity; (*objeto de arte raro y curioso*) curio; neatness, tidiness; care, carefulness
curio•so -sa *adj* curious; neat, tidy; careful || *mf* busybody || *m* (Ven) healer, medical man
currinche *m* cub reporter; hit playwright
cu•rro -rra *adj* flashy, sporty || *m* sport, dandy
curruca *f* (orn) whitethroat; **curruca de cabeza negra** blackcap, warbler
curruta•co -ca *adj* dudish, sporty; chubby || *m* dude, sport || *f* chic dame
cursa•do -da *adj* skilled, experienced; (*asignatura*) taken
cursante *mf* student
cursar *tr* (*una materia, estudios*) to take, study; (*conferencias*) attend; (*una carta*) forward; (*un paraje*) frequent, to haunt || *intr* to study; be current
cursear *intr* to have diarrhea
cursería *f* cheapness, flashiness, vulgarity; flashy lot of people
cursi *adj* cheap, flashy, vulgar, loud || *m* sporty guy || *f* flashy dame
cursien•to -ta *adj* diarrheic
cursilería *f* cheapness, flashiness, vulgarity; flashy lot of people
cursillo *m* refresher course; short course of lectures
cursi•vo -va *adj* cursive; italic || *f* cursive; italics
curso *m* course; academic year, school year; price, quotation, current rate; **curso académico** academic year; **curso legal** legal tender; **cursos** loose bowels; **dar curso a** to give way to; to forward
cursor *m* slide; sliding contact; **cursor de procesiones** marshal
curtiduría *f* tannery
curtiembre *f* tannery
curtir *tr* (*las pieles*) to tan; (*el cutis de una persona*) tan, sunburn; harden, inure; **estar curtido en** to be skilled in, be expert in || *ref* to become tanned, sunburned; become hardened; be weather-beaten
curva *f* curve; bend
curvadura *f* painful exhaustion
cur•vo -va *adj* curved, bent || *f* see **curva**
cusca *f* (Col) jag, drunk; (Mex) prostitute, slut
cúspide *f* (*de montaña*) peak; (*de diente*) cusp; apex, tip, top
custodia *f* custody, care; (*de un preso*) guard; (eccl) monstrance
custodiar *tr* to guard, watch over
custodio *m* custodian; guard
cususa *f* (CAm) rum
cu•tí *m* (*pl* **-tíes**) bedtick, ticking
cutícula *f* cuticle
cutio *m* work, labor
cu•tis *m* (*& f*) (*pl* **-tis**) skin, complexion; **cutis anserina** goose flesh
cu•yo -ya *adj rel* whose
c/v *abbr* **cuenta de venta**

Ch

Ch, ch (che) *f* fourth letter of the Spanish alphabet
chabacanada or **chabacanería** *f* crudeness, coarseness, vulgarity
chabaca•no -na *adj* crude, coarse, vulgar || *m* (Mex) apricot tree
chabola *f* shack, shanty; (mil) foxhole
chacal *m* jackal
chacanear *tr* (Chile) to spur, goad on; (Chile) to annoy, bother
chacare•ro -ra *mf* (SAm) farm laborer, field worker; (Col) quack doctor; (Urug) gossip
chacarrachaca *f* row, racket
chacolotear *intr* to clatter
chacota *f* laughter, racket; **hacer chacota de** to make fun of

chacotear *intr* to laugh and make a racket
chacra *f* farm house; small farm; sown field
chacua•co -ca *adj* ugly, crude, boorish || *m* (CAm) cigar butt; (CAm) cheap cigar
cháchara *f* chatter, idle talk; **cháchara**s trinkets, junk
chacharear *intr* to chatter
chafallar *tr* to botch
chafandín *m* conceited ass
chafar *tr* to rumple, muss; flatten; cut short; (Chile) to dismiss, send off
chafarrinar *tr* to blot, stain
chafarrinón *m* blot, stain; **echar un chafarrinón a** to insult, throw mud at
chaflán *m* chamfer
chaflanar *tr* to chamfer
chal *m* shawl
cha•lán -lana *adj* horse-dealing || *mf* horse dealer; horse trader || *m* broncobuster, horsebreaker || *f* scow, flatboat
chalanear *tr* (*un negocio*) to pull off shrewdly; (*un caballo*) break; (Arg) to take advantage of || *intr* to horse-trade
chalanería *f* horse trading
chalanes•co -ca *adj* horse-trading
chaleco *m* vest, waistcoat; **al chaleco** (Mex) by force; (Mex) for nothing; **chaleco salvavidas** life jacket
chalecón *m* (Mex) crook
chalupa *f* small two-master; launch, lifeboat; (Mex) corncake
chama•co -ca *mf* (Mex) youngster, urchin
chamago•so -sa *adj* (Mex) dirty, filthy; (Mex) botched
chamarasca *f* brushwood; brush fire
chamarille•ro -ra *mf* junk dealer, secondhand dealer || *m* gambler
chamari•llón -llona *mf* poor card player
chamarra *f* sheepskin jacket
chamarreta *f* loose jacket; square poncho
chamba *f* fluke, scratch; (Mex) work
chambelán *m* chamberlain; (Mex) atomizer, spray
chambergo *m* (orn) bobolink; (Arg) soft hat
chambe•rí *adj* (*pl* **-ríes**) (Peru) showy, flashy
cham•bón -bona *adj* awkward, clumsy; lucky
chambonada *f* awkwardness, clumsiness; stroke of luck
chambonear *intr* to foozle
chambra *f* blouse; (Ven) din, uproar
chambrana *f* trim (*around a door*)
chamburgo *m* (Col) stagnant water, puddle
chamico *m* jimson weed; **dar chamico a** (SAm) to bewitch
chamorrar *tr* to shear
champán *m* sampan; (coll) champagne
champaña *m* champagne
cham•pú *m* (*pl* **-púes**) shampoo
chamuchina *f* rabble; populace
chamuscar §73 *tr* to singe, scorch; (Mex) to undersell
chamusco *m* singe, scorch
chamusquina *f* singeing; fight, row, quarrel; **oler a chamusquina** to look like a fight; smack of heresy
chancar §73 *tr* to crush; beat, beat up; botch
chance *m* (SAm) opportunity, chance
chancear *intr & ref* to joke, jest
chance•ro -ra *adj* joking, jesting
canciller *m* chancellor
chancla *f* old shoe; house slipper
chancleta *mf* good-for-nothing || *f* slipper; (Ven) accelerator
chanclo *m* overshoe, rubber
chancha *f* cheat, lie; (Chile) slut; **hacer la chancha** (Bol, Col, Chile) to play hooky
chanche•ro -ra *mf* (Arg, Chile) pork butcher
chan•cho -cha *adj* dirty, filthy || *m* pig || *f* see **chancha**
chanchulle•ro -ra *mf* crook
chandal *m* or **chándal** *m* jump suit, gym suit
changador *m* (SAm) errand boy
changarro *m* (Mex) small shop
chan•go -ga *adj* (Chile) dull, stupid; (Mex) sly, crafty || *mf* (Mex) monkey || *m* (Arg) house boy
chan•guí *m* (*pl* **-guíes**) trick, deception
chantaje *m* blackmail
chantajista *mf* blackmailer
chantar *tr* to put on; (SAm) to throw hard; (Urug) to keep waiting || *ref* (*p.ej., el sombrero*) to clap on
chantre *m* cantor, precentor
chanza *f* joke, jest
chao *interj* (coll) good-by
chapa *f* sheet, plate; (*hoja fina de madera*) veneer; (*en las mejillas*) flush; (coll) good sense, judgment; (Chile) lock, bolt; **chapa de circulación** (aut) license plate; **chapas** flipping coins
chapa•do -da *adj* plated; veneered; **chapado a la antigua** old-fashioned
chapalear *intr* (*el agua; las manos y los pies en el agua*) to splash; (*la herradura floja*) clatter
chapar *tr* to cover or line with sheets of metal; veneer
chaparrear *intr* to pour
chapa•rro -rra *mf* (Mex) child, little one; (Mex) runt || *m* scrub oak
chaparrón *m* downpour
chapea•do -da *adj* lined with sheets of metal; veneered || *m* plywood; veneer
chapear *tr* to cover or line with sheets of metal; veneer
chapista *m* tinsmith, tinman
chapitel *m* (*remate de torre*) spire; (*capitel de columna*) capital
chapodar *tr* to trim, clear of branches; to curtail
chapotear *tr* to sponge, moisten || *intr* to splash
chapucear *tr & intr* to botch, bungle
chapuce•ro -ra *adj* crude, rough; clumsy, bungling || *mf* bungler; amateur || *m* blacksmith; junk dealer
chapurrar *tr & intr* to jabber
chapurreo *m* jabber
cha•puz *m* (*pl* **-puces**) duck, ducking
chapuzar §60 *tr, intr & ref* to duck
chaqué *m* cutaway coat, morning coat
chaqueta *f* jacket
chaquetilla *f* short jacket; (Ecuad) lady's vest
chaquetón *m* reefer, pea jacket

charamusca *f* brushwood, firewood; (Mex) candy twist
charanga *f* (mil) brass band
charangue•ro -ra *adj* crude, rough; bungling, clumsy || *mf* bungler
charca *f* pool
charco *m* puddle
charla *f* talk, chat; talk, lecture; chatter, prattle
charla•dor -dora *adj* garrulous; gossipy || *mf* chatterbox; gossip
charlar *intr* to talk, chat; chatter, prattle
charla•tán -tana *adj* garrulous; gossipy || *mf* chatterbox; gossip; charlatan
charlatanería *f* garrulity, loquacity
charlatanismo *m* charlatanism; garrulity, loquacity
charnela *f* (*de puerta; de molusco*) hinge; (mach) knuckle
charol *m* varnish; patent leather; lacquered tray; **calzarse las de charol** (Arg, Urug) to hit the jackpot; **darse charol** to blow one's own horn
charola•do -da *adj* shiny
charolar *tr* to varnish, lacquer
charpa *f* pistol belt; (*cabestrillo*) sling
charquear *tr* (*carne de vaca*) to jerk; slash, cut to pieces
charqui *m* jerked beef
charrada *f* country dance; boorishness; tawdry ornamentation
charretera *f* epaulet; garter; (*del aguador*) shoulder pad
charriada *f* (Mex) rodeo
cha•rro -rra *adj* coarse, ill-bred; flashy, loud, showy; Salamanca || *mf* peasant; Salamanca peasant || *m* broad-brimmed hat; Mexican cowboy
chasca *f* brushwood
chascar §73 *tr* (*la lengua*) to click; (*algún manjar*) crunch; (*engullir*) swallow || *intr* to crack, crackle
chascarrillo *m* funny story
chas•co -ca *adj* (Arg, Bol) crinkly, crinkly-haired || *m* joke, trick; disappointment; **dar un chasco a** to play a trick on; **llevar** or **llevarse (un) chasco** to be disappointed
chas•cón -cona *adj* (Bol, Chile) disheveled; (Bol, Chile) bushy-haired; (Bol, Chile) clumsy, unskilled
cha•sis *m* (*pl* **-sis**) chassis
chasquear *tr* (*un látigo*) to crack; play a trick on; disappoint || *intr* to crack || *ref* to be disappointed
chasqui *m* (SAm) messenger, courier
chasquido *m* crack; crackle
chata *f* barge, scow; flatcar; bedpan; (Mex) dear, darling
chatarra *f* iron slag; junk, scrap iron
chatarrería *f* junk yard
chatarre•ro -ra *mf* junk dealer, scrapiron dealer
cha•to -ta *adj* flat; flat-nosed; blunt; commonplace; disappointed || *m* wineglass || *f* see **chata**
chatre *adj* (Chile, Ecuad) all dressed up
chauvinismo *m* chauvinism
cha•val -vala *adj* (coll) young || *m* lad || *f* lass
chaveta *f* cotter pin; **perder la chaveta** to go out of one's head
chayote *m* chayote, vegetable pear; dunce, fool
chazar §60 *tr* (*la pelota*) to stop; (*el sitio donde paró la pelota*) to mark
che *interj* (SAm) say!, hey!
checar *tr* (Mex) to check
che•co -ca *adj & mf* Czech
checoeslova•co -ca *adj & mf* Czecho-Slovak
Checoeslovaquia *f* Czecho-Slovakia
checoslova•co -ca *adj & mf* Czecho-Slovak
Checoslovaquia *f* Czecho-Slovakia
chechén *m* (Mex) poison ivy
chécheres *mpl* trinkets, junk
chelín *m* shilling
cheque *m* check; **cheque de viajeros** traveler's check
chequear *tr* (CAm, W-I) to check
chequeo *m* control; checkup
chequera *f* checkbook
chévere *adj invar* terrific, fabulous; **¡que chévere!** terrific!
chica *f* lass, little girl; girl; my dear; **chica de cita** call girl; **chica de la vida alegre** party girl
chicalote *m* Mexican poppy
chicle *m* chewing gum
chiclear *intr* (Mex) to chew gum
chi•co -ca *adj* small, little; young || *mf* child, youngster || *m* lad, little boy; young fellow; old man; hand, turn || *f* see **chica**
chicolear *intr* to pay compliments, to flirt || *ref* (Arg, Peru) to enjoy oneself
chico•te -ta *mf* husky youngster || *m* cigar; cigar stub; whip
chicotear *tr* to beat up; kill
chicue•lo -la *adj* small, little || *m* little boy || *f* little girl
chicha *f* corn liquor; **no ser ni chicha ni limonada** to be good for nothing
chícharo *m* pea; (Col) poor cigar; (Mex) apprentice
chicharra *f* harvest fly; chatterbox; **cantar la chicharra** (coll) to be hot and sultry
chicharrón *m* residue of hog's fat; burnt meat; sunburned person; wrinkled person
chiche *adj invar* nice, pretty
chichear *tr & intr* to hiss
chi•chón -chona *adj* (CAm) easy; (SAm) joking; (Guat) large-breasted || *m* lump, bump on the head
chifla *f* hissing, whistling; paring knife; **estar de chifla** (Mex) to be in a bad humor
chifla•do -da *adj* (coll) daffy, nutty || *mf* crackbrain, nut
chifladura *f* daffiness, nuttiness; whim, wild idea
chiflar *tr* (*a un actor*) to hiss; (*vino o licor*) to gulp down; (*el cuero*) to pare || *intr* to whistle; (*las aves*) (Guat, Mex) to sing || *ref* to go crazy
chifle *m* whistle; (*para cazar aves*) bird call; powder flask
chiflido *m* whistle, hiss

chiflón *m* (SAm) cold blast of air; rapids; slide of loose stone
chilaba *f* jelab, jellaba
Chile *m* Chile
chile•no -na *adj & mf* Chilean
chilote *m* (CAm) ear of corn
chilla *f* fox call, hare call; clapboard; (Chile) small fox; (Mex) top gallery
chillar *intr* to shriek; to squeak; to hiss, sizzle; (*los colores*) to scream || *ref* to take offense
chillido *m* shriek, scream
chi•llón -llona *adj* shrill, high-pitched; screaming; (*color*) loud
chimenea *f* chimney, smokestack; fireplace, hearth; stovepipe hat; (naut) funnel
chimpancé *m* chimpanzee
china *f* Chinese woman; china, porcelain; pebble; nursemaid; (Col) spinning top || **China** *f* China
chinche *mf* bore, tiresome person || *m* (*clavito de cabeza chata*) thumbtack || *f* (*insecto*) bedbug; **caer** or **morir como chinches** to die like flies
chinchorre•ro -ra *adj* gossipy, mischievous
chincho•so -sa *adj* boring, tiresome
chinero *m* china closet
chines•co -ca *adj* Chinese || **chinescos** *mpl* (mus) bell tree
chingar **§44** *tr* to tipple; (CAm) to bob, dock; (CAm, Mex) to bother, annoy || *ref* to tipple; fail
chin•go -ga *adj* (CAm) short; (CAm) dull, blunt; (CAm) naked
chinguirito *m* cheap rum; swig of liquor
chi•no -na *adj & mf* Chinese || *m* (*idioma*) Chinese; (Col) boy, newsboy; (Mex) curl || *f* see **china**
chipichipi *m* drizzle, mist
Chipre *f* Cyprus
chiquero *m* pigsty; bull pen
chiquillada *f* childish prank
chiqui•to -ta *adj* small, little || *mf* little one || *m* (*de vino*) snifter; (Arg) moment, instant || *f* five cents; **no andarse con** or **en chiquitas** to talk right off the shoulder
chiquitura *f* trifle, small matter
chiribita *f* spark; daisy; **chiribitas** spots before the eyes
chiribitil *m* garret; cubbyhole
chirimbolos *mpl* utensils, vessels
chirimía *f* hornpipe
chiripa *f* (billiards) fluke, scratch; stroke of luck
chirivía *f* parsnip
chirle *adj* insipid, tasteless
chirlo *m* slash or scar on the face
chirlota *f* (Mex) meadow lark
chirona *f* jail, jug
chirriar §77 *intr* to creak, squeak; shriek; hiss, sizzle; sing or play out of tune || *ref* (Col) to go on a spree; (Col) to shiver
chirrido *m* creak, squeak; shriek; hiss, sizzle
chirrión *m* squeaky cart; (SAm) whip
chis *interj* sh-sh!; **¡chis, chis!** pst!
chischás *m* clash of swords
chisguete *m* swig of wine; squirt
chisme *m* piece of gossip; trinket; **chisme de vecindad** idle talker; **chismes** gossip; articles; **chismes de aseo** toilet articles
chismear *intr* to gossip
chismo•so -sa *adj* gossipy, catty || *mf* gossip
chispa *f* spark; (*pequeña cantidad*) drop; lightning; (fig) sparkle, wit; (coll) drunk, spree; (Col) rumor; **coger una chispa** to go on a drunk; **chispa de entrehierro** (elec) jump spark; **chispas** sprinkle (*of rain*); **dar chispa** (Guat, Mex) to work, to click; **echar chispas** to blow up, hit the ceiling
chispeante *adj* sparkling
chispar *tr* to throw (someone) out
chispear *intr* to spark; sparkle; drizzle, sprinkle
chis•po -pa *adj* tipsy || *m* swallow, drink || *f* see **chispa**
chisporrotear *intr* to spark, sputter
chispo•so -sa *adj* sputtering, sparking
chisquero *m* pocket lighter
chistar *intr* to speak, say something; **no chistar** to not say a word
chiste *m* joke; witticism; **caer en el chiste** to get the point; **dar en el chiste** to hit the nail on the head
chistera *f* fish basket; (coll) top hat
chisto•so -sa *adj* funny; witty || *mf* funny person; wit
chita *f* anklebone; quoits; **a la chita callando** quietly, secretly; **dar en la chita** to hit the nail on the head
chiticalla *mf* (*persona que no revela lo que sabe*) (coll) clam || *f* (coll) secret
chito *interj* hush!, sh-sh!
chivato *m* kid, young goat; (*soplón*) squealer; (Bol) apprentice, helper; (Chile) cheap rum
chi•vo -va *mf* kid || *m* billy goat; (Mex) day's wage; (Col, Ecuad, Ven) fit of rage || *f* nanny goat
chocante *adj* shocking; coarse, crude; (Col) annoying; (Mex) disagreeable
chocar **§73** *tr* to shock, annoy, irritate; surprise; (*vasos*) clink; please; **¡choque Vd. esos cinco!** shake! || *intr* to shock; collide; clash, fight
chocarre•ro -ra *adj* coarse, crude || *mf* crude joker
choclo *m* wooden overshoe; (Mex) low shoe; (SAm) tender ear of corn
chocolate *m* chocolate
chocha *f* woodcock
chochear *intr* to be in one's dotage; dote, be infatuated
chochera *f* dotage; (Arg, Peru) favorite
cho•chez *f* (*pl* **-checes**) dotage; doting act or remark
cho•cho -cha *adj* doting; doddering || *m* stick of cinnamon candy; **chochos** candy to quiet a child || *f* see **chocha**
chófer *m* chauffeur
chofeta *f* fire pan (*for lighting cigars*)
cho•lo -la *adj* half-breed (*Indian and white*) || *mf* Indian; half-breed; (Chile) coward; (SAm) darling
cholla *f* (coll) noodle, head; (coll) ability, brains

chomite *m* (Mex) coarse wool; (Mex) woolen skirt
chontal *m* uneducated person
chopo *m* black poplar; gun, rifle; **chopo de Italia** Lombardy poplar; **chopo del Canadá** or **de Virginia** cottonwood; **chopo lombardo** Lombardy poplar
choque *m* shock; collision, impact; clash, conflict, skirmish; (elec) choke, choke coil; **choque en cadena** (aut) pileup, mass collision
choricería *f* sausage shop
chorizo *m* smoked pork sausage
chorlito *m* plover, golden plover; scatterbrains
chorrea•do -da *adj* dirty; spotty
chorrear *intr* to gush, spurt, spout; drip; trickle
chorrera spout, channel; cut, gulley; rapids; lace front, jabot; (Arg) string, stream
chorrillo *m* constant stream; **irse por el chorrillo** to follow the current; **tomar el chorrillo de** to get the habit of
chorro *m* jet, spurt; stream, flow; **a chorros** in abundance; **chorro de arena** sandblast
chotaca•bras *m* (*pl* **-bras**) goatsucker
chotear *tr* to make fun of; (Guat) to keep an eye on
choteo *m* jeering, mocking
choza *f* hut, cabin, lodge
chubasco *m* squall, shower; (fig) temporary setback; **chubasco de agua** rainstorm; **chubasco de nieve** blizzard
chubasco•so -sa *adj* stormy, threatening
chucruta *f* sauerkraut
chucha *f* female dog, bitch; drunk, jag; (Col) opossum; (Col) body odor
chuchaque *m* (Ecuad) hangover
chuchear *tr* (*caza menor*) to trap || *intr* to whisper
chuchería *f* knickknack, trinket; delicacy, tidbit
chu•cho -cha *adj* (CAm) mean, stingy; (*fruto*) (Col) watery; (Col) wrinkled || *m* (coll) dog || *f* see **chucha**
chue•co -ca *adj* (Mex) twisted, bent; (SAm) bow-legged; (Mex) crippled || *m* (Mex) dealing in stolen goods || *f* stump; hockey; hockey ball
chufa *f* groundnut
chufletear *intr* to joke, jest
chula *f* flashy dame (*in lower classes of Madrid*)
chulada *f* light-hearted remark; vulgarity
chul•co -ca *mf* (Bol) baby (*youngest child*)
chulear *tr* to tease; (Mex) to flirt with
chuleta *f* chop, cutlet; slap, smack; (*de los estudiantes*) (coll) crib, pony; **chuleta de cerdo** pork chop; **chuleta de ternera** veal chop; **chuletas** sideburns, side whiskers
chu•lo -la *adj* flashy, sporty; foxy, slick; (Guat, Mex) pretty, cute || *m* sporty fellow (*in lower classes of Madrid*); pimp, procurer; gigolo; butcher's helper; (taur) attendant on foot || *f* see **chula**
chumbera *f* prickly pear
chume•ro -ra *mf* (CAm) apprentice
chunches *mpl* (CAm) junk, stuff
chunga *f* jest, fun
chunguear *ref* to jest, joke
chupa *f* frock, coat; (Arg) drunk, jag; (Arg) tobacco pouch
chupa•do -da *adj* thin, skinny; drunk; (*falda*) tight || *f* suck; pull (*on a cigar*)
chupador *m* teething ring, pacifier
chupaflor *m* (Mex, Ven) hummingbird
chupalla *f* straw hat
chupamirto *m* (Mex) hummingbird
chupar *tr* to suck; (*la hacienda ajena*) milk, sap; absorb || *intr* to suck || *ref* to get thin, lose strength; (*los labios*) smack
chupatin•tas *mf* (*pl* **-tas**) (coll) office drudge
chupete *m* (*para un niño*) pacifier; lollipop; **de chupete** fine, splendid
chu•pón -pona *mf* swindler || *m* (bot) sucker, shoot; (mach) plunger; baby bottle; pacifier
chupópte•ro -ra *mf* sponger
chuquisa *f* (Chile, Peru) prostitute
churrasco *m* barbecue
churrasquear *tr* to barbecue
churre *m* filth, dirt, grease
churrete *m* dirty spot (*on hands or face*)
churrigueres•co -ca *adj* churrigueresque; loud, flashy, tawdry
chu•rro -rra *adj* (*lana*) coarse; (*carnero*) coarse-wooled || *m* coarse-wooled sheep; fritter; botch
churrulle•ro -ra *adj* gossipy, loquacious || *mf* gossip, chatterbox
churrusco *m* burnt piece of bread
churumbela *f* hornpipe, flageolet; maté cup; (Col) worry, anxiety; (Col, Ecuad) pipe
churumo *m* (coll) substance (*money, brains, etc.*)
chus *interj* here! (*to call a dog*); **no decir chus ni mus** to not say boo
chus•co -ca *adj* droll, funny; (Peru) ill-mannered; (*perro*) (Peru) mongrel
chusma *f* galley slaves; mob, rabble
chuza *f* (Mex) strike (*in bowling*)

D

D, d (de) *f* fifth letter of the Spanish alphabet
D. *abbr* **don**
D.ª *abbr* **doña**
daca give me, hand over; **andar al daca y toma** to be at cross purposes
dactilógra•fo -fa *mf* typist || *m* typewriter
dactilograma *m* fingerprint
dádiva *f* gift, present
dadivo•so -sa *adj* liberal, generous
da•do -da *adj* given; **dado que** provided, as

long as || *m* die; **cargar los dados** to load the dice; **dados** dice; **el dado está tirado** the die is cast

daga *f* dagger

dalia *f* dahlia

dama *f* lady, dame; maid-in-waiting; (*en el juego de damas*) king; (*en el ajedrez y los naipes*) queen; (theat) leading lady; concubine, mistress; **dama joven** (theat) young lead; **damas** checkers; **señalar dama** (*en el juego de damas*) to crown a man

damajuana *f* demijohn

damasquina•do -da *adj & m* damascene

damasquinar *tr* to damascene

damasqui•no -na *adj* damascene

damero *m* checkerboard

damisela *f* young lady; courtesan

damnación *f* damnation

damnificar **§73** *tr* to damage, hurt

da•nés -nesa *adj* Danish || *mf* Dane || *m* (*idioma*) Danish

dáni•co -ca *adj* Danish

Danubio *m* Danube

danza *f* dance; dancing; dance team; **danza de cintas** Maypole dance; **danza de figuras** square dance; **meter en la danza** to drag in, involve

danza•dor -dora *mf* dancer

danzar **§60** *tr* to dance || *intr* to dance; butt in

danza•rín -rina *mf* dancer; meddler, scatterbrain

dañable *adj* harmful; reprehensible

daña•do -da *adj* bad, wicked; spoiled

dañar *tr* to hurt, damage, injure; spoil || *ref* to be damaged; spoil

dañi•no -na *adj* harmful, destructive, noxious; wicked

daño *m* damage, harm; (Arg) witchcraft; **a daño de** on the responsibility of; **daños y perjuicios** (law) damages; **en daño de** to the detriment of; **hacer daño** to be harmful; **hacer daño a** to hurt; **hacerse daño** to hurt oneself; to get hurt

daño•so -sa *adj* harmful, injurious

dar **§23** *tr* to give; cause; hit, strike; (*el reloj la hora*) strike; (*cartas*) deal; (*un paseo*) take; (*los buenos días*) wish; (*un film*) show; (*una capa de pintura*) put on, apply; **dar a conocer** to make known; **dar a luz** to bring out, publish; **dar cuerda a** (*un reloj*) to wind; **dar curso a** to circulate; **dar de beber a** to give something to drink to; **dar de comer a** to give something to eat to; **dar la razón a** to admit that (*someone*) is right; **dar prestado** to lend; **dar palmadas** to clap the hands; **dar por** to consider as; **dar que hablar** to cause talk; to stir up criticism; **dar que hacer** to cause annoyance or trouble; **dar que pensar** to give food for thought; to give rise to suspicion || *intr* to take place; to hit, strike; (*el reloj; dos, tres, etc. horas*) to strike; to tell, intimate; **dar a** to overlook; **dar con** to run into; **dar contra** to run against, strike against; **dar de sí** to stretch, to give; **dar en** to overlook; to hit; to run into; to fall into; to be bent on; (*un chiste*) to catch on to; **dar sobre** to overlook; **dar tras** to pursue hotly || *ref* to give oneself up; to give in, yield; to occur, be found; **darse a** to devote oneself to; **darse a conocer** to make a name for oneself, make oneself known; to get to know each other; **darse cuenta de** to realize, become aware of; **darse la mano** to shake hands; **dárselas de** to pose as; **darse por aludido** to take the hint; **darse por entendido** to show an understanding; to show appreciation; **darse por ofendido** to take offense; **darse por vencido** to give up, to acknowledge defeat

dardo *m* dart; cutting remark

dares y tomares *mpl* quarrels, disputes

dársena *f* basin, marina, inner harbor

darvinia•no -na *adj & mf* Darwinian, Darwinist

darvinismo *m* Darwinism

data *f* date; (*en una cuenta*) item; **de larga data** of long standing; **estar de mala data** to be in a bad humor

datar *tr & intr* to date; **datar de** to date from

dátil *m* date

datilera *f* date, date palm

dati•vo -va *adj & m* dative

dato *m* datum; basis, foundation

de *prep* of; from; about; **acompañado de** accompanied by; **cubierto de** covered with; **de noche** in the nighttime; **de no llegar nosotros a la hora** if we do not arrive on time; **más de** more than; **tratar de** to try to

deán *m* (eccl) dean

deanato *m* or **deanazgo** *m* deanship

debajo *adv* below, underneath; **debajo de** below, under

debate *m* debate; altercation, argument

debatir *tr & intr* to debate; fight, argue || *ref* to struggle

debe *m* debit

debelar *tr* to conquer, vanquish

deber *m* duty; (*deuda*) debt; homework, school work; **últimos deberes** last rites || *tr* to owe || *v aux* to have to, ought to, must, should; **deber de** must, most likely || *ref* to be committed; **deberse a** to be due to

debidamente *adv* duly

debi•do -da *adj* due, owed; proper, right; **debido a** due to

débil *adj* weak

debilidad *f* weakness, debility

debilitar *tr & ref* to weaken

débito *m* debt, debit; responsibility

debutante *mf* debutant(e), beginner

debutar *intr* to make one's start, appear for the first time

década *f* decade

decadencia *f* decadence

decadente *adj & mf* decadent

decaer **§15** *intr* to decay, decline, fail, weaken; (naut) to drift from the course

decampar *intr* (mil) to decamp

decanato *m* deanship

decano *m* dean

decanta•do -da *adj* puffed-up, overrated

decapitar *tr* to decapitate

decelerar *tr, intr, & ref* to decelerate
decencia *f* decency
decenio *m* decade
dece•no -na *adj & m* tenth
decentar §2 *tr* to cut the first slice of; begin to damage || *ref* to get bedsores
decente *adj* decent, proper; decent-looking
decepción *f* disappointment
decepcionar *tr* to disappoint
decidi•do -da *adj* decided, determined
decidir *tr* to decide; persuade || *intr & ref* to decide
deci•dor -dora *adj* facile, fluent, witty
decimal *adj & m* decimal
déci•mo -ma *adj & m* tenth
decimocta•vo -va *adj* eighteenth
decimocuar•to -ta *adj* fourteenth
decimono•no -na *adj* nineteenth
decimonove•no -na *adj* nineteenth
decimoquin•to -ta *adj* fifteenth
decimoséptí•mo -ma *adj* seventeenth
decimosex•to -ta *adj* sixteenth
decimoterce•ro -ra *adj* thirteenth
decimoter•cio -cia *adj* thirteenth
decir *m* say-so; **al decir de** according to || §24 *tr* to say; tell; (*disparates*) talk; **como si dijéramos** so to speak, in a manner of speaking; **decir entre sí** to say to oneself; **decirle a uno cuántas son cinco** to tell a person what's what; **decir para sí** to say to oneself; **decir por decir** to talk for talk's sake; **decir que no** to say no; **decir que sí** to say yes; **decírselo a una persona deletreado** to spell it out to a person; **es decir** that is to say; **mejor dicho** rather; **¡por algo te lo dije!** I told you so!; **por decirlo así** so to speak || *intr* to suit, fit; **¡diga!** (*al contestar el teléfono*) hello! || *ref* to be said; be called; **se dice** it is said, they say
decisión *f* decision
decisi•vo -va *adj* decisive
declamar *tr & intr* to declaim
declaración *f* declaration; (*en bridge*) bid; **declaración de renta** tax return
declarante *mf* declarant, deponent; (*en el juego de bridge*) bidder
declarar *tr* to declare; (*en bridge*) bid; (law) to depose || *ref* to declare oneself; break out, take place
declarati•vo -va *adj* declarative
declinación *f* declination; fall, drop; decline; (gram) declension
declinar *tr & intr* to decline
declive *m* descent, declivity, slope
declividad *f* declivity
decodificador *m* (telv) decoder
decollaje *m* (aer) take-off
decollar *intr* (aer) to take off
decomisar *tr* to seize, confiscate
decomiso *m* seizure, confiscation
decoración *f* decoration; memorizing; (theat) set, scenery; **decoraciones** (theat) scenery; **decoración interior** interior decoration
decorado *m* decoration; (theat) décor, scenery; memorizing
decora•dor -dora *mf* decorator
decorar *tr* to decorate; memorize
decoro *m* decorum; honor, respect; decency, propriety
decoro•so -sa *adj* decorous; respectful; decent
decrecer §22 *intr* to decrease, grow smaller, grow shorter
decrepitar *intr* to crackle
decrépi•to -ta *adj* decrepit
decretar *tr* to decree
decreto *m* decree
decurso *m* course; **en el decurso de** in the course of
dechado *m* sample, model, example; (*labor de las niñas*) sampler
dedada *f* touch, spot; **dar una dedada de miel a** to feed the hopes of
dedal *m* thimble
dedalera *f* foxglove
dedeo *m* (mus) finger dexterity
dedicación *f* dedication; (*aplicación*) diligence
dedicar §73 *tr* to dedicate; devote; autograph || *ref* to devote oneself
dedicatoria *f* dedication
dedil *m* fingerstall
dedillo *m* little finger; **saber** or **tener al dedillo** to have at one's finger tips, have a thorough knowledge of
dedo *m* finger; toe; bit; **alzar el dedo** (*en señal de dar palabra*) to raise one's hand; **cogerse los dedos** to burn one's fingers; **dedo auricular** little finger; **dedo cordial, de en medio,** or **del corazón** middle finger; **dedo gordo** thumb; big toe; **dedo índice** index finger, forefinger; **dedo meñique** little finger; **dedo mostrador** forefinger; **dedo pulgar** thumb; big toe; **estar a dos dedos de** to be within an ace of; **irse de entre los dedos** (coll) to slip between the fingers; **tener en la punta de los dedos** to have at one's fingertips
deducción *f* deduction; drawing off
deducir §19 *tr* (*concluir*) to deduce; (*rebajar*) deduct; (law) to allege
defecar §73 *intr* to defecate
defección *f* defection
defeccionar *intr & ref* (Chile) to defect
defecti•vo -va *adj* defective
defecto *m* defect; shortage, lack; **en defecto de** for lack of
defectuo•so -sa *adj* defective; lacking
defender §51 *tr* to defend; protect; delay, interfere with
defensa *f* defense; fender, guard; (*del toro*) horn; (*del elefante*) tusk; (*del automóvil*) bumper; **defensa marítima** (Arg) sea wall; **defensa propia** self-defense
defensi•vo -va *adj & f* defensive
defen•sor -sora *adj* defending || *mf* defender; (law) counsel for the defense
deferencia *f* deference
deferente *adj* deferential
deferir §68 *tr* to delegate || *intr* to defer
deficiencia *f* deficiency
deficiente *adj* deficient
défi•cit *m* (*pl* **-cits**) deficit
deficita•rio -ria *adj* deficit

definición *f* definition; decision, verdict
defini•do -da *adj* definite; sharp, defined
definir *tr* to define; settle, determine
definiti•vo -va *adj* definitive; **en definitiva** after all, in short
deflación *f* deflation
deflector *m* baffle
deformación *f* deformation; (rad) distortion
deformar *tr* to deform; disfigure; distort
deforme *adj* deformed
deformidad *f* deformity; gross error
defraudar *tr* to defraud, cheat; (*las esperanzas de una persona*) defeat; (*la claridad del día*) cut off
defuera *adv* outside; **por defuera** on the outside
defunción *f* decease, demise
degeneración *f* (*acción y efecto de degenerar*) degeneration; (*estado de degenerado; depravación*) degeneracy
degenera•do -da *adj & mf* degenerate
degenerar *intr* to degenerate
deglutir *tr & intr* to swallow
degollar §3 *tr* to cut the throat of; kill, massacre; (*un vestido*) cut low in the neck; (*el actor una obra dramática*) butcher, murder; become obnoxious to
degradante *adj* degrading
degradar *tr* to degrade; (mil) to break
degüello *m* throat-cutting; massacre; (*de un arma*) neck; **tirar a degüello** to try to harm
degustar *tr* (*probar*) to taste; (*percibir con deleite el sabor de*) to savor
dehesa *f* pasture land, meadow; (taur) range
deidad *f* deity
deificar §73 *tr* to deify
dejación *f* abandonment; (CAm, Chile, Col) negligence
dejadez *f* laziness; negligence; slovenliness; low spirits
deja•do -da *adj* lazy; negligent; slovenly; dejected
dejamiento *m* laziness; negligence; indolence, languor, indifference
dejar *tr* to leave; abandon; let, allow, permit; **dejar caer** to drop, let fall; **dejar feo** to slight; **dejar fresco** to leave in the lurch; **dejar por** + *inf* or **que** + *inf* to leave (*something*) to be + *pp*, e.g., **hemos dejado dos manuscritos por corregir** or **que corregir** we left two manuscripts to be corrected || *intr* to stop; **dejar de** to stop, cease; fail to || *ref* to be slovenly, neglect oneself; (*una barba*) grow; **dejarse de** (*disparates*) to cut out; (*preguntas*) stop asking; (*dudas*) put aside; **dejarse ver** to show up; be evident
dejillo *m* (*gusto que deja alguna comida*) aftertaste; (*acento regional*) local accent
dejo *m* (*gusto que deja alguna comida*) aftertaste; abandonment; slovenliness, neglect; local accent; (*placer o disgusto que queda después de hecha una cosa*) (fig) aftertaste
delación *f* accusation, denunciation
delantal *m* apron
delante *adv* before, ahead, in front; **delante de** before, ahead of, in front of
delantera *f* front; front row; advantage, lead; cowcatcher; **coger** or **tomar la delantera a** to get ahead of; get a start on; **delanteras** overalls
delante•ro -ra *adj* front, foremost, first || *m* — **delantero centro** (*fútbol*) center forward || *f* see **delantera**
delatar *tr* to accuse, denounce
delega•do -da *mf* delegate
delegar §44 *tr* to delegate
deleitable *adj* delectable, enjoyable
deleitar *tr & ref* to delight
deleite *m* delight
deleito•so -sa *adj* delightful
deletrear *tr & intr* to spell; decipher
deletreo *m* spelling
deleznable *adj* (*poco durable*) perishable; (*que se rompe fácilmente*) crumbly, fragile; (*que se desliza con facilidad*) slippery
delfín *m* (*primogénito del rey de Francia*) dauphin; (*mamífero cetáceo*) dolphin
delgadez *f* thinness, leanness; delicateness, lightness; perspicacity
delga•do -da *adj* thin, lean; delicate, light; sharp, perspicacious; (*terreno*) poor, exhausted || *adv* — **hilar delgado** to hew close to the line; split hairs
delgadu•cho -cha *adj* skinny; slight
deliberar *tr & intr* to deliberate
delicadeza *f* delicacy, delicateness; scrupulousness
delica•do -da *adj* delicate; scrupulous
delicia *f* delight
delicio•so -sa *adj* delicious, delightful
delicti•vo -va *adj* punishable; criminal
delincuencia *f* guilt, criminality
delincuente *adj* guilty, criminal || *mf* criminal
delineante *mf* designer || *m* draughtsman
delinquir §25 *intr* to transgress, be guilty
deliquio *m* faint, swoon; weakening
delirante *adj* delirious
delirar *intr* to be delirious, rant, rave; talk nonsense
delirio *m* delirium; nonsense
delito *m* crime; **delito de incendio** arson; **delito de lesa majestad** lese majesty; **delito de mayor cuantía** (law) felony; **delito de menor cuantía** (law) misdemeanor
deludir *tr* to delude
demacra•do -da *adj* emaciated, wasted, thin
demago•go -ga *mf* demagogue
demanda *f* demand, petition; charity box; lawsuit; undertaking; (*del Santo Grial*) quest; **demanda maxima** (elec) peak load; **en demanda de** in search of; **tener demanda** to be in demand
demanda•do -da *mf* (law) defendant
demandante *mf* (law) complainant, plaintiff
demandar *tr* to ask for, request; (law) to sue || *intr* (law) to sue, bring suit
demarcar §73 *tr* to demarcate
demás *adj* — **el demás . . .** the other. . . , the rest of the . . . ; **estar demás** to be useless, to be in the way; **lo demás** the

rest; **por lo demás** furthermore, besides || *pron* others; **los demás** the others, the rest || *adv* besides; **por demás** in vain; too, too much
demasía *f* excess, surplus; daring, boldness; evil, guilt, wrong; insolence; **en demasía** excessively, too much
demasia•do -da *adj & pron* too much; **demasia•dos -das** too many || **demasiado** *adv* too, too much, too hard
demasiar §77 *intr* to go too far
demediar *tr* to divide in half; use up half of; reach the middle of || *intr* to be divided in half
dementa•do -da *adj* insane; demented
demente *adj* insane || *mf* lunatic
democracia *f* democracy
demócrata *mf* democrat
democráti•co -ca *adj* democratic
demoler §47 *tr* to demolish
demolición *f* demolition
demonía•co -ca *adj* demoniacal
demonio *m* demon, devil; **estudiar con el demonio** to be full of devilishness
demora *f* delay
demorar *tr & ref* to delay
demostración *f* demonstration
demostra•dor -dora *mf* demonstrator || *m* hand (*of clock*)
demostrar §61 *tr* to demonstrate
demostrati•vo -va *adj* demonstrative
demudar *tr* to change, alter; disguise, cloak || *ref* to change countenance, color
denegación *f* denial, refusal
denegar §66 *tr* to deny, refuse
denegrecer §22 *tr* to blacken || *ref* to turn black
dengo•so -sa *adj* affected, finicky, overnice; (Col) strutting
dengue *m* affectation, finickiness, overniceness; (Col) strut, swagger
denguear *ref* (Col) to strut, swagger
denigrar *tr* to defame, revile; insult
denominación *f* denomination
denoda•do -da *adj* bold, daring
denostar §61 *tr* to abuse, insult, mistreat
denotar *tr* to denote
densidad *f* density; darkness, confusion
den•so -sa *adj* dense; dark, confused; crowded, thick, close
denta•do -da *adj* toothed; (*sello de correo*) perforated || *m* gear; teeth
dentadura *f* set of teeth; **dentadura artificial** or **postiza** denture
dental *adj & f* dental
dentellada *f* bite; tooth mark
dentellar *intr* (*los dientes*) to chatter
dentellear *tr* to nibble, nibble at
dentera *f* envy; eagerness; **dar dentera** to set the teeth on edge; make the mouth water
dentición *f* teething
dentífri•co -ca *adj* (*pasta, polvos*) tooth || *m* dentifrice
dentista *mf* dentist
dentistería *f* dentistry
dentística *f* (Chile) dentistry
dentro *adv* inside, within; **dentro de** inside, within; **dentro de poco** shortly; **por dentro** on the inside
denuedo *m* bravery, courage, daring
denuesto *m* abuse, insult, mistreatment
denuncia *f* denunciation; report; proclamation
denunciar *tr* to denounce; report; (*la guerra*) proclaim
deparar *tr* to furnish, provide; offer, present
departamento *m* department; (rr) compartment; (*piso*) apartment; naval district (*in Spain*)
departir *intr* to chat, converse
depauperación *f* impoverishment; exhaustion, weakening
depauperar *tr* to impoverish; exhaust, weaken
dependencia *f* dependence, dependency; branch, branch office; relationship, friendship; accessory; personnel
depender *intr* to depend; **depender de** to depend on; be attached to, belong to
dependienta *f* female employee, clerk
dependiente *adj* dependent; branch || *mf* employee, clerk
deplorable *adj* deplorable
deplorar *tr* to deplore
deponer §54 *tr* to depose; set aside, remove; (*las armas*) lay down || *intr* to depose; (*evacuar el vientre*) have a movement; (CAm, Mex) to vomit
deportación *f* deportation
deporta•do -da *mf* deportee
deportar *tr* to deport
deporte *m* sport; outdoor recreation
deportista *mf* sport fan || *m* sportsman || *f* sportswoman
deporti•vo -va *adj* sport, sports
depositante *mf* depositor
depositar *tr* to deposit; (*la esperanza, la confianza*) put, place; (*el equipaje*) check; (*a una persona en seguro*) commit; store || *ref* to deposit, settle
deposita•rio -ria *mf* trustee; (*de un secreto*) repository || *m* public treasurer
depósito *m* deposit; depot, warehouse; tank, reservoir; (*de libros en una biblioteca*) stack; (mil) depot; **depósito comercial** bonded warehouse; **depósito de agua** reservoir; **depósito de cadáveres** morgue; **depósito de cereales** grain elevator; **depósito de equipajes** (rr) checkroom; **depósito de gasolina** (aut) gas tank; **depósito de locomotoras** roundhouse; **depósito de municiones** munition dump
depravación *f* depravity, depravation
deprava•do -da *adj* depraved
depravar *tr* to deprave || *ref* to become depraved
deprecar §73 *tr* to entreat, implore
depreciación *f* depreciation
depreciar *tr & ref* to depreciate
depresión *f* depression; drop, dip; (*en un muro*) recess
deprimir *tr* to depress; press down; push in; belittle; humiliate || *ref* to be depressed; (*la frente de una persona*) recede

depurar *tr* to purify, cleanse; purge
derecha *f* right hand; right-hand side; (pol) right; **a la derecha** on the right, to the right
derechamente *adv* rightly; straight, direct; properly; wisely
derechazo *m* blow with the right; (box) right
dereche•ro -ra *adj* right, just
derechista *adj* rightist || *mf* rightist, right-winger
dere•cho -cha *adj* right; right-hand; right-handed; straight; upright, standing; (CAm) lucky || *m* right; law; exemption, privilege; road, path; (*de tela, papel, tabla*) right side; **derecho consuetudinario** common law; **derecho de gentes** law of nations, international law; **derecho de subscripción** (*a una nueva emisión de acciones*) (com) right; **derecho de tránsito** or **paso** right of way; **derecho internacional** international law; **derecho penal** criminal law; **derechos** dues, fees, taxes; (*de aduana*) duties; **derechos de almacenaje** storage, cost of storage; **derechos de autor** royalty; **derechos del hombre** rights of man; **derechos de propiedad literaria** or **derechos reservados** copyright; **derechos humanos** human rights; **según derecho** by right, by rights || *f* see **derecha** || **derecho** *adv* straight, direct; rightly
deriva (aer, naut) drift; **ir a la deriva** (naut) to drift, be adrift
derivado *m* by-product
derivar *tr* to derive || *intr & ref* to derive, be derived; (aer, naut) to drift
dermatitis *f* dermatitis
derogar §**44** *tr* to abolish, destroy, repeal
derrabar *tr* to dock, cut off the tail of
derrama•do -da *adj* extravagant, lavish
derramamiento *m* pouring, spilling; shedding; spreading; lavishing, wasting
derramar *tr* to pour, spill; (*sangre*) shed; spread, publish abroad; (*dinero*) lavish, waste || *ref* to run over, overflow; spread, scatter; (*una corriente, un río*) open, empty; (*la plumafuente*) leak
derrame *m* pouring, spilling; (*de sangre*) shed, shedding; spread, scattering; lavishing, wasting; overflow; leakage; slope; chamfering; (pathol) discharge, effusion
derrapada *f* or **derrapaje** *f* (aut) skidding
derredor *m* circumference; **al** or **en derredor** around, round about
derrelícto *m* (naut) derelict
derrelínquir §**25** *tr* to abandon, forsake
derrenga•do -da *adj* crooked, out of shape; crippled, lame
derrengar §**44** or §**66** *tr* to bend, make crooked; cripple
derreniego *m* curse
derreti•do -da *adj* madly in love; (*mantequilla*) drawn || *m* concrete
derretimiento *m* thawing, melting; intense love, passion
derretir §**50** *tr* to thaw, melt; (*la mantequilla*) draw; (*la hacienda*) squander || *ref* to thaw, melt; fall madly in love; be quite susceptible; be worried, be impatient
derribar *tr* to destroy, tear down, knock down; wreck; (*un árbol*) fell; bring down, shoot down; overthrow; humiliate || *ref* to fall down, tumble down; throw oneself on the ground
derribo *m* demolition, wrecking; (*de un árbol*) felling; overthrow; (*de un avión enemigo*) bringing down; **derribos** debris, rubble
derrocadero *m* rocky precipice
derrocar §**73** or §**81** *tr* to throw or hurl from a height; ruin, wreck, tear down; bring down, humble, overthrow
derrocha•dor -dora *mf* wastrel, squanderer
derrochar *tr* to waste, squander
derroche *m* wasting, squandering, extravagance
derrota *f* defeat, rout; road, route, way; (*de embarcación*) course
derrotadamente *adv* shabbily, poorly
derrotar *tr* to rout, put to flight; wear out; ruin || *ref* (naut) to drift from the course
derrotero *m* course, route; ship's course
derrotismo *m* defeatism
derrotista *adj & mf* defeatist
derrubiar *tr & ref* to wash away, wear away
derrubio *m* washout
derruir §**20** *tr* to tear down, demolish
derrumbadero *m* crag, precipice; hazard, risky business
derrumbamiento *m* headlong plunge; cave-in, collapse; **derrumbamiento de tierra** landslide
derrumbar *tr* to throw headlong || *ref* to plunge headlong; collapse, cave in, crumble
derrumbe *m* precipice; landslide; cave-in
derviche *m* dervish
desabonar *ref* to drop one's subscription
desabono *m* cancellation of subscription; discredit, disparagement
desabor *m* insipidity, tastelessness
desabotonar *tr* to unbutton || *intr* to blossom, bloom
desabri•do -da *adj* insipid, tasteless; gruff, surly; (*tiempo*) unsettled
desabrigar §**44** *tr* to uncover, bare || *ref* to bare oneself; undress
desabrir *tr* to give a bad taste to; displease, embitter
desabrochar *tr* to unclasp, unbutton, unfasten || *ref* to unbosom oneself
desacalorar *ref* to cool off
desacatamiento *m* incivility, disrespect
desacatar *tr* to treat disrespectfully
desacato *m* incivility, disrespect, contempt; (*para con las cosas sagradas*) profanation
desacelerar *tr & ref* to decelerate
desacerta•do -da *adj* mistaken, wrong
desacertar §**2** *intr* to be mistaken, be wrong
desacierto *m* error, mistake, blunder
desacomoda•do -da *adj* inconvenient; out of work; in straightened circumstances
desacomodar *tr* to inconvenience; discharge, dismiss
desacomodi•do -da *adj* (SAm) rude; impolite
desacomodo *m* discharge, dismissal

desaconseja•do -da *adj* ill-advised
desaconsejar *tr* to dissuade
desacordar §61 *tr* to put out of tune || *ref* to get out of tune; become forgetful
desacorde *adj* out of tune; incongruous
desacostumbra•do -da *adj* unusual
desacostumbrar *tr* to break of a habit
desacreditar *tr* to discredit; disparage
desacuerdo *m* discord, disagreement; error, mistake; unconsciousness; forgetfulness
desadaptación *f* maladjustment
desadeudar *tr* to free of debt || *ref* to get out of debt
desadormecer §22 *tr* to awaken; free of numbness || *ref* to get awake; shake off the numbness
desadorna•do -da *adj* unadorned, plain; bare, uncovered
desadverti•do -da *adj* unnoticed; inattentive
desadvertimiento *m* inadvertence
desafección *f* dislike
desafec•to -ta *adj* adverse, hostile; opposed || *m* dislike
desaferrar *tr* to unfasten, loosen; make (*a person*) change his mind; (*las áncoras*) weigh
desafiar §77 *tr* to challenge, defy, dare; rival, compete with
desafición *f* dislike
desaficionar *tr* to cause to dislike
desafilar *tr* to make dull || *ref* to become dull
desafina•do -da *adj* flat, out of tune
desafío *m* challenge, dare; rivalry, competition
desafora•do -da *adj* colossal, huge; disorderly, outrageous
desafortuna•do -da *adj* unfortunate
desafuero *m* excess, outrage
desagracia•do -da *adj* ungraceful, graceless
desagradable *adj* disagreeable
desagradar *tr & intr* to displease || *ref* to be displeased
desagradeci•do -da *adj* ungrateful
desagradecimiento *m* ungratefulness
desagrado *m* displeasure
desagraviar *tr* to make amends to, indemnify
desagravio *m* amends, indemnification
desagregación *f* disintegration
desagregar §44 *ref* to disintegrate
desaguadero *m* drain, outlet; (*ocasión de continuo gasto*) (fig) drain
desaguar §10 *tr* to drain, empty; squander, waste || *intr* to flow, empty || *ref* to drain, be drained
desagüe *m* drainage, sewerage; drain, outlet
desaguisa•do -da *adj* illegal || *m* offense, outrage, wrong
desahijar *tr* (*las crías del ganado*) to wean || *ref* (*las abejas*) to swarm
desahogadamente *adv* freely; comfortably, easily; impudently
desahoga•do -da *adj* brazen, forward; roomy; in comfortable circumstances
desahogar §44 *tr* to relieve, comfort; (*deseos, pasiones*) give free rein to || *ref* to take it easy, get comfortable; unbosom oneself, open up one's heart; get out of debt; **desahogarse en** (*denuestos*) to burst forth in
desahogo *m* brazenness; ample room; comfort; outlet, relief; comfortable circumstances
desahuciar *tr* to deprive of hope; evict, oust, dispossess || *ref* to lose all hope
desahucio *m* eviction, ousting, dispossession
desaira•do -da *adj* unattractive, unprepossessing; unsuccessful
desairar *tr* to slight, snub, disregard
desaire *m* slight, snub, disregard; unattractiveness, lack of charm
desajustar *tr* to put out of order || *ref* to get out of order; disagree
desalabanza *f* belittling, disparagement
desalabar *tr* to belittle, disparage
desala•do -da *adj* eager, in a hurry
desalar *tr* to desalt; clip the wings of || *ref* to hasten, rush; **desalarse por** to be eager to
desalentar §2 *tr* to put out of breath; discourage || *ref* to become discouraged
desalforjar *ref* to loosen one's clothing
desaliento *m* discouragement
desalinización *f* desalinization
desaliña•do -da *adj* slovenly, untidy; careless, slipshod
desaliño *m* slovenliness, untidiness; carelessness, neglect
desalma•do -da *adj* cruel, inhuman
desalojar *tr* to oust, evict; (*al enemigo*) to dislodge; (*el camino*) to clear || *intr* to leave, move away, move out
desalquila•do -da *adj* vacant, unrented
desalterar *tr* to calm, quiet
desalumbra•do -da *adj* dazzled, blinded; confused, unsure of oneself
desamable *adj* unlikeable, unlovable
desamar *tr* to dislike, hate, detest
desamarrar *tr* to untie, unfasten; (naut) to unmoor
desamistar *ref* to fall out, become estranged
desamor *m* dislike, coldness; hatred
desamorrar *tr* to make (*a person*) talk
desamparar *tr* to abandon, forsake; give up
desamparo *m* abandonment, desertion; helplessness
desamuebla•do -da *adj* unfurnished
desandar §5 *tr* to retrace, go back over
desandraja•do -da *adj* ragged, in tatters
desangrar *tr* to bleed; drain; (fig) to bleed, impoverish || *ref* to lose a lot of blood
desanimación *f* discouragement, downheartedness
desanima•do -da *adj* discouraged, downhearted; (*reunión*) lifeless, dull
desanimar *tr* to discourage, dishearten || *ref* to become discouraged
desánimo *m* discouragement
desanublar *tr & ref* to clear up, brighten up
desanudar *tr* to untie; disentangle
desapacible *adj* unpleasant, disagreeable
desapadrinar *tr* to disavow; disapprove
desaparecer §22 *intr & ref* to disappear
desapareci•do -da *adj* missing; extinct || **desaparecidos** *mpl* missing persons
desaparecimiento *m* disappearance

desaparejar *tr* to unharness, unhitch; (naut) to unrig
desaparición *f* disappearance; (Ven) death
desapasiona•do -da *adj* dispassionate, impartial
desapego *m* dislike, coolness, indifference
desapercibi•do -da *adj* unprepared; wanting; unnoticed
desapiada•do -da *adj* merciless, pitiless
desaplica•do -da *adj* idle, lazy
desapodera•do -da *adj* headlong, impetuous; violent, wild; excessive
desapoderar *tr* to dispossess; deprive of power || *ref* — **desapoderarse de** to lose possession of, give up possession of
desapolillar *tr* to free of moths || *ref* to expose oneself to the weather
desapreciar *tr* to depreciate
desaprecio *m* depreciation
desaprender *tr* to unlearn
desaprensión *f* composure, nonchalance
desapretar §2 *tr* to slacken, loosen; (typ) to unlock
desaprobación *f* disapproval
desaprobar §61 *tr & intr* to disapprove
desapropiar *tr* to divest || *ref*—**desapropiarse de** to divest oneself of
desaprovecha•do -da *adj* unproductive; indifferent, lackadaisical
desaprovechar *tr* to not take advantage of || *intr* to slip back
desarmable *adj* dismountable
desarmador *m* hammer (*of gun*); (Mex) screwdriver
desarmamiento *m* disarmament; arms reduction
desarmar *tr* to disarm; dismount, dismantle, take apart; (*la cólera*) temper, calm || *intr & ref* to disarm
desarme *m* disarmament; dismantling, dismounting
desarraigar §44 *tr* to uproot, dig up; expel, drive out
desarregla•do -da *adj* out of order; slovenly, disorderly; intemperate
desarrimo *m* lack of support; stand-offishness
desarrollar *tr & intr* to develop; unroll, unfold || *ref* to develop; unroll, unfold; take place
desarrollo *m* development; unrolling, unfolding; **ayuda al desarrollo** developmental aid
desarropar *tr & ref* to undress
desarrugar §44 *tr & ref* to unwrinkle
desarzonar *tr* to unsaddle, unhorse
desasea•do -da *adj* dirty, unclean, slovenly
desasentar §2 *tr* to remove; displease || *ref* to stand up
desaseo *m* dirtiness, uncleanliness, slovenliness
desasir §7 *tr* to let go, let go of || *ref* to come loose; let go; **desasirse de** to let go of; give up, get free of
desasosegar §66 *tr* to disquiet, worry, disturb
desasosiego *m* disquiet, worry
desastra•do -da *adj* disastrous; unfortunate, wretched; ragged, shabby
desastre *m* disaster; **ir al desastre** to go to rack and ruin
desastro•so -sa *adj* disastrous
desatacar §73 *tr* to unbuckle, untie
desatar *tr* to untie, undo, unfasten; solve, unravel || *ref* to come loose; free oneself; (*la tempestad*) break loose; forget oneself, go too far; **desatarse en** (*denuestos*) to burst forth in
desatascar §73 *tr* to pull out of the mud; (*un conducto obstruído*) unclog; (*a una persona de un apuro*) extricate
desataviar §77 *tr* to disarray, undress
desatavío *m* disarray, undress, slovenliness
desate *m* (*de palabras*) flood; **desate del vientre** loose bowels
desatención *f* inattention; discourtesy, disrespect
desatender §51 *tr* to slight, disregard, pay no attention to
desatenta•do -da *adj* wild, disorderly, extreme
desaten•to -ta *adj* inattentive; discourteous, disrespectful
desatina•do -da *adj* wild, disorderly; foolish, nonsensical || *mf* fool
desatinar *tr* to bewilder, confuse || *intr* to talk nonsense, act foolishly; lose one's bearings
desatino *m* folly, nonsense; awkwardness, loss of touch
desatolondrar *tr* to bring to || *ref* to come to one's senses
desatollar *tr* to pull out of the mud
desatornillador *m* screwdriver
desatornillar *tr* to unscrew
desatraillar §4 *tr* to unleash
desatrampar *tr* to unclog
desatrancar §73 *tr* to unbar, unbolt; unclog
desatufar *ref* to get out of the close air; cool off, quiet down
desautoriza•do -da *adj* unauthorized
desavenencia *f* disagreement, discord
desavenir §79 *tr* to cause disagreement among || *ref* to disagree; **desavenirse con** to differ with, disagree with
desaventura *f* misfortune
desaviar §77 *tr* to mislead, lead astray
desavisa•do -da *adj* unadvised; ill-advised; thoughtless, careless
desayuna•do -da *adj* — **estar desayunado** to have had breakfast
desayunar *intr* to breakfast || *ref* to breakfast; **desayunarse con** to have breakfast on; **desayunarse de** to get the first news of
desayuno *m* breakfast
desazón *f* insipidity, tastelessness; annoyance, displeasure; discomfort
desazonar *tr* to make tasteless; annoy, displease || *ref* to feel ill
desbancar §73 *tr* to win the bank from; cut out, to supplant
desbandada *f* — **a la desbandada** helter-skelter, in confusion
desbandar *ref* to run away; disband; desert

desbarajustar *tr* to put out of order || *ref* to get out of order, break down
desbarata•do -da *adj* debauched, corrupt || *mf* libertine
desbaratar *tr* to destroy, spoil, ruin; squander, waste; (mil) to rout, throw into confusion || *intr* to talk nonsense || *ref* to be unbalanced
desbarrancadero *m* precipice
desbastar *tr* to smooth off; waste, weaken; (*a una persona inculta*) polish || *ref* to become polished
desbautizar §60 *ref* to lose one's temper
desbeber *intr* (coll) to urinate
desbloquear *tr* to relieve the blockade of; (*crédito*) to unfreeze
desboca•do -da *adj* (*pieza de artillería*) wide-mouthed; (*herramienta*) nicked; (*caballo*) runaway; (*persona*) foul-mouthed
desbocar §73 *tr* to break the mouth of, break the spout of || *intr* (*un río*) to empty; (*una calle*) run, open, end || *ref* (*un caballo*) to run away, break loose; curse, swear
desbordamiento *m* overflow
desbordar *tr* to overwhelm || *intr & ref* to overflow
desbozalar *tr* to unmuzzle
desbravar *tr* to tame, break in || *intr & ref* to abate, moderate; cool off, calm down
desbrozar §60 *tr* to clear of underbrush, clear of rubbish
desbulla *f* oyster shell
desbulla•dor -dora *mf* oyster opener || *m* oyster fork
desbullar *tr* (*la ostra*) to open
descabal *adj* incomplete, imperfect
descabalgar §44 *intr* to dismount, alight from a horse
descabella•do -da *adj* disheveled; rash, wild
descabellar *tr* to muss, dishevel
descabeza•do -da *adj* crazy, rash, wild
descabezar §60 *tr* to behead; (*un árbol*) top; (*una dificultad*) get the best off; **descabezar el sueño** to doze, snooze || *intr* to border || *ref* to rack one's brains
descabullir §13 *ref* to sneak out, slip away; refuse to face the facts
descachalandra•do -da *adj* untidy; tattered
descacharra•do -da *adj* (CAm) dirty, slovenly, ragged
descaecer §22 *intr* to decline, lose ground
descaecimiento *m* weakness; depression, despondency
descalabazar §60 *ref* to rack one's brain
descalabra•do -da *adj* banged on the head; **salir descalabrado** to come out the loser, be worsted
descalabrar *tr* to bang on the head; knock down || *ref* to bang one's head
descalabro *m* misfortune, setback, loss
descalcificar §73 *tr* to decalcify
descalificar §73 *tr* to disqualify
descalzar §60 *tr* (*las botas, los guantes*) to take off; (*a una persona*) take the shoes or stockings off; undermine || *ref* to take one's shoes or stockings off; take one's gloves off; (*las botas, los guantes*) take off; (*el caballo*) lose a shoe
descal•zo -za *adj* barefooted; seedy, down at the heel
descamar *ref* to scale, scale off
descaminadamente *adv* off the road, on the wrong track
descaminar *tr* to mislead, lead astray || *ref* to get lost; run off the road
descamino *m* going astray; leading astray; nonsense; contraband, smuggled goods
descamisa•do -da *adj* shirtless, ragged || *m* wretch, ragamuffin
descampa•do -da *adj* free, open || *m* open country
descansadero *m* resting place, stopping place
descansa•do -da *adj* rested, refreshed; calm, restful
descansar *tr* to rest, relieve; (*la cabeza, el brazo*) rest, lean || *intr* to rest; lean; not worry; (*yacer en el sepulcro*) rest; **descansar en** to trust in
descanso *m* rest; peace, quiet; (*de la escalera*) landing; (theat) intermission; (Chile) toilet
descantillar *tr* to chip off; deduct
descañonar *tr* to pluck; shave against the grain; gyp
descapiruzar §60 *tr* (Col) to muss, rumple, crumple
descapotable *adj & m* (aut) convertible
descara•do -da *adj* barefaced, brazen, saucy
descarar *ref* to be impudent; **descararse a** to have the nerve to
descarga *f* unloading; (*de un arma de fuego*) discharge; (com) discount; (elec) discharge; **descarga de aduana** customhouse clearance
descargar §44 *tr* to unload; (*de una deuda u obligación*) free; (*un arma de fuego*) discharge; (*un golpe*) strike, deal; (elec) to discharge || *intr* to unload; (*un río*) empty; (*una calle, paseo*) open; (*una nube en lluvia*) burst || *ref* to unburden oneself; resign; **descargarse con** or **en uno de algo** to unload something on someone; **descargarse de** to get rid of; resign from; (*una imputación, un cargo*) clear oneself of
descargo *m* unloading; (*de una obligación*) discharge; (*del cargo que se hace a uno*) release, acquittal; receipt
descargue *m* unloading
descariño *m* coolness, indifference
descarnadamente *adv* right off the shoulder, bluntly
descarnar *tr* to remove the flesh from; chip; wear away; detach from earthly matters || *ref* to lose flesh
descaro *m* brazenness, effrontery
descarriar §77 *tr* to mislead, lead astray || *ref* to go wrong, go astray
descarrilamiento *m* derailment
descarrilar *intr* to jump the track; wander from the point || *ref* to jump the track
descartable *adj* disposable

descartar *tr* to cast aside, reject; discard || *ref* to shirk, evade; **descartarse de** (*un compromiso*) to shirk, evade
descarte *m* casting aside, rejection; discarding; (*cartas desechadas*) discard; shirking, evasion
descasar *tr* to divorce; disturb, disarrange
descascar §73 *tr* to husk, shell, peel || *ref* to break to pieces; jabber, talk too much
descascarar *tr* to shell, peel || *ref* to shell off, peel off
descascarillar *tr & ref* to shell, peel
descasta•do -da *adj* ungrateful, ungrateful to one's family
descaudalа•do -da *adj* ruined, penniless
descendencia *f* descent
descendente *adj* descendent, descending; (*tren*) down
descender §51 *tr* to bring down, lower; (*la escalera*) descend, go down || *intr* to descend, go down; flow, run; decline
descendiente *mf* descendant
descenso *m* descent; (*de temperatura*) drop; decline
descentralizar §60 *tr* to decentralize
desceñi•do -da *adj* loose-fitting, loose
descepar *tr* to pull up by the roots; extirpate, exterminate
descerebrar *tr* to brain
descerraja•do -da *adj* corrupt, evil, wicked
desciframiento *m* deciphering, decoding; resolving
descifrar *tr* to decipher, decode, figure out
desclasificar §73 *tr* to disqualify
descocer §16 *tr* to digest
descoco *m* impudence, insolence
descocholla•do -da *adj* (Chile) ragged
descolar *tr* to dock, crop; (*a un empleado*) (CAm) to discharge, fire; (Mex) to slight, snub
descolgar §63 *tr* to unhook; take down, lower; (*el auricular*) pick up || *ref* to come down, come off; to show up suddenly; **descolgarse con** to blurt out
descolón *m* (Mex) slight, snub
descolorar *tr & ref* to discolor, fade
descolori•do -da *adj* faded, off color
descollante *adj* prominent, outstanding; chief, main
descollar §61 *intr* to tower, stand out; (fig) to excel, stand out
descomedi•do -da *adj* immoderate, excessive; rude, discourteous
descomedir §50 *ref* to be rude, be discourteous
descomer *intr* to have a bowel movement
descómo•do -da *adj* inconvenient
descompasa•do -da *adj* extreme, excessive
descompletar *tr* to break (*a set or series*)
descomponer §54 *tr* to decompose; disturb, disorganize; put out of order; set at odds || *ref* to decompose; (*una persona, la salud de una persona*) fall to pieces; (*el tiempo*) change for the worse; (*el rostro*) become distorted; (*un aparato*) get out of order; to lose one's temper; **descomponerse con** to get angry with
descomposición *f* decomposition; disorder, disorganization; discord
descompostura *f* decomposition; disorder, untidiness; brazenness
descompresión *f* decompression
descompues•to -ta *adj* out of order; brazen, discourteous; irritated; drunk
descomulgar §44 *tr* to excommunicate
descomunal *adj* huge, colossal, enormous, extraordinary; (coll) humongous
desconcerta•do -da *adj* out of order; disconcerted, baffled, bewildered; slovenly; unbridled
desconcertar §2 *tr* to put out of order; disturb, upset; (*un hueso*) dislocate; disconcert, bewilder
desconcierto *m* disrepair; disorder; mismanagement; confusion; discomfiture; disagreement; lack of restraint; loose bowels
desconchabar *tr* to dislocate || *ref* to become dislocated; disagree, fall out
desconchado *m* scaly part of wall; (*en la porcelana*) chip
desconchar *tr & ref* to chip, chip off; scale off
desconectar *tr* to detach; disconnect
desconfia•do -da *adj* distrustful, suspicious
desconfianza *f* distrust
desconfiar §77 *intr* to lose confidence; **desconfiar de** to lose confidence in, to distrust
desconformar *intr* to dissent, disagree || *ref* to not go well together
descongelación *f* thaw, thawing out
descongelador *m* defroster
descongelar *tr* to melt; defrost; (com) to unfreeze
descongestión *f* decongestion; freeing up
descongestionar *tr* to decongest; free up
desconocer §22 *tr* to not know; disavow, disown; not recognize; slight, ignore; not see || *ref* to be unknown; be quite changed, be unrecognizable
desconocidamente *adv* unknowingly
desconoci•do -da *adj* unknown; strange, unfamiliar; ungrateful || *mf* unknown, unknown person
desconsentir §68 *tr* to not consent to
desconsidera•do -da *adj* ill-considered; inconsiderate
desconsola•do -da *adj* disconsolate, downhearted; (*estómago*) weak
desconsuelo *m* disconsolateness, grief; upset stomach
descontaminación *f* decontamination; **descontaminación de radiactividad** radioactive decontamination
descontar §61 *tr* to discount; deduct; take for granted; **dar por descontado que** to take for granted that
descontentadi•zo -za *adj* hard to please
desconten•to -ta *adj & m* discontent
descontinuar §21 *tr* to discontinue
descontrola•do -da *adj* uncontrolled; deregulated
descontrolar *tr* (com) deregulate; decontrol
desconvenar *tr* to call off

desconvenir §79 *intr* to disagree; not go together, not match; not be suitable || *ref* to disagree
desconvidar *tr* to cancel an invitation to; (*lo prometido*) take back
descopar *tr* to tcp (*a tree*)
descorazonar *tr* to discourage
descorchar *tr* to remove the bark from; (*una botella*) uncork; break into
descornar §61 *tr* to dehorn || *ref* to rack one's brains
descorrer *tr* to run back over; (*una cortina, un cerrojo*) draw || *intr & ref* to flow, run off
descortés *adj* discourteous, impolite
descortesía *f* discourtesy, impoliteness
descortezar §60 *tr* to strip the bark from; take the crust off; polish || *ref* to become polished
descoser *tr* to unstitch, rip || *ref* to loose one's tongue; (coll) to break wind
descosi•do -da *adj* disorderly, wild; indiscreet; desultory || *m* wild man; rip, open seam
descote *m* low neck
descoyuntar *tr* to dislocate; bore, annoy || *ref* (*p.ej., el brazo*) to throw out of joint
descrédito *m* discredit
descreer §43 *tr* to disbelieve; discredit || *intr* to disbelieve
descreí•do -da *adj* disbelieving, unbelieving || *mf* disbeliever, unbeliever
descriar §77 *ref* to spoil; waste away
describir §83 to describe
descripción *f* description
descripti•vo -va *adj* descriptive
descto. *abbr* **descuento**
descuadrar *intr* to disagree; **descuadrar con** (Mex) to displease
descuajar *tr* to liquefy, dissolve; uproot; discourage || *ref* to liquefy; drudge
descuartizar §60 *tr* to tear to pieces; quarter
descubierta *f* open pie; inspection; reconnoitering; (naut) scanning the horizon; **a la descubierta** openly; in the open; reconnoitering
descubiertamente *adv* clearly, openly
descubier•to -ta *adj* bareheaded; (*campo*) bare, barren; (*expuesto a reconvenciones*) under fire || *m* deficiency, shortage; exposition of the Holy Sacrament; **al descubierto** in the open; unprotected; (*sin tener disponibles las acciones que se venden*) short, e.g., **vender al descubierto** to sell short || *f* see **descubierta**
descubri•dor -dora *mf* discoverer || *m* (mil) scout
descubrimiento *m* discovery
descubrir §83 *tr* to discover; uncover, lay open, reveal; invent; (*p.ej., una estatua*) unveil || *ref* to take off one's hat, uncover; be discovered; open one's heart
descuello *m* excellence, superiority; great height; haughtiness
descuento *m* discount; deduction, rebate
descuerar *tr* (Chile) to skin, flay; (Chile) to discredit, flay
descuerno *m* slight, snub
descuida•do -da *adj* careless, negligent; slovenly, dirty; off guard
descuidar *tr* to overlook, neglect; divert, distract, relieve || *ref* to be careless, not bother; be diverted
descuide•ro -ra *mf* sneak thief
descuido *m* carelessness, negligence, neglect; slip, mistake, blunder; oversight; **al descuido** with studied carelessness; **en un descuido** when least expected
descuita•do -da *adj* carefree
deschavetar *intr* to get rattled; go mad; flip one's lid
desde *prep* since, from; after; **desde ahora** from now on; **desde entonces** since then, ever since; **desde hace** for, e.g., **estoy aquí desde hace cinco días** I've been here for five days; **desde luego** at once; of course; **desde que** since
desdecir §24 (*impv sg* **-dice**) *intr* to slip back; be out of harmony || *ref* — **desdecirse de** to take back, retract
desdén *m* scorn, disdain; **al desdén** with studied neglect
desdenta•do -da *adj* toothless
desdeñar *tr* to scorn, disdain || *ref* to be disdainful; **desdeñarse de** to loathe, despise; not deign to
desdeño•so -sa *adj* scornful, disdainful
desdicha *f* misfortune; indigence
desdicha•do -da *adj* unfortunate, unlucky; poor, wretched; backward, timid
desdinerar *tr* to impoverish
desdoblar *tr & intr* to unfold, spread open; split, divide
desdorar *tr* to remove the gold or gilt from; tarnish, sully; disparage
desdoro *m* tarnish, blemish, blot; disparagement
deseable *adj* desirable
desear *tr* to desire, wish
desecar §73 *tr & ref* to dry; drain
desechable *adj* disposable
desechar *tr* to discard, throw out, cast aside; underrate; blame, censure; (*la llave de una puerta*) turn
desecho *m* remainder; offal, rubbish; castoff; scorn, contempt; short cut; **desecho de hierro** scrap iron
desegregación *f* desegregation
desellar *tr* to unseal
desembalaje *m* unpacking
desembalar *tr* to unpack
desembarazar §60 *tr* to free, clear, empty, open || *ref* to free oneself; be cleared, emptied; **desembarazarse de** to get rid of
desembarazo *m* naturalness, lack of restraint; delivery, childbirth; **con desembarazo** naturally, readily
desembaracadero *m* wharf, pier, landing
desembarcar §73 *tr* to unload, debark, disembark || *intr* to land, debark, disembark; (*de un carruaje*) get out, alight; (*la escalera al plano bajo*) end || *ref* to land, debark, disembark

desembarco *m* landing, debarkation, disembarkation; (*de la escalera*) landing
desembarque *m* unloading, debarkation, disembarkation
desembocadura *f* (*de una calle*) opening, outlet; (*de un río*) mouth
desembocar §73 *intr* (*una calle*) open, to end; (*un río*) flow, empty
desembolsar *tr* to disburse, pay out
desembolso *m* disbursement, payment
desembragar §44 *tr* (*el motor*) to disengage || *intr* to throw the clutch out
desembrague *m* disengagement, clutch release
desembravecer §22 *tr* to tame; calm, quiet, pacify
desembriagar §44 *tr & ref* to sober up
desembrollar *tr* to untangle, unravel
desemejante *adj* — **desemejante de** dissimilar from or to, unlike; **desemejantes** dissimilar, unlike
desemejar *tr* to change, disfigure || *intr* to be different, not look alike
desempacar §73 *tr* to unpack, unwrap || *ref* to cool off, calm down
desempalagar §44 *tr* to rid of nausea || *ref* to get rid of nausea
desempañar *tr* (*el vidrio*) to wipe the steam or smear from; take the diaper off
desempapelar *tr* to unwrap; (*una pared, una habitación*) scrape the wallpaper from
desempaquetar *tr* to unpack; unwrap
desempatar *tr* to break the tie between; (*los votos*) break the tie in
desempate *m* breaking a tie
desempedrar §2 *tr* to remove the paving stones from; (*un sitio empedrado*) pound; **ir desempedrando la calle** to dash down the street
desempeñar *tr* (*un papel*) to play (*a rôle*); (*un cargo*) fill, perform; (*a uno de un empeño*) disengage; (*un deber*) discharge; free of debt; take out of hock || *ref* to get out of a jam; get out of debt
desempeño *m* acting, performance; disengagement; (*de un deber*) discharge; payment of a debt; taking out of hock
desempernar *tr* to unbolt
desemplea•do -da *adj & mf* unemployed
desempleo *m* unemployment; **desempleo en masa** mass unemployment
desempolvar *tr* to dust; renew, take up again || *ref* to brush up
desempolvorar *tr* to dust, dust off
desenamorar *tr* to alienate; *ref* to grow apart; **desenamorarse de** to get fed up with
desencadenar *tr* to unchain, unleash || *ref* to break loose
desencajar *tr* to dislocate; disconnect || *ref* to get out of joint; (*el rostro*) be contorted
desencaminar *tr* to lead astray, mislead
desencantamiento *m* disenchantment, disillusion
desencantar *tr* to disenchant, disillusion
desencantarar *tr* (*nombres o números*) to draw; (*un nombre o nombres*) exclude from balloting
desencanto *m* disenchantment, disillusion
desencarecer §22 *tr* to lower the price of || *intr & ref* to come down in price
desencerrar §2 *tr* to release, set free; disclose, reveal
desencoger §17 *tr* to unfold, spread out || *ref* to relax, shake off one's timidity
desencolar *tr* to unglue || *ref* to become unglued
desenconar *tr* to take the soreness out of; calm down
desenchufar *tr* to unplug, disconnect
desendiosar *tr* to bring down a peg
desenfadaderas *fpl* — **tener buenas desenfadaderas** to be resourceful
desenfada•do -da *adj* free, easy, unconstrained
desenfado *m* ease, naturalness; relaxation, calmness
desenfoca•do -da *adj* out of focus
desenfrena•do -da *adj* unbridled, wanton, licentious
desenfrenar *tr* to unbridle|| *ref* to yield to temptation; fly into a passion; (*la tempestad, el viento*) break loose
desenfreno *m* unruliness, wantonness, licentiousness
desenfundar *tr* to take out of its sheath, bag, pillowcase, etc.
desenganchar *tr* to unhook, uncouple, unfasten, disengage; to unhitch
desenganche *m* unhooking, disengaging; unhitching
desengañar *tr* to disabuse, undeceive; disillusion; disappoint
desengaño *m* disabusing; disillusionment; disappointment; plain fact, plain truth
desengrana•do -da *adj* out of gear
desengranar *tr* to unmesh; disengage, throw out of gear
desengraso *m* (Chile) dessert
desenlace *m* outcome, result; (*de un drama, novela, etc.*) dénouement
desenlazar §60 *tr* to untie; solve; (*el nudo de un drama*) unravel
desenmarañar *tr* to disentangle; (*una cosa obscura*) unravel
desenmascarar *tr* to unmask || *ref* to take one's mask off
desenojar *tr* to appease, free of anger || *ref* to calm down; be amused
desenredar *tr* to disentangle; clear up || *ref* to extricate oneself
desenredo *m* disentanglement; (*de un drama, novela, etc.*) dénouement
desenrollar *tr* to unroll, unwind, unreel
desensartar *tr* to unstring, unthread
desensillar *tr* to unsaddle (*a horse*)
desentablar *tr* to disrupt; break off (*a bargain, friendship, etc.*)
desentender §51 *ref* — **desentenderse de** to take no part in, not participate in; affect ignorance of, pretend to be unaware of
desenterrar §2 *tr* to dig up; disinter; (fig) to unearth, dig up; (fig) to recall to mind
desentona•do -da *adj* out of tune, flat

desentonar *tr* to humble, bring down a peg ‖ *intr* to be out of tune; be out of harmony ‖ *ref* to talk loud and disrespectfully
desentono *m* dissonance, false note; loud tone of voice
desentornillar *tr* to unscrew
desentrampar *ref* to get out of debt
desentrañar *tr* to disembowel; figure out, unravel ‖ *ref* to give away all that one has
desentrena•do -da *adj* out of training
desentronizar **§60** *tr* to dethrone; strip of influence
desentumecer **§22** *tr* to relieve of numbness ‖ *ref* to be relieved of numbness
desenvainar *tr* to unsheathe; (*las uñas el animal*) show, stretch out; bare, uncover
desenvoltura *f* naturalness, ease of manner, offhandedness; fluency; lewdness, boldness (*chiefly in women*)
desenvolver **§47 & §83** *tr* to unfold, unroll, unwrap; unwind; unravel, clear up; develop ‖ *ref* to unroll; unwind; develop, evolve; extricate oneself; be forward
desenvuel•to -ta *adj* free and easy, offhand; fluent; brazen, bold, lewd
deseo *m* desire, wish
deseo•so -sa *adj* desirous, anxious
desequilibra•do -da *adj* unbalanced
desequilibrar *tr* to unbalance ‖ *ref* to become unbalanced
desequilibrio *m* disequilibrium, imbalance; derangement, mental instability
deserción *f* desertion
desertar *tr & intr* to desert
desertor *m* deserter
deservicio *m* disservice
desesperación *f* despair; **ser una desesperación** to be unbearable
desespera•do -da *adj* despairing, desperate ‖ *mf* desperate person
desesperanza *f* hopelessness
desesperanza•do -da *adj* hopeless
desesperanzar **§60** *tr* to discourage ‖ *ref* to lose hope
desesperar *tr* to drive to despair; exasperate ‖ *intr* to lose hope; be exasperated ‖ *ref* to be desperate, lose all hope
desestancar **§73** *tr* to open up, unclog; make free of duty; open the market to
desestimar *tr* to hold in low regard; refuse, reject
deséxito *m* failure
desfachata•do -da *adj* brazen, impudent
desfachatez *f* brazenness, impudence
desfalcar **§73** *tr & intr* to embezzle
desfalco *m* embezzlement
desfallecer **§22** *tr* to weaken ‖ *intr* to grow weak; faint, faint away; lose courage
desfalleci•do -da *adj* weak; faint
desfallecimiento *m* weakness; fainting; discouragement
desfavorable *adj* unfavorable
desfigurar *tr* to disfigure; distort, misrepresent; disguise; change, alter ‖ *ref* to look different
desfiladero *m* defile, pass
desfilar *intr* to defile, parade, file by
desfile *m* review, parade
desflorar *tr* to deflower; mention in passing
desfogar **§44** *tr* (*un horno*) to vent; (*la cal*) slake; (*una pasión*) give free rein to ‖ *intr* (*una tempestad*) to break into rain and wind ‖ *ref* to give vent to one's anger
desfondar *tr* to stave in; (*una nave*) bilge; (agr) to trench-plow
desforestar *tr* to deforest
desgaire *m* slovenliness; disdain, scorn; **al desgaire** scornfully; carelessly, with affected carelessness
desgajar *tr* to tear off; split off ‖ *ref* to come off, come loose; arise, originate; separate, break away
desgana *f* lack of appetite; indifference; boredom; **a desgana** unwillingly, reluctantly
desgarba•do -da *adj* ungainly, uncouth
desgarrar *tr* to tear, rend; (*la flema*) cough up ‖ *ref* to tear oneself away
desgarro *m* tear, rent; brazenness, effrontery; boasting, bragging; (Chile, Col) phlegm, mucus
desgasta•do -da *adj* worn (out); eroded; (*llanta*) treadless; (*tela*) threadbare
desgastar *tr* to wear away, wear down; to weaken, spoil ‖ *ref* to wear away; grow weak, decline
desgaste *m* wear, wearing away
desgoberna•do -da *adj* ungovernable, uncontrollable
desgobernar **§2** *tr* to misgovern; (*un hueso*) dislocate ‖ *intr* (naut) to steer poorly ‖ *ref* to twist and turn in dancing
desgobierno *m* misgovernment; dislocation
desgonzar **§60** *tr* to unhinge; disconnect
desgracia *f* misfortune; (*acontecimiento adverso*) mishap; (*pérdida de favor*) disfavor, disgrace; (*aspereza en el trato*) gruffness; (*falta de gracia*) lack of charm; **correr con desgracia** to have no luck; **por desgracia** unfortunately
desgracia•do -da *adj* unfortunate; unattractive, unpleasant; disagreeable ‖ *mf* wretch, unfortunate
desgraciar *tr* to displease; spoil ‖ *ref* to spoil; fail; fall out, disagree
desgranar *tr* (*el maíz*) to shell; (*un racimo*) to pick the grapes from ‖ *ref* (*piezas ensartadas*) to come loose
desgreñar *tr* to dishevel ‖ *ref* to get disheveled; pull each other's hair
deshabita•do -da *adj* unoccupied
deshabituar **§21** *tr* to break of a habit
deshacer **§39** *tr* to undo; untie; take apart; wear away, consume, destroy; melt; put to flight, rout; (*un tratado o negocio*) violate ‖ *ref* to get out of order; vanish, disappear; **deshacerse de** to get rid of; **deshacerse en** (*cumplidos*) to lavish; (*lágrimas*) burst into; **deshacerse por** to strive hard to
desharrapa•do -da *adj* ragged, in rags
deshebillar *tr* to unbuckle
deshebrar *tr* to unravel, unthread
deshecha *f* sham, pretense; dismissal; **hacer la deshecha** to feign, pretend; (Mex) to pretend lack of interest

deshelar §2 *tr* to thaw, melt; defrost; (aer) to deice || *intr* to thaw, melt
deshereda•do -da *adj* disinherited; underprivileged
desheredar *tr* to disinherit || *ref* to be a disgrace to one's family
desherrar §2 *tr* to unchain, unshackle; (*a una caballería*) unshoe
desherrumbrar *tr* to remove the rust from
deshidratar *tr* to dehydrate
deshielo *m* thaw; defrosting; détente
deshilachar *ref* to fray
deshila•do -da *adj* in a file; **a la deshilada** in single file; secretly || *m* openwork, drawn work
deshilar *tr* to unweave; (*reducir a hilos*) shred || *ref* to fray; get thin
deshilvana•do -da *adj* disconnected, desultory
deshincar §73 *tr* to pull up, pull out
deshinchar *tr* to deflate; (*la cólera*) give vent to || *ref* (*un tumor*) to go down; (*una persona orgullosa*) become deflated
deshojar *tr* to strip of leaves; tear the pages out of || *ref* to lose the leaves
deshollejar *tr* (*la uva*) to peel, skin; (*las habichuelas*) shell
deshollina•dor -dora *mf* chimney sweep; curious observer || *m* long-handled brush or broom
deshones•to -ta *adj* immodest, indecent; improper
deshonor *m* dishonor; disgrace
deshonorar *tr* to dishonor; degrade; disfigure
deshonra *f* dishonor; disrespect; **tener a deshonra** to consider improper
deshonrabue•nos *mf* (*pl* **-nos**) slanderer; (coll) black sheep
deshonrar *tr* to disgrace; (*a una mujer*) seduce; insult
deshonro•so -sa *adj* disgraceful, improper, discreditable
deshora *f* wrong time; **a deshora** at the wrong time, inopportunely; suddenly, unexpectedly
deshuesar *tr* (*la carne de un animal*) to bone; (*la fruta*) stone, take the pits out of
deshumedecer §22 *tr* to dehumidify
desidia *f* laziness, indolence
desidio•so -sa *adj* lazy, indolent || *mf* lazy person
desier•to -ta *adj* desert; deserted || *m* desert; wilderness
designar *tr* to designate; (*un trabajo*) plan
designio *m* design, plan, scheme
desigual *adj* unequal; unlike; rough, uneven; difficult; inconstant
desigualar *tr* to make unequal || *ref* to become unequal; (*aventajarse*) get ahead
desigualdad *f* inequality; roughness, unevenness
desilusión *f* disillusionment; disappointment
desilusionar *tr* to disillusion; disappoint || *ref* to become disillusioned; be disappointed
desimanar or **desimantar** *tr* to demagnetize
desimpresionar *tr* to undeceive
desinclina•do -da *adj* disinclined
desinencia *f* (gram) termination, ending
desinfectante *adj & m* disinfectant
desinfectar or **desinficionar** *tr* to disinfect
desinflación *f* deflation
desinflamar *tr* to take the soreness out of
desinflar *tr* to deflate; let the air out of; (*a una persona*) deflate
desinhibición *f* loss of inhibitions
desinsectación *f* insect control
desinsectar *intr* to exterminate insects
desintegración *f* disintegration
desintegrar *tr & ref* to disintegrate
desinterés *m* disinterestedness
desinteresa•do -da *adj* (*imparcial*) disinterested; (*poco interesado*) uninterested
desinteresar *ref* to lose interest
desintonizar §60 *tr* (rad) to tune out; (rad) to put out of tune
desintoxicación *f* detoxification; sobering (up)
desintoxicar *tr* to detoxify; sober up
desistir *intr* to desist
desjarretar *tr* to hamstring; bleed to excess
desjuicia•do -da *adj* lacking judgment, senseless
desjuntar *tr* to disjoin, separate
deslabonar *tr* to unlink; disconnect || *ref* to come loose; withdraw
deslastrar *tr* to unballast
deslava•do -da *adj* faded, colorless; barefaced || *mf* barefaced person
deslavar *tr* to wash superficially; fade, take the life out of
desleal *adj* disloyal; unfair
deslealtad *f* disloyalty
deslechar *tr* (Col) to milk
desleír §58 *tr* to dissolve; dilute; (*los colores, la pintura*) thin; (*sus pensamientos*) express too diffusely || *ref* to dissolve; become diluted
deslengua•do -da *adj* foul-mouthed, shameless
desliar §77 *tr* to untie, undo; unravel || *ref* to come untied
desligar §44 *tr* to untie, unbind; disentangle; excuse || *ref* to come untied, come loose
deslindar *tr* to mark the boundaries of; distinguish; define, explain
des•liz *m* (*pl* **-lices**) sliding; (*superficie lisa*) slide; slip, blunder; peccadillo, indiscretion
deslizade•ro -ra *adj* slippery || *m* slippery place; launching way
deslizadi•zo -za *adj* slippery
deslizador *m* (aer) glider
deslizar §60 *tr* to slide; (*decir por descuido*) let slip || *intr* to slide; slip; glide || *ref* to slide; slip; glide; slip away, sneak away; (*un reparo*) slip out; (*caer en una flaqueza*) slide back, backslide
deslomar *tr* to break or strain the back of || *ref* to break or strain one's back; **no deslomarse** to not strain oneself
desluci•do -da *adj* quiet, lackluster; dull, undistinguished
deslucir §45 *tr* to tarnish; deprive of charm, deprive of distinction; discredit

deslumbramiento *m* dazzle, glare; bewilderment, confusion
deslumbrante *adj* dazzling; bewildering, confusing
deslumbrar *tr* to dazzle; bewilder, confuse
deslustra•do -da *adj* dull, flat, dingy; (*vidrio*) ground, frosted
deslustrar *tr* to tarnish; dull, dim; (*el vidrio*) frost; discredit || *ref* to tarnish
deslustre *m* tarnishing; dulling, dimming; discredit; (*del vidrio*) frosting
deslustro•so -sa *adj* ugly, unbecoming
desmadejar *tr* to enervate, weaken
desmagnetizar **§60** *tr* to demagnetize
desmán *m* excess, misconduct; misfortune, mishap
desmanchar *tr* (Chile) to clean of spots
desmanda•do -da *adj* disobedient, unruly
desmandar *tr* to cancel, countermand || *ref* to misbehave; go away, keep apart; get out of control
desmanear *tr* to unfetter, unshackle
desmantela•do -da *adj* dilapidated
desmantelar *tr* to dismantle; (naut) to unmast; (naut) to unrig
desmaña *f* awkwardness, clumsiness
desmaña•do -da *adj* awkward, clumsy
desmaquillar *tr & ref* to take makeup off
desmaya•do -da *adj* faint, languid, weak; unconscious; (*color*) dull
desmayar *tr* to depress, discourage || *intr* to lose heart, be discouraged; falter || *ref* to faint
desmayo *m* depression, discouragement; faint, fainting fit; weeping willow
desmedi•do -da *adj* excessive; boundless, limitless
desmedir **§50** *ref* to go too far, be impudent
desmedra•do -da *adj* weak, run-down
desmedrar *tr* to impair || *intr & ref* to decline, deteriorate
desmejorar *tr* to impair, spoil || *intr & ref* to decline, go into a decline
desmelenar *tr* to muss, dishevel, rumple
desmembrar **§2** *tr* to dismember
desmemoria *f* forgetfulness
desmemoria•do -da *adj* forgetful
desmemoriar *ref* to become forgetful
desmentida *f* contradiction; **dar una desmentida a** to give the lie to
desmentir **§68** *tr* to belie, give the lie to; conceal || *intr* to be out of line || *ref* to contradict oneself
desmenudear *tr & intr* (Col) to sell at retail
desmenuzar **§60** *tr* to crumble; chop up; examine in detail; criticize harshly || *ref* to crumb, crumble
desmerece•dor -dora *adj* unworthy
desmerecer **§22** *tr* to be unworthy of || *intr* to decline in value; **desmerecer de** to compare unfavorably with
desmesura *f* excess, lack of restraint
desmesura•do -da *adj* excessive, disproportionate; insolent || *mf* insolent person
desmigajar *tr & ref* to crumble, break up
desmigar **§44** *tr & ref* to crumble, crumb
desmilitarizar **§60** *tr* to demilitarize; **zona desmilitarizada** demilitarized zone
desmirria•do -da *adj* exhausted, emaciated, run-down
desmochar *tr* (*un árbol*) to top; (*al toro*) dehorn; (*una obra artística*) cut
desmodular *tr* to demodulate
desmola•do -da *adj* toothless
desmontable *adj* demountable
desmontar *tr* (*un terreno*) to level; (*un bosque*) clear; dismantle, dismount, take apart, knock down; (*las piezas de artillería del enemigo*) knock out; (*al jinete el caballo*) unhorse, to throw; (*un arma de fuego*) uncock || *ref* to dismount, alight
desmoralizar **§60** *tr* to demoralize
desmoronadi•zo -za *adj* crumbly
desmoronar *tr* to wear away || *ref* to wear away; crumble, decline
desmotadera *f* burler; **desmotadera de algodón** cotton gin
desmotar *tr* (*la lana*) to burl; (*el algodón*) gin
desmovilizar **§60** *tr* to demobilize
desmurador *m* mouser
desnatadora *f* cream separator
desnatar *tr* to skim; remove the slag from; take the choicest part of
desnaturalizar **§60** *tr* to denaturalize; (*el alcohol*) denature; alter, pervert
desnivel *m* unevenness; difference of level
desnivelar *tr* to make uneven || *ref* to become uneven
desnudar *tr* to undress; strip, lay bare; (*la espada*) draw || *ref* to undress, get undressed; become evident; **desnudarse de** to get rid of
desnudez *f* nakedness; bareness
desnu•do -da *adj* naked, nude; bare; destitute, penniless || **el desnudo** the nude
desnutrición *f* undernourishment, malnutrition
desnutri•do -da *adj* undernourished
desobedecer *tr & intr* to disobey
desobediencia *f* disobedience
desobediente *adj* disobedient
desocupación *f* unemployment; idleness, leisure
desocupa•do -da *adj* unemployed; idle; free, unoccupied, vacant, empty || *mf* unemployed person
desocupar *tr* to empty, vacate || *intr* (*una mujer*) to be delivered || *ref* to become empty, vacated; become unemployed, become idle
desodorante *adj & m* deodorant
desodorizar **§60** *tr* to deodorize
desoír **§48** *tr* to not hear, pretend not to hear
desolación *f* desolation
desola•do -da *adj* desolate, disconsolate
desolar **§61** *tr* to desolate, lay waste || *ref* to be desolate, be disconsolate
desoldar **§61** *tr* to unsolder || *ref* to come unsoldered
desolla•do -da *adj* brazen, impudent
desollar **§61** *tr* to skin, flay; harm, hurt; **desollar vivo** (*hacer pagar mucho más de*

lo justo) fleece, skin alive; (*murmurar acerbamente de*) (coll) to flay
desopilar *ref* to roar with laughter
desopinar *tr* to defame, discredit
desorbita•do -da *adj* popeyed; crazy
desorbitar *tr* to pop wide-open
desorden *m* disorder
desordena•do -da *adj* disorderly, unruly
desordenar *tr* to put out of order || *ref* to get out of order; be unruly; go too far
desoreja•do -da *adj* infamous, degraded; (*que canta mal*) (Peru) off tune; (Cuba) shameless; (Cuba) spendthrift, prodigal; (Guat) stupid; (Chile) without handles
desorganizar §60 *tr* to disorganize
desorientación *f* disorientation; confusedness; going astray
desorientar *tr* to lead astray; confuse
desovar *intr* to spawn
desove *m* spawning; spawning season
desovillar *tr* to unravel, disentangle; encourage
desoxidar *tr* to deoxidize; clean of rust
despabiladeras *fpl* snuffers
despabila•do -da *adj* wide-awake
despabilar *tr* (*una candela*) to snuff, trim; (*la hacienda*) dissipate; (*una comida*) dispatch; (*robar*) snitch; (*matar*) dispatch || *ref* to brighten up; wake up; leave, disappear
despacio *adv* slow, slowly; at leisure; (Arg, Chile) in a low voice
despacio•so -sa *adj* slow, easy-going
despachaderas *fpl* surly reply; resourcefulness
despacha•do -da *adj* brazen, impudent; quick, resourceful
despachante *m* (Arg) clerk; **despachante te de aduana** (Arg) customhouse broker
despachar *tr* to send, ship; dispatch, expedite; discharge, dismiss; decide, settle; sell; (*a los parroquianos*) wait on; (*la correspondencia*) attend to; hurry; (*matar*) dispatch, kill || *intr* to hurry; make up one's mind; work, be employed || *ref* to hurry; (*una mujer*) be delivered; speak out
despacho *m* shipping; dispatch, expedition; discharge, dismissal; (*tienda*) store, shop; (*aposento para el estudio*) study; (*aposento para los negocios*) office; (*comunicación por telégrafo o teléfono*) dispatch; (Chile) attic; **despacho de billetes** ticket office; **despacho de localidades** box office; **estar al despacho** to be pending; **tener buen despacho** to be expeditious
despachurrar *tr* to crush, smash, squash; (*dejar sin tener que replicar*) squelch; (*lo que uno trata de decir*) butcher, murder
despampanante *adj* stunning, terrific
despampanar *tr* (*las vides*) to prune, trim; astound || *intr* to give vent to one's feelings || *ref* to fall and hurt oneself
despancar §73 *tr* to husk (*corn*)
desparejar *tr* (*dos cosas que forman pareja*) to break, separate (*a pair*)
desparpajar *tr* to tear apart || *intr* to rant, rave || *ref* to rant, rave; (CAm, Mex, W-I) to wake up
desparramar *tr* to scatter, spread; (*el agua*) to spill; (*la hacienda*) squander || *ref* to scatter, spread; make merry
despartir *tr* to divide, part, separate; to reconcile
despatarrada *f* split (*in dancing*); **hacer la despatarrada** to stretch out on the floor pretending to be ill or injured
despatarrar *tr* to dumbfound || *ref* to open one's legs wide, fall down with legs outspread; lie motionless; be dumbfounded
despavori•do -da *adj* terrified
despea•do -da *adj* footsore
despear *ref* to get sore feet
despecti•vo -va *adj* contemptuous; (gram) pejorative
despecha•do -da *adj* spiteful, enraged
despechar *tr* to spite, enrage; (*destetar*) to wean || *ref* to be enraged; despair, lose hope
despecho *m* spite; despair; weaning; **a despecho de** despite, in spite of; **por despecho** out of spite
despechugar §44 *tr* to carve the breast of || *ref* (coll) to go with bare breast, bare one's breast
despedazar §60 *tr* to break to pieces; (*la honra de uno*) to ruin; (*el alma de una persona*) break || *ref* to break to pieces; **despedazarse de risa** to split one's sides laughing
despedida *f* farewell, leave-taking; (*de una carta*) close, conclusion; (*copla final*) envoi
despedir §50 *tr* to throw; emit, send forth; discharge, dismiss; (*al que sale de la casa*) see off; (*un mal pensamiento*) banish; **despedir en la puerta** to see to the door || *ref* to take leave, say good-by; give up one's job; **despedirse a la francesa** to take French leave; **despedirse de** to take leave of, say good-by to
despega•do -da *adj* gruff, surly
despegar §44 *tr* to loosen, unglue, unseal; open; separate, detach || *intr* (aer) to take off || *ref* to come off; **despegarse con** to be unbecoming to
despego *m* dislike, indifference
despegue *m* (aer) take-off; **despegue vertical** vertical take-off
despeina•do -da *adj* unkempt
despeja•do -da *adj* (*frente*) wide; (*día, cielo*) clear, cloudless; bright, sprightly; (*en el trato*) unconstrained
despejar *tr* to clarify, explain; free; (*una incógnita*) (math) to find || *ref* to brighten up, cheer up; (*el cielo, el tiempo; una situación dificultosa*) clear up; (*un borracho*) sober up
despejo *m* ease, naturalness; talent, intelligence, understanding
despelotar *ref* to disrobe
despeluzar §60 *tr* to muss the hair of; make the hair of (*a person*) stand on end || *ref* (*el pelo*) to stand on end
despeluznante *adj* hair-raising, horrifying
despellejar *tr* to skin, flay; slander, malign

despenalización *f* legalization
despenalizar §60 *tr* to legalize; condone
despenar *tr* to console; (coll) to kill; (Chile) to deprive of hope
despender *tr* to spend, squander; (*el tiempo*) to waste
despensa *f* pantry; food supplies; day's marketing; stewardship; (naut) storeroom
despensero *m* butler, steward; (naut) storekeeper
despeñadamente *adv* hastily; boldly
despeñade•ro -ra *adj* precipitous || *m* precipice; danger, risk
despeñadi•zo -za *adj* precipitous
despeñar *tr* to hurl, throw, push || *ref* to hurl oneself, jump; fall headlong; (*en vicios, pecados, pasiones*) plunge downward
despeño *m* plunge; headlong fall; ruin, failure, collapse; (coll) loose bowels
despepitar *tr* to seed, remove the seeds from || *ref* to rush around madly, go around screaming; **despepitarse por** to be mad about
desperdicia•do -da *adj* wasteful, prodigal || *mf* spendthrift, prodigal
desperdiciar *tr* to waste, squander; (*la ocasión de aprovechar una cosa*) miss, lose
desperdicio *m* waste, squandering; **desperdicios** waste; waste products; by-products; rubbish; **no tener desperdicio** to be excellent, be useful
desperdigar §44 *tr* to separate, scatter
desperecer §22 *ref* to long eagerly
desperezar §60 *ref* to stretch, stretch one's arms and legs
desperfecto *m* blemish, flaw, imperfection
desperna•do -da *adj* footsore, weary
desperta•dor -dora *mf* awakener || *m* alarm clock; warning
despertar §2 *tr* to awaken; arouse, stir || *intr & ref* to awaken, wake up
despestañar *tr* to pluck the eyelashes of || *ref* to look hard, strain one's eyes
despiada•do -da *adj* cruel, pitiless
despichar *tr* to squeeze dry; (Col, Chile) to crush, flatten || *intr* (coll) to croak, die
despidiente *m* stick placed between a hanging scaffold and wall; **despidiente de agua** flashing
despido *m* layoff, discharge
despier•to -ta *adj* wide-awake, alert; **soñar despierto** to daydream
despilfarra•do -da *adj* wasteful; ragged || *mf* prodigal; raggedy person
despilfarrar *tr* to squander, waste || *ref* to spend recklessly
despilfarro *m* squandering, waste, extravagance; slovenliness
despintar *tr* to remove the paint from; disfigure, distort, spoil; **no despintarle a uno los ojos** to not take one's eyes from a person || *intr* to decline, slip back; **despintar de** to be unworthy of || *ref* to fade, wash off; **no despintársele a uno** to not fade from one's memory
despiojar *tr* to delouse; (coll) to free from poverty
despique *m* revenge
despistar *tr* to outwit, throw off the track || *ref* to run off the track, run off the road
desplacer *m* displeasure || §22 *tr* to displease
desplantar *tr* to uproot; throw out of plumb || *ref* to get out of plumb; lose one's upright posture
desplaya•do -da *adj* broad, open, wide || *m* (Arg) wide sandy beach
desplayar *tr* to widen, spread out || *ref* (*el mar*) to recede from the beach
desplaza•do -da *adj* displaced || *mf* displaced person
desplazar §60 *tr* (*cierto peso de agua*) to displace; move, transport || *ref* to move
desplegar §66 *tr* to unfold, spread; display; explain; (mil) to deploy || *ref* to unfold, spread out; (mil) to deploy
despliegue *m* unfolding, spreading out; display; (mil) deployment
desplomar *tr* to throw out of plumb || *ref* to get out of plumb; collapse, tumble; fall down in a faint; (*un trono*) crumble; (aer) to pancake
desplome *m* leaning; collapse, tumbling; falling in a faint; downfall; (aer) pancaking
desplumar *tr* to pluck; (*dejar sin dinero*) fleece || *ref* to molt
despoblado *m* wilderness, deserted spot
despoblar §61 *tr* to depopulate; lay waste; clear, lay bare
despojar *tr* to strip, despoil, divest; dispossess || *ref* to undress; **despojarse de** to divest oneself of; (*ropa*) take off
despojo *m* dispoilment; dispossession; booty, plunder, spoils; prey, victim; **despojos** scraps, leavings; mortal remains; secondhand building materials
despolarizar §60 *tr* to depolarize
despolvar *tr* to dust
despolvorear *tr* to dust, dust off; scatter
desportillar *tr* to chip, nick || *ref* to chip, chip off
desposa•do -da *adj* handcuffed; newly married || *mf* newlywed
desposar *tr* to marry || *ref* to be betrothed, get engaged; get married
desposeer §43 *tr* to dispossess || *ref*—**desposeerse de** to divest oneself of
desposorios *mpl* betrothal, engagement; marriage, nuptials
despostar *tr* to cut up, carve; butcher
déspota *m* despot
despóti•co -ca *adj* despotic
despotismo *m* despotism
despotricar §73 *intr & ref* to rave, rant
despreciable *adj* contemptible, despicable
despreciar *tr* to scorn, despise; slight, snub; overlook, forgive; reject || *ref*—**despreciarse de** to not deign to
despreciati•vo -va *adj* contemptuous, scornful
desprecio *m* scorn, contempt; slight, snub
desprender *tr* to loosen, unfasten, detach; emit, give off; (chem) to liberate || *ref* to come loose, come off; issue, come forth;

desprenderse de to give up, part with; be deduced from
desprendi•do -da *adj* generous, disinterested
desprendimiento *m* loosening, detachment; emission, liberation; generosity, disinterestedness; landslide; (chem) liberation
despreocupación *f* relaxation; impartiality; indifference
despreocupa•do -da *adj* relaxed, unconcerned; impartial; indifferent
despreocupante *adj* relaxing
despreocupar *ref* to relax; **despreocuparse de** to forget about, be unconcerned about
desprestigiar *tr* to disparage, run down || *ref* to lose caste, lose one's standing, lose face
desprestigio *m* disparagement; loss of standing, discredit
despreveni•do -da *adj* off one's guard; **coger a uno desprevenido** to catch someone unawares
desproporciona•do -da *adj* disproportionate
despropósito *m* absurdity, nonsense; malapropism
desproveer §43 & §83 *tr* to deprive
desprovis•to -ta *adj* destitute; **desprovisto de** lacking, devoid of
después *adv* after, afterwards; **después de** after; **después (de) que** after
despuli•do -da *adj* ground (*glass*)
despumar *tr* to skim
despuntar *tr* to dull, blunt; (*un cabo o punta*) (naut) to double, round || *intr* to begin to sprout; (*empezar a amanecer*) dawn; stand out || *ref* to get dull
desquiciar *tr* to unhinge; shake loose, upset; unsettle, perturb; overthrow, undermine
desquitar *tr* to recover, retrieve; compensate || *ref* to retrieve a loss; get revenge, get even
desquite *m* recovery, retrieval; retaliation, revenge; (sport) return match
desrazonable *adj* unreasonable
desrielar *intr* to jump the track
destaca•do -da *adj* outstanding, distinguished
destacamiento *m* (mil) detachment; (mil) detail
destacar §73 *tr* to highlight, point up; emphasize; make stand out; (mil) to detach; (mil) to detail || *intr* to stand out, be conspicuous || *ref* to stand out, project; (fig) to stand out
destajar *tr* to arrange for, establish the terms for; (*la baraja*) cut; carve up
destaje•ro -ra or **destajista** *mf* pieceworker, jobber; free lance
destajo *m* piecework; job, contract; **a destajo** by the piece, by the job; freelancing; **hablar a destajo** to talk too much
destapar *tr* to open, uncover, take the lid off; uncock, unplug; reveal || *ref* to get uncovered; throw off the covers; unbosom oneself
destaponar *tr* to uncock, unplug; (*una botella; las fosas nasales*) unstop
destartala•do -da *adj* tumble-down, ramshackle
destazar §60 *tr* to carve up
destechar *tr* to unroof
destejar *tr* to remove the tiles from; leave unprotected
destejer *tr* to unbraid, unknit, unweave; upset, disturb
destellar *tr & intr* to flash
destello *m* flash, beam, sparkle
destempla•do -da *adj* disagreeable, unpleasant; inharmonious, out of tune; indisposed; (*clima; pulso*) irregular
destemplanza *f* unpleasantness; discord; indisposition; (*del pulso*) irregularity; (*del tiempo*) inclemency; excess
destemple *m* dissonance; indisposition; disorder, disturbance
desteñir §72 *tr* to discolor || *intr & ref* to fade
desternillante *adj* sidesplitting
desternillar *ref* — **desternillarse de risa** to split one's sides with laughter
desterra•do -da *adj* exiled || *mf* exile
desterrar §2 *tr* to exile, banish; (fig) to banish
destetar *tr* to wean || *ref* — **destetarse con** to have known since childhood
destete *m* weaning
destiempo *m* — **a destiempo** untimely
destiento *m* surprise, shock
destierro *m* exile; backwoods
destilación *f* distillation
destiladera *f* still; scheme, stratagem
destilar *tr* to distill; filter; exude || *intr* to drip
destilatorio *m* distillery; (*alambique*) still
destilería *f* distillery
destinación *f* destination
destinar *tr* to destine; assign, designate
destinata•rio -ria *mf* addressee; consignee; (*de homenaje, aplausos*) recipient
destino *m* (*lugar a donde va una persona o una remesa*) destination; (*suerte, encadenamiento fatal de los sucesos*) fate, destiny; employment; place of employment; **con destino a** bound for
destituir §20 *tr* to deprive; dismiss, discharge
destorcer §74 *tr* to untwist, straighten || *ref* to become untwisted; (naut) to drift
destornilla•do -da *adj* rash, reckless, out of one's head
destornillador *m* screwdriver
destornillar *tr* to unscrew || *ref* to lose one's head, go berserk
destoser *ref* to cough (*artificially, to attract attention*)
destrabar *tr* to loosen, untie, detach
destraillar §4 *tr* unleash
destral *m* hatchet
destreza *f* skill, dexterity
destripacuen•tos *m* (*pl* **-tos**) (coll) butter-in
destripar *tr* to disembowel, gut; crush, mangle; spoil (*a story by telling its outcome*)
destripaterro•nes *m* (*pl* **-nes**) (coll) clodhopper
destriunfar *tr* to force to play trump
destrocar §81 *tr* to swap back again
destronar *tr* to dethrone; overthrow
destroncar §73 *tr* to chop down; chop off; ruin; exhaust, wear out

destrozar §60 *tr* to shatter, break to pieces; destroy; squander; (*al ejército enemigo*) wipe out
destrozo *m* havoc, destruction; rout, annihilation, defeat
destrucción *f* destruction
destructi•vo -va *adj* destructive
destructor *m* (nav) destroyer
destruir §20 *tr* to destroy || *ref* (alg) to cancel each other
desuellaca•ras *m* (*pl* **-ras**) sloppy barber; scoundrel
desuello *m* skinning, flaying; shamelessness; (*precio excesivo*) (coll) highway robbery
desuncir §36 *tr* to unyoke
desunir *tr* to disunite; take apart || *ref* to disunite; come apart
desusa•do -da *adj* obsolete, out of use; uncommon, unusual; **estar desusado** (*perder la práctica*) to be rusty
desuso *m* disuse; **caído en desuso** obsolete
desvaí•do -da *adj* lank, ungainly; (*color*) dull
desvainar *tr* to shell
desvali•do -da *adj* helpless, destitute
desvalijar *tr* (*una valija, baúl, etc.*) to rifle; rob, wipe out
desvalorar *tr* to devalue
desvalorizar §60 *tr* to devalue
desván *m* garret, loft
desvanecedor *m* (phot) mask
desvanecer §22 *tr* to dispel, dissipate; (*una conspiración*) break up; (*la sospecha*) banish; (phot) to mask || *ref* to disappear, vanish, evanesce; evaporate; faint, faint away, swoon; (rad) to fade
desvanecimiento *m* disappearance, evanescence; dissipation; pride, vanity; faintness, fainting spell; (phot) masking; (rad) fading, fadeout
desvaria•do -da *adj* delirious, raving
desvariar §77 *intr* to be delirious, rave, rant
desvarío *m* delirium, raving; absurdity, nonsense, extravagance; whim, caprice; inconstancy
desvela•do -da *adj* wakeful, sleepless; watchful, vigilant; anxious, worried
desvelar *tr* to keep awake, not let sleep || *ref* to keep awake, go without sleep; be watchful, be vigilant; **desvelarse por** to be anxious about, be worried about
desvelo *m* wakefulness, sleeplessness; watchfulness, vigilance; anxiety, worry, concern
desvenar *tr* to strip (*tobacco*)
desvencija•do -da *adj* rickety, ramshackle
desvencijar *tr* to break, tear apart || *ref* to go to rack and ruin
desvendar *tr* to unbandage, undress
desventaja *f* disadvantage
desventaja•do -da *adj* disadvantaged; deprived
desventajo•so -sa *adj* disadvantageous
desventura *f* misfortune
desventura•do -da *adj* unfortunate; fainthearted; stingy
desvergonza•do -da *adj* shameless, impudent
desvergüenza *f* shamelessness, impudence
desvestir §50 *tr & ref* to undress
desviación *f* deviation, deflection; detour; (rad, telv) drift
desviacionismo *m* deviationism
desviacionista *mf* deviationist
desviadero *m* (rr) siding, turnout
desvia•do -da *adj* devious; (gone) astray; off track; lost
desviar §77 *tr* to deviate, deflect; turn aside; dissuade; parry, ward off; (rr) to switch || *ref* to deviate, deflect; turn aside; branch off; be dissuaded
desvío *m* deviation, deflection; coldness, indifference; detour; (rr) siding, sidetrack
desvirgar §44 *tr* to deflower, ravish
desvirtuar §21 *tr* to weaken, spoil, impair
desvivir *ref* — **desvivirse por** to be crazy about; **desvivirse por** + *inf* to be eager to + *inf*, to do one's best to + *inf*
desvolvedor *m* wrench
desvolver §47 & §83 *tr* to alter, change; (*la tierra*) turn up; (*una tuerca o tornillo*) loosen, unscrew
detall *m* — **al detall** at retail
detalladamente *adv* in detail
detallar *tr* to detail, tell in detail; retail, sell at retail
detalle *m* detail; retail; **ahí está el detalle** that's the point
detallista *mf* retailer; person fond of details
detección *f* detection
detectar *tr* to detect
detective *m* detective
detector *m* detector; **detector de mentiras** lie detector
detención *f* detention, detainment; delay; care, thoroughness
detener §71 *tr* to detain; stop; arrest; keep, retain; (*el aliento*) hold || *ref* to stop; linger, tarry
detenidamente *adv* carefully, thoroughly
deteni•do -da *adj* careful, thorough; hesitant, timid; stingy, mean || *mf* person held in custody
detenimiento *m* var of **detención**
detergente *adj & m* detergent
deteriorar *tr & ref* to deteriorate
deterioro *m* deterioration
determinación *f* determination; decision
determina•do -da *adj* determined, resolute; (*artículo*) (gram) definite
determinar *tr* to determine; cause, bring about || *ref* to decide
detestar *tr* to detest; curse; **detestar** + *inf* to hate to + *inf*
detonar *intr* to detonate
detraer §75 *tr* to withdraw, take away, detract; defame, vilify
detrás *adv* behind; **detrás de** behind, back of; **por detrás** behind; behind one's back; **por detrás de** behind the back of
detrimento *m* harm, detriment
deuda *f* debt; indebtedness
deu•do -da *mf* relative || *m* kinship || *f* see **deuda**
deu•dor -dora *adj* indebted || *mf* debtor; **deudor hipotecario** mortgagor; **deudor moroso** delinquent (*in payment*)

devalar *intr* (naut) to drift from the course
devaluación *f* devaluation
devanar *tr* to wind, roll; (*un cuento*) to unfold || *ref* (CAm, Mex, W-I) to roll with laughter; (CAm, Mex, W-I) to writhe in pain
devanear *intr* to talk nonsense; loaf around
devaneo *m* nonsense; loafing; flirtation
devastación *f* devastation
devastar *tr* to devastate
develar *tr* to reveal; (*p.ej., una estatua*) unveil
devengar §44 *tr* (*salarios*) to earn; (*intereses*) draw, earn
devoción *f* devotion
devolución *f* return, restitution
devolver §47 & §83 *tr* to return, give back, send back; pay back; (coll) to vomit || *ref* to return, come back
devorar *tr* to devour
devo•to -ta *adj* devout; devoted; devotional || *mf* devotee; devout person; **devoto del volante** car enthusiast || *m* object of worship
D.F. *abbr* **Distrito Federal**
d/f *abbr* **días fecha**
dho. *abbr* **dicho**
día *m* day; daytime; daylight; **al día** per day; up to date; **al otro día** on the following day; **buenos días** good morning; **dar los días a** to wish (*someone*) many happy returns of the day; **de día** in the daytime, in the daylight; **día de años** birthday; **día de ayuno** fast day; **día de carne** meat day; **día de engañabobos** December 28th, day when practical jokes are played on unsuspecting people; **día de inauguración** (fa) private view; **día de la raza** Columbus Day; **día del juicio** judgment day; **día de los caídos** Memorial Day; **día de los difuntos** All Souls' Day; **día de ramos** Palm Sunday; **día de Reyes** Epiphany; **día de todos los santos** All Saints' Day; **día de trabajo** workday; weekday; **día de vigilia** fast day; **día festivo** holiday; **día inhábil** day off; holiday; **día laborable** workday, weekday; **día lectivo** school day; **día puente** day off between two holidays; **el día de Año Nuevo** New Year's Day; **el día menos pensado** when least expected; **el mejor día** some fine day; **en cuatro días** in a few days; **en pleno día** in broad daylight; **en su día** in due time; **ocho días** a week; **poner al día** to bring up to date; **quince días** two weeks, a fortnight; **tener sus días** to be up in years; **un día sí y otro no** every other day; **vivir al día** to live from hand to mouth
diabetes *f* diabetes
diabéti•co -ca *adj & mf* diabetic
diablillo *m* imp
diablo *m* devil; (Chile) ox-drawn log drag; **ahí será el diablo** (coll) there will be the devil to pay; **diablo cojuelo** tricky devil; **diablos azules** delirium tremens
diablura *f* devilment, deviltry, mischief
diabóli•co -ca *adj* devilish, diabolical
diaconisa *f* deaconess
diácono *m* deacon
diacríti•co -ca *adj* diacritical
diadema *f* diadem; (*adorno femenino*) tiara
diáfa•no -na *adj* diaphanous
diafragma *m* diaphragm
diagno•sis *f* (*pl* **-sis**) diagnosis
diagnosticar §73 *tr* to diagnose
diagonal *adj* diagonal || *f* diagonal, bias
diagrama *m* diagram
dialecto *m* dialect
dialogar *intr* to talk
diálogo *m* dialogue
diamante *m* diamond
diametral or **diamétri•co -ca** *adj* diametrical
diámetro *m* diameter
diana *f* bull's-eye; (mil) reveille; **hacer diana** to hit the bull's-eye
diantre *m* devil || *interj* the devil!, the deuce!
diapasón *m* tuning fork; pitch pipe; (*p.ej., del violín*) finger board; **bajar el diapasón** to lower one's voice, to change one's tune
diapositiva *f* slide, lantern slide
dia•rio -ria *adj* daily || *m* diary; daily, daily paper; **diario hablado** newscast
diarismo *m* journalism
diarrea *f* diarrhea
diástole *f* diastole
diatermia *f* diathermy
dibujante *mf* sketcher, illustrator || *m* draftsman
dibujar *tr* to draw, sketch, design; outline || *ref* to be outlined; appear, show
dibujo *m* drawing, sketch, design; outline; **dibujo al carbón** charcoal drawing; **dibujo animado** animated cartoon; **no meterse en dibujos** to attend to one's business
di•caz *adj* (*pl* **-caces**) sarcastic, witty
dicción *f* diction; word
diccionario *m* dictionary
díceres *mpl* sayings; rumor(s)
diciembre *m* December
dicloruro *m* dichloride
dicotomía *f* dichotomy; (*entre médicos*) split fee
dictado *m* dictation; **escribir al dictado** to take dictation; (*lo que otro dicta*) to take down
dictador *m* dictator
dictadura *f* dictatorship
dictáfono *m* dictaphone
dictamen *m* dictum, judgment, opinion
dictar *tr* to dictate; (*una ley*) promulgate; inspire, suggest; (*una conferencia*) give, deliver (*a lecture*)
dicterio *m* taunt, insult
dicha *f* happiness; luck; **por dicha** by chance
dicharache•ro -ra *adj* obscene, vulgar
dicharacho *m* obscenity, vulgarity; wisecrack
di•cho -cha *adj* said; **dicho y hecho** no sooner said than done; **mejor dicho** rather; **tener por dicho** to consider settled || *m* saying; promise of marriage, one's word; witticism; insult; **dicho de las gentes** talk, hearsay, gossip || *f* see **dicha**

dicho•so -sa *adj* happy; lucky, fortunate; annoying, tiresome
didácti•co -ca *adj* didactic
diecinueve *adj & pron* nineteen ‖ *m* nineteen; (*en las fechas*) nineteenth
diecinuevea•vo -va *adj & m* nineteenth
dieciocha•vo -va *adj m* eighteenth
dieciocho *adj & pron* eighteen ‖ *m* eighteen; (*en las fechas*) eighteenth
dieciséis *adj & pron* sixteen ‖ *m* sixteen; (*en las fechas*) sixteenth
dieciseisa•vo -va *adj & m* sixteenth
diecisiete *adj & pron* seventeen ‖ *m* seventeen; (*en las fechas*) seventeenth
diecisietea•vo -va *adj & m* seventeenth
diente *m* tooth; (*de elefante y otros animales*) tusk, fang; (*de peine, sierra, rastrillo*) tooth; (*de rueda dentada*) cog; **dar diente con diente** to shake all over; **decir entre dientes** to mutter, to mumble; **diente canino** eyetooth, canine tooth; **diente de león** dandelion; **estar a diente** to be famished; **tener buen diente** to be a hearty eater; **traer entre dientes** to have a grudge against; to talk about
diére•sis *f* (*pl* **-sis**) diaeresis; (*señal que indica la metafonía*) umlaut
diesel *m* diesel motor
dieseleléctri•co -ca *adj* diesel-electric
dies•tro -tra *adj* right; handy, skillful; shrewd, sly; favorable; **a diestro y siniestro** wildly, right and left ‖ *m* expert fencer; bullfighter on foot; matador; halter, bridle ‖ *f* right hand; **juntar diestra con diestra** to join forces
dieta *f* diet; **dietas** per diem; **estar a dieta** to diet, be on a diet
dietario *m* family budget
dietista *mf* dietitian
diez *adj & pron* ten; **las diez** ten o'clock ‖ *m* ten; (*en las fechas*) tenth
diezmar *tr* (*causar gran mortandad en*) to decimate; (*pagar el diezmo de*) tithe
diezmo *m* tithe
difamación *f* defamation, vilification
difamar *tr* to defame, vilify
diferencia *f* difference; **a diferencia de** unlike; **partir la diferencia** to split the difference
diferenciar *tr* to differentiate ‖ *intr* (*discordar*) to differ, dissent ‖ *ref* (*distinguirse una cosa de otra*) to differ, be different
diferente *adj* different
diferir §68 *tr* to defer, postpone, put off ‖ *intr* to differ, be different
difícil *adj* difficult, hard; hard to please
difícilmente *adv* with difficulty
dificultad *f* difficulty; (*reparo que se opone a una opinión*) objection
dificultar *tr* to make difficult; consider difficult ‖ *intr* to raise objections ‖ *ref* to become difficult
dificulto•so -sa *adj* difficult, troublesome; objecting; (coll) ugly, homely
difidencia *f* distrust
difidente *adj* distrustful
difteria *f* diphtheria
difundir *tr* to diffuse; spread, disseminate; divulge, publish; broadcast ‖ *ref* to diffuse; spread
difun•to -ta *adj & mf* deceased; **difunto de taberna** dead-drunk ‖ *m* corpse
difu•so -sa *adj* diffuse; extended; wordy
digerible *adj* digestible
digerir §68 *tr* to digest; **no digerir** to not bear, not stand ‖ *intr* to digest
digestible *adj* digestible
digestión *f* digestion
digesti•vo -va *adj & m* digestive
digesto *m* (law) digest
dígito *m* digit
dignación *f* condescension
dignar *ref* to deign, condescend
dignatario *m* dignitary, official
dignidad *f* dignity; bishop, archbishop
dignificar §73 *tr* to dignify
dig•no -na *adj* worthy; fitting, suitable; (*grave, decoroso*) dignified
digresión *f* digression
dije *m* amulet, charm, trinket; (*persona de excelentes cualidades*) jewel; person all dressed-up; handy person
dilacerar *tr* to tear to pieces; (*la honra, el orgullo*) damage
dilación *f* delay
dilapidación *f* waste; squandering
dilapidar *tr* to squander
dilatación *f* expansion; serenity
dilatar *tr* to dilate, expand; defer, postpone; (*p.ej., la fama*) spread ‖ *ref* to dilate, expand; spread; be wordy; delay
dilección *f* true love
dilec•to -ta *adj* dearly beloved
dilema *m* dilemma
diletante *adj & mf* dilettante
diletantismo *m* dilettantism
diligencia *f* diligence; step, démarche; errand; dispatch, speed; stagecoach; **hacer una diligencia** to do an errand; to have a bowel movement
diligente *adj* diligent; quick, ready
dilucidación *f* explanation; enlightenment
dilucidar *tr* to elucidate, explain
dilución *f* dilution
diluí•do -da *adj* dilute
diluir §20 *tr* to dilute; thin ‖ *ref* to dilute; melt; dissolve
diluviar *intr* to rain hard, pour
diluvio *m* deluge
dimanar *intr* to spring up; **dimanar de** to spring from, originate in
dimensión *f* dimension
dimes *mpl* — **andar en dimes y diretes con** to bicker with
diminuti•vo -va *adj & m* (gram) diminutive
diminu•to -ta *adj* tiny, diminutive; defective
dimisión *f* resignation
dimisorias *fpl* — **dar dimisorias a** to discharge, fire
dimitir *tr* to resign, resign from ‖ *intr* to resign
din *m* (coll) dough, money
Dinamarca *f* Denmark

dinamar•qués -quesa *adj* Danish || *mf* Dane || *m* Danish (*language*)
dinámi•co -ca *adj* dynamic
dinamita *f* dynamite
dinamitar *tr* to dynamite
dínamo *f* dynamo
dinasta *m* dynast
dinastía f dynasty
dindán *m* ding-dong
dinerada *f* or **dineral** *m* large sum of money
dinero *m* money; currency; wealth; **dinero contante** cash; **dinero contante y sonante** ready cash, spot cash; **dinero de bolsillo** pocket money
dinero•so -sa *adj* moneyed, wealthy
dintel *m* lintel, doorhead
dióce•si *f* or **dióce•sis** *f* (*pl* **-sis**) diocese
diodo *m* diode
dios *m* god; **Dios mediante** God willing; **¡por Dios!** goodness!, for heaven's sake; **¡válgame Dios!** bless me!; **¡vaya con Dios!** off with you!
diosa *f* goddess
diploma *m* diploma
diplomacia *f* diplomacy
diploma•do -da *adj & mf* graduate
diplomar *tr & ref* to graduate
diplomáti•co -ca *adj* diplomatic || *mf* diplomat
diptongar §**44** *tr & ref* to diphthongize
diptongo *m* diphthong
diputación *f* congress; commission
diputa•do -da *mf* deputy, representative
diputar *tr* to commission, delegate; designate
dique *m* dike, jetty; dry dock; check, stop; **dique seco** dry dock
dirección *f* direction; (*señas en una carta*) address; administration, management; directorship; (aut) steering; **de dirección única** one-way; **dirección a la derecha** right-hand drive; **dirección a la izquierda** left-hand drive; **perder la dirección** to lose control of the car
directi•vo -va *adj* managing || *mf* director, manager || *f* management
direc•to -ta *adj* direct; straight
direc•tor -tora *adj* directing, guiding; managing, governing || *mf* director, manager; (*de un periódico*) editor; (*de una escuela*) principal; (*de una orquesta*) conductor; **director de escena** stage manager; **director de funeraria** funeral director; **director gerente** managing director
directorio *m* directorship; directory
dirigente *mf* leader, head, executive
dirigible *adj & m* dirigible
dirigir §**27** *tr* to direct; manage; (*un automóvil*) steer; (*una carta; la palabra*) address; (*una obra*) dedicate || *ref* to go, betake oneself; turn; **dirigirse a** to address; apply to
dirimir *tr* to dissolve, annul; (*una dificultad*) solve; (*una controversia*) settle, mediate
discar §**73** *tr & intr* to dial
disceptar *intr* to discuss, debate
discerniente *adj* discerning
discernir §**28** *tr* to discern; distinguish
disciplina *f* discipline; **disiplinas** scourge, whip
disciplina•do -da *adj* disciplined; (*flores*) many-colored
disciplinar *tr* to discipline; teach; scourge, whip
disciplinazo *m* lash
discípu•lo -la *mf* disciple; pupil
disco *m* disk; (*del gramófono*) record, disk; (sport) discus; **disco de cola** (rr) taillight; **disco de goma** (*para un grifo*) washer (*for a spigot*); **disco de identificación** identification tag; **disco de larga duración** long-playing record; **disco de señales** (rr) semaphore; **disco selector** (telp) dial; **disco vertebral** spinal disk; **siempre el mismo disco** the same old song
discóbolo *m* discus thrower
discófi•lo -la *mf* record lover, discophile
dísco•lo -la *adj* ungovernable, wayward
disconforme *adj* disagreeing
discontinuar §**21** *tr* to discontinue
discordancia *f* discordance
discordar §**61** *intr* to be out of tune; disagree
discorde *adj* discordant, disagreeing; (mus) discordant, out of tune
discordia *f* discord
discoteca *f* discothèque, disco; record cabinet; record library
discreción *f* discretion; wit; witticism; **a discreción** at discretion; (mil) unconditionally
discrepancia *f* discrepancy; dissent
discrepar *intr* to differ, disagree
discretear *intr* to try to be clever, try to sparkle
discre•to -ta *adj* (*juicioso*) discreet; (*discontinuo*) discrete; witty
discrimen *m* risk, hazard; difference
discriminación *f* discrimination
discriminar *tr* to discriminate against || *intr* to discriminate
discriminato•rio -ria *adj* discriminatory
disculpa *f* excuse, apology
disculpar *tr* to excuse; pardon, overlook || *ref* to apologize; **disculparse con** to apologize to; **disculparse de** to apologize for
discurrir *tr* to contrive, invent; guess, conjecture || *intr* to ramble, roam; occur, take place; discourse; reason; pass, elapse
discursis•to -ta *adj* long-winded; (coll) windy; *mf* windbag; big talker
discursi•vo -va *adj* meditative
discurso *m* discourse, speech; (*paso del tiempo*) course; **discurso de sobremesa** after-dinner speech
discusión *f* discussion
discutible *adj* debatable
discutir *tr* to discuss || *intr* to discuss; argue
disecar §**73** *tr* to dissect; (*un animal muerto*) stuff; (*una planta*) mount
diseminar *tr* to disseminate; scatter || *ref* to scatter
disensión *f* (*oposición*) dissent; (*contienda*) dissension
disentería *f* dysentery
disentir §**68** *intr* to dissent
diseñar *tr* to draw, sketch; design, outline

diseño *m* drawing, sketch; design, outline
disertar *intr* to discourse, discuss
diser•to -ta *adj* fluent, eloquent
disfavor *m* disfavor
disforme *adj* formless; monstrous, ugly
disforzar §35 *ref* (Peru) to be prudish, be finical
dis•fraz *m* (*pl* **-fraces**) disguise; (*traje de máscara*) costume, fancy dress
disfrazar §60 *tr* to disguise || *ref* to disguise oneself; wear fancy dress, masquerade, dress in costume
disfrutar *tr* to enjoy, to use || *intr* —**disfrutar de** to enjoy, use; **disfrutar con** to enjoy, take enjoyment in
disfrute *m* enjoyment, use
disfunción *f* dysfunction
disgregar §44 *tr & intr* to disintegrate, break up
disgusta•do -da *adj* tasteless, insipid; sad, sorrowful; disagreeable; (Mex) hard to please
disgustar *tr* to displease || *ref* to be displeased; fall out, become estranged
disgusto *m* displeasure; annoyance, unpleasantness; grief, sorrow; difference, quarrel; **a disgusto** against one's will
disidencia *f* dissidence; (*de una doctrina*) dissent
disidente *adj* dissident || *mf* dissident, dissenter
disidir *intr* to dissent
disíla•bo -ba *adj* dissyllabic || *m* dissyllable
disímil *adj* dissimilar
disimilar *tr & ref* to dissimilate
disimula•do -da *adj* sly, underhanded; **a lo disimulado** or **a la disimulada** underhandedly; **hacer la disimulada** to feign ignorance
disimular *tr* to dissemble, dissimulate, hide, conceal; overlook, pardon || *intr* to dissemble, dissimulate
disimulo *m* dissembling, dissimulation; indulgence
disipación *f* dissipation
disipa•do -da *adj* dissipated; spendthrift || *mf* debauchee; spendthrift
disipar *tr* to dissipate || *ref* to be dissipated; disappear, evanesce
dislate *m* nonsense
dislocar §73 *tr* to dislocate || *ref* to dislocate; be dislocated
disloque *m* tops, top notch
disminución *f* diminution; decrease; **disminución física** handicap, disability
disminuir §20 *tr, intr & ref* to diminish
disociar *tr* to dissociate
disolución *f* dissolution; disbandment; (*relajación de costumbres*) dissoluteness, dissipation
disolu•to -ta *adj* dissolute || *mf* debauchee
disolver §47 & §83 *tr* to dissolve; disband; destroy, ruin || *intr & ref* to dissolve
disonancia *f* dissonance
disonar §61 *intr* to be dissonant, lack harmony, disagree; cause surprise; sound bad
dispar *adj* unlike, different; (*que no hace juego*) odd
disparada *f* sudden flight; **a la disparada** like a shot, in mad haste; **de una disparada** (Arg) right away; **tomar la disparada** (Arg) to take to one's heels
disparadero *m* trigger
disparador *m* trigger; (*de reloj*) escapement; **poner en el disparador** to drive mad
disparar *tr* to throw, hurl; shoot, fire || *intr* to rant, talk nonsense || *ref* to dash away, rush away; (*un caballo*) run away; (*una escopeta*) to go off; be beside oneself
disparata•do -da *adj* absurd, nonsensical; frightful
disparatar *intr* to talk nonsense; act foolishly
disparate *m* folly, nonsense; blunder, mistake; outrage
dispare•jo -ja *adj* unequal, different, uneven, disparate; rough, broken
disparidad *f* disparity
disparo *m* shot, discharge; nonsense; (mach) release, trip; **cambiar disparos** to exchange shots
dispendio *m* waste, extravagance
dispendio•so -sa *adj* expensive
dispensar *tr* to excuse, pardon; exempt; dispense; dispense with
dispensario *m* dispensary; **dispensario de alimentos** soup kitchen
dispepsia *f* dyspepsia
dispersar *tr & ref* to disperse
displicente *adj* disagreeable; cross, fretful, peevish
disponer §54 *tr* to dispose, arrange; direct, order || *intr* to dispose; **disponer de** to dispose of, have at one's disposal || *ref* to prepare, get ready; get ready to die, make one's will
disponible *adj* available, disposable
disposición *f* disposition, arrangement, layout; inclination; preparation; disposal; predisposition; state of health; elegance; **estar a la disposición de** to be at the disposal of, be at the service of; **última disposición** last will and testament
dispositivo *m* appliance, device
dispues•to -ta *adj* ready, prepared; comely, graceful; clever, skillful; **bien dispuesto** well-disposed; well, in good health; **mal dispuesto** ill-disposed, unfavorable; ill, indisposed
disputa *f* dispute; fight, struggle; **sin disputa** beyond dispute
disputar *tr* to dispute, question; argue over; fight for || *intr* to dispute; debate, argue; fight
disquería *f* record shop
disque•ro -ra *mf* record dealer
distancia *f* distance; **a distancia** at a distance; **a larga distancia** long-distance; **tomar distancia** to stand aside, stand off
distante *adj* distant
distar *intr* to be distant, be far; be different
distender §51 *tr* to distend; (*p.ej., las piernas*) stretch || *ref* to distend; relax; (*un reloj*) run down

distensión *f* distension; relaxation of tension
distinción *f* (*honor, prerrogativa*) distinction; (*diferencia*) distinctness; **a distinción de** unlike
distingui•do -da *adj* distinguished; refined, urbane, smooth
distinguir §29 *tr* to distinguish; give distinction to; make out
distinti•vo -va *adj* distinctive || *m* badge, insignia; distinction; distinctive mark
distin•to -ta *adj* distinct; different; **distintos** various, several
distorsión *f* distortion
distorsionar *tr* to distort, twist, bend
distracción *f* distraction; (*licencia en las costumbres*) dissipation; (*substracción de fondos*) embezzlement
distraer §75 *tr* to distract; amuse, divert, entertain; seduce; embezzle
distraí•do -da *adj* absent-minded, distracted; licentious, dissolute; (Chile, Mex) untidy, careless
distribución *f* distribution; electric supply system; timing gears, valve gears
distribui•dor -dora *adj* distributing || *mf* distributor || *m* (aut) distributor; slide valve; **distribuidor automático** vending machine
distribuir §20 *tr* to distribute
distrito *m* district; (rr) section; **distrito electoral** precinct; **distrito postal** zone, postal zone
disturbar *tr* to disturb
disturbio *m* disturbance
disuadir *tr* to dissuade
disyunti•vo -va *adj* disjunctive || *f* dilemma
disyuntor *m* circuit breaker
dita *f* bond, surety
diuca *m* (Arg, Chile) teacher's pet || *f* (Arg, Chile) finch (*Fringilla diuca*)
diuréti•co -ca *adj & m* diuretic
diur•no -na *adj* day, daytime
diva *f* goddess; (mus) diva
divagación *f* digression; wandering
divagar §44 *intr* to digress; ramble, wander
diván *m* divan; **diván cama** day bed
divergir §27 *intr* to diverge
diversidad *f* diversity; abundance
diversificación *f* diversification
diversificar §73 *tr & ref* to diversify
diversión *f* diversion
diver•so -sa *adj* diverse, different; **diversos** several, various, divers
diverti•do -da *adj* amusing, funny; (Am) tipsy
divertimiento *m* diversion, amusement
divertir §68 *tr* to divert; amuse || *ref* to enjoy oneself, have a good time
dividendo *m* dividend
dividir *tr* to divide || *ref* to divide, be divided; separate
divieso *m* boil
divinidad *f* divinity; (*persona dotada de gran belleza*) beauty
divinizar §60 *tr* to deify; exalt, extol
divi•no -na *adj* divine
divisa *f* badge; emblem; motto; goal, ideal; currency, foreign exchange
divisar *tr* to descry, espy
división *f* division; (*deportes*) class, category; league
divisor *m* (math) divisor; **máximo común divisor** greatest common divisor; **divisor de voltaje** (rad) voltage divider
divisoria *f* dividing line; (geog) divide
di•vo -va *adj* godlike, divine || *m* god; (mus) opera star || *f* see **diva**
divorciar *tr* to divorce || *ref* to divorce, get divorced
divorcio *m* divorce; divergency (*in opinion*); (Col) jail for women
divulgación *f* divulging, disclosure; popularization
divulgar §44 *tr* to divulge, disclose; popularize
D.ⁿ *abbr* **don**
dobladillar *tr* to hem
dobladillo *m* hem
dobla•do -da *adj* rough, uneven; stocky, thickset; double-dealing || *m* (mov) dubbing
doblaje *m* (mov) dubbing
doblar *tr* to double; fold, crease; bend; (*una esquina*) turn, round; (*un promontorio*) double; (*una película, generalmente en otro idioma*) dub; (bridge) to double; (Mex) to shoot down || *intr* to turn; (*tocar a muerto*) toll; (mov, theat) to double, stand in; (bridge) to double || *ref* to double; fold, crease; bend; bow, stoop; give in, yield
doble *adj* double; heavy, thick; stocky, thickset; deceitful, two-faced || *adv* double, doubly || *mf* (mov, theat) double, stand-in || *m* double; fold, crease; (*toque de difuntos*) toll, knell; (*suma que se paga por la prórroga de una operación a plazos en la bolsa*) margin; **al doble** doubly
doblegar §44 *tr* to fold; bend; (*una espada*) brandish, flourish; sway, dominate || *ref* to fold; bend; give in, yield
doblete *adj* medium || *m* (*piedra falsa; cada una de dos palabras que poseen un mismo origen*) doublet; (bridge) doubleton
do•blez *m* (*pl* **-bleces**) fold, crease; (*del pantalón*) cuff; duplicity, double-dealing
doce *adj & pron* twelve; **las doce** twelve o'clock || *m* twelve; (*en las fechas*) twelfth
docea•vo -va *adj & m* twelfth
docena *f* dozen; **docena del fraile** baker's dozen
docencia *f* (Arg) teaching; (Arg) teaching staff
docente *adj* educational, teaching
dócil *adj* docile; soft, ductile
doc•to -ta *adj* learned || *mf* scholar
doc•tor -tora *mf* doctor || *f* (coll) bluestocking
doctorado *m* doctorate
doctoran•do -da *mf* candidate for the doctor's degree
doctorar *tr* to grant the doctor's degree to || *ref* to get the doctor's degree
doctrina *f* doctrine; teaching, instruction; learning; catechism; preaching the Gospel
doctrinar *tr* to teach, instruct

doctrino *m* orphan (*in orphanage*); **parecer un doctrino** to look scared
documentación *f* documentation; **documentación del buque** ship's papers
documental *adj* documentary || *m* (mov) documentary
documentar *tr* to document
documento *m* document; **documento de prueba** (law) exhibit
dogal *m* (*para atar las caballerías*) halter; (*para ahorcar a un reo*) noose, halter, hangman's rope; **estar con el dogal a la garganta** or **al cuello** to be in a tight spot
dogmáti•co -ca *adj* dogmatic
do•go -ga *mf* bulldog
dolamas *fpl* or **dolames** *mpl* hidden defects of a horse; complaints, aches and pains
dolar **§61** *tr* to hew
dólar *m* dollar
dolencia *f* ailment, complaint
doler **§47** *tr* to ache, pain; grieve, distress; **dolerle a uno el dinero** to hate to spend money || *intr* to ache, hurt, pain || *ref* to complain; feel sorry; repent
doliente *adj* sick, ill; aching, suffering; sad, sorrowful || *mf* sufferer, patient || *m* mourner
dolo *m* deceit, fraud, guile
dolor *m* ache, pain; grief, sorrow; regret, repentance; **dolor de cabeza** headache; **dolor de muelas** toothache; **dolor de oído** earache; **dolor de yegua** (CAm) lumbago; **estar con dolores** to be in labor
dolori•do -da *adj* sore, painful; grieving, disconsolate
doloro•so -sa *adj* painful; sorrowful, sad
dolo•so -sa *adj* deceitful, guileful
domador *m* horsebreaker; animal tamer
domar *tr* to tame, break; master
domeñar *tr* to master, subdue
domesticar **§73** *tr* to domesticate; tame
domésti•co -ca *adj* domestic, household || *mf* domestic, servant
domiciliar *tr* to domicile, settle; (*una carta*) (Mex) to address || *ref* to be domiciled, take up one's residence
domicilio *m* domicile, home; dwelling, house; **domicilio social** home office, company office
dominación *f* domination; (mil) eminence, high ground
dominante *adj* dominant; (*mandón*) domineering || *f* (mus) dominant
dominar *tr* to dominate; check, restrain, subdue; (*una ciencia, un idioma*) master || *intr* to dominate; (*mandar imperiosamente*) domineer || *ref* to restrain oneself
dómine *m* schoolmaster, Latin teacher; pedant
domingo *m* Sunday; **domingo de ramos** Palm Sunday; **domingo de resurrección** Easter Sunday; **guardar el domingo** to keep the Sabbath
dominguillo *m* tumbler
dominica•no -na *adj* & *mf* Dominican
dominio *m* dominion; domain; (*de una ciencia, de un idioma*) mastery; (*del aire*) supremacy
domi•nó *m* (*pl* **-nós**) (*traje*) domino; (*juego*) dominoes; (*fichas*) set of dominoes
dom.° *abbr* **domingo**
domo *m* dome
dompedro *m* four-o'clock
don *m* gift, present; talent, natural gift; Don (*Spanish title used before masculine Christian names*); **don de acierto** knack for doing the right thing; **don de errar** knack for doing the wrong thing; **don de gentes** charm, social grace; **don de lenguas** linguistic facility; **don de mando** ability to lead, generalship
dona *f* gift, present; **donas** wedding presents from the bridegroom to the bride
donación *f* gift, bequest; endowment
donada *f* lay sister
donado *m* lay brother
dona•dor -dora *mf* donor
donaire *m* charm, grace; witticism; cleverness
donairo•so -sa *adj* charming, graceful; witty; clever
donar *tr* to donate, give
doncel *adj* mild, mellow || *m* (*joven noble aun no armado caballero*) bachelor; (*hombre virgen*) virgin
doncella *f* maiden, virgin; housemaid; lady's maid; maid of honor; (Col, Ven) felon, whitlow
doncellez *f* maidenhood, virginity
doncellona *f* or **doncellueca** *f* unmarried woman, maiden lady
donde *conj* where; wherever; in which; **donde no** otherwise; **por donde quiera** anywhere, everywhere || *prep* at or to the house, office, or store of
dónde *adv* where; **a dónde** where, whither; **de dónde** from where, whence; **por dónde** which way; for what cause, for what reason
dondequiera *adv* anywhere; **dondequiera que** wherever
dondiego *m* four-o'clock; **dondiego de día** morning-glory; **dondiego de noche** four-o'clock
donillero *m* sharper, smoothy
donjuán *m* four-o'clock
donosidad *f* charm, grace, wit
dono•so -sa *adj* charming, graceful, witty
donostiarra *adj* San Sebastian || *mf* native or inhabitant of San Sebastian
donosura *f* charm, grace, wit
doña *f* Doña (*Spanish title used before feminine Christian names*)
doñear *intr* (coll) to hang around women
doquier or **doquiera** *conj* wherever; **por doquier** everywhere
dorada *f* (ichth) gilthead
doradillo *m* fine brass wire
dora•do -da *adj* golden; gilt || *m* gilt, gilding; **dorados** bronze trimmings (*on furniture*) || *f* see **dorada**

dorar *tr* to gold-plate; gild; (*tostar ligeramente*) brown; (*paliar*) sugar-coat || *ref* to turn golden; turn brown
dormi•lón -lona *adj* sleepy || *mf* sleepyhead || *f* reclining armchair; mimosa; (Mex) headrest; (Ven) sleeping gown; **dormilonas** pearl earrings
dormir §30 *tr* to put to sleep; (*p.ej., una borrachera*) sleep off || *intr* to sleep; spend the night || *ref* to sleep; fall asleep; (*entorpecerse, p.ej., el pie*) go to sleep
dormirlas *m* hide-and-seek
dormitar *intr* to doze, nap
dormitorio *m* bedroom; (*muebles propios de esta habitación*) bedroom suit
dorsal *m* (sport) number (*worn on shirt*)
dorso *m* back
dos *adj & pron* two; **las dos** two o'clock || *m* two; (*en las fechas*) second
dosal•bo -ba *adj* (*horse*) with two white feet
doscien•tos -tas *adj & pron* two hundred || **doscientos** *m* two hundred
dosel *m* canopy, dais
doselera *f* valance, drapery
dosificación *f* dosage
dosificar §73 *tr* (*un medicamento*) to dose, give in doses
do•sis *f* (*pl* **-sis**) dose
dos-pie•zas *m* (*pl* **-zas**) two-piece bathing suit
dotación *f* (*de una mujer; de una fundación*) endowment; (nav) complement; (aer) crew; (*de remeros*) (sport) crew; staff, personnel
dotar *tr* to give a dowry to; endow; (*un buque*) staff, man; (*una oficina*) staff; equip; fix the wages for
dote *m & f* dowry, marriage portion || *m* (*en el juego de naipes*) stack of chips || *f* endowment, talent, gift; **dotes de mando** leadership
dovela *f* voussoir
doza•vo -va *adj & m* twelfth
d/p *abbr* **días plazo**
dracma *f* (*moneda griega*) drachma; (*peso farmacéutico*) dram
draga *f* dredge; (*barco*) dredger
dragado *m* dredging
dragami•nas *m* (*pl* **-nas**) mine sweeper
dragar §44 *tr* to dredge
dragón *m* dragon; (*planta*) snapdragon; (*soldado*) dragoon
dragonear *intr* to flirt; boast; **dragonear de** to boast of being; pretend to be, pass oneself off as
drama *m* drama
dramáti•co -ca *adj* dramatic || *mf* (*autor*) dramatist; actor || *f* (*arte y género*) drama
dramatizar §60 *tr* to dramatize
dramaturgo *m* dramatist
drásti•co -ca *adj* drastic
dren *m* drain
drenaje *m* drainage
drenar *tr* to drain
driblar *tr & intr* to dribble
dril *m* drill; duck; **dril de algodón** denim
driza *f* (naut) halyard
dro. *abbr* **derecho**
droga *f* drug; annoyance, bother; deceit, trick; (Chile, Mex, Peru) bad debt; (Cuba) drug on the market; **drogas milagrosas** wonder drugs
drogadic•to -ta *adj* drug-addicted || *mf* drug addict
drogado *m* doping
drogar §44 *tr* to dope
droguería *f* drug store; drug business; (*comercio de substancias usadas en química, industria, medicina, bellas artes*) drysaltery (Brit)
drogue•ro -ra *mf* druggist; drysalter (Brit)
droguista *mf* druggist; (coll) crook, cheat; (Arg) toper, drunk
drolláti•co -ca *adj* droll, snappy
dromedario *m* dromedary; big heavy animal; brute (*person*)
druida *m* druid
dúa *f* (min) gang of workmen
dual *adj & m* dual
dualidad *f* duality; (Chile) tie vote
ducado *m* duchy, dukedom; (*moneda antigua*) ducat; **gran ducado** grand duchy
dúctil *adj* ductile; easy to handle
ducha *f* (*chorro de agua en una cavidad del cuerpo*) douche; (*chorro de agua sobre el cuerpo entero*) shower bath; (*lista en los tejidos*) stripe; **ducha en alfileres** needle bath
duchar *tr* to douche; give a shower bath to || *ref* to douche; take a shower bath
du•cho -cha *adj* experienced, expert, skillful || *f* see **ducha**
duda *f* doubt; **sin duda** doubtless, no doubt, without doubt
dudable *adj* doubtful
dudar *tr* to doubt; question || *intr* to hesitate; **dudar de** to doubt
dudo•so -sa *adj* doubtful; dubious
duela *f* stave (*of barrel*)
duelista *m* duelist
duelo *m* (*combate entre dos*) duel; grief, sorrow; bereavement, mourning; (*los que asisten a los funerales*) mourners; **batirse en duelo** to duel, to fight a duel; **duelos** hardships; **sin duelo** in abundance
duende *m* elf, goblin; gold cloth, silver cloth; (coll) restless daemon; **tener duende** to be burning within
due•ño -ña *mf* owner, proprietor; **dueño de sí mismo** one's own master; **ser dueño de** to be master of; be at liberty to, be free to || *m* master, landlord || *f* mistress, landlady, housekeeper; duenna; matron; **dueña de casa** housewife
duermevela *f* doze, light sleep; (*sueño fatigoso e interrumpido*) fitful sleep
dula *f* common pasture land; land irrigated from common ditch
dulce *adj* sweet; (*agua*) fresh; (*metal*) soft, ductile; gentle, mild, pleasant; (*manjar*) tasteless, insipid || *m* candy; piece of candy; preserves; **dulce de almíbar** preserved fruit; **dulces** candy
dulcera *f* candy dish, preserve dish
dulcería *f* candy store, confectionery store

dulce•ro -ra *adj* sweet-toothed || *mf* confectioner || *f* see **dulcera**
dulcificar §73 *tr* to sweeten; appease, mollify || *ref* to sweeten, turn sweet
dulcinea *f* sweetheart; ideal
dulzaina *f* flageolet
dulza•rrón -rrona *adj* cloying, sickening
dulzo•so -sa *adj* sweetish
dulzura *f* sweetness; pleasantness, kindliness; (*del clima*) mildness; endearment, sweet word
duna *f* dune
dun•do -da *adj* (CAm, Col) simple, stupid || *mf* (CAm, Col) simpleton
dúo *m* duet, duo
duodéci•mo -ma *adj & m* twelfth
duodeno *m* duodenum
duplica•do -da *adj & m* duplicate; **por duplicado** in duplicate
duplicar §73 *tr* to duplicate; double; repeat
duplicata *f* duplicate
duplicidad *f* (*falsedad*) duplicity; (*calidad de doble*) doubleness
du•plo -pla *adj & m* double
duque *m* duke; **gran duque** grand duke
duquesa *f* duchess; **gran duquesa** grand duchess
dura *f* durability; **de dura** or **de mucha dura** strong, durable
durable *adj* durable, lasting
duración *f* duration, endurance; (*espacio de tiempo del uso de una cosa*) life
durade•ro -ra *adj* durable, lasting
durante *prep* during, for
durar *intr* to last; remain; (*la ropa*) last, wear, wear well
durazno *m* peach; peach tree
dureza *f* hardness; harshness, roughness; **dureza de corazón** hardheartedness; **dureza de oído** hardness of hearing; **dureza de vientre** constipation
durmiente *adj* sleeping; **la Bella Durmiente** Sleeping Beauty || *mf* sleeper || *m* girder, sleeper, stringer; tie, railroad tie; (Ven) steel bar
du•ro -ra *adj* hard; (*huevo*) hard-boiled; harsh, rough; cruel; stubborn, obstinate; unbearable; strong, tough; stingy; (*tiempo*) stormy; **duro de corazón** hard-hearted; **duro de oído** hard of hearing; **duro de película** movie hero; **estar muy duro con** to be hard on; **ser duro de pelar** to be hard to put across; be hard to deal with || *m* dollar (*Spanish coin worth five pesetas*) || *f* see **dura** || **duro** *adv* hard
dux *m* (*pl* **dux**) doge
d/v *abbr* **días vista**

E

E, e (e) *f* sixth letter of the Spanish alphabet
e *conj* (used before words beginning with *i* or *hi* not followed by a vowel) and
ea *interj* hey!
ebanista *m* cabinetmaker, woodworker
ebanistería *f* cabinetmaking, woodwork; cabinetmaker's shop
ébano *m* ebony
ebriedad *f* drunkenness
e•brio -bria *adj* drunk; (*p.ej., de ira*) blind || *mf* drunk
ebrio•so -sa *adj* drinking || *mf* drinker
ebullición *f* boiling
ecléctí•co -ca *adj & mf* eclectic
eclesiásti•co -ca *adj & m* ecclesiastic
eclipsar *tr* to eclipse; (fig) to outshine || *ref* to be in eclipse; (fig) to disappear
eclipse *m* eclipse
eclip•sis *f* (*pl* **-sis**) var of **elipsis**
eclisa *f* (rr) fishplate
eco *m* echo; (*del tambor*) rumbling; **hacer eco** to echo; attract attention; **tener eco** to be well received, catch on
ecología *f* ecology
ecológi•co -ca *adj* ecologic(al)
ecologista *mf* or **ecólogo** *m* ecologist
economato *m* stewardship; commissary, company store, coöperative store
economía *f* economy; want, poverty; **economía política** economics; **economías** savings
económi•co -ca *adj* economic; (*que gasta poco; poco costoso*) economical; cheap; miserly, niggardly
economista *mf* economist
economizar §60 *tr* to economize, save; avoid || *intr* to economize, save; skimp
ecónomo *m* steward, trustee; supply priest
ecuación *f* equation
ecuador *m* equator || **el Ecuador** Ecuador
ecuánime *adj* calm, composed; impartial
ecuanimidad *f* equanimity; impartiality
ecuatoria•no -na *adj & mf* Ecuadoran, Ecuadorian
ecuestre *adj* equestrian
eculcorante *adj* sweetening || *m* sweetener
ecuméni•co -ca *adj* ecumenic(al)
eczema *m & f* eczema
echacan•tos *m* (*pl* **-tos**) good-for-nothing
echacuer•vos *m* (*pl* **-vos**) pimp, procurer; cheat
echada *f* cast, throw; man's length; (Arg, Mex) boast, hoax
echadero *m* place to stretch out
echadi•zo -za *adj* discarded, waste; spying || *mf* foundling || *m* spy

echa•do -da *adj* stretched out; (C-R) lazy, indolent; **estar echado** (CAm, Mex, P-R) to have an easy job (or easy life) || *f* see **echada**
echar *tr* to throw, throw away, throw out; issue, emit; publish; discharge, dismiss; swallow; (*p.ej., agua*) pour; (*p.ej., un cigarrillo*) smoke; (*la baraja*) deal; (*una partida de cartas*) play; (*una llave*) turn; (*un discurso*) deliver; (*un drama*) put on; (*maldiciones*) utter; (*pelo, dientes, renuevos*) grow, put forth; (*impuestos*) impose, levy; (*la buenaventura*) tell; (*precio, distancia, edad, etc.*) ascribe, attribute; (*una mirada*) cast; (*sangre*) shed; (*la culpa*) lay; (*una mano*) lend; **echar abajo** to demolish, destroy; overthrow; **echar a pasear** to dismiss unceremoniously; **echar a perder** to spoil, ruin; **echar a pique** to sink; **echar de menos** to miss; **echarla de** to claim to be, boast of being; **echarlo todo a rodar** to upset everything; hit the ceiling || *intr* — **echar a** to begin to; burst out (*e.g., crying*); **echar a perder** to spoil, ruin; **echar de ver** to notice, happen to see; **echar por** (*un empleo, un oficio*) to go into, take up; (*la derecha, la izquierda*) turn toward; (*un camino*) go down || *ref* to throw oneself; lie down, stretch out; (*el viento*) fall; (*un abrigo*) throw on; (*una gallina*) set; **echarse a** to begin to; **echarse a morir** to give up in despair; **echarse a perder** to spoil, be ruined; **echarse atrás** to back out; **echarse de ver** to be easy to see; **echárselas de** to claim to be, boast of being; **echarse sobre** to rush at, fall upon
echazón *f* jettison, jetsam
echiquier *m* Exchequer
edad *f* age; **edad crítica** change of life; **edad de quintas** draft age; **edad escolar** school age; **Edad Media** Middle Ages; **edad viril** prime of life; **mayor edad** majority; **menor edad** minority
edecán *m* aide-de-camp
edema *f* edema
edición *f* edition; publication; **la segunda edición de** the spit and image of
edicto *m* edict
edificación *f* construction, building; buildings; (*inspiración con el buen ejemplo*) edification, uplift
edificante *adj* edifying
edificar **§73** *tr* to construct, build; (*dar buen ejemplo a*) edify, uplift
edificio *m* edifice, building
editar *tr* to publish
edi•tor -tora *adj* publishing || *mf* publisher
editorial *adj* publishing; editorial || *m* editorial || *f* publishing house
editorialista *mf* editorial writer
editorializar **§60** *intr* (Urug) to editorialize
edredón *m* eider down
educación *f* education
educacional *adj* educational
educa•dor -dora *mf* educator
educan•do -da *mf* pupil, student
educar **§73** *tr* to educate; (*los sentidos*) train; (*al niño o el adolescente*) rear, bring up
educati•vo -va *adj* educational
EE.UU. *abbr* **Estados Unidos**
efectismo *m* sensationalism
efectista *adj* sensational, theatrical || *mf* sensationalist
efectivamente *adv* actually, really; as a matter of fact
efecti•vo -va *adj* actual, real; (*empleo, cargo*) regular, permanent; (*vigente*) effective; **hacer efectivo** to carry out; (*un cheque*) to cash; **hacerse efectivo** to become effective || *m* cash; **efectivo en caja** cash on hand
efecto *m* effect; end, purpose; article; (*en el juego de billar*) English; **a ese efecto** for that purpose; **al efecto** for the purpose; **con efecto** or **en efecto** indeed, as a matter of fact; **efecto útil** efficiency, output; **llevar a efecto** or **poner en efecto** to put into effect, carry out; **surtir efecto** to work, have the desired effect
efectuar **§21** *tr* to carry out, effect, effectuate || *ref* to take place
efervescencia *f* effervescence
efervescente *adj* effervescent
eficacia *f* efficacy
efi•caz *adj* (*pl* **-caces**) efficacious, effectual; efficient
eficiencia *f* efficiency
eficiente *adj* efficient
efigie *f* effigy
efíme•ro -ra *adj* ephemeral
efugio *m* evasion, subterfuge
efusión *f* effusion; (*manifestación de afectos muy viva*) warmth, effusiveness; **efusión de sangre** bloodshed
efusi•vo -va *adj* effusive
égida *f* aegis
egip•cio -cia *adj & mf* Egyptian
Egipto *m* Egypt
eglantina *f* sweetbriar
eglefino *m* haddock
égloga *f* eclogue
egoísmo *m* egoism
egoísta *adj* egoistic || *mf* egoist
egolatría *f* self-worship, self-glorification
egotismo *m* egotism
egotista *adj* egotistic(al) || *mf* egotist
egre•gio -gia *adj* distinguished, eminent
egresar *intr* to graduate
egreso *m* departure; graduation
eje *m* (*pieza alrededor de la cual gira un cuerpo*) axle, shaft; (*línea que divide en dos mitades; línea recta alrededor de la cual se supone que gira un cuerpo*) axis; (fig) core, crux; **eje de balancín** rocker, rockershaft; **eje de carretón** axletree; **eje motor** drive shaft; **eje tándem** dual axle; dual rear
ejecución *f* execution
ejecutante *mf* performer
ejecutar *tr* to execute; perform
ejecutivamente *adv* expeditiously
ejecuti•vo -va *adj* urgent, pressing; insistent; executive || *m* executive
ejecu•tor -tora *adj* executive || *mf* executor;

ejecutor de la justicia executioner; ejecutor testamentario executor (*of a will*) || *f*— ejecutora testamentaria executrix

ejemplar *adj* exemplary || *m* pattern, model; (*de una obra impresa*) copy; precedent; (*caso que sirve de escarmiento*) example; **ejemplar de cortesía** complimentary copy; **ejemplar muestra** sample copy; **sin ejemplar** unprecedented; as a special case

ejemplarizar §60 *tr* to set an example to; exemplify

ejemplificar §73 *tr* to exemplify

ejemplo *m* example, instance; **por ejemplo** for example, for instance; **sin ejemplo** unexampled

ejercer §78 *tr* (*la medicina*) to practice; (*la caridad*) show, exercise; (*una fuerza*) exert || *intr* to practice; **ejercer de** to practice as, work as

ejercicio *m* exercise; drill, practice; (*de un cargo u oficio*) tenure; (*uso constante*) exertion; (*año económico*) fiscal year; **hacer ejercicio** to take exercise; (mil) to drill

ejercitar *tr* to exercise; practice; drill, train || *ref* to exercise; practice

ejército *m* army; **ejército permanente** standing army; **los tres ejércitos** the three arms of the service

ejido *m* commons

ejote *m* (CAm, Mex) string bean

el, la (*pl* **los, las**) *art def* the || *pron dem* that, the one; **el que** who, which, that; he who, the one that

él *pron pers masc* he, it; him, it

elabora•do -da *adj* elaborate; finished

elaborar *tr* to elaborate; (*una teoría*) work out; (*el metal, la madera*) fashion, to work

elación *f* magnanimity, nobility; (*de estilo y lenguaje*) pomposity

elástica *f* knit undershirt; **elásticas** (Ven) suspenders

elasticidad *f* elasticity

elásti•co -ca *adj* elastic || *m* elastic; bedspring || *f* see **elástica**

eléboro *m* hellebore

elección *f* election; choice

electi•vo -va *adj* elective

elec•to -ta *adj* elect

electorado *m* electorate

electorero *m* henchman, heeler

electricidad *f* electricity

electricista *mf* electrician

eléctrico -ca *adj* electric(al)

electrificar §73 *tr* to electrify

electrizar §60 *tr* to electrify

electro *m* electromagnet

electroafeitadora *f* electric shaver

electrocutar *tr* to electrocute

electrodo *m* electrode

electrodomésti•co -ca *adj* electric-appliance || *m* electric appliance

electróge•no -na *adj* generating electricity || *m* electric generator

electroimán *m* electromagnet

electrólisis *f* electrolysis

electrólito *m* electrolyte

electromagnéti•co -ca *adj* electromagnetic

electromo•tor -tora or **-triz** *adj* (*pl* **-tores -toras -trices**) electromotive

electrón *m* electron

electróni•co -ca *adj* electronic || *f* electronics

electrostáti•co -ca *adj* electrostatic

electrotecnia *f* electrical engineering

electrotipar *tr* to electrotype

electrotipo *m* electrotype

elefante *m* elephant; **elefante blanco** (fig) (SAm) white elephant

elegancia *f* elegance; style, stylishness

elegante *adj* elegant; stylish || *mf* fashion plate

eleganto•so -sa *adj* elegant

elegía *f* elegy

elegía•co -ca *adj* elegiac

elegible *adj* eligible

elegir §57 *tr* to elect; choose, select

elemental *adj* (*primordial; simple, no compuesto*) elemental; (*que se refiere a los principios de una ciencia o arte; de fácil comprensión*) elementary

elemento *m* element; (*de una pila o batería*) cell; **elemento de compuestos** (gram) combining form; **elemento en rastro** trace element; **estar en su elemento** to be in one's element

elenco *m* catalogue, list, table; (theat) cast

elepé *adj* (*disco*) long-playing; LP || *m* long-playing record

elevación *f* elevation; **elevación a potencias** (math) involution

eleva•do -da *adj* elevated, high; lofty, sublime

elevador *m* elevator; **elevador de granos** grain elevator

elevar *tr* to elevate, lift; (math) to raise || *ref* to ascend, rise; be exalted; become conceited

elfo *m* elf

elidir *tr* to eliminate; (*una vocal*) elide

eliminar *tr* to eliminate; strike out || *ref* (Mex) to go away, leave

elipse *f* (geom) ellipse

elip•sis *f* (*pl* **-sis**) (gram) ellipsis

elípti•co -ca *adj* (geom & gram) elliptic(al)

elisión *f* elision

elitista *adj* & *mf* elitist

elocución *f* public speaking, elocution

elocuencia *f* eloquence

elocuente *adj* eloquent

elogiable *adj* praiseworthy

elogiar *tr* to praise, eulogize

elogio *m* praise, eulogy

elogio•so -sa *adj* laudatory, glowing

elote *m* (Mex, Guat) ear of corn; **coger asando elotes** (CAm) to catch in the act; **pagar los elotes** (CAm) to be the goat

elucidar *tr* to elucidate

eludir *tr* to elude, evade, avoid

elusi•vo -va *adj* evasive; elusive

ella *pron pers fem* she, it; her, it; (coll) the trouble

ello *pron pers neut* it; (coll) the trouble; **ello es que** the fact is that || *m* (psychoanalysis) id

E.M. *abbr* **Estado Mayor**
emancipar *tr* to emancipate
embadurnamiento *m* daub, daubing
embadurnar *tr* to daub
embaír §1 *tr* to deceive, take in, hoax
embajada *f* embassy; ambassadorship; (iron) fine proposition
embajador *m* ambassador; **embajadores** ambassador and wife
embajadora *f* ambassadress
embalaje *m* packing; package; (sport) sprint
embalar *tr* to pack || *intr* (sport) to sprint || *ref* (*el motor*) to race; (sport) to sprint
embaldosado *m* tile paving
embaldosar *tr* to pave with tile
embalsamar *tr* to embalm; perfume
embalsar *tr* to dam, dam up
embalse *m* dam; damming; backwater
embanastar *tr* to put in a basket; pack, jam, overcrowd
embanquetar *tr* (Mex) to line with sidewalks
embarazada *adj fem* pregnant || *f* pregnant woman
embarazar §60 *tr* (*estorbar*) to embarrass; obstruct; make pregnant || *ref* to be embarrassed, be encumbered; become pregnant
embarazo *m* embarrassment; obstruction; awkwardness; pregnancy
embarazo•so -sa *adj* embarrassing, troublesome
embarbillar *tr* to rabbet
embarcación *f* boat, ship; embarkation (*of passengers*)
embarcadero *m* pier, wharf; (rr) platform; **embarcadero de ganado** (Arg) loading chute; **embarcadero flotante** landing stage
embarcador *m* shipper
embarcar §73 *tr* to ship || *intr* to entrain || *ref* to embark, ship; get involved
embarco *m* embarkation (*of passengers*)
embargar §44 *tr* to embargo; paralyze; (law) to seize, attach
embargo *m* embargo; indigestion; (law) seizure, attachment; **sin embargo** however, nevertheless
embarnizar §60 *tr* to varnish
embarque *m* shipment, embarkation (*of freight*)
embarrada *f* blunder
embarrancar §73 *tr, intr & ref* to run into a ditch; (*una nave*) run aground
embarrar *tr* to splash with mud; smear, stain; (CAm, Mex) to involve in a shady deal; **embarrarla** (Arg) to spoil the whole thing
embarrilar *tr* to barrel, put in barrels
embarullar *tr* to muddle, make a mess of; bungle, botch
embastar *tr* to baste, stitch
embate *m* blow, attack; (*del mar*) beating, dashing; (*de viento*) gust; **embates de la fortuna** hard knocks
embauca•dor -dora *mf* trickster; impostor; con man
embaucar §73 *tr* to trick, bamboozle, swindle
embaula•do -da *adj* crowded, packed, jammed
embaular §8 *tr* to put in a trunk; jam, pack in
embayar *ref* (Ecuad) to fly into a rage
embazar §60 *tr* to dye brown; hinder, obstruct; astound, dumbfound || *ref* to get bored; be upset, get sick at the stomach
embebecer §22 *tr* to entertain, amuse, fascinate, enchant
embeber *tr* to absorb, soak up; soak; contain, include; embed; contract, shrink || *intr* to contract, shrink || *ref* to be enchanted, be enraptured; become absorbed or immersed; become well versed
embebi•do -da *adj* (*vocal*) elided; (*columna*) engaged
embelecar §73 *tr* to cheat, dupe, bamboozle
embeleco *m* cheating, fraud; bore; **embelecos** cuteness
embeleñar *tr* to dope, stupefy; enchant, bewitch
embelequería *f* (Col, Mex, W-I) fraud, swindle
embelesar *tr* to charm, enrapture, fascinate
embeleso *m* charm, fascination, delight
embellece•dor -dora *adj* embellishing, beautifying || *m* (aut) hubcap || *f* beautician
embellecer §22 *tr* to embellish, beautify
embellecimiento *m* embellishment, beautification
embermejecer §22 *tr* to dye red; make blush || *ref* to blush
emberrinchar *ref* to fly into a rage
embestida *f* attack, assault; (*detención intempestiva*) buttonholing
embesti•dor -dora *mf* beat, sponger
embestir §50 *tr* to attack, assail; to strike; buttonhole, waylay || *intr* to attack, charge, rush
embetunar *tr* to blacken; cover with tar
embicar §73 *tr* (Mex) to turn upside down, tilt || *intr* (Arg, Chile) to run aground
emblandecer §22 *tr* to soften; placate, mollify || *ref* to soften, yield
emblanquecer §22 *tr* to whiten; bleach || *ref* to turn white
emblema *m* emblem
emblemáti•co -ca *adj* emblematic(al)
embobar *tr* to amaze, fascinate || *ref* to stand gaping
embocadero *m* mouth, outlet
embocadura *f* nozzle; (*de río*) mouth; (*del freno; de instrumento de viento*) mouthpiece; (*de cigarrillo*) tip; (*del vino*) taste; stage entrance
embocar §73 *tr* to catch in the mouth; put in the mouth; take on, undertake; gulp down; try to put over || *intr & ref* to enter, pass
embolada *f* stroke
embolado *m* bull with wooden balls on horns; (theat) minor role; (coll) trick, hoax
embolar *tr* (*los cuernos del toro*) to put wooden balls on; (*el calzado*) to shine || *ref* (CAm, Mex) to get drunk
embolia *f* embolism
émbolo *m* (mach) piston; **émbolo buzo** (mach) plunger

embolsar *tr* to pocket, take in
embonar *tr* to fertilize; suit, be becoming to
emboquillar *tr* (*los cigarrillos*) to put tips on; (*una galería o túnel*) cut an entrance in; (*las junturas entre los ladrillos*) (Chile) to point, chink
emborrachar *tr* to intoxicate || *ref* to get drunk; (*los colores de una tela*) run
emborrar *tr* to stuff, pad, wad; gulp down
emborrascar §**73** *tr* to stir up, irritate || *ref* to get stormy; (*un negocio*) fail; (*la veta de una mina*) (Arg, CAm, Mex) to peter out
emborronar *tr* to blot; scribble
emboscada *f* ambush, ambuscade
emboscado *m* draft dodger
emboscar §**73** *tr* (*tropas para sorprender al enemigo*) to ambush || *ref* to ambush, lie in ambush; shirk, take an easy way out
embota•do -da *adj* blunt, dull; (Chile) black-pawed
embotadura *f* bluntness, dullness
embotar *tr* to blunt, dull; dull, weaken; (*el tabaco*) put in a jar
embotella•do -da *adj* (*discurso*) prepared || *m* bottling; (*del tráfico*) bottleneck
embotellamiento *m* bottling; traffic jam
embotellar *tr* to bottle; (*un negocio*) tie up; (nav) to bottle up
embotijar *tr* (*un suelo*) to underlay with jugs || *ref* to swell up with anger
embovedar *tr* to vault, vault over; put in a vault
emboza•do -da *adj* muffled up || *mf* person muffled up to eyes
embozar §**60** *tr* to muffle up to the eyes; (*p.ej., a un perro*) muzzle; disguise || *ref* to muffle oneself up to the eyes
embozo *m* muffler, cloak held over the face; fold back (*of bed sheet*); cunning, dissimulation; **quitarse el embozo** to drop one's mask
embragar §**44** *tr* (*el motor*) to engage || *intr* to throw the clutch in
embrague *m* clutch; engagement
embravecer §**22** *tr* to enrage, make angry || *ref* to get angry; (*el mar*) get rough
embraveci•do -da *adj* angry; rough, wild
embrear *tr* to tar, cover with tar; calk with tar
embregar §**44** *ref* to wrangle
embriagar §**44** *tr* to intoxicate, make drunk; enrapture || *ref* to get drunk
embriaguez *f* drunkenness; rapture
embridar *tr* to bridle; check, restrain
embriología *f* embryology
embrión *m* embryo
embroca *f* poultice
embrocar §**73** *tr* to empty; (*el toro al torero*) to catch between the horns || *ref* (C-R) to fall on one's face; (Mex) to put on over the head
embrollar *tr* to tangle, muddle, embroil
embrollo *m* entanglement, muddle, embroilment; deception, trick
embromar *tr* to joke with, play jokes on; bore, annoy || *ref* to be bored, be annoyed
embrujar *tr* to bewitch
embrutecer §**22** *tr* to brutify, stupefy
embrutecimiento *m* brutalization; coarsening
embuchado *m* pork sausage; subterfuge; (*de la urna electoral*) stuffing (of ballot box)
embudar *tr* to put a funnel in; trick, trap
embudista *adj* tricky, scheming || *mf* schemer
embudo *m* funnel; trick; (mil) shell hole; **embudo de bomba** (mil) bomb crater
embullar *tr* to stir up, excite, key up || *ref* to become excited, keyed up
emburujar *tr* to jumble, pile up || *ref* to wrap oneself up
embuste *m* lie, falsehood, trick; **embustes** baubles, trinkets; (*del niño*) cuteness
embuste•ro -ra *adj* lying, false, tricky || *mf* liar, cheat
embuti•do -da *adj* inlaid, flush || *m* inlay, marquetry; pork sausage; lace insertion
embutir *tr* to stuff, pack tight; insert; inlay; set flush; (*una hoja de metal*) fashion, hammer into shape || *ref* to squeeze in; stuff oneself
emergencia *f* emergence; incident
emerger §**17** *intr* to emerge; (*un submarino*) surface
emersión *f* emersion; (*de un submarino*) surfacing
eméti•co -ca *adj & m* emetic
emigración *f* emigration; migration
emigra•do -da *mf* émigré
emigrante *adj & mf* emigrant
emigrar *intr* to emigrate; migrate
eminencia *f* eminence
eminente *adj* eminent
emisa•rio -ria *mf* emissary || *m* outlet
emisión *f* (*acción de exhalar; acción de lanzar ondas luminosas, etc.*) emission; (*títulos creados de una vez*) (com) issue; (*acción de emitir títulos nuevos*) (com) issuance; (rad) broadcast; **emisión seriada** (rad) serial
emi•sor -sora *adj* emitting; broadcasting || *m* (rad) transmitter || *f* broadcasting station
emitir *tr* to emit, send forth; issue, give out; (*p.ej., opiniones*) utter, express; (com) to issue; (rad) to broadcast
emoción *f* emotion
emocional *adj* emotional
emocionante *adj* moving, touching; thrilling, exciting
emocionar *tr* to move, stir; thrill
emoti•vo -va *adj* emotional
empacadi•zo -za *adj* (Arg) touchy
empaca•do -da *adj* (Arg) gruff, grim
empacar §**73** *tr* to pack, crate || *ref* to be stubborn; (*un animal*) balk, get balky
empa•cón -cona *adj* stubborn; balky
empacha•do -da *adj* backward, fumbling
empachar *tr* to hinder, embarrass; disguise; surfeit, upset the stomach of || *ref* blush, be embarrassed; be upset, have indigestion
empacho *m* hindrance; embarrassment, bashfulness; indigestion
empacho•so -sa *adj* sickening; shameful
empadronar *tr* to register, take the census of || *ref* to register, be registered in the census

empalagar §44 *tr* to cloy, pall, surfeit; bore, weary

empalago•so -sa *adj* cloying, sickening, mawkish; boring, annoying; fawning

empalar *tr* impale

empalizada *f* palisade, stockade, fence

empalizar §60 *tr* to fence in

empalmar *tr* to splice, connect, join, couple; combine || *intr* to connect, make connections; **empalmar con** to connect with; follow, succeed

empalme *m* splice, connection, joint, coupling; combination; (elec) joint; (rr) connection, junction

empanada *f* pie; fraud

empanadilla *f* pie

empana•do -da *adj* unlighted, unventilated || *f* see **empanada**

empanar *tr* to crumb, bread; (*las tierras*) sow with wheat

empantanar *tr* to flood; obstruct

empaña•do -da *adj* dim, misty; blurred, fogged; (*voz*) flat

empañar *tr* (*a las criaturas*) to swaddle; blur, fog, dim, dull; tarnish, sully || *ref* to blur, fog, dim, dull

empañetar *tr* to plaster

empapar *tr* to soak; soak up, absorb; drench || *ref* to soak; be soaked; to become imbued; be surfeited

empapelado *m* papering, paper hanging; wallpaper; paper lining

empapela•dor -dora *mf* paper hanger

empapelar *tr* to wrap in paper; paper, line with paper; wallpaper; bring a criminal charge against

empaque *m* packing; look, appearance, mien; stiffness, stuffiness; brazenness

empaquetadura *f* gasket

empaquetar *tr* to pack; jam, stuff || *ref* to pack; pack in; dress up

empareda•do -da *mf* recluse || *m* sandwich

emparedar *tr* to wall in, confine

emparejar *tr* to pair, match; smooth, make level; even, make even; (*una puerta*) close flush || *intr* to come up, come abreast; **emparejar con** to catch up with || *ref* to pair, match

emparentar §2 *intr* to become related by marriage; **emparentar con** (*buena gente*) to marry into the family of; (*una familia rica*) marry into

emparrado *m* arbor, bower

emparrillar *tr* to grill

empasta•dor -dora *mf* bookbinder

empastadura *f* binding

empastar *tr* (*un diente*) to fill; (*un libro*) bind with stiff covers; convert into pasture land || *ref* (Chile) to be overgrown with weeds

empaste *m* (*de diente*) filling; stiff binding

empastelar *tr* (typ) to pie

empatar *tr* (*en la votación y los juegos*) to tie; join, connect; tie, fasten || *intr* to tie || *ref* to tie; **empatársela a una persona** to be a match for someone; **empatárselo a una persona** (Guat, Hond) to put it over on someone

empate *m* tie, draw; (Col) penholder; (Ven) waste of time

empatía *f* empathy

empavar *tr* (Ecuad) to annoy; (Peru) to kid, razz

empavesado *m* (naut) dressing, bunting

empavesar *tr* to bedeck with flags and bunting; (*un buque*) dress; (*un monumento*) veil || *ref* to become overcast

empavonar *tr* to blue; grease, spread grease over || *ref* (CAm) to dress up

empecina•do -da *adj* stubborn

empecinamiento *m* stubbornness; determination

empecinar *tr* to tar; dip in pitch || *ref* to be stubborn; persist

empederni•do -da *adj* hardened, inveterate; hard-hearted

empedra•do -da *adj* cloud-flecked; pock-marked; (*caballo*) dark-spotted || *m* stone paving

empedrar §2 *tr* to pave with stones; bespatter

empegado *m* tarpaulin

empegar §44 *tr* to coat with pitch, dip in pitch; (*el ganado lanar*) mark with pitch

empeine *m* instep; (*de la bota*) vamp; (*enfermedad cutánea*) tetter; (*región central del hipogastrio*) pubes

empelotar *ref* to get all tangled up; get into a row; take all one's clothes off; (Mex, W-I) to fall madly in love

empella *f* vamp

empellar *tr* to push, shove

empeller §31 *tr* to push, shove

empellón *m* push, shove; **a empellones** pushing, roughly

empenachar *tr* to adorn with plumes

empeña•do -da *adj* (*disputa*) bitter, heated; **no empeñado** noncommitted

empeñar *tr* (*dar en prenda*) to pawn; (*una lucha*) launch, begin; (*prendar, hipotecar*) pledge; (*la palabra*) pledge; force, compel || *ref* to commit oneself, bind oneself; go into debt; (*una lucha, una disputa*) begin, start; **empeñarse en** to engage in; persist in, insist on

empeñe•ro -ra *mf* (Mex) pawnbroker

empeño *m* pledge, engagement, commitment; (*prenda*) pawn; pawnshop; persistence, insistence; eagerness, perseverance; effort, endeavor; pledge, backer, patron; favor, protection; **con empeño** eagerly

empeño•so -sa *adj* eager, persistent

empeorar *tr* to impair, make worse || *intr & ref* to get worse, deteriorate

empequeñecer §22 *tr* (*hacer más pequeño*) to make smaller, dwarf; (*amenguar la importancia de*) belittle || *ref* to get smaller, dwarf

emperador *m* emperor; **los emperadores** the emperor and empress

empera•triz *f* (*pl* **-trices**) empress

emperchar *tr* to hang on a clothes rack

emperejilar *tr & ref* to dress up, spruce up

emperezar §60 *tr* to delay, put off || *intr & ref* to get lazy

empericar §73 *ref* (Col, Ecuad) to get drunk; (Mex) to blush
emperifollar *tr & ref* to dress up gaudily
empernar *tr* to bolt
empero *conj* but, however, yet
emperrar *ref* to get stubborn
empezar **§18** *tr & intr* to begin
empicar §73 *ref* to become infatuated
empicotar *tr* to pillory
empiema *m* empyema
empina•do -da *adj* high, lofty; steep; stiff, stuck-up || *f* (aer) zoom, zooming; **irse a la empinada** (*un caballo*) to rear
empinar *tr* to raise, lift; tip over; (*el codo*) crook; (aer) to zoom || *intr* to be a toper || *ref* to stand on tiptoe; (*un caballo*) rear; tower, rise high; (aer) to zoom
empingorota•do -da *adj* influential; proud, haughty
empingorotar *tr* to put on top || *ref* to climb up, get up; be stuck-up
empíre•o -a *adj & m* empyrean
empíri•co -ca *adj* empiric(al) || *mf* empiricist
empizarrado *m* slate roof
empizarrar *tr* to roof with slate
emplastar *tr* to put a plaster on; put make-up on; (*un negocio*) tie up, obstruct || *ref* to put make-up on; smear oneself up
emplásti•co -ca *adj* sticky
emplasto *m* plaster, poultice
emplazamiento *m* emplacement, location; (law) summons
emplazar **§60** *tr* to place, locate; summon, summons
emplea•do -da *mf* employee; (*de oficina, de tienda*) clerk; **empleado público** civil servant
emplear *tr* to employ; use; (*el dinero*) invest; **estarle a uno bien empleado** to serve someone right || *ref* to be employed; busy oneself; **empleárselo mal** to act up, misbehave
empleo *m* employ, employment; use; job, position, occupation
empleomanía *f* eagerness to hold public office
empleóma•no -na *mf* public officeholder, bureaucrat
emplomar *tr* to lead; line with lead; (*un techo*) cover with lead; put a lead seal on; (*un diente*) (Arg) to fill
emplumar *tr* to put a feather on; adorn with feathers; tar and feather; (Hond) to thrash; **emplumarlas** (Col) to beat it || *intr* to fledge, grow feathers
emplumecer **§22** *intr* to fledge, grow feathers
empobrecer **§22** *tr* to impoverish || *intr & ref* to become poor
empodrecer **§22** *intr & ref* to rot
empolva•do -da *adj* (Mex) rusty
empolvar *tr* to cover with dust; (*el rostro*) powder || *ref* to get dusty; (*el rostro*) powder; (Mex) to get rusty
empolla•do -da *adj* primed for an examination
empollar *tr* (*huevos*) to brood, hatch; (*estudiar con mucha detención*) bone up on || *intr* to grind, be a grind; **empollar sobre** to bone up on || *ref* to hatch; bone up on
empo•llón -llona *mf* (coll) grind
emponcha•do -da *adj* (SAm) poncho-wearing; (SAm) crafty, hypocritical; (SAm) suspicious-looking
emponzoñar *tr* to poison; corrupt
emporcar **§81** *tr* to soil, dirty
emporra•do -da *adj* (*drogas*) high
empotra•do -da *adj* built-in; recessed
empotrar *tr* to embed, recess, fasten in a wall || *intr & ref* to fit, interlock
emprende•dor -dora *adj* enterprising
emprender *tr* to undertake; **emprenderla con** to squabble with, have it out with; **emprenderla para** to set out for
empreñar *tr* to make pregnant || *ref* to become pregnant
empresa *f* enterprise, undertaking; company, concern, firm; device, motto; (*la parte patronal*) management; **empresa anunciadora** advertising agency; **empresa de tranvías** traction company; **pequeña empresa** small business
empresarial *adj* managerial
empresa•rio -ria *mf* contractor; business leader, industrialist; manager; promoter; theatrical manager; **empresario de circo** showman; **empresario de pompas fúnebres** undertaker; **empresario de publicidad** advertising man; **empresario de teatro** impresario, theater manager
emprestar *tr* to borrow
empréstito *m* loan, government loan
empujar *tr* to push, shove; replace || *intr* to push, shove
empujatierra *f* bulldozer
empuje *m* push; (*fuerza o presión ejercidas por una cosa sobre otra*) thrust; (*espíritu emprendedor*) enterprise, push
empujón *m* hard push, shove; **tratar a empujones** to push around
empuñadura *f* (*de la espada*) hilt; first words of a story; (*de bastón o paraguas*) handle
empuñar *tr* to seize, grasp, clutch; (*un empleo o puesto*) obtain; (*la mano*) (Chile) to clench; (Bol) to punch; **empuñar el bastón** (fig) to seize the reins
emular *tr & intr* to emulate; **emular con** to emulate, vie with
ému•lo -la *adj* emulous || *mf* rival
emulsión *f* emulsion
emulsionar *tr* to emulsify
en *prep* at; in; into; by; on; of, e.g., **pensar en** to think of
enaceitar *tr* to oil || *ref* to get oily, get rancid
enagua *f* petticoat; skirt; **enaguas** petticoat
enagüillas *fpl* kilt, short skirt
enajenación *f* alienation; estrangement; rapture; (*distracción*) absent-mindedness; **enajenación mental** mental derangement
enajenar *tr* (*la propiedad, el dominio; a un amigo*) to alienate, estrange; enrapture, transport || *ref* to be enraptured, be transported; **enajenarse de** to dispossess one-

self of; (*un amigo*) become alienated from
enaltecer §22 *tr* to exalt, extol
enamoradi•zo -za *adj* susceptible
enamora•do -da *adj* lovesick; (*propenso a enamorarse*) susceptible || *mf* sweetheart || *m* lover
enamorar *tr* to make love to; enamor, captivate || *ref* to fall in love
enamoricar §73 *ref* to trifle in love
enangostar *tr & ref* to narrow
ena•no -na *adj* dwarfish || *mf* dwarf
enarbolar *tr* to hoist, hang out; (*una espada*) brandish || *ref* to get angry; (*el caballo*) rear
enarcar §73 *tr* to arch; (*los toneles*) hoop || *ref* to become confused, be bashful; (*el caballo*) (Mex) to rear
enardecer §22 *tr* to inflame, excite || *ref* to get excited; (*una parte del cuerpo*) become inflamed, get sore
enarenar *tr* to throw sand on || *ref* (naut) to run aground
enastar *tr* (*una herramienta*) to put a handle on; (*una bandera*) put a shaft on
encabalgamiento *m* gun carriage; trestlework; (*en el verso*) enjambment
encabalgar §44 *tr* to provide with horses || *intr* to lean, rest
encaballar *tr* to overlap; (typ) to pie
encabezamiento *m* heading; (*fórmula con que comienza un documento*) opening words; tax list; tax rate; **encabezamiento de factura** billhead
encabezar §60 *tr* (*un escrito*) to put a heading or title on; head; register; (*vinos*) fortify
encabritar *ref* (*un caballo*) to rear; (*un buque*) shoot up, pitch up; (*un avión*) nose up
encadenar *tr* to chain, put in chains; brace, buttress; bind, tie together; tie down
encajar *tr* to fit, fit in, make fit; insert, put in; (*un golpe*) give, let go; (*dinero*) put away; (*un chiste*) tell at the wrong time; to palm off; throw, hurl; **encajar una cosa a uno** to foist something on someone, palm something off on someone || *intr* to fit; (*una puerta*) close right || *ref* to squeeze one's way; (*una prenda de vestir*) put on; butt in, intrude
encaje *m* (*tejido de mallas*) lace; (*labor de taracea*) inlay, mosaic; recess, groove; fitting, matching; insertion; appearance, look
encaje•ro -ra *mf* lacemaker; lace dealer
encajonado *m* cofferdam
encajonar *tr* to box, crate, case; squeeze in || *ref* (*un río*) to narrow, narrow down; squeeze in, squeeze through
encalambrar *ref* to get cramps
encalar *tr* (*espolvorear con cal*) to lime, sprinkle with lime; (*blanquear con cal*) whitewash
encalma•do -da *adj* (*mercado de valores*) dull, quiet; (*mar, viento*) becalmed
encalvecer §22 *intr* to get bald
encalladero *m* sand bank, shoal
encallar *intr* to run aground; fail, get stuck
encallecer §22 *intr* (*la piel*) to become callous || *ref* to become callous; (fig) to become callous, become hardened
encamar *tr* to spread out on the ground || *ref* to take to bed; (*el grano*) droop, bend over
encaminar *tr* to direct, show the way to; (*sus esfuerzos, su atención*) direct || *ref* to set out
encanalar *tr* to channel, pipe
encandecer §22 *tr* to make white-hot
encandila•do -da *adj* (*sombrero*) cocked; stiff, erect
encandilar *tr* to daze, befuddle; (*un fuego*) to stir || *ref* (*los ojos*) to flash
encanecer §22 *intr & ref* to turn gray; get old; become moldy
encanta•do -da *adj* absent-minded, distracted; (*casa*) rambling
encanta•dor -dora *adj* charming, enchanting || *mf* charmer || *f* enchantress
encantamiento *m* charm, enchantment
encantar *tr* to charm, enchant, bewitch
encante *m* auction sale; auction house
encanto *m* charm, enchantment, spell
encantusar *tr* to coax, wheedle
encañada *f* gorge, ravine
encañar *tr* (*el agua*) to pipe; (*las tierras*) drain; (*las plantas*) prop up; wind on a spool
encañizada *f* reed fence; weir
encañonar *tr* to pipe; wind on a spool; (*un pliego*) (typ) to tip in
encaperuzar §60 *tr* to put a hood on || *ref* to put on one's hood
encapotar *tr* to cloak || *ref* to frown; cloud over, become overcast
encaprichar *ref* to insist on getting one's way; become infatuated
encaracolado *m* spiral ornament, spiral work
encara•do -da *adj* — **bien encarado** well-featured; **mal encarado** ill-featured
encaramar *tr* to raise up, lift up; praise, extol; elevate, exalt || *ref* to climb, get on top; rise, tower; blush
encarar *tr* to aim, point; (*una dificultad*) face || *intr & ref* to come face to face
encarcelar *tr* to incarcerate, imprison, jail; (*piezas de madera recién encoladas*) clamp; plaster in || *ref* to stay indoors
encarecer §22 *tr* (*el precio*) to raise; raise the price of; extol; urge; overrate || *intr & ref* to rise, rise in price
encarecidamente *adv* earnestly, insistently, eagerly
encarga•do -da *mf* agent, representative; **encargado de negocios** chargé d'affaires
encargamiento *m* duty; obligation; charge
encargar §44 *tr* (*mercancías*) to order; (*confiar*) entrust; urge, warn || *ref* to take charge, be in charge
encargo *m* assignment, job, charge; (*pedido*) order; warning; **como de encargo** or **ni de encargo** just the thing, as if made to order
encariñamiento *m* endearment
encariñar *tr* to awaken love in || *ref* — **encariñarse con** to become fond of, become attached to

encarnación *f* incarnation, embodiment
encarna•do -da *adj* red; Caucasian-skin-("flesh")-colored; (*de forma humana*) incarnate
encarnar *tr* to incarnate, embody; (*el anzuelo*) bait || *intr* to become incarnate; (*una herida*) heal over
encarnecer §**22** *intr* to put on flesh
encarniza•do -da *adj* bloodshot; bloody, fierce, bitter, hard-fought
encarnizar §**60** *tr* to anger, provoke || *ref* to get angry; become fierce; **encarnizarse con** or **en** to be merciless to
encaro *m* aim; stare; blunderbuss
encarrilar *tr* to put back on the rails; set right, put on the right track; guide, direct
encarruja•do -da *adj* wrinkled; (*pelo*) kinky; (*terreno*) (Mex) rough
encartar *tr* to enroll, register; outlaw; (*un naipe*) slip in || *ref* to be unable to discard
encartonar *tr* to cover with cardboard; (*libros*) bind in boards
encasar *tr* (*un hueso dislocado*) to set (*a broken bone*)
encasillado *m* set of pigeonholes; (*lista de candidatos apoyados por el gobierno*) government slate; (SAm) checkerwork
encasillar *tr* to pigeonhole; sort out, classify; (*el gobierno a un candidato*) slate
encasquetar *tr* (*un sombrero*) to stick on the head; (*una idea*) drive in; force on
encasquillar *tr* to put a tip on; (*un caballo*) shoe || *ref* to stick, get stuck
encastilla•do -da *adj* haughty, proud
encastillar *tr* to fortify with castles; pile up || *ref* to stick, get stuck; take to the hills; stick to one's opinion
encastrar *tr* to engage, mesh
encastre *m* engaging, meshing; groove, socket; insert
encauchar *tr* to cover with rubber, line with rubber
encausar *tr* to prosecute, sue, bring to trial
encausticar §**73** *tr* to wax
encáustico *m* floor wax, furniture polish
encauzar §**60** *tr* (*una corriente*) to channel; guide, direct
encavar *ref* to hide, burrow
encebollado *m* beef stew with onions
encelar *tr* to make jealous || *ref* to get jealous; be in rut
encella *f* cheese mold
encenagar §**44** *ref* to get covered with mud; wallow in vice
encencerrar *tr* (*al ganado*) to put a bell on
encendajas *fpl* kindling, brush
encendedor *m* lighter; **encendedor de bolsillo** pocket lighter
encender §**51** *tr* to light, kindle; ignite, fire to; (*la luz, la radio*) turn on; (*la lengua*) burn; stir up, excite || *ref* to catch fire, ignite; become excited; blush
encendi•do -da *adj* bright, high-colored; red, flushed; keen, enthusiastic || *m* ignition
encenizar §**60** *tr* to cover with ashes || *ref* to get covered with ashes
encepar *tr* to put in the stocks || *intr & ref* to take deep root
encera•do -da *adj* wax, wax-colored; (*huevo*) boiled || *m* oilcloth; tarpaulin; (*pizarra*) blackboard
encerar *tr* to wax || *intr & ref* (*el grano*) to ripen, turn yellow
encerotar *tr* (*el hilo*) to wax
encerradero *m* sheepfold; (taur) bull pen
encerrar §**2** *tr* to shut in; lock in, lock up; contain, include; encircle; imply || *ref* to lock oneself in; go into seclusion; **encerrarse con** to be closeted with
encerrona *f* dilemma; tight spot; (coll) fix
encespedar *tr* to sod
encestar *tr* to put in a basket; (coll) to sink (*a basketball*)
encía *f* gum
encíclica *f* encyclical
enciclopedia *f* encyclopedia
enciclopédi•co -ca *adj* encyclopedic
encierro *m* locking up, confinement; inclusion; encirclement; lockup, prison; solitary confinement; retirement, retreat; (taur) bull pen
encima *adv* above, overhead, on top; at hand, here now; besides, in addition; **de encima** (Chile) in the bargain; **echarse encima** to take upon oneself; **encima de** on, upon; above, over; **por encima** hastily, superficially; **por encima de** above, over; in spite of; **quitarse de encima** to get rid of, shake off
encina *f* holm oak, evergreen oak
encinta *adj* pregnant; **dejar encinta** to make pregnant
encintado *m* curb
encintar *tr* to trim with ribbons; provide with curbs
enclaustrar *tr* to cloister; hide away
enclavar *tr* to nail; pierce, transfix; (*el pie del caballo*) prick; cheat
enclave *m* enclave
enclavijar *tr* to dowel; (*un instrumento*) to peg
enclenque *adj* sickly, feeble
enclíti•co -ca *adj & m* enclitic
enclocar §**81** *intr & ref* to brood
encofrado *m* planking, timbering; (*para el hormigón*) form
encoger §**17** *tr* to shrink, shrivel; discourage; draw in || *intr* to shrink, shrivel || *ref* to shrink, shrivel; be discouraged; be bashful; (*humillarse*) cringe; (*en la cama*) curl up; **encogerse de hombros** to shrug one's shoulders
encogi•do -da *adj* bashful, timid
encogimiento *m* shrinkage; crouch; bashfulness, timidity; **encogimiento de hombros** shrug
encojar *tr* to cripple, lame || *ref* to become lame; feign illness
encolar *tr* to glue; (*la superficie que ha de pintarse*) size; (*el vino*) clarify; (*p.ej., una pelota*) throw out of reach
encolerizar §**60** *tr* to anger || *ref* to get angry

encomendar §2 *tr* to commend, entrust, commit; knight || *ref* to commend oneself; send regards
encomiar *tr* to praise, extol
encomienda *f* charge, commission; commendation, praise; favor, protection; knight's cross; royal land grant (*with Indian inhabitants*); parcel post; (Mex) fruit stand
encomio *m* encomium
enconamiento *m* soreness; rancor, ill will
enconar *tr* to make sore, inflame; aggravate, irritate || *ref* to get sore, become inflamed; (*una herida; el ánimo de uno*) rankle, fester
enconchar *ref* to draw back into one's shell, keep aloof
encono *m* rancor, ill will; (Col, Chile, Mex, W-I) soreness
encono•so -sa *adj* sore, sensitive; harmful; rancorous
encontra•do -da *adj* opposite, facing; contrary; hostile; **estar encontrados** to be at odds
encontrar *tr* to encounter, meet; (*hallar*) find || *intr* to meet; collide || *ref* to meet, meet each other; be, be situated; find oneself; **encontrarse con** to meet, run into
encontrón *m* bump, jolt, collision
encopeta•do -da *adj* aristocratic, of noble descent; conceited, boastful
encorajar *tr* to encourage || *ref* to fly into a rage
encorajinar *ref* to fly into a rage; (Chile) to break up, go to ruin
encorchar *tr* (*botellas*) to cork; (*abejas*) to hive
encordar §61 *tr* (*un violín, una raqueta*) to string; wrap, wind up with rope
encordelar *tr* to string; tie with strings
encornudar *tr* to cuckold, make a cuckold of || *intr* to grow horns
encorralar *tr* to corral
encortinar *tr* to curtain
encorvada *f* stoop, bending over; **hacer la encorvada** to malinger
encorvar *tr* to bend over || *ref* to stoop, bend over; be partial, be biased
encovar §61 *tr* & *ref* to hide away
encrespar *tr* to curl; (*el pelo*) make stand on end; (*plumas*) ruffle; (*las olas*) stir up; irritate, anger || *ref* to curl; bristle, stand on end; (*el mar, las olas*) get rough; get involved; bristle, get angry
encresta•do -da *adj* proud, haughty
encrucijada *f* crossroads, street intersection; ambush, snare, trap
encrudecer §22 *tr* to make raw; aggravate
encuadernación *f* bookbinding; (*taller*) bindery; **encuadernación a la holandesa** half binding
encuaderna•dor -dora *mf* bookbinder
encuadernar *tr* to bind; **sin encuadernar** unbound
encuadrar *tr* (*encerrar en un marco o cuadro*) to frame; (*incluir dentro de sí*) encompass; (*encajar*) insert, fit in; (Arg) to summarize
encuadre *m* film adaptation; (mov & telv) frame
encubar *tr* to put in a cask or vat; (min) to shore up
encubierta *f* fraud, deception
encubrimiento *m* concealment; (law) complicity
encubrir §83 *tr* to hide, conceal || *ref* to hide; disguise oneself
encuentro *m* encounter, meeting; clash, collision; (*hallazgo*) find; (sport) game, match; **encuentro fronterizo** border clash; **llevarse de encuentro** (CAm, Mex, W-I) to knock down, run over; (CAm, Mex, W-I) to drag down to ruin; **mal encuentro** foul play; **salir al encuentro a** to go to meet; get ahead of; take a stand against
encuerar *tr* to strip of clothes; fleece || *ref* to strip, get undressed
encuesta *f* inquiry; **encuesta demoscópica** opinion poll; survey
encuestador *m* pollster
encuitar *ref* to grieve
encumbra•do -da *adj* high, lofty; sublime; influential
encumbramiento *m* height, elevation; exaltation
encumbrar *tr* to raise, elevate; exalt || *ref* to rise; be exalted; be proud; be flowery, use flowery speech; (*subir una cosa a mucha altura*) tower
encunar *tr* to cradle; catch between the horns
encurtido *m* pickle
encurtir *tr* to pickle
enchapado *m* veneer
enchapar *tr* to veneer
encharcar §73 *tr* to make a puddle of; (*el estómago*) upset || *ref* to turn into a puddle; wallow in vice
enchavetar *tr* to key
enchichar *ref* (SAm) to get drunk; (CAm) to get angry
enchilada *f* (Guat, Mex) corn cake with tomato sauce seasoned with chili
enchilado *m* (Cuba, Mex) shellfish stew with chili sauce
enchilo•so -sa *adj* (CAm, Mex) spicy, hot
enchinar *tr* to pave with pebbles; (Mex) to curl || *ref* (Mex) to get goose flesh
enchispar *tr* to make drunk || *ref* to get drunk
enchivar *ref* (Col, Ecuad, CAm) to fly into a rage
enchufar *tr* (*un tubo o caño*) to fit; (*dos tubos o caños*) connect, connect together; (*dos negocios*) merge; (elec) to connect, plug in || *intr* to fit || *ref* to merge
enchufe *m* fitting; (*de tubo o caño*) male end; (*de dos tubos*) joint; (elec) connector; (elec) plug; (elec) receptacle; sinecure, easy job; **tener enchufe** to have pull, have a drag
enchufismo *m* spoils system; wire pulling
enchufista *m* spoilsman
ende *adv* — **por ende** therefore
endeble *adj* feeble, weak; worthless
endecha *f* dirge
endechadera *f* hired mourner
endemia *f* endemic

endémi•co -ca *adj* endemic
endemonia•do -da *adj* possessed of the devil; furious, wild; (coll) devilish
endenantes *adv* recently
endentar §2 *tr & intr* to mesh
endentecer §22 *intr* to teethe
enderezar §60 *tr* to stand up; straighten; direct; put in order; regulate || *intr* to go straight || *ref* to stand up, straighten up; head, make one's way; go straight; (aer) to flatten out, level off
endeuda•do -da *adj* indebted
endeudamiento *m* indebtedness
endeudar *ref* to run into debt; acknowledge one's indebtedness
endevota•do -da *adj* pious, devout; fond, devoted
endiabla•do -da *adj* devilish; deformed, ugly; mean, wicked; (Arg) difficult, complicated
endilgar §44 *tr* to send, direct; to spring, unload
endiosar *tr* to deify || *ref* to get stuck-up; get absorbed
endominga•do -da *adj* Sunday; all dressed up
endomingar §44 *ref* to get dressed in one's Sunday best
endosante *mf* endorser
endosar *tr* (*un documento de crédito*) to endorse; (*una cosa poco grata*) unload
endosata•rio -ria *mf* endorsee
endoso *m* endorsement
endriago *m* fabulous monster
endri•no -na *adj* sloe-colored || *m* (*arbusto*) sloe, blackthron || *f* (*fruto*) sloe
endrogar §44 *ref* to run into debt
endulzar §60 *tr* to sweeten; make bearable
endura•dor -dora *adj* saving, stingy
endurar *tr* to harden; delay, put off; (*tolerar*) endure; save, spare || *ref* to get hard
endurecer §22 *tr* to harden; (*robustecer, acostumbrar*) inure
endureci•do -da *adj* hard, strong; inured; hard-hearted; tenacious, obstinate
enebrina *f* juniper berry
enebro *m* juniper
enecha•do -da *adj & mf* foundling
eneldo *m* dill
enema *f* enema
enemiga *f* enmity, hatred
enemi•go -ga *adj* enemy; hostile || *mf* enemy, foe; **el enemigo malo** the Evil One || *f* see **enemiga**
enemistad *f* enmity
enemistar *tr* to make an enemy of; make enemies of || *ref* to become enemies
energéti•co -ca *adj* energy; power
energía *f* energy; power; **energía atómica** atomic power (or energy); **energías alternas** alternate energy sources; **energía solar** solar energy
enérgi•co -ca *adj* energetic
energúme•no -na *adj* fiendish || *mf* crazy person, wild person
enero *m* January
enervar *tr* to enervate; weaken
enési•mo -ma *adj* nth
enfadadi•zo -za *adj* peevish, irritable
enfadar *tr* to annoy, bother; anger
enfado *m* annoyance, bother; anger
enfado•so -sa *adj* annoying, disagreeable
enfaldar *ref* to tuck up one's skirt
enfardar *tr* to bale, pack
énfa•sis *m* (*pl* **-sis**) emphasis; bombast, affected speech
enfasizar §60 *tr* to emphasize
enfáti•co -ca *adj* emphatic; affected
enfermar *tr* to make sick || *intr* to get sick
enfermedad *f* sickness, illness, disease
enfermera *f* nurse; **enfermera ambulante** visiting nurse
enfermería *f* infirmary
enfermero *m* male nurse
enfermi•zo -za *adj* sickly; (*clima*) unhealthy
enfer•mo -ma *adj* sick, ill; (*enfermizo*) sickly; **enfermo de amor** lovesick || *mf* patient
enfermo•so -sa *adj* sickly
enfiestar *ref* to have a good time
enfilar *tr* to line up; (*p.ej., perlas*) string; aim; go down, go up; (mil) to enfilade || *intr* to bear
enfisema *m* emphysema
enflaquecer §22 *tr* to make thin; weaken || *intr* to get thin; flag, slacken || *ref* to get thin, lose weight
enflauta•do -da *adj* pompous, inflated
enflautar *tr* to blow up, inflate; cheat
enfocar §73 *tr* to focus; (fig) to size up
enfoque *m* focus, focusing; (fig) approach (*to a problem*)
enfoscar §73 *tr* to trim with mortar; patch with mortar; darken, make dark || *ref* to become sullen, become grouchy; become absorbed in business; become overcast
enfrailar *tr* to make a friar or monk of || *ref* to become a friar or monk
enfranque *m* shank
enfrascar §73 *tr* to bottle || *ref* to become involved, intangled; be sunk in work; have a good time
enfrenar *tr* (*un caballo*) to bridle; (*un tren*) brake; check
enfrentamiento *m* (*policía, masas*) confrontation
enfrentar *tr* to put face to face; (*p.ej., al enemigo*) face || *intr* to be facing || *ref* to meet face to face; **enfrentarse con** to stand up to; cope with
enfrente *adv* opposite, in front; **enfrente de** opposite, in front of; opposed to
enfriadera *f* bottle cooler, ice pail
enfriar §77 *tr* to cool, chill; kill || *intr & ref* to cool off
enfundar *tr* to sheathe, put in a case; stuff; (*un tambor*) muffle
enfurecer §22 *tr* to infuriate, anger || *ref* to rage
enfurruñar *ref* to sulk
engalanar *tr* to adorn, deck out, dress
engalla•do -da *adj* straight, erect; haughty
engallador *m* checkrein
enganchar *tr* to hook; (*un caballo*) hitch; (*un coche de ferrocarril*) couple; recruit; inveigle || *intr* to get caught || *ref* to get caught; (mil) to enlist

enganche *m* hook; hooking; hitching; coupling; inveigling; recruiting; enlisting; (rr) coupler
engañabo•bos *mf* (*pl* **-bos**) bamboozler
engaña•dor -dora *adj* deceptive; (*simpático*) winsome
engañar *tr* to deceive, cheat, fool; (*el tiempo*) while away; (*el sueño, el hambre*) ward off; wheedle || *ref* to be mistaken
engañifa *f* deception, trick
engaño *m* deception, deceit, fraud; mistake; falsehood; **llamarse a engaño** to back out because of fraud
engaño•so -sa *adj* deceptive
engargantar *tr* (*un ave*) to stuff the throat of || *intr & ref* to mesh, engage
engarzar **§60** *tr* to link, string, wire; curl; enchase; (Col) to hook
engastar *tr* to enchase, mount, set
engaste *m* enchasing, mounting, setting
engatusar *tr* to coax, wheedle; inveigle
engendrar *tr* to beget, engender; (geom) to generate
engendro *m* foetus; botch, bungle; (*criatura informe*) runt, stunt; **mal engendro** (coll) young tough
engolfar *intr* to go far out in the ocean || *ref* to go far out in the ocean; become deeply involved; be lost in thought
engoma•do -da *adj* (Chile) all dressed up || *m* (CAm) hangover
engomar *tr* to gum || *ref* to have a hangover
engorda *f* fattening; animals being fattened
engordar *tr* to fatten || *intr* to get fat; (coll) to get fat, get rich
engorro *m* bother, nuisance, obstacle
engorro•so -sa *adj* annoying
engoznar *tr* to hinge, to hang on a hinge
engranaje *m* gear, gears, teeth; (fig) link, connection; **engranaje de distribución** (aut) timing gears; **engranaje de tornillo sin fin** worm gear
engranar *tr* to gear, mesh; throw into gear || *intr* to gear, mesh
engrandecer **§22** *tr* to amplify, enlarge, magnify; exalt, extol; enhance
engrane *m* gear; mesh
engranerar *tr* (*el grano*) to store
engrapa•dor -dora *mf* stapler
engrapar *tr* to clamp, cramp
engrasador *m* grease cup; **engrasador de pistón** grease gun
engrasar *tr* to grease; smear with grease
engrase *m* greasing; grease
engravar *tr* to spread gravel over
engredar *tr* to chalk, to clay
engreí•do -da *adj* conceited, vain
engreimiento *m* conceit, vanity
engreír **§58** *tr* to make conceited; spoil, pamper || *ref* to become conceited
engreña•do -da *adj* disheveled
engrescar **§73** *tr* to incite to fight; incite to merriment || *ref* to pick a fight; join in the fun
engrifar *tr* to curl, crisp || *ref* to curl up; stand on end; (*un caballo*) rear
engrillar *tr* to shackle, fetter || *ref* (*las patatas*) to sprout
engringar **§44** *ref* to act like a foreigner
engrosar **§61** *tr* to broaden; enlarge || *intr* to get fat || *ref* to broaden; swell, get bigger
engrudar *tr* to paste
engrudo *m* paste
engualdrapar *tr* to caparison
enguapear *ref* (Mex) to get drunk
enguirnaldar *tr* to garland, wreathe; trim, bedeck
engullir **§13** *tr* to gulp down
engurrio *m* sadness, melancholy
enhebrar *tr* (*una aguja*) to thread; (*perlas*) string; (*mentiras*) rattle off
enhestar **§2** *tr* to stand upright, erect; hoist, lift up
enhies•to -ta *adj* upright, straight, erect
enhilar *tr* to thread; direct; line up; (*ideas*) marshal || *intr* to set out
enhorabuena *adv* safely, luckily; **enhorabuena que** thank heavens that || *f* congratulations; **dar la enhorabuena a** to congratulate
enhoramala *adv* unluckily, under an unlucky star; **nacer enhoramala** to be born under an unlucky star; **vete enhoramala** go to the devil
enhornar *tr* to put into the oven
enigma *m* enigma, riddle, puzzle
enigmáti•co -ca *adj* enigmatic(al)
enjabonar *tr* to soap, lather; (*adular*) (coll) to soft-soap; (*reprender*) (coll) to upbraid
enjaezar **§60** *tr* to harness, put trappings on
enjalbegado *m* whitewashing
enjalbegar **§44** *tr* to whitewash; (*el rostro*) paint || *ref* to paint the face
enjambrar *intr* (*las abejas*) to swarm; to multiply in great numbers
enjambre *m* swarm
enjaretado *m* grating, lattice work
enjarrar *ref* (C-R, Mex) to stand with arms akimbo
enjaular *tr* to cage; jail, lock up
enjergar **§44** *tr* to launch, get started, start on a shoestring
enjoyar *tr* to adorn with jewels; set with precious stones; adorn
enjuagadien•tes *m* (*pl* **-tes**) mouthwash
enjuagar **§44** *tr* to rinse, rinse out
enjuague *m* rinse; rinsing water; mouthwash; rinsing cup; (coll) plot
enjugador *m* drier; clotheshorse
enjugama•nos *m* (*pl* **-nos**) towel, hand towel
enjugaparabri•sas *m* (*pl* **-sas**) windshield wiper
enjugar **§44** *tr* (*secar*) to dry; (*el sudor*) wipe, wipe off; (*lágrimas*) wipe away; (*deudas, un déficit*) wipe out || *ref* to lose weight
enjuiciamiento *m* procedure; prosecution, suit; trial; judgment, sentence
enjuiciar *tr* to prosecute, sue; try; judge
enjundio•so -sa *adj* fatty, greasy; solid, substantial
enju•to -ta *adj* (*tiempo, clima; ojos*) dry; lean, skinny; quiet, stolid || **enjutos** *mpl*

brushwood; (*para excitar la gana de beber*) tidbits
enlabiar *tr* to entice, take in; press one's lips against
enlace *m* connection, linking; relationship; betrothal, engagement; marriage; (mil, phonet) liaison; (rr) connection, junction
enlaciar *tr, intr & ref* to wither, wilt, shrivel; rumple
enladrillado *m* brickwork; bricklaying; brick paving
enladrillar *tr* to pave with bricks
enlajado *m* (Ven) flagstone
enlajar *tr* (Ven) to pave with flagstones
enlardar *tr* to baste
enlatado *m* canning
enlatar *tr* to can; roof with tin, line with tin
enlazar **§60** *tr* to connect, link; lace; (*un animal con el lazo*) lasso || *intr* (*p.ej., dos trenes*) to connect || *ref* to be connected, be linked; connect; get married; become related by marriage
enlechar *tr* to grout
enlistonado *m* lathing, lath
enlistonar *tr* to lath
enlodar *tr* to muddy, smear with mud; plaster with mud; seal with mud; (fig) to sling mud at
enloquecer **§22** *tr* to drive crazy || *intr* to go crazy
enloquecimiento *m* insanity, madness
enlosado *m* flagstone paving
enlosar *tr* to pave with flagstone
enlozar **§60** *tr* to enamel
enlozado *m* enamelware
enlucido *m* plaster, coat (*of plaster*)
enlucir **§45** *tr* (*una pared*) to plaster; (*la plata*) polish
enlutar *tr* to put in mourning, hang with crape; darken, sadden || *ref* to dress in mourning
enmaderar *tr* to cover with boards; build the framework for
enmagrecer **§22** *tr* to make thin || *intr & ref* to get thin
enmalecer **§22** *tr* to spoil || *ref* to get full of weeds, be overgrown with weeds
enmarañar *tr* to entangle; confuse || *ref* to become entangled; become overcast, get cloudy
enmarcar **§73** *tr* to frame
enmarchitar *tr & ref* to wither
enmaridar *intr & ref* to take a husband
enmarillecer **§22** *ref* to turn yellow, turn pale
enmasar *tr* (*tropas*) to mass
enmascarar *tr* to mask; camouflage || *ref* to put on a mask; masquerade
enmasillar *tr* to putty
enmendación *f* emendation
enmendar **§2** *tr* (*corregir*) to emend; (*reformar*) amend; (*resarcir*) make amends for || *ref* to amend, mend one's ways, go straight
enmienda *f* (*corrección*) emendation; (*propuesta de variante*) amendment; (*satisfacción del daño hecho*) amends
enmohecer **§22** *tr* to make moldy; rust; neglect || *ref* to get moldy; rust; (*la memoria*) get rusty; fade away
enmontar *ref* (CAm, Mex, Col, Ven) to become overgrown with brush
enmudecer **§22** *tr* to hush, silence || *intr* to hush up, keep quiet; become dumb, lose one's voice
enmuescar **§73** *tr* to notch; (carp) to mortise
ennegrecer **§22** *tr* to blacken, dye black || *ref* to turn black; (*el porvenir*) be black
ennoblecer **§22** *tr* to ennoble; glorify, enhance
ennoblecimiento *m* ennoblement; glory, splendor; (*grandeza de alma*) nobility
enodio *m* fawn, young deer
enojada *f* (Mex) fit of anger
enojadi•zo -za *adj* irritable, ill-tempered
enojar *tr* to anger; annoy, vex || *ref* to get angry; **enojarse con** or **contra** to get angry with (*a person*); **enojarse de** to get angry at (*a thing*)
enojo *m* anger; annoyance, bother
eno•jón -jona *adj* (Chile, Ecuad, Mex) irritable, ill-tempered
enojo•so -sa *adj* annoying, bothersome
enorgullecer **§22** *tr* to fill with pride, make proud || *ref* to be proud; **enorgullecerse de** to pride oneself on
enorme *adj* enormous, huge
enotecnia *f* wine making; oenology
enquiciar *tr* (*una puerta, una ventana*) to hang; fasten, make firm
enrabiar *tr* to enrage || *intr* to have rabies || *ref* to become enraged
enramar *tr* (*ramos*) to intertwine; adorn with branches || *intr* to sprout branches || *ref* to hide in the branches
enranciar *tr* to make rancid || *ref* to get rancid
enrarecer **§22** *tr* to rarefy; make scarce || *intr* to become scarce || *ref* to rarefy; become scarce
enrarecimiento *m* (*p.ej., del aire*) thinness; scarceness, scarcity
enrasar *tr* to make flush; grade, level || *intr* to be flush
enratonar *ref* to get sick from eating mice; (Ven) to have a hangover
enredadera *adj* (*planta*) climbing || *f* climbing plant, vine
enreda•dor -dora *mf* gossip, busybody
enredar *tr* to catch in a net; (*redes, una trampa*) set; tangle up; involve, entangle; (*una pelea*) start; intertwine, interweave; endanger, compromise || *intr* to romp around, be frisky || *ref* to get tangled up; get involved, become entangled; (coll) to have an affair
enredijo *m* entanglement
enredo *m* tangle; involvement, entanglement, complication; restlessness; friskiness; mischievous lie; (*de una novela, un drama*) plot; (*trato ilícito de hombre y mujer*) liaison
enre•dón -dona *adj* scheming || *mf* schemer

enredo•so -sa *adj* entangled, complicated, difficult
enrejado *m* grating, trellis, latticework; iron railing; grill; openwork embroidery
enrejar *tr* to grate, lattice; (*una ventana*) put a grate on; fence with an iron grating; (*ladrillos, tablas*) pile alternately crosswise; (Mex) to darn
enrielar *tr* to make into ingots; lay rails on; put on the tracks; put on the right track
enriquecer §22 *tr* to enrich || *intr & ref* to get rich
enrisca•do -da *adj* craggy, full of cliffs
enrizar §60 *tr & ref* to curl
enrocar §73 *tr & intr* (chess) to castle
enrodrigar §44 *tr* to prop, prop up
enrojar *tr* to redden, make red; (*el horno*) to heat up || *ref* to redden, turn red
enrojecer §22 *tr* to make red; make red-hot; make blush || *intr* to blush || *ref* to turn red; get red-hot; flush; get sore, get inflamed
enromar *tr* to make dull, make blunt
enronquecer §22 *tr* to make hoarse || *intr & ref* to get hoarse
enronquecimiento *m* hoarseness
enroque *m* (chess) castling
enroscar §73 *tr* to coil, twist, screw in || *ref* to coil, twist
enrubiar *tr* to bleach, make blond || *ref* to turn blond
enrubio *m* bleaching; bleaching lotion
enrular *tr & ref* (Arg) to curl
ensacar §73 *tr* to bag, put in a bag
ensaimada *f* twisted coffee cake
ensalada *f* salad; hodgepodge; fiasco, flop
ensaladera *f* salad bowl
ensalmar *tr* (*un hueso*) to set; treat or heal by incantation
ensalmo *m* incantation, spell; **como por ensalmo** as if by magic
ensalzar §60 *tr* to exalt, elevate, extol
ensamblar *tr* to assemble, join, fit together; **ensamblar a cola de milano** or **a cola de pato** to dovetail
ensanchador *m* glove stretcher
ensanchar *tr* to widen, enlarge; (*una prenda ajustada*) ease, let out; (*el corazón*) unburden || *intr & ref* to be proud and haughty
ensanche *m* widening, extension; (*de una calle*) extension; suburban development; allowance (*for enlargement of garment*)
ensandecer §22 *intr* to go crazy
ensangrenta•do -da *adj* bloody, gory
ensangrentar §2 *tr* to bathe in blood; stain with blood || *ref* to rage, go wild; (*p.ej., las manos*) bloody, make bloody
ensañar *tr* to anger, enrage || *ref* to be cruel, be merciless; (*una enfermedad*) rage
ensartar *tr* (*una aguja*) to thread; (*cuentas*) string; stick; rattle off || *ref* to squeeze in
ensayar *tr* to try, try on, try out; (*un espectáculo*) rehearse; (*minerales*) assay; teach, train; test || *ref* to practice
ensaye *m* assay
ensayista *mf* essayist; (Chile) assayer
ensayo *m* trying, trial; testing, test; (*género literario*) essay; (*de minerales*) assay; exercise, practice; (theat) rehearsal; **ensayo de choque** (aut) crash test; **ensayo general** dress rehearsal
ensenada *f* inlet, cove
enseña *f* standard, ensign
enseña•do -da *adj* trained, informed; (*perro de caza*) trained
enseñanza *f* teaching; education, instruction; (*ejemplo que sirve de experiencia*) lesson; **enseñanza superior** higher education
enseñar *tr* to teach; train; show, point out || *intr* to teach
enseñorear *ref* to control oneself; **enseñorearse de** to take possession of
enseres *mpl* utensils, equipment, household goods
enseriar *ref* to become serious
ensillar *tr* to saddle
ensimismamiento *m* absorption in thought, deep thought
ensimismar *ref* to become absorbed in thought; (Chile, Ecuad, Peru) to be proud, be boastful
ensoberbecer §22 to make proud || *ref* to become proud; (*el mar, las olas*) swell, get rough
ensoberbecimiento *m* haughtiness
ensombrecer §22 *tr* to darken || *ref* to get dark; become sad and gloomy
ensoña•dor -dora *adj* dreamy || *mf* dreamer
ensopar *tr* to dip, dunk; soak, drench
ensordece•dor -dora *adj* deafening
ensordecer §22 *tr* to deafen; (*una consonante sonora*) unvoice || *intr* to become deaf; play deaf, not answer || *ref* to unvoice
ensortijar *tr* to curl, make curly; (*la nariz de un animal*) ring, put a ring in || *ref* to curl
ensuciar *tr* to dirty, soil; stain, smear; defile, sully || *ref* to soil oneself; take bribes
ensueño *m* dream; daydream
entablado *m* flooring; wooden framework
entablar *tr* to board, board up; (*un hueso roto*) splint; (*una conversación*) start; (*p.ej., una batalla*) launch; (*un pleito*) bring; (*las piezas del ajedrez y de las damas*) set up || *ref* (*el viento*) to settle
entable *m* boarding; (*en los juegos de ajedrez y damas*) position of men; (Col) business, undertaking
entablillar *tr* (*un hueso roto*) to splint
enta•blón -blona *adj* (Peru) blustering, bragging || *mf* (Peru) bully
entalegar §44 *tr* to bag, put in a bag; (*dinero*) hoard
entalladura *f* carving, sculpture; engraving; slot, groove, mortise; cut, incision (*in a tree*)
entallar *tr* to carve, sculpture; engrave; notch; groove, mortise; (*un traje*) fit, tailor || *intr* to take shape; (*el vestido*) fit; go well, be fitting
entallecer §22 *intr & ref* to shoot, sprout
entapizar §60 *tr* to tapestry, hang with tapestry; cover with a fabric; overgrow, spread over
entarimado *m* parquet, inlaid floor, hardwood floor

entarimar *tr* to parquet, to put an inlaid floor on || *ref* to put on airs

entarugar **§44** *tr* to pave with wooden blocks || *ref* (*el sombrero*) (Ven) to stick on

ente *m* being; (coll) guy, odd fellow

enteca•do -da or **ente•co -ca** *adj* sickly, frail

enteleri•do -da *adj* shaking with cold, shaking with fright; sickly, frail

entena *f* lateen yard

entena•do -da *mf* stepchild || *m* stepson || *f* stepdaughter

entendederas *fpl* (coll) brains; **tener malas entendederas** (coll) to have no brains

entende•dor -dora *adj* understanding, intelligent || *mf* understanding person; **al buen entendedor, pocas palabras** a word to the wise is enough

entender *m* understanding, opinion || **§51** *tr* to understand; intend, mean || *intr*—**entender de** to be a judge of; be experienced as; **entender de razón** to listen to reason; **entender en** to be familiar with, deal with || *ref* to be understood; be meant; have a secret understanding; **entenderse con** to get along with; concern; (*una mujer*) have an affair with

entendi•do -da *adj* expert, skilled; informed; **no darse por entendido** to take no notice, pretend not to understand; **los entendidos** informed sources; **un entendido en** a well-informed person in

entendimiento *m* understanding

entenebrecer **§22** *tr* to darken; confuse || *ref* to get dark; become confused

entera•do -da *adj* informed, posted; (Chile) conceited; (Chile) intrusive, meddlesome || *mf* insider

enterar *tr* to inform, acquaint; to pay; (Arg, Chile) to complete || *intr* (Chile) to get better; (Chile) to drift along || *ref* to find out; to recover; **enterarse de** to find out about, become aware of

entereza *f* entirety, completeness; wholeness; perfection; fairness; constancy, fortitude; strictness

enteri•zo -za *adj* in one piece

enternece•dor -dora *adj* moving, touching

enternecer **§22** *tr* to move, touch || *ref* to be moved to pity

enternecimiento *m* pity, compassion

ente•ro -ra *adj* entire, whole, complete; honest, upright; firm, energetic; sound, vigorous; (*tela*) strong, heavy || *m* (arith) integer; payment; (Chile) balance; **por entero** entirely, wholly, completely

enterrador *m* gravedigger

enterramiento *m* burial, interment; (*hoyo*) grave; (*monumento*) tomb

enterrar **§2** *tr* to bury, inter; outlive, survive || *ref* to hide away

entesar **§2** *tr* to stretch, make taut

entibar *tr* to prop up, shore up || *intr* to rest, lean

entibiar *tr* to cool off; temper, moderate || *ref* to cool off, cool down

entidad *f* entity; importance, consequence, moment; body, organization

entierramuer•tos *m* (*pl* **-tos**) gravedigger

entierro *m* burial, interment; (*hoyo*) grave; (*monumento*) tomb; funeral; funeral cortege; buried treasure

entintar *tr* to ink; ink in; stain with ink; dye

entoldar *tr* to cover with awnings; adorn with hangings || *ref* to get cloudy, become overcast; swell with pride

entomología *f* entomology

entonación *f* intonation; blowing of bellows

entona•do -da *adj* arrogant; haughty; harmonious, in tune

entonar *tr* to intone; sing in tune; (*el órgano*) blow; (*colores*) harmonize; tone, tone up; (*alabanzas*) sound || *intr* to sing in tune || *ref* to be puffed up with pride

entonces *adv* then || *m*—**por aquel entonces** at that time

entonelar *tr* to put in barrels, put in casks

entongar **§44** *tr* (Mex, W-I) to pile up, pile in rows; (Col) to drive crazy

entono *m* intoning; arrogance, haughtiness

entontecer **§22** *tr* to make foolish, make stupid || *intr* & *ref* to become foolish, become stupid

entorchado *m* bullion; **ganar los entorchados** to win one's stripes

entorna•do -da *adj* ajar, half-closed

entornar *tr* to half-close; (*los ojos*) squint; (*una puerta*) leave ajar; (*volcar*) upset || *ref* to upset

entornillar *tr* to twist, screw up

entorno *m* environment

entorpecer **§22** *tr* to stupefy; obstruct, delay; benumb; (*una cerradura, una ventana*) make stick || *ref* to stick, get stuck

entortar **§61** *tr* to bend, make crooked; knock out the eye of || *ref* to bend, get crooked

entrada *f* entrance, entry; admission; arrival; income, receipts; admission ticket; entrance hall; (*número de personas que asisten a un espectáculo*) house; (*producto de cada función*) gate; (*amistad en alguna casa*) entree; (*naipes que guarda un jugador*) hand; (*de una comida*) entree; (*visita breve*) short call; (Col) down payment; (Mex) attack, onslaught; (elec) input; **dar entrada a** to admit; to give an opening to; (*un buque*) to give the right of entry to; **entrada de taquilla** gate; **entrada general** top gallery; **entrada llena** full house; **mucha entrada** good house, good turnout; **se prohibe la entrada** no admittance

entra•do -da *adj* (Chile) officious, self-assertive; **entrado en años** advanced in years || *f* see **entrada**

entra•dor -dora *adj* (*enamoradizo*) susceptible; (Mex) lively, energetic; (Chile) officious, self-assertive

entrama•do -da *adj* half-timbered || *m* timber framework

entram•bos -bas *adj* & *pron indef* both; **entrambos a dos** both

entrampar *tr* to ensnare, trap; trick, deceive; overload with debt || *ref* to get trapped; be tricked; run into debt

entrante *adj* entering; (*p.ej., tren*) inbound, incoming; (*próximo, que viene*) next || *mf* entrant; **entrantes y salientes** (coll) hangers-on

entraña *f* internal organ; (fig) heart, center; **entrañas** entrails; (fig) heart, feeling; (fig) disposition, temper

entrañable *adj* close, intimate

entrañar *tr* to put away deep, bury deep; involve; (*malos pensamientos*) harbor || *ref* to go deep into; be buried deep; be close, be intimate

entrapajar *tr* to wrap up, bandage

entrar *tr* to bring in; overrun, invade; influence || *intr* to enter, go in, come in; (*un río*) empty; (*el viento, la marea*) rise; attack; begin; **entrar a matar** (taur) to go in for the kill; **entrar en** to enter, enter into, go into; fit into; adopt, take up; **que entra** next

entre *prep* (*en medio de*) between; (*en el número de*) among; (*en el intervalo de*) in the course of; **entre manos** at hand; **entre mí** to myself; **entre que** while; **entre tanto** meanwhile; **entre Vd. y yo** between you and me

entreabier•to -ta *adj* half-open; (*puerta*) ajar

entreabrir **§83** *tr* to half-open; leave ajar

entreacto *m* entr'acte

entreca•no -na *adj* graying, grayish

entrecarril *m* (Ven) gauge

entrecejo *m* space between the eyebrows; frown; **fruncir el entrecejo** to frown; **mirar con entrecejo** to frown at

entrecoger **§17** *tr* to catch, seize; press hard, hold down

entrecoro *m* chancel

entrecorta•do -da *adj* broken, intermittent

entrecortar *tr* to break in on, keep interrupting

entre•cruz *m* (*pl* **-cruces**) interweaving

entrecruzar **§60** *tr & ref* to intercross; interweave, interlace; to interbreed

entrecubiertas *fpl* between-decks

entrechocar **§73** *ref* to collide, clash

entredicho *m* interdiction, prohibition; (law) injunction; (Bol) alarm bell; **poner en entredicho** to cast doubt upon

entredós *m* (*tira de encaje*) insertion; (typ) long primer

entrefilete *m* short feature, special item

entrefi•no -na *adj* medium

entrega *f* delivery; (*p.ej., de una plaza fuerte*) surrender; (*cuaderno de un libro que se vende suelto*) fascicle; (*de una revista*) issue, number; **por entregas** in instalments

entregar **§44** *tr* to deliver; hand over, surrender; fit in, insert; **entregarla** to die || *ref* to give in, surrender; abandon oneself; to devote oneself; **entregarse de** to take possession of, take charge of

entrehierro *m* (elec) spark gap; (phys) air gap

entrelazar **§60** *tr* to interlace, interweave

entremediar *tr* to put between

entremedias *adv* in between; in the meantime; **entremedias de** between; among

entremés *m* hors d'œuvre, side dish; short farce (*inserted in an auto or performed between two acts of a comedia*)

entremesear *tr* (*una conversación*) to enliven

entremeter *tr* to put in, insert || *ref* to meddle, intrude, butt in

entremeti•do -da *adj* meddling, meddlesome || *mf* meddler, intruder, busybody

entremezclar *tr & ref* to intermingle, intermix

entremorir **§30 & §83** *intr* to flicker, die out

entrenador *m* (sport) coach, trainer, handler

entrenamiento *m* (sport) coaching, training

entrenar *tr & ref* (sport) to coach, train

entrepaño *m* (*de una puerta*) panel; (*espacio entre dos columnas, etc.*) pier; shelf

entreparecer **§60** *ref* to show through

entrepiernas *fpl* crotch; patches in the crotch of trousers; (Chile) bathing trunks

entrepuentes *mpl* between-decks; (naut) steerage

entrerrenglón *m* interline; space between the lines

entrerrenglonar *tr* to write between the lines

entrerriel *m* gauge

entrerrisa *f* giggle

entrerrosca *f* (mach) nipple

entresacar **§73** *tr* to pick, pick out, select; cull, sift; (*árboles; el pelo*) thin out

entresemana *adv* (SAm) weekdays; workdays

entresijo *m* secret; mystery; **tener muchos entresijos** to be mysterious, be hard to figure out

entresuelo *m* mezzanine, entresol

entretallar *tr* to carve, engrave; carve in bas-relief; do openwork in; intercept

entretanto *adv* meantime, meanwhile || *m* meanwhile; **en el entretanto** in the meantime

entretecho *m* (Arg, Chile, Urug) attic, garret

entretejer *tr* to interweave

entretela *f* interlining

entretelar *tr* to interline

entretención *f* amusement, entertainment

entretener **§71** *tr* to amuse, entertain; (*el tiempo*) while away; maintain, keep up; put off, delay; (*el dolor*) allay; (*el hambre*) stave off (*by taking a bite before mealtime*); try to get one's mind off || *ref* to amuse oneself, be amused

entreteni•do -da *adj* amusing, entertaining; (rad) continuous, undamped || *f* kept woman; **dar la entretenida a** or **dar con la entretenida a** to stall off by constant talk

entretenimiento *m* amusement, entertainment; upkeep, maintenance

entretiempo *m* in-between season; **de entretiempo** spring-and-fall (*coat*)

entreventana *f* pier

entrever **§80** *tr* to glimpse, descry, catch a glimpse of; guess, suspect

entreverar *tr* to mix || *ref* (Arg) to get all mixed together; (*dos grupos de caballería*) (Arg) to clash in hand-to-hand combat

entrevía *f* gauge

entrevista *f* interview

entrevistar *ref* to have an interview
entristecer §22 *tr* to sadden, make sad || *ref* to sadden, become sad
entrojar *tr* to store in a granary
entrometer *tr & ref* var of **entremeter**
entrometi•do -da *adj & mf* var of **entremetido**
entronar *tr* to enthrone
entroncamiento *m* connection, relationship; (*de caminos, ferrocarriles*) junction
entroncar §73 *tr* to prove relationship between || *intr* to be related; (*dos caminos, ferrocarriles, etc.*) connect
entronerar *tr* (*una bola de billar*) to pocket
entronizar §60 *tr* to enthrone; exalt; popularize || *ref* to be puffed up with pride
entronque *m* connection, relationship; (*de caminos, ferrocarriles*) junction
entruchar *tr* to decoy, trick
entru•chón -chona *adj* tricky || *mf* trickster
entuerto *m* wrong, harm, injustice
entumecer §22 *tr* to make numb || *ref* (*un miembro*) to get numb, go to sleep; (*el mar*) swell, get rough
entupir *tr* to stop up, clog; pack tight || *ref* to get stopped up, get clogged
enturbiar *tr* to stir up, make muddy; confuse, upset
entusiasmar *tr* to enthuse, make enthusiastic || *ref* to enthuse, become enthusiastic
entusiasmo *m* enthusiasm; inspiration
entusiasta *adj* enthusiastic || *mf* enthusiast
entusiásti•co -ca *adj* enthusiastic
enumerar *tr* to enumerate
enunciar *tr* to enunciate, enounce
enunciati•vo -va *adj* (gram) declarative
envainar *tr* to sheathe
envalentonar *tr* to embolden, make bold || *ref* to pluck up, take courage
envanecer §22 *tr* to make vain || *ref* to become vain, get conceited
envanecimiento *m* vanity, conceit
envaramiento *m* stiffness
envarar *tr* to make numb, to stiffen || *ref* to get stiff; get numb
envasar *tr* (*p.ej., trigo*) to pack, sack; (*p.ej., vino*) bottle; (*p.ej., pescado*) can; (*una espada*) thrust, poke; (*mucho vino*) put away || *intr* to tipple
envase *m* container; bottle, jar; can; packing; bottling; canning; **envase de hojalata** tin can
envedijar *ref* to get tangled; come to blows
envejecer §22 *tr* to age, make old || *intr & ref* to age, grow old; get out of date
envejeci•do -da *adj* old, aged; experienced, tried
envenenar *tr* to poison; (*llenar de amargura*) envenom, embitter; (*las palabras o conducta de una persona*) put an evil interpretation on || *ref* to take poison
enverdecer §22 *intr* to turn green
envergadura *f* (*de las alas abiertas del ave*) spread; (*ancho de una vela*) breadth; (aer) span, wingspread; (fig) compass, spread, reach
envés *m* wrong side; (*del cuerpo humano*) back
enviado *m* envoy
enviar §77 *tr* to send; (*mercancías*) ship; **enviar a buscar** to send for; **enviar a paseo** to send on his way, dismiss without ceremony; **enviar por** to send for
enviciar *tr* to corrupt, vitiate; (*mimar*) spoil || *intr* to have many leaves and little fruit || *ref* to become addicted; **enviciarse con** or **en** to addict oneself to, become addicted to
envidar *tr* to bid against, bet against || *intr* to bid, bet
envidia *f* envy; desire
envidiable *adj* enviable
envidiar *tr* to envy, begrudge; desire, want
envidio•so -sa *adj* envious; greedy, covetous || *mf* envious person
envilecer §22 *tr* to debase, vilify, revile || *ref* to degrade oneself
envío *m* sending; (*de mercancías*) shipment; (*de dinero*) remittance; (*en una obra*) autograph, inscription
envirota•do -da *adj* stiff, stuck-up
envite *m* bet; bid, offer, invitation; push, shove; (*apuesta adicional a un lance o suerte*) side bet; **al primer envite** right off, at the start
enviudar *intr* (*una mujer*) to become a widow; (*un hombre*) become a widower
envoltorio *m* bundle; (*defecto en el paño*) knot
envoltura *f* cover, wrapper, envelope; swaddling clothes
envolver §47 **&** §83 *tr* to wrap, wrap up; (*hilo, cinta*) wind, roll up; (*al niño*) swaddle; imply, mean; involve; envelop; (*dejar cortado y sin salida en la disputa*) floor; (mil) to encircle || *ref* to become involved; have an affair
enyerbar *tr* (Col, Chile, Mex) to bewitch || *ref* to be covered with grass; (Mex) to fall madly in love; (Mex) to take poison
enyesar *tr* to plaster; put in a plaster cast; (*la tierra, el vino*) gypsum
enyugar §44 *tr* to yoke
enzima *f* enzyme
enzolvar *tr* (Mex) to clog, stop up
epazote *m* (CAm, Mex) Mexican tea
E.P.D. *abbr* **en paz descanse**
epénte•sis *f* (*pl* **-sis**) epenthesis
eperlano *m* smelt
épica *f* epic poetry
epice•no -na *adj* (gram) epicene, common
épi•co -ca *adj* epic || *m* epic poet || *f* see épica
epicúre•o -a *adj* epicurean || *mf* epicurean, epicure
epidemia *f* epidemic
epidémi•co -ca *adj* epidemic
epidemiología *f* epidemiology
epidermis *f* epidermis; **tener la epidermis fina** or **sensible** to be touchy
Epifanía *f* Epiphany, Twelfth-day
epígrafe *m* epigraph; inscription; headline, title; device, motto
epigrama *m* epigram
epilepsia *f* epilepsy

epilépti•co -ca *adj & mf* epileptic
epilogar §44 *tr* to sum up, summarize
episcopalista *adj & mf* Episcopalian
episodio *m* episode
epistemología *f* epistemology
epístola *f* epistle
epitafio *m* epitaph
epíteto *m* epithet
epitomar *tr* to epitomize
epítome *m* epitome
E.P.M. *abbr* **en propia mano**
época *f* epoch; **hacer época** to be epoch-making
epopeya *f* epic, epic poem
equidad *f* equity; (*templanza habitual*) equableness; (*moderación en el precio*) reasonableness
equiláte•ro -ra *adj* equilateral
equilibra•do -da *adj* balanced; (fig) sensible, even-tempered
equilibrar *tr* to balance, equilibrate; (*el presupuesto*) balance ‖ *ref* to balance, equilibrate
equilibrio *m* equilibrium, balance, equipoise; (*del presupuesto*) balancing; **equilibrio político** balance of power
equilibrista *mf* balancer, ropedancer
equinoccial *adj* equinoctial
equinoccio *m* equinox
equipaje *m* baggage; piece of baggage; equipment; (naut) crew; **equipaje de mano** hand baggage
equipar *tr* to equip
equiparar *tr* to compare
equi•pier *m* (*pl* **-piers**) teammate
equipo *m* equipment, outfit; crew, gang; (sport) team; **equipo de alta fidelidad** stereo system; hi-fi set; **equipo de novia** trousseau; **equipo de urgencia** first-aid kit
equitación *f* horsemanship, riding
equitati•vo -va *adj* fair, equitable; (*tranquilo*) equable
equivalente *adj & m* equivalent
equivaler §76 *intr* to be equal, be equivalent
equivocación *f* mistake; mistakenness
equivoca•do -da *adj* mistaken, wrong
equivocar §73 *tr* (*una cosa por otra*) to mistake, mix ‖ *ref* to be mistaken, make a mistake; be wrong; **equivocarse con** to be mistaken for; **equivocarse de** to be wrong in, take the wrong . . .
equívo•co -ca *adj* equivocal, ambiguous ‖ *m* equivocation, ambiguity; pun
equivoquista *mf* equivocator; punster
era *f* era, age; threshing floor; vegetable patch, garden bed
eral *m* two-year-old bull
erario *m* state treasury
erección *f* erection; foundation, establishment
eremita *m* hermit
ergástulo *m* dungeon, slave prison
ergio *m* erg
ergotismo *m* argumentativeness; (pathol) ergotism
ergotista *adj invar* argumentative; dogmatic; *mf* dogmatist; know-it-all
erguir §33 *tr* to raise; straighten up ‖ *ref* to straighten up; swell with pride
erial *adj* unplowed, uncultivated ‖ *m* unplowed land, uncultivated land
erigir §27 *tr* to erect, build; found, establish; (*a nueva condición*) elevate ‖ *ref*—**erigirse en** to be elevated to; set oneself up as
eriza•do -da *adj* bristling, bristly, spiny
erizar §60 *tr* to make stand on end, cause to bristle ‖ *ref* to stand on end, to bristle
erizo *m* (*mamífero*) hedgehog; (*zurrón espinoso de la castaña*) bur, thistle; (*púas de hierro que coronan lo alto de una muralla*) cheval-de-frise; (*persona de carácter áspero*) curmudgeon; **erizo de mar** (zool) sea urchin
ermita *f* hermitage
ermita•ño -ña *mf* hermit
erogación *f* (*de bienes o caudales*) distribution; expenditure; (Peru, Ven) gift, charity; (Mex) outlay
erogar §44 *tr* to distribute; (Ecuad) to contribute; (Mex) to cause
erosión *f* erosion
erosionar *tr & ref* to erode
erradicar §73 *tr* to eradicate
erra•do -da *adj* mistaken, wrong
errar §34 *tr* to miss ‖ *intr* to err, be mistaken, be wrong; wander ‖ *ref* to be mistaken, be wrong
errata *f* erratum; printer's error
erróne•o -a *adj* erroneous
error *m* error, mistake; **error de pluma** clerical error; **salvo error u omisión** barring error or omission
eructar *intr* to belch; (coll) to brag
eructo *m* belch, belching
erudición *f* erudition, learning
erudi•to -ta *adj* erudite, learned ‖ *mf* scholar, savant; **erudito a la violeta** egghead, highbrow
erugino•so -sa *adj* rusty
erumpir *intr* (*un volcán*) to erupt
erupción *f* eruption
esbel•to -ta *adj* slender, lithe, willowy
esbirro *m* bailiff, constable; (*el que ejecuta órdenes injustas*) myrmidon, henchman
esbozar §60 *tr* to sketch, outline
esbozo *m* sketch, outline
escabechar *tr* to pickle; (*el pelo, la barba*) dye; (*reprobar en un examen*) flunk; stab to death ‖ *ref* to dye one's hair; (*el pelo, la barba*) dye
escabeche *m* pickle; pickled fish; hair dye
escabel *m* stool; footstool; (*para medrar*) stepping stone
escabio•so -sa *adj* mangy
escabro•so -sa *adj* scabrous, risqué; scabrous, uneven, rough, harsh
escabuche *m* weeding hoe
escabullir §13 *ref* to slip away, sneak away; slip out, wiggle out
escafandra *f* diving suit; **escafandra espacial** space suit
escafandrista *mf* diver

escala *f* (*escalera de mano*) ladder, stepladder; (*línea graduada de instrumento*) scale; (*de buque*) call; (*de avión*) stop; (*puerto donde toca una embarcación*) port of call; (*serie de las notas musicales*) scale; **en escala de** on a scale of; **en grande escala** on a large scale; **escala móvil** (*de salarios*) sliding scale; **hacer escala** (naut) to call

escalada *f* scaling, climbing; breaking in; escalation

escalador *m* climber; (*ladrón*) burglar, housebreaker

escalación *f* escalation

escalafón *m* roster, roll, register

escalar *tr* (*subir, trepar*) to scale; break in, burglarize; (*la compuerta de la acequia*) open || *intr* to climb; (naut) to call || *ref* to escalate

escalato•rres *m* (*pl* **-rres**) steeplejack, human fly

escalda•do -da *adj* cautious, scared, wary; (*mujer*) lewd, loose

escaldar *tr* to scald; make red hot || *ref* to get scalded; chafe

escalera *f* stairs, stairway; (*la portátil*) ladder; (*de naipes*) sequence; (*en el póker*) straight; **de escalera abajo** from below stairs, from the servants; **escalera de caracol** winding stairway; **escalera de escape** fire escape; **escalera de husillo** winding stairway; **escalera de incendios** fire escape; **escalera de mano** ladder; **escalera de salvamento** fire escape; **escalera de tijera** or **escalera doble** ladder; **escalera excusada** or **falsa** private stairs; **escalera extensible** extension ladder; **escalera hurtada** secret stairway; **escalera mecánica, móvil** or **rodante** escalator, moving stairway

escalerilla *f* low step; car step; (*en las medias*) runner; (*de naipes*) sequence; thumb index

escalfar *tr* (*huevos*) to poach; (*el pan*) bake brown

escalinata *f* stone steps, front steps

escalo *m* burglary, breaking in

escalofria•do -da *adj* chilly

escalofrío *m* chill

escalón *m* step, rung; (*grada de la escalera*) tread; (fig) step, echelon, grade; (*paso con que uno adelanta sus pretensiones*) (fig) stepping stone; (mil) echelon; (rad) stage

escalonamiento *m* ranking; gradation

escalonar *tr* to space out, spread out; (*las horas de trabajo*) stagger; (mil) to echelon

escalope *m* (*loncha delgada de carne*) scallop (*thin slice of meat*)

escalpar *tr* to scalp

escalpelo *m* scalpel

escama *f* scale; fear, suspicion

escamar *tr* (*los peces*) to scale; (coll) to frighten || *ref* to be frightened

escamondar *tr* to trim, prune

escamo•so -sa *adj* scaly

escamotea•dor -dora *mf* prestidigitator; swindler

escamotear *tr* to whisk out of sight, cause to vanish; (*una carta*) palm; swipe, snitch

escampada *f* clear spell, break in rain

escampar *tr* to clear out || *intr* to stop raining; ease up; **¡ya escampa!** there you go again! || *ref* — **escamparse del agua** to get in out of the rain

escampavía *f* (naut) cutter, revenue cutter

escamujar *tr* (*un árbol, esp. un olivo*) to prune; (*ramas*) clear out

escanciar *tr* (*vino*) to pour, serve, drink || *intr* to drink wine

escandalizar §60 *tr* to scandalize || *ref* to be scandalized; be outraged, be exasperated

escándalo *m* scandal; **causar escándalo** to make a scene

escandalo•so -sa *adj* scandalous; noisy, riotous; loud, flashy

escandallo *m* (naut) sounding lead; (*del contenido de varios envases*) testing, sampling; cost accounting

escandina•vo -va *adj & mf* Scandinavian

escandir *tr* (*versos*) to scan

escansión *f* scansion; (telv) scanning

escaño *m* settle, bench with a back; (*en las Cortes*) seat; park bench; (Guat) nag

escañuelo *m* footstool

escapada *f* escape, flight; short trip, quick trip

escapar *tr* to free, save; (*un caballo*) drive hard || *intr* to escape; flee, run away; **escapar en una tabla** to have a narrow escape || *ref* to escape; flee, run away; (*el gas, el agua*) leak; **escapársele a uno** to let slip; not notice

escaparate *m* show window; (*armario con cristales*) cabinet; wardrobe, clothes closet; **escaparete de tienda** shop window

escaparatista *mf* window dresser

escapatoria *f* escape, getaway; (*de atenciones, deberes, etc.*) (fig) escape; (*efugio, pretexto*) (coll) evasion, subterfuge

escape *m* escape; flight; (*de gas, agua*) leak; (*de reloj*) escapement; (aut) exhaust valve; (aut) exhaust, exhaust pipe; **a escape** at full speed, on the run; **escape de rejilla** (rad) grid leak; **escape libre** (aut) cutout

escápula *f* shoulder blade, scapula

escaque *m* square; **escaques** chess

escarabajear *tr* to bother, worry, harass || *intr* to swarm, crawl; scrawl, scribble

escarabajo *m* black beetle; (*imperfección en los tejidos*) flaw; (*persona pequeña*) runt

escaramuza *f* skirmish

escaramuzar §60 *intr* to skirmish

escarapela *f* (*divisa en forma de lazo*) cockade; dispute ending in hair pulling

escarapelar *intr & ref* to quarrel, wrangle

escarbadien•tes *m* (*pl* **-tes**) toothpick

escarbar *tr* (*el suelo*) to scratch, scratch up; (*la lumbre*) poke; (*los dientes, los oídos*) pick; pry into

escarcha *f* frost, hoarfrost

escarchar *tr* (*confituras*) to frost, put frosting on; (*la tierra del alfarero*) dilute with water; spangle || *intr* — **escarcha** there is frost

escardar or **escardillar** *tr* to weed, weed out
escardillo *m* weeding hoe
escariar *tr* to ream
escarlata *adj* scarlet || *f* scarlet fever
escarlatina *f* scarlet fever
escarmentar §**2** *tr* to make an example of || *intr* to learn one's lesson
escarmiento *m* example, lesson, warning; caution, wisdom; punishment
escarnecer §**22** *tr* to scoff at, make fun of
escarnio *m* scoff, scoffing
escarola *f* endive
escarpa *f* scarp, escarpment; (Mex) sidewalk
escarpa•do -da *adj* steep; abrupt, craggy
escarpia *f* hooked spike
escarpín *m* pump
escasamente *adv* barely; hardly
escasear *tr* to give sparingly; cut down on, avoid; bevel || *intr* to be scarce
escase•ro -ra *adj* sparing; saving, frugal; stingy || *mf* skinflint
escasez *f* (*falta de una cosa*) scarcity; (*pobreza*) need, want; (*mezquindad*) stinginess
esca•so -sa *adj* (*poco abundante*) scarce; (*no cabal*) scant; (*muy económico*) parsimonious, frugal; (*tacaño*) stingy; (*oportunidad*) dim, slim, slight; **estar escaso de** to be short of
escatimar *tr & intr* to scrimp
escena *f* (*parte del teatro donde se representan las obras*) stage; (*subdivisión de un acto*) scene; incident, episode; **poner en escena** to stage
escenario *m* stage; (*disposición de la representación*) setting; (*guión de un cine*) scenario; (*antecedentes de una persona o cosa*) background
escenarista *mf* scenarist
escéni•co -ca *adj* scenic
escenificar §**73** *tr* to adapt for the stage
escépti•co -ca *adj* sceptic(al) || *mf* sceptic
Escila *f* Scylla; **entre Escila y Caribdis** between Scylla and Charybdis
Escipión *m* Scipio
escisión *f* (biol) fission; (surg) excision
esclarecer §**22** *tr* to light up, brighten; explain, elucidate; ennoble || *intr* to dawn
esclareci•do -da *adj* noble, illustrious
esclavitud *f* slavery
esclavización *f* enslavement
esclavizar §**60** *tr* to enslave
escla•vo -va *adj & mf* slave
escla•vón -vona *adj & mf* Slav
esclerosis múltiple *f* multiple sclerosis
esclusa *f* lock; floodgate; **esclusa de aire** caisson
esclusero *m* lock tender
escoba *f* broom
escobada *f* sweep; sweeping
escobar *tr* to sweep with a broom
escobazar §**60** *tr* to sprinkle with a wet broom
escobén *m* (naut) hawse
escobilla *f* brush, whisk; gold and silver sweepings; (elec) brush
escocer §**16** *intr* to smart, sting || *ref* to hurt; chafe, become chafed
esco•cés -cesa *adj* Scotch, Scottish || *mf* Scot || *m* Scotchman; (*whisky; dialecto*) Scotch; **los escoceces** the Scotch, the Scottish
Escocia *f* Scotland; **la Nueva Escocia** Nova Scotia
escofina *f* rasp
escofinar *tr* to rasp
escoger §**17** *tr* to choose, pick out
escogi•do -da *adj* choice, select
escolar *adj* school || *m* pupil
escolaridad *f* schooling, school attendance; curriculum
escolimo•so -sa *adj* impatient, gruff, restless
escolta *f* escort
escoltar *tr* to escort
escollar *intr* (Arg) to run aground on a reef; (Arg, Chile) to fail
escollera *f* jetty, breakwater
escollo *m* (*peñasco a flor de agua*) reef, rock; (*peligro*) pitfall; (*obstáculo*) stumbling block
escombrar *tr* to clear out
escombro *m* (*pez*) mackerel; **escombros** debris, rubble, rubbish
esconder *tr* to hide, conceal; harbor, contain || *ref* to hide; lurk
escondi•do -da *adj* hidden; **a escondidas** secretly; **a escondidas de** without the knowledge of
escondite *m* hiding place; (*juego de muchachos*) hide-and-seek; **jugar al escondite** to play hide-and-seek
escondrijo *m* hiding place
escopeta *f* shotgun; **escopeta blanca** gentleman hunter; **escopeta de caza** fowling piece; **escopeta de dos cañones** double-barreled shotgun; **escopeta de viento** air rifle; **escopeta negra** professional hunter
escopetazo *m* gunshot; gunshot wound; bad news, blow; (SAm) sarcasm; insult
escoplear *tr* to chisel
escoplo *m* chisel
escorbuto *m* scurvy
escoria *f* dross, scoria, slag; (fig) dross, dregs
escorial *m* cinder bank, slag dump
escorpión *m* scorpion; **Escorpión** *m* (astr) Scorpio
escorzar §**60** *tr* to foreshorten
escorzo *m* foreshortening
escota *f* (naut) sheet
escota•do -da *adj* low-neck || *m* low neck
escotadura *f* low neck, low cut in neck
escotar *tr* to cut to fit; draw water from, drain; cut low in the neck || *intr* to go Dutch
escote *m* low neck; (*encajes en el cuello de una vestidura*) tucker; **ir a escote** or **pagar a escote** to go Dutch
escotilla *f* (naut) hatchway, scuttle
escotillón *m* hatch, trap door, scuttle; (theat) trap door
escozor *m* burning, smarting, stinging; grief, sorrow
escriba *m* scribe
escribanía *f* court clerkship; desk; writing materials
escribano *m* court clerk; lawyer's clerk

escribiente *mf* clerk, office clerk; **escribiente a máquina** typist
escribir §**83** *tr & intr* to write || *ref* to enroll, enlist; write to each other; **no escribirse** to be impossible to describe
escriño *m* casket, jewel case; straw basket
escri•to -ta *adj* streaked || *m* writing; (law) brief, writ; **poner por escrito** to write down, put in writing
escri•tor -tora *mf* writer
escritorio *m* writing desk; office; **escritorio ministro** kneehole desk, office desk; **escritorio norteamericano** rolltop desk
escritura *f* writing; script, handwriting, longhand; (law) deed, indenture; (law) sworn statement; **escritura al tacto** touch typewriting || **Escritura** *f* Scripture; **Sagrada Escritura** Holy Scripture, Holy Writ
escriturar *tr* to notarize; (*p.ej., a un actor*) book || *ref* (taur) to sign up for a fight
escrnía. *abbr* **escribanía**
escrno. *abbr* **escribano**
escrófula *f* scrofula
escrúpulo *m* scruple
escrupulo•so -sa *adj* scrupulous; exact
escrutar *tr* to scrutinize; (*los votos*) count
escrutinio *m* scrutiny; counting of votes
escuadra *f* (*pequeño número de personas o de soldados*) squad; (*pieza de metal para asegurar las ensambladuras*) angle iron; (*de carpintero*) square; (*de dibujante*) triangle; (nav) squadron
escuadrar *tr* (carp) to square
escuadrilla *f* (aer) squadron
escuadrón *m* (mil) squadron
escualidez *f* squalor
escuáli•do -da *adj* squalid
escualor *m* squalor
escucha *mf* listener || *m* (mil) scout, vedette || *f* listening; (*en un convento*) chaperon; **escuchas telefónicas** listening in on telephone conversations; wiretapping; **estar de escucha** (coll) to eavesdrop
escuchar *tr* to listen to; (*atender a*) heed; (*radiotransmisiones*) monitor || *intr* to listen || *ref* to like the sound of one's own voice
escudar *tr* to shield
escudero *m* esquire; nobleman; lady's page
escudete *m* escutcheon; (*refuerzo en la ropa*) gusset; (*planchuela delante de la cerradura*) escutcheon, escutcheon plate
escudilla *f* bowl
escudo *m* shield; buckler; (*delante de la cerradura*) escutcheon plate; **escudo de armas** coat of arms; **escudo térmico** (*de una cápsula espacial*) heat shield
escudriñar *tr* to scrutinize
escuela *f* school; **escuela de artes y oficios** trade school; **escuela de párvulos** kindergarten; **escuela de verano** summer school; **escuela dominical** Sunday school; **Escuela Naval Militar** Naval Academy; **escuela preparatoria** prep school; **hacer escuela** to be the leader of a school (*of thought*)
escuelante *mf* (Mex) schoolteacher || *m* (Mex) schoolboy || *f* (Mex) schoolgirl
escuerzo *m* toad
escue•to -ta *adj* free, unencumbered; bare, unadorned
escuintle *adj* (Mex) sickly || *m* (*perro*) (Mex) mutt; (Mex) brat
esculcar §**73** *tr* to frisk
esculpir *tr & intr* to sculpture, carve; engrave
escultismo *m* outdoor activities
escultista *m* outdoorsman
escultor *m* sculptor
escultora *f* sculptress
escultura *f* sculpture
escultural *adj* sculptural; statuesque
escupidera *f* cuspidor; chamber pot
escupidura *f* spit; fever blister
escupir *tr & intr* to spit
escurrepla•tos *m* (*pl* **-tos**) dish rack
escurridero *m* drainpipe; drainboard; slippery spot
escurridi•zo -za *adj* slippery
escurri•do -da *adj* narrow-hipped; abashed, confused
escurridor *m* colander
escurriduras *fpl* dregs, lees
escurrir *tr* (*una vasija; un líquido; la vajilla*) to drain; to wring, wring out; **escurrir el bulto** to duck || *intr* to drip, ooze, trickle; slide, slip || *ref* to drip, ooze, trickle; slide, slip; slip away; (*un reparo*) slip out
esdrúju•lo -la *adj* accented on the antepenult || *m* word or verse accented on the antepenult
ese, esa *adj dem* (*pl* **esos, esas**) that (*near you*) || **ese** *f* sound hole (*of violin*); **hacer eses** to reel, stagger
ése, ésa *pron dem* (*pl* **ésos, ésas**) that (*near you*); **ésa** your city
esencia *f* essence; **esencia de pera** banana oil; **quinta esencia** quintessence
esencial *adj & m* essential
esfera *f* sphere; (*del reloj*) dial
esféri•co -ca *adj* spherical || *m* football
esfero *m* or **esferográfica** *f* (Col) ball-point pen
esfinge *f* sphinx; spiteful woman
esforza•do -da *adj* brave, vigorous, enterprising
esforzar §**35** *tr* to strengthen, invigorate; encourage || *ref* to exert oneself; strive
esfuerzo *m* effort, exertion, endeavor; courage, vigor, spirit
esfumar *tr* to stump || *ref* to disappear, fade away
esgarrar *tr* (*la flema*) to try to cough up || *intr* to clear the throat
esgrima *f* fencing
esgrimidura *f* fencing
esgrimir *tr* to wield, brandish; (*un argumento*) swing || *intr* to fence
esgrimista *mf* (Arg, Chile, Peru) fencer; (Chile) swindler, panhandler
esguazar §**60** *tr* to ford
esguazo *m* fording; ford
esguince *m* dodge, duck; (*gesto de disgusto*) frown; twist, sprain, wrench

eslabón *m* (*de cadena*) link; (*hierro acerado para sacar fuego de un pedernal; cilindro de acero para afilar cuchillos*) steel
eslabonar *tr* to link; link together, string together || *intr* to link
eslálom *m* slalom
esla•vo -va *adj* Slav, Slavic || *mf* Slav || *m* (*idioma*) Slavic
esla•vón -vona *adj & mf* Slav
eslogan *m* (*consigna usada en fórmulas publicitarias*) slogan
eslora *f* (naut) length
eslova•co -ca *adj & mf* Slovak
esmaltar *tr* to enamel; embellish
esmalte *m* enamel; **esmalte para las uñas** nail polish
esmera•do -da *adj* careful, painstaking
esmeralda *f* emerald
esmerar *tr* to polish, shine; examine, check || *ref* to take pains, do one's best
esmeril *m* emery
esmeriladora *f* emery wheel
esmerilar *tr* to grind or polish with emery
esmero *m* care, neatness
esmoladera *f* grindstone
esmoquin *m* tuxedo, dinner coat
esnifar *tr & intr* (*heroína*) to sniff
esnob *adj* snobbish || *mf* (*pl* **esnobs**) snob
esnobismo *m* snobbery, snobbishness
esnobista *adj* snobbish
eso *pron dem* that; **a eso de** about; **eso es** that's it; that is; **por eso** for that reason; therefore
esófago *m* esophagus
espabila•do -da *adj* intelligent; bright
espabilar *ref* to know the ropes; be well informed
espaciador *m* space bar
espacial *adj* space, spatial
espaciar §77 (Arg, Chile) & **regular** *tr* to space; spread, scatter || *ref* to expatiate; amuse oneself, relax
espacio *m* space; **espacio de chispa** spark gap; **espacio exterior** outer space; **espacio libre** (*entre dos cosas*) clearance; **espacio muerto** (*en el cilindro de un motor*) clearance; **por espacio de** in the space of
espacio•so -sa *adj* spacious, roomy; slow, deliberate
espada *m* swordsman; (taur) matador || *f* sword; playing card (*representing a sword*) equivalent to spade; **entre la espada y la pared** between the devil and the deep blue sea
espadachín *m* swordsman; (*amigo de pendencias*) bully
espadaña *f* cattail, bulrush, reed mace; (*campanario*) bell gable
espadilla *f* (*remo que se usa como timón*) scull; (*aguja para sujetar el pelo*) bodkin; red insignia of Order of Santiago
espadín *m* rapier
espadón *m* (coll) brass hat
espagueti *m* spaghetti
espalar *tr* to shovel
espalda *f* back; **a espaldas de uno** behind one's back; **de espaldas a** with one's back to; **tener buenas espaldas** to have broad shoulders; **volver las espaldas a** to turn a cold shoulder to
espaldar *m* (*de silla*) back; (*enrejado para plantas*) trellis, espalier
espaldarazo *m* slap on the back; (*ceremonia para armar caballero*) accolade; **dar el espaldarazo a** to accept, approve
espalera *f* trellis, espalier
espantada *f* (*de un animal*) sudden flight; (*desistimiento ocasionado por el miedo*) cold feet
espantadi•zo -za *adj* shy, skittish, scary
espantajo *m* scarecrow; (*persona fea*) fright
espantamos•cas *m* (*pl* **-cas**) (*para poner a los caballos*) fly net; (*aparato para asustar y alejar las moscas*) fly chaser
espantapája•ros *m* (*pl* **-ros**) scarecrow
espantar *tr* to scare, frighten; scare away || *ref* to get scared; be surprised, marvel
espanto *m* fright, terror; (*amenaza*) threat; ghost
espantosidad *f* fright; frightfulness; awfulness
espanto•so -sa *adj* frightening, terrifying
España *f* Spain; **la Nueva España** New Spain (*Mexico in the early days*)
espa•ñol -ñola *adj* Spanish; **a la española** in the Spanish manner || *mf* Spaniard || *m* (*idioma*) Spanish; **los españoles** the Spanish || *f* Spanish woman
españolería *f* Spanishness; hispanophilia
españolada *f* Spanish mannerism; Spanish remark
españolizar §60 *tr* to make Spanish, Hispanicize; translate into Spanish || *ref* to become Spanish
esparadrapo *m* sticking plaster
esparaván *m* spavin
esparavel *m* mortarboard
esparcimiento *m* spreading, scattering, dissemination; diversion, relaxation; frankness, openness
esparcir §36 *tr* to spread, scatter; divert, relax || *ref* to spread, scatter; disperse; take it easy, relax
espárrago *m* asparagus; (*perno*) stud bolt; awning pole
esparrancar §73 *ref* to spread one's legs wide apart
esparta•no -na *adj & mf* Spartan
esparto *m* esparto grass
espasmo *m* spasm
espasmódi•co -ca *adj* spasmodic
espásti•co -ca *adj* spastic
espato *m* spar; **espato flúor** fluor spar
espátula *f* spatula; putty knife
especia *f* spice
especia•do -da *adj* spicy
especial *adj* especial, special
especialidad *f* speciality; (*ramo a que se consagra una persona o negocio*) specialty
especialista *mf* specialist
especializar §60 *tr, intr & ref* to specialize
especiar *tr* to spice
especie *f* (*categoría de la clasificación biológica*) species; (*clase, género*) sort, kind;

(*caso, asunto*) matter; (*chisme, cuento*) news, rumor; appearance, pretext, show; remark; **en especie** in kind; **soltar una especie** to try to draw someone out
especie•ro -ra *mf* spice dealer ‖ *m* spice box
especificar §73 *tr* to specify; itemize
específi•co -ca *adj* specific ‖ *m* specific; patent medicine
espécimen *m* (*pl* **especímenes**) specimen
especio•so -sa *adj* (*engañoso*) specious; nice, neat, perfect
especiota *f* hoax, wild idea
espectáculo *m* spectacle; **dar un espectáculo** to make a scene; **espectáculo de atracciones** side show
especta•dor -dora *mf* witness; spectator
espectral *adj* ghostly
espectro *m* specter, phantom, ghost; (phys) spectrum
especular *tr* to check, examine; contemplate ‖ *intr* to speculate
espejear *intr* to sparkle
espejismo *m* mirage
espejo *m* mirror, looking glass; model; **espejo de cuerpo entero** full-length mirror, pier glass; **espejo de retrovisión** rear-view mirror; **espejo de vestir** full-length mirror, pier glass; **espejo retrovisor** rear-view mirror
espelunca *f* cave, cavern
espeluznante *adj* hair-raising
espera *f* wait, waiting; (*puesto para cazar*) blind, hunter's blind; composure, patience, respite; delay; (law) stay; **no tener espera** to be of the greatest urgency
esperanza *f* hope; **tener puesta su esperanza en** to pin one's faith on
esperanza•do -da *adj* hopeful (*having hope*)
esperanza•dor -dora *adj* hopeful (*giving hope*)
esperanzar §60 *tr* to give hope to
esperanzo•so -sa *adj* hopeful, full of hope
esperar *tr* (*aguardar*) to wait for, await; (*tener esperanza de conseguir*) expect, hope for; **ir a esperar** to go to meet ‖ *intr* to wait; hope; **esperar** + *inf* to hope to + *inf;* **esperar a que** to wait until; **esperar desesperando** to hope against hope; **esperar en** to put one's hope in; **esperar que** to hope that; **esperar sentado** to have a good wait
esperinque *m* smelt
esperma *f* sperm
esperpento *m* monstrosity; freak; nonsense
espesar *m* depth, thickness (*of woods*) ‖ *tr* to thicken; (*un tejido*) weave tighter ‖ *ref* to thicken, get thick or thicker
espe•so -sa *adj* thick; dirty, greasy
espesor *m* thickness; (*de un flúido, gas, masa*) density
espesura *f* thickness; (*matorral*) thicket; (*cabellera muy espesa*) shock of hair; dirtiness, greasiness
espetar *tr* to skewer; pierce, pierce through; **espetar algo a** to spring something on ‖ *ref* to be solemn, be pompous; settle down
espetón *m* (*hurgón*) poker; (*asador*) skewer, spit; jab, poke
espía *mf* spy; squealer ‖ *f* (naut) warping; (*cuerda*) (naut) warp
espiar §77 *tr* to spy on ‖ *intr* to spy; (naut) to warp
espichar *tr* to prick; (*dinero*) (Chile) to cough up; (Chile, Peru) to tap ‖ *intr* (coll) to die ‖ *ref* (Mex, W-I) to get thin
espiche *m* (*arma o instrumento puntiagudo*) prick; (naut) peg, bung
espichón *m* stab, prick
espiga *f* (bot) ear, spike; peg, pin, tenon; (*clavo sin cabeza*) brad; (*badajo*) clapper; (*de una llave*) stem
espigar §44 *tr* to glean; tenon, dowel ‖ *intr* (*los cereales*) to form ears ‖ *ref* to grow tall, shoot up
espigón *m* sharp point, spur; (*mazorca*) ear of corn; (*cerro puntiagudo*) peak; breakwater
espina *f* thorn, spine; (*de los peces*) fishbone; doubt, uncertainty; sorrow; (anat) spine; **dar mala espina a** to worry; **espina de pescado** herringbone; **espina de pez** fishbone; **espina dorsal** spinal column; **estar en espinas** to be on pins and needles
espinaca *f* spinach; **espinacas** spinach
espinal *adj* spinal
espinapez *m* herringbone; thorny matter, difficulty
espinar *m* thorny spot; (fig) thorny matter ‖ *tr* to prick; (*árboles*) protect with thornbushes; hurt, offend
espinazo *m* backbone; (*de un arco*) keystone
espinel *m* trawl, trawl line
espineta *f* spinet
espinilla *f* (*de la pierna*) shin, shinbone; (*granillo en la piel*) blackhead
espino *m* hawthorn; **espino artificial** barbed wire; **espino negro** blackthorn
espinochar *tr* (*el maíz*) to husk
espino•so -sa or **espinu•do -da** *adj* thorny; (*pez*) bony; (*difícil*) (fig) thorny, knotty
espiocha *f* pickaxe
espión *m* spy
espionaje *m* spying, espionage
espira *f* turn
espiración *f* breathing; exhalation
espiral *adj* spiral ‖ *f* (*línea curva que da vueltas alrededor de un punto*) spiral; (*del reloj*) hairspring; (*de humo*) curl, wreath
espirar *tr* to breath; encourage ‖ *intr* to breathe; exhale, expire; (*el viento*) (poet) to blow gently
espiritismo *m* spiritualism
espirito•so -sa *adj* spirited, lively; (*licor*) spirituous
espíritu *m* spirit; (*mente*) mind; (*aparecido, fantasma*) ghost, spirit; **espíritu de equipo** teamwork; **Espíritu Santo** Holy Ghost, Holy Spirit; **dar, despedir, exhalar** or **rendir el espíritu** to give up the ghost
espiritual *adj* spiritual; sharp, witty
espiritualismo *m* spiritualism
espita *f* tap, cock; (coll) tippler
espitar *tr* to tap
esplendidez *f* splendor, magnificence

esplén·di·do -da *adj* splendid, magnificent; generous, open-handed; (poet) brilliant, radiant
esplendor *m* splendor
esplendoro·so -sa *adj* resplendent
espliego *m* lavender
esplín *m* melancholy
espolada *f* prick with spur; **espolada de vino** shot of wine
espolear *tr* to spur, spur on
espoleta *f* fuse; (*hueso*) wishbone
espolón *m* (*del gallo, una montaña, un buque de guerra*) spur; dike, jetty, mole, cutwater; (*prominencia córnea de las caballerías*) fetlock; (*sabañón*) chilblain
espolvorear *tr* (*quitar el polvo de; esparcir el polvo sobre*) dust; (*el azúcar*) sprinkle
esponja *f* sponge; (*sablista*) sponge, sponger; **beber como una esponja** to drink like a fish; **tirar la esponja** to throw in (or up) the sponge
esponja·do -da *adj* proud, puffed-up; fresh, healthy
esponjar *tr* to puff up, make fluffy || *ref* to puff up, become fluffy; be puffed up, be conceited; look fresh and healthy
esponjo·so -sa *adj* spongy
esponsales *mpl* betrothal, engagement
espontanear *ref* to make a clean breast of it; open one's heart
espontáne·o -a *adj* spontaneous || *m* (taur) spectator who jumps into the ring to take on the bull
espora *f* spore
esporádi·co -ca *adj* sporadic
esposa *f* wife; **esposas** handcuffs, manacles
esposar *tr* to handcuff, manacle
espo·so -sa *mf* spouse || *m* husband || *f* see **esposa**
espuela *f* spur; **echar la espuela** (coll) to take a nightcap; **espuela de caballero** delphinium, rocket larkspur; **espuela de galán** nasturtium
espuelar *tr* (SAm) to spur, goad
espuerta *f* two-handled esparto basket
espulgar §44 *tr* to delouse; scrutinize
espuma *f* foam; (*en un vaso de cerveza; saliva parecida a la espuma*) froth; (*película de impurezas en la superficie de un líquido*) scum; **crecer como espuma** to grow like weeds; to have a meteoric rise; **espuma de caucho** foam rubber; **espuma de jabón** lather; **espuma de mar** meerschaum
espumadera *f* skimmer
espumajear *intr* to froth at the mouth
espumajo·so -sa *adj* foamy, frothy
espumante *adj* foaming; (*vino*) sparkling
espumar *tr* to skim || *intr* to foam, froth; (*el jabón*) lather; (*el vino*) sparkle; increase rapidly
espumarajo *m* froth, frothing at the mouth
espumilla *f* voile; (CAm, Ecuad) meringue
espumo·so -sa *adj* foamy, frothy; (*cubierto de una película*) scummy; (*jabonoso*) lathery; (*vino*) sparkling
espu·rio -ria *adj* spurious
espurrear or **espurriar** *tr* to squirt with water from the mouth
esputar *tr & intr* to spit
esputo *m* spit, saliva
esq. *abbr* **esquina**
esqueje *m* cutting, slip
esquela *f* note; announcement; death notice; **esquela amorosa** billet-doux
esqueléti·co -ca *adj* skeleton; skeletal, thin, wasted
esqueleto *m* skeleton; (CAm, Mex) blank form; (Chile) sketch, outline
esquema *m* scheme, diagram
es·quí *m* (*pl* **-quís**) ski; skiing; **esquí acuático** water ski; water skiing; **esquí remolcado** ski-joring
esquia·dor -dora *adj* ski || *mf* skier
esquiar §77 *intr* to ski
esquiciar *tr* to sketch
esquicio *m* sketch
esquifar *tr* (naut) to fit out, staff, man
esquife *m* skiff
esquiismo *m* skiing
esquila *f* sheepshearing; hand bell
esquilar *tr* to shear, fleece
esquilimo·so -sa *adj* fastidious, squeamish
esquilmar *tr* to harvest; (*las plantas el jugo de la tierra*) drain, exhaust; (*una fuente de riqueza*) drain, squander, use up; carry away, steal
esquilmo *m* harvest, farm produce; (Mex) farm scrapings
esquilmo·so -sa *adj* fastidious
esquimal *adj & mf* Eskimo
esquina *f* corner; (SAm) corner store; **a la vuelta de la esquina** around the corner; **doblar la esquina** to turn the corner; **hacer esquina** (*un edificio*) to be on the corner; **las cuatro esquinas** puss in the corner
esquina·do -da *adj* sharp-cornered; difficult, unsociable
esquinar *tr* to be on the corner of; put in the corner; alienate || *intr* — **esquinar con** to be on the corner of || *ref* — **esquinarse con** to fall out with
esquinazo *m* corner; (Arg, Chile) serenade; **dar esquinazo a** to give the slip to, to shake off
esquinencia *f* quinsy
esquinera *f* corner piece (*of furniture*)
esquirla *f* splinter
esquirol *m* scab, strikebreaker
esquisto *m* schist
esquite *m* (CAm, Mex) popcorn
esquivar *tr* to avoid, evade, shun; dodge || *ref* to withdraw; dodge
esquivez *f* aloofness, gruffness
esqui·vo -va *adj* aloof, gruff
estable *adj* stable, permanent; full-time || *mf* regular guest, permanent guest
establecer §22 *tr* to establish, institute || *ref* to settle, take up residence; start a business, open an office
establecimiento *m* establishment; place of business; decree, ordinance, statute
establo *m* stable

estaca *f* stake, picket, pale; cudgel, club; (*clavo largo*) spike; (hort) cutting
estacada *f* stockade, palisade; dueling ground; **dejar en la estacada** to leave in the lurch; **quedarse en la estacada** to succumb on the field of battle, fall in a duel; fail; lose out
estacar **§73** *tr* to stake, stake off; tie to a stake || *ref* to stand stiff
estación *f* (*cada una de las cuatro divisiones del año*) season; (*sitio en que paran los trenes; radioemisora*) station; (*lugar en que se hace alto en un paseo, etc.*) stop; **estación balnearia** bathing resort; **estación de cabeza** (rr) terminal; **estación de carga** freight station; **estación de empalme** junction; **estación de gasolina** gas station, filling station; **estación de la seca** dry season; **estación de paso** (rr) way station; **estación depuradora** sewage-disposal plant; **estación de radiodifusión** broadcasting station; **estación de seguimiento** tracking station; **estación de servicio** service station; **estación difusora** or **emisora** broadcasting station; **estación espacial** space station; **estación gasolinera** gas station, filling station; **estación meteorológica** weather station; **estación telefónica** telephone exchange
estacional *adj* seasonal
estacionamiento *m* stationing; parking; parking lot
estacionar *tr* to station; stand, park || *intr* to stand, park || *ref* to station oneself; be stationary; stand, park; **se prohibe estacionarse** no standing, no parking
estaciona•rio -ria *adj* stationary
estada *f* stay, stop
estadía *f* (*ante un pintor*) sitting; stop, stay; (com) demurrage
estadio *m* stadium; phase, stage; (*longitud*) furlong
estadista *mf* (*perito en estadística*) statistician || *m* statesman
estadística *f* statistics
estadísti•co -ca *adj* statistical || *m* statistician || *f* see **estadística**
estadiunense *adj* American, United States || *mf* American
estadi•zo -za *adj* (*aire*) heavy, stifling; (*agua*) stagnant
estado *m* state; state, condition, status; statement, report; **en estado de buena esperanza** or **en estado interesante** in the family way; **estado asistencial** welfare state; **estado civil** marital status; **estado de ánimo** state of mind; **estado de cuentas** (com) statement; **estado libre asociado** commonwealth; **estado llano** commons, common people; **estado mayor** (mil) staff; **estado mayor conjunto** joint chiefs of staff; **estado mayor general** general staff; **Estados Unidos** *msg* the United States; **estado tapón** buffer state; **estar en estado de guerra** to be under martial law; **los Estados Unidos** *mpl* the United States; **tomar estado** to take a wife; to go into the church
estado-policía *m* (*pl* **estados-policías**) police state
estadounidense or **estadunidense** *adj* American, United States || *mf* American
estafa *f* swindle, trick; (*estribo*) stirrup
estafar *tr* to swindle, trick; overcharge
estafeta *f* post, courier; post office; diplomatic mail
estallar *intr* to burst; explode; (*un incendio, una revolución; la guerra*) break out; (*la ira*) break forth
estallido *m* report, crash, explosion; crack; (*p.ej., de la guerra*) outbreak; **dar un estallido** to crash, explode
estambre *m* (*hebras de lana e hilo formado de ellas*) worsted; (bot) stamen; **estambre de la vida** course or thread of life
estampa *f* stamp, print, engraving; press, printing; footstep, track; aspect, appearance; **dar a la estampa** to publish, bring out; **parecer la estampa de la herejía** to be a sight, be a mess; **la propia estampa de** the very image of
estampado *m* printing, stamping; printed fabric, cotton print
estampar *tr* to stamp, print, engrave; (*en al ánimo*) fix, engrave; (*p.ej., el pie*) leave a mark of; (bb) to tool; (*arrojar con fuerza*) (coll) to dash, slam
estampida *f* report, crash, explosion; stampede
estampido *m* report, crash, explosion; **estampido sónico** (aer) sonic boom
estampilla *f* (*sello con letrero para estampar*) stamp; (*sello con una firma en facsímile*) rubber stamp; (*sello de correos o fiscal*) stamp
estampillar *tr* to stamp; rubber-stamp
estanca•do -da *adj* stagnant; (fig) stagnant, dead
estancar **§73** *tr* to stanch; stem, check; (*un negocio*) suspend, hold up; corner; monopolize || *ref* to become stagnant, become choked up
estancia *f* stay, sojourn; (*aposento*) living room; day in hospital; cost of day in hospital; (*estrofa*) stanza; (mil) bivouac; (Arg, Urug, Chile) cattle ranch; (Col) small country place; (Ven) truck farm
estanciero *m* rancher, cattle raiser
estan•co -ca *adj* stanch, watertight || *m* government monopoly; cigar store, government store (*for sale of tobacco, matches, postage stamps, etc.*); archives; (Ecuad) liquor store
estándar *m* standard
estandardizar **§60** or **estandarizar** **§60** *tr* to standardize
estandarte *m* banner, standard
estandartizar **§60** *tr* to standardize
estanque *m* basin, reservoir; pond, pool
estanque•ro -ra *mf* storekeeper, tobacconist; (Ecuad) saloonkeeper || *m* reservoir tender

estanquillo *m* cigar store, government store (*for sale of tobacco, matches, postage stamps, etc.*); (Col, Ecuad) bar, saloon; (Mex) booth, stand
estante *adj* located, being; settled, permanent || *m* shelf; shelving; bookcase, open bookcase
estantería *f* shelves, shelving; book stack
estañar *tr* to tin; tin-plate; solder; (Ven) to hurt, injure; (Ven) to fire
estaño *m* tin
estaquilla *f* peg, dowel, pin; (*clavo pequeño sin cabeza*) brad; (*clavo largo*) spike
estaquillar *tr* to peg, dowel; nail
estar §37 *v aux* (*to form progressive form*) to be, e.g., **están aprendiendo el español** they are learning Spanish || *intr* to be; be in, be home; be ready; **¿a cuántos estamos?** what day of the month is it?; **¡está bien!** O.K.!, all right!; **estar a** to cost, sell at; **estar bien** to be well; **estar bien con** to be on good terms with; **estar de** to be (*on a temporary basis*); **estar de más** to be in the way; be unnecessary; be idle; **estar de viaje** to be on a trip; **estar mal** to be sick, be ill; **estar mal con** to be on bad terms with; **estar para** to be about to; **estar por** to be for, be in favor of; to be about to; to have a mind to; to remain to be + *pp;* **estar sobre sí** to be wary, be on one's guard || *ref* (*p.ej., en casa*) to stay; (*p.ej., quieto*) to keep
estarcido *m* stencil
estarcir §36 *tr* to stencil
estatal *adj* state
estáti•co -ca *adj* static; dumbfounded, speechless
estatificar §73 *tr* to nationalize
estatizar §60 *tr* to nationalize
estatorreactor *m* ramjet (engine)
estatua *f* statue; **quedarse hecho una estatua** to stand aghast
estatuir §20 *tr* to order, decree; establish, prove
estatura *f* stature
estatuta•rio -ria *adj* statutory
estatuto *m* statute
estay *m* (naut) stay; **estay mayor** (naut) mainstay
este, esta *adj dem* (*pl* **estos, estas**) this || *m* east; east wind
éste, ésta *pron dem* (*pl* **éstos, éstas**) this one, this one here; the latter; **ésta** this city
estela *f* (*de un buque*) wake; (*de cohete, humo, cuerpo celeste, etc.*) trail
estenógrafo *m* (Cuba) ball-point pen
estenotipia *f* stenotypy; machine stenography
estepa *f* steppe
estera *f* mat; matting; **cargado de esteras** out of patience
esterar *tr* to cover with matting || *intr* to bundle up for the cold
estercolar *m* dunghill || §61 *tr* to dung, to manure
estercolero *m* manure pile, dunghill; manure collector
estereofóni•co -ca *adj* stereophonic, stereo
estereoscópi•co -ca *adj* stereoscopic, stereo
estereotipa•do -da *adj* stereotyped
estéril *adj* (*que no produce nada*) sterile; (*inútil, vano*) futile
esterilización *f* sterilization
esterilizar §60 *tr* to sterilize || *ref* to become sterile
esterlina *adj fem* (*libra*) sterling (*pound*)
esternón *m* breastbone
estero *m* tideland; estuary; (Arg) swamp, marsh; (Chile) stream; (Col, Ven) pool, puddle
esterto *m* death rattle; (*ruido en ciertas enfermedades, perceptible por la auscultación*) stertor, râle; **estertor agónico** death rattle
esteta *mf* aesthete || *f* beautician
estéti•co -ca *adj* aesthetic || *f* aesthetics
estetoscopio *m* stethoscope
estiaje *m* low water
estiba *f* (naut) stowage
estibador *m* stevedore, longshoreman
estibar *tr* to pack, stuff; (naut) to stow
estiércol *m* dung, manure
esti•gio -gia *adj* Stygian || **Estigia** *f* Styx
estigma *m* stigma
estigmatizar §60 *tr* to stigmatize
estilar *tr* (*una escritura*) to draw up in proper form; be given to || *intr & ref* to be in fashion
estilete *m* (*puñal*) stiletto
estilo *m* style; **por el estilo** like that, of the kind; **por el estilo de** like; **estilo directo** (gram) direct discourse; **estilo indirecto** (gram) indirect discourse
estilográfica *f* fountain pen
estima *f* esteem; (naut) dead reckoning
estimable *adj* estimable; considerable; appreciable, computable; esteemed
estimación *f* esteem, estimation; estimate, evaluation
estimar *tr* (*tener en buen concepto*) to esteem; (*apreciar, valuar*) estimate; think, believe; appreciate, thank; be fond of, like; **estimar en poco** to hold in low esteem
estimativa *f* judgment; instinct
estimulante *adj & m* stimulant
estimular *tr* to stimulate
estímulo *m* stimulus
estío *m* summer
estipendio *m* stipend; wages
estípti•co -ca *adj* styptic; constipated; mean, stingy
estipular *tr* to stipulate
estiradamente *adv* scarcely, hardly; violently
estira•do -da *adj* conceited, stuck-up; prim, neat; tight, closefisted
estirar *tr* to stretch; (*alambre, metal*) draw; (*planchar ligeramente*) iron lightly; (*un escrito, discurso, cargo, etc.*) (fig) to stretch out; (*el dinero*) (fig) to stretch || *ref* to stretch; put on airs
estirón *m* jerk, tug; **dar un estirón** to grow up in no time
estirpe *f* race, stock, lineage; (*linaje*) strain, pedigree
estitiquez *f* constipation
estival *adj* summer

esto *pron dem* that; **en esto** at this point; **por esto** for this reason

estocada *f* thrust, stab, lunge; (*herida*) stab, stab wound; (*cosa que ocasiona dolor*) blow

Estocolmo *f* Stockholm

estofa *f* brocade; quality, kind

estofado *m* stew

estoi•co -ca *adj & mf* stoic

estóli•do -da *adj* stupid, imbecile

estómago *m* stomach; **estómago de avestruz** iron digestion; **tener buen estómago** or **mucho estómago** to be thick-skinned; have an easy conscience

estopa *f* (*de lino o cáñamo*) tow; (*de calafatear*) (naut) oakum; **estopa de acero** steel wool; **estopa de algodón** cotton waste

estopilla *f* (*tela muy sutil*) lawn; (*tela ordinaria de algodón*) cheesecloth

estoque *m* rapier; sword lily, gladiola

estoquear *tr* to stab with a rapier

estor *m* blind, shade, window shade

estorbar *tr* to hinder, obstruct; inconvenience, bother, annoy ‖ *intr* to be in the way

estorbo *m* hindrance, obstruction; inconvenience, bother, annoyance

estorbo•so -sa *adj* hindering; bothersome, annoying

estornino *m* starling; **estornino de los pastores** grackle, myna

estornudar *intr* to sneeze

estornudo *m* sneeze, sneezing

estrado *m* (*tarima del trono*) dais; lecture platform; (archaic) lady's drawing room; **estrados** courtrooms, law courts; **citar para estrados** to subpoena

estrafala•rio -ria *adj* odd, eccentric; sloppy, sloppily dressed ‖ *mf* screwball

estragar **§44** *tr* to spoil, damage, vitiate

estrago *m* damage, ruin, havoc

estrambote *m* tail (*of sonnet*)

estrambóti•co -ca *adj* odd, weird

estrangul *m* (mus) reed, mouthpiece

estrangular *tr & ref* to strangle, choke

estraperlear *intr* to deal in the black market

estraperlista *adj* black-market ‖ *mf* black-market dealer

estraperlo *m* black market

estrapontín *m* folding seat, jump seat

estratagema *f* stratagem; craftiness

estratega *m* strategist

estrategia *f* strategy; **alta estrategia** grand strategy

estratégi•co -ca *adj* strategic(al) ‖ *m* strategist

estratificar **§73** *tr & ref* to stratify

estrato *m* stratum, layer

estratosfera *f* stratosphere

estraza *f* rag; brown paper

estrechar *tr* (*reducir a menor ancho*) narrow; (*apretar*) tighten; press, pursue; force, compel; hug, embrace; squeeze; **estrechar la mano a** to shake hands with ‖ *ref* to narrow down; contract; hug, embrace; (*reducir los gastos*) retrench; **estrecharse en** to squeeze in; **estrecharse la mano** (*dos personas*) to shake hands

estrechez *f* narrowness; rightness; (*amistad íntima*) closeness, intimacy; austerity, strictness; poverty, want, need; trouble, jam; **estrechez de miras** narrow outlook, narrow-mindedness; **hallarse en gran estrechez** to be in dire straits

estre•cho -cha *adj* narrow; tight; close, intimate; austere, strict; stingy, tight; poor, needy; mean ‖ *m* (*paso angosto en el mar*) strait; fix, predicament

estrechura *f* narrowness; tightness; closeness, intimacy; austerity, strictness; trouble, predicament

estregar **§66** *tr* to rub hard; scour

estregón *m* hard rub

estrella *f* star; (typ) asterisk, star; (mov & theat) star; (*hado, destino*) (fig) star; **estrella de los Alpes** edelweiss; **estrella de mar** starfish; **estrella de rabo** comet; **estrella filante** or **fugaz** shooting star; **estrella fulgurante** (astr) flare star; **estrella polar** pole-star; **estrella vespertina** evening star; **ver las estrellas** (fig) to see stars

estrella•do -da *adj* (*cielo*) starry; star-spangled; star-shaped; (*huevos*) fried

estrellamar *m* starfish

estrellar *adj* star ‖ *tr* to star, spangle with stars; (*huevos*) fry; shatter, dash to pieces ‖ *ref* to be spangled with stars; crash; **estrellarse con** to clash with

estrellón *m* large star; (*fuego artificial*) star; smash-up

estremecer **§22** *tr* to shake; (*el aire*) rend; (fig) to shake, upset ‖ *ref* to shake, tremble, shiver, shudder

estrena *f* (*regalo que se da en señal de agradecimiento*) handsel; first use

estrenar *tr* to use for the first time, wear for the first time; (*un drama*) perform for the first time; (*un cine*) show for the first time; try out for the first time ‖ *ref* to make the day's first transaction; appear for the first time; (*un drama, un cine*) open

estrenista *mf* first-nighter

estreno *m* beginning, debut; première, first performance; first use

estre•nuo -nua *adj* strenuous, vigorous, enterprising

estreñimiento *m* constipation

estreñir **§72** *tr* to constipate

estrépito *m* racket, crash; fuss, show

estrepito•so -sa *adj* loud, noisy, boisterous; notorious; shocking

estría *f* flute, groove

estriar **§77** *tr* to flute, groove

estribar *intr* to lean, rest; be based, depend

estriberón *m* stepping stone

estribillo *m* (*de un poema*) burden, refrain; pet word, pet phrase

estribo *m* (*de coche*) step; (*de automóvil*) running board; (*apoyo para el pie*) footboard; (*para el pie del jinete*) stirrup; abutment, buttress; (fig) foundation, support;

perder los estribos to fly off the handle; lose one's head
estribor *m* starboard
estricnina *f* strychnine
estricote *m* (Ven) riotous living; **al estricote** hither and thither
estric•to -ta *adj* strict, severe, rigorous; proper, punctual; (*sentido de una palabra*) narrow
estrictura *f* (pathol) stricture
estrige *f* barn owl; (*Athene noctua*) little owl
estro *m* poetic inspiration; (*de animal*) rut, heat
estrofa *f* strophe
estroncio *m* strontium
estropajo *m* mop; dishcloth; **servir de estropajo** to be forced to do the dirty work; be treated with indifference
estropajo•so -sa *adj* raggedy, slovenly; (*carne*) tough, leathery; spluttering
estropear *tr* to spoil, ruin, damage; abuse, mistreat; cripple, maim || *ref* to spoil, go to ruin; fail
estropicio *m* breakage; havoc, ruin; fracas, rumpus
estructura *f* structure
estruendo *m* noise, crash, boom; confusion, uproar; pomp, show; fame
estruendo•so -sa *adj* noisy, booming
estrujar *tr* to squeeze; press, crush, mash; bruise; rumple; drain, exhaust
estuante *adj* hot, burning
estuario *m* estuary; tideland
estucar §73 *tr* to stucco
estuco *m* stucco; **estuco de París** plaster of Paris
estuche *m* case, box; (*caja y utensilios que se guardan en ella*) kit; casket, jewel case; (*para tijeras*) sheath; **estuche de afeites** compact, vanity case; **ser un estuche** to be a handy fellow
estudia•do -da *adj* affected, studied
estudiantado *m* student body
estudiante *mf* student
estudiantil *adj* student
estudiar *tr* to study; (*la lección a una persona*) to hear (*someone's lesson*) || *intr* to study; **estudiar para . . .** to study to become . . .
estudio *m* study; (*aposento*) studio; (mus) étude; **altos estudios** advanced studies
estudio•so -sa *adj* studious || *m* student, scholar
estufa *f* stove; steam cabinet, steam room; foot stove; (*invernáculo*) hothouse
estul•to -ta *adj* stupid, silly, foolish
estupefac•to -ta *adj* stupefied, dumbfounded
estupen•do -da *adj* stupendous; famous, distinguished
estúpi•do -da *adj* stupid || *mf* dolt
estupor *m* stupor; surprise, amazement
estuprar *tr* to rape, violate
estupro *m* rape, violation
estuque *m* stucco
esturión *m* sturgeon
etapa *f* stage; **a etapas pequeñas** by easy stages
éter *m* ether
etére•o -a *adj* ethereal
eternidad *f* eternity
eternizar §60 *tr* to prolong endlessly || *ref* to be endless, be interminable
eter•no -na *adj* eternal
éti•co -ca *adj* ethical || *f* ethics
etileno *m* ethylene
etilo *m* ethyl
étimo *m* etymon
etimología *f* etymology; **etimología popular** folk etymology
etíope *adj & mf* Ethiopian
etiópi•co -ca *adj & m* Ethiopic
etiqueta *f* (*marbete*) tag, label; (*ceremonial que se debe observar*) etiquette; (*ceremonia en la manera de tratarse*) formality; **de etiqueta** formal, full-dress; **de etiqueta menor** semiformal; **estar de etiqueta** to have become cool toward each other
etiquetar *tr* to tag, label
etiquete•ro -ra *adj* formal, ceremonious; full of compliments
etiquez *f* (pathol) consumption
étni•co -ca *adj* ethnic(al); (gram) gentilic
etnografía *f* ethnography
etnología *f* ethnology
E.U.A. *abbr* **Estados Unidos de América**
eucalipto *m* eucalyptus
Eucaristía *f* Eucharist
eufemismo *m* euphemism
eufemísti•co -ca *adj* euphemistic
eufonía *f* euphony
eufóni•co -ca *adj* euphonic, euphonious
euforia *f* euphoria; endurance, fortitude
eufuísmo *m* euphuism
eufuísti•co -ca *adj* euphuistic
eugenesia *f* eugenics
eunuco *m* eunuch
euritmia *f* regular pulse
euro *m* east wind
Europa *f* Europe
europe•o -a *adj & mf* European
eutanasia *f* euthanasia
eutrapelia *f* moderation; lightheartedness; simple pastime
evacuación *f* evacuation; **evacuación de basuras** garbage disposal
evacuar §21 & **regular** *tr* to evacuate; (*un trámite*) transact; (*una visita*) pay; (*un encargo, un asunto*) do, carry out; **evacuar el vientre** to have a bowel movement || *intr* to evacuate; have a bowel movement
evadi•do -da *adj* escaped || *mf* escapee
evadir *tr* to avoid, evade, elude || *ref* to evade; escape, flee
evaluar §21 *tr* to evaluate; value
evangéli•co -ca *adj* evangelic(al)
evangelio *m* gospel, gospel truth || **Evangelio** *m* Gospel, Evangel
evangelista *m* Gospel singer or chanter; (Mex) public writer, penman || **Evangelista** *m* Evangelist
evaporar *tr & ref* to evaporate
evaporizar §60 *tr, intr & ref* to vaporize
evasión *f* (*efugio, evasiva*) evasion; (*fuga*) escape

evasi•vo -va *adj* evasive || *f* loophole, pretext, excuse
evento *m* chance, happening, contingency; (Col) sports event; **a todo evento** in any event
eventual *adj* contingent; (*emolumentos; gastos*) incidental
eventualidad *f* eventuality, contingency; uncertainty
evidencia *f* evidence, obviousness; (*prueba judicial*) evidence; **evidencia moral** moral certainty
evidenciar *tr* to show, make evident
evidente *adj* evident, obvious
evitable *adj* avoidable
evitación *f* avoidance; prevention
evitar *tr* to avoid, shun; (*p.ej., el polvo*) keep off; prevent; **evitar** + *inf* to avoid + *ger;* save from + *ger,* e.g., **la luz de la luna nos evitó tener que encender los faroles** the light of the moon saved us from having to light the lights
evo *m* (poet) age, aeon; (theol) eternity
evocar §73 *tr* to evoke; (*p.ej., los demonios*) invoke
evolución *f* evolution; change, development (*of one's point of view, plans, conduct, etc.*)
evolucionar *intr* to evolve; change, develop; (mil & nav) to maneuver
evolucionista *adj & mf* evolutionist; evolutionary
ex *adj* ex- (*former*), e.g., **el ex presidente** the ex-president
ex abrupto *adv* brashly || *m* brash remark
exacción *f* (*de impuestos, deudas, multas, etc.*) exaction, levy; (*cobro injusto*) extortion
exacerbar *tr* to exacerbate, aggravate
exactitud *f* exactness; punctuality
exac•to -ta *adj* exact; punctual, faithful || **exacto** *interj* right!
exactor *m* tax collector
exagerar *tr* to exaggerate
exalta•do -da *adj* exalted; extreme, hotheaded; wrought-up; radical
exaltar *tr* to exalt; extol || *ref* to be wrought-up, get excited
examen *m* examination; **examen de ingreso** entrance examination; **sufrir un examen** to take an examination
examinar *tr* to examine; inspect || *ref* to take an examination; **examinarse de ingreso** to take entrance examinations
exangüe *adj* bloodless; weak, exhausted; dead
exánime *adj* (*sin vida*) lifeless; (*desmayado*) faint, in a faint, lifeless
exasperar *tr* to exasperate
Exc.ª *abbr* **Excelencia**
excandecer §22 *tr* to incense, enrage
excarcelación *f* release
excarcelar *tr* (*a un preso*) to release
excavadora *f* power shovel
excavar *tr* to excavate; loosen soil around
excedente *adj* excess; excessive; on leave || *m* excess, surplus; **excedente de ganancia** profit margin
exceder *tr* (*ser mayor que*) to exceed; (*aventajar*) excel || *ref* to go too far, go to extremes; **excederse a sí mismo** to outdo oneself
excelencia *f* excellence, excellency; **por excelencia** par excellence; **Su Excelencia** Your Excellency
excelente *adj* excellent
excel•so -sa *adj* lofty, sublime || **el Excelso** the Most High
excéntrica *f* eccentric
excentricidad *f* eccentricity
excéntri•co -ca *adj* eccentric; (*barrio*) outlying || *mf* eccentric || *f* see **excéntrica**
excepción *f* exception; **a excepción de** with the exception of
excepcional *adj* exceptional
excepto *prep* except
exceptuar §21 *tr* to except; (*eximir*) exempt
excerpta or **excerta** *adj* excerpt
excesi•vo -va *adj* excessive; excess
exceso *m* excess; **exceso de equipaje** excess baggage; **exceso de peso** excess weight; **exceso de velocidad** speeding
excitable *adj* excitable
excitación *f* excitement; excitation
excitante *adj & m* stimulant
excitar *tr* to excite, stir up, stimulate || *ref* to become excited
exclamación *f* exclamation
exclamar *tr & intr* to exclaim
exclaustrar *tr* (*a un religioso*) to secularize
excluir §20 *tr* to exclude
exclusión *f* exclusion; **con exclusión de** to the exclusion of; **exclusión de contribución** tax deduction
exclusiva *f* rejection, turndown; sole right, monopoly; (*anticipación de una noticia por un periódico*) news beat
exclusive *adv* exclusively || *prep* exclusive of, not counting
exclusivista *adj* exclusive, clannish || *mf* snob
exclusi•vo -va *adj* exclusive || *f* see **exclusiva**
Exc.ᵐᵒ *abbr* **Excelentísimo**
ex combatiente *m* ex-serviceman
excomulgar §44 *tr* to excommunicate; ostracize, banish
excomunión *f* excommunication
excoriar *tr* to skin || *ref* to skin oneself; (*p.ej., el codo*) skin
excrementar *intr* to have a bowel movement
excremento *m* excrement
exculpar *tr* to exculpate, exonerate
excursión *f* excursion, outing
excursionista *mf* excursionist, tourist
excusa *f* excuse; **a excusa** secretly; **excusa es decir** it is unnecessary to say
excusabaraja *f* basket with lid
excusable *adj* excusable; avoidable
excusadamente *adv* unnecessarily
excusa•do -da *adj* exempt; unnecessary; private, set apart; (*puerta*) side || *m* toilet
excusa•lí *m* (*pl* **-líes**) small apron

excusar *tr* to excuse; exempt; avoid; prevent; make unnecessary; **excusar** + *inf* to not have to + *inf* || *ref* to excuse oneself; apologize; **excusarse de** + *inf* to decline to + *inf*
exención *f* exemption
exencionar *tr* to exempt
exentamente *adv* freely; frankly, simply
exentar *tr* to exempt
exen•to -ta *adj* exempt; open, unobstructed; free, disengaged
exequias *fpl* obsequies
exfolia•dor -dora *adj* tear-off
exhalación *f* exhalation; flash of lightning; shooting star; fume, vapor; **como una exhalación** like a flash of lightning
exhalar *tr* to exhale, emit; (*suspiros, quejas*) breathe forth; **exhalar el último suspiro** to breathe one's last || *ref* to exhale; (*con el ejercicio violento del cuerpo*) breathe hard; hurry; crave
exhausti•vo -va *adj* exhaustive
exhaus•to -ta *adj* exhausted; wasted away
exheredar *tr* to disinherit
exhibición *f* exhibition; exhibit; **exhibición repetida** (telv) rerun
exhibición-venta *f* sales exhibit
exhibir *tr* to exhibit; (Mex) to pay || *ref* to make oneself evident
exhilarante *adj* exhilarating; (*gas*) laughing
exhortar *tr* to exhort
exhumar *tr* to exhume
exigencia *f* exigency, requirement
exigente *adj* exigent, demanding
exigir §27 *tr* to exact, require, demand
exi•guo -gua *adj* meager, scanty
exila•do -da *adj & mf* exile
exi•mio -mia *adj* choice, select, superior; distinguished
eximir *tr* to exempt
existencia *f* existence; **en existencia** in stock; **existencias** (com) stock
existente *adj* existing, extant; in stock
existir *intr* to exist
exitazo *m* smash hit
exitista *adj* (Arg) me-too || *mf* (Arg) me-tooer
éxito *m* (*resultado feliz*) success; (*canción, cine, etc. que ha tenido mucho éxito*) hit; (*resultado de un negocio*) outcome, result; **éxito de librería** best seller; **éxito de taquilla** box-office hit, good box office; **éxito de venta** best seller; **éxito rotundo** smash hit
exito•so -sa *adj* (Arg) successful
ex li•bris *m* (*pl* **-bris**) bookplate
exobiología *f* exobiology
éxodo *m* exodus; **éxodo de técnicos** brain drain
exonerar *tr* to exonerate, relieve; discharge, dismiss; **exonerar el vientre** to have a bowel movement
exorar *tr* to beg, entreat
exorbitante *adj* exorbitant
exorcizar §60 *tr* to exorcise
exornar *tr* to adorn, embellish
exóti•co -ca *adj* exotic; striking, stunning, glamorous
expandir *tr & ref* (Arg, Chile) to expand, extend, spread
expansión *f* expansion; (*manifestación efusiva*) expansiveness; (*difusión de una opinión*) spread; rest, recreation
expansionar *ref* to expand; open one's heart; relax, take it easy
expansi•vo -va *adj* expansive
expatria•do -da *adj & mf* expatriate
expectación *f* expectancy; **expectación de vida** life expectancy
expectativa *f* expectation; **estar en la expectativa de** to be expecting, be on the lookout for
expectorar *tr & intr* to expectorate
expediar *tr* to expedite; handle without delay; rush, speed
expedición *f* (*excursión para realizar una empresa*) expedition; (*remesa*) shipment; (*de un certificado, títulos, etc.*) issuance; (*agilidad, facilidad*) expedition
expedi•dor -dora *mf* sender, shipper
expediente *m* expedient; makeshift, apology; (*agilidad, facilidad*) expedition; (*todos los papeles correspondientes a un asunto*) dossier; (law) action, proceedings; **expediente académico** (educ) record
expedienteo *m* red tape
expedir §50 *tr* to send, ship, remit; (*títulos*) issue; (*despachar, cursar*) expedite
expeditar *tr* to expedite
expediti•vo -va *adj* expeditious
expedi•to -ta *adj* ready; clear, open, unencumbered
expeler *tr* to expel, eject
expende•dor -dora *mf* dealer, retailer; ticket agent; **expendedor de moneda falsa** distributor of counterfeit money
expendeduría *f* cigar store (*for sale of state-monopolized articles*)
expender *tr* to spend; dispense; sell at retail; (*moneda falsa*) circulate
expendio *m* shop, store; retail; (Mex) cigar store
expensar *tr* (Chile, Guat, Mex) to pay the cost of
expensas *fpl* expenses
experiencia *f* (*enseñanza que se adquiere con la práctica o con el vivir; suceso en que uno ha participado, cosa que uno ha experimentado*) experience; (*ensayo, experimento*) experiment
experimenta•do -da *adj* experienced
experimentar *tr* to experience, undergo, feel; test, try, try out || *intr* to experiment
experimento *m* experiment; **experimento piloto** pilot test, pilot run
exper•to -ta *adj & m* expert
expiación *f* expiation, atonement; purification
expiar §77 *tr* to expiate, atone for; purify
expirar *intr* to expire
explanación *f* grading, leveling; explanation
explanada *f* esplanade
explanar *tr* to grade, level; explain
explayar *tr* to enlarge, extend || *ref* to spread out, extend; go for an outing; expatiate,

talk at length; **explayarse con** to unbosom oneself to
explicación *f* explanation
explicar §73 *tr* to explain; (*exponer*) expound; (*exculpar*) explain away; (*una clase*) teach || *intr* to explain || *ref* to explain oneself; understand, make out
explicati•vo -va *adj* explanatory
explíci•to -ta *adj* explicit
exploración *f* exploration; (mil) scouting; (telv) scanning
explora•dor -dora *mf* explorer || *m* boy scout; (mil) scout
explorar *tr* to explore; (mil) to scout; (telv) to scan
explosión *f* explosion; (*de gases en un motor*) combustion
explosi•vo -va *adj & m* explosive || *f* (phonet) explosive
explotación *f* operation, running; exploitation; **explotación abusiva** (geol) overexploitation (of resources)
explotar *tr* to operate, run; (*una mina*) work; exploit || *intr* to explode
exponente *m* exponent; (fig) interpreter, apologist
exponer §54 *tr* to expose; (*explicar*) expound; (*a un niño recién nacido*) abandon || *intr* to display, show, exhibit; (eccl) to expose the Host || *ref* to expose oneself; be on view
exportación *f* exportation, export; (*mercaderías que se exportan*) exports
exporta•dor -dora *mf* exporter
exportar *tr & intr* to export
exposición *f* exposition; (*a un peligro; con relación a los puntos cardinales*) exposure; (phot) exposure; (rhet) exposition; **exposición universal** world's fair
exposición-venta *f* sales exhibit
exposímetro *m* light meter
expósi•to -ta *mf* foundling
exposi•tor -tora *mf* exhibitor
exprés *m* express train; (Mex) express company
expresa•do -da *adj* above-mentioned
expresamente *adv* express, expressly
expresar *tr* to express || *ref* to express oneself
expresión *f* expression; (*acción de exprimir*) squeezing; (*zumo exprimido*) juice; **expresiones** regards
expresi•vo -va *adj* expressive; kind, affectionate
expre•so -sa *adj* express || *m* (*tren muy rápido; correo extraordinario*) express; express company
exprimidera *f* squeezer; **exprimidera de naranjas** orange squeezer
exprimi•do -da *adj* lean, skinny; stiff, stuck-up; affected, prim, prudish
exprimidor *m* wringer; squeezer; **exprimidor de ropa** clothes wringer
exprimir *tr* to squeeze, press; (*p.ej., la ropa blanca*) wring, wring out; (*extraer apretando*) express
ex profeso *adv* on purpose
expropiar *tr* to expropriate
expues•to -ta *adj* dangerous, hazardous
expugnar *tr* to take by storm
expulsanie•ves *m* (*pl* **-ves**) snowplow
expulsar *tr* to expel
expulsión *f* expulsion
expurgar §44 *tr* to expurgate
exquisi•to -ta *adj* exquisite
extasiar §77 & **regular** *ref* to go into ecstasy
éxta•sis *m* (*pl* **-sis**) ecstasy
extáti•co -ca *adj* ecstatic
extemporal *adj* unseasonable
extemporáne•o -a *adj* unseasonable; untimely, inopportune
extender §51 *tr* to extend, stretch out, spread out; spread; (*un documento*) draw up || *ref* to extend, stretch out; spread; **extenderse a** or **hasta** to amount to
extendidamente *adv* at length, in detail
extensión *f* extension; (*vasta superficie, p.ej., del océano*) expanse; (*alcance, importancia*) extent; extending
extensi•vo -va *adj* extensive; **hacer extensivos a** to extend (*e.g., good wishes*) to
exten•so -sa *adj* extensive, extended, vast; **por extenso** at length, in detail
extenuar §21 *tr* to weaken, emaciate
exterior *adj* exterior, outer, outside; foreign || *m* exterior, outside; appearance, bearing; **al exterior** or **a lo exterior** on the outside; outwardly; **del exterior** from abroad; **en el exterior** on the outside; abroad; **en exteriores** (mov) on location
exterioridad *f* externals, outward appearance; **exterioridades** pomp, show
exteriorista *adj* outgoing, outgiving || *mf* extrovert
exteriorizar §60 *tr* to reveal || *ref* to unbosom one's heart
exterminar *tr* to exterminate
exterminio *m* extermination
exter•no -na *adj* external || *mf* day pupil
extinción *f* extinction; cancellation, elimination
extinguidor *m* (SAm) (*incendios*) fire extinguisher
extinguir §29 *tr* to extinguish, put out; wipe out, put an end to; fulfil, carry out; (*un plazo, un tiempo*) spend, serve || *ref* to be extinguished, go out; come to an end
extin•to -ta *adj* (*volcán*) extinct; deceased || *mf* deceased
extintor *m* fire extinguisher; **extintor de espuma** foam extinguisher; **extintor de granada** fire grenade
extirpar *tr* to extirpate, eradicate
extorno *m* premium adjustment (*based on change in policy*)
extorsión *f* extortion; harm, damage
extorsionar *tr* to harm, damage; extort
extra *adj* extra; **extra de** in addition to, besides || *mf* (theat) extra || *m* (*de un periódico*) extra; extra, bonus
extracción *f* extraction; (*en la lotería*) drawing numbers; **extracción de raíces** (math) evolution
extractar *tr* (*un escrito*) to abstract

extracto *m* (*de un escrito*) abstract; (pharm) extract
extractor *m* extractor; remover; **extractor de aire** ventilator; **extractor de humos** smoke evacuator
extracurricular *adj* extracurricular
extradición *f* extradition
extraer §75 *tr* to extract; pull; (*la raíz*) (math) to extract
extrafuerte *adj* heavy-duty
extragalácti•co -ca *adj* extragalactic
extralimitar *ref* to go too far
extramural *adj* extramural
extanjerismo *m* borrowing
extranje•ro -ra *adj* foreign, alien || *mf* foreigner, alien; **extranjero enemigo** enemy alien || *m* foreign country; **al extranjero** abroad; **del extranjero** from abroad; **en el extranjero** abroad
extrañar *tr* to banish, expatriate; surprise; find strange; miss || *ref* to be surprised; refuse
extrañeza *f* strangeness, peculiarity; (*desavenencia*) estrangement; wonder, surprise
extra•ño -ña *adj* foreign; (*raro, singular*) strange; extraneous; **extraño a** unconnected with || *mf* foreigner
extraoficial *adj* unofficial
extraordina•rio -ria *adj* extraordinary; extra, special || *m* extra dish; special mail; (*de un periódico*) extra
extrapla•no -na *adj* extra-flat
extrapolar *tr & intr* to extrapolate
extrarradio *m* outer edge of town
extrasensorial *adj* extrasensory
extraterrestre *adj* extraterrestrial; otherworldly
extravagancia *f* (*singularidad, ridiculez*) extravagance, wildness, folly
extravagante *adj* (*singular, ridículo*) extravagant, wild, foolish; (*correspondencia en la casa de correos*) in transit
extravia•do -da *adj* lost, misplaced; astray, gone astray; (*lugar*) out-of-the-way
extraviar §77 *tr* to lead astray, mislead; mislay, misplace || *ref* to get lost, go astray; go wrong; get out of line
extravío *m* going astray; loss; misleading; misconduct; misplacement
extrema *f* (*escasez grande*) extremity; (*de la vida*) end, last moment
extremar *tr* to carry far, carry to the limit || *ref* to strive hard
extremaunción *f* extreme unction; last rites (*Roman Catholic*)
extreme•ño -ña *adj* frontier
extremidad *f* extremity; end, tip; **extremidades** (*pies y manos*) extremities; **la última extremidad** one's last moment
extremismo *m* extremism
extremista *mf* extremist
extre•mo -ma *adj* extreme; utmost; critical, desperate || *m* extremity; (*de la calle*) end; (*del dedo*) tip; (*punto último*) extreme; great care; (*de una conversación, una carta*) point; winter pasture; **al extremo de** to the point of; **de extremo a extremo** from one end to the other; **hacer extremos** to be demonstrative, gush || *f* see **extrema**
extremo•so -sa *adj* extreme, forthright; effusive, gushy, demonstrative
extrínse•co -ca *adj* extrinsic
extroversión *f* extroversion
extroverti•do -da *mf* extrovert
exuberante *adj* exuberant; luxuriant
exudar *tr & intr* to exude
exultante *adj* exultant
exultar *intr* to exult
exvoto *m* votive offering
eyacular *tr & intr* to ejaculate

F

F, f (efe) *f* seventh letter of the Spanish alphabet
f.a.b. *abbr* **franco a bordo**
fabada *f* pork-and-bean stew (*in Asturias*)
fábrica *f* factory, plant; building, masonry; (eccl) vestry
fabricación *f* manufacture; **fabricación en serie** mass production
fabricante *mf* manufacturer
fabricar §73 *tr* to manufacture; devise, invent; fabricate
fabril *adj* factory
fabriquero *m* manufacturer; charcoal burner; churchwarden
fábula *f* fable; (*p.ej., de un drama*) plot, story; rumor, gossip; (*mentira*) story, lie; (*objeto de murmuración*) talk of the town
fabulario *m* book of fables
fabulo•so -sa *adj* fabulous
facción *f* faction; feature; battle; **estar de facción** (mil) to be on duty; **facciones** features
facciona•rio -ria *adj* factional
faceta *f* facet
facetada *f* (Mex) flat joke
face•to -ta *adj* (Mex) affected; (Mex) finicky || *f* see **faceta**
facial *adj* facial
fácil *adj* easy; pliant, yielding; likely; loose, wanton
facilidad *f* facility, ease, easiness; **facilidades de pago** easy payments
facilitar *tr* to facilitate, expedite; furnish, supply

facili•tón -tona *adj* bumbling, brash || *mf* bumbler
facinero•so -sa *adj* wicked || *mf* villain
facistol *m* choir desk
facón *m* (Arg, Urug) gaucho knife
facsimilar *tr* to facsimile; copy
facsímile *m* facsimile
factible *adj* feasible
factor *m* factor; commission merchant; baggageman; freight agent
factoría *f* trading post; (Ecuad, Peru) foundry; (Mex) factory
factura *f* invoice, bill; workmanship; **factura simulada** pro forma invoice; **según factura** as per invoice
facturación *f* invoicing, billing (*del equipaje*) checking
facturar *tr* to invoice, bill; (*el equipaje*) check
facultad *f* faculty; (*de la universidad*) school; knowledge, skill; power; **facultad de altos estudios** graduate school
facultar *tr* to empower, authorize
facultati•vo -va *adj* faculty; optional || *m* doctor, physician
facundia *f* eloquence, fluency
facun•do -da *adj* eloquent, fluent
facha *mf* (*adefesio*) sight || *f* look, appearance; **facha a facha** face to face
fachada *f* façade; (*de un libro*) title page; look, build, bearing; **hacer fachada con** to overlook, to look out on
facha•do -da *adj* — **bien fachado** good-looking || *f* see *fachada*
fachenda *m* boaster, show-off || *f* boasting
fachendear *intr* to boast, show off
fachendista or **fachen•dón -dona** or **fachendo•so -sa** *adj* boastful || *mf* boaster, show-off
fachinal *m* (Arg) marshland
fada *f* fairy, witch
faena *f* work; toil; chore, task, job; (taur) windup; (taur) stunt, trick; (mil) fatigue, fatigue duty; (Guat, Mex, W-I) extra work, overtime; (Ecuad) morning work in the field; (Chile) gang of farm hands
faenero *m* (Chile) farm hand
Faetón *m* Phaëthon
fagot *m* bassoon
faisán *m* pheasant
faja *f* sash, girdle; bandage; band, strip; newspaper wrapper; (*de carretera*) lane; (*de tierra*) strip; **faja central** or **divisoria** median strip; **faja medical** supporter
fajar *tr* to wrap; bandage; swaddle; (*un periódico o revista*) put a wrapper on; beat, thrash; to attack || *ref* to put on a sash
fajardo *m* meat pie
fajín *m* sash
fajina *f* bundle of sticks; fire wood; (mil) call to quarters
fajo *m* bundle; (*de papel moneda*) roll; swig; (Mex) blow; (Mex) leather belt; **fajos** swaddling clothes
falacia *f* deception; deceitfulness
falange *f* phalanx
falangia *f* daddy-longlegs
fa•laz *adj* (*pl* **-laces**) deceitful; deceptive
falba•lá *m* (*pl* **-aes**) gore; flounce, ruffle
falce *m* sickle; falchion
falda *f* skirt, dress; (*regazo*) lap; flap; fold; (*del sombrero*) brim; foothill; (*mujer*) skirt; **cosido a las faldas de** tied to the apron strings of
falde•ro -ra *adj* skirt; (*perro*) lap; lady-loving || *m* lap dog
faldillas *fpl* skirts, coattails
faldón *m* coattail; shirttail; saddle flap
falible *adj* fallible
fáli•co -ca *adj* phallic
falo *m* penis, phallus
falsada *f* swoop (*of bird of prey*)
falsa•rio -ria *adj* lying || *mf* falsifier, crook; liar
falsear *tr* to falsify; counterfeit; forge; (*la verdad*) distort; (*una cerradura*) pick; bevel || *intr* to sag, buckle; give, give way
falsedad *f* falsity; (*mentira*) falsehood
falsete *m* falsetto; plug, tap; door (*between rooms*)
falsetista *f* falsetto
falsía *f* falsity, treachery; unsteadiness
falsificación *f* falsification; fake; counterfeit; forgery
falsificar **§73** *tr* to falsify; fake; counterfeit; forge
falsilla *f* guide lines
fal•so -sa *adj* false; counterfeit; (*caballo*) vicious || *m* patch; **coger en falso** (Mex) to catch in a lie; **envidar en falso** to bluff
falta *f* fault; lack, want; misdeed; absence; (*ausencia de la clase*) cut; (sport) fault; **a falta de** for want of; **echar en falta** to miss; **falta de ortografía** misspelling **hacer falta** to be needed; be lacking; **hacerle falta a uno** to need, e.g., **le hacen falta a Juan estos libros** John needs these books; to miss, e.g., **Vd. me hace mucha falta** I miss you very much; **sin falta** without fail
faltar *intr* to be missing, be lacking, be wanting; fall short; run out; be absent; fail; die; lack, need, e.g., **me falta dinero** I lack money, I need money; **faltar a la clase** to cut class; **faltar a la verdad** to fail to tell the truth; **faltar a una cita** to fail to keep an appointment; **faltar . . . para** to be . . . to, e.g., **faltan cinco minutos para las dos** it is five minutes to two; **faltar poco para** to come near; **faltar por** to remain to be, e.g., **faltan por escribir dos cartas** two letters remain to be written
fal•to -ta *adj* short, lacking; (*peso o medida*) short; (Arg) dull, stupid; (Col) proud, vain; **falto de** short of || *f* see **falta**
fal•tón -tona *adj* dilatory, remiss; (Arg) simple-minded
falto•so -sa *adj* addlebrained; (Col) quarrelsome; (CAm, Mex) disrespectful
faltriquera *f* pocket; handbag; **faltriquera de reloj** watch fob; **rascarse la faltriquera** to cough up
falúa *f* barge, tender
falucho *m* felucca

falla *f* failure, breakdown; defect; (geol) fault; (Mex) baby's bonnet
fallar *tr* to trump; judge, pass judgment on || *intr* to fail, miss; misfire; sag, weaken; break down; judge, pass judgment
falleba *f* espagnolette
fallecer §22 *intr* to die; fail, expire
falleci•do -da *adj* deceased, late
falli•do -da *adj* unsuccessful; bankrupt; (*deuda*) uncollectible
fallir §13 *intr* to fail; (Ven) to go bankrupt
fa•llo -lla *adj* (Chile) silly, simple; **estar fallo a** to be out of (*cards of a suit*) || *m* short suit; decision; judgment; verdict; **fallo humano** human error; **tener fallo a** or **de** to be out of || *f* see **falla**
fama *f* fame; reputation; rumor; (Chile) bull's-eye; **correr fama** to be rumored; **es fama** it is said, it is rumored
faméli•co -ca *adj* famished, starving
familia *f* family
familiar *adj* familiar; family; (*sin ceremonia*) informal; (*lenguaje, estilo*) colloquial || *m* member of the family; member of the household; acquaintance; **familiar dependiente** dependent
familiaridad *f* familiarity
familiarizar §60 *tr* to familiarize || *ref* to become familiar; become too familiar; familiarize oneself
famo•so -sa *adj* famous; (*excelente*) famous; (*formidable*) some, e.g., **famoso sujeto** some guy
fámu•lo -la *mf* servant
fanal *m* beacon, lighthouse; lantern; bell glass, bell jar; lamp shade
fanáti•co -ca *adj* fanatic(al) || *mf* fanatic; (sport) fan
fanatismo *m* fanaticism
fanega *f* 1.58 bu.; **fanega de tierra** 1.59 acres
fanfarria *f* fanfare; blustering
fanfa•rron -rrona *adj* blustering, bragging; flashy || *mf* blusterer, braggart
fanfarronada *f* bluster, bravado
fanfarronnear *intr* to bluster, brag
fanfarronería *f* blustering, bragging, sword rattling
fanfurriña *f* pet, peeve
fango *m* mud, mire; **llenar de fango** (fig) to sling mud at
fango•so -sa *adj* muddy; sticky, gooey
fanguero *m* (Cuba, Mex, P-R) mud, quagmire
fantasear *tr* to dream of || *intr* to fancy, to daydream; **fantasear de** to boast of being
fantasía *f* fantasy; fancy, conceit, vanity; imagery; **con fantasía** (Arg) hard; **de fantasía** fancy, imitation; **tocar por fantasía** (Ven) to play by ear
fantasio•so -sa *adj* vain, conceited
fantasma *m* phantom, ghost; stuffed shirt; (telv) ghost; **fantasma magnético** magnetic curves || *f* scarecrow, hobgoblin
fantas•món -mona *adj* (coll) conceited || *mf* conceited person || *m* stuffed shirt; (coll) scarecrow
fantásti•co -ca *adj* fantastic; fancy; conceited
fantoche *m* puppet, marionette; nincompoop, whippersnapper
faquín *m* street porter, errand boy
fara•lá *m* (*pl* **-laes**) ruffle, flounce; frill
faramalla *mf* cheat, swindler || *f* jabber, claptrap; bluff, fake; (Chile) bragging
faramalle•ro -ra or **farama•llón -llona** *adj* scheming, swindling || *mf* schemer, swindler
farándula *f* (*baile*) farandole; gossip, scheming; theater people; (*de gente*) (Arg) crush, milling
farandulear *intr* to boast, to show off
Faraón *m* Pharaoh
faraute *m* herald, messenger; interpreter; (*actor*) prologue; busybody
fardel *m* bag, bundle; sloppy person
fardo *m* bundle, package
farero *m* lighthouse keeper
farfa•lá *m* (*pl* **-laes**) ruffle, flounce
farfullar *tr* (*p.ej., una lección*) to sputter through; (*p.ej., una tarea*) stumble through || *intr* to sputter
faringe *f* pharynx
fariseo *m* pharisee; Pharisee; lanky good-for-nothing
farmacéuti•co -ca *adj* pharmaceutical || *mf* pharmacist
farmacia *f* pharmacy, drug store; **farmacia de guardia** drug store open all night
fármaco *m* drug, medicine
faro *m* lighthouse, beacon; floodlight; (aut) headlight; (fig) beacon; **faro piloto** (aut) spotlight; **faros de carretera** (aut) bright lights; **faros de cruce** (aut) dimmers; **faros de población** or **de situación** (aut) parking lights
farol *m* lamp, light; lantern; street light; (rr) headlight; (coll) conceited fellow; (Bol) bay window; **farol de tope** (naut) headlight
farola *f* lighthouse; street lamp, lamppost
farolear *intr* to boast, brag
farole•ro -ra *adj* boasting || *mf* boaster || *m* lamplighter
farolillo *m* heartseed; Canterbury bell; **farolillo veneciano** Chinese lantern, Japanese lantern
farota *f* minx, vixen
farotear *intr* (Col) to romp around, make a racket
faro•tón -tona *adj* brazen, cheeky || *mf* cheeky person
farra *f* salmon trout; (SAm) revelry
fárrago *m* hodgepodge
farraquista *m* scatterbrain; muddlehead
farrear *intr* to celebrate; (coll) to goof off
farro *m* grits
farru•co -ca *adj* bold, fearless; ill-humored || *mf* Galician abroad, Asturian abroad
farru•to -ta *adj* (Arg, Bol, Chile) sickly
farsa *f* farce; humbug
farsante *adj* & *mf* fake, fraud, humbug
fas — por fas o por nefas rightly or wrongly, in any event
fascinante *adj* fascinating

fascinar *tr* to fascinate, bewitch; cast a spell on, cast the evil eye on
fascismo *m* fascism
fascista *adj & mf* fascist
fase *f* phase
fastidiar *tr* to bore, annoy; cloy, sicken; disappoint || *ref* to get bored; suffer, be a victim
fastidio *m* boredom, annoyance; distaste, nausea
fastidio•so -sa *adj* boring, annoying; cloying, sickening; annoyed, displeased
fas•to -ta *adj* happy, blessed || *m* pomp, show
fastuo•so -sa *adj* vain, pompous; magnificent
fatal *adj* fatal; bad, evil; (law) unextendible
fatalidad *f* fatality; misfortune
fatalismo *m* fatalism
fatalista *mf* fatalist
fatalmente *adv* fatally; inevitably; unfortunately; badly, poorly
fatídi•co -ca *adj* ominous, fateful
fatiga *f* fatigue; hard breathing; **fatigas** hardship
fatigante *adj* tiresome; fatiguing
fatigar §44 *tr* to fatigue, tire, weary; annoy, bother || *ref* to get tired
fatigo•so -sa *adj* fatiguing, tiring; trying, tedious
fa•tuo -tua *adj* fatuous; conceited || *mf* simpleton
fauces *fpl* (anat) fauces; (fig) jaws, mouth
fauna *f* fauna
fauno *m* faun
faus•to -ta *adj* happy, fortunate || *m* pomp, magnificence
fausto•so -sa *adj* magnificent
fau•tor -tora *mf* abettor, accomplice
favor *m* favor; **a favor de** under cover of; by means of; in favor of; **hágame Vd. el favor de** do me the favor to; **por favor** please; **vender favores** to peddle influence
favorable *adj* favorable
favorecer §22 *tr* to favor; flatter
favoritismo *m* favoritism
favori•to -ta *adj & mf* favorite
fayanca *f* unstable posture
faz *f* (*pl* **faces**) face; aspect, look; (*de monedas o medallas*) obverse; **faces** cheeks; **faz a faz** face to face
F.C. *abbr* **ferrocarril**
fe *f* faith; testimony, witness; certificate; **¡a fe mía!** upon my faith!; **dar fe de** to certify; **en fe de lo cual** in witness whereof; **fe de erratas** list of errata; **hacer fe** to be valid; **la fe del carbonero** simple faith
fealdad *f* ugliness
Febe *f* Phoebe
feble *adj* weak, sickly; (*moneda, aleación*) lacking in weight or fineness
Febo *m* Phoebus
febrero *m* February
febril *adj* feverish
fécula *f* starch
feculen•to -ta *adj* starchy; fecal
fecundar *tr* to fecundate, to fertilize
fecun•do -da *adj* fecund, fertile
fecha *f* date; **con fecha de** under date of; **de larga fecha** of long standing; **hasta la fecha** to date
fechador *m* (Chile, Mex) canceler, postmark
fechar *tr* to date
fechoría *f* misdeed, villainy
federación *f* federation
federal *adj & mf* federal
federar *tr & ref* to federate
feéri•co -ca *adj* fairy
fehaciente *adj* authentic
feldespato *m* feldspar
felicidad *f* felicity, happiness; luck
felicitar *tr* to felicitate, congratulate, wish happiness to
feli•grés -gresa *mf* parishioner, church member
feligresía *f* parish; congregation
Felipe *m* Philip
fe•liz *adj* (*pl* **-lices**) happy; lucky; (*oportuno*) felicitous
fe•lón -lona *adj* perfidious, treacherous || *mf* wicked person
felonía *f* perfidy, treachery
felpa *f* plush; drubbing; severe reprimand
felpu•do -da *adj* plushy, downy || *m* mat, door mat
femenil *adj* feminine, womanly
femeni•no -na *adj* feminine; (*sexo*) female || *m* feminine
fementi•do -da *adj* false, treacherous
feminismo *m* feminism
fenecer §22 *tr* to finish, close || *intr* to come to an end; die
Fenicia *f* Phoenicia
feni•cio -cia *adj & mf* Phoenician || *f* see **Fenicia**
fé•nix *m* (*pl* **-nix** or **-nices**) phoenix
fenobarbital *m* phenobarbital
fenomenal *adj* phenomenal
fenómeno *m* phenomenon; monster, freak
fe•o -a *adj* ugly || *m* slight; **hacer un feo a** to slight || **feo** *adv* (Arg, Col, Mex) bad, e.g., **oler feo** to smell bad
feo•te -ta *adj* ugly, hideous
feral *adj* cruel, bloody
fe•raz *adj* (*pl* **-races**) fertile
féretro *m* bier
feria *f* weekday; market; fair; day off; (Mex) small change; (Mex) con man; (CAm, Mex) extra, tip, gratuity; **revolver la feria** to upset the applecart
ferial *adj* week (*day*); market (*day*) || *m* market; fair
feriante *adj* fair-going || *mf* fairgoer
feriar *tr* to buy, sell; give, present; (Mex) to give change for
feri•no -na *adj* wild, savage; (*tos*) whooping (*cough*)
fermentación *f* ferment; fermentation
fermentar *tr & intr* to ferment
fermento *m* ferment
ferocidad *f* ferocity, fierceness
ferósti•co -ca *adj* irritable; hideous
fe•roz *adj* (*pl* **-roces**) ferocious, fierce
férre•o -a *adj* iron
ferrería *f* ironworks, foundry
ferretear *tr* to trim with iron; work in iron

ferretería *f* ironworks; hardware; hardware store
ferrete•ro -ra *mf* hardware dealer
ferrocarril *m* railroad, railway; **ferrocarril de cremallera** rack railway, mountain railroad
ferrocarrile•ro -ra *adj* railroad, rail ‖ *m* railroader
ferrotipo *m* tintype
ferrovia•rio -ria *adj* railroad, rail ‖ *m* railroader
fértil *adj* fertile
fertilizar §60 *tr* to fertilize
férula *f* flexible splint; ferule; **estar bajo la férula de** to be under the thumb of
férvi•do -da *adj* fervid; (*fiebre; sed*) burning
ferviente *adj* fervent
fervor *m* fervor, zeal
fervoro•so -sa *adj* ardent, zealous
festejar *tr* to fete, honor, entertain; celebrate; court, woo; (Mex) to beat, thrash
festejo *m* feast, entertainment; celebration; courting, wooing; (Peru) revelry; **festejos** public festivities
festín *m* feast, banquet
festinar *tr* to hurry through; (CAm) to entertain
festival *m* festival, music festival
festividad *f* festivity; feast day, witticism
festi•vo -va *adj* festive, gay; witty; (*digno no de celebrarse*) solemn
festón *m* festoon
festonear *tr* to festoon
fetiche *m* fetish
féti•do -da *adj* fetid, foul
feto *m* fetus
feú•co -ca or **feú•cho -cha** *adj* hideous, repulsive
feudal *adj* feudal
feudalismo *m* feudalism
feudo *m* fief; **feudo franco** freehold
fiable *adj* trustworthy
fiado *m* — **al fiado** on credit; **en fiado** on bail
fia•dor -dora *mf* bail; **salir fiador por** to go bail for ‖ *m* fastener; catch, pawl; (Chile, Ecuad) chin strap
fiambre *adj* cold, cold-served; (*noticias*) old, stale ‖ *m* cold lunch, cold food; stale news; (Arg) dull party; **fiambres** cold cuts
fiambrera *f* dinner pail, lunch basket
fiambrería *f* (Arg) delicatessen store
fianza *f* guarantee, surety; bond; bail; **fianza carcelera** bail
fiar §77 *tr* to entrust, confide; guarantee; give credit to; sell on credit ‖ *intr & ref* to trust
fiasco *m* fiasco
fibra *f* fiber; (fig) fiber, strength, vigor; **fibras del corazón** heartstrings
fibro•so -sa *adj* fibrous
ficción *f* fiction
ficciona•rio -ria *adj* fictional
fice *m* (ichth) hake
ficti•cio -cia *adj* fictitious
ficha *f* chip; counter; domino; filing card; police record; (elec) plug; **ficha catalográfica** index card; **ficha perforada** punch card; **llevar ficha** to have a police record; **ser una buena ficha** to be a sly fox
ficha•dor -dora *mf* file clerk
fichar *tr* to file; play, move; black-list; (Cuba) to cheat ‖ *intr* (Col) to die
fichero *m* card index, filing cabinet
fidedig•no -na *adj* reliable, trustworthy
fideicomisa•rio -ria *mf* trustee
fideicomiso *m* trusteeship
fidelería *f* (Arg, Ecuad, Peru) vermicelli factory, noodle factory
fidelidad *f* fidelity; punctiliousness; **alta fidelidad** (rad) high fidelity
fideo *m* skinny person; (Arg) joke; (Arg) confusion, disorder; **fideos** vermicelli
Fidias *m* Phidias
fiducia•rio -ria *adj & mf* fiduciary
fiebre *f* fever; **fiebre del heno** hay fever; **fibre tifoidea** typhoid fever
fiel *adj* faithful; exact; punctilious; honest, trustworthy ‖ *m* inspector of weights and measures; (*en las balanzas*) pointer; (*de las tijeras*) pin; **fiel de romana** inspector of weights in a slaughterhouse; **los fieles** the faithful
fielato *m* inspector's office; octroi
fieltro *m* felt; felt hat; felt rug
fiera *f* wild animal; (*persona*) fiend; (taur) bull; **ser una fiera para** to be a fiend for
fierabrás *m* spitfire, little terror
fierecilla *f* shrew
fiereza *f* fierceness; cruelty; deformity
fie•ro -ra *adj* fierce, wild; cruel; deformed, ugly; huge, tremendous; **echar** or **hacer fieros** to bluster ‖ *f* see **fiera**
fierro *m* (SAm) branding iron
fierros *mpl* (Ecuad, Mex) tools
fiesta *f* feast, holy day; holiday; celebration, festivity; **estar de fiesta** (coll) to be in a holiday mood; **fiesta de la hispanidad** or **fiesta de la raza** Columbus Day; **fiesta de todos los santos** All Saints' Day; **fiesta onomástica** saint's day, birthday; **fiestas** holiday, vacation; **hacer fiesta** to take off (*from work*); **hacer fiestas a** to act up to, to fawn on; **la fiesta brava** bullfighting; **no estar para fiestas** to be in no mood for joking; **por fin de fiestas** to top it off; **se acabó la fiesta** let's drop it
fieste•ro -ra *adj* merry, cheerful ‖ *mf* merrymaker, party-goer
figón *m* cheap restaurant
figura *f* figure; face, countenance; (*naipe*) face card; (mus) note; (theat) character; **figura retórica** figure of speech; **hacer figura** to cut a figure
figuración *f* representation; (Arg) status, social standing
figura•do -da *adj* figurative
figurar *tr* to depict, trace, represent; feign ‖ *intr* to figure, be in the limelight ‖ *ref* to figure, imagine
figurati•vo -va *adj* figurative, representative
figurería *f* face, grimace
figurilla *mf* silly little runt ‖ *f* figurine
figurín *m* dummy, model; fashion plate
figurina *f* figurine

figurita *mf* silly little runt
figurón *m* stuffed shirt; **figurón de proa** (naut) figurehead
fija *f* hinge; trowel; (*caballo*) (Peru) sure bet; **la fija** sure thing
fijacarte•les *m* (*pl* **-les**) billposter
fijación *f* fixing, fastening; posting; **fijación de precios** price fixing
fijado *m* (phot) fixing
fija•dor -dora *adj* fixing || *m* carpenter who installs doors and windows; fixing bath; sprayer; (mas) pointer; hair set, hair spray
fijamárge•nes *m* (*pl* **-nes**) margin stop
fijapeína•dos *m* (*pl* **-dos**) hair set, hair spray
fijar *tr* to fix; fasten; (*carteles*) post; (*una fecha; los cabellos; una imagen fotográfica; los precios; la atención; una hora, una cita*) fix; (*residencia*) establish; paste, glue || *ref* to settle; notice; **fijarse en** to notice; pay attention to; be intent on
fijeza *f* firmness, stability; steadfastness; **mirar con fijeza** to stare at
fi•jo -ja *adj* fixed; firm, solid, secure, fast; sure, determined; **de fijo** surely || *f* see **fija**
fil *m* — **estar en fil** or **en un fil** to be alike; **fil derecho** leapfrog
fila *f* row, line; file; (*linea que los soldados forman de frente*) rank; dislike, hatred; **cerrar las filas** (mil) to close ranks; **en fila** in single file; **en filas** (mil) in active service; **fila india** single file, Indian file; **llamar a filas** (mil) to call to the colors; **pasarse a las filas de** to go over to; **romper filas** (mil) to break ranks
filamento *m* filament
filantropía *f* philanthropy
filántrop•po -pa *mf* philanthropist
filar *tr* (naut) to pay out slowly
filarmónica *f* (Mex) accordion
filarmóni•co -ca *adj* philharmonic
filatelia *f* philately
filatelista *mf* philatelist
filatería *f* fast talking; wordiness
filate•ro -ra *adj* fast-talking; wordy || *mf* fast talker; great talker
file•no -na *adj* cute, tiny
filete *m* (*de carne o pescado*) filet or fillet; (*asador*) spit; edge, rim; narrow hem; (*de tornillo*) thread; snaffle bit; (archit, bb) fillet; (typ) rule, fancy rule
filetear *tr* to fillet; (*un tornillo*) thread; (bb) to tool
filiación *f* filiation; description, characteristics; (mil) regimental register
filial *adj* filial || *f* affiliate, branch
filiar **§77** *tr* to register || *ref* to enroll
filibustero *m* filibuster, buccaneer
filigrana *f* filigree; (*en el papel*) watermark
filipi•no -na *adj* Filipine, Filipino || *mf* Filipino || **Filipinas** *fpl* Philippines
Filipo *m* Philip (*of Macedonia*)
Filis *f* Phyllis
filiste•o -a *adj* & *mf* Philistine || *m* tall, fat fellow
film *m* (*pl* **-films or filmes**) film
filmadora *f* movie camera
filmar *tr* to film, shoot
filo *m* edge; ridge; dividing line; (CAm, Mex) hunger; **al filo de** at, at about; **dar filo a** to sharpen; **filo del viento** direction of the wind; **pasar al filo de la espada** to put to the sword; **por filo** exactly
filobús *m* trolley bus, trackless trolley
filocommunista *adj* & *mf* procommunist
filología philology
filólo•go -ga *mf* philologist
filón *m* seam, vein; (fig) gold mine
filo•so -sa *adj* sharp
filosofía *f* philosophy
filosófi•co -ca *adj* philosophic(al)
filóso•fo -fa *mf* philosopher
filote *m* (Col) corn silk; (Col) ear of green corn
filtración *f* filtering; leak; (fig) leak, loss
filtrado *m* filtrate
filtrar *tr* to filter || *intr* to leak; ooze || *ref* to filter; (*el dinero*) leak away, disappear
filtro *m* filter; (*brebaje para conciliar el amor*) philter, love potion
filu•do -da *adj* (SAm) sharp-edged
filván *m* featheredge
fimo *m* dung, manure
fin *m* end; aim, purpose, end; **a fin de** to, in order to; **a fin de que** in order that, so that; **a fines de** toward the end of, late in; **al fin** finally; **al fin del mundo** far, far away; **al fin y a la postre** or **al fin y al cabo** after all, in the end; **dar fin a** to put an end to; **fin de semana** weekend; **por fin** finally, in short; **sin fin** endless; endlessly; **un sin fin de** no end of
fina•do -da *adj* deceased, late || *mf* deceased
final *adj* final || *m* end; (mus) finale; **por final** finally || *f* (sport) finals; **final de partido** windup
finalidad *f* end, purpose
finalista *mf* finalist
finalizar **§60** *tr* to end, terminate; (*una escritura*) (law) to execute || *intr* to end, terminate
financiación *f* financing
financiamiento *m* (SAm) financial backing
financiar *tr* to finance
financie•ro -ra *adj* financial || *mf* financier
finanzas *fpl* finances
finar *intr* to die || *ref* to yearn
finca *f* property, piece of real estate; farm, ranch; **buena finca** sly fellow
fincar **§73** *tr* (P-R) to cultivate, farm || *intr* to buy up real estate; (Col) to reside, rest, be based || *ref* to buy up real estate
fincha•do -da *adj* vain, conceited
fi•nés -nesa *adj* Finnic; Finnish || *mf* Finn || *m* (*idioma uraliano*) Finnic; (*idioma de Finlandia*) Finnish
fineza *f* fineness; kindness, courtesy; token of affection, favor
fingi•do -da *adj* fake, sham; false, deceitful
fingir **§27** *tr* & *intr* to feign, pretend, fake || *ref* to pretend to be
finiquitar *tr* (*una cuenta*) to settle, to close; finish, wind up
finiquito *m* settlement, closing; **dar finiquito a** to settle, close; finish, wind up

finíti•mo -ma *adj* bordering, neighboring
fini•to -ta *adj* finite
finlan•dés -desa *adj* Finnish || *mf* Finn, Finlander || *m* Finnish
Finlandia *f* Finland
fi•no -na *adj* fine; (*ligero, casi transparente*) sheer; (*esbelto*) thin, slender; (*paño, papel, etc.*) thin; (*agua*) pure; polite, courteous; shrewd, cunning
finta *f* feint
finura *f* fineness, excellence; politeness, courtesy
finústi•co -ca *adj* overobsequious
firma *f* signature; signing; firm; firm name; mail to be signed; **con mi firma** under my hand; **firma en blanco** blank check
firmamento *m* firmament
firmante *adj* signatory || *mf* signer, signatory
firmar *tr & intr* to sign
firme *adj* firm, steady; solid, hard; staunch, unswerving || *adv* firmly, steadily || *m* roadbed; **de firme** hard, e.g., **llover de firme** to rain hard
firmeza *f* firmness; constancy, fortitude
firmón *m* shyster who signs anything
fiscal *adj* fiscal, treasury || *m* treasurer; district attorney; busybody
fiscalizar §60 *tr* to control, inspect; prosecute; pry into
fisco *m* state treasury, exchequer
fisga *f* fish spear; prying, snooping; banter, raillery
fisgar §44 *tr* to harpoon, fish with a spear; pry into || *intr* to pry, snoop; mock, jeer || *ref* to mock, jeer
fis•gón -gona *mf* (coll) mocker, jester; (coll) snooper, busybody
físi•co -ca *adj* physical; (Mex, W-I) finicky, prudish || *mf* physicist || *m* physique || *f* physics; **física de las partículas** particle physics; **física del estado sólido** solid state physics; **física molecular** molecular physics
fisil *adj* fissionable
fisiología *f* physiology
fisiológi•co -ca *adj* physiological
fisión *f* fission
fisionable *adj* fissionable
fisonomía *f* physiognomy
fistol *m* sly fellow; (Mex) necktie pin
fisura *f* (anat, min) fissure; **fisura del paladar** cleft palate
fla•co -ca *adj* thin, skinny; feeble, weak, frail; insecure, unstable || *m* weak spot
flacu•cho -cha *adj* skinny
flagrante *adj* occurring, actual; **en flagrante** in the act
flamante *adj* bright, flaming; brand-new, spick-and-span
flameante *adj* flamboyant
flamear *intr* to flame; flare up (*with anger*); flutter, wave
flamen•co -ca *adj* Flemish; buxom; Andalusian gypsy; flashy, snappy, gypsyish || *mf* Fleming || *m* (*idioma*) Flemish; Andalusian gypsy dance, song, or music; (orn) flamingo
fláme•o -a *adj* flamelike
flamíge•ro -ra *adj* (poet) flaming; (archit) flamboyant
flan *m* custard
flanco *m* side, flank; **coger por el flanco** to catch off guard
Flandes *f* Flanders
flanquear *tr* to flank
flaquear *intr* to weaken, flag; become faint; become discouraged
flaqueza *f* thinness, skinniness; weakness; instability
flashback *m* (*retrospectiva*) flashback
flato *m* gas; gloominess, melancholy
flato•so -sa *adj* flatulent, windy; gloomy, melancholy
flauta *f* flute
flautín *m* piccolo
flautista *mf* flautist, flutist
flebitis *f* phlebitis
fleco *m* fringe; ragged edge; **flecos** bangs
flecha *f* arrow; (aer) sweepback
flechar *tr* (*el arco*) to draw; (*a una persona*) wound with an arrow, kill with an arrow; infatuate
flechero *m* archer, bowman
fleje *m* iron strap, iron hoop
flema *f* phlegm
flemáti•co -ca *adj* phlegmatic(al); (coll) cool
flemón *m* gumboil
flequillo *m* bangs
Flesinga *f* Flushing
fletante *m* shipowner; (Arg, Chile, Ecuad) conveyancer
fletar *tr* (*una nave*) to charter; (*ganado*) load; (*bestias de carga, carros, etc.*) (Arg, Chile, Ecuad, Mex) to hire || *ref* (Arg) to sneak in, slip in; (Cuba, Mex) to beat it, clear out
flete *m* (naut) freight, cargo; (Arg, Bol, Col, Urug) race horse; **salir sin flete** (Col, Ven) to beat it
flexible *adj* flexible; (*sombrero*) soft || *m* soft hat; (elec) flexible cord
flexo *m* gooseneck lamp
flinflanear *intr* to tinkle
flirt *m* or **flirtación** *f* flirting
flirtear *intr* to flirt
flojear *intr* to ease up, idle; flag, weaken
flojedad *f* slackness; looseness; limpness; laziness; weakness
flojel *m* fluff, nap; down, soft feathers
flo•jo -ja *adj* slack, loose; limp; languid; lazy; weak; (*precios*) sagging; (*viento*) light; lax, careless
flor *f* flower; (*de árbol frutal*) blossom; (*del cuero*) grain; (fig) compliment, bouquet; **a flor de** even with, flush with; **a flor de agua** at water level; **decir flores a** to flatter; to flirt with; **flor de la edad** bloom of youth; **flor de la vida** prime of life; **flor del campo** wild flower; **flor de lis** (*escudo de armas de Francia*) lily, fleur-de-lis; **flor de mano** paper flower, artificial flower; **la flor de la canela** the tops; **la flor y nata de** the cream of
flora *f* flora

floral *adj* floral
florcita *f* little flower; **andar de florcita** (Arg, Bol, Chile, Urug) to stroll around with a flower in one's buttonhole, take it easy
florear *tr* to flower, decorate with flowers; (*los naipes*) stack; (*harina*) bolt || *intr* (*la punta de la espada*) to quiver; twang away on a guitar; throw bouquets
florecer §22 *intr* to flower, blossom, bloom; (*prosperar*) flourish || *ref* to become moldy
floreciente *adj* flowering, florescent; flourishing
florenti•no -na *adj & mf* Florentine
floreo *m* idle talk; bright remark; (*de la punta de la espada*) quivering; (*de la guitarra*) twanging; (mus) flourish; **andarse con floreos** to beat about the bush
florera *f* flower girl
florería *f* flower shop
flore•ro -ra *adj* flattering, jesting || *mf* flatterer, jester; florist || *m* (*vaso para flores*) vase; (*maceta con flores*) flowerpot; flower stand, jardiniere; (*cuadro, pintura*) flower piece || *f* see **florera**
florescencia *f* florescence
floresta *f* woods, woodland; grove; rural setting; anthology
florete *m* (*esgrima*) fencing; (*espadín*) foil
floretear *tr* to decorate with flowers || *intr* to fence
flori•do -da *adj* flowery, full of flowers; choice, select
florilegio *m* anthology
floripondio *m* (SAm) angel's-trumpet
florista *mf* florist
floristería *f* flower shop
florón *m* large flower; finial; rosette; (typ) tailpiece, vignette
flota *f* fleet; **flota petrolera** tanker fleet
flotación *f* buoyancy
flotador *m* float
flotaje *m* log driving
flotante *adj* floating; (*barba*) flowing || *m* (Col) braggart
flotar *intr* to float; (*una bandera*) wave
flote *m* floating; **a flote** afloat
fluctuar §21 *intr* to fluctuate; bob up and down; wave; waver; be in danger
fluente *adj* fluent, flowing; (*hemorroides*) bleeding
fluidez *f* fluidity
flúi•do -da *adj* fluid; (*estilo, lenguaje*) fluent || *m* fluid
fluir §20 *intr* to flow
flujo *m* flow, flux; (*acceso de la marea*) floodtide; **flujo de risa** fit of noisy laughter; **flujo de vientre** loose bowels; **flujo y reflujo** ebb and flow
flúor *m* fluorine
fluorescencia *f* fluorescence
fluorescente *adj* fluorescent
fluorhídri•co -ca *adj* hydrofluoric
fluorización *f* fluoridation
fluorizar §60 *tr* to fluoridate
fluoroscopio *m* fluoroscope
fluoruro *m* fluoride
flux *m* (*en el póker*) flush; suit of clothes; **estar en flux** to be penniless; **hacer flux** to blow in everything without settling accounts; **tener flux** to be lucky
fluxión *f* (*acumulación morbosa de humores*) congestion; (*enrojecimiento de la cara y el cuello*) flush; (*constipado de narices*) cold in the head; **fluxión de muelas** swollen cheek; **fluxión de pecho** pneumonia
foca *f* seal
focal *adj* focal
foco *m* focus; (*de vicios*) center; (*de un absceso*) core; electric light
fodo•lí *adj* (*pl* **-líes**) meddlesome
fodon•go -ga *adj* (Mex) dirty, slovenly
fo•fo -fa *adj* soft, fluffy, spongy
fogaje *m* (*contribución*) hearth money; blush, flush; (Arg) fire, blaze; (Arg, Mex) rash, eruption
fogata *f* blaze, bonfire
fogón *m* cooking stove; (*de máquina de vapor*) firebox
fogonazo *m* powder flash
fogonero *m* fireman, stoker
fogosidad *f* fire, spirit, dash
fogo•so -sa *adj* fiery, spirited
fol. *abbr* **folio**
folgo *m* foot muff
foliar *tr* to folio
folio *m* folio; **al primer folio** right off; **de a folio** enormous; **en folio** folio
folklore *m* folklore
follaje *m* foliage; gaudy ornament; (*palabrería*) fustian
follar *tr* to shape like a leaf || §61 *tr* to blow with bellows
folletín *m* newspaper serial (*printed at bottom of page*); pamphlet
folleto *m* brochure, pamphlet, tract
fo•llón -llona *adj* careless, indolent, lazy; arrogant, cowardly || *mf* lazy loafer, knave || *m* noiseless rocket
fomentar *tr* to foment; foster, encourage, promote; warm
fonda *f* inn, restaurant; (Chile) refreshment stand
fondeadero *m* anchorage
fondea•do -da *adj* well-heeled
fondear *tr* (*un buque*) to search; scrutinize, examine closely || *intr* to cast anchor || *ref* to save up for a rainy day
fondillos *mpl* seat (*of trousers*)
fondista *mf* innkeeper
fondo *m* bottom; (*de un cuarto, una tienda*) back, rear; (*del mar, de una piscina, etc.*) floor; (*de un cilindro, barril, etc.*) head; background; (*de una casa*) depth; (*de un paño*) ground; (*caudal*) fund; (*lo esencial*) bottom; **a fondo** thoroughly; **bajos fondos sociales** underworld, scum of the earth; **colar a fondo** to sink; **dar fondo** to cast anchor; **echar a fondo** to sink; **en el fondo** at bottom; **estar en fondos** to have funds available; **fondo de amortización** sinking fund; **fondos** (*caudales, dinero*) funds; **irse a fondo** to go to the bottom; (*un negocio*)

to fail; **tener buen fondo** to be good-natured
fonducho *m* cheap eating house
fonéti•co -ca *adj* phonetic
foniatría *f* speech correction
fónica *f* phonics
fono *m* (Chile) earphone
fonoabsorbente *adj* sound-absorbent; sound-deadening
fonocaptor *m* pickup
fonógrafo *m* phonograph; record player
fonología *f* phonology
fontanería *f* plumbing; water-supply system
fontane•ro -ra *adj* fountain || *m* plumber, tinsmith
foque *m* (naut) jib; (coll) piccadilly collar
foraji•do -da *adj* fugitive || *mf* fugitive, outlaw, bandit
foráne•o -a *adj* foreign, strange; offshore
foraste•ro -ra *adj* outside, strange; foreign || *mf* outsider, stranger
forbante *m* freebooter
forcejar or **forcejear** *intr* to struggle, resist, contend
forceju•do -da *adj* strong, husky, robust
fór•ceps *m* (*pl* **-ceps**) forceps
forestal *adj* forest
forja *f* forge; forging; silversmith's forge; foundry, ironworks; mortar
forjar *tr* to forge; build with stone and mortar; roughcast; (*mentiras*) forge || *ref* to forge; hatch, think up
forma *f* form, shape; way; (*de un libro*) format; **de forma que** so that, with the result that; **tener buenas formas** to have a good figure
formación *f* formation; **formación de palabras** word formation
formal *adj* formal, ceremonious; express, definite; reliable; sedate; serious
formalidad *f* formality; reliability; seriousness
formar *tr* to form; to shape, fashion; train, educate || *intr* to form; form a line, stand in line || *ref* to form; form a line, stand in line; take form, grow, develop
formato *m* format
formidable *adj* formidable
formidolo•so -sa *adj* scared, frightened; frightful, horrible
fórmula *f* formula; prescription; **por fórmula** as a matter of form
formular *tr* to formulate
formulario *m* form, blank; **formulario de pedido** order blank
fornicación *f* fornication
fornicar *intr* to fornicate; to have sex
forni•do -da *adj* husky, sturdy, robust
foro *m* forum; (*abogacía*) bar; (*del escenario*) back, rear
forrado *m* lining; padding
forraje *m* forage, fodder
forrajear *tr & intr* to forage
forrar *tr* to line; (*un vestido*) face; (*un libro, un paraguas*) cover; (*un lienzo*) stretch || *ref* (Guat, Mex) to stuff oneself
forro *m* lining; cover, covering; (naut) sheathing, planking; **forro de freno** brake lining; **ni por el forro** not by a long shot
fortalecer **§22** *tr* to fortify, strengthen
fortaleza *f* fortitude; strength, vigor; fortress, stronghold
fortificación *f* fortification
fortificante *m* tonic
fortificar **§73** *tr* to fortify
fortín *m* small fort; bunker
fortui•to -ta *adj* fortuitous
fortuna *f* fortune; **correr fortuna** (naut) to ride the storm; **de fortuna** makeshift; **por fortuna** fortunately; **probar fortuna** to try one's luck
fortunón *m* windfall
forza•do -da *adj* forced; (*p.ej., entrada*) forcible; (*sonrisa*) (fig) forced; (*trabajos*) hard || *m* galley slave
forzar **§35** *tr* to force
forzo•so -sa *adj* unavoidable; strong, husky; (*trabajos*) hard; (*aterrizaje; marcha*) forced || *f* — **hacer la forzosa a** to put the squeeze on
forzu•do -da *adj* strong, husky, robust
fosa *f* grave; (aut) pit; **fosa de los leones** (Bib) lions' den
fosar *tr* to dig a ditch around
fos•co -ca *adj* dark; cross, sullen; (*tiempo*) threatening
fosfato *m* phosphate
fosforera *f* matchbox
fosforescente *adj* phosphorescent
fósforo *m* (*cuerpo simple*) phosphorus; match; **fósforo de seguridad** safety match
fósil *adj & m* fossil
foso *m* hole, pit; (*que rodea un castillo o fortaleza*) moat; (theat & aut) pit
fotingo *m* jalopy, jitney
foto *f* photo; **foto fija** still
fotocopia *f* photocopy
fotocopiador *m* or **fotocopiadora** *f* photocopier
fotocopiar *tr* to photocopy
fotodrama *m* photoplay
fotofija *m* photo-finish camera
fotogéni•co -ca *adj* photogenic
fotograbado *m* photoengraving
fotografía *f* (*arte*) photography; (*imagen, retrato*) photograph; photograph gallery; **fotografía aérea** aerial photograph(y)
fotografiar **§77** *tr & intr* to photograph
fotógra•fo -fa *mf* photographer
fotómetro *m* light meter
fotoperiodismo *m* photojournalism
fotopila *f* solar battery
fotostatar *tr & intr* to photostat
fotóstato *m* photostat
fototubo *m* phototube
fra. *abbr* **factura**
frac *m* (*pl* **-fraques**) full-dress coat, tails, swallow-tailed coat
fracasar *intr* to fail; break to pieces
fracaso *m* failure; breakdown, crash
fracción *f* fraction
fraccionar *tr* to divide up; break up
fracciona•rio -ria *adj* fractional

fractura *f* fracture; breaking open, breaking in
fracturar *tr* to fracture; break open, break in || *ref* (*p.ej., un brazo*) to fracture
fragancia *f* fragrance; good reputation
fragante *adj* fragrant; **en fragante** (archaic) in the act
fragata *f* frigate; **fragata ligera** corvette
frágil *adj* fragile; (*quebradizo; que cae fácilmente en el pecado*) frail; (Mex) poor, needy
fragmento *m* fragment
fragor *m* crash, roar, thunder
fragoro•so -sa *adj* noisy, thundering
fragosidad *f* roughness, unevenness; (*de un bosque*) thickness, denseness; rough road
frago•so -sa *adj* rough, uneven; thick, dense; noisy, thundering
fragua *f* forge
fraguar §10 *tr* to forge; hatch, scheme; (*mentiras*) forge || *intr* to forge; (*la cal, el cemento*) set
fraile *m* friar, monk; **fraile de misa y olla** friarling; **fraile rezador** praying mantis
frambesia *f* (pathol) yaws
frambuesa *f* raspberry
frambueso *m* raspberry bush
francachela *f* feast, spread; carousal, high time; (Arg) excessive familiarity
francalete *m* strap with buckle
fran•cés -cesa *adj* French; **despedirse a la francesa** to take French leave || *m* Frenchman; (*idioma*) French || *f* Frenchwoman
francesada *f* French remark; French invasion of Spain in 1808
francesilla *f* French roll; (bot) turban buttercup
Francia *f* France
francisca•no -na *adj & mf* Franciscan
francmasón *m* Freemason
francmasonería *f* Freemasonry
fran•co -ca *adj* generous, liberal; outspoken, candid, frank; (*camino*) free, open; (*suelo*) loamy; free, gratis; Frankish; **franco a bordo** free on board; **franco de porte** postpaid || *mf* Frank || *m* franc; (*idioma*) Frankish
francolín *m* black partridge
franco•te -ta *adj* frank, wholehearted
francotirador *m* sniper
franela *f* flannel
frangente *m* accident, mishap
frangir §27 *tr* to break up, break to pieces
frangollar *tr* to bungle, to botch
frangollo *m* porridge; mash for cattle; bungle, botch
franja *f* fringe; strip, band; (opt) fringe
franjar *tr* to fringe
franquear *tr* to exempt; cross, go over; grant; free, enfranchise; (*un camino*) open, clear; (*una carta*) frank, pay the postage for; **a franquear en destino** postage will be paid by addressee || *ref* to yield; **franquearse con** to open one's heart to
franqueo *m* freeing, liberation; postage; **franqueo concertado** postage permit
franqueza *f* generosity; candidness, frankness; freedom
franquía *f* (naut) sea room; **en franquía** (naut & fig) in the open
franquicia *f* franchise; exemption, tax exemption; **franquicia postal** franking privilege
franquista *mf* Francoist
frasca *f* leaves, twigs, brush; (Guat, Mex) high jinks
frasco *m* flask; (*p.ej., de aceitunas*) jar
frase *f* phrase; (*oración cabal*) sentence; idiom; **frase hecha** saying, proverb; cliché; **gastar frases** to talk all around the subject
frasear *tr* to phrase || *intr* to talk all around the subject
frasquera *f* bottle frame, liquor case
fratás *m* plastering trowel
fraternal *adj* brotherly, fraternal
fraternidad *f* fraternity, brotherhood
fraternizar §60 *intr* to fraternize
frater•no -na *adj* brotherly, fraternal
fraude *m* fraud; **fraude fiscal** tax evasion
fraudulen•to -ta *adj* fraudulent
fray *m* Fra
frecuencia *f* frequency; **alta frecuencia** high frequency; **baja frecuencia** low frequency; **con frecuencia** frequently
frecuentar *tr* (*ir con frecuencia a*) to frequent; keep up, repeat
frecuente *adj* frequent; (*usual*) common
fregadero *m* sink, kitchen sink
frega•do -da *adj* annoying, bothersome; cunning; (SAm) stubborn; (P-R) brazen || *m* scrubbing; mopping; mess
frega•dor -dora *mf* dishwasher
fregar §66 *tr* (*restregar*) to rub; (*restregar para limpiar*) scrub, scour; (*el pavimento*) mop; (*los platos*) wash; annoy, bother
fregasue•los *m* (*pl* **-los**) mop, floor mop
frega•triz *f* (*pl* **-trices**) var of **fregona**
fre•gón -gona *adj* annoying, bothersome; brazen || *f* (*criada que friega el pavimento*) scrub woman; (*criada que lava la vajilla*) dishwasher, scullery maid
freiduría *f* fried-fish shop
freír §58 & §83 *tr* to fry; bore to death || *intr* to fry; **dejarle a uno freír en su aceite** to let someone stew in his own juice || *ref* to fry; be bored to death; **freírsele a** to try to fool, scheme to deceive
fréjol *m* kidney bean
frenar *tr* to bridle, check, hold back; (*un automóvil, tren*) brake
frene•sí *m* (*pl* **-síes**) frenzy
frenéti•co -ca *adj* frantic; mad, furious; wild
frenillo *m* muzzle; **no tener frenillo en la lengua** to not mince one's words
freno *m* (*parte de la brida*) bit; (*aparato para parar el movimiento de los vehículos*) brake; (fig) brake, check, curb; **freno de contrapedal** coaster brake; **freno de disco** disk brake; **freno de tambor** drum brake; **morder el freno** to champ the bit
frenología *f* phrenology
frentazo *m* (Mex) rebuff
frente *m & f* (*de un edificio*) front || *m* (mil)

front, front line; **al frente de** at the head of, in charge of || *f* brow, forehead; face, front; head; **a frente** straight ahead; **arrugar la frente** to knit the brow; **de frente** straight ahead; abreast; **en frente de** in front of; against, opposed to; **frente a** in front of; compared with

freo *m* channel, strait

fresa *f* strawberry; (*de fresadora*) cutter

fresado *m* milling, millwork

fresadora *f* milling machine

fresal *m* strawberry patch

fresar *tr* to mill

fresca *f* fresh air; cool part of the day; blunt remark, piece of one's mind

fresca•chón -chona *adj* bouncing, buxom; (*viento*) brisk

fresca•les *mf* (*pl* **-les**) forward sort of person

frescamente *adv* recently; cheekily, brazenly

fres•co -ca *adj* (*acabado de hacer o suceder*) fresh; (*moderadamente frío*) cool; (*pintura*) fresh, wet; (*tela, vestido*) light; calm, unruffled; buxom, ruddy; cheeky, fresh; **estar fresco** to be in a fine pinch; **quedarse tan fresco** to show no offense, be indifferent or unconcerned || *m* coolness; fresh air; fresh bacon; (fa) fresco; cool drink; **al fresco** in the open air; in the night air; **hace fresco** it is cool; **tomar el fresco** to go out for some fresh air || *f* see **fresca**

frescor *m* freshness; cool, coolness

fresco•te -ta *adj* plump and rosy

frescura *f* freshness; cool, coolness; unconcern, offhand manner; sharp reply; cheek, impudence

fresno *m* ash tree; (*madera*) ash

fresquera *f* meat closet, food cabinet, icebox

fresquería *f* ice-cream parlor, soft-drink store

fresque•ro -ra *mf* fish dealer; (Peru) soft-drink vendor || *f* see **fresquera**

freudismo *m* Freudianism

freza *f* dung; spawning; hole made by game

frialdad *f* coldness; carelessness, laxity; stupidity; (pathol) frigidity; (pathol) impotence; (fig) coolness, coldness

friáti•co -ca *adj* chilly; awkward, stupid; (*ropa*) cold

fricar §73 *tr* to rub

fricasé *m* fricassee

fricción *f* rubbing; massage; (pharm) rubbing liniment; (phys) friction

friccionar *tr* to rub; massage

friega *f* rubbing, massage; annoyance, bother; flogging, whipping

frigidez *f* frigidity; coldness

frígi•do -da *adj* frigid; cold

frigorífero *m* freezing chamber

frigorífi•co -ca *adj* refrigerating; cold-storage || *m* refrigerator; (Arg, Urug) packing house, cold-storage plant

fríjol *m* bean, kidney bean; **fríjol de media luna** Lima bean; **¡fríjoles!** (W-I) absolutely no!

frijolear *tr* (Guat) to annoy, molest

frijolizar §60 *tr* (Peru) to bewitch

frí•o -a *adj* cold; dull, weak, colorless; (fig) cold, cool || *m* cold; **fríos** chills and fever; **coger frío** to catch cold; **hace frío** it is cold; **tener frío** (*una persona*) to be cold; **tomar frío** to catch cold

friole•ro -ra *adj* chilly || *f* trifle, trinket; snack, bite

frisar *tr* to rub; to fit, fasten; (naut) to calk || *intr* to agree, get along; **frisar con** or **en** to border on

friso *m* dado, wainscot; (archit) frieze

fri•són -sona *adj & mf* Frisian

fritada *f* fry

fri•to -ta *adj* fried; bored to death || *m* fry; (Ven) daily bread

fritura *f* fry

frívo•lo -la *adj* frivolous; trifling

fronda *f* leaf; (*de helecho*) frond; sling-shaped bandage; **frondas** frondage, foliage

frondo•so -sa *adj* leafy; woodsy

frontalera *f* yoke pad

frontera *f* frontier, border; front, façade

fronteri•zo -za *adj* frontier, border; facing, opposite

fronte•ro -ra *adj* frontier, border; facing, opposite; front || *f* see **frontera**

frontín *m* (Mex) flip, fillip

fron•tis *m* (*pl* **-tis**) front, façade

frontispicio *m* frontispiece; (coll) face

frontón *m* (*encima de puertas o ventanas*) gable, pediment; pelota court; pelota wall; handball court

frotamiento *m* rubbing; (phys) friction

frotar *tr* to rub; to chafe || *ref* to rub

fro•tis *m* (*pl* **-tis**) (bact) smear

fructuo•so -sa *adj* fruitful

frugal *adj* (*en comer y beber*) temperate; (*no muy abundante*) frugal

fruición *f* enjoyment, satisfaction; (*del mal ajeno*) evil satisfaction

fruiti•vo -va *adj* enjoyable

frunce *m* shirr, shirring, gathering

frunci•do -da *adj* grim, gruff, stern; (Chile) temperate; (Chile) sad, gloomy || *m* shirr, shirring, gathering

fruncir §36 *tr* to wrinkle, pucker, pleat; (*la frente*) knit; (*los labios*) curl, purse; (*la verdad*) twist, disguise; shirr, gather || *ref* to affect modesty, be shocked

fruslería *f* trifle, trinket; (coll) futility, triviality

frusle•ro -ra *adj* futile, trivial, trifling || *m* rolling pin

frustrar *tr* to frustrate, thwart

fruta *f* fruit; **fruta del tiempo** fruit in season; **fruta de sartén** fritter, pancake; **frutas** fruit; **frutas agrias** citrus fruit

frutal *adj* fruit || *m* fruit tree

frutería *f* fruit store

frute•ro -ra *adj* fruit || *mf* fruit dealer || *m* fruit dish; tray of imitation fruit

frutilla *f* (*del rosario*) bead; Chilean strawberry; gumdrop

fruto *m* (bot & fig) fruit; **fruto de bendición** legitimate offspring; **frutos** produce; **sacar fruto de** to derive benefit from

fu *interj* faugh! fie!; (*del gato*) spit!; **ni fu ni fa** neither this nor that

fucilazo *m* heat lightning, sheet lightning

fuego *m* fire; (*para encender un cigarrillo*) light; (*de arma de fuego*) firing; lighthouse, beacon; hearth, home; rash, eruption; sore, fever blister; **abrir fuego** to open fire; **echar fuego** to blow up, hit the ceiling; **¡fuego!** fire!; **fuego fatuo** will-o'-the-wisp; **fuego graneado** or **nutrido** drumfire; **fuegos artificiales** fireworks; **hacer fuego** to fire, shoot; **marcar a fuego** to brand; **pegar fuego a** to set fire to, set on fire; **poner a fuego y sangre** to lay waste; **prenderse fuego** to catch on fire; **romper fuego** to open fire; stir up a row; **tocar a fuego** to sound the fire alarm

fuelle *m* fold, pucker, wrinkle; (*instrumento para soplar*) bellows; (*cubierta de coche*) folding carriage top; wind clouds; (*persona soplona*) gossip, talebearer

fuente *f* fountain, spring; public hydrant; font, baptismal font; platter, tray; (fig) source; **beber en buenas fuentes** to have good sources of information; **fuente de gasolina** gasoline pump; **fuente de sodas** soda fountain; **fuente para beber** drinking fountain; **fuentes termales** hot springs

fuer *m* — **a fuer de** as a, by way of

fuera *adv* out, outside; away, out of town; **desde fuera** from the outside; **fuera de** outside of; away from; out of; aside from; in addition to; **fuera de que** aside from the fact that; **fuera de sí** beside oneself; **por fuera** on the outside

fuera-bordo *m* outboard motor

fuere•ño -ña *mf* (Mex) hick, stranger

fuero *m* law, statute; code of laws; jurisdiction; exemption, privilege; **fuero interior** conscience, inmost heart; **fueros** pride, arrogance

fuerte *adj* strong; hard; loud; heavy; **hacerse fuerte** to stick to one's guns; (mil) to hole up, to dig in || *adv* hard; loud || *m* fort, fortress; forte, strong point

fuerza *f* force, strength, power; (*de un ejército*) main body; literal meaning; (phys) force; **a fuerza de** by dint of, by force of; **a la fuerza** forcibly, by force; **a viva fuerza** by main strength; **fuerza aérea** air force; **fuerza de agua** water power; **fuerza de sangre** animal power; **fuerza mayor** (law) force majeure, act of God; **fuerza motriz** motive power; **fuerza pública** police; **fuerza viva** kinetic energy; **hacer fuerza** to strain, struggle; to carry weight; **por fuerza** perforce, necessarily; **ser fuerza** + *inf* to be necessary to + *inf*

fuete *m* whip

fufar *intr* (*el gato*) to spit

fuga *f* flight; (*salida de un gas o líquido*) leak; ardor, vigor; (mus) fugue; **darse a la fuga** to take flight, run away; **fuga de capitales** capital flight; **poner en fuga** to put to flight

fugar §44 *ref* to flee, escape, run away

fu•gaz *adj* (*pl* **-gaces**) fleeting, passing; (*estrella*) shooting

fugiti•vo -va *adj* & *mf* fugitive

fugui•llas *m* (*pl* **-llas**) (coll) hustler

fula•no -na *mf* so-and-so

fulcro *m* fulcrum

fulgor *m* brilliance, radiance

fulgurar *intr* to flash

fulmicotón *m* guncotton

fulminar *tr* to strike with lightning; strike dead; (*censuras, amenazas, etc.*) thunder; (*balas o bombas*) hurl

fullería *f* trickery, cheating

fulle•ro -ra *adj* crooked, cheating || *mf* crook, cheat; **fullero de naipes** cardsharp

fumada *f* puff, whiff

fumadero *m* smoking room; **fumadero de opio** opium den

fuma•dor -dora *adj* smoking || *mf* smoker

fumar *tr* to smoke || *intr* to smoke; **fumar en pipa** to smoke a pipe; **se prohibe fumar** no smoking || *ref* to squander; stay away from; (*la clase*) cut

fumarada *f* (*de humo*) puff; (*de tabaco*) pipeful

fumigación *f* fumigation; **fumigación aérea** crop dusting

fumigar §44 *tr* to fumigate

fumista *m* stove or heater repairman; stove or heater dealer

fumistería *f* stove or heater shop

fumo•so -sa *adj* smoky

funámbu•lo -la *mf* ropewalker

función *f* function; duty, office, function; (*espectáculo teatral*) show, performance; **entrar en funciones** to take office, take up one's duties; **función benéfica** charitable performance; **función de aficionados** amateur performance; **función de títeres** puppet show; **función secundaria** side show

funcional *adj* functional

funcionariado *m* bureaucracy

funcionario *m* functionary, public official, civil servant

funcione•ro -ra *adj* officious, fussy

fund. *abbr* **fundador**

funda *f* case, sheath, envelope, slip; (*para una espada*) scabbard; (*para proteger los muebles*) slip cover; **funda de almohada** pillowcase; **funda de asientos** seat cover; **funda de gafas** spectacle case

fundación *f* foundation

fundadamente *adv* with good reason; on good authority

funda•dor -dora *adj* founding || *mf* founder

fundamental *adj* fundamental

fundamentar *tr* to lay the foundations of

fundamento *m* foundation; (*razón, motivo*) grounds, reason; basis; reliability, sense; (Col) skirt

fundar *tr* to found, base || *ref* — **fundarse en** to be based on; base one's opinion on

fundente *adj* molten || *m* flux

fundería *f* foundry

fundible *adj* fusible

fundición *f* (*acción de fundir*) founding; (*fábrica*) foundry; (*herrería*) forge; (*hierro colado*) cast iron; (typ) font

fundi•do -da *adj* melted; (*individuo*) ruined; (elec) shorted, blown out

fundidor *m* founder, foundryman

fundillo *m* (Cuba, Mex) behind, buttocks
fundir *tr* (*p.ej., metales*) to found; (*campanas, estatuas*) cast; (*derretir para purificar*) smelt; (*colores*) mix; (*un filamento eléctrico*) burn out || *intr* to smelt || *ref* to melt; fuse; (*un filamento eléctrico*) burn out; fail, founder; (fig) to fuse, merge
fúnebre *adj* (*marcha, procesión*) funeral; (*triste*) funereal
funeral *adj* funeral; (*triste, lúgubre*) funereal || *m* funeral; **funerales** funeral
funerala — a la funerala (mil) with arms inverted (*as a token of mourning*)
funera•rio -ria *adj* funeral || *m* mortician, funeral director || *f* (*empresa*) undertaking establishment; (*local*) funeral home, funeral parlor
funes•to -ta *adj* ill-fated; sad, sorrowful; (*p.ej., influencia*) baneful
fungir §27 *intr* (CAm, Mex) to act, function
fungo *m* (pathol) fungus
fungo•so -sa *adj* fungous
funicular *adj & m* funicular
fuñique *adj* awkward; dull, tiresome
furgón *m* wagon, truck; (rr) freight car, boxcar; (rr) caboose
furgoneta *f* light truck, delivery truck
furia *f* fury
furibun•do -da *adj* furious, frenzied
furio•so -sa *adj* furious; (*muy grande*) terrific, tremendous
furor *m* rage, furor; **causar furor** to make a splash, cause a stir; **hacer furor** to be all the rage
furti•vo -va *adj* furtive; sneaky, poaching
furúnculo *m* boil
fusa *f* (mus) demisemiquaver
fus•co -ca *adj* dark
fusela•do -da *adj* streamlined
fuselaje *m* fuselage
fusible *adj* fusible || *m* (elec) fuse
fusil *m* gun, rifle
fusilar *tr* to shoot, execute; plagiarize
fusilazo *m* (*tiro de fusil*) gunshot, rifle shot; (*relámpago sin ruido*) heat lightning, sheet lightning
fusilería *f* rifle corps; rifles, guns; (*descarga*) fusillade
fusión *f* fusion; melting; **fusión de empresas** (com) merger
fusionar *tr & ref* to fuse, merge
fusta *f* brushwood, twigs; teamster's whip
fustán *m* fustian; cotton petticoat; (Ven) skirt
fuste *m* wood, timber; shaft, stem; (fig) importance, substance
fustigar §44 *tr* to whip, lash; rebuke harshly
fútbol *m* football; soccer, **fútbol asociación** soccer
fútil *adj* futile, trifling, inconsequential
futilidad *f* futility
futre *m* (SAm) dandy, dude
futu•ro -ra *adj* future || *m* future; (gram) future; fiancé; **futuros** (com) futures || *f* fiancée

G

G, g (ge) *f* eighth letter of the Spanish alphabet
G. *abbr* gracia
gaba•cho -cha *adj & mf* Pyrenean; (coll) Frenchy || *m* (coll) Frenchified Spanish (*language*)
gabán *m* overcoat
gabardina *f* gabardine; raincoat with belt
gabarra *f* barge, lighter
gabarro *m* (*en una piedra*) nodule; (*en un tejido*) flaw, defect; mistake
gabinete *m* cabinet; (*de médico, abogado, etc.*) office; studio, study; laboratory; (Col) glassed-in balcony; **de gabinete** armchair, theoretical; **gabinete de aseo** washroom; **gabinete de lectura** reading room
gablete *m* gable
gacela *f* gazelle
gaceta *f* government journal; newspaper; **mentir más que la gaceta** to lie like a trooper
gacetilla *f* town talk, gossip column; short item
gacetillero *m* gossip columnist
gacetista *mf* newspaper reader; newsmonger
gacilla *f* (CAm) safety pin
gacha *f* watery mass; (Col, Ven) earthenware bowl; **gachas** mush, pap; porridge; mud; **gachas de avena** oatmeal; **hacerse unas gachas** to be mushy
ga•cho -cha *adj* turned down; flopping; (*sombrero*) slouch; **a gachas** on all fours || *f* see **gacha**
gachumbo *m* (SAm) hard fruit shell
gachu•pín -pina *mf* (CAm, Mex) Spanish settler in Latin America
gaéli•co -ca *adj* Gaelic || *mf* Gael || *m* Gaelic (*language*)
gafa *f* clamp; (*enganche de los anteojos*) temple; **gafas** glasses; **gafas de sol** or **gafas para sol** sunglasses
gafe *m* jinx, hoodoo
ga•fo -fa *adj* claw-handed; foot-sore || *f* see **gafa**
gaguear *intr* to stutter
gaita *f* hornpipe; hurdy-gurdy; chore, hard task; neck; **gaita gallega** bagpipe
gaite•ro -ra *adj* flashy, gaudy || *m* piper, bagpipe player
gajes *mpl* wages, salary; **gajes del oficio** cares of office, occupational annoyances

gajo *m* broken branch; (*de un racimo de uvas*) small stem; (*división interior de ciertas frutas*) slice; (*de horca*) tine, prong; (*ramal de montes*) spur; curl
gala *f* fine clothes; (*lo más selecto*) choice, cream; tip, fee; **de gala** full-dress; **hacer gala de** to glory in; **llevarse la gala** to win approval
galafate *m* slick thief
galai•co -ca *adj* Galician
galán *m* good-looking fellow; lover, gallant, ladies' man; (*el que sirve de escolta a una dama*) escort, cavalier; (theat) leading man; **galán joven** (theat) juvenile; **primer galán** (theat) leading man
galancete *m* (theat) juvenile
gala•no -na *adj* elegant, graceful; spruce, smartly dressed; rich, tasteful
galante *adj* (*con las damas*) gallant; (*con los caballeros*) flirtatious; (*mujer*) wanton, loose
galantear *tr* to court, woo, make love to; sue, entreat
galantería *f* gallantry; charm, elegance; generosity
galanura *f* charm, elegance
galápago *m* pond tortoise; (*del arado*) moldboard; light saddle; ingot
galardón *m* reward, recompense
galardonar *tr* to reward, recompense
galaxia *f* galaxy
galbana *f* laziness; shiftlessness
galbano•so -sa *adj* lazy; phlegmatic
gale•no -na *adj* gentle; mild || *m* (coll) physician, doctor
galeón *m* (naut) galleon
galeote *m* galley slave
galera *f* covered wagon; women's jail; (*de hospital*) ward; (naut & typ) galley
galerada *f* wagonload; (typ) galley; (typ) galley proof
galería *f* gallery; **galería de tiro** shooting gallery; **galerías** department store; **hablar para la galería** to play to the gallery
galerna *f* stormy wind from the northwest (*on the northern coast of Spain*)
Gales *f* Wales; **el país de Gales** Wales; **la Nueva Gales del Sur** New South Wales
ga•lés -lesa *adj* Welsh || *m* Welshman; Welsh (*language*) || *f* Welsh woman
galguear *intr* (CAm, Mex, Arg) to be hungry
gal•go -ga *adj* (Col) sweet-toothed || *m* greyhound || *f* greyhound bitch; rolling stone; mange, rash
Galia, la Gaul
gálibo *m* template, pattern; (rr) gabarit
galicismo *m* Gallicism
gáli•co -ca *adj* Gallic || *m* syphilis; syphilitic
galillo *m* uvula; gullet
galimatí•as *m* (*pl* **-as**) gibberish, nonsense; confusion
galiparia *f* Frenchified Spanish
ga•lo -la *adj* Gaulish || *mf* Gaul || *m* Gaulish (*language*)
galocha *f* clog, wooden shoe
galón *m* braid, galloon; (*medida para líquidos*) gallon; (mil) chevron, stripe
galopar *intr* to gallop
galope *m* gallop; **a galope** at a gallop; in great haste; **a galope tendido** on the run
galopea•do -da *adj* hasty, sketchy || *m* beating, punching
galopear *intr* to gallop
galopillo *m* scullion, kitchen boy
galopín *m* ragamuffin; (*hombre taimado*) wise guy; (naut) cabin boy
galpón *m* (SAm) iron shed; (Col) tile works
galvanizar **§60** *tr* to electroplate; galvanize
galvanoplastia *f* electroplating
galladura *f* tread (*of egg*)
gallardete *m* streamer, pennant
gallardía *f* gallantry; elegance; nobility; generosity
gallar•do -da *adj* gallant; elegant; noble; generous; (*temporal*) fierce
gallear *intr* to stand out, excel; shout, yell, threaten
galle•go -ga *adj* & *mf* Galician
gallera *f* cockpit
galleta *f* hardtack, ship biscuit; cracker; little pitcher; slap
gallina *adj* chicken-hearted || *mf* chicken-hearted person || *f* hen; **estar como gallina en corral ajeno** to be like a fish out of water; **gallina ciega** blindman's buff; **gallina de Guinea** guinea fowl
gallinería *f* poultry shop; cowardice
galline•ro -ra *mf* poultry dealer || *m* hencoop, henhouse; poultry basket; top gallery; babel, madhouse
gallipavo *m* turkey; sour note
gallito *m* (*el que figura sobre los demás*) somebody; **gallito del lugar** cock of the walk
gallo *m* cock, rooster; false note, sour note; boss; frog in the throat; (box) bantamweight; (Col, C-R, Mex) strong man; **gallo de bosque** wood grouse; **gallo de pelea** gamecock; **tener mucho gallo** to be cocky
gallofa *f* vegetables; French roll; talk, gossip
gallofear *intr* to beg, bum, loaf around
gallofe•ro -ra *adj* begging, loafing || *mf* beggar, loafer
gama *f* doe, female fallow deer; (mus & fig) gamut
gamberrismo *m* gangsterism, rowdyism
gambe•rro -rra *adj* & *mf* libertine || *m* hoodlum, tough, rowdy
gambeta *f* crosscaper; caper, prance
gambito *m* gambit
gamo *m* buck, male fallow deer
gamón *m* asphodel
gamonal *m* field of asphodel; boss
gamuza *f* chamois
gana *f* desire; will; **darle a uno la gana de** to feel like, e.g., **le da la gana de trabajar** he feels like working; **de buena gana** willingly; **de gana** in earnest; willingly; **de mala gana** unwillingly; **tener ganas de** to feel like, to have a mind to
ganadería *f* cattle, livestock; brand, stock; cattle raising; cattle ranch
ganade•ro -ra *adj* cattle, livestock || *mf* cattle breeder; cattle dealer || *m* cattleman

ganado *m* cattle, livestock; **ganado caballar** horses; **ganado cabrío** goats; **ganado lanar** sheep; **ganado mayor** large farm animals (*cows, bulls, horses, and mules*); **ganado menor** small farm animals (*sheep, goats, pigs*); **ganado menudo** young cattle; **ganado moreno** swine; **ganado ovejuno** sheep; **ganado porcino** swine; **ganado vacuno** cattle
gana•dor -dora *adj* winning; earning; hard-working || *mf* winner; earner
ganancia *f* gain, profit; (Guat, Mex) extra, bonus; **ganancias y pérdidas** profit and loss
ganancial *adj* profit
gananció•so -sa *adj* gainful, profitable; earning || *mf* earner
ganapán *m* errand boy; boor
ganapierde *m & f* giveaway
ganar *tr* (*dinero trabajando*) to earn; (*la victoria luchando*) win; (*beneficios en los negocios*) gain; (*a una persona en una contienda*) beat, defeat; (*aventajar*) excel; (*la voluntad de una persona*) win over; (*alcanzar*) reach; **ganar algo a alguien** to win something from someone; **ganar de comer** to earn a living || *intr* to earn; (*mejorar*) improve || *ref* to win over; **ganarse la vida** to earn a livelihood
ganchero *m* log driver; (Chile) odd-jobber; (Ecuad) gentle mount
ganchillo *m* crochet needle; crochet, crochet work; **hacer ganchillo** to crochet
gancho *m* hook; shepherd's crook; coaxer; procurer, pimp; hairpin; (Col, Ecuad) lady's saddle; **gancho de botalones** (naut) gooseneck; **echar el gancho a** to hook in, to land; **tener gancho** (*una mujer*) to have a way with the men
gandaya *f* (coll) bumming, loafing
gandujar *tr* to pleat, shirr
gan•dul -dula *adj* loafing, idling || *mf* loafer, idler
gandulear *intr* to loaf, idle
ganfo•rro -rra *mf* scoundrel
ganga *f* bargain
ganglio *m* ganglion
gangocho *m* burlap
gango•so -sa *adj* snuffling, nasal
gangrena *f* gangrene
gangrenar *tr & ref* to gangrene
gángster *m* gunman, gangster
gangsteril *adj* gangster(like)
gangsterismo *m* gangsterism; mobsterism
ganguear *intr* to snuffle, talk through the nose
gangue•ro -ra *adj* bargain-hunting; self-seeking || *mf* bargain hunter
gano•so -sa *adj* desirous; (*caballo*) (Chile) spirited, fiery
gan•so -sa *mf* dope, dullard || *m* goose; gander; **ganso bravo** wild goose || *f* female goose
Gante Ghent
ganzúa *f* (*garfio*) picklock, lock pick; (*persona*) picklock; pumper (*of secrets*)
gañán *m* farm hand; rough, husky fellow
gañido *m* yelp; croak
gañir §12 *intr* (*el perro*) to yelp; (*p.ej., el cuervo*) croak
garabatear *tr* to scribble || *intr* to hook; beat about the bush; scribble
garabato *m* hook; pothook; scribbling; weeding hoe; (*bozal*) muzzle; (*de una mujer*) winsomeness; **garabato de carnicero** meat-hook; **garabatos** wiggling of hands and fingers
garabato•so -sa *adj* full of scrawls; winsome
garage *m* or **garaje** *m* garage
garagista *m* garbage man
garambaina *f* gaudy trimming; **garambainas** simpering, smirking; (coll) scribble
garante *adj* responsible || *mf* guarantor, voucher
garantía *f* guarantee, guaranty; warranty; **garantia anticorrosión** antirust warranty
garantir §1 *tr* to guarantee
garantizar §60 *tr* to guarantee
garañón *m* stud jackass; stud camel; stallion
garapiña *f* icing, sugar-coating; iced pineapple drink
garapiñar *tr* to ice, sugar-coat; candy
garapiñera *f* ice-cream freezer
garbanzo *m* chickpea; **garbanzo negro** (fig) black sheep
garbeo *m* walk; promenade
garbillar *tr* to sieve, screen riddle
garbillo *s* sieve, screen; riddled ore
garbo *m* jauntiness, grace, fine bearing; generosity
garbo•so -sa *adj* jaunty, graceful, spruce, sprightly; generous
gardu•ño -ña *mf* (archaic) sneak thief || *f* stone marten, beech marten
garete *m* — **al garete** (naut) adrift
garfa *f* claw
garfio *m* hook, gaff
gargajear *intr* to cough up phlegm, hawk
gargajo *m* phlegm
garganta *f* throat; (*de un río, una vasija, etc.*) neck, throat; (*del pie*) instep; (*entre montañas*) ravine, gorge; (*del arado*) sheath; (*de una polea*) groove; (archit) shaft; **tener buena garganta** to have a good voice
gargantear *intr* to warble
gargantilla *f* necklace
gárgara *f* gargling; **gárgaras** (*líquido*) gargle; **hacer gárgaras** to gargle
gargarear *intr* to gargle
gargarismo *m* gargling; (*líquido*) gargle
gargarizar §60 *intr* to gargle
gárgola *f* gargoyle
garguero *m* gullet; (*caña del pulmón*) windpipe
garita *f* sentry box; porter's lodge; (*de una fortificación*) watchtower; railroad-crossing box; privy (*with one seat*); **garita de centinela** sentry box; **garita de señales** (rr) signal tower
garito *m* gambling den
garlito *m* fish trap; trap, snare
garlopa *f* jack plane, trying plane
garnar *intr* to drizzle

garra *f* claw, talon; catch, hook; **caer en las garras de** to fall into the clutches of
garrafa *f* carafe, decanter; **garrafa corchera** demijohn
garrafal *adj* awful, terrible
garrafiñar *tr* to snatch
garrafón *m* carboy, demijohn
garramar *tr* to snitch
garranchuelo *m* crab grass
garrapata *f* cattle tick, sheep tick; (mil) disabled horse; (Chile) little runt; (Mex) slut
garrapatear *intr* to scrawl, scribble
garrapato *m* pothook, scrawl; **garrapatos** scrawl
garri•do -da *adj* handsome, elegant
garroba *f* carob bean
garrocha *f* goad; (sport) pole
garrotazo *m* blow with a club
garrote *m* club, cudgel; garrote (*method of execution; iron collar used for such execution*); (Mex) brake; **dar garrote a** to garrote
garrote•ro -ra *adj* (Chile) stingy || *m* (Mex) brakeman
garrotillo *m* croup
garrucha *f* pulley, sheave
gárru•lo -la *adj* chirping; (*hablador*) garrulous; (*arroyo*) babbling; (*viento*) rustling
garúa drizzle
garuar **§21** *intr* to drizzle
garulla *f* mob, rabble
garza *f* heron; **garza real** gray heron
gar•zo -za *adj* blue || *f* see **garza**
garzón *m* boy, youth; suitor; woman chaser
gas *m* gas; **gas de alumbrado** illuminating gas; **gas exhilarante** or **hilarante** laughing gas; **gas lacrimógeno** tear gas; **gas mostaza** mustard gas
gasa *f* gauze, chiffon; (*tira de gasa negra con que se rodea el sombrero en señal de luto*) hatband
Gascuña *f* Gascony
gasear *tr* to gas
gaseo•so -sa *adj* gaseous || *f* soda water, carbonated water
gasificar **§73** *tr* to gasify; exalt, elate || *ref* to gasify
gasista *m* gas fitter; (Chile) gasworker
gasoducto *m* gas pipe line
gasógeno *m* gas generator, gas producer; mixture of benzine and alcohol used for lighting and cleaning
gas-oil *m* diesel oil
gasolina *f* gasoline
gasolinera *f* motor boat; gas station, filling station
gasómetro *m* gasholder, gas tank
gastadero *m* waste
gasta•do -da *adj* worn-out; used up; spent; (*chiste*) crummy, corny
gasta•dor -dora *adj* & *mf* spendthrift || *m* convict; (mil) sapper, pioneer
gastadura *f* worn spot
gastar *tr* (*dinero, tiempo*) to spend; (*en cosas inútiles*) waste; (*echar a perder con el uso*) wear out; (*consumir*) use up; (*p.ej., una barba*) wear; (*un coche*) keep; **gastarlas** to act, behave || *intr* to spend || *ref* to wear; wear out; become used up; waste away
gasto *m* cost, expense; wear; **gastos de conservación** or **de entretenimiento** upkeep; **gastos de explotación** operating expenses; **gastos menudos** petty expenses; **hacer el gasto** to do most of the talking; to be the subject of conversation; **hacer frente a los gastos** to meet expenses; **meterse en gastos con** to go to the expense of
gasto•so -sa *adj* wasteful, extravagant
gástri•co -ca *adj* gastric
gastronomía *f* gastronomy
gastróno•mo -ma *mf* gourmet
gata *f* she-cat; low-hanging cloud; Madrid woman; (Mex) maid, servant girl; **a gatas** on all fours, on hands and knees
gatada *f* catty act
gatatumba *f* faked attention, fake emotion, faked pain
gatazo *m* gyp
gatea•do -da *adj* catlike; grained, striped || *m* crawling, climbing; scratching, clawing
gatear *tr* to scratch, claw; snitch || *intr* to crawl, climb
gatera *f* cathole; (naut) hawsehole
gatería *f* cats; gang of toughs; fake humility
gate•ro -ra *adj* full of cats || *mf* cat lover || *f* see **gatera**
gates•co -ca *adj* catlike, feline
gatillo *m* (*de arma de fuego*) trigger; little pickpocket
gato *m* cat; tomcat; (*instrumento para levantar pesos*) jack, lifting jack; sly fellow; sneak thief; native of Madrid; **gato montés** wildcat; **gato rodante** dolly; **vender gato por liebre** to gyp, cheat
gatopardo *m* cheetah
gauchada *f* (SAm) sly trick; (SAm) good turn
gauchaje *m* (SAm) gathering of Gauchos
gauches•co -ca *adj* Gaucho
gau•cho -cha *adj* (SAm) Gaucho; (Arg, Chile) sly, crafty || *m* (SAm) Gaucho; (SAm) good horseman || *m* (Arg) mannish woman; (Arg) loose woman
gaulteria *f* wintergreen
gaveta *f* drawer, till
gavia *f* ditch, drain; (*ave*) gull; (min) gang of basket passers; (naut) topsail
gavilán *m* sparrow hawk; (*de la pluma*) nib; (*en la escritura*) hair stroke; ingrowing nail
gavilla *f* sheaf, bundle; gang
gaviota *f* sea gull
gavota *f* gavotte
gaya *f* colored stripe; (*ave*) magpie
gayar *tr* to trim with colored stripes
ga•yo -ya *adj* cheerful, bright, showy || *m* (orn) jay || *f* see **gaya**
gayola *f* cage; jail
gayomba *f* Spanish broom
gazapa *f* lie
gazapatón *m* blunder, slip
gazapera *f* rabbit warren; gang, gang of thugs; brawl, row

gazapo *m* young rabbit; sly fellow; slip, boner, blunder; (*de actor*) fluff
gazmiar *tr* (*oliendo*) to sniff; (*comiendo*) nibble || *ref* to complain
gazmoñada *f* or **gazmoñería** *f* prudishness, priggishness
gazmoñe•ro -ra or **gazmo•ño -ña** *adj* prudish, priggish, strait-laced, demure || *mf* prude, prig
gaznápiro *m* gawk, boob, bumpkin
gaznate *m* gullet; (Mex) fritter
gazpacho *m* cold vegetable soup; (Hond) leftovers
gazuza *f* hunger
Gedeón *m* Gideon
gehena *m* Gehenna
géiser *m* geyser
gel *m* gel
gelatina *f* gelatine
gema *f* gem; (bot) bud
geme•lo -la *adj & mf* twin; **gemelos** twins; binoculars; cuff links; **gemelos de campo** field glasses; **gemelos de teatro** opera glasses || **Gemelos** *mpl* (astr) Gemini
gemido *m* moan, groan; wail, whine; howl, roar
Géminis *m* (astr) Gemini
gemiquear *intr* (Chile) to whine
gemir **§50** *intr* to moan, groan; wail, whine; howl, roar
gen *m* gene
genciana *f* gentian
gendarme *m* policeman
genealogía *f* genealogy
generación *f* generation
genera•dor -dora *adj* generating || *m* generator
general *adj* general; common, usual; **en general** or **por lo general** in general || *m* general; **capitán general de ejército** five-star general; **general de brigada** brigadier, brigadier general; **general de división** major general || **generales** *fpl* general information, personal data
generala *f* general's wife; call to arms
generalato *m* generalship
generalidad *f* generality; majority; **la generalidad de** the general run of
generalísimo *m* generalissimo
generalizar **§60** *tr & intr* to generalize || *ref* to become generalized
generar *tr* to generate
genéri•co -ca *adj* generic; (*artículo*) indefinite; (*nombre*) common; showing gender
género *m* kind, sort; way, manner; cloth, material; (biol, log) genus; (gram) gender; **de género** genre; **género chico** one-act play, one-act operetta; **género de punto** knit goods, knitwear; **género humano** humankind; **género ínfimo** light vaudeville; **género novelístico** fiction; **género picaresco** burlesque; **géneros** goods, merchandise, material; **géneros de pieza** yard goods; **géneros para vestidos** dress goods
genero•so -sa *adj* generous; highborn; noble, magnanimous; (*vino*) rich, full
géne•sis *f* (*pl* **-sis**) genesis || **el Génesis** (Bib) Genesis
genéti•co -ca *adj* genetic || *f* genetics
genial *adj* inspired, geniuslike; pleasant, agreeable; temperamental
geniazo *m* fiery temper
genio *m* (*índole, carácter*) temperament, disposition; (*don altísimo de invención; persona que lo posee; espíritu tutelar, deidad pagana*) genius; fire, spirit
genital *adj* genital || **genitales** *mpl* genitals
geniti•vo -va *adj* genitive
genitourina•rio -ria *adj* genitourinary
genocida *adj* genocidal || *mf* genocide
genocidio *m* genocide
Génova *f* Genoa
geno•vés -vesa *adj & mf* Genoese
gente *f* people; (*parentela, familia*) folks; race, nation; troops; **gente baja** lower classes, rabble; **gente bien** nice people; **gente de bien** decent people; **gente de capa parda** country people; **gente de coleta** bullfighters; **gente de color** colored people; **gente de la cuchilla** butchers; **genta de la vida airada** bullies; underworld; **gente del bronce** bright, lively people; **gente del rey** convicts; **gente de mal vivir** toughs, underworld; **gente de mar** seafaring people; **gente de paz** (*palabras con las cuales se contesta al que pregunta ¿quién?*) friend; **gente de pluma** (coll) clerks; **gente de su majestad** convicts; **gente de trato** tradespeople; **gente forzada** convicts; **gente menuda** small fry; common people
gentecilla *f* mob, rabble
gentil *adj* heathen, gentile; elegant, genteel; noble || *mf* heathen, pagan
gentileza *f* elegance, gentility, courtesy; gallantry; show, splendor; (*hidalguía*) nobility
gentilhombre *m* (*pl* **gentileshombres**) gentleman; messenger to the king; my good man; **gentilhombre de cámara** gentleman in waiting
gentili•cio -cia *adj* national; family; (gram) gentile
gentilidad *f* heathendom
gentío *m* crowd, mob
gentualla or **gentuza** *f* rabble, riffraff
genui•no -na *adj* genuine
geofísi•co -ca *adj* geophysical || *mf* geophysicist || *f* geophysics
geografía *f* geography
geográfi•co -ca *adj* geographic(al)
geógra•fo -fa *mf* geographer
geología *f* geology
geológi•co -ca *adj* geologic(al)
geólo•go -ga *mf* geologist
geómetra *mf* geometrician
geometría *f* geometry; **geometría del espacio** solid geometry
geométri•co -ca *adj* geometric(al)
geopolíti•co -ca *adj* geopolitical || *f* geopolitics
geranio *m* geranium
gerencia *f* management; manager's office
gerente *m* manager, director; **gerente de**

publicidad advertising manager; **gerente de ventas** sales manager
geriatría *f* geriatry
geriatra *adj* geriatrical || *mf* geriatrician
geriátri•co -ca *adj* geriatrical
germanía *f* gypsy slang, cant of thieves
germanizar **§60** *tr* to Germanize
germen *m* germ; **germen plasma** germ plasm
germicida *adj* germicidal || *m* germicide
germinal *adj* germ; germinal
germinar *intr* to germinate
gerontología *f* gerontology
gerundio *m* gerund; present participle; bombastic writer or speaker
gestación *f* gestation
gestear *intr* to make faces
gesticular *intr* to make a face, to make faces; (*hacer ademanes*) to gesticulate
gestión *f* step, measure; management; action, proceeding, negotiation
gestionar *tr* to promote, pursue; manage; negotiate
gesto *m* face; wry face, grimace; look, appearance; (*movimiento, ademán*) gesture
ges•tor -tora *adj* managing || *m* manager
gestu•do -da *adj* cross-looking
ghetto *m* ghetto
giba *f* hump; annoyance
giga *f* jig
giganta *f* giantess
gigante *adj* giant || *m* giant; (*en las procesiones*) giant figure
gigantes•co -ca *adj* gigantic
gigantez *f* giant size
gigantilla *f* large-headed masked figure; little fat woman
gigan•tón -tona *mf* huge giant || *m* giant figure
gigote *m* chopped-meat stew; **hacer gigote** to chop up
gilí *adj* foolish, stupid
gimnasia *f* gymnastics; **gimnasia sueca** Swedish movements, setting-up exercises
gimnasio *m* gymnasium; secondary school, academy
gimnasta *mf* gymnast
gimnásti•co -ca *adj* gymnastic || *f* gymnastics
gimotear *intr* to whine
gimoteo *m* whining
ginebra *f* gin; (*de voces*) buzz, din; confusion, disorder || **Ginebra** *f* Geneva
ginebri•no -na *adj* & *mf* Genevan
ginecología *f* gynecology
ginecológi•co -ca *adj* gynecologic(al)
ginecólo•go -ga *mf* gynecologist
ginesta *f* Spanish broom
gira *f* var of **jira**
gira•do -da *mf* drawee
gira•dor -dora *mf* drawer
giralda *f* weathercock (*in the form of person or animal*)
girándula *f* girandole
girar *tr* (*una visita*) to pay; (com) to draw || *intr* to turn; rotate, gyrate; trade; (com) to draw
girasol *m* sunflower, sycophant
girato•rio -ria *adj* revolving || *f* revolving bookcase
gi•ro -ra *adj* (Guat) drunk; (Mex) cocky || *m* turn; rotation; revolution; course, trend, turn; turn of phrase; boast, threat; gash, slash; line of business; trade; (com) draft; **giro a la vista** sight draft; **giro postal** money order || *f* see **gira**
giroflé *m* clove
giroscopio *m* gyroscope
gis *m* (Col) slate pencil
gitana *f* gypsy woman, gypsy girl
gitanada *f* gypsy trick; fawning, flattery
gitanería *f* band of gypsies; gypsy life; fawning, flattery
gitanes•co -ca *adj* gypsyish
gita•no -na *adj* gypsy; flattering; sly, tricky || *mf* gypsy || *m* Gypsy (*language*) || *f* see **gitana**
glaciación *f* freezing
glacial *adj* glacial; (*zona*) frigid; (fig) cold, indifferent
glaciar *m* glacier
glándula *f* gland; **glándula cerrada** ductless gland
glasé *m* glacé silk
glasea•do -da *adj* glossy, shiny
glicerina *f* glycerin
global *adj* total; global, world-wide
globo *m* globe; (*aparato que, lleno de un gas, se eleva en el aire*) balloon; (*bomba de lámpara*) globe, lamp shade; **globo de aire** (aut) air bag; **globo del ojo** eyeball; **globo sonda** trial balloon; **lanzar un globo sonda** (fig) to send up a trial balloon
glóbulo *m* globule; (physiol) corpuscle; **glóbulo rojo** red cell
gloria *f* glory; **ganar la gloria** to go to glory; **oler a gloria** to smell heavenly; **saber a gloria** to taste heavenly
gloriar **§77** *tr* to glorify || *intr* to recite the rosary || *ref* to glory
glorieta *f* arbor, bower, summerhouse; public square; traffic circle
glorificar **§73** *tr* to glorify || *ref* to glory
glorio•so -sa *adj* glorious; boastful
glosa *f* gloss
glosa•dor -dora *adj* commenting || *mf* commentator
glosar *tr* to gloss; audit; (Col) to scold || *intr* to find fault
glosario *m* glossary
glóti•co -ca *adj* glottal
glo•tón -tona *adj* gluttonous || *mf* glutton
glotonería *f* gluttony
glucosa *f* glucose
gluglú *m* (*del agua*) gurgle, glug; (*del pavo*) gobble; **hacer gluglú** to gurgle, to glug
gluglutear *intr* to gobble
gnomo *m* gnome
gob. *abbr* **gobierno**
gobernación *f* governing; government; department of the interior; (Arg) territory
gobernad•dor -dora *adj* governing || *m* governor
gobernalle *m* rudder, helm

gobernante *adj* governing || *mf* ruler || *m* self-appointed head
gobernar §2 *tr* to govern; guide, direct; control, rule; (*un buque*) steer || *intr* to govern; steer
goberno•so -sa *adj* orderly
gobierno *m* government; governor's office, governorship; management; control, rule; guidance; (*de un buque*) navigability; **de buen gobierno** (*buque*) navigable; **gobierno de monigotes** puppet government; **gobierno doméstico** housekeeping; **gobierno exilado** government in exile; **para su gobierno** for your guidance; **servir de gobierno** to serve as a guide
goce *m* enjoyment
go•do -da *adj* Gothic || *mf* Goth; Spanish noble; (Arg, Chile) Spaniard
gofio *m* roasted corn meal
gol *m* goal
gola *f* gullet
goldre *m* quiver
goleta *f* schooner
golf *m* golf
golfán *m* white water lily
golfista *mf* golfer
gol•fo -fa *mf* ragamuffin || *m* gulf; open sea; **golfo de Méjico** Gulf of Mexico; **golfo de Vizcaya** Bay of Biscay
Gólgota, el (Bib) Golgotha
golilla *f* gorget, ruff; magistrate's collar; pipe flange; (*de los caños de barro*) collar, sleeve; (*del gallo*) erectile bristles
golondrina *f* swallow; **empresa golondrina** fly-by-night outfit
golosina *f* delicacy, tidbit; eagerness, appetite; trifle
golosinear *intr* to go around eating candy
golo•so -sa *adj* sweet-toothed; (*glotón*) gluttonous; (*apetitoso*) tasty
golpe *m* blow, stroke, hit; bump, bruise; heartbeat; crowd, throng, flock; (*del bolsillo*) flap; (*pestillo*) bolt, latch; (*de licor*) shot; surprise, wonder; (*infortunio*) blow; witticism; **dar golpe** to make a hit; **de golpe** all at once, suddenly; **de golpe y porrazo** slambang; **de un golpe** at one stroke; **golpe de ariete** water hammer; **golpe de calor** heatstroke; **golpe de estado** coup d'état; **golpe de fortuna** stroke of fortune; **golpe de gracia** coup de grâce; **golpe de mano** surprise attack; **golpe de mar** surge; **golpe de ojo** glance; **golpe de teatro** dramatic turn of events; **golpe de tos** fit of coughing; **golpe de vista** glance, look; view; **golpe en vago** miss, flop; **golpe mortal** deathblow; **no dar golpe** to not raise a hand, not do a stroke of work
golpear *tr* to strike, hit, beat; bump, bruise || *intr* to beat, strike; (*el reloj*) tick; (*el motor de combustión interna*) knock
golpete *m* door catch, window catch
golpetear *tr & intr* to beat; rattle
golpismo *m* government by coup d'état
gollería *f* delicacy, dainty; **pedir gollerías** to ask for too much
gollete *m* throat, neck; (*de botella*) neck
goma *f* gum, rubber; (*tira de goma elástica*) rubber band; (*neumático*) tire; **goma arábiga** gum arabic; **goma de borrar** eraser, rubber; **goma de mascar** chewing gum; **goma espumosa** foam rubber; **goma laca** shellac
gomecillo *m* blind man's guide
gomia *f* bugaboo; waster; glutton
gomo•so -sa *adj* gum; gummy || *m* dude, dandy
góndola *f* gondola
gondolero *m* gondolier
gongo *m* gong
gonorrea *f* gonorrhea
gordal *adj* large-size
gordia•no -na *adj* Gordian
gordi•flón -flona or **gordin•flón -flona** *adj* chubby, pudgy, fatty || *mf* fatty
gor•do -da *adj* fat, plump; fatty, greasy; coarse; big, large; whopping big; (*agua*) hard || *m* fat, suet; first prize (*in lottery*) || **gordo** *adv* — **hablar gordo** to talk big
gordura *f* fatness, plumpness, stoutness, corpulence; fat, grease
gorgojo *m* grub, weevil; dwarf, runt; **gorgojo del algodón** boll weevil
gorgojo•so -sa *adj* grubby
gorgón *m* (Col) concrete
gorgonear *intr* (*el pavo*) to gobble
gorgoritear *intr* to trill
gorgorito *m* trill
gorgotear *intr* to burble, gurgle
gorgotero *m* peddler, hawker
gorigori *m* lugubrious funeral chant
gorila *f* gorilla; (coll) thug; strong-arm man
gorjear *intr* to warble, trill || *ref* (*el niño*) to gurgle
gorra *f* cap; bumming, sponging; **andar de gorra** to sponge; **colarse de gorra** (coll) to crash the gate; **gorra de visera** cap; **vivir de gorra** to live on other people
gorrada *f* tipping the hat
gorrear *intr* (Ecuad) to sponge
gorretada *f* tipping the hat
gorrión *m* sparrow; **gorrión triguero** bunting
gorrista *adj* sponging || *mf* sponger
gorro *m* cap, bonnet; baby's bonnet; **gorro de dormir** nightcap
go•rrón -rrona *adj* sponging || *mf* sponger || *m* pivot; journal, gudgeon
gota *f* drop; (pathol) gout; **gotas** touch of rum or brandy in coffee; **sudar la gota gorda** to work one's head off
gotear *intr* to drip, dribble; (*llover a gotas espaciadas*) sprinkle
gotera *f* drip, dripping; mark left by dripping; (*en el techo*) leak; (*adorno de una cama*) valance; **estar lleno de goteras** to be full of aches and pains; **es una gotera** it's a constant drain; **goteras** aches, pains; (Col) environs, outskirts
góti•co -ca *adj* Gothic; noble, illustrious || *m* Gothic
goto•so -sa *adj* gouty || *mf* gout sufferer
gozar §60 *tr* (*poseer*) to enjoy || *intr* to enjoy oneself; **gozar de** (*poseer*) to enjoy || *ref* to enjoy oneself; rejoice

gozne *m* hinge
gozo *m* joy, enjoyment; **no caber en sí de gozo** to be beside oneself with joy; **saltar de gozo** to leap with joy
gozo•so -sa *adj* joyful; **gozoso con** or **de** joyful over
gozque *m* or **gozquejo** *m* little yapping dog
grabación *f* (*de disco*) recording; **grabación sobre cinta** tape recording
grabado *m* engraving; print, cut, picture; (*de disco*) recording; **grabado en madera** wood engraving, woodcut; **grabado fuera de texto** inset, insert
graba•dor -dora *adj* recording || *mf* engraver || *f* recorder; **grabadora de cinta** tape recorder
grabador-reproductor *m* cassette recorder
grabadura *f* engraving
grabar *tr* to engrave; (*un sonido, una canción, un disco, etc.*) record; **grabar en** or **sobre cinta** to tape-record || *ref* to become engraved
gracejada *f* (CAm, Mex) cheap comedy, clownishness
gracejar *intr* to be engaging, witty; joke
gracejo *m* lightness, winsome manner, charm; (CAm, Mex) clown
gracia *f* witticism, witty remark, joke; grace; gracefulness; favor; pardon; (*de un chiste*) point; name; **caer en gracia a** to be pleasing to; **de gracia** gratis; **decir dos gracias a** to tell someone a thing or two; **en gracia a** because of; **gracia de Dios** daily bread; air and sunshine; **gracias** thanks; **¡gracias!** thanks!; **gracias a** thanks to; **¡gracias a Dios!** thank heavens!; **hacer gracia** to be pleasing; **hacer gracia de algo a uno** to exempt or free someone from something; **hacerle a uno gracia** to strike someone as funny; **¡linda gracia!** nonsense!; **tener gracia** to be funny, be surprising
graciable *adj* kind, gracious; easy to grant
grácil *adj* thin, small, slender
gracio•so -sa *adj* (*que tiene donaire, gracia*) graceful; (*afable, fino*) gracious; (*agudo, chistoso*) funny, witty; (*que se da de balde*) free, gratis || *mf* comic || *m* gracioso (*gay, comic character in Spanish comedy*)
grada *f* step, stair; row of seats; grandstand; altar step; (agr) harrow; (*plano inclinado sobre el cual se construyen los barcos*) slip; **gradas** stone steps; (Chile, Peru) atrium; **gradas al aire libre** bleachers
gradar *tr* (agr) to harrow
gradería *f* stone steps; row of seats; bleachers; **gradería cubierta** grandstand
gradiente *m* (phys) gradient || *f* slope, gradient
grado *m* step; grade; degree; (*título que se da en las universidades*) degree; (*sección en las escuelas*) grade, form, class; (mil) rank; **de buen grado** willingly; **de grado en grado** by degrees; **de grado o por fuerza** willy-nilly; **de mal grado** unwillingly; **en sumo grado** to a great extent; **mal de mi grado** unwillingly, against my wishes
graduación *f* graduation; (*de las bebidas espirituosas*) strength; (mil) rank
gradual *adj* gradual
graduan•do -da *mf* (*persona próxima a graduarse en la universidad*) graduate (*candidate for a degree*)
graduar §21 *tr* to graduate, grade; (*un grifo, una válvula, etc.*) regulate; appraise, estimate || *ref* to graduate
grafía *f* graph
gráfi•co -ca *adj* graphic(al); printing; illustrated; picture, camera || *m* diagram || *f* graph
grafito *m* graphite
grafospasmo *m* writer's cramp
gragea *f* colored candy; sugar-coated pill
grajear *intr* (*los cuervos*) to caw; (*los niños*) gurgle
grajien•to -ta *adj* foul-smelling
gra•jo -ja *mf* rook, crow; chatterbox || *m* body odor
gral. *abbr* **general**
gramática *f* grammar; **gramática parda** shrewdness, mother wit
gramatical *adj* grammatical
gramáti•co -ca *adj* grammatical || *mf* grammarian || *f* see **gramática**
gramil *m* marking gauge, gauge
gramo *m* gram
gramófono *m* gramophone
gramola *f* console phonograph; portable phonograph
gran *adj* apocopated form of **grande,** used only before nouns of both genders in the singular
grana *f* seed; seeding; seeding time; red; **dar en grana** to go to seed
granada *f* pomegranate; (*proyectil explosivo*) grenade; **granada de mano** hand grenade; **granada de metralla** shrapnel; **granada extintora** fire extinguisher, fire grenade
granadero *m* grenadier
granadilla *f* passionflower
granadina *f* grenadine
grana•do -da *adj* choice, select; mature, expert || *m* pomegranate; **granado blanco** rose of Sharon || *f* see **granada**
granalla *f* filings
granangular *adj* wide-angle
granate *m adj invar & m* garnet
Gran Bretaña, la Great Britain
grande *adj* big, large; great || *m* grandee
grandeza *f* bigness, largeness; greatness; (*tamaño*) size; (*magnificencia*) grandeur; grandees; grandeeship
grandi•llón -llona *adj* oversize, overgrown
grandio•so -sa *adj* grandiose, grand
grandor *m* size
granea•do -da *adj* spattered; (*fuego*) heavy and continuous
granear *tr* to sow; (*la pólvora; una piedra litográfica*) grain; stipple
granel — a granel in bulk, loose; at random; lavishly
granelar *tr* (*el cuero*) to grain
granero *m* granary
granete *m* center punch

graníſu•go -ga *adj* hail-dispersing
granito *m* granite
granizada *f* hailstorm; (Arg, Chile) iced drink
granizar **§60** *tr* (*p.ej., golpes*) to hail; sprinkle || *intr* to hail
granizo *m* hail
granja *f* farm, grange; dairy; country place
granjear *tr* to earn, gain; win, win over || *ref* to win, win over
granjería *f* husbandry; gain, profit
granje•ro -ra *mf* farmer; merchant, trader
grano *m* grain; (*baya*) berry; (*baya de la uva*) grape; (*tumorcillo en la piel*) pimple; (*peso*) grain; **grano de belleza** beauty spot; **grano de café** coffee bean; **granos** (*fruto de los cereales*) grain; **ir al grano** to come to the point
granuja *m* scoundrel; (*muchacho vagabundo*) waif || *f* loose grape; grapeseed
granujo *m* pimple
granular *adj* granular; pimply || *tr & ref* to granulate
gránulo *m* granule
grapa *f* clamp, clip, staple
grasa *f* fat, grease; (*polvo*) pounce; (Mex) shoe polish; **grasa de ballena** blubber; **grasas** slag
grasien•to -ta *adj* greasy
grasilla *f* pounce
gra•so -sa *adj* fatty, greasy || *m* fattiness, greasiness || *f* see **grasa**
grasones *mpl* wheat porridge
graso•so -sa *adj* greasy; (pathol) fatty
grata *f* wire brush; (*carta*) favor
gratificar **§73** *tr* to gratify; reward, recompense; tip, fee
gratín *m* — **al gratín** au gratin
gratis *adv* gratis
gratisda•to -ta *adj* free, gratis
gratitud *f* gratitude
gra•to -ta *adj* pleasing; free; (Bol, Chile) grateful || *f* see **grata**
gratuidad *f* cost exemption; exemption from fees
gratui•to -ta *adj* gratuitous; free, gratis
grava *f* gravel; crushed stone
gravamen *m* burden, obligation; encumbrance, lien; assessment
gravar *tr* to burden, encumber; assess || *ref* to get worse
grave *adj* grave, serious, solemn; hard, difficult; (*que pesa*) heavy; (*sonido*) grave, deep, low; (*música*) majestic, noble; (*negocio*) important; (*enfermedad*) serious; (*acento*) grave; paroxytone
gravedad *f* gravity; seriousness; **de gravedad** seriously; gravely; **gravedad nula** weightlessness, zero gravity
gravedo•so -sa *adj* heavy, pompous
gravidez *f* pregnancy
grávi•do -da *adj* pregnant
gravitación *f* gravitation
gravitar *intr* to gravitate; **gravitar sobre** to weigh down on
gravo•so -sa *adj* burdensome, onerous, costly; boring, tiresome
graznar *intr* to caw, croak; cackle; (*al cantar*) (fig) cackle
graznido *m* caw, croak; cackle; (*canto que disuena mucho*) (fig) cackle
Grecia *f* Greece
grecia•no -na *adj* Grecian
gre•co -ca *adj & mf* Greek
greda *f* clay, fuller's earth
grega•rio -ria *adj* (*que vive confundido con otros*) gregarious; slavish, servile
gregoria•no -na *adj* Gregorian
gremial *adj* guild; trade-union, union || *m* guildsman; union member
gremio *m* guild, corporation; trade union, union; association, society
greña *f* confusion, entanglement; (*de cabello*) shock, tangled mop; **andar a la greña** to get into a hot argument; (*dos mujeres*) to pull each other's hair
greñu•do -da *adj* bushy-headed, shock-headed
gres *m* sandstone; stoneware
gresca *f* tumult, uproar; row, quarrel
grey *f* (*de ganado menor*) flock; group, party; nation, people; (*de fieles*) flock, congregation
grie•go -ga *adj* Greek || *mf* Greek || *m* (*idioma*) Greek; **hablar en griego** to not make sense
grieta *f* crack, crevice, chink; (*en la piel*) chap
grieta•do -da *adj* crackled || *m* crackleware
grietar *ref* to crack, split; (*la piel*) become chapped
gri•fo -fa *adj* (*pelo*) kinky, tangled; (*letra*) script; (W-I) colored; (Mex) drunk; (Col) conceited || *mf* (W-I) person of color; (Mex) drunk || *m* faucet, spigot, tap, cock; (myth) griffin; (Peru) gas station, (Mex) marijuana || *f* (Mex) marijuana
grilla *f* female cricket; (rad) grid; (Col) fight, quarrel; (SAm) annoyance, bother; **¡ésa es grilla!** (coll) you expect me to believe that!
grillar *intr* (*el grillo*) to chirp || *ref* (*las semillas, bulbos, etc.*) to sprout
grillete *m* fetter, shackle
grillo *m* (*insecto*) cricket; (*brote tierno*) sprout, shoot; **grillos** fetters, shackles
grima *f* fright, horror; **dar grima** to grate on the nerves
grin•go -ga *mf* (disparaging) foreigner; (*anglosajón*) gringo || *m* gibberish; **hablar en gringo** to talk nonsense
griñón *m* (*toca de monja*) wimple; (*melocotón*) nectarine
gripe *f* grippe
gris *adj* gray; dull, gloomy || *m* gray; **hacer gris** (*el tiempo*) to be sharp, be brisk
grisáce•o -a *adj* grayish
gri•sú *m* (*pl* **-súes**) firedamp
grita *f* shouting; hubbub, uproar; **dar grita a** to hoot at
gritar *intr* to shout, cry out
gritería *f* shouting, outcry, uproar
grito *m* cry, shout; scream, shriek; **el último grito** the latest thing, all the rage; **poner el**

grito en el cielo to raise the roof, scream wildly
gro. *abbr* **género**
Groenlandia *f* Greenland
grosella *f* currant; **grosella silvestre** gooseberry
grosellero *m* currant bush; **grosellero silvestre** gooseberry bush
grosería *f* grossness, coarseness; churlishness, rudeness; stupidity; vulgarity
grose•ro -ra *adj* gross, coarse; churlish, rude; stupid; vulgar || *mf* churl, boor
grosor *m* thickness, bulk
grosura *f* fat, suet, tallow; meat diet; coarseness, vulgarity
grotes•co -ca *adj* grotesque
grúa *f* crane, derrick; **grúa de bote** (naut) davit; **grúa de auxilio** wrecking crane; **grúa de caballete** gantry crane
grúa-remolque *m* tow truck
grue•so -sa *adj* big, thick, bulky, heavy; coarse, ordinary; stout, fat; (*mar*) rough, heavy; **en grueso** in gross, in bulk || *f* (*doce docenas*) gross
grulla *f* (orn) crane
grumete *m* ship's boy, cabin boy
grumo *m* clot, curd; bunch, cluster
grumo•so -sa *adj* clotty, curdly
gruñido *m* (*de cerdo*) grunt; (*de perro cuando amenaza*) growl; (*de persona*) grumble; (*de puerta*) creak; grumble, scolding
gruñir §12 *intr* (*el cerdo*) to grunt; (*el perro*) growl; (*una persona*) grumble; (*una puerta*) creak
gru•ñón -ñona *adj* grumpy, grumbly || *mf* crosspatch
grupa *f* croup, rump
grupada *f* squall
grupal *adj* group
grupo *m* group; (mach & elec) unit
grupúsculo *m* splinter group
gruta *f* grotto
grutes•co -ca *adj & m* (fa) grotesque
Gruyère *m* Swiss cheese
gte. *abbr* **gerente**
guaca *f* (Bol, Peru) Indian tomb; hidden treasure
guacal *m* crate
guacama•yo -ya *adj* (P-R) flashy, sporty || *m* macaw
guachapear *tr* to splash with the feet; bungle, botch || *intr* to clank, clatter
guachinan•go -ga *adj* flattering, sly || *mf* (disparaging term used by Cubans) Mexican
gua•cho -cha *adj* (SAm) homeless, orphan; (SAm) odd, unmatched
guadal *m* bog, swamp; sand hill, dune
Guadalupe *f* Gaudeloupe
guadama•cí *m* (*pl* **-cíes**) embossed leather
guadaña *f* scythe
guadañadora *f* mowing machine
guadañar *tr* to cut with a scythe
guadarnés *m* harness room; harness man
guagua *f* trifle; (SAm) baby; (W-I) bus; (Col) paca
guagüita *f* (Cuba, P-R) station wagon
guajada *f* (Mex) nonsense, folly
guaje *adj* (Hond, Mex) foolish, stupid || *m* (Hond, Mex) calabash, gourd; (CAm) piece of junk
guaji•ro -ra *mf* (W-I) peasant, yokel
guajolote *m* turkey; (Mex) simpleton
gualda *f* (bot) weld, dyer's rocket
gual•do -da *adj* yellow || *f* see **gualda**
gualdrapa *f* housing, trappings; dirty rag hanging from clothes
gualdrapear *tr* to line up head to tail || *intr* (*las velas*) to flap
Gualterio *m* Walter
guanaco *m* (SAm) dope, simpleton; (SAm) tall lanky fellow; (zool) guanaco
guanajo *m* turkey; (W-I) boob, dunce
guano *m* palm tree; bird manure
guante *m* glove; **arrojar el guante** to throw down the gauntlet; **echar un guante** to pass the hat; **guantes** tip, fee; **recoger el guante** to take up the gauntlet; **salvo el guante** excuse my glove
guantelete *m* gauntlet
guantería *f* glove shop
guantón *m* box on the ear
guapear *intr* to bluster, swagger; dress to kill
guape•tón -tona *adj* handsome; flashy, sporty; bold, fearless || *m* bully, tough
guapeza *f* good looks; flashiness, sportiness; (coll) boldness, daring; bravado
gua•po -pa *adj* handsome, good-looking; flashy, sporty; bold, daring || *m* (*hombre pendenciero*) bully; gallant, lady's man
guapura *f* good looks
guarache *m* (Mex) leather sandal; (Mex) tire patch
guarapo *m* sugar-cane juice; fermented juice of sugar cane
guarda *mf* guard, custodian || *m* (Arg) trolley-car conductor; **guarda de la aduana** customhouse officer; **guarda forestal** forest ranger || *f* guard, custody; (*de la ley*) observance; (*de la espada*) guard; (*de la cerradura*) ward; (bb) flyleaf
guardabarrera *mf* (rr) gatekeeper
guardaba•rros *m* (*pl* **-rros**) fender, mudguard, dashboard
guardabosque *m* gamekeeper; forest ranger; shortstop
guardabrisa *m* windshield; (naut) glass candle shade
guardacantón *m* spur stone
guardacarril *m* (rr) railguard
guardacar•tas *m* (*pl* **-tas**) letter file
guardaco•ches *m* (*pl* **-ches**) car watcher
guardacos•tas *m* (*pl* **-tas**) revenue cutter, coast guard cutter; **guardacostas** *mpl* (*servicio*) coast guard
guarda•dor -dora *adj* guarding, protecting; mindful, observant; stingy || *m* guardian, keeper; observer
guardaespal•das *m* (*pl* **-das**) bodyguard
guardafango *m* fender, mudguard
guardafre•nos *m* (*pl* **-nos**) (rr) brakeman, flagman
guardafuego *m* fender, fireguard
guardagu•jas *m* (*pl* **-jas**) (rr) switchman

guardajo•yas *m* (*pl* **-yas**) jewel case
guardalado *m* railing, parapet
guardalmacén *m* warehouseman; (Cuba) country station master
guardamalleta *f* valance
guardameta *m* goalkeeper
guardamue•bles *m* (*pl* **-bles**) warehouse, furniture warehouse
guardanieve *m* snowshed
guardapelo *m* locket
guardapolvo *m* (*sobretodo ligero*) duster; (*resguardo para preservar del polvo*) cover, cloth; (*del reloj*) inner lid; (*sobre una puerta o ventana*) hood
guardapuerta *f* storm door
guardar *tr* to guard; watch over; protect; put away; show, observe; save, e.g., **¡Dios guarde a la Reina!** God save the Queen ‖ *intr* to keep, save; **¡guarda!** look out!, watch out! ‖ *ref* to be on one's guard; **guardarse de** to look out for, watch out for, guard against
guardarraya *f* (CAm, W-I) boundary line, property line
guardarropa *mf* keeper of the wardrobe ‖ *m* (*armario donde se guarda la ropa*) wardrobe; (*local destinado a la custodia de ropa en establecimientos públicos*) checkroom, cloakroom; check boy ‖ *f* check girl, hat girl
guardarropía *f* (theat) wardrobe
guardasilla *f* chair rail
guardaventana *f* storm window
guardavía *m* (rr) trackwalker, lineman
guardavida *m* lifeguard
guardavien•tos *m* (*pl* **-tos**) (*abrigo contra los vientos*) windbreak; (*mitra de chimenea*) chimney pot
guardavivo *m* bead, corner bead
guardería *f* guard, guardship; **guardería infantil** day nursery
guardesa *f* woman guard
guardia *m* guard, guardsman; **guardia civil** rural policeman; **guardia marina** midshipman, middy; **guardia urbano** policeman ‖ *f* (*cuerpo de hombres armados; manera de defenderse en la esgrima*) guard; (naut) watch; **de guardia** on duty; on guard; **guardia civil** rural police; **guardia de asalto** shock troops; **guardia de corps** (mil) bodyguard; **guardia de cuartillo** (naut) dogwatch; **guardia suiza** Swiss Guards
guar•dián -diana *mf* guardian ‖ *m* watchman
guardilla *f* attic; attic room
guardo•so -sa *adj* careful, neat, tidy; (*que ahorra mucho*) thrifty; (*mezquino*) stingy
guarecer §22 *tr* to take in, give shelter to; keep, preserve; (*a un enfermo*) treat ‖ *ref* to take refuge, take shelter
guarida *f* den, lair; shelter; haunt, hangout, hide-out
guarismo *m* cipher, figure
guarnecer §22 *tr* to trim, adorn; equip, provide; bind, edge; (*joyas*) set; stucco, plaster; (*frenos*) line; (*un cojinete*) bush; (*una plaza fuerte*) man, garrison; (culin) garnish
guarnición *f* trimming; equipping; binding, edging; (*de joyas*) setting; stuccoing, plastering; (*de la espada*) guard; (*de frenos*) lining; (*del émbolo*) packing; (*tropa que guarnece un lugar*) garrison; (culin) garnish; **guarniciones** fixtures, fittings; (*de la caballería*) harness
guarnicionar *tr* to garrison
guarnicionero *m* harness maker
guaro *m* (CAm) sugar-cane liquor
gua•rro -rra *mf* hog
guasa *f* heaviness, churlishness; joking, kidding
guasca *f* rawhide; whip; **dar guasca a** to whip, thrash
guasería *f* (SAm) coarseness, crudity; (Chile) timidity
gua•so -sa *adj* (SAm) coarse, crude, uncouth ‖ *mf* (Chile) peasant ‖ *f* see **guasa**
gua•són -sona *adj* heavy, churlish; funny, comical ‖ *mf* dullard, churl; joker, kidder
guata *f* wadding, padding; (Arg, Chile, Peru) belly, paunch; (*de una pared*) (Chile) bulging, warping; (Ecuad) boon companion; **echar guata** (Chile) to prosper
guatemalte•co -ca *adj* & *mf* Guatemalan
guáter *m* toilet, water closet
guau *m* (*ladrido del perro*) bowwow; (bot) woodbine, Virginia creeper; **guau guau** (*perro*) bowwow ‖ *interj* bowwow!
guay *interj* — **¡guay de mí!** (poet) woe is me!
guayaba *f* guava, guava apple
guayabo *m* guava tree; lie, trick
guayaco *m* lignum vitae
Guayana *f* Guyana
gubernamental *adj* governmental; (*defensor*) strong-government
gubernati•vo -va *adj* governmental
gubia *f* gouge
guedeja *f* shock of hair; lion's mane
guerra *f* war, warfare; billiards; **Gran guerra** Great War; **guerra a muerte** war to the death; **guerra bacteriana** or **bacteriológica** germ warfare; **guerra de guerrillas** guerrilla warfare; **guerra de las dos Rosas** War of the Roses; **guerra de los Cien Años** Hundred Years' War; **guerra del Transvaal** Boer War; **guerra de ondas** radio jamming; **guerra de Troya** Trojan War; **guerra fría** cold war; **Guerra Mundial** World War; **guerra nuclear** nuclear war; **guerra relámpago** blitzkrieg; **hacer la guerra** to wage war
guerrea•dor -dora *adj* warring ‖ *mf* warrior
guerrear *intr* to war, wage war, fight; struggle, resist
guerre•ro -ra *adj* war, warlike; warring; mischievous ‖ *mf* fighter ‖ *m* warrior, soldier, fighting man ‖ *f* tight-fitting military jacket

guerrilla *f* band of skirmishers; guerrilla band; guerrilla warfare
guerrillear *intr* to skirmish; wage guerrilla warfare
guerrillero *m* guerrilla
guía *mf* guide, leader; adviser || *m* (mil) guide || *f* guide; guidance; directory; (*del viajero*) guidebook; (*caballo*) leader; (*de la bicicleta*) handle bar; (*del bigote*) turned-up end; (*de la sierra*) fence; marker; shoot, sprout; (mach) guide; (rr) timetable; **guías** reins; **guía sonora** sound track; **guía telefónica** telephone directory; **guía turística** tourist guide
guiadera *f* (mach) guide
guiar §77 *tr* to guide, lead; (*un automóvil*) steer, drive; pilot; (*una planta, una vid*) train || *intr* to shoot, sprout || *ref*—**guiarse por** to be guided by, go by
guija *f* pebble; grass pea
guijarro *m* cobble, cobblestone
guije•ño -ña *adj* pebbly; hard-hearted
guijo *m* gravel
guijo•so -sa *adj* gravelly; pebbly
güila *f* (Mex) prostitute
guillame *m* rabbet plane
Guillermo *m* William
guillotina *f* guillotine; paper cutter
guillotinar *tr* to guillotine
guimbalete *m* pump handle
guinche *m* or **güinche** *m* (mach) crane
guinda *f* sour cherry
guindal *m* sour cherry tree
guindaleza *f* (naut) hawser
guindar *tr* to hoist, raise; win; (*ahorcar*) hang, string up
guindilla *m* policeman, cop; Guinea pepper
guindo *m* sour cherry tree
guindola *f* (naut) boatswain's chair; (naut) life buoy
guinea *f* (*moneda*) guinea
guineo *m* small banana
guinga *f* gingham
guiña *f* (Col, Ven) bad luck
guiñada *f* wink; (naut) yaw
guiñapo *m* rag, tatter; ragamuffin
guiñar *tr* (*el ojo*) to wink || *intr* to wink; (naut) to yaw || *ref* to wink at each other
guiño *m* wink; **hacer guiños a** to make eyes at; **hacerse guiños a** to make faces at each other
guión *m* banner, standard; cross (*carried before prelate in procession*); (*signo ortográfico*) hyphen; (*signo ortográfico largo*) dash; (mil) guidon; (mov & theat) scenario; (rad & telv) script; (mus) repeat sign; **guión de montaje** (mov) cutter's script; **guión de rodaje** (mov) shooting script
guionista *mf* (mov) scenarist; (mov) scriptwriter; (mov) subtitle writer
guirigay *m* gibberish; confusion, hubbub
guirindola *f* frill, jabot
guirlache *m* almond brittle, peanut brittle
guirnalda *f* garland, wreath
guisa *f* way, manner, wise; **a guisa de** in the manner of, like
guisado *m* stew, meat stew
guisante *m* pea; **guisante de olor** sweet pea
guisar *tr* to cook; stew; arrange, prepare || *intr* to cook
guiso *m* dish
guisote *m* hash
guita *f* twine; (coll) dough, money
guitarra *f* guitar
guitarrista *mf* guitarist
gui•tón -tona *mf* tramp, bum
gula *f* gluttony; gorging, guzzling
gulo•so -sa *adj* gluttonous; guzzling
gumía *f* Moorish poniard
gurrumi•no -na *adj* weak, puny || *m* henpecked husband || *f* uxoriousness
gusanear *intr* to swarm
gusanera *f* nest of worms; ruling passion
gusanien•to -ta *adj* wormy, grubby
gusanillo *m* small worm; twist stitch; (*de la barrena*) spur; **matar el gusanillo** to take a shot of liquor before breakfast
gusano *m* worm; **gusano de luz** glowworm; **gusano de seda** silk worm; **gusano de tierra** earthworm
gusano•so -sa *adj* wormy, grubby
gusarapo *m* waterworm, vinegar worm
gustación *f* tasting; taste
gustar *tr* to taste; try, sample; please, be pleasing to; like, e.g., **me gustan estas peras** I like these pears || *intr* to like e.g., **como Vd. guste** as you like; **gustar de** to like; like to
gustillo *m* slight taste, touch
gusto *m* taste; flavor; liking; caprice, whim; pleasure; **a gusto** as you like it; **con mucho gusto** with pleasure, gladly; **encontrarse a gusto** or **estar a gusto** to like it (*e.g., in the country*); **tanto gusto** so glad to meet you
gusto•so -sa *adj* tasty; agreeable, pleasant; ready, willing, glad
gutapercha *f* gutta-percha
gutural *adj* guttural

H

H, h (hache) *f* ninth letter of the Spanish alphabet
haba *f* bean, broad bean; (*simiente del café y el cacao*) bean; **ser habas contadas** to be a sure thing
Habana, La Havana

haber *m* salary, wages; credit, credit side; **haberes** property, wealth || *v* **§38** *tr* to have; get, get hold of || *v aux* to have, e.g., **lo he visto a menudo** I have seen it often; **haber de** + *inf* to be to + *inf,* e.g., **ha de llegar a mediodía** he is to arrive at noon || *v impers* there to be, e.g., **ha habido tres personas allí** there were three people there; **haber que** + *inf* to be necessary to + *inf;* **no hay de qué** you're welcome, don't mention it || *ref* to behave oneself; **habérselas con** to deal with; to have it out with

habichuela *f* kidney bean; **habichuela verde** string bean

hábil *adj* skillful, capable; (*día*) work

habilidad *f* skill, ability, capability; (*lo que se ejecuta con gracia*) feat; (*enredo, embuste*) scheme, trick

habilido•so -sa *adj* skillful

habilitación *f* qualification; backing, financing; equipping, outfitting; **habilitaciones** fixtures

habilitar *tr* to qualify; back, finance; equip, fit out; (*en un examen*) pass

habitabilidad *f* habitability; (aut) interior (space)

habitable *adj* inhabitable

habitación *f* habitation; (*edificio donde se habita*) house, home, dwelling; (*aposento de la casa o el hotel*) room; (*donde vive una especie vegetal o animal*) habitat

habitante *mf* (*de una casa*) dweller, occupant; (*de una población*) inhabitant

habitar *tr* to inhabit, live in; (*una casa, un piso*) occupy || *intr* to live

hábito *m* garment, dress; habit, custom; **ahorcar los hábitos** to doff the cassock, to leave the priesthood; to change jobs; **el hábito no hace al monje** clothes don't make the man

habitua•do -da *mf* habitué

habitual *adj* habitual; regular, usual

habituar **§21** *tr* to accustom || *ref* to become accustomed

habitud *f* relationship, connection; custom, habit

habla *f* speech; **al habla** speaking

hablada *f* talk, talking

habla•dor -dora *adj* talkative; gossipy || *mf* talker, chatterbox; gossip

habladuría *f* cut, sarcasm; **andar con habladurías** to go around gossiping

hablante *adj* speaking || *mf* speaker

hablar *tr* (*una lengua*) to speak, talk; (*disparates*) talk || *intr* to speak, talk; **es hablar por demás** it's wasted talk; **estar hablando** (*una pintura, una estatua*) to be almost alive; **hablar claro** to talk straight from the shoulder

hablilla *f* story, piece of gossip

hablista *mf* speaker, good speaker

hacede•ro -ra *adj* feasible, practicable

hacenda•do -da *adj* landed, property-owning || *mf* landholder, property owner; cattle rancher; plantation owner

hacendar **§2** *tr* (*el dominio de bienes raíces*) to pass on || *ref* to buy property in order to settle down

hacende•ro -ra *adj* thrifty

hacendista *m* economist, fiscal expert; man of independent means

hacendo•so -sa *adj* hard-working, thrifty

hacer **§39** *tr* (*crear, producir, formar*) to make; (*ejecutar, llevar a cabo*) do; (*un baúl*) pack; (*un papel*) play; (*un mandato*) give; (*un drama*) act, perform; pretend to be; (*una pregunta*) ask; **hace** ago, e.g., **hace un mes** a month ago; **hacer** + *inf* to have + *inf,* e.g., **le hice tomar un libro en la biblioteca** I had him get a book at the library; to make + *inf,* e.g., **el médico me hizo guardar cama** the doctor made me stay in bed; to have + *pp,* e.g., **hará construir una casa** he will have a house built; **hacer . . . que** to be . . . since, e.g., **hace un año que yo estuve aquí** it is a year since I was here; to be for. . . , e.g., **hace un año que estoy aquí** I have been here for a year; for expressions like **hacer frío** to be cold, see the noun || *intr* to act; **hacer a** to fit; **hacer al caso** (coll) to be to the purpose; **hacer como que** + *ind* to pretend to + *inf;* **hacer de** to act as, work as; **hacer por** to try to || *ref* to become, get to be, grow; **hacerse a** to become accustomed to; **hacerse a un lado** to step aside; **hacerse con** to make off with; **hacerse chiquito** to sing small; **hacérsele a uno difícil** to strike one as difficult; **hacerse viejo** to grow old; kill time

hacia *prep* toward; (*cierta hora o época*) about, near; **hacia abajo** downward; **hacia adelante** forward; **hacia arriba** upward; **hacia atrás** backward; the wrong way; **hacia dentro** inward; **hacia fuera** outward

hacienda *f* farmstead, landed estate, country property; property, possessions; ranch; (Arg) cattle, livestock; **hacienda pública** public finance, federal income; **haciendas** household chores

hacina *f* pile, heap; shock, stack

hacinar *tr* to pile, heap, stack

hacha *f* axe; (*hacha pequeña*) hatchet; torch, firebrand; four-wick wax candle; **hacha de armas** battleaxe

hachazo *m* blow with an axe

hachear *tr & intr* to hew, hack, or chop with an axe

hachero *m* torchbearer; (*candelero*) torch stand; (*leñador*) woodcutter

hachich *m* or **hachís** *m* hashish

hacho *m* torch; (*sitio elevado cerca de la costa*) beacon, beacon hill

hada *f* fairy; (*mujer que encanta por su belleza, gracia, etc.*) charmer; **hada madrina** fairy godmother

hadar *tr* (*determinar el hado*) to predestine, foreordain; (*pronosticar*) to foretell; (*encantar*) to charm, cast a spell on

hado *m* fate, destiny

haiga *m* (slang) flashy auto; (slang) sport

halagar **§44** *tr* (*lisonjear*) to flatter; (*demostrar cariño a*) cajole, fawn on; (*agradar*) gratify, please
halago *m* flattery; cajolery; gratification; **halagos** flattery, blandishments
halagüe•ño -ña *adj* flattering; fawning; gratifying, pleasing; bright, rosy, promising
halar *tr* (naut) to haul, pull
halcón *m* falcon
halconear *intr* (*la mujer*) to chase after men
halconería *f* falconry
halconero *m* falconer
halda *f* skirt; **poner haldas en cinta** to pull up one's skirts to run; roll up one's sleeves
halieto *m* fish hawk, osprey
hálito *m* breath; vapor; (poet) gentle breeze
halitosis *f* halitosis
halo *m* halo
haló *interj* (*teléfono*) hello!
halógeno *m* halogen
halterio *m* dumbbell
halterofilia *f* weight lifting
halterofilista *mf* weight lifter
haluro *m* halide
hallar *tr* to find; (*averiguar*) find out, discover || *ref* to find oneself; to be; **hallarse bien con** to be satisfied with; **hallárselo todo hecho** to never have to turn a hand; **no hallarse** to feel uncomfortable, not like it
hallazgo *m* (*cosa hallada*) find; (*acción de hallar*) finding, discovery; (*premio al que ha hallado una cosa perdida*) reward, finder's reward, e.g., **diez dólares de hallazgo** ten dollars reward
hallulla *f* bread baked on embers or hot stones; (Chile) fine bread
hamaca *f* hammock
hamamelina *f* witch hazel
hambre *f* hunger; (*escasez general de comestibles*) famine; **matar de hambre** to starve to death; **morir de hambre** to starve to death, die of starvation; **pasar hambre** to go hungry; **tener hambre** to be hungry
hambrear *tr & intr* to starve, famish
hambrien•to -ta *adj* hungry, starving
hambruna *f* (SAm) mad hunger; (Ecuad) starvation
hamburguesa *f* hamburger sandwich
hamo *m* fishhook
hampa *f* underworld life; denizens of the underworld
hampes•co -ca *adj* underworld
hampón *m* bully, tough
hangar *m* (aer) hangar
hara•gán -gana *adj* idling, loafing, lazy || *mf* idler, loafer
haraganear *intr* to idle, loaf, hang around
harapien•to -ta *adj* ragged, tattered
harapo *m* rag, tatter; **andar** or **estar hecho un harapo** (coll) to go around in rags
harapo•so -sa *adj* ragged, tattered
harén *m* harem
harina *f* (*especialmente del trigo*) flour; (*de cualquier grano*) meal; **estar metido en harina** to be deeply absorbed; to be fat and heavy; **harina de avena** oatmeal; **harina de maíz** corn meal; **ser harina de otro costal** to be a horse of another color
harine•ro -ra *adj* flour || *m* flour dealer; flour bin
harino•so -sa *adj* floury, mealy
harnear *tr* (Col, Chile) to sift
harnero *m* sieve
ha•rón -rona *adj* lazy || *mf* lazy loafer
harpillera *f* burlap, sackcloth
hartar *tr* to stuff, cram; satisfy, satiate; **tire**, bore; overwhelm, deluge || *intr* to have one's fill || *ref* to stuff; be satiated; tire, be bored
hartazgo *m* or **hartazón** *m* fill, bellyful; **darse un hartazgo** to eat one's fill; **darse un hartazgo de** to have or to get one's fill of
har•to -ta *adj* full, fed up; very much; **harto de** full of, fed up with, sick of || **harto** *adv* enough; very, quite
hartura *f* fill, satiety; full satisfaction; abundance
hasta *adv* even || *prep* until, till; to, as far as; down to, up to; as much as; **hasta ahora** up till now; **hasta aquí** so far; **hasta después** so long, good-by; **hasta la vista** or **hasta luego** so long, good-by; **hasta mañana** see you tomorrow; **hasta más no poder** to the utmost; **hasta no más** to the utmost; **hasta que** until, till
hastial *m* gable end; (*hombrón rústico*) bumpkin
hastiar **§77** *tr* to surfeit, sicken, cloy; (*fastidiar*) bother, annoy, bore
hastío *m* surfeit, loathing, disgust; bother, annoyance, boredom
hataca *f* large wooden ladle; (*cilindro para extender la masa*) rolling pin
hatajo *m* small herd, small flock; (*p.ej., de disparates*) lot, flock
hato *m* (*de ganado vacuno*) herd; (*de ovejas*) flock; (*de ropa*) pack, bundle; (*de gente*) clique, ring; (*de gente malvada*) gang; everyday outfit; (*de disparates*) flock, lot; cattle ranch; **liar el hato** to pack up, pack one's baggage; **revolver el hato** to stir up trouble
haya *f* beech tree; (*madera*) beech || **La Haya** The Hague
hayaca *f* (Ven) mince pie
hayo *m* (Col) coca; (Col) coca leaves (*mixed for chewing*)
hayuco *m* beechnut, mast
haz *m* (*pl* **haces**) bunch, bundle; (*de leña*) fagot; (*de mieses*) sheaf; (*de rayos*) beam, pencil; (*de soldados*) file || *f* (*pl* **haces**) face; (*de la tierra*) surface; (*de paño o tela*) right side; (*de un edificio*) façade, front; **a sobre haz** on the surface; **ser de dos haces** to be two-faced
hazaña *f* feat, exploit, deed
hazañería *f* fuss
hazañe•ro -ra *adj* fussy
hazaño•so -sa *adj* gallant, courageous
hazmerreír *m* laughingstock, butt
he *adv* behold, lo and behold; **he aquí** here is, here are; **he allí** there is, there are

hebilla *f* buckle
hebra *f* thread; fiber; (*en la madera*) grain; (*del discurso*) (fig) thread; **de una hebra** (Chile) all at once; **pegar la hebra** to strike up a conversation; to keep on talking
hebre•o -a *adj & mf* Hebrew || *m* (*idioma*) Hebrew
hebro•so -sa *adj* fibrous, stringy
hecatombe *f* hecatomb
hechicera *f* witch, sorceress; (*mujer que por su belleza cautiva*) enchantress
hechicería *f* witchcraft, sorcery, wizardry; (fig) fascination, charm
hechice•ro -ra *adj* bewitching, charming, enchanting; magic || *mf* sorcerer, magician; charmer, enchanter || *m* wizard, sorcerer || *f* see **hechicera**
hechizar §60 *tr* to bewitch, cast a spell on; (fig) to bewitch, charm, enchant || *intr* to practice sorcery; (fig) to be charming, enchant
hechi•zo -za *adj* fake, artificial; (*de quita y pon*) detachable; made, manufactured; (*producto*) local, home || *m* spell, charm; magic, sorcery; (fig) magic, sorcery, glamour; (fig) charmer; **hechizos** (*de una mujer*) charms
he•cho -cha *adj* accustomed; finished; turned into; (*traje*) ready-made; (*llegado a la edad adulta*) full-grown || *m* act, deed; fact; event; (*hazaña*) feat; **de hecho** in fact; **en hecho de verdad** as a matter of fact; **estar en el hecho de** to catch on to; **hecho consumado** fait accompli || **hecho** *interj* all right!, OK!
hechura *f* form, shape, cut, build; creation, creature; workmanship; (Chile) drink, treat; **hechuras** cost of making; **no tener hechura** to be impracticable
heder §51 *tr* to bore, annoy, tire || *intr* to stink, reek
hediondez *f* stench, stink
hedion•do -da *adj* stinking, smelly; annoying, boring; obscene, filthy, dirty || *m* bean trefoil; skunk
hedor *m* stench, stink
helada *f* freezing; (*escarcha*) frost; **helada blanca** hoarfrost
heladera *f* refrigerator; (Chile) ice-cream tray
heladería *f* ice-cream parlor
hela•do -da *adj* cold, icy; (*pasmado por el miedo, la sorpresa, etc.*) frozen; (*esquivo, indiferente*) cold, chilly; (*cubierto de azúcar*) (Ven) iced || *m* cold drink; (*manjar*) water ice; (*sorbete*) ice cream; **helado al corte** brick ice cream || *f* see **helada**
hela•dor -dora *adj* freezing || *f* ice-cream freezer
helar §2 *tr* to freeze; harden, congeal; dumbfound; discourage || *intr* to freeze || *ref* to freeze; harden, congeal, set; (*cubrirse de hielo*) to ice
helecho *m* fern
helléni•co -ca *adj* Hellenic
hele•no -na *adj* Hellenic || *mf* Hellene
helero *m* glacier
hélice *f* helix; (*de un buque*) screw, propeller; (*de un avión*) propeller
helicóptero *m* helicopter
helio *m* helium
heliotropo *m* heliotrope
helipuerto *m* heliport
hematíe *m* red cell
hembra *adj invar* (*animal, planta, herramienta*) female; weak, thin, delicate || *f* female; (*del corchete*) eye; (*tuerca*) nut; **hembra de terraja** (mach) die
hembraje *m* (SAm) females of a flock or herd
hembrilla *f* (mach) female part or piece; (*armella*) eyebolt
hemeroteca *f* periodical library
hemiciclo *m* (*semicírculo*) hemicycle; (*gradería semicircular*) amphitheater; (*espacio central del salón de sesiones de las Cortes*) floor
hemisferio *m* hemisphere
hemistiquio *m* hemistich
hemofilia *f* hemophilia
hemoglobina *f* hemoglobin
hemorragia *f* hemorrhage
hemorroides *fpl* hemorrhoids
hemóstato *m* hemostat
henal *m* hayloft
henar *m* hayfield
henchir §50 *tr* to fill; (*un colchón*) stuff; (*a una persona, p.ej., de favores*) heap, shower || *ref* to be filled; stuff, stuff oneself
hendedura *f* crack, split, cleft
hender §51 *tr* to crack, split, cleave; (*el aire, las ondas*) cleave; make one's way through || *ref* to crack, split
hendidura *f* crack, split, cleft
henil *m* hayloft, haymow
henna *f* henna
heno *m* hay
heñir §72 *tr* to knead; **hay mucho que heñir** there's still a lot of work to do
heraldía *f* heraldry
heráldi•co -ca *adj* heraldic || *f* heraldry
heraldo *m* herald
herbáce•o -a *adj* herbaceous
herbajar *tr & intr* to graze
herbaje *m* herbage
herba•rio -ria *adj* herbal || *m* (*libro*) herbal; (*colección*) herbarium
herbicida *m* weed killer
herbo•so -sa *adj* grassy
hercúle•o -a *adj* herculean
heredad *f* country estate
heredar *tr & intr* to inherit; **heredar a** to inherit from
herede•ro -ra *mf* heir, inheritor; owner of an estate; **heredero forzoso** heir apparent || *m* heir || *f* heiress
heredita•rio -ria *adj* hereditary
hereje *mf* heretic
herejía *f* heresy; insult, outrage; outrageous price

herencia *f* heritage, inheritance; (*transmisión de caracteres biológicos*) heredity; (*patrimonio de un difunto*) estate
heréti•co -ca *adj* heretic(al)
herida *f* injury, wound; insult, outrage; **renovar la herida** to open an old sore; **tocar en la herida** to sting to the quick
heri•do -da *adj* hurt, wounded; (*ofendido*) hurt || *mf* injured person, wounded person; **los heridos** the injured, the wounded || *f* see **herida**
herir §68 *tr* to injure, hurt, wound; (*ofender*) hurt; (*golpear*) strike; (*el sol sobre*) beat down upon; (*un instrumento de cuerda*) play; (*la cuerda de un instrumento*) pluck; touch, move
hermana *f* sister; **hermana de leche** foster sister; **hermana política** sister-in-law; **media hermana** half sister
hermanar *tr* to match, mate; combine, join; harmonize || *ref* to match; become attached as brothers or sisters or brother and sister
hermanastra *f* stepsister
hermanastro *m* stepbrother
hermandad *f* brotherhood; sisterhood; close friendship; close relationship
herma•no -na *adj* (*p.ej., idioma*) sister || *mf* companion, mate || *m* brother; **hermano de leche** foster brother; **hermano político** brother-in-law; **hermanos** brother and sister; brothers and sisters; **hermanos siameses** Siamese twins; **medio hermano** half brother; **primo hermano** first cousin || *f* see **hermana**
herméti•co -ca *adj* hermetic(al); air-tight; impenetrable; tight-lipped
hermosear *tr* to beautify, embellish
hermo•so -sa *adj* beautiful; (*caballero*) handsome
hermosura *f* beauty; (*mujer hermosa*) belle, beauty
hernia *f* hernia
héroe *m* hero
heroi•co -ca *adj* heroic; (*remedio*) desperate
heroína *f* heroine; (pharm) heroin
heroinómano *m* heroin addict
heroísmo *m* heroism
herrada *f* wooden bucket
herrador *m* horseshoer
herradura *f* horseshoe; **mostrar las herraduras** (*un caballo*) to kick, be vicious; (coll) to show one's heels
herraje *m* hardware, ironwork
herramental *adj* tool || *m* toolbox, tool bag
herramienta *f* tool; set of tools; (coll) teeth; (coll) horns
herrar §2 *tr* (*guarnecer con hierro*) to fit with hardware; (*un caballo*) to shoe; (*marcar con hierro candente*) to brand; (*un barril*) to hoop
herrería *f* forge, blacksmith shop; blacksmithing; ironworks; rumpus
herrero *m* blacksmith; **herrero de grueso** ironworker; **herrero de obra** steelworker
herrete *m* tip, metal tip
herretear *tr* to tip, put a metal tip on
herrín *m* rust
herón *m* (*tejo de hierro horadado*) quoit; (*arandela*) washer
herrumbre *f* rust; (*honguillo parásito*) rust, plant rot
herrumbro•so -sa *adj* rusty
herventar §2 *tr* to boil
hervidero *m* boiling; bubbling spring; (*en el pecho*) rattle; (*de gente*) swarm
hervidor *m* boiler, cooker
hervir §68 *intr* to boil; (*el mar; una persona encolerizada*) boil, seethe; swarm, teem
hervor *m* boil, boiling; (*de la juventud*) fire, restlessness; **alzar el hervor** to begin to boil
hervoro•so -sa *adj* ardent, fiery, impetuous
heterócli•to -ta *adj* irregular; unconventional
heterodinar *tr* to heterodyne
heterodi•no -na *adj* heterodyne
heterodo•xo -xa *adj* heterodox
heterogeneidad *f* heterogeneity
heterogéne•o -a *adj* heterogeneous
hexámetro *m* hexameter
hez *f* (*pl* **heces**) (fig) scum, dregs; **heces** lees, dregs; feces, excrement
hiato *m* hiatus
hibisco *m* hibiscus
hibridación *f* hybridization
hibridar *tr & intr* to hybridize
híbri•do -da *adj & m* hybrid
hidal•go -ga *adj* noble, illustrious || *m* nobleman || *f* noblewoman
hidalguez *f* or **hidalguía** *f* nobility
hidra *f* hydra
hidratar *tr & ref* to hydrate
hidrato *m* hydrate
hidráuli•co -ca *adj* hydraulic || *f* hydraulics
hidroala *m* (*vehículo mixto de buque y avión*) hydrofoil
hidroaleta *f* (*miembro alar del hidroala*) hydrofoil
hidroavión *m* hydroplane
hidrocarburo *m* hydrocarbon
hidroeléctri•co -ca *adj* hydroelectric
hidrófi•lo -la *adj* (*algodón*) absorbent (*cotton*)
hidrofobia *f* hydrophobia
hidrófu•go -ga *adj* waterproof
hidrógeno *m* hydrogen
hidropesía *f* dropsy
hidróxido *m* hydroxide
hiedra *f* ivy
hiel *f* bile, gall; (fig) gall, bitterness, sorrow; **echar la hiel** to strain, overwork
hielo *m* ice; (fig) coldness, coolness; **hielo flotante** drift ice, ice pack; **hielo seco** dry ice; **romper el hielo** (*quebrantar la reserva*) to break the ice
hiena *f* hyena
hienda *f* dung
hierba *f* grass; (*especialmente la que tiene propiedades medicinales*) herb; **hierba de la plata** honesty; **hierba del asno** evening primrose; **hierba de París** truelove; **hierba gatera** catnip; **hierba pastel** woad; **hierbas** grass, pasture; herb poison; years of age (*said of animals*); **mala hierba** weed; wayward young fellow

hierbabuena *f* mint

hierro *m* iron; (*marca candente que se pone a los ganados*) brand; **hierro colado** cast iron; **hierro colado en barras** pig iron; **hierro de desecho** scrap iron; **hierro de marcar** branding iron; **hierro dulce** wrought iron; **hierro fundido** cast iron; **hierro galvanizado** galvanized iron; **hierro ondulado** corrugated iron; **hierros** irons, fetters; **llevar hierro a Vizcaya** to carry coals to Newcastle

higa *f* baby's fist-shaped amulet; scorn, contempt; **dar higa** to misfire; **no dar dos higas por** to not give a rap for

hígado *m* liver; **echar los hígados** to strain, to overwork; **hígados** guts, courage; **malos hígados** hatred, grudge; **ser un hígado** to be a nuisance

higiene *f* hygiene

higiéni•co -ca *adj* hygienic

higo *m* fig; **higo chumbo** prickly pear; **higo paso** dried fig; **no valer un higo** to be not worth a continental

higuera *f* fig tree; **higuera chumba** prickly pear

hija *f* daughter; **hija política** daughter-in-law

hijas•tro -tra *mf* stepchild || *m* stepson || *f* stepdaughter

hi•jo -ja *mf* child; (*de un animal*) young; **hijo de bendición** legitimate child; good child; **hijo de la cuna** foundling; **hijo del amor** love child; **hijo de leche** foster child || *m* son; **cada hijo de vecino** every man Jack, every mother's son; **hijo del agua** good sailor; good swimmer; **hijo de su padre** chip off the old block; **hijo de sus propias obras** self-made man; **hijo político** son-in-law; **hijos** children; descendants || *f* see **hija**

hijodalgo *m* (*pl* **hijosdalgo**) nobleman

hijuela *f* little girl, little daughter; (*tira de tela*) gore; branch drain; side path

hijuelero *m* rural postman

hijuelo *m* shoot, sucker

hila *f* row, line; (*acción de hilar*) spinning; **a la hila** in single file; **hilas** (*hebras para curar heridas*) lint

hilacha *f* shred, fraying; **hilacha de acero** steel wool; **hilacha de algodón** cotton waste; **hilacha de vidrio** spun glass; **hilachas** lint; **mostrar la hilacha** (Arg) to show one's worst side

hilachen•to -ta *adj* tattered; in rags

hilachos *mpl* (Mex) rags, tatters

hilacho•so -sa *adj* frayed, raggedy

hilada *f* row, line; (mas) course

hilado *m* spinning; (*hilo*) yarn, thread

hila•dor -dora *adj* spinning || *mf* spinner || *f* spinning machine

hilandería *f* spinning; spinning mill

hilande•ro -ra *adj* spinning || *m* spinning mill

hilar *tr & intr* to spin; **hilar delgado** to hew close to the line; **hilar largo** to drag on

hilarante *adj* laughable; (*gas*) laughing

hilaza *f* yarn, thread; lint; **descubrir la hilaza** to show one's true nature

hilera *f* row, line; fine thread, fine yarn; (*parhilera*) ridgepole; (mil) file

hilo *m* thread; (*hebras retorcidas*) yarn; (*alambre*) wire; (*de perlas*) string; (*de agua*) thin stream; (*de luz*) beam; linen, linen fabric; (*de un discurso, de la vida*) (fig) thread; **hilo bramante** twine; **hilo de la muerte** end of life; **hilo de masa** (aut) ground wire; **hilo de medianoche** midnight sharp; **hilo dental** dental floss; **hilo de tierra** (elec) ground wire; **irse al hilo** or **tras el hilo de la gente** to follow the crowd; **manejar los hilos** to pull strings; **perder el hilo de** to lose the thread of

hilván *m* basting, tacking; basting stitch; (Chile) basting thread; (Ven) hem; **hablar de hilván** to jabber along

hilvanar *tr* to baste, tack; sketch, outline; (*hacer con precipitación*) hurry; (Ven) to hem || *intr* to baste, tack

himnario *m* hymnal, hymn book

himno *m* hymn; **himno nacional** national anthem

hin *m* neigh, whinny

hincadura *f* driving, thrusting, sticking

hincapié *m* stamping the foot; **hacer hincapié en** to lay great stress on, to emphasize

hincar §73 *tr* to drive, thrust, stick, sink; (*la rodilla*) go down on, fall on || *ref* to kneel, kneel down; **hincarse de rodillas** to go down on one's knees

hincha *mf* (sport) fan, rooter || *f* grudge, ill will

hinchable *adj* inflatable; (*goma de mascar*) bubble

hincha•do -da *adj* swollen; swollen with pride; (*estilo, lenguaje*) pompous, high-flown || *m* (*de un neumático*) inflation || *f* (sport) fans, rooters

hinchar *tr* to swell; inflate; (*un neumático*) pump up; exaggerate, embroider || *ref* to swell; swell up, become puffed up (*with pride*)

hinchazón *f* swelling; vanity, conceit; (*del estilo, lenguaje*) bombast

hinchismo *m* (sport) fans, rooters

hin•dú -dúa (*pl* **-dúes -dúas**) *adj & mf* Hindoo, Hindu

hiniesta *f* Spanish broom

hinojo *m* fennel; **de hinojos** on one's knees

hipar *intr* to hiccup; (*los perros cuando siguen la caza*) pant, snuffle; (*gimotear*) whimper; be worn out; **hipar por** to long for; long to

hiperacidez *f* hyperacidity

hipérbola *f* (geom) hyperbola

hipérbole *f* (rhet) hyperbole

hiperbóli•co -ca *adj* (geom & rhet) hyperbolic

hipersensible *adj* (*alérgico*) hypersensitive

hipertensión *f* hypertension, high blood pressure

hípica *f* (horseback) riding; equestrianism

hípi•co -ca *adj* horse, equine

hipnosis *f* hypnosis

hipnóti•co -ca *adj* hypnotic || *mf* hypnotic || *m* (*medicamento que provoca el sueño*) hypnotic
hipnotismo *m* hypnotism
hipnotista *mf* hypnotist
hipnotizar §60 *tr* to hypnotize
hipo *m* hiccup; longing, desire; **tener hipo contra** to have a grudge against; **tener hipo por** to desire eagerly
hipocondría•co -ca *adj & mf* hypochondriac
hipocresía *f* hypocrisy
hipócrita *adj* hypocritical || *mf* hypocrite
hipodérmi•co -ca *adj* hypodermic
hipódromo *m* hippodrome, race track
hipopótamo *m* hippopotamus
hiposulfito *m* hyposulfite
hipoteca *f* mortgage; **¡buena hipoteca!** you may believe it, if you want to!
hipotecar §73 *tr* to mortgage
hipoteca•rio -ria *adj* mortgage
hipotenusa *f* hypotenuse
hipóte•sis *f* (*pl* **-sis**) hypothesis; **hipótesis de guía** working hypothesis
hipotéti•co -ca *adj* hypothetic(al)
hiriente *adj* cutting, stinging
hirsu•to -ta *adj* hairy, bristly; (fig) brusque, gruff
hirviente *adj* boiling
hisopear *tr* to sprinkle with holy water
hisopo *m* (bot) hyssop; aspergillum, sprinkler of holy water; paint brush, shaving brush
hispalense *adj & mf* Sevillian
hispáni•co -ca *adj & mf* Hispanic
hispanista *mf* Hispanist
hispa•no -na *adj* Spanish; Spanish American || *mf* Spaniard; Spanish American
hispanohablante or **hispanoparlante** *adj* Spanish-speaking || *mf* speaker of Spanish
híspi•do -da *adj* bristly, spiny
histéri•co -ca *adj* hysterical
histerismo *m* hysteria
histología *f* histology
historia *f* history; story, tale; **de historia** notorious, infamous; **dejarse de historias** to come to the point; **historia de lagrimitas** (coll) sob story; **historias** gossip, meddling; **pasar a la historia** to become a thing of the past; **picar en historia** to turn out to be serious
historia•do -da *adj* richly adorned; overadorned; (*cuadro, dibujo*) storied
historial *adj* historical || *m* record, dossier
historiar §77 & regular *tr* to tell the history of; tell the story of; (*un suceso histórico*) (fa) to depict
históri•co -ca *adj* historic(al)
historieta *f* anecdote, brief story; **historieta gráfica** comic strip
histrión *m* actor; juggler, buffoon
histrióni•co -ca *adj* histrionic
hita *f* brad; landmark, milestone
hi•to -ta *adj* fixed, firm; (*casa, calle*) next; (*caballo*) black || *m* (*clavo fijado en la tierra*) peg, hob; (*juego*) quoits; (*blanco*) target; (*mojón*) landmark, milestone; **dar en el hito** to hit the nail on the head; **mirar de hito en hito** to eye up and down || *f* see **hita**
Hno. *abbr* **Hermano**
hoba•chón -chona *adj* lumpish
hocicar §73 *tr* to nuzzle, root; keep on kissing || *intr* to nuzzle, root; run into a snag; (*la proa*) (naut) to dip
hocico *m* snout; (*de una persona*) snout; sour face; **caer de hocicos** to fall on one's face; **meter el hocico en todo** to poke one's nose into everything; **poner hocico** to make a face
hogaño *adv* this year; at the present time
hogar *m* fireplace, hearth; furnace; home; family life; (*hoguera*) bonfire
hogare•ño -ña *adj* home-loving || *mf* homebody, stay-at-home
hogaza *f* large loaf of bread
hoguera *f* bonfire
hoja *f* (*de planta, libro, mesa, muelle, puerta plegadiza, etc.; pétalo de flor*) leaf; (*de planta acuática*) pad; (*de papel*) sheet; blank sheet; (*de cuchillo, sierra, espada, etc.*) blade; (*hojuela de metal*) foil; (*de persiana*) slat; (*del patín*) runner; **doblar la hoja** to change the subject; **hoja clínica** clinical chart; **hoja de afeitar** razor blade; **hoja de embalaje** packing slip; **hoja de encuadernador** (bb) end paper; **hoja de estaño** tin foil; **hoja de estudios** transcript; **hoja de guarda** (bb) flyleaf; **hoja del anunciante** tear sheet; **hoja de lata** tin, tin plate; **hoja de nenúfar** lily pad; **hoja de paga** pay roll; **hoja de parra** fig leaf; **hoja de pedidos** order blank; **hoja de rodaje** (mov) shooting record; **hoja de ruta** waybill; **hoja de servicios** service record; **hoja de trébol** cloverleaf (*intersection*); **hoja maestra** master blade (*of spring*); **hojas del autor** (typ) advance sheets; **hoja suelta** leaflet, handbill; (bb) flyleaf; **hoja volante** leaflet, handbill
hojalata *f* tin, tin plate
hojalatería *f* tinsmith's shop; tinwork
hojalatero *m* tinsmith, tinner
hojaldre *m & f* puff paste
hojarasca *f* dead leaves; trash, rubbish; bluff, vain show
hojear *tr* to leaf through || *intr* to scale off; (*las hojas de los árboles*) flutter
hojita *f* leaflet; **hojita de afeitar** razor blade
hojo•so -sa *adj* leafy
hojuela *f* (*hoja de otra compuesta*) leaflet; (*fruta de sartén*) pancake; (*hoja muy delgada de metal*) foil; **hojuela de estaño** tin foil
hola *interj* hey!, hello!
Holanda *f* Holland
holan•dés -desa *adj* Dutch; **a la holandesa** (*bb*) half-bound || *mf* Hollander || *m* Dutchman; (*idioma*) Dutch || *f* Dutch woman
holga•chón -chona *adj* lazy, idle || *mf* loafer, idler
holgadero *m* hangout
holga•do -da *adj* idle, unoccupied; (*vestido*) loose, full, roomy; (*que vive con bienestar*) fairly well-off

holganza *f* idleness, leisure; pleasure, enjoyment

holgar §63 *intr* to idle, be idle; take it easy, rest up; not fit, be too loose; be unnecessary, be of no use; be glad || *ref* to be glad; be amused

holga•zán -zana *adj* idle, lazy || *mf* idler, loafer

holgazanear *intr* to idle, loaf, bum around

hol•gón -gona *adj* pleasure-loving || *mf* loafer, lizard

holgorio *m* fun, merriment

holgura *f* looseness, fulness; enjoyment, merriment; comfort, easy circumstances; (mach) play

holocausto *m* holocaust

hollar §61 *tr* to tread on, to trample on

hollejo *m* hull, peel, skin

hollín *m* soot

hollinar *tr* (Chile) to cover with soot

hollinien•to -ta *adj* sooty

hombracho *m* big husky fellow

hombrada *f* manly act

hombradía *f* manliness, courage

hombre *m* man; husband, man; my boy, old chap; **buen hombre** good-natured fellow; **¡hombre al agua!** or **¡hombre a la mar!** man overboard!; **hombre bueno** arbiter, referee; **hombre de bien** honorable man; **hombre de buenas prendas** man of parts; **hombre de ciencia** scientist; **hombre de dinero** man of means; **hombre de estado** statesman; **hombre de letras** man of letters; **hombre de mundo** man of the world; **hombre de suposición** man of straw; **hombre hecho** grown man || *interj* man alive!, upon my word!

hombre-anuncio *m* sandwich man

hombrear *tr* (Arg) to carry on the shoulders; (Mex) to aid, back || *intr* to try to be somebody; (*una mujer*) to be mannish; **hombrear con** to try to be equal

hombrecillo *m* little man; (*lúpulo*) hop

hombrera *f* (*del vestido*) shoulder; shoulder pad; epaulet

hombre-rana *m* (*pl* **hombres-ranas**) frogman

hombría *f* manliness; **hombría de bien** honor, probity

hombrillo *m* (*de la camisa*) yoke; shoulder piece

hombro *m* shoulder; **arrimar el hombro** to lend a hand, put one's shoulder to the wheel; **encoger los hombros** to let one's shoulders droop; **encogerse de hombros** to shrug one's shoulders; to crouch, to shrink with fear; to not answer; **mirar por encima del hombro** to look down upon; **salir en hombros** to be carried off on the shoulders of the crowd

hombru•no -na *adj* mannish

homenaje *m* homage; (feud) homage; (Chile) gift, favor; **homenaje de boca** lip service; **rendir homenaje a** to swear allegiance to

homeópata *mf* homeopath

homeopatía *f* homeopathy

homicida *adj* homicidal || *mf* homicide

homicidio *m* homicide

homilía *f* homily

homogeneidad *f* homogeneity

homogeneizar §60 *tr* to homogenize

homogéne•o -a *adj* homogeneous

homologación *f* confirmation, ratification; (sport) validation

homologar §44 *tr* to confirm, ratify; (*un récord*) (sport) to validate

homólo•go -ga *adj* homologous || *m* colleague

homóni•mo -ma *adj* homonymous; of the same name || *mf* namesake || *m* homonym

homosexual *adj & mf* homosexual; gay

homúnculo *m* guy, little runt

honda *f* sling

hondazo *m* blow with a sling

hondear *tr* (naut) to sound

hondillos *mpl* patches in the crotch of pants

hon•do -da *adj* deep; (*terreno*) low || *m* bottom || *f* see **honda** || **hondo** *adv* deep

hondón *m* (*de la aguja*) eye; (*de un vaso*) bottom; lowland

hondonada *f* lowland, ravine

hondura *f* depth, profundity; **meterse en honduras** to go beyond one's depth

hondure•ño -ña *adj & mf* Honduran

honestidad *f* decency; chastity; modesty; honesty, probity; fairness, reasonableness

hones•to -ta *adj* decent; chaste, pure; modest; honest, upright; (*precio*) fair, reasonable

hongo *m* fungus, mushroom; (*sombrero*) bowler, derby

honor *m* honor; **en honor a la verdad** as a matter of fact, to tell the truth; **hacer honor a** to do honor to; (*la firma*) to honor

honorable *adj* honorable

honora•rio -ria *adj* honorary || *s* fee, honorarium

honorífi•co -ca *adj* honorific

honra *f* honor; **tener a mucha honra** to be proud of

honradez *f* honesty, integrity

honra•do -da *adj* honorable

honrar *tr* to honor || *ref* to feel honored

honrilla *f* — **por la negra honrilla** out of concern for what people will say

honro•so -sa *adj* honorable

hopo *m* tuft, shock (*of hair*); bushy tail; **seguir el hopo a** (coll) to keep right after

hora *f* hour; (*momento determinado para algo*) time; **a la hora** on time; **a la hora de ahora** right now; **a la hora en punto** on the hour; **a las pocas horas** within a few hours; **dar hora** to fix a time; **dar la hora** (*el reloj*) to strike; **de última hora** up-to-date; most up-to-date; (*noticias*) late; **en buen hora** or **en hora buena** safely, luckily; all right; **en mal hora** or **en hora mala** unluckily, in an evil hour; **fuera de horas** after hours; **hasta altas horas** until late into the night; **hora de acostarse** bedtime; **hora de aglomeración** rush hour; **hora de cierre** closing time; curfew; **hora de comer** mealtime; **hora deshorada** fatal hour; **hora de verano** daylight-saving time; **hora de verdad** (taur) kill; **hora legal** or

oficial standard time; **hora punta** peak hour; rush hour; **horas de afluencia** rush hour; **horas extra** overtime; **horas de consulta** office hours (*of a doctor*); **horas de ocio** leisure hours; **horas de punta** rush hour; **horas extraordinarias de trabajo** overtime

horadar *tr* to drill, bore, pierce

hora•rio -ria *adj* hour || *m* hour hand; clock; (*de ferrocarriles*) timetable; **horario escolar** roster

horca *f* (*para levantar la paja*) pitchfork; (*para ahorcar a un condenado*) gallows, gibbet; (*de ajos, cebollas, etc.*) string

horcajadas — a horcajadas astride, astraddle

horcajadillas — a horcajadillas astride, astraddle

horcajadura *f* crotch

horcajo *m* (*confluencia de dos ríos*) fork; (*para mulas*) yoke

horcón *m* pitchfork; forked prop (*for fruit trees*); upright, prop

horchata *f* orgeat

horda *f* horde

horero *m* (*reloj*) hour hand

horizontal *adj* & *f* horizontal

horizonte *m* horizon

horma *f* form, mold; shoe tree; hat block; **hallar la horma de su zapato** to meet one's match

hormiga *f* ant; (*enfermedad que causa comezón*) itch

hormigón *m* concrete; **hormigón armado** reinforced concrete

hormigonera *f* concrete mixer

hormigo•so -sa *adj* antlike; full of ants; ant-eaten; (*picante*) itchy

hormiguear *intr* (*ponerse en movimiento gente o animales*) to swarm; (*experimentar una sensación de hormigas corriendo por el cuerpo*) crawl, creep; abound, teem

hormiguero *m* anthill; (*de gente*) swarm, mob

hormillón *m* hat block

hormón *m* or **hormona** *f* hormone

hornacina *f* niche

hornada *f* (*cantidad que se cuece de una vez en un horno*) batch, bake; (*conjunto de individuos de una misma promoción*) crop

hornazo *m* Easter cake filled with hard-boiled eggs; Easter gift to Lenten preacher

horne•ro -ra *mf* baker

hornilla *f* kitchen grate; pigeonhole

hornillo *m* kitchen stove; hot plate; (*de la pipa de fumar*) bowl

horno *m* oven, furnace; (*para cocer ladrillos*) kiln; **alto horno** blast furnace; **horno de cal** limekiln; **horno de fundición** smelting furnace; **horno de ladrillero** brickkiln

horóscopo *m* horoscope; **sacar un horóscopo** to cast a horoscope

horqueta *f* pitchfork; fork, prop; (*ángulo agudo en un río*) (Arg) bend

horquilla *f* pitchfork; (*de bicicleta*) fork; (*de microteléfono*) cradle; (*alfiler para sujetar el pelo*) hairpin

horrar *tr* to save

hórreo *m* granary; (in Asturias and Galicia) crib or granary raised on pillars (*to protect grain from mice and dampness*)

horrible *adj* horrible

horripilante *adj* hair-raising, blood-curdling

horror *m* horror; **tener horror a** to have a horror of

horrorizar §60 *tr* to horrify

horroro•so -sa *adj* horrid; hideous, ugly

hortaliza *f* vegetable

hortela•no -na *adj* garden || *mf* gardener

hortera *m* clerk, helper || *f* wooden bowl

hortícola *adj* horticultural

horticul•tor -tora *mf* horticulturist

horticultura *f* horticulture

hos•co -ca *adj* dark, dark-skinned; sullen, grim, gloomy

hospedaje *m* lodging

hospedar *tr* to lodge || *ref* to lodge, stop, put up

hospedería *f* hospice; inn, hostelry

hospede•ro -ra *mf* innkeeper

hospicio *m* hospice; poorhouse; orphan asylum

hospital *m* hospital; **estar hecho un hospital** (*una persona*) to be full of aches and pains; (*una casa*) to be turned into a hospital; **hospital de la sangre** poor relations; **hospital de primera sangre** (mil) field hospital; **hospital robado** bare house

hospitala•rio -ria *adj* hospitable

hospitalidad *f* hospitality; (*estancia del enfermo en el hospital*) hospitalization

hospitalizar §60 *tr* to hospitalize

hosquedad *f* darkness; sullenness, grimness, gloominess

hostelería *f* restaurant and hotel business

hostería *f* inn, hostelry

hostia *f* sacrificial victim; wafer; (eccl) wafer, Host

hostigar §44 *tr* to scourge; harass; to pester; cloy, surfeit

hostigo•so -sa *adj* cloying, sickening

hostil *adj* hostile

hostilidad *f* hostility

hostilizar §60 *tr* to antagonize; (*al enemigo*) harry, harass

hotel *m* (*establecimiento donde se da comida y alojamiento por dinero*) hotel; (*casa particular lujosa*) mansion

hotele•ro -ra *adj* hotel || *mf* hotelkeeper

hoy *adv* & *s* today; **de hoy a mañana** any time now; **de hoy en adelante** from now on; **hoy día** nowadays

hoya *f* hole, pit, ditch; (*sepultura*) grave; valley; (*almáciga*) seedbed; river basin

hoyanca *f* potter's field

hoyo *m* hole; grave; pockmark

hoyo•so -sa *adj* full of holes

hoyuelo *m* dimple; (*juego de muchachos*) pitching pennies

hoz *f* (*pl* **hoces**) sickle; narrow pass, defile; **de hoz y de coz** headlong, recklessly

hozar **§60** *tr & intr* to nuzzle, root
hta. *abbr* **hasta**
huacal *m* var of **guacal**
huachinango *m* (Mex) red snapper
hucha *f* workingman's chest; (*alcancía*) toy bank; (*dinero ahorrado*) savings, nest egg
huchear *intr* to cry, shout
hue•co -ca *adj* hollow; (*mullido*) soft, fluffy, spongy; (*voz*) deep, resounding; vain, conceited; (*estilo, lenguaje*) affected, pompous ‖ *m* hollow; interval; (*en un muro, una hilera de coches, etc.*) opening; (*empleo sin proveer*) opening; **hueco de la axila** armpit; **hueco de escalera** stair well
huélfago *m* (vet) heaves
huelga *f* (*ocio*) rest, leisure, idleness; recreation; pleasant spot; (*cesación del trabajo en señal de protesta*) strike; (mach) play; **huelga de brazos caídos** sit-down strike; **huelga de hambre** hunger strike; **huelga general** general strike; **huelga patronal** lockout; **huelga por solidaridad** sympathy strike; **huelga sentada** sit-down strike; **ir a la huelga** or **ponerse en huelga** to go on strike
huelguista *mf* striker
huella *f* track, footprint; trace, mark; rut; (*acción de hollar*) tread, treading; (*peldaño en que se asienta el pie*) tread; **huella dactilar** or **digital** fingerprint; **huella de sonido** sound track; **seguir las huellas de** to follow in the footsteps of
huérfa•no -na *adj* orphan; orphaned; alone, deserted ‖ *mf* orphan; (Chile, Peru) foundling
hue•ro -ra *adj* rotten; (fig) empty, hollow; (Guat, Mex) blond; **salir huero** (coll) to flop, turn out bad ‖ *mf* (Guat, Mex) blond
huerta *f* vegetable garden; fruit garden; irrigated region
huerte•ro -ra *mf* (Arg, Peru) gardener
huerto *m* (*de árboles frutales*) orchard; (*de verduras*) kitchen garden
huesa *f* grave
huesear *intr* to beg (alms)
huesillo *m* (Chile, Peru) sun-dried peach
hueso *m* bone; (*de ciertas frutas*) stone, pit; drudgery; **a otro perro con ese hueso** tell that to the marines; **calarse hasta los huesos** to get soaked to the skin; **hueso de la alegría** crazy bone, funny bone; **hueso de la suerte** wishbone; **hueso duro de roer** a hard nut to crack; **la sin hueso** the tongue; **no dejarle a uno un hueso sano** to beat someone up; to pick someone to pieces; **no poder con sus huesos** to be all in; **soltar la sin hueso** to talk too much; to pour forth insults; **tener los huesos molidos** to be all fagged out
hueso•so -sa *adj* bony
hués•ped -peda *mf* (*persona alojada en casa ajena*) guest; (*persona que hospeda a otra en su casa*) host; (*mesonero*) innkeeper, host
hueste *f* followers; (*ejército*) army, host
huesu•do -da *adj* bony, big-boned
hueva *f* roe, fish roe
hueve•ro -ra *mf* egg dealer ‖ *f* eggcup; oviduct
huevo *m* egg; **huevo a la plancha** fried egg; **huevo al plato** shirred egg; **huevo del té** tea ball; **huevo de zurcir** darning egg or gourd; **huevo duro** hard-boiled egg; **huevo escalfado** poached egg; **huevo estrellado** or **frito** fried egg; **huevo pasado por agua** soft-boiled egg; **huevos revueltos** scrambled eggs
huída *f* flight; (*de un líquido*) leak; (*ensanche en un agujero*) flare, splay; (*de caballo*) shying
huidi•zo -za *adj* fugitive; evasive
huincha *f* (SAm) tape; (SAm) tape measure
huipil *m* (Mex) colorful poncho worn by Indian women
huir **§20** *tr* to flee, avoid, shun; (*el cuerpo*) duck ‖ *intr* to flee; (*el tiempo*) fly; (*de la memoria*) to slip ‖ *ref* to flee
hule *m* (*tela impermeable*) oilcloth; rubber; (taur) blood, goring
hulear *intr* (CAm) to gather rubber
hulla *f* coal; **hulla azul** tide power; wind power; **hulla blanca** white power; water power
hullera *f* colliery, coal mine
humanidad *f* humanity; fatness
humanista *adj & mf* humanist
humanita•rio -ria *adj & mf* humanitarian
huma•no -na *adj* (*perteneciente al hombre*) human; (*compasivo, misericordioso; civilizador*) humane
humareda *f* cloud of smoke
humeante *adj* smoking, smoky; steamy, reeking
humear *tr* (SAm) to fumigate ‖ *intr* to smoke; steam, reek; put on airs; (*reliquias de un alboroto, enemistad, etc.*) last, persist
humectador *m* humidifier
humedad *f* humidity, dampness, moisture
humedecer **§22** *tr* to humidify, dampen, moisten, wet
húme•do -da *adj* humid, damp, moist
humero *m* smokestack, chimney
húmero *m* humerus
humidificador *m* air humidifier
humildad *f* humility
humilde *adj* humble
humilladero *m* calvary, road shrine; priedieu
humillante *adj* humiliating
humillar *tr* (*abatir el orgullo de*) to humble; (*avergonzar*) humiliate; (*la cabeza*) bow; (*el cuerpo, las rodillas*) bend ‖ *ref* to humble oneself; cringe, grovel
humo *m* smoke; steam, fume; **a humo de pajas** lightly, thoughtlessly; **bajar los humos a** (coll) to humble, take down a peg; **echar más humo que una chimenea** to smoke like a chimney; **humos** airs, conceit; hearths, homes; **irse todo en humo** to go up in smoke; **tragar el humo** to inhale; **vender humos** to peddle influence

humor *m* humor; **de mal humor** out of humor; **estar de humor para** to be in the humor for; **seguir el humor a** to humor
humorismo *m* humor, humorousness
humorista *mf* humorist
humorísti•co -ca *adj* humorous
humo•so -sa *adj* smoky
hundible *adj* sinkable
hundir *tr* to sink; plunge; (*abrumar*) overwhelm; confound, confute; destroy, ruin || *ref* to sink; collapse; settle, cave in; come to ruin; disappear, vanish
húnga•ro -ra *adj & mf* Hungarian || *m* (*idioma*) Hungarian
Hungría *f* Hungary
hupe *m* punk
huracán *m* hurricane
hurañía *f* shyness, unsociability
hura•ño -ña *adj* shy, unsociable
hurgar **§44** *tr* to poke; (fig) to stir up, incite; **peor es hurgallo** (i.e., **hurgarlo**) better keep hands off || *intr* to poke || *ref* (*la nariz*) to pick
hurgón *m* poker; thrust, stab
hurgonazo *m* (*con hurgón*) poke; jab, stab, thrust
hurgonear *tr* to poke; to jab, to stab at
hurgonero *m* poker
hu•rón -rona *adj* shy, diffident || *mf* prier, snooper; shy person, diffident person || *m* ferret
huronear *tr* to ferret, hunt with a ferret; to ferret out
huronera *f* ferret hole; lair, hiding place
hurtadillas — a hurtadillas by stealth, on the sly; **a hurtadillas de** unbeknown to
hurtar *tr* to steal; (*en pesos y medidas*) cheat; (*el suelo*) wear away; plagiarize; **hurtar el cuerpo** to dodge, duck || *ref* to withdraw, hide
hurto *m* thieving; theft; **a hurto** stealthily, on the sly; **coger con el hurto en las manos** to catch with the goods; **hurto mayor** grand larceny
husma *f* snooping; **andar a la husma** to go around snooping
husmear *tr* to scent, smell out; pry into || *intr* (*la carne*) to smell bad, become gamy
husmo *m* gaminess, high odor; **estar al husmo** to wait for a chance
huso *m* (*para hilar*) spindle; (*para devanar*) bobbin; (*cilindro del torno*) drum; **huso horario** time zone; **ser más derecho que un huso** to be as straight as a ramrod
huta *f* hunter's blind
huy *interj* ouch!
huyente *adj* (*frente*) receding; (*ojeada*) shifty

I

I, i (i) *f* tenth letter of the Spanish alphabet
ib. *abbr* **ibídem**
ibéri•co -ca *adj* Iberian
ibe•ro -ra *adj & mf* Iberian
íbice *m* ibex
ice•berg *m* (*pl* **-bergs**) iceberg
iconoclasia *f* or **iconoclasmo** *m* iconoclasm
iconoclasta *mf* iconoclast.
iconoscopio *m* (telv) iconoscope
ictericia *f* jaundice
ictericia•do -da *adj* jaundiced
ictiología *f* ichthyology
ida *f* going; departure; rashness; sally; trail; **de ida y vuelta** round-trip; **idas y venidas** comings and goings
idea *f* idea; **mudar de idea** to change one's mind
ideal *adj & m* ideal
idealista *adj & mf* idealist
idealizar **§60** *tr* to idealize
idear *tr* to think up, devise
idemista *adj* yes-saying || *mf* yes sayer
idénti•co -ca *adj* identic(al); (*muy parecido*) very similar
identidad *f* identity, sameness
identificación *f* identification
identificar **§73** *tr* to identify
ideología *f* ideology
idíli•co -ca *adj* idyllic
idilio *m* idyll
idioma *m* language; (*modo particular de hablar*) idiom, speech
idiomáti•co -ca *adj* idiomatic; language, linguistic
idiosincrasia *f* idiosyncrasy
idiota *adj* idiotic || *mf* idiot
idiotez *f* idiocy
idiotismo *m* ignorance; (*idiotez*) idiocy; (gram) idiom
i•do -da *adj* wild, scatterbrained; drunk || **los idos** the dead || *f* see **ida**
idolatrar *tr* to idolize
idolatría *f* idolatry; (*amor excesivo a una persona*) idolization
ídolo *m* idol
idoneidad *f* fitness, suitability
idóne•o -a fit, suitable
idus *mpl* ides
iglesia *f* church; **entrar en la iglesia** to go into the church; **llevar a la iglesia** to lead to the altar
iglesie•ro -ra *adj* (Arg) church-going || *mf* (Arg) church goer
igna•ro -ra *adj* ignorant
ignominio•so -sa *adj* ignominious
ignorancia *f* ignorance
ignorante *adj* ignorant || *mf* ignoramus
ignorar *tr* to not know, be ignorant of

igno•to -ta *adj* unknown
igual *adj* equal; (*liso, llano*) smooth, even, level; (*no variable*) firm, constant, equable; indifferent; **me es igual** it makes no difference to me || *m* equal; equal sign; **al igual de** like, after the fashion of; **al igual que** as; while, whereas; **en igual de** instead of
iguala *f* equalization; agreement
igualización *f* equalization; agreement
igualar *tr* to equal; (*alisar, allanar*) smooth, even, level; make equal, match; deem equal || *intr & ref* to be equal
igualdad *f* equality; smoothness, evenness; **igualdad de ánimo** equanimity; **igualdad de oportunidades** equal opportunity
igualmente *adv* likewise; **igualmente que** the same as
ijada *f* (*de animal*) flank; (*del cuerpo humano*) loin; (*dolor en estas partes*) stitch; **tener su ijada** to have its weak side or point
ijadear *intr* to pant
ijar *m* flank; loin
ilegal *adj* illegal
ilegible *adj* illegible
ilegíti•mo -ma *adj* illegitimate
ile•so -sa *adj* unscathed, unharmed
iletra•do -da *adj* unlettered, uncultured
ilíci•to -ta *adj* illicit, unlawful
ilimita•do -da *adj* limitless
ilitera•to -ta *adj* illiterate
ilógi•co -ca *adj* illogical
ilote *m* ear of corn
iludir *tr* to elude, evade
iluminación *f* illumination
iluminador *m* lighting engineer
iluminar *tr* to illuminate, light, light up || *ref* to light up, brighten
ilusión *f* illusion; (*esperanza infundada*) delusion; enthusiasm, zeal; dream; **forjarse** or **hacerse ilusiones** to kid oneself, indulge in wishful thinking
ilusionar *tr* to delude || *ref* to have illusions, indulge in wishful thinking; be enraptured, be beguiled
ilusionista *mf* prestidigitator, magician
ilusi•vo -va *adj* illusive
ilu•so -sa *adj* deluded, misguided; (*propenso a ilusionarse*) visionary
iluso•rio -ria *adj* illusory
ilustración *f* illustration; enlightenment; illustrated magazine
ilustra•do -da *adj* illustrated; learned, informed; enlightened
ilustrar *tr* (*adornar con grabados alusivos al texto*) to illustrate; make illustrious, make famous; explain, elucidate; enlighten || *ref* to become famous; be enlightened
ilustre *adj* illustrious
imagen *f* image; picture
imaginación *f* imagination
imaginar *tr, intr & ref* to imagine
imagina•rio -ria *adj* imaginary
imaginati•vo -va *adj* imaginative || *f* imagination; understanding
imaginería *f* fancy colored embroidery; carving or painting of religious images
imán *m* magnet; (fig) lodestone; **imán de herradura** horseshoe magnet; **imán inductor** (elec) field magnet
imanar or **imantar** *tr* to magnetize
imbatible *adj* unbeatable
imbécil *adj & mf* imbecile
imbecilidad *f* imbecility
imberbe *adj* beardless
imbíbi•to -ta *adj* including; included
imbornal *m* drain hole
imborrable *adj* indelible; unforgettable
imbuir **§20** *tr* to imbue
imitación *adj invar* imitation || *f* imitation; **a imitación de** in imitation of; **de imitación** imitation, fake
imita•do -da *adj* imitated; mock, sham; imitation
imitar *tr* to imitate
impaciencia *f* impatience
impacientar *tr* to make impatient || *ref* to get impatient
impaciente *adj* impatient
impacto *m* impact, hit; (*señal que deja el proyectil*) mark; **impacto directo** direct hit
impar *adj* odd, uneven; (*que no tiene igual*) unmatched || *m* odd number
imparcial *adj* impartial; (*que no entra en ningún partido*) nonpartisan
impartir *tr* to distribute, impart; (*lecciones*) to give
impás *m* finesse
impasible *adj* impassible, impassive
impávi•do -da *adj* dauntless, fearless, intrepid
impecable *adj* impeccable
impedancia *f* impedance
impedi•do -da *adj* disabled, crippled
impedimento *m* impediment, obstacle, hindrance
impedir **§50** *tr* to hinder, prevent
impeler *tr* to impel; spur, incite
impenetrable *adj* impenetrable
impenitente *adj & mf* impenitent
impensable *adj* unthinkable
impensa•do -da *adj* unexpected
imperar *intr* to rule, reign, command
imperati•vo -va *adj & m* imperative
imperceptible *adj* imperceptible
imperdible *m* safety pin
imperdonable *adj* unpardonable, unforgivable
imperecede•ro -ra *adj* imperishable, undying
imperfección *f* imperfection
imperfec•to -ta *adj & m* imperfect
imperial *adj* imperial || *f* imperial, roof (*of a coach or bus*)
imperialista *adj & mf* imperialist
impericia *f* unskillfulness, inexpertness
imperio *m* empire; dominion, sway
imperio•so -sa *adj* (*que manda con imperio*) imperious; (*indispensable*) imperative
imperi•to -ta *adj* unskilled, inexpert
impermeable *adj* impermeable; water-proof || *m* raincoat
impersonal *adj* impersonal

impertérri•to -ta *adj* dauntless, intrepid
impertinencia *f* impertinence; irrelevance; fussiness
impertinente *adj* impertinent; (*que no viene al caso*) irrelevant; (*nimiamente susceptible*) fussy || **impertinentes** *mpl* lorgnette
impetrar *tr* to beg (for); obtain by entreaty
ímpetu *m* impetus; force; haste
impetuo•so -sa *adj* impetuous
impiedad *f* (*falta de religión*) impiety; (*falta de compasión*) pitilessness
impí•o -a *adj* (*irreligioso*) impious; (*falto de compasión*) pitiless
impla *f* wimple
implacable *adj* relentless
implantar *tr* to implant; introduce
implementos *mpl* implements; tools
implicar **§73** *tr* (*envolver*) to implicate; (*incluir en esencia*) imply || *intr* to stand in the way
implíci•to -ta *adj* implicit, implied
implorar *tr* to implore
implume *adj* featherless
imponente *adj* imposing || *mf* depositor, investor
imponer **§54** *tr* (*la voluntad de uno, silencio, tributos*) to impose; (*dinero a rédito*) invest; (*dinero en depósito*) deposit; instruct; impute falsely || *intr* to dominate, command respect || *ref* (*responsabilidades*) to assume; command attention, command respect; **imponerse a** to dominate, command the respect of; **imponerse de** to learn, to find out
imponible *adj* taxable
impopular *adj* unpopular
impopularidad *f* unpopularity
importación *f* importation; import; imports
importa•dor -dora *mf* importer
importancia *f* importance; (*extensión, tamaño*) size; **ser de la importancia de** to be the concern of
importante *adj* important; large
importar *tr* (*introducir en un país*) to import; amount to; involve, imply; concern || *intr* to import; be important; matter
importe *m* amount
importunar *tr* to importune
importu•no -na *adj* (*molesto*) importunate; (*fuera de sazón*) inopportune
imposibilita•do -da *adj* paralyzed, disabled
imposibilitar *tr* to make impossible || *ref* to become paralyzed, become disabled
imposible *adj* impossible
imposición *f* (*de la voluntad de uno*) imposition; burden; imposture; (*de dinero*) deposit; (typ) make-up
impos•tor -tora *mf* impostor; slanderer
impostura *f* imposture
impotable *adj* undrinkable
impotencia *f* impotence
impotente *adj* impotent
impracticable *adj* impracticable, impassable; impractical
impreci•so -sa *adj* imprecise; vague
impregnar *tr* to impregnate, saturate
impremedita•do -da *adj* unpremeditated
imprenta *f* printing; printing shop; (*lo que se publica impreso*) printed matter; (*máquina para imprimir o prensar; conjunto de periódicos o periodistas*) press
imprentar *tr* (*la ropa*) (Chile) to press, iron; (Ecuad) to mark
imprescindible *adj* indispensable, essential
impresentable *adj* unpresentable
impresión *f* (*efecto producido en el ánimo; señal que una cosa deja en otra por presión*) impression; (*acción de imprimir*) printing; (*los ejemplares de una edición*) edition, issue; (phot) print; **impresión dactilar** or **digital** fingerprint
impresionable *adj* impressionable
impresionante *adj* impressive
impresionar *tr* to impress; (*un disco fonográfico*) record; (phot) to expose || *intr* to make an impression || *ref* to be impressed
impreso *m* printed paper or book; **impreso derivado** (*ordenador*) printout; **impresos** printed matter
impre•sor -sora *mf* printer
imprevisible *adj* unforeseeable
imprevisión *f* improvidence, lack of foresight
imprevi•sor -sora *adj* improvident
imprevis•to -ta *adj* unforeseen, unexpected || **imprevistos** *mpl* emergencies, unforeseen expenses
imprimar *tr* to prime
imprimir *tr* (*respeto, miedo; movimiento*) to impart || **§83** *tr* to stamp, imprint, impress; (*un disco fonográfico*) press; (typ) to print
improbable *adj* improbable
improbar **§61** *tr* to disapprove
improbidad *f* dishonesty; hardness, arduousness
ímpro•bo -ba *adj* dishonest; (*trabajo*) arduous
improcedente *adj* wrong; unfit, untimely
improducti•vo -va *adj* unproductive; unemployed
impronunciable *adj* unpronounceable
improperar *tr* to insult, revile
improperio *m* insult, affront
impropi•cio -cia *adj* unpropitious
impro•pio -pia *adj* improper; (*ajeno*) foreign
impróspe•ro -ra *adj* unsuccessful
impróvi•do -da *adj* unprepared
improvisación *f* improvisation; meteoric rise; (mus) impromptu
improvisadamente *adv* suddenly, unexpectedly; extempore
improvisar *tr & intr* to improvise
improvi•so -sa *adj* unforeseen, unexpected
imprudencia *f* imprudence; **imprudencia temeraria** criminal negligence
imprudente *adj* imprudent
impudicia *f* immodesty
impúdi•co -ca *adj* immodest
impues•to -ta *adj* informed || *m* tax; **impuesto sobre el valor añadido** or **impuesto al valor agregado** value-added tax; **impuesto sobre la renta** income tax
impugnar *tr* to impugn, contest
impulsar *tr* to impel; drive

impulsión *f* impulse, drive
impulsi•vo -va *adj* impulsive
impulso *m* impulse
impune *adj* unpunished
impunidad *f* impunity
impureza *f* impurity
impu•ro -ra *adj* impure
imputar *tr* to impute; credit on account
inabordable *adj* unapproachable
inacabable *adj* endless, interminable
inaccesible *adj* inaccessible
inacción *f* inaction
inacentua•do -da *adj* unaccented
inactividad *f* inactivity
inacti•vo -va *adj* inactive
inadecua•do -da *adj* inadequate; unsuited
inadvertencia *f* inadvertence, oversight
inadverti•do -da *adj* inadvertent, unwitting; careless, thoughtless; unseen, unnoticed
inagotable *adj* inexhaustible
inaguantable *adj* unbearable
inalámbri•co -ca *adj* wireless
inalcanzable *adj* unattainable
inamisto•so -sa *adj* unfriendly
inamovible *adj* irremovable; undetachable; (*incorporado*) built-in
inamovilidad *f* irremovability; tenure, permanent tenure
inane *adj* inane
inanición *f* starvation
inanima•do -da *adj* inanimate, lifeless
inapelable *adj* unappealable; unavoidable
inapetencia *f* loss of appetite
inapreciable *adj* inappreciable; imperceptible
inarmóni•co -ca *adj* unharmonious
inarrugable *adj* wrinkle-free
inarticula•do -da *adj* inarticulate
inartísti•co -ca *adj* inartistic
inasequible *adj* unattainable; unobtainable
inastillable *adj* nonshatterable, shatter-proof
inatacable *adj* unattackable; **inatacable por** resistant to
inaudi•to -ta *adj* unheard-of; outrageous
inauguración *f* inauguration; (*de una estatua*) unveiling
inaugural *adj* inaugural
inaugurar *tr* to inaugurate; (*p.ej., una estatua*) unveil
inaveriguable *adj* unascertainable
inca *mf* Inca
incai•co -ca *adj* Inca, Incan
incalificable *adj* unqualifiable; (*infame, atroz*) unspeakable
incambiable *adj* unchangeable
incandescente *adj* incandescent
incansable *adj* untiring, indefatigable
incapacitar *tr* to incapacitate; (law) to declare incompetent
inca•paz *adj* (*pl* **-paces**) incapable, unable; not large enough; stupid; (law) incompetent; frightful, unbearable
incasable *adj* unmarriageable; opposed to marriage; (*por su fealdad*) unable to find a husband
incautar *ref* — **incautarse de** to hold until claimed; (law) to seize, attach
incau•to -ta *adj* unwary, heedless
incendajas *fpl* kindling
incendiar *tr* to set on fire || *ref* to catch fire
incendia•rio -ria *adj* incendiary || *mf* incendiary, firebug
incendio *m* fire; (fig) fire, passion
incensar §2 *tr* to incense, burn incense before; (fig) to flatter
incensario *m* censer, incense burner
incenti•vo -va *adj & m* incentive
inceremonio•so -sa *adj* unceremonious
incertidumbre *f* uncertainty, incertitude
incesante *adj* unceasing
incesto *m* incest
incestuo•so -sa *adj* incestuous
incidencia *f* incidence; **por incidencia** by chance
incidente *adj* incident; incidental || *m* incident
incidir *tr* to make an incision in || *intr* — **incidir en culpa** to fall into guilt; **incidir en** or **sobre** to strike, impinge on
incienso *m* incense; (*olíbano*) frankincense
incier•to -ta *adj* uncertain
incineración *f* incineration; (*de cadáveres*) cremation
incinerar *tr* to incinerate; (*cadáveres*) cremate
incipiente *adj* incipient
incisión *f* incision; (*mordacidad en el lenguaje*) incisiveness, sarcasm
incisi•vo -va *adj* incisive; biting, sarcastic
inci•so -sa *adj* (*estilo del escritor*) choppy || *m* comma; clause; sentence
incitar *tr* to incite
incivil *adj* rude, impolite
incivilizа•do -da *adj* uncivilized
inclemencia *f* inclemency; **a la inclemencia** in the open, without shelter
inclemente *adj* inclement
inclinación *f* inclination; bent, leaning, propensity; nod, bow
inclinar *tr, intr & ref* to incline; bend, bow
íncli•to -ta *adj* illustrious, renowned
incluir §20 *tr* to include; (*en una carta*) inclose
inclusa *f* foundling home
incluse•ro -ra *mf* foundling
inclusión *f* inclusion; friendship
inclusive *adv* inclusive, inclusively || *prep* including
inclusi•vo -va *adj* inclusive
inclu•so -sa *adj* inclosed || *f* see **inclusa** || **incluso** *adv* inclusively; (*hasta, aun*) even || **incluso** *prep* including
incobrable *adj* uncollectible; irrecoverable
incógni•to -ta *adj* (*no conocido*) unknown; (*que no se da a conocer*) incognito || *mf* (*persona*) incognito || *m* (*condición de no ser conocido*) incognito; **de incógnito** (*sin ser conocido*) incognito || *f* (math & fig) unknown quantity
incoherente *adj* incoherent
íncola *m* inhabitant
incolo•ro -ra *adj* colorless
incólume *adj* unharmed, safe

incombustible *adj* incombustible, fireproof; cold, indifferent
incomerciable *adj* unmarketable
incomible *adj* uneatable, inedible
incomodar *tr* to inconvenience, disturb
incomodidad *f* inconvenience; annoyance, discomfort
incómo•do -da *adj* inconvenient; annoying, uncomfortable || *m* inconvenience; discomfort
incomparable *adj* incomparable
incompartible *adj* unsharable
incompasi•vo -va *adj* pitiless, unsympathetic
incompatible *adj* incompatible; (*acontecimientos, citas, horas de clase, etc.*) conflicting
incompetente *adj* incompetent
incompetible *adj* unmatchable
incomple•to -ta *adj* incomplete
incomponible *adj* unmendable, beyond repair
incomprable *adj* unpurchasable
incomprensible *adj* incomprehensible
incomprensión *f* incomprehension
incomunicación *f* isolation, solitary confinement
incomunica•do -da *adj* incommunicado; in solitary confinement
inconcebible *adj* inconceivable
inconclu•so -sa *adj* unfinished
inconcluyente *adj* inconclusive
inconcu•so -sa *adj* undeniable
incondicional *adj* unconditional
incone•xo -xa *adj* unconnected; (*inaplicable*) irrelevant
inconfidente *adj* distrustful
inconformidad *f* nonconformity; disagreement
inconformista *mf* nonconformist
inconfundible *adj* unmistakable
incon•gruo -grua *adj* incongruous
inconocible *adj* unknowable
inconquistable *adj* unconquerable; (*que no se deja vencer con ruegos y dádivas*) unbending, unyielding
inconsciencia *f* unconsciousness; unawareness
inconsciente *adj* unconscious; unaware; **lo inconsciente** the unconscious
inconsecuencia *f* (*falta de consecuencia o correspondencia en dichos y hechos*) inconsistency
inconsecuente *adj* inconsistent; (*que no se deduce de otra cosa*) inconsequential
inconsidera•do -da *adj* inconsiderate
inconsiguiente *adj* inconsequential, illogical
inconsistencia *f* (*falta de cohesión*) inconsistency
inconsistente *adj* inconsistent
inconsolable *adj* inconsolable
inconstante *adj* inconstant
inconstitucional *adj* unconstitutional
inconsútil *adj* seamless
incontable *adj* countless, innumerable
incontenible *adj* irrepressible
incontestable *adj* incontestable
incontinente *adj* incontinent || *adv* at once, instantly
incontrastable *adj* invincible; inconvincible; (*argumento*) unanswerable
incontrovertible *adj* incontrovertible
inconveniencia *f* inconvenience; unsuitability; impoliteness; impropriety
inconveniente *adj* inconvenient; unsuitable; impolite; improper || *m* drawback; disadvantage; objection
incordio *m* bore, nuisance
incorporación *f* incorporation, embodiment
incorpora•do -da *adj* (*el que estaba echado*) sitting up; (*montado en la construcción*) built-in
incorporar *tr* to incorporate, embody || *ref* to incorporate; (*el que estaba echado*) sit up; **incorporarse a** to join
incorrec•to -ta *adj* incorrect
incrédu•lo -la *adj* incredulous || *mf* disbeliever, doubter
increíble *adj* incredible
incremento *m* increment, increase
increpar *tr* to chide, rebuke
incriminar *tr* to incriminate; (*un delito, falta, defecto*) exaggerate the gravity of
incruen•to -ta *adj* bloodless
incrustar *tr* to incrust; (*embutir por adorno*) inlay
incubadora *f* incubator
incubar *tr & intr* to incubate || *ref* (fig) to be brewing
incuestionable *adj* unquestionable
inculcar §73 *tr* to inculcate|| *ref* to become obstinate
inculpable *adj* blameless, guiltless
inculpar *tr* to accuse, blame
incultivable *adj* untillable
incul•to -ta *adj* uncultivated, untilled; uncultured; (*estilo*) coarse, sloppy
incumbencia *f* incumbency, duty, obligation, province
incumbir *intr* — **incumbir a** to be incumbent on
incumplimiento *m* nonfulfillment
incunable *m* incunabulum
incurable *adj & mf* incurable
incuria *f* carelessness, negligence
incurio•so -sa *adj* careless, negligent
incurrir *intr* — **incurrir en** to incur
incursión *f* incursion, inroad, raid
indagación *f* investigation, research
indagatorio *m* deposition of the accused
indagar §44 *tr* to investigate
indebidamente *adv* unduly
indebi•do -da *adj* undue; wrong
indecencia *f* indecency
indecente *adj* indecent
indecible *adj* unspeakable, unutterable
indeci•so -sa *adj* undecided, indecisive; (*contorno, forma*) vague, obscure
indeclinable *adj* unavoidable; (gram) indeclinable
indecoro•so -sa *adj* improper
indefectible *adj* unfailing
indefendible *adj* indefensible
indefen•so -sa *adj* defenseless, undefended

indefinible *adj* indefinable
indefini•do -da *adj* indefinite; limitless; vague
indeleble *adj* indelible
indelibera•do -da *adj* unpremeditated
indelica•do -da *adj* indelicate
indemne *adj* unharmed, undamaged
indemnidad *f* (*seguridad contra un daño*) indemnity
indemnización *f* (*compensación*) indemnity, indemnification; **indemnización por despido** severance pay
indemnizar §60 *tr* to indemnify
independencia *f* independence
independiente *adj* & *mf* independent
independizar §60 *tr* to free, emancipate || *ref* to become independent
indescriptible *adj* indescribable
indeseable *adj* & *mf* undesirable
indesea•do -da *adj* unwanted
indesmallable *adj* runproof
indestructible *adj* indestructible
indetermina•do -da *adj* indeterminate; (gram) indefinite
indevo•to -ta *adj* impious; not fond, not devoted
india *f* wealth, riches; **Indias Occidentales** West Indies; **la India** India
indiana *f* printed calico
india•no -na *adj* & *mf* Spanish American; East Indian; West Indian || *m* man back from America with great wealth; **indiano de hilo negro** (coll) skinflint || *f* see **indiana**
indicación *f* indication; **por indicación de** at the direction of
indica•do -da *adj* appropriate, advisable; **muy indicado** just the thing, just the person
indica•dor -dora *adj* indicating, pointing || *m* indicator; gauge; (*de tránsito*) traffic signal
indicar §73 *tr* to indicate
indicati•vo -va *adj* & *m* indicative
índice *m* index; **índice de libros prohibidos** (eccl) Index; **índice de materias** table of contents; **índice en el corte** thumb index
indiciar *tr* to betoken, indicate; surmise, suspect
indicio *m* sign, token, indication; **indicios vehementes** circumstantial evidence
indiferente *adj* indifferent; (*que no importa*) immaterial
indígena *adj* indigenous || *mf* native
indigente *adj* indigent
indigestar *ref* to be indigestible; be disliked, be unbearable
indigestible *adj* indigestible
indigestión *f* indigestion
indignación *f* indignation
indigna•do -da *adj* indignant
indignar *tr* to anger, provoke || *ref* to become indignant
indignidad *f* (*falta de mérito*) unworthiness; (*acción reprobable*) indignity
indig•no -na *adj* unworthy
índigo *m* indigo
in•dio -dia *adj* & *mf* Indian || *f* see **india**
indirec•to -ta *adj* indirect || *f* hint, innuendo; **indirecta del padre Cobos** broad hint
indiscernible *adj* indiscernible
indiscre•to -ta *adj* indiscreet
indiscrimina•do -da *adj* indiscriminate; nondiscriminating
indisculpable *adj* inexcusable
indiscutible *adj* undeniable
indisoluble *adj* indissoluble
indispensable *adj* unpardonable; indispensable
indisponer §54 *tr* (*alterar la salud de*) to indispose, upset; disturb, upset; **indisponer a uno con** to set someone against, prejudice someone against || *ref* to become indisposed; **indisponerse con** to fall out with
indisponible *adj* unavailable
indispues•to -ta *adj* indisposed
indistintamente *adv* indistinctly; indiscriminately, without distinction
indistin•to -ta *adj* indistinct
individual *adj* individual; (*habitación en un hotel; partido de tenis*) single
individualidad *f* individuality
indivi•duo -dua *adj* individual; indivisible || *mf* (*persona indeterminada*) (coll) individual || *m* (*cada persona*) individual; (*miembro de una corporación*) member, fellow
indócil *adj* unteachable; headstrong, unruly
indocumenta•do -da *adj* unidentified; unqualified || *mf* nobody (*person of no account*)
indochi•no -na *adj* & *mf* Indo-Chinese || **la Indochina** Indochina
indoeurope•o -a *adj* & *m* Indo-European
índole *f* kind, class; nature, disposition, temper
indolente *adj* stolid, impassive; (*perezoso*) indolent
indolo•ro -ra *adj* painless
indoma•do -da *adj* untamed
indone•sio -sia *adj* & *mf* Indonesian || **la Indonesia** Indonesia
inducción *f* induction
inducido *m* (*de dínamo o motor*) (elec) armature
inducir §19 *tr* to induce
inductor *m* (*de dínamo o motor*) (elec) field
indudable *adj* doubtless
indulgente *adj* indulgent
indultar *tr* to pardon; free, exempt
indulto *m* pardon; exemption
indumentaria *f* clothing, dress; historical study of clothing
indumento *m* clothing, dress
industria *f* industry; **de industria** on purpose
industrial *adj* industrial || *m* industrialist
industrializar §60 *tr* to industrialize
industriar *tr* to teach, instruct, train || *ref* to get along, manage
industrio•so -sa *adj* industrious
inédi•to -ta *adj* unpublished; new, novel, unknown
inefable *adj* ineffable
ineficacia *f* inefficacy

inefi•caz *adj* (*pl* **-caces**) inefficacious, ineffectual
inelegible *adj* ineligible
ineludible *adj* inescapable
inenarrable *adj* indescribable
inencogible *adj* unshrinkable
inencontrable *adj* unobtainable
inequidad *f* inequity
inequívo•co -ca *adj* unmistakable
inercia *f* inertia
inerme *adj* unarmed
inerte *adj* inert; slow, sluggish
inescrupulo•so -sa *adj* unscrupulous
inescrutable or **inescudriñable** *adj* inscrutable
inespera•do -da *adj* unexpected, unforeseen; unhoped for
inestable *adj* unstable
inevitable *adj* unavoidable, inevitable
inexactitud *f* inaccuracy, inexactness
inexac•to -ta *adj* inaccurate, inexact
inexcusable *adj* inexcusable, unpardonable; unavoidable; indispensable
inexistencia *f* nonexistence
inexorable *adj* inexorable
inexperiencia *f* inexperience
inexplicable *adj* inexplicable, unexplainable
inexplica•do -da *adj* unexplained, unaccounted for
inexplora•do -da *adj* unexplored; (*mar*) uncharted
inexpresable *adj* inexpressible
inexpues•to -ta *adj* (phot) unexposed
inexpugnable *adj* impregnable; firm, unshakable
inextinguible *adj* unextinguishable; perpetual, lasting; (*sed*) unquenchable; (*risa*) uncontrollable
inextirpable *adj* ineradicable
infalible *adj* infallible
infamación *f* defamation
infamar *tr* to defame, discredit
infame *adj* infamous; vile, frightful || *mf* scoundrel
infamia *f* infamy
infancia *f* infancy
infan•do -da *adj* odious, unmentionable
infanta *f* female child; infanta (*any daughter of a king of Spain; wife of an infante*)
infante *m* male child; infante (*any son of a king of Spain who is not heir to the throne*); (mil) infantryman; **infante de coro** choirboy
infantería *f* infantry; **infantería de marina** marines, marine corps
infantil *adj* infant, infantile, childlike; innocent
infarto *m* (heart) infarct
infatigable *adj* indefatigable
infatuar §21 *tr* to make vain || *ref* to become vain
infaus•to -ta *adj* fatal, unlucky
infección *f* infection
infeccionar *tr* to infect
infeccio•so -sa *adj* infectious
infectar *tr* to infect
infec•to -ta *adj* foul, corrupt; infected; fetid
infecun•do -da *adj* sterile, barren
infe•liz (*pl* **-lices**) *adj* unhappy; simple, goodhearted || *m* wretch, poor soul
inferior *adj* inferior; lower; **inferior a** inferior to; lower than; less than; smaller than || *m* inferior
inferioridad *f* inferiority
inferir §68 *tr* to infer; lead to, entail; (*una herida*) inflict; (*una ofensa*) cause, offer
infernáculo *m* hopscotch
infernal *adj* infernal
infernar §2 *tr* to damn; irritate, annoy
infernillo *m* chafing dish
infestar *tr* to infest || *ref* to become infested
inficionar *tr* to infect || *ref* to become infected
infidelidad *f* infidelity; (*conjunto de infieles*) unbelievers
infidente *adj* faithless, disloyal
infiel *adj* (*falto de fidelidad*) unfaithful; (*no exacto*) inaccurate, inexact; (*no cristiano*) infidel || *mf* infidel
infierno *m* hell; **en el quinto infierno** or **en los quintos infiernos** far, far away
infijo *m* (gram) infix
infiltrar *tr & ref* to infiltrate
ínfi•mo -ma *adj* lowest; humblest, most abject; meanest, vilest
infinidad *f* infinity
infiniti•vo -va *adj & m* infinitive
infini•to -ta *adj* infinite || *m* infinite; (math) infinity || **infinito** *adv* greatly, very much
infirme *adj* infirm
inflación *f* inflation; (*vanidad*) conceit
inflaciona•rio -ria *adj* inflationary
inflado *m* inflation (*of a tire*)
inflamable *adj* inflammable, flammable
inflamación *f* ignition, inflammation; ardor, enthusiasm; (pathol) inflammation
inflamar *tr* to set on fire; inflame || *ref* to catch fire; become inflamed
inflar *tr* to inflate; exaggerate; puff up with pride || *ref* to inflate; be puffed up with pride
inflexible *adj* inflexible; unyielding, unbending
inflexión *f* inflection; **inflexión vocálica** (*metafonía*) umlaut
inflexionar *tr* to umlaut
infligir §27 *tr* to inflict
influencia *f* influence
influenciar *tr* to influence
influenza *f* influenza
influir §20 *intr* to have influence; have great weight; **influir en** or **sobre** to influence
influjo *m* influence; rising tide
influyente *adj* influential
información *f* information; (law) judicial inquiry, investigation; **informaciones** testimonial
informal *adj* (*que no se ajusta a las reglas debidas*) informal; unreliable
informar *tr & intr* to inform || *ref* to inquire, find out
informática *f* computer science
informati•vo -va *adj* informational; (*sección de un periódico*) news

informe *adj* shapeless, formless; misshapen || *m* piece of information; report; **informes** information; **informes confidenciales** inside information
infortuna•do -da *adj* unfortunate, unlucky
infortunio *m* misfortune; (*acaecimiento desgraciado*) mishap
infracción *f* infraction, infringement
infraconsumo *m* underconsumption
infrac•to -ta *adj* unperturbable
infraestructura *f* substructure; (rr) roadbed
inframundo *m* underworld
infrarro•jo -ja *adj & m* infrared
infrascri•to -ta *adj* undersigned; hereinafter mentioned
infrecuente *adj* infrequent
infringir **§27** *tr* to infringe, break, violate
infructuo•so -sa *adj* fruitless, unfruitful
ínfulas *fpl* conceit, airs; **darse ínfulas** to put on airs
infunda•do -da *adj* unfounded, groundless, baseless
infundio *m* lie, fib
infundir *tr* to infuse, instill
infusión *f* infusion; (*acción de echar agua sobre el que se bautiza*) sprinkling; **estar en infusión para** to be all set for
ingeniar *tr* to think up || *ref* to manage; **ingeniarse a** or **para** to manage to; **ingeniarse para ir viviendo** to manage to get along
ingeniería *f* engineering; **ingeniería genética** genetic engineering
ingeniero *m* engineer; **ingeniero de caminos, canales y puertos** government civil engineer
ingenio *m* talent, creative faculty; talented person; cleverness, skill, wit; (*artificio mecánico*) apparatus, device; (*del encuadernador*) paper cutter; engine of war; **afilar** or **aguzar el ingenio** to sharpen one's wits; **ingenio de azúcar** sugar refinery
ingeniosidad *f* ingenuity; wittiness
ingenio•so -sa *adj* (*dotado de ingenio; hecho con ingenio*) ingenious; (*agudo, sutil*) witty
ingéni•to -ta *adj* innate, inborn
ingente *adj* huge, enormous
ingenuidad *f* ingenuousness
inge•nuo -nua *adj* ingenuous
ingerir **§68** *tr & ref* var of **injerir**
ingestión *f* (food) consumption; ingestion
Inglaterra *f* England
ingle *f* groin
in•glés -glesa *adj* English; **a la inglesa** in the English manner || *m* Englishman; (*idioma*) English; **el inglés medio** Middle English; **los ingleses** the English || *f* Englishwoman
ingramatical *adj* ungrammatical
ingratitud *f* ingratitude, ungratefulness
ingra•to -ta *adj* (*desagradecido*) ungrateful; (*desagradecido; desagradable, áspero; improductivo*) thankless || *mf* ingrate
ingravidez *f* lightness, tenuousness; (*gravedad nula*) weightlessness
ingrávi•do -da *adj* light, tenuous; weightless
ingrediente *m* ingredient
ingresa•do -da *mf* new student
ingresar *tr* to deposit || *intr* to enter, become a member; (*beneficios*) come in || *ref* (Mex) to enlist
ingreso *m* entrance; admission; **ingresos** income, revenue
íngri•mo -ma *adj* solitary, alone
inhábil *adj* unable; unskillful; unfit, unqualified
inhabilidad *f* inability; unskillfulness; unfitness
inhabilitar *tr* to disable, to disqualify, to incapacitate
inhabita•do -da *adj* uninhabited
inhabitua•do -da *adj* unaccustomed
inherente *adj* inherent
inhibir *tr* to inhibit
inhospitala•rio -ria *adj* inhospitable
inhóspi•to -ta *adj* inhospitable
inhumanidad *f* inhumanity
inhuma•no -na *adj* inhuman, inhumane; (Chile) filthy
iniciación *f* initiation
inicial *adj & f* initial
iniciar *tr* to initiate || *ref* to be initiated
iniciativa *f* initiative
ini•cuo -cua *adj* wicked, iniquitous
inigualable *adj* incomparable
iniguala•do -da *adj* unequaled
ininteligente *adj* unintelligent
ininteligible *adj* unintelligible
ininterrumpi•do -da *adj* uninterrupted
iniquidad *f* iniquity
injerencia *f* interference, meddling
injerir **§68** *tr* to insert, introduce; (*alimentos*) take in; (hort) to graft || *ref* to interfere, meddle, intrude
injertar *tr* (hort & surg) to graft
injerto *m* (hort & surg) graft; transplant
injuria *f* offense, insult; abuse, wrong; damage, harm
injuriar *tr* to offend, insult; abuse, wrong; harm, damage
injurio•so -sa *adj* offensive, insulting; abusive; harmful; (*lenguaje*) profane
injusticia *f* injustice
injustifica•do -da *adj* unjustified
injus•to -ta *adj* unjust
inmacula•do -da *adj* immaculate
inmanejable *adj* unmanageable; unhandy
inmarcesible *adj* unfading
inmaterial *adj* immaterial
inmaturo -ra *adj* immature
inmediación *f* immediacy; proximity, nearness; **inmediaciones** neighborhood, outskirts
inmediatamente *adv* immediately; **inmediatamente que** as soon as
inmedia•to -ta *adj* immediate; close, adjoining, next; next above; next below; (*pago*) prompt; **venir a las inmediatas** to get into the thick of the fight
inmejorable *adj* superb, unsurpassable
inmemorial *adj* immemorial
inmen•so -sa *adj* immense
inmensurable *adj* immeasurable
inmereci•do -da *adj* undeserved
inmergir **§27** *tr* to immerse

inmersión *f* immersion
inmigración *f* immigration
inmigrante *mf* immigrant
inmigrar *intr* to immigrate
inminente *adj* imminent
inmiscuir §20 & **regular** *tr* to mix || *ref* to meddle, interfere
inmobilia•rio -ria *adj* real-estate
inmoble *adj* motionless; firm, constant
inmodera•do -da *adj* immoderate
inmodes•to -ta *adj* immodest
inmódi•co -ca *adj* excessive
inmoral *adj* immoral
inmortal *adj* immortal, deathless || *mf* immortal
inmortalizar §60 *tr* to immortalize
inmotiva•do -da *adj* groundless; unmotivated
inmovilizar §60 *tr* to immobilize; (*un caudal*) tie up
inmueble *m* property, piece of real estate; **inmuebles** real estate
inmun•do -da *adj* dirty, filthy
inmune *adj* immune
inmunizar §60 *tr* to immunize
inmutar *tr* to change, alter; disturb, upset || *ref* to change, alter; change countenance; **sin inmutarse** without batting an eye
inna•to -ta *adj* innate, inborn; natural
innatural *adj* unnatural
innavegable *adj* (*río*) unnavigable; (*embarcación*) unseaworthy
innecesa•rio -ria *adj* unnecessary
innegable *adj* undeniable
innoble *adj* ignoble
innocuidad *f* harmlessness
inno•cuo -cua *adj* harmless
innovación *f* innovation
innovar *tr* to innovate
innumerable *adj* innumerable
inocencia *f* innocence
inocentada *f* simpleness; blunder; (Ecuad) April Fools' joke
inocente *adj & mf* innocent; **coger por inocente** to make an April fool of
inocen•tón -tona *adj* simple, gullible || *mf* gull, dupe
inoculación *f* inoculation
inocular *tr* to inoculate; contaminate, pervert
inodo•ro -ra *adj* odorless || *m* deodorizer; (*excusado que funciona con agua corriente*) toilet
inofensi•vo -va *adj* inoffensive
inolvidable *adj* unforgettable
inope *adj* impecunious
inopia *f* indigence
inoportu•no -na *adj* inopportune, untimely
inorgáni•co -ca *adj* inorganic
inortodo•xo -xa *adj* unorthodox
inoxidable *adj* (*acero*) stainless; inoxidizable
inquietante *adj* disquieting, upsetting
inquietar *tr* to disquiet, worry; stir up, excite
inquie•to -ta *adj* anxious, worried
inquietud *f* disquiet, worry, concern
inquili•no -na *mf* tenant, renter
inquina *f* aversion, dislike, ill will
inquirir §40 *tr* to inquire, inquire into
inquisición *f* inquiry; inquisition
insabible *adj* unknowable
insaciable *adj* insatiable
insania *f* insanity
insa•no -na *adj* insane; imprudent
insatisfacción *f* dissatisfaction
insatisfe•cho -cha *adj* unsatisfied
inscribir §83 *tr* to inscribe; (law) to record || *ref* to enroll, register
inscripción *f* inscription; enrollment, registration
insecticida *adj & m* insecticide
insecto *m* insect
insegu•ro -ra *adj* insecure, unsafe; uncertain
insensa•to -ta *adj* foolish, stupid
insensible *adj* callous, hard-hearted, unfeeling; imperceptible
inseparable *adj* inseparable; undetachable || *mf* inseparable || *m* lovebird
insepul•to -ta *adj* unburied
inserción *f* insertion
inserir §68 *tr* to insert; (*injertar*) graft, engraft
insertar *tr* to insert
inservible *adj* useless
insidia *f* snare, ambush; plotting
insidiar *tr* to ambush, waylay; trap, trick
insidio•so -sa *adj* insidious
insigne *adj* noted, famous, renowned
insignia *f* badge, decoration, insignia; banner, standard
insignificante *adj* insignificant
insince•ro -ra *adj* insincere
insinuación *f* insinuation, hint
insinuante *adj* engaging, slick, crafty
insinuar §21 *tr* to insinuate; suggest, hint at || *ref* to creep in, slip in; ingratiate oneself; flow, run; **insinuarse en** to work one's way in
insípi•do -da *adj* insipid, vapid
insistir *intr* to insist
ínsi•to -ta *adj* inbred, innate
insociable *adj* unsociable
insolencia *f* insolence
insolentar *tr* to make insolent || *ref* to become insolent
insolente *adj* insolent
insóli•to -ta *adj* unusual
insoluble *adj* insoluble
insolvencia *f* insolvency
insomne *adj* sleepless
insomnio *m* insomnia
insondable *adj* fathomless; inscrutable
insonorización *f* soundproofing
insonoriza•do -da *adj* soundproof
insonorizar §60 *tr* to soundproof
insono•ro -ra *adj* soundproof
insospecha•do -da *adj* unsuspected
insostenible *adj* untenable
inspección *f* inspection; inspectorship; **inspección técnica de vehículos** (**I.T.V.**) car inspection
inspeccionar *tr* to inspect
inspiración *f* inspiration; inhalation
inspirante *adj* inspiring
inspirar *tr & intr* to inspire; (*atraer a los pulmones*) inhale, breathe in || *ref* to be inspired

instalación *f* plant, factory; outfit, equipment; arrangements, fittings; installment; **instalación sanitaria** plumbing
instalar *tr* to install || *ref* to settle
instantáne•o -a *adj* instantaneous || *f* snapshot
instante *m* instant, moment; **al instante** right away, immediately; **por instantes** uninterruptedly; any time
instantemente *adv* insistently, urgently
instar *tr* to press, urge || *intr* to be pressing, be urgent
instaurar *tr* to restore; reestablish
instigar §44 *tr* to instigate
instilar *tr* to instill
instinti•vo -va *adj* instinctive
instinto *m* instinct
institución *f* institution; **instituciones** (*de un Estado*) constitution; (*de una ciencia, arte, etc.*) principles
instituir §20 *tr* to institute, found
instituto *m* institute; (*de una orden religiosa*) rule, constitution; **instituto de segunda enseñanza** or **de enseñanza media** high school
institu•triz *f* (*pl* **-trices**) governess
instrucción *f* instruction; education
instructi•vo -va *adj* instructive
instruc•tor -tora *mf* teacher, instructor || *m* (mil) drillmaster || *f* instructress
instruí•do -da *adj* well-educated; well-posted
instruir §20 *tr* to instruct; (*un proceso o expediente*) draw up
instrumentar *tr* to instrument
instrumentista *mf* instrumentalist
instrumento *m* instrument; (*persona que se emplea para alcanzar un resultado*) tool; **instrumento de cuerda** (mus) stringed instrument; **instrumento de viento** (mus) wind instrument
insubordina•do -da *adj* insubordinate
insubstituíble *adj* irreplaceable
insudar *intr* to drudge
insuficiente *adj* insufficient
insufrible *adj* insufferable
ínsula *f* island; one-horse town
insular *adj* insular || *mf* islander
insulina *f* insulin
insulsez *f* tastelessness; dullness, heaviness
insul•so -sa *adj* tasteless; dull, heavy
insultada *f* insult
insultar *tr* to insult || *ref* to faint, swoon
insulto *m* insult; fainting spell
insume *adj* expensive
insumergible *adj* unsinkable
insuperable *adj* insurmountable
insurgente *adj & mf* insurgent
insurrección *f* insurrection
intac•to -ta *adj* intact, untouched
intachable *adj* blameless, irreproachable
integración *f* integration
integridad *f* integrity; virginity
ínte•gro -gra *adj* integral, whole; honest
intelecto *m* intellect
intelectual *adj & mf* intellectual
intelectualidad *f* intellectuality; (*conjunto de los intelectuales de un país o región*) intelligentsia
inteligencia *f* intelligence; **estar en inteligencia con** to be in collusion with
inteligente *adj* intelligent; trained, skilled
inteligible *adj* intelligible
intemperancia *f* intemperance
intemperante *adj* intemperate
intemperie *f* inclement weather; **a la intemperie** in the open, unsheltered
intempesti•vo -va *adj* unseasonable, inopportune, untimely
intención *f* intention; (*cautelosa advertencia*) caution; (*instinto dañino de un animal*) viciousness; **con intención** deliberately, knowingly; **de intención** on purpose
intendencia *f* intendance; (SAm) mayoralty
intendente *m* intendant; quartermaster general; (SAm) mayor
intensar *tr & ref* to intensify
intensidad *f* intensity
intensificar §73 *tr & ref* to intensify
intensión *f* intensity
intensi•vo -va *adj* intensive
inten•so -sa *adj* intense
intentar *tr* to try, to attempt; intend; try out
intento *m* intent, purpose; **de intento** on purpose
intentona *f* rash attempt (*to rob, escape, etc.*)
interacción *f* interaction
interamerica•no -na *adj* inter-American
intercalar *tr* to intercalate, insert
intercambiar *tr & ref* to interchange
intercambio *m* interchange, exchange
interceder *intr* to intercede
interceptar *tr* to intercept
intercep•tor -tora *mf* interceptor || *m* trap; separator; (aer) interceptor
interdecir §24 *tr* to interdict, forbid
interés *m* interest; **intereses creados** vested interests; **poner a interés** to put out at interest
interesa•do -da *adj* interested || *mf* interested party
interesante *adj* interesting
interesar *tr* to interest; involve || *intr* to be interesting || *ref* — **interesarse en** or **por** to be interested in, take an interest in
interescolar *adj* interscholastic, intercollegiate
interfec•to -ta *adj* murdered || *mf* victim of murder
interferencia *f* interference
interferir §68 *tr* to interfere with || *intr* to interfere
interfono *m* intercom
ínterin *adv* meanwhile || *conj* while, as long as || *m* (*pl* **intérines**) temporary incumbency
interinar *tr* to fill temporarily, fill in an acting capacity
interi•no -na *adj* temporary, acting, interim
interior *adj* interior, inner, inside; home, domestic || *m* interior, inside; mind, soul; **interiores** entrails, insides

interioridad *f* inside; **interioridades** inside story, private matters
interjección *f* interjection
interlinear *tr* to interline; (typ) to space, lead
interlocu•tor -tora *mf* speaker, party; interviewer
intermedia•rio -ria *adj & mf* intermediary ‖ *m* (com) middleman
interme•dio -dia *adj* intermediate ‖ *m* interval, interim; (mus) intermezzo; (theat) intermission, entr'acte
intermitente *adj* intermittent ‖ *m* (aut) direction light, turning light
internacional *adj* international
internacionalizar **§60** *tr* to internationalize
interna•do -da *mf* (mil) internee ‖ *m* boarding school
internamiento *m* internment
internar *tr* to send inland; intern ‖ *intr* to move inland ‖ *ref* to move inland; take refuge, hide; insinuate oneself; **internarse en** to go deeply into
internista *mf* internist
inter•no -na *adj* internal; inside ‖ *mf* boarding-school student; **interno de hospital** intern
interpelar *tr* to seek the protection or aid of; interrogate; interpellate
interpolar *tr* to interpolate; interpose; interrupt briefly
interponer **§54** *tr* to interpose; appoint as mediator ‖ *ref* to intervene, intercede
interprender *tr* to take by surprise
interpresa *f* surprise action; surprise seizure
interpretar *tr* to interpret
intérprete *mf* interpreter
interrogación *f* interrogation; question mark
interrogar **§44** *tr & intr* to question, interrogate
interrumpir *tr* to interrupt
interruptor *m* (elec) switch; **interruptor automático** (elec) circuit breaker; **interruptor del encendido** (aut) ignition switch; **interruptor de resorte** (elec) snap switch
intersección *f* (geom) intersection
intersticio *m* interstice; interval
intervalo *m* interval
intervención *f* intervention; inspection; (*de cuentas*) audit, auditing; (surg) operation; **intervención de los precios** price control; **no intervención** nonintervention
intervenir **§79** *tr* to take up, work on; inspect, supervise; (*cuentas*) audit; (*un teléfono*) tap; (surg) operate on ‖ *intr* to mediate, intervene, intercede; participate; happen
interventor *m* election supervisor; (com) auditor
inter•viev *m* (*pl* **-vievs**) interview
intervievar *tr* to interview
intesta•do -da *adj & mf* intestate
intesti•no -na *adj* internal; domestic ‖ *m* intestine; **intestino delgado** small intestine; **intestino grueso** large intestine
intimación *f* announcement, notification
intimar *tr* to announce ‖ *intr & ref* to become well-acquainted, to become intimate
intimidad *f* intimacy; (*parte íntima o personal*) privacy
intimidar *tr* to intimidate
ínti•mo -ma *adj* intimate; (*más interno*) innermost
intitular *tr* to entitle ‖ *ref* to use a title; be called
intocable *mf* untouchable
intolerante *adj & mf* intolerant
inton•so -sa *adj* unshorn; ignorant; (*libro o revista*) uncut ‖ *mf* ignoramus
intoxicación *f* intoxication; poisoning
intoxicar **§73** *tr* to poison, intoxicate
intracruzamiento *m* inbreeding
intranquilidad *f* uneasiness, worry
intranquilizar **§60** *tr* to make uneasy, worry
intranqui•lo -la *adj* uneasy, worried
intransigente *adj & mf* intransigent, die-hard
intransiti•vo -va *adj* intransitive
intrascendente *adj* unimportant; nonessential
intratable *adj* unmanageable; impassable; unsociable
intrepidez *f* intrepidity
intrépi•do -da *adj* intrepid
intriga *f* intrigue
intrigar **§44** *tr* (*excitar la curiosidad de*) to intrigue ‖ *intr* to intrigue ‖ *ref* to be intrigued
intrinca•do -da *adj* intricate
intrincar **§73** *tr* to complicate; confuse, bewilder
intríngu•lis *m* (*pl* **-lis**) hidden motive, mystery
intrínse•co -ca *adj* intrinsic(al)
introducción *f* introduction
introducir **§19** *tr* to introduce; insert, put in ‖ *ref* to gain access; meddle, interfere, intrude
introito *m* (*de un escrito o una oración*) introduction; (*de un poema dramático*) prologue; (eccl) introit
introspecti•vo -va *adj* introspective
introverti•do -da *mf* introvert
intru•so -sa *adj* intrusive ‖ *mf* intruder, interloper
intuición *f* intuition
intuir **§20** *tr* to guess, sense
intuito *m* view, glance, look; **por intuito de** in view of
inundación *f* flood, inundation
inundar *tr* to flood, inundate
inurba•no -na *adj* discourteous, unmannerly
inusita•do -da *adj* (*no ordinario*) unusual; obsolete, out of use
inusual *adj* unusual
inútil *adj* useless
invadir *tr* to invade
invalidar *tr* to invalidate
invalidez *f* invalidity
inváli•do -da *adj & mf* invalid
invariable *adj* invariable
invasión *f* invasion
inva•sor -sora *mf* invader
invectiva *f* invective
invectivar *tr* to inveigh against
invencible *adj* invincible

invención *f* invention; finding, discovery; deception
invendible *adj* unsalable
inventar *tr* to invent
inventariar §77 & **regular** *tr* to inventory
inventario *m* inventory
inventi•vo -va *adj* inventive || *f* inventiveness
invento *m* invention
inven•tor -tora *adj* inventive || *mf* inventor
inverecun•do -da *adj* shameless, brazen
inverisímil *adj* improbable, unlikely
invernáculo *m* greenhouse, hothouse, conservatory
invernada *f* wintertime; (SAm) pasture land; (Ven) torrential rain
invernadero *m* greenhouse, hothouse; winter resort; winter pasture
invernal *adj* winter || *m* cattle shed (*in winter-pasture land*)
invernar §2 *intr* to winter; be winter
inverni•zo -za *adj* winter; wintery
inverosímil *adj* improbable, unlikely
inversión *f* inversion; (*de dinero*) investment; (gram) inverted order
inversionista *adj* investment || *mf* investor
inver•so -sa *adj* inverse, opposite; **a** or **por la inversa** on the contrary
inversor *m* investor
invertebra•do -da *adj* & *m* invertebrate
inverti•do -da *adj* inverted || *mf* invert
invertir §68 *tr* to invert; (*dinero*) invest; (*tiempo*) spend; reverse
investidura *f* investment, investiture; station, standing
investigación *f* investigation, research; **investigación mercológica** market research
investigar §44 *tr* to investigate || *intr* to research
investir §50 *tr* — **investir con** or **de** (*poner en posesión de*) to invest with
invetera•do -da *adj* inveterate, confirmed
invic•to -ta *adj* unconquered
invidencia *f* blindness
invidente *adj* blind || *mf* blind person
invierno *m* winter; rainy season
inviolabilidad *f* inviolability; undamageability
invisible *adj* invisible || *m* (Mex) hair net; **en un invisible** in an instant
invitación *f* invitation
invita•do -da *mf* guest
invitar *tr* to invite
invocar §73 *tr* to invoke
involunta•rio -ria *adj* involuntary
invulnerable *adj* invulnerable
inyección *f* injection; **inyección secundaria** booster shot
inyectable *adj* injectable || *m* ampule, phial
inyecta•do -da *adj* bloodshot, inflamed
inyectar *tr* to inject || *ref* to become congested; become inflamed
ionizar §60 *tr* to ionize || *ref* to be ionized
ionosfera *f* ionosphere
ir §41 *intr* to go; be becoming, fit, suit; be at stake; **ir a** + *inf* to be going to + *inf* (*to express futurity*); **ir a buscar** to go get, go for; **ir a parar en** to end up in; **ir con cuidado** to be careful; **ir con miedo** to be afraid; **ir con tiento** to watch one's step; **ir de caza** to go hunting; **ir de pesca** to go fishing; **lo que va de** so far (as); **¡qué va!** of course not!; **¡vaya!** the deuce!; what a. . . ! || *ref* to go away; leak; wear away; get old; break to pieces
ira *f* anger, wrath, ire
iracun•do -da *adj* angry, wrathful, irate
Irak, el Iraq
Irán, el Iran
ira•nés -nesa or **ira•nio -nia** *adj* & *mf* Iranian
ira•qués -quesa or **iraquiano -na** *adj* & *mf* Iraqi
iris *m* (*pl* **iris**) (*del ojo*) iris; rainbow
Irlanda *f* Ireland
irlan•dés -desa *adj* Irish || *m* Irishman; (*idioma*) Irish; **los irlandeses** the Irish || *f* Irishwoman
ironía *f* irony
iróni•co -ca *adj* ironic(al)
ironizar §60 *tr* to ridicule
irracional *adj* irrational
irradiar *tr* to radiate, irradiate; (*difundir*) broadcast || *intr* to radiate
irrazonable *adj* unreasonable
irreal *adj* unreal
irrealidad *f* unreality
irrebatible *adj* irrefutable
irreconocible *adj* unrecognizable
irrecuperable *adj* irretrievable
irrecusable *adj* unimpeachable
irredimible *adj* irredeemable
irreemplazable *adj* irreplaceable
irreflexión *f* rashness, thoughtlessness
irreflexi•vo -va *adj* rash, thoughtless
irregular *adj* irregular || *m* (mil) irregular
irregularidad *f* irregularity; embezzlement
irrelevante *adj* irrelevant
irreligio•so -sa *adj* irreligious
irrellenable *adj* nonrefillable
irremediable *adj* irremediable
irremisible *adj* unpardonable
irreparable *adj* irreparable
irreprimible *adj* irrepressible
irreprochable *adj* irreproachable
irresistible *adj* irresistible
irresoluble *adj* unworkable, unsolvable
irrespetuo•so -sa *adj* disrespectful
irresponsable *adj* irresponsible
irresuel•to -ta *adj* hesitant, wavering
irreverente *adj* irreverent
irrigación *f* irrigation
irrigar §44 *tr* to irrigate
irrisible *adj* laughable, absurd
irrisión *f* derision, ridicule; laughingstock
irritante *adj* & *m* irritant
irritar *tr* to irritate || *ref* to become exasperated
irrompible *adj* unbreakable
irrumpir *intr* to burst in; **irrumpir en** to burst into
irrupción *f* sudden attack; invasion
isi•dro -dra *mf* hick, jake, yokel
isla *f* island; (*manzana de casas*) block; **isla de peatones** or **isla de seguridad** safety zone (for pedestrians); **islas Baleares** Ba-

learic Islands; **islas Canarias** Canary Islands; **islas de Barlovento** Windward Islands; **islas de Sotavento** Leeward Islands; **islas Filipinas** Philippine Islands
Islam, el Islam
islan•dés -desa *adj* Icelandic || *mf* Icelander || *m* (*idioma*) Icelandic
Islandia *f* Iceland
isle•ño -ña *adj* island || *mf* islander; (Cuba) Canarian
isleta *f* isle
isométri•co -ca *adj* isometric
isométrica *f* isometrics
isósce•les *adj* (*pl* **-les**) isosceles
isótopo *m* isotope
israe•lí (*pl* **-líes**) *adj* & *mf* Israeli
israelita *adj* & *mf* Israelite
istmo *m* isthmus
Italia *f* Italy
italia•no -na *adj* & *mf* Italian
itáli•co -ca *adj* Italic; (typ) italic || *f* (typ) italics
itinera•rio -ria *adj* & *m* itinerary
izar **§60** *tr* (naut) to hoist, haul up
izquierda *f* left hand; left-hand side; (pol) left; **a la izquierda** left, on the left, to the left
izquierdear *intr* to go wild, go astray, go awry
izquierdista *adj* leftist || *mf* leftist, leftwinger
izquierdizante *adj* leftish
izquier•do -da *adj* left; left-hand; left-handed; crooked; **levantarse del izquierdo** to get out of bed on the wrong side || *f* see **izquierda**

J

J, j (jota) *f* eleventh letter of the Spanish alphabet
jabalcón *m* strut, brace
jaba•lí *m* (*pl* **-líes**) wild boar
jabalina *f* javelin; wild sow
jabardillo *m* (*de insectos*) noisy swarm; noisy throng
jabeque *m* (naut) xebec; gash in the face
jabón *m* soap; cake of soap; **dar jabón a** to softsoap; **dar un jabón a** (coll) to upbraid, to reprimand; **jabón de afeitar** shaving soap; **jabón de Castilla** Castile soap; **jabón de tocador** or **de olor** toilet soap; **jabón de sastre** soapstone, French chalk; **jabón en polvo** soap powder
jabonado *m* soaping; (*ropa lavada o por lavar*) wash
jabonadura *f* soaping; **dar una jabonadura a** to lambaste, upbraid; **jabonaduras** soapy water; soapsuds
jabonar *tr* to soap; reprimand
jaboncillo *m* cake of toilet soap; **jaboncillo de sastre** soapstone, French chalk
jabone•ro -ra *adj* soap; (*toro*) yellowish, dirty-white || *mf* soapmaker; soap dealer || *f* soap dish
jabonete *m* cake of toilet soap
jabono•so -sa *adj* soapy, lathery
jaca *f* pony, jennet
jacal *m* (Guat, Mex, Ven) hut, shack
jácara *f* merry ballad; cheerful song and dance; night revelers; story, argument; fake, hoax, lie; annoyance, bother
jacarear *intr* to go serenading, go singing in the street; be disagreeable
jáca•ro -ra *adj* & *m* braggart || *f* see **jácara**
jacinto *m* hyacinth
jaco *m* nag, jade; gray parrot
jactancia *f* boasting, bragging
jactancio•so -sa *adj* boastful, bragging
jactar *ref* to boast, brag; **jactarse de** to boast of
jade *m* jade
jadeante *adj* panting
jadear *intr* to pant
jadeo *m* panting
ja•ez *m* (*pl* **-eces**) harness, piece of harness; ilk, stripe, kind; **jaeces** trappings
jaguar *m* jaguar
jagüel *m* (Arg) reservoir
jaharrar *tr* to plaster
jalar *tr* to pull; flirt with || *intr* to get out, beat it || *ref* to get drunk
jalbegar **§44** *tr* to whitewash; (*el rostro*) to paint || *ref* to paint the face
jalbegue *m* whitewash; whitewashing; paint, make-up
jalda•do -da *adj* bright-yellow
jalea *f* jelly; **hacerse una jalea** to be madly in love
jalear *tr* (*a los que bailan y cantan*) to animate with clapping and shouting; (*a los perros*) to incite, urge on; (Chile) to tease, pester || *intr* to dance the jaleo || *ref* to have a noisy time; swing and sway
jaleo *m* cheering, shouting; jamboree; jaleo (*vivacious Spanish solo dance*)
jalis•co -ca *adj* (Guat, Mex) drunk || *m* (Mex) straw hat
jalma *f* small packsaddle
jalón *m* surveying rod, range pole; (Guat, Mex) swig of liquor; (CAm) beau; **jalón de mira** leveling rod
jalonar *tr* to stake out, mark out
jalonear *tr* (Mex) to pull, jerk
jalonero *m* (surv) rodman
jamaica *m* Jamaica rum || *f* (Mex) charity fair
jamaica•no -na or **jamaiqui•no -na** *adj* & *mf* Jamaican
jamar *tr* to eat
jamás *adv* never; ever

jamba *f* jamb
jambaje *m* doorframe, window frame
jamelgo *m* jade, nag
jamete *m* samite
jamón *m* ham
jamona *f* fat middle-aged woman
jamugas *fpl* mule chair
jánda•lo -la *adj & mf* Andalusian
Jantipa *f* or **Jantipe** *f* Xanthippe
Japón, el Japan
japo•nés -nesa *adj & mf* Japanese || *m* (*idioma*) Japanese
jaque *m* (*lance del ajedrez*) check; bully; **dar jaque a** to check; **dar jaque mate a** to checkmate; **en jaque** in check; **estar muy jaque** to be full of pep; **jaque mate** checkmate; **tener en jaque** to hold a threat over the head of || *interj* check!
jaquear *tr* to check; (*al enemigo*) harass
jaqueca *f* sick headache; **dar una jaqueca a** to bore to death
jacqueco•so -sa *adj* boring, tiresome
jaquemar *m* jack (*figure that strikes a clock bell*)
jarabe *m* syrup; sweet drink; **jarabe de pico** lip service, idle promise
jarana *f* merrymaking; rumpus; carousal, spree; trick, deceit; jest, joke; small guitar; **ir de jarana** to go on a spree
jaranear *tr* (CAm, Col) to swindle, cheat || *intr* to go on a spree; raise a rumpus; joke
jarane•ro -ra *adj* merrymaking; cheerful, merry || *mf* merrymaker, reveler
jarano *m* sombrero
jarcia *f* fishing tackle; jumble, mess; **jarcias** tackle, rigging; **jarcia trozada** junk (*old cable*)
jardín *m* garden, flower garden; (baseball) field, outfield; (naut) privy, latrine; **jardín central** (baseball) center field; **jardín de la infancia** kindergarten; **jardín derecho** (baseball) right field; **jardín izquierdo** (baseball) left field
jardinera *f* jardiniere, flower stand; basket carriage; summer trolley car, open trolley car
jardinería *f* gardening
jardine•ro -ra *mf* gardener; **jardinero adornista** landscape gardener || *m* (baseball) fielder, outfielder || *f* see **jardinera**
jardinista *mf* landscape gardener
jarea *f* (Mex) hunger
jarear *intr* (Bol) to stop for a rest || *ref* (Mex) to flee, run away; (Mex) to swing, sway; (Mex) to die of starvation
jareta *f* (sew) casing
jari•fo -fa *adj* showy, spruce, natty
jaro•cho -cha *adj* brusk, bluff || *m* insulting fellow; Veracruz peasant
jarope *m* syrup; nasty potion
jarra *f* jug, jar, water pitcher; **de jarras** or **en jarras** with arms akimbo
jarrete *m* hock, gambrel
jarretera *f* garter
jarro *m* pitcher; **echar un jarro de agua (fría) a** to pour cold water on
jarrón *m* (*vaso para adornar chimeneas, consolas, etc.*) vase; (*sobre un pedestal*) urn
jaspe *m* jasper
jaspea•do -da *adj* marbled, speckled || *m* marbling, speckling
jaspear *tr* to marble, speckle
jateo *m* foxhound
ja•to -ta *mf* calf
Jauja *f* Cockaigne; **¿estamos aquí o en Jauja?** where do you think you are?; **vivir en Jauja** to live in the lap of luxury
jaula *m* cage; (*embalaje de listones de madera*) crate; (Mex) open freight car; (Cuba, P-R) police wagon; **jaula de locos** insane asylum, madhouse
jauría *f* pack (*of hounds*)
java•nés -nesa *adj & mf* Javanese || *m* (*idioma*) Javanese
jazmín *m* jasmine; **jasmín de la India** gardenia
jazz *m* jazz
J.C. *abbr* **Jesucristo**
jebe *m* alum; (SAm) rubber
jedive *m* khedive
jefa *f* female head or leader; **jefa de ruta** hostess (*on a bus*)
jefatura *f* headship, leadership; (*de policía*) headquarters
jefe *m* chief, boss, head, leader; (*de una tribu*) chieftain; **jefe de cocina** chef; **jefe do coro** choirmaster; **jefe de equipajes** (rr) baggage master; **jefe de estación** stationmaster; **jefe del estado** chief of state; **jefe del gobierno** chief executive; **jefe de redacción** editor in chief; **jefe de ruta** guide; **jefe de tren** (rr) conductor; **jefe de tribu** chieftain; **quedar jefe** (Chile) to gamble away everything
jején *m* gnat, sandfly
jenabe *m* or **jenable** *m* mustard
jengibre *m* ginger
Jenofonte *m* Xenophon
jeque *m* sheik
jerarca *m* hierarch, head
jerarquía *f* hierarchy; **de jerarquía** important
jeremiada *f* jeremiad
jeremiquear *intr* to moan; pour out one's troubles
jerez *m* sherry
jerga *f* coarse cloth; straw mattress; (*lenguaje especial de ciertos oficios; lenguaje difícil de entender*) jargon
jergón *m* straw mattress; ill-fitting clothes; (*persona torpe y estúpida*) lummox
Jericó Jericho
jerife *m* shereef
jerigonza *f* (*lenguaje especial de ciertos oficios; lenguaje difícil de entender*) jargon; (*lenguaje vulgar, caló*) slang; piece of folly
jeringa *f* syringe; (*para inyectar materias blandas en una máquina*) gun; annoyance, plague; **jeringa de engrase** or **grasa** grease gun
jeringar §44 *tr* to syringe; inject; give an enema to; plague
jeringazo *m* injection, shot; squirt

jeringuilla *f* (*jeringa pequeña*) syringe; (bot) mock orange

Jerjes *m* Xerxes

jeroglífi•co -ca *adj & m* hieroglyphic

Jerónimo *m* Jerome

jer•sey *m* (*pl* **-seis**) jersey, sweater

Jerusalén Jerusalem

Jesucristo *m* Jesus Christ

jesuíta *adj & m* Jesuit

jesuíti•co -ca *adj* Jesuitic(al)

Jesús *m* Jesus; (*imagen del niño Jesús*) bambino; **en un decir Jesús** in an instant; **¡Jesús, María y José!** my gracious!

jeta *f* hog's snout, pig face; (*rostro de una persona*) phiz, mug; **estar con tanta jeta** to make a long face; **poner jeta** to pucker one's lips

jetu•do -da *adj* thick-lipped; grim, gruff

Jhs. *abbr* **Jesús**

jíba•ro -ra *mf* (W-I) white peasant

jibia *f* cuttlefish

jícara *f* chocolate cup; (CAm, Mex, W-I) calabash cup

jícaro *m* calabash (tree)

jifia *f* swordfish

jilguero *m* linnet, goldfinch

jilote *m* (Mex) green ear of corn

jineta *f* (zool) genet

jinete *m* rider, horseman

jinetear *tr* (*caballos cerriles*) to break in || *intr* to show off one's horsemanship

jinglar *intr* to swing, to rock

jingoísmo *m* jingoism

jingoísta *adj & mf* jingo

jipa•to -ta *adj* pale, wan; insipid, tasteless; (Guat) drunk

jipijapa *m* Panama hat || *f* jipijapa; strip of jipijapa straw

jira *f* strip of cloth; outing, picnic; trip, tour; swing, political trip

jirón *m* rag, tatter, shred; (*de una falda*) facing; pennant; bit, drop, shred; **hacer jirones** to tear to shreds

jitomate *m* (Mex) tomato

joco•so -sa *adj* jocose, jocular

jocotal *m* (CAm, Mex) Spanish plum (*tree*)

jocote *m* (CAm, Mex) Spanish plum (*fruit*)

jocoyote *m* (Mex) baby (*youngest child*)

jofaina *f* washbowl, basin

jolgorio *m* fun, merriment

jonrón *m* (baseball) home run

Jordán *m* Jordan (*river*); **ir al Jordán** to be born again

Jordania *f* Jordan (*country*)

jorda•no -na *adj & mf* Jordanian

jorguín *m* sorcerer, wizard

jorguina *f* sorceress, witch

jorguinería *f* sorcery, witchcraft

jornada *f* journey, trip, stage; day's journey; (*horas del trabajo diario del obrero*) workday; (*tiempo que dura la vida de un hombre*) lifetime; battle; (*muerte*) passing; summer residence of diplomat or diplomatic corps; event, occasion; undertaking; (mil) expedition; (*de un drama*) (archaic) act; **a grandes** or **largas jornadas** by forced marches; **al fin de la jornada** in the end; **caminar por sus jornadas** to proceed with circumspection; **hacer mala jornada** to get nowhere; **jornada ordinaria** full time; **jornada reducida** reduced working hours

jornal *m* day's work; day's pay; **a jornal** by the day; **jornal mínimo** minimum wage

jornalero *m* day laborer

joroba *f* hump; annoyance, bother

joroba•do -da *adj* humpbacked, hunchbacked; annoyed, bothered || *mf* humpback, hunchback

jorobar *tr* to annoy, pester

jorongo *m* (Mex) poncho; (Mex) woolen blanket

jota *f* (*letra del alfabeto*) J; jota (*Spanish folk dance and music*); jot, iota, tittle; vegetable soup; **sin faltar una jota** with not a whit left out

joven *adj* young; **ser joven de esperanzas** to have a bright future || *mf* youth, young person; **de joven** as a youth, as a young man, as a young woman

jovial *adj* jovial

joya *f* jewel; (*brocamantón*) diamond brooch; (*agasajo*) gift, present; (*persona o cosa de mucha valía*) (fig) jewel, gem; **joya de familia** heirloom; **joyas** jewelry; trousseau; **joyas de fantasía** costume jewelry

joyante *adj* glossy

joyelero *m* jewel case, casket

joyería *f* (*conjunto de joyas*) jewelry; jewelry shop; jewelry trade

joye•ro -ra *mf* jeweler || *m* jewel case, casket

Juan *m* John; **Buen Juan** sap, easy mark; **Juan Español** the Spanish people, the typical Spaniard; **San Juan Bautista** John the Baptist

Juana *f* Jane, Jean, Joan; **Juana de Arco** Joan of Arc, Jeanne d'Arc; **juanas** glove stretcher

juanete *m* bunion; high cheekbone

jubilación *f* retirement; (*renta de la persona jubilada*) pension, retirement annuity

jubila•do -da *adj* retired || *mf* retired person, pensioner

jubilar *tr* to retire, pension; throw out || *intr* to rejoice; retire, be pensioned || *ref* to rejoice; retire, be pensioned; (Col) to decline, go to pieces; (CAm, Ven) to play hooky; (Cuba, Mex) to become a past master

jubileo *m* much coming and going, great doings; (eccl) jubilee; **por jubileo** once in a long time

júbilo *m* jubilation

jubilo•so -sa *adj* jubilant, joyful

jubón *m* jerkin

judaísmo *m* Judaism

judería *f* (*raza judaica*) Jewry; (*barrio de los judíos*) ghetto

judía *f* Jewess; kidney bean, string bean; **judía de careta** black-eyed bean; **judía de la peladilla** Lima bean

judicatura *f* judicature; (*cargo de juez*) judgeship

judicial *adj* judicial, judiciary

judí•o -a *adj* Jewish || *mf* Jew || *f* see **judía**

juego *m* (*acción de jugar*) play, playing; (*ejercicio recreativo en el cual se gana o se pierde*) game; (*vicio de jugar*) gambling; (*lugar donde se ejecutan ciertos juegos*): (bowling) alley; (tennis) court; (baseball) field; (*tantos necesarios para ganar la partida*) game; (*de muebles*) suit, suite; (*de café*) service; (*de vajilla*) set; (*de luces, colores, aguas*) play; (mach) play; (*p.ej., de diplomacia*) (fig) game; **a juego** to match, e.g., **una silla a juego** a chair to match; **conocer el juego de** to see through, to have the number of; **en juego** at hand; **hacer juego** to match; **hacer juego con** to match, to go with; **juego de alcoba** bedroom suit; **juego de azar** game of chance; **juego de bolas** (mach) ball bearing; **juego de campanas** chimes; **juego de comedor** dining-room suit; **juego de envite** gambling game, game played for money; **juego de escritorio** desk set; **juego de la cuna** cat's cradle; **juego de la pulga** tiddlywinks; **juego del corro** ring-around-a-rosy; **juego del salto** leapfrog; **juego del tres en raya** tick-tack-toe played with movable counters or pebbles; **juego de manos** legerdemain, sleight of hand; roughhousing; **juego de niños** (*cosa muy fácil*) child's play; **juego de palabras** play on words, pun; **juego de pelota** ball game; pelota; **juego de piernas** footwork; **juego de por ver** (Chile) game played for fun; **juego de prendas** game of forfeits, forfeits; **juego de suerte** game of chance; **juego de tejo** shuffleboard; **juego de timbres** glockenspiel; **juego de vocablos** or **voces** play on words, pun; **juego limpio** fair play; **juego público** gambling house; **juegos de sociedad** parlor games; **juegos malabares** juggling; flimflam; **juego sucio** foul play; **no ser cosa de juego** to be no laughing matter; **por juego** in fun, for fun; **verle a uno el juego** to be on to someone

juerga *f* carousal, spree; **juerga de borrachera** drinking bout, binge; **ir de juerga** (coll) to go on a spree

juerguista *mf* carouser, reveler

jue•ves *m* (*pl* **-ves**) Thursday; **Jueves Santo** Maundy Thursday

juez *m* (*pl* **jueces**) judge; **juez de alzadas** appellate judge; **juez de guardia** coroner; **juez de instrucción** examining magistrate; **juez de paz** justice of the peace; **juez de salida** (sport) starter; **juez de tiempo** (sport) timekeeper

jugada *f* (*lance*) play, throw, stroke, move; **mala jugada** dirty trick

juga•dor -dora *mf* player; gambler; **jugador de manos** prestidigitator; **jugador de ventaja** sharper

jugar §42 *tr* (*p.ej., un naipe, una partida de juego*) to play; (*una espada*) wield; (*arriesgar*) stake, risk; (*las manos, los dedos*) move; **jugarle a uno las bebidas** to match someone for the drinks || *intr* to play; to gamble; (*hacer juego dos cosas*) match; (*intervenir*) figure, participate; **jugar a** (*p.ej., los naipes, el tenis*) to play; **jugar con** (*un contrario*) to play; (*una persona; los sentimientos de una persona*) toy with; match; **jugar en** to have a hand in || *ref* (*p.ej., la vida*) to risk; to be at stake; **jugarse el todo por el todo** to stake all, shoot the works

jugarreta *f* bad play, poor play; mean trick, dirty trick

juglar *m* minstrel, jongleur; (*bufón*) (archaic) juggler

juglaría *f* minstrelsy

jugo *m* (*p.ej., de la naranja*) juice; (*de la carne*) gravy; (*líquido orgánico*) juice; (fig) gist, essence, substance; **en su jugo** (culin) au jus; **jugo de muñeca** elbow grease

jugo•so -sa *adj* juicy; substantial, important

juguete *m* toy, plaything; (*burla*) joke, jest; (theat) skit; **de juguete** toy, e.g., **soldado de juguete** toy soldier; **juguete de movimiento** mechanical toy; **por juguete** for fun, in fun

juguetear *intr* to frolic, romp, sport

juguete•ro -ra *adj* toy || *mf* toy dealer || *m* whatnot, étagère

juguete-sorpresa *m* (*pl* **juguetes-sorpresa**) jack-in-the-box

jugue•tón -tona *adj* playful, frisky

juicio *m* judgment; (law) trial; **estar en su cabal juicio** to be in one's right mind; **estar fuera de juicio** to be out of one's mind; **juicio de Dios** (hist) ordeal; **pedir en juicio** (law) to sue

juicio•so -sa *adj* judicious, wise

julepe *m* julep; scolding; scare, fright

julepear *tr* to scold; whip; (SAm) to scare, frighten; (Mex) to weary, tire out

julio *m* July

julo *m* lead cow, lead mule

jumen•to -ta *mf* ass, donkey

juncal *adj* willowy, rushy; (fig) willowy, lissome

juncia *f* sedge; **vender juncia** to boast, brag

junco *m* (*embarcación china*) junk; (bot) rush, bulrush; **junco de Indias** (bot) rattan; **junco de laguna** (bot) rush, bulrush

junco•so -sa *adj* rushy, full of rushes

jungla *f* jungle

junio *m* June

junípero *m* juniper

junquera *f* rush, bulrush

junquillo *m* jonquil

junta *f* meeting, conference; board, council; junction, union; joint, seam; (*empaquetadura*) gasket; (*arandela*) washer; **junta de comercio** board of trade; **junta de charnela** (mach) knuckle; **junta de sanidad** board of health; **junta universal** (mach) universal joint

juntamente *adv* together; at the same time

juntar *tr* to join, unite; gather, gather together; (*una puerta*) half-close || *ref* to gather together; go along; copulate

jun•to -ta *adj* joined, united; **jun•tos -tas** together || *f* see **junta** || **junto** *adv* together;

at the same time; **junto a** near, close to; **junto con** along with, together with; **todo junto** at the same time, all at once
juntura *f* junction; (*p.ej., de una cañería; de un hueso*) joint; connection, coupling
jura *f* oath
jura•do -da *adj* (*enemigo*) sworn || *m* (*conjunto de cuidadanos encargados de determinar la culpabilidad del acusado; conjunto de examinadores de un certamen*) jury; (*cada uno de los expresados individuous*) juror; juryman
juramentar *tr* to swear in || *ref* to take an oath, be sworn in
juramento *m* oath; (*voto, reniego*) curse, swearword; **prestar juramento a** to swear to; **tomar juramento a** to swear in
jurar *tr* to swear; (*la verdad de una cosa*) swear to; swear allegiance to || *intr* (*pronunciar un juramento*) to swear, take an oath; (*echar votos o reniegos*) swear, curse; **jurar** + *inf* to swear to + *inf* || *ref* to swear; **jurársela** or **jurárselas a uno** to have it in for someone, swear to get even with someone
jure•ro -ra *mf* (SAm) false witness
jurídi•co -ca *adj* juridical
jurisconsulto *m* (*el que escribe sobre el derecho*) jurist; (*jurisperito*) legal expert
jurisdicción *f* jurisdiction
jurisperito *m* jurist, legal expert
jurisprudencia *f* jurisprudence
jurista *mf* jurist
juro *m* right of perpetual ownership; **de juro** inevitably, for sure
justa *f* joust, tournament
justamente *adv* just, just at that time; justly; (*ajustadamente*) tightly
justar *intr* to joust, to tilt
justicia *f* justice; (*castigo de muerte*) execution; **de justicia** justly, deservedly; **hacer justicia a** to do justice to; **ir por justicia** to go to court, to bring suit
justicie•ro -ra *adj* just, fair; stern, righteous
justificable *adj* justifiable
justifica•do -da *adj* (*hecho*) just, right; (*persona*) just, upright
justificante *m* voucher, proof
justificar **§73** *tr* to justify; (typ) to justify
justillo *m* jerkin, waist
justipreciar *tr* to estimate, appraise
jus•to -ta *adj* just; right, exact; (*apretado*) tight || *mf* just person || *f* see **justa** || **justo** *adv* just; right, in tune; tight; (*con estrechez*) in straitened circumstances
Jutlandia *f* Jutland
ju•to -ta *mf* Jute
juvenil *adj* juvenile, youthful
juventud *f* youth; young people
juzgado *m* court of law; courtroom; court of one judge
juzgar **§44** *tr & intr* to judge; **a juzgar por** judging by; **juzgar de** to judge, pass judgment on

K

K, k (ka) *f* twelfth letter of the Spanish alphabet
karate *m* or **karaté** *m* karate
karateka *m* karate expert
kermesse *f* var of **quermés**
keroseno *m* kerosene, coal oil
kg. *abbr* **kilogramo**
kilate *m* var of **quilate**
kilo *m* kilo, kilogram
kilociclo *m* kilocycle
kilogramo *m* kilogram
kilometraje *m* kilometrage, distance in kilometers
kilométri•co -ca *adj* kilometric; (coll) interminable, long-drawn-out
kilómetro *m* kilometer
kilovatio *m* kilowatt
kilovatio-hora *m* (*pl* **kilovatios-hora)** kilowatt-hour
kimono *m* var of **quimono**
kinescopio *m* (telv) kinescope
kiosco *m* var of **quiosco**
kirieleisón *m* dirge; **cantar el kirieleisón** to beg mercy
km. *abbr* **kilómetro**
kph. *abbr* **kilómetros por hora**
kv. *abbr* **kilovatio**
kv-h *abbr* **kilovatio-hora**

L

L, l (ele) thirteenth letter of the Spanish alphabet
la *art def fem* of **el** || *pron pers fem* her, it; you || *pron dem* that, the one; **la que** who, which, that; she who, the one that
laberinto *m* labyrinth, maze
labia *f* fluency, smoothness
labial *adj & f* labial
labio *m* lip; (fig) edge, lip; **chuparse los labios** to smack one's lips; **labio leporino** harelip; **leer en los labios** to lip read
labiolectura *f* lip reading

labio•so -sa *adj* fluent, smooth
labor *f* labor, work; (*cultivo de los campos*) farming, tilling; (*obra de coser, bordar, etc.*) needlework, fancywork, embroidery; **hacer labor** to match; **labor blanca** linen work, linen embroidery; **labor de ganchillo** crocheting
laborable *adj* workable; arable, tillable; (*día*) work
laborante *m* journeyman; political henchman
laborar *tr* to work || *intr* to scheme
laboratorio *m* laboratory; **laboratorio de idiomas** language laboratory; **laboratorio espacial** space laboratory; Skylab
laborio•so -sa *adj* (*trabajador*) laborious, industrious; (*trabajoso*) laborious, arduous
laborismo *m* British Labour Party
laborista *adj* Labour || *mf* Labourite
laborterapia *f* work therapy
labra *f* carving
labrada *f* fallow ground (*to be sown the following year*)
labrade•ro -ra *adj* arable, tillable
labra•do -da *adj* wrought, fashioned; carved; figured, embroidered || *m* carving; **labrado de madera** wood carving || *f* see **labrada**
labra•dor -dora *adj* work; farm || *mf* farmer; (*campesino*) peasant || *m* plowman; **el Labrador** Labrador
labrantí•o -a *adj* farm || *m* farmland
labranza *f* farming; farm, farmland
labrar *tr* to work, fashion; (*la piedra, la madera*) carve; (*arar*) plow; (*construir o mandar construir*) build; till, cultivate; cause, bring about || *intr* to make a lasting impression
labrie•go -ga *mf* peasant
laca *f* lacquer; shellac; **laca de uñas** nail polish; **lacas** lacquer ware
lacayo *m* lackey, footman
lacear *tr* to tie with a bow; adorn with bows; (*la caza*) drive within shot; (*la caza menor*) trap, snare
laceria *f* poverty, want; trouble, bother; leprosy
lacerio•so -sa *adj* poor, needy
lacero *m* lassoer; poacher; dogcatcher
la•cio -cia *adj* faded, withered; languid; (*cabello*) lank, straight
lacóni•co -ca *adj* laconic
lacra *f* fault, defect; (*señal dejada por una enfermedad*) mark, remains; sore; scab, scar
lacrimóge•no -na *adj* tear, tear-producing
lacrimo•so -sa *adj* lachrymose, tearful
lactar *tr* to suckle
lácte•o -a *adj* milky
lacustre *adj* lake
ladear *tr* to tip, tilt; bend, lean; (*un avión*) bank || *intr* to tip, tilt; bend, lean; turn away, turn off; (*la aguja de brújula*) deviate || *ref* to tip, tilt; bend, lean; be equal, be even; (Chile) to fall in love; **ladearse a** (*un dictamen, un partido*) to lean to or toward
ladeo *m* tipping, tilting; bending, leaning; inclination, bent
lade•ro -ra *adj* side, lateral || *f* hillside
ladilla *f* crab louse; **pegarse como ladilla** to stick like a leech
ladi•no -na *adj* crafty, sly, cunning; polyglot
lado *m* side; direction; (*del hilo telefónico*) end; **al lado** nearby; **dejar a un lado** to leave aside; **de lado** square, e.g., **diez centímetros de lado** ten centimeters square; **de otro lado** on the other hand; **de un lado** on the one hand; **echar a un lado** to cast aside; to finish up; **hacer lado** to make room; **hacerse a un lado** to step aside; **lados** backers, advisers; **mirar de lado** or **de medio lado** to look askance at; to sneak a look at; **ponerse al lado de** to take sides with; **por el lado de** in the direction of; **tirar por su lado** to pull for oneself
ladrar *tr* (*p.ej., injurias*) to bark || *intr* to bark
ladrido *m* bark, barking; slander, blame
ladrillador *m* bricklayer
ladrillal *m* brickyard
ladrillo *m* brick; (*azulejo*) tile; (*p.ej., de chocolate*) cake; **ladrillo de fuego** or **ladrillo refractario** firebrick
la•drón -drona *adj* thievish, thieving || *mf* thief || *m* sluice gate; **ladrón de corazones** heartbreaker, lady-killer
ladronera *f* den of thieves; thievery; (*alcancía*) child's bank
ladronerío *m* (Arg) gang of thieves; (Arg) wave of thieving
ladronzue•lo -la *mf* petty thief
lagaña *f* var of **legaña**
lagar *m* wine press; olive press; (*establecimiento*) winery
lagarta *f* female lizard; sly woman; (ent) gypsy moth
lagartija *f* green lizard; wall lizard
lagarto *m* lizard; sly fellow; (Mex) fop, dandy; **lagarto de Indias** alligator
lago *m* lake
lagotear *tr & intr* to flatter, wheedle
lágrima *f* tear; (*de cualquier licor*) drop; **beberse las lágrimas** to hold back one's tears; **deshacerse en lágrimas** to weep one's eyes out; **lágrimas de cocodrilo** crocodile tears; **llorar a lágrima viva** to shed bitter tears
lagrimear *intr* to weep easily, be tearful; (*los ojos*) fill
lagrimo•so -sa *adj* tearful; (*ojos*) watery
laguna *f* (*lago pequeño*) lagoon; (*hueco, omisión*) lacuna, gap
laical *adj* lay
laicismo *m* secularism
laja *f* slab, flagstone
lama *f* mud, ooze, slim; pond scum
lambrija *f* earthworm; skinny person
lamedero *m* salt lick
lame•dor -dora *adj* licking || *mf* licker || *m* syrup; **dar lamedor** to lose at first in order to take in one's opponent
lamedura *f* lick, licking
lamentable *adj* lamentable
lamentación *f* lamentation
lamentar *tr, intr & ref* to lament, mourn

lamento *m* lament
lamento•so -sa *adj* lamentable; plaintive
lamer *tr* to lick; lap, lap against; (*las llamas un tejado*) to lick || *ref* (*p.ej., los dedos*) to lick
lame•rón -rona *adj* (coll) sweet-toothed
lametada *f* lap, lick
lámina *f* sheet, plate, strip; (*plancha grabada*) engraving; (*pintura en cobre*) copper plate; (*figura estampada*) cut, picture, illustration
laminador *m* rolling mill
laminar *tr* to laminate; (*el hierro, el acero*) roll
lampadario *m* floor lamp
lámpara *f* lamp, light; (*mancha en la ropa*) grease spot, oil spot; (rad) vacuum tube; **atizar la lámpara** to fill up the glasses again; **lámpara de alcohol** spirit lamp; **lámpara de arco** arc lamp, arc light; **lámpara de bolsillo** flashlight; **lámpara de carretera** (aut) bright light; **lámpara de cruce** (aut) dimmer; **lámpara de pie** floor lamp; **lámpara de sobremesa** table lamp; **lámpara de socorro** trouble light; **lámpara de soldar** blowtorch; **lámpara de techo** ceiling light; (aut) dome light; **lámpara inundante** floodlight; **lámpara testigo** pilot light
lamparilla *f* rushlight; aspen
lampi•ño -ña *adj* beardless; hairless
lampista *mf* lamplighter || *m* tinsmith, plumber, glazier, electrician
lana *f* wool; (CAm) common person; (CAm) swindler; **lana de acero** steel wool; **lana de ceiba** kapoc; **lana de escorias** mineral wool, rock wool; **lana de vidrio** glass wool
lance *m* cast, throw; (*en la red*) catch, haul; (*accidente en el juego*) play, move, stroke; (*ocasión crítica*) chance, pass, juncture; incident, event; (*riña*) row, quarrel; (taur) capework; **de lance** cheap; secondhand; **echar buen lance** to have a break; **lance de honor** affair of honor, duel; **tener pocos lances** to be dull and uninteresting
lancero *m* lancer, spearman, pikeman
lanceta *f* (surg) lancet; (Mex, SAm) sting
lancinante *adj* piercing
lancha *f* barge, lighter; flagstone, slab; (naut) longboat; (nav) launch; (Ecuad) mist, fog; (Ecuad) frost; **lancha automóvil** launch, motor launch; **lancha de auxilio** lifeboat (*stationed on shore*); **lancha de carreras** speedboat; **lancha de desembarco** (nav) landing craft; **lancha salvavidas** lifeboat (*on shipboard*)
lanchar *intr* (Ecuad) to get foggy; (Ecuad) to freeze
lan•dó *m* (*pl* **-dós**) landau
landre *f* swollen gland; hidden pocket
lanería *f* wool shop; **lanerías** woolens, woolen goods
langosta *f* (*insecto*) locust; (*crustáceo*) lobster, spiny lobster
langostera *f* lobster pot
langostín *m* or **langostino** *m* prawn (*Peneus*)
langostón *m* green grasshopper
languidecer §22 *intr* to languish
languidez *f* languor
lángui•do -da *adj* languid, languorous
lano•so -sa *adj* woolly
lanu•do da *adj* woolly; (Ecuad, Ven) coarse, ill-bred
lanza *f* lance, pike; (*de la manguera*) nozzle; (*palo de coche*) wagon pole
lanzabom•bas *m* (*pl* **-bas**) (aer) bomb release; (mil) trench mortar
lanzacohe•tes *m* (*pl* **-tes**) rocket launcher
lanzadera *f* shuttle; **parecer una lanzadera** to buzz around
lanza•do -da *adj* sloping; (*salida de una carrera*) (sport) running (*start*)
lanza•dor -dora *mf* thrower; **lanzador de lodo** (fig) mudslinger || *m* launcher; (aer) jettison gear; (baseball) pitcher
lanzaespu•mas *m* (*pl* **-mas**) foam extinguisher
lanzalla•mas *m* (*pl* **-mas**) flame thrower
lanzamiento *m* throw, hurl, fling, launch; (*de un buque*) launching; (*de un cohete*) shot, launch; (*p.ej., de víveres*) (aer) airdrop; (*de bombas*) (aer) release; (*de paracaidistas*) (aer) jump; (law) dispossession; (naut) steeve
lanzami•nas *m* (*pl* **-nas**) (nav) mine layer
lanzapla•tos *m* (*pl* **-tos**) trap
lanzar §60 *tr* to throw, hurl, fling; (*un proyecto, un cohete, maldiciones, una ofensiva, un producto nuevo, un buque*) launch; (*una mirada*) cast; vomit, throw up; (*flores, hojas una planta*) put forth; (*una advertencia*) toss, toss out; (aer) to airdrop; (*bombas*) (aer) to release; (law) to dispossess || *ref* to launch, launch forth; throw oneself; dash, rush; (aer) to jump; (sport) to sprint
lanzatorpe•dos *m* (*pl* **-dos**) (nav) torpedo tube
laña *f* clamp; rivet
lañar *tr* to clamp; (*objetos de porcelana*) rivet
lapicero *m* pencil holder; mechanical pencil; ball-point pen; **lapicero fuente** fountain pen
lápida *f* tablet, stone; **lápida supulcral** gravestone
lapidar *tr* to stone to death
lá•piz *m* (*pl* **-pices**) (*grafito*) black lead; (*barrita que sirve para escribir*) pencil, lead pencil; **lápiz de bolilla** (Para) ball-point pen; **lápiz de labios** lipstick; **lápiz de pizarra** slate pencil; **lápiz de pasta** (Chile) ball-point pen; **lápiz de plomo** graphite; **lápiz estíptico** styptic pencil; **lápiz labial** lipstick
lapizar §60 *tr* to mark or line with a pencil
la•pón -pona *adj* Lapp || *mf* Lapp, Laplander || *m* (*idioma*) Lapp
Laponia *f* Lapland
lapso *m* lapse
laquear *tr* to lacquer
lardo•so -sa *adj* greasy, fatty
larga *f* long billiard cue; **dar largas a** to postpone, put off
largamente *adv* at length, extensively; in comfort; generously; long, for a long time
largar §44 *tr* to let go, release; ease, slack; utter; (*un golpe*) deal, strike, give; (naut) to

unfurl; (Col) to give || *ref* to move away; get away, sneak away, beat it; take to sea; (*el ancla*) to come loose

lar•go -ga *adj* long; abundant; liberal, generous; quick, ready; shrewd, cunning; (naut) loose, slack; **a la larga** in the long run, in the end; **a lo largo** lengthwise; at great length; far away; **a lo largo de** along; along with; throughout; in the course of; (*el mar*) far out in; **a lo más largo** at most; **hacerse a lo largo** to get out in the open sea; **largo de lengua** loose-tongued; **largo de uñas** light-fingered; **pasar de largo** to pass without stopping; take a quick look; miss; **ponerse de largo** to come out, make one's debut; **vestir de largo** to wear long clothes || *m* length || *f* see **larga** || **largo** *adv* at length, at great length; abundantly || **largo** *interj* get out of here!

largometraje *m* full-featured film, full-length movie

largor *m* length

larguero *m* (*palo, madero*) stringer; (*almohada larga*) bolster; (aer) longeron

largueza *f* length; liberality, generosity

larguiru•cho -cha *adj* gangling, lanky

largura *f* length

lárice *m* larch tree

laringe *f* larynx

laríngeo -a *adj* laryngeal

laringitis *f* laryngitis

laringoscopio *m* laryngoscope

larva *f* larva; mask; (*duende*) hobgoblin

lasca *f* advantage, benefit

lascar §73 *tr* (naut) to pay out, slacken; (Mex) to scratch, bruise; (*un objeto de porcelana*) (Mex) to chip

lascivia *f* lasciviousness

lasci•vo -va *adj* lascivious; playful

láser *m* laser

la•so -sa *adj* tired, exhausted; weak, wan

lástima *f* pity; (*quejido*) complaint; **contar lástimas** to tell a hard-luck story; **dar lástima** to be pitiful; **es lástima (que)** it is a pity (that); **estar hecho una lástima** to be a sorry sight; **hacer lástima** to be pitiful; **llorar lástimas** to put on a show of tears; **poner lástima** to be pitiful; **¡qué lástima!** what a pity!, what a shame!; **¡qué lástima de saliva!** what a waste of breath!

lastimar *tr* to hurt, injure; hurt, offend; bruise || *ref* to hurt oneself; bruise oneself; complain

lastime•ro -ra *adj* hurtful, injurious; pitiful, sad, doleful

lastimo•so -sa *adj* pitiful

lastra *f* slab, flagstone

lastrar *tr* (aer & naut) to ballast

lastre *m* (aer & naut) ballast; (fig) wisdom, maturity; (coll) food; (rr) (Chile) ballast

lat. *abrr* **latín, latitud**

lata *f* (*hojalata*) tin, tin plate; (*envase*) tin, tin can; (*madero sin pulir*) log; (*tabla delgada*) lath; annoyance, bore; **dar la lata a** (coll) to pester; **es una lata** that's terribly boring; **estar en la lata** (Col) to be penniless; **¡que lata!** what a nuisance! what a curse!

latebra *f* hiding place

latebro•so -sa *adj* furtive, secretive

latente *adj* latent

lateral *adj* lateral

latido *m* (*del perro*) yelp; (*del corazón*) beat, throb; (*dolor*) pang, twinge

latifundio *m* large neglected landed estate

latigazo *m* lash; crack of whip; (*reprensión áspera*) lashing

látigo *m* whip, horsewhip; cinch strap

latiguear *tr* to lash, whip || *intr* crack a whip

latiguillo *m* small whip; (*del actor u orador*) claptrap

latín *m* Latin; **latín de cocina** dog Latin, hog Latin; **latín rústico** or **vulgar** Vulgar Latin; **saber latín** or **mucho latín** to be very shrewd

latinajo *m* dog Latin, hog Latin; Latin word or phrase (*slipped into the vernacular*)

latinar or **latinear** *intr* to use Latin

lati•no -na *adj* Latin; (naut) lateen || *mf* Latin

Latinoamérica *f* Latin America

latinoamerica•no -na *adj* Latin-American || *mf* Latin American

latir *tr* (Ven) to annoy, bore, molest || *intr* (*el perro*) to bark, yelp; (*el corazón*) beat, throb; **me late que** (Mex) I have a hunch that

latitud *f* latitude

la•to -ta *adj* broad || *f* see **lata**

latón *m* brass; (Cuba) garbage pail

lato•so -sa *adj* annoying, boring || *mf* bore

latrocinio *m* thievery; thievishness

laucha *f* (Arg, Chile) mouse

laúd *m* (mus) lute; (zool) leatherback turtle

laudable *adj* laudable

láudano *m* laudanum

laudato•rio -ria *adj* laudatory

laudo *m* (law) finding, decision

láurea *f* laurel wreath

laurea•do -da *adj & mf* laureate

laurean•do -da *mf* graduate, candidate for a degree

laurear *tr* to trim or adorn with laurel; crown with laurel; decorate, honor, reward

laurel *m* laurel; (*de la victoria*) laurels; **dormirse sobre sus laureles** to rest or sleep on one's laurels

láure•o -a *adj* laurel || *f* see **láurea**

lauréola *f* crown of laurel, laurel wreath; (*aureola*) halo

lava *f* lava; (min) washing

lavable *adj* washable

lavabo *m* washstand; washroom, lavatory

lavaca•ras *mf* (*pl* **-ras**) fawner, flatterer, bootlicker

lavaco•ches *m* (*pl* **-ches**) car washer

lavada *f* wash(ing)

lavade•dos *m* (*pl* **-dos**) finger bowl

lavadero *m* laundry; (*tabla de lavar*) washboard; (*a orillas de un río*) washing place; (Guat, Mex, SAm) placer

lava•do -da *adj* brazen, fresh, impudent || *m* wash, washing; **lavado a seco** dry cleaning; **lavado cerebral** or **de cerebro** brainwashing; **lavado químico** dry cleaning

lava•dor -dora *mf* washer || *m* (phot) washer || *f* washing machine; **lavadora de platos** or **de vajilla** dishwasher
lavadura *f* washing; (*agua sucia; rozadura de una cuerda*) washings
lavafru•tas *m* (*pl* **-tas**) fruit bowl, finger bowl
lavama•nos *m* (*pl* **-nos**) (*pila con caño y llave*) washstand; (*jofaina*) washbowl
lavanda *f* lavender
lavandera *f* laundress, laundrywoman, washerwoman; (orn) sandpiper
lavandero *m* launderer, laundryman
lavándula *f* lavender
lavao•jos *m* (*pl* **-jos**) eyecup
lavaparabri•sas *m* (*pl* **-sas**) windshield washer
lavapla•tos (*pl* **-tos**) *mf* (*persona*) dishwasher || *m* (*aparato*) dishwasher; (Chile) kitchen sink
lavar *tr & ref* to wash
lavativa *f* enema; annoyance, bore
lavatorio *m* washing; washstand; toilet; washroom; (*ceremonia de lavar los pies*) maundy; (med) wash, lotion
lavavajillas *m* dishwasher
lavazas *fpl* dirty water, wash water
laxante *adj & m* laxative
laxar *tr* to ease, slack; (*el vientre*) loosen
la•xo -xa *adj* lax, slack; (fig) lax, loose
laya *f* spade; kind, quality
layar *tr* to spade, dig with a spade
lazada *f* bowknot
lazar **§60** *tr* to lasso
lazarillo *m* blind man's guide
lazari•no -na *adj* leprous || *mf* leper
lázaro *m* raggedy beggar; **estar hecho un lázaro** to be full of sores
lazo *m* bow, knot, tie; lasso, lariat; snare, trap; bond, tie; **armar lazo a** to set a trap for; **caer en el lazo** to fall into the trap; **lazo de amor** truelove knot; **lazo de unión** (fig) tie, bond
Ldo. *abbr* **Licenciado**
le *pron pers* to him, to her, to it; to you; him; you
leal *adj* loyal, faithful; reliable, trustworthy || *m* loyalist
lealtad *f* loyalty; reliability, trustworthiness
le•brel -brela *mf* whippet, small greyhound
lebrillo *m* earthen washtub
lebrón *m* large hare; coward; (Mex) slicker
lección *f* lesson; (*interpretación de un pasaje*) reading; **dar la lección** to recite one's lesson; **echar** or **señalar lección** to assign the lesson; **tomar una lección a** to hear the lesson of
leccionista *mf* private tutor
lecti•vo -va *adj* school (*e.g., day*)
lec•tor -tora *adj* reading || *mf* reader || *m* foreign-language teacher; (*empleado que anota el consumo registrado por el contador de agua, gas o electricidad*) meter reader; **lector mental** mind reader
lectura *f* reading; broad culture; public lecture; college subject; (*interpretación de un pasaje*) reading; (elec) playback; (typ) pica; **lectura de la mente** mind reading
lechada *f* grout; whitewash; (*para hacer papel*) pulp; (CAm, Mex, W-I) whitewash
lechar *tr* to milk; (CAm, Mex, W-I) to whitewash
leche *f* milk; (coll) sperm; **estar con la leche en los labios** to lack experience, to be young and inexperienced; **leche de manteca** buttermilk; **leche desnatada** skim milk; **leche en polvo** milk powder; **tener mala leche** to behave like a cad
lechecillas *fpl* sweetbread
lechera *f* milkmaid, dairymaid; (*vasija para guardar la leche*) milk can; (*vasija para servir la leche*) milk pitcher
lechería *f* dairy, creamery
leche•ro -ra *adj* (*que da leche*) milch; (*perteneciente a la leche*) milk; (*cicatero*) (coll) stingy || *m* milkman, dairyman; (coll) lucky dog || *f* see **lechera**
lecho *m* bed; (*especie de sofá*) couch; (*cauce de río*) bed; layer, stratum; **abandonar el lecho** to get up (*from illness*); **lecho de plumas** (fig) feather bed
le•chón -chona *adj* filthy, sloppy || *mf* suckling pig; (*persona sucia, desaseada*) pig || *m* pig || *f* sow
lecho•so -sa *adj* milky || *m* papaya (*tree*) || *f* papaya (*fruit*)
lechuga *f* lettuce; head of lettuce; (*fuelle formado en la tela*) frill; **lechuga romana** romaine lettuce
lechugui•no -na *adj* stylish, sporty || *m* dandy || *f* stylish young lady
lechuza *f* barn owl, screech owl; owllike woman
lechu•zo -za *adj* owlish; (*muleto*) yearling || *m* bill collector; summons server; owllike fellow || *f* see **lechuza**
leer **§43** *tr* to read || *intr* to read; lecture; **leer en** to read (*someone's thoughts*) || *ref* to read, e.g., **este libro se lee con facilidad** this book reads easily
leg. *abbr* **legal, legislatura**
lega *f* lay sister
legación *f* legation
legado *m* (*don que se hace por testamento*) legacy; (*enviado diplomático*) legate
legajo *m* file, docket, dossier
legal *adj* legal; faithful, prompt, right
legalidad *f* legality; faithfulness, promptness
legalizar **§60** *tr* to legalize; authenticate
légamo *m* slime, ooze
legamo•so -sa *adj.* slimy, oozy
legaña *f* gum (*on edge of eyelids*)
legaño•so -sa *adj* gummy
legar **§44** *tr* to bequeath, will
legata•rio -ria *mf* legatee
legenda•rio -ria *adj* legendary
legible *adj* legible
legión *f* legion
legislación *f* legislation
legisla•dor -dora *adj* legislating || *mf* legislator
legislar *intr* to legislate
legislati•vo -va *adj* legislative

legislatura *f* (session of a) legislature
legista *m* law professor; law student
legitimar *tr* to legitimate; legitimize
legitimidad *f* legitimacy
legíti•mo -ma *adj* legitimate
le•go -ga *adj* lay; uninformed || *m* layman; lay brother || *f* see **lega**
legua *f* league; **a leguas** far, far away
leguleyo *m* pettifogger
legumbre *f* (*hortaliza*) vegetable; (bot) legume; (Chile) vegetable stew
leíble *adj* legible, readable
leída *f* reading
leí•do -da *adj* well-read; **leído y escribido** (coll) posing as learned || *f* see **leída**
lejanía *f* distance, remoteness
leja•no -na *adj* distant, remote; (*pariente*) distant
lejía *f* lye; wash water; severe rebuke
lejiadora *f* washing machine
lejos *adv* far; **a lo lejos** in the distance; **de lejos** or **desde lejos** from a distance || *m* glimpse; look from afar; **tener buen lejos** to look good at a distance
le•lo -la *adj* stupid, inane
lema *m* motto, slogan; theme
len *adj* soft, flossy
lena *f* spirit, vigor; breathing
lencería *f* linen goods, dry goods; linen closet; dry-goods store
lence•ro -ra *mf* linen dealer, dry-goods dealer
lendrera *f* fine-toothed comb
lendro•so -sa *adj* nitty, lousy
lene *adj* (*suave al tacto*) soft; (*ligero*) light; kind, agreeable
lengua *f* (anat) tongue; (*idioma*) language, tongue; (*de tierra, de fuego, de zapato; badajo de campana; lengua de un animal usada como alimento*) tongue; **buscar la lengua a** to pick a fight with; **dar la lengua** to chew the rag; **hacerse lenguas de** to rave about; **írsele a** (*uno*) **la lengua** to blab; **lengua madre** or **matriz** mother tongue (*language from which another is derived*); **lengua materna** mother tongue (*language acquired by reason of nationality*); **morderse la lengua** to hold one's tongue; **tener en la lengua** to have on the tip of one's tongue; **tener la lengua gorda** to talk thick; to be drunk; **tener mala lengua** to be blasphemous; to have an evil tongue; **tener mucha lengua** to be a great talker; **tirar de la lengua a** to draw out; **tomar en lenguas** to gossip about; **tomar lengua** or **lenguas** to pick up news
lenguado *m* sole
lenguaje *m* language
lengua•raz (*pl* **-races**) *adj* foul-mouthed, scurrilous; polyglot || *mf* linguist
len•guaz *adj* (*pl* **-guaces**) garrulous
lengüeta *f* (*de la balanza*) pointer, needle; (*del zapato*) tongue; (anat) epiglottis; (carp) tongue; (*de un instrumento de viento*) (mus) reed; (Chile) paper cutter; (Mex) petticoat fringe; (SAm) chatterbox
lengüetada *f* licking, lapping
lengüetear *intr* to stick the tongue out; flicker, flutter; jabber, rant; lick
lengüilar•go -ga *adj* foul-mouthed, scurrilous
lengüisu•cio -cia *adj* (Mex, P-R) foul-mouthed, scurrilous
lenidad *f* lenience
lenocinio *m* pandering, procuring
lente *m & f* lens; **lente de aumento** magnifying glass; **lente de contacto** or **lente invisible** contact lens; **lentes** *mpl* nose glasses; **lentes de nariz** or **de pinzas** pince-nez; **lente telefotográfica** tele(photo)lens
lenteja *f* lentil; (*del reloj*) bob, pendulum bob
lentejuela *f* sequin, spangle
lentillas *fpl* contact lenses
lentitud *f* slowness
len•to -ta *adj* slow; sticky; (*fuego*) low
leña *f* firewood, kindling wood; **cargar de leña** to give a drubbing to; **llevar leña al monte** to carry coals to Newcastle
leña•dor -dora *mf* woodcutter || *m* woodsman
leñame *m* lumber, timber; stock of firewood
leñero *m* wood merchant; wood purchaser; (*sitio donde se guarda la leña*) woodshed
leño *m* (*madera*) wood; (*tronco de árbol, limpio de ramas*) log; sap, blockhead; (poet) ship, vessel; **dormir como un leño** to sleep like a log
leño•so -sa *adj* woody
Leo *m* (astr) Leo
león *m* lion
leona *f* lioness
leona•do -da *adj* tawny, fulvous
leonera *f* lion cage, den of lions; dive, gambling joint; junk room, lumber room
leonero *m* lion keeper; keeper of a gambling joint
leontina *f* watch chain
leopardo *m* leopard
leopoldina *f* watch fob; (mil) Spanish shako
leotardo *m* leotard
lépa•ro -ra *adj* (CAm, Mex) indecent, improper
lepe *m* (Ven) flip in the ear; **saber más que Lepe** to be wide-awake
leperada *f* (CAm, Mex) coarseness, vulgarity
lepisma *f* (ent) silver fish, fish moth
lepori•no -na *adj* hare, harelike
lepra *f* leprosy
leprosería *f* leper house
lepro•so -sa *adj* leprous || *mf* leper
lerdera *f* (CAm) laziness, apathy; (CAm) slowness
ler•do -da *adj* slow, dull; coarse, crude
lesbianismo *m* lesbianism
les•bio -bia *adj & mf* Lesbian || *f* (*mujer homosexual*) Lesbian, lesbian
lesión *f* harm, hurt; (pathol) lesion
lesionar *tr* to harm, hurt, injure
lesi•vo -va *adj* harmful, injurious
lesna *f* awl
le•so -sa *adj* hurt, harmed, injured; wounded; offended; perverted; (SAm) simple, foolish
leste *m* (naut) east
letal *adj* lethal, deadly
letame *m* manure
letanía *f* litany; (*enumeración seguida*) litany

letárgi•co -ca *adj* lethargic
letargo *m* lethargy
letargo•so -sa *adj* lethargic
le•tón -tona *adj* Lettish || *mf* Lett || *m* (*idioma*) Lettish, Lett
Letonia *f* Latvia
letra *f* (*del alfabeto*) letter; (*modo de escribir propio de una persona*) hand, handwriting; (*de una canción*) words, lyric; (com) draft; (typ) type; (*sentido material*) (fig) letter; **a la letra** (*al pie de la letra*) to the letter; **a letra vista** (com) at sight; **bellas letras** belles lettres; **cuatro letras** or **dos letras** (*esquela, cartita*) a line; **en letras de molde** in print; **escribir en letra de molde** to print; **las letras y las armas** the pen and the sword; **letra a la vista** (com) sight draft; **letra de cambio** (com) bill of exchange; **letra de imprenta** (typ) type; **letra de mano** handwriting; **letra de molde** printed letter; **letra menuda** fine print; (fig) cunning; **letra muerta** dead letter; **letra negrilla** (typ) boldface; **letra redonda** or **redondilla** (typ) roman; **letras** (*literatura*) letters; (coll) a few words, a line; **primeras letras** elementary education, three R's
letra•do -da *adj* learned, lettered; pedantic || *m* lawyer
letrero *m* sign, notice; (*p.ej., en una botella*) label
letrina *f* privy, latrine; (*cloaca*) sewer; (*cosa sucia*) (fig) cesspool
letrista *mf* lyricist, writer of lyrics (*for songs*); calligrapher, engrosser
leucemia *f* leukemia
leucorrea *f* leucorrhea
leudar *tr* to leaven, ferment with yeast || *ref* (*la masa con la levadura*) to rise
leu•do -da *adj* leavened, fermented
leva *f* weighing anchor; (mach) cam; (mil) levy; (CAm, Col) trick; (CAm, Col) swindle
levada *f* (*de la espada, el florete, etc.*) flourish; (*de los astros*) rise; (*del émbolo*) stroke
levadi•zo -za *adj* (*puente*) lift
levadura *f* leaven; leavening; yeast; (*tabla*) board; **levadura comprimida** yeast cake; **levadura de cerveza** brewer's yeast; **levadura en polvo** baking powder
levantaco•ches *m* (*pl* **-ches**) auto jack
levantada *f* rising, getting up (*from bed or from sickbed*)
levantamiento *m* rise, elevation; insurrection, revolt, uprising; **levantamiento del cadáver** inquest; **levantamiento del censo** census taking; **levantamiento de planos** surveying
levantar *tr* to raise, lift, elevate; agitate, rouse, stir up; (*una sesión*) adjourn; (*la mesa*) clear; (*la voz*) raise; (*el campo*) break; (*gente para el ejército; un sitio; fondos*) raise; (*el ancla*) weigh; straighten up; build, construct, erect; establish, found; **levantar casa** to break up housekeeping; **levantar planos** to make a survey || *ref* to rise; (*de la cama*) get up; (*de una silla*) stand up; straighten up; (*sublevarse*) rise up, rebel
levantaválvu•las *m* (*pl* **-las**) valve lifter
levantaventana *m* sash lift
levante *m* east; (*viento*) levanter; (CAm, P-R) slander, libel || **Levante** *m* (*países de la parte oriental del Mediterráneo*) Levant; northeastern Mediterranean shores of Spain, especially around Valencia, Alicante, and Murcia
levanti•no -na *adj* Levantine; of the northeastern Mediterranean shores of Spain || *mf* Levantine; native or inhabitant of the northeastern Mediterranean shores of Spain
levar *tr* (*el ancla*) to weigh || *ref* to set sail
leve *adj* (*de poco peso*) light; slight, trivial, trifling
levedad *f* lightness; trivialness
leviatán *m* (Bib & fig) leviathan
levita *m* deacon || *f* coat, frock coat
levitón *m* heavy frock coat
léxi•co -ca *adj* lexical || *m* lexicon; (*caudal de voces de un autor*) vocabulary; (*conjunto de vocablos de una lengua o dialecto*) wordstock
lexicografía *f* lexicography
lexicográfi•co -ca *adj* lexicographic(al)
lexicógra•fo -fa *mf* lexicographer
lexicología *f* lexicology
lexicón *m* lexicon
ley *f* law; loyalty, devotion; norm, standard; (*de un metal*) fineness; **a ley de caballero** on the word of a gentleman; **de buena ley** sterling, genuine; **ley de la selva** law of the jungle; **ley del menor esfuerzo** line of least resistance; **ley marcial** martial law; **ley seca** dry law; **tener** or **tomar ley a** to become devoted to; **venir contra una ley** to break a law
leyenda *f* legend
leyente *adj* reading || *mf* reader
lezna *f* awl
lía *f* plaited esparto rope; **lías** lees, dregs
lianza *f* (Chile) account, credit (*in a store*)
liar §77 *tr* to tie, bind; tie up, wrap up; (*un cigarillo*) roll; embroil, involve; **liarlas** to beat it; kick the bucket || *ref* to join together, be associated; have a liaison; become embroiled, become involved; **liárselos** to roll one's own (*i.e., cigarettes*)
libación *f* libation; (*acción de beber vino u otro licor*) libation
liba•nés -nesa *adj & mf* Lebanese
Líbano, el Lebanon
libar *tr* to suck; taste, sip || *intr* to pour out a libation; imbibe
libelo *m* lampoon, libel; (law) petition
libélula *f* dragonfly
liberación *f* liberation; (*cancelación de la carga que grava un inmueble*) redemption; (*de una cuenta*) settlement, closing; quittance
liberal *adj* liberal; (*expedito*) quick, ready; (pol) liberal; (*de amplias miras*) (Arg) liberal-minded || *mf* (pol) liberal
liberalidad *f* liberality
liberar *tr* to free

libertad *f* liberty, freedom; **libertad de cátedra** academic freedom; **libertad de cultos** freedom of worship; **libertad de empresa** free enterprise; **libertad de enseñanza** academic freedom; **libertad de imprenta** freedom of the press; **libertad de los mares** freedom of the seas; **libertad de palabra** freedom of speech, free speech; **libertad de reunión** freedom of assembly; **libertad vigilada** probation; **plena libertad** free hand; **tomarse la libertad de** to take the liberty to

liberta•do -da *adj* bold, daring; free, brash, unrestrained

liberta•dor -dora *mf* liberator

libertar *tr* to liberate, set free; (*de un peligro, la muerte, etc.*) save

liberta•rio -ria *adj* anarchistic

libertinaje *m* licentiousness, profligacy; impiety, ungodliness

liberti•no -na *adj & mf* libertine

liber•to -ta *mf* (law) probationer || *m* freedman || *f* freedwoman

libídine *f* lewdness, lust; (*impulso a las actividades sexuales*) libido

libidino•so -sa *adj* libidinous

libido *f* libido

libra *f* pound; **Libra** *f* (astr) Libra; **libra esterlina** pound sterling

libraco *m* or **libracho** *m* trashy book

libra•do -da *mf* (com) drawee

libra•dor -dora *mf* (com) drawer

libranza *f* (com) draft; **libranza postal** money order

librar *tr* to free; save, spare; (*la esperanza*) place; (*batalla*) give, join; (com) to draw || *intr* to be delivered, give birth; (*una religiosa*) receive a visitor in the locutory; (com) to draw; **librar bien** to come off well, succeed; **librar mal** to come off badly, fail || *ref* to free oneself; escape

libre *adj* free; free, brash, outspoken; free, unmarried; free, loose, licentious; innocent, guiltless; **libre de culpa** (*seguro, divorcio*) no-fault; **libre de porte** postage prepaid

librea *f* livery

librecambio *m* free trade

librecambista *mf* freetrader

librepensa•dor -dora *adj* freethinking || *mf* freethinker

librería *f* bookstore, bookshop; book business; (*mueble*) bookshelf; **librería de viejo** second-hand bookshop

libreril *adj* book

librero *m* bookseller; (*encuadernador*) bookbinder; (Cuba, Mex) bookshelf

libres•co -ca *adj* bookish

libreta *f* notebook; **libreta de banco** bankbook

libreto *m* (mus) libretto

librillo *m* earthen washtub; (*de papel de fumar, de sellos, etc.*) book

libro *m* book; **ahorcar los libros** to become a dropout; **a libro abierto** at sight; **hacer libro nuevo** to turn over a new leaf; **libro a la rústica** paperbound book; **libro de caballerías** romance of chivalry; **libro de cocina** cookbook; **libro de cheques** checkbook; **libro de chistes** joke book; **libro de lance** second-hand book; **libro de mayor venta** best seller; **libro de memoria** memo book; **libro de oro** guest book; **libro de recuerdos** scrapbook; **libro de teléfonos** telephone book; **libro de texto** textbook; **libro diario** day book; **libro en imágenes** picture book; **libro en rústica** paperbound book; **libro mayor** (com) ledger; **libro talonario** checkbook, stub book

libro-registro *m* (com) book

licencia *f* license; leave of absence; (mil) furlough; **licencia absoluta** (mil) discharge; **licencia por enfermedad** sick leave

licencia•do -da *adj* pedantic || *mf* licenciate || *m* lawyer; (mil) discharged soldier; university student (*wearing the long student gown*)

licenciar *tr* to license; allow, permit; confer the degree of licenciate or master on; (mil) to discharge || *ref* to receive the degree of licenciate or master; become dissolute; (mil) to be discharged

licenciatura *f* licenciate, master's degree; graduation with a licenciate or master's degree; work leading to a licenciate or master's degree

licencio•so -sa *adj* licentious

liceo *m* (*sociedad literaria, establecimiento de enseñanza popular*) lyceum; (*instituto de segunda enseñanza*) (Chile) lycée; (Mex) primary school

licitación *f* bidding

licita•dor -dora *mf* bidder

licitar *tr* to bid on; (Arg) to buy at auction, to sell at auction || *intr* to bid

líci•to -ta *adj* fair, just; licit, legal

licor *m* (*bebida espiritosa; cuerpo líquido*) liquor; (*bebida espiritosa preparada por mezcla de azúcar y substancias aromáticas*) liqueur

licorera *f* cellaret

licorista *mf* distiller; liquor dealer

licoro•so -sa *adj* spirituous, alcoholic; (*vino*) rich, generous

licuar §21 & **regular** *tr* to liquefy

lid *f* fight, combat; dispute, argument; **en buena lid** by fair means

líder *adj* leading || *m* leader

liderar *tr & intr* to lead, be the leader

lidia *f* fight; bullfight

lidiadera *f* (Ecuad) quarreling, bickering

lidia•dor -dora *mf* fighter || *ref* bullfighter

lidiar *tr* (*un toro*) to fight || *intr* to fight; **lidiar con** to fight with; have to put up with

liebre *f* hare; (*hombre cobarde*) coward

liendre *f* nit

lien•to -ta *adj* damp, dank

lienza *f* strip of cloth

lienzo *m* linen (cloth); linen handkerchief; (*de edificio o pared*) face, front; (*pintura sobre lienzo*) canvas

liga *f* (*cinta elástica para asegurar las medias*) garter; (*aleación*) alloy; (*materia pegajosa para cazar pájaros*) birdlime; (*confederación, alianza*) league; (*muérdago*) mistletoe; band; **liga de goma** rubber band
ligado *m* (mus & typ) ligature
ligadura *f* tie, bond; (mus) ligature, glide; (surg) ligature
ligamento *m* ligament
ligar §44 *tr* to tie, bind; join, combine; alloy; (*bebidas*) mix; (surg) to ligate || *ref* to league together; be committed; be bound or attached (*e.g., in friendship*)
ligereza *f* lightness; speed, rapidity; fickleness, inconstancy; tactlessness
lige•ro -ra *adj* light; (*té*) weak; (*tejido*) light, thin; quick; slight; **a la ligera** lightly; quickly; unceremoniously; **de ligero** thoughtlessly, rashly; **ligero de cascos** light-headed, scatter-brained; **ligero de lengua** loose-tongued; **ligero de pies** light-footed; **ligero de ropa** scantily clad || **ligero** *adv* fast, rapidly
lignito *m* lignite
ligustro *m* privet
lija *f* (*pez*) dogfish; (*papel que sirve para pulir*) sandpaper; **darse lija** (W-I) to boast, brag, pat oneself on the back
lijar *tr* to sand, sandpaper
lila *adj* silly, simple || *m* lilac (*color*) || *f* lilac (*plant and flower*)
li•lac *f* (*pl* **-laques**) lilac
liliputiense *adj & mf* Lilliputian
lima *f* (*herramienta*) file; sweet lime; sweet-lime tree; (*del tejado*) hip; hip rafter; correcting, polishing; **lima de uñas** nail file; **lima hoya** valley (*of roof*)
limadura *f* filing; (*partecillas*) filings
limalla *f* filings
limar *tr* to file; file down; polish, touch up; smooth, smooth over; (*cercenar*) curtail
limaza *f* (*babosa*) slug; (Ven) large file
limazo *m* slime, sliminess
limbo *m* (*borde*) edge; (theol) limbo; **estar en el limbo** to be quite distraught
limen *m* (physiol, psychol & fig) threshold
limenso *m* (Chile) honeydew melon
lime•ño -ña *adj & mf* Limean
limero *m* sweet-lime tree
limita•do -da *adj* limited; dull-witted
limitador *m* — **limitador de corriente** clock meter; slot meter
limitar *tr* to limit; cut down, reduce || *intr* — **limitar con** to border on
límite *m* limit; boundary, border
limítrofe *adj* bordering
limo *m* slime, mud
limón *m* lemon; lemon tree; (*de un coche o carro*) shaft
limonada *f* lemonade
limoncillo *m* citronella
limonera *f* shaft
limonero *m* lemon tree
limosna *f* alms
limosnear *intr* to beg
limosne•ro -ra *adj* almsgiving, charitable || *mf* almsgiver; beggar || *m* alms box
limo•so -sa *adj* slimy, muddy
limpia *f* cleaning
limpiaba•rros *m* (*pl* **-rros**) scraper, foot scraper
limpiabo•tas *m* (*pl* **-tas**) shoeshiner, bootblack; (fig) flatterer
limpiacrista•les *m* (*pl* **-les**) windshield washer
limpiachimene•as *m* (*pl* **-as**) chimney sweep
limpiadien•tes *m* (*pl* **-tes**) toothpick
limpia•dor -dora *adj* cleaning || *mf* cleaner
limpiadura *f* cleaning; **limpiaduras** cleanings, dirt
limpiama•nos *m* (*pl* **-nos**) (Guat, Hond) towel
limpiamente *adv* in a clean manner; with ease, skillfully; simply, sincerely; unselfishly
limpiameta•les *m* (*pl* **-les**) metal polish
limpianieve *m* snowplow
limpiaparabri•sas *m* (*pl* **-sas**) windshield wiper
limpia•piés *m* (*pl* **-piés**) (Mex) door mat
limpiapi•pas *m* (*pl* **-pas**) pipe cleaner
limpiaplu•mas *m* (*pl* **-mas**) penwiper
limpiar *tr* to clean; (*purificar*) cleanse; (*de culpas*) exonerate; (*un árbol*) clean out, prune; (*zapatos*) shine; (*hurtar*) snitch; (*a una persona en el juego*) clean out; (*dinero en el juego*) clean up; (mil) to mop up; **limpiarle a uno de** to clean someone out of || *ref* to clean, clean oneself
limpiaú•ñas *m* (*pl* **-ñas**) nail cleaner, orange stick
limpiaví•as *m* (*pl* **-as**) track cleaner
limpieza *f* (*acción de limpiar*) cleaning; (*calidad de limpio*) cleanness; (*hábito del aseo*) cleanliness; neatness, tidiness; honesty; chastity; ease, skill; (*observancia de las reglas en los juegos*) fair play; **limpieza de bolsa** emptiness of the pocketbook; **limpieza de la casa** house cleaning; **limpieza en seco** dry cleaning
lim•pio -pia *adj* clean; (*que tiene el hábito del aseo*) cleanly; neat, tidy; honest; chaste; clear, free; **dejar limpio** to clean out; **en limpio** (com) net; **estar limpio** to have no (criminal) record; be clean; **limpio de polvo y paja** free, for nothing; net, after deducting expenses; **poner en limpio** to make a clear or fair copy of; **quedar limpio** to be cleaned out; **sacar en limpio** to make a clear or clean copy of; deduce, understand || *f* see **limpia** || **limpio** *adv* fair; cleanly; **jugar limpio** to play fair
limpión *m* (*limpiadura ligera*) lick; (coll) cleaner; (Col) scolding; (Col, Ven) dustcloth; (Ecuad) dishcloth
limusina *f* limousine
lín. *abbr* **línea**
lina *f* (Chile) coarse wool
linaje *m* lineage; class, description; **linaje humano** mankind
linaju•do -da *adj* highborn || *mf* highborn person
linaza *f* flaxseed, linseed
lince *adj* keen, shrewd, discerning; (*ojos*) keen || *m* lynx; (fig) keen person
lincear *tr* to see into

linchamiento *m* lynching
linchar *tr* to lynch
lindante *adj* bordering, adjoining
lindar *intr* to border, be contiguous; **lindar con** to border on
linde *m & f* limit, boundary
linde•ro -ra *adj* bordering, adjoining || *m* edge; boundary stone, landmark || *f* limit, boundary; (bot) spicebush
lindeza *f* prettiness, niceness; elegance; witticism, funny remark; flirting; **lindezas** insults
lin•do -da *adj* pretty, nice; fine, perfect; **de lo lindo** a lot, a great deal; wonderfully || *m* dude, sissy
lindura *f* prettiness, niceness
línea *f* line; (*contorno de una figura, un vestido*) lines; figure, waistline; **conservar la línea** to keep one's figure; **leer entre líneas** to read between the lines; **línea de agua** water line; **línea de batalla** line of battle; **línea de empalme** (rr) branch line; **línea de flotación** water line; **línea de fuego** firing line; **línea de fuerza** (elec) power line; (phys) line of force; **línea del partido** party line; **línea de mira** line of sight; **línea de montaje** assembly line; **línea de puntos** dotted line; **línea de tiro** (mil) line of fire; **línea férrea** railway; **línea internacional de cambio de fecha** international date line; **línea suplementaria** (mus) added line, ledger line
lineal *adj* linear
lineamentos *mpl* lineaments
linfa *f* lymph; (poet) water
linfáti•co -ca *adj* lymphatic
lingote *m* ingot, slug; (naut) ballast bar
lingual *adj & f* lingual
lingüista *mf* linguist
lingüísti•co -ca *adj* linguistic || *f* linguistics
linimento *m* liniment
lino *m* flax; (*tela*) linen; (poet) sail
linóleo *m* linoleum
linón *m* lawn
linotipia *f* linotype
linotípi•co -ca *adj* linotype
linotipista *mf* linotype operator
linotipo *m* linotype
linterna *f* lantern; **linterna eléctrica** flashlight
lío *m* bundle; (*de papeles*) batch; muddle, mess; liaison, affair; **armar un lío** to raise a row; **hacerse un lío** to get into a jam
liofilización *f* freeze-drying
liofilizar **§60** *tr* to freeze-dry
lionesa — **a la lionesa** (culin) lyonnaise
liorna *f* hubbub, uproar || **Liorna** *f* Leghorn
lio•so -sa *adj* trouble-making; knotty, troublesome
liq.ⁿ *abbr* **liquidación**
líq.º *abbr* **líquido**
liquen *m* lichen
liquidación *f* (*de una cuenta*) sale
liquidar *tr* to liquefy; (com) to liquidate || *intr* (com) to liquidate || *ref* to liquefy
liquidez *f* liquidity
líqui•do -da *adj & m* liquid; (com) net || *f* (phonet) liquid
lira *f* (mus) lyre; (*numen de un poeta*) inspiration; poems, poetry
lírica *f* lyric poetry
líri•co -ca *adj* lyric(al); (*músico, operístico*) lyric; fantastic, utopian || *m* lyric poet; (Arg, Ven) visionary || *f* see **lírica**
lirio *m* (bot) iris; **lirio blanco** (*azucena*) Madonna lily; **lirio de agua** (bot) calla, calla lily; **lirio de los valles** (bot) lily of the valley
lirismo *m* lyricism; spellbinding; fancy, illusion
lirón *m* (bot) water plantain; (zool) dormouse; (coll) sleepyhead
lis *m* (bot) lily || *f* (bot) iris; (heral) fleur-de-lis
Lisboa *f* Lisbon
lisia•do -da *adj* hurt, injured; crippled; (*muy deseoso*) eager || *mf* cripple
lisiar *tr* to hurt, injure; cripple || *ref* to become crippled
lisimaquia *f* loosestrife
li•so -sa *adj* even, smooth; (*vestido*) plain, unadorned; (*franco, sincero*) simple, plain-dealing; brash, insolent; **liso y llano** simple, easy
lisonja *f* flattery
lisonjear *tr* to flatter; please || *intr* to flatter
lisonje•ro -ra *adj* flattering; pleasing || *mf* flatterer
lista *f* list; (*tira*) strip; (*en un tejido*) colored stripe; (*recuento en alta voz de las personas que deben estar en un lugar*) roll call; **lista de bajas** casualty list; **lista de comidas** bill of fare; **lista de correos** general delivery; **lista de espera** waiting list; **lista de frecuencia** frequency list; **lista de pagos** pay roll; **pasar lista** to call the roll
listar *tr* to list
listero *m* roll keeper, timekeeper
listín *m* telephone directory; (S-D) newspaper
lis•to -ta *adj* ready; quick, prompt; alert, wide-awake; **estar listo** to be ready; to be finished; **listo de manos** light-fingered; **pasarse de listo** to be shrewd, be clever || *f* see **lista**
listón *m* (*cinta*) ribbon, tape; (*pedazo de tabla angosta*) lath, strip of wood
listonado *m* lath, lathing
lisura *f* evenness, smoothness; plainness; candor; brashness, insolence
lit. *abbr* **literalmente**
lite *f* lawsuit
litera *f* (*vehículo llevado por hombres o por animales*) litter; (*cama fija en los camarotes*) berth; **litera alta** upper berth; **litera baja** lower berth
literal *adj* literal
litera•rio -ria *adj* literary
litera•to -ta *adj* literary || *mf* literary person; **literatos** literati
literatura *f* literature; **literatura de escape** or **de evasión** escape literature
litigación *s* litigation
litigante *adj & mf* litigant

litigar §44 *tr & intr* to litigate
litigio *m* litigation, lawsuit; dispute
litigio•so -sa *adj* litigious
litina *s* (chem) lithia
litio *m* (chem) lithium
litisexpensas *fpl* (law) costs
litografía *f* (*arte de grabar en piedra para la reproducción en estampa*) lithography; (*estampa*) lithograph
litografiar §77 *tr* to lithograph
litógra•fo -fa *mf* lithographer
litoral *adj* coastal, littoral || *m* coast, shore
litro *m* liter
liturgia *f* liturgy
litúrgi•co -ca *adj* liturgic(al)
liviandad *f* lightness; inconstancy, fickleness; lewdness
livia•no -na *adj* light; inconstant, fickle; lewd || *m* leading donkey; **livianos** lights, lungs
lívi•do -da *adj* livid
liza *f* combat, fight; (*campo para lidiar*) lists; **entrar en liza** to enter the lists
lo *art def neut* (used with *masc sg* form of *adj*) the, e.g., **lo bueno** the good; what is, e.g., **lo útil** what is useful; **lo mío** what is mine; (used with *adv* or inflected *adj*) the + noun, e.g., **lo aprisa que habla** the speed with which he speaks; **lo tacaños que son** the stinginess of them; how, e.g., **Vd., no sabe lo felices que son** you do not know how happy they are; **lo más** as . . . as, e.g., **lo más temprano posible** as early as possible || *pron pers masc* him, it; you; (with **estar, ser, parecer,** and the like, it stands for an adjective or noun understood and is either not translated or is translated by "so"), e.g., **Vd. está preparado pero ella no lo está** you are ready but she is not || *pron dem* that; **de lo que** + *verb* than + *verb*, e.g., **ese libro ha costado más dinero de lo que vale** that book cost more money than it is worth; **lo de** the matter of, the question of, e.g., **lo de sus deudas** the matter of your debts; **lo de que** the fact that, the statement that; **lo de siempre** the same old story; **lo que** what, that which; **todo lo que** all (that), e.g., **me dió todo lo que tenía** he gave me all he had
loa *f* praise; (*del teatro antiguo*) prologue; short dramatic poem
loable *adj* laudable, praiseworthy
loar *tr* to praise
loba *f* she-wolf; ridge
lobagante *m* lobster (*Homarus*)
lobanillo *m* wen, cyst
lobato *m* wolf cub
lo•bo -ba *adj & mf* (Mex) half-breed || *m* wolf; **coger** or **pillar un lobo** (coll) to go on a jag; **desollar** or **dormir un lobo** to sleep off a drunk; **lobo de mar** (ichth) sea wolf; (coll) old salt, sea dog; **lobo solitario** (fig) lone wolf || *f* see **loba**
lóbre•go -ga *adj* dark, dismal; gloomy
lobreguez *f* darkness; gloominess
lobu•no -na *adj* wolf, wolfish
locación *f* lease
local *adj* local || *m* quarters, place
localidad *f* (*lugar, sitio*) location, locality; (*plaza en un tren*) accommodations; (theat) seat
localización *f* localization; location; **localización de averías** trouble shooting
localizar §60 *tr* (*limitar a un punto determinado*) to localize; (*determinar el lugar de*) locate
locería *f* pottery
loción *f* wash; (pharm) lotion; **loción facial** after-shave lotion
lo•co -ca *adj* crazy, insane, mad; terrific, wonderful; **estar loco por** to be crazy about, to be mad about; **loco de amor** madly in love; **loco de atar** raving mad; **loco perenne** insane, demented; full of fun; **loco rematado** stark-mad; **volver loco** to drive crazy || *mf* crazy person, lunatic || *m* (*bufón*) fool
locomotora *f* engine, locomotive; **locomotora de maniobras** shifting engine
locro *m* (SAm) meat and vegetable stew
lo•cuaz *adj* (*pl* **-cuaces**) loquacious
locución *f* expression, locution; idiomatic phrase, idiom
locuela *f* speech, way of speaking
locue•lo -la *adj* wild, frisky || *f* see **locuela**
locura *f* insanity, madness; folly, madness
locu•tor -tora *mf* announcer, commentator
locutorio *m* (*en un convento de monjas*) parlor, locutory; telephone booth
lodazal *m* mudhole
lodo *m* mud, mire; (*substancia que sirve para cerrar junturas, tapar grietas, etc.*) (chem) lute
lodo•so -sa *adj* muddy
logaritmo *m* logarithm
logia *f* (*p.ej., de francmasones*) lodge; (archit) loggia
lógi•co -ca *adj* logical || *mf* logician || *f* logic
logísti•co -ca *adj* logistic(al) || *f* logistics
logopedía *f* speech correction
logrado -da *adj* successful
lograr *tr* to get, obtain; achieve, attain; **lograr** + *inf* to succeed in + *ger* || *ref* to be successful
logrear *intr* to be a moneylender; profiteer
logre•ro -ra *adj* moneylending; profiteering || *mf* moneylender; profiteer; (Chile) sponger
logro *m* attainment, success; gain, profit; usury; **dar** or **prestar a logro** to lend at usurious rates
loma *f* low hill, elevation
Lombardía *f* Lombardy
lombar•do -da *adj & mf* Lombard
lombriguera *f* wormhole in the ground; (bot) tansy
lom•briz *f* (*pl* **-brices**) worm, earthworm; (pathol) worm; (*persona muy alta y delgada*) beanpole; **lombriz de tierra** earthworm; **lombriz solitaria** tapeworm
lomera *f* (*de la guarnición*) backstrap; (*del tejado*) ridgepole; (bb) backing
lominhies•to -ta *adj* high-backed; conceited
lomo *m* (*de animal, libro, cuchillo*) back; (*tierra que levanta el arado*) ridge; (*carne

de lomo del animal) loin; (*pliegue del tejido*) crease; (bb) spine; **lomos** ribs
lona *f* canvas; sailcloth; (Mex) burlap
loncha *f* slab, flagstone; slice, strip
lonchería *f* snack bar
londinense *adj* London || *mf* Londoner
Londres *m* London; **el Gran Londres** Greater London
longáni•mo -ma *adj* long-suffering
longaniza *f* pork sausage
longevidad *f* longevity
longe•vo -va *adj* long-lived
longitud *f* length; (astr & geog) longitud
lonja *f* exchange, commodity exchange; grocery store; wool warehouse; (*de carne*) slice; (*de cuero*) strip; (*a la entrada de un edificio*) elevated parvis; (Arg) rawhide
lonjeta *f* bower, summerhouse
lonjista *mf* grocer
lontananza *f* (*de una pintura*) background; **en lontananza** in the distance, on the horizon
loor *m* praise
loquear *intr* to talk nonsense, play the fool; carry on, have a high time
loquera *f* insanity
loquería *f* (Chile) madhouse, insane asylum
loque•ro -ra *mf* guard in a mental hospital || *m* (Arg) confusion, pandemonium; (Arg) insane asylum
loques•co -ca *adj* crazy; funny, jolly
lorán *m* (naut) loran
lord *m* (*pl* **lores**) lord
lo•ro -ra *adj* dark-brown || *m* parrot; cherry laurel; (Chile) spy; (Chile) glass bedpan; (Chile) third degree
losa *f* slab, flagstone; tomb
losange *m* lozenge; (baseball) diamond
lote *m* lot, share, portion; lottery prize; (Cuba, Mex) remnant; (Arg) dunce, simpleton; (Col) swallow, swig; (*de terreno*) (Cuba, Mex) lot
lotear *tr* (Chile) to divide up, divide into lots
lotería *f* lottery; (*juego casero*) lotto; (*cosa insegura, riesgo*) gamble
lote•ro -ra *mf* vendor of lottery tickets
lotizar §60 *tr* (Peru) to divide into lots
loto *m* lotus
loza *f* (*barro cocido y barnizado*) porcelain; crockery, earthenware; **loza fina** china, chinaware
lozanear *intr* to be luxuriant; be full of life || *ref* (*deleitarse*) to luxuriate
lozanía *f* luxuriance, verdure; exuberance, vigor; pride, haughtiness
loza•no -na *adj* luxuriant, verdant; exuberant, vigorous; proud, haughty
lubricante *adj & m* lubricant
lubricar **§73** *tr* to lubricate
lúbri•co -ca *adj* (*resbaladizo; lascivo*) lubricous (*slippery; lewd*)
lubrificar §73 to lubricate
lucera *f* skylight
lucerna *f* large chandelier; (*abertura, tronera*) loophole
lucero *m* bright star; (*planeta*) Venus; (*ventanillo en un muro*) light; **lucero del alba** or **de la mañana** morning star; **lucero de la tarde** evening star; **luceros** (poet) eyes
luci•do -da *adj* generous, magnificent; brilliant, successful; sumptuous; (Arg) striking, dashing
lúci•do -da *adj* lucid
luciente *adj* bright, shining
luciérnaga *f* glowworm, firefly
lucifer *m* overbearing fellow || **Lucifer** *m* Lucifer
lucífe•ro -ra *adj* (poet) bright, dazzling || *m* morning star; (Col) match
lucimiento *m* brilliance, luster; show, dash; success; **quedar** or **salir con lucimiento** to come off with flying colors
lu•cio -cia *adj* shiny || *m* salt pool; (*pez*) pike, luce
lucir **§45** *tr* to light, light up; show, display; (*p.ej., un traje nuevo*) sport; help; plaster || *intr* to shine || *ref* to dress up; come off with great success; (*sobresalir, distinguirse*) shine; flop, e.g., **lucido me quedé** I was a flop
lucrar *tr* to get, obtain || *intr & ref* to profit, make money
lucrati•vo -va *adj* lucrative
lucro *m* gain, profit; **lucros y daños** profit and loss
lucro•so -sa *adj* lucrative
luctuo•so -sa *adj* sad, mournful, gloomy
lucha *f* fight; (*disputa*) quarrel; (*actividad forzada*) struggle; (*combate cuerpo a cuerpo*) wrestling; **lucha antipolución** antipollution movement (or campaign); **lucha de la cuerda** (sport) tug of war; **lucha por la vida** struggle for existence
lucha•dor -dora *mf* fighter, wrestler
luchar *intr* (*combatir*) to fight; (*disputar*) quarrel; (*esforzarse*) struggle; (*pelear cuerpo a cuerpo*) wrestle
ludibrio *m* derision, mockery, scorn
ludir *tr, intr & ref* to rub, rub together
luego *adv* next, then; therefore; soon; once in a while; **desde luego** right away; of course; **hasta luego** good-bye, so long; **luego como** as soon as; **luego de** after, right after; **luego que** as soon as
luen•go -ga *adj* long
lúes *f* pestilence; **lúes canina** distemper; **lúes venérea** syphilis
lugano *m* (orn) siskin
lugar *m* place; site, spot; job, position; (*espacio*) room, space; (*asiento*) seat; village, hamlet; (geom) locus; **dar lugar** to make room; **dar lugar a** to give cause for; give rise to; **en lugar de** instead of, in place of; **hacer lugar** to make room; **lugar común** (*expresión trivial*) commonplace; (*retrete*) toilet, water closet; **lugar de cita** tryst; **lugares estrechos** close quarters; **lugar geométrico** locus; **lugar religioso** place of burial
lugarejo *m* hamlet
lugare•ño -ña *adj* village || *mf* villager
lugarteniente *m* lieutenant
luge *m* sled
lúgubre *adj* dismal, gloomy, lugubrious

luir **§20** *tr* (naut) to gall, wear; (Chile) to muss, rumple; (*vasijas de barro*) (Chile) to polish || *ref* (Chile) to rub, wear away

luisa *f* (bot) lemon verbena

lujo *m* luxury; **de lujo** de luxe; **gastar mucho lujo** to live in high style; **lujo de** abundance of, excess of

lujo•so -sa *adj* luxurious

lujuria *f* lust, lechery

lujuriante *adj* (*lozano*) luxuriant, lush; (*libidinoso*) lustful

lujuriar *intr* to lust, be lustful; (*los animales*) copulate

lujurio•so -sa *adj* lustful, lecherous || *mf* lecher

lu•lo -la *adj* (Chile) lank, slender || *m* (Chile) bundle

lu•lú *m* (*pl* **-lúes**) spitz dog

lumbago *m* lumbago

lumbre *f* light; fire; (*para encender el cigarrillo*) light; (*hueco en un muro por donde entra la luz*) light; brightness, brilliance; knowledge, learning; **echar lumbre** to blow one's top; **lumbre del agua** surface of the water; **lumbres** tinderbox; **ni por lumbre** not for love or money; **ser la lumbre de los ojos de** to be the light of the eyes of

lumbrera *f* light, source of light; light, lamp; (*abertura por donde entran el aire y la luz*) louver; skylight; dormer window; air duct, ventilating shaft; (*persona insigne*) light, luminary; (mach) port; **lumbreras** eyes

luminar *m* luminary

luminiscente *adj* luminescent

lumino•so -sa *adj* luminous; (*idea*) bright

luminotecnia *f* lighting engineering

lun. *abbr* **lunes**

luna *f* moon; moonlight; (*tabla de cristal*) plate glass; (*espejo*) mirror; (*de los anteojos*) lens, glass; whim; **estar de buena luna** to be in a good mood; **estar de mala luna** to be in a bad mood; **luna de miel** honeymoon; **luna llena** full moon; **luna menguante** waning moon; **luna nueva** new moon; **media luna** half moon; (*figura de cuarto de luna creciente o menguante*) crescent; **quedarse a la luna de Valencia** to be disappointed

lunar *adj* lunar || *m* (*mancha de la piel*) mole; (*punto en un diseño de puntos*) polka dot; (fig) stain, blot, stigma; **lunar postizo** beauty spot

lunáti•co -ca *adj & mf* lunatic

lu•nes *m* (*pl* **-nes**) Monday; **hacer San Lunes** to knock off on Monday

luneta *f* (*de los anteojos*) lens, glass; orchestra seat; (aut) rear window

lunfardo *m* (Arg) thief; underworld slang

lupa *m* magnifying glass

lupanar *m* brothel, bawdyhouse

lupia *mf* (Hond) quack, healer || *f* wen, cyst; **lupias** (Col) small amount of money, small change

lúpulo *m* (*vid*) hop; (*flores desecadas de la vid*) hops

luquete *m* slice of orange or lemon used to flavor wine; (Chile) bald spot; (*en la ropa*) (Chile) spot, hole

lu•rio -ria *adj* (Mex) mad, crazy

lusitanismo *m* Lusitanism

lusita•no -na *adj & mf* Lusitanian, Portuguese

lustrabo•tas *m* (*pl* **-tas**) shoeshiner

lustrar *tr* to shine, polish || *intr* to wander, roam

lustre *m* shine, polish; luster, gloss; (*fama, gloria*) (fig) luster

lustrina *f* (Chile) shoe polish

lustro *m* five years; chandelier

lustro•so -sa *adj* shining, bright, lustrous

lutera•no -na *adj & mf* Lutheran

luto *m* (*señal exterior de duelo*) mourning; (*duelo, aflicción*) sorrow, bereavement; **estar de luto** to be in mourning; **lutos** crape; **luto riguroso** deep mourning

lutocar *m* (Chile) trash cart

luz *f* (*pl* **luces**) light; window, light; electricity; (*dinero*) money; cash; **a primera luz** at dawn; **a toda luz** or **a todas luces** everywhere; by all means; **dar a luz** to have a child; to give birth to; to bring out; to publish; **entre dos luces** at twilight; half-seas over; **luces de carretera** (aut) bright lights; **luces de cruce** (aut) dimmers; **luz de balizaje** (aer) marker light; **luz de magnesio** magnesium light; flash bulb, flashlight; **luz de matrícula** license-plate light; **luz de parada** stop light; **luz trasera** taillight; **sacar a luz** to bring to light; **salir a luz** to come to light; come out, be published; take place; **ver la luz** to see the light, see the light of day

Luzbel *m* Lucifer

Ll

Ll, ll (elle) *f* fourteenth letter of the Spanish alphabet

llaga *f* sore, ulcer; sorrow, grief; (*entre dos ladrillos*) (mas) seam, joint; (fig) ulcer

llagar **§44** *tr* to make sore; hurt

llama *f* flame, blaze; marsh, swamp; (zool) llama; (fig) fire, passion; **saltar de las llamas y caer en las brasas** to jump out of the frying pan into the fire

llamada *f* call; (*movimiento con que se llama la atención de uno*) sign, signal; knock, ring; reference, reference mark; (mil) call, call to arms; (Mex) cowardice; **batir** or **tocar a llamada** (mil) to sound the call to arms; **llamada a filas** (mil) call to the colors; **llamada a quintas** draft call; **llamada por cobrar** collect call

llamadera *f* goad

llama•do -da *adj* so-called || *f* see **llamada**

llama•dor -dora *mf* caller || *m* messenger; door knocker; push button

llamamiento *m* call; calling, vocation

llamar *tr* to call; (*dar nombre a*) name, call; summon; invoke, call upon; (*la atención*) attract || *intr* to call; (*golpear en la puerta*) knock; (*hacer sonar la campanilla*) ring; (*el viento*) (naut) to veer || *ref* to be called, be named; **se llama Juan** his name is John

llamarada *f* blaze, flare-up; (*encendimiento repentino del rostro*) flush; (fig) flare-up, outburst

llamarón *m* flare-up

llamati•vo -va *adj* showy, loud, flashy, gaudy; (*manjar*) thirst-raising

llamazar *m* swamp, marsh

llame *m* (Chile) bird net, bird trap

llamear *intr* to blaze, flame, flash

lla•món -mona *adj* (Mex) cowardly

llampo *m* (Chile) ore

llana *f* trowel, float; plain; **dar de llana** to smooth with the trowel

llanada *f* plain

llanero *m* ranger, plainsman

llaneza *f* plainness, simplicity; familiarity; sincerity

lla•no -na *adj* even, level, smooth; (*parecido a un plano geométrico*) plane; (*sencillo*) plain, simple; clear, evident; (*palabras*) frank; accented on the next to last syllable || *m* plain; (*de la escalera*) landing || *f* see **llana**

llanque *m* (Peru) rawhide sandal

llanta *f* (*cerco exterior de la rueda*) tire (*of iron or rubber*); (*borde exterior de la rueda*) rim; (*pieza de hierro más ancha que gruesa*) iron flat; **llanta de goma** rubber tire; **llanta de invierno** snow tire; **llanta de oruga** (*de un tractor de oruga*) track

llanto *m* weeping, crying; **en llanto** in tears

llanura *f* evenness, level, smoothness; (*terreno extenso y llano*) plain

llapan•go -ga *adj* (Ecuad) barefooted

llares *m* pothanger

llave *adj* key || *f* (*pieza para abrir y cerrar las cerraduras*) key; (*herramienta*) wrench; (*grifo*) faucet, spigot, cock; (*de arma de fuego*) cock; (elec) switch; (*de un instrumento de viento*) (mus) key; (*de un enigma, secreto, traducción, cifra; lugar estratégico más propicio*) key; **bajo llave** under lock and key; **echar la llave a** to lock; **llave de caja** socket wrench; **llave de caño** pipe wrench; **llave de cubo** socket wrench; **llave de chispa** flintlock; **llave de estufa** damper; **llave de mandíbulas dentadas** alligator wrench; **llave de paso** stopcock; passkey; **llave de purga** drain cock; **llave espacial** space key; **llave inglesa** monkey wrench; **llave maestra** master key, skeleton key; **llave para tubos** pipe wrench

llave•ro -ra *mf* keeper of the keys; (*carcelero*) turnkey || *m* key ring

llavín *m* latchkey

llegada *f* arrival

llegar §44 *tr* to bring up, bring close || *intr* to arrive; happen; **llegar a** to arrive at; reach; amount to; be equal to; **llegar a** + *inf* to come to + *inf;* succeed in + *ger;* **llegar a ser** to become || *ref* to come close

llena *f* flood

llenado *m* filling

llena•dor -dora *adj* (*alimento*) (Chile) filling

llenar *tr* to fill; (*un formulario*) fill out; (*ciertas condiciones*) fulfill; satisfy; (*colmar*) overwhelm || *intr* (*la luna*) to be full || *ref* to fill, fill up; stuff oneself; **llenarse a rebosar** to be filled to overflowing

llene *m* filling; full tank

lle•no -na *adj* full; **lleno a rebosar** full to overflowing; **lleno de goteras** full of aches and pains || *m* fill, plenty; fulness, full enjoyment; completeness; full moon; (*en el teatro*) full house || *f* see **llena**

lleva or **llevada** *f* carrying, conveying; ride; **lleva gratuita** free ride

llevade•ro -ra *adj* bearable, tolerable

llevar *tr* (*transportar*) to carry; (*traer consigo*) take; (*conducir*) lead; carry away, take away; (*cuentas, libros; la anotación en los naipes*) keep; (*la correspondencia con una persona*) carry on; (*un drama a la pantalla*) put on; (*buena o mala vida*) lead; (*aguantar*) bear, stand for; (*castigo*) suffer; get, obtain; win; (*cierto precio*) charge; (*traje, vestido*) wear; (*armas*) bear; (*cierto tiempo*) have been, e.g., **llevo ocho días en cama** I have been in bed for a week; (*ropa*) **a todo llevar** for all kinds of wear; **llevar** (*cierto tiempo*) **a** (*uno*) to be older than (*someone*) by (*a certain age*); (*cierta distancia*) **a** (*uno*) to be ahead of (*someone*) by (*a certain distance*); (*cierto peso*) **a** (*uno*) to be heavier than (*someone*) by (*a certain weight*); **llevar a las antenas** to put on the air; **llevarla hecha** to have it all figured out; **llevar puesto** to wear, to have on; **llevar** + *pp* to have + *pp,* e.g., **lleva conseguidas muchas victorias** he has won many victories || *ref* to carry away; take, take away; carry off; win; get along; **llevarse algo a alguien** to take something away from someone

lloradue•los *mf* (*pl* **-los**) crybaby, sniveler

lloralásti•mas *mf* (*pl* **-mas**) poverty-crying skinflint

llorar *tr* to weep over; mourn, lament || *intr* to weep, cry; (*los ojos*) water, run

llorera *f* crying; sobbing

lloriquear *intr* to whine, to whimper

lloriqueo *m* whining, whimpering

lloro *m* weeping, crying; tears

llo•rón -rona *adj* weeping, crying || *mf* weeper, crybaby || *m* weeping willow; pendulous plume || *f* hired mourner

lloro•so -sa *adj* weepy; sad, tearful

llovedi•zo -za *adj* (*agua*) rain; (*techo*) leaky

llover §47 *tr* (*enviar como lluvia*) to rain ||

intr to rain; **como llovido** unexpectedly; **llueva o no** rain or shine; **llueve** it is raining || *ref* (*el techo*) to leak
llovido *m* stowaway
llovizna *f* drizzle
lloviznar *intr* to drizzle
llovizno•so -sa *adj* moist, damp (*from drizzle*); drizzly
lluvia *f* rain; rain water; (*copia, muchedumbre*) (fig) shower, downpour; **lluvia ácida** acid rain; **lluvia radiactiva** fallout, radioactive fallout
lluvio•so -sa *adj* rainy

M

M, m (eme) *f* fifteenth letter of the Spanish alphabet
m. *abbr* **mañana, masculino, meridiano, metro, minuto, muerto**
maca *f* flaw, blemish; bruise (*on fruit*); spot, stain; hammock
maca•co -ca *adj* ugly, misshapen || *m* — **macaco de la India** rhesus
macadamizar §60 *tr* to macadamize
macadán *m* macadam
macana *f* cudgel, club; drug on the market; nonsense; (Arg) botch; (Arg) lie, trick
macanear *intr* to fib, lay it on; (Col, Ven) to manage (well)
macanu•do -da *adj* terrific, swell, grand; (Col, Ecuad) strong, husky
macarrón *m* macaroon; **macarrones** macaroni
macear *tr* to mace, hammer || *intr* to pester, bore
macelo *m* slaughterhouse
macero *m* macebearer
maceta *f* stone hammer; flowerpot; flower vase; (*de herramienta*) handle; (*de cantero*) hammer; (Mex) head
macfarlán *m* inverness cape
macilen•to -ta *adj* pale, wan, gaunt
macillo *m* hammer (*of piano*)
macis *m* mace (*spice*)
macizar §60 *tr* to fill in, fill up
maci•zo -za *adj* solid; massive || *m* solid; flower bed; bulk, mass; massif; wall space
macu•co -ca *adj* (Chile) sly, cunning; (Arg, Chile, Ven) important, notable; (Ecuad) old, worthless; (Arg, Chile, Peru) strong, husky || *m* (Arg, Bol, Col) overgrown boy
mácula *f* spot; stain; blemish; trick, deception
macha *f* (Bol) drunkenness; (Arg) joke; (Bol) mannish woman
machaca *mf* pest, bore || *f* crusher
machacar §73 *tr* to crush, mash, pound || *intr* to pester, bore
macha•cón -cona *adj* boring, tiresome, importunate || *mf* bore
machada *f* flock of billy goats; stupidity
machado *m* hatchet
machamartillo — **a machamartillo** solidly, firmly, lastingly
machaque•ro -ra *adj* tiresome, boring || *mf* bore
machar *tr* to crush, grind, pound || *ref* (Bol, Ecuad) to get drunk
machete *m* machete, cane knife
machi *mf* (Chile) quack, healer
machihembrar *tr* (*ensamblar a ranura y lengüeta*) to feather; (*ensamblar a caja y espiga*) mortise
machina *f* derrick, crane; pile driver; (P-R) merry-go-round
machismo *m* machismo; male chauvinism
machista *m* male chauvinist
macho *adj invar* (*animal, planta, herramienta*) male; strong, robust; dull, stupid || *m* sledge hammer; abutment, pillar; male; he-mule; dullard; (*del corchete*) hook; (mach) male piece; (coll) he-man; (C-R) blond foreigner; **macho cabrío** he-goat, billy goat; **macho de aterrajar** or **macho de terraja** (mach) tap, screw tap
machona *f* (Arg, Bol, Ecuad, Guat) mannish woman
macho•rro -rra *adj* barren, sterile || *f* barren woman; (Mex) mannish woman
machucar §73 *tr* to beat, pound, bruise
machu•cho -cha *adj* sedate, judicious; elderly
madamita *m* (coll) sissy
madeja *f* hank, skein; tangle of hair; (*hombre flojo*) jellyfish; **madeja sin cuenda** hopeless tangle
madera *m* Madeira wine || *f* wood; piece of wood; knack, flair; makings; **madera aserradiza** lumber; **madera contrachapada** plywood; **madera de sierra** lumber; **madera laminada** plywood; **tener madera de** to have what it takes to
maderada *f* raft, float
maderaje *m* or **maderamen** *m* woodwork
maderería *f* lumberyard
madere•ro -ra *adj* lumber || *m* lumberman; carpenter; log driver
madero *m* log, beam; ship, vessel; blockhead
madrastra *f* stepmother; bother
madraza *f* doting mother
madre *adj* mother || *f* mother; matron; womb; main sewer; river bed; dregs; sediment; **madre adoptiva** foster mother; **madre de leche** wet nurse; **madre patria** mother country, old country; **madre política** mother-in-law; stepmother; **sacar de madre** to annoy, to upset

madreperla *f* (*molusco*) pearl oyster; (*nácar*) mother-of-pearl
madreselva *f* honeysuckle
madriga•do -da *adj* twice-married; (*toro*) that has sired; worldly-wise
madriguera *f* burrow, lair, den
madrile•ño -ña *adj* Madrid || *mf* native or inhabitant of Madrid
madrina *f* godmother; patroness, protectress; prop, shore, brace; joke; leading mare; **madrina de boda** bridesmaid; **madrina de guerra** war mother
madrugada *f* early morning, dawn; early rising
madruga•dor -dora *adj* early-rising || *mf* early riser
madrugar **§44** *intr* to get up early; be out in front
madurar *tr* to ripen; mature; think out || *intr* to ripen; mature
madurez *f* ripeness; maturity
madu•ro -ra ripe; mature
maestra *f* teacher; elementary girls' school; **maestra de escuela** schoolmistress
maestranza *f* arsenal, armory; navy yard; order of equestrian knights
maestría *f* mastery; mastership
maes•tro -tra *adj* master; masterly; chief, main; (*perro*) trained || *m* master; teacher; (*en la música y la pintura*) maestro; **maestro de capilla** choirmaster; **maestro de ceremonias** master of ceremonies; **maestro de equitación** riding master; **maestro de escuela** elementary schoolteacher; **maestro de esgrima** fencing master; **maestro de obras** master builder || *f* see **maestra**
Magallanes *m* Magellan
magancear *intr* (Col, Chile) to loaf around
magan•to -ta *adj* dull, spiritless
magia *f* magic
magiar *adj* & *mf* Magyar; Hungarian
mági•co -ca *adj* magic || *mf* magician, wizard || *f* magic
magín *m* fancy, imagination
magisterio *m* teaching; teachers
magistrado *m* magistrate
magistral *adj* masterly
magnáni•mo -ma *adj* magnanimous
magnesio *m* magnesium; (phot) flashlight
magnéti•co -ca *adj* magnetic
magnetismo *m* magnetism
magnetizar **§60** *tr* magnetize
magneto *m* & *f* magneto
magnetofón *m* or **magnetófono** *m* tape recorder
magnetoscopia *f* video recorder
magnificar **§73** *tr* to magnify; exalt
magnífi•co -ca *adj* magnificent
magnitud *f* magnitude
mag•no -na *adj* great, e.g., **Alejandro Magno** Alexander the Great
mago *m* magician; soothsayer; (fig) wizard, expert; **Magos de Oriente** Wise Men of the East
ma•gro -gra *adj* lean, thin || *m* loin of pork || *f* slice of ham
maguar **§10** *ref* (Ven, W-I) to be disappointed
magüeta *f* heifer
magüeto *m* young bull
maguey *m* century plant
magullar *tr* to bruise || *ref* to get bruised
magullón *m* bruise; contusion
mahometa•no -na *adj* & *mf* Mohammedan
mahometismo *m* Mohammedanism
mahones *mpl* (P-R, S-D) blue jeans
mahonesa *f* mayonnaise
maído *m* meow
maitines *mpl* matins
maíz *m* maize, Indian corn; **comer maíz** to accept bribes; **maíz en la mazorca** corn on the cob
maizal *m* cornfield
maja *f* flashy dame
majada *f* sheepfold; dung, manure
majaderear *tr* to bother, annoy
majadería *f* nonsensical remark; bother, nuisance
majade•ro -ra *adj* pestiferous, stupid || *mf* bore, dunce || *m* pestle
majar *tr* to crush, mash, grind, pound; annoy, bother
majestad *f* majesty
majestuo•so -sa *adj* majestic
ma•jo -ja *adj* sporty; handsome, dashing; pretty, nice; all dressed up || *mf* sport || *m* bully || *f* see **maja**
mal *adj* apocopated form of **malo,** used only before nouns in masculine singular || *adv* badly, poorly; wrong; hardly, scarcely; **mal de** short of; **mal que le pese** in spite of him || *m* evil; damage, harm; wrong; sickness; misfortune; **mal de altura** mountain sickness; **mal de la tierra** homesickness; **mal de mar** seasickness; **mal de piedra** (pathol) stone; **mal de rayos** radiation sickness; **mal de vuelo** airsickness; **por mal de mis pecados** to my sorrow; **tener a mal** to object to; **¡mal haya . . . !** curses on . . . !
mala *f* mail; mailbag; mailboat
malabarista *mf* juggler; sneak thief
malacate *m* whim; (*hoisting machine*) (Mex, Hond) spindle
malaconseja•do -da *adj* ill-advised
malacrianza *f* var of **malcriadez**
malagradeci•do -da *adj* ungrateful
malandante *adj* unlucky, unfortunate
malandanza *f* bad luck, misfortune
malan•drín -drina *adj* evil, wicked || *mf* scoundrel, rascal
malaria *f* malaria
malaventura *f* misfortune
mala•yo -ya *adj* & *mf* Malay
mala•zo -za *adj* perverse; evil; wicked
malbaratar *tr* to undersell; squander
malcasa•do -da *adj* mismated; undutiful
malcasar *tr* to mismate || *intr* & *ref* to be mismated
malcaso *m* treachery
malconten•to -ta *adj* & *mf* malcontent
malcriadez *f* rudeness; bad manners
malcria•do -da *adj* ill-bred
malcriar **§77** *tr* to spoil, pamper

maldad *f* evil, wickedness
maldecir §11 *tr* to curse || *intr* to curse, damn; **maldecir de** to slander, vilify
maldición *f* malediction, curse; oath, curse
maldispues•to -ta *adj* ill, indisposed; unwilling, ill-disposed
maldi•to -ta *adj* damned, accursed; wicked; (Mex) coarse, crude, indecent; **no saber maldita la cosa de** to not know a single thing about || **el Maldito** the Evil One || *f* (coll) tongue; **soltar la maldita** to talk too much
maleante *adj* wicked, evil || *mf* crook, hoodlum, rowdy
malear *tr* to spoil; corrupt || *ref* to spoil, get spoiled; be corrupted
malecón *m* levee, dike, mole, jetty
maledicencia *f* calumny, slander
maleficiar *tr* to damage, harm; to curse, bewitch, cast a spell on
maleficio *m* curse, spell; witchcraft
maléfi•co -ca *adj* evil; harmful
malentender §51 *tr* to misunderstand
malentendido *m* misunderstanding, misapprehension
malestar *m* malaise, indisposition
maleta *m* bungler; ham bullfighter || *f* valise; **hacer la maleta** to pack up
maletín *m* satchel
malevolencia *f* malice, malevolence
malévo•lo -la *adj* malevolent
maleza *f* thicket, underbrush; weeds
malfuncionamiento *m* malfunction
malgasta•do -da *adj* ill-spent
malgastar *tr* to waste, squander
malgenio•so -sa *adj* ill-tempered, irritable
malhabla•do -da *adj* foul-mouthed
malhada•do -da *adj* ill-starred
malhe•cho -cha *adj* deformed || *m* misdeed
malhe•chor -chora *mf* malefactor || *f* malefactress
malherir §68 *tr* to injure badly
malhumora•do -da *adj* ill-humored
malicia *f* (*maldad*) evil; (*bellaquería, malevolencia*) malice; insidiousness, trickiness; suspicion
malicio•so -sa *adj* evil; malicious; insidious, tricky
malignar *tr* to corrupt, vitiate; spoil
malignidad *f* malignity
malig•no -na *adj* (*malévolo; pernicioso*) malign; (*malicioso; perjudicial*) malignant; (pathol) malignant
malintenciona•do -da *adj* ill-disposed, evil-minded
malmaridada *f* faithless wife
malmeter *tr* to lead astray, misguide; alienate, estrange
ma•lo -la *adj* bad, poor, evil; (*travieso*) naughty, mischievous; (*enfermo*) sick, ill; (*que no es como debiera ser*) wrong; (*inflamado, dolorido*) sore; **a la mala** (Cuba, P-R) by force; (Mex) insincere; (Mex) mean; **estar de malas** to be out of luck; **lo malo es que** the trouble is that; **malo con** or **para con** mean to; **por malas o por buenas** willingly or unwillingly; **ser malo de engañar** to be hard to trick || **el Malo** the Evil One || *f* see **mala**
malogra•do -da *adj* late, ill-fated
malograr *tr* to miss || *ref* to fail; come to an untimely end
malogro *m* failure, disappointment
maloliente *adj* malodorous, foul-smelling
malón *m* mean trick; (SAm) Indian incursion; (Chile) surprise party
malpara•do -da *adj* hurt; **salir malparado (de)** to fail (in), come out worsted (in)
malparar *tr* to mistreat
malparir *intr* to miscarry, have a miscarriage
malparto *m* miscarriage
malquerencia *f* dislike
malquerer §55 *tr* to dislike
malquistar *tr* to alienate, estrange || *ref* to become alienated
malquis•to -ta *adj* disliked, unpopular
malrotar *tr* to squander
malsa•no -na *adj* unhealthy
malsín *m* mischief-maker
malsonante *adj* obnoxious, odious
malsufri•do -da *adj* impatient
malta *m* malt || *f* asphalt, tar; dark beer; (Chile) premium beer
maltraer §75 *tr* to abuse, ill-treat; call down, scold
maltratar *tr* to abuse, ill-treat, maltreat; damage, spoil
maltre•cho -cha *adj* battered, damaged
malu•co -ca or malu•cho -cha *adj* sickish, upset
malva *f* mallow; **malva arbórea** hollyhock, rose mallow; **ser como una malva** to be meek and mild
malva•do -da *adj* evil, wicked || *mf* evildoer
malvarrosa *f* hollyhock, rose mallow
malvavisco *m* marsh mallow
malvender *tr* to sell at a loss
malversación *f* graft, embezzlement, misappropriation
malversar *tr & intr* to graft, embezzle
malvezar §60 *tr* to give bad habits to || *ref* to acquire bad habits
malla *f* mesh, meshing; (*de la armadura*) mail; (*traje*) tights; bathing suit
mallete *m* mallet
Mallorca *f* Majorca
mallor•quín -quina *adj & mf* Majorcan
mama *f* mamma
ma•má *f* (*pl* **-más**) mamma
mamada *f* suck; sucking; cinch; advantageous deal; easy profit
mama•lón -lona *adj* (Ven, W-I) loafing || *mf* (Cuba) sponger
mamama *f* (Hond) granny
mamamama *f* (Peru) granny
mamar *tr* to suck; learn as a child; swallow; wangle; **mamóla** he was taken in || *intr* to suck || *ref* to swallow; (*obtener sin mérito*) wangle; (SAm) to get drunk; **mamarse a uno** to get the best of someone; take someone in; (Col, Chile, Peru) to do away with someone
mamarracho *m* mess, sight; (*hombre ridículo*) milksop

mamelón *m* knoll, mound

mamífe•ro -ra *adj* mammalian || *m* mammal, mammalian

mamola *f* chuck (*under the chin*); **hacer la mamola a** to chuck under the chin; take in, make a fool of

ma•món -mona *adj* sucking; fond of sucking || *mf* suckling || *m* shoot, sucker; (Guat, Hond) club; (Mex) soft cake || *f* chuck (*under chin*)

mamonear *tr* (Guat, Hond) to beat, cudgel; (S-D) to put off, delay; (*el tiempo*) (S-D) to waste

mamotreto *m* memo book; batch of papers; hulk, bulk

mampara *f* screen; folding screen; (Peru) glass door

mamparo *m* bulkhead

mampostería *f* rubble, rubblework; masonry, stone masonry

ma•mut *m* (*pl* **-muts**) mammoth

manada *f* (*de ganado vacuno*) herd, drove; (*de ganado lanar*) flock; (*de lobos*) pack; (*de gente*) gang, troop; (*de hierba, trigo, etc.*) handful

manade•ro -ra *adj* flowing || *m* spring, source; shepherd

manantial *adj* flowing, running || *m* spring, source; (fig) source

manar *tr* to run with || *intr* to pour forth, run; abound

manaza *f* big hand

mancar §73 *tr* to maim, cripple || *intr* (*el viento*) (naut) to abate, subside

manca•rrón -rrona *adj* (*caballería*) skinny, worn-out; (Chile) tired out, exhausted || *m* old nag; (Chile, Peru) dam, dike

manceba *f* mistress, concubine

mancebía *f* bawdyhouse, brothel; wild oats; youth

mance•bo -ba *adj* youthful || *m* youngster; youth, young man; (*en una farmacia, barbería, etc.*) helper || *f* see **manceba**

mancerina *f* saucer with hook to hold chocolate cup

mancilla *f* spot, blemish

mancillar *tr* to spot, blemish

man•co -ca *adj* armless, one-armed; one-handed; defective, faulty || *mf* cripple || *m* (Chile) old nag

mancomún — **de mancomún** jointly, in common

mancomunar *tr* to unite, combine; (*fuerzas, caudales, etc.*) pool || *ref* to unite, combine

mancomunidad *f* association, union; (*asociación de provincias*) commonwealth

mancornar §61 *tr* (*un novillo*) to throw and hold on the ground; (*una res vacuna*) tie a horn and front leg of; (*dos reses*) tie together by the horns; (coll) to join, bring together

mancornas or **mancuernas** *fpl* (Mex) cuff links

mancuernillas *fpl* (Guat, Hond) cuff links

mancha *f* spot, stain; (*de vegetación*) patch; speckle; (fig) stain, blot; **mancha solar** sunspot

manchar *tr* to spot, stain; speckle; (fig) to stain, disgrace || *intr* to spot; **¡mancha!** wet paint!

manda *f* gift, offer; bequest, legacy

mandade•ro -ra *mf* messenger || *m* errand boy

mandado *m* order, command; errand; **hacer un mandado** to run an errand

manda•más *m* (*pl* **-mases**) (slang) big shot; (*jefe político*) (slang) boss

mandamiento *m* order, command; (Bib) commandment; (law) writ; **los cinco mandamientos** the five fingers of the hand

mandar *tr* to order, command; (*legar*) bequeath; (*enviar*) send; **mandar a distancia** to operate by remote control; **mandar** + *inf* to have + *inf*, e.g., **la mandé leer en voz alta** I had her read aloud || *intr* to be in command, be the boss; **mandar llamar** to send for; **mandar por** to send for; **mande Vd.** I beg your pardon || *ref* (*un enfermo*) to manage to get around; (*dos piezas*) be communicating; **mandarse con** (*otra pieza*) to communicate with; be rude to

mandarina *f* tangerine

mandatario *m* agent, proxy; chief executive

mandato *m* mandate; term (*of office*)

mandíbula *f* jaw, jawbone; **reír a mandíbula batiente** to roar with laughter

mandil *m* apron

mando *m* command; control, drive; **alto mando** (mil) high command; **mando a distancia** remote control; **mando a punta de dedo** finger-tip control; **mando de las válvulas** timing gears; **mando por botón** push-button control; **tener el mando y el palo** to be the boss, rule the roost

mandolina *f* mandolin

man•dón -dona *adj* bossy || *mf* domineering person || *m* (*en las minas*) boss, foreman; (*en las carreras de caballos*) (Chile) starter

mandrágora *f* mandrake

mandril *m* (mach) chuck

mandrilar *tr* to bore

manea *f* hobble

manear *tr* to hobble

manecilla *f* (*de reloj*) hand; clasp, book clasp; (bot) tendril; (typ) fist, index

manejable *adj* manageable

manejar *tr* to manage; handle, wield; (*un automóvil*) drive || *ref* to behave; get around, move about

manejo *m* management; handling; intrigue, scheming; horsemanship; driving; **manejo a distancia** remote control; **manejo doméstico** housekeeping

manera *f* manner, way; **a la manera de** in the manner of; like; **de manera que** so that; **en gran manera** to a great extent; extremely; **sobre manera** exceedingly

manga *f* (*parte del vestido*) sleeve; (*tubo de caucho*) hose; waterspout; (bridge) game; **en mangas de camisa** in shirt-sleeves; **ir de manga** to be in cahoots; **manga de**

agua waterspout; cloudburst; **manga de camisa** shirt-sleeve; **manga de riego** watering hose; **manga de viento** whirlwind; **manga marina** waterspout; **mangas** extras, profits
mangana *f* lasso
manganear *tr* to lasso; (Peru) to annoy, bother
manganeso *m* manganese
mango *m* handle; **mango de escoba** broomstick; (aer) stick, control stick
mangonear *tr* to plunder || *intr* to loaf around; meddle; dabble
mangosta *f* mongoose
mangote *m* sleeve protector
manguera *f* hose; (*tubo de ventilación*) funnel
mangueta *f* fountain syringe; door jamb
manguitero *m* furrier
manguito *m* muff; sleeve guard; coffee cake; (mach) sleeve
ma•ní *m* (*pl* **-níes** or **-nises**) peanut
manía *f* mania; craze, whim; grudge; **tener manía a** to dislike
maniabier•to -ta *adj* open-handed
manía•co -ca *adj* maniac(al) || *mf* maniac
maníaco-depresi•vo -va *adj* manic-depressive
maniatar *tr* to tie the hands of
maniáti•co -ca *adj* stubborn; queer, eccentric; (*entusiasta*) crazy || *mf* crank, eccentric
manicero *m* peanut vendor
manicomio *m* madhouse, insane asylum
manicor•to -ta *adj* closefisted, tight
manicu•ro -ra *mf* manicure, manicurist || *f* manicure, manicuring
mani•do -da *adj* shabby, worn; hackneyed; (culin) high || *f* haunt, hangout
manifestación *f* manifestation; (*reunión pública para dar a conocer un sentimiento u opinión*) demonstration
manifestante *mf* demonstrator
manifestar §2 *tr* to manifest; (*el Santísimo Sacramento*) expose || *intr* to demonstrate || *ref* to become manifest
manifies•to -ta *adj* manifest || *m* manifesto; (eccl) exposition of the Host; (naut) manifest
manigua *f* (Mex, W-I) thicket, jungle; **irse a la manigua** (W-I) to revolt
manija *f* handle; clamp; crank
manilar•go -ga *adj* ready-fisted; generous
manilla *f* bracelet; handcuff, manacle
manillar *m* handle bar
maniobra *f* handling; lever; maneuver; (naut) gear, tackle
maniobrar *intr* to work with the hands; maneuver; (rr) to shift
maniota *f* hobble
manipula•dor -dora *mf* manipulator || *m* (telg) key
manipular *tr* to manipulate
mani•quí *m* (*pl* **-quíes**) manikin, mannequin; (*para exponer prendas de ropa*) dress form; (*de pintores y escultores*) lay figure; (fig) puppet; **ir hecho un maniquí** to be a fashion plate || *f* (*mujer joven que luce los trajes de última moda*) mannequin, model
manirro•to -ta *adj* lavish, prodigal
manivací•o -a *adj* empty-handed
manivela *f* crank; **manivela de arranque** starting crank
manjar *m* dish, food, tidbit, delicacy; lift, recreation
mano *m* first to play, e.g., **soy mano** I'm first || *f* hand; (*de cuadrúpedo*) forefoot; (*de pintura*) coat; (*de papel*) quire; (*saetilla de reloj u otro instrumento*) hand; (*lance en un juego*) round, hand; (*del elefante*) trunk; pestle, masher; **a la mano** at hand, on hand; within reach; understandable; **a mano airada** violently; **asidos de la mano** hand in hand; **bajo mano** underhandedly; **caer en manos de** to fall into the hands of; **¡dame esa mano!** put it here!; **dar la mano** to lend a hand; **darse las manos** to join hands; to shake hands; **de las manos** hand in hand; **de primera mano** at first hand; first-hand; **de segunda mano** second-hand; **echar mano de** to resort to; **echar una mano** to lend a hand; to play a game; **en buena mano está** after you, you drink first; **escribir a la mano** to take dictation; **escribir a manos de** to write in care of; **estrecharse la mano** to shake hands; **ganarle a uno por la mano** to steal a march on someone; **lavarse las manos de** to wash one's hands of; **llegar a las manos** to come to blows; **malas manos** awkwardness; **mano de gato** cat's-paw; master hand, master touch; **mano de obra** labor; **mano derecha** right-hand man; **mano de santo** sure cure; **¡manos a la obra!** let's get to work!; **manos libres** outside work; **manos limpias** extras, perquisites; clean hands; **manos puercas** graft; **probar la mano** to try one's hand; **tener mano con** to have a pull with; **tener mano izquierda** to be on one's toes; **untar la mano a** to grease the palm of; **venir a las manos** to come to blows; **vivir de la mano a la boca** to live from hand to mouth
manojo *m* bunch, bundle, handful; **a manojos** in abundance
manopla *f* gauntlet; postilion's whip; (Chile) knuckles, brass knuckles
manosear *tr* to finger, paw; muss, rumple; fiddle with; pet || *ref* to spoon, neck
manotada *f* slap
manotear *tr* to slap, smack; (Arg, Mex) to steal, snitch; || *intr* to gesticulate
manquedad *f* lack of one or both hands or arms; disability; deficiency
mansalva — **a mansalva** without risk; without warning; **a mansalva de** safe from
mansarda *f* mansard, mansard roof
mansedumbre *f* gentleness, mildness, meekness; tameness
mansión *f* stay, sojourn; abode, dwelling; **hacer mansión** to stop, stay
man•so -sa *adj* gentle, mild, meek; tame || *m* bellwether; farm

manta *f* blanket; heavy shawl; (coll) beating, thrashing; (Chile, Ecuad) poncho; (Col, Mex, Ven) coarse cotton cloth; **a manta de Dios** copiously; **dar una manta a** to toss in a blanket; **manta de coche** lap robe; **manta de viaje** steamer rug; **tirar de la manta** to let the cat out of the bag

mantear *tr* to toss in a blanket; abuse, mistreat

manteca *f* (*grasa de los animales, esp. la del cerdo*) lard; butter; pomade; (*dinero*) (slang) dough; **como manteca** smooth as butter; **manteca de puerco** lard; **manteca de vaca** butter

mantecado *m* custard ice cream, French ice cream

mantecón *m* mollycoddle, milksop

mantel *m* tablecloth; altar cloth

mantelería *f* table linen

mantelillo *m* embroidered centerpiece

mantelito *m* lunch cloth

mantener **§71** *tr* to maintain; keep; keep up; sustain, defend || *ref* to keep, remain, continue

mantenida *f* kept woman

mantenido *m* (*hombre que vive a expensas de su mujer*) (Guat, Mex, W-I) gigolo; (Guat, Mex, W-I) sponger

mantenimiento *m* maintenance; food, support, living

manteo *m* mantle, cloak

mantequera *f* churn, butter churn; butter dish

mantequería *f* creamery; delicatessen

mantequilla *f* butter; **mantequilla azucarada** hard sauce; **mantequilla derretida** drawn butter

mantilla *f* mantilla (*silk or lace head scarf*); **mantillas** swaddling clothes

mantillo *m* humus, mold

manto *m* mantle, cloak; (*de chimenea*) mantel; (*ropa talar de algunos religiosos, catedráticos, alumnos*) robe, gown; (fig) cloak

mantón *m* shawl, kerchief

manuable *adj* handy

manual *adj* (*que se hace con las manos*) hand; (*fácil de manejar*) handy; easy; easy to understand; easy-going; manual || *m* manual, handbook; notebook

manubrio *m* handle; crank, winch

manuela *f* open hack (*in Madrid*)

manufactura *f* (*fábrica*) factory; (*obra fabricada*) manufacture

manufacturar *tr* to manufacture

manuscribir **§83** *tr* to write by hand

manuscri•to -ta *adj & m* manuscript

manutención *f* maintenance; care, upkeep; shelter, protection

manutener **§71** *tr* (law) to maintain, support

manzana *f* apple; (*conjunto aislado de varias casas contiguas*) block, city block; (*remate en un mueble*) knob, finial; **manzana de Adán** (Chile) Adam's apple

manzanar *m* apple orchard

manzanilla *f* camomile; (*aceituna pequeña; vino blanco*) manzanilla (*small olive; white wine*); (*remate en un mueble*) knob, finial

manzano *m* apple tree

maña *f* skill, dexterity; cunning, craftiness; bad habit, vice; (*de lino, cáñamo, etc.*) bunch; sister; **darse maña** to manage, contrive; **hacer maña** (Col) to fool around

mañana *adv* tomorrow; **¡hasta mañana!** see you tomorrow!; **pasado mañana** the day after tomorrow || *m* tomorrow; (*tiempo venidero*) morrow || *f* morning; **de mañana** in the morning; **muy de mañana** very early in the morning; **por la mañana** in the morning; **tomar la mañana** to get up early; have a shot of liquor before breakfast

mañanear *intr* to be in the habit of getting up early

mañane•ro -ra *adj* morning; early-rising

mañanica *f* early morning, break of day

mañanita *f* woman's bed jacket

mañear *tr* to manage craftily || *intr* to act with cunning

mañerear *intr* (Arg) to dawdle, dilly-dally

mañería *f* sterility

mañe•ro -ra *adj* clever, shrewd; simple, easy; skittish

ma•ño -ña *mf* (coll) Aragonese || *m* brother || *f* see **maña**

mañoso -sa *adj* skillful, clever; crafty, tricky; vicious

mañuela *f* craftiness, trickiness

mañue•las *mf* (*pl* **-las**) tricky person

mapa *m* map; **mapa itinerario** road map || *f* — **llevarse la mapa** to take the prize

mapache *m* coon, raccoon

mapamundi *m* map of the world; (coll) buttocks, behind

mapurite *m* (CAm) skunk

maque *m* lacquer

maquear *tr* to lacquer; (Mex) to varnish

maqueta *f* (*en tamaño reducido*) maquette; (*en tamaño natural*) mock-up; (*de un libro*) dummy

maquillador *m* (theat) make-up man

maquillaje *m* (theat) make-up

maquillar *tr & ref* to make up

máquina *f* machine; (*motor*) engine; locomotive; plan, project; (fig) machinery; (coll) heap, pile, lot; (Cuba) auto; (Chile) ganging up; **escribir a máquina** to typewrite; **máquina de afeitar** safety razor; **máquina de apostar** gambling machine; **máquina de componer** typesetter; **máquina de coser** sewing machine; **máquina de escribir** typewriter; **máquina de lavar** washing machine; **máquina de sumar** adding machine; **máquina de volar** flying machine; **máquina fotográfica** camera; **máquina sacaperras** slot machine

maquinación *f* machination, scheming

máquina-herramienta *f* (*pl* **máquinas-herramientas**) machine tool

maquinal *adj* mechanical

maquinar *tr* to plot, scheme

maquinaria *f* machinery; applied mechanics

maquinilla *f* windlass, winch; clippers; **maquinilla cortapelos** clippers, hair clippers; **maquinilla de afeitar** safety razor; **maquinilla de rizar** curling iron

maquinista *mf* (*persona que fabrica máquinas*) machinist; (*persona que dirige una máquina o locomotora*) engineer; **segundo maquinista** (naut) machinist

mar *m & f* sea; tide, flood; **alta mar** high seas; **a mares** abundantly, copiously; **arrojarse a la mar** to plunge, take great risks; **baja mar** low tide; **correr los mares** to follow the sea; **hablar de la mar** to talk wildly, talk on and on; **hacerse a la mar** to put to sea; **la mar de** (fig) oceans of, large numbers of; **mar alta** rough sea; **mar ancha** high seas; **mar bonanza** calm sea; **mar Caribe** Caribbean Sea, Caribbean; **mar de las Antillas** Caribbean Sea; **mar de las Indias** Indian Ocean; **mar de nubes** cloud bank; **mar Latino** Mediterranean Sea; **mar llena** high tide; **meter la mar en un pozo** to attempt the impossible; **meterse mar adentro** (fig) to go beyond one's depth

maraña *f* undergrowth, thicket; silk waste; (*de hilo, pelo, etc.*) tangle; trick, scheme; puzzle

marañón *m* cashew

maraño•so -sa *adj* scheming || *mf* schemer

maravilla *f* wonder, marvel; (bot) marigold, calendula; **a las maravillas** or **a las mil maravillas** magnificently; **a maravilla** wonderfully well; **por maravilla** rarely, occasionally

maravillar *tr* to astonish || *ref* to wonder, marvel; **maravillarse con** or **de** to marvel at, wonder at

maravillo•so -sa *adj* wonderful, marvelous

marbete *m* label, tag; baggage check; edge, border; **marbete engomado** sticker

marca *f* mark; (*tipo de producto*) make, brand; (*de tamaño*) standard; score; record; height-measuring device; **de marca** outstanding; **marca de agua** watermark; **marca de fábrica** trademark; **marca de reconocimiento** (naut) landmark, seamark; **marca de taquilla** box-office record; **marca registrada** registered trademark

marca•do -da *adj* marked, pronounced

marcaje *m* (sport) scoring; (sport) interfering; (telp) dialing

marcapaso *m* or **marcapasos** *m* (heart) pacemaker

marcar §73 *tr* to mark; brand; embroider; (*p.ej., un pañuelo*) initial; (*la hora un reloj*) show; (*un tanto*) make, score; (*el número telefónico*) dial || *ref* (*un buque*) to take bearings

marcear *tr* to shear || *ref* to be Marchlike

marcial *adj* martial; gallant, noble

marcia•no -na *adj & mf* Martian

marco *m* frame; framework; (*de pesas y medidas*) standard

marcha *f* march; (*funcionamiento*) running, operation; (*p.ej., de los astros*) course, path; (*desenvolvimiento de un asunto*) course, march, progress; (*grado de velocidad*) rate of speed; (*de los engranajes*) (aut) speed; **cambiar de marcha** to shift gears; **en marcha** on the march; underway; in motion; **marcha atrás** reverse; **marcha del hambre** hunger march; **marcha directa** high gear; **marcha forzada** (mil) forced march

marchamo *m* customhouse mark; (Arg, Bol) tax on slaughtered cattle

marchante *adj* commercial || *m* dealer, merchant; customer

marchapié *m* running board

marchar *intr* to march; run, work, go; leave, go away; come along, proceed; **marchar en vacío** to idle || *ref* to leave, go away

marchitar *tr* to wilt, wither || *ref* to wilt, wither; languish

marchi•to -ta *adj* withered, faded; (fig) languid

marea *f* tide; tideland; gentle sea breeze; dew; drizzle; **marea alta** high tide; **marea baja** low tide; **marea creciente** or **entrante** flood tide; **marea menguante** ebb tide; **marea muerta** neap tide; **marea viva** spring tide; **rendir la marea** to stem the tide

marea•do -da *adj* nauseated, sick, lightheaded; seasick

mareaje *m* navigation, seamanship; (*de un buque*) course

marear *tr* to sail; annoy, pester || *intr* to be annoying || *ref* to get sick, get giddy; get seasick; be damaged at sea; fade

marejada *f* heavy sea; (*de desorden*) stirring, undercurrent; **marejada de fondo** ground swell

maremagno *m* or **maremágnum** *m* big mess

mareo *m* nausea, dizziness, sickness; seasickness; annoyance

marfil *m* ivory

marfile•ño -ña *adj* ivory

mar•fuz -fuza *adj* (*pl* **-fuces -fuzas**) cast aside, rejected; deceptive

marga *f* marl

margar §44 *tr* to marl

margarita *f* pearl; (bot) daisy; **margarita de los prados** English daisy; **margarita** (*impresora*) (*ordenador*) daisy wheel

margen *m & f* margin; border, edge; marginal note; **al margen de** aloof from; outside of; independent of; aside from; **dar margen para** to give occasion for; **dejar al margen** to leave out; **quedar al margen** to be left out of

marginal *adj* marginal

mariache *m* Mexican band and singers

marica *m* sissy, milksop || *f* magpie

maricón *m* sissy

maridable *adj* marital

maridaje *m* married life; (fig) union

maridar *tr* to combine, unit || *intr* to get married; to live as man and wife

marido *m* husband

mariguana *f* marihuana

mariguanza *f* (Chile) hocus-pocus; (Chile) pirouette; **mariguanzas** (Chile) clowning; (Chile) powwowing

marimacho *m* mannish woman

marimandona *f* queen bee, bossy woman

marimarica *m* sissy

marimorena *f* fight, row
marina *f* navy; (*conjunto de buques*) marine, fleet; (*cuadro o pintura*) seascape; shore, seaside; sailing, navigation; **marina de guerra** navy; **marina mercante** merchant marine
marinar *tr* to marinate, salt; (*un buque*) staff, man || *intr* to be a sailor
marinera *f* sailor blouse; (*blusa de niño*) middy, middy blouse
marinería *f* sailoring; sailors
marine•ro -ra *adj* sea, marine; seaworthy; seafaring || *m* mariner, seaman, sailor; **marinero de agua dulce** (*el que ha navegado poco*) landlubber (*person unacquainted with the sea*); **marinero matalote** (*hombre de mar, rudo y torpe*) landlubber (*awkward and unskilled seaman*) || *f* see **marinera**
marines•co -ca *adj* sailor; sailorly
mari•no -na *adj* marine, sea || *m* mariner, seaman, sailor || *f* see **marina**
marioneta *f* marionette
mariposa *f* butterfly; butterfly valve; wing nut; rushlight; (Col) blindman's buff; **mariposa nocturna** moth
mariposear *intr* to flit about; be fickle
mariposón *m* (Cuba, Guat, Mex) fickle flirt
mariquita *m* sissy, milksop, popinjay || *f* (ent) ladybird
marisabidilla *f* bluestocking
mariscal *m* blacksmith; (mil) marshal; **mariscal de campo** (mil) field marshal
marisco *m* shellfish; **mariscos** seafood
marisma *f* swamp, marsh, salt marsh
marisquería *f* seafood store, seafood restaurant
maríti•mo -ma *adj* maritime; marine, sea
maritor•nes *f* (*pl* **-nes**) mannish maidservant, wench
marmita *f* pot, boiler, kettle
marmitón *m* kitchen scullion
mármol *m* marble
marmóre•o -a *adj* marble
marmosete *m* vignette
marmota *f* marmot; sleepyhead; worsted cap; **marmota de Alemania** hamster; **marmota de América** ground hog, woodchuck
maroma *f* hemp rope, esparto rope; acrobatic stunt
maromear *intr* to perform acrobatic stunts, walk the tight rope; wobble, sway from side to side (*e.g., in politics*); hesitate
marome•ro -ra *mf* acrobat, tightrope walker; weaseler; opportunist
marqués *m* marquis; **los marqueses** the marquis and marchioness
marquesa *f* marchioness, marquise; (*sobre la puerta de un hotel*) marquee
marquesina *f* cover over field tent; (*sobre la puerta de un hotel*) marquee; locomotive cab
marquetería *f* cabinetwork, woodwork; (*taracea*) marquetry
marra•jo -ja *adj* sly, tricky; (*toro*) vicious
marrana *f* sow; slattern, slut
marranada *f* piggishness, filth
marranalla *f* rabble, riffraff
marra•no -na *adj* base, vile; dirty, sloppy || *mf* hog || *m* male hog, boar; filthy person, hog; cad, cur || *f* see **marrana**
marrar *intr* to miss, fail; go astray
marras *adv* long ago; **hacer marras que** (Bol, Ecuad) to be a long time since
marro *m* game resembling quoits and played with a stone; (*juego de muchachos*) tag; (*ladeo*) dodge, duck; slip, miss
marrón *adj invar* maroon (*dark-red*); tan (*shoes*) || *m* maroon; candied chestnut; stone (*used as a sort of quoit*)
marro•quí (*pl* **-quíes**) *adj & mf* Moroccan || *m* morocco, morocco leather
marro•quín -quina *adj & mf* var of **marroquí**
marrubio *m* horehound
marrue•co -ca *adj & mf* Moroccan
Marruecos *m* Morocco
marrulle•ro -ra *adj* cajoling, wheedling || *mf* cajoler, wheedler
Marsella *f* Marseille
marsopa *f* or **marsopla** *f* porpoise
mart. *abbr* **martes**
marta *f* pine marten; **marta cebellina** sable, Siberian sable; **marta del Canadá** fisher
Marte *m* Mars
mar•tes *m* (*pl* **-tes**) Tuesday; **martes de carnaval** or **carnestolendas** Shrove Tuesday
martillar *tr* to hammer; pester, worry || *intr* to hammer
martillazo *m* blow with a hammer
martillear *tr & intr* var of **martillar**
martillero *m* (Chile) auctioneer
martillo *m* hammer; auction house; (*persona*) scourge; (mus) tuning hammer; (*de arma de fuego*) cock
martín *m* — **martín pescador** (*pl* **martín pescadores**) kingfisher
martinete *m* drop hammer; pile driver; (*del piano*) hammer
martinico *m* ghost, goblin
mártir *mf* martyr
martirio *m* martyrdom
márts. *abbr* **mártires**
marullo *m* surge, swell
marxista *adj & mf* Marxist or Marxian
marzo *m* March
mas *conj* but
más *adv* more; most; **a lo más** at most, at the most; **a más de** besides, in addition to; **como el que más** as the next one, as well as anybody; **cuando más** at the most; **de más** extra; too much, too many; **estar de más** to be in the way; be unnecessary; be superfluous; **los más de** most of, the majority of; **más bien** rather; **más de** + *número* more than; **más de lo que** + *verbo* more than; **más que** more than; better than; **no . . . más** no longer; **no . . . más nada** nothing more; **no . . . más que** only || *prep* plus || *m* more; (*signo de adición*) plus
masa *f* mass; (*pasta que se forma con agua y harina*) dough; (*masa aplastada*) mash;

nature, disposition; (Chile, Ecuad) puff paste; (*p.ej., de un automóvil*) (elec) ground; **las masas** the masses
masada *f* farm
masadero *m* farmer
masaje *m* massage; **masaje facial** facial
masajear *tr* to massage
masajista *m* masseur || *f* masseuse
masar *tr* to knead; massage
mascar §73 *tr* to chew; mumble, mutter || *ref* (*un cabo*) (naut) to gall
máscara *mf* (*persona*) mask, mummer || *f* mask; (*traje, disfraz*) masquerade; **máscara antigás** gas mask
mascarada *f* masquerade
mascarilla *f* half mask; false face; death mask
mascarón *m* false face; (*persona fea*) fright; (archit) mask; **mascarón de proa** (naut) figurehead
mascota *f* mascot
mascujar *tr & intr* to chew with difficulty; mumble
masculi•no -na *adj* masculine; (*sexo*) male; (*traje*) men's || *m* masculine
mascullar *tr & intr* to mumble, mutter; to chew with difficulty
masera *f* kneading trough
masilla *f* putty
masita *f* (mil) money withheld for clothing; (Arg, Bol) cake
masón *m* Mason
masonería *f* Masonry
masoquis•to -ta *adj* masochistic || *mf* masochist
mastelero *m* (naut) topmast
masticar §73 *tr* to chew, masticate; meditate on; mumble
mástil *m* (*de una embarcación*) mast; (*de un violín o guitarra*) neck; stalk; (*de pluma*) shaft, stem; upright
mas•tín -tina *mf* mastiff; **mastín danés** Great Dane
mastodonte *m* mastodon
mastuerzo *m* (bot) cress; dolt
masturbación *f* masturbation
masturbar *tr & ref* to masturbate
mat. *abbr* **matématica**
mata *f* bush, shrub; blade, sprig; brush, underbrush; **mata de pelo** crop of hair, head of hair; **mata parda** chaparro (*oak*); **saltar de la mata** to come out of hiding
mataca•bras *m* (*pl* **-bras**) cold blast from the north
matacán *m* dog poison
matacande•las *m* (*pl* **-las**) candle snuffer
matadero *m* abattoir, slaughterhouse; drudgery
mata•dor -dora *mf* killer || *m* matador; **matador de mujeres** lady-killer
matadura *f* sore, gall
matafue•gos *m* (*pl* **-gos**) fire extinguisher; (*oficial*) fireman
matalo•bos *m* (*pl* **-bos**) wolf's-bane
mata•lón -lona *mf* skinny old nag
matalotaje *m* (naut) ship stores; mess, hodgepodge
matamale•zas *m* (*pl* **-zas**) weed killer
matamari•dos *f* (*pl* **-dos**) many times a widow
matamo•ros *m* (*pl* **-ros**) bully
matamos•cas *m* (*pl* **-cas**) fly swatter; flypaper
matanza *f* slaughter, massacre; butchering; pork products; (CAm) butcher shop; (Ven) slaughterhouse
matape•rros *m* (*pl* **-rros**) harum-scarum, street urchin
matar *tr* to kill; butcher; (*el fuego, la luz*) put out; (*la cal*) slack; (*el metal*) mat; (*un color*) tone down; (*un naipe*) spot; play a card higher than; (*a un caballo*) gall; bore to death; (*el tiempo, el hambre, etc.*) (fig) to kill || *intr* to kill || *ref* to kill oneself; drudge, overwork; be disappointed; **matarse con** to quarrel with; **matarse por** to struggle for; struggle to
matarratas *m* rat poison; (*aguardiente de mala calidad*) rotgut
matarro•tos *m* (*pl* **-tos**) (Chile) pawnshop
matasa•nos *m* (*pl* **-nos**) quack doctor
matasellar *tr* to cancel, postmark
matase•llos *m* (*pl* **-llos**) postmark
matasie•te *m* (*pl* **-te**) bully, swashbuckler
matatí•as *m* (*pl* **-as**) moneylender, pawnbroker
matazar•zas *m* (*pl* **-zas**) weed killer
mate *adj* dull, flat || *m* checkmate; (SAm) maté; (SAm) maté gourd; **dar mate a** to checkmate; make fun of; **dar mate ahogado a** to stalemate; **mate ahogado** stalemate
matear *tr* to plant at regular intervals; make dull; (Chile) to checkmate || *ref* (*el trigo*) to sprout; (*un perro de caza*) hunt through the bushes
matemáti•co -ca *adj* mathematical || *mf* mathematician || *f* mathematics; **matemáticas** mathematics
materia *f* matter; material, stuff; **materia colorante** dyestuff; **materia de guerra** matériel; **materia prima** or **primera materia** raw material
material *adj* material; (*grosero*) crude || *m* material; (*conjunto de objetos necesario para un servicio*) matériel; (typ) matter, copy; **material de guerra** matériel; **material fijo** (rr) permanent way; **material móvil** or **rodante** (rr) rolling stock; **ser material** to be immaterial
materialismo *m* materialism
materialista *mf* materialist; (Mex) truck driver
materializar §60 *tr* (*beneficios*) to realize
maternal *adj* maternal, mother; (*afectos, cuidados, etc.*) motherly
maternidad *f* maternity; motherhood
mater•no -na *adj* maternal, mother
matinal *adj* morning
matinée *f* matinée; dressing gown, wrapper
ma•tiz *m* (*pl* **-tices**) shade, hue, nuance
matizar §60 *tr* (*diversos colores*) to blend; (*un color, un sonido*) shade; (*en cuanto al color*) match
matón *m* bully, browbeater

matorral *m* thicket, underbrush
matraca *f* rattle, noisemaker; taunting, bantering; bore, pest; **dar matraca a** to taunt, to tease
matraquear *intr* to make a racket; to taunt, tease
ma•traz *m* (*pl* **-traces**) flask
matre•ro -ra *adj* cunning, shrewd || *m* (SAm) cheat, swindler
matriarca *f* matriarch
matricida *adj* matricidal || *mf* matricide
matricidio *m* matricide
matrícula *f* register, roster, roll; license; registry
matricular *tr & ref* to matriculate
matrimonialmente *adv* as husband and wife
matrimoniar *intr* to marry, get married
matrimonio *m* marriage, matrimony; (*marido y mujer*) married couple; **matrimonio consensual** common-law marriage
ma•triz *adj* (*pl* **-trices**) main, first, mother || *f* matrix; (*de libro talonario*) stub; screw nut; first draft
matrona *f* matron; matronly lady
matronal *adj* matronly
matun•go -ga *adj* skinny, full of sores || *m* old nag
maturran•go -ga *adj* (SAm) poor, clumsy || *m* (SAm) stranger; (SAm) old nag || *f* trickery
Matusalén *m* Methuselah; **vivir más años que Matusalén** to be as old as Methuselah
matute *m* smuggling; smuggled goods; gambling den
matutear *intr* to smuggle
matute•ro -ra *mf* smuggler
matutinal or **matuti•no -na** *adj* morning
maula *mf* lazy loafer; poor pay; tricky person, cheat || *f* junk, trash; remnant; trickery
maulería *f* remnant shop; trickiness
maullar §8 *intr* to meow
maullido *m* or **maúllo** *m* meow
mausoleo *m* mausoleum
máxima *f* maxim; principle
máxime *adv* chiefly, mainly, especially
máxi•mo -ma *adj* maximum; top; superlative || *m* maximum || *f* see **máxima**
may. *abbr* **mayúscula**
maya *f* May queen; English daisy
mayal *m* flail
mayear *intr* to be Maylike
mayestáti•co -ca *adj* royal
mayido *m* meow
mayo *m* May; Maypole
mayonesa *f* mayonnaise
mayor *adj* greater; larger; older, elder; greatest; largest; oldest, eldest; major; elderly; (*calle*) main; (*altar; misa*) high; **hacerse mayor de edad** to come of age; **ser mayor de edad** to be of age || *m* chief, head, superior; **al por mayor** wholesale; **mayor de edad** (*persona de edad legal*) major; **mayores** elders; ancestors, forefathers; **mayor general** staff officer
mayoral *m* boss, foreman; head shepherd; stagecoach driver; (Arg) streetcar conductor
mayorazgo *m* primogeniture; entailed estate descending by primogeniture; first-born son
mayordoma *f* stewardess, housekeeper
mayordomo *m* steward, butler, majordomo
mayoreo *m* wholesale
mayoría *f* (*mayor edad; el mayor número, la mayor parte*) majority; superiority; **alcanzar su mayoría de edad** to come of age; **mayoría cómoda** solid majority; **mayoría de edad** majority
mayoridad *f* majority
mayorista *adj* (Arg, Chile) wholesale || *mf* (Arg, Chile) wholesaler
mayorita•rio -ria *adj* majority
mayormente *adv* chiefly, mainly, mostly
mayúscu•lo -la *adj* (*letra*) capital; awful, tremendous || *f* capital, capital letter
maza *f* mace; heavy drumstick; bore, pedant; **la maza y la mona** constant companions; **maza de gimnasia** Indian club
mazacote *m* barilla; concrete, cement; botched job; tough, doughy food; (coll) bore
mazar §60 *tr* to churn
mazmorra *f* dungeon
mazo *m* mallet, maul; bunch; (*de la campana*) clapper; (*hombre fastidioso*) bore, pest
mazonería *f* stone masonry; (*obra de relieve*) relief; gold or silver embroidery
mazorca *f* ear of corn; cocoa bean; (*husada*) spindleful; (*de un balustre*) spindle; **comer maíz de** or **en la mazorca** to eat corn on the cob
mazorral *adj* coarse, crude
m/c *abbr* **mi cargo, mi cuenta, moneda corriente**
m/cta *abbr* **mi cuenta**
m/cte *abbr* **moneda corriente**
me (used as object of verb) *pron pers* me, to me || *pron reflex* myself; to myself
meada *f* urination, water; urine stain
meadero *m* urinal
meados *mpl* urine
meaja *f* crumb; **meaja de huevo** tread
meandro *m* meander; wandering speech, wandering writing
mear *tr* to urinate on || *intr & ref* to urinate
Meca, La Mecca
¡mecachis! *interj* wow!, geez!
mecáni•co -ca *adj* mechanical; low, mean || *m* (*obrero perito en el arreglo de las máquinas*) mechanic; (*obrero que fabrica y compone máquinas*) machinist; workman, repairman; driver, chauffeur; **mecánicos** (CAm, Cuba, S-D) blue jeans || *f* mechanics; (*aparato que da movimiento a un artefacto*) machinery, works; meanness; **mecánicas** household chores
mecánico-dentista *m* dental technician
mecanismo *m* mechanism, machinery
mecanizar §60 *tr* to mechanize; motorize
mecanógrafa *f* typist
mecanografía *f* typewriting; **mecanografía al tacto** touch typewriting
mecanografiar §77 *tr & intr* to typewrite

mecanógra•fo -fa *mf* typist, typewriter
mecapale•ro -ra *m* (Mex) messenger, porter
mece•dor -dora *adj* swinging, rocking || *m* stirrer; (*columpio*) swing || *f* rocker, rocking chair
mecer §46 *tr* (*un líquido*) to stir; (*la cuna*) rock || *ref* to rock, swing
mecha *f* (*de vela o bujía*) wick; (*tubo de pólvora*) fuse; lock of hair; (*para mechar carne*) slice of bacon; bundle of thread; (Col, Ecuad, Ven) joke
mechar *tr* (*la carne*) to lard, interlard
mechera *f* shoplifter
mechero *m* (*p.ej., de cigarrillos*) lighter, pocket lighter; (*de aparato de alumbrado*) burner; (*de candelero*) socket; shoplifter; **mechero encendedor** pilot, pilot light
mechón *m* cowlick; (Guat) torch
medalla *f* medal; medallion
medallón *m* medallion; (*joya en que se colocan retratos, etc.*) locket
médano *m* dune, sandbank
media *f* stocking; (math) mean; **media corta** (Arg) sock; **media media** (Arg, Ecuad, Ven) sock; **y media** half past, e.g., **las dos y media** half past two
mediación *f* mediation
media•do -da *adj* half over; half-full; **a mediados de** about the middle of; **mediada la tarde** in the middle of the afternoon
media•dor -dora *mf* mediator
mediana *f* long billiard cue
medianería *f* party wall; party fence
mediane•ro -ra *adj* middle; mediating || *mf* mediator; partner; owner of a row house
medianía *f* average; (*persona que carece de dotes relevantes*) mediocrity
media•no -na *adj* middling, medium; average, fair; mediocre || *f* see **mediana**
medianoche *f* midnight; small meat pie
mediante *adj* interceding || *prep* by means of, by virtue of
mediar *intr* to be half over; be in the middle; intercede, mediate; elapse; take place
mediatinta *f* half-tone
medible *adj* measurable
medical *adj* medical
medicamento *m* medicine
medicamento•so -sa *adj* medicinal
medicastro *m* quack
medicina *f* medicine; **medicina general** general medicine
medicinar *tr* to treat || *ref* to take medicine
medición *f* measurement; metering
médi•co -ca *adj* medical || *mf* doctor, physician; **médico de cabecera** family physician; **médico de urgencia** emergency doctor; **médico general** general practitioner
medida *f* measurement; measure; caution, moderation; **a medida de** in proportion to; according to; **a medida que** in proportion as; **en la medida que** to the extent that; **hecho a la medida** custom-made; **medida para áridos** dry measure; **medida para líquidos** liquid measure; **tomarle a uno las medidas** to take someone's measure, size up someone
medidamente *adv* with moderation
medidor *m* measurer; (Mex, SAm) meter
medie•ro -ra *mf* hosier; partner
medieval *adj* medieval
medievalista *mf* medievalist
medievo *m* Middle Ages
me•dio -dia *adj* middle; medium; medieval; half; a half, e.g., **media libra** a half pound; half a, e.g., **media naranja** half an orange; average, mean; mid, in the middle of, e.g., **a media tarde** in mid afternoon, in the middle of the afternoon; **a medias** half; half-and-half; **ir a medias (con)** to go halves (with), go fifty-fifty (with) || *m* middle; medium, environment; step, measure; means; (*en el espiritismo*) medium; (baseball) shortstop; (arith) half; (*del ruedo*) (taur) center; **a medio** half; **en medio de** in the middle of; in the midst of; **justo medio** happy medium, golden mean; **medio ambiente** environment; situation; **medio centro** (*deporte*) center half; **medios de comunicación** mass media; **por medio de** by means of; **quitarse de en medio** to get out of the way || *f* see **media** || **medio** *adv* half
mediocre *adj* mediocre
mediocridad *f* mediocrity
mediodía *m* noon, midday; south; **en pleno mediodía** at high noon; **hacer mediodía** to stop for the noon meal
mediquillo *m* quack
medir §50 *tr* to measure || *intr* to measure || *ref* to act with moderation
meditabun•do -da *adj* meditative
meditar *tr* to meditate; plan, contemplate || *intr* to meditate
mediterráne•o -a *adj* inland || **Mediterráne•o -na** *adj & m* Mediterranean
mé•dium *m* (*pl* **-dium** or **diums**) medium
medra *f* growth, prosperity
medrana *f* fear
medrar *intr* to thrive, prosper, improve
medro *m* growth, prosperity; **medros** progress
medro•so -sa *adj* fearful, scared; frightful, terrible
médula *f* or **medula** *f* marrow, medulla; (bot) pith; (fig) pith, gist, essence; **médula espinal** spinal cord
medular *adj* pithy
medusa *f* jellyfish
mefistofél•ico -ca *adj* Mephistophelian
megaciclo *m* megacycle
megáfono *m* megaphone
me•go -ga *adj* meek, gentle, mild
megohmio *m* megohm
Méj. *abbr* **Méjico**
mejica•no -na *adj & mf* Mexican
Méjico *m* Mexico; **Nuevo Méjico** New Mexico
meji•do -da *adj* beaten with sugar and milk
mejilla *f* cheek
mejor *adj* better; best; (*licitador*) highest; **a lo mejor** unexpectedly; worse luck; perhaps, maybe; **el mejor día** some fine day || *adv* better; best; **mejor dicho** rather

mejora *f* growth, improvement; higher bid; alteration
mejoramiento *m* improvement
mejorana *f* sweet marjoram
mejorar *tr* to improve; (*los licitadores el precio de una cosa*) raise; **mejorando lo presente** present company excepted || *intr & ref* to improve, get better, recover; make progress; (*el tiempo*) to clear up; **¡que se mejore!** get well!
mejoría *f* improvement; (*en una enfermedad*) betterment, recovery
mejunje *m* brew, potion, mixture
mela•do -da *adj* honey-colored || *m* thick cane syrup
melancolía *f* (*tristeza vaga*) melancholy; (*depresión moral*) melancholia
melancóli•co -ca *adj* melancholy
melaza *f* molasses
melcocha *f* taffy, molasses candy
melchor *m* German silver
melena *f* hair falling over the eyes; long hair, loose hair; (*del león*) mane; (*del caballo*) forelock; **andar a la melena** to pull each other's hair; to get into a fight; **estar en melena** (coll) to have one's hair down
melga *f* ridge made by plow; (Col, Chile) plot of ground to be sown; (Hond) small piece of work to be finished
melindre *m* honey fritter; (*dulce de pasta de mazapán*) ladyfinger; narrow ribbon; prudery, finickiness
melindrear *intr* to be prudish, be finicky
melindro•so -sa *adj* prudish, finicky
melocotón *m* peach tree; peach
melocotonero *m* peach tree
melodía *f* melody
melodio•so -sa *adj* melodious
melodramáti•co -ca *adj* melodramatic
melón *m* melon; (*Cucumis melo*) muskmelon; blockhead; bald head; **melón de agua** watermelon
melo•so -sa *adj* sweet, honeyed; gentle, mild, mellow
mella *f* dent, nick, notch; gap, hollow; harm, injury; **hacer mella a** to have an effect on; **hacer mella en** to harm
mellar *tr* to dent, nick, notch; harm
melli•zo -za *adj & mf* twin
membrana *f* membrane; (*del teléfono, micrófono*) diaphragm
membrete *m* note, memo; letterhead; heading; written invitation
membrillero *m* quince tree
membrillo *m* quince; quince tree
membru•do -da *adj* brawny, burly
memeches — **a memeches** (CAm) on horseback
memela *f* (CAm, Mex) cornmeal pancake
me•mo -ma *adj* foolish, simple || *mf* fool, simpleton
memorán•dum *m* (*pl* **-dum**) memorandum book, notebook; (*sección en los periódicos*) professional services; (*papel con membrete*) letterhead
memorar *tr & ref* to remember
memoria *f* memory; (*exposición de ciertos hechos*) memoir; account, record; (*ordenador*) data storage, memory; **de memoria** by heart; **encomendar a la memoria** to commit to memory; **hablar de memoria** (coll) to say the first thing that comes to one's mind; **hacer memoria de** to bring up; **memorias** memoirs; regards
memorial *m* memorandum book; memorial, petition; (law) brief
memorizar §60 *tr* to memorize
mena *f* ore
menaje *m* household furniture; school supplies
mención *f* mention
mencionar *tr* to mention
men•daz *adj* (*pl* **-daces**) mendacious || *mf* liar
mendicante *adj & mf* mendicant
mendigante *adj* begging, mendicant || *mf* beggar, mendicant
mendigar §44 *tr* to beg for || *intr* to beg, go begging
mendi•go -ga *mf* beggar
mendiguez *f* begging
mendo•so -sa *adj* false, wrong
mendrugo *m* crumb, crust
menear *tr* to stir, shake; wiggle; (*la cola*) wag; (*un negocio*) manage; **peor es meneallo** (i.e., **menearlo**) better keep hands off || *ref* to shake; wiggle; wag; hustle, bestir oneself
meneo *m* stirring, shaking; wagging; hustling; drubbing, thrashing
menester *m* need; want, lack; job, occupation; **haber menester** to be necessary, to be need for; **menesteres** bodily needs; property; implements, tools; **ser menester** to be necessary
menestero•so -sa *adj* needy || *mf* needy person
menestra *f* vegetable soup
menes•tral -trala *mf* mechanic
meng. *abbr* **menguante**
mengua *f* want, lack; poverty; decline; decrease, diminution; **en mengua de** to the discredit of
mengua•do -da *adj* timid, cowardly; simple, silly; mean, stingy; wretched, miserable; poor, needy; fatal
menguante *adj* decreasing; declining; waning || *f* decrease; decline; low water; ebb tide; **menguante de la luna** wane, waning of the moon
menguar §10 *tr* to diminish, lessen; discredit || *intr* to diminish, lessen; decline; decrease; (*la luna*) wane; (*la marea*) fall
mengue *m* (coll) devil
menina *f* young lady in waiting
menino *m* noble page of the royal family
menor *adj* less, lesser; smaller; younger; least; smallest; youngest; slightest; minor || *m* minor; **al por menor** retail; **menor de edad** minor; **por menor** retail; in detail, minutely || *f* minor premise
Menorca *f* Minorca
menoría *f* inferiority, subordination; (*tiempo de menor edad*) minority

menorista *adj* (Arg, Chile) retail || *mf* (Arg, Chile) retailer
menor•quín -quina *adj & mf* Minorcan
menos *adv* less; fewer; least; fewest; **al menos** at least; **a lo menos** at least; **a menos que** unless; **echar de menos** to miss; **¡menos mal!** lucky break!; **menos mal que** it is a good thing that; **no poder menos de** + *inf* to not be able to help + *ger;* **por lo menos** at least; **tener en menos** to think little of; **venir a menos** to decline; become poor || *prep* less, minus; (*al decir la hora*) of, to, e.g., **las tres menos diez** ten minutes of (or to) three || *m* less; (*signo de resta o sustracción*) minus, minus sign
menoscabar *tr* to lessen, diminish, reduce; damage; discredit
menoscabo *m* lessening, reduction; damage; discredit; **con menoscabo de** to the detriment of
menoscuenta *f* part payment
menospreciable *adj* despicable, contemptible
menospreciar *tr* to underestimate, underrate; scorn, despise
menosprecio *m* underestimation; scorn
mensaje *m* message
mensajería *f* public conveyance; **mensajerías** transportation company; shipping line
mensaje•ro -ra *mf* messenger || *m* harbinger
men•so -sa *adj* (Mex) foolish, stupid
menstruar §21 *intr* to menstruate
menstruo *m* menses
mensual *adj* monthly
mensualidad *f* monthly pay, monthly installment
ménsula *f* bracket; elbow rest
mensurar *tr* to measure
menta *f* mint; **menta piperita** peppermint; **menta romana** or **verde** spearmint
menta•do -da *adj* famous, renowned
mentar §2 *tr* to mention
mente *f* mind
mentecatería or **mentecatez** *f* simpleness, folly
menteca•to -ta *adj* simple, foolish || *mf* simpleton, fool
mentidero *m* hangout; gossip column
mentir §68 *tr* to disappoint || *intr* to lie; be misleading; (*un color*) clash; **¡miento!** my mistake!
mentira *f* lie; error, mistake; **mentira inocente** or **oficiosa** white lie; **parece mentira** it's hard to believe
mentirilla *f* fib, white lie; **de mentirillas** for fun
mentirón *m* whopper
mentiro•so -sa *adj* lying; false, deceptive; full of errors || *mf* liar
men•tís *m* (*pl* **-tís**) insulting contradiction; **dar un mentís a** to give the lie to
mentón *m* chin
me•nú *m* (*pl* **-nús**) menu
menudamente *adv* in detail; at retail
menudear *tr* to make frequently; tell in detail; (Col) to sell at retail || *intr* to happen frequently, be frequent; go into detail; (Arg) to grow, increase
menudencia *f* smallness; trifle; meticulousness; **menudencias** pork products; (Col, Mex) giblets
menudeo *m* constant repetition; detailed accounting; **al menudeo** at retail
menudillos *mpl* giblets
menu•do -da *adj* small, slight, minute; futile, worthless; meticulous; common, vulgar; petty || *m* innards (*of fowl and other animals*); rice coal; **al menudo** at retail; **a menudo** often; **menudos** small change; **por menudo** in detail; at retail
meñique *adj* little, tiny; (*dedo*) little || *m* little finger
meollo *m* marrow; pith; (*seso*) brain; brains, intelligence; gist, marrow, essence
me•ón -ona *adj* (*niño*) piddling; (*niebla*) dripping
mequetrefe *m* whippersnapper
mercachifle *m* peddler; small dealer
mercadear *intr* to deal, trade
merca•der -dera *mf* merchant; **mercader de grueso** wholesale merchant
mercadería *f* merchandise, commodity; **mercaderías** goods, merchandise
mercado *m* market; **lanzar al mercado** to put on the market; **mercado de valores** stock market; **mercado negro** black market
mercaduría *f* commodity
mercancía *f* trade, commerce; merchandise; piece of merchandise; **mercancías** goods, merchandise || **mercancías** *msg* (*pl* **-as**) freight train
mercante *adj & m* merchant
mercantil *adj* mercantile
mercar §73 *tr* to buy || *intr* to trade
merced *f* pay, wages; favor, grace; **a merced de** at the mercy of; **merced a** thanks to; **merced de agua** distribution of irrigating water; **vuestra merced** your grace
mercena•rio -ria *adj* mercenary || *m* mercenary; day laborer, hireling
mercería *f* haberdashery, notions store; drygoods store; hardware store
mercología *f* marketing
mercurio *m* mercury
merecer §22 *tr* to deserve, merit; (*lo que se desea*) attain; (*alabanza*) win; (*cierta suma*) be worth; **merecer la pena** to be worthwhile || *intr* to be deserving; **merecer bien de** to deserve the gratitude of
mereci•do -da *adj* deserved || *m* just deserts; **llevar su merecido** to get what's coming to one
mereciente *adj* deserving
merecimiento *m* desert, merit
merendar §2 *tr* to lunch on, have for lunch; keep an eye on, peep at || *intr* to lunch || *ref* to manage to get; (*en el juego*) (Chile) to clean out
merendero *m* lunchroom; picnic grounds
merendona *f* fine spread
merengar §44 *tr* to whip (*cream*)
merengue *m* meringue

mere•triz *f* (*pl* **-trices**) harlot
meridiana *f* lounge, couch; afternoon nap; meridian line; **a la meridiana** at noon
meridia•no -na *adj* meridian; bright, dazzling || *m* meridian || *f* see **meridiana**
meridional *adj* southern || *mf* southerner
merienda *f* lunch, snack; hunchback
meri•no -na *adj* merino; (*cabello*) thick and curly || *mf* merino || *m* merino shepherd; merino wool
mérito *m* merit, desert; value, worth; **hacer mérito de** to make mention of; **hacer méritos** to try to please, put one's best foot forward
merito•rio -ria *adj* meritorious || *m* volunteer worker; unpaid learner, apprentice
merluza *f* (*pez*) hake; drunk, spree
merma *f* decrease, reduction; leakage, shrinkage
mermar *tr* to decrease, reduce || *intr* to decrease, shrink, dwindle
mermelada *f* marmalade
me•ro -ra *adj* mere, pure; (Col, Ven) alone || *m* grouper, jewfish || **mero** *adv* (CAm) almost, soon
merodea•dor -dora *adj* marauding || *m* marauder
merodear *intr* to maraud
mes *m* month; monthly pay; menses; **caer en el mes del obispo** to come at the right time
mesa *f* table; (*mostrador*) counter; (*escritorio*) desk; (*de arma blanca o herramienta*) flat side; (*de escalera*) landing; (*comida*) fare, food; (*conjunto de dirigentes*) board; **alzar la mesa** to clear the table; **hacer mesa limpia** to clean up (*in gambling*); **levantar la mesa** to clear the table; **mesa de batalla** sorting table; **mesa de extensión** extension table; **mesa de juego** gambling table; **mesa de milanos** scanty fare; **mesa de trucos** pool table; **mesa perezosa** drop table; **poner la mesa** to set or lay the table; **tener a mesa y mantel** to feed, support; **tener mesa** to keep open house
mesana *f* (naut) mizzen
mesar *tr* (*los cabellos*) to tear, pull out || *ref* — **mesarse los cabellos** to pull out one's hair; pull out each other's hair
mescolanza *f* jumble, hodgepodge, medley
meseguería *f* harvest watch
mesera *f* waitress
mesero *m* journeyman on monthly pay; waiter
meseta *f* plateau, tableland; (*de escalera*) landing
Mesías *m* Messiah
mesilla *f* mantel, mantelpiece; (*de escalera*) landing; window sill
mesita *f* stand, small table; **mesita portateléfono** telephone table
mesnada *f* armed retinue; band, company
mesón *m* inn, tavern; (Chile) bar; (Chile) counter
mesone•ro -ra *adj* inn, tavern || *mf* innkeeper, tavern keeper
mester *m* (archaic) craft, trade; (archaic) literary genre; **mester de clerecía** clerical verse of the Middle Ages; **mester de juglaría** popular minstrelsy of the Middle Ages
mesti•zo -za *adj* & *mf* half-breed; (*perro*) mongrel
mesura *f* dignity, gravity; calm, restraint; courtesy, civility
mesura•do -da *adj* dignified, sedate; calm, restrained; polite; moderate, temperate
mesurar *tr* to temper, moderate || *ref* to act with restraint
meta *f* goal
metafonía *f* umlaut
metáfora *f* metaphor
metafóri•co -ca *adj* metaphorical
metal *m* metal; money; (*de la voz*) timbre; condition, quality; (mus) brass; **el vil metal** filthy lucre; **metal blanco** nickel silver; **metal de imprenta** type metal
metale•ro -ra *adj* (Bol, Chile, Peru) metal || *m* (Bol, Chile, Peru) metalworker
metáli•co -ca *adj* metallic || *m* metalworker; cash, coin
metalistería *f* metalwork
metalizar **§60** *tr* to make metallic; put a metal coating on; turn into cash || *ref* to become mercenary
metaloide *m* nonmetal
metalurgia *f* metallurgy
metamorfo•sis *f* (*pl* **-sis**) metamorphosis
metano *m* methane
metástasis *f* metastasis
metate *m* (CAm, Mex) flat stone on which corn is ground
metáte•sis *f* (*pl* **-sis**) metathesis
mete•dor -dora *mf* smuggler
metedura *f* disgrace, shame
meteduría *f* smuggling
metemuer•tos *m* (*pl* **-tos**) stagehand; busybody, meddler
meteo *f* weather bureau, weather report
meteóri•co -ca *adj* meteoric
meteoro *m* or **metéoro** *m* meteor; atmospheric phenomenon
meteorología *f* meteorology
meter *tr* to put, place; insert; (*un ruido*) make; (*miedo*) cause; (*mentiras*) tell; (*chismes, enredos*) start; (*dinero en el juego*) stake; to smuggle; (*un golpe*) strike || *ref* to project; meddle, butt in; **meterse a** to set oneself up as; take it upon oneself to; **meterse con** to pick a quarrel with; **meterse en** to get into; to plunge into; empty into
meticulo•so -sa *adj* meticulous; shy, timid
meti•do -da *adj* close, tight; rich, abundant; meddlesome; **muy metido con** on close terms with; **muy metido en** deeply involved in || *m* push; punch; strong lye; loose leaf; (*tela*) seam
metódi•co -ca *adj* methodic(al)
metodista *adj* & *mf* Methodist
método *m* method
metraje *m* distance or length in meters; (*cine*) **de corto metraje** short; (*cine*) **de largo metraje** full-length
metralla *f* scrap iron; grapeshot; shrapnel
métri•co -ca *adj* metric(al) || *f* prosody

metro *m* meter; ruler; tape measure; subway; **metro plegadizo** folding rule
metrónomo *m* metronome
metrópoli *f* metropolis; mother country
metropolita•no -na *adj* metropolitan || *m* subway; (eccl) metropolitan
Méx. *abbr* **México**
mexcal *m* agave liquor
mexica•no -na *adj & mf* Mexican
México *m* Mexico; **Nuevo México** New Mexico
mezcal *m* var of **mexcal**
mezcla *f* mixture; (*argamasa*) mortar; (*tejido*) tweed
mezclar *tr* to mix; blend || *ref* to mix; (*introducirse uno entre otros*) mingle; intermarry; meddle
mezclilla *f* light tweed
mezcolanza *f* jumble, hodgepodge, medley
mezquinar *tr* to be stingy with || *intr* to be stingy
mezquindad *f* meanness, stinginess; need, poverty; smallness, tininess; wretchedness
mezqui•no -na *adj* mean, stingy; needy, poor; small, tiny; wretched
mezquita *f* mosque
mi *adj poss* my
mí (used as object of a preposition) *pron pers* me || *pron reflex* myself
miar §77 *intr* to meow
miau *m* meow
mica *f* mica; (Guat) flirt; **ponerse una mica** (CAm) to go on a jag
mico *m* long-tailed monkey; libertine; hoodlum; **dar mico** to not keep a date
microbio *m* microbe
microbiología *f* microbiology
microbús *m* (Chile) jitney
microfaradio *m* microfarad
microficha *f* microcard
micro•film *m* (*pl* **-films** or **-filmes**) microfilm
microfilmar *tr* to microfilm
micrófono *m* microphone
microonda *f* microwave
microordenador *m* microcomputer
micropelícula *f* microfilm
microprocesador *m* chip, microprocessor
microscópi•co -ca *adj* microscopic
microscopio *m* microscope
microsurco *adj invar* microgroove || *m* microgroove
microteléfono *m* handset, French telephone
mi•cho -cha *mf* pussy cat
miedo *m* fear, dread; **miedo cerval** great fear; **por miedo de** for fear of; **por miedo (de) que** for fear that; **tener miedo (a)** to be afraid (of); **tener miedo de** to be in fear of, be afraid of; be afraid to
miedo•so -sa *adj* fearful, afraid
miel *f* honey; (*jarabe saturado*) molasses; **dejar con la miel en los labios** to spoil the fun for; **hacerse de miel** to be peaches and cream
mielga *f* lucerne
miembro *m* member; (*extremidad del hombre y los animales*) member, limb
mientes *fpl* mind, thought; wish, desire; **caer en las mientes** or **en mientes** to come to mind; **parar** or **poner mientes en** to reflect on; **venírsele a uno a las mientes** to come to one's mind
mientras *conj* while; whereas; **mientras que** while; whereas; **mientras tanto** meanwhile
miérco•les *m* (*pl* **-les**) Wednesday; **miércoles de ceniza** Ash Wednesday
mies *f* cereal, grain; harvest time; **mieses** grain fields
miga *f* (*porción pequeña*) bit; (*parte más blanda del pan*) crumb; (fig) substance; **hacer buenas migas con** to get along well with; **migas** fried crumbs
migaja *f* bit, piece; (*de inteligencia*) smattering; **migajas** crumbs; leavings
migajón *m* crumb; substance
migar §44 *tr* (*el pan*) to crumb; (*p.ej., la leche*) put crumbs in
migrato•rio -ria *adj* migratory
miguelear *tr* (CAm) to make love to
miguele•ño -ña *adj* (Hond) impolite, discourteous
mijo *m* millet
mil *adj & m* thousand, a thousand, one thousand; **a las mil quinientas** at an unearthly hour
milagre•ro -ra *adj* superstitious; miracle-working
milagro *m* (*hecho sobrenatural*) miracle; (*cosa rara*) wonder; votive offering; **colgar el milagro a** to put the blame on; **vivir de milagro** to have a hard time getting along; have had a narrow escape
milagrón *m* fuss, excitement
milagro•so -sa *adj* miraculous; marvelous, wonderful
milano *m* burr, down; (orn) kite
mil•deu *m* (*pl* **-deues**) mildew
milena•rio -ria *adj* millennial || *m* millennium
milenio *m* millennium
milenrama *f* yarrow
milési•mo -ma *adj & m* thousandth
miliamperio *m* milliampere
milicia *f* militia; soldiery; warfare; military service
milicia•no -na *adj* military || *m* militiaman
miligramo *m* milligram
milímetro *m* millimeter
militante *adj* militant
militar *adj* military; army || *m* soldier, military man || *intr* to fight, go to war; struggle; serve in the army; (*surtir efecto*) militate
militarismo *m* militarism
militarista *adj & mf* militarist
militarizar §60 *tr* to militarize
mílite *m* soldier
milpa *f* (CAm, Mex) cornfield
milla *f* mile
millar *m* thousand
millarada *f* about a thousand; **echar millaradas** to boast about one's wealth
millo *m* millet
millón *m* million

millona•rio -ria *adj* of a million or more inhabitants || *mf* millionaire
mimar *tr* to fondle, pet; pamper, indulge, spoil
mimbre *m & f* (bot) osier; wicker, withe
mimbrear *intr & ref* to sway
mimbre•ño -ña *adj* willowy
mimbrera *f* (bot) osier, osier willow
mimbro•so -sa *adj* osier; (*hecho de mimbre*) wicker
mimeografiar §77 *tr* to mimeograph
mimeógrafo *m* mimeograph
mímica *f* mimicry; sign language
mimo *m* (*entre los griegos y romanos*) mime; fondling, petting; pampering
mimo•so -sa *adj* delicate, tender; finicky, fussy
mina *f* mine; (*de lápiz*) lead; (fig) mine, gold mine, storehouse; underground passage; (SAm) moll; **beneficiar una mina** to work a mine; **mina de carbón** or **mina hullera** coal mine; **voló la mina** the truth is out
minado *m* mine work; (nav) mining
mina•dor -dora *adj* (nav) mine-laying || *m* (mil) miner; (nav) mine layer
minar *tr* to mine; undermine; consume; plug away at || *intr* to mine
minarete *m* minaret
mineraje *m* mining; **mineraje a tajo abierto** strip mining
mineral *adj & m* mineral
mineralogía *f* mineralogy
minería *f* mining; mine operators
mine•ro -ra *adj* mining || *m* miner; mine operator; (fig) source, origin
mingitorio *m* street urinal
min•gón -gona *adj* (Ven) spoiled, pampered
miniar *tr* to paint in miniature; (*un manuscrito*) illuminate
miniatura *f* miniature
miniaturización *f* miniaturization
minifalda *f* miniskirt
míni•mo -ma *adj* minimum; tiny, small, minute; least, smallest || *m* minimum || *f* tiny bit
mini•no -na *mf* kitty, pussy
miniordenador *m* minicomputer
ministerial *adj* ministerial
ministerio *m* ministry, cabinet, government; **formar ministerio** to form a government; **ministerio de Hacienda** Treasury Department (U.S.A.); Treasury (Brit); **ministerio de la Gobernación** Department of the Interior (U.S.A.); Home Office (Brit); **ministerio del Ejército** Department of the Army (U.S.A.); War Office (Brit); **ministerio de Marina** Department of the Navy (U.S.A.); Board of Admiralty (Brit); **Ministerio de Relaciones Exteriores** State Department; Foreign Ministry; **ministerio radiofónico** (theol) radio ministry
ministrar *tr* to administer; furnish
ministro *m* minister; bailiff, constable; **ministro de asuntos exteriores** foreign minister; **ministro de Gobernación** Home Secretary (Brit); **ministro de Hacienda** Secretary of the Treasury (U.S.A.); Chancellor of the Exchequer (Brit); **ministro de Justicia** Attorney General (U.S.A.); **primer ministro** prime minister, premier
minorar *tr* to diminish, reduce; weaken
minorati•vo -va *adj & m* laxative
minoría *f* minority
minoridad *f* minority
minorista *m* retailer
minorita•rio -ria *adj* minority
minucia *f* trifle; **minucias** minutiae
minucio•so -sa *adj* minute, meticulous
minué *m* or **minuete** *m* minuet
minúscu•lo -la *adj* (*letra*) small; small, tiny || *f* small letter
minusvalía *f* (physical) handicap
minuta *f* first draft, rough draft; memorandum; menu, bill of fare; roll, list
minutero *m* minute hand
minu•to -ta *adj* minute || *m* minute || *f* see **minuta**
mí•o -a *adj poss* mine; of mine, e.g., **un amigo mío** a friend of mine || *pron poss* mine
miope *adj* near-sighted || *mf* near-sighted person
miopía *f* near-sightedness
mira *f* (*de arma de fuego, telescopio, etc.*) sight; aim, object, purpose; target; watchtower; **estar a la mira** to be on the lookout; **poner la mira en** to have designs on
mirada *f* glance, look; **apuñalar con la mirada** to look daggers at; **mirada de soslayo** side glance
miradero *m* (*lugar desde donde se mira*) lookout; (*persona o cosa que es objeto de la atención pública*) cynosure
mira•do -da *adj* cautious, circumspect; **bien mirado** highly regarded || *f* see **mirada**
mirador *m* belvedere; bay window, oriel
miramiento *m* considerateness, courtesy, regard; look; **miramientos** fuss, bother
miranda *f* eminence, vantage point
mirar *tr* to look at, watch; consider, contemplate; **mirar bien** to look with favor on; **mirar por encima** to glance at || *intr* to look, glance; **¡mira!** look out!; **mirar a** to look at, glance at; face, overlook; aim at; aim to; **mirar por** to look after || *ref* to look at oneself; look at each other; **mirarse en ello** to watch one's step; **mirarse en una persona** to be all wrapped up in a person
mirasol *m* sunflower
miríada *f* myriad
mirilla *f* peephole; (*para dirigir visuales*) target; (phot) finder
miriñaque *m* hoop skirt, crinoline; bauble, trinket; (Arg) cowcatcher
mirística *f* nutmeg tree
mirlar *ref* to try to look important
mirlo *m* blackbird; solemn look; **mirlo blanco** rare bird; **soltar el mirlo** to start to jabber
mirmidón *m* tiny fellow, nincompoop
mi•rón -rona *adj* onlooking; nosy || *mf* onlooker; (*de una partida de juego*) kibitzer; busybody

mirra *f* myrrh
mirto *m* myrtle
misa *f* mass; **cantar misa** to say mass; **como en misa** in dead silence; **misa cantada** High Mass; **misa de prima** early mass; **misa mayor** High Mass; **misa rezada** Low Mass
misal *m* missal
misantropía *f* misanthropy
misántropo *m* misanthrope
misar *intr* to say mass; to hear mass
misario *m* acolyte
misceláne•o -a *adj* miscellaneous || *f* miscellany
miserable *adj* miserable, wretched; mean, stingy; despicable, vile || *mf* cur, cad; wretch; miser
miseran•do -da *adj* pitiful
miserear *intr* to be stingy
miseria *f* misery, wretchedness; poverty; stinginess; trifle, pittance; **comerse de miseria** to live in great poverty
misericordia *f* compassion, mercy, pity
misericordio•so -sa *adj* merciful
míse•ro -ra *adj* miserable, wretched || *mf* wretch
mísil *m* missile; **mísil crucero** cruise missile; **mísil dirigible** guided missile
misión *f* mission; ration for harvesters; **ir a misiones** to go away as a missionary
misional *adj* missionary
misionario *m* missionary; envoy, messenger
misionero *m* missionary
misi•vo -va *adj* & *f* missive
mismísi•mo -ma *adj* very same, self-same
mis•mo -ma *adj* & *pron indef* same; own, very; -self, e.g., **ella misma** herself; myself, e.g., **yo mismo** I myself; yourself, himself, herself, itself; **así mismo** likewise, also; **casi lo mismo** much the same; **lo mismo** just the same; **lo mismo me da** it's all the same to me; **mismo . . . que** same . . . as; **por lo mismo** for that very reason || **mismo** *adv* right, e.g., **ahora mismo** right now; **aquí mismo** right here
mistela *f* flavored brandy; needled must, spiked must
misterio *m* mystery; **hablar de misterio** to talk mysteriously
misterio•so -sa *adj* mysterious
misticismo *m* mysticism
místi•co -ca *adj* mystic(al) || *mf* mystic
mistificación *f* hoax, mystification
mistificar **§73** *tr* to hoax, mystify
mistifori *m* hodgepodge
misturera *f* (Peru) flower girl
mita *f* mite, cheese mite; (SAm) Indian slave labor; (*turno en el trabajo*) (Arg, Chile) shift, turn
mitad *f* half; middle; **a (la) mitad de** halfway through; **cara mitad** better half; **en la mitad de** in the middle of; **la mitad de** half the; **mitad y mitad** half-and-half; **por la mitad** in half, in the middle
míti•co -ca *adj* mythical
mitigar **§44** *tr* to mitigate, appease, allay
mitin *m* (*pl* **mitins** or **mítines**) meeting, rally
mito *m* myth
mitología *f* mythology
mitológi•co -ca *adj* mythological
mitón *m* mitten
mitra *f* chimney pot; (eccl) miter
mixtificación *f* hoax, mystification
mixtificar **§73** *tr* to hoax, mystify
mixtifori *m* hodgepodge
mixtión *f* mixture
mix•to -ta *adj* mixed || *m* compound number; sulphur match; explosive compound
mixtura *f* mixture
mixturar *tr* to mix
mixturera *f* (Peru) flower girl
miz *interj* here, pussy!, here, kitty!
mízcalo *m* edible milk mushroom
m/l *abbr* **mi letra**
m/n *abbr* **moneda nacional**
mobilia•rio -ria *adj* personal (*property*) || *m* furniture, suite of furniture
moblaje *m* furniture, suite of furniture
moblar **§61** *tr* to furnish
moca *m* Mocha coffee || *f* (Ecuad) mudhole; (Mex) wineglass
mocador *m* handkerchief
mocar **§73** *tr* to blow the nose of || *ref* to blow one's nose
mocarro *m* snot
mocasín *m* moccasin
mocear *intr* to act young; sow one's wild oats
mocedad *f* youth; wild oats
mocerío *m* young people
mocero *adj masc* woman-crazy
mocetón *m* strapping young fellow
mocetona *f* buxom young woman
mocil *adj* youthful
moción *f* motion, movement; (*en junta deliberante*) motion; **hacer** or **presentar una moción** to make a motion
mocionante *mf* mover
mocionar *tr* & *intr* to move
moci•to -ta *adj* young || *mf* youngster
moco *m* (*humor segregado por una membrana mucosa*) mucus; (*mocarro*) snot; (*extremo del pabilo de una vela*) snuff; **a moco de candil** by candle light; **llorar a moco tendido** to cry like a baby; **moco de pavo** crest of a turkey; trifle; (bot) cockscomb
moco•so -sa *adj* snotty, snively; rude, ill-bred; flip, saucy; mean, worthless || *mf* brat
mochar *tr* to butt; chop off; (Arg) to rob; (Col) to fire
mochil *m* errand boy for farmers in the field
mochila *f* knapsack, haversack; tool bag; (mil) ration
mochín *m* (slang) executioner
mo•cho -cha *adj* blunt, stub, flat; (*árbol*) topped; stub-horned; mutilated; (Mex) reactionary || *m* butt end
mochuelo *m* (orn) little owl; (*de una o más palabras*) omission; **cargar con el mochuelo** or **tocarle a** (*uno*) **el mochuelo** to get the worst of a deal
moda *f* fashion, mode, style; **a la moda de** after the fashion of, in the style of; **alta**

moda haute couture; **de moda** in fashion; **fuera de moda** out of fashion; **pasar de moda** to go out of fashion
modales *mpl* manners
modalidad *f* manner, way, nature, kind
modelar *tr* to model; to form, shape; to mold || *ref* to model; **modelarse sobre** to pattern oneself after
modelo *adj invar* model, e.g., **ciudad modelo** model city || *mf* model, mannequin, fashion model || *m* model, pattern; form, blank; equal, peer; style; **modelo estrella** (aut) crest-line model
modera•do -da *adj* moderate
moderador *m* regulator; (*para retardar el efecto de los neutrones*) moderator
moderar *tr* to moderate, control, restrain || *ref* to moderate, control oneself, restrain oneself
modernizar §60 *tr* to modernize
moder•no -na *adj* modern
modestia *f* modesty
modes•to -ta *adj* modest
modicidad *f* moderateness, reasonableness
módi•co -ca *adj* moderate, reasonable
modificante *adj* modifying || *m* (gram) modifier
modificar §73 *tr* to modify
modismo *m* idiom
modista *f* dressmaker; **modista de sombreros** milliner
modistería *f* dressmaking; ladies' dress shop
modistilla *f* dressmaker's helper; unskilled dressmaker
modisto *m* ladies' tailor
modo *m* manner, mode, way; (gram) mood, mode; **al** or **a modo de** like, on the order of; **de buen modo** politely; **de ese modo** at that rate; **de tal modo que** with the result that; **de modo que** so that; and so; **de ningún modo** by no means; **de todos modos** anyhow, at any rate; **en cierto modo** after a fashion; **modo de empleo** usage; instructions for use; **modo de ser** nature, disposition; **por modo de** as, by way of; **sobre modo** extremely; **uno a modo de** a sort of, a kind of
modorra *f* drowsiness, heaviness
modorrar *tr* to make drowsy || *ref* to get drowsy, fall asleep; (*la fruta*) get squashy
modo•rro -rra *adj* drowsy, heavy; dull, stupid; (*fruta*) squashy || *f* see **modorra**
modo•so -sa *adj* quiet, well-behaved
modrego *m* boor, awkward fellow
modulación *f* modulation; **modulación de altura** or **de amplitud** amplitude modulation; **modulación de frecuencia** frequency modulation
modular *tr & intr* to modulate
módulo *m* module; **módulo lunar** lunar lander, lunar module
modulo•so -sa *adj* harmonious
mofa *f* jeering, scoffing, mockery
mofeta *f* skunk; (*gas pernicioso que se desprende de las minas*) blackdamp, firedamp
moflete *m* fat cheek, jowl
mofletu•do -da *adj* fat-cheeked
mo•gol -gola *adj & mf* Mongol, Mongolian
mogollón *m* — **comer de mogollón** (coll) to sponge
mo•gón -gona *adj* one-horned, broken-horned
mogote *m* knoll, hillock; stack of sheaves; budding antler
mohatra *f* fake sale; cheating
mohien•to -ta *adj* moldy, musty; (*hierro*) rusty
mohín *m* face, grimace
mohina *f* annoyance, displeasure
mohi•no -na *adj* sad, melancholy, moody; (*caballo, buey, vaca*) black, black-nosed || *mf* hinny || *m* blue magpie || *f* see **mohina**
moho *m* mold, must; (*del hierro*) rust; laziness; **no dejar criar moho** to keep in constant use, to use up quickly
moho•so -sa *adj* moldy, rusty; (*hierro*) rusty; (*chiste*) stale
Moisés *m* Moses
moja•do -da *adj* wet; (*p.ej., por la lluvia*) drenched, soaked; (*húmedo*) moist; (phonet) liquid || *m* (Mex) wetback
mojar *tr* to wet; (*la lluvia a una persona*) drench, soak; (*humedecer*) dampen, moisten; (*ensopar*) dunk; stab || *intr* — **mojar en** to get mixed up in || *ref* to get wet; get drenched, get soaked
mojarrilla *mf* jolly person
moje *m* or **mojete** *m* sauce, gravy
mojicón *m* muffin, bun; slap in the face
mojiganga *f* masquerade, mummery; clowning
mojigatería or **mojigatez** *f* hypocrisy; prudery, sanctimoniousness
mojiga•to -ta *adj* hypocritical; prudish, sanctimonious || *mf* hypocrite; prude, sanctimonious person
mojinete *m* (*de un muro*) coping; (*de un tejado*) ridge; (Arg) gable; (Chile) gable end
mojón *m* boundary stone, landmark; (*montón sin orden*) pile, heap; (*guía en desplobado*) road mark; (*porción de excremento humano*) turd
moldar *tr* to mold; put molding on
molde *m* mold; pattern; cast, stamp, matrix; (*persona*) model, ideal; (*letra*) **de molde** printed; **venir de molde** to be just right
moldear *tr* to mold; (*vaciar*) cast; put molding on
moldura *f* molding
moldurar *tr* to put molding on
mole *adj* soft || *m* (Mex) stew seasoned with chili sauce || *f* bulk, mass
molécula *f* molecule
molende•ro -ra *mf* miller, grinder || *m* chocolate grinder; (CAm) grinding table
moler §47 *tr* (*granos*) to grind, mill; annoy, harass, weary; tire out, fatigue; chew; **moler a palos** to beat up
molesquina *f* moleskin
molestar *tr* to disturb, molest; bother, annoy; tire, weary || *ref* to bother; be annoyed; **molestarse en** to take the trouble to

molestia *f* disturbance, discomfort; annoyance, bother, nuisance
moles•to -ta *adj* bothersome, troublesome; boring, tedious; bored, tired
molesto•so -sa *adj* bothersome
moleteado *m* knurl
moletear *tr* to knurl
molibdeno *m* molybdenum
molicie *f* softness; effeminacy; voluptuous living
moli•do -da *adj* ground; exhausted, worn out
molienda *f* grinding, milling; (*cantidad que se muele de una vez*) grist; (*molino*) mill; bore, annoyance; fatigue, weariness
molimiento *m* grinding; weariness
moline•ro -ra *adj* mill || *m* miller || *f* miller's wife
molinete *m* little mill; ventilating fan; (*juguete de papel*) windmill; (*movimiento que se hace con el bastón*) twirl; (*con la espada*) flourish; (naut) windlass; (*rueda de cohetes*) (Mex) pinwheel
molinillo *m* hand mill; **molinillo de café** coffee grinder
molino *m* mill; **luchar con los molinos de viento** to tilt at windmills; **molino de sangre** animal-driven mill; **molino de viento** windmill; **molino harinero** gristmill, flour mill
moloc *m* (Ecuad) mashed potatoes
molondrón *m* lazy bum; (Ven) large inheritance, much money
molusco *m* mollusk
mollar *adj* soft, tender; mushy, squashy; (*carne*) lean; profitable; gullible, easily taken in
mollear *intr* to give, yield; bend
molleja *f* gizzard; **criar molleja** to get lazy; **mollejas** sweetbread
mollejón *m* grindstone; big fat loafer; good-natured fellow
mollera *f* crown (*of the head*); brains, sense; **cerrado de mollera** stupid; **duro de mollera** stubborn
mollete *m* muffin
molli•no -na *adj* drizzly || *f* drizzle
mollizna *f* drizzle
momentáne•o -a *adj* momentary
momento *m* moment; **a cada momento** constantly, all the time; **al momento** at once; **de un momento a otro** at any moment
momería *f* clowning
mome•ro -ra *adj* clowning || *mf* clown
momia *f* mummy
momificar **§73** *tr* to mummify
mo•mio -mia *adj* lean, skinny || *m* extra; (*ganga*) bargain; sinecure || *f* see **momia**
momo *m* face, grimace; (coll) caress
mona *f* female monkey; Barbary ape; ape, copycat; drunkenness; (*persona*) drunk; (taur) guard for right leg; **dormir la mona** to sleep off a drunk; **pillar una mona** to go on a jag; **pintar la mona** to put on airs
monacal *adj* monachal
monacato *m* monkhood
monacillo *m* altar boy, acolyte
monada *f* monkeyshine; (*gesto*) face, grimace, monkey face; darling; cuteness; flattery; folly, childishness
monaguillo *m* altar boy, acolyte
monaquismo *m* monasticism
monarca *m* monarch
monarquía *f* monarchy
monárqui•co -ca *adj* monarchic(al) || *mf* monarchist
monasterio *m* monastery
monásti•co -ca *adj* monastic
monda *f* pruning, trimming; parings, peelings; beating, whipping
mondadien•tes *m* (*pl* **-tes**) toothpick
mondadura *f* pruning, trimming; **mondaduras** peelings
mondar *tr* to clean; prune, trim; peel, pare, hull, husk; (*quitar con engaño los bienes a*) fleece; beat, whip
mon•do -da *adj* clean; pure; **mondo y lirondo** pure, unadulterated || *f* see **monda**
mondonga *f* kitchen wench
mondongo *m* intestines, insides; (*del hombre*) guts
monear *intr* to act like a monkey; boast || *ref* (Hond) to plug away; (Hond) to punch each other
moneda *f* coin; money; **la Moneda** the government of Chile; **moneda corriente** currency; common knowledge; **moneda falsa** counterfeit; **moneda menuda** change; **moneda metálica** or **sonante** specie; **moneda suelta** change; **pagar en la misma moneda** to pay back in one's own coin
monedar *tr* to coin, mint
monedero *m* moneybag; **monedero falso** counterfeiter
monería *f* monkeyshine; cuteness; childishness
mones•co -ca *adj* apish
moneta•rio -ria *adj* monetary
mon•gol -gola *adj & mf* Mongol, Mongolian
monigote *m* lay brother; rag figure, stuffed form; botched painting, botched statue; sap, boob
monipodio *m* collusion, deal, plot
monís *m* trinket; **monises** money, dough
mónita *f* cunning, smoothness, slickness
monitor *m* monitor
monja *f* nun; **monjas** lingering sparks in burning paper
monje *m* monk
monjía *f* monkhood
monjil *adj* nunnish || *m* nun's dress
mono -na *adj* cute, nice; blond; (*cabello*) red || *m* monkey, ape; (*traje de faena*) coveralls; whippersnapper, squirt; (*drogas*) withdrawal symptom; (coll) clown; (taur) attendant of picador; (Chile) pyramid of fruit or vegetables; **estar de monos** to be on the outs; **mono de Gibraltar** Barbary ape || *f* **see mona**
monóculo *m* monocle
monogamia *f* monogamy
monografía *f* monograph
monograma *m* monogram
monolíti•co -ca *adj* monolithic

monologar §44 *intr* to soliloquize
monólogo *m* monologue
monomanía *f* monomania
monomio *m* monomial
mono•no -na *adj* cute, sweet
monopatín *m* scooter
monoplano *m* monoplane
monopolio *m* monopoly
monopolizar §60 *tr* to monopolize
monorriel *m* monorail
monosabio *m* (taur) attendant of picador
monosílabo *m* monosyllable
monoteísta *adj* monotheistic ‖ *mf* monotheist
monotipia *f* or **monotipo** *m* monotype
monotonía *f* monotony
monóto•no -na *adj* monotonous
monóxido *m* monoxide
monseñor *m* monseigneur; (eccl) monsignor
monserga *f* gibberish
monstruo *m* monster
monstruosidad *f* monstrosity
monstruo•so -sa *adj* monstrous
monta *f* sum, total; **de poca monta** of little account
montacar•gas *m* (*pl* **-gas**) hoist, freight elevator
montadero *m* horse block
montadura *f* mounting; (*de una caballería de silla*) harness; (*engaste*) setting, mount
montaje *m* montage; setting up; (mach) assembly; (rad) hookup
montanero *m* forest ranger
montante *m* post, upright; (*suma*) amount; (*hueco cuadrilongo sobre una puerta*) transom; (*espadón*) broadsword ‖ *f* flood tide
montaña *f* mountain; mountain country; **la Montaña** the Province of Santander, Spain; **montaña de hielo** iceberg; **montaña rusa** roller coaster
monta•ñés -ñesa *adj* mountain ‖ *mf* mountaineer, highlander
montaño•so -sa *adj* mountainous
montapla•tos *m* (*pl* **-tos**) dumbwaiter
montar *tr* to mount, get on; (*un caballo, una bicicleta, los hombros de una persona*) ride; (*un servicio*) set up, establish; (*un fusil*) cock; (*una piedra preciosa*) set, mount; (*el caballo a la yegua*) cover; (*un reloj*) wind; (elec) to hook up; (mach) to assemble, to mount; (*la guardia*) (mil) to mount; (*un cabo*) (naut) to round; (*un buque*) (naut) to command; (*importar*) amount to ‖ *intr* to mount; get on top; weigh, be important; **tanto monta** it's all the same ‖ *ref* to mount; get on top; **montarse en cólera** to fly into a rage
monta•raz *adj* (*pl* **-races**) backwoods; wild, untamed ‖ *m* forester, warden
monte *m* mountain, mount; woods, woodland; obstruction, interference; backwoods, wilds; bank, kitty; dirty head of hair; **andar al monte** to take to the woods; **monte alto** forest; **monte bajo** thicket, brushwood; **monte de piedad** pawnshop; **monte pío** pension fund for widows and orphans; mutual benefit society; **monte tallar** tree farm
montear *tr* to hunt, track down; make a working drawing of; arch, vault
montecillo *m* mound, hillock
montepío *m* pension fund for widows and orphans; mutual benefit society
montera *f* cloth cap; glass roof; wife of hunter; bullfighter's black bicorne; (Hond) drunk, jag
montería *f* hunting, big-game hunting; hunting party; (Bol, Ecuad) canoe to shoot the rapids; (Mex) lumberman's camp
monterilla *f* (naut) moonsail
montero *m* hunter, huntsman; (Mex) sawmill
montés or **montesi•no -na** *adj* wild (*e.g., goat*)
montículo *m* mound, hillock
montilla *f* montilla (*a pale dry sherry*)
monto *m* sum, total
montón *m* pile, heap; (*de gente*) crowd; lot, great deal, great many; **a, de,** or **en montón** taken together; **a montones** in abundance; **ser del montón** to be quite ordinary
montonera *f* heap, pile; band of mounted rebels
montonero *m* guerrilla
montu•no -na *adj* wooded; wild, untamed, rustic
montuo•so -sa *adj* wooded, woody; rugged, hilly
montura *f* (*cabalgadura*) mount; (*de una cabalgadura*) harness; seat, saddle; (*de una piedra preciosa, de un instrumento astronómico*) mounting; (*de gafas*) frame
monumento *m* monument
monzón *m* monsoon
moña *f* doll; mannequin; ribbon, hair ribbon; drunk, jag
moño *m* topknot; crest, top; (Col) caprice, whim; (*de caballo*) (Chile) forelock; **moños** frippery
moquear *intr* to snivel
moqueo *m* snivel, sniveling
moquero *m* handkerchief
moquete *m* punch in the nose
moquillo *m* runny nose; (vet) distemper
moquita *f* mucus, snivel
mor *m* — **por mor de** for love of; because of
mora *f* black mulberry; blackberry, brambleberry; white mulberry
morada *f* dwelling; stay, sojourn
mora•do -da *adj* purple, mulberry ‖ *f* see **morada**
moral *adj* moral ‖ *m* black mulberry tree ‖ *f* (*ciencia de la conducta; conducta*) morals; (*espíritu, confianza*) morale; (*p.ej., de una fábula*) moral
moraleja *f* moral
moralidad *f* morality; (*de una fábula*) moral
morar *intr* to live, dwell
moratoria *f* moratorium
mórbi•do -da *adj* (*perteneciente a la enfermedad*) morbid; soft, delicate, mellow
morbo *m* sickness, illness; **morbo gálico** syphilis; **morbo regio** jaundice
morbo•so -sa *adj* morbid, diseased

morcilla *f* blood pudding, black pudding; (*añadidura que mete un actor en su papel*) gag
mor•daz *adj* (*pl* **-daces**) mordant, mordacious, sharp, caustic
mordaza *f* (*pañuelo o instrumento que se pone en la boca para impedir el hablar*) gag; (*aparato que sirve para apretar*) clamp, jaw; pipe vise; **poner la mordaza a** to gag
mordedura *f* bite
morder §47 *tr* to bite; nibble at; wear away; gossip about, ridicule; (Mex, Ven, W-I) to cheat || *intr* to bite; take hold
mordicar §73 *tr & intr* to bite, sting
mordida *f* bite; (*para eludir una multa*) (Mex) payoff
mordiente *m* mordant
mordiscar §73 *tr* to nibble at || *intr* to nibble, gnaw away; champ
mordisco *m* nibble, bite; champ
more•no -na *adj* brown, dark-brown; dark, dark-complexioned; (*de la raza negra*) black; mulato || *mf* black person; mulato || *m* brunet || *f* brunette; loaf of brown bread; rick of new-mown hay
morería *f* Moorish quarter; Moorish land
moretón *m* black-and-blue mark
morfina *f* morphine
morfinomanía *f* morphine habit, drug habit
morfinóma•no -na *adj* addicted to morphine, addicted to drugs || *mf* morphine addict, drug addict
morfología *f* morphology
moribun•do -da *adj* moribund, dying || *mf* dying person
morillo *m* andiron, firedog
morir §30 & §83 *intr* to die; (*el fuego, la luz, etc.*) die away; **morir ahogado** to drown; **morir de risa** to die laughing; **morir de viejo** to die of old age; **morir helado** to freeze to death; **morir quemado** to burn to death; **morir vestido** to die a violent death || *ref* to die; be dying; die away, die out; (*una pierna, un brazo*) go to sleep; **morirse por** to be crazy about; be dying to
moris•co -ca *adj* Morisco, Moorish || *mf* Moor converted to Christianity (*after the Reconquest*); (*descendiente de mulato y española o de mulata y español*) (Mex) Morisco
mo•ro -ra *adj* Moorish; (*vino*) unwatered || *mf* Moor; **hay moros en la costa** there's trouble brewing; **moro de paz** man of peace || *f* see **mora**
moro•cho -cha *adj* strong, robust; (SAm) dark
morón *m* mound, knoll; moron
moron•do -da *adj* bare, stripped
moronga *f* (CAm, Mex) sausage
moro•so -sa *adj* slow, tardy; (*retrasado en el pago de deudas*) delinquent
morra *f* (*de la cabeza*) top, crown; (*de gato*) purr; **andar a la morra** to come to blows
morrada *f* slap, punch; (*golpe dado con la cabeza*) butt
morral *m* nose bag; (*saco de cazador*) game bag; (*de soldado, viandante, etc.*) knapsack; boor, lout
morralla *f* small fish; (*gente de escaso valor*) rabble, trash; (*mezcla de cosas inútiles*) junk, trash; (Mex) change, small change
morriña *f* blues, melancholy; **morriña de la tierra** homesickness
morriño•so -sa *adj* sickly; (coll) blue, melancholy
morrión *m* helmet; (mil) bearskin
morro *m* (*cosa redonda*) knob; (*monte redondo*) knoll; (*guijarro*) pebble; (*saliente que forman los labios*) snout; **beber a morro** (slang) to drink out of the bottle; **estar de morro** or **de morros** to be on the outs; **poner morro** to make a snout; **por el morro** just like that, simply so
morrocotu•do -da *adj* strong, thick, heavy; (*asunto, negocio*) weighty; big, enormous; (Col) rich, wealthy; (Chile) graceless, monotonous
morsa *f* walrus
mortaja *f* shroud, winding sheet; cigarette paper; (carp) mortise
mortal *adj* mortal; deadly; mortally ill; deathly pale; sure, conclusive || *m* mortal
mortalidad *f* mortality; death rate
mortandad *f* massacre, mortality, butchery
morteci•no -na *adj* dead; dying; failing, weak; **hacer la mortecina** to play dead, to play possum
mortero *m* (*vaso que sirve para machacar; argamasa*) mortar; (*en los molinos de aceite*) nether stone; (arti) mortar
mortífe•ro -ra *adj* deadly
mortificar §73 *tr* to vex, annoy, bother; mortify || *ref* (Mex) to be mortified, be embarrassed
mortual *m* (CAm, Mex) inheritance
mortuo•rio -ria *adj* mortuary, funeral; (*casa*) of the deceased || *m* (archaic) funeral
morueco *m* ram
moru•no -na *adj* Moorish
mosai•co -ca *adj* Mosaic || *m* tile, paving tile; mosaic; **mosaico de madera** marquetry
mosca *f* fly; (*barba*) imperial; cash, dough; disappointment; bore, nuisance; **aflojar la mosca** to shell out, to fork out; **mosca borriquera** horsefly; **mosca de las frutas** fruit fly; **mosca del vinagre** fruit fly; **mosca muerta** hypocrite; **moscas** sparks; **moscas volantes** spots before the eyes; **papar moscas** to gape, gawk
moscareta *f* (orn) flycatcher
moscona *f* hussy, brazen woman
Moscú Moscow
mosquear *tr* (*moscas*) to shoo; beat, whip; answer sharply || *intr* (Mex) to sneak a ride || *ref* to shake off annoyances; take offense
mosquero *m* flytrap; fly swatter
mosquete *m* musket
mosquetear *intr* (Arg, Bol) to snoop
mosquete•ro -ra *adj* idle || *mf* (Arg, Bol) bystander, snooper || *m* musketeer || *f* wallflower
mosquetón *m* snap hook

mosquitera *f* or **mosquitero** *m* mosquito net; fly net
mosquito *m* (*Culex pungens*) mosquito; (*insecto parecido al anterior*) gnat; (coll) tippler
mostacera *f* mustard jar
mostacho *m* mustache; spot on the face
mostachón *m* macaroon
mostaza *f* mustard; (*semilla; munición*) mustard seed; **subírsele a** (*uno*) **la mostaza a las narices** to fly into a rage
mosto *m* must; **mosto de cerveza** wort
mostrador *m* (*en las tiendas*) counter; (*en las tabernas*) bar; (*de reloj*) dial
mostrar **§61** *tr* to show || *ref* to show; show oneself to be
mostrear *tr* to spot, splash
mostren•co -ca *adj* ownerless, unclaimed; (*que no tiene casa ni hogar*) homeless; (*animal*) stray; slow, dull; fat, heavy || *mf* dolt, dullard
mota *f* mote, speck; (*en el paño*) burl, knot; hill, rise; defect, fault; (Mex, W-I) powder puff
mote *m* device, emblem, riddle; (*apodo*) nickname; (Chile) mistake; (SAm) stewed corn
motear *tr* to speck, speckle; dapple, mottle || *intr* (Peru) to eat stewed corn
motejar *tr* to call names; scoff at, make fun of; **motejar de** to brand as
motín *m* mutiny, riot
motinista *m* (Peru) rioter
motivar *tr* to explain, account for; rationalize
moti•vo -va *adj* motive || *m* motive, reason; (mus) motif; **con motivo de** because of; on the occasion of; **de su motivo propio** on his own accord; **motivo conductor** (mus) leitmotif; **motivos** grounds, reasons; (Chile) finickiness, prudery
moto *m* guidepost, landmark || *f* motorcycle
motobomba *f* fire truck, fire engine
motocarro *m* three-wheel delivery truck
motocicleta *f* motorcycle
motocine *m* drive-in theater
motogrúa *f* truck crane
motoli•to -ta *adj* simple, stupid; **vivir de motolito** to be a sponger, live on other people || *f* (orn) wagtail; (Ven) decent woman
motón *m* (naut) block, pulley
motonáuti•co -ca *adj* motorboat || *f* motorboating
motonaustismo *m* (sport) motorboating
motonave *f* motor launch; motor ship
motoneta *f* motor scooter; moped; light three-wheel delivery truck
mo•tor -tora *adj* motor, motive || *m* motor, engine; **motor a chorro** jet engine; **motor de arranque** (aut) starter, starting motor; **motor de cuatro tiempos** four-cycle engine; **motor de dos tiempos** two-cycle engine; **motor de explosión** internal-combustion engine; **motor de reacción** jet engine; **motor fuera de borda** outboard motor; **motor térmico** heat engine || *f* small motor boat
motorista *mf* motorist; motorcyclist; motorcycle racer || *m* motorcycle policeman; motorman
motorización *f* motorization
motorizar **§60** *tr* to motorize
motosegadora *f* power mower
motovelero *m* (naut) motor sailer
motriz *adj fem* (*fuerza*) motive
movedi•zo -za *adj* shaky, unsteady; fickle, inconstant; (*arena*) quick, shifting
mover **§47** *tr* to move; (*la cola el perro*) wag; (*discordia*) stir up || *intr* to move; abort, miscarry; bud, sprout || *ref* to move; be moved
movible *adj* movable; fickle, inconstant, changeable
móvil *adj* movable, mobile; fickle, changeable; moving || *m* moving body; cause, motive
movilizar **§60** *tr* to mobilize
movimiento *m* movement, motion; **movimiento feminista** women's liberation (movement)
moza *f* girl, lass; mistress, concubine; maid, kitchen maid; (*en algunos juegos de naipes*) last hand; wash bat; **buena moza** or **real moza** good-looking woman; **moza de fortuna** or **del partido** prostitute; **moza de taberna** barmaid
mozalbete *m* lad, young fellow
mozárabe *adj* Mozarabic || *mf* Mozarab
mo•zo -za *adj* young, youthful; single, unmarried || *m* youth, lad; (*camarero*) waiter; (*criado*) servant; porter; (*cuelgacapas*) cloak hanger; **buen mozo** or **real mozo** handsome fellow; **mozo de caballerías** hostler, stable boy; **mozo de café** waiter; **mozo de cámara** (naut) cabin boy; **mozo de ciego** blind man's guide; **mozo de cordel** street porter, public errand boy; **mozo de cuadra** stable boy; **mozo de cuerda** public errand boy; **mozo de espuelas** groom who walks in front of master's horse; **mozo de esquina** street porter, public errand boy; **mozo de estación** station porter; **mozo de estoques** (taur) sword handler; **mozo de hotel** porter, bellhop; **mozo de paja y cebada** hostler (*at an inn*); **mozo de restaurante** waiter || *f* see **moza**
mozue•lo -la *mf* youngster || *m* lad, young fellow || *f* lass, young woman
m/p *abbr* **mi pagaré**
m/r *abbr* **mi remesa**
Mro. *abbr* **Maestro**
M.S. *abbr* **manuscrito**
mtd. *abbr* **mitad**
mu *m* moo || *f* bye-bye; **ir a la mu** to go bye-bye
muaré *adj invar & m* moiré
muca•mo -ma *mf* (Arg, Urug) house servant || *f* (Arg, Chile, Urug) servant girl
muceta *f* (*de los doctores en los actos universitarios*) hood; (eccl) mozzetta
muco•so -sa *adj* mucous || *f* mucous membrane
múcura *f* (Bol, Col, Ven, W-I) water pitcher; (Col) thickhead

muchacha *f* girl; young woman; servant girl
muchachada *f* youthful prank
muchachez *f* boyishness, girlishness
mucha•cho -cha *adj* young, youthful || *mf* youth, young person; servant || *m* boy || *f* see **muchacha**
muchedumbre *f* crowd, multitude, flock
mu•cho -cha *adj* much, a lot of, a great deal of; (*tiempo*) a long || *pron* much, a lot, a great deal || **mu•chos -chas** *adj & pron* many || **mucho** *adv* much; (*más de lo regular*) hard; often; a long time; **con mucho** by far; **ni con mucho** or **ni mucho menos** not by a long shot; **por mucho que** however much; **sentir mucho** to be very sorry; **tener mucho de** to take after
muda *f* change; change of voice; change of clothes; (*cambio de plumas o de piel*) molt, molting; molting season; **estar de muda** to be changing one's voice; **estar en muda** (coll) to keep too quiet; **hacer la muda** to molt; **muda de ropa** change of clothing
mudable *adj* fickle, inconstant
mudada *f* change of clothing; move, change of residence
mudadi•zo -za *adj* fickle, inconstant
mudanza *f* change; (*cambio de domicilio*) moving; fickleness, inconstancy; (*en el baile*) figure
mudar *tr* to change || *intr* to change; **mudar de** to change || *ref* to change; change clothing; move; move away; have a bowel movement; **mudarse de** to change
mudez *f* muteness, dumbness; continued silence
mu•do -da *adj* dumb, mute; (phonet) voiceless, surd || *mf* mute || *f* see **muda**
mueblaje *m* furniture, suite of furniture
mueble *adj* movable || *m* piece of furniture; (*p.ej., de un aparato de radio*) cabinet; **muebles** furniture
mueblería *f* furniture shop
mueblista *mf* furniture dealer
mueca *f* face, grimace
muela *f* grindstone; knoll, mound; back tooth, grinder; **muela cordal** wisdom tooth; **muela de esmeril** emery wheel; **muela del juicio** wisdom tooth; **muela de molino** millstone
muellaje *m* dockage, wharfage
muelle *adj* soft; voluptuous || *m* (*pieza elástica de metal*) spring; (*obra en la orilla del mar o de un río*) dock, wharf, pier; (rr) freight platform; **muelle real** mainspring
muérdago *m* mistletoe
muérgano *m* (Col, Ven) piece of junk, drug on the market; (Col, Ecuad, Ven) boor, nobody
muermo *m* (vet) glanders
muerte *f* death; **cada muerte de obispo** once in a blue moon; **dar la muerte a** to put to death; **de mala muerte** crummy, not much of a; **estar a la muerte** to be at death's door; **muerte chiquita** nervous shudder
muer•to -ta *adj* dead; (*apagado, marchito*) flat, dull; (*cal, yeso*) slaked; **muerto de** dying of; **muerto por** crazy about || *mf* corpse, dead person || *m* (*en los naipes*) dummy; **hacerse el muerto** to play possum; play deaf; **tocar a muerto** to toll
muesca *f* nick, notch; (carp) mortise
muestra *f* (*porción de un producto que sirve para conocer su calidad*) sample; model, specimen; (*rótulo sobre una tienda u hotel*) sign; show, exhibition, indication; (*esfera de reloj*) dial, face; (*parada del perro para levantar la caza*) set; (*ademán, porte*) bearing; **dar muestras de** to show signs of
mugido *m* moo, low; bellow, roar
mugir §27 *intr* (*la res vacuna*) to moo, low; (*con ira*) bellow; (*el viento, el mar*) roar
mugre *f* dirt, filth, grime
mugrien•to -ta *adj* dirty, filthy, grimy
muguete *m* lily of the valley
mujer *f* woman; (*esposa*) wife; **mujer de gobierno** housekeeper; **mujer de su casa** good manager; **mujer fatal** vamp; **ser mujer** to be a grown woman
mujeren•go -ga *adj* (Arg, Urug, CAm) effeminate
mujerie•go -ga *adj* feminine, womanly; effeminate, womanish; fond of women; **a mujeriegas** sidesaddle || *m* flock of women
mujeril *adj* womanly; womanish
mújol *m* mullet, striped mullet
mula *f* mule, she-mule; junk, trash; (Arg) ingrate, traitor; (Arg) hoax; (C-R) jag, drunk; (Guat, Hond) anger, rage; (Mex) drug on the market; (Ven) flask; **devolver la mula** (CAm) to pay back in one's own coin; **echar la mula a** (Mex) to rake over the coals; **en mula de San Francisco** on shank's mare
mulada *f* drove of mules
muladar *m* dungheap, dunghill; dump, trash heap; filth
mula•to -ta *adj & mf* mulatto
muleta *f* (*palo para apoyarse al andar*) crutch; muleta (*cloth attached to a stick, used by matador*); support, prop; snack
muletilla *f* cross-handle cane; pet word, pet phrase; (taur) muleta
mulo *m* mule
multa *f* fine
multar *tr* to fine
multicopista *m* copying machine
multigrafiar §77 *tr* to multigraph
multígrafo *m* multigraph
multilateral *adj* multilateral
multiláte•ro -ra *adj* multilateral
multinacionales *mpl* multinational corporations
múltiple *adj* multiple, manifold || *m* manifold; **múltiple de admisión** intake manifold; **múltiple de escape** exhaust manifold; **múltiple de uso** multipurpose
multiplicar §73 *tr, intr & ref* to multiply
multiplicidad *f* multiplicity
múlti•plo -pla *adj* multiple, manifold || *m* (math) multiple
multitud *f* multitude
mulli•do -da *adj* soft, fluffy || *m* stuffing (*for cushions, pillows, etc.*) || *f* bedding, litter (*for animals*)

mullir **§13** *tr* to soften, fluff up; (*la cama*) beat up, shake up; (*la tierra*) loosen around a stalk || *ref* to get fluffy
munda•no -na *adj* mundane, worldly; (*mujer*) loose
mundial *adj* world-wide, world
mundillo *m* arched clotheshorse; cushion for making lace; warming pan; guelder-rose, cranberry tree; world (*of artists, scholars, etc.*)
mundo *m* world; **así va el mundo** so it goes; **desde que el mundo es mundo** since the world began; **echar al mundo** to bring into the world; to bring forth; **el otro mundo** the other world; **gran mundo** high society; **medio mundo** (*mucha gente*) half the world; **nada del otro mundo** nothing special, no great thing; **tener mucho mundo** to know one's way around; **todo el mundo** everybody; **ver mundo** to see the world, to travel
mundonuevo *m* peep show
munición *f* munition, ammunition; **de munición** (mil) government issue; (coll) done hurriedly
municionar *tr* to supply with munition
municipal *adj* municipal || *m* policeman
munícipe *m* citizen
municipio *m* municipality; town council
munidad *f* susceptibility to infection
munífi•co -ca *adj* munificent
muñeca *f* (*figurilla infantil con que juegan las niñas*) doll; (*parte del cuerpo humano en donde se articula la mano con el brazo*) wrist; manikin, dress form; tea bag; (*mujer linda; mozuela frívola*) doll; **muñeca de trapo** rag doll, rag baby; **muñeca parlante** talking doll
muñeco *m* doll (*representing a male child or animal*); dummy, manikin; fop, effeminate fellow; (fig) puppet; (coll) lad, little fellow
muñequera *f* strap for wrist watch
muñequilla *f* (mach) chuck; (Arg, Chile) young ear of corn
muñidor *m* heeler, henchman
muñir **§12** *tr* to convoke, summon; (pol) to fix, rig
muñón *m* (*p.ej., de un brazo cortado*) stump; (mach) journal, gudgeon; **muñón de cola** dock
mural *adj* mural
muralla *f* wall, rampart
murar *tr* to surround with a wall
murciélago *m* bat
murga *f* tin-pan band; trouble, bother; torment
muriente *adj* dying, faint
murmujear *tr & intr* to mumble
murmullar *intr* to murmur
murmullo *m* murmur; whisper; (*de aguas corrientes*) ripple; (*del viento*) rustle
murmurar *tr* to murmur, mutter; murmur at || *intr* to murmur, mutter; whisper; (*las aguas corrientes*) ripple, purl; (*el viento*) rustle; gossip
muro *m* wall; **muro del sonido** sound barrier
murria *f* (coll) blues, dejection
musa *f* muse; **las Musas** the Muses; **soplarle a uno la musa** to be inspired to write poetry; be lucky at games of chance
musaraña *f* shrew, shrewmouse; bug, worm; **mirar a las musarañas** to stare vacantly
músculo *m* muscle
musculo•so -sa *adj* muscular
muselina *f* muslin
museo *m* museum; **museo de cera** waxworks
muserola *f* noseband
mus•go -ga *adj* dark-brown || *m* moss
musgo•so -sa *adj* mossy, moss-covered
música *f* music; (*músicos que tocan juntos*) band; noise, racket; **con la música a otra parte** don't bother me, get out; **música celestial** nonsense; **música de fondo** background music; **poner en música** to set to music
musical *adj* musical
musicalidad *f* musicianship
music-hall *s* vaudeville theater, burlesque show
músi•co -ca *adj* musical || *mf* musician; **músico mayor** bandmaster || *f* see **música**
musicología *f* musicology
musicólo•go -ga *mf* musicologist
musiquero *m* music cabinet
musitar *tr & intr* to mutter, mumble
muslime *adj & mf* Muslim
muslo *m* thigh; (*de ave cocida*) leg, drumstick
mustiar *ref* to wither
mus•tio -tia *adj* sad, gloomy; (*marchito*) withered; (Mex) hypocritical; (Mex) standoffish
musul•mán -mana *adj & mf* Muslim
mutación *f* mutation; unsettled weather, change of weather; (biol) mutation, sport; (theat) change of scene
mutila•do -da *adj* crippled || *mf* cripple
mutilar *tr* to mutilate; cripple
múti•lo -la *adj* mutilated; crippled
mutis *m* (theat) exit; **hacer mutis** (theat) to exit; keep quiet
mutual *adj* mutual
mutualidad *f* mutuality; mutual benefit; mutual benefit association
mutualista *mf* member of a mutual benefit association
mu•tuo -tua *adj* mutual, reciprocal
muy *adv* very; very much; too, e.g., **es muy tarde para dar un paseo tan largo** it is too late to take such a long walk; **muy de noche** late at night; **Muy señor mío** Dear Sir

N

N, n (ene) *f* sixteenth letter of the Spanish alphabet
n/ *abbr* **nuestro**
N. *abbr* **Norte**
nabo *m* turnip; (naut) mast
Nabucodonosor *m* Nebuchadnezzar
nácar *m* mother-of-pearl
nacara•do -da *adj* mother-of-pearl
nacatamal *m* (CAm, Mex) meat-filled tamale
nacela *f* nacelle
nacencia *f* birth; growth, tumor
nacer **§22** *intr* to be born; bud, take rise, originate, appear; dawn || *ref* bud, shoot, sprout; (*abrirse la ropa por las costuras*) split
naci•do -da *adj* natural, innate; apt, proper, fit; **nacida** née or nee || *m* human being; growth, boil
naciente *adj* incipient; resurgent; (*sol*) rising || *m* east
nacimiento *m* birth; origin, beginning, fountainhead; descent, lineage; (*de agua*) spring, fountainhead; crèche
nación *f* nation
nacional *adj* national; domestic || *mf* national || *m* militiaman
nacionalidad *f* nationality
nacionalismo *m* nationalism
nacionalista *adj & mf* nationalist
nacionalizar **§60** *tr* to nationalize || *ref* to be naturalized; become a citizen
nacista *adj & mf* Nazi
naco *m* (Arg, Bol, Urug) black rolled leaf of chewing tobacco; (Arg) fear, scare; (Col) stewed corn; (Col) mashed potatoes
nada *pron indef* nothing, not . . . anything; **de nada** don't mention it, you're welcome || *adv* not at all
nadaderas *fpl* water wings
nada•dor -dora *adj* swimming, floating || *mf* swimmer || *m* (Chile) fishnet float
nadar *intr* to swim; float; fit loosely or too loosely; **nadar en** (*riqueza*) to be rolling in; (*suspiros*) be full of; (*sangre*) be bathed in
nadear *tr* to destroy, wipe out
nadería *f* trifle
nadie *pron indef* nobody, not . . . anybody; **nadie más** nobody else; **nadie más que** nobody but || *m* nobody; **un don nadie** a nonentity
nado — a nado swimming, floating; **echarse a nado** to dive in; **pasar a nado** to swim across
nafta *f* naphtha
nagual *m* (Guat, Hond) (*dícese de un animal*) inseparable companion; (Mex) sorcerer, wizard; (Mex) lie
nagualear *intr* (Mex) to lie; (Mex) to be out looking for trouble all night
naguas *fpl* petticoat
naipe *m* playing card; deck of cards; **naipe de figura** face card; **tener buen naipe** to be lucky
naire *m* mahout
nalgada *f* shoulder, ham; blow on or with the buttocks
nalgas *fpl* buttocks, rump
nana *f* grandma; lullaby, cradlesong; (CAm, Mex, W-I) child's nurse; (Arg, Chile, Urug) child's complaint
nao *f* ship, vessel
napoleóni•co -ca *adj* Napoleonic
Nápoles *f* Naples
napolita•no -na *adj & mf* Neapolitan
naranja *f* orange; **media naranja** (coll) sidekick, better half; **naranja cajel** Seville orange, sour orange; **¡naranjas!** nonsense!
naranjada *f* orangeade; orange juice; orange marmalade
naranjal *m* orange grove
naranjo *m* orange tree; boob, simpleton
narciso *m* narcissus; fop, dandy; **narciso trompón** daffodil || **Narciso** *m* Narcissus
narcóti•co -ca *adj & m* narcotic
narcotizar **§60** *tr* to dope, drug
narcotraficante *mf* drug dealer
narguile *m* hookah
narigada *f* (SAm) pinch of snuff
nari•gón -gona *adj* big-nosed || *m* big nose
narigu•do -da *adj* big-nosed; nose-shaped
nariguera *f* nose ring
na•riz *f* (*pl* **-rices**) nose; nostril; sense of smell; (*del vino*) bouquet; **nariz de pico de loro** hooknose; **sonarse las narices** to blow one's nose; **tabicarse las narices** to hold one's nose; **tener agarrado por las narices** to lead by the nose
narración *f* narration
narra•dor -dora *adj* narrating || *mf* narrator
narrar *tr* to narrate
narrati•vo -va *adj* narrative || *f* (*relato; habilidad en narrar*) narrative
narria *f* sled, sledge, drag
nasal *adj & f* nasal
nasalizar **§60** *tr* to nasalize
nata *f* cream; whipped cream; élite, choice; skim, scum
natación *f* swimming
natal *adj* natal; native || *m* birth; birthday
natali•cio -cia *adj* birth || *m* birthday
natalidad *f* birth rate
naterón *m* cottage cheese
natillas *fpl* custard
natividad *f* birth; Christmas; (*día; festividad; pintura*) Nativity
nati•vo -va *adj* native; natural; natural-born; innate
na•to -ta *adj* born, e.g., **criminal nato** born criminal || *f* see **nata**
natural *adj* natural; native; (mus) natural || *mf* native || *m* temper, disposition, nature; **al natural** au naturel; rough, unfinished; live; **del natural** from life, from nature
naturaleza *f* nature; disposition, temperament; nationality; **naturaleza muerta** still life
naturalidad *f* naturalness; nationality
naturalismo *m* naturalism
naturalista *mf* naturalist

naturalización *f* naturalization
naturalizar §60 *tr* to naturalize; acclimatize || *ref* to become naturalized; go native
naturalmente *adv* naturally; easily, readily
naturismo *m* nudism
naufragar §44 *intr* to be shipwrecked; fail
naufragio *m* shipwreck; failure, ruin
náufra•go -ga *adj* shipwrecked || *mf* shipwrecked person || *m* shark
náusea *f* nausea; **dar náuseas a** to nauseate; sicken, disgust; **tener náuseas** to be nauseated, be sick at one's stomach
nauseabun•do -da *adj* nauseating, nauseous, loathsome, sickening
nauta *m* mariner, sailor
náuti•co -ca *adj* nautical || *f* sailing, navigation
nava *f* hollow plain between mountains
navaja *f* folding knife; razor; penknife; tusk of wild boar; razor clam; evil tongue; **navaja barbera** straight razor
navajada *f* or **navajazo** *m* slash, gash
navajero *m* razor case; razor cloth
naval *adj* naval; nautical; **naval militar** naval
nava•rro -rra *adj & mf* Navarrese || **Navarra** *f* Navarre
navazo *m* garden in sandy marshland
nave *f* ship, vessel; (*de un taller, fábrica, tienda, iglesia, etc.*) aisle; commercial ground floor; hall, shed, bay, building; **nave central** or **principal** (archit) nave; **nave lateral** (archit) aisle
navegable *adj* navigable
navegación *f* navigation; sailing; sea voyage; **navegación a vela** sailing
navega•dor -dora or **navegante** *adj* navigating || *mf* navigator
navegar §44 *tr* to sail || *intr* to navigate, sail; move around; (Mex) to suffer, bear
navel *f* (*pl* **-vels**) navel orange
Navidad *f* Christmas; Christmas time; **¡Felices Navidades!** Merry Christmas!; **contar** or **tener muchas Navidades** to be pretty old
navidal *m* Christmas card
navide•ño -ña *adj* Christmas
navie•ro -ra *adj* ship, shipping || *m* shipowner; outfitter
navío *m* ship, vessel; **navío de guerra** warship
náyade *f* naiad
nazare•no -na *adj & mf* Nazarene || *m* penitent in Passion Week procession || **nazarenas** *fpl* (SAm) large gaucho spurs
nazi *adj & mf* Nazi
N.B. *abbr* **nota bene** (Lat) note well
nébeda *f* catnip
neblina *f* fog, mist
neblino•so -sa *adj* foggy, misty
nebulo•so -sa *adj* nebulous, cloudy, misty, hazy, vague; gloomy, sullen || *f* nebula
necedad *f* foolishness, stupidity, nonsense
necesa•rio -ria *adj* necessary || *f* water closet, privy
neceser *m* toilet case; sewing kit; **neceser de belleza** vanity case; **neceser de costura** workbasket
necesidad *f* necessity; need, want; starvation; **de necesidad** from weakness; of necessity; **necesidad mayor** bowel movement; **necesidad menor** urination
necesita•do -da *adj* necessitous, poor, needy; **estar necesitado de** to be in need of || *mf* needy person
necesitar *tr* to necessitate; need; **necesitar** + *inf* to have to, need to + *inf* || *intr* to be in need; **necesitar de** to be in need of, need || *ref* to be needed, be necessary
ne•cio -cia *adj* foolish, stupid; imprudent; stubborn; touchy || *mf* fool
necrología *f* necrology
necromancia *f* necromancy
néctar *m* nectar
neerlan•dés -desa *adj* Netherlandish, Dutch || *mf* Netherlander || *m* Dutchman; (*idioma*) Netherlandish or Dutch || *f* Dutchwoman
nefalista *mf* teetotaler
nefan•do -da *adj* base, infamous
nefas•to -ta *adj* ominous, fatal, tragic
negable *adj* deniable
negación *f* negation; denial; refusal
nega•do -da *adj* unfit, incompetent; dull, indifferent
negar §66 *tr* to deny; refuse; prohibit; disown; conceal || *intr* to deny || *ref* to avoid; refuse; deny oneself to callers; **negarse a** to refuse; **negarse a** + *inf* to refuse to + *inf*
negati•vo -va *adj* negative || *f* negative; denial; refusal
negligencia *f* negligence
negligente *adj* negligent
negociable *adj* negotiable
negociación *f* negotiation; deal, matter
negociado *m* department, bureau; affair, business; (SAm) illegal dealing; (Chile) store
negociante *m* dealer, trader
negociar *tr* to negotiate || *intr* to negotiate; deal, trade
negocio *m* business; affair, deal, transaction; profit; (SAm) store
negocio•so -sa *adj* businesslike
negrear *intr* to turn black; look black
negre•ro -ra *adj* slave-trading; (fig) slave-driving || *mf* slave trader; (fig) slave driver
negrilla *f* (typ) boldface
ne•gro -gra *adj* black, dark; gloomy; fatal, wicked; (coll) broke || *mf* black (person); dear, darling || *m* black; **negro de humo** lampblack
negror *m* or **negrura** *f* blackness
negruz•co -ca *adj* blackish
néme•sis *f* (*pl* **-sis**) (*justo castigo; castigador*) nemesis || **Némesis** Nemesis
nemoro•so -sa *adj* (poet) woody, sylvan
ne•ne -na *mf* baby; dear, darling || *m* rascal, villain
nenúfar *m* white water lily
neo *m* neon
neocelan•dés -desa *adj* New Zealand || *mf* New Zealander
neoesco•cés -cesa *adj & mf* Nova Scotian
neófi•to -ta *mf* neophyte

neologismo *m* neologism
neomejica•no -na *adj & mf* New Mexican
neomicina *f* neomycin
neón *m* neon
neoyorki•no -na *adj* New York || *mf* New Yorker
Nepal, el Nepal
nepa•lés -lesa *adj & mf* Nepalese
nepente *m* nepenthe
nepote *m* relative and favorite of the Pope || **Nepote** Nepos
neptunio *m* neptunium
Neptuno *m* Neptune
nereida *f* Nereid
Nerón *m* Nero
nervio *m* nerve; (*del ala del insecto*) rib; strength, vigor
nerviosidad *f* nervousness
nervio•so -sa *adj* nervous; energetic, vigorous, sinewy; (*célula; centro; tónico*) nerve; (*sistema; enfermedad; postración, colapso*) nervous
nervosidad *f* nervosity; ductility, flexibility; (*de un argumento*) force, cogency
nervo•so -sa *adj* var of **nervioso**
nervu•do -da *adj* vigorous, sinewy
nervura *f* backbone (*of book*)
nesga *f* gore
nesgar **§44** *tr* to gore
ne•to -ta *adj* net
neumáti•co -ca *adj* pneumatic; air || *m* tire
neumonía *f* pneumonia
neuralgia *f* neuralgia
neurología *f* neurology
neurona *f* neuron
neuro•sis *f* (*pl* **-sis**) neurosis; **neurosis de guerra** shell shock
neuróti•co -ca *adj & mf* neurotic
neutral *adj & mf* neutral
neutralidad *f* neutrality
neutralismo *m* neutralism
neutralista *adj & mf* neutralist
neutralizar **§60** *tr* to neutralize
neu•tro -tra *adj* neuter; (*que no es de un color ni de otro*) neutral; (bot, chem, elec, phonet, zool) neutral; (*verbo*) intransitive
neutrón *m* neutron
neva•do -da *adj* snow-covered; snow-white || *f* snowfall
nevar **§2** *tr* to make snow-white || *intr* to snow
nevasca *f* snowfall; snowstorm, blizzard
nevazón *f* (SAm) snowfall
nevera *f* icebox, refrigerator; icehouse; (P-R) jail
nevería *f* ice-cream parlor
neve•ro -ra *mf* ice-cream dealer || *m* place of perpetual snow; perpetual snow || *f* see **nevera**
nevisca *f* snow flurry
neviscar **§73** *intr* to snow lightly
nevo *m* mole; **nevo materno** birth mark
nevo•so -sa *adj* snowy
ni *conj* neither, nor; **ni . . . ni** neither . . . nor; **ni . . . siquiera** not even
niacina *f* niacin
nicaragüense or **nicaragüe•ño -ña** *adj & mf* Nicaraguan
Nicolás *m* Nicholas
nicotina *f* nicotine
nicho *m* niche
nidada *f* (*huevos en el nido*) nestful of eggs; (*pajarillos en el nido*) nest, brood, hatch
nidal *m* (*donde la gallina pone sus huevos*) nest; nest egg; haunt; source; basis, foundation
nido *m* nest; haunt; home; source; (*de ladrones*) nest, den
niebla *f* fog, mist, haze; mildew; fog, confusion; **hay niebla** it is foggy; **niebla artificial** smoke screen
nie•to -ta *mf* grandchild || *m* grandson; **nietos** grandchildren || *f* granddaughter
nieve *f* snow; water ice
nigromancia *f* necromancy
nihilismo *m* nihilism
nihilista *mf* nihilist
Nilo *m* Nile; **Nilo Azul** Blue Nile
nilón *m* nylon
nimbo *m* nimbus; halo
nimiedad *f* excess; fussiness, fastidiousness; timidity
ni•mio -mia *adj* excessive; fussy, fastidious; tiny
ninfa *f* nymph; **ninfa marina** mermaid
ninfea *f* white water lily
ningún *adj indef* apocopated form of **ninguno,** used only before masculine singular nouns and adjectives
ningu•no -na *adj indef* no, not any || *pron indef* none, not any; neither, neither one; **ninguno de los dos** neither one || **ninguno** *pron indef* nobody, no one
niña *f* child, girl; (*del ojo*) pupil; **niña del ojo** apple of one's eye; **niña exploradora** girl scout
niñada *f* childishness
niñera *f* nursemaid
niñería *f* childishness; trifle
niñero -ra *adj* fond of children || *f* see **niñera**
niñez *f* childhood; childishness; (fig) infancy
ni•ño -ña *adj* childlike, childish; young, inexperienced || *mf* child; (*persona joven e inexperta*) babe; **desde niño** from childhood; **niño expósito** foundling; **niño travieso** imp || *m* child, boy; **niño bonito** playboy; **niño de coro** choirboy; **niño de la bola** child Jesus; lucky fellow; **niño explorador** boy scout; **niño gótico** playboy || *f* see **niña**
niño-probeta *m* test-tube baby
ni•pón -pona *adj & mf* Nipponese
níquel *m* nickel
niquelar *tr* to nickel-plate
nirvana, el nirvana
níspero *m* medlar (*tree and fruit*)
níspola *f* medlar (*fruit*)
nitidez *f* brightness, clearness; sharpness
níti•do -da *adj* bright, clear; sharp
nitrato *m* nitrate
nítri•co -ca *adj* nitric
nitro *m* niter; **nitro de Chile** saltpeter
nitrógeno *m* nitrogen

nitroglicerina *f* nitroglycerine
nitro•so -sa *adj* nitrous
nitruro *m* nitride
nivel *m* level; **nivel de burbuja** spirit level; **nivel de vida** standard of living; **nivel sonoro** noise level
nivelar *tr* to level; even, make even, grade; survey
no *adv* not; no; **¿cómo no?** why not?; of course, certainly; **creer que no** to think not, believe not; **¿no?** is it not so?; **no bien** no sooner; **no más que** not more than; only; **no sea que** lest; **no . . . sino** only; **ya no** no longer
nobabia *f* (aer) dope
noble *adj* noble || *m* noble, nobleman
nobleza *f* nobility
noción *f* notion, idea; rudiment
nocividad *f* harmfulness
noci•vo -va *adj* noxious, harmful
noctur•no -na *adj* nocturnal; lonely, sad, melancholy; night, nighttime
noche *f* night, nighttime; darkness; **buenas noches** good evening; good night; **de la noche a la mañana** overnight; unexpectedly, suddenly; **de noche** at night, in the nighttime; **esta noche** tonight; **hacer noche en** to spend the night in; **hacerse de noche** to grow dark; **muy de noche** late at night; **por la noche** at night, in the nighttime; **noche buena** Christmas Eve; **noche de estreno** (theat) first night; **noche de uvas** New Year's Eve; **noche vieja** New Year's Eve; watch night
nochebuena *f* Christmas Eve
nochebueno *f* Christmas cake; Yule log
nochero *m* sleepwalker
nodo *m* (astr, med, phys) node
No-Do *m* (acronym for **Noticiario y Documentales**) newsreel; newsreel theater
nodriza *f* wet nurse; vacuum tank
Noé *m* Noah
nogal *m* walnut; **nogal de la brujería** witch hazel
nómada or **nómade** *adj & mf* nomad
nomádi•co -ca *adj* nomadic
nombradía *f* fame, renown, reputation
nombra•do -da *adj* famous
nombramiento *m* naming; appointment
nombrar *tr* to name; appoint
nombre *m* name; fame, reputation; nickname; watchword; noun; **del mismo nombre** (elec) like; **de nombres contrarios** (elec) unlike; **nombre comercial** firm name; **nombre de lugar** place name; **nombre de pila** first name, Christian name; **nombre de soltera** maiden name; **nombre substantivo** noun; **nombre supuesto** alias
nomeolvi•des *f* (*pl* **-des**) forget-me-not
nómina *f* list, roll; payroll
nominal *adj* nominal; noun
nominar *tr* to name; appoint
nominati•vo -va *adj & m* nominative
non *adj* odd, uneven || *m* odd number
nonada *f* trifle, nothing
no•no -na *adj & m* ninth
nopal *m* prickly pear
norcorea•no -na *adj & mf* North Korean
nordestada *f* or **nordeste** *m* (*viento*) northeaster (*wind*)
noria *f* chain pump; (*pozo*) draw well; Ferris wheel; treadmill, drudgery
norma *f* norm, standard; rule, method; (carp) square
normal *adj* normal; standard; perpendicular
Normandía *f* Normandy
norman•do -da *adj & mf* Norman || *m* Norseman
norte *m* north; north wind; (*guía*) (fig) polestar, lodestar
Norteamérica *f* North America; America, the United States
norteamerica•no -na *adj & mf* North American; (*estadunidense*) American
norte•ño -ña *adj* northern
norue•go -ga *adj & mf* Norwegian || **Noruega** *f* Norway
nos (used as object of verb) *pron pers* us; to us || *pron reflex* ourselves, to ourselves; each other, to each other
noso•tros -tras *pron pers* we; us; ourselves
nostalgia *f* nostalgia
nota *f* note; (*en la escuela*) mark, grade; (*en el restaurante*) check; (mus) note; **nota de adorno** grace note; **nota tónica** keynote
notables *mpl* notables; prominent persons; (coll) VIPs
notar *tr* to note; dictate; annotate; criticize; discredit
notario *m* notary, notary public
noticia *f* news; notice, information; notion, rudiment; knowledge; **noticias de actualidad** news of the day; **noticias de última hora** late news; **una noticia** a piece of news, a news item
noticiar *tr* to notify; give notice of
noticia•rio -ria *adj* news || *m* up-to-the-minute news; newsreel; newscast; **noticiario gráfico** picture page; **noticiario teatral** theater page
noticie•ro -ra *adj* news || *m* newsman, reporter; late news
noticio•so -sa *adj* informed; learned; well-informed; newsy || *m* news item
notificar §73 *tr* to notify; report on
no•to -ta *adj* known, well-known || *m* south wind || *f* see **nota**
notoriedad *f* general knowledge; fame
noto•rio -ria *adj* manifest, well-known
nov. *abbr* **noviembre**
novatada *f* hazing; beginner's blunder
nova•to -ta *adj* beginning || *mf* beginner; freshman
novecien•tos -tas *adj & pron* nine hundred || **novecientos** *m* nine hundred
novedad *f* newness, novelty; news; fashion; happening; change; failing health; **sin novedad** as usual; safe; well; without anything happening
novel *adj* new, inexperienced, beginning || *m* beginner

novela *f* novel; story, lie; **novela caballista** novel of western life; **novela policíaca** or **policial** detective story; **novela por entregas** serial
novele•ro -ra *adj* fond of novelty; fond of fiction; gossipy; fickle
noveles•co -ca *adj* novelistic, fictional; romantic, fantastic
novelista *mf* novelist
novelísti•co -ca *adj* fictional || *f* fiction
novelizar **§60** *tr* to fictionalize
nove•no -na *adj & m* ninth
noventa *adj, pron & m* ninety
noventa•vo -va *adj & m* ninetieth
novia *f* fiancée; bride; **novia de guerra** war bride
noviazgo *m* engagement, courtship
novi•cio -cia *adj & mf* novice
noviembre *m* November
novilunio *m* new moon
novilla *f* heifer
novillada *f* drove of young bulls; (taur) fight with young bulls by aspiring bullfighters
novillero *m* herdsman of young cattle; (taur) aspiring fighter, untrained fighter; truant
novillo *m* young bull; (coll) cuckold; (Mex, P-R) fiancé; **hacer novillos** to play truant
novio *m* suitor; fiancé; bridegroom; **novios** engaged couple; bride and groom, newlyweds
novocaína *f* novocaine
nro. *abbr* **nuestro**
N.S. *abbr* **Nuestro Señor**
ntro. *abbr* **nuestro**
nubada *f* local shower; abundance
nubarrón *m* storm cloud
nube *f* cloud; **andar** (*los precios*) **por las nubes** to be sky-high; **bajar de las nubes** to come back to or down to earth; **poner en** or **sobre las nubes** to praise to the skies
nube-hongo *f* mushroom cloud
nubla•do -da *adj* cloudy || *m* storm cloud; impending danger; abundance; **aguantar el nublado** to suffer resignedly
nublar *tr* to cloud, cloud over || *ref* to become cloudy
nu•blo -bla *adj* cloudy || *m* storm cloud
nublo•so -sa *adj* cloudy; adverse, unfortunate
nubosidad *f* clouding, clouds
nubo•so -sa *adj* cloudy
nuca *f* nape
nuclear *adj* nuclear
núcleo *m* nucleus; core; (*de nuez*) kernel; (*de la fruta*) stone; (*de un electroimán*) core
nudillo *m* knuckle; stocking stitch; plug (*in wall*)
nudo *m* knot; bond, tie, union; crux; tangle, plot; difficulty; (*en el drama*) crisis; center, juncture; (bot) node; (naut) knot; **cortar el nudo gordiano** to cut the Gordian knot; **hacérsele a** (*uno*) **un nudo en la garganta** to get a lump in one's throat
nudo•so -sa *adj* knotted, knotty
nuera *f* daughter-in-law
nues•tro -tra *adj poss* our || *pron poss* ours
nueva *f* news; piece of news; **nuevas** *fpl* news
Nueva York *m & f* New York; **el Gran Nueva York** Greater New York
Nueva Zelandia New Zealand
nueve *adj & pron* nine; **las nueve** nine o'clock || *m* nine; (*en las fechas*) ninth
nue•vo -va *adj* new; **de nuevo** again, anew; **nuevo flamante** brand-new; **¿qué hay de nuevo?** what's new? || *mf* novice; freshman || *f* see **nueva**
nuevomejica•no -na *adj & mf* New Mexican
Nuevo Méjico *m* New Mexico
nuez *f* (*pl* **nueces**) nut; walnut; Adam's apple; **nuez dura** (*árbol*) hickory; hickory nut; **nuez moscada** nutmeg
nulidad *f* nullity; incapacity; nobody
nu•lo -la *adj* null, void, worthless
núm. *abbr* **número**
numen *m* deity; inspiration
numeral *adj* numeral
numerar *tr* to number; count; numerate
numerario *m* cash, coin, specie
numéri•co -ca *adj* numerical
número *m* number; (*de un periódico*) copy, issue; (*de zapatos*) size; lottery ticket; **cargar** or **cobrar al número llamado** (telp) to reverse the charges; **de número** (*dícese de los individuos de una sociedad*) regular; **mirar por el número uno** to look out for number one; **número de serie** series number; **número equivocado** (telp) wrong number
numero•so -sa *adj* numerous
nunca *adv* never; **no . . . nunca** not . . . ever, never; **nunca jamás** nevermore
nupcial *adj* nuptial
nupcialidad *f* marriage rate
nupcias *fpl* nuptials, marriage; **casarse en segundas nupcias** to marry the second time
nutria *f* otter
nutrición *f* nutrition
nutri•do -da *adj* great, intense, robust, vigorous, steady; full, abounding, rich, heavy; (*carácter, letra*) thick; (*cañoneo*) heavy, sustained
nutrimento *m* or **nutrimiento** *m* nourishment, nutriment
nutrir *tr* to nourish, feed; supply, stock; support, back up; fill to overflowing
nu•triz *f* (*pl* **-trices**) wet nurse

Ñ

Ñ, ñ (eñe) *f* seventeenth letter of the Spanish alphabet
ñadi *m* (Chile) broad, shallow swamp
ñajú *m* okra, gumbo
ñámbar *m* Jamaica rosewood
ñame *m* yam; (W-I) blockhead, dunce
ñan•dú *m* (*pl* **-dúes**) nandu, American ostrich
ñaño -ña *adj* close, intimate; spoiled, overindulged || *m* elder brother || *f* elder sister; nursemaid; dear
ñapa *f* something thrown in, lagniappe; **de ñapa** in the bargain
ñaque *m* junk, pile of junk
ña•to -ta *adj* pug-nosed; (Arg) ugly, deformed
ñeque *adj* (Am) strong, vigorous; (*dícese de los ojos*) drooping || *m* slap, blow; pep
ñiqueñaque *m* (coll) trash
ñisca *f* bit, fragment; excrement
ñoclo *m* macaroon
ñolombre *m* old peasant; **¡viene ñolombre!** here comes the bogeyman
ñon•go -ga *adj* slow, lazy; foolish, stupid; tricky; suspicious
ñoñería *f* or **ñoñez** *f* timidity; inanity; dotage
ño•ño -ña *adj* timid; inane; doting

O

O, o (o) eighteenth letter of the Spanish alphabet
o *conj* or; **o . . . o** either . . . or
oa•sis *m* (*pl* **-sis**) oasis
ob. *abbr* **obispo**
obduración *f* obduracy
obedecer §22 *tr* (with personal **a**) to obey || *intr* to obey; **obedecer a** to yield to, be due to, be in keeping with, arise from
obediencia *f* obedience
obediente *adj* obedient
obelisco *m* obelisk; (typ) dagger
obertura *f* (mus) overture
obesidad *f* obesity
obe•so -sa *adj* obese
obispo *m* bishop
óbito *m* decease, demise
obituario *m* obituary
objeción *f* objection
objetable *adj* objectionable (*open to objection*)
objetar *tr* to object; (*dudas*) raise; (*una razón contraria*) set up, offer, present; object to
objeti•vo -va *adj* & *m* objective
objeto *m* object; subject matter; **objetos de cotillión** favors; **objeto volante no identificado (ovni)** unidentified flying object (UFO)
oblea *f* wafer; pill, tablet; **hecho una oblea** nothing but skin and bones
obli•cuo -cua *adj* oblique
obligación *f* obligation, duty; bond, debenture; **obligaciones** family responsibilities
obligacionista *mf* bondholder
obliga•do -da *adj* obliged, grateful; submissive; (mus) obbligato || *m* (mus) obbligato
obligar §44 *tr* to obligate; oblige
obliterar *tr* to cancel
oblon•go -ga *adj* oblong
oboe *m* oboe; oboist
oboísta *mf* oboist
óbolo *m* mite
obra *f* work; **obra de** a matter of; **obra de consulta** reference work; **obra maestra** masterpiece; **obra pía** charity; useful effort; **obra prima** shoemaking; **obras** construction, repairs, alterations; **obra segunda** shoe repairing; **poner por obra** to undertake, set to work on
obra•dor -dora *mf* worker || *m* workman; shop, workshop || *f* workingwoman
obraje *m* manufacture; processing
obrajero *m* foreman; (Arg) lumberman; (Bol) artisan
obrar *tr* to build; perform; work || *intr* to work; act, operate, proceed; have a movement of the bowels; **obra en mi poder** I have at hand, I have in my possession
obrera *f* workingwoman
obrerismo *m* labor; labor movement
obre•ro -ra *adj* working; labor || *m* workman; **los obreros** labor || *f* see **obrera**
obrero-patronal *adj* labor management
obscenidad *f* obscenity
obsce•no -na *adj* obscene
obscurecer §22 *tr* to darken; dim; discredit; cloud, confuse || *intr* to grow dark || *ref* to cloud over; become dimmed; fade away
obscuridad *f* obscurity; darkness
obscu•ro -ra *adj* obscure; dark; gloomy; uncertain, dangerous; **a obscuras** in the dark || *m* dark; (paint) shading
obsequia•do -da *mf* recipient; guest of honor
obsequiar *tr* to fawn over, flatter; present, give; court, woo
obsequio *m* flattery; gift; attention, courtesy; **en obsequio de** in honor of
obsequio•so -sa *adj* obsequious; obliging, courteous
observación *f* observation
observa•dor -dora *adj* observant || *mf* observer
observancia *f* observance; deference, respectfulness
observar *tr* to observe
observatorio *m* observatory
obsesión *f* obsession
obsesionar *tr* to obsess

obsole•to -ta *adj* obsolete
obstaculizar §60 *tr* to prevent; obstruct
obstáculo *m* obstacle
obstante *adj* standing in the way; **no obstante** however, nevertheless; in spite of
obstar *intr* to stand in the way; **obstar a** or **para** to hinder, check, oppose
obstetricia *f* obstetrics
obstétri•co -ca *adj* obstetrical || *mf* obstetrician
obstinación *f* obstinacy
obstina•do -da *adj* obstinate
obstinar *ref* to be obstinate
obstrucción *f* obstruction
obstruccionar *tr* to hinder, obstruct
obstruir §20 *tr* to obstruct; block; stop up
obtención *f* obtaining
obtener §71 *tr* to obtain; keep
obtenible *adj* obtainable
obturación *f* plugging up, sealing off
obturador *m* stopper, plug; (aut) choke; (aut) throttle; (phot) shutter; **obturador de guillotina** drop shutter
obtu•so -sa *adj* obtuse
obús *m* howitzer; shell; (*de válvula de neumático*) plunger
obvención *f* extra, bonus, incidental
obvencional *adj* incidental
obviar §77 & **regular** *tr* to obviate, prevent || *intr* to stand in the way
ob•vio -via *adj* obvious; unnecessary
oca *f* goose
ocasión *f* occasion; opportunity, chance; danger, risk; **aprovechar la ocasión** to improve the occasion; **aprovechar la ocasión de** to avail oneself of the opportunity to; **asir la ocasión por la melena** to take time by the forelock; **de ocasión** secondhand
ocasiona•do -da *adj* dangerous, risky; exposed, subject, liable; annoying
ocasionar *tr* to occasion, cause; stir up; endanger
ocasional *adj* occasional; causal; causing; (*causa*) responsible; accidental
ocaso *m* west; (*de un cuerpo celeste*) setting; sunset; decline; end, death
occidental *adj* western; occidental
occidente *m* occident
oceáni•co -ca *adj* oceanic
océano *m* ocean
ocio *m* idleness, leisure; distraction, pastime; spare time
ocio•so -sa *adj* idle; useless, needless
oclusión *f* occlusion
oclusi•vo -va *adj* & *f* occlusive
ocote *m* (Mex) torch pine
octava *f* octave
octavilla *f* handbill; eight-syllable verse
octavín *m* piccolo
octa•vo -va *adj* eighth || *mf* octoroon || *m* eighth || *f* see **octava**
oct.[e] *abbr* **octubre**
octogési•mo -ma *adj* & *m* eightieth
octubre *m* October
ocular *adj* ocular, eye || *m* eyepiece, eyeglass, ocular
oculista *mf* oculist; fawner, flatterer
ocultar *tr* & *ref* to hide
ocul•to -ta *adj* hidden, concealed; (*misterioso, sobrenatural*) occult
ocupación *f* occupation; occupancy; employment
ocupa•do -da *adj* busy; occupied; **ocupada** pregnant
ocupante *adj* occupying || *mf* occupant || **ocupantes** *mpl* occupying forces
ocupar *tr* to occupy; busy, keep busy; employ; bother, annoy; attract the attention of || *ref* to be occupied; be busy; be preoccupied; bother
ocurrencia *f* occurrence; witticism; bright idea
ocurrente *adj* witty
ocurrir *intr* to occur, happen; come; (*venir a la mente*) occur
ocha•vo -va *adj* eighth; octagonal || *m* eighth; octagon
ochenta *adj, pron* & *m* eighty
ochenta•vo -va *adj* & *m* eightieth
ocho *adj* & *pron* eight; **las ocho** eight o'clock || *m* eight; (*en las fechas*) eighth
ochocien•tos -tas *adj* & *pron* eight hundred || **ochocientos** *m* eight hundred
oda *f* ode
odiar *tr* to hate
odio *m* hate, hatred
odio-amor *m* love-hate
odio•so -sa *adj* odious, hateful
Odisea *f* Odyssey
Odiseo *m* Odysseus
odontología *f* odontology, dentistry
odontólo•go -ga *mf* odontologist, dentist
odre *m* goatskin wine bag; (coll) toper
OEA *f* OAS
oeste *m* west; west wind
ofender *tr* & *intr* to offend || *ref* to take offense
ofensa *f* offense
ofensi•vo -va *adj* & *f* offensive
ofen•sor -sora *adj* offending || *mf* offender
oferta *f* offer; gift, present; **oferta y demanda** supply and demand
oficial *adj* official || *m* official, officer; skilled workman; clerk, office worker; journeyman; commissioned officer; **oficial de derrota** navigator
oficiar *tr* to announce officially in writing; (*la misa*) celebrate; officiate at || *intr* to officiate; **oficiar de** to act as
oficina *f* office; shop; pharmacist's laboratory; **oficina de objetos perdidos** lost-and-found department
oficines•co -ca *adj* office, clerical; bureaucratic
oficinista *mf* clerk, office worker
oficio *m* office, occupation; function, rôle; craft, trade; memo, official note; (eccl) office, service; **de oficio** officially; professionally; **hacer oficios de** to function as; **tomar por oficio** to take to, keep at
oficio•so -sa *adj* diligent; obliging; officious, meddlesome; profitable; unofficial
ofrecer *tr* & *intr* to offer; (*una recepción*) give || *ref* to offer; offer oneself; happen

ofrecimiento *m* offer, offering; **ofrecimiento de presentación** introductory offer
ofrenda *f* offering; gift
ofrendar *tr* to make offerings of; contribute
oftalmología *f* ophthalmology
oftalmólo•go -ga *mf* ophthalmologist
ofuscación *f* obfuscation; (mental) derangement
ofuscar **§73** *tr* to obfuscate; dazzle
ogro *m* ogre
Oh *interj* O!, Oh!
ohmio *m* ohm
oíble *adj* audible
oída *f* hearing; **de** or **por oídas** by hearsay
oído *m* hearing; ear; **abrir tanto oído** to be all ears; **al oído** by listening; confidentially; **decir al oído** to whisper; **hacer** or **tener oídos de mercader** to turn a deaf ear
oír **§48** *tr* to hear; listen to; (*una conferencia*) attend; **oír** + *inf* to hear + *inf,* e.g., **oí entrar a mi hermano** I heard my brother come in; hear + *ger,* e.g., **oí cantar a la muchacha** I heard the girl singing; hear + *pp,* e.g., **oí tocar la campana** I heard the bell rung; **oír decir que** to hear that; **oír hablar de** to hear about || *intr* to hear; listen; **¡oíga!** say!, listen!; the idea!, the very idea!
ojada *f* (Col) skylight
ojal *m* buttonhole; eyelet; grommet
ojalá *interj* God grant . . . !, would to God . . . !; **¡ojalá que** would that . . . !, I hope that . . . !
ojeada *f* glimpse, glance; **buena ojeada** eyeful
ojear *tr* to eye, stare at; cast the evil eye on; (*la caza*) start, rouse; frighten, startle
ojera *f* eyecup, eyeglass; **ojeras** (*bajo los párpados inferiores*) rings, circles
ojeriza *f* grudge, ill will
ojero•so -sa *adj* with rings or circles under the eyes
ojete *m* eyelet, eyehole
ojienju•to -ta *adj* dry-eyed, tearless
ojituer•to -ta *adj* cross-eyed
ojiva *f* ogive, pointed arch
ojo *m* eye; (*de la escalera*) opening, well; (*del puente*) bay, span; (*de agua*) spring; **a ojos vistas** visibly, openly; **costar un ojo de la cara** to cost a mint, cost a fortune; **dar los ojos de la cara por** to give one's eyeteeth for; **hasta los ojos** up to one's ears; **mirar con ojos de carnero degollado** to make sheep's eyes at; **no pegar el ojo** to not sleep a wink; **ojo de buey** (archit, meteor, naut) bull's-eye; (bot) oxeye; **ojo de la cerradura** keyhole; **poner los ojos en blanco** to roll one's eyes; **saltar a los ojos** to be self-evident; **valer un ojo de la cara** to be worth a mint || *interj* beware!; look out!; attention!; **¡mucho ojo!** be careful!, watch out!; **¡ojo con . . . !** look out for . . . !; **¡ojo, mancha!** fresh paint!
ojota *f* (SAm) sandal; (SAm) tanned llama hide
ola *f* wave; (*de gente apiñada*) surge
ole *m* or **olé** *m* bravo || *interj* bravo!
oleada *f* big wave; (*de gente apiñada*) surge, swell
oleaje *m* surge, rush of waves
óleo *m* oil; holy oil; oil painting; **los santos óleos** extreme unction
oleoducto *m* pipe line
oler **§49** *tr* to smell; pry into; sniff out || *intr* to smell, smell fragrant, smell bad; **no oler bien** to look suspicious; **oler a** to smell of, smell like; smack of
olfatear *tr* to smell, scent, sniff; (*p.ej., un buen negocio*) scent, sniff out
olfato *m* smell, sense of smell; scent; keen insight
olíbano *m* frankincense
oliente *adj* smelling, odorous
oligarquía *f* oligarchy
Olimpíada *f* Olympiad
olímpi•co -ca *adj* Olympian; Olympic; haughty
oliscar **§73** *tr* to smell, scent, sniff; investigate || *intr* to smell bad
oliva *f* olive; olive tree; barn owl; olive branch, peace
olivar *m* olive grove
olivillo *m* mock privet
olivo *m* olive tree; **tomar el olivo** (taur) to duck behind the barrier; beat it
olmeda *f* or **olmedo** *m* elm grove
olmo *m* elm tree
olor *m* odor; promise, hope; trace, suspicion; **olores** (Chile, Mex) spice, condiment
oloro•so -sa *adj* odorous, fragrant
olote *m* (CAm & Mex) cob, corncob
olvidadi•zo -za *adj* forgetful; ungrateful
olvida•do -da *adj* forgetful; ungrateful
olvidar *tr & intr* to forget; **olvidar** + *inf* to forget to + *inf* || *ref* to forget oneself; **olvidarse de** to forget; **olvidarse de** + *inf* to forget to + *inf;* **olvidársele a uno** to forget, e.g., **se me olvidó mi pasaporte** I forgot my passport; **olvidársele a uno** + *inf* to forget to + *inf,* e.g., **se me olvidó cerrar la ventana** I forgot to close the window
olvido *m* forgetfulness; oblivion
olla *f* pot, kettle; stew; eddy, whirlpool; **olla a** or **de presión** pressure cooker
ollería *f* potter's shop
ollero *m* potter
ombligo *m* navel; (*centro, punto medio*) (fig) navel
omino•so -sa *adj* ominous
omisión *f* omission; oversight, neglect
omi•so -sa *adj* neglectful, remiss
omitir *tr* to omit; overlook, neglect
ómni•bus *adj* (*tren*) accommodation || *m* (*pl* **-bus**) bus, omnibus; **ómnibus de dos pisos** double-decker
omnímo•do -da *adj* all-inclusive
omnipotente *adj* omnipotent
omnisciente or **omnis•cio -cia** *adj* omniscient
omnívo•ro -ra *adj* omnivorous
omóplato *m* shoulder blade

once *adj & pron* eleven; **las once** eleven o'clock || *m* eleven; (*en las fechas*) eleventh
oncea•vo -va *adj & m* eleventh
once•no -na *adj & mf* eleventh
oncología *f* oncology
onda *f* wave; flicker; (*en el pelo*) wave; **onda portadora** (rad) carrier wave; **ondas entretenidas** (rad) continuous waves
ondear *tr* (*en el pelo*) to wave || *intr* to wave; ripple; flow; flicker; be wavy || *ref* to wave, sway, swing
ondo•so -sa *adj* wavy
ondulación *f* undulation; wave; wave motion
ondula•do -da *adj* wavy, ripply; rolling; corrugated || *m* (*en el pelo*) wave
ondular *tr* (*el pelo*) to wave || *intr* to undulate; (*una bandera*) wave, flutter; (*las ondas del mar*) billow; (*una culebra*) wriggle
onero•so -sa *adj* onerous, burdensome
ónice *m* or **ónique** *m* or **ónix** *m* onyx
onomásti•co -ca *adj* of proper names || *m* name day || *f* study of proper names
onomatopéyi•co -ca *adj* onomatopoeic
ONU *f* UN
onza *f* ounce; (zool) snow leopard
onza•vo -va *adj & m* eleventh
opa•co -ca *adj* opaque; sad, gloomy
ópalo *m* opal
opción *f* option, choice; **opción nula** or **opción cero** zero option
ópera *f* opera; **ópera semiseria** light opera; **ópera seria** grand opera
operación *f* operation; transaction; **operaciones** (*ordenador*) software
operar *tr* to operate on || *intr* to operate; work || *ref* to occur, come about; be operated on
opera•rio -ria *mf* worker || *m* workman || *f* working woman
opereta *f* operetta
operista *mf* opera singer
operísti•co -ca *adj* operatic
opia•to -ta *adj m & f* opiate
opinable *adj* moot
opinar *intr* to opine; think; pass judgment
opinión *f* opinion, view; reputation, public image
opio *m* opium
opípa•ro -ra *adj* sumptuous, lavish
oponer §54 *tr* to oppose; (*resistencia*) to offer, put up || *ref* to oppose each other; face each other; **oponerse a** to oppose, be opposed to; be against, resist; compete for
oporto *m* port, port wine
oportunidad *f* opportunity; opportuneness; **oportunidades** *fpl* witticisms
oportunista *adj* opportunistic || *mf* opportunist
oportu•no -na *adj* opportune, timely; proper; witty
oposición *f* opposition; competitive examination
oposi•tor -tora *adj* rivaling, competing || *mf* opponent; competitor
opresión *f* oppression
opresi•vo -va *adj* oppressive
opre•sor -sora *adj* oppressive || *mf* oppressor
oprimir *tr* to oppress; squeeze, press
oprobiar *tr* to defame, revile
oprobio *m* opprobrium
oprobio•so -sa *adj* opprobrious
optar *tr* to enter; assume || *intr* — **optar entre** to choose between; **optar por** to choose to
ópti•co -ca *adj* optical || *mf* optician || *f* optics
óptimamente *adv* to perfection
óptimismo *m* optimism
optimista *adj* optimistic || *mf* optimist
ópti•mo -ma *adj* fine, excellent
optometrista *mf* optometrist
opues•to -ta *adj* opposite, contrary
opugnar *tr* to attack; lay siege to; contradict
opulen•to -ta *adj* opulent
opúsculo *m* short work, opuscule
oquedad *f* hollow; hollowness
ora *conj* — **ora . . . ora** now . . . now, now . . . then
oración *f* oration, speech; prayer; sentence; **oración dominical** Lord's prayer; **ponerse en oración** to get down on one's knees
oráculo *m* oracle
ora•dor -dora *mf* orator, speaker; **orador de plazuela** soapbox orator; **orador de sobremesa** after-dinner speaker
oraje *m* rough weather, storm
oral *adj* oral
orangután *m* orang-outang
orar *intr* to pray; make a speech
orato•rio -ria *adj* oratorical || *m* oratorio; (*capilla privada*) oratory || *f* (*arte de la elocuencia*) oratory
orbe *m* orb; world
órbita *f* orbit
orca *f* killer whale
Órcadas *fpl* Orkney Islands
órdago — **de órdago** (coll) swell, real
orden *m & f* order; **hasta nueva orden** until further notice; **orden** *f* **de allanamiento** search warrant; **orden** *m* **de colocación** word order; **orden de pago** money order
ordenador *m* computer; **ordenador de viaje** on-board computer
ordenancista *adj* strict, severe || *mf* taskmaster, disciplinarian, martinet
ordenanza *m* errand boy; (mil) orderly || *f* ordinance; order, system; command; **ser de ordenanza** to be the rule
ordenar *tr* to order; put in order; ordain || *ref* to be ordained, take orders
ordeñadero *m* milk pail
ordeñar *tr* to milk
ordeño *m* milking
ordinal *adj* orderly; ordinal || *m* ordinal
ordinariez *f* coarseness, crudeness
ordina•rio -ria *adj* ordinary || *m* daily household expenses; delivery man
orear *tr* to air || *ref* to be aired; dry in the air; take an airing
orégano *m* pot or wild marjoram, winter sweet

oreja *f* ear; (*del zapato*) flap; (*de martillo*) claw; lug, flange, **aguzar las orejas** to prick up one's ears; **con las orejas caídas** crestfallen; **con las orejas tan largas** all ears; **descubrir** or **enseñar las orejas** to give oneself away

oreja•no -na *adj* (*res*) unbranded; (*animal*) skittish; shy; cautious

orejera *f* earflap, earmuff

orejeta *f* lug

ore•jón -jona *adj* coarse, uncouth; (Mex) skinny || *m* strip of dried peach; pull on the ear; (*de la hoja de un libro*) dog's-ear

oreju•do -da *adj* big-eared

oreo *m* breeze

orfanato *m* orphanage

orfandad *f* orphanage, orphanhood

orfebre *m* goldsmith; silversmith

orfelinato *m* (SAm) orphanage

Orfeo *m* Orpheus

orfeón *m* glee club, choral society

organ•dí *m* (*pl* **-díes**) organdy

orgáni•co -ca *adj* organic

organillero -ra *mf* organ-grinder

organillo *m* barrel organ, hand organ, hurdy-gurdy

organismo *m* organism; organization

organista *mf* organist

organización *f* organization; **Organización de las Naciones Unidas (ONU)** United Nations (UN); **Organización de los Estados Americanos (OEA)** Organization of American States (OAS); **Organización del Tratado del Sudeste Asiático (O.T.A.S.E.)** Southwest Asia Treaty Organization (SEATO); **Organización para el Tratado del Atlántico Norte (O.T.A.N.)** North Atlantic Treaty Organization (NATO)

organizar §60 *tr* to organize

órgano *m* organ; (*de una máquina*) part; (*medio, conducto*) organ; (mus) organ

orgasmo *m* orgasm

orgía *f* orgy

orgiásti•co -ca *adj* orgiastic

orgullo *m* haughtiness; pride

orgullo•so -sa *adj* haughty; proud

oriental *adj* eastern; oriental

orientar *tr* to orient; guide, direct; (*una vela*) trim || *ref* to orient oneself; find one's bearings

oriente *m* east; source, origin; east wind; youth || **Oriente** *m* Orient; **el Cercano Oriente** the Near East; **el Extremo Oriente** the Far East; **el Lejano Oriente** the Far East; **el Oriente Medio** the Middle East; **el Próximo Oriente** the Near East; **gran oriente** (*logia masónica central*) grand lodge

orificar §73 *tr* to fill with gold

orífice *m* goldsmith

orificio *m* orifice, aperture, hole

origen *m* origin; source

original *adj* original; strange, odd, quaint || *m* original; character; **de buen original** on good authority; **original de imprenta** copy

originar *tr & ref* to originate, start

orilla *f* border, edge; margin; bank, shore; sidewalk; breeze; **orillas** (Arg, Mex) outskirts; **salir a la orilla** to manage to get through

orillar *tr* to put a border or edge on; trim || *intr* to come up to the shore

orillo *m* selvage, list

orín *m* rust; **orines** urine; **tomarse de orines** to get rusty

orina *f* urine

orinal *m* chamber pot

orinar *tr* to pass, urinate || *intr & ref* to urinate

oriun•do -da *adj & mf* native; **ser oriundo de** to come from, hail from

orla *f* border, edge; trimming, fringe

orlar *tr* to border, put an edge on; trim, trim with a fringe

orn. *abbr* **orden**

ornamentar *tr* to ornament, adorn

ornamento *m* ornament, adornment

ornar *tr* to adorn

ornato *m* adornment, show

oro *m* gold; playing card (*representing a gold coin*) equivalent to diamond; **de oro y azul** all dressed up; **oro batido** gold leaf; **oro de ley** standard gold; **poner de oro y azul** to rake over the coals; **ponerle colores al oro** to gild the lily

oron•do -da *adj* big-bellied; hollow, spongy, puffed up; pompous, self-satisfied

oropel *m* tinsel; **gastar mucho oropel** to put up a big front

oropéndola *f* golden oriole

orozuz *m* licorice

orquesta *f* orchestra; **orquesta típica** regional orchestra

orquestar *tr* to orchestrate

órquide *f* or **orquídea** *f* orchid

ortiga *f* nettle; **ser como unas ortigas** to be a grouch

orto *m* rise (*of sun or star*)

ortodoncia *f* orthodontics; **aparato de ortodoncia** orthodontic appliance, braces

ortodo•xo -xa *adj* orthodox

ortografía *f* orthography; spelling

ortografiar §77 *tr & intr* to spell

oruga *f* caterpillar

orujo *m* bagasse of grapes or olives

orzuelo *m* sty

os *pron pers & reflex* (used as object of verb and corresponding to **vos** and **vosotros**) you, to you; yourself, to yourself; yourselves, to yourselves; each other, to each other

osa *f* she-bear; **Osa mayor** Great Bear; **Osa menor** Little Bear

osadía *f* boldness, daring

osa•do -da *adj* bold, daring

osamenta *f* skeleton; bones

osar *intr* to dare

osario *m* ossuary, charnel house

oscilar *intr* to oscillate; fluctuate; waver, hesitate

ósculo *m* kiss

oscurecer §22 *tr, intr & ref* var of **obscurecer**

oscuridad *f* var of **obscuridad**
oscu•ro -ra *adj & m* var of **obscuro**
osera *f* bear's den
osificar §73 *tr & ref* to ossify
oso *m* bear; **hacer el oso** to make a fool of oneself; to make love in the open; **oso blanco** polar bear; **oso hormiguero** ant bear; anteater; **oso lavador** raccoon
ostensorio *m* (eccl) monstrance
ostentar *tr* to show; make a show of || *ref* to show off; boast
ostentati•vo -va *adj* ostentatious
ostento *m* portent, prodigy
ostento•so -sa *adj* magnificent, showy
osteópata *mf* osteopath
osteopatía *f* osteopathy
ostión *m* large oyster
ostra *f* oyster; **ostras en su concha** oyster cocktail, oysters on the half shell
ostracismo *m* ostracism
ostral *m* oyster bed, oyster farm
ostrería *f* oysterhouse
ostre•ro -ra *adj* oyster || *m* oysterman; oyster bed, oyster farm
osu•do -da *adj* bony
osu•no -na *adj* bearish, bearlike
O.T.A.N., la NATO
O.T.A.S.E., la SEATO
otate *m* Mexican giant grass (*Guadua amplexifolia*); otate stick
otero *m* hillock, knoll
otomán *m* ottoman
otoma•no -na *adj & mf* Ottoman || *f* ottoman
otoñal *adj* autumnal
otoño *m* autumn, fall
otorgar §44 *tr* to agree to; grant, confer; (law) to execute
o•tro -tra *adj indef* other, another || *pron indef* other one, another one; **como dijo el otro** as someone said
ovación *f* ovation
ovacionar *tr* to give an ovation to
oval *adj* oval
óvalo *m* oval
ovante *adj* victorious, triumphant
ovario *m* ovary
oveja *f* ewe, female sheep; **oveja negra** (fig) black sheep; **oveja perdida** (fig) lost sheep
oveje•ro -ra *adj* sheep || *mf* sheep raiser
oveju•no -na *adj* sheep, of sheep
ove•ro -ra *adj* blossom-colored; egg-colored
overol *m* overall
Ovidio *m* Ovid
ovillar *tr* to wind up; sum up || *intr* to form into a ball || *ref* to curl up into a ball
ovillo *m* ball of yarn; ball, heap; tangled ball; **hacerse un ovillo** to cower, recoil; (*hablando*) get all tangled up
ovni *m* UFO
óvulo *m* ovule; ovum
oxear *tr & intr* to shoo
oxiacanta *f* hawthorn
oxidación *f* oxidation
oxidar *tr* to oxidize || *ref* to oxidize; get rusty
óxido *m* oxide; **óxido de carbono** carbon monoxide; **óxido de mercurio** mercuric oxide
oxígeno *m* oxygen
oxíto•no -na *adj* oxytone
oxte *interj* get out!, beat it!, **sin decir oxte ni moxte** without opening one's mouth
oyente *mf* hearer; (*a la radio*) listener; (*en la escuela*) auditor
ozono *m* ozone

P

P, p (pe) *f* nineteenth letter of the Spanish alphabet
P. *abbr* **Padre, Papa, Pregunta**
pabellón *m* pavilion; bell tent; flag, banner; (*de fusiles*) stack; canopy; summerhouse; (*de instrumento de viento*) bell
pabilo or **pábilo** *m* wick
Pablo *m* Paul
pábulo *m* food; support, encouragement, fuel
pacana *f* pecan
paca•to -ta *adj* mild, gentle
pacer §22 *tr* to pasture, graze; gnaw, eat away || *intr* to pasture, graze
paciencia *f* patience
paciente *adj & mf* patient
pacienzu•do -da *adj* long-suffering
pacificar §73 *tr* to pacify || *intr* to sue for peace || *ref* to calm down
pacífi•co -ca *adj* pacific
pacifismo *m* pacifism
pacifista *adj & mf* pacifist
pa•co -ca *adj* (Chile) bay, reddish || *m* paco, alpaca; Moorish sniper; sniper || **Paco** *m* Frank
pacotilla *f* trash, junk; (Chile) rabble, mob; **hacer su pacotilla** to make a cleanup; **ser de pacotilla** to be shoddy, be poorly made
pacotille•ro -ra *mf* (Chile, Ven) peddler
pactar *tr* to agree upon || *intr* to come to an agreement
pacto *m* pact, covenant
pacha•cho -cha *adj* (Chile) short-legged; (Chile) lax, lazy; (Chile) chubby
pa•chón -chona *adj* (CAm) shaggy, hairy, wooly || *m* (*perro*) pointer; (*hombre flemático*) sluggard
pachorra *f* sluggishness, indolence
pachotada *f* silliness
padecer §22 *tr* to suffer; be victim of || *intr* to suffer
padrastro *m* stepfather; hangnail

padre *adj* huge; (Peru) terrific || *m* father; stallion, sire; **padres** parents; ancestors; **tener el padre alcalde** to have pull, have a friend at court

padrina *f* godmother

padrinazgo *m* godfathership; sponsorship, patronage

padrino *m* godfather; sponsor; (*en un desafío*) second; **padrino de boda** best man; **padrinos** godparents

padrón *m* poll, census; pattern, model; memorial column; indulgent father; stallion; (Col) stock bull

padrote *m* stock animal; (Mex) pimp, procurer

paella *f* saffron-flavored stew of chicken, seafood, and rice with vegetables

paf *interj* bang!

pág. *abbr* **página**

paga *f* pay, payment; wages; fine; **como paga y señal** on account; as down payment

paga-alquiler *f* rent, rent money

pagadero -ra *adj* payable

paga•do -da *adj* pleased, cheerful; **estamos pagados** we are quits; **pagado de sí mismo** self-satisfied, conceited

paga•dor -dora *adj* paying || *mf* payer || *m* paymaster

paganismo *m* paganism

paga•no -na *adj & mf* pagan || *m* easy mark

pagar §44 *tr* to pay; pay for; (*una bondad, una visita*) return || *intr* to pay || *ref* to become fond; be flattered; boast; be satisfied

pagaré *m* promissory note, I.O.U.

página *f* page

paginar *tr* to page

pago *m* payment; (*de viñas u olivares*) district, region

pagote *m* easy mark

paila *f* large pan

pairar *intr* (naut) to lie to

país *m* country, land; landscape; **el país de Gales** Wales; **los Países Bajos** (*Bélgica, Holanda y Luxemburgo*) the Low Countries; (*Holanda*) The Netherlands; **países no alineados** nonaligned nations; Third World countries

paisaje *m* landscape

paisajista *mf* landscape painter

paisa•no -na *adj* of the same country || *mf* peasant; civilian; (Mex) Spaniard || *m* fellow countryman; **de paisano** in civies

paja *f* straw; chaff; trash, rubbish; **no dormirse en las pajas** to not let the grass grow under one's feet; **no levantar paja del suelo** to not lift a hand, not do a stroke of work

pájara *f* paper kite; paper rooster; bird; crafty female

pajarera *f* aviary; large bird cage

pajarería *f* flock of birds; bird store; pet shop

pajare•ro -ra *adj* bright, cheerful; bright-colored, gaudy || *m* bird dealer; bird fancier || *f* see **pajarera**

pajarita *f* paper kite; bow tie; wing collar, piccadilly

pájaro *m* bird; crafty fellow; expert; **pájaro bobo** penguin; motmot; **pájaro carpintero** woodpecker; **pájaro de cuenta** big shot; **pájaro mosca** hummingbird

pajarota *f* or **pajarotada** *f* hoax, canard

paje *m* page; valet; dressing table; (naut) cabin boy

pajilla *f* cornhusk cigarette; **pajilla de madera** excelsior

paji•zo -za *adj* straw; straw-colored; straw-thatched

pajuela *f* short straw; sulfur match or fuse; toothpick; (Bol) match

Pakistán, el var of **Paquistán**

pakista•ní (*pl* **-níes**) *adj & mf* var of **paquistaní**

pala *f* shovel; (*de remo, de la azada, etc.*) blade; (*del panadero*) peel; scoop; racket; (*del calzado*) upper; (*de excavadora*) bucket; shoulder strap; (coll) cunning, craftiness

palabra *f* word; speech; (*de una canción*) words; (*derecho para hablar en asambleas*) floor; **palabras mayores** words, angry words; **remojar la palabra** to wet one's whistle; **usar de la palabra** to speak, make a speech

palabre•ro -ra *adj* wordy, windy || *mf* windbag

palabrota *f* vulgarity, obscenity

palabru•do -da *adj* talkative; chattering

palacie•go -ga *adj* palace, court || *m* courtier

palacio *m* palace; mansion; **palacio municipal** city hall

palada *f* shovelful; (*de remo*) stroke

paladar *m* palate; taste; gourmet

paladear *tr* to taste, relish

paladín *m* champion, hero

palafrén *m* palfrey

palanca *f* lever; pole; crowbar; **palanca de mando** (aer) control stick; **palanca de mayúsculas** shift key

palancada *f* leverage

palangana *f* washbowl, basin

palanganear *intr* to brag, give oneself airs

palanganero *m* washstand

palangre *m* trawl, trawl line

palanqueta *f* jimmy; **palanquetas** (Arg) dumbbell

palatal *adj & f* palatal

palco *m* (theat) box

palear *tr* to beat, pound; shovel

palenque *m* paling, palisade; (SAm) hitching post; (C-R) Indian ranch; (Chile) pandemonium

paleta *f* palette; small shovel; trowel; (*de una rueda*) paddle; blade, bucket, vane; shoulder blade; (*dulce con un palito que sirve de mango*) lollipop

paletilla *f* shoulder blade

paleto *m* fallow deer; rustic, yokel

palia *f* altar cloth; (eccl) pall

paliacate *m* (Mex) bandanna

paliar §77 & regular *tr* to palliate

palidecer §22 *intr* to pale, to turn pale

palidez *f* paleness, pallor

páli•do -da *adj* pale, pallid

palillo *m* toothpick; drumstick; bobbin; **palillos** chopsticks; castanets; rudiments; trifles
palinodia *f* backdown; **cantar la palinodia** to eat crow, eat humble pie
palique *m* chit-chat, small talk
paliquear *intr* to chat, to gossip
paliza *f* beating, thrashing
palizada *f* fenced-in enclosure; stockade; embankment
palma *f* (*de la mano*) palm; (*árbol y hoja*) palm; **batir palmas** to clap, to applaud; **llevarse la palma** to carry off the palm
palmada *f* slap; hand, applause, clapping; **dar palmadas** to clap hands
palma•rio -ria *adj* clear, evident
palmatoria *f* candlestick
palmera *f* date palm
palmito *m* palmetto; woman's face; slender figure
palmo *m* span, palm; **dejar con un palmo de narices** to disappoint
palmotear *tr* to pat; clap, applaud || *intr* to clap, applaud
palo *m* stick; pole; staff; handle; tree; (*golpe*) whack; (*madera*) wood; (*grupo de naipes de la baraja*) suit; (naut) mast; **dar palos de ciego** to lay about, swing wildly; **de tal palo tal astilla** like father like son; **palo de escoba** broomstick; **palo en alto** (fig) big stick; **palo mayor** (naut) mainmast; **servir del palo** to follow suit
paloma *f* pigeon, dove; prostitute; (fig) dove, meek person; **paloma mensajera** carrier pigeon; **palomas** whitecaps
palomar *m* pigeon house, dovecot
palomilla *f* doveling; small butterfly; white horse; (*del caballo*) back; pillow block, journal bearing; (CAm, Mex) rabble, scum; **palomillas** whitecaps
palomita *f* doveling; (baseball) fly; **palomitas** popcorn
palpable *adj* palpable
palpar *tr* to touch, feel; grope through || *intr* to grope
palpitante *adj* throbbing; thrilling; (*cuestión*) burning
palpitar *intr* to palpitate, throb; (*un afecto*) flash, break forth
pálpito *m* (SAm) hunch
palta *f* (SAm) alligator pear, avocado (*fruit*)
palto *m* (SAm) alligator pear, avocado (*tree*)
palúdi•co -ca *adj* marshy; malarial
paludismo *m* malaria
palur•do -da *adj* rustic, boorish || *mf* rustic, boor
pallador *m* (SAm) Gaucho minstrel
pampa *f* pampa; **La Pampa** the Pampas
pámpana *f* vine leaf
pámpano *m* tendril; vine leaf
pan *m* bread; loaf; loaf of bread; wheat; food; livelihood; pie dough; (*de jabón, cera, etc.*) cake; gold foil or leaf; silver foil or leaf; **como el pan bendito** as easy as pie; **de pan llevar** arable, tillable; **llamar al pan pan y al vino vino** to call a spade a spade; **panes** grain, breadstuff; **venderse como pan bendito** to sell like hot cakes || **Pan** *m* Pan
pana *f* corduroy; (aut) breakdown
panacea *f* panacea
panadería *f* bakery; baking business
panade•ro -ra *mf* baker; (Chile) flatterer
panadizo *m* felon; sickly person
panal *m* honeycomb
pana•má *m* (*pl* **-maes**) Panama hat
paname•ño -ña *adj* & *mf* Panamanian
panamerica•no -na *adj* Pan-American
pancarta *f* placard, poster
pancista *adj* weaseling || *mf* weaseler
páncre•as *m* (*pl* **-as**) pancreas
pancho *m* paunch, belly
pandear *intr* & *ref* to warp, bulge, buckle, sag, bend
pandereta *f* tambourine
pandilla *f* party, faction; gang, band; picnic, excursion
pan•do -da *adj* bulging; slow-moving; slow, deliberate
pandorga *f* kite; fat, lazy woman
panecillo *m* roll, crescent
panfleto *m* pamphlet
paniaguado *m* servant, minion; protégé, favorite
páni•co -ca *adj* panic, panicky || *m* panic
panizo *m* Italian millet; (Chile) gangue; (Chile) abundance
panocha *f* ear of grain; ear of corn; pancake made of corn and cheese; (Mex) panocha (*brown sugar*)
panoja *f* ear of grain; ear of corn
panorama *m* panorama
pano•so -sa *adj* mealy
panqué *m* or **panqueque** *m* pancake
pantalán *m* pier, wooden pier
pantalón *m* trousers; **calzarse los pantalones** to wear the pants; **pantalones** trousers, pants; **pantalones azules** (CAm) blue jeans; **pantalones de mezclilla** (C-R, Mex) blue jeans
pantalla *f* lamp shade; fire screen; motion-picture screen; television screen; (*persona que encubre a otra*) blind; (*cine, arte del cine*) screen; fan; **llevar a la pantalla** to put on the screen; **pantalla acústica** loudspeaker; **pantalla de plata** silver screen; **pequeña pantalla** television screen; **servir de pantalla a** to be a blind for
pantano *m* bog, marsh, swamp; dam, reservoir; trouble, obstacle
pantano•so -sa *adj* marshy, swampy; muddy; knotty, difficult
panteísmo *m* pantheism
panteón *m* pantheon; cemetery
pantera *f* panther
pantomima *f* pantomime
pantoque *m* (naut) bilge
pantorrilla *f* calf (*of leg*)
pantufla *f* or **pantuflo** *m* house slipper
panty *m* panty hose
panza *f* paunch, belly
panzu•do -da *adj* paunchy, big-bellied
pañal *m* diaper; shirttail; **pañales** swaddling clothes; infancy; early stages

pañe•ro -ra *adj* dry-goods, cloth || *mf* dry-goods dealer, clothier
paño *m* cloth; rag; (*de agujas*) paper; (*ancho de la tela*) breadth; (*mancha en el rostro*) spot; (*en, p.ej., un espejo*) blur; sailcloth, canvas; **al paño** off-stage; **conocer el paño** to know one's business, to know the ropes; **paño de adorno** doily; **paño de cocina** washrag, dishcloth; **paño de lágrimas** helping hand, stand-by; **paño de mesa** tablecloth; **paño de tumba** crape; **paño mortuorio** pall; **paños menores** underclothing; **paños tibios** appeasement attempts
pañuelo *m* handkerchief; shawl; **pañuelo de hierbas** bandanna
papa *m* pope || *f* potato; fake, hoax; food, grub; snap, cinch; **ni papa** nothing
pa•pá *m* (*pl* **-pás**) papa, daddy
papada *f* double chin; (*de animal*) dewlap; (Guat) stupidity
papado *m* papacy
papagayo *m* parrot
papalina *f* sunbonnet; drunk
papana•tas *m* (*pl* **-tas**) simpleton, gawk
paparrucha *f* hoax; trifle
papel *m* paper; piece of paper; rôle, part; character, figure; **desempeñar** or **hacer un papel** to play a rôle; **papel alquitranado** tar paper; **papel cebolla** onionskin; **papel de empapelar** wallpaper; **papel de esmeril** emery paper; **papel de estaño** tin foil; **papel de excusado** toilet paper; **papel de fumar** cigarette paper; **papel de lija** sandpaper; **papel de oficio** foolscap; **papel de seda** tissue paper; **papel de segundón** (fig) second fiddle; **papel de tornasol** litmus paper; **papel filtrante** filter paper; **papel higiénico** toilet paper; **papel moneda** paper money; **papel pintado** wallpaper; **papel secante** blotting paper; **papel viejo** waste paper; **papel volante** handbill, printed leaflet
papelada *f* farce; ridiculous act
papeleo *m* red tape
papelera *f* paper case; writing desk; wastebasket; paper factory
papelería *f* stationery store; mess of papers, litter
papelerío *m* paper work
papele•ro -ra *adj* paper; boastful, showy || *mf* stationer; paper manufacturer; (Mex) paperboy || *f* see **papelera**
papeleta *f* slip of paper; card, file card; ticket; **papeleta de empeño** pawn ticket
papelista *m* paper maker, paper manufacturer; stationer; paper hanger
pape•lón -lona *adj* bluffing, four-flushing || *mf* bluffer, four-flusher || *m* thin cardboard
papelonear *intr* to bluff, to four-flush
papelote *m* worthless piece of paper; paper kite
papel-prensa *m* newsprint
papera *f* goiter; mumps
papilla *f* pap; guile, deceit
papiro *m* papyrus
papirote *m* fillip, flick; nincompoop
paq. *abbr* **paquete**
paquear *tr* to snipe at || *intr* to snipe
paque•te -ta *adj* self-important, pompous; (Arg) chic, dolled-up || *m* package, parcel, bundle, bale; sport, dandy; **darse paquete** (Guat, Mex) to put on airs; **en paquete aparte** under separate cover, in a separate package; **paquetes postales** parcel post
Paquistán, el Pakistan
paquista•ní (*pl* **-níes**) or **paquistano -na** *adj* & *mf* Pakistani
Paquita *f* Fanny
par *adj* like, similar, equal; (math) even || *m* pair, couple; peer; (elec, mech) couple; (math) even number; **a pares** in twos; **de par en par** wide-open; completely; overtly; **¿pares o nones?** odd or even? || *f* par; **a la par** equally; jointly; at the same time; at par; **bajo la par** below par, under par; **sobre la par** above par
para *prep* to, for; towards; compared to; (*antes de*) by; **para** + *inf* in order to + *inf;* **para con** towards; **para que** in order that, so that
parabién *m* congratulation
parábola *f* parable
parabri•sa *m* or **parabri•sas** *m* (*pl* **-sas**) windshield
paracaí•das *m* (*pl* **-das**) parachute; **lanzarse en paracaídas** to parachute; **salvarse en paracaídas** to parachute to safety
paracaidismo *m* parachute jumping; (sport) sky diving
paracaidista *mf* parachutist || *m* paratrooper
parachis•pas *m* (*pl* **-pas**) spark arrester
paracho•ques *m* (*pl* **-ques**) bumper
parachutar *intr* to parachute
parada *f* stop; end; stay; shutdown; (*en el juego*) stake; dam; (*para el ganado*) stall; stud farm; (*en la esgrima*) parry; (*tiro de caballerías de reemplazo*) relay; (mil) parade, dress parade, review; **parada de taxi** taxi stand
paradero *m* end; whereabouts; stopping place; wayside station
para•do -da *adj* slow, spiritless, witless; idle, unemployed; closed; proud, stiff; **quedar bien parado** to be lucky; **quedar mal parado** to be unlucky || *f* see **parada**
paradoja *f* paradox
paradóji•co -ca *adj* paradoxical
parador *m* inn, wayside inn; motel; **parador de carretera** drive-in restaurant
parafina *f* paraffin
paragol•pes *m* (*pl* **-pes**) buffer, bumper
para•guas *m* (*pl* **-guas**) umbrella
Paraguay, el Paraguay
paraguaya•no -na or **paragua•yo -ya** *adj* & *mf* Paraguayan
paragüero *m* umbrella man; umbrella stand
paraíso *m* paradise
paraje *m* place, spot; state, condition
paralela *f* parallel, parallel line; **paralelas** parallel bars
paralelizar §60 *tr* to parallel, compare
parale•lo -la *adj* parallel || *m* (geog) parallel || *f* see **paralela**

paráli•sis *f* (*pl* **-sis**) paralysis
paralíti•co -ca *adj & mf* paralytic
paralizar §60 *tr* to paralyze || *ref* to become paralyzed
parámetro *m* parameter; established boundary
páramo *m* high barren plain; bleak windy spot; (Bol, Col, Ecuad) cold drizzle
paranie•ves *m* (*pl* **-ves**) snow fence
paraninfo *m* assembly hall, auditorium
paranoi•co -ca *adj & mf* paranoiac
parapeto *m* parapet
paraplegia *f* paraplegia
parar *tr* to stop; check; change; prepare; put up, stake; parry; order; get, acquire; (*la atención*) fix; (*la caza*) point; (typ) to set || *intr* to stop; (*en un hotel*) put up; **parar en** to become; run to, run as far as || *ref* to stop; stop work; stand; turn, become; (*el perro de muestra*) point; (*el pelo*) stand on end; **pararse en** to pay attention to
pararra•yo *m* or **pararra•yos** *m* (*pl* **-yos**) (*barra metálica que sirve para preservar los edificios del rayo*) lightning rod; (*dispositivo que sirve para preservar una instalación eléctrica de la electricidad atmosférica o de las chispas que produce*) lightning arrester
parasíti•co -ca *adj* parasitic
parási•to -ta *adj* parasitic; (elec) stray || *m* parasite; **parásitos atmosféricos** atmospherics, static
parasol *m* parasol
parato•pes *m* (*pl* **-pes**) bumper
Parcas *fpl* Fates
parcela *f* particle; plot of ground
parcelar *tr* to parcel, divide into lots
parcial *adj* partial; partisan || *mf* partisan
par•co -ca *adj* frugal, sparing; moderate
parcómetro *m* parking meter
parchar *tr* to mend, patch
parche *m* plaster, sticking plaster; patch; drum; drumhead; daub, botch, splotch; **parche poroso** porous plaster
pardal *m* linnet; sly fellow
pardiez *interj* by Jove!
pardillo *m* linnet
par•do -da *adj* brown, drab; dark; cloudy; (*voz*) dull, flat; (*cerveza*) dark; mulatto || *mf* mulatto || *m* brown, drab; leopard
pardus•co -ca *adj* dark-brown, drabbish
parea•do -da *adj* rhymed || *m* couplet
parear *tr* to pair; match || *ref* to pair off
parecer *m* opinion; look, mien, countenance || *v* §22 *intr* to appear; show up; look, seem; **me parece que. . . .** I think that. . . . || *ref* to look alike, resemble each other; **parecerse a** to look like
pareci•do -da *adj* like, similar; **bien parecido** good-looking; **parecido a** like, e.g., **esta casa es parecida a la otra** this house is like the other one; **parecidos** alike, e.g., **estas casas son parecidas** these houses are alike || *m* similarity, resemblance, likeness; **tener un gran parecido** to be a good likeness
pared *f* wall; **dejar pegado a la pared** to nonplus; **paredes** house
pareja *f* pair, couple; dancing partner; **correr parejas** or **a las parejas** to be abreast, arrive together; go together, match, be equal; **correr parejas con** to keep up with, keep abreast of; **parejas** (*de naipes*) pair
pareje•ro -ra *adj* even, equal; servile, fawning; forward, overfamiliar || *m* race horse
pare•jo -ja *adj* equal, like; even, smooth || *m* (CAm) dancing partner || *f* see **pareja**
parentela *f* kinsfolk, relations
parentesco *m* relationship; bond, tie
paréntе•sis *m* (*pl* **-sis**) parenthesis; break, interval
parhilera *f* ridgepole
paria *mf* pariah, outcast
paridad *f* par, parity; comparison
parien•te -ta *adj* related || *mf* relative; (coll) spouse
parihuela *f* handbarrow; (*camilla*) stretcher
parir *tr* to bear, give birth to, bring forth || *intr* to give birth; come forth, come to light; talk well
parisiense *adj & mf* Parisian
parking *m* parking (space)
parlamentar *intr* to talk, chat; parley
parlamento *m* parliament; parley; speech; (theat) speech
parlan•chín -china *adj* jabbering || *mf* chatterbox
parlante *m* loudspeaker
parlar *intr* to speak with facility; chatter, talk too much; (*el loro*) talk
parle•ro -ra *adj* loquacious, garrulous; gossipy; (*ave*) singing, song; (*ojos*) expressive; (*arroyo, fuente*) babbling
parlotear *intr* to prattle, jabber, chin
parloteo *m* jabber, prattle
parnaso *m* (*colección de poesías*) Parnassus; **el Parnaso** Parnassus, Mount Parnassus
paro *m* shutdown, work stoppage; lockout; titmouse; (*de dados*) (SAm) throw; **paro forzoso** layoff
parodia *f* parody, travesty
parodiar *tr* to parody, travesty, burlesque
parón *m* stop; delay
paroxíto•no -na *adj & m* paroxytone
parpadear *intr* to blink, wink; flicker
parpadeo *m* blinking, winking; flicker
párpado *m* eyelid
parque *m* park; parking; parking lot; **parque de atracciones** amusement park
parqué *m* floor, inlaid floor
parqueadero *m* (Col) parking lot
parquear *tr* to park
parquímetro *m* parking meter
parra *f* grapevine; earthen jug
párrafo *m* paragraph; chat
parral *m* grape arbor
parranda *f* spree, party; (Col) large number; **andar de parranda** to go out on a spree, go out to celebrate
parricida *mf* patricide, parricide
parricidio *m* patricide, parricide

parrilla *f* grill, gridiron, broiler; grate, grating; grillroom, grill; **asar a la parrilla** to broil
párroco *m* parish priest
parroquia *f* parish; parish church; customers, clientele
parroquial *adj* parochial
parroquia•no -na *mf* parishioner; customer
parte *m* dispatch, communiqué; **parte meteorológico** weather report || *f* part; share; party; side; direction; (*papel de un actor*) role; (law) party; **de un mes a esta parte** for about a month past; **en ninguna otra parte** nowhere else; **en ninguna parte** nowhere; **ir a la parte** to go shares; **la mayor parte** most, the majority; **parte del león** lion's share; **parte de por medio** (theat) bit part, walk-on; **partes** parts, gifts, talent; faction; parts, genitals; **por otra parte** in another direction; elsewhere; on the other hand; **por todas partes** everywhere; **salva sea la parte** excuse me for not mentioning where
partea•guas *m* (*pl* **-guas**) divide, ridge
partear *tr* to deliver
parte•luz *m* (*pl* **-luces**) mullion, sash bar
Partenón *m* Parthenon
partera *f* midwife
partición *f* partition, division
participar *tr* to notify, inform; give notice of || *intr* to participate; partake
participio *m* participle
partícula *f* particle
particular *adj* particular; peculiar; private, personal || *m* particular; matter, subject; individual; **particular a particular** (telp) person-to-person
particulizar **§60** *tr* to itemize || *ref* to stand out; specialize
partida *f* departure; entry, item; certificate; party, group, band; band of guerrillas; game; (*de cartas*) hand; (*de tenis*) set; lot, shipment; behavior; **mala partida** mean trick; **partida de campo** picnic; **partida doble** (com) double entry; **partida sencilla** (com) single entry
partida•rio -ria or **partidista** *adj & mf* partisan
parti•do -da *adj* generous, open-handed || *m* (pol) party; decision; profit; advantage; step, measure; deal, agreement; protection, support; (*casamiento que elegir*) match; district, county; (sport) team; (sport) game, match; **partido de desempate** play-off; **tomar partido** to take a stand, take sides || *f* see **partida**
partir *tr* to divide; distribute; share; split, split open; break, crack; upset, disconcert || *intr* to start, depart, leave, set out; **a partir de** beginning with || *ref* to become divided; crack, split
partisa•no -na *mf* (mil) partisan
partitura *f* (mus) score
parto *m* childbirth, confinement; newborn child; offspring; **estar de parto** to be in labor, be confined; **parto del ingenio** brain child
parva *f* light breakfast (*on fast days*); heap of unthreshed grain; heap, pile
parvulario *m* nursery school; kindergarten
parvulista *mf* kindergarten teacher
párvu•lo -la *adj* small, tiny; simple, innocent; humble || *mf* child, tot; (*niño*) kindergartner
pasa *f* raisin; (*del pelo de los negros*) kink; **pasa de Corinto** currant
pasada *f* passage; passing; **de pasada** in passing, hastily; **mala pasada** mean trick
pasade•ro -ra *adj* passable || *f* stepping stone; walkway, catwalk
pasadizo *m* passage, corridor, hallway, alley; catwalk
pasa•do -da *adj* past; gone by; overripe, spoiled; overdone; stale; burned out; antiquated; faded || *m* past; **pasados** ancestors || *f* see **pasada**
pasa•dor -dora *mf* smuggler || *m* door bolt; bolt, pin; hatpin; brooch; stickpin; safety pin; strainer
pasaje *m* passage; fare; fares; passengers; **cobrar el pasaje** to collect fares
pasaje•ro -ra *adj* passing, fleeting; (*camino, calle*) common, traveled || *mf* passenger; hotel guest; **pasajero colgado** straphanger; **pasajero no presentado** no-show
pasamano *m* lace trimming; (*baranda*) handrail; (naut) gangway
pasamonta•ña *m* or **pasamonta•ñas** *m* (*pl* **-ñas**) ski mask, storm hood
pasaporte *m* passport
pasapuré *m* potato masher
pasar *m* livelihood || *tr* to pass; cross; take across; send, transfer, transmit; (*contrabando*) slip in; spend; swallow; excel; overlook, stand for; undergo, suffer; (*un libro*) go through; (*una película*) show; dry in the sun; tutor; study with or under; **pasarlo** to get along; live; (*dícese de la salud*) be; **pasar por alto** to disregard; omit, leave out, skip || *intr* to pass; go; pass away; pass over; happen; last; spread; get along; yield; come in, e.g., **pase Vd.** come in; **pasar de** to go beyond, exceed; to go above; be more than; **pasar por** to pass by, down, through, over, etc.; pass as, pass for; stop or call at; **pasar sin** to do without || *ref* to pass; go; excel; pass over; get along; pass away; take an examination; leak; go too far; become overripe, become overcooked; rot; melt; burn out; (*una llave, un tornillo*) not fit, be loose; forget; **pasarse por** to stop or call at; **pasarse sin** to do without
pasarela *f* footbridge; catwalk, gangplank
pasatiempo *m* pastime
pascua *f* Passover; Easter; Twelfth-night; Pentecost; Christmas; **dar las pascuas** to wish a Happy New Year; **estar como una pascua** or **unas pascuas** (coll) to be bubbling over with joy; **¡Felices Pascuas!** Merry Christmas!; **Pascua de flores** Easter; **Pascua del Espíritu Santo** Pentecost; **Pascua de Navidad** Christmas; **Pascua de Resurrección** or **Pascua florida** Easter; **Pascuas navideñas** Christmas

pase *m* (*permiso; billete gratuito; movimiento de las manos del mesmerista, el torero*) pass; (*en la esgrima*) feint; **pase de cortesía** complimentary ticket

paseante *adj* strolling || *mf* stroller

pasear *tr* to walk; promenade, show off || *intr* to take a walk; go for a ride || *ref* to take a walk; go for a ride; wander, ramble; take it easy

paseíllo *m* processional entrance of bullfighters

paseo *m* walk, stroll, promenade; ride; drive; avenue; **dar un paseo** to take a walk; take a ride; **enviar a paseo** to send on his way, dismiss without ceremony; **paseo de caballos** bridle path; **paseo de la cuadrilla** processional entrance of the bullfighters

pasillo *m* short step; passage, corridor; (theat) short piece, sketch

pasión *f* passion

pasi•vo -va *adj* passive; (*pensión*) retirement || *m* liabilities; debit side

pasmar *tr* to chill; frostbite; stun, benumb; dumbfound, astound || *ref* to chill; become frostbitten; be astounded; get lockjaw; (*los colores*) become dull or flat

pasmo *m* cold; lockjaw, tetanus; astonishment; wonder, prodigy

pasmo•so -sa *adj* astounding; awesome

paso *m* step; pace; (*de la escalera*) step; gait; walk; passing; passage; step, measure, démarche; pass, permit; strait; footstep, footprint; incident, happening; (*de hélice, tornillo*) pitch; (elec) pitch; (rad) stage; (theat) short piece, sketch, skit; **al paso** in passing, on the way; **al paso que** at the rate that; (*a la vez que, mientras*) while, whereas; **ceder el paso** to make way; to keep clear; **de paso** in passing; at the same time; **paso a nivel** grade crossing; **paso de ganado** cattle crossing; **paso de ganso** goose step

paspa *f* (SAm) crack in the lips

pasquín *m* lampoon

pasquinar *tr* to lampoon

pasta *f* paste, dough, pie crust, soup paste; mash; (*para hacer papel*) pulp; cardboard; board binding; (*de un diente*) filling; (*dinero*) (coll) dough; **pasta dentrífica** toothpaste; **pasta española** marbled leather binding, tree calf; **pastas** noodles, macaroni, spaghetti, etc.; **pasta seca** cookie

pastar *tr & intr* to graze

pastel *m* pie; pastry roll; pastel; settlement, pacification; cheat, trick; (typ) pi; (typ) smear; (coll) plot, deal; **pastel de cumpleaños** birthday cake

pastelería *f* pastry; pastry shop

pastele•ro -ra *mf* pastry cook

pastelillo *m* tart, cake; (*de mantequilla*) pat

pasterizar **§60** *tr* to pasteurize

pastilla *f* tablet, lozenge, drop; (*pequeña masa pastosa*) dab; (*de jabón, chocolate, etc.*) cake

pasto *m* pasture; grass; food, nourishment; **a pasto** to excess; in abundance; **a todo pasto** freely, without restriction; **de pasto** ordinary, everyday

pastor *m* shepherd; pastor

pastora *f* shepherdess

pastoral *adj & f* pastoral

pastorear *tr* (*a las ovejas o los fieles*) to shepherd; lie in ambush for; spoil, pamper; (Arg, Urug) to court

pasto•so -sa *adj* pasty, doughy; (*voz*) mellow; (Arg, Chile) grassy

pastura *f* pasture; fodder

pasu•do -da *adj* kinky

pata *f* paw, foot, leg; (*de un mueble*) leg; duck; **a cuatro patas** on all fours; **estirar la pata** to kick the bucket; **meter la pata** to butt in, to put one's foot in it; **pata de gallo** crow's-foot; blunder; piece of nonsense; **pata de palo** peg leg, wooden leg; **pata galana** game leg; lame person; **patas arriba** on one's back, upside down; topsy-turvy

patada *f* kick; stamp, stamping; step; footstep, track; **en dos patadas** in a jiffy

patalear *intr* to kick; stamp the feet

pataleta *f* fit; feigned fit or convulsion; (dial) tantrum

patán *m* churl, boor, lout; peasant

pataplún *interj* kerplunk!

patata *f* potato

patear *tr* to kick; trample on || *intr* to stamp one's foot; bustle around; kick

patentar *tr* to patent

patente *adj* patent, clear, evident || *f* grant, privilege, warrant; patent; **de patente** (Chile) excellent, first-class; **patente de circulación** owner's license; **patente de invención** patent; **patente de sanidad** bill of health

paternal *adj* paternal, fatherly

paternidad *f* paternity, fatherhood; **paternidad literaria** authorship

pater•no -na *adj* paternal

pateta *m* (coll) the devil; cripple

patéti•co -ca *adj* pathetic

patetismo *m* pathos

patibula•rio -ria *adj* hair-raising

patíbulo *m* scaffold

patiesteva•do -da *adj* bowlegged

patilla *f* small paw or foot; pocket flap; watermelon; (naut) compass; **patillas** sideburns, side whiskers

patín *m* small patio; skate; skid, slide, runner; (*ave marina*) petrel; **patín de cuchilla** or **de hielo** ice skate; **patín de ruedas** roller skate

patinada *f* (SAm) (aut) skidding

patinadero *m* skating rink

patina•dor -dora *mf* skater

patinaje *m* skating; skidding; **patinaje artístico** figure skating; **patinaje de fantasía** fancy skating; **patinaje de figura** figure skating

patinar *intr* to skate; skid; slip

patinazo *m* skid; slip; slip, blunder

patinete *m* scooter

patio *m* patio, court, yard; campus; (rr) yard, switchyard; **patio de recreo** playground

patituer•to -ta *adj* crooked-legged; crooked, lopsided
patizam•bo -ba *adj* knock-kneed
pato *m* duck, drake; **pagar el pato** to be the goat; **pato de flojel** eider duck
patochada *f* blunder, stupidity
patojo *m* (CAm) street urchin
patología *f* pathology
patota *f* (Arg, Urug) teen-age gang
patraña *f* fake, humbug, hoax
patria *f* country; mother country, fatherland, native land; birthplace; (*p.ej., de las artes*) home; **patria chica** native heath
patriarca *m* patriarch
patri•cio -cia *adj & mf* patrician
patrimonio *m* patrimony
pa•trio -tria *adj* native, home; paternal || *f* see **patria**
patriota *mf* patriot
patrióti•co -ca *adj* patriotic
patriotismo *m* patriotism
patrocinar *tr* to sponsor, patronize
patrocinio *m* sponsorship
patrón *m* sponsor, protector; patron saint; patron; landlord; owner, master; boss, foreman; host; (*de un barco*) skipper; pattern; standard; **patrón oro** gold standard; **patrón picado** stencil
patrona *f* patroness; landlady; owner, mistress; hostess
patronal *adj* management, employers
patronato *m* employers' association; foundation; board of trustees; patronage
patronear *tr* to skipper
patro•no -na *mf* sponsor, protector; employer || *m* patron; landlord; boss, foreman; lord of the manor; **los patronos** the management || *f* see **patrona**
patrulla *f* patrol; gang, band
patrullar *tr & intr* to patrol
paulati•no -na *adj* slow, gradual
pausa *f* pause; slowness, delay; (mus) rest
pausa•do -da *adj* slow, calm, deliberate || **pausado** *adv* slowly, calmly
pausar *tr & intr* to slow down
pauta *f* ruler; guide lines; guideline, rule, guide, standard, model
pava *f* turkey hen; **pelar la pava** to make love at a window
pavesa *f* ember, cinder, spark
pavimentar *tr* to pave
pavimento *m* pavement
pa•vo -va *adj* (coll) silly, stupid || *m* turkey; turkey cock; **comer pavo** to be a wallflower; **pavo real** peacock
pavón *m* bluing; peacock
pavonar *tr* to blue
pavonear *intr & ref* to strut, swagger
pavor *m* fear, terror, dread
pavoro•so -sa *adj* frightful, dreadful
payador *m* (SAm) gaucho minstrel
payasada *f* clownishness, clownish remark
payaso *m* clown; laughingstock
paz *f* (*pl* **paces**) peace; peacefulness; **dejar en paz** to leave alone, stop pestering; **estar en paz** to be even; to be quits; **hacer las paces con** to make peace with, to come to terms with; **salir en paz** to break even
pazgua•to -ta *adj* simple, doltish || *mf* simpleton, dolt
pazpuerca *f* slut, slattern
P.D. *abbr* **posdata**
peaje *m* toll
peatón *m* pedestrian; rural postman
pebete *m* punk, joss stick; fuse; (*cosa hedionda*) (coll) stinker
peca *f* freckle
pecado *m* sin
peca•dor -dora *adj* sinning, sinful || *mf* sinner
pecamino•so -sa *adj* sinful
pecar §73 *intr* to sin; **pecar de** to be too, e.g., **pecar de confiado** to be too trusting
pecera *f* fish globe, fish bowl
pecino•so -sa *adj* slimy
pecio *m* flotsam
pecíolo *m* leafstalk
pécora *f* head of sheep; **buena pécora** or **mala pécora** schemer, scheming woman
peco•so -sa *adj* freckly, freckle-faced
peculado *m* embezzlement, peculation
peculiar *adj* peculiar
pecunia•rio -ria *adj* pecuniary
pechada *f* bump or push with the chest; tossing an animal (*with a bump of horse's chest*); bumping contest between two horsemen
pechar *tr* to pay as a tax; fulfill; take on; drive one's horse against; bump with the chest; strike for a loan || *ref* (*dos jinetes*) to vie in a bumping contest
pechera *f* shirt front, shirt bosom; chest protector; (*del delantal*) bib; breast strap; (coll) bosom; **pechera postiza** dickey
pecho *m* chest; breast, bosom; heart, courage; **dar el pecho** to nurse, suckle; face it out; **de dos pechos** double-breasted; **de un solo pecho** single-breasted; **echar el pecho al agua** to put one's shoulder to the wheel; (coll) to speak out; **en pechos de camisa** in shirt sleeves; **tomar a pecho** to take to heart; **¡pecho al agua!** take heart!, put your shoulder to the wheel!
pechuga *f* (*del ave*) breast; slope, hill; brass, cheek; treachery, perfidy; (coll) bosom, breast
pechu•gón -gona *adj* big-chested; brazen || *mf* sponger || *m* slap or blow on the chest; fall on the chest
pedagogía *f* pedagogy
pedal *mf* pedal, treadle
pedalear *intr* to pedal
pedante *adj* pedantic || *mf* pedant
pedantería *f* pedantry
pedantes•co -ca *adj* pedantic
pedantismo *m* pedantry
pedazo *m* piece; **hacer pedazos** to break to pieces; **hacerse pedazos** (coll) to fall to pieces; to strain, to wear oneself out; **pedazo de alcornoque, de animal** or **de bruto** dolt, imbecile, good-for-nothing; **pedazo del alma, de las entrañas** or **del corazón** (*niño*) darling, apple of one's eye; **pedazo de pan** (*pequeña cantidad*) crumb; (*precio bajo*) song

pederastia *f* pederasty
pedernal *m* flint; flintiness; flint-hearted person
pedestal *m* pedestal
pedestre *adj* pedestrian
pedestrismo *m* pedestrianism; walking; foot racing; cross-country racing
pedíatra *mf* pediatrician
pediatría *f* pediatrics
pedido *m* request; (*encargo de mercancías*) order
pedigüe•ño -ña *adj* insistent, demanding, bothersome
pedir §50 *tr* to ask, ask for; request; demand, require; need; ask for the hand of; (*mercancías*) order; (gram) to govern; **pedir prestado a** to borrow from || *intr* to ask; beg; bring suit; **a pedir de boca** opportunely; as desired
pedorre•ro -ra *adj* flatulent || *f* flatulence; (orn) tody; **pedorreras** tights
pedrada *f* stoning; hit or blow with a stone; hint, taunt
pedregal *m* rocky ground; pile of rocks
pedrego•so -sa *adj* stony, rocky; suffering from gallstones || *mf* sufferer from gallstones
pedrejón *m* boulder
pedrera *f* quarry, stone quarry
pedrería *f* precious stones, jewelry
pedrusco *m* boulder
pedúnculo *m* stem, stalk
peer §43 *intr & ref* to break wind
pega *f* sticking; pitch varnish; drubbing; (*en un examen*) catch question; trick, joke; (W-I) work, jobs; **de pega** (coll) fake
pegadi•zo -za *adj* sticky; catching, contagious; sponging; fake, imitation
pegajo•so -sa *adj* sticky; contagious; tempting; soft, gentle; mushy
pegapega *f* glue
pegar §44 *tr* to stick, paste; fasten, attach, tie; (*carteles*) post; (*fuego*) set; (*una enfermedad*) transmit; (*un botón*) sew on; (*un grito*) let out; (*un salto*) take; (*un golpe, una bofetada*) let go; beat; **no pegar el ojo** to not sleep a wink || *intr* to stick, catch; take root, take hold; cling; join; fit, match; be fitting; pass, be accepted; beat; knock || *ref* to stick, catch; take root, take hold; hang on, stick around; (*una enfermedad*) be catching; **pegársela a uno** to make a fool of someone
pegatina *f* sticker (or tag)
pegotear *intr* to hang around, sponge
peina•do -da *adj* groomed; effeminate || *m* hairdo, coiffure; (*manera de componer el pelo*) hairstyle; (*policía, soldados*) search; **peinado al agua** finger wave
peina•dor -dora *mf* hairdresser || *m* wrapper, dressing gown; dressing table
peinar *tr* to comb; (*policía, soldados*) search || *ref* to comb oneself, comb one's hair
peine *m* comb; sly fellow
peineta *f* back comb
pelada *f* pelt, sheepskin
peladero *m* wasteland
peladilla *f* sugar almond; small pebble
peladillo *m* clingstone peach
pela•do -da *adj* bare; bald; barren; penniless; (*decena, centena, etc.*) even || *m* raggedy fellow; (W-I) haircut || *f* see **pelada**
pelafus•tán -tana *mf* derelict, good-for-nothing
pelaga•tos *m* (*pl* **-tos**) wretch, ragamuffin
pelaje *m* coat, fur; (*especie, calidad*) sort, stripe
pelar *tr* (*pelo*) to cut; (*pelo, plumas*) pluck, pull out; peel, skin, husk, hull, shell; (*los dientes*) show; (*en el juego*) clean out; beat, thrash || *ref* to peel off; lose one's hair; get a haircut; clear out, make a getaway; **pelárselas por** to crave; crave to
pelazón *f* poverty; misery
peldaño *m* step
pelea *f* fight; quarrel; struggle; **pelea de gallos** cockfight
pelear *intr* to fight; quarrel; struggle || *ref* to fight, fight each other
pele•ón -ona *adj* pugnacious, quarrelsome; (*vino*) cheap, ordinary || *mf* quarrelsome person || *m* cheap wine || *f* row, scuffle, fracas
peletería *f* furriery; fur shop; (Cuba) shoe store
pelete•ro -ra *mf* furrier; (Cuba) shoe dealer
peliagu•do -da *adj* furry, long-haired; arduous, ticklish
película *f* film; motion picture; **película de dibujos** animated cartoon; **película del Oeste** western; **película de terror** or **película horripilante** horror movie; **película sonora** sound film
pelicule•ro -ra *adj* moving-picture || *mf* scenario writer || *m* movie actor || *f* movie actress
peligrar *intr* to be in danger
peligro *m* danger, peril, risk; **ponerse en peligro de paz** to be alerted for war
peligro•so -sa *adj* dangerous
pelillo *m* trifle; **echar pelillos a la mar** to bury the hatchet; **no pararse en pelillos** to not bother about trifles, pay no attention to small matters; **no tener pelillos en la lengua** to speak right out
pelirro•jo -ja *adj* red-haired, redheaded || *mf* redhead
pelo *m* hair; (*en las frutas y el cuerpo humano*) down; (*del paño*) nap; (*de la madera*) grain; (*de un animal*) coat; (*en las piedras preciosas*) flaw; (*del caballo*) color; (*en el billar*) kiss; (*del reloj*) hairspring; hair trigger; fiber, filament; raw silk; **al pelo** with the hair, with the nap; perfectly, to the point; **con todos sus pelos y señales** chapter and verse; **en pelo** bareback; **escapar por un pelo** to escape by a hairbreadth, have a narrow escape; **no tener pelos en la lengua** to be outspoken, not mince words; **ponerle a uno los pelos de punta** to make one's hair stand on end; **tomar el pelo a** to make fun of, make a fool of; **venir a pelo** to come in handy

pe•lón -lona *adj* bald, hairless; dull, stupid; penniless
Pélope *m* Pelops
peloponense *adj & mf* Peloponnesian
Peloponeso *m* Peloponnesus
pelo•so -sa *adj* hairy
pelota *f* ball; ball game; handball; **en pelota** stripped; stark-naked; **pelota acuática** water polo; **pelota rodada** (baseball) grounder; **pelota vasca** pelota, jai alai
pelotari *mf* pelota player
pelotear *intr* to knock a ball around; wrangle, argue
pelotera *f* row, brawl
pelotón *m* large ball; gang, crowd; platoon; **pelotón de fusilamiento** firing squad; **pelotón de los torpes** awkward squad
peltre *m* pewter
peluca *f* wig
peluche *m* plush, pile
pelu•do -da *adj* hairy, furry; bushy
peluquear *tr* (Col, Ven) to cut the hair of || *intr* (Col, Ven) to get a haircut
peluquería *f* hairdresser's, barbershop
peluque•ro -ra *mf* hairdresser; barber; wigmaker
peluquín *m* hairpiece; toupee
pelusa *f* down; lint, fuzz; nap; jealousy, envy
pellejo *m* skin; pelt, rawhide; peel, rind; wineskin; (*la vida de uno*) (coll) hide, skin; (coll) sot, drunkard; **dar, dejar** or **perder el pellejo** to die
pellizcar §73 to pinch; nip; take a pinch of || *ref* to long, pine
pellizco *m* pinch; nip; bit, pinch
pena *f* punishment; penalty; pain, hardship, toil; sorrow, grief; effort, trouble; **a duras penas** hardly, with great difficulty; **de pena** of a broken heart; **pena privativa de libertad** imprisonment; **¡qué pena!** what a pity!; **so pena de** on pain of, under penalty of; **valer la pena** to be worthwhile (to)
penacho *m* crest; tuft, plume; arrogance; (bot) tassel
pena•do -da *adj* afflicted, grieved; difficult || *mf* convict
penalidad *f* trouble, hardship; (law) penalty
penalizar §60 *tr* to punish; penalize
penar *tr* to penalize; punish || *intr* to suffer; linger; **penar por** to pine for, long for || *ref* to grieve
penca *f* pulpy leaf; cowhide; **coger una penca** to get a jag on
penco *m* nag, jade; boor
pendejo *m* pubes; pubic hair; (coll) coward
pendencia *f* dispute, quarrel, fight; pending litigation
pendencie•ro -ra *adj* quarrelsome || *mf* wrangler
pender *intr* to hang, dangle; depend; be pending
pendiente *adj* pendent, hanging, dangling; pending; under way; expecting; **estar pendiente de** (*las palabras de una persona*) to hang on; depend on; be in the process of || *m* earring, pendant; watch chain || *f* slope, grade; dip, pitch
péndola *f* feather; pendulum; clock; pen, quill; queen post
pendolón *m* king post
pendón *m* banner, standard, pennon
péndulo *m* pendulum; clock
pene *m* penis
penetrar *tr* to penetrate; pierce; grasp, fathom || *intr* to penetrate || *ref* to grasp, fathom; realize; become convinced
penicilina *f* penicillin
península *f* peninsula
peninsular *adj & mf* peninsular; (*ibero*) Peninsular
penique *m* penny
penitencia *f* penitence; penance; **hacer penitencia** to do penance; eat sparingly; take potluck
penitente *adj & mf* penitent
penol *m* (naut) yardarm
peno•so -sa *adj* arduous, difficult; suffering; conceited; shy
pensa•dor -dora *adj* thinking || *mf* thinker
pensamiento *m* thought; (*planta y flor*) pansy
pensar §2 *tr* to think; think over; (*un naipe, un número, etc.*) think of; intend to; **pensar de** to think of, e.g., **¿qué piensa Vd. de este libro?** what do you think of this book? || *intr* to think; **pensar en** (*dirigir sus pensamientos a*) to think of (*to turn one's thoughts to*)
pensati•vo -va *adj* pensive, thoughtful
pensión *f* pension; annuity; allowance; boardinghouse; (*para ampliar estudios*) fellowship; **pensión completa** board and lodging
pensionar *tr* to pension
pensionista *mf* pensioner; boarder; boarding-school pupil; **medio pensionista** day boarder
pentagrama *m* staff, musical staff
Pentecostés, el Pentecost
penúlti•mo -ma *adj* penultimate; next to last || *f* penult
penumbra *f* penumbra; semidarkness, half-light
penuria *f* shortage
peña *f* rock, boulder; cliff; club, group, circle
peñasco *m* pinnacle; crag
peñasco•so -sa *adj* rocky, craggy
peñón *m* rock, spire; **peñón de Gibraltar** rock of Gibraltar
peón *m* laborer; pedestrian; foot soldier; farm hand; (*en el ajedrez*) pawn; (*en las damas*) man; top, peg top; spindle, axle; (taur) attendant; **peón de albañil** or **de mano** hod carrier
peor *adj & adv* worse; worst
pepa *f* (*de la manzana*) (Col) seed; (*del durazno*) (Arg) stone; (*canica*) (Arg) marble; (Col) lie, cheat, trick
pepe *mf* foundling || *m* bib; **Pepe** *m* Joe
pepinillo *m* gherkin
pepino *m* cucumber; **me importa un pepino** I couldn't care less
pepita *f* seed, pip; nugget; (vet) pip
peque *m* tot
pequén *m* (Chile) burrowing owl

peque•ñez *f* (*pl* **-ñeces**) smallness; infancy; trifle
peque•ño -ña *adj* little, small; young; low, humble
pequeño-burgués *adj* petit bourgeois
Pequín *m* Peking
pequi•nés -nesa *adj & mf* Pekinese
pera *f* pear; goatee; cinch, sinecure; pear-shaped bulb; pear-shaped switch
peral *m* pear tree
perca *f* (ichth) perch
percance *m* mischance, misfortune; **percances** perquisites
percatar *ref* — **percatarse de** to be aware of; beware of, guard against
percebe *m* barnacle; fool, sap
percepción *f* perception; collection
percibir *tr* to perceive; collect
percudir *tr* to tarnish, dull; spread through
percha *f* perch, pole, roost; clothes tree; coat hanger; coat hook; barber pole
perchero *m* rack, clothes rack, clothes hanger
perde•dor -dora *adj* losing || *mf* loser
perder §51 *tr* to lose; waste, squander; (*un tren, una ocasión*) miss; (*una asignatura*) flunk; ruin; spoil || *intr* to lose; fade || *ref* to get lost; miscarry; sink; become ruined; spoil; go to the dogs
perdición *f* perdition; loss; outrage; ruination
pérdida *f* loss; waste; ruination; **no tener pérdida** to be easy to find; **pérdida de reclamable** tax loss
perdi•do -da *adj* (*bala*) stray, wild; (*manga*) wide, loose; fruitless; (*horas*) off, spare, idle; distracted; inveterate; madly in love || *m* profligate, rake
perdido•so -sa *adj* unlucky; easily lost
perdigón *m* young partridge; profligate; heavy loser; (*alumno*) failure; **perdigones** (*granos de plomo*) shot; **perdigón zorrero** buckshot
per•diz *f* (*pl* **-dices**) partridge
perdón *m* pardon, forgiveness; **con perdón** by your leave
perdonable *adj* pardonable
perdonar *tr* to pardon, forgive, excuse; **no perdonar** to not miss, not omit
perdula•rio -ria *adj* careless, sloppy; incorrigible, vicious || *mf* good-for-nothing, profligate
perdurable *adj* long-lasting; everlasting
perdurar *intr* to last, last a long time, survive
perecede•ro -ra *adj* perishable; mortal || *m* extreme want
perecer §22 *intr* to perish; suffer; be in great want || *ref* to pine; **perecerse por** to be dying for; (*una mujer*) be mad about
peregrinación *f* peregrination; pilgrimage
peregri•no -na *adj* wandering, traveling; foreign; rare, strange; beautiful; mortal; (*ave*) migratory || *mf* pilgrim
perejil *m* parsley; (coll) frippery
perenne *adj* perennial
pereza *f* laziness; slowness
perezo•so -sa *adj* lazy; slow, dull, heavy || *mf* lazybones; sleepyhead || *m* (zool) sloth
perfección *f* perfection
perfeccionar *tr* to perfect, improve
perfec•to -ta *adj & m* perfect
perfidia *f* perfidy
pérfi•do -da *adj* perfidious
perfil *m* profile; side view; cross section; thin stroke; outline, sketch; **perfil aerodinámico** streamlining; **perfiles** finishing touches; courtesies
perfila•do -da *adj* (*cara*) long and thin; (*nariz*) well-formed; (*facciones*) delicate; streamlined
perfilar *tr* to profile, outline; perfect, polish, finish || *ref* to be outlined; show one's profile, stand sidewise; stand out; dress up
perforación *f* perforation; drilling; puncture; keypunching
perfora•dor -dora *adj* perforating; drilling || *f* pneumatic drill, rock drill
perforar *tr* to perforate; drill, bore; puncture; (*una tarjeta*) punch
perforista *mf* keypuncher
perfumar *tr* to perfume
perfume *m* perfume
pergamino *m* parchment
pergenio *m* rascal
pericia *f* skill, expertness
periclitar *intr* to be in jeopardy, be shaky
perico *m* (*pelo postizo*) periwig; parakeet; (slang) chamber pot; (CAm) compliment; **perico entre ellas** lady's man
periferia *f* periphery; surroundings
perifollos *mpl* finery, frippery, chiffons
perilla *f* pear-shaped ornament; goatee; knob, doorknob; (*del arzón*) pommel; (*de la oreja*) lobe; **de perilla** apropos, to the point
periodísti•co -ca *adj* newspaper, journalistic
periódi•co -ca *adj* periodic || *m* newspaper; periodical
periodismo *m* journalism
periodista *mf* journalist || *m* newspaperman || *f* newspaperwoman
período *m* period; compound sentence; (phys) cycle; **período lectivo** (*en la escuela*) term
peripues•to -ta *adj* dudish, all spruced up, sporty
periquete *m* jiffy; **en un periquete** in a jiffy
periquito *m* parakeet; **periquito de Australia** budgerigar
periscopio *m* periscope
peri•to -ta *adj* skilled, skillful; expert || *m* expert
perjudicar §73 *tr* to damage, impair, hurt, prejudice
perjudicial *adj* harmful, injurious, detrimental, prejudicial
perjuicio *m* harm, injury, damage, prejudice; **en perjuicio de** to the detriment of
perjurar *intr* to commit perjury; swear, be profane || *ref* to commit perjury; perjure oneself
perjurio *m* perjury
perla *f* pearl; **de perlas** perfectly
perlesía *f* palsy
permanecer §22 *intr* to stay, remain
permanencia *f* permanence; stay, sojourn

permanente *adj* permanent || *f* permanent wave
permiso *m* permission; permit; time off; (*en el monedaje*) tolerance; leave; **con permiso** excuse me; **permiso de circulación** owner's license; **permiso de conducir** driver's license
permitir *tr* to permit, allow || *ref* to be permitted; **no se permite fumar** no smoking
permutar *tr* to interchange; barter; to permute
pernear *intr* to kick; hustle; fuss, fret
pernera *f* trouser leg
pernicio•so -sa *adj* pernicious
pernil *m* trouser leg; (*anca y muslo*) ham
perno *m* bolt; **perno con anillo** ringbolt; **perno roscado** screw bolt
pernoctar *intr* to spend the night
pero *conj* but, yet || *m* but; fault, defect; **poner pero a** to find fault with
perogrullada *f* platitude, inanity
peroración *f* peroration; harangue
perorar *intr* to perorate; orate
peróxido *m* peroxide; **peróxido de hidrógeno** hydrogen peroxide
perpendicular *adj & f* perpendicular
perpetrar *tr* to perpetrate
perpetuar **§21** *tr* to perpetuate
perpe•tuo -tua *adj* perpetual; life
perplejidad *f* perplexity; worry, anxiety
perple•jo -ja *adj* perplexed; worried, anxious; baffling, perplexing
perra *f* bitch; tantrum; drunkenness
perrada *f* pack of dogs; dirty trick
perrera *f* kennel, doghouse; tantrum; toil, drudgery
perro *m* dog; **el perro del hortelano** dog in the manger; **perro caliente** (slang) hot dog; **perro cobrador** retriever; **perro de aguas** spaniel; **perro de lanas** poodle; **perro de muestra** pointer; **perro faldero** lap dog; **perro marino** dogfish, shark; **perro raposero** foxhound; **perro viejo** (coll) wise old owl
perro-lazarillo *m* (*pl* **perros-lazarillos**) Seeing Eye dog
persa *adj & mf* Persian
persecución *f* persecution; pursuit; annoyance, harassment
perseguir **§67** *tr* to persecute; pursue; annoy, harass
perseverar *intr* to persevere
persiana *f* slatted shutter; flowered silk; louver; Venetian blind; **persiana del radiador** (aut) louver
persistir *intr* to persist
persona *f* person; personage; **persona desplazada** displaced person; **personas** people; **por persona** per capita
personaje *m* personage; (theat) character; person of importance
personal *adj* personal || *m* personnel, staff, force
personalidad *f* personality
personificar **§73** *tr* to personify
perspectiva *f* perspective; outlook, prospect; appearance
perspi•caz *adj* (*pl* **-caces**) perspicacious, discerning; keen-sighted
persuadir *tr* to persuade
persuasión *f* persuasion
pertenecer **§22** *intr* to belong; pertain || *ref* to be independent, be free
perteneciente *adj* pertaining
pértiga *f* pole, rod, staff
perti•naz *adj* (*pl* **-naces**) pertinacious; (*dolor de cabeza*) persistent
pertinente *adj* pertinent, relevant
pertrechos *mpl* supplies, provisions, equipment; tools; **pertrechos de guerra** ordnance
perturbar *tr* to perturb; disturb; upset, disconcert; confuse, interrupt
Perú, el Peru
perua•no -na *adj & mf* Peruvian
perversidad *f* perversity
perversión *f* perversion
perver•so -sa *adj* perverse; wicked, depraved || *mf* profligate
perverti•do -da *mf* pervert
pervertir **§68** *tr* to pervert || *ref* to become perverted; go to the bad
pesa *f* weight; (CAm, Col, Ven) butcher shop
pesacar•tas *m* (*pl* **-tas**) letter scales
pesadez *f* heaviness; slowness; tiresomeness; harshness; (phys) gravity
pesadilla *f* nightmare
pesa•do -da *adj* heavy; slow; tiresome; harsh; boring
pesadumbre *f* sorrow, grief; trouble; weight, heaviness
pesaje *m* weighing; (sport) weigh-in
pésame *m* condolence; **dar el pésame a** to extend one's sympathy to
pesantez *f* (phys) gravity
pesar *m* sorrow, regret; **a pesar de** in spite of || *tr* to weigh; make sorry || *intr* to weigh; be heavy; cause regret, cause sorrow
pesaro•so -sa *adj* sorrowful, regretful
pesca *f* fishing; catch; **ir de pesca** to go fishing; **pesca de bajura** off-shore fishing; **pesca de gran altura** deep-sea fishing
pescadería *f* fish market; fish store; fish stand
pescade•ro -ra *mf* fish dealer, fishmonger
pescado *m* fish (*that has been caught*)
pesca•dor -dora *adj* fishing || *m* fisherman || *f* fisherwoman, fishwife
pescante *m* coach box; (*de una grúa*) jib; (aut) front seat; (naut) davit; (theat) trap door
pescar **§73** *tr* to fish; fish for; fish out; (*peces*) catch; (coll) to manage to get || *intr* to fish
pescozón *m* slap on the neck or head
pescuezo *m* neck
pesebre *m* crib, rack, manger; crèche
pesero *m* (CAm, Col, Ven) butcher; (Mex) shared taxi
pesimismo *m* pessimism
pesimista *adj* pessimistic || *mf* pessimist
pési•mo -ma *adj* very bad, abominable

peso *m* weight; scale, balance; burden, load; judgment, good sense; (*unidad monetaria*) peso; **caerse de su peso** to be self-evident; **llevar el peso de la batalla** to bear the brunt of the battle; **peso atómico** atomic weight; **peso molecular** molecular weight
pespuntar *tr & intr* to backstitch
pespunte *m* backstitch
pesquera *f* fishery; fishing grounds; (*presa para detener los peces*) weir
pesquería *f* fishing; fishery
pesque•ro -ra *adj* fishing || *m* fishing boat || *f* see **pesquera**
pesquis *m* acumen, keenness
pesquisa *m* (Arg) detective || *f* inquiry, investigation
pesquisar *tr* to investigate, inquire into
pestaña *f* eyelash; flange; fringe, edging; index tab
pestañear *intr* to wink, blink; **sin pestañear** without batting an eye
peste *f* pest, plague; epidemic; stink, stench; abundance; (Col, Peru) head cold; (Chile) smallpox; **pestes** insults
pesticida *m* pesticide
pestífe•ro -ra *adj* pestiferous; stinking
pestilencia *f* pestilence
pestillo *m* bolt; doorlatch
petaca *f* cigar case; cigarette case; tobacco pouch; leather-covered hamper
pétalo *m* petal
petardear *tr* to swindle || *intr* (aut) to backfire
petardeo *m* swindling; (aut) backfire
petardo *m* petard; bomb; swindle, cheat
petate *m* sleeping bag; bedding; luggage; cheat; poor soul; **liar el petate** to pack up and get out; to kick the bucket
petición *f* petition; request; plea; (law) claim, bill; **a petición de** at the request of; **petición de mano** formal betrothal
petimetre *m* dude, sport, dandy
petirrojo *m* redbreast, robin
Petrarca *m* Petrarch
petrificar **§73** *tr & ref* to petrify
petróleo *m* petroleum; **petróleo combustible** fuel oil
petrole•ro -ra *adj* oil, petroleum || *mf* oil dealer || *m* oil tanker
petroquími•co -ca *adj* petrochemical
petulancia *f* flippancy, pertness
petulante *adj* flippant, pert
pez *m* (*pl* **peces**) fish; reward, just desert; **como un pez en el agua** snug as a bug in a rug; **pez de plata** (ent) silverfish; **salga pez o salga rana** blindly, hit or miss || *f* pitch, tar
pezón *m* stem; nipple, teat
pezonera *f* linchpin
pezuña *f* hoof
piado•so -sa *adj* merciful; pitiful; pious
piafar *intr* (*el caballo*) to paw, to stamp
piano *m* piano; **piano de cola** grand piano; **piano de media cola** baby grand
piar **§77** *intr* to peep, chirp
pica *f* pike; pikeman; picador's goad; (Col) pique, resentment
picada *f* peck; bite; (Bol) knock at the door; (Arg, Bol, Urug) narrow ford; (SAm) path, trail
picadillo *m* (*carne, verduras, ajos, etc. reducidos a pequeños trozos*) hash; (*carne picada*) mincemeat
pica•do -da *adj* perforated; pitted; (*tabaco*) cut; (*hielo*) cracked; (*mar*) choppy; piqued || *m* mincemeat; (aer) dive; **picado con motor** (aer) power dive || *f* see **picada**
picador *m* horsebreaker; (*torero de a caballo*) picador (*mounted bullfighter*); chopping block; meat grinder
picadura *f* bite, prick, sting; nick; puncture; cut tobacco; (*en un diente*) cavity
picaflor *m* hummingbird
picahie•los *m* (*pl* **-los**) ice pick
picamade•ros *m* (*pl* **-ros**) green woodpecker
picante *adj* biting, pricking, stinging; piquant, juicy, racy; (SAm) highly seasoned || *m* mordancy; piquancy
pícap *m* (Bol, Chile, Col) var of **pick-up**
picapedrero *m* stonecutter
picaplei•tos *m* (*pl* **-tos**) troublemaker; shyster, pettifogger
picaporte *m* latch; latchkey; door knocker
picar **§73** *tr* to prick, pierce, puncture; sting; bite; burn; peck; nibble; pit, pock; mince, chop up, cut up; stick, poke; spur; goad; perforate; (*hielo*) crack; harass, pursue; tame; pique, annoy || *intr* to itch; (*el sol*) burn; nibble; have a smattering; be catching; (*los negocios*) pick up; (aer) to dive; (*caer en el lazo*) (coll) to bite; **picar en** to nibble at; dabble in; **picar muy alto** aim high, expect too much || *ref* to rot; (*la ropa*) be moth-eaten; (*el vino*) turn sour; (*un diente*) be decayed; (*el mar*) get rough; be offended; get drunk; (*drogas*) get a fix, shoot up; **picarse de** to boast of being
picardía *f* roguishness, knavery; crudeness, coarseness; mischief
picares•co -ca *adj* roguish, rascally; picaresque; rough, coarse, crude; witty, humorous
pícaro -ra *adj* roguish; scheming, tricky; low, vile; mischievous || *mf* rogue; schemer
picaza *f* magpie
picazón *f* itch, itching; annoyance
pícea *f* spruce tree
pick-up *m* pickup; phonograph
pico *m* beak, bill; (*de jarra*) spout; (*del yunque*) beak; (*del pañuelo*) corner; nib, tip; (*de la pluma de escribir*) point; peak; (*herramienta*) pick; (*de dinero*) pile, lot; talkativeness; (elec) peak; (naut) bow, prow; **callar el pico** to shut up; **darse el pico** (*las palomas*) to bill; **pico de oro** silver-tongue; **tener mucho pico** to talk too much; **y pico** odd, e.g., **trescientos y pico** three hundred odd; a little after, e.g., **a las tres y pico** a little after three o'clock
picor *m* (*del paladar*) smarting; itch, itching, burning
pico•so -sa *adj* pock-marked
picota *f* pillory; peak, point, spire
picotazo *m* peck

picotear *tr* to peck || *intr* (*el caballo*) to toss the head; chatter, jabber, gab; (*las mujeres*) wrangle

pichel *m* pewter tankard

pichón -chona *mf* darling || *m* young pigeon; **pichón de barro** clay pigeon

pie *m* foot; footing; foothold; base, stand; (*de copa*) stem; (*de la cama*) footboard; cause, origin, reason; (*de la página*) foot, bottom; (theat) cue; (Chile) down payment; **a cuatro pies** on all fours; **al pie de fábrica** at the factory; **al pie de la letra** literally; **al pie de la obra** (com) delivered; **a pie** on foot, walking; **buscar cinco** (or **tres**) **pies al gato** to be looking for trouble; **de pie** standing; up and about; firm, steady; firmly, steadily; **en pie de guerra** on a war footing; **ir a pie** to go on foot, to walk; **morir al pie del cañón** to die in the harness, to die with one's boots on; **nacer de pie** or **de pies** to be born with a silver spoon in one's mouth; **pie de atleta** athlete's foot; **pie de cabra** crowbar; **pie de imprenta** imprint, printer's mark; **pie derecho** upright, stanchion; **pie marino** sea legs; **pie plano** flatfoot; **pie quebrado** (*de verso*) short line; **vestirse por los pies** to be a man

piedad *f* (*devoción a las cosas santas*) piety; (*misericordia*) pity, mercy

piedra *f* stone; rock; (*pedernal*) flint; heavy hailstone; (pathol) stone; **piedra angular** cornerstone; (fig) cornerstone, keystone; **piedra arenisca** sandstone; **piedra azul** (chem) bluestone; **piedra de albardilla** copestone; **piedra de amolar** grindstone; **piedra de chispa** flint; **piedra de pipas** meerschaum; **piedra imán** loadstone; **piedra miliar** or **miliaria** milestone; **piedra movediza** rolling stone; **piedra pómez** pumice, pumice stone

piel *f* skin; hide, pelt; fur; leather; (*de las frutas*) peel, skin; **piel de cabra** goatskin; **piel de foca** sealskin; **piel de gallina** goose flesh || *m* — **piel roja** (*pl* **pieles rojas**) (*indio norteamericano*) redskin

pienso *m* feed, feeding; **ni por pienso** by no means, don't think of it

pierna *f* leg; post, upright; **dormir a pierna suelta** or **tendida** to sleep like a log; **estirar la pierna** to lie down on the job; kick the bucket; **estirar** or **extender las piernas** to stretch one's legs, go for a walk; **ser buena pierna** (Arg, Urug) to be a good-natured fellow

pieza *f* (*órgano de una máquina o artefacto; obra dramática; composición suelta de múscia; cañón; figura que sirve para jugar a las damas, al ajedrez, etc.; moneda*) piece; (*objeto; mueble; porción de tela*) piece or article; (*habitación, cuarto*) room; **buena pieza** hussy; sly fox; **pieza de recambio** or **de repuesto** spare part; **quedarse en una pieza** or **hecho una pieza** to be dumbfounded, stand motionless

pífano *m* fife; fifer

pifia *f* (billiards) miscue; (coll) miscue, slip

pifiar *intr* to miscue

pigmentar *tr & ref* to pigment

pigmento *m* pigment

pigme•o -a *adj & mf* pygmy

pijama *f* pajamas

pila *f* basin; trough; sink; font; pile, heap; (elec) battery, cell; (elec & phys) pile; **pila de linterna** flashlight battery

pilar *m* (*de una fuente*) basin, bowl; pillar; stone post, milestone; (*persona*) (fig) pillar || *tr* (*el grano*) to crush, pound

Pilatos *m* Pilate

píldora *f* pill; bad news; **píldora para dormir** sleeping pill

pileta *f* sink; basin, bowl; font; swimming pool

pilón *m* pylon; drinking trough; loaf of sugar; counterpoise; drop hammer; (Mex, Ven) tip, gratuity; **de pilón** in addition, on top of it

pilotar *tr* to pilot

pilote *m* pile

piloto *m* pilot; first mate; (Chile) hail fellow well met

pillar *tr* to pillage, plunder; catch

pi•llo -lla *adj* roguish, rascally; sly, crafty || *m* rogue, rascal; crafty fellow

pilluelo *m* scamp, little scamp

pimentero *m* pepper, black pepper; pepperbox

pimentón *m* cayenne pepper, red pepper; (*condimento preparado moliendo pimientos encarnados secos*) paprika

pimienta *f* pepper, black pepper; allspice, pimento; allspice tree

pimiento *m* (*planta*) pepper, black pepper; Guinea pepper

pimpante *adj* smart, spruce

pimpollo *m* sucker, shoot, sprout; rosebud; (*árbol nuevo*) sapling; handsome child; handsome young person

pina *f* fellow

pinacoteca *f* picture gallery

pináculo *m* pinnacle

pincel *m* brush; painter; painting; (*de luz*) pencil, beam

pincelada *f* brush stroke; touch, finish, flourish

pincelar *tr* to paint; picture; (med) to pencil

pincia•no -na *adj* Valladolid || *mf* native or inhabitant of Valladolid

pincha *f* kitchenmaid

pinchar *tr* to prick, jab, pierce, puncture; stir up, prod, provoke || *intr* to have a puncture; **no pinchar ni cortar** to have no say || *ref* (*drogas*) to get a fix, shoot up

pinchazo *m* prick, jab, puncture; provocation; **a prueba de pinchazos** puncture-proof

pinche *m* scullion, kitchen boy; helper

pincho *m* thorn, prick; snack; spike

Píndaro *m* Pindar

pingajo *m* rag, tatter

pingo *m* rag, tatter; ragamuffin; horse; **andar** or **ir de pingo** (*una mujer*) to gad about

pingüe *adj* oily, greasy, fat; abundant, rich; fertile; profitable

pingüino *m* penguin
pinito *m* first step, little step; **hacer pinitos** to begin to walk; (fig) to take the first steps
pino *m* pine tree; first step; **hacer pinos** to begin to walk; (fig) to take the first steps
pinocha *f* pine needle
pinta *m* scoundrel || *f* spot, mark, sign; dot; pint
pintacilgo *m* goldfinch
pintada *f* Guinea hen
pinta•do -da *adj* spotted, mottled; tipsy; accented; **el más pintado** the aptest one; the shrewdest one; the best one; **venir como pintado** to be just the thing || *m* (*acto de pintar*) painting || *f* see **pintada**
pintar *tr* to paint; (*una letra, un acento, etc.*) draw; picture, depict; put an accent mark on; **pintarla** to put it on, put on airs || *intr* to paint; begin to turn red, begin to ripen; show, turn out || *ref* to paint, put on make-up; begin to turn red, begin to ripen
pintarrajear *tr* to daub, smear
pin•to -ta *adj* speckled, spotted || *f* see **pinta**
pin•tor -tora *mf* painter; **pintor de brocha gorda** painter, house painter; dauber
pintores•co -ca *adj* picturesque
pintura *f* (*color preparado para pintar*) paint; (*arte; obra pintada*) painting; **hacer pinturas** to prance; **no poder ver ni en pintura** to not be able to stand the sight of
pinture•ro -ra *adj* showy, conceited || *mf* show-off
pinza *f* clothespin; (*de langosta, cangrejo, etc.*) claw; **pinzas** pliers; pincers; tweezers; forceps
pinzón *m* pump handle; (orn) finch
piña *f* fir cone, pine cone; knob; plug; cluster, knot; pineapple
piñonear *intr* (*un arma de fuego*) to click; reach the age of puberty; (coll) to be an old goat
piñoneo *m* click (*of a firearm*)
pí•o -a *adj* pious; merciful, compassionate; (*caballo*) pied, dappled || *m* peeping, chirping; keen desire
piocha *f* jeweled head adornment; artificial flower made of feathers; pick
piojo *m* louse
piojo•so -sa *adj* lousy; mean, stingy
piola *f* string, cord
pione•ro -ra *adj & mf* pioneer
pipa *f* (*para fumar tabaco*) pipe; (*medida para vinos*) butt; wine cask; (*simiente*) pip; (mus) pipe, reed; (coll) handgun; **pipa de espuma de mar** meerschaum pipe; **pipa de riego** watering cart; **pipa de tierra** clay pipe
pipí *m* (coll) pee, urine; **hacer pipí** to pee, urinate
pipiolo *m* (CAm, Mex) child
pique *m* pique, resentment; eagerness; (*insecto*) chigger; (*naipe*) spade; **a pique** steep; **a pique de** in danger of; on the verge of; **echar a pique** to sink; ruin; **irse a pique** to sink; go to ruin, be ruined
piquera *f* bung, bunghole; (Mex) dive, joint
piquete *m* sharp jab; small hole; stake, picket; (*de soldados, de huelguistas*) picket; **piquete de ejecución** firing squad; **piquete de salvas** firing squad
pira *f* pyre
piragua *f* pirogue; (sport) single shell
piragüismo *m* canoeing
piragüista *m* (sport) crewman
pirámide *f* pyramid
pirata *m* pirate; **pirata aéreo** hijacker
piratear *intr* to pirate, be a pirate
piratería *f* piracy; **piratería aérea** hijacking, skyjacking, air piracy
pirca *f* (SAm) dry stone wall
pirco *m* (Chile) succotash
Pireo, el Piraeus
pirine•o -a *adj* Pyrenean || **Pirineos** *mpl* Pyrenees
pirita *f* pyrites
pirófa•go -ga *adj* fire-eating || *mf* fire-eater
piropear *tr* to flatter, flirt with
piropo *m* garnet, carbuncle; flattery, compliment, flirtatious remark
piróscafo *m* steamship
pirotecnia *f* pyrotechnics
pirotécni•co -ca *adj* pyrotechnical || *m* powder maker, fireworks manufacturer
pirueta *f* pirouette; somersault; caper
piruetear *intr* to pirouette
pisada *f* tread; footstep; footprint; trampling
pisapape•les *m* (*pl* **-les**) paperweight
pisar *tr* to trample, tread on, step on; tamp, pack down; (*p.ej., uvas*) tread; cover part of; ram; (*una tecla*) strike; (mus) to pluck; (coll) to abuse, tread all over; **pisar algo a alguien** to snitch something from someone || *intr* to be right above; step || *ref* (Arg) to guess wrong, come out wrong
pisaverde *m* fop, dandy
piscina *f* swimming pool; fishpond
Piscis *m* (astr) Pisces
pisco *m* Peruvian brandy
pisicorre *f* (W-I) station wagon
piso *m* tread; floor; flooring; (*de una carretera*) surface; flat, apartment; **buscar piso** to be looking for a place to live; **piso alto** top floor; **piso bajo** street floor, ground floor; **piso principal** main floor, second floor
pisón *m* ram, tamper
pisotear *tr* to trample, tread on, tread under foot; abuse, tread all over
pisotón *m* stamp, tread
pista *f* track; trace, trail; clew; race track; (*de bolera*) alley; (*de cabaret*) floor; (aer) runway; **pista de esquí** ski run; **pista de patinar** skating rink
pisto *m* (*para los enfermos*) chicken broth; vegetable cutlet; jumbled speech or writing; mess; (CAm, Mex) money
pistola *f* pistol; sprayer; rock drill; **pistola de arzón** horse pistol; **pistola engrasadora** grease gun
pistolera *f* holster
pistolerismo *m* gangsterism
pistolero *m* gangster, gunman
pistón *m* piston

pistonear *intr* to knock
pistoneo *m* knock
pistonu•do -da *adj* stunning, swank
pita *f* century plant; hiss, hissing; glass marble; string, thread
pitar *tr* to pay, pay off; (*a un torero*) whistle disapproval of || *intr* to blow a whistle, whistle; blow the horn, honk; talk nonsense; **no pitar** to not be popular; **salir pitando** to run away, dash away
pitazo *m* blast, toot, honk, whistle (sound)
pitear *intr* to whistle
pitillera *f* cigarette maker; cigarette case
pitillo *m* cigarette
pito *m* whistle; horn; fife; fifer; cigarette; jackstone; (*insecto*) tick; woodpecker; (coll) continental, straw, tinker's damn
pitón *m* lump, sprig; tenderling; (*del cuerno*) tip; nozzle, spout; python
pitonisa *f* witch, siren; pythoness
pitu•so -sa *adj* tiny, cute || *mf* tot
piular *intr* to peep, chirp
pivotar *intr* to pivot
pivote *m* pivot; **pivote de dirección** (aut) kingpin
píxide *f* pyx
pizarra *f* slate; blackboard
pizarrero *m* roofer, slater
pizarrín *m* slate pencil
pizca *f* mite, whit, jot
placa *f* plaque, tablet; badge; plate; slab, sheet; scab; (anat, elec, electron, phot, zool) plate; **placa de matrícula** license plate; **placa giratoria** (*de ferrocarril; de gramófono*) turntable
placaminero *m* persimmon
placebo *m* placebo
pláceme *m* congratulation
placente•ro -ra *adj* pleasant, agreeable
placer *m* pleasure; sandbank, reef; **a placer** at one's convenience || *v* §52 *tr* to please
place•ro -ra *adj* public || *mf* market vendor; loafer, town gossip
pláci•do -da *adj* placid; pleasing
plaga *f* plague; pest; scourge; abundance; sore; clime, region
plagar §44 *tr* to plague, infest; (*de minas*) sow
plagiar *tr* to plagiarize
plagio *m* plagiarism; abduction, kidnaping
plan *m* plan; level, height; **plan de estudios** or **plan escolar** curriculum
plana *f* plain, flat country; trowel; cooper's plane; page
plancha *f* plate, sheet; iron, flatiron; gangplank; (coll) blunder; **a la plancha** grilled; (*huevo*) fried; **plancha de blindaje** armor plate
planchado *m* ironing; pressing
planchar *tr* (*la ropa interior blanca*) to iron; (*un traje de hombre*) to press || *intr* to be a wallflower
planchear *tr* to plate
planear *tr* to plan, outline; (*una tabla*) plane || *intr* to hover; (aer) to volplane, glide
planeta *m* planet
planicie *f* plain
planificar §73 *tr* to plan
planilla *f* list, roll, schedule; (*de candidatos para un puesto público*) (Mex) panel; (Mex) ballot; (Mex) commutation ticket
pla•no -na *adj* plane; level, smooth, even; flat || *m* plan; map; (*superficie*) plane; (aer) plane; **de plano** clearly, plainly, flatly; flat; **levantar un plano** to make a survey; **primer plano** foreground || *f* see **plana**
planta *f* (*del pie*) sole; foot; plan; project; floor plan; (*del personal de una oficina*) roster; plant, factory; (bot) plant; (sport) stance; **de planta** from the ground up; **echar plantas** to swagger, bully; **planta baja** ground floor; **planta del sortilegio** (bot) witch hazel; **tener buena planta** to make a fine appearance
plantar *tr* to plant; establish, found; (*un golpe*) plant; jilt; (*en la calle, en la cárcel*) throw || *ref* to take a stand; gang together; (*un animal*) balk; land, arrive
plantear *tr* to plan, outline; establish, execute, carry out; state, set up, expound, pose
plantel *m* nursery garden; educational establishment
plantificar §73 *tr* to plan, outline; (*un golpe*) plant; (*en la calle, la cárcel*) throw || *ref* to land, arrive
plantilla *f* plantlet, young plant; insole; reinforced sole; model, pattern, template; (*de empleados*) staff; (*del personal de una oficina*) roster; plan, design; (*bizcocho*) ladyfinger
plantío *m* planting; garden patch; tree nursery
plantón *m* (*que ha de ser transplantado*) shoot; graft; guard, watchman; waiting, standing around
plañide•ro -ra *adj* mournful, plaintive || *f* hired mourner
plañir §12 *tr* to lament, grieve over || *intr* to lament, grieve, bewail
plasma *m* plasma
plasmar *tr* to mold, shape
plasta *f* paste, soft mass; flattened object; poor job, bungle
plástica *f* (*arte de plasmar*) plastic; plastic arts
plásti•co -ca *adj* plastic || *m* (*substancia*) plastic || *f* see **plástica**
plata *f* silver; (*moneda o monedas*) silver; wealth; money; **en plata** briefly, to the point; plainly; **plata de ley** sterling silver
plataforma *f* platform; platform car; (*del ferrocarril*) roadbed; (*programa político*) platform; (*de lanzamiento de cohete*) pad; **plataforma giratoria** (rr) turntable
platal *m* piles of money, fortune
platanal *m* or **platanar** *m* banana plantation
plátano *m* banana; banana tree; plane tree; **plátano de occidente** buttonwood tree
platea *f* (theat) orchestra, parquet
platea•do -da *adj* silvered; silver-plated; (coll) well-to-do
platear *tr* to silver, coat or plate with silver
platero *m* silversmith; jeweler

plática *f* talk, chat; talk, informal lecture; sermon
platicar §73 *tr* to talk over, discuss || *intr* to talk, chat; discuss; preach
platillo *m* plate; saucer; (*de la balanza*) pan; (mus) cymbal; **platillo volador** or **volante** flying saucer
platino *m* platinum
plato *m* dish; plate; (*de una comida*) course; daily fare; **plato fuerte** main course; **plato giratorio** (*del gramófono*) turntable
pla•tó *m* (*pl* **-tós**) (mov) set
Platón *m* Plato
platu•do -da *adj* rich
plausible *adj* praiseworthy; acceptable
playa *f* beach, shore, strand; **playa infantil** sand pile
playera *f* fishwoman; beach shoe
plaza *f* plaza, square; market place; town, city; fortified town; space, room; yard; office, employment; character, reputation; seat; **sentar plaza** to enlist; **plaza de armas** parade ground; public square; **plaza de gallos** cockpit; **plaza de toros** bullring; **plaza mayor** main square
plazo *m* term; time; time limit; date of payment; instalment; **a plazo** on credit, on time; **en plazos** in installments
pleamar *f* high tide, high water
plebe *f* common people
plebe•yo -ya *adj & mf* plebeian
plegadi•zo -za *adj* folding; pliable
plegar §66 *tr* to fold; crease; pleat || *ref* to yield, give in
plegaria *f* prayer; noon call to prayer
pleito *m* litigation, lawsuit; dispute, quarrel; fight; **pleito de acreedores** bankruptcy proceedings; **pleito homenaje** (feud) homage; **pleito viciado** mistrial
plenilunio *m* full moon
plenitud *f* fullness, abundance
ple•no -na *adj* full; **en plena marcha** in full swing; **en pleno rostro** right in the face
pleuresía *f* pleurisy
pliego *m* (*de papel*) sheet; folder; cover, envelope; bid, specification; sealed letter; printer's proof
pliegue *m* fold, crease, pleat; **pliegue de tabla** box pleat
plisar *tr* to pleat
plomada *f* carpenter's lead pencil; plummet; plumb bob; sinker, sinkers; scourge tipped with lead balls
plomar *tr* to seal with lead
plomazo *m* (Guat, Mex, W-I) gunshot
plomería *f* lead roofing; leadwork, plumbing
plomero *m* lead worker; plumber
plomi•zo -za *adj* lead, leaden
plomo *m* lead; (*pedazo de plomo; bala*) lead; (elec) fuse; (coll) bore; **a plomo** plumb, perpendicularly; straight down; just right
pluma *f* feather; quill; plume; pen; faucet; (CAm) hoax; (Chile) crane, derrick; **pluma esferográfica** ball-point pen; **pluma estilográfica** or **pluma fuente** fountain pen
plumaje *m* plumage
plúmbe•o -a *adj* lead
plumero *m* (*caja o vaso para las plumas*) penholder; feather duster
plumífe•ro -ra *adj* (*escritor*) hack, second-rate; (poet) feathered || *m* padded or quilted jacket, ski jacket; hack writer; newshound
plumilla *f* small feather; (*de la pluma fuente*) point, tip; (Ven) ball-point pen
plumón *m* down; feather bed; (Mex) felt-tipped pen
plumo•so -sa *adj* downy, feathery
plural *adj & m* plural
pluriempleo *m* moonlighting
plus *m* extra, bonus
plusmarca *f* (sport) record
plusmarquista *mf* (sport) record breaker
plusvalía *f* appreciation (*in value*)
Plutarco *m* Plutarch
plutonio *m* plutonium
población *f* population; village, town, city
poblada *f* (SAm) riot, mob
pobla•do -da *adj* thick, bushy || *m* town, community || *f* see **poblada**
poblar §61 *tr* to people, populate; found, settle, colonize; (*un estanque, una colmena*) stock; (*con árboles*) plant || *intr* to settle, colonize; multiply, be prolific || *ref* to become full, covered, or crowded
pobre *adj* poor || *mf* pauper; beggar
pobreza *f* poverty, want; poorness
pocilga *f* pigpen
poción *f* potion, dose
po•co -ca *adj & pron* (*comp & super* **menos**) little; few, e.g., **poca gente** few people; **pocos** few; **unos pocos** a few || **poco** *adv* little; **a poco** shortly afterwards; **a poco de** shortly after; **dentro de poco** shortly; **por poco** almost, nearly; **tener en poco** to hold in low esteem, think little of; **un poco (de)** a little
po•cho -cha *adj* faded, discolored; overripe; rotten; (Chile) chubby
podar *tr* to prune, to trim
podenco *m* hound
poder *m* power; power of attorney, proxy; **el cuarto poder** the fourth estate; **obra en mi poder** I have at hand, I have in my possession; **poder adquisitivo** purchasing power || *v* §53 *intr* to be possible; be able, have power or strength; **a más no poder** as hard as possible; **no poder con** to not be able to stand, not be able to manage; **no poder más** to be exhausted, be all in; **no poder menos de** to not be able to keep from, not be able to help || *v aux* to be able to, may, can, might, could; **no poder ver** to not be able to stand
poderhabiente *mf* attorney, proxy
poderío *m* power, might; wealth, riches; sway, dominion
podero•so -sa *adj* powerful, mighty; wealthy, rich
podio *m* podium
podre *f* pus
podredumbre *f* corruption, putrefaction; pus; deep grief
poema *m* poem

poesía *f* poetry; poem; **bella poesía** (fig) fairy tale
poeta *m* poet
poéti•co -ca *adj* poetic(al) || *f* poetics
poetisa *f* poetess
pola•co -ca *adj* Polish || *mf* Pole || *m* (*idioma*) Polish
polaina *f* legging
polar *adj* pole; polar || *f* polestar
polarizar §60 *tr* to polarize
polea *f* pulley
poleame *m* (naut) tackle
polen *m* pollen
policía *m* policeman || *f* police; policing; politeness; cleanliness; neatness; **policía urbana** street cleaning
policía•co -ca or policial *adj* police; (*novela*) detective
polifacéti•co -ca *adj* many-sided
polígа•mo -ma *adj* polygamous || *mf* polygamist
poliglo•to -ta *adj* polyglot || *mf* polyglot, linguist
polígono *m* polygon
polígrafo *m* prolific writer; copying machine; ball-point pen; lie detector
polilla *f* moth
Polimnia *f* Polyhymnia
polinizar §60 *tr* to pollinate
polinomio *m* polynomial
polio *f* (path) polio
pólipo *m* polyp
polisón *m* bustle
polista *mf* poloist, polo player
politeísta *adj* polytheistic || *mf* polytheist
política *f* politics; policy; manners, politeness, courtesy; **política de café** parlor politics; **política del buen vecino** Good Neighbor Policy
políti•co -ca *adj* political; politic, tactful; polite, courteous; -in-law; e.g., **padre político** father-in-law || *mf* politician || *f* see **política**
polivalente *adj* manifold; (chem, bact) polyvalent
póliza *f* policy, contract; draft, check; customhouse permit; **póliza de seguro** insurance policy
polizón *m* bum, tramp; stowaway
polizonte *m* cop, policeman
polo *m* pole; popsicle; (*juego*) polo; **polo de agua** water polo; **polo de atracción popular** drawing card
pololear *tr* to bother, annoy; (Chile) to flirt with
polo•lo -la *adj* (Chile) youngster || *m* (Chile) flirt; side job
Polonia *f* Poland
pol•trón -trona *adj* idle, lazy, comfort-loving || *f* easy chair
polución *f* (*del ambiente*) pollution
polvareda *f* cloud of dust; rumpus
polvera *f* compact, powder case
polvo *m* dust; powder; pinch of snuff; **polvo dentífrico** tooth powder; **polvos** dust; powder; **polvos de la madre Celestina** hocus-pocus; **polvos de talco** talcum powder
pólvora *f* powder, gunpowder; fireworks; (*persona avispada*) live wire; **correr como pólvera en reguero** to spread like wildfire
polvorear *tr* to dust, sprinkle with dust or powder
polvorien•to -ta *adj* dusty; powdery
polvorín *m* powder magazine; powder flask; (*insecto*) tick; (Chile) spitfire
polvoro•so -sa *adj* dusty; **poner pies en polvorosa** to take to one's heels
polla *f* pullet; (*puesta en juegos de naipes*) stake, kitty; (coll) lassie
pollera *f* poultry woman; chicken coop; poultry yard; go-cart; (Arg, Chile) skirt
pollero *m* poulterer; poultry yard
polli•no -na *mf* donkey, ass
polli•to -ta *mf* chick; (*persona joven*) chick, chicken
pollo *m* chicken; (*persona joven*) chicken
pomada *f* pomade
pómez *f* pumice stone
pomo *m* pome; (*de la guarnición de la espada*) pommel; (*bola aromática*) pomander; (*frasco para perfume*) flacon; **pomo de puerta** doorknob
pompa *f* pomp; soap bubble; swell, bulge; (*de la ropa*) billowing, ballooning; (*de las alas del pavo real*) spread; (naut) pump; **pompa fúnebre** funeral
pompis *m* behind, butt, rear end
pompo•so -sa *adj* pompous; high-flown, highfalutin
pómulo *m* cheekbone
ponche *m* (*bebida*) punch; **ponche de huevo** eggnog
ponchera *f* punch bowl
pon•cho -cha *adj* lazy, careless, easy-going; (Col) chubby || *m* poncho; greatcoat
ponderar *tr* to weigh; ponder, ponder over; exaggerate; praise to the skies; balance; weight
ponencia *f* paper, report
poner §54 *tr* to put, place, lay, set; arrange, dispose; (*una observación*) put in; (*una pieza dramática*) put on; (*la mesa*) set; assume, suppose; (*una ley, un impuesto*) impose; wager, stake; (*huevos*) lay; (*por escrito*) set down, put down; (*tiempo*) take; (*p.ej., miedo*) cause; make, turn; (*la luz, la radio*) turn on; (*marcha directa*) (aut) to go in; **poner en acción** to set in motion; **poner en limpio** to make a clean copy of; **poner por encima** to prefer, put ahead || *ref* to put or place oneself; become, get, turn; (*el sol, los astros*) set; (*sombrero, saco, etc.*) put on; dress, dress up; get spotted; get, reach, arrive; **ponerse a** to set out to, begin to; **ponerse tan alto** to take offense, become hoity-toity
poniente *m* west; west wind
ponqué *m* poundcake
pontífice *m* pontiff
pontón *m* pontoon; pontoon bridge; (*buque viejo*) hulk
ponzoña *f* poison

ponzoño•so -sa *adj* poisonous
popa *f* poop, stern
popote *m* (Mex) straw for brooms; (*para tomar refrescos*) (Mex) straw
populache•ro -ra *adj* popular; cheap, vulgar; rabble-rousing || *mf* rabble-rouser
populacho *m* populace, mob, rabble
popular *adj* popular
popularizar §60 *tr* to popularize
populo•so -sa *adj* populous
popu•rrí *m* (*pl* **-rríes**) medley
poquedad *f* paucity, scantiness; scarcity; timidity; trifle
poqui•to -ta *adj* very little; timid, shy, backward
por *prep* by; through, over; via, by way of; in, e.g., **por la mañana** in the morning; for; because of; for the sake of; on account of; in exchange for; in order to; as; about, e.g., **por Navidad** about Christmastime; out of, e.g., **por ignorancia** out of ignorance; times, e.g., **tres por cuatro** four times three; **estar por** to be on the point of, be ready to; be still to be, e.g., **la carta está por escribir** the letter is still to be written; **ir por** to go for, to go after; to follow; **por ciento** per cent; **por entre** among, between; **por que** because; in order that; **por qué** why; **por** + *adj* or *adv* + **que** however
porcelana *f* porcelain, chinaware; (*usado por los plateros*) enamel; (Mex) washbowl
porcentaje *m* percentage
porción *f* portion
porche *m* porch, portico
pordiosear *intr* to beg, go begging
pordiose•ro -ra *mf* beggar
porfía *f* persistence, stubbornness, obstinacy; **a porfía** in emulation; insistently
porfia•do -da *adj* persistent, stubborn, obstinate; opinionated
porfiar §77 *intr* to persist; argue stubbornly
pórfido *m* porphyry
pormenor *m* detail, particular
pormenorizar §60 *tr* to detail, tell in detail; to itemize
poro *m* pore
poro•so -sa *adj* porous
poroto *m* (SAm) bean, string bean; (Chile) little runt
porque *conj* because; in order that
porqué *m* why; quantity, share; wherewithal, money
porquería *f* dirt, filth; trifle; crudity; (*alimento dañoso a la salud*) junk
porra *f* club, bludgeon; bore, nuisance; boasting; (*pelos enredados*) (Arg, Bol) knot, tangle; (Mex) claque
porrazo *m* clubbing; blow, bump, thump
porro *m* (*mariguana*) joint
porta *f* porthole
portaavio•nes *m* (*pl* **-nes**) aircraft carrier, flattop
portacandado *m* hasp
portada *f* front, façade; portal; title page; (*de una revista*) cover; **falsa portada** half title
portadis•cos *m* (*pl* **-cos**) turntable
porta•dor -dora *adj* (*onda*) (rad) carrier || *mf* bearer; carrier || *m* waiter's tray
portaequipaje *m* (aut) trunk
portaequipa•jes *m* (*pl* **-jes**) baggage rack
portaguan•tes *m* (*pl* **-tes**) (aut) glove compartment
portal *m* vestibule, entrance hall; porch, portico; arcade; city gate; (*de un túnel*) portal *m;* crèche
portalámpa•ras *m* (*pl* **-ras**) (elec) socket
portalón *m* gate, portal; (*en el costado del buque*) gangway
portamira *m* (surv) rodman
portamone•das *m* (*pl* **-das**) pocketbook
portanue•vas *mf* (*pl* **-vas**) newsmonger
portañuela *f* (*de los pantalones*) fly; (Col, Mex) carriage door
portapape•les *m* (*pl* **-les**) brief case
portaplu•mas *m* (*pl* **-mas**) penholder
portar *tr* to carry, bear; (hunt) to retrieve || *ref* to behave, conduct oneself
portase•nos *m* (*pl* **-nos**) brassiere
portátil *adj* portable
portatinte•ro *m* inkstand
portavian•das *m* (*pl* **-das**) dinner pail
porta•voz *m* (*pl* **-voces**) megaphone; mouthpiece, spokesperson
portazgo *m* toll, road toll
portazo *m* bang, slam
porte *m* portage; carrying charge, freight; postage; behavior, conduct; dress, bearing; size, capacity; (Chile) birthday present; **porte concertado** mailing permit; **porte pagado** postage prepaid, freight prepaid
portear *tr* to carry, transport || *intr* to slam || *ref* (*las aves*) to migrate
portento *m* prodigy, wonder
portento•so -sa *adj* portentous, extraordinary
porte•ño -ña *adj* Buenos Aires; Valparaiso; pertaining to any large South American city with a port || *mf* native or inhabitant of Buenos Aires, Valparaiso or any large South American city with a port
porte•ro -ra *mf* doorkeeper; gatekeeper; (sport) goalkeeper || *m* porter, janitor; doorman; **portero electrónico** automatic door opener || *f* portress, janitress
portezuela *f* small door; (*de un coche o automóvil*) door; pocket flap
pórtico *m* portico, porch; little gate
portilla *f* porthole; private cart road, private cattle pass
portillo *m* gap, opening; nick, notch; (*puerta chica en otra mayor*) wicket; gate; narrow pass; side entrance
portorrique•ño -ña *adj & mf* Puerto Rican
portua•rio -ria *adj* port, harbor, dock || *m* dock hand, dock worker
Portugal *m* Portugal
portu•gués -guesa *adj & mf* Portuguese
porvenir *m* future
pos — **en pos de** after, behind; in pursuit of
posa *f* knell, toll
posada *f* inn, wayside inn; lodging; boardinghouse; home, dwelling; camp; **posadas** (Mex) pre-Christmas celebration

posade•ro -ra *mf* innkeeper; **posaderas** buttocks
posar *tr* to put down || *intr* to put up, lodge; alight, perch; pose || *ref* to alight, perch; settle; rest
posbéli•co -ca *adj* postwar
posdata *f* postscript
pose *f* pose; (phot) exposure
poseer **§43** *tr* to own, possess, hold; have a mastery of || *ref* to control oneself
posesión *f* possession; **tomar posesión** (*un cargo*) to take up
posesionar *tr* to give possession to || *ref* to take possession
posesor *m* owner
poseta *f* (Ven) toilet, washroom
posfecha *f* postdate
posguerra *f* postwar period
posible *adj* possible; **hacer todo lo posible** to do one's best || **posibles** *mpl* means, income, property
posición *f* position; standing
positi•vo -va *adj* positive || *f* (phot) print, positive
poso *m* sediment, dregs; grounds; rest, quiet; **poso del café** coffee grounds
posponer **§54** *tr* to subordinate; think less of
posta *f* (*de caballos*) relay; posthouse; stage; stake, wager; slice; **a posta** on purpose; **por la posta** posthaste; **postas** buckshot
postal *adj* postal || *f* post card; **postal ilustrada** picture post card
poste *m* post, pillar, pole; **poste de alumbrado** or **de farol** lamppost; **poste de telégrafo** telegraph pole; (*persona muy alta y delgada*) beanpole; **poste indicador** road sign
póster *m* poster
postergar **§44** *tr* to delay, postpone; pass over
posteridad *f* posterity; posthumous fame
posterior *adj* back, rear; later, subsequent
postigo *m* (*puerta chica en otra mayor*) wicket; (*puertecilla en una ventana*) peep window; (*puerta excusada*) postern; shutter
posti•zo -za *adj* false, artificial; (*cuello*) detachable || *m* switch, false hair, rat
postóni•co -ca *adj* posttonic
postor *m* bidder; **el mejor postor** the highest bidder
postración *f* prostration
postrar *tr* to prostrate; weaken, exhaust || *ref* to collapse, be prostrated; prostrate oneself
postre *adj* last, final; **a la postre** at last; afterwards || *m* dessert; **postres** dessert
postulación *f* postulation; nomination
postulante *mf* applicant, candidate
póstu•mo -ma *adj* posthumous
postura *f* posture; attitude, stand; stake, wager; agreement, pact; egg, eggs; (*de huevos*) laying; **postura del sol** sunset
potabilizar **§60** *tr* to make drinkable
potable *adj* drinkable
potaje *m* pottage; jumble; (*bebida*) mixture; scheme; **potajes** vegetables
potasa *f* potash
potasio *m* potassium
pote *m* pot, jug; flowerpot; **a pote** in abundance
potencia *f* potency; power; **potencia de choque** striking power
potenciación *f* (math) involution
potencial *adj & m* potential
potenciar *tr* (*las aguas de un río; el entusiasmo de una persona*) to harness; (*elevar a una potencia*) (math) to raise
potentado *m* potentate
potente *adj* powerful; big, huge
potestad *f* power
potista *mf* toper, soak
potosí *m* great wealth, gold mine
potra *f* filly; hernia, rupture
potranca *f* young mare
potro *m* colt; pest, annoyance
pozal *m* bucket, pail
pozo *m* well; pit; whirlpool; (min) shaft; (naut) hold; (Chile, Col) pool, puddle; (Ecuad) spring, fountain; **pozo de ciencia** fountain of knowledge; **pozo de lanzamiento** launching silo; **pozo de lobo** (mil) foxhole; **pozo negro** cesspool
P.P. *abbr* **porte pagado, por poder**
p.p.do *abbr* **próximo pasado**
práctica *f* practice; method; skill; **prácticas** studies, training
prácticamente *adv* through practice, by experience
practicar **§73** *tr* to practice; bring about; (*un agujero*) make, cut
prácti•co -ca *adj* practical; skillful, practiced; practicing || *m* medical practitioner; (naut) pilot || *f* see **práctica**
pradera *f* meadowland; prairie
prado *m* meadow, pasture; promenade
Praga *f* Prague
pral. *abbr* **principal**
pralte. *abbr* **principalmente**
prángana —**estar en la prángana** (Mex, W-I) to be broke; (P-R) to be naked
preámbulo *m* preamble; evasion; **no andarse en preámbulos** to come to the point
prebéli•co -ca *adj* prewar
prebenda *f* prebend; sinecure
preca•rio -ria *adj* precarious
precaución *f* precaution
precaver *tr* to stave off, head off || *intr & ref* to be on one's guard; **precaverse contra** or **de** to guard against
precavido -da *adj* cautious
precedente *adj* preceding || *m* precedent
preceder *tr & intr* to precede
precepto *m* precept; order, injunction; **los preceptos** the Ten Commandments
preces *fpl* devotions; supplications
precia•do -da *adj* esteemed, valued; precious, valuable; boastful, proud
preciar *tr* to appraise, estimate || *ref* to boast
precintar *tr* to bind, strap; seal
precio *m* price; value, worth; esteem, credit; **a precio de quemazón** at a giveaway price; **precios de cierre** closing prices; **precio tope** ceiling price
preciosidad *f* preciousness; beauty, gem, jewel

precio•so -sa *adj* precious; valuable; witty; beautiful
preciosura *f* beauty; pretty woman
precipicio *m* precipice; destruction
precipitación *f* precipitation; **precipitación acuosa** rainfall; **precipitación radiactiva** fallout
precipitar *tr* to precipitate; rush, hurl, throw headlong || *ref* to rush, throw oneself headlong
precipito•so -sa *adj* precipitous, rash, reckless; risky, dangerous
precisar *tr* to state precisely, specify; fix; need; oblige, force; determine || *intr* to be necessary; be important; be urgent; **precisar de** to need
precisión *f* precision; necessity, obligation; (Chile) haste; **precisiones** data
preci•so -sa *adj* necessary; precise; (Ven) haughty
precita•do -da *adj* above-mentioned
precla•ro -ra *adj* illustrious, famous
preconizar **§60** *tr* to proclaim, commend publicly
pre•coz *adj* (*pl* **-coces**) precocious
predato•rio -ria *adj* predatory
predecir **§24** *tr* to predict, foretell
prédica *f* Protestant sermon; harangue
predicar **§73** *tr* to preach; praise to the skies; scold, preach to
predicción *f* prediction; **predicción del tiempo** weather forecasting
predilec•to -ta *adj* favorite, preferred
predio *m* property, estate
predisponer **§54** *tr* to predispose
predominante *adj* predominant
preeminente *adj* preëminent
preestreno *m* (mov) preview
prefabricar **§73** *tr* to prefabricate
prefacio *m* preface
preferencia *f* preference; **de preferencia** preferably
preferente *adj* preferable; favored; (*acciones*) preferred
preferible *adj* preferable
preferir **§68** *tr* to prefer
prefigurar *tr* to foreshadow
prefijar *tr* to prefix; prearrange
prefijo *m* prefix
pregón *m* proclamation, public announcement (*by town crier*)
pregonar *tr* to proclaim, announce publicly; hawk; reveal; outlaw; praise openly
pregonero *m* auctioneer; town crier
preguerra *f* prewar period
pregunta *f* question; **hacer una pregunta** to ask a question
preguntar *tr* to ask; to question || *intr* to ask, inquire; **preguntar por** to ask after or for || *ref* to ask oneself; wonder
pregun•tón -tona *adj* inquisitive || *mf* inquisitive person
prejudicio *m* or **prejuicio** *m* prejudgment; prejudice
prelado *m* prelate
preliminar *adj & m* preliminary; **preliminares** (*de un libro*) front matter
preludio *m* prelude
premeditar *tr* to premeditate
premiar *tr* to reward; give an award to
premio *m* reward, prize; premium; **a premio** at a premium; **premio de enganche** (mil) bounty; **premio gordo** first prize
premio•so -sa *adj* tight, close; bothersome; strict, rigid; slow, dull
premisa *f* premise; mark, token, clue
premura *f* pressure, haste, urgency
premuro•so -sa *adj* pressing, urgent
prenda *f* pledge; security; pawn; jewel, household article; garment, article of clothing; gift, talent; darling, loved one; **en prenda** in pawn; **en prenda de** as a pledge of; **prenda perdida** forfeit; **prendas** (*juego*) forfeits; **prendas interiores** underwear
prendar *tr* to pawn; pledge; charm, captivate || *ref* — **prendarse de** to take a liking for, fall in love with
prendedero *m* or **prendedor** *m* fillet, brooch; stickpin
prender *tr* to seize, grasp; catch; imprison; dress up; pin; fasten || *intr* to catch; catch fire; take root; turn out well || *ref* to dress up; be fastened; catch hold
prendería *f* second-hand shop
prende•ro -ra *mf* second-hand dealer
prenombra•do -da *adj* above-mentioned; foregoing
prensa *f* press; printing press; vise; press, newspapers; press, frame; **entrar en prensa** to go to press; **meter en prensa** to put the squeeze on; **prensa amarilla** yellow press; **prensa taladradora** drill press
prensado *m* pressing; (*lustre de los tejidos prensados*) sheen
prensador *m* (CAm) paper clip
prensar *tr* to press; squeeze
preña•do -da *adj* pregnant; sagging, bulging; full, charged
preñez *f* pregnancy; fullness; impending danger; inherent confusion
preocupación *f* (*posesión anticipada; cuidado, desvelo*) preoccupation; (*posesión anticipada*) preoccupancy; bias, prejudice
preocupar *tr* to preoccupy, worry || *ref* to become preoccupied, be worried
preparación *f* preparation
prepara•do -da *adj* ready, prepared || *m* (pharm) preparation
preparar *tr* to prepare || *ref* to prepare, get ready
preparati•vo -va *adj* preparatory || *m* preparation, readiness
preponderante *adj* preponderant
preposición *f* preposition
prepóste•ro -ra *adj* reversed, upset, out of order, inopportune
prerrogativa *f* prerogative
presa *f* capture, seizure; catch, prey; booty, spoils; dam; trench, ditch, flume; bit, morsel; fang, tusk, claw; fishweir; (sport) hold; **hacer presa** to seize; **ser presa de** to be a victim of; be prey to
presagiar *tr* to presage, forebode

presagio *m* presage, omen, token
présbita or **présbite** *adj* far-sighted || *mf* far-sighted person
presbiteria•no -na *adj & mf* Presbyterian
prescindir *intr* — **prescindir de** to leave aside, leave out, disregard; do without, dispense with; avoid
prescribir **§83** *tr & intr* to prescribe
presencia *f* presence; show, display; **presencia de ánimo** presence of mind
presenciar *tr* to witness, be present at
presentación *f* presentation; (*de una persona en el trato de otra u otras*) introduction; (*de un nuevo automóvil, libro, etc.*) appearance
presentador *m* or **presentadora** *f* (telv) moderator
presentar *tr* to present; introduce || *ref* to present oneself; appear, show up; introduce oneself
presente *adj* present; **hacer presente** to notify of, remind of; **tener presente** to bear or keep in mind || *interj* here!, present! || *m* present, gift; person present
presentimiento *m* presentiment, premonition
presentir **§68** *tr* to have a presentiment of
preservar *tr* to preserve, protect
preservati•vo -va *adj & m* preventive; preservative
presidencia *f* presidency; chairmanship
presidente *m* president; chairman; presiding judge
presidiario *m* convict
presidio *m* garrison; fortress; citadel; penitentiary; imprisonment; hard labor; aid, help
presidir *tr* to preside over; dominate || *intr* to preside
presilla *f* loop, fastener; clip; paper clip; shoulder strap
presión *f* pressure; (*cerveza*) **a presión** on draught; **presión de inflado** tire pressure
presionar *tr* to press; put pressure on || *intr* to press; **presionar sobre** to put pressure on
pre•so -sa *adj* seized; imprisoned || *mf* prisoner; convict; **preso preventivo** pretrial prisoner; *f* see **presa**
presta•do -da *adj* lent, loaned; **dar prestado** to lend; **pedir** or **tomar prestado** to borrow
prestamista *mf* moneylender; pawnbroker
préstamo *m* loan; **préstamo lingüístico** loan word, borrowing
prestar *tr* to lend, loan; (*oído; ayuda; noticias*) give; (*atención*) pay; (*un favor*) do; (*un servicio*) render; (*juramento*) take; (*silencio*) keep; (*paciencia*) show || *intr* (*un paño, la ropa*) give, yield; be useful || *ref* to lend oneself, lend itself
prestata•rio -ria *mf* borrower
presteza *f* speed, promptness, readiness
prestidigitación *f* sleight of hand
prestidigita•dor -dora *adj* captivating || *mf* magician; faker, impostor
prestigio *m* prestige; good standing; spell; illusion
prestigio•so -sa *adj* captivating, spellbinding; famous, renowned; illusory
pres•to -ta *adj* quick, prompt, ready; nimble || **presto** *adv* right away
presumi•do -da *adj* conceited, vain || *mf* would-be
presumir *tr* to presume || *intr* to boast, be conceited
presunción *f* presumption; conceit
presuntuo•so -sa *adj* conceited, vain
presuponer **§54** *tr* to presuppose; budget
presupuestar *tr* to budget; (*el coste de una obra*) estimate
presupuesto *m* budget; reason, motive; supposition; estimate
presuro•so -sa *adj* speedy, quick, hasty; zealous, persistent
pretencio•so -sa *adj* pretentious, showy; conceited, vain
pretender *tr* to claim, pretend to; try for, try to do; be a suitor for || *intr* to insist; **pretender** + *inf* to try to + *inf*
pretendiente *mf* pretender, claimant; office seeker || *m* suitor
pretensión *f* pretension; claim; pretense; presumption; effort, pursuit
pretéri•to -ta *adj & m* past
pretil *m* parapet, railing; walk along a parapet
pretina *f* girdle, belt; waistband
pretóni•co -ca *adj* pretonic
prevalecer **§22** *intr* to prevail; take root; thrive
prevaler **§76** *ref* — **prevalerse de** to avail oneself of, take advantage of
prevaricar **§73** *intr* to collude, connive; play false; transgress; rave, be delirious
prevención *f* preparation; prevention; foresight; warning; prejudice; stock, supply; jail, lockup; guardhouse; **a** or **de prevención** spare, emergency
preveni•do -da *adj* prepared, ready; foresighted, forewarned; stocked, full
prevenir **§79** *tr* to prepare, make ready; forestall, prevent, anticipate; overcome; warn; prejudice || *intr* (*una tempestad*) to come up || *ref* to get ready; come to mind
prever **§80** *tr* to foresee
pre•vio -via *adj* previous; preliminary; after, with previous, subject to, e.g., **previo acuerdo** subject to agreement; **cita previa** by appointment
previsión *f* prevision, foresight; foresightedness; forecast; **previsión del tiempo** weather forecasting
prie•to -ta *adj* dark, blackish; stingy, mean; tight, compact; dark-complexioned || *mf* (W-I) darling
prima *f* early morning; bonus, bounty; (ins) premium; (mil) first quarter of the night; (*cuerda*) (mus) treble
pri•mal -mala *adj & mf* yearling
prima•rio -ria *adj* primary || *m* (elec) primary
primavera *f* spring, springtime; cowslip, primrose; robin
primer *adj* apocopated form of **primero,** used only before masculine singular nouns and adjectives

prime•ro -ra *adj* first; former; early; primary; prime; (*materia*) raw || *m* first; **a primeros de** around the beginning of || **primero** *adv* first
primicia *f* first fruits
primige•nio -nia *adj* original, primitive
primiti•vo -va *adj* primitive
pri•mo -ma *adj* first; prime, excellent; skillful; (*materia*) raw || *mf* cousin; sucker, dupe; **primo carnal** or **primo hermano** first cousin, cousin-german || *f* see **prima** || **primo** *adv* in the first place
primogéni•to -ta *adj & mf* first-born
primor *m* care, skill, elegance; beauty
primoro•so -sa *adj* careful, skillful, elegant; fine, exquisite
princesa *f* princess; **princesa viuda** dowager princess
principal *adj* principal, main, chief; first, foremost; essential, important; famous, illustrious; (*piso*) second || *m* principal, head, chief
príncipe *m* prince; **portarse como un príncipe** to live like a prince; **príncipe de Asturias** heir apparent of the King of Spain; **príncipe de Gales** prince of Wales; **príncipes** prince and princess
principiante *adj* beginning || *mf* beginner, apprentice, novice
principiar *tr, intr & ref* to begin
principio *m* start, beginning; principle; origin, source; (culin) entree; **a principios de** around the beginning of; **en un principio** at the beginning; **principio de admiración** inverted exclamation point; **principio de interrogación** inverted question mark
pringar §44 *tr* to dip or soak in grease or fat; spot or stain with grease; make bleed; slander, run down; splash || *intr* to meddle; (CAm, Mex) to drizzle || *ref* to peculate
pringo•so -sa *adj* greasy, fatty
prioridad *f* priority; **de máxima prioridad** of the highest priority
prisa *f* hurry, haste; urgency; crush, crowd; **darse prisa** to hurry, make haste; **estar de prisa** or **tener prisa** to be in a hurry
prisión *f* seizure, capture; imprisonment; prison; **prisión celular** cell house; **prisiones** shackles, fetters
prisione•ro -ra *mf* prisoner; (*cautivo de una pasión o afecto*) captive || *m* setscrew; studbolt
prisma *m* prism
prismáticos *mpl* binoculars
priva•do -da *adj* private || *m* (*de un alto personaje*) favorite || *f* cesspool
privar *tr* to deprive; forbid, prohibit || *intr* to be in vogue; prevail; be in favor || *ref* to deprive oneself; **privarse de** to give up
privilegiar *tr* to grant a privilege to
privilegio *m* privilege
pro *m & f* profit, advantage; **¡buena pro!** good appetite!; **de pro** of note, of worth; **el pro y el contra** the pros and the cons; **en pro de** on behalf of
proa *f* (aer) nose; (naut) prow
probable *adj* probable, likely
probador *m* fitting room
probar §61 *tr* to prove; test; try; (*clothing*) try on; try out; sample; fit; suit; (*vino*) touch || *intr* to taste; **probar de** to take a taste of || *ref* to try on
probidad *f* probity, integrity, honesty
problema *m* problem
pro•caz *adj* (*pl* **-caces**) impudent, insolent, bold
procedencia *f* origin, source; point of departure
procedente *adj* coming, originating; proper
proceder *m* conduct, behavior || *intr* to proceed; originate; behave; be proper
procedimiento *m* procedure; proceeding; process
procelo•so -sa *adj* tempestuous, stormy
prócer *adj* high, lofty || *m* hero, leader
procesamiento *m* (data) processing
procesar *tr* to sue, prosecute; indict; try; (*ordenador*) to process, data-process
procesión *f* procession; origin, emergence
proceso *m* process; progress; suit, lawsuit; **proceso verbal** minutes
proclama *f* proclamation; marriage banns
proclamar *tr* to proclaim; acclaim
proclíti•co -ca *adj & m* proclitic
procurador *m* attorney, solicitor; proxy
procurar *tr* to strive for; manage as attorney; yield, produce; try to
prodigar §44 *tr* to lavish; squander; waste || *ref* to be a show-off
prodigio *m* prodigy
prodigio•so -sa *adj* prodigious, marvelous; fine, excellent
pródigo -ga *adj* prodigal; lavish || *mf* prodigal
producción *f* production; crop, yield, produce; **producción en masa** or **en serie** mass production
producir §19 *tr* to produce; yield, bear; cause, bring about || *ref* to explain oneself; come about; take place
producto *m* product; produce; proceeds
proeza *f* prowess; feat, stunt
prof. *abbr* **profeta**
profanar *tr* to profane
profa•no -na *adj* profane; indecent, immodest; worldly; lay || *mf* profane; worldly person; layman
profecía *f* prophecy || **las Profecías** (Bib) the Prophets
proferir §68 *tr* to utter
profesar *tr & intr* to profess
profesión *f* profession; **profesión de fe** confession of faith
profe•sor -sora *mf* teacher; professor
profeta *m* prophet
profetisa *f* prophetess
profetizar §60 *tr* to prophesy
profilácti•co -ca *adj & m* prophylactic; preventive || *f* hygiene
prófu•go -ga *adj & mf* fugitive || *m* slacker, draft dodger
profundidad *f* profundity; depth
profundizar §60 *tr* to deepen; fathom, get to the bottom of

profun•do -da *adj* profound; deep
progenie *f* descent, lineage, parentage
progno•sis *f* (*pl* **-sis**) prognosis; (*del tiempo*) forecast
programa *m* program; **programa continuo** (mov) continuous showing; **programa de estudios** curriculum; **programa (para ordenador)** program(me), software
programación *f* (*ordenador*) program(m)ing; (telv) scheduling
programador *m* or **programadora** *f* (*ordenador*) program(m)er
programar *tr* to program; (*ordenador*) program(me)
progresar *intr* to progress
progresista *adj & mf* (pol) progressive
progreso *m* progress; **hacer progresos** to make progress
prohibir *tr* to prohibit, forbid ‖ *ref* **se prohibe fijar carteles** post no bills
prohijar *tr* to adopt
prohombre *m* (*en los gremios de los artesanos*) master; leader, head; (coll) big shot
prójimo *m* fellow man, fellow creature, neighbor; fellow
pról. *abbr* **prólogo**
prole *f* progeny, offspring
proletariado *m* proletariat
proleta•rio -ria *adj & m* proletarian
proliferar *intr* to proliferate
prolífi•co -ca *adj* prolific
proli•jo -ja *adj* tedious, too long; fussy, fastidious; long-winded; tiresome
prologar **§44** *tr* to preface, write a preface for
prólogo *m* prologue; preface
prolongar **§44** *tr* to prolong, extend; (geom) to produce
promediar *tr* to divide into two equal parts; average ‖ *intr* to mediate; be half over
promedio *m* average, mean; middle
promesa *f* promise
promete•dor -dora *adj* promising
prometer *tr & intr* to promise ‖ *ref* to become engaged
prometi•do -da *adj* engaged, betrothed ‖ *m* promise; fiancé ‖ *f* fiancée
prominente *adj* prominent
promiso•rio -ria *adj* promissory
promoción *f* promotion; advancement; (*conjunto de individuos que obtienen un grado en un mismo año*) class, year, crop
promontorio *m* promontory, headland; unwieldy thing
promover **§47** *tr* to promote; advance, further
promulgar **§44** *tr* to promulgate
pronombre *m* pronoun
pronosticar **§73** *tr* to prognosticate, foretell
pronóstico *m* prognostic, forecast; almanac; (med) prognosis
pron•to -ta *adj* quick, speedy; prompt; ready ‖ *m* jerk; sudden impulse, fit of anger ‖ **pronto** *adv* right away, soon; early; promptly; **lo más pronto posible** as soon as possible; **tan pronto como** as soon as
pronunciación *f* pronunciation
pronuncia•do -da *adj* marked; (*curva*) sharp; (*pendiente*) steep; bulky
pronunciamiento *m* insurrection, uprising; (*golpe de estado militar*) pronunciamento; (law) decree
pronunciar *tr* to pronounce; utter; (*un discurso*) make, deliver; decide on ‖ *ref* to rebel; declare oneself
propaganda *f* propaganda; advertising
propagar **§44** *tr* to propagate; spread; broadcast
propalar *tr* to divulge, spread
proparoxíto•no -na *adj & m* proparoxytone
propasar *ref* to go too far, take undue liberty
propender *intr* to tend, incline, be inclined
propensión *f* propensity; predisposition
propen•so -sa *adj* inclined, disposed, prone
propiciar *tr* to propitiate; support, favor, sponsor
propi•cio -cia *adj* propitious, favorable
propiedad *f* property; ownership; naturalness, likeness; **es propiedad** copyrighted; **propiedad horizontal** one-floor ownership in an apartment house; **propiedad literaria** copyright
propieta•rio -ria *mf* owner ‖ *m* proprietor ‖ *f* proprietress
propina *f* tip, fee, gratuity
propinar *tr* (*algo a beber*) to offer; (*medicamentos*) prescribe or administer; (*palos, golpes, etc.*) give ‖ *ref* (*una bebida*) to treat oneself to
propin•cuo -cua *adj* near, close at hand
pro•pio -pia *adj* proper, suitable; peculiar, characteristic; natural; same; himself, herself, etc.; own ‖ *m* messenger; native; **propios** public lands
proponer **§54** *tr* to propose; propound; (*a una persona para un empleo*) name, present ‖ *ref* to plan; propose
proporción *f* proportion; opportunity
proporciona•do -da *adj* proportionate; fit, suitable
proporcionar *tr* to furnish, provide, supply, give; proportion; adapt, adjust
proposición *f* proposition; **proposición dominante** main clause
propósito *m* aim, purpose, intention; subject matter; **a propósito** by the way; apropos, fitting; in place; **a propósito de** apropos of; **de propósito** on purpose; **fuera de propósito** irrelevant, beside the point
propuesta *f* proposal, proposition
propulsar *tr* to propel, drive
propulsión *f* propulsion; **propulsión a chorro** jet propulsion; **propulsión a cohete** rocket propulsion
pror. *abbr* **procurador**
prorratear *tr* to prorate
prórroga *f* extension, renewal
prorrogar **§44** *tr* to defer, postpone, extend
prorrumpir *intr* to spurt, shoot forth; break forth, burst out
prosa *f* prose; chatter, idle talk
prosai•co -ca *adj* prose; prosaic, dull
proscribir **§83** *tr* to outlaw, proscribe
proscrip•to -ta *mf* exile, outlaw

prosecución *f* continuation, prosecution; pursuit
proseguir **§67** *tr* to continue, carry on || *intr* to continue
prosélito *m* proselyte
prosista *mf* prose writer; chatterbox
prosódi•co -ca *adj* (*acento*) stress
prospectar *tr & intr* to prospect
prosperar *tr* to make prosper || *intr* to prosper, thrive
prosperidad prosperity
próspe•ro -ra *adj* prosperous, thriving, successful
prosternar *ref* to prostrate oneself
prostituir **§20** *tr* to prostitute || *ref* to prostitute oneself; become a prostitute
prostituta *f* prostitute
prosu•do -da *adj* (Chile, Ecuad, Peru) pompous, solemn
protagonista *mf* protagonist
protagonizar **§60** *tr* to play the leading rôle of
protección *f* protection; **protección aduanera** protective tariff; **protección a la infancia** child welfare
proteger **§17** *tr* to protect
protegida *f* protégée
protegido *m* protégé
proteína *f* protein
proter•vo -va *adj* perverse
protesta *f* protest; pledge, promise
protestante *adj & mf* protestant; Protestant
protestar *tr* to protest, asseverate; (*la fe*) profess || *intr* to protest; **protestar de** (*aseverar con ahinco*) to protest (*to state positively*); **protestar contra** (*negar la validez de*) to protest (*to deny forcibly*)
protocolo *m* protocol
protoplasma *m* protoplasm
prototipo *m* prototype
protozoario *m* or **protozoo** *m* protozoön
provec•to -ta *adj* old, ripe
provecho *m* advantage, benefit; profit, gain; advance, progress; **¡buen provecho!** good luck!; good appetite!; **de provecho** useful; **provechos** perquisites
provecho•so -sa *adj* advantageous, beneficial; profitable; useful
proveedor -dora *mf* supplier, provider, purveyor; steward
proveer **§43 & §83** *tr* to provide, furnish; supply; resolve, settle || *intr* to provide; **proveer a** to provide for || *ref* to supply oneself; have a bowel movement
provenir **§79** *intr* to come, arise
Provenza, la Provence
provenzal *adj & mf* Provençal
proverbio *m* proverb
providencia *f* providence, foresight; step, measure
providencial *adj* providential
provincia *f* province
provisión *f* provision; supply, stock; **provisiones de boca** foodstuffs
proviso•rio -ria *adj* provisory, provisional
provocar **§73** *tr* to provoke; promote, bring about; incite, tempt, move || *intr* to provoke; vomit
proxeneta *mf* go-between
proximidad *f* proximity; **proximidades** neighborhood
próxi•mo -ma *adj* next; near; neighboring, close; early; **próximo pasado** last
proyección *f* projection; influence
proyectar *tr* to project; cast; design || *ref* to project, stick out; (*una sombra*) be projected, fall
proyectil *m* projectile; **proyectil buscador del blanco** homing missile; **proyectil dirigido** or **teleguiado** guided missile
proyecto *m* project; **proyecto de ley** bill
proyector *m* projector, searchlight; projection machine
prudencia *f* prudence
prudente *adj* prudent
prueba *f* proof; trial, test; examination; (*de un traje*) fitting; (*de un alimento o una bebida*) sample, sampling; evidence; acrobatics; sleight of hand; (sport) event; **a prueba** on approval, on trial; **a prueba de** proof against, -proof, e.g., **a prueba de escaladores** burglarproof; **a prueba de incendio** fireproof; **prueba de alcohol** alcohol-level test; **pruebas de planas** page proof; **pruebas de primeras** first proof (*for proofreader*); **pruebas de segundas** galley proof (*for author*)
pruebista *mf* acrobat
prurito *m* itching; eagerness, itch
psicoanálisis *m* psychoanalysis
psicoanalizar **§60** *tr* to psychoanalyze
psicodéli•co -ca *adj* psychedelic
psicología *f* psychology
psicológi•co -ca *adj* psychologic(al)
psicólo•go -ga *mf* psychologist
psicópata *mf* psychopath
psico•sis *f* (*pl* **-sis**) psychosis; **psicosis de guerra** war psychosis, war scare
psicoterapia *f* psychotherapy; **psicoterapia de grupo** group therapy
psicóti•co -ca *adj & mf* psychotic
psique *f* cheval glass || **Psique** *f* Psyche
psiquiatra *mf* psychiatrist
psiquiatría *f* psychiatry
psíqui•co -ca *adj* psychic
P.S.M. *abbr* **por su mandato**
pte. *abbr* **parte, presente**
púa *f* point; prick, barb; tine, prong; (*del fonógrafo*) needle; (*del peine*) tooth; thorn; (*del puerco espín*) spine, quill; sting; graft; plectrum; tricky person
pubertad *f* puberty
publicación *f* publication
publicar **§73** *tr* to publish; publicize
publicidad *f* publicity; advertising; **publicidad de lanzamiento** advance publicity
publicita•rio -ria *adj* publicity; advertising
públi•co -ca *adj & m* public
pucha *f* (W-I) small bouquet; (Mex) crescent roll
púcher *m* (*drogas*) pusher

puchero *m* pot, kettle; stew; daily bread; pouting; **hacer pucheros** to pout, screw up one's face
pucho *m* fag end, remnant; (*de cigarro*) stump; trifle, trinket; (*el hijo menor*) baby
puden•do -da *adj* ugly, shameful; obscene; (*partes*) private
pudiente *adj* powerful; well-off, well-to-do
pudín *m* pudding
pudor *m* modesty, shyness; chastity
pudoro•so -sa *adj* modest, shy; chaste
pudrición *f* rot, rotting
pudrir §83 *tr* to rot; worry || *intr* to be dead and buried || *ref* to rot; be worried; (*en la cárcel*) languish
pueblo *m* people; common people; town, village; **puebla de Dios** or **de Israel** children of Israel
puente *m* bridge; (dent, mus) bridge; (aut) axle, rear axle; **hacer puente** to take the intervening day off; **puente aéreo** airlift, air bridge; **puente colgante** suspension bridge; **puente de engrase** grease lift; **puente levadizo** drawbridge, lift bridge
puer•co -ca *adj* piggish, hoggish; dirty, filthy; slovenly; coarse, mean; lewd || *m* hog; **puerco espín** or **espino** porcupine || *f* sow; slattern, slut
puericia *f* childhood
puericultura *f* child rearing, infant care
pueril *adj* puerile, childish
puerilidad *f* puerility, childishness
puerro *m* leek; (*mariguana, hachich*) joint
puerta *f* door, doorway; gate, gateway; **a puerta cerrada** or **a puertas cerradas** behind closed doors
puerto *m* harbor, port; haven; mountain pass; **puerto aéreo** airport; **puerto brigantino** Corunna; **puerto de arribada** port of call; **puerto de mar** seaport; **puerto franco** free port; **puerto marítimo** dock, port; **puerto seco** frontier customhouse
puertorrique•ño -ña *adj & mf* Puerto Rican
pues *adv* then, well; yes, certainly; why; anyhow; **pues bien** well then; **pues que** since || *conj* for, since, because, inasmuch as || *interj* well!, then!
puesta *f* setting; laying; putting; (*dinero apostado*) stake; **a puesta del sol** or **a puestas del sol** at sunset; **puesta a punto** adjustment; carrying out, completion; **puesta a tierra** (elec) grounding; **puesta de largo** coming out, social debut
pues•to -ta *adj* dressed; **puesto que** since, inasmuch as || *m* place; booth, stand; office; station; barracks; (*para cazadores*) blind; **puesto a punto** (aut) tuning; **puesto de socorros** first-aid station || *f* see **puesta**
púgil *m* pugilist
pugilato *m* boxing; fist fight
pugilismo *m* pugilism
pugna *f* fight, battle; struggle, conflict; **en pugna con** at issue; **en pugna con** at odds with
pugnar *intr* to fight, struggle; strive, persist
pug•naz *adj* (*pl* **-naces**) pugnacious
pujante *adj* powerful, mighty, vigorous
pujar *tr* (*un proyecto*) to push; (*un precio*) raise, bid up || *intr* to struggle, strain; falter; (*por decir una cosa*) grope; snivel; **pujar para adentro** (CAm, W-I) to keep silent, say nothing
pul•cro -cra *adj* neat, tidy, trim; circumspect
pulga *f* flea; **de malas pulgas** peppery, hot-tempered; **hacer de una pulga un camello** or **un elefante** to make a mountain out of a molehill; **no aguantar pulgas** to stand for no nonsense
pulgada *f* inch
pulgar *m* thumb
puli•do -da *adj* pretty; neat; polished; clean, spotless
pulimentar *tr* to polish
pulimento *m* polish
pulir *tr* to polish; finish; give a polish to
pulmón *m* lung; **pulmón de acero** or **de hierro** iron lung
pulmonía *f* pneumonia
púlpito *m* pulpit
pulpo *m* octopus
pulque *m* (Mex) agave brandy
pulsación *f* pulsation, throb, beat; strike, striking; (*del pianista, el mecanógrafo*) touch
pulsar *tr* (*un botón*) to push; (*un piano, arpa, guitarra*) play; (*una tecla*) strike; feel or take the pulse of; sound out, examine || *intr* to pulsate, throb, beat
pulsear *intr* to hand-wrestle
pulsera *f* bracelet; wristlet, watch strap; **pulsera de pedida** engagement bracelet
pulso *m* pulse; steadiness, steady hand; tact, care, caution; bracelet; wrist watch; **a pulso** with hand and wrist; by main strength; (*dibujo*) freehand; **sacar a pulso** to carry out against odds; **tomar el pulso a** to take the pulse of
pulular *intr* to swarm; bud, sprout
pulverizar §60 *tr* to pulverize; atomize; spray
pulla *f* dig, cutting remark; filthy remark; witticism
pum *interj* bang!
puma *m* cougar
puna *f* (SAm) bleak tableland in the Andes; (SAm) mountain sickness
pundonor *m* point of honor; face
pundonoro•so sa *adj* punctilious, scrupulous; haughty, dignified
pungir §27 *tr* to prick; sting
punta *f* (*extremo agudo*) point; tip, end; (*del cigarro*) butt; nail; point, cape, headland; (*del toro*) horn; (*del asta del ciervo*) tine, prong; style, graver; touch, tinge, trace; (*del vino*) souring; (elec) point; **de punta** on end; on tiptoe; **de punta en blanco** in full armor; in full regalia; **estar de punta (con)** to be at odds (with); **punta de combate** (*del torpedo*) warhead; **punta de lanza** spearhead; **punta de París** wire nail; **sacar punta a** to put a point on, to sharpen; **tener en la punta de la lengua** to have on the tip of one's tongue
puntabola *f* (Bol) ball-point pen

puntada *f* hint; (sew) stitch; (*dolor agudo*) stitch, sharp pain
puntal *m* prop, support; stay, stanchion; backing, support; bite, snack; (naut) depth of hold
puntapié *m* kick; **echar a puntapiés** to kick out
puntear *tr* to dot, mark with dots; (*guitarra*) pluck; stipple; stitch || *intr* (naut) to tack
puntera *f* toe, toe patch; leather tip; (coll) kick
puntería *f* aim, aiming; marksmanship
puntero *m* pointer; (*del reloj*) hand; stonecutter's chisel; punch; leading animal
puntiagu•do -da *adj* sharp-pointed
puntilla *f* brad; narrow lace edging; (*de la pluma fuente*) point; (carp) tracing point; dagger; **de puntillas** on tiptoe; **puntilla francesa** finishing nail
puntillero *m* bullfighter who delivers coup de grace with dagger
puntillo•so -sa *adj* punctilious
punto *m* (*señal de dimensiones poco perceptibles*) point, dot; stitch, loop; mesh; (*rotura en un tejido de punto*) break; jot; cabstand, hackstand; (gram) period; (math, typ, sport, fig) point; **a buen punto** opportunely; **al punto** at once; **a punto de** on the point of; **a punto fijo** for certain; **de punto** knitted; **dos puntos** (gram) colon; **en punto** sharp, on the dot; **poner punto final a** to wind up, to bring to an end; **punto de admiración** exclamation mark or point; **punto de aguja** knitting; **punto de Hungría** herringbone; **punto de media** knitwork; **punto de mira** aim; center of attraction; **¡punto en boca!** mum's the word!; **punto interrogante** question mark; **punto menos** almost; **punto muerto** dead center; (aut) neuter; **puntos y rayas** dots and dashes; **punto y coma** *msg* semicolon
puntuación *f* punctuation; mark, grade; scoring
puntual *adj* punctual; certain, sure; exact, accurate
puntualizar **§60** *tr* to fix in the memory; give a detailed account of; finish; draw up
puntuar **§21** *tr & intr* to punctuate; score
puntura *f* puncture, prick
punzada *f* prick; shooting pain; (*del remordimiento*) pang
punzante *adj* sharp, pricking; barbed, biting, caustic
punzar **§60** *tr* to prick, puncture, punch; to sting; to grieve || *intr* to sting
punzón *m* punch; pick; burin, graver; budding horn, tenderling; **punzón de marcar** center punch
puñada *f* punch
puñado *m* handful, bunch
puñal *m* dagger, poniard
puñalada *f* stab; blow, sudden sorrow; **puñalada de misericordia** coup de grâce; **puñalada trapera** stab in the back
puñetazo *m* punch; bang with the fist
puño *m* fist; cuff; wristband; grasp; fistful, handful; hilt; (*p.ej., del paraguas*) handle; (*del bastón*) head; punch; **como un puño** whopping big; tiny, microscopic; close-fisted; **de su propio puño** or **de su puño y letra** in his own hand, in his own writing; **puño de herro** brass knuckles
pupa *f* pimple; fever blister
pupila *f* (*del ojo*) pupil
pupi•lo -la *mf* boarder; orphan, ward; pupil || *f* see **pupila**
pupitre *m* writing desk
puquio *m* (SAm) spring or pool of fresh, clear water
puré *m* purée; **puré de patatas** mashed potatoes; **puré de tomates** stewed tomatoes
purera *f* cigar case
pureza *f* purity
purga *f* purge; purgative; drain valve
purgante *adj & m* purgative
purgar **§44** *tr* to purge; physic; drain; purify, refine; expiate; (*pasiones*) control, check; (*sospechas*) clear away || *ref* to take a physic; unburden oneself
puridad *f* purity
purificar **§73** *tr* to purify
purita•no -na *adj & mf* puritan; Puritan
pu•ro -ra *adj* pure; sheer; (*cielo*) clear; out-and-out, outright; **de puro** completely, totally; because of being || *m* cigar
púrpura *f* purple
purpura•do -da *adj* purple || *m* (eccl) cardinal
purpúre•o -a *adj* purple
pusilánime *adj* pusillanimous
pústula *f* pustule
puta *f* whore
putañear or **putear** *intr* to whore around, chase after lewd women
putati•vo -va *adj* spurious
putrefac•to -ta *adj* rotten, putrid
pútri•do -da *adj* putrid, rotten
puya *f* steel point; (*del gallo*) spur

Q

Q, q (cu) *f* twentieth letter of the Spanish alphabet
q.b.s.m. *abbr* **que besa su mano**
q.e.p.d. *abbr* **que en paz descanse**
q.e.s.m. *abbr* **que estrecha su mano**
quántum *m* (*pl* **quanta**) quantum
que *pron rel* that, which; who, whom; **el que** he who; which, the one which; who, the one who || *adv* than || *conj* that; for, because; let, e.g., **que entre** let him come in; **a que** I'll bet that
qué *adj & pron interr* what, which; **¿qué tal?**

how?; hello, how's everything? || *interj* what!; what a!; how!

quebrada *f* gorge, ravine, gap; brook; failure, bankruptcy

quebradi•zo -za *adj* brittle, fragile; frail

quebra•do -da *adj* weakened; bankrupt; ruptured; rough; winding || *m* (math) fraction || *f* see **quebrada**

quebrantable *adj* breakable

quebrantar *tr* to break; break open; break out of; grind, crush; soften, mollify; (*un contrato; la ley; un hábito; un testamento; el corazón de una persona*) break || *ref* to break; become broken

quebrantaterro•nes *m* (*pl* **-nes**) clodhopper

quebranto *m* break, breaking; heavy loss; great sorrow; discouragement

quebrar **§2** *tr* to break; bend, twist; crush; overcome; temper, soften || *intr* to break; fail; weaken, give in || *ref* to break; weaken; become ruptured

queda *f* curfew

quedar *intr* to remain; stay; be left; be left over; stop, leave off; turn out; be; be found, be located; **quedar en** to agree on; agree to; **quedar por** + *inf* or **sin** + *inf* to remain to be + *pp* || *ref* to remain; stay; stop; be; be left; put up; **quedarse con** to keep, to take; **quedarse tan fresco** to show no offense

que•do -da *adj* quiet, still; gentle || *f* see **queda** || **quedo** *adv* softly, in a low voice; gropingly

quehacer *m* work, task, chore

queja *f* complaint, lament; whine, moan

quejar *ref* to complain, lament; whine, moan

quejido *m* complaint, whine, moan

quejumbre *f* complaining, whine, moan

quejumbro•so -sa *adj* complaining; whining, whiny

quema *f* fire; burning; **a quema ropa** point-blank; **de quema** distilled; **hacer quema** (Arg, Bol) to hit the mark

quemada *f* burnt brush; (Mex) fire

quemadero *m* incinerator; (*poste destinado para quemar a los condenados a la pena de fuego*) stake

quema•do -da *adj* burned; burnt out; angry || *m* burnt brush; **oler a quemado** to smell of fire; **saber a quemado** to taste burned || *f* see **quemada**

quema•dor -dora *adj* burning; incendiary || *m* burner

quemadura *f* burn; (agr) smut

quemar *tr* to burn; scald; set on fire; scorch; frostbite; sell too cheap; (CAm, Mex) to betray, inform against || *intr* to burn, be hot || *ref* to burn; be burning up; fret; (*estar cercano a lo que se busca*) be warm, be hot; **quemarse las cejas** to burn the midnight oil

quemarropa — **a quemarropa** point-blank

quemazón *f* burn; burning; intense heat; (*de un fusible*) blowout; itch; cutting remark; pique, anger; (hum) bargain sale; (Arg, Bol, Chile) mirage on the pampas

que•pis *m* (*pl* **-pis**) kepi

queque *m* cake

querella *f* complaint; dispute, quarrel

querellar *ref* to complain; whine

querencia *f* liking, affection; attraction; love of home; (*de animales*) haunt; favorite spot

querencio•so -sa *adj* homing; (*sitio*) favorite

querer *m* love, affection; liking, fondness || *v* **§55** *tr* to wish, want, desire; like; love; **como quiera** anyhow; anyway; **como quiera que** whereas; inasmuch as; no matter how; **cuando quiera** any time; **donde quiera** anywhere; **querer bien** to love; **sin querer** unwillingly; unintentionally || *v aux* to wish to, want to, desire to; will; be about to, be trying to, e.g., **quiere llover** it is trying to rain; **querer decir** to mean; **querer más** to prefer to, would rather

queri•do -da *adj* dear || *mf* lover; paramour; dearie || *f* mistress

quermés *f* or **quermese** *f* bazaar; village or country fair

queroseno *m* var of **keroseno**

querubín *m* cherub

quesadilla *f* cheesecake; sweet pastry

quese•ro -ra *adj* cheesy || *mf* cheesemonger; cheesemaker || *f* cheese board; cheese mold; cheese dish

queso *m* cheese; **queso de cerdo** headcheese; **queso helado** brick ice cream; **queso para extender** cheese spread

quevedos *mpl* nose glasses

quiá *interj* oh, no!

quicio *m* pivot hole (*of hinge*); **fuera de quicio** out of order; **sacar de quicio** to put out of order; unhinge

quiebra *f* crack; damage, loss; bankruptcy

quien *pron rel* who, whom; he who, she who; someone who, anyone who

quién *pron interr* who, whom

quienquiera *pron indef* anyone, anybody; **quienquiera que** whoever; **a quienquiera que** whomever

quie•to -ta *adj* quiet, calm; virtuous

quietud *f* quiet, calm, stillness

quijada *f* jaw, jawbone

quijotes•co -ca *adj* quixotic

quilate *m* carat

quilo *m* kilogram; **sudar el quilo** to slave, be a drudge

quilla *f* keel; (*de ave*) breastbone; **dar de quilla** (naut) to keel over

quimera *f* chimera; dispute, quarrel

química *f* chemistry

quími•co -ca *adj* chemical || *mf* chemist || *f* see **química**

quimicultura *f* tank farming

quimono *m* kimono

quimioterapia *f* chemotherapy

quina *f* cinchona, Peruvian bark

quincalla *f* hardware

quincallería *f* hardware store; hardware business; hardware factory

quincalle•ro -ra *mf* hardware merchant

quince *adj & pron* fifteen || *m* fifteen; (*en las fechas*) fifteenth

quincea•vo -va *adj & m* fifteenth

quince•no -na *adj & m* fifteenth || *f* fortnight, two weeks; two weeks' pay
quincuagési•mo -ma *adj & m* fiftieth
quiniela *f* pelota game of five; soccer lottery; daily double; (Arg, Urug) numbers game
quinien•tos -tas *adj & pron* five hundred || **quinientos** *m* five hundred
quinina *f* quinine
quinqué *m* student lamp, oil lamp
quinquenal *adj* five-year
quinta *f* villa, country house; draft, induction; **ir a quintas** to be drafted; **redimirse de las quintas** to be exempted from the draft
quintacolumnista *mf* fifth columnist
quintal *m* quintal, hundredweight
quintar *tr* to draft
quinteto *m* quintet
quintilla *f* five-line stanza of eight syllables and two rhymes; any five-line stanza with two rhymes
quintilli•zo -za *mf* quint, quintuplet
Quintín — **armar la de San Quintín** to raise a rumpus, raise a row
quin•to -ta *adj* fifth || *m* fifth; lot; pasture; draftee || *f* see **quinta**
quinza•vo -va *adj & m* fifteenth
quiosco *m* kiosk, summerhouse; stand; **quiosco de música** bandstand; **quiosco de necesidad** comfort station; **quiosco de periódicos** newsstand
quiquiri•quí *m* (*pl* **-quíes**) cock-a-doodle-doo; cock of the walk
quirófano *m* operating room
quiromancia *f* or **quiromancía** *f* palmistry
quiropodista *mf* chiropodist
quiropráctí•co -ca *adj* chiropractic || *mf* chiropractor
quirúrgi•co -ca *adj* surgical
quirurgo *m* surgeon
quiscal *m* grackle
quisicosa *f* puzzler
quisqui•do -da *adj* (Arg) constipated
quisquilla *f* trifle, triviality; **pararse en quisquillas** to bicker, make a fuss over trifles; **quisquillas** hairsplitting, quibbling
quisquillo•so -sa *adj* trifling; touchy; fastidious; hairsplitting
quiste *m* cyst
quis•to -ta *adj* — **bien quisto** well-liked, welcome; **mal quisto** disliked, unwelcome
quitaesmalte *m* nail-polish remover
quitaman•chas *mf* (*pl* **-chas**) (*persona*) clothes cleaner, spot remover || *m* (*substancia*) clothes cleaner, spot remover
quitamo•tas *mf* (*pl* **-tas**) bootlicker, apple polisher
quitanie•ve *m* or **quitanie•ves** *m* (*pl* **-ves**) snowplow
quitapie•dras *m* (*pl* **-dras**) cowcatcher
quitapintura *m* paint remover
quitapón *m* pompon for draft mules; **de quitapón** detachable, removable
quitar *tr* to remove; take away; (*la mesa*) clear; (*esfuerzo, trabajo*) save; (*tiempo*) take; free; parry; **quitar algo a algo** to take something off something, remove something from something; **quitar algo a uno** to remove something from someone; take something away from someone || *intr* — **de quita y pon** detachable, removable || *ref* (*el sombrero, una prenda de vestir*) to take off; (*el sombrero en señal de cortesía*) tip; (*una mancha*) come out, come off; (*un vicio*) give up; withdraw
quitasol *m* parasol
quite *m* removal; hindrance; dodge; (*en la esgrima*) parry; (taur) passes made with the cape to draw the bull away from the man in danger
quizá or **quizás** *adv* maybe, perhaps
quó•rum *m* (*pl* **-rum**) quorum

R

R, r (ere) *f* twenty-first letter of the Spanish alphabet
R. *abbr* **respuesta, Reverencia, Reverendo**
rabada *f* hind quarter, rump
rabadilla *f* base of the spine
rábano *m* radish; **rábano picante** or **rusticano** horseradish; **tomar el rábano por las hojas** to be on the wrong track
ra•bí *m* (*pl* **-bíes**) rabbi
rabia *f* anger, rage; (*hidrofobia*) rabies; **tener rabia a** to have a grudge against
rabiar *intr* to rage, rave; get mad; go mad, have rabies; **que rabia** like the deuce; **rabiar por** to be dying for; be dying to
rabieta *f* tantrum
rabillo *m* leafstalk; flower stalk; (*en los cereales*) mildew spot; (*del ojo*) corner
rabio•so -sa *adj* mad, rabid
rabo *m* tail; (*del ojo*) corner; (fig) tail, train; **rabo verde** (CAm) old rake
ra•bón -bona *adj* bobtail; (Chile) bare, naked; (Mex) mean, wretched || *f* camp follower; **hacer rabona** to play hooky
rabotada *f* swish of the tail; coarse remark
rabu•do -da *adj* long-tailed
racial *adj* racial
racimar *ref* to cluster, gather together
racimo *m* bunch; cluster; (*de perlas*) string
raciocinio *m* reasoning
ración *f* ration; allowance; **ración de hambre** starvation wages
racional *adj* rational
racionar *tr* to ration
racismo *m* racism

racista *adj & mf* racist
racha *f* split, crack; chip; squall, gust of wind; streak of luck
rada *f* (naut) road, roadstead
radar *m* radar
radiación *f* radiation
radiacti•vo -va *adj* radioactive
radia•dor -dora *adj* radiating || *m* radiator
radiante *adj* radiant; (*alegre, sonriente*) radiant
radiar *tr* to radiate; radio; broadcast; cross out, erase || *intr* to radiate
radicación *f* taking root; (math) evolution
radical *adj & m* radical
radicar §73 *intr* to take root; be located || *ref* to take root; settle; (*un negocio*) be based
radio *m* edge, outskirts; (*de una rueda*) spoke, rung; (*de acción*) radius; (chem) radium; (math) radius || *m & f* radio
radioaficiona•do -da *mf* radio amateur, radio fan
radiodifundir *tr & intr* to broadcast
radiodifusión *f* broadcasting
radioemisora *f* broadcasting station
radioescucha *mf* radio listener; radio monitor
radiofrecuencia *f* radio frequency
radiografiar §77 *tr* to X-ray; radio
radiograma *m* X-ray (*photograph*)
radiola *f* record player
radioperturbación *f* jamming
radioteléfono *m* radio(tele)phone
radioterapia *f* radiotherapy
radioyente *mf* radio listener
raer §56 *tr* to scrape, scrape off; smooth, level; wipe || *ref* to become frayed, wear away
ráfaga *f* gust, puff; gust of wind; flash of light; (*de ametralladora*) burst; **ráfaga violenta** (aer) wind shear
raí•do -da *adj* threadbare; barefaced
ra•íz *f* (*pl* **-íces**) root; **a raíz de** close to the root of; even with; right after, hard upon; **de raíz** by the root; completely; **echar raíces** to take root
raja *f* crack, split; splinter, chip; slice
rajar *tr* to crack, split; splinter, chip; slice || *intr* to boast; chatter || *ref* to crack, split; splinter, chip; (Mex, CAm, W-I) to back down, break one's promise
rajatabla —**a rajatabla** desperately, ruthlessly
ralea *f* kind, quality; breed, ilk
ralear *intr* to thin out; be true to form
ralentí *m* slow motion
ra•lo -la *adj* sparse, thin
rallador *m* grater
rallar *tr* to grate; grate on, annoy
rallo *m* grater; scraper; rasp; (*de la regadera*) spout, nozzle; unglazed porous jug (*for cooling water by evaporation*)
rama *f* branch, bough; **andarse por las ramas** to beat about the bush; **en rama** raw; unbound, in sheets; in the grain
ramaje *m* branches, foliage
ramal *m* (*de una cuerda*) strand; halter; branch; (rr) branch line
ramalazo *m* lash; (*señal en el cutis por un golpe o enfermedad*) spot, pock; sharp pain; blow, sudden sorrow
rambla *f* dry ravine; avenue, boulevard
ramera *f* whore, harlot
ramificar §73 *tr & ref* to ramify
ramillete *m* bouquet; centerpiece, epergne; (bot) cluster
ramo *m* branch, limb; bouquet, cluster; (*de géneros, negocios, etc.*) line; (*p.ej., de una ciencia*) branch; (*de una enfermedad*) touch, slight attack
ramojo *m* brushwood, dead wood
ramonear *intr* to trim twigs; browse
rampa *f* ramp; cramp; (aer) apron; (Bol) litter, stretcher; **rampa de lanzamiento** launching pad
ram•plón -plona *adj* (*zapato*) heavy, coarse; common, vulgar
ramplonería *f* coarseness, vulgarity
rana *f* frog; **no ser rana** to be a past master; **rana toro** bullfrog
ran•cio -cia *adj* rank, rancid, stale; (*vino*) old; old, ancient; old, old-fashioned
ranchar *ref* (Col, Ven) to balk
ranchear *tr* to sack, pillage || *intr & ref* to build huts, form a settlement
ranchera *f* (Ven) station wagon
ranchero *m* messman; rancher, ranchman
rancho *m* mess; meeting, gathering; camp; thatched hut; ranch; (naut) stock of provisions; (Arg) straw hat; **hacer rancho** to make room; **hacer rancho aparte** to be a lone wolf, go one's own way
randa *m* pickpocket || *f* lace trimming
rango *m* rank; class, nature; pomp, splendor; (*elevada condición social*) status, standing
ranura *f* groove; slot
rapagón *m* stripling
rapar *tr* to shave; crop; scrape; snatch, filch || *ref* to shave; (*una vida regalada*) lead
ra•paz (*pl* **-paces**) *adj* thievish; rapacious || *m* young boy, lad
rapaza *f* young woman, lass
rapé *m* snuff
rápi•do -da *adj* rapid || *m* (rr) express; **rápidos** (*de un río*) rapids
raposa *f* fox; female fox; (*persona*) (coll) fox
raposo *m* male fox; foxy fellow; slipshod fellow
raptar *tr* to abduct; kidnap
rapto *m* abduction; kidnaping; rapture; faint, swoon
raque *m* beachcombing; **andar al raque** to go beachcombing
raquear *intr* to beachcomb
raquero *m* priate; beachcomber
raqueta *f* racket; battledore; badminton; snowshoe; **raqueta y volante** battledore and shuttlecock
raquíti•co -ca *adj* (*que padece raquitis*) rickety; flimsy, weak, miserable
raquitis *f* rickets
raramente *adv* rarely, seldom; oddly
rareza *f* rareness; rarity; oddness, strangeness; peculiarity

ra•ro -ra *adj* rare; odd, strange; thin, sparse
ras *m* evenness; **a ras** close, even, flush; **a ras de** even with, flush with; **ras con ras** flush, at the same level; grazing
rasar *tr* to graze, skim || *ref* to clear up
rascacie•los *m* (*pl* **-los**) skyscraper
rascamoño *m* fancy hairpin; (bot) zinnia
rascar **§73** *tr* to scrape; scuff; scratch; scrape clean || *ref* (*una cicatriz, un grano*) to pick; get drunk
rasete *m* satinet
rasga•do -da *adj* (*boca; ventana*) wide-open; (*ojos*) large; outspoken; (Col) generous || *m* tear, rip, rent
rasgar **§44** *tr* to tear, rip || *ref* to become torn
rasgo *m* (*de una pluma de escribir*) flourish, stroke; trait, characteristic; feat, deed; flash of wit, bright remark; **a grandes rasgos** in bold strokes; **rasgos** (*de la cara*) features
rasguear *tr* to thrum on || *intr* to make a flourish
rasgón *m* tear, rip, rent
rasguñar *tr* to scratch; sketch, outline
rasguño *m* scratch; sketch, outline
ra•so -sa *adj* smooth, flat, level, even; common, plain; clear, cloudless; (coll) brazen, shameless || *m* flat country; satin; **al raso** in the open
raspa *f* stalk, stem; (*de mazorca de maíz*) beard; (*de pez*) spine, backbone; shell, rind; (CAm, Mex) dirty trick, nasty joke
raspadura *f* scraping; erasure; pan sugar
raspar *tr* to scrape, scrape off; scratch, scratch out; graze; (*el vino*) bite; take, steal; (W-I) to dismiss, fire; (W-I) to scold || *intr* (Ven) to go away; (Ven) to die
raspear *tr* (SAm) to scold || *intr* (*una pluma*) to scratch
rastra *f* rake; harrow; drag; track, trail; (*p.ej., de cebollas*) string; (naut) drag; **pescar a la rastra** to trawl
rastracuero *m* show-off; upstart; sharper, adventurer
rastreador *m* dredge; (nav) mine sweeper
rastrear *tr* to trail, track, trace; drag; dredge; check into || *intr* to rake; skim the ground, fly low
rastre•ro -ra *adj* dragging, trailing; creeping; low-flying; groveling, cringing; low, vile
rastrillar *tr* to rake; (*cáñamo, lino*) hatchel, comb; (Arg, Col) to shoot, to fire; (*un fósforo*) (Arg, Col) to strike (*a match*)
rastrillo *m* rake; hackle, hatchel, flax comb; (*de cerradura o llave*) ward; grating, iron grate; (rr) cowcatcher
rastro *m* rake; harrow; track, trail; scent; trace, vestige; slaughterhouse; wholesale meat market; rag fair; **rastro de condensación** (aer) contrail
rastrojo *m* stubble
rasura *f* shaving; scraping
rasurar *tr & ref* to shave
rata *f* rat; female rat; **rata del trigo** hamster
ratear *tr* to apportion; snitch
ratería *f* baseness, meanness, vileness; petty thievery; petty theft
rate•ro -ra *adj* thievish; trailing, dragging; base, vile || *mf* sneak thief
raticida *f* rat poison
ratificar **§73** *tr* to ratify
rato *m* time, while, little while; **a ratos** from time to time; **a ratos perdidos** in spare time, in one's leisure hours; **buen rato** pleasant time; large amount; **pasar el rato** to waste one's time; **un rato** awhile
ratón *m* mouse; (Ven) hangover; **ratón de biblioteca** bookworm
ratonera *f* (*trampa*) mousetrap; (*agujero*) mousehole; nest of mice; hut, shop
raudal *m* stream, torrent; abundance
rau•do -da *adj* rapid, swift, impetuous
raya *f* stripe; (*línea fina; pez*) ray; (*en la imprenta, la escritura y la telegrafía*) dash; (*de los pantalones*) crease; (*en los cabellos*) part; boundary line, limit; (*para impedir la comunicación del incendio en los campos*) firebreak; (*del espectro*) (phys) line; (Mex) pay, wages; **a rayas** striped; **hacerse la raya** to part one's hair; **pasar de la raya** to go too far; **tener a raya** to keep within bounds
raya•no -na *adj* bordering; borderline
rayar *tr* (*papel*) to rule, line; stripe; scratch, score, mark; cross out; underscore || *intr* to border; stand out; (*el alba, el día, la luz, el sol*) begin, arise, come forth; **rayar en** to verge on, border on || *ref* (Col) to get rich
rayo *m* (*de luz*) ray; (*de rueda*) spoke; lightning, flash of lightning, stroke of lightning, thunderbolt; (*persona*) (fig) live wire; **echar rayos** to blow up, hit the ceiling; **rayo mortífero** death ray; **rayos X** X rays
rayón *m* rayon
raza *f* race; breed, stock; crack, slit; quality; ray of light (*coming through a crack*)
razón *f* reason; right, justice; account, story; (*cantidad o grado medidos por otra cosa tomada como unidad*) rate; (math) ratio; **a razón de** at the rate of; **con razón o sin ella** right or wrong; **hacer la razón** to return a toast; join at table; **meterse en razón** to listen to reason; **no tener razón** to be wrong; **razón social** firm name, trade name; **tener razón** to be right; be in the right
razonable *adj* reasonable
razonar *tr* to reason, reason out; itemize || *intr* to reason
reabrir **§83** *tr & ref* to reopen
reacción *f* reaction; **reacción en cadena** chain reaction
reaccionar *intr* to react
reacciona•rio -ria *adj & mf* reactionary
rea•cio -cia *adj* stubborn, obstinate
reactivo *m* reagent
real *adj* real; royal; fine, splendid || *m* army camp; fairground; real (*old Spanish coin; Spanish money of account equal to a quarter of a peseta*)
realce *m* embossment, raised work; enhancement, lustre; emphasis; **bordar de realce** to embroider in relief; (fig) to embroider, to exaggerate

realeza *f* royalty
realidad *f* reality; truth; **hecho realidad** come true, e.g., **un sueño hecho realidad** a dream come true
realismo *m* realism
realista *mf* (*persona que tiende a ver las cosas como son*) realist; (*partidario de la monarquía*) royalist
realización *f* realization, fulfillment; achievement; sale; **realización de beneficios** profit taking
realizar **§60** *tr* to fulfill; carry out; turn into cash || *ref* to become fulfilled; be carried out
realquilar *tr* to sublet
realzar **§60** *tr* to raise, elevate; emboss; enhance, set off; emphasize
reanimar *tr* to revive, restore; cheer, encourage || *ref* to revive, recover one's spirits
reanudar *tr* to renew, resume
reaparecer **§22** *intr* to reappear
reata *f* rope to keep animals in single file; single file; **de reata** in single file; in blind submission; next, following
rebaba *f* burr, fin
rebaja *f* rebate; diminution
rebajar *tr* to lower; diminish, reduce; rebate; (*precios*) mark down; (*a una persona*) deflate; (carp) to rabbet || *ref* to stoop; humble oneself
rebajo *m* rabbet, groove; offset, recess
rebalsar *tr* to dam || *ref* to become dammed up; be checked; pile up, accumulate
rebanada *f* slice
rebanar *tr* to slice; cut through
rebañadera *f* grapnel
rebaño *m* flock
rebarbati•vo -va *adj* crabbed, surly
rebasar *tr* to exceed; overflow; sail past
rebatiña *f* grabbing, scramble; **andar a la rebatiña** to scramble
rebatir *tr* to repel, drive back; check; resist; strengthen; rebut, refute; deduct, rebate; beat hard
rebato *m* alarm, call to arms; alarm, excitement; (mil) surprise attack
rebeca *f* cardigan
rebelar *ref* to revolt, rebel; resist; break away
rebelde *adj* rebellious; stubborn || *mf* rebel
rebeldía *f* rebelliousness; defiance, stubbornness
rebelión *f* rebellion, revolt
rebe•lón -lona *adj* balky, restive
rebobinar *tr* to rewind; unwind
reborde *m* flange, rim, collar
rebosar *tr* to cause overflow || *intr* to overflow, run over; be in abundance; **rebosar de** or **en** to overflow with, burst with; be rich in; have an abundance of || *ref* to overflow, run over
rebotar *tr* to bend back; repel; annoy, worry || *intr* to bounce; bounce back, rebound || *ref* to become annoyed, become worried
rebote *m* bounce; rebound
rebozar **§60** *tr* (*la cara*) to muffle up; cover with batter || *ref* to muffle up, muffle oneself up
rebozo *m* muffling; muffler; shawl; **de rebozo** secretly; **sin rebozo** frankly, openly
rebulta•do -da *adj* bulky, massive
rebullicio *m* hubbub, loud uproar
rebullir **§13** *intr* to stir, begin to move; give signs of life || *ref* to stir, begin to move
rebusca *f* seeking, searching; gleaning; leavings, refuse
rebusca•do -da *adj* affected, unnatural, recherché
rebuscar **§73** *tr* to seek after; search into; to glean
rebuznar *intr* to bray; talk nonsense
rebuzno *m* braying; nonsense
recade•ro -ra *mf* messenger || *m* errand boy
recado *m* errand; message; gift, present; daily marketing; compliments, regards; safety, security; equipment, outfit; **mandar recado** to send word; **recado de escribir** writing materials
recaer **§15** *intr* to fall again; fall back; relapse; backslide; **recaer en** to fall to; **recaer sobre** to fall upon, devolve upon
recaída *f* relapse; backsliding
recalar *tr* to soak, saturate || *intr* to sight land
recalcar **§73** *tr* to press, squeeze; cram, pack, stuff; (*sus palabras*) stress || *intr* (naut) to list, heel; **recalcar en** to lay stress on || *ref* to harp on the same string; sprawl; (*p.ej., la muñeca*) sprain
recalentar **§2** *tr* to overheat; (*la comida*) to warm over
recalmón *m* (naut) lull
recamado *m* embroidery
recamar *tr* to embroider
recámara *f* dressing room; (*de un arma de fuego*) breech, chamber; reserve, caution; (Mex) bedroom
recamarera *f* (Mex) chambermaid
recambio *m* spare part; (*parte, rueda, etc.*) **de recambio** spare
recapacitar *tr* to run over in one's mind || *intr* to refresh one's memory; reflect
recargable *adj* rechargeable
recargar **§44** *tr* to reload; overload; recharge; overcharge; overadorn; (*una cuota de impuesto*) increase; (elec) to recharge || *ref* to become more feverish
recargo *m* new burden; extra charge; new charge; (*que paga el contribuyente moroso*) penalty; (pathol) rise in temperature; **recargo de tarifa** extra fare
recata•do -da *adj* cautious, circumspect; modest; shy
recatar *tr* to hide, conceal || *ref* to hide; be afraid to take a stand
recato *m* caution, reserve; modesty
recauchutaje *m* recapping, retreading
recauchutar *tr* to recap, retread
recaudar *tr* (*impuestos, tributos*) to gather, collect; guard, watch over
recaudo *m* tax collecting; care, precaution; bail, surety; **a buen recaudo** under guard, in safety
recelar *tr* to fear, distrust || *intr & ref* to fear, be afraid
recelo *m* fear, distrust

recelo•so -sa *adj* fearful, distrustful
recensión *f* review, book review
recepción *f* reception; reception desk
recepcionista *m* room clerk || *f* receptionist
receptáculo *m* receptacle; shelter, refuge
receptador *m* (coll) fence, holder of stolen goods
receptar *tr* to receive, welcome; (*delincuentes*) hide, conceal; (*cosas robadas*) receive
recepti•vo -va *adj* receptive; susceptible
receptor *m* receiver; **receptor de cabeza** headpiece; **receptor telefónico** receiver
receta *f* recipe; (pharm) prescription
recetar *tr* (*un medicamento*) to prescribe; request
recibí *m* receipt; received payment
recibida *f* reception; admission
recibi•dor -dora *mf* receiver; receiving teller; ticket collector || *m* reception room
recibimiento *m* reception; welcome; reception room; (*visita en que una persona recibe a sus amistades*) at-home
recibir *tr* to receive; (*visitas*) entertain || *intr* to receive; entertain || *ref* to be received, be admitted; **recibirse de** to be admitted to practice as; be graduated as
recibo *m* reception; receipt; hall; parlor; at-home; **acusar recibo de** to acknowledge receipt of; **estar de recibo** to be at home; **ser de recibo** to be acceptable
reciclable *adj* recyclable
reciclado *m* or **reciclaje** *m* recycling
reciclar *tr* to recycle
recién *adv* (used before past participles) recently, just, newly, e.g., **recién llegado** newly arrived; just now, recently
reciente *adv* recently
recinto *m* area, inclosure, place
re•cio -cia *adj* strong; thick, coarse, heavy; harsh; hard, bitter, arduous; (*tiempo*) severe; swift, impetuous || **recio** *adv* strongly; swiftly; hard; loud
reciprocidad *f* reciprocity
recípro•co -ca *adj* reciprocal
recital *m* (*de música o poesía*) recital
recitar *tr* to recite; (*un discurso*) deliver
reclamación *f* claim, demand; objection; protest, complaint
reclamar *tr* to claim, demand; (*un ave*) decoy, lure || *intr* to cry out, protest, complain
réclame *m & f* advertising
reclamo *m* bird call; decoy bird; (*para aves*) lure; allurement, attraction; advertisement; blurb, puff; reference; (typ) catchword; (SAm) complaint
reclinar *tr* (*p.ej., la cabeza*) to lean, bend || *ref* to recline
reclinatorio *m* prie-dieu; couch, lounge
recluir §20 *tr* to seclude, shut in; imprison || *ref* to go into seclusion
reclusión *f* seclusion; imprisonment
reclu•so -sa *adj* secluded; imprisoned || *mf* prisoner; inmate
recluta *m* recruit || *f* recruiting; (*del ganado disperso*) (Arg) roundup
reclutar *tr* to recruit; (Arg) to round up
recobrar *tr* to recover || *ref* to recover; come to
recobro *m* recovery; (*de un motor*) pickup
recodar *intr* to lean; bend, twist, turn, wind
recodo *m* bend, twist, turn
recoger §17 *tr* to pick up; gather, collect; harvest; shorten, draw in; keep; welcome; lock up || *ref* to take shelter, take refuge; withdraw; (*echarse en la cama*) retire; go home; cut down expenses
recogida *f* collection; withdrawal; suspension; **recogida de basuras** garbage collection
recogimiento *m* gathering, collecting; harvesting; seclusion, retreat; concentration; self-communion
recolectar *tr* to gather, gather in; (*el algodón*) pick
recombina•do -da *adj* (*genética*) recombinant
recomendable *adj* commendable
recomendar §2 *tr* to recommend; commend
recompensa *f* recompense, reward
recompensar *tr* to recompense, reward
recompostura *f* repair
recomprar *tr* to buy back, repurchase
reconcentrar *tr* to bring together; (*un sentimiento o afecto*) conceal, disguise || *ref* to come together; be absorbed in thought
reconciliar *tr* to reconcile || *ref* to become reconciled
recóndi•to -ta *adj* hidden, concealed
reconfortar *tr* to comfort, cheer
reconocer §22 *tr* to recognize; admit, acknowledge; examine; (mil) to reconnoiter || *intr* (mil) to reconnoiter || *ref* to be clear
reconoci•do -da *adj* grateful
reconocimiento *m* recognition; admission, acknowledgment; gratitude; reconnaissance; **reconocimiento médico** inquest
reconquista *f* reconquest
reconsiderar *tr* to reconsider
reconstruir §20 *tr* to reconstruct, rebuild, recast
recontar §61 *tr* (*volver a contar; narrar*) to recount (*to count again; narrate*)
reconvenir §79 *tr* to expostulate with, to remonstrate with
reconversión *f* reconversion
recopilar *tr* to compile
record *m* (*pl* **records**) (sport) record; **batir un record** to break a record; **establecer un récord** to make a record
recordar §61 *tr* to remember; remind || *intr* to remember; get awake; come to; **si mal no recuerdo** if I remember correctly
recordati•vo -va *adj* reminding, reminiscent || *m* reminder
recordatorio *m* reminder; memento
record•man (*pl* **-men**) record holder
recorrer *tr* to go over, go through; look over, look through; (*un libro*) run through; overhaul
recorrido *m* trip, run, route; (*del émbolo*) stroke; repair
recortado *m* cutout

recortar *tr* to trim, cut off; (*figuras en una tela, en un papel*) cut out; outline || *ref* to stand out
recorte *m* cutting; (*de un periódico*) clipping; dodge, duck; **recortes** cuttings, trimmings
recostar §61 *tr* to lean || *ref* to lean, lean back, sit back
recova *f* poultry business; poultry stand; (Arg) portico; (SAm) food market
recoveco *m* bend, turn, twist; subterfuge, trick
recreación *f* recreation
recreo *m* recreation; place of amusement
recrudecer §22 *intr & ref* to flare up, get worse
rectángu•lo -la *adj* right-angled || *m* rectangle
rectificar §73 *tr* to rectify; (*un cilindro de motor*) rebore
rec•to -ta *adj* straight; (*ángulo*) right; right, just, righteous || *m* rectum
rec•tor -tora *adj* governing, managing || *mf* principal, superior || *m* rector; (*de una universidad*) rector, president
recua *f* drove; (*de personas o cosas*) string, line
recuadro *m* panel, square; (*sección de un impreso encerrada dentro de un marco*) box
recubrir §83 *tr* to cover, cap, coat
recuento *m* count; recount; inventory
recuerdo *m* memory, remembrance; keepsake, souvenir
recuero *m* muleteer
recular *intr* to back up; (*un arma de fuego*) recoil; back down
reculón *m* backing; **a reculones** backing away, recoiling
recuperar *tr & ref* to recuperate, recover
recurrir *intr* to resort, have recourse; revert
recurso *m* recourse; resource; resort; appeal, petition
recusar *tr* to refuse, reject; (law) to challenge
rechazar §60 *tr* to refuse, reject; repel, drive back
rechazo *m* rejection; rebound, recoil
rechifla *f* catcall
rechiflar *tr & intr* to catcall, hiss || *ref* to make fun
rechinar *intr* to creak, grate, squeak; act with bad grace; (Mex) to rage
rechistar *intr* to stir, say a word; **sin rechistar** without protest
rechon•cho -cha *adj* chubby, tubby, plump
rechupete — **de rechupete** fine, wonderful
red *f* net; netting; network, system; baggage netting; (fig) net, snare, trap; **a red barredera** with a clean sweep; **red barredera** dragnet
redacción *f* writing; editing; editorial staff; newspaper office, city room
redactar *tr* to write up; edit
redac•tor -tora *mf* writer; editor, newspaper editor; **redactor publicitario** copy writer
redada *f* (*de peces*) catch, netful; (*p.ej., de criminales*) haul, roundup
redecilla *f* hair net
rededor *m* surroundings; **al rededor (de)** around
redención *f* redemption; help, recourse
reden•tor -tora *mf* redeemer
redición *f* constant repetition
redi•cho -cha *adj* overprecise
redil *m* sheepfold
redimir *tr* to redeem; ransom; buy back
rédito *m* income, revenue, yield
redituar §21 *tr* to yield, produce
redobla•do -da *adj* stocky, heavy-built; heavy, strong; (mil) double-quick
redoblar *tr* to double; clinch; repeat || *intr* (*un tambor*) to roll
redoble *m* doubling; clinching; repeating; roll of a drum
redoma *f* phial, flask
redoma•do -da *adj* sly, crafty
redonda *f* district, neighborhood; (mus) semibreve; **a la redonda** around, roundabout
redondear *tr* to round, make round; round off; round out || *ref* to be well-off; be out of debt
redondel *m* circle; round cloak; (*espacio destinado a la lidia*) (taur) ring
redondilla *f* eight-syllable quatrain with rhyme abba or abab
redon•do -da *adj* round; straightforward; (*terreno*) pasture; honest; stupid || *m* ring, circle; cash || *f* see **redonda**
redopelo *m* row, scuffle; **al redopelo** against the grain, the wrong way; roughly, violently
reducir §19 *tr & ref* to reduce; **reducirse a** to come to, amount to; be obliged to
reducto *m* (fort) redoubt
redundante *adj* redundant
redundar *intr* to redound; overflow; **redundar en** to redound to
reduplicación *f* doubling
reelección *f* reëlection
reembarcar §73 *tr, intr & ref* to reship, reëmbark
reembarco *m* reshipment (*of persons*), reëmbarkation
reembarque *m* reshipment (*of goods*)
reembolsar *tr* to reimburse; refund || *ref* to collect a debt, be reimbursed
reembolso *m* reimbursement; refund; **contra reembolso** collect on delivery; cash on delivery
reemplazar §60 *tr* to replace
reemplazo *m* replacement; (mil) replacements; (*hombre que sirve en lugar de otro*) (mil) replacement
reencuadernar *tr* (bb) to rebind
reencuentro *m* collision; (*de tropas*) clash
reenganchar *tr & ref* to reënlist
reentrada *f* reëntry
reestrenar *tr* (theat) to revive
reestreno *m* (theat) revival
reexamen *m* or **reexaminación** *f* reëxamination
reexpedición *f* forwarding, reshipment
reexpedir §50 *tr* to forward, reship
refacción *f* refreshment; allowance; repair, repairs; extra, bonus; spare part

refaccionar *tr* to finance; (SAm) to repair, renovate
refajo *m* underskirt, slip
referencia *f* reference; account, report
referi•do -da *adj* above-mentioned
referir §68 *tr* to refer; tell, report || *ref* to refer
refinamiento *m* refinement
refinar *tr* to refine; polish, perfect
refinería *f* refinery
reflejar *tr* to reflect; reflect on; show, reveal || *intr* to reflect
reflejo *m* glare; reflection; reflex; **reflejo acondicionado** conditioned reflex; **reflejo patelar** or **rotuliano** knee jerk
reflexión *f* reflection
reflexionar *tr* to reflect on or upon || *intr* to reflect
reflugo *m* ebb
refocilar *tr* to cheer; strengthen || *intr* (Arg, Urug) to lighten || *ref* to be cheered; take it easy
reforma *f* reform; reformation; alteration, renovation || **la Reforma** the Reformation
reformación *f* reformation
reformar *tr* to reform; mend, repair; alter, renovate; revise; reorganize || *ref* to reform; hold oneself in check
reforzar §35 *tr* to reinforce; strengthen; encourage
refracción *f* refraction
refracta•rio -ria *adj* rebellious, unruly, stubborn
refrán *m* proverb, saying
refregar §66 *tr* to rub; upbraid
refrenar *tr* to curb, rein; check, restrain
refrendar *tr* to countersign; authenticate; visé; repeat
refrescar **§73** *tr* to refresh; cool, refrigerate || *intr & ref* to refresh; refresh oneself; cool off; go out for fresh air; (*el viento*) (naut) to blow up
refresco *m* refreshment; cold drink, soft drink
refriega *f* fray, scuffle
refrigerador *m* refrigerator; ice bucket
refrigerio *m* coolness; relief; pick-me-up, light lunch
refuerzo *m* reinforcement
refugia•do -da *mf* refugee
refugiar *tr* to shelter || *ref* to take refuge
refugio *m* refuge; hospice; shelter; haunt; (*para peatones en medio de la calle*) safety zone; **refugio antiaéreo** air-raid shelter; **refugio antiatómico** fallout shelter
refundición *f* recast; revision; (*de una pieza dramática*) adaptation
refundir *tr* to recast; revise; (*una pieza dramática*) adapt || *intr* to redound
refunfuñar *intr* to grumble, growl
refutar *tr* to refute
regadera *f* watering can; street sprinkler
regadí•o -a or regadi•zo -za *adj* irrigable || *m* irrigated land
regala *f* gunwale
regala•do -da *adj* dainty, delicate; pleasing, pleasant; (*vida*) of ease
regalar *tr* to give; regale, entertain; treat; caress, fondle; indulge
regalía *f* privilege, perquisite; bonus; royalty; (Arg, Chile) muff
regaliz *m* licorice
regalo *m* gift, present; treat; joy, pleasure; **regalos de fiesta** favors
rega•lón -lona *adj* comfort-loving, pampered; (*vida*) soft, easy
regañar *tr* to scold || *intr* to growl, snarl; grumble; quarrel; scold
regaño *m* scolding; growl, snarl; grumble
regar §66 *tr* to water, sprinkle; irrigate; spread, sprinkle, strew
regate *m* dodge, duck; (fig) dodge, subterfuge
regatear *tr* to haggle over; sell at retail; avoid, shun || *intr* to haggle, bargain; duck, dodge; (naut) to race
regazo *m* lap
regenerar *tr & ref* to regenerate
regente *m* director, manager; registered pharmacist; (typ) foreman
regicida *mf* regicide
regicidio *m* regicide
regi•dor -dora *adj* ruling, governing || *m* alderman, councilman
régimen *m* (*pl* **regímenes**) regime; diet; rate; management; (gram) government; **régimen de hambre** starvation diet; **régimen de justicia** rule of law
regimental *adj* regimental
regimentar §2 *tr* to regiment
regimiento *m* regiment; rule, government; city council
re•gio -gia *adj* regal, royal; magnificent
región *f* region
regir §57 *tr* to rule, govern; control, manage; guide, steer; (gram) to govern || *intr* to prevail, be in force
registra•dor -dora *adj* registering; recording || *m* registrar, recorder; inspector || *f* cash register
registrar *tr* to register; record; examine, inspect || *ref* to register; be recorded; take place
registro *m* registration, registry; recording; examination, inspection; entry, record; bookmark; manhole; (*de chimenea*) damper; (*de reloj*) regulator; (*de órgano*) (mus) stop; (*de piano*) (mus) pedal
regla *f* rule; (*para trazar líneas*) ruler; measure, moderation; order; menstruation; **regla de cálculo** slide rule; **reglas** monthlies, menses
reglamenta•rio -ria *adj* prescribed, statutory
reglamento *m* rules, regulations
reglar *tr* to regulate; (*papel*) rule || *ref* to guide oneself, be guided
regleta *f* (typ) lead
regletear *tr* (typ) to lead, space
regocijar *tr* to cheer, delight || *ref* to rejoice
regocijo *m* cheer, delight, rejoicing
regoldar §3 *intr* to belch
regolfar *intr & ref* to surge back, flow back, back up
regorde•te -ta *adj* dumpy, plump

regresar *intr* to return
regreso *m* return; **estar de regreso** to be back
regüeldo *m* belch, belching
reguero *m* drip, trickle; (*señal que deja una cosa que se va vertiendo*) track; irrigating ditch; **ser un reguero de pólvora** to spread like wildfire
regulador *m* regulator; (*de locomotora*) throttle; (mach) governor
regular *adj* regular; fair, moderate, medium; **por lo regular** as a rule || *tr* to regulate; put in order; throttle
rehabilitación *f* rehabilitation
rehacer **§39** *tr* to remake, make over, do over; mend, repair, renovate || *ref* to recover, rally
rehén *m* hostage; **llevarse en rehenes** to carry off as a hostage; **toma de rehenes** hostage taking
rehilandera *f* pinwheel
rehilar *intr* to quiver; whiz by
rehilete *m* shuttlecock; (*que se lanza por diversión*) dart; dig, cutting remark; (taur) banderilla
rehuir **§20** *tr* to avoid, shun; shrink from; refuse; dislike || *intr & ref* to flee
rehusar *tr* to refuse, turn down
reimpresión *f* reprint
reimprimir **§83** *tr* to reprint
reina *f* queen; **reina Margarita** aster, China aster; **reina viuda** queen dowager
reinado *m* reign
reinar *intr* to reign; prevail
reincidir *intr* to backslide; repeat an offense
reingreso *m* reëntry
reino *m* kingdom; **Reino Unido** United Kingdom
reinstalar *tr* to reinstate, reinstall
reintegrar *tr* to refund, pay back
reintegro *m* refund, payment
reír **§58** *tr* to laugh at || *intr & ref* to laugh; **reír de** or **reírse de** to laugh at
reja *f* grate, grating, grille; plowshare, colter; **entre rejas** behind bars
rejilla *f* screen; grating; lattice, latticework; cane, cane upholstery; foot brasier; fire grate; (electron) grid; (*de acumulador*) (elec) grid; (rr) baggage rack
rejón *m* spear; dagger; (taur) lance
rejonear *tr* (*el jinete al toro*) (taur) to jab with a lance made to break off in the bull's neck
rejuvenecimiento *m* rejuvenation
relación *f* relation; account, list; (*en un drama*) speech; **relación de ciego** blind man's ballad; **relaciones** betrothal, engagement; **relaciones públicas** public relations
relacionar *tr* to relate || *ref* to be related
relai *m* or **relais** *m* (elec) relay
relajación *f* or **relajamiento** *m* relaxation; slackening; laxity; rupture, hernia
relajar *tr* to relax; slacken; debauch || *intr* to relax || *ref* to relax, become relaxed; become debauched; be ruptured
relamer *ref* to lick one's lips; gloat; to relish; boast; slick oneself up
relami•do -da *adj* prim, overnice
relámpago *m* flash of lightning; flash of wit; **relámpago fotogénico** flash bulb, flashlight; **relámpagos** lightning
relampaguear *intr* to lighten; flash
relatar *tr* to relate, report
relati•vo -va *adj* relative
relato *m* story; statement, report
relé *m* (elec) relay; **relé de televisión** television relay system
releer **§43** *tr* to reread
relegar **§44** *tr* to relegate; banish, exile; shelve, lay aside
relente *m* night dew, light drizzle
relevador *m* (elec) relay
relevancia *f* relevance; significance
relevante *adj* outstanding
relevar *tr* to emboss; make stand out; relieve; release; absolve; replace || *intr* to stand out in relief
relevo *m* (elec) relay; (mil) relief; **relevos** (sport) relay race
relicario *m* shrine; (*medallón*) locket
relieve *m* relief; merit, distinction; **en relieve** in relief; **poner de relieve** to point out; to make stand out; **relieves** scraps, leftovers
religión *f* religion
religio•so -sa *adj* religious
relinchar *intr* to neigh
relincho *m* neigh, neighing; cry of joy
reliquia *f* relic; trace, vestige; **reliquia de familia** heirloom
reloj *m* watch; clock; meter; **como un reloj** like clockwork; **conocer el reloj** to know how to tell time; **reloj de caja** grandfather's clock; **reloj de carillón** chime clock; **reloj de cuarzo** quartz watch; **reloj de cuclillo** cuckoo clock; **reloj de ocho días cuerda** eight-day clock; **reloj de pulsera** wrist watch; **reloj de sol** sundial; **reloj despertador** alarm clock; **reloj registrador** time clock; **reloj registrador de tarjetas** punch clock
relojera *f* watch case; watch pocket
relojería *f* watchmaking, clockmaking; watchmaker's shop
reloje•ro -ra *mf* watchmaker, clockmaker || *f* see **relojera**
reluciente *adj* shining, brilliant, flashing
relucir **§45** *intr* to shine
relumbrar *intr* to shine, dazzle, glare
relumbre *m* beam, sparkle; flash; dazzle, glare
relumbrón *m* flash, glare; tinsel; **de relumbrón** showy, tawdry
rellano *m* (*en la pendiente de un terreno*) level stretch; (*de escalera*) landing
rellenar *tr* to refill; fill up; stuff; pad; fill out; cram, stuff || *ref* to fill up; cram, stuff oneself
relle•no -na *adj* full, packed; stuffed || *m* refill; filling, stuffing; padding, wadding; (*en un escrito*) filler
remachar *tr* (*un clavo ya clavado*) to clinch; (*un roblón*) rivet; stress, emphasize || *ref* (Col) to maintain strict silence
remache *m* clinching; riveting; rivet
remanso *m* dead water, backwater

remar *intr* to row; toil, struggle
remata•do -da *adj* hopeless; **loco rematado** raving mad
rematador *m* auctioneer
rematar *tr* to finish, put an end to; finish off, kill off; (*en una subasta*) knock down || *intr* to end || *ref* to come to ruin
remate *m* end; crest, top, finial; closing; highest bid; (*en una subasta*) sale; **de remate** hopelessly
rembolsar *tr* to reimburse; repay; redeem
rembolso *m* reimbursement; **contra rembolso** C.O.D. (cash on delivery)
remecer **§46** *tr & ref* to shake, swing, rock
remedar *tr* to copy, imitate; ape, mimic; mock
remediar *tr* to remedy; help; prevent; (*del peligro*) free, save
remediava•gos *m* (*pl* **-gos**) short cut
remedio *m* remedy; help; recourse; **no hay remedio** or **no hay más remedio** it can't be helped; **no tener remedio** to be unavoidable
remedión *m* (theat) substitute performance
remedo *m* copy, imitation; poor imitation
remendar **§2** *tr* to patch, mend, repair; darn; emend, correct; touch up
remen•dón -dona *mf* mender, repairer; shoe mender; tailor (*who does mending*)
reme•ro -ra *mf* rower || *m* oarsman
remesa *f* remittance; shipment
remesar *tr* to remit; ship
remezón *m* hard shake; tremor
remiendo *m* patch; mending, repair; retouching; emendation, correction; job printing, job work; **a remiendos** piecemeal
remilga•do -da *adj* prim and finicky; affected, smirking
remilgar **§44** *intr* to be prim and finicky; smirk
remilgo *m* primness, affectation
remira•do -da *adj* circumspect, discreet
remisión *f* remission; reference
remitente *mf* sender, shipper
remitido *m* (*noticia de un particular a un periódico*) personal; letter to the editor
remitir *tr* to remit; forward, send, ship; refer; defer, postpone; pardon, forgive || *intr* to remit, let up; refer || *ref* to remit, let up; defer, yield
remo *m* oar; leg, arm, wing; toil, labor; (sport) rowing; **aguantar los remos** to lie or rest on one's oars
remoción *f* discharge, dismissal; removal
remodelación *f* remodeling
remodelar *tr* to remodel
remojar *tr* to soak, steep, dip; celebrate with a drink; **remojar la palabra** to wet one's whistle
remojo *m* soaking, steeping; **poner en remojo** to put off to a more suitable time
remolacha *f* beet; **remolacha azucarera** sugar beet
remolcador *m* tug, tugboat; towboat; tow car
remolcar **§73** *tr* to tow; take in tow
remoler **§47** *tr* to grind up; bore
remolinear *tr, intr & ref* to eddy, whirl about
remolino *m* eddy, whirlpool; swirl, whirl; disturbance, commotion; throng, crowd; cowlick
remo•lón -lona *adj* lazy, indolent || *mf* shirker, quitter
remolonear *intr* to refuse to budge
remolque *m* tow; towing; trailer; **a remolque** in tow
remontar *tr* to mend, repair; frighten away; elevate, raise up; (*p.ej., un río*) go up || *intr* (*en el tiempo*) go back || *ref* to rise, rise up; soar; (*en el tiempo*) go back
remontuar *m* stem-winder
remoquete *m* punch; nickname; sarcasm; flirting
rémora *f* hindrance, obstacle
remordimiento *m* remorse
remo•to -ta *adj* remote; unlikely; **estar remoto** to be rusty
remover **§47** *tr* to remove; shake; stir; disturb, upset; dismiss, discharge || *ref* to move away
remozar **§60** *tr* to rejuvenate || *ref* to become rejuvenated
rempujar *tr* to push, jostle
rempujón *m* push, jostle
remuda *f* change, replacement; change of clothes
remudar *tr* to change, replace; move around
remuneración *f* remuneration; **remuneración por rendimiento** piece wage
renacer **§22** *intr* to be reborn, be born again; recover
renacimiento *m* rebirth; renaissance
renacuajo *m* tadpole; (coll) shrimp, little squirt
Renania *f* Rhineland
ren•co -ca *adj* lame
rencor *m* rancor; **guardar rencor** to bear malice
rendición *f* surrender; submission; fatigue, exhaustion; yield
rendi•do -da *adj* tired, worn-out; submissive
rendija *f* crack, split, slit
rendimiento *m* submission; exhaustion; yield; output; (mech) efficiency
rendir **§50** *tr* to conquer; subdue; surrender; exhaust, wear out; return, give back; yield, produce; (*gracias, obsequios, homenaje*) render || *intr* to yield || *ref* to surrender; yield, give in; be exhausted, be worn out
renegar **§66** *tr* to deny vigorously; abhor, detest || *intr* to curse; be insulting; **renegar de** to deny; curse; abhor, detest
renegociación *f* renegotiation
Renfe, la acronym for **la Red Nacional de los Ferrocarriles Españoles** the Spanish National Railroad System
renglón *m* line; **a renglón sequido** right below; **leer entre renglones** to read between the lines
reniego *m* curse
reno *m* reindeer
renombra•do -da *adj* renowned, famous
renombre *m* renown, fame
renovar **§61** *tr* to renew; renovate; transform, restore; remodel

renquear *intr* to limp
renta *f* income; private income; annuity; public debt; rent; **renta nacional** gross national product
rentar *tr* to produce, yield
rentista *mf* bondholder; financier; person of independent means
renuente *adj* reluctant, unwilling
renuevo *m* sprout, shoot; renewal
renuncia *f* renunciation; resignation; (law) waiver
renunciar *tr* to renounce; resign || *intr* to renounce; (*no servir al palo que se juega*) renege; **renunciar a** to give up, renounce, waive
renuncio *m* slip, mistake; (*en juegos de naipes*) renege; lie
reñi•do -da *adj* on bad terms; bitter, hard-fought
reñir **§72** *tr* (*regañar*) to scold; (*una batalla, un desafío*) fight || *intr* to fight; be at odds, fall out
re•o -a *adj* guilty, criminal || **reo** *mf* offender, criminal; (law) defendant
reojo — **de reojo** askance, out of the corner of one's eye; hostilely
reorganizar **§60** *tr & ref* to reorganize
reorientación *f* reorientation
reóstato *m* rheostat
repanchigar or **repantigar** **§44** *ref* to sprawl, loll
reparar *tr* to repair, mend; make amends for; notice, observe; (*un golpe*) parry || *intr* to stop; **reparar en** to notice, pay attention to || *ref* to stop; refrain
reparo *m* repairing, repairs; notice, observation; doubt, objection; shelter; bashfulness
repa•rón -rona *adj* faultfinding || *mf* faultfinder
repartida *f* distribution; issuing
repartir *tr* to distribute; (*naipes*) deal
reparto *m* distribution; (*de naipes*) deal; (theat) cast; **reparto de acciones gratis** stock dividend
repasar *tr* to repass; retrace; review; revise; (*la ropa*) mend
repasata *f* scolding, reprimand
repaso *m* revision; (*de una lección*) review; mending; reprimand
repatriar **§77** *tr* to repatriate; send home || *intr & ref* to be repatriated; go or come home
repeler *tr* to repel, repulse
repente *m* start, sudden movement; **de repente** suddenly
repenti•no -na *adj* sudden, unexpected
repentista *mf* (mus) improviser; (mus) sight reader
repentizar **§60** *intr* to improvise; (mus) to sight-read, perform at sight
repercutir *intr* to rebound; reëcho, reverberate
repertorio *m* repertory
repetición *f* repetition; (mus) repeat
repetir **§50** *tr & intr* to repeat
repicar **§73** *tr* to mince, chop up; ring, sound; sting again || *intr* peal, ring out, resound || *ref* to boast, be conceited
repique *m* chopping, mincing; peal, ringing; squabble, quarrel
repiqueteo *m* pealing, ringing; beating, rapping
repisa *f* shelf, ledge; bracket; **repisa de chimenea** mantelpiece; **repisa de ventana** window sill
replantear *tr* to lay out again; reaffirm, reimplement
replegar **§66** *tr* to fold over and over || *ref* to fold, fold up; (mil) to fall back
reple•to -ta *adj* replete, full, loaded; fat, chubby
réplica *f* answer, retort; replica
replicar **§73** *tr* to argue against || *intr* to answer back, retort
repli•cón -cona *adj* saucy, flip
repliegue *m* fold, crease; (mil) falling back
repollo *m* cabbage; (*p.ej., de lechuga, col*) head
reponer **§54** *tr* to replace, put back; restore; (*una pieza dramática*) revive; **repuso** he replied || *ref* to recover; calm down
reportaje *m* reporting; news coverage; report
reportar *tr* to check, restrain; get, obtain; bring, carry; report || *ref* to restrain or control oneself
reporte *m* report, news report; gossip
repórter *m* reporter
reporte•ro -ra *mf* reporter
reposa cabezas *f* (aut) head rest
reposar *intr & ref* to rest, repose; take a nap; (*en la sepultura*) lie, be at rest; (*poso, sedimento*) settle
reposición *f* replacement; (*de la salud*) recovery; (theat) revival
reposo *m* rest, repose
repostar *tr, intr & ref* to stock up; refuel
repostería *f* pastry shop, confectionery; pantry
reposte•ro -ra *mf* pastry cook, confectioner
repregunta *f* (law) cross-examination
repreguntar *tr* (law) to cross-examine
reprender *tr* to reprehend, scold
represa *f* dam; damming; repression, check; (*de un buque*) recapture
represalia *f* reprisal; retaliation
represar *tr* to dam; repress, check; (*de un buque*) to recapture
representación *f* representation; dignity, standing; performance; **en representación de** representing; **representación exclusiva** sole dealership
representante *adj* representing || *mf* representative; actor, player; (com) agent, representative
representar *tr* to represent; show, express; state, declare; act, perform, play; (*determinada edad*) appear to be || *ref* to imagine
representati•vo -va *adj* representative
reprimenda *f* reprimand
reprimir *tr* to repress
reprobación *f* reproof; flunk, failure
reprobar **§61** *tr* to reprove; flunk, fail
reprochar *tr* to reproach

reproche *m* reproach
reproducción *f* reproduction; breeding
reproducir **§19** *tr & ref* to reproduce
repro•pio -pia *adj* balky
reptar *intr* to crawl; to cringe
reptil *m* reptile
república *f* republic
republica•no -na *adj & mf* republican || *m* patriot
repudiar *tr* to repudiate, disown, disavow
repues•to -ta *adj* secluded; spare, extra || *m* stock, supply; serving table; pantry; **de repuesto** spare, extra
repugnante *adj* repugnant, disgusting
repugnar *tr* to conflict with; contradict; object to, avoid; revolt, be repugnant to || *intr* to be repugnant
repujar *tr* to emboss
repulgar **§44** *tr* to hem, border
repulgo *m* hem, border
repuli•do -da *adj* highly polished; all dolled up
repulsar *tr* to reject, refuse
repulsi•vo -va *adj* repulsive
repuntar *tr* (*animales dispersos*) (Arg, Chile, Urug) to round up || *intr* to begin to appear; (naut) to begin to rise; (naut) to begin to ebb || *ref* to begin to turn sour; fall out
repuso see **reponer**
reputación *f* reputation, repute
reputar *tr* to repute; esteem
requebra•dor -dora *adj* flirtatious || *mf* flirt
requebrar **§2** *tr* to break into smaller pieces; flatter, flirt with
requemar *tr* to burn again; parch; overcook; inflame; bite, sting || *ref* to become tanned or sunburned; smolder, burn within
requerir **§68** *tr* to notify; summon; request; urge; check, examine; require; seek, look for; reach for; court, make love to
requesón *m* cottage cheese
requiebro *m* fine crushing; flattery, flattering remarks, flirtation
requisi•to -ta *adj* requisite || *m* requisite, requirement; accomplishment; **requisito previo** prerequisite
res *f* head of cattle; beast; **reses** cattle
resabio *m* unpleasant aftertaste; bad habit, vice
resabio•so -sa *adj* sly, crafty; (*caballo*) vicious
resaca *f* surge, surf; undertow; (com) redraft; (slang) hangover
resalir **§65** *intr* to jut out, project
resaltar *tr* to emphasize || *intr* to bounce, rebound; jut out, project; stand out
resanar *tr* to retouch, patch, repair
resarcir **§36** *tr* to indemnify, make amends to; (*un daño, un agravio*) repay; (*una pérdida*) make good; to mend, repair || *ref* — **resarcirse de** to make up for
resbaladi•zo -za *adj* slippery; skiddy; risky; (*memoria*) shaky
resbalar *intr* to slide; skid; slip || *ref* to slide; slip; (fig) to slip, to misstep
rescatar *tr* to ransom, redeem; rescue; (*el tiempo perdido*) make up for; relieve; atone for; (Mex) to resell
rescate *m* ransom, redemption; rescue; salvage; ransom money
rescindir *tr* to rescind
rescoldera *f* heartburn
rescoldo *m* embers; smoldering; doubt, scruple; **arder en rescoldo** to smolder
resenti•do -da *adj* resentful
resentimiento *m* resentment; sorrow, disappointment
resentir **§68** *ref* to be resentful; **resentirse de** to feel the bad effects of; resent; suffer from
reseña *f* outline; book review; newspaper account; (mil) review
reseñador *m* reviewer; critic
reseñar *tr* to outline; (*un libro*) review; (mil) to review
reserva *f* reserve; reservation; **con** or **bajo la mayor reserva** in strictest confidence; **reserva de caza** game preserve
reservar *tr* to reserve; put aside; postpone; exempt; keep secret || *ref* to save oneself, bide one's time; beware, be distrustful
resfriado *m* cold
resfriar **§77** *tr* to cool, chill || *intr* to turn cold || *ref* to catch cold; cool off, grow cold
resguardar *tr* to defend; protect, shield || *ref* to take shelter; protect oneself
resguardo *m* defense; protection; check, voucher; collateral; (naut) wide berth, sea room
residencia *f* residence; impeachment; **residencia de ancianos** nursing home; home for the aged
residenciar *tr* to call to account; impeach
residir *intr* to reside
residuo *m* residue, remains; remainder; **residuos radiactivos** radioactive waste
resignación *f* resignation
resignar *tr* to resign || *ref* to resign, become resigned; **resignarse con** (*p.ej., su suerte*) to be resigned to
resina *f* resin
resistencia *f* resistance; strength; **resistencia de rejilla** (electron) grid leak
resistente *adj* resistant; strong; (hort) hardy; **resistente al rayado** scratch-resistant
resistir *tr* to bear, stand; (*la tentación*) resist || *intr* to resist; hold out; **resistir a** (*la violencia; la risa*) resist; refuse to || *ref* to resist; struggle; **resistirse a** to refuse to
resma *f* ream
resobrina *f* grandniece, greatniece
resobrino *m* grandnephew, greatnephew
resolución *f* resolution; **en resolución** in brief, in a word
resolver **§47 & §83** *tr* to resolve; solve; decide on; dissolve || *ref* to resolve; make up one's mind
resollar **§61** *intr* to breathe; breathe hard, pant; stop for a rest
resonar **§61** *intr* to resound, echo
resoplar *intr* to puff; snort
resoplido *m* puffing; snort

resorte *m* spring; springiness; means; province, scope; rubber band; **resorte espiral** coil spring; **tocar resortes** to pull wires, pull strings
respailar *intr* — **ir respailando** to scurry along
respaldar *m* back; || *tr* to back; indorse || *ref* to lean back; sprawl
respaldo *m* back; backing; indorsement
respectar *tr* (with personal **a**) to concern; **por lo que respecta a . . .** as far as . . . is concerned
respecti•vo -va *adj* respective
respecto *m* respect, reference, relation; **al respecto** in the matter; **respecto a** or **de** with respect to, in or with regard to
respetable *adj* respectable
respetar *tr* to respect
respeto *m* respect; consideration; **campar por sus respetos** to be inconsiderate, go one's (his, her, etc.) own way; **de respeto** spare, extra
respetuo•so -sa *adj* respectful; awesome, impressive; humble, obedient
respigón *m* hangnail
respingar **§44** *intr* to balk, shy; (*elevarse el borde, p.ej., de la falda*) curl up; give in unwillingly
respin•gón -gona *adj* (*nariz*) snubby, upturned; surly, churlish
respirar *tr* to breathe || *intr* to breathe; breathe freely; breathe a sigh of relief; catch one's breath, stop for a rest; **no respirar** to not breathe a word; **sin respirar** without respite, without letup
respiro *m* breathing; respite, breather, breathing spell; (*para el pago de una deuda*) extension of time
resplandecer **§22** *intr* to shine; flash, glitter
resplandeciente *adj* brilliant; resplendent
resplandor *m* brilliance, radiance; resplendence; glare
responder *tr* to answer || *intr* to answer, respond; correspond; answer back; **responder de** (*una cosa*) to answer for; **responder por** (*una persona*) to answer for
respon•dón -dona *adj* (coll) saucy
responsable *adj* responsible; **responsable de** responsible for
responsabilizar *tr* to put in charge; hold responsible || *ref* to assume responsibility
respuesta *f* answer, response
resquebrajar *tr & ref* to crack, split
resquemar *tr & intr* to bite, sting || *ref* to be parched; (*resentirse sin manifestarlo*) smolder
resquemo *m* bite, sting
resquicio *m* crack, chink; chance, opportunity
restablecer **§22** *tr* to reëstablish, restore || *ref* to recover
restañar *tr* to retin; (*sangre*) stanch, stop the flow of
restar *tr* to deduct; reduce; take away; (*una pelota*) return; subtract || *intr* to remain, be left
restaurante *m* restaurant; **restaurante automático** automat
restaurar *tr* to restore; to recover
restitución *f* restitution, return
restituir **§20** *tr* to return, give back; restore || *ref* to return, come back
resto *m* rest, remainder, residue; (*en juegos de naipes*) stakes; (*de una pelota*) return; **a resto abierto** without limit; **echar el resto** to stake all, shoot the works; **restos** remains, mortal remains; **restos de serie** remnants
restregar **§66** *tr* to rub hard; scrub hard
restringir **§27** *tr* to restrict; constrict, to contract
resucitar *tr & intr* to resuscitate; resurrect; revive
resuel•to -ta *adj* resolute, resolved, determined; prompt, quick
resuello *m* breathing; hard breathing, panting
resulta *f* result; outcome; vacancy; **de resultas de** as a result of
resultado *m* result
resultar *intr* to result; prove to be, turn out to be; be, become
resumen *m* summary, résumé; **en resumen** in brief, in a word
resumir *tr* to summarize, sum up || *ref* to be reduced, be transformed
resurrección *f* resurrection
retaguardia *f* rearguard
retal *m* piece, remnant
retama *f* Spanish broom; **retama de escoba** furze
retar *tr* to challenge, dare; blame, find fault with
retardación *f* retardation
retardar *tr* to retard, slow down
retardo *m* retard, delay
retazo *m* piece, remnant; scrap, fragment
retén *m* store, stock, reserve; catch, pawl; (mil) reserve
retener **§71** *tr* to retain, keep, withhold; detain, arrest; (*el pago de un haber*) stop
retentiva *f* memory; recall
reticente *adj* deceptive, misleading; noncommital
retintín *m* jingle, tinkling; (*en el oído*) ringing; tone of reproach, sarcasm, mockery
retiñir **§12** *intr* to jingle, tinkle (*los oídos*) ring
retirada *f* retirement, withdrawal; place of refuge; (mil) retreat, retirement; (*toque*) (mil) retreat; **batirse en retirada** to beat a retreat
retirar *tr* to retire, withdraw; take away; pull back || *ref* to retire, withdraw; (mil) to retire
reto *m* challenge, dare; threat
retocar **§73** *tr* to retouch; touch up; (*un disco de fonógrafo*) play back
retoño *m* sprout, shoot, sucker
retorcer **§74** *tr* to twist; twist together; (*las manos*) wring; (fig) to twist, misconstrue || *ref* to twist; writhe
retóri•co -ca *adj* rhetorical || *f* rhetoric

retornar *tr* to return, give back; back, back up || *intr & ref* to return, go back
retorno *m* return; barter, exchange; reward, requital; **retorno terrestre** (elec) ground
retorta *f* (chem) retort
retozar **§60** *intr* to frolic, gambol, romp
retozo *m* frolic, gambol, romping; **retozo de la risa** giggle, titter
reto•zón -zona *adj* frolicsome, frisky
retracción *f* retraction; (pathol) atrophy
retractar *tr & ref* to retract
retráctil *adj* retractable
retraer **§75** *tr* to bring again, bring back; dissuade || *ref* to withdraw, retire; take refuge
retraí•do -da *adj* solitary; reserved, shy
retransmisión *f* rebroadcasting
retransmitir *tr* to rebroadcast
retrasa•do -da *adj* (mentally) retarded
retrasar *tr* to delay, retard; put off; (*un reloj*) set or turn back || *intr* to be too slow; (*en los estudios*) be or fall behind || *ref* to delay, be late, be slow, be behind time; (*un reloj*) go or be slow
retraso *m* delay; **tener retraso** to be late
retratar *tr* to portray; photograph; imitate || *ref* to sit for a portrait; have one's picture taken
retrato *m* portrait; photograph; copy, imitation; description; **el vivo retrato de** the living image of
retrepar *ref* to lean back, lean back in the chair
retreta *f* (mil) retreat, tattoo; outdoor band concert
retrete *m* toilet, lavatory
retribuir **§20** *tr* to repay, pay back
retroacti•vo -va *adj* retroactive
retroalimentación *f* feedback
retroceder *intr* to retrogress; back away; back down, back out
retroceso *m* retrogression; (*de un arma de fuego*) recoil; (*de una enfermedad*) flare-up; (mach, mov) rewind(ing)
retrocohete *m* retrorocket
retrodisparo *m* retrofiring
retropropulsión *f* (aer) jet propulsion
retrospecti•vo -va *adj* retrospective || *f* (mov) flashback
retrovisor *m* rear-view mirror
retrucar **§73** *intr* to answer, reply; (billiards) kiss
retruco *m* (billiards) kiss
retruécano *m* pun
retumbar *intr* to resound, rumble
retumbo *m* resounding, rumble, echo
reumáti•co -ca *adj & mf* rheumatic
reumatismo *m* rheumatism
reunificación *f* reunification
reunión *f* reunion, gathering, meeting; assemblage
reunir **§59** *tr* to join, unite; assemble, gather together, bring together; reunite; (*dinero*) raise || *ref* to unite; assemble, gather together, come together, meet; reunite
reválida *f* final examination (*for a higher degree*)
revalorar *tr* to revaluate
revalorizar **§60** *tr* to revaluate
revejecer **§22** *intr & ref* to grow old before one's time
revelación *f* revelation
revelado *m* (phot) development
revelador *m* (phot) developer
revelar *tr* to reveal; (phot) to develop
revender *tr* to resell; retail
reventa *f* resale
reventar **§2** *tr* to smash, crush; burst, blow out, explode; ruin; annoy, bore; (*a una persona*) work to death; (*a un caballo*) run to death || *intr* to burst, blow out, explode; (*las olas*) break; (*morir*) croak; (*de ira*) blow up, hit the ceiling; **reventar por** to be dying to || *ref* to burst, blow out, explode; be worked to death; (*un caballo*) be run to death
reventón *m* burst; (aut) blowout
rever **§80** *tr* to revise, review; (*un caso legal*) retry
reverberar *intr* to reverberate
reverbero *m* reflector; street lamp; chafing dish
reverencia *f* reverence; bow, curtsy
reverenciar *tr* to revere, reverence || *intr* to bow, curtsy
reveren•do -da *adj & m* reverend
reverso *m* back; wrong side; reverse
revertir **§68** *intr* to revert
revés *m* back, reverse; wrong side; backhand; (*desgracia, contratiempo*) reverse, setback; **al revés** wrong side out; inside out; upside down; backwards
revestir **§50** *tr* to put on, don; cover, coat, face, line, surface; assume, take on; disguise; (*un cuento*) adorn; invest || *ref* to put on vestments; be haughty; gird oneself
revirar *tr* to turn, twist; turn over
revisada *f* examination; revision
revisar *tr* to revise, review, check; audit
revisión *f* revision, review, check
revisionismo *m* revisionism
revisionista *adj & mf* revisionist
revisor *m* inspector, examiner; (rr) conductor, ticket collector
revista *f* review; (mil) review; (theat) review, revue; (law) new trial
revistar *tr* (mil) to review
revivir *tr & intr* to revive
revocar **§73** *tr* to revoke; dissuade; drive back, drive away; plaster, stucco
revocatoria *f* (SAm) recall; repeal; cancellation
revolar **§61** *intr & ref* to flutter, flutter around
revolcar **§81** *tr* to knock down; (*a un adversario*) floor; (*a un alumno en un examen*) flunk, fail || *ref* to wallow, roll around; be stubborn
revolotear *tr* to fling up || *intr* to flutter, flutter around, flit
revoltijo *m* or **revoltillo** *m* mess, jumble; stew

revolto•so -sa *adj* rebellious, riotous; (*niño*) unruly, mischievous; complicated; winding || *mf* troublemaker, rioter
revolución *f* revolution
revoluciona•rio -ria *adj & mf* revolutionary
revolver §47 & §83 *tr* to shake; stir; turn around; turn upside down; wrap up; mess up; disturb; (*sus pasos*) retrace; alienate, estrange || *intr* to retrace one's steps || *ref* to retrace one's steps; turn around; toss and turn; (*un astro en su órbita*) revolve; (*el mar*) get rough
revólver *m* revolver
revuelco *m* upset, tumble; wallowing
revuelo *m* whirl, flying around; stir, commotion
revuelta *f* revolution, revolt; disturbance; turning point; fight, row
rey *m* king; swineherd; **los Reyes Católicos** Ferdinand and Isabella; **los Reyes Magos** the Three Wise Men; **ni rey ni roque** nobody; **rey de zarza** wren; **reyes** king and queen; **Reyes** Twelfth-night
reyerta *f* quarrel, wrangle
reyezuelo *m* (orn) kinglet; **reyezuelo moñudo** goldcrest
rezaga•do -da *mf* straggler, laggard
rezagar §44 *tr* to outstrip, leave behind; postpone || *ref* to fall behind
rezar §60 *tr* (*una oración*) to pray; (*una oración; la misa*) say; (coll) to say, to read; (*anunciar*) (coll) to call for || *intr* to pray; grumble; (coll) to say, to read; **rezar con** to concern
rezo *m* prayer; devotions
rezón *m* grapnel
rezongar §44 *tr* (CAm) to scold || *intr* to grumble, growl
rezumar *intr* to ooze, seep || *ref* to ooze, seep; to leak; (*una especie*) leak out
ría *f* estuary, fiord
riachuelo *m* rivulet, streamlet
riada *f* flood, freshet
ribazo *m* slope, embarkment
ribera *f* bank, shore; riverside
ribere•ño -ña *adj* riverside
ribero *m* levee, dike
ribete *m* edge, trimming, border; (*a un cuento*) embellishment
ribetear *tr* to edge, trim, border, bind
ri•co -ca *adj* rich; dear, darling
ridiculizar §60 *tr* to ridicule
ridícu•lo -la *adj* ridiculous; touchy || *m* ridiculous situation; **poner en ridículo** to ridicule, expose to ridicule
riego *m* irrigation; watering
riel *m* ingot; curtain rod; rail
rielar *intr* to shimmer, gleam; (poet) to twinkle
rienda *f* rein; **a rienda suelta** swiftly, violently; with free rein
riente *adj* laughing; bright, cheerful
riesgo *m* risk, danger; **correr riesgo** to run or take a risk
riesgo•so -sa *adj* risky; dangerous
rifa *f* raffle; fight, quarrel
rifar *tr* to raffle, raffle off || *intr* to raffle; fight, quarrel
rígi•do -da *adj* rigid, stiff; strict, severe
riguro•so -sa *adj* rigorous; severe
rima *f* rhyme; **rimas** poems, poetry
rimar *tr & ref* to rhyme
rimbombante *adj* resounding; flashy
rímel *m* mascara
rimero *m* heap, pile
Rin *m* Rhine
rincón *m* corner; nook; piece of land; (coll) home
rinconera *f* corner piece of furniture; corner table; corner cupboard
ringla *f*, **ringle** *m* or **ringlera** *f* row, tier
ringorrango *m* curlicue; frill, frippery
rinoceronte *m* rhinoceros
riña *f* fight, scuffle
riñón *m* kidney; (fig) heart, center, interior; **tener bien cubierto el riñón** to be well-heeled
río *m* river; **pescar en río revuelto** to fish in troubled waters
riostra *f* brace, stay; guy wire
riostrar *tr* to brace, stay
ripia *f* shingle
ripio *m* debris; rubble; (*palabras inútiles empleadas para completar el verso*) padding; **no perder ripio** to not miss a trick
riqueza *f* riches, wealth; richness; **riquezas del subsuelo** mineral resources
risa *f* laugh, laughter
risco *m* cliff, crag; honey fritter
risible *adj* laughable
risotada *f* guffaw, horse laugh
ristra *f* string of onions, string of garlic; (coll) string, row, file
ristre *m* lance rest
risue•ño -ña *adj* smiling
rítmi•co -ca *adj* rhythmic(al)
ritmo *m* rhythm; **a gran ritmo** at great speed
rito *m* rite
rival *mf* rival
rivalidad *f* rivalry; enmity
rivalizar §60 *intr* to vie, compete; **rivalizar con** to rival
riza•do -da *adj* curly; ripply || *m* curl, curling; rippling
rizador *m* curling iron, hair curler
rizar §60 *tr & ref* to curl; (*la superficie del agua*) ripple
ri•zo -za *adj* curly || *m* curl, ringlet; ripple; (aer) loop; **rizar el rizo** (aer) to loop the loop
ro *interj* — **¡ro ro!** hushaby!, bye-bye!
roba•dor -dora *mf* robber, thief
róbalo or **robalo** *m* (*Labrax lupus*) bass; (*Centropomus undecimalis*) snook
robar *tr* to rob, steal; (*un naipe o ficha de dominó*) draw || *intr & ref* to steal
robinete *m* faucet, spigot, cock
roblar *tr* to clinch, rivet
roble *m* oak; (*Quercus robur*) British oak tree; husky fellow
roblón *m* rivet

robo *m* robbery, theft; (*naipe tomado del monte*) draw; **robo con escalamiento** burglary
ro•bot *m* (*pl* **-bots**) robot
robótica *f* robotics
robotización *f* use of robots; robotization
robus•to -ta *adj* robust
roca *f* rock
rocalla *f* pebbles; stone chips; large glass bead
rocallo•so -sa *adj* stony, pebbly
roce *m* rubbing; close contact
rociada *f* sprinkling; dew; (*de balas, piedras, etc.*) shower; (*de invectivas*) volley
rociadera *f* sprinkling can
rociar §77 *tr* to sprinkle; spray; bedew; scatter || *intr* to drizzle; **rocía** there is dew
rocín *m* hack, nag; work horse, draft horse; riding horse; rough guy
rocío *m* dew; drizzle; sprinkling
rocke•ro -ra *mf* rock singer
roco•so -sa *adj* rocky
rodada *f* rut, track
roda•do -da *adj* (*fácil, flúido*) rounded, fluent; (*tránsito*) vehicular || *f* see **rodada**
rodadura *f* rolling; rut; (*de neumático*) tread
rodaja *f* disk, caster; round slice
rodaje *m* wheels; (*de una película cinematográfica*) shooting, filming; **en rodaje** (aut) being run in; (mov) being filmed
rodamiento *m* bearing; (*de un neumático*) tread; **rodamientos** running gear
Ródano *m* Rhone
rodante *adj* rolling; on wheels; (Chile) wandering
rodapié *m* baseboard, washboard
rodar §61 *tr* to roll; (*una película cinematográfica*) shoot, film, take; screen, project; drag along; (*una llave*) turn; (*la escalera*) roll down; (*un nuevo coche*) run in; (*válvulas de un motor*) grind || *intr* to roll, roll along; roll down; rotate, revolve; tumble; roam, wander about; (*por medio de ruedas*) run; prowl
Rodas *f* Rhodes
rodear *tr* to surround; round up || *intr* to go around; go by a roundabout way; beat about the bush || *ref* to turn, twist, toss about
rodela *f* buckler, target; padded ring
rodeo *m* detour, roundabout way; dodge, duck; rodeo, roundup; **andar con rodeos** to beat about the bush; **dar un rodeo** to go a roundabout way
rodilla *f* knee; floor rag, mop; padded ring; **de rodillas** kneeling, on one's knees
rodillera *f* kneepad; baggy knee; (*de prenda de vestir*) knee; (*del órgano*) (mus) knee swell
rodillo *m* roller; rolling pin; road roller; inking roller; (*de la máquina de escribir*) platen
rodrigar §44 *tr* to prop, prop up, stake
rodrigón *m* prop, stake
roer §62 *tr* to gnaw, gnaw away at; (*un hueso*) pick; wear down
rogar §63 *tr & intr* to beg; pray; **hacerse de rogar** to like to be coaxed
roí•do -da *adj* miserly, stingy
ro•jo -ja *adj* red; ruddy; red-haired; Red || *mf* (*comunista*) Red || *m* red; **al rojo** to a red heat
rollar *tr* to roll, roll up
rolli•zo -za *adj* round, cylindrical; plump, stocky || *m* round log
rollo *m* roll, coil; roller, rolling pin; round log; yoke pad; rôle; (*de tela*) bolt
romadizo *m* cold in the head
romance *adj* (*neolatino*) Romance || *m* Romance language; Spanish language; romance of chivalry; octosyllabic verse with alternate lines in assonance; narrative poem in octosyllabic verse; ballad; **romance heroico** hendecasyllabic verse with alternate lines in assonance
romancero *m* collection of Old Spanish romances
romancillo *m* verse of less than eight syllables with alternate lines in assonance
románi•co -ca *adj* (*neolatino*) Romance, Romanic; (*arquitectura*) Romanesque || *m* Romanesque
roma•no -na *adj & mf* Roman
romanticismo *m* romanticism
románti•co -ca *adj* romantic
romanza *f* (mus) romance, romanza
romería *f* pilgrimage; crowd, gathering
rome•ro -ra *mf* pilgrim || *m* rosemary
ro•mo -ma *adj* blunt, dull; flat-nosed
rompeáto•mos *m* (*pl* **-mos**) atom smasher
rompecabe•zas *m* (*pl* **-zas**) riddle, puzzle; (*figura que ha sido cortada en trozos menudos y que hay que recomponer*) jigsaw puzzle
rompehie•los *m* (*pl* **-los**) iceboat, icebreaker
rompehuel•gas *m* (*pl* **-gas**) strikebreaker
rompeo•las *m* (*pl* **-las**) mole, breakwater
romper §83 *tr* to break; break through; break up; tear || *intr* to break; (*las flores*) break open, burst open; break down; **romper a** to start to, burst out
rompiente *m* reef, shoal; (*oleaje que choca contra las rocas*) breaker
rompope *m* eggnog
ron *m* rum; **ron de laurel** or **de malagueta** bay rum
ronca *f* (*época del celo*) rut; cry of buck in rutting season; bullying
roncar §73 *intr* to snore; (*el viento, el mar*) roar; cry in rutting season; bully
ronce•ro -ra *adj* slow, poky; grouchy
ron•co -ca *adj* hoarse; harsh || *f* see **ronca**
roncha *f* weal, welt; black-and-blue mark
ronchar *tr* to crunch
ronda *f* (*de un policía; de visitas; de cigarros o bebidas*) round; (*juego del corro*) (Chile) ring-around-a-rosy; **ronda negociadora** round of negotiations
rondar *tr* to go around; fly around; patrol; hang around; court || *intr* to patrol by night; gad about at nighttime; go serenading; prowl; (mil) to make the rounds
ronquedad *f* hoarseness; harshness

ronquera *f* hoarseness
ronquido *m* snore; rasping sound
ronronear *intr* to purr
ronroneo *m* purr, purring
ronzal *m* halter
ronzar **§60** *tr* to crunch, munch
roña *f* scab, mange; sticky dirt; pine bark; stinginess; spite, ill will; (Col) malingering; **jugar a roña** (Peru) to play for fun
roño•so -sa *adj* scabby, mangy; dirty, filthy; stingy; spiteful
ropa *f* clothing, clothes; dry goods; **a quema ropa** point-blank; **ropa blanca** linen; **ropa de cama** bed linen; bed-clothes; **ropa dominguera** Sunday best; **ropa hecha** ready-made clothes; **ropa interior** underwear; **ropa sucia** laundry
ropaje *m* clothes, clothing; gown, robe; drapery
ropaveje•ro -ra *mf* old-clothes dealer
rope•ro -ra *mf* ready-made clothier; wardrobe keeper || *m* wardrobe, clothes closet
roque *m* rook, castle
roque•ño -ña *adj* rocky; hard, flinty
rorro *m* baby; (Mex) doll
rosa *f* rose; **rosa de los vientos** or **rosa náutica** (naut) compass card; **rosas** popcorn; **verlo todo de color de rosa** to see everything through rose-colored glasses
rosa•do -da *adj* rose-colored, rosy; pink; flushed || *f* frost
rosaleda or **rosalera** *f* rose garden
rosario *m* rosary; (*de sucesos*) string; chain pump
ros•bif *m* (*pl* **-bifs**) roast beef
rosca *f* coil, spiral; (*de una espiral*) turn; twisted roll; (*de un tornillo*) thread; (Chile) padded ring
roscar **§73** *tr* to thread
roseta *f* sprinkling spout or nozzle; red spot on cheek; **rosetas** popcorn
rosetón *m* rose window
rosita *f* little rose; (Chile) earring; **rositas** popcorn
rosquilla *f* coffeecake, doughnut, cruller
rostro *m* face; snout; beak; (*retrato*) **de rostro entero** full-faced
rostropáli•do -da *mf* paleface
rota *f* rout, defeat; (naut) route, course
rotisería *f* fast-food restaurant; delicatessen
rotograbado *m* rotogravure
rótula *f* lozenge; kneecap; knuckle
rotulador *m* felt pen
rotular *tr* to label, title, letter
rótulo *m* label, title; poster, show bill
rotun•do -da *adj* round; rotund, sonorous, full; peremptory
rotura *f* break, breaking; breach, opening; tear, tearing
roturación *f* (agr) reclamation
roya *f* (agr) blight, rust
rozamiento *m* rubbing; friction; (*desavenencia*) (fig) friction
rozar **§60** *tr* to graze; scrape; border on; grub, stub; (*las tierras*) clear; (*la hierba*) nibble; (*leña menuda*) cut and gather || *intr* to graze by || *ref* to be on close terms, rub elbows, hobnob; falter, stammer; be alike
roznar *tr* to crunch || *intr* to bray
roznido *m* crunch, crunching noise; bray, braying
Rte. *abbr* **Remite**
ru•bí *m* (*pl* **-bíes**) ruby; (*de un reloj*) ruby, jewel
rubia *f* blonde; station wagon; peseta; **rubia oxigenada** peroxide blonde; **rubia platino** platinum blonde
rubia•les *mf* (*pl* **-les**) goldilocks
ru•bio -bia *adj* blond, fair; golden || *m* blond || *f* see **rubia**
rublo *m* ruble
rubor *m* bright red; blush, flush; bashfulness
ruborizar **§60** *tr* to make blush || *ref* to blush
rúbrica *f* title, heading; (*rasgo después de la firma de uno*) flourish
rubricación *f* listing; itemization
ru•bro -bra *adj* red || *m* title, heading; (Chile) (com) entry
rudimento *m* rudiment
ru•do -da *adj* coarse, rough; rude, crude; dull, stupid; hard, severe
rueca *f* distaff
rueda *f* wheel; caster, roller; (*de gente*) ring, circle; round slice; pinwheel; (*de la cola del pavo*) spread; sunfish; **hacer la rueda** (*el pavo*) to spread its tail; **hacer la rueda a** to play up to; **rueda de andar** treadmill; **rueda de cadena** sprocket, sprocket wheel; **rueda de escape** escapement wheel; **rueda de fuego** pinwheel; **rueda dentada** gearwheel; **rueda de paletas** paddle wheel; **rueda de prensa** press conference; **rueda de presos** line-up; **rueda de recambio** spare wheel; **rueda de tornillo sin fin** worm wheel; **rueda motriz** drive wheel
ruedo *m* turn, rotation; round mat; selvage; hemline; (taur) ring; **a todo ruedo** at all events
ruego *m* request, entreaty; prayer
ru•fián -fiana *mf* bawd, go-between || *m* cur, cad
ru•fo -fa *adj* sandy, sandy-haired; curly-haired
rugido *m* roar; (*de las tripas*) rumble
rugir **§27** *intr* to roar; rumble
rugo•so -sa *adj* rugged, wrinkled
ruibarbo *m* rhubarb
ruido *m* noise; rumor; row, rumpus
ruido•so -sa *adj* noisy; loud; sensational
ruin *adj* base, mean, vile; stingy; (*animal*) vicious
ruina *f* ruin
ruindad *f* baseness, meanness, vileness; stinginess; viciousness
ruino•so -sa *adj* tottery, run-down
ruiseñor *m* nightingale
ruleta *f* roulette; (CAm, Arg) tape measure
ruletero *m* (Mex) cruising taxi driver (*in search of fares*)
rulo *m* roll; rolling pin; (hair) curler
ruma•no -na *adj* & *mf* Rumanian

rumbo *m* bearing, course, direction; pomp, show; generosity; (CAm) noisy celebration; **por aquellos rumbos** in those parts; **rumbo a** bound for
rumbo•so -sa *adj* pompous, magnificent; generous
rumiar *tr & intr* to ruminate
rumor *m* rumor; (*de voces*) murmur, buzz; rumble
rumorear *tr* to rumor, circulate by a rumor || *intr* to murmur, buzz, rumble || *ref* to be rumored; **se rumorea que** it is rumored that
rumoro•so -sa *adj* noisy, loud, rumbling
runfla *f* or **runflada** *f* string, row; (*en los naipes*) sequence
ruptor *m* (elec) contact breaker
ruptura *f* rupture, break; crack, split; (*cesación de relaciones*) rupture
Rusia *f* Russia; **la Rusia Soviética** Soviet Russia
ru•so -sa *adj & mf* Russian
rúst. *abbr* **rústica**
rústi•co -ca *adj* rustic; coarse, crude, clumsy; (*latín*) Vulgar; **en rústica** paper-bound || *m* rustic, peasant
ruta *f* route; **ruta aérea** air lane
rutilante *adj* shining, sparkling
rutina *f* routine
rutina•rio -ria *adj* routine

S

S, s (ese) *f* twenty-second letter of the Spanish alphabet
S. *abbr* **San, Santo, sobresaliente, sur**
sábado *m* (*de los cristianos*) Saturday; (*de los judíos*) Sabbath
sábalo *m* shad
sabana *f* savanna, pampa; **ponerse en la sabana** (Ven) to get rich overnight
sábana *f* sheet; altar cloth
sabandija *f* insect, bug, worm; (*persona*) vermin; **sabandijas** (*animales o personas*) vermin
sabanilla *f* kerchief; altar cloth
sabañón *m* chilblain
sabe•dor -dora *adj* aware, informed
sabelotodo *m* (*pl* **sabelotodo**) know-it-all, wise guy
saber *m* knowledge, learning || *v* **§64** *tr & intr* to know; to find out; to taste; **a saber** namely, to wit; **me sabe mal** I'm sorry, I regret; **no saber dónde meterse** to not know which way to turn; **que yo sepa** as far as I know; **saber a** to taste of; smack of; **saber a poco** to be just a taste, taste like more; **saber de** to be aware of; hear from || *ref* to know; be or become known
sabidi•llo -lla *adj & mf* know-it-all
sabi•do -da *adj* well-informed; learned; **de sabido** certainly, surely
sabiduría *f* wisdom; knowledge, learning
sabiendas — **a sabiendas** knowingly, consciously; **a sabiendas de que** knowing that, aware that
sabihon•do -da *adj & mf* know-it-all
sa•bio -bia *adj* wise; learned; (*animal*) trained || *mf* wise person, scholar, scientist || *m* wise man, sage
sablazo *m* stroke with a saber, wound made by a saber; sponging; **dar un sablazo a** to hit for a loan
sable *m* saber, cutlass; (coll) sponging
sablear *tr* to hit for a loan, sponge on || *intr* to go around sponging
sablista *mf* sponger
sabor *m* taste, flavor
saborcillo *m* slight taste, touch
saborear *tr* to flavor; taste; savor; entice; || *ref* to smack one's lips; **saborearse de** to taste; to savor
sabotaje *m* sabotage
sabotear *tr & intr* to sabotage
sabro•so -sa *adj* tasty, savory, delicious
sabueso *m* bloodhound; sleuth
saburro•so -sa *adj* (*boca*) foul; (*lengua*) coated
sacaboca•do *m* or **sacaboca•dos** *m* (*pl* **-dos**) ticket punch; sure thing
sacabotas *m* (*pl* **-tas**) bootjack
sacacor•chos *m* (*pl* **-chos**) corkscrew
sacaman•chas *mf* (*pl* **-chas**) clothes cleaner, spot remover; dry cleaner; dyer
sacamue•las *m* (*pl* **-las**) tooth puller; quack, cheat
sacamuer•tos *m* (*pl* **-tos**) stagehand
sacapintura *m* paint remover
sacapun•tas *m* (*pl* **-tas**) pencil sharpener
sacar §73 *tr* (*un clavo, una espada, agua, una conclusión*) to draw; pull out; pull up; take out; extract, remove; show; bring out, publish; find out, solve; (*un secreto*) elicit, draw out; copy; (*una fotografía*) take; except, exclude; get, obtain; produce, invent, imitate; (*un premio*) win; (*una pelota*) serve; (*el pecho*) stick out; **sacar a bailar** to drag in; **sacar a relucir** to bring up unexpectedly; **sacar en claro** or **en limpio** to recopy clearly; deduce, clear up || *ref* (Mex) to make off
sacarina *f* saccharin
sacasi•llas *m* (*pl* **-llas**) stagehand
sacerdocio *m* priesthood
sacerdote *m* priest
saciar *tr* to satiate

saco *m* bag, sack; coat, jacket; sack, plunder, pillage; (*de mentiras*) pack; **saco de dormir** sleeping bag; **saco de noche** overnight bag
sacramento *m* sacrament
sacrificar §73 *tr* to sacrifice; slaughter || *intr* to sacrifice || *ref* to sacrifice; sacrifice oneself
sacrificio *m* sacrifice; **sacrificio del altar** Sacrifice of the Mass
sacrilegio *m* sacrilege
sacríle•go -ga *adj* sacrilegious
sacristán *m* sacristan; sexton; **sacristán de amén** yes man
sacristía *f* sacristy, vestry
sa•cro -cra *adj* sacred
sacudida *f* shake, jar, jolt, jerk, bump; (elec) shock
sacudi•do -da *adj* intractable; determined || *f* see **sacudida**
sacudir *tr* to shake; beat; jar, jolt; rock; shake off || *ref* to shake, to shake oneself; rock; **sacudirse bien** to wangle one's way out
sádi•co -ca *adj* sadistic || *mf* sadist
saeta *f* arrow, dart; (*del reloj*) hand; magnetic needle
saetilla *f* small arrow; (*del reloj*) hand; magnetic needle; (bot) arrowhead
saetín *m* flume, millrace
sa•gaz *adj* (*pl* **-gaces**) sagacious; keen-scented
Sagitario *m* (astr) Sagittarius
sagra•do -da *adj* sacred || *m* asylum, haven, sanctuary; **acogerse a sagrado** to take sanctuary
sagrario *m* sanctuary, shrine; ciborium
sahariana *f* tight-fitting military jacket
sahornar *ref* to skin oneself
sahumar *tr* to perfume with smoke or incense; (Chile) to gold-plate, silver-plate
sainete *m* one-act farce; flavor, relish, spice, zest; sauce, seasoning; tidbit
sa•jón -jona *adj & mf* Saxon
sal *f* salt; grace, charm; wit; (CAm) misfortune; **sal de sosa** washing soda; **sales aromáticas** smelling salts; **sal gema** rock salt
sala *f* hall; drawing room, living room, sitting room; **sala de batalla** sorting room; **sala de calderas** boiler room; **sala de enfermos** infirmary; **sala de espera** waiting room; **sala de estar** living room, sitting room; **sala de fiestas** night club; **sala del cine** moving-picture house; **sala de máquinas** engine room
saladillo *m* salted peanut
Salamina *f* Salamis
salar *tr* to salt; spoil, ruin; bring bad luck to
salario *m* wages, pay; **salario de hambre** starvation wages
salcochar *tr* to boil in salt water
salcocho *m* food boiled in salt water
salchicha *f* sausage
salchiche•ro -ra *mf* pork butcher
saldar *tr* to settle, liquidate; sell out
saldo *m* settlement; balance; remnant; bargain; **saldo de mercancías** job lot; **saldo deudor** debit balance
salero *m* saltshaker, saltcellar; salt lick; grace, charm, wit
salero•so -sa *adj* charming, winsome, lively; salty, witty
salgar §44 *tr* (*el ganado*) to salt
salida *f* start; departure; exit; outcome, result; subterfuge; pretext; outlay, expenditure; projection; outlying fields; (elec) output; (sport) start; (mil) sally, sortie; (coll) witticism, sally; **salida de baño** bathrobe; **salida del sol** sunrise; **salida de teatro** evening wrap; **salida de teatros** after-theater party; **salida de tono** irrelevancy, impropriety; **salida lanzada** (sport) running start; **tener salida** to sell well; (*una muchacha*) to be popular with the boys
saliente *adj* projecting; (*p.ej., tren*) outbound; (*sol*) rising || *m* east || *f* projection; (*de la carretera*) shoulder
salir §65 *intr* to go out, come out; leave, go away, depart; sail; run out, come to an end; appear, show up; (*una mancha*) come out, come off; (*p.ej., el sol*) rise; shoot, spring, come up; project, stick out; make the first move; result, turn out; be elected; **salga lo que saliere** come what may; **salir a** to amount to; open into; resemble, look like; **salir al, encuentro a** to go to meet; take a stand against; get ahead of; **salir bien en un examen** to pass an examination; **salir con bien** to be successful; **salir de** to depart from; cease being; get rid of; (*p.ej., su juicio, sentido*) lose; **salir disparado** to start like a shot; **salir pitando** to start off on a mad run; blow up, hit the ceiling; **salir reprobado** (*en un examen*) to fail || *ref* to slip out, escape; slip off, run off; leak; boil over; **salirse con la suya** to have one's own way; carry one's point
salitre *m* saltpeter
saliva *f* saliva; **gastar saliva** to rattle along; to waste one's breath
salmo *m* psalm
salmón *m* salmon
salmuera *f* brine, pickle; salty food or drink
salobre *adj* brackish, saltish
salón *m* salon, drawing room; (*de un buque*) saloon; meeting room; **salón de actos** auditorium; **salón de baile** ballroom; **salón de belleza** beauty parlor; **salón del automóvil** automobile show; **salón de refrescos** ice-cream parlor; **salón de tertulia** or **salón social** lounge
saloncillo *m* (*p.ej., de un teatro*) rest room
salpicadero *m* control panel; (aut) dashboard
salpicar §73 *tr* to splash; sprinkle
salpimentar §2 *tr* to salt and pepper, season with salt and pepper; (fig) to sweeten
salpullido *m* rash, eruption
salpullir §13 *tr* to cause a rash on; splotch || *ref* to break out
salsa *f* sauce, dressing, gravy; **salsa de ají** chili sauce; **salsa de tomate** catsup, ketchup; **salsa inglesa** Worcestershire sauce
salsera *f* gravy dish; small saucer (*to mix paints*)

saltaban•co *m* or **saltaban•cos** *m* (*pl* **-cos**) quack, mountebank; prestidigitator; nuisance
saltamon•tes *m* (*pl* **-tes**) grasshopper
saltar *tr* to jump, jump over; skip, skip over || *intr* to jump, leap, hop, skip; bounce; shoot up, spurt; come loose, come off; crack, break, burst; chip; project, stick out; **saltar a la vista** or **los ojos** to be self-evident; **saltar por** to jump over, jump out of || *ref* to skip; come off
saltatum•bas *m* (*pl* **-bas**) burying parson
salteador *m* highwayman, holdup man
saltear *tr* to attack, hold up, waylay; take by surprise
saltimbanco *m* var of **saltabanco**
salto *m* jump, leap, bound; skip; dive; fall, waterfall; leapfrog; **salto de altura** high jump; **salto de ángel** swan dive; **salto de cama** morning wrap, dressing gown; **salto de carpa** jackknife; **salto de esquí** ski jump; **salto de viento** (naut) sudden shift in the wind; **salto mortal** somersault; **salto ornamental** fancy dive
salubre *adj* healthful, salubrious
salud *f* health; welfare; salvation; greeting; **gastar, vender** or **verter salud** to radiate health || *interj* greetings!; **¡salud y pesetas!** health and wealth!
saludar *tr* to greet, salute, hail, bow to; give regards to || *intr* to salute; bow
saludo *m* greeting, salute, bow; salutation; **saludo final** conclusion
salutación *f* salutation, greeting, bow
salva *f* greeting, welcome; salvo; oath; tray; (*de aplausos; de una batería de artillería*) round
salvado *m* bran
salva•dor -dora *mf* savior, saver, rescuer || **el Salvador** the Saviour; (*país de la América Central*) El Salvador
salvadore•ño -ña *adj & mf* Salvadoran
salvaguardar *tr* to safeguard
salvaguardia *m* bodyguard, escort || *f* safeguard, safe-conduct; protection, shelter
salvaje *adj* wild, uncultivated; savage; stupid || *mf* savage; dolt
salvaji•no -na *adj* wild; (*de la carne de los animales monteses*) gamy || *f* wild animal; wild animals
salvamante•les *m* (*pl* **-les**) coaster
salvamento *m* salvation; lifesaving; rescue; salvage; place of safety
salvar *tr* to save, rescue; to salvage; (*una dificultad*) avoid, overcome; (*un obstáculo*) clear, get around; (*una distancia*) cover, get over; rise above; jump over; make an exception of; **salvar apariencias** to save face || *ref* to save oneself, escape danger; be saved; **sálvese el que pueda** every man for himself
salvavi•das *m* (*pl* **-das**) life preserver; lifeboat; (*empleado de una estación de salvamento*) lifeguard
salvedad *f* reservation, exception
salvia *f* (bot) sage
sal•vo -va *adj* safe; omitted; **a salvo** safe, out of danger; **a salvo de** safe from || **salvo** *prep* save, except for; **salvo error u omisión (s.e.u.o.)** barring error or omission; **salvo que** unless || *f* see **salva**
salvoconducto *m* safe-conduct
sámara *f* (bot) key, key fruit
san *adj* apocopated and unstressed form of **santo**
sanaloto•do *m* (*pl* **-do**) cure-all
sanar *tr* to cure, heal || *intr* to heal; recover
sanción *f* (*aprobación*) sanction; (*castigo, pena*) penalty
sancionar *tr* (*aprobar*) to sanction; (*imponer pena a*) penalize
sancochar *tr* to parboil
sandalia *f* sandal
sándalo *m* (yellow) sandalwood
san•dez *f* (*pl* **-deces**) folly, nonsense; piece of folly
sandía *f* watermelon
san•dio -dia *adj* foolish, nonsensical
saneamiento *m* sanitation, drainage; guarantee
sanear *tr* to guarantee; indemnify; make sanitary, drain, dry up
sangrar *tr* to bleed; drain; tap; (typ) to indent; (coll) to rob || *intr* to bleed; **estar sangrando** to be new or recent; be plain or obvious || *ref* to have oneself bled; (*los colores*) run
sangre *f* blood; **a sangre** by horsepower; **a sangre fría** in cold blood; **pura sangre** *m* thoroughbred; **sangre torera** bullfighting in the blood
sangría *f* bleeding; outlet, draining; ditch, trench; (*bebida*) sangaree; tap; tapping; (typ) indentation
sangrien•to -ta *adj* bloody; bleeding; cruel, sanguinary
sangrigor•do -da *adj* unpleasant
sangrilige•ro -ra *adj* nice, pleasant
sangripesa•do -da *adj* unpleasant
sangüesa *f* raspberry
sangüeso *m* raspberry bush
sanguijuela *f* leech
sanguina•rio -ria *adj* sanguinary, bloodthirsty
sanidad *f* healthiness; healthfulness; health; sanitation; **sanidad pública** health department
sanita•rio -ria *adj* sanitary
sa•no -na *adj* hale, healthy; healthful; sound; sane; earnest, sincere; safe, sure; whole, untouched, unharmed; **sano y salvo** safe and sound
santiague•ro -ra *adj* Santiago de Cuba || *mf* native or inhabitant of Santiago de Cuba
santia•gués -guesa *adj* Santiago de Compostela || *mf* native or inhabitant of Santiago de Compostela
santiagui•no -na *adj* Santiago de Chile || *mf* native or inhabitant of Santiago de Chile
santiamén *m* jiffy; **en un santiamén** in the twinkling of an eye
santidad *f* holiness, sanctity, saintliness; **su Santidad** his Holiness

santificar §73 *tr* to sanctify, hallow, consecrate; (*las fiestas*) keep; excuse, justify
santiguar §10 *tr* to bless, make the sign of the cross over; punish, slap, abuse || *ref* to cross oneself, make the sign of the cross
san•to -ta *adj* holy, saintly, blessed; (*día*) live-long; artless, simple; **santo y bueno** well and good || *mf* saint || *m* name day; image of a saint; **a santo de** because of; **desnudar a un santo para vestir a otro** to rob Peter to pay Paul; **írsele a uno el santo al cielo** to forget what one was up to; **santo y seña** password, watchword
Santo Domingo Hispaniola
santuario *m* sanctuary, shrine; (Col) buried treasure; (Col, Ven) Indian idol
santu•rrón -rrona *adj* sanctimonious || *mf* sanctimonious person
saña *f* fury, rage; cruelty
sañu•do -da *adj* furious, enraged; cruel
sapiente *adj* wise, intelligent
sapo *m* toad; (coll) stuffed shirt; (Chile) little runt
saque *m* (*en el tenis*) serve, service; server; service line; (Col) distillery; **tener buen saque** to be a heavy eater and drinker
saquear *tr* to sack, plunder, pillage, loot
sarampión *m* measles
sarao *m* soirée, evening party
sarape *m* (Guat, Mex) bright-colored woolen poncho
sarcasmo *m* sarcasm
sarcásti•co -ca *adj* sarcastic
sardina *f* sardine; **como sardinas en banasta** or **en lata** packed in like sardines
sar•do -da *adj & mf* Sardinian
sarga *f* serge
sargento *m* sergeant
sarmiento *m* vine shoot, running stem
sarna *f* itch, mange
sarno•so -sa *adj* itchy, mangy
sarrace•no -na *adj & mf* Saracen
sarracina *f* scuffle, free fight; bloody brawl
sarro *m* crust; (*p.ej., en la lengua*) fur; (*en los dientes*) tartar
sarta *f* string; line, fine, series
sartén *f* frying pan; **saltar de la sartén y dar en las brasas** to jump from the frying pan into the fire
sastre *m* tailor
satélite *m* satellite; **satélite de comunicaciones** communications satellite; **satélite espía** spy satellite
satelizar §60 *tr* to put into orbit; (pol) to make a satellite of || *ref* to go into orbit
satén *m* sateen
satíri•co -ca *adj* satiric(al) || *mf* satirist
satirizar §60 *tr & intr* to satirize
satisfacción *f* satisfaction
satisfacer §39 *tr & intr* to satisfy || *ref* to satisfy oneself, be satisfied, take satisfaction
satisfacto•rio -ria *adj* satisfactory
saturar *tr* to saturate; satiate
sauce *m* willow tree; **sauce de Babilonia** or **sauce llorón** weeping willow
saúco *m* elder, elderberry
savia *f* sap
saxofón *m* or **saxófono** *m* saxophone
saya *f* skirt; petticoat
sayo *m* smock frock, tunic; garment
sazón *f* ripeness; season; time, occasion; taste, seasoning; **a la sazón** at that time; **en sazón** in season, ripe; on time, opportunely
sazonar *tr* to ripen; season || *ref* to ripen, mature
s/c *abbr* **su cuenta**
S.E. *abbr* **Su Excelencia**
se *pron reflex* himself, to himself; herself, to herself; itself, to itself; themselves, to themselves; yourself, to yourself; yourselves, to yourselves; oneself, to oneself; each other, to each other || *pron pers* (used before the pronouns **lo, la, le,** etc.) to him, to her, to it, to them, to you
sebo *m* tallow; fat, suet
seca *f* drought; dry season
secador *m* drier, hair drier
secadora *f* clothes drier
secafir•mas *m* (*pl* **-mas**) blotter
secano *m* dry land, unwatered land
secansa *f* sequence
secante *m* blotting paper
secar §73 *tr* to dry, wipe dry; annoy, bore || *ref* to dry, get dry; dry oneself; wither; be dry, be thirsty; (*un pozo*) run dry
secarropa *f* clothes dryer; **secarropa de travesaños** clotheshorse
sección *f* section; cross section; **sección de fondo** editorial section
secesión *f* secession
se•co -ca *adj* dry; dried up, withered; lank, lean; harsh, sharp; (*bebida*) straight, indifferent; plain, unadorned || *f* see **seca**
secreta•rio -ria *adj* confidential, trusted || *mf* secretary
secreter *m* secretary (*writing desk*)
secre•to -ta *adj* secret || *m* secret; secrecy; hiding place, secret drawer; (*mecanismo oculto para abrir una cerradura*) key; **en el secreto de las cosas** on the inside
secta *f* sect
secta•rio -ria *adj & mf* sectarian
sector *m* sector; **sector de distribución** house current, power line
se•cuaz *adj* (*pl* **-cuaces**) partisan || *mf* partisan, follower
secuela *f* sequel, result
secuencia *f* sequence
secuestrar *tr* to kidnap; (*un avión*) to hijack; (law) to sequester
secular *adj* secular
secundar *tr* to second, back
secunda•rio -ria *adj* secondary || *m* (elec) secondary
sed *f* thirst; drought; **tener sed** to be thirsty
seda *f* silk; **como una seda** smooth as silk; easy as pie; sweet-natured; **seda encerada** dental floss
sedal *m* fish line
sedán *m* sedan; **sedán de reparto** delivery truck
sede *f* (*p.ej., del gobierno*) seat; (eccl) see; **Santa Sede** Holy See

senta•rio -ria *adj* sedentary
sede•ño -ña *adj* silk, silken
sedición *f* sedition
sedicio•so -sa *adj* seditious
sedien•to -ta *adj* thirsty; (*terreno*) dry; anxious, eager
sedimento *m* sediment
sedo•so -sa *adj* silky
seducción *f* seduction; charm, captivation
seducir §19 *tr* to seduce; tempt, lead astray; charm, captivate
seducti•vo -va *adj* seductive; tempting; charming, captivating
seduc•tor -tora *adj* seductive; tempting; charming || *mf* seducer; tempter; charmer
sefar•dí (*pl* **-fíes**) *adj* Sephardic || *mf* Sephardi
sega•dor -dora *adj* harvesting || *m* harvestman || *f* harvester; mowing machine; **segadora de césped** lawn mower; **segadora trilladora** combine
segar §66 *tr* to reap, harvest, mow; mow down || *intr* to reap, harvest, mow
segazón *f* harvest; harvest time
seglar *adj* secular, lay || *m* layman || *f* laywoman
segmento *m* segment; **segmento de émbolo** piston ring
segregacionista *mf* segregationist
segregar §44 *tr* to segregate
seguida *f* series, succession; **de seguida** without interruption, continuously; at once; in a row; **en seguida** at once, immediately
seguidilla *f* Spanish stanza made up of a quatrain and a tercet; **seguidillas** seguidilla (*Spanish dance and music*)
segui•do -da *adj* continued, successive; straight, direct; running, in a row; **todo seguido** straight ahead || *f* see **seguida**
seguimiento *m* chase, hunt, pursuit; continuation; (*de vehículos espaciales*) tracking
seguir §67 *tr* to follow; pursue; continue; dog, hound || *intr* to go on, continue; still be, be now; keep + *ger* || *ref* to follow, ensue; issue, spring
según *prep* according to, as per; **según que** according as || *conj* as, according as
segunda *f* double meaning; (aut & mus) second
segundero *m* second hand; **segundero central** sweep-second, center-second
segun•do -da *adj* second || *m* second; **ser sin segundo** to be second to none || *f* see **segunda**
segur *f* axe; sickle
segurador *s* security, bondsman
seguridad *f* security; safety; surety; certainty; assurance; confidence
segu•ro -ra *adj* sure, certain; secure, safe; reliable; constant; steady, unfailing || *m* assurance, certainty; safety; confidence; insurance; **a buen seguro** surely, truly; **seguro contra accidentes** accident insurance; **seguro de desempleo** or **desocupación** unemployment insurance; **seguro de enfermedad** health insurance; **seguro de incendios** fire insurance; **seguro sobre la vida** life insurance; **sobre seguro** without risk || **seguro** *adv* surely
seis *adj & pron* six; **las seis** six o'clock || *m* six; (*en las fechas*) sixth
seiscien•tos -tas *adj & pron* six hundred || **seiscientos** *m* six hundred
selección *f* selection
seleccionar *tr* to select, choose
selec•to -ta *adj* select, choice
selva *f* forest, woods; jungle
selváti•co -ca *adj* woodsy; rustic, wild
sellar *tr* to seal; stamp; close; finish up
sello *m* seal; stamp; signet; wafer; **sello aéreo** air-mail stamp; **sello de correo** postage stamp; **sello de urgencia** special-delivery stamp; **sello fiscal** revenue stamp
semáforo *m* semaphore; traffic light
semana *f* week; week's pay; **semana inglesa** working week of five and a half days
semanal *adj* weekly
semanalmente *adv* weekly
semana•rio -ria *adj & m* weekly
semánti•co -ca *adj* semantic || *f* semantics
semblante *m* face, mien, countenance; appearance, expression, look
semblanza *f* biographical sketch, portrait
sembrado *m* sown ground, grain field
sembrar §2 *tr* to seed, sow; scatter, spread, sprinkle
semejante *adj* like, similar; such; **semejante a** like; **semejantes** alike, e.g., **estas sillas son semejantes** these chairs are alike || *m* resemblance, likeness; fellow, fellow man
semejanza *f* similarity, resemblance; simile; **a semejanza de** like
semejar *tr* to resemble, be like || *intr & ref* to be alike; **semejar a** or **semejarse a** to resemble, be like
semen *m* semen
semental *adj* (*animal*) stud, breeding || *m* sire; stallion; stock bull
semestral *adj* semester
semestre *m* semester
semibola *f* little slam
semibreve *f* (mus) whole note
semiconductor *m* semiconductor
semiconsciente *adj* semiconscious
semicul•to -ta *adj* semilearned
semidifun•to -ta *adj* half-dead
semidormi•do -da *adj* half-asleep
semifinal *adj & f* (sport) semifinal
semilla *f* seed; **semilla de césped** grass seed
semillero *m* seedbed
seminario *m* seminary; seminar; nursery
semi-remolque *m* semitrailer
semita *mf* Semite || *m* (*idioma*) Semitic
semíti•co -ca *adj* Semitic
semivi•vo -va *adj* half-alive
semovientes *mpl* stock, livestock
sempiter•no -na *adj* everlasting
Sena *m* Seine
senado *m* senate
senador *m* senator
senaduría *f* senatorship
sencillez *f* simplicity, plainness, candor
senci•llo -lla *adj* simple, plain, candid; single || *m* change, loose change

senda *f* path, footpath
sendero *m* path, footpath, byway
sen•dos -das *adj pl* one each, one to each, e.g., **les dio sendos libros** he gave one book to each of them, he gave each of them a book
senectud *f* age, old age
senil *adj* senile
senilidad *f* senility
senilismo *m* (pathol) senility
seno *m* bosom, breast; lap; heart; womb; bay, gulf; cavity, hollow, recess; asylum, refuge
sensación *f* sensation
sensatez *f* good sense
sensa•to -ta *adj* sensible
sensibilizar **§60** *tr* to sensitize
sensible *adj* appreciable, perceptible, noticeable, sensible; considerable; sensitive; deplorable, regrettable
sensiblería *f* mawkishness
sensible•ro -ra *adj* mawkish
sensiti•vo -va *adj* (*de los sentidos*) sense, sensitive; sentient; stimulating
senso•rio -ria *adj* sensory
sensual *adj* sensual, sensuous
sentada *f* sitting; **de una sentada** at one sitting
senta•do -da *adj* seated; settled; stable, permanent; sedate; **dar por sentado** to take for granted || *f* see **sentada**
sentar **§2** *tr* to seat; settle; fit, suit; agree with || *ref* to sit, sit down; settle, settle down
sentencia *f* maxim; (law) sentence
sentenciar *tr* to sentence; (*una cuestión*) to decide; (*p.ej., un libro a la hoguera*) to consign
senti•do -da *adj* felt; deep-felt; sensitive; eloquent; **darse por sentido** to take offense || *m* sense, meaning; direction; consciousness; **sentido común** common sense
sentimiento *m* sentiment; feeling; sorrow, regret
sentir *m* feeling; opinion; judgment || **§68** *tr* to feel; hear; be or feel sorry for; sense || *intr* to feel; be sorry, feel sorry || *ref* to feel; feel oneself to be; be resentful; crack, be cracked; **sentirse de** to feel; have a pain in; resent
seña *f* sign, mark, token; password, watchword; **por las señas** to all appearances; **por más señas** or **por señas** as a greater proof; **seña de tráfico** traffic sign; **señas** address; description
señal *f* sign, mark, token; landmark; bookmark; trace, vestige; scar; signal; traffic light; representation; reminder; pledge; brand; down payment; **señal de ocupado** (telp) busy signal; **señal de tramo** (rr) block signal; **señal de vídeo** video signal; **señal digital** fingerprint; **señal para marcar** (telp) dial tone
señala *f* (Chile) earmark (*on livestock*)
señala•do -da *adj* noted, distinguished
señalar *tr* to mark; show, indicate; point at, point out; signal; brand; determine, fix; appoint; sign and seal; scar; threaten || *ref* to distinguish oneself, excel
señalizar **§60** *tr* to signal
señor *m* sir, mister; lord, master, owner; **muy señor mío** Dear Sir; **señores** Mr. and Mrs.; ladies and gentlemen
señora *f* madam, missus; mistress, owner; wife; **muy señora mía** Dear Madam; **Nuestra Señora** our Lady; **señora de compañía** chaperon
señorear *tr* to dominate, rule; master, control; seize, take control of; tower over; excel || *intr* to strut, swagger || *ref* to strut, swagger; control oneself; **señorearse de** to seize, take control of
señoría *f* lordship; ladyship; rule, sway
señoril *adj* lordly; haughty; majestic
señorío *m* dominion, sway, rule; mastery; arrogance, lordliness, majesty; gentry, nobility
señorita *f* young lady; miss
señorito *m* master; young gentleman; playboy
señuelo *m* decoy, lure; bait; enticement
separación *f* separation; **separación de poderes** (pol) separation of powers
separa•do -da *adj* separate; separated; apart; **por separado** separately; under separate cover
separar *tr* to separate; dismiss, discharge || *ref* to separate; resign
separata *f* reprint, offprint
sept.^{e} *abbr* **septiembre**
septeto *m* septet
sépti•co -ca *adj* septic
septiembre *m* September
sépti•mo -ma *adj & m* seventh
sepulcro *m* sepulcher, tomb, grave; **santo sepulcro** Holy Sepulcher
sepultar *tr* to bury; hide away
sepultura *f* burial; grave; **estar con un pie en la sepultura** to have one foot in the grave
sepulturero *m* gravedigger
sequedad *f* dryness, drought; gruffness, surliness
sequía *f* drought
séquito *m* retinue, suite; following, popularity
ser *m* being; essence; life || *v* **§69** *v aux* (to form passive voice) to be, e.g., **el discurso fue aplaudido por todos** the speech was applauded by everybody || *intr* to be; **a no ser por** if it were not for; **a no ser que** unless; **érase que se era** once upon a time there was; **es decir** that is to say; **sea lo que fuere** be that as it may; **ser de** to belong to; become of; be, e.g., **el reloj es de oro** the watch is gold; **ser de ver** to be worth seeing; **soy yo** it is me, it is I
serafín *m* seraph; great beauty (*person*)
serena *f* night love song; night dew, night air
serenar *tr* to calm; pacify; cool; settle
serenata *f* serenade
serenidad *f* serenity; **serenidad del espíritu** peace of mind

sere•no -na *adj* serene, calm; clear, cloudless || *m* night watchman; night dew, night air || *f* see **serena**
serial *adj* serial || *m* (telv) serial; **serial lacrimógeno** soap opera; **serial radiado** (rad) serial
serie *f* series; **de serie** serial; stock, e.g., **coche de serie** stock car; **en serie** mass; **fuera de serie** custom-built, special; outsize
seriedad *f* seriousness; reliability; sternness, severity; solemnity
se•rio -ria *adj* serious; reliable; stern; solemn
sermón *m* sermon
sermonear *tr & intr* to sermonize
serpear or **serpentear** *intr* to wind, meander; wriggle, squirm
serpentín *m* coil
serpiente *f* serpent, snake; **serpiente de cascabel** rattlesnake
serranía *f* range of mountains, mountainous country
serra•no -na *adj* highland, mountain || *mf* highlander, mountaineer
serrar §2 *tr* to saw
serrería *f* sawmill
serrín *m* sawdust
serrucho *m* handsaw
Servia *f* Serbia
servicial *adj* accommodating, obliging
servicio *m* service; (tennis) service, serve; (Am) toilet; **en acto de servicio** in the line of duty; **fuera de servicio** out of service; inoperative; (coll) down; **libre servicio** self-service; **servicio de grúa** (aut) towing service; **servicio postventa** customer service; **servicio telegráfico y telefónico** wire service
servi•dor -dora *mf* servant; humble servant; (tennis) server; **servidor de Vd.** your servant, at your service || *m* waiter; suitor || *f* waitress
servidumbre *f* servitude; servants, help; compulsion; (law) easement; **servidumbre de la gleba** serfdom; **servidumbre de paso** (law) right of way; **servidumbre de vía** (rr) right of way
servil *adj* servile
servilleta *f* napkin
servilletero *m* napkin ring
ser•vio -via *adj & mf* Serbian || *f* see **Servia**
servir §50 *tr* to serve; help, wait on; (*un pedido*) fill; (tennis) serve; **para servir a Vd.** at your service || *intr* to serve; (*en los naipes*) follow suit; **servir de** to serve as; be used as; **servir para** to be good for, be used for || *ref* to help oneself, serve oneself; have the kindness to, deign to; **servirse de** to use, make use of; **sírvase** please
serv.º *abbr* **servicio**
servocroata *adj & mf* Serbo-Croatian
servodirección *f* (aut) power steering
servoembrague *m* (aut) automatic clutch
servofreno *m* power brake
sésamo *m* sesame; **sésamo ábrete** open sesame
sesenta *adj, pron & m* sixty
sesenta•vo -va *adj & m* sixtieth
sesgar §44 *tr* (*el paño*) to cut on the bias; bevel, slant, slope
ses•go -ga *adj* beveled, slanting, sloped; oblique; stern; calm || *m* bevel; bias; slant, slope; turn; compromise; **al sesgo** obliquely; on the bias
sesión *f* session; sitting; meeting; (*cada representación de un drama o película*) show; **sesión continua** (mov) continuous showing; **sesión de espiritistas** séance, spiritualistic séance
sesionar *intr* to be in session
seso *m* brain; brains, intelligence; **calentarse** or **devanarse los sesos** to rack one's brain
sestear *intr* to take a siesta; (*el ganado*) rest in the shade
sesu•do -da *adj* brainy; (Chile) stubborn
seta *f* bristle; toadstool
setecien•tos -tas *adj & m* seven hundred || **setecientos** *m* seven hundred
setenta *adj, pron & m* seventy
setenta•vo -va *adj & m* seventieth
seto *m* fence; **seto vivo** hedge, quickset
seudónimo *m* pseudonym, pen name
s.e.u.o. *abbr* **salvo error u omisión**
seve•ro -ra *adj* severe; stern; strict
sevicia *f* ferocity, cruelty
sexo *m* sex; **el bello sexo** the fair sex; **el sexo feo** the sterner sex
sextante *m* sextant
sex•to -ta *adj & m* sixth
sexual *adj* sexual, sex
si *conj* if; whether; I wonder if; **por si acaso** just in case; **si acaso** if by chance; **si no** otherwise
sí *adv* yes; indeed; (gives emphasis to verb and is often equivalent to English auxiliary verb) **él sí habla español** he does speak Spanish || *pron reflex* himself, herself, itself, themselves; yourself, yourselves; oneself; each other || *m* (*pl* **-síes**) yes; **dar el sí** to say yes
sia•més -mesa *adj & mf* Siamese
siberia•no -na *adj & mf* Siberian
sibila *f* sibyl
sicalipsis *f* spiciness, suggestiveness
sicalípti•co -ca *adj* spicy, suggestive, sexy
Sicilia *f* Sicily
sicilia•no -na *adj & mf* Sicilian
sico. . . var of **psico. . .**
sicofanta *m* or **sicofante** *m* informer, spy; slanderer
sico•sis *f* (*pl* **-sis**) psychosis; (*afección de la piel*) sycosis
SIDA *abbr* **síndrome de inmunidad deficiente adquirida**
sideral or **sidére•o -a** *adj* sidereal
siderurgia *f* iron and steel industry
sidra *f* cider; **sidra achampañada** hard cider
siega *f* reaping, mowing; harvest; crop
siembra *f* sowing; seeding; seedtime; sown field

siempre *adv* always; **de siempre** usual; **para siempre** or **por siempre** forever; **por siempre jamás** forever and ever; **siempre que** whenever; provided
siempreviva *f* everlasting flower
sien *f* temple (*of head*)
sierpe *f* serpent, snake
sierra *f* saw; sierra, mountain range; **sierra circular** buzz saw; **sierra continua** band saw; **sierra de armero** hacksaw; **sierra de bastidor** bucksaw; **sierra de hilar** ripsaw; **sierra de vaivén** jig saw; **sierra sin fin** band saw
sier•vo -va *mf* slave; servant; **siervo de la gleba** serf
sieso *m* anus
siesta *f* siesta; hot time of day; **siesta del carnero** nap before lunch
siete *adj & pron* seven; **las siete** seven o'clock || *m* seven; (*en las fechas*) seventh; (coll) V-shaped tear or rip
sífilis *f* syphilis
sifón *m* siphon; siphon bottle; (*tubo doblemente acodado*) trap
sig.[e] *abbr* **siguiente**
sigilar *tr* to seal, stamp; conceal, keep silent
sigilo *m* seal; concealment, reserve; **sigilo sacramental** inviolable secrecy of the confessional
sigilo•so -sa *adj* tight-lipped; reserved
sigla *f* initial; abbreviation, symbol
siglo *m* (*cien años*) century; (*comercio de los hombres*) world; (*largo tiempo*) age; **siglo de la ilustración** or **de las luces** Age of Enlightenment
signar *tr* to mark; sign; make the sign of the cross over
signatura *f* library number; (mus & typ) signature
significado *m* meaning
significar **§73** *tr* to signify, mean; point out, make known || *intr* to be important
signo *m* sign; mark; sign of the cross; fate, destiny; **signo de admiración** exclamation mark; **signo de interrogación** question mark; **signo externo** status symbol
siguiente *adj* following; next
sílaba *f* syllable; **última sílaba** ultima
silbar *tr* (*p.ej., una canción*) to whistle; (*un silbato*) blow; (*a un actor*) hiss || *intr* to whistle; (*ir zumbando por el aire*) whiz, whiz by
silbato *m* whistle
silbido *m* whistle, whistling, hiss; (rad) howling, squealing; **silbido de oídos** ringing in the ears
silbo *m* whistle, hiss
silenciador *m* silencer; (aut) muffler
silencio *m* silence; (*toque que manda que cada cual se acueste*) (mil) taps; (mus) rest
silencio•so -sa *adj* silent, noiseless; quiet, still || *m* (aut) muffler
sílfide *f* sylph
silo *m* silo; cave, dark place
silogismo *m* syllogism
silueta *f* silhouette
silva *f* (*materias escritas sin orden*) miscellany; verse of iambic hendecasyllables intermingled with seven-syllable lines
silvestre *adj* wild; rustic, uncultivated
silvicultura *f* forestry
silla *f* chair; **silla alta** high chair; **silla de balanza** rocking chair; **silla de cubierta** deck chair; **silla de junco** rush-bottomed chair; **silla de manos** sedan chair; **silla de montar** saddle, riding saddle; **silla de ruedas** wheel chair; **silla de tijera** folding chair; **silla giratoria** swivel chair; **silla hamaca** (Arg) rocking chair; **silla plegadiza** folding chair; **silla poltrona** armchair, easy chair; **sillas apilables** chairs that can be stacked or nested
sillar *m* ashlar
silleta *f* bedpan
sillico *m* chamber pot, commode
sillín *m* saddle (*of bicycle*)
sillón *m* armchair, easy chair; **sillón de orejas** wing chair
sima *f* chasm, abyss
simbióti•co -ca *adj* symbiotic
simbóli•co -ca *adj* symbolic(al)
simbolizar **§60** *tr* to symbolize
símbolo *m* symbol; **Símbolo de la fe** or **de los Apóstoles** Apostles' Creed
simetría *f* symmetry
simétri•co -ca *adj* symmetric(al)
simiente *f* seed, sperm
símil *adj* like, similar || *m* similarity; (rhet) simile
similar *adj* similar
similigrabado *m* (typ) half-tone
similor *m* ormolu, similor; **de similor** fake, sham
simio *m* monkey
simpatía *f* affection, attachment, liking; friendliness; congeniality; **tomar simpatía a** to take a liking for
simpáti•co -ca *adj* agreeable, pleasant, likeable, congenial
simpatizar **§60** *intr* to be congenial, get on well together; **simpatizar con** to get on well with
simple *adj* simple; single || *mf* simpleton || *m* (*planta medicinal*) simple
simpleza *f* simpleness; stupidity
simplificar **§73** *tr* to simplify
simulacro *m* phantom, vision; idol, image; semblance, show; pretense; sham battle; **simulacro de ataque aéreo** air-raid drill; **simulacro de combate** sham battle
simula•do -da *adj* fake; (com) pro forma
simular *tr* to simulate, feign, fake || *intr* to malinger; pretend
simultanear *tr* to do simultaneously || *intr* to work simultaneously
simultáne•o -a *adj* simultaneous
sin *prep* without; **sin embargo** nevertheless, however; **sin que** + *subj* without + *ger*
sinagoga *f* synagogue
sinapismo *m* mustard plaster; bore, nuisance
sincerar *tr* to vindicate, justify
sinceridad *f* sincerity
since•ro -ra *adj* sincere

síncopa *f* (phonet) syncope
síncope *m* fainting spell
sincróni•co -ca *adj* synchronous
sincronizar **§60** *tr & intr* to synchronize
sindicar **§73** *tr & ref* to syndicate
sindicato *m* syndicate; labor union
síndico *m* trustee; (*en una quiebra*) receiver
sin•diós (*pl* **-diós**) *adj* godless || *mf* atheist
síndrome *m* syndrome; **síndrome de choque tóxico** toxic-shock syndrome; **síndrome de inmunidad deficiente adquirida (SIDA)** acquired immune-deficiency syndrome (AIDS)
sinecura *f* sinecure
sinfín *m* endless amount, number
sinfonía *f* symphony
sinfóni•co -ca *adj* symphonic
singladura *f* (naut) day's run
singular *adj* singular; special; single || *m* singular; **en singular** in particular
singularizar **§60** *tr* to distinguish, single out || *ref* to distinguish oneself, stand out
sinhueso *f* (coll) tongue
sinies•tro -tra *adj* evil, perverse; calamitous, disastrous || *m* calamity, disaster || *f* left hand, left-hand side
sinnúmero *m* great amount, great number
sino *conj* but, except; **no . . . sino** only; **no . . . sino que** only; **no solo . . . sino que** not only . . . but also || *m* fate, destiny
sinóni•mo -ma *adj* synonymous || *m* synonym
sinop•sis *f* (*pl* **-sis**) synopsis
sinrazón *f* wrong, injustice
sinsabor *m* displeasure; anxiety, trouble, worry
sinsonte *m* mockingbird
sinsostenismo *m* (coll) bra-less fashion
sintaxis *f* syntax
sínte•sis *f* (*pl* **-sis**) synthesis
sintéti•co -ca *adj* synthetic(al)
sintetizar **§60** *tr* to synthesize
síntoma *m* symptom; sign; **síntoma de abstinencia** withdrawal symptom
sintonía *f* (rad) tuning; (rad) theme song
sintonizar **§60** *tr* (*el aparato receptor*) to tune; (*la estación emisora*) tune in
sinuo•so -sa *adj* sinuous, winding; wavy; evasive
sinvergüenza *adj* brazen, shameless || *mf* scoundrel, rascal
sionismo *m* Zionism
siqui. . . var of **psiqui. . .**
siquiera *adv* even; at least || *conj* although, even though
sirena *f* siren; mermaid; **sirena de la playa** bathing beauty; **sirena de niebla** foghorn
sirga *f* towrope, towline
sirgar **§44** *tr* to tow
Siria *f* Syria
si•rio -ria *adj & mf* Syrian || **Sirio** *m* (astr) Sirius || *f* see **Siria**
sirvienta *f* maid, servant girl
sirviente *m* servant; waiter
sisa *f* petty theft; (*para fijar los panes de oro*) sizing
sisal *m* sisal, sisal hemp
sisar *tr* to filch, snitch; (*lo que se ha de dorar*) size
sisear *tr* to hiss || *intr* to hiss; sizzle
siseo *m* hiss, hissing; sizzle, sizzling
Sísifo *m* Sisyphus
sismógrafo *m* seismograph
sismología *f* seismology
sistema *m* system; **el Sistema** the Establishment, established order
sistematizar **§60** *tr* to systematize
sístole *f* systole
sitial *m* place of honor
sitiar *tr* to surround, hem in; siege, besiege
sitio *m* place, spot, room; location, site; country place; seat; cattle ranch; taxi stand; (mil) siege
si•to -ta *adj* situated, located
situación *f* situation, position; **pedir situación** (aer) to ask for bearings
situar **§21** *tr* to situate, locate, place; (*dinero*) place, invest; (*un pedido*) place || *ref* to take a position; settle; take place; (aer) to get one's bearings
s.l. *abbr* **sin lugar**
S.M. *abbr* **Su majestad**
smo•king *m* (*pl* **-kings**) tuxedo, dinner coat
so *prep* under, e.g., **so pena de** under penalty of || *interj* whoa!; you. . . !, e.g., **¡so animal!** you beast!
sobaco *m* armpit
sobajar *tr* to crush, to rumple; to humiliate
sobaquera *f* (*en el vestido*) armhole; (*para resguardar del sudor la parte del vestido correspondiente al sobaco*) shield
sobaquina *f* underarm odor
sobar *tr* to knead; massage; beat, slap; paw, pet, feel; annoy, be fresh to; flatter; (*un hueso dislocado*) (CAm) to set; (*la cabalgadura*) (Arg) to tire out; (Col) to flay, skin; (P-R) to bribe
soberanía *f* sovereignty
sobera•no -na *adj* sovereign; superb || *mf* sovereign || *m* (*moneda*) sovereign
sober•bio -bia *adj* proud, haughty; arrogant; magnificent, superb || *f* pride, haughtiness; arrogance; magnificence
so•bón -bona *adj* malingering; fresh, mushy, spoony
soborna•do -da *adj* twisted; out of shape
sobornar *tr* to bribe
soborno *m* bribery; (SAm) extra load; **de soborno** (Bol) in addition; **soborno de testigo** (law) subornation of perjury
sobra *f* extra, surplus; **sobras** leftovers, leavings; trash
sobradillo *m* penthouse
sobra•do -da *adj* excessive, superfluous; bold, daring; rich, wealthy || *m* attic, garret || **sobrado** *adv* too
sobrante *adj* remaining, leftover, surplus || *m* leftover, surplus
sobrar *tr* to exceed, surpass || *intr* to be more than enough; be in the way; be left, remain
sobre *prep* on, upon; over; above; about; near; after; in addition to; out of, e.g., **en nueve casos sobre diez** in nine out of ten

cases || *m* envelope; **sobre de ventanilla** window envelope
sobrealimentar *tr* to overfeed; supercharge
sobrecama *f* bedspread
sobrecarga *f* overload, extra load; overcharge; surcharge
sobrecargar §44 *tr* to overload, overburden; overcharge; surcharge; (aer) to pressurize
sobrecargo *m* (naut) supercargo; purser || *f* flight attendant, stewardess
sobrecejo *m* frown
sobreceño *m* frown
sobrecoger §17 *tr* to surprise, catch; scare, terrify || *ref* to be surprised; be scared; **sobrecogerse de** to be seized with
sobrecubierta *f* extra cover; (*de un libro*) jacket, dust jacket
sobredi•cho -cha *adj* above-mentioned
sobredosis *f* overdose
sobreestimar *tr* to overestimate
sobreexcitar *tr* to overexcite || *ref* to become overexcited
sobreexponer §54 *tr* to overexpose
sobreexposición *f* overexposure
sobregirar *tr & intr* to overdraw
sobregiro *m* overdraft
sobreherido *adj* slightly wounded
sobrehombre *m* superman
sobrehuma•no -na *adj* superhuman
sobrellevar *tr* to bear, carry; (*la carga de otra persona*) ease; (*los trabajos o molestias de la vida*) share; (*molestias*) suffer with patience
sobremanera *adv* exceedingly, beyond measure
sobremesa *f* tablecloth, table cover; **de sobremesa** desk, e.g., **reloj de sobremesa** desk clock; after-dinner, e.g., **discurso de sobremesa** after-dinner speech
sobremodo *adv* var of **sobremanera**
sobrenadar *intr* to float
sobrenatural *adj* supernatural
sobrenombrar *tr* to surname; nickname
sobrenombre *m* surname; nickname
sobrentender §51 *tr* to understand || *ref* to be understood, be implied
sobrepasar *tr* to excel, surpass, outdo; exceed; overtake || *ref* to outdo each other; go too far
sobrepeine *adv* slightly, briefly || *m* hair trimming
sobrepe•lliz *f* (*pl* **-llices**) surplice
sobreponer §54 *tr* to superpose, put on top; superimpose || *ref* to control oneself; triumph over adversity; **sobreponerse a** to overcome
sobreprecio *m* extra charge, surcharge
sobreproducción *f* overproduction
sobrepujar *tr* to excel, surpass
sobresaliente *adj* projecting; conspicuous, outstanding; (*en un examen*) distinguished || *mf* substitute; understudy
sobresalir §65 *intr* to project, jut out; stand out, excel
sobresaltar *tr* to assail, rush upon; startle, frighten || *intr* to stand out clearly || *ref* to be startled, be frightened; start, wince
sobresalto *m* fright, scare; start, shock, wince; **de sobresalto** suddenly, unexpectedly
sobrescribir §83 *tr* to address
sobrescrito *m* address
sobrestante *m* boss, foreman
sobresueldo *m* extra wages, extra pay
sobretiro *m* offprint
sobretodo *adv* especially || *m* overcoat, topcoat
sobrevenir §79 *intr* to happen, take place; supervene, set in; **sobrevenir a** to overtake
sobrevidriera *f* window screen; window grill; storm window
sobrevivencia *f* (Ecuad) survival
sobreviviente *adj* surviving || *mf* survivor
sobrevivir *intr* to survive; **sobrevivir a** to survive, outlive
sobrevolar §61 *tr* to overfly
sobriedad *f* sobriety, moderation
sobrina *f* niece
sobrino *m* nephew
so•brio -bria *adj* sober, moderate, temperate
socaire *m* (naut) lee; **al socaire de** (naut) under the lee of; (coll) under the shelter of; **estar al socaire** to shirk
socapa *f* subterfuge; **a socapa** clandestinely
socarrén *m* eaves
socarrar *tr* to singe, scorch
soca•rrón -rrona *adj* crafty, cunning, sly; sneering; roguish
socavar *tr* to undermine, dig under
socavón *m* cave-in; cave; (min) gallery
sociable *adj* sociable
social *adj* social; company, e.g., **edificio social** company building
socialismo *m* socialism
socialista *mf* socialist
sociedad *f* society; company, firm; **buena sociedad** (*mundo elegante*) society; **sociedad anónima** stock company; **sociedad de control** holding company; **Sociedad de las Naciones** League of Nations; **sociedad distribuidora** (wholesale) distributor
so•cio -cia *mf* partner; companion; member || *m* fellow; (scornful) guy
sociología *f* sociology
socorrer *tr* to aid, help, succor
socorri•do -da *adj* ready; handy, useful; hackneyed, trite, worn; well stocked
socorrismo *m* first aid
socorro *m* aid, help, succor
socoyote *m* (Mex) baby, youngest son
soda *f* soda; soda water
sodio *m* sodium
so•ez *adj* (*pl* **-eces**) base, mean, vile
so•fá *m* (*pl* **-fás**) sofa; **sofá cama** day bed
soflama *f* glow, flicker; blush; deceit, cheating
soflamar *tr* to flimflam; make blush || *ref* to become scorched
sofocar §73 *tr* to choke, suffocate, stifle, smother; quench, extinguish; make blush; bother, harass || *ref* to choke, suffocate; blush; get excited; get out of breath
sofoco *m* blush, embarrassment

sofrenar *tr* (*un caballo*) to check suddenly; (*una pasión*) control; chide, reprimand
soga *m* sly fellow || *f* rope, cord; **dar soga a** to make fun of; **hacer soga** to lag behind
soja *f* soy, soy bean
sojuzgar **§44** *tr* to subjugate, subdue
sol *m* sun; sunlight; sunny side; **de sol a sol** from sunrise to sunset; **hacer sol** to be sunny; **soles** (poet) eyes
solamente *adv* only
solana *f* sunny spot; sun porch
solanera *f* sunburn; sunny spot
solapa *f* lapel; pretext, pretense; flap
solapa•do -da *adj* overlapping; cunning, underhanded, sneaky
solapar *tr* to put lapels on; overlap; conceal, cover up || *intr* to overlap
solapo *m* lapel; flap; chuck under chin
solar *adj* solar; ancestral || *m* ground, plot; backyard; manor house, ancestral mansion; noble lineage; (Cuba) tenement || *v* **§61** *tr* to pave, floor; (*zapatos*) sole
solarie•go -ga *adj* ancestral; manorial
solario *m* sun porch
so•laz *m* (*pl* **-laces**) solace, consolation; recreation; **a solaz** with pleasure
soldada *f* wages, pay
soldadera *f* (Mex) camp follower
soldadesca *f* soldiery; undisciplined troops
soldado *m* soldier; **soldado de a pie** foot soldier; **soldado de juguete** toy soldier; **soldado de marina** marine; **soldado de plomo** tin soldier; **soldado de primera** private first class; **soldado raso** buck private
soldadura *f* solder; soldering; weld; welding; **soldadura al arco** arc welding; **soldadura autógena** welding; **soldadura a tope** butt welding; **soldadura por puntos** spot welding
soldar **§61** *tr* to solder; (*sin materia extraña*) weld || *ref* (*los huesos*) to knit
solear *tr* to sun || *ref* to sun, sun oneself
soledad *f* solitude, loneliness; longing, grieving; lonely spot
soledo•so -sa *adj* solitary, lonely; longing, grieving
solemne *adj* solemn; (*error, mentira, etc.*) downright
soler **§47** *intr* to be accustomed to
solera *f* crossbeam; lumber, timber; mother liquor, mother of the wine; blend of sherry; old vintage sherry; tradition, standing; (Chile) curb; (Mex) brick, tile, stone; **de solera** or **de rancia solera** of the good old school, of the good old times
solevantar *tr* to raise up; rouse, stir up, incite || *ref* to rise up; revolt
solevar *tr* to raise up; incite to rebellion || *ref* to rise up; revolt
solicitante *mf* petitioner; applicant
solicitar *tr* to solicit, ask for; apply for; woo, court; drive, pull; (*la atención*) attract; (phys) to attract
solíci•to -ta *adj* solicitous; careful, diligent; obliging; fond, affectionate
solicitud *f* solicitude; petition, request; application
solidar *tr* to harden; establish, prove
solida•rio -ria *adj* jointly liable; jointly binding; **solidario con** or **de** integral with
solidarizar **§60** *ref* to declare one's solidarity (with); identify (with)
solidez *f* solidity; strength, soundness; constancy
sóli•do -da *adj* solid; strong, sound || *m* solid
soliloquio *m* soliloquy
solista *adj* (*p.ej., instrumento*) (mus) solo || *mf* (mus) soloist
solita•rio -ria *adj* solitary; lonely || *mf* hermit, recluse, solitary || **en solitario** alone, solo || *m* (*juego y diamante*) solitaire || *f* tapeworm
sóli•to -ta *adj* accustomed, customary
soliviantar *tr* to rouse, stir up, incite
soliviar *tr* to lift, lift up
so•lo -la *adj* only, sole; alone; lonely; (*p.ej., whisky*) straight; (*café*) black; **a mis solas** alone, all by myself; **a solas** alone, unaided || *pron* only one || *m* (mus) solo
sólo *adv* only, solely
solomillo *m* sirloin
solomo *m* sirloin; loin of pork
solsticio *m* solstice
soltador *m* release; **soltador del margen** margin release
soltar **§61** *tr* to untie, unfasten, loosen; let go; let go of; (*una observación*) drop, let slip; (*el agua*) turn on || *ref* to get loose or free; come loose, come off; loosen **up**; burst out; thaw out, let oneself go
solte•ro -ra *adj* single, unmarried || *m* bachelor || *f* unmarried woman
solterona *f* older unmarried woman
soltura *f* looseness; agility, ease, freedom; fluency; dissoluteness; release
solución *f* solution
solucionar *tr* to solve, resolve
solventar *tr* (*lo que uno debe*) to settle, pay up; (*una dificultad*) solve
solvente *adj* solvent; (*fuente*) believable; reliable || *m* solvent
sollastre *m* scullion
sollozar **§60** *intr* to sob
sollozo *m* sob
sombra *f* (*falta de luz brillante*) shade; (*imagen obscura que proyecta un cuerpo opaco*) shadow; shady side; darkness; parasol; ignorance; ghost, spirit; grace, charm, wit; favor, protection; luck; **a la sombra** in the shade; in jail; **a sombra de tejado** stealthily, sneakingly; **ni por sombra** by no means; without any notice; **no ser su sombra** to be but a shadow of one's former self; **sombra (de ojos)** eye shadow; **tener buena sombra** to be likeable; to bring good luck
sombrear *tr* to shade; (*un dibujo*) hatch
sombrerera *f* bandbox, hatbox
sombrerería *f* hat store, hat factory; millinery shop
sombrere•ro -ra *mf* hatter, hat maker || *f* see **sombrerera**

sombrero *m* hat; **sombrero de copa** high hat, top hat; **sombrero de muelles** opera hat; **sombrero de paja** straw hat; **sombrero de pelo** high hat; **sombrero de tres picos** three-cornered hat; **sombrero gacho** slouch hat; **sombrero hongo** derby; **sombrero jarano** sombrero
sombrilla *f* parasol, sunshade; **sombrilla de playa** beach umbrella; **sombrilla protectora** (mil) umbrella
sombrí•o -a *adj* shady; somber; gloomy
sombro•so -sa *adj* shadowy, full of shadows; shady
some•ro -ra *adj* brief, summary; slight; superficial, shallow
someter *tr* to subdue, subject; (*razones, reflexiones; un negocio*) submit || *ref* to yield, submit, surrender
someti•do -da *adj* humble, submissive
sometimiento *m* subjection
somier *m* bedspring, spring mattress
somnolencia *f* sleepiness, drowsiness
somorgujar *tr* to plunge, submerge || *intr* to dive, || *ref* to plunge
son *m* sound; news, rumor; pretext, motive; manner, mode; **en son de** in the manner of, by way of; as
sona•do -da *adj* talked-about; famous, noted
sonaja *f* jingle
sonajero *m* rattle, child's rattle
sonámbu•lo -la *mf* sleepwalker, somnambulist
sonar §61 *tr* to sound, ring; (*un instrumento de viento, un silbato*) blow; (*un instrumento de viento*) play || *intr* to sound, ring; (*un reloj*) strike; seem; sound familiar; **sonar a** to sound like, have the appearance of || *ref* to be rumored; (*las narices*) blow
sonda *f* sounding; plummet, lead; drill; (surg) probe, sound
sondar or **sondear** *tr & intr* to sound, probe
sonetizar §60 *intr* to sonneteer
soneto *m* sonnet
sóni•co -ca *adj* sonic
sonido *m* sound; report, rumor
sonido silencioso ultrasound
sonoridad *f* sonority
sonorizar §60 *intr* (*una película cinematográfica*) to record sound effects on; (*una consonante sorda*) voice || *ref* to voice
sono•ro -ra *adj* sound; clear, loud, resounding
sonreír §58 *intr & ref* to smile
sonriente *adj* smiling
sonrisa *f* smile
sonrojar or **sonrojear** *tr* to make one blush || *ref* to blush
sonrojo *m* blush; word that causes blushing
sonrosar or **sonrosear** *tr* to rose-color; make blush || *ref* to become rose-colored; blush
sonsacar §73 *tr* to pilfer; entice away; elicit, draw out
son•so -sa *adj* stupid
sonsonete *m* rhythmical tapping; sing-song
soña•dor -dora *adj* dreamy || *mf* dreamer
soñar §61 *tr* to dream; **ni soñarlo** not even in a dream, by no means || *intr* to dream; **soñar con** to dream of; **soñar despierto** to daydream
soñolien•to -ta *adj* sleepy, dozy, drowsy, somnolent; lazy
sopa *f* (*pan u otra cosa empapada en un líquido*) sop; soup; **hecho una sopa** soaked to the skin, sopping wet; **sopa de pastas** noodle soup
sopapo *m* chuck under the chin; blow, slap
sopetear *tr* to dip, dunk; abuse
sopetón *m* slap, box; **de sopetón** suddenly
sopista *mf* beggar
soplar *tr* to blow; blow away; blow up, inflate; snitch, swipe; inspire; prompt; tip off; (*la dama a un rival*) cut out; squeal on || *intr* to blow; squeal || *ref* to be puffed up, be conceited; swill, gulp, gobble
soplete *m* blowpipe
soplillo *m* blower, fan; chiffon, silk gauze; light sponge cake
soplo *m* blowing, blast; breath; gust of wind; instant, moment; (*informe dado en secreto*) tip; squealing; squealer
so•plón -plona *adj* tattletale || *mf* tattletale, squealer
sopor *m* sleepiness, drowsiness; stupor
soporífico *m* soporific; nightcap
soportal *m* porch, portico, arcade
soportar *tr* to support, hold up, bear; endure, suffer
soporte *m* support, bearing, rest, standard; base, stand
soprano *mf* (*persona*) soprano || *m* (*voz*) soprano
sor *f* (used before names of nuns) Sister
sorber *tr* to sip; absorb, soak up
sorbete *m* sherbet, water ice
sorbetera *f* ice-cream freezer; high hat
sorbo *m* sip; gulp
sordera or **sordez** *f* deafness
sórdi•do -da *adj* sordid
sordina *f* silencer; (mus) mute; (mus) damper; **a la sordina** silently, on the quiet
sor•do -da *adj* deaf; silent, mute; muffled, dull; (*dolor, ruido*) dull || *mf* deaf person; **hacerse el sordo** to pretend to be deaf; turn a deaf ear
sordomu•do -da *adj* deaf and dumb || *mf* deaf-mute
sorgo *m* sorghum, broomcorn
sorna *f* slowness; sluggishness; cunning
sorochar *ref* to blush; (SAm) to become mountain-sick
soroche *m* flush, blush; (SAm) mountain sickness; (Bol, Chile) silver-bearing galena
sorprendente *adj* surprising
sorprender *tr* to surprise; catch; (*un secreto*) discover || *ref* to be surprised
sorpresa *f* surprise; surprise package
sorpresi•vo -va *adj* surprising
sortear *tr* to draw or cast lots for; choose by lot; dodge; duck through || *intr* to draw or cast lots
sorteo *m* drawing, casting of lots; choosing by lot; dodging; (taur) workout, performance

sortija *f* ring; curl; hoop; **sortija de sello** signet ring
sortilegio *m* sorcery, witchery
sortíle•go -ga *mf* fortuneteller || *m* sorcerer || *f* sorceress
sosa *f* soda
sosega•do -da *adj* calm, quiet, peaceful
sosegar §66 *tr* to calm, quiet, allay || *intr* to become calm, rest || *ref* to calm down, quiet down
sosiega *f* nightcap
sosiego *m* calm, quiet, serenity
sosla•yo -ya *adj* slanting, oblique; **al soslayo** or **de soslayo** slantingly; askance
so•so -sa *adj* insipid; tasteless; dull, inane || *f* see **sosa**
sospecha *f* suspicion
sospechar *tr* to suspect
sospecho•so -sa *adj* suspicious; suspect || *m* suspect
sostén *m* support; (*de un buque*) steadiness; brassiere
sostener §71 *tr* to support, hold up; sustain; maintain; bear, stand || *ref* to remain
sosteni•do -da *adj & m* (mus) sharp
sota *m* (Chile) boss, foreman || *f* (*en los naipes*) jack; jade, hussy
sotana *f* soutane, cassock
sótano *m* basement, cellar
sotavento *m* (naut) leeward
soterrar §2 *tr* to bury; hide away
soto *m* grove; brush, thicket, copse
so•viet *m* (*pl* **-viets**) soviet
soviéti•co -ca *adj* soviet, sovietic
sovoz — **a sovoz** sotto voce, in a low tone
soya *f* soybean
Sr. *abbr* **Señor**
Sra. *abbr* **Señora**
Srta. *abbr* **Señorita**
S.S.S. *abbr* **su seguro servidor**
ss.ss. *abbr* **seguros servidores**
stock *m* stock; inventory; **tener en stock** to carry; have in stock
su *adj poss* his, her, its, their, your, one's
suave *adj* suave, smooth, soft; gentle, mild, meek
suavizador *m* razor strop
suavizar §60 *tr* to smooth, ease, sweeten, soften, mollify; (*una navaja de afeitar*) strop
subalter•no -na *adj & mf* subaltern, subordinate
subasta *f* auction, auction sale; **sacar a pública subasta** to sell at auction
subastar *tr* to auction, sell at auction
subcampe•ón -ona *mf* (sport) runner-up
subcentral *f* (elec) substation
subconsciencia *f* subconscious, subconsciousness
subconsciente *adj* subconscious
subdesarrolla•do -da *adj* underdeveloped
súbdi•to -ta *adj & mf* subject
subentender §51 *tr* to understand || *ref* to be understood, be implied
subestimar *tr* to underestimate
subfusil *m* submachine gun
subi•do -da *adj* high, fine, superior; strong, intense; (*color*) bright; high, high-priced || *f* rise; ascent; (*p.ej., al trono*) accession
subir *tr* to raise; lift; carry up; (*p.ej., una escalera*) go up; (mus) to raise the pitch of || *intr* to go up, come up; rise; get worse; spread; **subir a** to climb; climb on; get in or into; get on, mount || *ref* to rise
súbi•to -ta *adj* sudden, unexpected; hurried; hasty, impetuous || **súbito** *adv* suddenly
subjeti•vo -va *adj* subjective
subjunti•vo -va *adj & m* subjunctive
sublevación *f* uprising, revolt
sublevado *m* rebel, insurrectionist
sublevar *tr* to incite to rebellion || *ref* to revolt
submarinista *mf* (sport) scuba diver; skin diver || *m* (nav) submariner
submari•no -na *adj* underwater, submarine || *m* submarine
subnormal *adj* (mentally) retarded
suboficial *m* sergeant major; noncommissioned officer
subordina•do -da *adj & mf* subordinate
subordinar *tr* to subordinate
subproducto *m* by-product
subrayar *tr* to underline; emphasize
subrepti•cio -cia *adj* surreptitious
subsanar *tr* to excuse, overlook; correct, repair
subscribir §83 *tr* to subscribe; subscribe to, endorse; subscribe to or for; sign; sign up || *ref* to subscribe
subseguir §67 *intr & ref* to follow next
subsidiar *tr* to subsidize
subsidiarias *fpl* feeder industries
subsidiario *m* subsidiary
subsidio *m* subsidy; aid, help
subsiguiente *adj* subsequent
subsistencia *f* subsistence, sustenance
subsistir *intr* to subsist
subsóni•co -ca *adj* subsonic
substancia *f* substance
substanciar *tr* to abstract, abridge
substanti•vo -va *adj & m* substantive
substitución *f* replacement; (chem, law, math) substitution
substitui•dor -dora *adj & mf* substitute
substituir §20 *tr* to replace; substitute for, take the place of || *intr* to take someone's place || *ref* to be replaced; relieve each other
substituti•vo -va *adj & m* substitute
substitu•to -ta *mf* substitute
substraer §75 *tr* to remove; deduct; rob, steal; subtract || *ref* to withdraw; **substraerse a** to evade, avoid, slip away from
subte *m* (Arg, Urug) subway
subteniente *m* second lieutenant
subterráne•o -a *adj* subterranean, underground || *m* subterranean; (Arg) subway
subtitular *tr* to subtitle
subtítulo *m* subtitle, subheading
suburbio *m* suburb; outlying slum
subvención *f* subvention, subsidy
subvencionar *tr* to subvention, subsidize

subvenir §79 *intr* to provide; **subvenir a** to provide for; (*gastos*) defray
subvertir §68 *tr* to subvert
subyugar §44 *tr* to subjugate, subdue
sucedàne•o -a *adj & m* substitute
suceder *tr* to succeed, follow || *intr* to happen; **suceder a** (*p.ej., el trono*) to succeed to || *ref* to follow one another
sucesi•vo -va *adj* successive; **en lo sucesivo** in the future
suceso *m* event, happening; issue, outcome; **sucesos de actualidad** current events
suciedad *f* dirt, filth; dirtiness, filthiness
su•cio -cia *adj* dirty, filthy; base, low; tainted; blurred; (sport) foul || **sucio** *adv* (sport) foully, unfairly
sucumbir *intr* to succumb
sucursal *f* branch, branch office
Sudamérica *f* South America
sudamerica•no -na *adj & mf* South American
sudar *tr* to sweat; cough up || *intr* to sweat; (*trabajar mucho*) sweat
sudario *m* shroud, winding sheet
sudcorea•no -na *adj & mf* South Korean
sudor *m* sweat; (fig) sweat, toil; **chorrear de sudor** to swelter
sudoro•so -sa *adj* sweaty
Suecia *f* Sweden
sue•co -ca *adj* Swedish || *mf* Swede || *m* (*idioma*) Swedish
suegra *f* mother-in-law
suegro *m* father-in-law
suela *f* sole; sole leather; (*fish*) sole
sueldacostilla *f* grape hyacinth
sueldo *m* salary, pay; **a sueldo** (*gángster*) on a contract, hired (to kill)
suelo *m* ground, soil, land; floor, flooring; pavement; (*p.ej., de una botella*) bottom; **no pisar en el suelo** to walk on air; **suelo franco** loam; **suelo natal** home country
suel•to -ta *adj* loose; free; easy; swift, agile, nimble; fluent; bold, daring; (*ejemplar*) single; (*verso*) blank; odd, separate; spare; bulk; **suelto de lengua** loose-tongued || *m* small change; news item
sueñecillo *m* nap; **descabezar un sueñecillo** to take a nap
sueño *m* sleep; dream; (*cosa de gran belleza*) (fig) dream; **conciliar el sueño** to manage to go to sleep; **ni por sueños** by no means; **no dormir sueño** to not sleep a wink; **tener sueño** to be sleepy; **último sueño** (*muerte*) last sleep; **sueño hecho realidad** dream come true; **sueños dorados** daydreams
suero *m* serum
suerte *f* fortune, luck; piece of luck; fate, lot; kind, sort; way, manner; feat, trick; (taur) play, suerte; (Peru) lottery ticket; **de esta suerte** in this way; **de suerte que** so that, with the result that; **la suerte está echada** the die is cast; **suerte de capa** (taur) capework
suerte•ro -ra *adj* fortunate, lucky || *m* (coll) lucky dog
sué•ter *m* (*pl* **-ters**) sweater
suficiente *adj* sufficient; adequate; fit, competent
sufijo *m* suffix
sufragar §44 *tr* to help, support, favor; defray || *intr* (SAm) to vote
sufragio *m* help, succor; benefit; (*voto*) suffrage
sufragismo *m* woman suffrage
sufragista *mf* woman-suffragist || *f* suffragette
sufri•do -da *adj* long-suffering; (*color*) serviceable; (*marido*) complaisant
sufrir *tr* to suffer; undergo, experience; support, hold up; tolerate; (*un examen*) take || *intr* to suffer
sugerencia *f* suggestion
sugerir §68 *tr* to suggest
sugestión suggestion
sugestionar *tr* to influence by suggestion
sugesti•vo -va *adj* suggestive; stimulating, striking, conspicuous
suicida *adj* suicidal || *mf* suicide
suicidar *ref* to commit suicide
suicidio *m* suicide
Suiza *f* Switzerland
sui•zo -za *adj & mf* Swiss || *f* see **Suiza**
sujeción *f* subjection; surrender; fastening; fastener
sujetador *m* bra(ssiere)
sujetahilo *m* (elec) binding post
sujetapape•les *m* (*pl* **-les**) paper clip
sujetar *tr* to subject; subdue; fasten, tighten || *ref* to subject oneself, submit; stick, adhere
suje•to -ta *adj* subject, liable; able, capable || *m* subject; fellow, individual; **buen sujeto** good egg
sulfato *m* sulfate
sulfito *m* sulfite
sulfúri•co -ca *adj* sulfuric
sulfuro *m* sulfide; **sulfuro de hidrógeno** hydrogen sulfide
sulfuro•so -sa *adj* sulfurous
sultán *m* sultan; (*galanteador*) sheik
suma *f* sum, addition; summary; sum and substance; **en suma** in short, in a word
sumadora *f* adding machine
sumamente *adv* extremely, exceedingly
sumar *tr* to add; sum up; amount to || *intr* to add; amount; **suma y sigue** add and carry || *ref* to add up; adhere
suma•rio -ria *adj & m* summary
sumergir §27 *tr* to submerge || *ref* to submerge; (*un submarino*) dive
sumersión *f* submersion; (*de un submarino*) dive
sumidad *f* top, apex, summit
sumidero *m* drain, sewer; sink
suministrar *tr* to provide, supply
suministro *m* provision, supply; **suministros** supplies
sumir *tr* to sink; press down; overwhelm || *ref* to sink; (*p.ej., los carrillos, el pecho*) be sunken; shrink, shrivel; cower; (*p.ej., el sombrero*) pull down
sumisión *f* submission (*sometimiento*) subjection
sumi•so -sa *adj* submissive

su•mo -ma *adj* high, great, extreme; supreme; **a lo sumo** at most, at the most || *f* see **suma**
suncho *m* hoop
suntuo•so -sa *adj* sumptuous
supeditar *tr* to hold down, oppress
superar *tr* to surpass, excel; conquer
superávit *m* (com) surplus
supercarburante *m* high-test fuel
supercheria *f* fraud, deceit
superficial *adj* superficial; surface
superficie *f* surface; exterior, outside; area; **superficie de sustentación** (aer) airfoil
super•fluo -flua *adj* superfluous
superhombre *m* superman
superintendente *mf* superintendent, supervisor; **superintendente de patio** (rr) yardmaster
superior *adj* superior; upper; higher; **superior a** superior to; higher than; more than; larger than || *m* superior
superiora *f* mother superior
superiordad *f* superiority; authorities
superlati•vo -va *adj & m* superlative
supermercado *m* supermarket
super•no -na *adj* highest, supreme
superpetrolero *m* supertanker
superpoblar §61 *tr* to overpopulate
superponer §54 *tr* to superpose
superproduction *f* overproduction
supersóni•co -ca *adj* supersonic || *f* supersonics
superstición *f* superstition
supersticio•so -sa *adj* superstitious
supertanquero *m* (SAm) supertanker
supervisar *tr* to supervise
supervivencia *f* survival; (law) survivorship
súpi•to -ta *adj* sudden; impatient; (Col) dumbfounded
suplantar *tr* to supplant by treachery; (*un documento*) to alter fraudulently
suplefal•tas *mf* (*pl* **-tas**) substitute, fill-in
suplemento *m* supplement; excess fare; **suplemento dominical** (*periódico*) Sunday supplement
súplica *f* entreaty, supplication; request
suplicante *adj & mf* suppliant
suplicar §73 *tr & intr* to entreat, implore; (law) to petition
suplicio *m* torture; punishment, execution; anguish
suplir *tr* to supplement, make up for; replace, take the place of; (*un defecto de otra persona*) cover up; (gram) to understand
suponer §54 *tr* to suppose; presuppose, imply; entail || *intr* to have weight, have authority
suposición *f* supposition; distinction; falsehood, imposture
supositorio *m* suppository
supradi•cho -cha *adj* above-mentioned
supre•mo -ma *adj* supreme
supresión *f* suppression, elimination, omission; cancellation; deletion
suprimir *tr* to suppress, eliminate, do away with; cancel; delete
supues•to -ta *adj* supposed, assumed, hypothetical; **supuesto que** since, inasmuch as || *m* assumption, hypothesis; **dar por supuesto** to take for granted; **por supuesto** of course, naturally
supurar *intr* suppurate, discharge pus
sur *m* south; south wind
Suramérica *f* South America
surcar §73 *tr* to furrow; plough; cut through; streak through
surco *m* furrow; wrinkle, rut, cut; (*del disco gramofónico*) groove; **echarse en el surco** to lie down on the job
surcorea•no -na *adj & mf* South Korean
sure•ño -ña *adj* southern || *mf* southerner
surestada *f* (Arg) southeaster
surgir §27 *intr* to spout, spurt; come forth, spring up; arise, appear
suripanta *f* (hum) chorus girl; (scornful) slut, jade
surti•do -da *adj* assorted || *m* assortment; supply, stock
surtidor *m* jet, spout, fountain; **surtidor de gasolina** gasoline pump
surtir *tr* to furnish, provide, supply || *intr* to spout, spurt, shoot up
susceptible *adj* susceptible; touchy
suscitar *tr* to stir up, provoke; (*dudas, una cuestión*) to raise
susodi•cho -cha *adj* above-mentioned
suspender *tr* to hang; suspend; astonish; postpone; fail, flunk || *ref* to be suspended
suspensión *f* suspension; astonishment; **suspensión de fuegos** cease fire
suspen•so -sa *adj* suspended, hanging; baffled, bewildered; (theat) closed || *m* flunk, condition
suspensores *mpl* suspenders
suspensorio *m* jockstrap, supporter
suspi•caz *adj* (*pl* **-caces**) suspicious, distrustful
suspirar *intr* to sigh
suspiro *m* sigh; ladyfinger; (mus) quarter rest
sustentación *f* support, prop; (aer) lift
sustentar *tr* to sustain, support, feed; maintain; (*una tesis*) defend
sustento *m* sustenance, support, food; maintenance
susto *m* scare, fright
susurrar *tr* to whisper || *intr* to whisper; murmur, rustle, purl, hum; be bruited about || *ref* to be bruited about
susurro *m* whisper; murmur, rustle, purling, hum
susu•rrón -rrona *adj* whispering || *mf* whisperer
sutil *adj* subtle; keen, observant; thin, delicate
su•yo -ya *adj poss* of his, of hers, of yours, of theirs, e.g., **un amigo suyo** a friend of his; *pron poss* his, hers, yours, theirs, its, one's; **hacer de las suyas** to be up to one's old tricks; **salirse con la suya** to have one's way; to carry one's point

T

T, t (te) *f* twenty-third letter of the Spanish alphabet
t. *abbr* **tarde**
taba *f* anklebone; (*del carnero*) knucklebone; (*juego*) knucklebones
tabaco *m* tobacco; cigar; snuff; (Cuba, CAm, Mex) punch; **tabaco en rama** leaf tobacco; **tabaco sin humo** smokeless tobacco
tabalada *f* bump, thump, heavy fall; slap
tabalear *tr* to rock, sway || *intr* to drum with the fingers
tabanazo *m* slap; slap in the face
tabanco *m* stand, stall, booth
tábano *m* horsefly, gadfly
tabanque *m* treadle wheel
tabaola *f* noise, hubbub
tabaquera *f* snuffbox; (*de la pipa de fumar*) bowl; (Arg, Chile) tobacco pouch
tabaquería *f* tobacco store, cigar store
tabaque•ro -ra *adj* tobacco || *mf* tobacconist; cigar maker || *m* (Bol) pocket handkerchief || *f* see **tabaquera**
tabardete *m* or **tabardillo** *m* sunstroke; harum-scarum
tabarra *f* bore, tiresome talk
taberna *f* tavern, saloon, barroom, pub
tabernáculo *m* tabernacle
tabernera *f* barmaid
tabernero *m* tavern keeper; bartender
tabica *f* (*para cubrir un hueco*) board; (*del frente de un escalón*) riser
tabicar §73 *tr* to close up, shut up; wall up
tabique *m* thin wall; partition wall, partition
tabla *f* (*de madera*) board; (*de metal*) sheet; (*de piedra*) slab; (*de tierra*) strip; (*cuadro pintado en una tabla*) panel; (*lista, catálogo; índice de materias*) table; **escapar** or **salvarse en una tabla** to have a narrow escape; **tabla de lavar** washboard; **tabla de planchar** ironing board; **tabla de salvación** lifesaver, helping hand; **tablas** draw, tie; (*escenario del teatro*) stage; (*de la plaza de toros*) barrier; **tener tablas** to have stage presence
tablado *m* flooring; scaffold; (*escenario del teatro*) stage
tablear *tr* to cut into boards; divide into plots or patches; level, grade
tablero *m* boarding; timber; table top; gambling table; cutting board; checkerboard, chessboard; counter; blackboard; **poner al tablero** to risk; **tablero de instrumentos** (aer) control panel; (aut) dashboard
tableta *f* small board; (*taco de papel; comprimido, pastilla*) tablet
tabletear *intr* to rattle
tabilla *f* tablet; splint; bulletin board
tablón *m* plank; beam
tabloncillo *m* (taur) seat in last row
ta•bú *m* (*pl* **-búes**) taboo
tabuco *m* hovel
tabulador *m* tabulator
tabular *tr* to tabulate
taburete *m* stool
tac *m* tick
tacada *f* stroke (*of a billiard cue*)
taca•ño -ña *adj* stingy
táci•to -ta *adj* tacit; silent
tacitur•no -na *adj* taciturn; melancholy
taco *m* bung, plug; wad, wadding; billiard cue; pad, tablet; drumstick; snack, bite; drink; oath, curse; heel; muddle, mess; (Mex) rolled-up tortilla with fillings, taco
tacón *m* heel
taconear *tr* (Chile) to fill, stuff || *intr* to click the heels; strut
taconeo *m* click, clicking (*of heels*)
tácti•co -ca *adj* tactical || *m* tactician || *f* tactics
tacto *m* (sense of) touch; (*del dactiló-grafo, el pianista, el instrumento*) touch; skill; tact
tacha *f* defect, fault, flaw
tachar *tr* to erase; strike out; blame, find fault with
tacho *m* tin sheet; (Arg) garbage can; (Arg) watch; (Arg, Chile) boiler; (Cuba) sugar pan
tachón *m* scratch, erasure; ornamental tack or nail; trimming
tachonar *tr* to adorn with ornamental tacks; trim with ribbon; spangle, stud
tachuela *f* tack; hobnail; (Chile, Mex) runt, half pint; (SAm) drinking cup
Tadeo *m* Thaddeus
tafetán *m* taffeta; **tafetanes** flags, colors; finery; **tafetán inglés** court plaster
tafilete *m* morocco leather; sweatband
tagarote *m* sparrow hawk; scrivener; lout; gentleman sponger
tagua *f* (Chile) mud hen; (*arbusto*) (SAm) ivory palm; (*fruto*) (SAm) ivory nut
taha•lí *m* (*pl* **-líes**) baldric
tahona *f* horse-driven flour mill; bakery
ta•hur -hura *adj* gambling; cheating || *mf* gambler; cheat; cardsharp
tailan•dés -desa *adj & mf* Thai
Tailandia *f* Thailand
taima•do -da *adj* sly, crafty; (Arg, Ecuad) lazy; (Chile) gruff, sullen
tajada *f* cut; slice; hoarseness; drunk
tajadero *m* chopping block
tajalá•piz *m* (*pl* **-pices**) pencil sharpener
tajamar *m* cutwater; dike, dam
tajar *tr* to cut; slice; (*un lápiz*) sharpen
tajo *m* cut; cutting edge; chopping block; execution block; steep cliff || **Tajo** *m* Tagus
tal *adj indef* such; such a || *pron indef* so-and-so; such a thing; someone || *adv* so; in such a way; **con tal (de) que** provided (that); **¿qué tal?** how?; hello!, how's everything?
talabarte *m* sword belt
talabartero *m* saddler, harness maker
talache *m* or **talacho** *m* (Mex) mattock
taladrar *tr* to bore, drill, pierce, perforate; (*un billete*) punch; (*un problema*) get to the bottom of
taladro *m* drill; auger; drill hole; drill press
tálamo *m* bridal bed

talán *m* ding-dong
talante *m* countenance, mien; desire, will, pleasure; way, manner
talar *adj* (*traje, vestidura*) long ‖ *tr* (*árboles*) to fell; destroy, lay waste
talco *m* tinsel; talc; **talco en polvo** talcum powder
talega *f* bag, sack; **talegas** money, wealth
talego *m* big bag, sack; slob; **tener talego** to have money tucked away
taleguilla *f* small bag; bullfighter's breeches
talento *m* talent
talento•so -sa *adj* talented
Tales *m* Thales
Talía *f* Thalia
talismán *m* talisman
talón *m* heel; (aut) lug, flange; check, voucher, coupon; (*de un cheque*) stub
talona•rio -ria *adj* stub ‖ *m* stub book, checkbook
talonear *intr* to dash along
talud *m* slope
talla *f* cut; carving; height, stature; size; ransom; reward; (*diamante*) cut, polish; (Arg) chatting, prattle; (CAm) fraud, lie; (Col) beating, thrashing
tallar *tr* to carve; (*una piedra preciosa*) cut; (*naipes*) deal; appraise; engrave; grind; size up; (Col) beat, thrash ‖ *intr* (Arg) to chat, converse; (Chile) to make love
tallarín *m* noodle
talle *m* shape, figure, stature; waist; fit; appearance, outline; bodice
taller *m* shop, workshop; factory, mill; atelier, studio; laboratory; **taller agremiado** closed shop; **taller carrocero** (aut) body shop; **taller franco** open shop; **taller penitenciario** workhouse
tallo *m* stem, stalk; shoot, sprout; (Col) cabbage
tamal *m* (CAm, Mex) tamale; (Chile) bundle; (coll) intrigue
tamañi•to -ta *adj* so small; very small; confused, disconcerted
tama•ño -ña *adj* so big; such a big; very big, very large; so small; **abrir tamaños ojos** to open one's eyes wide ‖ *m* size
tambaleante *adj* staggering
tambalear *intr & ref* to stagger, reel, totter
también *adv* also, too
tambo *m* (Arg, Chile) brothel; (SAm) roadside inn; (Arg, Urug) dairy
tambor *m* drum; (*persona que toca el tambor*) drummer; sieve, screen; eardrum, coffee roaster; **a tambor batiente** with drums beating; in triumph; **tambor mayor** drum major
tamborilear *tr* to praise to the skies ‖ *intr* to drum
Támesis *m* Thames
ta•miz *m* (*pl* **-mices**) sieve
tamizar §60 *tr* to sift, sieve
tamo *m* fuzz, fluff
tampoco *adv* neither, not either; **ni yo tampoco** nor I either
tampón *m* stamp pad
tan *adv* so; **tan . . . como** or **cuan** as . . . as; **tan siquiera** at least; **un tan** +*adj* such a +*adj* ‖ *m* boom (*of a drum*)
tanatología *f* thanatology
tanda *f* turn; shift, relay; task; coat, layer; game, match; flock, lot, pack; show; habit, bad habit
tangente *adj & f* tangent; **escaparse, irse** or **salir por la tangente** to evade the issue
Tánger *f* Tangier
tanguista *f* hostess (*in a night club*)
ta•no -na *adj & mf* (Arg) Neapolitan, Italian
tanque *m* tank; (dial) dipper, drinking cup
tantán *m* tom-tom; clanging; boom
tantear *tr* to compare; size up; probe, test, feel out; sketch, outline; keep the score of ‖ *intr* to keep score; to grope; **¡tantee Vd.!** just imagine!, fancy that!
tanteo *m* comparison; careful consideration; test, probe, trial; trial and error; score
tan•to -ta *adj & pron indef* so much; as much; **tanto . . . como** as much . . . as; both . . . and; **tan•tos -tas** so many; as many; **tantos . . . como** as many . . . as; **y tantos** odd, or more, e.g., **veinte y tantos** twenty odd, twenty or more ‖ *m* copy; counter, chip; point; portion, part; **apuntar los tantos** to keep score; **entre tanto** in the meantime; **estar al tanto de** to be aware of, to be or keep informed about; **poner al tanto de** to make aware of, to keep informed of; **por lo tanto** or **por tanto** therefore ‖ **tanto** *adv* so much; so hard; so often; so long; as much
tañer §70 *tr* (*un instrumento músico*) to play; (*una campana*) to ring ‖ *intr* to drum with the fingers
tañido *m* sound, tone; twang; ring, tang
tapa *f* lid, cover, top, cap; (*de un cilindro, un barril*) head; (*de una compuerta*) gate; (*de un libro*) board cover; shirt front; (aut) valve cap; **levantarse** or **saltarse la tapa de los sesos** to blow one's brains out; **tapas** appetizer, free lunch
tapabalazo *m* fly (*of trousers*)
tapabarro *m* (Chile) mudguard
tapaboca *f* slap in the mouth; muffler; squelch, squelcher
tapacu•bo *m* or **tapacu•bos** *m* (*pl* **-bos**) (aut) hubcap
tapadera *f* lid, cover, cap
tapagote•ras *m* (*pl* **-ras**) (Arg) roofing cement; (Col) roofer
tapaguje•ros *m* (*pl* **-ros**) (coll) bungling mason; substitute, replacement
tapar *tr* to cover; cover up, hide; plug, stop, stop up; conceal; obstruct; wrap up; (*un diente*) (Chile) to fill
tapara *f* (Ven) gourd; **vaciarse como una tapara** (Ven) to spill all one knows
taparrabo *m* loincloth; bathing trunks
tapera *f* (SAm) ruins; (SAm) shack
tapete *m* rug; runner; table scarf; **estar sobre el tapete** to be on the carpet, be under discussion; **tapete verde** card table, gambling table
tapia *f* mud wall, adobe wall
tapiar *tr* to wall up, wall in; close up

tapicería *f* tapestries; upholstery; tapestry shop; upholstery shop
tapicero *m* tapestry maker; upholsterer; carpet maker; carpet layer
ta•piz *m* (*pl* **-pices**) tapestry
tapizar §60 *tr* to tapestry; upholster; carpet; cover
tapon *m* stopper, cork; cap; bottle cap; bung, plug; (elec) fuse; (surg) tampon; **tapón de algodón** (surg) swab; **tapón de cubo** (aut) hubcap; **tapón de desagüe** drain plug; **tapón de tráfico** traffic jam; **tapón de vaciado** (aut) drain plug
taponar *tr* to plug, stop up; (surg) to tampon
taponazo *m* pop
taque *m* click; knock, rap
taqué *m* (aut) tappet
taquigrafía *f* shorthand, stenography
taquigrafiar §77 *tr* to take down in shorthand ‖ *intr* to take shorthand
taquígra•fo -fa *mf* stenographer
taquilla *f* ticket rack; ticket window; ticket office; box office; gate, take; file; (C-R) inn, tavern
taquille•ro -ra *adj* box-office ‖ *mf* ticket agent
taquimeca *mf* shorthand-typist
taquimecanógra•fo -fa *mf* shorthand-typist
tarabilla *f* millclapper; catch; turnbuckle; (*de la hebilla de la correa*) tongue; chatterbox; jabber; **soltar la tarabilla** to talk a blue streak
tarabita *f* (*clavillo de la hebilla*) tongue; (SAm) rope of rope bridge
taracea *f* marquetry, inlaid work
tarambana *adj & mf* (coll) crackpot
tararear *tr & intr* to hum
tarasca *f* dragon (*in Corpus Christi procession*); (*mujer fea*) hag
tarascada *f* bite; tart reply
tardanza *f* slowness, delay, tardiness
tardar *intr* to be long, be slow; be late; **a más tardar** at the latest; **tardar en** + *inf* to be late in + *ger* ‖ *ref* to be long, be slow; be late
tarde *adv* late; too late; **hacerse tarde** to grow late; **tarde o temprano** sooner or later ‖ *f* afternoon; evening; **de la tarde a la mañana** overnight; suddenly, in no time; unexpectedly
tardecer §22 *intr* to grow dark, grow late
tardí•do -a *adj* late, delayed; dilatory, tardy; slow
tar•do -da *adj* slow; late; slow, dull, dense
tar•dón -dona *mf* poke, slow poke
tarea *f* task, job; care, worry
tarifa *f* tariff; price list; rate; fare; (telp) toll; **tarifa recargada** extra fare
tarima *f* platform; stand; stool; low bench; (*entablado para dormir*) bunk
tarjeta *f* card; **tarjeta de buen deseo** or **de felicitación** greeting card; **tarjeta de crédito** credit card; **tarjeta de visita** calling card, visiting card; **tarjeta navideña** Christmas card; **tarjeta perforada** punch card; **tarjeta postal** post card, postal card
tarjetero *m* card case; card index
tarquín *m* mire, slime, mud
tarro *m* jar; milk pail; horn; (SAm) top hat
tarta *f* tart, cake; pan
tartajear *intr* to stutter
tartalear *intr* to stagger, sway; be speechless
tartamudear *intr* to stutter, stammer
tartamudeo *m* stuttering, stammering
tartamu•do -da *mf* stutterer, stammerer
tartán *m* Scotch plaid
tarugo *m* wooden plug; wooden paving block; (Guat, Mex) dolt, blockhead
tasa *f* appraisal; measure, standard; rate; ceiling price
tasación *f* appraisal; regulation
tasajo *m* jerked beef
tasar *tr* to appraise; regulate; hold down, keep within bounds; grudge
tasca *f* dive, joint; tavern; (Peru) surf, breakers
tata *m* daddy ‖ *f* nursemaid; little sister
tate *m* hashish; hashish user
tato *m* little brother
tatuaje *m* tattoo, tattooing
tatuar §21 *tr & ref* to tattoo
tauri•no -na *adj* bullfighting
Tauro *m* (astr) Taurus
taurófi•lo -la *mf* bullfight fan
tauromaquia *f* bullfighting
taxear *intr* (aer) to taxi
taxi *m* taxi, taxicab ‖ *f* taxi dancer
taxista *mf* taxi driver
taza *f* cup; (*de la fuente*) basin; (*del inodoro*) bowl
te *pron pers & reflex* thee, to thee; you, to you; thyself, to thyself; yourself, to yourself
té *m* tea; **té bailable** tea dance
tea *f* torch, firebrand
teatral *adj* theatrical
teatre•ro -ra *mf* theater-goer
teatro *m* theater; **dar teatro a** to bally-hoo; **teatro de estreno** first-run house; **teatro de repetorio** stock company
teatrólo•go -ga *mf* theater critic ‖ *m* actor ‖ *f* actress
Tebas *f* Thebes
tebe•o -a *adj & mf* Theban ‖ *m* comic book, funny paper
teca *f* teak
tecla *f* (*de piano, máquina de escribir, etc.*) key; touchy subject; **dar en la tecla** to get the knack of it; **tecla de cambio** shift key; **tecla de escape** margin release; **tecla de espacios** space bar; **tecla de retroceso** backspacer
teclado *m* keyboard; **teclado manual** (mus) manual
teclear *tr* to feel out ‖ *intr* to run over the keys; drum, thrum; (Chile) to be at death's door; (*un jugador*) (Chile) to be losing one's last cent
tecleo *m* fingering; touch; (*de la máquina de escribir*) click
técni•co -ca *adj* technical ‖ *m* technician; expert ‖ *f* technique; technics
tecolote *m* eagle owl (*of Central America*); (Mex) night policeman

techado *m* roof; **bajo techado** indoors
techar *tr* to roof
techo *m* ceiling; roof; (*sombrero*) hat; **techo de paja** thatched roof
techumbre *f* ceiling; roof
tedio *m* ennui, boredom
tedio•so -sa *adj* tedious, boresome
teja *f* roofing tile; shovel hat; yew tree; linden tree; **a toca teja** (coll) for cash; **teja de madera** shingle
tejadillo *m* cover, top; (*de coche*) roof
tejado *m* tile roof; roof; **tejado de vidrio** (fig) glass house
tejama•ní *m* (*pl* **-níes**) shake (*long shingle*)
tejar *m* tile works || *tr* to tile, roof with tiles
teja•roz *m* (*pl* **-roces**) eaves
teje•dor -dora *adj* weaving; scheming || *mf* weaver; schemer
tejer *tr & intr* to weave
tejido *m* weave, texture; web; fabric, textile; tissue; (biol & fig) tissue; **tejido adhesivo** friction tape; **tejido conjunctivo** (anat) connective tissue; **tejido de saco** (Mex) burlap; **tejido de punto** knitted fabric, jersey
tejo *m* disk; quoit; yew tree
tejón *m* badger
tela *f* cloth, fabric; (*de cebolla*) skin; (*del insecto*) web; film; (bb) cloth; (paint) canvas; (*dinero*) (slang) dough; **poner en tela de juicio** to question, doubt; **tela de alambre** wire screen; **tela de araña** spider web, cobweb; **tela emplástica** court plaster; **tela metálica** chicken wire; wire screen
telar *m* loom; frame; embroidery frame; (bb) sewing press
telaraña *f* spider web, cobweb
telecomedia serial *f* sitcom
telecontrol *m* remote control
telediario *m* daytime television news
teledifundir *tr & intr* to telecast
teledifusión *f* telecasting; telecast
telefonar *tr & intr* to telephone
telefonazo *m* telephone call
telefonear *tr & intr* to telephone
telefonema *m* telephone message
telefonista *mf* telephone operator
teléfono *m* telephone; **teléfono automático** dial telephone; **teléfono público** pay phone
teleg. *abbr* **telégrafo, telegrama**
telegrafiar §77 *tr & intr* to telegraph
telegrafista *mf* telegrapher
telégrafo *m* telegraph; **telégrafo de banderas** wigwagging; **telégrafo de máquinas** (naut) engine-room telegraph; **telégrafo sin hilos** wireless telegraph
telegrama *m* telegram
teleimpresor *m* teletype, teleprinter
Telémaco *m* Telemachus
telemando *m* remote control
telemetrar *tr* to telemeter
telemetría *f* telemetry
telémetro *m* telemeter; (mil) range finder
telen•do -da *adj* sprightly, lively
telerreceptor *m* television set
telescopar *tr & ref* to telescope
telescopio *m* telescope
telesilla *f* chair lift
telespecta•dor -dora *mf* viewer, televiewer; **telespectadores** television audience
telesquí *m* ski lift, ski tow
teleta *f* blotter, blotting paper
teletipo *m* teletype
teletubo *m* (telv) picture tube
televidente *mf* viewer, televiewer
televisar *tr* to televise
televisión *f* television; **televisión en circuito cerrado** closed-circuit television; **televisión en colores** color television; **televisión por cable** cable television
televi•sor -sora *adj* televising; television || *m* television set || *f* television transmitter
telón *m* drop curtain; **telón de acero** (fig) iron curtain; **telón de boca** (theat) front curtain; **telón de fondo** or **foro** (theat) backdrop
tema *m* theme, subject; exercise; (gram) stem; (mus) theme || *f* fixed idea; persistence; grudge; **a tema** in emulation
temario *m* agenda
temblar §2 *intr* to tremble, shake, quiver, shiver; **estar temblando** to teeter
tem•blón -blona *adj* shaking, tremulous || *m* aspen tree
temblor *m* temor, shaking, trembling; **temblor de tierra** earthquake
tembloro•so -sa *adj* trembling, shaking, tremulous
tem•bo -ba *adj* (Col) silly, stupid
temer *tr & intr* to fear
temera•rio -ria *adj* rash, reckless, foolhardy
temeridad *f* rashness, recklessness, foolhardiness, temerity
temero•so -sa *adj* frightful, dread; timid; fearful
temible *adj* dreadful, terrible, fearful
temor *m* fear, dread
témpano *m* small drum; drumhead; (*de barril*) head; (*de tocino*) flitch; (*de hielo*) iceberg, floe; (archit) tympan; (mus) kettledrum
temperamental *adj* temperamental
temperamento *m* temperament; conciliation, compromise; weather
temperar *tr* to temper, soften, moderate, calm; tune || *intr* to go to a warmer climate
temperatura *f* temperature; weather
temperie *f* weather, state of the weather
tempestad *f* storm, tempest; **tempestad de arena** sandstorm; **tempestades de risas** gales of laughter
tempesti•vo -va *adj* opportune, timely
tempestuo•so -sa *adj* stormy, tempestuous
templa•do -da *adj* temperate; moderate; lukewarm, medium; brave, courageous; drunk, tipsy; (SAm) in love; (CAm, Mex) clever
templanza *f* temperence; mildness
templar *tr* to temper; soften; ease, dilute; (*colores*) blend; (*velas*) trim || *intr* (*el tiempo*) to warm up || *ref* to temper; moderate; fall in love; die

temple *m* weather, state of the weather; temper, disposition; humor; average; dash, boldness; (*del acero, el vidrio, etc.*) temper

templo *m* temple

témpora *f* Ember days

temporada *f* season; period; (*p.ej., de buen tiempo*) spell; **de temporada** temporarily; vacationing

temporal *adj* temporal; temporary || *m* weather; storm, tempest; spell of rainy weather

temporáne•o -a or **tempora•rio -ria** *adj* temporary

temporizar §60 *intr* to temporize; putter around

temprane•ro -ra *adj* early

tempra•no -na *adj* early || **temprano** *adv* early

tenacidad *f* tenacity; persistence

tenacillas *fpl* sugar tongs; hair curler; tweezers; snuffers

te•naz *adj* (*pl* **-naces**) tenacious; persistent

tenazas *fpl* pincers, pliers; tongs

tenazón — a or **de tenazón** without taking aim; offhand

tenazuelas *fpl* tweezers

tendedera *f* clothesline; litter

tendedero *m* drier, frame for drying clothes; drying ground

tendencia *f* tendency

tender §51 *tr* to spread; stretch out; extend; reach out; offer, tender; (*la ropa*) hang out; (*con una capa de cal o yeso*) coat; (*un puente*) throw, build; (*una trampa*) set; (*conductores eléctricos, vías de ferrocarril, cañerías*) lay; (*la cama*) make; (*un cadáver*) lay out || *intr* to tend || *ref* to stretch out; throw one's cards on the table; run at full gallop

ténder *m* tender

tenderete *m* stand, booth

tende•ro -ra *mf* shopkeeper, storekeeper || *m* tent maker

tendido *m* (*p.ej., de un cable*) laying; (*de una cortina de humo*) spreading; (*de alambres*) hanging, stretching; wires; (*trecho de ferrocarril*) stretch; (*ropa que tiende la lavandera*) wash; (*de cal o yeso*) coat; (*del tejado*) slope; (*de panes*) batch; (taur) uncovered stand; (Col) bedclothes

tendón *m* tendon

tenducha *f* or **tenducho** *m* miserable old store

tenebro•so -sa *adj* dark, gloomy; (*negocio*) dark, shady; (*estilo*) obscure

tenedor *m* holder, bearer; fork, table fork; **tenedor de acciones** stockholder; **tenedor de bonos** bondholder; **tenedor de libros** bookkeeper

teneduría *f* bookkeeping

tenencia *f* tenure, tenancy; (mil & nav) lieutenancy

tener §71 *tr* to have; hold; keep; own, possess; consider; (*recibir*) get; esteem; stop; **no tenerlas todas consigo** to be alarmed, dismayed; **no tener nada que ver con** to have nothing to do with; **no tener sobre qué caerse muerto** to not have a cent to one's name; **tener que** to have to; for expressions like **tener hambre** to be hungry, see the noun || *ref* to stop; catch oneself, keep from falling; consider oneself; fit, go

tenería *f* tannery

tenida *f* meeting, session

teniente *adj* holding, owning; unripe; mean, miserly; hard of hearing || *m* lieutenant; **teniente coronel** lieutenant colonel; **teniente de navío** (nav) lieutenant

tenis *m* tennis

tenista *mf* tennis player

tenor *m* tenor, character, import, drift; (mus) tenor; **a tenor de** in accordance with

tenorio *m* lady-killer

tensión *f* tension, stress; (elec) tension, voltage; (mech) stress; **tensión arterial** or **sanguínea** blood pressure

ten•so -sa *adj* tense, tight, taut

tentación *f* temptation

tentáculo *m* tentacle, feeler

tenta•dor -dora *adj* tempting || *m* tempter

tentar §2 *tr* to touch; (*el camino*) feel; try, attempt; examine; try out, test; tempt; probe

tentati•vo -va *adj* tentative || *f* attempt; trial, feeler

tentempié *m* snack, bite, pick-me-up; (*juguete*) tumbler

tenue *adj* tenuous; light, soft; faint, subdued; (*estilo*) simple

teñir §72 *tr* to dye; stain; tinge, shade, color

teología *f* theology; **no meterse en teologías** to keep out of deep water; *teología liberacionista* liberation theology

teorema *m* theorem

teoría *f* theory; *teoría ondulatoria* wave theory

tepe *m* turf, sod

tequila *m* (Mex) tequila (*distilled liquor*)

terapéuti•co -ca *adj* therapeutic(al) || *f* therapeutics

terapia *f* therapy; *terapia vocacional* occupational therapy

tercena *f* government tobacco warehouse; (Ecuad) butcher shop

tercermundista *adj* Third World

terce•ro -ra *adj* third || *mf* third; mediator; go-between || *m* procurer, bawd; referee, umpire

Tercero Mundo *m* Third World; nonaligned nations

terceto *m* tercet; trio

terciar *tr* to place diagonally; divide into three parts; (*p.ej., la capa, el fusil*) to swing over one's shoulder; (*licor*) water || *intr* to intercede, mediate || *ref* to happen; be opportune

tercia•rio -ria *adj* tertiary

ter•cio -cia *adj* third || *m* third; (mil) corps; **hacer buen tercio a** to do a good turn

terciopelo *m* velvet

ter•co -ca *adj* stubborn; hard, resistant

Teresa *f* Theresa

tergiversar *tr* to slant, twist, distort
terliz *m* ticking
termal *adj* thermal; steam
termas *fpl* hot baths
térmi•co -ca *adj* temperature; steam; steam-generated
terminación *f* termination
terminal *adj* terminal || *m* (elec) terminal
terminante *adj* final, definitive, peremptory
terminar *tr* to end, terminate; finish || *intr* to end, terminate
término *m* end, limit; boundary; bearing, manner; term; **medio término** subterfuge, evasion; compromise; **primer término** foreground; (mov) close-up; **segundo término** middle distance; **término medio** average; **último término** background
termistor *m* (elec) thermistor
termite *m* termite
termoaislante *adj* heat-insulated
termodinámi•co -ca *adj* thermodynamic || *f* thermodynamics
termómetro *m* thermometer; **termómetro clínico** clinical thermometer
termonuclear *adj* thermonuclear
termopar *m* (elec) thermocouple
Termópilas, las Thermopylae
ter•mos *m* (*pl* **-mos**) thermos bottle; hot-water heater; **termos de acumulación** (elec) off-peak heater
termosifón *m* hot-water boiler
termóstato *m* thermostat
terna *f* trio
terne•jo -ja *adj* (Ecuad, Peru) peppy, energetic
ternera *f* calf; (*carne*) veal
terneza *f* tenderness; fondness; love; **ternezas** flirting, flirtation
ternilla *f* gristle
terno *m* suit of clothes; oath, curse; trio; piece of luck; (Col) cup and saucer; (W-I) set of jewelry
ternura *f* tenderness; fondness, love
terquedad *f* stubbornness; hardness, resistance
terraja *f* diestock
terral *adj* (*viento*) land || *m* land breeze
Terranova *m* (*perro*) Newfoundland (*dog*) || *f* (*isla y provincia*) Newfoundland (*island and province)*
terraplén *m* fill; embankment; terrace, platform; earthwork, rampart
terrateniente *mf* landholder, landowner
terraza *f* terrace; veranda; flat roof; (*de jardín*) border; edge; sidewalk cafe; glazed jar with two handles
terremoto *m* earthquake
terrenal *adj* earthly, mundane, worldly
terre•no -na *adj* terrestrial; mundane, worldly || *m* land, ground, terrain; lot, plot; (sport) field; (fig) field, sphere; **sobre el terreno** on the spot; with data in hand; **terreno echadizo** refuse dump
terre•ro -ra *adj* earthly; of earth; humble || *m* pile, heap; mark, target; terrace; public square; (min) dump
terrestre *adj* terrestrial; ground, land
terrible *adj* terrible; gruff, surly, ill-tempered
territorio *m* territory
terromontero *m* hill, butte
terrón *m* clod; lump, cake
terror *m* terror
terrorismo *m* terrorism, frightfulness
terrorista *adj & mf* terrorist
terro•so -sa *adj* earthly, dirty
terruño *m* piece of ground; soil; country, native soil
ter•so -sa *adj* smooth, glossy, polished; smooth, limpid, flowing
tertulia *f* party, social gathering; literary gathering; game room; **estar de tertulia** to sit around and talk
tertulia•no -na *mf* party-goer; regular member
Tesalia, la Thessaly
te•sis *f* (*pl* **-sis**) thesis
te•so -sa *adj* taut, tight, tense || *m* top of hill; (*en superficie lisa*) rough spot
tesón *m* grit, pluck, tenacity
tesone•ro -ra *adj* obstinate, stubborn, tenacious
tesorería *f* treasury
tesore•ro -ra *mf* treasurer
tesoro *m* treasure; treasury; treasure house; thesaurus
Tespis *m* Thespis
testa *f* head; front; head, brains; **testa coronada** crowned head
testaferro *m* dummy, figurehead, straw man
testamento *m* testament, will; **Antiguo Testamento** Old Testament; **Nuevo Testamento** New Testament; **Viejo Testamento** Old Testament
testar *tr* (Ecuad) to cross out || *intr* to make a will
testaru•do -da *adj* stubborn, pig-headed
testera *f* front; (*de animal*) forehead; (*de coche*) back seat
testículo *m* testicle
testificar **§73** *tr & intr* to testify
testigo *mf* witness; **testigo de vista, testigo ocular,** or **testigo presencial** eyewitness || *m* (*evidencia*) witness; (*en un experimento*) control
testimoniar *tr* to attest, testify to, bear witness to
testimonio *m* testimony; affidavit; false witness
tes•tuz *m* (*pl* **-tuces**) (*p.ej., de caballo*) face; nape
teta *f* teat; breast
tetera *f* teapot; teakettle
tetilla *f* nipple
tétri•co -ca *adj* dark gloomy; sad, sullen, gloomy
textil *adj & m* textile
texto *m* text; **fuera de texto** tipped-in
textura *f* texture
tez *f* complexion
ti *pron pers* thee; you
tía *f* aunt; old lady, old woman; bawd; **no hay tu tía** there's no chance; **tía abuela** grandaunt
tiara *f* tiara

tibante *adj* (Col) haughty, proud
tibia *f* shinbone; pipe, flute
ti•bio -bia *adj* tepid, lukewarm; (SAm) angry || *f* see **tibia**
tibor *m* large porcelain vase; chamber pot
tiburón *m* shark
Ticiano, El Titian
tictac *m* tick-tock
tiempo *m* time; weather; (gram) tense; (*de un motor de combustión interna*) cycle; (*de una sinfonía*) (mus) movement; (mus) tempo; **darse buen tiempo** to have a good time; **de cuatro tiempos** (mach) four-cycle; **de dos tiempos** (mach) two-cycle; **de un tiempo a esta parte** for some time now; **el Tiempo** Father Time; **fuera de tiempo** untimely, at the wrong time; **hacer buen tiempo** to be clear; **mucho tiempo** a long time; **tomarse tiempo** to bide one's time
tienda *f* store, shop; tent; **ir de tiendas** to go shopping; **tienda de campaña** army tent; camping tent; **tienda de modas** ladies' dress shop; **tienda de objetos de regalo** gift shop; **tienda de raya** (Mex) company store
tienta *f* cleverness; probe; (taur) testing the mettle of a young bull; **andar a tientas** to grope in the dark; feel one's way
tiento *m* touch; blind man's stick; ropewalker's pole; steady hand; care, caution; mahlstick; blow, hit; swig; **andarse con tiento** to watch one's step; **perder el tiento** to lose one's touch
tier•no -na *adj* tender; loving; tearful; soft
tierra *f* earth; ground; land; dirt; (elec) ground; **dar en tierra con** to upset, overthrow, ruin; **echar tierra a** to hush up; **en tierra, mar y aire** on land, on sea, and in the air; **irse a tierra** to topple, to collapse; **la tierra de nadie** (mil) no man's island; **tierra adentro** inland; **tierra de pan llevar** wheat land, cereal-growing land; **tierra firme** mainland; land, terra firma; **Tierra Firme** Spanish Main; **Tierra Santa** Holy Land; **tierra y escombros** landfill; **tomar tierra** to land; to fine one's way around; **venir** or **venirse a tierra** to topple, to collapse; **ver tierras** to see the world, to go traveling
tierral *m* cloud of dust
tie•so -sa *adj* stiff; tight, taut, tense; stubborn; bold, enterprising; strong, well; stiff, stuck-up; **tenérselas tiesas a** or **con** to stand up to || **tieso** *adv* hard
ties•to -ta *adj* stiff; tight, taut, tense; stubborn || *m* flowerpot; (*pedazo roto*) postherd || **tiesto** *adv* hard
tiesura *f* stiffness
ti•fo -fa *adj* full, satiated || *m* typhus; **tifo de América** yellow fever; **tifo de Oriente** bubonic plague
tifón *m* waterspout; typhoon
tigra *f* tigress; (female) jaguar
tigre *m* tiger; (male) jaguar
tijera *f* scissors, shears; sawbuck; **buena tijera** good cutter; good eater; gossip; **tijeras** scissors, shears
tijeretear *tr* to snip, clip, cut; meddle with || *intr* to gossip
tila *f* linden tree; linden-blossom tea
tildar *tr* to put a tilde or dash over; erase, strike out; **tildar de** to brand as
tilde *m & f* tilde; accent mark; superior dash; blemish, flaw; censure || *f* jot, tittle
tiliche *m* (CAm, Mex) trinket
tiliche•ro -ra *mf* (CAm) peddler
tilín *m* ting-a-ling
tilo *m* linden tree; linden-blossom tea
tilo•so -sa *adj* (CAm) dirty, filthy
timar *tr* to snitch; swindle || *ref* to make eyes at each other
timba *f* game of chance; gambling den; (CAm, Mex) belly
timbal *m* kettledrum; (*pastel relleno*) casserole
timbrar *tr* to stamp
timbre *m* stamp, seal; tax stamp; stamp tax; deed of glory; (phonet & phys) timbre; **timbre nasal** twang; **timbres** glockenspiel
tími•do -da *adj* timid, bashful
timo *m* theft, swindle; lie; catch phrase
timón *m* (*del arado*) beam; rudder; (fig) helm; **timón de dirección** (aer) vertical rudder; **timón de profundidad** (aer) elevator
timonel *m* helmsman, steersman
timonera *f* (naut) pilot house, wheelhouse
timora•to -ta *adj* God-fearing; chicken-hearted
tímpano *m* eardrum; kettledrum
tina *f* large earthen jar; wooden vat; bathtub
tinaja *f* large earthen jar
tincazo *m* (Arg, Ecuad) fillip
tinglado *m* shed; intrigue, trick; (zool) leatherback
tinieblas *fpl* darkness
tino *m* feel (*for things*); good aim; knack; insight, wisdom; **coger el tino** to get the knack of it
tinta *f* ink; tint, hue; dyeing; **de buena tinta** on good authority; **tinta china** India ink; **tinta simpática** invisible ink
tinte *m* dye; dyeing; dyer's shop; (fig) coloring, false appearance
tinterillo *m* clerk, lawyer's clerk; pettifogger
tintero *m* inkstand, inkwell
tintín *m* clink; jingle
tintinear *intr* to clink; jingle
tin•to -ta *adj* red || *m* red table wine || *f* see *tinta*
tintorería *f* dyeing; dyeing establishment; dry-cleaning establishment
tintore•ro -ra *mf* dyer; dry cleaner
tintura *f* dye; dyeing; rouge; tincture; (fig) smattering; **tintura de tornasol** litmus, litmus solution; **tintura de yodo** iodine
tiña *f* ringworm; stinginess
tiño•so -sa *adj* scabby, mangy; stingy
tío *m* uncle; old man; guy, fellow; **tío abuelo** granduncle; **tíos** uncle and aunt
tiovivo *m* merry-go-round, carrousel
tipiadora *f* (*máquina*) typewriter; (*mujer*) typist
tipiar *tr & intr* to type, typewrite

tipicista *adj* regional, local
típi•co -ca *adj* typical; regional; quaint
tipismo *m* quaintness
tipista *mf* typist, typewriter
tiple *mf* soprano (*person*); treble-guitar player || *m* soprano (*voice*); treble guitar
tipo *m* type; (*de descuento, de interés, de cambio*) rate; shape, figure, build; fellow, guy, specimen; **tener buen tipo** to have a good figure; **tipo de ensayo** or **prueba** eye-test chart; **tipo de impuesto** tax rate; **tipo de letra** typeface; **tipo menudo** small print
tipografía *f* typography
típula *f* (ent) daddy-longlegs
tira *m* (Arg, Chile, Col) detective || *f* strip; **hecho tiras** (Chile) in rags; **tira emplástica** (Arg) court plaster; **tira proyectable** film strip; **tiras cómicas** comics, funnies
tirabala *f* popgun
tirabuzón *m* corkscrew; corkscrew curl
tirada *f* throw; distance, stretch; time, period; printing; edition, issue; shooting party, hunting party; tirade; **de** or **en una tirada** at one stroke; **tirada aparte** reprint
tira•do -da *adj* dirt-cheap; (*letra*) cursive || *f* see **tirada**
tira•dor -dora *mf* shot, good shot || *m* knob; doorknob; pull chain; **tirador certero** sharpshooter; **tirador emboscado** sniper
tirafondo *m* wood screw
tiraje *m* draft; printing, edition
tiramira *f* long, narrow mountain range; (*de personas o cosas*) string; distance, stretch
tiranía *f* tyranny
tiráni•co -ca *adj* tyrannic(al)
tira•no -na *adj* tyrannous || *mf* tyrant
tirante *adj* tense, taut, tight; (fig) tense, strained || *m* (*de los arreos de una caballería*) trace; **tirantes** suspenders
tirantez *f* tenseness, tautness, tightness; strain
tirar *tr* to throw, cast, fling; throw away; shoot, fire; (*alambre*) draw, pull, stretch; (*una línea*) draw; (*una coz, un pellizco*) give; print; attract; tear down, knock down; (phot) to print || *intr* to pull; last; appeal, have an appeal; (*una chimenea*) draw; (*a la derecha, a la izquierda*) bear, turn; **ir tirando** to get along; **tirar a** to shoot at; (*la espada*) handle; shade into; tend to; aspire to; **tirar de** to pull, pull on; (*una espada*) draw; attract; boast of being; **tira y afloja** give and take; hot and cold || *ref* to rush, throw oneself; give oneself over; lie down; serve time (in prison)
tirilla *f* neckband; **tirilla de bota** bootstrap; **tirilla de camisa** collarband
tiritar *intr* to shiver
tiro *m* throw; shot; charge, load; (*estampido*) report; rifle range; (*p.ej., de chimenea*) draft; (*de caballos*) team; (*de escalera*) flight; (*de las guarniciones*) trace; (*de un paño*) length; pull cord, pull chain; reach; hurt, damage; trick; theft; (min) shaft; (sport) drive, shot; (*alusión desfavorable*) shot; (fig) shot, marksman; **a tiro de fusil** within gunshot; **a tiro de piedra** within a stone's throw; **matar a tiros** to shoot to death; **ni a tiros** not for love nor money; **poner el tiro muy alto** to hitch one's wagon to a star; **tiro al blanco** target practice; **tiro al vuelo** trapshooting; **tiro de la pesa** (sport) shot-put
tirón *m* tyro, novice; jerk; tug, pull; **de un tirón** all at once; at a stretch
tirotear *tr* to snipe at, blaze away at || *ref* to fire at each other; bicker
tirria *f* dislike, grudge; **tener tirria a** to have it in for
tisana *f* tea, infusion
tísi•co -ca *adj* tubercular || *mf* tubercular person, tubercular
tisis *f* consumption, tuberculosis
titanio *m* titanium
tít. *abbr* **título**
títere *m* marionette, puppet; fixed idea; whipper-snapper, nincompoop; **no dejar títere con cabeza** or **cara** to upset the applecart; **títeres** puppet show
titilar *tr* to titillate || *intr* to flutter, quiver; twinkle
titubear *intr* to stagger, totter; stammer, stutter; waver, hesitate
titular *m* bearer, holder; incumbent; headline || *f* capital letter || *tr* to title, entitle || *intr* to receive a title || *ref* to be called; call oneself
titulillo *m* running head
título *m* title; titled person; regulation; bond; certificate; degree; diploma; headline; **a título de** as a, by way of, on the score of; **títulos** credentials
tiza *f* chalk
tiznar *tr* to soil with soot; spot, stain; to defame || *ref* to become soiled; get spotted or stained; (Arg, Chile, CAm) to get drunk
tizne *m & f* soot || *m* firebrand
tiznón *m* smudge, spot of soot
tizón *m* brand, firebrand; wheat smut; brand, dishonor
tizonear *intr* to stir up the fire
tlapalería *f* (Mex) paint store
toalla *f* towel; **toalla rusa** Turkish towel; **toalla sin fin** roller towel
toallero *m* towel rack
toar *tr* (naut) to tow
tobar *tr* (Col) to tow
tobillera *f* anklet; (sport) ankle support; (coll) subdeb; (coll) flapper
tobillo *m* ankle
tobo *m* (Ven) bucket
tobogán *m* toboggan; chute, slide
toca *f* toque; headdress
tocadis•cos *m* (*pl* **-cos**) record player; **tocadiscos automático** record changer
toca•do -da *adj* (*echado a perder; medio loco*) touched; **tocado de la cabeza** touched in the head || *m* hairdo, coiffure; headdress
toca•dor -dora *mf* performer; player || *m* boudoir; dressing table; dressing case, toilet case
tocante *adj* touching; **tocante a** concerning, with reference to

tocar §73 *tr* to touch; touch on; feel; ring; toll; strike; come to know, suffer, feel; (*el cabello*) do; (*un tambor*) beat; (mus) to play; (paint) to touch up || *intr* to touch; **tocar a** to knock at; pertain to, concern; fall to the lot of; be the turn of; (*el fin*) approach; **tocar en** (*un puerto*) to touch at; (*tierra*) touch; touch on; approach, border on || *ref* to put one's hat on, cover one's head; touch each other; be related; make one's toilet; become mentally unbalanced; (*el sombrero*) tip; **tocárselas** to beat it

toca•yo -ya *mf* namesake

tocino *m* bacon; salt pork

tocón *m* stump

tocuyo *m* (SAm) coarse cotton cloth

tochimbo *m* (Peru) smelting furnace

to•cho -cha *adj* rough, coarse, crude

todavía *adv* still, yet; **todavía no** not yet

to•do -da *adj* all, whole, every; any || *m* whole; everything; **con todo** still, however; **del todo** wholly, entirely; **jugar el todo por el todo** to stake everything, shoot the works; **sobre todo** above all, especially; **todo el que** everybody who; **todo lo que** all that; **todos** all, everybody; **todos cuantos** all those who

todopodero•so -sa *adj* all-powerful, almighty

toga *f* (academic) gown

toldilla *f* poop, poop deck

toldería *f* (SAm) Indian camp, Indian village

toldo *m* awning; pride, haughtiness; (SAm) Indian hut

tole *m* hubbub, uproar; **tole tole** gossip, talk; **tomar el tole** to run away

tolerancia *f* tolerance; **por tolerancia** on sufferance

tolerar *tr* to tolerate

tolete *m* club, cudgel; raft; (Cuba) dunce

toletole *m* (Col) persistence, obstinacy; (Ven) merry life of a wanderer

tolon•dro -dra *adj* scatterbrained || *mf* scatterbrain || *m* bump, lump

tolva *f* hopper; chute

tolvanera *f* dust storm

tolla *f* quagmire; (Cuba) watering trough

tom. *abbr* **tomo**

toma *f* taking; seizure, capture; tap; intake; inlet; (elec) tap, outlet; (elec) plug; (elec) terminal; (*de rapé*) pinch; **toma de posesión** installation, induction; inauguration; **toma de tierra** (aer) landing; (rad) ground connection; **toma directa** high gear

toma-corrien•te *m* or **toma-corrien•tes** *m* (*pl* **-tes**) (elec) current collector; (elec) tap, outlet; (elec) plug

tomadero *m* handle; intake, inlet

toma•dor -dora *mf* (com) drawee; thief; drinker, toper

tomar *tr* to take; get; seize; take on; (*un resfriado*) catch; (*p.ej., el desayuno*) have, eat; (*el café, un trago*) take, drink; **tomar a bien** to take in the right spirit; **tomar a mal** to take offense at; **tomarla con** to pick a quarrel with; have a grudge against; **tomar prestado** to borrow; **tomar sobre sí** to take upon oneself || *intr* to take, turn || *ref* to take; (*p.ej., el desayuno*) have, eat; (*el café*) take, drink; get rusty

tomate *m* tomato; (*en medias, calcetines, etc.*) tear, run

tomavis•tas *m* (*pl* **-tas**) movie camera; cameraman

tómbola *f* raffle, charity raffle

tomillo *m* thyme

tomo *m* volume; bulk, importance, consequence; **de tomo y lomo** of consequence; bulky and heavy

ton. *abbr* **tonelada**

ton *m* — **sin ton ni son** without rhyme or reason

tonada *f* air, melody, song; singsong; (Cuba) hoax; (*pronunciación particular*) (Arg, Chile) accent

tonel *m* cask, barrel

tonelada *f* (*unidad de peso; unidad de volumen; unidad de desplazamiento*) ton; (*medida de capacidad para el vino*) tun

tonelaje *m* tonnage

tonele•ro -ra *mf* barrelmaker, cooper

tonga *f* coat, layer; (Arg, Col) task; (Col) sleep; (Cuba) heap, pile

tongonear *ref* to strut, swagger

tóni•co -ca *adj & m* tonic || *f* (mus) keynote

tonillo *m* singsong; (*pronunciación particular*) accent

tono *m* tone; tune; (mus) pitch; (mus) key; (*de un instrumento de bronce*) (mus) slide; **dar el tono** to set the standard; **darse tono** to put on airs; **de buen tono** stylish, elegant; **estar a tono** to be in style; **poner a tono** (*un motor de automóvil*) to tune up; **tono mayor** (mus) major key; **tono menor** (mus) minor key

tonsila *f* tonsil

tonsilitis *f* tonsilitis

tonsurar *tr* to shear, clip

tontear *intr* to talk nonsense, act foolishly

tontería *f* foolishness, nonsense

ton•to -ta *adj* foolish, stupid, silly; **a tontas y a locas** wildly, recklessly; in disorder, haphazardly || *mf* fool, dolt; **tonto de capirote** blatant fool

tonu•do -da *adj* (Arg) magnificent, showy, conceited

topacio *m* topaz

topar *tr* to butt; bump; run into, encounter || *intr* to butt; succeed; lie, be found; **topar con** or **en** to run into, encounter

tope *adj* (*precio*) top; (*fecha*) last || *m* butt; bumper; bump, collision; rub, difficulty; scuffle; masthead; **al tope** or **a tope** end to end; flush; **estar hasta el tope** or **los topes** to be loaded to the gunwales; be fed up; **tope de puerta** doorstop

topera *f* molehill

topetada *f* butt

topetar *tr* to butt || *intr* to butt; **topetar con** to bump, bump into; to run across

topetón *m* butt; bump, collision

tópi•co -ca *adj* local || *m* topic; (med) external application

topinera *f* molehill; **beber como una topinera** to drink like a fish

topo *m* mole; blunderer; stumbler, awkward person
topografía *f* topography
toque *m* touch; (*de una campana*) ringing; (*del tambor*) beat; sound; knock; stroke; check, test; (*punto esencial*) gist; (paint) touch; (coll) blow; **dar un toque a** to put to the test; feel out, sound out; **toque a muerto** knell, toll; **toque de diana** reveille; **toque de queda** curfew; **toque de retreta** (mil) tattoo; **toque de tambor** drumbeat
torada *f* drove of bulls
tó•rax *m* (*pl* **-rax**) thorax
torbellino *m* whirlwind; (*persona bulliciosa*) harum-scarum
torcecuello *m* (orn) wryneck
torcedura *f* twist; sprain; dislocation
torcer §74 *tr* to twist; bend; turn; sprain; (*la cara*) screw up; (*el tobillo*) wrench; turn; (*interpretar mal*) distort, misconstrue || *intr* to turn || *ref* to twist; bend; sprain, dislocate; turn sour; go crooked; fail
torci•do -da *adj* twisted; crooked; bent; (*ojos*) cross; (*persona o conducta*) crooked; (Guat) unlucky || *f* wick, lampwick; curlpaper
tor•do -da *adj* dapple-gray || *mf* dapple-gray horse || *m* thrush; starling
torear *tr* (*toros*) to fight; banter, tease, string along || *intr* to fight bulls, be a bullfighter
toreo *m* bullfighting; (taur) performance
tore•ro -ra *adj* bullfighting || *mf* bullfighter
toril *m* (taur) bull pen
tormenta *f* storm; adversity, misfortune
tormento *m* torment, torture; anguish
tormento•so -sa *adj* stormy; (*barco*) stormridden
torna *f* return; dam; tap; **se han vuelto las tornas** the luck has changed; **volver las tornas** to give tit for tat
tornar *tr* to return, give back; turn, make || *intr* to return; turn; **tornar a** + *inf* verb + again, e.g., **tornó a abrir la puerta** he opened the door again || *ref* to turn, become
tornasol *m* sunflower; litmus; iridescence
tornasola•do -da *adj* changeable, iridescent
tornavía *m* (rr) turntable
torna•voz *m* (*pl* **-voces**) sounding board; **hacer tornavoz** to cup one's hands to one's mouth
tornear *tr* to turn, turn up || *intr* to go around; tourney; muse, meditate
torneo *m* tourney; match, tournament; **torneo radiofónico** quiz program
tornillo *m* (*cilindro que entra en la tuerca*) screw; (*clavo con resalto helicoidal*) bolt; (*instrumento con dos mandíbulas*) vise; (mil) desertion; (CAm, Ven) screw tree; **apretar los tornillos a** to put the screws on; **tener flojos los tornillos** to have a screw loose; **tornillo de mariposa** or **de orejas** thumbscrew; **tornillo de presión** setscrew; **tornillo para metales** machine screw
torniquete *m* (*para contener hemorragias*) tourniquet; (*torno para cerrar un paso*) turnstile; **dar torniquete a** to twist the meaning of
torno *m* turn, revolution; (*máquina simple que consiste en un cilindro que gira sobre su eje*) winch, windlass; (*de alfarero*) potter's wheel; (*instrumento con dos mandíbulas*) vise; (*máquina herramienta que sirve para labrar metal o madera*) lathe; (*de coche*) brake; (*de un río*) bend, turn; revolving server; **en torno a** or **de** around; **torno de alfarero** potter's wheel; **torno de banco** bench vise; **torno de hilar** spinning wheel
toro *m* bull; **toro corrido** smart fellow; **toros** bullfight
torón *m* strand
toronja *f* grapefruit
toronjo *m* grapefruit (*tree*)
torpe *adj* slow, heavy; clumsy, awkward; stupid; lewd; crude, ugly
torpedear *tr* to torpedo
torpedo *m* torpedo; touring car
torpeza *f* torpidity, slowness; clumsiness, awkwardness; stupidity; lewdness; turpitude; crudeness, ugliness
torrar *tr* to toast
torre *f* tower; watchtower; (*en el ajedrez*) castle, rook; **torre del homenaje** donjon, keep; **torre de lanzamiento** launching tower; **torre de marfil** (fig) ivory tower; **torre de vigía** (naut) crow's-nest; **torre maestra** donjon, keep; **torre reloj** clock tower
torreja *f* (dial, Am) French toast
torrentada *f* flash flood
torrente *m* torrent
torreón *m* (archit) turret
torreta *f* (nav) turret
tórri•do -da *adj* torrid
torrija *f* French toast
torta *f* cake; (typ) font; slap; **ser tortas y pan pintado** to be a cinch; **torta a la plancha** hot cake, griddle cake
torticolis *m* or **tortícolis** *m* wryneck, stiff neck
tortilla *f* omelet; (CAm, Mex) tortilla (*cornmeal cake*); **tortilla a la española** potato omelet; **tortilla a la francesa** plain omelet; **tortilla de tomate** Spanish omelet
tórtola *f* turtledove
tortuga *f* tortoise, turtle
tortuo•so -sa *adj* winding; (fig) devious
tortura *f* torture
torturar *tr* to torture
tor•vo -va *adj* grim, stern
tos *f* cough; **tos ferina** whooping cough
tosca•no -na *adj* Tuscan || **la Toscana** Tuscany
tos•co -ca *adj* coarse, rough; uncouth
toser *intr* to cough
tósigo *m* poison; sorrow
tosiguero *m* poison ivy
tosquedad *f* coarseness, roughness; uncouthness

tostada *f* piece of toast; toast; **dar** or **pegar la tostada** or **una tostada a** to cheat, trick; **tostadas** toast
tosta•do -da *adj* brown; tan, sunburned || *m* toasting; roasting || *f* see **tostada**
tostador *m* toaster, roaster
tostar **§61** *tr & ref* to toast; roast; tan, burn
tostón *m* roasted chickpea; toast dipped in olive oil; roast pig; scorched food
total *adj & m* total || *adv* in a word
totalidad *f* totality; entirety; **en su totalidad** in its entirety
tóxi•co -ca *adj & m* toxic
toxicomanía *f* drug addiction
toxicóma•no -na *adj* drug-addicted || *mf* drug addict
tozu•do -da *adj* stubborn
tpo. *abbr* **tiempo**
traba *f* bond, tie; clasp, lock; hobble, clog; obstacle, hindrance
traba•do -da *adj* tied, fastened; joined, connected; robust, sinewy; (*sílaba*) checked; tongue-tied; (*ojos*) (Col) cross
trabaja•do -da *adj* overworked, worn-out; strained, forced, labored; busy
trabaja•dor -dora *adj* working; industrious, hard-working || *mf* worker, toiler || *m* workman, workingman || *f* workingwoman
trabajar *tr* to work; till; bother, disturb; (*a una persona*) work, drive || *intr* to work; strain; warp; **trabajar en** or **por** to strive to || *ref* to strive, exert oneself
trabajo *m* work; trouble; (*en contraposición de capital*) labor; **costar trabajo** + *inf* to be hard to + *inf;* **trabajo a destajo** piecework; **trabajo a domicilio** homework; **trabajo a jornal** timework; **trabajo de menores** child labor; **trabajo de oficina** clerical work; **trabajo de taller** shopwork; **trabajos** hardships, tribulations; **trabajos forzados** or **forzosos** hard labor, penal labor
trabajo•so -sa *adj* arduous, laborious; (*maganto*) wan, languid; (*falto de espontaneidad*) labored; unpleasant, annoying
trabalen•guas *m* (*pl* **-guas**) tongue twister, jawbreaker
trabar *tr* to join, unite; catch, seize; fasten; fetter; lock; begin; (*una batalla*) join; (*una conversación, amistad*) strike up || *intr* to take hold || *ref* to become entangled; jam; to foul; **trabársele a uno la lengua** to become tongue-tied
trabe *f* beam
trabilla *f* gaiter strap; belt loop; end stitch, loose stitch
trabuco *m* blunderbuss; popgun
trac *m* stage fright
tracale•ro -ra *adj* (CAm, Mex, W-I) cheating, tricky || *mf* (CAm, Mex, W-I) cheat, trickster
tracción *f* traction; **tracción delantera** front drive; **tracción trasera** rear drive
tractor *m* tractor; **tractor de oruga** caterpillar tractor
tradición *f* tradition
tradicionista *mf* folklorist
traducción *f* translation; **traducción automática** machine translation
traducir **§19** *tr* to translate; change
traduc•tor -tora *mf* translator
traer **§75** *tr* to bring; bring on; draw, pull; make, keep; wear; have, carry; **traer a mal traer** to abuse, mistreat || *intr* — **traer y llevar** to gossip || *ref* to dress; behave; **traérselas** to get worse and worse, cause a lot of trouble
tráfago *m* traffic, trade; toil, drudgery
trafa•gón -gona *adj* hustling, lively; slick, tricky || *mf* hustler, live wire
traficante *mf* dealer, merchant
traficar **§73** *intr* to deal, trade, traffic; travel about
tráfico *m* trade; traffic
tragaderas *fpl* gullibility; tolerance; **tener buenas tragaderas** to be too gullible
tragalda•bas *mf* (*pl* **-bas**) glutton; easy mark
tragale•guas *mf* (*pl* **-guas**) (coll) great walker
traga•luz *m* (*pl* **-luces**) skylight, bull's-eye; cellar window
tragamone•das *m* (*pl* **-das**) or **tragape•rras** *m* (*pl-* **-rras**) slot machine
tragar **§44** *tr* to swallow; swallow up; gulp down; (*creer fácilmente*) swallow; overlook; **no poder tragar** to not be able to stomach || *intr & ref* to swallow
tragasable *m* sword swallower
tragavenado *f* (SAm) anaconda
tragaviro•tes *m* (*pl* **-tes**) stuffed shirt
tragedia *f* tragedy
trági•co -ca *adj* tragic(al) || *m* tragedian
trago *m* swallow; swig; misfortune; **a tragos** slowly
tra•gón -gona *adj* gluttonous || *mf* glutton
traición *f* treachery, betrayal; (*delito contra la patria*) treason; treacherous act; **alta traición** high treason; **a traición** treacherously; **hacer traición a** to betray
traicionar *tr* to betray
traicione•ro -ra *adj* treacherous; treasonable || *mf* traitor
traída *f* conveyance, transfer; (Guat) sweetheart; **traída de aguas** water supply
traí•do -da *adj* worn, threadbare || *f* see **traída**
trai•dor -dora *adj* treacherous; treasonable || *mf* traitor; betrayer || *m* villain || *f* traitoress
traílla *f* leash; road scraper
traje *m* suit; clothes; dress; gown; **cortar un traje a** to gossip about; **traje a la medida** suit made to order; **traje de baño** bathing suit; **traje de calle** street clothes; **traje de ceremonia** or **de etiqueta** dress suit; full dress; evening clothes; **traje de faena** (mil) fatigue clothes; **traje de luces** bullfighter's costume; **traje de malla** tights; **traje de montar** riding habit; **traje de paisano** civilian clothes; **traje hecho** ready-made suit; **traje sastre** lady's tailor-made suit; **traje serio** formal dress; **vestir su primer traje largo** to come out, make one's debut
trajear *tr* to dress, clothe
trajín *m* carrying, transfer, conveyance; going and coming; bustle, commotion

trajinar *tr* to carry, convey; (Arg, Chile) to poke into; (Arg, Chile) to deceive; (Pan) to annoy || *intr* to bustle around
tralla *f* lash, whiplash, whipcord
trama *f* weft, woof; plot, scheme, machination; (*de un drama o novela*) plot
tramar *tr* to weave; plot, scheme; (*un enredo*) hatch (*a plot*)
trambucar §73 *intr* (Col, Ven) to be shipwrecked; (Col, Ven) to go out of one's mind
tramitación *f* transaction, negotiation; procedure, steps; **tramitación automática de datos** data processing
tramitar *tr* to transact, negotiate
trámite *m* step, procedure; proceeding; transaction
tramo *m* tract; stretch; (*de una escalera*) flight; (*de un puente*) span; (*de un canal entre dos esclusas*) level
tramontana *f* north; north wind; pride, haughtiness
tramoya *f* stage machinery; scheme
tramoyista *adj* scheming, tricky || *mf* schemer, impostor || *m* stagehand
trampa *f* trap; trap door; (*de un mostrador*) flap; (*de los pantalones*) fly; **armar una trampa a** to lay a trap for; **trampa explosiva** (mil) booby trap
trampear *tr* to trick, swindle || *intr* to cheat; manage to get along
trampilla *f* peephole in the floor; (*de los pantalones*) fly; (*de un secreter*) top, lid; (*de una mesa*) leaf, hinged leaf
trampolín *m* diving board; springboard; ski jump
trampo•so -sa *adj* tricky, crooked || *mf* cheat, swindler
tranca *f* beam, pole; crossbar; (Arg, Chile) drunk, spree; (P-R) dollar; **a trancas y barrancas** through fire and water
trancar §73 *tr* to bar || *intr* to stride along
trance *m* crisis; peril; trance; **a todo trance** at any cost; **último trance** (*de la vida*) last stage, end
tranco *m* long stride; threshold
tranquera *f* palisade, fence
tranquilidad *f* tranquillity
tranquilizante *m* tranquilizer
tranquilizar §60 *tr, intr & ref* to tranquilize, calm down
tranqui•lo -la *adj* tranquil, calm
tranquilla *f* feeler
tranquillo *m* knack
transacción *f* settlement, compromise; transaction
transaéreo *m* airliner
transar *tr* to settle || *intr* to yield, give in, compromise
transatlánti•co -ca *adj & m* transatlantic
transbordador *m* ferry; **transbordador espacial** space shuttle
transbordar *tr* to transship; transfer || *intr* to transfer, change trains
transbordo *m* transshipment; transfer
transcribir §83 *tr* to transcribe
transcripción *f* transcription
transcurrir *intr* to pass, elapse
transcurso *m* course (*of time*)
transepto *m* transept
transeúnte *adj* transient || *mf* transient; passer-by
transferencia *f* transfer
transferir §68 *tr* to transfer; postpone
transformador *m* transformer
transformar *tr* to transform || *ref* to transform, be transformed
tránsfuga *mf* turncoat; fugitive
transfusión *f* transfusion; **transfusión de sangre** transfusion, blood transfusion
transgredir §1 *tr* to transgress
transgresión *f* transgression
transi•do -da *adj* overcome, paralyzed; mean, cheap, stingy
transigencia *f* compromise; compromising
transigente *adj* compromising
transigir §27 *tr* to settle, compromise || *intr* to settle, compromise; agree
transistor *m* transistor
transistorizar §60 *tr* transistorize
transitable *adj* passable, practicable
transitar *intr* to go, walk; to travel
transiti•vo -va *adj* transitive
tránsito *m* transit; traffic; stop; passage; transfer
transito•rio -ria *adj* transitory
translúci•do -da *adj* translucent
transmisión *f* transmission; **transmisión del pensamiento** thought transference
transmisor *m* transmitter; **transmisor de órdenes** (naut) engine-room telegraph
transmitir *tr & intr* to transmit
transmudar *tr* to transfer; persuade, convince
transmutar *tr, intr & ref* to transmute
transparecer §22 *intr* to show through
transparencia *f* transparency; slide
transparentar *ref* to show through
transparente *adj* transparent || *m* curtain, window curtain; **transparente de resorte** window blind or shade
transpirar *intr* to transpire; (*dejarse conocer una cosa secreta*) transpire
transplantar *tr* to transplant
transponer §54 *tr* to transpose; disappear behind || *ref* (*ocultarse detrás del horizonte*) to set; get sleepy
transportar *tr* to transport; (mus) to transpose
transporte *m* transport; transportation; (aer & naut) transport; **transporte colectivo** public transportation
transportista *mf* transport worker
transvesti•do -da *adj & mf* transvestite
tranvestismo *m* transvestism
tranvía *m* trolley, trolley car, streetcar; **tranvía de sangre** horsecar
tranzar §60 *tr* to cut off, rip off; plait, braid
trapacear *tr* to chear, swindle
trapacería *f* cheating, swindling
trapace•ro -ra *adj* cheating, swindling || *mf* cheat, swindler
trapajo *m* rag, tatter

trápala *adj* chattering; cheating || *mf* chatterbox; cheat || *m* loquacity || *f* noise, uproar; (*del trote de un caballo*) clatter; cheating
trapear *tr* to mop
trapecio *m* (geom) trapezoid; (sport) trapeze
trapecista *mf* trapeze performer
trape•ro -ra *mf* ragpicker; junk dealer
trapiche *m* sugar mill; olive press; ore crusher
trapien•to -ta *adj* raggedy, in rags
trapío *m* flipness, pertness; (*del toro de lidia*) spirit
trapisonda *f* brawl, row; scheming
trapisondista *mf* schemer
trapo *m* rag; (naut) canvas, sails; bullfighter's bright-colored cape; (*de la muleta*) cloth; **a todo trapo** full sail; **poner como un trapo** to rake over the coals; **sacar los trapos a la colada, a relucir** or **al sol** to wash one's dirty linen in public; **soltar el trapo** to burst out crying, to burst out laughing; **trapos** rags, duds; **trapos de cristianar** Sunday best
trapo•so -sa *adj* raggedy, in rags
tráquea *f* trachea, windpipe
traquea•do -da *adj* (*sendero*) (Arg) beaten
traquear *tr* to shake, rattle; fool with || *intr* to crackle; rattle, chatter
traqueo *m* shake, rattle, chatter
traquetear *tr & intr* to rattle, jerk
tras *prep* after; behind; **tras de** behind; in addition to
trasatlánti•co -ca *adj & m* var of **transatlántico**
trasbordador *m* var of **transbordador**
trasbordar *tr & intr* var of **trasbordar**
trasbordo *m* var of **transbordo**
trascendencia *f* penetration, keenness; importance
trascendente *adj* penetrating; important
trascender **§51** *tr* to go into, dig up || *intr* to smell; come to be known, leak out
trascendi•do -da *adj* keen, perspicacious
trascocina *f* scullery
trascorral *m* back yard; backside
trascribir **§83** *tr* var of **transcribir**
trascripción *f* var of **transcripción**
trascuarto *m* back room
trascurrir *intr* var of **transcurrir**
trascurso *m* var of **transcurso**
trasegar **§66** *tr* to upset, turn topsy-turvy; decant, draw off
trase•ro -ra *adj* back, rear || *m* buttock, rump
trasferir **§68** *tr* var of **transferir**
trasformador *m* var of **transformador**
trasformar *tr & intr* var of **transformar**
trásfuga *mf* var of **tránsfuga**
trasfusión *f* var of **transfusión**
trasgo *m* goblin, hobgoblin; imp
trashojar *tr* to leaf through
trashumante *adj* nomadic, migrating
trasiego *m* upset, disorder; decantation
trasladar *tr* to transfer; postpone; copy, transcribe; transmit; move || *intr* to go; move
traslado *m* transfer; copy, transcript; moving
traslapar *tr, intr & ref* to overlap
traslapo *m* lap, overlap
traslúci•do -da *adj* var of **translúcido**
traslucir **§45** *tr* to guess || *intr* to leak out || *ref* to be translucent; leak out
traslumbrar *tr* to dazzle || *ref* to be dazzled; vanish
trasluz *m* diffused light; glint, gleam; **al trasluz** against the light
trasmisión *f* var of **transmisión**
trasmisor *m* var of **transmisor**
trasmitir *tr & intr* var of **transmitir**
trasmóvil *m* (Col) mobile unit, radio pickup
trasmudar *tr* var of **transmudar**
trasmundo *m* afterlife, future life
trasmutar *tr, intr & ref* var of **transmutar**
trasnocha•do -da *adj* stale; haggard, rundown; hackneyed || *f* last night; sleepless night; (mil) night attack
trasnocha•dor -dora *mf* night owl
trasnochar *tr* (*un problema*) to sleep over || *intr* to spend the night; spend a sleepless night; stay up late
trasoír **§48** *tr* to hear wrong
traspapelar *tr* to mislay || *ref* to become mislaid
trasparecer **§22** *intr* var of **transparecer**
trasparencia *f* var of **transparencia**
trasparente *adj & m* var of **transparente**
traspasar *tr* to cross, cross over; send; transfer; move; pierce, transfix; pain, grieve || *ref* to go too far
traspié *m* slip, stumble; trip
traspirar *intr* var of **transpirar**
trasplantar *tr* var of **transplantar**
trasponer **§54** *tr & ref* var of **transponer**
trasportar *tr* var of **transportar**
trasporte *m* var of **transporte**
trasportista *mf* var of **transportista**
traspunte *m* (theat) callboy
traspuntín *m* flap seat, folding seat, jump seat
trasquilar *tr* to crop, lop; (*las ovejas*) shear; curtail
trastazo *m* whack, blow
traste *m* fret; **dar al traste con** to throw away, ruin, spoil
trastera *f* attic, junk room
trastienda *f* back room
trasto *m* piece of furniture; piece of junk; good-for-nothing; **trastos** tools, implements, utensils; arms, weapons; junk; muleta and sword
trastornar *tr* to upset; overturn; disturb; perplex; daze, make dizzy; persuade
trastorno *m* upset; disturbance
trastrocar **§81** *tr* to turn around, reverse, change
trasudor *m* cold sweat
trasueño *m* blurred dream, vague recollection
trasuntar *tr* to copy; abstract, sum up
trasunto *m* copy; record; likeness
trasverter **§51** *intr* to run over, overflow
trasvolar **§61** *tr* to fly over
trata *f* traffic, trade, slave trade; **trata de blancas** white slavery; **trata de esclavos** slave trade
tratado *m* (*escrito, libro*) treatise; (*convenio entre gobiernos*) treaty; agreement

tratamiento *m* treatment; title; **apear el tratamiento** to leave off the title
tratante *mf* dealer, retailer
tratar *tr* to handle; deal with; treat; **tratar a uno de** to address someone as; charge someone with being || *intr* to deal; treat; try; **tratar de** to deal with; treat of; come in contact with; try to || *ref* to deal; behave; (*bien o mal*) live; **tratarse de** to deal with; be a question of
trate•ro -ra *mf* (Chile) pieceworker
trato *m* treatment; deal, agreement; manner; business; title; friendly relations; **tener buen trato** to be very nice, be very pleasant; **trato colectivo** collective bargaining; **trato doble** double-dealing; **¡trato hecho!** it's a deal!
través *m* bend, bias, turn; reverse, misfortune; (naut) beam; **al** or **a través de** through, across; **dar al través con** to do away with; **mirar de través** to squint; look at out of the corner of one's eye
travesaño *m* crosspiece; (*de cama*) bolster; (*p.ej., de una sila*) rung
travesear *intr* to romp, carry on; sparkle, be witty; lead a wild life
travesía *f* crossing, voyage; crossroad; distance, passage; cross wind; (Arg, Bol) wasteland; (Chile) west wind
travesura *f* prank, antic, caper; mischief; sparkle, wit; slick trick
traviesa *f* crossing, voyage; rafter; side bet; (rr) tie
travie•so -sa *adj* cross; keen, shrewd; restless, fidgety; naughty, mischievous; debauched || *f* see **traviesa**
trayecto *m* journey, passage, course; stretch, run
trayectoria *f* trajectory; path
traza *f* plan, design; scheme; means; appearance; mark, trace; footprint; streak, trait; **tener trazas de** to show signs of; look like
trazar **§60** *tr* to plan, design; outline; trace; (*una línea*) draw; lay out, plot
trazo *m* line, stroke; trace; outline
trebejo *m* implement; chessman
trébol *m* clover; (*naipe que corresponde al basto*) club
trece *adj & pron* thirteen || *m* thirteen; (*en las fechas*) thirteenth; **estarse, mantenerse** or **seguir en sus trece** to stand firm
trecea•vo -va *adj & m* thirteenth
trecho *m* stretch; while; **a trechos** at intervals
tregua *f* truce; respite, letup
treinta *adj & pron* thirty || *m* thirty; (*en las fechas*) thirtieth
treinta•vo -va *adj & m* thirtieth
tremar *intr* to tremble, shake
tremen•do -da *adj* frightful, terrible, tremendous; (*muy grande*) tremendous
trementina *f* turpentine
tremer *intr* to tremble, shake
tremolar *tr & intr* to wave
tren *m* (*de coches o vagones; de ondas*) train; outfit, equipment; following, retinue; show, pomp; (*de la vida*) way; **tren aerodinámico de lujo** (rr) streamliner; **tren ascendente** (rr) up train; **tren correo** (rr) mail train; **tren de aterrizaje** (aer) landing gear; **tren de laminadores** rolling mill; **tren de lavado** laundry; **tren de mercancías** freight train; **tren de mudadas** moving company; **tren descendente** (rr) down train; **tren de viajeros** passenger train; **tren ómnibus** (rr) accomodation train; **tren rápido** (rr) flyer
treno *m* dirge
trenza *f* braid, plait; tress; (*p.ej., de ajos*) string; **en trenzas** with her hair down
trenzar **§60** *tr* to braid, plait || *intr* to caper; prance
trepa•dor -dora *adj* climbing || *mf* climber || *f* (bot) climber
trepar *tr* to climb; drill, bore || *intr* to climb; **trepar por** to climb up || *ref* to lean back
trepidar *intr* to shake, vibrate; (Chile) to hesitate, waver
tres *adj & pron* three; **las tres** three o'clock || *m* three; (*en las fechas*) third
trescien•tos -tas *adj & pron* three hundred || **trescientos** *m* three hundred
tresillo *m* ombre; three-piece living-room suite; (mus) triplet
tresnal *m* (agr) shock
treta *f* trick, scheme; (*del esgrimidor*) feint
treza•vo -va *adj & m* thirteenth
triángulo *m* triangle
triar **§77** *tr* to sort
tribu *f* tribe
tribuna *f* tribune, rostrum, platform; grandstand; (*en la iglesia*) gallery; **tribuna de la prensa** press box; **tribuna del órgano** (mus) organ loft; **tribuna de los acusados** (law) dock
tribunal *m* tribunal, court; **tribunal de apelación** appellate court; **tribunal tutelar de menores** juvenile court
tributar *tr* (*contribuciones, impuestos, etc.*) to pay; (*admiración, gratitud, etc.*) render
tributario -ria *adj* tributary; tax; **ser tributario de** to be indebted to || *m* tributary
tributo *m* tribute; tax
tricornio *m* tricorn, three-cornered hat
trifocal *adj* trifocal
trifulca *f* wrangle, squabble
trigési•mo -ma *adj & m* thirtieth
trigo *m* wheat; (slang) dough, money; **trigo entero** whole wheat; **trigo sarraceno** buckwheat
trigonometría *f* trigonometry
trigue•ño -ña *adj* swarthy, olive-skinned
trilogía *f* trilogy
trilla *f* threshing
trilla•do -da *adj* (*sendero*) beaten; trite, commonplace
trilladora *f* threshing machine
trillar *tr* to thresh; mistreat; frequent
trilli•zo -za *mf* triplet
trillón *m* British trillion; quintillion (*in U.S.A.*)
trimestral *adj* quarterly
trimestre *m* quarter
trinado *m* trill, warble

trinar *intr* to trill, warble, quaver; get angry
trinca *f* trinity
trincar **§73** *tr* to bind, lash, tie fast; crush; (slang) to kill || *intr* to take a drink
trinchar *tr* to carve, slice
trinchera *f* cut; trench; trench coat
trineo *m* sleigh, sled
Trinidad *f* Trinity
trino *m* trill
trinquete *m* pawl, ratchet; (naut) foresail
trin•quis *m* (*pl* **-quis**) drink, swig
trío *m* sorting; trio; (mus) trio
tripa *f* gut, intestine; belly; (*del cigarro*) filler; **hacer de tripas corazón** to pluck up courage
triple *adj & m* triple
triplica•do -da *adj & m* triplicate; **por triplicado** in triplicate
triplicar **§73** *tr* to triplicate || *intr* to treble
trípode *m* tripod
tríptico *m* triptych
tripu•do -da *adj* big-bellied, potbellied
tripulación *f* crew
tripulante *m* crew member
tripular *tr* to man; fit out, equip
trique *m* crack, swish; **a cada trique** at every turn; **triques** (Mex) tools, implements
triquiñuela *f* chicanery, subterfuge
triquitraque *m* clatter; firecracker
tris *m* crackle; shave, inch; trice
trisar *tr* (Chile) to crack, chip || *intr* to chirp
triscar **§73** *tr* to mix; (*una sierra*) set || *intr* to stamp the feet; romp, frisk around; (Col) to gossip
trismo *m* lockjaw
triste *adj* sad; dismal, gloomy; (*despreciable, ridículo*) sorry
tristeza *f* sadness; gloominess
tris•tón -tona *adj* wistful, melancholy
tritón *m* eft, newt, triton; (*hombre experto en la natación*) merman
trituradora *f* crushing machine
triturar *tr* to grind, crush; abuse
triunfal *adj* triumphal
triunfante *adj* triumphant
triunfar *intr* to triumph; trump; **triunfar de** to triumph over; trump
triunfo *m* triumph; trump; **sin triunfo** no trump
trivial *adj* trivial; trite, commonplace; (*sendero*) beaten
trivialidad *f* triviality; triteness
triza *f* shred; **hacer trizas** to tear to pieces
trizar **§60** *tr* to tear to pieces
trocar **§81** *tr* to exchange, swap; barter; confuse, twist, distort || *intr* to swap || *ref* to change; change seats
trocha *f* trail, narrow path; gauge
trofeo *m* trophy; victory
troj *f* or **troje** *f* granary; olive bin
trole *m* trolley pole
trolebús *m* trolley bus, trackless trolley
tromba *f* (*de polvo, agua, etc.*) whirl, column; **tromba marina** waterspout; **tromba terrestre** tornado
trombón *m* trombone
trompa *f* (*del elefante*) trunk; waterspout; top; nozzle; (anat) duct, tube; (mus) horn; (Col, Chile) cowcatcher; **trompa de armonía** French horn; **trompa de Eustaquio** Eustachian tube
trompada *f* bump, collision; punch
trompar *intr* to spin a top
trompeta *f* trumpet; bugle, clarion; good-for-nothing; drunkenness
trompetear *intr* to trumpet, sound the trumpet
trompetilla *f* ear trumpet; Bronx cheer
trompicar **§44** *tr* to trip, make stumble || *intr* to stumble
trompicón *m* stumble
trompiza *f* fist fight
trompo *m* (*juguete*) top; (*en el ajedrez*) man; (*buque malo y pesado*) tub
tronada *f* thunderstorm
tronar **§61** *tr* (Mex) to shoot || *intr* to thunder; fail, collapse; **por lo que pueda tronar** just in case
troncar **§44** *tr* to cut off the head of; (*un escrito*) cut, shorten
tronco *m* (*del cuerpo, del árbol, de una familia, del ferrocarril*) trunk; (*leño*) log; (*de caballerías*) team; sap, fathead; **estar hecho un tronco** to be knocked out; be sound asleep
troncha *f* slice; cinch
tronchar *tr* to smash, split; chop off
tronera *m* madcap, roisterer || *f* embrasure, loophole; louver; (*de la mesa de billar*) pocket
tronido *m* thunderclap
trono *m* throne
tronquista *m* driver, teamster
tronzar **§60** *tr* to shatter, break to pieces; pleat; wear out
tropa *f* troop; herd, drove; **en tropa** straggling, without formation; **tropas de asalto** shock troops, storm troops
tropel *m* crowd, throng; rush, hurry; jumble; **de** or **en tropel** in a mad rush
tropelía *f* mad rush; outrage
tropero *m* (Arg) cowboy
tropezar **§18** *tr* to strike || *intr* to stumble; slip, blunder; **tropezar con** or **en** to stumble over, trip over; run into; come upon
trope•zón -zona *adj* stumbly || *m* stumble; stumbling place; **a tropezones** by fits and starts; falteringly; **dar un tropezón** to stumble, trip
tropical *adj* tropic(al)
trópico *m* tropic
tropiezo *m* stumble; stumbling block; slip, blunder, fault; obstacle; quarrel
tropilla *f* (Arg, Urug) drove of horses following a leading mare
troposfera *f* troposphere
troquel *m* die
trotaconven•tos *f* (*pl* **-tos**) procuress, bawd
trotamun•dos *m* (*pl* **-dos**) globetrotter
trotar *intr* to trot; to hustle
trote *m* trot; chore; **al trote** right away; **para todo trote** for everyday wear; **trote de perro** jog trot
trotona *f* chaperone

trovador *m* troubadour
trovadores•co -ca *adj* troubadour
trovero *m* trouvère
Troya *f* Troy; **ahí fué Troya** it's a shambles; **¡arda Troya!** come what may!
troya•no -na *adj & mf* Trojan
troza *f* log
trozar §60 *tr* to break to pieces; (*un tronco*) cut into logs
trozo *m* piece, fragment; block; excerpt, selection
truco *m* contrivance, device; trick; pocketing of ball; **truco de naipes** card trick; **trucos** pool
truculen•to -ta *adj* truculent
trucha *f* trout
trueno *m* thunder, thunderclap; shot, report; rake, roué; **trueno gordo** finale (*of fireworks*); big scandal; **truenos** (Ven) heavy shoes
trueque *m* barter; exchange, swap; trade-in; **a trueque de** in exchange for; **trueques** (Col) change
trufa *f* truffle; fib, lie
tru•hán -hana *adj* crooked; clownish || *mf* crook; clown
trujal *m* wine press; oil press
trulla *f* noise, bustle; crowd; trowel
truncar §73 *tr* to cut off the head of; (*palabras o frases*) cut, slash; cut off, interrupt
trusas *fpl* trunk hose; trunks
tu *adj poss* thy, your
tú *pron pers* thou, you
tubérculo *m* (*rizoma engrosado, p.ej., de la patata*) tuber; (*protuberancia*) tubercle
tuberculosis *f* tuberculosis
tubería *f* tubing; piping
tubo *m* tube; pipe; **tubo de desagüe** drainpipe; **tubo de ensayo** test tube; **tubo de humo** flue; **tubo de imagen** picture tube; **tubo de vacío** vacuum tube; **tubo digestivo** alimentary canal; **tubo sonoro** chime
tuerca *f* nut; **tuerca de aletas** wing nut
tuer•to -ta *adj* crooked, bent; one-eyed; **a tuertas** upside down; crosswise; **a tuertas o a derechas** rightly or wrongly; thoughtlessly || *mf* one-eyed person || *m* wrong, harm, injustice; **tuertos** afterpains
tuétano *m* marrow; pith; **hasta los tuétanos** through and through; head over heels
tufi•llas *mf* (*pl* **-llas**) touchy person
tufillo *m* whiff, smell
tufo *m* fume, vapor; sidelock; foul odor, foul breath; **tufos** airs, conceit
tugurio *m* shepherd's hut; hovel
tuición *f* protection, custody
tulipán *m* tulip
tullecer §22 *tr* to abuse, mistreat || *intr* to be crippled
tulli•do -da *adj* paralyzed, crippled || *mf* paralytic, cripple
tullir §13 *tr* to cripple, paralyze; abuse, mistreat || *ref* to become crippled or paralyzed
tumba *f* grave, tomb; tombstone; arched top; felling of trees
tumbacuarti•llos *mf* (*pl* **-llos**) old toper, rounder
tumbar *tr* to knock down; catch, trick; stun || *intr* to tumble; capsize || *ref* to lie down
tumbo *m* fall, tumble; boom, rumble; crisis; rise and fall of sea; rough surf
tumbona *f* hammock
tumor *m* tumor
túmulo *m* catafalque
tumulto *m* tumult
tuna *f* loafing, bumming; (bot) prickly pear
tunante *adj* bumming, loafing; crooked, tricky || *mf* bum, loafer; crook
tundidora *f* lawn mower
tuneci•no -na *adj & mf* Tunisian
túnel *m* tunnel; **túnel de lavado** automatic car wash
tunes *mpl* (Col) little steps, first steps
Túnez (*ciudad*) Tunis; (*país*) Tunisia
tungsteno *m* tungsten
túnica *f* tunic
tu•no -na *adj* crooked, tricky || *mf* crook || *f* see **tuna**
tupé *m* toupee; nerve, cheek, brass
tupi•do -da *adj* thick, dense, compact; dull, stupid; clogged up
tupir *tr* to pack tight || *ref* to stuff, stuff oneself
turba *f* crowd, mob; peat
turbamulta *f* job, rabble
turbar *tr* to disturb, trouble; stir up || *ref* to be confused
turbiedad *f* muddiness; confusion
turbina *f* turbine
tur•bio -bia *adj* turbid, muddy, cloudy; confused; obscure
turbión *m* squall, thunderstorm; (*p.ej., de balas*) (fig) hail
turbocompresor *m* turbocompressor
turbohélice *m* turboprop
turbopropulsor *m* turboprop (*engine*)
turborreactor *m* turbojet (*engine*)
turbosupercargador *m* turbosupercharger
turbulen•to -ta *adj* turbulent
tur•co -ca *adj* Turkish || *mf* Turk || *m* (*idioma*) Turkish || *f* (coll) binge; boozing; **coger una turca** to get drunk
turfista *adj* horsy || *m* turfman
turismo *m* touring; touring car
turista *mf* tourist
turísti•co -ca *adj* tourist; touring
turnar *intr* to alternate, take turns
tur•nio -nia *adj* (*ojos*) cross; cross-eyed; (*que mira con ceño*) cross-looking
turno *m* turn, shift; **aguardar turno** to wait one's turn; **por turno** in turn; **turno diurno** day shift
turón *m* polecat
turquesa *s* turquoise
Turquía *s* Turkey
turrón *m* nougat; plum
tusa *f* corncob; corn silk; (Chile) mane; (Col) pockmark; (CAm, W-I) trollop
tusar *tr* to shear, clip, cut
tutear *tr* to thou, address familiarly || *ref* to thou each other, address each other familiarly

tutela *f* guardianship; protection
tutelar *adj* guardian; protecting || *tr* to protect, shelter, guide
tu•tor -tora or **-triz** *mf* (*pl* **-trices**) guardian, tutor
tu•yo -ya *adj poss* of thee || *pron poss* thine, yours
tuza *f* gopher

U

U, u (u) *f* twenty-fourth letter of the Spanish alphabet
u *conj* (used before words beginning with *o* or *ho*) or
U. *abbr* **usted**
ubicar **§73** *tr* to locate, place || *intr & ref* to be situated
ubi•cuo -cua *adj* ubiquitous
ubre *f* udder
Ucrania *f* Ukraine
ucrania•no -na *adj & mf* Ukrainian
ucra•nio -nia *adj & mf* Ukrainian || *f* see **Ucrania**
Ud. *abbr* **usted**
Uds. *abbr* **ustedes**
ufanar *ref* — **ufanarse con** or **de** to boast of, be proud of
ufanía *f* pride, conceit; cheer, satisfaction; ease, smoothness
ufa•no -na *adj* proud, conceited; cheerful, satisfied; easy, smooth
ujier *m* doorman, usher
úlcera *f* ulcer, fester, sore; **úlcera de decúbito** bedsore
ulcerar *tr & ref* to ulcerate, fester
ulterior *adj* ulterior; subsequent
ulteriormente *adv* subsequently, later
últimamente *adv* finally; lately, recently
ultimar *tr* to finish, end, conclude, wind up; kill, finish off
ultimátum *m* (*pl* **-tums**) ultimatum; definite decision
últi•mo -ma *adj* last, latest; final; excellent, superior; (*precio*) lowest, final; most remote; (*piso*) top; (*hora*) late; **a la última** in the latest fashion; **a última hora** at the eleventh hour; **a últimos de** toward the end of, in the latter part of; **de última hora** last-minute; **estar a lo último** or **en las últimas** to be up to date, be well-informed; be on one's last-legs; **por último** at last, finally; **último suplicio** capital punishment
ultraatmosféri•co -ca *adj* outer (*space*)
ultraeleva•do -da *adj* (rad) ultrahigh
ultrajar *tr* to outrage, offend
ultraje *m* outrage, offense
ultrajo•so -sa *adj* outrageous, offensive
ultramar *m* country overseas
ultramari•no -na *adj* overseas || **ultramarinos** *mpl* groceries, delicatessen
ultranza — **a ultranza** to the death; unflinchingly
ultrarro•jo -ja *adj & m* infrared
ultratumba *adv* beyond the grave
ultraviola•do -da or **ultravioleta** *adj & m* ultraviolet
ululación *f* howl; whoop; (*del buho*) hoot; (*del disco del fonógrafo*) wow
ulular *intr* to howl; whoop; (*el buho*) hoot
ululato *m* howl; (*del buho*) hoot
umbilical *adj* umbilical
umbral *m* threshold, doorsill; (*madero que sostiene el muro encima de un vano*) lintel; (physiol, psychol & fig) threshold; **atravesar** or **pisar los umbrales** to cross the threshold; **estar en los umbrales de** to be on the threshold of
umbralada *f* (Col) threshold
umbrí•o -a *adj* shady || *f* shady side
umbro•so -sa *adj* shady
un, una (the apocopated form **un** is used before masculine singular nouns and adjectives and before feminine singular nouns beginning with stressed *a* or *ha*) *art indef* a || *adj* one
unánime *adj* unanimous
unanimidad *f* unanimity
unción *f* unction
uncir **§36** *tr* (*bueyes*) to yoke, hitch
undéci•mo -ma *adj & m* eleventh
undo•so -sa *adj* wavy
ungir **§27** *tr* to smear with ointment or with oil; anoint
ungüento *m* unguent, ointment, salve
únicamente *adv* only, solely
úni•co -ca *adj* only, sole; (*sin otro de su especie*) unique; one, e.g., **precio único** one price
unicornio *m* unicorn
unidad *f* (*concepto de una sola cosa o persona; cantidad que se toma como medida común de todas las demás de su clase; el número entero más pequeño*) unit; (*indivisión; armonía de conjunto; el número uno*) unity
uni•do -da *adj* united; smooth, even; close-knit
unifamiliar *adj casa* one-family
unificar **§73** *tr* to unify
uniformar *tr* to make uniform; provide with a uniform
uniforme *adj* uniform || *m* uniform; **uniforme de gala** (mil) full dress
uniformidad *f* uniformity
unilateral *adj* unilateral
unión *f* union; double ring; **Unión Soviética** Soviet Union
unir *tr & ref* to unite

unisonancia *f* (mus) unison; (*de un orador*) monotony
unísono — al unísono in unison; unanimously; **al unísono de** in unison with
unita•rio -ria *adj* unit
universal *adj* universal; all-purpose; (*teclado de máquina de escribir*) standard
universidad *f* university
universita•rio -ria *adj* university || *mf* university student, college student || *m* university professor
universo *m* universe
u•no -na *pron* one, someone; **a una** of one accord; **la una** one o'clock; **somos uno** we are one; **uno a otro, unos a otros** each other, one another; **uno que otro** one or more, a few; **u•nos -nas** some; pair of, e.g., **unas gafas** a pair of glasses; **unas tijeras** a pair of scissors; **unos cuantos** some; **uno y otro** both || *pron indef* one, e.g., **uno no sabe qué hacer aquí** one does not know what to do here || *m* (*unidad y signo que la representa*) one
untar *tr* to smear, grease; anoint; bribe || *ref* to get smeared; grease oneself; embezzle
unto *m* grease; (*gordura del cuerpo del animal*) fat; (Chile) shoe polish; **unto de Méjico** or **de rana** bribe money
untuo•so -sa *adj* unctuous, greasy, sticky
uña *f* nail, fingernail, toenail; (*pezuña*) hoof; (*del ancla*) fluke, bill; (mach) claw, gripper; **enseñar** or **mostrar las uñas** to show one's teeth; **ser largo de uñas** to have long fingers; **ser uña y carne** to be hand in glove; **tener en la uña** to have on the tip of one's fingers
uñada *f* scratch, nail scratch; (*impulso dado con la uña*) flip
uñero *m* ingrowing nail; (*inflamación del dedo en la raíz de la uña*) whitlow
ural *adj* Ural || **Urales** *mpl* Urals
uranio *m* uranium
urbanidad *f* urbanity
urbanismo *m* city planning
urbanista *mf* city planner
urbanísti•co -ca *adj* city-planning || *f* city planning
urbanizar §60 *tr* (*convertir en poblado*) to urbanize; refine; polish
urba•no -na *adj* urban, city; (*atento, cortés*) urbane || *m* policeman
urbe *f* metropolis
urdema•las *mf* (*pl* **-las**) schemer
urdimbre *f* warp; scheme, scheming; **estar en la urdimbre** (Chile) to be thin, be emaciated
urdir *tr* (*los hilos*) to beam; (*una conspiración*) hatch
urente *adj* burning, smarting
uretra *f* urethra
urgencia *f* urgency; **de urgencia** special-delivery
urgente *adj* urgent; (*correo*) special-delivery
urgir §27 *intr* to be urgent
urina•rio -ria *adj* urinary || *m* urinal
urna *f* glass case; ballot box; (*para guardar las cenizas de los cadáveres*) urn; **acudir** or **ir a las urnas** to go to the polls
urología *f* urology
urraca *f* magpie
U.R.S.S. *abbr* **Unión de Repúblicas Socialistas Soviéticas**
urticaria *f* hives
Uruguay, el Uruguay
urugua•yo -ya *adj & mf* Uruguayan
usa•do -da *adj* (*empleado; gastado por el uso; acostumbrado*) used; skilled, experienced; (*vocablo*) **poco usado** rare
usanza *f* use, usage, custom
usar *tr* to use, make use of; (*un cargo, un oficio*) follow || *intr* — **usar** + *inf* to be accustomed to + *inf;* **usar de** to use, have recourse to; **usar de la palabra** to speak, make a speech || *ref* to be the custom
usina *f* factory, plant; powerhouse; (*estación de tranvía*) (Arg) carbarn
uso *m* use; custom, usage; wear, wear and tear; habit, practice; **al uso** according to custom; **en buen uso** in good condition; **hacer uso de la palabra** to speak, make a speech
usted *pron pers* you
usual *adj* (*de uso común*) usual; (*que se usa con facilidad*) usable; sociable
usualmente *adv* usually
usua•rio -ria *mf* user
usufructo *m* use, enjoyment
usufructuar §21 *tr* to enjoy the use of
usura *f* usury; profit; **pagar con usura** to pay back a thousandfold
usurero *m* loan shark; profiteer
usurpar *tr* to usurp
utensilio *m* utensil
útero *m* uterus, womb
útil *adj* useful || **útiles** *mpl* utensils, tools, equipment
utilería *f* (Arg) properties, stage equipment
utilero *m* (Arg) property man
utilidad *f* utility, usefulness; profit, earnings
utilita•rio -ra *adj* utilitarian
utilizable *adj* usable
utilizar §60 *tr* to utilize, use || *ref* — **utilizarse con, de** or **en** to make use of; **utilizarse para** to be good for
utopía *f* utopia
utopista *adj & mf* utopian
UU. *abbr* **ustedes**
uva *f* grape; wart on eyelid; (*baya*) berry; **estar hecho una uva** to have a load on; **uva crespa** gooseberry; **uva de Corinto** currant; **uva de raposa** nightshade; **uva espín** or **espina** gooseberry; **uva pasa** raisin; **uvas verdes** (*de la fábula de Esopo*) sour grapes
uve *f* (*letra del alfabeto*) **V**
uxoricida *m* uxoricide (*husband*)
uxoricidio *m* uxoricide (*act*)
uxo•rio -ria *adj* uxorious

V

V, v (ve *or* uve) *f* twenty-fifth letter of the Spanish alphabet
V. *abbr* **usted, vease, venerable**
V.A. *abbr* **Vuestra Alteza**
vaca *f* cow; (*cuero*) cowhide; (*carne de vaca o de buey*) beef; gambling pool; **hacer vaca** (Peru) to play truant; **vaca de la boda** (coll) goat, laughingstock; friend in need; **vaca de leche** milch cow; **vaca de San Antón** (ent) ladybird
vacación *f* (*cargo que está sin proveer*) vacancy; **de vacaciones** on vacation; **vacaciones** vacation; **vacaiones retribuídas** vacation with pay
vacacionista *mf* vacationist
vacancia *f* vacancy
vacante *adj* vacant || *f* vacancy
vacar **§73** *intr* (*un empleo, un cargo*) to be vacant, be unfilled; take off, take a vacation; **vacar a** to attend to; **vacar de** to lack, be devoid of
vacia•do -da *adj* hollow-ground || *m* cast, casting; plaster cast
vaciante *f* ebb tide
vaciar **§77 & regular** *tr* to empty, drain; cast, mold; (*formar un hueco en*) hollow out; sharpen on a grindstone; copy, transcribe; explain in detail || *intr* to empty; flow; (*el agua en el río*) fall, go down || *ref* to blab
vacilación *f* vacillation; flickering; hesitancy, hesitation
vacilada *f* (Mex) spree, high time; (Mex) drunk
vacilante *adj* vacillating; (*luz*) flickering; (*irresoluto*) hesitant
vacilar *intr* to vacillate; (*la luz*) flicker; shake, wobble; (*estar irresoluto*) hesitate, waver
vací•o -a *adj* empty; (*hueco*) hollow; idle; useless, unsuccessful; (*vaca*) barren; presumptuous || *m* emptiness; (*laguna, abertura; vacante*) vacancy; (*espacio que no contiene ninguna materia*) void; (*espacio de que se ha extraído el aire*) vacuum; (*ijada*) side, flank; **de vacío** light, unloaded; **hacer el vacío a** to isolate
vacuidad *f* vacuity, emptiness
vacuna *f* (*enfermedad de las vacas*) cowpox; (*virus cuya inoculación preserva de una enfermedad determinada*) vaccine
vacunación *f* vaccination
vacunar *tr* to vaccinate
vacu•no -na *adj* bovine; cowhide || *f* see **vacuna**
va•cuo -cua *adj* vacant || *m* cavity, hollow
vadear *tr* (*un río*) to ford; wade through; overcome; sound out || *ref* to behave; manage
vado *m* ford; expedient, resource; **al vado o a la puente** one way or another; **no hallar vado** to see no way out; **tentar el vado** to feel one's way
vagabundaje *m* vagrancy
vagabundear *intr* to wander, roam; loaf around
vagabun•do -da *adj* vagabond || *mf* vagabond, tramp; wanderer
vagancia *f* loafing, vagrancy
vagar *m* leisure; **con vagar** slowly; **estar de vagar** to have nothing to do || **§44** *intr* to wander, roam; be idle; have plenty of leisure; (*una cosa*) lie around; (*p.ej., una sonrisa por los labios*) play
vagido *m* cry of a newborn baby
vagina *f* vagina
vagneria•no -na *adj & mf* Wagnerian
va•go -ga *adj* wandering, roaming; idle, loafing; lax, loose; hesitating, wavering; (*indefinido, indeciso*) vague; (*mirada*) blank || *m* vagabond; idler, loafer; **en vago** shakily; in vain; in the air; **poner en vago** to tilt
vagón *m* car, railroad car; **vagón cama** sleeping car; **vagón carbonero** coal car; **vagón cerrado** boxcar; **vagón cisterna** tank car; **vagón de carga** freight car; **vagón de cola** caboose; **vagón de mercancías** freight car; **vagón de plataforma** flatcar; **vagón frigorífico** refrigerator car; **vagón salón** chair car; **vagón tolva** hopper-bottom car; **vagón volquete** dump car
vagoneta *f* tip car; station wagon
vaguear *intr* to wander around
vaguedad *f* vagueness; vague remark
vaguido *m* faintness, fainting spell
vaharada *f* breath, exhalation
vahear *intr* to emit odors, give forth an aroma
vahido *f* faintness, fainting spell
vaho *m* odor, aroma, vapor, fume
vaina *f* sheath; scabbard; knife case; (*de ciertas semillas*) pod, husk; annoyance, bother; (Col) luck, stroke of luck
vainica *f* hemstitch
vainilla *f* vanilla
vainita *f* (Ven) string bean
vaivén *m* swing, seesaw, backward and forward motion; unsteadiness, inconstancy; risk, chance
vajilla *f* dishes, set of dishes; **lavar la vajilla** to wash the dishes; **vajilla de oro** gold plate; **vajilla de plata** silver plate, silverware; **vajilla de porcelana** chinaware
vale *m* promissory note; voucher; farewell; (Ven) chum, pal; **vale respuesta** reply coupon
valede•ro -ra *adj* valid, effective
vale•dor -dora *mf* defender, protector; (Mex) friend, companion
valedura *f* (Mex) favor, protection
valencia *f* (chem) valence
valentía *f* bravery, valor; feat, exploit; dash, boldness; boast; **pisar de valentía** to strut, swagger
valen•tón -tona *adj* arrogant, boastful || *mf* braggart, boaster || *f* bragging
valer *m* worth, merit, value || **§76** *tr* to defend, protect; favor, patronize; avail; yield; be worth, be valued at; be equal to; suit; **valer la pena** to be worthwhile (to);

valerle a uno + *inf* to help someone to + *inf*, to get someone to + *inf*; **valor lo que pesa** to be worth its (his, her, etc.) weight in gold; **valga lo que valiere** come what may; **¡válgame Dios!** bless my soul!, so help me God! || *intr* to have worth; be worthy; be valuable; be valid; prevail; hold, count; have influence; **hacer valer** (*sus derechos*) to assert; make felt; make good; turn to account; **más vale** it is better (to); **vale O.K.; valer para** to be useful for; **valer por** to be equal to || *ref* to help oneself, defend oneself; **valerse de** to make use of, avail oneself of

valero•so -sa *adj* valorous, brave; strong, active, effective

va•let *m* (*pl* **-lets**) (cards) jack

valía *f* value, worth; favor, influence; **mayor valía** or **plus valía** appreciation, increased value; unearned increment

validación *f* validation

validar *tr* to validate

validez *f* validity; strength, vigor

vali•do -da *adj* highly esteemed, influential || *m* court favorite; prime minister

váli•do -da *adj* valid; strong, robust

valiente *adj* valiant; strong, robust; fine, excellent; (*grande y excesivo*) terrific || *m* brave fellow; bully

valija *f* satchel, brief case; mailbag, mailpouch; mail; **valija diplomática** diplomatic pouch

valimiento *m* favor, protection; favor at court, favoritism

valio•so -sa *adj* valuable; influential; wealthy

va•lón -lona *adj* & *mf* Walloon

valor *m* value, worth; valor, courage; meaning, import; efficacy; equivalence; (*rédito*) income, return; effrontery; (*persona, cosa o cualidad dignas de ser poseídas*) (fig) asset; **¿cómo va ese valor?** how are you?; **valor de rescate** (ins) surrender value; **valores** securities

valoración *f* valuation, appraisal

valorar or **valorear** *tr* (*poner precio a*) to value, appraise; enhance the value of

valorizar **§60** *tr* to value; enhance the value of; sell of (*for quick realization*)

vals *m* waltz

valsar *intr* to waltz

valuación *f* valuation, appraisal

valuar **§21** *tr* to estimate

válvula *f* valve; **válvula corredize** slide valve; **válvula de admisión** intake valve; **válvula de escape** exhaust valve; **válvula de escape libre** cutout; **válvula de seguridad** safety valve; **válvula en cabeza** valve in the head, overhead valve

valla *f* fence, railing; barricade; hindrance, obstacle; (sport) hurdle; (W-I) cockpit; **valla paranieves** snow fence

vallado *m* barricade, stockade

valle *m* valley; river bed; valley dwellings; **valle de lágrimas** vale of tears

vampiresa *f* vampire

vampíri•co -ca *adj* vampire; ghoulish

vampiro *m* vampire; (*persona que se deleita con cosas horribles*) ghoul

vanadio *m* vanadium

vanagloriar **§77 & regular** *ref* to boast

vanaglorio•so -sa *adj* vainglorious, conceited, boastful

vanamente *adv* vainly

vandalismo *m* vandalism

vánda•lo -la *adj* & *mf* Vandal; (fig) vandal

vanguardia *f* (mil & fig) vanguard, van; **a vanguardia** in the vanguard

vanguardismo *m* avant-garde

vanguardista *adj* avant-garde || *mf* avant-gardist

vanidad *f* vanity; (*fausto*) pomp, show; **ajar la vanidad de** to take down a peg; **hacer vanidad de** to boast of

vanido•so -sa *adj* vain, conceited

va•no -na *adj* vain; hollow, empty; **en vano** in vain || *m* opening in a wall

vapor *m* steam; (*el visible: exhalación, vaho, niebla, etc.*) vapor; steamer, steamboat; **al vapor** at full speed; **vapores** gas (*belched*); blues; **vapor volandero** tramp steamer

vaporar *tr* & *ref* to evaporate

vaporizador *m* atomizer, sprayer

vaporizar **§60** *tr* to vaporize; spray || *ref* to vaporize

vaporo•so -sa *adj* vaporous

vapular or **vapulear** *tr* whip, flog

vaquería *f* drove of cattle; dairy; (Mex) party

vaqueri•zo -za *adj* cattle || *f* winter stable for cattle

vaque•ro -ra *adj* cattle || *mf* cattle tender; (Peru) truant || *m* cow hand; cowboy; **vaqueros** blue jeans

vaqueta *f* leather; (P-R) strop; **zurrarle a uno la vaqueta** to tan someone's hide

vaquillona *f* (Arg, Chile) heifer

vara *f* pole, rod, staff; (*de carruaje*) shaft; (*bastón de mando*) wand; measuring stick; (taur) thrust with goad; **tener vara alta** to have the upper hand; **vara alcándara** shaft; **vara alta** upper hand; **vara buscadora** divining rod (*ostensibly to discover water or metals*); **vara de adivinar** divining rod; **vara de oro** goldenrod; **vara de pescar** fishing rod; **vara de San José** goldenrod

vara-alta *m* boss

varada *f* beaching; running aground

varadero *m* repair dock

varapalo *m* long pole; setback, disappointment, reverse

varar *tr* (*una embarcación*) to beach || *intr* to run aground; (*un negocio*) come to a standstill

varear *tr* (*los frutos de los árboles*) to beat down, knock down; beat, strike; (taur) to goad; (*los caballos de carreras*) (SAm) to exercise, train || *ref* to lose weight, get thin

varec *m* (bot) wrack

varenga *f* (naut) floor, floor timber

vareta *f* twig, stick; lime twig for catching birds; colored stripe; cutting remark; hint; **irse de vareta** to have diarrhea

variable *adj* & *f* variable

variación *f* variation

varia•do -da *adj* varied; variegated
variante *adj & f* variant
variar §77 to vary, change || *intr* to vary, change; be different; **variar de** or **en opinión** to change one's mind
varice *f* or **várice** *f* varicose veins
varicela *f* chicken pox
varico•so -sa *adj* varicose
variedad *f* variety; **variedades** variety show, vaudeville
varilla *f* rod, stem, twig; (*bastón de mando*) wand; (*de paraguas, abanico, etc.*) rib; (*del corsé*) *stay;* (*de rueda*) wire spoke; jawbone; (Mex) peddler's wares; **varilla de nivel** dipstick; **varilla de virtudes** wand, magician's wand
varillaje *m* ribs, ribbing; (*de máquina de escribir*) type bars
varille•ro -ra *adj* (*caballo*) (Ven) race || *m* (Mex) peddler
va•rio -ria *adj* (*de diversos colores; que tiene variedad*) various, varied; fickle, inconstant; **varios** various; several
varón *adj* male, e.g., **hijo varón** male child || *m* man, male; grown man, adult male; man of standing; **santo varón** plain artless fellow
varonía *f* male issue
varonil *adj* manly, virile; courageous
Varsovia *f* Warsaw
vasa•llo -lla *adj & mf* vassal
vas•co -ca *adj & mf* Basque (*of Spain and France*) || *m* Basque (*language*)
vas•cón -cona *adj & mf* Basque (*of old Spain*)
vasconga•do -da *adj & mf* Basque (*of Spain*) || *m* Basque (*language*) || **las Vascongadas** the Basque Provinces
vascuence *adj & m* Basque (*language*) || *m* gibberish
vaselina *f* Vaseline
vasera *f* kitchen shelf; bottle rack, tumbler rack
vasija *f* container, vessel
vaso *m* tumbler, glass; vase, flower jar; (anat) duct, vessel; **vaso de engrase** (mach) grease cup; **vaso de noche** pot, chamber pot; **vaso graduado** measuring glass; **vaso sanguíneo** blood vessel
vástago *m* shoot, sapling; scion, offspring; rod, stem; **vástago de émbolo** piston rod; **vástago de válvula** valve stem
vastedad *f* vastness
vas•to -ta *adj* vast
vate *m* bard, seer, poet
váter *m* toilet, water closet
vataije *m* wattage
vaticinar *tr* to prophesy, predict
vaticinio *m* prophecy, prediction
vatídi•co -ca *adj* prophetical || *mf* prophet
vatímetro *m* wattmeter
vatio *m* watt
vatio-hora *m* (*pl* **vatios-hora**) watt-hour
vaya *f* jest, jeer
Vd. *abbr* **usted**
Vds. *abbr* **ustedes**
V.E. *abbr* **Vuestra Excelencia**
vece•ro -ra *adj* alternating; yielding in alternate years || *mf* person waiting his turn
vecinamente *adv* nearby
vecindad *f* neighborhood, vicinity; residency; residents; **hacer mala vecindad** to be a bad neighbor
vecindario *m* neighborhood, community; people, population
veci•no -na *adj* neighboring; like, similar || *mf* neighbor; resident, citizen
veda *f* prohibition; (*de la caza y la pesca*) closed season
vedado *m* game preserve
vedar *tr* to forbid, prohibit; hinder, stop; veto
vedija *f* fleece, tuft of wool; mat of hair; matted hair
vee•dor -dora *adj* curious, spying || *mf* busybody || *m* supervisor, overseer
vega *f* fertile plain; (Cuba) tobacco plantation
vegetación *f* vegetation; **vegetaciones adenoideas** adenoids
vegetal *adj & m* vegetable
vegetaria•no -na *adj & mf* vegetarian
vego•so -sa *adj* (Chile) damp, wet
vehemencia *f* vehemence
vehemente *adj* vehement
vehículo *m* vehicle; **vehículo espacial** space vehicle
veinta•vo -va *adj & m* twentieth
veinte *adj & pron* twenty; **a las veinte** late, untimely || *m* twenty; (*en las fechas*) twentieth
vientena *f* score, twenty
veintiún *adj* this apocopated form of **veintiuno** is used before masculine singular nouns and adjectives
veintiu•no -na *adj & pron* twenty-one || *m* twenty-one; (*en las fechas*) twenty-first || *f* (*juego de naipes*) twenty-one
vejación *f* vexation, annoyance
vejamen *m* vexation, annoyance; bantering, taunting
vejar *tr* to vex, annoy; taunt
vejestorio *m* old dodo
vejete *m* little old fellow
vejez *f* old age; oldness; dotage; platitude, old story; **a la vejez, viruelas** there's no fool like an old fool
vejiga *f* (*órgano que recibe la orina de los riñones*) bladder; (*ampolla*) blister; (*saco hecho de piel, goma, etc.*) bag, pouch, bladder; **vejiga de la bilis** or **de la hiel** gall bladder
vela *f* wakefulness; pilgrimage; evening; work in the evening; sail; sailboat; (*cilindro con una torcida que sirve para alumbrar*) candle; vigil (*before Eucharist*) awning; (Mex) scolding; **a toda vela** full sail; **a vela** under sail; **a vela llena** under full sail; **en vela** awake; **estar entre dos velas** to be halfseas over, have a sheet in the wind; **hacerse a la vela** to set sail; **vela latina** lateen sail; **vela mayor** mainsail; **vela romana** Roman candle
velada *f* evening party, soirée; vigil, watch
vela•do -da *adj* veiled, hidden; (phot) lightstruck || *f* see **velada**

velador *m* pedestal table, gueridon; wooden candlestick; watchman; (SAm) night table; (Mex) lamp globe
velaje *m* or **velamen** *m* (naut) canvas, sails
velar *adj & f* velar || *tr* to watch over; guard; (*la guardia*) keep; hold a wake over; (*cubrir con un velo*) veil; (phot) to fog; (fig) to veil, hide, conceal || *intr* to stay awake; stay awake working; keep vigil; (*el viento*) keep up all night; (*un escollo, un peñasco*) stick up out of the water; **velar por** or **sobre** to watch over || *ref* (phot) to fog, be light-struck
velatorio *m* wake
veleidad *f* whim, caprice; fickleness, flightiness
veleido•so -sa *adj* whimsical, capricious; fickle, flighty
vele•ro -ra *adj* swift-sailing || *m* sailboat
veleta *mf* (*persona inconstante*) weathercock || *f* vane, weathervane, weathercock; (*de un molino*) rudder vane; (*de la caña de pescar*) bob; streamer, pennant; **veleta de manga** (aer) air sleeve, air sock
velís *m* (Mex) valise
velita *f* little candle
velo *m* veil; taking the veil; confusion, perplexity; (*disfraz*) veil; (*de lágrimas*) mist; (phot) fog; **correr el velo** to pull aside the curtain, to dispel the mystery; **tomar el velo** to take the veil; **velo del paladar** soft palate
velocidad *f* (*rapidez*) speed, velocity; (mech) velocity; **en gran velocidad** (rr) by express; **en pequeña velocidad** (rr) by freight; **primera velocidad** (aut) low gear; **segunda velocidad** (aut) second; **tercera velocidad** (aut) high gear; **velocidad con respecto al suelo** (aer) ground speed; **velocidad de crucero** cruising speed; **velocidad permitida** speed limit
velocímetro *m* speedometer
velón *m* brass olive-oil lamp
velorio *m* evening party or bee; wake; wake for a dead child; dull party; come-on
ve•loz *adj* (*pl* **-loces**) swift, speedy; agile, quick
vello *m* down, fuzz
vellocino *m* fleece; **vellocino de oro** Golden Fleece
vellón *m* fleece; unsheared sheepskin; lock of wool; copper coin; copper-silver alloy
vello•so -sa *adj* downy, hairy, fuzzy
velludillo *m* velveteen
vellu•do -da *adj* shaggy, hairy, fuzzy || *m* (*felpa*) plush; (*terciopelo*) velvet
vena *f* vein; (*en piedras*) grain; (fig) poetical inspiration; **estar en vena** to be all set, be inspired; sparkle with wit; **vena de loco** fickle disposition
venablo *m* dart, javelin; **echar venablos** to burst forth in anger
venado *m* deer, stag; **pintar el venado** (Mex) to play hooky
venáti•co -ca *adj* fickle, unsteady; daffy, nutty
vence•dor -dora *adj* conquering, victorious || *mf* conqueror, victor
vencejo *m* band, string; (orn) European swift, black martin
vencer §78 *tr* to vanquish, conquer; excel, outdo; overcome, surmount || *intr* to conquer, be victorious; (*un plazo*) be up; (*un contrato*) expire; (*una letra*) mature, fall due || *ref* to control oneself; (*un camino*) bend, turn; (Chile) to wear out, become useless
vencetósigo *m* milkweed, tame poison
venci•do -da *adj* conquered; (com) due, mature, payable
vencimiento *m* (*acción de vencer*) victory; (*hecho de ser vencido*) defeat; (com) expiration, maturity
venda *f* (*para ligar un miembro herido*) bandage; (*para tapar los ojos*) blindfold
vendaje *m* bandage, dressing; **vendaje enyesado** plaster cast
vendar *tr* (*un miembro, una herida*) to bandage; (*los ojos*) blindfold; (*cegar*) (fig) to blind; (*engañar*) (fig) to hoodwink
vendaval *m* strong southeasterly wind from the sea; strong wind, gale
vendedera *f* saleswoman, saleslady
vende•dor -dora *adj* selling || *m* salesman || *f* saleslady, sales girl
vendehu•mos *mf* (*pl* **-mos**) influence peddler
vendeja *f* public sale
vender *tr* to sell; betray, sell out; **vender salud** to be the picture of health || *intr* to sell; **¡vendo, vendo, vendí!** going, going, gone! || *ref* to sell oneself; sell, be for sale; betray oneself, give oneself away; **venderse caro** to be hard to see; be quite a stranger; **venderse en** (*p.ej., cien pesetas*) to sell for; **venderse por** to pass oneself off as
ven•dí *m* (*pl* **-díes**) certificate of sale
vendible *adj* salable, marketable
vendimia *f* vintage; (fig) big profit
vendimia•dor -dora *mf* vintager
vendimiar *tr* (*la uva*) to gather, harvest; (*las viñas*) gather the grapes of; make off with; kill
venduta *f* public sale; (W-I) greengrocery
Venecia *f* (*ciudad*) Venice; (*provincia*) Venetia
venecia•no -na *adj & mf* Venetian
veneno *m* poison, venom
veneno•so -sa *adj* poisonous, venomous
venera *f* scallop shell; (*manantial de agua*) spring; **empeñar la venera** to go all out, spare no expense
venerable *adj* venerable
venerar *tr* to venerate, revere; worship
venére•o -a *adj* venereal || *m* venereal disease
venero *m* (*de agua*) spring; (*filón de mineral*) lode, vein; (fig) source
venezola•no -na *adj & mf* Venezuelan
Venezuela *f* Venezuela
venga•dor -dora *adj* avenging || *mf* avenger
venganza *f* vengeance, revenge
vengar §44 *tr* to avenge || *ref* to take revenge; **vengarse de** to take revenge on

vengati•vo -va *adj* vengeful, vindictive
venia *f* forgiveness, pardon; leave, permission; bow, greeting
venida *f* coming; return; flood, freshet
venide•ro -ra *adj* coming, future || **venideros** *mpl* successors, posterity
venir §79 *intr* to come; **que viene** coming, next; **venga lo que viniere** come what may; **venir** + *ger* to be + *ger;* **venir a** + *inf* to come to + *inf;* to amount to + *ger;* to happen to + *inf;* to finally + *inf,* e.g., **después de una larga enfermedad, vino a morir** after a long illness he finally died; **venir a ser** to turn out to be || *ref* to ferment; **venirse abajo** to collapse
veno•so -sa *adj* venous
venta *f* sale; roadside inn; (Chile) refreshment stand; (S-D) grocery store; **de venta** or **en venta** on sale, for sale; **ser una venta** to be an expensive place; **venta al descubierto** short sale
ventaja *f* advantage; (*en juegos o apuestas*) odds; extra pay
ventajo•so -sa *adj* advantageous
ventalla *f* valve
ventana *f* window; (*de la nariz*) nostril; **echar la casa por la ventana** to go to a lot of expense; **ventana batiente** casement; **ventana de guillotina** sash window; **ventana salediza** bay window
ventanal *m* church window; picture window
ventanear *intr* to be at the window all the time
ventanilla *f* (*de coche, de banco, de sobre*) window; ticket window; (*de la nariz*) nostril
ventanillo *m* (*postigo de puerta o ventana*) wicket; (*mirilla*) peephole
ventar §2 *tr* to sniff || *impers* — **vienta** it is windy
ventarrón *m* gale, windstorm
ventear *tr* to sniff; dry in the wind; snoop into || *intr* to snoop, pry around || *impers* — **ventea** it is windy || *ref* (*henderse*) to split; break wind; spend a lot of time in the open
vente•ro -ra *mf* innkeeper
ventilador *m* ventilator; fan; (naut) funnel; **ventilador aspirador** exhaust fan
ventilar *tr* to ventilate; (fig) to air, ventilate
ventisca *f* drift, snowdrift; (*borrasca*) blizzard
ventiscar §73 *intr* to snow and blow; (*la nieve*) drift
ventisquero *m* snowdrift; blizzard; snowcapped mountain; glacier
ventolera *f* blast of wind; (*molinete*) pinwheel; vanity, pride; wild idea; (Mex) wind
ventosa *f* vent, air hole; **pegar una ventosa a** to swindle
ventosear *intr* to break wind
vento•so -sa *adj* windy || *f* see **ventosa**
ventregada *f* brood, litter; outpouring, abundance
ventrículo *m* ventricle
ventrílo•cuo -cua *mf* ventriloquist
ventriloquia *f* or **ventriloquismo** *m* ventriloquism
ventura *f* happiness; luck, chance; danger, risk; **a la ventura** at random; at a risk; **por ventura** perhaps, perchance; **probar ventura** to try one's luck
venture•ro -ra *adj* adventurous; fortunate, lucky || *mf* adventurer
ventu•ro -ra *adj* future, coming || *f* see **ventura**
venturón *m* stroke of luck
venturo•so -sa *adj* fortunate, lucky
Venus *m* (astr) Venus || *f* (myth) Venus; (*mujer de belleza*) Venus
venus•to -ta *adj* beautiful, graceful
venza *f* goldbeater's skin
ver *m* (*vista*) sight; (*apariencia*) appearance; opinion; **a mi ver** in my opinion || **§80** *tr* to see; look at; (law) to hear, try; **no poder ver** to not be able to bear; **no tener nada que ver con** to have nothing to do with; **ver** + *inf* to see + *inf,* e.g., **ví entrar a mi hermano I** saw my brother come in; to see + *ger,* e.g., **ví bailar a la muchacha I** saw the girl dancing; to see + *pp.* e.g., **ví ahorcar al criminal I** saw the criminal hanged; **ver venir a uno** to see what someone is up to || *intr* to see; **a más ver** so long; **a ver** let's see; **hasta más ver** good-bye, so long; **ver de** to try to; **ver y creer** seeing is believing || *ref* to be seen; be obvious; see oneself; see each other; meet; (*encontrarse*) be, find oneself; **verse con** to see, have a talk with; **ya se ve** of course, certainly
vera *f* edge, border; **a la vera de** near, beside; **de veras** in truth; **jugar de veras** to play for keeps; **veras** truth, reality; earnestness
veracidad *f* veracity, truthfulness
veranda *f* verandah; bay window, closed porch
veraneante *mf* summer vacationist, summer resident
veranear *intr* to summer
veranie•go -ga *adj* summer; unimportant, insignificant
veranillo *m* Indian summer; **veranillo de San Martín** Indian summer
ve•raz *adj* (*pl* **-races**) veracious, truthful
verbena *f* fair, country fair, night festival; (bot) verbena
verbigracia *adv* for example
verbo *m* verb || **Verbo** *m* (theol) Word
verbo•so -sa *adj* verbose, wordy
verdacho *m* green earth
verdad *f* truth; **a la verdad** in truth, as a matter of fact; **de verdad** really; **la verdad desnuda** the plain truth; **¿no es verdad?** or **¿verdad?** isn't that so? La traducción al inglés de esta pregunta depende generalmente de la aseveración que la precede. Si la aseveración es afirmativa, la pregunta es negativa, p.ej., **Vd. vivió aquí. ¿No es verdad?** You lived here. Did you not?; Si la aseveración es negativa, la pregunta es afirmativa, p.ej., **Vd. no vivió aquí. ¿No**

es verdad? You did not live here? Did you? Si el sujeto de la aseveración es un nombre sustantivo, va representado en la pregunta con un pronombre personal, p.ej., **Juan no estuvo aquí anoche. ¿No es verdad?** John was not here last evening. Was he?; **ser verdad** to be true; **verdad trillada** truism

verdade•ro -ra *adj* true; real; (*que dice siempre la verdad*) truthful

verde *adj* green; young, youthful; (*viuda*) merry; (*cuento*) shady, off-color; **están verdes** they're hard to reach || *m* green; foliage, verdure

verdear *intr* to turn green, look green

verdecer §22 *intr* to turn green, grow green again

verdecillo *m* (orn) greenfinch

verdemar *m* sea green

verdete *m* verdigris

verdín *m* fresh green; (*capa verde de aguas estancadas*) mold, pond scum; (*cardenillo*) verdigris

verdise•co -ca *adj* half-dry

verdor *m* verdure; youth

verdo•so -sa *adj* greenish

verdugado *m* hoop skirt

verdugo *m* shoot, sucker; (*estoque*) rapier; (*azote*) scourge; (*roncha*) welt; executioner, hangman; torment; butcher bird, shrike

verdugón *m* wale, weal

verdulería *f* greengrocery

verdule•ro -ra *mf* greengrocer || *f* fishwife

verdura *f* greenness; (*color verde de las plantas*) verdure; (*obscenidad*) smuttiness; **verduras** vegetables, greens

verecundia *f* bashfulness, shyness

verecun•do -da *adj* bashful, shy

vereda *f* path, lane; sidewalk

veredicto *m* verdict

verga *f* (naut) yard

vergel *m* flower and fruit garden

vergonzo•so -sa *adj* (*que causa vergüenza*) shameful; (*que tiene vergüenza*) ashamed; (*que se avergüenza con facilidad*) bashful, shy; (*que causa humillación*) embarrassing; shabby, wretched || *mf* bashful person || *m* armadillo

vergüenza *f* (*arrepentimiento*) shame; (*oprobio*) shamefulness; (*pudor, timidez*) bashfulness, shyness; (*desconcierto, humillación*) embarrassment; (*pundonor*) dignity, face; public punishment; **¡qué vergüenza!** shame on you!; **tener vergüenza** to be ashamed; **vergüenzas** privates, genitals

vericueto *m* rough, rocky ground

verídi•co -ca *adj* truthful

verificación *f* verification; checking, testing, inspection; **verificación a la ventura** spot check

verifica•dor -dora *adj* verifying || *m* meter inspector

verificar §73 *tr* to verify, check; (*llevar a cabo*) carry out; (*los contadores de agua, gas y electricidad*) inspect || *ref* to prove true; take place

verja *f* iron gate, iron fence, grating

ver•mú *m* (*pl* **-mús**) vermouth; matinée

vernácu•lo -la *adj* vernacular

verónica *f* (bot) veronica; (taur) veronica (*graceful pass in which the bullfighter waits for the bull with open cape*)

veroniquear *intr* (taur) to perform veronicas

verosímil *adj* likely, probable

verraco *m* male hog, boar

verraquear *intr* to grunt, grumble; cry hard

verruga *f* wart; bore, nuisance

verrugo *m* miser

versal *adj* & *f* capital

versalilla or **versalita** *f* small capital

Versalles Versailles

versar *intr* — **versar acerca de** or **sobre** to deal with, treat of || *ref* — **versarse en** to be or become versed in

versátil *adj* fickle; versatile; (*arma*) multipurpose

versículo *m* verse (*in the Bible*)

versificación *f* versification

versificar §73 *tr* & *intr* to versify

versión *f* version; translation

verso *m* verse; (typ) verso; **versos pareados** rhymed couplet

vertebra•do -da *adj* & *m* vertebrate

vertedero *m* dump; weir, spillway

verter §51 *tr* (*un líquido, un polvo*) to pour; (*un recipiente*) empty; (*lágrimas; luz; sangre*) shed; (*descargar*) dump; translate || *intr* to flow || *ref* to run, empty

vertical *adj* & *f* vertical

vértice *m* vertex

vertiente *m* & *f* (*declive*) slope; (*colina por donde corre el agua*) shed || *f* (Arg, Col, Chile) spring, fountain

vertigino•so -sa *adj* dizzy

vértigo *m* vertigo, dizziness; fit of insanity

vesícula *f* vesicle; **vesícula biliar** gall bladder

veso *m* polecat

Véspero *m* Vesper

vesperti•no -na *adj* evening || *m* evening sermon

vestíbulo *m* vestibule; (theat) foyer, lobby

vestido *m* clothing, dress; (*de mujer*) gown, dress; (*de hombre*) suit; costume; **vestido de ceremonia** dress suit; **vestido de etiqueta** evening clothes; **vestido de etiqueta de mujer** or **vestido de noche** evening gown; **vestido de gala** (mil) full dress; **vestido de serio** evening clothes; **vestido de tarde-noche** cocktail dress

vestidura *f* clothing; (*del sacerdote*) vestment

vestigio *m* vestige, trace; track, footprint

vestir §50 *tr* to dress, clothe; adorn; cover up; disguise; (*tal o cual vestido*) wear; put on; **vestir el cargo** to look the part || *intr* to dress; (*una prenda o la materia*) be dressy; **vestir de** (*p.ej., blanco*) to dress in; **vestir de etiqueta** to dress in evening clothes; **vestir de paisano** to dress in civilian clothes || *ref* to dress, get dressed; dress oneself; (*de una enfermedad*) be up, be about; **vestirse de** (*nubes, flores, hierba, etc.*) to be covered with; (*importancia, humildad, etc.*) assume

vestuario *m* (*las prendas de uno*) wardrobe;

dressing room; bathhouse; checkroom, cloakroom; (mil) uniform; (theat) dressing room
Vesubio, el Vesuvius
veta *f* vein; streak, stripe; **descubrir la veta de** to be on to
vetar *tr* to veto
vetea•do -da *adj* veined, striped || *m* graining || *f* (Ecuad) whipping
vetear *tr* to grain, stripe; (Eucad) to whip, flog
veteranía *f* experience, know-how
vetera•no -na *adj & mf* veteran
veterina•rio -ria *adj* veterinary || *mf* veterinarian || *f* veterinary medicine
vetus•to -ta *adj* old, ancient
vez *f* (*pl* **veces**) time; (*tiempo de hacer una cosa por turno*) turn; **a la vez** at the same time; **a la vez que** while; **alguna vez** sometimes; ever; **a su vez** in turn; on his part; **a veces** at times, sometimes; **cada vez** every time; **cada vez más** more and more; **cuántas veces** how often; **de una vez** at one time; once and for all; **de vez en cuando** once in a while; **dos veces** twice; **en vez de** instead of; **esperar vez** to wait one's turn; **hacer las veces de** to take the place of; **las más veces** most of the time; **muchas veces** often; **otra vez** again; **raras veces** or **rara vez** seldom, rarely; **repetidas veces** over and over again; **tal vez** perhaps; **tomar la vez a** to get ahead of; **una que otra vez** once in a while; **una vez** once
veza *f* vetch, spring vetch
v.g. or **v.gr.** *abbr* **verbigracia**
vía *f* road, route, way; (*par de rieles y el suelo en que se asientan*) (rr) track; (*el mismo carril*) (rr) rail, track; (anat) passage, tract; (fig) way; **por la vía de** via; **por vía aérea** by air; **por vía bucal** by mouth; **vía aérea** airway; **vía ancha** (rr) broad gauge; **vía de agua** waterway; (naut) leak; **vía estrecha** (rr) narrow gauge; **vía férrea** railway; **vía fluvial** waterway; **Vía Láctea** Milky Way; **vía muerta** (rr) siding; **vía normal** (rr) standard gauge; **vía pública** thoroughfare; **vías de hecho** (law) assault and battery || *prep* via
viable *adj* feasible
viaducto *m* viaduct
viajante *adj* traveling || *mf* traveler || *m* drummer, traveling salesman
viajar *tr* to sell on the road; (*ciertas comarcas*) cover as salesman || *intr* to travel, journey
viaje *m* trip, journey; travel book; water supply; (*drogas*) trip; **¡buen viaje!** bon voyage!; **viaje de ida y vuelta** or **viaje redondo** round trip; **viaje de pruebas** shakedown cruise, trial cruise
viaje•ro -ra *adj* traveling || *mf* traveler; passenger
vial *adj* road, highway || *m* tree-lined road
vianda *f* food, viand; meal
viandante *mf* traveler; itinerant
vitático *m* travel allowance; (eccl) viaticum
víbora *f* viper
vibración *f* vibration
vibrar *tr* to vibrate; (*la voz; la r*) roll; (*una lanza*) hurl || *intr* to vibrate || *ref* to be thrilled
vicaría *f* vicarage
vicario *m* vicar
vicealmirante *m* vice-admiral
vicepresiden•te -ta *mf* vice-president
viceversa *adv* vice versa
viciar *tr* to vitiate; (*una proposición*) to slant || *ref* to become vitiated; give oneself up to vice; become addicted; (*una tabla*) warp
vicio *m* vice; pampering, spoiling; luxuriance, overgrowth; **hablar de vicio** to talk all the time, talk too much; **quejarse de vicio** to be a chronic complainer
vicio•so -sa *adj* vicious; faulty, defective; strong, robust; luxuriant, overgrown; dissolute; (*niño*) spoiled
víctima *f* victim, **víctima propiciatoria** scapegoat
victimar *tr* to kill, murder
victoria *f* victory
victorio•so -sa *adj* victorious
vid *f* vine, grapevine
vida *f* life; living, livelihood; **darse buena vida** to live high; live in comfort; **de por vida** for life; **en mi vida** never; **escapar con vida** to have a narrow escape; **ganar** or **ganarse la vida** to earn one's livelihood, make a living; **hacer por la vida** to get a bite to eat; **mudar de vida** to mend one's ways; **¡por vida mía!** upon my soul!; **vida airada** licentious living; **vida ancha** loose living; **vida de familia** or **de hogar** home life; **vida mía** my darling
vidalita *f* (Arg, Chile, Urug) mournful love song
vidente *mf* clairvoyant || *m* prophet, see || *f* seeress
videocasete *m* video cassette
videodisco *m* video disk
videograbación *f* video-tape recording
video-juego *m* video game
videoseñal *f* picture signal
videotocadiscos *m* video-disk player
vidria•do -da *adj* glazed; brittle || *m* glaze, glazing; glazed pottery; dishes
vidriar §77 **& regular** *tr* to glaze || *ref* (*los ojos*) to become glassy
vidriera *f* glass window, glass door; shopwindow, store window; **vidriera de colores** or **vidriera pintada** stained-glass window
vidriería *f* glassworks; glass store
vidriero *m* glass blower, glassworker; glazier; glass dealer
vidrio *m* glass; piece of glass; windowpane; **pagar los vidrios rotos** to take the blame, to be the goat; **vidrio cilindrado** plate glass; **vidrio de aumento** magnifying glass; **vidrio de color** stained glass; **vidrio deslustrado** ground glass; **vidrio tallado** cut glass
vidrio•so -sa *adj* glassy, vitreous; (*quebradizo*) brittle; (*resbaladizo*) slippery; (*que se*

resiente fácilmente) touchy; (*mirada, ojos*) (fig) glassy

vie•jo -ja *adj* old || *m* old man; **viejo verde** old goat, old rake || *f* old woman

vie•nés -nesa *adj & mf* Viennese

viento *m* wind; course, direction; (*cuerda que mantiene una cosa derecha*) guy; (*gases intestinales*) wind; **ceñir el viento** (naut) to sail close to the wind; **viento de cola** (aer) tail wind; **viento en popa** (naut) tail wind; **vientos alisios** trade winds

vientre *m* belly; (*parte de la ondulación entre dos nodos*) (phys) loop; **evacuar** or **exonerar el vientre** to have a bowel movement; **vientre flojo** loose bowels

vier•nes *m* (*pl* **-nes**) Friday; **Viernes santo** Good Friday

viertea•guas *m* (*pl* **-guas**) *m* flashing

vietna•més -mesa *adj & mf* Vietnamese

viga *f* beam, girder, rafter; **estar contando las vigas** to gaze blankly at the ceiling; **viga de celosía** lattice girder

vigencia *f* force, operation; (*de una póliza de seguro*) life; **en vigencia** in force, in effect

vigente *adj* effective, in force

vigési•mo -ma *adj & m* twentieth

vigía *m* lookout, watch; **vigía de incendios** firewarden || *f* watch; watchtower; (naut) rock, reef

vigiar §77 *tr* to watch over

vigilancia *f* vigilance, watchfulness; **bajo vigilancia médica** under the care of a physician

vigilante *adj* vigilant, watchful || *m* guard, watchman; **vigilante nocturno** night watchman

vigilar *tr* to watch over; look out for || *intr* to watch, keep guard

vigilia *f* vigil; wakefulness; night work, night study; (*víspera*) eve; (mil) guard, watch; **comer de vigilia** to fast, abstain from meat

vigor *m* vigor; **en vigor** in force; into effect

vigoriza•dor -dora *adj* invigorating || *m* tonic; **vigorizador del cabello** hair tonic

vigorizante *adj* invigorating

vigorizar §60 *tr* to invigorate; encourage

vigoro•so -sa *adj* vigorous

vigueta *f* small beam, small girder

vihuela *f* Spanish lute

vil *adj* vile, base, mean || *mf* scoundrel

vilano *m* bur, down

vileza *f* vileness, baseness

vilipendiar *tr* to scorn, despise

vilipendio•so -sa *adj* contemptible

vilo — en vilo in the air; (fig) up in the air

vilorta *f* reed hoop; (*arandela*) washer

villa *f* town; (*casa de recreo en el campo*) villa; **la Villa** the city (*Madrid*)

villancico *m* carol, Christmas carol

villanes•co -ca *adj* boorish, crude, rustic

villanía *f* humbleness, humble birth; vileness, meanness; foul remark

villa•no -na *adj* base, vile; rude, impolite || *mf* peasant; knave, scoundrel

villorrio *m* small country town

vinagre *m* vinegar; (*persona de genio áspero*) grouch

vinagrera *f* vinaigrette; (bot) sorrel; (SAm) heartburn; **vinagreras** cruet stand

vinagreta *f* French dressing, vinaigrette sauce

vinagro•so -sa *adj* vinegary

vinariego *m* vineyardist

vinatería *f* wine business; wine shop

vinate•ro -ra *adj* wine || *m* wine dealer, vintner

vincular *tr* to bind, tie, unite; continue, perpetuate; (*esperanzas*) found, base; (law) entail

vínculo *m* bond, tie; (law) entail

vindicar §73 *tr* (*vengar*) to avenge; (*exculpar*) vindicate

vindicta *f* revenge

vinicul•tor -tora *mf* winegrower

vinicultura *f* winegrowing

vinilo *m* vinyl

vino *m* wine; sherry reception, wine party; **tener mal vino** to be a quarrelsome drunk; **vino cubierto** dark-red wine; **vino de Jerez** sherry; **vino del terruño** local wine; **vino de mesa** table wine; **vino de Oporto** port wine; **vino de pasto** table wine; **vino de postre** after-dinner wine; **vino de segunda** second-run wine; **vino de solera** solera sherry; **vino tinto** red table wine

vinolen•to -ta *adj* too fond of wine

viña *f* vineyard; **ser una viña** to be a mine; **tener una viña** to have a sinecure

viña•dor -dora *mf* vineyardist, vinedresser || *m* guard of a vineyard

viñedo *m* vineyard

viñeta *f* vignette, headpiece

viola•do -da *adj & m* violet (*color*)

violar *m* bed of violets || *tr* to violate; ravish, rape; profane, desecrate; tamper with

violencia *f* violence

violentar *tr* to do violence to; (*p.ej., una casa*) break into || *ref* to force oneself

violen•to -ta *adj* violent

violeta *m* (*color; colorante*) violet || *f* (bot) violet

violín *m* violin; (billiards) bridge, cue rest; **embolsar el violín** (Arg, Ven) to cower, to slink away

violinista *mf* violinist

violón *m* (mus) bass viol; **tocar el violón** to talk nonsense

violoncelista *mf* cellist, violoncellist

violoncelo *m* (mus) cello, violoncello

violonchelista *mf* cellist, violoncellist

violonchelo *m* (mus) cello, violoncello

vira *f* welt; (*saetilla*) dart

virada *f* turn, change of direction; (naut) tack

virago *f* mannish woman

viraje *m* turn, swerve; (phot) toning

virar *tr* (naut) to wind; (naut) to tack, veer; (phot) to tone || *intr* to turn, swerve; (naut) to tack, veer

virgen *adj* virgin || *f* virgin, maiden

virginidad *f* virginity

Virgo *m* (astr) Virgo

vírgula *f* rod; thin line, light dash

virgulilla *f* fine line; diacritic mark

virilidad *f* virility

virin•go -ga *adj* (Col) naked

virolen•to -ta *adj* pock-marked; having smallpox
virología *f* virology
virote *m* (*saeta*) bolt; sporty young fellow; (coll) stuffed shirt
virrey *m* viceroy
virtual *adj* virtual
virtud *f* virtue
virtuosismo *m* virtuosity
virtuo•so -sa *adj* virtuous || *m* virtuoso
viruela *f* smallpox; pock mark; **viruelas locas** chicken pox
virulencia *f* virulence
virulen•to -ta *adj* virulent
vi•rus *m* (*pl* **-rus**) virus
viruta *f* shaving
virutilla *f* thin shaving; **virutillas de acero** steel wool
visado *m* visa
visaje *m* face, grimace
visar *tr* to visa; to O.K.; (arti & surv) to sight
vísceras *fpl* viscera
visco *m* birdlime
viscosa *f* viscose
viscosilla *f* rayon thread
visco•so -sa *adj* viscous || *f* see **viscosa**
visera *f* (*del yelmo, de las gorras, del parabrisas del automóvil, etc.*) visor; (*pequeña pantalla que se pone en la frente para resguardar la vista*) eyeshade; (W-I) blinder, blinker
visible *adj* visible; (*manifiesto*) evident; (*que llama la antención*) conspicuous
visigo•do -da *adj* Visigothic || *mf* Visigoth
visillo *m* window curtain, window shade
visión *f* vision; view; (*persona fea y ridícula*) sight, scarecrow; **ver visiones** to be seeing things; **visión negra** (*del aviador*) blackout
visionar *tr* to contemplate, look at
visiona•rio -ria *adj* & *mf* visionary
visir *m* vizier; **gran visir** grand vizier
visita *f* visit; visitor, caller; inspection; **ir de visitas** to go calling; **pagar la visita a** to return the call of; **tener visita** to have callers; **visita de cumplido** formal call; **visita de médico** short call
visita•dor -dora *mf* frequent caller || *m* inspector || *f* (Hond, Ven) enema
visitante *adj* visiting || *mf* visitor
visitar *tr* to visit; inspect
visite•ro -ra *adj* visiting; (*médico*) fond of making calls || *mf* visitor
vislumbrar *tr* to descry, glimpse; surmise, suspect || *ref* (*verse confusamente por la distancia*) glimmer; (*aparecer en la distancia*) loom
vislumbre *f* glimpse, glimmer; **vislumbres** inkling, notion
viso *m* sheen, gleam; (*de ciertas telas*) luster; streak, strain; appearance, thin veneer; elevation, height; colored material worn under transparent outer garment; **a dos visos** with a double purpose; **de viso** conspicuous; **hacer visos** to be iridescent
visón *m* mink
visor *m* (aer) bombsight; (phot) finder
víspera *f* eve, day before; **en vísperas de** on the eve of; **víspera de año nuevo** New Year's Eve; **víspera de Navidad** Christmas Eve; **vísperas** (eccl) vespers, evensong
vista *m* custom-house inspector || *f* (*sentido del ver*) vision, sight; (*paisaje que se ve desde un punto; estampa que representa un lugar*) view; (*panorama, perspectiva*) vista; comparison; purpose, design; (*ojeada*) glance, look; interview; eye; eyes; (law) hearing, trial; **a la vista** (com) at sight; **a vista de** in view of; compared with; **con vistas a** with a view to; **de vista** by sight; **doble vista** second sight; **hacer la vista gorda ante** to shut one's eyes to; **hasta la vista** good-bye, so long; **medir con la vista** to size up; **saltar a la vista** to be self-evident; **tener a la vista** to keep one's eyes on; (*p.ej., una carta*) to have at hand; **torcer la vista** to squint; **vista a ojo de pájaro** bird's-eye view; **vistas** (*aberturas de un edificio*) lights, openings; view, outlook; visible parts, parts that show
vistazo *m* look, glance
vistillas *fpl* eminence, height; **irse a las vistillas** to try to get a look at one's opponent's cards
vis•to -ta *adj* evident, obvious; in view of; **bien visto** looked upon with approval; **mal visto** looked upon with disapproval; **no visto** or **nunca visto** unheard-of; **por lo visto** apparently, judging from the facts; **visto bueno** approved, O.K.; **visto que** whereas, inasmuch as || *m* whereas || *f* see **vista**
visto•so -sa *adj* showy, flashy, loud
visual *adj* visual || *f* line of sight
vital *adj* vital
vitali•cio -cia *adj* life, lifetime || *m* life-insurance policy; life annuity
vitalidad *f* vitality
vitalizar **§60** *tr* to vitalize
vitamina *f* vitamin
vitan•do -da *adj* hateful, odious; being shunned
vitela *f* vellum
viticul•tor -tora *mf* grape grower, vineyardist
viticultura *f* grape growing
vitola *f* cigar size; mien, appearance; (Cuba) cigar band
vítor *interj* hurray! || *m* panegyric tablet; triumphal pageant
vitorear *tr* to cheer, acclaim
vitral *m* stained-glass window
vítre•o -a *adj* vitreous, glassy
vitrina *f* showcase, glass cabinet; shopwindow
vitrióli•co -ca *adj* (chem) vitriolic
vitrola *f* record player
vituallas *fpl* victuals
vituperable *adj* vituperable
vituperar *tr* to vituperate
viuda *f* widow; **viuda de marido vivo** or **viuda de paja** grass widow
viudedad *f* widowhood; dower; widow's pension

viudez *f* (*estado de viuda*) widowhood; (*estado de viudo*) widowerhood
viu•do -da *adj* left a widow; left a widower ‖ *m* widower ‖ *f* see **viuda**
viva *interj* viva!, long live! ‖ *m* viva
vivacidad *f* longevity; vivacity, liveliness; brightness, brilliance
vivande•ro -ra *mf* (mil) sutler, camp follower
vivaque *m* bivouac; guardhouse; police headquarters; **estar al vivaque** to bivouac
vivaquear *intr* to bivouac
vivar *m* warren, burrow; aquarium ‖ *tr* to cheer, acclaim
vivara•cho -cha *adj* vivacious, lively
vi•vaz *adj* (*pl* **-vaces**) long-lived; vivacious, lively; keen, perceptive; (bot) perennial
víveres *mpl* food, provisions, victuals
vivero *m* tree nursery; fishpond; (*origen de cosas perjudiciales*) (fig) hotbed
viveza *f* agility, briskness; ardor, vehemence; sharpness, keenness; perception; brightness, brilliance; witticism; (*de los ojos*) sparkle; (*acción o palabra poco consideradas*) thoughtlessness
vivide•ro -ra *adj* livable
vívi•do -da *adj* quick, perceptive; lively
vivienda *f* dwelling; life, way of life; **vivienda unifamiliar** one-family house
viviente *adj* living, alive
vivificar **§73** *tr* to vivify, enliven
vivir *m* life, living ‖ *tr* (*una experiencia o ventura*) to live; (*toda la vida; la vejez*) live out; (*habitar*) live in ‖ *intr* to live; **¿quién vive?** (mil) who goes there?; **vivir de** (*p.ej., carne*) to live on; **vivir para ver** to live and learn; **vivir y dejar vivir** to live and let live
vivisección *f* vivisection
vi•vo -va *adj* living, alive, live; (*lleno de vida; intenso*) live; (*sutil, agudo*) sharp, keen; (*dolor*) acute; (*carne*) raw; active, effective; (*luz*) bright, intense; (*pronto y ágil*) quick; (*idioma*) living, modern; **de viva voz** viva voce, by word of mouth; **herir en lo vivo** to cut or to sting to the quick ‖ *mf* living person; **los vivos y los muertos** the quick and the dead ‖ *m* edging, border; (vet) mange
Vizcaya *f* Biscay; **llevar hierro a Vizcaya** to carry coals to Newcastle
vizconde *m* viscount
vizcondesa *f* viscountess
V.M. *abbr* **Vuestra Majestad**
V.°B.° *abbr* **visto bueno**
vocablista *mf* punster
vocablo *m* word; **jugar del vocablo** to pun
vocabulario *m* vocabulary
vocación *f* vocation, calling
vocal *adj* vocal ‖ *mf* director ‖ *f* vowel
vocalista *mf* singer, vocalist
vocativo *m* vocative
voceador *m* town crier; (Col, Ecuad) paper boy
vocear *tr* to cry, shout; cheer, acclaim; call, page; boast about publicly ‖ *intr* to shout
vocería *f* shouting, outcry; spokesmanship
vocerío *m* shouting, outcry
vocero *m* spokesman, mouthpiece
vociferar *tr* (*injurias*) to shout; boast loudly about ‖ *intr* to vociferate, shout
vocingle•ro -ra *adj* loudmouthed; loud, talkative
vo•dú *m* (*pl* **-dúes**) voodoo
voduísta *adj & mf* voodoo
vol. *abbr* **volumen, voluntad**
volada *f* short flight; (*del jugador de billar*) (Arg) stroke; (Col, Ecuad) trick; (*noticia inventada*) (Mex) hoax
voladi•zo -za *adj* projecting ‖ *m* projection
vola•do -da *adj* (typ) superior ‖ *f* see **volada**
vola•dor -dora *adj* flying; hanging, dangling; swift, fast ‖ *m* rocket; flying fish
voladura *f* blast, explosion
volandas — **en volandas** in the air; fast
volante *adj* flying; unsettled ‖ *m* shuttlecock; battledore and shuttlecock; (*rueda que regula el movimiento de una máquina*) flywheel; (*rueda de mano para la dirección del automóvil*) steering wheel; (*pieza del reloj movida por la espiral*) balance wheel; flunkey, lackey; (*criado que iba a pie delante del coche o caballo*) outrunner; (*de papel*) slip, leaflet; (sew) flounce, ruffle; **un buen volante** a good driver
volan•tín -tina *adj* unsettled ‖ *m* fish line; kite
volantista *m* driver, man at the wheel
volan•tón -tona *mf* fledgling ‖ *f* (Ven) loose woman
volapié *m* (taur) stroke in which the matador moves in for the kill; **a volapié** half running, half flying; half walking, half swimming
volar **§61** *tr* (*llevar en un aparato de aviación*) to fly; blow up, explode; irritate; (*una letra, tipo o signo*) (typ) to raise ‖ *intr* to fly; fly away; disappear; jut out, project; (*una especie*) spread rapidly; (*p.ej., una torre*) rise in the air; **volar sin motor** (aer) to glide ‖ *ref* to fly away; fly off the handle
volatería *f* fowling with decoys; **de volatería** offhand
volátil *adj* volatile
volatilizar *tr & ref* to volatilize
volatín *m* ropewalker, acrobat, tumbler
volatine•ro -ra *mf* ropewalker, acrobat, tumbler
volcán *m* volcano
volcar **§81** *tr* to upset, overturn, dump; tip, tilt; (*a una persona un olor fuerte*) to make dizzy; change the mind of; irritate, tease ‖ *intr* to upset ‖ *ref* to turn upside down
volear *tr* (tennis) to volley
voleo *m* (tennis) volley; reeling punch; **del primer voleo** or **de un voleo** with a smash, all at once; **sembrar al voleo** to sow, broadcast
volframio *m* wolfram
volibol *m* volleyball
volquete *m* dumpcart, dump truck
voltai•co -ca *adj* voltaic
voltaje *m* voltage
volta•rio -ria *adj* fickle, inconstant; (Chile) willful; (Chile) sporty

voltea•do -da *mf* (Col) turncoat, deserter
voltear *tr* to upset, turn over; turn around; move, transform || *intr* to roll over, tumble
volteo *m* upset, overturning; tumbling; (P-R) scolding
voltereta *f* tumble; turning up card to determine trump
voltímetro *m* voltmeter
voltio *m* volt
volti•zo -za *adj* curled, twisted; fickle
voluble *adj* easily turned; fickle, inconstant
volumen *m* volume; **volumen sonoro** volume; (geom) volume
volumino•so -sa *adj* voluminous
voluntad *f* will; (*amor, cariño*) fondness, love; **a voluntad** at will; **buena voluntad** willingness; **de buena voluntad** willingly; **de mala voluntad** unwillingly; **de su propia voluntad** of one's own volition; **última voluntad** last will and testament; last wish; **voluntad de hierro** iron will
voluntariedad *f* willfulness
volunta•rio -ra *adj* (*que se hace por espontánea voluntad*) voluntary; (*que tiene voluntad obstinada*) willful; (*que se presta voluntariamente a hacer algo*) volunteer || *mfr* volunteer
voluntario•so -sa *adj* willful
voluptuo•so -sa *adj* (*que inspira complacencia en los placeres sensuales*) voluptuous; (*dado a los placeres sensuales*) voluptuary || *mf* voluptuary
voluta *f* (archit) scroll, volute; (*p.ej., de humo*) ring
volvedor *m* screwdriver; (Col) extra, something thrown in; **volvedor de machos** tap wrench
volver §47 & §83 *tr* to turn; turn upside down; turn inside out; return, send back, give back; (*una puerta*) push to, pull to; translate; vomit || *intr* to turn; return, come back; **volver a** + *inf* verb + again, e.g., **volvió a abrir la puerta** he opened the door again; **volver en sí** to come to; **volver por** to defend, stand up for || *ref* to become; turn around; return, come back; change one's mind; turn, turn sour; **volverse atrás** to back out; **volverse contra** to turn on
vomitar *tr* to vomit, throw up; (*fuego los cañones*) belch forth; (*maldiciones*) utter; (*un secreto*) let out; (*lo que uno retiene indebidamente*) cough up || *intr* to vomit, throw up; come across, disgorge
vómito *m* vomit, vomiting; **provocar a vómito** to nauseate; **vómitos del embarazo** morning sickness
voracidad *f* voracity
vorágine *f* whirlpool, vortex
vo•raz *adj* (*pl* **-races**) voracious
vormela *f* polecat
vórtice *m* vortex
vos *pron pers* (subject of verb and object of preposition; takes plural form of verb but is singular in meaning; used in addressing the Deity, the Virgin, etc., and distinguished persons; in Spanish America is much used instead of **tú**) you
voso•tros -tras *pron pers* (plural of **tú**) you
votación *f* vote, voting; **votación de desempate** runoff election
votante *adj* voting || *mf* voter
votar *tr* to vote for; (*sí, no*) vote; (*p.ej., un cirio a la Virgen*) vow || *intr* to vote; vow; swear, curse
voti•vo -va *adj* votive
voto *m* (*sufragio; derecho de votar; persona que da su voto*) vote; (*promesa solemne*) vow; (*exvoto*) votive offering; (*blasfemia*) oath, curse; wish, desire; **echar votos** to swear, to curse; **regular los votos** to tally the votes; **voto de amén** vote of a yes man; yes man; **voto de calidad** casting vote; **voto informativo** straw vote; **votos** good wishes; **¡voto va!** come now!
voz *f* (*pl* **voces**) voice; (*vocablo*) word; **aclarar la voz** to clear one's throat; **a una voz** with one voice; **a voces** shouting; **a voz en cuello** or **en grito** at the top of one's voice; **correr la voz que** to be rumored that; **dar voces** to shout, cry out; **de viva voz** viva voce, by word of mouth; **en alta voz** aloud, in a loud voice; **en voz baja** in a low voice; **llevar la voz cantante** to have the say, be the boss; **voces** outcry
voz-guía *f* (*diccionario*) entry word
vro. *abbr* **vuestro**
V.S. *abbr* **Vueseñoría**
vuelco *m* upset, overturn; **darle a uno un vuelco el corazón** to have a presentiment
vuelo *m* flight; flying; (*de una falda*) flare, fullness; projection; lace cuff trimming; **al vuelo** at once; on the wing; scattered at random; (chess) en passant; **alzar el vuelo** to take flight; to dash away; **echar a vuelo las campanas** to ring a full peal; **tirar al vuelo** to shoot on the wing; **tocar a vuelo las campanas** to ring a full peal; **vuelo a ciegas** (aer) blind flying; **vuelo de distancia** (aer) long-distance flight; **vuelo de enlace** connecting flight; **vuelo de ensayo** or **de prueba** (aer) test flight; **vuelo espacial tripulado** manned space flight; **vuelo planeado** (aer) volplane; **vuelo rasante** (aer) hedgehopping; **vuelo sin escala** (aer) nonstop flight; **vuelo sin motor** (aer) glide, gliding
vuelta *f* turn; (*regreso; devolución*) return; (*dinero sobrante de un pago*) change; (*de un camino*) bend, turn; (*del pantalón*) cuff; cuff trimming; (*paseo corto*) stroll; (*revés*) other side; (*paliza*) beating, whipping; (*en un cabo*) loop; (*en la media*) clock; (*mudanza*) change; **a la vuelta** on returning; please turn the page; **a la vuelta de** at the end of; at the turn of; (*la esquina*) around; **a vuelta de** about; **a vuelta de correo** by return mail; **dar cien vueltas a** to run rings around, be way ahead of; **dar la vuelta de campana** to turn somersault; **darse una vuelta a la redonda** to tend to one's own business; **dar una vuelta** to take a stroll, take a walk; take a look; change one's

ways; **dar vuelta** to turn around; (*el vino*) turn sour; **dar vuelta a** to reverse, turn around; **estar de vuelta** to be back; **quedarse con la vuelta** to keep the change; **vuelta de campana** somersault; **vuelta del mundo** trip around the world
vuelto *m* change
vues•tro -tra (corresponds to **vos** and **vosotros**) *adj poss* your || *pron poss* yours
vulcanizar **§60** *tr* to vulcanize
vulgacho *m* populace, mob
vulgar *adj* vulgar, popular, common, vernacular
vulgarismo *m* popular expression; (philol) popular word, popular form
vulgarizar **§60** *tr* to popularize; translate into the vernacular || *ref* to associate with the people
Vulgata *f* Vulgate
vulgo *adv* commonly || *m* common people; (*personas que en una materia sólo conocen la parte superficial*) laity
vulnerable *adj* vulnerable
vulnerar *tr* to hurt, injure; (*la reputación de una persona*) damage; (*una ley, un precepto*) break
vulpeja *f* she-fox, vixen
V.V. or **VV** *abbr* **ustedes**

X

X, x (equis) *f* twenty-sixth letter of the Spanish alphabet
xenia *f* xenia
xenofobia *f* xenophobia
xenófo•bo -ba *mf* xenophobe
xenón *m* xenon
xerografía *f* xerography
xerografiar §77 *tr* to xerograph || *intr* to make xerograph copies
xilófono *m* (mus) xylophone
xilografía *f* (*arte*) xylography; (*grabado*) xylograph
xpiano *abbr* **cristiano**
Xpo *abbr* **Cristo**
xptiano *abbr* **cristiano**
Xpto *abbr* **Cristo**
xunde *m* (Mex) reed basket, palm basket

Y

Y, y (ye) *f* twenty-seventh letter of the Spanish alphabet
y *conj* and
ya *adv* already; right away; now; **no ya** not only; **ya no** no longer; **ya que** since, inasmuch as
yac *m* (*bandera de proa*) (naut) jack; (*bóvido del Tibet*) yak
yacer **§82** *intr* to lie
yacija *f* bed, couch; (*sepultura*) grave
yacimiento *m* bed, field, deposit; **yacimiento de petróleo** oil field
yámbi•co -ca *adj* iambic
yambo *m* iamb, iambus
yanqui *adj & mf* Yankee
Yanquilandia *f* Yankeedom
yapa *f* bonus, extra, allowance; **de yapa** in the bargain, extra
yarda *f* yard, yardstick
yate *m* yacht
yedra *f* ivy
yegua *f* mare; (CAm) cigar butt
yeguada *f* stud
yelmo *m* helmet
yema *f* (*de huevo*) yolk; candied yolk; (*del invierno*) dead; (*renuevo*) bud; (fig) cream; **dar en la yema** to put one's finger on the spot; **yema del dedo** finger tip; **yema mejida** eggnog
yente — yentes y vinientes *mpl* habitués, frequenters
yerba *f* var of **hierba**
yer•mo -ma *adj* deserted, uninhabited; (*suelo*) unsown; (*mujer*) not pregnant || *m* desert, wilderness
yerno *m* son-in-law
yerro *m* error, mistake; **yerro de cuenta** miscalculation; **yerro de imprenta** printer's error
yer•to -ta *adj* stiff, rigid
yesca *f* punk, tinder; (*cosa que excita una pasión*) fuel; **echar una yesca** to strike **a** light
yeso *m* gypsum; plaster cast
yo *pron pers* **I; soy yo** it's me, it is **I**
yodhídri•co -ca *adj* hydriodic
yodo *m* iodine
yoduro *m* iodide
yoga *f* yoga
yogui *m* yogi
yogurt *m* yogurt
yola *f* shell (*boat*)
yonquí *m* (*drogas*) junkie, drug addict
yugo *m* yoke; **sacudir el yugo** to throw off the yoke

Yugoeslavia *f* Yugoslavia
yugoesla•vo -va *adj & mf* Yugoslav
yugular *adj & f* jugular || *tr* to cut off, nip in the bud
yunque *m* anvil; drudge, work horse
yunta *f* yoke, team
yute *m* jute
yuxtaponer §54 *tr* to juxtapose
yuyo *m* (Arg, Chile) weed; **yuyos** (Col, Ecuad, Peru) greens

Z

Z, z (zeda or zeta) *f* twenty-eighth letter of the Spanish alphabet
zabordar *intr* (naut) to run aground
zabullir §13 *tr* (*p.ej., a un perro*) to duck, give a ducking to; throw, hurl || *ref* (*meterse debajo del agua con ímpetu*) to dive; (*esconderse rápidamente*) duck
zacapela *f* or **zacapella** *f* row, rumpus
zacate *m* (CAm, Mex) hay, fodder; **zacate de empaque** excelsior
zacateca *m* (Cuba) undertaker, gravedigger
zacatín *m* old-clothes market
zacear *tr* (*al perro*) to chase away || *intr* to lisp
zafaduría *f* (Arg) brazenness, effrontery
zafar *tr* to adorn, bedeck; loosen, untie; clear, free; (*un buque*) lighten || *ref* to slip away; slip off, come off; **zafarse de** to get out of
zafarrancho *m* (naut) clearing the decks; (coll) havoc, ravage; (coll) scuffle, row; **zafarrancho de combate** (naut) clearing the deck for action
za•fio -fia *adj* rough, uncouth, boorish
zafiro *m* sapphire
za•fo -fa *adj* unhurt, intact; (naut) free, clear || **zafo** *prep* (Col) except
zafra *f* olive-oil can; drip jar; sugar crop; sugar making; sugar-making season; (min) rubbish, muck
zaga *f* rear; load carried in the rear; (mil) rearguard; **a la zaga, a zaga** or **en zaga** behind, in the rear; **no ir en zaga a** to not be behind, be as good as
zagal *m* young fellow; strapping young fellow; shepherd boy; footboy
zagala *f* lass, maiden; young shepherdess
zaguán *m* vestibule, hall, entry
zague•ro -ra *adj* back, rear || *m* (sport) back, backstop
zaherir §68 *tr* to upbraid, reproach; scold shamefully
zahones *mpl* chaps, hunting breeches
zaho•rí *m* (*pl* **-ríes**) keen observer; seer, clairvoyant
zahurda *f* pigpen
zai•no -na *adj* treacherous, false; (*caballo*) vicious; (*caballo*) dark-chestnut; **mirar a lo zaino** or **de zaino** to look askance at
za•lá *f* (*pl* **-laes**) Muslim prayer; **hacer la zalá a** to fawn on
zalagarda *f* ambush; skirmish; (*trampa para cazar animales*) trap; trick; row, rumpus; mock fight
zalamería *f* flattery, cajolery
zalame•ro -ra *adj* flattering, fawning || *mf* flatterer, fawner
zalea *f* unsheared sheepskin
zalear *tr* to drag around, shake; (*al perro*) chase away
zalema *f* salaam
zamacuco *m* blockhead; sullen fellow; drunkenness
zamacueca *f* cueca (*Chilean courtship dance*)
zamarra *f* undressed sheepskin; sheepskin jacket
zam•bo -ba *adj* knock-kneed
zambra *f* merrymaking, celebration; Moorish boat
zambucar §73 *tr* to slip away, hide away
zambullida *f* dive, plunge; (fencing) thrust to the breast
zambulli•dor -dora *adj* diving, plunging || *mf* diver, plunger || *m* (orn) diver, loon
zambullir §13 *tr* (*p.ej., a un perro*) to duck, give a ducking to; throw, hurl || *ref* (*meterse debajo del agua con ímpetu*) to dive; (*esconderse rápidamente*) duck
zampa *f* pile, bearing pile
zampacuarti•llos *mf* (*pl* **-llos**) toper, soak
zampalimos•nas *mf* (*pl* **-nas**) bum, ordinary bum
zampar *tr* to slip away, hide away; gobble down || *ref* to slip away, hide away
zampator•tas *mf* (*pl* **-tas**) glutton; boor
zampear *tr* (*el terreno*) to strengthen with piles and rubble
zampoña *f* shepherd's pipe, rustic flute; nonsense, folly
zampuzar §60 *tr* to duck, give a ducking to; slip away, hide away
zanahoria *f* carrot
zanca *f* long leg; (*de la escalera*) horse
zancada *f* long stride; **en dos zancadas** in a flash, in a jiffy
zancadilla *f* booby trap; **echar la zancadilla a** to stick out one's foot and trip
zancajo *m* heel; **no llegar a los zancajos a** to not come up to, not be equal to
zancajo•so -sa *adj* duck-toed; down-at-the-heel
zancarrón *m* dirty old fellow
zanco *m* stilt; **en zancos** from a vantage point

zancu•do -da *adj* long-legged; (orn) wading || *m* mosquito || *f* wading bird
zanfonía *f* hurdy-gurdy
zangala *f* buckram
zangamanga *f* trick
zanganada *f* impertinence, impudence
zanganear *intr* to loaf around
zángano *m* (ent) drone; (fig) drone, loafer; (CAm) scoundrel
zangarrear *intr* to thrum a guitar
zangolotear *tr* to jiggle || *intr* to fuss around || *ref* to jiggle, flop around, rattle
zangoloteo *m* jiggle, jiggling, rattle; fuss, bother
zanguanga *f* malingering; flattery; **hacer la zanguanga** to malinger
zanguan•go -ga *adj* slow, lazy || *mf* loafer || *f* see **zanguanga**
zanja *f* ditch, trench; (SAm) gully; **abrir las zanjas** to lay the foundations
zanquear *intr* to waddle; to rush around
zanquilar•go -ga *adj* leggy, long-legged
zanquituer•to -ta *adj* bandy-legged
zapa *f* spade; sharkskin, (mil) sap
zapapico *m* mattock, pickax
zapar *tr* (mil) to sap, mine, excavate
zaparrastrar *intr* — **ir zaparrastrando** to go along trailing one's clothes on the ground
zapateado *m* clog dance, tap dance
zapatear *tr* to hit with the shoe; tap with the feet; abuse, ill-treat || *intr* to tap-dance; (*las velas*) flap || *ref* — **zapatearse con** to hold out against
zapatería *f* shoemaking; shoemaker's shop; (*tienda*) shoe store
zapate•ro -ra *adj* poorly cooked || *mf* shoemaker; shoe dealer; **quedarse zapatero** to not take a trick; **¡zapatero, a tus zapatos!** stick to your last!; **zapatero de viejo** or **zapatero remendón** cobbler, shoemaker
zapatilla *f* slipper; (*escarpín*) pump; (*del grifo*) washer; (*del florete*) leather tip or button; cloven hoof
zapato *m* shoe, low shoe; **andar con zapatos de fieltro** to gumshoe; **como tres en un zapato** hard up; like sardines; **zapato de goma** overshoe; **zapato inglés** low shoe
zapatón *m* (Guat, SAm) overshoe
zapear *tr* (*al gato*) to scare away, chase away
zaque *m* wineskin; tippler, drunk
zaquiza•mí *m* (*pl* **-míes**) attic, garret; hovel, pigpen
zar *m* czar
zarabanda *f* (mus) saraband; noise, confusion, uproar; (Mex) beating, thrashing
zaragata *f* scuffle, row; **zaragatas** (W-I) flattery
Zaragoza *f* Saragossa
zaranda *f* sieve, screen; colander; (Ven) horn; (Ven) top
zarandajas *fpl* odds and ends, trinkets
zarandar *tr* to sift, screen; winnow, pick out, select; jiggle || *ref* to jiggle; swagger, strut
zaraza *f* chintz, printed cotton
zarcillo *m* eardrop; (bot) tendril
zarigüeya *f* opossum
zarina *f* czarina
zarpa *f* claw, paw; (naut) weighing anchor
zarpar *tr* (*el ancla*) (naut) to weigh (*anchor*) || *intr* (naut) to weigh anchor, set sail
zarpo•so -sa *adj* mud-splashed
zarracatería *f* cajolery, insincere flattery
zarracatín *m* sharp trader
zarramplín *m* botcher, bungler
zarrien•to -ta *adj* mud-splashed
zarza *f* blackberry, bramble (*bush*)
zarzamora *f* blackberry (*fruit*)
zarzaparrilla *f* sarsaparilla
zarzo *m* hurdle, wattle
zarzo•so -sa *adj* brambly
zarzuela *f* small bramble; (theat) zarzuela (*Spanish musical comedy*); **zarzuela grande** three-act zarzuela
zas *interj* bang!; **¡zas, zas!** bing, bang!
zascandilear *intr* to meddle, scheme
zepelín *m* zeppelin
Zeus *m* Zeus
zigzag *m* zigzag
zigzaguear *intr* to zigzag
zinc *m* (*pl* **zinces**) zinc
zipizape *m* scuffle, row, rumpus
ziszás *m* zigzag
zoca *f* public square
zócalo *m* (archit) socle; (*de una pared*) dado; (rad) socket; (Mex) public square, center square
zoca•to -ta *adj* (*fruto*) corky, pithy; **left**; left-handed || *mf* left-handed person
zoclo *m* clog, wooden shoe
zo•co -ca *adj* left; left-handed || *mf* left-handed person || *m* clog, wooden shoe; Moroccan market place; (archit) socle; **andar de zocos en colodros** to jump from the frying pan into the fire || *f* see **zoca**
zodíaco *m* zodiac
zofra *f* Moorish carpet, Moorish rug
zolo•cho -cha *adj* stupid, simple || *mf* simpleton
zollipar *intr* to sob
zollipo *m* sob
zona *m* (pathol) shingles || *f* zone; (*banda, faja*) belt, girdle; **zona a batir** target area; **zona desmilitarizada** demilitarized zone; **zona siniestrada** disaster area
zon•zo -za *adj* tasteless, insipid; dull, inane || *mf* dolt, dimwit
zoófito *m* zoöphyte
zoología *f* zoölogy
zoológi•co -ca *adj* zoölogic(al)
zoólo•go -ga *mf* zoölogist
zopen•co -ca *adj* dull, stupid || *mf* dullard, blockhead
zopilote *m* (Mex, CAm) turkey buzzard, turkey vulture
zo•po -pa *adj* crippled; awkward, gauche || *mf* cripple
zoquete *m* (*de madera*) block, chunk, end; (*de pan*) bit, crust; chump, lout
zoquetu•do -da *adj* coarse, crude
zorra *f* fox; female fox; cunning person; prostitute; drunkenness; dray, truck; **pillar una zorra** to get drunk

zorrera *f* (*cueva de zorros*) foxhole; smoke-filled room; worry, confusion
zorrería *f* foxiness, craftiness
zorre•ro -ra *adj* sly, foxy; slow, heavy, tardy || *f* see **zorrera**
zorrillo *m* skunk
zorro *m* male fox; (*piel*) fox; (*hombre taimado*) fox; **estar hecho un zorro** to be overwhelmed with sleep; be dull and sullen; **zorros** duster
zorral *m* (orn) fieldfare; sly fellow; (Chile) simpleton
zozobra *f* capsizing, sinking; anxiety
zozobrar *tr* (*un buque*) to sink; (*un negocio*) wreck || *intr* to capsize, sink; (*la embarcación en la tempestad*) wallow; (*un negocio*) be in great danger; be greatly worried || *ref* to capsize, sink
zueco *m* clog, wooden shoe, sabot
zulacar **§73** *tr* to waterproof
zulaque *m* waterproofing
zulú *adj* & *mf* (*pl* **-lús** o **-lúes**) Zulu
zullar *ref* to have a bowel movement; break wind
zullen•co -ca *adj* windy, flatulent
zumaque *m* sumach; wine
zumaya *f* (*autillo*) tawny owl; (*chotacabras*) goatsucker
zumba *f* bell worn by leading mule; (Mex) drunkenness; **hacer zumba a** to make fun of; **sin zumba** (Mex) in a rush, in a hurry
zumbador *m* buzzer; (Mex) pauraque; (Mex, CAm, W-I) hummingbird
zumbar *tr* to make fun of; (*un golpe, una bofetada*) let have || *intr* to buzz; zoom; (*los oídos*) ring; **zumbar a** (*frisar con*) to be close to, border on || *ref* (Cuba) to go too far, forget oneself; (P-R) to rush ahead; **zumbarse de** to make fun of
zumbido *m* buzz; zoom; blow, smack; **zumbido de ocupación** (telp) busy signal; **zumbido de oídos** ringing in the ears
zum•bón -bona *adj* waggish, playful || *mf* wag, jester
zumien•to -ta *adj* juicy
zumo *m* juice; advantage, profit; **zumo de cepas** or **de parras** fruit of the vine
zumo•so -sa *adj* juicy
zunchar *tr* to band, hoop
zuncho *m* band, hoop
zupia *f* (*del vino*) dregs; slop, wine full of dregs; (fig) junk, trash
zurcido *m* darning; darn; invisible mending
zurcir **§36** *tr* to darn; (*una mentira*) hatch, concoct; (*unas mentiras*) weave (*a tissue of lies*)
zurdazo *m* (box) left, blow with the left
zur•do -da *adj* left; left-handed; **a zurdas** with the left hand; the wrong way || *mf* left-handed person
zurear *intr* to coo
zuro *m* stripped corncob
zurra *f* dressing, currying; scuffle, quarrel; drubbing, thrashing; (*trabajo o estudio continuados*) grind
zurrapa *f* thread, filament; trash, rubbish; **con zurrapas** in a sloppy manner
zurrar *tr* (*el cuero*) to dress, curry; get the best of; (*censurar con dureza*) dress down; (*castigar con azotes*) drub, thrash || *ref* (*hacer sus necesidades involuntariamente*) to have an accident; be scared to death; (Arg) to break wind noiselessly
zurriagar **§44** *tr* to whip, horsewhip
zurriago *m* whip, lash
zurribanda *f* rain of blows; rumpus, scuffle
zurrir *intr* to buzz, grate
zurrón *m* shepherd's leather bag; leather bag; (*cáscara*) husk
zurrona *f* loose, evil woman
zurullo *m* soft roll; turd
zurupeto *m* unregistered broker; shyster notary
zuta•no -na *mf* so-and-so

Spanish Irregular Verbs

All simple tenses are shown in these tables if they contain one irregular form or more, except the conditional (which can always be derived from the stem of the future indicative) and the imperfect and future subjunctive (which can always be derived from the third plural preterit indicative minus the last syllable **-ron**).

The numbers are those that accompany the respective verbs and verbs of identical patterns where they are listed in their alphabetical places in this Dictionary. The letters (a) to (h) identify the tenses as follows:

(a)	gerund	(e)	present subjunctive
(b)	past participle	(f)	imperfect indicative
(c)	imperative	(g)	future indicative
(d)	present indicative	(h)	preterit indicative

§1 **abolir:** defective verb used only in forms whose endings contain the vowel **i**

§2 **acertar**
(c) **acierta,** acertad
(d) **acierto, aciertas, acierta,** acertamos, acertáis, **aciertan**
(e) **acierte, aciertes, acierte,** acertemos, acertéis, **acierten**

§3 **agorar:** like **§61** but with diaeresis on the **u** of **ue**
(c) **agüera,** agorad
(d) **agüero, agüeras, agüera,** agoramos, agoráis, **agüeran**
(e) **agüere, agüeres, agüere,** agoremos, agoréis, **agüeren**

§4 **airar**
(c) **aíra,** airad
(d) **aíro, aíras, aíra,** airamos, airáis, **aíran**
(e) **aíre, aíres, aíre,** airemos, airéis, **aíren**

§5 **andar**
(h) **anduve, anduviste, anduvo, anduvimos, anduvisteis, anduvieron**

§6 **argüir:** like **§20** but with diaeresis on **u** in forms with accented **i** in the ending
(a) **arguyendo**
(b) **argüído**
(c) **arguye,** argüid
(d) **arguyo, arguyes, arguye,** argüimos, argüís, **arguyen**
(e) **arguya, arguyas, arguya, arguyamos, arguyáis, arguyan**
(h) **argüí, argüiste, arguyó,** argüimos, argüisteis, **arguyeron**

§7 **asir**
(d) **asgo,** ases, ase, asimos, asís, asen
(e) **asga, asgas, asga, asgamos, asgáis, asgan**

§8 **aunar**
(c) **aúna,** aunad
(d) **aúno, aúnas, aúna,** aunamos, aunáis, **aúnan**
(e) **aúne, aúnes, aúne,** aunemos, aunéis, **aúnen**

§9 **avergonzar:** combination of **§3** and **§60**
(c) **avergüenza,** avergonzad
(d) **avergüenzo, avergüenzas, avergüenza,** avergonzamos, avergonzáis, **avergüenzan**
(e) **avergüence, avergüences, avergüence, avergoncemos, avergoncéis, avergüencen**
(h) **avergoncé,** avergonzaste, avergonzó, avergonzamos, avergonzasteis, avergonzaron

§10 **averiguar**
(e) **averigüe, averigües, averigüe, averigüemos, averigüéis, averigüen**
(h) **averigüé,** averiguaste, averiguó, averiguamos, averiguasteis, averiguaron

§11 **bendecir**
(a) **bendiciendo**
(c) **bendice,** bendecid
(d) **bendigo, bendices, bendice,** bendecimos, bendecís, **bendicen**
(e) **bendiga, bendigas, bendiga, bendigamos, bendigáis, bendigan**
(h) **bendije, bendijiste, bendijo, bendijimos, bendijisteis, bendijeron**

§12 **bruñir**
(a) **bruñendo**
(h) **bruñí, bruñiste, bruñó,** bruñimos, bruñisteis, **bruñeron**

§13 **bullir**
(a) **bullendo**
(h) **bullí, bulliste, bulló,** bullimos, bullisteis, **bulleron**

§14 **caber**
(d) **quepo,** cabes, cabe, cabemos, cabéis, caben
(e) **quepa, quepas, quepa, quepamos, quepáis, quepan**
(g) **cabré, cabrás, cabrá, cabremos, cabréis, cabrán**
(h) **cupe, cupiste, cupo, cupimos, cupisteis, cupieron**

§15 **caer**
(a) **cayendo**
(b) **caído**
(d) **caigo,** caes, cae, caemos, caéis, caen
(e) **caiga, caigas, caiga, caigamos, caigáis, caigan**
(h) caí, **caíste, cayó, caímos, caísteis, cayeron**

§16 **cocer:** combination of **§47** and **§78**
(c) **cuece,** coced
(d) **cuezo, cueces, cuece,** cocemos, cocéis, **cuecen**
(e) **cueza, cuezas, cueza, cozamos, cozáis, cuezan**

§17 **coger**
(d) **cojo,** coges, coge, cogemos, cogéis, cogen
(e) **coja, cojas, coja, cojamos, cojáis, cojan**

§18 **comenzar:** combination of **§2** and **§60**
(c) **comienza,** comenzad
(d) **comienzo, comienzas, comienza,** comenzamos, comenzáis, **comienzan**
(e) **comience, comiences, comience, comencemos, comencéis, comiencen**
(h) **comencé,** comenzaste, comenzó, comenzamos, comenzasteis, comenzaron

§19 **conducir**
(d) **conduzco,** conduces, conduce, conducimos, conducís, conducen
(e) **conduzca, conduzcas, conduzca, conduzcamos, conduzcáis, conduzcan**
(h) **conduje, condujiste, condujo, condujimos, condujisteis, condujeron**

§20 **construir**
(a) **construyendo**
(b) **construído**
(c) **construye,** construid
(d) **construyo, construyes, construye,** construimos, construís, **construyen**
(e) **construya, construyas, construya, construyamos, construyáis, construyan**
(h) construí, construiste, **construyó,** construimos, construisteis, **construyeron**

§21 **continuar**
(c) **continúa,** continuad
(d) **continúo, continúas, continúa,** continuamos, continuáis, **continúan**
(e) **continúe, continúes, continúe,** continuemos, continuéis, **continúen**

§22 **crecer**
(d) **crezco,** creces, crece, crecemos, crecéis, crecen
(e) **crezca, crezcas, crezca, crezcamos, crezcáis, crezcan**

§23 **dar**
(d) **doy,** das, da, damos, dais, dan
(e) **dé,** des, **dé,** demos, deis, den
(h) **dí, diste, dio, dimos, disteis, dieron**

§24 **decir**
(a) **diciendo**
(b) **dicho**
(c) **di,** decid
(d) **digo, dices, dice,** decimos, decís, **dicen**
(e) **diga, digas, diga, digamos, digáis, digan**
(g) **diré, dirás, dirá, diremos, diréis, dirán**
(h) **dije, dijiste, dijo, dijimos, dijisteis, dijeron**

§25 **delinquir**
(d) **delinco,** delinques, delinque, delinquimos, delinquís, delinquen
(e) **delinca, delincas, delinca, delincamos, delincáis, delincan**

§26 **desosar:** like **§61** but with **h** before **ue**
(c) **deshuesa,** desosad
(d) **deshueso, deshuesas, deshuesa,** desosamos, desosáis, **deshuesan**
(e) **deshuese, deshueses, deshuese,** desosemos, desoséis, **deshuesen**

§27 **dirigir**
(d) **dirijo,** diriges, dirige, dirigimos, dirigís, dirigen
(e) **dirija, dirijas, dirija, dirijamos, dirijáis, dirijan**

§28 **discernir**
(c) **discierne,** discernid
(d) **discierno, disciernes, discierne,** discernimos, discernís, **disciernen**
(e) **discierna, disciernas, discierna,** discernamos, discernáis, **disciernan**

§29 **distinguir**
(d) **distingo,** distingues, distingue, distinguimos, distinguís, distinguen
(e) **distinga, distingas, distinga, distingamos, distingáis, distingan**

§30 **dormir**
(a) **durmiendo**
(c) **duerme,** dormid
(d) **duermo, duermes, duerme,** dormimos, dormís, **duermen**
(e) **duerma, duermas, duerma, durmamos, durmáis, duerman**
(h) dormí, dormiste, **durmió,** dormimos, dormisteis, **durmieron**

§31 **empeller**
(a) **empellendo**
(h) empellí, empelliste, **empelló,** empellimos, empellisteis, **empelleron**

§32 **enraizar:** combination of **§4** and **§60**
(c) **enraíza,** enraizad
(d) **enraízo, enraízas, enraíza,** enraizamos, enraizáis, **enraízan**
(e) **enraíce, enraíces, enraíce, enraicemos, enraicéis, enraícen**
(h) **enraicé,** enraizaste, enraizó, enraizamos, enraizasteis, enraizaron

§33 **erguir:** combination of **§29** and **§50** or **§68**
(a) **irguiendo**
(c) **irgue** or **yergue,** erguid
(d) **irgo, irgues, irgue,** / **yergo, yergues, yergue,** } erguimos, erguís, { **irguen** / **yerguen**
(e) **irga, irgas, irga,** / **yerga, yergas, yerga,** } **irgamos, irgáis,** { **irgan** / **yergan**
(h) erguí, erguiste, **irguió,** erguimos, erguisteis, **irguieron**

§34 **errar:** like **§2** but with initial **ye** for **ie**
(c) **yerra,** errad
(d) **yerro, yerras, yerra,** erramos, erráis, **yerran**
(e) **yerre, yerres, yerre,** erremos, erréis, **yerren**

§35 **esforzar:** combination of §**60** and §**61**
(c) **esfuerza,** esforzad
(d) **esfuerzo, esfuerzas, esfuerza,** esforzamos, esforzáis, **esfuerzan**
(e) **esfuerce, esfuerces, esfuerce, esforcemos, esforcéis, esfuercen**
(h) **esforcé,** esforzaste, esforzó, esforzamos, esforzasteis, esforzaron

§36 **esparcir**
(d) **esparzo,** esparces, esparce, esparcimos, esparcís, esparcen
(e) **esparza, esparzas, esparza, esparzamos, esparzáis, esparzan**

§37 **estar**
(c) **está,** estad
(d) **estoy, estás, está,** estamos, estáis, **están**
(e) **esté, estés, esté,** estemos, estéis, **estén**
(h) **estuve, estuviste, estuvo, estuvimos, estuvisteis, estuvieron**

§38 **haber**
(c) **hé,** habed
(d) **he, has, ha, hemos,** habéis, **han** (*v impers*) **hay**
(e) **haya, hayas, haya, hayamos, hayáis, hayan**
(g) **habré, habrás, habrá, habremos, habréis, habrán**
(h) **hube, hubiste, hubo, hubimos, hubisteis, hubieron**

§39 **hacer**
(b) **hecho**
(c) **haz,** haced
(d) **hago,** haces, hace, hacemos, hacéis, hacen
(e) **haga, hagas, haga, hagamos, hagáis, hagan**
(g) **haré, harás, hará, haremos, haréis, harán**
(h) **hice, hiciste, hizo, hicimos, hicisteis, hicieron**

§40 **inquirir**
(c) **inquiere,** inquirid
(d) **inquiero, inquieres, inquiere,** inquirimos, inquirís, **inquieren**
(e) **inquiera, inquieras, inquiera,** inquiramos, inquiráis, **inquieran**

§41 **ir**
(a) **yendo**
(c) **vé, vamos,** id
(d) **voy, vas, va, vamos, vais, van**
(e) **vaya, vayas, vaya, vayamos, vayáis, vayan**
(f) **iba, ibas, iba, íbamos, ibais, iban**
(h) **fui, fuiste, fue, fuimos, fuisteis, fueron**

§42 **jugar:** like §**63** but with radical **u**
(c) **juega,** jugad
(d) **juego, juegas, juega,** jugamos, jugáis, **juegan**
(e) **juegue, juegues, juegue, juguemos, juguéis, jueguen**
(h) **jugué,** jugaste, jugó, jugamos, jugasteis, jugaron

§43 **leer**
(a) **leyendo**
(b) **leído**
(h) leí, **leíste, leyó, leímos, leísteis, leyeron**

§44 **ligar**
(e) **ligue, ligues, ligue, liguemos, liguéis, liguen**
(h) **ligué,** ligaste, ligó, ligamos, ligasteis, ligaron

§45 **lucir**
(d) **luzco,** luces, luce, lucimos, lucís, lucen
(e) **luzca, luzcas, luzca, luzcamos, luzcáis, luzcan**

§46 **mecer**
(d) **mezo,** meces, mece, mecemos, mecéis, mecen
(e) **meza, mezas, meza, mezamos, mezáis, mezan**

§47 mover
(c) **mueve,** moved
(d) **muevo, mueves, mueve,** movemos, movéis, **mueven**
(e) **mueva, muevas, mueva,** movamos, mováis, **muevan**

§48 oír
(a) **oyendo**
(b) **oído**
(c) **oye, oíd**
(d) **oigo, oyes, oye, oímos,** oís, **oyen**
(e) **oiga, oigas, oiga, oigamos, oigáis, oigan**
(h) oí, **oíste, oyó, oímos, oísteis, oyeron**

§49 oler: like §47 but with **h** before **ue**
(c) **huele,** oled
(d) **huelo, hueles, huele,** olemos, oléis, **huelen**
(e) **huela, huelas, huela,** olamos, oláis, **huelan**

§50 pedir
(a) **pidiendo**
(c) **pide,** pedid
(d) **pido, pides, pide,** pedimos, pedís, **piden**
(e) **pida, pidas, pida, pidamos, pidáis, pidan**
(h) pedí, pediste, **pidió,** pedimos, pedisteis, **pidieron**

§51 perder
(c) **pierde,** perded
(d) **pierdo, pierdes, pierde,** perdemos, perdéis, **pierden**
(e) **pierda, pierdas, pierda,** perdamos, perdáis, **pierdan**

§52 placer
(d) **plazco,** places, place, placemos, placéis, placen
(e) **plazca, plazcas, plazca, plazcamos, plazcáis, plazcan**
(h) plací, placiste, plació (or **plugo**), placimos, placisteis, placieron

§53 poder
(a) **pudiendo**
(c) (**puede,** poded)
(d) **puedo, puedes, puede,** podemos, podéis, **pueden**
(e) **pueda, puedas, pueda,** podamos, podáis, **puedan**
(g) **podré, podrás, podrá, podremos, podréis, podrán**
(h) **pude, pudiste, pudo, pudimos, pudisteis, pudieron**

§54 poner
(b) **puesto**
(c) **pon,** poned
(d) **pongo,** pones, pone, ponemos, ponéis, ponen
(e) **ponga, pongas, ponga, pongamos, pongáis, pongan**
(g) **pondré, pondrás, pondrá, pondremos, pondréis, pondrán**
(h) **puse, pusiste, puso, pusimos, pusisteis, pusieron**

§55 querer
(c) **quiere,** quered
(d) **quiero, quieres, quiere,** queremos, queréis, **quieren**
(e) **quiera, quieras, quiera,** queramos, queráis, **quieran**
(g) **querré, querrás, querrá, querremos, querréis, querrán**
(h) **quise, quisiste, quiso, quisimos, quisisteis, quisieron**

§56 raer
(a) **rayendo**
(b) **raído**
(d) **raigo** (or **rayo**), raes, rae, raemos, raéis, raen
(e) **raiga** (or **raya**), **raigas, raiga, raigamos, raigáis, raigan**
(h) **raí, raíste, rayó, raímos, raísteis, rayeron**

§57 **regir:** combination of **§27** and **§50**
(a) **rigiendo**
(c) **rige,** regid
(d) **rijo, riges, rige,** regimos, regís, **rigen**
(e) **rija, rijas, rija, rijamos, rijáis, rijan**
(h) regí, registe, **rigió,** regimos, registeis, **rigieron**

§58 **reír**
(a) **riendo**
(b) **reído**
(c) **ríe, reíd**
(d) **río, ríes, ríe, reímos,** reís, **ríen**
(e) **ría, rías, ría, riamos, riáis, rían**
(h) reí, **reíste, rió, reímos, reísteis, rieron**

§59 **reunir**
(c) **reúne,** reunid
(d) **reúno, reúnes, reúne,** reunimos, reunís, **reúnen**
(e) **reúna, reúnas, reúna,** reunamos, reunáis, **reúnan**

§60 **rezar**
(e) **rece, reces, rece, recemos, recéis, recen**
(h) **recé,** rezaste, rezó, rezamos, rezasteis, rezaron

§61 **rodar**
(c) **rueda,** rodad
(d) **ruedo, ruedas, rueda,** rodamos, rodáis, **ruedan**
(e) **ruede, ruedes, ruede,** rodemos, rodéis, **rueden**

§62 **roer**
(a) **royendo**
(b) **roído**
(d) **roo** (**roigo,** or **royo**), roes, roe, roemos, roéis, roen
(e) **roa** (**roiga,** or **roya**), roas, roa, roamos, roáis, roan
(h) roí, **roíste, royó, roímos, roísteis, royeron**

§63 **rogar:** combination of **§44** and **§61**
(c) **ruega,** rogad
(d) **ruego, ruegas, ruega,** rogamos, rogáis, **ruegan**
(e) **ruegue, ruegues, ruegue, roguemos, roguéis, rueguen**
(h) **rogué,** rogaste, rogó, rogamos, rogasteis, rogaron

§64 **saber**
(d) **sé,** sabes, sabe, sabemos, sabéis, saben
(e) **sepa, sepas, sepa, sepamos, sepáis, sepan**
(g) **sabré, sabrás, sabrá, sabremos, sabréis, sabrán**
(h) **supe, supiste, supo, supimos, supisteis, supieron**

§65 **salir**
(c) **sal,** salid
(d) **salgo,** sales, sale, salimos, salís, salen
(e) **salga, salgas, salga, salgamos, salgáis, salgan**
(g) **saldré, saldrás, saldrá, saldremos, saldréis, saldrán**

§66 **segar:** combination of **§2** and **§44**
(c) **siega,** segad
(d) **siego, siegas, siega,** segamos, segáis, **siegan**
(e) **siegue, siegues, siegue, seguemos, seguéis, sieguen**
(h) **segué,** segaste, segó, segamos, segasteis, segaron

§67 **seguir:** combination of **§29** and **§50**
(a) **siguiendo**
(c) **sigue,** seguid
(d) **sigo, siegues, sigue,** seguimos, seguís, **siguen**
(e) **siga, sigas, siga, sigamos, sigáis, sigan**
(h) seguí, seguiste, **siguió,** seguimos, seguisteis, **siguieron**

§68 sentir
(a) **sintiendo**
(c) **siente,** sentid
(d) **siento, sientes, siente,** sentimos, sentís, **sienten**
(e) **sienta, sientas, sienta, sintamos, sintáis, sientan**
(h) sentí, sentiste, **sintió,** sentimos, sentisteis, **sintieron**

§69 ser
(c) **sé,** sed
(d) **soy, eres, es, somos, sois, son**
(e) **sea, seas, sea, seamos, seáis, sean**
(f) **era, eras, era, éramos, erais, eran**
(h) **fui, fuiste, fue, fuimos, fuisteis, fueron**

§70 tañer
(a) **tañendo**
(h) tañí, tañiste, **tañó,** tañimos, tañisteis, **tañeron**

§71 tener
(c) **ten,** tened
(d) **tengo, tienes, tiene,** tenemos, tenéis, **tienen**
(e) **tenga, tengas, tenga, tengamos, tengáis, tengan**
(g) **tendré, tendrás, tendrá, tendremos, tendréis, tendrán**
(h) **tuve, tuviste, tuvo, tuvimos, tuvisteis, tuvieron**

§72 teñir: combination of **§12** and **§50**
(a) **tiñendo**
(c) **tiñe,** teñid
(d) **tiño, tiñes, tiñe,** teñimos, teñis, **tiñen**
(e) **tiña, tiñas, tiña, tiñamos, tiñáis, tiñan**
(h) teñi, teñiste, **tiñó,** teñimos, teñisteis, **tiñeron**

§73 tocar
(e) **toque, toques, toque, toquemos, toquéis, toquen**
(h) **toqué,** tocaste, tocó, tocamos, tocasteis, tocaron

§74 torcer: combination of **§47** and **§78**
(c) **tuerce,** torced
(d) **tuerzo, tuerces, tuerce,** torcemos, torcéis, **tuercen**
(e) **tuerza, tuerzas, tuerza, torzamos, torzáis, tuerzan**

§75 traer
(a) **trayendo**
(b) **traído**
(d) **traigo,** traes, trae, traemos, traéis, traen
(e) **traiga, traigas, traiga, traigamos, traigáis, traigan**
(h) **traje, trajiste, trajo, trajimos, trajisteis, trajeron**

§76 valer
(d) **valgo,** vales, vale, valemos, valéis, valen
(e) **valga, valgas, valga, valgamos, valgáis, valgan**
(g) **valdré, valdrás, valdrá, valdremos, valdréis, valdrán**

§77 variar
(c) **varía,** variad
(d) **varío, varías, varía,** variamos, variáis, **varían**
(e) **varíe, varíes, varíe,** variemos, variéis, **varíen**

§78 vencer
(d) **venzo,** vences, vence, vencemos, vencéis, vencen
(e) **venza, venzas, venza, venzamos, venzáis, venzan**

§79 venir
(a) **viniendo**
(c) **ven,** venid
(d) **vengo, vienes, viene,** venimos, venís, **vienen**
(e) **venga, vengas, venga, vengamos, vengáis, vengan**

(g) **vendré, vendrás, vendrá, vendremos, vendréis, vendrán**
(h) **vine, viniste, vino, vinimos, vinisteis, vinieron**

§80 **ver**
(b) **visto**
(d) **veo,** ves, ve, vemos, veis, ven
(e) **vea, veas, vea, veamos, veáis, vean**
(f) **veía, veías, veía, veíamos, veíais, veían**

§81 **volcar:** combination of **§61** and **§73**
(c) **vuelca,** volcad
(d) **vuelco, vuelcas, vuelca,** volcamos, volcáis, **vuelcan**
(e) **vuelque, vuelques, vuelque, volquemos, volquéis, vuelquen**
(h) **volqué,** volcaste, volcó, volcamos, volcasteis, volcaron

§82 **yacer**
(c) **yaz** (or yace), yaced
(d) **yazco (yazgo,** or **yago),** yaces, yace, yacemos, yacéis, yacen
(e) **yazca (yazga,** or **yaga), yazcas, yazca, yazcamos, yazcáis, yazcan**

§83 The following verbs, some of which are included in the foregoing table, and their compounds have irregular past participles:

abrir	**hacer**	**escrito**	**poner**	**ver**	**podrido**
cubrir	**imprimir**	**frito**	**proveer**	**volver**	**roto**
decir	**abierto**	**hecho**	**pudrir**	**muerto**	**suelto**
escribir	**cubierto**	**impreso**	**romper**	**puesto**	**visto**
freír	**dicho**	**morir**	**solver**	**provisto**	**vuelto**

Inglés-Español

A

A, a [e] primera letra del alfabeto inglés
a [e] *art indef* un
aback [ə'bæk] *adv* atrás; **to be taken aback** quedar desconcertado; **to take aback** desconcertar
abaft [ə'bæft] *adv* a popa, en popa; *prep* detrás de
abandon [ə'bændən] *s* abandono ‖ *tr* abandonar
abandonment [ə'bændənmənt] *s* abandono, abandonamiento; desembarazo
abase [ə'bes] *tr* degradar, humillar
abash [ə'bæʃ] *tr* avergonzar
abashed [ə'bæʃt] *adj* avergonzado; humillado
abate [ə'bet] *tr* disminuir, reducir; deducir ‖ *intr* disminuir, moderarse
aba•tis ['æbətɪs] *s* (*pl* **-tis**) abatida
abattoir ['æbə,twar] *s* matadero
abba•cy ['æbəsi] *s* (*pl* **-cies**) abadía
abbess ['æbɪs] *s* abadesa
abbey ['æbi] *s* abadía
abbot ['æbət] *s* abad *m*
abbreviate [ə'brivɪ,et] *tr* abreviar
abbreviation [ə,brivɪ'eʃən] *s* (*shortening*) abreviación; (*shortened form*) abreviatura
A B C [,e,bi'si] *s* abecé *m;* **A B C's** abecedario
abdicate ['æbdɪ,ket] *tr & intr* abdicar
abdomen ['æbdəmən] o [æb'domən] *s* abdomen *m*
abduct [æb'dʌkt] *tr* raptar, secuestrar
abduction [æb'dʌkʃən] *s* rapto; secuestro
abed [ə'bɛd] *adv* en cama, acostado
aberration [,æbɛ'reʃən] *s* aberración; (*mind*) extravío
abet [ə'bɛt] *v* (*pret & pp* **abetted;** *ger* **abetting**) *tr* incitar (*a una persona, esp. al mal*); fomentar (*el crimen*)
abeyance [ə'be•əns] *s* suspensión; **in abeyance** en suspenso
ab•hor [æb'hɔr] *v* (*pret & pp* **-horred;** *get* **-horring**) *tr* aborrecer, detestar
abhorrence [əb'hɔrəns] *s* aversión; aborrecimiento
abhorrent [æb'hɔrənt] *adj* aborrecible, detestable
abide [ə'baɪd] *v* (*pret & pp* **abode** o **abided**) *tr* esperar; tolerar ‖ *intr* permanecer; **to abide by** cumplir con; atenerse a
abili•ty [ə'bɪlɪti] *s* (*pl* **-ties**) habilidad, capacidad; talento
abject [æb'dʒɛkt] *adj* abyecto, servil
abjure [æb'dʒur] *tr* abjurar
ablative ['æblətɪv] *s* ablativo
ablaut ['æblaʊt] *s* apofonía
ablaze [ə'blez] *adj* brillante; ardiente; encolerizado ‖ *adv* en llamas, ardiendo
able ['ebəl] *adj* hábil, capaz; **to be able to** poder
able-bodied ['ebəl'bɑdid] *adj* sano; fornido; experto
abloom [ə'blum] *adj* floreciente ‖ *adv* en flor
abnormal [æb'nɔrməl] *adj* anormal
aboard [ə'bord] *adv* a bordo; al bordo; **all aboard!** ¡señores viajeros al tren!; **to go aboard** ir a bordo; **to take aboard** embarcar ‖ *prep* a bordo de; (*a train*) en
abode [ə'bod] *s* domicilio, residencia
abolish [ə'bɑlɪʃ] *tr* eliminar, suprimir
abolition [,æbə'lɪʃən] *s* abolición
A-bomb ['e,bɑm] *s* bomba atómica
abominable [ə'bɑmɪnəbəl] *adj* abominable
abomination [ə',bɑmɪ'neʃən] *s* abominación
aborigines [,æbə'rɪdʒɪ,niz] *spl* aborígenes *mf*
abort [ə'bɔrt] *tr & intr* abortar
abortion [ə'bɔrʃən] *s* aborto
abortionist [ə'bɔrʃənɪst] *s* abortista *mf*
abound [ə'baʊnd] *intr* abundar
about [ə'baʊt] *adv* casi; aquí; **to be about to** estar a punto de, estar para ‖ *prep* acerca de; con respecto a; cerca de; hacia, a eso de; **to be about** tratar de
above [ə'bʌv] *adj* antedicho ‖ *adv* arriba, encima ‖ *prep* sobre, encima de, más alto que; superior a; **above all** sobre todo
above-mentioned [ə'bʌv'mɛnʃənd] *adj* sobredicho, antedicho, susodicho, prenombrado
abrasive [ə'bresɪv] o [ə'breziv] *adj & s* abrasivo
abreast [ə'brɛst] *adj & adv* de frente; **to be abreast of** correr parejas con; estar al corriente de
abridge [ə'brɪdʒ] *tr* abreviar; disminuir; condensar, resumir
abroad [ə'brɔd] *adv* al extranjero; en el extranjero; fuera de casa
abrupt [ə'brʌpt] *adj* brusco; repentino; áspero; abrupto, escarpado
abscess ['æbsɛs] *s* absceso
abscond [æb'skɑnd] *intr* irse a hurtadillas; **to abscond with** alzarse con
absence ['æbsəns] *s* ausencia
absent ['æbsənt] *adj* ausente ‖ [æb'sɛnt] *tr*—**to absent oneself** ausentarse

absentee [,æbsən'ti] *s* ausente *mf*
absent-minded ['æbsənt'maɪndɪd] *adj* distraído, absorto
absinth ['æbsɪnθ] *s* (*plant*) absintio, ajenjo; (*drink*) absenta, ajenjo
absolute ['æbsə,lut] *adj & s* absoluto
absolutely 'æbsə,lutli] *adv* absolutamente ‖ [,æbsə'lutli] *adv* (coll) positivamente
absolution ['æbsə'luʃən] *s* absolución
absolve [æb'sɑlv] *tr* absolver
absorb [æb'sɔrb] *tr* absorber; **to be** or **become absorbed** ensimismarse
absorbent [æb'sɔrbənt] *adj* absorbente; (*cotton*) hidrófilo
absorbing [æb'sɔrbɪŋ] *adj* absorbente
absorption [æb'sɔrpʃən] *s* abstracción; embebecimiento; absorción
abstain [æb'sten] *intr* abstenerse
abstemious [æb'stimɪ•əs] *adj* abstemio, sobrio
abstinent ['æbstɪnənt] *adj* abstinente
abstract ['æbstrækt] *adj* abstracto ‖ *s* resumen *m*, sumario, extracto ‖ *tr* resumir, compendiar, extractar ‖ [æb'strækt] *tr* abstraer; quitar
abstruse [æb'strus] *adj* abstruso
absurd [æb'sʌrd] o [æb'zʌrd] *adj* absurdo
absurdi•ty [æb'sʌrdɪti] o [æb'zʌrdɪti] *s* (*pl* **-ties**) absurdidad, absurdo
abundance [ə'bʌndəns] *s* abundancia, copia; (CAm) bastedad
abundant [ə'bʌndənt] *adj* abundante
abuse [ə'bjus] *s* maltrato; injuria, insulto; (*bad practice; injustice*) abuso ‖ [ə'bjuz] *tr* maltratar; injuriar, insultar; (*to misapply, take unfair advantage of*) abusar de
abusive [ə'bjusiv] *adj* injurioso, insultante; abusivo
abut [ə'bʌt] *v* (*pret & pp* **abutted;** *ger* **abutting**) *intr*—**to abut on** confinar con, terminar en
abutment [ə'bʌtmənt] *s* confinamiento; estribo, contrafuerte *m*
abyss [ə'bɪs] *s* abismo
academic [,ækə'dɛmɪk] *adj* académico
academic costume *s* toga, traje *m* de catedrático
academic freedom *s* libertad de cátedra, libertad de enseñanza
academician [ə,kædə'mɪʃən] *s* académico
academic subjects *spl* materias no profesionales
academic year *s* año escolar
acade•my [ə'kædəmi] *s* (*pl* **-mies**) academia
accede [æk'sid] *intr* acceder; **to accede to** acceder a, condescender a; (*e.g., the throne*) ascender a, subir a
accelerate [æk'sɛlə,ret] *tr* acelerar ‖ *intr* acelerarse
accelerator [æk'sɛlə,retər] *s* acelerador *m*
accent ['æksɛnt] *s* acento ‖ ['æksɛnt] o [æk'sɛnt] *tr* acentuar
accent mark *s* acento ortográfico
accentuate [æk'sɛntʃʊ,et] *tr* acentuar
accept [æk'sɛpt] *tr* aceptar
acceptable [æk'sɛptəbəl] *adj* aceptable
acceptance [æk'sɛptəns] *s* aceptación
access ['æksɛs] *s* acceso
accessible [æk'sɛsɪbəl] *adj* accesible
accession [æk'sɛʃən] *s* accesión; (*to a dignity*) ascenso; (*of books in a library*) adquisición
accesso•ry [æk'sɛsəri] *adj* accesorio ‖ *s* (*pl* **-ries**) accesorio; (*to a crime*) cómplice *mf*
accident ['æksɪdənt] *s* accidente *m;* **by accident** por casualidad
accidental [,æksɪ'dɛntəl] *adj* accidental
acclaim [ə'klem] *s* aclamación ‖ *tr & intr* aclamar
acclimate ['æklɪ,met] *tr* aclimatar ‖ *intr* aclimatarse
accolade [,ækə'led] *s* acolada; elogio, premio
accommodate [ə'kɑmə,det] *tr* acomodar; alojar
accommodating [ə'kɑmə,detɪŋ] *adj* acomodadizo, servicial
accommodation [ə,kɑmə'deʃən] *s* acomodación; **accommodations** facilidades, comodidades; (*in a train*) localidad; (*in a hotel*) alojamiento
accommodation train *s* tren *m* omnibus
accompaniment [ə'kʌmpənɪmənt] *s* acompañamiento
accompanist [ə'kʌmpənɪst] *s* acompañante *m*
accompa•ny [ə'kʌmpəni] *v* (*pret & pp* **-nied**) *tr* acompañar
accomplice [ə'kɑmplɪs] *s* cómplice *mf*, codelincuente *mf*
accomplish [ə'kɑmplɪʃ] *tr* realizar, llevar a cabo
accomplished [ə'kɑmplɪʃt] *adj* realizado; culto, talentoso; (*fact*) consumado
accomplishment [ə'kɑmplɪʃmənt] *s* realización; **accomplishments** prendas, talentos
accord [ə'kɔrd] *s* acuerdo; **in accord with** de acuerdo con: **of one's own accord** de buen grado, voluntariamente; **with one accord** de común acuerdo ‖ *tr* conceder, otorgar ‖ *intr* concordar, avenirse
accordance [ə'kɔrdəns] *s* conformidad; **in accordance with** de acuerdo con
according [ə'kɔrdɪŋ] *adj* — **according as** según que; **according to** según
accordingly [ə'kɔrdɪŋli] *adv* en conformidad; por consiguiente
accordion [ə'kɔrdɪ•ən] *s* acordeón *m;* filarmónica (Mex)
accost [ə'kɔst] o [ə'kɑst] *tr* abordar, acercarse a
accouchement [ə'kuʃmənt] *s* alumbramiento, parto
accoucheur [,æku'ʃʌr] *s* comadrón *m*
accoucheuse [,æku'ʃuz] *s* comadrona
account [ə'kaʊnt] *s* informe *m*, relato; cuenta; estado de cuenta; importancia; **by all accounts** según el decir general; **of no account** de poca importancia; **on account** como paga y señal; **on account of** a causa de; **to bring to account** pedir cuentas a; **to buy on account** comprar a plazos; **to turn to account** sacar provecho de, hacer valer

|| *intr*—**to account for** explicar; responder de
accountable [ə'kaUntəbəl] *adj* responsable; explicable
accountant [ə'kaUntənt] *s* contador *m*, contable *m*
accounting [ə'kaUntɪŋ] *s* arreglo de cuentas; contabilidad
accouterments [ə'kutərmənts] *spl* equipo, avíos
accredit [ə'krɛdɪt] *tr* acreditar
accrue [ə'kru] *intr* acumularse; resultar
acct. *abbr* **account**
accumulate [ə'kjumjə,let] *tr* acumular || *intr* acumularse
accuracy ['ækjərəsi] *s* exactitud, precisión
accurate ['ækjərɪt] *adj* exacto
accusation [,ækjə'zeʃən] *s* acusación
accusative [ə'kjuzətɪv] *adj & s* acusativo
accuse [ə'kjuz] *tr* acusar
accustom [ə'kʌstəm] *tr* acostumbrar
ace [es] *s* as *m;* **to be within an ace of** estar a dos dedos de
acetate ['æsɪ,tet] *s* acetato
acetic acid [ə'sitɪk] *s* ácido acético
aceti•fy [ə'sɛtɪ,faɪ] *v* (*pret & pp* **-fied**) *tr* acetificar || *intr* acetificarse
acetone ['æsɪ,ton] *s* acetona
acetylene [ə'sɛtɪ,lin] *s* acetileno
acetylene torch *s* soplete oxiacetilénico
ache [ek] *s* achaque *m*, dolor *m* || *int* doler
achieve [ə'tʃiv] *tr* llevar a cabo; alcanzar, ganar, lograr
achievement [ə'tʃivmənt] *s* realización; (*feat*) hazaña
Achilles' heel [ə'kɪliz] *s* talón *m* de Aquiles
acid ['æsɪd] *adj* ácido; agrio, mordaz || *s* ácido
acidi•fy [ə'sɪdɪ,faɪ] *v* (*pret & pp* **-fied**) *tr* acidificar || *intr* acidificarse
acidi•ty [ə'sɪdɪti] *s* (*pl* **-ties**) acidez *f*
acid rain *s* lluvia ácida
acid test *s* prueba decisiva
ack•ack ['æk'æk] *s* (slang) artillería antiaérea; (slang) fuego antiaéreo
acknowledge [æk'nɑlɪdʒ] *tr* reconocer; acusar (*recibo de una carta*); agradecer (*p.ej., un favor*)
acknowledgment [æk'nɑlɪdʒmənt] *s* reconocimiento; (*of receipt of a letter*) acuse *m;* (*of a favor*) agradecimiento
acme ['ækmi] *s* auge *m*, colmo
acne ['ækni] *s* acne *f*
acolyte ['ækə,laɪt] *s* acólito
acorn ['ekɔrn] o ['ekərn] *s* bellota
acoustic [ə'kustɪk] *adj* acústico || **acoustics** *ssg* acústica
acquaint [ə'kwent] *tr* informar, poner al corriente; **to be acquainted** conocerse; **to be acquainted with** conocer; estar al corriente de
acquaintance [ə'kwentəns] *s* conocimiento; (*person*) conocido
acquiesce [,ækwɪ'ɛs] *intr* consentir, condescender, asentir
acquiescence [,ækwɪ'ɛsəns] *s* consentimiento, condescendencia, aquiescencia
acquire [ə'kwaɪr] *tr* adquirir
acquired im•mune'-de•fi'cien•cy syndrome (AIDS) *s* síndrome *m* de inmunidad deficiente adquirida (SIDA)
acquired taste *s* gusto adquirido
acquisition [,ækwɪ'zɪʃən] *s* adquisición
acquit [ə'kwɪt] *v* (*pret & pp* **acquitted;** *ger* **acquitting**) *tr* absolver, exculpar; **to acquit oneself** conducirse, portarse
acquittal [ə'kwɪtəl] *s* absolución, exculpación
acrid ['ækrɪd] *adj* acre, acrimonioso
acrobat ['ækrə,bæt] *s* acróbata *mf*
acrobatic [,ækrə'bætɪk] *adj* acrobático || **acrobatics** *ssg* (*profession*) acrobatismo; *spl* (*stunts*) acrobacia
acronym ['ækrənɪm] *s* acrónimo
acropolis [ə'krɑpəlɪs] *s* acrópolis *f*
across [ə'krɔs] o [ə'krɑs] *prep* al través de; al otro lado de; **to come across** encontrarse con; **to go across** atravesar
across'-the-board' *adj* comprensivo, general
acrostic [ə'krɔstɪk] o [ə'krɑstɪk] *s* acróstico
act [ækt] *s* acto; (law) decreto; **in the act** en flagrante || *tr* representar; desempeñar (*un papel*); **to act the fool** hacer el bufón; **to act the part of** hacer o desempeñar el papel de || *intr* actuar; funcionar, obrar; conducirse; **to act as if** hacer como que; **to act for** representar; **to act up** travesear; **to act up to** hacer fiestas a
acting ['æktɪŋ] *adj* interino || *s* actuación
action ['ækʃən] *s* acción; **to take action** tomar medidas
activate ['æktɪ,vet] *tr* activar
active ['æktɪv] *adj* activo
activi•ty [æk'tɪvɪti] *s* (*pl* **-ties**) actividad
act of God *s* fuerza mayor
actor ['æktər] *s* actor *m*
actress ['æktrɪs] *s* actriz *f*
actual ['æktʃu•əl] *adj* real, efectivo
actually ['æktʃu•əli] *adv* en realidad
actuar•y ['æktʃu,ɛri] *s* (*pl* **-ies**) actuario (de seguros)
actuate ['æktʃu,et] *tr* actuar; estimular, mover
acuity [ə'kju•ɪti] *s* agudeza
acumen [ə'kjumən] *s* cacumen *m*, perspicacia
acupuncture ['ækjə,pʌŋktʃər] *s* acupuntura
acute [ə'kjut] *adj* agudo
A.D. *abbr* **anno Domini** (Lat) **in the year of our Lord**
ad [æd] *s* (coll) anuncio
adage ['ædɪdʒ] *s* adagio, refrán *m*
Adam ['ædəm] *s* Adán *m;* **the old Adam** la inclinación al pecado
adamant ['ædəmənt] *adj* firme, inexorable
Adam's apple *s* nuez *f*
adapt [ə'dæpt] *tr* adaptar; refundir (*un drama*)
adaptation [,ædæp'teʃən] *s* adaptación; (*of a play*) refundición
add [æd] *tr* agregar, añadir; sumar || *intr* sumar; **to add up to** subir a; (coll) querer decir
added line *s* (mus) línea suplementaria

adder [ˈædər] *s* víbora; serpiente *f*
addict [ˈædɪkt] *s* enviciado; adicto, partidario ‖ [əˈdɪkt] *tr* enviciar; entregar; **to addict oneself to** enviciarse con o en; entregarse a
addiction [əˈdɪkʃən] *s* enviciamiento; adhesividad
adding machine *s* sumadora, máquina de sumar
addition [əˈdɪʃən] *s* adición; **in addition** de pilón; **in addition to** además de
additive [ˈædɪtɪv] *adj & s* aditivo
address [əˈdrɛs] o [ˈædrɛs] *s* dirección; consignación ‖ [əˈdrɛs] *s* alocución, discurso; **to deliver an address** hacer uso de la palabra ‖ *tr* dirigirse a; dirigir (*p.ej., una alocución, una carta*); consignar
addressee [ˌædrɛˈsi] *s* destinatario; (com) consignatario
addressing machine *s* máquina para dirigir sobres
adduce [əˈdjus] o [əˈdus] *tr* aducir
adenoids [ˈædəˌnɔɪdz] *spl* vegetaciones adenoides
adept [əˈdɛpt] *adj & s* experto, perito
adequate [ˈædɪkwɪt] *adj* suficiente
adhere [ædˈhɪr] *intr* adherir, adherirse; conformarse
adherence [ædˈhɪrəns] *s* adhesión
adherent [ædˈhɪrənt] *adj & s* adherente *m*
adhesion [ædˈhiʒən] *s* (*sticking*) adherencia; (*support, loyalty*) adhesión; (pathol) adherencia; (phys) adherencia o adhesión
adhesive [ædˈhisɪv] *adj* adhesivo
adhesive tape *s* tafetán adhesivo
adieu [əˈdju] o [əˈdu] *interj* ¡adiós! ‖ *s* (*pl* **adieus** o **adieux**) adiós *m;* **to bid adieu to** desperdirse de
adjacent [əˈdʒesənt] *adj* adyacente
adjective [ˈædʒɪktɪv] *adj & s* adjetivo
adjoin [əˈdʒɔɪn] *tr* lindar con ‖ *intr* colindar
adjoining [əˈdʒɔɪnɪŋ] *adj* colindante, contiguo
adjourn [əˈdʒʌrn] *tr* prorrogar, suspender ‖ *intr* prorrogarse, suspenderse; (coll) ir
adjournment [əˈdʒʌrnmənt] *s* prorrogación, suspensión
adjust [əˈdʒʌst] *tr* ajustar, arreglar; corregir, verificar; (ins) liquidar
adjustable [əˈdʒʌstəbəl] *adj* ajustable, arreglable
adjustment [əˈdʒʌstmənt] *s* ajuste *m,* arreglo; (ins) liquidación de la avería
adjutant [ˈædʒətənt] *s* ayudante *m*
ad•lib [ˌædˈlɪb] *v* (*pret & pp* **-libbed;** *ger* **-libbing**) *tr & intr* improvisar
Adm. *abbr* **Admiral**
administer [ædˈministər] *tr* administrar; **to administer an oath** tomar juramento ‖ *intr* — **to administer to** cuidar de
administrator [ædˈmɪnɪsˌtretər] *s* administrador *m*
admiral [ˈædmɪrəl] *s* almirante *m;* buque *m* almirante
admiral•ty [ˈædmɪrəlti] *s* (*pl* **-ties**) almirantazgo
admire [ædˈmaɪr] *tr* admirar
admirer [ædˈmaɪrər] *s* admirador *m;* enamorado
admissible [ædˈmɪsɪbəl] *adj* admisible
admission [ædˈmɪʃən] *s* admisión; (*in a school*) ingreso; (*reception*) recibida; precio de entrada; **to gain admission** lograr entrar
ad•mit [ædˈmɪt] *v* (*pret & pp* **-mitted;** *ger* **-mitting**) *tr* admitir ‖ *intr* dar entrada; **to admit of** admitir, permitir
admittance [ædˈmɪtəns] *s* admisión; derecho de entrar; **no admittance** acceso prohibido, se prohibe la entrada
admonish [ædˈmɑnɪʃ] *tr* amonestar
ado [əˈdu] *s* bulla, excitación
adobe [əˈdobi] *s* adobe *m;* casa de adobe
adolescence [ˌædəˈlɛsəns] *s* adolescencia
adolescent [ˌædəˈlɛsənt] *adj & s* adolescente *mf*
adopt [əˈdɑpt] *tr* adoptar
adoption [əˈdɑpʃən] *s* adopción
adorable [əˈdorəbəl] *adj* adorable
adore [əˈdor] *tr* adorar
adorn [əˈdɔrn] *tr* adornar
adornment [əˈdɔrnmənt] *s* adorno
adrenal gland [ædˈrinəl] *s* glándula suprarrenal
Adriatic [ˌedrɪˈætɪk] *adj & s* Adriático
adrift [əˈdrɪft] *adj & adv* al garete, a la deriva
adroit [əˈdrɔɪt] *adj* diestro
adult [əˈdʌlt] o [ˈædʌlt] *adj & s* adulto
adulterate [əˈdʌltəˌret] *tr* adulterar
adulterer [əˈdʌltərər] *s* adúltero
adulteress [əˈdʌltərɪs] *s* adúltera
adulter•y [əˈdʌltəri] *s* (*pl* **-ies**) adulterio
adulthood [əˈdʌltˌhud] *s* adultez *f*
advance [ædˈvæns] *adj* adelantado; anticipado ‖ *s* adelanto, avance *m;* aumento, subida; **advances** propuestas; requerimiento amoroso; propuesta indecente; préstamo; **in advance** de antemano, por anticipado ‖ *tr* adelantar ‖ *intr* adelantar; adelantarse
advanced [ædˈvænst] *adj* avanzado; **advanced in years** avanzado de edad, entrado en años
advanced standing *s* traspaso de matrículas, traspaso de crédito académico
advanced studies *spl* altos estudios
advancement [ædˈvænsmənt] *s* adelanto, avance *m;* subida; promoción
advance publicity *s* publicadad de lanzamiento
advantage [ædˈvæntɪdʒ] *s* ventaja; lasca; **to take advantage of** aprovecharse de; abusar de, engañar
advantageous [ˌædvənˈtedʒəs] *adj* ventajoso
advent [ˈædvɛnt] *s* advenimiento ‖ **Advent** *s* (eccl) Adviento
adventure [ædˈvɛntʃər] *s* aventura ‖ *tr* aventurar ‖ *intr* aventurarse
adventurer [ædˈvɛntʃərər] *s* aventurero
adventuresome [ædˈvɛntʃərsəm] *adj* aventurero
adventuress [ædˈvɛntʃərɪs] *s* aventurera
adventurous [ædˈvɛntʃərəs] *adj* aventurero

adverb [ˈædvʌrb] *s* adverbio
adversar•y [ˈædvər,sɛri] *s* (*pl* **-ies**) adversario
adversi•ty [ædˈvʌrsɪti] *s* (*pl* **-ties**) adversidad
advertise [ˈædvər,taiz] *tr & intr* anunciar
advertisement [,ædvərˈtaɪzmənt] o [ædˈvʌrtɪzmənt] *s* anuncio
advertiser [ˈædvər,taɪzər] *s* anunciante *mf*
advertising [ˈædvər,taɪzɪŋ] *s* propaganda, publicidad, anuncios; reclame *m & f*
advertising agency *s* empresa anunciadora
advertising campaign *s* campaña de publicidad
advertising man *s* empresario de publicidad
advertising manager *s* gerente *m* de publicidad
advice [ædˈvaɪs] *s* consejo; aviso, noticia; **a piece of advice** un consejo
advisable [ædˈvaɪzəbəl] *adj* aconsejable
advise [ædˈvaɪz] *tr* aconsejar, asesorar; advertir, avisar
advisement [ædˈvaɪzmənt] *s* consideración; **to take under advisement** someter a consideración
advisory [ædˈvaɪʒəri] *adj* consultivo
advocate [ˈædvə,ket] *s* defensor *m;* abogado ‖ *tr* abogar por
Aegean Sea [ɪˈdʒi•ən] *s* Archipiélago; (*of the ancients*) mar Egeo
aegis [ˈidʒɪs] *s* égida
aerate [ˈɛret] o [ˈe•ə,ret] *tr* airear
aerial [ˈɛrɪ•əl] *adj* aéreo ‖ *s* antena
aerialist [ˈɛrɪ•əlɪst] *s* volatinero
aerial photograph *s* fotografía aérea
aerodrome [ˈɛrə,drom] *s* aeródomo
aerodynamic [,ɛrodaɪˈnæmɪk] *adj* aerodinámico ‖ **aerodynamics** *ssg* aerodinámica
aeronaut [ˈɛrə,nɔt] *s* aeronauta *mf*
aeronautic [,ɛrəˈnɔtɪk] *adj* aeronáutico ‖ **aeronautics** *ssg* aeronáutica
aerosol [ˈɛrə,sol] *s* aerosol *m*
aerospace [ˈɛro,spes] *adj* aeroespacial
aesthete [ˈɛsθit] *s* esteta *mf*
aesthetic [ɛsˈθɛtɪk] *adj* estético ‖ **aesthetics** *ssg* estética
afar [əˈfar] *adv* lejos
affable [ˈæfəbəl] *adj* afable
affair [əˈfɛr] *s* asunto, negocio; lance *m;* amorío; encuentro, combate *m;* **affairs** negocios
affect [əˈfɛkt] *tr* influir en; impresionar, enternecer; (*to assume; to pretend*) afectar; aficionarse a
affectation [,æfɛkˈteʃən] *s* afectación
affected [əˈfɛktɪd] *adj* afectado
affection [əˈfɛkʃən] *s* afecto, cariño, afección; (pathol) afección
affectionate [əˈfɛkʃənɪt] *adj* afectuoso, cariñoso
affidavit [,æfɪˈdevɪt] *s* declaración jurada, acta notarial
affiliate [əˈfɪlɪ,et] *adj* afiliado ‖ *s* afiliado; filial *f* ‖ *tr* afiliar ‖ *intr* afiliarse
affini•ty [əˈfɪnɪti] *s* (*pl* **-ties**) afinidad
affirm [əˈfʌrm] *tr & intr* afirmar
affirmative [əˈfʌrmətɪv] *adj* afirmativo ‖ *s* afirmativa
affix [ˈæfɪks] *s* añadidura; (gram) afijo ‖ [əˈfɪks] *tr* añadir; atribuir (*p.ej., culpa*); poner (*una firma, sello, etc.*)
afflict [əflɪkt] *tr* afligir; **to be afflicted with** sufrir de, adolecer de
affliction [əˈflɪkʃən] *s* aflicción, desgracia; achaque *m*
affluence [ˈæflʊ•əns] *s* (*abundance*) afluencia; (*wealth*) opulencia
afford [əˈfɔrd] *tr* proporcionar; **to be able to afford (to)** poder darse el lujo de, poder permitirse
affray [əˈfre] *s* pendencia, riña
affront [əˈfrʌnt] *s* afrenta ‖ *tr* afrentar
Afghan [ˈæfgæn] *adj & s* afgano
Afghanistan [æfˈgænɪ,stæn] *s* el Afganistán
afire [əˈfaɪr] *adj & adv* ardiendo
aflame [əˈflem] *adj & adv* en llamas
afloat [əˈflot] *adj & adv* a flote; a bordo; inundado; sin rumbo; (*rumor*) en circulación
afoot [əˈfʊt] *adj & adv* a pie; en marcha
afoul [əˈfaʊl] *adj & adv* enredado; en colisión; **to run afoul of** enredarse con
afraid [əˈfred] *adj* asustado; **to be afraid** tener miedo
Africa [ˈæfrɪkə] *s* Africa
African [ˈæfrɪkən] *adj & s* africano
aft [æft] *adj & adv* en popa
after [ˈæftər] *adj* siguiente ‖ *adv* después ‖ *prep* después de; según; **after all** al fin y al cabo ‖ *conj* después de que
af'ter-din'ner speaker *s* orador *m* de sobremesa
after-dinner speech *s* discurso de sobremesa
af'ter•hours' *adv* después del trabajo
af'ter•life' *s* vida venidera; resto de la vida
aftermath [ˈæftər,mæθ] *s* segunda siega; consecuencias, consecuencias desastrosas
af'ter•noon' *s* tarde *f*
af'ter•shave' lotion *s* loción facial
af'ter•taste' *s* dejo, gustillo, resabio
af'ter•thought' *s* idea tardía, expediente tardío
afterward [ˈæftəwərd] *adv* después, luego
af'ter•while' *adv* dentro de poco
again [əˈgɛn] *adv* otra vez, de nuevo; además; **to** + *inf* + **again** volver a + *inf*, p.ej., **he will come again** volverá a venir
against [əˈgɛnst] *prep* contra; cerca de; en contraste con; por; para
agape [əˈgep] *adj* abierto de par en par ‖ *adv* con la boca abierta
agave [əˈgavi] *s* agave *f*
agave brandy *s* pulque *m* (Mex)
agave liquor *s* mexcal *m,* mezcal *m*
age [edʒ] *s* edad; (*old age*) vejez *f;* (*one hundred years; a long time*) siglo; edad mental; **of age** mayor de edad; **to come of age** alcanzar su mayoría de edad, llegar a mayor edad; **under age** menor de edad ‖ *tr* envejecer ‖ *intr* envejecer, envejecerse
age bracket *s* grupo de personas de la misma edad
aged [edʒd] *adj* de la edad de ‖ [ˈedʒɪd] *adj* anciano, viejo

ageism [ˈedʒɪzəm] *s* discriminación contra los ancianos
ageless [ˈedʒlɪs] *adj* eternamente joven
agen•cy [ˈedʒənsi] *s* (*pl* **-cies**) agencia; mediación
agenda [əˈdʒɛndə] *s* agenda, temario
agent [ˈədʒənt] *s* agente *m*
Age of Enlightenment *s* siglo de las luces
agglomeration [ə,glɑməˈreʃən] *s* aglomeración
aggrandizement [əˈgrændɪzmənt] *s* engrandecimiento
aggravate [ˈægrə,vet] *tr* agravar; (coll) exasperar, irritar
aggregate [ˈægrɪ,get] *adj* & *s* agregado || *tr* agregar, juntar; ascender a
aggression [əˈgrɛʃən] *s* agresión
aggressive [əˈgrɛsɪv] *adj* agresivo
aggressor [əˈgrɛsər] *s* agresor *m*
aghast [əˈgæst] *adj* horrorizado
agile [ˈædʒɪl] *adj* ágil
agitate [ˈædʒɪ,tet] *tr* & *intr* agitar
aglow [əˈglo] *adj* & *adv* fulgurante
agnostic [ægˈnɑstɪk] *adj* & *s* agnóstico
ago [əˈgo] *adv* hace, p.ej., **two days ago** hace dos días
ago•ny [ˈægəni] *s* (*pl* **-nies**) angustia, congoja; (*anguish; death struggle*) agonía
agrarian [əˈgrɛrɪ•ən] *adj* agrario || *s* agrariense *mf*
agree [əˈgri] *intr* estar de acuerdo, ponerse de acuerdo; sentar bien; (gram) concordar
agreeable [əˈgri•əbəl] *adj* (*to one's liking*) agradable; (*willing to consent*) acorde, conforme
agreement [əˈgrimənt] *s* acuerdo, convenio; concordancia; **in agreement** de acuerdo
agric. *abbr* **agriculture**
agriculture [ˈægrɪ,kʌltʃər] *s* agricultura
agronomy [əˈgrɑnəmi] *s* agronomía
aground [əˈgraʊnd] *adv* encallado, varado; **to run aground** encallar, varar
agt. *abbr* **agent**
ague [ˈegju] *s* escalofrío; fiebre *f* intermitente
ahead [əˈhɛd] *adj* & *adv* delante, al frente; **ahead of** antes de; delante de; al frente de; **to get ahead (of)** adelantarse (a)
ahoy [əˈhɔɪ] *interj* — **ship ahoy!** ¡ah del barco!
aid [ed] *s* ayuda, auxilio; (mil) ayudante *m* || *tr* ayudar, auxiliar; **to aid and abet** auxiliar e incitar, ser cómplice de || *intr* ayudar
aide [ed] *s* ayudante *m;* (mil) edecán *m*
aide-de-camp [ˈeddəˈkæmp] *s* (*pl* **aides-de-camp**) ayudante *m* de campo, edecán *m*
AIDS [edz] *abbr* **acquired immune-deficiency syndrome**
ail [el] *tr* inquietar; **what ails you?** ¿qué tiene Vd.? || *intr* sufrir, estar enfermo
aileron [ˈelə,rɑn] *s* alerón *m*
ailing [ˈelɪŋ] *adj* enfermo, achacoso
ailment [ˈelmənt] *s* enfermedad, achaque *m*
aim [em] *s* puntería; intento; punto de mira || *tr* apuntar, encarar; dirigir (*p.ej., una observación*) || *intr* apuntar
air [ɛr] *s* aire *m;* **by air** por vía aérea; **in the open air** al aire libre; **on the air** en antena, en la radio; **to let the air out of** desinflar; **to put on airs** darse aires; **to put on the air** llevar a las antenas; **to walk on air** no pisar en el suelo || *tr* airear, ventilar; radiodifundir; (fig) ventilar
air'-a•tom'ic *adj* aeroatómico
air bag *s* (aut) globo de aire, bolsa de aire
air'borne' *adj* aerotransportado
air brake *s* freno de aire comprimido
air castle *s* castillo en el aire
air'-condi'tion *tr* climatizar
air conditioner *s* acondicionador *m* de aire
air conditioning *s* acondicionamiento del aire, clima *m* artificial, climatización
air corps *s* cuerpo de aviación
air'craft' *ssg* máquina de volar; *spl* máquinas de volar
aircraft carrier *s* portaaviones *m*
airdrome [ˈɛr,drom] *s* aeródromo
air'drop' *s* lanzamiento || *tr* lanzar
air field *s* campo de aviación
air'foil' *s* superficie *f* de sustentación
air force *s* fuerza aérea, ejército del aire
air gap *s* (phys) entrehierro
air'-ground' *adj* aeroterrestre
air hostess *s* aeromoza, azafata
air humidifier *s* humidificador *m*
air lane *s* ruta aérea
air'lift' *s* puente aéreo
air liner *s* transaéreo, avión *m* de travesía
air mail *s* correo aéreo, aeroposta
air'-mail' letter *s* carta aérea, carta por avión
air-mail pilot *s* aviador *m* postal
air-mail stamp *s* sello aéreo
air•man [ˈɛrmən] *s* (*pl* **-men** [mən]) aviador *m*
air'plane' *s* avión *m*, aparato
airplane carrier *s* portaaviones *m*
air pocket *s* bache aéreo
air pollution *s* contaminación atmosférica
air'port' *s* aeropuerto
air raid *s* ataque aéreo
air'-raid' drill *s* simulacro de ataque aéreo
air-raid shelter *s* abrigo antiaéreo
air-raid warning *s* alarma aérea
air rifle *s* escopeta de viento, escopeta de aire comprimido
air'ship' *s* aeronave *f*
air'sick' *adj* mareado en el aire
air'sick'ness *s* mal *m* de vuelo
air sleeve o **sock** *s* veleta de manga
air'strip' *s* pista de despegue, pista de aterrizaje
air taxi *s* aerotaxi *m*
air'tight' *adj* herméticamente cerrado, estanco al aire
air'-traff'ic controller *s* controlador aéreo
air'waves' *spl* ondas de radio
air'way' *s* aerovía, vía aérea
airway lighting *s* balizaje *m*
air•y [ˈɛri] *adj* (*comp* **-ier;** *super* **-iest**) airoso; aireado; alegre; impertinente; (coll) afectado
aisle [aɪl] *s* (*in theater, movie, etc.*) pasillo; (*in a store, factory, etc.*) nave *f;* (archit) nave *f* lateral; (*any of the long passageways of a church*) (archit) nave *f*

ajar [ə'dʒɑr] *adj* entreabierto, entornado
akimbo [ə'kɪmbo] *adj & adv* — **with arms akimbo** en jarras
akin [ə'kɪn] *adj* emparentado; semejante
alabaster ['ælə,bæstər] *s* alabastro
alarm [ə'lɑrm] *s* alarma ‖ *tr* alarmar
alarm clock *s* reloj *m* despertador
alarmist [ə'lɑrmɪst] *s* alarmista *mf*
alas [ə'læs] o [ə'lɑs] *interj* ¡ay!, ¡ay de mí!
Albanian [æl'benɪ•ən] *adj & s* albanés *m*
albatross ['ælbə,trɔs] o ['ælbə,trɑs] *s* albatros *m*
album ['ælbəm] *s* álbum *m*
albumen [æl'bjumən] *s* albumen *m;* albúmina
alchemy ['ælkɪmi] *s* alquimia
alcohol ['ælkə,hɔl] o ['ælkə,hɑl] *s* alcohol *m*
alcoholic [,ælkə'hɔlɪk] o [,ælkə'hɑlɪk] *adj & s* alcohólico
al'co•hol-lev'el test *s* prueba de alcohol
alcove ['ælkov] *s* gabinete *m*, rincón *m;* (*in a bedroom*) trasalcoba; (*in a garden*) cenador *m*
alder ['ɔldər] *s* aliso
alder•man ['ɔldərmən] *s* (*pl* **-men** [mən]) concejal *m*
ale [el] *s* ale *f* (*cerveza inglesa, obscura, espesa y amarga*)
alembic [ə'lɛmbɪk] *s* alambique *m*
alert [ə'lʌrt] *adj* listo, vivo; vigilante ‖ *s* (aer) alarma; (mil) alerta *m;* **to be on the alert** estar sobre aviso, estar alerta ‖ *tr* alertar
Aleutian Islands [ə'luʃən] *spl* islas Aleutas, islas Aleutianas
Alexandrine [,ælɪg'zændrɪn] *adj & s* alejandrino
alg. *abbr* **algebra**
algae ['ældʒi] *spl* algas
algebra ['ældʒɪbrə] *s* álgebra
algebraic [,ældʒɪ'bre•ɪk] *adj* algebraico
Algeria [æl'dʒɪrɪ•ə] *s* Argelia
Algerian [æl'dʒɪrɪ•ən] *adj & s* argelino
Algiers [æl'dʒɪrz] *s* Argel *f*
alias ['elɪ•əs] *adv* alias ‖ *s* alias *m*, nombre supuesto
ali•bi ['ælɪ,baɪ] *s* (*pl* **-bis**) coartada; (coll) excusa
alien ['elɪ•ən] *adj & s* extranjero
alienate ['eljə,net] o ['elɪ•ə,net] *tr* enajenar, alienar; desenamorar
alight [ə'laɪt] *v* (*pret & pp* **alighted** o **alit** [ə'lɪt]) *intr* bajar, apearse; posarse (*un ave*)
align [ə'laɪn] *tr* alinear ‖ *intr* alinearse
alike [ə'laɪk] *adj* semejantes; **to look alike** parecerse ‖ *adv* igualmente
alimentary canal [,ælɪ'mɛntəri] *s* canal alimenticio, tubo digestivo
alimony ['ælɪ,moni] *s* alimentos
alive [ə'laɪv] *adj* vivo, viviente; animado; **alive to** despierto para, sensible a; **alive with** hormigueante en
alka•li ['ælkə,laɪ] *s* (*pl* **-lis** o **-lies**) álcali *m*
alkaline ['ælkə,laɪn] *adj* alcalino
all [ɔl] *adj indef* todo, todos; todo el, todos los ‖ *pron indef* todo; todos, todo el mundo; **after all** sin embargo; **all of** todo el, todos los; **all that** todo lo que, todos los que; **for all I know** que yo sepa; a lo mejor; **not at all** nada; no hay de qué ‖ *adv* enteramente; **all along** desde el principio; a lo largo de; **all at once** de golpe; **all right** bueno, corriente; **all too** excesivamente
Allah ['ælə] *s* Alá *m*
allay [ə'le] *tr* aliviar, calmar
all-clear ['ɔl'klɪr] *s* cese *m* de alarma
allege [ə'lɛdʒ] *tr* alegar
allegiance [ə'lidʒəns] *s* fidelidad, lealtad; homenaje *m;* **to swear allegiance to** jurar fidelidad a; rendir homenaje a
allegoric(al) [,ælɪ'gɑrɪk(əl)] o [,ælɪ'gɔrɪk(əl)] *adj* alegórico
allego•ry ['ælɪ,gori] *s* (*pl* **-ries**) alegoría
aller•gy ['ælərdʒi] *s* (*pl* **-gies**) alergia
alleviate [ə'livɪ,et] *tr* aliviar
alleviation [ə,livɪ'eʃən] *s* aligeramiento
alley ['æli] *s* callejuela; paseo arbolado, paseo de jardín; (bowling) pista; (tennis) espacio lateral
All Fools' Day *s* var of **April Fools' Day**
Allhallows [,ɔl'hæloz] *s* día *m* de todos los santos
alliance [ə'laɪ•əns] *s* alianza
alligator ['ælɪ,getər] *s* caimán *m*
alligator pear *s* aguacate *m*
alligator wrench *s* llave *f* de mandíbulas dentadas
alliteration [ə,lɪtə'reʃən] *s* aliteración
all-knowing ['ɔl'no•ɪŋ] *adj* omnisciente
allocate ['ælə,ket] *tr* asignar, distribuir
allot [ə'lɑt] *v* (*pret & pp* **allotted;** *ger* **allotting**) *tr* asignar, distribuir
all'-out' *adj* acérrimo
allow [ə'lau] *tr* dejar, permitir; admitir; conceder ‖ *intr* — **to allow for** tener en cuenta; **to allow of** permitir; admitir
allowance [ə'lau•əns] *s* permiso; concesión; ración; descuento, rebaja; tolerancia; **to make allowance for** tener en cuenta
alloy ['ælɔɪ] o [ə'lɔɪ] *s* aleación, liga ‖ [ə'lɔɪ] *tr* alear, ligar
all'-pow'er•ful *adj* todopoderoso
all'-pur'pose *adj* universal, para todo uso
All Saints' Day *s* día *m* de todos los santos
All Souls' Day *s* día *m* de los difuntos
allspice ['ɔl,spaɪs] *s* pimienta inglesa
all'-star' game *s* (sport) juego de estrellas
allude [ə'lud] *intr* aludir
allure [ə'lur] *s* tentación, encanto, fascinación ‖ *tr* tentar, encantar
alluring [ə'lurɪŋ] *adj* tentador, encantador, fascinante
allusion [ə'luʒən] *s* alusión
all'-weath'er *adj* para todo tiempo
al•ly ['ælaɪ] o [ə'laɪ] *s* (*pl* **-lies**) aliado ‖ [ə'laɪ] *v* (*pret & pp* **-lied**) *tr* aliar ‖ *intr* aliarse
almanac ['ɔlmə,næk] *s* almanaque *m*
almighty [ɔl'maɪti] *adj* todopoderoso, omnipotente
almond ['ɑmənd] o ['æmənd] *s* almendra
almond brittle *s* crocante *m*
almond tree *s* almendro
almost ['ɔlmost] o [ɔl'most] *adv* casi

alms [amz] *s* limosna
alms'house' *s* casa de beneficencia
aloe ['ælo] *s* áloe *m*
aloft [ə'lɔft] o [ə'lɑft] *adv* arriba; (aer) en vuelo; (naut) en la arboladura
alone [ə'lon] *adj* solo; **let alone** sin mencionar; y mucho menos; **to let alone** no molestar; no mezclarse en || *adv* solamente
along [ə'lɔŋ] o [ə'lɑŋ] *adv* conmigo, consigo, etc.; **all along** desde el principio; **along with** junto con || *prep* a lo largo de
along'side' *adv* a lo largo; (naut) al costado; **to bring alongside** acostar || *prep* a lo largo de; (naut) al costado de
aloof [ə'luf] *adj* apartado; reservado || *adv* lejos, a distancia
aloud [ə'laʊd] *adv* alto, en voz alta
alphabet ['ælfə,bɛt] *s* alfabeto
alpine ['ælpaɪn] *adj* alpestre, alpino
Alps [ælps] *spl* Alpes *mpl*
already [ɔl'rɛdi] *adv* ya
Alsace [æl'ses] o ['ælsæs] *s* Alsacia
Alsatian [æl'seʃən] *adj & s* alsaciano
also ['ɔlso] *adv* también
alt. *abbr* **alternate, altitude**
altar ['ɔltər] *s* altar *m;* **to lead to the altar** conducir al altar
altar boy *s* acólito, monaguillo
altar cloth *s* sabanilla, palia
al'tar•piece' *s* retablo
altar rail *s* comulgatorio
alter ['ɔltər] *tr* alterar || *intr* alterarse
alteration [,ɔltə'reʃən] *s* alteración; (*in a building*) reforma; (*in clothing*) arreglo
alternate ['ɔltərnɪt] o ['æltərnɪt] *adj* alterno || ['ɔltər,net] o ['æltər,net] *tr & intr* alternar
alternating current *s* corriente alterna o alternativa
although [ɔl'ðo] *conj* aunque
altimetry [æl'tɪmɪtri] *s* altimetría
altitude ['æltɪ,tjud] *s* altitud, altura
al•to ['ælto] *s* (*pl* **-tos**) contralto
altogether [,ɔltə'gɛðər] *adv* enteramente; en conjunto
altruist ['æltrʊ•ɪst] *s* altruísta *mf*
altruistic [,æltrʊ'ɪstɪk] *adj* altruísta
alum ['æləm] *s* alumbre *m*
aluminum [ə'lumɪnəm] *s* aluminio
alum•na [ə'lʌmnə] *s* (*pl* **-nae** [ni]) graduada
alum•nus [ə'lʌmnəs] *s* (*pl* **-ni** [naɪ]) graduado
alveo•lus [æl'vi•ələs] *s* (*pl* **-li** [,laɪ]) **alvéolo**
always ['ɔlwɪz] o ['ɔlwez] *adv* siempre
A.M. *abbr* **ante meridiem,** i.e., **before noon; amplitude modulation**
Am. *abbr* **America, American**
amalgam [ə'mælgəm] *s* amalgama *f*
amalgamate [ə'mælgə,met] *tr* amalgamar || *intr* amalgamarse
amass [ə'mæs] *tr* amontonar; amasar (*dinero*)
amateur ['æmətʃər] *adj & s* chapucero, principiante *mf;* aficionado
amateur performance *s* función de aficionados
amaze [ə'mez] *tr* asombrar, maravillar
amazing [ə'mezɪŋ] *adj* asombroso, maravilloso
Amazon ['æmə,zɑn] *s* Amazonas *m*
ambassador [æm'bæsədər] *s* embajador *m*
ambassadress [æm'bæsədrɪs] *s* embajadora
amber ['æmbər] *adj* ambarino || *s* ámbar *m*
ambigui•ty [,æmbɪ'gju•ɪti] *s* (*pl* **-ties**) ambigüedad
ambiguous [æm'bɪgju•əs] *adj* ambiguo
ambition [æm'bɪʃən] *s* ambición
ambitious [æm'bɪʃəs] *adj* ambicioso
amble ['æmbəl] *s* ambladura || *intr* amblar
ambulance ['æmbjələns] *s* ambulancia
ambush ['æmbʊʃ] *s* emboscada; **to lie in ambush** estar emboscado || *tr* (*to station in ambush*) emboscar; (*to lie in wait for and attack*) insidiar || *intr* emboscarse
ame•ba [ə'mibə] *s* (*pl* **-bas** o **-bae** [bi]) amiba
amelioration [ə,miljə'reʃən] *s* mejoramiento
amen ['e'mɛn] o ['a'mɛn] *interj* ¡amén! || *s* amén *m*
amenable [ə'minəbəl] o [ə'mɛnəbəl] *adj* dócil; responsable
amend [ə'mɛnd] *tr* enmendar || *intr* enmendarse || **amends** *spl* enmienda; **to make amends for** enmendar
amendment [ə'mɛndmənt] *s* enmienda
ameni•ty [ə'minɪti] o [ə'mɛnɪti] *s* (*pl* **-ties**) amenidad
America [ə'mɛrɪkə] *s* América
American [ə'mɛrɪkən] *adj & s* americano; norteamericano, estadounidense
Americanize [ə'mɛrɪkə,naɪz] *tr* americanizar
amethyst ['æmɪθɪst] *s* amatista
amiable ['emɪ•əbəl] *adj* amable, bonachón
amicable ['æmɪkəbəl] *adj* amigable
amid [ə'mɪd] *prep* en medio de
amidship [ə'mɪdʃɪp] *adv* en medio del navío
amiss [ə'mɪs] *adj* inoportuno; malo || *adv* inoportunamente; mal; **to take amiss** llevar a mal, tomar en mala parte
ami•ty ['æmɪti] *s* (*pl* **-ties**) amistad
ammeter ['æm,mitər] *s* anmetro, amperímetro
ammonia [ə'monɪ•ə] *s* amoníaco; agua amoniacal
ammunition [,æmjə'nɪʃən] *s* munición
amnes•ty ['æmnɪsti] *s* (*pl* **-ties**) amnistía || *v* (*pret & pp* **-tied**) *tr* amnistiar
amniocentesis [,æmnɪ•osen'tisɪs] *s* amniocentesis *f*
amoeba [ə'mibə] *s* var of **ameba**
among [ə'mʌŋ] *prep* entre, en medio de, en el número de
amorous ['æmərəs] *adj* amoroso; erótico, sensual, voluptuoso
amortize ['æmər,taɪz] *tr* amortizar
amount [ə'maʊnt] *s* cantidad, importe *m* || *intr* — **to amount to** ascender a; significar
amp. *abbr* **ampere, amperage**
ampere ['æmpɪr] *s* amperio
am'pere-hour' *s* amperio-hora *m*
amphibious [æm'fɪbɪ•əs] *adj* anfibio
amphitheater ['æmfɪ,θi•ətər] *s* anfiteatro
ample ['æmpəl] amplio; bastante, suficiente; abundante
amplifier ['æmplɪ,faɪ•ər] *s* amplificador *m*

ampli•fy ['æmplɪ,faɪ] *v* (*pret & pp* **-fied**) *tr* amplificar ‖ *intr* espaciarse
amplitude ['æmplɪ,tjud] *s* amplitud
amplitude modulation *s* modulación de amplitud
ampule ['æmpjul] *s* inyectable *m*
amputate ['æmpjə,tet] *tr* amputar
amt. *abbr* **amount**
amuck [ə'mʌk] *adv* frenéticamente; **to run amuck** atacar a ciegas
amulet ['æmjəlɪt] *s* amuleto
amuse [ə'mjuz] *tr* divertir, entretener
amusement [ə'mjuzmənt] *s* diversión, entretenimiento; pasatiempo, recreación; (*in a park or circus*) atracción
amusement park *s* parque *m* de atracciones
amusing [ə'mjuzɪŋ] *adj* divertido, gracioso
an [æn] o [ən] *art indef* (antes de sonido vocal) un
anachronism [ə'nækrə,nɪzəm] *s* anacronismo
anachronistic [ə,nækrə'nɪstɪk] *adj* anacrónico
anaemia [ə'nimɪ•ə] *s* anemia
anaemic [ə'nimɪk] *adj* anémico
anaesthesia [,ænɪs'θiʒə] *s* anestesia
anaesthetic [,ænɪs'θɛtik] *adj & s* anestésico
anaesthetize [æ'nɛsθɪ,taɪz] *tr* anestesiar
analogous [ə'næləgəs] *adj* análogo
analo•gy [ə'nælədʒi] *s* (*pl* **-gies**) analogía
analyse ['ænə,laɪz] *tr* analizar
analy•sis [ə'nælɪsɪs] *s* (*pl* **-ses** [,siz]) análisis *m & f*
analyst ['ænəlɪst] *s* analista *mf*
analytic(al) [,ænə'lɪtɪk(əl)] *adj* analítico
analyze ['ænə,laɪz] *tr* analizar
anarchist ['ænərkɪst] *s* anarquista *mf*
anarchy ['ænərki] *s* anarquía
anathema [ə'næθɪmə] *s* anatema *m & f*
anatomic(al) [,ænə'tɑmɪk(əl)] *adj* anatómico
anato•my [ə'nætəmi] *s* (*pl* **-mies**) anatomía
ancestor ['ænsɛstər] *s* antecesor *m*, antepasado
ances•try ['ænsɛstri] *s* (*pl* **-tries**) abolengo, alcurnia
anchor ['æŋkər] *s* ancla, áncora; (fig) áncora; **to cast anchor** echar anclas; **to weigh anchor** levar anclas ‖ *tr* sujetar con el ancla ‖ *intr* anclar, ancorar
ancho•vy ['æntʃovi] *s* (*pl* **-vies**) anchoa
ancient ['enʃənt] *adj* antiguo
and [ænd] o [ənd] *conj* y; **and so forth** y así sucesivamente
Andalusia [,ændə'luʒə] *s* Andalucía
Andalusian [,ændə'luʒən] *adj & s* andaluz *m*
Andean [æn'di•ən] *adj & s* andino
Andes ['ændiz] *spl* Andes *mpl*
andirons ['ænd,aɪ•ərnz] *spl* morillos
anecdote ['ænɪk,dot] *s* anécdota
anemia [ə'nimɪ•ə] *s* anemia
anemic [ə'nimɪk] *adj* anémico
aneroid barometer ['ænə,rɔɪd] *s* barómetro aneroide
anesthesia [,ænɪs'θiʒə] *s* anestesia
anesthetic [,ænɪs'θɛtɪk] *adj & s* anestésico
anesthetize [æ'nɛsθɪ,taɪz] *tr* anestesiar
aneurysm ['ænjə,rɪzəm] *s* aneurisma *m*
anew [ə'nju] o [ə'nu] *adv* de nuevo, nuevamente
angel ['endʒəl] *s* ángel *m;* (*financial backer*) caballo blanco
angelic(al) [æn'dʒɛlɪk(əl)] *adj* angélico, angelical
anger ['æŋgər] *s* cólera, ira ‖ *tr* encolerizar, airar
angina pectoris [æñ'dʒainə 'pɛktərɪs] *s* angina de pecho
angle ['æŋgəl] *s* ángulo; punto de vista ‖ *intr* pescar con caña; intrigar
angle iron *s* ángulo de hierro, hierro angular
angler ['æŋglər] *s* pescador *m* de caña; intrigante *mf*
Anglo-Saxon [,æŋglo'sæksən] *adj & s* anglosajón *m*
an•gry ['æŋgri] *adj* (*comp* **-grier;** *super* **-griest**) encolerizado, airado; (pathol) inflamado, irritado; **to become angry at** enojarse de; **to become angry with** enojarse con o contra
anguish ['æŋgwɪʃ] *s* angustia, congoja
angular ['æŋgjələr] *adj* angular; (*features*) anguloso
anhydrous [æn'haɪdrəs] *adj* anhidro
aniline dyes ['ænɪlɪn] o ['ænɪ,laɪn] *s* colores *mpl* de anilina
animal ['ænɪməl] *adj & s* animal *m*
animal spirits *spl* ardor *m*, vigor *m*, vivacidad
animated cartoon ['ænɪ,metɪd] *s* película de dibujos, dibujo animado
animation [,ænɪ'meʃən] *s* animación
animosi•ty [,ænɪ'mɑsɪti] *s* (*pl* **-ties**) animosidad
anion ['æn,aɪ•ən] *s* anión *m*
anise ['ænɪs] *s* anís *m*
aniseed ['ænɪ,sid] *s* grano de anís
anisette [,ænɪ'zɛt] *s* anisete *m*
ankle ['æŋkəl] *s* tobillo
an'kle•bone' *s* hueso del tobillo
ankle support *s* tobillera
anklet ['æŋklɪt] *s* ajorca; (*sock*) tobillera
annals ['ænəlz] *spl* anales *mpl*
anneal [ə'nil] *tr* recocer
annex ['ænɛks] *s* anexo; (*of a building*) pabellón *m* ‖ [ə'nɛks] *tr* anexar
annihilate [ə'naɪ•ɪ,let] *tr* aniquilar
anniversa•ry [,ænɪ'vʌrsəri] *adj* aniversario ‖ *s* (*pl* **-ries**) aniversario
annotate ['ænə,tet] *tr* anotar
announce [ə'naʊns] *tr* anunciar
announcement [ə'naʊnsmənt] *s* anuncio
announcer [ə'naʊnsər] *s* anunciador *m;* (rad) locutor *m*
annoy [ə'nɔɪ] *tr* fastidiar, molestar; majaderear; pololear; (Cuba, Mex) ciscar
annoyance [ə'nɔɪ•əns] *s* fastidio, molestia
annoying [ə'nɔɪ•ɪŋ] *adj* fastidioso, molesto
annual ['ænjʊ•əl] *adj* anual ‖ *s* publicación anual; planta anual
annui•ty [ə'nju•ɪti] o [ə'nu•ɪti] *s* (*pl* **-ties**) anualidad; renta vitalicia
an•nul [ə'nʌl] *v* (*pret & pp* **-nulled;** *ger* **-nulling**) *tr* anular, invalidar
anode ['ænod] *s* ánodo

anoint [ə'nɔɪnt] *tr* ungir, untar
anomalous [ə'nɑmələs] *adj* anómalo
anoma•ly [ə'nɑməli] *s* (*pl* **-lies**) anomalía
anon. *abbr* **anonymous**
anonymity [,ænə'nɪmɪti] *s* anónimo; **to preserve one's anonymity** guardar o conservar el anónimo
anonymous [ə'nɑnɪməs] *adj* anónimo
another [ə'nʌðər] *adj* & *pron indef* otro
ans. *abbr* **answer**
answer ['ænsər] *s* contestación, respuesta; solución || *tr* contestar, responder; resolver (*un problema o un enigma*) || *intr* contestar, responder; **to answer for** responder de (*una cosa*); responder por (*una persona*)
ant [ænt] *s* hormiga
antagonism [æn'tægə,nɪzəm] *s* antagonismo
antagonize [æn'tægə,naɪz] *tr* oponerse a; enemistar, enajenar
antarctic [ænt'ɑrktɪk] *adj* antártico || **the Antarctic** las Tierras Antárticas
antecedent [,æntɪ'sidənt] *adj* antecedente || *s* antecedente *m;* **antecedents** antecedentes *mpl;* antepasados
antechamber ['æntɪ,tʃembər] *s* antecámara
antedate ['æntɪ,det] *tr* antedatar; preceder
antelope ['æntɪ,lop] *s* antílope *m*
anten•na [æn'tɛnə] *s* (*pl* **-nae** [ni]) (ent) antena || *s* (*pl* **-nas**) (rad) antena
autepenult [,æntɪ'pinʌlt] *s* antepenúltima
anteroom ['æntɪ,rum] *s* antecámara
anthem ['ænθəm] *s* himno; antífona
ant'hill' *s* hormiguero
antholo•gy [æn'θɑlədʒi] *s* (*pl* **-gies**) antología
anthracite ['ænθrə,saɪt] *s* antracita
anthrax ['ænθræks] *s* ántrax *m*
anthropology [,ænθrə'pɑlədʒi] *s* antropología
anti-aircraft [,æntɪ'ɛr,kræft] *adj* antiaéreo
antibiotic [,æntɪbaɪ'ɑtɪk] *adj* & *s* antibiótico
antibod•y ['æntɪ,badi] *s* (*pl* **-ies**) anticuerpo
anticipate [æn'tɪsɪ,pet] *tr* esperar, prever; anticipar; (*to get ahead of*) anticiparse a; impedir; prometerse (*p.ej., un placer*); temerse (*algo desagradable*)
antics ['æntɪks] *spl* cabriolas, gracias, travesuras
antidote ['æntɪ,dot] *s* antídoto
antifreeze [,æntɪ'friz] *s* anticongelante *m*
antiglare [,æntɪ'glɛr] *adj* antideslumbrante
antiknock [,æntɪ'nɑk] *adj* & *s* antidetonante *m*
antilabor [,æntɪ'lebər] *adj* antiobrero
Antilles [æn'tɪliz] *spl* Antillas
antimatter ['æntɪ,mætər] *s* antimateria
antimissile [,æntɪ'mɪsɪl] *adj* antiproyectil
antimony ['æntɪ,moni] *s* antimonio
antipas•to [,ɑntɪ'pɑsto] *s* (*pl* **-tos**) aperitivo, entremés *m*
antipa•thy [æn'tɪpəθi] *s* (*pl* **-thies**) antipatía
antipollution movement [,æntɪpə'luʃən] *s* lucha antipolución
antiquar•y ['æntɪ,kwɛri] *s* (*pl* **-ies**) anticuario
antiquated ['æntɪ,kwetɪd] *adj* anticuado
antique [æn'tik] *adj* antiguo || *s* antigüedad
antique dealer *s* anticuario
antique store *s* tienda de antigüedades
antiqui•ty [æn'tɪkwɪti] *s* (*pl* **-ties**) antigüedad
anti-Semitic [,æntɪsɪ'mɪtɪk] *adj* antisemítico
antiseptic [,æntɪ'sɛptɪk] *adj* & *s* antiséptico
antislavery [,æntɪ'slevəri] *adj* antiesclavista
anti-Soviet [,æntɪ'sovɪ,ɛt] *adj* antisoviético
antitank [,æntɪ'tæŋk] *adj* antitanque
antiterrorist [,æntɪ'tɛrərɪst] *adj* & *s* antiterrorista *mf*
antithe•sis [æn'tɪθɪsɪs] *s* (*pl* **-ses** [,siz]) antítesis *f*
antitoxin [,æntɪ'tɑksɪn] *s* antitoxina
antitrust [,æntɪ'trʌst] *adj* anticartel
antiwar [,æntɪ'wɔr] *adj* antibélico
antler ['æntlər] *s* cuerna
antonym ['æntənɪm] *s* antónimo
Antwerp ['æntwərp] *s* Amberes *f*
anvil ['ænvɪl] *s* yunque *m*
anxie•ty [æŋ'zaɪ•əti] *s* (*pl* **-ties**) ansiedad, inquietud; ansia, anhelo
anxious ['æŋkʃəs] *adj* ansioso, inquieto; anhelante; **to be anxious to** tener ganas de
any ['ɛni] *adj indef* algún, cualquier; todo; **any place** dondequiera; **any time** cuando quiera; alguna vez || *pron indef* alguno, cualquiera || *adv* algo
an'y•bod'y *pron indef* alguno, alguien, cualquiera, quienquiera; todo el mundo; **not anybody** nadie
an'y•how' *adv* de cualquier modo; de todos modos; sin embargo
an'y•one' *pron indef* alguno, alguien, cualquiera
an'y•thing' *pron indef* algo, alguna cosa; cualquier cosa; todo cuanto; **anything at all** cualquier cosa que sea; **anything else** cualquier otra cosa; **anything else?** ¿algo más?; **not anything** nada
an'y•way' *adv* de cualquier modo; de todos modos; sin embargo; sin esmero, sin orden ni concierto
an'y•where' *adv* dondequiera; adondequiera; **not anywhere** en ninguna parte
apace [ə'pes] *adv* aprisa
apart [ə'pɑrt] *adv* aparte; en pedazos; **to fall apart** caerse a pedazos; desunirse; ir al desastre; **to live apart** vivir separados; vivir aislado; **to stand apart** mantenerse apartado; **to take apart** descomponer, desarmar, desmontar; **to tell apart** distinguir
apartment [ə'pɑrtmənt] *s* apartamento
apartment house *s* casa de pisos
apathetic [,æpə'θɛtɪk] *adj* apático
apa•thy ['æpəθi] *s* (*pl* **-ties**) apatía; lerdera
ape [ep] *s* mono || *tr* imitar, remedar
aperture ['æpərtʃər] *s* abertura, orificio
apex ['epɛks] *s* (*pl* **apexes** o **apices** ['æpɪ,siz]) ápex *m,* ápice *m*
aphorism ['æfə,rɪzəm] *s* aforismo
aphrodisiac [,æfrə'dɪzɪ,æk] *adj* & *s* afrodisíaco
apiar•y ['epɪ,ɛri] *s* (*pl* **-ies**) abejar *m,* colmenar *m*
apiece [ə'pis] *adv* cada uno; por persona
apish ['epɪʃ] *adj* monesco; tonto
aplomb [ə'plɑm] *s* aplomo, sangre fría
apogee ['æpə,dʒi] *s* apogeo

apologetic [ə,pɑlə'dʒɛtɪk] *adj* lleno de excusas

apologist [ə'pɑlədʒɪst] *s* defensor *m;* exponente *m*

apologize [ə'pɑlə,dʒaɪz] *intr* excusarse, disculparse; **to apologize for** disculparse de; **to apologize to** disculparse con

apology [ə'pɑlədʒi] *s* (*pl* **-gies**) excusa; (*makeshift*) expediente *m*

apoplectic [,æpə'plɛktɪk] *adj & s* apoplético

apoplexy ['æpə,plɛksi] *s* apoplejía

apostle [ə'pɑsəl] *s* apóstol *m*

apostrophe [ə'pɑstrəfi] *s* (*written sign*) apóstrofo; (*words addressed to absent person*) apóstrofe *m & f*

apothecar•y [ə'pɑθɪ,kɛri] *s* (*pl* **-ies**) boticario

apothecary's jar *s* bote *m* de porcelana

apothecary's shop *s* botica

appall [ə'pɔl] *tr* espantar, pasmar

appalling [ə'pɔlɪŋ] *adj* aterrador, espantoso, pasmoso

appara•tus [,æpə'retəs] o [,æpə'rætəs] *s* (*pl* **-tus** o **-tuses**) aparato

apparel [ə'pærəl] *s* indumentaria, vestido

apparent [ə'pærənt] *adj* aparente

apparition [,æpə'rɪʃən] *s* aparición

appeal [ə'pil] *s* súplica, instancia, solicitud; atracción, interés *m;* (law) apelación || *intr* ser atrayente; **to appeal to** (*to make an entreaty to*) suplicar; (*to be attractive to*) atraer, interesar; (law) apelar a

appear [ə'pɪr] *intr* (*to come into sight; to be in sight; to be published*) aparecer; (*to come into sight; to be in sight; to look; to seem*) parecer; (*to come before the public*) presentarse; (*to come before a court)* comparecer

appearance [ə'pɪrəns] *s* (*act of appearing*) aparición; (*outward look*) apariencia, aspecto; (law) comparecencia

appease [ə'piz] *tr* apaciguar

appeasement [ə'pizmənt] *s* apaciguamiento

appeasement attempts *spl* (coll) paños tibios *mpl*

appellate [ə'pɛlɪt] *adj* apelante

appellate court *s* tribunal *m* de apelación

appellate judge *s* juez *m* de alzadas

appendage [ə'pɛndɪdʒ] *s* apéndice *m*

appendicitis [ə,pɛndɪ'saɪtɪs] *s* apendicitis *f*

appen•dix [ə'pɛndɪks] *s* (*pl* **-dixes** o **-dices** [dɪ,siz]) apéndice *m*

appertain [,æpər'ten] *intr* relacionarse

appetite ['æpɪ,taɪt] *s* apetito

appetizer ['æpɪ,taɪzər] *s* aperitivo, apetite *m*

appetizing ['æpɪ,taɪzɪŋ] *adj* apetitoso

applaud [ə'plɔd] *tr & intr* aplaudir

applause [ə'plɔz] *s* aplauso, aplausos

apple ['æpəl] *s* manzana

ap'ple•jack' *s* aguardiente *m* de manzana

apple of the eye *s* niña del ojo

apple pie *s* pastel *m* de manzana

apple polisher *s* (slang) quitamotas *mf*

ap'ple•sauce' *s* compota de manzanas; (slang) música celestial

apple tree *s* manzano

appliance [ə'plaɪ•əns] *s* artificio, dispositivo, aparato; aplicación

applicant ['æplɪkənt] *s* aspirante *mf,* pretendiente *mf,* solicitante *mf*

ap•ply [ə'plaɪ] *v* (*pret & pp* **-plied)** *tr* aplicar || *intr* aplicarse; dirigirse; **to apply for** pedir, solicitar

appoint [ə'pɔɪnt] *tr* designar, nombrar; señalar; amueblar

appointment [ə'pɔɪntmənt] *s* designación, nombramiento; empleo, puesto; cita; **appointments** instalación, accesorios, adornos; **by appointment** cita previa

apportion [ə'porʃən] *tr* prorratear

appraisal [ə'prezəl] *s* tasación, valoración, apreciación

appraise [ə'prez] *tr* tasar, valorar, apreciar

appreciable [ə'priʃɪ•əbəl] *adj* apreciable; sensible

appreciate [ə'priʃɪ,et] *tr* apreciar; aprobar; comprender; estar agradecido por || *intr* subir de valor

appreciation [ə,priʃɪ'eʃən] *s* aprecio; agradecimiento; plusvalía, aumento de valor

appreciative [ə'priʃɪ,etɪv] *adj* apreciador; agradecido

apprehend [,æprɪ'hɛnd] *tr* aprehender, prender; comprender; temer

apprehension [,æprɪ'hɛnʃən] *s* aprehensión; (*fear, worry*) aprensión; comprensión

apprehensive [,æprɪ'hɛnsɪv] *adj* (*fearful, worried*) aprehensivo, aprensivo

apprentice [ə'prɛntɪs] *s* aprendiz *m,* meritorio; chumero, chumera (CAm) || *tr* poner de aprendiz

apprenticeship [ə'prɛntɪs,ʃɪp] *s* aprendizaje *m*

apprise o **apprize** [ə'praɪz] *tr* informar; apreciar, tasar

approach [ə'protʃ] *s* acercamiento; vía de entrada; proposición; (*to a problem*) enfoque *m* || *tr* abordar, acercarse a; (*to bring closer*) acercar || *intr* acercarse, aproximarse

approbation [,æprə'beʃən] *s* aprobación

appropriate [ə'proprɪ•ɪt] *adj* apropiado, a propósito || [ə'proprɪ,et] *tr* apropiarse; asignar, destinar (*el parlamento determinada suma a un determinado fin*)

approval [ə'pruvəl] *s* aprobación; **on approval** a prueba

approve [ə'pruv] *tr & intr* aprobar

approximate [ə'prɑksɪmɪt] *adj* aproximado || [ə'prɑksɪ,met] *tr* aproximar || *intr* aproximarse

apricot ['eprɪ,kɑt] o ['æprɪ,kɑt] *s* albaricoque *m*

apricot tree *s* albaricoquero

April ['eprɪl] *s* abril *m*

April fool *s* — **to make an April fool of** coger por inocente

April Fools' Day *s* día *m* de engañabobos, primer día de abril, en que se coge por inocente a la gente

apron ['eprən] *s* delantal *m;* (*of a workman*) mandil *m;* **tied to the apron strings of** cosido a las faldas de

apropos [,æprə'po] *adj* oportuno || *adv* a propósito; **apropos of** a propósito de
apse [æps] *s* ábside *m*
apt [æpt] *adj* apto; a propósito; dispuesto, inclinado
aptitude ['æptɪ,tjud] *s* aptitud
aquamarine [,ækwəmə'rin] *s* aguamarina
aquaplane ['ækwə,plen] *s* acuaplano || *intr* correr en acuaplano
aquari•um [ə'kwɛrɪ•əm] *s* (*pl* **-ums** o **-a** [ə]) acuario
Aquarius [ə'kwɛrɪ•əs] *s* (astr) Acuario
aquatic [ə'kwætɪk] o [ə'kwɑtɪk] *adj* acuático || **aquatics** *spl* deportes acuáticos
aqueduct ['ækwə,dʌkt] *s* acueducto
aquiline nose ['ækwɪ,laɪn] *s* nariz aguileña
Arab ['ærəb] *adj* árabe || *s* árabe *mf;* caballo árabe
Arabia [ə'rebɪ•ə] *s* la Arabia
Arabian [ə'rebɪ•ən] *adj* árabe; arábigo || *s* árabe *mf*
Arabic ['ærəbɪk] *adj* arábigo || *s* árabe *m,* arábigo
Aragon ['ærə,gɑn] *s* Aragón *m*
Arago•nese [,ærəgə'niz] *adj* aragonés || *s* (*pl* **-nese**) aragonés *m*
arbiter ['ɑrbɪtər] *s* árbitro
arbitrary ['ɑrbɪ,trɛri] *adj* arbitrario
arbitrate ['ɑrbɪ,tret] *tr & intr* arbitrar
arbitration [,ɑrbɪ'treʃən] *s* arbitraje *m*
arbor ['ɑrbər] *s* emparrado, glorieta
arbore•tum [,ɑrbə'ritəm] *s* (*pl* **-tums** o **-ta** [tə]) jardín botánico de árboles
arbor vitae ['ɑrbər 'vaɪti] *s* árbol *m* de la vida
arbutus [ɑr'bjutəs] *s* madroño
arc [ɑrk] *s* arco
arcade [ɑr'ked] *s* arcada, galería
arch. *abbr* **archaic, archaism, archipelago, architect**
arch [ɑrtʃ] *adj* astuto; travieso; principal || *s* arco || *tr* arquear, enarcar; atravesar
archaeology [,ɑrkɪ'ɑlədʒi] *s* arqueología
archaic [ɑr'ke•ɪk] *adj* arcaico
archaism ['ɑrke,ɪzəm] *s* arcaísmo
archangel ['ɑrk,endʒəl] *s* arcángel *m*
archbishop ['ɑrtʃ 'bɪʃəp] *s* arzobispo
archduke ['ɑrtʃ 'djuk] *s* archiduque *m*
archene•my ['ɑrtʃ,ɛnɪmi] *s* (*pl* **-mies**) archienemigo
archeology [,ɑrkɪ'ɑlədʒi] *s* arqueología
archer ['ɑrtʃər] *s* arquero, flechero
archery ['ɑrtʃəri] *s* tiro de flechas
archipela•go [,ɑrkɪ'pɛləgo] *s* (*pl* **-gos** o **-goes**) archipiélago
architect ['ɑrkɪ,tɛkt] *s* arquitecto
architectural [,ɑrkɪ'tɛktʃərəl] *adj* arquitectónico, arquitectural
architecture ['ɑrkɪ,tɛktʃər] *s* arquitectura
archives ['ɑrkaɪvz] *spl* archivo
arch'way' *s* arcada
arc lamp *s* lámpara de arco
arctic ['ɑrktɪk] *adj* ártico || **the Arctic** las Tierras Articas
arc welding *s* soldadura de arco
ardent ['ɑrdənt] *adj* ardiente
ardor ['ɑrdər] *s* ardor *m*
arduous ['ɑrdjʊ•əs] *adj* arduo, difícil; enérgico; (*steep*) escarpado
area ['ɛrɪ•ə] *s* área, superficie *f;* comarca, región; zona; patio
ar'ea•way' *s* entrada baja de un sótano
Argentina [,ɑrdʒən'tinə] *s* la Argentina
Argentine ['ɑrdʒən,tin] o ['ɑrdʒən,taɪn] *adj & s* argentino || **the Argentine** la Argentina
Argentinean [,ɑrdʒən'tɪnɪ•ən] *adj & s* argentino
Argonaut ['ɑrgə,nɔt] *s* argonauta *m*
argue ['ɑrgju] *tr* argüir; **to argue into** persuadir a + *inf;* **to argue out of** disuadir de + *inf* || *intr* argüir
argument ['ɑrgjəmənt] *s* argumento; disputa
argumentative [,ɑrgjə'mɛntətɪv] *adj* argumentador; ergotista *masc*
argumentativeness [,ɑrgjə'mɛntətɪvnɪs] *s* ergotismo
aria ['ɑrɪ•ə] o ['ɛrɪ•ə] *s* (mus) aria
arid ['ærɪd] *adj* árido
aridity [ə'rɪdɪti] *s* aridez *f*
Aries ['ɛriz] *s* (astr) Aries *m*
aright [ə'raɪt] *adv* acertadamente; **to set aright** rectificar
arise [ə'raɪz] *v* (*pret* **arose** [ə'roz]; *pp* **arisen** [ə'rɪzən]) *intr* levantarse; subir; aparecer; **to arise from** provenir de
aristocra•cy [,ærɪs'tɑkrəsi] *s* (*pl* **-cies**) aristocracia
aristocrat [ə'rɪstə,kræt] *s* aristócrata *mf*
aristocratic [ə,rɪstə'krætɪk] *adj* aristocrático
Aristotelian [,ærɪstə'tilɪ•ən] *adj & s* aristotélico
Aristotle ['ærɪs,tɑtəl] *s* Aristóteles *m*
arith. *abbr* **arithmetic**
arithmetic [ə'rɪθmətɪk] *s* aritmética
arithmetical [,ærɪθ'mɛtɪkəl] *adj* aritmético
arithmetician [ə,rɪθmə'tɪʃən] *s* aritmético
ark [ɑrk] *s* arca de Noé
ark of the covenant *s* arca de la alianza
arm [ɑrm] *s* brazo; (*weapon*) arma; **arm in arm** de bracero, asidos del brazo; **in arms** de pecho, de teta; **the three arms of the service** los tres ejércitos; **to be up in arms** estar en armas; **to keep at arm's length** mantener a distancia; mantenerse a distancia; **to lay down one's arms** rendir las armas; **to rise up in arms** alzarse en armas; **under arms** sobre las armas || *tr* armar || *intr* armarse
armament ['ɑrməmənt] *s* armamento
armature ['ɑrmə,tʃər] *s* armadura; (*of a dynamo or motor*) (elec) inducido
arm'chair' *adj* de gabinete || *s* butaca, sillón *m,* silla de brazos
Armenian [ɑr'minɪ•ən] *adj & s* armenio
armful ['ɑrm,fʊl] *s* brazado
arm'hole' *s* (*in clothing*) sobaquera
armistice ['ɑrmɪstɪs] *s* armisticio
armor ['ɑrmər] *s* armadura; coraza, blindaje *m* || *tr* acorazar, blindar
armored car *s* carro blindado
armorial bearings [ɑr'morɪ•əl] *spl* blasón *m,* escudo de armas
armor plate *s* plancha de blindaje

ar'mor-plate' *tr* acorazar, blindar
armor•y ['ɑrməri] *s* (*pl* **-ies**) arsenal *m;* (*arms factory*) armería
arm'pit' *s* sobaco, hueco de la axila
arm'rest' *s* apoyabrazos *m*
arms race *s* carrera armanentista
arms reduction *s* desarmamiento
ar•my ['ɑrmi] *adj* militar, castrense || *s* (*pl* **-mies**) ejército
army corps *s* cuerpo de ejército
aroma [ə'romə] *s* aroma *m,* fragancia
aromatic [,ærə'mætɪk] *adj* aromático
around [ə'raʊnd] *adv* alrededor, a la redonda; en la dirección opuesta || *prep* alrededor de, en torno a o de; cerca de; (*the corner*) a la vuelta de
arouse [ə'raʊz] *tr* despertar; excitar, incitar
arpeg•gio [ɑr'pɛdʒo] *s* (*pl* **-gios**) arpegio
arraign [ə'ren] *tr* acusar; presentar al tribunal
arrange [ə'rendʒ] *tr* arreglar, disponer; (mus) adaptar, refundir
array [ə're] *s* orden *m;* orden *m* de batalla; adorno, atavío || *tr* poner en orden; poner en orden de batalla; adornar, ataviar
arrears [ə'rɪrz] *spl* atrasos; **in arrears** atrasado en pagos
arrest [ə'rɛst] *s* arresto, prisión; detención; **under arrest** bajo arresto || *tr* arrestar; detener; atraer (*la atención*)
arresting [ə'rɛstɪŋ] *adj* impresionante
arrhythmia [ə'rɪθmi•ə] *s* arritmia
arrival [ə'raɪvəl] *s* llegada; (*person*) llegado
arrive [ə'raɪv] *intr* llegar; tener éxito
arrogance ['ærəgəns] *s* arrogancia
arrogant ['ærəgənt] *adj* arrogante
arrogate ['ærə,get] *tr* — **to arrogate to oneself** arrogarse
arrow ['æro] *s* flecha
ar'row-head' *s* punta de flecha; (bot) saetilla
arsenal ['ɑrsənəl] *s* arsenal *m*
arsenic ['ɑrsɪnɪk] *s* arsénico
arson ['ɑrsən] *s* incendio premeditado, delito de incendio
art [ɑrt] *s* arte *m & f*
arter•y ['ɑrtəri] *s* (*pl* **-ies**) arteria
artful ['ɑrtfəl] *adj* astuto, mañoso; diestro, ingenioso
arthritic [ɑr'θrɪtɪk] *adj & s* artrítico
arthritis [ɑr'θraɪtɪs] *s* artritis *f*
artichoke ['ɑrtɪ,tʃok] *s* alcachofa
article ['ɑrtɪkəl] *s* artículo; **an article of clothing** una prenda de vestir
articulate [ɑr'tɪkjəlɪt] *adj* claro, distinto; capaz de hablar || [ɑr'tɪkjə,let] *tr* articular
artifact ['ɑrtɪ,fækt] *s* artefacto
artifice ['ɑrtɪfɪs] *s* artificio
artificial [,ɑrtɪ'fɪʃəl] *adj* artificial
artillery [ɑr'tɪləri] *s* artillería
artillery•man [ɑr'tɪlərimən] *s* (*pl* **-men** [mən]) artillero
artisan ['ɑrtɪzən] *s* artesano
artist ['ɑrtɪst] *s* artista *mf*
artistic [ɑr'tɪstɪk] *adj* artístico
artistry ['ɑrtɪstri] *s* habilidad artística
artless ['ɑrtlɪs] *adj* sencillo, natural; ingenuo, inocente; (*crude, clumsy*) chabacano
arts and crafts *spl* artes y oficios
art•y ['ɑrti] *adj* (*comp* **-ier;** *super* **-iest**) (coll) ostentosamente artístico
Aryan ['ɛrɪ•ən] o ['ɑrjən] *adj & s* ario
as [æz] o [əz] *pron rel* que; **the same as** el mismo que || *adv* tan; **as . . . as** tan . . . como; **as for** en cuanto a; **as long as** mientras que; ya que; **as many as** tantos como; **as much as** tanto como; **as regards** en cuanto a; **as soon as** tan pronto como; **as soon as possible** cuanto antes, los más pronto posible; **as though** como si; **as to** en cuanto a; **as well** también; **as yet** hasta ahora || *conj* como; que; ya que; a medida que; **as it seems** por lo visto, según parece || *prep* por, como; **as a rule** por regla general
asbestos [æs'bɛstəs] *s* asbesto, amianto
ascend [ə'sɛnd] *tr* subir a (*p.ej., el trono*) || *intr* ascender
ascendancy [ə'sɛndənsi] *s* ascendiente *m*
ascension [ə'sɛnʃən] *s* ascensión
Ascension Day *s* fiesta de la Ascensión
ascent [ə'sɛnt] *s* ascensión, subida; ascenso, promoción
ascertain [,æsər'ten] *tr* averiguar
ascertainable [,æsər'tenəbəl] *adj* averiguable
ascetic [ə'sɛtɪk] *adj* ascético || *s* asceta *mf*
ascorbic acid [ə'skɔrbɪk] *s* ácido ascórbico
ascribe [ə'skraɪb] *tr* atribuir
aseptic [ə'sɛptɪk] o [e'sɛptɪk] *adj* aséptico
ash [æʃ] *s* ceniza; (*tree; wood*) fresno; **ashes** ceniza, cenizas; (*mortal remains*) cenizas
ashamed [ə'ʃemd] *adj* avergonzado; **to be ashamed** tener vergüenza
ashlar ['æʃlər] *s* sillar *m*
ashore [ə'ʃor] *adv* en tierra, a tierra
ash tray *s* cenicero
Ash Wednesday *s* miércoles *m* de ceniza
Asia ['eʒə] o ['eʃə] *s* Asia
Asia Minor *s* el Asia Menor
Asian ['eʒən] o ['eʃən] o **Asiatic** [,eʒɪ'ætɪk] o [,eʃɪ'ætɪk] *adj & s* asiático
aside [ə'saɪd] *adv* aparte; **aside from** además de; **to step aside** hacerse a un lado || *s* (theat) aparte *m*
asinine ['æsɪ,naɪn] *adj* tonto, necio
ask [æsk] o [ɑsk] *tr* (*to request*) pedir; (*to inquire of*) preguntar; hacer (*una pregunta*); invitar; **to ask in** invitar a entrar || *intr*—**to ask about, after,** or **for;** preguntar por; **to ask for** pedir
askance [ə'skæns] *adv* al sesgo, de soslayo; con desdén, sospechosamente
asleep [ə'slip] *adj* dormido; **to fall asleep** dormirse
asp [æsp] *s* áspid *m*
asparagus [ə'spærəgəs] *s* espárrago
aspect ['æspɛkt] *s* aspecto
aspen ['æspən] *s* tiemblo, álamo temblón
aspersion [ə'spʌrʒən] o [ə'spʌrʃən] *s* calumnia, difamación
asphalt ['æsfɔlt] *s* asfalto || *tr* asfaltar
asphyxiate [æs'fɪksɪ,et] *tr* asfixiar
aspirant [ə'spaɪrənt] o ['æspɪrənt] *s* pretendiente *mf,* candidato
aspire [ə'spaɪr] *intr* aspirar
aspirin ['æspɪrɪn] *s* aspirina

ass [æs] *s* asno
assail [ə'sel] *tr* asaltar, acometer
assassin [e'sæsɪn] *s* asesino
assassinate [ə'sæsɪ,net] *tr* asesinar
assassination [ə,sæsɪ'neʃən] *s* asesinato
assault [ə'sɔlt] *s* asalto || *tr* asaltar
assault and battery *s* vías de hecho, violencias
assay [ə'se] o ['æse] *s* ensaye *m;* muestra de ensaye || [ə'se] *tr* ensayar; apreciar
assemble [ə'sɛmbəl] *tr* reunir; (mach) armar, montar || *intr* reunirse
assem•bly [ə'sɛmbli] *s* (*pl* **-blies**) asamblea; reunión; (mach) armadura, montaje *m*
assembly hall *s* aula magna, paraninfo; salón *m* de sesiones
assembly line *s* línea de montaje
assembly plant *s* fábrica de montaje
assembly room *s* sala de reunión; (mach) taller *m* de montaje
assent [ə'sɛnt] *s* asentimiento, asenso || *intr* asentir
assert [ə'sʌrt] *tr* afirmar, aseverar, declarar; **to assert oneself** imponerse, hacer valer sus derechos
assertion [ə'sʌrʃən] *s* aserción, aseveración
assess [ə'sɛs] *tr* amillarar, gravar; fijar (*daños y perjuicios*); apreciar, estimar
assessment [ə'sɛsmənt] *s* amillaramiento, gravamen *m;* fijación; apreciación, estimación
asset ['æsɛt] *s* posesión, ventaja; (*person, thing, or quality worth having*) (fig) valor *m;* **assets** (com) activo
assiduous [ə'sɪdjʊ•əs] *adj* asiduo
assign [ə'saɪn] *tr* asignar
assignment [ə'saɪnmənt] *s* asignación, cometido; lección
assimilate [ə'sɪmɪ,let] *tr* asimilarse (*los alimentos, el conocimiento*) || *intr* asimilarse
assist [ə'sɪst] *tr* ayudar, asistir, auxiliar
assistant [ə'sɪstənt] *adj* & *s* auxiliar *mf,* ayudante *mf*
assistantship [ə'sɪstənt,ʃɪp] *s* ayudantía
assn. *abbr* **association**
associate [ə'soʃɪ•ɪt] *adj* asociado || *s* asociado, socio || [ə'soʃɪ,et] *tr* asociar || *intr* asociarse
association [ə,soʃɪ'eʃən] *s* asociación
assort [ə'sɔrt] *tr* clasificar, ordenar
assortment [ə'sɔrtmənt] *s* surtido; clase *f,* grupo
asst. *abbr* **assistant**
assume [ə'sum] o [ə'sjum] *tr* asumir (*p.ej., responsabilidades*); arrogarse; suponer, dar por sentado
assumption [ə'sʌmpʃən] *s* asunción; suposición
assurance [ə'ʃʊrəns] *s* aseguramiento; seguridad, confianza; (com) seguro
assure [ə'ʃʊr] *tr* asegurar; (com) asegurar
Assyria [ə'sɪrɪ•ə] *s* Asiria
Assyrian [ə'sɪrɪ•ən] *adj* & *s* asirio
astatine ['æstə,tin] *s* ástato
aster ['æstər] *s* (bot) aster *m;* (*China aster*) reina Margarita
asterisk ['æstə,rɪsk] *s* asterisco
astern [ə'stʌrn] *adv* por la popa
asthma ['æzmə] o ['æsmə] *s* asma *f*
astonish [ə'stɑnɪʃ] *tr* asombrar
astonishing [ə'stɑnɪʃɪŋ] *adj* asombroso
astound [ə'staʊnd] *tr* pasmar
astounding [ə'staʊndɪŋ] *adj* pasmoso
astraddle [ə'strædəl] *adv* a horcajadas
astray [ə'stre] *adv* por mal camino; **to go astray** extraviarse; **gone astray** desviado; **to lead astray** extraviar
astride [ə'straɪd] *adv* a horcajadas || *prep* a horcajadas de
astrology [ə'strɑlədʒi] *s* astrología
astronaut ['æstrə,nɔt] *s* astronauta *m*
astronautic [,æstrə'nɔtɪk] *adj* astronáutico || **astronautics** *s* astronáutica
astronavigation [,æstro,nævɪ'geʃən] *s* astronavigación
astronomer [ə'strɑnəmər] *s* astrónomo
astronomic(al) [,æstrə'nɑmɪk(əl)] *adj* astronómico
astronomy [ə'strɑnəmi] *s* astronomía
astrophysics [,æstro'fɪzɪks] *s* astrofísica
Asturian [ə'stʊrɪ•ən] *adj* & *s* asturiano
astute [ə'stjut] *adj* astuto, sagaz
asunder [ə'sʌndər] *adv* a pedazos, en dos
asylum [ə'saɪləm] *s* asilo
asymmetry [ə'sɪmɪtri] *s* asimetría
at [æt] o [ət] *prep* en, p.ej., **I saw her at the library** la ví en la biblioteca; a, p.ej., **at five o'clock** a las cinco; de, p.ej., **to be surprised at** estar sorprendido de; **to laugh at** reírse de; en casa de, p.ej., **at John's** en casa de Juan
atavistic [,ætə'vɪstɪk] *adj* atávico
atheism ['eθi,ɪzəm] *s* ateísmo
atheist ['eθi•ɪst] *s* ateísta *mf,* ateo
Athenian [ə'θinɪ•ən] *adj* & *s* ateniense *mf*
Athens ['æθɪnz] *s* Atenas *f*
athirst [ə'θʌrst] *adj* sediento
athlete ['æθlit] *s* atleta *mf*
athlete's foot *s* pie *m* de atleta
athletic [æθ'lɛtɪk] *adj* atlético || **athletics** *s* atletismo
Atlantic [æt'læntɪk] *adj* & *s* Atlántico
atlas ['ætləs] *s* atlas *m*
atmosphere ['ætməs,fɪr] *s* atmósfera
atmospheric [,ætməs'fɛrɪk] *adj* atmosférico || **atmospherics** *spl* parásitos atmosféricos
atom ['ætəm] *s* átomo
atom bomb *s* bomba atómica
atomic [ə'tɑmɪk] *adj* atómico
atomic bomb *s* bomba atómica
atomic weight *s* peso atómico
atomize ['ætə,maɪz] *tr* atomizar
atomizer ['ætə,maɪzər] *s* pulverizador *m,* vaporizador *m*
atom smasher *s* rompeátomos *m*
atone [ə'ton] *intr* dar reparación; **to atone for** dar reparación por, expiar
atonement [ə'tonmənt] *s* reparación, expiación
atop [ə'tɑp] *adv* encima || *prep* encima de
atrocious [ə'troʃəs] *adj* atroz; (coll) abominable, muy malo
atroci•ty [ə'trɑsɪti] *s* (*pl* **-ties**) atrocidad

atro•phy [ˈætrəfi] *s* (pathol) atrofia, retracción ‖ *v* (*pret & pp* **-phied**) *tr* atrofiar ‖ *intr* atrofiarse
attach [əˈtætʃ] *tr* atar, ligar; atribuir (*p.ej., importancia*); (law) embargar; **to be attached to** aficionarse a; (*to be officially associated with*) depender de
attaché [,ætəˈʃe] *s* agregado
attachment [əˈtætʃmənt] *s* atadura, enlace *m;* atribución; apego, cariño; accesorio; (law) embargo
attack [əˈtæk] *s* ataque *m* ‖ *tr & intr* atacar
attain [əˈten] *tr* alcanzar, lograr
attainment [əˈtenmənt] *s* consecución, logro; **attainments** dotes *fpl,* prendas
attempt [əˈtɛmpt] *s* tentativa; (*assault*) atentado, conato ‖ *tr* procurar, intentar; (*e.g., the life of a person*) atentar a o contra
attend [əˈtɛnd] *tr* atender, asistir; asistir a (*p.ej., la escuela*); auxiliar (*a un moribundo*) ‖ *intr* atender; **to attend to** atender a
attendance [əˈtɛndəns] *s* asistencia, concurrencia; **to dance attendance** hacer antesala
attendant [əˈtɛndənt] *adj & s* asistente *mf;* concomitante *m*
attention [əˈtɛnʃən] *s* atención; **to attract attention** llamar la atención; **to call attention to** hacer presente; **to pay attention to** hacer caso de
attentive [əˈtɛntɪv] *adj* atento
attenuate [əˈtɛnjʊ,et] *tr* adelgazar; debilitar ‖ *intr* debilitarse; desaparecer
attest [əˈtɛst] *tr* atestiguar; juramentar ‖ *intr* dar fe; **to attest to** dar fe de
attic [ˈætɪk] *s* buharda, guardilla, desván *m*
attire [əˈtaɪr] *s* atavío, traje *m* ‖ *tr* ataviar, vestir
attitude [ˈætɪ,tjud] o [ˈætɪ,tud] *s* actitud, ademán *m*
attorney [əˈtʌrni] *s* abogado; procurador *m*
attract [əˈtrækt] *tr* atraer; llamar (*la atención*)
attraction [əˈtrækʃən] *s* atracción; (*personal charm*) atractivo
attractive [əˈtræktɪv] *adj* atractivo; (*agreeable, interesting*) atrayente
attribute [ˈætrɪ,bjut] *s* atributo ‖ [əˈtrɪbjʊt] *tr* atribuir
atty. *abbr* **attorney**
auburn [ˈɔbərn] *adj & s* castaño rojizo
auction [ˈɔkʃən] *s* almoneda, remate *m,* subasta ‖ *tr* rematar, subastar
auctioneer [,ɔkʃənˈɪr] *s* subastador *m,* rematador *m* ‖ *tr & intr* rematar, subastar
auction house *s* martillo
audacious [ɔˈdeʃəs] *adj* audaz
audaci•ty [ɔˈdæsɪti] *s* (*pl* **-ties**) audacia
audience [ˈɔdɪ•əns] *s* (*hearing; formal interview*) audiencia; público, auditorio
audio frenquency [ˈɔdɪ,o] *s* audiofrecuencia
audiometer [,ɔdɪˈɑmɪtər] *s* audiómetro
audit [ˈɔdɪt] *s* intervención ‖ *tr* intervenir
audition [ɔˈdɪʃən] *s* audición ‖ *tr* dar audición a
auditor [ˈɔdɪtər] *s* oyente *mf;* (com) interventor *m*
auditorium [,ɔdɪˈtorɪ•əm] *s* auditorio, anfiteatro, paraninfo
auger [ˈɔgər] *s* barrena
augment [ɔgˈmɛnt] *tr & intr* aumentar
augur [ˈɔgər] *s* augur *m* ‖ *tr & intr* augurar; **to augur well** ser de buen agüero
augu•ry [ˈɔgəri] *s* (*pl* **-ries**) augurio
august [ɔˈgʌst] *adj* augusto ‖ **August** [ˈɔgəst] *s* agosto
aunt [ænt] o [ɑnt] *s* tía
aurora [eˈrorə] *s* aurora
auspice [ˈɔspɪs] *s* auspicio; **under the auspices of** bajo los auspicios de
austere [ɔsˈtɪr] *adj* austero
Australia [ɔˈstreljə] *s* Australia
Australian [ɔˈstreljən] *adj & s* australiano
Austria [ˈɔstrɪ•ə] *s* Austria
Austrian [ˈɔstrɪ•ən] *adj & s* austríaco
authentic [ɔˈθɛntɪk] *adj* auténtico
authenticate [ɔˈθɛntɪ,ket] *tr* autenticar
author [ˈɔθər] *s* autor *m*
authoress [ˈɔθərɪs] *s* autora
authoritarian [ɔ,θɔrɪˈtɛrɪ•ən] *adj & s* autoritario
authoritative [ɔˈθɔrɪ,tetɪv] *adj* autorizado; (*dictatorial*) autoritario
authori•ty [ɔˈθɔrɪti] *s* (*pl* **-ties**) autoridad; **on good authority** de buena tinta, de fuente fidedigna
authorize [ˈɔθə,raɪz] *tr* autorizar
authorship [ˈɔθər,ʃɪp] *s* paternidad literaria
autistic [ɔˈtɪstɪk] *s* autístico
au•to [ˈɔto] *s* (*pl* **-tos**) (coll) auto, coche *m*
autobiogra•phy [,ɔtobaɪˈɑgrəfi] *s* (*pl* **-phies**) autobiografía
autobus [ˈɔto,bʌs] *s* autobús *m*
autocratic(al) [,ɔtəˈkrætɪk(əl)] *adj* autocrático
autograph [ˈɔtə,græf] *adj & s* autógrafo ‖ *tr* autografiar
autograph seeker *s* cazaautógrafos *m*
automat [ˈɔtə,mæt] *s* restaurante automático
automatic [,ɔtəˈmætɪk] *adj* automático
automatic car wash *s* túnel *m* de lavado
automatic clutch *s* servoembrague *m*
automation [,ɔtəˈmeʃən] *s* automación, automatización
automa•ton [ɔˈtɑmə,tɑn] *s* (*pl* **-tons** o **-ta** [tə]) autómata
automobile [,ɔtəmoˈbil] u [,ɔtəˈmobil] *s* automóvil *m*
automobile show *s* salón *m* del automóvil
autonomous [ɔˈtɑnəməs] *adj* autónomo
autonomy [ɔˈtɑnəmi] *s* autonomía
autop•sy [ˈɔtɑpsi] *s* (*pl* **-sies**) autopsia
autumn [ˈɔtəm] *s* otoño
autumnal [əˈtʌmnəl] *adj* otoñal
auxilia•ry [ɔgˈzɪljəri] *adj* auxiliar ‖ *s* (*pl* **-ries**) auxiliar *mf;* **auxiliaries** tropas auxiliares
av. *abbr* **avenue, average, avoirdupois**
avail [əˈvel] *s* provecho, utilidad ‖ *tr* beneficiar; **to avail oneself of** aprovecharse de, valerse de ‖ *intr* aprovechar
available [əˈveləbəl] *adj* disponible; **to make available to** poner a la disposición de
avalanche [ˈævə,læntʃ] *s* alud *m,* avalancha

avant-garde [ə,vɑnt'gɑrd] *adj* vanguardista ‖ *s* vanguardismo
avant-guardist [ə,vɑnt'gɑrdist] *s* vanguardista *mf*
avarice ['ævərɪs] *s* avaricia
avaricious [,ævə'rɪʃəs] *adj* avaricioso, avariento
Ave. *abbr* **Avenue**
avenge [ə'vɛndʒ] *tr* vengar; **to avenge oneself on** vengarse en
avenue ['ævə,njʊ] o ['ævə,nu] *s* avenida
aver [ə'vʌr] *v* (*pret & pp* **averred;** *ger* **averring**) *tr* afirmar, declarar
average ['ævərɪdʒ] *adj* común, mediano, ordinario ‖ *s* promedio, término medio; (naut) avería ‖ *tr* calcular el término medio de; prorratear; ser de un promedio de
averse [ə'vʌrs] *adj* renuente, contrario
aversion [ə'vʌrʒen] *s* aversión, antipatía; cosa aborrecida
avert [ə'vʌrt] *tr* apartar, desviar; impedir
aviar•y ['evɪ,ɛri] *s* (*pl* **-ies**) avería, pajarera
aviation [,evɪ'eʃən] *s* aviación
aviation medicine *s* aeromedicina
aviator ['evɪ,etər] *s* aviador *m*
avid ['ævɪd] *adj* ávido
avidity [ə'vɪdɪti] *s* avidez *f*
avocado [,ævə'kɑdo] *s* aguacate *m*
avocation [,ævə'keʃən] *s* distracción, diversión
avoid [ə'vɔid] *tr* evitar
avoidable [ə'vɔɪdəbəl] *adj* evitable
avoidance [ə'vɔɪdəns] *s* evitación
avow [ə'vaʊ] *tr* admitir, confesar
avowal [ə'vaʊ•əl] *s* admisión, confesión
await [ə'wet] *tr* aguardar, esperar
awake [ə'wek] *adj* despierto ‖ *v* (*pret & pp* **awoke** [ə'wok] o **awaked**) *tr & intr* despertar
awaken [ə'wekən] *tr & intr* despertar
awakening [ə'wekəniŋ] *s* despertamiento; desilusión
award [ə'wɔrd] *s* premio; condecoración; adjudicación ‖ *tr* conceder; adjudicar
aware [ə'wɛr] *adj* enterado; **to become aware of** enterarse de, darse cuenta de
awareness [ə'wɛrnɪs] *s* conciencia
away [ə'we] *adj* ausente; distante ‖ *adv* lejos; a lo lejos; **away from** lejos de; **to do away with** deshacerse de; **to get away** escapar; **to go away** irse; **to make away with** robar, hurtar; **to run away** fugarse; **to send away** enviar; despedir; **to take away** llevarse; quitar
awe [ɔ] *s* temor *m* reverencial ‖ *tr* infundir temor reverencial a
awesome ['ɔsəm] *adj* imponente
awestruck ['ɔ,strʌk] *adj* espantado
awful ['ɔfəl] *adj* atroz, horrible; impresionante; (coll) muy malo, muy feo, enorme
awfully ['ɔfəli] *adv* atrozmente, horriblemente; (coll) muy, excesivamente
awfulness ['ɔfəlnɪs] *s* espantosidad (SAm)
awhile [ə'hwaɪl] *adv* un rato, algún tiempo
awkward ['ɔkwərd] *adj* desmañado, torpe, lerdo; embarazoso, delicado
awkward squad *s* pelotón *m* de los torpes
awl [ɔl] *s* alesna, lezna
awning ['ɔnɪŋ] *s* toldo
ax [æks] *s* hacha
axiom ['æksɪ•əm] *s* axioma *m*
axiomatic [,æksɪ•ə'mætɪk] *adj* axiomático
axis ['æksɪs] *s* (*pl* **axes** ['æksiz]) *s* eje *m*
axle ['æksəl] *s* eje *m*, árbol *m*
axle load *s* carga por eje
ax'le•tree' *s* eje *m* de carretón
ay [aɪ] *adv & s* sí ‖ [e] *adv* siempre; **for ay** por siempre ‖ [e] *interj* ¡ay!
aye [aɪ] *adv & s* sí ‖ [e] *adv* siempre; **for aye** por siempre
azimuth ['æzɪməθ] *s* acimut *m*
Azores [ə'zorz] o ['ezorz] *spl* Azores *fpl*
Aztec ['æztɛk] *adj & s* azteca *mf*
azure ['æʒər] o ['eʒər] *adj & s* azul *m*

B

B, b [bi] segunda letra del alfabeto inglés
b. *abbr* **bass, bay, born, brother**
baa [bɑ] *s* be *m*, balido ‖ *intr* balar
babble ['bæbəl] *s* barboteo; charla; (*of a brook*) murmullo ‖ *tr* barbotar; decir indiscretamente ‖ *intr* barbotar; murmurar (*un arroyo*)
babe [beb] *s* rorro, criatura; (*innocent, gullible person*) niño; (slang) chica, chica hermosa
baboon [bæ'bun] *s* babuíno
ba•by ['bebi] *s* (*pl* **-bies**) rorro, criatura, bebé *m;* (*the youngest child*) benjamín *m* ‖ *v* (*pret & pp* **-bied**) *tr* mimar; tratar como niño
baby carriage *s* cochecillo para niños
baby grand *s* piano de media cola
babyhood ['bebi,hʊd] *s* primera infancia, niñez *f*
babyish ['bebi•ɪʃ] *adj* aniñado, infantil
Babylon ['bæbɪlən] o ['bæbɪ,lɑn] *s* Babilonia (*ciudad*)
Babylonia [,bæbɪ'lonɪ•ə] *s* Babilonia (*imperio*)
Babylonian [,bæbɪ'lonɪ•ən] *adj & s* babilonio
baby sitter *s* niñera tomada por horas
baccalaureate [,bækə'lɔrɪ•ɪt] *s* bachillerato
bachelor ['bætʃələr] *s* (*unmarried man*) soltero; (*holder of bachelor's degree*) bachiller *mf;* (*apprentice knight*) doncel *m*
bachelorhood ['bætʃələr,hʊd] *s* celibato, soltería (*del hombre*)

bacil•lus [bə'sɪləs] *s* (*pl* **-li** [laɪ]) bacilo
back [bæk] *adj* trasero, posterior; atrasado ‖ *adv* atrás, detrás; de vuelta; (*ago*) hace; **back of** detrás de; **to go back to** remontarse a; **to send back** devolver ‖ *s* espalda; dorso; (*of a coin*) reverso; (*of a chair*) espaldar *m,* respaldo; (*of an animal, of a book*) lomo; (*of a hall, a room*) fondo; (*of a writing, a book*) final *m;* **behind one's back** a espaldas de uno; **on one's back** postrado, en cama; a cuestas ‖ *tr* mover hacia atrás; apoyar, respaldar ‖ *intr* moverse hacia atrás; **to back down** u **out** volverse atrás, echarse atrás; **to back up** retroceder; regolfar (*el agua*)
back'ache' *s* dolor *m* de espalda
back'bone' *s* espinazo; (*of a book*) nervura; firmeza, resistencia
back'break'ing *adj* deslomador
back'down' *s* palinodia, retractación
back'drop' *s* telón *m* de fondo o de foro
backer ['bækər] *s* sostenedor *m,* defensor *m;* (*of a business venture*) impulsador *m*
back'fire' *s* (aut) petardeo ‖ *intr* (aut) petardear
back'ground' *s* fondo; antecedentes *mpl;* conocimientos, educación; (*of a painting*) lontananza
background music *s* música de fondo
backing ['bækɪŋ] *s* apovo, sostén *m;* garantía, respaldo; financiamiento; (bb) lomera
back'lash' *s* (mach) contragolpe *m;* (mach) juego; (fig) reacción violenta
back'log' *s* (com) reserva de pedidos pendientes; (*e.g., of work*) acumulación
back number *s* número atrasado; (coll) persona anticuada
back pay *s* sueldo retrasado
back seat *s* puesto secundario; **to take a back seat** perder influencia
back'side' *s* espalda; trasero
back'slide' *v* (*pret & pp* **-slid** [,slɪd]) *intr* reincidir
backspacer ['bæk,spesər] *s* tecla de retroceso
back'stage' *adv* detrás del telón; entre bastidores
back'stairs' *adj* indirecto, secreto
back stairs *spl* escalera trasera; medios indirectos
back'stitch' *s* pespunte *m* ‖ *tr & intr* pespuntar
back'stop' *s* reja o red *f* para detener la pelota
back'swept' wing *s* (aer) ala en flecha
back talk *s* respuesta insolente
backward ['bækwərd] *adj* atrasado, tardío; tímido ‖ *adv* de atrás; de espaldas; al revés; cada vez peor; para atrás, hacia atrás
back'wa'ter *s* remanso; (fig) atraso, yermo
back'woods' *spl* monte *m,* región alejada de los centros de población
back yard *s* patio trasero, corral trasero
bacon ['bekən] *s* tocino
bacteria [bæk'tɪrɪ•ə] *pl de* **bacterium**
bacterial [bæk'tɪrɪ•əl] *adj* bacteriano
bacteriologist [bæk,tɪrɪ'ɑlədʒɪst] *s* bacteriólogo
bacteriology [bæk,tɪrɪ'ɑlədʒi] *s* bacteriología
bacteri•um [bæk'tɪrɪ•əm] *s* (*pl* **-a** [ə]) bacteria
bad [bæd] *adj* (*comp* **worse** [wʌrs]; *super* **worst** [wʌrst]) malo; (*money*) falso; (*debt*) incobrable; **from bad to worse** de mal en peor; **to be in bad** (coll) caer en desgracia; **to be too bad** ser lástima; **to go to the bad** (coll) ir por mal camino; (coll) arruinarse; **to look bad** tener mala cara
bad breath *s* mal aliento
badge [bædʒ] *s* divisa, insignia
badger ['bædʒər] *s* tejón *m*
badly ['bædli] *adv* mal; con urgencia; gravemente
badly off *adj* malparado; muy enfermo
badminton ['bædmɪntən] *s* juego del volante
baffle ['bæfəl] *s* deflector *m;* (rad) pantalla acústica ‖ *tr* confundir; burlar, frustrar
baffling ['bæflɪŋ] *adj* perplejo, desconcertador
bag [bæg] *s* saco; saquito de mano; (*in clothing*) bolsa; (*purse*) bolso; (*take of game*) caza; **to be in the bag** (slang) ser cosa segura ‖ *v* (*pret & pp* **bagged;** *ger* **bagging**) *tr* ensacar; coger, cazar ‖ *intr* hacer bolsa (*un vestido*)
baggage ['bægɪdʒ] *s* equipaje *m;* (mil) bagaje *m*
baggage car *s* furgón *m* de equipajes
baggage check *s* contraseña de equipajes
baggage rack *s* red *f* de equipajes
baggage room *s* sala de equipajes
bag'pipe' *s* gaita, cornamusa
bag'pi'per *s* gaitero
bail [bel] *s* caución, fianza; **to go bail for** salir fiador por ‖ *tr* caucionar, afianzar; achicar (*la embarcación; el agua*); **to bail out** salir fiador por; achicar ‖ *intr* achicar; **to bail out** lanzarse en paracaídas
bailiff ['belɪf] *s* algualcil *m,* corchete *m*
bailiwick ['belɪwɪk] *s* alguacilazgo; **to be in the bailiwick of** ser de la pertenencia de
bait [bet] *s* carnada, cebo; señuelo; **to swallow the bait** tragar el anzuelo ‖ *tr* cebar, encarnar (*el anzuelo*); tentar, seducir; (*to pester*) hostigar
baize [bez] *s* bayeta
bake [bek] *tr* cocer al horno; cocer (*loza, gres, etc.*)
bakelite ['bekə,laɪt] *s* baquelita
baker ['bekər] *s* panadero, hornero
baker's dozen *s* docena del fraile
baker•y ['bekəri] *s* (*pl* **-ies**) panadería
baking powder ['bekɪŋ] *s* levadura en polvo
baking soda *s* bicarbonato de sosa
bal. *abbr* **balance**
balance ['bæləns] *s* (*instrument for weighing*) balanza; (*state of equilibrium*) equilibrio; (*amount left over*) resto; (*amount still owed*) saldo; (*statement of debits and credits*) balance *m;* **to lose one's balance** perder el equilibrio; **to strike a balance** hacer o pasar balance ‖ *tr* balancear; equilibrar; equilibrar, nivelar (*el presupuesto*) ‖ *intr* equilibrarse; (*to waver*) balancear

balanced [ˈbælənst] *adj* equilibrado
balance of payments *s* balanza de pagos
balance of power *s* equilibrio político
balance sheet *s* balance *m*, avanzo
balco•ny [ˈbælkəni] *s* (*pl* **-nies**) balcón *m;* (*in a theater*) galería, paraíso
bald [bɔld] *adj* calvo; franco, directo
baldness [ˈbɔldnɪs] *s* calvicie *f*
baldric [ˈbɔldrɪk] *s* tahalí *m*
bale [bel] *s* bala || *tr* embalar
Balearic [,bælɪˈærɪk] *adj* balear
Balearic Islands *spl* islas Baleares
baleful [ˈbelfəl] *adj* funesto, maligno
balk [bɔk] *tr* burlar, frustrar || *intr* emperrarse, resistirse
Balkan [ˈbɔlkən] *adj* balcánico || **the Balkans** los Balcanes
balk•y [ˈbɔki] *adj* (*comp* **-ier;** *super* **-iest**) rebelón, repropio
ball [bɔl] *s* bola, pelota; esfera, globo; (*of wool, yarn*) ovillo; (*of finger*) yema; (*projectile*) bala; (*dance*) baile *m*
ballad [ˈbæləd] *s* balada
ballade [bəˈlɑd] *s* (mus) balada
ballast [ˈbæləst] *s* (aer, naut) lastre *m;* (rr) balasto || *tr* lastrar; balastar
ball bearing *s* cojinete *m* de bolas
ballerina [,bæləˈrinə] *s* bailarina
ballet [ˈbæle] *s* ballet *m*, baile *m*
ballistic [bəˈlɪstɪk] *adj* balístico
balloon [bəˈlun] *s* globo
ballot [ˈbælət] *s* balota; sufragio || *intr* balotar
ballot box *s* urna electoral
ball′play′er *s* pelotari *m;* beisbolero
ball′-point′ pen *s* bolígrafo, pluma estilográfica; biro (Arg); birome *f* (Arg, Urug); puntabola, punto bola (Bol); lapicero (CAm, Col); lápiz *m* de pasta (Chile); esferográfica, esfero (Col); estenógrafo (Cuba); lápiz *m* de bolilla (Peru); plumilla (Ven)
ball′room′ *s* salón *m* de baile
ballyhoo [ˈbælɪ,hu] *s* alharaca, bombo || *tr* dar teatro a, dar bombo a
balm [bɑm] *s* bálsamo
balm•y [ˈbɑmi] *adj* (*comp* **-ier;** *super* **-iest**) bonancible, suave
baloney [bəˈloni] *interj* (coll) ¡aprieta!
balsam [ˈbɔlsəm] *s* bálsamo
Baltic [ˈbɔltɪk] *adj* báltico
Baltimore oriole [ˈbɔltɪ,mor] *s* cacique veranero
baluster [ˈbæləstər] *s* balaustre *m*
bamboo [bæmˈbu] *s* bambú *m*
bamboozle [bæmˈbuzəl] *tr* (coll) embaucar, engañar
bamboozler [bæmˈbuzlər] *s* (coll) embaucador *m*, engañabobos *mf*
ban [bæn] *s* prohibición; excomunión, entredicho; (*of marriage*) amonestación || *v* (*pret & pp* **banned;** *ger* **banning**) *tr* prohibir; excomulgar
banana [bəˈnænə] *s* banana, plátano; (*tree*) banano, bananero, plátano
banana oil *s* esencia de pera
band [bænd] *s* banda; (*of people*) cuadrilla; (*of a hat*) cintillo; (*of a cigar*) anillo; liga de goma; (mus) banda, música, charanga || *intr* abanderizarse
bandage [ˈbændɪdʒ] *s* venda || *tr* vendar
bandanna [bænˈdænə] *s* pañuelo de hierbas
band′box′ *s* sombrerera
bandit [ˈbændɪt] *s* bandido
band′mas′ter *s* músico mayor
bandoleer [,bændəˈlɪr] *s* bandolera
band saw *s* sierra continua, sierra sin fin
band′stand′ *s* quiosco de música
baneful [ˈbenfəl] *adj* nocivo, venenoso; (*e.g., influence*) funesto
bang [bæŋ] *adv* de golpe || *interj* ¡pum! || *s* golpazo; (*of a door*) portazo; **bangs** flequillo || *tr* golpear con ruido; cerrar (*p.ej., una puerta*) de golpe || *intr* hacer estrépito
banish [ˈbænɪʃ] *tr* desterrar; despedir (*p.ej., miedo*)
banishment [ˈbænɪʃmənt] *s* destierro
banister [ˈbænɪstər] *s* balaustre *m*
bank [bæŋk] *s* banco; (*in certain games*) banca; (*small container for coins*) alcancía; (*of a river*) ribera, orilla; (*of earth, snow, clouds*) montón *m* || *tr* depositar o guardar (*dinero*) en un banco; amontonar; cubrir (*un fuego*) con cenizas || *intr* depositar dinero; **to bank on** (coll) contar con
bank account *s* cuenta de banco
bank′book′ *s* libreta de banco
banker [ˈbæŋkər] *s* banquero
banking [ˈbæŋkɪŋ] *adj* bancario || *s* banca
bank note *s* billete *m* de banco
bank roll *s* lío de papel moneda
bankrupt [ˈbæŋkrʌpt] *adj & s* bancarrotero; **to go bankrupt** hacer bancarrota || *tr* hacer quebrar; arruinar
bankrupt•cy [ˈbæŋkrʌptsi] *s* (*pl* **-cies**) bancarrota
banner [ˈbænər] *s* bandera, estandarte *m*
banner cry *s* grito de combate
banquet [ˈbæŋkwɪt] *s* banquete *m* || *tr & intr* banquetear
bantamweight [ˈbæntəm,wet] *s* (box) gallo
banter [ˈbæntər] *s* burla, chanza || *intr* burlar, chancear
baptism [ˈbæptɪzəm] *s* bautismo, bautizo; (fig) bautismo
Baptist [ˈbæptɪst] *adj & s* baptista *mf*, bautista *mf*
baptister•y [ˈbæptɪstəri] *s* (*pl* **-ies**) baptisterio, bautisterio
baptize [ˈbæptaɪz] *tr* bautizar
bar. *abbr* **barometer, barrel, barrister**
bar [bɑr] *s* barra; (*of door or window*) tranca; (*of jail*) reja; barrera; (*legal profession*) abogacía; (*members of legal profession*) curia; (*of public opinion*) tribunal *m;* (mus) barra; (*unit between two bars*) (mus) compás *m;* **behind bars** entre rejas || *prep* salvo; **bar none** sin excepción || *v* (*pret & pp* **barred;** *ger* **barring**) *tr* barrear, atrancar; impedir; prohibir; excluir
bar association *s* colegio de abogados
barb [bɑrb] *s* púa, lengüeta; (*of a pen*) barbilla

Barbados [bɑr'bedoz] *s* la Barbada
barbarian [bɑr'bɛrɪ•ən] *s* bárbaro
barbaric [bɑr'bærɪk] *adj* bárbaro
barbarism ['bɑrbə,rɪzəm] *s* barbaridad *f;* (gram) barbarismo
barbari•ty [bɑr'bærɪti] *s* (*pl* **-ties**) barbarie *f*
barbarous ['bɑrbərəs] *adj* bárbaro
Barbary ape ['bɑrbəri] *s* mono de Gibraltar
barbed [bɑrbd] *adj* armado de púas; mordaz, punzante
barbed wire *s* alambre *m* de espino, alambre de púas
barber ['bɑrbər] *adj* barberil || *s* barbero, peluquero
barber pole *s* percha de barbero
bar'ber•shop' *s* barbería, peluquería
bard [bɑrd] *s* bardo; (*horse armor*) barda || *tr* bardar
bare [bɛr] *adj* desnudo; (*head*) descubierto; (*unfurnished*) desamueblado; (*wire*) sin aislar; mero, sencillo, puro || *tr* desnudar; descubrir
bare'back' *adj & adv* en pelo, sin silla
barefaced ['bɛr,fest] *adj* desvergonzado
bare'foot' *adj* descalzo || *adv* con los pies desnudos
bareheaded ['bɛr,hɛdɪd] *adj* descubierto || *adv* con la cabeza descubierta
barelegged ['bɛr,lɛgɪd] o ['bɛr,lɛgd] *adj* con las piernas desnudas
barely ['bɛrli] *adv* aspenas; escasamente
bargain ['bɑrgɪn] *s* (*deal*) convenio, trato; (*cheap purchase*) ganga; **in the bargain** de añadidura || *tr* — **to bargain away** vender regalado || *intr* negociar; (*to haggle*) regatear
bargain counter *s* baratillo
bargain sale *s* venta de saldos
barge [bɑrdʒ] *s* gabarra, lanchón *m;* bongo (SAm) || *intr* moverse pesadamente; **to barge in** entrar sin pedir permiso, entrar sin llamar a la puerta
barium ['bɛrɪ•əm] *s* bario
bark [bɑrk] *s* (*of tree*) corteza; (*of dog*) ladrido; (*boat*) barca || *tr* ladrar (*p.ej., injurias*) || *intr* ladrar
barley ['bɑrli] *s* cebada
barley water *s* hordiate *m*
bar magnet *s* barra imantada
bar'maid' *s* moza de taberna
barn [bɑrn] *s* granero, troje *m;* caballeriza, establo; cochera
barnacle ['bɑrnəkəl] *s* cirrópodo
barn owl *s* lechuza, oliva
barn'yard' *s* corral *m*
barnyard fowl *spl* aves *fpl* de corral
barometer [bə'rɑmɪtər] *s* barómetro
baron ['bærən] *s* barón *m*
baroness ['bærənɪs] *s* baronesa
baroque [bə'rok] *adj & s* barroco
barracks ['bærəks] *spl* cuartel *m*
barrage [bə'rɑʒ] *s* (*dam*) presa; (mil) barrera de fuego
barrel ['bærəl] *s* barril *m*, tonel *m;* (*of a gun, pen, etc.*) cañón *m*
barrel organ *s* organillo
barren ['bærən] *adj* árido, estéril
barricade [,bærɪ'ked] *s* barrera || *tr* barrear
barrier ['bærɪ•ər] *s* barrera
barrier reef *s* barrera de arrecifes
barrister ['bærɪstər] *s* (Brit) abogado
bar'room' *s* bar *m*, cantina
bar'tend'er *s* cantinero, tabernero, barman *m*
barter ['bɑrtər] *s* trueque *m* || *tr* trocar
base [bes] *adj* bajo, humilde; infame, vil; (*metal*) bajo de ley || *s* base *f;* (*of electric light or vacuum tube; of projectile*) culote *m;* (mus) bajo || *tr* basar
base'ball' *s* beisbol *m;* pelota de beisbol
baseball player *s* beisbolero, beisbolista *m*
base'board' *s* rodapié *m*
Basel ['bɑzəl] *s* Basilea
baseless ['beslɪs] *adj* infundado
basement ['besmənt] *s* sótano
bashful ['bæʃfəl] *adj* encogido, tímido
basic ['besɪk] *adj* básico
basic commodities *spl* artículos de primera necesidad
basilica [bə'sɪlɪkə] *s* basílica
basin ['besɪn] *s* jofaina, palangana; (*of a fountain*) tazón *m;* (*of a river*) cuenca; (*of a harbor*) dársena
ba•sis ['besɪs] *s* (*pl* **-ses** [siz]) base *f;* **on the basis of** a base de
bask [bæsk] o [bɑsk] *intr* asolearse, calentarse
basket ['bæskɪt] *s* cesta; (*large basket*) cesto; (*with two handles*) canasta; (*with lid*) excusabaraja; (*sport*) cesto, red *f*
bas'ket•ball' *s* baloncesto, basquetbol *m*
Basle [bɑl] *s* Basilea
Basque [bæsk] *adj & s* (*of Spain*) vascongado; (*of Spain and France*) vasco; (*of old Spain*) vascón *m*
bas-relief [,bɑrɪ'lif] *s* bajo relieve
bass [bes] *adj & s* (mus) bajo || [bæs] *s* (ichth) róbalo; (ichth) micróptero
bass drum *s* bombo
bass horn *s* tuba
bas•so ['bæso] *s* (*pl* **-sos** o **-si** [si]) (mus) bajo
bassoon [bə'sun] *s* bajón *m*
bass viol ['vaɪ•əl] *s* violón *m*, contrabajo
bastard ['bæstərd] *adj & s* bastardo
bastard title *s* anteportada
baste [best] *tr* (*to sew slightly*) hilvanar; (*to moisten with drippings while roasting*) enlardar; (*to thrash*) azotar; (*to scold*) regañar
bat. *abbr* **battalion, battery**
bat [bæt] *s* palo; (coll) golpe *m;* (zool) murciélago || *v* (*pret & pp* **batted;** *ger* **batting)** *tr* golpear; batear (*una pelota*); **without batting an eye** sin inmutarse, sin pestañear || *intr* golpear
batch [bætʃ] *s* (*of bread*) hornada; (*of papers*) lío
bath [bæθ] *s* baño
bathe [beð] *tr* bañar || *intr* bañarse; **to go bathing** ir a bañarse
bather ['beðər] *s* bañista *mf*
bath'house' *s* casa de baños; caseta de baños
bathing beach *s* playa de baños
bathing beauty *s* sirena de la playa
bathing resort *s* estación balnearia
bathing suit *s* traje *m* de baño, bañador *m*

bathing trunks *spl* taparrabo
bath'robe' *s* albornoz *m*, bata de baño; bata, peinador *m*
bath'room' *s* baño, cuarto de baño
bathroom fixtures *spl* aparatos sanitarios
bath'tub' *s* bañera, baño
bathyscaphe [ˈbæθəˌskæf] *s* batiscafo
baton [bæˈtɑn] *s* bastón *m;* (mus) batuta
battalion [bəˈtæljən] *s* batallón *m*
batter [ˈbætər] *s* pasta, batido; (*baseball*) bateador *m* ‖ *tr* magullar, estropear
battering ram *s* ariete *m*
batter•y [ˈbætəri] *s* (*pl* **-ies**) batería; (*primary*) (elec) pila; (*secondary*) (elec) acumulador *m;* (law) violencia
battle [ˈbætəl] *s* batalla; **to do battle** librar batalla ‖ *tr* batallar
battle array *s* orden *m* de batalla
battle cry *s* grito de combate
battledore [ˈbætəlˌdor] *s* raqueta; **battledore and shuttlecock** raqueta y volante
bat'tlefield' *s* campo de batalla
battle front *s* frente *m* de combate
battlement [ˈbætəlmənt] *s* almenaje *m*
battle piece *s* (paint) batalla
bat'tle•ship' *s* acorazado
battue [bæˈtu] o [bæˈtju] *s* batida
bauble [ˈbɔbəl] *s* chuchería; cetro de bufón
Bavaria [bəˈvɛrɪ•ə] *s* Baviera
Bavarian [bəˈvɛrɪ•ən] *adj & mf* bávaro
bawd [bɔd] *s* alcahuete *m*, alcahueta
bawd•y [ˈbɔdi] *adj* (*comp* **-ier;** *super* **-iest**) indecente, obsceno
bawd'y•house' *s* mancebía, lupanar *m*
bawl [bɔl] *s* voces *fpl*, gritos ‖ *tr* — **to bawl out** (slang) regañar ‖ *intr* vocear, gritar; llorar ruidosamente
bay [be] *adj* bayo ‖ *s* bahía; aullido, ladrido; caballo bayo; (bot) laurel *m;* **to keep at bay** tener a raya ‖ *intr* aullar, ladrar
Bay of Biscay *s* golfo de Vizcaya
bayonet [ˈbe•ənɪt] *s* bayoneta ‖ *tr* herir o matar con bayoneta
bay rum *s* ron *m* de laurel, ron de malagueta
bay window *s* ventana salediza, mirador *m*
bazooka [bəˈzukə] *s* bazuca
bbl. *abbr* **barrel, barrels**
B.C. *abbr* **before Christ**
bd. *abbr* **board**
be [bi] *v* (*pres* **am** [æm], **is** [ɪz] **are** [ɑr]; *pret* **was** [wɑz] o [wʌz], **were** [wʌr]; *pp* **been** [bɪn]) *intr* estar; ser; tener, p.ej., **to be cold** tener frío; **to be wrong** no tener razón; tener la culpa; **here is** o **here are** aquí tiene Vd.; **there is** o **there are** hay ‖ *v aux* estar, p.ej., **he is studying** está estudiando; ser, p.ej., **she was hit by a car** fué atropellada por un coche; deber, p.ej., **what am I to do?** ¿qué debo hacer? ‖ *v impers* ser, p.ej., **it is necessary to get up early** es necesario levantarse temprano; haber, p.ej., **it is sunny** hay sol; hacer, p.ej., **it is cold** hace frío
beach [bitʃ] *s* playa
beach'comb' *intr* raquear; **to go beachcombing** andar al raque
beach'comb'er *s* raquero; vago de playa
beach'head' *s* cabeza de playa
beach robe *s* albornoz *m*
beach shoe *s* playera
beach umbrella *s* sombrilla de playa
beach wagon *s* rubia, coche *m* rural
beacon [ˈbikən] *s* señal luminosa; (*lighthouse*) faro; (*hill overlooking sea*) hacho; radiofaro; (*guide*) faro ‖ *tr* iluminar, guiar ‖ *intr* brillar
bead [bid] *s* cuenta; (*of glass*) abalorio; (*of sweat*) gota; (*moulding on corner of wall*) guardavivo; **to say** o **tell one's beads** rezar el rosario
beadle [ˈbidəl] *s* bedel *m*
beagle [ˈbigəl] *s* sabueso
beak [bik] *s* pico; cabo, promontorio
beam [bim] *s* (*of wood*) viga; (*of light, heat, etc.*) rayo; (naut) bao; (*direction perpendicular to the keel*) (naut) través *m;* (*of hope*) (fig) rayo; **on the beam** siguiendo el haz del radiofaro; (coll) siguiendo el buen camino ‖ *tr* emitir (*luz, ondas*) ‖ *intr* brillar; sonreír alegremente
bean [bin] *s* haba (*Vicia faba*); alubia, judía (*Phaseolus vulgaris*); (*of coffee, cocoa*) haba; (slang) cabeza
bean'pole' *s* rodrigón *m* para frijoles; (*tall, skinny person*) (coll) poste *m* de telégrafo
bear [bɛr] *s* oso; (*in stock market*) bajista *mf* ‖ *v* (*pret* **bore** [bor]; *pp* **borne** [born]) *tr* cargar; traer; llevar (*armas*); apoyar; aguantar; sentir, experimentar; producir, rendir (*frutos; interés*); (*to give birth to*) parir; tener (*amor, odio*); **to bear out** confirmar ‖ *intr* dirigirse, volver; **to bear on** referirse a; **to bear up** no perder la esperanza; **to bear with** ser indulgente para con
beard [bɪrd] *s* barba; (*of wheat*) arista
beardless [ˈbɪrdlɪs] *adj* imberbe
bearer [ˈbɛrər] *s* portador *m*
bearing [ˈbɛrɪŋ] *s* porte *m*, presencia; referencia, relación; (mach) cojinete *m;* **bearings** orientación; **to lose one's bearings** desorientarse
bearish [ˈbɛrɪʃ] *adj* bajista
bear'skin' *s* piel *f* de oso; (*military cap*) morrión *m*
beast [bist] *s* bestia
beast•ly [ˈbistli] *adj* (*comp* **-lier;** *super* **-liest**) bestial; (coll) muy malo ‖ *adv* (coll) muy mal
beast of burden *s* bestia de carga, acémila
beat [bit] *s* golpe *m;* (*of heart*) latido; (*of rhythm*) compás *m;* marca del compás; (mus) tiempo; (phys) batimiento; (rad) batido; (*of a policeman*) ronda; (*sponger*) (slang) embestidor *m* ‖ *v* (*pret* **beat;** *pp* **beat** o **beaten**) *tr* azotar, pegar; batir; sacudir (*una alfombra*); aventajar; llevar (*el compás*); tocar (*un tambor*); (*a una persona en una contienda*) ganar; **to beat it** (slang) largarse; **to beat up** batir (*p.ej., huevos*); (slang) aporrear ‖ *intr* batir; latir (*el corazón*); **to beat against** azotar
beaten path [ˈbitən] *s* camino trillado
beater [ˈbitər] *s* batidor *m;* (*mixer*) batidora

beati•fy [bɪ'ætɪ,faɪ] *v* (*pret & pp* **-fied**) *tr* beatificar
beating ['bitɪŋ] *s* golpeo; (*of wings*) aleteo; (*with a whip*) paliza; (*defeat*) derrota
beau [bo] *s* (*pl* **beaus** o **beaux** [boz]) galán *m*, cortejo; novio; elegante *m*
beautician [bju'tɪʃən] *s* embellecedora, esteta *mf*, esteticista *mf*
beautiful ['bjutɪfəl] *adj* bello, hermoso
beauti•fy ['bjutɪ,faɪ] *v* (*pret & pp* **-fied**) *tr* hermosear, embellecer
beau•ty ['bjuti] *s* (*pl* **-ties**) beldad *f*, belleza; (*person*) preciosura
beauty contest *s* concurso de belleza
beauty parlor *s* salón *m* de belleza
beauty queen *s* reina de la belleza
beauty sleep *s* primer sueño (*antes de medianoche*)
beauty spot *s* lunar postizo; sitio pintoresco
beaver ['bivər] *s* castor *m;* piel *f* de castor
becalm [bɪ'kɑm] *tr* calmar, serenar
because [bɪ'kɔz] *conj* porque; **because of** por, por causa de
beck [bɛk] *s* seña (*con la cabeza o la mano*); **at the beck and call of** a la disposición de
beckon ['bɛkən] *s* seña (*con la cabeza o la mano*) || *tr* llamar por señas; atraer, tentar || *intr* hacer señas
be•come [bɪ'kʌm] *v* (*pret* **-came;** *pp* **-come**) *tr* convenir, sentar bien || *intr* hacerse; llegar a ser; ponerse, volverse; convertirse en; **to become of** ser de, p.ej., **what will become of the soldier?** ¿qué será del soldado? hacerse, p.ej., **what became of his pencil?** ¿qué se ha hecho su lápiz?
becoming [bɪ'kʌmɪŋ] *adj* conveniente, decente; que sienta bien
bed [bɛd] *s* cama; (*of a river*) cauce *m;* (*of flower garden*) macizo; **to go to bed** acostarse; **to take to bed** encamarse
bed and board *s* pensión completa, casa y comida
bed'bug' *s* chinche *f*
bed'cham'ber *s* alcoba, cuarto de dormir
bed'clothes' *spl* ropa de cama
bed'cov'er *s* cubrecama, cobertor *m*
bedding ['bɛdɪŋ] *s* ropa de cama; (*for animals*) cama
bedev•il [bɪ'dɛvəl] *v* (*pret & pp* **-iled** o **-illed;** *ger* **-iling** o **-illing**) *tr* atormentar, confundir
bed'fast' *adj* postrado en cama
bed'fel'low *s* compañero o compañera de cama
bedlam ['bɛdləm] *s* confusión, desorden *m*, tumulto
bed linen *s* ropa de cama
bed'pan' *s* silleta
bed'post' *s* pilar *m* de cama
bedridden ['bɛd,rɪdən] *adj* postrado en cama
bed'room' *s* alcoba, cuarto de dormir
bed'side' *s* cabecera
bed'sore' *s* úlcera de decúbito; **to get bedsores** decentarse
bed'spread' *s* sobrecama, cobertor *m*
bed'spring' *s* colchón *m* de muelles, somier *m*
bed'stead' *s* cuja
bed'straw' *s* paja de jergón
bed'tick' *s* cutí *m*
bed'time' *s* hora de acostarse
bed warmer *s* calientacamas *m*
bee [bi] *s* abeja
beech [bitʃ] *s* haya
beech'nut' *s* hayuco
beef [bif] *s* carne *f* de vaca; ganado vacuno de engorde; (coll) fuerza muscular; (slang) queja || *tr* — **to beef up** (coll) reforzar || *intr* (slang) quejarse; (slang) soplar
beef cattle *s* ganado vacuno de engorde
beef'steak' *s* biftec *m*
bee'hive' *s* colmena
bee'line' *s* — **to make a beeline for** ir en línea recta hacia, ir derecho a
beer [bɪr] *s* cerveza; **dark beer** cerveza parda, cerveza negra; **light beer** cerveza clara
beeswax ['bɪz,wæks] *s* cera de abejas || *tr* encerar
beet [bit] *s* remolacha
beetle ['bitəl] *s* escarabajo
beetle-browed ['bitəl,braud] *adj* cejijunto; (*sullen*) ceñudo
beet sugar *s* azúcar *m* de remolacha
be•fall [bɪ'fɔl] *v* (*pret* **-fell** ['fɛl]; *pp* **-fallen** ['fɔlən]) *tr* acontecer a || *intr* acontecer
befitting [bɪ'fɪtɪŋ] *adj* conveniente; decoroso
before [bɪ'for] *adv* antes; delante, enfrente || *prep* (*in time*) antes de; (*in place*) delante de; (*in the presence of*) ante || *conj* antes (de) que
before'hand' *adv* de antemano, con anticipación
befriend [bɪ'frɛnd] *tr* ofrecer amistad a, amparar, proteger
befuddle [bɪ'fʌdəl] *tr* aturdir, confundir
beg [bɛg] *v* (*pret & pp* **begged;** *ger* **begging**) *tr* pedir, rogar, solicitar; mendigar; huesar || *intr* mendigar; **to beg off** excusarse
be•get [bɪ'gɛt] *v* (*pret* **-got** ['gɑt]; *pp* **-gotten** o **-got;** *ger* **-getting**) *tr* engendrar
beggar ['bɛgər] *s* mendigo; pobre *mf;* pícaro, bribón *m;* sujeto, tipo
be•gin [bɪ'gɪn] *v* (*pret* **-gan** ['gæn]; *pp* **-gun** ['gʌn]; *ger* **-ginning**) *tr & intr* comenzar, empezar; **beginning with** a partir de
beginner [bɪ'gɪnər] *s* principiante *mf;* iniciador *m*
beginning [bɪ'gɪnɪŋ] *s* comienzo, principio
begrudge [bɪ'grʌdʒ] *tr* dar de mala gana; envidiar
beguile [bɪ'gaɪl] *tr* engañar; divertir, entretener; engañar (*el tiempo*)
behalf [bɪ'hæf] — **on behalf of** en nombre de; a favor de
behave [bɪ'hev] *intr* conducirse, comportarse; portarse bien; funcionar
behavior [bɪ'hevjər] *s* conducta, comportamiento; funcionamiento
behaviorism [bɪ'hevjə,rɪzəm] *s* comportamentismo
behead [bɪ'hɛd] *tr* decapitar, descabezar
behind [bɪ'haɪnd] *adv* detrás; hacia atrás; con retraso; **to stay behind** quedarse atrás ||

prep detrás de; **behind the back of** a espaldas de; **behind the times** astrasado de noticias; **behind time** tarde || *s* (slang) trasero, pompis *m*
behold [bɪˈhold] *v* (*pret & pp* **-held** [ˈhɛld]) *tr* contemplar || *interj* ¡he aquí!
behoove [bɪˈhuv] *tr* convenir, tocar
being [ˈbi•ɪŋ] *adj* existente; **for the time being** por ahora, por el momento || *s* ser, ente *m*
belch [bɛltʃ] *s* eructo, regüeldo || *tr* vomitar (*p.ej., llamas, injurias*) || *intr* eructar, regoldar
beleaguer [bɪˈligər] *tr* sitiar, cercar
bel•fry [ˈbɛlfri] *s* (*pl* **-fries**) campanario
Belgian [ˈbɛldʒən] *adj & s* belga *mf*
Belgium [ˈbɛldʒəm] *s* Bélgica
be•lie [bɪˈlaɪ] *v* (*pret & pp* **-lied** [ˈlaɪd]; *ger* **-lying** [ˈlaɪ•ɪŋ]) *tr* desmentir
belief [bɪˈlif] *s* creencia
believable [bɪˈlivəbəl] *adj* creíble; (*source*) solvente
believe [bɪˈliv] *tr & intr* creer
believer [bɪˈlivər] *s* creyente *mf*
belittle [bɪˈlɪtəl] *tr* empequeñecer, despreciar
bell [bɛl] *s* campana; (*electric bell*) timbre *m*, campanilla; (*ring of bell*) campanada || *intr* bramar, berrear
bell′boy′ *s* botones *m*
belle [bɛl] *s* beldad *f*, belleza
belles-lettres [,bɛlˈlɛtrə] *spl* bellas letras
bell gable *s* espadaña
bell glass *s* fanal *m*
bell′hop′ *s* (slang) botones *m*
bellicose [ˈbɛlɪ,kos] *adj* belicoso
belligerent [bəˈlɪdʒərənt] *adj & s* beligerante *mf*
bellow [ˈbɛlo] *s* bramido; **bellows** fuelle *m*, barquín *m* || *tr* gritar || *intr* bramar
bell ringer *s* campanero
bellwether [ˈbɛl,wɛðər] *s* manso
bel•ly [ˈbɛli] *s* (*pl* **-lies**) barriga, vientre *m;* estómago || *v* (*pret & pp* **-lied**) *intr* hacer barriga; hacer bolso (*las velas*)
bel′ly•ache′ *s* (slang) dolor *m* de barriga || *intr* (slang) quejarse
belly button *s* (coll) ombligo
belly dance *s* (coll) danza del vientre
bellyful [ˈbɛlɪ,ful] *s* (slang) panzada
bel′ly-land′ *intr* (aer) aterrizar de panza
belong [bɪˈlɔŋ] *intr* pertenecer; deber estar
belongings [bɪˈlɔŋɪŋz] *spl* pertenencias, efectos; corotos
beloved [bɪˈlʌvɪd] o [bɪˈlʌvd] *adj & s* querido, amado
below [bɪˈlo] *adv* abajo; (*in a text*) más abajo; bajo cero, p.ej., **ten below** diez grados bajo cero || *prep* debajo de; inferior a
belt [bɛlt] *s* cinturón *m;* (aer, mach) correa; (geog) faja, zona; **to tighten one's belt** ceñirse
bemoan [bɪˈmon] *tr* deplorar, lamentar
bench [bɛntʃ] *s* banco; (law) tribunal *m*
bend [bɛnd] *s* curva; (*in a road, river, etc.*) recodo, vuelta || *v* (*pret & pp* **bent** [bɛnt]) *tr* encorvar; doblar (*un tubo; la rodilla*); inclinar (*la cabeza*); dirigir (*sus esfuerzos*) || *intr* encorvarse; doblarse; inclinarse
beneath [bɪˈniθ] *adv* abajo || *prep* debajo de; inferior a
benediction [,bɛnɪˈdɪkʃən] *s* bendición *f*
benefaction [,bɛnɪˈfækʃən] *s* beneficio
benefactor [ˈbɛnɪ,fæktər] o [,bɛnɪˈfæktər] *s* bienhechor *m*
benefactress [ˈbɛnɪ,fæktrɪs] o [,bɛnɪˈfæktrɪs] *s* bienhechora
beneficence [bɪˈnɛfɪsəns] *s* beneficencia
beneficent [bɪˈnɛfɪsənt] *adj* bienhechor
beneficial [,bɛnɪˈfɪʃəl] *adj* beneficioso
beneficiar•y [,bɛnɪˈfɪʃɪ,ɛri] *s* (*pl* **-ies**) beneficiario
benefit [ˈbɛnɪfɪt] *s* beneficio; lasca; **for the benefit of** a beneficio de || *tr* beneficiar
benefit performance *s* beneficio
benevolence [bɪˈnɛvələns] *s* benevolencia
benevolent [bɪˈnɛvələnt] *adj* benévolo; (*e.g., institution*) benéfico
benign [bɪˈnaɪn] *adj* benigno
benigni•ty [bɪˈnɪgnɪti] *s* (*pl* **-ties**) benignidad
bent [bɛnt] *adj* encorvado, doblado, torcido; **bent on** resuelto a, empeñado en; **bent over** cargado de espaldas || *s* encorvadura; inclinación *f*, propensión *f*
benzedrine [ˈbɛnzə,drin] *s* bencedrina
benzine [bɛnˈzin] *s* bencina
bequeath [bɪˈkwið] o [bɪˈkwiθ] *tr* legar
bequest [bɪˈkwɛst] *s* manda, legado
berate [bɪˈret] *tr* regañar, reñir
be•reave [bɪˈriv] *v* (*pret & pp* **-reaved** o **-reft** [ˈrɛft]) *tr* despojar, privar; desconsolar
bereavement [bɪˈrivmənt] *s* despojo, privación *f;* desconsuelo
berkelium [bərˈkilɪ•əm] *s* berkelio
Berliner [bərˈlɪnər] *s* berlinés *m*
ber•ry [ˈbɛri] *s* (*pl* **-ries**) baya; (*of coffee plant*) grano, haba
berserk [ˈbʌrsʌrk] *adj* frenético || *adv* frenéticamente
berth [bʌrθ] *s* (*bed*) litera; (*room*) camarote *m;* (*for a ship*) amarradero; (coll) empleo, puesto
beryllium [bəˈrɪlɪ•əm] *s* berilio
be•seech [bɪˈsitʃ] *v* (*pret & pp* **-sought** [ˈsɔt] o **-seeched**) *tr* suplicar
be•set [bɪˈsɛt] *v* (*pret & pp* **-set;** *ger* **-setting**) *tr* acometer, acosar; cercar, sitiar
beside [bɪˈsaɪd] *adv* además, también || *prep* cerca de, junto a; en comparación de; excepto; **beside oneself** fuera de sí; **beside the point** incongruente
besiege [bɪˈsidʒ] *tr* asediar, sitiar
besmirch [bɪˈsmʌrtʃ] *tr* ensuciar, manchar
bespatter [bɪˈspætər] *tr* salpicar
be•speak [bɪˈspik] *v* (*pret* **-spoke** [ˈspok]; *pp* **-spoken**) *tr* apalabrar, pedir de antemano
best [bɛst] *adj super* mejor; óptimo || *adv super* mejor; **had best** debería || *s* (lo) mejor; (lo) más; **at best** a lo más; **to do one's best** hacer lo mejor posible; **to get the best of** aventajar, sobresalir; **to make the best of** sacar el mejor partido de
best girl *s* (coll) amiga preferida, novia

be•stir [bɪ'stʌr] *v* (*pret & pp* **-stirred;** *ger* **-stirring**) *tr* excitar, incitar; **to bestir oneself** esforzarse, afanarse
best man *s* padrino de boda
bestow [bɪ'sto] *tr* otorgar, conferir; dedicar
best seller *s* éxito de venta, campeón *m* de venta; éxito de librería
bet. *abbr* **between**
bet [bɛt] *s* apuesta || *v* (*pret & pp* **bet** o **betted;** *ger* **betting**) *tr & intr* apostar; **I bet** a que, apuesto a que; **to bet on** apostar por; **you bet** (slang) ya lo creo
be•take [bɪ'tek] *v* (*pret* **-took** ['tʊk]; *pp* **-taken**) *tr* — **to betake oneself** dirigirse; darse, entregarse
be•think [bɪ'θɪŋk] *v* (*pret & pp* **-thought** ['θɔt]) *tr* — **to bethink oneself of** considerar, acordarse de
Bethlehem ['bɛθlɪ,hɛm] *s* Belén *m*
betide [bɪ'taɪd] *tr* presagiar; acontecer a || *intr* acontecer
betoken [bɪ'tokən] *tr* anunciar, indicar, presagiar
betray [bɪ'tre] *tr* traicionar; descubrir, revelar
betrayal [bɪ'tre•əl] *s* traición; descubrimiento, revelación
betroth [bɪ'troð] o [bɪ'trɔθ] *tr* prometer en matrimonio; **to become betrothed** desposarse
betrothal [bɪ'troðəl] o [bɪ'trɔθəl] *s* desposorios, esponsales *mpl*
betrothed [bɪ'troðd] o [bɪ'trɔθt] *s* prometido, novio
better ['bɛtər] *adj comp* mejor; **it is better to** más vale; **to grow better** mejorarse; **to make better** mejorar || *adv comp* mejor; más; **had better** debería; **to like better** preferir || *s* superior; ventaja; **to get the better of** llevar la ventaja a || *tr* aventajar; mejorar; **to better oneself** mejorar su posición
better half *s* (coll) cara mitad
betterment ['bɛtərmənt] *s* mejoramiento; (*in an illness*) mejoría
between [bɪ'twin] *adv* en medio, entremedias || *prep* entre; **between you and me** entre Vd. y yo; acá para los dos
be•tween'-decks' *s* entrecubiertas, entrepuentes *mpl*
between decks *adv* entrecubiertas
bev•el ['bɛvəl] *adj* biselado || *s* (*instrument*) cartabón *m;* (*sloping part*) bisel *m* || *v* (*pret & pp* **-eled** o **-elled;** *ger* **-eling** o **-elling**) *tr* biselar
beverage ['bɛvərɪdʒ] *s* bebida
bev•y ['bɛvi] *s* (*pl* **-ies**) (*of birds*) bandada; (*of girls*) grupo
bewail [bɪ'wel] *tr & intr* lamentar
beware [bɪ'wɛr] *tr* guardarse de || *intr* tener cuidado; **beware of . . . !** ¡ojo con . . . !, ¡cuidado con . . . !; **to beware of** guardarse de
bewilder [bɪ'wɪldər] *tr* aturdir, dejar perplejo, desatinar
bewilderment [bɪ'wɪldərmənt] *s* aturdimiento, perplejidad

beyond [bɪ'jɑnd] *adv* más allá, más lejos || *prep* más allá de; además de; no capaz de; **beyond a doubt** fuera de duda; **beyond the reach of** fuera del alcance de || *s* — **the great beyond** el más allá, el otro mundo
bg. *abbr* **bag**
bias ['baɪ•əs] *s* sesgo, diagonal *f;* prejuicio; (electron) polarización de rejilla || *tr* predisponer, prevenir
Bib. *abbr* **Bible, Biblical**
bib [bɪb] *s* babero; pepe *m;* (*of apron*) pechera
Bible ['baɪbəl] *s* Biblia
Biblical ['bɪblɪkəl] *adj* bíblico
bibliographer [,bɪblɪ'ɑgrəfər] *s* bibliógrafo
bibliogra•phy [,bɪblɪ'ɑgrəfi] *s* (*pl* **-phies**) bibliografía
bibliophile ['bɪblɪ•ə,faɪl] *s* bibliófilo
bicameral [baɪ'kæmərəl] *adj* bicameral
bicarbonate [baɪ'kɑrbə,net] *s* bicarbonato
bicker ['bɪkər] *s* discusión ociosa || *intr* discutir ociosamente
bicycle ['baɪsɪkəl] *s* bicicleta
bid [bɪd] *s* oferta, postura; (*in bridge*) declaración || *v* (*pret* **bade** [bæd] o **bid;** *ger* **bidden** ['bɪdən]) *tr & intr* ofrecer, pujar, licitar; (*in bridge*) declarar
bidder ['bɪdər] *s* postor *m;* (*in bridge*) declarante *mf;* **the highest bidder** el mejor postor
bidding ['bɪdɪŋ] *s* mandato, orden *f;* postura; (*in bridge*) declaración
bide [baɪd] *tr* — **to bide one's time** esperar la hora propicia
biennial [baɪ'ɛnɪ•əl] *adj* bienal
bier [bɪr] *s* féretro, andas
bifocal [baɪ'fokəl] *adj* bifocal || **bifocals** *spl* anteojos bifocales
big [bɪg] *adj* (*comp* **bigger;** *super* **biggest**) grande; (*considerable*) importante; (*grown-up*) adulto; **big with child** preñada || *adv* (coll) con jactancia; **to talk big** (coll) hablar gordo
bigamist ['bɪgəmɪst] *s* bígamo
bigamous ['bɪgəməs] *adj* bígamo
bigamy ['bɪgəmi] *s* bigamia
big-bellied ['bɪg,bɛlɪd] *adj* panzudo
Big Dipper *s* Carro mayor
big game *s* caza mayor
big-hearted ['bɪg,hɑrtɪd] *adj* magnánimo, generoso
bigot ['bɪgət] *s* intolerante *mf,* fanático
bigoted ['bɪgətɪd] *adj* intolerante, fanático
bigot•ry ['bɪgətri] *s* (*pl* **-ries**) intolerancia, fanatismo
big shot *s* (slang) pájaro de cuenta, señorón *m,* capitoste *m*
big stick *s* palo en alto
big toe *s* dedo gordo o grande (*del pie*)
bikini [bɪ'kini] *s* bikini *m*
bile [baɪl] *s* bilis *f*
bilge [bɪldʒ] *s* pantoque *m* || *tr* desfondar
bilge pump *s* bomba de sentina
bilge water *s* agua de pantoque
bilge ways *spl* anguilas
bilingual [baɪ'lɪŋgwəl] *adj* bilingüe

bilious [ˈbɪljəs] *adj* bilioso
bilk [bɪlk] *tr* estafar, trampear
bill [bɪl] *s* (*statement of charges for goods or service*) cuenta, factura; (*paper money*) billete *m;* (*poster*) cartel *m,* aviso; cartel de teatro; (*draft of law*) proyecto de ley; (*handbill*) hoja suelta; (*of bird*) pico; (com) giro, letra de cambio ‖ *tr* facturar; cargar en cuenta a; anunciar por carteles ‖ *intr* darse el pico (*las palomas*); acariciarse (*los enamorados*); **to bill and coo** acariciarse y arrullarse
bill'board' *s* cartelera
billet [ˈbɪlɪt] *s* (mil) boleta; (mil) alojamiento ‖ *tr* (mil) alojar
billet-doux [ˈbɪleˈdu] *s* (*pl* **billets-doux** [ˈbɪleˈduz]) esquela amorosa
bill'fold' *s* cartera de bolsillo, billetero
bill'head' *s* encabezamiento de factura
billiards [ˈbɪljərdz] *s* billar *m*
billion [ˈbɪljən] *s* (U.S.A.) mil millones; (Brit) billón *m*
bill of exchange *s* letra de cambio
bill of fare *s* lista de comidas, menú *m*
bill of lading [ˈledɪŋ] *s* conocimiento de embarque
bill of sale *s* escritura de venta
billow [ˈbɪlo] *s* oleada, ondulación ‖ *intr* ondular, hincharse
bill'post'er *s* fijacarteles *m,* fijador *m* de carteles
bil•ly [ˈbɪli] *s* (*pl* **-lies**) cachiporra
billy goat *s* macho cabrío
bin [bɪn] *s* arcón *m,* hucha
bind [baɪnd] *v* (*pret & pp* **bound** [baʊnd]) *tr* ligar, atar; juntar, unir; (*with a garland*) enguirlandar; ribetear (*la orilla del vestido*); agavillar (*las mieses*); vendar (*una herida*); encuadernar (*un libro*); estreñir (*el vientre*)
binder•y [ˈbaɪndəri] *s* (*pl* **-ies**) taller *m* de encuadernación
binding [ˈbaɪndɪŋ] *s* atadura; (*of a book*) encuadernación
binding post *s* borne *m,* sujetahilo
binge [bɪndʒ] *s* (slang) borrachera; turca; **to go on a binge** (slang) pegarse una mona, coger una turca
binnacle [ˈbɪnəkəl] *s* bitácora
binoculars [bɪˈnɑkjələrz] o [baɪˈnɑkjələrz] *spl* gemelos, prismáticos
biochemical [ˌbaɪ•əˈkɛmɪkəl] *adj* bioquímico
biochemist [ˌbaɪ•əˈkɛmɪst] *s* bioquímico
biochemistry [ˌbaɪ•əˈkɛmɪstri] *s* bioquímica
biodegradable [ˌbaɪ•ədɪˈgredəbəl] *adj* biodegradable
biog. *abbr* **biographical, biography**
biographer [baɪˈɑgrəfər] *s* biógrafo
biographic(al) [ˌbaɪ•əˈgræfɪk(əl)] *adj* biográfico
biogra•phy [baɪˈɑgrəfi] *s* (*pl* **-phies**) biografía
biologist [baɪˈɑlədʒɪst] *s* biólogo
biology [baɪˈɑlədʒi] *s* biología
biophysical [ˌbaɪ•əˈfɪzɪkəl] *adj* biofísico
biophysics [ˌbaɪ•əˈfɪzɪks] *s* biofísica
bioplasm [ˈbaɪ•əˌplæzəm] *s* bioplasma
biopsy [ˈbaɪ•ɑpsi] *s* biopsia
biped [ˈbaɪpɛd] *adj & s* bípedo
birch [bʌrtʃ] *s* abedul *m* ‖ *tr* azotar, varear
bird [bʌrd] *s* ave *f,* pájaro
bird cage *s* jaula
bird call *s* reclamo
bird'lime' *s* liga
bird of passage *s* ave *f* de paso
bird of prey *s* ave *f* de rapiña
bird'seed' *s* alpiste *m,* cañamones *mpl*
bird's'-eye' view *s* vista a ojo de pájaro
bird shot *s* perdigones *mpl*
birth [bʌrθ] *s* nacimiento; (*childbirth*) parto; origen *m*
birth certificate *s* partida de nacimiento
birth control *s* limitación de la natalidad, control de la natalidad, control de los nacimientos
birth'day' *s* cumpleaños *m,* natal *m;* (*of any event*) aniversario; **to have a birthday** cumplir años
birthday cake *s* pastel *m* de cumpleaños
birthday present *s* regalo de cumpleaños
birth'mark' *s* antojo, nevo materno
birth'place' *s* suelo natal, patria, lugar *m* de nacimiento
birth rate *s* natalidad
birth'right' *s* derechos de nacimiento; primogenitura
Biscay [ˈbɪske] *s* Vizcaya
biscuit [ˈbɪskɪt] *s* panecillo redondo; bizcocho
bisect [baɪˈsɛkt] *tr* bisecar ‖ *intr* empalmar (*dos caminos*)
bishop [ˈbɪʃəp] *s* obispo; (*in chess*) alfil *m*
bismuth [ˈbɪzməθ] *s* bismuto
bison [ˈbaɪsən] *s* bisonte *m*
bit [bɪt] *s* poquito, pedacito; (*of food*) bocado; (*of time*) ratito; (*part of bridle*) bocado, freno; (*for drilling*) barrena; **a good bit** una buena cantidad
bitch [bɪtʃ] *s* (*dog*) perra; (*fox*) zorra; (*wolf*) loba; (vulg) mujer *f* de mal genio
bite [baɪt] *s* mordedura; (*of bird or insect*) picadura; (*burning sensation on tongue*) resquemo; (*of food*) bocado; (*snack*) (coll) tentempié *m,* refrigerio ‖ *v* (*pret* **bit** [bɪt]; *pp* **bit** o **bitten** [ˈbɪtən]) *tr* morder; picar (*los peces, los insectos*); resquemar (*la lengua los alimentos*); comerse (*las uñas*) ‖ *intr* morder; picar; resquemar; (*to be caught by a trick*) (slang) picar
biting [ˈbaɪtɪŋ] *adj* penetrante; mordaz, picante
bitter [ˈbɪtər] *adj* amargo; (*e.g., struggle*) encarnizado; **to the bitter end** hasta el extremo; hasta la muerte
bitter almond *s* almendra amarga
bitterness [ˈbɪtərnɪs] *s* amargura
bitumen [bɪˈtjumən] *s* betún *m*
bivou•ac [ˈbɪvʊˌæk] *s* vivaque *m* ‖ *v* (*pret & pp* **-acked; ger -acking**) *intr* vivaquear
bizarre [bɪˈzɑr] *adj* original, raro
bk. *abbr* **bank, block, book**
bkg. *abbr* **banking**
bl. *abbr* **barrel**
b.l. *abbr* **bill of lading**

blabber ['blæbər] *tr & intr* barbullar
black [blæk] *adj* negro || *s* negro; luto; **to wear black** ir de luto
black'-and-blue' *adj* encardenalado, amoratado
black'-and-white' *adj* en blanco y negro
black'ber'ry *s* (*pl* **-ries**) (*bush*) zarza; (*fruit*) zarzamora
black'bird' *s* mirlo
black'board' *s* encerado, pizarra
black box *s* registrador *m* de vuelo
black'damp' *s* mofeta
blacken ['blækən] *tr* ennegrecer; (*to defame*) desacreditar, denigrar
blackguard ['blægɑrd] *s* bribón *m*, canalla *m* || *tr* injuriar, vilipendiar
black'head' *s* espinilla, comedón *m*
black hole *s* (astr) agujero negro
blackish ['blækɪʃ] *adj* negruzco
black'jack' *s* (*club*) cachiporra; (*flag*) bandera negra (*de pirata*) || *tr* aporrear
black'mail' *s* chantaje *m* || *tr* amenazar con chantaje
blackmailer ['blæk,melər] *s* chantajista *mf*
Black Maria [mə'raɪ•ə] *s* (coll) coche *m* celular
black market *s* estraperlo, mercado negro
blackness ['blæknɪs] *s* negror *m*, negrura
black'out' *s* (*in wartime*) apagón *m;* (*in theater*) apagamiento de luces; (*of aviators*) visión negra; pérdida de la memoria; cegura
black sheep *s* (fig) oveja negra, garbanzo negro
black'smith' *s* (*man who works with iron*) herrero; (*man who shoes horses*) herrador *m*
black'thorn' *s* espino negro, endrino
black tie corbata de smoking; smoking *m*
bladder ['blædər] *s* vejiga
blade [bled] *s* (*of a knife, sword*) hoja; (*of a propeller*) aleta; (*of a fan*) paleta; (*of an oar*) pala; (*of an electric switch*) cuchilla; (*sword*) espada; tallo de hierba; (coll) gallardo joven
blame [blem] *s* culpa || *tr* culpar
blameless ['blemlɪs] *adj* inculpable, irreprochable
blanch [blæntʃ] *tr* blanquear || *intr* palidecer
bland [blænd] *adj* apacible; suave; (*character; weather*) blando
blandish ['blændɪʃ] *tr* engatusar, lisonjear
blank [blæŋk] *adj* en blanco; blanco, vacío; (*stare, look*) vago || *s* blanco; papel blanco; formulario
blank check *s* firma en blanco; (fig) carta blanca
blanket ['blæŋkɪt] *adj* general, comprensivo || *s* manta, frazada; (fig) capa, manto || *tr* cubrir con manta; cubrir, obscurecer
blasé [blɑ'ze] *adj* hastiado
blaspheme [blæs'fim] *tr* blasfemar contra || *intr* blasfemar
blasphemous ['blæsfɪməs] *adj* blasfemo
blasphe•my ['blæsfɪmi] *s* (*pl* **-mies**) blasfemia
blast [blæst] *s* (*of wind*) ráfaga; (*of air, sand, water*) chorro; (*of bellows*) soplo; (*of a horn*) toque *m;* carga de pólvora; voladura, explosión; **full blast** en plena marcha || *tr* (*to blow up*) volar; arruinar; infamar, maldecir
blast furnace *s* alto horno
blast'off' *s* lanzamiento de cohete
blatant ['bletənt] *adj* ruidoso; vocinglero; intruso; chillón, cursi
blaze [blez] *s* llamarada; (*fire*) incendio; (*bonfire*) hoguera; luz *f* brillante || *tr* encender, inflamar; **to blaze a trail** abrir una senda || *intr* encenderse; resplandecer
bldg. *abbr* **building**
bleach [blitʃ] *s* blanqueo || *tr* blanquear; colar (*la ropa*)
bleachers ['blitʃərz] *spl* gradas al aire libre
bleak [blik] *adj* desierto, yermo, frío, triste
bleat [blit] *s* balido || *intr* balar
bleed [blid] *v* (*pret & pep* **bled** [blɛd]) *tr & intr* sangrar
blemish ['blɛmɪʃ] *s* mancha || *tr* manchar
blend [blɛnd] *s* mezcla; armonía || *v* (*pret & pp* **blended** o **blent** [blɛnt]) *tr* mezclar; armonizar; fusionar || *intr* mezclarse; armonizar; fusionarse
bless [blɛs] *tr* bendecir; **to be blessed with** estar dotado de
blessed ['blɛsɪd] *adj* bendito, santo
blessedness ['blɛsɪdnɪs] *s* bienaventuranza
blessing ['blɛsɪŋ] *s* bendición
blight [blaɪt] *s* niebla, roya; ruina || *tr* anublar; arruinar
blimp [blɪmp] *s* dirigible pequeño
blind [blaɪnd] *adj* ciego || *s* (*window shade*) estor *m*, transparente *m* de resorte; (*Venetian blind*) persiana; pretexto, subterfugio || *tr* cegar; (*to dazzle*) deslumbrar; (*to deceive*) cegar, vendar
blind alley *s* callejón *m* sin salida
blind date *s* cita a ciegas
blinder ['blaɪndər] *s* anteojera
blind flying *s* (aer) vuelo a ciegas
blind'fold' *adj* vendado de ojos || *s* venda || *tr* vendar los ojos a
blind landing *s* aterrizaje *m* a ciegas
blind man *s* ciego
blind'man's' buff *s* gallina ciega
blindness ['blaɪndnɪs] *s* ceguedad
blink [blɪŋk] *s* guiñada, parpadeo || *tr* guiñar (*el ojo*) || *intr* guiñar, parpadear, pestañear; oscilar (*la luz*)
blip [blɪp] *s* bache *m*
bliss [blɪs] *s* bienaventuranza, felicidad
blissful ['blɪsfəl] *adj* bienaventurado, feliz
blister ['blɪstər] *s* ampolla, vejiga || *tr* ampollar || *intr* ampollarse
blithe [blaɪð] *adj* alegre, animado
blitzkrieg ['blɪts,krig] *s* guerra relámpago
blizzard ['blɪzərd] *s* ventisca, chubasco de nieve
bloat [blot] *tr* hinchar || *intr* hincharse, abotagarse
block [blɑk] *s* bloque *m;* (*of hatter*) horma; (*of houses*) manzana; (*for chopping meat*)

tajo; estorbo, obstáculo || *tr* cerrar, obstruir; conformar (*un sombrero*)
blockade [bla'ked] *s* bloqueo || *tr* bloquear
blockade runner *s* forzador *m* de bloqueo
block and tackle *s* aparejo de poleas
block'bust'er *s* (coll) bomba rompedora
block'head' *s* tonto, zoquete *m*
block signal *s* (rr) señal *f* de tramo
blond [bland] *adj* rubio, blondo || *s* rubio (*hombre rubio*)
blonde [bland] *s* rubia (*mujer rubia*)
blood [blʌd] *s* sangre *f;* **in cold blood** a sangre fría
bloodcurdling ['blʌd,kʌrdlɪŋ] *adj* horripilante
blood'hound' *s* sabueso
blood poisoning *s* envenenamiento de la sangre
blood pressure *s* presión arterial
blood pudding *s* morcilla
blood relation *s* pariente consanguíneo
blood'shed' *s* efusión de sangre
blood'shot' *adj* inyectado en sangre, encarnizado
blood'stream' *s* corriente *f* sanguínea
blood test *s* análisis *m* de sangre
blood'thirst'y *adj* sanguinario
blood transfusion *s* transfusión de sangre
blood vessel *s* vaso sanguíneo
blood•y ['blʌdi] *adj* (*comp* **-ier;** *super* **-iest**) sangriento || *v* (*pret & pp* **-ied**) *tr* ensangrentar
bloom [blum] *s* florecimiento; flor *f* || *intr* florecer
blossom ['blasəm] *s* brote *m*, flor *f;* **in blossom** en cierne || *intr* cerner, florecer
blot [blat] *s* borrón *m* || *v* (*pret & pp* **blotted;** *ger* **blotting**) *tr* (*to smear*) borrar; secar con papel secante; **to blot out** borrar || *intr* borrarse; echar borrones (*una pluma*)
blotch [blatʃ] *s* manchón *m;* (*in the skin*) erupción
blotter ['blatər] *s* teleta, secafirmas *m*
blotting paper *s* papel *m* secante
blouse [blaus] *s* blusa
blow [blo] *s* (*hit, stroke*) golpe; (*blast of air*) soplo, soplido; (*blast of wind*) ventarrón *m;* (*of horn*) toque *m*, trompetazo; (*sudden sorrow*) estocada, ramalazo; (*boaster*) (slang) fanfarrón *m;* **to come to blows** venir a las manos || *v* (*pret* **blew** [blu]; *pp* **blown**) || *tr* soplar; sonar, tocar (*un instrumento de viento*); silbar (*un silbato*); sonarse (*las narices*); quemar (*un fusible*); (slang) malgastar (*dinero*); **to blow out** apagar soplando; quemar (*un fusible*); **to blow up** (*with air*) inflar; (*e.g., with dynamite*) volar, hacer saltar; ampliar (*una foto*) || *intr* soplar; (*to pant*) jadear, resoplar; fundirse (*un fusible*); (slang) fanfarronear; **to blow out** apagarse con el aire; quemarse, fundirse (*un fusible*); reventar (*un neumático*); **to blow up** volarse; (*to fail*) fracasar; (*with anger*) (slang) estallar, reventar
blow'out' *s* (aut) reventón *m;* (*of a fuse*) quemazón *f;* (slang) tertulia concurrida, festín *m*
blowout patch *s* parche *m* para neumático
blow'pipe' *s* (*torch*) soplete *m;* (*peashooter*) cerbatana
blow'torch' *s* antorcha a soplete, lámpara de soldar
blubber ['blʌbər] *s* grasa de ballena; lloro ruidoso || *intr* llorar ruidosamente
bludgeon ['blʌdʒən] *s* cachiporra || *tr* aporrear; intimidar
blue [blu] *adj* azul; abatido, triste || *s* azul *m;* **the blues** la murria, la morriña || *tr* azular; añilar (*la ropa blanca*) || *intr* azularse
blue'ber'ry *s* (*pl* **-ries**) mirtilo
blue chip *s* valor *m* de primera fila
blue'jay' *s* cianocita
blue jeans *spl* blujins *mpl*, vaqueros; pantalones de mezclilla (C-R, Mex); mecánicos (CAm, Cuba, S-D); pantalones azules (CAm); azulones (El Salv); mahones (P-R, S-D)
blue moon *s* cosa muy rara; **once in a blue moon** cada muerte de obispo, de Pascuas a Ramos
Blue Nile *s* Nilo Azul
blue'-pen'cil *tr* marcar o corregir con lápiz azul
blue'print' *s* cianotipo || *tr* copiar a la cianotipia
blue'stock'ing *s* (coll) marisabidilla
blue streak *s* (coll) rayo; **to talk a blue streak** (coll) soltar la tarabilla
bluff [blʌf] *adj* escarpado || *s* risco, peñasco escarpado; (*deception*) farol *m*, blof *m;* **to call someone's bluff** cogerle la palabra a uno || *intr* farolear, papelonear
blunder ['blʌndər] *s* disparate *m*, desatino || *intr* disparatar, desatinar
blunt [blʌnt] *adj* despuntado, embotado; brusco, franco, directo || *tr* despuntar, embotar
bluntness ['blʌntnɪs] *s* embotadura; brusquedad, franqueza
blur [blʌr] *s* borrón *m*, mancha || *v* (*pret & pp* **blurred;** *ger* **blurring**) *tr* empañar; obscurecer (*la vista*) || *intr* empañarse
blurb [blʌrb] *s* anuncio efusivo
blurt [blʌrt] *tr* — **to blurt out** soltar abrupta e impulsivamente
blush [blʌʃ] *s* rubor *m*, sonrojo || *intr* ruborizarse, sonrojarse
bluster ['blʌstər] *s* tumulto, gritos; jactancia || *intr* soplar con furia (*el viento*); bravear, fanfarronear
blustery ['blʌstəri] *adj* tempestuoso; (*wind*) violento; (*swaggering*) fanfarrón
blvd. *abbr* **boulevard**
boar [bor] *s* (*male swine*) verraco; (*wild hog*) jabalí *m*
board [bord] *s* tabla; (*to post announcements*) tablillo; (*table with meal*) mesa; (*daily meals*) pensión; (*organized group*) junta, consejo; (naut) bordo; **in boards** (bb) en cartoné; **on board** en el tren; (naut) a bordo || *tr* entablar; subir a (*un tren*);

embarcarse en (*un buque*) || *intr* hospedarse; estar de pupilo
board and lodging *s* mesa y habitación, pensión completa
boarder [ˈbordər] *s* pensionista *mf*, pupilo
boarding house *s* pensión, casa de huéspedes
boarding school *s* escuela de internos
board of health *s* junta de sanidad
board of trade *s* junta de comercio
board of trustees *s* consejo de administración
board'walk' *s* paseo entablado a la orilla del mar
boast [bost] *s* jactancia, baladronada || *intr* jactarse, baladronear, bravatear
boastful [ˈbostfəl] *adj* jactancioso
boat [bot] *s* barco, buque *m*, nave *f*; (*small boat*) bote *m*; **to be in the same boat** correr el mismo riesgo
boat hook *s* bichero
boat'house' *s* casilla para botes
boating [ˈbotɪŋ] *s* paseo en barco
boat•man [ˈbotmən] *s* (*pl* **-men** [mən]) barquero, lanchero
boat race *s* regata
boatswain *s* [ˈbosən] *s* contramaestre *m*
boatswain's chair *s* guindola
boatswain's mate *s* segundo contramaestre
bob [bɑb] *s* (*of pendulum of clock*) lenteja; (*of plumb line*) plomo; (*of a fishing line*) corcho; (*of a horse*) cola cortada; (*of a girl*) pelo cortado corto; (*jerky motion*) sacudida || *v* (*pret & pp* **bobbed**; *ger* **bobbing**) *tr* cortar corto || *intr* agitarse, menearse; **to bob up and down** subir y bajar con sacudidas cortas
bobbin [ˈbɑbɪn] *s* broca, canilla, bobina
bobby pin [ˈbɑbi] *s* horquillita para el pelo
bob'by•socks' *spl* (coll) tobilleras (*de jovencita*)
bobbysoxer [ˈbɑbɪˌsɑksər] *s* (coll) tobillera
bobolink [ˈbɑbəˌlɪŋk] *s* chambergo
bob'sled' *s* doble trineo articulado
bob'tail' *s* animal *m* rabón; cola corta; cola cortada
bob'white' *s* colín *m* de Virginia
bock beer [bɑk] *s* cerveza de marzo
bode [bod] *tr & intr* anunciar, presagiar; **to bode ill** ser un mal presagio; **to bode well** ser un buen presagio
bodice [ˈbɑdɪs] *s* jubón *m*, corpiño
bodily [ˈbɑdɪli] *adj* corporal, corpóreo || *adv* en persona; en conjunto
bodkin [ˈbɑdkɪn] *s* (*needle*) aguja roma; (*for lady's hair*) espadilla; (*to make holes in cloth*) punzón *m*
bod•y [ˈbɑdi] *s* (*pl* **-ies**) cuerpo; (*of a carriage or auto*) caja, carrocería
bod'y•guard' *s* (mil) guardia de corps; guardaespaldas *m*
body shop *s* taller *m* carrocero
Boer [bor] o [bur] *s* bóer *mf*
Boer War *s* guerra del Transvaal
bog [bɑg] *s* pantano || *v* (*pret & pp* **bogged**; *ger* **bogging**) *intr* — **to bog down** atascarse, hundirse
bogey [ˈbogi] *s* duende *m*, coco
bo'gey•man' *s* (*pl* **-men** [ˌmɛn]) duende *m*, espantajo
bogus [ˈbogəs] *adj* (coll) fingido, falso
bo•gy [ˈbogi] *s* (*pl* **-gies**) duende *m*, demonio, coco
Bohemian [boˈhimɪ•ən] *adj & s* bohemio
boil [bɔɪl] *s* hervor *m*, ebullición; (pathol) divieso, furúnculo || *tr* hacer hervir, herventar || *intr* hervir, bullir; **to boil over** salirse (*un líquido*) al hervir
boiler [ˈbɔɪlər] *s* caldera; (*for cooking*) marmita, olla
boil'er•mak'er *s* calderero
boiler room *s* sala de calderas
boiling [ˈbɔɪlɪŋ] *adj* hirviente, hirviendo || *s* hervor *m*, ebullición
boiling point *s* punto de ebullición
boisterous [ˈbɔɪstərəs] *adj* bullicioso, ruidoso, estrepitoso
bold [bold] *adj* audaz, arrojado, osado; descarado, impudente; temerario
bold'face' *s* negrilla
boldness [ˈboldnɪs] *s* audacia, arrojo, osadía; descaro, impudencia; temeridad
Bolivia [boˈlɪvɪ•ə] *s* Bolivia
Bolivian [boˈlɪvɪ•ən] *adj & s* boliviano
boll weevil [bol] *s* gorgojo del algodón
Bologna [bəˈlonjə] *s* Bolonia
Bolshevik [ˈbɑlʃəvɪk] o [ˈbolʃəvɪk] *adj & s* bolchevique *mf*
Bolshevism [ˈbɑlʃəˌvɪzəm] o [ˈbolʃəˌvɪzəm] *s* bolchevismo
bolster [ˈbolstər] *s* (*of bed*) larguero, travesaño; refuerzo, soporte *m* || *tr* apoyar, sostener; animar, alentar
bolt [bolt] *s* perno; (*to fasten a door*) cerrojo, pasador *m*; (*arrow*) cuadrillo; (*of lightning*) rayo; (*of cloth or paper*) rollo || *tr* empernar; acerrojar; deglutir de una vez; cribar, tamizar; disidir de (*un partido político*) || *intr* salir de repente; disidir; desbocarse (*un caballo*)
bolter [ˈboltər] *s* disidente *mf*; (*sieve*) criba, tamiz *m*
bolt from the blue *s* rayo en cielo sin nubes; suceso inesperado
bomb [bɑm] *s* bomba || *tr* bombear, bombardear
bombard [bɑmˈbɑrd] *tr* bombardear; (*e.g., with questions*) asediar
bombardment [bɑmˈbɑrdmənt] *s* bombardeo
bombast [ˈbɑmbæst] *s* ampulosidad
bombastic [bɑmˈbæstɪk] *adj* ampuloso
bomb crater *s* (mil) embudo de bomba
bomber [ˈbɑmər] *s* bombardero
bomb'proof' *adj* a prueba de bombas
bomb release *s* lanzabombas *m*
bomb'shell' *s* bomba; **to fall like a bombshell** caer como una bomba
bomb shelter *s* refugio antiaéreo
bomb'sight' *s* mira de bombardeo, visor *m*
bona fide [ˈbonəˌfaɪdə] *adj & adv* de buena fe
bonbon [ˈbɑnˌbɑn] *s* bombón *m*, confite *m*
bond [bɑnd] *s* (*tie, union*) enlace *m*, vínculo, lazo de unión; (*interest-bearing certificate*)

bono, obligación; (*surety*) fianza; (mas) aparejo; **bonds** cadenas, grillos; **in bond** en depósito bajo fianza
bondage [ˈbɑndɪdʒ] *s* cautiverio, servidumbre
bonded warehouse *s* depósito comercial
bond'hold'er *s* obligacionista *mf*, tenedor *m* de bonos
bonds•man [ˈbɑndzmən] *s* (*pl* **-men** [mən]) fiador *m*
bone [bon] *s* hueso; (*of fish*) espina; **bones** esqueleto; (*mortal remains*) huesos; castañuelas; (*dice*) (coll) dados; **to have a bone to pick with** tener una queja con; **to make no bones about** no andarse con rodeos en ‖ *tr* desosar; quitar la espina a; emballenar (*un corsé*) ‖ *intr* — **to bone up on** (coll) empollar, estudiar con ahinco
bone'head' *s* (coll) mentecato, zopenco
boneless [ˈbonlɪs] *adj* mollar, desosado; (*fish*) sin espinas
boner [ˈbonər] *s* (coll) patochada, plancha, gazapo
bonfire [ˈbɑn,faɪr] *s* hoguera
bonnet [ˈbɑnɪt] *s* gorra; (*sunbonnet*) papalina; (*of auto*) cubierta, capó *m*
bonus [ˈbonəs] *s* prima, plus *m;* dividendo extraordinario
bon•y [ˈboni] *adj* (*comp* **-ier;** *super* **-iest**) osudo; descarnado; (*fish*) espinoso
boo [bu] *s* rechifla; **not to say boo** no decir ni chus ni mus ‖ *tr & intr* abuchear, rechiflar
boo•by [ˈbubi] *s* (*pl* **-bies**) bobalicón *m*, zopenco; el peor jugador
booby prize *s* premio al peor jugador
booby trap *s* (*mine*) trampa explosiva; (*trick*) zancadilla
boogie-woogie [ˈbʊgiˈwʊgi] *s* bugui-bugui *m*
book [bʊk] *s* libro; (*bankbook*) libreta; (*book containing records of business transactions*) libro-registro; (*of cigaret paper, stamps, etc.*) librillo; **to keep books** llevar libros ‖ *tr* reservar (*un pasaje*); escriturar (*a un actor*)
bookbinder [ˈbʊk,baɪndər] *s* encuadernador *m*
book'bind'er•y *s* (*pl* **-ies**) encuadernación (*taller*)
book'bind'ing *s* encuadernación (*acción, arte*)
book'case' *s* armario para libros, estante *m* para libros
book end *s* apoyalibros *m*
bookie [ˈbʊki] *s* (coll) corredor *m* de apuestas
booking [ˈbʊkɪŋ] *s* (*of passage*) reservación; (*of an actor*) escritura
booking clerk *s* taquillero (*que despacha pasajes o localidades*)
bookish [ˈbʊkɪʃ] *adj* libresco
book'keep'er *s* tenedor *m* de libros
book'keep'ing *s* teneduría de libros, contabilidad
book'mak'er *s* corredor *m* de apuestas
book'mark' *s* registro
book'plate' *s* ex libris *m*
book review *s* reseña
book'sell'er *s* librero
book'shelf' *s* (*pl* **-shelves** [,ʃɛlvz] estante *m* para libros
book'stand' *s* (*rack*) atril *m;* mostrador *m* para libros; puesto de venta para libros
book'store' *s* librería
book'worm' *s* polilla que roe los libros; (fig) ratón *m* de biblioteca
boom [bum] *s* (*sudden prosperity*) auge *m*, boom *m;* (*noise*) estampido, trueno; (*of a crane*) aguilón *m;* (naut) botalón *m* ‖ *intr* hacer estampido, tronar; estar en auge
boomerang [ˈbumə,ræŋ] *s* bumerán *m*
boom town *s* pueblo en bonanza
boon [bun] *s* bendición, dicha
boon companion *s* buen compañero
boor [bʊr] *s* patán *m*, rústico
boorish [ˈbʊrɪʃ] *adj* rústico, zafio
boost [bust] *s* empujón *m* hacia arriba; (*in price*) alza; alabanza; ayuda ‖ *tr* empujar hacia arriba; alzar (*el precio*); alabar; ayudar
booster [ˈbustər] *s* cohete *m* lanzador; primera etapa de un cohete lanzador; (*enthusiastic backer*) bombista *mf*
booster shot *s* inyección secundaria
boot [but] *s* bota; **to boot** de añadidura, además; **to die with one's boots on** morir al pie del cañón ‖ *tr* dar un puntapié a; **to boot out** (slang) poner en la calle
boot'black' *s* limpiabotas *m*
booth [buθ] *s* casilla, quiosco; (*to telephone, to vote, etc.*) cabina; (*at a fair or market*) puesto
boot'jack' *s* sacabotas *m*
boot'leg' *adj* contrabandista; de contrabando ‖ *s* contrabando de licores ‖ *v* (*pret & pp* **-legged;** *ger* **-legging**) *tr* pasar de contrabando ‖ *intr* contrabandear en bebidas alcohólicas
bootlegger [ˈbut,lɛgər] *s* destilador *m* clandestino, contrabandista *m*
boot'leg'ging *s* contrabando en bebidas alcohólicas
bootlicker [ˈbut,lɪkər] *s* (slang) quitamotas *mf*, lavacaras *mf*
boot'strap' *s* tirilla de bota
boo•ty [ˈbuti] *s* (*pl* **-ties**) botín *m*, presa
booze [buz] *s* (coll) bebida alcohólica ‖ *intr* borrachear
bor. *abbr* **borough**
borax [ˈboræks] *s* bórax *m*
Bordeaux [bɔrˈdo] *s* Burdeos
border [ˈbɔrdər] *adj* frontero, fronterizo ‖ *s* borde *m*, margen *m & f;* frontera; **borders** bambalinas ‖ *tr* bordear; deslindar ‖ *intr* confinar
border clash *s* encuentro fronterizo
bor'der•line' *adj* incierto, indefinido ‖ *s* frontera
bore [bor] *s* (*drill hole*) barreno; (*size of hole*) calibre *m;* (*of firearm*) alma, ánima; (*of cylinder*) alesaje *m;* (*wearisome person*) latoso, machaca *mf;* fastidio ‖ *tr* aburrir, fastidiar; barrenar, hacer (*un agujero*)
boredom [ˈbordəm] *s* aburrimiento, fastidio
boring [ˈborɪŋ] *adj* aburrido, pesado; **that's terribly boring** es una lata

born [bɔrn] *adj* nacido; (*natural, by birth*) nato, innato; **to be born** nacer

borough [ˈbʌro] *s* (*town*) villa; distrito electoral de municipio

borrow [ˈbɑro] o [ˈbɔro] *tr* pedir o tomar prestado; apropiarse (*p.ej., una idea*); incorporar (*un elemento lingüístico extranjero*); **to borrow trouble** tomarse una molestia sin motivo alguno

borrower [ˈbɑro•ər] o [ˈbɔro•ər] *s* prestatario

borrowing [ˈbɑro•ɪŋ] o [ˈbɔro•ɪŋ] *s* préstamo; préstamo lingüístico, extranjerismo

bosom [ˈbʊzəm] *s* seno; (*of shirt*) pechera; corazón *m*, pecho

bosom friend *s* amigo de la mayor confianza

Bosporus [ˈbɑspərəs] *s* Bósforo

boss [bɔs] o [bɑs] *s* (coll) amo, capataz *m*, mandamás *m*, jefe *m;* (*in politics*) (coll) cacique *m;* protuberancia || *tr* (coll) mandar, dominar

bossism [ˈbɔsɪzəm] *s* caciquismo

boss•y [ˈbɔsi] *adj* (*comp* **-ier;** *super* **-iest**) mandón

botanical [bəˈtænɪkəl] *adj* botánico

botanist [ˈbɑtənɪst] *s* botánico

botany [ˈbɑtəni] *s* botánica

botch [bɑtʃ] *s* remiendo chapucero || *tr* remendar chapuceramente

both [boθ] *adj & pron* ambos || *adv* igualmente || *conj* a la vez; **both . . . and** tanto . . . como, así . . . como

bother [ˈbɑðər] *s* incomodidad, molestia, majadería, murga || *tr* incomodar, molestar, majaderear, pololear || *intr* molestarse

bothersome [ˈbɑðərsəm] *adj* incómodo, molesto, fastidioso

bottle [ˈbɑtəl] *s* botella, frasco || *tr* embotellar; **to bottle up** (nav) embotellar

bot'tle•neck' *s* gollete *m;* (*in traffic*) embotellado

bottle opener [ˈopənər] *s* abrebotellas *m*

bottom [ˈbɑtəm] *adj* (*price*) (el) más bajo; (*e.g., dollar*) último || *s* fondo; (*of a chair*) asiento; (*of jar*) culo; (coll) trasero; **at bottom** en el fondo; **to go to the bottom** irse a pique

bottomless [ˈbɑtəmlɪs] *adj* sin fondo, insondable

boudoir [buˈdwɑr] *s* tocador *m*

bough [baʊ] *s* rama

bouillon [ˈbʊljɑn] *s* caldo

boulder [ˈboldər] *s* pedrejón *m*

boulevard [ˈbʊlə,vɑrd] *s* bulevar *m*

bounce [baʊns] *s* rebote *m* || *tr* hacer botar; (slang) despedir || *intr* botar, rebotar; saltar; **to bounce along** dar saltos al andar

bouncer [ˈbaʊnsər] *s* cosa grande; (slang) apagabroncas *m*

bouncing [ˈbaʊnsɪŋ] *adj* frescachón, vigoroso; (*baby*) gordinflón

bound [baʊnd] *adj* atado, ligado; (*book*) encuadernado; dispuesto, propenso; puesto en aprendizaje; **bound for** con destino a, con rumbo a; **bound in boards** (bb) encartonado, en cartoné; **bound up in** entregado a, muy adicto a; absorto en || *s* salto; (*of a ball*) bote *m;* límite *m*, confín *m;* **bounds** región, comarca; **out of bounds** fuera de los límites; **within bounds** a raya

bounda•ry [ˈbaʊndəri] *s* (*pl* **-ries**) límite *m*, frontera; (*established*) parámetro

boundary mark *s* (*annotation*) acotamiento

boundary stone *s* mojón *m*

bounder [ˈbaʊndər] *s* persona vulgar y malcriada

boundless [ˈbaʊndlɪs] *adj* ilimitado, inmenso, infinito

bountiful [ˈbaʊntɪfəl] *adj* generoso, liberal; abundante

boun•ty [ˈbaʊnti] *s* (*pl* **-ties**) generosidad, liberalidad; don *m*, favor *m;* galardón *m*, premio; (*bonus*) prima; (mil) premio de enganche

bouquet [buˈke] *s* ramillete *m;* (*aroma of a wine*) nariz *f*

bourgeois [ˈbʊrʒwɑ] *adj & s* burgués *m*

bourgeoisie [,bʊrʒwɑˈzi] *s* burguesía

bout [baʊt] *s* encuentro; rato; (*of an illness*) ataque *m*

bow [baʊ] *s* inclinación, reverencia; (*of a ship*) proa || *tr* inclinar (*la cabeza*) || *intr* inclinarse; **to bow and scrape** hacer reverencias obsequiosas; **to bow to** saludar, inclinarse delante || [bo] *s* (*for shooting an arrow*) arco; lazo, nudo; (mus) arco; (*stroke of bow*) (mus) arqueada || *tr* (mus) tocar con arco || *intr* arquearse

bowdlerize [ˈbaʊdlə,raɪz] *tr* expurgar

bowel [ˈbaʊ•əl] *s* intestino; **bowels** intestinos; (*inner part*) entrañas

bowel movement *s* evacuación del vientre; **to have a bowel movement** evacuar el vientre

bower [ˈbaʊ•ər] *s* emparrado, glorieta

bower•y [ˈbaʊ•əri] *adj* frondoso, sombreado || *s* (*pl* **-ies**) finca, granja

bowknot [ˈbo,nɑt] *s* lazada

bowl [bol] *s* (*for soup or broth*) escudilla, cuenco; (*for washing hands*) jofaina, palangana; (*of toilet*) cubeta, taza; (*of fountain*) tazón *m;* (*of spoon*) paleta; (*of pipe*) hornillo; (*hollow place*) concavidad, cuenco || *tr* — **to bowl over** tumbar || *intr* jugar a los bolos; **to bowl along** rodar

bowlegged [ˈbo,lɛgd] o [ˈbo,lɛgɪd] *adj* patiestevado

bowler [ˈbolər] *s* jugador *m* de bolos; (Brit) sombrero hongo

bowling [ˈbolɪŋ] *s* juego de bolos, boliche *m*

bowling alley *s* bolera, boliche *m*

bowling green *s* bolera encespada

bowshot [ˈbo,ʃɑt] *s* tiro de flecha

bowsprit [ˈbaʊsprɪt] o [ˈbosprɪt] *s* bauprés *m*

bow tie [bo] *s* corbata de mariposa, pajarita

bowwow [ˈbaʊ,waʊ] *interj* ¡guau! || *s* guau guau *m*

box [bɑks] *s* caja; (*slap*) bofetada; (*plant*) boj *m;* (*in newspaper*) recuadro; (theat) palco || *tr* encajonar; (*to slap*) abofetear; (naut) cuartear (*la aguja*) || *intr* boxear

box'car' *s* vagón *m* de carga cerrado

boxer ['bɑksər] *s* embalador *m;* (sport) boxeador *m*
boxing ['bɑksɪŋ] *s* embalaje *m;* (sport) boxeo
boxing gloves *spl* guantes *mpl* de boxeo
box office *s* taquilla, despacho de localidades; boletería
box'-of'fice hit *s* éxito de taquilla
box-office record *s* marca de taquilla
box-office sale *s* venta de localidades en taquilla
box pleat *s* pliegue *m* de tabla
box seat *s* asiento de palco
box'wood' *s* boj *m*
boy [bɔɪ] *s* muchacho; (*servant*) mozo; (coll) compadre *m*
boycott ['bɔɪkɑt] *s* boicoteo ‖ *tr* boicotear
boyhood ['bɔɪhʊd] *s* muchachez *f;* muchachería
boyish ['bɔɪ•ɪʃ] *adj* amuchachado, muchachil
boy scout *s* niño explorador
Bp. *abbr* **bishop**
b.p. *abbr* **bills payable, boiling point**
br. *abbr* **brand, brother**
b.r. *abbr* **bills receivable**
bra [brɑ] *s* (coll) portasenos *m,* sostén *m,* sujetador *m*
brace [bres] *s* riostra; berbiquí *m;* **braces** (Brit) tirantes *mpl;* (*on teeth*) aparato de ortodoncia ‖ *tr* arriostrar; asegurar, vigorizar; **to brace oneself** (coll) cobrar ánimo ‖ *intr* — **to brace up** (coll) cobrar ánimo
brace and bit *s* berbiquí y barrena
bracelet ['breslɪt] *s* brazalete *m,* pulsera
bracer ['bresər] *s* (coll) trago de licor
bracing ['bresɪŋ] *adj* fortificante, tónico
bracket ['brækɪt] *s* puntal *m,* soporte *m;* ménsula, repisa; (*mark used in printing*) corchete *m;* clase *f,* categoría ‖ *tr* acorchetar; agrupar
brackish ['brækɪʃ] *adj* salobre
brad [bræd] *s* clavito, estaquilla
brag [bræg] *s* jactancia ‖ *v* (*pret & pp* **bragged;** *ger* **bragging**) *intr* jactarse, bravatear, palanganear
braggart ['brægərt] *s* fanfarrón *m*
braid [bred] *s* (*flat strip of cotton, silk, etc.*) cinta, galón *m;* (*something braided*) trenza ‖ *tr* encintar, galonear; trenzar
brain [bren] *s* cerebro; **brains** cerebro, inteligencia; **to rack one's brains** devanarse los sesos ‖ *tr* descerebrar
brain child *s* parto del ingenio
brain drain *s* (coll) éxodo de técnicos
brainless ['brenlɪs] *adj* tonto, sin seso
brain power *s* capacidad mental
brain'storm' *s* acceso de locura; confusión mental; buena idea, hallazgo
brain trust *s* grupo de peritos
brain'wash'ing *s* lavado cerebral
brain wave *s* onda encefálica; (coll) buena idea, hallazgo
brain'work' *s* trabajo intelectual
brain•y ['breni] *adj* (*comp* **-ier;** *super* **-iest**) (coll) inteligente, sesudo
braise [brez] *tr* soasar y cocer (*la carne*) a fuego lento en vasija bien tapada
brake [brek] *s* freno; breque *m;* (*for dressing flax*) agramadera; (*thicket*) matorral *m;* (*fern*) helecho común ‖ *tr* frenar; brequear; agramar (*el lino o el cañamo*)
brake band *s* cinta de freno
brake drum *s* tambor *m* de freno
brake lining *s* forro o cinta de freno
brake•man ['brekmən] *s* (*pl* **-men** [mən]) guardafrenos *m*
brake shoe *s* zapata de freno
bramble ['bræmbəl] *s* frambueso, zarza
bram•bly ['bræmbli] *adj* (*comp* **-blier;** *super* **-bliest**) zarzoso
bran [bræn] *s* afrecho, salvado
branch [bræntʃ] *s* (*of tree*) rama; (*smaller branch; branch cut from tree; of a science, etc.*) ramo; (*of vine*) sarmiento; (*of road, railroad*) ramal *m;* (*of candlestick, river, etc.*) brazo; (*of a store, bank*) sucursal *f* ‖ *intr* ramificarse; **to branch out** extender sus actividades
branch line *s* ramal *m,* línea de empalme
branch office *s* sucursal *f*
brand [brænd] *s* (*kind, make*) marca; (*trademark*) marca de fábrica; (*branding iron*) hierro de marcar; (*mark stamped with hot iron*) hierro; (*dishonor*) tizón *m* ‖ *tr* poner marca de fábrica en; herrar con hierro candente; tiznar (*la reputación de una persona*); **to brand as** tildar de
brandied ['brændid] *adj* macerado en aguardiente
branding iron *s* hierro de marcar; fierro
brandish ['brændɪʃ] *tr* blandear
brand'-new' *adj* nuevecito, flamante
bran•dy ['brændi] *s* (*pl* **-dies**) aguardiente *m*
brash [bræʃ] *adj* atrevido, impetuoso; descarado, respondón ‖ *s* acceso, ataque *m*
brass [bræs] *s* latón *m;* (*in army and navy*) (slang) los mandamases; (coll) descaro; **brasses** (mus) cobres *mpl*
brass band *s* banda, charanga
brass hat *s* (slang) espadón *m,* mandamás *m*
brassiere [brə'zɪr] *s* portasenos *m,* sostén *m,* sujetador *m*
brass knuckles *spl* llave inglesa, bóxer *m*
brass tack *s* clavito dorado de tapicería; **to get down to brass tacks** (coll) entrar en materia
brass winds *spl* (mus) cobres *mpl,* instrumentos músicos de metal
brass•y ['bræsi] *adj* (*comp* **-ier;** *super* **-iest**) hecho de latón; metálico; descarado
brat [bræt] *s* rapaz *m,* mocoso, braguillas *m*
brava•do [brə'vɑdo] *s* (*pl* **-does** o **-dos**) bravata
brave [brev] *adj* bravo, valiente ‖ *s* valiente *m;* guerrero indio norteamericano ‖ *tr* hacer frente a, arrostrar; desafiar, retar
bravery ['brevəri] *s* bravura, valor *m*
bra•vo ['brɑvo] *interj* ¡bravo! ‖ *s* (*pl* **-vos**) bravo
brawl [brɔl] *s* pendencia, reyerta; alboroto ‖ *intr* armar pendencia; alborotar
brawler ['brɔlər] *s* pendenciero; alborotador *m*
brawn [brɔn] *s* fuerza musculosa

brawn•y [ˈbrɔni] *adj* (*comp* **-ier;** *super* **-iest**) fornido, musculoso

bray [bre] *s* rebuzno || *intr* rebuznar

braze [brez] *s* soldadura de latón || *tr* soldar con latón; cubrir de latón; adornar con latón

brazen [ˈbrezən] *adj* de latón; descarado || *tr* — **to brazen through** llevar a cabo descaradamente

brazier [ˈbreʒər] *s* brasero

Brazil [brəˈzɪl] *s* el Brasil

Brazilian [brəˈzɪljən] *adj & s* brasileño

Brazil nut *s* castaña de Pará

breach [britʃ] *s* (*opening*) abertura; (*in a wall*) brecha; abuso, violación || *tr* abrir brecha en

breach of faith *s* falta de fidelidad

breach of peace *s* perturbación del orden público

breach of promise *s* incumplimiento de la palabra de matrimonio

breach of trust *s* abuso de confianza

bread [brɛd] *s* pan *m* || *tr* empanar

bread and butter *s* pan *m* con mantequilla; (coll) pan de cada día

bread crumbs *spl* pan rallado

breaded [ˈbrɛdɪd] *adj* empanado

bread line *s* cola del pan

breadth [brɛdθ] *s* anchura; alcance *m*, extensión; (*e.g., of judgment*) amplitud *f*

bread'win'ner *s* sostén *m* de la familia

break [brek] *s* rompimiento; interrupción; intervalo, pausa; (*split*) hendidura, grieta; (*in prices*) baja; (*in clouds*) claro; (*from jail*) evasión, huída; (*among friends*) ruptura; (*luck, good or bad*) (slang) suerte *f;* (slang) disparate *m;* **to give someone a break** abrirle a uno la puerta || *v* (*pret* **broke** [brok]; *pp* **broken**) *tr* romper, quebrar; cambiar (*un billete*); comunicar (*una mala noticia*); suspender (*relaciones*); faltar a (*la palabra*); batir (*un récord*); cortar (*un circuito*); quebrantar (*un testamento; un hábito*); romper (*una ley*); levantar (*el campo*); (mil) degradar; **to break in** forzar (*una puerta*); **to break open** abrir por la fuerza || *intr* romperse, quebrarse; reventar; aclarar (*el tiempo*); bajar (*los precios*); quebrantarse (*la salud*); **to break down** perder la salud; prorrumpir en llanto; **to break even** salir sin ganar ni perder; **to break in** entrar por fuerza; irrumpir en; **to break loose** desprenderse; escaparse; desbocarse (*un caballo*); desencadenarse (*una tempestad*); **to break out** estallar, declararse; (*in laughter, weeping*) romper; (*on the skin*) brotar granos; **to break through** abrirse paso; abrir paso por entre; **to break up** desmenuzarse; levantarse (*una reunión*); **to break with** romper con

breakable [ˈbrekəbəl] *adj* rompible

breakage [ˈbrekɪdʒ] *s* estropicio; indemnización por objetos rotos

break'down' *s* mal éxito; avería, pana; (*in health*) colapso; (*in negotiations*) ruptura; análisis *m*

breaker [ˈbrekər] *s* cachón *m*, rompiente *m*

breakfast [ˈbrɛkfəst] *s* desayuno || *intr* desayunar

breakfast food *s* cereal *m* para el desayuno

break'neck' *adj* vertiginoso; **at breakneck speed** a mata caballo

break of day *s* alba, amanecer *m*

break'through' *s* (mil) brecha, ruptura; (fig) descubrimiento sensacional

break'up' *s* disolución, dispersión; desplome *m;* (*in health*) postración

break'wa'ter *s* rompeolas *m*, escollera

breast [brɛst] *s* pecho, seno; (*of fowl*) pechuga; (*of garment*) pechera; **to make a clean breast of it** confesarlo todo

breast'bone' *s* esternón *m;* (*of fowl*) quilla

breast drill *s* berbiquí *m* de pecho

breast'pin' *s* alfiler *m* de pecho

breast stroke *s* brazada de pecho

breath [brɛθ] *s* aliento, respiración; **out of breath** sin aliento; **short of breath** corto de resuello; **to gasp for breath** respirar anhelosamente; **under one's breath** por lo bajo, en voz baja

breathe [brið] *tr* respirar; **to breathe one's last** dar el último suspiro || *intr* respirar; **to breathe freely** cobrar aliento; **to breathe in** aspirar; **to breathe out** espirar

breathing spell *s* respiro, rato de descanso

breathless [ˈbrɛθlɪs] *adj* falto de aliento, jadeante; intenso, vivo; sin aliento

breath'tak'ing *adj* conmovedor, imponente

breech [britʃ] *s* culata, recámara; **breeches** [ˈbrɪtʃɪz] calzones *mpl;* (coll) pantalones *mpl;* **to wear the breeches** (coll) calzarse los pantalones

breed [brid] *s* casta, raza; clase *f*, especie *f* || *v* (*pret & pp* **bred** [brɛd]) *tr* criar || *intr* criar; criarse

breeder [ˈbridər] *s* (*of animals*) criador *m;* (*animal*) reproductor *m*

breeding [ˈbridɪŋ] *s* cría; crianza, modales *mpl;* **bad breeding** mala crianza; **good breeding** buena crianza

breeze [briz] *s* brisa

breez•y [ˈbrizi] *adj* (*comp* **-ier;** *super* **-iest**) airoso; animado, vivo; (coll) desenvuelto, vivaracho

brevi•ty [ˈbrɛvɪti] *s* (*pl* **-ties**) brevedad

brew [bru] *s* calderada de cerveza; mezcla || *tr* fabricar (*cerveza*); preparar (*té*); (fig) tramar, urdir || *intr* amenazar (*una tormenta*)

brewer [ˈbru•ər] *s* cervecero

brewer's yeast *s* levadura de cerveza

brewer•y [ˈbru•əri] *s* (*pl* **-ies**) cervecería, fábrica de cerveza

bribe [braɪb] *s* soborno; **to take bribes** comer maíz || *tr* sobornar

briber•y [ˈbraɪbəri] *s* (*pl* **-ies**) soborno

bric-a-brac [ˈbrɪkə,bræk] *s* chucherías, curiosidades *fpl*

brick [brɪk] *s* ladrillo; (coll) buen sujeto || *tr* enladrillar

brick'bat' *s* pedazo de ladrillo; (coll) palabra hiriente

brick ice cream *s* queso helado, helado al corte
brickkiln [ˈbrɪk,kɪln] *s* horno de ladrillero
bricklayer [ˈbrɪk,le•ər] *s* ladrillador *m*
brick'yard' *s* ladrillal *m*
bridal [ˈbraɪdəl] *adj* nupcial; de novia
bridal wreath *s* corona nupcial
bride [braɪd] *s* desposada, novia
bride'groom' *s* desposado, novio
bridesmaid [ˈbraɪdz,med] *s* madrina de boda
bridge [bridʒ] *s* puente *m;* (*of nose*) caballete *m;* (*card game*) bridge *m* ‖ *tr* tender un puente sobre; salvar (*un obstáculo*); colmar, llenar (*un vacío*)
bridge'head' *s* (mil) cabeza de puente
bridle [ˈbraɪdəl] *s* brida ‖ *tr* embridar ‖ *intr* engallarse, erguirse
bridle path *s* camino de herradura
brief [brif] *adj* breve, corto, conciso ‖ *s* resumen *m;* (law) escrito; **in brief** en resumen ‖ *tr* resumir; dar consejos anticipados a; dar informes a
brief case *s* cartera
briefing [ˈbrifɪŋ] *s* órdenes *fpl;* (*of the press*) informe *m*
brier [ˈbraɪ•ər] *s* zarza; brezo blanco
brig [brɪg] *s* (naut) bergantín *m;* prisión en buque de guerra
brigade [brɪˈged] *s* brigada
brigadier [,brɪgəˈdɪr] *s* general *m* de brigada
brigand [ˈbrɪgənd] *s* bandolero
brigantine [ˈbrɪgən,tin] *s* (naut) bergantín *m* goleta
bright [braɪt] *adj* brillante; (*e.g., day*) claro; (*color*) subido; listo, inteligente, despierto; (*idea, thought*) luminoso; (*disposition*) alegre, vivo
brighten [ˈbraɪtən] *tr* abrillantar; alegrar, avivar ‖ *intr* avivarse; alegrarse; despejarse (*el cielo*)
bright lights *spl* luces *fpl* brillantes; (aut) faros o luces de carretera
brilliance [ˈbrɪljəns] o **brilliancy** [ˈbrɪljənsi] *s* brillantez *f*, brillo
brilliant [ˈbrɪljənt] *adj* brillante
brillantine [ˈbrɪljəntin] *s* brillantina
brim [brɪm] *s* borde *m;* (*of hat*) ala
brim'stone' *s* azufre *m*
brine [braɪn] *s* salmuera, agua salobre
bring [brɪŋ] *v* (*pret & pp* **brought** [brɔt]) *tr* traer; llevar; **to bring about** efectuar; **to bring back** devolver; **to bring down** abatir; **to bring forth** sacar a luz; **to bring in** traer a colación; servir (*una comida*); introducir, presentar; **to bring into play** poner en juego; **to bring on** causar, producir; **to bring out** sacar; presentar al público; **to bring suit** poner pleito; **to bring to** sacar de un desmayo; **to bring together** reunir; confrontar; reconciliar; **to bring to pass** efectuar, llevar a cabo; **to bring up** arrimar (*p.ej., una silla*); educar, criar; traer a colación; **to bring upon oneself** atraerse (*un infortunio*)
bringing-up [ˈbrɪŋɪŋˈʌp] *s* educación, crianza
brink [brɪŋk] *s* borde *m*, margen *m;* **on the brink of** al borde de
brisk [brɪsk] *adj* animado, vivo, vivaz
bristle [ˈbrɪsəl] *s* cerda ‖ *intr* erizarse, encresparse; (*to be visibly annoyed*) encresparse
bris•tly [ˈbrɪsli] *adj* (*comp* **-tlier;** *super* **-tliest**) cerdoso, erizado
Britannic [brɪˈtænɪk] *adj* británico
British [ˈbrɪtɪʃ] *adj* británico ‖ **the British** los britanos
Britisher [ˈbrɪtɪʃər] *s* britano
Briton [ˈbrɪtən] *s* britano
Brittany [ˈbrɪtəni] *s* Bretaña
brittle [ˈbrɪtəl] *adj* quebradizo, frágil
bro. *abbr* **brother**
broach [brotʃ] *s* (*skewer*) asador *m*, espetón *m;* (*ornamental pin*) broche *m*, prendedero ‖ *tr* sacar a colación
broad [brɔd] *adj* ancho; liberal, tolerante; (*day, noon, etc.*) pleno
broad'cast' *s* radiodifusión; audición, programa radiotelefónico ‖ *v* (*pret & pp* **-cast**) *tr* difundir, esparcir ‖ (*pret & pp* **-cast** o **-casted**) *tr* radiodifundir, radiar, emitir
broadcasting station *s* emisora, estación de radiodifusión
broad'cloth' *s* paño fino
broaden [ˈbrɔdən] *tr* ensanchar ‖ *intr* ensancharse
broad'loom' *adj* tejido en telar ancho y en color sólido
broad-minded [ˈbrɔdˈmaɪndɪd] *adj* tolerante, de amplias miras
broad-shouldered [ˈbrɔdˈʃoldərd] *adj* ancho de espaldas
broad'side' *s* (naut) costado; (naut) andanada; (coll) torrente *m* de injurias
broad'sword' *s* espada ancha
brocade [broˈked] *s* brocado
broccoli [ˈbrɑkəli] *s* brécol *m*, brécoles *mpl*
brochure [broˈʃʊr] *s* folleto
brogue [brog] *s* acento irlandés
broil [brɔɪl] *tr* asar a la parrilla ‖ *intr* asarse
broiler [ˈbrɔɪlər] *s* parrilla; pollo para asar a la parrilla
broken [ˈbrokən] *adj* roto, quebrado; agotado; amansado; (*accent*) chapurrado; suelto
bro'ken-down' *adj* abatido; descompuesto; destartalado
broken-hearted [ˈbrokənˈhartɪd] *adj* abrumado por el dolor
broker [ˈbrokər] *s* corredor *m*
brokerage [ˈbrokərɪdʒ] *s* corretaje *m*
bromide [ˈbromaɪd] *s* bromuro; (slang) trivialidad
bromine [ˈbromin] *s* bromo
bronchitis [brɑŋˈkaɪtɪs] *s* bronquitis *f*
bron•co [ˈbrɑŋko] *s* (*pl* **-cos**) potro cerril
bron'co•bust'er *s* domador *m* de potros; vaquero
bronze [brɑnz] *adj* bronceado ‖ *s* bronce *m* ‖ *tr* broncear ‖ *intr* broncearse
brooch [brotʃ] o [brutʃ] *s* alfiler *m* de pecho, prendedero, pasador *m*

brood [brud] *s* cría; nidada; casta, raza || *tr* empollar || *intr* enclocar; **to brood on** meditar con preocupación
brook [brUk] *s* arroyo || *tr* — **to brook no** no tolerar, no aguantar
broom [brum] o [brUm] *s* escoba; (bot) hiniesta
broom'corn' *s* sorgo
broom'stick' *s* palo de escoba
bros. *abbr* **brothers**
broth [brɔθ] o [braθ] *s* caldo
brothel ['brɑθəl] o ['braðəl] *s* burdel *m;* (Mex) congal *m*
brother ['brʌðər] *s* hermano
brotherhood ['brʌðər,hud] *s* hermandad
broth'er-in-law' *s* (*pl* **brothers-in-law**) cuñado, hermano político; (*husband of one's wife's or husband's sister*) concuñado
brotherly ['brʌðərli] *adj* fraternal
brow [braU] *s* (*forehead*) frente *f;* (*eyebrow*) ceja; **to knit one's brow** fruncir las cejas
brow'beat' *v* (*pret* **-beat;** *pp* **beaten**) *tr* intimidar con mirada ceñuda
brown [braUn] *adj* pardo, castaño, moreno; (*race*) cobrizo; tostado del sol || *s* castaño, moreno || *tr* poner moreno; tostar, quemar, broncear; (culin) dorar
brownish ['braUnɪʃ] *adj* que tira a moreno
brown study *s* absorción, pensamiento profundo, ensimismamlento
brown sugar *s* azúcar terciado
browse [braUz] *intr* (*to nibble at twigs*) ramonear; (*to graze*) pacer; hojear un libro ociosamente; **to browse about** o **around** curiosear
bruise [bruz] *s* contusión, magulladura, magullón *m* || *tr* contundir, magullar || *intr* contundirse, magullarse
brunet [bru'nɛt] *adj* moreno || *s* moreno (*hombre moreno*)
brunette [bru'nɛt] *s* morena (*mujer morena*)
brunt [brʌnt] *s* fuerza, choque *m,* empuje *m;* (*e.g., of a battle*) peso, (lo) más reñido
brush [brʌʃ] *s* brocha, cepillo, escobilla; (*stroke*) brochada; (*light touch*) roce *m;* (*brief encounter*) encuentro, escaramuza; (*growth of bushes*) maleza; (elec) escobilla || *tr* acepillar; (*to graze*) rozar; **to brush aside** echar a un lado || *intr* pasar ligeramente; **to brush up on** repasar
brush'-off' *s* (slang) desaire *m;* **to give the brush-off to** (slang) despedir noramala
brush'wood' *s* broza, ramojo
brusque [brʌsk] *adj* brusco, rudo
brusqueness ['brʌsknɪs] *s* brusquedad
Brussels ['brʌsəlz] *s* Bruselas
Brussels sprouts *spl* bretones *mpl,* col *f* de Bruselas
brutal ['brutəl] *adj* brutal, bestial
brutali•ty [bru'tælɪti] *s* (*pl* **-ties**) brutalidad, crueldad
brutalization [,brutələ'zeʃən] *s* embrutecimiento
brute [brut] *adj* bruto; (*force*) inconsciente, ciego || *s* bruto
brutish ['brutɪʃ] *adj* abrutado, estúpido
bu. *abbr* **bushel**
bubble ['bʌbəl] *s* burbuja; ampolla; ilusión, quimera || *intr* burbujear; **to bubble over** desbordar, rebosar
buck [bʌk] *s* (*goat*) cabrón *m;* (*deer*) gamo; (*rabbit*) conejo; (*of a horse*) corveta, encorvada; (*youth*) pisaverde *m;* (slang) dólar *m;* **to pass the buck** (coll) echar la carga a otro || *tr* hacer frente a, resistir a; (*to butt*) acornear, topetar; colar (*la ropa*); **to buck up** (coll) alentar, animar || *intr* botarse, encorvarse; **to buck against** embestir contra
bucket ['bʌkɪt] *s* balde *m,* cubo; (*of a well*) pozal *m;* **to kick the bucket** (slang) estirar la pata, liar el petate
bucket seat *s* baquet *m*
buckle ['bʌkəl] *s* hebilla; (*bend, bulge*) alabeo, pandeo || *tr* abrochar con hebilla || *intr* (*to bend, bulge*) alabearse, pandear; **to buckle down to** (coll) dedicarse con empeño a
buck private *s* (slang) soldado raso
buckram ['bʌkrəm] *s* zangala; (bb) bocací *m,* bucarán *m*
buck'saw' *s* sierra de bastidor
buck'shot' *s* postas
buck'tooth' *s* (*pl* **-teeth**) diente *m* saliente
buck'wheat' *s* alforfón *m,* trigo sarraceno
bud [bʌd] *s* botón *m,* brote *m;* **to nip in the bud** cortar de raíz || *v* (*pret & pp* **budded;** *ger* **budding**) *intr* abotonar, brotar
bud•dy ['bʌdi] *s* (*pl* **-dies**) (coll) camarada *m,* cumpa *m* (coll) muchachito
budge [bʌdʒ] *tr* mover || *intr* moverse
budget ['bʌdʒɪt] *s* presupuesto || *tr* presuponer, presupuestar
budgetary ['bʌdʒɪ,tɛri] *adj* presupuestario
buff [bʌf] *adj* de ante || *s* (*leather*) ante *m;* color *m* de ante; chaqueta de ante; rueda pulidora; (coll) piel desnuda; aficionado || *tr* dar color de ante a; pulimentar
buffa•lo ['bʌfə,lo] *s* (*pl* **-loes** o **-los**) búfalo || *tr* (slang) intimidar
buffer ['bʌfər] *s* amortiguador *m* de choques; tope *m,* paragolpes *m;* pulidor *m*
buffer state *s* estado tapón
buffet [bu'fe] *s* (*piece of furniture*) aparador *m;* restaurante *m* de estación || ['bʌfɪt] *tr* abofetear, golpear, pegar
buffet car *s* coche *m* bar
buffet lunch *s* servicio de bufet
buffet supper *s* ambigú *m,* bufet *m*
buffoon [bə'fun] *s* bufón *m,* payaso
buffooner•y [bə'funəri] *s* (*pl* **-ies**) bufonada, chocarrería
bug [bʌg] *s* insecto, bicho, sabandija; microbio; (*bedbug*) (Brit) chinche *f;* (coll) defecto; (slang) micrófono escondido; (slang) loco; (slang) entusiasta *mf* || *v* (*pret & pp* **bugged;** *ger* **bugging**) *tr* (slang) esconder un micrófono en
bug'bear' *s* espantajo; aversión
bug•gy ['bʌgi] *adj* (*comp* **-gier;** *super* **-giest**) infestado de bichos; (slang) loco || *s* (*pl* **-gies**) calesa
bug'house' *adj* (slang) loco || *s* (slang) manicomio, casa de locos

bugle [ˈbjugəl] *s* corneta
bugle call *s* toque *m* de corneta
bugler [ˈbjuglər] *s* corneta *m*
build [bɪld] *s* forma, hechura, figura; (*of human being*) talle *m* || *v* (*pret & pp* **built** [bɪlt]) *tr* construir, edificar; componer; establecer, fundar; crearse (*p.ej., una clientela*)
builder [ˈbɪldər] *s* constructor *m;* aparejador *m,* maestro de obras
building [ˈbɪldɪŋ] *s* construcción; edificio; (*one of several in a group*) pabellón *m*
building and loan association *s* sociedad *f* de crédito para la construcción
building lot *s* solar *m*
building site *s* terreno para construir
building trades *spl* oficios de edificación
build'-up' *s* acumulación, formación; (coll) propaganda anticipada
built'in' *adj* integrante, incorporado, empotrado
built'-up' *adj* armado, montado; (*land*) aglomerado
bulb [bʌlb] *s* (*of plant*) bulbo; (*of thermometer*) bola, cubeta; (*of syringe*) pera; (*of electric light*) ampolla, bombilla
Bulgaria [bʌlˈgɛrɪ•ə] *s* Bulgaria
Bulgarian [bʌlˈgɛrɪ•ən] *adj & s* búlgaro
bulge [bʌldʒ] *s* protuberancia, bulto, bombeo; **to get the bulge on** (coll) llevar la ventaja a || *intr* hacer bulto, bombearse
bulimia [bjuˈlimi•ə] *s* bulimia
bulk [bʌlk] *s* bulto, volumen *m;* (*main mass*) grueso; **in bulk** a granel || *intr* abultar, hacer bulto; tener importancia
bulk'head' *s* mamparo; tabique hermético
bulk•y [ˈbʌlki] *adj* (*comp* **-ier;** *super* **-iest**) abultado, voluminoso, grueso
bull [bul] *s* toro; (*in stockmarket*) alcista *m;* (*papal document*) bula; disparate *m;* **to take the bull by the horns** asir al toro por las astas || *tr* — **to bull the market** jugar al alza
bull'dog' *s* dogo
bulldoze [ˈbul,doz] *tr* coaccionar, intimidar con amenazas
bulldozer [ˈbul,dozər] *s* explanadora de empuje, empujatierra
bullet [ˈbulɪt] *s* bala
bulletin [ˈbulətɪn] *s* boletín *m;* comunicado; (*of a school*) anuario
bulletin board *s* tablilla
bul'let•proof' *adj* a prueba de balas, blindado
bull'fight' *s* corrida de toros
bull'fight'er *s* torero
bull'fight'ing *adj* torero || *s* toreo
bull'finch' *s* (orn) camachuelo
bull'frog' *s* rana toro
bull-headed [ˈbul,hɛdɪd] *adj* obstinado, terco
bullion [ˈbuljən] *s* oro en barras, plata en barras; (*twisted fringe*) entorchado
bullish [ˈbulɪʃ] *adj* obstinado; (*market*) en alza; (*speculator*) alcista; optimista
bullock [ˈbulək] *s* buey *m*
bull'pen' *s* (taur) toril *m;* (*jail*) (coll) prevención
bull'ring' *s* plaza de toros
bull's-eye [ˈbulz,aɪ] *s* (*of a target*) diana; (archit, meteor, naut) ojo de buey; **to hit the bull's-eye** hacer diana
bul•ly [ˈbuli] *adj* (coll) excelente, magnífico || *s* (*pl* **-lies**) matón *m,* valentón *m* || *v* (*pret & pp* **-lied**) *tr* intimidar, maltratar
bulrush [ˈbul,rʌʃ] *s* junco; junco de laguna; (*Typha*) anea, espadaña; (Bib) papiro
bulwark [ˈbulwərk] *s* baluarte *m* || *tr* abaluartar; defender, proteger
bum [bʌm] *s* (slang) holgazán *m;* (slang) vagabundo; (slang) mendigo || *v* (*pret & pp* **bummed;** *ger* **bumming**) *tr* (slang) mendigar || *intr* holgazanear; (slang) vagabundear; (slang) mendigar
bumblebee [ˈbʌmbəl,bi] *s* abejorro
bump [bʌmp] *s* (*collision*) topetón *m;* (*shake*) sacudida; (*on falling*) batacazo; (*of plane in rough air*) rebote *m;* (*swelling*) hinchazón *f,* chichón *m;* protuberancia || *tr* dar contra, topar; (*to bruise*) abollar || *intr* chocar; dar sacudidas; **to bump into** tropezar con; encontrarse con
bumper [ˈbʌmpər] *adj* (coll) abundante, grande || *s* tope *m,* paratopes *m;* (aut) amortiguador *m,* parachoques *m;* vaso lleno
bumpkin [ˈbʌmpkɪn] *s* patán *m,* palurdo
bumptious [ˈbʌmpʃəs] *adj* engreído, presuntuoso
bump•y [ˈbʌmpi] *adj* (*comp* **-ier;** *super* **-iest**) (*ground*) desigual, áspero; (*air*) agitado
bun [bʌn] *s* buñuelo, bollo; (*of hair*) castaña
bunch [bʌntʃ] *s* manojo, puñado; (*of grapes, bananas, etc.*) racimo; (*of flowers*) ramillete *m;* (*of people*) grupo || *tr* agrupar, juntar || *intr* agruparse; arracimarse
bundle [ˈbʌndəl] *s* atado, bulto, lío, paquete *m;* (*of papers*) legajo; (*of wood*) haz *m* || *tr* atar, liar, empaquetar, envolver; **to bundle off** despedir precipitadamente; **to bundle up** arropar || *intr* — **to bundle up** arroparse
bung [bʌŋ] *s* bitoque *m,* tapón *m*
bungalow [ˈbʌŋgə,lo] *s* bungalow *m,* casa de una sola planta
bung'hole' *s* piquera, boca de tonel
bungle [ˈbʌŋgəl] *s* chapucería || *tr & intr* chapucear
bungler [ˈbʌŋglər] *s* chapucero
bungling [ˈbvŋglɪŋ] *adj* chapucero || *s* chapucería
bunion [ˈbʌnjən] *s* juanete *m*
bunk [bʌŋk] *s* tarima; (slang) palabrería vana, música celestial
bunker [ˈbʌŋkər] *s* carbonera; (mil) fortín *m*
bun•ny [ˈbʌni] *s* (*pl* **-nies**) conejito
bunting [ˈbʌntɪŋ] *s* banderas colgadas como adorno; (*of a ship*) empavesado; (orn) gorrión triguero
buoy [bɔɪ] o [ˈbu•i] *s* boya; boya salvavidas, guindola || *tr* — **to buoy up** mantener a flote; animar, alentar
buoyancy [ˈbɔɪ•ənsi] o [ˈbujənsi] *s* flotación; alegría, animación
buoyant [ˈbɔɪ•ənt] o [ˈbujənt] *adj* boyante; alegre, animado

bur [bʌr] *s* erizo, vilano
burble [ˈbʌrbəl] *s* burbujeo ‖ *intr* burbujear
burden [ˈbʌrdən] *s* carga; (*of a speech*) tema *m;* (*of a poem*) estribillo ‖ *tr* cargar; agobiar, gravar
burden of proof *s* peso de la prueba
burdensome [ˈbʌrdənsəm] *adj* gravoso, oneroso
burdock [ˈbʌrdak] *s* bardana, cadillo
bureau [ˈbjʊro] *s* cómoda; despacho, oficina; departamento, negociado
bureaucra•cy [bjʊˈrɑkrəsi] *s* (*pl* **-cies**) burocracia; funcionariado
bureaucrat [ˈbjʊrə,kræt] *s* burócrata *mf*
bureaucratic [,bjʊrəˈkrætɪk] *adj* burocrático
burgess [ˈbʌrdʒɪs] *s* burgués *m,* ciudadano; alcalde *m* de un pueblo o villa
burglar [ˈbʌrglər] *s* escalador *m*
burglar alarm *s* alarma de ladrones
bur'glar•proof' *adj* a prueba de escaladores; antirrobo
burglar•y [ˈbʌrgləri] *s* (*pl* **-ies**) robo con escalamiento
Burgundian [bərˈgʌndɪ•ən] *adj* & *s* borgoñón *m*
Burgundy [ˈbʌrgəndi] *s* la Borgoña; (*wine*) borgoña *m*
burial [ˈbɛrɪ•əl] *s* entierro
burial ground *s* cementerio
burlap [ˈbʌrlæp] *s* arpillera
burlesque [bərˈlɛsk] *adj* burlesco, festivo ‖ *s* parodia ‖ *tr* parodiar
burlesque show *s* espectáculo de bailes y cantos groseros, music-hall *m;* bataclán *m* (SAm)
bur•ly [ˈbʌrli] *adj* (*comp* **-lier;** *super* **-liest**) fornido, corpulento, membrudo
Burma [ˈbʌrmə] *s* Birmania
Bur•mese [bərˈmiz] *adj* birmano ‖ *s* (*pl* **-mese**) birmano
burn [bʌrn] *s* quemadura, quemazón *f* ‖ *v* (*pret & pp* **burned** o **burnt** [bʌrnt]) *tr* quemar ‖ *intr* quemar, quemarse; estar encendido (*p.ej., un faro*); **to burn out** quemarse (*un fusible*); fundirse (*una bombilla*); **to burn within** requemarse
burner [ˈbʌrnər] *s* (*of furnace*) quemador *m;* (*of gas fixture or lamp*) mechero
burning [ˈbʌrnɪŋ] *adj* ardiente ‖ *s* quema, incendio
burning question *s* cuestión palpitante
burnish [ˈbʌrnɪʃ] *s* bruñido ‖ *tr* bruñir ‖ *intr* bruñirse
burnoose [bərˈnus] *s* albornoz *m*
burnt almond [bʌrnt] *s* almendra tostada
burr [bʌr] *s* (*of plant*) erizo; (*of cut in metal*) rebaba
burrow [ˈbʌro] *s* madriguera, conejera ‖ *tr* hacer madrigueras en; socavar ‖ *intr* amadrigarse; esconderse
bursar [ˈbʌrsər] *s* tesorero universitario
burst [bʌrst] *s* explosión, reventón *m,* estallido; (*of machine gun*) ráfaga; salida brusca ‖ *v* (*pret & pp* **burst**) *tr* reventar ‖ *intr* reventar, reventarse; partirse (*el corazón*); **to burst into** irrumpir en (*un cuarto*); desatarse en (*amenazas*); prorrumpir en (*lágrimas*); **to burst out crying** deshacerse en lágrimas; **to burst with laughter** reventar de risa
bur•y [ˈbɛri] *v* (*pret & pp* **-ied**) *tr* enterrar; **to be buried in thought** estar absorto en meditación; **to bury the hatchet** hacer la paz, echar pelillos a la mar
burying ground *s* cementerio
bus. *abbr* **business**
bus [bʌs] *s* (*pl* **busses** o **buses**) autobús *m* ‖ *tr* llevar en un autobús
bus boy *s* ayudante *m* de camarero
bus•by [ˈbʌzbi] *s* (*pl* **-bies**) morrión *m* de húsar, colbac *m*
bush [bʊʃ] *s* arbusto; (*scrubby growth*) matorral *m,* monte *m;* **to beat about the bush** andar con rodeos
bushel [ˈbʊʃəl] *s* medida para áridos (*35,23 litros en E.U.A. y 36,35 litros en Inglaterra*)
bushing [ˈbʊʃɪŋ] *s* buje *m,* forro
bush•y [ˈbʊʃi] *adj* (*comp* **-ier;** *super* **-iest**) arbustivo; peludo, lanudo; espeso
business [ˈbɪznɪs] *adj* comercial, de negocios ‖ *s* negocio, comercio; (*company, concern*) empresa; (*job, employment*) empleo, oficio; (*matter*) asunto, cuestión; (*duty*) obligación; (*right*) derecho; **on business** por negocios; **to have no business to** no tener derecho a; **to make it one's business to** proponerse; **to mean business** (coll) obrar en serio, hablar en serio; **to mind one's own business** no meterse en lo que no le importa a uno; **to send about one's business** mandar a paseo
business district *s* barrio comercial
businesslike [ˈbɪznɪs,laɪk] *adj* práctico, sistemático, serio
business•man [ˈbɪznɪs,mæn] *s* (*pl* **-men** [,mɛn]) comerciante *m,* hombre *m* de negocios
business suit *s* traje *m* de calle
bus•man [ˈbʌsmən] *s* (*pl* **-men** [mən]) conductor *m* de autobús
buss [bʌs] *s* (coll) beso sonado ‖ *tr* dar besos sonados a ‖ *intr* dar besos sonados; darse besos sonados
bust [bʌst] *s* busto; (*of woman*) pecho; (slang) fracaso, borrachera ‖ *tr* (slang) reventar, romper; (slang) arruinar; (slang) golpear, pegar ‖ *intr* (slang) reventar, fracasar
buster [ˈbʌstər] *s* muchachito
bustle [ˈbʌsəl] *s* (*of woman's dress*) polisón *m;* alboroto, bullicio ‖ *intr* ajetrearse, menearse
bus•y [ˈbɪzi] *adj* (*comp* **-ier;** *super* **-iest**) ocupado; (*e.g., street*) concurrido; (*meddling*) intruso, entremetido ‖ *v* (*pret & pp* **-ied**) *tr* ocupar; **to busy oneself with** ocuparse de
busybod•y [ˈbɪzɪ,badi] *s* (*pl* **-ies**) entremetido, fisgón *m*
busy signal *s* (telp) señal *f* de ocupado
but [bʌt] *adv* sólo, solamente, no . . . más que; **but for** a no ser por; **but little** muy poco ‖ *prep* excepto, salvo; **all but** casi ‖

conj pero; sino, p.ej., **nobody came but John** no vino sino Juan
butcher [ˈbutʃər] *s* carnicero; pesero (CAm, Col, Ven) ‖ *tr* matar (*reses para el consumo*); dar muerte a; (*to bungle*) chapucear
butcher knife *s* cuchilla de carnicero
butcher shop *s* carnicería; pesa (CAm, Col, Ven)
butcher•y [ˈbʌtʃəri] *s* (*pl* **-ies**) (*slaughterhouse*) matadero; (*wanton slaughter*) matanza, carnicería
butler [ˈbʌtlər] *s* despensero, mayordomo
butt [bʌt] *s* (*of gun*) culata; (*of cigaret*) colilla, punta; (*of horned animal*) cabezada, topetada, topetón *m;* (*target*) blanco; hazmerreír *m;* (*large cask*) pipa; (*rear end*) pompis *m* ‖ *tr* topar, topetar; acornear ‖ *intr* dar cabezadas; **to butt against** confinar con; **to butt in** (slang) entremeterse
butter [ˈbʌtər] *s* mantequilla ‖ *tr* untar con mantequilla; **to butter up** (coll) adular, lisonjear
but'ter•cup' *s* botón *m* de oro
butter dish *s* mantequillera
but'ter•fly' *s* (*pl* **-flies**) mariposa
butter knife *s* cuchillo mantequillero
but'ter•milk' *s* leche *f* de manteca
butter sauce *s* mantequilla fundida
but'ter•scotch' *s* bombón *m* escocés, bombón hecho con azúcar terciado y mantequilla
buttocks [ˈbʌtəks] *spl* nalgas; fundillo (Cuba, Mex)
button [ˈbʌtən] *s* botón *m* ‖ *tr* abotonar, abrocharse
but'ton•hole' *s* ojal *m* ‖ *tr* detener con conversación
but'ton•hook *s* abotonador *m*
but'ton•wood' tree *s* plátano de occidente
buttress [ˈbʌtrɪs] *s* contrafuerte *m;* (fig) apoyo, sostén *m* ‖ *tr* estribar; (fig) apoyar, sostener
butt weld *s* soldadura a tope
buxom [ˈbʌksəm] *adj* rolliza, frescachona
buy [baɪ] *s* (coll) compra; (*bargain*) (coll) ganga ‖ *v* (*pret & pp* **bought** [bɔt]) *tr* comprar; **to buy back** recomprar; **to buy off** comprar, sobornar; **to buy out** comprar la parte de (*un socio*); **to buy up** acaparar
buyer [ˈbaɪ•ər] *s* comprador *m*
buzz [bʌz] *s* zumbido ‖ *intr* zumbar; **to buzz about** ajetrearse, cazcalear
buzzard [ˈbʌzərd] *s* alfaneque *m*
buzz bomb *s* bomba volante
buzzer [ˈbʌzər] *s* zumbador *m*
buzz saw *s* sierra circular
bx. *abbr* **box**
by [baɪ] *adv* cerca; a un lado; **by and by** luego ‖ *prep* por; cerca de, al lado de; (*not later than*) para; **by far** con mucho; **by the way** de paso; a propósito
by-and-by [ˈbaɪ•əndˈbaɪ] *s* porvenir *m*
bye-bye [ˈbaɪˈbaɪ] *s* mu *f;* **to go bye-bye** ir a la mu ‖ *interj* (coll) ¡adiosito!; (*to a child*) ¡ro ro!
bygone [ˈbaɪ,gɔn] o [ˈbaɪ,gɑn] *adj* pasado ‖ *s* pasado; **let bygones be bygones** olvidemos lo pasado
bylaw [ˈbaɪ,lɔ] *s* reglamento, estatuto
bypass [ˈbaɪ,pæs] *s* desviación; tubo de paso ‖ *tr* desviar; eludir
by'-prod'uct *s* subproducto, derivado
bystander [ˈbaɪ,stændər] *s* asistente *mf,* circunstante *mf*
byway [ˈbaɪ,we] *s* camino apartado
byword [ˈbaɪ,wʌrd] *s* objeto de oprobio; refrán *m,* muletilla; apodo
Byzantine [ˈbɪzən,tin] o [bɪˈzæntin] *adj & s* bizantino
Byzantium [bɪˈzænʃɪ•əm] o [bɪˈzæntɪ•əm] *s* Bizancio

C

C, c [si] tercera letra del alfabeto inglés
c. *abbr* **cent, center, centimeter**
C. *abbr* **centigrade, Congress, Court**
cab [kæb] *s* coche *m* de plaza o de punto; taxi *m;* (*of a truck*) casilla
cabaret [,kæbəˈre] *s* cabaret *m*
cabbage [ˈkæbɪdʒ] *s* col *f,* berza
cab driver *s* cochero de plaza; taxista *mf*
cabin [ˈkæbɪn] *s* (*hut, cottage*) cabaña; (aer) cabina; (naut) camarote *m*
cabin boy *s* mozo de cámara
cabinet [ˈkæbɪnɪt] *s* (*piece of furniture for displaying objects*) escaparate *m,* vitrina; (*for a radio*) caja, mueble *m;* (*closet*) armario; (*private room; ministry of a government*) gabinete *m*
cab'inet•ma'ker *s* ebanista *m*
cab'inet•ma'king *s* ebanistería
cable [ˈkebəl] *adj* cablegráfico ‖ *s* cable *m;* cablegrama *m* ‖ *tr & intr* cablegrafiar
cable address *s* dirección cablegráfica
cable car *s* tranvía *m* de tracción por cable
cablegram [ˈkebəl,græm] *s* cablegrama *m*
cable television *s* televisión por cable
caboose [kəˈbus] *s* (rr) furgón de cola
cab'stand' *s* punto de coches, punto de taxis
cache [kæʃ] *s* escondrijo; víveres escondidos ‖ *tr* depositar en un escondrijo; ocultar
cachet [kæˈʃe] *s* sello
cackle [ˈkækəl] *s* (*of a hen*) cacareo; (*idle talk*) charla ‖ *intr* cacarear; charlar
cac•tus [ˈkæktəs] *s* (*pl* **-tuses** o **-ti** [taɪ]) cacto
cad [kæd] *s* sinvergüenza *mf;* **to behave like a cad** tener mala leche

cadaver [kə'dævər] *s* cadáver *m*
cadaverous [kə'dævərəs] *adj* cadavérico
caddie ['kædi] *s* caddie *m* (*muchacho que lleva los utensilios en el juego de golf*) ‖ *intr* servir de caddie
cadence ['kedəns] *s* cadencia
cadet [kə'dɛt] *s* hermano menor, hijo menor; (*student at military school*) cadete *m*
cadmium ['kædmɪ•əm] *s* cadmio
cadre ['kædri] *s* (mil) cuadro
Caesar ['sizər] *s* César *m*
café [kæ'fe] *s* bar *m*, cabaret *m;* restaurante *m*
café society *s* gente *f* del mundo elegante que frecuenta los cabarets de moda
cafeteria [,kæfə'tɪrɪ•ə] *s* cafetería
cage [kedʒ] *s* jaula ‖ *tr* enjaular
cageling ['kedʒlɪŋ] *s* pájaro enjaulado
ca•gey ['kedʒi] *adj* (*comp* **-gier;** *super* **-giest**) (coll) astuto
cahoots [kə'huts] *s* — **to be in cahoots** (slang) confabularse (*dos o más personas*); **to go cahoots** (slang) entrar por partes iguales
Cain [ken] *s* Caín *m;* **to raise Cain** (slang) armar camorra
Cairo ['kaɪro] *s* El Cairo
caisson ['kesən] *s* cajón *m* de aire comprimido, esclusa de aire
cajole [kə'dʒol] *tr* adular, lisonjear, halagar
cajoler•y [kə'dʒoləri] *s* (*pl* **-ies**) adulación, lisonja, halago
cake [kek] *s* pastel *m*, bollo, queque *m;* (*small cake*) pastelillo; (*sponge cake*) bizcocho; (*of fish*) fritada; (*of earth*) terrón *m;* (*of soap*) pan *m*, pastilla; (*of ice*) témpano; **to take the cake** (coll) ser el colmo ‖ *intr* apelmazarse, aterronarse
calabash ['kælə,bæʃ] *s* calabacera; jícaro; (*fruit*) calabaza
calamitous [kə'læmɪtəs] *adj* calamitoso
calami•ty [kə'læmɪti] *s* (*pl* **-ties**) calamidad
calci•fy ['kælsɪ,faɪ] *v* (*pret & pp* **-fied**) calcificar ‖ *intr* calcificarse
calcium ['kælsɪ•əm] *s* calcio
calculate ['kælkjə,let] *tr* calcular; (*to reckon*) (coll) calcular ‖ *intr* calcular; **to calculate on** contar con
calculating ['kælkjə,letɪŋ] *adj* de calcular; astuto, intrigante
calculating machine *s* calculadora, máquina de calcular
calcu•lus ['kælkjələs] *s* (*pl* **-luses** o **-li** [,laɪ]) (math, pathol) cálculo
caldron ['kɔldrən] *s* calderón *m*
calendar ['kæləndər] *s* calendario, almanaque *m*
calf [kæf] o [kɑf] *s* (*pl* **calves** [kævz] o [kɑvz]) ternero; (*of the leg*) pantorrilla
calf'skin' *s* becerro, becerrillo
caliber ['kælɪbər] *s* calibre *m*
calibrate ['kælɪ,bret] *tr* calibrar
cali•co ['kælɪ,ko] *s* (*pl* **-coes** o **-cos**) calicó *m*, indiana
California [,kælɪ'fɔrnɪ•ə] *s* California
calipers ['kælɪpərz] *spl* calibrador *m*, compás *m* de calibres
caliph ['kelɪf] o ['kælɪf] *s* califa *m*
caliphate ['kælɪ,fet] *s* califato
calisthenic [,kælɪs'θɛnɪk] *adj* calisténico ‖ **calisthenics** *spl* calistenia
calk [kɔk] *tr* calafatear
calking ['kɔkɪŋ] *s* calafateo
call [kɔl] *s* llamada; visita; (*of a boat or airplane*) escala; vocación; **within call** al alcance de la voz ‖ *tr* llamar; convocar (*p.ej., una huelga*); **to call back** mandar volver; **to call down** (coll) reprender, regañar; **to call in** hacer entrar; (*from circulation*) retirar; **to call off** aplazar, suspender; desconvocar; **to call out** llamar (*a uno*) que salga; **to call together** convocar, reunir; **to call up** llamar por teléfono; evocar, recordar ‖ *intr* llamar, gritar; hacer una visita; (naut) hacer escala; **to call on** acudir a; visitar; **to call out** gritar; **to go calling** ir de visitas
calla lily ['kælə] *s* cala, lirio de agua
call bell *s* timbre *m* de llamada
call'boy' *s* (*in a hotel*) botones *m;* (theat) traspunte *m*
caller ['kɔlər] *s* visitante *mf*
call girl *s* chica de cita
calling ['kɔlɪŋ] *s* profesión, vocación
calling card *s* tarjeta de visita
calliope [kə'laɪ•əpi] o ['kælɪ•op] *s* (mus) órgano de vapor ‖ **Calliope** [kə'laɪ•əpi] *s* Calíope *f*
call number *s* número de teléfono; (*of a book*) número de clasificación
callous ['kæləs] *adj* calloso; (fig) duro, insensible
call to arms *s* — **to sound the call to arms** (mil) batir o tocar a llamada
call to the colors *s* (mil) llamada a filas
callus ['kæləs] *s* callo
calm [kɑm] *adj* tranquilo, quieto; (*sea*) bonancible ‖ *s* tranquilidad, calma ‖ *tr* tranquilizar, calmar ‖ *intr* — **to calm down** tranquilizarse, calmarse; abonanzar, calmar (*el viento, el tiempo*)
calmness ['kɑmnɪs] *s* tranquilidad, calma
calorie ['kæləri] *s* caloría
calum•ny ['kæləmni] *s* (*pl* **-nies**) calumnia
calva•ry ['kælvəri] *s* (*pl* **-ries**) (*at the entrance to a town*) humilladero ‖ **Calvary** *s* Calvario
calyp•so [kə'lɪpso] *s* (*pl* **-sos**) calipso ‖ **Calypso** *s* Calipso *f*
cam [kæm] *s* leva
cambric ['kembrɪk] *s* batista
camel ['kæməl] *s* camello
came•o ['kæmɪ•o] *s* (*pl* **-os**) camafeo
camera ['kæmərə] *s* cámara fotográfica, máquina fotográfica
camera•man ['kæmərə,mæn] *s* (*pl* **-men** [,mɛn]) camarógrafo, tomavistas *m*
camomile ['kæmə,maɪl] *s* manzanilla
camouflage ['kæmə,flɑʒ] *s* camuflaje *m* ‖ *tr* camuflar
camp [kæmp] *s* campamento ‖ *intr* acampar
campaign [kæm'pen] *s* campaña ‖ *intr* hacer campaña
campaigner [kæm'penər] *s* propagandista *mf;* veterano

camp'fire' *s* hoguera de campamento
camphor ['kæmfər] *s* alcanfor *m*
camp'stool' *s* silla de tijera, catrecillo
campus ['kæmpəs] *s* terrenos, recinto (*de la universidad*)
cam'shaft' *s* árbol *m* de levas
can [kæn] *s* bote *m*, envase *m*, lata ‖ *v* (*pret & pp* **canned;** *ger* **canning**) *tr* envasar, enlatar ‖ *v* (*pret & cond* **could**) *v aux* **he can come tomorrow** puede venir mañana; **can you swim?** ¿sabe Vd. nadar?
Canada ['kænədə] *s* el Canadá
Canadian [kə'nedɪ•ən] *adj & s* canadiense
canal [kə'næl] *s* canal *m*
canar•y [kə'nɛri] *s* (*pl* **-ies**) canario ‖ **Canaries** *spl* Canarias
can•cel ['kænsəl] *v* (*pret & pp* **-celed** o **-celled;** *ger* **-celing** o **-celling**) *tr* cancelar, eliminar, suprimir; matasellar, obliterar (*sellos de correo*)
canceler ['kænsələr] *s* matasellos *m*
cancellation [,kænsə'leʃən] *s* cancelación, eliminación, supresión; revocatoria; (*of stamps*) obliteración
cancer ['kænsər] *s* cáncer *m;* **Cancer** *s* (astr) Cáncer *m*
cancerous ['kænsərəs] *adj* canceroso
candela•brum [,kændə'lebrəm] *s* (*pl* **-bra** [brə] o **-brums**) candelabro
candid ['kændɪd] *adj* franco, sincero; imparcial
candida•cy ['kændɪdəsi] *s* (*pl* **-cies**) candidatura
candidate ['kændɪ,det] *s* candidato; (*for a degree*) graduando
candid camera *s* cámara indiscreta
candle ['kændəl] *s* bujía, candela, vela
can'dle•hold'er *s* candelero
can'dle•light' *s* luz *f* de vela; crepúsculo
candle power *s* bujía
can'dle•stick' *s* palmatoria
candor ['kændər] *s* franqueza, sinceridad; imparcialidad
can•dy ['kændi] *s* (*pl* **-dies**) bombón *m*, confite *m*, dulce *m;* dulces *mpl* ‖ *v* (*pret & pp* **-died**) *tr* almibarar, confitar, garapiñar ‖ *intr* almibararse
candy box *s* bombonera, confitera
candy store *s* confitería, dulcería
cane [ken] *s* (*plant; stem*) caña; (*walking stick*) bastón *m;* (*for chair seats*) junco, mimbre *m*, rejilla
cane seat *s* asiento de rejilla
cane sugar *s* azúcar *m* de caña
canine ['kenaɪn] *adj* canino ‖ *s* (*tooth*) canino; perro
canned goods *spl* conservas alimenticias
canner•y ['kænəri] *s* (*pl* **-ies**) conservera, fábrica de conservas
cannibal ['kænɪbəl] *adj & s* caníbal *mf*
canning ['kænɪŋ] *adj* conservero ‖ *s* conservería
cannon ['kænən] *s* cañón *m;* cañones
cannonade [,kænə'ned] *s* cañoneo ‖ *tr* cañonear
cannon ball *s* bala de cañón
cannon fodder *s* carne *f* de cañón
can•ny ['kæni] *adj* (*comp* **-nier;** *super* **-niest**) cauteloso, cuerdo; astuto
canoe [kə'nu] *s* canoa; bongo (SAm)
canoeing [kə'nu•ɪŋ] *s* piraguismo
canoeist [kə'nu•ɪst] *s* canoero
canon ['kænən] *s* canon *m;* (*priest*) canónigo
canonical [kə'nɑnɪkəl] *adj* canónico; aceptado, auténtico, establecido ‖ **canonicals** *spl* vestiduras sacerdotales
canonize ['kænə,naɪz] *tr* canonizar
canon law *s* cánones *mpl*, derecho canónico
canon•ry ['kænənri] *s* (*pl* **-ries**) canonjía
can opener ['opənər] *s* abrelatas *m*
cano•py ['kænəpi] *s* (*pl* **-pies**) dosel *m*, pabellón *m;* (*over an entrance*) marquesina; (*for electrical fixtures*) campana
canopy of heaven *s* bóveda celeste
cant [kænt] *s* hipocresía; jerga, jerigonza
cantaloupe ['kæntə,lop] *s* cantalupo
cantankerous [kæn'tæŋkərəs] *adj* de mal genio, pendenciero
canteen [kæn'tin] *s* (*shop*) cantina; (*water flask*) cantimplora; (mil) centro de recreo
canter ['kæntər] *s* medio galope ‖ *intr* ir a medio galope
canticle ['kæntɪkəl] *s* cántico
cantilever ['kæntɪ,livər] *adj* voladizo ‖ *s* viga voladiza
cantle ['kæntəl] *s* arzón trasero
canton [kæn'tɑn] *tr* acantonar
cantonment [kæn'tɑnmənt] *s* acantonamiento
cantor ['kæntər] *s* chantre *m;* (*in a synagogue*) cantor *m* principal
canvas ['kænvəs] *s* cañamazo, lona; (naut) vela, lona; (*painting*) lienzo; **under canvas** (mil) en tiendas; (naut) con las velas izadas
canvass ['kænvəs] *s* pesquisa, escrutinio; (*of votes*) solicitación ‖ *tr* escrutar, solicitar; discutir detenidamente
canyon ['kænjən] *s* cañón *m*
cap. *abbr* **capital, capitalize**
cap [kæp] *s* gorra, gorra de visera; (*of academic costume*) birrete *m;* (*of bottle*) cápsula; (*e.g., of a fountain pen*) capuchón *m* ‖ *v* (*pret & pp* **capped;** *ger* **capping**) *tr* cubrir con gorra; capsular (*una botella*); **to cap the climax** ser el colmo
capabili•ty [,kepə'bɪlɪti] *s* (*pl* **-ties**) habilidad, capacidad
capable ['kepəbəl] *adj* hábil, capaz
capacious [kə'peʃəs] *adj* espacioso, capaz
capaci•ty [kə'pæsɪti] *s* (*pl* **-ties**) (*room, space; ability, aptitude*) capacidad; (*status, function*) calidad; **in the capacity of** en calidad de
cap and bells *spl* caperuza de bufón; cetro de la locura
cap and gown *s* birrete y toga
caparison [kə'pærɪsən] *s* caparazón *m* ‖ *tr* engualdrapar
cape [kep] *s* cabo, promontorio; (*garment*) capa, esclavina
Cape Colony *s* la Colonia del Cabo
Cape Horn *s* el Cabo de Hornos
Cape of Good Hope *s* Cabo de Buena Esperanza

caper [ˈkepər] *s* (*gay jump*) cabriola; (*prank*) travesura; **to cut capers** dar cabriolas; hacer travesuras || *intr* cabriolear; retozar
Cape'town' o **Cape Town** *s* El Cabo, la Ciudad del Cabo
cape'work' *s* (taur) suerte *f* de capa, lance *m*
capital [ˈkæpɪtəl] *adj* capital || *s* (*money*) capital *m;* (*city*) capital *f;* (*top of a column*) capitel *m;* **to make capital out of** sacar beneficio de
capital flight *s* fuga de capitales
capitalism [[ˈkæpɪtə,lɪzəm] *s* capitalismo
capitalize [ˈkæpɪtə,laɪz] *tr* escribir con mayúscula; capitalizar || *intr* — **to capitalize on** aprovecharse de
capital letter *s* letra mayúscula
capital punishment *s* pena capital, último suplicio
capitol [ˈkæpɪtəl] *s* capitolio
capitulate [kəˈpɪtʃə,let] *intr* capitular
capon [ˈkepɑn] *s* capón *m*
caprice [kəˈpris] *s* capricho, antojo; veleidad
capricious [kəˈprɪʃəs] *adj* caprichoso, antojadizo
Capricorn [ˈkæprɪ,kɔrn] *s* (astr) Capricornio
capsize [ˈkæpsaɪz] *tr* volcar || *intr* volcar; tumbar, zozobrar (*un barco*)
capstan [ˈkæpstən] *s* cabrestante *m*
cap'stone' *s* coronamiento
capsule [ˈkæpsəl] *s* cápsula
Capt. *abbr* **Captain**
captain [ˈkæptən] *s* capitán *m* || *tr* capitanear
captain•cy [ˈkæptənsi] *s* (*pl* **-cies**) capitanía
caption [ˈkæpʃən] *s* título; (*in a movie*) subtítulo
captivate [ˈkæptɪ,vet] *tr* cautivar, encantar
captive [ˈkæptɪv] *adj* & *s* cautivo
captivi•ty [kæpˈtɪvɪti] *s* (*pl* **-ties**) cautividad, cautiverio
captor [ˈkæptər] *s* aprenhensor *m*
capture [ˈkæptʃər] *s* apresamiento, captura; (*of a stronghold*) toma || *tr* apresar, capturar; tomar (*una plaza*); captar (*p.ej., la atención de una persona*)
Capuchin nun [ˈkæpjʊtʃɪn] o [ˈkæpjʊʃɪn] *s* capuchina
car [kɑr] *s* coche *m;* (*of an elevator*) caja, carro
carafe [kəˈræf] *s* garrafa
caramel [ˈkærəməl] o [ˈkɑrməl] *s* (*burnt sugar*) caramelo; bombón *m* de caramelo
carat [ˈkærət] *s* quilate *m*
caravan [ˈkærə,væn] *s* caravana
caravansa•ry [,kærəˈvænsəri] *s* (*pl* **-ries**) caravanera
caraway [ˈkærə,we] *s* alcaravea
car'barn' *s* cochera de tranvías
carbide [ˈkɑrbaɪd] *s* carburo
carbine [ˈkɑrbaɪn] *s* carabina
carbolic acid [kɑrˈbɑlɪk] *s* ácido carbólico
car bomb *s* coche bomba
carbon [ˈkɑrbən] *s* (*chemical element*) carbono; (*pole of arc light or battery*) carbón *m;* papel *m* carbón; (*in auto cylinders*) carbonilla
carbon copy *s* copia al carbón
carbon dioxide *s* dióxido de carbono
carbon monoxide *s* óxido de carbono, monóxido de carbono
carbon paper *s* papel *m* carbón
car'boy' *s* bombona, garrafón *m*
carbuncle [ˈkɑrbʌŋkəl] *s* (*stone*) carbunclo, carbúnculo; (pathol) carbunclo, carbunco
carburetor [ˈkɑrbə,retər] *s* carburador *m*
car caller *s* avisacoches *m*
carcass [ˈkɑrkəs] *s* res muerta, cadáver *m*
carcinogen [kɑrˈsɪnəjən] *s* carcinógeno
carcinoma [,kɑrsəˈnomə] *s* carcinoma
card [kɑrd] s tarjeta; (*for playing games*) naipe *m*, carta; (*for filing*) ficha; (*person*) (coll) sujeto, tipo
card'board' *s* cartón *m*
cardboard binding *s* encuadernación en pasta
card case *s* tarjetero
card catalogue *s* catálogo de fichas
cardiac [ˈkɑrdɪ,æk] *adj* cardíaco || *s* (*medicine; sufferer*) cardíaco
cardigan [ˈkɑrdɪgən] *s* albornoz *m*, rebeca
cardinal [ˈkɑrdɪnəl] *adj* cardinal; purpurado || *s* (*prelate; bird*) cardenal *m;* número cardinal
card index *s* fichero, tarjetero
card party *s* tertulia de baraja
card'sharp' *s* fullero, tahur *m*
card trick *s* truco de naipes
care [kɛr] *s* (*worry*) inquietud, ansiedad; (*watchful attention*) esmero; (*charge*) cargo, custodia; **care of** suplicada en casa de; **to take care of oneself** cuidarse || *intr* inquietarse, preocuparse; **to care for** cuidar de; amar, querer; **to care to** tener ganas de; **I couldn't care less** me importe un pepino
careen [kəˈrin] *intr* inclinarse; mecerse precipitadamente
career [kəˈrɪr] *adj* de carrera || *s* carrera
care'free' *adj* despreocupado, libre de cuidados
careful [ˈkɛrfəl] *adj* (*acting with care*) cuidadoso; (*done with care*) esmerado; **to be careful to** cuidarse de
careless [ˈkɛrlɪs] *adj* descuidado, negligente
carelessness [ˈkɛrlɪsnɪs] *s* descuido, negligencia
car enthusiast *s* devoto del volante
caress [kəˈrɛs] *s* caricia || *tr* acariciar || *intr* acariciarse
caretaker [ˈkɛr,tekər] *s* curador *m*, guardián *m*, custodio
care'worn' *adj* fatigado, rendido
car'fare' *s* pasaje *m* de tranvía o autobús
car•go [ˈkɑrgo] *s* (*pl* **-goes** o **-gos**) carga, cargamento
cargo boat *s* barco de carga
Caribbean [,kærɪˈbi•ən] o [kəˈrɪbɪ•ən] *adj* caribe || *s* mar *m* Caribe
caricature [ˈkærɪkətʃər] *s* caricatura || *tr* caricaturizar
caricaturist [ˈkærɪkətʃərɪst] *s* caricaturista *mf*
carillon [ˈkærɪ,lɑn] o [kəˈrɪljən] *s* carillón *m*
car'load' *s* furgonada, vagonada

carnage [ˈkɑrnɪdʒ] *s* carnicería, matanza
carnation [kɑrˈneʃən] *adj* encarnado ‖ *s* clavel *m,* clavel reventón
carnival [ˈkɑrnɪvəl] *adj* carnavalesco ‖ *s* (*period before Lent*) carnaval *m;* verbena, espectáculo de atracciones
car•ol [ˈkærəl] *s* canción alegre, villancico ‖ *v* (*pret & pp* **-oled** o **-olled;** *ger* **-oling** o **-olling**); *tr* celebrar con villancicos ‖ *intr* cantar con alegría
carom [ˈkærəm] *s* carambola ‖ *intr* carambolear
carousal [kəˈraʊzəl] *s* juerga, borrachera, jarana
carouse [kəˈraʊz] *intr* emborracharse, jaranear
carp [kɑrp] *s (pez)* carpa ‖ *intr* quejarse
carpenter [ˈkɑrpəntər] *s* carpintero
carpentry [ˈkɑrpəntri] *s* carpintería
carpet [ˈkɑrpɪt] *s* alfombra; **to be on the carpet** estar sobre el tapete ‖ *tr* alfombrar
carpet sweeper *s* barredora de alfombras
car'-rent'al service *s* alquiler *m* de coches
carriage [ˈkærɪdʒ] *s* carruaje *m;* (*cost of carrying*) porte *m,* transporte *m;* (*bearing*) porte *m,* continente *m;* (mach) carro
carrier [ˈkærɪ•ər] *s* portador *m,* transportador *m;* portador de gérmenes; empresa de transportes; (*mailman*) cartero; vendedor *m* de periódicos; portaaviones *m;* (rad) onda portadora
carrier pigeon *s* paloma mensajera
carrier wave *s* (rad) onda portadora
carrion [ˈkærɪ•ən] *adj* carroño; inmundo ‖ *s* carroña; inmundicia
carrot [ˈkærət] *s* zanahoria
carrousel [ˌkærəˈzɛl] *s* caballitos, tiovivo
car•ry [ˈkæri] *v* (*pret & pp* **-ried**) *tr* llevar, portar, traer; transportar; sostener (*una carga*); **to carry away** llevarse; encantar, entusiasmar; **to carry into effect** llevar a cabo; **to carry one's point** salirse con la suya; **to carry out** llevar a cabo; **to carry the day** quedar victorioso, ganar la palma; **to carry weight** ser de peso ‖ *intr* tener alcance; **to carry on** continuar, perseverar; (coll) travesear; (coll) comportarse de un modo escandaloso; (coll) hacer locuras
cart [kɑrt] *s* carreta, carro ‖ *tr* carretear
carte blanche [ˈkɑrtˈblɑnʃ] *s* carta blanca
cartel [kɑrˈtɛl] *s* cartel *m*
Carthage [ˈkɑrθɪdʒ] *s* Cartago
Carthaginian [ˌkɑrθəˈdʒɪnɪ•ən] *adj & s* cartaginés *m*
cart horse *s* caballo de tiro
cartilage [ˈkɑrtɪlɪdʒ] *s* cartílago
cartoon [kɑrˈtun] *s* caricatura; (*comic strip*) tira cómica; (*film*) película de dibujos ‖ *tr* caricaturizar
cartoonist [kɑrˈtunɪst] *s* caricaturista *mf*
cartridge [ˈkɑrtrɪdʒ] *s* cartucho
cartridge belt *s* canana
carve [kɑrv] *tr* trinchar (*carne*); esculpir, tallar
carving knife [ˈkɑrvɪŋ] *s* cuchillo de trinchar
car washer *s* lavacoches *m*
caryatid [ˌkærɪˈætɪd] *s* cariátide *f*
cascade [kæsˈked] *s* cascada
case [kes] *s* (*instance; form of a word*) caso; (*box*) caja; (*small container*) estuche *m;* (*for cigarettes*) pitillera; (*sheath*) vaina, funda; (law) causa, pleito; **in case** caso que; **in no case** de ninguna manera ‖ *tr* encajonar, enfundar
casement [ˈkesmənt] *s* ventana batiente; bastidor *m* (*de la ventana*)
cash [kæʃ] *s* dinero contante; pago al contado; **cash on delivery** contra reembolso, pago contra entrega; **to pay cash** pagar al contado ‖ *tr* cobrar (*un cheque el portador*); abonar, pagar (*un cheque el banco*) ‖ *intr* — **to cash in on** (coll) sacar provecho de
cash and carry *s* pago al contado con transporte a cargo del comprador
cash'box' *s* caja
cashew [ˈkæʃu] *s* anacardo, marañón *m*
cashew nut *s* anacardo, nuez *f* de marañón
cashier [kæˈʃɪr] *s* cajero ‖ *tr* destruir; (*in the army*) degradar
cashier's check *s* cheque *m* de caja
cashier's desk *s* caja
cashmere [ˈkæʃmɪr] *s* casimir *m,* cachemir *m*
cash on hand *s* efectivo en caja
cash payment *s* pago al contado
cash purchase *s* compra al contado
cash register *s* caja registradora
casing [ˈkesɪŋ] *s* caja, cubierta, envoltura; (*of door or window*) marco, cerco; (*of tire*) cubierta; (sew) jareta
cask [kæsk] o [kɑsk] *s* casco, pipa, tonel *m*
casket [ˈkæskɪt] *s* (*box for valuables*) cajita, joyero; (*coffin*) caja, ataúd *m*
cassava [kəˈsɑvə] *s* cazabe *m,* casabe *m*
casserole [ˈkæsəˌrol] *s* cacerola; (*dish cooked in a casserole*) timbal *m*
cassette [kæˈsɛt] *s* casete *m*
cassette player *s* grabador-reproductor *m*
cassock [ˈkæsək] *s* balandrán *m,* sotana
cast [kæst] *s* echada, tiro; forma, molde *m;* aire *m,* semblante *m;* matiz *m,* tinte *m;* (*of actors*) reparto ‖ *v* (*pret & pp* **cast**) *tr* echar, tirar; volver (*los ojos*); proyectar (*una sombra*); colar, fundir (*metales*); depositar (*votos*); echar (*suertes*); (theat) repartir (*papeles*); **to cast aside** desechar; **to cast loose** soltar; **to cast out** arrojar, echar fuera; despedir, desterrar ‖ *intr* echar los dados; arrojar el sedal o el anzuelo; **to cast about** revolver proyectos; **to cast off** (naut) soltar las amarras
castanet [ˌkæstəˈnɛt] *s* castañuela, castañeta
cast'a•way' *adj & s* proscrito, réprobo; náufrago
caste [kæst] *s* casta; **to lose caste** desprestigiarse
caster [ˈkæstər] *s* ruedecilla de mueble; (*cruet stand*) angarillas, vinagreras; frasco
Castile [kæsˈtil] *s* Castilla
Castile soap *s* jabón *m* de Castilla
Castilian [kæsˈtɪljən] *adj & s* castellano
casting [ˈkæstɪŋ] *s* fundición, pieza fundida; (theat) reparto
casting vote *s* voto de calidad

cast iron *s* hierro colado, hierro fundido
cast'-i'ron *adj* de hierro colado; fuerte, endurecido; duro, inflexible
castle ['kæsəl] *s* castillo; (chess) roque *m*, torre *f* || *tr & intr* (chess) enrocar
castle in Spain o **castle in the air** *s* castillo en el aire
cast'off' *adj* abandonado, desechado; (*clothing*) de desecho || *s* desecho
castor oil ['kæstər] *s* aceite *m* de ricino
castrate ['kæstret] *tr* capar, castrar
casual ['kæʒu•əl] *adj* casual, fortuito; descuidado, indiferente
casual•ty ['kæʒu•əlti] *s* (*pl* **-ties**) desgracia, accidente *m;* accidentado, víctima; (*in war*) baja
casualty list *s* lista de bajas
cat. *abbr* **catalogue, catechism**
cat [kæt] *s* gato; mujer maligna; **to bell the cat** ponerle cascabel al gato; **to let the cat out of the bag** revelar el secreto
catacomb ['kætə,kom] *s* catacumba
Catalan ['kætə,læn] *adj & s* catalán *m*
catalogue ['kætə,lɔg] o ['kætə,lɑg] *s* catálogo || *tr* catalogar
Catalonia [,kætə'lonɪ•ə] *s* Cataluña
Catalonian [,kætə'lonɪ•ən] *adj & s* catalán *m*
catapult ['kætə,pʌlt] *s* catapulta || *tr* catapultar
cataract ['kætə,rækt] *s* catarata; (pathol) catarata
catarrh [kə'tɑr] *s* catarro
catastrophe [kə'tæstrəfi] *s* catástrofe *f*
cat'call' *s* rechifla || *tr & intr* rechiflar
catch [kætʃ] *s* (*of a ball*) cogida; (*of fish*) pesca; (*of a lock*) cerradera, pestillo; (*booty*) botín *m*, presa; (*fastener*) broche *m;* (*good match*) buen partido || *v* (*pret & pp* **caught** [kɔt]) *tr* asir, coger, atrapar; llegar a oír; coger (*un resfriado*); (*to come upon suddenly*) sorprender; comprender; capturar (*al delincuente*); **to catch fire** encenderse; **to catch hold of** agarrar, coger; apoderarse de; **to catch it** (coll) merecerse un regaño; **to catch oneself** contenerse; recobrar el equilibrio; **to catch sight of** alcanzar a ver; **to catch up** arrebatar; coger al vuelo; (*in a mistake*) cazar || *intr* pegarse (*una enfermedad*); enredarse; encenderse; **to catch at** agarrarse a, tratar de asir; **to catch on** prender en (*p.ej., un gancho*); comprender, coger el tino; **to catch up** salir del atraso; (*in one's debts*) ponerse al día; **to catch up with** emparejar con
catcher ['kætʃər] *s* (baseball) receptor, parador *m*
catching ['kætʃɪŋ] *adj* pegajoso, contagioso; atrayente, cautivador
catch question *s* pega
catchup ['kætʃəp] *s* salsa de tomate condimentada
catch'word' *s* lema *m*, palabra de efecto; (*actor's cue*) pie *m;* (typ) reclamo
catch•y ['kætʃi] *adj* (*comp* **-ier;** *super* **-iest**) (*tune*) animado, vivo; (*title of a book*) impresionante, llamativo; (*question*) intrincado; (*breathing*) espasmódico
catechism ['kætɪ,kɪzəm] *s* catecismo
catego•ry ['kætɪ,gori] *s* (*pl* **-ries**) categoría; (*sports*) division
cater ['ketər] *tr & intr* abastecer, proveer; **to cater to** proveer a
cater-cornered ['kætər,kɔrnərd] *adj* diagonal || *adv* diagonalmente
caterer ['ketərər] *s* abastecedor *m*, proveedor *m* de alimentos (*esp. para fiestas caseras*)
caterpillar ['kætər,pɪlər] *s* oruga
caterpillar tractor *s* tractor *m* de oruga
cat'fish' *s* bagre *m*
cat'gut' *s* (mus) cuerda de tripa; (surg) catgut *m*
Cath. *abbr* **Catholic**
cathartic [kə'θɑrtɪk] *adj & s* catártico
cathedral [kə'θidrəl] *s* catedral *f*
catheter ['kæθɪtər] *s* catéter *m*
catheterize ['kæθɪtə,raɪz] *tr* cateterizar
cathode ['kæθod] *s* cátodo
catholic ['kæθəlɪk] *adj* católico || **Catholic** *adj & s* católico
catkin ['kætkɪn] *s* candelilla, amento
cat nap *s* sueñecito
catnip ['kætnɪp] *s* hierba gatera, nébeda
cat-o'-nine-tails [,kætə'naɪn,telz] *s* azote *m* con nueve ramales
cat's cradle *s* juego de la cuna
cat's-paw o **catspaw** ['kæts,pɔ] *s* mano *f* de gato, instrumento
catsup ['kætsəp] o [kɛtʃəp] *s* salsa de tomate condimentada
cat'tail' *s* anea, espadaña; amento
cattle ['kætəl] *s* ganado vacuno
cattle crossing *s* paso de ganado
cattle•man ['kætəlmən] *s* (*pl* **-men** [mən]) *s* ganadero
cattle raising *s* ganadería
cattle ranch *s* hacienda de ganado
cat•ty ['kæti] *adj* (*comp* **-tier;** *super* **-tiest**) (*like a cat*) felino, gatuno; (*spiteful*) malicioso; (*gossipy*) chismoso
cat'walk' *s* pasadero, pasarela
Caucasian [kɔ'keʒən] *adj & s* caucasiano, caucásico
Caucasus ['kɔkəsəs] *s* Cáucaso
caucus ['kɔkəs] *s* junta de políticos
cauliflower ['kɔlɪ,flau•ər] *s* coliflor *f*
cause [kɔz] *s* causa; (*person*) causante *mf* || *tr* causar
cause'way' *s* (*highway*) calzada; calzada elevada
caustic ['kɔstɪk] *adj* cáustico
cauterize ['kɔtə,raɪz] *tr* cauterizar
caution ['kɔʃən] *s* (*carefulness*) cautela; (*warning*) advertencia, amonestación || *tr* advertir, amonestar
cautious ['kɔʃəs] *adj* cauteloso, cauto
Cav. *abbr* **Cavalry**
cavalcade [,kævəl'ked] o ['kævəl,ked] *s* cabalgata
cavalier [,kævə'lɪr] *adj* (*haughty*) altivo, desdeñoso; (*offhand*) alegre, desenvuelto, inceremonioso || *s* (*horseman*) caballero; (*lady's escort*) galán *m*
caval•ry ['kævəlri] *s* (*pl* **-ries**) caballería

cavalry•man [ˈkævəlrimən] *s* (*pl* **-men** [mən]) soldado de caballería
cave [kev] *s* cueva, caverna || *intr* — **to cave in** hundirse; (*to give in, yield*) (coll) ceder, rendirse
cave′-in′ *s* hundimiento, derrumbe *m*, socavón *m*
cave man *s* hombre grosero
cavern [ˈkævərn] *s* caverna
cav•il [ˈkævɪl] *v* (*pret & pp* **-iled** o **-illed;** *ger* **-iling** o **-illing**) *intr* buscar quisquillas
cavi•ty [ˈkævɪti] *s* (*pl* **-ties**) cavidad; (*in a tooth*) picadura
cavort [kəˈgɔrt] *intr* (coll) cabriolar
caw [kɔ] *s* graznido || *intr* graznar
CB *abbr* **citizens band**
cc. *abbr* **cubic centimeter**
CD *abbr* **compact disk**
cease [sis] *tr* parar, suspender || *intr* cesar; cesar de, dejar de + *inf*
cease′fire′ *s* cese *m* de fuego || *intr* suspender hostilidades
ceaseless [ˈsislɪs] *adj* incesante, continuo
cedar [ˈsidər] *s* cedro
cede [sid] *tr* ceder, traspasar
ceiling [ˈsilɪŋ] *s* techo, cielo raso; (aer) techo, cielo máximo
ceiling price *s* precio tope
celebrant [ˈsɛlɪbrənt] *s* celebrante *m*
celebrate [ˈsɛlɪ,bret] *tr* celebrar || *intr* (*to say mass*) celebrar; divertirse, festejarse; farrear
celebrated [ˈsɛlɪ,bretɪd] *adj* célebre, renombrado
celebration [,sɛlɪˈbreʃən] *s* celebración; diversión, festividad
celebri•ty [sɪˈlɛbrɪti] *s* (*pl* **-ties**) (*fame; famous person*) celebridad
celery [ˈsɛləri] *s* apio
celestial [sɪˈlɛstʃəl] *adj* celeste, celestial
celiba•cy [ˈsɛlɪbəsi] *s* (*pl* **-cies**) celibato
celibate [ˈsɛlɪbɪt] *adj & s* célibe *mf*
cell [sɛl] *s* (*of convent or jail*) celda; (*of honeycomb*) celdilla; (*of electric battery*) elemento; (*of plant or animal; of photoelectric device; of political group*) célula
cellar [ˈsɛlər] *s* sótano; (*for wine*) bodega
cellaret [,sɛləˈrɛt] *s* licorera
cell house *s* prisión celular
cellist o **'cellist** [ˈtʃɛlɪst] *s* violoncelista *mf*
cel•lo o **'cel•lo** [ˈtʃɛlo] *s* (*pl* **-los**) violoncelo
cellophane [ˈsɛlə,fen] *s* celofán *m*
celluloid [ˈsɛljə,lɔɪd] *s* celuloide *m*
Celt [sɛlt] o [kɛlt] *s* celta *mf*
Celtic [ˈsɛltɪk] o [ˈkɛltɪk] *adj* céltico || *s* (*language*) celta *m*
cement [sɪˈmɛnt] *s* cemento || *tr* revestir con cemento; (*la amistad*) consolidar
cemeter•y [ˈsɛmɪ,tɛri] *s* (*pl* **-ies**) cementerio
cen. *abbr* **central**
censer [ˈsɛnsər] *s* incensario
censor [ˈsɛnsər] *s* censor *m* || *tr* censurar
censure [ˈsɛnʃər] *s* censura || *tr* censurar
census [ˈsɛnsəs] *s* censo; **to take the census** levantar el censo
cent. *abbr* **centigrade, central, century**
cent [sɛnt] *s* centavo
centaur [ˈsɛntɔr] *s* centauro
centennial [sɛnˈtɛnɪ•əl] *adj & s* centenario
center [ˈsɛntər] *adj* centrista || *s* centro || *tr* centrar
center half *s* (*ball games*) medio centro
cen′ter•piece′ *s* centro de mesa
center punch *s* granete *m*, punzón *m* de marcar
centigrade [ˈsɛntɪ,gred] *adj* centígrado
centimeter [ˈsɛntɪ,mitər] *s* centímetro
centipede [ˈsɛntɪ,pid] *s* ciempiés *m*
central [ˈsɛntrəl] *adj* central || *s* (telp) central *f*, central de teléfonos; (*operator*) telefonista *mf*
Central America *s* Centro América, la América Central
Central American *adj & mf* centroamericano
centralize [ˈsɛntrə,laɪz] *tr* centralizar || *intr* centralizarse
centrifuge [ˈsɛntrəfjudʒ] *s* centrifugadora
centu•ry [ˈsɛntʃəri] *s* (*pl* **-ries**) siglo
century plant *s* pita, maguey *m*
ceramic [sɪˈræmɪk] *adj* cerámico
cereal [ˈsɪrɪ•əl] *adj & s* cereal *m*
ceremonious [,sɛrɪˈmonɪ•əs] *adj* ceremonioso, etiquetero
ceremo•ny [ˈsɛrɪ,moni] *s* (*pl* **-nies**) ceremonia; **to stand on ceremony** hacer ceremonias, ser etiquetero
certain [ˈsʌrtən] *adj* cierto; **a certain** cierto; **for certain** por cierto
certainly [ˈsɛrtənli] *adj* ciertamente; (*gladly*) con mucho gusto
certain•ty [ˈsʌrtənti] *s* (*pl* **-ties**) certeza; **with certainty** a ciencia cierta
certificate [sərˈtɪfɪkɪt] *s* certificación, certificado; (*of birth, death, etc.*) partida, fe *f;* (*document representing financial assets*) título || [sərˈtɪfɪ,ket] *tr* certificar
certified public accountant [ˈsʌrtɪ,faɪd] *s* contador público, censor jurado de cuentas
certi•fy [ˈsʌrtɪ,faɪ] *v* (*pret & pp* **-fied**) *tr* certificar
cervix [ˈsʌrvɪks] *s* (*pl* **cervices** [sərˈvaɪsiz]) cerviz *f*
cessation [sɛˈseʃən] *s* cesación
cessation of hostilities *s* suspensión de hostilidades
cesspool [ˈsɛs,pul] *s* pozo negro; (fig) sitio inmundo
Ceylon [sɪˈlɑn] *s* Ceilán
Ceylo•nese [,siləˈniz] *adj* ceilanés || *s* (*pl* **-nese**) ceilanés *m*
cf. *abbr* **confer,** i.e., **compare**
C.F.I., c.f.i. *abbr* **cost, freight, and insurance**
cg. *abbr* **centigram**
ch. *abbr* **chapter, church**
chafe [tʃef] *s* fricción, roce *m;* desgaste *m;* irritación || *tr* (*to rub*) frotar; (*to rub and make sore*) escocer; (*to wear*) desgastar; irritar || *intr* escocerse; desgastarse; irritarse
chaff [tʃæf] *s* barcia; paja menuda; broza, desperdicio
chafing dish [ˈtʃefɪŋ] *s* cocinilla, infernillo

chagrin [ʃə'grɪn] *s* desazón *f,* disgusto || *tr* desazonar, disgustar
chain [tʃen] *s* cadena || *tr* encadenar
chain gang *s* cadena de presidiarios, collera, cuerda de presos
chain reaction *s* reacción en cadena
chain'smoke' *intr* fumar un pitillo tras otro
chain store *s* empresa con una cadena de tiendas; tienda de una cadena de tiendas
chair [tʃɛr] *s* silla; (*de catedrático*) cátedra; presidencia; **to take the chair** presidir la reunión; abrir la sesión || *tr* presidir (*una reunión*)
chair lift *s* telesilla
chair•man ['tʃɛrmən] *s* (*pl* **-men** [mən]) presidente *m*
chairmanship ['tʃɛrmən,ʃɪp] *s* presidencia
chair rail *s* guardasilla
chalice ['tʃælɪs] *s* cáliz *m*
chalk [tʃɔk] *s* (*soft white limestone*) creta; (*piece used for writing*) tiza || *tr* marcar o escribir con tiza; **to chalk up** apuntar; marcar (*un tanto*)
challenge ['tʃælɪndʒ] *s* desafío; (law) recusación || *tr* desafiar; (law) recusar
chamber ['tʃembər] *s* cámara; (*of a gun*) recámara; dormitorio; **chambers** oficina de juez
chamberlain ['tʃembərlɪn] *s* chambelán *m*
cham'ber•maid' *s* camarera
chamber pot *s* orinal *m*
chameleon [kə'milɪ•ən] *s* camaleón *m*
chamfer ['tʃæmfər] *s* chaflán *m* || *tr* chaflanar
cham•ois ['ʃæmi] *s* (*pl* **-ois**) gamuza
champ [tʃæmp] *s* mordisco; (slang) campeón *m* || *tr & intr* mordiscar; (*el freno*) morder
champagne [ʃæm'pen] *s* champaña *m*
champion ['tʃæmpɪ•ən] *s* campeón *m* || *tr* defender
championess ['tʃæmpɪ•ənɪs] *s* campeona
championship ['tʃæmpɪ•ən,ʃɪp] *s* campeonato
chance [tʃæns] o [tʃɑns] *adj* casual, imprevisto || *s* oportunidad, ocasión; casualidad, suerte *f;* probabilidad; peligro, riesgo; chance *m* (SAm); **by chance** por casualidad; **to not stand a chance** no tener probabilidad de éxito; **to take a chance** probar fortuna; comprar un billete de lotería; **to take chances** probar fortuna; **to wait for a chance** esperar la oportunidad || *intr* acontecer; **to chance on** o **upon** tropezar con; **to chance to** acertar a
chancel ['tʃænsəl] o ['tʃɑnsəl] *s* entrecoro
chanceller•y ['tʃænsələri] o ['tʃɑnsələrɪ] *s* (*pl* **-ies**) cancillería
chancellor ['tʃænsələr] *s* canciller *m*
chandelier [,ʃændə'lɪr] *s* araña de luces
change [tʃendʒ] *s* cambio, mudanza; suelto, moneda suelta; (*surplus money returned with a purchase*) vuelta; (*of clothing*) muda; **for a change** por variedad; **to keep the change** quedarse con la vuelta; || *tr* cambiar, mudar; cambiar de, mudar de; reemplazar; **to change clothes** cambiar de ropa; **to change gears** cambiar de velocidades; **to change hands** cambiar de dueño; **to change money** cambiar moneda; **to change one's mind** cambiar de parecer; **to change trains** cambiar de tren, transbordar || *intr* cambiar, mudar; corregirse
changeable ['tʃendʒəbəl] *adj* cambiable; inconstante, cambiante, mudable
change of clothing *s* muda de ropa
change of heart *s* arrepentimiento, conversión
change of life *s* cesación natural de las reglas
change of voice *s* muda
chan•nel ['tʃænəl] *s* (*body of water joining two others*) canal *m;* (*bed of river*) álveo, cauce *m;* (*means of communication*) vía; (*passage*) conducto; (*groove*) ranura, surco; (telv) canal *m;* **the Channel** el Canal de la Mancha || *v* (*pret & pp* **-neled** o **-nelled;** *ger* **-neling** o **-nelling**) *tr* acanalar; canalizar (*esfuerzos, dinero, etc.*)
chant [tʃænt] *s* (*song*) canción; (*song sung in a monotone*) canto || *tr & intr* cantar
chanter ['tʃæntər] *s* cantor *m;* (*priest*) chantre *m*
chanticleer ['tʃæntɪ,klɪr] *s* el gallo
chaos ['ke•ɑs] *s* caos *m*
chaotic [ke'ɑtɪk] *adj* caótico
chap. *abbr* **chaplain, chapter**
chap [tʃæp] *s* (*jaw*) mandíbula; (*cheek*) mejilla; (*crack in the skin*) grieta; chico, tipo; **chaps** zahones *mpl* || *v* (*pret & pp* **chapped;** *ger* **chapping**) *tr* agrietar, rajar || *intr* agrietarse, rajarse
chapel ['tʃæpəl] *s* capilla
chaperon o **chaperone** ['ʃæpə,ron] *s* carabina, señora de compañía || *tr* acompañar (*una señora a una o más señoritas*)
chaplain ['tʃæplɪn] *s* capellán *m*
chaplet ['tʃæplɪt] *s* (*wreath for head*) guirnalda; rosario
chapter ['tʃæptər] *s* capítulo; (*of the Scriptures*) capítula; (*of a cathedral*) cabildo
chapter and verse *adv* con todos sus pelos y señales
char [tʃɑr] *v* (*pret & pp* **charred;** *ger* **charring**) *tr* carbonizar; (*to scorch*) socarrar
character ['kærɪktər] *s* carácter *m;* (*conspicuous person; person in a play or novel*) personaje *m;* (*part or role in a play*) papel *m;* (*fellow*) (coll) tipo, sujeto
character assassination *s* asesinato de carácter
characteristic [,kærɪktə'rɪstɪk] *adj* característico || *s* característica
characterize ['kærɪktə,raɪz] *tr* caracterizar
char'coal' *s* carbón *m* de leña; (*for sketching*) carboncillo; (*sketch*) dibujo al carbón
charcoal burner *s* (*person*) carbonero; horno para hacer carbón de leña
charge [tʃɑrdʒ] *s* (*of an explosive, of electricity, of soldiers against the enemy; responsibility*) carga; (*accusation; amount owed; recording of amount owed*) cargo; encargamiento; (heral) blasón *m;* (*attack*) embestida; **in charge of** a cargo de; **to put in charge** responsabilizar; **to reverse the charges** (telp) cargar al número llamado; **to take charge of** hacerse cargo de || *tr*

cargar; cobrar (*cierto precio*); (*to order*) encargar, mandar; cargar (*un acumulador; al enemigo*); **to charge to the account of someone** cargarle a uno en cuenta; **to charge with** cargar de ‖ *intr* embestir
charge account *s* cuenta corriente
chargé d'affaires [ʃɑr'ʒe də'fɛr] *s* (*pl* **chargés d'affaires**) encargado de negocios
charger ['tʃɑrdʒər] *s* caballo de guerra; (*of a battery*) cargador *m*
chariot ['tʃærɪ•ət] *s* carro romano
charioteer [,tʃærɪ•ə'tɪr] *s* carretero, auriga *m*
charisma [kə'rɪzmə] *s* carisma
charismatic [,kɑrɪz'mætɪk] *adj* carismático
charitable ['tʃærɪtəbəl] *adj* caritativo
chari•ty ['tʃærɪti] *s* (*pl* **-ties**) caridad; asociación de beneficencia, obra pía; **charity begins at home** la caridad bien ordenada empieza por uno mismo
charity performance *s* función benéfica
charlatan ['ʃɑrlətən] *s* charlatán *m*
charlatanism ['ʃɑrlətən,ɪzəm] *s* charlatanismo
Charlemagne ['ʃɑrlə,men] *s* Carlomagno
Charles [tʃɑrlz] *s* Carlos *m*
charlotte ['ʃɑrlət] *s* carlota ‖ **Charlotte** *s* Carlota
charlotte russe ['ʃɑrlət 'rus] *s* carlota rusa
charm [tʃɑrm] *s* encanto, hechizo; (*trinket*) amuleto, dije *m* ‖ *tr* encantar, hechizar
charming ['tʃɑrmɪŋ] *adj* encantador
charnel ['tʃɑrnəl] *adj* cadavérico, horrible ‖ *s* carnero, osario
charnel house *s* carnero, osario
chart [tʃart] *s* mapa geográfico; (naut) carta de marear; cuadro, diagrama *m* ‖ *tr* bosquejar; **to chart a course** trazar una ruta
charter ['tʃɑrtər] *s* carta (de privilegio) ‖ *tr* alquilar (*un autobús*); fletar (*un barco*)
charter member *s* socio fundador
char•woman ['tʃɑr,wʊmən] *s* (*pl* **-women** [,wɪmɪn]) alquilona, asistenta
Charybdis [kə'rɪbdɪs] *s* Caribdis *f*
chase [tʃes] *s* caza, persecución ‖ *tr* cazar, perseguir; **to chase away** ahuyentar
chasm ['kæzəm] *s* abismo
chas•sis ['tʃæsi] *s* (*pl* **-sis** [siz]) chasis *m*
chaste [tʃest] *adj* casto; (*style*) castizo
chasten ['tʃesən] *tr* castigar, corregir
chastise [tʃæs'taɪz] *tr* castigar
chastity ['tʃæstɪti] *s* castidad
chasuble ['tʃæzjəbəl] *s* casulla
chat [tʃæt] *s* charla, plática ‖ *v* (*pret & pp* **chatted;** *ger* **chatting**) *intr* charlar, platicar
chatelaine ['ʃætə,len] *s* castellana
chattels ['tʃætəlz] *spl* bienes *mpl* muebles, enseres *mpl*
chatter ['tʃætər] *s* (*talk*) cháchara; (*rattling*) traqueo; (*of teeth*) castañeteo; (*of birds*) chirrido ‖ *intr* chacharear; traquear; castañetear, dentellar (*los dientes*)
chat'ter•box' *s* charlador *m*, tarabilla
chattering ['tʃætərɪŋ] *adj* palabrudo
chauffeur ['ʃofər] o [ʃo'fʌr] *s* chófer *m*
chauvinism ['ʃovinɪzəm] *s* chauvinismo
cheap [tʃip] *adj* barato; (*charging low prices*) no carero, baratero; (*flashy*) cursi; baladí; **to feel cheap** sentirse avergonzado ‖ *adv* barato
cheapen ['tʃipən] *tr* abaratar
cheapness ['tʃipnɪs] *s* baratura; baratía; (*flashiness*) cursilería
cheat [tʃit] *s* trampa, fraude *m;* (*person*) trampista *mf*, defraudador *m* ‖ *tr* trampear, defraudar
check [tʃɛk] *s* (*of bank*) cheque *m;* (*for baggage*) talón *m*, contraseña; (*in a restaurant*) cuenta; (*in theater or movie*) contraseña, billete *m* de salida; (*restraint*) freno; (*to hold a door*) amortiguador *m;* (*in chess*) jaque *m;* inspección; comprobación, verificación; (*cloth*) paño a cuadros; **in check** en jaque; **to hold in check** contener, refrenar ‖ *interj* ¡jaque! ‖ *tr* parar súbitamente; contener, refrenar; amortiguar; facturar (*equipajes*); inspeccionar; comprobar, verificar; marcar, señalar; chequear; (*in chess*) jaquear, dar jaque a; **to check up** comprobar, verificar ‖ *intr* pararse súbitamente; corresponder punto por punto; **to check in** (*at a hotel*) llegar e inscribirse; **to check out** pagar la cuenta y despedirse; (slang) morir
check'book' *s* talonario (de cheques), chequera
checker ['tʃɛkər] *s* inspector *m;* cuadro; dibujo a cuadros; (*in game of checkers*) ficha, pieza; **checkers** damas, juego de damas ‖ *tr* marcar con cuadros; diversificar, variar
check'er•board' *s* damero, tablero
check girl *s* moza de guardarropa
checking account *s* cuenta corriente
check'mate' *s* mate *m*, jaque *m* mate ‖ *tr* dar mate a, dar jaque mate a; (fig) derrotar completamente
check'out' *s* (*from a hotel*) salida; hora de salida; (*in a self-service retail store*) revisión y pago
checkout counter *s* mostrador *m* de revisión
check'point' *s* punto de inspección
check'rein' *s* engallador *m*
check'room' *s* guardarropa *m;* (rr) consigna, depósito de equipajes
check'up' *s* verificación rigurosa; chequeo; (*of an automobile*) revisión; (med) reconocimiento general
cheek [tʃik] *s* mejilla, carrillo; (coll) descaro, frescura
cheek'bone' *s* pómulo
cheek by jowl *adv* cara a cara, en estrecha intimidad
cheek•y ['tʃiki] *adj* (*comp* **-ier;** *super* **-iest**) (coll) descarado, fresco
cheer [tʃɪr] *s* alegría, regocijo; (*shout*) viva *m*, aplauso; **what cheer?** ¿qué tal? ‖ *tr* alegrar, animar; aplaudir, vitorear; dar la bienvenida a, con vivas y aplausos ‖ *intr* alegrarse, animarse; **cheer up!** ¡ánimo!
cheerful ['tʃɪrfəl] *adj* alegre
cheerio ['tʃɪrɪ,o] *interj* (coll) ¡hola! ¡qué tal!; (coll) ¡adiós! ¡hasta la vista!
cheerless ['tʃɪrlɪs] *adj* sombrío, triste
cheese [tʃiz] *s* queso

cheese'cloth' *s* estopilla
cheese spread *s* queso para extender
cheetah ['tʃitə] *s* gatopardo; leopardo indio
chef [ʃɛf] *s* primer cocinero, jefe *m* de cocina
chem. *abbr* **chemical, chemist, chemistry**
chemical ['kɛmɪkəl] *adj* químico || *s* producto químico, substancia química
chemise [ʃə'miz] *s* camisa (de mujer)
chemist ['kɛmɪst] *s* químico
chemistry ['kɛmɪstri] *s* química
chemotherapy [,kimo'θɛrəpi] *s* quimioterapia
cherish ['tʃɛriʃ] *tr* acariciar; (*a hope*) abrigar, acariciar
cher•ry ['tʃɛri] *s* (*pl* **-ries**) (*fruit; color*) cereza; (*tree*) cerezo
cher•ub ['tʃɛrəb] *s* (*pl* **-ubim** [əbɪm]) querubín *m* || *s* (*pl* **-ubs**) niño angelical
chess [tʃɛs] *s* ajedrez *m*
chess'board' *s* tablero de ajedrez
chess•man ['tʃɛs,mæn] *s* (*pl* **-men** [,mɛn]) pieza de ajedrez, trebejo
chess player *s* ajedrecista *mf*
chess set *s* ajedrez *m*
chest [tʃɛst] *s* (*part of body*) pecho; (*receptacle*) cajón *m*, cofre *m;* (*piece of furniture*) cómoda
chestnut ['tʃɛsnət] *s* (*tree, wood, color*) castaño; (*fruit*) castaña
chest of drawers *s* cómoda
cheval glass [ʃə'væl] *s* psique *f*
chevalier [,ʃɛvə'lɪr] *s* caballero
chevron ['ʃɛvrən] *s* galón *m* en forma de V invertida
chew [tʃu] *s* mascadura || *tr* mascar; **to chew gum** chiclear; **to chew the rag** (slang) dar la lengua || *intr* mascar
chewing gum *s* goma de mascar, chicle *m*
chg. *abbr* **charge**
chic [ʃik] *adj & s* chic *m*
chicaner•y [ʃɪ'kenəri] *s* (*pl* **-ies**) triquiñuela
chick [tʃɪk] *s* pollito; (slang) polla
chicken ['tʃɪkən] *s* pollo; (*young person*) pollo; (*young girl*) polla
chicken coop *s* pollera
chicken feed *s* (coll) calderilla
chickenhearted ['tʃɪkən,hɑrtɪd, varicela] *adj* gallina
chicken pox *s* viruelas locas, varicela
chicken wire *s* alambrada, tela metálica
chick'pea' *s* garbanzo
chico•ry ['tʃɪkəri] *s* (*pl* **-ries**) achicoria
chide [tʃaɪd] *v* (*pret* **chided** o **chid** [tʃɪd]; *pp* **chided, chid** o **chidden** ['tʃɪdən]) *tr* reprender, regañar
chief [tʃif] *adj* principal || *s* jefe *m;* (*of American Indians*) cacique *m*
chief executive *s* jefe *m* del gobierno
chief justice *s* presidente *m* de sala; presidente del tribunal supremo
chiefly ['tʃifli] *adv* principalmente, mayormente
chief of staff *s* jefe *m* de estado mayor
chief of state *s* jefe *m* del estado
chieftain ['tʃiftən] *s* (*of a clan or tribe*) jefe *m;* adalid *m*, caudillo
chiffon [ʃɪ'fɑn] *s* gasa, soplillo; **chiffons** atavíos, perifollos
chiffonier [,ʃɪfə'nɪr] *s* cómoda alta
chignon ['ʃinjɑn] *s* castaña, moño
chilblain ['tʃɪl,blen] *s* sabañón *m*
child [tʃaɪld] *s* (*pl* **children** ['tʃɪldrən]) *s* (*infant, youngster*) niño; pipiolo (CAm, Mex); (*one's offspring*) hijo; descendiente *mf;* **with child** encinta, embarazada
child'birth' *s* alumbramiento, parto
childhood ['tʃaɪldhʊd] *s* niñez *f*, puericia; **from childhood** desde niño
childish ['tʃaɪldɪʃ] *adj* aniñado, pueril
childishness ['tʃaɪldɪʃnɪs] *s* puerilidad
child labor *s* trabajo de menores
childless ['tʃaɪldlɪs] *adj* sin hijos
child'like' *adj* aniñado
child'-rear'ing *s* puericultura
child's play *s* juego de niños
child welfare *s* protección a la infancia
Chile ['tʃɪli] *s* Chile *m*
Chilean ['tʃɪlɪ•ən] *adj & s* chileno
chili sauce ['tʃɪli] *s* ají *m*, salsa de ají
chill [tʃɪl] *adj* frío || *s* frío desapacible; (*sensation of cold*) escalofrío; (*lack of cordiality*) frialdad || *tr* enfriar || *intr* calofriarse
chill•y ['tʃɪli] *adj* (*comp* **-ier;** *super* **-iest**) (*causing shivering*) frío; (*sensitive to cold*) escalofriado, friolero; (*indifferent*) (fig) frío
chime [tʃaɪm] *s* campaneo, repique *m;* tubo sonoro; **chimes** juego de campanas || *tr & intr* campanear, repicar
chime clock *s* reloj *m* de carillón
chimera [kaɪ'mɪrə] o [kɪ'mɪrə] *s* quimera
chimney ['tʃɪmni] *s* chimenea; (*for a lamp*) tubo
chimney cap *s* caperuza
chimney flue *s* cañón *m* de chimenea
chimney pot *s* mitra, guardavientos *m*
chimney sweep *s* limpiachimeneas *m*, deshollinador *m*
chimpanzee [tʃɪm'pænzi] o [,tʃɪmpæn'zi] *s* chimpancé *m*
chin [tʃɪn] *s* barba, mentón *m;* **to keep one's chin up** (coll) no desanimarse || *v* (*pret & pp* **chinned;** *ger* **chinning**) *intr* (coll) charlar
china ['tʃaɪnə] *s* china, porcelana || **China** *s* China
china closet *s* chinero
China•man ['tʃaɪnəmən] *s* (*pl* **-men** [mən]) (offensive) chino
chi'na•ware' *s* porcelana, vajilla de porcelana
Chi•nese [tʃaɪ'niz] *adj* chino || *s* (*pl* **-nese**) chino
Chinese gong *s* batintín *m*
Chinese lantern *s* farolillo veneciano
Chinese puzzle *s* problema embrollado
chink [tʃɪŋk] *s* grieta, hendidura; sonido metálico
chin strap *s* barboquejo, carrillera
chintz [tʃɪnts] *s* zaraza
chip [tʃɪp] *s* astilla, brizna; (*in china*) desconchado; (*in poker*) ficha; **chip off the old block** hijo de su padre || *v* (*pret & pp* **chipped;** *ger* **chipping**) *tr* astillar (*la ma-*

dera); desconchar (*la porcelana*); **to chip in** contribuir con su cuota || *intr* astillarse; desconcharse
chipmunk ['tʃɪp,mʌŋk] *s* ardilla listada
chipper ['tʃɪpər] *adj* (coll) alegre, jovial, vivo
chiropodist [kaɪ'rɑpədɪst] o [kɪ'rɑpədɪst] *s* quiropodista *mf*
chiropractor ['kaɪrə,præktər] *s* quiropráctico
chirp [tʃʌrp] *s* chirrido, gorjeo || *intr* chirriar, gorjear; hablar alegremente
chis•el ['tʃɪzəl] *s* (*for wood*) escoplo, formón *m;* (*for stone and metal*) cincel *m* || *v* (*pret & pp* **-eled** o **-elled;** *ger* **-eling** o **-elling**) *tr* escoplear; cincelar; (slang) estafar
chit-chat ['tʃɪt,tʃæt] *s* charla, palique *m;* habliIla, chismes *mpl*
chivalric ['ʃɪvəlrɪk] o [ʃɪ'vælrɪk] *adj* caballeresco
chivalrous ['ʃɪvəlrəs] *adj* caballeroso
chivalry ['ʃɪvəlri] *s* (*knighthood*) caballería; (*gallantry, gentlemanliness*) caballerosidad
chloride ['kloraɪd] *s* cloruro
chlorine ['klorin] *s* cloro
chloroform ['klorə,fɔrm] *s* cloroformo || *tr* cloroformizar
chlorophyll ['klorəfɪl] *s* clorofila
chock-full ['tʃɑk'fʊl] *adj* de bote en bote, colmado
chocolate ['tʃɑkəlɪt] *s* chocolate *m*
choice [tʃɔɪs] *adj* escogido, selecto, superior || *s* elección, selección; lo más escogido; **to have no choice** no tener alternativa
choir [kwaɪr] *s* coro
choir'boy' *s* niño de coro, infante *m* de coro
choir desk *s* facistol *m*
choir loft *s* coro
choir'mas'ter *s* jefe *m* de coro, maestro de capilla
choke [tʃok] *s* estrangulación; (*of carburetor*) cierre *m,* obturador *m;* (elec) choque *m* || *tr* ahogar, sofocar, estrangular; obstruir, tapar; (aut) obturar; **to choke down** atragantar || *intr* sofocarse; atragantarse; **to choke on** atragantarse con
choke coil *s* (elec) bobina de reacción, choque *m*
cholera ['kɑlərə] *s* cólera *m*
choleric ['kɑlərɪk] *adj* colérico
cholesterol [kə'lɛstə,rol] *s* colesterol *m*
choose [tʃuz] *v* (*pret* **chose** [tʃoz]; *pp* **chosen** ['tʃozən]) *tr* escoger, elegir || *intr* — **to choose between** optar entre; **to choose to** optar por
chop [tʃɑp] *s* golpe *m* cortante; (*of meat*) chuleta; **chops** boca, labios || *v* (*pret & pp* **chopped;** *ger* **chopping**) *tr* cortar, tajar; picar (*la carne*); **to chop off** tronchar; **to chop up** desmenuzar
chop'house' *s* restaurante *m,* figón *m,* colmado
chopper ['tʃɑpər] *s* (*person*) tajador *m;* (*tool*) hacha; (*of butcher*) cortante *m;* (slang) helicóptero
chopping block *s* tajo
chop•py ['tʃɑpi] *adj* (*comp* **-pier;** *super* **-piest**) (*sea*) agitado, picado; (*wind*) variable; (*style*) cortado, inciso
chop'sticks' *spl* palillos
choral ['korəl] *adj* coral
chorale [ko'rɑl] *s* coral *m*
choral society *s* orfeón *m*
chord [kɔrd] *s* (*harmonious combination of tones*) (mus) acorde *m;* (aer, anat, geom) cuerda
chore [tʃor] *s* tarea, quehacer *m*
choreography [,korɪ'ɑgrəfi] *s* coreografía
chorine [ko'rin] *s* (slang) corista, suripanta
chorus ['korəs] *s* coro; (*refrain of a song*) estribillo
chorus girl *s* corista, conjuntista
chorus man *s* corista *m,* conjuntista *m*
chowder ['tʃaudər] *s* estofado de almejas o pescado
Chr. *abbr* **Christian**
Christ [kraɪst] *s* Cristo
christen ['krɪsən] *tr* bautizar
Christendom ['krɪsəndəm] *s* cristiandad
christening ['krɪsənɪŋ] *s* bautismo, bautizo
Christian ['krɪstʃən] *adj & s* cristiano
Christianity [,krɪstʃɪ'ænɪti] *s* cristianismo
Christianize ['krɪstʃə,naɪz] *tr* cristianizar
Christian name *s* nombre *m* de pila
Christmas ['krɪsməs] *adj* navideño || *s* Navidad, Pascua de Navidad
Christmas card *s* aleluya navideña
Christmas carol *s* villancico
Christmas Eve *s* nochebuena
Christmas gift *s* aguinaldo, regalo de Navidad
Christmas tree *s* árbol *m* de Navidad
Christopher ['krɪstəfər] *s* Cristóbal *m*
chrome [krom] *adj* cromado || *s* cromo || *tr* cromar
chromium ['kromɪ•əm] *s* cromo
chro•mo ['kromo] *s* (*pl* **-mos**) (*colored picture*) cromo; (*piece of junk*) (slang) trasto
chromosome ['kromə,som] *s* cromosoma *m*
chron. *abbr* **chronological, chronology**
chronic ['krɑnɪk] *adj* crónico
chronicle ['krɑnɪkəl] *s* crónica || *tr* narrar en una crónica; narrar, contar
chronicler ['krɑnɪklər] *s* cronista *mf*
chronolo•gy [krə'nɑlədʒi] *s* (*pl* **-gies**) cronología
chronometer [krə'nɑmɪtər] *s* cronómetro
chrysanthemum [krɪ'sænθɪməm] *s* crisantemo
chub•by ['tʃʌbi] *adj* (*comp* **-bier;** *super* **-biest**) rechoncho, regordete
chuck [tʃʌk] *s* (*throw*) echada, tirada; (*under the chin*) mamola; (*of a lathe*) mandril *m* || *tr* arrojar; **to chuck under the chin** hacer la mamola a
chuckle ['tʃʌkəl] *s* risa ahogada || *intr* reírse con risa ahogada
chug [tʃʌg] *s* ruido explosivo sordo; (*of a locomotive*) resoplido || *v* (*pret & pp* **chugged;** *ger* **chugging**) *intr* hacer ruidos explosivos sordos, moverse con ruidos explosivos sordos

chum [tʃʌm] *s* (coll) compinche *mf;* compañero de cuarto || *v* (*pret & pp* **chummed;** *ger* **chumming**) *intr* (coll) ser compinche, ser compinches; (coll) compartir un cuarto
chum•my [ˈtʃʌmi] *adj* (*comp* **-mier;** *super* **-miest**) muy amigable, íntimo
chump [tʃʌmp] *s* tarugo, zoquete *m;* (coll) estúpido, tonto
chunk [tʃʌnk] *s* trozo, pedazo grueso
church [tʃʌrt] *s* iglesia
churchgoer [ˈtʃʌrtʃ,go•ər] *s* persona que frecuenta la iglesia
church•man [ˈtʃʌrtʃmən] *s* (*pl* **-men** [mən]) sacerdote *m,* eclesiástico; feligrés *m*
church member *s* feligrés *m*
Church of England *s* Iglesia Anglicana
church'ward'en *s* capiller *m*
church'yard' *s* patio de iglesia; cementerio
churl [tʃʌrl] *s* palurdo, patán *m*
churlish [ˈtʃʌrlɪʃ] *adj* palurdo, insolente
churn [tʃʌrn] *s* mantequera || *tr* mazar (*leche*); hacer (*mantequilla*) en una mantequera; agitar, revolver || *intr* revolverse
chute [ʃut] *s* cascada, salto de agua; rápidos; conducto inclinado; (*e.g., into a swimming pool*) tobogán *m;* (*e.g., for grain*) tolva; paracaídas *m*
cibori•um [sɪˈborɪ•əm] *s* (*pl* **-a** [ə]) (*canopy*) ciborio, baldaquín *m;* (*cup*) copón *m*
Cicero [ˈsɪsə,ro] *s* Cicerón *m*
cider [ˈsaɪdər] *s* sidra
C.I.F., c.i.f. *abbr* **cost, insurance, and freight**
cigar [sɪˈgɑr] *s* cigarro, puro
cigar band *s* anillo de cigarro
cigar case *s* cigarrera, petaca
cigar cutter *s* cortacigarros *m*
cigaret o **cigarette** [,sɪgəˈrɛt] *s* cigarrillo, pitillo
cigarette case *s* pitillera
cigarette holder *s* boquilla
cigarette lighter *s* mechero, encendedor *m* de bolsillo
cigarette paper *s* papel *m* de fumar
cigar holder *s* boquilla
cigar store *s* estanco, tabaquería
cinch [sɪntʃ] *s* (*of saddle*) cincha; (*sure grip*) (coll) agarro; (*something easy*) (slang) breva || *tr* cinchar; (coll) agarrar
cinder [ˈsɪndər] *s* ceniza; (*coal burning without flame*) pavesa
cinder bank *s* escorial *m*
Cinderella [,sɪndəˈrɛlə] *s* la Cenicienta
cinder track *s* pista de cenizas
cinema [ˈsɪnəmə] *s* cine *m*
cinematograph [,sɪnəˈmætə,græf] o [,sɪnəˈmætə,grɑf] *s* cinematógrafo || *tr & intr* cinematografiar
cinnabar [ˈsɪnə,bɑr] *s* cinabrio
cinnamon [ˈsɪnəmən] *s* canela
cipher [ˈsaɪfər] *s* cifra; cero; (*nonentity*) cero a la izquierda; (*key to a cipher*) clave *f* || *tr* cifrar; calcular
circle [ˈsʌrkəl] *s* círculo || *tr* circundar; dar la vuelta a; girar alrededor de
circuit [ˈsʌrkɪt] *s* circuito
circuit breaker *s* disyuntor *m*
circuitous [sərˈkju•ɪtəs] *adj* indirecto, tortuoso
circular [ˈsʌrkjələr] *adj* tortuoso || *s* circular *f,* carta circular
circularize [ˈsʌrkjələ,raɪz] *tr* anunciar por circular; enviar circulares a
circulate [ˈsʌrkjə,let] *tr & intr* circular
circumcise [ˈsʌrkəm,saɪz] *tr* circuncidar
circumference [sərˈkʌmfərəns] *s* circunferencia
circumflex [ˈsʌrkəm,flɛks] *adj* circunflejo
circumlocution [,sʌrkəmloˈkjuʃən] *s* circunlocución, circunloquio
circumnavigate [,sʌrkəmˈnævɪ,get] *tr* circunnavegar
circumnavigation [,sʌrkəm,nævɪˈgeʃən] *s* circunnavegación
circumscribe [,sʌrkəmˈskraɪb] *tr* circunscribir
circumspect [ˈsʌrkəm,spɛkt] *adj* circunspecto
circumstance [ˈsʌrkəm,stæns] *s* circunstancia; ceremonia, ostentación; **in easy circumstances** acomodado; **under no circumstances** de ninguna manera, ni a bala
circumstantial [,sʌrkəmˈstænʃəl] *adj* (*derived from circumstances*) circunstancial; (*detailed*) circunstanciado
circumstantial evidence *s* (law) indicios vehementes
circumstantiate [,sʌrkəmˈstænʃɪ,et] *tr* apoyar con pruebas y detalles; (*to describe in detail*) circunstanciar
circumvent [,sʌrkəmˈvɛnt] *tr* (*to catch by a trick*) entrampar, embaucar; (*to outwit*) burlar; (*to keep away from, get around*) evitar
circus [ˈsʌrkəs] *s* circo
cistern [ˈsɪstərn] *s* cisterna, aljibe *m*
citadel [ˈsɪtədəl] *s* ciudadela
citation [saɪˈteʃən] *s* (*of a text*) cita; (*before a court of law*) citación; (*for gallantry*) mención
cite [saɪt] *tr* (*to quote; to summon*) citar; (*for gallantry*) mencionar
citizen [ˈsɪtɪzən] *s* ciudadano; (*civilian*) paisano
citizen•ry [ˈsɪtɪzənri] *s* (*pl* **-ries**) conjunto de ciudadanos
citizens band *s* banda ciudadana
citizenship [ˈsɪtɪzən,ʃɪp] *s* ciudadanía
citron [ˈsɪtrən] *s* (*fruit*) cidra; (*tree*) cidro; (*candied rind*) cidrada
citronella [,sɪtrəˈnɛlə] *s* limoncillo (*Andropogon nardus*); aceite *m* de limoncillo
citrus fruit [ˈsɪtrəs] *s* agrios, frutas cítricas
cit•y [ˈsɪti] *s* (*pl* **-ies**) ciudad
city clerk *s* archivero
city council *s* ayuntamiento
city editor *s* redactor de periódico encargado de noticias locales
city fathers *spl* concejales *mpl*
city hall *s* casa consistorial
city plan *s* plano de la ciudad
city planner *s* urbanista *mf*
city planning *s* urbanismo
city room *s* redacción

cit'y-state' *s* ciudad-estado *f*
civic ['sɪvɪk] *adj* cívico || **civics** *s* estudio de los deberes y derechos del ciudadano
civic-mindedness ['maɪndɪdnɪs] *s* civismo
civies ['sɪviz] *spl* (coll) traje *m* de paisano; **in civies** (coll) de paisano
civil ['sɪvɪl] *adj* civil
civilian [sɪ'vɪljən] *adj* civil || *s* civil *mf*, paisano
civilian clothes *spl* traje *m* de paisano
civili•ty [sɪ'vɪlɪti] *s* (*pl* **-ties**) civilidad
civilization [,sɪvɪlɪ'zeʃən] *s* civilización
civilize ['sɪvɪ,laɪz] *tr* civilizar
civil servant *s* funcionario del estado
claim [klem] *s* demanda, pretensión, reclamación || *tr* demandar, pretender, reclamar; afirmar, declarar; **to claim to** + *inf* pretender + *inf*
claim check *s* comprobante *m*
clairvoyance [klɛr'vɔɪ•əns] *s* clarividencia
clairvoyant [klɛr'vɔɪ•ənt] *adj* & *s* clarividente *mf*
clam [klæm] *s* almeja; (*tight-lipped person*) (coll) chiticalla *m* || *intr* — **to clam up** (coll) callarse la boca
clamber ['klæmər] *intr* — **to clamber up** subir gateando
clamor ['klæmər] *s* clamor *m*, clamoreo || *intr* clamorear
clamorous ['klæmərəs] *adj* clamoroso
clamp [klæmp] *s* abrazadera, grapa; (*vise-like device*) mordaza || *tr* agrapar, afianzar con abrazadera; sujetar en una mordaza || *intr* — **to clamp down on** (coll) apretar los tornillos a
clan [klæn] *s* clan *m*
clandestine [klæn'dɛstɪn] *adj* clandestino
clang [klæŋ] *s* tantán *m*, sonido metálico resonante || *tr* hacer sonar fuertemente || *intr* sonar fuertemente
clank [klæŋk] *s* sonido metálico seco || *tr* hacer sonar secamente || *intr* sonar secamente
clannish ['klænɪʃ] *adj* exclusivista
clap [klæp] *s* golpe seco; (*of the hands*) palmada; (*of thunder*) estampido || *v* (*pret* & *pp* **clapped;** *ger* **clapping**) *tr* batir (*palmas*); palmotear, aplaudir; **to clap shut** cerrar de golpe || *intr* palmotear, dar palmadas
clap of thunder *s* estampido de trueno
clapper ['klæpər] *s* palmoteador *m;* (*of a bell*) badajo; (*to cause grain to slide*) tarabilla
clap'trap' *s* faramalla; (*of an actor*) latiguillo
claque [klæk] *s* (*paid clappers*) claque *f;* (*crush hat*) clac *m*
claret ['klærɪt] *s* clarete *m*
clari•fy ['klærɪ,faɪ] *v* (*pret* & *pp* **-fied**) *tr* clarificar; encolar (*el vino*)
clarinet ['klærɪ'net] *s* clarinete *m*
clarion ['klærɪ•ən] *adj* claro, brillante || *s* clarín *m*
clarity ['klærɪti] *s* claridad
clash [klæʃ] *s* choque *m*, encontrón *m;* estruendo, ruido || *intr* chocar, entrechocarse
clasp [klæsp] *s* (*fastener*) abrazadera, cierre *m;* (*for, e.g., a necktie*) broche *m;* (*buckle*) hebilla; (*embrace*) abrazo; (*grip*) agarro || *tr* abrochar; abrazar; agarrar, apretar (*la mano*); apretarse (*la mano*)
class. *abbr* **classical**
class [klæs] *s* clase *f;* ó (slang) elegancia, buen tono; (*sports*) división || *tr* clasificar || *intr* clasificarse
class consciousness *s* sentimiento de clase
classic ['klæsɪk] *adj* & *s* clásico; **the classics** las obras clásicas
classical ['klæsɪkəl] *adj* clásico
classical scholar *s* erudito en las lenguas clásicas
classicist ['klæsɪsɪst] *s* clasicista *mf*
classified ['klæsɪ,faɪd] *adj* clasificado; clasificado como secreto
classified ads *spl* anuncios clasificados en secciones
classi•fy ['klæsɪ,faɪ] *v* (*pret* & *pp* **-fied**) *tr* clasificar
class'mate' *s* compañero de clase
class'room' *s* aula, sala de clase
class struggle *s* lucha de clases
class•y ['klæsi] *adj* (*comp* **-ier;** *super* **-iest**) (slang) elegante
clatter ['klætər] *s* estruendo confuso; algazara, gresca; (*of hoofs*) trápala || *intr* caer o moverse con estruendo confuso; hablar rápida y ruidosamente; **to clatter down the stairs** bajar la escalera ruidosamente
clause [klɔz] *s* (*article in a legal document*) cláusula; (gram) oración dependiente
clavichord ['klævɪ,kɔrd] *s* clavicordio
clavicle ['klævɪkəl] *s* clavícula
clavier ['klævɪ•ər] o [klə'vɪr] *s* teclado || [klə'vɪr] *s* instrumento musical con teclado
claw [klɔ] *s* garra, uña; (*of lobster, crab, etc.*) pinza; (*of hammer, wrench, etc.*) oreja; (coll) dedos, mano *f* || *tr* (*to clutch*) agarrar; (*to scratch*) arañar; (*to tear*) desgarrar
clay [kle] *adj* arcilloso || *s* arcilla
clay pigeon *s* pichón *m* de barro
clay pipe *s* pipa de tierra
clean [klin] *adj* limpio; distinto, neto, nítido; completo || *adv* completamente; **to come clean** (slang) confesarlo todo || *tr* limpiar; (*to tidy up*) asear; **to be cleaned out** (*of money*) (slang) quedar limpio; **to clean out** limpiar; (slang) dejar limpio || *intr* limpiarse; asearse; **to clean up** limpiarse; (coll) llevárselo todo; (*in gambling*) (slang) hacer mesa limpia; **to clean up after someone** limpiar lo que alguno ha ensuciado
clean bill of health *s* patente limpia de sanidad
cleaner ['klinər] *s* limpiador *m;* (*dry cleaner*) tintorero; (*preparation*) quitamanchas *m;* **to send to the cleaners** (slang) dejar limpio
cleaning ['klinɪŋ] *s* limpieza
cleaning fluid *s* quitamanchas *m*
cleaning woman *s* criada que hace la limpieza, alquilona

cleanliness [ˈklɛnlɪnɪs] *s* limpieza
clean•ly [ˈklɛnli] *adj* (*comp* **-lier;** *super* **-liest**) limpio (*que tiene el hábito del aseo*)
cleanse [klɛnz] *tr* limpiar, lavar, depurar
clean-shaven [ˈklinˈʃevən] *adj* lisamente afeitado
clean'up' *s* limpieza general; **to make a cleanup** (slang) hacer su pacotilla
clear [klɪr] *adj* claro; (*cloudless*) despejado; (*of debts, etc.*) libre ‖ *adv* claro, claramente; **clear through** de parte a parte ‖ *tr* despejar (*un bosque*); clarificar (*lo que estaba turbio*); (*to make less dark*) aclarar; saltar por encima de; (*to prove the innocence of*) absolver; sacar (*una ganancia neta*); abonar, acreditar; liquidar (*una cuenta*); (*in the customhouse*) despachar; salvar (*un obstáculo*); levantar (*la mesa*); desmontar (*un terreno*); **to clear the way** abrir camino ‖ *intr* clarificarse; aclararse; **to clear away** irse, desaparecer; **to clear up** abonanzarse (*el tiempo*); despejarse (*el cielo, el tiempo*)
clearance [ˈklɪrəns] *s* aclaración; abono, acreditación; espacio libre; (*in a cylinder*) espacio muerto; (com) compensación
clearance sale *s* venta de liquidación
clearing [ˈklɪrɪŋ] *s* (*in a woods*) claro; (com) compensación
clearing house *s* cámara de compensación
clear-sighted [ˈklɪrˈsaɪtɪd] *adj* clarividente, perspicaz
clear'sto'ry *s* (*pl* **-ries**) var of **clerestory**
cleat [klit] *s* abrazadera, listón *m*
cleavage [ˈklivɪdʒ] *s* división, hendidura; (fig) desunión
cleave [kliv] *v* (*pret & pp* **cleft** [klɛft] o **cleaved**) *tr* rajar, partir; hender (*las aguas un buque, los aires una flecha*) ‖ *intr* adherirse, pegarse; apegarse, ser fiel
cleaver [ˈklivər] *s* cortante *m*, cuchilla de carnicero
clef [klɛf] *s* (mus) clave *f*
cleft palate [klɛft] *s* fisura del paladar
clematis [ˈklɛmətɪs] *s* clemátide *f*
clemen•cy [ˈklɛmənsi] *s* (*pl* **-cies**) clemencia; (*of the weather*) benignidad
clement [ˈklɛmənt] *adj* clemente; (*weather*) benigno
clench [klɛntʃ] *s* agarro ‖ *tr* agarrar; apretar, cerrar (*el puño, los dientes*)
clerest•ory [ˈklɪr,stori] *s* (*pl* **-ries**) claraboya
cler•gy [ˈklɛrdʒi] *s* (*pl* **-gies**) clerecía, clero
clergy•man [ˈklɛrdʒimən] *s* (*pl* **-men** [mən]) clérigo, pastor *m*
cleric [ˈklɛrɪk] *s* clérigo
clerical [ˈklɛrɪkəl] *adj* (*of clergy*) clerical; (*of office work*) oficinesco ‖ *s* clérigo, eclesiástico; (*supporter of power of clergy*) clerical *m;* **clericals** (coll) hábitos clericales
clerical error *s* error *m* de pluma
clerical work *s* trabajo de oficina
clerk [klʌrk] *s* (*in a store*) dependiente *mf;* (*in an office*) oficinista *mf;* (*in a city hall*) archivero; (*in a church*) lego, seglar *m;* (*in law office, in court*) escribano
clever [ˈklɛvər] *adj* hábil, diestro, mañoso; inteligente
cleverness [ˈklɛvərnɪs] *s* habilidad, destreza, maña; inteligencia
clew [klu] *s* indicio, pista
cliché [kliˈʃe] *s* (*printing plate*) clisé *m;* (*trite expression*) cliché *m*
click [klɪk] *s* golpecito; (*of typewriter*) tecleo; (*of firearm*) piñoneo; (*of heels*) taconeo; (*of tongue*) claqueo, chasquido ‖ *tr* hacer sonar con un golpecito seco; chascar (*la lengua*); **to click the heels** taconear; cuadrarse (*un soldado*) ‖ *intr* sonar con un golpecito seco; piñonear (*el gatillo de un arma de fuego*); claquear (*la lengua*)
client [ˈklaɪ•ənt] *s* cliente *mf;* cliente de abogado
clientele [,klaɪ•ənˈtɛl] *s* clientela
cliff [klɪf] *s* acantilado, escarpa, risco
climate [ˈklaɪmɪt] *s* clima *m*
climax [ˈklaɪmæks] *s* colmo; orgasmo; **to cap the climax** ser el colmo
climb [klaɪm] *s* subida, trepa ‖ *tr & intr* escalar, subir, trepar
climber [ˈklaɪmər] *s* trepador *m;* ambicioso de figurar; (bot) enredadera, trepadora
clinch [klɪntʃ] *s* agarro, abrazo; (*of a nail*) remache *m* ‖ *tr* afianzar, sujetar; agarrar, abrazar; apretar (*el puño*); remachar (*un clavo ya clavado*); resolver decisivamente
cling [klɪŋ] *v* (*pret & pp* **clung** [klʌŋ]) *intr* adherirse, pegarse; **to cling to** agarrarse a, asirse de
cling'stone' peach *s* albérchigo, peladillo
clinic [ˈklɪnɪk] *s* clínica
clinical [ˈklɪnɪkəl] *adj* clínico
clinical chart *s* hoja clínica
clinician [klɪˈnɪʃən] *s* clínico
clink [kliŋk] *s* tintín *m* ‖ *tr* hacer tintinear; chocar (*vasos, copas*) ‖ *intr* tintinear
clinker [ˈklɪŋkər] *s* escoria de hulla
clip [klɪp] *s* tijereteo, esquileo; grapa, pinza; (*to fasten papers*) sujetapapeles *m*, presilla de alambre; **at a good clip** a buen paso ‖ *v* (*pret & pp* **clipped;** *ger* **clipping**) *tr* tijeretear, esquilar; (*to fasten with a clip*) afianzar, sujetar; recortar (*p.ej., un cupón*) ‖ *intr* moverse con rapidez
clipper [ˈklɪpər] *s* tijera, cizalla; **clippers** maquinilla cortapelos; tijeras podadoras
clipping [ˈklɪpɪŋ] *s* tijereteo, esquileo; (*from a newspaper*) recorte *m*
clique [klik] *s* pandilla, corrillo ‖ *intr* — **to clique together** apandillarse
cliquish [ˈklikɪʃ] *adj* exclusivista
clk. *abbr* **clerk, clock**
cloak [klok] *s* capote *m;* (*disguise, excuse*) capa ‖ *tr* encapotar; disimular, encubrir
cloak-and-dagger [ˈklokənˈdægər] *adj* de capa y espada (*dícese de duelos, espionaje, etc.*)
cloak-and-sword [ˈklokənˈsord] *adj* de capa y espada (*dícese, p.ej., de las costumbres caballerescas*)
cloak hanger *s* cuelgacapas *m*
cloak'room' *s* guardarropa *m;* (Brit) excusado

clock [klɑk] *s* reloj *m* (de pared o de mesa); (*in a stocking*) cuadrado || *tr* registrar; (sport) cronometrar
clock'mak'er *s* relojero
clock tower *s* torre *f* reloj
clock'wise' *adj* & *adv* en el sentido de las agujas del reloj
clock'work' *s* mecanismo de relojería; **like clockwork** como un reloj
clod [klɑd] *s* terrón *m*
clod'hop'per *s* destripaterrones *m*, quebrantaterrones *m;* **clodhoppers** zapatos fuertes de trabajo
clog [klɑg] *s* estorbo, obstáculo; (*wooden shoe*) zueco; (*dance*) zapateado; (*hobble on animal*) traba || *v* (*pret* & *pp* **clogged;** *ger* **clogging**) *tr* atascar || *intr* atascarse; bailar el zapateado
clog dance *s* zapateado
cloister [ˈklɔɪstər] *s* claustro || *tr* enclaustrar
cloistral [ˈklɔɪstrəl] *adj* claustral
close [klos] *adj* cercano, próximo; casi igual; (*translation*) fiel, exacto; (*fabric*) compacto; (*weather, atmosphere*) pesado, sofocante; (*stingy*) tacaño; (*battle, race, election*) reñido; (*friend*) íntimo; (*shut in, enclosed*) cerrado; (*narrow*) estrecho || *adv* cerca; **close to** cerca de || [kloz] *s* fin *m*, terminación; (*of business, of stock market*) cierre *m;* **at the close of day** a la caída de la tarde; **to bring to a close** poner término a; **to come to a close** tocar a su fin || *tr* cerrar; (*to cover*) tapar; (*to finish*) concluir; saldar (*una cuenta*); cerrar (*un trato*); **to close in** cerrar, encerrar; **to close ranks** cerrar las filas || *intr* cerrar, cerrarse; **to close in on** cerrar con (*el enemigo*)
close call [klos] *s* (coll) escape *m* por un pelo
closed car [klozd] *s* coche cerrado, conducción interior
closed chapter *s* asunto concluído
closed season *s* veda
closed shop *s* taller agremiado
closefisted [ˈklosˈfɪstɪd] *adj* cicatero, tacaño, manicorto
close-fitting [ˈklosˈfɪtɪŋ] *adj* ajustado, ceñido al cuerpo
close-lipped [ˈklosˈlɪpt] *adj* callado, reservado
closely [ˈklosli] *adv* de cerca; estrechamente; fielmente; atentamente
close quarters [klos] *spl* lugar muy estrecho, lugares estrechos
close shave [klos] *s* afeitado a ras; (coll) escape *m* por un pelo
closet [ˈklɑzɪt] *s* (*wall*) alacena, closet *m;* (*wardrobe*) armario; (*small private room*) aposento, gabinete *m;* (*for keeping clothing*) guardarropa *m;* (*toilet*) retrete *m* || *tr* — **to be closeted with** encerrarse con
close-up [ˈklos,ʌp] *s* (*moving picture*) vista de cerca; fotografía de cerca
closing [ˈklozɪŋ] *s* cerradura, cierre *m*
closing prices *spl* precios de cierre
closing time *s* hora de cierre
clot [klɑt] *s* grumo, coágulo || *v* (*pret* & *pp* **clotted;** *ger* **clotting**) *intr* engrumecerse, coagularse
cloth [klɔθ] o [klɑθ] *s* paño, tela; ropa clerical; (*canvas, sails*) lona, trapo, vela; (*for binding books*) tela; **the cloth** la clerecía
clothe [kloð] *v* (*pret* & *pp* **clothed** o **clad** [klæd]) *tr* trajear, vestir; cubrir; (*e.g., with authority*) investir
clothes [kloz] o [kloθz] *spl* ropa, vestidos; ropa de cama
clothes'bas'ket *s* cesto de la ropa, cesto de la colada
clothes'brush' *s* cepillo de ropa
clothes closet *s* ropero
clothes dryer *s* secadora de ropa, secarropa
clothes hanger *s* colgador *m*, perchero
clothes'horse' *s* enjugador *m*, secarropa de travesaños
clothes'line' *s* cordel *m* para tender la ropa, tendedera
clothes'pin' *s* pinza, alfiler *m* de madera
clothes tree *s* percha
clothes wringer *s* exprimidor *m* de ropa
clothier [ˈklooјər] *s* (*person who sells ready-made clothes*) ropero; (*dealer in cloth*) pañero
clothing [ˈkloðɪŋ] *s* ropa, vestidos, ropaje *m*
cloud [klaʊd] *s* nube *f* || *tr* anublar || *intr* — **to cloud over** anublarse
cloud bank *s* mar *m* de nubes
cloud'burst' *s* aguacero, chaparrón *m*
cloud-capped [ˈklaʊd,kæpt] *adj* coronado de nubes
cloudless [ˈklaʊdlɪs] *adj* despejado, sin nubes
cloud of dust *s* polvareda, nube *f* de polvo
cloud•y [ˈklaʊdi] *adj* (*comp* **-ier;** *super* **-iest**) nuboso, nublado; (*muddy, turbid*) turbio; confuso, obscuro; melancólico, sombrío
clove [klov] *s* (*flower*) clavo de especia; (*spice*) clavo
clover [ˈklovər] *s* trébol *m;* **to be in clover** vivir en el lujo
clo'ver•leaf' *s* (*pl* **-leaves** [,livz]) *s* cruce *m* en trébol
clove tree *s* clavero
clown [klaʊn] *s* bufón *m*, payaso; (*rustic*) patán *m* || *intr* hacer el payaso
clownish [ˈklaʊnɪʃ] *adj* bufonesco; rústico
cloy [klɔɪ] *tr* hastiar, empalagar
club [klʌb] *s* porra, clava; (*playing card*) basto, trébol *m;* club *m*, casino || *v* (*pret* & *pp* **clubbed;** *ger* **clubbing**) *tr* aporrear || *intr* — **to club together** unirse; formar club
club car *s* coche *m* club, coche bar
club'house' *s* casino, club *m*
club•man [ˈklʌbmən] *s* (*pl* **-men** [mən]) clubista *m*
club•woman [ˈklʌb,wʊmən] *s* (*pl* **-women** [,wɪmɪn]) clubista *f*
cluck [klʌk] *s* cloqueo, clo clo || *intr* cloquear, hacer clo clo
clue [klu] *s* indicio, pista
clump [klʌmp] *s* (*of earth*) terrón *m;* (*of trees or shrubs*) grupo; pisada fuerte || *intr* — **to clump along** andar pesadamente

clum•sy [ˈklʌmzi] *adj* (*comp* **-sier;** *super* **-siest**) (*worker*) chapucero, desmañado, torpe; (*work*) chapucero, tosco, grosero
cluster [ˈklʌstər] *s* grupo; (*of grapes or other things growing or joined together*) racimo || *intr* arracimarse; **to cluster around** reunirse en torno a; **to cluster together** agruparse
clutch [klʌtʃ] *s* (*grasp, grip*) agarro, apretón *m* fuerte; (aut) embrague *m;* (aut) pedal *m* de embrague; **to fall into the clutches of** caer en las garras de; **to throw the clutch in** embragar; **to throw the clutch out** desembragar || *tr* agarrar, empuñar
clutter [ˈklʌtər] *tr* — **to clutter up** cubrir o llenar desordenadamente
cm. *abbr* **centimeter**
cml. *abbr* **commercial**
Co. *abbr* **Company, County**
coach [kotʃ] *s* coche *m,* diligencia; (aut) coche cerrado; (rr) coche de viajeros, coche ordinario *m;* (sport) entrenador *m* || *tr* aleccionar; (sport) entrenar || *intr* entrenarse
coach house *s* cochera
coaching [ˈkotʃɪŋ] *s* lecciones *fpl* particulares; (sport) entrenamiento
coach•man [ˈkotʃmən] *s* (*pl* **-men** [mən]) *s* cochero
coagulate [koˈægjə,let] *tr* coagular || *intr* coagularse
coal [kol] *s* carbón *m,* hulla || *tr* proveer de carbón || *intr* proveerse de carbón
coal'bin' *s* carbonera
coal bunker *s* carbonera
coal car *s* vagón carbonero
coal'deal'er *s* carbonero
coaling [ˈkolɪŋ] *adj* carbonero || *s* toma de carbón
coalition [,ko•əˈlɪʃən] *s* unión; (*alliance between states or factions*) coalición
coal mine *s* mina de carbón
coal oil *s* aceite *m* mineral
coal scuttle *s* cubo para carbón
coal tar *s* alquitrán *m* de hulla
coal'yard' *s* carbonería
coarse [kors] *adj* (*of inferior quality*) basto, burdo; (*composed of large particles*) grueso; (*crude in manners*) grosero, rudo, vulgar
coarseness [ˈkorsnɪs] *s* bastedad
coast [kost] *s* costa; **the coast is clear** ya no hay peligro || *tr* costear || *intr* deslizarse cuesta abajo; **to coast along** avanzar sin esfuerzo
coastal [ˈkostəl] *adj* costero
coaster [ˈkostər] *s* salvamanteles *m*
coaster brake *s* freno de contrapedal
coast guard *s* guardacostas *mpl;* guardia *m* de los guardacostas
coast guard cutter *s* escampavía de los guardacostas
coasting trade *s* cabotaje *m*
coast'land' *s* litoral *m*
coast'line' *s* línea de la costa
coast'wise' *adj* costanero || *adv* a lo largo de la costa
coat [kot] *s* (*jacket*) americana, saco; (*topcoat*) abrigo, sobretodo; (*of an animal*) lana, pelo; (*of paint*) capa, mano *f* || *tr* cubrir, revestir; dar una capa de pintura a
coated [ˈkotɪd] *adj* revestido; (*tongue*) saburroso
coat hanger *s* colgador *m*
coating [ˈkotɪŋ] *s* revestimiento; (*of paint*) capa; (*of plaster*) enlucido
coat of arms *s* escudo de armas
coat'room' *s* guardarropa *m*
coat'tail' *s* faldón *m*
coax [koks] *tr* engatusar
cob [kɑb] *s* zuro; **to eat corn on the cob** comer maíz en la mazorca
cobalt [ˈkobɔlt] *s* cobalto
cobbler [ˈkɑblər] *s* remendón *m,* zapatero de viejo
cob'ble•stone' *s* guijarro
cob'web' *s* telaraña
cocaine [koˈken] *s* cocaína; (slang) coca
cock [kɑk] *s* (*rooster*) gallo; (*faucet, valve*) espita, grifo; (*of firearm*) martillo; (*weathervane*) veleta; caudillo, jefe *m* || *tr* amartillar (*un arma de fuego*); ladear (*la cabeza*); enderezar, levantar
cockade [[kɑˈked] *s* cucarda, escarapela
cock-a-doodle-doo [ˈkɑkə,dudəlˈdu] *s* quiquiriquí *m*
cock-and-bull story [ˈkɑkəndˈbʊl] *s* cuento absurdo, cuento increíble
cocked hat [kɑkt] *s* sombrero de candil, sombrero de tres picos; **to knock into a cocked hat** (slang) apabullar
cockeyed [ˈkɑk,aɪd] *adj* bisojo, bizco; (coll) encorvado, torcido; (slang) disparatado, extravagante
cock'fight' *s* pelea de gallos
cockney [ˈkɑkni] *s* londinense *mf* de la clase pobre que habla un dialecto característico; dialecto de la clase pobre de Londres
cock of the walk *s* quiquiriquí *m,* gallito del lugar
cock'pit' *s* gallera; (aer) carlinga
cock'roach' *s* cucaracha
cockscomb [ˈkɑks,kom] *s* cresta de gallo; gorro de bufón; (bot) cresta de gallo, moco de pavo
cock'sure' *adj* muy seguro de sí mismo
cock'tail' *s* coctel *m;* (*of fruit, oysters, etc.*) aperitivo
cocktail party *s* coctel *m*
cocktail shaker [ˈʃekər] *s* coctelera
cock•y [ˈkɑki] *adj* (*comp* **-ier;** *super* **-iest**) (coll) arrogante, hinchado; **to be cocky** (coll) tener mucho gallo
cocoa [ˈkoko] *s* cacao; (*drink*) chocolate *m*
cocoanut o **coconut** [ˈkokə,nʌt] *s* coco
cocoanut palm o **tree** *s* cocotero
cocoon [kəˈkun] *s* capullo
C.O.D., c.o.d. *abbr* **collect on delivery;** (Brit) **cash on delivery**
cod [kɑd] *s* abadejo, bacalao
coddle [ˈkɑdəl] *tr* consentir, mimar
code [kod] *s* (*of laws; of manners; of signals*) código; (*of telegraphy*) alfabeto; (*secret system of writing*) cifra, clave *f;* (com)

cifrario; **in code** en cifra || *tr* (*to put in code*) cifrar
code word *s* clave telegráfica
codex [ˈkodɛks] *s* (*pl* **codices** [ˈkodɪ,siz] o [ˈkɑdɪ,siz]) *s* códice *m*
cod'fish' *s* abadejo, bacalao
codger [ˈkɑdʒər] *s* — **old codger** (coll) anciano, tío
codicil [ˈkɑdɪsɪl] *s* codicilo; apéndice *m*
codi•fy [ˈkɑdɪ,faɪ] o [ˈkodɪ,faɪ] *v* (*pret & pp* **-fied**) *tr* codificar
cod'-liv'er oil *s* aceite *m* de hígado de bacalao
coed o **co-ed** [ˈko,ɛd] *s* alumna de una escuela coeducativa
coeducation [,ko,ɛdʒəˈkeʃən] *s* coeducación
coefficient [,ko•ɪˈfɪʃənt] *adj & s* coeficiente *m*
coerce [koˈʌrs] *tr* forzar, coactar
coercion [koˈʌrʃən] *s* compulsión, coacción
coeval [koˈivəl] *adj & s* coetáneo
coexist [,ko•ɪgˈzɪst] *intr* coexistir
coexistence [,ko•ɪgˈzɪstəns] *s* coexistencia
coffee [ˈkɔfi] o [ˈkɑfi] *s* café *m;* (*plant*) cafeto; **black coffee** café solo; **to drink coffee** cafetear
coffee bean *s* grano de café
cof'fee•cake' *s* rosquilla (que se come con el café)
coffee dealer *s* cafetalero
coffee grinder *s* molinillo de café
coffee grounds *spl* poso del café
coffee mill *s* molinillo de café
coffee plantation *s* cafetal *m*
coffee planter *s* cafetalero
coffee pot *s* cafetera
coffee tree *s* cafeto
coffer [ˈkɔfər] o [ˈkɑfər] *s* arca, cofre *m;* **coffers** tesoro, fondos
cof'fer•dam' *s* ataguía, encajonado
coffin [ˈkɔfɪn] o [ˈkɑfɪn] *s* ataúd *m*
C. of S. *abbr* **Chief of Staff**
cog [kɑg] *s* diente *m* (*de rueda dentada*); rueda dentada; **to slip a cog** equivocarse
cogency [ˈkodʒənsi] *s* fuerza (*de un argumento*)
cogent [ˈkodʒənt] *adj* fuerte, convincente
cogitate [ˈkɑdʒɪ,tet] *tr & intr* cogitar, meditar
cognac [ˈkɑnjæk] *s* coñac *m*
cognizance [ˈkɑgnɪzəns] o [ˈkɑnɪzəns] *s* conocimiento; **to take cognizance of** enterarse de
cognizant [ˈkɑgnizənt] o [ˈkɑnɪzənt] *adj* sabedor, enterado
cog'wheel' *s* rueda dentada
cohabit [koˈhæbɪt] *intr* cohabitar
coheir [koˈɛr] *s* coheredero
cohere [koˈhɪr] *intr* adherirse, pegarse; conformarse, corresponder
coherent [koˈhɪrənt] *adj* coherente
cohesion [koˈhiʒən] *s* cohesión
coiffeur [kwɑˈfʌr] *s* peluquero
coiffure [kwɑˈfjʊr] *s* peinado, tocado
coil [kɔɪl] *s* (*something wound in a spiral*) rollo; (*single turn of spiral*) vuelta; (*of a still*) serpentín *m;* (*of hair*) rizo; (*of a spring*) espiral *f;* (elec) carrete *m* || *tr* arrollar, enrollar; (naut) adujar || *intr* arrollarse, enrollarse; (*like a snake*) serpentear
coil spring *s* resorte *m* espiral
coin [kɔɪn] *s* moneda; (*wedge*) cuña; **to pay back in one's own coin** pagar en la misma moneda; **to toss a coin** echar a cara o cruz || *tr* acuñar; forjar, inventar (*palabras o frases*); **to coin money** (coll) ganar mucho dinero
coincide [,ko•ɪnˈsaɪd] *intr* coincidir
coincidence [koˈɪnsɪdəns] *s* coincidencia
coition [koˈɪʃən] o **coitus** [ˈko•ɪtəs] *s* coito
coke [kok] *s* coque *m*, cok *m*
col. *abbr* **colored, colony, column**
colander [ˈkʌləndər] o [ˈkɑləndər] *s* colador *m*, escurridor *m*
cold [kold] *adj* frío; **to be cold** (*said of a person*) tener frío; (*said of the weather*) hacer frío || *s* frío; (*indisposition*) resfriado; **to catch cold** resfriarse, coger un resfriado
cold blood *s* — **in cold blood** a sangre fría
cold chisel *s* cortafrío
cold comfort *s* poca consolación
cold cream *s* colcrén *m*
cold cuts *spl* fiambres *mpl*
cold feet *spl* (coll) desánimo, miedo
cold'heart'ed *adj* duro, insensible
cold meat *s* carne *f* fiambre
coldness [ˈkoldnɪs] *s* frialdad
cold shoulder *s* — **to turn a cold shoulder on** (coll) tratar con suma frialdad
cold snap *s* corto rato de frío agudo
cold storage *s* conservación en cámara frigorífica
cold war *s* guerra fría
coleslaw [ˈkol,slɔ] *s* ensalada de col
colic [ˈkɑlɪk] *adj & s* cólico
coliseum [,kɑlɪˈsi•əm] *s* coliseo
colitis [kəˈlaɪtɪs] *s* colitis *f*
coll. *abbr* **colleague, collection, college, colloquial**
collaborate [kəˈlæbə,ret] *intr* colaborar
collaborationist [kə,læbəˈreʃənɪst] *s* colaboracionista *mf*
collaborator [kəˈlæbə,retər] *s* colaborador *m*
collapse [kəˈlæps] *s* desplome *m;* (*in business*) fracaso; (pathol) colapso || *intr* desplomarse; fracasar; postrarse, sufrir colapso
collapsible [kəˈlæpsɪbəl] *adj* abatible, plegable, desmontable
collar [ˈkɑlər] *s* cuello; (*of dog, horse*) collar *m;* (mach) collar
col'lar•band' *s* tirilla de camisa
col'lar•bone' *s* clavícula
collate [kəˈlet] o [ˈkɑlet] *tr* colacionar, cotejar
collateral [kəˈlætərəl] *adj* colateral || *s* (*relative*) colateral *mf;* (com) colateral *m*
collation [kəˈleʃən] *s* (*act of comparing; light meal*) colación
colleague [ˈkɑlig] *s* colega *mf;* homólogo
collect [ˈkɑlɛkt] *s* (eccl) colecta || [kəˈlɛkt] *tr* acumular, reunir; colectar, recaudar (*impuestos*); coleccionar (*sellos de correo, antiguallas*); recolectar (*cosechas*); cobrar (*pasajes*); recoger (*billetes; el correo*); **to**

collect oneself reponerse || *intr* acumularse; **collect on delivery** contra reembolso, cobro contra entrega
collect call *s* llamada por cobrar
collected [kə'lɛktɪd] *adj* sosegado, dueño de sí mismo
collection [kə'lɛkʃən] *s* colección; (*of taxes*) recaudación; (*of mail*) recogida
collection agency *s* agencia de cobros de cuentas
collective [kə'lɛktɪv] *adj* colectivo
collector [kə'lɛktər] *s* (*of stamps, antiques*) coleccionista *mf;* (*of taxes*) recaudador *m;* (*of tickets*) cobrador *m*
college ['kɑlɪdʒ] *s* colegio universitario; (*of cardinals, electors, etc.*) colegio
collide [kə'laɪd] *intr* chocar; **to collide with** chocar con
collie ['kɑli] *s* perro pastoril escocés
collier ['kɑljər] *s* barco carbonero; minero de carbón
collier•y ['kɑljəri] *s* (*pl* **-ies**) mina de carbón
collision [kə'lɪʒən] *s* colisión
colloid ['kɑlɔɪd] *adj & s* coloide *m*
colloquial [kə'lokwɪ•əl] *adj* coloquial, familiar
colloquialism [kə'lokwɪ•ə,lɪzəm] *s* coloquialismo
collo•quy ['kɑləkwi] *s* (*pl* **-quies**) coloquio
collusion [kə'luʒən] *s* colusión, confabulación; **to be in collusion with** estar en inteligencia con
cologne [kə'lon] *s* agua de colonia, colonia || **Cologne** *s* Colonia
colon ['kolən] *s* (anat) colon *m;* (gram) dos puntos
colonel ['kʌrnəl] *s* coronel *m*
colonel•cy ['kʌrnəlsi] *s* (*pl* **-cies**) coronelía
colonial [kə'lonɪ•əl] *adj* colonial || *s* colono
colonize ['kɑlə,naɪz] *tr & intr* colonizar
colonnade [,kɑlə'ned] *s* columnata
colo•ny ['kɑləni] *s* (*pl* **-nies**) colonia
colophon ['kɑlə,fɑn] *s* colofón *m*
color ['kʌlər] *s* color; **the colors** los colores, la bandera; **to call to the colors** llamar a filas: **to give** o **to lend color to** dar visos de probabilidad a; **under color of** so color de, bajo pretexto de; **with flying colors** con banderas desplegadas || *tr* colorar, colorear; (*to excuse, palliate*) colorear; (*to dye*) teñir || *intr* sonrojarse, ponerse colorado, demudarse
col'or-blind' *adj* ciego para los colores
colored ['kʌlərd] *adj* de color; (*specious*) colorado
colorful ['kʌlərfəl] *adj* colorido; pintoresco
coloring ['kʌlərɪŋ] *adj & s* colorante *m*
colorless ['kʌlərlɪs] *adj* incoloro; (fig) insulso
color photography *s* fotografía en colores
color salute *s* (mil) saludo con la bandera
color sergeant *s* sargento abanderado
color screen *s* (phot) pantalla de color
color television *s* televisión en colores
colossal [kə'lɑsəl] *adj* colosal
colossus [kə'lɑsəs] *s* coloso
colt [kolt] *s* potro

Columbus [kə'lʌmbəs] *s* Colón *m*
Columbus Day *s* día *m* de la raza, fiesta de la hispanidad
column ['kɑləm] *s* columna
columnist ['kɑləmɪst] *s* columnista *mf*
com. *abbr* **comedy, commerce, common**
Com. *abbr* **Commander, Commissioner, Committee**
coma ['komə] *s* (pathol) coma *m*
comb [kom] *s* peine *m;* (*currycomb*) almohaza; (*of rooster*) cresta; cresta de ola || *tr* peinar; explorar con minuciosidad
com•bat ['kɑmbæt] *s* combate *m* || ['kɑmbæt] o [kəm'bæt] *v* (*pret & pp* **-bated** o **-batted;** *ger* **-bating** o **-batting)** *tr & intr* combatir
combatant ['kɑmbətənt] *adj & s* combatiente *m*
combat duty *s* servicio de frente
combination [,kɑmbɪ'neʃən] *s* combinación
combine ['kɑmbaɪn] *s* monopolio; segadora trilladora; (coll) combinación || [kəm'baɪn] *tr* combinar || *intr* combinarse
combining form *s* (gram) elemento de compuestos
combustible [kəm'bʌstɪbəl] *adj* combustible; (fig) ardiente, impetuoso || *s* combustible *m*
combustion [kəm'bʌstʃən] *s* combustión
combustion chamber *s* cámara de combustión
come [kʌm] *v* (*pret* **came** [kem]; *pp* **come)** *intr* venir; **to come about** suceder; **to come across** encontrarse con; **to come after** venir detrás de; venir después de; venir por, venir en busca de; **to come again** volver; **to come apart** desunirse, desprenderse; **to come around** restablecerse; volver en sí; rendirse; ponerse de acuerdo; cambiar de dirección; **to come at** alcanzar; **to come back** volver; rehabilitarse; **to come before** anteponerse; **to come between** interponerse; desunir, separar; **to come by** conseguir; **to come down** bajar; (*in social position, etc.*) descender; (*from one person to another*) ser transmitido; **to come downstairs** bajar (*de un piso a otro*); **to come down with** enfermarse de; **to come for** venir por, venir en busca de; **to come forth** salir; aparecer; **to come forward** avanzar; presentarse; **to come from** venir de; provenir de; **to come in** entrar; entrar en; empezar; ponerse en uso; **to come in for** conseguir, recibir; **to come into one's own** ser reconocido; **to come off** desprenderse; acontecer; **to come out** salir; salir a luz; ponerse de largo (*una joven*); divulgarse (*una noticia*); **to come out for** anunciar su apoyo de; **to come out with** descolgarse con; **to come over** dejarse persuadir; pasar, p.ej., **what's come over him?** ¿qué le ha pasado?; **to come through** salir bien, tener éxito; ganar; **to come to** volver en sí; **to come together** juntarse, reunirse; **to come true** hacerse realidad; **to come up** subir; presentarse; **to come upstairs** subir (*de un piso a otro*); **to come up to** acercarse a;

subir a; estar a la altura de; **to come up with** proponer
come'back' *s* rehabilitación; (slang) respuesta aguda; **to stage a comeback** rehabilitarse
comedian [kə'midɪ•ən] *s* cómico, comediante *m;* autor *m* de comedias
comedienne [kə,midɪ'ɛn] *s* cómica, comedianta
come'down' *s* humillación, revés *m*
come•dy ['kɑmədi] *s* (*pl* **-dies**) comedia cómica; (*comicalness*) comicidad
come•ly ['kʌmli] *adj* (*comp* **-lier;** *super* **-liest**) (*attractive*) donairoso, gracioso; (*decorous*) conveniente, decente
comet ['kɑmɪt] *s* cometa *m*
comfort ['kʌmfərt] *s* comodidad, confort *m;* (*encouragement, consolation*) confortación; (*person*) confortador *m;* (*bed cover*) colcha, cobertor *m* || *tr* confortar
comfortable ['kʌmfərtəbəl] *adj* cómodo, confortable; (*fairly well off*) holgado; (*salary*) (coll) suficiente || *s* colcha, cobertor *m*
comforter ['kʌmfərtər] *s* confortador *m,* consolador *m;* colcha, cobertor *m;* bufanda de lana
comforting ['kʌmfərtɪŋ] *adj* confortante
comfort station *s* quiosco de necesidad
comfrey ['kʌmfri] *s* consuelda
comic ['kɑmɪk] *adj* cómico || *s* cómico; periódico cómico; **comics** tiras cómicas
comical ['kɑmɪkəl] *adj* cómico
comic book *s* tebeo
comic opera *s* ópera cómica
comic strip *s* tira cómica
coming ['kʌmɪŋ] *adj* que viene, venidero; prometedor || *s* venida
coming out *s* (*of stocks, bonds, etc.*) emisión; (*of a young girl*) puesta de largo, entrada en sociedad
comma ['kɑmə] *s* coma
command [kə'mænd] *s* (*commanding*) dominio, mando; (*order, direction*) mandato, orden *f;* (*e.g., of a foreign language*) dominio; (mil) comando; **to be in command of** estar al mando de; **to take command** tomar el mando || *tr* mandar, ordenar; dominar (*un idioma extranjero*); merecer (*p.ej., respeto*); (mil) comandar || *intr* mandar
commandant [,kɑmən'dænt] o [,kɑmən'dɑnt] *s* comandante *m*
commandeer [,kɑmən'dɪr] *tr* reclutar forzosamente; expropiar; (coll) apoderarse de
commander [kə'mændər] *s* comandante *m;* (*of a military order*) comendador *m*
commandment [,kə'mændmənt] *s* (Bib) mandamiento
commemorate [kə'mɛmə,ret] *tr* conmemorar
commence [kə'mɛns] *tr & intr* comenzar, empezar
commencement [kə'mɛnsmənt] *s* comienzo, principio; día *m* de graduación; ceremonia de graduación
commend [kə'mɛnd] *tr* (*to entrust*) encargar, encomendar; (*to recommend*) recomendar; (*to praise*) alabar, elogiar
commendable [kə'mɛndəbəl] *adj* recomendable
commendation [,kɑmən'deʃən] *s* encargo, encomienda; recomendación; alabanza, elogio
comment ['kɑmɛnt] *s* comentario, comento || *intr* comentar; **to comment on** comentar
commentar•y ['kɑmən,tɛri] *s* (*pl* **-ies**) comentario
commentator ['kɑmən,tetər] *s* comentarista *mf*
commerce ['kɑmərs] *s* comercio
commercial [kə'mʌrʃəl] *adj* comercial || *s* anuncio publicitario radiofónico o televisivo; (rad & telv) programa publicitario
commercial traveler *s* agente viajero
commiserate [kə'mɪzə,ret] *intr* — **to commiserate with** condolerse de
commiseration [kə,mɪzə'reʃən] *s* conmiseración
commissar [,kɑmɪ'sɑr] *s* comisario (*en Rusia*)
commissar•y ['kɑmɪ,sɛri] *s* (*pl* **-ies**) (*deputy*) comisario; (*store*) economato
commission [kə'mɪʃən] *s* comisión; (mil) nombramiento; **to put in commission** poner en uso; poner (*un buque*) en servicio activo; **to put out of commission** inutilizar, descomponer; retirar (*un buque*) del servicio activo || *tr* comisionar; poner en uso; poner (*un buque*) en servicio activo; (mil) nombrar
commissioned officer *s* oficial *m*
commissioner [kə'mɪʃənər] *s* comisario; (*person authorized by a commission*) comisionado
com•mit [kə'mɪt] *v* (*pret & pp* **-mitted;** *ger* **-mitting**) *tr* cometer (*un crimen, una falta; un negocio a una persona*); (*to hand over*) confiar, entregar; dar, empeñar (*la palabra*); (*to bind, pledge*) comprometer; internar (*a un demente*); (*to memory*) encomendar; **to commit oneself** comprometerse, empeñarse; **to commit to writing** poner por escrito
commitment [kə'mɪtmənt] *s* (*act of committing*) comisión; (*to an asylum*) internación; (*written, order*) auto de prisión; compromiso, cometido, empeño
committee [kə'mɪti] *s* comité *m,* comisión
commode [kə'mod] *s* (*chest of drawers*) cómoda; (*washstand*) lavabo; (*chamber pot*) sillico
commodious [kə'modɪ•əs] *adj* espacioso, holgado
commodi•ty [kə'mɑdɪti] *s* (*pl* **-ties**) artículo de consumo, mercancía
commodity exchange *s* lonja, bolsa mercantil
common ['kɑmən] *adj* común || *s* campo común, ejido; **commons** estado llano; (*of a school*) refectorio; **the Commons** (Brit) los Comunes
common carrier *s* empresa de transportes públicos
commoner ['kɑmənər] *s* plebeyo; (Brit) miembro de la Cámara de los Comunes

common law *s* derecho consuetudinario
com'mon-law' marriage *s* matrimonio consensual
com'mon•place' *adj* común, trivial, ordinario || *s* lugar *m* común, trivialidad
common sense *s* sentido común
com'mon-sense' *adj* cuerdo, razonable
common stock *s* acción ordinaria; acciones ordinarias
commonweal ['kɑmən,wil] *s* bien público
com'mon•wealth' *s* estado, nación; república; (*state of U.S.A.*) estado; (*self-governing associated country*) estado libre asociado; (*association of states*) mancomunidad
commotion [kə'moʃən] *s* conmoción
commune [kə'mjun] *intr* conversar; (eccl) comulgar
communicant [kə'mjunɪkənt] *s* comunicante *mf;* (eccl) comulgante *mf*
communicate [kə'mjunɪ,ket] *tr* comunicar || *intr* comunicarse
communicating [kə'mjunɪ,ketɪŋ] *adj* comunicador
communication [kə,mjunə'keʃən] *s* comunicación
communications satellite *s* satélite *m* de comunicaciones
communicative [kə'mjunɪ,ketɪv] *adj* comunicativo
communion [kə'mjunjən] *s* comunión; **to take communion** comulgar
communion rail *s* comulgatorio
communiqué [kə,mjunɪ'ke] o [kə'mjunɪ,ke] *s* comunicado, parte *m*
communism ['kɑmjə,nɪzəm] *s* comunismo
communist ['kɑmjənɪst] *s* comunista *mf*
communi•ty [kə'mjunɪti] *s* (*pl* **-ties**) vecindario; (*group of people living together*) comunidad
communize ['kɑmjə,naɪz] *tr* comunizar
commutation ticket [,kɑmjə'teʃən] *s* billete *m* de abono
commutator ['kɑmjə,tetər] *s* (elec) colector *m*
commute [kə'mjut] *tr* conmutar || *intr* viajar con billete de abono
commuter [kə'mjutər] *s* abonado al ferrocarril
comp. *abbr* **compare, comparative, composer, composition, compound**
compact [kəm'pækt] *adj* compacto; breve, preciso || ['kɑmpækt] *s* convenio, pacto; estuche *m* de afeites
compact disk *s* disco compacto
companion [kəm'pænjən] *s* compañero
companionable [kəm'pænjənəbəl] *adj* afable, sociable, simpático
companionship [kəm'pænjən,ʃɪp] *s* compañerismo
companionway [kəm'pænjən,we] *s* (naut) escalera de cámara
compa•ny ['kʌmpəni] *s* (*pl* **-nies**) compañía; visita, visitas, invitado, invitados; (naut) tripulación; **to be good company** ser compañero alegre; **to keep company** ir juntos (*un hombre y una mujer*); **to keep some-one company** hacerle compañía a una persona; **to part company** separarse; enemistarse
company building *s* edificio social
company office *s* domicilio social
comparative [kəm'pærətɪv] *adj & s* comparativo
compare [kəm'pɛr] *s* — **beyond compare** sin comparación, sin par || *tr* comparar
comparison [kəm'pærɪsən] *s* comparación
compartment [kəm'pɑrtmənt] *s* compartimiento; (rr) departamento
compass ['kʌmpəs] *s* brújula, compás *m;* ámbito, recinto; alcance *m,* extensión; **compass** o **compasses** (*for drawing circles*) compás *m*
compass card *s* (naut) rosa náutica, rosa de los vientos
compassion [kəm'pæʃən] *s* compasión
compassionate [kəm'pæʃənɪt] *adj* compasivo
com•pel [kəm'pɛl] *v* (*pret & pp* **-pelled;** *ger* **-pelling**) *tr* forzar, obligar, compeler; imponer (*respeto, silencio*)
compendious [kəm'pɛndɪ•əs] *adj* compendioso
compendi•um [kəm'pɛndɪ•əm] *s* (*pl* **-ums** o **-a** [ə]) compendio
compensate ['kɑmpən,set] *tr & intr* compensar; **to compensate for** compensar
compensation [,kɑmpən'seʃən] *s* compensación
compete [kəm'pit] *intr* competir
competence ['kɑmpɪtəns] o **competency** ['kɑmpɪtənsi] *s* (*aptitude; legal capacity*) competencia; (*sufficient means to live comfortably*) buen pasar *m*
competent ['kɑmpɪtənt] *adj* competente
competition [,kɑmpɪ'tɪʃən] *s* (*rivalry*) competencia; (*in a match, examination, etc.*) certamen *m,* concurso; (*in business*) concurrencia
competitive [kəm'pɛtɪtɪv] *adj* — **to be competitive** poder competir
competitive examination *s* oposición
competitiveness [kəm'pɛtɪtɪvnɪs] *s* capacidad competiva
competitive prices *spl* precios de competencia
competitor [kəm'pɛtɪtər] *s* competidor *m*
compilation [,kɑmpɪ'leʃən] *s* compilación, recopilación
compile [kəm'paɪl] *tr* compilar, recopilar
complacence [kəm'plesəns] o **complacency** [kəm'plesənsi] *s* (*quiet satisfaction*) complacencia; satisfacción de sí mismo
complacent [kəm'plesənt] *adj* (*willing to please*) complaciente; satisfecho de sí mismo
complain [kəm'plen] *intr* quejarse
complainant [kəm'plenənt] *s* (law) demandante *mf*
complaint [kəm'plent] *s* queja; reclamo; (*grievance*) agravio; (*illness*) enfermedad, mal *m;* (law) demanda, querella
complaisance [kəm'plezəns] o ['kɑmplɪ,zæns] *s* amabilidad, cortesía
complaisant [kəm'plezənt] o ['kɑmplɪ,zænt] *adj* amable, cortés

complement [ˈkɑmplɪmənt] *s* complemento; (nav) dotación ‖ *tr* complementar
complete [kəmˈplit] *adj* completo ‖ *tr* completar, terminar, realizar
completion [kəmˈpliʃən] *s* terminación, realización
complex [kəmˈplɛks] o [ˈkɑmplɛks] *adj* (*not simple*) complexo; (*composite*) complejo; (*intricate*) complicado ‖ [ˈkɑmplɛks] *s* complejo; (psychol) complejo; (coll) obsesión
complexion [kəmˈplɛkʃən] *s* (*constitution*) complexión; (*texture of skin, esp. of face*) tez *f;* aspecto general, índole *f*
compliance [kəmˈplaɪ•əns] *s* condescendencia; sumisión, rendimiento; **in compliance with** de acuerdo con, en conformidad con
complicate [ˈkɑmplɪ,ket] *tr* complicar
complicated [ˈkɑmplɪ,ketɪd] *adj* complicado
complication [ˈkɑmplɪ,keʃən] *s* complicación
complici•ty [kəmˈplɪsɪti] *s* (*pl* **-ties**) complicidad, codelincuencia
compliment [ˈkɑmplɪmənt] *s* (*show of courtesy*) cumplimiento; (*praise*) alabanza, halago; perico (CAm); **compliments** saludos, recuerdos ‖ [ˈkɑmplɪ,mɛnt] *tr* cumplimentar; alabar, halagar
complimentary copy [,kɑmplɪˈmɛntəri] *s* ejemplar *m* de cortesía
complimentary ticket *s* billete *m* de regalo, pase *m* de cortesía
com•ply [kəmˈplaɪ] *v* (*pret & pp* **-plied**) *intr* conformarse; **to comply with** conformarse con, obrar de acuerdo con
component [kəmˈponənt] *adj* componente ‖ *m* componente *m*
compose [kəmˈpoz] *tr* componer; **to be composed of** estar compuesto de
composed [kəmˈpozd] *adj* sosegado, tranquilo
composer [kəmˈpozer] *s* componedor *m;* (mus) compositor *m;* autor *m*
composing stick *s* componedor *m*
composite [kəmˈpɑzɪt] *adj & s* compuesto
composition [,kɑmpəˈzɪʃən] *s* composición
compositor [kəmˈpɑzɪtər] *s* cajista *mf,* componedor *m*
composure [kəmˈpoʒər] *s* serenidad, sosiego
compote [ˈkɑmpot] *s* (*stewed fruit*) compota; (*dish*) compotera
compound [ˈkɑmpaʊnd] *adj* compuesto ‖ *s* compuesto; (gram) vocablo compuesto ‖ [kɑmˈpaʊnd] *tr* componer, combinar; (*interest*) capitalizar
comprehend [,kɑmprɪˈhɛnd] *tr* comprender
comprehensible [,kɑmprɪˈhɛnsɪbəl] *adj* comprensible
comprehension [,kɑmprɪˈhɛnʃən] *s* comprensión
comprehensive [,kɑmprɪˈhɛnsɪv] *adj* comprensivo, inclusivo, completo
compress [ˈkɑmprɛs] *s* (med) compresa, bilma ‖ [kəmˈprɛs] *tr* comprimir
compression [kəmˈprɛʃən] *s* compresión
comprise o **comprize** [kəmˈpraɪz] *tr* abarcar, comprender, incluir
compromise [ˈkɑmprə,maɪz] *s* (*adjustment*) componenda, transigencia, transacción; (*endangering*) comprometimiento ‖ *tr* (*by mutual concessions*) componer, transigir; (*to endanger*) comprometer, exponer ‖ *intr* transigir, avenirse
comptroller [kənˈtrolər] *s* contralor *m,* interventor *m*
compulsory [kəmˈpʌlsəri] *adj* obligatorio
computable [kəmˈpjutəbəl] *adj* calculable
computation [,kɑmpjuˈteʃən] *s* cálculo, cómputo
compute [kəmˈpjut] *tr & intr* computar, calcular
computer [kəmˈpjutər] *s* ordenador *m,* computador *m;* (*person*) computador *m,* calculador *m*
computer dating *s* citas computerizadas
computer science *s* informática
comrade [ˈkɑmræd] o [ˈkɑmrɪd] *s* camarada *m*; cumpa *m* (SAm)
con. *abbr* **conclusion, consolidated, contra**
con [kɑn] *s* (*opposite opinion*) contra *m*; (*slang*) engaño ‖ *v* (*pret & pp* **conned;** *ger* **conning**) *tr* leer con atención, aprender de memoria; (*slang*) engañar
concave [ˈkɑnkev] o [kɑnˈkev] *adj* cóncavo
conceal [kənˈsil] *tr* encubrir, ocultar
concealment [kənˈsilmənt] *s* encubrimiento, ocultación; (*place*) escondite *m*
concede [kənˈsid] *tr* conceder
conceit [kənˈsit] *s* (*vanity*) orgullo, engreimiento; (*witty expression*) concepto, dicho ingenioso
conceited [kənˈsitɪd] *adj* orgulloso, engreído
conceivable [kənˈsivəbəl] *adj* concebible
conceive [kənˈsiv] *tr & intr* concebir
concentrate [ˈkɑnsən,tret] *tr* concentrar ‖ *intr* concentrarse; **to concentrate on** o **upon** reconcentrarse en
concentric [kənˈsɛntrɪk] *adj* concéntrico
concept [ˈkɑnsɛpt] *s* concepto
conception [kənˈsɛpʃən] *s* concepción
concern [kənˈsʌrn] *s* (*business establishment*) empresa, casa comercial, razón *f* social; (*worry*) inquietud, preocupación; (*relation, reference*) concernencia; (*matter*) asunto, negocio ‖ *tr* atañer, concernir; interesar; **as concerns** respecto de; **to whom it may concern** a quien pueda interesar, a quien corresponda
concerning [kənˈsʌrnɪŋ] *prep* respecto de, tocante a
concert [ˈkɑnsərt] *s* concierto ‖ [kənˈsʌrt] *tr & intr* concertar
con'cert•mas'ter *s* concertino
concer•to [kənˈtʃɛrto] *s* (*pl* **-tos** o **-ti** [ti]) concierto
concession [kənˈsɛʃən] *s* concesión
concessive [kənˈsɛsɪv] *adj* concesivo
concierge [,kɑnsɪˈʌrʒ] *s* conserje *m*
conciliate [kənˈsɪlɪ,et] *tr* conciliar; conciliarse (*el respeto, la estima*)
conciliatory [kənˈsɪlɪ•ə,tori] *adj* conciliador
concise [kənˈsaɪs] *adj* conciso
conclude [kənˈklud] *tr & intr* concluir
concluding [kənˈkludɪŋ] *adj* final

conclusion [kən'kluʒən] *s* conclusión; (*of a letter*) despedida
conclusive [kən'klusɪv] *adj* concluyente
concoct [kən'kakt] *tr* confeccionar; (*a story*) forjar, inventar
concomitant [kən'kamɪtənt] *adj & s* concomitante *m*
concord ['kaŋkɔrd] *s* concordia; (gram, mus) concordancia
concordance [kən'kɔrdəns] *s* concordancia
concourse ['kaŋkors] *s* (*of people*) concurso; (*of streams*) confluencia; bulevar *m,* gran vía; (*of railroad station*) gran salón *m*
concrete ['kankrit] o [kan'krit] *adj* concreto; de hormigón || *s* hormigón *m*
concrete block *s* bloque *m* de hormigón
concrete mixer *s* hormigonera, mezcladora de hormigón
concubine ['kaŋkjə,baɪn] *s* concubina
con•cur [kən'kʌr] *v* (*pret & pp* **-curred;** *ger* **-curring**) *intr* concurrir
concurrence [kən'kʌrəns] *s* (*happening together*) concurrencia; (*agreement*) acuerdo
concussion [kən'kʌʃən] *s* concusión
condemn [kən'dɛm] *tr* condenar
condemnation [,kandɛm'neʃən] *s* condenación
condense [kən'dɛns] *tr* condensar || *intr* condensarse
condescend [,kandɪ'sɛnd] *intr* dignarse
condescending [,kandɪ'sɛndɪŋ] *adj* condescendiente con inferiores
condescension [,kandɪ'sɛnʃən] *s* dignación, aire *m* protector
condiment ['kandɪmənt] *s* condimento
condition [kən'dɪʃən] *s* condición; **on condition that** a condición (de) que || *tr* acondicionar
conditional [kən'dɪʃənəl] *adj* condicional
conditioned reflex [kən'dɪʃənd] *s* reflejo acondicionado
condole [kən'dol] *intr* condolerse
condolence [kən'doləns] *s* condolencia
condominium [,kandə'mɪni•əm] *s* condominio
condone [kən'don] *tr* condonar; (*legally*) despenalizar
condor ['kandər] *s* cóndor *m*
conduce [kən'djus] *intr* conducir
conducive [kən'djusɪv] *adj* conducente, contribuyente
conduct ['kandʌkt] *s* conducta || [kən'dʌkt] *tr* conducir; **to conduct oneself** conducirse, comportarse
conductor [kən'dʌktər] *s* conductor *m,* guía *mf;* (elec & phys) conductor *m,* conductora *f;* (rr) revisor *m;* (*on trolley or bus*) cobrador *m*
conduit ['kandɪt] o ['kandu•ɪt] *s* canal *f* para alambres o cables
cone [kon] *s* cono; (*of pastry*) barquillo; (*of paper*) cucurucho
confectioner•y [kən'fɛkʃə,nɛri] *s* (*pl* **-ies**) (*shop*) confitería; (*sweetmeats*) dulces *mpl,* confites *mpl,* confituras
confedera•cy [kən'fɛdərəsi] *s* (*pl* **-cies**) confederación; (*for unlawful purpose*) conjuración
confederate [kən'fɛdərɪt] *s* confederado; cómplice *mf* || [kən'fɛdə,ret] *tr* confederar || *intr* confederarse
con•fer [kən'fʌr] *v* (*pret & pp* **-ferred;** *ger* **-ferring**) *tr* conferir || *intr* conferenciar, consultar
conference ['kanfərəns] *s* conferencia, coloquio
confess [kən'fɛs] *tr* confesar || *intr* confesar, confesarse
confession [kən'fɛʃən] *s* confesión
confessional [kən'fɛʃənəl] *s* confesonario
confession of faith *s* profesión de fe
confessor [kən'fɛsər] *s* (*person who confesses*) confesante *mf;* (*Christian, esp. in spite of persecution; priest*) confesor *m*
confide [kən'faɪd] *tr* confiar || *intr* confiar, confiarse; **to confide in** confiarse en
confidence ['kanfɪdəns] *s* confianza; (*secret*) confidencia; **in strictest confidence** bajo la mayor reserva
confident ['kanfɪdənt] *adj* seguro || *s* confidente *m,* confidenta
confidential [,kanfɪ'dɛnʃəl] *adj* confidencial
confine ['kanfaɪn] *s* confín *m;* **the confines** los confines || [kən'faɪn] *tr* (*to keep within limits*) limitar, restringir; (*to keep shut in*) encerrar; **to be confined** estar de parto; **to be confined to bed** tener que guardar cama
confinement [kən'faɪnmənt] *s* limitación; encierro; parto, sobreparto
confirm [kən'fʌrm] *tr* confirmar
confirmed [kən'fʌrmd] *adj* confirmado; empedernido, inveterado
confiscate ['kanfɪs,ket] *tr* confiscar
conflagration [,kanflə'greʃən] *s* conflagración
conflict ['kanflɪkt] *s* conflicto; (*of interests, class hours, etc.*) incompatibilidad || [kən'flɪkt] *intr* chocar, desavenirse
conflicting [kən'flɪktɪŋ] *adj* contradictorio; (*events, appointments, class hours, etc.*) incompatible, conflictivo
confluence ['kanflu•əns] *s* confluencia
conform [kən'fɔrm] *intr* conformar, conformarse
conformance [kən'fɔrməns] *s* conformidad
conformi•ty [kən'fɔrmɪti] *s* (*pl* **-ties**) conformidad
confound [kan'faund] *tr* confundir || ['kan'faund] *tr* maldecir; **confound it!** ¡maldito sea!
confounded [kan'faundɪd] *adj* confundido; aborrecible; maldito
confrere ['kanfrɛr] *s* colega *m*
confront [kən'frʌnt] *tr* (*to face boldly*) confrontarse con, hacer frente a; (*to meet face to face*) encontrar cara a cara; (*to bring face to face; to compare*) confrontar
confrontation [,kanfrʌn'teʃən] *s* enfrentamiento
confuse [kən'fjuz] *tr* confundir
confusedness [kən'fjuzɪdnɪs] *s* desorientación

confusion [kən'fjuʒən] *s* confusión
confute [kən'fjut] *tr* confutar
Cong. *abbr* **Congregation, Congressional**
congeal [kən'dʒil] *tr* congelar || *intr* congelarse
congenial [kən'dʒinjəl] *adj* simpático; agradable; compatible; (*having the same nature*) congenial
congenital [kən'dʒɛnɪtəl] *adj* congénito
conger eel ['kaŋgər] *s* congrio
congest [kən'dʒɛst] *tr* congestionar || *intr* congestionarse
congestion [kən'dʒɛstʃən] *s* congestión
congratulate [kən'grætʃə,let] *tr* congratular, felicitar
congratulation [kən,grætʃə'leʃən] *s* congratulación, felicitación
congregate ['kaŋgrɪ,get] *intr* congregarse
congregation [,kaŋgrɪ'geʃən] *s* congregación; feligresía, fieles *mf* (*de una iglesia*)
congress ['kaŋgrɪs] *s* congreso
congress•man ['kaŋgrɪsmən] *s* (*pl* **-men** [mən]) congresista *m*
conical ['kanɪkəl] *adj* cónico
conj. *abbr* **conjugation, conjunction**
conjecture [kən'dʒɛktʃər] *s* conjetura || *tr & intr* conjeturar
conjugal ['kandʒəgəl] *adj* conyugal
conjugate ['kandʒə,get] *tr* conjugar
conjugation [,kandʒə'geʃən] *s* conjugación
conjunction [kən'dʒʌŋkʃən] *s* conjunción
conjuration [,kandʒə'reʃən] *s* (*superstitious invocation*) conjuro; (*magic spell*) hechizo
conjure [kən'dʒʊr] *tr* (*to appeal to solemnly*) conjurar || ['kʌndʒər] o ['kandʒər] *tr* (*to exorcise, drive away*) conjurar; **to conjure away** conjurar; **to conjure up** evocar; crear, suscitar (*dificultades*)
con man [kan] *s* (coll) embaucador *m*, embaucadora
connect [kə'nɛkt] *tr* conectar; asociar, relacionar || *intr* enlazarse; asociarse, relacionarse; empalmar, enlazar (*dos trenes*)
connecting flight *s* vuelo de enlace
connecting rod *s* biela
connection [kə'nɛkʃən] *s* conexión; (*relative*) pariente *mf;* (*of trains*) combinación, enlace *m*, empalme *m;* (*in subway*) correspondencia; **in connection with** con respecto a; juntamente con
connective tissue [kə'nɛktɪv] *s* (anat) tejido conjunctivo
conning tower ['kanɪŋ] *s* torreta de mando
conniption [kə'nɪpʃən] *s* pataleta, berrinche *m*
connive [kə'naɪv] *intr* confabularse, estar en connivencia
conquer ['kaŋkər] *tr* vencer; (*by force of arms*) conquistar || *intr* triunfar
conqueror ['kaŋkərər] *s* conquistador *m*, vencedor *m*
conquest ['kaŋkwɛst] *s* conquista
conscience ['kanʃəns] *s* conciencia; **in all conscience** en conciencia
conscientious [,kanʃɪ'ɛnʃəs] *adj* concienzudo
conscientious objector [ab'dʒɛktər] *s* objetante *m* de conciencia
conscious ['kanʃəs] *adj* (*aware of one's own existence*) consciente; (*deliberate*) intencional; (*self-conscious*) encogido, tímido; **to become conscious** volver en sí
consciousness ['kanʃəsnɪs] *s* conciencia, conocimiento
consciousness raising *s* concienciación
conscript ['kanskrɪpt] *s* conscripto, quinto || [kən'skrɪpt] *tr* reclutar
conscription [kən'skrɪpʃən] *s* conscripción, quinta
consecrate ['kansɪ,kret] *tr* consagrar
consecutive [kən'sɛkjətɪv] *adj* (*successive*) consecutivo; (*continuous*) consecuente
consensus [kən'sɛnsəs] *s* consenso; **the consensus of opinion** la opinión general
consent [kən'sɛnt] *s* consentimiento; **by common consent** de común acuerdo || *intr* consentir; **to consent to** consentir en
consequence ['kansɪ,kwɛns] *s* consecuencia; aires *mpl* de importancia
consequential [,kansɪ'kwɛnʃəl *adj* consiguiente; importante; altivo, pomposo
consequently ['kansɪ,kwɛntli] *adv* por consiguiente
conservation [,kansər'veʃən] *s* conservación
conservatism [kən'sʌrvə,tɪzəm] *s* conservadurismo
conservative [kən'sʌrvətɪv] *adj* (*preservative*) conservativo; (*disposed to maintain existing views and institutions*) conservador; cauteloso, moderado || *s* preservativo; conservador *m*
conservato•ry [kən'sʌrvə,tori] *s* (*pl* **-ries**) (*school of music*) conservatorio; (*greenhouse*) invernadero
consider [kən'sɪdər] *tr* considerar
considerable [kən'sɪdərəbəl] *adj* considerable
considerate [kən'sɪdərɪt] *adj* considerado
consideration [kən,sɪdə'reʃən] *s* consideración; **for a consideration** por un precio; **in consideration of** en consideración de; en cambio de; **on no consideration** bajo ningún concepto; **out of consideration for** por respeto a; **without due consideration** sin reflexión
considering [kən'sɪdərɪŋ] *adv* (coll) teniendo en cuenta las circunstancias || *prep* en vista de, en razón de || *conj* en vista de que
consign [kən'saɪn] *tr* consignar
consignee [,kansaɪ'ni] *s* consignatario
consignment [kən'saɪnmənt] *s* consignación
consist [kən'sɪst] *intr* — **to consist in** consistir en; **to consist of** consistir en, constar de
consisten•cy [kən'sɪstənsi] *s* (*pl* **-cies**) (*firmness, amount of firmness*) consistencia; (*logical connection*) consecuencia
consistent [kən'sɪstənt] *adj* (*holding firmly together*) consistente; (*agreeing with itself or oneself*) consecuente; **consistent with** (*in accord with*) compatible con
consisto•ry [kən'sɪstəri] *s* (*pl* **-ries**) consistorio
consolation [,kansə'leʃən] *s* consolación, consuelo

console [ˈkɑnsol] *s* consola; mesa de consola || [kənˈsol] *tr* consolar
consommé [,kɑnsəˈme] *s* consumado, consommé *m*
consonant [ˈkɑnsənənt] *adj & s* consonante *f*
consort [ˈkɑnsɔrt] *s* consorte *mf;* embarcación que acompaña a otra || [kənˈsɔrt] *tr* asociar || *intr* asociarse; armonizar, concordar
consorti•um [kənˈsɔrʃɪ•əm] *s* (*pl* **-a** [ə]) consorcio
conspicuous [kənˈspɪkjʊ•əs] *adj* manifiesto, claro, evidente; llamativo, vistoso, sugestivo; conspicuo, notable
conspira•cy [kənˈspɪrəsi] *s* (*pl* **-cies**) conspiración, conjuración
conspire [kənˈspaɪr] *intr* conspirar, conjurar
constable [ˈkɑnstəbəl] o [ˈkʌnstəbəl] *s* policía *m,* guardia *m,* alguacil *m*
constancy [ˈkɑnstənsi] *s* constancia; fidelidad
constant [ˈkɑnstənt] *adj* constante; incesante; fiel || *s* constante *f*
constellation [,kɑnstəˈleʃən] *s* constelación
constipate [ˈkɑnstɪ,pet] *tr* estreñir
constipation [,kɑnstɪˈpeʃən] *s* estreñimiento, estitiquez *f*
constituen•cy [kənˈstɪtʃʊ•ənsi] *s* (*pl* **-cies**) votantes *mpl;* clientela; comitentes *mpl;* distrito electoral
constituent [kənˈstɪtʃʊ•ənt] *adj* constitutivo, componente; (*having power to create or revise a constitution*) constituyente || *s* constitutivo, componente *m;* (*person who appoints another to act for him*) comitente *m*
constitute [ˈkɑnstɪ,tjut] *tr* constituir
constitution [,kɑnstɪˈtjuʃən] *s* constitución
constrain [kənˈstren] *tr* constreñir; detener, encerrar; restringir
construct [kənˈstrʌkt] *tr* construir
construction [kənˈstrʌkʃən] *s* construcción; interpretación
construe [kənˈstru] *tr* interpretar; deducir, inferir; traducir; (*to combine syntactically*) construir; (*to explain the syntax of*) analizar
consul [ˈkɑnsəl] *s* cónsul *m*
consular [ˈkɑnsələr] *adj* consular
consulate [ˈkɑnsəlɪt] *s* consulado
consulship [ˈkɑnsəl,ʃɪp] *s* consulado
consult [kənˈsʌlt] *tr & intr* consultar
consultant [kənˈsʌltənt] *s* consultor *m*
consultation [,kɑnsəlˈteʃən] *s* (*consulting*) consulta; (*meeting*) consulta, consultación
consume [kənˈsum] o [kənˈsjum] *tr* consumir; (*to absorb the interest of*) preocupar; || *intr* consumirse
consumer [kənˈsumər] *s* consumidor *m;* (*of gas, electricity, etc.*) abonado
consumer credit *s* crédito consuntivo
consumer goods *spl* bienes *mpl* de consumo
consumerism [kənˈsumə,rɪzəm] *s* consumerismo
consummate [kənˈsʌmɪt] *adj* consumado || [ˈkɑnsə,met] *tr* consumar
consumption [kənˈsʌmpʃən] *s* consunción, consumo; (pathol) consunción, tisis *f*
consumptive [kənˈsʌmptɪv] *adj* consuntivo; (path) tísico || *s* tísico
cont. *abbr* **contents, continental, continued**
contact [ˈkɑntækt] *s* contacto; (elec) contacto; (elec) toma de corriente || *tr* (coll) ponerse en contacto con || *intr* contactar
contact breaker *s* (elec) ruptor *m*
contact lens *s* lente *m* de contacto, lente invisible, lentilla
contagion [kənˈtedʒən] *s* contagio
contagious [kənˈtedʒəs] *adj* contagioso
contain [kənˈten] *tr* contener; **to contain oneself** contenerse, refrenarse
container [kənˈtenər] *s* continente *m,* recipiente *m,* vaso, caja, envase *m,* contenedor *m*
containment [kənˈtenmənt] *s* contención, refrenamiento
contaminate [kənˈtæmɪ,net] *tr* contaminar
contamination [kən,tæmɪˈneʃən] *s* contaminación
contd. *abbr* **continued**
contemplate [ˈkɑntəm,plet] *tr & intr* contemplar; pensar, proyectar
contemplation [,kɑntəmˈpleʃən] *s* contemplación; intención, propósito
contemporaneous [kən,tɛmpəˈrenɪ•əs] *adj* contemporáneo
contemporar•y [kənˈtɛmpə,rɛri] *adj* contemporáneo, coetáneo || *s* (*pl* **-ies**) contemporáneo, coetáneo
contempt [kənˈtɛmpt] *s* desprecio; (law) contumacia
contemptible [kənˈtɛmptɪbəl] *adj* despreciable
contemptuous [kənˈtɛmptʃʊ•əs] *adj* despreciativo, desdeñoso
contend [kənˈtɛnd] *tr* sostener, mantener || *intr* contender
contender [kənˈtɛndər] *s* contendiente *mf,* concurrente *mf*
content [kənˈtɛnt] *adj & s* contento || [ˈkɑntɛnt] *s* contenido; **contents** contenido || [kənˈtɛnt] *tr* contentar
contented [kənˈtɛntɪd] *adj* contento, satisfecho
contentedness [kənˈtɛndɪdnɪs] *s* contentamiento, satisfacción
contention [kənˈtɛnʃən] *s* (*strife; dispute*) contención; (*point argued for*) argumento
contentious [kənˈtɛnʃəs] *adj* contencioso
contentment [kənˈtɛntmənt] *s* contentamiento, contento
contest [ˈkɑntɛst] *s* (*struggle, fight*) contienda; (*competition*) competencia, concurso || [kənˈtɛst] *tr* disputar; tratar de conseguir || *intr* contender
contestant [kənˈtɛstənt] *s* contendiente *mf*
context [ˈkɑntɛkst] *s* contexto
contiguous [kənˈtɪgjʊ•əs] *adj* contiguo
continence [ˈkɑntɪnəns] *s* continencia
continent [ˈkɑntɪnənt] *adj & s* continente *m;* **the Continent** la Europa continental
continental [,kɑntɪˈnɛntəl] *adj* continental || **Continental** *s* habitante *mf* del continente europeo

contingen•cy [kən'tɪndʒənsi] *s* (*pl* **-cies**) contingencia
contingent [kən'tɪndʒənt] *adj & s* contingente *m*
continual [kən'tɪnjʊ•əl] *adj* continuo
continue [kən'tɪnjʊ] *tr & intr* continuar; **to be continued** continuará
continui•ty [,kɑntɪ'nju•ɪti] o [,kɑntɪ'nu•ɪti] *s* (*pl* **-ties**) continuidad; (mov, rad, telv) guión *m;* (rad, telv) comentarios o anuncios entre las partes de un programa
continuous [kən'tɪnjʊ•əs] *adj* continuo
continuous showing *s* (mov) sesión continua
continuous waves *spl* (rad) ondas entretenidas
contortion [kən'tɔrʃən] *s* contorsión
contour ['kɑntʊr] *s* contorno
contr. *abbr* **contracted, contraction**
contraband ['kɑntrə,bænd] *adj* contrabandista || *s* contrabando
contrabass ['kɑntrə,bes] *s* contrabajo
contraceptive [,kɑntrə'sɛptɪv] *adj & s* anticonceptivo, contraceptivo
contract ['kɑntrækt] *s* contrato; **on a contract (to kill)** a sueldo || ['kɑntrækt] o [kən'trækt] *tr* contraer (*p.ej., matrimonio* || *intr* (*to shrink*) contraerse; (*to enter into an agreement*) comprometerse; **to contract for** contratar
contraction [kən'trækʃən] *s* contracción
contractor [kən'træktər] *s* contratista *mf*
contradict [,kɑntrə'dɪkt] *tr* contradecir
contradiction [,kɑntrə'dɪkʃən] *s* contradicción
contradictory [,kɑntrə'dɪktəri] *adj* (*involving contradiction*) contradictorio; (*inclined to contradict*) contradictor
contrail ['kɑn,trel] *s* (aer) estela de vapor, rastro de condensación
contral•to [kən'trælto] *s* (*pl* **-tos**) (*person*) contralto *mf;* (*voice*) contralto *m*
contraption [kən'træpʃən] *s* (coll) artilugio, dispositivo
contra•ry ['kɑntrɛri] *adv* contrariamente || *adj* contrario || [kən'trɛri] *adj* obstinado, terco || ['kɑntrɛri] *s* (*pl* **-ries**) contrario; **on the contrary** al contrario
contrast ['kɑntræst] *s* contraste *m* || [kən'træst] *tr* comparar; poner en contraste || *intr* contrastar
contravene [,kɑntrə'vin] *tr* contradecir; contravenir a (*una ley*)
contribute [kən'trɪbjʊt] *tr* contribuir || *intr* contribuir; (*to a newspaper, conference, etc.*) colaborar
contribution [,kɑntrɪ'bjuʃən] *s* contribución; (*to a newspaper, conference, etc.*) colaboración
contributor [kən'trɪbjʊtər] *s* contribuidor *m,* contribuyente *mf;* colaborador *m*
contrite [kən'traɪt] *adj* contrito
contrition [kən'trɪʃən] *s* contrición
contrivance [kən'traɪvəns] *s* aparato, dispositivio; idea, plan *m,* designio
contrive [kən'traɪv] *tr* (*to devise*) idear, inventar; (*to scheme up*) maquinar, tramar; (*to bring about*) efectuar; **to contrive to** + *inf* ingeniarse a + *inf* || *intr* maquinar
con•trol [kən'trol] *s* gobierno, mando; chequeo; (*of a scientific experiment*) contrarregistro, control *m;* **controls** mandos; **to get under control** conseguir dominar (*un incendio*) || *v* (*pret & pp* **-trolled;** *ger* **-trolling**) *tr* gobernar, mandar; comprobar, controlar; **to control oneself** dominarse
controlling interest *s* (el) mayor porcentaje de acciones
control panel *s* (aer) tablero de instrumentos
control stick *s* (aer) mango de escoba, palanca de mando
controversial [,kɑntrə'vʌrʃəl] *adj* controvertible, disputable; disputador
controver•sy ['kɑntrə,vʌrsi] *s* (*pl* **-sies**) controversia, polémica
controvert ['kɑntrə,vʌrt] o [,kɑntrə'vʌrt] *tr* (*to argue against*) contradecir; (*to argue about*) controvertir
contumacious [,kɑntju'meʃəs] *adj* contumaz
contuma•cy ['kɑntjʊməsi] *s* (*pl* **-cies**) contumacia
contume•ly ['kɑntjʊmɪli] *s* (*pl* **-lies**) contumelia
contusion [kən'tjuʒən] *s* contusión; magullón *m*
conundrum [kə'nʌndrəm] *s* acertijo, adivinanza; problema complicado
convalesce [,kɑnvə'lɛs] *intr* convalecer
convalescence [,kɑnvə'lɛsəns] *s* convalecencia
convalescent [,kɑnvə'lɛsənt] *adj & s* convaleciente *mf*
convalescent home *s* clínica de reposo
convene [kən'vin] *tr* convocar || *intr* convenir, reunirse
convenience [kən'vinjəns] *s* comodidad, conveniencia; **at your earliest convenience** a la primera oportunidad que Vd. tenga
convenient [kən'vinjənt] *adj* cómodo, conveniente; próximo
convent ['kɑnvɛnt] *s* convento; convento de religiosas
convention [kən'vɛnʃən] *s* (*agreement*) convención, conveniencia; (*accepted usage*) costumbre *f,* conveniencia social, convención; (*meeting*) congreso, convención
conventional [kən'vɛnʃənəl] *adj* convencional
conventionali•ty [kən,vɛnʃə'nælɪti] *s* (*pl* **-ties**) precedente *m* convencional
converge [kən'vʌrʒ] *intr* convergir
conversant [kən'vʌrsənt] *adj* familiarizado, versado
conversation [,kɑnvər'seʃən] *s* conversación
conversational [,kɑnvər'seʃənəl] *adj* conversacional
converse ['kɑnvʌrs] *adj & s* contrario || [kən'vʌrs] *intr* conversar
conversion [kən'vʌrʒən] *s* conversión; (*unlawful appropriation*) malversación
convert ['kɑnvʌrt] *s* convertido, converso || [kən'vʌrt] *tr* convertir || *intr* convertirse
convertible [kən'vʌrtɪbəl] *adj* convertible || *s* (aut) convertible *m,* descapotable *m*

convex [ˈkɑnvɛks] o [kɑnˈvɛks] *adj* convexo
convey [kənˈve] *tr* llevar, transportar; comunicar, participar (*informes*); transferir, traspasar (*bienes de una persona a otra*)
conveyance [kənˈve•əns] *s* transporte *m;* comunicación, participación; vehículo; (*transfer of property*) traspaso; escritura de traspaso
convict [ˈkɑnvɪkt] *s* reo convicto, presidiario ‖ [kənˈvɪkt] *tr* probar la culpabilidad de; declarar convicto (*a un acusado*)
conviction [kənˈvɪkʃən] *s* convencimiento; condena, fallo de culpabilidad
convince [kənˈvɪns] *tr* convencer
convincing [kənˈvɪnsɪŋ] *adj* convincente
convivial [kənˈvɪvɪ•əl] *adj* jovial
convocation [ˌkɑnvəˈkeʃən] *s* asamblea
convoke [kənˈvok] *tr* convocar
convoy [ˈkɑnvɔɪ] *s* convoy *m,* conserva ‖ *tr* convoyar
convulse [kənˈvʌls] *tr* convulsionar; agitar; **to convulse with laughter** mover a risas convulsivas
coo [ku] *intr* arrullar
cook [kʊk] *s* cocinero ‖ *tr* cocer, cocinar, guisar; **to cook up** (coll) falsificar; (coll) maquinar, tramar ‖ *intr* cocer, cocinar
cook'book' *s* libro de cocina
cookie [ˈkʊki] *s* var de **cooky**
cooking [ˈkʊkɪŋ] *s* cocina, arte *m* de cocinar
cook'stove' *s* cocina económica
cook•y [ˈkʊki] *s* (*pl* **-ies**) pasta seca, pastelito dulce
cool [kul] *adj* fresco; frío, indiferente ‖ *s* fresco ‖ *tr* refrescar; moderar ‖ *intr* refrescarse; moderarse; **to cool off** refrescarse; serenarse
cooler [ˈkulər] *s* heladera, refrigerador *m;* refrigerante *m;* cárcel *f*
cool'-head'ed *adj* sereno, tranquilo, juicioso
coolie [ˈkuli] *s* culí *m*
coolish [ˈkulɪʃ] *adj* fresquito
coolness [ˈkulnɪs] *s* fresco, frescura; (fig) frialdad
coon [kun] *s* mapache *m,* oso lavandero
coop [kup] *s* gallinero; (*for fattening capons*) caponera; jaula, redil *m;* (*jail*) (slang) caponera; **to fly the coop** (slang) escabullirse ‖ *tr* encerrar en un gallinero; enjaular; **to coop up** emparedar
coöp. *abbr* **cooperative**
cooper [ˈkupər] *s* barrilero, tonelero
coöperate [koˈɑpəˌret] *intr* cooperar
coöperation [koˌɑpəˈreʃən] *s* cooperación
coöperative [koˈɑpəˌretɪv] *adj* cooperativo
coöpt [koˈɑpt] *tr* cooptar
coördinate [koˈɔrdɪnɪt] *adj* coordenado; (gram) coordinante ‖ *s* (math) coordenada ‖ [koˈɔrdɪˌnet] *tr & intr* coordinar
cootie [ˈkuti] *s* (slang) piojo
cop [kɑp] *s* (slang) polizonte *m* ‖ *v* (*pret & pp* **copped;** *ger* **copping**) *tr* (slang) hurtar
copartner [koˈpɑrtnər] *s* consocio, copartícipe *mf*
cope [kop] *intr* — **to cope with** hacer frente a, enfrentarse con
cope'stone' *s* piedra de albardilla
copier [ˈkɑpɪ•ər] *s* (*person who copies*) copiante *mf,* copista *mf,* imitador *m;* (*apparatus*) copiador *m,* copiadora
copilot [ˈkoˌpaɪlət] *s* copiloto
coping [ˈkopɪŋ] *s* albardilla
copious [ˈkopɪ•əs] *adj* copioso
copper [ˈkɑpər] *adj* cobreño; (*in color*) cobrizo ‖ *s* cobre *m;* (*coin*) calderilla, vellón *m;* (slang) polizonte *m*
cop'per•head' *s* víbora de cabeza de cobre
cop'per•smith' *s* cobrero
coppery [ˈkɑpəri] *adj* cobreño; (*in color*) cobrizo
coppice [ˈkɑpɪs] o **copse** [kɑps] *s* soto, monte bajo
copulate [ˈkɑpjəˌlet] *intr* copularse
cop•y [ˈkɑpi] *s* (*pl* **-ies**) copia; (*of a book*) ejemplar *m;* (*of a magazine*) número; (*document to be reproduced in print*) original *m,* manuscrito ‖ *v* (*pret & pp* **-ied**) *tr* copiar
cop'y•book' *s* cuaderno de escritura
copyist [ˈkɑpɪ•ɪst] *s* copiante *mf,* copista *mf;* imitador *m*
cop'y•right' *s* (derechos de) propiedad literaria ‖ *tr* registrar en el registro de la propiedad literaria
copy writer *s* escritor publicitario
co•quet [koˈkɛt] *v* (*pret & pp* **-quetted;** *ger* **-quetting**) *intr* coquetear; burlarse
coquet•ry [ˈkokətri] o [koˈkɛtri] *s* (*pl* **-ries**) coquetería; burla
coquette [koˈkɛt] *s* coqueta
coquettish [koˈkɛtɪʃ] *adj* coqueta
cor. *abbr* **corner, coroner, correction, corresponding**
coral [ˈkɑrəl] o [ˈkɔrəl] *adj* coralino ‖ *s* coral *m*
coral reef *s* arrecife *m* de coral
cord [kɔrd] *s* cordón *m;* piola ‖ *tr* acordonar
cordial [ˈkɔrdʒəl] *adj* cordial ‖ *s* licor tónico; (*medicine*) cordial *m*
cordiali•ty [kɔrˈdʒælɪti] *s* (*pl* **-ties**) cordialidad
corduroy [ˈkɔrdəˌrɔɪ] *s* pana; **corduroys** pantalones *mpl* de pana
core [kor] *s* corazón *m;* (*of an electromagnet*) núcleo
corespondent [ˌkorɪsˈpɑndənt] *s* cómplice *mf* del demandado en juicio de divorcio
Corinth [ˈkɔrinθ] *s* Corinto *f*
cork [kɔrk] *s* corcho; corcho, tapón *m* de corcho; tapón (*de cualquier materia*) ‖ *tr* encorchar, tapar con corcho
corking [ˈkɔrkɪŋ] *adj* (slang) brutal, extraordinario
cork oak *s* alcornoque *m*
cork'screw' *s* sacacorchos *m,* tirabuzón *m*
cormorant [ˈkɔrmərənt] *s* cormorán *m,* cuervo marino
corn [kɔrn] *s* (*in U.S.A.*) maíz *m;* (*in England*) trigo; (*in Scotland*) avena; grano (*de maíz, trigo*); (*on the foot*) callo; (coll) aguardiente *m;* (slang) trivialidad
corn bread *s* pan *m* de maíz
corn'cake' *s* tortilla de maíz
corn'cob' *s* mazorca de maíz, carozo

corncob pipe *s* pipa de fumar hecha de una mazorca de maíz
corn′crib′ *s* granero para maíz
corn cure *adj* callicida *m*
cornea [ˈkɔrnɪ•ə] *s* córnea
corner [ˈkɔrnər] *s* ángulo; (*esp. where two streets meet*) esquina; (*inside angle formed by two or more surfaces; secluded place; region, quarter*) rincón *m;* (*of eye*) comisura, rabillo; (*of lips*) comisura; (*awkward position*) apuro, aprieto; monopolio; **around the corner** a la vuelta de la esquina; **to turn the corner** doblar la esquina; pasar el punto más peligroso ‖ *tr* arrinconar; monopolizar
corner cupboard *s* rinconera
corner room *s* habitación de esquina
cor′ner•stone′ *s* piedra angular; (*of a new building*) primera piedra
cornet [kɔrˈnɛt] *s* corneta
corn exchange *s* bolsa de granos
corn′field′ *s* (*in U.S.A.*) maizal *m;* (*in England*) trigal *m;* (*in Scotland*) avenal *m*
corn flour *s* harina de maíz
corn′flow′er *s* cabezuela
corn′husk′ *s* perfolla
cornice [ˈkɔrnɪs] *s* cornisa
Cornish [ˈkɔrnɪʃ] *adj & s* córnico
corn liquor *s* chicha
corn meal *s* harina de maíz
corn on the cob *s* maíz *m* en la mazorca
corn plaster *s* emplasto para los callos
corn silk *s* cabellos, barbas del maíz
corn′stalk′ *s* tallo de maíz
corn′starch′ *s* almidón *m* de maíz
cornucopia [,kɔrnəˈkopɪ•ə] *s* cornucopia
Cornwall [ˈkɔrn,wɔl] *s* Cornualles
corn•y [ˈkɔrni] *adj* (*comp* **-ier;** *super* **-iest**) de maíz; (coll) gastado, trivial, pesado
corollar•y [ˈkɑrə,lɛri] o [ˈkɔrə,lɛri] *s* (*pl* **-ies**) corolario
coronation [,kɑrəˈneʃən] o [,kɔrəˈneʃən] *s* coronación
coroner [ˈkɑrənər] o [ˈkɔrənər] *s* juez *m* de guardia
coroner's inquest *s* pesquisa dirigida por el juez de guardia
coronet [ˈkɑrə,nɛt] o [ˈkɔrə,nɛt] *s* (*worn by members of nobility*) corona; (*ornamental band of jewels worn on head*) diadema *f*
Corp. *abbr* **Corporation**
corporal [ˈkɔrpərəl] *adj* corporal ‖ *s* (mil) cabo
corporation [,kɔrpəˈreʃən] *s* (*provincial, municipal, or service entity*) corporación; sociedad anónima por acciones
corps [kor] *s* (*pl* **corps** [korz]) cuerpo; (mil) cuerpo
corps de ballet [kɔr də bæˈlɛ] *s* cuerpo de baile
corpse [kɔrps] *s* cadáver *m*
corpulent [ˈkɔrpjələnt] *adj* corpulento
corpuscle [ˈkɔrpəsəl] *s* corpúsculo, partícula; (physiol) glóbulo
corr. *abbr* **correspondence, corresponding**
cor•ral [kəˈræl] *s* corral *m* ‖ *v* (*pret & pp* **-ralled;** *ger* **-ralling**) *tr* acorralar

correct [kəˈrɛkt] *adj* correcto; (*proper*) cumplido ‖ *tr* corregir
correction [kəˈrɛkʃən] *s* corrección
corrective [kəˈrɛktɪv] *adj & s* correctivo
correctness [kəˈrɛktnɪs] *s* corrección; cumplimiento, cumplido
correlate [ˈkɔrə,let] *tr* correlacionar ‖ *intr* correlacionarse
correlation [,kɔrəˈleʃən] *s* correlación
correlative [kəˈrɛlətɪv] *adj & s* correlativo
correspond [,kɑrɪˈspɑnd] o [,kɔrɪˈspɑnd] *intr* corresponder; (*to communicate by writing*) corresponderse
correspondence [,kɑrɪˈspɑndəns] o [,kɔrɪˈspɑndəns] *s* correspondencia
correspondence school *s* escuela por correspondencia
correspondent [,kɑrɪˈspɑndənt] o [,kɔrɪˈspɑndənt] *adj* correspondiente ‖ *s* correspondiente *mf;* (*for a newspaper*) corresponsal *mf*
corresponding [,kɑrɪˈspɑndɪŋ] o [,kɔrɪˈspɑndɪŋ] *adj* correspondiente
corridor [ˈkɑrɪdər] o [ˈkɔrɪdər] *s* corredor *m,* pasillo
corroborate [kəˈrɑbə,ret] *tr* corroborar
corrode [kəˈrod] *tr* corroer ‖ *intr* corroerse
corrosion [kəˈroʒən] *s* corrosión
corrosive [kəˈrosɪv] *adj & s* corrosivo
corrugated [ˈkɑrə,getɪd] o [ˈkɔrə,getɪd] *adj* acanalado, ondulado
corrupt [kəˈrʌpt] *adj* corrompido ‖ *tr* corromper ‖ *intr* corromperse
corruption [kəˈrʌpʃən] *s* corrupción
corsage [kɔrˈsɑʒ] *s* (*bodice*) corpiño, jubón *m;* (*bouquet*) ramillete *m* que se lleva en el pecho o la cintura
corsair [ˈkɔr,sɛr] *s* corsario
corset [ˈkɔrsɪt] *s* corsé *m*
corset cover *s* cubrecorsé *m*
Corsica [ˈkɔrsɪkə] *s* Córcega
Corsican [ˈkɔrsɪkən] *adj & s* corso
cortege [kɔrˈteʒ] *s* procesión; (*retinue*) cortejo, séquito
cor•tex [ˈkɔr,tɛks] *s* (*pl* **-tices** [tɪ,siz]) corteza; corteza cerebral
cortisone [ˈkɔrtɪ,son] *s* cortisona
corvette [kɔrˈvɛt] *s* corbeta
cosmetic [kɑzˈmɛtɪk] *adj & s* cosmético
cosmic [ˈkɑzmɪk] *adj* cósmico
cosmonaut [ˈkɑzmə,nɔt] *s* cosmonauta *mf*
cosmopolitan [,kɑzməˈpɑlɪtən] *adj & s* cosmopolita *mf*
cosmos [ˈkɑzməs] *s* cosmos *m;* (bot) cosmos
Cossack [ˈkɑ,sæk] *adj & s* cosaco
cost [kɔst] o [kɑst] *s* coste *m,* costo; **at cost** a coste y costas; **at all costs** a toda costa; **costs** (law) costas ‖ *v* (*pret & pp* **cost**) *intr* costar; **cost what it may** cueste lo que cueste
cost accounting *s* escandallo
Costa Rican [ˈkɑstə ˈrikən] o [ˈkɔste ˈrikən] *adj & s* costarricense *mf,* costarriqueño
cost′-ben′e•fit analysis *s* análisis costebeneficio
cost exemption *s* gratuidad

cost, insurance, and freight costo, seguro y flete

cost•ly [ˈkɔstli] o [ˈkɑstli] *adj* (*comp* **-lier;** *super* **-liest**) costoso, dispendioso; (*lavish*) pródigo; (*magnificent*) suntuoso

cost of living *s* costo de la vida, carestía de la vida

costume [ˈkɑstjum] *s* traje *m;* (*garb worn on stage, at balls, etc.*) disfraz *m,* traje de época

costume ball *s* baile *m* de trajes

costume jewelry *s* joyas de fantasía, bisutería

cot [kɑt] *s* catre *m*

coterie [ˈkotəri] *s* círculo, grupo; (*clique*) corrillo

cottage [ˈkɑtɪdʒ] *s* cabaña; casita de campo

cottage cheese *s* naterón *m,* requesón *m*

cotter pin [ˈkɑtər] *s* chaveta

cotton [ˈkɑtən] *s* algodón *m* || *intr* — **to cotton up to** (coll) aficionarse a

cotton field *s* algodonal *m*

cotton gin *s* desmotadera de algodón

cotton picker [ˈpɪkər] *s* recogedor *m* de algodón; máquina para recolectar el algodón

cot'ton•seed' *s* semilla de algodón

cottonseed oil *s* aceite *m* de algodón

cotton waste *s* hilacha de algodón, estopa de algodón

cot'ton•wood' *s* chopo del Canadá, chopo de Virginia

cottony [ˈkɑtəni] *adj* algodonoso

couch [kaʊtʃ] *s* canapé *m,* sofá *m* || *tr* expresar

cougar [ˈkugər] *s* puma *m*

cough [kɔf] o [kɑf] *s* tos *f* || *tr* — **to cough up** arrojar por la boca; (slang) sudar, entregar || *intr* toser; (*artificially, to attract attention*) destoserse

cough drop *s* pastilla para la tos

cough syrup *s* jarabe *m* para la tos

could [kʊd] *v aux* pude, podía; podría

council [ˈkaʊnsəl] *s* (*deliberative or legislative assembly*) consejo; (*of a municipality*) concejo; (eccl) concilio

council•man [ˈkaʊnsəlmən] *s* (*pl* **-men** [mən]) concejal *m*

councilor [ˈkaʊnsələr] *s* consejero

coun•sel [ˈkaʊnsəl] *s* consejo; (*advisor*) consejero; (*consultant*) consultor *m;* (*lawyer*) abogado consultor; **to keep one's own counsel** no revelar sus intenciones || *v* (*pret & pp* **-seled** o **-selled; ger -seling** o **-selling**) *tr* aconsejar || *intr* aconsejarse

counselor [ˈkaʊnsələr] *s* consejero; abogado

count [kaʊnt] *s* (*act of counting*) cuenta, recuento; (*result of counting*) suma, total *m;* (*nobleman*) conde *m;* (*charge*) (law) cargo; **to take the count** (box) dejarse contar diez || *tr* contar; **to count off** separar contando; **to count out** no incluir; (sport) declarar vencido || *intr* contar; (*to be worth consideration*) valer; **to count for** valer; **to count on** contar con

countable [ˈkaʊntəbəl] *adj* contable

count'-down' *s* cuenta a cero, cuenta atrás

countenance [ˈkaʊntɪnəns] *s* cara, rostro, semblante *m;* (*composure*) compostura, serenidad; **to keep one's countenance** contenerse; **to lose countenance** conturbarse; **to put out of countenance** avergonzar, confundir || *tr* aprobar, apoyar, favorecer

counter [ˈkaʊntər] *adj* contrario || *adv* en el sentido opuesto; **counter to** a contrapelo de || *s* contador *m;* (*piece of wood or metal for keeping score*) ficha; (*board in shop over which business is transacted*) mostrador *m;* (box) contragolpe *m* || *tr* oponerse a; contradecir || *intr* (box) dar un contragolpe; **to counter with** replicar con

coun'ter•act' *tr* contrarrestar, contrariar

coun'ter•attack' *s* contraataque *m* || **coun'ter•attack'** *tr & intr* contraatacar

coun'ter•bal'ance *s* contrabalanza, contrapeso || **coun'ter•bal'ance** *tr* contrabalancear, contrapesar

coun'ter•clock'wise' *adj & adv* en el sentido contrario al de las agujas del reloj

coun'ter•cul'ture *s* contracultura

coun'ter•es'pionage *s* contraespionaje *m*

counterfeit [ˈkaʊntərfɪt] *adj* contrahecho, falsificado || *s* contrahechura, falsificación; moneda falsa || *tr* contrahacer, falsificar

counterfeiter [ˈkaʊntər,fɪtər] *s* contrahacedor *m,* falsificador *m;* monedero falso

counterfeit money *s* moneda falsa

countermand [ˈkaʊntər,mænd] o [ˈkaʊntər,mɑnd] *s* contramandato || *tr* contramandar; hacer volver

coun'ter•march' *s* contramarcha || *intr* contramarchar

coun'ter•offen'sive *s* contraofensiva

coun'ter•pane' *s* cubrecama

coun'ter•part' *s* contraparte *f;* copia, duplicado

coun'ter•plot' *s* contratreta || *v* (*pret & pp* **-plotted;** *ger* **-plotting**) *tr* complotar contra (*la treta de otro u otros*)

coun'ter•point' *s* contrapunto

Counter Reformation *s* Contrarreforma

coun'ter•rev'olu'tion *s* contrarrevolución

coun'ter•sign' *s* contraseña || *tr* refrendar

coun'ter•sink' *v* (*pret & pp* **-sunk**) *tr* avellanar

coun'ter•spy' *s* (*pl* **-spies**) contraespía *mf*

coun'ter•stroke' *s* contragolpe *m*

coun'ter•weight' *s* contrapeso

countess [ˈkaʊntɪs] *s* condesa

countless [ˈkaʊntlɪs] *adj* incontable, innumerable

countrified [ˈkʌntrɪ,faɪd] *adj* campesino, rústico

coun•try [ˈkʌntri] *s* (*pl* **-tries**) (*territory of a nation*) país *m;* (*land of one's birth*) patria; (*not the city*) campo

country club *s* club *m* campestre

country cousin *s* isidro

country estate *s* heredad, hacienda de campo

coun'try•folk' *s* gente *f* del campo, campesinos
country gentleman *s* propietario acomodado de finca rural
country house *s* casa de campo, quinta
country jake [dʒek] *s* (coll) patán *m*
country life *s* vida rural
country•man [ˈkʌntrimən] *s* (*pl* **-men** [mən]) compatriota *m;* campesino
country people *s* gente *f* del campo, gente de capa parda
coun'try•side' *s* campiña
coun'try•wide' *adj* nacional
country•woman [ˈkʌntrɪ,wʊmən] *s* (*pl* **-women** [,wɪmɪn]) compatriota *f;* campesina
coun•ty [ˈkaʊnti] *s* (*pl* **-ties**) (*small political unit*) partido; (*domain of a count*) condado
county seat *s* cabeza de partido
coup [ku] *s* golpe *m*
coup de grâce [ku də ˈgrɑs] *s* puñalada de misericordia, golpe *m* de gracia
coup d'état [ku deˈtɑ] *s* golpe *m* de estado
coupé [kuˈpe] *s* cupé *m*
couple [ˈkʌpəl] *s* par *m;* (*man and wife*) matrimonio; (*two people dancing together*) pareja; (elec, mech) par *m;* (*two more or less*) (coll) par *m* ‖ *tr* acoplar, juntar, unir ‖ *intr* juntarse, unirse
coupler [ˈkʌplər] *s* (rr) enganche *m*
couplet [ˈkʌplɪt] *s* copla, pareado
coupon [kuˈpɑn] o [kjuˈpɑn] *s* (*of a bond*) cupón *m;* (*piece detached from larger piece*) talón *m*
courage [ˈkʌrɪdʒ] *s* valor *m,* ánimo; firmeza, resolución; **to have the courage of one's convictions** ajustarse abiertamente con su conciencia; **to pluck up courage** hacer de tripas corazón
courageous [kəˈredʒəs] *adj* valiente, animoso
courier [ˈkʌrɪ•ər] o [ˈkʊrɪ•ər] *s* estafeta, mensajero; guía *m*
course [kors] *s* (*onward movement*) curso; (*of a ship*) derrota, rumbo; (*of time*) transcurso; (*of events*) marcha; (*in school*) asignatura, curso; (*of a meal*) plato; campo de golf; (mas) hilada; **in the course of** en el decurso de; **of course** por supuesto, naturalmente
court [kort] *s* (*of justice*) tribunal *m;* (*of a king*) corte *f;* (*open space enclosed by a building*) atrio, patio; (*for tennis*) cancha, pista; **to pay court to** hacer la corte a ‖ *tr* cortejar; buscar, solicitar
courteous [ˈkʌrtɪ•əs] *adj* cortés
courtesan [ˈkʌrtɪzən] o [ˈkortɪzən] *s* cortesana
courte•sy [ˈkʌrtɪsi] *s* (*pl* **-sies**) cortesía
court'house' *s* palacio de justicia
courtier [ˈkortɪ•ər] *s* cortesano, palaciego
court jester *s* bufón *m*
court•ly [ˈkortli] *adj* (*comp* **-lier;** *super* **-liest**) cortés, cortesano; (*pertaining to the court*) cortesano
court'-mar'tial *s* (*pl* **courts-martial**) consejo de guerra ‖ *v* (*pret & pp* **-tialed** o **-tialled;** *ger* **-tialing** o **-tialling**) *tr* someter a consejo de guerra
court plaster *s* tafetán *m* inglés
court'room' *s* sala de justicia, tribunal *m*
courtship [ˈkortʃɪp] *s* cortejo, galanteo; noviazgo
court'yard' *s* atrio, patio
cousin [ˈkʌzɪn] *s* primo
cove [kov] *s* cala, ensenada
covenant [ˈkʌvənənt] *s* convenio, pacto; contrato; (Bib) alianza ‖ *tr & intr* pactar
cover [ˈkʌvər] *s* cubierta; (*of a magazine*) portada; (*place for one person at table*) cubierto; (*for a bed*) cobertor *m;* **to take cover** ocultarse; **under cover** bajo cubierto, bajo techado; oculto; disfrazado; **under cover of** (*e.g., the night*) a cubierto de; so capa de; **under separate cover** bajo cubierta separada, por separado ‖ *tr* cubrir; (*to line, to coat*) recubrir, revestir; recorrer (*cierta distancia*); cubrirse (*la cabeza*); tapar (*una olla*) ‖ *intr* cubrirse
coverage [ˈkʌvərɪdʒ] *s* (*amount or space covered*) alcance *m;* (*of news*) reportaje *m;* (*funds to meet liabilities*) cobertura
coveralls [ˈkʌvər,ɔlz] *s* mono
cover charge *s* precio del cubierto
covered [ˈkʌvərd] *adj* cubierto; (*wire*) forrado; (*bridge*) cubierto
covered wagon *s* carromato
cover girl *s* (coll) muchacha hermosa en la portada de una revista
covering [ˈkʌvərɪŋ] *s* cubierta, envoltura
covert [ˈkʌvərt] *adj* disimulado, secreto
cov'er•up' *s* efugio, subterfugio
covet [ˈkʌvɪt] *tr* codiciar
covetous [ˈkʌvɪtəs] *adj* codicioso
covetousness [ˈkʌvɪtəsnɪs] *s* codicia
covey [ˈkʌvi] *s* (*brood*) nidada; (*in flight*) bandada; corro, grupo
cow [kaʊ] *s* vaca ‖ *tr* acobardar, intimidar
coward [ˈkaʊ•ərd] *s* cobarde *mf*
cowardice [ˈkaʊ•ərdɪs] *s* cobardía; llamada (Mex)
cowardly [ˈkaʊ•ərdli] *adj* cobarde; correlón (Col, Mex); llamón (Mex) ‖ *adv* cobardemente
cow'bell' *s* cencerro
cow'boy' *s* vaquero; gaucho (Arg)
cowcatcher [ˈkaʊ,kætʃər] *s* quitapiedras *m,* rastrillo; trompa (Col, Chile)
cower [ˈkaʊ•ər] *intr* agacharse
cow'herd' *s* vaquero, pastor *m* de ganado vacuno
cow'hide' *s* cuero; (*whip*) zurriago ‖ *tr* zurriagar
cowl [kaʊl] *s* capucha, cogulla; (aer) cubierta del motor; (aut) cubretablero, bóveda
cow'lick' *s* mechón *m,* remolino (*pelos que se levantan sobre la frente*)
cowpox [ˈkaʊ,pɑks] *s* vacuna
coxcomb [ˈkɑks,kom] *s* petimetre *m,* mequetrefe *m*
coxswain [ˈkɑksən] o [ˈkɑk,swen] *s* timonel *m;* contramaestre *m*
coy [kɔɪ] *adj* recatado, modesto; coquetón

co•zy [ˈkozi] *adj* (*comp* **-zier;** *super* **-ziest)** cómodo || *s* (*pl* **-zies**) cubretetera
cp. *abbr* **compare**
c.p. *abbr* **candle power**
C.P.A. *abbr* **certified public accountant**
cpd. *abbr* **compound**
cr. *abbr* **credit, creditor**
crab [kræb] *s* cangrejo; (*grouch*) cascarrabias *mf*
crab apple *s* manzana silvestre
crabbed [ˈkræbɪd] *adj* avinagrado, ceñudo
crab grass *s* garranchuelo
crab louse *s* ladilla
crack [kræk] *adj* (coll) de primera clase; (*shot*) (coll) certero || *s* grieta, hendidura; (*noise*) crujido, estallido; (coll) instante *m,* momento; (*joke*) (slang) chiste *m;* **at the crack of dawn** al romper el alba || *tr* agrietar, hender; chasquear (*un látigo*); abrir (*una caja fuerte*) por la fuerza; cascar (*nueces*); descifrar (*un código*); (slang) decir (*un chiste*); (slang) descubrir (*un secreto*); **to crack a smile** (slang) sonreír; **to crack up** (coll) alabar, elogiar || *intr* agrietarse; crujir; cascarse (*la voz de una persona*); enloquecerse; ceder, someterse; **to crack up** fracasar; perder la salud; estrellarse (*un avión*)
cracked [krækt] *adj* agrietado; (*ice*) picado; (coll) mentecato, loco
cracker [ˈkrækər] *s* galleta
crack'le•ware' *s* grietado
crack'pot' *adj & s* (slang) excéntrico, tarambana *mf*
crack'up' *s* fracaso; colisión; derrota; (aer) aterrizaje violento; (coll) colapso
cradle [ˈkredəl] *s* cuna; (*of handset*) horquilla || *tr* acunar
cra'dle•song' *s* canción de cuna, arrullo
craft [kræft] o [krɑft] *s* arte *m,* arte manual; astucia, maña; nave *f* || *spl* naves
craftiness [ˈkræftɪnɪs] *s* astucia
crafts•man [ˈkræftsmən] *s* (*pl* **-men** [mən]) artesano; artista *m*
craftsmanship [ˈkræftsmən,ʃɪp] *s* artesanía
craft•y [ˈkræfti] o [ˈkrɑfti] *adj* (*comp* **-ier;** *super* **-iest)** astuto, mañoso
crag [kræg] *s* peñasco, despeñadero
cram [kræm] *v* (*pret & pp* **crammed;** *ger* **cramming)** *tr* atascar, atracar, embutir; (coll) aprender apresuradamente || *intr* atracarse; (*to study hard*) (coll) empollar
cramp [kræmp] *s* (*metal bar*) grapa, laña; (*clamp*) abrazadera; (*painful contraction of muscle*) calambre *m;* **cramps** retortijón *m* de tripas || *tr* engrapar, lañar; apretar; dar calambre a
cranber•ry [ˈkræn,bɛri] *s* (*pl* **-ries**) arándano agrio
crane [kren] *s* (*bird*) grulla; (*derrick*) grúa, guinche *m,* güinche *m* || *tr* estirar (*el cuello*) || *intr* estirar el cuello
crani•um [ˈkrenɪ•əm] *s* (*pl* **-a** [ə]) cráneo
crank [kræŋk] *s* manivela, manubrio; (coll) estrafalario || *tr* hacer girar (*el motor*) con la manivela
crank'case' *s* caja de cigüeñal, cárter *m* del cigüeñal
crank'shaft' *s* cigüeñal *m*
crank•y [ˈkræŋki] *adj* (*comp* **-ier;** *super* **-iest)** malhumorado; (*queer*) estrafalario
cran•ny [ˈkræni] *s* (*pl* **-nies**) hendidura, grieta, rendija
crape [krep] *s* crespón *m;* crespón fúnebre, crespón negro
crape'hang'er *s* (slang) aguafiestas *mf*
craps [kræps] *s* juego de dados; **to shoot craps** jugar a los dados
crash [kræʃ] *s* caída, desplome *m;* colisión, choque *m;* estallido, estrépito; fracaso; crac financiero; lienzo grueso; (aer) aterrizaje violento || *tr* romper con estrépito, estrellar; **to crash a party** (slang) asistir a una fiesta sin invitación; **to crash the gate** (slang) colarse de gorra || *intr* caer, desplomarse; romperse con estrépito, estallar; (*in business*) quebrar; aterrizar violentamente, estrellarse (*un avión*); **to crash into** chocar con
crash dive *s* sumersión instantánea (*de submarino*)
crash landing *s* aterrizaje violento
crash program *s* programa intensivo
crash test *s* (aut) ensayo de choque
crass [kræs] *adj* espeso, tosco; (*ignorance, mistake*) craso
crate [kret] *s* (*box made of slats*) jaula; (*basket*) banasta, cuévano || *tr* embalar en jaula, embalar con listones
crater [ˈkretər] *s* cráter *m*
cravat [krəˈvæt] *s* corbata
crave [krev] *tr* anhelar, ansiar; pedir (*indulgencia*) || *intr* — **to crave for** anhelar, ansiar; pedir con insistencia
craven [ˈkrevən] *adj & s* cobarde *mf*
craving [ˈkrevɪŋ] *s* anhelo, ansia, deseo ardiente
craw [krɔ] *s* buche *m*
crawl [krɔl] *s* arrastre *m;* gateado || *intr* reptar, arrastarse, gatear; (*to have a feeling of insects on skin*) hormiguear; **to crawl along** andar paso a paso; **to crawl up** trepar
crayon [ˈkre•ən] *s* creyón *m*
craze [krez] *s* boga, moda; locura, manía || *tr* enloquecer
cra•zy [ˈkrezi] *adj* (*comp* **-zier;** *super* **-ziest)** loco; (*rickety*) desvencijado; achacoso, débil; **crazy as a bedbug** (slang) loco de atar; **to be crazy about** (coll) estar loco por; **to drive crazy** volver loco
crazy bone *s* hueso de la alegría
creak [krik] *s* crujido, rechinamiento || *intr* crujir, rechinar
creak•y [ˈkriki] *adj* (*comp* **-ier;** *super* **-iest)** crujidero, rechinador
cream [krim] *s* crema; (*e.g., of society*) crema, nata y flor || *tr* desnatar (*la leche*)
creamer•y [ˈkriməri] *s* (*pl* **-ies**) mantequería, quesería, lechería
cream puff *s* bollo de crema
cream separator *s* desnatadora

cream•y [ˈkrimi] *adj* (*comp* **-ier;** *super* **-iest**) cremoso
crease [kris] *s* arruga, pliegue *m;* (*in trousers*) raya ‖ *tr* arrugar, plegar
create [kriˈet] *tr* crear
creation [kriˈeʃən] *s* creación
creative [kriˈetɪv] *adj* creativo
creator [kriˈetər] *s* creador *m*
creature [ˈkritʃər] *s* criatura; (*being, strange being*) ente *m;* animal *m*
credence [ˈkridəns] *s* creencia; **to give credence to** dar fe a
credentials [krɪˈdɛnʃəlz] *spl* credenciales *fpl*
credible [ˈkrɛdɪbəl] *adj* creíble
credit [ˈkrɛdɪt] *s* crédito; **to take credit for** atribuirse el mérito de ‖ *tr* acreditar; **to credit a person with** atribuirle a una persona el mérito de
creditable [ˈkrɛdɪtəbəl] *adj* honorable, estimable
credit card *s* tarjeta de crédito
creditor [ˈkrɛdɪtər] *s* acreedor *m*
cre•do [ˈkrido] o [ˈkredo] *s* (*pl* **-dos**) credo
credulous [ˈkrɛdʒələs] *adj* crédulo; creído
creed [krid] *s* credo
creek [krik] *s* arroyo, riachuelo
creep [krip] *v* (*pret & pp* **crept** [krɛpt]) *intr* arrastrarse; (*on all fours*) gatear; (*to climb*) trepar; (*with a sensation of insects*) hormiguear; **to creep up on** acercarse insensiblemente a
creeper [ˈkripər] *s* planta rastrera, planta trepadora
creeping [ˈkripɪŋ] *adj* lento, progresivo; (*plant*) rastrero ‖ *s* arrastramiento
cremate [ˈkrimet] *tr* incinerar
cremation [krɪˈmeʃən] *s* cremación, incineración
cremato•ry [ˈkriməˌtori] *adj* crematorio ‖ *s* (*pl* **-ries**) crematorio
crème de menthe [krɛm də ˈmɑ̃t] *s* crema de menta
Creole [ˈkri•ol] *adj & s* criollo
crescent [ˈkrɛsənt] *s* (*moon in first or last quarter*) creciente *f* de la luna; (*shape of moon in either of these phases*) media luna; panecillo (*en forma de media luna*)
cress [krɛs] *s* mastuerzo
crest [krɛst] *s* cresta
crestfallen [ˈkrɛstˌfɔlən] *adj* cabizbajo
crest'-line' model *s* (aut) modelo estrella
Cretan [ˈkritən] *adj & s* cretense *mf*
Crete [krit] *s* Creta
cretonne [krɪˈtɑn] *s* cretona
crevice [ˈkrɛvɪs] *s* grieta
crew [kru] *s* equipo; (*of a ship*) dotación, tripulación; (*group, esp. of armed men*) banda, cuadrilla
crew cut *s* corte *m* de pelo a cepillo
crib [krɪb] *s* pesebre *m;* camita de niño; (coll) plagio; (*student's pony*) (coll) chuleta ‖ *v* (*pret & pp* **cribbed;** *ger* **cribbing**) *tr & intr* (coll) hurtar
cricket [ˈkrɪkɪt] *s* (ent) grillo; (sport) cricquet *m;* (coll) juego limpio
crier [ˈkraɪ•ər] *s* pregonero
crime [kraɪm] *s* crimen *m,* delito
criminal [ˈkrɪmɪnəl] *adj & s* criminal *mf;* delictivo
criminal code *s* código penal
criminal law *s* derecho penal
criminal negligence *s* imprudencia temeraria
criminology [ˌkrɪməˈnɑlədʒi] *s* criminología
crimp [krɪmp] *s* rizado, rizo; **to put a crimp in** (coll) estorbar, impedir ‖ *tr* rizar
crimple [ˈkrɪmpəl] *tr* arrugar, rizar ‖ *intr* arrugarse, rizarse
crimson [ˈkrɪmzən] *adj & s* carmesí *m* ‖ *intr* enrojecerse
cringe [krɪndʒ] *intr* arrastrarse, reptar, encogerse
crinkle [ˈkrɪŋkəl] *s* arruga, pliegue *m;* (*in the water*) rizo u onda ‖ *tr* arrugar, plegar ‖ *intr* arrugarse
cripple [ˈkrɪpəl] *s* zopo, lisiado ‖ *tr* lisiar, estropear; dañar, perjudicar
cri•sis [ˈkraɪsɪs] *s* (*pl* **-ses**) [siz]) crisis *f*
crisp [krɪsp] *adj* frágil, quebradizo; (*air, weather*) refrescante; decisivo
criteri•on [kraɪˈtɪrɪ•ən] *s* (*pl* **-a** [ə]) u **-ons**) criterio
critic [ˈkrɪtɪk] *s* crítico; (*reviewer*) reseñador; (*faultfinder*) criticón *m*
critical [ˈkrɪtɪkəl] *adj* crítico; (*faultfinding*) criticón
criticism [ˈkrɪtɪˌsɪzəm] *s* crítica
criticize [ˈkrɪtɪˌsaɪz] *tr & intr* criticar
critique [krɪˈtik] *s* (*art of criticism*) crítica; ensayo crítico
croak [krok] *s* (*of raven*) graznido; canto de ranas ‖ *intr* graznar (*el cuervo*); croar (*la rana*); (*morir*) (slang) reventar
Croat [ˈkro•æt] *s* (*native or inhabitant*) croata *mf;* (*language*) croata *m*
Croatian [kroˈeʃən] *adj & mf* croata *mf*
cro•chet [kroˈʃe] *s* croché *m* ‖ *v* (*pret & pp* **-cheted** [ˈʃed]; *ger* **-cheting** [ˈʃe•ɪŋ]) *tr* trabajar con aguja de gancho ‖ *intr* hacer croché
crocheting [kroˈʃə•ɪŋ] *s* labor *f* de ganchillo
crochet needle *s* aguja de gancho
crock [krɑk] *s* cacharro, vasija de barro cocido
crockery [ˈkrɑkəri] *s* loza
crocodile [ˈkrɑkəˌdaɪl] *s* cocodrilo
crocodile tears *spl* lágrimas de cocodrilo
crocus [ˈkrokəs] *s* azafrán *m,* croco
crone [kron] *s* vieja acartonada, vieja arrugada
cro•ny [ˈkroni] *s* (*pl* **-nies**) compinche *mf*
crook [krʊk] *s* gancho, garfio; curva; (*of shepherd*) cayado; (coll) fullero, ladrón *m;* chalecón *m* (Mex) ‖ *tr* encorvar; (slang) empinar (*el codo*) ‖ *intr* encorvarse
crooked [ˈkrʊkɪd] *adj* encorvado, torcido; (*person or his conduct*) torcido; **to go crooked** (coll) torcerse
croon [krun] *intr* cantar con voz suave, cantar con melancolía exagerada
crooner [ˈkrunər] *s* cantor de voz suave, cantor melancólico
crop [krɑp] *s* cosecha; (*head of hair*) cabellera; cabello corto; (*of a bird*) buche *m;* (*whip*) látigo; (*of appointments, promo-*

tions, heroes, etc.) hornada || *v* (*pret & pp* **cropped;** *ger* **cropping**) *tr* desmochar (*un árbol*); desorejar (*a un animal*); esquilar, trasquilar || *intr* — **to crop out** o **up** aflorar; asomar, dejarse ver, manifestarse inesperadamente

crop dusting *s* aerofumigación, fumigación aérea

croquet [kro'ke] *s* crocquet *m*

croquette [kro'kɛt] *s* croqueta

crosier ['kroʒər] *s* báculo pastoral, cayado

cross [krɑs] o [krɔs] *adj* transversal, travieso; (*breed*) cruzado; malhumorado, enfadado || *s* cruz *f;* (*of races; of two roads*) cruce *m;* **to take the cross** (*to join a crusade*) cruzarse || *tr* cruzar; (*to oppose*) contrariar, frustrar; **to cross off** u **out** borrar; **to cross oneself** hacerse la señal de la cruz; **to cross one's mind** ocurrírsele a uno; **to cross one's t's** poner travesaño a las tes, poner el palo a las tes || *intr* cruzar; cruzarse; **to cross over** atravesar de un lado a otro

cross'bones' *spl* huesos cruzados (*símbolo de la muerte*)

cross'bow' *s* ballesta

cross'breed' *v* (*pret & pp* **-bred** [,brɛd]) *tr* cruzar (*animales o plantas*)

cross'coun'try *adj* a campo traviesa; a través del país

cross'cur'rent contracorriente *f;* (fig) tendencia encontrada

cross'-exam'i•na'tion *s* interrogatorio riguroso; (law) repregunta

cross'ex•am'ine *tr* interrogar rigurosamente; (law) repreguntar

cross-eyed ['krɑs,aɪd] *adj* bisojo, bizco, ojituerto

crossing ['krɑsɪŋ] *s* (*of lines, streets, etc.*) cruce *m;* (*of the ocean*) travesía; (*of a river*) vado; (rr) crucero, paso a nivel

crossing gate *s* barrera, barrera de paso a nivel

crossing point *s* punto de cruce

cross'patch' *s* (coll) gruñón *m*

cross'piece' *s* travesaño

cross reference *s* contrarreferencia, remisión

cross'road' *s* vía transversal; **crossroads** encrucijada, cruce *m;* **at the crossroads** en el momento crítico

cross section *s* corte *m* transversal; (fig) sección representativa

cross street *s* calle traviesa, calle de travesía

cross'word' puzzle *s* crucigrama *m*

crotch [krɑtʃ] *s* (*forked piece*) horcajadura, bifurcación; (*between legs*) entrepierna, bragadura, horcajadura

crotchety ['krɑtʃɪti] *adj* caprichoso, estrambótico, de mal genio

crouch [krautʃ] *s* posición agachada || *intr* agacharse, acuclillarse

croup [krup] *s* garrotillo, crup *m;* (*of horse*) anca, grupa

croupier ['krupɪ•ər] *s* crupié *m*

crouton ['krutɑn] *s* corteza de pan

crow [kro] *s* corneja, grajo, chova; (*cry of the cock*) quiquiriquí *m;* (*crowbar*) alzaprima; **as the crow flies** a vuelo de pájaro; **to eat crow** (coll) cantar la palinodia; **to have a crow to pick with** (coll) tener que habérselas con || *intr* cantar (*el gallo*); jactarse; **to crow over** jactarse de

crow'bar' *s* alzaprima, pie *m* de cabra

crowd [kraud] *s* gentío, multitud; (*flock of people*) caterva, tropel *m;* (*mob, common people*) populacho, vulgo; (*clique, set*) corrillo, grupo || *tr* apiñar, apretar, atestar; (*to push*) empujar || *intr* apiñarse, apretarse, atestarse; (*to mill around*) arremolinarse

crowded ['kraudɪd] *adj* atestado, concurrido

crown [kraun] *s* corona; (*of hat*) copa || *tr* coronar; (checkers) coronar; (slang) golpear en la cabeza

crowned head *s* testa coronada

crown prince *s* príncipe heredero

crown princess *s* princesa heredera

crow's'-foot' *s* (*pl* **-feet'**) pata de gallo

crow's'-nest' *s* (naut) cofa de vigía, torre *f* de vigía

crucial ['kruʃəl] *adj* crucial; difícil, penoso

crucible ['krusɪbəl] *s* crisol *m*

crucifix ['krusɪfɪks] *s* crucifijo

crucifixion [,krusɪ'fɪkʃən] *s* crucifixión

cruci•fy ['krusɪ,faɪ] *v* (*pret & pp* **-fied**) *tr* crucificar

crude [krud] *adj* (*raw, unrefined*) crudo; (*lacking culture*) grosero, tosco; (*unfinished*) basto, sin labrar

crudi•ty ['krudɪti] *s* (*pl* **-ties**) crudeza; grosería, tosquedad; bastedad

cruel ['kru•əl] *adj* cruel

cruel•ty ['kru•əlti] *s* (*pl* **-ties**) crueldad

cruet ['kru•ɪt] *s* ampolleta

cruet stand *s* angarillas, vinagreras

cruise [kruz] *s* viaje *m* por mar; (aer, naut) crucero || *tr* (naut) cruzar || *intr* cruzar; (coll) andar de un lado a otro

cruise missile *s* misil *m* crucero

cruiser ['kruzər] *s* (nav) crucero

cruising ['kruzɪŋ] *adj* de crucero || *s* (aer, naut) crucero

cruising radius *s* autonomía

cruising speed *s* velocidad de crucero

cruller ['krʌlər] *s* buñuelo

crumb [krʌm] *s* migaja; (*soft part of bread*) miga; (*given to a beggar*) mendrugo || *tr* desmigar (*el pan*); (culin) empanar, cubrir con pan rallado; limpiar (*la mesa*) de migajas || *intr* desmigarse, desmenuzarse

crumble ['krʌmbəl] *tr* desmenuzar || *intr* desmenuzarse; (*to fall to pieces gradually*) desmoronarse

crum•my ['krʌmi] *adj* (*comp* **-mier;** *super* **-miest**) (slang) desaseado, sucio; (slang) de mal gusto, de mala muerte

crumple ['krʌmpəl] *tr* arrugar, ajar, chafar || *intr* arrugarse, ajarse

crunch [krʌntʃ] *tr* ronchar, ronzar || *intr* crujir

crusade [kru'sed] *s* cruzada || *intr* hacer una cruzada

crusader [kru'sedər] *s* cruzado

crush [krʌʃ] *s* aplastamiento; (*of people*) aglomeración, bullaje *m;* **to have a crush on**

(slang) estar perdido por || *tr* aplastar, machacar, magullar; (*to grind*) moler; bocartear (*el mineral*); (*to oppress, grieve*) abrumar

crush hat *s* clac *m*

crust [krʌst] *s* corteza; corteza de pan; (*scab*) costra

crustacean [krʌsˈteʃən] *s* crustáceo

crustaceous [krʌsˈteʃəs] *adj* crustáceo

crust•y [ˈkrʌsti] *adj* (*comp* **-ier;** *super* **-iest**) (*scabby*) costroso; áspero, grosero, rudo

crutch [krʌtʃ] *s* muleta

crux [krʌks] *s* punto capital; enigma *m*

cry [kraɪ] *s* (*pl* **cries**) grito; (*weeping*) lloro, llorera; (*of peddler*) pregón *m;* (*of wolf*) aullido; (*of bull*) bramido; **in full cry** en plena persecución; **to have a good cry** desahogarse en lágrimas abundantes || *v* (*pret & pp* **cried**) *tr* decir a gritos; (*to announce publicly*) pregonar; **to cry one's eyes** o **heart out** llorar amargamente; **to cry out** decir a gritos; pregonar || *intr* gritar; (*to weep*) llorar; aullar (*el lobo*); bramar (*el toro*); **to cry for** clamar por; **to cry for joy** llorar de alegría; **to cry out** clamar; **to cry out against** clamar contra; **to cry out for** clamar, clamar por

cry'ba'by *s* (*pl* **-bies**) llorón *m*, llorona, lloraduelos *mf*

crypt [krɪpt] *s* cripta

cryptic(al) [ˈkrɪptɪk(əl)] *adj* enigmático, misterioso

crystal [ˈkrɪstəl] *s* cristal *m*

crystal ball *s* bola de cristal

crystalline [ˈkrɪstəlɪn] o [ˈkrɪstə,laɪn] *adj* cristalino

crystallize [ˈkrɪstə,laɪz] *tr* cristalizar || *intr* cristalizarse

C.S. *abbr* **Christian Science, Civil Service**

ct. *abbr* **cent**

cu. *abbr* **cubic**

cub [kʌb] *s* cachorro

Cuban [ˈkjubən] *adj & s* cubano

cubbyhole [ˈkʌbɪ,hol] *s* chiribitil *m*

cube [kjub] *adj* (*root*) cúbico || *s* cubo; (*of ice*) cubito || *tr* cubicar

cubic [ˈkjubɪk] *adj* cúbico

cub reporter *s* (coll) reportero novato

cuckold [ˈkʌkəld] *adj & s* cornudo || *tr* encornudar

cuckoo [ˈkʊkʊ] *adj* (slang) mentecato, loco || *s* cuclillo, cuco; (*call of cuckoo*) cucú *m*

cuckoo clock *s* reloj *m* de cuclillo

cucumber [ˈkjukəmbər] *s* pepino

cud [kʌd] *s* bolo alimenticio; **to chew the cud** rumiar

cuddle [ˈkʌdəl] *s* abrazo cariñoso || *tr* abrazar con cariño || *intr* estar abrazados, arrimarse cariñosamente

cudg•el [ˈkʌdʒəl] *s* garrote *m*, porra; **to take up the cudgels for** salir a la defensa de || *v* (*pret & pp* **-eled** o **-elled;** *ger* **-eling** o **-elling**) *tr* apalear, aporrear

cue [kju] *s* señal *f*, indicación; (*hint*) indirecta; (*rôle*) papel *m;* (*rod used in billiards*) taco; (*of hair*) coleta; (*of people in line*) cola; (theat) apunte *m*

cuff [kʌf] *s* (*of shirt*) puño; (*of trousers*) doblez *f*, vuelta; (*blow*) bofetada || *tr* abofetear

cuff links *spl* gemelos

cuirass [kwɪˈræs] *s* coraza

cuisine [kwɪˈzin] *s* cocina (*arte culinario*)

culinary [ˈkjulɪ,nɛri] *adj* culinario

cull [kʌl] *tr* (*to choose, pick*) entresacar, escoger; (*to gather, pluck*) coger, recoger

culm [kʌlm] *s* (*coal dust*) cisco; (*stalk of grasses*) caña, tallo

culminate [ˈkʌlmɪ,net] *intr* culminar; **to culminate in** conducir a, terminar en

culpable [ˈkʌlpəbəl] *adj* culpable

culprit [ˈkʌlprɪt] *s* acusado; reo

cult [kʌlt] *s* culto; secta

cultivate [ˈkʌltɪ,vet] *tr* cultivar

cultivated [ˈkʌltɪ,vetɪd] *adj* culto, cultivado

cultivation [,kʌltɪˈveʃən] *s* (*of the land, the arts, one's memory, etc.*) cultivo; (*refinement*) cultura

culture [ˈkʌltʃər] *s* cultura

cultured [ˈkʌltʃərd] *adj* culto

culvert [ˈkʌlvərt] *s* alcantarilla

cumbersome [ˈkʌmbərsəm] *adj* incómodo, molesto; (*clumsy*) pesado, inmanejable

cunning [ˈkʌnɪŋ] *adj* (*sly*) astuto; (*clever*) hábil; (*attractive*) gracioso, mono || *s* astucia; habilidad, destreza

cup [kʌp] *s* taza; (*of thermometer*) cubeta; (mach) vaso de engrase; (sport) copa; (*of sorrow*) (fig) copa; **in one's cups** borracho || *v* (*pret & pp* **cupped;** *ger* **cupping**) *tr* ahuecar dando forma de taza o copa a; poner ventosa a

cupboard [ˈkʌbərd] *s* alacena, aparador *m*, armario

cupidity [kjʊˈpɪdɪti] *s* codicia

cupola [ˈkjupələ] *s* cúpula

cur [kʌr] *s* perro mestizo, perro de mala raza; (*despicable fellow*) canalla *m*

curate [ˈkjurɪt] *s* cura *m*

curative [ˈkjurətɪv] *adj* curativo || *s* curativa

curator [kjʊˈretər] *s* conservador *m*

curb [kʌrb] *s* (*of sidewalk*) encintado; (*of well*) brocal *m;* (*of bit*) barbada; (*market*) bolsín *m;* (*check, restraint*) freno; (vet) corva || *tr* contener, refrenar

curb'stone' *s* piedra de encintado; brocal *m* de pozo

curd [kʌrd] *s* cuajada || *tr* cuajar || *intr* cuajarse

curdle [ˈkʌrdəl] *tr* cuajar; **to curdle the blood** horrorizar || *intr* cuajar

cure [kjʊr] *s* cura, curación || *tr* curar || *intr* curar; curarse

cure'-all' *s* sanalotodo

curfew [ˈkʌrfju] *s* queda, cubrefuego; toque *m* de queda; hora de cierre

curi•o [ˈkjʊrɪ,o] *s* (*pl* **-os**) curiosidad

curiosi•ty [,kjʊrɪˈɑsɪti] *s* (*pl* **-ties**) curiosidad

curious [ˈkjʊrɪ•əs] *adj* curioso

curl [kʌrl] *s* bucle *m*, rizo; (*spiral-shaped curl*) tirabuzón *m;* (*of smoke*) espiral *f;* (*curling*) rizado || *tr* encrespar, ensortijar, rizar; (*to coil, to roll up*) arrollar; fruncir (*los labios*) || *intr* encresparse, ensortijarse, rizarse; arrollarse; **to curl up** arrollarse; (*in bed*) encogerse; (*to break up, collapse*) (coll) desplomarse

curler [ˈkʌrlər] *s* (*hair*) rulo, bigudí *m*

curlicue [ˈkʌrlɪ,kju] *s* ringorrango

curling iron *s* rizador *m*, maquinilla de rizar

curl'pa'per *s* torcida, papelito para rizar el pelo

curl•y [ˈkʌrli] *adj* (*comp* **-ier;** *super* **-iest**) crespo, rizo

curmudgeon [kərˈmʌdʒən] *s* cicatero, tacaño, erizo

currant [ˈkʌrənt] *s* pasa de Corinto; (*Ribes alpinum*) calderilla

curren•cy [ˈkʌrənsi] *s* (*pl* **-cies**) moneda corriente, dinero en circulación; uso corriente

current [ˈkʌrənt] *adj* corriente || *s* corriente *f;* (elec) corriente *f*

current account *s* cuenta corriente

current events *spl* actualidades, sucesos de actualidad

curricu•lum [kəˈrɪkjələm] *s* (*pl* **-lums** o **-la** [lə]) plan *m* de estudios

cur•ry [ˈkʌri] *s* (*pl* **-ries**) cari *m* || *v* (*pret & pp* **-ried**) *tr* curtir (*las pieles*); almohazar (*el caballo*); **to curry favor** procurar complacer

cur'ry•comb' *s* almohaza || *tr* almohazar

curse [kʌrs] *s* maldición; (*profane oath*) reniego, voto; (*evil, misfortune*) calamidad || *tr* maldecir || *intr* jurar, echar votos; echar carnes (Mex)

cursed [ˈkʌrsɪd] o [kʌrst] *adj* maldito; aborrecible

cursive [ˈkʌrsɪv] *adj* cursivo || *s* cursiva

cursory [ˈkʌrsəri] *adj* apresurado, rápido, superficial, de paso

curt [kʌrt] *adj* áspero, brusco; corto, conciso

curtail [kərˈtel] *tr* acortar, abreviar, cercenar

curtain [ˈkʌrtən] *s* cortina; (theat) telón *m;* **to draw the curtain** correr la cortina; **to drop the curtain** (theat) bajar el telón || *tr* encortinar; separar con cortina; cubrir, ocultar

curtain call *s* llamada a la escena para recibir aplausos

curtain raiser [ˈrezər] *s* (theat) pieza preliminar

curtain ring *s* anilla

curtain rod *s* riel *m*

curt•sy [ˈkʌrtsi] *s* (*pl* **-sies**) cortesía, reverencia || *v* (*pret & pp* **-sied**) *intr* hacer una cortesía

curve [kʌrv] *s* curva || *tr* encorvar || *intr* encorvarse; volver, virar

curved [kʌrvd] *adj* curvo, encorvado; (*crooked*) combo

cushion [ˈkʊʃən] *s* cojín *m*, almohada; (*of billiard table*) baranda || *tr* amortiguar

cusp [kʌsp] *s* cúspide *f*

cuspidor [ˈkʌspɪ,dɔr] *s* escupidera

custard [ˈkʌstərd] *s* flan *m*, natillas

custodian [kəsˈtodɪ•ən] *s* custodio; (*of a house or building*) casero

custo•dy [ˈkʌstədi] *s* (*pl* **-dies**) custodia; **in custody** en prisión; **to take into custody** prender

custom [ˈkʌstəm] *s* costumbre; (*customers*) parroquia, clientela; **customs** aduana; derechos de aduana

customary [ˈkʌstə,mɛri] *adj* acostumbrado, de costumbre

cus'tom-built' *adj* hecho por encargo, fuera de serie

customer [ˈkʌstəmər] *s* parroquiano, cliente *mf;* (*of a café or restaurant*) consumidor *m;* (coll) individuo, sujeto, tipo

customer service *s* servicio postventa

cus'tom•house' *adj* aduanero || *s* aduana

cus'tom-made' *adj* hecho a la medida

customs clearance *s* despacho de aduana

customs officer *s* aduanero

custom tailor *s* sastre *m* a la medida

custom work *s* trabajo hecho a la medida

cut [kʌt] *s* corte *m;* (*piece cut off*) tajada; (*wound*) cuchillada; (*for a canal, highway, etc.*) desmonte *m;* (*shortest way*) atajo; (*in prices, wages, etc.*) reducción; (*of a garment*) corte *m*, hechura; (*in winnings, earnings, etc.*) parte *f;* (*diamond*) talla; (typ) estampa, grabado; (tennis) golpe *m* cortante; (*absence from school*) (coll) falta de asistencia; (*snub*) (coll) desaire *m;* (coll) palabra hiriente || *v* (*pret & pp* **cut;** *ger* **cutting**) *tr* cortar; practicar (*un agujero*); reducir (*gastos*); capar, castrar; desleír, diluir; (coll) ausentarse de, faltar a (*la clase*); (coll) desairar; (coll) herir; **to cut down** cortar; derribar cortando; castigar (*gastos*); **to cut off** cortar; desheredar; amputar (*una pierna*); (elec) cortar (*la corriente, la ignición*); cerrar (*el carburador*); **to cut open** abrir cortando; **to cut out** cortar; sacar cortando; labrar; suprimir, omitir; (*to take the place of*) desbancar; soplar (*la dama a un rival*); (slang) dejarse de (*disparates*); **to cut short** terminar de repente; interrumpir, chafar; **to cut teeth** endentecer; **to cut up** desmenuzar, despedazar; criticar severamente; (coll) afligir || *intr* cortar; cortarse; salir (*los dientes*); (coll) fumarse la clase; **to cut in** entrar de repente; interrumpir; (*in a dance*) cortar o separar la pareja; **to cut under** vender a menor precio que; **to cut up** (slang) travesear, hacer travesuras; (slang) jaranear

cut-and-dried [ˈkʌtənˈdraɪd] *adj* dispuesto de antemano; monótono, poco interesante

cutaway coat [ˈkʌtə,we] *s* chaqué *m*

cut'back' *s* reducción; discontinuación, incumplimiento; (mov) retorno a una época anterior

cute [kjut] *adj* (coll) mono, monono; (coll) astuto, listo

cut glass *s* cristal tallado

cuticle [ˈkjutɪkəl] *s* cutícula

cutlass [ˈkʌtləs] *s* alfanje *m*

cutler [ˈkʌtlər] *s* cuchillero

cutlery [ˈkʌtləri] *s* cuchillería; (*knives, forks, and spoons*) cubierto

cutlet [ˈkʌtlɪt] *s* chuleta; croqueta

cut'out' *s* (*design to be cut out*) recortado; (aut) escape *m* libre, válvula de escape libre

cut'-rate' *adj* de precio reducido
cutter ['kʌtər] *s* cortador *m;* (*machine*) cortadora; (naut) escampavía
cut'throat' *adj* asesino; implacable || *s* asesino
cutting ['kʌtɪŋ] *adj* cortante; hiriente, mordaz || *s* corte *m;* (*from a newspaper*) recorte *m;* (hort) esqueje *m*
cutting edge *s* canto de corte
cuttlefish ['kʌtəl,fɪʃ] *s* jibia
cut'wa'ter *s* espolón *m,* tajamar *m*
cwt. *abbr* **hundredweight**
cyanamide [saɪ'ænə,maɪd] *s* cianamida; cianamida de calcio
cyanide ['saɪ•ə,naɪd] *s* cianuro
cybernetics [,saɪbər'nɛtɪks] *s* cibernética
cycle ['saɪkəl] *s* ciclo; bicicleta; (*of an internal-combustion engine*) tiempo; (phys) periódo || *intr* montar en bicicleta
cyclic(al) ['saɪklɪk(əl)] o ['sɪklɪk(əl)] *adj* cíclico
cyclone ['saɪklon] *s* ciclón *m*
cyl. *abbr* **cylinder, cylindrical**
cylinder ['sɪlɪndər] *s* cilindro
cylinder block *s* bloque *m* de cilindros
cylinder bore *s* alesaje *m*
cylinder head *s* (*of steam engine*) tapa del cilindro; (*of gas engine*) culata del cilindro
cylindric(al) [sɪ'lɪndrɪk(əl)] *adj* cilíndrico
cymbal ['sɪmbəl] *s* címbalo, platillo
cynic ['sɪnɪk] *adj & s* cínico
cynical ['sɪnɪkəl] *adj* cínico
cynicism ['sɪnɪ,sɪzəm] *s* cinismo
cynosure ['saɪnə,ʃʊr] o ['sɪnə,ʃʊr] *s* blanco de las miradas; guía, norte *m*
cypress ['saɪprəs] *s* ciprés *m*
Cyprus ['saɪprəs] *s* Chipre *f*
Cyrillic [sɪ'rɪlɪk] *adj* cirílico
Cyrus ['saɪrəs] *s* Ciro
cyst [sɪst] *s* quiste *m*
czar [zɑr] *s* zar *m;* (fig) autócrata *m*
czarina [zɑ'rinə] *s* zarina
Czech [tʃɛk] *adj & s* checo
Czecho-Slovak ['tʃɛko'slovæk] *adj & s* checoeslovaco o checoslovaco
Czecho-Slovakia [,tʃɛkoslo'vækɪ•ə] *s* Checoeslovaquia o Checoslovaquia

D

D, d [di] cuarta letra del alfabeto inglés
d. *abbr* **date, day, dead, degree, delete, diameter, died, dollar, denarius (penny)**
D. *abbr* **December, Democrat, Duchess, Duke, Dutch**
D.A. *abbr* **District Attorney**
dab [dæb] *s* toque ligero; masa pastosa || *v* (*pret & pp* **dabbed;** *ger* **dabbing)** *tr* tocar ligeramente, frotar suavemente
dabble ['dæbəl] *tr* salpicar || *intr* chapotear; **to dabble in** meterse en; jugar a (*la Bolsa*); especular en (*granos*)
dad [dæd] *s* (coll) papá *m*
dad•dy ['dædi] *s* (*pl* **-dies**) (coll) papá *m*
daffodil ['dæfədɪl] *s* narciso trompón
daff•y ['dæfi] *adj* (*comp* **-ier;** *super* **-iest)** (coll) chiflado
dagger ['dægər] *s* daga, puñal *m;* (typ) cruz *f,* obelisco; **to look daggers at** apuñalar con la mirada
dahlia ['dæljə] *s* dalia
dai•ly ['deli] *adj* cotidiano, diario || *adv* diariamente || *s* (*pl* **-lies**) diario
dain•ty ['denti] *adj* (*comp* **-tier;** *super* **-tiest)** delicado || *s* (*pl* **-ties**) golosina
dair•y ['dɛri] *s* (*pl* **-ies**) lechería, vaquería
dais ['de•ɪs] *s* estrado
dai•sy ['dezi] *s* (*pl* **-sies**) margarita
daisy wheel *s* (*computer*) margarita (*impresora*)
dal•ly ['dæli] *v* (*pret & pp* **-lied)** *intr* juguetear, retozar; tardar, malgastai el tiempo
dam [dæm] *s* represa, embalse *m;* (*female quadruped*) madre *f;* (dent) dique *m* || *v* (*pret & pp* **dammed;** *ger* **damming)** *tr* represar, embalsar; cerrar, tapar, obstruir
damage ['dæmɪdʒ] *s* daño, perjuicio; (*to one's reputation*) desdoro; (com) avería; **damages** daños y perjuicios || *tr* dañar, perjudicar; averiar
damascene ['dæmə,sin] o [,dæmə'sin] *adj* damasquino || *s* ataujía, damasquinado || *tr* ataujiar, damasquinar
dame [dem] *s* dama, señora; (coll) mujer *f*
damn [dæm] *s* terno; **I don't give a damn** (slang) maldito lo que me importa; **that's not worth a damn** (slang) eso no vale un pito || *tr* condenar (a pena eterna); condenar; maldecir || *intr* maldecir, echar ternos
damnation [dæm'neʃən] *s* damnación; (theol) condenación
damned [dæmd] *adj* condenado (a pena eterna); abominable, detestable || **the damned** los malditos, los condenados (a pena eterna)
damp [dæmp] *adj* húmedo, mojado || *s* humedad; (*firedamp*) grisú *m* || *tr* humedecer, mojar; (*to deaden, muffle*) amortecer, amortiguar; (*to discourage*) abatir, desalentar; (elec) amortiguar (*ondas electromagnéticas*)
dampen ['dæmpən] *tr* humedecer, mojar; amortecer, amortiguar; abatir, desalentar
damper ['dæmpər] *s* (*of chimney*) registro; (*of piano*) apagador *m,* sordina
damsel ['dæmzəl] *s* señorita, muchacha
dance [dæns] *s* baile *m,* danza || *tr & intr* bailar, danzar
dance band *s* orquesta de jazz

dance floor *s* pista de baile
dance hall *s* salón *m* de baile
dancer ['dænsər] *s* bailador *m*, danzador *m;* (*professional*) bailarín *m*
dancing partner *s* pareja (de baile)
dandelion ['dændɪ,laɪ•ən] *s* diente *m* de león
dandruff ['dændrəf] *s* caspa
dan•dy ['dændi] *adj* (*comp* **-dier;** *super* **-diest**) (coll) excelente, magnífico || *s* (*pl* **-dies**) currutaco, petimetre *m;* lagarto (Mex)
Dane [den] *s* danés *m*, dinamarqués *m*
danger ['dendʒər] *s* peligro
dangerous ['dendʒərəs] *adj* peligroso; riesgoso
dangle ['dæŋgəl] *tr & intr* colgar flojamente, colgar en el aire
Danish ['denɪʃ] *adj & s* danés *m*, dinamarqués *m*
dank [dæŋk] *adj* húmedo, liento
Danube ['dænjʊb] *s* Danubio
dapper ['dæpər] *adj* aseado, apuesto
dapple ['dæpəl] *adj* habado, rodado || *tr* motear
dare [dɛr] *s* desafío, reto || *tr* retar; **to dare to** (*to challenge to*) desafiar a || *intr* osar, atreverse; **I dare say** talvez; **to dare to** (*to have the courage to*) atreverse a
dare'dev'il *s* calavera *m*, temerario
daring ['dɛrɪŋ] *adj* atrevido, osado || *s* atrevimiento, osadía
dark [dɑrk] *adj* obscuro; (*in complexion*) moreno; secreto, oculto; (*gloomy*) lóbrego; (*beer*) pardo || *s* obscuridad, tinieblas; noche *f;* **in the dark** a obscuras
Dark Ages *spl* edad media; principios de la edad media
dark-complexioned ['darkkəm'plɛkʃənd] *adj* moreno
darken ['dɑrkən] *tr* obscurecer; entristecer; cegar || *intr* obscurecerse
dark horse *s* caballo desconocido; candidato nombrado inesperadamente
darkly ['dɑrkli] *adv* obscuramente; secretamente, misteriosamente
dark meat *s* carne *f* del ave que no es la pechuga
darkness ['dɑrknɪs] *s* obscuridad
dark'room' *s* (phot) cuarto obscuro
darling ['dɑrlɪŋ] *adj & s* querido, amado; predilecto; (*as address*) chata (Mex)
darn [dɑrn] *tr & intr* zurcir; (coll) maldecir
darnel ['dɑrnəl] *s* cizaña
darning ['dɑrnɪŋ] *s* zurcido
darning needle *s* aguja de zurcir
dart [dɑrt] *s* dardo; (*small missile used in a game*) rehilete *m* || *intr* lanzarse, precipitarse; volar como dardo
Darwinian [dɑr'wɪni•ən] *adj* darviniano
Darwinism ['dɑrwə,nɪzəm] *s* darvinismo
Darwinist ['dɑrwənɪst] *s* darviniano
dash [dæʃ] *s* arranque *m;* (*splash*) rociada; carrera corta; (*spirit*) brío; pequeña cantidad; (*in printing, writing, telegraphy*) raya || *tr* lanzar; estrellar, romper; frustrar (*las esperanzas de uno*); rociar, salpicar; **to dash off** escribir de prisa; **to dash to pieces** hacer añicos || *intr* estrellarse (*las olas del mar*); lanzarse, precipitarse; **to dash by** pasar corriendo; **to dash in** entrar como un rayo
dash'board' *s* tablero de instrumentos; cuadro de mando; (aut) guardabarros *m*, salpicadero
dashing ['dæʃɪŋ] *adj* brioso; ostentoso, vistoso || *s* (*of waves*) embate *m*
dastard ['dæstərd] *adj & s* vil *mf*, miserable *mf*, cobarde *mf*
data bank ['detə] *s* banco de datos, almacenamiento
da'ta-proc'ess *tr & intr* procesar
data processing *s* procesamiento; tramitación automática de datos
data storage *s* memoria, almacenamiento
date [det] *s* (*time*) fecha, data; (*palm*) datilera; (*fruit*) dátil *m;* (*appointment*) (coll) cita; **out of date** anticuado, fuera de moda; **to date** hasta la fecha; **under date of** con fecha de || *tr* fechar, datar; (coll) tener cita con || *intr* —**to date from** datar de
date line *s* línea de cambio de fecha
date palm *s* palmera (datilera)
dative ['detɪv] *adj & s* dativo
datum ['detəm] o ['dætəm] *s* (*pl* **data** ['detə] o ['dætə]) dato
dau. *abbr* **daughter**
daub [dɔb] *s* embadurnamiento || *tr* embadurnar
daughter ['dɔtər] *s* hija
daughter-in-law ['dɔtərɪn,lɔ] *s* (*pl* **daughters-in-law**) nuera, hija política
daunt [dɔnt] *tr* asustar, espantar; desanimar, acobardar
dauntless ['dɔntlɪs] *adj* atrevido, intrépido, impávido
dauphin ['dɔfɪn] *s* delfín *m*
davenport ['dævən,port] *s* sofá *m* cama
davit ['dævɪt] *s* (naut) pescante *m*, grúa de bote
daw [dɔ] *s* corneja
dawdle ['dɔdəl] *intr* malgastar el tiempo, haronear
dawn [dɔn] *s* amanecer *m*, alba || *intr* amanecer; despuntar (*el día, la mañana*); empezar a mostrarse; **to dawn on** empezar a hacerse patente a
day [de] *adj* diurno || *s* día *m;* (*of travel, work, worry, etc.*) jornada; (*from noon to noon*) (naut) singladura; **any day now** de un día para otro; **by day** de día; **the day after** el día siguiente; **the day after tomorrow** pasado mañana; **the day before** la víspera; la víspera de; **the day before yesterday** anteayer; **to call it a day** (coll) dejar de trabajar; **to win the day** ganar la jornada
day bed *s* sofá *m* cama, diván *m* cama
day'break' *s* amanecer *m*
day coach *s* (rr) coche *m* de viajeros
day'dream' *s* ensueño || *intr* soñar despierto
day laborer *s* jornalero
day'light' *s* luz *f* del día; amanecer *m;* **in broad daylight** en pleno día; **to see daylight** comprender; ver el fin de una tarea difícil

day'light'-sav'ing time *s* hora de verano
day nursery *s* guardería infantil
day off *s* asueto
day of reckoning *s* día *m* de ajustar cuentas
day shift *s* turno diurno
day'time' *adj* diurno ‖ día *m*
daze [dez] *s* aturdimiento; **in a daze** aturdido ‖ *tr* aturdir
dazzle ['dæzəl] *s* deslumbramiento ‖ *tr* deslumbrar
dazzling ['dæzlɪŋ] *adj* deslumbrante
deacon ['dikən] *s* diácono
deaconess ['dikənɪs] *s* diaconisa
dead [dɛd] *adj* muerto; (coll) cansado ‖ *adv* (coll) completamente, muy ‖ *s* — **in the dead of night** en plena noche; **the dead** los muertos; **the dead of winter** lo más frío del invierno
dead beat *s* (slang) gorrón *m;* (slang) holgazán *m*
dead bolt *s* cerrojo dormido
dead calm *s* calma chicha, calmazo
dead center *s* punto muerto
dead'drunk' *adj* difunto de taberna
deaden ['dɛdən] *tr* amortiguar, amortecer
dead end *s* callejón *m* sin salida
dead'latch' *s* aldaba dormida
dead'-let'ter office *s* departamento de cartas no reclamadas
dead'line' *s* línea vedada; fin *m* del plazo
dead'lock' *s* cerradura dormida; desacuerdo insuperable ‖ *tr* estancar
dead•ly ['dɛdli] *adj* (*comp* **-lier;** *super* **-liest**) mortal; (*sin*) capital; abrumador
dead pan *s* (slang) semblante *m* sin expresión
dead reckoning *s* (naut) estima
dead ringer ['rɪŋər] *s* segunda edición
dead'wood' *s* leña seca; cosa inútil, gente *f* inútil
deaf [dɛf] *adj* sordo; **to turn a deaf ear** hacerse el sordo, hacer oídos de mercader
deaf and dumb *adj* sordomudo
deafen ['dɛfən] *tr* asordar, ensordecer
deafening ['dɛfənɪŋ] *adj* ensordecedor
deaf'-mute' *s* sordomudo
deafness ['dɛfnɪs] *s* sordera
deal [dil] *s* negocio, trato; (*of cards*) mano *f;* turno de dar; (*share*) parte *f,* porción; (coll) convenio secreto; **a good deal (of)** o **a great deal (of)** mucho; **to make a great deal of** hacer fiestas a ‖ *v* (*pret & pp* **dealt** [dɛlt]) *tr* asestar (*un golpe*); repartir (*la baraja*) ‖ *intr* negociar, comerciar; intervenir; (*in card games*) ser mano; **to deal with** entender en; tratar de; tratar con
dealer ['dilər] *s* comerciante *mf,* concesionario; (*of cards*) repartidor *m*
dean [din] *s* decano; (eccl) deán *m*
deanship ['dinʃɪp] *s* decanato, deanato, deanazgo
dear [dɪr] *adj* (*beloved*) caro; (*expensive*) caro; (*charging high prices*) carero; **dear me!** ¡Dios mío! ‖ *s* queriao
dearie ['dɪri] *s* (coll) queridito
dearth [dʌrθ] *s* carestía
death [dɛθ] *s* muerte *f;* **to bleed to death** morir desangrado; **to bore to death** matar de aburrimiento; **to burn to death** morir quemado; **to choke to death** morir atragantado; **to die a violent death** morir vestido; **to freeze to death** morir helado; **to put to death** dar la muerte a; **to shoot to death** matar a tiros; **to stab to death** escabechar; **to starve to death** matar de hambre; morir de hambre
death'bed' *s* lecho de muerte
death'blow' *s* golpe *m* mortal
death certificate *s* fe *f* de óbito, partida de defunción
death house *s* capilla (*de los reos de muerte*)
deathless ['dɛθlɪs] *adj* inmortal, eterno
deathly ['dɛθli] *adj* mortal, de muerte ‖ *adv* mortalmente; excesivamente
death penalty *s* pena de muerte
death rate *s* mortalidad
death rattle *s* estertor agónico
death ray *s* rayo mortífero
death warrant *s* sentencia de muerte; fin *m* de toda esperanza
death'watch' *s* vela de un difunto; guardia de un reo de muerte
debacle [de'bɑkəl] *s* desastre *m,* ruina, derrota; (*in a river*) deshielo
de•bar [dɪ'bɑr] *v* (*pret & pp* **-barred;** *ger* **-barring**) *tr* excluir; prohibir
debark [dɪ'bɑrk] *tr & intr* desembarcar
debarkation [,dibɑr'keʃən] *s* (*of passengers*) desembarco; (*of freight*) desembarque *m*
debase [dɪ'bes] *tr* degradar; falsificar
debatable [dɪ'betəbəl] *adj* disputable
debate [dɪ'bet] *s* debate *m* ‖ *tr* debatir ‖ *intr* debatir; deliberar
debauchee [,dɛbɔ'ʃi] o [,dɛbɔ'tʃi] *s* libertino, disoluto
debaucher•y [dɪ'bɔtʃəri] *s* (*pl* **-ies**) libertinaje *m,* crápula
debenture [dɪ'bɛntʃər] *s* (*bond*) obligación; (*voucher*) vale *m*
debilitate [dɪ'bɪlɪ,tet] *tr* debilitar
debili•ty [dɪ'bɪlɪti] *s* (*pl* **-ties**) debilidad
debit ['dɛbɪt] *s* debe *m;* (*entry on debit side*) cargo ‖ *tr* adeudar, cargar
debit balance *s* saldo deudor
debonair [,dɛbə'nɛr] *adj* alegre; cortés
debris [de'bri] *s* despojos, ruinas
debt [dɛt] *s* deuda; **to run into debt** endeudarse, entramparse
debtor ['dɛtər] *s* deudor *m*
debut [de'bju] o ['debju] *s* estreno, debut *m,* **to make one's debut** estrenarse, debutar; ponerse de largo, entrar en sociedad (*una joven*)
debutante [,dɛbjʊ'tɑnt] o ['dɛbjə,tænt] *s* joven *f* que se pone de largo; debutante *f*
dec. *abbr* **deceased**
decade ['dɛked] *s* decenio, década
decadence [dɪ'kedəns] *s* decadencia
decadent [dɪ'kedənt] *adj & s* decadente *mf*
decanter [dɪ'kæntər] *s* garrafa
decapitate [dɪ'kæpɪ,tet] *tr* decapitar
decay [dɪ'ke] *s* (*decline*) decaimiento, descaecimiento; (*rotting*) podredumbre; (*of teeth*) caries *f* ‖ *tr* pudrir ‖ *intr* pudrirse; decaer; cariarse (*los dientes*)

decease [dɪ'sis] *s* fallecimiento || *intr* fallecer
deceased [dɪ'sist] *adj & s* difunto
deceit [dɪ'sit] *s* engaño, fraude *m*
deceitful [dɪ'sitfəl] *adj* engañoso, fraudulento
deceive [dɪ'siv] *tr & intr* engañar
decelerate [dɪ'sɛlə,ret] *tr* desacelerar || *intr* desacelerarse
December [dɪ'sɛmbər] *s* diciembre *m*
decen•cy ['disənsi] *s* (*pl* **-cies**) decencia, honestidad; (*propriety*) conveniencia
decent ['disənt] *adj* decente, honesto; (*proper*) conveniente
decentralize [dɪ'sɛntrə,laɪz] *tr* descentralizar
deception [dɪ'sɛpʃən] *s* engaño
deceptive [dɪ'sɛptɪv] *adj* engañoso
decide [dɪ'saɪd] *tr & intr* decidir
decimal ['dɛsɪməl] *adj & s* decimal *m*
decimal point *s* (*in Spanish the comma is used to separate the decimal fraction from the integer*) coma
decimate ['dɛsɪ,met] *tr* diezmar
decipher [dɪ'saɪfər] *tr* descifrar
deciphering [dɪ'saɪfərɪŋ] *s* desciframiento
decision [dɪ'sɪʒən] *s* decisión
decisive [dɪ'saɪsɪv] *adj* decisivo; determinado, resuelto
deck [dɛk] *s* (*of cards*) baraja; (*of ship*) cubierta; **between decks** (naut) entre cubiertas || *tr* — **to deck out** adornar, engalanar
deck chair *s* silla de cubierta
deck hand *s* marinero de cubierta
deck'-land' *intr* apontizar
deck'-land'ing *s* apontizaje *m*
deckle edge ['dɛkəl] *s* barba
declaim [dɪ'klem] *tr & intr* declamar
declaration [,dɛklə'reʃən] *s* declaración
declarative [dɪ'klærətɪv] *adj* declarativo; (gram) enunciativo
declare [dɪ'klɛr] *tr & intr* declarar
declension [dɪ'klɛnʃən] *s* declinación
declination [,dɛklɪ'neʃən] *s* declinación
decline [dɪ'klaɪn] *s* bajada, declinación; (*in prices*) baja; (*in health, wealth, etc.*) bajón *m;* (*of sun*) ocaso || *tr & intr* declinar; rehusar
declivi•ty [dɪ'klɪvɪti] *s* (*pl* **-ties**) declividad, declive *m*
decode [di'kod] *tr* descifrar
decoder [di'kodər] *s* (telv) decodificador *m*
decoding [di'kodɪŋ] *s* desciframiento
décolleté [,dekɑl'te] *adj* escotado
decompose [,dikəm'poz] *tr* descomponer || *intr* descomponerse
decomposition [,dikɑmpə'zɪʃən] *s* descomposición
decompression [,dikəm'prɛʃən] *s* descompresión
decongest [,dikən'dʒɛst] *tr* descongestionar
decongestion [,dikən'dʒɛstʃən] *s* descongestión
decontamination [,dikəm,tæmɪ'neʃən] *s* descontaminación; **radioactive decontamination** descontaminación de radiactividad
decon•trol [,dikən'trol] *v* (*pret & pp* **-trolled;** *ger* **-trolling**) descontrolar

décor [de'kɔr] *s* decoración; (theat) decorado
decorate ['dɛkə,ret] *tr* decorar; (*with medal, badge*) condecorar
decoration [,dɛkə'reʃən] *s* decoración; (*medal, badge*) condecoración
decorator ['dɛkə,retər] *s* decorador *m;* (*of interiors*) adornista *mf*
decorous ['dɛkərəs] o [dɪ'korəs] *adj* decoroso
decorum [dɪ'korəm] *s* decoro
decoy [dɪ'kɔɪ] o ['dikɔɪ] *s* añagaza, señuelo; (*person*) entruchón *m* || [dɪ'kɔɪ] *tr* atraer con señuelo; entruchar
decoy pigeon *s* cimbel *m*
decrease ['dikris] *s* disminución || [dɪ'kris] *tr* disminuir || *intr* disminuir, disminuirse
decree [dɪ'kri] *s* decreto || *tr* decretar
decrepit [dɪ'krɛpɪt] *adj* decrépito
de•cry [dɪ'kraɪ] *v* (*pret & pp* **-cried**) *tr* censurar, denigrar
dedicate ['dɛdɪ,ket] *tr* dedicar
dedication [,dɛdɪ'keʃən] *s* dedicación; (*inscription in a book*) dedicatoria
deduce [dɪ'djus] *tr* deducir (*inferir, concluir; derivar*)
deduct [dɪ'dʌkt] *tr* deducir (*rebajar, substraer*)
deduction [dɪ'dʌkʃən] *s* deducción
deed [did] *s* acto, hecho; (*feat, exploit*) hazaña; (law) escritura || *tr* traspasar por escritura
deem [dim] *tr & intr* creer, juzgar
deep [dip] *adj* profundo; (*sound*) grave; (*color*) subido; de hondo, p.ej., **two meters deep** dos metros de hondo; **deep in debt** cargado de deudas; **deep in thought** absorto en la meditación || *adv* hondo; **deep into the night** muy entrada la noche
deepen ['dipən] *tr* profundizar || *intr* profundizarse
deep-laid ['dip,led] *adj* concebido con astucia
deep mourning *s* luto riguroso
deep-rooted ['dip,rutɪd] *adj* profundamente arraigado
deep'-sea' fishing *s* pesca de gran altura
deep-seated ['dip,sitɪd] *adj* profundamente arraigado
deer [dɪr] *s* ciervo, venado
deer'skin' *s* piel *f* de ciervo
def. *abbr* **defendant, deferred, definite**
deface [dɪ'fes] *tr* desfigurar
de facto [di'fækto] *adv* de hecho
defamation [,dɛfə'meʃən] o [,difə'meʃən] *s* difamación
defame [dɪ'fem] *tr* difamar
default [dɪ'fɔlt] *s* falta, incumplimiento; **by default** (sport) por no presentarse; **in default of** por falta de || *tr* dejar de cumplir; no pagar || *intr* faltar; (sport) perder por no presentarse
defeat [dɪ'fit] *s* derrota || *tr* derrotar, vencer
defeatism [dɪ'fitɪzəm] *s* derrotismo
defeatist [dɪ'fitɪst] *adj & s* derrotista *mf*
defecate ['dɛfɪ,ket] *intr* defecar
defect [dɪ'fɛkt] o ['difɛkt] *s* defecto, imperfección || [dɪ'fɛkt] *intr* desertar

defection [dɪˈfɛkʃən] *s* defección; (*lack, failure*) falta
defective [dɪˈfɛktɪv] *adj* defectivo, defectuoso
defend [dɪˈfɛnd] *tr* defender
defendant [dɪˈfɛndənt] *s* (law) demandado, acusado
defender [dɪˈfɛndər] *s* defensor *m*
defense [dɪˈfɛns] *s* defensa
defenseless [dɪˈfɛnslɪs] *adj* indefenso
defensive [dɪˈfɛnsɪv] *adj* defensivo || *s* defensiva
de•fer [dɪˈfʌr] *v* (*pret & pp* **-ferred;** *ger* **-ferring**) *tr* aplazar, diferir || *intr* deferir
deference [ˈdɛfərəns] *s* deferencia
deferential [ˌdɛfəˈrɛnʃəl] *adj* deferente
deferment [dɪˈfʌrmənt] *s* aplazamiento, dilación
defiance [dɪˈfaɪ•əns] *s* oposición; desafío, provocación; **in defiance of** sin mirar a, a despecho de
defiant [dɪˈfaɪ•ənt] *adj* provocante, hostil
deficien•cy [dɪˈfɪʃənsi] *s* (*pl* **-cies**) carencia, deficiencia; (com) descubierto
deficient [dɪˈfɪʃənt] *adj* deficiente, defectuoso
deficit [ˈdɛfɪsɪt] *adj* deficitario || *s* déficit *m*
defile [dɪˈfaɪl] o [ˈdifaɪl] *s* desfiladero || [dɪˈfail] *tr* corromper, manchar || *intr* desfilar
define [dɪˈfaɪn] *tr* definir
definite [ˈdɛfɪnɪt] *adj* definido
definition [ˌdɛfɪˈnɪʃən] *s* definición
definitive [dɪˈfɪnɪtɪv] *adj* definitivo
deflate [dɪˈflet] *tr* desinflar
deflation [dɪˈfleʃən] *s* desinflación; (*of prices*) deflación
deflect [dɪˈflɛkt] *tr* desviar || *intr* desviarse
deflower [diˈflaʊ•ər] *tr* desflorar
deforest [diˈfɑrɛst] o [diˈfɔrɛst] *tr* desforestar, despoblar
deform [dɪˈfɔrm] *tr* deformar
deformed [dɪˈfɔrmd] *adj* deforme
deformi•ty [dɪˈfɔrmɪti] *s* (*pl* **-ties**) deformidad
defraud [dɪˈfrɔd] *tr* defraudar
defray [diˈfre] *tr* sufragar, subvenir a
defrost [diˈfrɔst] *tr* descongelar, deshelar
defroster [diˈfrɔstər] *s* descongelador *m*
deft [dɛft] *adj* diestro, hábil
defunct [dɪˈfʌŋkt] *adj* difunto
de•fy [dɪˈfaɪ] *v* (*pret & pp* **-fied**) *tr* desafiar, provocar
deg. *abbr* **degree**
degeneracy [dɪˈdʒɛnərəsi] *s* degeneración
degenerate [dɪˈdʒɛnərɪt] *adj & s* degenerado || [dɪˈdʒɛnəˌret] *intr* degenerar
degrade [dɪˈgred] *tr* degradar
degrading [dɪˈgredɪŋ] *adj* degradante
degree [dɪˈgri] *s* grado; **by degrees** de grado en grado; **to take a degree** graduarse, recibir un grado o título
dehumidifier [ˌdihjuˈmɪdɪˌfaɪ•ər] *s* deshumedecedor *m*
dehydrate [diˈhaɪdret] *tr* deshidratar
deice [diˈaɪs] *tr* deshelar
dei•fy [ˈdi•ɪˌfaɪ] *v* (*pret & pp* **-fied**) *tr* deificar
deign [den] *intr* dignarse
dei•ty [ˈdi•ɪti] *s* (*pl* **-ties**) deidad; **the Deity** Dios *m*
dejected [dɪˈdʒɛktɪd] *adj* abatido
dejection [dɪˈdʒɛkʃən] *s* abatimiento
del. *abbr* **delegate, delete**
delay [dɪˈle] *s* retraso, tardanza; parón || *tr* retrasar || *intr* demorarse
delectable [dɪˈlɛktəbəl] *adj* deleitable
delegate [ˈdɛlɪgɪt] *s* diputado, delegado; (*to a convention*) congresista *mf* || [ˈdɛlɪˌget] *tr* delegar
delete [dɪˈlit] *tr* borrar, suprimir
deletion [dɪˈliʃən] *s* supresión
deliberate [dɪˈlɪbərɪt] *adj* pensado, reflexionado; (*slow in deciding*) cauto, circunspecto; (*slow in moving*) espacioso, lento || [dɪˈlɪbəˌret] *tr & intr* deliberar
delica•cy [ˈdɛlɪkəsi] *s* (*pl* **-cies**) delicadeza; (*choice food*) golosina
delicatessen [ˌdɛlɪkəˈtɛsən] *s* colmado, tienda de ultramarinos || *spl* ultramarinos
delicious [dɪˈlɪʃəs] *adj* delicioso, sabroso
delight [dɪˈlaɪt] *s* deleite *m*, delicia || *tr* deleitar || *intr* deleitarse
delightful [dɪˈlaɪtfəl] *adj* deleitoso, ameno, exquisito
delinquen•cy [dɪˈlɪŋkwənsi] *s* (*pl* **-cies**) culpa; (*in payment of debt*) morosidad; (*debt in arrears*) atrasos
delinquent [dɪˈlɪŋkwənt] *adj* culpado; (*in payment*) moroso, atrasado; no pagado || *s* culpado; deudor moroso
delirious [dɪˈlɪrɪ•əs] *adj* delirante
deliri•um [dɪˈlɪrɪ•əm] *s* (*pl* **-ums** o **-a** [ə]) delirio
deliver [dɪˈlɪvər] *tr* entregar; asestar (*un golpe*); pronunciar, recitar (*un discurso*); transmitir, rendir (*energía*); partear (*a la mujer que está de parto*)
deliver•y [dɪˈlɪvəri] *s* (*pl* **-ies**) entrega; (*of mail*) distribución, reparto; (*of a speech*) declamación; (*childbirth*) alumbramiento, parto
delivery•man [dɪˈlɪvərimən] *s* (*pl* **-men** [mən]) mozo de reparto
delivery room *s* sala de alumbramiento
delivery service *s* servicio a domicilio
delivery truck *s* sedán *m* de reparto
dell [dɛl] *s* vallecito
delouse [diˈlaʊs] *tr* despiojar
delphinium [dɛlˈfɪnɪ•əm] *s* (*Delphinium ajacis*) espuela de caballero; (*Delphinium consolida*) consuelda real
delude [dɪˈlud] *tr* deludir, engañar
deluge [ˈdɛljudʒ] *s* diluvio || *tr* inundar
delusion [dɪˈluʃən] *s* engaño, decepción
de luxe [dɪˈlʌks] *adj & adv s* de lujo
delve [dɛlv] *intr* cavar; **to delve into** cavar en
demagnetize [diˈmægnɪˌtaɪz] *tr* desimantar
demagogue [ˈdɛməˌgɑg] *s* demagogo
demand [dɪˈmænd] o [dɪˈmɑnd] *s* demanda; **to be in demand** tener demanda || *tr* demandar perentoriamente
demanding [dɪˈmændɪŋ] *adj* exigente
demarcate [dɪˈmɑrket] o [ˈdimɑrˌket] *tr* demarcar

démarche [de'marʃ] *s* diligencia, gestión, paso
demeanor [dɪ'minər] *s* conducta, porte *m*
demented [dɪ'mɛntɪd] *adj* demente, dementado
demigod ['dɛmɪ,gɑd] *s* semidiós *m*
demijohn ['dɛmɪ,dʒɑn] *s* damajuana
demilitarize [di'mɪlɪtə,raɪz] *tr* desmilitarizar
demilitarized zone *s* zona desmilitarizada
demimonde ['dɛmɪ,mɑnd] *s* mujeres de vida alegre
demise [dɪ'maɪz] *s* fallecimiento
demisemiquaver [,dɛmɪ'sɛmɪ,kwevər] *s* (mus) fusa
demitasse ['dɛmɪ,tæs] o ['dɛmɪ,tɑs] *s* taza pequeña
demobilize [di'mobɪ,laɪz] *tr* desmovilizar
democra•cy [dɪ'mɑrkrəsi] *s* (*pl* **-cies**) democracia
democrat ['dɛmə,kræt] *s* demócrata *mf*
democratic [,dɛmə'krætɪk] *adj* democrático
demodulate [di'mɑdjə,let] *tr* desmodular
demolish [dɪ'mɑlɪʃ] *tr* demoler
demolition [,dɛmə'lɪʃən] o [,dimə'lɪʃən] *s* demolición
demon ['dimən] *s* demonio
demoniacal [,dimə'naɪ•əkəl] *adj* demoníaco
demonstrate ['dɛmən,stret] *tr* demostrar ‖ *intr* demostrar; (*to show feelings in public gatherings*) manifestar
demonstration [,dɛmən'streʃən] *s* demostración; (*public show of feeling*) manifestación
demonstrative [dɪ'mɑnstrətɪv] *adj* demostrativo; (*giving open exhibition of emotion*) extremoso
demonstrator ['dɛmən,stretər] *s* demostrador *m;* manifestante *mf*
demoralize [dɪ'mɔrə,laɪz] *tr* desmoralizar
demote [dɪ'mot] *tr* degradar
demotion [dɪ'moʃən] *s* degradación
de•mur [dɪ'mʌr] *v* (*pret & pp* **-murred;** *ger* **-murring**) *intr* poner reparos
demure [dɪ'mjʊr] *adj* modesto, recatado; grave, serio
demurrage [dɪ'mʌrɪdʒ] *s* (com) estadía
den [dɛn] *s* (*of animals, thieves*) madriguera; (*dirty little room*) cuchitril *m;* lugar *m* de retiro; cuarto de estudio; (*of lions*) (Bib) fosa
denaturalize [di'nætjərə,laɪz] *tr* desnaturalizar
denatured alcohol [di'netʃərd] *s* alcohol desnaturalizado
denial [dɪ'naɪ•əl] *s* denegación; negación, desmentida
denim ['dɛnɪm] *s* dril *m* de algodón
denizen ['dɛnɪzən] *s* habitante *mf,* vecino
Denmark ['dɛnmɑrk] *s* Dinamarca
denomination [dɪ,nɑmɪ'neʃən] *s* denominación; categoría, clase *f;* secta, confesión, comunión
denote [dɪ'not] *tr* denotar
dénoument [denu'mã] *s* desenlace *m*
denounce [dɪ'naʊns] *tr* denunciar
dense [dɛns] *adj* denso; estúpido
densi•ty ['dɛnsɪti] *s* (*pl* **-ties**) densidad
dent [dɛnt] *s* abolladura, mella ‖ *tr* abollar, mellar ‖ *intr* abollarse, mellarse
dental ['dɛntəl] *adj & s* dental *f*
dental floss *s* hilo dental, seda encerada
dental technician *s* mecánico-dentista *m*
dentrifrice ['dɛntɪfrɪs] *s* dentífrico
dentist ['dɛntɪst] *s* dentista *mf*
dentistry ['dɛntɪstri] *s* odontología
denture ['dɛntʃər] *s* dentadura artificial
denunciation [dɪ,nʌnsɪ'eʃən] o [dɪ,nʌnʃɪ'eʃən] *s* denuncia
de•ny [dɪ'naɪ] *v* (*pret & pp* **-nied**) *tr* (*to declare not to be true*) negar; (*to refuse*) denegar; **to deny oneself to callers** negarse ‖ *intr* negar; denegar
deodorant [di'odərənt] *adj & s* desodorante *m*
deodorize [di'odə,raɪz] *tr* desodorizar
deoxidize [di'ɑksɪ,daɪz] *tr* desoxidar
dep. *abbr* **department, departs, deputy**
depart [dɪ'pɑrt] *intr* partir, salir, irse; desviarse
department [dɪ'pɑrtmənt] *s* departamento; (*of government*) ministerio
department store *s* grandes almacenes *mpl*
departure [dɪ'pɑrtʃər] *s* partida, salida; desviación
depend [dɪ'pɛnd] *intr* depender; **to depend on** depender de
dependable [dɪ'pɛndəbəl] *adj* confiable, fidedigno
dependence [dɪ'pɛndəns] *s* dependencia
dependen•cy [dɪ'pɛndənsi] *s* (*pl* **-cies**) dependencia; (*country, territory*) posesión
dependent [dɪ'pɛndənt] *adj* dependiente ‖ *s* carga de familia, familiar *m* dependiente
depict [dɪ'pɪkt] *tr* describir, representar, pintar
deplete [dɪ'plit] *tr* agotar, depauperar
deplorable [dɪ'plorəbəl] *adj* deplorable
deplore [dɪ'plor] *tr* deplorar
deploy [dɪ'plɔɪ] *tr* (mil) desplegar ‖ *intr* (mil) desplegarse
deployment [dɪ'plɔɪmənt] *s* (mil) despliegue *m*
depolarize [di'polə,raɪz] *tr* despolarizar
depopulate [di'pɑpjə,let] *tr* despoblar
deport [dɪ'port] *tr* deportar; **to deport oneself** conducirse, portarse
deportation [,dipor'teʃən] *s* deportación
deportee [,dipor'ti] *s* deportado
deportment [dɪ'portmənt] *s* conducta, comportamiento
depose [dɪ'poz] *tr & intr* deponer
deposit [dɪ'pɑzɪt] *s* depósito; (*down payment*) señal *f,* pago anticipado; (min) yacimiento ‖ *tr* depositar ‖ *intr* depositarse
deposit account *s* cuenta corriente
depositor [dɪ'pɑzɪtər] *s* cuentacorrentista *mf,* imponente *mf*
depot ['dipo] o ['dɛpo] *s* almacén *m,* depósito; (mil) depósito; (rr) estación
depraved [dɪ'prevd] *adj* depravado
depravi•ty [dɪ'prævɪti] *s* (*pl* **-ties**) depravación
deprecate ['dɛprɪ,ket] *tr* desaprobar

depreciate [dɪˋpriʃɪ,et] *tr* (*to lower value or price of*) depreciar; (*to disparage*) desapreciar ‖ *intr* depreciarse
depreciation [dɪ,priʃɪˋeʃən] *s* (*drop in value*) depreciación; (*disparagement*) desaprecio
depress [dɪˋprɛs] *tr* deprimir; desanimar, desalentar; bajar (*los precios*)
depression [dɪˋprɛʃən] *s* depresión; desaliento; (*slump*) crisis *f*
deprive [dɪˋpraɪv] *tr* privar
deprived [dɪˋpraɪvd] *adj* desventajado
dept. *abbr* **department**
depth [dɛpθ] *s* profundidad; (*of a house, of a room*) fondo; **in the depth of night** en mitad de la noche; **in the depth of winter** en pleno invierno; **to go beyond one's depth** meterse en agua demasiado profunda; (fig) meterse en honduras
depth of hold *s* (naut) puntal *m*
depu•ty [ˋdɛpjəti] *s* (*pl* **-ties**) diputado
derail [dɪˋrel] *tr* hacer descarrilar ‖ *intr* descarrilar
derailment [dɪˋrelmənt] *s* descarrilamiento
derange [dɪˋrendʒ] *tr* desarreglar, descomponer; trastornar el juicio a
derangement [dɪˋrendʒmənt] *s* desarreglo, descompostura; locura; obfuscación
der•by [ˋdʌrbi] *s* (*pl* **-bies**) sombrero hongo
deregulate [diˋrɛgjə,let] *tr* descontrolar
derelict [ˋdɛrɪlɪkt] *adj* abandonado; negligente ‖ *s* pelafustán *m;* (naut) derrelicto
deride [dɪˋraɪd] *tr* burlarse de, ridiculizar
derision [dɪˋrɪʒən] *s* burla, irrisión
derive [dɪˋraɪv] *tr & intr* derivar
dermatitis [,dʌrməˋtaɪtɪs] *s* dermatitis *f*
derogatory [dɪˋrɑgə,tori] *adj* despreciativo
derrick [ˋdɛrɪk] *s* grúa; (min) castillete *m*
dervish [ˋdʌrvɪʃ] *s* derviche *m*
desalinization [dɪ,selɪnɪˋzeʃən] *s* desalinización
desalt [diˋsɔlt] *tr* desalar
descend [dɪˋsɛnd] *tr* bajar, descender (*la escalera*) ‖ *intr* bajar, descender; **to descend on** caer sobre, invadir
descendant [dɪˋsɛndənt] *adj* descendente ‖ *s* descendiente *mf*
descendent [dɪˋsɛndənt] *adj* descendente
descent [dɪˋsɛnt] *s* (*passing from higher to lower state*) descenso; (*extraction; lineage*) descendencia; cuesta, bajada; invasión
describe [dɪˋskraɪb] *tr* describir
description [dɪˋskrɪpʃən] *s* descripción
descriptive [dɪˋskrɪptɪv] *adj* descriptivo
de•scry [dɪˋskraɪ] *v* (*pret & pp* **-scried**) *tr* avistar, divisar; descubrir
desecrate [ˋdɛsɪ,kret] *tr* profanar
desegregation [di,sɛgrɪˋgeʃən] *s* desegregación
desert [ˋdɛzərt] *adj & s* desierto, yermo ‖ [dɪˋzʌrt] *s* mérito; **he received his just deserts** llevó su merecido ‖ *tr* desertar de ‖ *intr* desertar
deserter [dɪˋzʌrtər] *s* desertor *m*
desertion [dɪˋzʌrʃən] *s* deserción; abandono de cónyuge
deserve [dɪˋzʌrv] *tr & intr* merecer
deservedly [dɪˋzʌrvɪdli] *adv* merecidamente
design [dɪˋzaɪn] *s* diseño; (*combination of details; art of designing*) dibujo; (*plan, scheme*) designio; **to have designs on** poner la mira en ‖ *tr* deseñar, dibjuar; idear, proyectar ‖ *intr* diseñar, dibujar
designate [ˋdɛzɪg,net] *tr* designar
designing [dɪˋzaɪnɪŋ] *adj* intrigante, maquinador
desirable [dɪˋzaɪrəbəl] *adj* deseable
desire [dɪˋzaɪr] *s* deseo ‖ *tr* desear
desirous [dɪˋzaɪrəs] *adj* deseoso
desist [dɪˋzɪst] *intr* desistir
desk [dɛsk] *s* bufete *m*, escritorio; (*lectern*) atril *m;* (*clerk's counter in a hotel*) caja
desk clerk *s* cajero, recepcionista *m*
desk set *s* juego de escritorio
desolate [ˋdɛsəlɪt] *adj* (*hopeless*) desolado; despoblado, yermo, desierto; solitario; (*dismal*) lúgubre ‖ [ˋdɛsə,let] *tr* desconsolar; (*to lay waste*) desolar, devastar; despoblar
desolation [,dɛsəˋleʃən] *s* (*devastation; great affliction*) desolación; (*dreariness*) lobreguez *f*
despair [dɪˋspɛr] *s* desesperación ‖ *intr* desesperar, desesperarse
despairing [dɪˋspɛrɪŋ] *adj* desesperado
despera•do [,dɛspəˋredo] o [,dɛspəˋrɑdo] *s* (*pl* **-does** o **-dos**) criminal dispuesto a todo
desperate [ˋdɛspərɪt] *adj* dispuesto a todo; (*bitter, excessive*) encarnizado; (*hopeless*) desesperado; (*remedy*) heroico
despicable [ˋdɛspɪkəbəl] *adj* despreciable, ruin
despise [dɪˋspaɪz] *tr* despreciar, desdeñar
despite [dɪˋspaɪt] *prep* a despecho de
desponden•cy [dɪˋspɑndənsi] *s* (*pl* **cies**) abatimiento, desaliento
despondent [dɪˋspɑndənt] *adj* abatido, desalentado
despot [ˋdɛspɑt] *s* déspota *m*
despotic [dɛsˋpɑtɪk] *adj* despótico
despotism [ˋdɛspə,tɪzəm] *s* despotismo
dessert [dɪˋzʌrt] *s* postre *m*
destination [,dɛstɪˋneʃən] *s* (*end of a journey or shipment*) destino; (*purpose*) destinación
destine [ˋdɛstɪn] *tr* destinar
desti•ny [ˋdɛstɪni] *s* (*pl* **-nies**) destino
destitute [ˋdɛstɪ,tjut] *adj* (*being in complete poverty*) indigente; (*lacking, deprived*) desprovisto
destitution [,dɛstɪˋtjuʃən] *s* indigencia
destroy [dɪˋstrɔi] *tr* destruir
destroyer [dɪˋstrɔɪ•ər] *s* (nav) destructor *m*
destruction [dɪˋstrʌkʃən] *s* destrucción
destructive [dɪˋstrʌktɪv] *adj* destructivo
desultory [ˋdɛsəl,tori] *adj* deshilvanado, descosido
detach [dɪˋtætʃ] *tr* desprender, separar; (mil) destacar
detachable [dɪˋtætʃəbəl] *adj* desprendible, separable; (*collar*) postizo
detached [dɪˋtætʃt] *adj* separado, suelto; imparcial, desinteresado
detachment [dɪˋtætʃmənt] *s* desprendimiento, separación; imparcialidad, desinterés *m;* (mil) destacamento

detail [dɪ'tel] o ['ditel] *s* detalle *m*, pormenor *m;* (mil) destacamento || [dɪ'tel] *tr* detallar; (mil) destacar
detain [dɪ'ten] *tr* detener; tener preso
detect [dɪ'tɛkt] *tr* detectar
detection [dɪ'tɛkʃən] *s* detección
detective [dɪ'tɛktɪv] *s* detective *m*
detective story *s* novela policíaca o policial
detector [dɪ'tɛktər] *s* detector *m*
detention [dɪ'tɛnʃən] *s* detención
de•ter [dɪ'tʌr] *v* (*pret & pp* **-terred;** *ger* **-terring**) *tr* impedir, refrenar
detergent [dɪ'tʌrdʒənt] *adj & s* detergente *m*
deteriorate [dɪ'tɪrɪ•ə'ret] *tr* deteriorar || *intr* deteriorarse
determination [dɪ,tʌrmə'neʃən] *s* resolución; empecinamiento
determine [dɪ'tʌrmɪn] *tr* determinar
deterrent [dɪ'tʌrənt] *s* impedimento, refrenamiento
detest [dɪ'tɛst] *tr* detestar, aborrecer
dethrone [dɪ'θron] *tr* destronar
detonate ['dɛtə,net] o ['ditə,net] *tr* hacer estallar || *intr* detonar
detour ['ditʊr] o [dɪ'tʊr] *s* desvío; rodeo, vuelta; manera indirecta || *tr* desviar (*el tráfico*) || *intr* desviarse
detoxification [di,tɑksəfə'keʃən] *s* desintoxicación
detoxi•fy [di'tɑksə,faɪ] *v* (*pret & pp* **-fied**) *tr* desintoxicar
detract [dɪ'trækt] *tr* detraer || *intr* — **to detract from** disminuir, rebajar
detriment ['dɛtrɪmənt] *s* perjuicio, detrimento; **to the detriment of** en perjuicio de
detrimental [,dɛtrɪ'mɛntəl] *adj* perjudicial
deuce [djus] o [dus] *s* (*in cards*) dos *m;* **the deuce!** ¡demonio!
devaluation [di,vælju'eʃən] *s* desvalorización, devaluación
devastate ['dɛvəs,tet] *tr* devastar
devastation [,dɛvəs'teʃən] *s* devastación
develop [dɪ'vɛləp] *tr* desarrollar, desenvolver; (phot) revelar; explotar (*una mina*) || *intr* desarrollarse, desenvolverse; evolucionar, manifestarse
developer [dɪ'vɛləpər] *s* fomentador *m;* (phot) revelador *m*
development [dɪ'vɛləpmənt] *s* desarrollo, desenvolvimiento; (phot) revelado; (*of a mine*) explotación; acontecimiento nuevo
developmental aid [dɪ,vɛləp'mɛntəl] *s* ayuda al desarrollo
deviate ['divɪ,et] *tr* desviar || *intr* desviarse
deviation [,divɪ'eʃən] *s* desviación
deviationism [,divɪ'eʃə,nɪzəm] *s* desviacionismo
deviationist [,divɪ'eʃənɪst] *s* desviacionista *mf*
device [dɪ'vaɪs] *s* dispositivo, aparato; (*trick*) ardid *m*, treta; (*motto*) lema *m*, divisa; **to leave someone to his own devices** dejarle a uno que haga lo que se le antoje
dev•il ['dɛvəl] *s* diablo; **between the devil and the deep blue sea** entre la espada y la pared; **to raise the devil** (slang) armar un alboroto || *v* (*pret & pp* **iled** o **-illed;** *ger* **-iling** o **illing**) *tr* condimentar con picantes; (coll) acosar, molestar
devilish ['dɛvəlɪʃ] *adj* diabólico
devilment ['dɛvəlmənt] *s* (*mischief*) diablura; (*evil*) maldad
devil•try ['dɛvəltri] *s* (*pl* **-tries**) maldad, crueldad; (*mischief*) diablura
devious ['dɪvɪ•əs] *adj* (*straying*) desviado, extraviado; (*roundabout; shifty*) tortuoso
devise [dɪ'vaɪz] *tr* idear, inventar; (law) legar
devoid [dɪ'vɔɪd] *adj* desprovisto
devote [dɪ'vot] *tr* dedicar
devoted [dɪ'votɪd] *adj* (*zealous, ardent*) devoto; dedicado
devotee [,dɛvə'ti] *s* devoto
devotion [dɪ'voʃən] *s* devoción; (*to study, work, etc.*) dedicación; **devotions** oraciones, preces *fpl*
devour [dɪ'vaʊr] *tr* devorar
devout [dɪ'vaʊt] *adj* devoto; cordial, sincero
dew [dju] o [du] *s* rocío
dew'drop' *s* gota de rocío
dew'lap' *s* papada
dew•y ['dju•i] o ['du•i] *adj* rociado
dexterity [dɛks'tɛrɪti] *s* destreza
D.F. *abbr* **Defender of the Faith**
diabetes [,daɪ•ə'bitɪs] *s* diabetes *f*
diabetic [,daɪ•ə'bɛtɪk] *adj & s* diabético
diabolic(al) [,daɪ•ə'bɑlɪk(əl)] *adj* diabólico
diacritical [,daɪ•ə'krɪtɪkəl] *adj* diacrítico
diadem ['daɪ•ə,dɛm] *s* diadema *f*
diaere•sis [daɪ'ɛrɪsɪs] *s* (*pl* **-ses** [,siz]) diéresis *f*
diagnose [,daɪ•əg'nos] *tr* diagnosticar
diagno•sis [,daɪ•əg'nosɪs] *s* (*pl* **-ses** [siz]) diagnosis *f*, diagnóstico
diagonal [daɪ'ægənəl] *adj & s* diagonal *f*
diagram ['daɪ•ə,græm] *s* diagrama *m*
dial. *abbr* **dialect**
dial ['daɪ•əl] *s* (*of radio*) cuadrante *m;* (*of watch*) cuadrante *m*, esfera, muestra; (*of telephone*) disco selector || *tr* sintonizar (*el radiorreceptor*); marcar (*el número telefónico*); llamar (*a una persona*) por teléfono automático || *intr* (telp) marcar
dialect ['daɪ•ə,lɛkt] *s* dialecto
dialing ['daɪ•əlɪŋ] *s* (telp) marcaje *m*
dialogue ['daɪ•ə,lɔg] *s* diálogo
dial telephone *s* teléfono automático
dial tone *s* (telp) señal *f* para marcar
diam. *abbr* **diameter**
diameter [daɪ'æmɪtər] *s* diámetro
diametric(al) [,daɪ•ə'mɛtrɪk(əl)] *adj* diamétrico
diamond ['daɪmənd] *s* diamante *m;* (*figure of a rhombus*) losange *m;* (*playing card*) carró *m*, diamante *m;* (baseball) losange *m*
diaper ['daɪpər] *s* pañal *m*
diaphanous [daɪ'æfənəs] *adj* diáfano
diaphragm ['daɪ•ə,fræm] *s* diafragma *m*
diarrhea [,daɪ•ə'ri•ə] *s* diarrea; **to have diarrhea** cursear
dia•ry ['daɪ•əri] *s* (*pl* **-ries**) diario
diastole [daɪ'æstəli] *s* diástole *f*
diathermy ['daɪ•ə,θʌrmi] *s* diatermia

dice [daɪs] *spl* dados; (*small cubes*) cubitos; **to load the dice** cargar los dados || *tr* cortar en cubos
dice'box' *s* cubilete *m*
dichloride [daɪˈkloraɪd] *s* dicloruro
dichoto•my [daɪˈkɑtəmi] *s* (*pl* **-mies**) dicotomía
dickey [ˈdɪki] *s* camisolín *m*, pechera postiza; babero de niño
dict. *abbr* **dictionary**
dictaphone [ˈdɪktə,fon] *s* dictáfono
dictate [ˈdɪktet] *s* mandato || [ˈdɪktet] o [dɪkˈtet] *tr* dictar; mandar
dictation [dɪkˈteʃən] *s* dictado; (*orders; giving orders*) mandato; **to take dictation** escribir al dictado
dictator [ˈdɪktetər] o [dɪkˈtetər] *s* dictador *m*
dictatorship [dɪkˈtetərʃɪp] *s* dictadura
diction [ˈdɪkʃən] *s* dicción
dictionar•y [ˈdɪkʃən,ɛri] *s* (*pl* **-ies**) diccionario
dic•tum [ˈdɪktəm] *s* (*pl* **-ta** [tə]) dictamen *m;* aforismo, sentencia
didactic(al) [daɪˈdæktɪk(əl)] o [dɪˈdæktɪk(əl)] *adj* didáctico
die [daɪ] *s* (*pl* **-dice** [daɪs]) dado; **the die is cast** la suerte está echada || *s* (*pl* **dies**) (*for stamping coins, medals, etc.*) troquel *m;* (*for cutting threads*) hembra de terraja || *v* (*pret & pp* **died;** *ger* **dying**) *intr* morir; **to be dying** estar agonizando; **to die laughing** morir de risa
die'hard' *adj & s* intransigente *mf*
die'sel-elec'tric [ˈdizəl] *adj* dieseleléctrico
diesel engine *s* diesel *m*
diesel oil *s* gas-oil *m*
die'stock' *s* terraja
diet [ˈdaɪ•ət] *s* dieta, régimen alimenticio || *intr* estar a dieta
dietitian [,daɪ•əˈtɪʃən] *s* dietista *mf*
diff. *abbr* **difference, different**
differ [ˈdɪfər] *intr* (*to be different*) diferir, diferenciarse; (*to dissent*) diferenciar; **to differ with** desavenirse con
difference [ˈdɪfərəns] *s* diferencia; **to make no difference** no importar; **to split the difference** partir la diferencia
different [ˈdɪfərənt] *adj* diferente
differentiate [,dɪfəˈrɛnʃɪ,et] *tr* diferenciar || *intr* diferenciarse
difficult [ˈdɪfɪ,kʌlt] *adj* difícil
difficul•ty [ˈdɪfɪ,kʌlti] *s* (*pl* **-ties**) dificultad
diffident [ˈdɪfɪdənt] *adj* apocado, tímido
diffuse [dɪˈfjus] *adj* difuso || [dɪˈfjuz] *tr* difundir || *intr* difundirse
dig [dɪg] *s* (*poke*) empuje *m;* (*jibe*) pulla, palabra hiriente || *v* (*pret & pp* **dug** [dʌg] o **digged;** *ger* **digging**) *tr* cavar, excavar; **to dig up** desenterrar || *intr* cavar, excavar; **to dig in** (coll) poner manos a la obra; (mil) antrincherarse; **to dig under** socavar
digest [ˈdaɪdʒɛst] *s* compendio, resumen *m;* (law) digesto || [dɪˈdʒɛst] o [daɪˈdʒɛst] *tr & intr* digerir
digestible [dɪˈdʒɛstɪbəl] o [daɪˈdʒɛstɪbəl] *adj* digerible, digestible
digestion [dɪˈdʒɛstʃən] o [daɪˈdʒɛstʃən] *s* digestión
digestive [dɪˈdʒɛstɪv] o [daɪˈdʒɛstɪv] *adj & s* digestivo
digit [ˈdɪdʒɪt] *s* dígito
digital telephone [ˈdɪdʒətəl] *s* teléfono digital
dignified [ˈdɪgnɪ,faɪd] *adj* digno, grave, decoroso
digni•fy [ˈdɪgnɪ,faɪ] *v* (*pret & pp* **-fied**) *tr* dignificar; engrandecer el mérito de
dignitar•y [ˈdɪgnɪ,tɛri] *s* (*pl* **-ies**) dignatario
digni•ty [ˈdɪgnɪti] *s* (*pl* **-ties**) dignidad; **to stand upon one's dignity** ponerse tan alto
digress [dɪˈgrɛs] o [daɪˈgrɛs] *intr* divagar
digression [dɪˈgrɛʃən] o [daɪˈgrɛʃən] *s* digresión, divagación
dike [daɪk] *s* dique *m;* (*bank of earth thrown up in digging*) montón *m;* (*causeway*) arrecife *m*, malecón *m*
dilapidated [dɪˈlæpɪ,detɪd] *adj* destartalado, desvencijado
dilate [daɪˈlet] *tr* dilatar || *intr* dilatarse
dilatory [ˈdɪlə,tori] *adj* tardío
dilemma [dɪˈlɛmə] *s* dilema *m*, disyuntiva; encerrona
dilettan•te [,dɪləˈtænti] *adj* diletante || *s* (*pl* **-tes** o **-ti** [ti]) diletante *mf*
diligence [ˈdɪlɪdʒəns] *s* diligencia; dedicación
diligent [ˈdɪlɪdʒənt] *adj* diligente
dill [dɪl] *s* eneldo
dillydal•ly [ˈdɪlɪ,dæli] *v* (*pret & pp* **-lied**) *intr* malgastar el tiempo, haraganear
dilute [dɪˈlut] o [daɪˈlut] *adj* diluído || [dɪˈlut] *tr* diluir || *intr* diluirse
dilution [dɪˈluʃən] *s* dilución
dim. *abbr* **diminutive**
dim [dɪm] *adj* (*comp* **dimmer;** *super* **dimmest**) débil, indistinto, confuso; obscuro, poco claro; (*chance*) escaso; (*not clearly understanding*) torpe, lerdo; **to take a dim view of** mirar escépticamente || *v* (*pret & pp* **dimmed;** *ger* **dimming**) *tr* amortiguar (*la luz*); poner (*un faro*) a media luz; disminuir || *intr* obscurecerse
dime [daɪm] *s* moneda de diez centavos
dimension [dɪˈmɛnʃən] *s* dimensión
diminish [dɪˈmɪnɪʃ] *tr* disminuir || *intr* disminuir, disminuirse
diminution [,dɪməˈnuʃən] *s* disminución
diminutive [dɪˈmɪnjətɪv] *adj* (*tiny*) diminuto; (gram) diminutivo || *s* diminutivo
dimi•ty [ˈdɪmɪti] *s* (*pl* **-ties**) cotonía
dimly [ˈdɪmli] *adv* indistintamente
dimmer [ˈdɪmər] *s* amortiguador *m* de luz; (aut) lámpara de cruce, luz *f* de cruce
dimple [ˈdɪmpəl] *s* hoyuelo
dimwit [ˈdɪm,wɪt] *s* (slang) mentecato, bobo
dim•witted [ˈdɪm,wɪtɪd] *adj* (slang) mentecato, bobo
din [dɪn] *s* estruendo, ruido ensordecedor || *v* (*pret & pp* **dinned;** *ger* **dinning**) *tr* ensordecer con mucho ruido; repetir insistentemente; impresionar con repetición ruidosa || *intr* sonar estrepitosamente

dine [daɪn] *tr* dar de comer a; obsequiar con una cena o comida || *intr* cenar, comer; **to dine out** cenar fuera de casa
diner [ˈdaɪnər] *s* invitado a una cena, convidado a una comida; coche-comedor *m*
ding-dong [ˈdɪŋ,dɔŋ] *s* dindán *m*
din•gy [ˈdɪndʒi] *adj* (*comp* **-gier;** *super* **-giest**) deslustrado, sucio
dining car *s* coche-comedor *m*
dining room *s* comedor *m*
din'ing-room' suite *s* juego de comedor
dinner [ˈdɪnər] *s* cena, comida; (*formal meal*) banquete *m*
dinner coat o **jacket** *s* smoking *m*
dinner pail *s* fiambrera, portaviandas *m*
dinner set *s* vajilla
dinner time *s* hora de la cena o comida
dint [dɪnt] *s* abolladura; **by dint of** a fuerza de || *tr* abollar
diocese [ˈdaɪ•əˈsis] o [ˈdaɪ•əsis] *s* diócesi *f* o diócesis *f*
diode [ˈdaɪ•od] *s* diodo
dioxide [daɪˈɑksaɪd] *s* dióxido
dip [dɪ] *s* zambullida, inmersión; baño corto; (*in a road*) depresión; (*of magnetic needle*) inclinación || *v* (*pret & pp* **dipped;** *ger* **dipping**) *tr* sumergir; sacar con cuchara; (*bread*) sopetear; **to dip the colors** saludar con la bandera || *intr* sumergirse; inclinarse hacia abajo; desaparecer súbitamente; **to dip into** hojear (*un libro*); meterse en (*un comercio*); **to dip into one's purse** gastar dinero
diphtheria [dɪfˈθɪrɪ•ə] *s* difteria
diphthong [ˈdɪfθɔŋ] *s* diptongo
diphthongize [ˈdɪfθɔŋ,gaɪz] *tr* diptongar || *intr* diptongarse
diploma [dɪˈplomə] *s* diploma *m*
diploma•cy [dɪˈploməsi] *s* (*pl* **-cies**) diplomacia
diplomat [ˈdɪplə,mæt] *s* diplomático
diplomatic [,dɪpləˈmætɪk] *adj* diplomático
diplomatic pouch *s* valija diplomática
dipper [ˈdɪpər] *s* cazo, cucharón *m*
dip'stick' *s* varilla de nivel
dire [daɪr] *adj* horrendo, espantoso
direct [dɪˈrɛkt] o [daɪˈrɛkt] *adj* directo; franco, sincero || *tr* dirigir; mandar, ordenar
direct current *s* corriente continua
direct discourse *s* (gram) estilo directo
direct hit *s* blanco directo, impacto directo
direction [dɪˈrɛkʃən] o [daɪˈrɛkʃən] *s* dirección; instrucción; **directions** (*for use*) modo de empleo
direction light *s* (aut) intermitente *m*
direct object *s* (gram) complemento directo
director [dɪˈrɛktər] o [daɪˈrɛktər] *s* director *m,* administrador *m;* (*member of a governing body*) vocal *m*
directorship [dɪˈrɛktər,ʃɪp] o [daɪˈrɛktər,ʃɪp] *s* dirección, directorio
directo•ry [dɪˈrɛktəri] o [daɪˈrɛktəri] *s* (*pl* **-ries**) (*list of names and addresses; board of directors*) directorio; anuario telefónico, guía telefónica
dirge [dʌrdʒ] *s* endecha, canto fúnebre, treno; (eccl) misa de réquiem
dirigible [ˈdɪrɪdʒɪbəl] *adj & s* dirigible *m*
dirt [dʌrt] *s* (*soil*) tierra, suelo; (*dust*) polvo; (*mud*) barro, lodo; excremento; (*accumulation of dirt*) suciedad; (*moral filth*) suciedad, porquería, obscenidad; (*gossip*) chismes *mpl*
dirt'cheap' *adj* tirado, muy barato
dirt road *s* camino de tierra
dirt•y [ˈdʌrti] *adj* (*comp* **-ier;** *super* **-iest**) puerco, sucio; berroso, enlodado; polvoriento; (*obscene*) hediondo; bajo, vil || *v* (*pret & pp* **-tied**) *tr* ensuciar
dirty linen *s* ropa sucia; **to air one's dirty linen in public** sacar los trapos sucios a relucir
dirty trick *s* (slang) perrada, mala partida
disabili•ty [,dɪsəˈbɪlɪti] *s* (*pl* **-ties**) incapacidad, inhabilidad; disminución (*física*)
disable [dɪsˈebəl] *tr* incapacitar, inhabilitar, lisiar; (law) descalificar
disabled veteran *s* lisiado de guerra
disabuse [,dɪsəˈbjuz] *tr* desengañar
disadvantage [,dɪsədˈvæntɪdʒ] o [,dɪsədˈvɑntɪdʒ] *s* desventaja
disadvantaged [,dɪsədˈvæntɪdʒd] *adj & s* desventajado
disadvantageous [dɪs,ædvənˈteʒəs] *adj* desventajoso
disagree [,dɪsəˈgri] *intr* desavenirse, desconvenirse; (*to quarrel*) altercar, contender; **to disagree with** no estar de acuerdo con; no sentar bien
disagreeable [,dɪsəˈgri•əbəl] *adj* desagradable
disagreement [,dɪsəˈgrimənt] *s* desavenencia, desacuerdo; disensión; inconformidad
disappear [,dɪsəˈpɪr] *intr* desaparecer, desaparecerse
disappearance [,dɪsəˈpɪrəns] *s* desaparecimiento, desaparición
disappoint [,dɪsəˈpɔɪnt] *tr* decepcionar, desilusionar, chasquear; **to be disappointed** chasquearse, llevarse chasco
disappointment [,dɪsəˈpɔɪntmənt] *s* decepción, desilusión, chasco
disapproval [,dɪsəˈpruvəl] *s* desaprobación
disapprove [,dɪsəˈpruv] *tr & intr* desaprobar
disarm [dɪsˈɑrm] *tr* desarmar || *intr* desarmar, desarmarse
disarmament [dɪsˈɑrməmənt] *s* desarme *m,* desarmamiento
disarming [dɪsˈɑrmɪŋ] *adj* congraciador, simpático
disarray [,dɪsəˈre] *s* desorden *m;* (*in apparel*) desatavío || *tr* desordenar; desataviar
disaster [dɪˈzæstər] desastre *m,* siniestro
disaster area *s* zona siniestrada
disastrous [dɪˈzæstrəs] *adj* desastroso, desastrado
disavow [,dɪsəˈvaʊ] *tr* desconocer, negar, repudiar
disband [dɪsˈbænd] *tr* disolver (*una asamblea*); licenciar (*tropas*) || *intr* desbandarse
dis•bar [dɪsˈbɑr] *v* (*pret & pp* **-barred;** *ger* **-barring**) *tr* (law) expulsar del foro

disbelief ['dɪsbɪ'lif] *s* incredulidad
disbelieve ['dɪsbɪ'lig] *tr & intr* descreer
disburse [dɪs'bʌrs] *tr* desembolsar
disbursement [dɪs'bʌrsmənt] *s* desembolso
disc. *abbr* **discount, discoverer**
disc [dɪsk] *s* disco
discard [dɪs'kɑrd] *s* descarte *m;* **to put into the discard** desechar || *tr* descartar; desechar
discern [dɪ'zʌrn] o [dɪ'sʌrn] *tr* discernir, percibir
discerning [dɪ'zʌrnɪŋ] o [dɪ'sʌrnɪŋ] *adj* discerniente, perspicaz
discharge [dɪs'tʃɑrdʒ] *s* (*of a gun, of a battery*) descarga; (*of a prisoner*) liberación; (*of a duty*) desempeño; (*of a debt, of an obligation*) descargo; (*from a job*) despedida, remoción; (mil) certificado de licencia; (pathol) derrame *m* || *tr* descargar; desempeñar (*un deber*); libertar (*a un preso*); despedir, remover (*a un empleado*); (*from the hospital*) dar de alta; (mil) licenciar || *intr* descargar (*un tubo, río, etc.*); descargarse (*un arma de fuego*)
disciple [dɪ'saɪpəl] *s* discípulo
disciplinarian [,dɪsɪplɪ'nɛrɪ•ən] *s* ordenancista *mf*
discipline ['dɪsɪplɪn] *s* disciplina; castigo || *tr* disciplinar; castigar
disclaim [dɪs'klem[*tr* desconocer, negar
disclose [dɪs'kloz] *tr* divulgar, revelar; descubrir
disclosure [dɪs'kloʒər] *s* divulgación, revelación; descubrimiento
disco ['dɪsko] *abbr* **discotheque**
discolor [dɪs'kʌlər] *tr* descolorar || *intr* descolorarse
discomfiture [dɪs'kʌmfɪtʃər] *s* desconcierto; frustración
discomfort [dɪs'kʌmfərt] *s* incomodidad || *tr* incomodar
disconcert [,dɪskən'sʌrt] *tr* desconcertar, confundir
disconnect [,dɪskə'nɛkt] *tr* desunir, separar; desconectar
disconsolate [dɪs'kɑnsəlɪt] *adj* desconsolado, desolado
discontent [,dɪskən'tɛnt] *adj & s* descontento || *tr* descontentar
discontented [,dɪskən'tɛntɪd] *adj* descontento
discontinue [,dɪskən'tɪnjʊ] *tr* descontinuar
discord ['dɪskɔrd] *s* desacuerdo, discordia; discordancia
discordance [dɪs'kɔrdəns] *s* discordancia
discotheque [,dɪsko'tɛk] *s* discoteca
discount ['dɪskaʊnt] *s* descuento || ['dɪskaʊnt] o [dɪs'kaʊnt] *tr* descontar; descontar por exagerado
discount rate *s* tipo de descuento; tipo de redescuento
discourage [dɪs'kʌrɪdʒ] *tr* desalentar, desanimar; desaprobar; disuadir
discouragement [dɪs'kʌrɪdʒmənt] *s* desaliento; desaprobación; disuasión
discourse ['dɪskors] o [dɪs'kors] *s* discurso || [dɪs'kors] *intr* discurrir
discourteous [dɪs'kʌrtɪ•əs] *adj* descortés
discourte•sy [dɪs'kʌrtəsi] *s* (*pl* **-sies**) descortesía
discover [dɪs'kʌvər] *tr* descubrir
discover•y [dɪs'kʌvəri] *s* (*pl* **-ies**) descubrimiento
discredit [dɪs'krɛdɪt] *s* descrédito || *tr* desacreditar
discreditable [dɪs'krɛdɪtəbəl] *adj* deshonroso
discreet [dɪs'krit] *adj* discreto
discrepan•cy [dɪs'krɛpənsi] *s* (*pl* **-cies**) discrepancia
discrete [dɪs'krit] *adj* discreto
discretion [dɪs'krɛʃən] *s* discreción; **at discretion** a discreción
discriminate [dɪs'krɪmɪ,net] *intr* discriminar; **to discriminate against** discriminar
discrimination [dɪs,krɪmɪ'neʃən] *s* discriminación
discriminatory [dɪs'krɪmɪnə,tori] *adj* discriminatorio
discus ['dɪskəs] *s* (sport) disco
discuss [dɪs'kʌs] *tr & intr* discutir
discussion [dɪs'kʌʃən] *s* discusión
discus thrower ['θro•ər] *s* discóbolo
disdain [dɪs'den] *s* desdén *m* || *tr* desdeñar
disdainful [dɪs'denfəl] *adj* desdeñoso
disease [dɪ'ziz] *s* enfermedad
diseased [dɪ'zizd] *adj* morboso
disembark [,dɪsɛm'bɑrk] *tr & intr* desembarcar
disembarkation [dɪs,ɛmbɑr'keʃən] *s* (*of passengers*) desembarco; (*of freight*) desembarque *m*
disembowel [,dɪsɛm'baʊ•əl] *tr* desentrañar
disenchant [,dɪsɛn'tʃænt] *tr* desencantar
disenchantment [,dɪsɛn'tʃæntmənt] *s* desencanto
disengage [,dɪsɛn'gedʒ] *tr* (*from a pledge*) desempeñar; (*to disconnect*) desenganchar; desembragar (*el motor*)
disengagement [,dɪsɛn'gedʒmənt] *s* desempeño; desenganche *m;* desembrague *m*
disentangle [,dɪsɛn'tæŋgəl] *tr* desenredar
disentanglement [,dɪsɛn'tæŋgəlmənt] *s* desenredo
disestablish [,dɪsɛs'tæblɪʃ] *tr* separar (*la Iglesia*) del Estado
disfavor [dɪs'fevər] *s* disfavor *m*
disfigure [dɪs'fɪgjər] *tr* desfigurar
disfranchise [dɪs'fræntʃaɪz] *tr* privar de los derechos de ciudadanía
disgorge [dɪs'gɔrdʒ] *tr & intr* vomitar
disgrace [dɪs'gres] *s* deshonra, vergüenza; disfavor *m;* metedura || *tr* deshonrar, avergonzar; despedir con ignominia
disgraceful [dɪs'gresfəl] *adj* deshonroso, vergonzoso
disgruntle [dɪs•grʌntəl] *tr* disgustar, enfadar
disguise [dɪs'gaɪz] *s* disfraz *m* || *tr* disfrazar
disgust [dɪs'gʌst] *s* asco, repugnancia || *tr* dar asco a, repugnar
disgusting [dɪs'gʌstɪŋ] *adj* asqueroso, repugnante; bofe (CAm)
dish [dɪʃ] *s* (*any container used at table*) vasija; (*shallow, circular dish; its contents*) plato; **to wash the dishes** lavar la vajilla || *tr* servir en un plato; (slang) arruinar

dish'cloth' *s* albero
dishearten [dɪs'hartən] *tr* descorazonar, desalentar, desanimar
dishev•el [dɪ'ʃɛvəl] *v* (*pret & pp* **-eled** o **-elled;** *ger* **-eling** o **-elling**) desgreñar, desmelenar
dishonest [dɪs'anɪst] *adj* no honrado, ímprobo
dishones•ty [dɪs'anɪsti] *s* (*pl* **-ties**) falta de honradez, improbidad
dishonor [dɪs'anər] *s* deshonra, deshonor *m* || *tr* deshonrar, deshonorar; (com) no aceptar, no pagar
dishonorable [dɪs'anərəbəl] *adj* ignominioso, deshonroso
dish'pan' *s* paila de lavar la vajilla
dish rack *s* escurreplatos *m*
dish'rag' *s* albero
dish'tow'el *s* paño para secar platos
dish'wash'er *s* (*person*) fregona; (*machine*) lavaplatos *m*, lavavajillas *m*
dish'wa'ter *s* agua de lavar platos, agua sucia
disillusion [,dɪsɪ'luʒən] *s* desilusión || *tr* desilusionar
disillusionment [,dɪsɪ'luʒənmənt] *s* desilusión
disinclination [dɪs,ɪnklɪ'neʃən] *s* aversión, desafición
disinclined [,dɪsɪn'klaɪnd] *adj* desinclinado
disinfect [,dɪsɪn'fɛkt] *tr* desinfectar, desinficionar
disinfectant [,dɪsɪn'fɛktant] *adj & s* desinfectante *m*
disingenuous [,dɪsɪn'dʒɛnjʊ•əs] *adj* insincero, poco ingenuo
disinherit [,dɪsɪn'hɛrɪt] *tr* desheredar
disintegrate [dɪs'ɪntɪ,gret] *tr* desagregar, desintegrar || *intr* desagregarse, desintegrarse
disintegration [dɪs,ɪntɪ'greʃən] *s* desagregación, desintegración
disin•ter [,dɪsɪn'tʌr] *v* (*pret & pp* **-terred;** *ger* **-terring**) *tr* desenterrar
disinterested [dɪs'ɪntə,rɛstɪd] o [dɪs'ɪntrɪstɪd] *adj* desinteresado
disinterestedness [dɪs'ɪntə,rɛstɪdɪnɛs] o [dɪs'ɪntrɪstɪdnɪs] *s* desinterés *m*
disjunctive [dɪs'dʒʌŋktɪv] *adj* disyuntivo
disk [dɪsk] *s* disco
disk brake *s* freno de disco
disk jockey *s* (rad) locutor *m* de un programa de discos
dislike [dɪs'laɪk] *s* aversión, antipatía; **to take a dislike for** cobrar aversión a || *tr* desamar
dislocate ['dɪslo,ket] *tr* dislocar, dislocarse (*un hueso*)
dislodge [dɪs'ladʒ] *tr* desalojar
disloyal [dɪs'lɔɪ•əl] *adj* desleal
disloyal•ty [dɪs'lɔɪ•əlti] *s* (*pl* **-ties**) deslealtad
dismal ['dɪzməl] *adj* lúgubre, tenebroso; terrible, espantoso
dismantle [dɪs'mæntəl] *tr* desarmar, desmontar
dismay [dɪs'me] *s* consternación || *tr* consternar
dismember [dɪs'mɛmbər] *tr* desmembrar
dismiss [dɪs'mɪs] *tr* despedir, destituir; desechar; alejar del pensamiento, echar en olvido
dismissal [dɪs'mɪsəl] *s* despedida, destitución
dismount [dɪs'maʊnt] *tr* desmontar || *intr* desmontarse
disobedience [,dɪsə'bidɪ•əns] *s* desobediencia
disobedient [,dɪsə'bidɪ•ənt] *adj* desobediente
disobey [,dɪsə'be] *tr & intr* desobedecer
disorder [dɪs'ɔrdər] *s* desorden *m* || *tr* desordenar
disorderly [dɪs'ɔrdərli] *adj* desordenado; alborotador, revoltoso
disorderly conduct *s* conducta contra el orden público
disorderly house *s* burdel *m*, lupanar *m*
disorganize [dɪs'ɔrgə,naɪz] *tr* desorganizar
disorientation [dɪs,ɔrien'teʃən] *s* desorientación
disown [dɪs'on] *tr* desconocer, repudiar
disparage [dɪs'pærɪdʒ] *tr* desacreditar, desdorar
disparagement [dɪs'pærɪdʒmənt] *s* descrédito, desdoro
disparate ['dɪspərɪt] *adj* disparejo
dispari•ty [dɪs'pærɪti] *s* (*pl* **-ties**) disparidad
dispassionate [dɪs'pæʃənɪt] *adj* desapasionado
dispatch [dɪs'pætʃ] *s* despacho || *tr* despachar; (coll) despabilar (*una comida*)
dis•pel [dɪs'pɛl] *v* (*pret & pp* **-pelled;** *ger* **-pelling**) *tr* desvanecer, disipar
dispensa•ry [dɪs'pɛnsəri] *s* (*pl* **-ries**) dispensario
dispense [dɪs'pɛns] *tr* dispensar (*medicamentos*); administrar (*justicia*); expender (*p.ej., gasolina*); (*to exempt*) eximir || *intr* **— to dispense with** deshacerse de; pasar sin, prescindir de
disperse [dɪs'pʌrs] *tr* dispersar || *intr* dispersarse
displace [dɪs'ples] *tr* remover, trasladar; despedir, deponer; reemplazar; desplazar (*un volumen de agua*)
displaced person *s* persona desplazada
display [dɪs'ple] *s* despliegue *m;* exhibición, exposición; ostentación || *tr* (*to unfold; to reveal*) desplegar; (*to exhibit, show*) exhibir, exponer; (*to show ostentatiously*) ostentar
display cabinet *s* vitrina, escaparate *m*
display window *s* escaparate *m* de tienda
displease [dɪs'pliz] *tr* desagradar, disgustar, desplacer
displeasing [dɪs'plizɪŋ] *adj* desagradable
displeasure [dɪs'plɛʒər] *s* desagrado, disgusto, desplacer *m*
disposable [dɪs'pozəbəl] *adj* (available for any use) disponible; (*made to be thrown away after serving its purpose*) desechable, descartable
disposal [dɪs'pozəl] *s* disposición; donación, liquidación, venta; **at the disposal of** a la disposición de; **to have at one's disposal** disponer de

dispose [dɪs'poz] *tr* disponer; inducir, mover || *intr* disponer; **to dispose of** disponer de; deshacerse de; dar, vender; acabar con
disposition [,dɪspə'zɪʃən] *s* disposición; índole *f*, genio, natural *m;* ajuste *m*, arreglo; venta
dispossess [,dɪspə'zɛs] *tr* desposeer; (*to evict, oust*) desahuciar
disproof [dɪs'pruf] *s* confutación, refutación
disproportionate [,dɪsprə'porʃənɪt] *adj* desproporcionado
disprove [dɪs'pruv] *tr* confutar, refutar
dispute [dɪs'pjut] *s* disputa; **beyond dispute** sin disputa; **in dispute** disputado || *tr & intr* disputar
disquali•fy [dɪs'kwɑlɪ,faɪ] *v* (*pret & pp* **-fied**) *tr* descalificar, desclasificar
disquiet [dɪs'kwaɪ•ət] *s* desasosiego, inquietud || *tr* desasosegar, inquietar
disregard [,dɪsrɪ'gɑrd] *s* desatención, desaire *m* || *tr* desatender, desairar, pasar por alto
disrepair [,dɪsrɪ'pɛɛr] *s* desconcierto, descompostura
disreputable [dɪs'rɛpjətəbəl] *adj* desacreditado, de mala fama; raído, usado, desaliñado
disrepute [,dɪsrɪ'pjut] *s* descrédito, mala fama; **to bring into disrepute** desacreditar, dar mala fama a
disrespect [,dɪsrɪ'spɛkt] *s* desacato || *tr* desacatar
disrespectful [,dɪsrɪ'spɛktfəl] *adj* irrespetuoso
disrobe [dɪs'rob] *tr* desnudar || *intr* desnudarse, despelotarse
disrupt [dɪs'rʌpt] *tr* romper; (*to throw into disorder*) desbaratar
dissatisfaction [,dɪssætɪs'fækʃən] *s* desagrado, descontento, insatisfacción
dissatisfied [dɪs'sætɪs,faɪd] *adj* descontento
dissatis•fy [dɪs'sætɪs,faɪ] *v* (*pret & pp* **-fied**) *tr* descontentar
dissect [dɪ'sɛkt] *tr* disecar
dissemble [dɪ'sɛmbəl] *tr* disimular || *intr* disimular; obrar hipócritamente
disseminate [dɪ'sɛmɪ,net] *tr* diseminar, difundir
dissension [dɪ'sɛnʃən] *s* disensión
dissent [dɪ'sɛnt] *s* disensión; (*nonconformity*) disidencia || *intr* disentir; (*from doctrine or authority*) disidir
dissenter [dɪ'sɛntər] *s* disidente *mf*
disservice [dɪ'sʌrvɪs] *s* deservicio
dissidence ['dɪsɪdəns] *s* disidencia
dissident ['dɪsɪdənt] *adj & s* disidente *mf*
dissimilar [dɪ'sɪmɪlər] *adj* disímil, desemejante
dissimilate [dɪ'sɪmɪ,let] *tr* disimilar || *intr* disimilarse
dissimulate [dɪ'sɪmjə,let] *tr & intr* disimular
dissipate ['dɪsɪ,pet] *tr* disipar || *intr* disiparse; entregarse a la disipación
dissipated ['dɪsɪ,petɪd] *adj* disipado, disoluto
dissipation [,dɪsɪ'peʃən] *s* disipación
dissociate [dɪ'soʃɪ,et] *tr* disociar
dissolute ['dɪsə,lut] *adj* disoluto
dissolution [,dɪsə'luʃən] *s* disolución
dissolve [dɪ'zɑlv] *tr* disolver || *intr* (*to have the power of dissolving*) disolver; (*to pass into a liquid*) disolverse
dissonance ['dɪsənəns] *s* disonancia
dissuade [dɪ'swed] *tr* disuadir
dissyllabic [,dɪssɪ'læbɪk] *adj* disílabo, disilábico
dissyllable [dɪ'sɪləbəl] *s* disílabo
dist. *abbr* **distance, distinguish, district**
distaff ['dɪstæf] o ['dɪstɑf] *s* rueca
distaff side *s* rama femenina de la familia
distance ['dɪstəns] *s* distancia; **at a distance** a distancia; **in the distance** a lo lejos; **to keep at a distance** no permitir familiaridades; **to keep one's distance** mantenerse a distancia
distant ['dɪstənt] *adj* distante; (*relative*) lejano; (*not familiar*) frío, indiferente
distaste [dɪs'test] *s* aversión, repugnancia
distasteful [dɪs'testfəl] *adj* desagradable, repugnante
distemper [dɪs'tɛmpər] *s* enfermedad; (*of dogs*) moquillo
distend [dɪs'tɛnd] *tr* ensanchar, distender || *intr* ensancharse, distender
distension [dɪs'tɛnʃən] *s* ensanche *m*, distensión
distill [dɪs'tɪl] *tr* destilar
distillation [,dɪstɪ'leʃən] *s* destilación
distiller•y [dɪs'tɪləri] *s* (*pl* **-ies**) destilería, destilatorio
distinct [dɪs'tɪŋkt] *adj* distinto; cierto, indudable; (*not blurred*) nítido, bien definido
distinction [dɪs'tɪŋkʃən] *s* distinción; (*distinguishing characteristic*) distintivo
distinctive [dɪs'tɪŋktɪv] *adj* distintivo
distinguish [dɪs'tɪŋgwɪʃ] *tr* distinguir
distinguished [dɪs'tɪŋgwɪʃt] *adj* distinguido
distort [dɪs'tɔrt] *tr* deformar, torcer; distorsionar; (*the truth*) falsear
distortion [dɪs'tɔrʃən] *s* deformación, torcimiento; (*of the truth*) falseamiento; (rad) deformación, distorsión
distract [dɪs'trækt] *tr* distraer
distraction [dɪs'trækʃən] *s* distracción
distraught [dɪs'trɔt] *adj* trastornado, perplejo, aturdido
distress [dɪs'trɛs] *s* pena, aflicción, angustia; infortunio, peligro || *tr* apenar, afligir, angustiar
distressing [dɪs'trɛsɪŋ] *adj* penoso, angustioso
distress signal *s* señal *f* de socorro
distribute [dɪs'trɪbjʊt] *tr* distribuir, repartir
distribution [,dɪstrɪ'bjuʃən] *s* distribución, repartimiento, repartida
distributor [dɪs'trɪbjətər] *s* distribuidor *m;* (aut) distribuidor
district ['dɪstrɪkt] *s* comarca, región; (*of a city*) barrio; (*administrative division*) distrito || *tr* dividir en distritos
district attorney *s* fiscal *m*
distrust [dɪs'trʌst] *s* desconfianza || *tr* desconfiar de
distrustful [dɪs'trʌstfəl] *adj* desconfiado
disturb [dɪs'tʌrb] *tr* disturbar, incomodar, molestar; desordenar, revolver; inquietar,

dejar perplejo; perturbar (*el orden público*)

disturbance [dɪs'tʌrbəns] *s* disturbio, molestia; desorden *m;* inquietud; tumulto, trastorno

disuse [dɪs'jus] *s* desuso

ditch [dɪtʃ] *s* zanja || *tr* zanjar; echar en una zanja; (slang) deshacerse de || *intr* amarar forzosamente

ditch reed *s* carrizo

dither ['dɪðər] *s* agitación, temblor; **to be in a dither** (coll) estar muy agitado

dit•to ['dɪto] *s* (*pl* **-tos**) ídem *m;* (*ditto symbol*) íd.; copia, duplicado || *tr* copiar, duplicar

ditto mark *s* la sigla " (*es decir:* íd.)

dit•ty ['dɪti] *s* (*pl* **-ties**) cancioneta

diuretic [,daɪə'rɛtɪk] *adj & s* diurético

div. *abbr* **dividend, division**

diva ['divɑ] *s* (mus) diva

divan ['daɪvæn] o [dɪ'væn] *s* diván *m*

dive [daɪv] *s* zambullida; (*of a submarine*) sumersión; (aer) picado; (coll) leonera, tasca || *v* (*pret & pp* **dived** o **dove** [dov]) *intr* zambullirse; (*to work as a diver*) bucear; sumergirse (*un submarino*); (aer) picar

dive'-bomb' *tr & intr* bombardear en picado

dive bombing *s* bombardeo en picado

diver ['daɪvər] *s* zambullidor *m;* buceador; (*person who works under water*) escafandrista *mf,* buzo; (orn) zambullidor *m*

diverge [dɪ'vʌrdʒ] o [daɪ'vʌrdʒ] *intr* divergir

divers ['daɪvərz] *adj* diversos, varios

diverse [dɪ'vʌrs] o [daɪ'vʌrs] *adj* (*different*) diverso; (*of various kinds*) variado

diversification [dɪ'vʌrsɪfɪ'keʃən] o [daɪ,vʌrsɪfɪ'keʃən] *s* diversificación

diversi•fy [dɪ'vʌrsɪ,faɪ] o [daɪ'vʌrsɪ,faɪ] *v* (*pret & pp* **-fied**) *tr* diversificar || *intr* diversificarse

diversion [dɪ'vʌrʒən] o [daɪ'vʌrʒən] *s* diversión

diversi•ty [dɪ'vʌrsɪti] o [daɪ'vʌrsɪti] *s* (*pl* **-ties**) diversidad

divert [dɪ'vʌrt] o [daɪ'vʌrt] *tr* apartar, divertir; (*to entertain*) divertir, entretener; (mil) divertir

diverting [dɪ'vʌrtɪŋ] o [daɪ'vʌrtɪŋ] *adj* divertido

divest [dɪ'vɛst] o [daɪ'vɛst] *tr* desnudar; despojar, desposeer; **to divest oneself of** desposeerse de

divide [dɪ'vaɪd] *s* (geog) divisoria || *tr* dividir || *intr* dividirse

dividend ['dɪvɪ,dɛnd] *s* dividendo

dividers [dɪ'vaɪdərz] *spl* compás *m* de división

divination [,dɪvɪ'neʃən] *s* adivinación

divine [dɪ'vaɪn] *adj* divino || *s* sacerdote *m,* clérigo || *tr* adivinar

diving ['daɪvɪŋ] *s* zambullida; buceo

diving bell *s* campana de buzo

diving board *s* trampolín *m*

diving suit *s* escafandra

divining rod [dɪ'vaɪnɪŋ] *s* vara de adivinar; (*ostensibly to discover water or metals*) vara buscadora

divini•ty [dɪ'vɪnɪti] *s* (*pl* **-ties**) divinidad; teología; **the Divinity** Dios *m*

division [dɪ'vɪʒən] *s* división

divisor [dɪ'vaɪzər] *s* (math) divisor *m*

divorce [di'vors] *s* divorcio; **to get a divorce** divorciarse || *tr* divorciar (*los cónyuges*); divorciarse de (*la mujer o el marido*) || *intr* divorciarse

divorcee [dɪvor'si] *s* persona divorciada; mujer divorciada

divulge [dɪ'vʌldʒ] *tr* divulgar, revelar

dizziness ['dɪzɪnɪs] *s* vértigo; confusión, perplejidad

diz•zy ['dɪzi] *adj* (*comp* **-zier;** *super* **-ziest**) (*suffering or causing dizziness*) vertiginoso; confuso, perplejo; aturdido, incauto; (coll) tonto

do. *abbr* **ditto**

do [du] *v* (*tercera persona* **does** [dʌz]; *pret* **did** [dɪd]; *pp* **done** [dʌn]) *tr* hacer; resolver (*un problema*); recorrer (*cierta distancia*); cumplir con (*un deber*); aprender (*una lección*); componer (*la cama*); tocar (*el cabello*); rendir (*homenaje*); **to do one's best** hacer todo lo posible; **to do over** volver a hacer; repetir; renovar; **to do right by** tratar bien; **to do someone out of something** (coll) defraudar algo a alguien; **to do to death** despachar, matar; **to do up** empaquetar; poner en orden; almidonar y planchar (*una camisa*) || *intr* actuar, obrar; conducirse; servir, ser suficiente; estar, hallarse; **how do you do?** ¿cómo está Vd.?; **that will do** eso sirve, eso es bastante; no digas más; **to have done** haber terminado; **to have done with** no tener más que ver con; **to have nothing to do with** no tener nada que ver con; **to have to do with** tratar de; **to do away with** suprimir; matar; **to do for** servir para; **to do well** salir bien; **to do without** pasar sin || *v aux* úsase 1) en oraciones interrogativas: **Do you speak Spanish?** ¿Habla Vd. español?; 2) en oraciones negativas; **I do not speak Spanish** No hablo español; 3) para substituir a otro verbo en oraciones elípticas; **Did you go to church this morning? Yes, I did** ¿Fué Vd. a la iglesia esta mañana? Sí, fuí; 4) para dar más energía a la oración; **I do believe what you told me** Yo sí creo lo que me dijo Vd.; 5) en inversiones después de ciertos adverbios; **Seldom does he come to see me** él rara vez viene a verme; 6) en tono suplicante con el imperativo; **Do come in** pase Vd., por favor

docile ['dɑsɪl] *adj* dócil

dock [dɑk] *s* (*wharf*) muelle *m;* (*waterway between two piers*) dársena; (*area including piers and waterways*) puerto de mar; muñón *m* de cola; (law) tribuna de los acusados || *tr* (naut) atracar en el muelle; derrabar, descolar (*a un animal*); reducir o suprimir (*el salario*) || *intr* (naut) atracar

dockage ['dɑkɪdʒ] *s* entrada en un puerto; (*charges*) muellaje *m*

docket [ˈdɑkɪt] *s* actas, orden *m* del día; lista de causas pendientes; **on the docket** (coll) pendiente, entre manos
dock hand *s* portuario
dock'yard' *s* arsenal *m*, astillero
doctor [ˈdɑktər] *s* doctor *m;* (*physician*) médico ‖ *tr* medicinar; (coll) componer, reparar ‖ *intr* (coll) ejercer la medicina; (coll) tomar medicinas
doctorate [ˈdɑktərɪt] *s* doctorado
doctrine [ˈdɑktrɪn] *s* doctrina
document [ˈdɑkjəmənt] *s* documento ‖ [ˈdɑkjə,mɛnt] *tr* documentar
documenta•ry [,dɑkjəˈmɛntəri] *adj* documental ‖ *s* (*pl* **-ries**) documental *m*
documentation [,dɑkəmɛnˈteʃən] *s* documentación
doddering [ˈdɑdərɪŋ] *adj* chocho, temblón
dodge [dɑdʒ] *s* esguince *m*, regate *m;* (fig) regate ‖ *tr* evitar (*un golpe*); (fig) evitar mañosamente ‖ *intr* regatear, hurtar el cuerpo; **to dodge around the corner** voltear la esquina
do•do [ˈdodo] *s* (*pl* **-dos** o **-does**) (coll) inocente *m* de ideas anticuadas
doe [do] *s* cierva, gama, coneja
doeskin [ˈdo,skɪn] *s* ante *m*, piel *f* de ante; tejido fino de lana
doff [dɑf] o [dɔf] *tr* quitarse (*el sombrero, la ropa*)
dog [dɔg] o [dɑg] *s* perro; **to go to the dogs** darse al abandono; **lucky dog** (coll) lechero, suertero; **to put on the dog** (coll) darse ínfulas ‖ *v* (*pret & pp* **dogged;** *ger* **dogging**) *tr* acosar, perseguir
dog'catch'er *s* lacero
dog days *spl* canícula, canicularse *mpl*
doge [dodʒ] dux *m*
dogged [ˈdɔgɪd] *adj* tenaz, terco
doggerel [ˈdɔgərəl] *s* coplas de ciego
dog•gy [ˈdɔgi] *adj* (*comp* **-gier;** *super* **-giest**) emperejilado ‖ *s* (*pl -gies*) perrito
dog'house' *s* perrera
dog in the manger *s* el perro del hortelano
dog Latin *s* latinajo, latín *m* de cocina
dogmatic [dɑgˈmætɪk] *adj* dogmático; ergotista
dog racing *s* carreras de galgos
dog's-ear [ˈdɔgzəɪr] *s* orejón *m*
dog show *s* exposición canina
dog's life *s* vida miserable
Dog Star *s* Canícula
dog'-tired' *adj* cansadísimo
dog'tooth' *s* (*pl* **-teeth** [,tiθ] colmillo
dog track *s* galgódromo
dog'watch' *s* (naut) guardia de cuartillo
dog'wood' *s* cornejo
doi•ly [ˈdɔɪli] *s* (*pl* **-lies**) pañito de adorno
doings [ˈdu•ɪŋz] *spl* acciones, obras, actividad
doldrums [ˈdɑldrəmz] *spl* (naut) calmas ecuatoriales; desanimación, inactividad
dole [dol] *s* limosna; subsidio a los desocupados ‖ *tr* — **to dole out** distribuir en pequeñas porciones
doleful [ˈdolfəl] *adj* triste, lúgubre
doll [dɑl] *s* muñeca ‖ *intr* — **to doll up** (slang) emperejilarse
dollar [ˈdɑlər] *s* dólar *m*
dollar mark *s* signo del dólar
dol•ly [ˈdɑli] *s* (*pl* **-lies**) muñequita; (*low, wheeled frame for moving heavy loads*) gato rodante
dolphin [ˈdɑlfɪn] *s* delfín *m*
dolt [dolt] *s* bobalicón *m*
doltish [ˈdoltɪʃ] *adj* bobalicón
dom. *abbr* **domestic, dominion**
domain [doˈmen] *s* dominio, heredad, propiedad; (*of learning*) campo
dome [dom] *s* cúpula, domo
dome light *s* (aut) lámpara de techo
domestic [dəˈmɛstɪk] *adj & s* doméstico
domesticate [dəˈmɛstɪ,ket] *tr* domesticar
domicile [ˈdɑmɪsɪl] o [ˈdɑmɪ,saɪl] *s* domicilio ‖ *tr* domiciliar
dominance [ˈdɑmɪnəns] *s* dominación
dominant [ˈdɑmɪnənt] *adj & s* dominante *f*
dominate [ˈdɑmɪ,net] *tr & intr* dominar
domination [,dɑmɪˈneʃən] *s* dominación
domineer [,dɑmɪˈnɪr] *intr* dominar
domineering [,dɑmɪˈnɪrɪŋ] *adj* dominante, mandón
Dominican [dəˈmɪnɪkən] *adj & s* dominicano
dominion [dəˈmɪnjən] *s* dominio
domi•no [ˈdɑmɪ,no] *s* (*pl* **-noes** o **-nos**) (*costume*) dominó *m;* antifaz *m;* persona que lleva dominó; ficha (*del juego de dominó*); **dominoes** *ssg* dominó (*juego*)
don [dɑn] *s* caballero, señor *m*, personaje *m* de alta categoría; (coll) preceptor *m*, socio de uno de los colegios de las Universidades de Oxford y Cambridge ‖ *v* (*pret & pp* **donned;** *ger* **donning**) *tr* ponerse (*el sombrero, la ropa*)
donate [ˈdonet] *tr* dar, donar
donation [doˈneʃən] *s* donación
done [dʌn] *adj* hecho, terminado; cansado, rendido; bien asado
done for *adj* (coll) cansado, rendido, agotado; (coll) arruinado, destruído; (coll) fuera de combate; (coll) muerto
donjon [ˈdʌndʒən] *s* torre *f* del homenaje
donkey [ˈdɑŋki] *s* asno, burro
donnish [ˈdɑnɪʃ] *adj* magistral, pedantesco
donor [ˈdonər] *s* donador *m*
doodle [ˈdudəl] *tr & intr* borrajear
doom [dum] *s* ruina, perdición, muerte *f;* condena, juicio; juicio final; hado, destino ‖ *tr* condenar; sentenciar a muerte; predestinar a la ruina, a la muerte
doomsday [ˈdumz,de] *s* día *m* del juicio final; día del juicio
door [dor] *s* puerta; (*of a carriage or automobile*) portezuela; (*one part of a double door*) hoja, batiente *m;* **behind closed doors** a puertas cerradas; **to see to the door** acompañar a la puerta
door'bell' *s* campanilla de puerta, timbre *m* de puerta
door check *s* amortiguador *m*, cierre *m* de puerta

door'frame' *s* bastidor *m* de puerta, marco de puerta
door'head' *s* dintel *m*
door'jamb' *s* jamba de puerta
door'knob' *s* botón *m* de puerta, pomo de puerta
door knocker *s* aldaba
door latch *s* pestillo
door•man [ˈdɔrmən] *s* (*pl* *-men* [mən]) portero; (*one who helps people in and out of cars*) abrecoches *m*
door'mat' *s* felpudo de puerta
door'nail' *s* clavo de adorno para puertas; **dead as a doornail** (coll) muerto sin duda alguna
door'post' *s* jamba de puerta
door scraper *s* limpiabarros *m*
door'sill' *s* umbral *m*
door'step' *s* escalón *m* delante de la puerta; escalera exterior
door'stop' *s* tope *m* de puerta
door'way' *s* puerta, portal *m*
dope [dop] *s* grasa lubricante; (aer) barniz *m*, nobabia; (slang) bobo, tonto; (slang) informes *mpl;* (slang) narcótico || *tr* (slang) narcotizar, drogar; **to dope out** (slang) descifrar
dope fiend *s* (slang) toxicómano
dope sheet *s* (slang) hoja confidencial sobre los caballos de carreras
dormant [ˈdɔrmənt] *adj* durmiente, latente
dormer window [ˈdɔrmər] *s* buharda, buhardilla
dormito•ry [ˈdɔrmɪ,tori] *s* (*pl* **-ries**) dormitorio común
dor•mouse [ˈdɔr,maʊs] *s* (*pl* **-mice** [,maɪs]) lirón *m*
dosage [ˈdosɪdʒ] *s* dosificación
dose [dos] *s* dosis *f;* (coll) mal trago || *tr* medicinar; dosificar (*un medicamento*)
dossier [ˈdɑsɪ,e] *s* expediente *m*
dot [dɑt] *s* punto; **on the dot** (coll) en punto || *v* (*pret & pp* **dotted;** *ger* **dotting**) *tr* (*to make with dots*) puntear; poner punto a; **to dot one's i's** poner los puntos sobre las íes
dotage [ˈdotɪdʒ] *s* chochera, chochez *f;* **to be in one's dotage** chochear
dotard [ˈdotərd] *s* viejo chocho
dote [dot] *intr* chochear; **to dote on** estar chocho por
doting [ˈdotɪŋ] *adj* chocho
dots and dashes *spl* (telg) puntos y rayas
dotted line [ˈdɑtɪd] *s* línea de puntos; **to sign on the dotted line** firmar ciegamente
double [ˈdʌbəl] *adj* doble || *adv* doble; dos juntos || *s* doble *m*, duplo; (mov, theat) doble *mf;* **doubles** (tennis juego de dobles || *tr* doblar; ser el doble de; (bridge) doblar || *intr* doblarse; (mov, theat, bridge) doblar; **to double up** doblarse en dos; ocupar una misma habitación, dormir en una misma cama (*dos personas*)
double-barreled [ˈdʌbəlˈbærəld] *adj* de dos cañones; (fig) para dos fines
double bass [bes] *s* contrabajo
double bassoon *s* contrabajón *m*
double bed *s* cama de matrimonio
double-breasted [ˈdʌbəlˈbrɛstɪd] *adj* cruzado, de dos pechos
double chin *s* papada
dou'ble-cross' *tr* traicionar (*a un cómplice*)
double date *s* cita de dos parejas
doub'le-deal'er *s* persona doble
double-edged [ˈdʌbəlˈɛdʒd] *adj* de dos filos
double entry *s* (com) partida doble
double feature *s* (mov) programa *m* doble, programa de dos películas de largo metraje
doubleheader [ˈdʌbəlˈhɛdər] *s* tren *m* con dos locomotoras; (baseball) dos partidos jugados sucesivamente
double-jointed [ˈdʌbəlˈdʒɔɪntɪd] *adj* de articulaciones dobles
dou'ble-park' *tr & intr* aparcar en doble fila
dou'ble-quick' *adj & adv* a paso ligero || *s* paso ligero || *intr* marchar a paso ligero
doublet [ˈdʌblɪt] *s* (*close-fitting jacket*) jubón *m;* (*counterfeit stone; each of two words having the same origin*) doblete *m*
double talk *s* (coll) galimatías *m;* (coll) habla ambigua para engañar
double time *s* pago doble por horas extraordinarias de trabajo; (mil) paso redoblado
doubleton [ˈdʌbəltən] *s* doblete *m*
double track *s* doble vía
doubling [ˈdʌblɪŋ] *s* reduplicación
doubt [daʊt] *s* duda; **beyond doubt** sin duda; **if in doubt** en caso de duda; **no doubt** sin duda || *tr* dudar, dudar de || *intr* dudar
doubter [ˈdaʊtər] *s* incrédulo
doubtful [ˈdaʊtfəl] *adj* dudoso
doubtless [ˈdaʊtlɪs] *adj* indudable || *adv* sin duda; probablemente
douche [duʃ] *s* ducha; (*instrument*) jeringa || *tr* duchar || *intr* ducharse
dough [do] *s* masa, pasta; (*money*) (slang) pasta
dough'boy' *s* (coll) soldado norteamericano de infantería
dough'nut' *s* rosquilla, buñuelo
dough•ty [ˈdaʊti] *adj* (*comp* **-tier;** *super* **-tiest**) (hum) fuerte, valiente
dough•y [ˈdo•i] *adj* (*comp* **-ier;** *super* **-iest**) pastoso
dour [daʊr] o [dʊr] *adj* triste, melancólico, austero
douse [daʊs] *tr* empapar, mojar, salpicar; (slang) apagar (*la luz*)
dove [dʌv] *s* paloma
dovecote [ˈdʌv,kot] *s* palomar *m*
dove'tail' *s* cola de milano, cola de pato || *tr* ensamblar a cola de milano, ensamblar a cola de pato; (*to make fit*) encajar || *intr* (*to fit*) encajar; concordar, corresponder
dowager [ˈdaʊ•ədʒər] *s* viuda con título o bienes que proceden del marido, p.ej., **dowager duchess** duquesa viuda; (coll) matrona, señora anciana respetable
dow•dy [ˈdaudi] *adj* (*comp* **-dier;** *super* **-diest**) desaliñado
dow•el [ˈdaʊ•əl] *s* clavija || *v* (*pret & pp* **-eled** o **-elled;** *ger* **-eling** o **-elling**) *tr* enclavijar
dower [ˈdaʊ•ər] *s* (*widow's portion*) viudedad; (*marriage portion*) dote *m & f*; (*natu-*

ral gift) prenda || *tr* señalar viudedad a; dotar

down [daʊn] *adj* descendente; abatido, triste; enfermo, malo; acostado, echado; (*money, payment*) anticipado; (*storage battery*) agotado; (mach) (coll) fuera de servicio || *adv* abajo; hacia abajo; en tierra; al sur; por escrito; al contado; **down and out** arruinado; sin blanca; **down from** desde; **down on one's knees** de rodillas; **down to** hasta; **down under** entre los antípodas; **down with . . . !** ¡abajo . . . !; **to get down to work** aplicarse resueltamente al trabajo; **to go down** bajar; **to lie down** acostarse; **to sit down** sentarse || *prep* bajando; **down the river** río abajo; **down the street** calle abajo || *s* (*of fruit and human body*) vello; (*of birds*) plumón *m;* descenso, revés *m* de fortuna; (*sand hill*) duna || *tr* derribar; (coll) tragar

down'cast' *adj* cariacontecido

down'fall' *s* caída, ruina; chaparrón *m;* nevazo

down'grade' *adj* (coll) pendiente, en declive || *adv* (coll) cuesta abajo || *s* bajada, declive *m;* **to be on the downgrade** decaer, declinar || *tr* disminuir la categoría de

downhearted ['daʊn,hɑrtɪd] *adj* abatido, desanimado

down'hill' *adj* pendiente || *adv* cuesta abajo; **to go downhill** ir cabeza abajo

down'pour' *s* aguacero, chaparrón *m*

down'right' *adj* absoluto, categórico; franco; claro || *adv* absolutamente

down'stairs' *adj* de abajo || *adv* abajo || *s* piso inferior, pisos inferiores; (*the help*) la servidumbre

down'stream' *adv* aguas abajo, río abajo

down'stroke' *s* carrera descendente

down'town' *adj* céntrico || *adv* al centro de la ciudad, en el centro de la ciudad || *s* barrios céntricos, calles céntricas

down train *s* tren *m* descendente

down'trend' *s* tendencia a la baja

downtrodden ['daʊn,trɑdən] *adj* pisoteado, oprimido

downward ['daʊnwərd] *adj* descendente || *adv* hacia abajo; hacia una época posterior

down•y ['daʊni] *adj* (*comp* **-ier;** *super* **-iest**) plumoso, felpudo, velloso; suave, blando

dow•ry ['daʊri] *s* (*pl* **-ries**) dote *m & f*

doz. *abbr* **dozen**

doze [doz] *s* duermevela, sueño ligero || *intr* dormitar

dozen ['dʌzən] *s* docena

dozy ['dozi] *adj* soñoliento

D.P. *abbr* **displaced person**

dpt. *abbr* **department**

dr. *abbr* **debtor, drawer, dram**

Dr. *abbr* **debtor, Doctor**

drab [dræb] *adj* (*comp* **drabber;** *super* **drabbest**) gris amarillento; monótono || *s* gris amarillento; ramera; mujer desaliñada

drach•ma ['drækmə] *s* (*pl* **-mas** o **-mae** [mi]) dracma

draft [dræft] *s* corriente *f* de aire; (*pulling; current of air in a chimney*) tiro; (*sketch, outline*) bosquejo; (*first form of a writing*) borrador *m;* (*drink*) bebida, trago; (com) giro, letra de cambio, libranza; aire inspirado; (naut) calado; (mil) conscripción, quinta; **drafts** damas, juego de damas; **on draft** a presión; **to be exempted from the draft** redimirse de las quintas || *tr* dibujar; bosquejar; hacer un borrador de; redactar (*un documento*); (mil) quintar; **to be drafted** (mil) ir a quintas

draft age *s* edad *f* de quintas

draft beer *s* cerveza a presión

draft board *s* (mil) junta de reclutamiento

draft call *s* llamada a quintas

draft dodger ['dɑdʒər] *s* emboscado

draftee [,dræf'ti] *s* conscripto, quinto

draft horse *s* caballo de tiro

drafting room *s* sala de dibujo

drafts•man ['dræftsmən] *s* (*pl* **-men** [mən]) dibujante *m;* (*man who draws up documents*) redactor *m;* (*in checkers*) peón *m*

draft treaty *s* proyecto de convenio

draft•y ['dræfti] *adj* (*comp* **-ier;** *super* **-iest**) airoso, con corrientes de aire

drag [dræg] *s* (*sledge for conveying heavy bodies*) narria; (*on a cigarette*) chupada; fumada; (naut) rastra; (aer) resistencia al avance; (fig) estorbo, impedimento; **to have a drag** (slang) tener buenas aldabas, tener enchufe || *v* (*pret & pp* **dragged;** *ger* **dragging**) *tr* arrastrar; (naut) rastrear || *intr* arrastrarse por el suelo; avanzar muy lentamente; decaer (*el interés*); **to drag on** ser interminable, prolongarse interminablemente

drag'net' *s* red barredera

dragon ['drægən] *s* dragón *m*

drag'on-fly' *s* (*pl* **-flies**) caballito del diablo, libélula

dragoon [drə'gun] *s* (*soldier*) dragón *m* || *tr* tiranizar; forzar, constreñir

drain [dren] *s* dren *m,* desaguadero, desagüe *m;* (surg) dren *m;* (*source of continual expense*) (fig) desaguadero || *tr* drenar, desaguar; avenar (*terrenos húmedos*); escurrir (*una vasija; un líquido*) || *intr* desaguarse; escurrirse

drainage ['drenɪdʒ] *s* drenaje *m,* desagüe *m*

drain'board' *s* escurridero

drain cock *s* llave *f* de purga

drain'pipe' *s* tubo de desagüe, escurridero

drain plug *s* tapón *m* de desagüe; (aut) tapón de vaciado

drake [drek] *s* pato

dram [dræm] *s* dracma; trago de aguardiente

drama ['drɑmə] o ['dræmə] *s* drama *m;* (*art and genre*) dramática

dramatic [drə'mætɪk] *adj* dramático || **dramatics** *ssg* representación de aficionados; *spl* obras representadas por aficionados

dramatist ['dræmətɪst] *s* dramático

dramatize ['dræmə,taɪz] *tr* dramatizar

dram'shop' *s* bar *m,* taberna

drape [drep] *s* cortina, colgadura; (*hang of a curtain, skirt, etc.*) caída || *tr* cubrir con colgaduras; adornar con colgaduras; dis-

poner los pliegues de (*una colgadura, una prenda de vestir*)
draper•y [ˈdrepəri] *s* (*pl* **-ies**) colgaduras, ropaje *m*
drastic [ˈdræstɪk] *adj* drástico
draught [dræft] *s & tr* var de **draft**
draught beer *s* cerveza a presión
draw [drɔ] *s* (*in a game or other contest*) empate *m;* (*in chess or checkers*) tablas; (*in a lottery*) sorteo; (*card drawn from the bank*) robo; (*of a drawbridge*) compuerta; (*of a chimney*) tiro ‖ *v* (*pret* **drew** [dru]; *pp* **drawn** [drɔn]) *tr* tirar (*una línea; alambre*); (*to attract*) tirar; (*to pull*) tirar de; derretir (*la mantequilla*); sacar (*un clavo, una espada, agua, una conclusión*); atraerse (*aplausos*); atraer (*a la gente*); aspirar (*el aire*); llamar (*la atención*); dar (*un suspiro*); correr (*una cortina*); cobrar (*un salario*); sacarse (*un premio*); empatar (*una partida*); robar (*fichas, naipes*); levantar (*un puente levadizo*); calar (*un buque cierta profundidad*); hacer (*una comparación*); consumir (*amperios*); (*to sketch in lines*) dibujar; (*to sketch in words*) redactar; (com) girar, librar; (com) devengar (*interés*); **to draw forth** hacer salir; **to draw off** sacar, extraer; trasegar (*un líquido*); **to draw on** ocasionar, provocar; ponerse (*p.ej., los zapatos*); (com) girar a cargo de; **to draw oneself up** enderezarse con dignidad; **to draw out** (*to persuade to talk*) sonsacar, tirar de la lengua a; **to draw up** redactar (*un documento*); (mil) ordenar para el combate ‖ *intr* tirar, tirar bien (*una chimenea*); empatar; echar suertes; atraer mucha gente; dibujar; **to draw aside** apartarse; **to draw back** retroceder, retirarse; **to draw near** acercarse; acercarse a; **to draw to a close** estar para terminar; **to draw together** juntarse, unirse
draw'back' *s* desventaja, inconveniente *m*
draw'bridge' *s* puente levadizo
drawee [,drɔˈi] *s* girado, librado
drawer [ˈdrɔ•ər] *s* dibujante *mf;* (com) girador *m,* librador *m* ‖ [drɔr] *s* cajón *m,* gaveta; **drawers** calzoncillos
drawing [ˈdrɔ•ɪŋ] *s* dibujo; (*in a lottery*) sorteo
drawing board *s* tablero de dibujo
drawing card *s* polo de atracción popular
drawing room *s* sala, salón *m*
draw'knife' *s* (*pl* **-knives** [,naɪvz]) cuchilla de dos mangos
drawl [drɔl] *s* habla lenta y prolongada ‖ *tr* decir lenta y prolongadamente ‖ *intr* hablar lenta y prolongadamente
drawn butter [drɔn] *s* mantequilla derretida
drawn work *s* calado, deshilado
dray [dre] *s* carro fuerte, camión *m;* (*sledge*) narria
drayage [ˈdre•ɪdʒ] *s* acarreo
dread [drɛd] *adj* espantoso, terrible ‖ *s* pavor *m,* terror *m* ‖ *tr & intr* temer
dreadful [ˈdrɛdfəl] *adj* espantoso, terrible; (coll) feo, desagradable
dread'naught' *s* (nav) gran buque acorazado
dream [drim] *s* sueño, ensueño; (*thing of great beauty*) sueño; (*fancy, illusion*) ensueño; **dream come true** sueño hecho realidad ‖ *v* (*pret & pp* **dreamed** o **dreamt** [drɛmt]) *tr* soñar; **to dream up** (coll) imaginar, inventar; ‖ *intr* soñar; **to dream of** soñar con
dreamer [ˈdrimər] *s* soñador *m*
dream'land' *s* reino del ensueño
dream'world' *s* tierra de la fantasía
dream•y [ˈdrimi] *adj* (*comp* **-ier;** *super* **-iest**) soñador; visionario; vago
drear•y [ˈdrɪri] *adj* (*comp* **-ier;** *super* **-iest**) sombrío, triste; monótono, pesado
dredge [drɛdʒ] *s* draga ‖ *tr* dragar, rastrear; (culin) enharinar
dredger [ˈdrɛdʒər] *s* draga (*barco*)
dredging [ˈdrɛdʒɪŋ] *s* dragado
dregs [drɛgz] *spl* heces *fpl;* (*of society*) hez *f*
drench [drɛntʃ] *tr* mojar, empapar
dress [drɛs] *s* ropa, vestidos; vestido de mujer; (*skirt*) falda; traje *m* de etiqueta; (*of a bird*) plumaje *m* ‖ *tr* vestir; (*to provide with clothing*) trajear; peinar (*el pelo*); curar (*una herida*); zurrar (*el cuero*); empavesar (*un barco*); adornar, ataviar; aderezar, aliñar (*los manjares*); **to dress down** (coll) reprender; **to get dressed** vestirse ‖ *intr* (*to put one's clothing on*) vestirse; (*to wear clothes*) vestir; (mil) alinearse; **to dress up** vestirse de etiqueta; ponerse de veinticinco alfileres; disfrazarse
dress ball *s* baile *m* de etiqueta
dress coat *s* frac *m*
dresser [ˈdrɛsər] *s* tocador *m;* cómoda con espejo; (*sideboard*) aparador *m;* **to be a good dresser** vestir con elegancia
dress form *s* maniquí *m*
dress goods *spl* géneros para vestidos
dressing [ˈdrɛsɪŋ] *s* adorno; (*for food*) aliño, salsa; (*stuffing for fowl*) relleno; (*fertilizer*) abono; (*for a wound*) vendaje *m*
dress'ing-down' *s* (coll) repasata, regaño
dressing gown *s* bata, peinador *m*
dressing room *s* cuarto de vestir; (theat) camarín *m*
dressing station *s* (mil) puesto de socorro
dressing table *s* tocador *m*; peinador *m*
dress'mak'er *s* costurera, modista
dress'mak'ing *s* costura, modistería
dress rehearsal *s* ensayo general
dress shirt *s* camisa de pechera almidonada, camisa de pechera de encaje
dress shop *s* casa de modas
dress suit *s* traje *m* de etiqueta
dress tie *s* corbata de smoking, corbata de frac
dress•y [ˈdrɛsi] *adj* (*comp* **-ier;** *super* **-iest**) (coll) elegante; (*showy*) acicalado, vistoso, peripuesto
dribble [ˈdrɪbəl] *s* goteo; (coll) llovizna ‖ *tr* (sport) driblar ‖ *intr* gotear; (*at the mouth*) babear; (sport) driblar
driblet [ˈdrɪblɪt] *s* gotita; pedacito
dried beef [draɪd] *s* cecina
dried fig *s* higo paso
dried peach *s* orejón *m*

drier [ˈdraɪ•ər] *s* enjugador *m; (for hair)* secador *m; (for clothes)* secadora; *(rack for drying clothes)* tendedero (de ropa)
drift [drɪft] *s* movimiento; *(of sand, snow)* montón *m; (movement of snow)* ventisca; tendencia, dirección; intención, sentido; (aer, naut) deriva; (rad, telv) desviación ‖ *intr* flotar a la deriva; amontonarse *(la nieve)*; ventiscar; (aer, naut) derivar, ir a la deriva; (fig) vivir sin rumbo
drift ice *s* hielo flotante
drift'wood' *s* madera flotante; madera llevada por el agua; madera arrojada a la playa por el agua; *(people)* vagos
drill [drɪl] *s* taladro; instrucción; *(fabric)* dril *m;* (mil) ejercicio ‖ *tr* taladrar; instruir; (mil) enseñar el ejercicio a ‖ *intr* adiestrarse; (mil) hacer el ejercicio
drill'mas'ter *s* amaestrador *m;* (mil) instructor *m*
drill press *s* prensa taladradora
drink [drɪŋk] *s* bebida; **the drinks are on the house!** ¡convida la casa! ‖ *v (pret* **drank** [dræŋk]; *pp* **drunk** [drʌŋk]) *tr* beber; beberse *(su sueldo)*; **to drink down** beber de una vez; **to drink in** beber *(las palabras de una persona)*; beberse *(un libro)*; aspirar *(el aire)* ‖ *intr* beber; **to drink out of** beber de o en; **to drink to the health of** beber a o por la salud de
drinkable [ˈdrɪŋkəbəl] *adj* bebedizo, potable
drinker [ˈdrɪŋkər] *s* bebedor *m*
drinking [ˈdrɪŋkɪŋ] *s* (el) beber
drinking cup *s* taza para beber
drinking fountain *s* fuente *f* para beber
drinking song *s* canción báquica, canción de taberna
drinking spree *s* bebezón *m;* bimba (Mex)
drinking trough *s* abrevadero
drinking water *s* agua para beber
drip [drɪp] *s* goteo; gotas ‖ *v (pret & pp* **dripped;** *ger* **dripping)** *intr* caer gota a gota, gotear
drip coffee *s* café *m* de maquinilla
drip'-dry' *adj* de lava y pon
drip pan *s* colector *m* de aceite
drive [draɪv] *s* paseo en coche; calzada; fuerza, vigor *m;* urgencia; campaña vigorosa; venta a bajo precio; (aut) tracción *(delantera o trasera)*; (mach) transmisión, mando ‖ *v (pret* **drove** [drov]; *pp* **driven** [ˈdrɪvən]) *tr* conducir, guiar, manejar *(un automóvil)*; clavar, hincar *(un clavo)*; arrear *(a las bestias)*; *(in a carriage or auto)* llevar *(a una persona)*; empujar, impeler; estimular; forzar, compeler; obligar a trabajar mucho; (sport) golpear con gran fuerza; **to drive away** ahuyentar; **to drive away** ahuyentar; **to drive back** rechazar; **to drive mad** volver loco ‖ *intr* ir en coche; **to drive at** aspirar a; querer decir; **to drive hard** trabajar mucho; **to drive in** entrar en coche; entrar en *(un sitio)* en coche; **to drive on the right** circular por la derecha; **to drive out** salir en coche; **to drive up** llegar en coche
drive-in restaurant [ˈdraɪv,ɪn] *s* parador *m* de carretera
drive-in theater *s* auto-teatro, motocine *m;* autocine *m* (Chile, Cuba); autocínema *f* (Mex)
driv•el [ˈdrɪvəl] *s (slobber)* baba; *(nonsense)* bobería ‖ *v (pret* **-eled** o **-elled;** *ger* **eling** o **-elling)** *intr* babear; *(to talk nonsense)* bobear
driver [ˈdraɪvər] *s* conductor *m; (of a carriage)* cochero; *(of a locomotive)* maquinista *m; (of pack animals)* arriero
driver's license *s* carnet *m* de chófer, permiso de conducir
drive shaft *s* árbol *m* de mando, eje *m* motor
drive'way' *s* calzada; camino de entrada para coches
drive wheel *s* rueda motriz
drive'-your•self' service *s* alquiler *m* sin chófer
driving school *s* auto-escuela
drizzle [ˈdrɪzəl] *s* llovizna ‖ *intr* lloviznar, garnar
droll [drol] *adj* chusco, gracioso
dromedar•y [ˈdrɑmə,dɛri] *s (pl* **-ies)** dromedario
drone [dron] *s* zángano; *(buzz, hum)* zumbido; *(of bagpipe)* bordón *m,* roncón *m;* avión radiodirigido ‖ *tr* decir monótonamente ‖ *intr* hablar monótonamente; *(to live in idleness)* zanganear; *(to buzz, hum)* zumbar
drool [drul] *s (slobber)* baba; (slang) bobería ‖ *intr* babear; (slang) bobear
droop [drup] *s* inclinación ‖ *intr* caer, colgar; inclinarse; marchitarse; abatirse; encamarse *(el grano)*
drooping [ˈdrupɪŋ] *adj (eyelid, shoulder)* caído
drop [drɑp] *s* gota; *(slope)* pendiente *f; (earring)* pendiente *m; (in temperature)* descenso; *(of supplies from an airplane)* lanzamiento; *(trap door)* escotillón *m; (gallows)* horca; *(lozenge)* pastilla; *(small amount)* chispa; *(slit for letters)* buzón *m; (curtain)* telón *m;* **a drop in the bucket** una gota en el mar ‖ *v (pret & pp* **dropped;** *ger* **dropping)** *tr* dejar caer; echar *(una carta)* al buzón; bajar *(una cortina)*; soltar *(una indirecta)*; escribir *(una esquela)*; omitir, suprimir; abandonar, dejar; echar *(el ancla)*; borrar de la lista *(a un alumno)*; lanzar *(bombas o suministros de un avión)* ‖ *intr* caer; bajar; cesar, terminar; **to drop dead** caer muerto; **to drop in** entrar al pasar, visitar de paso; **to drop off** desaparecer; quedarse dormido; morir de repente; **to drop out** desaparecer; retirarse; darse de baja
drop curtain *s* telón *m*
drop hammer *s* martinete *m*
drop'-leaf' table *s* mesa de hoja plegadiza
drop'light' *s* lámpara colgante
drop'out' *s* fracasado, desertor *m* escolar; **to become a dropout** ahorcar los libros
dropper [ˈdrɑpər] *s* cuentagotas *m*
drop shutter *s* obturador *m* de guillotina

dropsical [ˈdrɑpsɪkəl] *adj* hidrópico
dropsy [ˈdrɑpsi] *s* hidropesía
drop table *s* mesa perezosa
dross [drɔs] o [drɑs] *s* (*of metals*) escoria; (fig) escoria, hez *f*
drought [draʊt] *s* (*long period of dry weather*) sequía; (*dryness*) sequedad
drove [drov] *s* manada, rebaño, hato; gentío, multitud
drover [ˈdrovər] *s* ganadero
drown [draʊn] *tr* anegar, ahogar ‖ *intr* anegarse, ahogarse
drowse [draʊz] *intr* adormecerse, amodorrarse
drow•sy [ˈdraʊzi] *adj* (*comp* **-sier;** *super* **-siest**) soñoliento, modorro
drub [drʌb] *v* (*pret & pp* **drubbed;** *ger* **drubbing**) *tr* apalear, pegar, tundir; derrotar completamente
drudge [drʌdʒ] *s* yunque *m*, esclavo del trabajo ‖ *intr* afanarse
drudger•y [ˈdrʌdʒəri] *s* (*pl* **-ies**) trabajo penoso
drug [drʌg] *s* droga, medicamento; narcótico; **drug on the market** macana, artículo invendible ‖ *v* (*pret & pp* **drugged;** *ger* **drugging**) *tr* narcotizar; mezclar con drogas
drug addict *s* toxicómano, drogadicto; (coll) yonquí *m*
drug'-ad•dict'ed *adj* drogadicto
drug addiction *s* toxicomania
drug dealer *s* narcotraficante *mf*
druggist [ˈdrʌgɪst] *s* boticario, farmacéutico; (*dealer in drugs, chemicals, dyes, etc.*) droguero
drug habit *s* vicio de los narcóticos
drug store *s* farmacia, botica, droguería
drug traffic *s* contrabando de narcóticos
druid [ˈdru•ɪd] *s* druida *m*
drum [drʌm] *s* (*cylinder; instrument of percussion*) tambor *m;* (*container for oil, gasoline, etc.*) bidón *m* ‖ *v* (*pret & pp* **drummed;** *ger* **drumming**) *tr* reunir a toque de tambor; **to drum up trade** fomentar ventas ‖ *intr* tocar el tambor; (*with the fingers*) teclear
drum'beat' *s* toque *m* de tambor
drum brake *s* freno de tambor
drum corps *s* banda de tambores
drum'fire' *s* fuego graneado, fuego nutrido
drum'head' *s* parche *m* de tambor
drum major *s* tambor *m* mayor
drummer [ˈdrʌmər] *s* tambor *m*, baterista *mf*, tamborilero; agente viajero
drum'stick' *s* baqueta, palillo; (coll) muslo (*de ave cocida*)
drunk [drʌŋk] *adj* borracho; bolo (CAm, Mex); **to get drunk** emborracharse; coger una turca; embolarse (CAm, Mex) enchicharse (SAm) ‖ *s* (coll) borracho; (*spree*) (coll) borrachera
drunkard [ˈdrʌŋkərd] *s* borrachín *m*
drunken [ˈdrʌŋkən] *adj* borracho
drunken driving *s* — **to be arrested for drunken driving** ser arrestado por conducir en estado de embriaguez
drunkenness [ˈdrʌŋkənnɪs] *s* embriaguez *f;* bimba (Mex)
dry [draɪ] *adj* (*comp* **drier;** *super* **driest**) seco; (*thirsty*) sediento; (*dull, boring*) árido ‖ *s* (*pl* **drys**) (*prohibitionist*) (coll) seco ‖ *v* (*pret & pp* **dried**) *tr* secar; (*to wipe dry*) enjugar ‖ *intr* secarse; **to dry up** secarse completamente; (slang) callar, dejar de hablar
dry battery *s* pila seca; (*group of dry cells*) batería seca
dry cell *s* pila seca
dry'-clean' *tr* lavar en seco, limpiar en seco
dry cleaner *s* tintorero
dry cleaning *s* lavado a seco, limpieza en seco
dry'-clean'ing establishment *s* tintorería
dry dock *s* dique seco
dryer [ˈdraɪ•ər] *s* var de **drier**
dry'eyed' —*adj* ojienjuto
dry farming *s* cultivo de secano
dry goods *spl* mercancías generales (*tejidos, lencería, pañería, sedería*)
dry ice *s* carbohielo, hielo seco
dry law *s* ley seca
dry measure *s* medida para áridos
dryness [ˈdraɪnɪs] *s* sequedad; (*e.g., of a speaker*) aridez *f*
dry nurse *s* ama seca
dry season *s* estación de la seca
dry wash *s* ropa lavada y secada pero no planchada
d.s. *abbr* **days after sight, daylight saving**
D.S.T. *abbr* **Daylight Saving Time**
dual [ˈdju•əl o [ˈdu•əl] *adj & s* dual *m*
dual axle *s* eje tandem
duali•ty [djuˈælɪti] *s* (*pl* **-ties**) dualidad
dub [dʌb] *s* (slang) jugador *m* torpe ‖ *v* (*pret & pp* **dubbed;** *ger* **dubbing**) *tr* apellidar; armar caballero; (mov) doblar
dubbing [ˈdʌbɪŋ] *s* doblado, doblaje *m*
dubious [ˈdubɪ•əs] *adj* dudoso
ducat [ˈdʌkət] *s* ducado
duchess [ˈdʌtʃɪs] *s* duquesa
duch•y [ˈdʌtʃi] *s* (*pl* **-ies**) ducado
duck [dʌk] *s* pato; (*female*) pata; agachada rápida; (*in the water*) zambullida; **ducks** (coll) pantalones *mpl* de dril ‖ *tr* bajar rápidamente (*la cabeza*); (*in water*) chapuzar; (coll) esquivar, evitar (*un golpe*) ‖ *intr* chapuzar; **to duck out** (coll) escabullirse
duck'-toed' *adj* zancajoso
duct [dʌkt] *s* conducto, canal *m*
ductile [ˈdʌktɪl] *adj* dúctil
ductless gland [ˈdʌktlɪs] *s* glándula cerrada
duct'work' *s* canalización
dud [dʌd] *s* (slang) bomba que no estalla; (slang) fracaso; **duds** (coll) trapos, prendas de vestir
dude [dud] *s* caballerete *m*
due [dju] o [du] *adj* debido; aguardado, esperado; pagadero; **due to** debido a; **to fall due** vencer; **when is the train due?** ¿a qué hora debe llegar el tren? ‖ *adv* directa-

mente, derecho || *s* deuda; **dues** derechos; (*of a member*) cuota; **to get one's due** llevar su merecido; **to give the devil his due** ser justo hasta con el diablo
duel [ˈdju•əl] o [ˈdu•əl] *s* duelo; **to fight a duel** batirse en duelo || *v* (*pret & pp* **dueled** o **duelled;** *ger* **dueling** o **duelling**) *intr* batirse en duelo
duelist o **duellist** [ˈdju•əlɪst] o [ˈduəlɪst] *s* duelista *m*
dues-paying [ˈdjuz,pe•ɪŋ] o [ˈduz,peɪŋ] *adj* cotizante
duet [djuˈɛt] o [duˈɛt] *s* dúo
duke [djuk] *s* duque *m*
dukedom [ˈdjukdəm] *s* ducado
dull [dʌl] *adj* (*not sharp*) embotado, romo; (*color*) apagado; (*sound; pain*) sordo; (*stupid*) lerdo, torpe; (*business*) inactivo, muerto; (*boring*) aburrido, tedioso; (*flat*) deslucido, deslustrado || *tr* embotar, enromar; deslucir, deslustrar; enfriar (*el entusiasmo*) || *intr* embotarse, enromarse; deslucirse, deslustrarse
dullard [ˈdʌlərd] *s* estúpido
duly [ˈdjuli] o [ˈduli] *adv* debidamente
dumb [dʌm] *adj* (*lacking the power to speak*) mudo; (coll) estúpido, torpe
dumbˈbellˈ *s* halterio; (slang) estúpido, tonto
dumb creature *s* animal *m*, bruto
dumb show *s* pantomima
dumbˈwaitˈer *s* montaplatos *m*
dumfound [,dʌmˈfaʊnd] *tr* pasmar, dejar sin habla
dum•my [ˈdʌmi] *adj* falso, fingido, simulado || *s* (*pl* **-mies**) (*dress form*) maniquí *m;* cabeza para pelucas; (*in card games*) muerto; cartas del muerto; (*figurehead, straw man*) testaferro; (*skeleton copy of a book*) maqueta; imitación, copia; (slang) estúpido
dump [dʌmp] *s* basurero, vertedero; montón *m* de basuras; (mil) depósito de municiones; (min) terrero; **to be down in the dumps** (coll) tener murria || *tr* descargar, verter; vaciar de golpe; vender en grandes cantidades y a precios inferiores a los corrientes
dumping [ˈdʌmpɪŋ] *s* descarga; venta en grandes cantidades y a precios inferiores a los corrientes
dumpling [ˈdʌmplɪŋ] *s* bola de pasta rellena de fruta o carne
dump truck *s* camión *m* volquete
dump•y [ˈdʌmpi] *adj* (*comp* **-ier;** *super* **-iest**) regordete, rollizo
dun [dʌn] *adj* bruno, pardo, castaño || *s* acreedor importuno; (*demand for payment*) apremio || *v* (*pret & pp* **dunner;** *ger* **dunning**) *tr* importunar para el pago, apremiar (*a un deudor*)
dunce [dʌns] *s* zopenco, bodoque *m*
dunce cap *s* capirote *m* que se le pone al alumno torpe
dune [djun] o [dun] *s* duna, médano
dung [dʌŋ] *s* estiércol *m* || *tr* estercolar
dungarees [,dʌŋgəˈriz] *spl* pantalones *mpl* de trabajo de tela basta de algodón
dungeon [ˈdʌndʒən] *s* calabozo, mazmorra; (*fortified tower of medieval castle*) torre *f* del homenaje
dungˈhillˈ *s* estercolar *m;* lugar inmundo
dunk [dʌŋk] *tr* sopetear, ensopar
duo [ˈdju•o] o [ˈdu•o] *s* dúo
duode•num [,du•əˈdinəm] *s* (*pl* **-na** [nə]) duodeno
dupe [djup] o [dup] *s* víctima, primo, inocentón *m* || *tr* embaucar, engañar
duplex house [ˈduplɛks] *s* casa para dos familias
duplicate [ˈduplɪkɪt] *adj & s* duplicado; **in duplicate** por duplicado || [ˈduplɪ,ket] *tr* duplicar
duplici•ty [djuˈplɪsɪti] *s* (*pl* **-ties**) duplicidad
durable [ˈdjʊrəbəl] o [ˈdʊrəbəl] *adj* durable, duradero
durable goods *spl* artículos duraderos
duration [djʊˈreʃən] o [dʊˈreʃən] *s* duración
during [ˈdjʊrɪŋ] *prep* durante
dusk [dʌsk] *s* crepúsculo
dust [dʌst] *s* polvo || *tr* (*to free of dust*) desempolvar; (*to sprinkle with dust*) polvorear; **to dust off** desempolvar
dust bowl *s* cuenca de polvo
dustˈclothˈ *s* trapo para quitar el polvo
dust cloud *s* nube *f* de polvo, polvareda
duster [ˈdʌstər] *s* paño, plumero; (*light overgarment*) guardapolvo
dust jacket *s* sobrecubierta
dustˈpanˈ *s* pala para recoger la basura
dust rag *s* trapo para quitar el polvo
dust storm *s* tolvanera
dust•y [ˈdʌsti] *adj* (*comp* **-ier;** *super* **-iest**) polvoriento; (*grayish*) grisáceo
Dutch [dʌtʃ] *adj* holandés; (slang) alemán || *s* (*language*) holandés *m;* (*language*) (slang) alemán *m;* **in Dutch** (slang) en la desgracia; (slang) en un apuro; **the Dutch** los holandeses; (slang) los alemanes; **to go Dutch** (coll) pagar a escote
Dutch•man [ˈdʌtʃmən] *s* (*pl* **-men** [mən]) holandés *m;* (slang) alemán *m*
Dutch treat *s* (coll) convite *m* a escote
dutiable [ˈdjutɪ•əbəl] *adj* sujeto a derechos de aduana
dutiful [ˈdjutɪfəl] *adj* obediente, sumiso, solícito
du•ty [ˈdjuti] *s* (*pl* **-ties**) deber *m;* (*task*) faena, quehacer *m;* derechos de aduana; **in the line of duty** en acto de servicio; **off duty** libre; **on duty** de servicio, de guardia; **to do one's duty** cumplir con su deber; **to take up one's duties** entrar en funciones
duˈty-freeˈ *adj* libre de derechos
D.V. *abbr* **Deo volente,** i.e., **God willing**
dwarf [dwɔrf] *adj & s* enano || *tr* achicar, empequeñecer || *intr* achicarse, empequeñecerse
dwarfish [ˈdwɔrfɪʃ] *adj* enano, diminuto
dwell [dwɛl] *v* (*pret & pp* **dwelled** o **dwelt** [dwɛlt]) *intr* vivir, morar; **to dwell on** o **upon** hacer hincapié en
dwelling [ˈdwɛlɪŋ] *s* morada, vivienda
dwelling house *s* casa, domicilio

dwindle ['dwɪndəl] *intr* disminuir; decaer, consumirse
dwt. *abbr* **pennyweight**
dye [daɪ] *s* tinte *m*, tintura, color *m* || *v* (*pret & pp* **dyed;** *ger* **dyeing**) *tr* teñir
dyed-in-the-wool ['daɪdɪnðə,wul] *adj* intransigente
dyeing ['daɪ•ɪŋ] *s* tinte *m*, tintura
dyer ['daɪ•ər] *s* tintorero
dye'stuff' *s* materia, colorante
dying ['daɪ•ɪŋ] *adj* moribundo
dynamic [daɪ'næmɪk] o [dɪ'næmɪk] *adj* dinámico
dynamite ['daɪnə,maɪt] *s* dinamita || *tr* dinamitar
dyna•mo ['daɪnə,mo] *s* (*pl* **-mos**) dínamo *f*
dynast ['daɪnæst] *s* dinasta *m*
dynas•ty ['daɪnəsti] *s* (*pl* **-ties**) dinastía
dysentery ['dɪsən,tɛri] *s* disentería
dysfunction [dɪs'fʌŋʃən] *s* disfunción
dyspepsia [dɪs'pɛpsɪ•ə] o [dɪs'pɛpʃə] *s* dispepsia
dz. *abbr* **dozen**

E

E, e [i] quinta letra del alfabeto inglés
ea. *abbr* **each**
each [itʃ] *adj indef* cada || *pron indef* cada uno; **each other** nos, se; uno a otro, unos a otros || *adv* cada uno; por persona
eager ['igər] *adj* (*enthusiastic*) ardiente, celoso; **eager for** muy deseoso de; **eager to** + *inf* muy deseoso de + *inf*
eagerness ['igərnɪs] *s* ardor *m*, celo; deseo ardiente, empeño
eagle ['igəl] *s* águila
eagle owl *s* buho
ear [ɪr] *s* (*organ and sense of hearing*) oído; (*external part*) oreja; (*of corn*) mazorca; (*of wheat*) espiga; **all ears** con las orejas tan largas; **to be all ears** ser todo oídos, abrir tanto oído; **box on the ear** guantón *m;* **to prick up one's ears** aguzar las orejas; **to turn a deaf ear** hacer o tener oídos de mercader
ear'ache' *s* dolor *m* de oído
ear'drop' *s* arete *m*
ear'drum' *s* tímpano
ear'flap' *s* orejera
earl [ʌrl] *s* conde *m*
earldom ['ʌrldəm] *s* condado
ear•ly ['ʌrli] (*comp* **-lier;** *super* **-liest**) *adj* (*occurring before customary time*) temprano; (*first in a series*) primero; (*far back in time*) primero, remoto, antiguo; (*occurring in near future*) cercano, próximo || *adv* temprano; al principio; en los primeros tiempos; **as early as** (*a certain time of day*) ya a; (*a certain time or date*) ya en; **as early as possible** lo más pronto posible; **early in** (*e.g., the month of December*) ya en; **early in the morning** muy de mañana; **early in the year** a principios del año; **to rise early** madrugar
early bird *s* (coll) madrugador *m*
early mass *s* misa de prima
early riser *s* madrugador *m*
ear'mark' *s* señal *f*, distintivo || *tr* destinar, poner aparte (*para un fin determinado*)
ear'muff' *s* orejera
earn [ʌrn] *tr* ganar, ganarse; (*to get as one's due*) merecerse; (com) devengar (*intereses*) || *intr* ganar; rendir
earnest ['ʌrnɪst] *adj* serio, grave; **in earnest** en serio, de buena fe || *s* arras
earnest money *s* arras
earnings ['ʌrnɪŋz] *s* ganancia; salario
ear of corn *s* ilote *m;* chilote (CAm); **green ear of corn** jilote (Mex)
ear'phone' *s* audífono
ear'piece' *s* auricular *m*
ear'ring' *s* arete *m*
ear'shot' *s* alcance *m* del oído; **within earshot** al alcance del oído
ear'split'ting' *adj* ensordecedor
earth [ʌrθ] *s* tierra; **to come back to** o **down to earth** bajar de las nubes
earthen ['ʌrθən] *adj* de tierra; de barro
ear'then•ware' *s* loza, vasijas de barro
earthly ['ʌrθli] *adj* terrenal; concebible, posible; **to be of no earthly use** no servir para nada
earth'quake' *s* terremoto, temblor *m* de tierra
earth'work' *s* terraplén *m*
earth'worm' *s* lombriz *f* de tierra
earth•y ['ʌrθi] *adj* (*comp* **-ier;** *super* **-iest**) terroso; (*worldly*) mundanal; (*unrefined*) grosero; franco, sincero
ear trumpet *s* trompetilla
ear'wax' *s* cera de los oídos
ease [iz] *s* facilidad; (*readiness, naturalness*) desenvoltura, soltura; (*comfort, wellbeing*) comodidad, bienestar *m;* **with ease** con facilidad || *tr* facilitar; aligerar (*un peso*); (*to let up on*) aflojar, soltar; aliviar, mitigar || *intr* aliviarse, mitigarse, disminuir; moderar la marcha
easel ['izəl] *s* caballete *m*
easement ['izmənt] *s* alivio; (law) servidumbre
easily ['izɪli] *adv* fácilmente; suavemente; sin duda; probablemente
easiness ['izɪnɪs] *s* facilidad; desenvoltura, soltura; (*e.g., of motion of a machine*) suavidad; indiferencia
east [ist] *adj* oriental, del este || *adv* al este, hacia el este || *s* este *m*

Easter [ˈistər] *s* Pascua de flores, Pascua de Resurrección, Pascua florida
Easter egg *s* huevo duro decorado o huevo de imitación que se da como regalo en el día de Pascua de Resurrección
Easter Monday *s* lunes *m* de Pascua de Resurrección
eastern [ˈistərn] *adj* oriental
East'er•tide' *s* alelyua *m,* tiempo de Pascua
eastward [ˈistwərd] *adv* hacia el este
eas•y [ˈizi] *adj* (*comp* **-ier;** *super* **-iest**) fácil; (*conducive to ease*) cómodo; (*not tight*) holgado; (*amenable*) manejable; (*not forced or hurried*) lento, pausado, moderado; **to have an easy job** (o **life**) estar echado (CAm, Mex, P-R) ‖ *adv* (coll) fácilmente; (coll) despacio; **to take it easy** (coll) descansar, holgar; (coll) ir despacio
easy chair *s* poltrona, silla poltrona
eas'y•go'ing *adj* despacioso, comodón
easy mark *s* (coll) víctima, inocentón *m*
easy money *s* dinero ganado sin pena; (com) dinero abundante
easy payments *spl* facilidades de pago
eat [it] *v* (*pret* **ate** [et]; *pp* **eaten** [ˈitən]) *tr* comer; **to eat away** corroer; **to eat up** comerse ‖ *intr* comer
eatable [ˈitəbəl] *adj* comestible ‖ **eatables** *spl* comestibles *mpl*
eaves [ivz] *spl* alero, socarrén *m,* tejaroz *m*
eaves'drop' *v* (*pret & pp* **-dropped;** *ger* **-dropping**) *intr* escuchar a escondidas, estar de escucha
ebb [ɛb] *s* reflujo; decadencia ‖ *intr* bajar (*la marea*); decaer
ebb and flow *s* flujo y reflujo
ebb tide *s* marea menguante
ebon•y [ˈɛbəni] *s* (*pl* **-ies**) ébano
ebullient [ɪˈbʌljənt] *adj* hirviente; entusiasta
eccentric [ɛkˈsɛntrɪk] *adj* excéntrico ‖ *m* (*odd person*) excéntrico; (*device*) excéntrica
eccentrici•ty [ˌɛksɛnˈtrɪsɪti] *s* (*pl* **-ties**) excentricidad
ecclesiastic [ɪˌkliziˈæstɪk] *adj & s* eclesiástico
echelon [ˈɛʃəˌlɑn] *s* escalón *m;* (mil) escalón ‖ *tr* (mil) escalonar
ech•o [ˈɛko] *s* (*pl* **-oes**) eco ‖ *tr* repetir (*un sonido*); imitar ‖ *intr* hacer eco
éclair [eˈklɛr] *s* bollo de crema
eclectic [ɛkˈlɛktɪk] *adj & s* ecléctico
eclipse [ɪˈklɪps] *s* eclipse *m* ‖ *tr* eclipsar
eclogue [ˈɛklɔg] o [ˈɛklɑg] *s* égloga
ecologic(al) [ˌikəˈlɑdʒɪk(əl)] *adj* ecológico
ecologist [iˈkɑlədʒɪst] *s* ecologista *mf,* ecólogo
ecology [iˈkɑlədʒi] *s* ecología
economic [ˌikəˈnɑmɪk] *adj* económico (*perteneciente a la economía*)
economical [ˌikəˈnɑmɪkəl] *adj* económico (*ahorrador; poco costoso*)
economics [ˌikəˈnɑmɪks] *s* economía política
economist [ɪˈkɑnəmɪst] *s* economista *mf*
economize [ɪˈkɑnəˌmaɪz] *tr & intr* economizar
econo•my [ɪˈkɑnəmi] *s* (*pl* **-mies**) economía
ecsta•sy [ˈɛkstəsi] *s* (*pl* **-sies**) éxtasis *m*
ecstatic [ˈɛkˈstætɪk] *adj* extático
Ecuador [ˈɛkwəˌdɔr] *s* el Ecuador
Ecuadoran [ˌɛkwəˈdorən] o; **Ecuadorian** [ˌɛkwhəˈdorɪ•ən] *adj & s* ecuatoriano
ecumenic(al) [ˌɛkjəˈmɛnɪk(əl)] *adj* ecuménico
eczema [ˈɛksɪmə] o [ɛgˈzimə] *s* eczema *m & f,* eccema *m & f*
ed. *abbr* **edited, edition, editor**
ed•dy [ˈɛdi] *s* (*pl* **-dies**) remolino ‖ *v* (*pret & pp* **-died**) *tr & intr* remolinear
edelweiss [ˈedəlˌvaɪs] *s* estrella de los Alpes
edema [ɪˈdimə] *s* edema
edge [ɛdʒ] *s* (*of a knife, sword, etc.*) filo, corte *m;* (*of a cup, glass, piece of paper, piece of cloth, an abyss, etc.*) borde *m;* (*of a piece of cloth; of a body of water*) orilla; (*of a table*) canto; (*of a book*) corte *m;* (*of clothing*) ribete *m;* (slang) ventaja; **on edge** de canto; (fig) nervioso; **to have the edge on** (coll) llevar ventaja a; **to set the teeth on edge** dar dentera ‖ *tr* afilar, aguzar; bordear; ribetear (*un vestido*) ‖ *intr* avanzar de lado; **to edge in** lograr entrar
edgeways [ˈɛdʒˌwez] *adv* de filo, de canto; **to not let a person get a word in edgeways** no dejarle a una persona decir ni una palabra
edging [ˈɛdʒɪŋ] *s* orla, pestaña
edgy [ˈɛdʒi] *adj* agudo, angular; nervioso, irritable
edible [ˈɛdɪbəl] *adj & s* comestible *m*
edict [ˈidɪkt] *s* edicto
edification [ˌɛdɪfɪˈkeʃən] *s* edificación
edifice [ˈɛdɪfɪs] *s* edificio
edi•fy [ˈɛdɪˌfaɪ] *v* (*pret & pp* **-fied**) *tr* edificar
edifying [ˈɛdɪˌfaɪ•ɪŋ] *adj* edificante
edit. *abbr* **edited, edition, editor**
edit [ˈɛdɪt] *tr* preparar para la publicación; dirigir, redactar (*un periódico*)
edition [ɪˈdɪʃən] *s* edición
editor [ˈɛdɪtər] *s* (*of a newspaper or magazine*) director *m,* redactor *m;* (*of a manuscript*) revisor *m;* (*of an editorial*) cronista *mf*
editorial [ˌɛdɪˈtorɪ•əl] *adj* editorial ‖ *s* editorial *m,* artículo de fondo
editorial staff *s* redacción, cuerpo de redacción
editor in chief *s* jefe *m* de redacción
educate [ˈɛdʒʊˌket] *tr* educar, instruir
education [ˌɛdʒʊˈkeʃən] *s* educación, instrucción
educational [ˌɛdʒʊˈkeʃənəl] *adj* educativo, educacional
educational institution *s* centro docente
educator [ˈɛdʒʊˌketər] *s* educador *m*
eel [il] *s* anguila; **to be as slippery as an eel** escurrirse como una anguila
ee•rie o **ee•ry** [ˈɪri] *adj* (*comp* **-rier;** *super* **-riest**) espectral, misterioso
efface [ɪˈfes] *tr* destruir; borrar; **to efface oneself** retirarse, no dejarse ver
effect [ɪˈfɛkt] *s* efecto; **in effect** vigente; en efecto, en realidad; **to feel the effects of** resentirse de; **to go into effect** o **to take**

effect hacerse vigente, entrar en vigor; **to put into effect** poner en vigor || *tr* efectuar
effective [ɪˈfɛktɪv] *adj* eficaz; (*actually in effect*) efectivo; (*striking*) impresionante; **to become effective** hacerse efectivo, entrar en vigencia
effectual [ɪˈfɛktʃu•əl] *adj* eficaz
effectuate [ɪˈfɛktʃu,et] *tr* efectuar
effeminacy [ɪˈfɛmɪnəsi] *s* afeminación
effeminate [ɪˈfɛmɪnɪt] *adj* afeminado
effervesce [,ɛfərˈvɛs] *intr* estar en efervescencia
effervescence [,ɛfərˈvɛsəns] *s* efervescencia
effervescent [,ɛfərˈvɛsənt] *adj* efervescente
effete [ɪˈfit] *adj* estéril, infructuoso
efficacious [,ɛfɪˈkeʃəs] *adj* eficaz
effica•cy [ˈɛfɪkəsi] *s* (*pl* **-cies**) eficacia
efficien•cy [ɪˈfɪʃənsi] *s* (*pl* **-cies**) eficiencia; (mech) rendimiento, efecto útil
efficient [ɪˈfɪʃənt] *adj* eficiente, eficaz; (*person*) competente; (mech) de buen rendimiento
effi•gy [ˈɛfɪdʒi] *s* (*pl* **-gies**) efigie *f*
effort [ˈɛfɔrt] *s* esfuerzo, empeño
effronter•y [ɪˈfrʌntəri] *s* (*pl* **-ies**) desfachatez *f*, descaro
effusion [ɪˈfjuʒən] *s* efusión
effusive [ɪˈfjusɪv] *adj* efusivo, expansivo
e.g. *abbr* **exempli gratia,** i.e., **for example**
egg [ɛg] *s* huevo; (slang) buen sujeto || *tr* — **to egg on** incitar, instigar
egg beat'er *s* batidor *m* de huevos
egg'cup' *s* huevera
egg'head' *s* intelectual *mf*, erudito
eggnog [ˈɛg,nɑg] *s* caldo de la reina, yema mejida
egg'plant' *s* berenjena
egg'shell' *s* cascarón *m*, cáscara de huevo
egoism [ˈɛgo,ɪzəm] o [ˈigo,ɪzəm] *s* egoísmo
egoist [ˈɛgo•ɪst] o [ˈigo•ɪst] *s* egoísta *mf*
egotism [ˈɛgo,tɪzəm] o [ˈigo,tɪzəm] *s* egotismo
egotist [ˈɛgotɪst] o [ˈigotɪst] *s* egotista *mf*
egregious [ɪˈgridʒəs] *adj* enorme, escandaloso
egress [ˈgrɛs] *s* salida
Egypt [ˈedʒɪpt] *s* Egipto
Egyptian [ɪˈdʒɪpʃən] *adj & s* egipcio
eider [ˈaɪdər] *s* pato de flojel
eid'erdown' *s* edredón *m*
eight [et] *adj & pron* ocho || *s* ocho; **eight o'clock** las ocho
eight'-day' clock *s* reloj *m* de ocho días cuerda
eighteen [ˈetˈtin] *adj, pron & s* dieciocho, diez y ocho
eighteenth [ˈetˈtinθ] *adj & s* (*in a series*) decimoctavo; (*part*) dieciochavo || *s* (*in dates*) dieciocho, diez y ocho
eighth [etθ] *adj & s* octavo, ochavo || *s* (*in dates*) ocho
eight hundred *adj & pron* ochocientos || *s* ochocientos *m*
eightieth [ˈetɪ•ɪθ] *adj & s* (*in a series*) octogésimo; (*part*) ochentavo
eigh•ty [ˈeti] *adj & pron* ochenta || *s* (*pl* **-ties**) ochenta *m*
either [ˈiðər] o [ˈaɪðər] *adj* uno u otro, cada . . . (de los dos), cualquier . . . de los dos; ambos || *pron* uno u otro, cualquiera de los dos || *adv* — **not either** tampoco, no . . . tampoco || *conj* — **either . . . or** o . . . o
ejaculate [ɪˈdʒækjə,let] *tr & intr* exclamar; (physiol) eyacular
eject [ɪˈdʒɛkt] *tr* arrojar, expulsar, echar; (*to evict*) desahuciar
ejection [ɪˈdʒɛkʃən] *s* expulsión; (*of a tenant*) desahucio
ejection seat *s* (aer) asiento lanzable
eke [ik] *tr* — **to eke out** ganarse (*la vida*) con dificultad
elaborate [ɪˈlæbərɪt] *adj* (*done with great care*) elaborado; (*detailed, ornate*) primoroso, recargado || [ɪˈlæbə,ret] *tr* elaborar || *intr* — **to elaborate on** o **upon** explicar con más detalles
elapse [ɪˈlæps] *intr* pasar, transcurrir
elastic [ɪˈlæstɪk] *adj & s* elástico
elasticity [,ilæsˈtɪsɪti] *s* elasticidad
elated [ɪˈletɪd] *adj* alborozado, regocijado
elation [ɪˈleʃən] *s* alborozo, regocijo
elbow [ˈɛlbo] *s* codo; (*in a river*) recodo; (*of a chair*) brazo; **at one's elbow** a la mano; **out at the elbows** andrajoso, enseñando los codos; **to crook the elbow** empinar el codo; **to rub elbows** codearse, rozarse; **up to the elbows** hasta los codos || *tr* — **to elbow one's way** abrirse paso a codazos || *intr* codear
elbow grease *s* (coll) muñeca, jugo de muñeca
elbow patch *s* codera
elbow rest *s* ménsula
el'bow•room' *s* espacio suficiente; libertad de acción
elder [ˈɛldər] *adj* mayor, más antiguo || *s* mayor, señor *m* mayor; (eccl) anciano; (*plant*) saúco
el'der•ber'ry *s* (*pl* **-ries**) saúco; baya del saúco
elderly [ˈɛldərli] *adj* viejo, anciano
elder statesman *s* veterano de la política
eldest [ˈɛldɪst] *adj* (el) mayor, (el) más antiguo
elec. *abbr* **electrical, electricity**
elect [ɪˈlɛkt] *adj* (*chosen*) escogido; (*selected but not yet installed*) electo || *s* elegido; **the elect** los elegidos || *tr* elegir
election [ɪˈlɛkʃən] *s* elección
electioneer [ɪ,lɛkʃəˈnɪr] *intr* solicitar votos
elective [ɪˈlɛktɪv] *adj* electivo || *s* asignatura electiva
electorate [ɪˈlɛktərɪt] *s* electorado
electric(al) [ɪˈlɛktrɪk(əl)] *adj* eléctrico
electric appliance *s* electrodoméstico
electric fan *s* ventilador eléctrico
electrician [,ɛlɛkˈtrɪʃən] *s* electricista *mf*
electricity [,ɛlɛkˈtrɪsɪti] *s* electricidad
electric percolator *s* cafetera eléctrica
electric shaver *s* electroafeitadora
electric tape *s* cinta aislante
electri•fy [ɪˈlɛktrɪ,faɪ] *v* (*pret & pp* **-fied**) *tr* (*to provide with electric power*) electrifi-

car; (*to communicate electricity to; to thrill*) electrizar
electrocute [ɪˈlɛktrə,kjut] *tr* electrocutar
electrode [ɪˈlɛktrod] *s* electrodo
electrolysis [,ɛlɛkˈtrɑlɪsɪs] *s* electrólisis *f*
electrolyte [ɪˈlɛktrə,laɪt] *s* electrólito
electromagnet [ɪ,lɛktrəˈmægnɪt] *s* electro, electroimán *m*
electromagnetic [ɪ,lɛktrəmægˈnɛtɪk] *adj* electromagnético
electromotive [ɪ,lɛktrəˈmotɪv] *adj* electromotor
electron [ɪˈlɛktrɑn] *s* electrón *m*
electronic [,ɛlɛkˈtrɑnɪk] *adj* electrónico ‖ **electronics** *s* electrónica
electroplating [ɪˈlɛktrə,pletɪŋ] *s* galvanoplastia
electrostatic [ɪ,lɛktrəˈstætɪk] *adj* electrostático
electrotype [ɪˈlɛktrə,taɪp] *s* electrotipo ‖ *tr* electrotipar
eleemosynary [,ɛlɪˈmɑsɪ,nɛri] *adj* limosnero
elegance [ˈɛlɪgəns] *s* elegancia
elegant [ˈɛlɪgənt] *adj* elegante, elegantoso
elegiac [,ɛlɪˈdʒaɪ•æk] o [ɪˈlidʒɪ,æk] *adj* elegíaco
ele•gy [ˈɛlɪdʒi] *s* (*pl* **-gies**) elegía
element [ˈɛlɪmənt] *s* elemento; **to be in one's element** estar en su elemento
elementary [,ɛlɪˈmɛntəri] *adj* elemental
elephant [ˈɛlɪfənt] *s* elefante *m*
elevate [ˈɛlɪ,vet] *tr* elevar
elevated [ˈɛlɪ,vetɪd] *adj* elevado ‖ *s* (coll) ferrocarril aéreo o elevado
elevation [,ɛlɪˈveʃən] *s* elevación
elevator [ˈɛlɪ,vetər] *s* ascensor *m;* elevador *m* (Am); (*for freight*) montacargas *m;* (*for hoisting grain*) elevador de granos; (*warehouse for storing grain*) depósito de cereales; (aer) timón *m* de profundidad
eleven [ɪˈlɛvən] *adj & pron* once ‖ *s* once *m;* **eleven o'clock** las once
eleventh [ɪˈlɛvənθ] *adj & s* (*in a series*) undécimo, onceno; (*part*) onzavo ‖ *s* (*in dates*) once *m*
eleventh hour *s* último momento
elf [ɛlf] *s* (*pl* **elves** [elvz]) elfo, trasgo; enano
elicit [ɪˈlɪsɪt] *tr* sacar, sonsacar
elide [ɪˈlaɪd] *tr* elidir
eligible [ˈɛlɪdʒɪbəl] *adj* elegible; deseable, aceptable
eliminate [ɪˈlɪmɪ,net] *tr* eliminar
elision [ɪˈlɪʒən] *s* elisión
elite [eˈlit] *adj* selecto ‖ *s* — **the elite** la élite
elitist [eˈlitɪst] *adj & s* elitista *mf*
elk [ɛlk] *s* alce *m*
ellipse [ɪˈlɪps] *s* (geom) elipse *f*
ellip•sis [ɪˈlɪpsɪs] *s* (*pl* **-ses** [siz]) (gram) elipsis *f*
elliptic(al) [ɪˈlɪptɪk(əl)] *adj* (geom & gram) elíptico
elm tree [ɛlm] *s* olmo
elope [ɪˈlop] *intr* fugarse con un amante
elopement [ɪˈlopmənt] *s* fuga con un amante
eloquence [ˈɛləkwəns] *s* elocuencia
eloquent [ˈɛləkwənt] *adj* elocuente
else [ɛls] *adj* — **nobody else** ningún otro, nadie más; **nothing else** nada más; **somebody else** algún otro, otra persona; **something else** otra cosa; **what else** qué más, qué otra cosa; **who else** quién más; **whose else** de qué otra persona ‖ *adv* de otro modo; **how else** de qué otro modo; **or else** si no, o bien; **when else** en qué otro tiempo; a qué otra hora; **where else** en qué otra parte
else'where' *adv* en otra parte, a otra parte
elucidate [ɪˈlusɪ,det] *tr* elucidar
elude [ɪˈlud] *tr* eludir
elusive [ɪˈlusɪv] *adj* fugaz, efímero; evasivo; elusivo; (*baffling*) deslumbrador
emaciated [ɪˈmeʃɪ,etɪd] *adj* enflaquecido, macilento
emancipate [ɪˈmænsɪ,pet] *tr* emancipar
embalm [ɛmˈbɑm] *tr* embalsamar
embankment [ɛmˈbæŋkmənt] *s* terraplén *m*
embar•go [ɛmˈbɑrgo] *s* (*pl* **-goes**) embargo ‖ *tr* embargar
embark [ɛmˈbɑrk] *intr* embarcarse
embarkation [,ɛmbɑrˈkeʃən] *s* (*of passengers*) embarco; (*of freight*) embarque *m*
embarrass [ɛmˈbærəs] *tr* (*to make feel self-conscious*) avergonzar; (*to put obstacles in the way of*) embarazar; poner en apuros de dinero
embarrassing [ɛmˈbærəsɪŋ] *adj* desconcertante, vergonzoso; embarazoso
embarrassment [ɛmˈbærəsmənt] *s* desconcierto, vergüenza; (*interference; perplexity*) embarazo; (*financial difficulties*) apuros
embas•sy [ˈɛmbəsi] *s* (*pl* **-sies**) embajada
em•bed [ɛmˈbɛd] *v* (*pret & pp* **-bedded;** *ger* **-bedding**) *tr* empotrar, encajar
embellish [ɛmˈbɛlɪʃ] *tr* embellecer
embellishment [ɛmˈbɛlɪʃmənt] *s* embellecimiento
ember [ˈɛmbər] *s* ascua, pavesa; **embers** rescoldo
Ember days *spl* témpora
embezzle [ɛmˈbɛzəl] *tr & intr* desfalcar, malversar
embezzlement [ɛmˈbɛzəlmənt] *s* desfalco, malversación
embezzler [ɛmˈbɛzlər] *s* malversador *m*
embitter [ɛmˈbɪtər] *tr* blasonar; (fig) blasonar
emblem [ˈɛmbləm] *s* emblema *m*
emblematic(al) [,ɛmbləˈmætɪk(əl)] *adj* emblemático
embodiment [ɛmˈbɑdɪmənt] *s* incorporación; personificación, encarnación
embod•y [ɛmˈbɑdi] *v* (*pret & pp* **-ied**) *tr* incorporar; personificar, encarnar
embolden [ɛmˈboldən] *tr* envalentonar
embolism [ˈɛmbə,lɪzəm] *s* embolia
emboss [ɛmˈbɔs] o [ɛmˈbɑs] *tr* (*to raise in relief*) realzar; abollonar (*metal*); repujar (*cuero*)
embrace [ɛmˈbres] *s* abrazo ‖ *tr* abrazar ‖ *intr* abrazarse
embrasure [ɛmˈbreʒər] *s* alféizar *m*
embroider [ɛmˈbrɔɪdər] *tr* bordar, recamar

embroider•y [ɛmˈbrɔɪdəri] *s* (*pl* **-ies**) bordado, recamado
embroil [ɛmˈbrɔɪl] *tr* embrollar; (*to involve in contention*) envolver
embroilment [ɛmˈbrɔɪlmənt] *s* embrollo; (*in contention*) envolvimiento
embry•o [ˈɛmbrɪ,o] *s* (*pl* **-os**) embrión *m*
embryology [,ɛmbrɪˈɑlədʒi] *s* embriología
emend [ɪˈmɛnd] *tr* enmendar
emendation [,imɛnˈdeʃən] *s* enmienda
emerald [ˈɛmərəld] *s* esmeralda
emerge [ɪˈmʌrdʒ] *intr* emerger
emergence [ɪˈmʌrdʒəns] *s* emergencia (*acción de emerger*)
emergen•cy [ɪˈmʌrdʒənsi] *s* (*pl* **-cies**) emergencia (*caso urgente*)
emergency exit *s* salida de auxilio
emergency landing *s* aterrizaje forzoso
emergency landing field *s* aeródromo de urgencia
emergency physician *s* médico de urgencia
emersion [ɪˈmʌrʒən] o [ɪˈmʌrʃən] *s* emersión
emery [ˈɛməri] *s* esmeril *m*
emery cloth *s* tela de esmeril
emery wheel *s* esmeriladora, rueda de esmeril, muela de esmeril
emetic [ɪˈmɛtɪk] *adj & s* emético
emigrant [ˈɛmɪgrənt] *adj & s* emigrante *mf*
emigrate [ˈɛmɪ,gret] *intr* emigrar
émigré [emiˈgre] o [ˈɛmɪ,gre] *s* emigrado
eminence [ˈɛmɪnəns] *s* eminencia
eminent [ˈɛmɪnənt] *adj* eminente
emissar•y [ˈɛmɪ,sɛri] *s* (*pl* **-ies**) emisario
emission [ɪˈmɪʃən] *s* emisión
emit [ɪˈmɪt] *v* (*pret & pp* **emitted;** *ger* **emitting**) *tr* emitir
emotion [ɪˈmoʃən] *s* emoción
emotional [ɪˈmoʃənəl] *adj* emocional, emotivo
emperor [ˈɛmpərər] *s* emperador *m*
empathy [ˈɛmpəθi] *s* empatía
empha•sis [ˈɛmfəsɪs] *s* (*pl* **-ses** [,siz]) énfasis *m*
emphasize [ˈɛmfə,saɪz] *tr* acentuar, hacer hincapié en
emphatic [ɛmˈfætɪk] *adj* enfático
emphysema [,ɛmfɪˈsimə] *s* enfisema *m*
empire [ˈɛmpaɪr] *s* imperio
empiric(al) [ɛmˈpɪrɪk(əl)] *adj* empírico
empiricist [ɛmˈpɪrɪsɪst] *s* empírico
emplacement [ɛmˈplesmənt] *s* emplazamiento
employ [ɛmˈplɔɪ] *s* empleo ‖ *tr* emplear
employee [ɛmˈplɔɪ•i] o [,ɛmplɔɪˈi] *s* empleado
employer [ɛmˈplɔɪ•ər] *s* patrono
employment [ɛmˈplɔɪmənt] *s* empleo, colocación
employment agency *s* agencia de colocaciones
empower [ɛmˈpaʊ•ər] *tr* autorizar, facultar; habilitar, permitir
empress [ˈɛmprɪs] *s* emperatriz *f*
emptiness [ˈɛmptɪnɪs] *s* vaciedad, vacuidad
emp•ty [ˈɛmpti] *adj* (*comp* **-tier;** *super* **-tiest**) vacío; (coll) hambriento ‖ *v* (*pret & pp* **-tied**) *tr & intr* vaciar
empty-handed [ˈɛmptiˈhændɪd] *adj* manivacío
empty-headed [ˈɛmptiˈhɛdɪd] *adj* tonto, ignorante
empye•ma [,ɛmpɪˈimə] *s* (*pl* **-mata** [mətə]) empiema *m*
empyrean [,ɛmpɪˈri•ən] *adj & s* empíreo
emulate [ˈɛmjə,let] *tr & intr* emular
emulator [ˈɛmjə,letər] *s* émulo
emulous [ˈɛmjələs] *adj* émulo
emulsi•fy [ɪˈmʌlsɪ,faɪ] *v* (*pret & pp* **-fied**) *tr* emulsionar
emulsion [ɪˈmʌlʃən] *s* emulsión
enable [ɛnˈebəl] *tr* habilitar, facilitar
enact [ɛnˈækt] *tr* decretar, promulgar; hacer el papel de
enactment [ɛnˈæktmənt] *s* ley *f;* (*of a law*) promulgación; (*of a play*) representación
enam•el [ɛnˈæməl] *s* esmalte *m* ‖ *v* (*pret & pp* **-eled** o **-elled;** *ger* **-eling** o **-elling**) *tr* esmaltar
enam'el•ware' *s* utensilios de cocina de hierro esmaltado
enamor [ɛnˈæmər] *tr* enamorar
encamp [ɛnˈkæmp] *tr* acampar ‖ *intr* acampar, acamparse
encampment [ɛnˈkæmpmənt] *s* acampamiento
enchant [ɛnˈtʃænt] *tr* encantar
enchanting [ɛnˈtʃæntɪŋ] *adj* encantador
enchantment [ɛnˈtʃæntmənt] *s* encanto
enchantress [ɛnˈtʃæntrɪs] *s* encantadora
enchase [ɛnˈtʃes] *tr* engastar
encircle [ɛnˈsʌrkəl] *tr* encerrar, rodear; (mil) envolver
enclitic [ɛnˈklɪtɪk] *adj & s* enclítico
enclose [ɛnˈkloz] *tr* encerrar; (*in a letter*) adjuntar, incluir; **to enclose herewith** remitir adjunto
enclosure [ɛnˈkloʒər] *s* recinto; cosa inclusa, carta inclusa
encomi•um [ɛnˈkomɪ•əm] *s* (*pl* **-ums** o **-a** [ə]) encomio
encompass [ɛnˈkʌmpəs] *tr* encuadrar, abarcar
encore [ˈɑnkor] *s* bis *m* ‖ *interj* ¡bis!, ¡que se repita! ‖ *tr* pedir la repetición de (*p.ej., de una pieza o canción*); pedir la repetición **a** (*un actor*)
encounter [ɛnˈkaʊntər] *s* encuentro ‖ *tr* encontrar, encontrarse con ‖ *intr* batirse, combatirse
encourage [ɛnˈkʌrɪdʒ] *tr* animar, alentar; (*to foster*) fomentar
encouragement [ɛnˈkʌrɪdʒmənt] *s* ánimo, aliento; fomento
encroach [ɛnˈkrotʃ] *intr* — **to encroach on** o **upon** pasar los límites de; abusar de; invadir, entremeterse en
encumber [ɛnˈkʌmbər] *tr* embarazar, estorbar, impedir; (*to load with debts, etc.*) gravar
encumbrance [ɛnˈkʌmbrəns] *s* embarazo; estorbo; gravamen *m*
ency. o **encyc.** *abbr* **encyclopedia**
encyclical [ɛnˈsɪklɪkəl] o [ɛnˈsaɪklɪkəl] *s* encíclica

encyclopedia [ɛn,saɪklə'pidɪ•ə] *s* enciclopedia

encyclopedic [ɛn,saɪklə'pidɪk] *adj* enciclopédico

end [ɛnd] *s* (*in time*) fin *m;* (*in space*) extremo, remate *m;* (*e.g., of the month*) fines *mpl;* (*small piece*) cabo, pieza, fragmento; (*purpose*) intento, objeto, fin, mira; **at the end of** al cabo de; a fines de; **in the end** al fin; **no end of** (coll) un sin fin de; **to make both ends meet** pasar con lo que se tiene; **to no end** sin efecto; **to stand on end** poner de punta; ponerse de punta; erizarse, encresparse (*el pelo*); **to the end that** a fin de que || *tr* acabar, terminar || *intr* acabar, terminar; desembocar (*p.ej., una calle*); **to end up** acabar, morir; **to end up as** acabar siendo, parar en (*p.ej., ladrón*)

endanger [ɛn'dendʒər] *tr* poner en peligro

endear [ɛn'dɪr] *tr* hacer querer; **to endear oneself to** hacerse querer por

endearment [ɛn'dɪrmənt] *s* encariñamento

endeavor [ɛn'dɛvər] *s* esfuerzo, empeño || *intr* esforzarse, empeñarse

endemic [ɛn'dɛmɪk] *adj* endémico || *s* endemia

ending ['ɛndɪŋ] *s* fin *m,* terminación; (gram) desinencia, terminación

endive ['ɛndaɪv] *s* escarola

endless ['ɛndlɪs] *adj* interminable; (*chain, screw, etc.*) sin fin

end'most' *adj* último, extremo

endorse [ɛn'dɔrs] *tr* endosar; (fig) apoyar, aprobar

endorsee [,ɛndɔr'si] *s* endosatario

endorsement [ɛn'dɔrsmənt] *s* endoso; (fig) apoyo, aprobación

endorser [ɛn'dɔrsər] *s* endosante *mf*

endow [ɛn'daʊ] *tr* dotar

endowment [ɛn'daʊmənt] *adj* dotal || *s* (*of an institution*) dotación; (*gift, talent*) dote *f,* prenda

end paper *s* hoja de encuadernador

endurance [ɛn'djʊrəns] o [ɛn'dʊrəns] *s* aguante *m,* paciencia; (*ability to hold out*) resistencia, fortaleza; (*lasting time*) duración

endure [ɛn'djʊr] o [ɛn'dʊr] *tr* aguantar, tolerar, sufrir || *intr* durar; sufrir con paciencia

enduring [ɛn'djʊrɪŋ] o [ɛn'dʊrɪŋ] *adj* duradero, permanente, resistente

enema ['ɛnəmə] *s* enema, ayuda; (*liquid and apparatus*) lavativa

ene•my ['ɛnəmi] *adj* enemigo || *s* (*pl* **-mies**) enemigo

enemy alien *s* extranjero enemigo

energetic [,ɛnər'dʒɛtɪk] *adj* enérgico, vigoroso

ener•gy ['ɛnərdʒi] *s* (*pl* **-gies**) energía; **alternate energy sources** energías alternas

energy crisis *s* crisis energética

enervate ['ɛnər,vet] *tr* enervar

enfeeble [ɛn'fibəl] *tr* debilitar

enfold [ɛnfold] *tr* arrollar, envolver

enforce [ɛn'fors] *tr* hacer cumplir, poner en vigor; obtener por fuerza; (*e.g., obedience*) imponer; (*an argument*) hacer valer

enforcement [ɛn'forsmənt] *s* compulsión; (*e.g., of a law*) ejecución

enfranchise [ɛn'fræntʃaɪz] *tr* franquear, libertar; conceder el derecho de sufragio a

eng. *abbr* **engineer, engraving**

engage [ɛn'gedʒ] *tr* ocupar, emplear; alquilar, reservar; atraer (*p.ej., la atención de una persona*); engranar con; trabar batalla con; **to be engaged, to be engaged to be married** estar prometido, estar comprometido para casarse; **to engage someone in conversation** entablar conversación con una persona || *intr* empeñarse, comprometerse; empotrar, encajar; engranar; **to engage in** ocuparse en

engaged [ɛn'gedʒd] *adj* comprometido, prometido; (*column*) embebido, entregado

engagement [ɛn'gedʒmənt] *s* ajuste *m,* contrato, empeño; esponsales *mpl,* palabra de casamiento; (*duration of betrothal*) noviazgo; (*appointment*) cita; (mil) acción, batalla

engagement ring *s* anillo de compromiso, anillo de pedida

engaging [ɛn'gedʒɪŋ] *adj* agraciado, simpático

engender [ɛn'dʒɛndər] *tr* engendrar

engine ['ɛndʒɪn] *s* máquina; (*of automobile*) motor *m;* (rr) máquina, locomotora

engine driver *s* maquinista *m*

engineer [,ɛndʒə'nɪr] *s* ingeniero; (*engine driver*) maquinista *m* || *tr* dirigir o construir como ingeniero; llevar a cabo con acierto

engineering [,ɛndʒə'nɪrɪŋ] *s* ingeniería

engine house *s* cuartel *m* de bomberos

engine•man ['ɛndʒɪnmən] *s* (*pl* **-mən** [mən]) maquinista *m,* conductor *m* de locomotora

engine room *s* sala de máquinas; (naut) cámara de las máquinas

en'gine-room' telegraph *s* (naut) transmisor *m* de órdenes, telégrafo de máquinas

England ['ɪŋglənd] *s* Inglaterra

Englander ['ɪŋgləndər] *s* natural *m* inglés

English ['ɪŋglɪʃ] *adj* inglés || *s* inglés *m;* (*in billiards*) efecto; **the English** los ingleses

English Channel *s* Canal *m* de la Mancha

English daisy *s* margarita de los prados

English horn *s* (mus) corno inglés, cuerno inglés

English•man ['ɪŋglɪʃmən] *s* (*pl* **-men** [mən]) inglés *m*

Eng'lish-speak'ing *adj* de habla inglesa, angloparlante

Eng'lish•wom'an *s* (*pl* **-wom'en**) inglesa

engraft [ɛn'græft] *tr* (hort & surg) injertar; (fig) implantar

engrave [ɛn'grev] *tr* grabar; (*in the memory*) grabar

engraver [ɛn'grevər] *s* grabador *m*

engraving [ɛn'grevɪŋ] *s* grabado

engross [ɛn'gros] *tr* absorber; poner en limpio; copiar califgáficamente

engrossing [ɛn'grosɪŋ] *adj* acaparador, absorbente

engulf [ɛn'gʌlf] *tr* hundir, inundar
enhance [ɛn'hæns] *tr* realzar
enhancement [ɛn'hænsmənt] *s* realce *m*
enigma [ɪ'nɪgmə] *s* enigma *m*
enigmatic(al) [,ɪnɪg'mætɪk(əl)] *adj* enigmático
enjambment [ɛn'dʒæmmənt] o [ɛn'dʒæmbmənt] *s* encabalgamiento
enjoin [ɛn'dʒɔɪn] *tr* encargar, ordenar
enjoy [ɛn'dʒɔɪ] *tr* gozar; **to enjoy** + *ger* gozarse en + *inf;* **to enjoy oneself** divertirse
enjoyable [ɛn'dʒɔɪ•əbəl] *adj* agradable, deleitable
enjoyment [ɛn'dʒɔɪmənt] *s* (*pleasure*) placer *m;* (*pleasurable use*) goce *m*
enkindle [ɛn'kɪndəl] *tr* encender
enlarge [ɛn'lɑrdʒ] *tr* agrandar, aumentar; (phot) ampliar || *intr* agrandarse, aumentar; (*to talk at length*) explayarse; exagerar; **to enlarge on** o **upon** tratar con más extensión; exagerar
enlargement [ɛn'lɑrdʒmənt] *s* agrandamiento, aumento; (phot) ampliación
enlighten [ɛn'laɪtən] *tr* ilustrar, instruir
enlightenment [ɛn'laɪtənmənt] *s* ilustración, instrucción; dilucidación
enlist [ɛn'lɪst] *tr* alistar; ganar (*a una persona; el favor, los servicios de una persona*) || *intr* alistarse; **to enlist in** (*a cause*) poner empeño en
enliven [ɛn'laɪvən] *tr* avivar, animar
enmesh [ɛn'mɛʃ] *tr* enredar
enmi•ty ['ɛnmɪti] *s* (*pl* **-ties**) enemistad
ennoble [ɛn'nobəl] *tr* ennoblecer
ennui ['ɑnwi] *s* aburrimiento, tedio
enormous [ɪ'nɔrməs] *adj* enorme
enough [ɪ'nʌf] *adj, adv & s* bastante *m* || *interj* ¡basta!, ¡no más!
enounce [ɪ'naʊns] *tr* enunciar; pronunciar
en passant [,ɑn pæ'sɑnt] *adv* (chess) al vuelo
enrage [ɛn'redʒ] *tr* enrabiar, encolerizar
enrapture [ɛn'ræptʃər] *tr* embelesar, transportar, arrebatar
enrich [ɛn'rɪtʃ] *tr* enriquecer
enroll [ɛn'rol] *tr* alistar, inscribir; (*to wrap up*) envolver, enrollar || *intr* alistarse, inscribirse
en route [ɑn 'rut] *adv* en camino; **en route to** camino de, rumbo a
ensconce [ɛn'skɑns] *tr* esconder, abrigar; **to ensconce oneself** instalarse cómodamente
ensemble [ɑn'sɑmbəl] *s* conjunto; grupo de músicos que tocan o cantan juntos; traje armonioso
ensign ['ɛnsaɪn] *s* (*standard*) enseña, bandera; (*badge*) divisa, insignia || ['ɛnsən] o ['ɛnsaɪn] *s* (nav) alférez *m* de fragata
enslave [ɛn'slev] *tr* esclavizar
enslavement [ɛn'slevmənt] *s* esclavización
ensnare [ɛn'snɛr] *tr* entrampar
ensue [ɛn'su] *intr* seguirse; resultar
ensuing [ɛn'su•ɪŋ] *adj* siguiente; resultante
ensure [ɛn'ʃʊr] *tr* asegurar, garantizar
entail [ɛn'tel] *s* (law) vínculo || *tr* acarrear, ocasionar; (law) vincular
entangle [ɛn'tæŋgəl] *tr* enmarañar, enredar
entanglement [ɛn'tæŋgəlmənt]*s* enmarañamiento, enredo
enter ['ɛntər] *tr* entrar en (*una habitación*); entrar por (*una puerta*); (*in the customhouse*) declarar; (*to make a record of*) registrar, asentar; matricular (*a un alumno*); matricularse en; hacer miembro a; hacerse miembro de; (*to undertake*) emprender; asentar (*un pedido*); **to enter one's head** metérsele a uno en la cabeza || *intr* entrar; (theat) entrar en escena, salir; **to enter into** entrar en; celebrar (*p.ej., un contrato*); **to enter on** o **upon** emprender
enterprise ['ɛntər,praɪz] *s* (*undertaking*) empresa; (*spirit, push*) empuje *m*
enterprising ['ɛntər,praɪzɪŋ] *adj* emprendedor
entertain [,ɛntər'ten] *tr* entretener, divertir; (*to show hospitality to*) recibir; considerar, abrigar (*esperanzas, ideas, etc.*) || *intr* recibir
entertainer [,ɛntər'tenər] *s* (*host*) anfitrión *m;* (*in public*) actor *m*, bailador *m*, músico, vocalista *mf* (*esp. en un café cantante*)
entertaining [,ɛntər'tenɪŋ] *adj* entretenido
entertainment [,ɛntər'tenmənt] *s* entretenimiento, diversión; atracción, espectáculo; buen recibimiento; (*of hopes, ideas, etc.*) consideración, abrigo
enthrall [ɛn'θrɔl] *tr* cautivar, encantar; esclavizar, sojuzgar
enthrone [ɛn'θron] *tr* entronizar
enthuse [ɛn'θuz] o [ɛn'θjuz] *tr* (coll) entusiasmar || *intr* (coll) entusiasmarse
enthusiasm [ɛn'θuzɪ,æzəm] *s* entusiasmo
enthusiast [ɛn'θuzi,æst] *s* entusiasta *mf;* devoto
enthusiastic [ɛn,θuzɪ'æstɪk] *adj* entusiástico
entice [ɛn'taɪs] *tr* atraer, tentar; inducir al mal, extraviar
enticement [ɛn'taɪsmənt] *s* atracción, tentación; extravío
entire [ɛn'taɪr] *adj* entero
entirely [ɛn'taɪrli] *adv* enteramente; (*exclusively*) solamente
entire•ty [ɛtaɪrti] *s* (*pl* **-ties**) entereza; conjunto, totalidad
entitle [ɛn'taɪtəl] *tr* dar derecho a; (*to give a name to; to honor with a title*) intitular
enti•ty ['ɛntɪti] *s* (*pl* **-ties**) entidad
entomb [ɛn'tum] *tr* sepultar
entombment [ɛn'tummənt] *s* sepultura
entomology [,ɛntə'mɑlədʒi] *s* entomología
entourage [,ɑntu'rɑʒ] *s* cortejo, séquito
entrails ['ɛntrelz] *spl* entrañas
entrain [ɛn'tren] *tr* despachar en el tren || *intr* embarcar, salir en el tren
entrance ['ɛntrəns] *s* entrada, ingreso; (theat) entrada en escena || [ɛn'træns] *tr* arrebatar, encantar
entrance examination *s* examen *m* de ingreso; **to take entrance examinations** examinarse de ingreso
entrancing [ɛn'trænsɪŋ] *adj* arrebatador, encantador
entrant ['ɛntrənt] *s* entrante *mf;* (sport) concurrente *mf*

en•trap [ɛnˈtræp] *v* (*pret & pp* **-trapped;** *ger* **-trapping**) *tr* entrampar
entreat [ɛnˈtrit] *tr* rogar, suplicar
entreat•y [ɛnˈtriti] *s* (*pl* **-ies**) ruego, súplica
entree [ˈɑntre] *s* entrada, ingreso; (culin) entrada, principio
entrench [ɛnˈtrɛntʃ] *tr* atrincherar ‖ *intr* — **to entrench on** o **upon** infringir, violar
entrust [ɛnˈtrʌst] *tr* confiar
en•try [ˈɛntri] *s* (*pl* **-tries**) entrada; (*item*) partida, entrada; (*in a dictionary*) artículo; (sport) concurrente *mf*
entry word *s* (*in dictionary*) voz-guía *f*
entwine [ɛnˈtwaɪn] *tr* entretejer, entrelazar
enumerate [ɪˈnumə,ret] *tr* enumerar
enunciate [ɪˈnʌnsɪ,et] o [ɪˈnʌnʃɪ,et] *tr* enunciar; pronunciar
envelop [ɛnˈvɛləp] *tr* envolver
envelope [ˈɛnvə,lop] o [ˈɑnvə,lop] *s* (*for a letter*) sobre *m;* (*wrapper*) envoltura
envenom [ɛnˈvɛnəm] *tr* envenenar
enviable [ˈɛnvɪ•əbəl] *adj* envidiable
envious [ˈɛnvɪ•əs] *adj* envidioso
environment [ɛnˈvaɪrənmənt] *s* medio ambiente; entorno; (*surroundings*) inmediaciones
environmental [ɛn,vaɪrənˈmɛntəl] *adj* ambiental
environmental pollution *s* contaminación ambiental
environs [ɛnˈvaɪrəns] *spl* inmediaciones, alrededores *mpl*
envisage [ɛnˈvɪzɪdʒ] *tr* (*to look in the face of*) encarar; considerar, representarse
envoi [ˈɛnvɔɪ] *s* despedida (*copla al fin de una composición poética*)
envoy [ˈɛnvɔɪ] *s* (*diplomatic agent*) enviado; (*short concluding stanza*) despedida
en•vy [ˈɛnvi] *s* (*pl* **-vies**) envidia ‖ *v* (*pret & pp* **-vied**) *tr* envidiar
enzyme [ˈɛnzaɪm] *s* enzima *f*
epaulet o **epaulette** [ˈɛpə,lɛt] *s* charretera
epenthe•sis [ɛˈpɛnθɪsɪs] *s* (*pl* **-ses** [,siz]) epéntesis *f*
epergne [ɪˈpʌrn] o [eˈpɛrn] *s* ramillete *m,* centro de mesa
ephemeral [ɪˈfɛmərəl] *adj* efímero
epic [ˈɛpɪk] *adj* épico ‖ *s* epopeya
epicure [ˈɛpɪ,kjʊr] *s* epicúreo
epicurean [,ɛpɪkjʊˈri•ən] *adj & s* epicúreo
epidemic [,ɛpɪˈdɛmɪk] *adj* epidémico ‖ *s* epidemia
epidemiology [,ɛpɪ,dimɪˈɑlədʒi] *s* epidemiología
epidermis [,ɛpɪˈdʌrmɪs] *s* epidermis *f*
epigram [ˈɛpɪ,græm] *s* epigrama *m*
epilepsy [ˈɛpɪ,lɛpsi] *s* epilepsia
epileptic [,ɛpɪˈlɛptɪk] *adj & s* epiléptico
Epiphany [ɪˈpɪfəni] *s* Epifanía
Episcopalian [ɪ,pɪskəˈpelɪ•ən] *adj & s* episcopalista *mf*
episode [ˈɛpɪ,sod] *s* episodio
epistemology [ɪ,pɪstɪˈmɑlədʒi] *s* epistemología
epistle [ɪˈpɪsəl] *s* epístola
epitaph [ˈɛpɪ,tæf] *s* epitafio
epithet [ˈɛpɪ,θɛt] *s* epíteto
epitome [ɪˈpɪtəmi] *s* epítome *m;* (fig) esencia, personificación
epitomize [ɪˈpɪtə,maɪz] *tr* epitomar; (fig) encarnar, personificar
epoch [ˈɛpək] o [ˈipɑk] *s* época
epochal [ˈɛpəkəl] *adj* memorable, trascendental
ep'och-mak'ing *adj* que hace época
equable [ˈɛkwəbəl] o [ˈikwəbəl] *adj* constante, uniforme; sereno
equal [ˈikwəl] *adj* igual; **equal to** a la altura de ‖ *s* igual *mf* ‖ *v* (*pret & pp* **equaled** o **equalled;** *ger* **equaling** o **equalling**) *tr* (*to be equal to*) igualarse a o con; (*to make equal*) igualar
equali•ty [ɪˈkwɑlɪti] *s* (*pl* **-ties**) igualdad
equalize [ˈikwə,laɪz] *tr* igualar; (*to make uniform*) equilibrar
equally [ˈikwəli] *adv* igualmente
equal opportunity *s* igualdad de oportunidades
equanimity [,ikwəˈnɪmɪti] *s* ecuanimidad, igualdad de ánimo
equate [iˈkwet] *tr* poner en ecuación; considerar equivalente(s)
equation [iˈkweʃən] *s* ecuación
equator [iˈkwetər] *s* ecuador *m*
equer•ry [ˈɛkwəri] o [ɪˈkwɛri] *s* (*pl* **-ries**) caballerizo
equestrian [ɪˈkwɛstrɪ•ən] *adj* ecuestre ‖ *m* jinete *m,* caballista *m*
equestrian sport *s* hípica
equilateral [,ikwɪˈlætərəl] *adj* equilátero
equilibrium [,ikwɪˈlɪbrɪ•əm] *s* equilibrio
equinoctial [,ikwɪˈnɑkʃəl] *adj* equinoccial
equinox [ˈikwɪ,nɑks] *s* equinoccio
equip [ɪˈkwɪp] *v* (*pret & pp* **equipped;** *ger* **equipping**) *tr* equipar
equipment [ɪˈkwɪpmənt] *s* equipo, avíos, pertrechos; aptitud, capacidad
equipoise [ˈikwɪ,pɔɪz] o [ˈɛkwɪ,pɔɪz] *s* equilibrio; contrapeso ‖ *tr* equilibrar; equipesar
equitable [ˈɛkwɪtəbəl] *adj* equitativo
equi•ty [ˈɛkwɪti] *s* (*pl* **-ties**) (*fairness*) equidad; valor líquido
equivalent [ɪˈkwɪvələnt] *adj & s* equivalente *m*
equivocal [ɪˈkwɪvəkəl] *adj* equívoco
equivocate [ɪˈkwɪvə,ket] *intr* usar de equívocos para engañar, mentir
equivocation [ɪ,kwɪvəˈkeʃən] *s* equívoco
era [ˈɪrə] o [ˈirə] *s* era
eradicate [ɪˈrædɪ,ket] *tr* erradicar
erase [ɪˈres] *tr* borrar
eraser [ɪˈresər] *s* goma de borrar; (*for blackboard*) cepillo
erasure [ɪˈreʃər] o [ɪˈreʒər] *s* borradura, tachón *m*
ere [ɛr] *prep* antes de ‖ *conj* antes de que; más bien que
erect [ɪˈrɛkt] *adj* derecho, enhiesto, erguido; (*hair*) erizado ‖ *tr* (*to set in upright position*) erguir, enhestar; erigir (*un edificio*); armar, montar (*una máquina*)
erection [ɪˈrɛkʃən] *s* erección
erg [ʌrg] *s* ergio

ermine [ˈʌrmɪn] *s* armiño; (fig) toga, judicatura
erode [ɪˈrod] *tr* erosionar || *intr* erosionarse
erosion [ɪˈroʒən] *s* erosión
err [ʌr] *intr* errar, equivocarse, marrar; pecar, marrar
errand [ˈɛrənd] *s* mandado, recado, comisión; **to run an errand** hacer un mandado
errand boy *s* recadero, mandadero
erratic [ɪˈrætɪk] *adj* irregular, inconstante, variable; excéntrico
erra•tum [ɪˈretəm] o [ɪˈrɑtəm] *s* (*pl* **-ta** [tə]) errata
erroneous [ɪˈronɪ•əs] *adj* erróneo
error [ˈɛrər] *s* error *m;* **human error** fallo humano
erudite [ˈɛrʊ,daɪt] *adj* erudito
erudition [,ɛrʊˈdɪʃən] *s* erudición
erupt [ɪˈrʌpt] *intr* hacer erupción (*la piel, los dientes de un niño*); erumpir (*un volcán*)
eruption [ɪˈrʌpʃən] *s* erupción
escalate [ˈɛskə,let] *intr* escalarse
escalation [,ɛskə,ˈleʃən] *s* escalada, escalación
escalator [ˈɛskə,letər] *s* escalera mecánica, móvil o rodante
escallop [ˈɛsˈkæləp] *s* concha de peregrino; (*on edge of cloth*) festón *m* || *tr* hornear a la crema y con migajas de pan; cocer (*p.ej., ostras*) en su concha; festonear
escapade [,ɛskəˈped] *s* calaverada, aventura atolondrada; (*flight*) escapada
escape [ɛsˈkep] *s* (*getaway*) escape *m*, escapatoria; (*from responsibilities, duties, etc.*) escapatoria || *tr* evitar, eludir; **to escape someone** escapársele a uno; olvidársele a uno || *intr* escapar, escaparse; **to escape from** escaparse a (*una persona*); escaparse de (*la cárcel*)
escapee [,ɛskəˈpi] *s* evadido
escape literature *s* literatura de escape o de evasión
escapement [ɛsˈkepmənt] *s* escape *m*
escapement wheel *s* rueda de escape
escarpment [ɛsˈkɑrpmənt] *s* escarpa
eschew [ɛsˈtʃu] *tr* evitar, rehuir
escort [ˈɛskɔrt] *s* escolta; (*man or boy who accompanies a woman or girl in public*) acompañante *m*, caballero, galán *m* || [ɛsˈkɔrt] *tr* escoltar
escutcheon [ɛsˈkʌtʃən] *s* escudo de armas; (*plate in front of lock on door*) escudo, escudete *m*
Eski•mo [ˈɛskɪ,mo] *adj* esquimal || *s* (*pl* **-mos** o **-mo**) esquimal *mf*
esopha•gus [iˈsɑfəgəs] *s* (*pl* **-gi** [,dʒaɪ]) esófago
esp. *abbr* **especially**
espalier [ɛsˈpæljər] *s* espaldar *m*, espalera
especial [ɛsˈpɛʃəl] *adj* especial
espionage [ˈɛspɪ•ənɪdʒ] o [,ɛspɪ•əˈnɑʒ] *s* espionaje *m*
esplanade [,ɛspləˈned] *s* explanada
espousal [ɛsˈpaʊzəl] *s* desposorios; (*of a cause*) adhesión
espouse [ɛsˈpaʊz] *tr* casarse con; (*to advocate, adopt*) abogar por, adherirse a
Esq. *abbr* **Esquire**
esquire [ɛsˈkwaɪr] o [ˈɛskwaɪr] *s* escudero || **Esquire** *s* título de cortesía que se escribe después del apellido y que se usa en vez de **Mr.**
essay [ˈɛse] *s* ensayo
essayist [ˈɛse•ɪst] *s* ensayista *mf*
essence [ˈɛsəns] *s* esencia
essential [ɛˈsɛnʃəl] *adj & s* esencial *m*
est. *abbr* **established, estate, estimated**
establish [ɛsˈtæblɪʃ] *tr* establecer
establishment [ɛsˈtæblɪʃmənt] *s* establecimiento; **the Establishment** (*established order*) el Sistema
estate [ɛsˈtet] *s* estado; situación social; (*landed property*) finca, hacienda, heredad; (*a person's possessions*) bienes *mpl*, propiedad; (*left by a decedent*) herencia, bienes relictos
esteem [ɛsˈtim] *s* estima || *tr* estimar
esthete [ˈɛsθit] *s* esteta *mf*
esthetic [ɛsˈθɛtɪk] *adj* estético || **esthetics** *ssg* estética
estimable [ˈɛstɪməbəl] *adj* estimable
estimate [ˈɛstɪmɪt] *s* (*calculation of value, judgment of worth*) estimación; (*statement of cost of work to be done*) presupuesto || [ˈɛstɪ,met] *tr* (*to judge, deem*) estimar; presupuestar (*el coste de una obra*)
estimation [,ɛstɪˈmeʃən] *s* estimación
estrangement [ɛsˈtrendʒmənt] *s* extrañeza
estuar•y [ˈɛstʃʊ,ɛri] *s* (*pl* **-ies**) estero
etc. *abbr* **et cetera**
etch [ɛtʃ] *tr & intr* grabar al agua fuerte
etcher [ˈɛtʃər] *s* aguafortista *mf*
etching [ˈɛtʃɪŋ] *s* aguafuerte *f*
eternal [ɪˈtʌrnəl] *adj* eterno
eterni•ty [ɪˈtʌrnɪti] *s* (*pl* **-ties**) eternidad
ether [ˈiθər] *s* éter *m*
ethereal [ɪˈθɪrɪ•əl] *adj* etéreo
ethical [ˈɛθɪkəl] *adj* ético
ethics [ˈɛθɪks] *ssg* ética
Ethiopian [,iθɪˈopɪ•ən] *adj & s* etíope *mf*
Ethiopic [,iθɪˈopɪk] *adj & s* etiópico
ethnic(al) [ˈɛθnɪk(əl)] *adj* étnico
ethnography [ɛθˈnɑgrəfi] *s* etnografía
ethnology [ɛθˈnɑlədʒi] *s* etnología
ethyl [ˈɛθɪl] *s* etilo
ethylene [ˈɛθɪ,lin] *s* etileno
etiquette [ˈɛtɪ,kɛt] *s* etiqueta
et seq. *abbr* **et sequens, et sequentes, et sequentia** (Lat) **and the following**
étude [eˈtjud] *s* (mus) estudio
etymology [,ɛtɪˈmɑlədʒi] *s* etimología
ety•mon [ˈɛtɪ,mɑn] *s* (*pl* **-mons** o **-ma** [mə]) étimo
eucalyp•tus [,jukəˈlɪptəs] *s* (*pl* **-tuses** o **-ti** [taɪ]) eucalipto
Eucharist [ˈjukərɪst] *s* Eucaristía
euchre [ˈjukər] *s* juego de naipes || *tr* (coll) ser más listo que
eugenics [jʊˈdʒɛnɪks] *s* eugenesia
eulogistic [,juləˈdʒɪstɪk] *adj* elogiador
eulogize [ˈjulə,dʒaɪz] *tr* elogiar
eulo•gy [ˈjulədʒi] *s* (*pl* **-gies**) elogio
eunuch [ˈjunək] *s* eunuco
euphemism [ˈjufɪ,mɪzəm] *s* eufemismo

euphemistic [,jufɪ'mɪstɪk] *adj* eufemístico
euphonic [ju'fɑnɪk] *adj* eufónico
eupho•ny ['jufəni] *s* (*pl* **-nies**) eufonía
euphoria [ju'forɪ•ə] *s* euforia
euphuism ['jufju,ɪzəm] *s* eufuísmo
euphuistic [,jufju'ɪstɪk] *adj* eufuístico
Europe ['jʊrəp] *s* Europa
European [,jʊrə'pi•ən] *adj & s* europeo
euthanasia [,juθə'neʒə] *s* eutanasia
evacuate [ɪ'vækjʊ,et] *tr & intr* evacuar
evacuation [ɪ,vækjʊ'eʃən] *s* evacuación
evade [ɪ'ved] *tr* evadir ‖ *intr* evadirse
evaluate [ɪ'væljʊ,et] *tr* evaluar
Evangel [ɪ'vændʒəl] *s* Evangelio
evangelic(al) [,ivæn'dʒɛlɪk(əl)] o [,ɛvən-'dʒɛlɪk(əl)] *adj* evangélico
Evangelist [ɪ'vændʒəlɪst] *s* Evangelista *m*
evaporate [ɪ'væpə,ret] *tr* evaporar ‖ *intr* evaporarse
evasion [ɪ'veʒən] *s* evasión, evasiva
evasive [ɪ'vesɪv] *adj* evasivo; elusivo
eve [iv] *s* víspera; **on the eve of** en vísperas de
even ['ivən] *adj* (*smooth*) parejo, llano, liso; (*number*) par; constante, uniforme, invariable; (*temperament*) apacible, sereno; exacto, igual; **even with** al nivel de; **to be even** estar en paz; no deber nada a nadie; **to get even** desquitarse ‖ *adv* aun, hasta; sin embargo; también; exactamente, igualmente; **even as** así como; **even if** aunque, aun cuando; **even so** aun así; **even though** aunque, aun cuando; **even when** aun cuando; **not even** ni . . . siquiera; **to break even** salir sin ganar ni perder; (*in gambling*) salir en paz ‖ *tr* allanar, igualar
evening ['ivnɪŋ] *adj* vespertino ‖ *s* tarde *f*
evening clothes *spl* traje *m* de etiqueta
evening gown *s* vestido de noche (*de mujer*)
evening primrose *s* hierba del asno
evening star *s* estrella vespertina, lucero de la tarde
evening wrap *s* salida de teatro
e'ven•song' *s* canción de la tarde; (eccl) vísperas
event [ɪ'vɛnt] *s* acontecimiento, suceso; (*outcome*) resultado; (*public function*) acto; (sport) prueba; **at all events** o **in any event** en todo caso; **in the event that** en caso que
e'ven-tem'pered *adj* equilibrado
eventful [ɪ'vɛntfəl] *adj* lleno de acontecimientos; importante, memorable
eventual [ɪ'vɛntʃu•əl] *adj* final
eventuali•ty [ɪ'vɛntʃu'ælɪti] *s* (*pl*-**ties**) eventualidad
eventually [ɪ'vɛntʃʊ•əli] *adv* finalmente, con el tiempo
eventuate [ɪ'vɛntʃʊ,et] *intr* concluir, resultar
ever ['ɛvər] *adv* (*at all times*) siempre; (*at any time*) jamás, nunca, alguna vez; **as ever** como siempre; **as much as ever** tanto como antes; **ever since** (*since that time*) desde entonces; después de que; **ever so** muy; **ever so much** muchísimo; **hardly ever** o **scarcely ever** casi nunca; **not . . . ever** no . . . nunca
ev'er•glade' *s* tierra pantanosa cubierta de hierbas altas
ev'er•green' *adj* siempre verde ‖ *s* planta siempre verde; **evergreens** ramas colgadas como adorno
ev'er•last'ing *adj* sempiterno; (*lasting indefinitely*) duradero; (*wearisome*) aburrido, cansado ‖ *s* eternidad; (bot) siempreviva
ev'er•more' *adv* eternamente; **for evermore** para siempre jamás
every ['ɛvri] *adj* todos los; (*each*) cada, todo; (*being each in a series*) cada, p.ej., **every three days** cada tres días; **every bit** (coll) todo, p.ej., **every bit a man** todo un hombre; **every now and then** de vez en cuando; **every once in a while** una que otra vez; **every other day** cada dos días, un día sí y otro no; **every which way** (coll) por todas partes; (coll) en desarreglo
ev'ery•bod'y *pron indef* todo el mundo
ev'ery•day' *adj* de todos los días; cotidiano, diario; común, ordinario
every man Jack o **every mother's son** *s* cada hijo de vecino
ev'ery•one' o **every one** *pron indef* cada uno, todos, todo el mundo
ev'ery•thing' *pron indef* todo
ev'ery•where' *adv* en o por todas partes; a todas partes
evict [ɪ'vɪkt] *tr* desahuciar
eviction [ɪ'vɪkʃən] *s* desahucio
evidence ['ɛvɪdəns] *s* evidencia; (law) prueba
evident ['ɛvɪdənt] *adj* evidente
evil ['ɛivəl] *adj* malo, malvado, malazo, maléfico ‖ *s* mal *m,* maldad
e'vil•do'er *s* malhechor *m,* malvado
e'vil•do'ing *s* malhecho, maldad
evil eye *s* mal *m* de ojo
evil-minded ['ivəl'maɪndɪd] *adj* mal pensado, malintencionado
Evil One, the el enemigo malo
evince [ɪ'vɪns] *tr* manifestar, mostrar
evoke [ɪ'vok] *tr* evocar
evolution [,ɛvə'luʃən] *s* evolución; (math) extracción de raíces, radicación
evolutionary [,ɛvə'luʃə,nɛri] o **evolutionist** [,ɛgə'luʃənɪst] *s* evolucionista *mf*
evolve [ɪ'vɑlv] *tr* desarrollar; desprender (*olores, gases, calor*) ‖ *intr* evolucionar
ewe [ju] *s* oveja
ewer ['ju•ər] *s* aguamanil *m*
ex. *abbr* **examination, example, except, exchange, executive**
ex [ɛks] *prep* sin incluir, sin participación en
exact [ɛg'zækt] *adj* exacto ‖ *tr* exigir
exacting [ɛg'zæktɪŋ] *adj* exigente
exaction [ɛg'zækʃən] *s* exacción
exactly [ɛg'zæktli] *adv* exactamente; (*sharp, on the dot*) en punto
exactness [ɛg,zæktnɪs] *s* exactitud
exaggerate [ɛg'zædʒə,ret] *tr* exagerar
exalt [ɛg'zɔlt] *tr* exaltar, ensalzar
exam [ɛg'zæm] *s* (coll) examen *m*
examination [ɛg,zæmɪ'neʃən] *s* examen *m;* **to take an examination** sufrir un examen, examinarse
examine [ɛg'zæmɪn] *tr* examinar

example [ɛg'zæmpəl] o [ɛg'zɑmpəl] *s* ejemplo; (*case serving as a warning to others*) ejemplar *m;* (*of mathematics*) problema *m;* **for example** por ejemplo
exasperate [ɛg'zæspə,ret] *tr* exasperar
excavate ['ɛkskə,vet] *tr* excavar
exceed [ɛk'sid] *tr* exceder; sobrepasar (*p.ej., el límite de velocidad*)
exceedingly [ɛk'sidɪŋli] *adv* sumamente, sobremanera
ex•cel [ɛk'sɛl] *v* (*pret & pp* **-celled;** *ger* **-celling**) *tr* aventajar ‖ *intr* sobresalir
excellence ['ɛksələns] *s* excelencia
excellen•cy ['ɛksələnsi] *s* (*pl* **-cies**) excelencia; **Your Excellency** Su Excelencia
excelsior [ɛk'sɛlsɪ•ər] *s* pajilla de madera, virutas de madera
except [ɛk'sɛpt] *prep* excepto; **except for** sin; **except that** a menos que ‖ *tr* exceptuar
exception [ɛk'sɛpʃən] *s* excepción; **to take exception** poner reparos, objetar; ofenderse; **with the exception of** a excepción de
exceptional [ɛk'sɛpʃənəl] *adj* excepcional
excerpt ['ɛksʌrpt] *s* excerta, selección ‖ [ɛk'sʌrpt] *tr* escoger
excess ['ɛksɛs] o [ɛk'sɛs] *adj* excedente, sobrante ‖ [ɛk'sɛs] *s* (*amount or degree by which one thing exceeds another*) exceso, excedente *m;* (*excessive amount; immoderate indulgence, unlawful conduct*) exceso; **in excess of** más que, superior a
excess baggage *s* exceso de equipaje
excess fare *s* suplemento
excessive [ɛk'sɛsɪv] *adj* excesivo
ex'cess-prof'its tax *s* impuesto sobre beneficios extraordinarios
excess weight *s* exceso de peso
exchange [ɛks'tʃendʒ] *s* (*of greetings, compliments, blows, etc.*) cambio; (*of prisoners, merchandise, newspapers, credentials, etc.*) canje *m;* periódico de canje; (*place for buying and selling*) bolsa, lonja; estación telefónica, central *f* de teléfonos; **in exchange for** en cambio de, a trueque de ‖ *tr* cambiar; canjear (*prisioneros, mercancías, etc.*); darse, hacerse (*cortesías*); **to exchange greetings** saludarse; **to exchange shots** cambiar disparos
exchequer [ɛks'tʃɛkər] o ['ɛkstʃɛkər] *s* tesorería; fondos nacionales
excise tax [ɛk'saɪz] o ['ɛksaɪz] *m* impuesto sobre ciertas mercancías de comercio interior
excitable [ɛk'saɪtəbəl] *adj* excitable
excite [ɛk'saɪt] *tr* excitar
excitement [ɛk'saɪtmənt] *s* excitación
exciting [ɛk'saɪtɪŋ] *adj* emocionante, conmovedor; (*stimulating*) excitante
exclaim [ɛks'klem] *tr & intr* exclamar
exclamation [,ɛksklə'meʃən] *s* exclamación
exclamation mark o **point** *s* punto de admiración
exclude [ɛks'klud] *tr* excluir
exclusion [ɛks'kluʒən] *s* exclusión; **to the exclusion of** con exclusión de
exclusive [ɛks'klusɪv] *adj* exclusivo; (*clannish*) exclusivista; (*expensive*) (coll) carero; (*fashionable*) (coll) muy de moda; **exclusive of** con exclusión de
excommunicate [,ɛkskə'mjunɪ,ket] *tr* excomulgar
excommunication [,ɛkskə,mjunɪ'keʃən] *s* excomunión
excoriate [ɛks'korɪ,et] *tr* (fig) desollar, vituperar
excrement ['ɛkskrəmənt] *s* excremento
excruciating [ɛks'kruʃɪ,etɪŋ] *adj* atroz, agudísimo, vivísimo
exculpate ['ɛkskʌl,pet] o [ɛks'kʌlpet] *tr* exculpar
excursion [ɛks'kʌrʒən] *s* excursión
excursionist [ɛks'kʌrʒənɪst] *s* excursionista *mf*
excusable [ɛks'kjusəbəl] *adj* excusable
excuse [ɛks'kjus] *s* excusa ‖ [ɛks'kjuz] *tr* excusar, disculpar; dispensar, perdonar
execute ['ɛksɪ'kjut] *tr* ejecutar; (law) celebrar, finalizar (*una escritura*)
execution [,ɛksɪ'kjuʃən] *s* ejecución
executioner [,ɛksɪ'kjuʃənər] *s* ejecutor *m* de la justicia, verdugo
executive [ɛg'zɛkjətɪv] *adj* ejecutivo ‖ *m* poder ejecutivo; (*of a school, business, etc.*) dirigente *mf*
Executive Mansion *s* (U.S.A.) palacio presidencial
executor [ɛg'zɛkjətər] *s* albacea *m,* ejecutor testamentario
executrix [ɛg'zɛkjətrɪks] *s* albacea *f,* ejecutora testamentaria
exemplary [ɛg'zɛmpləri] o ['ɛgzəm,plɛri] *adj* ejemplar
exempli•fy [ɛg'zɛmplɪ,faɪ] *v* (*pret & pp* **-fied**) *tr* ejemplificar
exempt [ɛg'zɛmpt] *adj* exento ‖ *tr* eximir, exentar
exemption [ɛg'zɛmpʃən] *s* exención
exercise ['ɛksər,saɪz] *s* ejercicio; ceremonia; **to take exercise** hacer ejercicio ‖ *tr* ejercer (*p.ej., caridad, influencia*); ejercitar (*un arte, profesión, etc.; adiestrar con el ejercicio*); inquietar, preocupar; poner (*cuidado*) ‖ *ref* ejercitarse
exert [ɛg'zʌrt] *tr* ejercer (*una fuerza*); **to exert oneself** esforzarse
exertion [ɛg'zʌrʃən] *s* esfuerzo, empeño; (*active use*) ejercicio
exhalation [,ɛks•hə'leʃən] *s* (*of gas, vapors, etc.*) exhalación; (*of air from lungs*) espiración
exhale [ɛks'hel] o [ɛg'zel] *tr* exhalar (*gases, vapores*); espirar (*el aire aspirado*) ‖ *intr* exhalarse; espirar
exhaust [ɛg'zɔst] *s* escape *m;* tubo de escape ‖ *tr* (*to wear out, fatigue; to use up*) agotar; hacer el vacío en; apurar (*todos los medios*)
exhaust fan *s* ventilador *m* aspirador
exhaustion [ɛg'zɔstʃən] *s* agotamiento
exhaustive [ɛg'zɔstɪv] *adj* exhaustivo; comprensivo
exhaust manifold *s* múltiple *m* de escape
exhaust pipe *s* tubo de escape

exhaust valve *s* válvula de escape
exhibit [ɛg'zɪbit] *s* exhibición; (law) documento de prueba || *tr* exhibir
exhibition [,ɛksɪ'bɪʃən] *s* exhibición
exhibitor [ɛg'zɪbɪtər] *s* expositor *m*
exhilarating [ɛg'zɪlə,retɪŋ] *adj* alegrador, regocijador, alborozador
exhort [ɛg'zɔrt] *tr* exhortar
exhume [ɛks'hjum] *tr* exhumar
exigen•cy ['ɛksɪdʒənsi] *s* (*pl* **-cies**) exigencia
exigent ['ɛksɪdʒənt] *adj* exigente
exile ['ɛgzaɪl] o ['ɛksaɪl] *s* destierro; (*person*) desterrado || *tr* desterrar
exist [ɛg'zɪst] *intr* existir
existence [ɛg'zɪstəns] *s* existencia
existing [ɛg'zɪstɪŋ] *adj* existente
exit ['ɛgzɪt] o ['ɛksɪt] *s* salida || *intr* salir
exobiology [,ɛksobaɪ'ɑlədʒi] *s* exobiología
exodus ['ɛksədəs] *s* éxodo
exonerate [ɛg'zɑnə,ret] *tr* (*to free from blame*) exculpar; (*to free from an obligation*) exonerar
exorbitant [ɛg'zɔrbɪtənt] *adj* exorbitante
exorcise ['ɛksɔr,saɪz] *tr* exorcizar
exotic [ɛg'zɑtɪk] *adj* exótico
exp. *abbr* **expenses, expired, export, express**
expand [ɛks,pænd] *tr* dilatar (*un gas, el metal*); (*to enlarge, develop*) ampliar, ensanchar; (*to unfold, stretch out*) desplegar, extender; (math) desarrollar (*una ecuación*) || *intr* dilatarse; amplíarse, ensancharse; desplegarse, extenderse
expanse [ɛks'pæns] *s* extensión
expansion [ɛks'pænʃən] *s* expansión
expansive [ɛks'pænsɪv] *adj* expansivo
expatiate [ɛks'peʃɪ,et] *intr* espaciarse, explayarse
expatriate [ɛks'petrɪ•ɪt] *adj & s* expatriado
expect [ɛks'pɛkt] *tr* esperar; (coll) creer, suponer
expectan•cy [ɛks'pɛktənsi] *s* (*pl* **-cies**) expectación
expectant mother [ɛks'pɛktənt] *s* futura madre
expectation [,ɛks'pɛkteʃən] *s* expectativa
expectorate [ɛks'pɛktə,ret] *tr & intr* expectorar
expedien•cy [ɛks'pidɪ•ənsi] *s* (*pl* **-cies**) conveniencia, oportunidad; ventaja personal
expedient [ɛks'pidɪ•ənt] *adj* conveniente, oportuno; egoísta, ventajoso; (*acting with self-interest*) ventajista || *s* expediente *m*
expedite ['ɛkspɪ,daɪt] *tr* apresurar, despachar; expediar; dar curso a (*un documento*)
expedition [,ɛkspɪ'dɪʃən] *s* expedición
expeditious [,ɛkspɪ'dɪʃəs] *adj* expeditivo
expeditiously [,ɛkspɪ'dɪʃəsli] *adv* ejecutivamente
ex•pel [ɛks'pɛl] *v* (*pret & pp* **-pelled;** *ger* **-pelling**) *tr* expeler, expulsar
expend [ɛks'pɛnd] *tr* gastar, consumir
expendable [ɛks'pɛndəbəl] *adj* gastable; (*to be thrown away after use*) desechable; (*soldier*) sacrificable
expenditure [ɛks'pɛndɪtʃər] *s* gasto, consumo
expense [ɛks'pɛns] *s* gasto; **expenses** gastos, expensas; **to go to the expense of** meterse en gastos con; **to meet expenses** hacer frente a los gastos
expense account *s* cuenta de gastos
expensive [ɛks'pɛnsɪv] *adj* caro, costoso, dispendioso; (*charging high prices*) carero
experience [ɛks'pɪrɪ•əns] *s* experiencia || *tr* experimentar
experienced [ɛksɪ'ənst] *adj* experimentado
experiment [ɛks'perɪmənt] *s* experiencia, experimento || [ɛks'pɛrɪ,mɛnt] *intr* experimentar
expert ['ɛkspərt] *adj & s* experto
expiate ['ɛkspɪ,et] *tr* expiar
expiation [,ɛkspɪ'eʃən] *s* expiación
expire [ɛks'paɪr] *tr* expeler (*el aire de los pulmones*) || *intr* expirar (*expeler el aire de los pulmones; acabarse, p.ej., un plazo; fallecer*)
explain [ɛks'plen] *tr* explicar; **to explain away** descartar con explicaciones; (*to make excuse for*) explicar || *intr* explicar, explicarse
explanation [,ɛksplə'neʃən] *s* explicación; dilucidación
explanatory [ɛks'plænə,tori] *adj* explicativo
explicit [ɛks'plɪsɪt] *adj* explícito
explode [ɛks'plod] *tr* volar, hacer saltar; desacreditar (*una teoría*) || *intr* explotar, estallar, reventar
exploit ['ɛksplɔɪt] *s* hazaña, proeza || [ɛks'plɔɪt] *tr* explotar
exploitation [,ɛksplɔɪ'teʃən] *s* explotación
exploration [,ɛksplə'reʃən] *s* exploración
explore [ɛks'plor] *tr* explorar
explorer [ɛks'plorər] *s* explorador *m*
explosion [ɛks'ploʒən] *s* explosión; (*of a theory*) refutación
explosive [ɛks'plosɪv] *adj* explosivo || *s* explosivo; (phonet) explosiva
exponent [ɛks'ponənt] *s* exponente *m*, expositor *m;* (math) exponente *m*
export ['ɛksport] *adj* de exportación || *s* exportación; **exports** (*articles exported*) exportación || [ɛks'port] o ['ɛksport] *tr & intr* exportar
exportation [,ɛkspor'teʃən] *s* exportación
exporter [ɛksportər] *s* exportador *m*
expose [ɛks'poz] *tr* exponer; (*to unmask*) desenmascarar; (*the Host*) manifestar, exponer; (phot) impresionar
exposé [,ɛkspo'ze] *s* desenmascaramiento
exposition [,ɛkspə'zɪʃən] *s* exposición; (rhet) exposición
expostulate [ɛks'pɑstʃə,let] *intr* protestar; **to expostulate with** reconvenir
exposure [ɛks'poʒər] *s* (*to a danger; position with respect to points of compass*) exposición; (*unmasking*) desenmascaramiento; (phot) exposición
expound [ɛks'paʊnd] *tr* exponer
express [ɛks'prɛs] *adj* expreso || *adv* (*for a special purpose*) expresamente; por expreso || *s* expreso; **by express** (rr) en gran velocidad || *tr* expresar; (*to squeeze out*)

exprimir; enviar por expreso; **to express oneself** expresarse
express company *s* compañía de transportes rápidos
expression [ɛks'prɛʃən] *s* expresión
expressive [ɛks'prɛsɪv] *adj* expresivo
expressly [ɛks'prɛsli] *adv* expresamente
express•man [ɛks'prɛsmən] *s* (*pl* **-men** [mən]) (U.S.A.) empleado del servicio de transportes rápidos
express train *s* tren expreso
express'way' *s* carretera de vía libre
expropriate [ɛks'proprɪ,et] *tr* expropiar
expulsion [ɛks'pʌlʃən] *s* expulsión
expunge [ɛks'pʌndʒ] *tr* borrar, cancelar, arrasar
expurgate ['ɛkspər,get] *tr* expurgar
exquisite ['ɛkskwɪzɪt] o [ɛks'kwɪzɪt] *adj* exquisito; agudo, vivo; sensible
ex-service•man [,ɛks'sʌrvɪs,mæn] *s* (*pl* **-men** [,mɛn]) ex militar *m*, ex combatiente *m*
extant ['ɛkstənt] o [ɛks'tænt] *adj* existente
extemporaneous [ɛks,tɛmpə'renɪ•əs] *adj* sin preparación; (*made for the occasion*) provisional
extempore [ɛks'tɛmpəri] *adj* improvisado || *adv* improvisadamente
extemporize [ɛks'tɛmpə,raɪz] *tr* & *intr* improvisar
extend [ɛks'tɛnd] *tr* extender; dar, ofrecer; hacer extensivos (*p.ej., vivos deseos*); prorrogar (*un plazo*) || *intr* extenderse
extended [ɛks'tɛndɪd] *adj* extenso; prolongado
extension [ɛks'tɛnʃən] *s* extensión; prolongación
extension ladder *s* escalera extensible
extension table *s* mesa de extensión
extensive [ɛks'tɛnsɪv] *adj* (*having great extent*) extenso; (*characterized by extension*) extensivo
extent [ɛks'tɛnt] *s* extensión; **to a certain extent** hasta cierto punto; **to a great extent** en sumo grado; **to the full extent** en toda su extensión
extenuate [ɛks'tɛnjʊ,et] *tr* (*to make seem less serious*) atenuar; (*to underrate*) menospreciar, no dar importancia a
exterior [ɛks'tɪrɪ•ər] *adj* & *s* exterior *m*
exterminate [ɛks'tʌrmɪ,net] *tr* exterminar; (*insects*) desinsectar
external [ɛks'tʌrnəl] *adj* externo || **externals** *spl* exterioridad
extinct [ɛks'tɪŋkt] *adj* desaparecido; (*volcano*) extinto
extinguish [ɛkstɪŋgwɪʃ] *tr* extinguir
extinguisher [ɛks'tɪŋgwɪʃər] *s* apagador *m*, extintor *m*
extirpate ['ɛkstər,pet] o [ɛks'tʌrpet] *tr* extirpar
ex•tol [ɛks'tol] o [ɛks'tɑl] *v* (*pret* & *pp* **-tolled;** *ger* **-tolling**) *tr* ensalzar
extort [ɛks'tɔrt] *tr* obtener por amenazas, fuerza o engaño
extortion [ɛks'tɔrʃən] *s* extorción
extra ['ɛkstrə] *adj* extra; (*spare*) de repuesto || *adv* extraordinariamente || *s* (*of a newspaper*) extra *m;* pieza de repuesto; (*something additional*) extra *m;* (theat) extra *mf*
extract ['ɛkstrækt] *s* selección; (pharm) extracto || [ɛks'trækt] *tr* (*to pull out, remove*) extraer; seleccionar (*pasajes de un libro*); (math) extraer
extraction [ɛks'trækʃən] *s* extracción
extracurricular [,ɛkstrəkə'rɪkjələr] *adj* extracurricular
extradition [,ɛkstrə'dɪʃən] *s* extradición
extra fare *s* recargo de tarifa, tarifa recargada
ex'tra-flat' *adj* extraplano
extragalactic [,ɛkstrəgə'læktɪk] *adj* extragaláctico
extramural [,ɛkstrə'mjʊrəl] *adj* extramural
extraneous [ɛks'trenɪ•əs] *adj* ajeno, extraño
extraordinary [,ɛkstrə'ɔrdɪ,nɛri] o [ɛks'trɔrdɪ,nɛri] *adj* extraordinario
extrapolate [ɛks'træpə,let] *tr* & *intr* extrapolar
extrasensory [,ɛkstrə'sɛnsəri] *adj* extrasensorio
extraterrestrial [,ɛkstrətə'rɛstrɪ•əl] *adj* extraterrestre
extravagance [ɛks'trævəgəns] *s* derroche *m*, prodigalidad, gasto excesivo; (*wildness, folly*) extravagancia
extravagant [ɛks'trævəgənt] *adj* derrochador, pródigo, gastador; (*wild, foolish*) extravagante
extreme [ɛks'trim] *adj* & *s* extremo; **in the extreme** en sumo grado; **to go to extremes** excederse, propasarse
extremely [ɛks'trimli] *adv* extremadamente, sumamente
extreme unction *s* extremaunción
extremism [ɛks'trimɪzəm] *s* extremismo
extremi•ty [ɛks'trɛmɪti] *s* (*pl* **-ties**) extremidad; (*great want*) extrema necesidad; **extremities** medidas extremas; (*hands and feet*) extremidades
extricate ['ɛskstrɪ,ket] *tr* desembarazar, desenredar
extrinsic [ɛks'trɪnsɪk] *adj* extrínseco
extroversion [,ɛkstrə'vʌrʒən] *s* extroversión
extrovert ['ɛkstrə,vʌrt] *s* extrovertido
extrude [ɛks'trud] *intr* resaltar, sobresalir
exuberant [ɛg'zubərənt] *adj* exuberante
exude [ɛg'zud] o [ɛk'sud] *tr* & *intr* exudar
exult [ɛg'zʌlt] *intr* exultar, gloriarse
exultant [ɛg'zʌltənt] *adj* exultante
eye [aɪ] *s* ojo, (*of hook and eye*) hembra, corcheta; **to catch one's eye** llamar la atención a uno; **to feast one's eyes on** deleitar la vista en; **to lay eyes on** alcanzar a ver; **to make eyes at** hacer guiños a; **to roll one's eyes** poner los ojos en blanco; **to see eye to eye** estar completamente de acuerdo; **to shut one's eyes to** hacer la vista gorda ante; **without batting an eye** sin pestañear, sin inmutarse || *v* (*pret* & *pp* **eyed;** *ger* **eying** o **eyeing**) *tr* ojear; **to eye up and down** mirar de hito en hito
eye'ball' *s* globo del ojo
eye'bolt' *s* armella, cáncamo
eye'brow' *s* ceja; **to raise one's eyebrows** arquear las cejas

eye'cup' *s* ojera, lavaojos *m*
eyeful ['aɪfʊl] *s* (coll) buena ojeada
eye'glass' *s* (*of optical instrument*) ocular *m;* (*eyecup*) ojera, lavaojos *m;* **eyeglasses** gafas, anteojos
eye'lash' *s* pestaña
eyelet ['aɪlɪt] *s* ojete *m,* ojal *m;* (*hole to look through*) mirilla
eye'lid' *s* párpado
eye of the morning *s* sol *m*
eye opener ['opənər] *s* noticia asombrosa o inesperada; (coll) trago de licor
eye'piece' *s* ocular *m*
eye'shade' *s* visera
eye shadow *s* crema para los párpados; sombra (de ojos)
eye'shot' *s* alcance *m* de la vista
eye'sight' *s* vista; (*range*) alcance *m* de la vista
eye socket *s* cuenca del ojo
eye'sore' *s* cosa que ofende la vista
eye'strain' *s* vista fatigada
eye'-test' chart *s* escala tipográfica oftalmométrica, tipo de ensayo, tipo de prueba
eye'tooth' *s* (*pl* **teeth'**) colmillo, diente canino; **to cut one's eyeteeth** (coll) tener el colmillo retorcido; **to give one's eyeteeth for** (coll) dar los ojos de la cara por
eye'wash' *s* colirio; (slang) halago para engañar
eye'wit'ness *s* testigo ocular, testigo presencial
ey•rie o **ey•ry** ['ɛri] *s* (*pl* **-ries**) nido de águilas, nido de aves de rapiña; (fig) altura, morada elevada

F

F, f [ɛf] sexta letra del alfabeto inglés
f. *abbr* **feminine, folio**
F. *abbr* **Fahrenheit, Friday**
fable ['febəl] *s* fábula
fabric ['fæbrɪk] *s* tejido; textura; (*structure*) fábrica
fabricate ['fæbrɪ,ket] *tr* fabricar
fabrication [,fæbrɪ'keʃən] *s* fabricación; mentira
fabulous ['fæbjələs] *adj* fabuloso
façade [fə'sɑd] *s* fachada
face [fes] *s* cara, rostro; (*of cloth*) haz *f;* (*of earth*) faz *f;* (*grimace*) mueca; (*of watch*) esfera, muestra; (*impudence*) descaro; **in the face of** en presencia de; **to keep a straight face** contener la risa; **to lose face** desprestigiarse; **to save face** salvar las apariencias; **to show one's face** dejarse ver || *tr* volver la cara hacia; arrostrar; revestir (*un muro*); forrar (*un vestido*); **facing** cara a || *intr* — **to face about** volver la mirada; dar media vuelta; cambiar de opinión; **to face on** dar a o sobre; **to face up to** encararse con
face card *s* figura, naipe *m* de figura
face lifting *s* cirugía estética
face powder *s* polvos de tocador
facet ['fæsɪt] *s* faceta
facial ['feʃəl] *adj* facial || *s* masaje *m* facial
facilitate [fə'sɪlɪ,tet] *tr* facilitar
facili•ty [fə'sɪlɪti] *s* (*pl* **-ties**) facilidad
facing ['fesɪŋ] *s* revestimiento, paramento
facsimile [fæk'sɪmɪli] *s* facsímile *m* || *tr* facsimilar
fact [fækt] *s* hecho; **in fact** en realidad; **the fact is that** ello es que
faction ['fækʃən] *s* facción; discordia
factional ['fækʃənəl] *adj* faccionario
factionalism ['fækʃənə,lɪzəm] *s* parcialidad, partidismo
factor ['fæktər] *s* factor *m* || *tr* descomponer en factores
facto•ry ['fæktəri] *s* (*pl* **-ries**) fábrica
factual ['fæktʃʊ•əl] *adj* verdadero, objetivo
facul•ty ['fækəlti] *s* (*pl* **-ties**) facultad
fad [fæd] *s* afición pasajera, moda pasajera
fade [fed] *tr* desteñir || *intr* desteñir, desteñirse; apagarse (*un sonido*); (rad) desvanecerse
fade'out' *s* desaparición gradual; (rad) desvanecimiento
fag [fæg] *s* (*drudge*) yunque *m;* (coll) cigarrillo || *tr*—**to fag out** cansar
fagot ['fægət] *s* haz *m* de leña
fail [fel] *s*—**without fail** sin falta || *tr* faltar a; reprobar, suspender (a *un alumno*); salir mal en (*un examen*) || *intr* malograrse, fracasar; salir mal (*un alumno*); fallar (*un motor*); (com) quebrar, hacer bancarrota; **to fail to** dejar de
failure ['feljər] *s* malogro, fracaso, mal éxito; (*student*) perdigón *m;* (com) quiebra
faint [fent] *adj* débil; **to feel faint** sentirse desfallecido || *s* desmayo || *intr* desmayarse
faint-hearted ['fent'hɑrtɪd] *adj* cobarde, tímido, apocado
fair [fɛr] *adj* justo, imparcial; regular, ordinario; favorable, propicio; (*hair*) rubio; (*complexion*) blanco; (*sky*) despejado; (*weather*) bueno, bonancible || *adv* imparcialmente; **to play fair** jugar limpio || *s* (*exhibition*) feria; (*carnival*) quermese *m,* verbena
fair'ground' *s* real *m,* campo de una feria
fairly ['fɛrli] *adv* justamente; bastante
fair-minded ['fɛr'maɪndɪd] *adj* justo, imparcial
fairness ['fɛrnɪs] *s* justicia, imparcialidad; (*of weather*) serenidad; (*of complexion*) blancura
fair play *s* juego limpio, limpieza

fair sex *s* bello sexo
fair to middling *adj* bastante bueno, mediano
fair'weath'er *adj*—**a fair-weather friend** amigo del buen viento
fair•y [ˈfɛri] *adj* feérico || *s* (*pl* **-ies**) hada
fairy godmother *s* hada madrina
fair'y•land' *s* tierra de las hadas
fairy ring *s* corro de brujas
fairy tale *s* cuento de hadas; (fig) bella poesía
faith [feθ] *s* fe *f;* **to break faith with** faltar a la palabra dada a; **to keep faith with** cumplir la palabra dada a; **to pin one's faith on** tener puesta su esperanza en; **upon my faith!** ¡a fe mía!
faithful [ˈfeθfəl] *adj* fiel, leal || **the faithful** los fieles
faithless [ˈfeθlɪs] *adj* infiel, desleal
fake [fek] *adj* (coll) falso, fingido || *s* impostura, patraña; (*person*) farsante *mf* || *tr & intr* falsificar, fingir
faker [ˈfekər] *s* (coll) impostor *m,* patrañero; (*peddler*) (coll) buhonero
falcon [ˈfɔkən] o [ˈfɔlkən] *s* halcón *m*
falconer [ˈfɔkənər] o [ˈfɔlkənər] *s* cetrero, halconero
falconry [ˈfɔkənri] o [ˈfɔlkənri] *s* cetrería, halconería
fall [fɔl] *adj* otoñal || *s* caída; (*of water*) catarata, salto de agua; (*of prices*) baja; (*autumn*) otoño; **falls** catarata, caída de agua || *v* (*pret* **fell** [fɛl]; *pp* **fallen** [ˈfɔlən]) *intr* caer, caerse; **to fall apart** caerse a pedazos; **to fall back** (mil) replegarse; **to fall behind** quedarse atrás; **to fall down** caerse; **to fall due** vencer (*una letra*); **to fall flat** caer tendido; no tener éxito; **to fall for** (slang) ser engañado por; (slang) enamorarse de; **to fall in** desplomarse (*un techo*); ponerse de acuerdo; **to fall in with** trabar amistades con; ponerse de acuerdo con; **to fall off** caer de; disminuir; **to fall out** desavenirse; **to fall out of** caerse de; **to fall out with** esquinarse con; **to fall over** caerse; (coll) adular, halagar; **to fall through** fracasar, malograrse; **to fall to** recaer (*la herencia, la elección*) en; **to fall under** estar comprendido en
fallacious [fəˈleʃəs] *adj* erróneo, engañoso
falla•cy [ˈfæləsi] *s* (*pl* **-cies**) error *m,* equivocación
fall guy *s* (slang) cabeza de turco
fallible [ˈfælɪbəl] *adj* falible
falling star *s* estrella fugaz
fall'out' *s* caída radiactiva, precipitación radiactiva
fallout shelter *s* refugio antiatómico
fallow [ˈfælo] *adj* barbechado; **to lie fallow** estar en barbecho (*tierra labrantía*); (fig) quedar sin emplear, quedar sin ejecutar (*una cosa provechosa*) || *s* barbecho || *tr* barbechar
false [fɔls] *adj* falso; (*hair, teeth, etc.*) postizo || *adv* falsamente; **to play false** traicionar
false colors *spl* pretextos falsos
false face *s* mascarilla; (*ugly false face*) carantamaula
false-hearted [ˈfɔlsˈhɑrtɪd] *adj* pérfido
falsehood [ˈfɔls•hʊd] *s* falsedad
false pretenses *spl* impostura, falsas apariencias
false return *s* declaración falsa
falset•to [fɔlˈsɛto] *s* (*pl* **-tos**) (*voice*) falsete *m;* (*person*) falsetista *m*
falsi•fy [ˈfɔlsɪ,faɪ] *v* (*pret & pp* **-fied**) *tr* falsificar; (*to disprove*) refutar || *intr* falsificar; mentir
falsi•ty [ˈfɔlsɪti] *s* (*pl* **-ties**) falsedad
falter [ˈfɔltər] *s* vacilación; (*in speech*) balbuceo || *intr* vacilar; balbucear
fame [fem] *s* fama
famed [femd] *adj* afamado
familiar [fəˈmɪljər] *adj* familiar; conocido; común; **familiar with** familiarizado con
familiari•ty [fə,mɪlɪˈærɪti] *s* (*pl* **-ties**) familiaridad; conocimiento
familiarize [fəˈmɪljə,raɪz] *tr* familiarizar
fami•ly [ˈfæmɪli] *adj* familiar; **in the family way** (coll) en estado de buena esperanza || *s* (*pl* **-lies**) familia
family man *s* padre *m* de familia; hombre casero
family name *s* apellido
family physician *s* médico de cabecera
family tree *s* árbol genealógico
famish [ˈfæmɪʃ] *tr & intr* hambrear
famished [ˈfæmɪʃt] *adj* famélico
famous [ˈfeməs] *adj* famoso; (*notable, excellent*) (coll) famoso
fan [fæn] *s* abanico; ventilador *m;* (slang) hincha *mf,* aficionado || *v* (*pret & pp* **fanned;** *ger* **fanning**) *tr* abanicar; (*to winnow*) aventar; ahuyentar con abanico; avivar (*el fuego*); excitar (*las pasiones*); (slang) azotar || *intr* abanicarse; **to fan out** salir (*un camino*) en todas direcciones
fanatic [fəˈnætɪk] *adj & s* fanático
fanatical [fəˈnætɪkəl] *adj* fanático
fanaticism [fəˈnætɪ,sɪzəm] *s* fanatismo
fancied [ˈfænsid] *adj* imaginario
fancier [ˈfænsɪ•ər] *s* aficionado; visionario; (*of animals*) criador aficionado
fanciful [ˈfænsɪfəl] *adj* fantástico, extravagante; imaginativo
fan•cy [ˈfænsi] *adj* (*comp* **-cier;** *super* **-ciest**) de fantasía, de imitación; fino, de lujo, precioso; ornamental; primoroso; fantástico, extravagante || *s* (*pl* **-cies**) fantasía; afición, gusto; **to take a fancy to** aficionarse a, prendarse de || *v* (*pret & pp* **-cied**) *tr* imaginar
fancy ball *s* baile *m* de trajes
fancy dive *s* salto ornamental
fancy dress *s* traje *m* de fantasía
fancy foods *spl* comestibles *mpl* de lujo
fan'cy-free' *adj* libre del poder del amor
fancy jewelry *s* joyas de fantasía
fancy skating *s* patinaje *m* de fantasía
fan'cy•work' *s* (sew) labor *f*
fanfare [ˈfænfɛr] *s* fanfarria
fang [fæŋ] *s* colmillo; (*of reptile*) diente *m*
fan'light' *s* abanico

fantastic(al) [fæn'tæstɪk(əl)] *adj* fantástico
fanta•sy ['fæntəsi] *s* (*pl* **-sies**) fantasía
far [fɑr] *adj* lejano; **on the far side of** del otro lado de || *adv* lejos; **as far as** hasta; en cuanto; **as far as I am concerned** por lo que a mí me toca; **as far as I know** que yo sepa; **by far** con mucho; **far and near** por todas partes; **far away** muy lejos; **far be it from me** no lo permita Dios; **far better** mucho mejor; **far different** muy diferente; **far from** lejos de; **far from it** ni con mucho; **far into** hasta muy adentro de; hasta muy tarde de; **far more** mucho más; **far off** a gran distancia; **how far** cuán lejos; **how far is it?** ¿cuánto hay de aquí?; **in so far as** en cuanto; **thus far** hasta ahora; **thus far this year** en lo que va del año; **to go far towards** contribuir mucho a
faraway ['fɑrə,we] *adj* lejano, distante; abstraído, preocupado
farce [fɑrs] *s* farsa; (*ridiculous act*) papelada
farcical ['fɑrsɪkəl] *adj* ridículo
fare [fɛr] *s* pasaje *m;* pasajero; alimento; comida; **to collect fares** cobrar el pasaje || *intr* pasarlo, p.ej., **how did you fare?** ¿cómo lo pasó Vd.?
Far East *s* Extremo Oriente, Lejano Oriente
fare'well' *s* despedida; **to bid farewell to** o **to take farewell of** despedirse de || *interj* ¡adiós!
far•fetched ['far'fɛtʃt] *adj* traído por los pelos
far-flung ['fɑr'flʌŋ] *adj* de gran alcance, vasto
farm [fɑrm] *adj* agrícola; agropecuario || *s* granja; terreno agrícola || *tr* cultivar, labrar (*la tierra*) || *intr* cultivar la tierra y criar animales
farmer ['fɑrmər] *s* granjero; agricultor *m,* labrador *m*
farm hand *s* peón *m,* mozo de granja
farm'house' *s* alquería, cortijo
farming ['fɑrmɪŋ] *s* agricultura, labranza
farm'yard' *s* corral *m* de granja
far'-off' *adj* lejano, distante
far-reaching ['fɑr'ritʃɪŋ] *adj* de mucho alcance
far-sighted ['fɑr'saɪtɪd] *adj* longividente; precavido; présbita
farther ['fɑrðər] *adj* más lejano; adicional || *adv* más lejos, más allá; además, también; **farther on** más adelante
farthest ['fɑrðɪst] *adj* (el) más lejano; último || *adv* más lejos; más
farthing ['fɑrðɪŋ] *s* (Brit) cuarto de penique
Far West *s* (U.S.A.) Lejano Oeste
fascinate ['fæsɪ,net] *tr* fascinar
fascinating ['fæsɪ,netɪŋ] *adj* fascinante, cautivador
fascism ['fæʃɪzəm] *s* fascismo
fascist ['fæʃɪst] *adj & s* fascista *mf*
fashion ['fæʃən] *s* moda, boga; estilo, manera; alta sociedad; **after a fashion** en cierto modo; **in fashion** de moda; **out of fashion** fuera de moda; **to go out of fashion** pasar de moda || *tr* labrar, forjar
fashion designing *s* alta costura
fashion plate *s* figurín *m;* (*person*) (coll) figurín *m,* elegante *mf;* **to be a fashion plate** (coll) ir hecho un maniquí
fashion show *s* desfile *m* de modas
fast [fæst] *adj* rápido, veloz; (*clock*) adelantado; fijado; disipado; (*friend*) fiel || *adv* aprisa, rápidamente; firmemente; (*asleep*) profundamente; **to hold fast** mantenerse firme; **to live fast** vivir de una manera disipada || *s* ayuno; **to break one's fast** romper el ayuno || *intr* ayunar
fast day *s* día *m* de ayuno
fasten ['fæsən] *tr* fijar; atar; abrochar; cerrar con llave; (*one's belt*) ajustarse; (*blame*) aplicar || *intr* fijarse
fastener ['fæsənər] *s* asilla; (*snap, clasp*) cierre *m;* (*for papers*) sujetapapeles *m*
fast'-food' restaurant *s* rotisería
fast forward *s* (mach, mov) avance rápido
fastidious [fæs'tɪdɪ•əs] *adj* esquilmoso, quisquilloso, descontentadizo
fasting ['fæstɪŋ] *s* ayuno
fat [fæt] *adj* (*comp* **fatter;** *super* **fattest**) gordo; poderoso; opulento; (*profitable*) pingüe; (*spark*) caliente; **to get fat** engordar || *s* grasa; (*suet*) gordo, sebo
fatal ['fetəl] *adj* fatal
fatalism ['fetə,lɪzəm] *s* fatalismo
fatalist ['fetəlɪst] *s* fatalista *mf*
fatali•ty [fə'tælɪti] *s* (*pl* **-ties**) fatalidad; (*in accidents, war, etc.*) muerte *f*
fate [fet] *s* sino, hado; **the Fates** las Parcas || *tr* condenar, predestinar
fated ['fetɪd] *adj* hadado, predestinado
fateful ['fetfəl] *adj* fatídico; fatal
fat'head' *s* (coll) tronco, estúpido
father ['fɑðər] *s* padre *m;* (*an elderly man*) (coll) tío || *tr* servir de padre a; engendrar; inventar
fatherhood ['fɑðər,hʊd] *s* paternidad
fa'ther-in-law' *s* (*pl* **fathers-in-law**) suegro
fa'ther•land' *s* patria
fatherless ['fɑðərlɪs] *adj* huérfano de padre, sin padre
fatherly ['fɑðərli] *adj* paternal
Father's Day *s* día *m* del padre
Father Time *s* el Tiempo
fathom ['fæðəm] *s* braza || *tr* sondear; profundizar
fathomless ['fæðəmlɪs] *adj* insondable
fatigue [fə'tig] *s* fatiga; (mil) faena || *tr* fatigar, cansar
fatigue clothes *spl* (mil) traje *m* de faena
fatigue duty *s* faena
fatten ['fætən] *tr & intr* engordar
fat•ty ['fæti] *adj* (*comp* **-tier;** *super* **-tiest**) graso; (pathol) grasoso; (*chubby*) (coll) gordiflón || *s* (*pl* **-ties**) (coll) gordiflón *m*
fatuous ['fætʃʊ•əs] *adj* fatuo; irreal, ilusivo
faucet ['fɔsɪt] *s* grifo
fault [fɔlt] *s* (*misdeed, blame*) culpa; (*defect*) falta; (geol) falla; (sport) falta; **it's your fault Vd.** tiene la culpa; **to a fault** excesivamente; **to find fault with** culpar, echar la culpa a; hallar defecto en
fault'find'er *s* criticón *m,* reparón *m*

fault'find'ing *adj* criticón, reparón || *s* manía de criticar
faultless ['fɔltlɪs] *adj* perfecto, impecable
fault•y ['fɔlti] *adj* (*comp* **-ier;** *super* **-iest**) defectuoso, imperfecto
faun [fɔn] *s* fauno
fauna ['fɔnə] *s* fauna
favor ['fevər] *s* favor *m;* (*letter*) atenta, grata; **do me the favor to** hágame Vd. el favor de; **by your favor** con permiso de Vd.; **favors** regalos de fiesta, objetos de cotillón; **to be in favor with** disfrutar del favor de; **to be out of favor** caer en desgracia || *tr* favorecer; (coll) parecerse a
favorable ['fevərəbəl] *adj* favorable
favorite ['fevərɪt] *adj & s* favorito
favoritism ['fevərɪ,tɪzəm] *s* favoritismo
fawn [fɔn] *s* cervato || *intr*—**to fawn on** adular servilmente; hacer fiestas a
faze [fez] *tr* (coll) molestar, desanimar
FBI [,ɛf,bi'aɪ] *s* (letterword) **Federal Bureau of Investigation**
fear [fɪr] *s* miedo; **for fear of** por miedo de, por temor de; **for fear that** por miedo (de) que; **no fear** no hay peligro; **to be in fear of** tener miedo de || *tr & intr* temer
fearful ['fɪrfəl] *adj* medroso; (coll) enorme, muy malo
fearless ['fɪrlɪs] *adj* arrojado, intrépido
feasible ['fɪsɪbəl] *adj* factible, viable
feast [fist] *s* fiesta; (*sumptuous meal*) festín *m,* banquete *m* || *tr & intr* banquetear; **to feast on** regalarse con
feat [fit] *s* hazaña, proeza
feather ['fɛðər] *s* pluma; (*plume; arrogance*) penacho; clase *f,* género; **in fine feather** de buen humor; en buena salud || *tr* emplumar; (carp) machihembrar; **to feather one's nest** hacer todo para enriquecerse
feather bed *s* colchón *m* de plumas; (*comfortable situation*) lecho de plumas
feath'er•bed'ding *s* empleo de más obreros de lo necesario (*exigido por los sindicatos*)
feath'er•brain' *s* cascabelero
feath'er•edge' *s* (*of board*) bisel *m;* (*of sharpened tool*) filván *m*
feathery ['fɛðəri] *adj* plumoso
feature ['fitʃər] *s* facción; característica, rasgo distintivo; película principal; artículo principal; **features** facciones || *tr* delinear; ofrecer como cosa principal; (coll) destacar, hacer resaltar
feature writer *s* articulista *mf*
February ['fɛbru,ɛri] *s* febrero
feces ['fisiz] *spl* heces *fpl,* excremento
feckless ['fɛklɪs] *adj* abatido, sin valor; débil
federal ['fɛdərəl] *adj & s* federal *mf*
federate ['fɛdə,ret] *adj* federado || *tr* federar || *intr* federarse
federation [,fɛdə'reʃən] *s* federación
fedora [fɪ'dorə] *s* sombrero de fieltro suave con ala vuelta
fed up [fɛd] *adj* harto; **to get fed up with** desenamorarse de
fee [fi] *s* honorarios; (*for admission, tuition, etc.*) cuota, precio; (*tip*) propina || *tr* pagar; dar propina a
feeble ['fibəl] *adj* débil; caedizo
feeble-minded ['fibəl'maɪndɪd] *adj* imbécil; irresoluto, vacilante
feed [fid] *s* alimento, comida; (mach) dispositivo de alimentación || *v* (*pret & pp* **fed** [fɛd]) *tr* alimentar || *intr* alimentarse
feed'back' *s* regeneración, realimentación, retroalimentación; comentarios *fpl;* informaciones *fpl;* comentario privado y confidencial
feed bag *s* cebadera, morral *m*
feeder industries *spl* subsidiarias *fpl*
feed pump *s* bomba de alimentación
feed trough *s* comedero
feed wire *s* (elec) conductor *m* de alimentación
feel [fil] *s* sensación; (*sense of what is right*) tino || *v* (*pret & pp* **felt** [fɛlt]) *tr* sentir; (*e.g., with the hands*) palpar, tentar; tomar (*el pulso*); tantear (*el camino*) || *intr* (*sick, tired, etc.*) sentirse; palpar; **to feel bad** sentirse mal; condolerse; **to feel cheap** avergonzarse; **to feel comfortable** sentirse a gusto; **to feel for** buscar tentando; condolerse de; **to feel like** tener ganas de; **to feel safe** sentirse a salvo; **to feel sorry** sentir; arrepentirse; **to feel sorry for** compadecer; arrepentirse de
feeler ['filər] *s* (*something said to draw someone out*) buscapié *m,* tranquilla; **feelers** (*of insect*) anténulas, palpos; (*of mollusk*) tentáculos
feeling ['filɪŋ] *s* (*with senses*) sensación; (*impression, emotion*) sentimiento; presentimiento; parecer *m*
feign [fen] *tr* aparentar, fingir || *intr* fingir; **to feign to be** fingirse
feint [fent] *s* (*threat*) finta; (*of fencer*) pase *m,* treta || *intr* hacer una finta
feldspar ['fɛld,spɑr] *s* feldespato
felicitate [fə'lɪsɪ,tet] *tr* felicitar
felicitous [fə'lɪsɪtəs] *adj* (*opportune*) feliz; elocuente
fell [fɛl] *adj* cruel, feroz, mortal || *tr* talar (*árboles*)
felloe ['fɛlo] *s* aro de la rueda; (*part of this*) pina
fellow ['fɛlo] *s* (coll) mozo, tipo, sujeto; (coll) pretendiente *m;* prójimo; (*of a society*) socio, miembro; (*holder of fellowship*) pensionista *mf*
fellow being *s* prójimo
fellow citizen *s* conciudadano
fellow countryman *s* compatriota *mf*
fellow man *s* prójimo
fellow member *s* consocio
fellowship ['fɛlo,ʃɪp] *s* compañerismo; (*for study*) pensión
fellow traveler *s* compañero de viaje
felon ['fɛlən] *s* delincuente *mf* de mayor cuantía; (pathol) panadizo
felo•ny ['fɛləni] *s* (pl **-nies**) delito de mayor cuantía; **to compound a felony** aceptar dinero para no procesar
felt [fɛlt] *s* fieltro
felt'-tipped' pen *s* rotulador *m;* plumón *m* (Mex)

female [ˈfimel] *adj* (*sex*) femenino; (*animal, plant, piece of a device*) hembra ‖ *s* hembra
feminine [ˈfɛmɪnɪn] *adj & s* femenino
feminism [ˈfɛmɪˌnɪzəm] *s* feminismo
fen [fɛn] *s* pantano
fence [fɛns] *s* cerca, cercado; (*for stolen goods*) alcahuete *m;* receptador; (*of a saw*) guía; **on the fence** (coll) indeciso ‖ *tr* cercar ‖ *intr* esgrimir
fencing [ˈfɛnsɪŋ] *s* (*art*) esgrima; (*act*) esgrimidura
fencing academy *s* escuela de esgrima
fend [fɛnd] *tr*—**to fend off** apartar, resguardarse de ‖ *intr*—**to fend for oneself** (coll) tirar por su lado
fender [ˈfɛndər] *s* (*mudguard*) guardafango, guardabarros *m;* (*of locomotive*) quitapiedras *m;* (*of trolley car*) salvavidas *m;* (*of fireplace*) guardafuego
fennel [ˈfɛnəl] *s* hinojo
ferment [ˈfʌrmɛnt] *s* fermento; fermentación ‖ [fərˈmɛnt] *tr & intr* fermentar
fern [fʌrn] *s* helecho
ferocious [fəˈroʃəs] *adj* feroz
feroci•ty [fəˈrɑsɪti] *s* (*pl* **-ties**) ferocidad
ferret [ˈfɛrɪt] *s* hurón *m* ‖ *tr*—**to ferret out** huronear ‖ *intr* huronear
Ferris wheel [ˈfɛrɪs] *s* rueda de feria, noria
fer•ry [ˈfɛri] *s* (*pl* **-ries**) bote *m* de paso, ferry-boat *m* ‖ *v* (*pret & pp* **-ried**) *tr* pasar (*viajeros, mercancías*) a través del río ‖ *intr* cruzar el río en barco
fer'ry•boat' *s* bote *m* de paso, ferry-boat *m*
fertile [ˈfʌrtɪl] *adj* fértil
fertilize [ˈfʌrtɪˌlaɪz] *tr* abonar, fertilizar; (*to impregnate*) fecundar
fervid [ˈfʌrvɪd] *adj* férvido, vehemente
fervor [ˈfʌrvər] *s* fervor *m*
fervent [ˈfʌrvənt] *adj* ferviente, fervoroso
fester [ˈfɛstər] *s* úlcera ‖ *tr* enconar ‖ *intr* enconarse (*una herida; el ánimo de uno*)
festival [ˈfɛstɪvəl] *adj* festivo ‖ *s* fiesta; (*of music*) festival *m*
festive [ˈfɛstɪv] *adj* festivo
festivi•ty [fɛsˈtɪvɪti] *s* (*pl* **-ties**) festividad
festoon [fɛsˈtun] *s* festón *m* ‖ *tr* festonear
fetch [fɛtʃ] *tr* ir por, hacer venir, traer; venderse a, venderse por
fetching [ˈfɛtʃɪŋ] *adj* (coll) encantador, atractivo
fete [fet] *s* fiesta ‖ *tr* festejar
fetid [ˈfɛtɪd] o [ˈfitɪd] *adj* fétido
fetish [ˈfitɪʃ] o [ˈfɛtɪʃ] *s* fetiche *m*
fetlock [ˈfɛtlɑk] *s* espolón *m;* (*tuft of hair*) cerneja
fetter [ˈfɛtər] *s* grillete *m,* grillo ‖ *tr* engrillar; impedir
fettle [ˈfɛtəl] *s* estado, condición; **in fine fettle** en buena condición
fetus [ˈfitəs] *s* feto
feud [fjud] *s* odio hereditario, enemistad de larga duración
feudal [ˈfjudəl] *adj* feudal
feudalism [ˈfjudəˌlɪzəm] *s* feudalismo
fever [ˈfivər] *s* fiebre *f,* calentura
fever blister *s* escupidura, fuegos en los labios
feverish [ˈfivərɪʃ] *adj* febril, calenturiento
few [fju] *adj & pron* pocos, no muchos; **a few** unos pocos, unos cuantos; **quite a few** muchos
fiancé [ˌfi•ɑnˈse] *s* novio, prometido; novillo (Mex, P-R)
fiancée [ˌfi•ɑnˈse] *s* novia, prometida
fias•co [fɪˈæsko] *s* (*pl* **-cos** o **-coes**) fiasco
fib [fɪb] *s* mentirilla ‖ *v* (*pret & pp* **fibbed;** *ger* **fibbing**) *intr* decir mentirillas, macanear
fiber [ˈfaɪbər] *s* fibra; carácter *m,* índole *f*
fibrous [ˈfaɪbrəs] *adj* fibroso
fickle [ˈfɪkəl] *adj* inconstante, veleidoso
fiction [ˈfɪkʃən] *s* (*invention*) ficción; (*branch of literature*) novelística; **pure fiction!** ¡puro cuento!
fictional [ˈfɪkʃənəl] *adj* novelesco
fictionalize [ˈfɪkʃənəˌlaɪz] *tr* novelizar
fictitious [ˈfɪkˈtɪʃəs] *adj* ficticio
fiddle [ˈfɪdəl] *s* violín *m* ‖ *tr* tocar (*un aire*) con el violín; **to fiddle away** (coll) malgastar ‖ *intr* tocar el violín; **to fiddle with** manosear
fiddler [ˈfɪdlər] *s* (coll) violinista *mf*
fiddling [ˈfɪdlɪŋ] *adj* (coll) despreciable, insignificante
fideli•ty [fɪˈdɛlɪti] *s* (*pl* **-ties**) fidelidad
fidget [ˈfɪdʒɪt] *intr* agitarse, menearse; **to fidget with** manosear
fidgety [ˈfɪdʒɪti] *adj* inquieto, nervioso
fiduciar•y [fɪˈdjuʃɪˌɛri] *adj* fiduciario ‖ *s* (*pl* **-ies**) fiduciario
fie [faɪ] *interj* ¡qué vergüenza!
fief [fif] *s* feudo
field [fild] *adj* (mil) de campaña ‖ *s* campo; (*sown with grain*) sembrado; (baseball) jardín *m;* (elec) campo magnético; (*of motor or dynamo*) (elec) inductor *m*
fielder [ˈfildər] *s* (baseball) jardinero
field glasses *spl* gemelos de campo
field hockey *s* hockey *m* sobre hierba
field magnet *s* imán *m* inductor
field marshal *s* (mil) mariscal *m* de campo
field'piece' *s* cañón *m* de campaña
fiend [find] *s* diablo; (*person*) fiera; **to be a fiend for** ser una fiera para
fiendish [ˈfindɪʃ] *adj* diabólico
fierce [fɪrs] *adj* feroz, fiero; (*wind*) furioso; (coll) muy malo
fierceness [ˈfɪrsnɪs] *s* ferocidad, fiereza; furia
fier•y [ˈfaɪri] *adj* (*comp* **-ier;** *super* **-iest**) ardiente, caliente; brioso
fife [faɪf] *s* pífano
fifteen [ˈfɪfˈtin] *adj, pron & s* quince *m*
fifteenth [ˈfɪfˈtinθ] *adj & s* (*in a series*) decimoquinto; (*part*) quinzavo ‖ *s* (*in dates*) quince *m*
fifth [fɪfθ] *adj & s* quinto ‖ *s* (*in dates*) cinco
fifth column *s* quinta columna
fifth columnist *s* quintacolumnista *mf*
fiftieth [ˈfɪftɪ•ɪθ] *adj & s* (*in a series*) quincuagésimo; (*part*) cincuentavo
fif•ty [ˈfɪfti] *adj & pron* cincuenta ‖ *s* (*pl* **-ties**) cincuenta *m*

fif'ty-fif'ty *adv*—**to go fifty-fifty** (coll) ir a medias

fig. *abbr* **figure, figuratively**

fig [fɪg] *s* higo, breva; (*tree*) higuera; (*merest trifle*) bledo

fight [faɪt] *s* lucha, pelea; ánimo, brío; **to pick a fight with** meterse con, buscar la lengua a || *tr* luchar con; dar (*batalla*); lidiar (*al toro*) || *intr* luchar, pelear; **to fight shy of** tratar de evitar

fighter [ˈfaɪtər] *s* luchador *m,* peleador *m;* (*warrior*) combatiente *m;* (*game person*) porfiador *m;* (aer) avión *m* de combate, caza *m*

fig leaf *s* hoja de higuera; (*on statues*) hoja de parra

figment [ˈfɪgmənt] *s* ficción, invención

figurative [ˈfɪgjərətɪv] *adj* figurado; (*representing by a likeness*) figurativo

figure [ˈfɪgjər] *s* figura; (*bodily form*) talle *m;* precio; **to be good at figures** ser listo en aritmética; **to cut a figure** hacer figura; **to have a good figure** tener buen tipo; **to keep one's figure** conservar la línea || *tr* adornar con figuras; figurarse, imaginar; suponer, calcular; **to figure out** descifrar || *intr* figurar; **to figure on** contar con

fig'ure•head' *s* (naut) figurón *m* de proa, mascarón *m* de proa; (*straw man*) testaferro

figure of speech *s* figura retórica

figure skating *s* patinaje artístico

figurine [,fɪgjəˈrin] *s* figurilla, figurina

filament [ˈfɪləmənt] *s* filamento

filch [fɪltʃ] *tr* birlar, ratear

file [faɪl] *s* fila, hilera; (*tool*) lima; (*collection of papers*) archivo; (*cabinet*) archivador *m,* fichero || *tr* poner en fila; limar; archivar, clasificar; anotar || *intr* desfilar; **to file for** solicitar

file case *s* fichero

file clerk *s* fichador *m*

filet [fɪˈle] o [ˈfɪle] *s* filete *m* || *tr* cortar en filetes

filial [ˈfɪlɪ•əl] o [ˈfɪljəl] *adj* filial

filiation [,fɪlɪˈeʃən] *s* filiación

filibuster [ˈfɪlɪ,bʌstər] *s* obstrucción (*de la aprobación de una ley*); obstruccionista *mf;* (*buccaneer*) filibustero || *tr* obstruir (*la aprobación de una ley*)

filigree [ˈfɪlɪ,gri] *adj* afiligranado || *s* filigrana || *tr* afiligranar

filing [ˈfaɪlɪŋ] *s* (*of documents*) clasificación; limadura; **filings** limadura, limalla

filing cabinet *s* archivador *m,* clasificador *m*

filing card *s* ficha

Filipi•no [,fɪlɪˈpino] *adj* filipino || *s* (*pl* **-nos**) filipino

fill [fɪl] *s* (*sufficiency*) hartazgo; (*place filled with earth*) terraplén *m;* **to have** o **get one's fill of** darse un hartazgo de || *tr* llenar; rellenar; despachar (*un pedido*); tapar (*un agujero*); empastar (*un diente*); inflar (*un neumático*); llenar, ocupar (*un puesto*); colmar (*lagunas*); **to fill out** llenar (*un formulario*) || *intr* llenarse; rellenarse; **to fill in** hacer de suplente; **to fill up** ahogarse de emoción

filler [ˈfɪlər] *s* relleno; (*of cigar*) tripa; *sizing* aparejo; (*in a writing*) relleno

fillet [ˈfɪlɪt] *s* cinta, tira; (*for hair*) prendedero; (archit, bb) filete *m* || *tr* filetear || [ˈfɪle] o [ˈfɪlɪt] *s* (*of meat or fish*) filete *m* || *tr* cortar en filetes

filling [ˈfɪlɪŋ] *s* (*of a tooth*) empaste *m;* (*e.g., of a turkey*) relleno; (*of cigar*) tripa

filling station *s* estación gasolinera

fillip [ˈfɪlɪp] *s* aguijón *m,* estímulo; (*with finger*) capirotazo

fil•ly [ˈfɪli] *s* (*pl* **-lies**) potra; (coll) muchacha retozona

film [fɪlm] *s* película; (mov) película, film *m;* (phot) película || *tr* filmar

film library *s* cinemateca

film star *s* estrella de la pantalla

film strip *s* tira proyectable

film•y [ˈfɪlmi] *adj* (*comp* **-ier;** *super* **-iest**) delgadísimo, diáfano, sutil

filter [ˈfɪltər] *s* filtro || *tr* filtrar || *intr* filtrarse

filtering [ˈfɪltərɪŋ] *s* filtración

filter paper *s* papel *m* filtrante

filter tip *s* embocadura de filtro

filth [fɪlθ] *s* suciedad, porquería

filth•y [ˈfɪlθi] *adj* (*comp* **-ier;** *super* **-iest**) sucio, puerco

filthy lucre [ˈlukər] *s* (coll) el vil metal (*dinero, raíz de muchos males*)

filtrate [ˈfɪltret] *s* filtrado || *tr* filtrar || *intr* filtrarse

fin. *abbr* **finance**

fin [fɪn] *s* aleta

final [ˈfaɪnəl] *adj* final; (*last in a series*) último; decisivo, terminante || *s* examen *m* final; **finals** (sport) final *f*

finale [fɪˈnɑli] *s* (mus) final *m*

finalist [ˈfaɪnəlɪst] *s* finalista *mf*

finally [ˈfaɪnəli] *adv* finalmente, por último

finance [ˈfaɪnæns] *s* financiación; **finances** finanzas || *tr* financiar

financial [faɪˈnænʃəl] *adj* financiero

financier [,faɪnənˈsɪr] *s* financiero

financing [ˈfaɪnænsɪŋ] *s* financiación, financiamiento

finch [fɪntʃ] *s* pinzón *m*

find [faɪnd] *s* hallazgo || *v* (*pret & pp* **found** [faʊnd]) *tr* hallar, encontrar; **to find out** averiguar, darse cuenta de || *intr* (*law*) pronunciar fallo; **to find out about** informarse de

finder [ˈfaɪndər] *s* (*of camera*) visor *m;* (*of microscope*) portaobjeto cuadriculado

finding [ˈfaɪndɪŋ] *s* descubrimiento; (law) laudo, fallo

fine [faɪn] *adj* fino; (*weather*) bueno; divertido || *adv* (coll) muy bien; **to feel fine** (coll) sentirse muy bien de salud || *s* multa || *tr* multar

fine arts *spl* bellas artes

fineness *s* fineza; (*of metal*) ley *f*

fine print *s* letra menuda, tipo menudo

finer•y [ˈfaɪnəri] *s* (*pl* **-ies**) adorno, galas, atavíos

fine-spun [ˈfaɪn,spʌn] *adj* estirado en hilo finísimo; (fig) alambicado

finesse [fɪˈnɛs] *s* sutileza; (*in bridge*) impás *m* || *tr* hacer el impás con || *intr* hacer un impás
fine-toothed comb [ˈfaɪn,tuθt] *s* lendrera, peine *m* de púas finas; **to go over with a fine-toothed comb** escudriñar minuciosamente
finger [ˈfɪŋgər] *s* dedo; **to burn one's fingers** cogerse los dedos; **to put one's finger on the spot** poner el dedo en la llaga; **to slip between the fingers** irse de entre los dedos; **to snap one's fingers at** tratar con desprecio; **to twist around one's little finger** manejar a su gusto || *tr* manosear; (slang) acechar, espiar; (slang) identificar
finger board *s* (*of guitar*) diapasón *m;* (*of piano*) teclado
finger bowl *s* lavadedos *m,* lavafrutas *m*
finger dexterity *s* (mus) dedeo
fingering [ˈfɪŋgərɪŋ] *s* manoseo; (mus) digitación
fin'ger•nail' *s* uña
fingernail polish *s* esmalte *m* para las uñas
fin'ger•print' *s* huella digital, dactilograma *m* || *tr* tomar las huellas digitales de
finger tip *s* punta del dedo; **to have at one's finger tips** tener en la punta de los dedos, saber al dedillo
finial [ˈfɪnɪ•əl] *s* florón *m*
finical [ˈfɪnɪkəl] o **finicky** [ˈfɪnɪki] *adj* delicado, melindroso
finish [ˈfɪnɪʃ] *s* acabado; fin *m,* conclusión || *tr* acabar; **to be finished** estar listo || *intr* acabar; **to finish** + *ger* acabar de + *inf;* **to finish by** + *ger* acabar por + *inf*
finishing nail *s* puntilla francesa
finishing school *s* escuela particular de educación social para señoritas
finishing touch *s* toque *m* final, última mano
finite [ˈfaɪnaɪt] *adj* finito
finite verb *s* forma verbal flexional
Finland [ˈfɪnlənd] *s* Finlandia
Finlander [ˈfɪnləndər] *s* finlandés *m*
Finn [fɪn] *s* (*member of a Finnish-speaking group of people*) finés *m;* (*native or inhabitant of Finland*) finlandés *m*
Finnish [ˈfɪnɪʃ] *adj* finlandés || *s* (*language*) finlandés *m*
fir [fʌr] *s* abeto
fire [faɪr] *s* fuego; (*destructive burning*) incendio; **through fire and water** a trancos y barrancos; **to be on fire** estar ardiendo; **to be under enemy fire** estar expuesto al fuego del enemigo; **to catch fire** encenderse; **to hang fire** estar en suspensión; **to open fire** abrir fuego, romper el fuego; **to set on fire, to set fire to** pegar fuego a; **under fire** bajo el fuego del enemigo; acusado, inculpado || *interj* (mil) ¡fuego! || *tr* encender; calentar (*el horno*); cocer (*ladrillos*); disparar (*un arma de fuego*); pegar (*un tiro*); excitar (*la imaginación*); (coll) despedir (*a un empleado*) || *intr* encenderse; **to fire on** hacer fuego sobre; **to fire up** cargar el horno; calentar el horno
fire alarm *s* alarma de incendios, avisador *m* de incendios; **to sound the fire alarm** tocar a fuego
fire'arm' *s* arma de fuego
fire'ball' *s* bola de fuego; (*lightning*) rayo en bola
fire'bird' *s* cacique veranero
fire'boat' *s* buque *m* con mangueras para incendios
fire'box' *s* caja de fuego, fogón *m*
fire'brand' *s* tizón *m;* (*hothead*) botafuego
fire'break' *s* raya
fire'brick' *s* ladrillo refractario
fire brigade *s* cuerpo de bomberos
fire'bug' *s* (coll) incendiario
fire company *s* cuerpo de bomberos; compañía de seguros
fire'crack'er *s* triquitraque *m*
fire'damp' *s* grisú *m,* mofeta
fire department *s* servicio de bomberos
fire'dog' *s* morillo
fire drill *s* ejercicio para caso de incendio
fire engine *s* coche *m* bomba, bomba de incendios, motobomba
fire escape *s* escalera de salvamento
fire extinguisher *s* extintor *m,* apagafuegos *m,* extinguidor *m*
fire'fly' *s* (*pl* **-flies**) luciérnaga
fire'guard' *s* guardafuego
fire hose *s* manguera para incendios
fire'house' *s* cuartel *m* de bomberos, estación de incendios
fire hydrant *s* boca de incendio
fire insurance *s* seguro contra incendios
fire irons *spl* badil *m* y tenazas
fireless cooker [ˈfaɪrlɪs] *s* cocinilla sin fuego
fire•man [ˈfaɪrmən] *s* (*pl* **-men** [mən]) (*man who stokes fires*) fogonero; (*man who extinguishes fires*) bombero
fire'place' *s* chimenea, chimenea francesa
fire plug *s* boca de agua
fire power *s* (mil) potencia de fuego
fire'proof' *adj* incombustible; a prueba de incendio || *tr* hacer incombustible
fire sale *s* venta de mercancías averiadas en un incendio
fire screen *s* pantalla de chimenea
fire ship *s* brulote *m*
fire shovel *s* badil *m*
fire'side' *s* hogar *m*
fire'trap' *s* edificio sin medios adecuados de escape en caso de incendio
fire wall *s* cortafuego
fire'ward'en *s* vigía *m* de incendios
fire'wa'ter *s* aguardiente *m*
fire'wood' *s* leña
fire'works' *spl* fuegos artificiales
firing [ˈfaɪrɪŋ] *s* encendimiento; (*of bricks*) cocción; (*of a gun*) disparo; (*of soldiers*) tiroteo; (*of an internal-combustion engine*) encendido; (*of an employee*) (coll) despedida
firing line *s* línea de fuego, frente *m* de batalla
firing order *s* (aut) orden *m* del encendido
firing squad *s* (*for saluting at a burial*) piquete *m* de salvas; (*for executing*) pelo-

tón *m* de fusilamiento, piquete *m* de ejecución
firm [fʌrm] *adj* firme || *s* empresa, casa comercial
firmament [ˈfʌrməmənt] *s* firmamento
firm name *s* razón *f* social
firmness [ˈfʌrmnɪs] *s* firmeza
first [fʌrst] *adj* primero || *adv* primero; **first of all** ante todo || *s* primero; (aut) primera (velocidad); (mus) voz *f* principal; **at first** al principio; en primer lugar; **from the first** desde el principio
first aid *s* cura de urgencia, primeros auxilios
first′-aid′kit *s* botiquín *m*, equipo de urgencia
first-aid station *s* puesto de socorro, puesto de primera intención
first′-born′ *adj & s* primogénito
first′-class′ *adj* de primera, de primera clase || *adv* en primera clase
first cousin *s* primo hermano
first draft *s* borrador *m*
first finger *s* dedo índice, dedo mostrador
first floor *s* piso bajo
first fruits *spl* primicia
first lieutenant *s* teniente
firstly [ˈfʌrstli] *adv* en primer lugar
first mate *s* (naut) piloto
first name *s* nombre *m* de pila
first night *s* (theat) noche *f* de estreno
first′-night′er *s* (theat) estrenista *mf*
first officer *s* (naut) piloto
first quarter *s* cuarto creciente (*de la luna*)
first′-rate′ *adj* de primer orden; (coll) excelente || *adv* (coll) muy bien
first′-run′ house *s* teatro de estreno
fiscal [ˈfɪskəl] *adj* (*pertaining to public treasury*) fiscal; económico || *s* (*public prosecutor*) fiscal *m*
fiscal year *s* año económico, ejercicio
fish [fɪʃ] *s* pez *m;* (*that has been caught, that is ready to eat*) pescado; **to be like a fish out of water** estar como gallina en corral ajeno; **to be neither fish nor fowl** no ser carne ni pescado; **to drink like a fish** beber como una topinera, beber como una esponja || *tr* pescar || *intr* pescar; **to fish for compliments** buscar alabanzas; **to go fishing** ir de pesca; **to take fishing** llevar de pesca
fish′bone′ *s* espina de pez
fish bowl *s* pecera
fisher [ˈfɪʃər] *s* pescador *m;* embarcación de pesca; (zool) marta del Canadá
fisher•man [ˈfɪʃərmən] *s* (*pl* **-men** [mən]) pescador *m;* barco pesquero
fisher•y [ˈfɪʃəri] *s* (*pl* **-ies**) (*activity*) pesca; (*business*) pesquería; (*grounds*) pesquera
fish glue *s* cola de pescado
fish hawk *s* halieto
fish′hook′ *s* anzuelo
fishing [ˈfɪʃɪŋ] *adj* pesquero || *s* pesca
fishing ground *s* pesquería, pesquera
fishing reel *s* carrete *m*
fishing rod *s* caña de pescar
fishing tackle *s* aparejo de pescar, avíos de pescar
fishing torch *s* candelero
fish line *s* sedal *m*
fish market *s* pescadería
fish′plate′ (rr) eclisa
fish′pool′ *s* piscina
fish spear *s* fisga
fish story *s* (coll) andaluzada, patraña; **to tell fish stories** (coll) mentir por la barba
fish′tail′ *s* (aer) coleadura || *intr* (aer) colear
fish′wife′ *s* (*pl* **-wives** [ˌwaɪvz]) pescadera; (*foul-mouthed woman*) verdulera
fish′worm′ *s* lombriz *f* de tierra (*cebo para pescar*)
fish•y [ˈfɪʃi] *adj* (*comp* **-ier;** *super* **-iest**) que huele o sabe a pescado; (coll) dudoso, inverosímil
fission [ˈfɪʃən] *s* (biol) escisión; (phys) fisión
fissionable [ˈfɪʃənəbəl] *adj* fisionable; físil
fissure [ˈfɪʃər] *s* hendidura, grieta; (anat, min) fisura
fist [fɪst] *s* puño; (typ) manecilla; **to shake one's fist at** amenazar con el puño
fist fight *s* pelea con los puños
fisticuff [ˈfɪstɪˌkʌf] *s* puñetazo; **fisticuffs** pelea a puñetazos
fit [fɪt] *adj* (*comp* **-fitter;** *super* **-fittest**) apropiado, conveniente; apto; sano; **fit to be tied** (coll) impaciente, encolerizado; **fit to eat** bueno de comer; **to feel fit** gozar de buena salud; **to see fit** juzgar conveniente || *s* ajuste *m*, talle *m;* (*of one piece with another*) encaje *m;* (*of coughing*) acceso, ataque *m;* (*of anger*) arranque *m*, chivo; **by fits and starts** intermitentemente || *v* (*pret & pp* **-fitted;** *ger* **fitting**) *tr* ajustar, entallar; cuadrar, sentar; encajar; cuadrar con (*p.ej., las señas de una persona*); equipar, preparar; servir para; estar de acuerdo con (*p.ej., los hechos*); **to fit out** o **up** pertrechar || *intr* ajustar; encajar; sentar; **to fit in** caber en; encajar en
fitful [ˈfɪtfəl] *adj* caprichoso; intermitente, vacilante
fitness [ˈfɪtnɪs] *s* conveniencia; aptitud; tempestividad; buena salud
fitter [ˈfɪtər] *s* ajustador *m;* (*of machinery*) montador *m;* (*of clothing*) probador *m*
fitting [ˈfɪtɪŋ] *adj* apropiado, conveniente, justo || *s* ajuste *m;* encaje *m;* (*of a garment*) prueba; tubo de ajuste; **fittings** accesorios, avíos; (*iron trimmings*) herraje *m*
fitting room *s* probador *m*
five [faɪv] *adj & pron* cinco || *s* cinco; **five o'clock** las cinco
five hundred *adj & pron* quinientos || *s* quinientos *m*
five′-year′plan *s* plan *m* quinquenal
fix [fɪks] *s*—**in a tight fix** (coll) en calzas prietas; **to be in a fix** (coll) hallarse en un aprieto; **to get a fix** (*drugs*) picarse, pincharse || *tr* arreglar, componer, reparar; fijar (*una fecha; los cabellos; una imagen fotográfica; los precios; la atención; una hora, una cita*); calar (*la bayoneta*); (coll) desquitarse con; (pol) muñir || *intr* fijarse; **to fix on** decidir, escoger
fixed [fɪkst] *adj* fijo

fixing [ˈfɪksɪŋ] *adj* fijador || *s* (*fastening*) fijación; (phot) fijado
fixing bath *s* fijador *m*
fixture [ˈfɪkstʃər] *s* accesorio, artefacto; (*of a lamp*) guarnición; **fixtures** (*e.g., of a store*) instalaciones
fizz [fɪz] *s* ruido sibilante; bebida gaseosa; (Brit) champaña || *intr* hacer un ruido sibilante
fizzle [ˈfɪzəl] *s* (coll) fracaso || *intr* chisporrotear débilmente; (coll) fracasar
fl. *abbr* **flourished, fluid**
flabbergast [ˈflæbər,gæst] *tr* (coll) dejar sin habla, dejar estupefacto
flab•by [ˈflæbi] *adj* (*comp* **-bier;** *super* **-biest)** flojo, lacio
flag [flæg] *s* bandera || *v* (*pret & pp* **flagged;** *ger* **flagging**) *tr* hacer señal a (*una persona*) con una bandera; hacer señal de parada a (*un tren*) || *intr* aflojar, flaquear
flag captain *s* (nav) capitán *m* de bandera
flageolet [,flædʒəˈlɛt] *s* chirimía, dulzaina
flag•man [ˈflægmən] *s* (*pl* **-men** [mən]) (rr) guardafrenos *m;* (rr) guardavía *m*
flag of truce *s* bandera de parlamento
flag'pole' *s* asta de bandera; (surv) jalón *m*
flagrant [ˈflegrənt] *adj* enorme, escandaloso
flag'ship' *s* (nav) capitana
flag'staff' *s* asta de bandera
flag'stone' *s* losa
flag stop *s* (rr) apeadero
flail [flel] *s* mayal *m* || *tr* golpear con mayal; golpear, azotar
flair [flɛr] *s* instinto, perspicacia
flak [flæk] *s* fuego antiaéreo
flake [flek] *s* (*thin piece*) hojuela; (*of snow*) copo || *intr* desprenderse en hojuelas; caer en copos pequeños
flak•y [ˈfleki] *adj* (*comp* **-ier;** *super* **-iest)** escamoso, laminoso
flamboyant [flæmˈbɔɪ•ənt] *adj* flameante; llamativo; rimbombante; (archit) flameante, flamígero
flame [flem] *s* llama || *tr* (*to sterilize with a flame*) llamear || *intr* flamear
flame thrower [ˈθro•ər] *s* lanzallamas *m*
flaming [ˈflemɪŋ] *adj* llameante; flamante, resplandeciente; apasionado
flamin•go [fləˈmɪŋgo] *s* (*pl* **-gos** o **-goes)** flamenco
flammable [ˈflæməbəl] *adj* inflamable
Flanders [ˈflændərz] *s* Flandes *f*
flange [flændʒ] *s* pestaña
flank [flæŋk] *s* flanco; *tr* flanquear
flannel [ˈflænəl] *s* franela
flap [flæp] *s* (*fold in clothing; of a hat*) falda; (*of a pocket*) cartera; (*of a table*) hoja plegadiza; (*of shoe*) oreja; (*of an envelope*) tapa; (*of wings*) aletazo; (*of the counter in a store*) trampa || *v* (*pret & pp* **flapped;** *ger* **flapping**) *tr* golpear con ruido seco; batir, sacudir (*las alas*) || *intr* aletear; flamear con ruido
flare [flɛr] *s* llamarada, destello; cohete *m* de señales; (aer) bengala; (*outward curvature*) abocinamiento; (*of a dress*) vuelo || *tr* abocinar || *intr* arder con gran llamarada, destellar; (*to spread outward*) abocinarse; **to flare up** inflamarse; recrudecer (*una enfermedad*); encolerizarse
flare star *s* (astr) estrella fulgurante
flare'-up' *s* llamarada; (*of an illness*) retroceso; (coll) llamarada, arrebato de cólera
flash [flæʃ] *s* (*of light*) relumbrón *m*, ráfaga; (*of lightning*) relámpago; (*of hope*) rayo; (*of joy*) acceso; (*of insight*) rasgo; mensaje *m* urgente || *tr* quemar (*pólvora*); enviar (*un mensaje*) como un rayo || *intr* destellar, centellear; relampaguear (*los ojos*); **to flash by** pasar como un rayo
flash'back' *s* (mov) retrospectiva, flashback *m*
flash bulb *s* luz *f* de magnesio; bombilla de destello
flash flood *s* torrentada, avenida repentina
flashing [ˈflæʃɪŋ] *s* despidiente *m* de agua, vierteaguas *m*
flash'light' *s* linterna eléctrica, lámpara eléctrica de bolsillo; (*of a lighthouse*) luz *f* intermitente, fanal *m* de destellos; (*for taking photographs*) flash *m*, relámpago
flashlight battery *s* pila de linterna
flashlight bulb *s* bombilla de linterna
flashlight photography *s* fotografía instantánea de relámpago
flash sign *s* anuncio intermitente
flash•y [ˈflæʃi] *adj* (*comp* **-ier;** *super* **-iest)** chillón, llamativo
flask [flæsk] *s* frasco; frasco de bolsillo; (*for laboratory use*) matraz *m*, redoma
flat [flæt] *adj* (*comp* **flatter;** *super* **flattest)** plano; (*nose; boat*) chato; (*surface*) mate, deslustrado; (*beer*) muerto; (*tire*) desinflado; (*e.g., denial*) terminante; (mus) bemol || *adv*—**to fall flat** caer de plano; (fig) no surtir efecto, no tener éxito || *s* banco, bajío; (*apartment*) piso; (mus) bemol *m;* (coll) neumático desinflado
flat'boat' *s* chalana
flat'car' *s* vagón *m* de plataforma
flat'foot' *s* pie plano
flat-footed [ˈflæt,fʊtɪd] *adj* de pies planos; (coll) inflexible
flat'head' *s* (*of a bolt*) cabeza chata; clavo, tornillo o perno de cabeza chata; (coll) tonto, mentecato
flat'i'ron *s* plancha
flatten [ˈflætən] *tr* allanar, aplanar; chafar, aplastar; achatar || *intr* allanarse, aplanarse; aplastarse; achatarse; **to flatten out** ponerse horizontal, enderezarse
flatter [ˈflætər] *tr* lisonjear; cepillar (*to make more attractive than is*) favorecer || *intr* lisonjear
flatterer [ˈflætərər] *s* lisonjero; (coll) limpiabotas *m*
flattering [ˈflætərɪŋ] *adj* lisonjero
flatter•y [ˈflætəri] *s* (*pl* **-ies**) lisonja
flat'top' *s* portaaviones *m*
flatulence [ˈflætʃələns] *s* flatulencia
flat'ware' *s* vajilla de plata; vajilla de porcelana
flaunt [flɔnt] *tr* ostentar, hacer gala de
flautist [ˈflɔtɪst] *s* flautista *mf*

flavor [ˈflevər] *s* sabor *m,* gusto; condimento, sazón *f;* (*of ice cream*) clase *f* || *tr* saborear; condimentar, sazonar; aromatizar, perfumar
flavoring [ˈflevərɪŋ] *s* condimento, sainete *m*
flaw [flɔ] *s* defecto, imperfección; (*crack*) grieta
flawless [ˈflɔlɪs] *adj* perfecto, entero
flax [flæks] *s* lino
flaxen [ˈflæksən] *adj* blondo, rubio
flax'seed' *s* linaza
flay [fle] *tr* desollar
flea [fli] *s* pulga
flea'bite' *s* picadura de pulga; molestia insignificante
fleck [flɛk] *s* pinta, punto; partícula, pizca || *tr* puntear
fledgling [ˈflɛdʒlɪŋ] *s* pajarito, volantón *m;* (fig) novato, novel *m*
flee [fli] *v* (*pret & pp* **fled** [flɛd]) *tr & intr* huir
fleece [flis] *s* (*coat of wool*) lana; (*wool shorn at one time; tuft of wool or hair*) vellón *m* || *tr* esquilar; (*to strip of money*) desplumar
fleec•y [ˈflisi] *adj* (*comp* **-ier;** *super* **-iest**) lanudo; (*clouds*) aborregado
fleet [flit] *adj* veloz || *s* armada; (*of merchant vessels, airplanes, automobiles*) flota
fleeting [ˈflitɪŋ] *adj* fugaz, efímero; transitorio
Fleming [ˈflɛmɪŋ] *s* flamenco
Flemish [ˈflɛmɪʃ] *adj & s* flamenco
flesh [flɛʃ] *s* carne *f;* **in the flesh** en persona; **to lose flesh** perder carnes; **to put on flesh** cobrar carnes
flesh and blood *s* (*relatives*) carne y sangre; el cuerpo humano
fleshiness [ˈflɛʃɪnɪs] *s* carnosidad
fleshless [ˈflɛʃlɪs] *adj* descarnado
flesh'pot' *s* olla, marmita; **fleshpots** vida regalona; suntuosos nidos de vicios
flesh wound *s* herida superficial
flesh•y [ˈflɛʃi] *adj* (*comp* **-ier;** *super* **-iest**) carnoso
flex [flɛks] *tr* doblar || *intr* doblarse
flexible [ˈflɛksɪbəl] *adj* flexible
flexible cord *s* (elec) flexible *m*
flick [flɪk] *s* (*with finger*) papirote *m;* (*with whip*) latigazo; ruido seco || *tr* golpear rápida y ligeramente
flicker [ˈflɪkər] *s* llama trémula; (*of eyelids*) parpadeo; (*of emotion*) temblor momentáneo || *intr* flamear con llama trémula; aletear
flier [ˈflaɪ•ər] *s* aviador *m;* tren rápido; (coll) negocio arriesgado; (coll) hoja volante
flight [flaɪt] *s* fuga, huída; (*of an airplane*) vuelo; (*of birds*) bandada; (*of stairs*) tramo; (*of fancy*) arranque *m;* **to put to flight** poner en fuga; **to take flight** darse a la fuga
flight attendant *s* sobrecargo, sobrecarga
flight deck *s* (nav) cubierta de vuelo
flight•y [ˈflaɪti] *adj* (*comp* **-ier;** *super* **-iest**) veleidoso; casquivano
flim•flam [ˈflɪm,flæm] *s* (coll) engaño, trampa; (coll) tontería || *v* (*pret & pp* **-flammed;** *ger* **-flamming**) *tr* (coll) engañar, trampear
flim•sy [ˈflɪmzi] *adj* (*comp* **-sier;** *super* **-siest**) débil, endeble, flojo
flinch [flɪntʃ] *intr* encogerse de miedo
fling [flɪŋ] *s* echada, tiro; baile escocés muy vivo; **to go on a fling** echar una cana al aire; **to have a fling at** ensayar, probar; **to have one's fling** correrla, mocear || *v* (*pret & pp* **flung** [flʌŋ]) *tr* arrojar; (*e.g., on the floor, out the window, in jail*) echar; **to fling open** abrir de golpe; **to fling shut** cerrar de golpe
flint [flɪnt] *s* pedernal *m*
flint'lock' *s* llave *f* de chispa; trabuco de chispa
flint•y [ˈflɪnti] *adj* (*comp* **-ier;** *super* **-iest**) pedernalino; (fig) empedernido
flip [flɪp] *adj* (*comp* **flipper;** *super* **flippest**) (coll) petulante || *s* capirotazo || *v* (*pret & pp* **flipped;** *ger* **flipping**) *tr* echar de un capirotazo, mover de un tirón; **to flip a coin** echar a cara o cruz; **to flip one's lid** (coll) deschavetar; **to flip shut** cerrar de golpe (*p. ej., un abanico*)
flippancy [ˈflɪpənsi] *s* petulancia
flippant [ˈflɪpənt] *adj* petulante
flip side *s* contraportada (*del disco*)
flirt [flʌrt] *s* (*woman*) coqueta; (*man*) galanteador *m* || *intr* coquetear (*una mujer*); galantear (*un hombre*); **to flirt with** flirtear con; pololear (Chile); acariciar (*una idea*); jugar con (*la muerte*)
flit [flɪt] *v* (*pret & pp* **flitted;** *ger* **flitting**) *intr* revolotear, volar; pasar rápidamente
flitch [flɪtʃ] *s* hoja de tocino
float [flot] *s* (*raft*) balsa; (*of fishing line*) flotador *m;* (*of mason*) llana; carroza alegórica, carro alegórico || *tr* poner a flote; lanzar (*una empresa*); emitir (*acciones, bonos, etc.*) || *intr* flotar
floating [ˈflotɪŋ] *adj* flotante
flock [flɑk] *s* (*of birds*) bandada; (*of sheep*) grey *f,* rebaño, manada; (*of people*) muchedumbre; (*e.g., of nonsense*) hatajo; (*of faithful*) grey *f,* rebaño || *intr* congregarse, reunirse; llegar en tropel
floe [flo] *s* banquisa, témpano
flog [flɑg] *v* (*pret & pp* **flogged;** *ger* **flogging**) *tr* azotar, fustigar
flood [flʌd] *s* inundación; (*caused by heavy rain*) diluvio; (*sudden rise of river*) crecida; (*of tide*) pleamar *f;* (*of words, etc.*) diluvio, torrente *m* || *tr* inundar; (*to overwhelm*) abrumar || *intr* desbordar, rebosar; entrar a raudales
flood'gate' *s* (*of a dam*) compuerta; (*of a canal*) esclusa
flood'light' *s* faro de inundación || *tr* iluminar con faro de inundación
flood tide *s* pleamar *f,* marea montante
floor [flor] *s* (*inside bottom surface of room*) piso, suelo; (*story of a building*) piso, alto; (*of the sea, a swimming pool, etc.*) fondo; (*of an assembly hall*) hemiciclo; (naut) varenga; **to ask for the floor** pedir la palabra; **to have the floor** tener la palabra; **to take the floor** tomar la palabra || *tr* entarimar; derribar, echar al suelo; (coll)

confundir, envolver, revolcar (*al adversario en controversia*); (coll) vencer
floor lamp *s* lámpara de pie
floor mop *s* fregasuelos *m*, estropajo
floor plan *s* planta
floor show *s* espectáculo de cabaret
floor timber *s* (naut) varenga
floor'walk'er *s* jefe *m* de sección
floor wax *s* cera de pisos
flop [flɑp] *s* fracaso, caída; (*person*) berzas *m*, berzotas *m*; **to take a flop** caerse ‖ *v* (*pret & pp* **flopped**; *ger* **flopping**) *intr* agitarse; caerse; venirse abajo; fracasar; **to flop over** volcarse; cambiar de partido
flora ['florə] *s* flora
floral ['florəl] *adj* floral
Florentine ['flɔrən,tin] *adj & s* florentino
florescence [flo'rɛsəns] *s* florescencia
florid ['flɔrɪd] *adj* (*complexion*) encarnado; (*showy, ornate*) florido
Florida Keys ['flɔrɪdə] *s* Cayos de la Florida
florist ['florɪst] *s* florero, florista *mf*
floss [flɑs] *s* cadarzo; (*of corn*) cabellos
floss silk *s* seda floja sin torcer
floss•y ['flɑsi] *adj* (*comp* **-ier**; *super* **-iest**) ligero, velloso; (slang) cursi, vistoso
flotsam ['flɑtsəm] *s* pecio
flotsam and jetsam *s* pecios, despojos; (*trifles*) baratijas; gente *f* trashumante, gente perdida
flounce [flaʊns] *s* faralá *m*, volante *m* ‖ *tr* adornar con faralaes o volantes ‖ *intr* moverse airadamente
flounder ['flaʊndər] *s* platija ‖ *intr* forcejear, obrar torpemente, andar tropezando
flour [flaʊr] *adj* harinero ‖ *s* harina
flourish ['flʌrɪʃ] *s* (*with the sword*) molinete *m*; (*with the pen*) plumada, rasgo; (*as part of signature*) rúbrica; (mus) floreo ‖ *tr* blandir (*la espada*) ‖ *intr* florecer, prosperar
flourishing ['flʌrɪʃɪŋ] *adj* floreciente, próspero
flour mill *s* molino de harina
floury ['flaʊri] *adj* harinoso
flout [flaʊt] *tr* mofarse de, burlarse de ‖ *intr* mofarse, burlarse
flow [flo] *s* flujo ‖ *intr* fluir; subir (*la marea*); ondear (*el pelo en el aire*); **to flow into** desaguar en, desembocar en; **to flow over** rebosar; **to flow with** nadar en, abundar en
flower ['flaʊ•ər] *s* flor *f* ‖ *tr* florear ‖ *intr* florecer
flower bed *s* macizo, parterre *m*
flower garden *s* jardín *m*
flower girl *s* florera; (*at a wedding*) damita de honor
flower piece *s* ramillete *m*; (*painting*) florero
flow'er•pot' *s* tiesto, maceta
flower shop *s* floristería
flower show *s* exposición de flores
flower stand *s* florero
flowery ['flaʊ•əri] *adj* florido, cubierto de flores
flu [flu] *s* (coll) gripe *f*, influenza
fluctuate ['flʌktʃʊ,et] *intr* fluctuar
flue [flu] *s* cañón *m* de chimenea; tubo de humo
fluency ['flu•ənsi] *s* afluencia, facundia
fluent ['flu•ənt] *adj* (*flowing*) fluente; afluente, facundo, flúido
fluently ['flu•əntli] *adv* corrientemente
fluff [flʌf] *s* pelusa, tamo; vello, pelusilla; (*of an actor*) gazapo ‖ *tr* esponjar, mullir ‖ *intr* esponjarse
fluff•y ['flʌfi] *adj* (*comp* **-ier**; *super* **-iest**) fofo, esponjoso, mullido; velloso
fluid ['flu•ɪd] *adj & s* flúido
fluidity [flu'ɪdɪti] *s* fluidez *f*
fluke [fluk] *s* (*of anchor*) uña; (*in billiards*) chiripa
flume [flum] *s* caz *m*, saetín *m*
flunk [flʌŋk] *s* (coll) reprobación ‖ *tr* (coll) reprobar, dar calabazas a; perder (*un examen o asignatura*) ‖ *intr* (coll) fracasar, salir mal; **to flunk out** (coll) tener que abandonar los estudios por no poder aprobar
flunk•y ['flʌŋki] *s* (*pl* **-ies**) lacayo; adulador *m*
fluor ['flu•ɔr] *s* fluorita
fluorescence [,flu•ə'rɛsəns] *s* fluorescencia
fluorescent [,flu•ə'rɛsənt] *adj* fluorescente
fluoridate ['flu•ərɪ,det] *tr* fluorizar
fluoridation ['flu•ərɪ'deʃən] *s* fluorización
fluoride ['flu•ə,raɪd] *s* fluoruro
fluorine ['flu•ə,rin] *s* flúor *m*
fluorite ['flu•ə,raɪt] *s* fluorita
fluoroscope ['flu•ərə,skop] *s* fluoroscopio
fluor spar *s* espato flúor
flur•ry ['flʌri] *s* (*pl* **-ries**) agitación; (*of wind*) racha, ráfaga; (*of rain*) chaparrón *m*; (*of snow*) nevisca ‖ *v* (*pret & pp* **-ried**) *tr* agitar
flush [flʌʃ] *adj* rasante, nivelado; (*set in, in order to be flush*) embutido; abundante; robusto, vigoroso; próspero, bien provisto; coloradote; (*in printing*) justificado; **flush with** a ras de ‖ *adv* ras con ras, al mismo nivel ‖ *s* (*of water*) flujo repentino; (*in the cheeks*) rubor *m*; sonrojo; (*in the springtime*) floración repentina; (*of joy*) acceso; (*of youth*) vigor *m*; chorro del inodoro; (*in poker*) flux *m* ‖ *tr* (*to cause to blush*) abochornar; limpiar con un chorro de agua; hacer saltar (*una liebre*) ‖ *intr* abochornarse, estar encendido (*el rostro*); (*to gush*) brotar
flush outlet *s* (elec) caja de enchufe embutida
flush switch *s* (elec) llave embutida
flush tank *s* depósito de limpia
flush toilet *s* inodoro con chorro de agua
fluster ['flʌstər] *s* confusión, aturdimiento ‖ *tr* confundir, aturdir
flute [flut] *s* (*of a column*) estría; (mus) flauta ‖ *tr* estriar, acanalar
flutist ['flutɪst] *s* flautista *mf*
flutter ['flʌtər] *s* aleteo, revoloteo; confusión, turbación ‖ *intr* aletear, revolotear; flamear, ondear; agitarse; alterarse (*el pulso*); palpitar (*el corazón*)
flux [flʌks] *s* (*flow; flowing of tide*) flujo; (*for fusing metals*) flujo, fundente *m*

fly [flaɪ] *s* (*pl* **flies**) mosca; (*of trousers*) portañuela, bragueta; (*for fishing*) mosca artificial; **flies** (theat) bambalinas; **to die like flies** morir como chinches || *v* (*pret* **flew** [flu]; *pp* **flown** [flon]) *tr* hacer volar (*una cometa*); dirigir (*un avión*); (*to carry in an airship*) volar; atravesar en avión; desplegar, llevar (*una bandera*) || *intr* volar; huir; ondear (*una bandera*); **to fly off** salir volando; desprenderse; **to fly open** abrirse de repente; **to fly over** trasvolar; **to fly shut** cerrarse de repente

fly ball *s* (baseball) palomita

fly'blow' *s* cresa

fly'-by-night' *adj* indigno de confianza

fly'catch'er *s* moscareta, papamoscas *m*

fly chaser *s* espantamoscas *m*

flyer ['flaɪ•ər] *s* var de **flier**

fly'-fish' *tr & intr* pescar con moscas artificiales

flying ['flaɪ•ɪŋ] *adj* volante; rápido, veloz || *s* aviación

flying boat *s* hidroavión *m*

flying buttress *s* arbotante *m*

flying colors *spl* gran éxito

flying field *s* campo de aviación

flying saucer *s* platillo volante

flying sickness *s* mal *m* de altura

flying time *s* horas de vuelo

fly in the ointment *s* mosca muerta que malea el perfume

fly'leaf' *s* (*pl* **-leaves'**) guarda, hoja de guarda

fly net *s* (*for a bed*) mosquitero; (*for a horse*) espantamoscas *m*

fly'pa'per *s* papel *m* matamoscas

fly'speck' *s* mancha de mosca

fly'swatter ['swɑtər] *s* matamoscas *m*

fly'trap' *s* atrapamoscas *m*

fly'wheel' *s* volante *m*

fm. *abbr* **fathom**

F.M. *abbr* **frequency modulation**

foal [fol] *s* potro || *intr* parir (*la yegua*)

foam [fom] *s* espuma || *intr* espumar

foam extinguisher *s* lanzaespumas *m*, extintor *m* de espuma

foam rubber *s* caucho esponjoso, espuma de caucho

foam•y ['fomi] *adj* (*comp* **-ier;** *super* **-iest**) espumoso, espumajoso

fob [fɑb] *s* faltriquera de reloj; (*chain*) leopoldina; (*ornament*) dije *m*

F.O.B. *abbr* **free on board**

focal ['fokəl] *adj* focal

fo•cus ['fokəs] *s* (*pl* **-cuses** o **-ci** [saɪ]) foco; **in focus** enfocado; **out of focus** desenfocado || *v* (*pret & pp* **-cused** o **-cussed;** *ger* **-cusing** o **-cussing**) *tr* enfocar; fijar (*la atención*) || *intr* enfocarse

fodder ['fɑdər] *s* forraje *m*

foe [fo] *s* enemigo

fog [fɑg] o [fɔg] *s* niebla; (phot) velo || *v* (*pret & pp* **fogged;** *ger* **fogging**) *tr* envolver en niebla; (*to blur*) empañar; (phot) velar || *intr* empañarse; (phot) velarse

fog bank *s* banco de nieblas

fog bell *s* campana de nieblas

fog'bound' *adj* atascado en la niebla, envuelto en la niebla

fog•gy ['fɑgi] o ['fɔgi] *adj* (*comp* **-gier;** *super* **-giest**) neblinoso, brumoso; confuso; (phot) velado; **it is foggy** hay neblina

fog'horn' *s* sirena de niebla

foible ['fɔɪbəl] *s* flaqueza, lado flaco

foil [fɔɪl] *s* (*thin sheet of metal*) hojuela, laminilla; (*of mirror*) azogado, plateado; contraste *m*, realce *m;* (*sword*) florete *m* || *tr* frustrar; azogar, platear (*un espejo*)

foist [fɔɪst] *tr* — **to foist something on someone** encajar una cosa a uno

fol. *abbr* **folio, following**

fold [fold] *s* pliegue *m*, doblez *m;* arruga; (*for sheep*) aprisco, redil *m;* (*of the faithful*) rebaño || *tr* plegar, doblar; cruzar (*los brazos*); **to fold up** doblar (*p.ej., un mapa*) || *intr* plegarse, doblarse

folder ['foldər] *s* (*covers for holding papers*) carpeta; (*pamphlet*) folleto

folderol ['fɑldə,rɑl] *s* tontería, necedad; bagatela

folding ['foldɪŋ] *adj* plegadizo, plegable; plegador

folding camera *s* cámara de fuelle

folding chair *s* silla de tijera, silla plegadiza; (*of canvas*) catrecillo

folding cot *s* catre *m* de tijera

folding door *s* puerta plegadiza

folding rule *s* metro plegadizo

foliage ['folɪ•ɪdʒ] *s* follaje *m*

foli•o ['folɪ•o] *adj* en folio || *s* (*pl* **-os**) (*sheet*) folio; infolio, libro en folio || *tr* foliar

folk [fok] *adj* popular, tradicional, del pueblo || *s* (*pl* **folk** o **folks**) gente *f;* **folks** (coll) gente (*familia*)

folk etymology *s* etimología popular

folk'lore' *s* folkore *m*

folk music *s* música folklórica

folk song *s* canción típica, canción tradicional

folk•sy ['foksi] *adj* (*comp* **-sier;** *super* **-siest**) (coll) sociable, tratable; (*like common people*) (coll) plebeyo

folk'way' *s* costumbre tradicional

follicle ['fɑlɪkəl] *s* folículo

follow ['fɑlo] *tr* seguir; sequir el hilo de; interesarse en (*las noticias del día*) || *intr* seguir; resultar; **as follows** como sigue; **it follows** síguese

follower ['fɑlo•ər] *s* seguidor *m;* secuaz *mf*, partidario; imitador *m;* discípulo

following ['fɑlo•ɪŋ] *adj* siguiente || *s* séquito; partidarios

fol'low-up' *adj* consecutivo; recordativo || *s* carta recordativa, circular recordativa

fol•ly ['fɑli] *s* (*pl* **-lies**) desatino, locura; empresa temeraria; **follies** revista teatral

foment [fo'ment] *tr* fomentar

fond [fɑnd] *adj* afectuoso, cariñoso; **to become fond of** encariñarse con, aficionarse a o de

fondle ['fɑndəl] *tr* acariciar, mimar

fondness ['fɑndnɪs] *s* afición, cariño

font [fɑnt] *s* (*source; source of water*) fuente *f;* (*for holy water*) pila; (*of type*) fundición

food [fud] *adj* alimenticio || *s* comida, alimento; **food for thought** cosa en qué pensar
food store *s* tienda de comestibles, colmado
food'stuffs' *spl* comestibles *mpl*, víveres *mpl*
fool [ful] *s* tonto, necio; (*jester*) bufón *m;* (*person imposed on*) inocente *mf*, víctima; **to make a fool of** poner en ridículo; **to play the fool** hacer el tonto || *tr* embaucar, engañar; **to fool away** malgastar (*tiempo, dinero*) || *intr* tontear; **to fool around** (coll) malgastar el tiempo; **to fool with** (coll) ajar, manosear
fooler•y [ˈfuləri] *s* (*pl* **-ies**) locura, tontería, babosada
fool'har'dy *adj* (*comp* **-dier;** *super* **-diest**) temerario
fooling [ˈfulɪŋ] *s* broma; engaño; **no fooling** hablando en serio
foolish [ˈfulɪʃ] *adj* tonto; ridículo; gilí
fool'proof' *adj* (coll) a prueba de mal trato; (coll) infalible
fools'cap' *s* gorro de bufón; papel *m* de oficio
fool's errand *s* caza de grillos
fool's scepter *s* cetro de locura
foot [fut] *s* (*pl* **feet** [fit]) pie *m;* **to drag one's feet** ir a paso de caracol; **to have one foot in the grave** estar con un pie en la sepultura; **to put one's best foot forward** (coll) hacer méritos; **to put one's foot in it** (coll) meter la pata; (coll) tirarse una plancha; **to stand on one's own feet** volar con sus propias alas; **to tread under foot** hollar || *tr* pagar (*la cuenta*); **to foot it** andar a pie; bailar
footage [ˈfutɪdʒ] *s* distancia o largura en pies
foot'ball' *s* (*game*) balompié *m*, fútbol *m*; (*ball*) balón *m*
foot'board' *s* (*support for foot*) estribo; (*of bed*) pie *m*
foot'bridge' *s* pasarela, puente *m* para peatones
foot'fall' *s* paso
foot'hill' *s* colina al pie de una montaña
foot'hold' *s* arraigo, pie *m;* **to gain a foothold** ganar pie
footing [ˈfutɪŋ] *s* pie *m*, p.ej., **he lost his footing** perdió el pie; **on a friendly footing** en relaciones amistosas; **on an equal footing** en pie de igualdad; **on a war footing** en pie de guerra
foot'lights' *spl* candilejas, batería; (fig) tablas, escena
foot'loose' *adj* libre, no comprometido
foot•man [ˈfutmən] *s* (*pl* **-men** [mən]) lacayo, criado de librea
foot'mark' *s* huella
foot'note' *s* nota al pie de la página
foot'path' *s* senda para peatones
foot'print' *s* huella
foot race *s* carrera a pie
foot'rest' *s* apoyapié *m*, descansapié *m*
foot rule *s* regla de un pie
foot soldier *s* soldado de a pie
foot'sore' *adj* despeado
foot'step' *s* paso; **to follow in the footsteps of** seguir los pasos de
foot'stone' *s* lápida al pie de una sepultura
foot'stool' *s* escabel *m*, escañuelo
foot warmer *s* calientapiés *m*
foot'wear' *s* calzado
foot'work' *s* juego de piernas
foot'worn' *adj* (*road*) trillado; (*person*) despeado
foozle [ˈfuzəl] *s* chambonada; (coll) chambón *m*, torpe *m* || *tr* chafallar; errar (*un golpe*) de manera torpe || *intr* chambonear
fop [fɑp] *s* currutaco, petimetre *m;* lagarto (Mex)
for [fər] *prep* para; por; como, p.ej., **he uses his living room for an office** usa la sala como oficina; de, p.ej., **time for bed** hora de acostarse; desde hace, p.ej., **he has been here for a week** está aquí desde hace una semana; en honor de; a pesar de || *conj* pues, porque
for. *abbr* **foreign**
forage [ˈfɔrɪdʒ] *adj* forrajero || *s* forraje *m* || *tr & intr* forrajear; saquear
foray [ˈfɑre] o [ˈfɔre] *s* correría; saqueo || *intr* hacer correrías
for•bear [fɔrˈbɛr] *v* (*pret* **-bore** [ˈbor]; *pp* **-borne** [ˈborn]) *tr* abstenerse de || *intr* contenerse
forbearance [fɔrˈbɛrəns] *s* abstención; paciencia
for•bid [fɔrˈbɪd] *v* (*pret* **-bade** [ˈbæd] o **-bad** [ˈbæd]; *pp* **-bidden** [ˈbɪdən]; *ger* **-bidding**) *tr* prohibir
forbidding [fɔrˈbɪdɪŋ] *adj* repugnante, repulsivo
force [fors] *s* fuerza; (*staff of workers*) personal *m;* (*of soldiers, police, etc.*) cuerpo; (phys) fuerza; **by force** a la mala (Cuba, P-R); **by force of** a fuerza de; **by main force** con todas sus fuerzas; **in force** vigente, en vigor; en gran número; **to join forces** juntar diestra con diestra || *tr* forzar; obligar; **to force back** hacer retroceder; **to force open** abrir por fuerza; **to force through** llevar a cabo por fuerza
forced [forst] *adj* forzado
forced air *s* aire *m* a presión
forced landing *s* aterrizaje forzado o forzoso
forced march *s* marcha forzada
forceful [ˈforsfəl] *adj* enérgico, eficaz
for•ceps [ˈfɔrsəps] *s* (*pl* **-ceps** o **-cipes** [sɪ,piz]) (dent, surg) pinzas; (obstet) fórceps *m*
force pump *s* bomba impelente
forcible [ˈforsɪbəl] *adj* eficaz, convincente; forzado
ford [ford] *s* vado || *tr* vadear
fore [for] *adj* anterior; (naut) de proa || *adv* antes, anteriormente; delante; (naut) avante || *interj* ¡ojo!, ¡cuidado! || *s* delantera; **to the fore** destacado; a mano; vivo
fore and aft *adv* de popa a proa
fore'arm' *s* antebrazo || **fore•arm'** *tr* armar de antemano; prevenir
fore'bear' *s* antepasado
forebode [forˈbod] *tr* (*to portend*) presagiar; (*to have a presentiment of*) presentir, prever

foreboding [for'bodɪŋ] *s* presagio; presentimiento
fore'cast' *s* pronóstico ‖ *v* (*pret & pp* **-cast** o **-casted**) *tr* pronosticar
forecastle ['foksəl], ['for,kæsəl], o ['for,kɑsəl] *s* castillo de proa
fore•close' *tr* excluir; extinguir el derecho de redimir (*una hipoteca*); privar del derecho de redimir una hipoteca
fore•doom' *tr* condenar de antemano, predestinar al fracaso
fore edge *s* canal *f*
fore'fa'ther *s* antepasado
fore'fin'ger *s* dedo índice, dedo mostrador
fore'front' *s* puesto delantero; sitio de actividad más intensa; **in the forefront** a vanguardia
fore•go' *v* (*pret* **-went'**; *pp* **-gone'**) *tr & intr* preceder
foregoing ['for,go•ɪŋ] o [for'go•ɪŋ] *adj* anterior, precedente, prenombrado
fore'gone' conclusion *s* resultado inevitable; decisión adoptada de antemano
fore'ground' *s* primer plano, primer término
forehanded ['for,hændɪd] *adj* (*thrifty*) ahorrado; hecho de antemano
forehead ['fɑrɪd] o ['fɔrɪd] *s* frente *f*
foreign ['fɑrɪn] *adj* extranjero, exterior; **foreign to** (*not belonging to or connected with*) ajeno a
foreign affairs *spl* asuntos exteriores
for'eign-born' *adj* nacido en el extranjero
foreigner ['fɑrɪnər] *s* extranjero
foreign exchange *s* cambio extranjero; (*currency*) divisa
foreign minister *s* ministro de asuntos exteriores
foreign ministry *s* ministerio de relaciones exteriores
foreign office *s* ministerio de asuntos exteriores
foreign service *s* servicio diplomático y consular; servicio militar extranjero
foreign trade *s* comercio extranjero
fore'leg' *s* brazo, pata delantera
fore'lock' *s* mechón *m* de pelo sobre la frente; (*of a horse*) copete *m;* **to take time by the forelock** asir la ocasión por la melena
fore•man ['formən] *s* (*pl* **-men** [mən]) capataz *m*, mayoral *m*, sobrestante *m;* (*in a machine shop*) contramaestre *m;* presidente *m* de jurado
foremast ['forməst], ['for,mæst], o ['for,mɑst] *s* palo de trinquete
foremost ['for,most] *adj* primero, principal, más eminente
fore'noon' *adj* matinal ‖ *s* mañana
fore'part' *s* parte delantera; primera parte
fore'paw' *s* pata delantera
fore'quar'ter *s* cuarto delantero
fore'run'ner *s* precursor *m;* predecesor *m;* antepasado; anuncio, presagio
fore•sail ['forsəl] o ['for,sel] *s* trinquete *m*
fore•see' *v* (*pret* **-saw'**; *pp* **-seen'**) *tr* prever
foreseeable [for'si•əbəl] *adj* previsible
fore•shad'ow *tr* presagiar, prefigurar
fore•short'en *tr* escorzar
fore•short'ening *s* escorzo
fore'sight' *s* previsión, presciencia
fore'sight'ed *adj* previsor, presciente
fore'skin' *s* prepucio
forest ['fɑrɪst] o 'fɔrɪst] *adj* forestal ‖ *s* bosque *m*
fore•stall' *tr* impedir, prevenir; anticipar; acaparar
forest ranger ['rendʒər] *s* guarda *m* forestal, montanero
forestry ['fɑrɪstri] o ['fɔrɪstri] *s* silvicultura, ciencia forestal
fore'taste' *s* goce anticipado, conocimiento anticipado
fore•tell' *v* (*pret & pp* **-told'**) *tr* predecir; presagiar
fore'thought' *s* premeditación; providencia, previsión
forever [fɔr'ɛvər] *adv* por siempre; siempre
fore•warn' *tr* prevenir, poner sobre aviso
fore'word' *s* advertencia, prefacio
forfeit ['fɔrfɪt] *adj* perdido ‖ *s* multa, pena; prenda perdida; **forfeits** (*game*) prendas ‖ *tr* perder el derecho a
forfeiture ['fɔrfɪtʃər] *s* multa, pena; prenda perdida
forgather [fɔr'gæðər] *intr* reunirse; encontrarse; **to forgather with** asociarse con
forge [fordʒ] *s* fragua; (*blacksmith shop*) herrería; ‖ *tr* fraguar, forjar; falsificar (*la firma de otra persona*); fraguar, forjar (*mentiras*) ‖ *intr* fraguar, forjar; **to forge ahead** avanzar despacio y con esfuerzo
forger•y ['fordʒəri] *s* (*pl* **-ies**) falsificación
for•get [fɔr'gɛt] *v* (*pret* **-got** [gɑt]; *pp* **-got** o **-gotten;** *ger* **-getting**) *tr* olvidar, olvidarse de, olvidársele a uno, p.ej., **he forgot his overcoat** se le olvidó su abrigo; **forget it!** ¡no se preocupe!; **to forget oneself** no pensar en sí mismo; ser distraído; propasarse
forgetful [fɔr'gɛtfəl] *adj* olvidado, olvidadizo; descuidado
forgetfulness [fɔr'gɛtfəlnɪs] *s* olvido; descuido
for•get'-me-not' *s* nomeolvides *m*
forgivable [fɔr'gɪvəbəl] *adj* perdonable
for•give [fɔr'gɪv] *v* (*pret* **-gave'**; *pp* **-giv'en**) *tr* perdonar
forgiveness (fɔr'gɪvnɪs] *s* perdón *m;* misericordia
forgiving [fɔr'gɪvɪŋ] *adj* perdonador, misericordioso, clemente
for•go [fɔr'go] *v* (*pret* **-went'**; *pp* **-gone'**) *tr* privarse de
fork [fɔrk] *s* horca; (*of a gardener; of bicycle*) horquilla; (*of two rivers*) horcajo; (*of railroad*) ramal *m;* (*of a tree*) horqueta; (*for eating*) tenedor *m* ‖ *tr* ahorquillar; cargar con horquilla; (*in chess*) amenazar (*dos piezas*); **to fork out** (slang) entregar, sudar ‖ *intr* bifurcarse
forked [fɔrkt] *adj* ahorquillado
forked lightning *s* relámpago en zigzag
fork'lift' truck *s* carretilla elevadora de horquilla

forlorn [fɔr'lɔrn] *adj* desamparado; desesperado; miserable
forlorn hope *s* empresa desesperada
form [fɔrm] *s* forma; (*paper to be filled out*) formulario; (*construction to give shape to cement*) encofrado; (*type in a frame*) molde *m* || *tr* formar || *intr* formarse
formal ['fɔrməl] *adj* formal, ceremonioso; etiquetero
formal attire *s* vestido de etiqueta
formal call *s* visita de cumplido
formali•ty [fɔr'mælɪti] *s* (*pl* **-ties**) (*standard procedure*) formalidad; ceremonia, etiqueta
formal party *s* reunión de etiqueta
formal speech *s* discurso de aparato
format ['fɔrmæt] *s* formato
formation ['fɔr'meʃən] *s* formación
former ['fɔrmər] *adj* (*preceding*) anterior; (*long past*) antiguo; primero (*de dos*); **the former** aquél
formerly ['fɔrmərli] *adv* antes, en tiempos pasados
form'-fit'ting *adj* ceñido al cuerpo
formidable ['fɔrmɪdəbəl] *adj* formidable
formless ['fɔrmlɪs] *adj* informe
form letter *s* carta general
formu•la ['fɔrmjələ] *s* (*pl* **-las** o **-lae** [,li] fórmula
formulate ['fɔrmjə,let] *tr* formular
fornicate ['fɔrnə,ket] *intr* fornicar
fornication [,fɔrnə'keʃən] *s* fornicación
for•sake [fɔr'sek] *v* (*pret* **-sook** ['sʊk]; *pp* **-saken** ['sekən]) *tr* abandonar, desamparar; dejar
fort [fort] *s* fuerte *m*, fortaleza
forte [fort] *s* (*strong point*) fuerte *m*, caballo de batalla || ['forte] *adj* (mus) fuerte
forth [forθ] *adv* adelante; **and so forth** y así sucesivamente; **from this day forth** de hoy en adelante; **to go forth** salir
forth'com'ing *adj* próximo, venidero
forth'right' *adj* directo, franco, sincero || *adv* derecho; sinceramente, francamente; en seguida
forth'with' *adv* inmediatamente
fortieth ['fɔrtɪ•ɪθ] *adj* & *s* (*in a series*) cuadragésimo; (*part*) cuarentavo
fortification [,fɔrtɪfɪ'keʃən] *s* fortificación
forti•fy ['fɔrtɪ,faɪ] *v* (*pret* & *pp* **-fied**) *tr* fortificar; encabezar (*vinos*)
fortitude ['fɔrtɪ,tjud] *s* fortaleza, firmeza
fortnight ['fɔrtnaɪt] *s* quincena, dos semanas
fortress ['fɔrtrɪs] *s* fortaleza
fortuitous [fɔr'tju•ɪtəs] *adj* fortuito
fortunate ['fɔrtʃənɪt] *adj* afortunado
fortune ['fɔrtjən] *s* fortuna; (*money*) platal *m;* **to make a fortune** enriquecerse; **to tell someone his fortune** decirle a uno la buenaventura
fortune hunter *s* cazador *m* de dotes
for'tune•tel'ler *s* adivino, agorero
for•ty ['fɔrti] *adj* & *pron* cuarenta || *s* (*pl* **-ties**) cuarenta *m*
fo•rum ['forəm] *s* (*pl* **-rums** o **-ra** [rə]) foro; (*e.g., of public opinion*) tribunal *m*
forward ['fɔrwərd] *adj* delantero; precoz; atrevido, impertinente || *adv* hacia adelante; **to bring forward** pasar a cuenta nueva; **to come forward** adelantarse; **to look forward to** esperar con placer anticipado || *tr* cursar, hacer seguir, reexpedir; fomentar, patrocinar
fossil ['fɑsɪl] *adj* & *s* fósil *m*
foster ['fɑstər] o ['fɔstər] *adj* adoptivo, de leche, de crianza || *tr* fomentar
foster brother *s* hermano de leche
foster home *s* hogar *m* de adopción
foster mother *s* madre adoptiva; (*nurse*) ama de leche
foster sister *s* hermana de leche
foul [faʊl] *adj* sucio, puerco; (*air*) viciado; (*wind*) contrario; (*weather*) malo; obsceno; pérfido; (*breath*) fétido; (baseball) fuera del cuadro
foul-mouthed ['faʊl'maʊðd] o ['faʊl'maʊθt] *adj* deslenguado
foul play *s* mal encuentro; (sport) juego sucio
foul'spo'ken *adj* malhablado
found [faʊnd] *tr* fundar; (*to melt, to cast*) fundir
foundation [faʊn'deʃən] *s* fundación; (*endowment*) dotación; (*basis*) fundamento; (*masonry support*) cimiento
founder ['faʊndər] *s* fundador *m;* (*of metals*) fundidor *m* || *intr* despearse (*un caballo*); hundirse, irse a pique (*un buque*); (*to fail*) fracasar
foundling ['faʊndlɪŋ] *s* niño expósito; pepe *mf*
foundling hospital *s* casa de expósitos
found•ry ['faʊndri] *s* (*pl* **-ries**) fundición
foundry•man ['faʊndrɪmən] *s* (*pl* **-men** [mən]) fundidor *m*
fount [faʊnt] *s* fuente *f*
fountain ['faʊntən] *s* fuente *f*, manantial *m*
foun'tain•head' *s* nacimiento
fountain pen *s* pluma estilográfica, pluma fuente
fountain syringe *s* mangueta
four [for] *adj* & *pron* cuatro || *s* cuatro; **four o'clock** las cuatro; **on all fours** a gatas
four'-cy'cle *adj* (mach) de cuatro tiempos
four'-cyl'inder *adj* (mach) de cuatro cilindros
four'-flush' *intr* (coll) bravear, papelonear
fourflusher ['for,flʌʃər] *s* bravucón *m*
four-footed ['for'fʊtɪd] *adj* cuadrúpedo
four hundred *adj* & *pron* cuatrocientos || *s* cuatrocientos *m;* **the four hundred** la alta sociedad
four'-in-hand' *s* corbata de nudo corredizo; coche tirado por cuatro caballos
four'-lane' *adj* cuadriviario
four'-leaf' *adj* cuadrifoliado
four-legged ['for'lɛgɪd] o ['for'lɛgd] *adj* de cuatro patas; (*schooner*) de cuatro mástiles
four'-let'ter word *s* palabra impúdica de cuatro letras
four'-mo'tor plane *s* cuadrimotor *m*
four'-o'clock' *s* dondiego
four'post'er *s* cama imperial
four'score' *adj* cuatro veintenas de
foursome ['forsəm] *s* cuatrinca; cuatro jugadores; juego de cuatro

fourteen [ˈforˈtin] *adj, pron & s* catorce *m*
fourteenth [ˈforˈtinθ] *adj & s* (*in a series*) decimocuarto; (*part*) catorzavo || *s* (*in dates*) catorce *m*
fourth [forθ] *adj & s* cuarto || *s* (*in dates*) cuatro
fourth estate *s* cuarto poder
four'-way' *adj* de cuatro direcciones; (elec) de cuatro terminales
fowl [faʊl] *s* ave *f;* aves; gallina; gallo; carne *f* de ave
fowling piece *s* escopeta de caza
fox [fɑks] *s* zorra; (*fur*) zorro; (*cunning person*) (fig) zorro || *tr* (coll) engañar con astucia
fox'glove' *s* dedalera
fox'hole' *s* zorrera; (mil) pozo de lobo
fox'hound' *s* perro raposero, perro zorrero
fox hunt *s* caza de zorras
fox terrier *s* fox-terrier *m* (*casta de perro de talla pequeña*)
fox trot *s* trote corto (*de caballo*); fox-trot *m* (*baile de compás cuaternario*)
fox•y [ˈfɑksi] *adj* (*comp* **-ier;** *super* **-iest**) (coll) hermosa y erótica; zorrero, astuto, taimado
foyer [ˈfɔɪ•ər] *s* (*of a private house*) vestíbulo; (theat) salón *m* de entrada, vestíbulo
fr. *abbr* **fragment, franc, from**
Fr. *abbr* **Father, French, Friday**
Fra [frɑ] *s* fray *m*
fracas [ˈfrekəs] *s* alboroto, riña
fraction [ˈfrækʃən] *s* fracción; porción muy pequeña
fractional [ˈfrækʃənəl] *adj* fraccionario; insignificante
fractious [ˈfrækʃəs] *adj* reacio, rebelón; quisquilloso, regañón
fracture [ˈfræktʃər] *s* fractura || *tr* fracturar; (*e.g., an arm*) fracturarse; *intr* fracturarse
fragile [ˈfrædʒɪl] *adj* frágil
fragment [ˈfrægmənt] *s* fragmento
fragrance [ˈfregrəns] *s* fragancia
fragrant [ˈfregrənt] *adj* fragante
frail [frel] *adj* (*not robust*) débil; (*easily broken; morally weak*) frágil || *s* cesto de junco
frail•ty [ˈfrelti] *s* (*pl* **-ties**) debilidad; (*moral weakness*) fragilidad
frame [frem] *s* (*of a picture, mirror*) marco, (*of glasses*) montura, armadura; (*structure*) armazón *f,* esqueleto; (*for embroidering*) bastidor *m; (of government*) sistema *m;* (mov, telv) encuadre *m;* (naut) cuaderna || *tr* (*to put in a frame*) enmarcar; formar, forjar; construir; redactar, formular; (slang) incriminar (*a un inocente*)
frame house *s* casa de madera
frame of mind *s* manera de pensar
frame'-up' *s* (slang) treta, trama para incriminar a un inocente
frame'work' *s* armazón *f,* esqueleto, entramado
franc [fræŋk] *s* franco
France [fræns] o [frɑns] *s* Francia
franchise [ˈfræntʃaɪz] *s* franquicia, privilegio; (*right to vote*) sufragio
Franciscan [frænˈsɪskən] *adj & s* franciscano
frank [fræŋk] *adj* franco, sincero || *s* carta franca, envío franco; franquicia postal; sello de franquicia || *tr* franquear || **Frank** *s* (*member of a Frankish tribe*) franco; (*masculine name*) Paco
frankfurter [ˈfræŋkfərtər] *s* salchicha de carne de vaca y de cerdo
frankincense [ˈfræŋkɪn,sɛns] *s* olíbano
Frankish [ˈfræŋkɪʃ] *adj & s* franco
frankness [ˈfræŋknɪs] *s* franqueza, abertura, sinceridad
frantic [ˈfræntɪk] *adj* frenético
frappé [fræˈpe] *adj* helado || *s* refresco helado de zumo de frutas
frat [fræt] *s* (slang) club *m* de estudiantes
fraternal [frəˈtʌrnəl] *adj* fraternal
fraterni•ty [frəˈtʌrnɪti] *s* (*pl* **-ties**) (*brotherliness*) fraternidad; cofradía; asociación secreta; (U.S.A.) club *m* de estudiantes
fraternize [ˈfrætər,naɪz] *intr* fraternizar
fraud [frɔd] *s* fraude *m;* embelequería (Col, Mex, W-I); (*person*) (coll) impostor *m*
fraudulent [ˈfrɔdjələnt] *adj* fraudulento
fraught [frɔt] *adj*—**fraught with** cargado de, lleno de
fray [fre] *s* combate *m,* riña, batalla || *intr* deshilacharse, raerse
freak [frik] *s* (*sudden fancy*) capricho, antojo; (*person, animal*) fenómeno, esperpento
freakish [ˈfrikɪʃ] *adj* caprichoso, antojadizo; raro, fantástico
freckle [ˈfrɛkəl] *s* peca
freckle-faced [ˈfrɛkəl,fest] *adj* pecoso
freckly [ˈfrɛkli] *adj* pecoso
free [fri] *adj* (*comp* **freer** [ˈfri•ər]; *super* **freest** [ˈfri•ɪst]) libre; gratis, franco; liberal, generoso; **to be free with** dar abundantemente; **to set free** libertar || *adv* libremente; en libertad; de balde, gratis || *v* (*pret & pp* **freed** [frid]; *ger* **freeing** [ˈfri•ɪŋ]) *tr* libertar, poner en libertad; soltar; exentar, eximir
free and easy *adj* despreocupado
freebooter [ˈfri,butər] *s* forbante *m,* filibustero, pirata *m*
free'born' *adj* nacido libre; propio de un pueblo libre
freedom [ˈfridəm] *s* libertad
freedom of speech *s* libertad de palabra
freedom of the press *s* libertad de imprenta
freedom of the seas *s* libertad de los mares
freedom of worship *s* libertad de cultos
free enterprise *s* libertad de empresa
free fight *s* sarracina, riña tumultuaria
free'-for-all' *s* concurso abierto a todo el mundo; sarracina, riña tumultuaria
free hand *s* plena libertad, carta blanca
free'hand' drawing *s* dibujo a pulso
freehanded [ˈfri,hændɪd] *adj* dadivoso, generoso
free'hold' *s* (law) feudo franco
free lance *s* soldado mercenario; periodista *mf* sin empleo fijo; (*writer not on regular salary*) destajista *mf*

free lunch *s* tapas, enjutos
free•man ['frimən] *s* (*pl* **-men** [mən]) hombre *m* libre; ciudadano
Free'ma'son *s* francmasón *m*
Free'ma'sonry *s* francmasonería
free of charge *adj* gratis, de balde
free on board *adj* franco a bordo
free port *s* puerto franco
free ride *s* llevada gratuita
free service *s* servicio post-venta
free'-spo'ken *adj* franco, sin reserva
free'stone' *adj & s* abridero
free'think'er *s* librepensador *m*
free thought *s* librepensamiento
free trade *s* librecambio
free'trad'er *s* librecambista *mf*
free'way' *s* autopista
free will *s* libre albedrío
freeze [friz] *s* helada || *v* (*pret* **froze** [froz]; *pp* **frozen**) *tr* helar; congelar (*créditos, fondos, etc.*) || *intr* helarse; congelarse; helársele a uno la sangre (*p.ej., de miedo*)
freeze'-dry' *v* (*pret & pp* **-dried**) *tr* liofilizar
freeze drying *s* liofilización
freezer ['frizər] *s* heladora, sorbetera
freezing ['frizɪŋ] *s* glaciación
freight [fret] *s* carga; (naut) flete *m;* **by freight** como carga; (rr) en pequeña velocidad || *tr* enviar por carga
freight car *s* vagón *m* de carga, vagón de mercancías
freighter ['fretər] *s* buque *m* de carga, carguero
freight platform *s* (rr) muelle *m*
freight station *s* (rr) estación de carga
freight train *s* mercancías *msg,* tren *m* de mercancías
freight yard *s* (rr) patio de carga
French [frɛntʃ] *adj & s* francés *m;* **the French** los franceses
French chalk *s* jaboncillo de sastre
French doors *spl* puertas vidrieras dobles
French dressing *s* salsa francesa, vinagreta
French fried potatoes *spl* patatas fritas en trocitos
French horn *s* (mus) trompa de armonía
French horsepower *s* caballo de fuerza, caballo de vapor
French leave *s* despedida a la francesa; **to take French leave** despedirse a la francesa
French•man ['frɛntʃmən] *s* (*pl* **-men** [mən]) francés *m*
French telephone *s* microteléfono
French toast *s* torrija
French window *s* puerta ventana
French'wom'an *s* (*pl* **-wom'en**) francesa
frenzied ['frɛnzid] *adj* frenético
fren•zy ['frɛnzi] (*pl* **-zies**) frenesí *m*
frequen•cy ['frikwənsi] *s* (*pl* **-cies**) frecuencia
frequency list *s* lista de frecuencia
frequency modulation *s* modulación de frecuencia
frequent ['frikwənt] *adj* frecuente || [frɪ'kwɛnt] o ['frikwənt] *tr* frecuentar
frequently ['frikwəntli] *adv* con frecuencia, frecuentemente
fres•co ['frɛsko] *s* (*pl* **-coes** o **-cos**) fresco || *tr* pintar al fresco
fresh [freʃ] *adj* fresco; (*water*) dulce; (*wind*) fresquito; novicio, inexperto; (*cheeky*) (slang) fresco; (*toward women*) (slang) atrevido; **fresh paint!** ¡ojo mancha! || *adv* recientemente, recién; **fresh in** (coll) recién llegado, acabado de llegar; **fresh out** (coll) recién agotado
freshen ['frɛʃən] *tr* refrescar || *intr* refrescarse
freshet ['frɛʃɪt] *s* avenida, crecida
fresh•man ['frɛʃmən] *s* (*pl* **-men** [mən]) novato; estudiante *mf* de primer año
freshness ['frɛʃnɪs] *s* frescura; (*cheek*) (slang) frescura
fresh'-wa'ter *adj* de agua dulce; no acostumbrado a navegar; de poca monta
fret [frɛt] *s* (*interlaced design*) calado; (mus) ceja, traste *m;* queja || *v* (*pret & pp* **fretted;** *ger* **fretting**) *tr* adornar con calados || *intr* irritarse, quejarse, agitarse
fretful ['frɛtfəl] *adj* irritable, enojadizo, displicente
fret'work' *s* calado
Freudianism ['frɔɪdɪ•ə,nɪzəm] *s* freudismo
friar ['fraɪ•ər] *s* fraile *m* **friar•y** ['fraɪ•əri] *s* (*pl* **-ies**) convento de frailes
fricassee [,frikə'si] *s* fricasé *m*
friction ['frikʃən] *s* fricción, rozamiento; (fig) desavenencia, rozamiento
friction tape *s* cinta aislante
Friday ['fraɪdi] *s* viernes *m*
fried [fraɪd] *adj* frito
fried egg *s* huevo a la plancha, huevo frito o estrellado
friend [frɛnd] *s* amigo; (*in answer to "Who is there?"*) gente *f* de paz; **to be friends with** ser amigo de; **to make friends** trabar amistades; **to make friends with** hacerse amigo de
friend•ly ['frɛndli] *adj* (*comp* **-lier;** *super* **-liest**) amigo, amistoso, amigable
friendship ['frɛndʃɪp] *s* amistad
frieze [friz] *s* (archit) friso
frigate ['frɪgɪt] *s* fragata
fright [fraɪt] *s* susto, espanto; (*grotesque or ridiculous person*) (coll) espantajo; **to take fright at** asustarse de
frighten ['fraɪtən] *tr* asustar, espantar; **to frighten away** espantar, ahuyentar || *intr* asustarse
frightful ['fraɪtfəl] *adj* espantoso, horroroso; (coll) feúcho, repugnante; (coll) enorme, tremendo
frightfulness ['fraɪtfəlnɪs] *s* espanto, horror *m;* terrorismo; espantosidad (SAm)
frigid ['frɪdʒɪd] *adj* frío; (fig) frío; (*zone*) glacial
frigidity [frɪ'dʒɪdɪti] *s* frialdad; (pathol) frialdad; (fig) frialdad, frigidez *f*
frill [fril] *s* lechuga; (*of birds and other animals*) collarín *m;* (*frippery*) (coll) ringorrango; (*in dress, speech etc.*) (coll) afectación
fringe [frɪndʒ] *s* franja, orla; (opt) franja || *tr* franjar, orlar

fringe benefits *spl* beneficios accesorios; beneficios sociales
fripper•y [ˈfrɪpəri] *s* (*pl* **-ies**) (*flashiness*) cursilería; (*flashy clothes*) perejil *m*, perifollos
frisk [frɪsk] *tr* (slang) cachear; (slang) registrar y robar || *intr* retozar
frisk•y [ˈfrɪski] *adj* (*comp* **-ier;** *super* **-iest**) juguetón, retozón; (*horse*) fogoso
fritter [ˈfrɪtər] *s* fruta de sartén; fragmento || *tr*—**to fritter away** desperdiciar, malgastar poco a poco
frivolous [ˈfrɪvələs] *adj* frívolo
friz [frɪz] *s* (*pl* **frizzes**) rizo, pelo rizado apretadamente || *v* (*pret & pp* **frizzed;** *ger* **frizzing**) *tr* rizar, rizar apretadamente
frizzle [ˈfrɪzəl] *s* rizo apretado; chirrido, siseo || *tr* rizar apretadamente; asar o freír en parrilla || *intr* chirriar, sisear
friz•zly [ˈfrɪzli] *adj* (*comp* **-zlier;** *super* **-zliest**) muy ensortijado
fro [fro] *adv*—**to and fro** de acá para allá; **to go to and fro** ir y venir
frock [frɑk] *s* vestido; bata, blusa; (*of priest*) vestido talar
frock coat *s* levita
frog [frɑg] o [frɔg] *s* rana; (*button and loop on a garment*) alamar *m;* (*in throat*) ronquera, gallo
frog'man' *s* (*pl* **-men'**) hombre-rana *m*
frol•ic [ˈfrɑlɪk] *s* juego alegre, travesura; fiesta, holgorio || *v* (*pret & pp* **-icked;** *ger* **-icking**) *intr* juguetear, travesear, jaranear
frolicsome [ˈfrɑlɪksəm] *adj* juguetón, travieso
from [frʌm], [frɑm] o [frəm] *prep* de; desde; de parte de; según; a, p.ej., **to take something away from someone** quitarle algo a alguien
front [frʌnt] *adj* delantero; anterior || *s* frente *m & f;* (*of a shirt*) pechera; (*of a book*) principio; apariencia falsa (*p.ej., de riqueza*); ademán estudiado; (mil) frente *m;* **in front of** delante de, frente a, en frente de; **to put on a front** (coll) gastar mucho oropel; **to put up a bold front** (coll) hacer de tripas corazón || *tr* (*to face*) dar a; (*to confront*) afrontar, arrostrar; (*to supply with a front*) poner frente o fachada a || *intr*—**to front on** dar a; **to front towards** mirar hacia
frontage [ˈfrʌntɪdʒ] *s* fachada, frontera; terreno frontero
front door *s* puerta de entrada
front drive *s* (aut) tracción delantera
frontier [frʌnˈtɪr] *adj* fronterizo || *s* frontera
frontiers•man [frʌnˈtɪrzmən] *s* (*pl* **-men** [mən]) hombre *m* de la frontera, explorador *m*
frontispiece [ˈfrʌntɪs,pis] *s* (*of book*) portada; (archit) frontispicio
front matter *s* preliminares *mpl* (*de un libro*)
front page *s* primera plana
front porch *s* soportal *m*
front room *s* cuarto que da a la calle
front row *s* primera fila
front seat *s* asiento delantero
front steps *spl* escalones *mpl* de acceso a la puerta de entrada
front view *s* vista de frente
frost [frɔst] o [frɑst] *s* (*freezing*) helada; (*frozen dew*) escarcha; (slang) fracaso || *tr* cubrir de escarcha; escarchar (*confituras*); helar (*el frío las plantas*); deslustrar (*el vidrio*)
frost'bit'ten *adj* dañado por la helada; quemado por la helada o la escarcha
frosted glass *s* vidrio deslustrado
frosting [ˈfrɔstɪŋ] o [frɑstɪŋ] *s* garapiña; (*of glass*) deslustre *m*
frost•y [ˈfrɔsti] o [ˈfrɑsti] *adj* (*comp* **-ier;** *super* **-iest**) cubierto de escarcha; escarchado; frío, poco amistoso; canoso, gris
froth [frɔθ] o [frɑθ] *s* espuma; frivolidad, vanidad || *intr* espumar, echar espuma; (*at the mouth*) espumajear
froth•y [ˈfrɔθi] o [ˈfrɑθi] *adj* (*comp* **-ier;** *super* **-iest**) espumoso; frívolo, vano
froward [ˈfrowərd] *adj* díscolo, indócil
frown [fraʊn] *s* ceño, entrecejo || *intr* fruncir el entrecejo; to frown at *u* on mirar con ceño, desaprobar
frows•y o **frowz•y** [ˈfraʊzi] *adj* (*comp* **-ier;** *super* **-iest**) desaseado, desaliñado; maloliente; mal peinado
frozen foods [ˈfrozən] *spl* viandas congeladas
frt. *abbr* **freight**
frugal [ˈfrugəl] *adj* (*moderate in the use of things*) parco; (*not very abundant*) frugal
fruit [frut] *adj* (*tree*) frutal; (*boat, dish*) frutero || *s* (*such as apple, pear, strawberry*) fruta; frutas, p.ej., **I like fruit** me gustan las frutas; (*part containing seed*) fruto; (*effect, result*) (fig) fruto
fruit cake *s* torta de frutas
fruit cup *s* compota de frutas picadas
fruit fly *s* mosca del vinagre; mosca de las frutas
fruitful [ˈfrutfəl] *adj* fructuoso
fruition [fruˈɪʃən] *s* buen resultado, cumplimiento; **to come to fruition** lograrse cumplidamente
fruit jar *s* tarro para frutas
fruit juice *s* jugo de frutas
fruitless [ˈfrutlɪs] *adj* infructuoso
fruit of the vine *s* zumo de cepas o de parras
fruit salad *s* ensalada de frutas, macedonia de frutas
fruit stand *s* puesto de frutas
fruit store *s* frutería
frumpish [ˈfrʌmpɪʃ] *adj* basto, desgarbado, desaliñado
frustrate [ˈfrʌstret] *tr* frustrar
fry [fraɪ] *s* (*pl* **fries**) fritada || *v* (*pret & pp* **fried**) *tr & intr* freír
frying pan [ˈfraɪ•ɪŋ] *s* sartén *f;* **to jump from the frying pan into the fire** saltar de la sartén y dar en las brasas
ft. *abbr* **foot, feet**
fudge [fʌdʒ] *s* dulce *m* de chocolate
fuel [ˈfju•əl] *s* combustible *m;* (fig) pábulo; **alternate fuel** combustible alternativo || *v* (*pret & pp* **fueled** o **fuelled;** *ger* **fueling** o

fuelling) *tr* aprovisionar de combustible ‖ *intr* aprovisionarse de combustible
fuel cell *s* cámara de combustible, célula electrógena
fuel oil *s* aceite *m* combustible
fuel tank *s* depósito de combustible
fugitive [ˈfjudʒɪtɪv] *adj & s* fugitivo
fugue [fjug] *s* (mus) fuga
ful•crum [ˈfʌlkrəm] *s* (*pl* **-crums** o **-cra** [krə]) fulcro
fulfill [fʊlˈfɪl] *tr* (*to carry out*) cumplir, realizar; cumplir con (*una obligación*); llenar (*una condición*)
fulfillment [fʊlˈfɪlmənt] *s* cumplimiento, realización
full [fʊl] *adj* lleno; (*dress, garment*) amplio, holgado; (*formal dress*) de etiqueta; (*voice*) sonoro, fuerte; (*of food*) harto; **full of aches and pains** lleno de goteras; **full of fun** muy divertido, muy chistoso; **full of play** muy juguetón; **full to overflowing** lleno a rebosar ‖ *adv* completamente; **full many (a)** muchísimos; **full well** muy bien, perfectamente ‖ *s* colmo; **in full** por completo; sin abreviar; **to the full** completamente ‖ *tr* abatanar
full-blooded [ˈfʊlˈblʌdɪd] *adj* vigoroso; completo, pletórico; de raza
full-blown [ˈfʊlˈblon] *adj* (*flower, blossom*) abierto; desarrollado, maduro
full-bodied [ˈfʊlˈbɑdid] *adj* fuerte, espeso, consistente; aromático
full dress *s* traje *m* de etiqueta; (mil) uniforme *m* de gala
full′-dress′ coat *s* frac *m*
full-faced [ˈfʊlˈfest] *adj* carilleno; (*view*) de cuadrado; (*portrait*) de rostro entero
full-fledged [ˈfʊlˈflɛdʒd] *adj* hecho y derecho, nada menos que
full-grown [ˈfʊlˈgron] *adj* crecido, completamente desarrollado
full house *s* lleno, entrada llena; (poker) fulján *m*
full′-length′ mirror *s* espejo de cuerpo entero, espejo de vestir
full-length movie *s* largometraje *m*, cinta de largo metraje
full load *s* plena carga; (aer) peso total
full moon *s* luna llena, plenilunio
full name *s* nombre *m* y apellidos
full′-page′ *adj* a página entera
full powers *spl* plenos poderes, amplias facultades
full sail *adv* a todo trapo
fulll′-scale′ *adj* de tamaño natural; total, completo; pleno
full-sized [ˈfʊlˈsaɪzd] *adj* de tamaño natural
full speed *adv* a toda velocidad
full stop *s* parada completa; (gram) punto
full swing *s* plena actividad
full tilt *adv* a toda velocidad
full′-time′ *adj* a tiempo completo
full′-view′ *adj* de vista completa
full volume *s* (rad) máximo de volumen
fully [ˈfuli] o [ˈfulli] *adv* completamente; cabalmente; por lo menos
fulsome [ˈfʊlsəm] *adj* bajo, craso, de mal gusto
fumble [ˈfʌmbəl] *tr* no coger (*la pelota*), dejar caer (*la pelota*) desmañadamente; manosear desmañadamente ‖ *intr* revolver papeles; titubear; andar a tientas; (*in one's pockets*) buscar con las manos
fume [fjum] *s* humo, vapor *m*, gas *m*, vaho ‖ *tr* (*to treat with fumes*) ahumar ‖ *intr* (*to give off fumes*) humear; (*to show anger*) echar pestes; **to fume at** echar pestes contra
fumigate [ˈfjumɪˌget] *tr* fumigar
fumigation [ˌfjumɪˈgeʃən] *s* fumigación
fun [fʌn] *s* divertimiento; broma, chacota; **to be fun** ser divertido; **to have fun** divertirse; **to make fun of** reírse de, burlarse de
function [ˈfʌŋkʃən] *s* función ‖ *intr* funcionar
functional [ˈfʌŋkʃənəl] *adj* funcional
functionar•y [ˈfʌŋkʃəˌnɛri] *s* (*pl* **-ies**) funcionario
fund [fʌnd] *s* fondo; **funds** fondos ‖ *tr* consolidar (*una deuda*)
fundamental [ˌfʌndəˈmɛntəl] *adj* fundamental ‖ *s* fundamento
funeral [ˈfjunərəl] *adj* funeral; (*march, procession*) fúnebre; (*expense*) funerario ‖ *s* funeral *m*, funerales *mpl*, pompa fúnebre (*de cuerpo presente*); **it's not my funeral** (slang) no corre a mi cuidado
funeral director *s* empresario de pompas fúnebres
funeral home o **parlor** *s* funeraria
funeral service *s* oficio de difuntos, misa de cuerpo presente
funereal [fjuˈnɪrɪ•əl] *adj* fúnebre
fungous [ˈfʌŋgəs] *adj* fungoso
fungus [ˈfʌŋgəs] *s* (*pl* **funguses** o **fungi** [ˈfʌndʒaɪ]) hongo; (pathol) fungo
funicular [fjuˈnɪkjələr] *adj & s* funicular *m*
funk [fʌŋk] *s* (coll) miedo, cobardía; cobarde *mf*; **in a funk** asustado
fun•nel [ˈfʌnəl] *s* embudo; (*smokestack*) chimenea; (*tube for ventilation*) manguera, ventilador *m* ‖ *v* (*pret & pp* **-neled** o **-nelled**; *ger* **-neling** o **-nelling**) *tr* verter por medio de un embudo
funnies [ˈfʌniz] *spl* páginas cómicas, tiras cómicas, tebeo
fun•ny [ˈfʌni] *adj* (*comp* **-nier**; *super* **-niest**) cómico; divertido, chistoso; (coll) extraño, raro; **to strike someone as funny** hacerle a uno gracia
funny bone *s* hueso de la alegría
funny paper *s* páginas cómicas
fur. *abbr* **furlong, furnished**
fur [fʌr] *s* piel *f*; abrigo de pieles; (*on the tongue*) sarro
furbelow [ˈfʌrbəˌlo] *s* (*ruffle*) faralá *m*; (*frippery*) ringorrango
furbish [ˈfʌrbɪʃ] *tr* acicalar, limpiar; **to furbish up** renovar
furious [ˈfjʊrɪ•əs] *adj* furioso
furl [fʌrl] *tr* enrollar; (naut) aferrar
fur-lined [ˈfʌrˌlaɪnd] *adj* forrado con pieles
furlong [ˈfʌrlɔŋ] o [ˈfʌrlɑŋ] *s* estadio

furlough ['fʌrlo] *s* licencia || *tr* dar licencia a
furnace ['fʌrnɪs] *s* horno; (*to heat a house*) calorífero
furnish ['fʌrnɪʃ] *tr* amueblar; proporcionar, suministrar
furnishings ['fʌrnɪʃɪŋz] *spl* muebles *mpl;* (*things to wear*) artículos
furniture ['fʌrnɪtʃər] *s* muebles *mpl,* mobiliario; (naut) aparejo; **a piece of furniture** un mueble
furniture dealer *s* mueblista *mf*
furniture store *s* mueblería
furrier ['fʌrɪ•ər] *s* peletero
furrier•y ['fʌrɪ•əri] *s* (*pl* **-ies**) peletería
furrow ['fʌro] *s* surco || *tr* surcar
further ['fʌrðər] *adj* adicional; nuevo; más lejano || *adv* además; más lejos || *tr* adelantar, promover, fomentar
furtherance ['fʌrðərəns] *s* adelantamiento, promoción, fomento
furthermore ['fʌrðər,mor] *adv* además
furthest ['fʌrðɪst] *adj* (el) más lejano || *adv* más lejos
furtive ['fʌrtɪv] *adj* furtivo
fu•ry ['fjʊri] *s* (*pl* **-ries**) furia
furze [fʌrz] *s* aulaga; retama de escoba
fuse [fjuz] *s* (tube or wick filled with explosive material) mecha; (*device for detonating an explosive charge*) espoleta; (elec) fusible *m,* cortacircuitos *m,* tapón *m;* **to burn out a fuse** quemar un fusible || *tr* fundir; (*to unite*) fusionar || *intr* fundirse; fusionarse
fuse box *s* caja de fusibles
fuselage ['fjuzəlɪdʒ] *s* fuselaje *m*
fusible ['fjuzɪbəl] *adj* fundible, fusible
fusillade [,fjuzɪ'led] *s* fusilería; (*e.g., of questions*) andanada || *tr* atacar o matar con una descarga de fusilería, fusilar
fusion ['fjuʒən] *s* fusión
fuss [fʌs] *s* alharaca, hazañería; (coll) disputa por ligero motivo; **to make a fuss** hacer alharacas; **to make a fuss over** hacer fiestas a; disputar sobre || *tr* atolondrar, inquietar, confundir || *intr* hacer alharacas, inquietarse por bagatelas
fuss•y ['fʌsi] *adj* (*comp* **-ier;** *super* **-iest**)] alharaquiento, alborotado; descontentadizo, quisquilloso, melindroso; funcionero, hazañero; muy adornado
fustian ['fʌstʃən] *s* (*coarse cloth*) fustán *m;* (*sort of velveteen*) pana; (*bombast*) cultedad, follaje *m*
fust•y ['fʌsti] *adj* (*comp* **-ier;** *super* **-iest**) mohoso, rancio; que huele a cerrado; pasado de moda
futile ['fjutɪl] *adj* (*unproductive*) estéril; (*unimportant*) fútil
futili•ty [fju'tɪlɪti] *s* (*pl* **-ties**) esterilidad; futilidad
future ['fjutʃər] *adj* futuro || *s* futuro, porvenir *m;* (gram) futuro; **futures** (com) futuros; **in the future** en el futuro; **in the near future** en un futuro próximo
fuze [fjuz] *s* (*tube or wick filled with explosive material*) mecha; (*device for detonating an explosive charge*) espoleta; (elec) fusible *m* || *tr* poner la espoleta a
fuzz [fʌz] *s* (*as on a peach*) pelusa, vello; (*in pockets and corners*) borra, tamo; **the fuzz** (slang) policía *m,* guardia *m* urbano
fuzz•y ['fʌzi] *adj* (*comp* **-ier;** *super* **-iest**) cubierto de pelusa, velloso; polvoriento; (*indistinct*) borroso

G

G, g [dʒi] *s* séptima letra del alfabeto inglés
G. *abbr* **German, Gulf**
g. *abbr* **gender, genitive, gram**
gab [gæb] *s* (coll) cotorreo || (*pret & pp* **gabbed;** *ger* **gabbing**) *intr* (coll) cotorrear
gabardine ['gæbər ,din] *s* gabardina
gabble ['gæbəl] *s* cotorreo, parloteo || *intr* cotorrear, parlotear
gable ('gebəl] *s* (*of roof*) aguilón *m;* (*over a door or window*) gablete *m,* frontón *m*
gable end *s* hastial *m*
gable roof *s* tejado de dos aguas
gad [gæd] *v* (*pret & pp* **gadded;** *ger* **gadding**) *intr* callejear, andar de acá para allá; **to gad about** pindonguear (*una mujer*)
gad'a•bout' *adj* callejero || *s* cirigallo; (*woman*) pindonga
gad'fly' *s* (*pl* **-flies**) tábano
gadget ['gædʒɪt] *s* adminículo, chisme *m,* artilugio
Gael [gel] *s* gaélico
Gaelic ['gelɪk] *adj & s* gaélico
gaff [gæf] *s* garfio, arpón *m;* **to stand the gaff** (slang) tener aguante
gag [gæg] *s* mordaza; (*interpolation by an actor*) morcilla; (*joke*)) chiste *m,* payasada || *v* (*pret & pp* **gagged;** *ger* **gagging**) *tr* amordazar; dar bascas a || *intr* sentir bascas, arquear
gage [gedʒ] *s* (*pledge*) prenda; (*challenge*) desafío
gaie•ty ['ge•ɪti] *s* (*pl* **-ties**) alegría, algazara, diversión; (*of colors*) viveza
gaily ['geli] *adv* alegremente
gain [gen] *s* ganancia; (*increase*) aumento || *tr* ganar; (*to reach*) alcanzar || *intr* ganar terreno; mejorar (*un enfermo*); adelantarse (*un reloj*); **to gain on** ir alcanzando
gainful ['genfəl] *adj* ganancioso, provechoso
gain'say' *v* (*pret & pp* **-said** ['sed] o ['sɛd]) *tr* negar; contradecir; prohibir
gait [get] *s* paso, manera de andar
gaiter ['getər] *s* polaina corta
gal. *abbr* **gallon**

gala [ˈgelə] *adj* de gala ‖ *s* fiesta
galax•y [ˈgæləksi] *s* (*pl* **-ies**) galaxia
gale [gel] *s* ventarrón *m;* **gales of laughter** tempestades de risas; **to weather the gale** correr el temporal; (fig) ir tirando
Galician [gəˈlɪʃən] *adj & s* gallego
gall [gɔl] *s* bilis *f,* hiel *f;* vejiga de la bilis; (*something bitter*) (fig) hiel *f;* rencor *m,* odio; (*gallnut*) agalla; (*audacity*) (coll) descaro ‖ *tr* lastimar rozando; irritar ‖ *intr* raerse; (naut) mascarse (*un cabo*)
gallant [ˈgælənt] *adj* (*attentive to women*) galante; (*pertaining to love*) amoroso ‖ [ˈgælənt] *adj* (*stately, grand*) gallardo; (*spirited, daring*) hazañoso; (*showy, gay*) vistoso, festivo ‖ *s* hombre *m* valiente; (*man attentive to women*) galán *m*
gallant•ry [ˈgæləntri] *s* (*pl* **-ries**) galantería; gallardía
gall bladder *s* vejiga de la bilis, vesícula biliar
gall duct *s* conducto biliar
galleon [ˈgælɪ•ən] *s* (naut) galeón *m*
galler•y [ˈgæləri] *s* (*pl* **-ies**) galería; (*in church, theater, etc.*) tribuna; (*cheapest seats in theater*) gallinero; **to play to the gallery** (coll) hablar para la galería
galley [ˈgæli] *s* (naut & typ) galera; (naut) cocina
galley proof *s* (typ) galerada, pruebas de segundas
galley slave *s* galeote *m;* (*drudge*) esclavo del trabajo
Gallic [ˈgælɪk] *adj* gálico
galling [ˈgɔlɪŋ] *adj* irritante, ofensivo
gallivant [ˈgælɪ,vænt] *intr* andar a placer
gall'nut' *s* agalla
gallon [ˈgælən] *s* galón *m* (*medida*)
galloon [gəˈlun] *s* galón *m* (*cinta*)
gallop [ˈgæləp] *s* galope *m;* **at a gallop** a galope ‖ *tr* hacer galopar ‖ *intr* galopar; **to gallop through** (fig) hacer muy aprisa
gal•lows [ˈgæloz] *s* (*pl* **-lows** o **-lowses**) horca
gallows bird *s* (coll) carne *f* de horca
gall'stone' *s* cálculo biliar
galore [gəˈlor] *adv* en abundancia
galosh [gəˈlɑʃ] *s* chanclo alto
galvanize [ˈgælvə,naɪz] *tr* galvanizar
galvanized iron *s* hierro galvanizado
gambit [ˈgæmbɪt] *s* gambito
gamble [ˈgæmbəl] *s* (coll) empresa arriesgada ‖ *tr* aventurar en el juego; **to gamble away** perder en el juego ‖ *intr* jugar; (*in the stock market*) especular, aventurarse
gambler [ˈgæmblər] *s* jugador *m;* especulador *m*
gambling [ˈgæmblɪŋ] *s* juego
gambling den *s* garito
gambling house *s* casa de juego, juego público
gambling table *s* mesa de juego
gam•bol [ˈgæmbəl] *s* cabriola, retozo, salto ‖ *v* (*pret & pp* **-boled** o **-bolled;** *gen* **-boling** o **-bolling)** *intr* cabriolar, retozar, saltar
gambrel [ˈgæmbrəl] *s* corvejón *m*
gambrel roof *s* techo a la holandesa
game [gem] *adj* bravo, peleón; dispuesto, resuelto; (*leg*) cojo; de caza ‖ *s* (*form of play*) juego; (*single contest*) partida; (*score*) tantos; (*in bridge*) manga; (*any sport*) deporte *m;* (*animal or bird hunted for sport or food*) caza; (*any pursuit*) actividad; (*pursuit of diplomacy*) juego; **the game is up** estamos frescos; **to make game of** burlarse de; **to play the game** jugar limpio
game bag *s* morral *m*
game bird *s* ave *f* de caza
game'cock' *s* gallo de pelea
game'keep'er *s* guardabosque *m*
game of chance *s* juego de azar
game preserve *s* vedado
game warden *s* guardabosque *m*
gamut [ˈgæmət] *s* (mus & fig) gama
gam•y [ˈgemi] *adj* (*comp* **-ier;** *super* **-iest)** (*having flavor of uncooked game*) salvajino; bravo, peleón
gander [ˈgændər] *s* ganso
gang [gæŋ] *adj* múltiple ‖ *s* (*of workmen*) brigada, cuadrilla; (*of thugs*) pandilla ‖ *intr* — **to gang up** acuadrillarse; **to gang up against** u **on** atacar juntos; conspirar contra
gangling [ˈgæŋglɪŋ] *adj* larguirucho
gangli•on [ˈgæŋglɪ•ən] *s* (*pl* **-ons** o **-a** [ə]) ganglio
gang'plank' *s* plancha, pasarela
gangrene [ˈgæŋgrin] *s* gangrena ‖ *tr* gangrenar ‖ *intr* gangrenarse
gangster [ˈgæŋstər] *adj* gangsteril ‖ *s* gángster *m,* pistolero
gangsterism [ˈgæŋstə,rɪzəm] *s* gangsterismo; acciones de los gangsters
gang'way' *s* (*passageway*) pasillo; (*gangplank*) plancha, pasarela; (*in ship's side*) portalón *m* ‖ *interj* ¡abran paso!, ¡paso libre!
gantlet [ˈgɔntlɪt] *s* (rr) vía traslapada
gan•try [ˈgæntri] *s* (*pl* **-tries**) caballete *m,* poíno; (rr) puente *m* transversal de señales
gantry crane *s* grúa de caballete
gap [gæp] *s* (*break, open space*) laguna; (*in a wall*) boquete *m;* (*between mountains*) garganta, quebrada; (*between two points of view*) sima
gape [gep] o [gæp] *s* abertura, brecha; (*yawn*) bostezo; mirada de asombro; **the gapes** ganas de bostezar ‖ *intr* estar abierto de par en par; bostezar; embobarse; **to gape at** mirar embobado; **to stand gaping** embobarse
G.A.R. *abbr* **Grand Army of the Republic**
garage [gəˈrɑʒ] *s* garage *m*
garb [gɑrb] *s* vestidura ‖ *tr* vestir
garbage [ˈgɑrbɪdʒ] *s* basuras, desperdicios, bazofia
garbage can *s* cubo para bazofia, latón *m* de la basura
garbage collection *s* recogida de basuras
garbage disposal *s* evacuación de basuras
garbage heap *s* basural *m* (CAm)
garble [ˈgɑrbəl] *tr* mutilar (*un texto*)
garden [ˈgɑrdən] *s* (*of vegetables*) huerto; (*of flowers*) jardín *m*

gardener [ˈgɑrdənər] *s* (*of vegetables*) hortelano; (*of flowers*) jardinero

gardenia [gɑrˈdinɪ•ə] *s* gardenia, jazmín *m* de la India

gardening [ˈgɑrdənɪŋ] *s* horticultura; jardinería

garden party *s* fiesta que se da en un jardín o parque

gargle [ˈgɑrgəl] *s* gargarismo ‖ *intr* gargarizar

gargoyle [ˈgɑrgɔɪl] *s* gárgola

garish [ˈgɛrɪʃ] *adj* charro, chillón, cursi

garland [ˈgɑrlənd] *s* guirnalda

garlic [ˈgɑrlɪk] *s* ajo

garment [ˈgɑrmənt] *s* prenda de vestir

garner [ˈgɑrnər] *tr* (*to gather, collect*) acopiar; adquirir; (*cereales*) entrojar

garnet [ˈgɑrnɪt] *adj* & *s* granate *m*

garnish [ˈgɑrnɪʃ] *s* adorno; (culin) aderezo, condimento de adorno ‖ *tr* adornar; (culin) aderezar; (law) embargar

garret [ˈgærɪt] *s* buhardilla, desván *m*

garrison [ˈgærɪsən] *s* plaza fuerte; (*troops*) guarnición ‖ *tr* guarnecer, guarnicionar (*una plaza fuerte*); guarnecer una plaza fuerte de (*tropas*)

garrote [gəˈrɑt] o [gəˈrot] *s* estrangulación para robar; (*method of execution; iron collar used for such execution*) garrote *m* ‖ *tr* estrangular; estrangular para robar; agarrotar, dar garrote a

garrulous [ˈgærələs] *adj* gárrulo, locuaz

garter [ˈgɑrtər] *s* liga, jarretera

garth [gɑrθ] *s* patio de claustro

gas [gæs] *s* gas *m;* gasolina; (coll) palabrería ‖ *v* (*pret* & *pp* **gassed;** *ger* **gassing**) *tr* abastecer de gas; (*to attack, asphyxiate, or poison with gas*) gasear; abastecer de gasolina ‖ *intr* despedir gas; (slang) charlar

gas'bag' *s* (aer) cámara de gas; (slang) charlatán *m*

gas burner *s* mechero de gas

Gascony [ˈgæskəni] *s* Gascuña

gas engine *s* motor *m* a gas

gaseous [ˈgæsɪ•əs] *adj* gaseoso

gas fitter *s* gasista *m*

gas generator *s* gasógeno

gash [gæʃ] *s* cuchillada, chirlo ‖ *tr* acuchillar

gas heat *s* calefacción por gas

gas'hold'er *s* gasómetro

gasi•fy [ˈgæsɪˌfaɪ] *v* (*pret* & *pp* **-fied**) *tr* gasificar ‖ *intr* gasificarse

gas jet *s* mechero de gas; llama de gas

gasket [ˈgæskɪt] *s* empaquetadura

gas'light' *s* luz *f* de gas

gas main *s* cañería de gas

gas mask *s* careta antigás

gas meter *s* contador *m* de gas

gasohol [ˈgæsəˌhɔl] *s* alconafta

gasoline [ˈgæsəˌlin] o [ˌgæsəˈlin] *s* gasolina

gasoline pump *s* poste *m* distribuidor *m* de gasolina, surtidor *m* de gasolina

gasp [gæsp] *s* respiración entrecortada; (*of death*) boqueada ‖ *tr* decir con voz entrecortada ‖ *intr* boquear

gas producer *s* gasógeno

gas range *s* cocina a gas

gas station *s* estación gasolinera

gas stove *s* cocina a gas

gas tank *s* gasómetro; **(aut) depósito** de gasolina

gastric [ˈgæstrɪk] *adj* gástrico

gastronomy [gæsˈtrɑnəmi] *s* gastronomía

gas'works' *s* fábrica de gas

gate [get] *s* puerta; (*in fence or wall; of bird cage*) portillo; (*of sluice or lock*) compuerta; (*number of people paying admission; amount they pay*) entrada, taquilla; (rr) barrera; (fig) entrada, camino; **to crash the gate** (coll) colarse de gorra

gate'keep'er *s* portero; (rr) guardabarrera *mf*

gate'post' *s* poste *m* de una puerta de cercado

gate'way' *s* entrada, paso, camino

gather [ˈgæðər] *tr* recoger, reunir; recolectar (*la cosecha*); coger (*leña, flores, etc.*); cubrirse de (*polvo*); recoger (*una persona sus pensamientos*); (bb) alzar; (sew) fruncir; (*to deduce*) (fig) calcular, deducir; **to gather oneself together** componerse ‖ *intr* reunirse; amontonarse; saltar (*lágrimas*)

gathering [ˈgæðərɪŋ] *s* reunión; recolección; (bb) alzado; (sew) frunce *m*

gaud•y [ˈgɔdi] *adj* (*comp* **-ier;** *super* **-iest**) cursi, chillón, llamativo

gauge [gedʒ] *s* medida, norma; calibre *m;* (*of liquid in a container*) nivel *m;* (*of carpenter*) gramil *m;* (*of gasoline*) medidor *m;* (rr) ancho de vía, entrevía ‖ *tr* medir; calibrar; graduar; aforar (*la cantidad de agua de una coriente*); arquear (*una nave*)

gauge glass *s* tubo indicador, vidrio de nivel

Gaul [gɔl] *s* la Galia; (*native*) galo

Gaulish [ˈgɔlɪʃ] *adj* & *s* galo

gaunt [gɔnt] o [gɑnt] *adj* desvaído, macilento; hosco, tétrico

gauntlet [ˈgɔntlɪt] o [ˈgɑntlɪt] *s* guantelete *m;* guante con puño abocinado; carrera de baquetas; (rr) vía traslapada; **to run the gauntlet** correr baquetas, pasar por baquetas; **to take up the gauntlet** recoger el guante; **to throw down the gauntlet** arrojar el guante

gauze [gɔz] *s* gasa, cendal *m*

gavel [ˈgævəl] *s* mazo, martillo

gavotte [gəˈvɑt] *s* gavota

gawk [gɔk] *s* (coll) palurdo, papanatas *m* ‖ *intr* (coll) mirar de modo impertinente; papar moscas, mirar embobado

gawk•y [ˈgɔki] *adj* (*comp* **-ier;** *super* **-iest**) desgarbado, torpe, bobo

gay [ge] *adj* homosexual; alegre, festivo; (*brilliant*) vistoso; amigo de los placeres

gaye•ty [ˈge•ɪti] *s* var de **gaiety**

gaze [gez] *s* mirada fija ‖ *intr* mirar fijamente

gazelle [gəˈzɛl] *s* gacela

gazette [gəˈzɛt] *s* periódico; anuncio oficial

gazetteer [ˌgæzəˈtɪr] *s* diccionario geográfico

gear [gɪr] *s* pertrechos, utensilios; (*of transmission, steering, etc.*) mecanismo, aparato; rueda dentada; (*two or more toothed wheels meshed together*) engranaje *m;* **out of gear** desengranado; (fig) descompuesto; **to throw into gear** engranar; **to throw out**

of **gear** desengranar; (fig) descomponer || *tr & intr* engranar
gear'box' *s* caja de engranajes; (aut) caja de velocidades
gear case *s* caja de engranajes
gear'shift' *s* cambio de marchas, cambio de velocidades
gearshift lever *s* palanca de cambio de marchas
gear'wheel' *s* rueda dentada
gee [dʒi] *interj* ¡caramba!; **gee up!** (*get up!, said to a horse*) ¡arre!; **geez!** ¡mecachis!
Gehenna [gɪ'hɛnə] *s* gehena *m*
Geiger counter ['gaɪgər] *s* contador *m* de Geiger
gel [dʒɛl] *s* gel *m* || *v* (*pret & pp* **gelled;** *ger* **gelling**) *intr* cuajarse en forma de gel
gelatine ['dʒɛlətɪn] *s* gelatina
geld [gɛld] *v* (*pret & pp* **gelded** o **gelt** [gɛlt]) *tr* castrar
gem [dʒɛm] *s* gema, piedra preciosa; (fig) joya, preciosidad
Gemini ['dʒɛmɪ,naɪ] *s* (*constellation*) Géminis *m* o Gemelos; (*sign of zodiac*) Géminis *m*
gen. *abbr* **gender, general, genitive, genus**
gender ['dʒɛndər] *s* (gram) género; (coll) sexo
genealo•gy [,dʒɛnɪ'ælədʒi] *s* (*pl* **-gies**) genealogía
general ['dʒɛnərəl] *adj & s* general *m;* **general of the army** capitán general de ejército; **in general** en general o por lo general
general delivery *s* lista de correos
generalissi•mo [,dʒɛnərə'lɪsɪmo] *s* (*pl* **-mos**) generalísimo
generali•ty [,dʒɛnə'rælɪti] *s* (*pl* **-ties**) generalidad
generalize ['dʒɛnərə'laɪz] *tr & intr* generalizar
generally ['dʒɛnərəli] *adv* por lo general
general medicine *s* medicina general
general practitioner *s* médico general
generalship ['dʒɛnərəl,ʃɪp] *s* generalato; don *m* de mando
general staff *s* estado mayor general
general strike *s* huelga general
generate ['dʒɛnə,ret] *tr* (*to beget*) engendrar; generar (*electricidad*); (geom) engendrar
generating station *s* central *f*
generation ['dʒɛnə'reʃən] *s* generación
generator ['dʒɛnə,retər] *s* generador *m*
generic [dʒɪ'nɛrɪk] *adj* genérico
generous ['dʒɛnərəs] *adj* generoso; abundante, grande
gene•sis ['dʒɛnɪsɪs] *s* (*pl* **-ses** [,siz]) génesis *f* || **Genesis** *s* (Bib) el Génesis
genetic [dʒɪ'nɛtɪk] *adj* genético
genetic engineering *s* ingeniería genética
genetics [dʒɪ'nɛtɪks] *s* genética
Geneva [dʒɪ'nivə] *s* Ginebra
Genevan [dʒɪ'nivən] *adj & s* ginebrino
genial ['dʒinɪ•əl] *adj* afable, complaciente
genie ['dʒini] *s* genio
genital ['dʒɛnɪtəl] *adj* genital || **genitals** *spl* genitales *mpl*, órganos genitales
genitive ['dʒɛnɪtɪv] *adj & s* genitivo
genitourinary [,dʒɛnəto'jʊrɪ,nɛrɪ] *adj* genitourinario
genius ['dʒinjəs] o ['dʒinɪ•əs] *s* (*pl* **geniuses**) (*great inventive gift; person possessing it*) genio || *s* (*pl* **genii** ['dʒinɪ,aɪ]) (*guardian spirit; pagan deity*) genio
Genoa ['dʒɛno•ə] *s* Génova
genocidal [,dʒɛnə'saɪdəl] *adj* genocida
genocide ['dʒɛnə'saɪd] *s* (*act*) genocidio; (*person*) genocida *mf*
Geno•ese [,dʒɛno'iz] *adj* genovés || *s* (*pl* **-ese**) genovés *m*
genre ['ʒɑnrə] *adj* de género
gent. o **Gent.** *abbr* **gentleman, gentlemen**
genteel [dʒɛn'til] *adj* gentil, elegante; cortés, urbano
gentian ['dʒɛnʃən] *s* genciana
gentile ['dʒɛntɪl] o ['dʒɛntaɪl] *adj* gentilicio; (gram) gentilicio || ['dʒɛntaɪl] *adj & s* no judío; cristiano; (*pagan*) gentil *mf*
gentili•ty [dʒɛn'tɪlɪti] *s* (*pl* **-ties**) gentileza
gentle ['dʒɛntəl] *adj* apacible, benévolo; dulce, manso, suave; cortés, fino; (*e.g., tap on the shoulder*) ligero
gen'tle•folk' *s* gente bien nacida
gentle•man ['dʒɛntəlmən] *s* (*pl* **-men** [mən]) *s* caballero; (*attendant to a person of high rank*) gentilhombre *m*
gentleman in waiting *s* gentilhombre *m* de cámara
gentlemanly ['dʒɛntəlmənli] *adj* caballeroso
gentleman of leisure *s* señor *m* que vive sin trabajar, caballero de vida holgada
gentleman of the road *s* salteador *m* de caminos
gentleman's agreement *s* acuerdo verbal
gentle sex *s* bello sexo, sexo débil
gentry ['dʒɛntri] *s* gente bien nacida
genuine ['dʒɛnjʊ•ɪn] *adj* genuino; sincero, franco
genus ['dʒinəs] *s* (*pl* **genera** ['dʒɛnərə] o **genuses**) (biol, log) género
geog. *abbr* **geography**
geographer [dʒɪ'ɑgrəfər] *s* geógrafo
geographic(al) [,dʒi•ə'græfɪk(əl)] *adj* geográfico
geogra•phy [dʒɪ'ɑgrəfi] *s* (*pl* **-phies**) geografía
geol. *abbr* **geology**
geologic(al) [,dʒi•ə'lɑdʒɪk(əl)] *adj* geológico
geologist [dʒɪ'ɑlədʒɪst] *s* geólogo
geology [dʒɪ'ɑlədʒi] *s* (*pl* **-gies**) geología
geom. *abbr* **geometry**
geometric(al) [,dʒi•ə'mɛtrɪk(əl)] *adj* geométrico
geometrician [dʒɪ,ɑmɪ'trɪʃən] *s* geómetra *mf*
geome•try [dʒɪ'ɑmɪtri] *s* (*pl* **-tries**) geometría
geophysics [,dʒi•ə'fɪzɪks] *s* geofísica
geopolitics [,dʒi•ə'pɑlɪtɪks] *s* geopolítica
George [dʒɔrdʒ] *s* Jorge *m*
geranium [dʒɪ'renɪ•əm] *s* geranio
geriatrical [,dʒɛrɪ'ætrɪkəl] *adj* geriátrico
geriatrician [,dʒɛrɪ•ə'trɪʃən] *s* geriatra *mf*
geriatrics [,dʒɛrɪ'ætrɪks] *s* geriatría
germ [dʒʌrm] *s* germen *m*
German ['dʒʌrmən] *adj & s* alemán *m*

germane [dʒər'men] *adj* pertinente, relacionado
Germanize ['dʒʌrmə,naɪz] *tr* germanizar
German measles *s* rubéola
German silver *s* melchor *m,* alpaca
Germany ['dʒʌrməni] *s* Alemania
germ carrier *s* portador *m* de gérmenes
germ cell *s* célula germen
germicidal [,dʒʌrmɪ'saɪdəl] *adj* germicida
germicide ['dʒʌrmɪ,saɪd] *s* germicida *m*
germinate ['dʒʌrmɪ,net] *intr* germinar
germ plasm *s* germen *m* plasma
germ theory *s* teoría germinal
germ warfare *s* guerra bacteriana, guerra bacteriológica
gerontology [,dʒeran'talədʒi] *s* gerontología
gerund ['dʒerənd] *s* gerundio
gerundive [dʒɪ'rʌndɪv] *s* gerundio adjetivo
gestation [dʒes'teʃən] *s* gestación
gesticulate [dʒes'tɪkjə,let] *intr* accionar, manotear
gesticulation [dʒes,tɪkjə'leʃən] *s* ademán *m,* manoteo
gesture ['dʒestʃər] *s* ademán *m,* gesto; demostración, muestra || *intr* hacer ademanes, hacer gestos
get [get] *v* (*pret* **got** [gat]; *pp* **got** o **gotten** ['gatən]; *ger* **getting**) *tr* conseguir, obtener; recibir; ir por, buscar; tomar (*p.ej., un billete*); alcanzar; encontrar, hallar; hacer (*p.ej., la comida*); resolver (*un problema*); aprender de memoria; captar (*una estación emisora*); **to get across** hacer aceptar; hacer comprender; **to get back** recobrar; **to get down** descolgar; (*to swallow*) tragar; **to get off** quitar (*p.ej., una mancha*); **to get someone to** + *inf* lograr que alguien + *subj;* **to get** + *pp* hacer + *inf;* **to have got** (coll) tener; **to have got to** + *inf* (coll) tener que + *inf* || *intr* (*to become*) hacerse, ponerse, volverse; (*to arrive*) llegar; **get up!** (*to an animal*) ¡arre!; **to get about** estar levantado (*un convaleciente*); **to get along** seguir andando; irse; ir tirando; tener éxito; llevarse bien; **to get along in years** ponerse viejo; **to get along with** congeniar con; **to get angry** enfadarse; **to get around** divulgarse; salir mucho, ir a todas partes; eludir; manejar (*a una persona*); **to get away** conseguir marcharse; evadirse; **to get away with** llevarse, escaparse con; (coll) hacer impunemente; **to get back** volver, regresar; **to get back at** (coll) desquitarse con; **to get behind** quedarse atrás; apoyar, abogar por; **to get by** lograr pasar; (*to manage to shift*) (coll) arreglárselas; **to get going** ponerse en marcha; **to get in** entrar; volver a casa; llegar (*un tren*); **to get in with** llegar a ser amigo de; **to get married** casarse; **to get off** apearse; marcharse; **to get old** envejecer; **to get on** subir; llevarse bien; **to get out** salir, marcharse, divulgarse; **to get out of** bajar de (*un coche*); librarse de; perder (*la paciencia*); **to get out of the way** quitarse de en medio; **to get run over** ser atropellado; **to get through** pasar por entre; terminar; **to get to be** llegar a ser; **to get under way** ponerse en camino; **to get up** levantarse; **to not get over it** (coll) no volver de su asombro
get'a•way' *s* escapatoria, escape *m;* (*of an automobile*) arranque *m*
get'-to•geth'er *s* reunión, tertulia
get'-up' *s* (coll) disposición, presentación; (coll) atavío, traje *m*
gewgaw ['gjugɔ] *adj* cursi, charro, chillón || *s* fruslería, chuchería; adorno, charro
geyser ['gaɪzər] *s* géiser *m* || ['gizər] *s* (Brit) calentador *m* de agua
ghast•ly ['gæstli] o ['gastli] *adj* (*comp* **-lier;** *super* **-liest**) cadavérico, espectral; espantoso, horrible
Ghent [gent] *s* Gante
gherkin ['gʌrkɪn] *s* pepinillo
ghet•to ['geto] *s* (*pl* **-tos**) ghetto
ghost [gost] *s* espectro, fantasma *m;* (telv) fantasma *m;* **not a ghost of a** ni sombra de; **to give up the ghost** entregar el alma, rendir el alma
ghost•ly ['gostli] *adj* (*comp* **-lier;** *super* **-liest**) espectral
ghost story *s* cuento de fantasmas
ghost writer *s* colaborador anónimo, escritor anónimo de obras firmadas por otra persona
ghoul [gul] *s* demonio que se alimenta de cadáveres; ladrón *m* de tumbas; (*person who revels in horrible things*) vampiro
ghoulish ['gulɪʃ] *adj* vampírico, horrible
G.H.Q. *abbr* **General Headquarters**
GI ['dʒi'aɪ] *s* (*pl* **GI's**) (coll) soldado raso (*del ejército norteamericano*)
giant ['dʒaɪ•ənt] *adj & s* gigante *m*
giantess ['dʒaɪ•əntɪs] *s* giganta
gibberish ['dʒɪbərɪʃ] o ['gɪbərɪʃ] *s* guirigay *m*
gibbet ['dʒɪbɪt] *s* horca || *tr* ahorcar; poner a la vergüenza
gibe [dʒaɪb] *s* remoque *m,* mofa || *intr* mofarse; **to gibe at** mofarse de
giblets ['dʒɪblɪts] *spl* menudillos
giddiness ['gɪdɪnɪs] *s* vértigo, vahido; falta de juicio
gid•dy ['gɪdi] *adj* (*comp* **-dier;** *super* **-diest**) vertiginoso; mareado; casquivano, ligero de cascos
Gideon ['gɪdɪ•ən] *s* (Bib) Gedeón *m*
gift [gɪft] *s* regalo; (*natural ability*) don *m,* dote *f,* prenda
gifted ['gɪftɪd] *adj* talentoso; muy inteligente
gift horse *s* **—never look a gift horse in the mouth** a caballo regalado no se le mira el diente
gift of gab *s* (coll) facundia, labia
gift shop *s* comercio de objetos de regalo, tienda de regalos
gift'wrap' *v* (*pret & pp* **-wrapped;** *ger* **-wrapping**) *tr* envolver en paquete regalo
gigantic [dʒaɪ'gæntɪk] *adj* gigantesco
giggle ['gɪgəl] *s* risita, risa ahogada, retozo de la risa || *intr* reírse bobamente

gigo•lo [ˋdʒɪgə ,lo] *s* (*pl* **-los**) acompañante *m* profesional de mujeres; (*man supported by a woman*) mantenido

gild [gɪld] *v* (*pret & pp* **gilded** o **gilt** [gɪlt]) *tr* dorar

gilding [ˋgɪldɪŋ] *s* dorado

gill [gɪl] *s* (*of fish*) agalla; (*of cock*) barba || [dʒɪl] *s* cuarta parte de una pinta

gillyflower [ˋdʒɪlɪ,flaʊ•ər] *s* alhelí *m*

gilt [gɪlt] *adj & s* dorado

gilt-edged [ˋgɪlt,ɛdʒd] *adj* de toda confianza, de lo mejor que hay

gilt'head' *s* dorada

gimcrack [ˋdʒɪm ,kræk] *adj* de oropel || *s* chuchería

gimlet [ˋgɪmlɪt] *s* barrena de mano

gimmick [ˋgɪmɪk] *s* (slang) adminículo; (slang) adminículo mágico

gin [dʒɪn] *s* (*alcoholic liquor*) ginebra; desmotadera de algodón; trampa; (*fish trap*) garlito; torno de izar || *v* (*pret & pp* **ginned;** *ger* **ginning**) *tr* desmotar

gin fizz *s* ginebra con gaseosa

ginger [ˋdʒɪndʒər] *s* jenjibre *m;* (coll) energía, viveza

ginger ale *s* cerveza de jengibre gaseosa

gin'ger•bread' *s* pan *m* de jengibre; adorno charro

gingerly [ˋdʒɪndʒərli] *adj* cauteloso, cuidadoso || *adv* cautelosamente

gin'ger•snap' *s* galletita de jengibre

gingham [ˋgɪŋəm] *s* guinga

giraffe [dʒɪˋræf] *s* jirafa

girandole [ˋdʒɪrən,dol] *s* girándula

gird [gʌrd] *v* (*pret & pp* **girt** [gʌrt] o **girded**) *tr* ceñir; (*to equip*) dotar; (*to prepare*) aprestar; (*to surround, hem in*) rodear, encerrar

girder [ˋgʌrdər] *s* viga, trabe *f*

girdle [ˋgʌrdəl] *s* faja; corsé pequeño || *tr* ceñir; circundar, rodear

girl [gʌrl] *s* muchacha, niña, chica; (*servant*) moza

girl friend *s* (coll) amiguita

girlhood [ˋgʌrlhʊd] *s* muchachez *f;* juventud femenina

girlish [gʌrlɪʃ] *adj* de muchacha; juvenil

girl scout *s* niña exploradora

girth [gʌrθ] *s* (*band*) cincha; (*waistband*) pretina; circunferencia

gist [dʒɪst] *s* esencia

give [gɪv] *s* elasticidad || *v* (*pret* **gave** [gev]; *pp* **given** [ˋgɪvən] *tr* dar; ocasionar (*molestia, trabajo, etc.*); representar (*una obra dramática*); (*lessons*) impartir; pronunciar (*un discurso*); **to give away** dar de balde; revelar; llevar (*a la novia*); (coll) traicionar; **to give back** devolver; **to give forth** despedir (*p.ej. olores*); **to give oneself up** entregarse; **to give up** abandonar, dejar (*un empleo*); renunciar || *intr* dar; dar de sí; romperse (*p.ej., una cuerda*); **to give in** ceder, rendirse; **to give out** agotarse; no poder más; **to give up** darse por vencido

give'-and-take' *s* concesiones mutuas; conversación sazonada de burlas

give'a•way' *s* (coll) revelación involuntaria; (coll) traición; (*e.g., in checkers*) (coll) ganapierde *m & f*

given [ˋgɪvən] *adj* dado; (math) conocido; **given that** dado que, suponiendo que

given name *s* nombre *m* de pila

giver [ˋgɪvər] *s* dador *m*, donador *m*

gizzard [ˋgɪzərd] *s* molleja

glacial [ˋgleʃəl] *adj* glacial

glacier [ˋgleʃər] *s* glaciar *m*, helero

glad [glæd] *adj* (*comp* **gladder;** *super* **gladdest**) alegre, contento; **to be glad (to)** alegrarse (de)

gladden [ˋglædən] *tr* alegrar

glade [gled] *s* claro, claro herboso (*en un bosque*)

glad hand *s* (coll) acogida efusiva

gladiola [,glædɪˋolə] *s* estoque *m*

gladly [ˋglædli] *adv* alegremente; de buena gana, con mucho gusto

gladness [ˋglædnɪs] *s* alegría, regocijo

glad rags *spl* (slang) trapitos de cristianar; (slang) vestido de etiqueta

glamorous [ˋglæmərəs] *adj* fascinador, elegante

glamour [ˋglæmər] *s* fascinación, elegancia, hechizo

glamour girl *s* belleza exótica

glance [glæns] *s* ojeada, vistazo, golpe *m* de vista; **at a glance** de un vistazo; **at first glance** a primera vista || *intr* lanzar una mirada; **to glance at** lanzar una mirada a; examinar de paso; **to glance off** desviarse de soslayo; desviarse de, al chocar; **to glance over** mirar por encima

gland [glænd] *s* glándula

glanders [ˋglændərz] *spl* muermo

glandulous [ˋglændʒələs] *adj* glanduloso

glare [glɛr] *s* fulgor *m* deslumbrante, luz intensa; mirada feroz, mirada de indignación || *intr* relumbrar; lanzar miradas feroces; **to glare at** echar una mirada feroz a

glaring '[ˋglɛrɪŋ] *adj* deslumbrante, relumbrante; (*look*) feroz, penetrante; manifiesto, que salta a la vista

glass [glæs] *s* vidrio, cristal *m;* (*tumbler*) vaso, copa; (*mirror*) espejo; (*glassware*) vajilla de cristal; **glasses** anteojos

glass blower [ˋblo•ər] *s* soplador *m* de vidrio, vidriero

glass case *s* vitrina

glass cutter *s* cortavidrios *m*

glass door *s* puerta vidriera

glassful [ˋglæsfʊl] *s* vaso

glass'house' *s* invernadero; (fig) tejado de vidrio

glassine [glæˋsin] *s* papel *m* cristal

glass'ware' *s* cristalía, vajilla de vidrio

glass wool *s* cristal hilado

glass'works' *s* cristalería vidriería

glass'work'er *s* vidriero

glass•y [ˋglæsi] *adj* (*comp* **-ier;** *super* **-iest**) vidiroso

glaze [glez] *s* vidriado, esmalte *m;* (*of ice*) capa resbaladiza || *tr* vidriar, esmaltar; garapiñar (*golosinas*)

glazier [ˋgleʒər] *s* vidriero

gleam [glim] *s* destello, rayo de luz; luz *f* tenue; (*of hope*) rayo || *intr* destellar; brillar con luz tenue
glean [glin] *tr* espigar; (*to gather bit by bit, e.g., out of books*) espigar
glee [gli] *s* alegría, regocijo
glee club *s* orfeón *m*
glib [glɪb] *adj* (*comp* **glibber;** *super* **glibbest**) locuaz; (*tongue*) suelto; fácil e insincero
glide [glaɪd] *s* deslizamiento; (aer) vuelo sin motor, planeo; (mus) ligadura || *intr* deslizarse; (aer) volar sin motor, planear; **to glide along** pasar suavemente
glider [ˈglaɪdər] *s* (aer) planeador *m*, deslizador *m*
glimmer [ˈglɪmər] *s* luz *f* tenue; (*faint perception*) vislumbre *f* || *intr* brillar con luz tenue; (*to appear faintly*) vislumbrarse
glimmering [ˈglɪmərɪŋ] *adj* tenue, trémulo || *s* luz *f* tenue; vislumbre *f*
glimpse [glɪmps] *s* vislumbre *f;* **to catch a glimpse of** entrever, vislumbrar || *tr* vislumbrar
glint [glɪnt] *s* destello, rayo || *intr* destellar
glisten [ˈglɪsən] *s* centelleo || *intr* centellear
glitter [ˈglɪtər] *s* resplandor *m*, brillo || *intr* resplandecer, brillar
gloaming [ˈglomɪŋ] *s* crepúsculo vespertino
gloat [glot] *intr* relamerse; **to gloat over** mirar con satisfacción maligna
globe [glob] *s* globo
globetrotter [ˈglob,trɑtər] *s* trotamundos *m*
globule [ˈglɑbjʊl] *s* glóbulo
glockenspiel [ˈglɑkən,spil] *s* juego de timbres, órgano de campanas
gloom [glum] *s* lobreguez *f* tinieblas, obscuridad; abatimiento, tristeza; aspecto abatido
gloom•y [ˈglumi] *adj* (*comp* **-ier;** *super* **-iest**) (*dark; sad*) lóbrego; pesimista
glori•fy [ˈglorɪ,faɪ] *v* (*pret & pp* **-fied**) *tr* glorificar; (*to enhance*) realzar
glorious [ˈglorɪ•əs] *adj* glorioso; espléndido, magnífico; (coll) alegre
glo•ry [ˈglori] *s* (*pl* **-ries**) gloria; **to go to glory** ganar la gloria; (slang) fracasar || *v* (*pret & pp* **-ried**) *intr* gloriarse
gloss [glɑs] *s* brillo, lustre *m;* (*note, commentary*) glosa; glosario || *tr* (*to annotate*) glosar; lustrar, satinar; **to gloss over** disculpar, paliar
glossa•ry [ˈglɑsəri] *s* (*pl* **-ries**) glosario
gloss•y [ˈglɑsi] *adj* (*comp* **-ier;** *super* **-iest**) brillante, lustroso; (*silk*) joyante
glottal [ˈglɑtəl] *adj* glótico
glove [glʌv] *s* guante *m*
glove compartment *s* portaguantes *m*
glove stretcher *s* ensanchador *m*, *juanas*
glow [glo] *s* (*light of incandescence*) resplandor *m;* (*e.g., of sunset*) brillo, esplendor *m;* sensación de calor; color *m* en las mejillas || *intr* brillar sin llama; estar encendido (*el rostro, el cielo*); estar muy animado
glower [ˈglaʊ•ər] *s* ceño, mirada ceñuda || *intr* mirar con ceño
glowing [ˈglo•ɪŋ] *adj* ardiente, encendido; radiante; entusiasta, elogioso
glow'worm' *s* gusano de luz, luciérnaga
glucose [ˈglukos] *s* glucosa
glue [glu] *s* cola; pegapega || *tr* encolar; pegar fuertemente
glue pot *s* cazo de cola
gluey [ˈglu•i] *adj* (*comp* **gluier;** *super* **gluiest**) pegajoso; (*smeared with glue*) encolado
glug [glʌg] *s* gluglú *m* || *v* (*pret & pp* **glugged;** *ger* **glugging**) *intr* hacer gluglú (*el agua*)
glum [glʌm] *adj* (*comp* **glummer;** *super* **glummest**) hosco
glut [glʌt] *s* abundancia, gran acopio; exceso; **to be a glut on the market** abarrotarse || *v* (*pret & pp* **glutted;** *ger* **glutting**) *tr* hartar, saciar; inundar (*el mercado*); obstruir
glutton [ˈglʌtən] *adj & s* glotón *m*
gluttonous [ˈglʌtənəs] *adj* glotón
glutton•y [ˈglʌtəni] *s* (*pl* **-ies**) glotonería, gula
glycerine [ˈglɪsərɪn] *s* glicerina
G.M. *abbr* **general manager, Grand Master**
G-man [ˈdʒi,mæn] *s* (*pl* **-men** [,mɛn]) (coll) agente *m* de la policía federal
G.M.T. *abbr* **Greenwich mean time**
gnarl [nɑrl] *s* nudo || *tr* torcer || *intr* gruñir
gnarled [nɑrld] *adj* nudoso, retorcido
gnash [næʃ] *tr* hacer rechinar (*los dientes*) || *intr* hacer rechinar los dientes
gnat [næt] *s* jején *m*
gnaw [nɔ] *tr* roer; practicar (*un agujero*) royendo
gnome [nom] *s* gnomo
go [go] *s* (*pl* **goes**) ida; (coll) energía, ímpetu *m;* (coll) boga; (coll) ensayo; (*for traffic*) paso libre; **it's a go** (coll) es un trato hecho; **it's all the go** (coll) hace furor; **it's no go** (coll) es imposible; **on the go** (coll) en continuo movimiento; **to make a go of** (coll) lograr éxito en || *v* (*pret* **went** [wɛnt]; *pp* **gone** [gɔn] o [gɑn]) *tr* (coll) soportar, tolerar; **to go it alone** obrar sin ayuda || *intr* ir; (*to work, operate*) funcionar, marchar; andar (*p.ej., desnudo*); volverse (*p.ej., loco);* **going, going, gone!** ¡vendo, vendo, vendí!; **so it goes** así va el mundo; **to be going to** + *inf* ir a + *inf;* **to be gone** haber ido; haberse agotado; haber dejado de ser; **to go against** ir en contra de; **to go ahead** seguir adelante; **to go away** irse, marcharse; **to go back** volver; **to go by** pasar por; guiarse por; atenerse a; **to go down** bajar; hundirse (*un buque*); **to go fishing** ir de pesca; **to go for** ir por; **to go get** ir por, ir a buscar; **to go house hunting** ir a buscar casa; **to go hunting** ir de caza; **to go in** entrar; entrar en; (*to fit in*) caber en; **to go in for** dedicarse a, interesarse por; **to go into** entrar en; investigar; (aut) poner (*p.ej., primera*); **to go in with** asociarse con; **to go off** irse, marcharse; llevarse a cabo; estallar (*p.ej., una bomba*); dispararse (*un fusil*); **to go on** seguir adelante; ir tirando; **to go on** + *ger* seguir + *ger;* **to go on with** continuar; **to**

go out salir; pasar de moda; apagarse (*un fuego, una luz*); declararse en huelga; (*for entertainment, etc.*) salir; **to go over** tener éxito; releer; examinar, revisar; pasar por encima de; **to go over to** pasarse a las filas de; **to go through** pasar por; llegar al fin de; agotar (*una fortuna*); **to go with** ir con, acompañar; salir con (*una muchacha*); hacer juego con; **to go without** andarse sin, pasarse sin
goad [god] *s* aguijada, aguijón *m* || *tr* aguijonear; (SAm) espuelar
go'-a•head' *adj* (coll) emprendedor || *s* (coll) señal *f* para seguir adelante, luz *f* verde
goal [gol] *s* meta; (*in football*) gol *m*
goal'keep'er *s* guardameta *m*, portero
goal line *s* raya de la meta
goal post *s* poste *m* de la meta
goat [got] *s* cabra; (*male goat*) macho cabrío; (coll) víctima inocente; **to be the goat** (slang) pagar el pato; **to get the goat of** (slang) tomar el pelo a; **to ride the goat** (coll) ser iniciado en una sociedad secreta
goatee (go'ti] *s* perilla
goat'herd' *s* cabrero
goat'skin' *s* piel *f* de cabra
goat'suck'er *s* chotacabras *m*
gob [gɑb] *s* (coll) masa informe y pequeña; (coll) marinero de guerra
gobble ['gɑbəl] *s* gluglú *m* || *tr* engullir; **to gobble up** engullirse ávidamente; (coll) asir de repente, apoderarse ávidamente de || *intr* engullir; gluglutear, gorgonear (*el pavo*)
gobbledegook ['gɑbəldɪ,gʊk] *s* (coll) lenguaje obscuro e incomprehensible, galimatías *m*
go'-be•tween' *s* (*intermediary*) medianero; (*in promoting marriages*) casamentero; (*in shady love affairs*) alcahuete *m*, alcahueta
goblet ['gɑblɪt] *s* copa
goblin ['gɑblɪn] *s* duende *m*, trasgo
go'-by' *s* (coll) desaire *m*; **to give someone the go-by** (coll) negarse al trato de alguien
go'cart' *s* andaderas; cochecito para niños; carruaje ligero
god [gɑd] *s* dios *m*; **God forbid** no lo quiera Dios; **God grant** permita Dios; **God willing** Dios mediante
god'child' *s* (*pl* **chil'dren**) ahijado, ahijada
god'daugh'ter *s* ahijada
goddess ['gɑdɪs] *s* diosa
god'fa'ther *s* padrino
God'-fear'ing *adj* timorato; devoto, pío
God'for•sak'en *adj* dejado de la mano de Dios; (coll) desolado, desierto
god'head' *s* divinidad || **Godhead** *s* Dios *m*
godless ['gɑdlɪs] *adj* infiel, impío; desalmado, malvado
god•ly ['gɑdli] *adj* (*comp* **-lier;** *super* **-liest**) devoto, pío
god'moth'er *s* madrina
God's acre *s* campo santo
god'send' *s* cosa llovida del cielo, bendición
god'son' *s* ahijado
God'speed' *s* bienandanza, buena suerte, buen viaje *m*
go'-get'ter *s* (slang) buscavidas *mf*, persona emprendedora
goggle ['gɑgəl] *intr* volver los ojos; abrir los ojos desmesuradamente
goggle-eyed ['gɑgəl,aɪd] *adj* de ojos saltones
goggles ['gɑgəlz] *spl* anteojos de camino, gafas contra el polvo
going ['go•ɪŋ] *adj* en marcha, funcionando; **going on** casi, p.ej., **it is going on nine o'clock** son casi las nueve || *s* ida, partida
going concern *s* empresa que marcha
goings on *spl* actividades; bulla, jarana
goiter ['gɔɪtər] *s* bocio
gold [gold] *adj* áureo, de oro; dorado || *s* oro
gold'beat'er *s* batidor *m* de oro, batihoja *m*
goldbeater's skin *s* venza
gold brick *s* — **to sell a gold brick** (coll) vender gato por liebre
gold'crest' *s* reyezuelo moñudo
gold digger ['dɪgər] *s* (slang) extractora de oro
golden ['goldən] *adj* áureo, de oro; (*gilt*) dorado; (*hair*) rubio; excelente, favorable, floreciente
golden age *s* edad de oro, siglo de oro
golden calf *s* becerro de oro
Golden Fleece *s* vellocino de oro
golden mean *s* justo medio
golden plover *s* chorlito
gold'en•rod' *s* vara de oro, vara de San José
golden rule *s* regla de la caridad cristiana
golden wedding *s* bodas de oro
gold-filled ['gold,fɪld] *adj* empastado en oro
gold'finch' *s* jilguero, pintacilgo
gold'fish' *s* carpa dorada, pez *m* de color
goldilocks ['goldɪ ,lɑks] *s* rubiales *mf*
gold leaf *s* pan *m* de oro
gold mine *s* mina de oro; **to strike a gold mine** (fig) encontrar una mina
gold plate *s* vajilla de oro
gold'-plate' *tr* dorar
gold'smith' *s* orfebre *m*
gold standard *s* patrón *m* oro
golf [gɑlf] *s* golf *m* || *intr* jugar al golf
golf club *s* palo de golf; asociación de jugadores de golf
golfer ['gɑlfər] *s* golfista *mf*
golf links *spl* campo de golf
Golgotha ['gɑlgəθə] *s* el Gólgota
gondola ['gɑndələ] *s* góndola
gondolier [,gɑndə'lɪr] *s* gondolero
gone [gɔn] o [gɑn] *adj* agotado; arruinado; desaparecido; muerto; **gone on** (coll) enamorado de
gong [gɔŋ] o [gɑŋ] *s* batintín *m*
gonorrhea [,gɑnə'ri•ə] *s* gonorrea
goo [gu] *s* (slang) substancia pegajosa
good [gʊd] *adj* (*comp* **better;** *super* **best**) bueno; **good and . . .** (coll) muy, p.ej., **good and cheap** muy barato; **good for** bueno para; capaz de hacer; capaz de pagar; capaz de vivir (*cierto tiempo*); **to be good at** tener talento para; **to be no good** (coll) no servir para nada; (coll) ser un perdido; **to make good** tener éxito; cumplir (*sus promesas*); pagar (*una deuda*); responder de (*los daños*) || *s* bien *m*, prove-

cho, utilidad; **for good** para siempre; **for good and all** de una vez para siempre; **goods** efectos; géneros, mercancías; **the good** lo bueno; los buenos; **to catch with the goods** (slang) coger en flagrante; **to deliver the goods** (slang) cumplir lo prometido; **to do good** hacer el bien; dar salud o fuerzas a; **to the good** de sobra, en el haber; **what is the good of . . . ?** ¿para qué sirve . . . ?

good afternoon *s* buenas tardes

good'by' o **good'bye'***s* adiós *m* || *interj* ¡adiós!

good day *s* buenos días

good evening *s* buenas noches, buenas tardes

good fellow *s* (coll) buen chico, buen sujeto

good fellowship *s* compañerismo

good'-for-noth'ing *adj* inútil, sin valor || *s* pelafustán *m* perdido

Good Friday *s* Viernes santo

good graces *spl* favor *m,* estimación

good-hearted [ˋgʊdˋhɑrtɪd] *adj* de buen corazón

good-humored [ˋgʊdˋjumərd] *adj* de buen humor; afable

good-looking [ˋgʊdˋlʊkɪŋ] *adj* guapo, bien parecido

good looks *spl* hermosura, guapeza

good•ly [ˋgʊdli] *adj* (*comp* **-lier;** *super* **-liest**) considerable; bien parecido, hermoso; bueno, excelente

good morning *s* buenos días

good-natured [ˈgʊdˋnetʃərd] *adj* bonachón, afable

Good Neighbor Policy *s* política del buen vecino

goodness [ˋgʊdnɪs] *s* bondad; **for goodness' sake!** ¡por Dios!; **goodness knows!** ¡quién sabe! || *interj* ¡válgame Dios!

good night *s* buenas noches

good sense *s* buen sentido, sensatez *f*

good-sized [ˋgʊdˋsaɪzd] *adj* bastante grande, de buen tamaño

good speed *s* adiós *m* y buena suerte

good-tempered [ˋgʊdˋtɛmpərd] *adj* de natural apacible

good time *s* rato agradable; **to have a good time** divertirse; **to make good time** ir a buen paso; llegar en poco tiempo

good turn *s* favor *m,* servicio

good way *s* buen trecho

good will *s* buena voluntad; (com) buen nombre *m,* clientela

good•y [ˋgʊdi] *adj* (coll) beatuco, santurrón || *s* (*pl* **-ies**) (coll) golosina || *interj* (coll) ¡qué bien!, ¡qué alegría!

gooey [ˋgu•i] *adj* (*comp* **gooier;** *super* **gooiest**) (slang) pegajoso, fangoso

goof [guf] *s* (slang) tonto || *tr & intr* (slang) chapucear || *intr* — **to goof off** farrear

goof•y [ˋgufi] *adj* (*comp* **-ier;** *super* **-iest**) (slang) tonto, mentecato

goon (gun] *s* (*roughneck*) (coll) gamberro, canalla *m*; (coll) terrorista *m* de alquiler; (slang) estúpido

goose [gus] *s* (*pl* **geese** [gis] ánsar *m,* ganso, oca; **the goose hangs high** todo va a pedir de boca; **to cook one's goose** malbaratarle a uno los planes; **to kill the goose that lays the golden eggs** matar la gallina de los huevos de oro || *s* (*pl* **gooses**) plancha de sastre

goose'ber'ry *s* (*pl* **-ries**) (*plant*) grosellero silvestre; (*fruit*) grosella silvestre

goose egg *s* huevo de oca; (slang) cero

goose flesh *s* carne *f* de gallina

goose'neck' *s* cuello de cisne; (naut) gancho de botalones

goose pimples *spl* carne *f* de gallina

goose step *s* (mil) paso de ganso

G.O.P. *abbr* **Grand Old Party**

gopher [ˋgofər] *s* ardilla de tierra, ardillón *m;* (*Geomys*) tuza

Gordian knot [ˋgɔrdɪ•ən] *s* nudo gordiano; **to cut the Gordian knot** cortar el nudo gordiano

gore [gor] *s* sangre derramada, sangre cuajada; (*insert in a piece of cloth*) cuchillo, nesga || *tr* (*to pierce with a horn*) acornar; poner cuchillo o nesga a; nesgar

gorge [gɔrdʒ] *s* garganta, desfiladero; (*in a river*) atasco de hielo || *tr* atiborrar || *intr* atiborrarse

gorgeous [ˋgɔrdʒəs] *adj* primoroso, brillante, magnífico, suntuoso

gorilla [gəˋrɪlə] *s* gorila

gorse [gɔrs] *s* aulaga

gor•y [ˋgori] *adj* (*comp* **-ier;** *super* **-iest**) ensangrentado, sangriento

gosh [gɑʃ] *interj* ¡caramba!

goshawk [ˋgɑs,hɔk] *s* azor *m*

gospel [ˋgɑspəl] *s* evangelio || **Gospel** *s* Evangelio

gospel truth *s* evangelio, pura verdad

gossamer [ˋgɑsəmər] *s* telaraña flotante; gasa sutilísima; tela impermeable muy delgada; impermeable *m* de tela muy delgada

gossip [ˋgɑsɪp] *s* chismes *m;* (*person*) chismoso, bocaza; **piece of gossip** chisme *m* || *intr* chismear

gossip column *s* mentidero

gossip columnist *s* gacetillero, cronista *mf* social

gossipy [ˋgɑsɪpɪ] *adj* chismoso

Goth [gɑθ] *s* godo; (fig) bárbaro

Gothic [ˋgɑθɪk] *adj & s* gótico

gouge [gaʊdʒ] *s* gubia; (*cut made with a gouge*) muesca; (coll) estafa || *tr* excavar con gubia; (coll) estafar

goulash [ˋgulɑʃ] *s* puchero húngaro

gourd [gord] o [gʊrd] *s* calabaza

gourmand [ˋgʊrmənd] *s* gastrónomo; glotón *m,* goloso

gourmet [ˋgʊrme] *s* gastrónomo delicado

gout [gaʊt] *s* gota

gout•y [gaʊti] *adj* (*comp* **-ier;** *super* **-iest**) gotoso

gov. *abbr* **governor, government**

govern [ˋgʌvərn] *tr* gobernar; (gram) regir || *intr* gobernar

governess [ˋgʌvərnɪs] *s* aya, institutriz *f*

government [ˋgʌvərnmənt] *s* gobierno; (gram) régimen *m*

governmental [,gʌvərn'mɛntəl] *adj* gubernamental, gubernativo
government in exile *s* gobierno exilado
governor ['gʌvərnər] *s* gobernador *m;* (*of a jail, castle, etc.*) alcaide *m;* (mach) regulador *m*
governorship ['gʌvərnər,ʃɪp] *s* gobierno
govt. *abbr* **government**
gown [gaʊn] *s* (*of a woman*) vestido; (*of a professor, judge, etc.*) toga; (*of a priest*) traje *m* talar; (*dressing gown*) bata, peinador *m;* (nightgown) camisa de dormir
G.P.O. *abbr* **General Post Office, Government Printing Office**
gr. *abbr* **gram, grams, grain, grains, gross**
grab [græb] *s* asimiento, presa; (coll) robo ‖ *v* (*pret & pp* **grabbed**; *ger* **grabbing**) *tr* asir, agarrar; arrebatar ‖ *intr* — **to grab at** tratar de asir
grace [gres] *s* (*charm; favor; pardon*) gracia; (*prayer at table*) benedícite *m;* (*extension of time*) demora; **to be in the good graces of** gozar del favor de; **to say grace** rezar el benedícite; **with good grace** de buen talante ‖ *tr* adornar, engalanar; favorecer
graceful ['gresfəl] *adj* agraciado, gracioso
grace note *s* apoyatura, nota de adorno
gracious ['greʃəs] *adj* graciable, gracioso; misericordioso ‖ *interj* ¡válgame Dios!
grackle ['grækəl] *s* (*myna*) estornino de los pastores; (*purple grackle*) quiscal *m*
grad. *abbr* **graduate**
gradation [gre'deʃən] *s* (*gradual change*) paso gradual; (*arrangement in grades*) graduación; (*step in a series*) paso, grado
grade [gred] *s* grado; (*slope*) pendiente *f;* (*mark for work in class*) calificación, nota; **to make the grade** lograr subir la cuesta; vencer los obstáculos ‖ *tr* graduar, calificar; dar nota a (*un alumno*); explanar, nivelar
grade crossing *s* (rr) paso a nivel, cruce *m* a nivel
grade school *s* escuela elemental
gradient ['gredɪ•ənt] *adj* pendiente ‖ *s* pendiente *f;* (phys) gradiente *m*
gradual ['grædʒʊ•əl] *adj* paulatino
gradually [grædʒʊ•əli] *adv* paulatinamente, gradualmente, poco a poco
graduate ['grædʒʊ•ɪt] *adj* graduado ‖ *s* graduado; (*candidate for a degree*) graduando; vasija graduada ‖ ['grædʒʊ,et] *tr* graduar ‖ *intr* graduarse
graduate school *s* facultad de altos estudios
graduate student *s* estudiante graduado
graduate work *s* altos estudios
graduation [,grædʒʊ'eʃən] *s* graduación, ceremonia de graduación
graft [græft] *s* (hort & surg) injerto; (coll) soborno político, ganancia ilegal ‖ *tr & intr* (hort & surg) injertar; (coll) malversar
graham bread ['gre•əm] *s* pan *m* integral
graham flour *s* harina de trigo sin cerner
grain [gren] *s* (*small seed; tiny particle of sand, etc.; small unit of weight*) grano; (*cereal seeds*) granos; (*in stone*) vena; (*in wood*) fibra; **against the grain** a contrapelo ‖ *tr* granear (*la pólvora; una piedra litográfica*); crispir, vetear (*la madera*); granular (*una piel*)
grain elevator *s* elevador *m* de granos; (*tall building where grain is stored*) depósito de cereales
grain'field' *s* sembrado
graining ['grenɪŋ] *s* veteado
gram [græm] *s* gramo
grammar ['græmər] *s* gramática
grammarian [grə'mɛrɪ•ən] *s* gramático
grammar school *s* escuela pública elemental
grammatical [grə'mætɪkəl] *adj* gramático
gramophone ['græmə,fon] *s* (trademark) gramófono
grana•ry ['grænəri] *s* (*pl* **-ries**) granero
grand [grænd] *adj* espléndido, grandioso; importante, principal
grand'aunt' *s* tía abuela
grand'child' *s* (*pl* **chil'dren**) nieto, nieta
grand'daugh'ter *s* nieta
grand duchess *s* gran duquesa
grand duchy *s* gran ducado
grand duke *s* gran duque *m*
grandee [græn'di] *s* grande *m* de España
grandeur ['grændʒər] o ['grændʒʊr] *s* grandeza, magnificencia
grand'fa'ther *s* abuelo; (*forefather*) antepasado
grandfather's clock *s* reloj *m* de caja
grandiose ['grændɪ,os] *adj* grandioso; hinchado, pomposo
grand jury *s* jurado de acusación
grand larceny *s* hurto mayor
grand lodge *s* gran oriente *m*
grandma ['grænd ,mɑ], ['græm ,mɑ], o ['græmə] *s* (coll) abuela, abuelita
grand'moth'er *s* abuela
grand'neph'ew *s* resobrino
grand'niece *s* resobrina
grand opera *s* ópera seria
grandpa ['grænd,pɑ], ['græn,pɑ], o ['græmpə] *s* (coll) abuelo, abuelito
grand'par'ent *s* abuelo, abuela
grand piano *s* piano de cola
grand slam *s* (bridge) bola
grand'son' *s* nieto
grand'stand' *s* gradería cubierta, tribuna
grand strategy *s* alta estrategia
grand total *s* gran total *m*, suma de totales
grand'un'cle *s* tío abuelo
grand vizier *s* gran visir *m*
grange [grendʒ] *s* (*farm with barns, etc.*) granja; (*organization of farmers*) cámara agrícola
granite ['grænɪt] *s* granito
grant [grænt] o [grɑnt] *s* concesión; donación, subvención; traspaso de propiedad ‖ *tr* conceder; dar (*permiso, perdón*); transferir (*bienes inmuebles*); **to take for granted** dar por sentado; tratar con indiferencia
grantee [græn'ti] o [grɑn'ti] *s* cesionario
grant'-in-aid' *s* (*pl* **grants-in-aid**) subvención concedida por el gobierno para obras de utilidad pública; pensión para estimular

conocimientos científicos, literarios, artísticos
grantor [græn'tɔr] or [grɑn'tɔr] *s* cesionista *mf,* otorgante *mf*
grant winner *s* bequista *mf* (CAm, Cuba)
granular ['grænjələr] *adj* granular
granulate ['grænjə,let] *tr* granular || *intr* granularse
granule ['grænjʊl] *s* gránulo
grape [grep] *s* (*fruit*) uva; (*vine*) vid *f*
grape arbor *s* parral *m*
grape'fruit' *s* (*fruit*) toronja; (*tree*) toronjo
grape hyacinth *s* sueldacostilla
grape juice *s* zumo de uva
grape'shot' *s* metralla
grape'vine' *s* vid *f,* parra; **by the grapevine** por vías secretas, por vías misteriosas
graph [græf] *s* (*diagram*) gráfica; (gram) grafía
graphic(al) ['græfɪk(əl)] *adj* gráfico
graphite ['græfaɪt] *s* grafito
graph paper *s* papel cuadriculado
grapnel ['græpnəl] *s* rebañadera; (*anchor*) rezón *m*
grapple ['græpəl] *s* asimiento, presa; lucha cuerpo a cuerpo || *tr* asir, agarrar || *intr* agarrarse; luchar a brazo partido; **to grapple with** luchar a brazo partido con; tratar de resolver
grappling iron *s* arpeo
grasp [græsp] *s* asimiento; (*power, reach*) poder *m,* alcance *m;* (fig) comprensión; **to have a good grasp of** saber a fondo; **within the grasp of** al alcance de || *tr* (*with hand*) empuñar; (*to get control of*) apoderarse de; (fig) comprender || *intr* — **to grasp at** tratar de asir; aceptar con avidez
grasping ['græspɪŋ] *adj* avaro, codicioso
grass ['græs] *s* hierba; (*pasture land*) pasto; (*lawn*) césped *m;* **to go to grass** ir a pacer; disfrutar de una temporada de descanso; gastarse, arruinarse; morir; **to not let the grass grow under one's feet** no dormirse en las pajas
grass court *s* cancha de césped
grass'hop'per *s* saltamontes *m*
grass pea *s* almorta, guija
grass'-roots' *adj* de la gente común
grass seed *s* semilla de césped
grass widow *s* viuda de paja, viuda de marido vivo
grass•y ['græsi] *adj* (*comp* **-ier;** *super* **-iest**) herboso
grate [gret] *s* (*at a window*) reja; (*for cooking*) parrilla || *tr* (*to put a grate on*) enrejar; rallar (*p.ej., queso*) || *intr* crujir, rechinar; **to grate on** (fig) rallar
grateful ['gretfəl] *adj* agradecido; (*pleasing*) agradable
grater ['gretər] *s* rallador *m*
grati•fy ['grætɪ,faɪ] *v* (*pret & pp* **-fied**) *tr* complacer, gratificar
gratifying ['grætɪ,faɪ•ɪŋ] *adj* grato, satisfactorio
grating ['gretɪŋ] *adj* áspero, irritante; (*sound*) chirriante || *s* enrejado
gratis ['gretɪs] o ['grætɪs] *adj* gracioso, gratuito || *adv* gratis, de balde
gratitude ['grætɪ,tjud] *s* gratitud, reconocimiento
gratuitous [grə'tju•ɪtəs] o [grə'tu•ɪtəs] *adj* gratuito
gratui•ty [grə'tju•ɪti] *s* (*pl* **-ties**) propina; feria (CAm, Mex)
grave [grev] *adj* (*serious, dangerous; important*) grave; solemne; (*sound; accent*) grave || *s* sepulcro, sepultura; **to have one foot in the grave** estar con un pie en la sepultura
gravedigger ['grev ,dɪgər] *s* enterrador *m,* sepulturero, entierramuertos *m*
gravel ['grævəl] *s* grava, cascajo
graven image ['grevən] *s* ídolo
grave'stone' *s* lápida sepulcral
grave'yard' *s* camposanto
gravitate ['grævɪ,tet] *intr* gravitar; ser atraído
gravitation [,grævɪ'teʃən] *s* gravitación
gravi•ty ['grævɪti] *s* (*pl* **-ties**) gravedad
gravure [grə'vjʊr] *s* fotograbado
gra•vy ['grevi] *s* (*pl* **-vies**) (*juice from cooking meat*) jugo; (*sauce made with this juice*) salsa; (slang) ganga, breva
gravy dish *s* salsera
gray [gre] *adj* gris; (*gray-haired*) cano, canoso || *s* gris *m;* traje *m* gris || *intr* encanecer
gray'beard' *s* anciano, viejo
gray-haired ['gre,hɛrd] *adj* canoso
gray'hound' *s* galgo
grayish ['gre•ɪʃ] *adj* grisáceo; (*person; hair*) entrecano
gray matter *s* substancia gris; (*intelligence*) (coll) materia gris
graze [grez] *tr* (*to touch lightly*) rozar; (*to scratch lightly in passing*) raspar; pacer (*la hierba*); apacentar (*el ganado*); (*to lead to the pasture*) pastar || *intr* pacer, pastar
grease [gris] *s* grasa || [gris] o [griz] *tr* engrasar; (slang) sobornar
grease cup [gris] *s* vaso de engrase
grease gun [gris] *s* engrasador *m* de pistón, jeringa de engrase, bomba de engrase
grease lift [gris] *s* puente *m* de engrase
grease paint [gris] *s* maquillaje *m*
grease pit [gris] *s* fosa de engrase
grease spot [gris] *s* lámpara, mancha de grasa
greas•y ['grisi] o ['grizi] *adj* (*comp* **-ier;** *super* **-iest**) grasiento, pringoso
great [gret] *adj* grande; (coll) excelente || **the great** los grandes
great'-aunt' *s* tía abuela
Great Bear *s* Osa Mayor
Great Britain ['brɪtən] *s* la Gran Bretaña
great'coat' *s* gabán *m* de mucho abrigo
Great Dane *s* mastín *m* danés
Greater London *s* el Gran Londres
Greater New York *s* el Gran Nueva York
great'-grand'child' *s* (*pl* **-chil'dren**) bisnieto, bisnieta
great'-grand'daugh'ter *s* bisnieta
great'-grand'fa'ther *s* bisabuelo
great'-grand'moth'er *s* bisabuela
great'-grand'par'ent *s* bisabuelo, bisabuela

great'-grand'son' *s* bisnieto
greatly ['gretli] *adj* grandemente
great'-neph'ew *s* resobrino
greatness ['gretnɪs] *s* grandeza
great'-niece' *s* resobrina
great'-un'cle *s* tío abuelo
Great War *s* Gran guerra
Grecian ['griʃən] *adj & s* griego
Greece [gris] *s* Grecia
greed [grid] *s* codicia, avaricia; (*in eating and drinking*) glotonería
greed•y ['gridi] *adj* (*comp* **-ier;** *super* **-iest**) codicioso, avaro; glotón
Greek [grik] *adj & s* griego
green [grin] *adj* verde; inexperto ‖ *s* verde *m;* (*lawn*) césped *m;* **greens** verduras
green'back' *s* (U.S.A.) billete *m* de banco (*de dorso verde*)
green corn *s* maíz tierno
green earth *s* verdacho
greener•y ['grinəri] *s* (*pl* **-ies**) (*foliage*) verdura; (*hothouse*) invernáculo
green-eyed ['grin,aɪd] *adj* de ojos verdes; celoso
green'gage' *s* ciruela claudia
green grasshopper *s* langostón *m*
green'gro'cer *s* verdulero
green'gro'cer•y *s* (*pl* **-ies**) verdulería
green'horn' *s* novato; (*dupe*) primo, inocentón *m;* papanatas *m,* isidro; colegial *mf* (Mex)
green'house' *s* invernáculo
greenish ['grinɪʃ] *adj* verdoso
Greenland ['grinlənd] *s* Groenlandia
greenness ['grinnɪs] *s* verdura, verdor *m;* falta de experiencia
green'room' *s* saloncillo; chismería de teatro
greensward ['grin,swɔrd] *s* césped *m*
green thumb *s* pulgares *mpl* verdes (*don de criar plantas*)
green vegetables *spl* verduras
green'wood' *s* bosque *m* verde, bosque frondoso
greet [grit] *tr* saludar; acoger, recibir; presentarse a (*los ojos u los oídos de uno*)
greeting ['gritɪŋ] *s* saludo; acogida, recibimiento ‖ **greetings** *interj* ¡salud!
greeting card *s* tarjeta de buen deseo
gregarious [grɪ'gɛrɪ•əs] *adj* (*living in the midst of others*) gregario; (*fond of the company of others*) sociable
Gregorian [grɪ'gorɪ•ən] *adj* gregoriano
grenade [grɪ'ned] *s* granada; (*to put out fires*) granada extintora
grenadier [,grɛnə'dɪr] *s* granadero
grenadine [,grɛnə'din] *s* granadina
grey [gre] *adj, s & intr* var de **gray**
grid [grɪd] *s* parrilla, rejilla; (*electron*) rejilla; (*of a storage battery*) (elec) rejilla
griddle ['grɪdəl] *s* plancha
grid'dle•cake' *s* tortada (de harina) a la plancha
grid'i'ron *s* parrilla; campo de fútbol
grid leak *s* (electron) resistencia de rejilla, escape *m* de rejilla

grief [grif] *s* aflicción, pesar *m;* (coll) desgracia, disgusto; **to come to grief** fracasar, arruinarse
grievance ['grivəns] *s* agravio, injusticia; despecho, disgusto; motivo de queja
grieve [griv] *tr* afligir, penar ‖ *intr* afligirse, apenarse; **to grieve over** añorar
grievous ['grivəs] *adj* doloroso, penoso; atroz, cruel; (*deplorable*) lastimoso
griffin ['grɪfɪn] *s* (myth) grifo
grill [grɪl] *s* parrilla ‖ *tr* emparrillar; someter (*a un acusado*) a un interrogatorio muy apremiante
grille [grɪl] *s* reja, verja; (*of an automobile*) parrilla, rejilla
grill'room' *s* parrilla
grim [grɪm] *adj* (*comp* **grimmer;** *super* **grimmest**) (*fierce*) cruel, feroz; (*repellent*) horrible, siniestro; (*unyielding*) formidable, implacable; (*stern-looking*) ceñudo
grimace ['grɪməs] o [grɪ'mes] *s* mueca, gesto ‖ *intr* hacer muecas, gestear
grime [graɪm] *s* mugre *f;* (*soot*) tizne *m & f*
grim•y ['graɪmi] *adj* (*comp* **-ier;** *super* **-iest**) mugriento; tiznado
grin [grɪn] *s* sonrisa bonachona; mueca (*mostrando los dientes*) ‖ *v* (*pret & pp* **grinned;** *ger* **grinning**) *intr* sonreírse bonachonamente; hacer una mueca (*mostrando los dientes*)
grind [graɪnd] *s* molienda; (*long hard work or study*) (coll) zurra; (*student*) (coll) empollón *m* ‖ *v* (*pret & pp* **ground** [graʊnd]) *tr* moler; (*to sharpen*) afilar, amolar; tallar (*lentes*); pulverizar; picar (*carne*); rodar (*las válvulas de un motor*); dar vueltas a (*un manubrio*) ‖ *intr* hacer molienda; molerse; rechinar; (coll) echar los bofes
grinder ['graɪndər] *s* (*to sharpen tools*) muela, esmoladera; (*to grind coffee, pepper, etc.*) molinillo; (*back tooth*) muela
grind'stone' *s* esmoladera, piedra de amolar; **to keep one's nose to the grindstone** trabajar con ahinco
grin•go ['grɪŋgo] *s* (*pl* **-gos**) (disparaging) gringo
grip [grɪp] *s* (*grasp*) asimiento; (*withhand*) apretón *m;* (*handle*) asidero; saco de mano; **to come to grips (with)** luchar cuerpo a cuerpo (con); arrostrarse (con) ‖ *v* (*pret & pp* **gripped;** *ger* **gripping**) *tr* asir, agarrar; tener asido; absorber (*la atención*); absorber la atención a (*una persona*)
gripe [graɪp] *s* (coll) queja; **gripes** retortijón *m* de tripas ‖ *intr* (coll) quejarse, refunfuñar
grippe [grɪp] *s* gripe *f*
gripping ['grɪpɪŋ] *adj* conmovedor, impresionante
gris•ly ['grɪzli] *adj* (*comp* **-lier;** *super* **-liest**) espantoso, espeluznante
grist [grɪst] *s* (*batch of grain for one grinding*) molienda; (*grain that has been ground*) harina; (coll) acopio, acervo; **to be grist to one's mill** (coll) serle a uno de mucho provecho

gristle [ˈgrɪsəl] *adj* (*comp* **-tlier;** *super* **-tliest**) cartilaginoso, ternilloso
grist'mill' *s* molino harinero
grit [grɪt] *s* arena, guijo fino; (fig) ánimo, valentía; **grits** farro, sémola ‖ *v* (*pret & pp* **gritted;** *ger* **gritting**) *tr* hacer rechinar (*los dientes*); cerrar fuertemente (*los dientes*)
grit•ty [ˈgrɪti] *adj* (*comp* **-tier;** *super* **-tiest**) arenoso; (fig) valiente, resuelto
griz•zly [ˈgrɪzli] *adj* (*comp* **-zlier;** *super* **-zliest**) grisáceo; canoso ‖ *s* (*pl* **-zlies**) oso gris
grizzly bear *s* oso gris
groan [gron] *s* gemido, quejido ‖ *intr* gemir, quejarse; estar muy cargado, crujir por exceso de peso
grocer [ˈgrosər] *s* abacero, tendero de ultramarinos
grocer•y [ˈgrosəri] *s* (*pl* **-ies**) abacería, tienda de ultramarinos, colmado; **groceries** víveres *mpl,* ultramarinos
grocery store *s* abacería, tienda de ultramarinos, colmado
grog [grɑg] *s* grog *m*
grog•gy [ˈgrɑgi] *adj* (*comp* **-gier;** *super* **-giest**) (coll) inseguro, vacilante; (*shaky, e.g., from a blow*) (coll) atontado; (coll) borracho
groin [grɔɪn] *s* (anat) ingle *f;* (archit) arista de encuentro
groom [grum] *s* (*bridegroom*) novio; mozo de caballos ‖ *tr* asear, acicalar; almohazar (*caballos*); enseñar (*a un político*) para presentarse como candidato
grooms•man [ˈgrumzmən] *s* (*pl* **-men** [mən]) padrino de boda
groove [gruv] *s* ranura; (*of a pulley*) garganta; (*of a phonograph record*) surco; (*mark left by a wheel*) rodada; (coll) rutina, hábito arraigado ‖ *tr* ranurar, acanalar
grope [grop] *intr* andar a tientas; (*for words*) pujar; **to grope for** buscar a tientas, buscar tentando; **to grope through** palpar (*p.ej., la obscuridad*)
gropingly [ˈgropɪŋli] *adv* a tientas
grosbeak [ˈgros ˌbik] *s* pico duro
gross [gros] *adj* (*dense, thick*) denso, espeso; (*coarse; vulgar*) grosero; (*fat, burly*) grueso; (*with no deductions*) bruto ‖ *s* conjunto, totalidad; (*twelve dozen*) gruesa; **in gross** en grueso ‖ *tr* obtener un ingreso bruto de
grossly [ˈgrosli] *adv* aproximadamente
gross national product *s* renta nacional
grotesque [groˈtɛsk] adj (*ridiculous, extravagant*) grotesco; (fa) grutesco ‖ *s* (fa) grutesco
grot•to [ˈgrɑto] *s* (*pl* **-toes** o **-tos**) gruta
grouch [graʊtʃ] *s* (coll) mal humor *m;* (*person*) (coll) cascarrabias *mf,* vinagre *m* ‖ *intr* (coll) refunfuñar
grouch•y [ˈgraʊtʃi] *adj* (*comp* **-ier;** *super* **-iest**) (coll) gruñón, malhumorado
ground [graʊund] *adj* molido ‖ *s* (*earth, soil, land*) tierra; (*piece of land*) terreno; (*basis foundation*) causa, fundamento; motivo, razón *f;* (elec) tierra; (*body of automobile corresponding to ground*) (elec) masa; (elec) borne *m* de tierra; **ground for complaint** motivo de queja; **grounds** terreno; jardines *mpl;* causa, fundamento; (*of coffee*) posos; **on the ground of** con motivo de; **to break ground** empezar la excavación; **to fall to the ground** fracasar, abandonarse; **to gain ground** ganar terreno; **to give ground** ceder terreno; **to lose ground** perder terreno; **to stand one's ground** mantenerse firme; **to yield ground** ceder terreno ‖ *tr* establecer, fundar; (elec) poner a tierra; **to be grounded** estar sin volar (*un avión*); **to be well grounded** ser muy versado ‖ *intr* (naut) encallar, varar
ground connection *s* (rad) toma de tierra
ground crew *s* (aer) personal *m* de tierra
grounder [ˈgraʊndər] *s* (baseball) pelota rodada
ground floor *s* piso bajo
ground glass *s* vidrio deslustrado
ground hog *s* marmota de América
ground lead [lid] *s* (elec) conductor *m* a tierra
groundless [ˈgraʊndlɪs] *adj* infundado; inmotivado
ground plan *s* primer proyecto; (*of a building*) planta
ground speed *s* (aer) velocidad con respecto al suelo
ground swell *s* marejada de fondo
ground troops *spl* (mil) tropas terrestres
ground wire *s* (rad) alambre *m* de tierra; (aut) hilo de masa
ground'work' *s* infraestructura
group [grup] *adj* grupal; colectivo ‖ *s* grupo ‖ *tr* agrupar ‖ *intr* agruparse
group therapy *s* psicoterapia de grupo
grouse [graʊs] *s* perdiz blanca, bonasa americana, gallo de bosque; (slang) refunfuño ‖ *intr* (slang) refunfuñar
grout [graʊt] *s* lechada ‖ *tr* enlechar
grove [grov] *s* arboleda, bosquecillo
grov•el [ˈgrʌvəl] o [ˈgrɑvəl] *v* (*pret & pp* **-eled** o **-elled;** *ger* **-eling** o **-elling**) *intr* arrastrarse servilmente; rebajarse servilmente; deleitarse en vilezas
grow [gro] *v* (*pret* **grew** [gru]; *pp* **grown** [gron] *tr* cultivar (*plantas*); criar (*animales*); dejarse (*la barba*) ‖ *intr* crecer; cultivarse; criarse; brotar, nacer; (*to become*) hacerse, ponerse, volverse; **to grow angry** enfadarse; **to grow old** envejecerse; **to grow out of** tener su origen en; perder (*p.ej., la costumbre*); **to grow together** adherirse el uno al otro; **to grow up** crecer, desarrollar
growing child [ˈgro•ɪŋ] *s* muchacho de creces
growl [graʊl] *s* gruñido; refunfuño ‖ *intr* gruñir (*el perro*); refunfuñar
grown'up' *adj* adulto; juicioso ‖ *s* (*pl* **grown-ups**) adulto; **grown-ups** personas mayores
growth [groθ] *s* crecimiento; desarrollo; aumento; (*of trees, grass, etc.*) cobertura; (pathol) tumor *m*
growth stock *s* acción crecedera

grub [grʌb] *s* (*drudge*) esclavo del trabajo; (*larva*) gorgojo; (coll) comida, alimento ‖ *v* (*pret & pp* **grubbed;** *ger* **grubbing**) *tr* arrancar (*tocones*); desmalezar (*un terreno*) ‖ *intr* cavar; trabajar como esclavo
grub•by [ˈgrʌbi] *adj* (*comp* **-bier;** *super* **-biest**) gorgojoso; sucio, roñoso
grudge [grʌdʒ] *s* rencor *m*, inquina; **to have a grudge against** guardar rencor a, tener inquina a ‖ *tr* dar de mala gana; envidiar
grudgingly [ˈgrʌdʒɪŋli] *adv* de mala gana
gru•el [ˈgru•əl] *s* avenate *m* ‖ *v* (*pret & pp* **-eled** o **-elled;** *ger* **-elling** o **-elling**) *tr* agotar, castigar cruelmente
gruesome [ˈgrusəm] *adj* espantoso, horripilante
gruff [grʌf] *adj* áspero, brusco, rudo; (*voice, tone*) ronco
grumble [ˈgrʌmbəl] *s* gruñido, refunfuño; ruido sordo y prolongado ‖ *intr* gruñir, refunfuñar; retumbar
grump•y [ˈgrʌmpi] *adj* (*comp* **-ier;** *super* **-iest**) gruñón, malhumorado
grunt [grʌnt] *s* gruñido ‖ *intr* gruñir
G-string [ˈdʒi,strɪŋ] *s* (*loincloth*) taparrabo; (*worn by women entertainers*) cubresexo
gt. *abbr* **great; gutta** (Lat) **drop**
g.u. *abbr* **genitourinary**
Guadeloupe [,gwɑdəˈlup] *s* Guadalupe *f*
guarantee [,gaerənˈti] *s* garantía; (*guarantor*) garante *mf;* persona de quien otra sale fiadora ‖ *tr* garantizar
guarantor [ˈgærən,tɔr] *s* garante *mf*
guaran•ty [ˈgærənti] *s* (*pl* **-ties**) garantía ‖ *v* (*pret & pp* **-tied**) *tr* garantizar
guard [gɑrd] *s* (*act of guarding; part of handle of sword*) guarda; (*person who guards or takes care of something*) guarda *mf;* (*group of armed men; posture in fencing*) guardia; (*member of group of armed men*) guardia *m;* (*in front of trolley car*) salvavidas *m;* (sport) coraza; (rr) guardabarrera *mf;* (rr) guardafrenos *m;* **off guard** desprevenido; **on guard** alerta, prevenido; de centinela; **to mount guard** montar la guardia; **under guard** a buen recaudo ‖ *tr* guardar ‖ *intr* estar de centinela; **to guard against** guardarse de, precaverse contra o de
guard'house' *s* cuartel *m* de la guardia; prisión militar
guardian [ˈgɑrdɪ•ən] *adj* tutelar ‖ *s* guardián *m;* (law) curador *m*, tutor *m*
guardian angel *s* ángel *m* custodio, ángel de la guarda
guardianship [ˈgɑrdɪ•ən,ʃɪp] *s* amparo, protección; (law) curaduría, tutela
guard'rail' *s* baranda; (naut) barandilla; (rr) contracarril *m*
guard'room' *s* cuarto de guardia; cárcel *f* militar
guards•man [ˈgɑrdzmən] *s* (*pl* **-men** [mən]) guardia *m*, soldado de guardia
Guatemalan [,gwɑtɪˈmɑlən] *adj & s* guatemalteco
guerrilla [gəˈrɪlə] *s* guerrillero; montonero
guerrilla warfare *s* guerra de guerrillas
guess [gɛs] *s* conjetura, suposición; adivinación ‖ *tr & intr* conjeturar, suponer; (*to judge correctly*) acertar, adivinar; (coll) creer, suponer; **I guess so** (coll) creo que sí, me parece que sí
guess'work' *s* conjetura; **by guesswork** por conjeturas
guest [gɛst] *s* convidado; (*lodger*) huésped *m;* (*of a boarding house*) pensionista *mf;* (*of a hotel*) cliente *mf;* (*caller*) vista
guest book *s* libro de oro
guest room *s* cuarto de reserva
guffaw [gəˈfɔ] *s* risotada, carcajada ‖ *intr* risotear, reír a carcajadas
guidance [ˈgaɪdəns] *s* guía, gobierno, dirección; **for your guidance** para su gobierno
guide [gaɪd] *s* (*person*) guía *mf;* (*book*) guía; (*guidance*) guía; dirección; poste *m* indicador; (mach) guía, guiadera; (mil) guía *m* ‖ *tr* guiar
guide'board' *s* señal *f* de carretera
guide'book' *s* guia *m*, guía del viajero
guided missile [ˈgaɪdɪd] *s* proyectil dirigido o teleguiado; misil *m* dirigible
guide dog *s* perro-lazarillo
guide'line' *s* cuerda de guía; norma, pauta, directorio
guide'post' *s* poste *m* indicador
guidon [ˈgaɪdən] *s* (mil) guión *m;* (mil) portaguión *m*
guild [gɪld] *s* (*medieval association of craftsmen*) gremio; asociación benéfica
guild'hall' *s* casa consistorial
guile [gaɪl] *s* astucia, dolo, maña
guileful [ˈgaɪlfəl] *adj* astuto, doloso, mañoso
guileless [ˈgaɪllɪs] *adj* cándido, inocente, sencillo
guillotine [ˈgɪlə,tin] *s* guillotina ‖ [,gɪləˈtin] *tr* guillotinar
guilt [gɪlt] *s* culpa
guiltless [ˈgɪltlɪs] *adj* inocente, libre de culpa
guilt•y [ˈgɪlti] *adj* (*comp* **-ier;** *super* **-iest**) culpable; (*charged with guilt*) culpado; (*found guilty*) reo
guimpe [gɪmp] o [gæmp] *s* canesú *m*
guinea [ˈgɪni] *s* (*monetary unit*) guinea; gallina de Guinea
guinea fowl *s* pintada, gallina de Guinea
guinea hen *s* pintada, gallina de Guinea (*hembra*)
guinea pig *s* conejillo de Indias; (fig) cobayo
guise [gaɪz] *s* traje *m;* aspecto, semejanza; **under the guise of** so capa de
guitar [gɪˈtɑr] *s* guitarra
guitarist [gɪˈtɑrɪst] *s* guitarrista *mf*
gulch [gʌltʃ] *s* barranco, quebrada
gulf [gʌlf] *s* golfo
Gulf of Mexico *s* golfo de Méjico
Gulf Stream *s* Corriente *f* del Golfo
gull [gʌl] *s* gaviota; (coll) bobo ‖ *tr* estafar, engañar
gullet [ˈgʌlɪt] *s* gaznate *m*, garguero; esófago
gullible [ˈgʌlɪbəl] *adj* crédulo; creído; **to be too gullible** tener buenas tragaderas
gul•ly [ˈgʌli] *s* (*pl* **-lies**) barranca, arroyada; (*channel made by rain water*) badén *m*

gulp [gʌlp] *s* trago ‖ *tr* — **to gulp down** engullir; reprimir (*p.ej., sollozos*) ‖ *intr* respirar entrecortadamente

gum [gʌm] *s* goma; chanclo de goma; (*firm flesh around base of teeth*) encía; (*mucous on edge of eyelid*) legaña ‖ *v* (*pret & pp* **gummed;** *ger* **gumming**) *tr* engomar ‖ *intr* exudar goma

gum arabic *s* goma arábiga

gum'boil' *s* flemón *m*

gum boot *s* bota de agua

gum'drop' *s* frutilla

gum•my ['gʌmi] *adj* (*comp* **-mier;** *super* **-miest**) gomoso; (*eyelid*) legañoso

gumption ['gʌmpʃən] *s* ánimo, iniciativa, empuje *m*, fuerza; juicio, seso

gum'shoe' *s* chanclo de goma; (coll) detective *m* ‖ *v* (*pret & pp* **-shoed;** *ger* **-shoeing**) *intr* (slang) andar con zapatos de fieltro

gun [gʌn] *s* escopeta, fusil *m;* cañón *m;* (*for injections*) jeringa; (coll) revólver *m;* **to stick to one's guns** mantenerse en sus trece ‖ *v* (*pret & pp* **gunned;** *ger* **gunning**) *tr* hacer fuego sobre; (slang) acelerar rápidamente (*un motor, un avión*) ‖ *intr* andar a caza; disparar; **to gun for** ir en busca de; buscar para matar

gun'boat' *s* cañonero

gun carriage *s* cureña, encabalgamiento

gun'cot'ton *s* fulmicotón *m*, algodón *m* pólvora

gun'fire' *s* fuego (*de armas de fuego*); cañoneo

gun•man ['gʌnmən] *s* (*pl* **-men** [mən]) bandido armado, pistolero; gángster *m*

gun metal *s* bronce *m* de cañón; metal pavonado

gunnel ['gʌnəl] *s* (naut) borda, regala

gunner ['gʌnər] *s* artillero; cazador *m*

gunnery ['gʌnəri] *s* artillería

gunny sack ['gʌni] *s* saco de yute

gun'pow'der *s* pólvora

gun'run'ner *s* contrabandista *m* de armas de fuego

gun'run'ning *s* contrabando de armas de fuego

gun'shot' *s* escopetazo, tiro de fusil; alcance *m* de un fusil; **within gunshot** a tiro de fusil

gunshot wound *s* escopetazo

gun'smith' *s* armero

gun'stock' *s* caja de fusil

gunwale ['gʌnəl] *s* (naut) borda, regala

gup•py ['gʌpi] *s* (*pl* **-pies**) lebistes *m*

gurgle ['gʌrgəl] *s* gorgoteo, gluglú *m;* (*of a child*) gorjeo ‖ *intr* gorgotear, hacer gluglú; gorjearse (*el niño*)

gush [gʌʃ] *s* borbollón *m*, chorro ‖ *intr* surgir, salir a borbollones; (coll) hacer extremos, ser extremoso

gusher ['gʌʃər] *s* pozo de chorro de petróleo; (coll) personal extremosa

gushing ['gʌʃɪŋ] *adj* surgente; (coll) extremoso ‖ *s* borbollón *m*, chorro; (coll) efusión, extremos

gush•y ['gʌʃi] *adj* (*comp* **-ier;** *super* **-iest**) (coll) efusivo, extremoso

gusset ['gʌsɪt] *s* escudete *m*

gust [gʌst] *s* (*of wind*) ráfaga; (*of rain*) aguacero; (*of smoke*) bocanada; (*of noise*) explosión; (*of anger or enthusiasm*) arrebato

gusto ['gʌsto] *s* deleite *m*, entusiasmo; **with gusto** con sumo placer

gust•y ['gʌsti] *adj* (*comp* **-ier;** *super* **-iest**) tempestuoso, borrascoso

gut [gʌt] *s* tripa; cuerda de tripa; **guts** tripas; (slang) agallas ‖ *v* (*pret & pp* **gutted;** *ger* **gutting**) *tr* destripar; destruir lo interior de

gutta-percha ['gʌtə'pʌrtʃə] *s* gutapercha

gutter ['gʌtər] *s* (*on side of road*) cuneta; (*in street*) arroyo; (*of roof*) canal *f;* (*ditch formed by rain water*) badén *m;* barrios bajos

gut'ter-snipe' *s* pilluelo, hijo de la miseria; gamberro

guttural ['gʌtərəl] *adj* gutural ‖ *s* sonido gutural

guy [gaɪ] *s* viento, cable *m* de retén; (coll) tipo, tío, sujeto ‖ *tr* (coll) burlarse de

Guyana [gaɪ'ænə] *s* Guayana

guy wire *s* cable *m* de retén

guzzle ['gʌzəl] *tr & intr* beber con exceso

guzzler ['gʌzlər] *s* borrachín *m*

gym [dʒɪm] *s* (coll) gimnasio

gymnasi•um [dʒɪm'nezɪ•əm] *s* (*pl* **-ums** o **-a** [ə]) gimnasio

gymnast ['dʒɪmnæst] *s* gimnasta *mf*

gymnastic [dʒɪm'næstɪk] *adj* gimnástico ‖ **gymnastics** *spl* gimnasia, gimnástica

gym suit *s* chandal *m*, chándal *m*

gynecologic(al) [,gaɪnəko'lɑdʒɪk(əl)] or [,dʒaɪnəko'lɑdʒɪk(əl)] *adj* ginecológico

gynecologist [,gaɪnə'kɑlədʒɪst] or [,dʒaɪnə'kɑlədʒɪst] *s* ginecólogo

gynecology [,gaɪnə'kɑlədʒi] or [,dʒaɪnə'kɑlədʒi] *s* ginecología

gyp [dʒɪp] *s* (slang) estafa, timo; (*person*) (slang) estafador *m*, timador *m* ‖ *v* (*pret & pp* **gypped;** *ger* **gypping**) *tr* (slang) estafar, timar

gypsum ['dʒɪpsəm] *s* yeso, aljez *m*

gyp•sy ['dʒɪpsi] *adj* gitano ‖ *s* (*pl* **-sies**) gitano ‖ **Gypsy** *s* gitano (*idioma*)

gypsyish ['dʒɪpsɪ•ɪʃ] *adj* gitanesco

gypsy moth *s* lagarta

gyrate ['dʒaɪret] *intr* girar

gyroscope ['dʒaɪrə,skop] *s* giroscopio

H

H, h [etʃ] octava letra del alfabeto inglés
h. *abbr* **harbor, high, hour, husband**
haberdasher [ˈhæbər ˌdæʃər] *s* camisero; (*dealer in notions*) mercero
haberdasher•y [ˈhæbər ˌdæʃəri] *s* (*pl* **-ies**) camisería, tienda de artículos para hombres; artículos para hombres
habit [ˈhæbɪt] *s* costumbre *f,* hábito; (*costume*) traje *m;* **to be in the habit of** acostumbrar
habitat [ˈhæbɪˌtæt] *s* habitación
habitation [ˌhæbɪˈteʃən] *s* habitación
habit-forming [ˈhæbɪt ˌfɔrmɪŋ] *adj* enviciador
habitual [həˈbɪtʃu•əl] *adj* habitual
habitué [həˌbɪtʃuˈe] *s* habituado
hack [hæk] *s* (*cut*) corte *m;* (*notch*) mella; (*cough*) tos seca; coche *m* de alquiler; caballo de alquiler; caballo de silla; (*old nag*) rocín *m;* escritor *m* a sueldo ‖ *tr* cortar, machetear
hack•man [ˈhækmən] *s* (*pl* **-men** [mən]) cochero de punto
hackney [ˈhækni] *s* caballo de silla; coche *m* de alquiler; esclavo del trabajo
hackneyed [ˈhæknid] *adj* trillado, gastado
hack'saw' *s* sierra de armero, sierra de cortar metales
haddock [ˈhædək] *s* eglefino
haem ... [hɛm] o [him] = **hemo ...**
haft [hæft] o [hɑft] *s* mango, puño
hag [hæg] *s* (*ugly old woman*) tarasca; (*witch*) bruja
haggard [ˈhægərd] *adj* ojeroso, macilento, trasnochado
haggle [ˈhægəl] *intr* regatear
Hague,The [heg] La Haya
hail [hel] *s* (*frozen rain*) granizo; (*greeting*) saludo; **within hail** al alcance de la voz ‖ *interj* ¡salud!, ¡salve! ‖ *tr* saludar; dar vivas a, acoger con vivas; aclamar; granizar (*p.ej., golpes*) ‖ *intr* granizar; **to hail from** venir de, ser oriundo de
hail'-fel'low well met *s* compañero muy afable y simpático
Hail Mary *s* avemaría
hail'stone' *s* piedra de granizo
hail'storm' *s* granizada
hair [hɛr] *s* pelo, cabellos; **to a hair** con la mayor exactitud; **to cut the hair of** peluquear; **to get in one's hair** (slang) enojarle a uno; **to have one's hair down** estar en melena; **to let one's hair down** (slang) hablar con mucha desenvoltura; **to make one's hair stand on end** ponerle a uno los pelos de punta; **to not turn a hair** no inmutarse; **to split hairs** pararse en quisquillas
hair'breadth' *s* (el) grueso de un pelo, casi nada; **to escape by a hairbreadth** escapar por un pelo
hair'brush' *s* cepillo de cabeza
hair'cloth' *s* tela de crin; (*worn as a penance*) cilicio
hair curler [ˈkʌrlər] *s* rizador *m,* tenacillas, bigudí *m,* rulo
hair'cut' *s* corte *m* de pelo; **to get a haircut** cortarse el pelo, peluquear
hair'do' *s* (*pl* **-dos**) peinado, tocado
hair'dress'er *s* peinador *m,* peluquero
hair dryer *s* secador *m*
hair dye *s* tinte *m* para el pelo
hairless [ˈhɛrlɪs] *adj* pelón
hair net *s* redecilla
hair piece *s* peluquín *m*
hair'pin' *s* horquilla
hair-raising [ˈhɛrˌrezɪŋ] *adj* (coll) espeluznante, horripilante
hair restorer [rɪˈstorər] *s* crecepelo
hair ribbon *s* cinta para el cabello
hair set *s* fijapeinados *m*
hair shirt *s* calicio
hairsplitting [ˈhɛrˌsplɪtɪŋ] *adj* quisquilloso ‖ *s* quisquillas
hair spray *s* laca
hair'spring' *s* espiral *f*
hair'style' *s* peinado
hair tonic *s* vigorizador *m* del cabello
hair•y [ˈhɛri] *adj* (*comp* **-ier;** *super* **-iest**) peludo, cabelludo
hake [hek] *s* merluza; (genus: *Urophycis*) fice *m*
halberd [ˈhælbərd] *s* alabarda
halberdier [ˌhælbərˈdɪr] *s* alabardero
halcyon days [ˈhælsɪ•ən] *s* días tranquilos, época de paz
hale [hel] *adj* sano, robusto; **hale and hearty** sano y fuerte ‖ *tr* llevar a la fuerza
half [hæf] *adj* medio; **a half** o **half a** medio; **half the** la mitad de ‖ *adv* medio, p.ej., **half asleep** medio dormido; a medio, p.ej., **half finished** a medio acabar; a medias, p.ej., **half owner** dueño a medias; **half past** y media, p.ej., **half past three** las tres y media; **half . . . half** medio . . . medio ‖ *s* (*pl* **halves** [hævz]) mitad; (arith) medio; **in half** por la mitad; **to go halves** ir a medias
half'-and-half' *adj* mitad y mitad; indeterminado ‖ *adv* a medias, en partes iguales ‖ *s* mezcla de leche y crema; mezcla de dos cervezas inglesas
half'back' *s* (football) medio
half-baked [ˈhæfˌbekt] *adj* a medio cocer; incompleto; poco juicioso, inexperto
half binding *s* (bb) encuadernación a la holandesa, media pasta
half'-blood' *s* mestizo; medio hermano
half boot *s* bota de media caña
half'-bound' *adj* (bb) a la holandesa
half'-breed' *s* mestizo
half brother *s* medio hermano
half-cocked [ˈhæfˈkakt] *adv* (coll) con precipitación; **to go off half-cocked** obrar precipitadamente y antes del momento propio
half fare *s* medio billete
half'-full' *adj* mediado
half-hearted [ˈhæfˌhartɪd] *adj* indiferente, frío

half holiday *s* mañana o tarde *f* de asueto
half hose *spl* calcetines *mpl*
half'-hour *s* media hora; **on the half-hour** a la media en punto, cada media hora
half leather *s* (bb) encuadernación a la holandesa, media pasta
half'-length' *adj* de medio cuerpo
half'-mast' *s* — **at half mast** a media asta
half moon *s* media luna
half mourning *s* medio luto
half note *s* (mus) nota blanca
half pay *s* media paga; medio sueldo
halfpen•ny ['hepəni] o ['hepni] *s* (*pl* **-nies**) medio penique
half pint *s* media pinta; (*little runt*) (slang) gorgojo, mirmidón *m*
half'-seas' over *adj* — **to be half-seas over** (slang) estar entre dos velas, estar entre dos luces
half shell *s* (*either half of a bivalve*) concha; (*oysters*) **on the half shell** en su concha
half sister *s* media hermana
half sole *s* media suela
half'-sole' *tr* poner media suela a
half'-staff' *s* — **at half-staff** a media asta
half through *prep* a la mitad de
half-timbered ['hæf,tɪmbərd] *adj* entramado
half title *s* anteportada, falsa portada
half'tone' *s* (phot & paint) mediatinta; (typ) similigrabado
half'-track' *s* media oruga, semitractor *m*
half'-truth' *s* verdad a medias
half'way' *adj* a medio camino; incompleto, hecho a medias || *adv* a medio camino; **halfway through** a la mitad de; **to meet halfway** partir el camino con; partir la diferencia con; hacer concesiones mutuas (*dos personas*)
half-witted ['hæf ,wɪtɪd] *adj* imbécil; necio, tonto
halibut ['hælɪbət] *s* halibut *m*
halide ['hælaɪd] o ['helaɪd] *s* (chem) haluro
halitosis [,hælɪ'tosɪs] *s* halitosis *f,* aliento fétido
hall [hɔl] (*passageway*) corredor *m;* (*entranceway*) vestíbulo, zaguán *m;* (*large meeting room*) sala, salón *m;* (*assembly room of a university*) paraninfo; (*building, e.g., of a university*) edificio
halleluiah o **hallelujah** [,hælɪ'lujə] *s* aleluya *m & f* || *interj* ¡aleluya!
hall'mark' *s* marca de constraste; (*distinguishing feature*) (fig) sello
hal•lo [hə'lo] *s* (*pl* **-los**) grito || *interj* ¡hola!; (*to incite dogs in hunting*) ¡sus! || *intr* gritar
hallow ['hælo] *tr* santificar
hallowed ['hælod] *adj* santo, sagrado
Halloween o **Hallowe'en** [,hælo'in] *s* víspera de Todos los Santos
hallucination [hə,lusɪ'neʃən] *s* alucinación
hallucinogenic [hə,lusɪno'dʒɛnɪk] *adj* alucinante
hall'way' *s* corredor *m;* vestíbulo, zaguán *m*
ha•lo ['helo] *s* (*pl* **-los** o **-loes**) halo
halogen ['hælədʒən] *s* halógeno
halt [hɔlt] *adj* cojo, renco || *s* alto, parada; **to call a halt** mandar hacer alto; **to come to a halt** pararse, detenerse, interrumpirse || *tr* parar, detener || *intr* hacer alto
halter ['hɔltər] *s* (*for leading or fastening horse*) cabestro, ronzal *m,* dogal *m;* (*noose*) dogal *m,* cuerda de ahorcar; muerte *f* en la horca
halting ['hɔltɪŋ] *adj* cojo, renco; vacilante
halve [hæv] *tr* partir en dos, partir por la mitad
halyard ['hæljərd] *s* (naut) driza
ham [hæm] *s* (*part of leg behind knee*) corva; (*thigh and buttock*) pernil *m;* (*cured meat from hog's hind leg*) jamón *m;* (slang) comicastro; (slang) aficionado (*a la radio*); **hams** nalgas
ham and eggs *spl* huevos con jamón
hamburger ['hæm,bʌrgər] *s* hamburguesa
hamlet ['hæmlɪt] *s* aldehuela, caserío
hammer ['hæmər] *s* martillo; (*of piano*) macillo, martinete *m;* **to go under the hammer** venderse en pública subasta || *tr* martillar; **to hammer out** formar a martillazos; sacar en limpio a fuerza de mucho esfuerzo|| *intr* martillar; **to hammer away** trabajar asiduamente
hammock ['hæmək] *s* hamaca
hamper ['hæmpər] *s* canasto, cesto grande con tapa || *tr* estorbar, impedir
hamster ['hæmstər] *s* marmota de Alemania, rata del trigo
ham•string ['hæm,strɪŋ] *v* (*pret & pp* **-strung**) *tr* desjarretar; (fig) estropear, incapacitar
hand [hænd] *adj* (*done or operated with the hands*) manual || *s* mano *f;* (*workman*) obrero, peón *m;* (*way of writing*) escritura, puño y letra; (signature) firma; (*clapping of hands*) salva de aplausos; (*of clock or watch*) mano *f;* manecilla; (*all the cards in one's hand*) juego; (*a round of play*) mano *f;* (*player*) jugador *m;* (*source, origin*) fuente *f;* (*skill*) destreza; **all hands** (naut) toda la tripulación; (coll) todas; **at first hand** de primera mano; directamente, de buena tinta; **at hand** disponible; **hand in glove** uña y carne; **hand in hand** asidos de la mano; juntos; **hands up!** ¡arriba las manos! **hand to hand** cuerpo a cuerpo; **in hand** entre manos; **in his own hand** de su propio puño; **on hand** entre manos; disponible; **on hands and knees** (*crawling*) a gatas; (*beseeching*) de rodillas; **on the one hand** por una parte; **on the other hand** por otra parte; **out of hand** luego, en seguida; desmandado; **to be at hand** obrar en mi (nuestro) poder (*una carta*); **to change hands** mudar de manos; **to clap hands** batir palmas; **to eat out of one's hand** aceptar dócilmente la autoridad de uno; **to fall into the hands of** caer en manos de; **to have a hand in** tomar parte en; **to have one's hands full** estar ocupadísimo; **to hold hands** tomarse de las manos; **to hold up one's hands** (*as a sign of surrender*) alzar las manos; **to join hands** darse las manos; casarse; **to keep one's hands off** no tocar, no meterse en; **to lend a hand**

echar una mano; **to live from hand to mouth** vivir al día, vivir de la mano a la boca; **to not lift a hand** no levantar paja del suelo; **to play into the hands of** hacer el caldo gordo a; **to raise one's hand** (*in taking an oath*) alzar el dedo; **to shake hands** estrecharse la mano; **to show one's hand** descubrir su juego; **to take in hand** hacerse cargo de; tratar, estudiar (*una cuestión*); **to throw up one's hands** darse por vencido; **to try one's hand** probar la mano; **to turn one's hand to** dedicarse a, ocuparse en; **to wash one's hands of** lavarse las manos de; **under my hand** con mi firma, bajo mi firma, de mi puño y letra; **under the hand and seal of** firmado y sellado por || *tr* dar, entregar; **to hand in** entregar; **to hand on** transmitir; **to hand out** repartir

hand'bag' *s* saco de noche; bolso de señora

hand baggage *s* equipaje *m* de mano

hand'ball' *s* pelota; juego de pelota a mano

hand'bill' *s* hoja volante

hand'book' manual *m;* guía de turistas; registro para apuestas

hand'breadth' *s* palmo menor

hand'car' *s* (rr) carrito de mano

hand'cart' *s* carretilla de mano

hand control *s* mando a mano

hand'cuff' *s* manilla; **handcuffs** manillas, esposas || *tr* poner esposas a

handful ['hænd,ful] *s* puñado, manojo

hand glass *s* espejo de mano; lupa

hand grenade *s* granada de mano

hand gun *s* (coll) pipa

hand'-held' calculator *s* calculador a mano

handi·cap ['hændɪ,kæp] *s* desventaja, obstáculo; (sport) handicap *m;* (med) disminución, minusvalía || *v* (*pret & pp* **-capped;** *ger* **-capping**) *tr* poner trabas a; (sport) handicapar

handicraft ['hændɪ,kræft] *s* destreza manual; arte mecánica

handiwork ['hændɪ,wʌrk] *s* hechura, trabajo; obra manual

handkerchief ['hæŋkərtʃɪf] *s* pañuelo

handle ['hændəl] *s* (*of a basket, crock, pitcher*) asa; (*of a shovel, rake, etc.*) mango; (*of an umbrella, sword*) puño; (*of a door, drawer*) tirador *m;* (*of a hand organ*) manubrio; (*of a water pump*) guimbalete *m;* (*opportunity, pretext*) asidero; **to fly off the handle** (slang) salirse de sus casillas || *tr* manosear, manipular; dirigir, manejar, gobernar; comerciar en || *intr* manejarse

handle bar *s* manillar *m,* guía

handler ['hændlər] *s* (sport) entrenador *m*

hand'made' *adj* hecho a mano

hand'maid' o **hand'maid'en** *s* criada, sirvienta

hand'-me-down' *s* (coll) prenda de vestir de segunda mano

hand organ *s* organillo

hand'out' *s* comida que se da de limosna; comunicado de prensa

hand-picked ['hænd ,pɪkt] *adj* escogido a mano; escogido escrupulosamente; escogido con motivos ocultos

hand'rail' *s* barandilla, pasamano

hand'saw' *s* serrucho, sierra de mano

hand'set' *s* microteléfono

hand'shake' *s* apretón *m* de manos

handsome ['hænsəm[*adj* hermoso, elegante, guapo; considerable

hand'spring' *s* voltereta sobre las manos

hand'-to-hand' *adj* cuerpo a cuerpo

hand'-to-mouth' *adj* inseguro, precario; impróvido

hand'work' *s* trabajo a mano

hand'-wres'tle *intr* pulsear

hand'-writ'ing *s* escritura; (*writing by hand which characterizes a particular person*) letra

hand·y ['hændi] *adj* (*comp* **-ier;** *super* **-iest)** (*easy to handle*) manuable; (*within easy reach*) próximo, a la mano; (*skillful*) diestro, hábil; **to come in handy** venir a pelo

handy man *s* dije *m,* factótum *m*

hang [hæŋ] *s* (*of a dress, curtain, etc.*) caída; (*skill; insight*) tino; **I don't care a hang** (coll) no me importa un bledo; **to get the hang of it** (coll) coger el tino || *v* (*pret & pp* **hung** [hʌŋ]) *tr* colgar; tender (*la ropa mojada*); pegar (*el papel pintado*); fijar (*un cartel, un letrero*); enquiciar (*una puerta, una ventana*); bajar (*la cabeza*); **hang it!** (coll) ¡caramba!; **to hang up** colgar (*el sombrero*); impedir los progresos de || *intr* colgar, pender; estar agarrado; vacilar; **to hang around** esperar sin hacer nada; haraganear; rondar; **to hang on** colgar de; depender de; estar pendiente de (*las palabras de una persona*); estar sin acabar de morir; agarrarse; **to hang out** asomarse; (slang) recogerse, alojarse; **to hang over** (*to threaten*) cernerse sobre; **to hang together** mantenerse unidos; **to hang up** (telp) colgar || *v* (*pret* **hanged** o **hung**) *tr* ahorcar || *intr* ahorcarse

hangar ['hæŋər] o ['hæŋgɑr] *s* cobertizo; (aer) hangar *m*

hang'bird' *s* pájaro de nido colgante; (*Baltimore oriole*) cacique veranero

hanger ['hæŋər] *s* colgador *m,* suspensión; (*hook*) colgadero

hang'er·on' *s* (*pl* **hangers-on**) secuaz *mf;* parásito; (*sponger*) pegote *m*

hanging ['hæŋɪŋ] *adj* colgante, pendiente || *s* ahorcadura, muerte *f* en la horca; **hangings** colgaduras

hang·man ['hæŋmən] *s* (*pl* **-men** [mən]) verdugo

hang'nail' *s* padrastro, respigón *m*

hang'out' *s* guarida, querencia; (*place to loaf and gossip*) mentidero

hang'o'ver *s* (slang) resaca

hank [hæŋk] *s* madeja

hanker ['hæŋkər] *intr* sentir anhelo

Hannibal [hænɪbəl] *s* Aníbal *m*

haphazard [,hæp'hæzərd] *adj* casual, fortuito, impensado || *adv* al acaso, **a** la ventura

hapless ['hæplɪs] *adj* desgraciado, desventurado
happen ['hæpən] *intr* acontecer, suceder; (*to turn out*) resultar; (*to be the case by chance*) dar la casualidad; **to happen in** entrar por casualidad; **to happen on** encontrarse con; **to happen to** hacerse de; **to happen to** + *inf* por casualidad + *ind,* p.ej., **I happened to see her at the theater** por casualidad la ví en el teatro
happening ['hæpənɪŋ] *s* acontecimiento, suceso
happily ['hæpɪli] *adv* felizmente
happiness ['hæpɪnɪs] *s* felicidad
hap•py ['hæpi] *adj* (*comp* **-pier;** *super* **-piest**) feliz; (*pleased*) contento; **to be happy to** alegrarse de, tener gusto en
hap'py-go-luck'y *adj* irresponsable, imprόvido ‖ *adv* a la buenaventura
happy medium *s* justo medio
Happy New Year *interj* ¡Feliz Año Nuevo!
harangue [hə'ræŋ] *s* arenga ‖ *tr & intr* arengar
harass ['hærəs] o [hə'ræs] *tr* acosar, hostigar; molestar, vejar
harbinger ['hɑrbɪndʒər] *s* precursor *m;* anuncio, presagio ‖ *tr* anunciar, presagiar
harbor ['hɑrbər] *adj* portuario ‖ *s* puerto ‖ *tr* albergar; alcahuetar, encubrir (*delincuentes u objetos robados*); guardar (*sentimientos de odio*)
harbor master *s* capitán *m* de puerto
hard [hɑrd] *adj* duro; (*difficult) difícil;* (*water*) crudo, duro; (*solder*) fuerte; (*work*) asiduo; (*drinker*) empedernido; espiritoso, fuertemente alcohólico; **to be hard on** (*to treat severely*) ser muy duro con; (*to wear out fast*) gastar, echar a perder ‖ *adv* duro; fuerte; mucho; **hard upon** a raíz de; **to drink hard** beber de firme; **to rain hard** llover de firme
hard and fast *adj* inflexible, riguroso ‖ *adv* firmemente
hard-bitten ['hɑrd'bɪtən] *adj* terco, tenaz, inflexible
hard-boiled ['hɑrd'bɔɪld] *adj* (*egg*) duro, muy cocido; duro, inflexible
hard candy *s* caramelos
hard cash *s* dinero contante y sonante
hard cider *s* sidra muy fermentada
hard coal *s* antracita
hard-earned ['hɑrd'ʌrnd] *adj* ganado a pulso
harden ['hɑrdən] *tr* endurecer ‖ *intr* endurecerse
hardening ['hɑrdənɪŋ] *s* endurecimiento
hard facts *spl* realidades
hard-fought ['hɑrd'fɔt] *adj* reñido
hard-headed ['hɑrd'hɛdɪd] *adj* astuto, sagaz; terco, tozudo
hard-hearted ['hɑrd'hɑrtɪd] *adj* duro de corazón
hardihood ['hɑrdɪ, hʊd] *s* audacia, resolución; descaro, insolencia
hardiness ['hɑrdɪnɪs] *s* fuerza, robustez; audacia, resolución
hard labor *s* trabajos forzados
hard luck *s* mala suerte
hard'-luck' story *s* (coll) cuento de penas; **to tell a hard-luck story** (coll) contar lástimas
hardly ['hɑrdli] *adv* apenas; escasamente; casi no; (*with great difficulty*) a duras penas; (*grievously*) penosamente; **hardly ever** casi nunca
hardness ['hɑrdnɪs] *s* dureza; (*of water*) crudeza
hard of hearing *adj* duro de oído, teniente
hard-pressed ['hɑrd'prɛst] *adj* acosado; (*for money*) apurado, alcanzado
hard rubber *s* vulcanita
hard sauce *s* mantequilla azucarada
hard'-shell' clam *s* almeja redonda
hard'-shell' crab *s* cangrejo de cáscara dura
hardship ['hɑrdʃɪp] *s* penalidad, infortunio, apuro
hard'tack' *s* galleta, sequete *m*
hard times *spl* período de miseria, apuros
hard to please *adj* difícil de contentar
hard up *adj* (coll) apurado, alcanzado
hard'ware' *s* ferretería, quincalla; (*metal trimmings*) herraje *m;* (*computer*) ordenador *m*
hardware•man ['hɑrd,wɛrmən] *s* (*pl* **-men** [mən]) ferretero, quincallero
hardware store *s* ferretería, quincallería
hard-won ['hɑrd,wʌn] *adj* ganado a pulso
hard'wood' *s* madera dura; árbol *m* de madera dura
hardwood floor *s* entarimado
har•dy ['hɑrdi] *adj* (*comp* **-dier;** *super* **-diest**) fuerte, robusto; audaz, resuelto; (*rash*) temerario; (hort) resistente
hare [hɛr] *s* liebre *f*
harebrained ['hɛr,brend] *adj* atolondrado
hare'lip *s* labio leporino
harelipped ['hɛr ,lɪpt] *adj* labiohendido
harem ['hɛrəm] *s* harén *m*
hark [hɑrk] *intr* escuchar; **to hark back** volver (*la jauría*) sobre la pista; **to hark back to** volver a, recordar
harken ['hɑrkən] *intr* escuchar, atender
harlequin ['hɑrləkwɪn] *s* arlequín *m*
harlot ['hɑrlət] *s* meretriz *f*
harm [hɑrm] *s* daño, perjuicio ‖ *tr* dañar, perjudicar, hacer daño a
harmful ['hɑrmfəl] *adj* dañoso, perjudicial; maléfico; (*e.g., pests*) dañino
harmfulness ['hɑrmfəlnɪs] *s* nocividad
harmless ['hɑrmlɪs] *adj* innocuo, inofensivo
harmlessness ['hɑrmlɪsnɪs] *s* innocuidad
harmonic [hɑr'mɑnɪk] *adj & s* armónico
harmonica [hɑr'mɑnɪkə] *s* armónica
harmonious [hɑr'monɪ•əs] *adj* armonioso
harmonize ['hɑrmə,naɪz] *tr & intr* armonizar
harmo•ny ['hɑrməni] *s* (pl **-nies**) armonía
harness ['hɑrnɪs] *s* arreos, guarniciones; **to get back in the harness** volver a la rutina; **to die in the harness** morir al pie del cañón ‖ *tr* enjaezar, poner las guarniciones a; enganchar; captar (*las aguas de un río*)
harness maker *s* guarnicionero
harness race *s* carrera con sulky
harp [hɑrp] *s* arpa ‖ *intr* — **to harp on** repetir porfiadamente

harpist [ˈhɑrpɪst] *s* arpista *mf*
harpoon [hɑrˈpun] *s* arpón *m* || *tr & intr* arponear
harpsichord [ˈhɑrpsɪ ˌkɔrd] *s* clave *m*
har•py [ˈhɑrpi] *s* (*pl* **-pies**) arpía
harrow [ˈhæro] *s* (agr) grada || *tr* (agr) gradar; atormentar
harrowing [ˈhæro•ɪŋ] *adj* horripilante, espantoso
har•ry [ˈhæri] *v* (*pret & pp* **-ried**) *tr* acosar, hostilizar, hostigar; atormentar, molestar
harsh [hɑrʃ] *adj* (*to touch, taste, eyes, hearing*) áspero; duro, cruel
harshness [ˈhɑrʃnɪs] *s* aspereza; dureza, crueldad
hart [hɑrt] *s* ciervo
harum-scarum [ˈhɛrəmˈskɛrəm] *adj* atolondrado || *adv* atolondradamente || *s* mataperros *m*
harvest [ˈhɑrvɪst] *s* cosecha; corte *m* || *tr & intr* cosechar
harvester [ˈhɑrvɪstər] *s* cosechero; (*helper*) agostero; (*machine*) segadora
harvest home *s* entrada de los frutos; fiesta de segadores; canción de segadores
harvest moon *s* luna de la cosecha
has-been [ˈhæzˈbɪn] *s* (coll) antigualla
hash [hæʃ] *s* picadillo || *tr* picar
hash house *s* bodegón *m*
hashish [ˈhæʃiʃ] *s* hachich *m;* (coll) tate *m*
hashish user *s* (coll) tate *m*
hasp [hæsp] o [hɑsp] *s* portacandado; (*of book covers*) broche *m*
hassle [ˈhæsəl] *s* (coll) riña, disputa
hassock [ˈhæsək] *s* cojín *m* (*para los pies o las rodillas*)
haste [hest] *s* prisa; **in haste** de prisa; **to make haste** darse prisa
hasten [ˈhesən] *tr* apresurar; apretar (*el paso*) || *intr* apresurarse
hast•y [ˈhesti] *adj* (*comp* **-ier;** *super* **-iest**) apresurado, inconsiderado, impulsivo, colérico
hat [hæt] *s* sombrero; **to keep under one's hat** (coll) callar, no divulgar; **to throw one's hat in the ring** (coll) decidirse a bajar a la arena
hat'band' *s* cintillo; (*worn to show mourning*) gasa
hat block *s* horma, conformador *m*
hat'box' *s* sombrerera
hatch [hætʃ] *s* (*brood*) cría, nidada; (*trap door*) escotillón *m;* (*lower half of door*) media puerta; (*opening in ship's deck*) escotilla; (*lid for opening in ship's deck*) cuartel *m* || *tr* empollar (*huevos*); sombrear (*un dibujo*); maquinar, tramar || *intr* empollarse; salir del huevo
hat'-check' girl *s* guardarropa
hatchet [ˈhætʃɪt] *s* destral *m,* hacha pequeña; **to bury the hatchet** envainar la espada
hatch'way' *s* (*trap door*) escotillón *m;* (*opening in ship's deck*) escotilla
hate [het] *s* odio, aborrecimiento || *tr & intr* odiar, aborrecer, detestar
hateful [ˈhetfəl] *adj* odioso, aborrecible
hat'pin' *s* aguja de sombrero, pasador *m*
hat'rack' *s* percha
hatred [ˈhetrɪd] *s* odio, aborrecimiento
hat shop *s* bonetería
hatter [ˈhætər] *s* sombrerero
haughtiness [ˈhɔtɪnɪs] *s* altanería, altivez *f*
haugh•ty [ˈhɔti] *adj* (*comp* **-tier;** *super* **-iest**) altanero, altivo
haul [hɔl] *s* (*pull, tug*) tirón *m;* (*amount caught*) redada; (*distance transported*) trayecto, recorrido; (*roundup, e.g., of thieves*) redada || *tr* acarrear, transportar; (naut) halar
haunch [hɔntʃ] o [hɑntʃ] *s* (*hip*) cadera; (*hind quarter of an animal*) anca; (*leg of animal used for food*) pierna
haunt [hɔnt] o [hɑnt] *s* guarida, nidal *m,* querencia || *tr* andar por, vagar por; frecuentar; inquietar, molestar; perseguir (*las memorias a una persona*)
haunted house *s* casa de fantasmas
haute couture [ot kuˈtyr] *s* alta moda
Havana [həˈvænə] *s* La Habana
have [hæv] *v* (*pret & pp* **had** [hæd]) *tr* tener; (*to get, to take*) tomar; **to have and to hold** (úsase sólo en el infinitivo) para ser poseído en propiedad; **to have got** (coll) tener, poseer; **to have got to** + *inf* (coll) tener que + *inf;* **to have it in for** (coll) tener tirria a; **to have it out with** (coll) habérselas con, emprenderla con; **to have on** llevar puesto; **to have** (*something*) **to do with** tener que ver con; **to have what it takes to** tener madera de; **to have** + *inf* hacer, mandar + *inf,* p.ej., **I had him go out that door** le hice salir por esa puerta; **to have** + *pp* hacer, mandar + *inf,* p.ej., **I had my watch repaired** hice componer mi reloj || *intr* — **to have at** atacar, embestir; **to have to** + *inf* tener que + *inf;* **to have to do with** (*to be concerned with*) tratar de; (*to have connections with*) tener relaciones con || *v aux* haber, p.ej., **he has studied his lesson** ha estudiado su lección
havelock [ˈhævlɑk] *s* cogotera
haven [ˈhevən] *s* puerto; abrigo, asilo, buen puerto
have-not [ˈhævˌnɑt] *s* — **the haves and the have-nots** (coll) los ricos y los desposeídos
haversack [ˈhævərˌsæk] *s* barjuleta; (*of soldier*) mochila
havoc [ˈhævək] *s* estrago, estragos; **to play havoc with** hacer grandes estragos en
haw [hɔ] *s* (*of hawthorn*) baya, simiente *f;* (*in speech*) vacilación || *interj* ¡a la izquierda! || *tr & intr* volver a la izquierda
haw'-haw' *s* carcajada
hawk [hɔk] *s* halcón *m,* gavilán *m,* cernícalo; (*mortarboard*) esparavel *m;* (*sharper*) (coll) fullero || *tr* pregonar; **to hawk up** arrojar tosiendo || *intr* carraspear, gargajear
hawker [ˈhɔkər] *s* buhonero
hawksbill turtle [ˈhɔksˌbɪl] *s* carey *m*
hawse [hɔz] *s* (naut) muz *m;* (*hole*) (naut) escobén *m;* (naut) longitud de cadenas
hawse'hole' *s* (naut) escobén *m*
hawser [ˈhɔzər] *s* (naut) guindaleza
haw'thorn' *s* espino, oxiacanta

hay [he] *s* heno; **to hit the hay** (slang) acostarse; **to make hay while the sun shines** hacer su agosto
hay fever *s* fiebre *f* del heno
hay'field' *s* henar *m*
hay'fork' *s* horca; (*machine*) elevador *m* de heno
hay'loft' *s* henil *m*, henal *m*
hay'mak'er *s* (box) golpe *m* que pone fuera de combate
haymow ['he,maʊ] *s* henil *m;* acopio de heno
hay'rack' *s* pesebre *m*
hayrick ['he,rɪk] *s* almiar *m*
hay ride *s* paseo de placer en carro de heno
hay'seed' *s* simiente *f* de heno; (coll) patán *m*, campesino
hay'stack' *s* almiar *m*
hay'wire' *adj* (slang) descompuesto; (slang) destornillado, loco ‖ *s* alambre *m* para embalar el heno
hazard ['hæzərd] *s* peligro, riesgo; (*chance*) acaso, azar *m;* (golf) obstáculo; **at all hazards** por grande que sea el riesgo ‖ *tr* arriesgar; aventurar (*una opinión*)
hazardous ['hæzərdəs] *adj* peligroso, arriesgado
haze [hez] *s* calina, bruma; (fig) confusión, vaguedad ‖ *tr* dar novatada a
hazel ['hezəl] *adj* castaño claro ‖ *s* avellano
ha'zel•nut *s* avellana
hazing ['hezɪŋ] *s* novatada
ha•zy ['hezi] *adj* (*comp* **-zier;** *super* **-ziest**) calinoso, brumoso; confuso, vago
H-bomb ['etʃ,bɑm] *s* bomba de hidrógeno
H.C. *abbr* **House of Commons**
hd. *abbr* **head**
hdqrs. *abbr* **headquarters**
H.E. *abbr* **His Eminence, His Excellency**
he [hi] *pron pers* (*pl* **they**) él ‖ *s* (*pl* **hes**) macho, varón *m*
head [hɛd] *s* cabeza; (*of a bed*) cabecera; (*caption*) encabezamiento; (*of a boil*) centro; (*on a glass of beer*) espuma; (*of a drum*) parche *m;* (*of a cane*) puño; (*of a barrel, cylinder, etc.*) fondo, tapa; (*of cylinder of automobile engine*) culata; crisis *f*, punto decisivo; **at the head of** al frente de; **from head to foot** de pies a cabeza; **head over heels** en un salto mortal; hasta los tuétanos; precipitadamente; **heads** (*of a coin*) cara; **heads or tails?** ¿cara o cruz?; ¿águila o sol? (Mex); **over one's head** fuera del alcance de uno; (*going to a higher authority*) por encima de uno; **to be out of one's head** (coll) delirar; **to come into one's head** pasarle a uno por la cabeza; **to go to one's head** subírsele a uno a la cabeza; **to keep one's head;** no perder la cabeza; **to keep one's head above water** no dejarse vencer; **to put heads together** consultarse entre sí; **to not make head or tail of** no ver pies ni cabeza a ‖ *tr* acaudillar, dirigir, mandar; estar a la cabeza de (*p.ej., la clase*); venir primero en (*una lista*) ‖ *intr* — **to head towards** dirigirse hacia
head'ache' *s* dolor *m* de cabeza
head'band' *s* cinta para la cabeza; (*of a book*) cabezada
head'board' *s* cabecera de cama
head'cheese' *s* queso de cerdo
head'dress' *s* (*style of hair*) tocado; prenda para la cabeza
header ['hɛdər] *s* — **to take a header** (coll) caerse de cabeza
head'first' *adv* de cabeza; precipitadamente
head'gear' *s* sombrero; (*for protection*) casco
head'hunt'er *s* cazador *m* de cabezas
heading ['hɛdɪŋ] *s* encabezamiento; (*of a letter*) membrete *m;* (*of a chapter of a book*) cabecera
headland ['hɛdlənd] *s* promontorio
headless ['hɛdlɪs] *adj* sin cabeza; sin jefe; estúpido
head'light' *s* (aut) faro; (naut) farol *m* de tope; (rr) farol *m*
head'line' *s* (*of newspaper*) cabecera; (*of a page of a book*) titulillo, título de página ‖ *tr* poner cabecera a; (slang) destacar, dar cartel a (*un actor*)
head'lin'er *s* (slang) atracción principal
head'long' *adj* de cabeza; precipitado ‖ *adv* de cabeza; precipitadamente
head•man ['hɛd,mæn] *s* (*pl* **-men** [,mɛn]) caudillo, jefe *m*
head'mas'ter *s* director *m* de un colegio
head'most' *adj* delantero, primero
head office *s* oficina central
head of hair *s* cabellera
head'-on' *adj & adv* de frente; **head-on collision** colisión de frente
head'phone' *s* auricular *m* de casco, receptor *m* de cabeza
head'piece' *s* (*any covering for head*) casco, yelmo, morrión *m;* (*brains, judgment*) cabeza, juicio; cabecera de cama; (*headset*) auricular *m* de casco, receptor *m* de cabeza; (typ) cabecera, viñeta
head'quar'ters *s* centro de dirección; (*of police*) jefatura; (mil) cuartel *m* general
head'rest' *s* apoyo para la cabeza; (aut) reposa cabezas
head'set' *s* auricular *m* de casco, receptor *m* de cabeza
head'ship' *s* jefatura, dirección
head'stone' *s* (*cornerstone*) piedra angular; (*on a grave*) lápida sepulcral
head'stream' *s* afluente *m* principal
head'strong' *adj* cabezudo, terco
head'wait'er *s* jefe *m* de camareros, encargado de comedor
head'wa'ters *spl* cabecera
head'way' *s* avance *m*, progreso; espacio libre; **to make headway** avanzar, progresar
head'wear' *s* prendas de cabeza
head wind *s* viento de frente, viento por la proa
head'work' *s* trabajo intelectual
head•y ['hɛdi] *adj* (*comp* **-ier;** *super* **-iest**) excitante, emocionante; impetuoso, violento; (*intoxicating*) cabezudo; (*clever*) sesudo

heal [hil] *tr* curar, sanar; cicatrizar; remediar (*un daño*) || *intr* curar, sanar; cicatrizarse; remediarse
healer [ˈhilər] *s* curador *m*, sanador *m*
health [hɛlθ] *s* salud *f;* **to be in good health** estar bien de salud; **to be in poor health** estar mal de salud; **to drink to the health of** beber a la salud de; **to radiate health** verter salud; **to your health!** ¡a su salud!
healthful [ˈhɛlθfəl] *adj* saludable; sano
health insurance *s* seguro de enfermedad
health•y [ˈhɛlθi] *adj* (*comp* **-ier;** *super* **-iest**) sano; saludable
heap [hip] *s* montón *m* || *tr* amontonar, apilar; (*to supply with, e.g., favors*) colmar; (*to bestow in great quantity*) dar generosamente || *intr* amontonarse, apilarse
hear [hɪr] *v* (*pret & pp* **heard** [hʌrd]) *tr* oír; **to hear it said** oírlo decir || *intr* oír; **hear! hear!** ¡bravo!; **to hear about;** oír hablar de; **to hear from** tener noticias de; **to hear of** oír hablar de; **to hear tell of** oír hablar de; **to hear that** oír decir que
hearer [ˈhɪrər] *s* oyente *mf*
hearing [ˈhɪrɪŋ] *s* (*sense*) oído; (*act*) oída; audiencia; **in the hearing of** en presencia de; **within hearing** al alcance del oído
hearing aid *s* aparato auditivo
hear'say' *s* rumor *m;* **by hearsay** de o por oídas
hearse [hʌrs] *s* coche *m* fúnebre, carroza fúnebre
heart [hɑrt] *s* corazón *m;* (*e.g., of lettuce*) cogollo; **after one's heart** enteramente del gusto de uno; **by heart** de memoria; **heart and soul** de todo corazón; **to break the heart of** partir el corazón de; **to die of a broken heart** morir de pena; **to eat one's heart out** sufrir en silencio; **to get to the heart of** llegar al fondo de; **to have one's heart in one's work;** trabajar con entusiasmo; **to have one's heart in the right place** tener buenas intenciones; **to lose heart** descorazonarse; **to open one's heart to** descubrirse con; **to take heart** cobrar aliento; **to take to heart** tomar a pecho; **to wear one's heart on one's sleeve** llevar el corazón en la mano; **with all one's heart** con toda el alma de uno; **with one's heart in one's mouth** con el credo en la boca
heart'ache' *s* angustia, congoja
heart attack *s* ataque *m* de corazón, ataque cardíaco
heart'beat' *s* latido del corazón
heart'break' *s* angustia, dolor *m* abrumador
heart'break'er *s* ladrón *m* de corazones
heartbroken [ˈhɑrt,brokən] *adj* transido de dolor, muerto de pena
heart'burn' *s* acedía, rescoldera; (*jealousy*) celos
heart disease *s* enfermedad del corazón
hearten [ˈhɑrtən] *tr* alentar, animar
heart failure *s* debilidad coronaria; (*death*) paro del corazón; (*faintness*) desfallecimiento, desmayo
heartfelt [ˈhɑrt,fɛlt] *adj* cordial, sentido, sincero
hearth [hɑrθ] *s* hogar *m*
hearth'stone' *s* solera del hogar; (*home*) hogar *m*
heartily [ˈhɑrtɪli] *adv* cordialmente; con buen apetito; de buena gana; bien, mucho
heartless [ˈhɑrtlɪs] *adj* cruel, inhumano
heart pacemaker *s* marcapaso, marcapasos *m*
heart-rending [ˈhɑrt,rɛndɪŋ] *adj* angustioso, que parte el corazón
heart'seed' *s* farolillo
heart'sick' *adj* afligido, desconsolado
heart'strings' *spl* fibras del corazón, entretelas
heart'-to-heart' *adj* franco, sincero
heart trouble *s* — **to have heart trouble** enfermar del corazón
heart'wood' *s* madera de corazón
heart•y [ˈhɑrti] *adj* (*comp* **-ier;** *super* **-iest**) cordial, sincero; sano, fuerte; (*meal*) abundante; (*laugh*) bueno; (*eater*) grande
heat [hit] *adj* térmico || *s* calor *m;* (*warming of a room, house, etc.*) calefacción; (*rut of animals*) celo; (*in horse racing*) carrera de prueba; (fig) ardor *m*, ímpetu *m;* **in heat** encelo || *tr* calentar; calefaccionar (*p.ej., una casa*); (fig) acalorar, excitar || *intr* calentarse; (fig) acalorarse, excitarse
heated [ˈhitɪd] *adj* acalorado
heater [ˈhitər] *s* calentador *m;* (*for central heating*) calorífero; (electron) calefactor *m*
heater man *s* calefactor *m*
heath [hiθ] *s* (*shrub*) brezo; (*tract of land*) brezal *m*
hea•then [ˈhiðən] *adj* gentil, pagano; irreligioso || *s* (*pl* **-then** o **-thens**) gentil *mf*, pagano
heathendom [ˈhiðəndəm] *s* gentilidad
heather [ˈhɛðər] *s* brezo
heating [ˈhitɪŋ] *adj* calentador || *s* calefacción
heat'-in'su•lat•ed *adj* termoaislante
heat lightning *s* fucilazo, relámpago de calor
heat shield *s* blindaje térmico, escudo térmico
heat'stroke' *s* insolación; golpe *m* de calor
heat wave *s* (phys) onda calorífica; (coll) ola de calor
heave [hiv] *s* esfuerzo para levantar; esfuerzo para levantarse; **heaves** (vet) huélfago || *v* (*pret & pp* **heaved** o **hov** [hov]) *tr* alzar, levantar; arrojar, lanzar; exhalar (*un suspiro*) || *intr* levantarse y bajar alternativamente; palpitar (*el pecho*); elevarse; hacer esfuerzos por vomitar
heaven [ˈhɛvən] *s* cielo; **for heaven's sake!** o **good heavens!** ¡válgame Dios!; **heavens** (*firmament*) cielo || **Heaven** *s* cielo (*mansión de los bienaventurados*)
heavenly [ˈhɛvənli] *adj* (*body*) celeste; (*life, home*) celestial; (fig) celestial
heavenly body *s* astro, cuerpo celeste
heav•y [ˈhɛvi] *adj* (*comp* **-ier;** *super* **-iest**) (*of great weight*) pesado; (*liquid*) espeso, denso; (*cloth, paper, sea, line*) grueso;

(*traffic*) denso; (*crop, harvest*) abundante, copioso; (*expense*) fuerte; (*rain*) recio; (*features*) basto; (*eyes*) agravado; (*gunfire*) fragoroso; (*heart*) abatido, triste; (*drinker*) grande; (*stock market*) postrado; (*clothing*) de mucho abrigo || *adv* pesadamente; **to hang heavy;** pasar (*el tiempo*) con gran lentitud

heav'y•du'ty *adj* extrafuerte

heavy-hearted ['hɛvi'hɑrtɪd] *adj* afligido, acongojado

heav'y•set' *adj* costilludo, espaldudo

heav'y•weight' *s* (box) peso pesado

Hebrew ['hibru] *adj & s* hebreo

hecatomb ['hɛkə,tom] *s* hecatombe *f*

heckle ['hɛkəl] *tr* interrumpir (*a un orador*) con preguntas impertinentes

hectic ['hɛktɪk] *adj* (coll) agitado, turbulento

hedge [hedʒ] *s* cercado, vallado; (*of bushes*) seto vivo; apuesta compensatoria; (*in stock market*) operación compensatoria || *tr* cercar con vallado; cercar con seto vivo; **to hedge in** encerrar, rodear || *intr* no querer comprometerse; hacer apuestas compensatorias; hacer operaciones compensatorias

hedge'hog' *s* erizo; (*porcupine*) puerco espín *m*

hedge'hop' *v* (*pret & pp* **-hopped;** *ger* **-hopping**) *intr* (aer) volar rasando el suelo

hedgehopping ['hɛdʒ,hɑpɪŋ] *s* (aer) vuelo rasante

hedge'row' *s* cercado de arbustos, seto vivo

heed [hid] *s* atención, cuidado; **to take heed** ir con cuidado || *tr* atender a, hacer caso de || *intr* atender, hacer caso

heedless ['hidlɪs] *adj* desatento, descuidado

heehaw ['hi,hɔ] *s* (*of donkey*) rebuzno; risotada || *intr* rebuznar; reír groseramente

heel [hil] *s* (*of foot*) calcañar *m,* talón *m;* (*of stocking or shoe*) talón *m;* (*raised part of shoe below heel*) tacón *m;* (slang) sinvergüenza *mf;* **down at the heel** desaliñado, mal vestido; **to cool one's heels** (coll) hacer antesala; **to kick up one's heels** (slang) mostrarse alegre; **to show a clean pair of heels** o **to take to one's heels** poner pies en polvorosa

heeler ['hilər] *s* (slang) muñidor *m*

heft•y ['hɛfti] *adj* (*comp* **-ier;** *super* **-iest**) (*heavy*) pesado; (*strong*) fuerte, fornido

hegemo•ny [hɪ'dʒɛməni] o ['hedʒɪ-,moni] *s* (*pl* **-nies**) hegemonía

hegira [hɪ'dʒəɪrə] o ['hɛdʒɪrə] *s* fuga, huída

heifer ['hɛfər] *s* novilla, vaquilla

height [hɑɪt] *s* altura; (*e.g., of folly*) colmo

heighten ['haɪtən] *tr* hacer más alto; (*to increase the amount of*) aumentar; (*to set off, bring out*) realzar || *intr* aumentarse

heinous ['henəs] *adj* atroz, nefando

heir [ɛr] *s* heredero

heir apparent *s* (*pl* **heirs apparent**) heredero forzoso

heirdom ['ɛrdəm] *s* herencia

heiress ['ɛrɪs] *s* heredera

heirloom ['ɛr,lum] *s* joya de familia, reliquia de familia

helicopter ['hɛlɪ,kɑptər] *s* helicóptero

heliotrope ['hilɪ•ə,trop] *s* heliotropo

heliport ['hɛlɪ,port] *s* helipuerto

helium ['hilɪ•əm] *s* helio

helix ['hilɪks] *s* (*pl* **helixes** o **helices** ['hɛlɪ,siz]) hélice *f*

hell [hɛl] *s* infierno

hell-bent ['hɛl'bɛnt] *adj* (slang) muy resuelto; **hell-bent on** (slang) empeñado en

hell'cat' *s* (*bad-tempered woman*) arpía, mujer perversa; (*witch*) bruja

hellebore ['hɛlɪ,bor] *s* eléboro

Hellene ['hɛlin] *s* heleno

Hellenic [hɛ'lɛnik] *adj* helénico

hell'fire' *s* fuego del infierno

hellish ['hɛlɪʃ] *adj* infernal

hel•lo [hɛ'lo] *s* saludo || *interj* ¡qué tal!; (*on telephone*) ¡diga!

hello girl *s* (coll) chica telefonista

helm [hɛlm] *s* barra del timón; rueda del timón; (fig) timón *m* || *tr* dirigir, gobernar

helmet ['hɛlmɪt] *s* casco; (*of ancient armor*) yelmo

helms•man ['hɛlmzmən] *s* (*pl* **-men** [mən]) timonel *m*

help [hɛlp] *s* ayuda, socorro; (*of food*) ración; (*relief*) remedio, p.ej., **there's no help for it** no hay remedio; criados; empleados; obreros; **to come to the help of** acudir en socorro de || *interj* ¡socorro! || *tr* ayudar, socorrer; aliviar, mitigar; (*to wait on*) servir; **it can't be helped** no hay remedio; **so help me God!** ¡así Dios me salve!; **to help down** ayudar a bajar; **to help a person with his coat** ayudarle a una persona a ponerse el abrigo; **to help oneself** valerse por sí mismo; servirse; **to help up** ayudar a subir; ayudar a levantarse; **to not be able to help** + *ger* no poder menos de + *inf,* p.ej., **he can't help laughing** no puede menos de reír || *intr* ayudar

helper ['helpər] *s* ayudante *mf;* (*in a drug store, barbershop, etc.*) mancebo

helpful ['hɛlpfəl] *adj* útil, provechoso; servicial

helping [['hɛlpɪŋ] *s* ración (*de alimento*)

helpless ['hɛlplɪs] *adj* (*weak*) débil; (*powerless*) impotente; (*penniless*) desvalido; (*confused*) perplejo; (*situation*) irremediable

help'meet' *s* compañero; (*wife*) compañera

helter-skelter ['hɛltər'skɛltər] *adj, adv & s* cochite hervite *m*

hem [hɛm] *s* tos fingida; (*of a garment*) bastilla, dobladillo || *interj* ¡ejem! || *v* (*pret & pp* **hemmed;** *ger* **hemming**) *tr* bastillar, dobladillar; **to hem in** encerrar, rodear || *intr* destoserse; vacilar; **to hem and haw** vacilar al hablar; ser evasivo

hemisphere ['hɛmɪ,sfɪr] *s* hemisferio

hemistich ['hɛmɪ,stɪk] *s* hemistiquio

hem'line' *s* ruedo de la falda, borde *m* de la falda

hem'lock' *s* (*Tsuga canadensis*) abeto del Canadá; (*herb and poison*) cicuta

hemoglobin [,hɛmə'globɪn] o [,himə'globɪn] *s* hemoglobina

hemophilia [,hɛmə'fɪlɪ•ə] o [,himə'fɪlɪ•ə] *s* hemofilia
hemorrhage ['hɛmərɪdʒ] *s* hemorragia
hemorrhoids ['hɛmə,rɔɪdz] *spl* hemorroides *fpl*
hemostat ['hɛmə,stæt] o ['himə,stæt] *s* hemóstato
hemp [hɛmp] *s* cáñamo
hemstitch ['hɛm,stɪtʃ] *s* vainica ‖ *tr* hacer vainica en ‖ *intr* hacer vainica
hen [hɛn] *s* gallina
hence [hɛns] *adv* de aquí; desde ahora; por lo tanto, por consiguiente; de aquí a, p.ej., **three weeks hence** de aquí a tres semanas
hence'forth' *adv* de aquí en adelante
hench•man ['hɛntʃmən] *s* (*pl* **-men** [mən]) secuaz *m*, servidor *m;* (*political schemer*) muñidor *m*
hen'coop' *s* gallinero
hen'house' *s* gallinero
henna ['hɛnə] *s* alcana, alheña; (*dye*) henna *f* ‖ *tr* alheñarse (*el pelo*)
hen'peck' *tr* dominar (*la mujer al marido*)
henpecked husband *s* calzonazos *m*, gurrumino
hep [hɛp] *adj* (slang) enterado; **to be hep to** (slang) estar al corriente de
her [hʌr] *adj poss* su; el . . . de ella ‖ *pron pers* la; ella; **to her** le; a ella
herald ['hɛrəld] *s* heraldo; anunciador *m* ‖ *tr* anunciar; ser precursor de
heraldic [hɛ'rældɪk] *adj* heráldico
herald•ry ['hɛrəldri] *s* (*pl* **-ries**) (*office or duty of herald*) heraldía; (*science of armorial bearings*) blasón *m*, heráldica; (*heraldic device; coat of arms*) blasón; pompa heráldica
herb [ʌrb] o [hʌrb] *s* hierba; hierba aromática; hierba medicinal
herbaceous [hʌr'beʃəs] *adj* herbáceo
herbage ['ʌrbɪdʒ] o ['hʌrbɪdʒ] *s* herbaje *m*
herbal ['ʌrbəl] o ['hʌrbəl] *adj & s* herbario
herbalist ['hʌrbəlɪst] o ['ʌrbəlɪst] *s* herbolario
herbari•um [hʌr'bɛrɪ•əm] *s* (*pl* **-ums** o **-a** [ə]) herbario
herb doctor *s* herbolario
herculean [hʌr'kulɪ•ən] *adj* (*hard to perform*) penoso, laborioso; (*strong, big*) hercúleo
herd [hʌrd] *s* manada, rebaño, hato; (*of people*) chusma, multitud ‖ *tr* reunir en manada; reunir ‖ *intr* reunirse en manada; reunirse, ir juntos
herds•man ['hʌrdzmən] *s* (*pl* **-men** [mən]) manadero; (*of sheep*) pastor *m;* (*of cattle*) vaquero
here [hɪr] *adj* presente ‖ *adv* aquí; **here and there** acá y allá; **here is** o **here are** aquí tiene Vd.; **that's neither here nor there** eso no viene al caso ‖ *s* — **the here and the hereafter** esta vida y la futura ‖ *interj* ¡presente!
hereabouts ['hɪrə,baʊts] *adv* por aquí, cerca de aquí
here•af'ter *adv* de aquí en adelante; en lo sucesivo; en la vida futura ‖ **the hereafter** la otra vida, el más allá
here•by' *adv* por esto; por la presente
hereditary [hɪ'rɛdɪ,tɛri] *adj* hereditario
heredi•ty [hɪ'rɛdɪti] *s* (*pl* **-ties**) herencia
here•in' *adv* aquí dentro; en este asunto
here•of' *adv* de esto
here•on' *adv* en esto, sobre esto
here•sy ['hɛrəsi] *s* (*pl* **-sies**) herejía
heretic ['hɛrətɪk] *adj* herético ‖ *s* hereje *mf*
heretical [hɪ'rɛtɪkəl] *adj* herético
heretofore [,hɪtrʊ'for] *adv* antes, hasta ahora
here'u•pon' *adv* en esto, sobre esto; en seguida
here•with' *adv* adjunto, con la presente; de este modo
heritage ['hɛrɪtɪdʒ] *s* herencia
hermetic(al) [hʌr'mɛtɪk(əl)] *adj* hermético
hermit ['hʌrmɪt] *s* eremita *m*, ermitaño
hermitage ['hʌrmɪtɪdʒ] *s* ermita
herni•a ['hʌrnɪ•ə] *s* (*pl* **-as** o **-ae** [,i]) hernia
he•ro ['hɪro] *s* (*pl* **-roes**) héroe *m*
heroic [hɪ'ro•ɪk] *adj* heroico ‖ **heroics** *spl* verso heroico; lenguaje rimbombante
heroin ['hɛro•ɪn] *s* heroína (*polvo cristalino*); (slang) caballo
heroin addict *s* heroinómano
heroine ['hɛro•ɪn] *s* heroína (*mujer*)
heroism ['hɛro,ɪzəm] *s* heroísmo
heron ['hɛrən] *s* garza; (*Ardea cinerea*) airón *m*, garza real
herring ['hɛrɪŋ] *s* arenque *m*
her'ring•bone *s* (*in fabrics*) espina de pescado; (*in hardwood floors*) espinapez *m*, punto de Hungría
hers [hʌrz] *pron poss* el suyo, el de ella; suyo
herself [hʌr'sɛlf] *pron pers* ella misma; sí, sí misma; se, p.ej., **she enjoyed herself** se divirtió; **with herself** consigo
hesitan•cy ['hɛzɪtənsi] *s* (*pl* **-cies**) vacilación
hesitant ['hɛzɪtənt] *adj* vacilante
hesitate ['hɛzɪ,tet] *intr* vacilar, titubear; (*to stutter*) titubear
hesitation [,hɛzɪ'teʃən] *s* vacilación
heterodox ['hɛtərə,dɑks] *adj* heterodoxo
heterodyne ['hɛtərə,daɪn] *adj* heterodino ‖ *tr* heterodinar
heterogenei•ty [,hɛtərədʒɪ'ni•ɪti] *s* (*pl* **-ties**) heterogeneidad
heterogeneous [,hɛtərə'dʒinɪ•əs] *adj* heterogéneo
hew [hju] *v* (*pret* **hewed;** *pp* **hewed** o **hewn**) *tr* cortar, tajar; (*with an ax*) hachear; labrar (*madera*); picar (*piedra*); **to hew down** derribar a hachazos ‖ *intr* — **to hew close to the line** (coll) hilar delgado
hex [hɛks] *s* (coll) bruja; (coll) hechizo ‖ *tr* (coll) embrujar
hexameter [hɛks'æmɪtər] *s* hexámetro
hey [he] *interj* ¡oye!, ¡oiga!
hey'day' *s* época de mayor prosperidad
hf. *abbr* **half**
H.H. *abbr* **His Highness, Her Highness; His Holiness**
hia•tus [haɪ'etəs] *s* (*pl* **-tuses** o **-tus**) (*gap*) abertura, laguna; (*in a text; in verse*) hiato

hibernate ['haɪbər,net] *intr* invernar; estar inactivo
hibiscus [hɪ'bɪskəs] o [haɪ'bɪskəs] *s* hibisco
hiccough o **hiccup** ['hɪkəp] *s* hipo || *intr* hipar
hick [hɪk] *adj & s* (coll) campesino, palurdo
hicko•ry ['hɪkəri] *s* (*pl* **-ries**) nuez encarcelada, nuez dura (*árbol*)
hickory nut *s* nuez encarcelada, nuez dura (*fruto*)
hidden ['hɪdən] *adj* escondido, oculto; obscuro
hide [haɪd] *s* cuero, piel *f;* **hides** corambre *f;* **neither hide nor hair** ni un vestigio; **to tan someone's hide** (coll) zurrarle a uno la badana || *v* (*pret* **hid** [hɪd]; *pp* **hid** o **hidden** ['hɪdən]) *tr* esconder, ocultar || *intr* esconderse, ocultarse; **to hide out** (coll) recatarse
hide'-and-seek' *s* escondite *m;* **to play hide-and-seek** jugar al escondite
hide'bound' *adj* fanático, obstinado, dogmático
hideous ['hɪdɪ•əs] *adj* (*very ugly*) feote; (*heinous*) atroz, nefando; (*distressingly large*) brutal, enorme
hide'-out' *s* (coll) guarida, refugio, escondrijo
hiding ['haɪdɪŋ] *s* ocultación; (*place of concealment*) escondite *m,* escondrijo; **in hiding** escondido, oculto; (*in ambush*) emboscado
hiding place *s* escondite *m,* escondrijo
hie [haɪ] *v* (*pret & pp* **hied;** *ger* **hieing** o **hying**) *tr* — **hie thee home** apresúrate a volver a casa || *intr* apresurarse, ir volando
hierar•chy ['haɪ•ə,rɑrki] *s* (*pl* **-chies**) jerarquía
hieroglyphic [,haɪ•ərə'glɪfɪk] *adj & s* jeroglífico
hi-fi ['haɪ'faɪ] *adj* de alta fidelidad || *s* alta fidelidad
hi-fi fan *s* aficionado a la alta fidelidad
hi-fi set *s* equipo de alta fidelidad
higgledy-piggledy ['hɪgəldi'pɪgəldi] *adj* confuso, revuelto || *adv* confusamente, revueltamente
high [haɪ] *adj* alto; (*river*) crecido; (*sound*) agudo; (*wind*) fuerte; (coll) borracho; (*intoxicated*) embriagado; (*drugs*) emporrado; (culin) manido; **high and dry** abandonado, desamparado; **high and mighty** (coll) muy arrogante || *adv* en sumo grado; a gran precio; **to aim high** poner el tiro muy alto; **to come high** venderse caro || *s* (aut) marcha directa; **on high** en el cielo
high altar *s* altar *m* mayor
high'ball' *s* highball *m*
high blood pressure *s* hipertensión arterial
high'born' *adj* linajudo, de ilustre cuna
high'boy' *s* cómoda alta con patas altas
high'brow' *adj & s* (slang) erudito
high chair *s* silla alta
high command *s* alto mando
high cost of living *s* carestía de la vida
higher education *s* enseñanza superior
higher-up [,haɪ•ər'ʌp] *s* (coll) superior jerárquico
high explosive *s* explosivo rompedor
highfalutin [,haɪfə'lutən] *adj* (coll) pomposo, presuntuoso
high fidelity *s* alta fidelidad
high'-fre'quency *adj* de alta frecuencia
high gear *s* marcha directa, toma directa
high'-grade' *adj* de calidad superior
high-handed ['haɪ'hændɪd] *adj* arbitrario
high hat *s* sombrero de copa
high'-hat' *adj* (coll) copetudo, esnob; **to be high-hat** tener mucho copete || **high'-hat'** *v* (*pret & pp* **-hatted;** *ger* **-hatting**) *tr* desairar
high-heeled shoe ['haɪ,hild] *s* zapato de tacón alto
high horse *s* ademán *m* arrogante
high'jack' *tr* var de **hijack**
high jinks [dʒɪŋks] *spl* (slang) jarana, payasada
high jump *s* salto de altura
highland ['haɪlənd] *s* región montañosa; **highlands** montañas, tierras altas
high life *s* alta sociedad, gran mundo
high'light' *s* elemento sobresaliente || *tr* destacar
highly ['haɪli] *adv* altamente; en sumo grado; a gran precio; con aplauso general; **to speak highly of** decir mil bienes de
High Mass *s* misa cantada, misa mayor
high-minded ['haɪ'maɪndɪd] *adj* noble, magnánimo
highness ['haɪnɪs] *s* altura || **Highness** *s* Alteza
high noon *s* pleno mediodía
high-pitched ['haɪ'pɪtʃt] *adj* agudo; tenso, impresionable
high-powered ['haɪ'paʊ•ərd] *adj* de alta potencia
high'-pres'sure *adj* de alta presión; (fig) emprendedor, enérgico || *tr* (coll) apremiar
high-priced ['haɪ'praɪst] *adj* de precio elevado
high priest *s* sumo sacerdote
high rise *s* edificio de muchos pisos
high'road' *s* camino real
high school *s* escuela de segunda enseñanza
high sea *s* mar gruesa; **high seas** alta mar
high society *s* alta sociedad, gran mundo
high'-speed' *adj* de alta velocidad
high-spirited ['haɪ'spɪrɪtɪd] *adj* animoso; vivaz; (*horse*) fogoso
high spirits *spl* alegría, buen humor *m,* animación
high-strung ['haɪ'strʌŋ] *adj* tenso, impresionable
high'-test' fuel *s* supercarburante *m*
high tide *s* pleamar *f,* marea alta; (fig) punto culminante
high time *s* hora, p.ej., **it is high time for you to go** ya es hora de que Vd. se marche; (slang) jarana, parranda
high treason *s* alta traición
high water *s* aguas altas; pleamar *f,* marea alta
high'way' *s* carretera

highway•man [ˈhaɪ,wemən] *s* (*pl* **-men** [mən]) salteador *m* de caminos
hijack [ˈhaɪ,dʒæk] *tr* (coll) robar (*a un contrabandista de licores*); (coll) robar (*el licor a un contrabandista*)
hijacker [ˈhaɪ,dʒækər] *s* pirata aéreo
hijacking [ˈhaɪ,dʒækɪŋ] *s* piratería aérea
hike [haɪk] *s* caminata, marcha; (*increase, rise*) aumento ‖ *tr* elevar de un tirón; aumentar ‖ *intr* dar una caminata
hiker [ˈhaɪkər] *s* caminador *m*, aficionado a las caminatas
hilarious [hɪˈlɛrɪ•əs] o [haɪˈlɛrɪ•əs] *adj* jubiloso, regocijado
hill [hɪl] *s* colina, collado ‖ *tr* aporcar (*las hortalizas*)
hillbil•ly [ˈhɪl,bɪli] *s* (*pl* **-lies**) (coll) rústico montañés (*del sur de los EE.UU.*)
hillock [ˈhɪlək] *s* altozano, montecillo
hill'side' *s* ladera
hill'top' *s* cumbre *f*, cima
hill•y [ˈhɪli] *adj* (*comp* **-ier;** *super* **-iest**) colinoso; (*steep*) empinado
hilt [hɪlt] *s* empuñadura, puño; **up to the hilt** completamente
him [hɪm] *pron pers* le, lo; él; **to him** le; a él
himself [hɪmˈsɛlf] *pron pers* él mismo; sí, sí mismo; se, p.ej., **he enjoyed himself** se divirtió; **with himself** consigo
hind [haɪnd] *adj* posterior, trasero ‖ *s* cierva
hinder [ˈhɪndər] *tr* estorbar, impedir; obstruccionar
hindmost [ˈhaɪnd,most] *adj* postrero, último
Hindoo [ˈhɪndu] *adj & s* hindú *m*
hind'quar'ter *s* cuarto trasero
hindrance [ˈhɪndrəns] *s* estorbo, impedimento, obstáculo
hind'sight' *s* (*of a firearm*) mira posterior; percepción tardía, sabiduría tardía
Hindu [ˈhɪndu] *adj & s* hindú *m*
hinge [hɪndʒ] *s* (*of a door*) charnela, gozne *m*, bisagra; (*of a mollusk*) charnela; (bb) cartivana; punto capital ‖ *tr* engoznar ‖ *intr* — **to hinge on** depender de
hin•ny [ˈhɪni] *s* (*pl* **-nies**) burdégano, mohino
hint [hɪnt] *s* indirecta, insinuación; **to take the hint** darse por aludido ‖ *tr & intr* insinuar; indicar; **to hint at** aludir indirectamente a
hinterland [ˈhɪntər,lænd] *s* región interior
hip [hɪp] *s* cadera; (*of a roof*) caballete *m*, lima
hip'bone' *s* cía, hueso de la cadera
hipped [hɪpt] *adj* (*livestock*) renco; (*roof*) a cuatro aguas; **hipped on** (coll) obsesionado por
hippety-hop [ˈhɪpɪtɪˈhɑp] *adv* (coll) a coxcojita
hip•po [ˈhɪpo] *s* (*pl* **-pos**) (coll) hipopótamo
hippodrome [ˈhɪpə,drom] *s* hipódromo
hippopota•mus [,hipəˈpɑtəməs] *s* (*pl* **-muses** o **-mi** [,maɪ]) hipopótamo
hip roof *s* tejado a cuatro aguas
hire [haɪr] *s* alquiler *m;* precio; salario; **for hire** de alquiler ‖ *tr* alquilar (*p.ej., un coche*); ajustar (*p.ej., a un criado*) ‖ *intr* —**to hire out** ajustarse
hired girl *s* criada
hired man *s* (coll) mozo de campo
hireling [ˈhaɪrlɪŋ] *adj & s* alquiladizo
his [hɪz] *adj poss* su; el . . . de él ‖ *pron poss* el suyo, el de él; suyo
Hispanic [hɪsˈpænɪk] *adj & s* hispánico
Hispaniola [,hɪspənˈjolə] *s* Santo Domingo
hispanist [ˈhɪspənɪst] *s* hispanista *mf*
hispanophilia [hɪs,pænoˈfɪli•ə] *s* españolería
hiss [hɪs] *s* siseo, silbido ‖ *tr* sisear, silbar (*p.ej., una escena, a un actor por malo*) ‖ *intr* sisear, silbar
hist. *abbr* **historian, history**
histology [hɪsˈtɑlədʒi] *s* histología
historian [hɪsˈtorɪ•ən] *s* historiador *m*
historic(al) [hɪsˈtɔrɪk(əl)] *adj* histórico
histo•ry [ˈhɪstəri] *s* (*pl* **-ries**) historia
histrionic [,hɪstrɪˈɑnɪk] *adj* histriónico; teatral ‖ **histrionics** *s* actitud teatral, modales *mpl* teatrales
hit [hɪt] *s* golpe *m;* (*of a bullet*) impacto; (*blow that hits its mark*) tiro certero; (*sarcastic remark*) censura acerba; (baseball) batazo; (coll) éxito; **to make a hit** (coll) dar golpe; **to make a hit with** caer en la gracia de (*una persona*) ‖ *v (pret & pp* **hit;** *ger* **hitting**) *tr* golpear, pegar; dar con, dar contra, chocar con; dar en (*p.ej., el blanco*); censurar acerbamente; (*to run over in a car*) atropellar; afectar mucho (*un acontecimiento a una persona*) ‖ *intr* chocar; **to hit against** dar contra; **to hit on** dar con (*lo que se busca*)
hit'-and-run' *adj* que atropella y se da a la huída
hitch [hɪtʃ] *s* (*jerk*) tirón *m;* dificultad; obstáculo; **without a hitch** a pedir de boca, sin tropiezo ‖ *tr (to tie)* atar, sujetar; enganchar (*un caballo*); uncir (*bueyes*); (slang) casar
hitch'hike' *intr* (coll) hacer autostop, viajar en autostop
hitch'hik'er *s* autostopista *mf*
hitching post *s* poste *m* para atar a las cabalgaduras
hither [ˈhɪðər] *adv* acá, hacia acá; **hither and thither** acá y allá
hith'er•to' *adv* hasta ahora, hasta aquí
hit'-or-miss' *adj* descuidado, casual
hit parade *s* (rad) canciones que gozan de más popularidad en la actualidad
hit record *s* (coll) disco de mucho éxito
hit'-run' *adj* que atropella y se da a la huída
hive [haɪv] *s* (*box for bees*) colmena; (*swarm*) enjambre *m;* **hives** urticaria ‖ *tr* encorchar (*abejas*)
H.M. *abbr* **Her Majesty, His Majesty**
H.M.S. *abbr* **Her Majesty's Ship, His Majesty's Ship**
hoard [hord] *s* (*of money, provisions, etc.*) cúmulo; tesoro escondido ‖ *tr* acumular secretamente; atesorar (*dinero*) ‖ *intr* guardar víveres, atesorar dinero
hoarding [ˈhordɪŋ] *s* acumulación secreta; atesoramiento
hoar'frost' *s* helada blanca, escarcha
hoarse [hors] *adj* ronco

hoarseness [ˈhorsnɪs] *s* ronquedad; (*from a cold*) ronquera

hoar•y [ˈhori] *adj* (*comp* **-ier;** *super* **-iest**) cano, canoso; (*old*) vetusto

hoax [hoks] *s* pajarota, mistificación ‖ *tr* mistificar

hob [hɑb] *s* repisa interior del hogar; **to play hob with** (coll) trastornar

hobble [ˈhɑbəl] *s* (*limp*) cojera; (*rope used to tie legs of animal*) manea, traba ‖ *tr* dejar cojo; manear, trabar; dificultar ‖ *intr* cojear; tambalear

hobble skirt *s* falda de medio paso

hob•by [ˈhɑbi] *s* (*pl* **-bies**) comidilla, afición favorita, trabajo preferido; **to ride a hobby** entregarse demasiado al tema favorito

hob′by•horse′ *s* (*stick with horse's head*) caballito; (*rocking horse*) caballo mecedor

hob′gob′lin *s* duende *m*, trasgo; (*bogy*) bu *m*, coco

hob′nail′ *s* tachuela ‖ *tr* clavetear con tachuelas; (fig) atropellar

hob•nob [ˈhɑb,nɑb] *v* (*pret & pp* **-nobbed;** *ger* **-nobbing**) *intr* codearse, rozarse; beber juntos

ho•bo [ˈhobo] *s* (*pl* **-bos** o **-boes**) vagabundo

Hobson's choice [ˈhɑbsənz] *s* alternativa entre la cosa ofrecida o ninguna

hock [hɑk] *s* jarrete *m*, corvejón *m* ‖ *tr* (*to hamstring*) desjarretar; (coll) empeñar

hockey [ˈhɑki] *s* hockey *m*, chueca

hock′shop′ *s* (slang) casa de empeños, monte *m* de piedad

hocus-pocus [ˈhokəsˈpokəs] *s* (*meaningless formula*) abracadabra *m;* burla, engaño; juego de manos

hod [hɑd] *s* capacho, cuezo; cubo para carbón

hod carrier *s* peón *m* de albañil, peón de mano

hodgepodge [ˈhɑdʒ,pɑdʒ] *s* baturrillo

hoe [ho] *s* azada, azadón *m* ‖ *tr & intr* azadonar

hog [hɑg] o [hɔg] *s* cerdo, puerco ‖ *v* (*pret & pp* **hogged;** *ger* **hogging**) *tr* (slang) tragarse lo mejor de

hog′back′ *s* cuchilla

hoggish [ˈhɑgɪʃ] o [ˈhɔgɪʃ] *adj* comilón; glotón; egoísta

hog Latin *s* latín *m* de cocina

hogs′head′ *s* pipa de 63 galones o más; medida de capacidad de 63 galones

hog′wash′ *s* bazofia

hoist [hɔɪst] *s* (*apparatus for lifting*) montacargas *m*, torno izador, grúa; empujón *m* hacia arriba ‖ *tr* alzar, levantar; enarbolar (*p.ej., una bandera*); (naut) izar

hoity-toity [ˈhɔɪtiˈtɔɪti] *adj* frívolo, veleidoso; arrogante, altanero; **to be hoity-toity** ponerse tan alto

hokum [ˈhokəm] *s* (coll) música celestial, tonterías

hold [hold] *s* (*grip*) agarro; (*handle*) asa, mango; autoridad, dominio; (*in wrestling*) presa; (aer) cabina de carga; (mus) calderón *m;* (naut) bodega; **to take hold of** agarrar, coger; apoderarse de ‖ *v* (*pret & pp* **held** [hɛld]) *tr* tener, retener; (*to hold up, support*) apoyar, sostener; (*e.g., with a pin*) sujetar; contener, tener cabida para; ocupar (*un cargo, puesto, etc.*); celebrar (*una reunión*); sostener (*una opinión*); (mus) sostener (*una nota*); **to hold back** detener; retener; contener; **to hold in** refrenar; **to hold one's own** mantenerse firme, no perder terreno; **to hold over** aplazar, diferir; **to hold up** apoyar, sostener; (*to rob*) (coll) atracar ‖ *intr* ser valedero, seguir vigente; pegarse; **hold on!** ¡un momento!; **to hold back** refrenarse; **to hold forth** poner cátedra; **to hold off** esperar; mantenerse a distancia; **to hold on** agarrarse bien; **to hold on to** asirse de; **to hold out** no cejar; ir tirando; **to hold out for** insistir en

holder [ˈholdər] *s* tenedor *m*, posesor *m;* (*for a cigar or cigaret*) boquilla; (*to hold, e.g., a hot plate*) cojinillo; (*e.g., of a passport*) titular *m;* asa, mango

holding [ˈholdɪŋ] *s* tenencia, posesión; **holdings** valores habidos

holding company *s* sociedad de control, compañía tenedora

hold′up′ *s* (*stop, delay*) detención; atraco, asalto; precio excesivo

holdup man *s* atracador *m*, salteador *m*

hole [hol] *s* agujero; (*in cheese, bread, etc.*) ojo; (*in a road*) bache *m;* (*den of animals; den of vice*) guarida; (*dirty, disorderly dwelling*) cochitril *m;* **in the hole** adeudado, perdidoso; **to burn a hole in one's pocket** írsele a uno (*el dinero*) de entre las manos; **to pick holes in** (coll) poner reparos a ‖ *intr* — **to hole up** encovarse; buscar un rincón cómodo

holiday [ˈhɑlɪ,de] *s* día festivo; vacación

holiday attire *s* trapos de cristianar

holiness [ˈholɪnɪs] *s* santidad; **his Holiness** su Santidad

Holland [ˈhɑlənd] *s* Holanda

Hollander [ˈhɑləndər] *s* holandés *m*

hollow [ˈhɑlo] *adj* hueco; (*voice*) ahuecado, sepulcral; (*eyes, cheeks*) hundido; falso, engañoso ‖ *adv* — **to beat all hollow** (coll) derrotar completamente ‖ *s* hueco, cavidad; (*small valley*) vallecito ‖ *tr* ahuecar, excavar

hol•ly [ˈhɑli] *s* (*pl* **-lies**) acebo

hol′ly•hock′ *s* malva arbórea

holm oak [hom] *s* encina

holocaust [ˈhɑlə,kɔst] *s* holocausto

holster [ˈholstər] *s* pistolera

ho•ly [ˈholi] *adj* (*comp* **-lier;** *super* **-liest**) santo; (*e.g., writing*) sagrado; (*e.g., water*) bendito

Holy Ghost *s* Espíritu Santo

holy orders *spl* órdenes sagradas; **to take holy orders** recibir las órdenes sagradas, ordenarse

holy rood [rud] *s* crucifijo ‖ **Holy Rood** *s* Santa Cruz

Holy Scripture *s* Sagrada Escritura

Holy See *s* Santa Sede

Holy Sepulcher *s* santo sepulcro

holy water *s* agua bendita
Holy Writ *s* Sagrada Escritura
homage [ˈhɑmɪdʒ] o [ˈɑmɪdʒ] *s* homenaje *m;* (feud) homenaje, pleito homenaje
home [hom] *adj* casero, doméstico; nacional ‖ *s* casa, domicilio, hogar *m;* (*native heath*) patria chica; (*of the arts, etc.*) patria; (*for the sick, poor, etc.*) asilo; (sport) meta; **at home** en casa; en su propio país; (*ready to receive callers*) de recibo; (*at ease, comfortable*) a gusto; (sport) en campo propio; **away from home** fuera de casa; **make yourself at home** está Vd. en su casa ‖ *adv* en casa; a casa; **to see home** acompañar a casa; **to strike home** dar en lo vivo
home'bod'y *s* (*pl* **-ies**) hogareño
homebred [ˈhom,brɛd] *adj* doméstico; sencillo, inculto, tosco
home'brew' *s* cerveza o vino caseros
homecoming [ˈhom,kʌmɪŋ] *s* regreso al hogar
home country *s* suelo natal
home delivery *s* distribución a domicilio
home front *s* frente doméstico
home'land' *s* tierra natal, patria
homeless [ˈhomlɪs] *adj* sin casa, sin hogar
home life *s* vida de familia
home-loving [ˈhom,lʌvɪŋ] *adj* casero, hogareño
home•ly [ˈhomli] *adj* (*comp* **-lier;** *super* **-liest**) (*not attractive or good-looking*) feo; (*plain, not elegant*) sencillo, llano
homemade [ˈhomˈmed] *adj* casero, hecho en casa
homemaker [ˈhom,mekər] *s* ama de casa
home office *s* domicilio social, oficina central ‖ **Home Office** *s* (Brit) ministerio de la Gobernación
homeopath [ˈhomɪ•ə,pæθ] o [ˈhɑmɪ•ə,pæθ] *s* homeópata *mf*
homeopathy [,homɪˈɑpəθi] o [,hɑmɪˈɑpəθi] *s* homeopatía
home plate *s* (baseball) puesto meta
home port *s* puerto de origen
home rule *s* autonomía, gobierno autónomo
home run *s* (baseball) jonrón *m,* cuadrangular *m*
home'sick' *adj* nostálgico; **to be homesick (for)** sentir nostalgia (de)
home'sick'ness *s* nostalgia, mal *m* de la tierra
homespun [ˈhom,spʌn] *adj* hilado en casa; sencillo, llano
home'stead' *s* casa y terrenos, heredad
home stretch *s* esfuerzo final, último trecho
home town *s* ciudad natal
homeward [ˈhomwərd] *adj* de regreso ‖ *adv* hacia casa; hacia su país
home'work' *s* trabajo a domicilio; (*of a student*) deber *m,* trabajo escolar
homey [ˈhomi] *adj* (*comp* **homier;** *super* **homiest**) (coll) íntimo, cómodo
homicidal [,hɑmɪˈsaɪdəl] *adj* homicida
homicide [ˈhɑmɪ,saɪd] *s* (*act*) homicidio; (*person*) homicida *mf*
homi•ly [ˈhɑmɪli] *s* (*pl* **-lies**) homilía
homing [ˈhomɪŋ] *adj* (*animal*) querencioso; (*weapon*) buscador del blanco
homing pigeon *s* paloma mensajera
hominy [ˈhɑmɪni] *s* maíz molido
homogenei•ty [,hɑmədʒɪˈni•ɪti] *s* (*pl* **-ties**) homogeneidad
homogeneous [,hɑməˈdʒinɪ•əs] *adj* homogéneo
homogenize [həˈmɑdʒə,naɪz] *tr* homogeneizar
homonym [ˈhɑmənɪm] *s* homónimo
homonymous [həˈmɑnɪməs] *adj* homónimo
homosexual [,hɑməˈsɛkʃʊ•əl] *adj & s* homosexual *mf*
hon. *abbr* **honorary**
Hon. *abbr* **Honorable**
Honduran [hɑnˈdʊrən] *adj & s* hondureño
hone [hon] *s* piedra de afilar ‖ *tr* afilar, amolar, asentar
honest [ˈɑnɪst] *adj* honrado, probo, recto; (*money*) bien adquirido; sincero; genuino
honesty [ˈɑnɪsti] *s* honradez *f,* probidad, rectitud; (bot) hierba de la plata
hon•ey [ˈhʌni] *adj* meloso, dulce; (coll) querido ‖ *s* miel *f;* (coll) vida mía; **it's a honey** (slang) es una preciosidad ‖ *v* (*pret & pp* **-eyed** o **-ied**) *tr* enmelar, endulzar con miel; adular, lisonjear
hon'ey•bee' *s* abeja doméstica, abeja de miel
hon'ey•comb' *s* panal *m* ‖ *tr* (*to riddle*) acribillar; llenar, penetrar
hon'ey•dew' melon *s* melón muy dulce, blanco y terso
honeyed [ˈhʌnid] *adj* dulce, enmelado; melodioso; adulador
honey locust *s* acacia de tres espinas
hon'ey•moon' *s* luna de miel; viaje *m* de bodas ‖ *intr* pasar la luna de miel
honeysuckle [ˈhʌni,sʌkəl] *s* madreselva
honk [hɑŋk] *s* (*of wild goose*) graznido; (*of automobile horn*) bocinazo ‖ *tr* tocar (*la bocina*) ‖ *intr* graznar (*el ganso silvestre*); tocar la bocina
honkytonk [ˈhɑŋki,tɑŋk] *s* (slang) sala de fiestas de mala muerte
honor [ˈɑnər] *s* (*distinction; award for distinction; integrity*) honor *m;* (*good reputation; chastity*) honor, honra ‖ *tr* honrar; hacer honor a (*su firma*); aceptar y pagar (*una letra*)
honorable [ˈɑnərəbəl] *adj* (*behaving with honor; performed with honor*) honrado; (*bringing honor; associated with honor*) honroso; (*worthy, of honor*) honorable
honorary [ˈɑnə,rɛri] *adj* honorario
honorific [,ɑnəˈrɪfɪk] *adj* honorífico ‖ *s* antenombre *m*
honor system *s* acatamiento voluntario del reglamento
hood [hʊd] *s* capilla; (*one with a point*) caperuza; (*one which covers the face*) capirote *m;* (*worn with academic gown*) muceta, capirote *m;* (*of a chimney*) sombrerete *m;* (aut) capó *m,* cubierta; (slang) gamberro ‖ *tr* encapirotar; ocultar
hoodlum [ˈhudləm] *s* (coll) gamberro, maleante *m*

hoodoo ['hudu] *s* (*body of primitive rites*) vudú *m;* (coll) mala suerte || *tr* traer mala suerte a
hood'wink' *tr* burlar, engañar, vendar
hooey ['hu•i] *s* (slang) música celestial
hoof [huf] o [hʊf] *s* casco, pezuña; **on the hoof** (*cattle*) vivo, en pie || *tr & intr* (coll) caminar; **to hoof it** (coll) caminar, ir a pie; (coll) bailar
hoof'beat' *s* pisada, ruido de la pisada (*de animal ungulado*)
hook [hʊk] *s* gancho; (*for fishing*) anzuelo; (*to join two things*) enganche *m;* (*bend, curve*) ángulo, recodo; (box) crochet *m,* golpe *m* de gancho; (*of hook and eye*) corchete *m,* macho; **by hook or by crook** por fas o por nefas; **to swallow the hook;** tragar el anzuelo || *tr* enganchar; (*to bend*) encorvar, doblar; coger, pescar (*un pez*); (*to wound with the horns*) acornar || *intr* engancharse; encorvarse, doblarse
hookah ['hʊkə] *s* narguile *m*
hook and eye *s* broche *m,* corchete *m* (*macho y hembra*)
hook and ladder *s* carro de escaleras de incendio
hooked rug *s* tapete *m* de crochet
hook'nose' *s* nariz *f* de pico de loro
hook'up' *s* montaje *m*
hook'worm' *s* anquilostoma *m*
hooky ['hʊki] *s* — **to play hooky** hacer novillos
hooligan ['hulɪgən] *s* gamberro
hooliganism ['hulɪgən,ɪzəm] *s* gamberrismo
hoop [hup] o [hʊp] *s* aro || *tr* herrar, enarcar, enzunchar
hoop skirt *s* miriñaque *m*
hoot [hut] *s* resoplido, ululato; grito || *tr* reprobar a gritos; echar a gritos (*p.ej., a un cómico*) || *intr* resoplar, ulular; **to hoot at** dar grita a
hoot owl *s* autillo, cárabo
hop [hɑp] *s* saltito; (coll) vuelo en avión; (coll) sarao; (coll) baile *m;* lúpulo, hombrecillo; **hops** (*dried flowers of hop vine*) lúpulo || *v* (*pret & pp* **hopped;** *ger* **hopping**) *tr* cruzar de un salto; (coll) atravesar (*p.ej., el mar*) en avión; (coll) subir a (*un tren, taxi, etc.*) || *intr* saltar, brincar; (*on one foot*) saltar a la pata coja
hope [hop] *s* esperanza || *tr & intr* esperar; **to hope for** esperar
hope chest *s* ajuar *m* de novia
hopeful ['hopfəl] *adj* (*feeling hope*) esperanzado; (*giving hope*) esperanzador
hopeless ['hoplɪs] *adj* desesperanzado, (*situation*) desesperado
hopper ['hɑpər] *s* (*funnel-shaped container*) tolva; (*of blast furnace*) tragante *m*
hopper car *s* (rr) vagón *m* tolva
hop'scotch' *s* infernáculo
horde [hord] *s* horda
horehound ['hor,haʊnd] *s* marrubio; extracto de marrubio
horizon [hə'raɪzən] *s* horizonte *m*
horizontal [,hɑrɪ'zɑntəl] o [,hɔrɪ'zɑntəl] *adj & s* horizontal *f*
hormone ['hɔrmon] *s* hormón *m* u hormona
horn [hɔrn] *s* (*bony projection on head of certain animals*) cuerno; (*of bull*) asta, cuerno; (*of moon, anvil, etc.*) cuerno; (*of automobile*) bocina; (mus) cuerno; (*French horn*) (mus) trompa de armonía; **to blow one's own horn** cantar sus propias alabanzas; **to pull in one's horns** contenerse, volverse atrás || *intr* — **to horn in** (slang) entrometerse (en)
hornet ['hɔrnɪt] *s* crabrón *m,* avispón *m*
hornet's nest *s* panal *m* del avispón; **to stir up a hornet's nest** (coll) armar camorra, armar cisco
horn of plenty *s* cuerno de la abundancia
horn'pipe' *s* chirimía
horn-rimmed glasses ['hɔrn'rɪmd] *spl* anteojos de concha
horn•y ['hɔrni] *adj* (*comp* **-ier;** *super* **-iest**) córneo; (*callous*) calloso; (*having hornlike projections*) cornudo
horoscope ['hɑrə,skop] o ['hɔrə,skop] *s* horóscopo; **to cast a horoscope** sacar un horóscopo
horrible ['hɑrɪbəl] o ['hɔrɪbəl] *adj* horrible; (coll) muy desagradable
horrid ['hɑrɪd] o ['hɔrɪd] *adj* horroroso; (coll) muy desagradable
horri•fy ['hɑrɪ,faɪ] o ['hɔrɪ,faɪ] *v* (*pret & pp* **-fied**) *tr* horrorizar
horror ['hɑrər] o ['hɔrər] *s* horror *m;* **to have a horror of** tener horror a
horror movie *s* película de terror, película horripilante
hors d'oeuvre [ɔr 'dʌrv] *s* (*pl* **hors d'oeuvres** [ɔr 'dʌrvz]) *s* entremés *m*
horse [hɔrs] *s* caballo; (*of carpenter*) caballete *m;* **hold your horses** (coll) pare Vd. el carro; **to back the wrong horse** (coll) jugar a la carta mala; **to be a horse of another color** (coll) ser harina de otro costal
horse'back' *s* — **on horseback** a caballo || *adv* — **to ride horseback** montar a caballo
horseback riding *s* hípica
horse blanket *s* manta para caballo
horse block *s* montadero
horse'break'er *s* domador *m* de caballos
horse'car' *s* tranvía *m* de sangre
horse chestnut *s* (*tree*) castaño de Indias; (*nut*) castaña de Indias
horse collar *s* collera
horse dealer *s* chalán *m*
horse doctor *s* veterinario
horse'fly' *s* (*pl* **-flies**) mosca borriquera, tábano
horse'hair' *s* crines *fpl* de caballo; (*fabric*) tela de crin
horse'hide' *s* cuero de caballo
horse laugh *s* risotada
horse•man ['hɔrsmən] *s* (*pl* **-men** [mən]) jinete *m,* caballista *m*
horsemanship ['hɔrsmən,ʃɪp] *s* equitación, manejo
horse meat *s* carne *f* de caballo
horse opera *s* (U.S.A.) melodrama *m* del Oeste

horse pistol *s* pistola de arzón
horse'play' *s* chanza pesada, payasada
horse'pow'er *s* caballo de vapor inglés
horse race *s* carrera de caballos
horse'rad'ish *s* (*plant*) rábano picante o rusticano; (*condiment*) mostaza de los alemanes
horse sense *s* (coll) sentido común
horse'shoe' *s* herradura
horseshoe magnet *s* imán *m* de herradura
horseshoe nail *s* clavo de herrar
horse show *s* concurso hípico
horse'tail' *s* cola de caballo
horse thief *s* abigeo, cuatrero
horse'-trade' *intr* chalanear
horse trading *s* chalanería
horse'-trad'ing *adj* chalanesco
horse'whip' *s* látigo ‖ *v* (*pret & pp* **-whipped;** *ger* **-whipping)** *tr* dar latigazos a
horse•woman ['hɔrs,wʊmən] *s* (*pl* **-women** [,wɪmɪn]) amazona, caballista *f*
hors•y ['hɔrsi] *adj* (*comp* **-ier;** *super* **-iest)** caballar, hípico; (*interested in horses and horse racing*) carrerista, turfista; (coll) desmañado
horticultural [,hɔrtɪ'kʌltʃərəl] *adj* hortícola
horticulture ['hɔrtɪ,kʌltʃər] *s* horticultura
horticulturist [,hɔrtɪ'kʌltʃərɪst] *s* horticultor *m*
hose [hoz] *s* (*stocking*) media; (*sock*) calcetín *m;* (*flexible tube*) manguera ‖ **hose** *spl* calzas
hosier ['hoʒər] *s* mediero, calcetero
hosiery ['hoʒəri] *s* calcetas; calcetería
hospice ['hɑspɪs] *s* hospicio
hospitable ['hɑspɪtəbəl] o [hɑs'pɪtəbəl] *adj* hospitalario
hospital ['hɑspɪtəl] *s* hospital *m*
hospitali•ty [,hɑspɪ'tælɪti] *s* (*pl* **-ties)** hospitalidad
hospitalize ['hɑspɪtə,laɪz] *tr* hospitalizar
host [host] *s* anfitrión *m;* (*at an inn*) huésped *m,* mesonero; (*army*) hueste *f;* multitud, sinnúmero ‖ **Host** *s* (eccl) hostia
hostage ['hɑstɪdʒ] *s* rehén *m;* **to be held a hostage** quedar en rehenes
hostage taking *s* toma de rehenes
hostel•ry ['hɑstəlri] *s* (*pl* **-ries)** parador *m,* hostería
hostess ['hostɪs] *s* anfitriona; dueña, patrona; (*in a night club*) tanguista; (aer) azafata, aeromoza; (*e.g., on a bus*) jefa de ruta
hostile ['hɑstɪl] *adj* hostil
hostili•ty [hɑs'tɪlɪti] *s* (*pl* **-ties)** hostilidad
hostler ['hɑslər] o ['ɑslər] *s* mozo de cuadra, mozo de paja y cebada
hot [hɑt] *adj* (*comp* **hotter;** *super* **hottest)** (*water, air, coffee, etc.*) caliente; (*climate, country; taste*) cálido; (*fiery, excitable*) caluroso; (*pursuit*) enérgico; (*in rut*) caliente; (coll) muy radiactivo; **to be hot** (*said of a person*) tener calor; (*said of the weather*) hacer calor; **to make it hot for** (coll) hostilizar
hot air *s* (slang) palabrería, música celestial
hot'-air' furnace *s* calorífero de aire
hot and cold running water *s* circulación de agua fría y caliente
hot baths *spl* caldas, termas
hot'bed' *s* (hort) almajara; (*e.g., of vice*) sementera, semillero
hot-blooded ['hɑt'blʌdɪd] *adj* apasionado; temerario, irreflexivo
hot cake *s* torta a la plancha; **to sell like hot cakes** (coll) venderse como pan bendito
hot dog *s* (slang) perro caliente
hotel [ho'tɛl] *adj* hotelero ‖ *s* hotel *m*
ho•tel'-keep'er *s* hotelero
hot'head' *s* botafuego
hot-headed ['hɑt'hɛdɪd] *adj* caliente de cascos
hot'house' *s* estufa, invernáculo
hot plate *s* hornillo, calientaplatos *m*
hot springs *spl* fuentes *fpl* termales
hot-tempered ['hɑt'tɛmpərd] *adj* irascible
hot water *s* — **to be in hot water** (coll) estar en calzas prietas
hot'-wa'ter boiler *s* termosifón *m*
hot-water bottle *s* bolsa de agua caliente
hot-water heater *s* calentador *m* de acumulación
hot-water heating *s* calefacción por agua caliente
hot-water tank *s* depósito de agua caliente
hound [haʊnd] *s* podenco, perro de caza; **to follow the hounds** o **to ride the hounds** cazar a caballo con jauría ‖ *tr* acosar, hostigar
hour [aʊr] *s* hora; **by the hour** por horas; **in an evil hour** en hora mala; **on the hour** a la hora en punto cada hora; **to keep late hours** acostarse tarde; **to work long hours** trabajar muchas horas cada día
hour'glass' *s* reloj *m* de arena
hour hand *s* horario, horero
hourly ['aʊrli] *adj* de cada hora; por hora ‖ *adv* cada hora; muy a menudo
house [haʊs] *s* (*pl* **houses** ['haʊzɪz]) casa; (*legislative body*) cámara; teatro; (*size of audience*) entrada, p.ej., **a good house** mucha entrada; **to keep house** tener casa puesta; hacer los quehaceres domésticos; **to put one's house in order** arreglar sus asuntos ‖ [haʊz] *tr* domiciliar, alojar, hospedar
house arrest *s* arresto domiciliario
house'boat' *s* barco vivienda
house'break'er *s* escalador *m*
housebreaking ['haʊs,brekɪŋ] *s* escalo, allanamiento de morada
housebroken ['haʊs,brokən] *adj* (*perro o gato*) enseñado (*a hábitos de limpieza*)
house cleaning *s* limpieza de la casa
house coat *s* bata
house current *s* sector *m* de distribución, canalización de consumo
house'fly' *s* (*pl* **-flies)** mosca doméstica
houseful ['haʊs,fʊl] *s* casa llena
house'fur'nishings *spl* menaje *m,* enseres domésticos
house'hold' *adj* casero, doméstico ‖ *s* casa, familia

house'hold'er *s* dueño de la casa; jefe *m* de familia
house'-hunt' *intr* — **to go house-hunting** ir a buscar casa
house'keep'er *s* ama de llaves, mujer *f* de gobierno
house'keep'ing *s* manejo doméstico, gobierno doméstico; **to set up housekeeping** poner casa
housekeeping apartment *s* apartamento con cocina
house'maid' *s* criada de casa
house meter *s* contador *m* de abonado
house'moth'er *s* mujer encargada de una residencia de estudiantes
house of cards *s* castillo de naipes
house of ill fame *s* lupanar *m*, casa de prostitución
house painter *s* pintor *m* de brocha gorda
house physician *s* médico residente
house'top' *s* tejado; **to shout from the housetops** pregonar a los cuatro vientos
housewarming [ˈhaʊsˌwɔrmɪŋ] *s* fiesta para celebrar el estreno de una casa; **to have a housewarming** estrenar la casa
house'wife' *s* (*pl* **-wives**) ama de casa, madre *f* de familia
house'work' *s* quehaceres domésticos
housing [ˈhaʊzɪŋ] *s* (*of a horse*) gualdrapa; (aut) cárter *m;* (mach) caja, bastidor *m*
housing shortage *s* crisis *f* de viviendas
hovel [ˈhʌvəl] *s* casucha, choza; (*shed for cattle, tools, etc.*) cobertizo
hover [ˈhʌvər] *intr* cernerse (*un ave*); (*to hesitate; to be in danger*) fluctuar; asomar (*p.ej., una sonrisa en los labios de uno*)
how [haʊ] *adv* cómo; (*at what price*) a cómo; **how early** cuándo, a qué hora; **how else** de qué otra manera; **how far** hasta dónde; cuánto, p.ej., **how far is it to the airport?** ¿cuánto hay de aquí al aeropuerto?; **how long** cuánto tiempo; **how many** cuántos; **how much** cuánto; lo mucho que; **how often** cuántas veces; **how old are you?** ¿cuántas años tiene Vd.?; **how soon** cuándo, a qué hora; **how** + *adj qué* + *adj*, p.ej., **how beautiful she is!** ¡qué hermosa es!; lo + *adj*, p.ej., **you know how intelligent he is** Vd. sabe lo inteligente que es; **to know how to** + *inf* saber + *inf*
howdah [ˈhaʊdə] *s* castillo
how•ev'er *adv* no obstante, sin embargo; por muy . . . que, por mucho . . . que
howitzer [ˈhaʊ•ɪtsər] *s* cañón *m* obús
howl [haʊl] *s* aullido; chillido; risa muy aguda; (*of wind*) bramido ‖ *tr* decir a gritos; **to howl down** imponerse a gritos a (*una persona*) ‖ *intr* aullar; chillar; reír a más no poder; bramar (*el viento*)
howler [ˈhaʊlər] *s* aullador *m;* (coll) plancha, desacierto
hoyden [ˈhɔɪdən] *s* muchacha traviesa, tunantuela
H.P. *abbr* **horsepower**
hr. *abbr* **hour**
H.R.H. *abbr* **Her** (o **His**) **Royal Highness**
ht. *abbr* **height**
hub [hʌb] *s* cubo; (fig) centro, eje *m*
hubbub [ˈhʌbəb] *s* gritería, alboroto
hub'cap' *s* tapacubo, embellecedor *m*
huck'ster [ˈhʌkstər] *s* (*peddler*) buhonero; vendedor *m* ambulante de hortalizas; vil traficante *m*, sujeto ruin
huddle [ˈhʌdəl] *s* (coll) reunión secreta; **to go into a huddle** (coll) conferenciar en secreto ‖ *intr* acurrucarse, arrimarse
hue [hju] *s* matiz *m;* gritería; **hue and cry** vocería de indignación
huff [hʌf] *s* arrebato de cólera; **in a huff** encolerizado, ofendido
hug [hʌg] *s* abrazo ‖ *v* (*pret & pp* **hugged;** *ger* **hugging**) *tr* abrazar; apretar con los brazos; ahogar entre los brazos; navegar muy cerca de (*la costa*); ceñirse a (*p.ej., un muro*) ‖ *intr abrazarse*
huge [hjudʒ] *adj* enorme, descomunal
huh [hʌ] *interj* ¡eh!
hulk [hʌlk] *s* (*body of an old ship*) casco; (*clumsy old ship*) carcamán *m*, carraca; (*old ship tied up at a wharf and used as a warehouse, prison, etc.*) pontón *m;* (*shell of an old building, piece of furniture, machine, etc.; heavy, unwieldy person*) armatoste *m*
hulking [ˈhʌlkɪŋ] *adj* grueso, pesado
hull [hʌl] *s* (*of ship or hydroplane*) casco; (*of a dirigible*) armazón *f;* (*of certain vegetables*) hollejo, vaina ‖ *tr* deshollejar, desvainar; mondar, pelar
hullabaloo [ˈhʌləbəˌlu] o [ˌhʌləbəˈlu] *s* alboroto, gritería, tumulto
hum [hʌm] *s* canturreo, tarareo; (*of a bee, machine, etc.*) zumbido ‖ *interj* ¡ejem! ‖ *v* (*pret & pp* **hummed;** *ger* **humming**) *tr canturrear, tararear* ‖ *intr* canturrear, tararear; (*to buzz*) zumbar; (coll) estar muy activo
human [ˈhjumən] *adj* humano (*perteneciente al hombre*)
human being *s* ser humano
humane [hjuˈmen] *adj* humano (*compasivo*)
humanist [ˈhjumənɪst] *adj & s* humanista *mf*
humanitarian [hjuˌmænɪˈtɛrɪ•ən] *adj & s* humanitario
humani•ty [hjuˈmænɪti] *s* (*pl* **-ties**) humanidad
hu'man•kind' *s* género humano
humble [ˈhʌmbəl] *adj* humilde ‖ *tr* humillar
humble pie *s* — **to eat humble pie** cantar la palinodia
hum'bug' *s* patraña; (*person*) patrañero ‖ *v* (*pret & pp* **-bugged;** *ger* **-bugging**) *tr* embaucar, engaitar
hum'drum' *adj* monótono, tedioso
humer•us [ˈhjumərəs] *s* (*pl* **-i** [ˌaɪ]) húmero
humid [ˈhjumɪd] *adj* húmedo
humidifier [hjuˈmɪdɪˌfaɪ•ər] *s* humectador *m*
humidi•fy [hjuˈmɪdɪˌfaɪ] *v* (*pret & pp* **-fied**) *tr* humedecer
humidity [hjuˈmɪdɪti] *s* humedad
humiliate [hjuˈmɪlɪˌet] *tr* humillar
humiliating [hjuˈmɪlɪˌetɪŋ] *adj* humillante
humili•ty [hjuˈmɪlɪti] *s* (*pl* **-ties**) humildad

hummingbird [ˈhʌmɪŋ,bʌrd] *s* colibrí *m,* pájaro mosca

humongous [hjuˈmʌŋəs] *adj* (coll) descomunal

humor [ˈhjumər] o [ˈjumər] *s* humor *m;* **out of humor** de mal humor; **to be in the humor for** estar de humor para ‖ *tr* seguir el humor a; manejar con delicadeza

humorist [ˈhjumərɪst] *s* humorista *mf*

humorous [ˈhjumərəs] *adj* humorístico

hump [hʌmp] *s* corcova, joroba; (*in the ground*) montecillo

hump′back′ *s* corcova, joroba; (*person*) corcovado, jorobado

humus [ˈhjuməs] *s* mantillo

hunch [hʌntʃ] *s* corcova, joroba; (*premonition*) (coll) corazonada ‖ *tr* encorvar ‖ *intr* encorvarse

hunch′back′ *s* corcova, joroba; (*person*) corcovado, jorobado

hundred [ˈhʌndrəd] *adj* cien ‖ *s* ciento, cien; **a hundred** u **one hundred** ciento; cien; **by the hundreds** a centenares

hundredth [ˈhʌndredθ] *adj & s* centésimo

hun′dred•weight′ *s* quintal *m*

Hundred Years' War *s* guerra de los Cien Años

Hungarian [hʌŋˈgɛrɪ•ən] *adj & s* húngaro

Hungary [ˈhʌŋgəri] *s* Hungría

hunger [ˈhʌŋgər] *s* hambre *f* ‖ *intr* hambrear; **to hunger for** tener hambre de

hunger march *s* marcha del hambre

hunger strike *s* huelga de hambre

hun•gry [ˈhʌŋgri] *adj* (*comp* **-grier;** *super* **-griest**) hambriento; **to be hungry** tener hambre; galguear (Arg, CAm, Mex); **to go hungry** pasar hambre

hunk [hʌŋk] *s* (coll) buen pedazo, pedazo grande

hunt [hʌnt] *s* (*act of hunting*) caza; (*hunting party*) cacería; (*a search*) busca; **on the hunt for** a caza de ‖ *tr* cazar; (*to seek, look for*) buscar ‖ *intr* cazar; buscar; **to go hunting** ir de caza; **to hunt for** buscar; **to take hunting** llevar de caza

hunter [ˈhʌntər] *s* cazador *m;* perro de caza

hunting [ˈhʌntiŋ] *adj* de caza ‖ *s* (*act*) caza; (*art*) cacería, montería

hunting dog *s* perro de caza

hunting ground *s* cazadero

hunt′ing•horn′ *s* cuerno de caza

hunting jacket *s* cazadora

hunting lodge *s* casa de montería

hunting season *s* época de caza

huntress [ˈhʌntrɪs] *s* cazadora

hunts•man [ˈhʌntsmən] *s* (*pl* **-men** [mən]) cazador *m,* montero

hurdle [ˈhʌrdəl] *s* (*hedge over which horses must jump*) zarzo; (*wooden frame over which runners and horses must jump*) valla; (fig) obstáculo; **hurdles** carrera de vallas ‖ *tr* saltar por encima de

hurdle race *s* carrera de vallas

hurdy-gur•dy [ˈhʌrdiˈgʌrdi] *s* (*pl* **-dies**) organillo

hurl [hʌrl] *s* lanzamiento ‖ *tr* lanzar

hurrah [huˈrɑ] o **hurray** [huˈre] *s* viva *m* ‖ *interj* ¡viva!; **hurrah for. . . !** ¡viva. . . ! ‖ *tr aplaudir, vitorear* ‖ *intr* dar vivas

hurricane [ˈhʌrɪ,ken] *s* huracán *m*

hurried [ˈhʌrid] *adj* apresurado; hecho de prisa

hur•ry [ˈhʌri] *s* (*pl* **-ries**) prisa; **to be in a hurry** tener prisa, estar de prisa ‖ *v* (*pret & pp* **-ried**) *tr* apresurar, dar prisa a ‖ *intr* apresurarse, darse prisa; **to hurry after** correr en pos de; **to hurry away** marcharse de prisa; **to hurry back** volver de prisa; **to hurry up** darse prisa

hurt [hʌrt] *adj* (*injured*) lastimado, herido; (*offended*) resentido, herido ‖ *s* (*harm*) daño; (*injury*) herida; (*pain*) dolor *m* ‖ *v* (*pret & pp* **hurt**) *tr* (*to harm*) dañar, perjudicar; (*to injure*) lastimar, herir; (*to offend*) ofender, herir; (*to pain*) doler ‖ *intr* doler

hurtle [ˈhʌrtəl] *intr* lanzarse con violencia, pasar con gran estruendo

husband [ˈhʌzbənd] *s* marido, esposo ‖ *tr* manejar con economía

husband•man [ˈhʌzbəndmən] *s* (*pl* **-men** [mən]) agricultor *m,* granjero

husbandry [ˈhʌzbəndri] *s* agricultura, labranza; buena dirección, buen gobierno (*de la hacienda de uno*)

hush [hʌʃ] *s* silencio ‖ *interj* ¡chito! ‖ *tr* callar; **to hush up** echar tierra a (*un escándalo*) ‖ *intr* callarse

hushaby [ˈhʌʃə,baɪ] *interj* ¡ro ro!

hush′-hush′ *adj* muy secreto

hush money *s* precio del silencio

husk [hʌsk] *s* cáscara, hollejo, vaina; (*of corn*) perfolla ‖ *tr* descascarar, deshollejar, desvainar; espinochar (*el maíz*)

husk•y [ˈhʌski] *adj* (*comp* **-ier;** *super* **-iest**) fortachón, fornido; (*voice*) ronco

hus•sy [ˈhʌzi] o [ˈhʌsi] *s* (*pl* **-sies**) buena pieza, moza descarada; mujer desvergonzada

hustle [ˈhʌsəl] *s* (coll) energía, vigor *m* ‖ *tr* apresurar; echar a empellones ‖ *intr* apresurarse; (coll) menearse, trabajar con gran ahinco

hustler [ˈhʌslər] *s* trafagón *m,* buscavidas *mf*

hut [hʌt] *s* casucha, choza

hyacinth [ˈhaɪ•əsɪnθ] *s* jacinto

hybrid [ˈhaɪbrɪd] *adj & s* híbrido

hybridization [,haɪbrɪdɪˈzeʃən] *s* hibridación

hybridize [ˈhaɪbrɪ,daɪz] *tr & intr* hibridar

hy•dra [ˈhaɪdrə] *s* (*pl* **-dras** o **-drae** [dri]) hidra

hydrant [ˈhaɪdrənt] *s* boca de agua, boca de riego; (*water faucet*) grifo

hydrate [ˈhaɪdret] *s* hidrato ‖ *tr* hidratar ‖ *intr* hidratarse

hydraulic [haɪˈdrɔlɪk] *adj* hidráulico ‖ **hydraulics** *s* hidráulica

hydraulic ram *s* ariete hidráulico

hydriodic [,haɪdrɪˈɑdɪk] *adj* yodhídrico

hydrobromic [,haɪdrəˈbromɪk] *adj* bromhídrico

hydrocarbon [,haɪdrəˈkɑrbən] *s* hidrocarburo

hydrochloric [,haɪdrəˈklorɪk] *adj* clorhídrico

hydroelectric [,haɪdro•ɪ'lɛktrɪk] *adj* hidroeléctrico
hydrofluoric [,haɪdrəflu'ɔrɪk] *adj* fluorhídrico
hydrofoil ['haɪdrə,fɔɪl] *s* superficie hidrodinámica; (*wing designed to lift vessel*) hidroaleta; (*vessel*) hidroala *m*
hydrogen ['haɪdrədʒən] *s* hidrógeno
hydrogen bomb *s* bomba de hidrógeno
hydrogen peroxide *s* peróxido de hidrógeno
hydrogen sulfide *s* sulfuro de hidrógeno
hydrometer [haɪ'drɑmɪtər] *s* areómetro
hydrophobia [,haɪdrə'fobɪ•ə] *s* hidrofobia
hydroplane ['haɪdrə,plen] *s* hidroavión *m*
hydroxide [haɪ'drɑksaɪd] *s* hidróxido
hyena [haɪ'inə] *s* hiena
hygiene ['haɪdʒin] *s* higiene *f*
hygienic [,haɪdʒɪ'ɛnɪk] *adj* higiénico
hymn [hɪm] *s* himno
hymnal ['hɪmnəl] *s* himnario
hyp. *abbr* **hypotenuse, hypothesis**
hyperacidity [,haɪpərə'sɪdɪti] *s* hiperacidez *f*
hyperbola [haɪ'pʌrbələ] *s* (geom) hipérbola
hyperbole [haɪ'pʌrbəli] *s* (rhet) hipérbole *f*
hyperbolic [,haɪpər'bɑlɪk] *adj* (geom & rhet) hiperbólico
hypersensitive [,haɪpər'sɛnsɪtɪv] *adj* extremadamente sensible; (*allergic*) hipersensible
hypertension [,haɪpər'tɛnʃən] *s* hipertensión
hyphen ['haɪfən] *s* guión *m*
hyphenate ['haɪfə,net] *tr* unir con guión; escribir con guión
hypno•sis [hɪp'nosɪs] *s* (*pl* **-ses** [siz]) hipnosis *f*
hypnotic [hɪp'nɑtɪk] *adj* hipnótico || *s* (*person; sedative*) hipnótico
hypnotism ['hɪpnə,tizəm] *s* hipnotismo
hypnotist ['hɪpnətɪst] *s* hipnotista *mf*
hypnotize ['hɪpnə,taɪz] *tr* hipnotizar
hypochondriac [,haɪpə'kɑndrɪ,æk] *s* hipocondríaco
hypocri•sy [hɪ'pɑkrəsi] *s* (*pl* **-sies**) hipocresía
hypocrite ['hɪpəkrɪt] *s* hipócrita *mf*
hypocritical [,hɪpə'krɪtɪkəl] *adj* hipócrita
hypodermic [,haɪpə'dʌrmɪk] *adj* hipodérmico
hyposulfite [,haɪpə'sʌlfaɪt] *m* hiposulfito
hypotenuse [haɪ'pɑtɪ,nus] *s* hipotenusa
hypothe•sis [haɪ'pɑθɪsɪs] *s* (*pl* **-ses** [,siz] hipótesis *f*
hypothetic(al) [,haɪpə'θɛtɪk(əl)] *adj* hipotético
hyssop ['hɪsəp] *s* (bot) hisopo
hysteria [hɪs'tɪrɪ•ə] *s* histerismo, histeria
hysteric [hɪs'tɛrɪk] *adj* histérico || **hysterics** *s* paroxismo histérico
hysterical [hɪs'tɛrɪkəl] *adj* histérico

I

I, i [aɪ] novena letre del alfabeto inglés
I. *abbr* **Island**
I [aɪ] *pron pers* (*pl* **we** [wi]) yo; **it is I** soy yo
iambic (aɪ'æmbɪk] *adj* yámbico
iam•bus [aɪ'æmbəs] *s* (*pl* **-bi** [baɪ]) yambo
ib. *abbr* **ibidem**
Iberian [aɪb'ɪrɪ•ən] *adj* ibérico || *s* ibero
ibex ['aɪbɛks] *s* (*pl* **ibexes** o **ibices** ['ɪbɪ,siz]) íbice *m*, cabra montés
ibid. *abbr* **ibidem**
ice [aɪs] *s* hielo; **to break the ice** (*to overcome reserve*) romper el hielo; **to cut no ice** (coll) no importar nada; **to skate on thin ice** (coll) buscar el peligro || *tr* helar; enfriar con hielo; (*to cover with icing*) garapiñar || *intr* helarse
ice age *s* época glacial
ice bag *s* bolsa para hielo
iceberg ['aɪs,bʌrg] *s* banquisa, iceberg *m*
ice'boat' *s* cortahielos *m*, rompehielos *m;* trineo con vela para deslizarse sobre el hielo
ice'bound' *adj* rodeado de hielo; de tenido por el hielo
ice'box' *s* nevera, fresquera
ice'break'er *s* cortahielos *m*, rompehielos *m*
ice'cap' *s* bolsa para hielo; manto de hielo
ice cream *s* helado
ice'-cream' cone *s* cucurucho de helado, barquillo de helado
ice-cream freezer *s* heladora, garapiñera
ice-cream parlor *s* salón *m* de refrescos, tienda de helados
ice-cream soda *s* agua gaseosa con helado
ice cube *s* cubito de hielo
ice hockey *s* hockey *m* sobre patines
Iceland ['aɪslənd] *s* Islandia
Icelander ['aɪs,lændər] *s* islandés *m*
Icelandic [aɪs'lændɪk] *adj* islandés || *s* islandés *m* (*idioma*)
ice•man ['aɪs,mæn] *s* (*pl* **-men** [,mɛn]) vendedor *m* de hielo, repartidor *m* de hielo
ice pack *s* hielo flotante; bolsa de hielo
ice pail *s* enfriadera
ice pick *s* picahielos *m*
ice skate *s* patín *m* de cuchilla, patín de hielo
ice skating *s* patinaje *m* sobre hielo
ice tray *s* bandejita de hielo
ice water *s* agua helada
ichthyology [,ɪkθɪ'ɑlədʒi] *s* ictiología
icicle ['aɪsɪkəl] *s* carámbano
icing ['aɪsɪŋ] *s* garapiña, capa de azúcar; (aer) formación de hielo
iconoclasm [aɪ'kɑnə,klæzəm] *s* iconoclasia, iconoclasmo
iconoclast [aɪ'kɑnə,klæst] *s* iconoclasta *mf*

icy [ˈaɪsi] *adj* (*comp* **icier;** *super* **iciest**) cubierto de hielo; (*slippery*) resbaladizo; (fig) frío
id. *abbr* **idem**
id [ɪd] *s* (psychoanalysis) ello
I.D. *abbr* **identity card**
idea [aɪˈdi•ə] *s* idea
ideal [aɪˈdi•əl] *adj & s* ideal *m*
idealist [aɪˈdi•əlɪst] *adj & s* idealista *mf*
idealize [aɪˈdi•ə,laɪz] *tr* idealizar
identic(al) [aɪˈdɛntɪk(əl)] *adj* idéntico
identification [aɪ,dɛntɪfɪˈkeʃən] *s* identificación
identification tag *s* disco de identificación
identify [aɪˈdɛntɪ,faɪ] *v (pret & pp* **-fied**) *tr* identificar ‖ *intr* — **to identify with** solidarizar con
identi•ty [aɪˈdɛntɪti] *s* (*pl* **-ties**) identidad
identity card *s* carta de identificación
ideolo•gy [,aɪdɪˈɑlədʒi] o [,ɪdɪˈɑlədʒi] *s* (*pl* **-gies**) ideología
ides [aɪdz] *spl* idus *mpl*
idio•cy [ˈɪdɪ•əsi] *s* (*pl* **-cies**) idiotez *f*
idiom [ˈɪdɪ•əm] *s* (*expression that is contrary to the usual patterns of the language*) modismo; (*style of language*) idioma *m*, lenguaje *m;* (*style of an author*) estilo; (*character of a language*) índole *f*
idiomatic [,ɪdɪ•əˈmætɪk] *adj* idiomático
idiosyncra•sy [,ɪdɪ•əˈsɪnkrəsi] *s* (*pl* **-sies**) idiosincrasia
idiot [ˈɪdɪ•ət] *s* idiota *mf*
idiotic [,ɪdɪ•ˈɑtɪk] *adj* idiota
idle [ˈaɪdəl] *adj* desocupado, ocioso; **at idle moments** a ratos perdidos; **to run idle** marchar en ralentí ‖ *tr* — **to idle away** gastar ociosamente (*el tiempo*) ‖ *intr* estar ocioso, holgar; marchar (*un motor*) en ralentí
idleness [ˈaɪdəlnɪs] *s* desocupación, ociosidad
idler [ˈaɪdlər] *s* haragán *m*, ocioso
idol [ˈaɪdəl] *s* ídolo
idola•try [aɪˈdɑlətri] *s* (*pl* **-tries**) idolatría
idolize [ˈaɪdə,laɪz] *tr* idolatrar
idyll [ˈaɪdəl] *s* idilio
idyllic [aɪˈdɪlɪk] *adj* idílico
if [ɪf] *conj* si; **as if** como si; **even if** aunque; **if so** si es así; **if true** si es cierto
ignis fatuus [ˈɪgnɪsˈfætʃʊ•əs] *s* (*pl* **ignes fatui** [ˈɪgnizˈfætʃʊ,aɪ]) fuego fatuo
ignite [ɪgˈnaɪt] *tr* encender ‖ *intr* encenderse
ignition [ɪgˈnɪʃən] *s* inflamación; (aut) encendido
ignition switch *s* (aut) interruptor *m* de encendido
ignoble [ɪgˈnobəl] *adj* innoble
ignominious [,ɪgnəˈmɪnɪ•əs] *adj* ignominioso
ignoramus [,ɪgnəˈreməs] *s* ignorante *mf*
ignorance [ˈɪgnərəns] *s* ignorancia
ignorant [ˈɪgnərənt] *adj* ignorante
ignore [ɪgˈnor] *tr* no hacer caso de, pasar por alto
ilk [ɪlk] *s* especie *f*, jaez *m*
ill. *abbr* **illustrated, illustration**
ill [ɪl] *adj* (*comp* **worse** [wʌrs]; *super* **worst** [wʌrst]) enfermo, malo ‖ *adv* mal; **to take ill** tomar a mal; caer enfermo
ill-advised [ˈɪlədˈvaɪzd] *adj* desaconsejado, malaconsejado, desavisado
ill at ease *adj* inquieto, incómodo
ill-bred [ˈɪlˈbrɛd] *adj* malcriado
ill-considered [ˈɪlkənˈsɪdərd] *adj* des considerado, mal considerado
ill-disposed [ˈɪldɪsˈpozd] *adj* malintencionado, maldispuesto
illegal [ɪˈligəl] *adj* ilegal
illegible [ɪˈlɛdʒɪbəl] *adj* ilegible
illegitimate [,ɪlɪˈdʒɪtɪmɪt] *adj* ilegítimo
ill fame *s* mala fama, reputación de inmoral
ill-fated [ˈɪlˈfetɪd] *adj* aciago, funesto
ill-gotten [ˈɪlˈgɑtən] *adj* mal ganado
ill health *s* mala salud
ill-humored [ˈɪlˈhjumərd] *adj* malhumorado
illicit [ɪˈlɪsɪt] *adj* ilícito
illitera•cy [ɪˈlɪtərəsi] *s* (*pl* **-cies**) ignorancia; analfabetismo
illiterate [ɪˈlɪtərɪt] *adj* (*uneducated*) iliterato; (*unable to read or write*) analfabeto ‖ *s* analfabeto
ill-mannered [ˈɪlˈmænərd] *adj* de malos modales
illness [ˈɪlnɪs] *s* enfermedad
illogical [ɪˈlɑdʒɪkəl] *adj* ilógico
ill-spent [ˈɪlˈspɛnt] *adj* malgastado
ill-starred [ˈɪlˈstɑrd] *adj* malhadado
ill-tempered [ˈɪlˈtɛmpərd] *adj* de mal genio
ill-timed [ˈɪlˈtaɪmd] *adj* inoportuno, intempestivo
ill′-treat′ *tr* maltratar
illuminate [ɪˈlumɪ,net] *tr* alumbrar, iluminar; miniar (*un manuscrito*)
illuminating gas *s* gas *m* de alumbrado
illumination [ɪ,lumɪˈneʃən] *s* iluminación
illusion [ɪˈluʒən] *s* ilusión
illusive [ɪˈlusɪv] *adj* ilusivo
illusory [ɪˈlusəri] *adj* ilusorio
illustrate [ˈɪləs,tret] o [ɪˈlʌstret] *tr* ilustrar
illustration [,ɪləsˈtreʃən] *s* ilustración
illustrious [ɪˈlʌstrɪ•əs] *adj* ilustre
ill will *s* mala voluntad
image [ˈɪmɪdʒ] *s* imagen *f;* **the very image of** la propia estampa de
image•ry [ˈɪmɪdʒri] *s* (*pl* **-ries**) (*formation of mental images; product of the imagination*) fantasía; (*images collectively*) imágenes *fpl*
imaginary [ɪˈmædʒɪ,nɛri] *adj* imaginario
imagination [ɪ,mædʒɪˈneʃən] *s* imaginación
imagine [ɪˈmædʒɪn] *tr & intr* imaginar; (*to conjecture*) imaginarse
imbecile [ˈɪmbɪsɪl] *adj & s* imbécil *mf*
imbecili•ty [,ɪmbɪˈsɪlɪti] *s* (*pl* **-ties**) imbecilidad
imbibe [ɪmˈbaɪb] *tr* (*to drink*) beber; (*to absorb*) embeber; (*to become absorbed in*) embeberse de o en ‖ *intr* beber, empinar el codo
imbue [ɪmˈbju] *tr* imbuir
imitate [ˈɪmɪ,tet] *tr* imitar
imitation [,ɪmɪˈteʃən] *adj* (*e.g., jewelry*) imitado, imitación, de imitación ‖ *s* imitación; **in imitation of** a imitación de

immaculate [ɪˈmækjəlɪt] *adj* inmaculado
immaterial [,ɪməˈtɪrɪ•əl] *adj* inmaterial; poco importante
immature [,ɪməˈtjʊr] *adj* inmaturo
immeasurable [ɪˈmɛʒərəbəl] *adj* inmensurable
immediacy [ɪˈmidɪ•əsi] *s* inmediación
immediate [ɪˈmidɪ•ɪt] *adj* inmediato
immediately [ɪˈmidɪ•ɪtli] *adv* inmediatamente, en seguida
immemorial [,ɪmɪˈmorɪ•əl] *adj* inmemorial
immense [ɪˈmɛns] *adj* inmenso; (coll) excelente
immerge [ɪˈmʌrdʒ] *intr* sumergirse
immerse [ɪˈmʌrs] *tr* sumergir, inmergir
immersion [ɪˈmʌrʃən] o [ɪˈmʌrʒən] *s* sumersión, inmersión
immigrant [ˈɪmɪgrənt] *adj & s* inmigrante *mf*
immigrate [ˈɪmɪ,gret] *intr* inmigrar
immigration [,ɪmɪˈgreʃən] *s* inmigración
imminent [ˈɪmɪnənt] *adj* inminente
immobile [ɪˈmobɪl] *adj* inmoble, inmóvil
immobilize [ɪˈmobɪ,laɪz] *tr* inmovilizar
immoderate [ɪˈmɑdərɪt] *adj* inmoderado
immodest [ɪˈmɑdɪst] *adj* inmodesto
immoral [ɪˈmɔrəl] *adj* inmoral
immortal [ɪˈmɔrtəl] *adj & s* inmortal *mf*
immortalize [ɪˈmɔrtə,laɪz] *tr* inmortalizar
immune [ɪˈmjun] *adj* inmune
immunize [ˈɪmjə,naɪz] *tr* inmunizar
imp [ɪmp] *s* diablillo; (*child*) niño travieso
impact [ˈɪmpækt] *s* impacto
impair [ɪmˈpɛr] *tr* empeorar, deteriorar
impan•el [ɪmˈpænəl] *v* (*pret & pp* **-eled** o **-elled;** *ger* **-eling** o **-elling**) *tr* inscribir en la lista de los jurados; elegir (*un jurado*)
impart [ɪmˈpɑrt] *tr* (*to make known*) dar a conocer, hacer saber; (*to transmit, communicate*) imprimir
impartial [ɪmˈpɑrʃəl] *adj* imparcial
impassable [ɪmˈpæsəbəl] *adj* intransitable, impracticable
impasse [ɪmˈpæs] o [ˈɪmpæs] *s* callejón *m* sin salida
impassible [ɪmˈpæsɪbəl] *adj* impasible
impassioned [ɪmˈpæʃənd] *adj* ardiente,vehemente
impassive [ɪmˈpæsɪv] *adj* impasible
impatience [ɪmˈpeʃəns] *s* impaciencia
impatient [ɪmˈpeʃənt] *adj* impaciente
impeach [ɪmˈpɪtʃ] *tr* residenciar
impeachment [ɪmˈpitʃmənt] *s* residencia
impeccable [ɪmˈpɛkəbəl] *adj* impecable
impecunious [,ɪmpɪˈkjunɪ•əs] *adj* inope
impedance [ɪmˈpidəns] *s* impedancia
impede [ɪmˈpid] *tr* estorbar, dificultar
impediment [ɪmˈpɛdɪmənt] *s* impedimento; (*e.g., in speech*) defecto
im•pel [ɪmˈpɛl] *v* (*pret & pp* **-pelled;** *ger*-**pelling**) *tr* impeler, impulsar
impending [ɪmˈpɛndɪŋ] *adj* inminente
impenetrable [ɪmˈpɛnətrəbəl] *adj* impenetrable
impenitent [ɪmˈpɛnɪtənt] *adj & s* impenitente *mf*
imperative [ɪmˈpɛrɪtɪv] *adj* (*commanding*) imperativo; (*urgent, absolutely necessary*) imperioso ‖ *s* imperativo
imperceptible [,ɪmpərˈsɛptɪbəl] *adj* imperceptible, inapreciable
imperfect [ɪmˈpʌrfɪkt] *adj & s* imperfecto
imperfection [,ɪmpərˈfɛkʃən] *s* imperfección
imperial [ɪmˈpɪrɪ•əl] *adj* imperial; majestuoso ‖ *s* (*goatee*) perilla; (*top of coach*) imperial *f*
imperialist [ɪmˈpɪrɪ•əlɪst] *adj & s* imperialista *mf*
imper•il [ɪmˈpɛrɪl] *v* (*pret & pp* **-iled** o **-illed;** *ger* **-iling** o **-illing**) *tr* poner en peligro
imperious [ɪmˈpɪrɪ•əs] *adj* imperioso
imperishable [ɪmˈpɛrɪʃəbəl] *adj* imperecedero
impersonal [ɪmˈpʌrsənəl] *adj* impersonal
impersonate [ɪmˈpʌrsə,net] *tr* personificar; hacer el papel de
impertinence [ɪmˈpʌrtɪnəns] *s* impertinencia
impertinent [ɪmˈpʌrtɪnənt] *adj & s* impertinente *mf*
impetuous [ɪmˈpɛtʃʊ•əs] *adj* impetuoso
impetus [ˈɪmpɪtəs] *s* ímpetu *m*
impie•ty [ɪmˈpaɪ•əti] *s* (*pl* **-ties**) impiedad
impinge [ɪmˈpɪndʒ] *intr* — **to impinge on** o **upon** incidir eno sobre, herir; infringir, violar
impious [ˈɪmpɪ•əs] *adj* impío
impish [ˈɪmpɪʃ] *adj* endiablado, travieso
implant [ɪmˈplænt] *tr* implantar
implement [ˈɪmplɪmənt] *s* instrumento, utensilio, herramienta; **implements** implementos *mpl* ‖ [ˈɪmplɪ,mɛnt] *tr* poner por obra, llevar a cabo; (*to provide with implements*) pertrechar
implicate [ˈɪmplɪ,ket] *tr* implicar, comprometer, enredar
implicit [ɪmˈplɪsɪt] *adj* implícito; (*unquestioning*) absoluto, ciego
implied [ɪmˈplaɪd] *adj* implícito, sobrentendido
implore [ɪmˈplor] *tr* implorar, suplicar
im•ply [ɪmˈplaɪ] *v* (*pret & pp* **-plied**) *tr* dar a entender; implicar, incluir en esencia
impolite [,ɪmpəˈlaɪt] *s* descortés; desacomodido (SAm)
import [ˈɪmport] *s* importación; artículo importado; importancia, significación ‖ *tr* importar; significar ‖ *intr* importar
importance [ɪmˈpɔrtəns] *s* importancia
important [ɪmˈpɔrtənt] *adj* importante
importation [,ɪmporˈteʃən] *s* importación
importer [ɪmˈportər] *s* importador *m*
importunate [ɪmˈpɔrtʃənɪt] *adj* importuno
importune [,ɪmpɔrˈtjun] *tr* importunar
impose [ɪmˈpoz] *tr* imponer ‖ *intr* — **to impose on** o **upon** abusar de
imposing [ɪmˈpozɪŋ] *adj* imponente
imposition [,ɪmpəˈzɪʃən] *s* (*of someone's will*) imposición; abuso, engaño
impossible [ɪmˈpɑsɪbəl] *adj* imposible
impostor [ɪmˈpɑstər] *s* impostor *m*, embaucador *m*
imposture [ɪmˈpɑstʃər] *s* impostura
impotence [ˈɪmpətəns] *s* impotencia

impotent [ˈɪmpətənt] *adj* impotente
impound [ɪmˈpaʊnd] *tr* acorralar, encerrar; rebalsar (*agua*); (law) embargar, secuestrar
impoverish [ɪmˈpɑvərɪʃ] *tr* empobrecer
impracticable [ɪmˈpræktɪkəbəl] *adj* impracticable; (*intractable*) intratable
impractical [ɪmˈpræktkəl] *adj* impracticable; soñador, utópico
impregnable [ɪmˈprɛgnəbəl] *adj* inexpugnable
impregnate [ɪmˈprɛgnet] *tr* (*to make pregnant*) empreñar; (*to soak*) empapar; (*to fill the interstices of*) impregnar; (*to infuse, infect*) imbuir
impresari•o [,ɪmprɪˈsɑrɪ,o] *s* (*pl* **-os**) empresario, empresario de teatro
impress [ɪmˈprɛs] *tr* (*to have an effect on the mind or emotions of*) impresionar; (*to mark by using pressure*) imprimir; (*on the memory*) grabar; (mil) enganchar
impression [ɪmˈprɛʃən] *s* impresión
impressionable [ɪmˈprɛʃənəbəl] *adj* impresionable
impressive [ɪmˈprɛsɪv] *adj* impresionante
imprint [ˈɪmprɪnt] *s* impresión; (typ) pie *m* de imprenta ‖ [ɪmˈprɪnt] *tr* imprimir
imprison [ɪmˈprɪzən] *tr* encarcelar
imprisonment [ɪmˈprɪzənmənt] *s* encarcelamiento; pena privativa de libertad
improbable [ɪmˈprɑbəbəl] *adj* improbable
impromptu [ɪmˈprɑmptju] o [ɪmˈprɑmptu] *adj* improvisado ‖ *adv* de improviso ‖ *s* improvisación; (mus) impromptu *m*
improper [ɪmˈprɑpər] *adj* impropio; (*contrary to good taste or decency*) indecoroso
improve [ɪmˈpruv] *tr* perfeccionar, mejorar; aprovechar (*la oportunidad*) ‖ *intr* perfeccionarse, mejorar; **to improve on** o **upon** mejorar
improvement [ɪmˈpruvmənt] *s* perfecionamiento, mejoramiento; (*e.g., in health*) mejoría; (*useful employment, e.g., of time*) aprovechamiento
improvident [ɪmˈprɑvɪdənt] *adj* imprevisor
improvise [ˈɪmprə,vaɪz] *tr & intr* improvisar
imprudent [ɪmˈprudənt] *adj* imprudente
impudence [ˈɪmpjədəns] *s* insolencia, descaro, impertinencia
impudent [ˈɪmpjədənt] *adj* insolente, descarado, impertinente
impugn [ɪmˈpjun] *tr* poner en tela de juicio
impulse [ˈɪmpʌls] *s* impulso
impulsive [ɪmˈpʌlsɪv] *adj* impulsivo
impunity [ɪmˈpjunɪti] *s* impunidad
impure [ɪmˈpjʊr] *adj* impuro
impuri•ty [ɪmˈpjʊrɪti] *s* (*pl* **-ties**) impureza, impuridad
impute [ɪmˈpjut] *tr* imputar
in [ɪn] *adj* interior ‖ *adv* dentro; en casa, en la oficina; **in here** aquí dentro; **in there** allí dentro; **to be in** estar en casa; **to be in for** estar expuesto a; **to be in with** gozar del favor de ‖ *prep* en; (*within*) dentro de; (*over, through*) por; (*a period of the day*) en o por; **dressed in . . .** vestido de . . . ; **in so far as** en tanto que; **in that** en que, por cuanto ‖ *s* — **ins and outs** recovecos, pormenores minuciosos
inability [,ɪnəˈbɪlɪti] *s* inhabilidad, incapacidad
inaccessible [,ɪnækˈsɛsɪbəl] *adj* inaccesible
inaccura•cy [ɪnˈækjərəsi] *s* (*pl* **-cies**) inexactitud, incorrección
inaccurate [ɪnˈækjərɪt] *adj* inexacto, incorrecto
inaction [ɪnˈækʃən] *s* inacción
inactive [ɪnˈæktɪv] *adj* inactivo
inactivity [,ɪnækˈtɪvɪti] *s* inactividad
inadequate [ɪnˈædɪkwɪt] *adj* insuficiente, inadecuado
inadvertent [,ɪnədˈvʌrtənt] *adj* inadvertido
inadvisable [,ɪnədˈvaɪzəbəl] *adj* poco aconsejable, imprudente
inane [ɪnˈen] *adj* inane
inanimate [ɪnˈænɪmɪt] *adj* inanimado
inappreciable [,ɪnəˈpriʃɪ•əbəl] *adj* inapreciable
inappropriate [,ɪnəˈpropri•ɪt] *adj* no apropiado, no a propósito
inarticulate [,ɪnɑrˈtɪkjəlɪt] *adj* (*sounds, words*) inarticulado; (*person*) incapaz de expresarse
inartistic [,ɪnɑrˈtɪstɪk] *adj* antiartístico, inartístico
inasmuch as [,ɪnəzˈmʌtʃ,æz] *conj* ya que, puesto que; en cuanto, hasta donde
inattentive [,ɪnəˈtɛntɪv] *adj* desatento
inaugural [ɪnˈɔgjərəl] *adj* inaugural ‖ *s* discurso inaugural
inaugurate [ɪnˈɔgjə,ret] *tr* inaugurar
inauguration [ɪn,ɔgjəˈreʃən] *s* (*formal initiation or opening*) inauguración; (*investiture of a head of government*) toma de posesión
inborn [ˈɪnˈbɔrn] *adj* innato, ingénito
inbreeding [ˈɪn,bridɪŋ] *s* intracruzamiento
inc. *abbr* **inclosure, included, including, incorporated, increase**
Inca [ˈɪŋkə] *adj* incaico ‖ *s* inca *mf*
incandescent [,ɪnkənˈdɛsənt] *adj* incandescente
incapable [ɪnˈkepəbəl] *adj* incapaz
incapacitate [,ɪnkəˈpæsɪ,tet] *tr* incapacitar, inhabilitar
incapaci•ty [,ɪnkəˈpæsɪti] *s* (*pl* **-ties**) incapacidad
incarcerate [ɪnˈkɑrsə,ret] *tr* encarcelar
incarnate [ɪnˈkɑrnɪt] *adj* encarnado ‖ [ɪnˈkɑrnet] *tr* encarnar
incarnation [,ɪnkɑrˈneʃən] *s* encarnación
incendiarism [ɪnˈsɛndɪ•ə,rɪzəm] *s* incendio intencionado; incitación al desorden
incendiar•y [ɪnˈsɛndɪ,ɛri] *adj* incendiario ‖ *s* (*pl* **-ies**) incendiario
incense [ˈɪnsɛns] *s* incienso ‖ *tr* (*to burn incense before*) incensar ‖ [ɪnˈsɛns] *tr* exasperar, encolerizar
incense burner *s* incensario
incentive [ɪnˈsɛntɪv] *adj & s* incentivo
inception [ɪnˈsɛpʃən] *s* principio, comienzo
incertitude [ɪnˈsʌrt,tjud] *s* incertidumbre
incessant [ɪnˈsɛsənt] *adj* incesante
incest [ˈɪnsɛst] *s* incesto
incestuous [ɪnˈsɛstʃʊ•əs] *adj* incestuoso

inch [ɪntʃ] *s* pulgada; **to be within an inch of** estar a dos dedos de ‖ *intr* — **to inch ahead** avanzar poco a poco
incidence [ˈɪnsɪdəns] *s* incidencia; (*range of occurrence*) extensión
incident [ˈɪnsɪdənt] *adj & s* incidente *m*
incidental [ˌɪnsɪˈdɛntəl] *adj* incidente; (*incurred in addition to the regular amount*) obvencional ‖ *s* elemento incidental; **incidentals** gastos menudos
incidentally [ˌɪnsɪˈdɛntəli] *adv* incidentemente; a propósito
incipient [ɪnˈsɪpɪ•ənt] *adj* incipiente
incision [ɪnˈsɪʒən] *s* incisión
incisive [ɪnˈsaɪsɪv] *adj* incisivo
incite [ɪnˈsaɪt] *tr* incitar
incl. *abbr* **inclosure, inclusive**
inclemen•cy [ɪnˈklɛmənsi] *s* (*pl* **-cies**) inclemencia
inclement [ɪnˈklɛmənt] *adj* inclemente
inclination [ˌɪnklɪˈneʃən] *s* inclinación
incline [ˈɪnklaɪn] o [ɪnˈklaɪn] *s* declive *m*, pendiente *f* ‖ [ɪnˈklaɪn] *tr* inclinar ‖ *intr* inclinarse
inclose [ɪnˈkloz] *tr* encerrar; (*in a letter*) adjuntar, incluir; **to inclose herewith** remitir adjunto
inclosure [ɪnˈkloʒər] *s* recinto; cosa inclusa, carta inclusa
include [ɪnˈklud] *tr* incluir, comprender
including [ɪnˈkludɪŋ] *prep* incluso, inclusive; imbíbito (Guat, Mex)
inclusive [ɪnˈklusɪv] *adj* inclusivo; **inclusive of** comprensivo de ‖ *adv* inclusive
incogni•to [ɪnˈkɑgnɪˌto] *adj* incógnito ‖ *adv* de incógnito ‖ *s* (*pl* **-tos**) incógnito
incoherent [ˌɪnkoˈhɪrənt] *adj* incoherente
incombustible [ˌɪnkəmˈbʌstɪbəl] *adj* incombustible
income [ˈɪnkʌm] *s* renta, ingreso, utilidad
income tax *s* impuesto sobre rentas
in'come-tax' return *s* declaración de impuesto sobre rentas
in'com'ing *adj* de entrada, entrante; (*tide*) ascendente ‖ *s* entrada
incommunicado [ˌɪnkəˌmjunəˈkɑdo] *adj* incomunicado
incomparable [ɪnˈkɑmpərəbəl] *adj* incomparable; inigualable
incompatible [ˌɪnkəmˈpætɪbəl] *adj* incompatible
incompetent[ɪnˈkɑmpɪtənt] *adj* incompetente
incomplete [ˌɪnkəmˈplit] *adj* incompleto
incomprehensible [ˌɪnkɑmprɪˈhɛnsɪbəl] *adj* incomprehensible
incomprehension [ɪnˌkɑmprɪˈhɛnʃən] *s* incomprensión
inconceivable [ˌɪnkənˈsivəbəl] *adj* inconcebible
inconclusive [ˌɪnkənˈklusɪv] *adj* inconcluyente
incongruous [ɪnˈkɑŋgrʊ•əs] *adj* incongruo
inconsequential [ɪnˌkɑnsɪˈkwɛnʃəl] *adj* (*lacking proper sequence of thought or speech*) inconsecuente; (*trivial*) de poca importancia
inconsiderate [ˌɪnkənˈsɪdərɪt] *adj* desconsiderado, inconsiderado
inconsisten•cy [ˌɪnkənˈsɪstənsi] *s* (*pl* **-cies**) (*lack of coherence*) inconsistencia; (*lack of logical connection or uniformity*) inconsecuencia
inconsistent [ˌɪnkənˈsɪstənt] *adj* (*lacking coherence of parts*) inconsistente; (*not agreeing with itself or oneself*) inconsecuente
inconsolable [ˌɪnkənˈsoləbəl] *adj* inconsolable
inconspicuous [ˌɪnkənˈspɪkjʊ•əs] *adj* poco impresionante, poco aparente
inconstant [ɪnˈkɑnstənt] *adj* inconstante
incontinent [ɪnˈkɑntɪnənt] *adj* incontinente
incontrovertible [ˌɪnkɑntrəˈvʌrtɪbəl] *adj* incontrovertible
inconvenience [ˌɪnkənˈvinɪ•əns] *s* incomodidad, inconveniencia, molestia ‖ *tr* incomodar, molestar
inconvenient [ˌɪnkənˈvzinɪ•ənt] *adj* incómodo, inconveniente, molesto
incorporate [ɪnˈkɔrpəˌret] *tr* incorporar; constituir en sociedad anónima ‖ *intr* incorporarse; constituirse en sociedad anónima
incorporation [ɪnˈkɔrpəˈreʃən] *s* incorporación; constitución en sociedad anónima
incorrect [ˌɪnkəˈrɛkt] *adj* incorrecto
increase [ˈɪnkris] *s* aumento; ganancia, interés *m;* **to be on the increase** ir en aumento ‖ [ɪnˈkris] *tr* aumentar; (*by propagation*) multiplicar ‖ *intr* aumentar; multiplicarse
increasingly [ɪnˈkrisɪŋli] *adv* cada vez más
incredible [ɪnˈkrɛdɪbəl] *adj* increíble
incredulous [ɪnˈkrɛdʒələs] *adj* incrédulo
increment [ˈɪnkrɪmənt] *s* incremento
incriminate [ɪnˈkrɪmɪˌnet] *tr* acriminar, incriminar
incrust [ɪnˈkrʌst] *tr* incrustar
incubate [ˈɪnkjəˌbet] *tr & intr* incubar
incubator [ˈɪnkjəˌbetər] *s* incubadora
inculcate [ɪnˈkʌlket] o [ˈɪnkʌlˌket] *tr* inculcar
incumben•cy [ɪnˈkʌmbənsi] *s* (*pl* **-cies**) incumbencia
incumbent [ɪnˈkʌmbənt] *adj* — **to be incumbent on** incumbir a ‖ *s* titular *m*
incunabula [ˌɪnkjʊˈnæbjələ] *spl* (*beginnings*) orígenes *mpl;* (*early printed books*) incunables *mpl*
in•cur [ɪnˈkʌr] *v* (*pret & pp* **-curred;** *ger* **-curring**) *tr* incurrir en; (*a debt*) contraer
incurable [ɪnˈkjʊrəbəl] *adj & s* incurable *mf*
incursion [ɪnˈkʌrʒən] *s* incursión, correría
ind. *abbr* **independent, industrial**
indebted [ɪnˈdɛtɪd] *adj* adeudado; obligado
indebtedness [ɪnˈdɛtɪdnɪs] *s* endeudamiento
indecen•cy [ɪnˈdisənsi] *s* (*pl* **-cies**) indecencia, deshonestidad
indecent [ɪnˈdisənt] *adj* indecente, deshonesto; lépero (CAm, Mex)
indecisive [ˌɪndɪˈsaɪsɪv] *adj* indeciso
indeclinable [ˌɪndɪˈklaɪnəbəl] *adj* (gram) indeclinable
indeed [ɪnˈdid] *adv* verdaderamente, claro ‖ *interj* ¡de veras!
indefatigable [ˌɪndɪˈfætɪgəbəl] *adj* incansable, infatigable

indefensible [,ɪndɪ'fɛnsɪbəl] *adj* indefendible
indefinable [,ɪndɪ'fainəbəl] *adj* indefinible
indefinite [ɪn'dɛfɪnɪt] *adj* indefinido
indelible [ɪn'dɛlɪbəl] *adj* indeleble
indelicate [ɪn'dɛlɪkɪt] *adj* indelicado
indemnification [ɪn,dɛmnɪfɪ'keʃən] *s* indemnización
indemni•fy [ɪn'dɛmnɪ,faɪ] *v* (*pret & pp* **-fied**) *tr* indemnizar
indemni•ty [ɪn'dɛmnɪti] *s* (*pl* **-ties**) (*security against loss*) indemnidad; (*compensation*) indemnización
indent [ɪn'dɛnt] *tr* dentar, mellar; (typ) sangrar
indentation [,ɪndɛn'teʃən] *s* mella, muesca; (typ) sangría
indenture [ɪn'dɛntʃər] *s* escritura, contrato; contrato de aprendizaje || *tr* obligar por contrato
independence [,ɪndɪ'pɛndəns] *s* independencia
independen•cy [,ɪndɪ'pɛndənsi] *s* (*pl* **-cies**) independencia; país *m* independiente
independent [,ɪndɪ'pɛndənt] *adj & s* independiente *mf*
indescribable [,ɪndɪ'skraɪbəbəl] *adj* indescriptible
indestructible [,ɪndɪ'strʌktɪbəl] *adj* indestructible
indeterminate [,ɪndɪ'tʌrmɪnɪt] *adj* indeterminado
index ['ɪndɛks] *s* (*pl* **indexes** o **indices** ['ɪndɪ,siz] *s* índice *m;* (typ) manecilla || *tr* poner índice a; poner en un índice || **Index** *s Índice de los libros prohibidos*
index card *s* ficha catalográfica
index finger *s* dedo índice
index tab *s* pestaña
India ['ɪndɪ•ə] *s* la India
India ink *s* tinta china
Indian ['ɪndɪ•ən] *adj & s* indio
Indian club *s* maza de gimnasia
Indian corn *s* maíz *m,* panizo
Indian file *s* fila india || *adv* en fila india
Indian Ocean *s* mar *m* de las Indias, océano Índico
Indian summer *s* veranillo de San Martín
India paper *s* papel *m* de China
India rubber *s* caucho
indicate ['ɪndɪ,ket] *tr* indicar
indication [,ɪndɪ'keʃən] *s* indicación
indicative [ɪn'dɪkətɪv] *adj & s* indicativo
indicator ['ɪndɪ,ketər] *s* indicador *m*
indict [ɪn'daɪt] *tr* (law) acusar, procesar
indictment [ɪn'daɪtmənt] *s* acusación, procesamiento; auto de acusación formulado por el gran jurado
indifferent [ɪn'dɪfərənt] *adj* indiferente; (*not particularly good*) pasadero, mediano
indigenous [ɪn'dɪdʒɪnəs] *adj* indígena
indigent ['ɪndɪdʒənt] *adj* indigente
indigestible [,ɪndɪ'dʒɛstɪbəl] *adj* indigestible
indigestion [,ɪndɪ'dʒɛstʃən] *s* indigestión
indignant [ɪn'dɪgnənt] *adj* indignado
indignation [,ɪndɪg'neʃən] *s* indignación
indigni•ty [ɪn'dɪgnɪti] *s* (*pl* **-ties**) indignidad
indi•go ['ɪndɪgo] *adj* azul de añil || *s* (*pl* **-gos** o **-goes**) índigo
indirect [,ɪndɪ'rɛkt] *adj* indirecto
indirect discourse *s* estilo indirecto
indiscernible [,ɪndɪ'zʌrnɪbəl] o [,ɪndɪ'sʌrnɪbəl] *adj* indiscernible
indiscreet [,ɪndɪs'krit] *adj* indiscreto
indiscriminate [,ɪndɪs'krɪmənɪt] *adj* indiscriminado
indispensable ['ɪndɪs'pɛnsəbəl] *adj* indispensable, imprescindible
indispose [,ɪnds'poz] *tr* indisponer
indisposed [,ɪndɪs'pozd] *adj* (*disinclined*) maldispuesto; (*somewhat ill*) indispuesto
indissoluble [,ɪndɪ'sɑljəbəl] *adj* indisoluble
indistinct [,ɪndɪ'stɪŋkt] *adj* indistinto
indite [ɪn'daɪt] *tr* redactar, poner por escrito
individual [,ɪndɪ'vɪdʒu•əl] *adj* individual || *s* individuo
individuali•ty [,ɪndɪ,vɪdʒu,'ælɪti] *s* (*pl* **-ties**) individualidad; (*person of distinctive character*) personaje *m*
Indochina ['ɪndo'tʃaɪnə] *s* la Indochina
Indo-Chi•nese ['ɪndotʃaɪ'niz] *adj* indochino || *s* (*pl* **-nese**) indochino
indoctrinate [ɪn'dɑktrɪ,net] *tr* adoctrinar
Indo-European ['ɪndo,jurə'pi•ən] *adj & s* indoeuropeo
indolent ['ɪndələnt] *adj* indolente
Indonesia [,ɪndo'niʃə] o [,ɪndo'niʒə] *s* la Indonesia
Indonesian [,ɪndo'niʃən] o [,ɪndo'niʒən] *adj & s* indonesio
indoor ['ɪn,dor] *adj* interior, de puertas adentro; (*inclined to stay in the house*) casero
indoors ['ɪn'dorz] *adv* dentro, en casa, bajo techado, bajo cubierto
indorse [ɪn'dɔrs] *tr* endosar; (fig) apoyar, aprobar
indorsee [,ɪndɔr'si] *s* endosatario
indorsement [ɪn'dɔrsmənt] *s* endoso; (fig) apoyo, aprobación
indorser [ɪn'dɔrsər] *s* endosante *mf*
induce [ɪn'djus] *tr* inducir; causar, ocasionar
inducement [ɪn'djusmənt] *s* aliciente *m, estímulo, incentivo*
induct [ɪn'dʌkt] *tr* instalar; introducir, iniciar; (mil) quintar
induction [ɪn'dʌkʃən] *s* instalación; introducción; (elec & log) inducción; (mil) quinta
indulge [ɪn'dʌldʒ] *tr* gratificar (*p.ej., los deseos de uno*); mimar (*a un niño*) || *intr* abandonar; **to indulge in** entregarse a, permitirse el placer de
indulgence [ɪn'dʌldʒəns] *s* gusto, inclinación; intemperancia, desenfreno; (*leniency*) indulgencia
indulgent [ɪn'dʌldʒənt] *adj* indulgente
industrial [ɪn'dʌstrɪ•əl] *adj* industrial
industrialist [ɪn'dʌstrɪ•əlɪst] *s* industrial *m*
industrialize [ɪn'dʌstrɪ•ə,laɪz] *tr* industrializar
industrious [ɪn'dʌstrɪ•əs] *adj* industrioso, aplicado
indus•try ['ɪndəstri] *s* (*pl* **-tries**) industria
inebriation [ɪn,ibrɪ'eʃən] *s* embriaguez *f*
inedible [ɪn'ɛdɪbəl] *adj* incomible

ineffable [ɪn'ɛfəbəl] *adj* inefable
ineffective [,ɪnɪ'fɛktɪv] *adj* ineficaz; (*person*) incapaz
ineffectual [,ɪnɪ'fɛktʃu•əl] *adj* ineficaz, fútil
inefficacy [ɪn'ɛfɪkəsi] *s* ineficacia
inefficient [,ɪnɪ'fɪʃənt] *adj* de mal rendimiento
ineligible [ɪn'ɛlɪdʒɪbəl] *adj* inelegible
inequali•ty [,ɪnɪ'kwɑlɪti] *s* (*pl* **-ties**) desigualdad
inequi•ty [ɪn'ɛkwɪti] *s* (*pl* **-ties**) inequidad
ineradicable [,ɪnɪ'rædɪkəbəl] *adj* inextirpable
inertia [ɪn'ʌrʃə] *s* inercia
inescapable [,ɪnɛs'kepəbəl] *adj* ineludible
inevitable [ɪn'ɛvɪtəbəl] *adj* inevitable
inexact [,ɪnɛg'zækt] *adj* inexacto
inexcusable [,ɪnɛks'kjuzəbəl] *adj* indisculpable, inexcusable
inexhaustible [,ɪnɛg'zɔstɪbəl] *adj* inagotable
inexorable [ɪn'ɛksərəbəl] *adj* inexorable
inexpedient [,ɪnɛk'spidɪ•ənt] *adj* malaconsejado, inoportuno
inexpensive [,ɪnɛk'spɛnsɪv] *adj* barato, poco costoso
inexperience [,ɪnɛk'spɪrɪ•əns] *s* inexperiencia
inexplicable [ɪn'ɛksplɪkəbəl] *adj* inexplicable
inexpressible [,ɪnɛk'sprɛsɪbəl] *adj* inexpresable
Inf. *abbr* **Infantry**
infallible [ɪn'fælɪbəl] *adj* infalible
infamous ['ɪnfəməs] *adj* infame
infa•my ['ɪnfəmi] *s* (*pl* **-mies**) infamia
infan•cy ['ɪnfənsi] *s* (*pl* **-cies**) infancia
infant ['ɪnfənt] *adj* infantil; (*in the earliest stage*) (fig) naciente || *s* criatura, nene *m*
infant care *s* puericultura
infantile ['ɪnfən,taɪl] o ['ɪnfəntɪl] *adj* infantil; (*childish*) aniñado
infan•try ['ɪnfəntri] *s* (*pl* **-tries**) infantería
infantry•man ['ɪnfəntrimən] *s* (*pl* **-men** [mən]) infante *m*, soldado de infantería
infarct [ɪn'fɑrkt] *s* infarto
infatuated [ɪn'fætʃu,etɪd] *adj* apasionado, locamente enamorado
infect [ɪn'fɛkt] *tr* inficionar, infectar; influir sobre
infection [ɪn'fɛkʃən] *s* infección
infectious [ɪn'fɛkʃəs] *adj* infeccioso
in•fer [ɪn'fʌr] *v* (*pret & pp* **-ferred;** *ger* **-ferring**) *tr* inferir; (coll) conjeturar, suponer
inferior [ɪn'fɪrɪ•ər] *adj & s* inferior *m*
inferiority [ɪn,fɪrɪ'ɑrɪti] *s* inferioridad
inferiority complex *s* complejo de inferioridad
infernal [ɪn'fʌrnəl] *adj* infernal
infest [ɪn'fɛst] *tr* infestar
infidel ['ɪnfɪdəl] *adj & s* infiel *mf*
infideli•ty [,ɪnfɪ'dɛlɪti] *s* (*pl* **-ties**) infidelidad
in'field' *s* (baseball) cuadro interior
infiltrate ['ɪnfɪl,tret] *tr* infiltrar; infiltrarse en || *intr* infiltrarse
infinite ['ɪnfɪnɪt] *adj & s* infinito
infinitive [ɪn'fɪnɪtɪv] *adj & s* infinitivo
infini•ty [ɪn'fɪnɪti] *s* (*pl* **-ties**) infinidad; (math) infinito
infirm [ɪn'fʌrm] *adj* infirme, achacoso; (*unsteady*) inestable, inseguro; poco firme, poco sólido
infirma•ry [ɪn'fʌrməri] *s* (*pl* **-ries**) enfermería
infirmi•ty [ɪn'fʌrmɪti] *s* (*pl* **-ties**) achaque *m;* inestabilidad
in'fix *s* (gram) infijo
inflame [ɪn'flem] *tr* inflamar
inflammable [ɪn'flæməbəl] *adj* inflamable
inflammation [,ɪnflə'meʃən] *s* inflamación
inflate [ɪn'flet] *tr* inflar || *intr* inflarse
inflation [ɪn'fleʃən] *s* inflación; (*of a tire*) inflado
inflationary [ɪn'fleʃən,ɛri] *adj* inflacionario
inflect [ɪn'flɛkt] *tr* doblar, torcer; modular (*la voz*); (gram) modificar por inflexión
inflection [ɪn'flɛkʃən] *s* inflexión
inflexible [ɪn'flɛksɪbəl] *adj* inflexible
inflict [ɪn'flɪkt] *tr* infligir
influence ['ɪnflu•əns] *s* influencia || *tr* influir sobre, influenciar
influential [,ɪnflu'ɛnʃəl] *adj* influyente
influenza [,ɪnflu'ɛnzə] *s* influenza
inform [ɪn'fɔrm] *tr* informar, avisar, enterar || *intr* informar
informal [ɪn'fɔrməl] *adj* (*not according to established rules*) informal; (*unceremonious; colloquial*) familiar
information [,ɪnfər'meʃən] *s* información, informes *mpl*
informational [,ɪnfər'meʃənəl] *adj* informativo
informed sources *spl* los entendidos
infraction [ɪn'frækʃən] *s* infracción
infrared [,ɪnfrə'rɛd] *adj & s* infrarrojo
infrequent [ɪn'frikwənt] *adj* infrecuente
infringe [ɪn'frɪndʒ] *tr* infringir || *intr*—**to infringe on** o **upon** invadir, abusar de
infringement [ɪn'frɪndʒmənt] *s* infración
infuriate [ɪn'fjʊrɪ,et] *tr* enfurecer
infuse [ɪn'fjuz] *tr* infundir
infusion [ɪn'fjuʒən] *s* infusión
ingenious [ɪn'dʒinjəs] *adj* ingenioso
ingenui•ty [,ɪndʒɪ'nju•ɪti] o [,ɪndʒɪ'nu•ɪti] *s* (*pl* **-ties**) ingeniosidad
ingenuous [ɪn'dʒɛnjʊ•əs] *adj* ingenuo
ingenuousness [ɪn'dʒɛnjʊ•əsnɪs] *s* ingenuidad
ingest [ɪn'dʒɛst] *tr* injerir
in'go'ing *adj* entrante
ingot ['ɪngət] *s* lingote *m*
ingraft [ɪn'græft] *tr* (hort & surg) injertar; (fig) implantar
ingrate ['ɪngret] *s* ingrato
ingratiate [ɪn'greʃɪ,et] *tr*—**to ingratiate oneself with** congraciarse con
ingratiating [ɪn'greʃɪ,etɪŋ] *adj* atrayente, obsequioso
ingratitude [ɪn'grætɪ,tjud] *s* ingratitud, desagradecimiento
ingredient [ɪn'gridɪ•ənt] *s* ingrediente *m*
in'grow'ing nail *s* uñero
ingulf [ɪn'gʌlf] *tr* hundir, inundar
inhabit [ɪn'hæbɪt] *tr* habitar, poblar

inhabitant [ɪn'hæbɪtənt] *s* habitante *mf*
inhale [ɪn'hel] *tr* aspirar, inspirar || *intr* aspirar, inspirar; tragar el humo
inherent [ɪn'hɪrənt] *adj* inherente
inherit [ɪn'hɛrɪt] *tr & intr* heredar
inheritance [ɪn'hɛrɪtəns] *s* herencia; mortual *m* (CAm, Mex)
inheritor [ɪn'hɛrɪtər] *s* heredero
inhibit [ɪn'hɪbɪt] *tr* inhibir, prohibir
inhospitable [ɪn'hɑspɪtəbəl] o [,ɪnhɑs'pɪtəbəl] *adj* inhospitalario; (*affording no shelter or protection*) inhóspito
inhuman [ɪn'hjumən] *adj* inhumano
inhumane [,ɪnhju'men] *adj* inhumano
inhumani•ty [,inhju'mænɪti] *s* (*pl* **-ties**) inhumanidad
inimical [ɪ'nɪmɪkəl] *adj* enemigo
iniqui•ty [ɪ'nɪkwɪti] *s* (*pl* **-ties**) iniquidad
ini•tial [ɪ'nɪʃəl] *adj & s* inicial *f* || *v* (*pret* **-tialed** o **-tialled;** *ger* **-tialing** o **tialling**) *tr* firmar con sus iniciales; marcar (*p.ej., un pañuelo*)
initiate [ɪ'nɪʃɪ,et] *tr* iniciar
initiation [ɪ,nɪʃɪ'eʃən] *s* iniciación
initiative [ɪ'nɪʃɪ•ətɪv] o [ɪ'nɪʃətɪv] *s* iniciativa
inject [ɪn'dʒɛkt] *tr* inyectar; introducir (*una especie, una advertencia*)
injection [ɪn'dʒɛkʃən] *s* inyección
injudicious [,ɪndʒu'dɪʃəs] *adj* imprudente
injunction [ɪn'dʒʌŋkʃən] *s* admonición, mandato; (law) entredicho
injure ['ɪndʒər] *tr* (*to harm*) dañar, hacer daño a; (*to wound*) herir, lisiar, lastimar; (*to offend*) agraviar
injurious [ɪn'dʒʊrɪ•əs] *adj* dañoso, perjudicial; (*offensive*) agravioso
inju•ry ['ɪndʒəri] *s* (*pl* **-ries**) (*harm*) daño; (*wound*) herida, lesión; (*offense*) agravio
injustice [ɪn'dʒʌstɪs] *s* injusticia
ink [ɪŋk] *s* tinta || *tr* entintar
inkling ['ɪŋklɪŋ] *s* sospecha, indicio, noción vaga, vislumbre *f*
ink'stand' *s* (*cuplike container*) tintero; (*stand for ink, pens, etc.*) portatintero
ink'well' *s* tintero
ink•y ['ɪŋki] *adj* (*comp* **-ier;** *super* **-iest**) entintado; negro
inlaid ['ɪn,led] o [,ɪn'led] *adj* embutido, taraceado
inland ['ɪnlənd] *adj & s* interior *m* || *adv* tierra adentro
in'-law' *s* (coll) pariente político
in•lay ['ɪn,le] *s* embutido || [ɪn'le] o ['ɪn,le] *v* (*pret & pp* **-laid**) *tr* embutir, taracear
in'let *s* ensenada, cala, caleta
in'mate' *s* (*in a hospital or home*) asilado, recluso, acogido; (*in a jail*) presidiario, preso
inn [ɪn] *s* mesón *m*, posada
innate [ɪ'net] o ['ɪnet] *adj* ingénito, innato
inner ['ɪnər] *adj* interior; secreto
in'ner•spring' mattress *s* colchón *m* de muelles interiores
inner tube *s* cámara (de neumático)
inning ['ɪnɪŋ] *s* mano *f*, entrada, turno
inn'keep'er *s* mesonero, posadero
innocence ['ɪnəsəns] *s* inocencia
innocent ['ɪnəsənt] *adj & s* inocente *mf*
innovate ['ɪnə,vet] *tr* innovar
innovation [,ɪnə'veʃən] *s* innovación
innuen•do [,ɪnjʊ'ɛndo] *s* (*pl* **-does**) indirecta, insinuación
innumerable [ɪ'numərəbəl] *adj* innumerable, incontable
inoculate [ɪn'ɑkjə,let] *tr* inocular; (fig) imbuir
inoculation [ɪn,ɑkjə'leʃən] *s* inoculación
inoffensive [,ɪnə'fɛnsɪv] *adj* inofensivo
inoperative [ɪn'ɑpərətɪv] *adj* fuera de servicio
inopportune [ɪn,ɑpər'tjun] *adj* inoportuno
inordinate [ɪn'ɔrdɪnɪt] *adj* excesivo; (*unrestrained*) desenfrenado
inorganic [,ɪnɔr'gænɪk] *adj* inorgánico
in'put' *s* gasto, consumo; (elec) entrada; (mech) potencia consumida
inquest ['ɪnkwɛst] *s* encuesta; (*of coroner*) pesquisa judicial, levantamiento del cadáver
inquire [ɪn'kwaɪr] *tr* averiguar, inquirir || *intr* preguntar; **to inquire about, after** o **for** preguntar por; **to inquire into** averiguar, inquirir
inquir•y [ɪn'kwaɪri] o ['ɪnkwɪri] *s* (*pl* **-ies**) averiguación, encuesta; pregunta
inquisition [,ɪnkwɪ'zɪʃən] *s* inquisición
inquisitive [ɪn'kwɪzɪtɪv] *adj* curioso, preguntón
in'road' *s* incursión
ins. *abbr* **insulated, insurance**
insane [ɪn'sen] *adj* loco, insano, dementado
insane asylum *s* manicomio, casa de locos
insani•ty [ɪn'sænɪti] *s* (*pl* **-ties**) demencia, locura, insania, loquera
insatiable [ɪn'seʃəbəl] *adj* insaciable
inscribe [ɪn'skraɪb] *tr* inscribir; dedicar (*una obra literaria*)
inscription [ɪn'skrɪpʃən] *s* inscripción; (*of a book*) dedicatoria
inscrutable [ɪn'skrutəbəl] *adj* inescrutable
insect ['ɪnsɛkt] *s* insecto
insect control *s* desinsectación
insecticide [ɪn'sɛktɪ,saɪd] *adj & s* insecticida *m*
insecure [,ɪnsɪ'kjʊr] *adj* inseguro
inseparable [ɪn'sɛpərəbəl] *adj* inseparable
insert ['ɪnsʌrt] *s* inserción || [ɪn'sʌrt] *tr* insertar
insertion [ɪn'sʌrʃən] *s* inserción; (*strip of lace*) entredós *m*
in•set ['ɪn,sɛt] *s* intercalación || [ɪn'sɛt] o ['ɪn,sɛt] *v* (*pret & pp* **-set;** *ger* **-setting**) *tr* intercalar, encastrar
in'shore' *adj* cercano a la orilla || *adv* cerca de la orilla; hacia la orilla
in'side' *adj* interior; interno; secreto || *adv* dentro, adentro; **inside of** dentro de; **to turn inside out** volver al revés; volverse al revés || *prep* dentro de || *s* interior *m;* **insides** (coll) entrañas; **on the inside** (coll) en el secreto de las cosas
inside information *s* informes *mpl* confidenciales
insider [,ɪn'saɪdər] *s* persona enterada

insidious [ɪn'sɪdɪ•əs] *adj* insidioso
in'sight' *s* penetración
insigni•a [ɪn'sɪgnɪ•ə] *s* (*pl* **-a** o **-as**) insignia
insignificant [,ɪnsɪg'nɪfɪkənt] *adj* insignificante
insincere [,ɪnsɪn'sɪr] *adj* insincero; malo (Mex)
insinuate [ɪn'sɪnjʊ,et] *tr* insinuar
insipid [ɪn'sɪpɪd] *adj* insípido
insist [ɪn'sɪst] *intr* insistir
insofar as [,ɪnso'fɑr,æz] *conj* en cuanto
insolence ['ɪnsələns] *s* insolencia
insolent ['ɪnsələnt] *adj* insolente
insoluble [ɪn'sɑljəbəl] *adj* insoluble
insolven•cy [ɪn'sɑlvənsi] *s* (*pl* **-cies**) insolvencia
insomnia [ɪn'sɑmnɪ•ə] *s* insomnio
insomuch [,ɪnso'mʌtʃ] *adv* hasta tal punto; **insomuch as** ya que, puesto que; **insomuch that** hasta el punto que
inspect [ɪn'spɛkt] *tr* inspeccionar
inspection [ɪn'spɛkʃən] *s* inspección
inspiration [,ɪnspɪ're∫ən] *s* inspiración
inspire [ɪn'spaɪr] *tr & intr* inspirar
inspiring [ɪn'spaɪrɪŋ] *adj* inspirante
inst. *abbr* **instant** (*i.e.*, **present month**)
Inst. *abbr* **Institute, Institution**
install [ɪn'stɔl] *tr* instalar
installment [ɪn'stɔlmənt] *s* instalación; entrega; **in installments** por entregas; a plazos
installment buying *s* compra a plazos
installment plan *s* pago a plazos, compra a plazos; **on the installment plan** con facilidades de pago
instance ['ɪnstəns] *s* caso, ejemplo; **for instance** por ejemplo
instant ['ɪnstənt] *adj* instantáneo ‖ *s* instante *m*, momento; mes *m* corriente
instantaneous [,ɪnstən'tenɪ•əs] *adj* instantáneo
instantly ['ɪnstəntli] *adv* al instante
instead [ɪn'stɛd] *adv* preferiblemente; en su lugar; **instead of** en vez de, en lugar de
in'step' *s* empeine *m*
instigate ['ɪnstɪ,get] *tr* instigar
in•still' *tr* instilar
instinct ['ɪnstɪŋkt] *s* instinto
instinctive [ɪn'stɪŋktɪv] *adj* instintivo
institute ['ɪnstɪ,tjut] *s* instituto ‖ *tr* instituir
institution [,ɪnstɪ'tjuʃən] *s* institución
instruct [ɪn'strʌkt] *tr* instruir
instruction [ɪn'strʌkʃən] *s* instrucción
instructions for use *spl* modo de empleo
instructive [ɪn'strʌktɪv] *adj* instructivo
instructor [ɪn'strʌktər] *s* instructor *m*
instrument ['ɪnstrəmənt] *s* instrumento ‖ ['ɪnstrə,mɛnt] *tr* instrumentar
instrumentalist [,ɪnstrə'mɛntəlɪst] *s* instrumentista *mf*
instrumentali•ty [,instrəmən'tælɪti] *s* (*pl* **-ties**) agencia, mediación
instrument panel *s* cuadro de mando; salpicadero
insubordinate [,ɪnsə'bɔrdɪnɪt] *adj* insubordinado
insufferable [ɪn'sʌfərəbel] *adj* insufrible
insufficient [,insə'fɪʃənt] *adj* insuficiente
insular ['ɪnsələr] o ['ɪnsjʊlər] *adj* insular; (fig) de miras estrechas
insulate ['ɪnsə,let] *tr* aislar
insulation [,ɪnsə'leʃən] *s* aislación
insulator ['ɪnsə,lətər] *s* aislador *m*
insulin ['ɪnsəlɪn] *s* insulina
insult ['ɪnsʌlt] *s* insulto, insultada, escopetazo ‖ [ɪn'sʌlt] *tr* insultar
insurable [ɪn'ʃʊrəbəl] *adj* asegurable
insurance [ɪn'ʃʊrəns] *s* seguro
insure [ɪn'ʃʊr] *tr* asegurar
insurer [ɪn'ʃʊrər] *s* asegurador *m*
insurgent [ɪn'sʌrdʒənt] *adj & s* insurgente *mf*
insurmountable [,ɪnsər'maʊntəbəl] *adj* insuperable
insurrection [,ɪnsə'rɛkʃən] *s* insurrección
insusceptible [,ɪnsə'sɛptɪbəl] *adj* insusceptible
int. *abbr* **interest, interior, internal, international**
intact [ɪn'tækt] *adj* intacto, ileso
in'take' *s* (*place of taking in*) entrada; (*act or amount*) toma; (mach) admisión
intake manifold *s* múltiple *m* de admisión, colector *m* de admisión
intake valve *s* válvula de admisión
intangible [ɪn'tændʒɪbəl] *adj* intangible; vago, indefinido
integer ['ɪntɪdʒər] *s* (arith) entero
integral ['ɪntɪgrəl] *adj* íntegro; **integral with** solidario de ‖ *s* conjunto
integration [,ɪntɪ'greʃən] *s* integración
integrity [ɪŋ'tɛgrɪti] *s* integridad
intellect ['ɪntə,lɛkt] *s* intelecto; (*person*) intelectual *mf*
intellectual [,ɪntə'lɛktʃʊ•əl] *adj & s* intelectual *mf*
intellectuali•ty [,ɪntə,lɛktʃʊ'ælɪti] *s* (*pl* **-ties**) intelectualidad
intelligence [ɪn'tɛlɪdʒəns] *s* inteligencia; información
intelligence bureau *s* departamento de inteligencia
intelligence quotient *s* cociente *m* intelectual
intelligent [ɪn'tɛlɪdʒənt] *adj* inteligente; espabilado
intelligentsia [ɪn,tɛlɪ'dʒəntsɪ•ə] o [ɪn,tɛlɪ'gɛntsɪ•ə] *s* intelectualidad (*conjunto de los intelectuales de un país o región*)
intelligible [ɪn'tɛlɪdʒɪbəl] *adj* inteligible
intemperance [ɪn'tɛmpərəns] *s* intemperancia
intemperate [ɪn'tɛmpərɪt] *adj* intemperante; (*climate*) riguroso
intend [ɪn'tɛnd] *tr* pensar, proponerse, intentar; (*to mean for a particular purpose*) destinar; (*to signify*) querer decir
intendance [ɪn'tɛndəns] *s* intendencia
intendant [ɪn'tɛndənt] *s* intendente *m*
intended [ɪn'tɛndɪd] *adj & s* (coll) prometido, prometida
intense [ɪn'tɛns] *adj* intenso

intensi•fy [ɪn'tɛnsɪ,faɪ] *v* (*pret & pp* **-fied**) *tr* intensificar, intensar; (phot) reforzar || *intr* intensificarse, intensarse
intensi•ty [ɪn'tɛnsɪti] *s* (*pl* **-ties**) intensidad
intensive [ɪn'tɛnsiv] *adj* intensivo
intent [ɪn'tɛnt] *adj* atento; resuelto; intenso; **intent on** resuelto a || *s* (*purpose*) intento; (*meaning*) acepción, sentido; **to all intents and purposes** en realidad de verdad
intention [ɪn'tɛnʃən] *s* intención
intentional [ɪn'tɛnʃənəl] *adj* intencional, deliberado
in•ter [ɪn'tʌr] *v* (*pret & pp* **-terred;** *ger* **-terring**) *tr* enterrar
interact ['ɪntər,ækt] *s* (theat) entreacto || [,ɪntər'ækt] *intr* obrar recíprocamente
interaction [,ɪntər'ækʃən] *s* interacción
inter-American [,ɪntərə'mɛrɪkən] *adj* interamericano
inter•breed [,ɪntər'brid] *v* (*pret & pp* **-bred** ['brɛd]) *tr* entrecruzar || *intr* entrecruzarse
intercalate [ɪn'tʌrkə,let] *tr* intercalar
intercede [,ɪntər'sid] *intr* interceder
intercept [,ɪntər'sɛpt] *tr* interceptar
interceptor [,ɪntər'sɛptər] *s* interceptor *m*
interchange ['ɪntər,tʃendʒ] *s* intercambio; (*on a highway*) correspondencia || [,ɪntər-'tʃendʒ] *tr* intercambiar || *intr* intercambiarse
intercollegiate [,ɪntərkə'lidʒɪ•ɪt] *adj* interescolar
intercom ['ɪntər,kɑm] *s* interfono
intercourse ['ɪntər,kors] *s* comunicación, trato; (*interchange of products, ideas, etc.*) intercambio; (*copulation*) cópula, comercio; **to have intercourse** juntarse
intercross [,ɪntər'krɔs] o [,ɪntər'krɑs] *tr* entrecruzar || *intr* entrecruzarse
interdict ['ɪntər,dɪkt] *s* entredicho || [,ɪntər'dɪkt] *tr* interdecir
interest ['ɪntərɪst] *s* interés *m;* **the interests** las grandes empresas, el grupo influyente; **to put out at interest** poner a interés || *tr* interesar
interested ['ɪntə,rɛstɪd] *adj* interesado
interesting ['ɪntə,rɛstɪŋ] *adj* interesante
interface ['ɪntər,fes] *s* (*computer*) interfase
interfere [,ɪntər'fɪr] *intr* inmiscuirse, injerirse, interferir; (sport) parar una jugada; **to interfere with** dificultar, impedir, interferir
interference [,ɪntər'fɪrəns] *s* injerencia, interferencia
interim ['ɪntərɪm] *adj* interino || *s* intermedio, intervalo; **in the interim** entretanto
interior [ɪn'tɪrɪ•ər] *adj & s* interior *m*
interject [,ɪntər'dʒɛkt] *tr* interponer || *intr* interponerse
interjection [,ɪntər'dʒekʃən] *s* interposición; exclamación; (gram) interjección
interlard [,ɪntər'lɑrd] *tr* interpolar; mechar (*la carne*)
interline [,ɪntər'laɪn] *tr* interlinear; entretelar (*una prenda de vestir*)
interlining ['ɪntər,laɪnɪŋ] *s* (*of a garment*) entretela
interlink [,ɪntər'lɪŋk] *tr* eslabonar
interlock [,ɪntər'lɑk] *tr* trabar || *intr* trabarse
interlope [,ɪntər'lop] *intr* entremeterse; traficar sin derecho
interloper [,ɪntər'lopər] *s* intruso
interlude ['ɪntər,lud] *s* intervalo; (mus) interludio; (theat) intermedio
intermarriage [,ɪntər'mærɪdʒ] *s* casamiento entre parientes; casamiento entre personas de distintas razas, castas, etc.
intermediar•y [,ɪntər'midɪ,ɛri] *adj* intermediario || *s* (*pl* **-ies**) intermediario
intermediate [,ɪntər'midɪ•ɪt] *adj* intermedio
in•ter•me'di•ate-range' missile *s* cohete *m* de alcance medio
interment [ɪn'tʌrmənt] *s* entierro
intermez•zo [,ɪntər'mɛtso] o [,ɪntərmɛdzo] *s* (*pl* **-zos** o **-zi** [tsi] o [dzi]) (mus) intermedio, intermezzo
intermingle [,ɪntər'mɪŋgəl] *tr* entremezclar || *intr* entremezclarse
intermittent [,ɪntər'mɪtənt] *adj* intermitente
intermix [,ɪntər'mɪks] *tr* entremezclar || *intr* entremezclarse
intern ['ɪntʌrn] *s* interno de hospital || [ɪn'tʌrn] *tr* internar, recluir
internal [ɪn'tʌrnəl] *adj* interno
inter'nal-combus'tion engine *s* motor *m* de explosión
internal revenue *s* rentas internas
international [,ɪntər'næʃənəl] *adj* internacional
international date line *s* línea internacional de cambio de fecha
internationalize [,ɪntər'næʃənə,laɪz] *tr* internacionalizar
internecine [,ɪntər'nisɪn] *adj* sanguinario
internee [,ɪntʌr'ni] *s* (mil) internado
internist [ɪn'tʌrnɪst] *s* internista *mf*
internment [ɪn'tʌrnmənt] *s* internamiento
internship ['intʌrn,ʃɪp] *s* residencia de un médico en un hospital
interpellate [,ɪntər'pɛlet] o [ɪn'tʌrpɪ,let] *tr* interpelar
interplay ['ɪntər,ple] *s* interacción
interpolate [ɪn'tʌrpə,let] *tr* interpolar
interpose [,ɪntər'poz] *tr* interponer
interpret [ɪn'tʌrprɪt] *tr* interpretar
interpreter [ɪn'tʌrprɪtər] *s* intérprete *mf;* (fig) exponente *mf*
interrogate [ɪn'tɛrə,get] *tr & intr* interrogar
interrogation [ɪn,tɛrə'geʃən] *s* interrogación
interrogation mark o **point** *s* signo de interrogación
interrupt [,ɪntə'rʌpt] *tr* interrumpir
interscholastic [,ɪntərskə'læstɪk] *adj* interescolar
intersection [,ɪntər'sɛkʃən] *s* (*of streets, roads, etc.*) cruce *m,* bocacalle *f;* cruza (SAm); (geom) intersección
intersperse [,ɪntər'spʌrs] *tr* entremezclar, esparcir
interstice [ɪn'tʌrstɪs] *s* intersticio
intertwine [,ɪntər'twaɪn] *tr* entrelazar || *intr* entrelazarse
interval ['ɪntərvəl] *s* intervalo; **at intervals** (*now and then*) de vez en cuando; (*here and there*) de trecho en trecho

intervene [ˌɪntərˈvin] *intr* intervenir
intervening [ˌɪntərˈvinɪŋ] *adj* intermedio
intervention [ˌɪntərˈvɛnʃən] *s* intervención
interview [ˈɪntərˌvju] *s* entrevista, interview *m* || *tr* entrevistarse con
inter•weave [ˌɪntərˈwiv] *v* (*pret* **-wove** [ˈwov] o **-weaved;** *pp* **-wove, woven** o **weaved**) *tr* entretejer
intestate [ɪnˈtɛstet] *adj & s* intestado
intestine [ɪnˈtɛstɪn] *s* intestino
inthrall [ɪnˈθrɔl] *tr* cautivar, encantar; esclavizar, sojuzgar
inthrone [ɪnˈθron] *tr* entronizar
intima•cy [ˈɪntɪməsi] *s* (*pl* **-cies**) intimidad
intimate [ˈɪntɪmɪt] *adj* íntimo || *s* amigo íntimo || [ˈɪntɪˌmet] *tr* insinuar, intimar
intimation [ˌɪntɪˈmeʃən] *s* insinuación
intimidate [ɪnˈtɪmɪˌdet] *tr* intimidar
intitle [ɪnˈtaɪtəl] *tr* dar derecho a; (*to give a name to; to honor with a title*) intitular
into [ˈɪntu] o [ˈɪntʊ] *prep* en; hacia; hacia el interior de
intolerant [ɪnˈtalərənt] *adj & s* intolerante *mf*
intomb [ɪnˈtum] *tr* sepultar
intombment [ɪnˈtummənt] *s* sepultura
intonation [ˌɪntoˈneʃən] *s* entonación
intone [ɪnˈton] *tr* entonar
intoxicant [ɪnˈtɑksɪkənt] *s* bebida alcohólica
intoxicate [ɪnˈtɑksɪˌket] *tr* embriagar, emborrachar; (*to exhilarate*) alegrar, excitar; (*to poison*) envenenar, intoxicar
intoxication [ɪnˌtɑksɪˈkeʃən] *s* embriaguez *f;* alegría, excitación; (*poisoning*) envenenamiento, intoxicación
intractable [ɪnˈtræktəbəl] *adj* intratable
intransigent [ɪnˈtrænsɪdʒənt] *adj & s* intransigente *mf*
intransitive [ɪnˈtrænsɪtɪv] *adj* intransitivo
intrench [ɪnˈtrɛntʃ] *tr* atrincherar || *intr*—**to intrench on** o **upon** infringir, violar
intrepid [ɪnˈtrɛpɪd] *adj* intrépido
intrepidity [ˌɪntrɪˈpɪdɪti] *s* intrepidez *f*
intricate [ˈɪntrɪkɪt] *adj* intrincado
intrigue [ɪnˈtrig] *s* intriga; intriga amorosa, enredo amoroso || *tr* (*to arouse the curiosity of*) intrigar || *intr* intrigar; tener intrigas amorosas
intrinsic(al) [ɪnˈtrɪnsɪk(əl)] *adj* intrínseco
introd. *abbr* **introduction**
introduce [ˌɪntrəˈdjus] *tr* introducir; (*to make acquainted*) presentar
introduction [ˌɪntrəˈdʌkʃən] *s* introducción; (*of one person to another or others*) presentación
introductory offer [ˌɪntrəˈdʌktəri] *s* ofrecimiento de presentación, oferta preliminar
introit [ˈɪntro•ɪt] *s* (eccl) introito
introspective [ˌɪntrəˈspɛktɪv] *adj* introspectivo
introvert [ˈɪntrəˌvʌrt] *s* introvertido
intrude [ɪnˈtrud] *intr* injerirse, entremeterse
intruder [ɪnˈtrudər] *s* intruso, entremetido
intrusive [ɪnˈtrusɪv] *adj* intruso
intrust [ɪnˈtrʌst] *tr* confiar
intuition [ˌɪntjʊˈɪʃən] *s* intuición
inundate [ˈɪnənˌdet] *tr* inundar
inundation [ˌɪnənˈdeʃən] *s* inundación
inure [ɪnˈjʊr] *tr* acostumbrar, endurecer, aguerrir || *intr* ponerse en efecto; **to inure to** redundar en
inv. *abbr* **inventor, invoice**
invade [ɪnˈved] *tr* invadir
invader [ɪnˈvedər] *s* invasor *m*
invalid [ɪnˈvælɪd] *adj* inválido (*nulo, de ningún valor*) || [ˈɪnvəlɪd] *adj* inválido (*por viejo o por enfermo*) || [ˈɪnvəlɪd] *s* inválido
invalidate [ɪnˈvælɪˌdet] *tr* invalidar
invalidity [ˌɪnvəˈlɪdɪti] *s* invalidez *f*
invaluable [ɪnˈvælju•əbəl] *adj* inestimable, inapreciable
invariable [ɪnˈvɛrɪ•əbəl] *adj* invariable
invasion [ɪnˈveʒən] *s* invasión
invective [ɪnˈvɛktɪv] *s* invectiva
inveigh [ɪnˈve] *intr*—**to inveigh against** lanzar invectivas contra
inveigle [ɪnˈvegəl] o [ɪnˈvigəl] *tr* engatusar
invent [ɪnˈvɛnt] *tr* inventar
invention [ɪnˈvɛnʃən] *s* invención, invento
inventive [ɪnˈvɛntɪv] *adj* inventivo
inventiveness [ɪnˈvɛntivnɪs] *s* inventiva
inventor [ɪnˈvɛntər] *s* inventor *m*
invento•ry [ˈɪnvənˌtori] *s* (*pl* **-ries**) inventario; stock *m* || *v* (*pret & pp* **-ried**) *tr* inventariar
inverse [ɪnˈvʌrs] *adj* inverso
inversion [ɪnˈvʌrʒən] o [ɪnˈvʌrʃən] *s* inversión
invert [ˈɪnvʌrt] *s* invertido || [ɪnˈvʌrt] *tr* invertir
invertebrate [ɪnˈvʌrtɪˌbret] o [ɪnˈvʌrtɪbrɪt] *adj & s* invertebrado
inverted exclamation point *s* principio de admiración
inverted question mark *s* principio de interrogación
invest [ɪnˈvɛst] *tr* (*to vest, to install*) investir; invertir (*dinero*); (*to besiege*) cercar, sitiar; (*to surround, envelop*) cubrir, envolver
investigate [ɪnˈvɛstɪˌget] *tr* investigar
investigation [ɪnˌvɛstɪ•geʃən] *s* investigación
investment [ɪnˈvɛstmənt] *s* (*of money*) inversión; (*with an office or dignity*) investidura; (*siege*) cerco, sitio
investment capital *s* capital *m* de inversión
investor [ɪnˈvɛstər] *s* inversionista *mf;* inversor *m*
inveterate [ɪnˈvɛtərɪt] *adj* inveterado, empedernido
invidious [ɪnˈvɪdɪ•əs] *adj* irritante, odioso, injusto
invigorate [ɪnˈvɪgəˌret] *tr* vigorizar
invigorating [ɪnˈvɪgəˌretɪŋ] *adj* vigorizador, vigorizante
invincible [ɪnˈvɪnsɪbəl] *adj* invencible
invisible [ɪnˈvɪzɪbəl] *adj* invisible
invisible ink *s* tinta simpática
invitation [ˌɪnvɪˈteʃən] *s* invitación, convite *m*
invite [ɪnˈvaɪt] *tr* invitar, convidar
inviting [ɪnˈvaɪtɪŋ] *adj* atractivo, seductor; (*e.g., food*) apetitoso
invoice [ˈɪnvɔɪs] *s* factura; **as per invoice** según factura || *tr* facturar

invoke [ɪn'vok] *tr* invocar; evocar, conjurar (*p.ej., los demonios*)
involuntary [ɪn'vɑlən,tɛri] *adj* involuntario
involution [,ɪnvə'luʃən] *s* (math) elevación a potencias, potenciación
involve [ɪn'vɑlv] *tr* envolver, comprometer
invulnerable [ɪn'vʌlnərəbəl] *adj* invulnerable
inward ['ɪnwərd] *adj* interior ‖ *adv* interiormente, hacia dentro
iodide ['aɪ•ə,daɪd] *s* yoduro
iodine ['aɪ•ə,din] *s* yodo ‖ ['aɪ•ə,daɪn] *s* tintura de yodo
ion ['aɪ•ən] o ['aɪ•ɑn] *s* ion *m*
ionize ['aɪ•ə,naɪz] *tr* ionizar
ionosphere [aɪ'ɑnə,sfɪr] *s* ionosfera
IOU ['aɪ,o'ju] *s* (letterword) pagaré *m*
I.Q. ['aɪ'kju] *abbr & s* (letterword) **intelligence quotient**
Iran [ɪ'rɑn] o [aɪ'ræn] *s* el Irán
Iranian [ɪ'reni•ən] o [aɪ'renɪ•ən] *adj & s* iranés *m* o iranio
Iraq [ɪ'rɑk] *s* el Irak
Ira•qi [ɪ'rɑki] *adj* iraqués o iraquiano ‖ *s* (*pl* **-qis**) iraqués *m* o iraquiano
irate ['aɪret] o [aɪ'ret] *adj* airado
ire [aɪr] *s* ira, cólera
Ireland ['aɪrlənd] *s* Irlanda
iris ['aɪrɪs] *s* (*of the eye*) iris *m;* (*rainbow*) iris, arco iris; (bot) lirio
Irish ['aɪrɪʃ] *adj* irlandés ‖ *s* (*language*) irlandés *m;* whisky *m* de Irlanda; **the Irish** los irlandeses
Irish•man ['aɪrɪʃmən] *s* (*pl* **-men** [mən]) irlandés *m*
Irish stew *s* guisado de carne con patatas y cebollas
I'rish•wom'an *s* (*pl* **-wom'en**) irlandesa
irk [ʌrk] *tr* fastidiar, molestar
irksome ['ʌrksəm] *adj* fastidioso, molesto
iron ['aɪ•ərn] *adj* férreo ‖ *s* hierro; (*implement used to press or smooth clothes*) plancha; **irons** (*fetters*) hierros, grilletes *mpl;* **strike while the iron is hot** a hierro caliente batir de repente ‖ *tr* planchar (*la ropa*); **to iron out** allanar (*una dificultad*)
i'ron-bound' *adj* zunchado con hierro; (*unyielding*) férreo, duro, inflexible; (*rock-bound*) escabroso, rocoso
ironclad ['aɪ•ərn'klæd] *adj* acorazado, blindado; inflexible, exigente
iron curtain *s* (fig) telón *m* de hierro, cortina de hierro
iron digestion *s* estómago de avestruz
ironhanded ['aɪ•ərn,hændɪd] *adj* severo; rigoroso; de mano férrea
iron horse *s* (coll) locomotora
ironic(al) [aɪ'rɑnɪk(əl) *adj* irónico
ironing ['aɪ•ərnɪŋ] *s* planchado; ropa planchada; ropa por planchar
ironing board *s* tabla de planchar
iron lung *s* pulmón *m* de acero o de hierro
i'ron•ware' *s* ferretería
iron will *s* voluntad de hierro
i'ron•work' *s* herraje *m;* **ironworks** ferrería, herrería
i'ron•work'er *s* herrero de grueso; (*metalworker*) cerrajero
iro•ny ['aɪrəni] *s* (*pl* **-nies**) ironía
irradiate [ɪ'redɪ,et] *tr* irradiar; (med) someter a radiación ‖ *intr* irradiar
irrational ['ɪræʃənəl] *adj* irracional
irrecoverable [,ɪrɪ'kʌvərəbəl] *adj* incobrable, irrecuperable
irredeemable [,ɪrɪ'diməbəl] *adj* irredimible
irrefutable [,ɪrɪ'fjutəbəl] o [ɪ'rɛfjutəbəl] *adj* irrebatible
irregular [ɪ'rɛgələr] *adj* irregular ‖ *s* (mil) irregular *m*
irrelevance [ɪ'rɛləvəns] *s* impertinencia, inaplicabilidad
irrelevant [ɪ'rɛləvənt] *adj* impertinente, inaplicable; irrelevante
irreligious [,ɪrɪ'lɪdʒəs] *adj* irreligioso
irremediable [,ɪrɪ'midɪ•əbəl] *adj* irremediable
irremovable [,ɪrɪ'muvəbəl] *adj* inamovible
irreparable [ɪ'rɛpərəbəl] ɪadj irreparable
irreplaceable [,ɪrɪ'plesəbəl] *adj* insubstituíble, irreemplazable
irrepressible [,ɪrɪ'prɛsɪbəl] *adj* irreprimible, incontenible
irreproachable [,ɪrɪ'protʃəbəl] *adj* irreprochable
irresistible [,ɪrɪ'zɪstɪbəl] *adj* irresistible
irrespective [,ɪrɪ'spɛktɪv] *adj* — **irrespective of** sin hacer caso de, independiente de
irresponsible [,ɪrɪ'spɑnsɪbəl] *adj* irresponsable
irretrievable [,ɪrɪ'trivəbəl] *adj* irrecuperable
irreverent [ɪ'rɛvərənt] *adj* irreverente
irrevocable [ɪ'rɛvəkəbəl] *adj* irrevocable
irrigate ['ɪrɪ,get] *tr* irrigar
irrigation [,ɪrɪ'geʃən] *s* irrigación
irritant ['ɪrɪtənt] *adj & s* irritante *m*
irritate ['ɪrɪ,tet] *tr* irritar
irruption [ɪ'rʌpʃən] *s* irrupción
is. *abbr* **island**
isinglass ['aɪzɪŋ,glæs] o ['aɪzɪŋ,glɑs] *s* (*form of gelatine*) cola de pescado, colapez *f;* mica
isl. *abbr* **island**
Islam ['ɪsləm] o [ɪs'lɑm] *s* el Islam
island ['aɪlənd] *adj* isleño ‖ *s* isla
islander ['aɪləndər] *s* isleño
isle [aɪl] *s* isleta
isolate ['aɪsə,let] aislar
isolated ['aɪsə,letɪd] *adj* aislado; insulado; alejado
isolation [,aɪsə'leʃən] *s* aislamiento
isolationist [,aɪsə'leʃənɪst] *s* aislacionista *mf*
isometric [,aɪsə'mɛtrɪk] *adj* isométrico
isometrics *s* isométrica
isosceles [aɪ'sɑsə,liz] *adj* isosceles
isotope ['aɪsə,top] *s* isótopo
Israe•li [iz'reli] *adj* israelí ‖ *s* (*pl* **-lis** [liz] israelí *mf*
Israelite ['ɪzrɪ•ə,laɪt] *adj & s* israelita *mf*
issuance ['ɪʃʊ•əns] *s* emisión, expedición
issue ['ɪʃʊ] *s* (*outgoing; outlet*) salida; (*result*) consecuencia, resultado; (*offspring*) descendencia, sucesión; (*of a magazine*) edición, impresión, tirada, número; (*e.g.,*

of a bond) emisión; (*yield, profit*) beneficios, producto; punto en disputa; (*distribution*) repartida; (pathol) flujo; **at issue** en disputa; **to face the issue** afrontar la situación; **to force the issue** forzar la solución; **to take issue with** llevar la contraria a || *tr* publicar, dar a luz (*un nuevo libro, una revista, etc.*); emitir, expedir (*títulos, obligaciones, etc.*); distribuir (*ropa, alimento*) || *intr* salir; **to issue from** provenir de

isthmus [ˈɪsməs] *s* istmo

it [ɪt] *pron pers* (aplícase a cosas inanimadas, a niños de teta, a animales cuyo sexo no se conoce; y muchas veces no se traduce) él, ella; lo, la; **it is I** soy yo; **it is snowing** nieva; **it is three o'clock** son las tres

ital. *abbr* **italics**

Ital. *abbr* **Italian, Italy**

Italian [ɪˈtæljən] *adj & s* italiano

italic [ɪˈtælɪk] *adj* (typ) itálico || **italics** *s* (typ) itálica, bastardilla || **Italic** *adj* itálico

italicize [ɪˈtælɪ,saɪz] *tr* imprimir en bastardilla; subrayar

Italy [ˈɪtəli] *s* Italia

itch [ɪtʃ] *s* comezón *f;* (pathol) sarna; (*eagerness*) (fig) comezón, prurito || *tr* dar comezón a || *intr* picar; **to itch to** tener prurito por

itch•y [ˈɪtʃi] *adj* (*comp* **-ier;** *super* **-iest**) picante, hormigoso; (pathol) sarnoso

item [ˈaɪtəm] *s* artículo; noticia, suelto; (*in an account*) partida

itemization [,aɪtəmaɪˈzeʃən] *s* rubricación

itemize [ˈaɪtə,maɪz] *tr* particularizar, especificar, pormenorizar

itinerant [aɪˈtɪnərənt] o [ɪˈtɪnərənt] *adj* ambulante, errante || *s* viandante *mf*

itinerar•y][aɪˈtɪnə,rɛri] o [ɪˈtɪnə,rɛri] *adj* itinerario || *s* (*pl* **-ies**) itinerario

its [ɪts] *adj poss su* || *pron poss* el suyo; suyo

itself [ɪtˈsɛlf] *pron pers* mismo; sí, sí mismo; se

ivied [ˈaɪvid] *adj* cubierto de hiedra

ivo•ry [ˈaɪvəri] *adj* marfileño || *s* (*pl* **-ries**) marfil *m;* **ivories** (slang) teclas del piano; (slang) bolas de billar; (*dice*) (slang) dados; (slang) dientes *mpl*

ivory tower *s* (fig) torre *f* de marfil; (fig) inocencia

ivy [ˈaɪvi] *s* (*pl* **-ivies**) hiedra

J

J. j [dʒe] décima letra del alfabeto inglés

J. *abbr* **Judge, Justice**

jab [dʒæb] *s* hurgonazo; (*prick*) pinchazo; (*with elbow*) codazo || *v* (*pret & pp* **jabbed;** *ger* **jabbing**) *tr* hurgonear; dar un codazo a || *intr* hurgonear

jabber [ˈdʒæbər] *s* chapurreo || *tr & intr* chapurrear

jabot [dʒæˈbo] o [ˈdʒæbo] *s* chorrera

jack [dʒæk] *s* (*for lifting heavy objects*) gato, cric *m;* (*fellow*) mozo, sujeto, (*jackass*) asno, burro; (*in card games*) sota, valet *m;* (*small ball for bowling*) boliche *m;* (*jackstone*) cantillo; (*device for turning a spit*) torno de asador; (*figure which strikes a clock bell*) jaquemar *m;* (*to remove a boot*) sacabotas *m;* marinero; (*flag at the bow*) (naut) yac *m;* (rad & telv) jack *m;* (elec) caja de enchufe; (slang) dinero; **every man Jack** cada hijo de vecino; **jacks** cantillos, juego de los cantillos || *tr* — **to jack up** alzar con el gato; (coll) subir (*sueldos, precios, etc.*); (coll) recordar su obligación a

jackal [ˈdʒækɔl] *s* chacal *m*

jackanapes [ˈdʒækə,neps] *s* mequetrefe *m*

jack'ass' *s* asno, burro

jack'daw' *s* corneja

jacket [ˈdʒækɪt] *s* chaqueta; (*folded paper*) cubierta, envoltura; (*paper cover of a book*) sobrecubierta; (*metal caing*) camisa

jack'ham'mer *s* martillo perforador

jack'-in-the-box' *s* caja de sorpresa, jugete-sorpresa *m,* muñeco en una caja de resorte

jack'knife' *s* (*pl* **-knives'**) navaja de bolsillo; (*fancy dive*) salto de carpa

jack of all trades *s* hombre que hace toda clase de oficios dije *m*

jack-o'-lantern [ˈdʒækə,læntərn] *s* fuego fatuo; linterna hecha con una calabaza cortado de modo que remede una cabeza humana

jack pot *s*—**to hit the jack pot** (slang) ponerse las botas

jack rabbit *s* liebre grande norteamericana

jack'screw' *s* cric *m* o gato de tornillo

jack'stone' *s* cantillo; **jackstones** cantillos, juego de los cantillos

jack'-tar' *s* (coll) marinero

jade [dʒed] *adj* verdoso como el jade || *s* (*ornamental stone*) jade *m;* verde *m* de jade; (*worn-out horse*) jamelgo; picarona, mujerzuela || *tr* cansar, ahitar, saciar

jaded [ˈdʒedɪd] *adj* ahito, saciado

jag [dʒæg] *s* diente *m,* púa; **to have a jag on** (slang) estar borracho

jagged [ˈdʒægɪd] *adj* dentado, mellado; rasgado en sietes

jaguar [ˈdʒægwɑr] *s* jaguar *m*

jail [dʒel] *s* cárcel *f;* **to break jail** escaparse de la cárcel || *tr* encarcelar

jail'bird' *s* (coll) preso, encarcelado; (coll) infractor *m* habitual

jail'break' *s* escapatoria de la cárcel

jail delivery *s* evasión de la cárcel

jailer [ˈdʒelər] *s* carcelero

jalop•y [dʒə'lɑpi] *s* (*pl* **-ies**) automóvil viejo y ruinoso
jam [dʒæm] *s* apiñadura, apretura; (*e.g., in traffic*) embotellamiento, bloqueo; (*preserve*) compota, conserva; (*difficult situation*) (coll) aprieto, apuros || *v* (*pret & pp* **jammed;** *ger* **jamming**) *tr* apiñar, apretujar; machucarse (*p.ej., un dedo*); (rad) perturbar, sabotear; **to jam on the brakes** frenar de golpe
Jamaican [dʒə'mekən] *adj & s* jamaicano; jamaiquino (Am)
jamb [dʒæm] *s* jamba
jamboree [,dʒæmbɔ'ri] *s* (coll) francachela, holgorio; reunión de niños exploradores
jamming ['dʒæmɪŋ] *s* radioperturbación
jam nut *s* contratuerca
jam-packed ['dʒæm'pækt] *adj* (coll) apiñado, apretujado, atestado
jam session *s* reunión de músicos de jazz para tocar improvisaciones
jangle ['dʒæŋgəl] *s* cencerreo; altercado, riña || *tr* hacer sonar con ruido discordante || *intr* cencerrear; reñir
janitor ['dʒænɪtər] *s* portero, conserje *m*
janitress ['dʒænɪtrɪs] *s* portera
January ['dʒænju,ɛri] *s* enero
Ja•pan [dʒə'pæn] *s* laca japonesa; obra japonesa laqueada; aceite *m* secante japonés || *v* (*pret & pp* **-panned;** *ger* **-panning**) *tr* barnizar, charolar, laquear con laca japonesa || **Japan** *s* el Japón
Japa•nese [,dʒæpə'niz] *adj* japonés || *s* (*pl* **-nese**) japonés *m*
Japanese beetle *s* escarabajo japonés
Japanese lantern *s* farolillo veneciano
Japanese persimmon *s* caqui *m*
jar [dʒɑr] *s* tarro; (*e.g., of olives*) frasco; (*of a storage battery*) recipiente *m;* (*jolt*) sacudida; ruido desapacible; sorpresa desagradable; **on the jar** (*said of a door*) entreabierto, entornado || *v* (*pret & pp* **jarred;** *ger* **jarring**) *tr* sacudir; chocar; (*with a noise*) traquetear || *intr* sacudirse; traquetear; disputar; **to jar on** irritar
jardiniere [,dʒɑrdɪ'nɪr] *s* (*stand*) jardinera; (*pot, bowl*) florero
jargon ['dʒɑrgən] *s* jerga, jerigonza
jasmine ['dʒæsmɪn] *s* jazmín *m*
jasper ['dʒæspər] *s* jaspe *m*
jaundice ['dʒɔndɪs] o ['dʒɑndɪs] *s* ictericia; (fig) envidia, celos, negro humor
jaundiced ['dʒɔndɪst] o ['dʒɑndɪst] *adj* ictericiado; (fig) avinagrado
jaunt [dʒɔnt] o [dʒɑnt] *s* caminata, excursión, paseo
jaun•ty ['dʒɔnti] o ['dʒɑnti] *adj* (*comp* **-tier;** *super* **-tiest**) airoso, gallardo, vivo; elegante, de buen gusto
Java•nese [,dʒævə'niz] *adj* javanés || *s* (*pl* **-nese**) javanés *m*
javelin ['dʒævlɪn] o ['dʒævəlɪn] *s* jabalina
jaw [dʒɔ] *s* mandíbula, quijada; **into the jaws of death** a las garras de la muerte; **jaws** boca, garganta || *tr* (slang) regañar || *intr* (slang) regañar; (slang) chacharear, chismear
jaw'bone' *s* mandíbula, quijada
jaw'break'er *s* (*word*) (coll) trabalenguas *m;* (*candy*) (coll) hinchabocas *m;* (mach) trituradora de quijadas
jay [dʒe] *s* (orn) arrendajo; (coll) tonto, necio
jay'walk' *intr* (coll) cruzar la calle descuidadamente
jay'walk'er *s* (coll) peatón descuidado
jazz [dʒæz] *s* (mus) jazz *m;* (coll) animación, viveza || *tr*—**to jazz up** (coll) animar, dar viveza a
jazz band *s* orquesta de jazz
J.C. *abbr* **Jesus Christ, Julius Caesar**
jct. *abbr* **junction**
jealous ['dʒɛləs] *adj* celoso; envidioso; (*watchful in keeping or guarding something*) solícito, vigilante
jealous•y ['dʒɛləsi] *s* (*pl* **-ies**) celosía, celos; envidia; solicitud, vigilancia
jean [dʒin] *s* dril *m;* **jeans** pantalones *mpl* de dril
Jeanne d'Arc [,ʒɑn'dɑrk] *s* Juana de Arco
jeep [dʒip] *s* jip *m,* pequeño automóvil de propulsión total
jeer [dʒɪr] *s* befa, mofa, vaya || *tr* befar || *intr* mofarse; **to jeer at** befar, mofarse de
jelab [dʒə'lɑb] *s* chilaba
jell [dʒɛl] *s* jalea || *intr* (*to become jellylike*) cuajarse; (*to take hold, catch on*) (fig) cuajar
jel•ly ['dʒɛli] *s* (*pl* **-lies**) jalea || *v* (*pret & pp*) *tr* convertir en jalea || *intr* convertirse en jalea
jel'ly'bean' *s* frutilla
jel'ly•fish' *s* aguamala, medusa; (*weak person*) (coll) calzonazos *m*
jeopardize ['dʒɛpər,daɪz] *tr* arriesgar, exponer, poner en peligro
jeopardy ['dʒɛpərdi] *s* riesgo, peligro
jeremiad [,dʒɛrɪ'maɪ•æd] *s* jeremiada
Jericho ['dʒɛrɪ,ko] *s* Jericó
jerk [dʒʌrk] *s* arranque *m,* estirón *m,* tirón *m;* tic *m,* espasmo muscular; **by jerks** a sacudidas || *tr* mover de un tirón; arrojar de un tirón; atasajar (*carne*) || *intr* avanzar a tirones
jerked beef *s* tasajo
jerkin ['dʒʌrkɪn] *s* jubón *m,* justillo
jerk'wa'ter train *s* (coll) tren de ferrocarril económico
jerk•y ['dʒʌrki] *adj* (*comp* **-ier;** *super* **-iest**) (*road; style*) desigual; que va dando tumbos, que anda a tirones
jersey ['dʒʌrsi] *s* jersey *m,* chaqueta de punto
Jerusalem [dʒɪ'rusələm] *s* Jerusalén
jest [dʒɛst] *s* broma, chanza, chiste *m;* cosa de risa; **in jest** en broma || *intr* bromear
jester ['dʒɛstər] *s* bromista *mf,* burlón *m;* (*professional fool of medieval rulers*) bufón *m*
Jesuit ['dʒɛʒʊ•ɪt] o ['dʒɛzj,•ɪt] *adj & s* jesuíta *m*
Jesuitic(al) [,dʒɛʒʊ'ɪtɪk(əl)] o [,dʒɛzjʊ-'ɪtɪk(əl)] *adj* jesuítico
Jesus ['dʒizəs] *s* Jesús *m*
Jesus Christ *s* Jesucristo

jet [dʒɛt] *adj* de azabache; azabachado || *s* (*of a fountain*) surtidor *m;* (*of gas*) mechero; (*stream shooting forth from nozzle, etc.*) chorro; avión *m* a reacción, avión de chorro; (*hard black mineral; lustrous black*) azabache *m* || *v* (*pret & pp* **jetted;** *ger* **jetting**) *tr* arrojar en chorro || *intr* chorrear, salir en chorro; volar en avión de chorro

jet age *s* era de los aviones de chorro

jet'-black' *adj* azabachado

jet bomber *s* bombardero de reacción a chorro

jet coal *s* carbón *m* de bujía, carbón de llama larga

jet engine *s* motor *m* a chorro, motor de reacción

jet fighter *s* caza *m* de reacción, cazarreactor *m*

jet'lin'er *s* avión *m* de travesía con propulsión a chorro

jet plane *s* avión *m* de chorro

jet propulsion *s* propulsión a chorro, propulsión de escape

jetsam [ˈdʒɛtsəm] *s* (naut) echazón *f;* cosas desechadas

jet set *s* gente acomodada que viajan mucho por avión

jet stream *s* escape *m* de un motor cohete; (meteor) chorros de viento (*que soplan de oeste a este a la altura de 10 kilómetros*)

jettison [ˈdʒɛtɪsən] *s* (naut) echazón *f* || *tr* (naut) echar al mar; desechar, rechazar

jettison gear *s* (aer) lanzador *m*

jet•ty [ˈdʒɛti] *s* (*pl* **-ties**) (*structure projecting into sea to protect harbor*) excollera, malecón *m;* (*wharf*) muelle *m,* desembarcadero

Jew [dʒu] *s* judío

jewel [ˈdʒu•əl] *s* piedra preciosa; (*valuable personal ornament*) alhaja, joya; (*of a watch*) rubí *m;* (*article of costume jewelry*) joya de imitación; (*highly prized person or thing*) alhaja, joya

jewel case *s* guardajoyas *m,* estuche *m,* joyero

jeweler o **jeweller** [ˈdʒu•ələr] *s* joyero; relojero

jewelry [ˈdʒu•əlri] *s* joyería, joyas

jewelry shop *s* joyería; relojería

Jewess [ˈdʒu•ɪs] *s* judía

jew'fish' *s* mero

Jewish [ˈdʒu•ɪʃ] *adj* judío

Jew•ry [ˈdʒu•ri] *s* (*pl* **-ries**) judería

jews'-harp o **jew's-harp** [ˈdjuz,hɑrp] *s* birimbao

jib [dʒɪb] *s* (*of a crane*) aguilón *m,* pescante *m;* (naut) foque *m*

jib boom *s* (naut) botalón *m* de foque

jibe [dʒaɪb] *s* remoque *m,* mofa || *intr* mofarse; (coll) concordar (*dos cosas*); **to jibe at** mofarse de

jif•fy [ˈdʒɪfi] *s* (*pl* **-fies**)—**in a jiffy** (coll) en un santiamén

jig [dʒɪg] *s* (*dance and music*) giga; **the jig is up** (slang) ya se acabó todo, estamos perdidos

jigger [ˈdʒɪgər] *s* (*for fishing*) anzuelo de cuchara; (*for separating ore*) criba de vaivén; (*flea*) nigua; (*gadget*) cosilla, chisme *m,* dispositivo; vasito para medir el licor de un coctel (*onza y media*)

jiggle [ˈdʒɪgəl] *s* zangoloteo || *tr* zangolotear || *intr* zangolotearse

jig saw *s* sierra de vaivén

jig'saw' puzzle *s* rompecabezas *m* (*figura que ha sido cortada caprichosamente en trozos menudos y que hay que recomponer*)

jilt [dʒɪlt] *tr* dar calabazas a (*un novio*)

jim•my [ˈdʒɪmi] *s* (*pl* **-mies**) palanqueta || *v* (*pret & pp* **-mied**) *tr* forzar con palanqueta; **to jimmy open** abrir con palanqueta

jingle [ˈdʒɪŋgəl] *s* (*small bell*) cascabel *m;* (*of tambourine*) sonaja; (*sound*) cascabeleo; rima infantil; (rad) anuncio rimado y cantado || *tr* hacer sonar || *intr* cascabelear

jin•go [ˈdʒɪŋgo] *adj* jingoísta || *s* (*pl* **-goes**) jingoísta *mf;* **by jingo!** (coll) ¡caramba!

jingoism [ˈdʒɪŋgo,ɪzəm] *s* jingoísmo

jinx [dʒɪŋks] *s* gafe *m* || *tr* (coll) traer mala suerte a

jitters [ˈdʒɪtərz] *spl* (coll) inquietud, nerviosidad; **to give the jitters to** (coll) poner nervioso; **to have the jitters** (coll) ponerse nervioso

jittery [ˈdʒɪtəri] *adj* (coll) nervioso

Joan of Arc [ˈdʒon əv ˈɑrk] *s* Juana de Arco

job [dʒɑb] *s* (*piece of work*) trabajo; (*task, chore*) quehacer *m,* tarea; (*work done by contract*) destajo; (*employment*) empleo, oficio; (coll) robo; **by the job** a destajo; **on the job** trabajando de aprendiz; (slang) vigilante, atento a sus obligaciones; **to be out of a job** estar desocupado, estar sin trabajo; **to lie down on the job** (slang) echarse en el surco, estirar la pierna

job analysis *s* análisis *m* ocupacional

jobber [ˈdʒɑbər] *s* comerciante medianero; (*pieceworker*) destajero; (*dishonest official*) agiotista *m*

job'hold'er *s* empleado; (*in the government*) burócrata *mf*

jobless [ˈjɑblɪs] *adj* desocupado, sin empleo

job lot *s* saldo de mercancías

job market *s* oportunidades *fpl* de empleo

job printer *s* impresor *m* de remiendos

job printing *s* remiendo

job security *s* garantía de empleo continuo

jock [dʒɑk] *s* (slang) atleta *m*

jockey [ˈdʒɑki] *s* jockey *m* || *tr* montar (*un caballo*) en la pista; maniobrar; embaucar

jockstrap [ˈdʒɑk,stræp] *s* suspensorio (*para sostener el escroto*)

jocose [dʒoˈkos] *adj* jocoso

jocular [ˈdʒɑkjələr] *adj* jocoso, festivo

jodhpurs [ˈdʒɑdpərz] *spl* pantalones *mpl* de equitación

jog [dʒɑg] *s* golpecito; (*to the memory*) estímulo; trote corto || *v* (*pret & pp* **jogged;** *ger* **jogging**) *tr* empujar levemente; estimular (*la memoria*) || *intr*—**to jog along** avanzar al trote corto

jogging [ˈdʒɑgɪŋ] *s* trote *m* corto

jog trot *s* trote *m* de perro; (fig) rutina

john [dʒɑn] *s* (slang) retrete *m;* inodoro
John Bull *s* el inglés típico, el pueblo inglés
John Hancock [ˈhænkɑk] *s* (coll) la firma de uno
johnnycake [ˈdʒɑni,kek] *s* pan *m* de maíz
John'ny-come'-late'ly *s* recién llegado
John'ny-jump'-up' *s* (*pansy*) pensamiento, trinitaria, violeta
John'ny-on-the-spot' *s* (coll) el que está siempre presente y listo
John the Baptist *s* San Juan Bautista
join [dʒɔɪn] *tr* juntar, unir, ensamblar; asociarse a, unirse a; incorporarse a, ingresar en; abrazar (*un partido*); hacerse socio de (una asociación); alistarse en (*el ejército*); trabar (*batalla*); desaguar en (*el océano*) || *intr* juntarse, unirse; confluir (*p.ej., dos ríos*)
joiner [ˈdʒɔɪnər] *s* carpintero; (coll) el que tiene la manía de incorporarse a muchas asociaciones
joint [dʒɔɪnt] *s* (*in a pipe*) empalme *m,* juntura, (*of bones*) articulación, juntura, coyuntura; (*backbone of book*) nervura; (*hinge of book*) cartivana; (*in woodwork*) emsambladura; (*of meat*) tajada; (*marijuana*) porro, puerro; (elec) empalme *m;* (*gambling den*) (slang) garito; (slang) restaurante *m* de mala muerte; **out of joint** desencajado, descoyuntado; (fig) en desorden, desbarajustado; **to throw out of joint** descoyuntarse (*p.ej., el brazo*)
joint account *s* cuenta en común
Joint Chiefs of Staff *spl* (U.S.A.) Estado mayor conjunto
jointly [ˈdʒɔɪntli] *adv* juntamente, en común
joint owner *s* condueño
joint session *s* sesión conjunta
joint'-stock' company *s* sociedad anónima, compañía por acciones
jointure [ˈdʒɔɪntʃər] *s* bienes *mpl* parafernales
joist [dʒɔɪst] *s* viga
joke [dʒok] *s* broma, chiste *m;* (*trifling matter*) cosa de reír; (*person laughed at*) bufón *m,* hazmerreír *m;* **no joke** cosa seria; **to tell a joke** contar un chiste, **to play a joke on** gastar una broma a || *tr*—**to joke one's way into** conseguir (*p.ej., un empleo*) burla burlando || *intr* bromear, hablar en broma; **joking aside** o **no joking** burlas aparte
joke book *s* libro de chistes
joker [ˈdʒokər] *s* bromista *mf;* (*wise guy*) sábelotodo; (*playing card*) comodín *m;* (*hidden provision*) cláusula engañadora
jol•ly [ˈdʒɑli] *adj* (*comp* **-lier;** *super* **-liest**) alegre, festivo || *adv* (coll) muy, harto || *v* (*pret & pp* **-lied**) *tr* (coll) candonguear
jolt [dʒolt] *s* sacudida || *tr* sacudir || *intr* dar tumbos
Jonah [ˈdʒonə] *s* Jonás *m;* (fig) ave *f* de mal agüero
jongleur [ˈdʒɑŋglər] *s* juglar *m,* trovador *m*
jonquil [ˈdʒɑŋkwɪl] *s* junquillo
Jordan [ˈdʒɔrdən] *s* (*country*) Jordania; (*river*) Jordán *m*
Jordan almond *s* almendra de Málaga
Jordanian [dʒɔrˈdenɪ•ən] *adj & s* jordano
josh [dʒɑʃ] *tr* (coll) dar broma a || *intr* dar broma
jostle [ˈdʒɑsəl] *s* empellón *m,* empujón *m* || *tr* empellar, empujar || *intr* chocar, encontrarse; avanzar a fuerza de empujones o codazos
jot [dʒɑt] *s* —**I don't care a jot for** no se me da un bledo de *s v* (*pret & pp* **jotted;** *ger* **jotting**) *tr*—**to jot down** apuntar, anotar
jounce [dʒaʊns] *s* sacudida || *tr* sacudir || *intr* dar tumbos
journal [ˈdʒʌrnəl] *s* (*newspaper*) periódico; (*magazine*) revista; (*daily record*) diario; (com) libro diario; (naut) cuaderno de bitácora; (mach) gorrón *m,* muñón *m*
journalese [,dʒʌrnəˈliz] *s* lenguaje periodístico
journalism [ˈdʒʌrnə,lɪzəm] *s* periodismo
journalist [ˈdʒʌrnəlɪst] *s* periodista *mf*
journalistic [,dʒʌrnəˈlɪstɪk] *adj* periodístico
journey [ˈdʒʌrni] *s* viaje *m* || *intr* viajar
journey•man [ˈdʒʌrnimən] *s* (*pl* **-men** [mən]) oficial *m*
joust [dʒʌst] o [dʒust] o [dʒaust] *s* justa || *intr* justar
jovial [ˈdʒovɪ•əl] *adj* jovial
joviality [,dʒovɪˈælɪti] *s* jovialidad
jowl [dʒaʊl] *s* (*cheek*) moflete *m;* (*jawbone*) quijada; (*of cattle*) papada; (*of fowl*) barba
joy [dʒɔɪ] *s* alegría, regocijo; **to leap with joy** saltar de gozo
joyful [ˈdʒɔɪfəl] *adj* alegre; **joyful over** gozoso con o de
joyless [ˈdʒɔɪlɪs] *adj* triste, sin alegría
joyous [ˈdʒɔɪ•əs] *adj* alegre
joy ride *s* (coll) paseo de recreo en coche; (coll) paseo alocado en coche
J.P. *abbr* **Justice of the Peace**
Jr. *abbr* **junior**
jubilant [ˈdʒubɪlənt] *adj* jubiloso
jubilation [,dʒubɪˈleʃən] *s* júbilo, viva alegría
jubilee [ˈdʒubɪ,li] *s* (*jubilation*) júbilo; aniversario; quincuagésimo aniversario; (eccl) jubileo
Judaism [ˈdʒude,ɪzəm] *s* judaísmo
judge [dʒʌdʒ] *s* juez *m;* **to be a good judge of** ser buen juez de o en || *tr & intr* juzgar; **judging by** a juzgar por
judge advocate *s* (*in the army*) auditor *m* de guerra; (*in the navy*) auditor de marina
judgeship [ˈdʒʌdʒʃɪp] *s* judicatura
judgment [ˈdʒʌdʒmənt] *s* juicio; (*legal decision*) sentencia, fallo
judgment day *s* día *m* del juicio
judgment seat *s* tribunal *m*
judicature [ˈdʒudɪkətʃər] *s* judicatura
judicial [dʒuˈdɪʃəl *adj* judicial; (*becoming a judge*) crítico, juicioso
judiciar•y [dʒuˈdɪʃɪ,ɛri] *adj* judicial || *s* (*pl* **-ies**) (*judges of a city, country, etc.*) judicatura; (*branch of government that administers justice*) poder *m* judicial
judicious [dʒuˈdɪʃəs] *adj* juicioso
jug [dʒʌg] *s* botija, jarra, cántaro; (*jail*) (slang) chirona

juggle [ˈdʒʌgəl] *s* juego de manos; (*trick, deception*) trampa ‖ *tr* hacer suertes con (*p.ej., bolas*); alterar fraudulentamente, falsear (*cuentas, documentos, etc.*); **to juggle away** escamotear ‖ *intr* hacer suertes; hacer trampas

juggler [ˈdʒʌglər] *s* malabarista *mf;* impostor *m*

juggling [ˈdʒʌglɪŋ] *s* juegos malabares

Jugoslav [ˈjugoˈslɑv] *adj & s* yugoeslavo

Jugoslavia [ˈjugoˈslɑvɪ•ə] *s* Yugoeslavia

jugular [ˈdʒʌgjələr] *adj & s* yugular *f*

juice [dʒus] *s* jugo, zumo; (*natural fluid of an animal body*) jugo; (slang) electricidad; (slang) gasolina; **to stew in one's own juice** (coll) freír en su aceite

juic•y [ˈdʒusi] *adj* (*comp* **-ier;** *super* **-iest**) jugoso, zumoso; (*interesting, spicy*) picante

jukebox [ˈdʒuk,bɑks] *s* tocadiscos *m* tragamonedas

julep [ˈdʒulɪp] *s* julepe *m*

julienne [,dʒulɪˈɛn] *s* sopa juliana

July [dʒuˈlaɪ] *s* julio

jumble [ˈdʒʌmbəl] *s* revoltijo, masa confusa ‖ *tr* emburujar, revolver

jum•bo [ˈdʒʌmbo] *adj* (coll) enorme, colosal ‖ *s* (*pl* **-bos**) (*large clumsy person*) (coll) elefante *m;* (coll) objeto enorme

jump [dʒʌmp] *s* salto; (*in a parachute*) lanzamiento; (*of prices*) alza repentina; **to be always on the jump** (coll) andar siempre de aquí para allí; **to get** o **to have the jump on** (slang) ganar la ventaja a ‖ *tr* saltar; hacer saltar (*a un caballo*); (*in checkers*) comer; salir (*un tren*) fuera de (*el carril*) ‖ *intr* saltar; (*in a parachute from an airplane*) lanzarse; pasar del tope (*el carro de la máquina de escribir*); **to jump at** apresurarse a aceptar (*un convite*); apresurarse a aprovechar (*la oportunidad*); **to jump on** saltar a (*un tren*); (slang) regañar, criticar; **to jump over** saltar por, pasar de un salto; saltar (*la página de un libro*); **to jump to a conclusion** sacar una conclusión precipitadamente

jumper [ˈdʒʌmpər] *s* saltador *m;* blusa de obrero; **jumpers** traje holgado de juego para niños

jumping jack [ˈdʒʌmpɪŋ] *s* títere *m*

jump'ing-off' place *s* fin *m* del camino

jump seat *s* estrapontín *m*, traspuntín *m*

jump spark *s* (elec) chispa de entrehierro

jump suit *s* vestido unitario (*como de paracaidista*)

jump wire *s* (elec) alambre *m* de cierre

jump•y [ˈdʒʌmpi] *adj* (*comp* **-ier;** *super* **-iest**) saltón; asustadizo, nervioso

junc. *abbr* **junction**

junction [ˈdʒʌŋkʃən] *s* juntura, unión; (*of pieces of wood*) ensambladura; (*of two rivers*) confluencia; (*rail connection*) empalme *m;* (rr) estación de empalme

juncture [ˈdʒʌŋktʃər] *s* juntura, unión; (*time, occasion*) coyuntura; **at this juncture** a esta sazón, a estas alturas

June [dʒun] *s* junio

jungle [ˈdʒʌŋgəl] *s* jungla, selva; revoltijo, maraña

junior [ˈdʒunjər] *adj* menor, de menor edad; joven; del penúltimo año; hijo, p.ej., **John Jones, Junior** Juan Jones, hijo ‖ *s* menor *m;* socio menor; alumno del penúltimo año

junior college *s* escuela de estudios universitarios de primero y segundo años

junior high school *s* escuela intermedia entre la primaria y la secundaria

juniper [ˈdʒunɪpər] *s* enebro; (*red cedar*) cedro de Virginia

juniper berry *s* enebrina

junk [dʒʌŋk] *s* chatarra, hierro viejo; ropa vieja; (*useless stuff*) (coll) trastos viejos, baratijas viejas; (*old cable*) jarcia trozada; (*Chinese ship*) junco; (naut) carne salada ‖ *tr* (slang) echar a la basura; reducir a hierro viejo

junk dealer *s* chatarrero, chapucero

junket [ˈdʒʌŋkɪt] *s* manjar *m* de leche, cuajo y azúcar; (*outing*) viaje *m* de recreo; (*trip paid out of public funds*) jira ‖ *intr* hacer un viaje de recreo; ir de jira

junkie [ˈdʒʌŋki] *s* (slang) toxicómano, narcotómano, yonquí *m*

junk•man [ˈdʒʌŋk,mæn] *s* (*pl* **-men** [,mɛn]) chatarrero, chapucero; ropavejero; tripulante *m* de junco

junk room *s* leonera, trastera

junk shop o **junk store** *s* tienda de trastos viejos; baratío (CAm); barata (Col, Mex)

junk yard *s* chatarrería

juridical [dʒʊˈrɪdɪkəl] *adj* jurídico

jurisdiction [,dʒʊrɪsˈdɪkʃən] *s* jurisdicción

jurisprudence [,dʒʊrɪsˈprudəns] *s* jurisprudencia

jurist [ˈdʒʊrɪst] *s* jurista *mf*

juror [ˈdʒʊrər] *s* (*individual*) jurado

ju•ry [ˈdʒʊri] *s* (*pl* **-ries**) (*group*) jurado

jury box *s* tribuna del jurado

jury•man [ˈdʒʊrimən] *s* (*pl* **-men** [mən]) (*individual*) jurado

jury-rig [ˈdʒʊri,rɪg] *v* (*pret & pp* **-rigged;** *ger* **-rigging**) *tr* (naut) aparejar temporariamente

Jus. P. *abbr* **justice of the peace**

just [dʒʌst] *adj* justo ‖ *adv* justamente, justo; hace poco, apenas; sólo; (coll) absolutamente; **just** + *pp* acabado de + *inf*, p.ej., **just received** acabado de recibir; recién + *pp*, p.ej., **just arrived** recién llegado; **just as** como; en el momento en que; tal como, lo mismo que; **just beyond** un poco más allá (de); **just now** hace poco; ahora mismo; **just out** acabado de aparecer, recién publicado; **to have just** + *pp* acabar de + *inf*, p.ej., **I have just arrived** acabo de llegar; **I had just arrived** acababa de llegar

justice [ˈdʒʌstɪs] *s* justicia; (*judge*) juez *m;* (*just deserts*) premio merecido; **to bring to justice** aprehender y condenar por justicia; **to do justice to** hacer justicia a; apreciar debidamente

justice of the peace *s* juez *m* de paz

justifiable [ˈdʒʌstɪ,faɪ•əbəl] *adj* justificable

justi•fy [ˈdʒʌstɪˌfaɪ] *v* (*pret & pp* **-fied**) *tr* justificar; (typ) justificar
justly [ˈdʒʌstli] *adj* justamente, debidamente
jut [dʒʌt] *v* (*pre & pp* **jutted;** *ger* **jutting)** *intr*—**to jut out** resaltar, proyectarse
jute [dʒut] *s* yute *m* ‖ **Jute** *m* juto
Jutland [ˈdʒʌtlənd] *s* Jutlandia
juvenile [ˈdʒuvənɪl] o [ˈdʒuvəˌnaɪl] *adj* juvenil; para jóvenes ‖ *s* joven *mf*, mocito; libro para niños; (theat) galán *m*, galancete *m*
juvenile court *s* tribunal *m* tutelar de menores
juvenile delinquency *s* delincuencia de menores
juvenile lead [lid] *s* (theat) papel *m* de galancete; (theat) galancete *m*
juvenilia [ˌdʒuvəˈnɪlɪ•ə] *spl* obras de juventud
juxtapose [ˌdʒʌkstəˈpoz] *tr* yuxtaponer

K

K, k [ke] undécima letra del alfabeto inglés
k. *abbr* **karat, kilogram**
K. *abbr* **King, Knight**
kale [kel] *s* col *f*, berza; (slang) dinero, pasta
kaleidoscope [keˈlaɪdəˌskop] *s* calidoscopio
kangaroo [ˌkæŋgəˈru] *s* canguro
kapok [ˈkepɑk] *s* capoc *m*, lana de ceiba
kaput [kəˈpʊt] *adj* (slang) roto; gastado; inútil
karate [kəˈrɑti] *m* karate *m*, karaté *m*
karate expert *s* karateka *m*
katydid [ˈketidɪd] *s* saltamontes *m* cuyo macho emite un sonido chillón
kayak [ˈkaɪæk] *s* kayak *m*
kc. *abbr* **kilocycle**
kedge [kɛdʒ] *s* (naut) anclote *m*
keel [kil] *s* quilla ‖ *intr*—**to keel over** (naut) dar de quilla; volcarse; (coll) desmayarse
keelson [ˈkɛlsən] o [ˈkilsən] *s* (naut) sobrequilla
keen [kin] *adj* (*having a sharp edge*) agudo, afilado; (*sharp, cutting*) mordaz, penetrante; (*sharp-witted*) sutil, astuto, perspicaz; (*eager, much interested*) entusiasta; intenso, vivo; (slang) maravilloso; **to be keen on** ser muy aficionado a
keep [kip] *s* manutención, subsistencia; (*of medieval castle*) torre *f* del homenaje; **for keeps** (coll) de veras; (coll) para siempre; **to earn one's keep** (coll) ganarse la vida ‖ *v* (*pret & pp* **kept** [kɛpt] *tr* guardar, conservar; (*deciding to make a purchase*) quedarse con; cumplir, guardar (*su palabra, su promesa*); llevar (*cuentas*); apuntar (*los tantos*); tener (*criados, caballos, huéspedes*); cultivar (*una huerta*); dirigir (*un hotel, una escuela*); celebrar (*una fiesta*); hacer tardar (*a una persona*); **to keep away** tener alejado; **to keep back** retener; beberse (*las lágrimas*); reservar, no divulgar; **to keep down** reprimir; reducir (*los gastos*) al mínimo; **to keep** (*a person*) **from** + *ger* no dejarle (*a una persona*) + *inf;* **to keep in** no dejar salir; **to keep off** tener a distancia; no dejar penetrar (*p.ej., la lluvia*); evitar (*p.ej., el polvo*); **to keep out** no dejar entrar; no dejar penetrar; **to keep someone informed (about)** ponerle a uno al corriente (de); **to keep someone waiting** hacerle a uno esperar; **to keep up** mantener, conservar ‖ *intr* permanecer, quedarse; conservarse, no echarse a perder; **to keep** + *ger* seguir + *ger;* **to keep away** mantenerse a distancia; no dejarse ver; **to keep from** + *ger* abstenerse de + *inf;* **to keep informed (about)** ponerse al corriente (de); **to keep in with** (coll) congraciarse con, no perder el favor de; **to keep off** no acercarse a; no pisar (*el césped*); **to keep on** + *ger* seguir + *ger;* **to keep on with** continuar con; **to keep out** mantenerse fuera, no entrar; **to keep out of** no entrar en; no meterse en; evitar (*el peligro*); **to keep quiet** estarse quieto; **to keep to** seguir por, llevar (*la derecha, la izquierda*); **to keep to oneself** quedarse a solas; **to keep up** continuar; no rezagarse; **to keep up with** correr parejas con; llevar adelante, proseguir
keeper [ˈkipər] *s* guardián *m*, custodio; (*of a game preserve*) guardabosque *m;* (*of a magnet*) armadura, culata
keeping [ˈkipɪŋ] *s* custodia, cuidado; (*of a holiday*) celebración; **in keeping with** de acuerdo con, en armonía con; **in safe keeping** en lugar seguro, a buen recaudo; **out of keeping with** en desacuerdo con
keep'sake' *s* recuerdo
keg [kɛg] *s* cuñete *m*, cubeto
ken [kɛn] *s* alcance *m* de la vista, alcance del saber; **beyond the ken of** fuera del alcance de
kennel [ˈkɛnəl] *s* perrera
kep•i [ˈkepi] o [ˈkɛpi] *s* (*pl* **-is**) quepis *m*
kept woman [kɛpt] *s* entretenida, manceba
kerchief [ˈkʌrtʃɪf] *s* pañuelo, mantón *m*
kerchoo [kərˈtʃu] *interj* ¡ah-chís!
kernel [ˈkʌrnəl] *s* (*inner part of a nut or fruit stone*) almendra núcleo; (*of wheat or corn*) grano; (fig) medula
kerosene [ˈkɛrəˌsin] o [ˌkɛrəˈsin] *s* keroseno
kerosene lamp *s* lámpara de petróleo
kerplunk [kərˈplʌŋk] *interj* ¡pataplún!
ketchup [ˈkɛtʃəp] *s* salsa de tomate condimentada

kettle [ˈkɛtəl] *s* caldera, marmita; (*teakettle*) tetera

ket'tle•drum' *s* timbal *m,* tímpano

key [ki] *adj* clave ‖ *s* (*of door, trunk, etc.*) llave *f;* (*of piano, typewriter, etc.*) tecla; (*wedge or cotter used to lock parts together*) clavija, cuña, chaveta; (*reef or low island*) cayo; (bot) sámara; (*tone of voice*) tono; (mus) clave *f* o llave *f;* (telg) manipulador *m;* (*to a puzzle, secret, translation, code*) (fig) clave o llave; (*place giving control to a region*) (fig) llave *f;* (fig) persona principal; **off key** desafinado; desafinadamente ‖ *tr* acuñar, enchavetar; **to key up** alentar, excitar

key'board' *s* teclado

key fruit *s* sámara

key'hole' *s* ojo de la cerradura; (*of a clock*) agujero de cuerda

key money *s* pago ilícito al casero

key'note' *s* (mus) tónica, nota tónica; (fig) idea fundamental

keynote speech *s* discurso de apertura (*en que se expone el programa de un partido político*)

key'punch'er *s* perforista *mf*

key ring *s* llavero

key'stone' *s* clave *f,* espinazo; (fig) piedra angular

Key West *s* Cayo Hueso

key word *s* palabra clave

kg. *abbr* **kilogram**

K.G. *abbr* **Knight of the Garter**

kha•ki [ˈkɑki] o [ˈkæki] *adj* caqui ‖ *s* (*pl* **-kis**) caqui *m*

khedive [kəˈdiv] *s* jedive *m*

kibitz [ˈkɪbɪts] *intr* (coll) dar consejos molestos a los jugadores

kibitzer [ˈkɪbɪtsər] *s* (coll) mirón molesto (*de una partida de juego*); (coll) entremetido

kiblah [ˈkɪblɑ] *s* alquibla

kibosh [ˈkaɪbɑʃ] o [kɪˈbɑʃ] *s* (coll) música celestial; **to put the kibosh on** (coll) desbaratar, imposibilitar

kick [kɪk] *s* puntapié *m;* (*of an animal*) coz *f;* (*of a gun*) coz, culatazo; (*complaint*) (slang) queja, protesta; (*of liquor*) (slang) fuerza, estímulo; (*thrill*) gusto, placer intenso; **to get a kick out of** (slang) hallar mucho placer en ‖ *tr* acocear, dar de puntapiés a; sacudir (*los pies*); **to kick out** (coll) echar a puntapiés a la calle; (coll) echar, despedir; **to kick the bucket** (coll) morir; **to kick up a row** (slang) armar un bochinche ‖ *intr* cocear; dar culetazos (*un arma de fuego*); (coll) quejarse; **to kick about** (coll) quejarse de; **to kick against the pricks** dar coces contra el aguijón; **to kick off** (football) dar el golpe de salida

kick'back' *s* (coll) contragolpe *m;* (slang) devolución a un cómplice de una parte de lo robado

kick'off' *s* (football) golpe *m* de salida, puntapié *m* inicial

kid [kɪd] *s* (*young goat*) cabrito; (*leather*) cabritilla; (coll) chiquillo, chico; **kids** guantes *mpl* o zapatos de cabritilla ‖ *v* (*pret & pp* **kidded;** *ger* **kidding**) *tr* (slang) embromar, tomar el pelo a; **to kid oneself** (slang) forjarse ilusiones ‖ *intr* (slang) decirlo en broma

kidder [ˈkɪdər] *s* (slang) bromista *mf*

kid gloves *spl* guantes *mpl* de cabritilla; **to handle with kid gloves** tratar con suma discreción o cautela

kid'nap' *v* (*pret & pp* **-naped** o **-napped;** *ger* **naping** o **-napping**) *tr* secuestrar

kidnaper o **kidnapper** [ˈkɪd,næpər] *s* secuestrador *m,* ladrón *m* de niños

kidney [ˈkɪdni] *s* riñon *m;* (coll) clase *f,* *especie f;* (coll) carácter *m*

kidney bean *s* judía

kidney stone *s* cálculo renal

kill [kɪl] *s* matanza; (*of a wild beast, an army, a pack of hounds*) ataque *m* final; (*creek*) arroyo, riachuelo; **for the kill** para el golpe final ‖ *tr* matar; ahogar (*un proyecto de ley*); quitar (*el sabor*); producir una impresión irresistible en

killer [ˈkɪlər] *s* matador *m*

killer whale *s* orca

killing [ˈkɪlɪŋ] *adj* matador; (*exhausting*) abrumador; (coll) muy divertido, de lo más ridículo ‖ *s* matanza; (*game killed on a hunt*) cacería, piezas; (coll) gran ganancia; **to make a killing** (coll) enriquecerse de golpe

kill'-joy' *s* aguafiestas *mf*

kiln [kɪl] o [kɪln] *s* horno

kil•o [ˈkɪlo] o [ˈkilo] *s* (*pl* **-os**) kilo, kilogramo; kilómetro

kilocycle [ˈkɪlə,saɪkəl] *s* kilociclo

kilogram [ˈkɪlə,græm] *s* kilogramo

kilometer [ˈkɪlə,mitər] *s* kilómetro (*distancia*); **kilometer** [kɪˈlɑmətər] *s* kilómetro (*instrumento*)

kilometric [,kɪləˈmɛtrɪk] *adj* kilométrico

kilowatt [ˈkɪlə,wɑt] *s* kilovatio

kilowatt-hour [ˈkɪlə,wɑtˈaʊr] *s* (*pl* **kilowatt-hours**) kilovatio-hora

kilt [kɪlt] *s* enagüillas, falda corta

kilter [ˈkɪltər] *s*—**to be out of kilter** (coll) estar descompuesto

kimo•no [kɪˈmonə] *s* (*pl* **-nos**) quimono

kin [kɪn] *s* (*family relationship*) parentesco; (*relatives*) deudos; **near of kin** muy allegado; **of kin** allegado; **the next of kin** el pariente más próximo, los parientes próximos

kind [kaɪnd] *adj* bueno, bondadoso; (*greeting*) afectuoso; **kind to** bueno para con ‖ *s* clase *f,* especie *f,* suerte *f,* género; **a kind of** uno a modo de; **all kinds of** (coll) gran cantidad de; **in kind** en especie; en la misma moneda; **kind of** (coll) algo, más bien; **of a kind** de una misma clase; (*poor, mediocre*) de poco valor, de mala muerte; **of the kind** por el estilo

kindergarten [ˈkɪndər,gɑrtən] *s* parvulario, escuela de párvulos, jardín *m* de la infancia

kindergartner [ˈkɪndər,gɑrtnər] *s* (*child*) párvulo; (*teacher*) parvulista *mf*

kind-hearted [ˈkaɪndˈhɑrtɪd] *adj* bondadoso, de buen corazón

kindle [ˈkɪndəl] *tr* encender ‖ *intr* encenderse
kindling [ˈkɪndlɪŋ] *s* encendajas
kindling wood *s* leña
kind•ly [ˈkaɪndli] *adj* (*comp* **-lier;** *super* **-liest**) (*kind-hearted*) bondadoso; apacible, benigno; favorable ‖ *adv* bondadosamente; cordialmente; con gusto; por favor; **to not take kindly to** no aceptar de buen grado
kindness [ˈkaɪndnɪs] *s* bondad; **have the kindness to** tenga Vd. la bondad de
kindred [ˈkɪndrɪd] *adj* emparentado; afín, semejante ‖ *s* parentela; semejanza, afinidad
Kinescope [ˈkɪnɪ,skop] *s* (trademark) cinescopio, kinescopio
kinetic [kɪˈnɛtɪk] *adj* cinético ‖ **kinetics** *s* cinética
kinetic energy *s* fuerza viva, energía cinética
kinfolk [ˈkin,fok] *s* (coll) pariente(s)
king [kɪŋ] *s* rey *m;* (cards, chess, & fig) rey; (checkers) dama
king'bolt' *s* pivote *m* central
kingdom [ˈkɪŋdəm] *s* reino
king'fish'er *s* martín *m* pescador
king•ly [ˈkɪŋli] *adj* (*comp* **-lier;** *super* **-liest**) real, regio; (*stately*) majestuoso ‖ *adv* regiamente
king'pin' *s* (bowling) bolo delantero; pivote *m* central; (aut) pivote de dirección; (coll) persona principal; (coll) jefe *m* de criminales
king post *s* pendolón *m*
king's evil *s* escrófula
kingship [ˈkɪŋʃɪp] *s* dignidad real
king'-size' *adj* de tamaño largo
king's ransom *s* riquezas de Creso
kink [kɪŋk] *s* (*twist, e.g., in a rope*) enroscadura, coca; (*e.g., in hair*) pasa; (*soreness in neck*) tortícolis *m;* (*flaw, difficulty*) estorbo, traba; (*mental twist*) chifladura, manía ‖ *tr* enroscar ‖ *intr* enroscarse
kink•y [ˈkɪŋki] *adj* (*comp* **-ier;** *super* **-iest**) encarrujado, ensortijado; (coll) perverso, raro
kinsfolk [ˈkɪnz,fok] *s* parentela, familia, deudos
kinship [ˈkɪnʃɪp] *s* parentesco; semejanza, afinidad
kins•man [ˈkɪnzmən] *s* (*pl* **-men** [mən]) pariente *m*
kins•woman [ˈkɪnz,wʊmən] *s* (*pl* **-women** [,wɪmɪn]) *s* parienta
kipper [ˈkɪpər] *s* arenque acecinado, salmón acecinado ‖ *tr* acecinar (*el arenque o el salmón*)
kiss [kɪs] *s* beso; (billiards) retruco; (*confection*) dulce *m*, merengue *m* ‖ *tr* besar; **to kiss away** borrar con besos (*las pensas de una persona*) ‖ *intr* besar; besarse; (billiards) retrucar
kit [kɪt] *s* cartera de herramientas; (*case and its contents for various purposes*) estuche *m;* (*of a soldier*) equipo, pertrechos; (*of a traveler*) equipaje *m;* (*pail, tub*) balde *m*
kitchen [ˈkɪtʃən] *s* cocina
kitchenette [,kɪtʃəˈnɛt] *s* cocinilla
kitchen garden *s* huerto
kitch'en•maid' *s* ayudanta de cocina, pincha
kitchen police *s* (mil) trabajo de cocina; soldados que están de cocina
kitchen range *s* cocina económica
kitchen sink *s* fregadero; **everything but the kitchen sink** sin faltar apenas nada; completísimo
kitch'en-ware' *s* utensilios de cocina
kite [kaɪt] *s* cometa; (orn) milano; **to fly a kite** hacer volar una cometa
kith and kin [kɪθ] *spl* parientes *mpl;* parientes y amigos
kitten [ˈkɪtən] *s* gatito, minino
kittenish [ˈkɪtənɪʃ] *adj* juguetón, retozón; (*coy, flirtatious*) coquetón
kit•ty [ˈkɪti] *s* (*pl* **-ties**) gatito, minino; (*in card games*) polla, puesta ‖ *interj* ¡miz!
kleptomaniac [,klɛptəˈmenɪ,æk] *s* cleptómano
km. *abbr* **kilometer**
knack [næk] *s* tino, tranquillo, maña
knapsack [ˈnæp,sæk] *s* mochila
knave [nev] *s* bribón *m*, pícaro; (cards) sota
knaver•y [ˈnevəri] *s* (*pl* **-ies**) bribonería, picardía
knead [nid] *tr* amasar, sobar
knee [ni] *s* rodilla; (*of animal*) codillo; (*e.g., of trousers*) rodillera; (mach) ángulo, codo; **to bring** (*someone*) **to his knees** rendir, vencer; **to go down on one's knees** hincarse de rodillas, caer de rodillas; **to go down on one's knees to** implorar de rodillas
knee breeches [ˈbrɪtʃɪz] *spl* pantalones cortos
knee'cap' *s* rótula; (*protective covering*) rodillera
knee'-deep' *adj* metido hasta las rodillas
knee'high' *adj* que llega hasta la rodilla
knee'-hole' *s* hueco para acomodar las rodillas
knee jerk *s* reflejo rotuliano
kneel [nil] *v* (*pret & pp* **knelt** [nɛlt] o **kneeled**) *intr* arrodillarse; estar de rodillas
knee'pad' *s* rodillera
knee'pan' *s* rótula
knee swell *s* (*of organ*) (mus) rodillera
knell [nɛl] *s* doble *m*, toque *m* de difuntos; mal agüero; **to toll the knell of** anunciar la muerte de, anunciar el fin de ‖ *intr* doblar, tocar a muerto; sonar tristemente
knickers [ˈnɪkərz] *spl* pantalones *mpl* de media pierna
knickknack [ˈnɪk,næk] *s* chuchería,bujería, baratija
knife [naɪf] *s* (*pl* **-knives** [naɪvz] cuchillo; (*of a paper cutter or other instrument*) cuchilla; **to go under the knife** (coll) hacerse operar ‖ *tr* acuchillar; (slang) traicionar
knife sharpener *s* afilador *m*, afilón *m*
knife switch *s* (elec) interruptor *m* de cuchilla
knight [naɪt] *s* caballero; (chess) caballo ‖ *tr* armar caballero
knight-errant [ˈnaɪtˈɛrənt] *s* (*pl* **knights-errant**) caballero andante
knight-errant•ry [ˈnaɪtˈɛrəntri] *s* (*pl* **-ries**) caballería andante; (*quixotic behavior*) quijotada

knighthood [ˈnaɪt•hʊd] *s* caballería
knightly [ˈnaɪtli] *adj* caballeroso, caballeresco
Knight of the Rueful Countenance *s* Caballero de la triste figura (*Don Quijote*)
knit [nɪt] *v* (*pret & pp* **knitted** o **knit;** *ger* **knitting**) *tr* tejer a punto de aguja; enlazar, unir; fruncir (*las cejas*) arrugar (*la frente*) ‖ *intr* hacer calceta, hacer malla; trabarse, unirse; soldarse (*un hueso*)
knit goods *spl* géneros de punto
knitting [ˈnɪtɪŋ] *s* punto de media, trabajo de punto
knitting machine *s* máquina de hacer tejidos de punto
knitting needle *s* aguja de hacer media
knit'wear' *s* géneros de punto
knob [nɑb] *s* (*lump*) bulto, protuberancia; (*of a door*) botón *m,* tirador *m;* (*of a radio set*) botón, perilla; (*ornament on furniture*) manzana; colina o montaña redondeada
knock [nɑk] *s* golpe *m;* (*e.g., on a door*) toque *m,* llamada; (*with a door knocker*) aldabazo; (*of an internal-combustion engine*) pistoneo; (slang) censura, crítica ‖ *tr* golpear; (*repeatedly*) golpetear; (slang) censurar, criticar; **to knock down** (*with a blow, punch, etc.*) derribar; (*to the highest bidder*) rematar; desarmar, desmontar (*un aparato o máquina*); **to knock off** hacer saltar con un golpe; suspender (*el trabajo*); poner fin a; (slang) matar; **to knock out** agotar; (box) poner fuera de combate ‖ *intr* tocar, llamar; golpear, pistonear (*el motor de combustión interna*); (slang) censurar, criticar; **to knock about** andar vagando; **to knock against** dar contra, tropezar con; **to knock at** tocar a, llamar a (*la puerta*); **to knock off** dejar de trabajar
knocker [ˈnɑkər] *s* (*on a door*) aldaba; (coll) criticón *m*
knock-kneed [ˈnɑk,nid] *adj* patizambo, zambo
knock'out' *s* golpe decisivo, puñetazo decisivo; (box) (el) fuera de combate; (elec) destapadero; real moza
knockout drops *spl* (slang) gotas narcóticas
knoll [nol] *s* loma, otero
knot [nɑt] *s* nudo; (*worn as ornament*) lazo; corrillo, grupo; (*difficult matter; bond or tie*) nudo; nudo o lazo de matrimonio; (*protuberance in a fabric*) envoltorio; (naut) nudo; **to tie the knot** (coll) casarse ‖ *v* (*pret & pp* **knotted;** *ger* **knotting**) *tr* anudar; fruncir (*las cejas*) ‖ *intr* anudarse
knot'hole' *s* agujero en la madera (*que deja un nudo al desprenderse*)
knot•ty [ˈnɑti] *adj* (*comp* **-tier;** *super* **-tiest**) nudoso; (fig) espinoso, difícil
know [no] *s* **—to be in the know** estar enterado, tener informes secretos ‖ *v* (*pret* **knew** [nju] o [nu]; *pp* **known**) *tr & intr* (*by reasoning or learning*) saber; (*by the senses or by perception; through acquaintance or recognition*) conocer; **as far as I know** que yo sepa; **to know about** saber de; **to know best** ser el mejor juez, saber lo que más conviene; **to know how to** + *inf* saber + *inf;* **to know it all** (coll) sabérselo todo; **to know what one is doing** obrar con conocimiento de causa; **to know what's what** (coll) saber cuántas son cinco; **you ought to know better** deberías tener vergüenza
knowable [ˈno•əbəl] *adj* conocible
know'-how' *s* conocimiento, destreza, habilidad
knowingly [ˈno•ɪŋli] *adv* a sabiendas, con conocimiento de causa; (*on purpose*) adrede
know'-it-all' *adj & s* (coll) sabidillo, sabelotodo *mf*
knowledge [ˈnɑlɪdʒ] *s* (*faculty*) ciencia, conocimientos, el saber; (*awareness, acquaintance, familiarity*) conocimiento; **to have a thorough knowledge of** conocer a fondo; **to my knowledge** que yo sepa; **to the best of my knowledge** según mi leal saber y entender; **with full knowledge** con conocimiento de causa; **without my knowledge** sin saberlo yo
knowledgeable [ˈnɑlɪdʒəbəl] *adj* (coll) conocedor, inteligente
know'-noth'ing *s* ignorante *mf*
knuckle [ˈnʌkəl] *s* nudillo; (*of a quadruped*) jarrete *m;* (*mach*) junta de charnela; **knuckles** bóxer *m* ‖ *intr*—**to knuckle down** someterse, darse por vencido; aplicarse con empeño al trabajo
knurl [nʌrl] *s* moleteado ‖ *tr* moletear, cerrillar (*p.ej., las piezas de moneda*)
k.o. *abbr* **knockout**
kook [kuk] *s* (coll) tipo raro; excéntrico
Koran [koˈrɑn] o [koˈræn] *s* Corán *m*
Korea [koˈri•ə] *s* Corea
Korean [koˈri•ən] *adj & s* coreano
kosher [ˈkoʃər] *adj* autorizado por la ley judía; (coll) genuino, auténtico
kowtow [ˈkaʊˌtaʊ] o [ˈkoˌtaʊ] *intr* arrodillarse y tocar el suelo con la frente; doblegarse servilmente, mostrarse servilmente obsequioso
Kt. *abbr* **Knight**
kudos [ˈkjudɑs] o [ˈkudɑs] *s* (coll) gloria, renombre *m,* fama
kw. *abbr* **kilowatt**
K.W.H. *abbr* **kilowatt-hour**

L

L, l [ɛl] duodécima letra del alfabeto inglés
l. *abbr* **liter, line, league, length**
L. *abbr* **Latin, Low**
la•bel [ˈlebəl] *s* etiqueta, marbete *m*, rótulo; (*descriptive word*) calificación || *v* (*pret & pp* **-beled** o **-belled;** *ger* **-beling** o **-belling**) *tr* poner etiqueta o marbete a, rotular; calificar
labial [ˈlebɪ•əl] *adj & s* labial *f*
labor [ˈlebər] *adj* obrero || *s* trabajo, labor *f;* (*job, task*) tarea, faena; (*manual work involved in an undertaking; the wages for such work*) mano *f* de obra; (*wage-earning workers as contrasted with capital and management*) los obreros; (*childbirth*) parto; **labors** esfuerzos; **to be in labor** estar de parto || *intr* trabajar; (*to exert oneself*) forcejar; estar de parto; moverse penosamente; cabecear y balancear (*un buque*); **to labor under** ser víctima de
labor and management *spl* los obreros y los patronos
laborato•ry [ˈlæbərə,tori] *s* (*pl* **-ries**) laboratorio
labored [ˈlebərd] *adj* penoso, dificultoso; artificial, forzado
laborer [ˈlebərər] *s* trabajador *m*, obrero; (*unskilled worker*) bracero, jornalero, peón *m*
laborious [ləˈborɪ•əs] *adj* laborioso
la'bor-man'agement *adj* obrero-patronal
labor union *s* gremio obrero, sindicato
Labourite [ˈlebə,raɪt] *s* laborista *mf*
Labrador [ˈlæbrə,dɔr] *s* el Labrador
labyrinth [ˈlæbɪrɪnθ] *s* laberinto
lace [les] *s* encaje *m;* (*string to tie shoe, corset, etc.*) cordón *m*, lazo; (*braid*) galón *m* de oro o plata || *tr* adornar con encaje; atar (*los zapatos, el corsé*); (coll) dar una paliza a
lace trimming *s* randa
lace'work' *s* encaje *m*, obra de encaje
lachrymose [ˈlækrɪ,mos] *adj* lacrimoso
lacing [ˈlesɪŋ] *s* cordón *m;* lazo; galón *m;* (coll) paliza
lack [læk] *s* carencia, falta; (*complete lack*) defecto || *tr* carecer de, necesitar || *intr* (*to be lacking*) faltar
lackadaisical [,lækəˈdezɪkəl] *adj* desaprovechado, indiferente
lackey [ˈlæki] *s* lacayo; secuaz *m* servil
lacking [ˈlækɪŋ] *prep* sin, carente de
lack'lus'ter *adj* delustrado, deslucido
laconic [ləˈkɑnɪk] *adj* lacónico
lacquer [ˈlækər] *s* laca || *tr* laquear
lacquer ware *s* lacas, objetos de laca
lacu•na [ləˈkjunə] *s* (*pl* **-nas** o **-nae** [ni]) laguna
lac•y [ˈlesi] *adj* (*comp* **-ier;** *super* **-iest**) de encaje; (fig) diáfano
lad [læd] *s* muchacho, chico
ladder [ˈlædər] *s* escalera; (*stepladder*) escala, escalera de mano; (*two ladders fastened together at the top with hinges*) escalera de tijera; (*stepping stone*) (fig) escalón *m*
ladder truck *s* carro de escaleras de incendio
ladies' room *s* cuarto tocador
ladle [ˈledəl] *s* cazo; (*for soup*) cucharón *m;* (*of tinsmith*) cucharilla || *tr* servir con cucharón; sacar con cucharón
la•dy [ˈledi] *s* (*pl* **-dies**) señora, dama
la'dy-bird' o **la'dy•bug'** *s* mariquita, vaca de San Antón
la'dy•fin'ger *s* melindre *m*
lady-in-waiting *s* camarera de la reina
la'dy-kil'ler *s* ladrón *m* de corazones
la'dy•like' *adj* elegante; **to be ladylike** ser muy dama
la'dy•love' *s* amada, amiga querida
lady of the house *s* ama de casa
ladyship [ˈledi,ʃɪp] *s* señoría
lady's maid *s* doncella
lady's man *s* perico entre ellas
lag [læg] *s* retraso || *v* (*pret & pp* **lagged;** *ger* **lagging**) *intr* retrasarse; **to lag behind** quedarse atrás, rezagarse
lager beer [ˈlɑgər] *s* cerveza reposada
laggard [ˈlægərd] *s* perezoso, rezagado
lagoon [ləˈgun] *s* laguna
laid paper [led] *s* papel vergueteado
laid up *adj* almacenado, ahorrado; (naut) inactivo; (coll) encamado por estar enfermo
lair [lɛr] *s* cubil *m*
lai•ty [ˈle•ɪti] *s* legos
lake [lek] *adj* lacustre || *s* lago
lamb [læm] *s* cordero; carne *f* de cordero; piel *f* de cordero; (*meek person*) (fig) cordero
lambaste [læmˈbest] *tr* (*to thrash*) (coll) dar una paliza a; (*to reprimand harshly*) (coll) dar una jabonadura a
lamb chop *s* chuleta de cordero
lambkin [ˈlæmkɪn] *s* corderito; (fig) nenito
lamb'skin' *s* piel *f* de cordero, corderina; (*dressed with its wool*) corderillo
lame [lem] *adj* cojo; (*sore*) dolorido; (*e.g., excuse*) débil, pobre || *tr* encojar
lament [ləˈmɛnt] *s* lamento; (*dirge*) elegía || *tr* lamentar || *intr* lamentarse
lamentable [ˈlæməntəbəl] *adj* lamentable
lamentation [,læmənˈteʃən] *s* lamentación
laminate [ˈlæmɪ,net] *tr* laminar
laminated glass *s* cristal laminado
lamp [læmp] *s* lámpara
lamp'black' *s* negro de humo
lamp chimney *s* tubo de lámpara
lamp'light' *s* luz *f* de lámpara
lamp'light'er *s* farolero
lampoon [læmˈpun] *s* pasquín *m*, libelo || *tr* pasquinar
lamp'post' *s* poste *m* de farol
lamp shade *s* pantalla de lámpara
lamp'wick' *s* mecha de lámpara, torcida
lance [læns] o [lɑns] *s* lanza; (surg) lanceta || *tr* alancear; (surg) abrir con lanceta
lance rest *s* ristre *m*
lancet [ˈlænsɪt] *s* (surg) lanceta

land [lænd] *adj* terrestre; (*wind*) terral || *s* tierra; **on land, on sea, and in the air** en tierra, mar y aire; **to make land** atracar a tierra; **to see how the land lies** medir el terreno, ver el cariz que van tomando las cosas || *tr* desembarcar; conducir (*un avión*) a tierra; coger (*un pez*); (coll) conseguir || *intr* desembarcar; (*to reach land*) arribar, aterrar; aterrizar (*un avión*); (*to arrive or come to rest*) ir a dar, ir a parar; **to land on one's feet** caer de pies; **to land on one's head** caer de cabeza

landau ['lændɔ] o ['lændaʊ] *s* landó *m*

land breeze *s* terral *m*

landed ['lændɪd] *adj* (*owning land*) hacendado; (*real-estate*) inmobiliario; **landed property** bienes *mpl* raíces

land'fall' *s* (*sighting land*) aterrada; (*landing of ship or plane*) aterraje *m;* tierra vista desde el mar; (*landslide*) derrumbe *m*

land'fill' *s* tierra y escombros

land grant *s* donación de tierras

land'hold'er *s* terrateniente *mf,* hacendado

landing ['lændɪŋ] *s* (*of ship or plane*) aterraje *m;* (*of passengers*) desembarco; (*place where passengers and goods are landed*) desembarcadero; (*of stairway*) desembarco, descanso

landing beacon *s* (aer) radiofaro de aterrizaje

landing craft *s* (nav) lancha de desembarco

landing field *s* (aer) pista de aterrizaje

landing force *s* (nav) compañía de desembarco

landing gear *s* (aer) tren *m* de aterrizaje

landing stage *s* embarcadero flotante

landing strip *s* (aer) faja de aterrizaje

land'la'dy *s* (*pl* **-dies**) (*e.g., of an apartment*) casera, dueña; (*of a lodging house*) ama, patrona; (*of an inn*) mesonera, posadera

landlocked ['lænd,lɑkt] *adj* rodeado de tierra

land'lord' *s* (*e.g., of an apartment*) casero, dueño; (*of a lodging house*) amo, patrón *m;* (*of an inn*) mesonero, posadero

land'lub'ber *s* (*person unacquainted with the sea*) marinero de agua dulce; (*awkward and unskilled seaman*) marinero matalote

land'mark' *s* (*boundary stone*) mojón *m;* (*feature of landscape that marks a location*) guía; suceso que hace época; (naut) marca de reconocimiento

land office *s* oficina del catastro

land'-of'fice business *s* (coll) negocio de mucho movimiento

land'own'er *s* terrateniente *mf,* hacendado

landscape ['lænd,skep] *s* paisaje *m* || *tr* ajardinar

landscape architect *s* arquitecto paisajista

landscape gardener *s* jardinero adornista, jardinista *mf*

landscape painter *s* paisajista *mf*

landscapist ['lænd,skepɪst] *s* paisajista *mf*

land'slide' *s* derrumbe *m,* derrumbamiento de tierra, corrimiento; (fig) mayoría de votos abrumadora; (fig) victoria arrolladora

landward ['lændwərd] *adv* hacia tierra, hacia la costa

land wind *s* terral *m*

lane [len] *s* (*narrow street or passage*) callejuela; (*path*) carril *m;* (*of an automobile highway*) faja; (*of an air or ocean route*) derrotero, vía

langsyne ['læŋ'saɪn] *adv* (Scotch) hace mucho tiempo || *s* (Scotch) tiempo de antaño

language ['læŋgwɪdʒ] *s* idioma *m,* lengua; (*way of speaking or writing, style; figurative or poetic expression; communication of meaning said to be employed by flowers, birds, art, etc.*) lenguaje *m;* (*of a special group of people*) jerga

language laboratory *s* laboratorio de idiomas

languid ['læŋgwɪd] *adj* lánguido

languish ['læŋgwɪʃ] *intr* languidecer; afectar languidez

languor ['læŋgər] *s* languidez *f*

languorous ['læŋgərəs] *adj* lánguido; (*causing languor*) enervante

lank [læŋk] *adj* descarnado, larguirucho; (*hair*) lacio

lank•y ['læŋki] *adj* (*comp* **-ier;** *super* **-iest**) descarnado, larguirucho

lantern ['læntərn] *s* linterna

lantern slide *s* diapositiva, tira de vidrio

lanyard ['lænjərd] *s* (naut) acollador *m*

lap [læp] *s* (*of human body or clothing*) regazo; (*loose fold*) caída, doblez *f;* (*overlap of garment*) traslapo; (*with the tongue*) lametada; (*of the waves*) chapaleteo; (*in a race*) (sport) etapa, vuelta; **to live in the lap of luxury** llevar una vida regalada || *v* (*pret & pp* **lapped;** *ger* **lapping**) *tr* beber con la lengua; lamer (*las olas la playa*); (*to overlap*) traslapar; juntar a traslapo; **to lap up** tragar a lengüetadas; (coll) aceptar con entusiasmo || *intr* traslapar; traslaparse (*dos o más cosas*); **to lap against** lamer (*las olas la playa*); **to lap over** salir fuera, rebosar

lap'board' *s* tabla faldera

lap dog *s* perro de falda

lapel [lə'pɛl] *s* solapa

Lap'land' *s* Laponia

Laplander ['læp,lændər] *s* lapón *m* (*habitante*)

Lapp [læp] *s* lapón *m* (*habitante; idioma*)

lap robe *s* manta de coche

lapse [læps] *s* (*passing of time; slipping into guilt or error*) lapso; (*fall, decline*) caída, caída en desuso; (*e.g., of an insurance policy*) invalidación || *intr* caer en culpa o error; decaer, pasar (*p.ej., el entusiasmo*); caducar (*p.ej., una póliza de seguro*)

lap'wing' *s* ave fría

larce•ny ['lɑrsəni] *s* (*pl* **-nies**) hurto, robo

larch [lɑrtʃ] *s* alerce *m,* lárice *m*

lard [lɑrd] *s* cochevira, manteca de puerco || *tr* (culin) mechar

larder ['lɑrdər] *s* despensa

large ['lɑrdʒ] *adj* grande; **at large** en libertad

large intestine *s* intestino grueso

largely ['lɑrdʒli] *adj* por la mayor parte

largeness ['lɑrdʒnɪs] *s* grandeza

large'-scale' *adj* en grande escala, grande escala

lariat ['lærɪ•ət] *s* (*for catching animals*) lazo; (*for tying grazing animals*) cuerda, soga
lark [lɑrk] *s* alondra; (coll) parranda; **to go on a lark** (coll) andar de parranda, echar una cana al aire
lark'spur' *s* (*rocket larkspur*) espuela de caballero; (*field larkspur*) consuelda real
lar•va ['lɑrvə] *s* (*pl* **-vae** [vi]) larva
laryngeal [lə'rɪndʒɪ•əl] *adj* laríngeo
laryngitis [,lærɪn'dʒaɪtɪs] *s* laringitis *f*
laryngoscope [lə'rɪŋgə,skop] *s* laringoscopio
larynx ['lærɪŋks] *s* (*pl* **larynxes** o **larynges** [lə'rɪndʒiz]) laringe *f*
lascivious [lə'sɪvɪ•əs] *adj* lascivo
lasciviousness [lə'sɪvɪ•əsnɪs] *s* lascivia
laser ['lezər] *s* láser *m*
lash [læʃ] *s* (*cord on end of whip*) tralla; (*blow with whip; scolding*) latigazo; (*e.g., of animal's tail*) coletazo; (*of waves*) embate *m;* (*eyelash*) pestaña || *tr* (*to beat, whip*) azotar; (*to bind, tie*) atar; (*to shake, to switch*) agitar, sacudir; (*to attack with words*) increpar, reñir || *intr* lanzarse, pasar rápidamente; **to lash out at** azotar; embestir; vituperar
lashing ['læʃɪŋ] *s* atadura; paliza, zurra; (*severe scolding*) latigazo
lass [læs] *s* muchacha, chica; amada
las•so ['læso] o [læ'su] *s* (*pl* **-sos** o **-soes**) lazo || *tr* lazar
last [læst] o [lɑst] *adj* (*after all others; the only remaining; utmost, extreme*) último; (*most recent*) pasado; **before last** antepasado; **every last one** todos sin excepción; **last but one** penúltimo || *adv* después de todos; por último; por última vez || *s* última persona; última cosa; fin *m;* (*for holding shoe*) horma; **at last** por fin; **at long last** al fin y al cabo; **stick to your last!** ¡zapatero, a tus zapatos!; **the last of the month** a fines del mes; **to breathe one's last** dar el último suspiro; **to see the last of** no volver a ver; **to the last** hasta el fin || *intr* durar; resistir; dar buen resultado (*p.ej., una prenda de vestir*); seguir así
lasting ['læstɪŋ] *adj* perdurable, duradero
lastly ['læstli] *adv* finalmente, por último
last'-min'ute news *s* noticias de última hora
last name *s* apellido
last night *adv* anoche
last quarter *s* cuarto menguante
last rites *spl* (theol) extremaunción
last sleep *s* último sueño
last straw *s* acabóse *m,* colmo
Last Supper, the la Cena
last will and testament *s* última disposición, última voluntad
last word *s* última palabra; (*latest style*) (coll) última palabra
lat. *abbr* **latitude**
Lat. *abbr* **Latin**
latch [lætʃ] *s* picaporte *m* || *tr* cerrar con picaporte
latch'key' *s* llavín *m*
latch'string' *s* cordón *m* de aldaba; **the latchstring is out** ya sabe Vd. que ésta es su casa
late [let] *adj* (*happening after the usual time*) tardío; (*person*) atrasado; (*hour of the night*) avanzado; (*news*) de última hora; (*party, meeting, etc.*) que termina tarde; (*coming toward the end of a period of time*) de fines de; (*incumbent of an office*) anterior; (*deceased*) difunto, fallecido; **of late** recientemente, últimamente; **to be late** ser tarde; tardar (*p.ej., el tren*); **to be late in** + *ger* tardar en + *inf;* **to grow late** hacerse tarde || *adv* tarde; **late in** (*the week, the month, etc.*) a fines de, hacia fines de; **late in life** a una edad avanzada
late-comer ['let,kʌmər] *s* recién llegado; (*one who arrives late*) rezagado
lateen sail [læ'tin] *s* vela latina
lateen yard *s* entena
lately ['letli] *adv* recientemente, últimamente
latent ['letənt] *adj* latente
lateral ['lætərəl] *adj* lateral
lath [læθ] o [lɑθ] *s* lata, listón; enlistonado || *tr* enlistonar
lathe [leð] *s* torno (*máquina que sirve para labrar madera, hierro, etc. con un movimiento circular*)
lather ['læðər] *s* espuma de jabón; espuma de sudor || *tr* enjabonar; (coll) tundir, zurrar || *intr* espumar
lathery ['læðəri] *adj* espumoso, jabonoso
lathing ['læθɪŋ] *s* enlistonado
Latin ['lætɪn] o ['lætən] *adj* latino || *s* (*language*) latín *m;* (*person*) latino
Latin America *s* Latinoamérica, América Latina
Latin American *s* latinoamericano
Lat'in-Amer'ican *adj* latinoamericano
latitude ['lætɪ,tjud] *s* latitud
latrine [lə'trin] *s* letrina
latter ['lætər] *adj* (*more recent*) posterior; segundo (*de dos*); **the latter** éste; **the latter part of** fines *mpl* de (*p.ej., el siglo*)
lattice ['lætɪs] *s* enrejado || *tr* enrejar
lattice girder *s* viga de celosía
lat'tice•work' *s* enrejado
Latvia ['lætvɪ•ə] *s* Letonia, Latvia
laudable ['lɔdəbəl] *adj* laudable
laudanum ['lɔdənəm] o ['lɔdnəm] *s* láudano
laudatory ['lɔdə,tori] *adj* laudatorio
laugh [læf] *s* risa || *tr*—**to laugh away** ahogar en risas; **to laugh off** tomar a risa || *intr* reír, reírse
laughable ['læfəbəl] *adj* risible
laughing ['læfɪŋ] *adj* reidor; **to be no laughing matter** no ser cosa de risa || *s* risa, (el) reír
laughing gas *s* gas *m* hilarante
laugh'ing•stock' *s* hazmerreír *m*
laughter ['læftər] *s* risa, risas
launch [lɔntʃ] *s* (*of a ship*) botadura; (*of a rocket*) lanzamiento; (*open motorboat*) lancha automóvil; (nav) lancha || *tr* botar, lanzar (*un buque*); (*to throw; to start, set going, send forth*) lanzar || *intr* lanzarse
launching ['lɔntʃɪŋ] *s* lanzamiento
launching pad *s* plataforma de lanzamiento
launching tower *s* torre *f* de lanzamiento

launder [ˈlɔndər] *tr* lavar y planchar || *intr* resistir el lavado
launderer [ˈlɔndərər] *s* lavandero
laundress [ˈlɔndrɪs] *s* lavandera
laun•dry [ˈlɔndri] *s* (*pl* **-dries**) lavadero; lavado de la ropa; ropa lavada o para lavar
laundry•man [ˈlɔndrimən] *s* (*pl* **-men** [mən]) lavandero
laun'dry•wom'an *s* (*pl* **-wom'en**) lavandera
laureate [ˈlɔrɪ•ɪt] *adj* laureado || *s* laureado; poeta laureado
lau•rel [ˈlɔrəl] *s* laurel *m;* **laurels** laurel (*de la victoria*); **to rest** o **sleep on one's laurels** dormirse sobre sus laureles || *v* (*pret & pp* **-reled** o **-relled;** *ger* **-reling** o **-relling**) *tr* laurear, coronar de laurel
lava [ˈlɑvə] o [ˈlævə] *s* lava
lavato•ry [ˈlævə,tori] *s* (*pl* **-ries**) (*room equipped for washing hands and face*) lavabo; (*bowl with running water*) lavamanos *m; (toilet)* excusado
lavender [ˈlævəndər] *s* alhucema, espliego, lavanda
lavender water *s* agua de alhucema, agua de lavanda
lavish [ˈlævɪʃ] *adj* pródigo || *tr* prodigar
law [lɔ] *s* (*of man, of nature, of science*) ley *f; (branch of knowledge concerned with law; body of laws; study of law; profession of law*) derecho; **to enter the law** hacerse abogado; **to go to law** recurrir a la ley; **to lay down the law** dar órdenes terminantes; **to maintain law and order** mantener la paz; **to practice law** ejercer la profesión de abogado; **to read law** estudiar derecho
law-abiding [ˈlɔ•ə,baɪdɪŋ] *adj* observante de la ley
law'break'er *s* infractor *m* de la ley
law court *s* tribunal *m* de justicia
lawful [ˈlɔfəl] *adj* legal, legítimo
lawless [ˈlɔlɪs] *adj* ilegal; (*unbridled*) desenfrenado, licencioso
law'mak'er *s* legislador *m*
lawn [lɔn] *s* césped *m; (fabric)* linón *m*
lawn mower *s* cortacésped *m,* tundidora de césped
law office *s* bufete *m,* despacho de abogado
law of nations *s* derecho de gentes
law of the jungle *s* ley *f* de la selva
law student *s* estudiante *mf* de derecho
law'suit' *s* pleito, proceso, litigio
lawyer [ˈlɔjər] *s* abogado
lax [læks] *adj* (*in morals, discipline, etc.*) laxo, relajado; vago, indeterminado; (*loose, not tense*) laxo, flojo, suelto
laxative [ˈlæksətɪv] *adj & s* laxante *m*
lay [le] *adj* (*not belonging to clergy*) lego, seglar; (*not having special training*) lego, profano || *s* situación, orientación || *v* (*pret & pp* **laid** [led]) *tr* poner, colocar; dejar en el suelo; tender (*un cable*); echar (*los cimientos; la culpa*); situar (*la acción de un drama*); asentar (*el polvo*); poner (*huevos la gallina; la mesa una criada*); formar (*planes*); hacer (*una apuesta*); **to be laid in** ser (*la escena*) en; **to lay aside** echar a un lado; ahorrar; **to lay down** afirmar, declarar; dar (*la vida*); deponer (*las armas*); **to lay low** abatir, derribar; obligar a guardar cama; matar; **to lay off** despedir (*a obreros*); (*to mark off the boundaries of*) marcar, trazar; **to lay open** descubrir, revelar; (*to a risk or danger*) exponer; **to lay out** extender, tender; marcar (*una tarea, un trabajo*); gastar (*dinero*); amortajar (*a un difunto*); **to lay up** obligar a guardar cama; ahorrar; (naut) desarmar || *intr* poner (*las gallinas*); **to lay about** dar palos de ciego; **to lay for** acechar; **to lay off** (coll) dejar de trabajar; (coll) dejar de molestar; **to lay over** detenerse durante un viaje; **to lay to** (naut) capear
lay brother *s* donado, lego
lay day *s* (naut) día *m* de estadía
layer [ˈle•ər] *s* (*e.g., of paint*) capa; (*e.g., of bricks*) camada; (*e.g., of coal, rocks*) estrato, capa; (hort) codadura || *tr* (hort) acodar
layer cake *s* bizcocho de varias camadas
layette [leˈɛt] *s* canastilla
lay figure *s* maniquí *m*
laying [ˈle•ɪŋ] *s* colocación; (*of eggs*) postura; (*of a cable*) tendido
lay•man [ˈlemən] *s* (*pl* **-men** [mən]) (*person who is not a clergyman*) lego, seglar *m; (person who has no special training*) lego, profano
lay'off' *s* (*dismissal of workmen*) despido; (*period of unemployment*) paro forzoso
lay of the land *s* cariz *m* que van tomando las cosas
lay'out' *s* plan *m; (of tools*) equipo; disposición, organización; (coll) banquete *m,* festín *m*
lay'o'ver *s* parada en un viaje
lay sister *s* donada
laziness [ˈlezɪnɪs] *s* pereza; lerdera; (coll) galbana
la•zy [ˈlezi] *adj* (*comp* **-zier;** *super* **-ziest**) perezoso; (coll) galbanoso
la'zy•bones' *s* (coll) perezoso
lb. *abbr* **pound**
l.c. *abbr* **lower case; loco citato (Lat) in the place cited**
Ld. *abbr* **Lord**
lea [li] *s* prado
lead [lɛd] *adj* plomizo || *s* plomo; (*of lead pencil*) mina, (*for sounding depth*) (naut) escandallo; (typ) interlínea, regleta || [lɛd] *v* (*pret & pp* **leaded;** *ger* **leading**) *tr* emplomar; (typ) interlinear, regletear || *s* [lid] *s* (*foremost place*) primacía; (*guidance*) conducta, guía, dirección; indicación; ejemplo; (cards) salida; (*leash*) traílla; (*of a newspaper article*) primer párrafo; (elec) conductor *m;* (elec & mach) avance *m;* (min) filón *m;* (rad) alambre *m* de entrada; (theat) papel *m* principal; (theat) galán *m;* (theat) dama; **to take the lead** tomar la delantera || [lid] *v* (*pret & pp* **led** [lɛd]) *tr* conducir, llevar; liderar; (*to command*) acaudillar, mandar; estar a la cabeza de; dirigir (*p.ej., una orquesta*); llevar

(*buena o mala vida*); salir con (*cierto naipe*); (elec & mach) avanzar; **to lead someone to** + *inf* llevar a alguien a + *inf* ‖ **intr** ir delante, enseñar el camino; ser el primero; tener el mando; (cards) salir, ser mano; (mus) llevar la batuta; **to lead up to** conducir a, llevar a; llevar la conversación a

leaded gasoline [ˈlɛdɪd] *s* gasolina con plomo

leaden [ˈlɛdən] *adj* (*of lead; like lead*) plomizo; (*heavy as lead*) plúmbeo; (*sluggish*) tardo, indolente; (*with sleep*) cargado; triste, lóbrego

leader [ˈlidər] *s* caudillo, jefe *m*, líder *m;* (*ringleader*) cabecilla *m;* (*of an orchestra*) director *m;* (*in a dance; among animals*) guión *m;* (*horse*) guía; (*in a newspaper*) artículo de fondo

leader dog *s* perro-lazarillo

leadership [ˈlidər,ʃɪp] *s* caudillaje *m*, jefatura; dotes *fpl* de mando

leading [ˈlidɪŋ] *adj* primero, principal; preeminente; delantero; líder

leading article *s* artículo de fondo

leading edge *s* (aer) borde *m* de ataque

leading lady *s* primera actriz, dama

leading man *s* primer actor *m*, primer galán *m*

leading question *s* pregunta tendenciosa

leading strings *spl* andadores *mpl*

lead-in wire [ˈlid,ɪn] *s* (rad) bajada de antena, alambre *m* de entrada

lead pencil [lɛd] *s* lápiz *m*

leaf [lif] *s* (*pl* **leaves** [livz]) hoja; (*of vine*) pámpano; (*hinged leaf of table*) trampilla; **to shake like a leaf** temblar como un azogado; **to turn over a new leaf** hacer libro nuevo ‖ *intr* echar hojas; **to leaf through** hojear, trashojar

leafless [ˈliflɪs] *adj* deshojado

leaflet [ˈliflɪt] *s* hoja suelta, hoja volante; (*blade of compound leaf*) hojuela

leaf'stalk' *s* pecíolo

leaf•y [ˈlifi] *adj* (*comp* **-ier;** *super* **-iest**) hojoso, frondoso

league [lig] *s* (*unit of distance*) legua; (*association, alliance*) liga; (*sports*) división ‖ *tr* asociar ‖ *intr* asociarse, ligarse

League of Nations *s* Sociedad de las Naciones

leak [lik] *s* (*in a roof*) gotera; (*in a ship*) agua, vía de agua; (*of water, gas, electricity, steam*) escape *m*, fuga, salida; agujero, grieta, raja (*por donde se escapa el agua, etc.*); (*of money, news, etc.*) filtración; **to spring a leak** tener un escape; (naut) empezar a hacer agua ‖ *tr* dejar escapar, dejar salir (*el agua, gas, etc.*); dejar filtrar (*una noticia*) ‖ *intr* rezumarse (*un barril*); escaparse, salirse (*el agua, gas, etc.*); (naut) hacer agua; **to leak away** filtrarse (*el dinero*); **to leak out** rezumarse (*una especie*); trascender (*un hecho que estaba oculto*)

leakage [ˈlikɪdʒ] *s* escape *m*, fuga, salida; (com) merma

leak•y [ˈliki] *adj* (*comp* **-ier;** *super* **-iest**) agujereado, roto; (*roof*) llovedizo; (naut) que hace agua; (coll) indiscreto

lean [lin] *adj* magro, mollar; (*thin*) flaco; (*gasoline mixture*) pobre; **lean years** años de carestía ‖ *v* (*pret & pp* **leaned** o **leant** [lɛnt] *tr* inclinar, ladear, arrimar ‖ *intr* inclinarse, ladearse, arrimarse; (fig) inclinarse, tender; **to lean against** arrimarse a, estar arrimado a; **to lean back** retreparse, recostarse; **to lean on** apoyarse en; (*with the elbows*) acodarse sobre; **to lean out (of)** asomarse (a); **to lean over backwards** (coll) extremar la imparcialidad; **to lean toward** (fig) inclinarse a, ladearse a

leaning [ˈlinɪŋ] *adj* inclinado ‖ *s* inclinación; (fig) inclinación, tendencia

lean'-to' *s* (*pl* **-tos**) colgadizo

leap [lip] *s* salto; **by leaps and bounds** a pasos agigantados; **leap in the dark** salto a ciegas, salto en vago ‖ *v* (*pret & pp* **leaped** o **leapt** [lɛpt]) *tr* saltar *s* ‖ *intr* saltar; dar un salto (*el corazón de uno*)

leap day *s* día *m* intercalar

leap'frog' *s* fil derecho, juego del salto; **to play leapfrog** jugar a la una la mula

leap year *s* año bisiesto

learn [lʌrn] *v* (*pret & pp* **learned** o **learnt** [lʌrnt]) *tr* aprender; oír decir; saber (*una noticia*) ‖ *intr* aprender

learned [ˈlʌrnɪd] *adj* docto, erudito; (*e.g., word*) culto

learned journal *s* revista científica

learned society *s* sociedad de eruditos

learned word *s* cultismo, voz culta

learned world *s* mundo de la erudición

learner [ˈlʌrnər] *s* principiante *mf*, aprendiz *m*, estudiante *mf*

learning [ˈlʌrnɪŋ] *s* (*act and time devoted*) aprendizaje *m;* (*scholarship*) erudición

lease [lis] *s* arrendamiento, locación; **to give a new lease on life to** renovar completamente; volver a hacer feliz ‖ *tr* arrendar ‖ *intr* arrendarse

lease'hold' *adj* arrendado ‖ *s* arrendamiento; bienes raíces arrendados

leash [liʃ] *s* traílla; **to strain at the leash** sufrir la sujeción con impaciencia ‖ *tr* atraillar

least [list] *adj* (el) menor, mínimo, más pequeño ‖ *adv* menos ‖ *s* (el) menor; (lo) menos; **at least** o **at the least** al menos, a los menos, por lo menos; **not in the least** de ninguna manera

leather [ˈlɛðər] *s* cuero

leath'er•back' turtle *s* laúd *m*

leath'er•neck' *s* (slang) soldado de infantería de marina de los EE.UU.

leathery [ˈlɛðəri] *adj* correoso, coriáceo

leave [liv] *s* (*permission*) permiso; (*permission to be absent*) licencia; (*farewell*) despedida; **on leave** con licencia; **to give leave to** dar licencia a; **to take leave (of)** despedirse (de) ‖ *v* (*pret & pp* **left** [lɛft]) *tr* (*to let stay; to stop, give up; to disregard*) dejar; (*to go away from*) salir de; (*to bequeath*) legar; **leave it to me!** ¡déjemelo a mí!; **to be left** quedar p.ej., **the letter was left unanswered** la carta quedó sin contestar; **to leave alone** dejar en paz, dejar tranquilo; **to leave no stone unturned** no dejar piedra por mover; **to leave off** dejar; no ponerse (*una prenda de vestir*); **to leave out** omitir; **to leave things as they are** dejarlo como está || *intr* irse, marcharse; eliminarse (Mex); salir (*un avión, un tren, un vapor*)

leaven [ˈlɛvən] *s* levadura; (fig) influencia || *tr* leudar; (fig) transformar

leavening [ˈlɛvənɪŋ] *s* levadura

leave of absence *s* licencia

leave′-tak′ing *s* despedida

leavings [ˈlivɪŋz] *spl* desperdicios, sobras

Leba•nese [,lɛbəˈniz] *adj* libanés || *s* (*pl* **-nese**) libanés *m*

Lebanon [ˈlɛbənən] *s* el Líbano

Lebanon Mountains *spl* cordillera del Líbano

lecher [ˈlɛtʃər] *s* libertino, lujurioso

lecherous [ˈlɛtʃərəs] *adj* lascivo, lujurioso

lechery [ˈlɛtʃəri] *s* lascivia, lujuria

lectern [ˈlɛktərn] *s* atril *m*

lecture [ˈlɛktʃər] *s* conferencia; (*tedious reprimand*) sermoneo || *tr* instruir por medio de una conferencia; sermonear || *intr* dar una conferencia, dar conferencias

lecturer [ˈlɛktʃərər] *s* conferenciante *mf*

ledge [lɛdʒ] *s* (*projection in a wall*) retallo; cama de roca; arrecife *m*

ledger [ˈlɛdʒər] *s* (com) libro mayor

ledger line *s* (mus) línea suplementaria

lee [li] *s* (*shelter*) (naut) socaire *m;* (*quarter sheltered from the wind*) sotavento; **lees** heces *fpl*

leech [litʃ] *s* sanguijuela; **to stick like a leech** pegarse como ladilla

leek [lik] *s* puerro

leer [lɪr] *s* mirada de soslayo, mirada lujuriosa || *intr*—**to leer at** mirar de soslayo, mirar lujuriosamente

leery [ˈlɪri] *adj* (coll) receloso, suspicaz

leeward [ˈliwərd] o [ˈlu•ərd] *adj* (naut) de sotavento || *adv* (naut) a sotavento || *s* (naut) sotavento

Leeward Islands [ˈliwərd] *spl* islas de Sotavento

lee′way′ *s* (aer & naut) deriva; (coll) tiempo de sobra, espacio de sobra, dinero de sobra; (coll) libertad de acción

left [lɛft] *adj* izquierdo || *adv* hacia la izquierda || *s* (*left hand*) izquierda; (box) zurdazo; (pol) izquierda; **on the left** a la izquierda

left field *s* (baseball) jardín izquierdo

left′-hand′ drive *s* conducción o dirección a la izquierda

left-handed [ˈlɛftˈhændɪd] *adj* (*individual*) zurdo; (*clumsy*) desmañado, torpe; insincero; contrario a las agujas del reloj

leftish [ˈlɛftɪʃ] *adj* izquierdizante

leftist [ˈlɛftɪst] *adj & s* izquierdista *mf*

left′o′ver *adj & s* sobrante *m;* **leftovers** *spl* sobras

left′-wing′ *adj* izquierdista

left-winger [ˈlɛftˈwɪŋər] *s* (coll) izquierdista *mf*

leg. *abbr* **legal, legislature**

leg [lɛg] *s* (*of man or animal*) pierna; (*of animal, table, chair, etc.*) pata; (*of boot or stocking*) caña; (*of trousers*) pernera; (*of a cooked fowl*) muslo; (*of a journey*) etapa, trecho; **to be on one's last legs** estar sin recursos; estar en las últimas; **to not have a leg to stand on** (coll) no tener justificación alguna, no tener disculpa alguna; **to pull the leg of** (coll) tomar el pelo a; **to shake a leg** (coll) darse prisa; (*to dance*) (coll) bailar; **to stretch one's legs** estirar las piernas, dar un paseíto

lega•cy [ˈlɛgəsi] *s* (*pl* **-cies**) legado

legal [ˈligəl] *adj* legal

legali•ty [lɪˈgælɪti] *s* (*pl* **-ties**) legalidad

legalization [,ligələˈzeʃən] *s* legalización despenalización

legalize [ˈligə,laɪz] *tr* legalizar; despenalizar

legal tender *s* curso legal

legate [ˈlɛgɪt] *s* legado

legatee [,lɛgəˈti] *s* legatario

legation [lɪˈgeʃən] *s* legación

legend [ˈlɛdʒənd] *s* leyenda

legendary [ˈlɛdʒən,dɛri] *adj* legendario

legerdemain [,lɛdʒərdɪˈmen] *s* juego de manos, prestidigitación; (*cheating, trickery*) trapacería

legging [ˈlɛgɪŋ] *s* polaina

leg•gy [ˈlɛgi] *adj* (*comp* **-gier;** *super* **-giest**) zanquilargo; de piernas largas y elegantes

leg′horn′ *s* sombrero de paja de Italia || **Leghorn** *s* Liorna

legible [ˈlɛdʒɪbəl] *adj* legible

legion [ˈlidʒən] *s* legión

legislate [ˈlɛdʒɪs,let] *tr* imponer mediante legislación || *intr* legislar

legislation [ˈlɛdʒɪsˈleʃən] *s* legislación

legislative [ˈlɛdʒɪs,letɪv] *adj* legislativo

legislator [ˈlɛdʒɪs,letər] *s* legislador *m*

legislature [ˈlɛdʒɪs,letʃər] *s* asamblea legislativa, cuerpo legislativo

legitimacy [lɪˈdʒɪtɪməsi] *s* legitimidad

legitimate [lɪˈdʒɪtɪmɪt] *adj* legítimo || [lɪˈdʒɪtɪ,met] *tr* legitimar

legitimate drama *s* drama serio (*a distinción del cine o el melodrama*)

legitimize [lɪˈdʒɪtɪ,maɪz] *tr* legitimar

leg′work′ *s* (coll) el mucho caminar

leisure [ˈliʒər] o [ˈlɛʒər] *s* desocupación, ocio; **at leisure** desocupado, libre; **at one's leisure** a la comodidad de uno, cuando uno pueda

leisure activities *spl* recreos pasatiempos

leisure class *s* gente acomodada

leisure hours *spl* horas de ocio, ratos perdidos

leisurely [ˈliʒərli] o [ˈlɛʒərli] *adj* lento, pausado || *adv* lentamente, despacio, sin prisa

leisure wear *s* ropa de recreo, traje *m* informal

lemon [ˈlɛmən] *s* limón *m;* (slang) artículo de fábrica defectuosa

lemonade [,lɛməˈned] *s* limonada

lemon squeezer *s* exprimidera de limón

lemon verbena *s* luisa
lend [lɛnd] *s* (*pret & pp* **lent** [lɛnt]) *tr* prestar
lending library *s* biblioteca de préstamo
length [lɛŋθ] *s* largura, largo; (*of time*) extensión; (naut) eslora; **at length** por fin; largamente; **to go to any length** hacer cuanto esté de su parte; **to keep at arm's length** mantener a distancia; mantenerse a distancia
lengthen [ˈlɛŋθən] *tr* alargar || *intr* alargarse
length'wise' *adj* longitudinal || *adv* longitudinalmente
length•y [ˈlɛŋθi] *adj* (*comp* **-ier;** *super* **-iest**) muy largo, prolongado
leniency [ˈlinɪ•ənsi] *s* clemencia, indulgencia, lenidad
lenient [ˈlinɪ•ənt] *adj* clemente, indulgente
lens [lɛnz] *s* lente *m & f;* (*of the eye*) cristalino
Lent [lɛnt] *s* cuaresma *f*
Lenten [ˈlɛntən] *adj* cuaresmal
lentil [ˈlɛntəl] *s* lenteja
Leo [ˈli•o] *s* (astr) Leo
leopard [ˈlɛpərd] *s* leopardo
leotard [ˈli•ə,tɑrd] *s* leotardo
leper [ˈlɛpər] *s* leproso
leper house *s* leprosería
leprosy [ˈlɛprəsi] *s* lepra
leprous [ˈlɛprəs] *adj* leproso; (*covered with scales*) escamoso
Lesbian [ˈlɛzbɪ•ən] *adj* lesbio || *s* lesbio; (*female homosexual*) lesbia
lesbianism [ˈlɛzbɪ•ə,nɪzəm] *s* lesbianismo
lese majesty [ˈlizˈmædʒɪsti] *s* delito de lesa majestad
lesion [ˈliʒən] *s* lesión
less [lɛs] *adj* menor || *adv* menos; **less and less** cada vez menos; **less than** menos que; (*followed by numeral*) menos de; (*followed by verb*) menos de lo que || *s* menos *m*
lessee [lɛsˈi] *s* arrendatario
lessen [ˈlɛsən] *tr* disminuir, reducir a menos; quitar importancia a || *intr* disminuirse, reducirse; amainar (*el viento*)
lesser [ˈlɛsər] *adj* menor, más pequeño
lesson [ˈlɛsən] *s* lección
lessor [ˈlɛsər] *s* arrendador *m*
lest [lɛst] *conj* no sea que, de miedo que
let [lɛt] *v* (*pret & pp* **let;** *ger* **letting**) *tr* dejar, permitir; alquilar, arrendar; **let** + *inf* que + *subj,* p.ej., **let him come in** que entre; **let alone** y mucho menos; **let good enough alone** bueno está lo bueno; **let us** + *inf* vamos a + *inf,* p.ej., **let us eat** vamos a comer, comamos; **to let** se alquila; **to let alone** dejar en paz, dejar tranquilo; **to let be** no tocar; dejar en paz; **to let by** dejar pasar; **to let down** dejar bajar; desilusionar, traicionar; dejar plantado; **to let fly** disparar; (fig) disparar, soltar (*palabras injuriosas*); **to let go** soltar, desasirse de; vender; **to let in** dejar entrar, dejar entrar en; **to let it go at that** no hacer o decir nada más; **to let know** hacer saber; **to let loose** soltar; **to let on** (coll) dar a entender; **to let out** dejar salir; revelar, publicar; dar, soltar (*p.ej., más cuerda*); dar (*un grito*); ensanchar (*un vestido que aprieta*); dar en arrendamiento; (coll) despedir; **to let through** dejar pasar, dejar pasar por; **to let up** dejar subir; dejar levantarse || *intr* alquilarse, arrendarse; **to let down** (coll) ir más despacio; **to let go** desasirse; **to let go of** desasirse de; **to let on** (coll) fingir; **to let out** (coll) despedirse, cerrarse (*p.ej., la escuela*); **to let up** (coll) desistir; (coll) aflojar, amainar
let'down' *s* disminución; aflojamiento; desilusión, decepción; humillación
lethal [ˈliθəl] *adj* letal
lethargic [lɪˈθɑrdʒɪk] *adj* (*affected with lethargy*) letárgico; (*producing lethargy*) letargoso
lethar•gy [ˈlɛθərdʒi] *s* (*pl* **-gies**) letargo
Lett [lɛt] *s* letón *m*
letter [ˈlɛtər] *s* (*written message*) carta; (*of the alphabet*) letra; (*literal meaning*) (fig) letra; **letters** (*literature*) letras; **to the letter** al pie de la letra || *tr* estampar o marcar con letras
letter box *s* buzón *m* (*caja*)
letter carrier *s* cartero
letter drop *s* buzón *m* (*agujero*)
letter file *s* guardacartas *m*
let'ter•head' *s* membrete *m*; (*paper with printed heading*) memorándum *m*
lettering [ˈlɛtərɪŋ] *s* inscripción; letras
letter of credit *s* carta de crédito
letter opener [ˈopənər] *s* abrecartas *m*
letter paper *s* papel *m* de cartas
let'ter-per'fect *adj* que tiene bien aprendido su papel; correcto, exacto
let'ter•press' *s* impresión tipográfica; texto (*a distinción de los grabados*)
letter scales *spl* pesacartas *m*
Lettish [ˈletɪʃ] *adj* letón || *s* letón *m*
lettuce [ˈlɛtɪs] *s* lechuga
let'up' *s* (coll) calma, interrupción; **without letup** (coll) sin cesar
leucorrhea [,lukəˈri•ə] *s* leucorrea
leukemia [luˈkimɪ•ə] *s* leucemia
Levant [lɪˈvænt] *s* Levante *m* (*países de la parte oriental del Mediterráneo*)
Levantine [ˈlɛvən,tin] o [lɪˈvæntin] *adj & s* levantino
levee [ˈlɛvi] *s* (*embankment to hold back water*) ribero; (*reception at court*) besamanos *m*
lev•el [ˈlɛvəl] *adj* raso, llano; nivelado; (coll) sensato, juicioso; **level with** al nivel de, a flor de, a ras de || *s* (*device for determining horizontal position; degree of elevation*) nivel *m;* (*flat and even area of land*) terreno llano, llanura; (*part of a canal between two locks*) tramo; **to be on the level** obrar sin engaño, decir la pura verdad; **to find one's level** hallar su propio nivel || *v* (*pret & pp* **-eled** o **-elled;** *ger* **-eling** o **-elling**) *tr* nivelar; (*to smooth, flatten out*) arrasar, allanar; (*to bring down*) derribar, echar por tierra; apuntar (*un arma de fuego*); (fig) allanar (*dificultades*) || *intr*—**to level off** (aer) enderezarse para aterrizar

level-headed [ˈlɛvəlˈhɛdɪd] *adj* sensato, juicioso
leveling rod *s* (surv) jalón *m* de mira
lever [ˈlivər] o [lɛvər] *s* palanca ‖ *tr* apalancar
leverage [ˈlivərɪdʒ] o [ˈlɛvərɪdʒ] *s* palancada; poder *m* de una palanca; (fig) influencia, poder *m*
leviathan [lɪˈvaɪ•əθən] *s* (Bib & fig) leviatán *m;* buque *m* muy grande
levitation [,lɛvɪˈteʃən] *s* levitación
levi•ty [ˈlɛvɪti] *s* (*pl* **-ties**) frivolidad; (*fickleness*) ligereza
lev•y [ˈlɛvi] *s* (*pl* **-ies**) (*of taxes*) exación, recaudación; dinero recaudado; (mil) leva, enganche *m,* recluta ‖ *v* (*pret & pp* **-ied**) *tr* exigir, recaudar (*impuestos*); (mil) enganchar, reclutar; hacer (*la guerra*)
lewd [lud] *adj* lascivo, lujurioso; obsceno
lewdness [ˈludnɪs] *s* lascivia, lujuria; obscenidad
lexical [ˈlɛksɪkəl] *adj* léxico
lexicographer [,lɛksɪˈkɑgrəfər] *s* lexicógrafo
lexicographic(al) [,lɛksɪkəˈgræfɪk(əl)] lexicográfico
lexicography [,lɛksɪˈkɑgrəfi] *s* lexicografía
lexicology [,lɛksɪˈkɑlədʒi] *s* lexicología
lexicon [ˈlɛksɪkən] *s* léxico, lexicón *m*
liabili•ty [,laɪ•əˈbɪlɪti] *s* (*pl* **-ties**) (*e.g., to disease*) propensión; responsabilidad, obligación; desventaja; **liabilities** deudas; (*as detailed in balance sheet*) pasivo
liability insurance *s* seguro de responsabilidad civil
liable [ˈlaɪ•əbəl] *adj* (*e.g., to disease*) propenso, expuesto; responsable; **to be liable to** + *inf* (coll) amenazar + *inf*
liaison [ˈli•ə,zɑn] o [liˈezən] *s* enlace *m,* unión; (*illicit relationship between a man and woman*) amancebamiento, enredo, lío; (mil, nav & phonet) enlace *m*
liaison officer *s* (mil) oficial *m* de enlace
liar [ˈlaɪ•ər] *s* mentiroso
lib. *abbr* librarian, library
libation [laɪˈbeʃən] *s* libación; (*drink*) libación
li•bel [ˈlaɪbəl] *s* calumnia, difamación; levante (CAm, P-R); (*defamatory writing*) libelo ‖ *v* (*pret & pp* **-beled** o **-belled;** *ger* **-beling** o **-belling**) *tr* calumniar, difamar
libelous [ˈlaɪbələs] *adj* calumniador
liberal [ˈlɪbərəl] *adj* (*generous; done or given generously*) liberal; (*open-minded*) tolerante, de amplias miras; (*translation*) libre; (pol) liberal ‖ *s* liberal *mf*
liberali•ty [,lɪbəˈrælɪti] *s* (*pl* **-ties**) liberalidad
liberal-minded [ˈlɪbərəlˈmaɪndɪd] *adj* tolerante, de amplias miras
liberate [ˈlɪbə,ret] *tr* libertar; (*to disengage from a combination*) (chem) desprender
liberation [,lɪbəˈreʃən] *s* liberación; (chem) desprendimiento
liberation theology *s* teología liberacionista
liberator [ˈlɪbə,retər] *s* libertador *m*
libertine [ˈlɪbər,tin] *adj & s* libertino
liber•ty [ˈlɪbərti] *s* (*pl* **-ties**) libertad; **to take the liberty to** tomarse la libertad de
liberty-loving [ˈlɪbərtiˈlʌvɪŋ] *adj* amante de la libertad
libidinous [lɪˈbɪdɪnəs] *adj* libidinoso
libido [lɪˈbido] o [lɪˈbaɪdo] *s* libídine *f,* libido *f*
Libra [ˈlibrə] *s* (astr) Libra
librarian [laɪˈbrɛrɪ•ən] *s* bibliotecario
librar•y [ˈlaɪ,brɛri] o [ˈlaɪbrəri] *s* (*pl* **-ies**) biblioteca
library number *s* signatura
library school *s* escuela de bibliotecarios
library science *s* bibliotecnia; biblioteconomía
libret•to [lɪˈbrɛto] *s* (*pl* **-tos**) (mus) libreto
license [ˈlaɪsəns] *s* licencia ‖ *tr* licenciar
license number *s* número de matrícula
license plate o **tag** *s* chapa de circulación, placa de matrícula
licentious [laɪˈsɛnʃəs] *adj* licencioso, disoluto
lichen [ˈlaɪkən] *s* liquen *m*
lick [lɪk] *s* lamedura; (*place where animals go to lick*) lamedero; (*blow*) (coll) bofetón *m*; (*speed*) (coll) velocidad; (*beating*) (coll) zurra; (*quick cleaning*) (coll) limpión *m;* **to give a lick and a promise to** (coll) hacer rápida y superficialmente ‖ *tr* lamer; lamerse (*p.ej., los dedos*); lamer (*las llamas un tejado*); (*to beat, thrash*) (coll) zurrar; (*to conquer*) (coll) vencer ‖ *intr* lengüetear
licorice [ˈlɪkərɪs] *s* regaliz *m,* orozuz *m;* dulce *m* de regaliz
lid [lɪd] *s* (*of a box, trunk, chest, etc.*) tapa, tapadera; (*of a dish, pot, etc.*) cobertera; (*eyelid*) párpado; (*hat*) (slang) techo
lie [laɪ] *s* mentira; **to catch in a lie** coger en una mentira; **to give the lie to** dar un mentís a ‖ *v* (*pret & pp* **lied;** *ger* **lying**) *tr*—**to lie oneself out of** o **to lie one's way out of** librarse de un aprieto mintiendo ‖ *intr* mentir ‖ *v* (*pret* **lay** [le]; *pp* **lain** [len]; *ger* **lying**) *intr* estar echado; hallarse, estar situado; (*e.g., in the grave*) yacer, estar enterrado; **to lie down** echarse, acostarse
lie detector *s* detector *m* de mentiras
lien [lin] o [ˈli•ən] *s* gravamen *m,* derecho de retención
lieu [lu] *s*—**in lieu of** en lugar de, en vez de
lieutenant [luˈtɛnənt] *s* lugarteniente *m;* (mil) teniente *m;* (nav) teniente de navío
lieutenant colonel *s* (mil) teniente coronel *m*
lieutenant commander *s* (nav) capitán *m* de corbeta
lieutenant governor *s* (U.S.A.) vicegobernador *m* (*de un Estado*)
lieutenant junior grade *s* (nav) alférez *m* de navío
life [laɪf] *adj* (*animate*) vital; (*lifelong*) perpetuo; (*annuity, income*) vitalicio; (*working from nature*) (fa) del natural ‖ *s* (*pl* **lives** [laɪvz]) vida; (*of an insurance policy*) vigencia; **for life** de por vida; **for the life of me** así me maten; **the life and soul of** (*e.g., a party*) la alegría de; **to come to life** volver a la vida; **to depart this life** partir de esta vida; **to run for one's life** salvarse por los pies

life annuity *s* renta vitalicia
life belt *s* cinturón *m* salvavidas
life'boat' *s* bote *m* de salvamento, bote salvavidas; (*for shore-based rescue services*) lancha de auxilio
life buoy *s* boya salvavidas, guindola
life expectancy *s* expectación de vida
life float *s* balsa salvavidas
life'guard' *s* salvavidas *m*, guardavida *m*
life imprisonment *s* cadena perpetua
life insurance *s* seguro sobre la vida
life jacket *s* chaleco salvavidas
lifeless ['laɪflɪs] *adj* muerto, sin vida; (*in a faint*) desmayado, exánime; (*dull, colorless*) deslucido
life'like' *adj* natural, vivo
life line *s* cuerda salvavidas; cuerda de buzo
life'long' *adj* perpetuo, de toda la vida
life of leisure *s* vida de ocio
life of Riley ['raɪli] *s* (slang) vida regalada
life of the party *s* (coll) alegría de la fiesta, alma de la fiesta
life preserver [prɪ'zʌrvər] *s* chaleco salvavidas
lifer ['laɪfər] *s* (slang) presidiario de por vida
life'sav'er *s* salvador *m* (*de vidas*); (*something that saves a person from a predicament*) (coll) tabla de salvación
lifesaving ['laɪf,sevɪŋ] *adj* de salvamento || *s* salvamento (*de vidas*)
life sentence *s* condena a cadena perpetua
life'-size' *adj* de tamaño natural
life span *s* período de vida
life'time' *adj* vitalicio || *s* vida, curso de la vida, jornada
life'work' *s* obra principal de la vida de uno
lift [lɪft] *s* elevación, levantamiento; ayuda (*para levantar una carga*); (aer) sustentación; **to give a lift to** invitar (*a un peatón*) a subir a un coche; llevar en un coche; (fig) reanimar || *tr* elevar, levantar; quitarse (*el sombrero*); (naut) izar (*velas, vergas, etc.*); (fig) reanimar, exaltar; (coll) robar; (coll) plagiar || *intr* elevarse, levantarse; disiparse (*las nubes, las nieblas, la obscuridad, etc.*)
lift bridge *s* puente levadizo
lift'-off *s* despegue *m* vertical
lift truck *s* carretilla elevadora
ligament ['lɪgəmənt] *s* ligamento
ligature ['lɪgətʃər] *s* (mus & surg) ligadura; (mus & typ) ligado
light [laɪt] *adj* (*in weight*) ligero, leve, liviano; (*having illumination; whitish*) claro; (*hair*) blondo, rubio; (*complexion*) blanco; (*oil*) flúido; (*beer*) claro; (*reading*) poco serio; (*heart*) alegre, despreocupado; (*carrying a small cargo or none at all*) (naut) boyante; **light in the head** (*dizzy*) aturdido, mareado; (*simple, silly*) tonto, necio; **to make light of** no dar importancia a, no tomar en serio || *adv* sin carga; sin equipaje || *s* luz *f*; (*to light a cigarette*) lumbre *f*, fuego; (*to control traffic*) luz, señal *f*; (*window or other opening in a wall*) luz, claro, hueco; (*example, shining figure*) lumbrera; **according to one's lights** según Dios le da a uno a entender; **against the light** al trasluz; **in this light** desde este punto de vista; **lights** noticias; (*of sheep, etc.*) bofes *mpl*; **to come to light** salir a luz, descubrirse; **to shed** o **throw light on** echar luz sobre; **to strike a light** echar una yesca; encender un fósforo || *v* (*pret & pp* **lighted** o **lit** [lɪt] *tr* (*to furnish with illumination*) alumbrar, iluminar; (*to set afire, ignite*) encender; **to light up** iluminar || *intr* alumbrarse; encenderse; posar (*un ave*); (*from an auto*) bajar; **to light into** (*to attack*) (slang) arremeter contra; (*to scold, berate*) (slang) poner de oro y azul; **to light out** (slang) poner pies en polvorosa; **to light upon** tropezar con, hallar por casualidad
light bulb *s* (elec) bombilla
light complexion *s* tez blanca
lighten ['laɪtən] *tr* (*to make lighter in weight*) aligerar; iluminar; (*to cheer up*) alegrar, regocijar || *intr* (*to become less dark*) iluminarse; (*to give off flashes of lightning*) relampaguear; (fig) iluminarse (*los ojos, la cara de una persona*)
lighter ['laɪtər] *s* (*to light a cigarette*) encendedor *m*; (*flat-bottomed barge*) alijador *m*
light-fingered ['laɪt'fiŋgərd] *adj* largo de uñas, listo de manos
light-footed ['laɪt'fʊtɪd] *adj* ligero de pies
light-headed ['laɪt'hɛdɪd] *adj* (*dizzy*) aturdido, mareado; (*simple, silly*) tonto, necio, ligero de cascos
light-hearted ['laɪt'hɑrtɪd] *adj* alegre, libre de cuidados
light'house' *s* faro
lighthouse keeper *s* farero
lighting ['laɪtɪŋ] *s* alumbrado, iluminación
lighting engineer *s* iluminador *m*
lighting fixtures *spl* artefactos de alumbrado
lightly ['laɪtli] *adj* ligeramente
light meter *s* exposímetro
lightness ['laɪtnɪs] *s* (*in weight*) ligereza; (*in illumination*) claridad
lightning ['laɪtnɪŋ] *s* relámpagos, relampagueo || *intr* relampaguear
lightning arrester [ə'rɛstər] *s* pararrayos *m*
lightning bug *s* luciérnaga
lightning rod *s* pararrayos *m*
light opera *s* opereta
light'ship' *s* buque *m* fanal, buque faro
light•struck ['laɪt,strʌk] *adj* velado
light'weight' *adj* ligero; de entretiempo, p.ej., **lightweight coat** abrigo de entretiempo
light'-year' *s* año luz
lignite ['lɪgnaɪt] *s* lignito
lignum vitae ['lɪgnəm'vaɪti] *s* guayaco, palo santo
likable ['laɪkəbəl] *adj* simpático
like [laɪk] *adj* parecido, semejante; parecido a, semejante a, p.ej., **this hat is like mine** este sombrero es parecido al mío; (elec) del mismo nombre; **like father like son** de tal palo tal astilla; **to feel like** + *ger* tener ganas de + *inf*; **to look like** parecerse a; parecer que, p.ej., **it looks like rain** parece que va a llover || *adv* como; **like enough**

(coll) probablemente; **nothing like** ni con mucho ‖ *prep* a semejanza de ‖ *conj* (coll) del mismo modo que; (coll) que, p.ej., **it seems like he is right** parece que tiene razón ‖ *s* (*liking*) gusto, preferencia; (*fellow, fellow man*) prójimo, semejante *m;* **and the like** y cosas por el estilo; **to give like for like** pagar en la misma moneda ‖ *tr* gustar de, p.ej., **I like music** gusto de la música; gustar p.ej., **Mary likes peaches** a María le gustan los melocotones; **to like best** o **better** preferir; **to like it in** encontrarse a gusto en (*p.ej., el campo*); **to like to** + *inf* gustarle a uno + *inf,* p.ej., **I like to travel** me gusta viajar; gustarle a uno que + *subj,* p.ej., **I should like him to come to see me** me gustaría que él viniese a verme ‖ *intr* querer, p.ej., **as you like** como Vd. quiera; **if you like** si Vd. quiere

likelihood [ˈlaɪklɪ,hʊd] *s* probabilidad

like•ly [ˈlaɪkli] *adj* (*comp* **-lier;** *super* **-liest**) probable; a propósito; prometedor; **to be likely to** + *inf* ser probable que + *ind,* p.ej., **Mary is likely to come to see us tomorrow** es probable que María vendrá a vernos mañana ‖ *adv* probablemente

like-minded [ˈlaɪkˈmaɪndɪd] *adj* del mismo parecer; de natural semejante

liken [ˈlaɪkən] *tr* asemejar, comparar

likeness [ˈlaɪknɪs] *s* (*picture or image*) retrato; (*similarity*) semejanza, parecido; forma, aspecto, apariencia

like'wise' *adv* igualmente, asimismo; **to do likewise** hacer lo mismo

liking [ˈlaɪkɪŋ] *s* gusto, afición, simpatía; **to be to the liking of** ser del gusto de; **to have a liking for** aficionarse a

lilac [ˈlaɪlək] *adj* de color lila ‖ *s* lilac *m,* lila

Lilliputian [,lɪlɪˈpjuʃən] *adj & s* liliputiense *mf*

lilt [lɪlt] *s* paso airoso, movimiento airoso; canción cadenciosa, música alegre

lil•y [ˈlɪli] *s* (*pl* **-ies**) (*Lilium candidum*) azucena, lirio blanco; cala, lirio de agua; (*fleur-de-lis, the royal arms of France*) flor *f* de lis; **to gild the lily** ponerle colores al oro

lily of the valley *s* lirio de los valles, muguete *m*

lily pad *s* hoja de nenúfar

lima bean [ˈlaɪmə] *s* judía de la peladilla, frijol *m* de media luna

limb [lɪm] *s* (*arm or leg*) miembro; (*of a tree*) rama; (*of a cross; of the sea*) brazo; **to be out on a limb** (coll) estar en un aprieto

limber [ˈlɪmbər] *adj* ágil; flexible ‖ *intr*—**to limber up** agilitarse

lim•bo [ˈlɪmbo] *s* (*pl* **-bos**) lugar *m* de olvido; (theol) limbo

lime [laɪm] *s* (*calcium oxide*) cal *f;* (*Citrus aurantifolia*) limero agrio; (*its fruit*) lima agria; (*linden tree*) tila o tilo

lime'kiln' *s* calera, horno de cal

lime'light' *s* —**to be in the limelight** estar a la vista del público

limerick [ˈlɪmərɪk] *s* quintilla jocosa

lime'stone' *adj* calizo ‖ *s* caliza, piedra caliza

limit [ˈlɪmɪt] *s* límite *m;* **to be the limit** (slang) ser el colmo; **to go the limit** no dejar piedra por mover ‖ *tr* limitar

lim'ited-ac'cess high'way *s* carretera de vía libre

limited monarchy *s* monarquía constitucional

limitless [ˈlɪmɪtlɪs] *adj* ilimitado

limousine [ˈlɪmə,zin] o [,lɪməˈzin] *s* (aut) limusina

limp [lɪmp] *adj* flojo, débil, flexible ‖ *s* cojera ‖ *intr* cojear

limpid [ˈlɪmpɪd] *adj* diáfano, cristalino

linage [ˈlaɪnɪdʒ] *s* (typ) número de líneas

linchpin [ˈlɪntʃ,pɪn] *s* pezonera

linden [ˈlɪndən] *s* tila, tilo

line [laɪn] *s* línea; (*of people, houses, etc.*) hilera; (*rope, string*) cuerda, cordel *m;* (*wrinkle*) arruga; (*for fishing*) sedal *m;* (*written or printed line; line of goods*) renglón *m;* manera (*de pensar*); (*of the spectrum*) (phys) raya; **all along the line** por todas partes; desde cualquier punto de vista; **in line** alineado; dispuesto, preparado; **in line with** de acuerdo con; **out of line** desalineado; en desacuerdo; **to bring into line** poner de acuerdo; **to draw the line at** no ir más allá de; **to fall in line** conformarse; formar cola; alinearse; **to have a line on** (coll) estar enterado de; **to read between the lines** leer entre líneas; **to stand in line** hacer cola; **to toe the line** obrar como se debe; **to wait in line** hacer cola, esperar vez ‖ *tr* alinear, rayar; arrugar (*p.ej., la cara*); formar hilera a lo largo de (*la acera, la calle*); forrar (*un vestido*); guarnecer (*un freno*) ‖ *intr*—**to line up** ponerse en fila; hacer cola

lineage [ˈlɪnɪ•ɪdʒ] *s* linaje *m*

lineaments [ˈlɪnɪ•əmənts] *spl* lineamentos

linear [ˈlɪnɪ•ər] *adj* lineal

line•man [ˈlaɪnmən] *s* (*pl* **-men** [mən]) (elec) celador *m,* recorredor *m* de la línea; (rr) guardavía *m;* (surv) cadenero

linen [ˈlɪnən] *adj* de lino ‖ *s* (*fabric*) lienzo, lino; (*yarn*) hilo de lino; ropa blanca, ropa de cama

linen closet *s* armario para la ropa blanca

line of battle *s* línea de batalla

line of fire *s* (mil) línea de tiro

line of least resistance *s* ley *f* del menor esfuerzo; **to follow the line of least resistance** seguir la corriente, no oponer resistencia

line of sight *s* visual *f;* (*of firearm*) línea de mira

liner [ˈlaɪnər] *s* vapor *m* de travesía; (baseball) pelota rasa, lineazo

line'-up' *s* agrupación, formación; (*of prisoners*) rueda

linger [ˈlɪŋgər] *intr* estarse, quedarse; (*to be tardy*) demorar, tardar; tardar en marcharse; tardar en morirse; pasearse con paso lento; **to linger over** contemplar, reflexionar

lingerie [,lænʒə'ri] *s* ropa interior de mujer
lingering ['lɪŋgərɪŋ] *adj* prolongado
lingual ['lɪŋgwəl] *adj & s* lingual *f*
linguist ['lɪŋgwɪst] *s* (*person skilled in several languages*) poligloto; (*specialist in linguistics*) lingüista *mf*
linguistic [lɪŋ'gwɪstɪk] *adj* lingüístico || **linguistics** *s* lingüística
liniment ['lɪnɪmənt] *s* linimento
lining ['laɪnɪŋ] *s* (*of a coat*) forro, forrado; (*of auto brake*) guarnición; (*of a furnace*) camisa; (*of a wall*) revestimiento
link [lɪŋk] *s* eslabón *m;* **links** campo de golf || *tr* eslabonar || *intr* eslabonarse
linkup ['liŋk,ʌp] *s* conexión; (*in space*) acoplamiento
linnet ['lɪnɪt] *s* pardillo
linoleum [lɪ'nolɪ•əm] *s* linóleo
linotype ['laɪnə,taɪp] (trademark) *adj* linotípico || *s* (*machine*) linotipia; (*matter produced by machine*) linotipo || *tr* componer con linotipia
linotype operator *s* linotipista *mf*
linseed ['lɪn,sid] *s* linaza
linseed oil *s* aceite *m* de linaza
lint [lɪnt] *s* borra, pelusa, hilaza; (*used to dress wounds*) hilas
lintel ['lɪntəl] *s* dintel *m*, umbral *m*
lion ['laɪ•ən] *s* león *m;* (*man of strength and courage*) (fig) león; (fig) celebridad muy solicitada; **to beard the lion in his den** ir a desafiar la cólera de un jefe; **to put one's head in the lion's mouth** meterse en la boca del lobo
lioness ['laɪ•ənɪs] *s* leona
lion-hearted ['laɪ•ən,hɑrtɪd] *adj* valiente
lionize ['laɪ•ə,naɪz] *tr* agasajar
lions' den *s* (Bib) fosa de los leónes
lion's share *s* (la) parte *f* del león
lip [lɪp] *s* labio; (slang) lenguaje *m* insolente; **to hang on the words of** estar pendiente de las palabras de; **to smack one's lips** chuparse los labios
lip'-read' *v* (*pret & pp* **-read** [,rɛd]) *tr & intr* leer en los labios
lip reading *s* labiolectura
lip service *s* homenaje *m* de boca, jarabe *m* de pico
lip'stick' *s* lápiz *m* de labios, lápiz labial
liq. *abbr* **liquid, liquor**
lique•fy ['lɪkwɪ,faɪ] *v* (*pret & pp* **-fied**) *tr* liquidar || *intr* liquidarse
liqueur [lɪ'kʌr] *s* licor *m*
liquid ['lɪkwɪd] *adj* líquido || *s* líquido; (phonet) líquida
liquidate ['lɪkwɪ,det] *tr & intr* liquidar
liquidity [lɪ'kwɪdɪti] *s* liquidez *f*
liquid measure *s* medida para líquidos
liquor ['lɪkər] *s* licor *m*
Lisbon ['lɪzbən] *s* Lisboa
lisle [laɪl] *s* hilo fino de algodón, muy retorcido, sedalina
lisp [lɪsp] *s* ceceo || *intr* cecear
lissome ['lɪsəm] *adj* flexible, elástico; ágil, ligero
list [lɪst] *s* lista; (*strip*) lista, tira; (*border*) orilla; (*selvage*) orillo; (naut) ladeo; **lists** liza; **to enter the lists** entrar en liza; **to have a list** (naut) irse a la banda || *tr* alistar, listar; registrar || *intr* (naut) irse a la banda
listen ['lɪsən] *intr* escuchar; obedecer; **to listen in** escuchar a hurtadillas; escuchar por radio; **to listen to** escuchar; obedecer; **to listen to reason** meterse en razón
listener ['lɪsənər] *s* oyente *mf;* radioescucha *mf*, radioyente *mf*
listening post ['lɪsənɪŋ] *s* puesto de escucha
listing ['lɪstɪŋ] *s* (*items*) rubricación
listless ['lɪstlɪs] *adj* distraído, desatento, indiferente
listlessness ['lɪstlɪsnɪs] *s* apatía; indiferencia
list price *s* precio de catálogo, precio de tarifa
lit. *abbr* **liter, literal, literature**
lita•ny ['lɪtəni] *s* (*pl* **-nies**) letanía; (*repeated series*) (fig) letanía
liter ['litər] *s* litro
literacy ['lɪtərəsi] *s* capacidad de leer y escribir; instrucción
literal ['lɪtərəl] *adj* literal
literary ['lɪtə,rɛri] *adj* literario; (*individual*) literato
literate ['lɪtərɪt] *adj* que sabe leer y escribir; (*well-read*) literato, muy leído; (*educated*) instruído || *s* persona que sabe leer y escribir; literato, erudito
literati [,lɪtə'rɑti] *spl* literatos
literature ['lɪtərətʃər] *s* literatura; impresos, escritos de publicidad
lithe [laiθ] *adj* flexible, cimbreño
lithia ['lɪθ•ə] *s* (chem) litina
lithium ['lɪθɪ•əm] *s* (chem) litio
lithograph ['lɪθə,græf] *s* litografía || *tr* litografiar
lithographer [lɪ'θɑgrəfər] *s* litógrafo
lithography [lɪ'θɑgrəfi] *s* litografía
litigant ['lɪtɪgənt] *adj & s* litigante *mf*
litigate ['lɪtɪ,get] *tr & intr* litigar
litigation [,lɪtɪ'geʃən] *s* litigación; (*lawsuit*) litigio
litigious [lɪ'tɪdʒəs] *adj* litigioso
litmus ['lɪtməs] *s* tornasol *m*
litmus paper *s* papel *m* de tornasol
litter ['lɪtər] *s* desorden *m;* (*scattered rubbish*) basura, papelería; (*young brought forth at one birth*) camada, ventregada; (*bedding for animals*) cama, paja; (*vehicle carried by men or animals*) litera; (*stretcher*) camilla, parihuela || *tr* esparcir papeles por; esparcir (*desechos, papeles, etc.*); cubrir (*el suelo*) con paja || *intr* parir
lit'ter•bug' *s* persona que ensucia las calles tirando papeles rotos
littering ['lɪtərɪŋ] *s*—**no littering** se prohibe tirar papeles rotos
little ['lɪtəl] *adj* (*in size*) pequeño; (*in amount*) poco, p.ej., **little money** poco dinero; **a little** un poco de, p.ej., **a little money** un poco de dinero || *adv* poco; **little by little** poco a poco || *s* poco; **a little** un poco; (*somewhat*) algo; **to make little of** no dar importancia a, no tomar en serio; **to think little of** tener en poco; no vacilar en

Little Bear *s* Osa menor
Little Dipper *s* Carro menor
little finger *s* dedo auricular, dedo meñique; **to twist around one's little finger** manejar con suma facilidad
lit'tle•neck' *s* almeja redonda (*Venus mercenaria*)
little owl *s* mochuelo (*Athene noctua*)
little people *spl* hadas; gente menuda
Little Red Ridinghood [ˈraɪdɪŋ,hʊd] *s* Caperucita Roja
little slam *s* (bridge) semibola
liturgic(al) [lɪˈtʌrdʒɪk(əl)] *adj* litúrgico
litur•gy [ˈlɪtərdʒi] *s* (*pl* **-gies**) liturgia
livable [ˈlɪvəbəl] *adj* habitable, vividero; llevadero, tolerable
live [laɪv] *adj* (*living; full of life; intense*) vivo; (*coals; flame*) ardiente; de actualidad; (elec) cargado ‖ [lɪv] *tr* llevar (*tal o cual vida*); vivir (*una experiencia, una aventura; un actor sus personajes*); **to live down** borrar (*una falta*); **to live out** vivir (*toda la vida*); salir con vida de (*un desastre, una guerra*) ‖ *intr* vivir; **to live and learn** vivir para ver; **to live and let live** vivir y dejar vivir; **to live high** darse buena vida; **to live on** seguir viviendo; vivir de (*p.ej., carne*); vivir a expensas de; **to live up to** cumplir (*lo prometido*); gastar (*todas sus rentas*)
live coal *s* ascua
livelihood [ˈlaɪvlɪ,hʊd] *s* vida; **to earn one's livelihood** ganarse la vida
livelong [ˈlɪv,lɔŋ] o [ˈlɪv,lɑŋ] *adj*—**all the livelong day** todo el santo día
live•ly [ˈlaɪvli] *adj* (*comp* **-lier;** *super* **-liest**) animado, vivaz; alegre, festivo; (*active, keen*) vivo; (*resilient*) elástico
liven [ˈlaɪvən] *tr* animar, regocijar ‖ *intr* animarse, regocijarse
liver [ˈlɪvər] *s* vividor *m;* habitante *mf;* (anat) hígado
liver•y [ˈlɪvəri] *s* (*pl* **-ies**) librea
livery•man [ˈlɪvərimən] *s* (*pl* **-men** [mən]) dueño de una cochera; mozo de cuadra
livery stable *s* cochera de carruajes de alquiler
live'stock' *adj* ganadero ‖ *s* ganadería
live wire *s* (elec) alambre cargado; (slang) trafagón *m*
livid [ˈlɪvɪd] *adj* lívido, amoratado; encolerizado; pálido
living [ˈlɪvɪŋ] *adj* vivo, viviente ‖ *s* vida; **to earn** o **to make a living** ganarse la vida
living quarters *spl* aposentos, habitaciones
living room *s* sala, sala de estar
living wage *s* jornal *m* suficiente para vivir
lizard [ˈlɪzərd] *s* lagarto; (slang) holgón *m*
load [lod] *s* carga; **loads** (coll) muchísimo; **loads of** (coll) gran cantidad de; **to get a load of** (slang) escuchar, oír; (slang) mirar; **to have a load on** (slang) estar borracho ‖ *tr* cargar ‖ *intr* cargar; cargarse
loaded [ˈlodɪd] *adj* cargado; (slang) muy borracho; (slang) muy rico
loaded dice *spl* dados cargados
load'stone' *s* piedra imán; (fig) imán *m*
loaf [lof] *s* (*pl* **loaves** [lovz]) pan *m;* (*of sugar*) pilón *m* ‖ *intr* haraganear
loafer [ˈlofər] *s* haragán *m*
loam [lom] *s* suelo franco; (*mixture used in making molds*) tierra de moldeo
loamy [ˈlomi] *adj* franco
loan [lon] *s* (*among individuals*) préstamo; (*between companies or governments*) empréstito; **to hit for a loan** (coll) dar un sablazo a ‖ *tr* prestar
loan shark *s* (coll) usurero
loan word *s* préstamo lingüístico
loath [loθ] *adj* poco dispuesto; **nothing loath** de buena gana
loathe [loð] *tr* abominar, detestar
loathing [ˈloðɪŋ] *s* abominación, detestación
loathsome [ˈloðsəm] *adj* abominable, asqueroso
lob [lɑb] *v* (*pret & pp* **lobbed;** *ger* **lobbing**) *tr* (tennis) volear desde muy alto
lob•by [ˈlɑbi] *s* (*pl* **-bies**) salón *m* de entrada, vestíbulo; cabilderos ‖ *v* (*pret & pp* **-bied**) *intr* cabildear
lobbying [ˈlɑbɪ•ɪŋ] *s* cabildeo
lobbyist [ˈlɑbɪ•ɪst] *s* cabildero
lobster [ˈlɑbstər] *s* (*spiny lobster*) langosta; (*Homarus*) bogavante *m*
lobster pot *s* langostera
local [ˈlokəl] *adj* local ‖ *s* tren suburbano; (*branch of a union*) junta local; noticia de interés local
locale [loˈkæl] *s* localidad
locali•ty [loˈkælɪti] *s* (*pl* **-ties**) localidad
localize [ˈlokə,laɪz] *tr* localizar
local option *s* derecho local de legislar sobre la venta de bebidas alcohólicas
locate [loˈket] o [ˈloket] *tr* (*to discover the location of*) localizar; (*to place, to settle*) colocar, establecer; (*to ascribe a particular location to*) situar ‖ *intr* establecerse
location [loˈkeʃən] *s* (*place, position*) localidad; (*act of placing*) colocación; (*act of finding*) localización; **on location** (mov) en exteriores
loc. cit. *abbr* **loco citato** (Lat) **in the place cited**
lock [lɑk] *s* cerradura; (*of a canal*) esclusa; (*of hair*) bucle *m;* (*of a firearm*) llave *f;* **lock, stock, and barrel** (coll) del todo, por completo; **under lock and key** bajo llave ‖ *tr* echar la llave a, cerrar con llave; (*to key*) acuñar; hacer pasar (*un buque*) por la esclusa; abrazar, enlazar; **to lock in** encerrar, poner debajo de llave; **to lock out** cerrar la puerta a, dejar en la calle; dejar sin trabajo (*a los obreros*); **to lock up** encerrar poner debajo de llave; encarcelar
locker [ˈlɑkər] *s* armario cerrado con llave
locket [ˈlɑkɪt] *s* guardapelo, medallón *m*
lock'jaw' *s* trismo, oclusión forzosa de la boca
lock nut *s* contratuerca
lock'out' *s* huelga patronal
lock'smith' *s* cerrajero
lock step *s* marcha en fila apretada
lock stitch *s* punto encadenado
lock tender *s* esclusero

lock'up' *s* cárcel *f*
lock washer *s* arandela de seguridad
locomotive [,lokə'motɪv] *s* locomotora
lo•cus ['lokəs] *s* (*pl* **-ci** [saɪ]) sitio, lugar *m;* lugar (geométrico)
locust ['lokəst] *s* (ent) langosta (*Pachytylus*); (ent) cigarra (*Cicada*); (bot) acacia falsa
lode [lod] *s* filón *m,* venero, veta
lode'star' *s* (astr) estrella polar; estrella de guía; (*guide, direction*) guía, norte *m*
lodge [lɑdʒ] *s* casa de guarda; casa de campo; (*e.g., of Masons*) logia || *tr* alojar, hospedar; depositar, colocar; presentar (*una queja*) || alojarse, hospedarse; quedar colgado, ir a parar
lodger ['lɑdʒər] *s* inquilino (*en parte de una casa*)
lodging ['lɑdʒɪŋ] *s* alojamiento, hospedaje *m;* (*without meals*) cobijo
loft [lɔft] *s* (*attic*) desván *m,* sobrado; (*hayloft*) henal *m,* pajar *m;* (*in theater or church*) galería; (*in a store or office building*) piso alto
loft•y ['lɔfti] *adj* (*comp* **-ier;** *super* **-iest**) (*towering; sublime*) encumbrado; (*haughty*) altivo, orgulloso
log. *abbr* **logarithm**
log [lɔg] *s* leño, tronco; (*log chip*) (naut) barquilla; (*chip and line*) (naut) corredera; (aer) diario de vuelo; **to sleep like a log** dormir como un leño || *v* (*pret & pp* **logged;** *ger* **logging**) *tr* registrar; recorrer (*cierta distancia*)
logarithm ['lɔgə,rɪðəm] *s* logaritmo
log'book' *s* (aer) libro de vuelo; (naut) cuaderno de bitácora
log cabin *s* cabaña de troncos
log chip *s* (naut) barquilla
log driver *s* ganchero, maderero
log driving *s* flotaje *m*
logger ['lɔgər] o ['lɑgər] *s* leñador *m,* maderero; grúa de troncos; tractor *m*
log'ger•head' *s* mentecato; **at loggerheads** reñidos
loggia ['lodʒə] *s* (archit) logia
logic ['lɑdʒɪk] *s* lógica
logical ['lɑdʒɪkəl] *adj* lógico
logician [lo'dʒɪʃən] *s* lógico
logistic(al) [lo'dʒɪstɪk(əl)] *adj* logístico
logistics [lo'dʒɪstɪks] *s* logística
log'jam' *s* atasco de rollizos; (fig) estancación
log line *s* (naut) corredera
log'roll' *intr* trocar favores políticos
log'wood' *s* campeche *m*
loin [lɔɪn] *s* lomo; **to gird up one's loins** apercibirse para la acción
loin'cloth' *s* taparrabo
loiter ['lɔɪtər] *tr*—**to loiter away** malgastar (*el tiempo*) || *intr* holgazanear, rezagarse
loiterer ['lɔɪtərər] *s* holgazán *m,* rezagado
loll [lɑl] *intr* colgar flojamente; arrellanarse, repantigarse
lollipop ['lɑli,pɑp] *s* paleta (*dulce en el extremo de un palito*)
Lombard ['lɑmbɑrd] *adj & s* lombardo
Lombardy ['lɑmbərdi] *s* Lombardía
Lombardy poplar *s* álamo de Italia, chopo lombardo
lon. *abbr* **longitude**
London ['lʌndən] *adj* londinense || *s* Londres *m*
Londoner ['lʌndənər] *s* londinense *mf*
lone [lon] *adj* solo, solitario; (*sole, single*) único
loneliness ['lonlinɪs] *s* soledad
lone•ly ['lonli] *adj* (*comp* **-lier;** *super* **-liest**) soledoso
lonesome ['lonsəm] *adj* soledoso; (*spot, atmosphere*) solitario
lone wolf *s* (fig) lobo solitario
long. *abbr* **longitude**
long [lɔŋ] o [lɑŋ] (*comp* **longer** ['lɔŋgər] o ['lɑŋgər]; *super* **longest** ['lɔŋgɪst] o ['lɑŋgɪst]) *adj* largo; de largo, p.ej., **two meters long** dos metros de largo || *adv* mucho tiempo, largo tiempo; **as long as** mientras; (*provided*) con tal de que; (*inasmuch as*) puesto que; **before long** dentro de poco; **how long** cuánto tiempo; **long ago** hace mucho tiempo; **long before** mucho antes; **longer** más tiempo; **long since** desde hace mucho tiempo; **no longer** ya no; **so long!** (coll) ¡hasta luego!; **so long as** con tal de que || *intr* anhelar, suspirar; **to long for** anhelar por, ansiar
long'boat' *s* (naut) lancha
long'-dis'tance call *s* (telp) llamada a larga distancia
long-distance flight *s* (aer) vuelo a distancia
long'-drawn'-out' *adj* prolongado, pesado
longeron ['lɑndʒərən] *s* larguero
longevity [lɑn'dʒɛvɪti] *s* longevidad
long face *s* (coll) cara triste
long'hair' *adj & s* intelectual *mf;* aficionado a la música clásica
long'hand' *s* escritura a mano
longing ['lɔŋɪŋ] *adj* anhelante || *s* anhelo, ansia
longitude ['lɑndʒɪ,tjud] *s* longitud
long johns *spl* ropa interior que cubre brazos y piernas
long-lived ['lɔŋ'laɪvd] o (coll) ['lɔŋ'lɪvd] *adj* longevo, de larga vida
long-playing record ['lɔŋ'ple•ɪŋ] *s* disco de larga duración; elepé *m*
long primer ['prɪmər] *s* (typ) entredós *m*
long'-range' *adj* de largo alcance
longshore•man ['lɔŋ,ʃormən] *s* (*pl* **-men** [mən]) *s* estibador *m,* portuario
long'-stand'ing *adj* que existe desde hace mucho tiempo
long'-suf'fering *adj* longánimo, sufrido
long suit *s* (cards) palo fuerte; (fig) fuerte *m*
long'-term' *adj* a largo plazo
long'-wind'ed *adj* difuso, palabrero; discursisto
look [lʊk] *s* (*appearance*) aspecto, apariencia; (*glance*) mirada; (*search*) búsqueda; **looks** aspecto, apariencia; **to take a look at** echar una mirada a || *tr* expresar con la mirada; representar (*la edad que uno tiene*); **to look daggers at** apuñalar con la mirada; **to look the part** vestir el cargo; **to look up**

(*e.g., in a dictionary*) buscar; ir a visitar, venir a ver || *intr* mirar; buscar; parecer; **look out!** ¡cuidado!, ¡ojo!; **to look after** mirar por; ocuparse en; **to look at** mirar; **to look back** mirar hacia atrás; (fig) mirar el pasado; **to look down on** mirar por encima del hombro; **to look for** buscar; creer, p.ej., **I look for rain** creo que va á llover; **to look forward to** esperar con placer anticipado; **to look ill** tener mala cara; **to look in on** pasar por la casa o la oficina de; **to look into** averiguar, estudiar; **to look like** parecerse a; amenazar, p.ej., **it looks like rain** amenaza lluvia, parece que va a llover; **to look oneself** parecer el mismo; tener buena cara; **to look out** tener cuidado; mirar por (*p.ej., la ventana*); **to look out for** mirar por, cuidar de; guardarse de; **to look out on** dar a; **to look through** mirar por; hojear (*un libro*); **to look toward** dar a; **to look up to** admirar, mirar con respeto; **to look well** tener buena cara

lookalike [ˈlʊkəˌlaɪk] *adj & s* doble; parecido

looker-on [ˌlʊkərˈɑn] *s* (*pl* **lookers-on**) mirón *m*, espectador *m*

looking glass [ˈlʊkɪŋ] *s* espejo

look'out' *s* vigilancia; (*tower*) atalaya; (*person keeping watch*) vigilante *mf;* (*man watching from lookout tower*) atalaya *m;* (*care, concern*) (coll) cuidado; **to be on the lookout for** estar a la mira de

loom
[lum] *s* telar *m* || *intr* (*to appear indistinctly*) vislumbrarse; amenazar, parecer inevitable

loon [lun] *s* tonto, bobo; (orn) zambullidor *m*

loon•y [ˈluni] *adj* (*comp* **-ier;** *super* **-iest**) (slang) loco || *s* (*pl* **-ies**) (slang) loco

loop [lup] *s* lazo; (*in a cable or rope*) vuelta; (*of a river*) meandro; (*of a road*) recoveco; (*for fastening a button*) presilla; (aer) rizo; (elec) circuito cerrado; (*part of vibrating body between two nodes*) vientre *m;* **to loop the loop** (aer) rizar el rizo || *tr* hacer lazos en; enlazar || *intr* formar lazo; (aer) hacer el rizo

loop'hole' *s* (*narrow opening in wall*) lucerna; (*means of evasion*) efugio, escapatoria

loose [lus] *adj* (*dress, tooth, screw, bowels*) flojo; (*fitting, thread, wire, rivet, tongue, bowels*) suelto; (*sleeve*) perdido; (*earth, soil*) desmenuzado; (*unpackaged*) a granel, sin envase; (*unbound papers*) sin encuadernar; (*pulley*) loco; (*translation*) libre; (*life, morals*) relajado; (*woman*) fácil, frágil; **to become loose** desatarse, aflojarse; **to break loose** ponerse en libertad; **to turn loose** soltar || *s*—**to be on the loose** ser libre, estar sin trabas; estar de juerga || *tr* soltar; desatar, desencadenar

loose end *s* cabo suelto; **at loose ends** desarreglado, indeciso

loose'-leaf' notebook *s* cuaderno de hojas cambiables, cuaderno de hojas sueltas

loosen [ˈlusən] *tr* desatar, aflojar, desapretar; aflojar, laxar (*el vientre*) || *intr* desatarse, aflojarse, desapretarse

looseness [ˈlusnɪs] *s* flojedad, soltura; (*in morals*) relajamiento

loose'strife' *s* lisimaquia; salicaria

loose-tongued [ˈlusˈtʌŋd] *adj* largo de lengua, ligero de lengua

loot [lut] *s* botín *m*, presa || *tr* saquear, pillar

lop [lɑp] *v* (*pret & pp* **lopped;** *ger* **lopping**) *tr* dejar caer (*p.ej., los brazos*); **to lop off** cortar; podar (*un árbol, una vid*) || *intr* colgar

lopsided [ˈlɑpˈsaɪdɪd] *adj* ladeado, sesgado; desproporcionado, asimétrico, patituerto

loquacious [loˈkweʃəs] *adj* locuaz

loran [ˈlɔræn] *s* (naut) lorán *m*

lord [lɔrd] *s* señor *m;* (Brit) lord *m;* (hum & poet) marido || *tr*—**to lord it over** dominar despóticamente, imponerse a

lord•ly [ˈlɔrdli] *adj* (*comp* **-lier;** *super* **-liest**) señoril; magnífico; despótico, imperioso; altivo, arrogante

Lord's Day, the el domingo

lordship [ˈlɔrdʃɪp] *s* señoría, excelencia

Lord's Prayer *s* oración dominical, padrenuestro

Lord's Supper *s* sagrada comunión; Cena del Señor

lore [lor] *s* ciencia, saber *m;* ciencia popular, saber *m* popular

lorgnette [lɔrnˈjɛt] *s* (*eyeglasses*) impertinentes *mpl;* (*opera glasses*) gemelos de teatro con manija

lor•ry [ˈlɑri] o [ˈlɔri] *s* (*pl* **-ries**) carro de plataforma; (Brit) autocamión *m;* (Brit) vagoneta

lose [luz] *v* (*pret & pp* **lost** [lɔst] o [lɑst]) *tr* perder; no lograr salvar (*el médico al enfermo*); **to lose heart** desalentarse; **to lose oneself** perderse, errar el camino; ensimismarse || *intr* perder; quedar vencido; retrasarse (*el reloj*)

loser [ˈluzər] *s* perdedor *m*

losing [ˈluzɪŋ] *adj* perdedor || **losings** *spl* pérdidas, dinero perdido

loss [lɔs] o [lɑs] *s* pérdida; **to be at a loss** estar perplejo, no saber qué hacer; **to be at a loss to** + *inf* no saber como + *inf;* **to sell at a loss** vender con pérdida

loss leader *s* artículo vendido a gran descuento

loss of face *s* pérdida de prestigio, desprestigio

lost [lɔst] o [lɑst] *adj* perdido; (fig) desviado; **lost in thought** ensimismado, abismado; **lost to** perdido para; insensible a

lost'-and-found' department *s* oficina de objetos perdidos

lost sheep *s* oveja perdida

lot [lɑt] *s* (*for building*) solar *m*, parcela; (*fate, destiny*) suerte *f;* (*portion, parcel*) lote *m;* (*of people*) grupo; (coll) gran cantidad, gran número; (coll) sujeto, tipo; **a lot (of)** o **lots of** (coll) mucho, muchos; **to cast** o **to throw in one's lot with** compartir la suerte de; **to draw** o **to cast lots** echar suertes

lotion [ˈloʃən] *s* loción

lotter•y [ˈlɑtəri] *s* (*pl* **-ies**) lotería

lotto [ˈlɑto] *s* lotería
lotus [ˈlotəs] *s* loto
loud [laʊd] *adj* alto; (*noisy*) ruidoso; (*voice*) fuerte; (*garish*) chillón, llamativo; (*conspicuously vulgar*) charro, cursi; (*foul-smelling*) apestoso, maloliente ‖ *adv* alto, en voz alta; ruidosamente
loud'mouth' *s* bocaza, bocona, bocón *m*
loudmouthed [ˈlaʊd,maʊθt] o [ˈlaʊd,maʊðd] *adj* vocinglero
loud'speak'er *s* altavoz *m*, parlante *m*, pantalla acústica
lounge [laʊndʒ] *s* diván *m*, sofá *m* cama; salón *m* de descanso, salón social ‖ *intr* repantigarse a su sabor, recostarse cómodamente; **to lounge around** estar arrimado a la pared, pasearse perezosamente
lounge lizard *s* (slang) holgón *m*
louse [laʊs] *s* (*pl* **lice** [laɪs]) piojo
lous•y [ˈlaʊzi] *adj* (*comp* **-ier**; *super* **-iest**) piojoso; (*mean*) vil, ruin; (*filthy*) asqueroso, sucio; (*bungling*) chapucero; **lousy with** (slang) colmado de (*p.ej.*, *dinero*)
lout [laʊt] *s* patán *m*
louver [ˈluvər] *s* (*opening to let in air and light*) lumbrera; tablilla de persiana; (aut) persiana del radiador
lovable [ˈlʌvəbəl] *adj* amable
love [lʌv] *s* amor *m*; (*tennis*) cero, nada; **not for love nor money** ni a tiros; **to be in love (with)** estar enamorado (de); **to fall in love (with)** enamorarse (de); **to make love to** cortejar, galantear ‖ *tr* amar, querer; gustar de, tener afición a
love affair *s* amores *mpl*, amorío
love'bird' *s* inseparable *m*; **lovebirds** recién casados muy enamorados
love child *s* hijo del amor
love feast *s* ágape *m*
love'-hate' *s* odio-amor *m*
loveless [ˈlʌvlɪs] *adj* abandonado, sin amor; (*feeling no love*) desamado
lovelorn [ˈlʌv,lɔrn] *adj* abandonado por su amor, herido de amor
love•ly [ˈlʌvli] *adj* (*comp* **-lier**; *super* **-liest**) bello, hermoso; adorable, precioso; (coll) encantador, gracioso
love match *s* matrimonio de amor
love potion *s* filtro, filtro de amor
lover [ˈlʌvər] *s* amante *mf*; (*e.g.*, *of hunting, sports*) aficionado; (*e.g.*, *of work*) amigo
love seat *s* confidente *m*
love'sick' *adj* enfermo de amor
love'sick'ness *s* mal *m* de amor
love song *s* canción de amor
loving [ˈlʌvɪŋ] *adj* amoroso, afectuoso
lov'ing-kind'ness *s* bondad infinita, misericordia
low [lo] *adj* bajo; (*diet; visibility; opinion*) malo; (*dress, waist*) escotado; (*depressed*) abatido; gravemente enfermo; (*fire*) lento; **to lay low** dejar tendido, derribar; matar; **to lie low** no dejarse ver ‖ *adv* bajo ‖ *s* punto bajo; precio más bajo, precio mínimo; (*moo of cow*) mugido; (aut) primera marcha, primera velocidad; (meteor) depresión ‖ *intr* mugir (*la vaca*)
low'born' *adj* de humilde cuna
low'boy' *s* cómoda baja con patas cortas
low'brow' *adj* & *s* (slang) ignorante *mf*
low'-cost' housing *s* casas baratas
Low Countries, the los Países Bajos
low'-down' *adj* (coll) bajo, vil, ruin ‖ **low'-down'** *s* (slang) informes *mf* confidenciales, hechos verdaderos
lower [ˈlo•ər] *adj* bajo, inferior ‖ *tr* & *intr* bajar ‖ [ˈlaʊ•ər] *intr* poner mala cara, fruncir el entrecejo; encapotarse (*el cielo*)
lower berth [ˈlo•ər] *s* litera baja, cama baja
Lower California [ˈlo•ər] *s* la Baja California
lower case [ˈlo•ər] *s* (typ) caja baja
lower middle class [ˈlo•ər] *s* pequeña burguesía
lowermost [ˈlo•ər,most] *adj* (el) más bajo
low'-fre'quency *adj* de baja frecuencia
low gear *s* primera marcha, primera velocidad
low'-key' *adj* modesto; moderado
lowland [ˈlolənd] *s* tierra baja ‖ **Lowlands** *spl* Tierra Baja (*de Escocia*)
low life *s* gentuza
low•ly [ˈloli] *adj* (*comp* **-lier**; *super* **-liest**) humilde; (*in growth or position*) bajo
Low Mass *s* misa rezada
low-minded [ˈloˈmaɪndɪd] *adj* vil, ruin
low neck *s* escote *m*, escotado
low-necked [ˈloˈnɛkt] *adj* escotado
low-pitched [ˈloˈpɪtʃt] *adj* (*sound*) grave; (*roof*) de poco declive
low'-pres'sure *adj* de baja presión
low-priced [ˈloˈpraɪst] *adj* barato, de precio bajo
low shoe *s* zapato inglés
low'-speed' *adj* de baja velocidad
low-spirited [ˈloˈspɪrɪtɪd] *adj* abatido
low spirits *spl* abatimiento
low tide *s* bajamar *f*, marea baja; (fig) punto más bajo
low visibility *s* (aer) poca visibilidad
low water *s* (*of a river*) nivel mínimo; (*because of drought*) estiaje *m*; bajamar *f*, marea baja
loyal [ˈlɔɪ•əl] *adj* leal
loyalist [ˈlɔɪ•əlɪst] *s* leal *m*
loyal•ty [ˈlɔɪ•əlti] *s* (*pl* **-ties**) lealtad
lozenge [ˈlɑzɪndʒ] *s* losange *m*; (*candy cough drop*) pastilla, tableta
LP [ˈɛlˈpi] *s* (letterword) (trademark) disco de larga duración; elepé *m*
Ltd. *abbr* **limited**
lubricant [ˈlubrɪkənt] *adj* & *s* lubricante *m*
lubricate [ˈlubrɪ,ket] *tr* lubricar
lubricous [ˈlubrɪkəs] *adj* (*slippery; lewd*) lúbrico (*resbaladizo; lascivo*); incierto, inconstante
lucerne [luˈsʌrn] *s* mielga
lucid [ˈlusɪd] *adj* claro, inteligible; (*rational, sane*) lúcido; (*bright, shining*) luciente; (*clear, transparent*) cristalino
Lucifer [ˈlusɪfər] *s* Lucifer *m*
luck [lʌk] *s* (*good or bad*) suerte *f*; (*good*) suerte, buena suerte; **down on one's luck** de mala suerte, de malas; **in luck** de buena

suerte, de buenas; **out of luck** de mala suerte, de malas; **to bring luck** traer buena suerte; **to try one's luck** probar fortuna; **worse luck** desgraciadamente
luckily [ˈlʌkɪli] *adj* afortunadamente
luckless [ˈlʌklɪs] *adj* desgraciado
luck•y [ˈlʌki] *adj* (*comp* **-ier;** *super* **-iest**) afortunado; derecho (CAm); (*supposed to bring luck*) de buen agüero; **to be lucky** tener suerte; quedar bien parado
lucky hit *s* (coll) golpe *m* de fortuna
lucrative [ˈlukrətɪv] *adj* lucrativo
ludicrous [ˈludɪkrəs] *adj* absurdo, ridículo
lug [lʌg] *s* orejeta; (*pull, tug*) estirón *m,* esfuerzo ‖ *v* (*pret & pp* **lugged;** *ger* **lugging**) *tr* tirar con fuerza de; (*to bring up irrelevantly*) (coll) traer a colación
luggage [ˈlʌgɪdʒ] *s* equipaje *m*
lugubrious [lʊˈgubrɪ•əs] o [lʊˈgjubrɪ•əs] *adj* lúgubre
lukewarm [ˈluk,wɔrm] *adj* tibio, templado
lull [lʌl] *s* momento de calma, momento de silencio; (naut) recalmón *m* ‖ *tr* adormecer; calmar, aquietar; apaciguar
lulla•by [ˈlʌlə,baɪ] *s* (*pl* **-bies**) arrullo, canción de cuna
lumbago [lʌmˈbego] *s* lumbago
lumber [ˈlʌmbər] *s* madera aserrada, madera aserradiza, madera de sierra; trastos viejos ‖ *intr* andar pesadamente
lum'ber•jack' *s* leñador *m,* hachero
lumber•man [ˈlʌmbərmən] *s* (*pl* **-men** [mən]) (*dealer*) maderero; (*man who cuts down lumber*) leñador *m,* hachero
lumber room *s* leonera, trastera
lum'ber•yard' *s* maderería, depósito de maderas
luminar•y [ˈlumɪ,nɛri] *s* (*pl* **-ies**) luminar *m,* lumbrera
luminescent [,lumɪˈnɛsənt] *adj* luminiscente
luminous [ˈlumɪnəs] *adj* luminoso
lummox [ˈlʌməks] *s* (coll) jergón *m*
lump [lʌmp] *s* terrón *m;* (*swelling*) chichón *m,* bulto, hinchazón *m;* (*stupid person*) (coll) bodoque *m;* **in the lump** en grueso, por junto; **to get a lump in one's throat** hacérsele a (*uno*) un nudo en la garganta ‖ *tr* juntar, mezclar; (*to make into lumps*) aterronar; (coll) aguantar, tragar (cosa repulsiva)
lumpish [ˈlʌmpɪʃ] *adj* hobachón, torpe, pesado
lump sum *s* suma global, suma total
lump•y [ˈlʌmpi] *adj* (*comp* **-ier;** *super* **-iest**) aterronado, borujoso; torpe, pesado; (*sea*) agitado
luna•cy [ˈlunəsi] *s* (*pl* **-cies**) demencia, locura
lunar [ˈlunər] *adj* lunar
lunar lander o **lunar module** *s* módulo lunar
lunar landing *s* alunizaje *m*
lunatic [ˈlunətɪk] *adj & s* lunático, loco
lunatic asylum *s* manicomio
lunatic fringe *s* minoría fanática
lunch [lʌnʃ] *s* (*regular midday meal*) almuerzo; (*light meal*) colación, merienda ‖ *intr* almorzar; merendar, tomar una colación
lunch basket *s* fiambrera
lunch cloth *s* mantelito
luncheon [ˈlʌntʃən] *s* almuerzo; almuerzo de ceremonia
lunch'room' *s* cantina, merendero
lung [lʌŋ] *s* pulmón *m*
lung cancer *s* cáncer *m* pulmonar
lunge [lʌndʒ] *s* arremetida, embestida; (*with a sword*) estocada ‖ *intr* arremeter, lanzarse; **to lunge at** arremeter contra
lurch [lʌrtʃ] *s* sacudida, tumbo; (naut) bandazo; **to leave in the lurch** dejar en la estacada, dejar colgado ‖ *intr* dar una sacudida, dar un tumbo; (naut) dar un bandazo
lure [lʊr] *s* (*decoy*) cebo, señuelo; (fig) aliciente *m,* señuelo ‖ *tr* atraer con cebo, atraer con señuelo; (fig) atraer, tentar, seducir; **to lure away** llevarse con señuelo; (*from one's obligations*) desviar
lurid [ˈlʊrɪd] *adj* sensacional; (*gruesome*) espeluznante; (*fiery*) ardiente, encendido
lurk [lʌrk] *intr* acechar, andar furtivamente
luscious [ˈlʌʃəs] *adj* delicioso; lujoso; voluptuoso
lush [lʌʃ] *adj* jugoso, lozano; lujuriante; lujoso
Lusitanian [,lusɪˈtenɪ•ən] *adj & s* lusitano
lust [lʌst] *s* deseo vehemente; (*greed*) codicia; (*strong sexual appetite*) lujuria; entusiasmo ‖ *intr* lujuriar; **to lust after** o **for** codiciar; desear con lujuria
luster [ˈlʌstər] *s* (*gloss*) lustre *m;* (*of certain fabrics*) viso; (*fame, glory*) (fig) lustre
lus'ter•ware' *s* loza con visos metálicos
lustful [ˈlʌstfəl] *adj* lujurioso
lustrous [ˈlʌstrəs] *adj* lustroso
lust•y [ˈlʌsti] *adj* (*comp* **-ier;** *super* **-iest**) fuerte, robusto, lozano
lute [lut] *s* (mus) laúd *m;* (*substance used to close or seal a joint*) (chem) lodo
Lutheran [ˈluθərən] *adj & s* luterano
luxuriance [lʌgˈʒʊrɪ•əns] *s* lozanía
luxuriant [lʌgˈʒʊrɪ•ənt] *adj* lozano, lujuriante; (*overornamented*) recargado
luxuriate [lʌgˈʒʊrɪ,et] o [lʌkˈʃʊrɪ,et] *intr* crecer con lozanía; entregarse al lujo; (*to find keen pleasure*) lozanearse
luxurious [lʌgˈʒʊrɪ•əs] o [lʌkˈʃʊrɪ•əs] *adj* lujoso
luxu•ry [ˈlʌkʃəri] o [ˈlʌgʒəri] *s* (*pl* **-ries**) lujo
lye [laɪ] *s* lejía
lying [ˈlaɪ•ɪŋ] *adj* mentiroso ‖ *s* el mentir
ly'ing-in' hospital *s* casa de maternidad, clínica de parturientas
lymph [lɪmf] *s* linfa
lymphatic [lɪmˈfætɪk] *adj* linfático
lynch [lɪntʃ] *tr* linchar
lynching [ˈlɪntʃɪŋ] *s* linchamiento
lynch law *s* justicia de la soga
lynx [lɪŋks] *s* lince *m*
lynx-eyed [ˈlɪŋks,aɪd] *adj* de ojos linces
lyonnaise [,laɪ•əˈnez] *adj* (culin) a la lionesa
lyre [laɪr] *s* (mus) lira
lyric [ˈlɪrɪk] *adj* lírico ‖ *s* poema lírico; (*words of a song*) (coll) letra
lyrical [ˈlɪrɪkəl] *adj* lírico
lyricism [ˈlɪrɪ,sɪzəm] *s* lirismo
lyricist [ˈlɪrɪsɪst] *s* (*writer of words for songs*) letrista *mf;* (*poet*) poeta lírico

M

M, m [ɛm] decimotercera letra del alfabeto inglés
m. *abbr* **married, masculine, meter, midnight, mile, minute, month**
ma'am [mæm] o [mɑm] *s* (coll) señora
macadam [mə'kædəm] *s* macadán *m*
macadamize [mə'kædə,maɪz] *tr* macadamizar
macaro•ni [,mækə'roni] *s* (*pl* **-nis** o **-nies**) macarrones *mpl*
macaroon [,mækə'run] *s* mostachón *m*, almendrado
macaw [mə'kɔ] *s* aracanga, guacamayo
mace [mes] *s* maza; (*spice*) macis *m*
mace'bear'er *s* macero
machination [,mækɪ'neʃən] *s* maquinación
machine [mə'ʃin] *s* máquina; automóvil *m*, coche *m*; (*of a political party*) camarilla ‖ *tr* trabajar a máquina
machine gun *s* ametralladora
ma•chine'-gun' *tr* ametrallar
ma•chine'-made' *adj* hecho a máquina
machiner•y [mə'ʃinəri] *s* (*pl* **-ies**) maquinaria
machine screw *s* tornillo para metales
machine shop *s* taller mecánico
machine stenography *s* estenotipia
machine tool *s* máquina-herramienta
machine translation *s* traducción automática
machinist [mə'ʃinɪst] *s* (*person who makes machines*) maquinista *mf*; (*person who operates machines*) mecánico; (naut) segundo maquinista; (theat) maquinista *mf*, tramoyista *mf*
mackerel ['mækərəl] *s* caballa, escombro
mackerel sky *s* cielo aborregado
mackintosh ['mækɪn,tɑʃ] *s* impermeable *m*
mad [mæd] *adj* (*comp* **madder;** *super* **maddest**) (*angry*) enojado, furioso; (*crazy*) loco; (*foolish*) tonto, necio; (*rabid*) rabioso; **to be mad about** (coll) estar loco por; **to drive mad** volver loco; **to go mad** volverse loco; rabiar (*un perro*)
madam ['mædəm] *s* señora
mad'cap' *s* alocado, tarambana *mf*
madden ['mædən] *tr* (to make angry) enojar, enfurecer; (*to make insane*) enloquecer
made-to-order ['medtə'ɔrdər] *adj* hecho de encargo; (*clothing*) hecho a la medida
made'-up' *adj* inventado, ficticio; (*artificial*) postizo; (*face*) pintado
mad'house' *s* casa de locos, manicomio
madman ['mæd,mæn] *s* (*pl* **-men** [,mɛn]) loco
madness ['mædnɪs] *s* furia, rabia; locura; (*of a dog*) rabia
Madonna lily [mə'dɑnə] *s* azucena
maelstrom ['melstrəm] *s* remolino
mag. *abbr* **magazine**
magazine ['mægə,zin] o [,mægə'zin] *s* (*periodical*) revista, magazine *m;* (*warehouse*) almacén *m;* (*for cartridges*) cámara; (*for powder*) polvorín *m;* (naut) santabárbara; (phot) almacén *m*
Magellan [mə'dʒələn] *s* Magallanes *m*
maggot ['mægət] *s* cresa
Magi ['medʒaɪ] *spl* magos de Oriente, Reyes Magos
magic ['mædʒɪk] *adj* mágico ‖ *s* magia; ilusionismo, prestidigitación; **as if by magic** como por encanto
magician [mə'dʒɪʃən] *s* (*entertainer with sleight of hand*) ilusionista *mf*, prestidigitador *m;* (*sorcerer*) mágico
magistrate ['mædʒɪs,tret] *s* magistrado
magnanimous [mæg'nænɪməs] *adj* magnánimo
magnesium [mæg'niʃɪ•əm] o [mæg'nɪʒɪ•əm] *s* magnesio
magnet ['mægnɪt] *s* imán *m*
magnetic [mæg'nɛtɪk] *adj* magnético; (fig) atrayente, cautivador
magnetic curves *spl* fantasma magnético
magnetic field *s* campo magnético
magnetism ['mægnɪ,tɪzəm] *s* magnetismo
magnetize ['mægnɪ,taɪz] *tr* magnetizar, imanar
magne•to [mæg'nito] *s* (*pl* **-tos**) magneto *m & f*
magnificent [mæg'nɪfɪsənt] *adj* magnífico
magni•fy ['mægnɪ,faɪ] *v* (*pret & pp* **-fied**) *tr* magnificar; exagerar
magnifying glass *s* lupa, vidrio de aumento
magnitude ['mægnɪ,tjud] *s* magnitud
magpie ['mæg,paɪ] *s* picaza, urraca
Magyar ['mægjɑr] *adj & s* magiar *mf*
mahlstick ['mɑl,stɪk] o ['mɔl,stɪk] *s* tiento
mahoga•ny [me'hɑgəni] *s* (*pl* **-nies**) caoba
Mahomet [mə'hɑmɪt] *s* Mahoma *m*
mahout [mə'haʊt] *s* naire *m*, cornaca *m*
maid [med] *s* (*female servant*) criada, moza; (*young girl; housemaid*) doncella; gata (Mex); (*spinster*) soltera
maiden ['medən] *s* doncella
maid'en•hair' *s* (bot) cabello de Venus
maid'en•head' *s* himen *m*
maidenhood ['medən,hʊd] *s* doncellez *f*
maiden lady *s* soltera
maiden name *s* apellido de soltera
maiden voyage *s* primera travesía
maid'-in-wait'ing *s* (*pl* **maids-in-waiting**) dama
maid of honor *s* (*at a wedding*) primera madrina de boda; (*attendant on a princess*) doncella de honor; (*attendant on a queen*) dama de honor
maid'serv'ant *s* criada, doméstica
mail [mel] *s* correspondencia, correo; (*of armor*) malla; **by return mail** a vuelta de correo ‖ *tr* echar al correo
mail'bag' *s* valija
mail'boat' *s* vapor *m* correo
mail'box' *s* buzón *m*
mail car *s* carro correo, coche-correo, ambulancia de correos
mail carrier *s* cartero
mailing list *s* lista de envío
mailing permit *s* porte concertado
mail•man ['mel,mæn] *s* (*pl* **-men** [,mɛn]) cartero
mail order *s* pedido postal

mail'-or'der house *s* casa de ventas por correo
mail'plane' *s* avión-correo
mail train *s* tren *m* correo
maim [mem] *tr* estropear, mutilar
main [men] *adj* principal, primero, maestro, mayor || *s* cañería maestra; **in the main** mayormente
main clause *s* proposición dominante
main course *s* plato principal, plato fuerte
main deck *s* cubierta principal
mainland ['men,lænd] o ['menlənd] *s* continente *m,* tierra firme
main line *s* (rr) tronco, línea principal
mainly ['menli] *adv* principalmente, en su mayor parte
mainmast ['menməst], o ['men,mæst] o ['men,mɑst] *s* palo mayor
mainsail ['mensəl] o ['men,sel] *s* vela mayor
main'spring' *s* (*of watch*) muelle *m* real; (fig) móvil *m,* origen *m*
main'stay' *s* (naut) estay *m* mayor; (fig) soporte *m* principal
main'stream' *s* vía principal
main street *s* calle *f* mayor
maintain [men'ten] *tr* mantener; (*to support*) (law) manutener
maintenance ['mentɪnəns] *s* mantenimiento; (*upkeep*) conservación; gastos de conservación
maître d'hôtel [,metər do'tɛl] *s* (*butler*) mayordomo; (*headwaiter*) jefe *m* de comedor
maize [mez] *s* maíz *m*
majestic [mə'dʒəstɪk] *adj* majestuoso
majes•ty ['mædʒɪsti] *s* (*pl* **-ties**) majestad
major ['medʒər] *adj* (*greater*) mayor; (*elder*) mayor de edad; (mus) mayor || *s* (educ) especialización; (mil) comandante *m* || *intr* (educ) especializarse
Majorca [mə'dʒɔrkə] *s* Mallorca
Majorcan [mə'dʒɔrkən] *adj & s* mallorquín *m*
major•do•mo [,medʒər'domo] *s* (*pl* **-mos**) mayordomo
major general *s* general *m* de división
majori•ty [mə'dʒɔrɪti] *adj* mayoritario || *s* (*pl* **-ties**) (*being of full age; larger number or part*) mayoría; (*full age*) mayoridad; (mil) comandancia
make [mek] *s* (*brand*) marca; (*form, build*) hechura; carácter *m,* natural *m;* **on the make** (slang) buscando provecho || *v* (*pret & pp* **made** [med]) *tr* hacer; cometer (*un error*); efectuar (*un pago*); ganar (*dinero; una baza*); coger (*un tren*); dar (*dinero una empresa*); pronunciar (*un discurso*); cerrar (*un circuito*); poner (*a uno, p.ej., nervioso*); ser, p.ej., **she will make a good wife** será una buena esposa; **to make** + *inf* hacer + *inf,* p.ej., **she made him study** le hizo estudiar; **to make into** convertir en; **to make known** declarar; dar a conocer; **to make of** pensar de; **to make oneself known** darse a conocer; **to make out** distinguir, vislumbrar; descifrar; escribir (*una receta*); llenar (*un cheque*); **to make over** convertir; rehacer (*un traje*); (com) transferir; **to make up** preparar, confeccionar; inventar (*un cuento*); recobrar (*el tiempo perdido*); (theat) maquillar || *intr* estar (*p.ej., seguro*); **to make away with** llevarse; deshacerse de; matar; **to make believe** fingir, p.ej., **he made believe he knew me** fingió conocerme; **to make for** ir hacia; embestir contra; contribuir a (*p.ej., mejores relaciones*); **to make much of** (coll) hacer fiestas a, mostrar cariño a; **to make off** largarse; **to make off with** llevarse, hacerse con; **to make out** arreglárselas; **to make toward** encaminarse a; **to make up** maquillarse, pintarse; componerse, hacer las paces; **to make up for** suplir; compensar por (*una pérdida*); **to make up to** (coll) tratar de congraciarse con
make'-be•lieve' *adj* simulado || *s* pretexto, simulación, fantasía
maker ['mekər] *s* constructor *m,* fabricante *mf*
make'shift' *adj* de fortuna, provisional || *s* expediente *m;* (*person*) tapagujeros *m*
make'-up' *s* composición, constitución; afeite *m,* maquillaje *m;* (typ) imposición
make-up man *s* (theat) maquillador *m*
make'weight' *s* contrapeso; suplente *mf*
making ['mekɪŋ] *s* fabricación; material necesario; causa del éxito; **makings** elementos, materiales *mpl;* (*personal qualities necessary for some purpose*) madera
malachite ['mælə,kaɪt] *s* malaquita
maladjustment [,mælə'dʒʌstmənt] *s* desadaptación
mala•dy ['mælədi] *s* (*pl* **-dies**) dolencia, enfermedad
malaise [mæ'lez] *s* indisposición, malestar *m*
malapropism [,mælæ'prɑp,ɪzəm] *s* despropósito
malapropos [,mælæprə'po] *adj* impropio || *adv* fuera de propósito
malaria [mə'lɛrɪ•ə] *s* malaria, paludismo
Malay ['mele] o [mə'le] *adj & s* malayo
malcontent ['mælkən,tɛnt] *adj & s* malcontento
male [mel] *adj* (*sex*) masculino; (*animal, plant, piece of a device*) macho; (*human being*) varón, p.ej., **male child** hijo varón || *s* macho; varón *m*
male chauvinism *s* machismo
male chauvinist *s* machista *m*
malediction [,mælɪ'dɪkʃən] *s* maldición
malefactor ['mælɪ,fæktər] *s* malhechor *m*
male nurse *s* enfermero
malevolent [mə'lɛvələnt] *adj* malévolo
malfunction [,mæl'fʌŋkʃən] *s* malfuncionamiento *s intr* ir de través; estropearse
malice ['mælɪs] *s* malicia, malevolencia; **to bear malice** guardar rencor; **with malice prepense** [prɪ'pɛns] (law) con malicia y premeditación
malicious [mə'lɪʃəs] *adj* malicioso, malévolo
malign [mə'laɪn] *adj* maligno || *tr* calumniar
malignant [mə'lɪgnənt] *adj* maligno
maligni•ty [mə'lɪgnɪti] *s* (*pl* **-ties**) malignidad

malinger [mə'lɪŋgər] *intr* hacer la zanguanga, fingirse enfermo
mall [mɔl] o [mæl] *s* alameda, paseo de árboles
mallet ['mælɪt] *s* (*wooden hammer*) mazo; (*for croquet and polo*) mallete *m*
mallow ['mælo] *s* malva
malnutrition [,mælnju'trɪʃən] *s* desnutrición
malodorous [mæl'odərəs] *adj* maloliente
malt [mɔlt] *s* malta *m;* (coll) cerveza
maltreat [mæl'trit] *tr* maltratar
mamma ['mɑmə] o [mə'mɑ] *s* mama o mamá *f*
mammal ['mæməl] *s* mamífero
mammalian [mæ'melɪ•ən] *adj & s* mamífero
mammoth ['mæməθ] *adj* gigantesco, enorme ‖ *s* mamut *m*
man [mæn] *s* (*pl* **-men** [mɛən]) *s* hombre *m;* (*in chess*) pieza; (*in checkers*) pieza, peón *m;* **a man** uno, p.ej., **a man can't get work in this town** uno no puede obtener empleo en este pueblo; **as one man** unánimamente; **man alive!** ¡hombre!; **man and wife** marido y mujer; **to be one's own man** no depender de nadie ‖ *v* (*pret & pp* **manned;** *ger* **manning**) *tr* dotar, tripular (*un buque*); guarnecer (*una fortaleza*); servir (*los cañones*)
man about town *s* bulevardero, hombre *m* de mucho mundo
manacle ['mænəkəl] *s* manilla; **manacles** esposas ‖ *tr* poner esposas a
manage ['mænɪdʒ] *tr* manejar ‖ *intr* arreglárselas; **to manage to** ingeniarse a o para; **to manage to get along** ingeniarse para ir viviendo
manageable ['mænɪdʒəbəl] *adj* manejable
management ['mænɪdʒmənt] *s* manejo, dirección, gerencia; (*group who manage a business*) la empresa, la parte patronal, los patronos
manager ['mænədʒər] *s* director *m,* administrador *m,* gerente *mf;* empresario; (sport) manager *m*
managerial [,mænə'dʒɪrɪ•əl] *adj* empresarial
mandate ['mændet] *s* mandato ‖ *tr* asignar por mandato
mandolin ['mændəlɪn] *s* mandolina
mandrake ['mændrek] *s* mandrágora
mane [men] *s* (*of horse*) crines *fpl;* (*of lion, of person*) melena
maneuver [mə'nuvər] *s* maniobra ‖ *tr* hacer maniobrar ‖ *intr* maniobrar
manful ['mænfəl] *adj* varonil, resuelto
manganese ['mæŋgə,nis] o ['mæŋgə,niz] *s* manganeso
mange [mendʒ] *s* sarna
manger ['mendʒər] *s* pesebre *m*
mangle ['mæŋgəl] *tr* lacerar, aplastar
man•gy ['mendʒi] *adj* (*comp* **-gier;** *super* **-giest**) sarnoso; (*dirty, squalid*) roñoso
man'han'dle *tr* maltratar
man'hole' *s* caja de registro, pozo de inspección
manhood ['mænhʊd] *s* virilidad; hombres *mpl*
man hunt *s* caza al hombre
mania ['menɪ•ə] *s* manía
maniac ['menɪ,æk] *adj & s* maníaco
manic-depressive ['mænɪkdɪ'prɛsɪv] *adj & s* maníaco-depresivo
manicure ['mænɪ,kjʊr] *s* (*care of hands*) manicura; (*person*) manicuro, manicura ‖ *tr* hacer la manicura a (*una persona*); hacer (*las manos y las uñas*)
manicurist ['mænɪ,kjʊrɪst] *s* manicuro, manicura
manifest ['mænɪ,fɛst] *adj* manifiesto ‖ *s* (naut) manifiesto ‖ *tr* manifestar
manifes•to [,mænɪ'fɛsto] *s* (*pl* **-toes**) manifiesto
manifold ['mænɪ,fold] *adj* múltiple, vario; polivalente ‖ *s* copia, ejemplar *m;* (*pipe with outlets or inlets*) colector *m,* múltiple *m*
manikin ['mænɪkɪn] *s* maniquí *m;* (*dwarf*) enano
man in the moon *s* cara o cuerpo de hombre imaginarios en la luna llena
manioc ['mæniɑk] *s* cazabe *m,* casabe *m*
manipulate [mə'nɪpjə,let] *tr* manipular
man'kind' *s* el género humano ‖ **man'kind'** *s* el sexo masculino, los hombres
manliness ['mænlɪnɪs] *s* masculinidad, virilidad
man•ly ['mænli] *adj* (*comp* **-lier;** *super* **-liest**) masculino, varonil
manned spaceship [mænd] *s* astronave tripulada
mannequin ['mænɪkɪn] *s* maniquí *m;* (*young woman employed to exhibit clothing*) maniquí *f*
manner ['mænər] *s* manera; **bad manners** malcriadez *f,* malacrianza; **by all manner of means** de todos modos; **in a manner of speaking** como si dijéramos; **in the manner of** a la manera de; **manners** modales *mpl,* crianza; **to the manner born** avezado desde la cuna
mannish ['mænɪʃ] *adj* hombruno
man of letters *s* hombre *m* de letras
man of means *s* hombre *m* de dinero
man of parts *s* hombre *m* de buenas prendas
man of straw *s* hombre *m* de suposición
man of the world *s* hombre *m* de mundo
man-of-war [,mænəv'wɔr] *s* (*pl* **men-of-war** [,mɛnəv'wɔr]) *s* buque *m* de guerra
manor ['mænər] *s* señorío
manor house *s* casa solariega
man overboard *interj* ¡hombre al agua!
man'pow'er *s* número de hombres; personal *m* competente; (mil) fuerzas nacionales
mansard ['mænsɑrd] *s* mansarda; piso de mansarda
man'serv'ant *s* (*pl* **men'serv'ants**) criado
mansion ['mænʃən] *s* hotel *m,* palacio; (*manor house*) casa solariega
man'slaugh'ter *s* (law) homicidio sin premeditación
mantel ['mæntəl] *s* manto (*de chimenea*); (*shelf above it*) mesilla, repisa de chimenea
man'tel•piece' *s* mesilla, repisa de chimenea

mantle ['mæntəl] *s* capa, manto || *tr* vestir con manto; cubrir, tapar; ocultar || *intr* encenderse (*el rostro*)
manual ['mænjʊ•əl] *adj* manual || *s* (*book*) manual *m;* (mil) ejercicio; (mus) teclado manual
manual training *s* enseñanza de los artes y oficios
manufacture [,mænjə'fæktjər] *s* fabricación; obraje *m;* (*thing manufactured*) manufactura || *tr* fabricar, manufacturar
manufacturer [,mænjə'fæktjərər] *s* fabricante *mf*
manure [mə'njʊr] o [mə'nʊr] *s* estiércol *m* || *tr* estercolar
manuscript ['mænjə,skrɪpt] *adj & s* manuscrito
many ['mɛni] *adj & pron* muchos; **a good many** o **a great many** un buen número; **as many as** tantos como; hasta, p.ej., **as many as twenty** hasta veinte; **how many** cuántos; **many a** muchos, p.ej., **many a person** muchas personas; **many another** muchos otros; **many more** muchos más; **so many** tantos; **too many** demasiados; **twice as many as** dos veces más que
many-sided ['mɛni,saɪdɪd] *adj* multilátero; (*having many interests or capabilities*) polifacético
map [mæp] *s* mapa *m;* (*of a city*) plano || *v* (*pret & pp* **mapped;** *ger* **mapping**) *tr* trazar el mapa de; indicar en el mapa; **to map out** trazar el plan de
maple ['mepəl] *s* arce *m*
maquette [mɑ'kɛt] *s* maqueta
Mar. *abbr* **March**
mar [mɑr] *v* (*pret & pp* **marred;** *ger* **marring**) *tr* desfigurar, estropear; frustrar
maraud [mə'rɔd] *tr* saquear || *intr* merodear
marauder [mə'rɔdər] *s* merodeador *m*
marble ['mɑrbəl] *adj* marmóreo || *s* mármol *m;* (*little ball of glass, etc.*) canica; **marbles** (*game*) canica || *tr* crispir, jaspear
march [mɑrtʃ] *s* marcha; (*frontier, territory*) marca; **to steal a march on someone** ganarle a uno por la mano || *tr* hacer marchar || *intr* marchar || **March** *s* marzo
marchioness ['mɑrʃənɪs] *s* marquesa
mare [mɛr] *s* (*female horse*) yegua; (*female donkey*) asna
margarine ['mɑrdʒərɪn] *s* margarina
margin ['mɑrdʒɪn] *s* margen *m & f;* (*collateral deposited with a broker*) doble *m*
marginal ['mɑrdʒɪnəl] *adj* marginal
margin release *s* tecla de escape
margin stop *s* fijamárgenes *m,* cierrarrenglón *m,* cortarrenglón *m*
marigold ['mærɪ,gold] *s* clavelón *m;* (*Calendula*) maravilla, flamenquilla
marihuana o **marijuana** [,mɑrɪ'hwɑnə] *s* mariguana; grifa, grifo (Mex)
marina [mə'rinə] *s* dársena
marinate ['mærɪ,net] *tr* escabechar, marinar
marine [mə'rin] *adj* marino, marítimo || *s* marina; soldado de infantería de marina; **marines** infantería de marina; **tell that to the marines** (coll) cuénteselo a su abuela, a otro perro con ese hueso
mariner ['mærɪnər] *s* marino
marionette [,mærɪ•ə'nɛt] *s* marioneta, títere *m*
marital status ['mærɪtəl] *s* estado civil
maritime ['mærɪ,taɪm] *adj* marítimo
marjoram ['mɑrdʒərəm] *s* orégano; mejorana
mark [mɑrk] *s* marca, señal *f;* (*label*) marbete *m;* (*of punctuation*) punto; (*in an examination*) calificación, nota; (*used instead of signature by an illiterate person*) cruz *f,* signo; (*spot, stain*) mancha; (*coin*) marco; (*starting point in a race*) raya; (*target to shoot at*) blanco; **to be beside the mark** no venir al caso; **to hit the mark** dar en el blanco; **to leave one's mark** dejar memoria de sí; **to make one's mark** llegar a ser célebre; **to miss the mark** errar el tiro; **to toe the mark** ponerse en la raya; obedecer rigurosamente || *tr* marcar, señalar; dar nota a (*un alumno*); calificar (*un examen*); advertir, notar; **to mark down** poner por escrito; rebajar el precio de
mark'down' *s* reducción de precio
market ['mɑrkɪt] *s* mercado; **to bear the market** jugar a la baja; **to bull the market** jugar al alza; **to play the market** jugar a la bolsa; **to put on the market** lanzar al mercado || *tr* llevar al mercado; vender
marketable ['mɑrkɪtəbəl] *adj* comerciable, vendible
market basket *s* cesta para compras
marketing ['mɑrkɪtɪŋ] *s* mercología, mercadotecnia
market place *s* plaza del mercado
market price *s* precio corriente
market research *s* investigación mercológica
marking gauge ['mɑrkɪŋ] *s* gramil *m*
marks•man ['mɑrksmən] *s* (*pl* **-men** [mən]) tirador *m;* **a good marksman** un buen tiro
marksmanship ['mɑrksmən,ʃɪp] *s* puntería
mark'up' *s* aumento de precio
marl [mɑrl] *s* marga || *tr* margar
marmalade ['mɑrmə,led] *s* mermelada
marmot ['mɑrmət] *s* marmota
maroon [mə'run] *adj & s* marrón *m,* castaño obscuro || *tr* dejar abandonado (*en una isla desierta*)
marquee [mɑʃr'ki] *s* marquesina
marquess ['mɑrkwɪs] *s* marqués *m*
marque•try ['mɑrkətri] *s* (*pl* **-tries**) marquetería (*taracea*)
marquis ['mɑrkwɪs] *s* marqués *m*
marquise [mɑr'kiz] *s* marquesa; (*over the entrance to a hotel*) marquesina
marriage ['mærɪdʒ] *s* casamiento, matrimonio; (*married life; intimate union*) maridaje *m*
marriageable ['mærɪdʒəbəl] *adj* casadero
marriage portion *s* dote *m & f*
marriage rate *s* nupcialidad
married life ['mærid] *s* vida conyugal
marrow ['mæro] *s* médula, tuétano
mar•ry ['mæri] *v* (*pret & pp* **-ried**) *tr* casar (*el sacerdote o el juez a un hombre y una*

mujer); (*to take in marriage*) casar con, casarse con; (*to unite intimately*) maridar; **to get married to** casar con, casarse con || *intr* casar, casarse; **to marry into** emparentar con (*p.ej., una familia rica*); **to marry the second time** casarse en segundas nupcias

Mars [mɑrz] *s* Marte *m*

Marseille [mɑr'sɛ:j] *s* Marsella

marsh [mɑrʃ] *s* ciénaga, pantano

mar•shal ['mɑrʃəl] *s* cursor *m* de procesiones, maestro de ceremonias; (mil) mariscal *m;* (U.S.A.) oficial *m* de justicia || *v* (*pret & pp* **-shaled** o **-shalled;** *ger* **-shaling** o **-shalling**) *tr* conducir con ceremonia; ordenar, reunir (*los hechos de una argumentación*)

marsh mallow *s* (bot) malvavisco

marsh'mal'low *s* bombón *m* de merengue y gelatina; bombón de malvavisco

marsh•y ['mɑrʃi] *adj* (*comp* **-ier;** *super* **-iest**) pantanoso, palúdico

marten ['mɑrtən] *s* (*pine marten*) marta; (*beech marten*) garduña

martial ['mɑrʃəl] *adj* marcial

martial law *s* ley *f* marcial; **to be under martial law** estar en estado de guerra

Martian ['mɑrʃən] *adj & s* marciano

martin ['mɑrtɪn] *s* (orn) avión *m*

martinet [,mɑrtɪ'nɛt] o ['mɑrtɪ,nɛt] *s* ordenancista *mf*

martyr ['mɑrtər] *s* mártir *mf*

martyrdom ['mɑrtərdəm] *s* martirio

mar•vel ['mɑrvəl] *s* maravilla || *v* (*pret & pp* **-veled** o **-velled;** *ger* **-veling** o **-velling**) *intr* maravillarse; **to marvel at** maravillarse con o de

marvelous ['mɑrvələs] *adj* maravilloso

Marxist ['mɑrksɪst] *adj & s* marxista *mf*

masc. *abbr* **masculine**

mascara [mæs'kærə] *s* tinte *m* para las pestañas; rímel *m*

mascot ['mæskɑt] *s* mascota

masculine ['mæskjəlɪn] *adj & s* masculino

mash [mæʃ] *s* (*crushed mass*) masa; (*to form wort*) masa de cebada || *tr* machacar, majar

mashed potatoes [mæʃt] *spl* puré *m* de patatas

masher ['mæʃər] *s* (*device*) mano *f;* (slang) galanteador atrevido

mask [mæsk] o [mɑsk] *s* máscara; (*of beekeeper*) carilla; (*made from a corpse*) mascarilla; (*person*) máscara *mf;* (phot) desvanecedor *m* || *tr* enmascarar; (phot) desvanecer || *intr* enmascararse

masked ball [mæskt] *s* baile *m* de máscaras

masochism ['mæsə,kɪzəm] *s* masoquismo

masochist ['mæsəkɪst] *s* masoquista *mf*

masochistic [,mæsə'kɪstɪk] *adj* masoquista

mason ['mesən] *s* albañil *m* || **Mason** *s* masón *m*

mason•ry ['mesənri] *s* (*pl* **-ries**) albañilería || **Masonry** *s* masonería

masquerade [,mæskə'red] o [,mɑskə'red] *s* mascarada; (*costume, disguise*) máscara; (*false show*) farsa || *intr* enmascararse; **to masquerade as** disfrazarse de

masquerade ball *s* baile *m* de máscaras

mass [mæs] *s* masa; gran cantidad; (*bulk, heap*) mole *f; (something glimpsed, e.g., in the fog*) bulto informe; (*big splotch in a painting*) gran mancha; (*celebration of the Eucharist*) misa; **the masses** las masas || *tr* juntar, reunir; enmasar (*tropas*) || *intr* juntarse, reunirse

massacre ['mæsəkər] *s* carnicería, matanza || *tr* degollar, matar

massage [mə'sɑʒ] *s* masaje *m* || *tr* masar, masajear

masseur [mæ'sœr] *s* masajista *m*

masseuse [mæ'sœz] *s* masajista *f*

massive ['mæsɪv] *adj* macizo; sólido, imponente

mass media *spl* medios *spl* de comunicación

mass meeting *s* mitin *m* popular

mass production *s* fabricación en serie

mast [mæst] o [mɑst] *s* (*for a flag*) palo; (*of a ship*) palo, mástil *m;* (*food for swine*) bellotas, hayucos; **before the mast** como simple marinero

master ['mæstər] o ['mɑstər] *s* (*employer*) dueño, patrón *m;* (*male head of household*) amo; (*man who possesses some special skill; teacher*) maestro; (*commander of merchant vessel*) capitán *m;* (*title of respect for a boy*) señorito || *tr* dominar

master bedroom *s* alcoba de respeto

master blade *s* hoja maestra (*de una ballesta*)

master builder *s* maestro de obras

masterful ['mæstərfəl] o ['mɑstərfəl] *adj* hábil, experto; dominante, imperioso

master key *s* llave maestra

masterly ['mæstərli] o ['mɑstərli] *adj* magistral || *adv* magistralmente

master mechanic *s* maestro mecánico

mas'ter•mind' *s* mente directora || *tr* dirigir con gran acierto

master of ceremonies *s* maestro de ceremonias; (*in a night club, radio, etc.*) animador *m*

mas'ter•piece' *s* obra maestra

master stroke *s* golpe maestro

mas'ter•work' *s* obra maestra

master•y ['mæstəri] o ['mɑstəri] *s* (*pl* **-ies**) (*command, as of a subject*) dominio; ventaja, superioridad; (*skill*) maestría

mast'head' *s* (*of a newspaper*) cabecera editorial; (naut) tope *m*

masticate ['mæstɪ,ket] *tr* masticar

mastiff ['mæstɪf] o ['mɑstɪf] *s* mastín *m*

masturbate ['mæstər,bet] *tr* masturbar || *intr* masturbarse

masturbation [,mæstər'beʃən] *s* masturbación

mat [mæt] *s* (*for floor*) estera; (*for a cup, vase, etc.*) esterilla, ruedo; (*before a door*) felpudo; (*around a picture*) borde *m* de cartón || *v* (*pret & pp* **matted;** *ger* **matting**) *tr* (*to cover with matting*) esterar; enmarañar || *intr* enmarañarse

match [mætʃ] *s* fósforo; (*wick*) mecha; (*counterpart*) compañero; (*suitable partner in marriage*) partido; (*suitably associated* *pair*) pareja; (*game, contest*) match *m*, partido; **to be a match for** poder con, poder vencer; **to meet one's match** hallar la horma de su zapato || *tr* igualar; aparear, emparejar; hacer juego con; **to match someone for the drinks** jugarle a uno las bebidas || *intr* hacer juego, correr parejas; **to match** a juego, p.ej., **a chair to match** una silla a juego

match'box' *s* fosforera; (*of wax matches*) cerillera

matchless [ˈmætʃlɪs] *adj* incomparable, sin par

matchmaker [ˈmætʃ,mekər] *s* casamentero

mate [met] *s* compañero; (*e.g., of a shoe*) compañero, hermano; (*husband or wife*) cónyuge *mf;* (*to a female*) macho; (*to a male*) hembra; (*in chess*) mate *m;* (*naut*) piloto || *tr* aparear, casar; (*in chess*) dar jaque mate a; **to be well mated** hacer una buena pareja || *intr* aparearse, casarse

material [məˈtɪrɪ•əl] *adj* material; importante || *s* material *m;* (*what a thing is made of*) materia; (*cloth, fabric*) tela, género

materialism [məˈtɪrɪ•ə,lɪzəm] *s* materialismo

materialist [məˈtɪrɪ•əlɪst] *s* materialista *mf*

materialize [məˈtɪrɪ•ə,laɪz] *intr* realizarse

matériel [mə,tɪrɪˈɛl] *s* material *m;* material de guerra

maternal [məˈtʌrnəl] *adj* materno; (*motherly*) maternal

maternity [məˈtʌrnɪti] *s* maternidad

maternity hospital *s* casa de maternidad

math. *abbr* **mathematics**

mathematical [,mæθɪˈmætɪkəl] *adj* matemático

mathematician [,mæθɪməˈtɪʃən] *s* matemático

mathematics [,mæθɪˈmætɪks] *s* matemática, matemáticas

matinée [,mætɪˈne] *s* matinée *f*, función de tarde

mating season *s* época de celo

matins [ˈmætɪnz] *spl* maitines *mpl*

matriarch [ˈmetrɪ•ɑrk] *s* matriarca

matricidal [,metrɪˈsaɪdəl] *adj* matricida

matricide [ˈmetrɪ,saɪd] *s* (*act*) matricidio; (*person*) matricida *mf*

matriculate [məˈtrɪkjə,let] *tr* matricular || *intr* matricularse

matrimo•ny [ˈmætrɪ,moni] *s* (*pl* **-nies**) matrimonio

matron [ˈmetrən] *s* matrona

matronly [ˈmetrənli] *adj* matronal

matter [ˈmætər] *s* (*physical substance; pus*) materia; (*subject talked or written about*) asunto; (*reason, ground*) motivo; (*copy for printer*) material *m;* (*printed material*) impresos; **a matter of** cosa de, obra de; **for that matter** en cuanto a eso; **in the matter** al respecto; **no matter** no importa; **no matter when** cuando quiera; **no matter where** dondequiera; **what is the matter?** ¿qué hay?; **what is the matter with you?** ¿qué tiene Vd.? || *intr* importar

matter of course *s* cosa de cajón; **as a matter of course** por rutina

matter of fact *s*—**as a matter of fact** en realidad, en honor a la verdad

matter-of-fact [ˈmætərəv,fækt] *adj* prosaico, práctico, de poca imaginación

mattock [ˈmætək] *s* zapapico

mattress [ˈmætrɪs] *s* colchón *m*

mature [məˈtʃʊr] o [məˈtʊr] *adj* maduro; (*due*) pagadero, vencido || *tr* madurar || *intr* madurar; (*to become due*) (com) vencer

maturity [məˈtʃʊrɪti] o [məˈtʊrɪti] *s* madurez *f;* (com) vencimiento

maudlin [ˈmɔdlɪn] *adj* lacrimoso, sensiblero; chispo y lloroso

maul [mɔl] *tr* aporrear, maltratar

maulstick [ˈmɔl,stɪk] *s* tiento

maundy [ˈmɔndi] *s* lavatorio

Maundy Thursday *s* Jueves Santo

mausole•um [,mɔsəˈli•əm] *s* (*pl* **-ums** o **-a** [ə]) mausoleo

maw [mɔ] *s* (*of fowl*) buche *m;* (*of fish*) vejiga de aire

mawkish [ˈmɔkɪʃ] *adj* (*sickening*) empalagoso; (*sentimental*) sensiblero

max. *abbr* **maximum**

maxim [ˈmæksɪm] *s* máxima

maximum [ˈmæksɪməm] *adj & s* máximo

may *v aux* **it may be** puede ser; **may I come in?** ¿puedo entrar? **may you be happy!** ¡que seas feliz! || **May** *s* mayo

maybe [ˈmebi] o [ˈmebɪ] *adv* acaso, quizá, tal vez

May Day *s* primero de mayo; fiesta del primero de mayo

Mayday [ˈme,de] *interj* (*ships, airplanes*) ¡socorro!

mayhem [ˈmehɛm] o [ˈme•əm] *s* (law) mutilación criminal

mayonnaise [,me•əˈnez] *s* mayonesa

mayor [ˈme•ər] o [mɛr] *s* alcalde *m*

mayoress [ˈme•ərɪs] o [ˈmɛrɪs] *s* alcaldesa

May'pole' *s* mayo

Maypole dance *s* danza de cintas

May queen *s* maya

maze [mez] *s* laberinto

M.C. *abbr* **Master of Ceremonies, Member of Congress**

mdse. *abbr* **merchandise**

me [mi] *pron pers* me; mí; **to me** me; a mí; **with me** conmigo

meadow [ˈmɛdo] *s* prado, vega

mead'ow•land' *s* pradera

meager [ˈmigər] *adj* escaso, pobre; flaco, magro

meal [mil] *s* (*regular repast*) comida; (*edible grain coarsely ground*) harina

meal'time' *s* hora de comer

mean [min] *adj* (*intermediate*) medio; (*low in station or rank*) humilde, obscuro; (*shabby*) andrajoso, raído; (*stingy*) mezquino, tacaño; (*of poor quality*) inferior, pobre; (*small-minded*) vil, ruin, innoble; insignificante; (*vicious, as a horse*) arisco, mal intencionado; (coll) indisupuesto; (coll) avergonzado; (coll) de mal genio; **no mean** famoso, excelente || *s* promedio, término medio; **by all means** sí, por cierto, sin falta; **by means of** por medio de; **by no means** de ningún modo, en ningún caso; **means** bienes *mpl* de fortuna; (*agency*) medio, medios; **means to an end** paso para lograr un fin; **to live on one's means** vivar de sus rentas || *v* (*pret & pp* **meant** [mɛnt]) *tr* significar, querer decir; **to mean to** pensar || *intr*—**to mean well** tener buenas intenciones

meander [mɪ'ændər] *s* meandro || *intr* serpentear; vagar

meaning ['minɪŋ] *s* sentido, significado

meaningful ['minɪŋfəl] *adj* significativo

meaningless ['minɪŋlɪs] *adj* sin sentido

meanness ['minnɪs] *s* bajeza, vileza, ruindad; (*stinginess*) mezquindad; (*lowliness*) humildad, pobreza

mean'time' *adv* entretanto, mientras tanto || *s* medio tiempo; **in the meantime** entretanto, mientras tanto

mean'while' *adv & s* var de **meantime**

measles ['mizəlz] *s* sarampión *m;* (*German measles*) rubéola

mea•sly ['mizli] *adj* (*comp* **-slier;** *super* **-sliest**) sarampioso; (slang) despreciable, mezquino

measurable ['mɛʒərəbəl] *adj* medible

measure ['mɛʒər] *s* medida; (*step, procedure*) paso, gestión; (*legislative bill*) proyecto de ley; (*of verse*) pie *m;* (mus) compás *m;* **beyond measure** con exceso; **in a measure** hasta cierto punto; **in great measure** en gran parte; (*suit*) **to measure** hecho a la medida; **to take measures** tomar las medidas necesarias; **to take someone's measure** tomarle a uno las medidas || *tr* medir; recorrer (*cierta distancia*); **to measure out** medir; distribuir || *intr* medir

measurement ['mɛʒərmənt] *s* (*act of measuring*) medición; (*measuring; dimension*) medida

measuring glass *s* vaso graduado

meat [mit] *s* carne *f;* (*food in general*) manjar *m,* vianda; (*substance, gist*) meollo

meat ball *s* albóndiga

meat grinder *s* picador *m*

meat'hook' *s* garabato de carnicero

meat market *s* carnicería

meat•y ['miti] *adj* (*comp* **-ier;** *super* **-iest**) carnoso; (fig) jugoso, substancioso

Mecca ['mɛkə] *s* La Meca

mechanic [mɪ'kænɪk] *s* mecánico

mechanical [mɪ'kænɪkəl] *adj* mecánico, maquinal; (*machinelike*) (fig) maquinal

mechanical toy *s* juguete *m* de movimiento

mechanics [mɪ'kænɪks] *ssg* mecánica

mechanism ['mɛkə,nɪzəm] *s* mecanismo

mechanize ['mɛkə,naɪz] *tr* mecanizar

med. *abbr* **medicine, medieval**

medal ['mɛdəl] *s* medalla

medallion [mɪ'dæljən] *s* medallón *m*

meddle ['mɛdəl] *intr* meterse, entremeterse

meddler ['mɛdlər] *s* entremetido

meddlesome ['mɛdəlsəm] *adj* entremetido

media ['midɪ•ə] *abbr* **mass media**

median ['midɪ•ən] *adj* intermedio, medio || *s* punto medio, número medio

median strip *s* faja central o divisoria

mediate ['midɪ,et] *tr* dirimir (*una controversia*); reconciliar || *intr* (*to be in the middle*) mediar; (*to intervene to settle a dispute*) intervenir

mediation [,midɪ'eʃən] *s* mediación

mediator ['midɪ,etər] *s* mediador *m*

medical ['mɛdɪkəl] *adj* médico

medical student *s* estudiante *mf* de medicina

medicine ['mɛdɪsɪn] *s* (*science and art*) medicina; (*remedy, treatment*) medicina, medicamento

medicine cabinet *s* armario botiquín

medicine kit *s* botiquín *m*

medicine man *s* curandero, hechicero (*entre los pieles rojas*)

medieval [,midɪ'ivəl] o [,mɛdɪ'ivəl] *adj* medieval

medievalist [,midɪ'ivəlɪst] o [,mɛdɪ'ivəlɪst] *s* medievalista *mf*

mediocre ['midɪ,okər] o [,midɪ'okər] *adj* mediocre

mediocri•ty [,midɪ'ɑkrɪti] *s* (*pl* **-ties**) mediocridad

meditate ['mɛdɪ,tet] *tr & intr* meditar

Mediterranean [,mɛdɪtə'renɪ•ən] *adj & s* Mediterráneo

medi•um ['midɪ•əm] *adj* intermedio; a medio asar || *s* (*pl* **-ums** o **-a** [ə]) medio; (*in spiritualism*) medio, médium *m;* (*publication*) órgano; **through the medium of** por medio de

me'dium-range' *adj* de alcance medio

medlar ['mɛdlər] *s* (*tree and fruit*) níspero; (*fruit*) níspola

medley ['mɛdli] *s* mescolanza; (mus) popurrí *m*

medul•la [mɪ'dʌlə] *s* (*pl* **-lae** [li]) médula

meek [mik] *adj* dócil, manso

meekness ['miknɪs] *s* docilidad, mansedumbre

meerschaum ['mɪrʃəm] *s* ['mɪrʃɔm] *s* espuma de mar; pipa de espuma de mar

meet [mit] *adj* conveniente, a propósito || *s* concurso deportivo || *v* (*pret & pp* **met** [mɛt]) *tr* encontrar, encontrarse con; (*to make the acquaintance of*) conocer; empalmar con (*otro tren o autobús*); ir a esperar; honrar, pagar (*una letra*); hacer frente a (*gastos*); cumplir (*sus obligaciones*); batirse con; hallar (*la muerte*); tener (*mala suerte*); aparecer a (*la vista*) || *intr* encontrarse; reunirse; conocerse; **till we meet again** hasta la vista; **to meet with** encontrarse con; reunirse con; empalmar (*un tren*) con (*otro tren*); tener (*un accidente*)

meeting ['mitɪŋ] *s* junta, sesión; reunión; encuentro; (*of two rivers or roads*) confluencia; desafío, duelo

meeting of the minds *s* concierto de voluntades

meeting place *s* lugar *m* de reunión

megabucks ['mɛgə,bʌks] *s* (slang) vastas cantidades de dinero

megacycle ['mɛgə,saɪkəl] *s* megaciclo

megaphone ['mɛgə,fon] *s* megáfono

megohm ['mɛg,om] *s* megohmio

melancholia [,mɛlən'kolɪ•ə] *s* melancolía
melanchol•y ['mɛlən,kɑli] *adj* melancólico || *s* (*pl* **-ies**) melancolía
melee ['mele] o ['mɛle] *s* refriega, reyerta
mellow ['mɛlo] *adj* maduro, jugoso; suave, meloso; melodioso || *tr* suavizar || *intr* suavizarse
melodious [mɪ'lodɪ•əs] *adj* melodioso
melodramatic [,mɛlədrə'mætɪk] *adj* melodramático
melo•dy ['mɛlədi] *s* (*pl* **-dies**) melodía
melon ['mɛlən] *s* melón *m*
melt [mɛlt] *tr* derretir; fundir (*metales*); ablandar, aplacar || *intr* derretirse; fundirse; ablandarse, aplacarse; **to melt away** desvanecerse; **to melt into** convertirse gradualmente en; deshacerse en (*lágrimas*)
melt'down' *s* fusión; (*atomic reactor*) fusión del combustible por fisión no controlada
melting pot *s* crisol *m;* (fig) caldero de razas
member ['mɛmbər] *s* miembro
membership ['mɛmbər,ʃɪp] *s* asociación; (*e.g., of a club*) personal *m;* número de miembros
membrane ['mɛmbren] *s* membrana
memen•to [mɪ'mɛnto] *s* (*pl* **-tos** o **-toes**) recordatorio, prenda de recuerdo
mem•o ['mɛmo] *s* (*pl* **-os**) (coll) apunte *m,* membrete *m*
memoir ['mɛmwɑr] *s* memoria; biografía; **memoirs** memorias
memoran•dum [,mɛmə'rændəm] *s* (*pl* **-dums** o **-da** [də]) apunte *m,* membrete *m*
memorial [mɪ'morɪ•əl] *adj* conmemorativo || *s* monumento conmemorativo; (*petition*) memorial *m*
memorial arch *s* arco triunfal
Memorial Day *s* día *m* de los caídos
memorialize [mɪ'morɪ•ə,laɪz] *tr* conmemorar
memorize ['mɛmə,raɪz] *tr* aprender de memoria
memo•ry ['mɛməri] *s* (*pl* **-ries**) memoria; (*recall*) retentiva; (*computer*) memoria, almacenaje *m* o almacenamiento (de datos) **to commit to memory** encomendar a la memoria
menace ['mɛnɪs] *s* amenaza || *tr & intr* amenazar
ménage [me'naʒ] *s* casa, hogar *m;* economía doméstica
menagerie [mə'næʒəri] o [mə'nædʒəri] *s* casa de fieras; colección de fieras
mend [mɛnd] *s* remiendo; **to be on the mend** ir mejorando || *tr* (*to repair*) componer, reparar; (*to patch*) remendar; (*to improve*) reformar, mejorar || *intr* mejorar
mendacious [mɛn'deʃəs] *adj* mendaz
mendicant ['mɛndɪkənt] *adj & s* mendicante *mf*
mending ['mɛndɪŋ] *s* remiendo, zurcido
menfolk ['mɛn,fok] *spl* hombres *mpl*
menial ['minɪ•əl] *adj* bajo, servil || *s* criado, doméstico
menses ['mɛnsiz] *spl* menstruo
men's furnishings *spl* artículos para caballeros
men's room *s* lavabo para caballeros
menstruate ['mɛnstrʊ,et] *intr* menstruar
mental case *s* (coll) paciente *mf* mental; estrafalario
mental giant *s* (coll) genio
mental hygiene *s* higiene *f* mental
mental illness ['mɛntəl] *s* enfermedad mental
mental reservation *s* reserva mental
mental test *s* prueba de inteligencia
mention ['mɛnʃən] *s* mención || *tr* mencionar; **don't mention it** no hay de qué; **not to mention** sin contar
menu ['mɛnju] o ['menju] *s* menú *m,* lista de comidas; comida
meow [mɪ'aʊ] *s* maullido || *intr* maullar
Mephistophelian [,mɛfɪstə'filɪ•ən] *adj* mefistofélico
mercantile ['mʌrkən,til] o ['mʌrkən,taɪl] *adj* mercantil
mercenar•y ['mʌrsə,nɛri] *adj* mercenario || *s* (*pl* **-ies**) mercenario
merchandise ['mʌrtʃən,daɪz] *s* mercancías, mercaderías
merchant ['mʌrtʃənt] *adj* mercante || *s* mercante *m,* mercader *m*
merchant•man ['mʌrtʃəntmən] *s* (*pl* **-men** [mən]) buque *m* mercante
merchant marine *s* marina mercante
merchant vessel *s* buque *m* mercante
merciful ['mʌrsɪfəl] *adj* misericordioso
merciless ['mʌrsɪlɪs] *adj* despiadado, cruel, implacable
mercu•ry ['mʌrkjəri] *s* (*pl* **-ries**) mercurio, azogue *m;* columna de mercurio
mer•cy ['mʌrsi] *s* (*pl* **-cies**) misericordia; (*discretionary power*) merced *f;* **at the mercy of** a merced de
mere [mir] *adj* mero, puro; nada más que
meretricious [,mɛrɪ'trɪʃəs] *adj* postizo, de oropel; cursi, llamativo
merge [mʌrdʒ] *tr* enchufar, fusionar || *intr* enchufarse, fusionarse; convergir (*p.ej., dos caminos*); **to merge into** convertirse gradualmente en
merger ['mʌrdʒər] *s* fusión de empresas
meridian [mə'rɪdɪ•ən] *adj* meridiano; (el) más elevado || *s* meridiano; (fig) auge *m,* apogeo
meringue [mə'ræŋ] *s* merengue *m*
meri•no [mə'rino] *adj* merino || *s* (*pl* **-nos**) merino
merit ['mɛrɪt] *s* mérito || *tr* merecer
merlon ['mʌrlən] *s* almena, merlón *m*
mermaid ['mʌr,med] *s* sirena; (*girl who swims well*) ninfa marina
mer•man ['mʌr,mæn] *s* (*pl* **-men** [,mɛn]) tritón *m;* (*good swimmer*) tritón
merriment ['mɛrɪmənt] *s* alegría, regocijo
mer•ry ['mɛri] *adj* (*comp* **-rier;** *super* **-riest**) alegre, regocijado; **to make merry** divertirse
Merry Christmas *interj* ¡Felices Pascuas!, ¡Felices Navidades!
mer'ry-go-round' *s* tiovivo, caballito; serie ininterrumpida (de fiestas, tertulias, etc.)
mer'ry•mak'er *s* fiestero, jaranero
mesh [mɛʃ] *s* (*net, network*) red *f;* (*each open space of net*) malla; (*engagement of gears*)

engrane *m;* **meshes** celada, red *f* || *tr* enredar; (mach) engranar || *intr* enredarse; (mach) engranar

mess [mɛs] *s* (*dirty condition*) cochinería; fregado, lío, embrollo; (*meal for a group of people; such a group*) rancho; (*refuse*) bazofia; **to get into a mess** meterse en un lío; **to make a mess of** ensuciar, echar a perder || *tr* ensuciar; desarreglar; estropear, echar a perder || *intr* comer; **to mess around** (coll) ocuparse en fruslerías

message [ˈmɛsɪdʒ] *s* mensaje *m;* recado

messenger [ˈmɛsəndʒər] *s* mensajero; (*one who goes on errands*) mandadero; precursor *m*

mess hall *s* sala de rancho; comedor *m* de militares

Messiah [məˈsaɪ•ə] *s* Mesías *m*

mess kit *s* utensilios de rancho

mess'mate' *s* comensal *mf,* compañero de rancho

mess of pottage [ˈpɑtɪdʒ] *s* (Bib) plato de lentejas; cosa de ningún valor

Messrs. [ˈmɛsərz] *pl* de **Mr.**

mess•y [ˈmɛsi] *adj* (*comp* **-ier;** *super* **-iest**) desaliñado, desarreglado; sucio

met. *abbr* **metropolitan**

metal [ˈmɛtəl] *adj* metálico || *s* metal *m;* (fig) brío, ánimo

metallic [mɪˈtælɪk] *adj* metálico

metallurgy [ˈmɛtə,lʌrdʒi] *s* metalurgia

metal polish *s* limpiametales *m*

met'al•work' *s* metalistería

metamorpho•sis [,mɛtəˈmɔrfəsɪs] *s* (*pl* **-ses** [,siz]) metamorfosis *f*

metaphor [ˈmɛtə,fɔr] *s* metáfora

metaphorical [,mɛtəˈfɑrɪkəl] o [,mɛtəˈfɔrɪkəl] *adj* metafórico

metastasis [məˈtæstəsɪs] *s* metástasis *f*

metathe•sis [mɪˈtæθɪsɪs] *s* (*pl* **-ses** [,siz]) metátesis *f*

mete [mit] *tr*—**to mete out** repartir

meteor [ˈmitɪ•ər] *s* estrella fugaz; (*atmospheric phenomenon*) meteoro

meteorology [,mitɪ•əˈrɑlədʒi] *s* meteorología

meter [ˈmitər] *s* (*unit of measurement; verse*) metro; (*instrument for measuring gas, electricity, water*) contador *m;* (mus) compás *m,* tiempo || *tr* medir (con contador)

metering [ˈmitərɪŋ] *s* medición

meter reader *s* lector *m* (del contador)

methane [ˈmɛθen] *s* metano

method [ˈmɛθəd] *s* método

methodic(al) [mɪˈθɑdɪk(əl)] *adj* metódico

Methodist [ˈmɛθədɪst] *adj & s* metodista *mf*

Methuselah [miˈθuzələ] *s* Matusalén *m;* **to be as old as Methuselah** vivir más años que Matusalén

meticulous [mɪˈtɪkjələs] *adj* meticuloso, minucioso

metric(al) [ˈmɛtrɪk(əl)] *adj* métrico

metronome [ˈmɛtrə,nom] *s* metrónomo

metropolis [mɪˈtrɑpəlɪs] *s* metrópoli *f*

metropolitan [,mɛtrəˈpɑlɪtən] *adj* metropolitano || *s* (eccl) metropolitano

mettle [ˈmɛtəl] *s* ánimo, brío; **on one's mettle** dispuesto a hacer todo el esfuerzo posible

mettlesome [ˈmɛtəlsəm] *adj* animoso, brioso

mew [mju] *s* maullido; (orn) gaviota; **mews** (Brit) caballerizas alrededor de un corral

Mexican [ˈmɛksɪkən] *adj & s* mejicano

Mexico [ˈmɛksɪ,ko] *s* Méjico

mezzanine [ˈmɛzə,nin] *s* entresuelo

mfr. *abbr* **manufacturer**

mi. *abbr* **mile**

mica [ˈmaɪkə] *s* mica

microbe [ˈmaɪkrob] *s* microbio

microbiology [,maɪkrəbaɪˈɑlədʒi] *s* microbiología

microcard [ˈmaɪkrə,kɑrd] *s* microficha

microcomputer [ˈmaɪkrəkəm,pjutər] *s* microordenador *m*

microfarad [,maɪkrəˈfæræd] *s* microfaradio

microfilm [ˈmaɪkrə,fɪlm] *s* microfilm *m,* micropelícula || *tr* microfilmar

microgroove [ˈmaɪkrə,gruv] *adj* microsurco || *s* microsurco; disco microsurco

microphone [ˈmaɪkrə,fon] *s* micrófono

microprocessor [ˈmaɪkrə,prɑsɛsər] *s* microprocesador *m*

microscope [ˈmaɪkrə,skop] *s* microscopio

microscopic [,maɪkrəˈskɑpɪk] *adj* microscópico

microwave [ˈmaɪkrə,wev] *s* microonda

mid [mɪd] *adj* medio, p.ej., **in mid course** a medio camino

mid'day' *adj* del mediodía || *s* mediodia *m*

middle [ˈmɪdəl] *adj* medio || *s* centro, medio; (*of the human body*) cintura; **about the middle of** a mediados de; **in the middle of** en medio de

middle age *s* mediana edad || **Middle Ages** *spl* Edad Media

middle class *s* burguesía, clase media

Middle East *s* Oriente Medio

Middle English *s* el inglés medio

middle finger *s* dedo cordial, de en medio o del corazón

mid'dle•man' *s* (*pl* **-men** [,mɛn]) intermediario

middling [ˈmɪdlɪŋ] *adj* mediano, regular, pasadero || *adv* (coll) medianamente; (coll) así, así || *s* (*coarsely ground wheat*) cabezuela; **middlings** artículos de calidad o precio medianos

mid•dy [ˈmɪdi] *s* (*pl* **-dies**) (coll) aspirante *m* de marina; (*child's blouse*) marinera

middy blouse *s* marinera

midget [ˈmɪdʒɪt] *s* enano, liliputiense *mf*

midland [ˈmɪdlənd] *adj* de tierra adentro || *s* región central

mid'night' *adj* de medianoche; **to burn the midnight oil** quemarse las cejas || *s* medianoche *f*

midriff [ˈmɪdrɪf] *s* (anat) diafragma *m;* talle *m*

midship•man [ˈmɪd,ʃɪpmən] *s* (*pl* **-men** [mən]) guardia marina *m,* aspirante *m* de marina

midst [mɪdst] *s* centro; **in the midst of** en medio de; en lo más recio de

mid'stream' *s*—**in midstream** en pleno río
mid'sum'mer *s* pleno verano
mid'way' *adj* situado a mitad del camino || *adv* a mitad del camino || *s* mitad del camino; (*of a fair or exposition*) avenida central
mid'week' *s* mediados de la semana
mid'wife' *s* (*pl* **-wives**) partera, comadrona
mid'win'ter *s* pleno invierno
mid'year' *adj* de mediados del año || *s* mediados del año; **midyears** (coll) examen *m* de mediados del año escolar
mien [min] *s* aspecto, semblante *m*, porte *m*
miff [mɪf] *s* (coll) desavenencia || *tr* (coll) ofender
might [maɪt] *s* fuerza, poder *m;* **with might and main** con todas sus fuerzas, a más no poder || *v aux* se emplea para formar el modo potencial, p.ej., **she might not come** es posible que no venga
might•y ['maɪti] *adj* (*comp* **-ier;** *super* **-iest**) potente, poderoso; (*of great size*) grandísimo || *adv* (coll) muy
migrant worker ['maɪgrənt] *s* bracero migratorio
migrate ['maɪgret] *intr* emigrar
migratory ['maɪgrə,tori] *adj* migratorio
mil *abbr* **military, militia**
milch [mɪltʃ] *adj* lechero
mild [maɪld] *adj* blando, suave; dócil, manso; leve, ligero; (*climate*) templado
mildew ['mɪl,dju] *s* (*mold*) moho; (*plant disease*) mildeu *m*
mile [maɪl] *s* milla inglesa
mileage ['maɪlɪdʒ] *s* recorrido en millas
mileage ticket *s* billete contado por millas, semejante al billete kilométrico
mile'post' *s* poste miliario
mile'stone' *s* piedra miliaria; **to be a milestone** hacer época
milieu [mɪl'jʊ] *s* ambiente *m*, medio
militancy ['mɪlɪtənsi] *s* belicosidad
militant ['mɪlɪtənt] *adj* militante, belicoso
militarism ['mɪlɪtə,rɪzəm] *s* militarismo
militarist ['mɪlɪtərɪst] *adj & s* militarista *mf*
militarize ['mɪlɪtə,raɪz] *tr* militarizar
military ['mɪlɪ,tɛri] *adj* militar || *s* (los) militares
Military Academy *s* (U.S.A.) Academia General Militar
military police *s* policía militar
militate ['mɪlɪ,tet] *intr* militar
militia [mɪ'lɪʃə] *s* milicia
militia•man ['mɪ'lɪʃəmən] *s* (*pl* **-men** [mən]) miliciano
milk [mɪlk] *adj* lechero, de leche || *s* leche *f* || *tr* ordeñar; chupar (*los bienes de uno*); abusar de, explotar || *intr* dar leche
milk can *s* lechera
milk diet *s* régimen lácteo
milking ['mɪlkɪŋ] *s* ordeño
milk'maid' *s* lechera
milk•man ['mɪlk,mæn] *s* (*pl* **-men** [,mɛn]) lechero
milk of human kindness *s* compasión, humanidad
milk pail *s* ordeñadero
milk shake *s* batido de leche
milk'sop' *s* calzonazos *m*, marica *m*
milk'weed' *s* algodoncillo, vencetósigo
milk•y ['mɪlki] *adj* (*comp* **-ier;** *super* **-iest**) lechoso, lácteo
Milky Way *s* Vía Láctea
mill [mɪl] *s* (*for grinding grain*) molino; (*for making fabrics*) hilandería; (*for cutting wood*) aserradero; (*for refining sugar*) ingenio; (*for producing steel*) fábrica; (*to grind coffee*) molinillo; (*part of a dollar*) milésima; **to put through the mill** (coll) poner a prueba, someter a un entrenamiento riguroso || *tr* moler (*granos*); acordonar, cerrillar (*monedas*); laminar (*el acero*); triturar (*mena*); (*with a milling cutter*) fresar; batir (*chocolate*) || *intr*—**to mill about** o **around** arremolinarse
mill end *s* retal *m* de hilandería
millennial [mɪ'lɛnɪ•əl] *adj* milenario
millenni•um [mɪ'lɛnɪ•əm] *s* (*pl* **-ums** o **-a** [ə]) milenario, milenio
miller ['mɪlər] *s* molinero; (ent) polilla blanca
millet ['mɪlɪt] *s* mijo, millo
milliampere [,mɪlɪ'æmpɪr] *s* miliamperio
milligram ['mɪlɪ,græm] *s* miligramo
millimeter ['mɪlɪ,mitər] *s* milímetro
milliner ['mɪlɪnər] *s* modista *mf* de sombreros
millinery ['mɪlɪ,nɛri] o ['mɪlɪnəri] *s* artículos para sombreros de señora; confección de sombreros de señora; venta de sombreros de señora
millinery shop *s* sombrerería
milling ['mɪlɪŋ] *s* (*of grain*) molienda; (*of coins*) acordonamiento, cordoncillo; fresado
milling machine *s* fresadora
million ['mɪljən] *adj* millón de, millones de || *s* millón *m*
millionaire [,mɪljən'ɛr] *s* millonario
millionth ['mɪljənθ] *adj & s* millonésimo
millivolt ['mɪlɪ,volt] *s* vmilivoltio
mill'pond' *s* represa de molino
mill'race' *s* caz *m*
mill'stone' *s* muela de molino; (fig) carga pesada
mill wheel *s* rueda de molino
mill'work' *s* carpintería de taller
mime [maɪm] *s* mimo || *tr* remedar
Mimeograph ['mɪm•ə,græf] o ['mɪmɪ•ə,grɑf] *s* (trademark) mimeógrafo || *tr* mimeografiar
mim•ic ['mɪmɪk] *s* imitador *m*, remedador *m* || *v* (*pret & pp* **-icked;** *ger* **-icking)** *tr* imitar, remedar
mimic•ry ['mɪmɪkri] *s* (*pl* **-ries**) mímica, remedo
min. *abbr* **minimum, minute**
minaret [,mɪnə'rɛt] o ['mɪnə,rɛt] *s* alminar *m*, minarete *m*
mince [mɪns] *tr* desmenuzar; picar (*carne*) || *intr* andar remilgadamente; hablar remilgadamente
mince'meat' *s* cuajado, picadillo
mince pie *s* pastel relleno de carne picada con frutas

mind [maɪnd] *s* mente *f*, espíritu *m;* **to bear in mind** tener presente; **to be not in one's right mind** no estar en sus cabales; **to be of one mind** estar de acuerdo; **to be out of one's mind** estar fuera de juicio; **to change one's mind** mudar de parecer; **to go out of one's mind** volverse loco; **to have a mind to** tener ganas de; **to have in mind to** pensar en; **to have on one's mind** preocuparse con; **to lose one's mind** perder el juicio; **to make up one's mind** resolverse; **to my mind** a mi parecer; **to say whatever comes into one's mind** decir lo que se le viene a la boca; **to set one's mind on** resolverse a; **to slip one's mind** escaparse de la memoria; **to speak one's mind** decir su parecer; **with one mind** unánimamente || *tr* (*to take care of*) cuidar, estar al cuidado de; obedecer; fijarse en; sentir molestia por; **do you mind the smoke?** ¿le molesta el humo?; **mind your own business** no se meta Vd. en lo que no le toca || *intr* tener inconveniente; tener cuidado; **never mind** no se preocupe, no se moleste

mind'-bend'ing *adj* (coll) alucinante

mind'-blow'ing *adj* (coll) alucinante en exceso

mind'-bog'gling *adj* deslumbrante; abrumador

mindful ['maɪndfəl] *adj* atento; **mindful of** atento a, cuidadoso de

mind reader *s* adivinador *m* del pensamiento ajeno, lector *m* mental

mind reading *s* adivinación del pensamiento ajeno, lectura de la mente

mine [maɪn] *pron poss* el mío; mío || *s* mina; **to work a mine** beneficiar una mina || *tr* minar; beneficiar (*un terreno*); extraer (*mineral, carbón, etc.*) || *intr* minar; abrir minas

mine field *s* campo de minas

mine layer *s* buque *m* portaminas, lanzaminas *m*

miner ['maɪnər] *s* minero; (mil, nav) minador *m*

mineral ['mɪnərəl] *adj & s* mineral *m*

mineralogy [,mɪnə'rælədʒi] *s* mineralogía

mineral resources *spl* riquezas del subsuelo

mineral wool *s* lana de escorias

mine sweeper *s* dragaminas *m*

mingle ['mɪŋgəl] *tr* mezclar, confundir || *intr* mezclarse, confundirse; asociarse

miniature ['mɪnɪ•ətʃər] o ['mɪnɪtʃər] *s* miniatura; **to paint in miniature** miniar, pintar de miniatura

miniaturization [,mɪnɪ•ətʃərɪ'zeʃən] o [,mɪnɪtʃərɪ'zeʃən] *s* miniaturización

minicomputer ['mɪnɪkəm,pjutər] *s* miniordenador *m*

minimal ['mɪnɪməl] *adj* mínimo

minimize ['mɪnɪ,maɪz] *tr* empequeñecer

minimum ['mɪnɪməm] *adj & s* mínimo

minimum wage *s* jornal mínimo

mining ['maɪnɪŋ] *adj* minero || *s* mineraje *m*, minería; (nav) minado

minion ['mɪnjən] *s* paniaguado

minion of the law *s* esbirro, polizonte *m*

miniskirt ['mɪnɪ,skʌrt] *s* minifalda

minister ['mɪnɪstər] *s* ministro; pastor *m* protestante || *tr & intr* ministrar

ministerial ['mɪnɪs'tɪrɪ•əl] *adj* ministerial

minis•try ['mɪnɪstri] *s* (*pl* **-tries**) ministerio

mink [mɪŋk] *s* visón *m*

minnow ['mɪno] *s* pececillo; (ichth) foxino

minor ['maɪnər] *adj* (*smaller*) menor; de menor importancia; (*younger*) menor de edad; (mus) menor || *s* menor *m* de edad; (educ) asignatura secundaria

Minorca [mɪ'nɔrkə] *s* Menorca

Minorcan [mɪ'nɔrkən] *adj & s* menorquín *m*

minori•ty [maɪ'nɔrɪti] *adj* minoritario || *s* (*pl* **-ties**) (*being under age; smaller number or part*) minoría; (*less than full age*) minoridad

minstrel ['mɪnstrəl] *s* (*retainer who sang and played for his lord*) ministril *m;* (*medieval musician and poet*) juglar *m*, trovador *m;* (U.S.A.) cantor cómico disfrazado de negro

minstrel•sy ['mɪnstrəlsi] *s* (*pl* **-sies**) juglaría; compañía de juglares; poesía trovadoresca

mint [mɪnt] *s* casa de moneda; (*plant*) menta, hierbabuena; montón *m* de dinero; fuente *f* inagotable || *tr* acuñar; (fig) inventar

minuet [,mɪnju'ɛt] *s* minué *m*, minuete *m*

minus ['maɪnəs] *adj* menos || *prep* menos; falto de, sin || *s* menos *m*

minute [maɪ'njut] o [maɪ'nut] *adj* diminuto, menudo || ['mɪnɪt] *s* minuto; (*short space of time*) momento; **minutes** acta; **to write up the minutes** levantar acta; **up to the minute** al corriente; de última hora

minute hand ['mɪnɪt] *s* minutero

minutiae [mɪ'njuʃɪ,i] o [mɪ'nuʃɪ,i] *spl* minucias

minx [mɪŋks] *s* moza descarada

miracle ['mɪrəkəl] *s* milagro

miracle play *s* auto

miraculous [mɪ'rækjələs] *adj* milagroso

mirage [mɪ'rɑʒ] *s* espejismo

mire [maɪr] *s* fango, lodo

mirror ['mɪrər] *s* espejo; (aut) retrovisor *m* || *tr* reflejar

mirth [mʌrθ] *s* alegría, regocijo

mir•y ['maɪri] *adj* (*comp* **-ier;** *super* **-iest**) fangoso, lodoso; sucio

misadventure [,mɪsəd'vɛntʃər] *s* desgracia, contratiempo

misanthrope ['mɪsən,θrop] *s* misántropo

misanthropy [mɪs'ænθrəpi] *s* misantropía

misapprehension [,mɪsæprɪ'hɛnʃən] *s* malentendido

misappropriation [,mɪsə,proprɪ'eʃən] *s* malversación

misbehave [,mɪsbɪ'hev] *intr* conducirse mal, portarse mal

misbehavior [,mɪsbɪ'hevɪ•ər] *s* mala conducta, mal comportamiento

misc. *abbr* **miscellaneous, miscellany**

miscalculation [,mɪskælkjə'leʃən] *s* mal cálculo

miscarriage [mɪs'kærɪdʒ] *s* aborto, malparto; fracaso, malogro; (*of a letter*) extravío

miscar•ry [mɪs'kæri] *v* (*pret & pp* **-ried**) *intr* abortar, malparir; malograrse; extraviarse (*una carta*)
miscellaneous [,mɪsə'lenɪ•əs] *adj* misceláneo
miscella•ny ['mɪsə,leni] *s* (*pl* **-nies**) miscelánea
mischief ['mɪstʃɪf] *s* (*harm*) daño, mal *m; (disposition to annoy*) malicia; (*prankishness*) travesura
mis'chief-mak'er *s* malsín *m,* cizañero
mischievous ['mɪstʃɪvəs] *adj* dañoso, malo; malicioso; travieso
misconception [,mɪskən'sɛpʃən] *s* concepto erróneo, mala interpretación
misconduct [mɪs'kɑndəkt] *s* mala conducta
misconstrue [,mɪskən'stru] o [mɪs'kɑnstru] *tr* interpretar mal
miscount [mɪs'kaʊnt] *s* cuenta errónea || *tr & intr* contar mal
miscue [mɪs'kju] *s* (*in billiards*) pifia; (*slip*) pifia || *intr* pifiar; (theat) equivocarse de apunte
misdate [mɪs'det] *tr* fechar erróneamente
mis•deal ['mɪs,dil] *s* repartición errónea || [mɪs'dil] *v* (*pret & pp* **-dealt** ['dɛlt]) *tr & intr* repartir mal
misdeed [mɪs'did] o ['mɪs,did] *s* malhecho, fechoría
misdemeanor [,mɪsdɪ'minər] *s* mala conducta; (law) delito de menor cuantía
misdirect [,mɪsdɪ'rɛkt] o [,mɪsdaɪ'rɛkt] *tr* dirigir erradamente; hacer perder el camino
misdoing [mɪs'du•ɪŋ] *s* mala acción
miser ['maɪzər] *s* avaro, verrugo; codo (Guat, Mex)
miserable ['mɪzərəbəl] *adj* miserable; (coll) achacoso, indispuesto
miserly ['maɪzərli] *adj* avariento, mezquino
miser•y ['mɪzəri] *s* (*pl* **-ies**) miseria; pelazón *f*
misfeasance [mɪs'fizəns] *s* (law) fraude *m*
misfire [mɪs'faɪr] *s* falla de tiro; (*of internal-combustion engine*) falla de encendido || *intr* fallar (*un arma de fuego, el encendido de un motor*)
mis•fit ['mɪs,fɪt] *s* vestido mal cortado; cosa que no encaja bien; persona mal adaptada a su ambiente || [mɪs'fɪt] *v* (*pret & pp* **-fitted;** *ger* **-fitting**) *tr & intr* encajar mal, sentar mal
misfortune [mɪs'fɔrtʃən] *s* desgracia
misgiving [mɪs'gɪvɪŋ] *s* mal presentimiento, rescoldo
misgovern [mɪs'gʌvərn] *tr* desgobernar
misguidance [mɪs'gaɪdəns] *s* error *m,* extravío
misguided [mɪs'gaɪdɪd] *adj* descarriado, malaconsejado
mishap ['mɪshæp] o [mɪs'hæp] *s* accidente *m,* percance *m*
mishmash ['mɪʃ,mæʃ] *s* baturillo; mezcolanza
misinform [,mɪsɪn'fɔrm] *tr* dar informes erróneos a
misinterpret [,mɪsɪn'tɛrprɪt] *tr* interpretar mal
misjudge [mɪs'dʒʌdʒ] *tr & intr* juzgar mal
mis•lay [mis'le] *v* (*pret & pp* **-laid** [,led]) *tr* extraviar, perder; (*among one's papers*) traspapelar
mis•lead [mɪs'lid] *v* (*pret & pp* **-led** [,lɛd]) *tr* (*to lead astray*) extraviar, descaminar; (*to lead into wrongdoing*) seducir, inducir al mal; (*to deceive*) engañar
misleading [mɪs'lɪdɪŋ] *adj* engañoso
mismanagement [mɪs'mænɪdʒmənt] *s* mala administración, desgobierno
misnomer [mɪs'nomər] *s* nombre impropio, mal nombre
misplace [mɪs'ples] *tr* colocar fuera de su lugar; colocar mal; (*to mislay*) (coll) extraviar, perder
misprint ['mɪs,prɪnt] *s* errata de imprenta || [mɪs'prɪnt] *tr* imprimir con erratas
mispronounce [,mɪsprə'naʊns] *tr* pronunciar mal
mispronunciation [,mɪsprə,nʌnsɪ'eʃən] o [,mɪsprə,nʌnʃɪ'eʃən] *s* pronunciación incorrecta
misquote [mɪs'kwot] *tr* citar equivocadamente
misrepresent [,mɪsrɛprɪ'zɛnt] *tr* tergiversar
miss [mɪs] *s* falta, error *m;* fracaso, malogro; tiro errado; jovencita, muchacha || *tr* echar de menos; perder (*el tren, la función, la oportunidad*); errar (*el blanco; la vocación*); no entender, no comprender; omitir; no ver; no dar con, no encontrar; librarse de (*p.ej., la muerte*); escapársele a uno, p.ej., **I missed what you said** se me escapó lo que dijo Vd.; por poco, p.ej., **the car missed hitting me** el coche por poco me atropella || *intr* fallar; errar el blanco; malograrse || **Miss** *s* señorita
missal ['mɪsəl] *s* misal *m*
misshapen [mɪs'ʃepən] *adj* deforme, contrahecho
missile ['mɪsɪl] *adj* arrojadizo || *s* arma arrojadiza; proyectil *m;* proyectil dirigido, misil *m*
missile gap *s* desigualidad de armas proyectiles poseídas por dos potencias
missil(e)ry ['mɪsəlri] *s* cohetería; ciencia de las armas proyectiles
missing ['mɪsɪŋ] *adj* extraviado, perdido; desaparecido; ausente; **to be missing** hacer falta; haber desaparecido
missing link *s* hombre *m* mono
missing persons *spl* desaparecidos
mission ['mɪʃən] *s* misión; casa de misión
missionar•y ['mɪʃən,ɛri] *adj* misional || *s* (*pl* **-ies**) (*one sent to work to propagate his faith*) misionario, misionero; (*on a political or diplomatic mission*) misionario
missive ['mɪsɪv] *adj* misivo || *s* misiva
mis•spell [mɪs'spɛl] *v* (*pret & pp* **-spelled** o **-spelt** ['spɛlt]) *tr & intr* deletrear mal, escribir mal
misspelling [mɪs'spɛlɪŋ] *s* falta de ortografía
misspent [mɪs'spɛnt] *adj* malgastado
misstatement [mɪs'stetmənt] *s* relación equivocada, relación falsa
misstep [mɪs'stɛp] *s* paso falso; (*slip in conduct*) resbalón *m*

miss•y [ˈmɪsi] *s* (*pl* **-ies**) (coll) señorita
mist [mɪst] *s* neblina; (*of tears*) velo; (*fine spray*) vapor *m*
mis•take [mɪsˈtek] *s* error *m*, equivocación; **and no mistake** sin duda alguna; **by mistake** por descuido; **to make a mistake** equivocarse || *v* (*pret* **-took** [ˈtʊk]; *pp* **-taken**) *tr* tomar (*por otro; por lo que no es*); entender mal; **to be mistaken for** equivocarse con
mistaken [mɪsˈtekən] *adj* (*person*) equivocado; (*idea*) erróneo; (*act*) desacertado
mistakenly [mɪsˈtekənli] *adv* equivocadamente, por error
mistletoe [ˈmɪsəl,to] *s* (*Viscum album*) muérdago; (*Phoradendron flavescens, used in Christmas decorations in the U.S.A.*) cabellera
mistreat [mɪsˈtrit] *tr* maltratar
mistreatment [mɪsˈtritmənt] *s* maltratamiento
mistress [ˈmɪstrɪs] *s* (*of a household*) ama, dueña; moza, querida, manceba; (Brit) maestra de escuela
mistrial [mɪsˈtraɪ•əl] *s* pleito viciado de nulidad
mistrust [mɪsˈtrʌst] *s* desconfianza || *tr* desconfiar de || *intr* desconfiar
mistrustful [mɪsˈtrʌstfəl] *adj* desconfiado
mist•y [ˈmɪsti] *adj* (*comp* **-ier;** *super* **-iest**) brumoso, neblinoso; indistinto
misunder•stand [,mɪsʌndərˈstænd] *v* (*pret & pp* **-stood** [ˈstʊd]) *tr* no comprender, entender mal
misunderstanding [,mɪsʌndərˈstændɪŋ] *s* malentendido; (*disagreement*) desavenencia
misuse [mɪsˈjus] *s* abuso, mal uso; (*of funds*) malversación || [mɪsˈjuz] *tr* abusar de, emplear mal; malversar (*fondos*)
misword [mɪsˈwʌrd] *tr* redactar mal
mite [maɪt] *s* (*small contribution*) óbolo; (*small amount*) pizca; (ent) ácaro
miter [ˈmaɪtər] *s* mitra; (carp) inglete *m* || *tr* cortar ingletes en; juntar con junta a inglete
miter box *s* caja de ingletes
mitigate [ˈmɪtɪ,get] *tr* mitigar, atenuar, paliar
mitten [ˈmɪtən] *s* confortante *m*, mitón *m*
mix [mɪks] *tr* mezclar; amasar (*una torta*); aderezar (*ensalada*); **to mix up** equivocar, confundir || *intr* mezclarse; asociarse
mixed [mɪkst] *adj* mixto, mezclado; (*e.g., candy*) variados; (coll) confundido
mixed company *s* reunión de personas de ambos sexos
mixed drink *s* bebida mezclada
mixed feelings *s* concepto vacilante
mixer [ˈmɪksər] *s* (*of concrete*) mezcladora, hormigonera; **to be a good mixer** (coll) tener don de gentes
mixture [ˈmɪkstʃər] *s* mezcla, mixtura
mix'-up' *s* confusión; enredo, lío; (*of people*) equivocación
mizzen [ˈmɪzən] *s* mesana
mo. *abbr* **month**
M.O. *abbr* **money order**
moan [mon] *s* gemido || *intr* gemir
moat [mot] *s* foso
mob [mɑb] *s* chusma, populacho; (*crowd bent on violence*) muchedumbre airada || *v* (*pret & pp* **mobbed;** *ger* **mobbing**) *tr* asaltar, atropellar
mobile [ˈmobɪl] o [ˈmobil] *adj* móvil
mobility [moˈbɪlɪti] *s* movilidad
mobilization [,mobɪlɪˈzeʃən] *s* movilización
mobilize [ˈmobɪ,laɪz] *tr* movilizar || *intr* movilizar, movilizarse
mob rule *s* gobierno del populacho
mobster [ˈmɑbstər] *s* (slang) gamberro, pandillero, gángster
mobsterism [ˈmɑbstə,rɪzəm] *s* gangsterismo; acciones de los gangsters
moccasin [ˈmɑkəsɪn] *s* mocasín *m*
Mocha coffee [ˈmokə] *s* moca *m*, café *m* de moca
mock [mɑk] *adj* simulado, fingido || *s* burla, mofa || *tr* burlarse de, mofarse de; despreciar; engañar || *intr* mofarse; **to mock at** mofarse de
mocker•y [ˈmɑkəri] *s* (*pl* **-ies**) burla, mofa, escarnio; (*subject of derision*) hazmerreír *m;* (*poor imitation*) mal remedo; (*e.g., of justice*) negación
mock'ing•bird' *s* burlón *m*, sinsonte *m*
mock orange *s* jeringuilla, celinda
mock privet *s* olivillo
mock turtle soup *s* sopa de cabeza de ternera
mock'-up' *s* maqueta
mode [mod] *s* modo, manera; (*fashion*) moda; (gram) modo
mod•el [ˈmɑdəl] *adj* modelo, p.ej., **model city** ciudad modelo || *s* modelo || *v* (*pret & pp* **-eled** o **-elled;** *ger* **-eling** o **-elling**) *tr* (*to fashion in clay, wax, etc.*) modelar || *intr* modelarse; servir de modelo
model airplane *s* aeromodelo
mod'el-air'plane builder *s* aeromodelista *mf*
model-airplane building *s* aeromodelismo
model sailing *s* navegación de modelos a vela
moderate [ˈmɑdərɪt] *adj* moderado; (*tiempo*) templado; (*precio*) módico || [mɑdə,ret] *tr* moderar; presidir (*una asamblea*) || *intr* moderarse
moderator [ˈmɑdə,retər] *s* (*over an assembly*) presidente *m;* (*mediator*) árbitro; (telv) presentador *m*, presentadora; (*for slowing down neutrons*) moderador *m*
modern [mɑdərn] *adj* moderno
modernize [ˈmɑdər,naɪz] *tr* modernizar
modest [ˈmɑdɪst] *adj* modesto
modes•ty [ˈmɑdɪsti] *s* (*pl* **-ties**) modestia
modicum [ˈmɑdɪkəm] *s* pequeña cantidad
modifier [ˈmɑdɪ,faɪ•ər] *s* (gram) modificante *m*
modi•fy [ˈmɑdɪ,faɪ] *v* (*pret & pp* **-fied**) *tr* modificar
modish [ˈmodɪʃ] *adj* de moda, elegante
modulate [ˈmɑdʒə,let] *tr & intr* modular
modulation [,mɑdʒəˈleʃən] *s* modulación
mohair [ˈmo,hɛr] *s* mohair *m* (*pelo de cabra de Angora*)
Mohammedan [moˈhæmɪdən] *adj & s* mahometano

Mohammedanism [mo'hæmɪdə,nɪzəm] *s* mahometismo
moist [mɔɪst] *adj* húmedo, mojado; (*weather*) lluvioso; (*eyes*) lagrimoso
moisten ['mɔɪsən] *tr* humedecer ‖ *intr* humedecerse
moisture ['mɔɪstʃər] *s* humedad
molar ['molər] *s* diente *m* molar
molasses [mə'læsɪz] *s* melaza
molasses candy *s* melcocha
mold [mold] *s* molde *m;* cosa moldeada; (*shape*) forma; (*fungus*) moho; (*humus*) mantillo; (fig) carácter *m,* índole *f* ‖ *tr* amoldar, moldear; (*to make moldy*) enmohecer ‖ *intr* enmohecerse
molder ['moldər] *s* moldeador *m* ‖ *intr* convertirse en polvo, consumirse
molding ['moldɪŋ] *s* moldeado; (*cornice, shaped strip of wood, etc.*) moldura
mold•y ['moldi] *adj* (*comp* **-ier;** *super* **-iest**) (*overgrown with mold*) mohoso; (*stale*) rancio, pasado
mole [mol] *s* (*breakwater*) rompeolas *m;* (*inner harbor*) dársena; (*spot on skin*) lunar *m;* (*small mammal*) topo
molecular physics [mə'lɛkjələr] *s* física molecular
molecular weight *s* peso molecular
molecule ['malɪ,kjul] *s* molécula
mole'hill' *s* topinera
mole'skin' *s* piel *f* de topo, molesquina
molest [mə'lɛst] *tr* molestar; faltar al respeto a (*una mujer*)
moll [mal] *s* (slang) mujer *f* del hampa; (slang) ramera
molli•fy ['malɪ,faɪ] *v* (*pret & pp* **-fied**) *tr* apaciguar, aplacar
mollusk ['maləsk] *s* molusco
mollycoddle ['malɪ,kadəl] *s* mantecón *m,* marica *m* ‖ *tr* consentir, mimar
molt [molt] *s* muda ‖ *intr* hacer la muda
molten ['moltən] *adj* fundido, derretido; fundido, vaciado
molybdenum [mə'lɪbdɪnəm] o [,malɪb'dinəm] *s* molibdeno
moment ['momənt] *s* momento; **at any moment** de un momento a otro
momentary ['momən,tɛri] *adj* momentáneo
momentous [mo'mɛntəs] *adj* importante, grave
momen•tum [mo'mɛntəm] *s* (*pl* **-tums** o **-ta** [tə]) ímpetu *m;* (mech) cantidad de movimiento
monarch ['manərk] *s* monarca *m*
monarchic(al) [mə'narkɪk(əl)] *adj* monárquico
monarchist ['manərkɪst] *adj & s* monárquico, monarquista *mf*
monar•chy ['manərki] *s* (*pl* **-chies**) monarquía
monaster•y ['manəs,tɛri] *s* (*pl* **-ies**) monasterio
monastic [mə'næstɪk] *adj* monástico
monasticism [mə'næstɪ,sɪzəm] *s* monaquismo
Monday ['mʌndi] *s* lunes *m*
monetary ['manɪ,tɛri] *adj* monetario; pecuniario
money ['mʌni] *s* dinero; **to make money** ganar dinero; dar dinero (*una empresa*)
mon'ey•bag' *s* monedero, talega; **moneybags** (*wealth*) (coll) talegas; (*wealthy person*) (coll) ricacho
moneychanger ['mʌni,tʃendʒər] *s* cambista *mf*
moneyed ['mʌnid] *adj* adinerado
moneylender ['mʌni,lɛndər] *s* prestamista *mf*
mon'ey•mak'er *s* acaudalador *m;* (fig) manantial *m* de beneficios
money order *s* giro postal, orden *m* de pago
Mongol ['maŋgəl] *adj & s* mogol *mf*
Mongolian [maŋ'golɪ•ən] *adj & s* mogol *mf*
mon•goose ['maŋgus] *s* (*pl* **-gooses**) mangosta
mongrel ['mʌŋgrəl] *adj & s* mestizo
monitor ['manɪtər] *s* monitor *m* ‖ *tr* controlar (*la señal*); escuchar (*radio-transmisiones*); superentender
monk [mʌŋk] *s* monje *m*
monkey ['mʌŋki] *s* mono; simio; **to make a monkey of** tomar el pelo a ‖ *intr*—**to monkey around** haraganear; **to monkey with** ajar, manosear
mon'key•shine' *s* (slang) monería, monada, payasada
monkey wrench *s* llave inglesa
monkhood ['maŋkhud] *s* monacato; los monjes
monkshood ['maŋks•hud] *s* cogulla de fraile
monocle ['manəkəl] *s* monóculo
monogamy [mə'nagəmi] *s* monogamia
monogram ['manə,græm] *s* monograma *m*
monograph ['manə,græf] *s* monografía
monolithic [,manə'lɪθɪk] *adj* monolítico
monologue ['manə,lɔg] *s* monólogo
monomania [,manə'menɪ•ə] *s* monomanía
monomial [mə'nomɪ•əl] *s* monomio
monopolize [mə'napə,laɪz] *tr* monopolizar; acaparar (*p.ej., la conversación*)
monopo•ly [mə'napəli] *s* (*pl* **-lies**) monopolio
monorail ['manə,rel] *s* monorriel *m*
monosyllable ['manə,sɪləbəl] *s* monosílabo
monotheist ['manə,θi•ɪst] *adj & s* monoteísta *mf*
monotonous [me'nətənəs] *adj* monótono
monotony [me'nətəni] *s* monotonía
monotype ['manə,taɪp] *s* (*machine; method*) monotipia; (*machine*) monotipo
monotype operator *s* monotipista *mf*
monoxide [mə'naksaɪd] *s* monóxido
monseigneur [,mansen'jœr] *s* monseñor *m*
monsignor [man'sinjər] *s* (*pl* **monsignors** o **monsignori** [,mɔnsi'njori]) (eccl) monseñor *m*
monsoon [man'sun] *s* monsón *m*
monster ['manstər] *adj* monstruoso ‖ *s* monstruo
monstrance ['manstrəns] *s* custodia, ostensorio
monstrosi•ty [man'strasɪti] *s* (*pl* **-ties**) monstruosidad; esperpento
monstrous ['manstrəs] *adj* monstruoso

month [mʌnθ] *s* mes *m*
month•ly [ˈmʌnθli] *adj* mensual ‖ *adv* mensualmente ‖ *s* (*pl* **-lies**) revista mensual; **monthlies** (coll) reglas
monument [ˈmɑnjəmənt] *s* monumento
moo [mu] *s* mugido ‖ *intr* mugir
mood [mud] *s* humor *m*, genio; (gram) modo; **moods** accesos de mal humor
mood•y [ˈmudi] *adj* (*comp* **-ier;** *super* **-iest**) triste, hosco, melancólico; caprichoso, veleidoso
moon [mun] *s* luna
moon'beam' *s* rayo lunar
moon'light' *s* claror *m* de luna, luz *f* de la luna
moon'light'ing *s* multiempleo, pluriempleo
moon'sail' *s* (naut) monterilla
moon'shine' *s* luz *f* de la luna; (*idle talk*) cháchara, música celestial; (coll) whisky destilado ilegalmente
moon shot *s* lanzamiento a la Luna
moor [mʊr] *s* brezal *m*, páramo ‖ *tr* (naut) amarrar ‖ *intr* (naut) echar las amarras ‖ **Moor** *s* moro
Moorish [ˈmʊrɪʃ] *adj* moro
moor'land' *s* brezal *m*
moose [mus] *s* (*pl* **moose**) alce *m* de América
moot [mut] *adj* discutible, dudoso
mop [mɑp] *s* aljofifa, fregasuelos *m*, estropajo; (*of hair*) espesura ‖ *v* (*pret & pp* **mopped;** *ger* **mopping**) *tr* aljofifar; enjugarse (*la frente con un pañuelo*); **to mop up** limpiar de enemigos
mope [mop] *intr* andar abatido, entregarse a la melancolía
moped [ˈmopɛd] *s* motoneta
mopish [ˈmopɪʃ] *adj* abatido, melancólico
moral [ˈmɑrəl] o [ˈmɔrəl] *adj* moral ‖ *s* (*of a fable*) moraleja, moral *f;* **morals** (*ethics; conduct*) moral *f*
moral certainty *s* evidencia moral
morale [məˈræl] o [məˈrɑl] *s* moral *f* (*estado de ánimo, confianza en sí mismo*)
morali•ty [məˈrælɪti] *s* (*pl* **-ties**) moralidad
morals charge *s* acusación por delito sexual
morass [məˈræs] *s* pantano
moratori•um [,mɔrəˈtorɪ•əm] o [,mɑrəˈtorɪ•əm] *s* (*pl* **-ums** o **-a** [ə]) *s* moratoria
morbid [ˈmɔrbɪd] *adj* (*feelings, curiosity*) malsano; (*gruesome*) horripilante; (*pertaining to disease; pathologic*) morboso
mordacious [mɔrˈdeʃəs] *adj* mordaz
mordant [ˈmɔrdənt] *adj* mordaz ‖ *s* mordiente *m*
more [mor] *adj & adv* más; **more and more** cada vez más; **more than** más que; (*followed by numeral*) más de; (*followed by verb*) más de lo que ‖ *s* más *m*
more•o'ver *adv* además, por otra parte
Moresque [moˈrɛsk] *adj* moro; (archit) árabe ‖ *s* estilo árabe
morgue [mɔrg] *s* depósito de cadáveres
moribund [ˈmɔri,bʌnd] o [ˈmɑrɪ,bʌnd] *adj* moribundo
Moris•co [məˈrɪsko] *adj* morisco, moro ‖ *s* (*pl* **-cos** o **-coes**) moro; moro de España; (*offspring of mulatto and Spaniard, in Mexico*) morisco
morning [ˈmɔrnɪŋ] *adj* matinal ‖ *s* mañana; (*time between midnight and dawn*) madrugada; **in the morning** de mañana, por la mañana
morning coat *s* chaqué *m*
morn'ing•glo'ry *s* (*pl* **-ries**) dondiego de día
morning sickness *s* vómitos del embarazo
morning star *s* lucero del alba
Moroccan [məˈrɑkən] *adj & s* marroquí *mf* o marroquín *m*
morocco [məˈrɑko] *s* (*leather*) marroquí *m* o marroquín *m* ‖ **Morocco** *s* Marruecos *m*
moron [ˈmorɑn] *s* (*person of arrested intelligence*) morón *m;* (coll) imbécil *mf*
morose [məˈros] *adj* adusto, hosco, malhumorado
morphine [ˈmɔrfin] *s* morfina
morphology [mɔrˈfɑlədʒi] *s* morfología
Morris chair [ˈmɑrɪs] o [ˈmɔrɪs] *s* poltrona extensible
morrow [ˈmɑro] o [ˈmɔro] *s* (*future time*) mañana *m;* (*time following some event*) día *m* siguiente; **on the morrow** en el día de mañana; el día siguiente
morsel [ˈmɔrsəl] *s* bocadito; pedacito
mortal [ˈmɔrtəl] *adj & s* mortal *m*
mortality [mɔrˈtælɪti] *s* mortalidad; (*death or destruction on a large scale*) mortandad
mortar [ˈmɔrtər] *s* (*bowl used for crushing; mixture of lime, etc.*) mortero; (arti) mortero
mor'tar•board' *s* esparavel *m;* gorro académico cuadrado
mortgage [ˈmɔrgɪdʒ] *s* hipoteca ‖ *tr* hipotecar
mortgagee [,mɔrgɪˈdʒi] *s* acreedor hipotecario
mortgagor [ˈmɔrgɪdʒər] *s* deudor hipotecario
mortician [mɔrˈtɪʃən] *s* empresario de pompas fúnebres
morti•fy [ˈmɔrtɪ,faɪ] *v* (*pret & pp* **-fied**) *tr* humillar; mortificar (*el cuerpo, las pasiones*); **to be mortified** avergonzarse
mortise [ˈmɔrtɪs] *s* mortaja, muesca ‖ *tr* amortajar, enmuescar
mortise lock *s* cerradura embutida
mortuar•y [ˈmɔrtʃʊ,ɛri] *adj* mortuorio ‖ *s* (*pl* **-ies**) depósito de cadáveres; funeraria
mosaic [moˈze•ɪk] *m* mosaico
Moscow [ˈmɑskaʊ] o [ˈmɑsko] *s* Moscú
Moses [ˈmozɪz] o [ˈmozɪs] *s* Moisés *m*
Mos•lem [ˈmɑzləm] o [ˈmɑsləm] *adj & s* var of **Muslim,** musulmán *m*
mosque [mɑsk] *s* mezquita
mosqui•to [məsˈkito] *s* (*pl* **-toes** o **-tos**) mosquito
mosquito net *s* mosquitero
moss [mɔs] o [mɑs] *s* musgo
moss'back' *s* (coll) reaccionario; (*old-fashioned person*) (coll) fósil *m*
moss•y [ˈmɔsi] o [ˈmɑsi] *adj* (*comp* **-ier;** *super* **-iest**) musgoso
most [most] *adj* más; la mayor parte de, los más de ‖ *adv* más; muy, sumamente; (coll) casi ‖ *s* la mayor parte, el mayor número,

los más; **most of** la mayor parte de, el mayor número de; **to make the most of** sacar el mejor partido de
mostly [ˈmostli] *adv* por la mayor parte, mayormente; casi
moth [mɔθ] o [mɑθ] *s* mariposa nocturna; (*clothes moth*) polilla
moth ball *s* bola de alcanfor, bola de naftalina
moth'-ball' fleet *s* (nav) flota en conserva
moth'-eat'en *adj* apolillado; (fig) anticuado
mother [ˈmʌðər] *adj* (*love*) maternal; (*tongue*) materno; (*country*) madre; (*church*) metropolitano ‖ *s* madre *f;* (*an elderly woman*) (coll) tía ‖ *tr* servir de madre a
mother country *s* madre patria
Mother Goose *s* supuesta autora o narradora de una colección de cuentos infantiles (in Spain: *Cuentos de Calleja*)
motherhood [ˈmʌðər,hʊd] *s* maternidad
moth'er-in-law' *s* (*pl* **mothers-in-law**) suegra
moth'er•land' *s* patria
motherless [ˈmʌðərlɪs] *adj* huérfano de madre, sin madre
motherly [ˈmʌðərli] *adj* maternal
mother-of-pearl [ˈmʌðərəvˈpʌrl] *adj* nacarado ‖ *s* nácar *m*
Mother's Day *s* día *m* de la madre
mother superior *s* superiora
mother tongue *s* (*language naturally acquired by reason of nationality*) lengua materna; (*language from which another language is derived*) lengua madre, lengua matriz
mother wit *s* gracia natural, chispa
moth hole *s* apolilladura
moth•y [ˈmɔθi] o [ˈmɑθi] *adj* (*comp* **-ier;** *super* **-iest**) apolillado
motif [moˈtif] *s* motivo
motion [ˈmoʃən] *s* movimiento; (*signal, gesture*) seña, indicación; (*in a deliberating assembly*) moción; **to set in motion** poner en acción ‖ *intr* hacer señas con la mano o la cabeza
motionless [ˈmoʃənlɪs] *adj* inmoble, inmóvil
motion picture *s* película cinematográfica
mo'tion-pic'ture *adj* cinematográfico
motivate [ˈmotɪ,vet] *tr* animar, incitar, mover
motive [ˈmotɪv] *adj* (*promoting action*) motivo; (*producing motion*) motor ‖ *s* motivo
motive power *s* fuerza motriz, potencia motora o motriz; (rr) conjunto de locomotoras de un ferrocarril
motley [ˈmɑtli] *adj* abigarrado; mezclado, variado
motor [ˈmotər] *adj* motor ‖ *s* motor *m;* motor eléctrico; automóvil *m* ‖ *intr* viajar en automóvil
mo'tor•boat' *s* gasolinera, canoa automóvil
mo'tor•bus' *s* autobús *m*
motorcade [ˈmotər,ked] *s* caravana de automóviles
mo'tor•car' *s* automóvil *m*
mo'tor•cy'cle *s* motocicleta
motorist [ˈmotərɪst] *s* motorista *mf,* automovilista *mf*
motorize [ˈmotə,raɪz] *tr* motorizar
motor launch *s* lancha automóvil
motor•man [ˈmotərmən] *s* (*pl* **-men** [mən]) conductor *m* de tranvía, conductor de locomotora eléctrica
motor sailer [ˈselər] *s* motovelero
motor scooter *s* motoneta
motor ship *s* motonave *f*
motor truck *s* autocamión *m*
motor vehicle *s* vehículo motor, autovehículo
mottle [ˈmɑtəl] *tr* abigarrar, jaspear, motear
mot•to [ˈmɑto] *s* (*pl* **-toes** o **-tos**) lema *m,* divisa
mould [mold] *s, tr, & intr* var de **mold**
moulder [ˈmoldər] *s & intr* var de **molder**
moulding [ˈmoldɪŋ] *s* var de **molding**
mouldy [ˈmoldi] *adj* var de **moldy**
mound [maʊnd] *s* montón *m* de tierra; montecillo
mount [maʊnt] *s* (*hill, mountain*) monte *m;* (*horse for riding*) montura; (*setting for a jewel*) montadura; soporte *m;* cartón *m,* tela (*en que está pegada una fotografía*); (mach) montaje *m* ‖ *tr* subir (*una escalera, una cuesta*); subir a (*una plataforma*); escalar (*una muralla*); montar (*un servicio; una piedra preciosa*); poner a caballo; pegar (*vistas, pruebas*); (mil) montar (*la guardia*) ‖ *intr* montar, montarse; aumentar, subir (*los precios*)
mountain [ˈmaʊntən] *s* montaña; **to make a mountain out of a molehill** hacer de una pulga un camello
mountain climbing *s* alpinismo, montañismo
mountaineer [,maʊntəˈnɪr] *s* montañés *m*
mountainous [ˈmaʊntənəs] *adj* montañoso
mountain railroad *s* ferrocarril *m* de cremallera
mountain range *s* cordillera, sierra
mountain sickness *s* mal *m* de las montañas
mountebank [ˈmaʊntɪ,bæŋk] *s* saltabanco
mounting [ˈmaʊntɪŋ] *s* (*of a precious stone, of an astronomical instrument*) montura; papel *m* de soporte; papel o tela (*en que está pegada una fotografía*); (mach) montaje *m*
mourn [morn] *tr* llorar (*p.ej., la muerte de una persona*); lamentar (*una desgracia*) ‖ *intr* lamentarse; vestir de luto
mourner [ˈmornər] *s* doliente *mf;* (*person who makes a public profession of penitence*) penitente *mf;* (*person hired to attend a funeral*) plañidera; **mourners** duelo
mourners' bench *s* banco de los penitentes
mournful [ˈmornfəl] *adj* (*sorrowful*) doloroso; (*gloomy*) lúgubre
mourning [ˈmornɪŋ] *s* luto; **to be in mourning** estar de luto
mourning band *s* crespón *m* fúnebre, brazal *m* de luto
mouse [maʊs] *s* (*pl* **mice** [maɪs]) ratón *m*
mouse'hole' *s* ratonera
mouser [ˈmaʊzər] *s* desmurador *m*
mouse'trap' *s* ratonera

moustache [məs'tæʃ] o [məs'tɑʃ] *s* bigote *m*, mostacho

mouth [mauθ] *s* (*pl* **mouths** [mauðz]) boca; (*of a river*) desembocadura, embocadura; **by mouth** por vía bucal; **to be born with a silver spoon in one's mouth** nacer de pie; **to make one's mouth water** hacérsele a uno la boca agua; **to not open one's mouth** no decir esta boca es mía

mouthful ['mauθ,fʊl] *s* bocado

mouth organ *s* armónica de boca

mouth'piece' *s* (*of wind instrument*) boquilla; (*of bridle*) embocadura; (*spokesman*) portavoz *m*

mouth'wash' *s* enjuague *m*, enjuagadientes *m*

movable ['muvəbəl] *adj* movible, móvil

move [muv] *s* movimiento; (*démarche*) acción, gestión, paso; (*from one house to another*) mudanza; **on the move** en marcha, en movimiento; **to get a move on** (slang) menearse, darse prisa; **to make a move** dar un paso; hacer una jugada || *tr* mover; evacuar (*el vientre*); (*to stir, excite the feelings of*) conmover, enternecer; **to move up** adelantar (*una fecha*) || *intr* moverse; desplazarse (*un viajante; un planeta*); mudarse, mudar de casa; (*e.g., to another store, to another city*) trasladarse; hacer una jugada; hacer una moción; venderse, tener salida (*una mercancía*); evacuarse, moverse (*el vientre*); **to move away** apartarse; marcharse; mudarse de casa; **to move in** instalarse; alternar con, frecuentar (*la buena sociedad*); **to move off** alejarse

movement ['muvmənt] *s* movimiento; aparato de relojería; (*of the bowels*) evacuación; (*e.g., of a symphony*) tiempo

movie ['muvi] *s* película, cinta

movie camera *s* filmadora, cámara cinematográfica

movie•goer ['movi,go•ər] *s* aficionado al cine

movie house *s* cineteatro

mov'ie•land' *s* (coll) cinelandia

movie star *s* cineasta *m*

moving ['muvɪŋ] *adj* conmovedor, impresionante || *s* movimiento; (*from one house to another*) mudanza

moving picture *s* película cinematográfica

moving spirit *s* alma (*de una empresa*)

moving stairway *s* escalera mecánica, móvil o rodante

mow [mo] *v* (*pret* **mowed;** *pp* **mowed** o **mown**) *tr* segar; **to mow down** matar (*soldados*) con fuego graneado || *intr* segar

mower ['mo•ər] *s* segador *m;* segadora mecánica

mowing machine *s* segadora mecánica

Mozarab [mo'zærəb] *s* mozárabe *mf*

Mozarabic [mo'zærəbɪk] *adj* mozárabe

M.P. *abbr* **Member of Parliament, Military Police**

m.p.h. *abbr* **miles per hour**

Mr. ['mɪstər] *s* (*pl* **Messrs.** ['mɛsərz]) señor *m* (*tratamiento*)

Mrs. ['mɪsɪz] *s* señora (*tratamiento*)

MS. o **ms.** *abbr* **manuscript**

Mt. *abbr* **Mount**

much [mʌtʃ] *adj & pron* mucho; **too much** demasiado || *adv* mucho; **however much** por mucho que; **how much** cuánto; **too much** demasiado; **very much** muchísimo

mucilage ['mjusɪlɪdʒ] *s* goma para pegar; (*gummy secretion in plants*) mucílago

muck [mʌk] *s* estiércol húmedo; suciedad, porquería; (min) zafra

muck'rake' *intr* (coll) exponer ruindades

mucous ['mjukəs] *adj* mucoso

mucus ['mjukəs] *s* moco

mud [mʌd] *s* barro, fango, lodo; **to sling mud at** llenar de fango

muddle ['mʌdəl] *s* confusión, embrollo || *tr* confundir, embrollar; atontar, aturdir || *intr* obrar torpemente; **to muddle through** salir del paso a pesar suyo

mud'dle•head' *s* farraguista *mf*, cajón *m* de sastre

mud•dy ['mʌdi] *adj* (*comp* **-dier;** *super* **-diest**) barroso, fangoso, lodoso; (*obscure*) turbio || *v* (*pret & pp* **-died**) *tr* embarrar, enturbiar

mud'guard' *s* guardabarros *m*

mud'hole' *s* atolladero, ciénaga

mudslinger ['mʌd,slɪŋər] *s* (fig) lanzador *m* de lodo

muezzin [mju'ɛzɪn] *s* almuecín *m*, almuédano

muff [mʌf] *s* manguito || *tr & intr* chapucear

muffin ['mʌfɪn] *s* mollete *m*

muffle ['mʌfəl] *tr* arropar; (*about the face*) embozar; amortiguar (*un ruido*); enfundar (*un tambor*)

muffler ['mʌflər] *s* bufanda, tapaboca; (aut) silenciador *m*, silencioso

mufti ['mʌfti] *s* traje *m* de paisano

mug [mʌg] *s* pichel *m;* (slang) jeta, hocico || *v* (*pret & pp* **mugged;** *ger* **mugging**) *tr* (slang) fotografiar; (slang) atacar || *intr* (slang) hacer muecas

mugger ['mʌgər] *s* ladron *m* asaltador

mug•gy ['mʌgi] *adj* (*comp* **-gier;** *super* **-giest**) bochornoso, sofocante

mulat•to [mjʊ'læto] o [mə'læto] *s* (*pl* **-toes**) mulato

mulber•ry ['mʌl,bɛri] *s* (*pl* **-ries**) (*tree*) moral *m;* (*fruit*) mora

mulct [mʌlkt] *tr* defraudar

mule [mjul] *s* mulo, macho; (*slipper*) babucha

mule chair *s* artolas, jamugas

muleteer [,mjulə'tɪr] *s* mulatero

mulish ['mjulɪʃ] *adj* terco, obstinado

mull [mʌl] *tr* calentar (*vino*) con especias || *intr*—**to mull over** reflexionar sobre

mullion ['mʌljən] *s* parteluz *m*

Multigraph ['mʌltɪ,græf] o ['mʌltɪ,grɑf] *s* (trademark) multígrafo || *tr* multigrafiar

multilateral [,mʌltɪ'lætərəl] *adj* (*having many sides*) multilátero; (*participated in by more than two nations*) multilateral

multinational corporations *spl* multinacionales *mpl*

multiple ['mʌltɪpəl] *adj* múltiple, múltiplo || *s* (math) múltiplo

multiple sclerosis *s* esclerosis *f* múltiple
multiplex [ˈmʌltɪ,plɛks] *adj* múltiple
multiplici•ty [,mʌltɪˈplɪsɪti] *s* (*pl* **-ties**) multiplicidad
multi•ply [ˈmʌltɪ,plaɪ] *v* (*pret & pp* **-plied**) *tr* multiplicar ‖ *intr* multiplicar, multiplicarse
multipurpose [,mʌltɪˈpʌrpəs] *adj* múltiple de uso; versátil
multitude [ˈmʌltɪ,tjud] o [ˈmʌltɪ,tud] *s* multitud
mum [mʌm] *adj* callado; **mum's the word!** ¡punto en boca!; **to keep mum about** callar ‖ *interj* ¡chitón!
mumble [ˈmʌmbəl] *tr & intr* mascullar, mascujar
mummer•y [ˈmʌməri] *s* (*pl* **-ies**) mojiganga
mum•my [ˈmʌmi] *s* (*pl* **-mies**) momia
mumps [mʌmps] *s* papera
munch [mʌntʃ] *tr* ronzar
mundane [ˈmʌnden] *adj* mundano
municipal [mjuˈnɪsɪpəl] *adj* municipal
municipali•ty [mju,nɪsɪˈpælɪti] *s* (*pl* **-ties**) municipio
munificent [mjuˈnɪfɪsənt] *adj* munífico
munition [mjuˈnɪʃən] *s* munición ‖ *tr* municionar
munition dump *s* depósito de municiones
mural [ˈmjʊrəl] *adj* mural ‖ *s* pintura mural; decoración mural
murder [ˈmʌrdər] *s* asesinato, homicidio ‖ *tr* asesinar; (*to spoil, mar*) (coll) estropear
murderer [ˈmʌrdərər] *s* asesino
murderess [ˈmʌrdərɪs] *s* asesina
murderous [ˈmʌrdərəs] *adj* asesino; cruel, sanguinario
murk•y [ˈmʌrki] *adj* (*comp* **-ier;** *super* **-iest**) (*hazy*) calinoso; (*gloomy*) lóbrego
murmur [ˈmʌrmər] *s* murmullo ‖ *tr & intr* murmurar
mus. *abbr* **museum, music**
muscle [ˈmʌsəl] *s* músculo; (fig) fuerza muscular
muscular [ˈmʌskjələr] *adj* musculoso
muse [mjuz] *s* musa; **the Muses** las Musas ‖ *intr* meditar, reflexionar; **to muse on** contemplar
museum [mjuˈzi•əm] *s* museo
mush [mʌʃ] *s* gachas; (coll) sentimentalismo exagerado, sensiblería
mush'room' *s* hongo, seta ‖ *intr* aparecer de la noche a la mañana; **to mushroom into** convertirse rápidamente en
mushroom cloud *s* nube-hongo *f*
mush•y [ˈmʌʃi] *adj* (*comp* **-ier;** *super* **-iest**) mollar, pulposo; (coll) sensiblero, sobón; (*with women*) (coll) baboso; **to be mushy** (coll) hacerse unas gachas
music [ˈmjuzɪk] *s* música; **to face the music** (coll) afrontar las consecuencias; **to set to music** poner en música
musical [ˈmjuzɪkəl] *adj* musical, músico
musical comedy *s* comedia musical
musicale [,mjuzɪˈkæl] *s* velada musical, concierto casero
music box *s* caja de música
music cabinet *s* musiquero
music hall *s* salón *m* de conciertos; (Brit) teatro de variedades
musician [mjuˈzɪʃən] *s* músico
musicianship [mjuˈzɪʃən,ʃɪp] *s* musicalidad
musicologist [,mjuzɪˈkɑlədʒɪst] *s* musicólogo
musicology [,mjuzɪˈkɑlədʒi] *s* musicología
music rack o **music stand** *s* atril *m*
musk [mʌsk] *s* almizcle *m;* olor *m* de almizcle
musk deer *s* almizclero
musket [ˈmʌskɪt] *s* mosquete *m*
musketeer [,mʌskɪˈtɪr] *s* mosquetero
musk'mel'on *s* melón *m*
musk'rat' *s* almizclera
Muslim [ˈmʌzləm] o [ˈmʌsləm] *adj* muslime, islámico, mahometano ‖ *s* muslime *mf,* musulmán *m*
muslin [ˈmʌzlɪn] *s* muselina
muss [mʌs] *tr* (*the hair*) (coll) descabellar, desarreglar; (*clothing*) (coll) chafar, arrugar
muss•y [ˈmʌsi] *adj* (*comp* **-ier;** *super* **-iest**) desaliñado, desgreñado
must [mʌst] *s* mosto; (*mold*) moho; cosa que debe hacerse ‖ *v aux* **I must study my lesson** debo estudiar mi lección; **he must work tomorrow** tiene que trabajar mañana; **she must be ill** estará enferma
mustache [məsˈtæʃ], [məsˈtɑʃ], o [ˈmʌstæʃ] *s* bigote *m,* mostacho
mustard [ˈmʌstərd] *s* mostaza
mustard gas *s* gas *m* mostaza
mustard plaster *s* sinapismo, cataplasma *f*
muster [ˈmʌstər] *s* asamblea; matrícula de revista; **to pass muster** pasar revista; ser aceptable ‖ *tr* llamar a asamblea; reunir para pasar revista; reunir, acumular; **to muster in** alistar; **to muster out** dar de baja a; **to muster up courage** cobrar ánimo
muster roll *s* lista de revista
mus•ty [ˈmʌsti] *adj* (*comp* **-tier;** *super* **-tiest**) (*moldy*) mohoso; (*stale*) trasnochado; anticuado, pasado de moda
mutation [mjuˈteʃən] *s* mutación
mute [mjut] *adj & s* mudo ‖ *tr* poner sordina a
mutilate [ˈmjutɪ,let] *tr* mutilar
mutilated *adj* mútilo, mutilado, mocho
mutineer [,mjutɪˈnɪr] *s* amotinado
mutinous [ˈmjutɪnəs] *adj* amotinado
muti•ny [ˈmjutɪni] *s* (*pl* **-nies**) motín *m* ‖ *v* (*pret & pp* **-nied**) *intr* amotinarse
mutt [mʌt] *s* (slang) perro cruzado; (slang) bobo, tonto
mutter [ˈmʌtər] *tr & intr* murmurar
mutton [ˈmʌtən] *s* carnero, carne *f* de carnero
mutton chop *s* chuleta de carnero
mutual [ˈmutʃʊ•əl] *adj* mutual, mutuo
mutual aid *s* apoyo mutuo
mutual benefit association *s* mutualidad
mutual fund *s* sociedad inversionista mutualista
muzzle [ˈmʌzəl] *s* (*projecting part of head of animal*) hocico; (*device to keep animal from biting*) bozal *m;* (*of firearm*) boca ‖ *tr*

abozalar; (*to keep from speaking*) amordazar
my [maɪ] *adj poss* mi
myriad [ˈmɪrɪ•əd] *s* miríada
myrrh [mʌr] *s* mirra
myrtle [ˈmʌrtəl] *s* arrayán *m*, mirto
myself [maɪˈsɛlf] *pron pers* yo mismo; mí, mí mismo; me, p.ej., **I enjoyed myself** me divertí; **with myself** conmigo
mysterious [mɪsˈtɪrɪ•əs] *adj* misterioso
myster•y [ˈmɪstəri] *s* (*pl* **-ies**) misterio
mystic [ˈmɪstɪk] *adj & s* místico
mystical [ˈmɪstɪkəl] *adj* místico
mysticism [ˈmɪstɪ,sɪzəm] *s* misticismo
mystification [,mɪstɪfɪˈkeʃən] *s* confusión, mistificación
mysti•fy [ˈmɪstɪ,faɪ] *v* (*pret & pp* **-fied**) *tr* rodear de misterio; (*to hoax*) confundir, mistificar
myth [mɪθ] *s* mito
mythical [ˈmɪθɪkəl] *adj* mítico
mythological [,mɪθəˈlɑdʒɪkəl] *adj* mitológico
mytholo•gy [mɪˈθɑlədʒi] *s* (*pl* **-gies**) mitología

N

N, n [ɛn] decimocuarta letra del alfabeto inglés
n. *abbr* **neuter, nominative, noon, north, noun, number**
N. *abbr* **Nationalist, Navy, Noon, North, November**
N.A. *abbr* **National Academy, National Army, North America**
nab [næb] *v* (*pret & pp* **nabbed;** *ger* **nabbing**) *tr* (slang) agarrar, coger; (slang) poner preso, prender
nag [næg] *s* caballejo, jaco; pequeño caballo de silla ‖ *v* (*pret & pp* **nagged;** *ger* **nagging**) *tr* importunar regañando ‖ *intr* regañar
naiad [ˈne•æd] o [ˈnaɪ•æd] *s* náyade *f;* (fig) nadadora
nail [nel] *s* (*of finger*) uña; (*to fasten wood, etc.*) clavo; **to hit the nail on the head** dar en el clavo ‖ *tr* clavar
nail brush *s* cepillo de uñas
nail clippers *spl* cortauñas *m*
nail file *s* lima para las uñas
nail polish *s* esmalte *m* para las uñas, laca de uñas
nailset [ˈnel,sɛt] *s* contrapunzón *m*
naïve [nɑˈiv] *adj* cándido, ingenuo
naked [ˈnekɪd] *adj* desnudo; **to go naked** ir desnudo, andar a la cordobana; **to strip naked** desnudar; desnudarse; **with the naked eye** a simple vista
name [nem] *s* nombre *m;* (*first name*) nombre de pila; (*last name*) apellido; fama, reputación, renombre *m;* linaje, *m*, raza; **to call someone names** maltratar a uno de palabra; **to go by the name of** ser conocido por el nombre de; **to make a name for oneself** darse a conocer, hacerse un nombre; **what is your name?** ¿cómo se llama Vd.? ‖ *tr* nombrar; fijar (*un precio*)
name day *s* santo
nameless [ˈnemlɪs] *adj* sin nombre, anónimo
namely [ˈnemli] *adv* a saber, es decir
namesake [ˈnem,sek] *s* homónimo, tocayo
nanny goat [ˈnæni] *s* (coll) cabra
nap [næp] *s* lanilla, flojel *m;* sueñecillo; **to take a nap** descabezar un sueñecillo ‖ *v* (*pret & pp* **napped;** *ger* **napping**) *intr* echar un sueñecillo; estar desprevenido; **to catch napping** coger desprevenido
napalm [ˈnepɑm] *s* (mil) gelatina incendiaria
nape [nep] *s* cogote *m*, nuca
naphtha [ˈnæfθə] *s* nafta
napkin [ˈnæpkɪn] *s* servilleta; (*of a baby*) (Brit) pañal *m*
napkin ring *s* servilletero
Naples [ˈnepəlz] *s* Nápoles
Napoleonic [nə,polɪˈɑnɪk] *adj* napoleónico
narc [nɑrk] *s* (slang) agente *m* de policía antidroga
narcissus [nɑrˈsɪsəs] *s* (bot) narciso ‖ **Narcissus** *s* Narciso
narcotic [nɑrˈkɑtɪk] *adj & s* narcótico
narrate [næˈret] *tr* narrar
narration [næˈreʃən] *s* narración
narrative [ˈnærətɪv] *adj* narrativo ‖ *s* (*story, tale; art of telling stories*) narrativa
narrator [næˈretər] *s* narrador *m*
narrow [ˈnæro] *adj* angosto, estrecho; intolerante; minucioso; (*sense of a word*) estricto ‖ **narrows** *spl* angostura, paso estrecho ‖ *tr* enangostar, estrechar; reducir, limitar ‖ *intr* enangostarse, estrecharse; reducirse, limitarse
narrow escape *s* trance *m* difícil; **to have a narrow escape** escapar por un pelo, salvarse en una tabla
narrow gauge *s* trocha angosta, vía estrecha
narrow-minded [ˈnæroˈmaɪndɪd] *adj* intolerante, de miras estrechas, poco liberal
nasal [ˈnezəl] *adj & s* nasal *f*
nasalize [ˈnezə,laɪz] *tr* nasalizar ‖ *intr* ganguear
nasturtium [nəˈstʌrʃəm] *s* capuchina, espuela de galán
nas•ty [ˈnæsti] *adj* (*comp* **-tier;** *super* **-tiest**) asqueroso, sucio; desagradable; desvergonzado; amenazador; horrible
natatorium [,netəˈtorɪ•əm] *s* piscina de natación
nation [ˈneʃən] *s* nación

national [ˈnæʃənəl] *adj & s* nacional *mf*
national anthem *s* himno nacional
national hero *s* benemérito de la patria
national holiday *s* fiesta nacional
nationalism [ˈnæʃənə,lɪzəm] *s* nacionalismo
nationalist [ˈnæ,ʃənəlɪst] *adj & s* nacionalista *mf*
nationali•ty [ˈnæ,ʃən,ælɪti] *s* (*pl* **-ties**) nacionalidad, naturalidad
nationalize [ˈnæʃənə,laɪz] *tr* nacionalizar
na'tion-wide' *adj* de toda la nación
native [ˈnetɪv] *adj* nativo, natural; indígena; (*language*) materno; **to go native** vivir como los indígenas || *s* natural *mf;* indígena *mf*
native land *s* patria
nativi•ty [nəˈtɪvɪti] *s* (*pl* **-ties**) nacimiento || **Nativity** *s* (*day; festival; painting*) natividad
NATO [ˈneto] *s* (acronym) la O.T.A.N.
nat•ty [ˈnæti] *adj.* (*comp* **-tier;** *super* **-tier;** *super* **-tiest**) elegante, garboso
natural [ˈnætʃərəl] *adj* natural; (mus) natural || *s* imbécil *mf;* (mus) tono natural, nota natural; (*sign*) (mus) becuadro; (mus) tecla blanca; (coll) cosa de éxito certero
naturalism [ˈnætʃərə,lɪzəm] *s* naturalismo
naturalist [ˈnætʃərəlɪst] *s* naturalista *mf*
naturalization [,nætʃərəlɪˈzəʃən] *s* naturalización
naturalization papers *spl* carta de naturaleza
naturalize [ˈnætʃərə,laɪz] *tr* naturalizar
naturally [ˈnætʃərəli] *adv* naturalmente; claro, desde luego, por supuesto
nature [ˈnetʃər] *s* naturaleza; **from nature** del natural
naught [nɔt] *s* nada; cero; **to bring to naught** anular, invalidar, destruir; **to come to naught** reducirse a nada, frustrarse
naugh•ty [ˈnɔti] *adj* (*comp* **-tier;** *super* **-tiest**) desobediente, pícaro; desvergonzado; (*story, tale*) verde
nausea [ˈnɔʃɪ•ə] o [ˈnɔsɪ•ə] *s* náusea
nauseate [ˈnɔʃɪ,et] o [ˈnɔsɪ,et] *tr* dar náuseas a || *intr* nausear, marearse
nauseating [ˈnɔʃɪ,etɪŋ] o [ˈnɔsɪ,etɪŋ] *adj* nauseabundo, asqueroso
nauseous [ˈnɔ,ʃɪ•əs] o [ˈnɔsɪ•əs] *adj* nauseabundo
nautical [ˈnɔtɪkəl] *adj* náutico, marino, naval
nav. *abbr* **naval, navigation**
naval [ˈnevəl] *adj* naval, naval militar
Naval Academy *s* (U.S.A.) Escuela Naval Militar
naval officer *s* oficial *m* de marina
naval station *s* apostadero
nave [nev] *s* (*of a church*) nave *f* central, nave principal; (*of a wheel*) cubo
navel [ˈnevəl] *s* ombligo; (*center point, middle*) (fig) ombligo
navel orange *s* navel *f,* naranja de ombligo
navigability [,nævɪgəˈbɪlɪti] *s* (*of a river*) navegabilidad; (*of a ship*) buen gobierno
navigable [ˈnævɪgəbəl] *adj* (*river, canal, etc.*) navegable; (*ship*) marinero, de buen gobierno
navigate [ˈnævɪ,get] *tr & intr* navegar
navigation [ˈnævɪ,geʃən] *s* navegación
navigator [ˈnævɪ,getər] *s* navegador *m,* navegante *m;* (*he who is in charge of course of ship or plane*) oficial *m* de derrota; (Brit) peón *m*
nav•vy [ˈnævi] *s* (*pl* **-vies**) (Brit) bracero, peón *m*
na•vy [ˈnevi] *adj* azul oscuro || *s* (*pl* **-vies**) marina de guerra; (*personnel*) marina; azul oscuro
navy bean *s* frijol blanco común
navy blue *s* azul marino, azul oscuro
navy yard *s* arsenal *m* de puerto
Nazarene [,næzəˈrin] *adj & s* nazareno
Nazi [ˈnɑtsi] o [ˈnætsi] *adj & s* nazi *mf,* nacista *mf*
n.b. *abbr* **nota bene** (Lat) **note well**
N-bomb [ˈɛn,bɑm] *s* bomba de neutrones
Neapolitan [,ni•əˈpɑlitən] *adj & s* napolitano
neap tide [nip] *s* marea muerta
near [nɪr] *adj* cercano, próximo; íntimo; imitado || *adv* cerca; íntimamente || *prep* cerca de; hacia, por || *tr* acercarse a || *intr* acercarse
nearby [ˈnɪr,baɪ] *adj* cercano, próximo || *adv* cerca
Near East *s* Cercano Oriente, Próximo Oriente
nearly [ˈnɪrli] *adv* casi; de cerca; íntimamente; por poco, p.ej., **he nearly fell** por poco se cae
near-sighted [ˈnɪrˈsaɪtɪd] *adj* miope
near-sightedness *s* miopía
neat [nit] *adj* aseado, pulcro; pulido; diestro, primoroso; puro, sin mezcla || *ssg* res vacuna || *spl* ganado vacuno
neat's'-foot'oil *s* aceite *m* de pie de buey
Nebuchadnezzar [,nɛbjəkədˈnɛzər] *s* Nabucodonosor *m*
nebu•la [ˈnɛbjələ] *s* (*pl* **-lae** [,li] o **-las**) nebulosa
nebular [ˈnɛbjələr] *adj* nebular
nebulous [ˈnɛbjələs] *adj* nebuloso
necessary [ˈnɛsɪ,sɛri] *adj* necesario
necessitate [nɪˈsɛsɪ,tet] *tr* necesitar, exigir
necessitous [nɪˈsɛsɪtəs] *adj* necesitado
necessi•ty [nɪˈsɛsɪti] *s* (*pl* **-ties**) necesidad
neck [nɛk] *s* cuello; (*of a bottle*) gollete *m;* (*of violin or guitar*) mástil *m;* istmo, península; estrecho; **neck and neck** parejos; **to break one's neck** (coll) matarse trabajando; **to stick one's neck out** (coll) descubrir el cuerpo || *intr* (slang) acariciarse (*dos enamorados*)
neck'band' *s* tirilla de camisa
necklace [ˈnɛklɪs] *s* gargantilla, collar *m*
necktie [ˈnɛk,taɪ] *s* corbata
necktie pin *s* alfiler *m* de corbata
necrology [nɛˈkrɑlədʒi] *s* necrología
necromancy [ˈnɛkrə,mænsi] *s* necromancia, nigromancia
nectarine [,nɛktəˈrin] *s* griñón *m*
née o nee [ne] *adj* nacida o de soltera, p.ej., **Mary Wilson, née Miller** Maria Wilson, nacida Miller o María Wilson, de soltera Miller

need [nid] *s* necesidad; pobreza; **in need** necesitado || *tr* necesitar || *intr* estar necesitado; ser necesario || *v aux*—**if need be** si fuere necesario; **to need** + *inf* deber, tener que + *inf*

needful [ˈnidfəl] *adj* necesario || **the needful** lo necesario; (slang) el dinero

needle [ˈnidəl] *s* aguja; **to look for a needle in a haystack** buscar una aguja en un pajar || *tr* coser con aguja; (coll) aguijonear, incitar; (coll) añadir alcohol a (*la cerveza o el vino*)

needle bath *s* ducha en alfileres

needle'case' *s* alfiletero

needle point *s* bordado al pasado; encaje *m* de mano

needless [ˈnidlɪs] *adj* innecesario, inútil

needle'work' *s* costura, labor *f*

needs [nidz] *adv* necesariamente, forzosamente

need•y [ˈnidi] *adj* (*comp* **-ier;** *super* **-iest**) necesitado, indigente || **the needy** los necesitados

ne'er-do-well [ˈnɛrdu,wɛl] *adj & s* holgazán, perdido

negation [nɪˈgeʃən] *s* negación

negative [ˈnɛgətɪv] *adj* negativo || *s* negativa; electricidad negativa, borne negativo; (gram) negación; (math) término negativo; (phot) prueba negativa || *tr* desaprobar; anular

neglect [nɪˈglɛkt] *s* negligencia, descuido || *tr* descuidar; **to neglect to** dejar de, olvidarse de

neglectful [nɪˈglɛktfəl] *adj* negligente, descuidado

négligée o **negligee** [,nɛglɪˈʒe] *s* bata de mujer, traje *m* de casa

negligence [ˈnɛglɪdʒəns] *s* negligencia, descuido

negligent [ˈnɛglɪdʒənt] *adj* negligente, descuidado

negligible [ˈnɛglɪdʒɪbəl] *adj* insignificante, imperceptible

negotiable [nɪˈgoʃɪ•əbəl] *adj* negociable; transitable

negotiate [nɪˈgoʃɪ,et] *tr* negociar; (coll) salvar, vencer || *intr* negociar

negotiation [nɪ,goʃɪˈeʃən] *s* negociación; trámite *m;* **round of negotiations** ronda negociadora

Ne•gro [ˈnigro] *adj* (*usually offensive*) negro || *s* (*pl* **-groes**) (*usually offensive*) negro

neigh [ne] *s* relincho || *intr* relinchar

neighbor [ˈnebər] *adj* vecino || *s* vecino; (*fellow man*) prójimo || *tr* ser vecino de; ser amigo de || *intr* estar cercano; tener relaciones amistosas

neighborhood [ˈnebər,hʊd] *s* vecindad, vecindario, cercanías; **in the neighborhood of** en las inmediaciones de; (coll) cerca de, aproximadamente

neighboring [ˈnebərɪŋ] *adj* vecino, colindante

neighborly [ˈnebərli] *adj* buen vecino, amable, sociable

neither [ˈniðər] o [ˈnaɪðər] *adj indef* ninguno . . . (de los dos); **neither one** ninguno de los dos || *pron indef* ninguno (de los dos); ni uno ni otro, ni lo uno ni lo otro || *conj* ni; tampoco, ni . . . tampoco, p.ej., **neither do I** yo tampoco, ni yo tampoco; **neither . . . nor** ni . . . ni

neme•sis [ˈnɛmɪsɪs] *s* (*pl* **-ses** [,siz]) (*someone or something that punishes*) némesis *f* || **Nemesis** *s* Némesis *f*

neologism [niˈɑlə,dʒɪzəm] *s* neologismo

neomycin [,ni•əˈmaɪsɪn] *s* neomicina

neon [ˈni•ɑn] *s* neo, neón *m*

neophyte [ˈni•ə,faɪt] *s* neófito

Nepal [nɪˈpɔl] *s* el Nepal

Nepa•lese [,nɛpəˈliz] *adj* nepalés || *s* (*pl* **-lese**) nepalés *m*

nepenthe [nɪˈpɛnθi] *s* nepente *m*

nephew [ˈnɛfju] o [ˈnɛvju] *s* sobrino

Nepos [ˈnipɑs] o [ˈnɛpɑs] *s* Nepote *m*

Neptune [ˈnɛptʃun] o [ˈnɛptjun] *s* Neptuno

neptunium [nɛpˈtʃunɪ•əm] o [nɛpˈtjunɪ•əm] *s* neptunio

nerd [nʌrd] *s* (slang) tipo insípido; sujeto estúpido

Nereid [ˈnɪrɪ•ɪd] *s* nereida

Nero [ˈnɪro] *s* Nerón *m*

nerve [nʌrv] *adj* (*center; system; tonic; disease; prostration; breakdown*) nervioso || *s* nervio; ánimo, valor *m;* audacia; (coll) descaro; **nerves** excitabilidad nerviosa; **to get on one's nerves** irritar los nervios a uno; **to strain every nerve** esforzarse al máximo

nerve-racking [ˈnʌrv,rækɪŋ] *adj* irritante, exasperante

nervous [ˈnʌrvəs] *adj* nervioso

nervous breakdown *s* colapso nervioso

nervousness [ˈnʌrvəsnɪs] *s* nerviosidad

nervous shudder *s* muerte chiquita

nerv•y [ˈnʌrvi] *adj* (*comp* **-ier;** *super* **-iest**) (*strong, vigorous*) nervioso; atrevido, audaz; (coll) descarado

nest [nɛst] *s* nido; (*where hen lays eggs*) nidal *m;* (*birds in a nest*) nidada; (*set of things fitting within each other*) juego; (*of, e.g., thieves*) nido; **to feather one's nest** hacer todo para enriquecerse || *tr* colocar en un nido || *intr* anidar

nest egg *s* (*eggs left in a nest to induce hen to lay more*) nidal *m;* ahorros, hucha

nestle [ˈnɛsəl] *tr* poner en un nido; arrimar afectuosamente || *intr* anidar; arrimarse cómodamente; **to nestle up to** arrimarse a

net [nɛt] *adj* neto, líquido || *s* red *f;* precio neto, peso neto, ganancia líquida || *v* (*pret & pp* **netted;** *super* **netting**) *tr* enredar, tejer; coger con red; producir (*cierta ganancia líquida*)

nether [ˈnɛðər] *adj* inferior, más bajo

Netherlander [ˈnɛðər,lændər] o [ˈnɛðərləndər] *s* neerlandés *m*

Netherlandish [ˈnɛðər,lændɪʃ] o [ˈnɛðərləndɪʃ] *adj* neerlandés || *s* neerlandés *m*

Netherlands, The [ˈnɛðərləndz] los Países Bajos (*Holanda*)

netting [ˈnɛtɪŋ] *s* red *f*
nettle [ˈnɛtəl] *s* ortiga ‖ *tr* irritar, provocar
net'work' *s* red *f;* (rad & telv) cadena
neuralgia [njʊˈrældʒə] *s* neuralgia
neurology [njʊˈrɑlədʒi] *s* neurología
neuron [ˈnjʊrɑn] o [ˈnurɑn] *s* neurona
neuro•sis [njʊˈrosɪs] *s* (*pl* **-ses** [siz]) neurosis *f*
neurotic [njʊˈrɑtɪk] *adj & s* neurótico
neut. *abbr* **neuter**
neuter [ˈnjutər] *adj* neutro ‖ *s* género neutro; (aut) punto muerto
neutral [ˈnjutrəl] *adj* (*on neither side in a quarrel or war*) neutral; (*having little or no color*) neutro; (bot, chem, elec, phonet, zool) neutro ‖ *s* neutral *mf;* (aut) punto neutral, punto muerto
neutralism [ˈnjutrə,lɪzəm] *s* neutralismo
neutralist [ˈnjutrəlɪst] *adj & s* neutralista *mf*
neutrality [njuˈtrælɪti] *s* neutralidad
neutralize [ˈnjutrə,laɪz] *tr* neutralizar
neutron [ˈnjutrɑn] *s* neutrón *m*
neutron bomb *s* bomba de neutrones, bomba neutrónica
never [ˈnɛvər] *adv* nunca; en mi vida; de ningún modo; **never fear** no hay cuidado; **never mind** no importa
nev'er•more' *adv* nunca más
nevertheless [,nɛvərðəˈlɛs] *adv* no obstante, sin embargo
new [nju] o [nu] *adj* nuevo; **what's new?** ¿qué hay de nuevo?
new arrival *s* recién llegado; recién nacido
new'born' *adj* recién nacido; renacido
New Castile *s* Castilla la Nueva
New'cas'tle *s*—**to carry coals to Newcastle** echar agua al mar, llevar hierro a Vizcaya, llevar leña al monte
newcomer [ˈnju,kʌmər] *s* recién llegado, recién venido
New England *s* la Nueva Inglaterra
newfangled [ˈnju,fæŋgəld] *adj* de última moda, recién inventado
Newfoundland [ˈnjufənd,lænd] *s* (*island and province*) Terranova ‖ [njuˈfaʊndlənd] *s* (*dog*) Terranova *m*
newly [ˈnjuli] *adv* nuevamente; **newly** + *pp* recién + *pp*
new'ly•wed' *s* recién casado
New Mexican *adj & s* neomejicano, nuevomejicano
New Mexico *s* Nuevo Méjico
new moon *s* luna nueva, novilunio
news [njuz] o [nuz] *s* noticias; periódico; **a news item** una noticia; **a piece of news** una noticia
news agency *s* agencia de noticias
news beat *s* exclusiva, anticipación de una noticia por un periódico
news'boy' *s* vendedor *m* de periódicos
news'cast' *s* noticiario radiofónico ‖ *tr* radiodifundir (*noticias*) ‖ *intr* radiodifundir noticias
news'cast'er *s* cronista *mf* de radio
news conference *s* var de **press conference**
news coverage *s* reportaje *m*
news'let'ter *s* circular *f* noticiera
news•man [ˈnjuzmən] *s* (*pl* **-men** [mən]) noticiero
New South Wales *s* la Nueva Gales del Sur
news'pa'per *adj* periodístico ‖ *s* periódico
newspaper•man [ˈnjuz,pepər,mæn] *s* (*pl* **-men** [,mɛn]) periodista *m*
news'print' *s* papel-prensa *m*
news'reel' *s* actualidades, noticiario cinematográfico
news'stand' *s* quiosco de periódicos, puesto de periódicos
news'week'ly *s* (*pl* **-lies**) semanario de noticias
news'wor'thy *adj* de gran actualidad, de interés periodístico
news•y [ˈnjuzi] *adj* (*comp* **-ier;** *super* **-iest**) (coll) informativo
new'-world' *adj* del Nuevo Mundo
New Year's card *s* tarjeta de felicitación de Año Nuevo
New Year's Day *s* el Día de Año Nuevo
New Year's Eve *s* la noche vieja, la víspera de año nuevo
New York [jɔrk] *adj* neoyorkino ‖ *s* Nueva York
New Yorker [ˈjɔrkər] *s* neoyorkino
New Zealand [ˈzilənd] *adj* neocelandés ‖ *s* Nueva Zelanda
New Zealander [ˈziləndər] *s* neocelandés *m*
next [nɛkst] *adj* próximo, siguiente; de al lado; venidero, que viene ‖ *adv* luego, después; la próxima vez; **next to** junto a; después de; **next to nothing** casi nada; **the next best** lo mejor después de eso; **to come next** venir después, ser el que sigue
next door *s* la casa de al lado; **next door to** en la casa siguiente de; (coll) casi
next'door' *adj* siguiente, de al lado
next of kin *s* (*pl* **next of kin**) pariente más cercano
niacin [ˈnaɪ•əsɪn] *s* niacina
Niagara Falls [naɪˈægərə] *spl* las Cataratas del Niágara
nibble [ˈnɪbəl] *s* mordisco ‖ *tr & intr* mordiscar; picar (*un pez*); **to nibble at** picar de o en
Nicaraguan [,nɪkəˈrɑgwən] *adj & s* nicaragüense, nicaragüeño
nice [naɪs] *adj* delicado, fino, sutil; primoroso, pulido, refinado; dengoso, melindroso; atento, cortés, culto; escrupuloso, esmerado; agradable, simpático; decoroso, conveniente; complaciente; preciso; satisfactorio; (*weather*) bueno; (*attractive*) bonito; **nice and . . .** (coll) muy, mucho; **not nice** (coll) feo
nice-looking [ˈnaɪsˈlʊkɪŋ] *adj* hermoso, guapo, bien parecido
nicely [ˈnaɪsli] *adv* con precisión; escrupulosamente; satisfactoriamente; (coll) muy bien
nice•ty [ˈnaɪsəti] *s* (*pl* **-ties**) precisión; sutileza; finura; **to a nicety** con la mayor precisión
niche [nɪtʃ] *s* hornacina, nicho; colocación conveniente
Nicholas [ˈnɪkələs] *s* Nicolás *m*

nick [ˈnɪk] *s* mella, muesca; **in the nick of time** en el momento crítico || *tr* mellar, hacer muescas en; cortar
nickel [ˈnɪkəl] *s* níquel *m;* (U.S.A.) moneda de cinco centavos || *tr* niquelar
nick'el-plate' *tr* niquelar
nicknack [ˈnɪk,næk] *s* chuchería, friolera
nick'name' *s* apodo, mote *m* || *tr* apodar
nicotine [ˈnɪkə,tin] *s* nicotina
niece [nis] *s* sobrina
nif•ty [ˈnɪfti] *adj* (*comp* **-tier;** *super* **-tiest**) (slang) elegante; (slang) excelente
niggard [ˈnɪgərd] *adj & s* tacaño
night [naɪt] *adj* nocturno || *s* noche *f;* **at** o **by night** de noche or por la noche; **night before last** anteanoche; **to make a night of it** (coll) divertirse hasta muy entrada la noche
night'cap' *s* gorro de dormir; trago antes de acostarse, sosiega
night club *s* cabaret *m,* café *m* cantante, sala de fiestas
night driving *s* conducción de noche
night'fall' *s* anochecer *m,* caída de la noche
night'gown' *s* camisa de dormir
nightingale [ˈnaɪtən,gel] *s* ruiseñor *m*
night latch *s* cerradura de resorte
night letter *s* carta telegráfica nocturna
night'long' *adj* de toda la noche || *adv* durante toda la noche
nightly [ˈnaɪtli] *adj* nocturno; de cada noche || *adv* de noche, por la noche; cada noche
night'mare' *s* pesadilla
nightmarish [ˈnaɪt,mɛrɪʃ] *adj* espeluznante, horroroso
night owl *s* buho nocturno; (coll) anochecedor *m,* trasnochador *m*
night'shirt' *s* camisa de dormir
night'time' *adj* nocturno || *s* noche *f*
night'walk'er *s* vagabundo nocturno; ladrón nocturno; ramera callejera nocturna; sonámbulo
night watch *s* guardia de noche, ronda de noche; sereno; (mil) vigilia
night watchman *s* vigilante nocturno
nihilism [ˈnaɪ•ɪ,lɪzəm] *s* nihilismo
nihilist [ˈnaɪ•ɪlɪst] *s* nihilista *mf*
nil [nɪl] *s* nada
Nile [naɪl] *s* Nilo
nimble [ˈnɪmbəl] *adj* ágil, ligero; listo, vivo
nim•bus [ˈnɪmbəs] *s* (*pl* **-buses** o **-bi** [baɪ]) nimbo
Nimrod [ˈnɪmrɑd] *s* Nemrod *m*
nincompoop [ˈnɪnkəm,pup] *s* badulaque *m,* papirote *m*
nine [naɪn] *adj & pron* nueve || *s* nueve *m;* equipo de béisbol; **nine o'clock** las nueve; **the Nine** las nueve musas
nine hundred *adj & pron* novecientos || *s* novecientos *m*
nineteen [ˈnaɪnˈtin] *adj, pron & s* diecinueve *m,* diez y nueve *m*
nineteenth [ˈnaɪnˈtinθ] *adj & s* (*in a series*) decimonono; (*part*) diecinueveavo || *s* (*in dates*) diecinueve *m*
ninetieth [ˈnaɪntɪ•ɪθ] *adj & s* (*in a series*) nonagésimo; (*part*) noventavo
nine•ty [ˈnaɪnti] *adj & pron* noventa || *s* (*pl* **-ties**) noventa *m*
ninth [ˈnaɪnθ] *adj & s* nono, noveno || *s* (*in dates*) nueve *m*
nip [nɪp] *s* mordisco, pellizco; helada, escarcha; traguito; **nip and tuck** a quién ganará || *v* (*pret & pp* **nipped;** *ger* **nipping**) *tr* mordiscar, pellizcar; helar, escarchar; (slang) asir, coger; **to nip in the bud** atajar en el principio || *intr* beborrotear
nipple [ˈnɪpəl] *s* (*of female*) pezón *m;* (*of male; of nursing bottle*) tetilla; (mach) tubo roscado de unión, entrerrosca
Nippon [nɪˈpɑn] *s* el Japón
Nippon•ese [,nɪpəˈniz] *adj* nipón || *s* (*pl* **-ese**) nipón *m*
nip•py [ˈnɪpi] *adj* (*comp* **-pier;** *super* **-piest**) mordaz, picante; frío, helado; (Brit) ágil, ligero
nirvana [nɪrˈvɑnə] *s* el nirvana
nit [nɪt] *s* piojito; (*egg of insect*) liendre *f*
niter [ˈnaɪtər] *s* nitro; (agr) nitro de Chile
nitrate [ˈnaɪtret] *s* nitrato; (agr) nitrato de potasio, nitrato de sodio
nitric acid [ˈnaɪtrɪk] *s* ácido nítrico
nitride [ˈnaɪtraɪd] *s* nitruro
nitrogen [ˈnaɪtrədʒən] *s* nitrógeno
nitroglycerin [,naɪtrəˈglɪsərɪn] *s* nitroglicerina
nitrous oxide [ˈnaɪtrəs] *s* óxido nitroso
nitwit [ˈnɪt,wɪt] *s* (slang) bobalicón *m*
no [no] *adj indef* ninguno; **no admittance** no se permite la entrada; **no matter** no importa; **no parking** se prohibe estacionarse; **no smoking** se prohibe fumar; **no thoroughfare** prohibido el paso; **no use** inútil; **with no** sin || *adv* no; **no good** de ningún valor; ruin, vil; **no longer** ya no; **no sooner** no bien
Noah [ˈno•ə] *s* Noé *m*
nob•by [ˈnɑbi] *adj* (*comp* **-bier;** *super* **-biest**) (slang) elegante; (slang) excelente
nobili•ty [noˈbɪlɪti] *s* (*pl* **-ties**) nobleza; (*of sentiments, character, etc.*) nobleza, ennoblecimiento
noble [ˈnobəl] *adj & s* noble *m*
noble•man [ˈnobəlmən] *s* (*pl* **-men** [mən]) noble *m,* hidalgo
nobod•y [ˈno,bɑdi] o [ˈnobədi] *pron indef* nadie, ninguno; **nobody but** nadie más que; **nobody else** nadie más, ningún otro || *s* (*pl* **-ies**) nadie *m,* don nadie
nocturnal [nɑkˈtʌrnəl] *adj* nocturno
nod [nɑd] *s* inclinación de cabeza; seña con la cabeza; (*of a person going to sleep*) cabezada || *v* (*pret & pp* **nodded;** *ger* **nodding**) *tr* inclinar (*la cabeza*); indicar con una inclinación de cabeza || *intr* inclinar la cabeza; (*in going to sleep*) cabecear
node [nod] *s* bulto, protuberancia; nudo, enredo; (astr, med & phys) nodo; (bot) nudo
no'-fault' *adj* (*divorce, insurance*) libre de culpa
nohow [ˈno,haʊ] *adv* (coll) de ninguna manera
noise [nɔɪz] *s* ruido || *tr* divulgar
noiseless [ˈnɔɪzlɪs] *adj* silencioso, sin ruido

noise level *s* nivel sonoro
nois•y ['nɔɪzi] *adj* (*comp* **-ier;** *super* **-iest**) ruidoso; bullero; (*boisterous*) estrepitoso
nom. *abbr* **nominative**
nomad ['nomæd] *adj & s* nómada *mf*
nomadic [no'mædɪk] *adj* nomádico
no man's land *s* terreno sin reclamar; (mil) la tierra de nadie
nominal ['nɑmɪnəl] *adj* nominal; (*price*) módico
nominate ['nɑmɪ,net] *tr* postular como candidato; (*to appoint*) nombrar, designar
nomination [,nɑmɪ' neʃən] *s* postulación
nominative ['nɑmɪnətɪv] *adj & s* nominativo
nominee [,nɑmɪ'ni] *s* propuesto, candidato
nonaligned nations [,nɑnə'laɪnd] *spl* países no alineados; países no comprometidos
nonbelligerent [,nɑnbə'lɪdʒərənt] *adj & s* no beligerante *m*
nonbreakable [nɑn'brekəbəl] *adj* irrompible
nonchalance ['nɑnʃələns] *s* indiferencia, desenvoltura
nonchalant ['nɑnʃələnt] *adj* indiferente, desenvuelto
noncom ['nɑn,kɑm] *s* (coll) clase, suboficial *m*
noncombatant [nɑn'kɑmbətənt] *adj & s* no combatiente *m*
noncommissioned officer [,nɑnkə'mɪʃənd] *s* clase, suboficial *m*
noncommittal [,nɑnkə'mɪtəl] *adj* evasivo, reticente
noncommitted [,nɑnkə'mɪtɪd] *adj* no empeñado
non compos mentis ['nɑn'kɑmpəs'mɛntɪs] *adj* falto de juicio, loco
nonconformist [,nɑnkən'fɔrmɪst] *s* disidente *mf;* inconformista *mf*
nonconformity [,nɑnkən'fɔrmɪti] *s* inconformidad
nondelivery [,nɑndɪ'lɪvəri] *s* falta de entrega
nondescript ['nɑndɪ,skrɪpt] *adj* inclasificable, indefinido
nondiscriminating [,nɑndɪs'krɪmɪ,netɪŋ] *adj* indiscriminado
none [nʌn] *pron indef* nadie, ninguno, ningunos; **none of** ninguno de; nada de; **none other** ningún otro || *adv* nada, de ninguna manera; **none the less** sin embargo, no obstante
nonenti•ty [nɑn'ɛntɪti] *s* (*pl* **-ties**) cosa inexistente; (*person*) nulidad
nonessential [,nɑnɛ'sɛnʃəl] *adj* intrascendente
nonexistence [,nɑnɛg'zɪstəns] *s* inexistencia
nonfiction [nɑn'fɪkʃən] *s* literatura no novelesca
nonfulfillment [,nɑnfʊl'fɪlmənt] *s* incumplimiento
nonintervention [,nɑnɪntər'vɛnʃən] *s* no intervención
nonmetal ['nɑn,mɛtəl] *s* metaloide *m*
nonpartisan [nɑn'pɑrtɪzən] *adj* imparcial
nonpayment [nɑn'pemənt] *s* falta de pago
non•plus ['nɑnplʌs] o [nɑn'plʌs] *s* estupefacción || *v* (*pret & pp* **-plused** o **-plussed;** *ger* **-plusing** o **-plussing**) *tr* dejar estupefacto, dejar pegado a la pared
nonprofit [nɑn'prɑfɪt] *adj* sin fin lucrativo
nonrefillable [,nɑnrɪ'fɪləbəl] *adj* irrellenable
nonresident [nɑn'rɛzɪdənt] *s* transeúnte *mf*
nonresidential [nɑn,rɛzɪ'dɛnʃəl] *adj* comercial
nonscientific [nɑn,saɪ•ən'tɪfɪk] *adj* anticientífico
nonsectarian [,nɑnsɛk'tɛrɪ•ən] *adj* no sectario
nonsense ['nɑnsɛns] *s* disparate *m*, tontería; esperpento; **to talk nonsense** hablar en gringo
nonsensical [nɑn'sɛnsɪkəl] *adj* disparatado, tonto
nonskid ['nɑn'skɪd] *adj* antideslizante
nonstop ['nɑn'stɑp] *adj & adv* sin parar, sin escala
nonsupport [,nɑnsə'port] *s* falta de manutención
noodle ['nudəl] *s* tallarín *m;* (slang) mentecato, tonto; (slang) cabeza
noodle soup *s* sopa de pastas, sopa de fideos
nook [nʊk] *s* rinconcito
noon [nun] *s* mediodía *m;* **at high noon** en pleno mediodía
no one o **no-one** ['no,wʌn] *pron indef* nadie, ninguno; **no one else** nadie más, ningún otro
noontime ['nun,taɪm] *s* mediodía *m*
noose [nus] *s* lazo corredizo; (*to hang a criminal*) dogal *m;* trampa || *tr* lazar; hacer un lazo corredizo en
nor [nɔr] *conj* ni
Nordic ['nɔrdɪk] *adj & s* nórdico
norm [nɔrm] *s* norma
normal ['nɔrməl] *adj* normal
Norman ['nɔrmən] *adj & s* normando
Normandy ['nɔrməndi] *s* Normandía
Norse [nɔrs] *adj* nórdico; noruego || *s* (*ancient Scandinavian language*) nórdico; (*language of Norway*) noruego; **the Norse** los nórdicos; los noruegos
Norse•man ['nɔrsmən] *s* (*pl* **-men** [mən]) normando
north [nɔrθ] *adj* septentrional, del norte || *adv* al norte, hacia el norte || *s* norte *m*
North America *s* Norteamérica, la América del Norte
North American *adj & s* norteamericano
north'east'er *s* (*wind*) nordestada, nordeste *m* (*viento*)
northern ['nɔrðərn] *adj* septentrional; (*Hemisphere*) boreal
North Korea *s* la Corea del Norte
North Korean *adj & s* norcoreano
northward ['nɔrθwərd] *adv* hacia el norte
north wind *s* norte *m*, aquilón *m*
Norway ['nɔrwe] *s* Noruega
Norwegian [nɔr'widʒən] *adj & s* noruego
nos. *abbr* **numbers**
nose [noz] *s* nariz *f;* (aer) proa; **to blow one's nose** sonarse las narices; **to count noses** averiguar cuántas personas hay; **to follow one's nose** seguir todo derecho; avanzar guiándose por el instinto; **to hold one's**

nose tabicarse las narices; **to lead by the nose** llevar por la barba, tener agarrado por las narices; **to look down one's nose at** mirar por encima del hombro; **to pay through the nose** pagar un precio escandaloso; **to pick one's nose** hurgarse las narices; **to poke one's nose into** meter las narices en; **to speak through the nose** ganguear; **to thumb one's nose at** señalar (*a una persona*) poniendo el pulgar sobre la nariz en son de burla; tratar con sumo desprecio; **to turn up one's nose at** mirar con desprecio; **under the nose of** en las narices de, en las barbas de || *tr* olfatear || *intr* ventear; **to nose about** curiosear; **to nose over** capotar (*un avión*); **to nose up** encabritarse (*un buque, un avión*)

nose bag *s* cebadera, morral *m*

nose'band' *s* muserola, sobarba

nose'bleed' *s* hemorragia nasal

nose cone *s* cono de proa

nose dive *s* (aer) descenso de picado; (fig) descenso precipitado

nose'-dive' *intr* (aer) picar; (fig) descender precipidamente

nosegay [ˈnoz,ge] *s* ramillete *m*

nose ring *s* nariguera

no'-show' *s* pasajero no presentado

nostalgia [nɑˈstældʒə] *s* nostalgia

nostril [ˈnɑstrɪl] *s* nariz *f*, ventana

nos•y [ˈnozi] *adj* (*comp* **-ier;** *super* **-iest**) (coll) curioso, husmeador

not [nɑt] *adv* no; **not at all** nada, de ningún modo; **not yet** todavía no; **to think not** creer que no; **why not?** ¿cómo no?

notable [ˈnotəbəl] *adj & s* notable *m*

notarize [ˈnotə,raɪz] *tr* abonar con fe notarial

nota•ry [ˈnotəri] *s* (*pl* **-ries**) notario

notch [nɑtʃ] *s* muesca, mella, corte *m;* (U.S.A.) desfiladero, paso; (coll) grado || *tr* hacer muescas en, mellar

note [not] *s* nota; apunte *m;* esquela, cartita; marca, señal *f;* (com) pagaré *m,* vale *m;* canto, melodía; acento, voz *f;* (mus) nota || *tr* notar, apuntar; marcar, señalar

note'book' *s* cuaderno, libro de apuntes

noted [ˈnotɪd] *adj* aramado, conocido

note paper *s* papel *m* de cartas

note'wor'thy *adj* notable, digno de notarse

nothing [ˈnʌθɪŋ] *pron indef* nada; **for nothing** inútilmente; de balde, gratis; **nothing doing** (slang) ni por pienso; **nothing else** nada más; **that's nothing to me** eso nada me importa; **to make nothing of** no hacer caso de; no aprovecharse de; no entender; despreciar; **to think nothing of** no hacer caso de; tener por fácil; despreciar || *adv* nada, de ninguna manera; **nothing daunted** sin temor alguno || *s* nada; nadería, friolera

notice [ˈnotɪs] *s* atención, reparo, advertencia; aviso, noticia; letrero; mención, reseña; llamada; notificación; **on short notice** con poco tiempo de aviso; **to escape one's notice** pasarle inadvertido a uno; **to serve notice** dar noticia, hacer saber || *tr* notar, observar, reparar, reparar en; mencionar

noticeable [ˈnotɪsəbəl] *adj* sensible, perceptible; notable

noti•fy [ˈnotɪ,faɪ] *v* (*pret & pp* **-fied**) *tr* notificar, avisar, hacer saber

notion [ˈnoʃən] *s* noción; capricho; **notions** mercería, artículos menudos; **to have a notion to** + *inf* pensar + *inf*, tener ganas de + *inf*

notorie•ty [,noˈtəˈraɪ•əti] *s* (*pl* **-ties**) mala reputación; (*condition of being well known*) notoriedad; (*person*) notable *mf*

notorious [noˈtorɪ•əs] *adj* reputado, mal reputado; bien conocido

no'-trump' *adj & s* sin triunfo; **a no-trump hand** un sin triunfo

notwithstanding [,nɑtwɪðˈstændɪŋ] o [,nɑtwiθˈstændɪŋ] *adv* no obstante || *prep* a pesar de || *conj* a pesar de que

nougat [ˈnugət] *s* turrón *m*

noun [naʊn] *s* nombre, nombre sustantivo

nourish [ˈnʌrɪʃ] *tr* alimentar, nutrir; abrigar (*p.ej., esperanzas*)

nourishing [ˈnʌrɪʃɪŋ] *adj* alimenticio, nutritivo

nourishment [ˈnʌrɪʃmənt] *s* alimento, nutrimento

Nov. *abbr* **November**

Nova Scotia [ˈnovəˈskoʃə] *s* la Nueva Escocia

Nova Scotian [ˈnovəˈskoʃən] *adj & s* neoescocés *m*

novel [ˈnɑvəl] *adj* nuevo; insólito, extraño, original || *s* novela

novelist [ˈnɑvəlɪst] *s* novelista *mf*

novel•ty [ˈnɑvəlti] *s* (*pl* **-ties**) novedad, innovación; **novelties** bisutería, baratijas

November [noˈvɛmbər] *s* noviembre *m*

novice [ˈnɑvɪs] *s* novicio

novocaine [ˈnovə,ken] *s* novocaína

now [naʊ] *adv* ahora; ya; entonces; **from now on** de ahora en adelante; **how now?** ¿cómo?; **just now** hace un momento; **now and again** o **now and then** de vez en cuando; **now . . . now** ora . . . ora, ya . . . ya; **now that** ya que; **now then** ahora bien || *interj* ¡vamos! || *s* actualidad

nowadays [ˈnaʊ•ə,dez] *adv* hoy en día, hoy día

no'way' o **no'ways'** *adv* de ningún modo

no'where' *adv* en ninguna parte, a ninguna parte; **nowhere else** en ninguna otra parte

noxious [ˈnɑkʃəs] *adj* nocivo

nozzle [ˈnɑzəl] *s* (*of hoe*) lanza; (*of sprinkling can*) rallow, roseta; (*of candlestick*) cubo; (slang) nariz *f*

N.T. *abbr* **New Testament**

nth [ɛnθ] *adj* n^{mo} (*enésimo*); **to the nth degree** elevado a la potencia *n;* a más no poder

nuance [njuˈɑns] o [ˈnju•ɑns] *s* matiz *m*

nub [nʌb] *s* protuberancia; pedazo; (coll) meollo

nuclear [ˈnuklɪ•ər] *adj* nuclear

nu'cle•ar-pow'ered *adj* accionado por energía nuclear

nuclear test ban *s* proscripción de las pruebas nucleares
nuclear war *s* guerra nuclear
nucle•us [ˈnuklɪ•əs] *s* (*pl* **-i** [ˌaɪ] o **-uses**) núcleo
nude [njud] o [nud] *adj* desnudo ‖ *s*—**in the nude** desnudo; **the nude** el desnudo
nudism [ˈnjudɪzəm] o [ˈnudɪzəm] *s* (des)nudismo; naturismo
nudge [nʌdʒ] *s* codazo suave ‖ *tr* dar un codazo suave a, empujar suavemente
nugget [ˈnʌgɪt] *s* pedazo; (*of, e.g., gold*) pepita; preciosidad
nuisance [ˈnjusəns] o [ˈnusəns] *s* molestia, estorbo; majadería; persona o cosa fastidiosas; **to be a nuisance** ser un higado
nuke [njuk] o [nuk] *s* (slang) arma atómica ‖ *tr* (slang) atacar con arma atómica; aniquilar
null [nʌl] *adj* nulo; **null and void** nulo, írrito, nulo y sin valor
nulli•ty [ˈnʌlɪti] *v* (*pl* **-ties**) nulidad
nulli•fy [ˈnʌlifaɪ] *v* (*pret & pp* **-fied**) anular, invalidor
numb [nʌm] *adj* entumecido; **to get numb** envararse ‖ *tr* entumecer
number [ˈnʌmbər] *s* número; **a number of** varios ‖ *tr* numerar; ascender a (*cierto número*); **his days are numbered** tiene sus días contados o sus horas contadas; **to be numbered among** hallarse entre; **to number among** contar entre
numberless [ˈnʌmbərlɪs] *adj* innumerable
numeral [ˈnjumərəl] o [ˈnumərəl] *adj* numeral ‖ *s* número
numerical [njuˈmɛrɪkəl] o [nuˈmɛrɪkəl] *adj* numérico
numerous [ˈnjumərəs] o [ˈnumərəs] *adj* numeroso
numskull [ˈnʌmˌskʌl] *s* (coll) bodoque *m*, mentecato
nun [nʌn] *s* monja, religiosa
nuptial [ˈnʌpʃəl] *adj* nupcial ‖ **nuptials** *spl* nupcias, bodas
nurse [nʌrs] *s* enfermera; (*to suckle a child*) ama de cría, nodriza; (*to take care of a child*) niñera ‖ *tr* cuidar (*a una persona enferma*); amamantar; alimentar, criar; tratar de curarse de (*p.ej., un resfriado*); abrigar (*p.ej., odio*) ‖ *intr* ser enfermera
nurser•y [ˈnʌrsəri] *s* (*pl* **-ies**) cuarto de los niños; (*of plants*) criadero, plantel *m*, semillero; (fig) semillero
nursery•man [ˈnʌrsərɪmən] *s* (*pl* **-men** [mən]) cultivador *m* de semillero
nursery rhymes *spl* versos para niños
nursery tales *spl* cuentos para niños
nursing bottle *s* biberón *m*
nursing home *s* clínica de reposo; (*for the aged*) residencia de ancianos
nurture [ˈnʌrtʃər] *s* alimentación, nutrimento; crianza, educación ‖ *tr* alimentar, nutrir; criar, educar; acariciar (*p.ej., una esperanza*)
nut [nʌt] *s* nuez *f*; (*to screw on a bolt*) tuerca; (slang) estrafalario; **a hard nut to crack** (coll) hueso duro de roer
nut′crack′er *s* cascanueces *m*
nutmeg [ˈnʌtˌmɛg] *s* nuez moscada; (*tree*) mirística
nutriment [ˈnjutrɪmənt] *s* nutrimento
nutrition [njuˈtrɪʃən] *s* nutrición
nutritious [njuˈtrɪʃəs] *adj* nutricioso, nutritivo
nuts *adj* (slang) loco; estrafalario ‖ *interj* (slang) ¡no!, ¡niego!, ¡de ninguna manera!
nut′shell′ *s* cáscara de nuez; **in a nutshell** en pocas palabras
nut•ty [ˈnʌti] *adj* (*comp* **-tier;** *super* **-tiest**) abundante en nueces; que sabe a nueces; (slang) chiflado, loco; **nutty about** (slang) loco por
nuzzle [ˈnʌzəl] *tr* hocicar, hozar ‖ *intr* hocicar; arrimarse cómodamente; arroparse bien
nylon [ˈnaɪlɑn] *s* nilón *m;* **nylons** medias de nilón
nymph [nɪmf] *s* ninfa

O

O, o [o] decimoquinta letra del alfabeto inglés
O *interj* ¡oh!; ¡ay!, p.ej., **how pretty she is!** ¡Ay qué linda!; **O that. . . !** ¡Ojalá que. . . !
oaf [of] *s* zoquete *m*, zamacuco; niño contrahecho
oak [ok] *s* roble *m*
oaken [ˈokən] *adj* hecho de roble
oakum [ˈokəm] *s* estopa, estopa de calafatear
oar [or] *s* remo; **to lie** o **rest on one's oars** aguantar los remos; aflojar en el trabajo ‖ *tr* conducir a remo ‖ *intr* remar, bogar
oars•man [ˈorzmən] *s* (*pl* **-men** [mən]) remero
OAS [ˈoˈeˈɛs] *s* (*letterword*) OEA *f*
oa•sis [oˈesɪs] *s* (*pl* **-ses** [siz]) oasis *m*
oat [ot] *s* avena; **oats** (*edible grain*) avena; **to feel one's oats** (slang) estar fogoso y brioso; (slang) estar muy pagado de sí mismo; **to sow one's wild oats** correrla, pasar las mocedades
oath [oθ] *s* juramento; **on oath** bajo juramento; **to take an oath** prestar juramento
oat′meal′ *s* harina de avena; gachas de avena
ob. *abbr* **obiit** (Lat) **died**
obbligato [ˌɑblɪˈgɑto] *adj & s* obligado
obduracy [ˈɑbdjərəsi] *s* obduración

obdurate ['ɑbdjərɪt] *adj* obstinado, terco; empedernido
obedience [o'bidɪ•əns] *s* obediencia
obedient [o'bidɪ•ənt] *adj* obediente
obeisance [o'besəns] u [o'bisəns] *s* saludo respetuoso; homenaje *m*, respeto
obelisk ['ɑbəlɪsk] *s* obelisco
obese [o'bis] *adj* obeso
obesity [o'bisɪti] *s* obesidad
obey [o'be] *tr & intr* obedecer
obfuscate [ɑb'fʌsket] o ['ɑbfəs,ket] *tr* ofuscar
obituar•y [o'bɪtʃu,ɛri] *adj* necrológico ‖ *s* (*pl* **-ies**) necrología
obj. *abbr* **object, objection, objective**
object ['ɑbdʒɪkt] *s* objeto ‖ [ɑb'dʒɛkt] *tr* objetar ‖ *intr* hacer objeciones
objection [ɑb'dʒɛkʃən] *s* reparo, objeción; **to have no objections to make** no tener nada que objetar
objectionable [ɑb'dʒɛkʃənəbəl] *adj* desagradable, reprensible; (*causing disapproval*) objetable
objective [ɑb'dʒɛktɪv] *adj & s* objetivo
obl. *abbr* **oblique, oblong**
obligate [ɑblɪ,get] *tr* obligar
obligation [,ɑblɪ'geʃən] *s* obligación; encargamiento
oblige [ə'blaɪdʒ] *tr* obligar; complacer; **much obliged** muchas gracias
obliging [ə'blaɪdʒɪŋ] *adj* complaciente, condescendiente, servicial
oblique [ə'blik] *adj* oblicuo; indirecto, evasivo
obliterate [ə'blɪtə,ret] *tr* borrar; arrasar, destruir
oblivion [ə'blɪvɪ•ən] *s* olvido
oblivious [ə'blɪvɪ•əs] *adj* olvidadizo
oblong ['ɑblɔŋ] o ['ɑblɑŋ] *adj* oblongo
obnoxious [əb'nɑkʃəs] *adj* detestable, ofensivo
oboe ['obo] *s* oboe *m*
oboist ['obo•ɪst] *s* oboísta *mf*
obs. *abbr* **obsolete**
obscene [ɑb'sin] *adj* obsceno
obsceni•ty [ɑb'sɛnɪti] o [ɑb'sinɪti] *s* (*pl* **-ties**) obscenidad
obscure [əb'skjʊr] *adj* obscuro; (*vowel*) relajado, neutro
obscuri•ty [əb'skjʊrɪti] *s* (*pl* **-ties**) obscuridad
obsequies ['ɑbsɪkwiz] *spl* exequias
obsequious [əb'sikwɪ•əs] *adj* obsequioso, servil, rastrero
observance [əb'zʌrvəns] *s* observancia; ceremonia, rito
observant [əb'zʌrvənt] *adj* observador
observation [,ɑbzər'veʃən] *s* observación; observancia
observato•ry [əb'zʌrvə,tori] *s* (*pl* **-ries**) observatorio
observe [əb'zʌrv] *tr* observar; (*a holiday; silence*) guardar
observer [əb'zʌrvər] *s* observador *m*
obsess [əb'sɛs] *tr* obsesionar
obsession [əb'sɛʃən] *s* obsesión
obsolescent [,ɑbsə'lɛsənt] *adj* arcaizante
obsolete ['ɑbsə,lit] *adj* desusado, caído en desuso; obsoleto
obstacle ['ɑbstəkəl] *s* obstáculo
obstetrical [ɑb'stɛtrɪkəl] *adj* obstétrico
obstetrics [ɑb'stɛtrɪks] *ssg* obstetricia
obstina•cy ['ɑbstɪnəsi] *s* (*pl* **-cies**) obstinación
obstinate ['ɑbstɪnɪt] *adj* obstinado
obstruct [ɑb'strʌkt] *tr* obstruir; obstruccionar
obstruction [əb'strʌkʃən] *s* obstrucción
obtain [əb'ten] *tr* obtener ‖ *intr* existir, prevalecer
obtrusive [əb'trusɪv] *adj* entremetido, intruso
obtuse [əb'tjus] o [əb'tus] *adj* obtuso
obviate ['ɑbvɪ,et] *tr* obviar
obvious ['ɑbvɪ•əs] *adj* obvio
occasion [ə'keθən] *s* ocasión; **to improve the occasion** aprovechar la ocasión
occasional [ə'keʒənəl] *adj* raro, poco frecuente; alguno que otro; de circunstancia
occasionally [ə'keʒənəli] *adv* ocasionalmente, de vez en cuando
occident ['ɑksɪdənt] *s* occidente *m*
occidental [,ɑksɪ'dɛntəl] *adj* occidental
occlusive [ə'klusɪv] *adj* oclusivo ‖ *s* oclusiva
occult [ə'kʌlt] o ['ɑkʌlt] *adj* oculto
occupancy ['ɑkjepənsi] *s* ocupación
occupant ['ɑkjepənt] *s* ocupante *mf;* inquilino
occupation [,ɑkjə'peʃən] *s* ocupación
occupational therapy *s* terapia vocacional
occu•py ['ɑkjə,paɪ] *v* (*pret & pp* **-pied**) *tr* ocupar; habitar
oc•cur [ə'kʌr] *v* (*pret & pp* **-curred;** *ger* **-curring**) *intr* ocurrir, acontecer, suceder; encontrarse; (*to come to mind*) ocurrir
occurrence [ə'kʌrəns] *s* acontecimiento; caso, aparición
ocean ['oʃən] *s* océano
o'cean-go'ing *adj* transoceánico
oceanic [,oʃɪ'ænɪk] *adj* oceánico
ocean liner *s* buque transoceánico
o'clock [ə'klɑk] *adv* por el reloj; **it is one o'clock** es la una; **it is two o'clock** son las dos; **what o'clock is it?** ¿qué hora es?
Oct. *abbr* **October**
octave ['ɑktɪv] o ['ɑktev] *s* octava
October [ɑk'tobər] *s* octubre *m*
octo•pus ['ɑktəpəs] *s* (*pl* **-puses** o **-pi** [,paɪ]) pulpo
octoroon [,ɑktə'run] *s* octavo
ocular ['ɑkjələr]*adj & s* ocular *m*
oculist ['ɑkjəlɪst] *s* oculista *mf*
O.D. *abbr* **officer of the day, olive drab, overdose**
odd [ɑd] *adj* suelto; (*number*) impr; (*that doesn't match*) dispar; libre, de ocio; sobrante; extraño, raro, singular; y pico, y tantos, p.ej., **two hundred odd** doscientos y pico ‖ **odds** *ssg* o *spl* (*in betting*) ventaja; apuesta desigual; puntos de ventaja; **at odds** de monos, riñendo; **by all odds** muy probablemente, sin duda alguna; **it makes no odds** lo mismo da; **the odds are** lo probable es; la ventaja es de; **to be at odds** estar de punta, estar encontrados; **to set at odds** enemistar, malquistar

odd'ball' *adj & s* excéntrico; disente
oddi•ty [ˈɑdɪti] *s* (*pl* **-ties**) rareza, cosa rara
odd jobs *spl* pequeñas tareas
odd lot *s* lote *m* inferior al centenar
odds and ends *spl* pedacitos varios, cajón *m* de sastre
ode [od] *s* oda
odious [ˈodɪ•əs] *adj* odioso, abominable
odor [ˈodər] *s* olor *m;* **to be in bad odor** tener mala fama
odorless [ˈodərlɪs] *adj* inodoro
odorous [ˈodərəs] *adj* oloroso
Odysseus [oˈdɪsjus] u [oˈdɪsɪ•əs] *s* Odiseo
Odyssey [ˈɑdɪsi] *s* Odisea
Oedipus [ˈɛdɪpəs] o [ˈidɪpəs] *s* Edipo
oenology [iˈnɑlədʒi] *s* enotecnia
of [ɑv] o [əv] *prep* de, p.ej., **the top of the mountain** la cima de la montaña; a: **to smell of** oler a; con: **to dream of** soñar con; en: **to think of** pensar en; menos: **a quarter of two** las dos menos un cuarto
off. *abbr* **office, officer, official**
off [ɔf] o [ɑf] *adj* malo, p.ej., **off day** día, malo; (*account, sum*) errado; más distante; libre; sin trabajo; quitado; apagado; (*electric current*) cortado; de descuento, de rebaja; de la parte del mar; (*season*) muerto ‖ *adv* fuera, a distancia, lejos; allá; **off of** (coll) de; (coll) a expensas de; **to be off** ponerse en marcha ‖ *prep* de, desde, al lado de, a nivel de; fuera de; libre de; (naut) a la altura de ‖ *tr* (slang) matar, asesinar
offal [ˈɑfəl] u [ˈɔfəl] *s* (*of butchered meat*) carniza; basura, desperdicios
off and on *adv* unas veces sí y otras no
off'beat' *adj* (slang) insólito, chocante, original
off'chance' *s* posibilidad poco probable
off'-col'or *adj* descolorido; indispuesto; (*indecent, risqué*) colorado, subido de color
offend [əˈfɛnd] *tr & intr* ofender
offender [əˈfɛndər] *s* ofensor *m*
offense [əˈfɛns] *s* ofensa; **to take offense (at)** ofenderse (de)
offensive [əˈfɛnsɪv] *adj* ofensivo ‖ *f* ofensiva
offer [ˈɔfər] o [ˈɑfər] *s* ofrecimiento, oferta ‖ *tr* ofrecer; rezar (*oraciones*); oponer (*resistencia*)
offering [ˈɔfərɪŋ] o [ˈɑfərɪŋ] *s* ofrecimiento; (*gift, present*) oferta; (*presentation in worship*) ofrenda
off'hand' *adj* hecho de improviso; brusco, desenvuelto ‖ *adv* de improviso, súbitamente; bruscamente
office [ˈɔfɪs] o [ˈɑfɪs] *s* oficina, despacho; función, oficio; cargo, ministerio; (*of a lawyer*) bufete *m;* (*of a doctor*) consultorio
office boy *s* mandadero
office desk *s* escritorio ministro
of'fice•hold'er *s* funcionario, burócrata *m*
office hours *spl* horas de oficina; (*of a doctor*) horas de consulta
officer [ˈɔfɪsər] o [ˈɑfɪsər] *s* jefe *m,* director *m;* (*of army, an order, a society, etc.*) oficial *m;* agente *m* de policía
office seeker [ˈsikər] *s* aspirante *m,* pretendiente *m*
office supplies *spl* suministros para oficinas
official [əˈfɪʃəl] *adj* oficial ‖ *s* jefe *m,* director *m;* (*of a society*) dignatario
officiate [əˈfɪʃɪ,et] *intr* oficiar
officious [əˈfɪʃəs] *adj* oficioso
off'-peak' *adj* (*hours, stop, etc.*) de valle; de menor tránsito
off-peak heater *s* (elec) termos *m* de acumulación
off-peak load *s* (elec) carga de las horas de valle
off'print' *s* sobretiro
off,set' *s* compensación; (typ) offset *m* ‖ **off'set'** *v* (*pret & pp* **-set;** *ger* **-setting**) *tr* compensar; imprimir por offset
off'shoot' *s* (*of plant*) retoño, renuevo; (*of a family or race*) descendiente *mf;* (*branch*) ramal *m;* consecuencia
off'shore' *adj* (*wind*) terral; (*fishing*) de bajura; (*said of islands*) costero; **offshore drilling rig** barca perforador ‖ *adv* a lo largo
off'spring' *s* descendencia, sucesión; hijo, hijos
off'-stage' *adj* de entre bastidores
off'-the-rec'ord *adj* extraoficial, confidencial
often [ˈɔfən] o (ɑfən] *adv* a menudo, muchas veces; **how often?** ¿cuántas veces?; **not often** pocas veces
ogive [ˈodʒaɪv] u [oˈdʒaɪv] *s* ojiva
ogle [ˈogəl] *tr & intr* ojear; mirar amorosamente
ogre [ˈogər] *s* ogro
ohm [om] *s* ohmio
oil [ɔɪl] *adj* (*burner; field; well*) de petróleo; (*pump; stove*) de aceite; (*company, tanker*) petrolero; (*land*) petrolífero ‖ *s* aceite *m;* (*consecrated oil; painting*) óleo; **to burn the midnight oil** quemarse las cejas; **to pour oil on troubled waters** mojar la pólvora; **to strike oil** encontrar una capa de petróleo; (fig) enriquecerse de súbito ‖ *tr* aceitar; lubricar; lisonjear; (*to bribe*) untar ‖ *intr* proveerse de petróleo (*un buque*)
oil'can' *s* aceitera
oil'cloth' *s* encerado, hule *m*
oil field *s* yacamiento de petróleo
oil gauge indicador *m* del nivel de aceite
oil pan *s* colector *m* de aceite
oil shortage *s* carestía (*or* escasez *f*) de petróleo
oil tanker *s* petrolero
oil•y [ˈɔɪli] *adj* (*comp* **-ier;** *super* **-iest**) aceitoso; liso, resbaladizo; zalamero
ointment [ˈɔɪntmənt] *s* ungüento
O.K. [ˈoˈke] *adj* (coll) aprobado, conforme ‖ *adv* (coll) muy bien, está bien ‖ *s* (coll) aprobación ‖ *v* (*pret & pp* **O.K.'d;** *ger* **O.K.'ing**) *tr* (coll) aprobar
okra [ˈokrə] *s* quingombó *m*
old [old] *adj* viejo; antiguo; (*wine*) añejo; **how old is . . . ?** ¿cuántos años tiene . . . ?; **of old** de antaño, antiguamente; **to be . . . years old** tener . . . años

old age *s* ancianidad, vejez *f;* **to die of old age** morir de viejo
old boy *s* viejo; graduado; **the Old Boy** (slang) el diablo
Old Castile *s* Castilla la Vieja
old-clothes•man ['old'kloðz,mæn] *s* (*pl* **-men** [mɛn]) ropavejero
old country *s* madre patria
old-fashioned ['old'fæʃənd] *adj* chapado a la antigua; anticuado, fuera de moda
old fo•gey u **old fo•gy** ['fogi] *s* (*pl* **-gies**) persona un poco ridícula por sus ideas o costumbres atrasadas
Old Glory *s* la bandera de los Estados Unidos
Old Guard *s* (U.S.A.) bando conservador del partido republicano
old hand *s* practicón *m,* veterano
old maid *s* solterona
old master *s* (paint) gran maestro; obra de un gran maestro
old moon *s* luna menguante
old salt *s* lobo de mar
old school *s* gente chapada a la antigua
old'-time' *adj* del tiempo viejo
old-timer ['old'taɪmər] *s* (coll) antiguo residente, veterano; (coll) persona chapada a la antigua
old wives' tale *s* cuento de viejas
old'-world' *adj* del Viejo Mundo
oleander [,olɪ'ændər] *s* adelfa
oligar•chy ['ɑlɪ,gɑrki] *s* (*pl* **-chies**) oligarquía
olive ['ɑlɪv] *adj* aceitunado ‖ *s* aceituna
olive branch *s* ramo de olivo; (*peace*) oliva; hijo, vástago
olive grove *s* olivar *m*
olive oil *s* aceite *m, aceite de oliva*
olive tree *s* aceituno, olivo
Olympiad [o'lɪmpɪ,æd] *s* Olimpíada
Olympian [o'lɪmpɪ•ən] *adj* olímpico ‖ *s* dios griego
Olympic [o'lɪmpɪk] *adj* olímpico
omelet u **omelette** ['ɑmələt] o ['ɑmlɪt] *s* tortilla (de huevos)
omen ['omən] *s* agüero
ominous ['ɑmɪnəs] *adj* ominoso
omission [o'mɪʃən] *s* omisión
omit [o'mɪt] *v* (*pret & pp* **omitted;** *ger* **omitting**) *tr* omitir
omnibus ['ɑmnɪ,bʌs] o ['ɑmnɪbəs] *adj* general; (*volume*) colecticio ‖ *s* ómnibus *m*
omnipotent [ɑm'nɪpətənt] *adj* omnipotente
omniscient [ɑm'nɪʃənt] *adj* omnisciente
omnivorous [ɑm'nɪvərəs] *adj* omnívoro
on [ɑn] u [ɔn] *adj* puesto, p.ej., **with his hat on** con el sombrero puesto; principiando; en funcionamiento; encendido; conectado; **the deal is on** ya está concertado el trato; **the game is on** ya están jugando; **the race is on** allá van los corredores; **what is on at the theater this evening?** ¿qué representan esta noche? ‖ *adv* adelante; encima; **and so on** y así sucesivamente; **come on!** ¡anda, anda!; **farther on** más allá, más adelante; **later on** más tarde, después; **to be on to a person** (coll) conocerle a uno el juego; **to have on** tener puesto; **to . . . on** sequir + *ger,* **he played on** siguió tocando ‖ *prep* en, sobre, encima de; a, p.ej., **on foot** a pie; **on my arrival** a mi llegada; bajo, p.ej., **on my responsibility** bajo mi responsabilidad; contra, p.ej., **an attack on liberty** un ataque contra la libertad; de, p.ej., **on good authority** de buena tinta; **on a journey** de viaje; hacia, p.ej., **to march on the capital** marchar hacia la capital; por, p.ej., **on all sides** por todos lados; tras, p.ej., **defeat on defeat** derrota tras derrota; **on** + *ger* al + *inf,* p.ej., **on arriving** al llegar
on and on *adv* continuamente, sin cesar, sin parar
on'-board' computer *s* ordenador de viaje
once [wʌns] *adv* una vez; antes, p.ej., **once so happy** antes tan feliz; alguna vez, p.ej., **if this once becomes known** si esto llega a saberse alguna vez; **all at once** de súbito, de repente; **at once** en seguida; a la vez en el mismo momento; **for once** una vez por lo menos; **once and again** repetidas veces; **once in a blue moon** cada muerte de obispo; **once in a while** de vez en cuando; luego; **once more** otra vez; una vez más; **once upon a time there was** érase una vez, érase que se era ‖ *conj* una vez que ‖ *s* una vez; vez, p.ej., **this once** esta vez
once'-o'ver *s* (slang) examen rápido; **to give a thing the once-over** (coll) examinar una cosa superficialmente
oncology [ɑŋ'kɑlədʒi] *s* oncología
one [wʌn] *adj* un, uno; un tal, p.ej., **one Smith** un tal Smith; único, p.ej., **one price** precio único ‖ *pron* uno, p.ej., **one does not know what to do here** uno no sabe qué hacer aquí; se, p.ej., **how does one go to the station?** ¿cómo se va a la estación?; **I for one** yo por lo menos; **it's all one and the same to me** me es igual; **my little one** mi chiquito; **of one another** el uno del otro, los unos de los otros, p.ej., **we took leave of one another** nos despedimos el uno del otro; **one and all** todos; **one another** se, p.ej., **they greeted one another** se saludaron; uno a otro, unos a otros, p.ej., **they looked at one another** se miraron uno a otro; **one by one** uno a uno; **one o'clock** la una; **one or two** unos pocos; **one's** su, el . . . de uno; **the blue book and the red one** el libro azul y el rojo; **the one and only** el único; **the one that** el que, la que; **this one** éste; **that one** ése, aquél; **to make one** unir; casar ‖ *s* uno
one'-fam'i•ly house *s* vivienda unifamiliar
one'-horse' *adj* de un solo caballo, tirado por un solo caballo; (coll) insignificante, de poca monta
onerous ['ɑnərəs] *adj* oneroso
one'self' *pron* uno mismo; sí, sí mismo; se; **to be oneself** tener dominio de sí mismo; conducirse con naturalidad
one-sided ['wʌn'saɪdɪd] *adj* de un solo lado; injusto, parcial; desigual; unilateral
one'-track' *adj* de carril único; (coll) con un solo interés

one'-way' *adj* de una solo dirección, de dirección única; (*ticket*) sencillo, de ida
onion ['ʌnjən] *s* cebolla
on'ion•skin' *s* papel *m* de seda, papel cebolla
on'look'er *s* mirón *m*, espectador *m*
only ['onlɪ] *adj* solo, único || *adv* solamente, sólo, únicamente; no . . . más que; **not only . . . but also** no sólo . . . sino también || *conj* sólo que, pero
onomatopoeic [,ɑnə,mætə'pi•ɪk] *adj* onomatopéyico
on'set' *s* arremetida, embestida; (*of an illness*) principio
onward ['ɑnwərd] u **onwards** ['ɑnwərdz] *adv* adelante, hacia adelante
onyx ['ɑnɪks] *s* ónice *m* u ónix *m*
ooze [uz] *s* chorro suave; cieno; limo, lama || *tr* rezumar || *intr* rezumar, rezumarse; manar suavemente (*p.ej., la sangre de una herida*); agotarse poco a poco
op. *abbr* **opera, operation, opus, opposite**
opal ['opəl] *s* ópalo
opaque [o'pek] *adj* opaco; (*writer's style*) obscuro; estúpido
open ['opən] *adj* abierto; descubierto, destapado; sin tejado; vacante; (*hour*) libre; discutible, pendiente; (*hand*) liberal; (*hunting season*) legal; **to break** o **to crack open** abrir con violencia, abrir por la fuerza; **to throw open** abrir de par en par || *s* abertura; (*in the woods*) claro; **in the open** al aire libre; a campo raso; en alta mar; abiertamente || *tr* abrir; desbullar (*una ostra*) || *intr* abrir; abrirse; estrenarse (*un drama*); **to open into** desembocar en; **to open on** dar a; **to open up** descubrirse; descubrir el pecho
o'pen-air' *adj* al aire libre, a cielo abierto
open-eyed ['opən,aɪd] *adj* alerta, vigilante; con ojos asombrados; hecho con los ojos abiertos
open-handed ['opən'hændɪd] *adj* maniabierto, liberal
open-hearted (opən'hɑrtɪd] *adj* franco, sincero
open house *s* coliche *m;* **to keep open house** recibir a todos, gustar de tener siempre convidados en casa
opening ['opənɪŋ] *s* abertura; (*of, e.g., school*) apertura; (*in the woods*) claro; (*vacancy*) hueco, vacante *f; (chance to say something*) ocasión
opening night *s* noche *f* de estreno
opening number *s* primer número
opening price *s* primer curso, precio de apertura
open-minded ['opən'maɪndɪd] *adj* receptivo, razonable, imparcial
open secret *s* secreto a voces
open shop *s* taller franco
o'pen•work' *s* calado
opera ['ɑpərə] *s* ópera
opera glasses *spl* gemelos de teatro
opera hat *s* clac *m*, sombrero de muelles
opera house *s* teatro de la ópera
operate ['ɑpə,ret] *tr* hacer funcionar; dirigir, manejar; explotar || *intr* funcionar; operar; **to operate on** operar (*p.ej., una hernia; a un niño*)
operatic [,ɑpə'rætɪk] *adj* operístico
operating expenses *spl* gastos de explotación
operating room *s* quirófano
operating table *s* mesa operatoria
operation [,ɑpə,reʃən] *s* operación; funcionamiento; explotación
operator ['ɑpə,retər] *s* operador *m*, maquinista *m;* (com) empresario; (coll) corredor *m* de bolsa; (surg, telp) operador *m*
operetta [,ɑpə'rɛtə] *s* opereta
opiate ['opɪ•ɪt] u ['op,et] *adj & s* opiato
opinion [ə'pɪnjən] *s* opinión; **in my opinion** a mi parecer; **to have a high opinion of** tener buen concepto de
opinionated [ə'pɪnjə,netɪd] *adj* porfiado en su parecer, dogmático
opinion poll *s* encuesta demoscópica
opium ['opɪ•əm] *s* opio
opium den *s* fumadero de opio
opossum [ə'pɑsəm] *s* zarigüeya
opponent [ə'ponənt] *s* contrario
opportune [,ɑpər'tjun] *adj* oportuno
opportunist [,ɑpər'tjunɪst] *s* oportunista *mf;* maromero
opportuni•ty [,ɑpər'tjunɪti] *s* (*pl* **-ties**) oportunidad, ocasión
oppose [ə'poz] *tr* oponerse a
opposite ['ɑpəsɪt] *adj* opuesto; de enfrente, p.ej., **the house opposite** la casa de enfrente || *prep* enfrente de || *s* contrario
opposite number *s* igual *mf*, doble *mf*
opposition [,ɑpə'zɪʃən] *s* oposición
oppress [ə'prɛs] *tr* oprimir
oppression [ə'prɛʃən] *s* opresión
oppressive [ə'prɛsɪv] *adj* opresivo; sofocante, bochornoso
opprobrious [ə'probrɪ•əs] *adj* oprobioso
opprobrium [ə'probrɪ•əm] *s* oprobio
optic ['ɑptɪk] *adj* óptico || *s* (coll) ojo; **optics** *ssg* óptica
optical ['ɑptɪkəl] *adj* óptico
optician [ɑp'tɪʃən] *s* óptico
optimism ['ɑptɪ,mɪzəm] *s* optimismo
optimist ['ɑptɪmɪst] *s* optimista *mf*
optimistic [,ɑptɪ'mɪstɪk] *adj* optimístico
optimize ['ɑptə,maɪz] *tr* mejorar en todo lo posible
option ['ɑpʃən] *s* opción
optional ['ɑpʃənəl] *adj* facultativo, potestativo
optometrist [ɑp,tɑmɪtrɪst] *s* optometrista *mf*
opulent ['ɑpjələnt] *adj* opulento
or [ɔr] *conj* o, u
oracle ['ɑrəkəl] u ['ɔrəkəl] *s* oráculo
oracular [o'rækjələr] *adj* sentencioso; ambiguo, misterioso; fatídico; sabio
oral ['orəl] *adj* oral
orange ['ɑrɪndʒ] u ['ɔrɪndʒ] *adj* anaranjado || *s* naranja
orangeade [,ɑrɪndʒ'ed] u [,ɔrɪndʒ'ed] *s* naranjada
orange blossom *s* azahar *m*
orange grove *s* naranjal *m*
orange juice *s* zumo de naranja
orange squeezer *s* exprimidera de naranjas

orange tree *s* naranjo
orang-outang [o'ræŋʊ,tæŋ] *s* orangután *m*
oration [o'reʃən] *s* oración, discurso
orator ['ɑrətər] u ['ɔrətər] *s* orador *m*
oratorical [,ɔrə'tɔrɪkəl] *adj* oratorio
oratori•o [,ɔrə'torɪ,o] *s* (*pl* **-os**) oratorio
orato•ry ['ɔrə,tori] *s* (*pl* **-ries**) (*art of public speaking*) oratoria; (*small chapel*) oratorio
orb [ɔrb] *s* orbe *m*
orbit ['ɔrbɪt] *s* órbita; **to go into orbit** entrar en órbita || *tr* poner en órbita; moverse en órbita alrededor de || *intr* moverse enorbita
orbiter ['ɔrbɪtər] *s* satélite *m* (artificial)
orchard ['ɔrtʃərd] *s* huerto
orchestra ['ɔkɪstrə] *s* orquesta; (*parquet*) platea
orchestrate ['ɔrkɪs,tret] *tr* orquestar
orchid ['ɔrkɪd] *s* orquídea
ordain [ɔr'den] *tr* (eccl) ordenar; destinar; mandar
ordeal [ɔr'dil] u [ɔr'di•əl] *s* prueba rigurosa o penosa; (hist) juicio de Dios
order ['ɔrdər] *s* (*way one thing follows another; formal or methodical arrangement; peace, quiet; class, category*) orden *m;* (*command; honor society; monastic brotherhood; fraternal organization*) orden *f;* tarea, p.ej., **a big order** una tarea peliaguda; (com) pedido; (com) giro, libranza; (*formation*) (mil) orden Im; (*command*) (mil) orden *f;* **in order that** para que, a fin de que; **in order to** + *inf* para + *inf,* a fin de + *inf;* **to get out of order** descomponerse; **to give an order** dar una orden; (com) hacer un pedido || *tr* ordenar; mandar; encargar, pedir; mandar hacer; **to order around** ser muy mandón con; **to order someone away** mandar a uno que se marche
order blank *s* hoja de pedidos
order•ly ['ɔrdərli] *adj* ordenado, gobernoso; tranquilo, obediente || *s* (*pl* **-lies**) asistente *m* en un hospital; (mil) ordenanza *m*
ordinal ['ɔrdɪnəl] *adj & s* ordinal *m*
ordinance ['ɔrdɪnəns] *s* ordenanza
ordinary ['ɔrdɪ,nɛri] *adj* ordinario
ordnance ['ɔrdnəns] *s* artillería, cañones *mpl;* pertrechos de guerra
ore [or] *s* mena, mineral metalífero
organ ['ɔrgən] *s* órgano
organ•dy ['ɔrgəndi] *s* (*pl* **-dies**) organdí *m*
or'gan-grind'er *s* organillero
organic [ɔr'gænɪk] *adj* orgánico
organism ['ɔrgə,nɪzəm] *s* organismo
organist ['ɔrgənɪst] *s* organista *mf*
organize ['ɔrgə,naɪz] *tr* organizar
organ loft *s* tribuna del órgano
orgasm ['ɔrgæzəm] *s* orgasmo
orgiastic [,ɔrdʒi'æstɪk] *adj* orgiástico
or•gy ['ɔrdʒi] *s* (*pl* **-gies**) orgía
orient ['orɪ•ənt] *s* oriente *m* || **Orient** *s* oriente || **orient** ['orɪ,ɛnt] *tr* orientar
oriental [,orɪ'ɛntəl] *adj* oriental
orifice ['ɔrɪfɪs] *s* orificio
origin ['ɔrɪdʒɪn] *s* origen *m*
original [ə'rɪdʒɪnəl] *adj & s* original *m*
originate [ə'rɪdʒɪ,net] *tr* originar || *intr* originarse
oriole ['orɪ,ol] *s* oropéndola
Orkney Islands ['ɔrkni] *spl* Órcadas
ormolu ['ɔrmə,lu] *s* (*gold powder used in gilding*) oro molido; (*alloy of zinc and copper*) similor m; bronce dorado
ornament ['ɔrnəmənt] *s* ornamento || ['ɔrnə,mɛnt] *tr* ornamentar
ornate [ɔr'net] u ['ɔrnet] *adj* muy ornado; (*style*) florido
orphan ['ɔrfən] *adj & s* huérfano || *tr* dejar huérfano
orphanage ['ɔrfənɪdʒ] *s* (*institution*) orfanato; órfelinato (SAm); (*state, condition*) orfandad
orphan asylum *s* asilo de huérfanos
Orpheus ['ɔrfjus] u ['ɔrfɪ•əs] *s* Orfeo
orthodontic appliance [,ɔrθə'dɑntɪk] *s* aparato de ortodoncia
orthodontics [,ɔrθə'dɑntɪks] *s* ortodoncia
orthodox ['ɔrθə,dɑks] *adj* ortodoxo
orthogra•phy [ɔr'θɑgrəfi] *s* (*pl* **-phies**) ortografía
oscillate ['ɑsɪ,let] *intr* oscilar
osier ['oʒər] *s* mimbre *m & f;* sauce mimbrero
ossi•fy ['ɑsɪ,faɪ] *v* (*pret & pp* **-fied**) *tr* osificar || *intr* osificarse
ostensible [ɑs'tɛnsɪbəl] *adj* aparente, pretendido, supuesto
ostentatious [,ɑstɛn'teʃəs] *adj (pretentious)* ostentativo; (*showy*) ostentoso
osteopath ['ɑstɪ•ə,pæθ] *s* osteópata *mf*
osteopathy [,ɑstɪ'ɑpəθi] *s* osteopatía
ostracism ['ɑstrə,sɪzəm] *s* ostracismo
ostrich ['ɑstrɪtʃ] *s* avestruz *m*
O.T. *abbr* **Old Testament**
other ['ʌðər] *adj & pron indef* otro || *adv*—**other than** de otra manera que
otherwise ['ʌðər,waɪz] *adv* otramente, de otra manera; en otras circunstancias; fuera de eso; si no, de otro modo
otherworldly ['ʌðər,wʌrldli] *adj* extraterrestre
otter ['ɑtər] *s* nutria
ottoman ['ɑtəmən] *s* (*corded fabric*) otomán *m;* (*sofa*) otomana; escañuelo con cojín || **Ottoman** *adj & s* otomano
ouch [aʊtʃ] *interj* ¡ax!
ought [ɔt] *s* alguna cosa; cero; **for ought I know** por lo que yo sepa || *v aux* se emplea para formar el modo potencial, p.ej., **he ought to go at once** debiera salir en seguida
ounce [aʊns] *s* onza
our [aʊr] *adj poss* nuestro
ours [aʊrz] *pron poss* el nuestro; nuestro
ourselves [aʊr'sɛlvz] *pron pers* nosotros mismos; nos, p.ej., **we enjoyed ourselves** nos divertimos
oust [aʊst] *tr* echar fuera, desposeer; desahuciar (*al inquilino*)
out [aʊt] *adj* ausente; apagado; exterior; divulgado; publicado; (*size*) poco común || *adv* afuera, fuera; al aire libre; hasta el fin; **out for** buscando; **out of** de; entre; de

entre; fuera de; más allá de; (*kindness, fear, etc.*) por; (*money*) sin; (*a suit of cards*) fallo a; sobre, p.ej., **in nine out of ten cases** en nueve casos sobre diez; **out to** + *inf* esforzándose por + *inf* || *prep* por; allá en || *interj* ¡fuera de aquí! || *s* cesante *mf;* **to be at outs** u **on the outs** estar de monos

out and away *adv* con mucho

out'-and-out' *adj* perfecto, verdadero, rematado || *adv* completamente

out'-and-out'er *s* intransigente *mf;* extremista *mf*

out•bid' *v* (*pret* **-bid;** *pp* **-bid** o **-bidden;** *ger* **-bidding**) *tr* pujar más que (*otra persona*); (bridge) sobrepasar

out'board' motor *s* motor *m* fuera de borda, fuera-bordo *m*

out'break' *s* tumulto, motín *m; (of anger*) arranque *m;* (*of war*) estallido; (*of an epidemic*) brote *m*

out'build'ing *s* dependencia, edificio accesorio

out'burst' *s* explosión, arranque *m;* **outburst of laughter** carcajada

out'cast' *s* proscripto, paria *mf;* vagabundo

out'come' *s* resultado

out'cry' *s* (*pl* **-cries**) grito; gritería, clamoreo

out•dat'ed *adj* fuera de moda, anticuado

out•do' *v* (**-did;** *pp* **-done**) *tr* exceder; **to outdo oneself** excederse a sí mismo

out'door' *adj* al aire libre

out'doors' *adv* al aire libre, fuera de casa || *s* aire *m* libre, campo raso

outer space [ˈaʊtər] *s* espacio exterior

out'field' *s* (baseball) jardín *m*

out'field'er *s* (baseball) jardinero

out'fit *s* equipo; traje *m;* juego de herramientas; (*of soldiers*) cuerpo; (*of a bride*) ajuar *m;* (com) compañía || *v* (*pret & pp* **-fitted;** *ger* **-fitting**) *tr* equipar

out'go'ing *adj* de salida; cesante; (*tide*) descendente; (*nature, character*) exteriorista || *s* salida

out•grow' *v* (*pret* **-grew;** *pp* **-grown**) *tr* crecer más que; ser ya grande para; ser ya viejo para; ser ya más apto que; dejar (*las cosas de los niños; a los amigos de la niñez, etc.*) || *intr* extenderse

out'growth' *s* excrecencia, bulto; (*of leaves in springtime*) nacimiento; consecuencia, resultado

outing [ˈaʊtɪŋ] *s* jira, excursión al campo

outlandish [aʊtˈlændɪʃ] *adj* estrafalario; de aspecto extranjero; de acento extranjero

out•last' *tr* durar más que; sobrevivir a

out'law' *s* forajido, bandido; prófugo, proscrito || *tr* proscribir; declarar ilegal

out'lay' *s* desembolso || **out•lay'** *v* (*pret & pp* **-laid**) *tr* desembolsar

out'let *s* salida; desaguadero; orificio de salida; (elec) caja de enchufe; (*tap*) (elec) toma de corriente *m*

out'line' *s* contorno; trazado; esquema *m;* esbozo, bosquejo; compendio || *tr* contornar; trazar; trazar el esquema de; esbozar, bosquejar; compendiar

out•live' *tr* sobrevivir a; durar más que

out'look' *s* perspectiva; expectativa; concepto de la vida, punto de vista; atalaya

out'ly'ing *adj* remoto, circundante, de las afueras

out•mod'ed *adj* fuera de moda

out•num'ber *tr* exceder en número, ser más numeroso que

out'-of-date' *adj* fuera de moda, anticuado

out'-of-door' *adj* al aire libre

out'-of-doors' *adj* al aire libre || *adv* al aire libre, fuera de casa || *s* aire *m* libre, campo raso

out'-of-print' *adj* agotado

out'-of-the-way' *adj* apartado, remoto; poco usual, poco común

out of tune *adj* desafinado || *adv* desafinadamente

out of work *adj* desempleado, sin trabajo

out'pa'tient *s* paciente *mf* de consulta externa

out'post' *s* avanzada

out'put' *s* rendimiento; (elec) salida; (mech) rendimiento de trabajo, efecto útil

out'rage *s* atrocidad; ultraje *m* || *tr* maltratar; ultrajar; escandalizar

outrageous [aʊtˈredʒəs] *adj* (*grossly offensive*) ultrajoso; (*shocking, fierce*) atroz; (*extreme*) extravagante

out•rank' *tr* exceder en rango o grado

out'rid'er *s* carrerista *m;* (Brit) viajante *m* de comercio

out'right' *adj* cabal, completo; franco, sincero || *adv* enteramente; de una vez; sin rodeos; en seguida

out'run'ner *s* volante *m* (*criado*)

out'set' *s* principio

out'side' *adj* exterior; superficial; ajeno; (*price*) (el) máximo || *adv* fuera, afuera; **outside of** fuera de || *prep* fuera de; más allá de; (coll) a excepción de || *s* exterior *m;* superficie *f;* apariencia

outsider [ˌaʊtˈsaɪdər] *s* forastero; intruso

out'skirts' *spl* afueras

out'spo'ken *adj* boquifresco, franco

out•stand'ing *adj* sobresaliente; prominente; sin pagar, sin cobrar

outward [ˈaʊtwərd] *adj* exterior; superficial || *adv* exteriormente, hacia fuera

out•weigh' *tr* pesar más que; contrapesar, compensar

out•wit' *v* (*pret & pp* **-witted;** *ger* **-witting**) *tr* burlar, ser más listo que; despistar (*al perseguidor*)

oval [ˈovəl] *adj* oval || *s* óvalo

ova•ry [ˈovəri] *s* (*pl* **-ries**) ovario

ovation [oˈveʃən] *s* ovación

oven [ˈʌvən] *s* horno

over [ˈovər] *adj* acabado, concluído; superior; adicional; excesivo || *adv* encima; al otro lado, a la otra orilla; hacia abajo; al revés; patas arriba; otra vez, de nuevo; de añadidura; (*at the bottom of a page*) a la vuelta; acá, p.ej., **hand over the money** déme acá el dinero; **over again** una vez más; **over against** enfrente de; a distinción de; en contraste con; **over and over** repetidas veces; **over here** acá; **over in** allá en; **over there** allá || *prep* sobre, encima de, por encima de; por; de un extremo a otro de; al otro lado de; más allá de; desde; (*a certain number*) más de; acerca de; por causa de; durante; **over and above** además de, en exceso de

o'ver•all' *adj* cabal, completo; extremo, total || **overalls** *spl* pantalones *mf* de trabajo; overol *m*

o'ver•bear'ing *adj* altanero, imperioso

o'ver•board' *adv* al agua; **man overboard!** ¡hombre al agua!; **to throw overboard** arrojar, echar o tirar por la borda

o'ver•cast' *adj* encapotado, nublado || *s* cielo encapotado || *v* (*pret & pp* **-cast**) *tr* nublar

o'ver•charge' *s* cargo excesivo; recargo de precio; sobrecarga; (elec) carga excesiva || **o'ver•charge'** *tr* hacer pagar más del valor, cobrar demasiado a; cargar (*p.ej., 50 pesetas*) de más; (elec) poner una carga excesiva a

o'ver•coat' *s* abrigo, gabán *m*, sobretodo

o'ver•come' *v* (*pret* **-came;** *pp* **-come**) *tr* vencer; rendir; superar (*dificultades*)

o'ver•crowd' *tr* atestar, apiñar; poblar con exceso

o'ver•do *v* (*pret* **-did;** *pp* **-done**) *tr* exagerar; agobiar; asurar, requemar || *intr* cansarse mucho, excederse en el trabajo

o'ver•dose' *s* sobredosis *f*, dosis excesiva || *intr* tomar una dosis excesiva

o'ver•draft *s* sobregiro, giro en descubierto

o'ver•draw' *v* (*pret* **-drew;** *pp* **-drawn**) *tr & intr* sobregirar

o'ver•due' *adj* atrasado; vencido y no pagado

o'ver•eat' *v* (*pret* **-ate;** *pp* **-eaten**) *tr & intr* comer con exceso

o'ver•es'ti•mate *tr* sobreestimar

o'ver•exer'tion *s* esfuerzo excesivo

o'ver•ex'ploi•ta'tion *s* (*of resources*) explotación abusiva

o'ver•expose' *tr* sobreexponer

o'ver•expo'sure *s* sobreexposición

o'ver•flow' *s* desbordamiento, rebosamiento, derrame *m;* caño de reboso || **o'ver•flow** *intr* desbordar, rebosar

o'ver•fly' *v* (*pret* **-flew;** *pp* **-flown**) *tr* sobrevolar

o'ver•grown' *adj* demasiado grande para su edad; denso, frondoso

o'ver•hang' *v* (*pret & pp* **-hung**) *tr* sobresalir por encima de, estar pendiente o colgando sobre, salir fuera del nivel de; amenazar || *intr* estar pendiente, estar colgando

o'ver•haul' *tr* examinar, registrar, revisar; ir alcanzando, alcanzar; componer, rehabilitar, reacondicionar

o'ver•head' *adj* de arriba; aéreo, elevado; general, de conjunto || **o'ver•head'** *adv* por encima de la cabeza; arriba, en lo alto || **o'ver•head'** *s* gastos generales

o'ver•hear *v* (*pret & pp* **-heard**) *tr* oír por casualidad; acertar a oír, alcanzar a oír

o'ver•heat *tr* recalentar || *intr* recalentarse

overjoyed [,over'dʒɔɪd] *adj* lleno de alegría; **to be overjoyed** no caber de contento

o'ver•kill' *s* exceso de potencia; exceso de eficacia || *intr* exceder lo necesario

overland ['ovər,lænd] u ['ovərlənd] *adj & adv* por tierra, por vía terrestre

o'ver•lap' *v* (*pret & pp* **-lapped;** *ger* **-lapping**) *tr* solapar, traslapar || *intr* solapar, traslapar; traslaparse (*dos o más cosas*); suceder (*dos hechos*) en parte al mismo tiempo

o'ver•load' *s* sobrecarga || **o'ver•load'** *tr* sobrecargar

o'ver•look' *tr* dominar con la vista; pasar por alto, no hacer caso de; perdonar, tolerar; espiar, vigilar; cuidar de, dirigir; dar a, p.ej., **the window overlooks the garden** la ventana da al jardín

o'ver•lord' *s* jefe supremo || **o'ver•lord'** *tr* dominar despóticamente, imponerse a

overly ['ovərli] *adv* (coll) excesivamente, demasiado

o'ver•night' *adv* toda la noche; de la tarde a la mañana; **to stay overnight** pasar la noche

overnight bag *s* saco de noche

o'ver•pass' *s* viaducto

o'ver•pop'u•late' *tr* superpoblar

o'verpow'er *tr* dominar, supeditar, subyugar; colmar, dejar estupefacto

overpowering *adj* abrumador, arrollador, irresistible

o'ver•produc'tion *s* superproducción, sobreproducción

o'ver•rate' *tr* exagerar el valor de

o'ver•run' *v* (*pret* **-ran;** *pp* **-run;** *ger* **-running**) *tr* cubrir enteramente; infestar; exceder; **to overrun one's time** quedarse más de lo justo; hablar más de lo justo

o'ver•sea' u **o'ver•seas'** *adj* de ultramar || **o'ver•sea'** u **o'ver•seas'** *adv* allende los mares, en ultramar

o'ver•seer' *s* director *m*, superintendente *mf*

o'ver•shad'ow *tr* sombrear; (fig) eclipsar

o'ver•shoe' *s* chanclo, zapato de goma

o'ver•shoot' *v* (*pret & pp* **-shot**) *tr* tirar por encima de o más allá de; **to overshoot oneself** pasarse de listo, excederse

o'ver•sight' *s* inadvertencia, descuido

o'ver•sleep' *v* (*pret & pp* **-slept**) *intr* dormir demasiado tarde

o'ver•step' *v* (*pret & pp* **-stepped;** *ger* **-stepping**) *tr* exceder, traspasar

o'ver•stock' *tr* abarrotar

o'ver•sup•ply' *s* (*pl* **-plies**) provisión excesiva || **o'ver•sup•ply'** *v* (*pret* **-plied**) *tr* proveer en exceso

overt ['ovərt] u [o'vʌrt] *adj* abierto, manifiesto; premeditado

o'ver•take' *v* (*pret* **-took;** *pp* **-taken**) *tr* alcanzar; sobrepasar; sorprender; sobrevenir a

o'ver-the-count'er *adj* vendido directamente al comprador; vendido en tienda al por mayor

o'ver•throw' *s* derrocamiento; trastorno || **o'ver•throw'** *v* (*pret* **-threw;** *pp* **-thrown**) *tr* derrocar; trastornar

o'ver•time' *adj & adv* en exceso de las horas regulares || *s* horas extraordinarias de trabajo, horas extra
o'ver•trump *s* contrafallo ||
o'ver•trump' *tr & intr* contrafallar
overture ['ovərtʃər] *s* insinuación, proposición; (mus) obertura
o'ver•turn' *s* vuelco; movimiento de mercancías || **o'ver•turn'** *tr* volcar; trastornar; derrocar || *intr* volcar; trastornarse
overweening [,ovər'winɪŋ] *adj* arrogante, presuntuoso
o'ver•weight' *adj* excesivamente gordo o grueso || *s* sobrepeso; exceso de peso; peso de añadidura
overwhelm [,ovər'hwɛlm] *tr* abrumar; inundar; anonadar; (*with favors, gifts, etc.*) colmar
o'ver•work' *s* trabajo excesivo, exceso de trabajo; trabajo fuera de las horas regulares || **o'ver•work'** *tr* hacer trabajar demasiado; oprimir con el trabajo || *intr* trabajar demasiado
Ovid ['ɑvɪd] *s* Ovidio
ovum ['ovəm] *s* óvulo
ow [aʊ] *interj* ¡ax!
owe [o] *tr* deber, adeudar || *intr* tener deudas
owing ['o•ɪŋ] *adj* adeudado; debido, pagadero; **owing to** debido a, por causa de
owl [aʊl] *s* buho, lechuza, mochuelo
own [on] *adj* propio, p.ej., **my own brother** mi propio hermano || *s* suyo, lo suyo; **on one's own** (coll) por su propia cuenta; (*without taking advice from anyone*) por su cabeza; (*without help from anyone*) de su cabeza; **to come into one's own** entrar en posesión de lo suyo; tener el éxito merecido, recibir el honor merecido; **to hold one's own** no aflojar, no cejar, mantenerse firme || *tr* poseer; reconocer || *intr* confesar; **to own up to** (coll) confesar de plano (*una culpa, un delito, etc.*)
owner ['onər] *s* amo, dueño, poseedor *m*, posesor *m*, proprietario
ownership ['onər,ʃɪp] *s* posesión, propiedad
owner's license *s* permiso de circulación, patente *f* de circulación
ox [ɑks] *s* (*pl* **oxen**) ['ɑksən] buey *m*
ox'cart' *s* carreta de bueyes
oxide ['ɑksaɪd] *s* óxido
oxidize ['ɑksɪ,daɪz] *tr* oxidar || *intr* oxidarse
oxygen ['ɑksɪdʒən] *s* oxígeno
oxygen tent *s* cámara o tienda de oxígeno
oxytone ['ɑksɪ,ton] *adj & s* oxítono
oyster ['ɔɪstər] *adj* ostrero || *s* ostra
oyster bed *s* ostrero
oyster cocktail *s* ostras en su concha
oyster fork *s* desbullador *m*
oys'ter•house' *s* ostrería
oys'ter•knife' *s* abreostras *m*
oyster•man ['ɔɪstərmən] *s* (*pl* **-men** [mən]) ostrero
oyster opener ['opənər] *s* desbullador *m*
oyster shell *s* desbulla, concha de ostra
oyster stew *s* sopa de ostras
oz. *abbr* **ounce, ounces**
ozone ['ozon] *s* ozono; (coll) aire fresco
ozone layer *s* capa de ozono
ozs. *abbr* **ounces**

P

P, p [pi] decimosexta letra del alfabeto inglés
p. *abbr* **page, participle**
P.A. *abbr* **Passenger Agent, power of attorney, Purchasing Agent**
pace [pes] *s* paso; **to keep pace with** ir, andar o avanzar al mismo paso que; **to put through one's paces** poner (*a uno*) a prueba; dar a (*uno*) ocasión de lucirse; **to set the pace** establecer el paso; dar el ejemplo || *tr* establecer el paso para; medir a pasos; recorrer a pasos; **to pace the floor** pasearse desesperadamente por la habitación || *intr* andar a pasos regulares
pace'mak'er *s* (med) marcapaso, marcapasos *m*
pacific [pə'sɪfɪk] *adj* pacífico || **Pacific** *adj & s* Pacífico
pacifier ['pæsɪ,faɪ•ər] *s* pacificador *m*, chupon *m*; (*teething ring*) chupador *m*
pacifism ['pæsɪ,fɪzəm] *s* pacifismo
pacifist ['pæsɪfɪst] *adj & s* pacifista *mf*
paci•fy ['pæsɪ,faɪ] *v* (*pret & pp* **-fied**) *tr* pacificar
pack [pæk] *s* lío, fardo; paquete *m;* (*of hounds*) jauría; (*of cattle*) manada; (*of evildoers*) pandilla; (*of lies*) sarta, montón *m;* (*of playing cards*) baraja; (*of cigarettes*) cajetilla; (*of floating ice*) témpano; (med) compresa || *tr* empaquetar; embaular; encajonar; hacer (*el baúl, la maleta*); conservar en latas; apretar, atestar; cargar (*una acémila*); escoger de modo fraudulento (*un jurado*); **to be packed in** (coll) estar como sardinas en banasta || *intr* empaquetarse; hacer el baúl, hacer la maleta; consolidarse, formar masa compacta
package ['pækɪdʒ] *s* paquete *m* || *tr* empaquetar
pack animal *s* acémila, animal *m* de carga
packing box o **case** *s* caja de embalaje
packing house *s* frigorífico
packing slip *s* hoja de embalaje
pack'sad'dle *s* albarda
pack'thread' *s* bramante *m*
pack train *s* recua
pact [pækt] *s* pacto

pad [pæd] *s* conjincillo, almohadilla; (*of writing paper*) bloc *m;* (*for inking*) tampón *m;* (*of an aquatic plant*) hoja; (*for launching a rocket*) plataforma *f;* (*sound of footsteps*) pisada || *v* (*pret & pp* **padded;** *ger* **padding**) *tr* acolchar, rellenar; meter mucho ripio en (*un escrito*) || *intr* andar, caminar; caminar despacio y pesadamente

paddle [ˈpædəl] *s* (*of a canoe*) canalete *m;* (*of a wheel*) pala, paleta; (*for spanking*) palo || *tr* impulsar con canalete; (*to spank*) apalear || *intr* remar con canalete; remar suavemente; (*to splash*) chapotear

paddle wheel *s* rueda de paletas

paddock [ˈpædək] *s* dehesa; (*at a racecourse*) paddock *m*

paddy wagon [ˈpædi] *s* (coll) camión *m* de policía

pad'lock' *s* candado || *tr* cerrar con candado; (*to lock up officially*) condenar (*una habitación, un teatro*)

pagan [ˈpegən] *adj & s* pagano

paganism [ˈpegə,nɪzəm] *s* paganismo

page [pedʒ] *s* (*of a book*) página; (*boy attendant*) paje *m;* (*in a hotel or club*) botones *m* || *tr* paginar; buscar llamando

pageant [ˈpædʒənt] *s* espectáculo público

pageant•ry [ˈpædʒəntri] *s* (*pl* **-ries**) pompa, fausto; (*empty display*) bambolla

pail [pel] *s* balde *m,* cubo

pain [pen] *s* dolor *m;* **on pain of** so pena de; **pains** esmero, trabajo; dolores de parto; **to take pains** esmerarse || *tr & intr* doler

painful [ˈpenfəl] *adj* doloroso; penoso

pain'kill'er *s* analgésico; calmante *m* del dolor

painless [ˈpenlɪs] *adj* sin dolor, indoloro; fácil, sin trabajo

pains'tak'ing *adj* esmerado

paint [pent] *s* pintura|| *tr* pintar || *intr* pintar; pintarse, repintarse

paint'box' *s* caja de colores

paint'brush' *s* brocha, pincel *m*

painter [ˈpentər] *s* pintor *m*

painting [ˈpentɪŋ] *s* pintura

paint remover [rɪˈmuvər] *s* sacapintura *m,* quitapintura *m*

pair [pɛr] *s* par *m;* (*of people*) pareja; (*of cards*) parejas || *tr* aparear || *intr* aparearse

pair of scissors *s* tijeras

pair of trousers *s* pantalones *mpl*

pajamas [peˈdʒɑməz] o [peˈdʒæməz] *spl* pijama

Pakistan [,pɑkɪˈstɑn] *s* el Paquistán

Pakistani [,pɑkɪˈstɑni] *adj & s* paquistano, paquistaní *mf*

pal [pæl] *s* (coll) compañero; cumpa *m* (SAm) || *v* (*pret & pp* **palled;** *ger* **palling**) *intr* (coll) ser compañeros

palace [ˈpælɪs] *s* palacio

palatable [ˈpælətəbəl] *adj* sabroso, apetitoso

palatal [ˈpælətəl] *adj & s* palatal *f*

palate [pælɪt] *s* paladar *m*

pale [pel] *adj* pálido; (*color*) claro || *s* estaca; palizada; límite *m,* término || *intr* palidecer

pale'face' *s* rostropálido

palette [ˈpælɪt] *s* paleta

palfrey [ˈpɔlfri] *s* palafrén *m*

palisade [,pælɪˈsed] *s* estaca; estacada; (*line of cliffs*) acantilado

pall [pɔl] *s* paño de ataúd, paño mortuorio; (eccl) palia || *tr* hartar, saciar; quitar el sabor a || *intr* perder el sabor; **to pall on** hartar, saciar

pall'bear'er *s* acompañante *m* de un cadáver; portador *m* del féretro

palliate [ˈpælɪ,et] *tr* paliar

pallid [ˈpælɪd] *adj* pálido

pallor [ˈpælər] *s* palidez *f,* palor *m*

palm [pɑm] *s* (*of the hand*) palma; (*measure*) palmo; (*tree and leaf*) palma; **to carry off the palm** llevarse la palma; **to grease the palm of** (slang) untar la mano a; **to yield the palm to** reconocer por vencedor || *tr* esconder en la mano; escamotear (*una carta*); **to palm off something on someone** encajarle una cosa a uno

palmet•to [pælˈmɛto] *s* (*pl* **-tos** o **-toes**) palmito

palmist [ˈpɑmɪst] *s* quiromántico

palmistry [ˈpɑmɪstri] *s* quiromancia

palm leaf *s* palma, hoja de la palmera

palm oil *s* aceite *m* de palma; (slang) propina; (slang) soborno

Palm Sunday *s* domingo de ramos

palpable [ˈpælpəbəl] *adj* palpable

palpitate [ˈpælpɪ,tet] *intr* palpitar

pal•sy [ˈpɔlzi] *s* (*pl* **-sies**) perlesía || *v* (*pret & pp* **-sied**) *tr* paralizar

pal•try [ˈpɔltri] *adj* (*comp* **-trier;** *super* **-triest**) vil, ruin, mezquino

pamper [ˈpæmpər] *tr* mimar, consentir

pamphlet [ˈpæmflɪt] *s* folleto, panfleto

pan [pæn] *s* cacerola, cazuela, sartén *f;* caldera, perol *m* || *v* (*pret & pp* **panned;** *ger* **panning**) *tr* cocer, freír; separar (*el oro*) en la gamella; (coll) criticar ásperamente || *intr* separar el oro en la gamella; dar oro; **to pan out well** (coll) tener éxito, dar buen resultado ||

Pan *s* Pan

panacea [,pænəˈsi•ə] *s* panacea

Panama Canal [ˈpænə,mɑ] *s* canal *m* de Panamá

Panama Canal Zone *s* Zona del Canal

Panama hat *s* panamá *m*

Panamanian [,pænəˈmenɪ•ən] *adj & s* panameño

Pan-American [,pænəˈmɛrɪkən] *adj* panamericano

pan'cake' *s* hojuela, panqueque *m* || *intr* (aer) desplomarse

pancake landing *s* aterrizaje aplastado, aterrizaje en desplome

pancreas [ˈpænkrɪ•əs] *s* páncreas *m*

panda [ˈpændə] *s* panda *mf*

pander [ˈpændər] *s* alcahuete *m* || *intr* alcahuetear; **to pander to** gratificar

pane [pen] *s* cristal *m,* vidrio, hoja de vidrio

pan•el [ˈpænəl] *s* panel *m,* entrepaño, cuarterón *m;* grupo de personas en discusión cara al público; (aut, elec) tablero, panel *m;* (law) lista de personas que pueden servir como jurados || *v* (pret & pp **peled** o **-elled;**

ger **-elling** o **-elling**) *tr* adornar con cuarterones, labrar en cuarterones; artesonar (*un techo o bóveda*)
panel discussion *s* coloquio cara al público
panelist [ˈpænəlɪst] *s* coloquiante *mf* cara al público
panel lights *spl* luces *fpl* del tablero
pang [pæŋ] *s* dolor agudo; (*of remorse*) punzada; (*of death*) agonía
pan′han′dle *s* mango de sartén || *intr* (slang) mendigar, pedir limosna
pan•ic [ˈpænɪk] *adj & s* pánico || *v* (*pret & pp* **-icked;** *ger* **-icking**) *tr* sobrecoger de pánico || *intr* sobrecogerse de pánico
pan′ic-strick′en *adj* muerto de miedo, sobrecogido de terror
pano•ply [ˈpænəpli] *s* (*pl* **-plies**) panoplia, traje *m* ceremonial
panorama [,pænəˈræmə] o [,pænəˈrɑmə] *s* panorama *m*
pan•sy [ˈpænzi] *s* (*pl* **-sies**) pensamiento
pant [pænt] *s* jadeo; palpitación; **pants** pantalones *mpl;* **to wear the pants** (coll) calzarse los pantalones || *intr* jadear; palpitar
pantheism [ˈpænθɪ,ɪzəm] *s* panteísmo
pantheon [ˈpænθɪ,ɑn] *s* panteón *m*
panther [ˈpænθər] *s* pantera; puma
panties [ˈpæntiz] *spl* pantaloncillos de mujer
pantomime [ˈpæntə,maɪm] *s* pantomima
pan•try [ˈpæntri] *s* (*pl* **-tries**) despensa
panty hose *s* panty *m*
pap [pæp] *s* papilla, papas
papa•cy [ˈpepəsi] *s* (*pl* **-cies**) papado
paper [ˈpepər] *s* papel *m;* (*newspaper*) periódico; (*of needles*) paño || *tr* empapelar
pa′per•back′ *s* libro en rústica
pa′per•boy′ *s* vendedor *m* de periódicos
paper clip *s* clip *m,* sujetapapelas *m;* presilla; prensador (CAm); gancho de papel (Col)
paper cone *s* cucurucho
paper cutter *s* cortapapeles *m,* guillotina
paper doll *s* muñeca de papel
paper hanger *s* empapelador *m,* papelista *mf*
paper knife *s* cortapapeles *m*
paper mill *s* fábrica de papel
paper money *s* papel *m* moneda
paper profits *spl* ganancias no realizadas sobre valores no vendidos
paper tape *s* cinta perforada
pa′per•weight′ *s* pisapapeles *m*
paper work *s* preparación o comprobación de escritos; papelerío
paprika[pæˈprikə] o [ˈpæprɪkə] *s* pimentón *m*
papy•rus [peˈpaɪrəs] *s* (*pl* **-ri** [raɪ]) papiro
par. *abbr* **paragraph, parallel, parenthesis, parish**
par [pɑr] *adj* a la par; nominal; normal || *s* paridad; valor *m* nominal; **above par** sobre la par; con beneficio; con premio; **below par** o **under par** bajo la par; con pérdida; (coll) indispuesto; **to be on a par with** correr parejas con
parable [ˈpærəbəl] *s* parábola
parachute [ˈpærə,ʃut] *s* paracaídas *m* || *intr* parachutar, lanzarse en paracaídas; **to parachute to safety** salvarse en paracaídas
parachute jump *s* salto en paracaídas
parachutist [ˈpærə,ʃutɪst] *s* paracaidista *mf*
parade [pəˈred] *s* desfile *m;* paseo; ostentación || *tr* ostentar, pasear || *intr* desfilar, pasar por las calles; (mil) formar en parada
paradise [ˈpærə,daɪs] *s* paraíso
paradox [ˈpærə,dɑks] *s* paradoja; persona o cosa incomprensibles
paradoxical [,pærəˈdɑksɪkəl] *adj* paradójico
paraffin [ˈpærəfɪn] *s* parafina
paragon [ˈpærə,gɑn] *s* dechado
paragraph [ˈpærə,græf] *s* párrafo
Paraguay *s* el Paraguay
Paraguayan [,pærəˈgwaɪ•ən] *adj & s* paraguayano, paraguayo
parakeet [ˈpærə,kit] *s* perico, periquito
paral•lel [ˈpærə,lɛl] *adj* paralelo || *s* (línea) paralela; (plano) paralelo; (geog) paralelo; **parallels** (typ) doble raya vertical || *v* (*pret & pp* **-leled** o **-lelled;** *ger* **-leling** o **-lelling**) *tr* ser paralelo a; poner en dirección paralela; correr parejas con; (*to compare*) paralelizar
parallel bars *spl* paralelas, barras paralelas
paraly•sis [pəˈrælɪsɪs] *s* (*pl* **-ses** [,siz]) parálisis *f*
paralytic [,pærəˈlɪtɪk] *adj & s* paralítico
paralyze [ˈpærə,laɪz] *tr* paralizar
parameter [pəˈræmətər] *s* parámetro
paramount [ˈpærə,maʊnt] *adj* capital, supremo, principalísimo
paranoiac [,pærəˈnɔɪ•æk] o **paranoid** [pærə-,nɔɪd] *adj & s* paranoico
parapet [,pærə,pɛt] *s* parapeto
paraphernalia [,pærəfərˈnelɪ•ə] *spl* trastos, atavíos
paraplegia [,pærəˈplidʒə] *s* paraplegia
parasite [ˈpærə,saɪt] *s* parásito
parasitic(al) [,pærəˈsɪtɪk(el)] *adj* parasítico, parasitario
parasol [ˈpærə,sɔl] *s* quitasol *m,* parasol *m*
pa′ra•troop′er *s* paracaidista *m*
pa′ra•troops′ *spl* tropas paracaidistas
parboil [ˈpɑr,bɔɪl] *tr* sancochar; calentar con exceso
par•cel (pɑrsəl] *s* paquete *m,* atado, bulto || *v* (*pret & pp* **-celed** o **-celled;** *ger* **-celing** o **-celling**) *tr* empaquetar; parcelar (*el terreno*); **to parcel out** repartir
parcel post *s* paquetes *mpl* postales
parch [pɑrtʃ] *tr* abrasar, tostar; **to be parched** tener mucha sed
parchment [ˈpɑrtʃmənt] *s* pergamino
pardon [ˈpɑrdən] *s* perdón *m;* (*remission of penalty by the state*) indulto; **I beg your pardon** dispense Vd. || *tr* perdonar, dispensar; indultar
pardonable [ˈpɑrdənəbəl] *adj* perdonable
pardon board *s* junta de perdones
pare [pɛr] *tr* mondar (*fruta*); pelar (*patatas*); cortar (*callos, uñas*); despalmar (*la palma córnea de los animales*); adelgazar; reducir (*gastos*)
parent [ˈpɛrənt] *adj* madre, matriz, principal || *s* padre o madre; autor *m,* fuente *f,* origen *m;* **parents** padres *mpl*

parentage ['pɛrəntɪdʒ] *s* paternidad o maternidad; abolengo, linaje *m*
parent company compañía matriz
parenthe•sis [pə'rɛnθɪsɪs] *s* (*pl* **-ses** [,siz]) paréntesis *m*
parenthood ['pɛrənt,hud] *s* paternidad o maternidad
pariah [pə'raɪ•ə] o ['parɪ•ə] *s* paria *mf*
paring knife ['pɛrɪŋ] *s* cuchillo para mondar
parish ['pærɪʃ] *s* parroquia, feligresía
parishioner [pə'rɪʃənər] *s* parroquiano, feligrés *m*
Parisian [pə'rɪʒən] *adj & s* parisiense *mf*
parity ['pærɪti] *s* paridad
park [park] *s* parque *m* || *tr* estacionar, parquear; (coll) colocar, dejar || *intr* estacionar, parquear
parking ['parkɪŋ] *s* aparcamiento, estacionamiento; (*space*) parking *m;* **no parking** se prohibe estacionarse
parking lights *spl* (aut) faros de situación
parking lot *s* parque *m* de estacionamiento
parking meter *s* reloj *m* de estacionamiento, parquímetro, parcómetro
parking ticket *s* aviso de multa
park'way *s* gran via adornado con árboles
parley ['parli] *s* parlamento || *intr* parlamentar
parliament ['parlɪmənt] *s* parlamento
parlor ['parlər] *s* sala; parlatorio, locutorio
parlor car *s* coche-salón *m*
parlor politics *spl* política de café
Parnassus [par'næsəs] *s* (*collection of poems*) parnaso; el Parnaso; **to try to climb Parnassus** hacer pinos en poesía
parochial [pə'rokɪ•əl] *adj* parroquial; estrecho, limitado
paro•dy ['pærədi] *s* (*pl* **-dies**) parodia || *v* (*pret & pp* **-died**) *tr* parodiar
parole [pə'rol] *s* palabra de honor; libertad bajo palabra || *tr* dejar libre bajo palabra
paroyxytone [pær'aksɪ,ton] *adj & s* paroxítono
par•quet [par'ke] *s* entarimado; (theat) platea || *v* (*pret & pp* **-queted** ['ked]); *ger* **-queting** ['ke•ɪŋ] *tr* entarimar
parricide ['pærɪ,saɪd] *s* (*act*) parricidio; (*person*) parricida *mf*
parrot ['pærət] *s* papagayo, loro; (fig) papagayo || *tr* repetir o imitar como loro
par•ry ['pæri] *s* (*pl* **-ries**) parada, quite *m* || *v* (*pret & pp* **-ried**) *tr* parar; defenderse de
parse [pars] *tr* analizar (*una oración*) gramaticalmente; describir (*una palabra*) gramaticalmente
parsley ['parsli] *s* perejil *m*
parsnip ['parsnɪp] *s* chirivía
parson ['parsən] *s* cura *m,* párroço; clérigo; pastor *m* protestante
part [part] *s* parte *f;* (*of a machine*) pieza; (*of the hair*) raya; (theat) parte *f,* papel *m;* **part and parcel** parte esencial, parte inseparable, elemento esencial; **parts** partes *fpl;* prendas, dotes *fpl;* **to do one's part** cumplir con su obligación; **to look the part** vestir el cargo; **to take the part of** tomar el partido de, defender; desempeñar el papel de || *tr* dividir, partir, separar; **to part the hair** hacerse la raya || *intr* separarse; **to part with** deshacerse de, abandonar; despedirse de
par•take [par'tek] *v* (*pret* **-took** ['tuk]; *pp* **-taken**) *tr* compartir; comer; beber || *intr* participar
Parthenon ['parθɪ,nan] *s* Partenón *m*
partial ['parʃəl] *adj* parcial; aficionado
participate [par'tɪsɪ,pet] *intr* participar
participle ['partɪ,sɪpəl] *s* participio
particle ['partɪkəl] *s* partícula, corpúsculo
particle physics *s* física de las partículas
particular [pər'tɪkjələr] *adj* particular; difícil, exigente, quisquilloso; esmerado; minucioso; **a particular . . .** cierto . . . || *s* particular *m*
partisan ['partɪzən] *adj & s* partidario, partidista *mf;* (mil) partisano
partition [par'tɪʃən] *s* partición, distribución; división; proción; tabique *m* || *tr* repartir; dividir en cuartos, aposentos; tabicar
partner ['partnər] *s* compañero; (*wife or husband*) cónyuge *mf;* (*in a dance*) pareja *f;* (*in business*) socio
partnership ['partnər,ʃɪp] *s* asociación; consorcio, vida en común; (com) sociedad, asociación comercial
partridge ['partrɪdʒ] *s* perdiz *f*
part'-time' *adj* por horas, parcial
par•ty ['parti] *adj* de partido; de gala || *s* (*pl* **-ties**) convite *m,* reunión, fiesta, tertulia, recepción; (*for fishing, hunting, etc.; of armed men*) partida; cómplice *mf,* interesado; (pol) partido; (coll) persona, individuo
party girl *s* chica de vida alegre
party-goer ['parti,go•ər] *s* tertuliano; fiestero
party line *s* (*between two properties*) linde *m,* lindero; (*of communist party*) línea del partido; (telp) línea compartida
party politics *s* política de partido
pass. *abbr* **passenger, passive**
pass [pæs] o [pas] *s* paso; (*permit; free ticket; movement of hands of mesmerist, of bullfighter*) pase *m;* (*in an examination*) aprobación; nota de aprobación || *tr* pasar; pasar de largo (*una luz roja*); aprobar (*un proyecto de ley; un examen; a un alumno*); ser aprobado en (*un examen*); dejar atrás; cruzarse con; expresar (*una opinión*); pronunciar (*una sentencia*), dar (*la palabra*); dejar sin protestar; no pagar (*un dividendo*); **to pass off** colar, pasar, hacer aceptar (*una moneda falsa*); disimular (*p.ej., una ofensa con una risa*); **to pass over** omitir, pasar por alto; excusar; desdeñar; dejar sin protestar; postergar (*a un empleado*) || *intr* pasar; pasarse (*introducirse*); aprobar; **to bring to pass** llevar a cabo; **to come to pass** suceder; **to pass as** pasar por; **to pass away** pasar, pasar a mejor vida; **to pass off** pasar (*una enfermedad, una tempestad, etc.*); tener lugar; **to pass out** salir; (slang) desmayarse; **to pass over to** pasarse a (p.ej., el enemigo)

passable ['pæsəbəl] o ['pɑsəbəl] *adj* pasadero; (*law*) promulgable
passage ['pæsɪdʒ] *s* pasaje *m;* paso; pasillo; (*of time*) transcurso; (*of bowels*) evacuación
pass'book' *s* cartilla, libreta de banco
passenger ['pæsəndʒer] *adj* de viajeros || *s* pasajero, viajero
passer-by ['pæsər'baɪ] o ['pɑsər'baɪ] *s* (*pl* **passers-by**) transeúnte *mf*
passing ['pæsɪŋ] o ['pɑsɪŋ] *adj* pasajero; corriente; de aprobado || *s* (*act of passing; death*) paso; (*in an examination*) aprobación
passion ['pæʃən] *s* pasión
passionate ['pæʃənɪt] *adj* apasionado
passive ['pæsɪv] *adj* pasivo || *s* voz pasiva, verbo pasivo
pass'key' *s* llave *f* de paso
Pass'o'ver *s* pascua (*de los hebreos*)
pass'port' *s* pasaporte *m*
pass'word' *s* santo y seña
past [pæst] o [pɑst] *adj* pasado; último; que fué, p.ej., **past president** presidente que fué; acabado, concluído || *adv* más allá; por delante || *prep* más allá de; más de; por delante de; fuera de; después de, p.ej., **past two o'clock** después de las dos; **past belief** increíble; **past cure** incurable; **past hope** sin esperanza || *s* pasado
paste [pest] *s* (*dough; spaghetti, etc.*) pasta; (*for sticking things together*) engrudo || *tr* engrudar, pegar con engrudo
paste'board' *s* cartón *m*
pasteurize ['pæstə,raɪz] *tr* pasterizar
pastime ['pæs,taɪm] *s* pasatiempo
pastor ['pæstər] *s* pastor *m,* clérigo, cura *m*
pastoral ['pæstərəl] *adj & s* pastoral *f*
pas•try ['pestri] *s* (*pl* **-tries**) pastelería
pastry cook *s* pastelero, repostero
pastry shop *s* pastelería, repostería
pasture ['pæstər] *s* pasto, pastura, dehesa || *tr* apacentar, pacer || *intr* apacentarse, pacer
past•y ['pesti] *adj* (*comp* **-ier;** *super* **-iest**) pastoso; flojo, fofo, pálido
pat [pæt] *s* golpecito, palmadita; ruido de pasos ligeros; (*of butter*) pastelillo || *v* (*pret & pp* **patted;** *ger* **patting**) *tr* dar golpecitos a, golpear ligeramente; palmotear, acariciar con la mano; **to pat on the back** elogiar, cumplimentar
patch [pætʃ] *s* remiendo, parche *m;* terreno, pedazo de terreno; mancha; lunar postizo || *tr* remendar; **to patch up** componer (*una desavenencia*); componer lo mejor posible (*una cosa descompuesta*); hacer aprisa y mal
patent ['petənt] *adj* patente; abierto || ['pætənt] *adj* de patentes || *s* patente *f,* patente de invención; propiedad industrial; **patent applied for** se ha solicitado patente || *tr* patentar
patent leather ['pætənt] *s* charol *m*
patent medicine ['pætənt] *s* medicamento de patente
patent rights ['pætənt] *spl* derechos de patente
paternal [pə'tʌrnəl] *adj* paterno; (*affection*) paternal
paternity [pe'tʌrnɪti] *s* paternidad
path [pæθ] *s* senda, sendero; trayectoria
pathetic [pə'θɛtɪk] *adj* patético
path'find'er baquiano; explorador *m*
patholo•gy [pə'θɑlədʒi] *s* patología
pathos ['peθɑs] *s* patetismo
path'way' *s* senda, sendero
patience ['peʃəns] *s* paciencia
patient ['peʃənt] *adj* paciente || *s* paciente *mf,* enfermo
patriarch ['petrɪ,ɑrk] *s* patriarca *m*
patrician [pə'trɪʃən] *adj & s* patricio
patricide ['pætrɪ,saɪd] *s* (*act*) parricidio; (*person*) parricida *mf*
Patrick ['pætrɪk] *s* Patricio
patrimo•ny ['pætrɪ,moni] *s* (*pl* **-nies**) patrimonio
patriot ['petrɪ•ət] *s* patriota *mf*
patriotic [,petrɪ'ɑtɪk] *adj* patriótico
patriotism ['petrɪ•ə,tɪzəm] *s* patriotismo
pa•trol [pə'trol] *s* patrulla || *v* (*pret & pp* **-troled** o **-trolled;** *ger* **-troling** o **-trolling**) *tr & intr* patrullar
patrol•man [pə'trolmən] *s* (*pl* **-men** [mən]) guardia *m* municipal, vigilante *m* de policía
patrol wagon *s* camion *m* de policía; carropatrulla *m* (SAm)
patron ['petrən] *adj* tutelar || *s* parroquiano; patrocinador *m*
patronize ['petrə,naɪz] *tr* ser parroquiano de (*un tendero*); comprar de costumbre en; patrocinar; tratar con aire protector
patron saint *s* patrón *m,* santo titular
patter ['pætər] *s* golpeteo; (*of rain*) chapaleteo; charla, parloteo || *intr* golpetear; charlar, parlotear
pattern ['pætərn] *s* patrón *m;* modelo
P.A.U. *abbr* **Pan American Union**
paucity ['pɔsɪti] *s* corto número; falta, escasez *f, insuficiencia*
Paul [pɔl] *s* Pablo; (*name of popes*) Paulo
paunch [pɔntʃ] *s* panza
paunchy ['pɔntʃi] *adj* panzudo
pauper ['pɔpər] *s* pobre *mf,* indigente *mf*
pause [pɔz] *s* pausa; (mus) calderón *m;* **to give pause (to)** dar que pensar (a) || *intr* hacer pausa, detenerse brevemente; vacilar
pave [pev] *tr* pavimentar; (*with flagstones*) enlosar; (*with bricks*) enladrillar; (*with pebbles*) enchinar; **to pave the way (for)** preparar el terreno (para), abrir el camino (a)
pavement ['pevmənt] *s* pavimento; (*of brick*) enladrillado; (*of flagstone*) enlosado; (*sidewalk*) acera
pavilion [pə'vɪljən] *s* pabellón *m*
paw [pɔ] *s* pata; garra, zarpa; (coll) mano *f* || *tr* dar zarpazos a, restregar con las uñas; golpear, patear (*el suelo los caballos*); (coll) manosear; (*to handle overfamiliarly*) (coll) sobar || *intr* piafar (*el caballo*)
pawn [pɔn] *s* (*in chess*) peón *m;* (*security, pledge*) prenda; (*tool of another person*) instrumento; víctima || *tr* empeñar, dar en prenda

pawn'bro'ker *s* prestamista *mf*
pawn'shop' *s* casa de empeños, monte *m* de piedad
pawn ticket *s* papeleta de empeño
pay [pe] *s* paga; recompensa; castigo merecido || *v* (*pret & pp* **paid** [ped]) *tr* pagar; prestar o poner (*atención*); dar (*cumplidos*); dar (*dinero una actividad comercial*); dar dinero a, ser provechoso a; pagar en la misma moneda; pagar con creces; sufrir (*el castigo de una ofensa*); hacer (*una visita*); cubrir (*los gastos*); **to pay back** devolver; pagar en la misma moneda; **to pay off** pagar y despedir (*a un empleado*); pagar todo lo adeudado a; vengarse de; redimir (*una hipoteca*) || *intr* pagar; ser provechoso, valer la pena; **pay as you enter** pague a la entrada; **pay as you go** pagar el impuesto de utilidades con descuentos anticipados; **pay as you leave** pague a la salida
payable [ˈpe•əbəl] *adj* pagadero
pay boost *s* aumento de salario
pay'check' *s* cheque *m* en pago del sueldo; sueldo
pay'day' *s* día *m* de pago
payee [peˈi] *s* portador *m* o tenedor *m* (*de un giro*)
pay envelope *s* sobre *m* con el jornal; jornal *m*, salario
payer [ˈpe•ər] *s* pagador *m*
pay load *s* carga útil
pay'mas'ter *s* pagador *m*
payment [ˈpemənt] *s* pago; castigo
pay roll *s* nómina, hoja de paga
pay station *s* teléfono público
pd. *abbr* **paid**
p.d. *abbr* **per diem, potential difference**
pea [pi] *s* guisante *m*, chícharo
peace [pis] *s* paz *f;* **to make peace with** hacer las paces con
peaceable [ˈpisəbəl] *adj* pacífico
Peace Corps *s* Cuerpo de Paz
peaceful [ˈpɪsfəl] *adj* tranquilo, pacífico, sosegado
peace'mak'er *s* iris *m* de paz
peace of mind *s* serenidad del espíritu
peace pipe *s* pipa ceremonial (*de los pieles rojas*)
peach [pitʃ] *s* melocotón *m;* (slang) persona o cosa admirables
peach tree *s* melocotonero
peach•y [ˈpitʃi] *adj* (*comp* **-ier;** *super* **-iest**) (slang) estupendo, magnífico
pea'cock' *s* pavo real, pavón *m;* (fig) pinturero
peak [pik] *s* pico, cima, cumbre *f;* punta, extremo; máximo; (*of a cap*) visera; (*of a curve*) cresta; (elec) pico
peak hour *s* hora punta
peak load *s* (elec) carga de punta; demanda máxima
peal [pil] *s* fragor *m;* estruendo; (*of bells*) repique *m;* juego de campanas || *intr* repicar; resonar
peal of laughter *s* carcajada
peal of thunder *s* trueno
pea'nut' *s* cacahuete *m*, aráquida; **to work for peanuts** recibir poco sueldo
peanut vendor *s* manicero
pear [pɛr] *s* pera
pearl [pʌrl] *s* margarita, perla; (*of running water*) murmullo || *tr* alijofarar
pearl oyster *s* madreperla
pear tree *s* peral *m*
peasant [ˈpɛzənt] *adj & s* campesino, rústico
pea'shoot'er *s* cerbatana, bodoquera
pea soup *s* sopa de guisantes; (coll) neblina espesa y amarillenta
peat [pit] *s* turba
pebble [ˈpɛbəl] *s* china, guija || *tr* agranelar (*el cuero*)
peck [pɛk] *s* medida de áridos (*nueve litros*); montón *m;* picotazo; beso dado de mala gana || *tr* picotear || *intr* picotear; (coll) comer melindrosamente; **to peck at** querer picar; regañar constantemente; (coll) comer melindrosamente
peculate [ˈpɛkjə,let] *tr & intr* malversar
peculiar [pɪˈkjuljər] *adj* peculiar; singular, raro; excéntrico
pedagogue [ˈpɛdə,gɑg] *s* pedagogo; dómine *m*, pedante *m*
pedagogy [ˈpɛdə,godʒi] o [ˈpɛdə,gɑdʒi] *s* pedagogía
ped•al [ˈpɛdəl] *s* pedal *m* || *v* (*pret & pp* **-aled** o **-alled;** *ger* **-aling** o **-alling**) *tr* impulsar pedaleando || *intr* pedalear
pedant [ˈpɛdənt] *s* pedante *mf*
pedantic [pɪˈdæntɪk] *adj* pedantesco
pedant•ry [ˈpɛdəntri] *s* (*pl* **-pries**) pedantería
peddle [ˈpɛdəl] *tr* ir vendiendo de puerta en puerta; traer y llevar (*chismes*); vender (*favores*) || *intr* ser buhonero
peddler [ˈpɛdlər] *s* buhonero
pederasty [ˈpɛdə,ræsti] *s* pederastia
pedestal [ˈpɛdɪstəl] *s* pedestal *m*
pedestrian [pɪˈdɛstrɪ•ən] *adj* pedestre || *s* peatón *m*
pediatrician [,pidɪ•əˈtrɪʃən] *s* pedíatra *mf*
pediatrics [,pidɪˈætrɪks] *ssg* pediatría
pedigree [ˈpɛdɪ,gri] *s* árbol genealógico; ascendencia; fuente *f*, origen *m*
pediment [ˈpɛdɪmənt] *s* frontón *m*
pee [pi] *s* (coll) pipí *m* || *intr* (coll) hacer pipí
peek [pik] *s* mirada rápida y furtiva || *intr* mirar a hurtadillas
peel [pil] *s* cáscara, pellejo || *tr* pelar || *intr* pelarse
peep [pip] *s* mirada a hurtadillas; (*of chickens*) pío || *intr* mirar a hurtadillas; piar (*los pollos*)
peep'hole' *s* atisbadero; (*in a door*) mirilla, ventanillo
peep show *s* mundonuevo; (slang) vistas sicalípticas
peer [pir] *s* par *m* || *intr* mirar fijando la vista de cerca; **to peer at** mirar con ojos de miope; **to peer into** mirar hacia lo interior de, escudriñar
peerless [ˈpɪrlɪs] *adj* sin par
peeve [piv] *s* (coll) cojijo || *tr* (coll) enojar, irritar
peevish [ˈpivɪʃ] *adj* cojijoso, displicente

peg [pɛg] *s* clavija, claveta, estaquilla; **to take down a peg** (coll) bajar los humos a || *v* (*pret & pp* **pegged;** *ger* **pegging**) *tr* enclavijar; señalar con clavijas; fijar (*precios*) || *intr* trabajar con ahinco; **to peg away at** afanarse en

peg leg *s* pata de palo

peg top *s* peonza; **peg tops** pantalones anchos de caderas y perniles ajustados

Peking [ˈpiˈkɪŋ] *s* Pequín

Peking•ese [,pikɪˈniz] *adj* pequinés || *s* (*pl* **-ese**) pequinés *m*

pelf [pɛlf] *s* dinero mal ganado

pell-mell [ˈpɛlˈmɛl] *adj* tumultuoso || *adv* atropelladamente

Peloponnesian [,pɛləpəˈniʃən] *adj & s* peloponense *mf*

Peloponnesus [,pɛləpəˈnisəs] *s* Peloponeso

Pelops [ˈpilɑps] *s* Pélope *m*

pelota [pɛˈlotə] *s* pelota vasca

pelt [pɛlt] *s* pellejo; golpe violento; (*of a person*) (hum) pellejo || *tr* golpear violentamente; apedrear || *intr* golpear violentamente; caer con fuerza (*el granizo, la lluvia, etc.*); apresurarse

pen. *abbr* **peninsula**

pen [pɛn] *s* pluma; corral *m*, redil *m;* **the pen and the sword** las letras y las armas || *v* (*pret & pp* **penned;** *ger* **penning**) *tr* escribir (*con pluma*); redactar || *v* (*pret & pp* **penned** o **pent** [pɛnt]) *tr* acorralar, encerrar

penalize [ˈpinə,laɪz] *tr* penar; penalizar; (sport) sancionar

penal•ty [ˈpɛnəlti] *s* (*pl* **-ties**) pena; (*for late payment*) recargo; (sport) sanción; **under penalty of** so pena de

penance [ˈpɛnəns] *s* penitencia; **to do penance** hacer penitencia

penchant [ˈpɛnʃənt] *s* afición, inclinación, tendencia

pen•cil [ˈpɛnsəl] *s* lápiz *m;* (*of light*) pincel *m*, haz *m* || *v* (*pret & pp* **-ciled** o **-cilled;** *ger* **-ciling** o **-cilling**) *tr* marcar con lápiz; (med) pincelar

pencil sharpener *s* afilalápices *m*, cortalápices *m*

pendent [ˈpɛndənt] *adj* pendiente; sobresaliente || *s* medallón *m;* (*earring*) pendiente *m*

pending [ˈpɛndɪŋ] *adj* pendiente || *prep* hasta; durante

pendulum [ˈpɛndʒələm] *s* péndulo; (*of a clock*) péndola

pendulum bob *s* lenteja

penetrate [ˈpɛnɪ,tret] *tr & intr* penetrar

penguin [ˈpɛŋgwɪn] *s* pingüino, pájaro bobo

pen'hold'er *s* (*handle*) portaplumas *m;* (*box*) plumero

penicillin [,pɛnɪˈsɪlɪn] *s* penicilina

peninsula [pəˈnɪnsələ] *s* península

peninsular [pəˈnɪnsələr] *adj & s* peninsular *mf* || **Peninsular** *adj & s* (*Iberian*) peninsular *mf*

penis [ˈpinəs] *s* pene *m*, falo

penitence [ˈpɛnɪtəns] *s* penitencia

penitent [ˈpɛnɪtənt] *adj & s* penitente *mf*

pen'knife' *s* (*pl* **-knives**) navaja, cortaplumas *m*

penmanship [ˈpɛnmən,ʃɪp] *s* caligrafía; (*hand of a person*) letra

pen name *s* seudónimo

pennant [ˈpɛnənt] *s* gallardete *m*

penniless [ˈpɛnɪlɪs] *adj* pelón, sin dinero

pennon [ˈpɛnən] *s* pendón *m*

pen•ny [ˈpɛni] *s* (*pl* **-nies**) (U.S.A.) centavo || *s* (*pl* **pence** [pɛns]) (Brit) penique *m*

pen'ny•weight' *s* peso de 24 granos

pen pal *s* (coll) amigo por correspondencia

pen point *s* punta de la pluma; puntilla de la pluma fuente

pension [ˈpɛnʃən] *s* pensión, jubilación || *tr* pensionar, jubilar

pensioner [ˈpɛnʃənər] *s* pensionista *mf;* **pensioners** clases pasivas

pensive [ˈpɛnsɪv] *adj* pensativo; melancólico

Pentecost [ˈpɛntɪ,kɔst] *s* el Pentecostés

penthouse [ˈpɛnt,haʊs] *s* alpende *m*, colgadizo; casa de azotea

pent-up [ˈpɛnt,ʌp] *adj* contenido, reprimido

penult [ˈpinʌlt] *s* penúltima

penum•bra [pɪˈnʌmbrə] *s* (*pl* **-brae** [bri] o **-bras**) penumbra

penurious [pɪˈnʊrɪ•əs] *adj* (*stingy*) tacaño, mezquino; (*poor*) pobre, indigente

penury [ˈpɛnjəri] *s* tacañería, mezquindad; pobreza, miseria

pen'wip'er *s* limpiaplumas *m*

people [ˈpipəl] *spl* gente *f;* personas; gente del pueblo; se, p.ej., **people say** se dice || *ssg* (*pl* **peoples**) pueblo, nación || *tr* poblar

pep [pɛp] *s* (slang) ánimo, brío, vigor *m* || *v* (*pret & pp* **pepped;** *ger* **pepping**) *tr*—**to pep up** (slang) animar, dar vigor a

pepper [ˈpɛpər] *s* (*spice*) *pimienta;* (*plant and fruit*) pimiento || *tr* sazonar con pimienta; (*with bullets*) acribillar; salpicar

pep'per•box' *s* pimentero

pep'per•mint' *s* (*plant*) menta piperita; esencia de menta; pastilla de menta

pep talk *s* palabras alentadoras

per [pʌr] *prep* por; **as per** según

perambulator [pərˈæmbjə,letər] *s* cochecillo de niño

per capita [pər ˈkæpɪtə] por cabeza, por persona

perceive [pərˈsiv] *tr* percibir

per cent o **percent** [pərˈsɛnt] por ciento

percentage [pərˈsɛntɪdʒ] *s* porcentaje *m;* (slang) provecho, ventaja

perception [pərˈsɛpʃən] *s* percepción; comprensión, penetración

perch [pʌrtʃ] *s* percha, rama, varilla; sitio o posición elevada; (*fish*) perca || *tr* colocar en un sitio algo elevado *intr* sentarse en un sitio algo elevado; posar (*un ave*)

percolator [ˈpʌrkə,letər] *s* cafetera filtradora

per diem [pərˈdaɪ•əm] por día

perdition [pərˈdɪʃən] *s* perdición

perennial [pəˈrɛnɪ•əl] *adj* perenne; (bot) vivaz || *s* planta vivaz

perfect [ˈpʌrfɛkt] *adj & s* perfecto || [pərˈfɛkt] *tr* perfeccionar

perfidious [pərˈfɪdɪ•əs] *adj* pérfido

perfi•dy [ˈpʌrfɪdi] *s* (*pl* **-dies**) perfidia
perforate [ˈpʌrfə,ret] *tr* perforar
perforce [pərˈfors] *adv* por fuerza, necesariamente
perform [pərˈfɔrm] *tr* ejecutar; (theat) representar ‖ *intr* ejecutar; funcionar (*p.ej., una máquina*)
performance [pərˈfɔrməns] *s* ejecución; representación; funcionamiento; (theat) función
performer [pərˈfɔrmər] *s* ejecutante *mf;* actor *m;* acróbata *mf*
perfume [ˈpʌrfjum] *s* perfume *m* ‖ [pərˈfjum] *tr* perfumar
perfunctory [pərˈfʌŋktəri] *adj* hecho sin cuidado, hecho a la ligera; indiferente, negligente
perhaps [pərˈhæps] *adv* acaso, tal vez, quizá
per•il [ˈpɛrəl] *s* peligro ‖ *v* (*pret & pp* **-iled** o **-illed;** *ger* **-iling** o **-illing**) *tr* poner en peligro
perilous [ˈpɛrɪləs] *adj* peligroso
period [ˈpɪrɪ•əd] *s* período; (*in school*) hora; (gram) punto; (sport) division
period costume *s* traje *m* de época
periodic [,pɪrɪˈɑdɪk] *adj* periódico
periodical [,pɪrɪˈɑdɪkəl] *adj* periódico ‖ *s* periódico, revista periódica
peripher•y [pəˈrɪfəri] *s* (*pl* **-ies**) periferia
periscope [ˈpɛrɪ,skop] *s* periscopio
perish [ˈpɛrɪʃ] *intr* perecer
perishable [ˈpɛrɪʃəbəl] *adj* perecedero; (*merchandise*) corruptible
periwig [ˈpɛrɪ,wɪg] *s* perico
perjure [ˈpʌrdʒər] *tr* hacer (*a una persona*) quebrantar el juramento; **to perjure oneself** perjurarse
perju•ry [ˈpʌrdʒəri] *s* (*pl* **-ries**) perjurio
perk [pʌrk] *tr* alzar (*la cabeza*); aguzar (*las orejas*) ‖ *intr* pavonearse; engalanarse; **to perk up** reanimarse, sentirse mejor
permanence [ˈpʌrmənəns] *s* permanencia
permanency [ˈpʌrmənənsi] *s* (*pl* **-cies**) permanencia; persona, cosa o posición permanentes
permanent [ˈpʌrmənənt] *adj* permanente ‖ *s* permanente *f,* ondulación permanente
permanent tenure *s* inamovilidadperversión
permanent way *s* (rr) material fijo
permeate [ˈpʌrmɪ,et] *tr & intr* penetrar
permission [pərˈmɪʃən] *s* permisión
per•mit [ˈpʌrmɪt] *s* permiso; cédula de aduana ‖ [pərˈmɪt] *v* (*pret & pp* **-mitted;** *ger* **-mitting**) *tr* permitir
permute [perˈmjut] *tr* permutar
pernicious [pərˈnɪʃəs] *adj* pernicioso
pernickety [perˈnɪkɪti] *adj* (coll) descontentadizo, quisquilloso
perorate [ˈpɛrə,ret] *intr* perorar
peroration [,pɛrəˈreʃən] *s* peroración
peroxide [pərˈɑksaɪd] *s* peróxido; peróxido de hidrógeno
peroxide blonde *s* rubia oxigenada
perpendicular [,pʌrpənˈdɪkjələr] *adj & s* perpendicular *f*
perpetrate [ˈpʌrpɪ,tret] *tr* perpetrar
perpetual [pərˈpɛtʃʊ•əl] *adj* perpetuo
perpetuate [pərˈpɛtʃʊ,et] *tr* perpetuar
perplex [pərˈplɛks] *tr* dejar perplejo
perplexed [pərˈplɛkst] *adj* perplejo
perplexi•ty [pərˈplɛksɪti] *s* (*pl* **-ties**) perplejidad; problema *m*
per se [per ˈsi] por sí mismo, en sí mismo, esencialmente
persecute [ˈpʌrsɪ,kjut] *tr* perseguir
persecution [,pʌrsɪˈkjuʃən] *s* persecución
persevere [,pʌrsɪˈvɪr] *intr* perseverar
Persian [ˈpʌrʒən] *adj & s* persa *mf*
persimmon [pərˈsɪmən] *s* placaminero
persist [pərˈsɪst] o [pərˈzɪst] *intr* persistir; empecinarse
persistent [pərˈsɪstənt] o [pərˈzɪstənt] *adj* persistente; (*insistent*) porfiado; (*e.g., headache*) pertinaz
person [ˈpʌrsən] *s* persona; **no person** nadie
personage [ˈpʌrsənɪdʒ] *s* personaje *m;* persona
personal [ˈpʌrsənəl] *adj* personal; de uso personal ‖ *s* nota de sociedad; (*in a newspaper*) remitido
personali•ty [,pʌrsəˈnælɪti] *s* (*pl* **-ties**) personalidad
personality cult *s* culto a la personalidad
personal property *s* bienes *mpl* muebles
personi•fy [pərˈsɑnɪ,faɪ] *v* (*pret pp* **-fied**) *tr* personificar
personnel [,pʌrsəˈnɛl] *s* personal *m*
perˈson-to-perˈson *adv* (telp) particular a particular
perspective [pərˈspɛktɪv] *s* perspectiva
perspicacious [,pʌrspɪˈkeʃəs] *adj* perspicaz
perspire [pərˈspaɪr] *intr* sudar, transpirar
persuade [pərˈswed] *tr* persuadir
persuasion [pərˈsweʒən] *s* persuasión; creencia religiosa; creencia fuerte
pert [pʌrt] *adj* atrevido, descarado; (coll) animado, vivo
pertain [pərˈten] *intr* pertenecer; **pertaining to** perteneciente a
pertinacious [,pʌrtɪˈneʃəs] *adj* pertinaz
pertinent [ˈpʌrtɪnənt] *adj* pertinente
perturb [pərˈtʌrb] *tr* perturbar
Peru [pəˈru] *s* el Perú
perusal [pəˈruzəl] *s* lectura cuidadosa
peruse [pəˈruz] *tr* leer con atención
Peruvian [pəruvɪ•ən] *adj & s* peruano
pervade [pərˈved] *tr* penetrar, esparcirse por, extenderse por
perverse [pərˈvʌrs] *adj* perverso; avieso, díscolo; contumaz; malazo
perversion [pərˈvʌrʒən] *s* perversión
perversi•ty [pərˈvʌrsɪti] *s* (*pl* **-ties**) perversidad; indocilidad; contumacia
pervert [ˈpʌrvərt] *s* renegado, apóstata; pervertido ‖ [pərˈvʌrt] *tr* pervertir; emplear mal (*p.ej., los talentos que uno tiene*)
pes•ky [ˈpɛski] *adj* (*comp* **-kier;** *super* **-kiest**) (coll) cargante, molesto
pessimism [ˈpɛsɪ,mɪzəm] *s* pesimismo
pessimist [ˈpɛsɪmɪst] *s* pesimista *mf*
pessimistic [,pɛsɪˈmɪstɪk] *adj* pesimista
pest [pɛst] *s* peste *f;* insecto nocivo; (*misfortune*) plaga; (*annoying person, bore*) machaca *mf*
pester [ˈpɛstər] *tr* molestar, importunar

pest'house' *s* lazareto, hospital *m* de contagiosos
pesticide ['pɛstɪ,saɪd] *s* pesticida *m*
pestiferous [pɛs'tɪfərəs] *adj* pestifero; (coll) engorroso, molesto
pestilence ['pɛstɪləns] *s* pestilencia
pestle ['pɛsəl] *s* mano *f* de almirez
pet [pɛt] *s* animal mimado, animal casero; niño mimado; favorito; enojo pasajero || *v* (*pret & pp* **petted;** *ger* **petting**) *tr* acariciar, mimar || *intr* (slang) besuquearse
petal [pɛtəl] *s* pétalo
petard [pɪ'tɑrd] *s* petardo
pet'cock' *s* llave *f* de desagüe, llave de purga
Peter ['pitər] *s* Pedro; **to rob Peter to pay Paul** desnudar a un santo para vestir a otro
petit-bourgeois [pə'ti'burʒwɑ] *adj* pequeñoburgués
petition [pɪ'tɪʃəŋ] *s* petición; (*formal request signed by a number of people*) memorial *m*, instancia, solicitud || *tr* suplicar; dirigir una instancia a, solicitar
pet name *s* nombre *m* de cariño
Petrarch ['pitrɑrk] *s* Petrarca *m*
petri•fy ['pɛtrɪ,faɪ] *v* (*pret & pp* **-fied**) *tr* petrificar || *intr* petrificarse
petrochemical [,pɛtro'kɛmɪkəl] *adj* petroquímico
petrol ['pɛtrəl] *s* (Brit) gasolina
petroleum [pɪ'trolɪ•əm] *s* petróleo
pet shop *s* pajarería
petticoat ['pɛtɪ,kot] *s* enaguas; (*woman, girl*) (slang) falda
pet•ty ['pɛti] *adj* (*comp* **-tier;** *super* **-tiest**) insignificante, pequeño; mezquino; intolerante
petty cash *s* caja de menores, efectivo para gastos menores
petty larceny *s* ratería, hurto
petty officer *s* (naut) suboficial *m*
petulant ['pɛtjələnt] *adj* malhumorado, enojadizo
pew [pju] *s* banco de iglesia
pewter ['pjutər] *s* peltre *m;* vajilla de peltre
Phaëthon ['fe•ɪθən] *s* Faetón *m*
phalanx ['felæŋks] *s* falange *f*
phallic ['fælɪk] *adj* fálico
phallus ['fæləs] *s* falo
phantasm ['fæntæzəm] *s* fantasma *m*
phantom ['fæntəm] *s* fantasma *m*
Pharaoh ['fɛro] *s* Faraón *m*
pharisee ['færɪ,si] *s* fariseo || **Pharisee** *s* fariseo
pharmaceutical [,fɑrmə'sutɪkəl] *adj* farmacéutico
pharmacist ['fɑrməsɪst] *s* farmacéutico
pharma•cy ['fɑrməsi] *s* (*pl* **-cies**) farmacia
pharynx ['færɪŋks] *s* faringe *f*
phase [fez] *s* fase *f* || *tr* poner en fase; llevar a cabo a etapas uniformes; (coll) inquietar, molestar; **to phase out** deshacer paulatinamente
pheasant ['fɛzənt] *s* faisán *m*
phenobarbital [,fino'bɑrbɪ,tæl] *s* fenobarbital *m*
phenomenal [fɪ'nɑmɪ,nɑn] *s* (*pl* **-na** [nə]) fenómenal
phial ['faɪ•əl] *s* frasco pequeño; inyectable *m*
Phidias ['fɪdɪ•əs] *s* Fidias *m*
philanderer [fɪ'lændərər] *s* galanteador *m*, tenorio
philanthropist [fɪ'lænθrəpɪst] *s* filántropo
philanthro•py [fɪ'lænθrəpi] *s* (*pl* **-pies**) filantropía
philatelist [fɪ'lætəlɪst] *s* filatelista *mf*
philately [fɪ'lætəli] *s* filatelia
Philip ['fɪlɪp] *s* Felipe *m;* (*of Macedon*) Filipo
Philippine ['fɪlɪ,pin] *adj* filipino || **Philippines** *spl* Islas Filipinas
Philistine [fɪ'lɪstin] o ['fɪlɪ,stin] o ['fɪlɪ,staɪn] *adj & s* filisteo
philologist [fɪ'lɑlədʒɪst] *s* filólogo
philology [fɪ'lɑlədʒi] *s* filología
philosopher [fɪ'lɑsəfər] *s* filósofo
philosophic(al) [,fɪləsɑfɪk(əl)] *adj* filosófico
philoso•phy [fɪ'lɑsəfi] *s* (*pl* **-phies**) filosofía
philter ['fɪltər] *s* filtro
phlebitis [flɪ'baɪtɪs] *s* flebitis *f*
phlegm [flɛm] *s* flema *f*, gargajo; **to cough up phlegm** gargajear
phlegmatic(al) [flɛg'mætɪk(əl)] *adj* flemático; (coll) galbanoso
Phoebe ['fibi] *s* Febe *f*
Phoebus ['fibəs] *s* Febo
Phoenicia [fɪ'nɪʃə] o [fɪ'niʃə] *s* Fenicia
Phoenician [fɪ'nɪʃən] o [fɪ'niʃən] *adj & s* fenicio
phoenix ['finɪks] *s* fénix *m*
phone [fon] *s* (coll) teléfono; **to come** o **to go to the phone** acudir al teléfono, ponerse al aparato || *tr & intr* (coll) telefonear
phone call *s* llamada telefónica
phoneme ['fonim] *s* fonema
phonetic [fo'nɛtɪk] *adj* fonético
phonics ['fɑnɪks] *s* fónica
phonograph ['fonə,græf] *s* fonógrafo
phonology [fə'nɑlədʒi] *s* fonología
pho•ny ['foni] *adj* (*comp* **-nier;** *super* **-niest**) falso, contrahecho || *s* (*pl* **-nies**) (slang) farsa; (coll) farsante *mf*
phosphate ['fɑsfet] *s* fosfato
phosphorescent [,fɑsfə'rɛsənt] *adj* fosforescente
phospho•rus ['fɑsfərəs] *s* (*pl* **-ri** [,raɪ]) fósforo
pho•to ['foto] *s* (*pl* **-tos**) foto *f*
photocopier ['foto,kɑpɪ•ər] *s* fotocopiador *m;* fotóstato *m*
pho'to•cop'y *s* fotocopia || *v* (*pret & pp* **-ied**) *tr* fotocopiar
photoengraving [,foto•ɛn'grevɪŋ] *s* fotograbado
photo finish *s* (sport) llegada a la meta, determinada mediante el fotofija
pho'to•fin'ish camera *s* fotofija *m*
photogenic [,foto'dʒɛnɪk] *adj* fotogénico
photograph ['fotə,græf] *s* fotografía || *tr & intr* fotografiar
photographer [fə'tɑgrəfər] *s* fotógrafo
photography [fə'tɑgrəfi] *s* fotografía

photojournalism [ˌfotəˈdʒʌrnəˌlɪzəm] *s* fotoperiodismo
pho'to•play' *s* fotodrama *m*
photostat [ˈfotəˌstæt] *s* fotóstato ‖ *tr & intr* fotostatar
phototube [ˈfotəˌtjub] fototubo
phrase [frez] *s* frase *f* ‖ *tr* frasear
phrenology [frɪˈnɑlədʒi] *s* frenología
phys. *abbr* **physical, physician, physics, physiology**
phys•ic [ˈfɪzɪk] *s* medicamento; purgante *m* ‖ *v* (*pret & pp* **-icked;** *ger* **-icking**) *tr* curar; purgar
physical [ˈfɪzɪkəl] *adj* físico
physician [fɪˈzɪʃən] *s* médico
physicist [ˈfɪzɪsɪst] *s* físico
physics [ˈfɪzɪks] *s* física
physiognomy [ˌfɪzɪˈɑgnəmi] o [ˌfɪzɪˈɑnəmi] *s* fisonomía
physiological [ˌfɪzɪ•əˈlɑdʒɪkəl] *adj* fisiológico
physiology [ˌfɪzɪˈɑlədʒi] *s* fisiología
physique [fɪˈzik] *s* físico, talle *m*, exterior *m*
pi [paɪ] *s* (math) pi *f;* (typ) pastel *m* ‖ *v* (*pret & pp* **pied;** *ger* **piing**) *tr* (typ) empastelar
pian•o [pɪˈæno] *s* (*pl* **-os**) piano
picaresque [ˌpɪkəˈrɛsk] *adj* picaresco
picayune [ˌpɪkəˈjun] *adj* de poca monta, mezquino
piccadil•ly [ˌpɪkəˈdɪli] *s* (*pl* **-lies**) cuello de pajarita
picco•lo [ˈpɪkəˌlo] *s* (*pl* **-los**) flautín *m*
pick [pɪk] *s* (*tool*) pico; (*choice*) selección; (*choicest*) flor *f* ‖ *tr* escoger; recoger (*p.ej.*, *flores*); recolectar (*p.ej.*, *algodón*); romper (*el hielo*) con un picahielos; escarbarse (*los dientes*); descañonar, desplumar (*un ave*); hurgarse (*la nariz*); rescarse (*una cicatriz, un grano*); roer (*un hueso*); mondar (*las frutas*); falsear, forzar (*una cerradura*); armar (*una pendencia*); herir (*las cuerdas de un instrumento*); buscar (*defectos*); hurtar de (*los bolsillos*); **to pick out** entresacar; **to pick someone to pieces** (coll) no dejarle a uno un hueso sano; **to pick up** recoger; recobrar (*ánimo; velocidad*); descolgar (*el receptor*); hallar por casualidad; aprender con la práctica; aprender de oidas; invitar a subir a un coche; entablar conservación con (*sin presentación previa*); captar (*una señal de radio*) ‖ *intr* comer melindrosamente; escoger esmeradamente; **to pick at** comer melindrosamente; tomarla con, regañar; **to pick on** escoger; (coll) regañar; (coll) molestar; **to pick over** ir revolviendo y examinando; **to pick up** (coll) ir mejor, sentirse mejor; recobrar velocidad
pick'ax' *s* zapapico
picket [ˈpɪkɪt] *s* (*stake, pale*) piquete *m;* (*of strikers; of soldiers*) piquete *m* ‖ *tr* poner un cordón de piquetes a ‖ *intr* servir de piquete
picket fence *s* cerca de estacas
picket line *s* línea de piquetes
pickle [ˈpɪkəl] *s* encurtido; escabeche *m*, salmuera; (coll) apuro, aprieto ‖ *tr* encurtir; escabechar
pick-me-up [ˈpɪkmiˌʌp] *s* (coll) tentempié *m;* (coll) trago fortificante
pick'pock'et *s* carterista *m*, ratero; bolsero (Mex)
pick'up' *s* recolección; (*of a motor*) recobro; (*of an automobile*) aceleración; (elec) pickup, fonocaptor *m*
pic•nic [ˈpɪknɪk] *s* jira, partida de campo ‖ *v* (*pret & pp* **-nicked;** *ger* **-nicking**) *intr* hacer una jira al campo, merendar en el campo
pictorial [pɪkˈtorɪ•əl] *adj* gráfico; ilustrado ‖ *s* revista ilustrada
picture [ˈpɪktʃər] *s* cuadro; retrato; imagen *f;* lámina, grabado; fotografía; película; pintura ‖ *tr* dibujar; pintar; describir; **to picture to oneself** representarse
picture book *s* libro en imágenes
picture gallery *s* galería de pinturas
picture post card *s* postal ilustrada
picture show *s* exhibición de pinturas; cine *m*
picture signal *s* videoseñal *f*
picturesque [ˌpɪktjəˈrɛsk] *adj* pintoresco
picture tube *s* tubo de imagen, tubo de televisión
picture window *s* ventana panorámica
piddling [ˈpɪdlɪŋ] *adj* de poca monta, insignificante
pie [paɪ] *s* pastel *m;* (*bird*) picaza; (typ) pastel *m* ‖ *v* (*pret & pp* **pied;** *ger* **pieing**) *tr* (typ) empastelar
piece [pis] *s* (*fragment; section of cloth*) pedazo; (*part of a machine; drama; single composition of music; coin; figure or block used in checkers, chess, etc.*) pieza; (*of land*) lote *m*, parcela; **a piece of advice** un consejo; **a piece of baggage** un bulto; **a piece of furniture** un mueble; **to break to pieces** despedazar, hacer pedazos; despedazarse; **to fall to pieces** desbaratarse, caer en ruina; **to give someone a piece of one's mind** decirle a uno su parecer con toda franqueza; **to go to pieces** desvencijarse; darse a la desesperación; ir al desastre (*un negocio*); sufrir un ataque de nervios; perder por completo la salud; **to pick someone to pieces** (coll) no dejarle a uno un hueso sano ‖ *tr* formar juntando piezas; remendar ‖ *intr* (coll) comer a deshora
piece goods *spl* géneros de pieza
piece'work' *s* destajo, trabajo a destajo
piece'work'er *s* destajero, destajista *mf*
pier [pɪr] *s* muelle *m;* (*of a bridge*) estribo, sostén *m;* (*of a harbor*) rompeolas *m;* (*wall between two openings*) (archit) entrepaño
pierce [pɪrs] *tr* agujerear, horadar, taladrar; atravesar, traspasar; picar; pinchar, punzar; (fig) traspasar (*de dolor*) ‖ *intr* penetrar, entrar a la fuerza
piercing [ˈpɪrsɪŋ] *adj* agudo, penetrante, desgarrador; (*pain*) lancinante
pier glass *s* espejo de cuerpo entero
pie•ty [ˈpaɪ•əti] *s* (*pl* **-ties**) piedad, devoción
piffle [ˈpɪfəl] *s* (coll) disparates *mpl*, música celestial
pig [pɪg] *s* cerdo; (*young hog*) lechón *m;* (*domestic hog*) puerco, cochino; carne *f* de

puerco; (metal) lingote *m;* (*person who acts like a pig*) (coll) marrano, cochino
pigeon ['pidʒən] *s* paloma
pi'geon•hole' *s* hornilla, casilla de paloma; casilla || *tr* encasillar
pigeon house *s* palomar *m*
piggish ['pɪgɪʃ] *adj* glotón, voraz
pig'gy•back' *adv* a cuestas, en hombros
pig'-head'ed *adj* terco, cabezudo
pig iron *s* arrabio, hierro en lingotes
pigment ['pɪgmənt] *s* pigmento || *tr* pigmentar || *intr* pigmentarse
pig'pen' *s* pocilga; (fig) pocilga, corral *m* de vacas
pig'skin' *s* piel *f* de cerdo; (coll) balón *m* (*con que se juega al fútbol*)
pig'sty' *s* (*pl* **-sties**) pocilga
pig'tail' *s* coleta, trenza; (*of tobacco*) andullo
pike [paɪk] *s* pica; (*of an arrow*) punta; carretera; camino de barrera; (*fish*) lucio
piker ['paɪkər] *s* (slang) persona de poco fuste
Pilate ['paɪlət] *s* Pilatos *m*
pile [paɪl] *s* pila, montón *m;* (*stake*) pilote *m;* lanilla, pelusa; pira; (elec, phys) pila; (coll) caudal *m;* **piles** almorranas || *tr* apilar, amontonar || *intr* apilarse, amontonarse; **to pile in** o **into** entrar atropelladamente en; entrar todos en; subir todos a (*p.ej., un coche*)
pile driver *s* martinete *m*
pileup ['paɪl,ʌp] *s* (*collision*) choque en cadena
pilfer ['pɪlfər] *tr & intr* ratear
pilgrim ['pɪlgrɪm] *s* peregrino, romero
pilgrimage ['pɪlgrɪmɪdʒ] *s* peregrinación, romería
pill [pɪl] *s* píldora; mal trago, sinsabor *m;* (coll) persona molesta
pillage ['pɪlɪdʒ] *s* pillaje *m,* saqueo || *tr & intr* pillar, saquear
pillar ['pɪlər] *s* pilar *m;* **from pillar to post** de acá para allá sin objeto determinado
pillo•ry ['pɪləri] *s* (*pl* **-ries**) picota || *v* (*pret & pp* **-ried**) *tr* empicotar; (fig) motejar, poner en ridículo
pillow ['pɪlo] *s* almohada
pil'low•case' o **pil'low•slip'** *s* funda de almohada
pilot ['paɪlət] *s* piloto; (*of a harbor*) práctico; (*of a gas range*) mechero encendedor; (rr) trompa, delantera || *tr* pilotar; conducir
pilot run o **pilot test** *s* experimento piloto
pimp [pɪmp] *s* alcahuete *m*
pimple ['pɪmpəl] *s* barro, grano
pim•ply ['pɪmpli] *adj* (*comp* **-plier;** *super* **-pliest**) granujoso
pin [pɪn] *s* alfiler *m;* (*e.g., for a necktie*) prendedero; (*peg*) clavija; (*e.g., to hold scissors together*) clavillo, clavito; (bowling) bolo; **to be on pins and needles** estar en espinas || *v* (*pret & pp* **pinned;** *ger* **pinning**) *tr* alfilerar; clavar, fijar, sujetar; **to pin something on someone** (coll) acusarle a uno de una cosa; **to pin up** recoger y apuntar con alfileres; fijar en la pred con alfileres
pinafore ['pɪnə,for] *s* delantal *m* de niño
pin'ball' *s* billar romano, bagatela
pince-nez ['pæns,ne] *s* lentes *mpl* de nariz, lentes de pinzas
pincers ['pɪnsərz] *ssg* o *spl* pinzas
pinch [pɪntʃ] *s* pellizco; (*of hunger*) tormento; (slang) arresto; (slang) hurto, robo; **in a pinch** en un aprieto; en caso necesario || *tr* pellizcar; cogerse (*los dedos, p.ej., en una puerta*); apretar (*p.ej., el zapato a una persona*); contraer (*el frío la cara de uno*); limitar los gastos de; (slang) arrestar, prender; (slang) hurtar, robar || *intr* apretar; economizar, privarse de lo necesario
pinchers ['pɪntʃərz] *ssg* o *spl* var of **pincers**
pin'cush'ion *s* acerico
Pindar ['pɪndər] *s* Píndaro
pine [paɪn] *s* pino || *intr* languidecer; **to pine away** consumirse; **to pine for** penar por
pine'ap'ple *s* ananás *m,* piña
pine cone *s* piña
pine needle *s* pinocha
ping [pɪŋ] *s* silbido de bala || *intr* silbar (*una bala*); silbar como una bala
pin'head' *s* cabecilla de alfiler; cosa muy pequeña o insignificante; (coll) bobalicón *m*
pink [pɪŋk] *adj* rosado, sonrosado || *s* estado perfecto; comunistoide *mf;* (bot) clavel *m,* clavellina
pin money *s* alfileres *mpl*
pinnacle ['pɪnəkəl] *s* pináculo
pin'point' *adj* exacto, preciso || *s* punta de alfiler || *tr & intr* señalar con precisión
pin'prick' *s* alfilerazo
pinup girl ['pɪn,ʌp] *s* guapa
pin'wheel' *s* rueda de fuego, rueda giratoria de fuegos artificiales; molinete *m* (Mex); (*child's toy*) rehilandera, ventolera
pioneer [,paɪ•ə'nɪr] *s* pionero; (mil) zapador *m* || *intr* abrir nuevos caminos, explorar
pious ['paɪ•əs] *adj* pío, piadoso; mojigato; respetuoso
pip [pɪp] *s* (*seed*) pepita; (*on a card, dice, etc.*) punto; (vet) pepita
pipe [paɪp] *s* caño, conducto, tubo; (*to smoke tobacco*) pipa; (mus) pipa, caramillo, zampoña; (*of an organ*) cañón *m* || *tr* conducir por medio de tubos o cañerías; proveer de tuberías o cañerías || *intr* tocar el caramillo; **to pipe down** (slang) callarse
pipe cleaner *s* limpiapipas *m*
pipe dream *s* esperanza imposible, castillo en el aire
pipe line *s* cañería; tubería; oleoducto; fuente *f* de informes confidenciales
pipe organ *s* (mus) órgano
piper ['paɪpər] *s* flautista *m;* gaitero; **to pay the piper** pagar los vidrios rotos
pipe wrench *s* llave *f* para tubos
pippin ['pɪpɪn] *s* (*apple*) camuesa; (*tree*) camueso; (slang) real moza
piquancy ['pikənsi] *s* picante *m*
piquant ['pikənt] *adj* picante
pique [pik] *s* pique *m,* resentimiento || *tr* picar, enojar; despertar, excitar
piracy ['paɪrəsi] *s* piratería

Piraeus [paɪˈri•əs] *s* el Pireo
pirate [ˈpaɪrɪt] *s* pirata *m* || *tr* pillar, robar; publicar fraudulentamente || *intr* piratear
pirouette [ˌpɪruˈɛt] *s* pirueta || *intr* piruetear
Pisces [ˈpaɪsiz] *s* (astr) Piscis *m*
pistol [ˈpɪstəl] *s* pistola
piston [ˈpɪstən] *s* (mach) émbolo, pistón *m;* (mus) pistón *m*
piston displacement *s* cilindrada
piston ring *s* anillo de émbolo, aro de émbolo, segmento de émbolo
piston rod *s* vástago de émbolo
piston stroke *s* carrera de émbolo
pit [pɪt] *s* hoyo; (*in the skin*) cacaraña; (*of certain fruit*) hueso; (*for cockfights, etc.*) cancha, reñidero; (*of the stomach*) boca; abismo, infierno; (min) pozo; (theat) foso || *v* (*pret & pp* **pitted;** *ger* **pitting**) *tr* marcar con hoyos; dejar hoyoso (*el rostro*); deshuesar (*p.ej., una ciruela*)
pitch [pɪtʃ] *s* (*black sticky substance*) pez *f;* echada, lanzamiento; cosa lanzada; pelota lanzada; (*of a boat*) arfada, cabezada; (*of a roof*) pendiente *f;* (*of, e.g., a screw*) paso; (*of a winding*) (elec) paso; (mus) tono, altura; (fig) grado, extremo; (coll) bombo, elogio || *tr* echar, lanzar; elevar (*el heno*) con la horquilla; armar o plantar (*una tienda de campaña*); embrear; (mus) graduar el tono de || *intr* caerse, caer de cabeza; bajar en declive, inclinarse; arfar, cabecear (*un buque*); **to pitch in** (coll) poner manos a la obra; (coll) comenzar a comer
pitch accent *s* acento de altura
pitcher [ˈpɪtʃər] *s* jarro; (*in baseball*) lanzador *m*
pitch′fork′ *s* horca, horquilla; **to rain pitchforks** (coll) llover a cántaros
pitch pipe *s* (mus) diapasón *m*
pit′fall′ *s* callejo, trampa; (*danger for the unwary*) escollo, atascadero
pith [pɪθ] *s* médula; (*essential part*) (fig) médula; (fig) fuerza, vigor *m*
pith•y [ˈpɪθi] *adj* (*comp* **-ier;** *super* **-iest**) medular; enérgico, expresivo
pitiful [ˈpɪtɪfəl] *adj* lastimoso; compasivo; despreciable
pitiless [ˈpɪtɪlɪs] *adj* despiadado, empedernido, incompasivo
pit-y [ˈpɪti] *s (pl* **-ies**) piedad, compasión, lástima; **for pity's sake!** ¡por piedad!; **to have** o **to take pity on** tener piedad de, apiadarse de; **what a pity!** ¡qué lástima!, !qué pena! || *v* (*pret & pp* **-ied**) *tr* apiadarse de, compadecer
pivot [ˈpɪvət] *s* pivote *m*, gorrón *m*, eje *m* de rotación; (fig) eje *m* || *intr* pivotar; **to pivot on** girar sobre; depender de
placard [ˈplækɑrd] *s* cartel *m* || *tr* fijar carteles en; fijar (*un anuncio*) en sitio público; publicar por medio de carteles
place [ples] *s* sitio, lugar *m;* (*of business*) local *m;* (*job*) puesto; grado, rango; **in no place** en ninguna parte; **in place of** en lugar de; **out of place** fuera de su lugar; fuera de propósito; **to be looking for a place to live** buscar piso; **to take place** tener lugar; situar || *tr* poner, colocar; acordarse bien de; dar empleo a; prestar (*dinero*) a interés || *intr* colocarse (*un caballo en las carreras*)
place•bo [pləˈsibo] *s* (*pl* **-bos** o **-boes**) placebo
place card *s* tarjetita con el nombre (*que indica la colocación de uno en la mesa*)
placement [ˈplesmənt] *s* colocación
place name *s* nombre *m* de lugar, topónimo
placid [ˈplæsɪd] *adj* plácido, tranquilo
plagiarism [ˈpledʒəˌrɪzəm] *s* plagio
plagiarize [ˈpledʒəˌraɪz] *tr* plagiar
plague [pleg] *s* peste *f*, plaga; (*great public calamity*) plaga || *tr* apestar, plagar; atormentar, molestar
plaid [plæd] *s* (*cloth*) tartán *m;* cuadros a la escocesa
plain [plen] *adj* llano, claro, evidente; abierto, franco; ordinario; feo; humilde; solo, natural; **in plain English** sin rodeos; **in plain sight** o **view** en plena vista || *s* llano, llanura
plain clothes *spl* traje *m* de calle, traje de paisano
plainclothesman [ˈplenˈkloðzˌmæn] *s* (*pl* **-men** [ˌmɛn]) policía *m* que lleva traje de paisano
plain omelet *s* tortilla a la francesa
plains•man [ˈplenzmən] *s* (*pl* **-men** [mən]) llanero
plaintiff [ˈplentɪf] *s* (law) demandante *mf*
plaintive [ˈplentɪv] *adj* quejumbroso
plan [plæn] *s* plan *m*, intento, proyecto; (*drawing, diagram*) plan *m*, plano; **to change one's plans** cambiar de proyecto || *v* (*pret & pp* **planned;** *ger* **planning**) *tr* planear, planificar; **to plan to** proponerse || *intr* hacer proyectos
plane [plen] *adj* plano || *s* (*surface*) plano; aeroplano, avión *m;* (*of an airplane*) plano; (carp) cepillo; (*tree*) plátano || *tr* cepillar || *intr* viajar en aeroplano
plane sickness *s* mareo del aire, mal *m* de vuelo
planet [ˈplænɪt] *s* planeta *m*
plane tree *s* plátano
planing mill [ˈplenɪŋ] *s* taller *m* de cepillado
plank [plæŋk] *s* tabla gruesa, tablón *m;* artículo de un programa político || *tr* entablar, entarimar
plant [plænt] *s* fábrica, taller *m;* (*of an automobile*) grupo motor; (*educational establishment*) plantel *m;* (bot) planta || *tr* plantar; sembrar (*semillas*); inculcar (*doctrinas*); (slang) ocultar (*géneros robados*)
plantation [plænˈteʃən] *s* plantación, campo de plantas; (*estate cultivated by workers living on it*) hacienda
planter [ˈplæntər] *s* plantador *m*, cultivador *m*
plasma [ˈplæzmə] *s* plasma *m*
plaster [ˈplæstər] *s* (*gypsum*) yeso; (*mixture of lime, sand, water, etc.*) argamasa; (*coating*) enlucido; (*poultice*) emplasto || *tr* en-

yesar; argamasar; enlucir; emplastar; embadurnar; pegar (*anuncios*)
plas'ter•board' *s* cartón *m* de yeso y fieltro
plaster cast *s* (surg) vendaje enyesado; (sculp) yeso
plaster of Paris *s* estuco de París
plastic ['plæstɪk] *adj* plástico || *s* (*substance*) plástico; (*art of modeling*) plástica
plate [plet] *s* (*dish*) plato; (*sheet of metal, etc.*) chapa, placa; vajilla de oro, vajilla de plata; dentadura postiza, base *f* de la dentadura postiza; (baseball) puesto meta, puesto del batter; (anat, elec, electron, phot, zool) placa; (typ) clisé *m* || *tr* chapear, planchear; blindar; platear, dorar, niquelar (*por la galvanoplastia*); (typ) clisar
plateau [plæ'to] *s* meseta
plate glass *s* vidrio o cristal cilindrado
platen ['plætən] *s* rodillo
platform ['plæt,fɔrm] *s* plataforma *f;* (*of passenger station*) andén *m;* (*of freight station*) cargadero; (*of a speaker*) tribuna; (*political program*) plataforma
platform car *s* plataforma *f*
platinum ['plætɪnəm] *s* platino
platinum blonde *s* rubia platino
platitude ['plætɪ,tjud] o ['plætɪ,tud] *s* perogrullada, trivialidad
Plato ['pleto] *s* Platón *m*
platoon [plə'tun] *s* pelotón *m*
platter ['plætər] *s* fuente *f;* (slang) disco de fonógrafo
plausible ['plɔzɪbəl] *adj* aparente, especioso; bien hablado; (coll) creíble
play [ple] *s* juego; (*act or move in a game*) jugada; (*drama*) pieza; (*of water, colors, lights*) juego; (mach) huelgo, juego; **to give full play to** dar rienda suelta a || *tr* jugar (*p.ej., un naipe, una partida de juego*); jugar **a** (*p.ej., los naipes*); jugar con (*un contrario*); dar (*un chasco*); gastar (*una broma*); hacer (*una mala jugada*); dirigir (*agua, una manguera*); desempeñar (*un papel*); desempeñar el papel de; representar (*una obra dramática, un film*); apostar por (*un caballo*); tocar (*un instrumento, una pieza, un disco de fonógrafo*) || *intr* jugar; desempeñar un papel, representar; correr (*una fuente*); rielar (*la luz en la superficie del agua*); vagar (*p.ej., una sonrisa por los labios*); **to play out** rendirse; agotarse; acabarse; **to play safe** tomar sus precauciones; **to play sick** hacerse el enfermo; **to play up to** hacer la rueda a
play'back' *s* lectura; aparato de lectura
play'bill' *s* (*poster*) cartel *m;* (*of a play*) programa *m*
player piano ['ple•ər] *s* autopiano
playful ['plefəl] *adj* juguetón, retozón; dicho en broma
playgoer ['ple,go•ər] *s* aficionado al teatro
play'ground' *s* campo de juego; patio de recreo
play'house' *s* casita de muñecas; teatro
playing card ['ple•ɪŋ] *s* naipe *m*
playing field *s* campo de deportes
play'mate' *s* compañero de juego
play'-off' *s* partido de desempate
play'pen' *s* parque *m,* corral *m* (*para bebés*)
play'thing' *s* juguete *m*
play'time' *s* hora de recreo, hora de juego
playwright ['ple,raɪt] *s* dramaturgo, autor dramático; comediógrafo
play'writ'ing *s* dramaturgia, dramática
plea [pli] *s* ruego, súplica; disculpa, excusa; (law) contestación a la demanda
plead [plid] *v* (*pret & pp* **pleaded** o **pled** [plɛd]) *tr* defender (*una causa*) || *intr* suplicar; abogar; **to plead guilty** confesarse culpable; **to plead not guilty** negar la acusación, declararse inocente
pleasant ['plɛzənt] *adj* agradable; simpático; sangriligero
pleasant•ry ['plɛzəntri] *s* (*pl* **-ries**) broma, chiste *m,* dicho gracioso
please [pliz] *tr & intr* gustar; **as you please** como Vd. quiera; **if you please** si me hace el favor; **please** + *inf* hágame Vd. el favor de + *inf;* **to be pleased to** alegrarse de, complacerse en; **to be pleased with** estar satisfecho de o con
pleasing ['plizɪŋ] *adj* agradable, grato
pleasure ['plɛʒər] *s* placer *m,* gusto; **what is your pleasure?** ¿en qué puedo servirle?, ¿qué es lo que Vd. desea?; **with pleasure** con mucho gusto
pleasure seeker ['sikər] *s* amigo de los placeres
pleat [plit] *s* pliegue *m,* plisado || *tr* plegar, plisar
plebeian [plɪ'bi•ən] *adj & s* plebeyo
pledge [plɛdʒ] *s* empeño, prenda; (*vow*) voto, promesa; (*toast*) brindis *m;* **as a pledge of** en prenda de; **to take the pledge** comprometerse a no tomar bebidas alcohólicas || *tr* empeñar, prendar; dar (*la palabra*); brindar por
plentiful ['plɛntɪfəl] *adj* abundante, copioso
plenty ['plɛnti] *adv* (coll) completamente || *s* abundancia, copia; suficiencia
pleurisy ['plʊrɪsi] *s* pleuresía
pliable ['plaɪ•əbəl] *adj* flexible, plegable; dócil
pliers ['plaɪ•ərz] *ssg* o *spl* alicates *mpl*
plight [plaɪt] *s* estado, situación; apuro, aprieto; compromiso solemne || *tr* dar o empeñar (*su palabra*); **to plight one's troth** prometer fidelidad; dar palabra de casamiento
plod [plad] *v* (*pret & pp* **plodded;** *ger* **plodding**) *tr* recorrer (*un camino*) pausada y pesadamente || *intr* caminar pausada y pesadamente; trabajar laboriosamente
plot [plat] *s* complot *m,* conspiración; (*of a play or novel*) argumento, trama, parcela, solar *m;* cuadro de flores; cuadro de hortalizas; plano, mapa *m* || *v* (*pret & pp* **plotted;** *ger* **plotting**) *tr* fraguar, tramar, urdir, maquinar; dividir en parcelas o solares; trazar el plano de; trazar, tirar (*líneas*) || *intr* conspirar
plough [plaʊ] *s, tr & intr* var de **plow**
plover ['plʌvər] o ['plovər] *s* chorlito

plow [plaʊ] *s* arado; quitanieve *m* || *tr* arar; surcar; quitar o barrer (*la nieve*); **to plow back** reinvertir (*ganancias*) || *intr* arar; avanzar como un arado
plow•man [ˈplaʊmən] *s* (*pl* **-men** [mən]) arador *m*, yuguero
plow'share' *s* reja de arado
pluck [plʌk] *s* ánimo, coraje *m*, valor *m;* tirón *m* || *tr* arrancar; coger (*flores*); desplumar (*un ave*); puntear (*p.ej., una guitarra*) || *intr* dar un tirón; **to pluck up** recobrar ánimo
pluck•y [ˈplʌki] *adj* (*comp* **-ier;** *super* **-iest**) animoso, valiente
plug [plʌg] *s* taco, tarugo; boca de agua; tableta de tabaco; (*hat*) (slang) chistera; (elec) clavija, toma, ficha; (aut) bujía; (coll) rocín; (slang) elogio incidental || *v* (*pret & pp* **plugged;** *ger* **plugging**) *tr* atarugar; calar (*un melón*); **to plug in** (elec) enchufar || *intr* (coll) trabajar con ahinco
plum [plʌm] *s* (*tree*) ciruelo; (*fruit*) ciruela; (slang) turrón *m*, pingüe destino
plumage [ˈplumɪdʒ] *s* plumaje *m*
plumb [plʌm] *adj* vertical; (coll) completo || *adv* a plomo; (coll) verticalmente; (coll) directamente || *tr* aplomar; sondear
plumb bob *s* plomada
plumber [ˈplʌmər] *s* fontanero; (*worker in lead*) plomero
plumbing [ˈplʌmɪŋ] *s* instalación sanitaria; conjunto de cañerías; (*working in lead*) plomería; sondeo
plumbing fixtures *spl* artefactos sanitarios
plumb line *s* cuerda de plomada
plum cake *s* pastel aderezado con pasas de Corinto y ron
plume [plum] *s* (*of a bird*) pluma; (*tuft of feathers worn as ornament*) penacho || *tr* emplumar; componerse (*las plumas*); **to plume oneself on** enorgulleclerse de
plummet [ˈplʌmɪt] *s* plomada || *intr* caer a plomo, precipitarse
plump [plʌmp] *adj* rechoncho, regordete; brusco, franco || *adv* de golpe; francamente || *s* (coll) caída pesada; (coll) ruido sordo || *intr* caer a plomo
plum pudding *s* pudín *m* inglés con pasas de Corinto, corteza de limón, huevos y ron
plum tree *s* ciruelo
plunder [ˈplʌndər] *s* pillaje *m;* botín *m* || *tr* pillar, saquear
plunge [plʌndʒ] *s* zambullida; caída a plomo; sacudida violenta; salto; baño de agua fría; (*of a boat*) cabeceo || *tr* zambullir; sumergir; hundir (*p.ej., un puñal*) || *intr* zambullirse; sumergirse; hundirse (*p.ej., en la tristeza*); caer a plomo; arrojarse, precipitarse; cabecear (*un buque*); (slang) entregarse al juego, entregarse a las especulaciones
plunger [ˈplʌndʒər] *s* zambullidor *m;* émbolo buzo; (*of a tire valve*) obús *m;* (slang) jugador o especulador desenfrenado
plunk [plʌŋk] *adv* (coll) con un golpe seco, con un ruido de golpe seco || *tr* (coll) arrojar, empujar o dejar caer pesadamente || *intr* sonar o caer con un ruido de golpe seco
plural [ˈplʊrəl] *adj & s* plural *m*
plus [plʌs] *adj* más; y pico; **to be plus** (coll) tener por añadidura || *prep* más || *s* (*sign*) más *m;* añadidura
plush [plʌʃ] *adj* afelpado; (coll) lujoso, suntuoso || *s* felpa; peluche *m*
Plutarch [ˈplutɑrk] *s* Plutarco
plutonium [pluˈtonɪ•əm] *s* plutonio
ply [plaɪ] *s* (*pl* **plies**) (*e.g., of a cloth*) capa, doblez *m;* (*of a cable*) cordón *m* || *v* (*pret & pp* **plied**) *tr* manejar (*la aguja, etc.*); ejercer (*un oficio*); batir (*el agua con los remos*); importunar; navegar por (*p.ej., un río*) || *intr* avanzar; **to ply between** hacer (*un barco*) el servicio entre
ply'wood' *s* chapeado, madera laminada
P.M. *abbr* **Postmaster, post meridiem** (Lat) **afternoon**
pneumatic [njuˈmætɪk] o [nuˈmætɪk] *adj* neumático
pneumatic drill *s* perforadora de aire comprimido
pneumonia [njuˈmonɪ•ə] o [nuˈmonɪ•ə] *s* neumonía o pulmonía
P.O. *abbr* **post office**
poach [potʃ] *tr* escalfar (*huevos*) || *intr* cazar o pescar en vedado
poacher [ˈpotʃər] *s* cazador furtivo, pescador furtivo
pock [pɑk] *s* cacaraña, hoyuelo
pocket [ˈpɑkɪt] *s* bolsillo, faltriquera; (*in billiards*) tronera; (aer) bolsa de aire; (mil) bolsón *m* || *tr* embolsar; entronerar (*una bola de billar*); tragarse (*injurias*)
pock'et•book' *s* portamonedas *m;* (*of a woman*) bolsa
pocket calculator *s* bolsicalculadora, calculadora de bolsillo
pocket handkerchief *s* pañuelo de bolsillo o de mano
pock'et•knife' *s* (*pl* **-knives**) navaja, cortaplumas *m*
pocket money *s* alfileres *mpl*, dinero de bolsillo
pock'mark' *s* cacaraña, hoyuelo
pod [pɑd] *s* vaina
podium [ˈpodi•əm] *s* podio
poem [ˈpo•ɪm] *s* poema *m*, poesía
poet [ˈpo•ɪt] *s* poeta *m*
poetess [ˈpo•ɪtɪs] *s* poetisa
poetic [poˈɛtɪk] *adj* poético || **poetics** *ssg* poética
poetry [ˈpo•ɪtri] *s* poesía
pogrom [ˈpogrəm] *s* levantamiento contra los judíos
poignancy [ˈpɔɪnyənsi] *s* picante *m*, viveza, intensidad
poignant [ˈpɔɪnyənt] *adj* picante, vivo, intenso
point [pɔɪnt] *s* (*of a sword, pencil; of land*) punta; (*of pen*) pico; (*of fountain pen*) puntilla; (*mark of imperceptible dimensions*) punto; (*of a joke*) gracia; (elec) punta; (math, typ, sport, fig) punto; (coll) indirecta, insinuación; **beside the point**

fuera de propósito; **on the point of** a punto de; **to carry one's point** salirse con la suya; **to come to the point** venir al caso o al grano; **to get to the point** caer en la cuenta ‖ *tr* aguzar, sacar punta a; apuntar (*p.ej., un arma de fuego*); resanar (*una pared*); **to point one's finger at** señalar con el dedo; **to point out** señalar, indicar, hacer notar ‖ *intr* apuntar; pararse (*el perro de muestra*); **to point at** señalar con el dedo

point'blank' *adj & adv* a quemarropa

pointed [ˈpɔɪntɪd] *adj* puntiagudo; picante; acentuado, directo

pointer [ˈpɔɪntər] *s* puntero; indicador *m; (of a clock)* manecilla; perro de muestra; (mas) fijador *m;* (coll) indicación, dirección

poise [pɔɪz] *s* aplomo, equilibrio ‖ *tr* equilibrar; considerar ‖ *intr* equilibrarse; estar suspendido

poison [ˈpɔɪzən] *s* veneno, ponzoña ‖ *tr* envenenar

poison ivy *s* tosiguero

poisonous [ˈpɔɪzənəs] *adj* venenoso

poi'son-pen' letter *s* carta calumniosa

poke [pok] *s* (*push*) empuje *m,* empujón *m;* (*thrust*) hurgonazo; (*with elbow*) codazo; (*slow person*) tardón *m* ‖ *tr* empujar; hacer (*un agujero*) a empujones; abrirse (*paso*) a empujones; atizar, hurgar (*el fuego*); **to poke fun at** burlarse de; **to poke one's nose into** entremeterse en ‖ *intr* fisgar, husmear; andar perezosamente

poker [ˈpokər] *s* hurgón *m;* (*card game*) póker *m,* pócar *m*

poker face *s* cara de jugador de póker; **to keep a poker face** disfrazar la expresión del rostro, mantener una expresión imperturbable

pok•y [ˈpoki] *adj* (*comp* **-ier;** *super* **-iest**) (coll) tardo, roncero

Poland [ˈpolənd] *s* Polonia

polar bear [ˈpolər] *s* oso blanco

polarize [ˈpolə,raɪz] *tr* polarizar

pole [pol] *s* (*long rod or staff*) pértiga; (*of a flag*) asta; (*upright support*) poste *m;* (*to push a boat*) botador *m;* (astr, biol, elec, geog, math) polo ‖ *tr* impeler (*un barco*) con botador ‖ **Pole** *s* polaco

pole'cat' *s* turón *m,* veso

pole'star' *s* estrella polar; (*guide*) norte *m;* (*center of interest*) miradero

pole vault *s* salto con garrocha o con pértiga

police [pəˈlis] *s* policía ‖ *tr* poner o mantener servicio de policía en; (mil) limpiar

police car *s* carro-patrulla *m*

police•man [pəˈlismən] *s* (*pl* **-men** [mən]) policía *m,* guardia urbano

police record *s* ficha

police state *s* estado-policía *m*

police station *s* cuartel *m* o estación de policía

poli•cy [ˈpalɪsi] *s* (*pl* **-cies**) política; (ins) póliza

polio [ˈpolɪ•o] *s* (coll) polio *f*

polish [ˈpalɪʃ] *s* pulimento; cera de lustrar; (*for shoes*) bola, betún *m,* lustre *m;* (*diamond*) talla; elegancia; cultura, urbanidad ‖ *tr* pulimentar, pulir; embolar, dar betún a (*los zapatos*); **to polish off** (coll) terminar de prisa; (slang) engullir (*la comida, un trago*) ‖ **Polish** [ˈpolɪʃ] *adj & s* polaco

polisher [ˈpalɪʃər] *s* pulidor *m;* (*machine*) pulidora; (*for floors, tables, etc.*) enceradora

polite [pəˈlaɪt] *adj* cortés, fino, urbano; culto

politeness [pəˈlaɪtnɪs] *s* cortesía, fineza, urbanidad; cultura

politic [ˈpalɪtɪk] *adj* prudente, sagaz; astuto; juicioso

political [pəˈlɪtɪkəl] *adj* político

politician [,palɪˈtɪʃən] *s* político; (*politician seeking personal or partisan gain*) politiquero

politics [ˈpalɪtɪks] *ssg* o *spl* política

poll [pol] *s* (*questionnaire to determine opinion*) encuesta; votación; lista electoral; cabeza; **polls** urnas electorales; **to go to the polls** acudir a las urnas; **to take a poll** hacer una encuesta ‖ *tr* dar (*un voto*); recibir (*votos*)

pollen [ˈpalən] *s* polen *m*

pollinate [ˈpalɪ,net] *tr* polinizar

polling booth [ˈpolɪŋ] *s* cabina o caseta de votar

polliwog [ˈpalɪ,wag] *s* renacuajo; (slang) persona que atraviesa el ecuador en un barco por primera vez

pollster [ˈpolstʌr] *s* encuestador *m*

poll tax *s* capitación, impuesto por cabeza

pollutant [pəˈlutənt] *s* contaminante *m*

pollute [pəˈlut] *tr* contaminar, corromper, ensuciar

pollution [pəˈluʃən] *s* contaminación; (*of the environment*) polución; (fig) corrupción

polo [ˈpolo] *s* polo

polo player *s* polista *mf,* jugador *m* de polo

polygamist [pəˈlɪgəmɪst] *s* polígamo

polygamous [pəˈlɪgəməs] *adj* polígamo

polyglot [ˈpalɪ,glat] *adj & s* poligloto

polygon [ˈpalɪ,gan] *s* polígono

Polyhymnia [,palɪˈhɪmnɪ•ə] *s* Polimnia

polynomial [,palɪˈnomɪ•əl] *s* polinomio

polyp [ˈpalɪp] *s* pólipo

polytheist [ˈpalɪ,θi•ɪst] *s* politeísta *mf*

polytheistic [,palɪθiˈɪstɪk] *adj* politeísta

polyvalent [,paliˈvelənt] *adj* (chem, bact) polivalente

pomade [pəˈmed] *s* pomada

pomegranate [ˈpam,grænɪt] *s* (*shrub*) granado; (*fruit*) granada

pom•mel [ˈpʌməl] o [ˈpaməl] *s* (*on hilt of sword*) pomo; (*on saddle*) perilla ‖ *v* (*pret & pp* **-meled** o **-melled;** *ger* **-meling** o **-melling**) *tr* apuñear, aporrear

pomp [pamp] *s* pompa, fausto

pompadour [ˈpampə,dur] *s* copete *m*

pompous [ˈpampəs] *adj* pomposo, faustoso

pon•cho [ˈpantʃo] *s* (*pl* **-chos**) capote *m* de monte, poncho

pond [pand] *s* estanque *m,* charca

ponder [ˈpandər] *tr* ponderar ‖ *intr* meditar; **to ponder over** ponderar, considerar con cuidado

ponderous ['pandərəs] *adj* pesado, inmanejable; tedioso, fastidioso
pond scum *s* lama, verdín *m*
poniard ['panjərd] *s* puñal *m*
pontiff ['pantɪf] *s* pontífice *m*
pontoon [pan'tun] *s* pontón *m*
po•ny ['poni] *s* (*pl* **-nies**) jaca, caballito; (*for drinking liquor*) (coll) pequeño vaso; (*translation used dishonestly in school*) (coll) chuleta
poodle ['pudəl] *s* perro de lanas
pool [pul] *s* (*small puddle*) charco; (*for swimming*) piscina; (*game*) trucos; (*in certain games*) polla, puesta; combinación de intereses; caudales unidos para un fin ‖ *tr* mancomunar
pool'room' *s* sala de trucos
pool table *s* mesa de trucos
poop [pup] *s* popa; (*deck*) toldilla
poor [pʊr] *adj* (*having few possessions; arousing pity*) pobre; (*not good, inferior*) malo
poor box *s* cepillo, caja de limosnas
poor'house' *s* asilo de pobres, casa de caridad
poorly ['pʊrli] *adv* mal
poor white *s* pobre *mf* de la raza blanca (*en el sur de los EE.UU.*)
pop. *abbr* **popular, population**
pop [pap] *s* estallido, taponazo; bebida gaseosa ‖ *v* (*pret & pp* **popped;** *ger* **popping**) *tr* hacer estallar; **to pop the question** (coll) hacer una declaración de amor ‖ *intr* estallar
pop'corn' *s* rosetas, palomitas (de maíz)
pope [pop] *s* papa *m*
popeyed ['pap,aɪd] *adj* de ojos saltones; (*with fear, surprise, etc.*) desorbitado
pop'gun' *s* tirabala
poplar ['paplər] *s* álamo, chopo
pop•py ['papi] *s* (*pl* **-pies**) amapola
pop'py•cock' *s* (coll) necedad, tontería
popsicle ['papsɪkəl] *s* polo
populace ['papjəlɪs] *s* populacho; chamuchina
popular ['papjələr] *adj* popular
popularize ['papjələ,raɪz] *tr* popularizar, vulgarizar
populous ['papjələs] *adj* populoso
porcelain ['pɔrsəlɪn] *s* porcelana
porch [portʃ] *s* porche *m*, pórtico
porcupine ['pɔrkjə,paɪn] *s* puerco espín
pore [por] *s* poro ‖ *intr*—**to pore over** estudiar larga y detenidamente
pork [pork] *s* carne *f* de cerdo
pork chop *s* chuleta de cerdo
pornography [pɔr'nagræfi] *s* pornografía
pornographic [,pɔrnə'græfɪk] *adj* pornográfico
porno queen ['pɔrno] *s* (slang) actriz *f* de películas pornográficas
porous ['porəs] *adj* poroso
porous plaster *s* parche poroso
porphy•ry ['pɔrfɪri] *s* (*pl* **-ries**) pórfido
porpoise ['pɔrpəs] *s* marsopa, puerco de mar; (*dolphin*) delfín *m*
porridge ['pɔrɪdʒ] *s* gachas
port [port] *adj* portuario ‖ *s* puerto; (*opening in ship's side*) portilla; (*left side of ship or airplane*) babor *m;* oporto, vino de Oporto; (mach) lumbrera
portable ['portəbəl] *adj* portátil
portal ['portəl] *s* portal *m*
portend [por'tɛnd] *tr* anunciar de antemano, presagiar
portent ['portent] *s* augurio, presagio
portentous [por'tɛntəs] *adj* portentoso, extraordinario; amenazante, ominoso
porter ['portər] *s* (*doorkeeper*) portero, conserje *m;* (*in hotels and trains*) mozo de servicio; pórter *m* (*cerveza de Inglaterra de color obscuro*)
portfoli•o [port'folɪ,o] *s* (*pl* **-os**) cartera
port'hole' *s* porta, portilla
porti•co ['portɪ,ko] *s* (*pl* **-coes o -cos**) pórtico
portion ['porʃən] *s* porción; (*dowry*) dote *m & f*
port•ly ['portli] *adj* (*comp* **-lier;** *super* **-liest**) corpulento; grave, majestuoso
port of call *s* escala
portrait ['portret] o ['portrɪt] *s* retrato; **to sit for a portrait** retratarse
portray [por'tre] *tr* retratar
portrayal [por'tre•əl] *s* representación gráfica; retrato, descripción acertada
Portugal ['portʃəgəl] *s* Portugal *m*
Portu•guese ['portʃə,giz] *adj* portugués ‖ *s* (*pl* **-guese**) portugués *m*
port wine *s* vino de Oporto
pose [poz] *s* pose *f* ‖ *tr* plantear (*una pregunta, cuestión, etc.*) ‖ *intr* posar (*para retratarse; como modelo*); tomar una postura afectada; **to pose as** hacerse pasar por
posh [paʃ] *adj* (slang) elegante; (slang) lujoso, suntuoso
position [pə'zɪʃən] *s* posición; empleo, puesto; opinión; **to be in a position to** estar en condiciones de
positive ['pazɪtɪv] *adj* positivo ‖ *s* positiva
possess [pə'zɛs] *tr* poseer
possession [pə'zɛʃən] *s* posesión
possible ['pasɪbəl] *adj* posible
possum ['pasəm] *s* zarigüeya; **to play possum** hacer la mortecina
post [post] *s* (*piece of wood, metal, etc. set upright*) poste *m;* (*position*) puesto; (*job*) puesto, cargo; casa de correos ‖ *tr* fijar (*carteles*); echar al correo; apostar, situar; tener al corriente; **post no bills** se prohibe fijar carteles
postage ['postɪdʒ] *s* porte *m*, franqueo; **postage will be paid by addressee** a franquear en destino
postage meter *s* franqueadora
postage stamp *s* sello de correo; estampilla, timbre *m* (Am)
postal ['postəl] *adj* postal ‖ *s* postal *f*
postal card *s* tarjeta postal
postal permit *s* franqueo concertado
postal savings bank *s* caja postal de ahorros
post card *s* tarjeta postal
post'date' *s* posfecha ‖ **post'date'** *tr* posfechar

poster ['postər] *s* cartel *m*, cartelón *m*, letrero; póster *m*
posterity [pɑs'tɛrɪti] *s* posteridad
postern ['postərn] *s* postigo, portillo
post'haste' *adv* por la posta, a toda prisa
posthumous ['pɑstʃuməs] *adj* póstumo
post•man ['postmən] *s* (*pl* **-men** [mən]) cartero
post'mark' *s* matasellos *m*, timbre *m* de correos || *tr* matasellar, timbrar
post'mas'ter *s* administrador *m* de correos
post-mortem [,post'mɔrtəm] *adj* posterior a la muerte || *s* examen *m* de un cadáver
post office *s* casa de correos
post'-of'fice box *s* apartado de correos, casilla postal
postpaid ['post,ped] *adj* con porte pagado, franco de porte
postpone [post'pon] *tr* aplazar
postscript ['post,skrɪpt] *s* posdata
posttonic [post'tɑnɪk] *adj* postónico
posture ['pɑstʃər] *s* postura || *intr* adoptar una postura
post'war' *adj* de la posguerra
po•sy ['pozi] *s* (*pl* **-sies**) flor *f*, ramillete *m*
pot [pɑt] *s* pote *m*; (*for flowers*) tiesto; (*for the kitchen*) caldera, olla, puchero; vaso de noche, orinal *m*; (*in gambling*) puesta; (slang) mariguana
potash ['pɑt,æʃ] *s* potasa
potassium [pə'tæsɪ•əm] *s* potasio
pota•to [pə'teto] *s* (*pl* **-toes**) patata, papa; (*sweet potato*) batata, buniato
potato masher *s* pasapuré *m*
potato omelet *s* tortilla a la española
potbellied ['pɑt'bɛlid] *adj* barrigón, panzudo
poten•cy ['potənsi] *s* (*pl* **-cies**) potencia
potent ['potənt] *adj* potente
potentate ['potən,tet] *s* potentado
potential [pə'tɛnʃəl] *adj* & *s* potencial *m*
pot'hang'er *s* llares *fpl*
pot'hook' *s* garabato
potion ['poʃən] *s* poción
pot'luck *s* lo que hay de comer; **to take potluck** hacer penitencia
pot shot *s* tiro a corta distancia
potter ['pɑtər] *s* alfarero; ollero || *intr* ocuparse en fruslerías
potter's clay *s* arcilla figulina
potter's field *s* cementerio de los pobres, hoyanca
potter's shop *s* ollería
potter's wheel *s* torno de alfarero
potter•y ['pɑtəri] *s* (*pl* **-ies**) alfarería; cacharros (de alfarería)
pouch [pautʃ] *s* bolsa, saquillo; (*of kangaroo*) bolsa; (*for tobacco*) petaca; valija
poulterer ['poltərər] *s* pollero
poultice ['poltɪs] *s* cataplasma *f*
poultry ['poltri] *s* aves *fpl* de corral
pounce [pauns] *intr*—**to pounce on** saltar sobre, precipitarse sobre
pound [paund] *s* (*weight*) libra; (*for stray animals*) corral *m* de concejo || *tr* golpear; machacar, moler; encerrar en el corral de concejo; bombardear incesantemente; (*to keep walking over*) desempedrar || *intr* golpear
pound'cake' *s* pastel *m* en que entra una libra de cada ingrediente; ponqué *m* (Am)
pound sterling *s* libra esterlina
pour [por] *tr* vaciar, verter, derramar; echar, servir (*p.ej., té*); escanciar (*vino*) || *intr* fluir rápidamente; llover a torrentes; **to pour out of** salir a montones de (*p.ej., el teatro*)
pout [paut] *s* mala cara, puchero || *intr* poner mala cara, hacer pucheros
poverty ['pɑvərti] *s* pobreza; pelazón *f*
POW *abbr* **prisoner of war**
powder ['paudər] *s* polvo; (*for face*) polvos; (*explosive*) pólvora || *tr* pulverizar; (*to sprinkle with powder*) empolvar, polvorear
powder puff *s* borla para empolvarse
powder room *s* cuarto tocador, cuarto de aseo
powdery ['paudəri] *adj* (*like powder*) polvoriento; (*sprinkled with powder*) empolvado; (*crumbly*) quebradizo
power ['pau•ər] *s* (*ability to act or do something; possession*) poder *m*; (*control, influence; wealth*) poderío; (*influential nation; energy, force, strength*) potencia; **the powers that be** las autoridades, los que mandan || *tr* accionar, impulsar
power brake *s* servofreno
power dive *s* (aer) picado con motor
power failure *s* interrupción de fuerza
powerful ['pau•ərfəl] *adj* poderoso
pow'er•house' *s* central eléctrica
powerless ['pau•ərlɪs] *adj* impotente
power line *s* (elec) sector *m* de distribución
power mower *s* motosegadora
power of attorney *s* poder *m*
power plant *s* (aer) grupo motopropulsor; (aut) grupo motor; (elec) central eléctrica, estación generadora
power steering *s* (aut) servodirección
power tool *s* herramienta motriz
pp. *abbr* **pages**
p.p. *abbr* **parcel post, postpaid**
pr. *abbr* **pair, present, price**
P.R. *abbr* **public relations**
practical ['præktɪkəl] *adj* práctico
practically ['præktɪkəli] *adv* poco más o menos
practice ['præktɪs] *s* práctica; uso, costumbre; ensayo; (*of a profession*) ejercicio; (*of a doctor*) clientela || *tr* practicar; ejercitar (*p.ej., la caridad*); ejercer (*una profesión*); estudiar (*p.ej., el piano*); tener por costumbre || *intr* ejercitarse; practicar la medicina; ensayarse; entrenarse, adiestrarse; **to practice as** ejercer de (*p.ej., abogado*)
practitioner [præk'tɪʃənər] *s* (*medical doctor*) práctico
Prague [prɑg] o [preg] *s* Praga
prairie ['prɛri] *s* pradera, llanura, pampa
prairie dog *s* ardilla ladradora
prairie wolf *s* coyote *m*
praise [prez] *s* alabanza, elogío || *tr* alabar, elogiar
praise'wor'thy *adj* laudable, plausible

pram [præm] *s* cochecillo de niño
prance [præns] o [prɑns] *s* cabriola, trenzado || *intr* cabriolar, trenzar
prank [præŋk] *s* travesura
prate [pret] *intr* charlar, parlotear
prattle [ˈprætəl] *s* charla, parloteo || *intr* charlar, parlotear, balbucear (*un niño*)
pray [pre] *tr* implorar, rogar, suplicar; rezar (*una oración*) || *intr* orar, rezar; **pray tell me** sírvase decirme
prayer [prɛr] *s* ruego, súplica; oración, rezo
prayer book *s* devocionario
preach [pritʃ] *tr* predicar; aconsejar (*p.ej., la paciencia*) || *intr* predicar
preacher [ˈpritʃər] *s* predicador *m*
preamble [ˈpri,æmbəl] *s* preámbulo
prebend [ˈprɛbənd] *s* prebenda
precarious [priˈkɛrɪ•əs] *adj* precario
precaution [priˈkɔʃən] *s* precaución
precede [priˈsid] *tr & intr* preceder
precedent [ˈprɛsɪdənt] *s* precedente *m*
precept [ˈprisɛpt] *s* precepto
precinct [ˈprisɪŋkt] *s* barriada; distrito electoral
precious [ˈprɛʃəs] *adj* precioso; caro, amado; (coll) considerable || *adv* (coll) muy, p.ej., **precious little** muy poco
precipice [ˈprɛsɪpɪs] *s* precipicio
precipitate [prɪˈsɪpɪ,tet] *adj & s* precipitado || *tr* precipitar || *intr* precipitarse
precipitous [prɪˈsɪpɪtəs] *adj* empinado, escarpado; (*hurried, reckless*) precipitoso
precise [prɪˈsaɪs] *adj* preciso; meticuloso
precision [prɪˈsɪʒən] *s* precisión
preclude [prɪˈklud] *tr* excluir, imposibilitar
precocious [prɪˈkoʃəs] *adj* precoz
predatory [ˈprɛdə,tori] *adj* predatorio
predicament [prɪˈdɪkəmənt] *s* apuro, situación difícil
predict [prɪˈdɪkt] *tr* predecir
prediction [prɪˈdɪkʃən] *s* predicción
predispose [,pridɪsˈpoz] *tr* predisponer
predominant [prɪˈdɑmɪnənt] *adj* predominante
preëminent [prɪˈɛmɪnənt] *adj* preeminente
preëmpt [prɪˈɛmpt] *tr* apropiarse o apropiarse de
preen [prin] *tr* arreglarse (*las plumas*) con el pico; **to preen oneself** componerse, vestirse cuidadosamente
pref. *abbr* **preface, preferred, prefix**
prefabricate [priˈfæbrɪ,ket] *tr* prefabricar
preface [ˈprɛfɪs] *s* prefacio, advertencia || *tr* introducir, empezar
pre•fer [prɪˈfʌr] *v* (*pret & pp* **-ferred;** *ger* **-ferring**) *tr* preferir; presentar; promover
preferable [ˈprɛfərəbəl] *adj* preferible
preference [ˈprɛfərəns] *s* preferencia
prefix [ˈprifɪks] *s* prefijo || *tr* prefijar
pregnan•cy [ˈprɛgnənsi] *s* (*pl* **-cies**) preñez *f*, embarazo
pregnant [ˈprɛgnənt] *adj* preñado; encinta; **to make pregnant** dejar encinta
prejudice [ˈprɛdʒədɪs] *s* prejuicio; (*detriment*) perjuicio; **to the prejudice of** con perjuicio de; **without prejudice** (law) sin detrimento de sus propios derechos || *tr* predisponer, prevenir; (*to harm*) perjudicar
prejudicial [,prɛdʒəˈdɪʃəl] *adj* perjudicial
prelate [ˈprɛlɪt] *s* prelado
pre-Lenten [priˈlɛntən] *adj* carnavalesco
prelim [priˈlɪm] *s* (coll) examen *m* preliminar
preliminar•y [prɪˈlɪmɪ,nɛri] *adj* preliminar || *s* (*pl* **-ies**) preliminar *m*
prelude [ˈprɛljud] o [ˈprilud] *s* preludio || *tr* preludiar
premeditate [priˈmɛdɪ,tet] *tr* premeditar
premier [prɪˈmɪr] o [ˈpriˈmɪr] *s* primer ministro, presidente *m* del consejo
première [preˈmjɛr] o [ˈprimɪ•ər] *s* estreno; actriz *f* principal
premise [ˈprɛmɪs] *s* premisa; **on the premises** en el local mismo; **premises** predio, local *m*
premium [ˈprimɪ•əm] *s* premio; (ins) prima
premonition [,priməˈnɪʃən] *s* presagio; presentimiento
preoccupancy [priˈɑkjəpənsi] *s* preocupación
preoccupation [priˈɑkjəˈpeʃən] *s* preocupación
preoccu•py [priˈɑkjə,paɪ] *v* (*pret & pp* **-pied**) *tr* preocupar
prepaid [priˈped] *adj* pagado por adelantado; con porte pagado
preparation [,prɛpəˈreʃən] *s* preparación; (*e.g., for a trip*) preparativo; (pharm) preparado
preparatory [prɪˈpærə,torɪ] *adj* preparativo, preparatorio
prepare [prɪˈpɛr] *tr* preparar || *intr* prepararse
preparedness [prɪˈpɛrɪdnɪs] o [prɪˈpɛrdnɪs] *s* preparación; preparación militar
pre•pay [priˈpe] *v* (*pret & pp* **-paid**) *tr* pagar por adelantado
preponderant [prɪˈpɑndərənt] *adj* preponderante
preposition [,prɛpəˈzɪʃən] *s* preposición
prepossessing [,pripəˈzɛsɪŋ] *adj* atractivo, simpático
preposterous [prɪˈpɑstərəs] *adj* absurdo, ridículo
prep school [prɛp] *s* (coll) escuela preparatoria
prerecorded [,prirɪˈkɔrdɪd] *adj* (rad & telv) grabado de antemano
prerequisite [,priˈrɛkwɪzɪt] *s* requisito previo
prerogative [prɪˈrɑgətɪv] *s* prerrogativa
Pres. *abbr* **Presbyterian, President**
presage [ˈprɛsɪdʒ] *s* presagio || [prɪˈsedʒ] *tr* presagiar
Presbyterian [,prɛzbɪˈtɪrɪ•ən] *adj & s* presbiteriano
prescribe [prɪˈskraɪb] *tr & intr* prescribir
prescription [prɪˈskrɪpʃən] *s* prescripción; (pharm) receta
presence [ˈprɛzəns] *s* presencia
present [ˈprɛzənt] *adj* presente || *s* presente *m*, regalo || [prɪˈzɛnt] *tr* presentar, obsequiar
presentable [prɪˈzɛntəbəl] *adj* bien apersonado
presentation [,prɛzənˈteʃən] o [,prizənˈteʃən] *s* presentación

presentation copy *s* ejemplar *m* de cortesía con dedicatoria del autor
presentiment [prɪˈzɛntɪmənt] *s* presentimiento
presently [ˈprɛzəntli] *adv* luego, dentro de poco
preserve [prɪˈzʌrv] *s* conserva, compota; (*for game*) vedado ‖ *tr* conservar; preservar, proteger
preserved fruit *s* dulce *m* de almíbar
preside [prɪˈzaɪd] *intr* presidir; **to preside over** presidir
presiden•cy [ˈprɛzɪdənsi] *s* (*pl* **-cies**) presidencia
president [ˈprɛzɪdənt] *s* presidente *m;* (*of a university*) rector *m*
pres'i•dent-e•lect' *s* presidente *m* electo (*todavía sin gobierno*)
press [prɛs] *s* apretón *m,* empujón *m;* (*e.g., of business*) urgencia; muchedumbre; (*machine for printing, for making wine; newspapers and newspapermen*) prensa; (*printing*) imprenta; (*closet*) armario; **to go to press** entrar en prensa ‖ *tr* apretar (*p.ej., un botón*); (*in a press*) prensar; planchar (*la ropa*); imprimir (*discos de fonógrafo*); oprimir (*una tecla*); apresurar; abrumar; apremiar, instar; insistir en
press agent *s* agente *m* de publicidad
press conference *s* conferencia de prensa, rueda de prensa
pressing [ˈprɛsɪŋ] *adj* apremiante, urgente ‖ *s* planchado
press release *s* comunicado de prensa
pressure [ˈprɛʃər] *s* presión; premura, urgencia
pressure cooker [ˈkʊkər] *s* olla de presión, cocina de presión
pressurize [ˈprɛʃə,raɪz] *tr* (aer) sobrecargar
prestige [prɛsˈtiʒ] o [ˈprɛstɪdʒ] *s* prestigio
presumably [prɪˈzuməbli] *adv* probablemente, verosímilmente
presume [prɪˈzjum] *tr* presumir; suponer; **to presume to** tomar la libertad de ‖ *intr* suponer; **to presume on** o **upon** abusar de
presumption [prɪˈzʌmpʃən] *s* presunción; pretensión
presumptuous [prɪˈzʌmptʃʊ•əs] *adj* confianzudo, desenvuelto
presuppose [,prisəˈpoz] *tr* presuponer
pretend [prɪˈtɛnd] *tr* aparentar, fingir ‖ *intr* fingir; **to pretend to** pretender (*p.ej., el trono*)
pretender [prɪˈtɛndər] *s* pretendiente *mf*
pretense [prɪˈtɛns] o [ˈpritɛns] *s* pretensión; fingimiento; **under false pretenses** con apariencias fingidas; **under pretense of** so pretexto de
pretentious [prɪˈtɛnʃəs] *adj* pretencioso, aparatoso; ambicioso, vasto
pretonic [prɪˈtɑnɪk] *adj* pretónico
pretrial prisoner *s* preso preventivo
pret•ty [ˈprɪti] *adj* (*comp* **-tier;** *super* **-tiest**) bonito, lindo; (coll) bastante, considerable ‖ *adv* algo; bastante; muy
prevail [prɪˈvel] *intr* prevalecer, reinar; **to prevail on** o **upon** persuadir
prevailing [prɪˈvelɪŋ] *adj* prevaleciente, reinante; común, corriente
prevalent [ˈprɛvələnt] *adj* común, corriente, en boga
prevaricate [prɪˈværɪ,ket] *intr* mentir
prevent [prɪˈvɛnt] *tr* impedir ‖ *intr* obstar
prevention [prɪˈvɛnʃən] *s* (el) impedir; medidas de precaución
preventive [prɪˈvɛntɪv] *adj & s* preservativo
preview [ˈpri,vju] *s* vista anticipada; (*private showing*) (mov) preestreno; (*showing of brief scenes for advertising*) (mov) avance *m*
previous [ˈprivɪ•əs] *adj* previo, anterior ‖ *adv* previamente; **previous to** con anterioridad a, antes de
prewar [ˈpri,wɔr] *adj* prebélico, de preguerra
prey [pre] *s* presa; víctima; **to be prey to** ser presa de ‖ *intr* cazar; **to prey on** o **upon** apresar y devorar; pillar, robar; tener preocupado
price [praɪs] *s* precio ‖ *tr* apreciar, estimar; fijar el precio de, poner precio a; pedir el precio de
price control *s* intervención de precios
price cutting *s* reducción de precios
price fixing *s* fijación de precios
price freezing *s* congelación de precios
priceless [ˈpraɪslɪs] *adj* inapreciable, sin precio; (coll) absurdo, divertido
price war *s* guerra de precios
prick [prɪk] *s* (*pointed weapon or instrument*) espiche *m;* (*sharp point*) púa; (*small hole made with sharp point*) agujerillo; (*spur*) aguijón *m;* (*jab; sharp pain*) pinchazo, punzada; **to kick against the pricks** dar coces contra el aguijón ‖ *tr* pinchar; marcar con agujerillos; dar una punzada a; (*to sting*) punzar; **to prick up** aguzar (*las orejas*)
prick•ly [ˈprɪkli] *adj* (*comp* **-lier;** *super* **-liest**) espinoso, puado, punzante
prickly heat *s* salpullido causado por el calor
prickly pear *s* (*plant*) chumbera; (*fruit*) higo chumbo
pride [praɪd] *s* orgullo; arrogancia; **the pride of** la flor y nata de ‖ *tr*—**to pride oneself on** o **upon** enorgullecerse de
priest [prist] *s* sacerdote *m*
priesthood [ˈprist•hʊd] *s* sacerdocio
priest•ly [ˈpristli] *adj* (*comp* **-lier;** *super* **-liest**) sacerdotal
prig [prɪg] *s* gazmoño, pedante *mf*
prim [prɪm] *adj* (*comp* **primmer;** *super* **primmest**) estirado, relamido
primary [ˈpraɪ,mɛri] o [ˈpraɪməri] *adj* primario ‖ *s* (*pl* **-ries**) elección preliminar; (elec) primario
prime [praɪm] *adj* primero, principal; (*of the best quality*) primo ‖ *s* flor *f,* juventud, primavera; alba, aurora; (la) flor y nata; (*of a degree*) (phys) minuto; (typ) virgulilla; **prime of life** edad viril, flor *f* de edad ‖ *tr* informar de antemano; cebar (*un arma de fuego, una bomba, un carburador*); (*for painting*) imprimar; poner la primera capa o la primera mano a; poner virgulilla a

prime minister *s* primer ministro
primer [ˈprɪmər] *s* cartilla ‖ [ˈpraɪmər] *s* (*for paint*) aprestado *m;* (mach) cebador *m*
primitive [ˈprɪmɪtɪv] *adj* primitivo
primp [prɪmp] *tr* acicalar, engalanar ‖ *intr* acicalarse, engalanarse
prim'rose' *s* primavera
primrose path *s* vida dada a los placeres de los sentidos
prin. *abbr* **principal**
prince [prɪns] *s* príncipe *m;* **to live like a prince** portarse como un príncipe
Prince of Wales *s* príncipe *m* de Gales
princess [ˈprɪnsɪs] *s* princesa
principal [ˈprɪnsɪpəl] *adj* principal ‖ *s* principal *m,* jefe *m;* (*of a school*) director *m;* criminal *mf;* (*main sum, not interest*) capital *m*
principle [ˈprɪnsɪpəl] *s* principio
print [prɪnt] *s* marca, impresión; (*printed cloth*) estampado; (*design in printed cloth*) diseño; grabado, lámina; letras de molde; (*act of printing*) impresión; edición; tirada; (phot) impresión; **in print** impreso, publicado; **out of print** agotado ‖ *tr* imprimir; estampar; hacer imprimir; publicar; escribir en caracteres de imprenta; (phot) tirar, imprimir; (fig) imprimir o grabar (*en la memoria*)
printed matter *s* impresos
printer [ˈprɪntər] *s* impresor *m*
printer's devil *s* aprendiz *m* de imprenta
printer's ink *s* tinta de imprenta
printer's mark *s* pie *m* de imprenta
printing [ˈprɪntɪŋ] *s* impresión; caracteres impresos; edición; tirada; letras de mano imitación de las impresas; (phot) tiraje *m*
printout [ˈprɪnt,aʊt] *s* (*computer*) impreso derivado
prior [ˈpraɪ•ər] *adj* anterior ‖ *adv* anteriormente; **prior to** antes de
priori•ty [praɪˈɔrɪti] *s* (*pl* **-ties**) prioridad; **of the highest priority** de máxima prioridad
prism [ˈprɪzəm] *s* prisma *m*
prison [ˈprɪzən] *s* cárcel *f,* prisión ‖ *tr* encarcelar
prisoner [ˈprɪzənər] o [ˈprɪznər] *s* preso; (mil) prisionero
prison van *s* coche *m* celular
pris•sy [ˈprɪsi] *adj* (*comp* **-sier;** *super* **-siest**) (coll) remilgado, melindroso
priva•cy [ˈpraɪvəsi] *s* (*pl* **-cies**) aislamiento, retiro; secreto, reserva
private [ˈpraɪvɪt] *adj* particular, privado; confidencial; ‖ *s* soldado raso; **in private** privadamente; en secreto; **privates** partes pudendas
private first class *s* soldado de primera, aspirante *m* a cabo
private hospital *s* clínica, casa de salud
private property *s* bienes *mpl* particulares
private view *s* día *m* de inauguración
privet [ˈprɪvɪt] *s* aligustre *m*
privilege [ˈprɪvɪlɪdʒ] *s* privilegio
priv•y [ˈprɪvi] *adj* privado; **privy to** enterado secretamente de ‖ *s* (*pl* **-ies**) letrina
prize [praɪz] *s* premio; (*something captured*) presa ‖ *tr* apreciar, estimar
prize fight *s* partido de boxeo profesional
prize fighter *s* boxeador *m* profesional
prize ring *s* cuadrilátero de boxeo
pro [pro] *prep* en pro de ‖ *s* (*pl* **pros**) voto afirmativo; (coll) deportista *mf* profesional; **the pros and the cons** el pro y el contra
probabili•ty [,prɑbəˈbɪlɪti] *s* (*pl* **-ties**) probabilidad; acontecimiento probable; tiempo probable
probable [ˈprɑbəbəl] *adj* probable
probation [proˈbeʃən] *s* libertad vigilada; período de prueba
probe [prob] *s* encuesta, indagación; (*instrument*) sonda ‖ *tr* indagar; sondar
problem [ˈprɑbləm] *s* problema *m*
procedure [proˈsidʒər] *s* procedimiento
proceed [proˈsid] *intr* proceder ‖ **proceeds** [ˈprosidz] *spl* producto, ganancia
proceeding [proˈsidɪŋ] *s* procedimiento; **proceedings** actas; diligencias
process [ˈprɑsɛs] *s* procedimiento; proceso, progreso; **in the process of time** con el tiempo ‖ *tr* elaborar; (*electronic data*) procesar
processing [ˈprɑsɛsɪŋ] *s* (*electronic data*) procesamiento
process server [ˈsʌrvər] *s* entregador *m* de la citación
proclaim [proˈklem] *tr* proclamar
proclitic [proˈklɪtɪk] *adj & s* proclítico
procommunist [proˈkɑmjənɪst] *adj & s* filocomunista *mf*
procrastinate [proˈkræstɪ,net] *tr* diferir de un día para otro ‖ *intr* tardar, no decidirse
procure [proˈkjʊr] *tr* conseguir, obtener ‖ *intr* alcahuetear
prod [prɑd] *s* aguijada; empuje *m* ‖ *v* (*pret & pp* **prodded;** *ger* **prodding**) *tr* aguijar, pinchar; aguijonear, estimular
prodigal [ˈprɑdɪgəl] *adj & s* pródigo
prodigious [proˈdɪdʒəs] *adj & s* prodigioso, maravilloso; enorme, inmenso
prodi•gy [ˈprɑdɪdʒi] *s* (*pl* **-gies**) prodigio
produce [ˈprodjus] o [ˈprodus] *s* producto; productos agrícolas ‖ [proˈdjus] o [proˈdus] *tr* producir; presentar (*p.ej., un drama*) al público; (geom) prolongar
product [ˈprɑdəkt] *s* producto
production [proˈdʌkʃən] *s* producción
profane [proˈfen] *adj* profano; (*language*) injurioso, blasfemo ‖ *s* profano ‖ *tr* profanar
profani•ty [proˈfænɪti] *s* (*pl* **-ties**) blasfemia
profess [proˈfɛs] *tr & intr* profesar
profession [proˈfɛʃən] *s* profesión
professor [proˈfɛsər] *s* profesor *m,* catedrático; (coll) profesor, maestro
proffer [ˈprɑfər] *s* oferta, propuesta ‖ *tr* ofrecer, proponer
proficient [proˈfɪʃənt] *adj* perito, diestro, hábil
profile [ˈprofaɪl] *s* perfil *m* ‖ *tr* perfilar
profit [ˈprɑfɪt] *s* provecho, beneficio, utilidad, ganancia; **at a profit** con ganancia ‖ *tr* servir, ser de utilidad a ‖ *intr* sacar

provecho, ganar; adelantar, mejorar; **to profit by** aprovechar, sacar provecho de

profitable [ˈprɑfɪtəbəl] *adj* provechoso

profit and loss *s* ganancias y pérdidas

profiteer [ˌprɑfɪˈtɪr] *s* logrero, explotador *m* ‖ *intr* logrear, explotar

profit margin *s* excedente *m* de ganancia

profit taking *s* realización de beneficios

profligate [ˈprɑflɪgɪt] *adj* & *s* libertino; pródigo

pro forma invoice [pro ˈfɔrmə] *s* factura simulada

profound [proˈfaʊnd] *adj* profundo

profuse [proˈfjus] *adj* (*extravagant*) pródigo; (*abundant*) profuso

proge•ny [ˈprɑdʒeni] *s* (*pl* **-nies**) prole *f*

progno•sis [prɑgˈnosɪs] *s* (*pl* **-ses** [siz]) pronóstico

progno•sis [prɑgˈnɑstɪk] *s* pronóstico

program [ˈprogræm] *s* programa *m; (computer)* **program(me)** programa (para ordenador) ‖ *tr* programar; (*computer*) **program(me)** programar

program(m)er [ˈprogræmər] *s* (*computer*) programador *m*, programadora

program(m)ing [ˈprogræmɪŋ] *s* (*computer*) programación (de ordenadores)

progress [ˈprɑgrɛs] *s* progreso; progresos; **to make progress** hacer progresos ‖ [prəˈgrɛs] *intr* progresar

progressive [prəˈgrɛsɪv] *adj* progresivo; (pol) progresista ‖ *s* (pol) progresista *mf*

prohibit [proˈhɪbɪt] *tr* prohibir

project [ˈprɑdʒɛkt] *s* proyecto ‖ [prəˈdʒɛkt] *tr* proyectar ‖ *intr* proyectarse

projectile [prəˈdʒɛktɪl] *s* proyectil *m*

projection [prəˈdʒɛkʃən] *s* proyección

projector [prəˈdʒɛktər] *s* proyector *m*

proletarian [ˌprolɪˈtɛrɪ•ən] *adj* & *s* proletario

proletariat [ˌprolɪˈtɛrɪ•ət] *s* proletariado

proliferate [prəˈlɪfəˌret] *intr* proliferar

prolific [prəˈlɪfɪk] *adj* prolífico

prolix [ˈprolɪks] o [proˈlɪks] *adj* difuso, verboso

prologue [ˈprolɔg] *s* prólogo

prolong [proˈlɔŋ] *tr* prolongar

promenade [ˌprɑmɪˈned] *s* paseo; garbeo; baile *m* de gala ‖ *intr* pasear o pasearse

promenade deck *s* (naut) cubierta de paseo

prominent [ˈprɑmɪnənt] *adj* prominente

promise [ˈprɑmɪs] *s* promesa ‖ *tr* & *intr* prometer

promising young man *s* joven *m* de esperanzas

promissory [ˈprɑmɪˌsori] *adj* promisorio

promissory note *s* pagaré *m*

promonto•ry [ˈprɑmənˌtori] *s* (*pl* **-ries**) promontorio

promote [prəˈmot] *tr* promover; fomentar

promotion [prəˈmoʃən] *s* promoción; fomento

prompt [prɑmpt] *adj* pronto, puntual; listo, dispuesto ‖ *tr* incitar, mover; inspirar, sugerir; (theat) apuntar

prompter [ˈprɑmptər] *s* (theat) apuntador *m*

prompter's box *s* (theat) concha

promulgate [ˈprɑməlˌget] o [proˈmʌlget] *tr* promulgar

prone [pron] *adj* postrado boca abajo; extendido sobre el suelo; dispuesto, propenso

prong [prɔŋ] o [prɑŋ] *s* punta (*de un tenedor, horquilla, etc.*)

pronoun [ˈpronaʊn] *s* pronombre *m*

pronounce [prəˈnaʊns] *tr* pronunciar

pronouncement [prəˈnaʊnsmənt] *s* declaración; decisión, opinión

pronunciamen•to [prəˌnʌnsɪ•əˈmɛnto] *s* (*pl* **-tos**) pronunciamiento

pronunciation [prəˌnʌnsɪˈeʃən] o [prəˌnʌnʃɪˈeʃən] *s* pronunciación

proof [pruf] *adj* de prueba; **proof against** a prueba de ‖ *s* prueba

proof'read'er *s* corrector *m* de pruebas

prop [prɑp] *s* apoyo, puntal *m;* (*to hold up a plant*) rodrigón *m;* **props** (theat) accesorios ‖ *v* (*pret & pp* **propped;** *ger* **propping**) *tr* apoyar, apuntalar; poner un rodrigón a

propaganda [ˌprɑpəˈgændə] *s* propaganda

propagate [ˈprɑpəˌget] *tr* propagar

proparoxytone [ˌpropærˈɑksɪˌton] *adj* & *s* proparoxítono

pro•pel [prəˈpɛl] *v* (*pret & pp* **-pelled;** *ger* **-pelling**) *tr* propulsar, impeler

propeller [prəˈpɛlər] *s* hélice *f*

propensi•ty [prəˈpɛnsɪti] *s* (*pl* **-ties**) propensión

proper [ˈprɑpər] *adj* propio, conveniente; decente, decoroso; exacto, justo

proper•ty [ˈprɑpərti] *s* (*pl* **-ties**) propiedad; **properties** (theat) accesorios

property owner *s* propietario de bienes raíces

prophe•cy [ˈprɑfɪsi] *s* (*pl* **-cies**) profecía

prophe•sy [ˈprɑfɪˌsaɪ] *v* (*pret & pp* **-sied**) *tr* profetizar

prophet [ˈprɑfɪt] *s* profeta *m*

prophetess [ˈprɑfɪtɪs] *s* profetisa

prophylactic [ˌprofɪˈlæktɪk] *adj* & *s* profiláctico

propitiate [prəˈpɪʃɪˌet] *tr* propiciar

propitious [prəˈpɪʃəs] *adj* propicio

prop'jet *s* turbohélice *m*

proportion [prəˈporʃən] *s* proporción; **in proportion as** a medida que; **out of proportion** desproporcionado ‖ *tr* proporcionar

proportionate [prəˈporʃənɪt] *adj* proporcionado

proposal [prəˈpozəl] *s* propuesta; oferta de matrimonio

propose [prəˈpoz] *tr* proponer ‖ *intr* proponer matrimonio; **to propose to** pedir la mano a; proponerse a + *inf*

proposition [ˌprɑpəˈzɪʃən] *s* proposición, propuesta

propound [prəˈpaʊnd] *tr* proponer

proprietor [prəˈpraɪ•ətər] *s* propietario

proprietress [prəˈpraɪ•ətrɪs] *s* propietaria

proprie•ty [prəˈpraɪ•əti] *s* (*pl* **-ties**) corrección, conducta decorosa, conveniencia; **proprieties** cánones *mpl* sociales, convenciones

propulsion [prəˈpʌlʃən] *s* propulsión

prorate [proˈret] *tr* prorratear

prosaic [pro'ze•ɪk] *adj* prosaico
proscribe [pro'skraɪb] *tr* proscribir
prose [proz] *adj* prosaico || *s* prosa
prosecute ['prɑsɪ,kjut] *tr* llevar a cabo; (law) procesar
prosecutor ['prɑsɪ,kjutər] *s* acusador *m*, demandante *mf*; (*lawyer*) fiscal *m*
proselyte ['prɑsɪ,laɪt] *s* prosélito
prose writer *s* prosista *mf*
prosody ['prɑsədi] *s* métrica
prospect ['prɑspɛkt] *s* vista; esperanza; probabilidad de éxito; cliente *mf* o comprador *m* probable || *tr* & *intr* prospectar; **to prospect for** buscar (*p.ej., oro, petróleo*)
prosper ['prɑspər] *tr* & *intr* prosperar
prosperi•ty [prɑs'pɛrɪti] *s* (*pl* **-ties**) prosperidad
prosperous ['prɑspərəs] *adj* próspero
prostitute ['prɑstɪ,tjut] *s* prostituta; güila (Mex) || *tr* prostituir
prostrate ['prɑstret] *adj* postrado, prosternado || *tr* postrar
prostration [prɑs'treʃən] *s* postración
Prot. *abbr* **Protestant**
protagonist [pro'tægənɪst] *s* protagonista *mf*
protect [prə'tɛkt] *tr* proteger
protection [prə'tɛkʃən] *s* protección
protégé ['protə,ʒe] *s* protegido
protégée ['protə,ʒe] *s* protegida
protein ['proti•ɪn] o ['protin] *s* proteína
pro-tempore [pro'tɛmpəri] *adj* interino
protest ['protɛst] *s* protesta || [pro'tɛst] *tr* & *intr* protestar
protestant ['prɑtɪstənt] *adj* & *s* protestante *mf* || **Protestant** *adj* & *s* protestante *mf*
prothonotar•y [pro'θɑnə,tɛri] *s* (*pl* **-ies**) escribano principal (*de un tribunal*)
protocol ['protə,kɑl] *s* protocolo
protoplasm ['protə,plæzəm] *s* protoplasma *m*
prototype ['protə,taɪp] *s* prototipo
protozoön [,protə'zo•ɑn] *s* protozoo
protract [pro'trækt] *tr* prolongar
protrude [pro'trud] *intr* resaltar
proud [praud] *adj* orgulloso; soberbio; glorioso
proud flesh *s* carnosidad, bezo
prov. *abbr* **provincialism**
prove [pruv] *v* (*pret* **proved**; *pp* **proved** o **proven**) *tr* probar || *intr* resultar; **to prove to be** venir a ser, resultar
proverb ['prɑvərb] *s* proverbio
provide [prə'vaɪd] *tr* proporcionar, suministrar || *intr*—**to provide for** proveer a; asegurarse (*el porvenir*)
provided [prə'vaɪdɪd] *conj* a condición (de) que, con tal (de) que
providence ['prɑvɪdəns] *s* providencia
providential [,prɑvɪ'dɛnʃəl] *adj* providencial
providing [prə'vaɪdɪŋ] *conj* var de **provided**
province ['prɑvɪns] *s* provincia; (*sphere of activity or knowledge*) competencia
proving ground ['pruvɪŋ] *s* campo de ensayos
provision [prə'vɪʒən] *s* provisión; condición, estipulación
provi•so [prə'vaɪzo] *s* (*pl* **-sos** o **-soes**) condición, estipulación, salvedad
provoke [prə'vok] *tr* provocar
provoking [prə'vokɪŋ] *adj* provocador, irritante
prow [prau] *s* proa
prowess ['prau•ɪs] *s* proeza; destreza
prowl [praul] *intr* cazar al acecho, rodar, vagabundear
prowler ['praulər] *s* rondador *m*; ladrón *m*
proximity [prɑk'sɪmɪti] *s* proximidad
prox•y ['prɑksi] *s* (*pl* **-ies**) poder *m*, poderhabiente *mf*
prude [prud] *s* mojigato, gazmoño
prudence ['prudəns] *s* prudencia
prudent ['prudənt] *adj* prudente
pruder•y ['prudəri] *s* (*pl* **-ies**) mojigatería, gazmoñería
prudish ['prudɪʃ] *adj* mojigato, gazmoño
prune [prun] *s* ciruela pasa || *tr* podar, escamondar
pry [praɪ] *v* (*pret* & *pp* **pried**) *tr*—**to pry open** forzar con la alzaprima o palanca; **to pry out of** arrancar (*p.ej., un secreto*) a (*una persona*) || *intr* entremeterse; **to pry into** entremeterse en
P.S. *abbr* **postscript, Privy Seal**
psalm [sɑm] *s* salmo
Psalter ['sɔltər] *s* Salterio
pseudo ['sudo] o ['sjudo] *adj* supuesto, falso, fingido
pseudonym ['sudənɪm] o ['sjudənɪm] *s* seudónimo
Psyche ['saɪki] *s* Psique *f*
psychedelic [,saɪkə'dɛlɪk] *adj* psicodélico
psychiatrist [saɪ'kaɪ•ətrɪst] *s* psiquiatra *mf*
psychiatry [saɪ'kaɪ•ətri] *s* psiquiatria
psychic ['saɪkɪk] *adj* psíquico; mediúmnico || *s* médium *mf*
psychoanalysis [,saɪko•ə'nælɪsɪs] *s* psicoanálisis *m*
psychoanalyze [,saɪko'ænə,laɪz] *tr* psicoanalizar
psychologic(al) [,saɪkə'lɑdʒɪk(əl)] *adj* psicológico
psychologist [saɪ'kɑlədʒɪst] *s* psicólogo
psychology [saɪ'kɑlədʒi] *s* psicología
psychopath ['saɪkə,pæθ] *s* psicópata *mf*
psycho•sis [saɪ'kosɪs] *s* (*pl* **-ses** [siz]) psicosis *f*; estado mental
psychotherapy [,saɪkə'θɛrəpi] *s* psicoterapia
psychotic [saɪ'kɑtɪk] *adj* & *s* psicótico
pt. *abbr* **part, pint, point**
pub [pʌb] *s* (Brit) taberna
puberty ['pjubərti] *s* pubertad
public ['pʌblɪk] *adj* & *s* público
publication [,pʌblɪ'keʃən] *s* publicación
public conveyance *s* vehículo de servicio público
publicity [pʌb'lɪsɪti] *s* publicidad
publicize ['pʌblɪ,saɪz] *tr* publicar
public library *s* biblioteca municipal
public relations *spl* relaciones publicas
public school *s* (U.S.A.) escuela pública; (Brit) internado privado con dote
public speaking *s* elocución, oratoria

public spirit *s* celo patriótico del buen ciudadano
public toilet *s* quiosco de necesidad
public transportation *s* transporte colectivo
public utility *s* empresa de servicio público; **public utilities** acciones emitidas por empresas de servicio público
publish [ˈpʌblɪʃ] *tr* publicar
publisher [ˈpʌblɪʃər] *s* editor *m*
publishing house *s* casa editorial
pucker [ˈpʌkər] *s* (*small fold*) frunce *m;* pliego mal hecho ‖ *tr* fruncir (*una tela; la frente*); plegar mal ‖ *intr* plegarse mal
pudding [ˈpʊdɪŋ] *s* budín *m,* pudín *m*
puddle [ˈpʌdəl] *s* aguazal *m,* charco
pudg•y [ˈpʌdʒi] *adj* (*comp* **-ier;** *super* **-iest**) gordinflón, rechoncho
puerile [ˈpju•ərɪl] *adj* pueril
puerili•ty [ˌpju•əˈrɪlɪti] *s* (*pl* **-ties**) puerilidad
Puerto Rican [ˈpwɛrto ˈrikən] *adj & s* puertorriqueño
puff [pʌf] *s* soplo vivo; (*of smoke*) bocanada; (*in clothing*) bullón *m;* borla de polvos; pastelillo de crema o jalea; alabanza exagerada; ráfaga, ventolera ‖ *tr* soplar; hinchar; alabar exageradamente ‖ *intr* soplar; hincharse; enorgullecerse exageradamente
puff paste *s* hojaldre *m & f*
pugilism [ˈpjudʒɪˌlɪzəm] *s* pugilismo
pugilist [ˈpjudʒɪlɪst] *s* pugilista *m*
pug-nosed [ˈpʌgˌnozd] *adj* braco
puke [pjuk] *s* (slang) vómito ‖ *tr & intr* (slang) vomitar
pull [pʊl] *s* estirón *m,* tirón *m; (on a cigar*) chupada; (*of a door*) tirador *m,* (slang) enchufe *m,* buenas aldabas ‖ *tr* tirar de; torcer (*un ligamento*); (typ) sacar (*una impresión a prueba*); **to pull down** demoler, derribar; bajar (*p.ej., la cortinilla*); abatir, degradar; **to pull oneself together** componerse, recobrar la calma ‖ *intr* tirar; moverse despacio, moverse con esfuerzo; **to pull at** tirar de (*p.ej., la corbata*); chupar (*p.ej., un cigarro*); **to pull for** (slang) abogar por, ayudar; **to pull for oneself** tirar por su lado; **to pull in** llegar (*un tren*) a la estación; **to pull out** partir (*un tren*) de la estación; **to pull strings** usar enchufe; **to pull through** salir a flote; recobrar la salud
pullet [ˈpʊlɪt] *s* polla
pulley [ˈpʊli] *s* polea
pulp [pʌlp] *s* pulpa; (*to make paper*) pasta; (*of tooth*) bulbo
pulpit [ˈpʊlpɪt] *s* púlpito
pulsate [ˈpʌlset] *intr* pulsar; vibrar
pulsation [pʌlˈseʃən] *s* pulsación; vibracion
pulse [pʌls] *s* pulso; **to feel** o **take the pulse of** tomar el pulso a
pulverize [ˈpʌlvəˌraɪz] *tr* pulverizar
pumice stone [ˈpʌmɪs] *s* pómez *f,* piedra pómez
pum•mel [ˈpʌməl] *v* (*pret & pp* **-meled** o **-melled;** *ger* **-meling** o **-melling**) *tr* apuñear, aporrear
pump [pʌmp] *s* bomba; (*slipperlike shoe*) escarpín *m,* zapatilla ‖ *tr* elevar o sacar (*agua*) por medio de una bomba; (coll) tirar de la lengua a (*una persona*); **to pump up** hinchar, inflar (*un neumático*)
pump handle *s* guimbalete *m*
pumpkin [ˈpʌmpkɪn] o [ˈpʊŋkɪn] *s* calabaza común; **some pumpkins** persona de muchas campanillas
pump-priming [ˈpʌmpˌpraɪmɪŋ] *s* inyección económica (*por parte del gobierno*)
pun [pʌn] *s* equívoco, retruécano ‖ *v* (*pret & pp* **punned;** *ger* **punning**) *intr* decir equívocos, jugar del vocablo
punch [pʌntʃ] *s* puñetazo; (*tool*) punzón *m;* (*for tickets*) sacabocado; (*drink*) ponche *m* ‖ *tr* dar un puñetazo a; taladrar, perforar (*un billete, una tarjeta*)
punch bowl *s* ponchera
punch card *s* tarjeta perforada, ficha perforada
punch clock *s* reloj *m* registrador de tarjetas
punch'-drunk' *adj* atontado (*p.ej., por una tunda de golpes*); completamente aturdido
punched tape *s* cinta perforada
punching bag *s* punching *m,* boxibalón *m*
punch line *s* broche *m* de oro, colofón *m* del artículo
punctilious [pʌŋkˈtɪlɪ•əs] *adj* puntilloso, pundonoroso
punctual [ˈpʌŋktʃʊ•əl] *adj* puntual
punctuate [ˈpʌŋktʃʊˌet] *tr* puntuar; acentuar, destacar; interrumpir ‖ *intr* puntuar
punctuation [ˌpʌŋktʃʊˈeʃən] *s* puntuación
punctuation mark *s* signo de puntuación
puncture [ˈpʌŋktʃər] *s* puntura; (*of a tire*) picadura, pinchazo ‖ *tr* pinchar, picar, perforar
punc'ture-proof' *adj* a prueba de pinchazos
pundit [ˈpʌndɪt] *s* erudito, sabio
pungent [ˈpʌndʒənt] *adj* picante; estimulante
punish [ˈpʌnɪʃ] *tr* castigar; penalizar; (coll) maltratar
punishable [ˈpʌnɪʃəbəl] *adj* delictivo
punishment [ˈpʌnɪʃmənt] *s* castigo; (coll) maltrato
punk [pʌŋk] *adj* (slang) malo, de mala calidad ‖ *s* yesca, pebete *m;* (*decayed wood*) hupe *m;* (slang) pillo, gamberro
punster [ˈpʌnstər] *s* equivoquista *mf,* vocablista *mf*
pu•ny [ˈpjuni] *adj* (*comp* **-nier;** *super* **-niest**) encanijado, débil; insignificante, mezquino
pup [pʌp] *s* cachorro
pupil [ˈpjupəl] *s* alumno; (*of the eye*) pupila
puppet [ˈpʌpɪt] *s* títere *m;* (*doll*) muñeca; (*person controlled by another*) maniquí *m*
puppet government *s* gobierno de monigotes
puppet show *s* función de títeres
puppy love [ˈpʌpi] *s* (coll) primeros amores
purchase [ˈpʌrtʃəs] *s* compra; agarre *m* firme ‖ *tr* comprar
purchasing power *s* poder adquisitivo
pure [pjʊr] *adj* puro
purgative [ˈpʌrgətɪv] *adj & s* purgante *m*
purge [pʌrdʒ] *s* purga ‖ *tr* purgar
puri•fy [ˈpjʊrɪˌfaɪ] *v* (*pret & pp* **-fied**) *tr* purificar
puritan [ˈpjʊrɪtən] *adj & s* puritano ‖ **Puritan** *adj & s* puritano

purity [ˈpjʊrɪti] *s* pureza
purloin [pərˈlɔɪn] *tr & intr* robar, hurtar
purple [ˈpʌrpəl] *adj* purpurado, rojo morado || *m* púrpura, rojo morado
purport [ˈpʌrport] *s* significado, idea principal || [pərˈport] *tr* significar, querer decir
purpose [ˈpʌrpəs] *s* intención, propósito; fin *m,* objeto; **for the purpose** al efecto; **for what purpose?** ¿con qué fin?; **on purpose** adrede, de propósito; **to good purpose** con buenos resultados; **to no purpose** sin resultado; **to serve one's purpose** servir para el caso
purposely [ˈpʌrpəsli] *adv* adrede, de propósito
purr [pʌr] *s* ronroneo || *intr* ronronear
purse [pʌrs] *s* bolsa; (*money collected for charity*) colecta || *tr* fruncir
purser [ˈpʌrsər] *s* contador *m* de navío, comisario de a bordo
purse snatcher [ˈsnætʃər] *s* carterista *mf*
purse strings *spl* cordones *mpl* de la bolsa; **to hold the purse strings** tener las llaves de la caja
pursue [pərˈsu] o [pərˈsju] *tr* perseguir (*al que huye*); proseguir (*lo empezado*); seguir (*una carrera*); dedicarse a
pursuit [pərˈsut] o [pərˈsjut] *s* persecución; prosecución; (*e.g., of happiness*) busca o búsqueda; empleo
pursuit plane *s* caza *m,* avión *m* de caza
purvey [pərˈve] *tr* proveer, suministrar
pus [pʌs] *s* pus *m*
push [pʊʃ] *s* empuje *m,* empujón *m* || *tr* empujar; pulsar (*un botón*); extender (*p.ej., conquistas*); **to push around** (coll) tratar a empujones; **to push aside** hacer a un lado; **to push through** forzar (*p.ej., una resolución*) || *intr* empujar; **to push off** (coll) irse, salir; (naut) desatracarse
push button *s* botón *m* de llamada, botón interruptor
push'-but'ton control *s* mando por botón
push'cart' *s* carretilla de mano
pusher [ˈpʊʃər] *s* (*drugs*) púcher *m*
pushing [ˈpʊʃɪŋ] *adj* emprendedor; entremetido, agresivo
pushy [ˈpʊʃi] *adj* (coll) agresivo; presumido
pusillanimous [ˌpjusɪˈlænɪməs] *adj* pusilánime
puss [pʊs] *interj* ¡miz! || *s* micho; chica, muchacha; (slang) cara, boca
puss in the corner *s* las cuatro esquinas
puss•y [ˈpʊsi] *s* (*pl* **-ies**) michito
pussy willow *s* sauce norteamericano de amentos muy sedosos
pustule [ˈpʌstʃʊl] *s* pústula
put [pʊt] *v* (*pret & pp* **put;** *ger* **putting)** *tr* poner, colocar; arrojar, echar, lanzar; hacer (*una pregunta);* **to put across** llevar a cabo; hacer aceptar; **to put aside** poner aparte; rechazar; ahorrar (*dinero*); **to put down** anotar, apuntar; sofocar (*una insurrección*); rebajar (*los precios*); **to put off** posponer; deshacerse de; **to put on** ponerse (*la ropa*); poner en escena; llevar (*p.ej., un drama a la pantalla*); accionar (*un freno*); cargar (*impuestos*); fingir; atribuir; **to put oneself out** incomodarse, molestarse; afanarse, desvivirse; **to put out** extender (*la mano*); apagar (*el fuego, la luz*); poner en la calle; dar a luz, publicar; decepcionar; (sport) sacar fuera de la partida; **to put over** o **through** (coll) llevar a cabo; **to put up** construir, edificar; abrir (*un paraguas*); conservar (*fruta, legumbres*); (coll) incitar || *intr* dirigirse; **to put on** fingir; **to put up** parar, hospedarse; **to put up with** aguantar, tolerar
put'-out' *adj* contrariado, enojado
putrid [ˈpjutrɪd] *adj* pútrido; corrompido, perverso
putsch [pʊtʃ] *s* intentona de sublevación; sublevación; cuartelazo
putter [ˈpʌtər] *intr* trabajar sin orden ni sistema; **to putter around** ocuparse en fruslerías, temporizar
put•ty [ˈpʌti] *s* (*pl* **-ties**) masilla || *v* (*pret & pp* **-tied**) *tr* enmasillar
putty knife *s* cuchillo de vidriero, espátula
put'-up' *adj* (coll) premeditado con malicia
puzzle [ˈpʌzəl] *s* enigma *m;* acertijo, rompecabezas *m* || *tr* confundir, poner perplejo; **to puzzle out** descifrar || *intr* estar perplejo; **to puzzle over** tratar de descifrar
puzzler [ˈpʌzlər] *s* quisicosa
PW *abbr* **prisoner of war**
pyg•my [ˈpɪgmi] *adj* pigmeo || *s* (*pl* **-mies)** pigmeo
pylon [ˈpaɪlɑn] *s* pilón *m*
pyramid [ˈpɪrəmɪd] *s* pirámide *f* || *tr* aumentar (*su dinero*) comprando o vendiendo al crédito y empleando las ganancias para comprar o vender más
pyre [paɪr] *s* pira
Pyrenean [ˌpɪrɪˈni•ən] *adj* pirineo
Pyrenees [ˈpɪrɪˌniz] *spl* Pirineos
pyrites [paɪˈraɪtiz] o [ˈpaɪraɪts] *s* pirita
pyrotechnical [ˌpaɪrəˈtɛknɪkəl] *adj* pirotécnico
pyrotechnics [ˌpaɪrəˈtɛknɪks] *spl* pirotecnia
python [ˈpaɪθən] *s* pitón *m*
pythoness [pɑɪθənɪs] *s* pitonisa
pyx [pɪks] *s* píxide *f,* copón *m*

Q

Q, q [kju] decimoséptima letra del alfabeto inglés
Q. *abbr* **quarto, queen, question, quire**
Q.M. *abbr* **quartermaster**
qr. *abbr* **quarter, quire**
qt. *abbr* **quantity, quart**

qu. *abbr* **quart, quarter, quarterly, queen, query, question**
quack [kwæk] *adj* falso ‖ *s* graznido del pato; charlatán *m;* medicastro, curandero ‖ *intr* parpar (*el pato*)
quacker•y ['kwækəri] *s* (*pl* **-ies**) charlatanismo
quadrangle ['kwɑd,ræŋgəl] *s* cuadrángulo; patio cuadrangular
quadrant ['kwɑdrənt] *s* cuadrante *m*
quadroon [kwɑd'run] *s* cuarterón *m*
quadruped ['kwɑdrʊ,pɛd] *adj & s* cuadrúpedo
quadruple ['kwɑdrʊpəl] o [kwɑd'rupəl] *adj & s* cuádruple *m* ‖ *tr* cuadruplicar ‖ *intr* cuadruplicarse
quadruplet ['kwɑdrʊ,plɛt] o [kwɑd'ruplɛt] *s* cuatrillizo
quaff [kwɑf] o [kwæf] *s* trago grande ‖ *tr & intr* beber en gran cantidad
quail [kwel] *s* codorniz *f* ‖ *intr* acobardarse
quaint [kwent] *adj* curioso, raro; afectado, rebuscado; fantástico, singular
quake [kwek] *s* temblor *m,* terremoto ‖ *intr* temblar
Quaker ['kwekər] *adj & s* cuáquero
Quaker meeting *s* reunión de cuáqueros; reunión en que hay poca conversación
quali•fy ['kwɑlɪ,faɪ] *v* (*pret & pp* **-fied**) *tr* calificar; capacitar, habilitar ‖ *intr* capacitarse, habilitarse
quali•ty ['kwɑlɪti] *s* (*pl* **-ties**) (*characteristic; virtue*) calidad; (*property, attribute*) cualidad; (*of a sound*) timbre *m*
quality of life *s* calidad de vida
qualm [kwɑm] *s* escrúpulo de conciencia; duda, inquietud; (*nausea*) basca
quanda•ry ['kwɑndəri] *s* (*pl* **-ries**) incertidumbre, perplejidad
quanti•ty ['kwɑntɪti] *s* (*pl* **-ties**) cantidad
quan•tum ['kwɑntəm] *adj* cuántico ‖ *s* (*pl* **-ta** [tə]) cuanto, quántum *m*
quantum theory *s* teoría cuántica
quarantine ['kwɑrən,tin] o ['kwɔrən,tin] *s* cuarentena; estación de cuarentena ‖ *tr* poner en cuarentena
quar•rel ['kwɑrəl] o ['kwɔrəl] *s* disputa, riña, pelea; **to have no quarrel with** no estar en desacuerdo con; **to pick a quarrel with** tomarse con ‖ v (*pret & pp* **-reled** o **-relled;** *ger* **-reling** o **-relling**) *intr* disputar, reñir, pelear
quarrelsome ['kwɑrəlsəm] o ['kwɔrəlsəm] *adj* pendenciero
quar•ry ['kwɑri] o ['kwɔri] *s* (*pl* **-ries**) cantera, pedrera; caza, presa ‖ *v* (*pret & pp* **-ried**) *tr* sacar de una cantera; extraer, sacar
quart [kwɔrt] *s* cuarto de galón
quarter ['kwɔrtər] *adj* cuarto ‖ *s* cuarto, cuarta parte; (*three months*) trimestre *m;* moneda de 25 centavos; cuarto de luna; barrio; región, lugar *m;* (*clemency*) (mil) cuartel *m;* **quarters** morada, vivienda; local *m;* (mil) cuarteles *mpl;* **to take up quarters** alojarse ‖ *tr* descuartizar
quar'ter•deck' *s* alcázar *m*
quar'ter-hour' *s* cuarto de hora; **on the quarter-hour** al cuarto en punto cada cuarto de hora
quarter•ly ['kwɔrtərli] *adj* trimestral ‖ *adv* trimestralmente ‖ *s* (*pl* **-lies**) publicación o revista trimestral
quar'ter•mas'ter *s* (mil) comisario; (nav) cabo de brigadas
quartet [kwɔr'tɛt] *s* cuarteto
quartz [kwɔrts] *s* cuarzo
quartz watch *s* reloj de cuarzo
quasar ['kwesɑr] *s* (astr) objeto del espacio, fuente *f* cuasiestelar de radio
quash [kwɑʃ] *tr* sofocar, reprimir; anular, invalidar
quaver ['kwevər] *s* temblor *m,* estremecimiento; (mus) trémolo ‖ *intr* temblar, estremecerse
quay [ki] *s* muelle *m,* desembarcadero
queen [kwin] *s* reina; (*in chess*) dama o reina; (*in cards*) dama (*que corresponde al caballo*); abeja reina
queen bee *s* abeja reina, abeja maestra; (slang) marimandona, la que lleva la voz cantante
queen dowager *s* reina viuda
queen•ly ['kwinli] *adj* (*comp* **-lier;** *super* **-liest**) de reina; como reina; regio
queen mother *s* reina madre
queen olive *s* aceituna de la reina, aceituna gordal
queen post *s* péndola
queen's English *s* inglés castizo
queer [kwɪr] *adj* curioso, raro; estrambótico, estrafalario; aturdido, indispuesto; (coll) sospechoso, misterioso ‖ *tr* (slang) echar a perder; (slang) comprometer
quell [kwɛl] *tr* sofocar, reprimir; mitigar (*una pena o dolor*)
quench [kwɛntʃ] *tr* apagar (*el fuego; la sed*); sofocar, reprimir; (electron) amortiguar
que•ry ['kwɪri] *s* (*pl* **-ries**) pregunta; signo de interrogación; duda ‖ *v* (*pret & pp* **-ried**) *tr* interrogar; marcar con signode interrogación; dudar
ques. *abbr* **question**
quest [kwɛst] *s* búsqueda; (*of the Holy Grail*) demanda; **in quest of** en busca de
question ['kwɛstʃən] *s* pregunta; (*problem for discussion*) cuestión; asunto, proposición; **beside the question** que no viene al caso; **beyond question** fuera de duda; **out of the question** imposible, indiscutible; **to ask a question** hacer una pregunta; **to be a question of** tratarse de, ser cuestión de; **to call in question** poner en duda; **without question** sin duda ‖ *tr* interrogar; cuestionar (*poner en tela de juicio*)
questionable ['kwɛstʃənəbəl] *adj* cuestionable
question mark *s* punto interrogante, signo de interrogación
questionnaire [,kwɛstʃən'ɛr] *s* cuestionario
queue [kju] *s* (*of hair*) coleta; (*of people*) cola ‖ *intr* hacer cola
quibble [kwɪbəl] *intr* sutilizar

quick [kwɪk] *adj* rápido, veloz; ágil, vivo; despierto, listo; **the quick and the dead** los vivos y los muertos; **to cut** o **to sting to the quick** herir en lo vivo, tocar en la herida

quicken [ˈkwɪkən] *tr* acelerar, avivar; animar || *intr* acelerarse; animarse

quick'lime' *s* cal viva

quick lunch *s* servicio de la barra, servicio rápido

quick'sand' *s* arena movediza

quick'sil'ver *s* azogue *m*

quiet [ˈkwaɪ•et] *adj* (still) quieto; silencioso; (*market*) (com) encalmado; **to keep quiet** callarse || *s* quietud; silencio; **on the quiet** a las calladas || *tr* aquietar; acallar || *intr* aquietarse; callarse; **to quiet down** calmarse || *interj* ¡silencio!

quill [kwɪl] *s* pluma de ave; cañón *m* de pluma; (*of hedgehog, porcupine*) púa

quilt [kwɪlt] *s* edredón *m,* colcha || *tr* acolchar

quince [kwɪns] *s* membrillo

quinine [ˈkwaɪnaɪn] *s* quinina

quinsy [ˈkwɪnzi] *s* cinanquia, esquinencia

quintessence [kwɪnˈtɛsəns] *s* quintaesencia

quintet [kwɪnˈtɛt] *s* quinteto

quintuplet [kwɪnˈtjuplɛt] o [kwɪnˈtuplɛt] *s* quintillizo

quip [kwɪp] *s* chufleta, pulla || *v* (*pret & pp* **quipped;** *ger* **quipping**) *tr* decir en son de burla || *intr* echar pullas

quire [kwaɪr] *s* mano *f* de papel; (bb) alzado

quirk [kwʌrk] *s* excentricidad, rareza; sutileza; vuelta repentina

quit [kwɪt] *adj* libre, descargado; **to be quits** estar desquitados; **to call it quits** no seguir; descontinuar; **to cry quits** pedir treguas || *v* (*pret & pp* **quit** o **quitted;** *ger* **quitting**) *tr* dejar || *intr* irse; (coll) dejar de trabajar

quite [kwaɪt] *adv* enteramente; verdaderamente; (coll) bastante, muy

quitter [ˈkwɪtər] *s* remolón *m;* (*of a cause*) desertor *m*

quiver [ˈkwɪvər] *s* temblor *m;* (*to hold arrows*) aljaba, carcaj *m* || *intr* temblar

quixotic [kwɪksˈɑtɪk] *adj* quijotesco

quiz [kwɪz] *s* (*pl* **quizzes**) examen *m;* interrogatorio || *v* (*pret & pp* **quizzed;** *ger* **quizzing**) *tr* examinar; interrogar

quiz game *s* torneo de preguntas y respuestas

quiz program *s* programa *m* de preguntas y respuetas, torneo radiofónico

quiz section *s* grupo de práctica

quizzical [ˈkwɪzɪkəl] *adj* curioso; cómico; burlón

quoin [kɔɪn] o [kwɔɪn] *s* esquina; piedra angular; (*wedge*) cuña || *tr* (typ) acuñar

quoit [kwɔɪt] o [kɔɪt] *s* herrón *m,* tejo; **quoits** *ssg* hito

quondam [ˈkwɑndæm] *adj* antiguo, de otro tiempo

quorum [ˈkworəm] *s* quórum *m*

quota [ˈkwotə] *s* cuota

quotation [kwoˈteʃən] *s* (*from a book*) cita; (*of prices*) cotización

quotation marks *spl* comillas

quote [kwot] *s* (coll) cita; (coll) cotización; **close quote** fin de la cita; **quotes** (coll) comillas || *tr & intr* citar; cotizar; **quote** cito

quotient [ˈkwoʃənt] *s* cociente *m*

q.v. *abbr* **quod vide** (Lat) **which see**

R

R, r [ɑr] decimoctava letra del alfabeto inglés

r. *abbr* **railroad, railway, road, rod, ruble, rupee**

R. *abbr* **railroad, railway, Regina** (Lat) **Queen; Republican, response, Rex** (Lat) **King; River, Royal**

rabbet [ˈræbɪt] *s* barbilla, rebajo || *tr* embarbillar, rebajar

rab•bi [ˈræbaɪ] *s* (*pl* **-bis** o **-bies**) rabino

rabbit [ˈræbɪt] *s* conejo

rabbit ears *spl* (telv, rad) antena de conejo

rabble [ˈræbəl] *s* canalla, gentuza, palomilla, chamuchina

rabble rouser [ˈraʊzər] *s* populachero, alborotapueblos *mf*

rabies [ˈrebiz] o [ˈrebɪ,iz] *s* rabia

raccoon [ræˈkun] *s* mapache *m,* oso lavador

race [res] *s* (*people of same stock*) raza; (*contest in speed, etc.*) carrera; (*channel to lead water*) caz *m* || *tr* competir con, en una carrera; hacer correr de prisa; hacer funcionar (*un motor*) a velocidad excesiva || *intr* correr de prisa; correr en una carrera; competir en una carrera; embalarse (*un motor*); (naut) regatear

race horse *s* caballo de carreras

race riot *s* disturbio racista

race track *s* pista de carreras

racial [ˈreʃəl] *adj* racial

racing car *s* coche *m* de carreras

racism [ˈresizəm] *s* racismo

racist [ˈresist] *adj & s* racista

rack [ræk] *s* (*sort of shelf*) estante *m;* (*to hang clothes*) percha; (*for fodder for cattle*) pesebre *m;* (*for baggage*) red *f* de equipaje; (*for guns*) armero; (*bar made to gear with a pinion*) cremallera; **to go to rack and ruin** desvencijarse; ir al desastre || *tr* estirar, forzar; atormentar; despedazar; oprimir, agobiar; **to rack off** trasegar (*el vino*); **to rack one's brains** calentarse la cabeza, devanarse los sesos

racket [ˈrækɪt] *s* raqueta; (*noise*) baraúnda, alboroto; (slang) trapisonda, trapacería; **to raise a racket** armar un alboroto
racketeer [,rækɪˈtir] *s* trapisondista *mf*, trapacista *mf* || *intr* trapacear
rack railway *s* ferrocarril *m* de cremallera
rac•y [ˈresi] *adj* (*comp* **-ier;** *super* **-iest**) espiritoso, chispeante; perfumado; (*somewhat indecent*) picante
radar [ˈredɑr] *s* radar *m*
radar scanner *s* explorador *m* de radar
radiant [ˈredɪ•ənt] *adj* radiante, resplandeciente; (*cheerful, smiling*) radiante
radiate [ˈredɪ,et] *tr* radiar; difundir (*p.ej., felicidad*) || *intr* radiar, irradiar
radiation [,redɪˈeʃən] *s* radiación
radiation sickness *s* enfermedad de radiación, mal *m* de rayos
radiator [ˈredɪ,etər] *s* radiador *m*
radiator cap *s* tapón *m* de radiador
radical [ˈrædɪkəl] *adj & s* radical *m*
radi•o [ˈredɪ,o] *s* (*pl* **-os**) radio *f;* radiograma *m* || *tr* radiodifundir
radioactive [,redɪ•oˈæktɪv] *adj* radiactivo
radioactive waste *s* residuos radiactivos
radio amateur *s* radioaficionado
radio announcer *s* locutor *m* de radio
raˈdio•broadˈcastˈing *s* radiodifusión
radio frequency *s* radiofrecuencia
radio listener *s* radioescucha *mf*, radioyente *mf*
radiology [,redɪˈɑlədʒi] *s* radiología
radio ministry *s* (theol) ministerio radiofóŋco
radio network *s* red *f* de emisoras
radio newscaster *s* cronista *mf* de radio
radio receiver *s* radiorreceptor *m*
radio set *s* aparato de radio
raˈdio•(telˈe)phoneˈ *s* radioteléfono
raˈdi•o•therˈapy *s* radioterapia
radish [ˈrædɪ] *s* rábano
radium [redɪ•əm] *s* radio
radi•us [ˈredɪ•əs] *s* (*pl* **-i** [,ɑɪ] o **-uses**) radio; (*range of operation*) radio; **within a radius of en** . . . a la redonda
raffle [ˈræfəl] || *tr & intr* rifar
raft [ræft] *s* armadía, balsa; (coll) gran número
rafter [ˈræftər] *s* cabrio, contrapar *m*, traviesa
rag [ræg] *s* trapo; **to chew the rag** (slang) dar la lengua; **in rags** hilachento
ragamuffin [ˈrægə,mʌfɪn] *s* pelagatos *m*; golfo, chiquillo haraposo
rag baby o **rag doll** *s* muñeca de trapo
rage [redʒ] *s* rabia; **to be all the rage** estar en boga, hacer furor; **to fly into a rage** montar en cólera
ragged [ˈrægɪd] *adj* andrajoso; (*edge*) cortado en dientes
ragpicker [ˈræg,pɪkər] *s* andrajero, trapero
ragˈweedˈ *s* ambrosía
raid [red] *s* incursión, invasión; ataque de sorpresa; ataque aéreo || *tr* invadir; atacar inesperadamente; capturar (*p.ej., la policía un garito*)
rail [rel] *s* carrill *m*, riel *m*; (*railing*) barandilla; (*of a bridge*) guardalado; (*at a bar*) apoyo para los pies; palo; **by rail** por ferocarril; **rails** títulos o valores de ferrocarril || *tr* poner barandilla a || *intr* quejarse amargamente; **to rail at** injuriar, ultrajar
rail fence *s* cerca hecha de palos horizontales
railˈheadˈ *s* (rr) cabeza de línea
railing [ˈrelɪŋ] *s* barandilla, pasamano
railˈroadˈ *adj* ferroviario || *s* ferrocarril *m* || *tr* (coll) llevar a cabo con demasiada precipitación; (slang) encarcelar falsamente || *intr* trabajar en el ferrocarril
railroad crossing *s* paso a nivel
railˈwayˈ *adj* ferroviario || *s* ferrocarril *m*
raiment [ˈremənt] *s* prendas de vestir, indumentaria
rain [ren] *s* lluvia; **rain or shine** llueva o no, con buen o mal tiempo || *tr & intr* llover
rainˈbowˈ *s* arco iris
rainˈcoatˈ *s* impermeable *m*
rainˈfallˈ *s* lluvia repentina; precipitación acuosa
rain•y [ˈreni] *adj* (*comp* **-ier;** *super* **-iest**) lluvioso
rainy day *s* día lluvioso; tiempo futuro de posible necesidad
raise [rez] *s* aumento || *tr* levantar; aumentar; criar (*a niños, animales*); cultivar (*plantas*); reunir (*dinero*); suscitar (*una duda*); resucitar (*a los muertos*); dejarse (*barba, bigote*); poner (*una objeción*); plantear (*una pregunta*); levantar (*tropas; un sitio*); (math) elevar; (*to come in sight of*) (naut) avistar
raisin [ˈrezən] *s* pasa, uva seca
rake [rek] *s* rastro, rastrillo; (*person*) calavera *m*, libertino || *tr* rastrillar; **to rake together** acumular (*dinero*)
rakeˈ-offˈ *s* (slang) dinero obtenido ilícitamente
rakish [ˈrekɪʃ] *adj* airoso, gallardo; listo, vivo; libertino
ral•ly [ˈræli] *s* (*pl* **-lies**) reunión popular, reunión política; recuperación, recobro || *v* (*pret & pp* **-lied**) *tr* reunir; reanimar; recobrar (*la fuerza, la salud, el ánimo*) || *intr* reunirse; recobrarse (*p.ej., los precios en la Bolsa*); recobrar la fuerza, la salud, el ánimo; **to rally to the side of** acudir a, ir en socorro de
ram [rœm] *s* (*male sheep*) morucco, carnero padre; (*device for battering, crushing, etc.*) pisón *m* || *v* (*pret & pp* **rammed;** *ger* **ramming**) *tr* dar contra, chocar en; atestar, rellenar || *intr* chocar; **to ram into** chocar en
ramble [ˈræmbəl] *s* paseo || *intr* pasear; serpentear (*p.ej., un río*); extenderse serpenteando (*las enredaderas*); (*to wander aimlessly; to talk in an aimless way*) divagar
rami•fy [ˈræmɪ,faɪ] *v* (*pret & pp* **-fied**) *tr* ramificar || *intr* ramificarse
ramˈjetˈ(engine) *s* motor *m* autorreactor; estatorreactor *m*
ramp [ræmp] *s* rampa

rampage [ˈræmpedʒ] *s* alboroto; **to go on a rampage** alborotar, comportarse como un loco
rampart [ˈræmpɑrt] *s* muralla, terraplén *m;* amparo, defensa
ram'rod' *s* atacador *m*, baqueta
ram'shack'le *adj* desvencijado, destartalado
ranch [ræntʃ] *s* granja, hacienda
rancid [ˈrænsɪd] *adj* rancio
rancor [ˈræŋkər] *s* rencor *m*
random [ˈrændəm] *adj* casual, fortuito; **at random** al azar, a la ventura
range [rendʒ] *s* (*row, line*) fila, hilera; (*scope, reach*) alcance *m*; (*of speeds, prices, etc.*) escala; campo de tiro; terreno de pasto; (*of a boat or airplane*) autonomía; (*of the voice*) extensión; (*of colors*) gama, serie *f;* (*stove*) cocina económica; **within range of** al alcance de ‖ *tr* alinear; recorrer (*un terreno*); ir a lo largo de (*la costa*); arreglar, ordenar ‖ *intr* fluctuar, variar (*entre ciertos límites*); extenderse; divagar, errar; **to range over** recorrer
range finder *s* telémetro
rank [ræŋk] *adj* exuberante, lozano; denso, espeso; grosero; maloliente; excesivo; incorregible, rematado; indecente, vulgar ‖ *s* categoría, rango; condición, posición; distinción; (*line of soldiers standing abreast*) fila; (mil) empleo, grado ‖ *tr* alinear; ordenar; tener grado o posición más alta que ‖ *intr* ocupar el último grado; **to rank high** ocupar alta posición; ser tenido en alta estima; sobresalir; **to rank low** ocupar baja posición; **to rank with** estar al nivel de; tener el mismo grado que
rank and file *s* soldados de fila; pueblo, gente *f* común
rankle [ˈræŋkəl] *tr* enconar, irritar ‖ *intr* enconarse
ransack [ˈrænsæk] *tr* registrar, escudriñar; robar, saquear
ransom [ˈrænsəm] *s* rescate *m* ‖ *tr* rescatar
rant [rænt] *intr* desvariar, despotricar
rap [ræp] *s* golpe corto y seco; (*noise*) taque *m*; (coll) ardite *m*, bledo; (slang) crítica mordaz; **to take the rap** (slang) pagar la multa; sufrir las consecuencias ‖ *v* (*pret & pp* **rapped;** *ger* **rapping**) *tr* golpear con golpe corto y seco; decir vivamente; (slang) criticar mordazmente ‖ *intr* golpear con golpe corto y seco; **to rap at the door** tocar a la puerta
rapacious [rəˈpeʃəs] *adj* rapaz
rape [rep] *s* rapto; (*of a woman*) estupro, violación ‖ *tr* raptar; estuprar, violar
rapid [ˈræpɪd] *adj* rápido ‖ **rapids** *spl* (*of a river*) rápidos
rap'id-fire' *adj* de tiro rápido; hecho vivamente
rapier [ˈrepɪ•ər] *s* estoque *m*, espadín *m*
rapt [ræpt] *adj* arrebatado, extático, transportado; absorto
rapture [ˈræptʃər] *s* embeleso, éxtasis *f*, rapto
rare [rɛr] *adj* raro; (*word*) poco usado; (*meat*) poco asado; (*gem*) precioso
rare bird *s* mirlo blanco
rare•fy [ˈrɛrɪ,faɪ] *v* (*pret & pp* **-fied**) *tr* enrarecer ‖ *intr* enrarecerse
rarely [ˈrɛrli] *adv* rara vez
rascal [ˈræskəl] *s* bellaco, bribón *m*, pícaro; pergenio
rash [ræʃ] *adj* temerario ‖ *s* brote *m*, salpullido, erupción
rasp [ræsp] o [rɑsp] *s* escofina; (*sound of a rasp*) sonido áspero ‖ *tr* escofinar; irritar, molestar; decir con voz ronca ‖ *intr* hacer sonido áspero
raspber•ry [ˈræz,bɛri] o [ˈrɑz,bɛri] *s* (*pl* **-ries**) frambuesa, sangüesa
raspberry bush *s* frambueso, sangüeso
rat [ræt] *s* rata; (*false hair*) (coll) postizo; **to smell a rat** (coll) olerse una trama, sospechar una intriga
ratchet [ˈrætʃɪt] *s* trinquete *m*
rate [ret] *s* (*amount or degree measured in proportion to something else*) razón *f;* (*of interest*) tipo; velocidad; precio; **at any rate** de todos modos; **at the rate of** a razón de ‖ *tr* valuar; estimar, juzgar; clasificar ‖ *intr* ser considerado, ser tenido; estar clasificado
rate of exchange *s* tipo de cambio
rate table *s* baremo
rather [ˈræðər] o [ˈrɑðər] *adv* algo, un poco; bastante; antes, más bien; mejor dicho; por el contrario; muy, mucho; **rather than** antes que, más bien que ‖ *interj* ¡ya lo creo!
rati•fy [ˈrætɪ,faɪ] *v* (*pret & pp* **-fied**) *tr* ratificar
ra•tio [ˈreʃo] o [ˈreʃɪ,o] *s* (*pl* **-tios**) (math) razón *f;* (math) cociente *m*
ration [ˈreʃən] o [ˈræʃən] *s* ración ‖ *tr* racionar
ration book *s* cartilla de racionamiento
ration coupon *s* cupón *m* de racionamiento
rational [ˈræʃənəl] *adj* racional
rat poison *s* matarratas *m*; raticida
rat race *s* (coll) lucha diaria por ganarse el pan
rattle [ˈrætəl] *s* (*number of short, sharp sounds*) traqueteo; (*noise-making device*) carraca, matraca; (*child's toy*) sonajero; baraúnda; (*in the throat*) estertor *m* ‖ *tr* tabletear, traquetear; (*to confuse*) (coll) atortolar, desconcertar; **to rattle off** decir rápidamente ‖ *intr* tabletear, traquetear
rat'tle•snake' *s* serpiente *f* de cascabel
rat'trap' *s* ratonera; trance apurado, atolladero
raucous [ˈrɔkəs] *adj* ronco
ravage [ˈrævɪdʒ] *s* destrucción, estrago, ruina ‖ *tr* destruir, estragar, arruinar
rave [rev] *intr* desvariar, delirar; bramar, enfurecerse; **to rave about** hacerse lenguas de, deshacerse en elogios de
raven [ˈrevən] *s* cuervo
ravenous [ˈrævənəs] *adj* famélico, hambriento, voraz; rapaz
ravine [rəˈvin] *s* cañón *m*, hondonada
ravish [ˈrævɪʃ] *tr* encantar, entusiasmar; raptar; violar (*a una mujer*)
ravishing [ˈrævɪʃɪŋ] *adj* encantador

raw [rɔ] *adj* crudo; (*cotton, silk*) en rama; inexperto, principiante; ulceroso; (*weather, day*) crudo
raw deal *s* (slang) mala pasada
raw'hide' *s* cuero en verde; látigo hecho de cuero en verde
raw material *s* primera materia, materia prima
ray [re] *s* (*of light*) rayo; (*fine line; fish*) raya
rayon ['re•ɑn] *s* rayón *m*
raze [rez] *tr* arrasar, asolar
razor ['rezər] *s* navaja de afeitar
razor blade *s* hoja u hojita de afeitar
razor strop *s* asentador *m*, suavizador *m*
razz [ræz] *s* (slang) irrisión || *tr* (slang) mofarse de
R.C. *abbr* **Red Cross, Reserve Corps, Roman Catholic**
R.D. *abbr* **Rural Delivery**
reach [ritʃ] *s* alcance *m;* extensión; **out of reach (of)** fuera del alcance (de); **within reach of** al alcance de || *tr* alcanzar; extender; entregar con la mano; llegar a; ponerse en contacto con; influenciar; cumplir (*cierto número de años*) || *intr* alcanzar; extender la mano o el brazo; **to reach after** o **for** esforzarse por coger
react [rɪ'ækt] *intr* reaccionar
reaction [rɪ'ækʃən] *s* reacción
reactionar•y [rɪ'ækʃən,ɛri] *adj* reaccionario; mocho (Mex) || *s* (*pl* **-ies**) reaccionario
read [rid] *v* (*pret & pp* **read** [rɛd]) *tr* leer; recitar (*poesía*); estudiar (*derecho*); leer en, adivinar (*el pensamiento ajeno*); **to read over** recorrer, repasar || *intr* leer; rezar, p.ej., **this page reads thus** esta página reza así; leerse, p.ej., **this book reads easily** este libro se lee con facilidad; **to read on** seguir leyendo
reader ['ridər] *s* lector *m;* libro de lectura
readily ['rɛdɪli] *adv* de buena gana; fácilmente
reading ['ridɪŋ] *s* lectura; recitación
reading desk *s* atril *m*
reading glass *s* lente *f* para leer, vidrio de aumento; **reading glasses** anteojos para la lectura
reading lamp *s* lámpara de sobremesa
reading room *s* gabinete *m* de lectura; sala de lectura
read•y ['rɛdi] *adj* (*comp* **-ier;** *super* **-iest**) listo, preparado, pronto; ágil, diestro; vivo; disponible; **to make ready** preparar; prepararse || *v* (*pret & pp* **-ied**) *tr* preparar || *intr* prepararse
ready cash *s* dinero a la mano, dinero contante y sonante
read'y-made' clothing *s* ropa hecha
ready-made suit *s* traje hecho
reagent [rɪ'edʒənt] *s* reactivo
real ['ri•əl] *adj* real, verdadero
real estate *s* bienes *mpl* raíces, bienes inmuebles
re'al-es•tate' *adj* inmobiliario
realism ['ri•ə,lɪzəm] *s* realismo
realist ['ri•əlɪst] *s* realista *mf*
reali•ty [rɪ'ælɪti] *s* (*pl* **-ties**) realidad
realize ['ri•ə,laɪz] *tr* darse cuenta de; realizar, llevar a cabo; adquirir (*ganancias*); reportar (*ganancias*) || *intr* (*to sell property for ready money*) realizar
realm [rɛlm] *s* reino
Realtor ['ri•əl,tɔr] o ['ri•əltər] *s* corredor *m* de bienes raíces
realty ['ri•əlti] *s* bienes *mpl* raíces, bienes inmuebles
ream [rim] *s* resma; **reams** (coll) montones *mpl* || *tr* escariar
reap [rip] *tr & intr* (*to cut*) segar; (*to gather*), cosechar
reaper ['ripər] *s* (*person*) segador *m;* máquina segadora
reappear [,ri•ə'pɪr] *intr* reaparecer
reapportionment [,ri•ə'porʃənmənt] *s* nuevo prorrateo
rear [rɪr] *adj* posterior, trasero; de atrás || *s* espalda; (*of a room*) fondo; (*of a row; of an automobile*) cola; retaguardia; (slang) culo, trasero || *tr* levantar; edificar; criar, educar || *intr* encabritarse (*un caballo*)
rear admiral *s* contraalmirante *m*
rear drive *s* tracción trasera
rear end *s* (*buttocks*) nalgas, pompis *m*
rearmament [ri'ɑrməmənt] *s* rearme *m*
rear'-view' mirror *s* retrovisor *m*, espejo de retrovisión
rear window *s* (aut) luneta, luneta posterior
reason ['rizən] *s* razón *f;* **by reason of** con motivo de, a causa de; **to listen to reason** meterse en razón; **to stand to reason** ser razonable || *tr & intr* razonar
reasonable ['rizənəbəl] *adj* razonable
reassessment [,ri•ə'sɛsmənt] *s* nuevo amillaramiento; nueva estimación
reassure [,ri•ə'ʃur] *tr* volver a asegurar; tranquilizar
reawaken [,ri•ə'wekən] *tr* volver a despertar || *intr* volver a despertarse
rebate ['ribet] o [rɪ'bet] *s* rebaja || *tr* rebajar
rebel ['rɛbəl] *adj & s* rebelde *mf* || **re•bel** [rɪ'bɛl] *v* (*pret & pp* **-belled;** *ger* **-belling)** *intr* rebelarse
rebellion [rɪ'bɛljən] *s* rebelión
rebellious [rɪ'bɛljəs] *adj* rebelde
re•bind [ri'baɪnd] *v* (*pret & pp* **-bound** ['baund]) reatar; (*to edge, to border*) ribetear; (bb) reencuadernar
rebirth ['ribʌrθ] o [ri'bʌrθ] *s* renacimiento
rebore [ri'bor] *tr* rectificar
rebound ['ri,baʊnd] o [ri'baʊnd] *s* rebote *m* || [ri'baʊnd] *intr* rebotar
rebroad•cast [ri'brɔd,kæst] *s* retransmisión || *v* (*pret & pp* **-cast** o **-casted**) *tr* retransmitir
rebuff [rɪ'bʌf] *s* desaire *m*, rechazo || *tr* desairar, rechazar
re•build [ri'bɪld] *v* (*pret & pp* **-built** ['bɪlt]) *tr* reconstruir, reedificar
rebuke [rɪ'bjuk] *s* reprensión || *tr* reprender
re•but [rɪ'bʌt] *v* (*pret & pp* **-butted;** *ger* **-butting)** *tr* rebatir, refutar
rebuttal [rɪ'bʌtəl] *s* rebatimiento, refutación
rec. *abbr* **receipt, recipe, record, recorder**
recall [rɪ'kɔl] o ['rikɔl] *s* llamada; (*memory*) recordación, retentiva; (*repeal*) revocación,

revocatoria; (*of a diplomat*) retirada || [rɪ'kɔl] *tr* hacer volver, mandar volver; recordar; revocar; retirar (*a un diplomático*)

recant [rɪ'kænt] *tr* retractar || *intr* retractarse

re•cap ['ri,kæp] o [ri'kæp] *v* (*pret & pp* **-capped;** *ger* **-capping**) *tr* recauchutar

recapitalization [ri,kæpɪtəlɪ'zeʃən] *s* recapitalización

recapitulation [,rikə,pɪtʃə'leʃən] *s* recapitulación

re•cast ['ri,kæst] *s* refundición; (*of a sentence*) reconstrucción || [ri'kæst] *v* (*pret & pp* **-cast**) *tr* refundir; reconstruir (*p.ej., una frase*)

recd. o **rec'd.** *abbr* **received**

recede [rɪ'sid] *intr* (*to move back*) retroceder; (*to move away*) alejarse, retirarse; deprimirse (*p.ej., la frente de una persona*)

receipt [rɪ'sit] *s* recepción; (*acknowledgment*) recibo; (*acknowledgment of payment*) recibí *m;* (*recipe*) receta; **receipt in full** finiquito; **receipts** entradas, ingresos || *tr* poner el recibí a

receive [rɪ'siv] *tr* recibir; receptar (*cosas que son materia de delito*); **received payment** recibí || *intr* recibir

receiver [rɪ'sivər] *s* receptor *m;* (*in bankruptcy*) contador *m*, síndico; receptor telefónico

receivership [rɪ'sivər,ʃɪp] *s* (law) sindicatura

receiving set *s* aparato receptor

receiving teller *s* recibidor *m* (*de un banco*)

recent ['risənt] *adj* reciente

recently ['risəntli] *adv* recientemente; endenantes; recién, p.ej., **recently arrived** recién llegado

receptacle [rɪ'sɛptəkəl] *s* receptáculo

reception [rɪ'sɛpʃən] *s* recepción; recibida (*welcome*) recibimiento

reception desk *s* recepción

receptionist [rɪ'sɛpʃənɪst] *s* recepcionista *f*

receptive [rɪ'sɛptɪv] *adj* receptivo

recess [rɪ'sɛs] o ['risɛs] *s* intermisión; descanso; hora de recreo; (*in a surface*) depresión; (*in a wall*) hueco, nicho; escondrijo || [rɪ'sɛs] *tr* ahuecar; empotrar; deprimir || *intr* prorrogarse, suspenderse

recession [rɪ'sɛʃən] *s* retroceso, retirada; (*e.g., in a wall*) depresión; procesión de vuelta; contracción económica

rechargeable [rɪ'tʃɑrdʒəbəl] *adj* recargable

recipe ['rɛsɪ,pi] *s* receta (*de cocina*)

reciprocal [rɪ'sɪprəkəl] *adj* recíproco

reciprocity [,rɛsɪ'prɑsɪti] *s* reciprocidad

recital [rɪ'saɪtəl] *s* narración; (*of music or poetry*) recital *m*

recite [rɪ'saɪt] *tr* narrar; (*formally*) recitar

reckless ['rɛklɪs] *adj* atolondrado, temerario

reckon ['rɛkən] *tr* calcular; considerar; (coll) calcular, conjeturar || *intr* calcular; **to reckon on** contar con; **to reckon with** tener en cuenta

reclaim [rɪ'klem] *tr* hacer utilizable; hacer labrantío (*un terreno*); ganar (*terreno*) a la mar; recuperar (*materiales usados*); conducir, guiar (*a los que hacen mala vida*)

reclamation [,rɪklə'meʃən] *s* (agr) roturación

recline [rɪ'klaɪn] *intr* reclinarse

recluse [rɪ'klus] o ['rɛklus] *s* solitario, ermitaño

recognize ['rɛkəg,naɪz] *tr* reconocer

recoil [rɪ'kɔɪl] *s* reculada; (*of a firearm*) reculada, culetazo || *intr* recular, apartarse; recular (*un arma de fuego*)

recollect [,rɛkə'lɛkt] *tr & intr* recordar

recombinant [rɪ'kɑmbɪnənt] *adj* (*genetics*) recombinado

recommend [,rɛkə'mɛnd] *tr* recomendar

recompense ['rɛkəm,pɛns] *s* recompensa || *tr* recompensar

reconcile ['rɛkən,saɪl] *tr* reconciliar; **to reconcile oneself** resignarse

reconnaissance [rɪ'kɑnɪsəns] *s* reconocimiento

reconnoiter [,rɛkə'nɔɪtɛr] o [,rikɛ'nɔɪtɛr] *tr & intr* reconocer

reconquest [ri'kɑŋkwɛst] *s* reconquista

reconsider [,rikən'sɪdər] *tr* reconsiderar

reconstruct [,rikən'strʌkt] *tr* reconstruir

reconversion [,rikən'vʌrʒən] *s* reconversión

record ['rɛkərd] *s* anotación; ficha, historial *m*, historia personal; (*of a notary*) protocolo; (*of a phonograph*) disco; (educ) expediente académico; (sport) record *m*, plusmarca; **off the record** confidencialmente; **records** anales *mpl*, memorias; archivo; **to break a record** batir un record; **to have no (criminal) record** (coll) estar limpio; **to make a record** establecer un record; grabar un disco || [rɪ'kɔrd] *tr* asentar; registrar; inscribir; grabar (*un sonido, una canción, un disco fonográfico, etc.*)

record breaker *s* plusmarquista *mf*

record changer ['tʃendʒər] *s* cambiadiscos *m*, tocadiscos automático

record holder s (sport) recordman *m*

recording [rɪ'kɔrdɪŋ] *adj* registrador; (wire or tape) magnetofónico || *s* registro; (*of phonograph records*) grabación o grabado

recording secretary *s* secretario escribiente, secretario de actas

record player *s* tocadiscos *m*, pícap *m*, fonógrafo, vitrola, radiola

record store *s* disquería

recount ['ri,kaʊnt] *tr* (*to count again*) recontar || [rɪ'kaʊnt] *tr* (*to narrate*) recontar

recourse [rɪ'kors] o ['rikors] *s* recurso; (*helping hand*) paño de lágrimas; **to have recourse to** recurrir a

recover [rɪ'kʌvər] *tr* recobrar; rescatar; **to recover consciousness** recobrar el conocimiento, volver en sí || *intr* recobrarse; recobrar la salud; ganar un pleito

recover•y [rɪ'kʌvəri] *s* (*pl* **-ies**) recobro, recuperación; **past recovery** sin remedio

recreant ['rɛkrɪ•ənt] *adj & s* cobarde *mf*, traidor *m*

recreation [,rɛkrɪ'eʃən] *s* recreación

recruit [rɪ'krut] *s* recluta *m* || *tr* reclutar || *intr* alistar reclutas; ganar reclutas; restablecerse, reponerse

rect. *abbr* **receipt, rector, rectory**

rectangle ['rɛk,tæŋgəl] *s* rectángulo

recti•fy [ˈrɛktɪ,faɪ] *v* (*pret & pp* **-fied**) *tr* rectificar
rec•tum [ˈrɛktəm] *s* (*pl* **-ta** [tə]) recto
recumbent [rɪˈkʌmbənt] *adj* reclinado, recostado
recuperate [rɪˈkjupə,ret] *tr* recuperar; restablecer, reponer || *intr* recuperarse, recobrarse
re•cur [rɪˈkʌr] *v* (*pret & pp* **-curred;** *ger* **-curring**) *intr* volver a ocurrir; volver a presentarse (*a la memoria*); volver (*a un asunto*)
recurrent [rɪˈkʌrənt] *adj* repetido; periódico; (*illness*) recurrente
recyclable [rɪˈsaɪkləbəl] *adj* reciclable
recycling [rɪˈsaɪklɪŋ] *s* reciclado, reciclaje *m*
red [rɛd] *adj* (*comp* **redder;** *super* **reddest**) rojo, colorado; (*wine*) tinto; enrojecido, inflamado || *s* rojo; **in the red** (coll) endeudado; **to see red** (coll) enfurecerse || **Red** *adj & s* (*communist*) rojo
red'bait' *tr* motejar (*a uno*) de rojo o comunista
red'bird' *s* cardenal *m;* piranga
red-blooded [ˈrɛd,blʌdɪd] *adj* fuerte, valiente, vigoroso
red'breast' *s* petirrojo
red'bud' *s* ciclamor *m* del Canadá
red'cap' *s* (Brit) policía militar; (U.S.A.) mozo de estación
red cell *s* glóbulo rojo, hematíe *m*
red'coat' *s* (hist) soldado inglés
redden [ˈrɛdən] *tr* enrojecer || *intr* enrojecerse
redeem [rɪˈdim] *tr* redimir; cumplir (*una promesa*)
redeemer [rɪˈdimər] *s* redentor *m*
redemption [rɪˈdɛmpʃən] *s* redención
red-haired [ˈrɛd,hɛrd] *adj* pelirrojo
red'head' *s* pelirrojo
red herring *s* artificio para distraer la atención del asunto de que se trata
red'-hot' *adj* candente, calentado al rojo; ardiente, entusiasta; fresco, nuevo
rediscount rate [rɪˈdɪskaʊnt] *s* tipo de redescuento
rediscover [,ridɪsˈkʌvər] *tr* redescubrir
red'-let'ter day *s* día *m* memorable
red'-light' district *s* barrio de los lupanares, barrio de mala vida
red man *s* piel roja *m*
re•do [ˈriˈdu] *v* (*pret* **-did** [ˈdɪd]; *pp* **-done** [ˈdʌn]) *tr* rehacer, repetir; refundir; reformar
redolent [ˈrɛdələnt] *adj* fragante, perfumado; **redolent of** que huele a
redoubt [rɪˈdaʊt] *s* (fort) reducto
redound [rɪˈdaʊnd] *intr* redundar; **to redound to** redundar en
red pepper *s* pimentón *m*
redress [rɪˈdrɛs] o [ˈridrɛs] *s* reparación; remedio || [rɪˈdrɛs] *tr* repara; remediar
Red Ridinghood [ˈraɪdɪŋ,hʊd] *s* Caperucita Roja
red'skin' *s* piel roja *m*
red tape *s* expedienteo, papeleo
reduce [rɪˈdjus] o [rɪˈdus] *tr* reducir; (mil) degradar || *intr* reducirse; reducir peso
reducing exercises *spl* ejercicios físicos para reducir peso
redundant [rɪˈdʌndənt] *adj* redundante
red'wood' *s* secoya
reed [rid] *adj* (*organ, musical instrument*) de lengüeta || *s* (*stalk*) caña; (*plant*) carrizo, caña; (mus) instrumento de lengüeta; (*of instrument*) lengüeta
reëdit [riˈɛdɪt] *tr* refundir
reef [rif] *s* arrecife *m*, escollo; (min) filón *m*, veta || *tr* (naut) arrizar
reefer [ˈrifər] *s* chaquetón *m;* (slang) pitillo de mariguana
reek [rik] *intr* vahear, humear; estar bañado en sudor; estar mojado con sangre; **to reek of** o **with** oler a
reel [ril] *s* (*spool*) carrete *m;* (*of a shuttle*) broca; (*of motion pictures*) cinta; (*sway, staggering*) tambaleo; **off the reel** (coll) fácil y prestamente || *tr* aspar, devanar; **to reel off** (coll) narrar fácil y prestamente || *intr* tambalear; cejar (*p.ej., el enemigo*)
reëlection [,ri•ɪˈlɛkʃən] *s* reelección
reënlist [,ri•ɛnˈlɪst] *tr* reenganchar || *intr* reengancharse
reën•try [rɪˈɛntri] *s* (*pl* **-tries**) reingreso, nueva entrada; (*return to earth's atmosphere*) reentrada
reëxamination [,ri•ɛg,zæmɪˈneʃən] *s* reexaminación
ref. *abbr* **referee, reference, reformation**
re•fer [rɪˈfʌr] *v* (*pret & pp* **-ferred;** *ger* **-ferring**) *tr* referir || *intr* referirse
referee [,rɛfəˈri] *s* árbitro || *tr & intr* arbitrar
reference [ˈrɛfərəns] *adj* (*library, book, work*) de consulta || *s* referencia
referen•dum [,rɛfəˈrɛndəm] *s* (*pl* **-da** [də]) *s* referéndum *m*
refill [ˈrifɪl] *s* relleno || [riˈfɪl] *tr* rellenar
refine [rɪˈfaɪn] *tr* refinar
refinement [rɪˈfaɪnmənt] *s* refinamiento; buena crianza, cultura
refiner•y [rɪˈfaɪnəri] *s* (*pl* **-ies**) refinería
reflect [rɪˈflɛkt] *tr* reflejar; (*to meditate*) reflexionar; **to reflect on** o **upon** reflexionar en o sobre; perjudicar
reflection [rɪˈflɛkʃən] *s* (*thinking*) reflexión; (*reflected light; image*) reflejo
reflex [ˈriflɛks] *s* reflejo
reforestation [,rifɑrɪsˈteʃən] o [,rifarɪsˈteʃən] *s* reforestación
reform [rɪˈfɔrm] *s* reforma || *tr* reformar || *intr* reformarse
reformation [,rɛfərˈmeʃən] *s* reformación || **the reformation** la Reforma
reformato•ry [rɪˈfɔrmə,tori] *s* (*pl* **-ries**) reformatorio
reform school *s* casa de corrección
refraction [rɪˈfrækʃən] *s* refracción
refrain [rɪˈfren] *s* estribillo || *intr* abstenerse
refresh [rɪˈfrɛʃ] *tr* refrescar || *intr* refrescarse
refreshing [rɪˈfrɛʃɪŋ] *adj* confortante, restaurante
refreshment [rɪˈfrɛʃmənt] *s* refresco

refrigerator [rɪ'frɪdʒəretər] *s* heladera, nevera, refrigerador *m*
refrigerator car *s* carro o vagón frigorífico
refuel [ri'fjul] *tr & intr* repostar
refuge ['rɛfjudʒ] *s* refugio; expediente *m*, subterfugio; **to take refuge (in)** refugiarse (en)
refugee [,rɛfju'dʒi] *s* refugiado
refund ['rifʌnd] *s* reembolso || [rɪ'fʌnd] *tr* reembolsar || [ri'fʌnd] *tr* consolidar
refurnish [ri'fʌrnɪʃ] *tr* amueblar de nuevo
refusal [rɪ'fjuzəl] *s* negativa
refuse ['rɛfjus] *s* basura, desecho, desperdicios || [rɪ'fjuz] *tr* rehusar; rechazar, no querer aceptar; **to refuse to** negarse a
refute [rɪ'fjut] *tr* refutar
reg. *abbr* **register, registrar, registry, regular**
regain [rɪ'gen] *tr* recobrar, recuperar; volver a alcanzar; **to regain consciousness** recobrar el conocimiento, volver en sí
regal ['rigəl] *adj* regio
regale [rɪ'gel] *tr* regalar, agasajar
regalia [rɪ'gelɪ•ə] *spl* (*of an office or order*) distintivos; galas, trajes *mpl* de lujo
regard [rɪ'gɑrd] *s* consideración, miramiento; (*esteem*) respeto; (*particular matter*) respecto; (*look*) mirada; **in regard to** respecto a o de; **regards** recuerdos; **without regard to** sin hacer caso de; **with regard to** respecto a o de || *tr* considerar; mirar; tocar a, referirse a; **as regards** en cuanto a
regarding [rɪ'gɑrdɪŋ] *prep* tocante a, respecto a o de
regardless [rɪ'gɑrdlɪs] *adj* desatento, indiferente || *adj* (coll) pese a quien pese, cueste lo que cueste; **regardless of** sin hacer caso de; a pesar de
regenerate [rɪ'dʒɛnə,ret] *tr* regenerar || *intr* regenerarse
regent [,ridʒənt] *s* regente *mf*
regicide ['rɛdʒɪ,saɪd] *s* (*act*) regicidio; (*person*) regicida *mf*
regime o **régime** [re'ʒim] *s* régimen *m*
regiment ['rɛdʒɪmənt] *s* regimiento || ['rɛdʒɪ,mɛnt] *tr* regimentar
regimental [,rɛdʒɪ,mɛntəl] *adj* regimental || **regimentals** *spl* uniforme *m* militar
region ['ridʒən] *s* región, comarca
register ['rɛdʒɪstər] *s* (*record; book for keeping such a record*) registro; reja regulable de calefacción; (*of the voice or an instrument*) extensión || *tr* (*to indicate by a record; to show, as on a scale*) registrar; empadronar (*los vecinos en el padrón*); manifestar, dar a conocer; certificar (*envíos por correo*); inscribir || *intr* registrarse; empadronarse; inscribirse
registered letter *s* carta certificada
registrar ['rɛdʒɪs,trɑr] *s* registrador *m*, archivero
registration fee [,rɛdʒɪs'treʃən] *s* derechos de matrícula
re•gret [rɪ'grɛt] *s* pesar *m*, sentimiento; pesadumbre, remordimiento; **regrets** excusas || *v* (*pret & pp* **-gretted;** *ger* **-gretting**) *tr* sentir, lamentar; lamentar la pérdida de; arrepentirse de; **I regret** (*apology*) lo siento; me sabe mal; **to regret to** sentir
regrettable [rɪ'grɛtəbəl] *adj* lamentable
regular ['rɛgjələr] *adj* regular; (coll) cabal, completo, verdadero || *s* obrero permanente; parroquiano regular; **regulars** tropas regulares
regulate ['rɛgjə,let] *tr* regular
rehabilitate [,rihə'bɪlɪ,tet] *tr* rehabilitar
rehabilitation [,rihə,bɪlɪ'teʃən] *s* rehabilitación
rehearsal [rɪ'hʌrsəl] *s* ensayo
rehearse [rɪ'hʌrs] *tr* ensayar || *intr* ensayarse
reign [ren] *s* reinado || *intr* reinar
reimburse [,ri•ɪm'bʌrs] *tr* reembolsar, rembolsar
rein [ren] *s* rienda; **to give free rein to** dar rienda suelta a || *tr* dirigir por medio de riendas; contener, refrenar, gobernar
reincarnation [,ri•ɪnkɑr'neʃən] *s* reencarnación
reindeer ['ren,dɪr] *s* reno
reinforce [,ri•ɪn'fors] *tr* reforzar; armar (*el hormigón*)
reinforcement [,ri•ɪn'forsmənt] *s* refuerzo
reinstate [,ri•ɪn'stet] *tr* reinstalar
reiterate [ri'ɪtə,ret] *tr* reiterar
reject [rɪ'dʒɛkt] *tr* rechazar
rejection [rɪ'dʒɛkʃən] *s* rechazamiento
rejoice [rɪ'dʒɔɪs] *intr* regocijarse
rejoinder [rɪ'dʒɔɪndər] *s* contestación; (law) contrarréplica
rejuvenation [rɪ,dʒuvɪ'neʃən] *s* rejuvenecimiento
rel. *abbr* **relating, relative, religion, religious**
relapse [rɪ'læps] *s* recaída || *intr* recaer
relate [rɪ'let] *tr* (*to establish relationship between*) relacionar; (*to narrate*) contar, relatar
relation [rɪ'leʃən] *s* (*connection; narration*) relación; (*narration*) relato; (*relative*) pariente *mf;* (*kinship*) parentesco; **in relation to** o **with** tocante a, respecto a o de
relationship [rɪ'leʃən,ʃɪp] *s* (*connection*) relación; (*kinship*) parentesco
relative ['rɛlətɪv] *adj* relativo || *s* deudo, pariente *mf*
relax [rɪ'læks] *tr & intr* relajar
relaxation [,rilæks'eʃən] *s* relajación; despreocupación
relaxation of tension *s* disminución de tensión; disminución de la tirantez internacional
relaxing [rɪ'læksɪŋ] *adj* relajador; despreocupante, tranquilizador
relay ['rile] o [rɪ'le] *s* (elec) relais *m*, relevador *m*, relevo; (mil & sport) relevo; (sport) carrera de relevos || *v* (*pret & pp* **-layed**) transmitir relevándose; transmitir con un relais; retransmitir (*una emisión*); reexpedir (*un radiotelegrama*) || [rɪ'le] *v* (*pret & pp* **-laid**) *tr* volver a colocar, volver a tender
relay race *s* carrera de relevos
release [rɪ'lis] *s* liberación; (*from jail*) excarcelación; alivio; permiso de publicación, venta, etc.; obra o pieza lista para la pub-

licación, venta, etc.; (aer) lanzamiento; (mach) escape *m*, disparador *m* || *tr* soltar; libertar; excarcelar (*a un preso*); permitir la publicación, venta, etc. de; (aer) lanzar (*una bomba*)
relent [rɪ'lɛnt] *intr* ablandarse, aplacarse
relentless [rɪ'lɛntlɪs] *adj* implacable
relevance ['rɛlɪvəns] *s* relevancia
relevant ['rɛlɪvənt] *adj* pertinente
reliable [rɪ'laɪ•əbəl] *adj* confiable, fidedigno; (*source*) solvente
reliance [rɪ'laɪ•əns] *s* confianza
relic ['rɛlɪk] *s* reliquia
relief [rɪ'lif] *s* alivio; caridad; (*projection of figures; elevation*) relieve *m;* (mil) relevo; **in relief** en relieve; **on relief** viviendo de socorro, recibiendo auxilio social
relieve [rɪ'liv] *tr* (*to release from a post*) relevar; aliviar; auxiliar (*a los necesitados*); (mil) relevar
religion [rɪ'lɪdʒən] *s* religión
religious [rɪ'lɪdʒəs] *adj* religioso
relinquish [rɪ'lɪŋkwɪʃ] *tr* abandonar, dejar
relish ['rɛlɪʃ] *s* buen sabor, gusto; condimento, sazón *f;* entremés *m;* buen apetito || *tr* gustar de; comer o beber con placer
relocate [ri'loket] *tr* trasladar || *intr* trasladarse
relocation [,rilo'keʃən] *s* traslado
reluctance [rɪ'lʌktəns] *s* renuencia, aversión
reluctant [rɪ'lʌktənt] *adj* renuente, maldispuesto
re•ly [rɪ'laɪ] *v* (*pret & pp* **-lied**) *intr* depender, confiar; **to rely on** depender de, confiar en
remain [rɪ'men] *intr* permanecer, quedarse || **remains** *spl* desechos, restos, restos mortales; obra póstuma
remainder [rɪ'mendər] *s* resto, residuo; libro casi invendible || *tr* saldar (*libros que ya no se venden*)
re•make [ri'mek] *v* (*pret & pp* **-made** ['med]) *tr* rehacer
remark [rɪ'mɑrk] *s* observación || *tr & intr* observar; **to remark on** aludir a, comentar
remarkable [rɪ'mɑrkəbəl] *adj* notable, extraordinario
remar•ry [ri'mæri] *v* (*pret & pp* **-ried**) *intr* volver a casarse
reme•dy ['rɛmɪdi] *s (pl* **-dies**) remedio || *v* (*pret & pp* **-died**) *tr* remediar
remember [rɪ'mɛmbər] *tr* acordarse de, recordar; dar recuerdos de parte de, p.ej., **remember me to your brother** déle Vd. a su hermano recuerdos de mi parte || *intr* acordarse, recordar; **if I remember correctly** si mal no me acuerdo
remembrance [rɪ'mɛmbrəns] *s* recuerdo
remind [rɪ'maɪnd] *tr* recordar
reminder [rɪ'maɪndər] *s* recordatorio, recordativo
reminisce [,rɛmɪ'nɪs] *intr* entregarse a los recuerdos, contar sus recuerdos
remiss [rɪ'mɪs] *adj* descuidado, negligente
re•mit [rɪ'mɪt] *v* (*pret & pp* **-mitted;** *ger* **-mitting**) *tr* (*to send, to ship; to pardon*) remitir
remittance [rɪ'mɪtəns] *s* remesa
remnant ['rɛmnənt] *s* (*something left over*) remanente *m;* (*of cloth*) retal *m*, retazo; (*piece of cloth to be sold at reduced price*) saldo; vestigio
remod•el [ri'mɑdəl] *v* (*pret & pp* **-eled** o **-elled;** *ger* **-eling** o **-elling**) *tr* modelar de nuevo; rehacer, reconstruir; convertir, transformar; remodelar
remodeling [ri'mɑdəlɪŋ] *s* remodelación
remonstrate [rɪ'mɑnstret] *intr* protestar; **to remonstrate with** reconvenir
remorse [rɪ'mɔrs] *s* remordimiento
remorseful [rɪ'mɔrsfəl] *adj* compungido, arrepentido
remote [rɪ'mot] *adj* remoto
remote control *s* comando a distancia, telecontrol *m*, control remoto; **to operate by remote control** (co)mandar a distancia
removable [rɪ'muvəbəl] *adj* amovible
removal [rɪ'muvəl] *s* remoción; mudanza, traslado; (*dismissal*) deposición
remove [rɪ'muv] *tr* remover; quitar de en medio, apartar matando || *intr* removerse
remuneration [rɪ,mjunər'eʃən] *s* remuneración
renaissance [,rɛnə'sɑns] o [rɪ'nesəns] *s* renacimiento
rend [rɛnd] *v* (*pret & pp* **rent** [rɛnt]) *tr* (*to tear*) desgarrar; (*to split*) hender, rajar; estremecer (*un ruido el aire*)
render ['rɛndər] *tr* rendir (*gracias, obsequios, homenaje*); prestar, suministrar (*ayuda*); pagar (*tributo*); desempeñar (*un papel*); traducir (*sentimientos*); (*from one language to another*) verter; hacer (*justicia*); ejecutar (*una pieza de música*); derretir (*cera, manteca*); extraer la grasa o el sebo de; poner, volver
rendezvous ['rɑndə,vu] *s* (*pl* **-vous** [,vuz]) cita; (*in space*) encuentro, reunión || *v* (*pret & pp* **-voused** [,vud]; *ger* **-vousing** [,vu•ɪŋ]) *intr* reunirse en una cita
rendition [rɛn'dɪʃən] *s* rendición; traducción; (mus) ejecución
renege [rɪ'nɪg] *s* renuncio || *intr* renunciar; (coll) volverse atrás
renegotiation [,rinɪ,goʃɪ'eʃən] *s* renegociación
renew [rɪ'nju] o [rɪ'nu] *tr* renovar || *intr* renovarse
renewable [rɪ'nju•əbəl] o [rɪ'nu•əbəl] *adj* renovable
renewal [rɪ'nju•əl] o [rɪ'nu•əl] *s* renovación
renounce [rɪ'naʊns] *tr* renunciar; renunciar a (*p.ej., el mundo*) || *intr* renunciar
renovate ['rɛnə,vet] *tr* renovar; refaccionar; reformar (*p.ej., una tienda, una casa*)
renown [rɪ'naʊn] *s* renombre *m*
renowned [rɪ'naʊnd] *adj* renombrado
rent [rɛnt] *adj* desgarrado || *s* alquiler *m*, arriendo; (*tear, slit*) desgarro || *tr* alquilar, arrendar || *intr* alquilarse, arrendarse
rental ['rɛntəl] *s* alquiler *m*, arriendo
renunciation [rɪ,nʌnsɪ'eʃən] o [rɪ,nʌnʃɪ'eʃən] *s* renunciación
reopen [ri'opən] *tr* reabrir || *intr* reabrirse

reorganize [ri'ɔrgə,naɪz] *tr* reorganizar ‖ *intr* reorganizarse
reorientation [ri,orɪ•ən'teʃən] *s* reorientación
rep. *abbr* **report, reporter, representative, republic**
repair [rɪ'pɛr] *s* reparación; recompostura; **in repair** en buen estado ‖ *tr* reparar; refaccionar ‖ *intr* dirigirse; volver
repaper [ri'pepər] *tr* empapelar de nuevo
reparation [,rɛpə'reʃən] *s* reparación
repartee [,rɛpɑr'ti] *s* respuesta viva; agudeza y gracia en responder
repast [rɪ'pæst] o [rɪ'pɑst] *s* comida, comilona
repatriate [ri'petrɪ,et] *tr* repatriar
re•pay [rɪ'pe] *v* (*pret & pp* **-paid** ['ped]) *tr* reembolsar, rembolsar; resarcir (*un daño, una injuria*); compensar
repayment [rɪ'pemənt] *s* reembolso; resarcimiento; compensación
repeal [rɪ'pil] *s* abrogación, revocación; revocatoria ‖ *tr* abrogar, revocar
repeat [rɪ'pit] *s* repetición ‖ *tr & intr* repetir
re•pel [rɪ'pɛl] *v* (*pret & pp* **-pelled;** *ger* **-pelling**) *tr* rechazar, repeler; repugnar
repent [rɪ'pɛnt] *tr* arrepentirse de ‖ *intr* arrepentirse
repentance [rɪ'pɛntəns] *s* arrepentimiento
repentant [rɪ'pɛntənt] *adj* arrepentido
repertory theater ['rɛpər,tori] *s* teatro de repertorio
repetition [,rɛpɪ'tɪʃən] *s* repetición
repine [rɪ'paɪn] *intr* afligirse, quejarse
replace [rɪ'ples] *tr* (*to put back*) reponer; (*to take the place of*) reemplazar
replacement [rɪ'plesmənt] *s* reposición; reemplazo; pieza de repuesto; soldado reemplazante
replenish [rɪ'plɛnɪʃ] *tr* rellenar; reaprovisionar
replete [rɪ'plit] *adj* repleto
replica ['rɛplɪkə] *s* réplica
re•ply [rɪ'plaɪ] *s* (*pl* **-plies**) contestación, respuesta; contesto (Mex) ‖ *v* (*pret & pp* **-plied**) *tr & intr* contestar, responder
reply coupon *s* vale *m* respuesta
report [rɪ'port] *s* relato, informe *m;* voz *f*, rumor *m;* (*e.g., of a firearm*) detonación, tiro; denuncia ‖ *tr* relatar, informar acerca de; denunciar ‖ *intr* hacer un relato; redactar un informe; ser repórter; presentarse; **to report on** dar cuenta de, notificar
report card *s* certificado escolar
reportedly [rɪ'portɪdli] *adv* según se informa
reporter [rɪ'portər] *s* repórter *m*
reporting [rɪ'portɪŋ] *s* reportaje *m*
repose [rɪ'poz] *s* descanso ‖ *tr* descansar; poner (*confianza*) ‖ *intr* descansar
reprehend [,rɛprɪ'hɛnd] *tr* reprender
represent [,rɛprɪ'zɛnt] *tr* representar
representative [,rɛprɪ'zɛntətɪv] *adj* representativo ‖ *s* representante *mf*
repress [rɪ'prɛs] *tr* reprimir
reprieve [rɪ'priv] *s* suspensión temporal de un castigo, suspensión temporal de la pena de muerte; respiro, alivio temporal ‖ *tr* suspender temporalmente el castigo de o la pena de muerte de; aliviar temporalmente
reprimand ['rɛprɪ,mænd] *s* reprimenda ‖ *tr* reconvenir, reprender
reprint ['ri,prɪnt] *s* reimpresión; tirada aparte ‖ [ri'prɪnt] *tr* reimprimir
reprisal [rɪ'praɪzəl] *s* represalia
reproach [rɪ'protʃ] *s* reproche *m;* oprobio ‖ *tr* reprochar; oprobiar
reproduce [,riprə'djus] *tr* reproducir ‖ *intr* reproducirse
reproduction [,riprə'dʌkʃən] *s* reproducción
reproof [rɪ'pruf] *s* reprobación
reprove [rɪ'pruv] *tr* reprobar
reptile ['rɛptɪl] *s* reptil *m*
republic [rɪ'pʌblɪk] *s* república
republican [rɪ'pʌblɪkən] *adj & s* republicano
repudiate [rɪ'pjudɪ,et] *tr* repudiar; no reconocer (*p.ej., una deuda*)
repugnant [rɪ'pʌgnənt] *adj* repugnante
repulse [rɪ'pʌls] *s* repulsión, rechazo ‖ *tr* repeler, rechazar
repulsive [rɪ'pʌlsɪv] *adj* repulsivo
reputation [,rɛpjə'teʃən] *s* reputación; buena reputación
repute [rɪ'pjut] *s* reputación; buena reputación ‖ *tr* reputar
reputedly [rɪ'pjutɪdli] *adv* según la opinión común
request [rɪ'kwɛst] *s* petición, solicitud; **at the request of** a petición de ‖ *tr* pedir
require [rɪ'kwaɪr] *tr* exigir, requerir
requirement [rɪ'kwaɪrmənt] *s* requisito; necesidad
requisite ['rɛkwɪzɪt] *adj & s* requisito
requital [rɪ'kwaɪtəl] *s* compensación, retorno
requite [rɪ'kwaɪt] *tr* corresponder a (*los beneficios, el amor, etc.*); corresponder con (*el bienhechor*)
re•read [ri'rid] *v* (*pret & pp* **-read** ['rɛd]) *tr* releer
rerun ['ri,rʌn] *s* (*film, play, etc.*) exhibición repetida, programa *m* repetido
resale ['ri,sel] o [ri'sel] *s* reventa
rescind [rɪ'sɪnd] *tr* rescindir
rescue ['rɛskju] *s* salvación, rescate *m*, liberación; **to go to the rescue of** acudir al socorro de ‖ *tr* salvar, rescatar, libertar
rescue party *s* pelotón *m* de salvamento
research [rɪ'sʌrtʃ] o ['risʌrtʃ] *s* investigación ‖ *intr* investigar
re•sell [ri'sɛl] *v* (*pret & pp* **-sold** ['sold]) *tr* revender; rescatar (Mex)
resemblance [rɪ'zɛmbləns] *s* parecido, semejanza
resemble [rɪ'zɛmbəl] *tr* parecerse a, asemejarse a
resent [rɪ'zɛnt] *tr* resentirse de o por
resentful [rɪ'zɛntfəl] *adj* resentido
resentment [rɪ'zɛntmənt] *s* resentimiento
reservation [,rɛzər'veʃən] *s* reserva
reserve [rɪ'zʌrv] *s* reserva ‖ *tr* reservar
reservoir ['rɛzər,vwɑr] *s* depósito; (*where water is dammed back*) embalse *m*, pantano; (*of wisdom*) fondo
re•ship [ri'ʃɪp] *v* (pret & pp **-shipped;** *ger* **-shipping**) *tr* reenviar, reexpedir; (*on a ship*) reembarcar ‖ *intr* reembarcarse

reshipment [ri'ʃɪpmənt] *s* reenvío, reexpedición; (*of persons*) reembarco; (*of goods*) reembarque *m*
reside [rɪ'zaɪd] *intr* residir
residence ['rɛzɪdəns] *s* residencia
resident ['rɛzɪdənt] *adj & s* residente *mf*, vecino
residue ['rɛzɪ,dju] *s* residuo
resign [rɪ'zaɪn] *tr* dimitir, resignar, renunciar || *intr* dimitir; (*to yield, submit*) resignarse; **to resign to** resignarse con (*p.ej., su suerte*)
resignation [,rɛzig'neʃən] *s* (*from a job, etc.*) dimisión; (*state of being submissive*) resignación
resin ['rɛzɪn] *s* resina
resist [rɪ'zɪst] *tr* resistir (*la tentación*); resistir a (*la violencia; la risa*) || *intr* resistirse
resistance [rɪ'zɪstəns] *s* resistencia; **without resistance** sin rechistar
resole [ri'sol] *tr* sobresolar
resolute ['rɛzə,lut] *adj* resuelto
resolution [,rɛzə'luʃən] *s* resolución; **good resolutions** buenos propósitos
resolve [rɪ'zɔlv] *s* resolución || *tr* resolver || *intr* resolverse
resort [rɪ'zɔrt] *s* lugar muy frecuentado; (*e.g., for vacations*) estación; (*for help or support*) recurso; **as a last resort** como último recurso || *intr* recurrir
resound [rɪ'zaʊnd] *intr* resonar
resource [rɪ'sors] o ['risors] *s* recurso
resourceful [rɪ'sorsfəl] *adj* ingenioso
respect [rɪ'spɛkt] *s* (*deference, esteem*) respeto; (*reference, relation; detail*) respecto; **respects** recuerdos, saludos; **to pay one's respects (to)** ofrecer sus respetos (a); **with respect to** respecto a o de || *tr* respetar
respectable [rɪ'spɛktəbəl] *adj* respetable; decente, presentable
respectful [rɪ'spɛktfəl] *adj* respetuoso
respectfully [rɪ'spɛktfəli] *adj* respetuosamente; **respectfully yours** de Vd. atento y seguro servidor
respecting [rɪ'spɛktɪŋ] *prep* con respecto a, respecto de
respective [rɪ'spɛktɪv] *adj* respectivo
respire [rɪ'spaɪr] *tr & intr* respirar
respite ['rɛspɪt] *s* (*temporary relief*) respiro; (*postponement, especially of death sentence*) suspensión; **without respite** sin respirar
resplendent [rɪ'splɛndənt] *adj* resplandeciente
respond [rɪ'spɑnd] *intr* responder
response [rɪ'spɑns] *s* respuesta
responsibility [rɪ,spɑnsɪ'bɪlɪti] *s* responsabilidad; **to assume responsibility** responsabilizarse
responsible [rɪ'spɑnsɪbəl] *adj* responsable; (*job, position*) de confianza; **to hold responsible** responsabilizar; **responsible for** responsable de
rest [rɛst] *s* (*after exertion or work; sleep*) descanso; (*lack of motion*) reposo; (*of the dead*) paz *f;* (*what remains*) resto; (mus) pausa; **at rest** (*not moving*) en reposo; tranquilo; dormido; (*dead*) muerto; **the rest** lo demás; los demás; **to come to rest** venir a parar; **to lay to rest** enterrar || *tr* descansar; parar; poner (*p.ej., confianza*) || *intr* descansar; estar, hallarse; **to rest assured (that)** estar seguro, tener la seguridad (de que); **to rest on** descansar en o sobre, estribar en
restaurant ['rɛstərənt] *s* restaurante *m*
rest cure *s* cura de reposo
restful ['rɛstfəl] *adj* descansado, tranquilo, reposado
rest home *s* casa de reposo
resting place *s* lugar *m* de descanso; (*of a staircase*) descansadero; (*of the dead*) última morada
restitution [,rɛstɪ'tjuʃən] *s* restitución
restless ['rɛstlɪs] *adj* intranquilo; (sleepless) insomne
restock [ri'stɑk] *tr* reaprovisionar; repoblar (*p.ej., un acuario*)
restore [rɪ'stor] *tr* restaurar; (*to give back*) devolver
restrain [rɪ'stren] *tr* contener, refrenar; aprisionar
restraint [rɪ,'strent] *s* restricción; comedimiento, moderación
restrict [rɪ'strɪkt] *tr* restringir
rest room *s* sala de descanso; excusado, retrete *m;* (*of a theater*) saloncillo
result [rɪ'zʌlt] *s* resultado; **as a result of** de resultas de || *intr* resultar; **to result in** dar por resultado, parar en
resume [rɪ'zum] o [rɪ'zjum] *tr* reasumir; reanudar (*el viaje, el vuelo, etc.);* volver a tomar (*su asiento*) || *intr* continuar; recomenzar; reanudar el hilo del discurso
résumé [,rɛzʊ'me] *s* resumen *m*
resurface [ri'sʌrfɪs] *tr* dar nueva superficie a || *intr* volver a emerger (*un submarino*)
resurrect [,rɛzə'rɛkt] *tr & intr* resucitar
resurrection [,rɛzə'rɛkʃən] *s* resurrección
resuscitate [rɪ'sʌsɪ,tet] *tr & intr* resucitar
retail ['ritel] *adj & adv* al por menor || *s* venta al por menor || *tr* detallar, vendor al por menor || *intr* vender al por menor; venderse al por menor
retailer ['ritelər] *s* detallista *mf*, minorista *m*, comerciante *mf* al por menor
retain [rɪ'ten] *tr* retener; contratar (*a un abogado*)
retaliate [rɪ'tælɪ,et] *intr* desquitarse, vengarse
retaliation [rɪ,tælɪ'eʃən] *s* desquite *m*, venganza
retard [rɪ'tɑrd] *s* retardo || *tr* retardar
retardation [,ritɑr'deʃən] *s* retardación
retarded [rɪ'tɑrdɪd] *adj* subnormal, atrasado, retrasado
retch [rɛtʃ] *tr* vomitar || *intr* arquear, esforzarse por vomitar
retching ['rɛtʃɪŋ] *s* arcadas
ret'd. *abbr* **returned**
reticence ['rɛtɪsəns] *s* reserva, circunspección, sigilo
reticent ['rɛtɪsənt] *adj* reservado, circunspecto
retinue ['rɛtɪ,nju] *s* comitiva, séquito

retire [rɪ'taɪr] *tr* retirar; jubilar (*a un empleado*) || *intr* retirarse; jubilarse; (*to go to bed*) recogerse; (mil) retirarse
retirement [rɪ'taɪrmənt] *s* retiro; (*of an employee with pension*) jubilación; (mil) retirada
retirement annuity *s* jubilación
retort [rɪ'tɔrt] *s* respuesta pronta y aguda, réplica; (chem) retorta || *intr* replicar
retouch [ri'tʌtʃ] *tr* retocar
retrace [rɪ'tres] *tr* repasar; **to retrace one's steps** volver sobre sus pasos
retract [rɪ'trækt] *tr* retractarse de, desdecirse de (*lo que se ha dicho*) || *intr* retractarse, desdecirse
retractable [rɪ'træktəbəl] *adj* retráctil
retraction [rɪ'trækʃən] *s* retracción
re•tread ['ri,trɛd] *s* neumático recauchutado; neumático ranurado || [ri'trɛd] *v* (*pret & pp* **-treaded**) *tr* recauchutar; volver a ranurar || *v* (*pret* **-trod** ['trɑd]; *pp* **-trod** o **-trodden**) *tr* desandar || *intr* volverse atrás
retreat [rɪ'trit] *s* (*act of withdrawing; place of seclusion*) retiro; (eccl) retiro; (mil) retreta, retirada; (*signal*) (mil) retreta; **to beat a retreat** retirarse; (mil) batirse en retirada || *intr* retirarse
retrench [rɪ'trɛntʃ] *tr* cercenar || *intr* recogerse
retribution [,rɛtrɪ'bjuʃən] *s* justo castigo; (theol) juicio final
retrieve [rɪ'triv] *tr* cobrar; reparar (*p.ej., un daño*); desquitarse de (*una pérdida, una derrota*); (hunt) cobrar, portar || *intr* (hunt) cobrar, portar
retriever [rɪ'trivər] *s* perro cobrador, perro traedor
retroactive [,rɛtro'æktɪv] *adj* retroactivo
retrofiring [,rɛtro'faɪrɪŋ] *s* retrodisparo
retrogress ['rɛtrə,grɛs] *intr* retroceder; empeorar
retrorocket [,rɛtro'rɑkɪt] *s* retrocohete *m*
retrospect ['rɛtrə,spɛkt] *s* retrospección; **in retrospect** retrospectivamente
retrospective [,rɛtrə,spɛktɪv] *adj* retrospectivo
re•try [ri'traɪ] *v* (*pret & pp* **-tried**) *tr* reensayar; rever (*un caso legal*); procesar de nuevo (*a una persona*)
return [rɪ'tʌrn] *adj* repetido; de vuelta; **by return mail** a vuelta de correo || *s* vuelta; devolución; recompensa; respuesta; informe *m*, noticia; ganancia, beneficio, rédito; (*of an election*) resultado; (*of income tax*) declaración; **in return (for)** en cambio (de); **many happy returns of the day!** ¡que cumpla muchos más! || *tr* devolver; dar en cambio; corresponder a (*un favor*); dar (*una respuesta, las gracias*) || *intr* volver; responder
return address *s* dirección del remitente
return bout o **engagement** *s* (box) combate *m* revancha
return game *s* desquite *m*
return ticket *s* billete *m* de vuelta; billete de ida y vuelta
return trip *s* viaje *m* de vuelta
reunification [ri,junɪfɪ'keʃən] *s* reunificación
reunion [ri'junjən] *s* reunión
reunite [,rijʊ'naɪt] *tr* reunir || *intr* reunirse
rev. *abbr* **revenue, reverse, review, revised, revision, revolution**
Rev. *abbr*. **Revelation, Reverend**
rev [rev] *s* revolución || *v* (*pret & pp* **revved;** *ger* **revving**) *tr* cambiar la velocidad de; **to rev up** acelerar || *intr* acelerarse
revaluate [ri'væljʊ,et] *tr* revalorar, revalorizar, revaluar
revamp [ri'væmp] *tr* componer, renovar, remendar
reveal [rɪ'vil] *tr* revelar
reveille ['rɛvəli] *s* diana, toque *m* de diana
rev•el ['rɛvəl] *s* jarana, regocijo tumultuoso || *v* (*pret & pp* **-eled** o **-elled;** *ger* **-eling** o **-elling**) *intr* jaranear; deleitarse
revelation [,rɛvə'leʃən] *s* revelación
revel•ry ['rɛvəlri] *s* (*pl* **-ries**) jarana, diversión tumultuosa
revenge [rɪ'vɛndʒ] *s* venganza || *tr* vengar
revengeful [rɪ'vɛndʒfəl] *adj* vengativo
revenue ['rɛvə,nju] *s* renta, rédito; rentas públicas
revenue cutter *s* escampavía
revenue stamp *s* sello fiscal, timbre *m* del estado
reverberate [rɪ'vʌrbə,ret] *intr* reverberar
revere [rɪ'vɪr] *tr* reverenciar, venerar
reverence ['rɛvərəns] *s* reverencia || *tr* reverenciar
reverend ['rɛvərənd] *adj & s* reverendo
reverie ['rɛvəri] *s* ensueño
reversal [rɪ'vʌrsəl] *s* inversión (*e.g., of opinion*) cambio
reverse [rɪ'vʌrs] *adj* invertido; contrario; de marcha atrás || *s* (*opposite or rear*) revés *m;* contrario; contramarcha, marcha atrás; (*check, defeat*) revés *m*, contratiempo || *tr* invertir; dar vuelta a; poner en marcha atrás; **to reverse oneself** cambiar de opinión; **to reverse the charges** cobrar al destinatario; (telp) cobrar al número llamado || *intr* invertirse
reverse lever *s* palanca de marcha atrás
revert [rɪ'vʌrt] *intr* revertir; saltar atrás; **to revert to one's old tricks** volver a las andadas
review [rɪ'vju] *s* (*reëxamination; survey; magazine; musical show*) revista; (*of a book*) reseña, revista; (*of a lesson*) repaso; (mil) reseña, revista || *tr* rever, revisar; reseñar (*un libro*); repasar (*una lección*); (mil) revistar
reviewer [rɪ'vju•ər] *s* (*critic*) reseñador *m*
revile [rɪ'vaɪl] *tr* ultrajar, vilipendiar
revise [rɪ'vaɪz] *s* revisión; refundición; (typ) segunda prueba || *tr* rever, revisar; refundir (*un libro*); enmendar
revision [rɪ'vɪʒən] *s* revisión; revisada; (*of a book*) refundición; enmienda
revisionism [rɪ'vɪʒə,nɪzəm] *s* revisionismo
revisionist [rɪ'vɪʒənɪst] *adj & s* revisionista
revival [rɪ'vaɪvəl] *s* resucitación; reanimación; (*e.g., of learning*) renacimiento; de-

spertamiento religioso; (theat) reestreno, reposición
revive [rɪ'vaɪv] *tr* revivir; (theat) reestrenar, reponer || *intr* revivir; volver en sí, recordar
revoke [rɪ'vok] *tr* revocar
revolt [rɪ'volt] *s* rebelión, sublevación || *tr* dar asco a, repugnar || *intr* rebelarse, sublevarse
revolting [rɪ'voltiŋ] *adj* asqueroso, repugnante; rebelde
revolution [,rɛvə'luʃən] *s* revolución
revolutionar•y [,rɛvə'luʃə,nɛri] *adj* revolucionario || *s* (*pl* **-ies**) revolucionario
revolve [rɪ'valv] *tr* hacer girar; (*in one's mind*) revolver || *intr* girar; revolverse (*un astro en su órbita*)
revolver [rɪ'valvər] *s* revólver *m*
revolving bookcase *s* giratoria
revolving door *s* puerta giratoria
revolving fund *s* fondo rotativo
revue [rɪ'vju] *s* (theat) revista
revulsion [rɪ'vʌlʃən] *s* aversión, repugnancia; reacción fuerte
reward [rɪ'wɔrd] *s* premio, recompensa; (*money used to recapture or recover*) rescate *m;* hallazgo, p.ej., **five dollars reward** cinco dólares de hallazgo || *tr* premiar, recompensar
rewarding [rɪ'wɔrdɪŋ] *adj* remunerador, provechoso, agradecido
re•wind ['ri,waɪnd] *s* (mach, mov) retroceso || [ri'waɪnd] *v* (*pret & pp* **-wound** [waʊnd] *tr* (mach, mov) rebobinar
re•write [ri'raɪt] *v* (*pret* **-wrote** ['rot]; *pp* **-written** ['rɪtən]) *tr* escribir de nuevo; refundir (*un escrito*); redactar (*un escrito de otra persona*)
R.F. *abbr* **radio frequency**
R.F.D. *abbr* **Rural Free Delivery**
R.H. *abbr* **Royal Highness**
rhapso•dy ['ræpsədi] *s* (*pl* **-dies**) rapsodia
rheostat ['ri•ə,stæt] *s* reóstato
rhesus ['risəs] *s* macaco de la India
rhetoric ['rɛtərɪk] *s* retórica
rhetorical [rɪ'tɔrɪkəl] *adj* retórico
rheumatic [ru'mætɪk] *adj & s* reumático
rheumatism ['rumə,tɪzəm] *s* reumatismo
Rhine [raɪn] *s* Rin *m*
Rhineland ['raɪn,lænd] *s* Renania
rhine'stone' *s* diamante de imitación hecho de vidrio
rhinoceros [raɪ'nɑsərəs] *s* rinoceronte *m*
Rhodes [rodz] *s* Rodas *f*
Rhone [ron] *s* Ródano
rhubarb ['rubɑrb] *s* ruibarbo
rhyme [raɪm] *s* rima; **without rhyme or reason** sin ton ni son || *tr & intr* rimar
rhythm ['rɪðəm] *s* ritmo
rhythmic(al) ['rɪðmɪk(əl)] *adj* rítmico
rial•to [rɪ'ælto] *s* (*pl* **-tos**) mercado || **the Rialto** el puente del Rialto; el centro teatral de Nueva York
rib [rɪb] *s* costilla; (*of a fan or umbrella*) varilla; (*of a tire*) cuerda; (*in cloth*) canilla; (*of the wing of an insect*) nervio || *v* (*pret & pp* **ribbed;** *ger* **ribbing**) *tr* proveer de costillas; hacer canillas en; (slang) tomar el pelo a
ribald ['rɪbəld] *adj* grosero y obsceno
ribbon ['rɪbən] *s* cinta
rice [raɪs] *s* arroz *m*
rich [rɪtʃ] *adj* rico; (coll) platudo; (*color*) vivo; (*voice*) sonoro; (*wine*) generoso; azucarado, condimentado; (coll) divertido; (coll) ridículo; **to strike it rich** descubrir un buen filón || **riches** *spl* riquezas; **the rich** los ricos
rickets ['rɪkɪts] *s* raquitis *f*
rickety ['rɪkɪti] *adj* (*object*) destartalado, desvencijado; (*person*) tambaleante, vacilante; (*suffering from rickets*) raquítico
rid [rɪd] *v* (*pret & pp* **rid;** *ger* **ridding**) *tr* desembarazar; **to get rid of** desembarazarse de, deshacerse de; matar
riddance ['rɪdəns] *s* supresión, libramiento; **good riddance!** ¡adiós, gracias!, ¡de buena me he librado!
riddle ['rɪdəl] *s* acertijo, adivinanza; (*person or thing hard to understand*) enigma *m;* criba gruesa || *tr* acribillar; destruir (*un argumento; la reputación de una persona*); **to riddle with bullets** acribillar a balazos; **to riddle with questions** acribillar a preguntas
ride [raɪd] *s* paseo || *v* (*pret* **rode** [rod]; *pp* **ridden** ['rɪdən]) *tr* montar (*un caballo*); montar sobre (*los hombros de una persona*); recorrer a caballo; flotar sobre (*las olas*); dominar, tiranizar; (coll) burlarse de; **to ride down** atropellar; vencer; **to ride out** luchar felizmente con (*una tempestad*); aguantar con buen éxito (*una desgracia*) || *intr* montar; pasear en coche o carruaje; **to let ride** (slang) dejar correr; **to take riding** llevar de paseo
rider ['raɪdər] *s* jinete *m;* pasajero
ridge [rɪdʒ] *s* (*of a roof; of earth between two furrows*) caballete *m;* (*of a fabric*) cordoncillo; (*of mountains*) cordillera; (*of two plane surfaces*) arista
ridge'pole' *s* parhilera
ridicule ['rɪdɪ,kjul] *s* irrisión; **to expose to ridicule** poner en ridículo || *tr* ridiculizar
ridiculous [rɪ'dɪkjələs] *adj* ridículo
riding academy *s* escuela de equitación
riding boot *s* bota de montar
riding habit *s* amazona, traje *m* de montar
rife [raɪf] *adj* común, corriente, general; abundante, lleno; **rife with** abundante en, lleno de
riffraff ['rɪf,ræf] *s* bahorrina, canalla
rifle ['raɪfəl] *s* rifle *m*, fusil *m* || *tr* hurtar, robar; escudriñar y robar; desnudar, despojar
rifle range *s* tiro de rifle
rift [rɪft] *s* abertura, raja; desacuerdo, desavenencia
rig [rɪg] *s* equipaje *m;* carruaje *m* con caballo o caballos; traje extraño; (naut) aparejo || *v* (*pret & pp* **rigged;** *ger* **rigging**) *tr* equipar; aprestar, disponer; improvisar; vestir de una manera extraña; arreglar de una manera fraudulenta; (naut) aparejar

rigging [ˈrɪgɪŋ] *s* avíos, instrumentos, equipo; (naut) aparejo, cordaje *m*

right [raɪt] *adj* derecho; verdadero; exacto; conveniente; favorable; sano, normal; bien, correcto; señalado; correspondiente; que se busca, p.ej., **this is the right house** ésta es la casa que se busca; que se necesita, p.ej., **this is the right train** éste es el tren que se necesita; que debe, p.ej., **he is going the right way** sigue el camino que debe; **right or wrong** con razón o sin ella, bueno o malo; **to be all right** estar bien; estar bien de salud; **to be right** tener razón || *adv* derechamente; directamente; correctamente; exactamente; favorablemente; en orden, en buen estado; hacia la derecha; completamente; (coll) muy; mismo, p.ej., **right here** aquí mismo; **all right** muy bien || *interj* ¡bien! || *s* (*justice, reason*) derecho; (*right hand*) derecha; (box) derechazo; (com) derecho; (pol) derecha; **by right** según derecho; **on the right** a la derecha; **to be in the right** tener razón || *tr* enderezar; corregir, rectificar; hacer justicia a; deshacer (*un entuerto*) || *intr* enderezarse

righteous [ˈraɪtʃəs] *adj* recto, justo; virtuoso

right field *s* (baseball) jardín derecho

rightful [ˈraɪtfəl] *adj* justo; legítimo

right'-hand' drive *s* conducción o dirección a la derecha

right-hand man *s* mano derecha, brazo derecho

rightist [ˈraɪtɪst] *adj & s* derechista *mf*

rightly [ˈraɪtli] *adv* derechamente; correctamente; con razón; convenientemente; **rightly or wrongly** con razón o sin ella; **rightly so** a justo título

right mind *s* entero juicio

right of way *s* derecho de tránsito o de paso; (law) servidumbre de paso; (rr) servidumbre de vía; **to yield the right of way** ceder el paso

rights of man *spl* derechos del hombre

right'-wing' *adj* derechista

right-winger [ˈraɪtˈwɪŋər] *s* (coll) derechista *mf*

rigid [ˈrɪdʒɪd] *adj* rígido

rigmarole [ˈrɪgmə,rol] *s* galimatías *m*

rigorous [ˈrɪgərəs] *adj* riguroso

rile [raɪl] *tr* (coll) exasperar

rill [rɪl] *s* arroyuelo

rim [rɪm] *s* canto, borde *m;* (*of a wheel*) llanta; (*of a tire*) aro

rime [raɪm] *s* (*in verse*) rima; (*frost*) escarcha; **without rime or reason** sin ton ni son || *tr & intr* rimar

rind [raɪnd] *s* cáscara, corteza

ring [rɪŋ] *s* (*circular band, line, or mark*) anillo; (*for the finger*) sortija; (*for curtains; for gymnastics*) anilla; (*for nose of animal*) argolla; (*for fruit jars*) círculo de goma; (*for some sport or exhibition*) circo; (*for boxing*) cuadrilátero, ruedo; (*for bullfight*) redondel *m*, ruedo; boxeo; (*of a group of people*) corro; (*of evildoers*) pandilla; (*under the eyes*) ojera; (*of the anchor*) arganeo; (*sound of a bell, of a clock*) campanada; (*of a small bell; of the glass of glassware*) tintineo; (*to summon a person*) llamada; (*character, nature, spirit*) tono; **to be in the ring (for)** ser candidato (a); **to run rings around** dar cien vueltas a || *v* (*pret & pp* **ringed**) *tr* cercar, rodear; (*to put a ring on*) anillar || *intr* formar círculo o corro || *v* (*pret* **rang** [ræŋ]; *pp* **rung** [rʌŋ] *tr* tañer, tocar; (*to peal, ring out*) repicar; llamar al timbre; dar (*las horas la campana del reloj);* llamar por teléfono; **to ring up** llamar por teléfono; marcar (*una compra*) con el timbre || *intr* sonar (*una campana, un timbre, el teléfono*); tintinear (*el choque de copas, una campanilla*); resonar, retumbar; llamar; zumbar (*los oídos*); **to ring for** llamar, llamar al timbre; **to ring off** terminar una llamada por teléfono; **to ring up** llamar por teléfono

ring-around-a-rosy [ˈrɪŋə,raʊŋdəˈrozi] *s* juego del corro

ringing [ˈrɪŋɪŋ] *adj* resonante, retumbante || *s* anillamiento; campaneo, repique *m;* (*of the glass of glassware*) tintineo; (*in the ears*) retintín *m*, silbido

ring'lead'er *s* cabecilla *m*

ring'mas'ter *s* hombre encargado de los ejercicios ecuestres y acrobáticos de un circo

ring'side' *s* lugar junto al cuadrilátero; lugar desde el cual se puede ver de cerca

ring'worm' *s* tiña

rink [rɪŋk] *s* patinadero

rinse [rɪns] *s* aclaración, enjuague *m* || *tr* aclarar, enjuagar

riot [ˈraɪ•ət] *s* alboroto, tumulto; regocijos ruidosos; (*of colors*) exhibición brillante; **to run riot** desenfrenarse; crecer lozanamente (*las plantas*) || *intr* alborotarse, amotinarse

rioter [ˈraɪ•ətər] *s* alborotador *m*, amotinado

riot squad *s* pelotón *m* de asalto

rip [rɪp] *s* rasgón *m*, siete *m;* (*open seam*) descosido || *v* (*pret & pp* **ripped;** *ger* **ripping**) *tr* desgarrar, rasgar; descoser (*lo que estaba cosido*) || *intr* desgarrarse, rasgarse; (coll) adelantar o moverse de prisa o con violencia; **to rip out with** (coll) decir con violencia

ripe [raɪp] *adj* maduro; acabado, hecho; dispuesto, preparado; (*boil, tumor*) madurado; (*olive*) negro

ripen [ˈraɪpən] *tr & intr* madurar

ripoff [ˈrɪp,ɔf] *s* (slang) estafa; timo

ripple [ˈrɪpəl] *s* temblor *m*, rizo; (*sound*) murmullo, susurro || *tr* rizar || *intr* rizarse; murmurar, susurrar

rise [raɪz] *s* (*of temperature, prices, a road*) subida; (*of ground, of the voice*) elevación; (*of a heavenly body*) salida; (*of a step*) altura; (*in one's employment*) ascenso; (*of water*) crecida; (*of a source of water*) nacimiento; (*of a valve*) levantamiento; **to get a rise out of** (slang) sacar una réplica mordaz a; **to give rise to** dar origen a || *v* (*pret* **rose** [roz]; *pp* **risen** [ˈrɪzən]) *intr* subir; levantarse; salir (*un astro*); asomar (*un* *peligro*); brotar (*un manantial, una planta*); (*in someone's esteem*) ganar; resucitar; **to rise above** alzarse por encima de; mostrarse superior a; **to rise early** madrugar; **to rise to** ponerse a la altura de

riser ['raɪzər] *s* contraescalón *m*, contrahuella; **early riser** madrugador *m;* **late riser** dormilón *m*

risk [rɪsk] *s* riesgo; **to run** o **take a risk** correr riesgo, correr peligro || *tr* arriesgar; arriesgarse en (*una empresa dudosa*)

risk•y ['rɪski] *adj* (*comp* **-ier;** *super* **-iest**) arriesgado; riesgoso; escabroso

risqué [rɪs'ke] *adj* escabroso

rite [raɪt] *s* rito; **last rites** honras fúnebres

ritual ['rɪtʃu•əl] *adj & s* ritual *m*

riv. *abbr* **river**

ri•val ['raɪvəl] *s* rival *mf* || *v* (*pret & pp* **-valed** o **-valled;** *ger* **-valing** o **-valling**) *tr* rivalizar con

rival•ry ['raɪvəlri] *s* (*pl* **-ries**) rivalidad

river ['rɪvər] *s* río; **down the river** río abajo; **up the river** río arriba

river basin *s* cuenca de río

river bed *s* cauce *m*

river front *s* orilla del río

riv'er•side' *adj* ribereño || *s* ribera

rivet ['rɪvɪt] *s* roblón *m*, remache *m;* (*e.g., to hold scissors together*) clavillo || *tr* remachar; clavar (*p.ej., los ojos en una persona*)

rm. *abbr* **ream, room**

R.N. *abbr* **registered nurse, Royal Navy**

roach [rotʃ] *s* cucaracha

road [rod] *adj* itinerario, caminero || *s* camino; (naut) rada; **to be in the road** estorbar el paso; incomodar; **to get out of the road** quitarse de en medio

road'bed' *s* (*of a highway*) firme *m;* (rr) infraestructura

road'block' *s* (mil) barricada; (fig) obstáculo

road'house' *s* posada en el camino

road laborer *s* peón caminero

road map *s* mapa itinerario

road service *s* auxilio en carretera

road'side' *s* borde *m* del camino, borde de la carretera

roadside inn *s* posada en el camino

road sign *s* señal *f* de carretera, poste *m* indicador

road'stead' *s* rada

road'way' *s* camino, vía

roam [rom] *s* vagabundeo || *tr* vagar por, recorrer a la ventura || *intr* vagar, andar errante

roar [ror] *s* bramido, rugido || *intr* bramar, rugir; reírse a carcajadas

roast [rost] *s* asado; café tostado || *tr* asar; tostar (*café*); (coll) despellejar || *intr* asarse; tostarse

roast beef *s* rosbif *m*

roast of beef *s* carne de vaca asada o para asar

roast pork *s* carne de cerdo asada

rob [rɑb] *v* (*pret & pp* **robbed;** *ger* **robbing**) *tr & intr* robar

robber ['rɑbər] *s* robador *m*, ladrón *m*

robber•y ['rɑbəri] *s* (*pl* **-ies**) robo

robe [rob] *s* manto; abrigo; (*of a woman*) traje *m*, vestido; (*of a professor, judge, etc.*) toga, túnica; (*of a priest*) traje *m* talar; (*dressing gown*) bata; (*for lap in a carriage*) manta || *tr* vestir || *intr* vestirse

robin ['rɑbɪn] *s* (*in Europe*) petirrojo; (*in North America*) primavera

robot ['robɑt] *s* robot *m*

robotics [ro'bɑtɪks] *s* robótica

robust [ro'bʌst] *adj* robusto; vigoroso

rock [rɑk] *s* roca; (*sticking out of water*) escollo; (*one that is thrown*) piedra; (slang) diamante *m*, piedra preciosa; **on the rocks** arruinado, en pobreza extrema; (*said of hard liquor*) (coll) sobre hielo || *tr* acunar, mecer; (*to sleep*) arrullar; sacudir; **to rock to sleep** adormecer meciendo || *intr* mecerse; sacudirse || *abbr* **—rock-'n'-roll**

rock'-bot'tom *adj* (el) mínimo, (el) más bajo

rock candy *s* azúcar *m* cande

rock crystal *s* cristal *m* de roca

rocker ['rɑkər] *s* (*chair*) mecedora; (*curved piece at bottom of rocking chair or cradle*) arco; (mach) balancín *m;* (mach) eje *m* de balancín

rocket ['rɑkɪt] *s* cohete *m* || *intr* subir como un cohete

rocket bomb *s* bomba cohete

rocket launcher [lɔntʃər] *s* lanzacohetes *m*

rocket ship *s* aeronave *f* cohete

rock garden *s* jardín *m* entre rocas

rocking chair *s* mecedora, sillón *m* de hamaca

rocking horse *s* caballo mecedor

rock-'n'-roll ['rɑkən'rol] *s* rock *m*

Rock of Gilbraltar [dʒɪ'brɔltər] *s* peñón *m* de Gibraltar

rock salt *s* sal *f* de compás, sal gema

rock singer *s* rockero, rockera

rock wool *s* lana mineral

rock•y ['rɑki] *adj* (*comp* **-ier;** *super* **-iest**) rocoso, roqueño; (slange) débil, poco firme

rod [rɑd] *s* vara; varilla; barra; (*authority*) vara alta; opresión, tiranía; (*of the retina*) bastoncillo; (*elongated microörganism*) bastoncito; (mach) vástago; (surv) jalón *m;* (Bib) linaje *m*, raza, vástago; (slang) revólver *m*, pistola; **to spare the rod** excusar la vara

rodent ['rodənt] *adj & s* roedor *m*

rod•man ['rɑdmən] *s* (*pl* **-men** [mən]) jalonero, portamira *m*

roe [ro] *s* (*deer*) corzo; (*of fish*) hueva

rogue [rog] *s* bribón *m*, pícaro

rogues' gallery *s* colección de retratos de malhechores para uso de la policía

roguish ['rogɪʃ] *adj* bribón, pícaro; travieso, retozón

rôle o **role** [rol] *s* papel *m;* **to play a rôle** desempeñar un papel

roll [rol] *s* (*of cloth, film, paper, fat, etc.*) rollo; (*roller*) rodillo; (*cake of bread*) panecillo; (*of dice*) echada; (*of a boat*) balance *m;* (*of a drum*) redoble *m;* (*of thunder*) retumbo; bamboleo; ondulación; rol *m;* lista; (*of paper money*) fajo; **to call the roll**

pasar lista || *tr* hacer rodar; empujar hacia adelante; cilindrar, laminar; (*to wrap up with rolling motion*) arrollar; alisar con rodillo; liar (*un cigarrillo*); mover de un lado a otro; poner (*los ojos*) en blanco; tocar redobles con (*el tambor*); vibrar (*la voz; la r*); **to roll one's own** liárselos; **to roll up** arremangar (*p.ej., las mangas*); amontonar (*p.ej., una fortuna*) || *intr* rodar; bambolear; balancear (*un barco*); girar; retumbar (*el trueno*); redoblar (*un tambor*); **to roll around** revolcarse
roll call *s* lista, (el) pasar lista
roller ['rolər] *s* rodillo; (*of a piece of furniture*) ruedecilla; (*of a skate*) rueda; ola larga y creciente
roller bearing *s* cojinete *m* de rodillos
roller coaster *s* montaña rusa
roller skate *s* patín *m* de ruedas
roller towel *s* toalla sin fin
rolling mill ['rolɪŋ] *s* taller *m* de laminación; tren *m* de laminadores
rolling pin *s* rodillo, hataca, rulo
rolling stock *s* (rr) material *m* móvil, material rodante
rolling stone *s* piedra movediza
roll'-top' desk *s* escritorio norteamericano, escritorio de cortina corrediza
roly-poly ['roli'poli] *adj* regordete, rechoncho
Rom. *abbr* **Roman, Romance**
roman ['romən] *adj* (typ) redondo || *s* (typ) letra redonda || **Roman** *adj & s* romano
Roman candle *s* vela romana
Roman Catholic *adj & s* católico romano
romance [ro'mæns] o ['romæns] *s* (*tale of chivalry*) roman *m;* cuento de aventuras; cuento de amor; intriga amorosa; novela sentimental; (mus) romanza || [ro'mæns] *intr* contar o escribir romances, cuentos de aventuras o cuentos de amor; pensar o hablar de un modo romántico; exagerar, mentir || **Romance** ['romæns] o [ro'mæns] *adj* (*Neo-Latin*) romance o románico
romance languages *spl* lenguas romances *or* románicas
romance of chivalry *s* libro de caballerías
Roman Empire *s* Imperio romano
Romanesque [,romən'ɛsk] *adj & s* románico
Roman nose *s* nariz aguileña
romantic [ro'mæntɪk] *adj* romántico; (*spot, place*) encantador
romanticism [ro'mæntɪ,sɪzəm] *s* romanticismo
romp [rɑmp] *intr* corretear, triscar
rompers ['rɑmpərz] *spl* traje holgado de juego
roof [ruf] o [rʊf] *s* (*top outer covering of a house*) tejado; (*of a car or bus*) imperial *f*, tejadillo; (*of the mouth*) paladar *m;* (*of heaven*) bóveda; (*home, dwelling*) (fig) techo; **to raise the roof** (slang) poner el grito en el cielo || *tr* techar
roofer ['rufər] o ['rʊfər] *s* techador *m*, pizarrero
roof garden *s* (*garden on the roof*) pérgola, azotea de baile y diversión
rook [rʊk] *s* (*bird*) grajo; (*in chess*) roque *m* || *tr* trampear
rookie ['rʊki] *s* (slang) bisoño, novato
room [rum] o [rʊm] *s* aposento, cuarto, habitación, pieza; espacio, sitio, lugar *m;* ocasión; **to make room** abrir paso, hacer lugar || *intr* alojarse
room and board *s* pensión completa
room clerk *s* empleado en la recepción, encargado de las reservas
roomer ['rumər] *s* inquilino
rooming house *s* casa donde se alquilan cuartos
room'mate' *s* compañero de cuarto
room•y ['rumi] *adj* (*comp* **-ier;** *super* **-iest)** amplio, espacioso
roost [rust] *s* percha de gallinero; gallinero; lugar *m* de descanso; **to rule the roost** ser el amo del cotarro, tener el mando y el palo || *intr* descansar (*las aves*) en la percha; estar alojado; pasar la noche
rooster ['rustər] *s* gallo
root [rut] o [rʊt] *s* raíz *f;* **to get to the root of** profundizar; **to take root** echar raíces || *tr* hocicar, hozar || *intr* arraigar; **to root for** (slang) gritar alentando
rooter ['rutər] o ['rʊtər] *s* (slang) hincha *mf*
rope [rop] *s* cuerda; (*of a hangman*) dogal *m;* (*to catch an animal*) lazo; **to jump rope** saltar a la comba; **to know the ropes** (slang) saber todas las tretas; espabilarse || *tr* atar con una cuerda; coger con lazo; **to rope in** (slang) embaucar, engañar
rope'walk'er *sl* funámbulo, volatinero
rosa•ry ['rozəri] *s* (*pl* **-ries)** rosario
rose [roz] *adj* de color de rosa || *s* rosa
rose'bud' *s* pimpollo, capullo de rosa
rose'bush' *s* rosal *m*
rose'-col'ored *adj* rosado; **to see everything through rose-colored glasses** verlo todo de color de rosa
rose garden *s* rosaleda, rosalera
rose hip *s* (bot) cinarrodón *m;* eterio
rosemar•y ['roz,mɛri] *s* (*pl* **-ies)** romero
rose of Sharon ['ʃɛrən] *s* granado blanco, rosa de Siria
rose window *s* rosetón *m*
rose'wood' *s* palisandro
rosin ['rɑzɪn] *s* colofonia, brea seca
roster ['rɑstər] *s* catálogo, lista; horario escolar, horas de clase
rostrum ['rɑstrəm] *s* tribuna
ros•y ['rozi] *adj* (*comp* **-ier;** *super* **-iest)** rosado, sonrosado; alegre
rot [rɑt] *s* podredumbre; (slang) tontería || *v* (*pret & pp* **rotted;** *ger* **rotting)** *tr* pudrir || *intr* pudrirse
rotate ['rotet] o [ro'tet] *tr* hacer girar; alternar || *intr* girar; alternar
rote [rot] *s* rutina, repetición maquinal; **by rote** de memoria, maquinalmente
rot'gut' *s* (slang) matarratas *m*
rotogravure [,rotəgrə'vjʊr] o [,rotə'grevjʊr] *s* rotograbado
rotten ['rɑtən] *adj* putrefacto, pútrido; corrompido

rotund [roˈtʌnd] *adj* redondo de cuerpo; (*language*) redondo
rouge [ruʒ] *s* arrebol *m*, colorete *m* || *tr* arrebolar, pintar || *intr* arrebolarse, pintarse
rough [rʌf] *adj* áspero; (*sea*) agitado, picado; (*crude, unwrought*) tosco, grosero; aproximado || *tr* —**to rough it** vivir sin comodidades, hacer vida campestre
rough'cast' *s* modelo tosco; mezcla gruesa || *v* (*pret & pp* **-cast**) *tr* (*to prepare in rough form*) bosquejar; dar a (*la pared*) una capa de mezcla gruesa
rough copy *s* borrador *m*
roughly [ˈrʌfli] *adv* asperamente; brutalmente; aproximadamente
roulette [ruˈlɛt] *s* ruleta
round [raund] *adj* redondo || *adv* redondamente; alrededor; de boca en boca; por todas partes || *prep* alrededor de; (*e.g., the corner*) a la vuelta de; cerca de; acá y allá en || *s* camino, circuito; (*of a policeman; of visits; of drinks or cigars*) ronda; (*of applause; discharge of guns*) salva; (*discharge of a single gun*) disparo, tiro; (*of people*) corro, círculo; (*of golf*) partido; rutina, serie *f*, sucesión; redondez *f;* revolución; (box) asalto; **to go the rounds** ir de boca en boca; ir de mano en mano || *tr* (*to make round*) redondear; cercar, rodear; doblar (*una esquina, un promontorio*); **to round off** u **out** redondear; acabar, completar, perfeccionar; **to round up** juntar, recoger; rodear (*el ganado*)
roundabout [ˈraundəˌbaut] *adj* indirecto || *s* curso indirecto; (Brit) tío vivo; (Brit) glorieta de tráfico
rounder [ˈraundər] *s* (coll) pródigo; (coll) catavinos *m*, borrachín habitual
round'house' *s* cocherón *m*, casa de máquinas, depósito de locomotoras
round-shouldered [ˈraundˌʃoldərd] *adj* cargado de espaldas
Round Table *s* Tabla Redonda
round'-trip' ticket *s* billete *m* de ida y vuelta
round'up' *s* (*of cattle*) rodeo; (*of criminals*) redada; (*of old friends*) reunión
rouse [rauz] *tr* despertar; excitar, provocar; levantar (*la caza*) || *intr* despertarse, despabilarse
rout [raut] *s* derrota; fuga desordenada || *tr* derrotar; poner en fuga desordenada; arrancar hozando || *intr* hozar
route [rut] o [raut] *s* ruta; itinerario || *tr* encaminar
routine [ruˈtin] *adj* rutinario || *s* rutina
rove [rov] *intr* andar errante, vagar
row [rau] *s* (coll) camorra, pendencia, riña; (coll) alboroto, bullicio; (coll) balumba; **to raise a row** (coll) armar camorra || [ro] *s* fila, hilera; (*of houses*) crujía; **in a row** seguidos, p.ej., **five hours in a row** cinco horas seguidas || *intr* remar
rowboat [ˈroˌbot] *s* bote *m*, bote de remos
row•dy [ˈraudi] *adj* (*comp* **-dier;** *super* **-diest**) gamberro || *s* (*pl* **-dies**) gamberro
rower [ˈro•ər] *s* remero
royal [ˈrɔɪ•əl] *adj* real; (*magnificent, splendid*) regio
royalist [ˈrɔɪ•əlɪst] *s* realista *mf*
royal•ty [ˈrɔɪ•əlti] *s* (*pl* **-ties**) realeza; personaje *m* real, personajes reales; derechos de autor; derechos de inventor
r.p.m. *abbr* **revolutions per minute**
R.R. *abbr* **railroad, Right Reverend**
rub [rʌb] *s* frotación, roce *m;* **there's the rub** ahí está el busilis || *v* (*pret & pp* **rubbed;** *ger* **rubbing**) *tr* frotar; **to rub elbows with** rozarse mucho con; **to rub out** borrar; (slang) asesinar || *intr* frotar; **to rub off** quitarse frotando; borrarse
rubber [ˈrʌbər] *s* caucho, goma; goma de borrar; chanclo, zapato de goma; (*in bridge*) robre *m* || *intr* (slang) estirar el cuello o volver la cabeza para ver
rubber band *s* liga de goma
rubber plant *s* árbol *m* del caucho
rubber plantation *s* cauchal *m*
rubber stamp *s* cajetín *m*, sello de goma; (*with a person's signature*) estampilla; (coll) persona que aprueba sin reflexionar
rub'ber-stamp' *tr* estampar con un sello de goma; (*with a person's signature*) estampillar; (coll) aprobar sin reflexionar
rubbish [ˈrʌbɪʃ] *s* basura, desecho, desperdicios; (coll) disparate *m*, tontería
rubble [ˈrʌbəl] *s* (*broken stone*) ripio; (*masonry*) mampostería
rub'down' *s* masaje *m*, fricción
rube [rub] *s* (slang) isidro, rústico
ruble [ˈrubəl] *s* rublo
ru•by [ˈrubi] *s* (*pl* **-bies**) rubí *m*
rudder [ˈrʌdər] *s* timón *m*, gobernalle *m*
rud•dy [ˈrʌdi] *adj* (*comp* **-dier;** *super* **-diest**) coloradote, rubicundo;
rude [rud] *adj* rudo; desacomodido (SAm)
rudiment [ˈrudɪmənt] *s* rudimento
rudeness [ˈrudnɪs] *s* malcriadez *f*, malacrianza
rue [ru] *tr* lamentar, arrepentirse de
rueful [ˈrufəl] *adj* lamentable; triste
ruffian [ˈrʌfɪ•ən] *s* hombre grosero y brutal
ruffle [ˈrʌfəl] *s* arruga; (*of drum*) redoble *m;* (sew) volante *m* || *tr* arrugar; agitar, descomponer; enojar, molestar; confundir; redoblar (*el tambor*); (sew) fruncir un volante en, adornar o guarnecer con volante
rug [rʌg] *s* alfombra; alfombrilla; (*lap robe*) manta
rugged [ˈrʌgɪd] *adj* áspero, rugoso; recio, vigoroso; tempestuoso
ruin [ˈru•ɪn] *s* ruina || *tr* arruinar; estropear; echar a perder
rule [rul] *s* regla; autoridad, mando; regla de imprenta; (*reign*) reinado; (*of a court of law*) decisión, fallo; **as a rule** por regla general; **to be the rule** ser lo que se hace || *tr* gobernar, regir; dirigir, guiar; contener, reprimir; (*to mark with lines*) reglar; (law) decidir, determinar; **to rule out** excluir, rechazar || *intr* gobernar, regir; prevalecer; **to rule over** gobernar, regir
rule of law *s* régimen *m* de justicia

ruler [ˈrulər] *s* gobernante *mf;* soberano; (*for ruling lines*) regla
ruling [ˈrulɪŋ] *adj* gobernante, dirigente, imperante || *s* (*of a court or judge*) decisión, fallo; (*of paper*) rayado
rum [rʌm] *s* ron *m;* (*any alcoholic drink*) (U.S.A.) aguardiente *m*
Rumanian [ruˈmenɪ•ən] *adj & s* rumano
rumble [ˈrʌmbəl] *s* retumbo; (*of the intestines*) rugido; (slang) riña entre pandillas || *intr* retumbar; avanzar retumbando
ruminate [ˈrumɪ,net] *tr & intr* rumiar
rummage [ˈrʌmɪdʒ] *tr & intr* buscar revolviéndolo todo
rummage sale *s* venta de prendas usadas
rumor [ˈrumər] *s* rumor *m;* (coll) díceres *mpl;* bolado (CAm) || *tr* rumorear; **it is rumored that** se rumorea que
rump [rʌmp] *s* anca, nalga; (*cut of beef*) cuarto trasero
rumple [ˈrʌmpəl] *s* arruga || *tr* arrugar, ajar, chafar || *intr* arrugarse
rumpus [ˈrʌmpəs] *s* (coll) batahola, alboroto; **to raise a rumpus** (coll) armar la de San Quintín
run [rʌn] *s* carrera; clase *f,* tipo; arroyo; (*e.g., in a stocking*) carrera; (*on a bank by depositors*) asedio; (*of consecutive performances of a play*) serie *f;* (baseball & mus) carrera; **in the long run** a la larga; **on the run** a escape; en fuga desordenada; **the common run of people** el común de las gentes; **the general run of** la generalidad de; **to have a long run** permanecer en cartel durante mucho tiempo; **to have the run of** hallar el secreto de; tener libertad de ir y venir por || *v* (*pret* **ran** [ræn]; *pp* **run;** *ger* **running)** *tr* hacer funcionar; dirigir, manejar; trazar, tirar (*una línea*); exhibir (*un cine*); hacer (*mandados*); tener como candidato; burlar, violar (*un bloqueo*); tener (*calentura*); correr (*un caballo; un riesgo*); **to run down** cazar y matar; derribar; atropellar (*a un peatón*); (coll) denigrar, desacreditar; **to run in** rodar (*un nuevo coche*); **to run off** tocar (*una pieza de música*); tirar, imprimir; **to run up** (coll) aumentar (*gastos*) || *intr* correr; (*on wheels*) rodar; darse prisa; trepar (*la vid*); ir y venir (*un vapor*); supurar (*una llaga*); colar (*un líquido*); correrse (*un color o tinte*); presentar su candidatura; andar, funcionar, marchar; deshilarse (*las medias*); migrar (*los peces*); estar en fuerza; (*to be worded or written*) rezar; **to run across** dar con, tropezar con; **to run away** correr, huir; desbocarse (*un caballo*); **to run down** escurrir, gotear (*un líquido*); descargarse (*un acumulador*); distenderse (*el muelle de un reloj*); acabarse la cuerda, p.ej., **the watch ran down** se acabó la cuerda; **to run for** presentar su candidatura a; **to run in the family** venir de familia; **to run into** tropezar con; chocar con, topar con; **to run off the track** descarrilar (*un tren*); **to run out** salir; expirar, terminar; acabarse; agotarse; **to run out of** acabársele a uno, e.g., **I have run out of money** se me ha acabado el dinero; **to run over** atropellar (*a un peatón*); registrar a la ligera; pasar por encima; leer rápidamente; rebosar (*un líquido*); **to run through** disipar rápidamente (*una fortuna*); registrar a la ligera; estar difundido en
run'a•way' *adj* fugitivo; (*horse*) desbocado || *s* fugitivo; caballo desbocado; fuga
run'-down' *adj* desmedrado; desmantelado; inculto; (*clock spring*) sin cuerda, distendido; (*storage battery*) descargado
rung [rʌŋ] *s* (*of ladder or chair*) travesaño; (*of wheel*) radio, rayo
runner [ˈrʌnər] *s* corredor *m;* caballo de carreras; mensajero; (*of an ice skate*) cuchilla; (*of a sleigh*) patín *m;* (*long narrow rug*) pasacaminos *m;* (*strip of cloth for table top*) tapete *m;* (*in stockings*) carrera
run'ner-up' *s* (*pl* **runners-up**) subcampeón *m*
running [ˈrʌnɪŋ] *adj* corredor; (*expenses; water*) corriente; (*knot*) corredizo; (*sore*) supurante; (*writing*) cursivo; continuo; consecutivo; en marcha; (*start*) (*sport*) lanzado || *s* carrera, corrida; administración, dirección; marcha, funcionamiento; **to be in the running** tener esperanzas o posibilidades de ganar
running board *s* estribo
running head *s* titulillo
running start *s* (*sport*) salida lanzada
run'off e•lec'tion *s* votación de desempate
run-of-mine coal [ˈrʌnəvˈmaɪn] *s* carbón *m* tal como sale
run'-of-the-mill' *adj* (coll) ordinario; mediocre
run'proof' *adj* indesmallable
runt [rʌnt] *s* enano, hombrecillo; (*little child*) redrojo; animal achaparrado
run'way' *s* (*of a stream*) cauce *m;* senda trillada; (aer) pista de aterrizaje
rupture [ˈrʌptʃər] *s* ruptura; (*pathol*) quebradura; (*break in relations*) ruptura || *tr* romper; causar una hernia en || *intr* romperse; padecer hernia
rural free delivery [ˈrʊrəl] *s* distribución gratuita del correo en el campo
rural police *s* guardia civil
rural policeman *s* guardia civil *m*
ruse [ruz] *s* astucia, artimaña
rush [rʌʃ] *adj* urgente || *s* prisa grande, precipitación; agolpamiento de gente; (bot) junco; **in a rush** de prisa || *tr* empujar con violencia o prisa; despachar con prontitud; (slang) cortejar insistentemente (*a una mujer*); **to rush through** ejecutar de prisa, despachar rápidamente; expediar || *intr* lanzarse, precipitarse; venir de prisa, ir de prisa; actuar con prontitud; **to rush through** lanzarse a través de, lanzarse por entre
rush-bottomed chair [ˈrʌʃˈbɑtəmd] *s* silla de junco
rush hour *s* hora de aglomeración, horas de punta, horas de afluencia
rush'light' *s* mariposa, lamparilla

rush order *s* pedido urgente
russet ['rʌsɪt] *adj* canelo
Russia ['rʌʃə] *s* Rusia
Russian ['rʌʃən] *adj & s* ruso
rust [rʌst] *s* orín *m*, moho, herrumbre; (agr) roña, roya; color rojizo o anaranjado || *tr* aherrumbrar || *intr* aherrumbrarse
rustic ['rʌstɪk] *adj* rústico; sencillo, sin artificio || *s* rústico
rustle ['rʌsəl] *s* susurro, crujido || *tr* hacer susurrar, hacer crujir; hurtar (*ganado*) || *intr* susurrar, crujir; (slang) trabajar con ahinco
rusty ['rʌsti] *adj* (*comp* **-ier;** *super* **-iest)** herrumbroso, mohoso; rojizo; (*out of practice*) empolvado, desusado, remoto
rut [rʌt] *s* (*track, groove in road*) rodada, bache *m;* hábito arraigado; (*sexual excitement in animals*) celo; (*period of this excitement*) brama
ruthless ['ruθlɪs] *adj* despiadado, cruel
Ry. *abbr* **railway**
rye [raɪ] *s* centeno; whisky de centeno

S

S, s [ɛs] decimonona letra del alfabeto inglés
s *abbr* **second, shilling, singular**
Sabbath ['sæbəθ] *s* (*of Jews*) sábado; (*of Christians*) domínica; **to keep the Sabbath** observar el descanso dominical, guardar el domingo
saber ['sebər] *s* sable *m*
sable ['sebəl] *adj* negro || *s* marta cebellina; **sables** vestidos de luto
sabotage ['sæbə,tɑʒ] *s* sabotaje *m* || *tr & intr* sabotear
saccharin ['sækərɪn] *s* sacarina
sachet ['sæʃe] o [sæ'ʃe] *s* polvo oloroso; saquito de perfumes
sack [sæk] *s* saco; vino blanco generoso; (mil) saqueo, saco; (*of an employee*) (slang) despedida || *tr* ensacar; saquear, pillar; (slang) despedir (*a un empleado*)
sack'cloth' *s* harpillera; (*worn for penitence*) cilicio
sacrament ['sækrəmənt] *s* sacramento
sacred ['sekrəd] *adj* sagrado
sacrifice ['sækrɪ,faɪs] *s* sacrificio; **at a sacrifice** con pérdida || *tr* sacrificar; (*to sell at a loss*) malvender || *intr* sacrificar; sacrificarse
Sacrifice of the Mass *s* sacrificio del altar
sacrilege ['sækrɪlɪdʒ] *s* sacrilegio
sacrilegious [,sækrɪ'lɪdʒəs] o [,sækrɪ'lidʒəs] *adj* sacrílego
sacristan ['sækrɪstən] *s* sacristán *m*
sacris•ty ['sækrɪsti] *s* (*pl* **-ties**) sacristía
sad [sæd] *adj* (*comp* **sadder;** *super* **saddest)** triste; (slang) malo
sadden ['sædən] *tr* entristecer || *intr* entristecerse
saddle ['sædəl] *s* silla de montar; (*of a bicycle*) sillín *m* || *tr* ensillar; **to saddle with** echar a cuestas a
sad'dle•bags' *spl* alforjas
sad'dle•bow' [,bo] *s* arzón delantero
sad'dle•tree' *s* arzón *m*
sadist ['sædɪst] *s* sádico
sadistic ['sæ'dɪstɪk] *adj* sádico
sadness ['sædnɪs] *s* tristeza
safe [sef] *adj* seguro, ileso, salvo; cierto, digno de confianza; sin peligro, a salvo; **safe and sound** sano y salvo; **safe from** a salvo de || *s* caja fuerte, caja de caudales
safe'-con'duct *s* salvoconducto
safe'-crack'er *s* ladrón *m* de cajas de caudales
safe'-depos'it box *s* caja de seguridad
safe'guard' *s* salvaguardia, medida de seguridad || *tr* salvaguardar
safe•ty ['sefti] *adj* de seguridad || *s* (*pl* **-ties)** seguridad; **to parachute to safety** lanzarse en paracaídas; **to reach safety** ponerse a salvo, llegar a lugar seguro
safety belt *s* (aer, aut) correa de seguridad, cinturón *m* de seguridad; (naut) cinturón *m* salvavidas; **retractable safety belt** cinturón *m* retráctil
safety match *s* fósforo de seguridad
safety pin *s* imperdible *m*, alfiler *m* de seguridad, gacilla
safety rail *s* guardarriel *m*
safety razor *s* maquinilla de seguridad
safety valve *s* válvula de seguridad
safety zone *s* (*for pedestrians*) isla de peatones *or* de seguridad
saffron ['sæfrən] *adj* azafranado || *s* azafrán *m* || *tr* azafranar
sag [sæg] *s* comba, combadura; (*e.g., of a cable*) flecha || *v* (*pret & pp* **sagged;** *ger* **sagging)** *intr* combarse; (*to slacken, yield*) aflojar, ceder, doblegarse; bajar (*los precios*)
sagacious [sə'geʃəs] *adj* sagaz
sage ['sedʒ] *adj* sabio, cuerdo || *s* sabio; (bot) salvia; (bot) artemisa
sage'brush' *s* (bot) artemisa
Sagittarius [,sædʒə'tɛri•əs] *s* (astr) Sagitario
sail [sel] *s* vela; barco de vela; paseo en barco de vela; **to set sail** hacerse a la vela; **under full sail** a vela llena || *tr* gobernar (*un barco de vela*); navegar (*un mar, río, etc.*) || *intr* navegar, navegar a la vela; salir, salir de viaje; deslizarse, flotar, volar; **to sail into** (slang) atacar, regañar, reñir

sail'boat' *s* barco de vela, buque *m* de vela, velero
sail'cloth' *s* lona, paño
sailing ['selɪŋ] *adj* de salida ‖ *s* paseo en barco de vela; navegación; salida
sailing vessel *s* buque velero
sailor ['selər] *s* (*one who makes a living sailing*) marinero; (*an enlisted man in the navy*) marino
saint [sent] *adj & s* santo ‖ *tr* (coll) canonizar
saintliness ['sentlɪnɪs] *s* santidad
Saint Vitus's dance ['vaɪtəsəs] *s* (pathol) baile *m* de San Vito
sake [sek] *s* respeto, bien, amor *m;* **for his sake** por su bien; **for the sake of** por, por motivo de, por amor a; **for your own sake** por su propio bien
salaam [sə'lɑm] *s* zalema ‖ *tr* saludar con zalemas, hacer zalemas a
salable ['seləbəl] *adj* vendible
salad ['sæləd] *s* ensalada
salad bowl *s* ensaladera
salad oil *s* aceite *m* de comer
Salamis ['sæləmɪs] *s* Salamina
sala•ry ['sæləri] *s* (*pl* **-ries**) sueldo
sale [sel] *s* venta; (*auction*) almoneda, subasta; **for sale** de venta; se vende(n)
sales'clerk' *s* dependiente *mf* de tienda
sales exhibit *s* exhibición-venta, exposición-venta
sales'la'dy *s* (*pl* **-dies**) venedora
sales•man ['selzmən] *s* (*pl* **-men** [mən]) vendedor *m*, dependiente *m* de tienda
sales manager *s* gerente *m* de ventas
sales'man•ship' *s* arte de vender
sales'room' *s* salón *m* de ventas; salón de exhibición
sales talk *s* argumento para inducir a comprar
sales tax *s* impuesto sobre ventas
saliva [sə'laɪvə] *s* saliva
sallow ['sælo] *adj* cetrino
sal•ly ['sæli] *s* (*pl* **-lies**) paseo, viaje *m;* ímpetu *m*, arranque *m;* salida, ocurrencia; (mil) salida, surtida ‖ *v*, (*pret & pp* **-lied**) *intr* salir, hacer una salida; ir de paseo; **to sally forth** salir, avanzar con denuedo
salmon ['sæmən] *s* salmón *m*
salon [sæ'lɑn] *s* salón *m*
saloon [sə'lun] *s* cantina, taberna; (*on a steamer*) salón *m*
saloon'keep'er *s* tabernero
salt [sɔlt] *s* sal *f;* **to be not worth one's salt** no valer (*uno*) el pan que come ‖ *tr* salar; (*to preserve with salt*) salpresar; marinar (*el pescado*); salgar (*al ganado*); **to salt away** (slang) ahorrar, guardar para uso futuro
salt'cel'lar *s* salero
salted peanuts *spl* saladillos
saltine [sɔl'tin] *s* galletita salada
saltish ['sɔltɪʃ] *adj* salobre
salt lick *s* salero, lamedero
salt of the earth, the lo mejor del mundo
salt'pe'ter *s* (*potassium nitrate*) salitre *m;* (*sodium nitrate*) nitro de Chile
salt'sha'ker *s* salero
salt•y ['sɔlti] *adj* (*comp* **-ier;** *super* **-iest**) salado
salubrious [sə'lubrɪ•əs] *adj* salubre
salutation [,sæljə'teʃən] *s* salutación
salute [sə'lut] *s* saludo ‖ *tr* saludar
Salvadoran [,sælvə'dorən] o **Salvadorian** [,sælvə'dorɪ•ən] *adj & s* salvadoreño
salvage ['sælvɪdʒ] *s* salvamento ‖ *tr* salvar; recobrar
Salvation Army [sæl'veʃən] *s* ejército de Salvación
salve [sæv] o [sɑv] *s* ungüento ‖ *tr* curar con ungüento; preservar; aliviar
sal•vo ['sælvo] *s* (*pl* **-vos** o **-voes**) salva
Samaritan [sə'mærɪtən] *adj & s* samaritano
same [sem] *adj & pron indef* mismo; **it's all the same to me** lo mismo me da; **just the same** lo mismo, sin embargo; **same . . . as** mismo . . . que
samite ['sæmaɪt] o ['semaɪt] *s* jamete *m*
sample ['sæmpəl] *s* muestra ‖ *tr* catar, probar
sample copy *s* ejemplar *m* muestra
sancti•fy ['sæŋktɪ,faɪ] *v* (*pret & pp* **-fied**) *tr* santificar
sanctimonious [,sæŋktɪ'monɪ•əs] *adj* santurrón
sanction ['sæŋkʃən] *s* sanción ‖ *tr* sancionar
sanctuar•y ['sæŋktʃu,ɛri] *s* (*pl* **-ies**) santuario; asilo, refugio; **to take sanctuary** acogerse a sagrado
sand [sænd] *s* arena ‖ *tr* enarenar; lijar con papel de lija
sandal ['sændəl] *s* sandalia; cacle *m* (Mex)
san'dal•wood' *s* (bot) sándalo
sand'bag' *s* saco de arena
sand'bank' *s* banco de arena
sand bar *s* barra de arena
sand'blast' *s* chorro de arena ‖ *tr* limpiar con chorro de arena
sand'box' *s* (rr) arenero
sand dune *s* duna, médano
sand'glass' *s* reloj *m* de arena, ampolleta
sand' pa'per *s* papel *m* de lija ‖ *tr* lijar
sand'stone' *s* piedra arenisca
sand'storm' *s* tempestad de arena
sandwich ['sændwɪtʃ] *s* emparedado, sandwich *m* ‖ *tr* intercalar
sandwich man *s* hombre-anuncio
sand•y ['sændi] *adj* (*comp* **-ier;** *super* **-iest**) arenoso; (*hair*) rufo; cambiante, movible
sane [sen] *adj* cuerdo, sensato; (*principles*) sano
sanguinary ['sæŋgwɪn,ɛri] *adj* sanguinario
sanguine ['sæŋgwɪn] *adj* confiado, esperanzado; (*countenance*) coloradote
sanitary ['sænɪ,tɛri] *adj* sanitario
sanitary napkin *s* compresa higiénica
sanitation [,sænɪ'teʃən] *s* (*sanitary measures*) sanidad; (*drainage*) saneamiento
sanity ['sænɪti] *s* cordura, sensatez *f*
Santa Claus ['sæntə,klɔz] *s* el Papá Noel, San Nicolás
sap [sæp] *s* savia; (mil) zapa; (coll) necio, tonto ‖ *v* (*pret & pp* **sapped;** *ger* **sapping**) *tr* agotar, debilitar; zapar, socavar
sap'head' *s* (coll) cabeza de chorlito

sapling [ˈsæplɪŋ] *s* árbol *m* muy joven, pimpollo; jovenzuelo, mozuelo
sapphire [ˈsæfaɪr] *s* zafiro
saraband [ˈsærə,bænd] *s* zarabanda
Saracen [ˈsærəsən] *adj & s* sarraceno
Saragossa [,særəˈgɑsə] *s* Zaragoza
sarcasm [ˈsɑrkæzəm] *s* sarcasmo; escopetazo (SAm)
sarcastic [sɑrˈkæstɪk] *adj* sarcástico
sardine [sɑrˈdin] *s* sardina; **packed in like sardines** como sardinas en banasta o en lata
Sardinia [sɑrˈdɪnɪ•ə] *s* Cerdeña
Sardinian [sɑrˈdɪnɪ•ən] *adj & s* sardo
sarsaparilla [,sɑrsəpəˈrɪlə] *s* zarzaparrilla
sash [sæʃ] *s* banda, faja; (*of a window*) marco
sash window *s* ventana de guillotina
satchel [ˈsætʃəl] *s* maletín *m;* (*of a schoolboy*) cartapacio
sateen [sæˈtin] *s* satén *m*
satellite [ˈsætə,laɪt] *s* satélite *m*
satellite country *s* país *m* satélite
satiate [ˈseʃɪ,et] *adj* ahito, harto ‖ *tr* saciar
satin [ˈsætən] *s* raso
satinet [,sætɪˈnɛt] *s* rasete *m*
satiric(al) [səˈtɪrɪk(əl)] *adj* satírico
satirist [ˈsætɪrɪst] *s* satírico
satirize [ˈsætɪ,raɪz] *tr & intr* satirizar
satisfaction [,sætɪsˈfækʃən] *s* satisfacción
satisfactory [,sætɪsˈfæktəri] *adj* satisfactorio
satis•fy [ˈsætɪs,faɪ] *v* (*pret & pp* **-ified**) *tr & intr* satisfacer
saturate [ˈsætʃə,ret] *tr* saturar
Saturday [ˈsætərdi] *s* sábado
sauce [sɔs] *s* salsa; moje *f*, mojete *m;* (*of fruit*) compota; (*of chocolate*) crema; gracia, viveza; (coll) insolencia, lenguaje descomedido ‖ *tr* condimentar ‖ [sɔs] o [sæs] *tr* (coll) ser respondón con
sauce'pan' *s* cacerola
saucer [ˈsɔsər] *s* platillo
sau•cy [ˈsɔsi] *adj* (*comp* **-cier;** *super* **-ciest**) descarado, insolente; gracioso, vivo
sauerkraut [ˈsaur,kraut] *s* chucruta
saunter [ˈsɔntər] *s* paseo tranquilo y alegre ‖ *intr* dar un paseo tranquilo y alegre; pasear tranquila y alegremente
sausage [ˈsɔsɪdʒ] *s* salchicha, embutido; moronga (Mex)
savage [ˈsævidʒ] *adj & s* salvaje, *mf*
savant [ˈsævənt] *s* sabio, erudito
save [sev] *prep* salvo, excepto, menos ‖ *tr* salvar (*p.ej., una vida, un alma*); ahorrar (*dinero*); conservar, guardar, horrar; proteger, amparar; **God save the Queen!** ¡Dios guarde a la Reina!; **to save face** salvar las apariencias
saving [ˈseviŋ] *prep*, salvo, excepto; con el debido respeto a ‖ *adj* económico ‖ **savings** *spl* ahorros, economías
savings account *s* cuenta de ahorros
savings bank *s* banco de ahorros, caja de ahorros
savior [ˈsevjər] *s* salvador *m*
Saviour [ˈsevjər] *s* Salvador *m*
savor [ˈsevər] *s* sabor *m* ‖ *tr* saborear ‖ *intr* oler; **to savor of** oler a, saber a
savor•y [ˈsevəri] *adj* (*comp* **-ier;** *super* **-iest**) sabroso; picante; fragante ‖ *s* (*pl* **-ies**) (bot) ajedrea
saw [sɔ] *s* (*tool*) sierra; proverbio, refrán *m* ‖ *tr* aserrar, serrar
saw'buck' *s* cabrilla, caballete *m*
saw'dust' *s* aserrín *m*, serrín *m*
saw'horse' *s* cabrilla, caballete *m*
saw'mill' *s* aserradero, serrería; montero (Mex)
Saxon [ˈsæksən] *adj & s* sajón *m*
saxophone [ˈsæksə,fon] *s* saxofón *m*
say [se] *s* decir *m;* **to have one's say** decir su parecer ‖ *v* (*pret & pp* **said** [sɛd] *tr* decir; **I should say so!** ¡ya lo creo!; **it is said** se dice; **no sooner said than done** dicho y hecho; **that is to say** es decir, esto es; **to go without saying** caerse de su peso
saying [ˈse•ɪŋ] *s* dicho; proverbio, refrán *m;* **sayings** (*rumor*) díceres *mpl*
sc. *abbr* **scene, science, scruple, scilicet** (Lat) **namely**
scab [skæb] *s* costra; (*strikebreaker*) esquirol *m;* (slang) bribón *m*, golfo
scabbard [ˈskæbərd] *s* funda, vaina
scab•by [ˈskæbi] *adj* (*comp* **-bier;** *super* **-biest**) costroso; (coll) ruin, vil
scabrous [ˈskæbrəs] *adj* escabroso
scads [skædz] *spl* (slang) montones *mpl*
scaffold [ˈskæfəld] *s* andamio; (*to execute a criminal*) cadalso, patíbulo
scaffolding [ˈskæfəldɪŋ]*s* andamiaje *m*
scald [skɔld] *tr* escaldar
scale [skel] *s* escama; balanza; platillo de balanza; (*e.g., of a map*) escala; (mus) escala; **on a scale of** en escala de; **on a large scale** en grande escala; **scales** balanza ‖ *tr* escamer; descortezar, descostrar; escalar, subir, trepar; graduar ‖ *intr* descamarse; descortezarse, descostrarse; subir, trepar
scallop [ˈskɑləp] o [ˈskæləp] *s* concha de peregrino; (*shell or dish for serving fish*) concha; (*thin slice of meat*) escalope *m;* (*on edge of cloth*) festón ‖ *tr* cocer (*p.ej., ostras*) en su concha; festonear
scalp [skælp] *s* cuero cabelludo ‖ *tr* escalpar; comprar y revender (*billetes de teatro*) a precios extraoficiales
scalpel [ˈskælpəl] *s* escalpelo
scal•y [ˈskeli] *adj* (*comp* **-ier;** *super* **-iest**) escamoso
scamp [skæmp] *s* bribón *m*, golfo
scamper [ˈskæmpər] *intr* escaparse precipitadamente; **to scamper away** escaparse precipitadamente
scan [skæn] *v* (*pret & pp* **scanned;** *ger* **scanning**) *tr* escudriñar; escandir (*versos*); (telv) explorar; (coll) dar un vistazo a
scandal [ˈskændəl] *s* escándalo
scandalize [ˈskændə,laɪz] *tr* escandalizar
scandalous [ˈskændələs] *adj* escandaloso
Scandinavian [,skændɪˈnevɪ•ən] *adj & s* escandinavo
scanning [ˈskænɪŋ] *s* (telv) escansión, exploración
scansion [ˈskænʃən] *s* escansión

scant [skænt] *adj* escaso, insuficiente; solo, apenas suficiente || *tr* escatimar
scant•y ['skænti] *adj* (*comp* **-ier;** *super* **-iest**) escaso, insuficiente, poco suficiente; (*clothing*) ligero
scape'goat' *s* cabeza de turco, víctima propiciatoria
scar [skɑr] *s* cicatriz *f*, señal *f*, lacra || *v* (*pret & pp* **scarred;** *ger* **scarring**) *tr* señalar, marcar || *intr* cicatrizarse
scarce [skɛrs] *adj* escaso, raro; **to make oneself scarce** (coll) no dejarse ver
scarcely ['skɛrsli] *adv* apenas; probablemente no; ciertamente no; **scarcely ever** raramente
scarci•ty ['skɛrsɪti] *s* (*pl* **-ties**) escasez *f*, carestía
scare [skɛr] *s* susto, alarma || *tr* asustar, espantar; **to scare away** espantar, ahuyentar; **to scare up** (coll) juntar, recoger (*dinero*)
scare'crow' *s* espantajo, espantapájaros *m*
scarf [skɑrf] *s* (*pl* **scarfs** o **scarves** [skɑrvz]) bufanda; pañuelo para el cuello; (*cover for a table, bureau, etc.*) tapete *m;* corbata
scarf'pin' *s* alfiler *m* de corbata
scarlet ['skɑrlɪt] *adj* escarlata
scarlet fever *s* escarlata
scar•y ['skɛri] *adj* (*comp* **-ier;** *super* **-iest**) (*easily frightened*) (coll) asustadizo, espantadizo; (*causing fright*) (coll) espantoso
scathing ['skeðɪŋ] *adj* acerbo, duro
scatter ['skætər] *tr* esparcir, dispersar || *intr* esparcirse, dispersarse
scatterbrain ['skætər,bren] *s* (coll) farraquista *m*
scatterbrained *adj* (coll) alegre de cascos, casquivano
scattered showers *spl* lluvias aisladas
scenari•o [sɪ'nɛrɪ,o] o [sɪ'nɑrɪ,o] *s* (*pls* **-os**) guión *m*, escenario
scenarist [sɪ'nɛrɪst] o [sɪ'nɑrɪst] *s* guionista *mf*, escenarista *mf*
scene [sin] *s* (*view*) paisaje *m;* (*in literature, art, the theater, the movie*) escena; escándalo, demostración de pasión; **behind the scenes** entre bastidores; **to make a scene** causar escándalo
scener•y ['sinəri] *s* (*pl* **-ies**) paisaje *m;* (theat) decoraciones
scene shifter ['ʃɪftər] *s* tramoyista *m*
scenic ['sinɪk] o ['sɛnɪk] *adj* pintoresco; (*representing an action graphically*) gráfico; (*pertaining to the stage*) escénico
scent [sɛnt] *s* olor *m;* perfume *m;* (*sense of smell*) olfato; (*trail*) rastro, pista || *tr* oler; perfumar; olfatear, ventear; sospechar
scepter ['sɛptər] *s* cetro
sceptic ['skɛptɪk] *adj & s* escéptico
sceptical ['skɛptɪkəl] *adj* escéptico
schedule ['skɛdjʊl] *s* catálogo, cuadro, lista; plan *m*, programa *m;* (*of trains, planes, etc.*) horario || *tr* catalogar; proyectar; fijar la hora de
scheme [skim] *s* esquema *m;* plan *m*, proyecto; (*trick*) ardid *m*, treta; (*plot*) intriga, trama || *tr & intr* proyectar; tramar
schemer ['skimər] *s* proyectista *mf;* intrigante *mf*
scheming ['skimɪŋ] *adj* astuto, mañoso, intrigante || *s* intriga
schism ['sɪzəm] *s* cisma *m;* facción cismática
schist [ʃɪst] *s* esquisto
scholar ['skɑlər] *s* (*pupil*) alumno; (*scholarship holder*) becario; (*learned person*) sabio, erudito
scholarly ['skɑkərli] *adj* sabio, erudito
scholarship ['skɑlər,ʃɪp] *s* erudición; (*grant to study*) beca
scholarship holder *s* bequista *mf* (CAm, Cuba)
school [skul] *s* escuela; (*of a university*) facultad; (*of fish*) banco, cardume *m* || *tr* enseñar, instruir, disciplinar
school age *s* edad escolar
school attendance *s* escolaridad
school board *s* junta de instrucción pública
school'boy' *s* alumno de escuela
school day *s* día lectivo
school'girl' *s* alumna de escuela
school'house' *s* escuela
schooling ['skulɪŋ] *s* instrucción, enseñanza; experiencia
school'mate' *s* compañero de escuela
school'room' *s* aula, sala de clase
school'teach'er *s* maestro de escuela
school year *s* año lectivo
schooner ['skunər] *s* goleta
sci. *abbr* **science, scientific**
science ['saɪ•əns] *s* ciencia
science fiction *s* ciencia-ficción; novela científica
scientific [,saɪ•ən'tɪfɪk] *adj* científico
scientist ['saɪ•əntɪst] *s* científico, sabio, hombre *m* de ciencia
sci-fi ['saɪ'faɪ] *s* (slang) *abbr* **science fiction**
scil. *abbr* **scilicet** (Lat) **namely**
scimitar ['sɪmɪtər] *s* cimitarra
scintillate ['sɪntɪ,let] *intr* chispear, centellear
scion ['saɪ•ən] *s* vástago
Scipio ['sɪpɪ,o] *s* Escipión *m*
scissors ['sɪzərz] *ssg* o *spl* tijeras
scoff [skɔf] o [skɑf] *s* burla, mofa || *intr* burlarse, mofarse; **to scoff at** burlarse de, mofarse de
scold [skold] *s* regañón *m*, regañona || *tr & intr* regañar
scoop [skup] *s* (*instrument like a spoon*) cuchara, cucharón *m;* (*tool like a shovel*) pala; (*kitchen utensil*) paleta; (*for water*) achicador *m;* cucharada, palada, paletada; (*hollow made by a scoop*) hueco; (*big haul*) (coll) buena ganancia || *tr* sacar con cuchara, pala, paleta; achicar (*agua*); **to scoop out** ahuecar, vaciar
scoot [skut] *s* (coll) carrera precipitada || *intr* (coll) correr precipitadamente
scooter ['skutər] *s* monopatín *m*, patinete *m*
scope [skop] *s* alcance *m*, extensión; campo, espacio; **to give free scope to** dar campo libre a
scorch [skɔrtʃ] *s* chamusco || *tr* chamuscar; (*to dry, wither*) abrasar; criticar acerbamente || *intr* chamuscarse; abrasarse

scorching [ˈskɔrtʃɪŋ] *adj* abrasador; acerbo, duro, mordaz
score [skor] *s* (*in a game*) cuenta, tantos; (*in an examination*) nota; entalladura, muesca; línea, raya; (*twenty*) veintena; (mus) partitura; **on the score of** a título de; **to keep score** apuntar los tantos ‖ *tr* anotar (*los tantos*); ganar, tantear (*tantos*); rayar, señalar; regañar acerbamente; (mus) instrumentar ‖ *intr* ganar tantos; marcar los tantos
score board *s* marcador *m*, cuadro indicador
scorn [skɔrn] *s* desdén *m*, desprecio ‖ *tr & intr* desdeñar, despreciar; **to scorn to** no dignarse
scornful [ˈskɔrnfəl] *adj* desdeñoso
Scorpio [ˈskɔrpɪ•o] *s* (astr) Escorpión *m*
scorpion [ˈskɔrpɪ•ən] *s* alacrán *m*, escorpión *m*
Scot [skɑt] *s* escocés *m*
Scotch [skɑtʃ] *adj* escocés ‖ *s* (*dialect*) escocés *m;* whiskey *m* escocés; **the Scotch** los escoceses
Scotch•man [ˈskɑtʃmən] *s* (*pl* **-men** [mən]) escocés *m*
Scotland [ˈskɑtlənd] *s* Escocia
Scottish [ˈskɑtɪʃ] *adj* escocés ‖ *s* (*dialect*) escocés *m;* **the Scottish** los escoceses
scoundrel [ˈskaʊndrəl] *s* bribón *m*, pícaro
scour [skaʊr] *tr* fregar, estregar; recorrer, explorar detenidamente
scourge [skʌrdʒ] *s* azote *m* ‖ *tr* azotar
scout [skaʊt] *s* (mil) escucha, explorador *m;* niño explorador, niña exploradora; exploración, reconocimiento; (slang) individuo, sujeto, tipo ‖ *tr* explorar, reconocer (*un territorio*); observar (*al enemigo*); negarse a creer
scout'mas'ter *s* jefe *m* de tropa de niños exploradores
scowl [skaʊl] *s* ceño, semblante ceñudo ‖ *intr* mirar con ceño, poner mal gesto, poner mala cara
scramble [ˈskræmbəl] *s* arrebatiña ‖ *tr* arrebatar; recoger de prisa; revolver; hacer un revoltillo de (*huevos*); trepar ‖ *intr* luchar; trepar
scrambled eggs *spl* revoltillo, huevos revueltos
scrap [skræp] *s* fragmento, pedacito; desecho; chatarra; (slang) riña, contienda; **scraps** desperdicios, desechos; (*from the table*) sobras ‖ *v* (*pret & pp* **scrapped;** *ger* **scrapping**) *tr* desechar, descartar, echar a la basura; reducir a hierro viejo ‖ *intr* (slang) reñir, pelear
scrap'book' *s* álbum *m* de recortes, libro de recuerdos
scrape [skrep] *s* raspadura; (*place scratched*) raspaza; aprieto, enredo; ‖ *tr* raspar; (*to gather together with much difficulty*) arañar ‖ *intr* raspar; **to scrape along** ir tirando; **to scrape through** aprobar justo
scrap heap *s* montón *m* de cachivaches
scrap iron *s* chatarra, desecho de hierro
scrap paper *s* papel *m* para apuntes; papel de desecho
scratch [skrætʃ] *s* arañazo, rasguño; marca, raya, garrapato; (billiards) chiripa; (sport) línea de partida; **to start from scratch** empezar desde el principio, empezar de cero; **up to scratch** en buena condición ‖ *tr* arañar, rasguñar; borrar, rasgar (*lo escrito*); garrapatear; (sport) borrar (*a un corredor o caballo*) ‖ *intr* arañar, rasguñar; garrapatear; raspear (*una pluma*)
scratch pad *s* cuadernillo de apuntes
scratch paper *s* papel *m* para apuntes
scratch'-re•sist'ant *adj* resistente al rayado
scrawl [skrɔl] *s* garrapatos ‖ *tr & intr* garrapatear
scraw•ny [ˈskrɔni] *adj* (*comp* **-nier;** *super* **-niest**) huesudo, flaco
scream [skrim] *s* chillido, grito ‖ *tr* vociferar ‖ *intr* chillar, gritar; reírse a gritos
screech [skritʃ] *s* chillido ‖ *intr* chillar
screech owl *s* buharro; (*barn owl*) lechuza
screen [skrin] *s* mampara, biombo; (*in front of chimney*) pantalla; (*to keep flies out*) alambrera; (*to sift sand*) tamiz *m;* (mov, phys, telv) pantalla; **to put on the screen** llevar a la pantalla, llevar al celuloide ‖ *tr* defender, proteger; cubrir, ocultar; cinematografiar; rodar, proyectar (*una película*); adaptar para el cine; tamizar (*p.ej., arena*)
screen grid *s* (electron) rejilla blindada
screen'play' *s* cinedrama *m*
screw [skru] *s* tornillo; (*internal or female screw*) rosca, tuerca; (*of a boat*) hélice *f;* **to have a screw loose** (slang) tener flojos los tornillos; **to put the screws on** apretar los tornillos a ‖ *tr* atornillar; (*to twist, twist in*) enroscar; **to screw up** torcer (*el rostro*); ‖ *intr* atornillarse
screw'ball' *s* (slang) estrafalario, excéntrico
screw'driv'er *s* destornillador *m*, desatornillador *m*
screw eye *s* armella
screw jack *s* gato de tornillo
screw propeller *s* hélice *f*
scribal error [ˈskraɪbəl] *s* error *m* de escribiente
scribble [ˈskrɪbəl] *s* garrapatos ‖ *tr & intr* garrapatear
scribe [skraɪb] *s* (*teacher of Jewish law*) escriba *m;* escribiente *mf;* copista *mf;* autor *m*, escritor *m* ‖ *tr* arañar, rayar; trazar con punzón
scrimp [skrɪmp] *tr & intr* escatimar
script [skrɪpt] *s* escritura, letra cursiva; manuscrito, texto; (*of a play, movie, etc.*) palabras; (rad, telv) guión *m;* (typ) plumilla inglesa
scripture [ˈskrɪptʃər] *s* escrito sagrado ‖ **Scripture** *s* Escritura
script'writ'er *s* guionista *mf*, cinematurgo
scrofula [ˈskrɑfjələ] *s* escrófula
scroll [skrol] *s* rollo de papel, rollo de pergamino; (archit) voluta
scroll'work' *s* obra de volutas, adornos de voluta
scrub [skrʌb] *s* chaparral *m*, monte bajo; animal achaparrado; persona de poca monta; (*act of scrubbing*) fregado; (sport)

jugador *m* no oficial || *v* (*pret & pp* **scrubbed;** *ger* **scrubbing**) *tr* fregar, restregar

scrub oak *s* chaparro

scrub woman *s* fregona

scruff [skrʌf] *s* nuca; piel *f* que cubre la nuca; capa, superficie *f;* espuma

scruple [ˈskrupəl] *s* escrúpulo

scrupulous [ˈskrupjələs] *adj* escrupuloso

scrutinize [ˈskrutɪˌnaɪz] *tr* escudriñar, escrutar

scruti•ny [ˈskrutɪni] *s* (*pl* **-nies**) escudriñamiento, escrutinio

scubadiver [ˈskubəˌdɪvər] *s* submarinista *mf*

scuff [skʌf] *s* rascadura, desgaste *m* || *tr* rascar, desgastar

scuffle [ˈskʌfəl] *s* lucha, sarracina || *intr* forcejear, luchar

scull [skʌl] *s* espadilla|| *tr* impulsar con espadilla || *intr* remar con espadilla

sculler•y [ˈskʌləri] *s* (*pl* **-ies**) trascocina

scullery maid *s* fregona

scullion [ˈskʌljən] *s* pinche *m*

sculptor [ˈskʌlptər] *s* escultor *m*

sculptress [ˈskʌlptrɪs] *s* escultora

sculpture [ˈskʌlptʃər] *s* escultura || *tr & intr* esculpir

scum [skʌm] *s* espuma, nata; (*on metals*) escoria; (fig) escoria, canalla, gente baja; palomilla || *v* (*pret & pp* **scummed;** *ger* **scumming**) *tr & intr* espumar

scum•my [ˈskʌmi] *adj* (*comp* **-mier;** *super* **-miest**) espumoso; (fig) vil, ruin

scurf [skʌrf] *s* (*shed by the skin*) caspa; (*shed by any surface*) costra

scurrilous [ˈskʌrɪləs] *adj* chocarrero, grosero, insolente, difamatorio

scur•ry [ˈskʌri] *v* (*pret & pp* **-ried**) *intr* echar a correr, escabullirse; **to scurry around** menearse; **to scurry away** ir respailando

scur•vy [ˈskʌril] *adj* (*comp* **-vier;** *super* **-viest**) despreciable, ruin, vil || *s* escorbuto

scuttle [ˈskʌtəl] *s* (*bucket for coal*) cubo, balde *m;* (*trap door*) escotillón *m;* fuga, paso acelerado; (naut) escotilla || *tr* barrenar, dar barreno a || *intr* echar a correr

Scylla [ˈsɪlə] *s* Escila; **between Scylla and Charybdis** entre Escila y Caribdis

scythe [saɪð] *s* dalle *m,* guadaña

sea [si] *s* mar *m & f;* **at sea** en el mar; confuso, perplejo; **by the sea** a la orilla del mar; **to follow the sea** correr los mares, ser marinero; **to put to sea** hacerse a la mar

sea′board′ *adj* costanero, costero || *s* costa del mar, litoral *m*

sea breeze *s* brisa de mar

sea′coast′ *s* costa marítima, litoral *m*

sea dog *s* (*seal*) foca; (coll) marinero viejo, lobo de mar

seafarer [ˈsiˌfɛrər] *s* marinero; viajero por mar

sea′food′ *s* mariscos

seagoing [ˈsiˌgo•ɪŋ] *adj* de alta mar

sea gull *s* gaviota

seal [sil] *s* (*raised design; stamp; mark*) sello; (*sea animal*) foca || *tr* sellar; cerrar herméticamente; decidir irrevocablemente; (*with sealing wax*) lacrar

sea legs *spl* pie marino

sea level *s* nivel *m* del mar

sealing wax *s* lacre *m*

seal′skin′ *s* piel *f* de foca

seam [sim] *s* costura; (*edges left after making a seam*) metido; (*mark, line*) arruga; (*scar*) costurón *m;* grieta, juntura; (min) filón *m,* veta

sea•man [ˈsimən] *s* (*pl* **-men** [mən]) marinero; (nav) marino

sea mile *s* milla náutica

seamless [ˈsimlɪs] *adj* inconsútil, sin costura

seamstress [ˈsimstrɪs] *s* costurera; (*dressmaker's helper*) modistilla

seam•y [ˈsimi] *adj* (*comp* **-ier;** *super* **-iest**) lleno de costuras; tosco, burdo; vil, soez; miserable

séance [ˈse•ɑns] *s* sesión de espiritistas

sea′plane′ *s* hidroavión *m*, hidroplano

sea′port′ *s* puerto de mar

sea power *s* potencia naval

sear [sɪr] *adj* seco, marchito; gastado, raído || *s* chamusco, socarra || *tr* chamuscar, socarrar; quemar; marchitar; cauterizar

search [sʌrtʃ] *s* busca; pesquisa, indagación; (*frisking a person*) cacheo; (*police, soldiers*) peinado; **in search of** en busca de || *tr* averiguar, explorar; registrar || *intr* buscar; (*police, soldiers*) peinar; **to search for** buscar; **to search into** indagar, investigar

search′light′ *s* reflector *m*, proyector *m*

search warrant *s* auto de registro domiciliario, orden *f* de allanamiento

sea′scape′ *s* vista del mar; (*painting*) marina

sea shell *s* concha marina

sea′shore′ *s* costa, playa, ribera del mar

sea′sick′ *adj* mareado

sea′sick′ness *s* mareo

sea′side′ *s* orilla del mar, ribera del mar, playa

season [ˈsizən] *s* (*one of four parts of year*) estación; (*period of the year; period marked by certain activities*) temporada; (*opportune time; time of maturity, of ripening*) sazón *f;* **in season** en sazón; **in season and out of season** en tiempo y a destiempo; **out of season** fuera de sazón || *tr* condimentar, sazonar; curar (*la madera*); moderar, templar

seasonal [ˈsizənəl] *adj* estacional

seasoning [ˈsizənɪŋ] *s* aderezo, aliño, condimento; (*of wood*) cura; (fig) sal *f*, chiste *m*

season ticket *s* billete *m* de abono

seat [sit] *s* asiento; (*of trousers*) fondillos; morada; sitio, lugar *m;* (*e.g., of government*) sede *f;* (*in parliament*) escaño; (*e.g., of a war*) teatro; (*e.g., of learning*) centro; (*of a saddle*) batalla; (*of human body*) nalgas; (theat) localidad; **reclining seat** (*as in car*) asiento abatible; || *tr* sentar; tener asientos para; poner asiento a (*una silla*); echar fondillos a (*pantalones*); arraigar, establecer; **to be seated** estar sentado; **to seat oneself** sentarse

seat belt *s* cinturón *m* de asiento
seat cover *s* funda de asiento, cubreasiento
SEATO [ˈsito] *s* (acronym) la O.T.A.S.E.
sea wall *s* dique marítimo
sea'way' *s* ruta marítima; avance *m* de un buque por mar; vía de agua interior para buques de alta mar; mar gruesa
sea'weed' *s* alga marina; plantas marinas
sea wind *s* viento que sopla del mar
sea'wor'thy *adj* marinero, en condiciones de navegar
sec. *abbr* **secant, second, secondary, secretary, section, sector**
secede [sɪˈsid] *intr* separarse, retirarse
secession [sɪˈsɛʃən] *s* secesión
seclude [sɪˈklud] *tr* recluir
secluded [sɪˈkludɪd] *adj* aislado, apartado, solitario
seclusion [sɪˈkluʒən] *s* reclusión, soledad
second [ˈsɛkənd] *adj* segundo; **to be second to none** ser tan bueno como el que más, no tener segundo ‖ *adv* en segundo lugar ‖ *s* segundo; artículo de segunda calidad; (*in dates*) dos *m;* (*in a challenge*) padrino; (aut) segunda (velocidad); (mus) segunda ‖ *tr* secundar; apoyar (*una moción*)
secondar•y [ˈsɛkən,dɛri] *adj* secundario ‖ *s* (*pl* **-ies**) (elec) secundario
sec'ond-best' *adj* (el) mejor después del primero
sec'ond-class' *adj* de segunda clase
second hand *s* segundero
sec'ond-hand' *adj* de segunda mano, de ocasión
second-hand bookshop *s* librería de viejo
second lieutenant *s* alférez *m*, subteniente *m*
sec'ond•rate' *adj* de segundo orden; de calidad inferior
second sight *s* doble vista
second wind *s* nuevo aliento
secre•cy [ˈsikrəsi] *s* (*pl* **-cies**) secreto; **in secrecy** en secreto
secret [ˈsikrɪt] *adj & s* secreto; **in secret** en secreto
secretar•y [ˈsɛkrɪ,tɛri] *s* (*pl* **-ies**) secretario; (*desk*) secreter *m*, escritorio
secrete [sɪˈkrit] *tr* encubrir, esconder; (physiol) secretar
secretive [sɪˈkritɪv] *adj* callado, reservado
sect [sɛkt] *s* secta, comunión
sectarian [sɛkˈtɛrɪ•ən] *adj & s* sectario
section [ˈsɛkʃən] *s* sección; (*of a country*) región; (*of a city*) barrio; (*of a law*) artículo; (*department, bureau*) negociado; (rr) tramo
secular [ˈsɛkjələr] *adj* secular, seglar ‖ *s* clérigo secular
secularism [ˈsɛkjələ,rɪzəm] *s* laicismo
secure [sɪˈkjʊr] *adj* seguro ‖ *tr* asegurar; conseguir, obtener
securi•ty [sɪˈkjʊrɪti] *s* (*pl* **-ties**) seguridad; (*person*) segurador *m;* **securities** valores *mpl*, obligaciones, títulos
secy. o **sec'y.** *abbr* **secretary**
sedan [sɪˈdæn] *s* silla de manos; (aut) sedán *m*
sedate [sɪˈdet] *adj* sentado, sosegado
sedative [ˈsɛdətɪv] *adj & s* sedativo
sedentary [ˈsɛdən,tɛri] *adj* sedentario
sedge [sɛdʒ] *s* juncia
sediment [ˈsɛdɪmənt] *s* sedimento
sedition [sɪˈdɪʃən] *s* sedición
seditious [sɪˈdɪʃəs] *adj* sedicioso
seduce [sɪˈdjus] *tr* seducir
seducer [sɪˈdjusər] *s* seductor *m*
seduction [sɪˈdʌkʃən] *s* seducción
seductive [sɪˈdʌktɪv] *adj* seductivo
sedulous [ˈsɛdjələs] *adj* cuidadoso, diligente
see [si] *s* (eccl) sede *f* ‖ *v* (*pret* **saw** [sɔ]; *pp* **seen** [sin] *tr* ver; **to see off** ir a despedir; **to see through** llevar a cabo; ayudar en un trance difícil ‖ *intr* ver; **see here!** ¡mire Vd.!; **to see into** o **to see through** conocer el juego de
seed [sid] *s* semilla, simiente *f;* **to go to seed** dar semilla; echarse a perder ‖ *tr* sembrar; (*to remove the seeds from*) despepitar ‖ *intr* sembrar; dejar caer semillas
seed'bed' *s* semillero
seedling [ˈsidlɪŋ] *s* planta de semilla; árbol *m* de pie
seed•y [ˈsidi] *adj* (*comp* **-ier;** *super* **-iest**) lleno de granos; (coll) andrajoso, raído
seeing [ˈsi•ɪŋ] *adj* vidente ‖ *s* vista, visión ‖ *conj* visto que
Seeing Eye dog *s* perro-lazarillo
seek [sik] *v* (*pret & pp* **sought** [sɔt] *tr* buscar; recorrer buscando; dirigirse a ‖ *intr* buscar; **to seek after** tratar de obtener; **to seek to** esforzarse por
seem [sim] *intr* parecer
seemingly [ˈsimɪŋli] *adv* aparentemente, al parecer
seem•ly [ˈsimli] *adj* (*comp* **-lier;** *super* **-liest**) decente, decoroso, correcto; bien parecido
seep [sip] *intr* escurrirse, rezumarse
seer [sɪr] *s* profeta *m*, vidente *m*
see'saw' *s* balancín *m*, columpio de tabla; (*motion*) vaivén *m* ‖ *intr* columpiarse; alternar; vacilar
seethe [sið] *intr* hervir
segment [ˈsɛgmənt] *s* segmento
segregate [ˈsɛgrɪ,get] *tr* segregar
segregationist [,sɛgrɪˈgeʃənɪst] *s* segregacionista *mf*
Seine [sen] *s* Sena *m*
seismograph [ˈsaɪzmə,græf] *s* sismógrafo
seismology [saɪzˈmɑlədʒi] *s* sismología
seize [siz] *tr* agarrar, asir, coger; atar, prender, sujetar; apoderarse de; comprender; (law) embargar, secuestrar; aprovecharse de (*una oportunidad*)
seizure [ˈsiʒər] *s* prendimiento, prisión; captura, toma; (*of an illness*) ataque *m;* (law) embargo, secuestro
seldom [ˈsɛldəm] *adv* raramente, rara vez
select [sɪˈlɛkt] *adj* escogido, selecto ‖ *tr* seleccionar
selectee [sɪ,lɛkˈti] *s* (mil) quinto
selection [sɪˈlɛkʃən] *s* selección; trozo escogido; (*of goods for sale*) surtido
self [sɛlf] *adj* mismo ‖ *pron* sí mismo ‖ *s* (*pl* **selves** [sɛlvz]) uno mismo; ser *m;* yo; **all by one's self** sin ayuda de nadie

self'-abuse' *s* abuso de sí mismo; masturbación
self'-addressed' envelope *s* sobre *m* con el nombre y dirección del remitente
self'-cen'tered *adj* egocéntrico
self'-con'scious *adj* cohibido, apocado, tímido
self'-con•trol' *s* dominio de sí mismo; autodisciplina
self'-de•fense' *s* autodefensa; **in self-defense** en defensa propia
self'-de•ni'al *s* abnegación
self'-de•ter'mi•na'tion *s* autodeterminación
self'-dis'cipline *s* autodisciplina
self'-ed'u•cat'ed *adj* autodidacto
self'-em•ployed' *adj* que trabaja por su propia cuenta
self'-ev'i•dent *adj* patente, manifiesto
self'-ex•plan'a•tor'y *adj* que se explica por sí mismo
self'-glor'i•fi•ca'tion *s* egolatría
self'-gov'ernment *s* autogobierno, autonomía; dominio sobre sí mismo
self'-im•por'tant *adj* altivo, arrogante
self'-in•dul'gence *s* intemperancia, desenfreno
self'-in'terest *s* egoísmo, interés *m* personal
selfish ['sɛlfɪʃ] *adj* egoísta
selfishness ['sɛlfɪʃnɪs] *s* egoísmo
selfless ['sɛlflɪs] *adj* desinteresado
self'-liq'ui•dat'ing *adj* autoamortizable
self'-love' *s* amor propio, egoísmo
self'-made' man *s* hijo de sus propias obras
self'-por'trait *s* autorretrato
self'-pos•sessed' *adj* dueño de sí mismo
self'-pres'er•va'tion *s* propia conservación
self'-re•li'ant *adj* confiado en sí mismo
self'-re•spect'ing *adj* lleno de dignidad, decoroso
self'-right'eous *adj* santurrón
self'-sac'ri•fice' *s* sacrificio de sí mismo
self'-same' *adj* mismísimo
self'-sat'is•fied' *adj* pagado de sí mismo
self'-seal'ing *adj* autopegado
self'-seek'ing *adj* egoísta || *s* egoísmo
self'-ser'vice restaurant *s* restaurante *m* de libre servicio, restaurante de autoservicio
self'-start'er *s* arranque automático
self'-sup•port' *s* mantenimiento económico propio
self'-taught' *adj* autodidacto
self'-willed' *adj* obstinado, terco
self'-wind'ing clock *s* reloj *m* de cuerda automática, reloj de autocuerda
self'-wor'ship *s* egolatría
sell [sɛl] *v* (*pret & pp* **sold** [sold] *tr* vender; **to sell out** realizar, saldar; (*to betray*) vender || *intr* venderse, estar de venta; **to sell for** venderse a o en (*p.ej., cien pesetas*); **to sell off** bajar (*el mercado de valores*); **to sell out** venderlo todo, realizar
seller ['sɛlər] *s* vendedor *m*
sell'out' *s* (slang) realización, saldo; (slang) traición
Seltzer water ['sɛltsər] *s* agua de seltz
selvage ['sɛlvɪdʒ] *s* orillo, vendo
semantic [sɪ'mæntɪk] *adj* semántico || **semantics** *s* semántica
semaphore ['sɛmə,for] *s* semáforo; (rr) disco de señales
semblance ['sɛmbləns] *s* apariencia, imagen *f*, simulacro
semen ['simɛn] *s* semen *m*
semester [sɪ'mɛstər] *adj* semestral || *s* semestre *m*
semester hour *s* hora semestral
sem'ico'lon *s* punto y coma
sem'iconduc'tor *s* semiconductor *m*
sem'icon'scious *adj* semiconsciente
sem'ifi'nal *adj & s* (sport) semifinal *f*
sem'ilearn'ed *adj* semiculto
sem'imonth'ly *adj* quincenal || *s* (*pl* **-lies**) periódico quincenal
seminar ['sɛmɪ,nɑr] *s* seminario
seminar•y ['sɛmɪ,nɛri] *s* (*pl* **-ies**) seminario
sem'ipre'cious *adj* semiprecioso, fino
Semite ['sɛmaɪt] o ['simaɪt] *s* semita *mf*
Semitic [sɪ'mɪtɪk] *adj* semítico || *s* semita *mf;* (*language*) semita *m*
sem'itrail'er *s* semi-remolque *m*
sem'iweek'ly *adj* bisemanal || *s* (*pl* **-lies**) periódico bisemanal
sem'iyear'ly *adj* semestral
Sen. o **sen.** *abbr* **Senate, Senator, Senior**
senate ['sɛnɪt] *s* senado
senator ['sɛnətər] *s* senador *m*
senatorship ['sɛnətər,ʃɪp] *s* senaduría
send [sɛnd] *v* (*pret & pp* **sent** [sɛnt]) *tr* enviar, mandar; expedir, remitir; lanzar (*una bola, flecha, etc.*); **to send back** devolver, reenviar; **to send packing** despedir con cajas destempladas || *intr* (rad) transmitir; **to send for** enviar por, enviar a buscar
sender ['sɛndər] *s* remitente *mf;* (telg) transmisor *m*
send'-off' *s* (coll) despedida afectuosa
senile ['sinaɪl] o ['sinɪl] *adj* senil
senility [sɪ'nɪlɪti] *s* senilidad; (pathol) senilismo
senior ['sinjər] *adj* mayor, de mayor edad; viejo; del último año; padre, p.ej., **John Jones, Senior** Juan Jones, padre || *s* mayor *m;* socio más antiguo; alumno del último año
senior citizens *spl* gente *f* de edad
seniority [sin'jɔrɪti] *s* antigüedad; precedencia, prioridad
sensation [sɛn'seʃən] *s* sensación
sense [sɛns] *s* sentido; **to make sense out of** comprender, explicarse || *tr* intuir, sentir, sospechar; comprender
senseless ['sɛnslɪs] *adj* falto de sentido; desmayado; insensato, necio
sense of guilt *s* cargo de conciencia
sense of humor *s* sentido de humor
sense organ *s* órgano sensorio
sensibili•ty [,sɛnsɪ'bɪlɪti] *s* (*pl* **-ties**) sensibilidad; **sensibilities** sentimientos delicados
sensible ['sɛnsɪbəl] *adj* cuerdo, sensato; perceptible, sensible; equilibrado
sensitive ['sɛnsɪtɪv] *adj* sensible; (*of the senses*) sensorio, sensitivo

sensitize [ˈsɛnsɪ,taɪz] *tr* sensibilizar
sensory [ˈsɛnsəri] *adj* sensorio
sensual [ˈsɛnʃʊ•əl] *adj* sensual, voluptuoso
sensuous [ˈsɛnʃʊ•əs] *adj* sensual
sentence [ˈsɛntəns] *s* (gram) frase *f*, oración; (law) sentencia || *tr* sentenciar, condenar
sentiment [ˈsɛntɪmənt] *s* sentimiento
sentimentali•ty [,sɛntɪmənˈtælɪti] *s* (*pl* **-ties**) sentimentalismo
sentinel [ˈsɛntɪnəl] *s* centinela *m* or *f;* **to stand sentinel** estar de centinela, hacer centinela
sen•try [ˈsɛntri] *s* (*pl* **-tries**) centinela *m* or *f*
sentry box *s* garita de centinela
separate [ˈsɛpərɪt] *adj* separado; suelto || [ˈsɛpə,ret] *tr* separar || *intr* separarse
separation [,sɛpəˈreʃən] *s* separación
separation of powers *s* (pol) separación de poderes
Sephardic [sɪˈfɑrdɪk] *adj* sefardí, sefardita
Sephardim [sɪˈfɑrdɪm] *spl* sefardíes *mpl*
September [sɛpˈtɛmbər] *s* septiembre *m*
septet [sɛpˈtɛt] *s* septeto
septic [ˈsɛptɪk] *adj* séptico
sepulcher [ˈsɛpəlkər] *s* sepulcro
seq. *abbr* **sequentia** (Lat) **the following**
sequel [ˈsikwəl] *s* resultado, secuela; continuación
sequence [ˈsikwəns] *s* serie *f*, sucesión; (cards) secansa, escalera, runfla; (gram, mov & mus) secuencia
sequester [sɪˈkwɛstər] *tr* apartar, separar; (law) secuestrar
sequin [ˈsikwɪn] *s* lentejuela
ser•aph [ˈsɛrəf] *s* (*pl* **-aphs** o **-aphim** [əfɪm]) serafín *m*
Serb [sʌrb] *adj & s* servio
Serbia [ˈsʌrbɪ•ə] *s* Servia
Serbian [ˈsʌrbɪ•ən] *adj & s* servio
Serbo-Croatian [,sʌrbokroˈeʃən] *adj & s* servocroata *mf*
sere [sɪr] *adj* seco, marchito
serenade [,sɛrəˈned] *s* serenata || *tr* dar serenata a || *intr* dar serenatas
serene [sɪˈrin] *adj* sereno
serenity [sɪˈrɛnɪti] *s* serenidad
serf [sʌrf] *s* siervo de la gleba
serfdom [ˈsʌrfdəm] *s* servidumbre de la gleba
serge [sʌrdʒ] *s* sarga
sergeant [ˈsɑrdʒənt] *s* sargento
serˈgeant•at-armsˈ *s* (*pl* **sergeants-at-arms**) oficial *m* de orden
sergeant major *s* (*pl* **sergeant majors**) sargento mayor
serial [ˈsɪrɪ•əl] *adj* serial; publicado por entregas || *s* cuento o novela por entregas; (rad) serial *m*, serial radiado, emisión seriada
serially [ˈsɪrɪ•əli] *adv* en serie, por series; por entregas
serial number *s* número de serie
se•ries [ˈsɪriz] *s* (*pl* **-ries**) serie *f*
serious [ˈsɪrɪ•əs] *adj* (*e.g., person, face, matter*) serio; (*e.g., condition, illness*) grave
sermon [ˈsʌrmən] *s* sermón *m*
sermonize [ˈsʌrmə,naɪz] *tr & intr* sermonear
serpent [ˈsʌrpənt] *s* serpiente *f*
se•rum [ˈsɪrəm] *s* (*pl* **-rums** o **-ra** [rə]) suero
servant [ˈsʌrvənt] *s* criado, sirviente *m*
servant girl *s* criada, sirvienta
servant problem *s* crisis *f* del servicio doméstico
serve [sʌrv] *s* (*in tennis*) saque *m*, servicio || *tr* servir; (*to supply*) abastecer, proporcionar; cumplir (*una condena*); (*in tennis*) servir; **it serves me right** bien me lo merezco || *intr* servir; **to serve as** servir de
service [ˈsʌrvɪs] *s* servicio; **at your service** para servir a Vd.; **out of service** fuera de servicio; **the services** las fuerzas armadas || *tr* instalar; mantener, reparar
serviceable [ˈsʌrvɪsəbəl] *adj* útil; duradero; cómodo
serviceman [ˈsʌrvis,mæn] *s* (*pl* **-men** [,mən]) reparador *m*, mecánico; militar *m*
service record *s* hoja de servicios
service station *s* estación de servicio, taller *m* de reparaciones
service stripe *s* galón *m* de servicio
servile [ˈsʌrvɪl] *adj* servil
servitude [ˈsʌrvi,tjud] *s* servidumbre; trabajos forzados
sesame [ˈsɛsəmi] *s* sésamo; **open sesame** sésamo ábrete
session [ˈsɛʃən] *s* sesión; **to be in session** sesionar
set [sɛt] *adj* determinado, resuelto; inflexible, obstinado; fijo, firme; estudiado, meditado || *s* (*of books, chairs, etc.*) juego; (*of gears*) tren *m;* (*of horses*) pareja; (*of diamonds*) aderezo; (*of tennis*) partida; (*of dishes*) servicio; (*of kitchen utensils*) batería; clase *f*, grupo; equipo; porte *m*, postura; (*of a garment*) caída, ajuste *m;* (*of glue*) endurecimiento; (*of cement*) fraguado; (*of artificial teeth*) caja; (mov) plató *m;* (rad) aparato; (theat) decoración || *v* (*pret & pp* **set;** *ger* **setting**) *tr* asentar; colocar, poner; establecer, instalar; arreglar, preparar; adornar; apostar; poner (*un reloj*) en hora; (*in bridge*) reenvidar; poner, meter, pegar (*fuego*); fijar (*el precio*); engastar, montar (*una piedra preciosa*); encasar (*un hueso dislocado*); disponer (*los tipos*); triscar (*una sierra*); armar, colocar (*una trampa*); fijar (*el peinado*); poner (*la mesa*); dar (*un ejemplo*); **to set back** parar; poner obstáculos a; hacer retroceder; atrasar, retrasar (*el reloj*); **to set forth** exponer, dar a conocer; **to set one's heart on** tener la esperanza puesta en; **to set store by** dar mucha importancia a; **to set up shop** poner tienda; **to set up the drinks** (coll) convidar a beber || *intr* ponerse (*el Sol, la Luna, etc.*); cuajarse (*un líquido*); endurecerse (*la cola*); fraguar (*el cemento, el yeso*); empollar (*una gallina*); caer, sentar (*una prenda de vestir*); **to set about** ponerse a; **to set out** ponerse en camino; emprender un negocio, **to set out to** ponerse a; **to set to work** poner manos a la obra; **to set upon** acometer, atacar
setˈbackˈ *s* revés *m*, contrariedad
setˈscrewˈ *s* tornillo de presión

settee [sɛˈti] *s* sofá *m*, canapé *m*
setting [ˈsɛtɪŋ] *s* (*environment*) ambiente *m;* (*of a gem*) engaste *m*, montadura; (*of cement*) fraguado; (*e.g., of the sun*) puesta, ocaso; (theat) escena; (theat) puesta en escena, decoración
set'ting-up' exercises *spl* ejercicios sin aparatos, gimnasia sueca
settle [ˈsɛtəl] *tr* asentar, colocar; asegurar, fijar; componer, conciliar; calmar, moderar; matar (*el polvo*); casar; poblar, colonizar; ajustar, arreglar (*cuentas*) ‖ *intr* asentarse (*un líquido, un edificio*); establecerse; componerse; calmarse, moderarse; solidificarse; **to settle down to work** ponerse seriamente a trabajar; **to settle on** escoger; fijar (*p.ej., una fecha*)
settlement [ˈsɛtəlmənt] *s* establecimiento; colonia, caserío; decisión; (*of accounts*) arreglo, ajuste *m;* traspaso; casa de beneficencia
settler [ˈsɛtlər] *s* fundador *m;* poblador *m;* colono; árbitro, conciliador *m*
set'up' *s* porte *m*, postura; (*e.g., of the parts of a machine*) disposición; (coll) organización; (slang) invitación a beber
seven [ˈsɛvən] *adj & pron* siete ‖ *s* siete *m;* **seven o'clock** las siete
seven hundred *adj & pron* setecientos ‖ *s* setecientos *m*
seventeen [ˈsɛvənˈtin] *adj, pron & s* diecisiete *m*, diez y siete
seventeenth [ˈsɛvənˈtinθ] *adj & s* (*in a series*) decimoséptimo; (*part*) diecisieteavo ‖ *s* (*in dates*) diecisiete *m*
seventh [ˈsɛvənθ] *adj & s* séptimo ‖ *s* (*in dates*) siete *m*
seventieth [ˈsɛvəntɪ•ɪθ] *adj & s* (*in a series*) septuagésimo; (*part*) setentavo
seven•ty [ˈsɛvənti] *adj & pron* setenta ‖ *s* (*pl* **-ties**) setenta *m*
sever [ˈsɛvər] *tr* desunir, separar; romper (*relaciones*) ‖ *intr* desunirse, separarse
several [ˈsɛvərəl] *adj* diversos, varios; distintos, respectivos ‖ *spl* varios; algunos
severance pay [ˈsɛvərəns] *s* indemnización por despido
severe [sɪˈvɪr] *adj* severo; (*weather*) riguroso; recio, violento; (*look*) adusto; (*pain*) agudo; (*illness*) grave
sew [so] *v* (*pret* **sewed;** *pp* **sewed** o **sewn**) *tr & intr* coser
sewage [ˈsu•ɪdʒ] o [ˈsju•ɪdʒ] *s* agua de albañal, aguas cloacales
sew'age-dis•pos'al plant *s* estación depuradora
sewer [ˈsu•ər] o [ˈsju•ər] *s* albañal *m*, cloaca, alcantarilla ‖ *tr* alcantarillar
sewerage [ˈsu•ərɪdʒ] o [ˈsju•ərɪdʒ] *s* desagüe *m;* (*system*) alcantarillado; aguas de albañal
sewing basket [ˈso•ɪŋ] *s* cesta de costura
sewing machine *s* máquina de coser
sex [sɛks] *s* sexo; **the fair sex** el bello sexo; **the sterner sex** el sexo feo
sex appeal *s* atracción sexual; encanto femenino
sexism [ˈsɛksɪzəm] *s* sexismo
sexist [ˈsɛksɪst] *adj & s* sexista
sextant [ˈsɛkstənt] *s* sextante *m*
sextet [sɛksˈtɛt] *s* sexteto
sexton [ˈsɛkstən] *s* sacristán *m*
sexual [ˈsɛkʃu•əl] *adj* sexual
sex•y [ˈsɛksi] *adj* (*comp* **-ier;** *super* **-iest**) (slang) sicalíptico, erótico
shab•by [ˈʃæbi] *adj* (*comp* **-bier;** *super* **-biest**) gastado, raído, usado; andrajoso, desaseado; ruin, vil
shack [ʃæk] *s* casucha, choza
shackle [ˈʃækəl] *s* grillete *m;* (*to tie an animal*) maniota; (fig) impedimento, traba; **shackles** cadenas, esposas, grillos ‖ *tr* poner grilletes a; poner esposas a; encadenar; (fig) trabar
shad [ʃæd] *s* sábalo, alosa
shade [ʃed] *s* sombra; (*of a lamp*) pantalla; (*of a window*) cortina, estor *m*, visillo, cortina de resorte; (*for the eyes*) visera; (*hue; slight difference*) matiz *m;* **shades** (slang) gafas *fpl* de sol; **the shades** las tinieblas; (*of the dead*) las sombras ‖ *tr* sombrear; obscurecer; rebajar ligeramente (*el precio*)
shadow [ˈʃædo] *s* sombra ‖ *tr* sombrear; simbolizar; acechar, espiar (*a una persona*); **to shadow forth** representar vagamente, representar de un modo profético
shadowy [ˈʃædo•i] *adj* sombroso; ligero, vago; imaginario; simbólico
shad•y [ˈʃedi] *adj* (*comp* **-ier;** *super* **-iest**) sombrío, umbroso; (coll) sospechoso; (coll) de mala fama; (*story*) (coll) verde; **to keep shady** (slang) no dejarse ver
shaft [ʃæft] *s* dardo, flecha, saeta; (*of an arrow; of a feather*) astil *m;* (*of light*) rayo; (*of a wagon*) vara alcándara, limonera; (*of a mine; of an elevator*) pozo; (*of a column*) fuste *m*, caña; (*of a flag*) asta; (*of a motor*) árbol *m;* (*to make fun of someone*) dardo
shag•gy [ˈʃægi] *adj* (*comp* **-gier;** *super* **-giest**) hirsuto, peludo, veludo; lanudo; áspero
shake [ʃek] *s* sacudida; (coll) apretón *m* de manos; (slang) instante *m*, momento ‖ *v* (*pret* **shook** [ʃuk]; *pp* **shaken**) *tr* sacudir; agitar; apretar, estrechar (*la mano a uno*); inquietar, perturbar; (*to get rid of*) (slang) dar esquinazo a, zafarse de ‖ *intr* sacudirse; agitarse; temblar; inquietarse, perturbarse; (*from cold*) tiritar; **shake!** (coll) ¡choque Vd. esos cinco!, ¡vengan esos cinco!
shake'down' *s* (slang) exacción, concusión
shakedown cruise *s* viaje *m* de pruebas
shake'-up' *s* profunda conmoción; cambio de personal, reorganización completa
shak•y [ˈʃeki] *adj* (*comp* **-ier;** *super* **-iest**) trémulo, vacilante, movedizo; indigno de confianza
shall [ʃæl] *v* (*cond* **should** [ʃud]) *v aux* empléase para formar (1) el fut de ind, p.ej., **I shall do it** lo haré; (2) el fut perf de ind, p.ej., **I shall have done it** lo habré hecho; (3) el modo potencial, p.ej., **what shall I do?** ¿qué he de hacer?, ¿qué debo hacer?

shallow [ˈʃælo] *adj* bajo, poco profundo; (fig) frívolo, superficial

sham [ʃæm] *adj* falso, fingido; postizo || *s* fingimiento, falsificación, engaño; (*person*) (coll) farsante *mf;* || *v* (*pret & pp* **shammed;** *ger* **shamming**) *tr & intr* fingir

sham battle *s* simulacro de combate

shambles [ˈʃæmbəlz] *s* destrucción, ruina; (*confusion, mess*) lío, revoltijo

shame [ʃem] *s* vergüenza; deshonra; (*disgrace*) metedura; **shame on you!** ¡qué vergüenza!; **what a shame!** ¡qué lástima! || *tr* avergonzar; deshonrar

shameful [ˈʃemfəl] *adj* vergonzoso

shameless [ˈʃemlɪs] *adj* descarado, desvergonzado

shampoo [ʃæmˈpu] *s* champú *m* || *tr* lavar (*la cabeza*); lavar la cabeza a

shamrock [ˈʃæmrɑk] *s* trébol *m* irlandés

shanghai [ˈʃæŋhaɪ] o [ʃæŋˈhaɪ] *tr* embarcar emborrachando, embarcar narcotizando; llevarse con violencia, llevarse con engaño

shank [ʃæŋk] *s* (*of the leg*) caña, canilla; (*of an animal*) pierna; (*of a bird*) zanca; (*of an anchor*) caña; (*of the sole of a shoe*) enfranque *m;* astil *m*, caña, fuste *m;* extremidad, remate *m;* **to go** o **to ride on shank's mare** caminar en coche de San Francisco

shan•ty [ˈʃænti] *s* (*pl* **-ties**) chabola, choza

shape [ʃep] *s* forma; **in bad shape** (coll) arruinado; (coll) muy enfermo; **out of shape** deformado; descompuesto; (*twisted*) sobornado || *tr* formar, dar forma a; amoldar || *intr* formarse; **to shape up** tomar forma; desarrollarse bien

shapeless [ˈʃeplɪs] *adj* informe

shape•ly [ˈʃepli] *adj* (*comp* **-lier:** *super* **-liest**) bien formado, esbelto

share [ʃɛr] *s* parte *f*, porción; (*of stock in a company*) acción; **to go shares** ir a la parte || *tr* (*to enjoy jointly*) compartir; (*to apportion*) repartir || *intr* participar, tener parte

share'hold'er *s* accionista *mf*

shark [ʃɑrk] *s* tiburón *m;* (*swindler*) estafador *m;* (slang) experto, perito

sharp [ʃɑrp] *adj* afilado, agudo; anguloso; (*curve, slope, etc.*) fuerte, pronunciado; (*photograph*) nítido; (*hearing*) fino; (*step, gait*) rápido; atento, despierto; picante, mordaz; listo, vivo; (mus) sostenido; (slang) elegante; **sharp features** facciones bien marcadas || *adv* agudamente; en punto, p.ej., **at four o'clock sharp** a las cuatro en punto || *s* (mus) sostenido

sharpen [ˈʃɑrpən] *tr* aguzar; sacar punta a (*un lápiz*) || *intr* afilarse

sharper [ˈʃɑrpər] *s* fullero, jugador *m* de ventaja

sharp'shoot'er *s* tirador certero; (mil) tirador distinguido

shatter [ˈʃætər] *tr* hacer astillas, romper de un golpe; quebrantar (*la salud*); destruir, destrozar; agitar, perturbar || *intr* hacerse pedazos, romperse

shat'ter•proof' *adj* inastillable

shave [ʃev] *s* afeitado; rebanada delgada; **to have a close shave** (coll) escapar en una tabla || *tr* afeitar (*la cara*); raer, raspar; (*to graze; to cut close*) rozar; (*to slice thin*) rebanar; (carp) cepillar || *intr* afeitarse

shaving [ˈʃevɪŋ] *adj* de afeitar, para afeitar, p.ej., **shaving soap** jabón *m* de o para afeitar || *s* afeitado; **shavings** acepilladuras, virutas

shaving lotion *s* loción facial

shawl [ʃɔl] *s* chal *m*, mantón *m*

she [ʃi] *pron pers* (*pl* **they**) ella || *s* (*pl* **shes**) hembra

sheaf [ʃif] *s* (*pl* **sheaves** [ʃivz] gavilla; (*of paper*) atado

shear [ʃɪr] *s* hoja de la tijera; **shears** tijeras grandes); (*to cut metal*) cizallas || *v* (*pret* **sheared;** *pp* **sheared** o **shorn** [ʃorn]) *tr* esquilar, trasquilar (*las ovejas*); cizallar; quitar cortando; tundir (*paño*)

sheath [ʃiθ] *s* (**sheaths** [ʃiðz]) envoltura, estuche *m*, funda; (*for a sword*) funda, vaina

sheathe [ʃið] *tr* enfundar, envainar

shed [fɛd] *s* cobertizo; (*line from which water flows in two directions*) vertiente *m & f* || *v* (*pret & pp* **shed;** *ger* **shedding**) *tr* derramar, verter (*p.ej., sangre*); dar, echar, esparcir (*luz*); mudar (*la pluma, el pellejo*)

sheen [ʃin] *s* brillo, lustre *m;* (*of pressed cloth*) prensado

sheep [ʃip] *s* (*pl* **sheep**) carnero; (*female*) oveja; tonto; **to make sheep's eyes (at)** mirar con ojos de carnero degollado

sheep dog *s* perro ovejero, perro de pastor

sheep'fold' *s* aprisco, redil *m*

sheepish [ˈʃipɪʃ] *adj* avergonzado, corrido; tímido, tonto

sheep'skin' *s* (*undressed*) zalea; (*dressed*) badana; (coll) diploma *m*

sheer [ʃɪr] *adj* delgado, fino, ligero; casi transparente; escarpado; puro, sin mezcla; completo || *intr* desviarse

sheet [ʃit] *s* (e.g., for the bed) sábana; (*of paper*) hoja; (*of metal*) hoja, lámina; (*of water*) extensión; hoja impresa; periódico; (naut) escota

sheet lightning *s* fucilazo

sheet metal *s* metal laminado

sheet music *s* música en hojas sueltas

sheik [ʃik] *s* jeque *m;* (*great lover*) (slang) sultán *m*

shelf [ʃɛlf] *s* (*pl* **shelves** [ʃɛlvz]) estante *m*, anaquel *m;* bajío, banco de arena; **on the shelf** arrinconado, desechado, olvidado

shell [ʃɛl] *s* (*of an egg, nut, etc.*) cáscara; (*of a crustacean*) caparazón *m*, concha; (*of a vegetable*) vaina; (*of a cartridge*) cápsula; (*of a boiler*) cuerpo; armazón *f*, esqueleto; bomba, proyectil *m;* (*long, narrow racing boat*) (sport) yola || *tr* descascarar; desgranar, desvainar (*legumbres*); bombardear, cañonear; **to shell out** (coll) entregar (*dinero*)

shel•lac [ʃəˈlæk] *s* laca, goma laca || *v* (*pret & pp* **-lacked;** *ger* **-lacking**) *tr* barnizar con goma laca; (slang) azotar, zurrar; (slang) derrotar

shell'fish' *s* marisco, mariscos

shell hole *s* (mil) embudo

shell shock *s* neurosis *f* de guerra
shelter [ˈʃɛltər] *s* abrigo, asilo, amparo, refugio; **to take shelter** abrigarse, refugiarse || *tr* abrigar, amparar, proteger
shelve [ʃɛlv] *tr* poner sobre un estante; proveer de estantes; arrinconar, dejar a un lado; diferir indefinidamente
shepherd [ˈʃɛpərd] *s* pastor *m* || *tr* pastorear (*a las ovejas o los fieles*)
shepherd dog *s* perro ovejero, perro de pastor
shepherdess [ˈʃɛpərdɪs] *s* pastora
sherbet [ˈʃʌrbət] *s* sorbete *m*
shereef [ʃɛˈrif] *s* jerife *m*
sheriff [ˈʃɛrɪf] *s* alguacil *m* mayor
sher•ry [ˈʃɛri] *s* (*pl* **-ries**) jerez *m*, vino de Jerez
shield [ʃild] *s* escudo; (*for armpit*) sobaquera; (elec) blindaje *m* || *tr* amparar, defender, escudar; (elec) blindar
shift [ʃɪft] *s* cambio; (*order of work or other activity*) turno; (*group of workmen*) tanda; maña, subterfugio || *tr* cambiar; deshacerse de; echar (*la culpa*); (aut) cambiar de (*marcha*) || *intr* cambiar, cambiar de puesto; mañear; (naut) correrse (*el lastre*); (rr) maniobrar; **to shift for oneself** ayudarse, ingeniarse
shift key *s* tecla de cambio, palanca de mayúsculas
shiftless [ˈʃɪftlɪs] *adj* desidioso, perezoso
shiftlessness [ˈʃɪftlɪsnɪs] *s* galbana
shift•y [ˈʃɪfti] *adj* (*comp* **-ier;** *super* **-iest**) ingenioso, mañoso; evasivo, tramoyista; (*glance*) huyente
shilling [ˈʃɪlɪŋ] *s* chelín *m*
shimmer [ˈʃɪmər] *s* luz trémula || *intr* rielar
shin [ʃɪn] *s* espinilla || *v* (*pret & pp* **shinned;** *ger* **shinning**) *tr & intr* trepar
shin'bone' *s* espinilla
shine [ʃaɪn] *s* brillo, luz *f;* bruñido, lustre *m;* buen tiempo; (*on shoes*) (coll) lustre *m;* **to take a shine to** (slang) tomar simpatía a || *v* (*pret & pp* **shined**) *tr* pulir, lustrar; (coll) embolar, limpiar (*el calzado*) || *v* (*pret & pp* **shone** [ʃon]) *intr* brillar, lucir, resplandecer; hacer sol, hacer buen tiempo; (*to be distinguished, to stand out*) (fig) brillar, lucir
shingle [ˈʃɪŋgəl] *s* ripia, teja de madera; tejamaní *m* (Am); pelo a la garçonne; (coll) letrero de oficina; **shingles** (pathol) zona; **to hang out one's shingle** (coll) abrir una oficina; (coll) abrir un consultorio médico || *tr* cubrir con ripias; cortar (*el pelo*) a la garçonne
shining [ˈʃaɪnɪŋ] *adj* brillante, luciente
shin•y [ˈʃaɪni] *adj* (*comp* **-ier;** *super* **-iest**) brillante, lustroso; (*paper*) glaseado; (*from much wear*) brilloso
ship [ʃɪp] *s* nave *f*, buque *m*, barco, navío; (*steamer*) vapor *m;* aeronave *f* || *v* (*pret & pp* **shipped;** *ger* **shipping**) *tr* embarcar; enviar, remitir, remesar; armar (*los remos*); embarcar (*agua*) || *intr* embarcarse
ship'board' *s* bordo; **on shipboard** a bordo
ship'build'er *s* arquitecto naval, constructor *m* de buques
ship'build'ing *s* arquitectura naval, construcción de buques
ship'mate' *s* camarada *m* de a bordo
shipment [ˈʃɪpmənt] *s* embarque *m* (*por agua*); envío, expedición, remesa
shipper [ˈʃɪpər] *s* embarcador *m;* expedidor *m*, remitente *mf*
shipping memo [ˈʃɪpɪŋ] *s* nota de remisión
ship'shape' *adj & adv* en buen orden
ship'side' *adj & adv* al costado del buque || *s* zona de embarque y desembarque; muelle *m*
ship's papers *spl* documentación del buque
ship's time *s* hora local del buque
ship'wreck' *s* naufragio; barco náufrago || *tr* hacer naufragar || *intr* naufragar
ship'yard' *s* astillero, varadero
shirk [ʃʌrk] *tr* evitar (*el trabajo*); faltar a (*un deber*) || *intr* escurrir el hombro
shirred eggs [ʃʌrd] *spl* huevos al plato
shirt [ʃʌrt] *s* camisa; **to keep one's shirt on** (slang) quedarse sereno; **to lose one's shirt** (slang) perder hasta la camisa
shirt'band' *s* cuello de camisa
shirt front *s* pechera de camisa, cami solín *m*
shirt sleeve *s* manga de camisa; **in shirt sleeves** en mangas de camisa
shirt'tail' *s* faldón *m*, pañal *m*
shirt'waist' *s* blusa (*de mujer*)
shiver [ˈʃɪvər] *s* estremecimiento, tiritón *m* || *intr* estremecerse, tiritar
shoal [ʃol] *s* bajío, banco de arena
shock [ʃak] *s* (*sudden and violent blow or encounter*) choque *m;* (*sudden agitation of mind or emotions*) sobresalto; temblor *m* de tierra; (*of hair*) greña; (agr) tresnal *m;* (elec) sacudida; (med) choque *m;* (*profound depression*) (pathol) choque *m;* (coll) parálisis *f* || *tr* chocar; sobresaltar; dar una sacudida eléctrica a; chocar, escandalizar
shock absorber [æbˈsɔrbər] *s* amortiguador *m*
shocker [ˈʃakər] *s* (slang) novelucha; película horripilante
shocking [ˈʃakɪŋ] *adj* chocante, escandalizador
shock troops *spl* tropas de asalto
shod•dy [ˈʃadi] *adj* (*comp* **-dier;** *super* **-diest**) falso, de imitación
shoe [ʃu] *s* (*which goes above the ankle*) bota, botina; (*which does not go above the ankle*) zapato; (*of a tire*) cubierta; **to put on one's shoes** calzarse || *v* (*pret & pp* **shod** [ʃad]) *tr* calzar; herrar (*un caballo*)
shoe'black' *s* limpiabotas *m*
shoe'horn' *s* calzador *m*
shoe'lace' *s* cordón *m* de zapato, lazo de zapato
shoe'mak'er *s* zapatero; zapatero remendón
shoe mender [ˈmɛndər] *s* zapatero remendón
shoe polish *s* betún *m*, bola
shoe'shine' *s* brillo, lustre *m;* limpiabotas *m*
shoe store *s* zapatería

shoe'string' *s* cordón *m* de zapato, lazo de zapato; **on a shoestring** con muy poco dinero
shoe tree *s* horma
shoo [ʃu] *tr & intr* oxear
shoot [ʃut] *s* (*sprout, twig*) renuevo, vástago; conducto inclinado; (*for grain, sand, etc.*) tolva; tiro al blanco, cortamen *m* de tiradores; (*hunting party*) partida de caza ‖ *v* (*pret & pp* **shot** [ʃɑt]) *tr* tirar, disparar (*un arma*); herir o matar con arma; (*to execute with a discharge of rifles*) fusilar; fotografiar; (*to take a moving picture of*) rodar, filmar; echar (*los dados*); medir la altura de (*p.ej., el Sol*); **to shoot down** derribar (*un avión*); **to shoot up** (slang) destrozar echando balas a diestra y siniestra; (*drugs*) picarse, pincharse ‖ *intr* tirar; nacer, brotar; lanzarse, precipitarse, moverse rápidamente; punzar (*un dolor, una llaga*); **to shoot at** tirar a; (*to strive for*) (coll) poner el tiro en
shooting gallery *s* galería de tiro al blanco
shooting match *s* certamen *m* de tiro al blanco; (slang) conjunto, totalidad
shooting star *s* estrella fugaz, estrella filante
shoot'out' *s* balaceo, balacera (SAm)
shop [ʃɑp] *s* (*store*) tienda; (*workshop*) taller *m;* **to talk shop** hablar de su oficio, hablar del propio trabajo (*fuera de tiempo*) ‖ *v* (*pret & pp* **shopped;** *ger* **shopping**) *intr* ir de compras, ir de tiendas; **to go shopping** ir de compras, ir de tiendas; **to send shopping** mandar a la compra; **to shop around** ir de tienda en tienda buscando gangas
shop'girl' *s* muchacha de tienda
shop'keep'er *s* tendero, baratero
shoplifter ['ʃɑp,lɪftər] *s* mechera, ratero de tiendas
shopper ['ʃɑpər] *s* comprador *m*
shopping center *s* centro comercial (*grupo de establecimientos minoristas, con aparcamiento*)
shopping district *s* barrio comercial
shop'win'dow *s* escaparate *m* (de tienda); aparador *m* (Mex)
shop'work' *s* trabajo de taller
shop'worn' *adj* desgastado con el trajín de la tienda
shore [ʃor] *s* orilla, ribera; costa, playa; **shores** (poet) clima *m*, región ‖ *tr* acodalar, apuntalar
shore dinner *s* comida de pescado y mariscos
shore leave *s* (nav) permiso para ir a tierra
shore line *s* línea de la playa; línea de buques costeros
shore patrol *s* (nav) patrulla en tierra
short [ʃɔrt] *adj* (*in space, time, and quantity*) corto; (*in time*) breve; (*in stature*) bajo; (fig) corto, sucinto; (fig) brusco, seco; **in a short time** dentro de poco; **in short** en fin; **on short notice** con poco tiempo de aviso; **to be short of** estar escaso de; **short of breath** corto de resuello ‖ *adv* brevemente; bruscamente; (*without possessing the stock sold*) al descubierto, p.ej., **to sell short** vender al descubierto; **to run short of** acabársele a uno, p.ej., **I am running short of gasoline** se me acaba la gasolina; **to stop short** parar de repente ‖ *s* (elec) cortocircuito; (mov) cortometraje *m;* **shorts** calzones cortos, calzoncillos ‖ *tr* (elec) poner en cortocircuito ‖ *intr* (elec) ponerse en cortocircuito
shortage ['ʃɔrtɪdʒ] *s* carestía, escasez *f*, falta; déficit *m;* (*from pilfering*) substracción
short'cake' *s* torta de frutas; torta quebradiza
short'change' *tr* (coll) no devolver la vuelta debida a
short circuit *s* (elec) cortocircuito
short'cir'cuit *tr* (elec) cortocircuitar ‖ *intr* (elec) cortocircuitarse
short'com'ing *s* falta, defecto, desperfecto
short cut *s* atajo; (*method*) remediavagos *m*
shorten ['ʃɔrtən] *tr* acortar, abreviar ‖ *intr* acortarse, abreviarse
short'hand' *adj* taquigráfico ‖ *s* taquigrafía; **to take shorthand** taquigrafiar
short-lived ['ʃɔrt'laɪvd] o (coll) ['ʃɔrt'lɪvd] *adj* de breve vida, de breve duración
shortly ['ʃɔrtli] *adv* en breve, luego; descortésmente; **shortly after** poco tiempo después (de)
short'-range' *adj* de poco alcance
short sale *s* (coll) venta al descubierto
short-sighted ['ʃɔrt'saɪtɪd] *adj* miope; (fig) falto de perspicacia
short'stop' *s* (baseball) medio; guardabosque *m*, torpedero (Am)
short story *s* cuento
short-tempered ['ʃɔrt'tɛmpərd] *adj* de mal genio
short'-term' *adj* a corto plazo
shot [ʃɑt] *s* tiro, disparo; (*hit or wound made with a bullet*) balazo; (*distance*) alcance *m;* (*in certain games*) jugada, tirada, golpe *m;* (*of a rocket into space*) lanzamiento; conjetura, tentativa; fotografía, instantánea; (*small pellets of lead*) perdigones *mpl;* munición; (*marksman*) tiro; (*heavy metal ball*) (sport) pesa; (*hypodermic injection*) (slang) jeringazo; (*drink of liquor*) (slang) trago; **not by a long shot** ni con mucho, ni por pienso; **to start like a shot** salir disparado
shot'gun' *s* escopeta
shot'-put' *s* (sport) tiro de la pesa
should [ʃʊd] *v aux* empléase para formar (1) el pres de cond, *p.ej.*, **if I should wait for him, I should miss the train** si yo le esperase, perdería el tren; (2) el perf de cond, *p.ej.*, **if I had waited for him, I should have missed the train** si yo le hubiese esperado, habría, perdido el tren; y (3) el modo potencial, *p.ej.*, **he should go at once** debiera salir en seguida; **he should have gone at once** debiera haber salido en seguida
shoulder ['ʃoldər] *s* hombro; (*of slaughtered animal*) brazuelo; (*of a garment*) hombrera; **across the shoulder** en bandolera; **to put one's shoulders to the wheel** arrimar el hombro, echar el pecho al agua; **to turn a cold shoulder to** volver las espaldas

a || *tr* cargar sobre las espaldas; tomar sobre sí, hacerse responsable de; empujar con el hombro para abrirse paso
shoulder blade *s* escápula, omóplato
shoulder strap *s* (*of underwear*) presilla; (mil) charretera
shout [ʃaʊt] *s* grito, voz *f* || *tr* gritar, vocear; **to shout down** hacer callar a gritos || *intr* gritar, dar voces
shove [ʃʌv] *s* empujón *m* || *tr* empujar || *intr* dar empujones, avanzar a empujones; **to shove off** alejarse de la costa; (slang) ponerse en marcha, salir
shov•el [ˈʃʌvəl] *s* pala || *v* (*pret & pp* **-eled** o **-elled;** *ger* **-eling** o **-elling**) *tr* traspalar; espalar (*p.ej., la nieve*) || *intr* trabajar con pala
show [ʃo] *s* exhibición, exposición, muestra; espectáculo; (*in the theater*) función; (*each performance of a play or movie*) sesión; demostración, prueba; indicación, señal *f*, signo; apariencia; (*e.g., of confidence*) alarde *m;* (coll) ocasión, oportunidad; ostentación; espectáculo ridículo, hazmerreír *m;* **to make a show of** hacer gala de; **to steal the show from** robar la obra a (*otro actor*) || *tr* mostrar, enseñar; demostrar, probar; poner, proyectar (*un film*); (*e.g., to the door*) acompañar; **to show up** (coll) desenmascarar || *intr* mostrarse, aparecer, asomar; salir (*p.ej., las enaguas*); **to show off** fachendear; **to show through** clarearse, transparentarse; **to show up** (coll) presentarse, dejarse ver
show bill *s* cartel *m*
show business *s* comercio de los espectáculos
show'case' *s* vitrina (de exposición)
show'down' *s* cartas boca arriba; (coll) revelación forzosa, arreglo terminante
shower [ˈʃaʊ•ər] *s* (*sudden fall of rain*) aguacero, chaparrón *m;* (*shower bath*) ducha; (*e.g., of bullets*) rociada; despedida de soltera || *tr* regar; **to shower with** colmar de || *intr* llover
shower bath *s* ducha, baño de ducha
show girl *s* (theat) corista *f*, conjuntista *f*
show•man [ˈʃomən] *s* (*pl* **-men** [mən]) empresario de teatro, empresario de circo
show'-off' *s* (coll) pinturero
show'piece' *s* objeto de arte sobresaliente
show'place' *s* sitio o edificio que se exhibe por su belleza o lujo
show'room' *s* sala de muestras, sala de exhibición
show window *s* escaparate *m* (de tienda); aparador *m* (Mex)
show•y [ˈʃo•i] *adj* (*comp* **-ier;** *super* **-iest**) aparatoso, cursi, ostentoso
shrapnel [ˈʃræpnəl] *s* granada de metralla
shred [ʃrɛd] *s* jirón *m*, tira, triza; fragmento, pizca; **to tear to shreds** hacer trizas || *v* (*pret & pp* **shredded** o **shred;** *ger* **shredding**) *tr* desmenuzar, hacer trizas; deshilar (*carne*)
shrew [ʃru] *s* (*nagging woman*) arpía, fierecilla; (*animal*) musaraña
shrewd [ʃrud] *adj* astuto; despierto; listo
shriek [ʃrik] *s* chillido, grito agudo; risotada chillona || *intr* chillar
shrill [ʃrɪl] *adj* agudo, chillón
shrimp [ʃrɪmp] *s* camarón *m;* (*little insignificant person*) renacuajo
shrine [ʃraɪn] *s* relicario; sepulcro de santo; lugar sagrado
shrink [ʃrɪŋk] *v* (*pret* **shrank** [ʃræŋk] o **shrunk** [ʃrʌŋk]; *pp* **shrunk** o **shrunken**) *tr* contraer, encoger || *intr* contraerse, encogerse; moverse hacia atrás; rehuirse, retirarse
shrinkage [ˈʃrɪŋkɪdʒ] *s* contracción, encogimiento; disminución, reducción; merma, pérdida
shriv•el [ˈʃrɪvəl] *v* (*pret & pp* **-eled** o **-elled;** *ger* **-eling** o **-elling**) *tr* arrugar, marchitar, fruncir || *intr* arrugarse, marchitarse, fruncirse; **to shrivel up** avellanarse
shroud [ʃraʊd] *s* mortaja, sudario; cubierta, velo || *tr* amortajar; cubrir, velar
Shrove Tuesday [ʃrov] *s* martes *m* de carnaval
shrub [ʃrʌb] *s* arbusto
shrubber•y [ˈʃrʌbəri] *s* (*pl* **-ies**) arbustos; plantío de arbustos
shrug [ʃrʌg] *s* encogimiento de hombros || *v* (*pret & pp* **shrugged;** *ger* **shrugging**) *tr* contraer; **to shrug one's shoulders** encogerse de hombros || *intr* encogerse de hombros
shudder [ˈʃʌdər] *s* estremecimiento || *intr* estremecerse
shuffle [ˈʃʌfəl] *s* (*of cards*) barajadura; turno de barajar; (*of feet*) arrastramiento; evasiva; recomposición || *tr* barajar (*naipes*); arrastrar (*los pies*); mezclar, revolver || *intr* barajar; caminar arrastrando los pies; bailar arrastrando los pies; moverse rápidamente de un lado a otro; **to shuffle along** ir arrastrando los pies; ir tirando; **to shuffle off** irse arrastrando los pies
shuf'fle•board' *s* juego de tejo
shun [ʃʌn] *v* (*pret & pp* **shunned;** *ger* **shunning**) *tr* esquivar, evitar, rehuir
shunt [ʃʌnt] *tr* apartar, desviar; (elec) poner en derivación; (rr) desviar
shut [ʃʌt] *adj* cerrado || *v* (*pret & pp* **shut;** *ger* **shutting**) *tr* cerrar; **to shut in** encerrar; **to shut off** cortar (*electricidad, gas, etc.*); **to shut up** cerrar bien; aprisionar; (coll) hacer callar || *intr* cerrarse; **to shut up** (coll) callarse la boca
shut'down' *s* cierre *m*, paro
shutter [ˈʃʌtər] *s* celosía, persiana; (*outside a window*) contraventana; (*outside a show window*) cierre metálico; (phot) obturador *m*
shuttle [ˈʃʌtəl] *s* (*used in sewing*) lanzadera || *intr* hacer viajes cortos de ida y vuelta
shuttle train *s* tren *m* lanzadera
shy [ʃaɪ] *adj* (*comp* **shyer** o **shier;** *super* **shyest** o **shiest**) arisco, recatado, tímido; (*fearful*) asustadizo; escaso, pobre; **I am shy a dollar** me falta un dólar || *v* (*pret & pp* **shied**) *intr* esquivarse, hacerse a un

lado; espantarse, respingar; **to shy away** alejarse asustado
shyster [ˈʃaɪstər] *s* (coll) abogado trampista
Sia•mese [ˌsaɪ•əˈmiz] *adj* siamés ‖ *s* (*pl* **-mese**) siamés *m*
Siamese twins *spl* hermanos siameses
Siberian [saɪˈbɪrɪ•ən] *adj & s* siberiano
sibilant [ˈsɪbɪlənt] *adj & s* sibilante *f*
sibling [ˈsɪblɪŋ] *s* hermano o hermana
sibyl [ˈsɪbɪl] *s* sibila
Sicilian [sɪˈsɪljən] *adj & s* siciliano
Sicily [ˈsɪsɪli] *s* Sicilia
sick [sɪk] *adj* enfermo, malo; nauseado; (coll) mórbido, perverso; **sick and tired of** (coll) harto y cansado de; **sick at heart** afligido de corazón; **to be sick at one's stomach** tener náuseas; **to take sick** caer enfermo ‖ *tr* azuzar (*a un perro*)
sick′bed′ *s* lecho de enfermo
sicken [ˈsɪkən] *tr & intr* enfermar
sickening [ˈsɪkənɪŋ] *adj* repelente, repugnante, nauseabundo
sick headache *s* jaqueca con náuseas
sickle [ˈsɪkəl] *s* hoz *f*
sick leave *s* licencia por enfermedad
sick•ly [ˈsɪkli] *adj* (*comp* **-lier;** *super* **-liest**) enfermizo
sickness [ˈsɪknɪs] *s* enfermedad; náusea
side [saɪd] *adj* lateral ‖ *s* lado; (*of a solid; of a phonograph record*) cara; (*of a hill*) falda; (*of human body, of a ship*) costado; facción, partido ‖ *intr* tomar partido; **to side with** tomar el partido de
side arms *spl* armas de cinto
side′board′ *s* aparador *m*
side′burns′ *spl* patillas
side dish *s* plato de entrada
side door *s* puerta lateral; puerta excusada
side effect *s* efecto secundario perjudicial (*de ciertos medicamentos*)
side glance *s* mirada de soslayo
side issue *s* cuestión secundaria
side′kick′ *s* (slang) compañero regular
side line *s* negocio accesorio; **on the side lines** sin tomar parte
sidereal [saɪˈdɪrɪ•əl] *adj* sidéreo
side′sad′dle *adv* a asentadillas, a mujeriegas
side show *s* función secundaria, espectáculo de atracciones
side′split′ting *adj* desternillante
side′track′ *s* apartadero, desviadero, vía muerta ‖ *tr* desviar (*un tren*); echar a un lado
side view *s* perfil *m*, vista de lado
side′walk′ *s* acera; banqueta (Guat, Mex); vereda (Arg, Cuba, Peru)
sidewalk café *s* terraza, café *m* en la acera
sideward [ˈsaɪdwərd] *adj* oblicuo, sesgado ‖ *adv* de lado, hacia un lado
side′ways′ *adj* oblicuo, sesgado ‖ *adv* de lado, hacia un lado; a través
side whiskers *spl* patillas
side′wise′ *s* oblicuo, sesgado ‖ *adv* de lado, hacia un lado; a través
siding [ˈsaɪdɪŋ] *s* (rr) apartadero, desviadero, vía muerta
sidle [ˈsaɪdəl] *intr* ir de lado; **to sidle up to** acercarse de lado a (*una persona*) para no ser visto
siege [sidʒ] *s* sitio, cerco; **to lay siege to** poner sitio o cerco a; (fig) asediar (*p.ej., el corazón de una mujer*)
sieve [sɪv] *s* cedazo, tamiz *m* ‖ *tr* cerner, tamizar
sift [sɪft] *tr* cerner, cribar; escudriñar, examinar; (*to screen, separate*) entresacar; (*to scatter with or as with a sieve*) empolvar
sigh [saɪ] *s* suspiro; **to breathe a sigh of relief** respirar ‖ *tr* decir con suspiros ‖ *intr* suspirar; **to sigh for** suspirar por
sight [saɪt] *s* vista; cosa digna de verse; (*of a firearm, telescope, etc.*) mira; (coll) gran cantidad, montón *m;* (coll) horror *m*, atrocidad; **at first sight** a primera vista; **at sight** a primera vista; (*translation*) a libro abierto; (com) a la vista; **out of sight** fuera del alcance de la vista; (*prices*) por las nubes; **to catch sight of** alcanzar a ver; **to know by sight** conocer de vista; **to not be able to stand the sight of** no poder ver ni en pintura; **to see the sights** visitar los puntos de interés ‖ *tr* avistar, alcanzar con la vista ‖ *intr* apuntar con una mira; (arti & surv) visar
sight draft *s* (com) giro a la vista, letra a la vista
sightless [ˈsaɪtlɪs] *adj* ciego
sight′-read′ *v* (*pret & pp* **-read** [ˌrɛd]) *tr* leer a libro abierto; (mus) ejecutar a la primera lectura ‖ *intr* leer a libro abierto; (mus) repentizar
sight reader *s* lector *m* a libro abierto; (mus) repentista *mf*
sight′see′ing *s* turismo, visita de puntos de interés; **to go sightseeing** ir a ver los puntos de interés
sightseer [ˈsaɪtˌsi•ər] *s* turista *mf*, excursionista *mf*
sign [saɪn] *s* signo; señal *f*, marca; huella, vestigio; letrero, muestra; **to show signs of** dar muestras de, tener trazas de; **to make the sign of the cross** hacerse la señal de la cruz ‖ *tr* firmar; contratar; ceder, traspasar ‖ *intr* firmar; usar el alfabeto de los sordomudos; **to sign off** (rad) terminar la transmisión; **to sign up** (coll) firmar el contrato
sig•nal [ˈsɪgnəl] *adj* señalado, notable ‖ *s* señal *f* ‖ *v* (*pret & pp* **-naled** o **-nalled;** *ger* **-naling** o **-nalling**) *tr* señalar ‖ *intr* hacer señales
signal tower *s* (rr) garita de señales
signato•ry [ˈsɪgnɪˌtori] *s* (*pl* **-ries**) firmante *mf*
signature [ˈsɪgnətʃər] *s* firma; (mus & typ) signatura
sign′board′ *s* cartelón *m*, letrero
signer [ˈsaɪnər] *s* firmante *mf*
signet ring [ˈsɪgnɪt] *s* anillo sigilar, sortija de sello
significance [sɪgˈnɪfəkəns] *s* significado, significación; relevancia
signi•fy [ˈsɪgnɪˌfaɪ] *v* (*pret & pp* **-fied**) *tr* significar
sign′post′ *s* hito, poste *m* de guía

silence [ˈsaɪləns] *s* silencio || *tr* acallar; (mil) apagar el fuego de; (mil) apagar (*el fuego del enemigo*)
silent [ˈsaɪlənt] *adj* silencioso
silent movie *s* cine mudo
silhouette [ˌsɪluˈɛt] *s* silueta || *tr* siluetear
silk [sɪlk] *adj* sedeño || *s* seda; **to hit the silk** (slang) lanzarse en paracaídas
silken [ˈsɪlkən] *adj* sedeño
silk hat *s* sombrero de copa
silk'-stock'ing *adj* aristocrático || *s* aristócrata *mf*
silk'worm' *s* gusano de seda
silk•y [ˈsɪlki] *adj* (*comp* **-ier;** *super* **-iest**) sedoso, asedado
sill [sɪl] *s* travesaño; (*of a door*) umbral *m;* (*of a window*) antepecho
silliness [ˈsɪlinɪs] tontería, simpleza, pachotada
sil•ly [ˈsɪli] *adj* (*comp* **-lier;** *super* **-liest**) necio, tonto; (coll) pavo
si•lo [ˈsaɪlo] *s* (*pl* **-los**) silo || *tr* asilar
silt [sɪlt] *s* cieno, sedimento
silver [ˈsɪlvər] *ad* de plata; (*voice*) argentino; elocuente || *s* plata || *tr* platear; azogar (*un espejo*)
sil'ver•fish' *s* (ent) pez *m* de plata
silver foil *s* hoja de plata
silver lining *s* aspecto agradable de una condición desgraciada o triste
silver plate *s* vajilla de plata
silver screen *s* pantalla de plata
sil'ver•smith' *s* platero, orfebre *m*
silver spoon *s* riqueza heredada; **to be born with a silver spoon in one's mouth** nacer de pie
sil'ver-tongue' *s* (coll) pico de oro
sil'ver•ware' *s* plata, vajilla de plata; plata; cubertería
similar [ˈsɪmɪlər] *adj* similar, semejante, análogo
simile [ˈsɪmɪli] *s* (rhet) símil *m*
simmer [ˈsɪmər] *tr* cocer a fuego lento || *intr* cocer a fuego lento; (coll) estar a punto de estallar; **to simmer down** (coll) tranquilizarse lentamente
simoon [sɪˈmun] *s* simún *m*
simper [ˈsɪmpər] *s* sonrisa boba || *intr* sonreír bobamente
simple [ˈsɪmpəl] *adj* simple, sencillo || *s* (*medicinal plant*) simple *m*
simple-minded [ˈsɪmpəlˈmaɪndɪd] *adj* candoroso, ingenuo; idiota, mentecato; estúpido, ignorante
simple substance *s* (chem) cuerpo simple
simpleton [ˈsɪmpəltən] *s* simple *mf*, bobo, mentecato
simulate [ˈsɪmjəˌlet] *tr* simular
simultaneous [ˌsaɪməlˈtenɪ•əs] o [ˌsɪməlˈtenɪ•əs] *adj* simultáneo || *adv*—**to do simultaneously** simultanear
sin [sɪn] *s* pecado || *v* (*pret & pp* **sinned;** *ger* **sinning**) *intr* pecar
since [sɪns] *adv* desde entonces, después || *prep* desde; después de || *conj* desde que; después (de) que; ya que, puesto que
sincere [sɪnˈsɪr] *adj* sincero
sincerity [sɪnˈsɛrɪti] *s* sinceridad
sinecure [ˈsaɪnɪˌkjur] *s* sinecura
sinew [ˈsɪnju] *s* tendón *m;* (fig) fibra, nervio, vigor *m*
sinful [ˈsɪnfəl] *adj* (*person*) pecador; (*act, intention, etc.*) pecaminoso
sing [sɪŋ] *v* (*pret* **sang** [sæŋ] o **sung** [sʌŋ]; *pp* **sung**) *tr* cantar; **to sing to sleep** arrullar || *intr* cantar
singe [sɪndʒ] *v* (*ger* **singeing**) *tr* chamuscar, socarrar
singer [ˈsɪŋər] *s* cantante *mf; (in a night club)* vocalista *mf*
single [ˈsɪŋgəl] *adj* solo, único; simple, sencillo; particular; (*e.g., room in a hotel*) individual; (*copy*) suelto; (*unmarried*) soltero; solteril, de soltero || *tr* escoger, elegir; **to single out** singularizar
single blessedness *s* el bendito celibato
single-breasted [ˈsɪŋgəlˈbrɛstɪd] *adj* sin cruzar, de un solo pecho
single entry *s* (com) partida simple
single file *s* fila india; **in single file** de reata
single-handed [ˈsɪŋgəlˈhændɪd] *adj* solo, sin ayuda
single life *s* vida de soltero
sin'gle-track' *adj* de vía única; (coll) de cortos alcances
sing'song' *adj* monótono || *s* sonsonete *m*
singular [ˈsɪŋgjələr] *adj & s* singular *m*
sinister [ˈsɪnɪstər] *adj* amenazante, ominoso, funesto
sink [sɪŋk] *s* fregadero, pila || *v* (*pret* **sank** [sæŋk] o **sunk** [sʌŋk]; *pp* **sunk**) *tr* hundir, sumergir; echar a pique; abrir, cavar (*un pozo*); hincar (*los dientes*); invertir (*mucho dinero*) perdiéndolo todo; (*basketball*) encestar || *intr* hundirse; irse a pique; hundirse (*p.ej., el Sol en el horizonte*); descender, desaparecer; decaer (*un enfermo; una llama*); (*e.g., in a chair*) dejarse caer
sinking fund *s* fondo de amortización
sinless [ˈsɪnlɪs] *adj* impecable
sinner [ˈsɪnər] *s* pecador *m*
sinuous [ˈsɪnju•əs] *adj* sinuoso
sinus [ˈsaɪnəs] *s* seno
sip [sɪp] *s* sorbo, trago || *v* (*pret & pp* **sipped;** *ger* **sipping**) *tr* sorber, beber a tragos
siphon [ˈsaɪfən] *s* sifón *m* || *tr* sacar con sifón, trasegar con sifón
siphon bottle *s* sifón *m*
sir [sʌr] *s* señor *m;* (*British title*) sir *m;* **Dear Sir** Muy señor mío, Estimado señor
sire [saɪr] *s* padre *m*, semental *m;* caballo padre || *tr* engendrar
siren [ˈsaɪrən] *s* sirena
Sirius [ˈsɪrɪ•əs] *s* (astr) Sirio
sirloin [ˈsʌrlɔɪn] *s* solomillo
sirup [ˈsɪrəp] o [ˈsʌrəp] *s* var de **syrup**
sissi•fy [ˈsɪsɪˌfaɪ] *v* (*pret & pp* **-fied**) *tr* (coll) afeminar
sis•sy [ˈsɪsi] *s* (*pl* **-sies**) (coll) hermanita; (coll) maricón *m*, santito
sister [ˈsɪstər] *adj* (*ship*) gemelo; (*language*) hermano || *s* hermana

sis'ter-in-law' *s* (*pl* **sisters-in-law**) cuñada, hermana política; (*wife of one's husband's or wife's brother*) concuñada
Sisyphus [ˈsɪsɪfəs] *s* Sísifo
sit [sɪt] *v* (*pret & pp* **sat** [sæt]; *ger* **sitting**) *intr* estar sentado; sentarse; echarse (*un ave sobre los huevos*); reunirse, celebrar junta; descansar; **to sit down** sentarse; **to sit still** estarse quieto; **to sit up** incorporarse (*el que estaba echado*)
sitcom [ˈsɪt,kɑm] *s* (coll) telecomedia serial
sit'-down' strike *s* hulega de sentados, huelga de brazos caídos
site [saɪt] *s* sitio, paraje *m*
sit'-in' *s* manifestación pacífica a modo de bloqueo
sitting [ˈsɪtɪŋ] *s* (*period one remains seated*) sentada; (*before a painter*) estadía; (*of a court or legislature*) sesión; **at one sitting** de una sentada
sitting duck *s* pato sentado en el agua (*fácil de matar a tiro de escopeta*); (coll) blanco de fácil alcance
sitting room *s* sala de estar
situate [ˈsɪtʃu,et] *tr* situar
situation [,sɪtʃuˈeʃən] *s* situación; colocación, puesto; medio ambiente
sitz bath [sɪts] *s* baño de asiento
six [sɪks] *adj & pron* seis || *s* seis *m;* **at sixes and sevens** en confusión, en desacuerdo; **six o'clock** las seis
six hundred *adj & pron* seiscientos || *s* seiscientos *m*
sixteen [ˈsɪksˈtin] *adj, pron & s* dieciséis *m*, diez y seis
sixteenth [ˈsɪksˈtinθ] *adj & s* (*in a series*) decimosexto; (*part*) dieciseisavo || *s* (*in dates*) dieciséis *m*
sixth [sɪksθ] *adj & s* sexto || *s* (*in dates*) seis *m*
sixtieth [ˈsɪkstɪ•ɪθ] *adj & s* (*in a series*) sexagésimo; (*part*) sesentavo
six•ty [ˈsɪksti] *adj & pron* sesenta || *s* (*pl* **-ties**) sesenta *m*
sizable [ˈsaɪzəbəl] *adj* considerable, bastante grande
size [saɪz] *s* tamaño; (*of a person or garment*) talla; (*of a pipe, a wire*) diámetro; (*for gilding*) sisa, cola de retazo; (coll) verdadera situación || *tr* clasificar según tamaño; sisar, encolar; **to size up** enfocar (*un problema*); medir con la vista
sizzle [ˈsɪzəl] *s* siseo || *intr* sisear
S.J. *abbr* **Society of Jesus**
skate [sket] *s* patín *m;* (slang) adefesio, tipo || *intr* patinar; **to skate on thin ice** buscar el peligro
skating rink *s* patinadero, pista de patinar
skein [sken] *s* madeja; enredo, maraña
skeleton [ˈskɛlɪtən] *adj* esquelético || *s* esqueleto
skeleton key *s* llave maestra
skeptic [ˈskɛptɪk] *adj & s* escéptico
skeptical [ˈskɛptɪkəl] *adj* escéptico
sketch [skɛtʃ] *s* boceto, dibujo; bosquejo, esbozo; drama corto, pieza corta || *tr* dibujar; bosquejar, esbozar
sketch'book' *s* libro de bocetos; libro de esbozos literarios
skewer [ˈskju•ər] *s* broqueta || *tr* espetar; traspasar con aguja
ski [ski] *s* (*pl* **skis** o **ski**) esquí *m* *intr* esquiar
skid [skɪd] *s* (*of an auto*) resbalón *m;* (*of a wheel*) patinaje *m*, patinazo; calzo || *v* (*pret & pp* **skidded;** *ger* **skidding**) *tr* calzar || *intr* resbalar (*un coche*); patinar (*una rueda*)
skid chain *s* cadena antirresbaladiza
skidding *s* (aut) patinada, derrapada, derrapaje *m*
skid row *s* barrio de mala vida
skier [ˈski•ər] *s* esquiador *m*
skiff [skɪf] *s* esquife *m*
skiing [ˈski•ɪŋ] *s* esquiismo
ski jacket *s* plumífero
skijoring [skiˈdʒorɪŋ] *s* esquí remolcado
ski jump *s* salto de esquí; cancha de esquiar; trampolín *m*
ski lift *s* telesquí *m*
skill [skɪl] *s* destreza, habilidad, pericia
skilled [skɪld] *adj* hábil, experimentado, experto
skillet [ˈskɪlɪt] *s* cacerola de mango largo; sartén *f*
skillful [ˈskɪlfəl] *adj* diestro, hábil
skim [skɪm] *v* (*pret & pp* **skimmed;** *ger* **skimming**) *tr* desnatar (*la leche*); espumar (*el caldo, el almíbar*); (*to graze*) rasar, rozar; examinar ligeramente || *intr* rozar; **to skim over** pasar rozando; examinar **a** la ligera
ski mask *s* pasamontaña *m*
skimmer [ˈskɪmər] *s* (*utensil*) espumadera; (*straw hat*) canotié *m*
skim milk *s* leche desnatada
skimp [skɪmp] *tr* escatimar; chapucear || *intr* economizar, apretarse; chapucear
skimp•y [ˈskɪmpi] *adj* (*comp* **-ier;** super **-iest**) escaso; tacaño, mezquino
skin [skɪn] *s* piel *f;* (*of an animal, of fruit*) pellejo; **to be nothing but skin and bones** estar hecho un costal de huesos, estar en los huesos; **to get soaked to the skin** calarse hasta los huesos; **to save one's skin** salvar el pellejo || *v* (*pret & pp* **skinned;** *ger* **skinning**) *tr* pelar, desollar; escoriarse (*p.ej., el codo*); (coll) timar; **to skin alive** (coll) desollar vivo; (coll) vencer completamente
skin'-deep' *adj* superficial
skin diver *s* submarinista *mf*
skin diving *s* submarinismo
skin'flint' *s* escasero, avaro
skin game *s* (slang) fullería
skin•ny [ˈskɪni] *adj* (*comp* **-nier;** *super* **-niest**) flaco, enjuto, magro, seco, delgaducho
skin'-tight' *adj* ajustado al cuerpo
skip [skɪp] *s* salto || *v* (*pret & pp* **skipped;** *ger* **skipping**) *tr* saltar || *intr* saltar; saltar espacios (*la máquina de escribir*); moverse saltando; irse precipitadamente
skip bombing *s* (aer) bombardeo de rebote

ski pole *s* bastón *m* de esquiar
skipper ['skɪpər] *s* caudillo, jefe *m;* (*of a boat*) patrón *m;* gusano del queso || *tr* patronear
skirmish ['skʌrmɪʃ] *s* escaramuza || *intr* escaramuzar
skirt [skʌrt] *s* falda; borde *m*, orilla; (*woman*) (slang) falda || *tr* seguir el borde de; moverse a lo largo de
ski run *s* pista de esquí
ski stick *s* bastón *m* de esquiar
skit [skɪt] *s* boceto burlesco, paso cómico
skittish ['skɪtɪʃ] *adj* caprichoso; asustadizo; tímido; (*bull*) abanto
skulduggery [skʌl'dʌgəri] *s* (coll) trampa, embuste *m*
skull [skʌl] *s* cráneo, calavera
skull'cap' *s* casquete *m*
skunk [skʌŋk] *s* mofeta; (*person*) (coll) canalla *m*
sky [skaɪ] *s* (*pl* **skies**) cielo; **to praise to the skies** poner por las nubes, poner en el cielo
sky'div'ing *s* paracaidismo con plomada suelta inicial
Skylab ['skaɪ,læb]*s* laboratorio espacial
sky'lark' *s* alondra || *intr* jaranear
sky'light' *s* tragaluz *m*, claraboya
sky'line' *s* línea del horizonte, línea de los edificios contra el cielo
sky'rock'et *s* cohete *m* || *intr* subir como un cohete
sky'scrap'er *s* rascacielos *m*
sky'writ'ing *s* escritura aérea
slab [slæb] *s* losa; plancha, tabla
slack [slæk] *adj* flojo; perezoso; negligente; inactivo || *s* flojedad; inactividad; estación muerta, temporada inactiva; **slacks** pantalones flojos || *tr* aflojar; apagar (*la cal*) || *intr* atrasarse; descuidarse; **to slack up** aflojar el paso
slacker ['slækər] *s* perezoso; (mil) prófugo
slag [slæg] *s* escoria
slake [slek] *tr* aplacar, calmar; apagar (*la cal*)
slalom ['slɑləm] *s* eslálom *m*
slam [slæm] *s* golpe *m;* (*of a door*) portazo; (coll) crítica acerba || *v* (*pret & pp* **slammed;** *ger* **slamming**) *tr* cerrar de golpe; golpear o empujar estrepitosamente; (coll) criticar acerbamente || *intr* cerrarse de golpe
slam'-bang' *adv* (coll) de golpe y porrazo
slander ['slændər] *s* calumnia, difamación; levante (CAm, P-R) || *tr* calumniar, difamar
slanderous ['slændərəs] *adj* calumnioso, difamatorio
slang [slæŋ] *s* caló *m*, jerigonza
slant [slænt] *s* inclinación; parecer *m*, punto de vista || *tr* inclinar, sesgar; deformar, tergiversar (*un informe*) || *intr* inclinarse, sesgarse
slap [slæp] *s* manazo, palmada; (*in the face*) bofetada; (*in the back*) espaldarazo; desaire *m*, insulto || *v* (*pret & pp* **slapped;** *ger* **slapping**) *tr* dar una palmada a; abofetear
slash [slæʃ] *s* cuchillada || *tr* acuchillar; hacer fuerte rebaja de (*precios, sueldos, etc.*)
slat [slæt] *s* lámina, tablilla
slate [slet] *s* pizarra; candidatura, lista de candidatos || *tr* empizarrar; designar, destinar; poner en la lista de candidatos
slate pencil *s* pizarrín *m*
slate roof *s* empizarrado
slattern ['slætərn] *s* mujer desaliñada, pazpuerca
slaughter ['slɔtər] *s* carnicería, matanza || *tr* matar
slaughter house *s* matadero
Slav [slɑv] o [slæv] *adj & s* eslavo
slave [slev] *adj & s* esclavo || *intr* trabajar como esclavo
slave driver *s* negrero; (fig) negrero
slave'hold'er *s* dueño de esclavos
slavery ['slevəri] *s* esclavitud
slave trade *s* trata de esclavos
slave trader *s* negrero
Slavic ['slɑvɪk] o ['slævɪk] *adj & s* eslavo
slay [sle] *v* (*pret* **slew** [slu]; *pp* **slain** [slen]) *tr* matar
slayer ['sle•ər] *s* matador *m*
sled [slɛd] *s* luge *m* || *v* (*pret & pp* **sledded;** *ger* **sledding**) *intr* deslizarse en luge o trineo
sledge hammer [slɛdʒ] *s* acotillo
sleek [slik] *adj* liso y brillante || *tr* alisar y pulir; suavizar
sleep [slip] *s* sueño; **to be overcome with sleep** caerse de sueño; **to go to sleep** dormirse; dormirse, morirse (*un miembro*); **to put to sleep** adormecer; matar por anestesia || *v* (*pret & pp* **slept** [slɛpt]) *tr* pasar durmiendo; **to sleep it off** dormir la mona; **to sleep it over** consultar con la almohada; **to sleep off** dormir (*p.ej., una borrachera*) || *intr* dormir
sleeper ['slipər] *s* (*person*) durmiente *mf;* (*girder*) durmiente *m*
sleeping bag *s* saco de dormir
Sleeping Beauty *s* la Bella Durmiente
sleeping car *s* coche-cama *m*
sleeping pill *s* píldora para dormir
sleepless ['sliplɪs] *adj* insomne, desvelado; pasado en vela
sleep'walk'er *s* sonámbulo; nochero
sleep•y ['slipi] *adj* (*comp* **-ier;** *super* **-iest**) soñoliento; **to be sleepy** tener sueño
sleep'y•head' *s* dormilón *m*
sleet [slit] *s* cellisca || *intr* cellisquear
sleeve [sliv] *s* manga; (mach) manguito; **to laugh in** o **up one's sleeve** reírse para sí
sleigh [sle] *s* trineo || *intr* pasearse en trineo
sleigh bell *s* cascabel *m*
sleigh ride *s* paseo en trineo
sleight of hand [slaɪt] *s* juego de manos, prestidigitación
slender ['slɛndər] *adj* esbelto, flaco, delgado; escaso, insuficiente
sleuth [sluθ] *s* sabueso
slew [slu] *s* (coll) montón *m*
slice [slaɪs] *s* rebanada, tajada; (*of an orange*) gajo || *tr* rebanar, tajar; dividir; cortar
slick [slɪk] *adj* liso y brillante; meloso, suave; (coll) astuto, mañoso || *s* lugar aceitoso y lustroso (*en el agua*)

slicker ['slɪkər] *s* impermeable *m* de hule; (coll) embaucador *m*

slide [slaɪd] *s* resbalón *m;* (*slippery place*) resbaladero; (*slippery surface*) desliz *m;* derrumbamiento de tierra; (*image for projection*) diapositiva, transparencia; (*of a microscope*) plaquilla de vidrio; (*piece of a device that slides*) cursor *m;* (*of a trombone*) corredera (tubular) || *v* (*pret & pp* **slid** [slɪd]) *tr* deslizar || *intr* deslizar, resbalar; **to let slide** dejar pasar, no hacer caso de

slide fastener *s* cierre *m* cremallera, cierre relámpago

slide rule *s* regla de cálculo

slide valve *s* corredera, válvula corrediza

sliding contact *s* cursor *m*

sliding door *s* puerta de corredera

sliding scale *s* regla de cálculo; (*of salaries*) escala móvil

slight [slaɪt] *adj* delgado; leve; pequeño; escaso; delgaducho || *s* desatención, descuido; desaire *m*, menosprecio || *tr* desatender, descuidar; desairar

slim [slɪm] *adj* (*comp* **slimmer;** *super* **slimmest**) delgado, esbelto; débil, leve, pequeño, escaso

slime [slaɪm] *s* légamo; (*of snakes, fish, etc.*) baba

slim•y ['slaɪmi] *adj* (*comp* **-ier;** *super* **-iest**) legamoso; baboso, viscoso; puerco, sucio

sling [slɪŋ] *s* (*to shoot stones*) honda; (*to hold up a broken arm*) cabestrillo || *v* (*pret & pp* **slung** [slʌŋ]) *tr* lanzar con una honda; lanzar, tirar; poner en cabestrillo; colgar flojamente

sling'shot' *s* honda

slink [slɪŋk] *v* (*pret & pp* **slunk** [slʌŋk]) *intr* andar furtivamente; **to slink away** escabullirse, salir con el rabo entre piernas

slip [slɪp] *s* resbalón *m*, desliz *m;* falta, error *m*, desliz *m;* lapso; embarcadero; (*cover for a pillow, for furniture*) funda; (*piece of paper*) papeleta; (*cutting from a plant*) sarmiento; (*piece of underclothing*) combinación; (*of a dog*) traílla; huída, evasión; mozuelo, mozuela; **to give the slip to** burlar la vigilancia de || *v* (*pret & pp* **slipped;** *ger* **slipping**) *tr* poner rápidamente; quitar rápidamente; pasar por alto; eludir, evadir; **to slip off** (coll) quitarse de prisa; **to slip on** (coll) ponerse de prisa; **to slip one's mind** olvidársele a uno || *intr* deslizarse; patinar (*el embrague*); errar, equivocarse; (coll) declinar, deteriorarse; **to let slip** dejar pasar; decir inadvertidamente; **to slip away** escurrirse; **to slip by** pasar inadvertido; pasar rápidamente (*el tiempo*); **to slip out of one's hands** escurrirse de entre las manos; **to slip up** (coll) errar, equivocarse

slip cover *s* funda

slip of the pen *s* error *m* de pluma

slip of the tongue *s* error *m* de lengua

slipper ['slɪpər] *s* zapatilla, babucha

slippery ['slɪpəri] *adj* deslizadizo, resbaladizo; astuto, zorro, evasivo

slip'-up' *s* (coll) error *m*, equivocación

slit [slɪt] *s* hendidura, raja; cortada, incisión || *v* (*pret & pp* **slit;** *ger* **slitting**) *tr* hender, rajar; cortar

slob [slɑb] *s* (slang) sujeto desaseado, puerco

slobber ['slɑbər] *s* baba; sensiblería || *intr* babear; hablar con sensiblería

sloe [slo] *s* (*shrub*) endrino; (*fruit*) endrina

slogan ['slogən] *s* lema *m*, mote *m;* grito de combate; (*striking phrase used in advertising*) eslogan *m*

sloop [slup] *s* balandra

slop [slɑp] *s* gacha, zupia, agua sucia || *v* (*pret & pp* **slopped;** *ger* **slopping**) *tr* salpicar, ensuciar || *intr* derramarse; chapotear

slope [slop] *s* cuesta, pendiente *f;* (*of a continent or a roof*) vertiente *m & f* || *tr* inclinar || *intr* inclinarse

slop•py ['slɑpi] *adj* (*comp* **-pier;** *super* **-piest**) mojado y sucio; (*in one's dress*) desgalichado; (*in one's work*) chapucero

slot [slɑt] *s* ranura; (*for letters*) buzón *m*

sloth [sloθ] o [slɔθ] *s* pereza; (zool) perezoso

slot machine *s* tragamonedas *m*, máquina sacaperras

slot meter *s* contador automático

slouch [slaʊtʃ] *s* postura relajada; persona torpe de movimientos || *intr* agacharse, andar caído de hombros; **to slouch in a chair** repanchigarse

slouch hat *s* sombrero gacho

slough [slaʊ] *s* cenagal *m*, fangal *m;* estado de abandono moral || [slʌf] *s* (*of a snake*) camisa; (pathol) escara || *tr* mudar, echar de sí || *intr* caerse, desprenderse

Slovak ['slovæk] o [slo'væk] *adj & s* eslovaco

sloven•ly ['slʌvənli] *adj* (*comp* **-lier;** *super* **-liest**) desaseado, desaliñado

slow [slo] *adj* lento; (*sluggish*) cachazudo, despacioso; (*clock, watch*) atrasado; (*in understanding*) lerdo, tardo, torpe || *adv* despacio || *tr* retrasar; atrasar (*un reloj*) || *intr* retardarse, ir más despacio; atrasarse (*un reloj*)

slow'down' *s* huelga de brazos caídos

slow motion *s* (*film*) ralentí *m;* **in slow motion** al ralentí, a cámara lenta

slow'-mo'tion *adj* a cámara lenta

slowness ['slonɪs] lentitud, lerdera

slow'poke' *s* tardón *m*

slug [slʌg] *s* (*heavy piece of metal*) lingote *m;* (*metal disk used as a coin*) ficha; (zool) limaza, babosa; (coll) porrazo, puñetazo || *v* (*pret & pp* **slugged;** *ger* **slugging**) *tr* (coll) aporrear, apuñear

sluggard ['slʌgərd] *s* pachón *m*, perezoso

sluggish ['slʌgɪʃ] *adj* inactivo, indolente, tardo; pachorrudo, perezoso

sluice [slus] *s* canal *m;* (*floodgate*) compuerta; (*dam; flume*) presa

sluice gate *s* compuerta de presa

slum [slʌm] *s* barrio bajo || *v* (*pret & pp* **slummed;** *ger* **slumming**) *intr* visitar los barrios bajos

slumber ['slʌmbər] *s* sueño ligero, sueño tranquilo || *intr* dormir; dormitar

slump [slʌmp] *s* depresión, crisis económica; (*in prices, stocks, etc.*) baja repentina || *intr* hundirse, desplomarse; bajar repentinamente (*los precios, valores, etc.*)
slur [slʌr] *s* pronunciación indistinta; reparo crítico; (mus) ligado || *v* (*pret & pp* **slurred**; *ger* **slurring**) *tr* comerse (*sonidos, sílabas*); despreciar, insultar; (mus) ligar
slush [slʌʃ] *s* fango muy blando, aguanieve fangosa, nieve *f* a medio derretir; sentimentalismo tonto
slut [slʌt] *s* perra; (*slovenly woman*) pazpuerca; ramera, mala mujer
sly [slaɪ] *adj* (*comp* **slyer** o **slier**; *super* **slyest** o **sliest**) furtivo, secreto; astuto, socarrón; travieso; **on the sly** a hurtadillas
smack [smæk] *adv* (coll) de golpe, de sopetón || *s* dejo, gustillo; palmada, manotada; golpe *m;* beso sonado; (*of a whip*) chasquido || *tr* dar una manotada a; golpear; hacer chasquidos con (*un látigo*); besar sonoramente; **to smack one's lips** chuparse los labios || *intr*—**to smack of** saber a, oler a
small [smɔl] *adj* pequeño, chico; (*short in stature*) bajo; pobre, obscuro, humilde; (typ) minúsculo
small arms *spl* armas ligeras
small beer *s* cerveza floja; bagatela; persona de poca monta
small business *s* pequeña empresa
small capital *s* versalilla o versalita
small change *s* suelto, dinero menudo
small fry *s* gente menuda; gente de poca monta
small'-fry' *adj* de niños, para niños; de poca monta
small hours *spl* primeras horas (*de la mañana*)
small intestine *s* intestino delgado
small-minded [ˈsmɔlˈmaɪndɪd] *adj* tacaño, mezquino; intolerante
smallpox [ˈsmɔl,pɑks] *s* viruela
small print *s* tipo menudo
small talk *s* palique *m*, charlas frívolas
small'-time' *adj* de poca monta
small'-town' *adj* lugareño, apegado a cosas lugareñas
smart [smɑrt] *adj* listo, vivo, inteligente; agudo, penetrante; astuto; elegante, majo; picante, punzante; (coll) grande, considerable || *s* escozor *m;* dolor vivo || *intr* escocer, picar; padecer, sufrir
smart aleck [ˈælɪk] *s* (coll) fatuo, sabihondo
smart money *s* (fig) inversionistas *mpl/fpl* astutos; gente *f* bien informada
smart set *s* gente *f* chic, gente de buen tono
smash [smæʃ] *s* rotura violenta; fracaso, ruina; quiebra, bancarrota; (coll) choque violento, tope violento || *tr* romper con fuerza; arruinar, destrozar; aplastar || *intr* romperse con fuerza; arruinarse, destrozarse; aplastarse; **to smash into** chocar con, topar con
smash hit *s* (coll) éxito rotundo
smash'-up' *s* colisión violenta; ruina, desastre *m;* quiebra, bancarrota
smattering [ˈsmætərɪŋ] *s* barniz *m*, tintura, migaja
smear [smɪr] *s* embarradura; calumnia; (bact) frotis *m* || *tr* embarrar; calumniar || *intr* embarrarse
smear campaign *s* campaña de calumnias
smell [smɛl] *s* olor *m;* (*sense*) olfato; fragancia, perfume *m* || *v* (*pret & pp* **smelled** o **smelt** [smɛlt]) *tr* oler, olfatear || *intr* oler; heder, oler mal; **to smell of** oler a
smelling salts *spl* sales aromáticas
smell•y [ˈsmɛli] *adj* (*comp* **-ier**; *super* **-iest**) hediondo, maloliente
smelt [smɛlt] *s* (*fish*) eperlano, esperinque *m* || *tr & intr* fundir
smile [smaɪl] *s* sonrisa || *intr* sonreír, sonreírse
smiling [ˈsmaɪlɪŋ] *adj* risueño
smirk [smʌrk] *s* sonrisa fatua y afectada || *intr* sonreír fatua y afectadamente
smite [smaɪt] *v* (*pret* **smote** [smot]; *pp* **smitten** [ˈsmɪtən] o **smit** [smɪt]) *tr* golpear o herir súbitamente y con fuerza; caer con fuerza sobre; apenar, afligir; castigar
smith [smɪθ] *s* forjador *m*, herrero
smith•y [ˈsmɪθi] *s* (*pl* **-ies**) herrería
smitten [ˈsmɪtən] *adj* afligido; muy enamorado
smock [smɑk] *s* bata
smock frock *s* blusa de obrero
smog [smɑg] *s* mezcla de humo y niebla
smoke [smok] *s* humo; **to go up in smoke** irse todo en humo || *tr* (*to cure or treat with smoke*) ahumar; fumar (*tabaco*); **to smoke out** ahuyentar con humo, dar humazo a; descubrir || *intr* humear; fumar; hacer humo (*una chimenea dentro de la habitación*)
smoked glasses *spl* gafas ahumadas
smoke evacuator *s* extractor de humos
smokeless powder [ˈsmoklɪs] *s* pólvora sin humo
smokeless tobacco *s* tabaco sin humo
smoker [ˈsmokər] *s* fumador *m;* (*room*) fumadero; (rr) coche-fumador *m;* reunión de fumadores
smoke rings *spl* anillos de humo; **to blow smoke rings** sacar humo formando anillos
smoke screen *s* cortina de humo
smoke'stack' *s* chimenea
smoking [ˈsmokɪŋ] *s* el fumar; **no smoking** se prohibe fumar
smoking car *s* coche-fumador *m*, vagón *m* de fumar
smoking jacket *s* batín *m*
smoking room *s* fumadero, saloncito para fumadores
smok•y [ˈsmoki] *adj* (*comp* **-ier**; *super* **-iest**) humoso; (*emitting smoke*) humeante
smolder [ˈsmoldər] *s* fuego lento sin llama y con mucho humo || *intr* arder en rescoldo, arder sin llamas; (fig) estar latente; (*to burn within*) (fig) requemarse; (fig) expresar (*p.ej., los ojos*) una ira latente
smooth [smuð] *adj* liso, terso, suave; plano, llano; igual; acaramelado, afable, blando, meloso; (*water*) tranquilo; (*style*) fluido;

smooth as butter como manteca || *tr* alisar, suavizar; allanar; facilitar; **to smooth away** quitar (*p.ej., obstáculos*) suavemente; **to smooth down** ablandar, calmar
smooth-faced ['smuð,fest] *adj* barbilampiño
smooth-spoken ['smuθ,spokən] *adj* meloso, lisonjero
smooth•y ['smuði] *s* (*pl* **-ies**) galante *m;* elegante *m;* adulador *m*
smother ['smʌðər] *tr* ahogar, sofocar; suprimir; reprimir
smudge [smʌdʒ] *s* tiznón *m;* mancha || *tr* tiznar; manchar; ahumar, fumigar (*una huerta*)
smug [smʌg] *adj* (*comp* **smugger;** *super* **smuggest**) pagado de sí mismo; compuesto, pulcro; relamido
smuggle ['smʌgəl] *tr* meter de contrabando || *intr* contrabandear
smuggler ['smʌglər] *s* contrabandista *mf*
smuggling ['smʌglɪŋ] *s* contrabando
smut [smʌt] *s* tiznón *m;* obscenidad; (agr) carbón *m*, tizón *m*
smut•ty ['smʌti] *adj* (*comp* **-tier;** *super* **-tiest**) tiznado, manchado; obsceno; (agr) atizonado
snack [snæk] *s* parte *f*, porción; bocadillo, tentempié *m*
snack bar *s* lonchería
snag [snæg] *s* (*of a tree*) tocón *m;* (*of a tooth*) raigón *m;* obstáculo, tropiezo; **to strike** o **to hit a snag** tropezar con un obstáculo
snail [snel] *s* caracol *m;* (*slow person*) pachón *m;* **at a snail's pace** a paso de caracol, a paso de tortuga
snake [snek] *s* culebra, serpiente *f*
snake in the grass *s* traidor *m*, amigo pérfido
snap [snæp] *s* (*crackling sound*) chasquido, estallido; (*of the fingers*) castañetazo; (*bite*) mordisco; (*cracker*) galletita; (*of cold weather*) corto período; (*catch or fastener*) broche *m* de presión; (phot) instantánea; (coll) brío, vigor *m;* (slang) breva, cosa fácil || *v* (*pret & pp* **snapped;** *ger* **snapping**) *tr* asir, cerrar, etc. de golpe; castañetear (*los dedos*); chasquear (*el látigo*); fotografiar instantáneamente; tomar (*una instantánea*); **to snap one's fingers at** tratar con desprecio; **to snap up** aceptar con avidez, comprar con avidez; cortar la palabra a || *intr* chasquear, estallar; (*to crack*) saltar; (*from fatigue*) estallar; **to snap at** querer morder; asir (*una oportunidad*); **to snap out of it** (slang) cambiarse repentinamente; **to snap shut** cerrarse de golpe
snap'drag'on *s* (bot) boca de dragón
snap fastener *s* corchete *m* de presión
snap judgment *s* decisión atolondrada
snap•py ['snæpi] *adj* (*comp* **-pier;** *super* **-piest**) mordaz; (coll) elegante, garboso; (coll) enérgico, vivo; (*food*) acre, picante
snap'shot' *s* instantánea
snap switch *s* (elec) interruptor *m* de resorte
snare [snɛr] *s* lazo, trampa: (*of a drum*) bordón *m*, tirante *m*
snare drum *s* caja clara
snarl [snɑrl] *s* gruñido; regaño; maraña, enredo || *tr* decir con un gruñido; enmarañar, enredar || *intr* gruñir; regañar; enmarañarse, enredarse
snatch [snætʃ] *s* arrebatamiento; pedacito, trocito; ratito || *tr & intr* arrebatar; **to snatch at** tratar de asir o agarrar; **to snatch from** arrebatar a
sneak [snik] *adj* furtivo || *s* sujeto solapado || *tr* mover a hurtadillas || *intr* andar furtivamente, moverse a hurtadillas
sneaker ['snikər] *s* sujeto solapado; (coll) zapato blando, zapato de lona
sneak thief *s* ratero, descuidero
sneak•y ['sniki] *adj* (*comp* **-ier;** *super* **-iest**) solapado, furtivo
sneer [snɪr] *s* expresión de desprecio || *intr* hablar con desprecio, echar una mirada de desprecio; **to sneer at** mofarse de
sneeze [sniz] *s* estornudo || *intr* estornudar; **not to be sneezed at** (coll) no ser despreciable
snicker ['snɪkər] *s* risa tonta || *intr* reírse tontamente
sniff [snɪf] *s* husmeo, venteo; sorbo por las narices || *tr* husmear, ventear; sorber por las narices; (fig) husmear, averiguar; (fig) sospechar; (*heroin*) esnifar (*caballo*) || *intr* ventear; **to sniff at** husmear; menospreciar
sniffle ['snɪfəl] *s* resuello fuerte y repetido; **the sniffles** ataque *m* de resoplidos || *intr* resollar fuerte y repetidamente
snip [snɪp] *s* tijeretada; recorte *m*, pedacito; (coll) persona pequeña e insignificante || *v* (*pret & pp* **snipped;** *ger* **snipping**) *tr* tijeretear
snipe [snaɪp] *s* agachadiza, becacín *m* || *intr* paquear, tirar desde un escondite
sniper ['snaɪpər] *s* paco, tirador emboscado
snippet ['snɪpɪt] *s* recorte *m;* (coll) persona pequeña e insignificante
snip•py ['snɪpi] *adj* (*comp* **-pier;** *super* **-piest**) (coll) arrogante, desdeñoso; (coll) acre, brusco
snitch [snɪtʃ] *tr & intr* (slang) escamotear, ratear; manotear (Arg, Mex)
sniv•el ['snɪvəl] *s* gimoteo, lloriqueo; moqueo || *v* (*pret & pp* **-eled** o **-elled;** *ger* **-eling** o **-elling**) *intr* gimotear, lloriquear; (*to have a runny nose*) moquear
snob [snɑb] *s* esnob *mf*
snobbery ['snɑbəri] *s* esnobismo
snobbish ['snɑbɪʃ] *adj* esnob, esnobista
snoop [snup] *s* buscavidas *mf*, curioso || *intr* curiosear, ventear
snoopy ['snupi] *adj* curioso, entremetido
snoot [snut] *s* (slang) cara, narices *fpl*
snoot•y ['snuti] *adj* (*comp* **-ier;** *super* **-iest**) (slang) esnob
snooze [snuz] *s* (coll) sueñecito || *intr* echar un sueñecito
snore [snor] *s* ronquido || *intr* roncar
snort [snɔrt] *s* bufido || *intr* bufar
snot [snɑt] *s* (slang) mocarro
snot•ty ['snɑti] *adj* (*comp* **-tier;** *super* **-tiest**) mocoso; asqueroso, sucio; (slang) engreído

snout [snaut] *s* hocico; (*something shaped like the snout of an animal*) morro; (*of a person*) (coll) hocico
snow [sno] *s* nieve *f* || *intr* nevar
snow'ball' *s* bola de nieve || *tr* lanzar bolas de nieve a || *intr* aumentar rápidamente
snow'-blind' *adj* cegado por reflejos de la nieve
snow-capped ['sno,kæpt] *adj* coronado de nieve
snow'drift' *s* ventisquero, masa de nieve
snow'fall' *s* nevada
snow fence *s* valla paranieves
snow'flake' *s* copo de nieve, ampo
snow flurry *s* nevisca
snow job *s* (slang) decepción; engaño
snow line o **limit** *s* límite *m* de las nieves perpetuas
snow man *s* figura de nieve
snow'plow' *s* expulsanieves *m*, quitanieves *m*
snow'shoe' *s* raqueta de nieve
snow'storm' *s* nevasca, fuerte nevada
snow tire *s* llanta de invierno
snow'-white' *adj* blanco como la nieve
snow•y ['sno•i] *adj* (*comp* **-ier;** *super* **-iest**) nevoso
snowy owl *s* lechuza blanca
snub [snʌb] *s* desaire *m* || *v* (*pret & pp* **snubbed;** *ger* **snubbing**) *tr* desairar
snub•by ['snʌbi] *adj* (*comp* **-bier;** *super* **-biest**) (*nose*) respingona
snuff [snʌf] *s* rapé; (*of a candlewick*) moco; **up to snuff** (slang) en buena condición; (slang) difícil de engañar || *tr* husmear, olfatear; sorber por la nariz; despabilar (*una candela*); **to snuff out** apagar, extinguir
snuff'box' *s* tabaquera
snuffers ['snʌfərz] *spl* despabiladeras
snug [snʌg] *adj* (*comp* **snugger;** *super* **snuggest**) cómodo; (*garment*) ajustado, ceñido; (*well-off*) acomodado; (*in hiding*) escondido
snuggle ['snʌgəl] *intr* apretarse, arrimarse; dormir bien abrigado; **to snuggle up to** arrimarse a
so [so] *adv* así; tan + *adj* o *adv;* por tanto; también; **and so** así pues; también, lo mismo; **and so on** y así sucesivamente; **or so** más o menos; **to think so** creer que sí; **so as to** + *inf* para + *inf;* **so far** hasta aquí; hasta ahora; **so long** hasta la vista; **so many** tantos; **so much** tanto; **so so** tal cual, así así; **so that** de modo que, de suerte que, así que; para que; con tal de que; **so to speak** por decirlo así || *conj* as que || *interj* ¡bien!; ¡verdad!
soak [sok] *s* mojada; (*toper*) (coll) potista *mf* || *tr* empapar, remojar; embeber; (slang) aporrear; (slang) hacer pagar un precio exorbitante; **to soak up** absorber, embeber; (fig) entender; **soaked to the skin** calado hasta los huesos || *intr* empaparse, remojarse
so'-and-so' *s* (*pl* **-sos**) fulano, fulano de tal; tal cosa
soap [sop] *s* jabón *m* || *tr* jabonar
soap'box' *s* caja de jabón; tribuna callejera
soapbox orator *s* orador *m* de plazuela
soap bubble *s* burbuja de jabón, pompa de jabón
soap dish *s* jabonera
soap flakes *spl* copos de jabón
soap'mak'er *s* jabonero
soap opera *s* (coll) telenovela; serial lacrimógeno
soap powder *s* jabón *m* en polvo, polvo de jabón
soap'stone' *s* jaboncillo de sastre
soap'suds' *spl* jabonaduras
soap•y ['sopi] *adj* (*comp* **-ier;** *super* **-iest**) jabonoso
soar [sor] *intr* encumbrarse, subir muy alto, volar a gran altura; aspirar, pretender; (aer) planear
sob [sɑb] *s* sollozo || *v* (*pret & pp* **sobbed;** *ger* **sobbing**) *tr* decir o expresar sollozando || *intr* sollozar
sobbing *s* llorera
sober ['sobər] *adj* sobrio; no embriagado; grave, serio; cuerdo, sensato; sereno, tranquilo; (*color*) apagado || *tr* poner sobrio; desemborrachar; **to sober up** desintoxicar || *intr* volverse sobrio; desemborracharse; **to sober down** calmarse, sosegarse; **to sober up** desemborracharse
sobriety [so'braɪ•əti] *s* sobriedad, moderación; gravedad, seriedad; cordura, sensatez; serenidad
sobriquet ['sobrɪ,ke] *s* apodo
sob sister *s* (slang) periodista llorona
sob story *s* (slang) historia de lagrimitas
soc. o **Soc.** *abbr* **society**
so'-called' *adj* llamado, así llamado; supuesto
soccer ['sɑkər] *s* fútbol *m* asociación
sociable ['soʃəbəl] *adj* sociable
social ['soʃəl] *adj* social || *s* reunión social
social climber ['klaɪmər] *s* ambicioso de figurar
socialism ['soʃə,lɪzəm] *s* socialismo
socialist ['soʃəlɪst] *s* socialista *mf*
socialite ['soʃə,laɪt] *s* (coll) personaje *m* de la buena sociedad
social register *s* guía *m* social, registro de la buena sociedad
socie•ty [sə'saɪ•əti] *s* (*pl* **-ties**) sociedad; (*companionship or company*) compañía; buena sociedad, mundo elegante
society editor *s* cronista *mf* de la vida social
sociology [,sosɪ'ɑlədʒi] o [,soʃɪ'ɑlədʒi] *s* sociología
sock [sɑk] *s* calcetín *m;* (slang) golpe *m* fuerte || *tr* (slang) golpear con fuerza
socket ['sɑkɪt] *s* (*of the eyes*) cuenca; (*of a tooth*) alvéolo; (*of a candlestick*) cañón *m;* (*of a socket wrench*) cubo; (elec) portalámparas; (rad) zócalo
socket wrench *s* llave *f* de caja, llave de cubo
sod [sɑd] *s* césped *m;* terrón *m* de césped || *v* (*pret & pp* **sodded;** *ger* **sodding**) *tr* encespedar
soda ['sodə] *s* soda, sosa; (*drink*) soda
soda fountain *s* fuente *f* de sodas

soda water *s* agua gaseosa
sodium ['sodɪ•əm] *adj* sódico, de sodio || *s* sodio
sofa ['sofə] *s* sofá *m*
soft [sɔft] o [sɑft] *adj* blando, muelle; (*skin*) suave; (*iron*) dulce; (*hat*) flexible; (*solder*) tierno; (coll) fácil
soft-boiled egg ['sɔft'bɔɪld] o ['sɑft'bɔɪld] *s* huevo pasado por agua
soft coal *s* hulla grasa
soft drink *s* bebida no alcohólica, refresco
soften ['sɔfən] o ['sɑfən] *tr* ablandar; **to soften up** (*by bombardment*) ablandar || *intr* ablandarse
soft'-ped'al *tr* (mus) disminuir la intensidad de, por medio del pedal suave; (slang) moderar
soft soap *tr* jabón blando o graso; (coll) adulación
soft'-soap' *s* (coll) enjabonar, dar jabón a
soft'ware' *s* (*computer*) programa *m* (para ordenador), operaciones *fpl*
sog•gy ['sɑgi] *adj* (*comp* **-gier;** *super* **-giest**) remojado, ensopado
soil [sɔɪl] *s* suelo; país *m*, región; (*spot, stain*) mancha; (fig) mancha, deshonra || *tr* manchar, ensuciar; manchar, deshonrar; viciar, corromper || *intr* mancharse, ensuciarse
soil pipe *s* tubo de desagüe sanitario
soiree o **soirée** [swɑ're] *s* sarao, velada
sojourn ['sodʒʌrn] *s* estancia, permanencia || ['sodʒʌrn] o [so'dʒʌrn] *intr* estarse, permanecer
soil. *abbr* **soluble, solution**
solace ['sɑlɪs] *s* solaz *m*, consuelo || *tr* solazar, consolar
solar ['solər] *adj* solar
solar battery *s* fotopila
solder ['sɑdər] *s* soldadura || *tr* soldar
soldering iron *s* cautín *m*, soldador *m*
soldier ['soldʒər] *s* (*enlisted man as distinguished from an officer*) soldado; (*man in military service*) militar *m* || *intr* servir como soldado
soldier of fortune *s* aventurero militar
soldier•y ['soldʒəri] *s* (*pl* **-ies**) soldadesca
sold out [sold] *adj* agotado; **the theater is sold out** todas las localidades están vendidas; **we are sold out of those neckties** se nos han agotado esas corbatas
sole [sol] *adj* solo, único; exclusivo || *s* (*of foot*) planta; (*of shoe*) suela; (*fish*) lenguado || *tr* solar
solely ['solli] *adv* solamente, únicamente
solemn ['sɑləm] *adj* solemne
solicit [sə'lɪsɪt] *tr* solicitar; intentar seducir
solicitor [sə'lɪsɪtər] *s* solicitador *m*, agente *m;* (law) procurador *m*
solicitous [sə'lɪsɪtəs] *adj* solícito
solicitude [sə'lɪsɪ,tjud] o [sə'lɪsɪ,tud] *s* solicitud
solid ['sɑlɪd] *adj* sólido; unánime; (*sound, good*) sólido, macizo; (*e.g., clouds*) denso; (*without pause or interruption*) entero; (*e.g., gold*) puro || *s* sólido
solidarity [,sɑlɪ'derɪtɪ] *s* solidaridad; **to declare one's solidarity with** solidarizar con
solid geometry *s* geometría del espacio
solidity [sə'lɪdɪti] *s* (*pl* **-ties**) solidez *f*
solid majority *s* mayoría cómoda
sol'id-state' *adj* transistorizado
solid-state physics *s* física del estado sólido
solid tire *s* (aut) macizo
solilo•quy [sə'lɪləkwi] *s* (*pl* **-quies**) soliloquio
solitaire ['sɑlɪ,tɛr] *s* (*game and diamond*) solitario; sortija solitario
solitar•y ['sɑlɪ,tɛri] *adj* solitario; **in solitary confinement** incomunicado || *s* (*pl* **-ies**) solitario
solitary confinement *s* incomunicación, aislamiento penal
solitude ['sɑlɪ,tjud] o ['sɑlɪ,tud] *s* soledad
so•lo ['solo] *adj* (*instrument*) solista; a solas, hecho a solas || *s* (*pl* **-los**) (mus) solo
soloist ['solo•ɪst] *s* solista *mf*
solstice ['sɑlstɪs] *s* solsticio
solution [sə'luʃən] *s* solución
solve [sɑlv] *tr* resolver, solucionar; adivinar (*un enigma*)
solvent ['sɑlvənt] *adj & s* solvente *m*
somber ['sɑmbər] *adj* sombrío
some [sʌm] *adj indef* algún; un poco de; unos; (coll) grande, bueno, famoso || *pron indef pl* algunos, unos
some'bod'y *pron indef* alguien; **somebody else** algún otro, otra persona || *s* (*pl* **-ies**) (coll) personaje *m*
some'day' *adv* algúna día
some'how' *adv* de algún modo, de alguna manera; **somehow or other** de un modo u otro
some'one' *pron indef* alguien; **someone else** algún otro, otra persona
somersault ['sʌmər,sɔlt] *s* salto mortal || *intr* dar un salto mortal
something ['sʌmθɪŋ] *adv* algo, un poco; (coll) muy, excesivamente || *pron indef* alguna cosa, algo; **something else** otra cosa
some'time' *adj* antiguo, de otro tiempo || *adv* alguna vez; antiguamente
some'times' *adv* a veces, algunas veces
some'way' *adv* de algún modo
some'what' *adv* algo, un poco || *s* alguna cosa, algo
some'where' *adv* en alguna parte, a alguna parte; en algún tiempo; **somewhere else** en otra parte, a otra parte
somnambulist [sɑm'næmbjəlɪst] *s* sonámbulo
somnolent ['sɑmnələnt] *adj* soñoliento
son [sʌn] *s* hijo
song [sɔŋ] o [sɑŋ] *s* canción, canto; **for a song** muy barato; **to sing the same old song** volver a la misma canción
song'bird' *s* ave canora
Song of Songs *s* Cantar *m* de los Cantares
song writer *s* cantautor *m*
sonic ['sɑnɪk] *adj* sónico
sonic boom *s* (aer) estampido sónico
son'-in-law' *s* (*pl* **sons-in-law**) yerno, hijo político
sonnet ['sɑnɪt] *s* soneto

sonneteer [,sɑnɪ'tɪr] *s* sonetista *mf;* poetastro || *intr* sonetizar
son•ny ['sʌni] *s* (*pl* **-nies**) hijito
sonori•ty [sə'nɔrɪti] *s* (*pl* **-ties**) sonoridad
soon [sun] *adv* pronto, en breve; temprano; de buena gana; **as soon as** así que, en cuanto, luego que, tan pronto como; **as soon as possible** cuanto antes, lo más pronto posible; **had sooner** preferiría; **how soon?** ¿cuándo?; **soon after** poco después, poco después de; **sooner or later** tarde o temprano
soot [sʊt] o [sut] *s* hollín *m*
soothe [suð] *tr* aliviar, calmar, sosegar
soothsayer ['suθ,se•ər] *s* adivino
soot•y ['sʊti] o ['suti] *adv* (*comp* **-ier;** *super* **-iest**) holliniento, tiznado
sop [sɑp] *s* (*food soaked in milk, etc.*) sopa; regalo (*para acallar, apaciguar o sobornar*) || *v* (*pret & pp* **sopped;** *ger* **sopping**) *tr* empapar, ensopar; **to sop up** absorber
sophisticated [sə'fɪstɪ,ketɪd] *adj* mundano, falto de simplicidad, corrido
sophomore ['sɑfə,mor] *s* estudiante *mf* de segundo año
sopping ['sɑpɪŋ] *adj* empapado; **sopping wet** hecho una sopa
sopran•o [sə'prǽno] o [sə'prɑno] *adj* de soprano; para soprano || *s* (*pl* **-os**) soprano *mf*
sorcerer ['sɔrsərər] *s* brujo, hechicero
sorceress ['sɔrsərɪs] *s* bruja, hechicera
sorcer•y ['sɔrsəri] *s* (*pl* **-ies**) brujería, hechicería, sortilegio
sordid ['sɔrdɪd] *adj* sórdido
sore [sor] *adj* enrojecido, inflamado; (coll) resentido, picado; **to be sore at** (coll) estar enojado con || *s* llaga, úlcera; pena, dolor *m*, aflicción; **to open an old sore** renovar la herida
sorely ['sorli] *adv* penosamente; con urgencia
sore throat *s* dolor *m* de garganta
sorori•ty [sə'rɔrɪti] *s* (*pl* **-ties**) hermandad de estudiantas
sorrel ['sɔrəl] *adj* alazán
sorrow ['sɔro] *s* dolor *m*, pena pesar *m;* arrepentimiento || *intr* dolerse, apenarse, sentir pena; arrepentirse; **to sorrow for** añorar
sorrowful ['sɔrəfəl] *adj* doloroso, pesaroso, acongojado
sor•ry ['sɑri] o ['sɔri] *adj* (*comp* **-rier;** *super* **-riest**) afligido, apenado, pesaroso; arrepentido; malo, pésimo; despreciable, ridículo; **to be** o **feel sorry** sentir; arrepentirse; **to be** o **feel sorry for** compadecer; arrepentirse de; **I am sorry** lo siento, me sabe mal
sort [sɔrt] *s* clase *f*, especie *f;* modo, manera; **a sort of** uno a modo de; **out of sorts** de mal humor; **sort of** (coll) algo, en cierta medida || *tr* clasificar, separar; escoger, entresacar
so'-so' *adj* mediano, regular, talcualillo || *adv* así así, tal cual
sot [sɑt] *s* borracho
sotto voce ['sɑto 'votʃə] *adv* a sovoz, en voz baja
soubrette [su'brɛt] *s* (theat) confidenta de comedia; (theat) doncella coquetona
soul [sol] *s* alma; **upon my soul!** ¡por vida mía!
sound [saʊnd] *adj* sano: sólido, firme; solvente; sonoro; (*sleep*) profundo; prudente; legal, válido || *adv* profundamente || *s* sonido; ruido; (*passage of water*) estrecho, brazo de mar; (surg) sonda, tienta; **within sound of** al alcance de || *tr* sonar; tocar (*p.ej., campanas*); tantear, sondear; auscultar (*p.ej., los pulmones*); entonar (*p.ej., alabanzas*) || *intr* sonar, resonar; sondar; parecer; **to sound like** sonar a, sonar como
sound'-ab•sorb'ent *adj* fonoabsorbente
sound barrier *s* muro del sonido, barrera de sonido, barrera sónica
sound'-dead'en•ing *adj* fonoabsorbente
sound film *s* película sonora
soundly ['saʊndli] *adv* sanamente; profundamente; a fondo, completamente
sound'proof' *adj* antisonoro; insonorizado || *tr* insonorizar
soundproofing ['saʊnd,prufɪŋ] *s* insonorización
soup [sup] *s* sopa
soup kitchen *s* comedor *m* de beneficencia, dispensario de alimentos
soup spoon *s* cuchara de sopa
sour [saʊr] *adj* agrio || *tr* agriar || *intr* agriarse
source [sors] *s* fuente *f*, manantial *m*
source material *s* fuentes *fpl* originales
sour cherry *s* (*tree*) guindo; (*fruit*) guinda
sour grapes *interj* ¡están verdes las uvas!
south [saʊθ] *adj* meridional, del sur || *adv* al sur, hacia el sur || *s* sur *m*, mediodía *m*
South America *s* Sudamérica, la América del Sur
South American *adj & s* sudamericano
southern ['sʌðərn] *adj* meridional
Southern Cross *s* Cruz *f* del Sur
southerner ['sʌðərnər] *s* meridional *mf;* sureño (Am)
South Korea *s* la Corea del Sur
South Korean *adj & s* surcoreano
south'paw' *adj & s* (slang in sport) zurdo
South Pole *s* polo sur, polo antártico
southward ['saʊθwərd] *adv* hacia el sur
south wind *s* austro, noto
souvenir [,suvə'nɪr] o ['suvə,nɪr] *s* recuerdo, memoria
sovereign ['sɑvrɪn] o ['sʌvrɪn] *adj* soberano || *s* (*king; coin*) soberano; (*queen*) soberana
sovereign•ty ['sɑvrɪnti] o ['sʌvrɪnti] *s* (*pl* **-ties**) soberanía
soviet ['sovɪ,ɛt] o [,sovɪ'ɛt] *adj* soviético || *s* soviet *m*
sovietize ['sovɪ•ɛ,taɪz] *tr* sovietizar
Soviet Russia *s* la Rusia Soviética
Soviet Union *s* Unión Soviética
sow [saʊ] *s* puerca || [so] *v* (*pret* **sowed;** *pp* **sown** o **sowed**) *tr* sembrar; (*with mines*) plagar
soybean ['sɔɪ,bin] *s* soja; soya; semilla de soja
sp. *abbr* **special, species, specific, specimen, spelling**

spa [spɑ] *s* caldas, balneario
space [spes] *adj* espacial, del espacio || *s* espacio; **in the space of** por espacio de || *tr* espaciar
space bar *s* espaciador *m*, tecla de espacios
space'craft' *s* astronave *f*, cosmonave *f*
space flight *s* vuelo espacial
space key *s* llave *f* espacial
space•man ['spes,mæn] *s* (*pl* **-men** [,mɛn]) navegador *m* del espacio; astronauta *m;* visitante *m* a la Tierra del espacio exterior
space'ship' *s* nave *f* del espacio
space shuttle *s* transbordador *m* espacial
space station *s* apostadero espacial
space suit *s* escafandra espacial
space travel *s* cosmonavegación
space vehicle *s* vehículo espacial
spacious ['speʃəs] *adj* espacioso
spade [sped] *s* laya; (*playing card*) pique *m;* **to call a spade a spade** llamar al pan pan y al vino vino
spade'work' *s* trabajo preliminar
spaghetti [spə'gɛti] *s* espagueti *m*
Spain [spen] *s* España
span [spæn] *s* palmo, cuarta, llave *f* de la mano; espacio, lapso, trecho; (*of horses*) pareja; (*of a bridge*) ojo; (aer) envergadura || *v* (*pret & pp* **spanned;** *ger* **spanning**) *tr* medir a palmos; atravesar, extenderse sobre
spangle ['spæŋgəl] *s* lentejuela || *tr* adornar con lentejuelas; (*to stud with bright objects*) estrellar || *intr* brillar
Spaniard ['spænjərd] *s* español *m*
spaniel ['spænjəl] *s* perro de aguas
Spanish ['spænɪʃ] *adj & s* español *m;* **the Spanish** los españoles
Spanish America *s* la América Española, Hispanoamérica
Spanish broom *s* retama
Spanish fly *s* abadejo, cantárida
Spanish Main *s* Costa Firme, Tierra Firme; mar *m* Caribe
Spanish moss *s* barba española
Spanish omelet *s* tortilla de tomate
Span'ish-speak'ing *adj* de habla española, hispanohablante, hispanoparlante
spank [spæŋk] *tr* azotar, zurrar
spanking ['spæŋkɪŋ] *adj* rápido; fuerte; (coll) muy grande, muy hermoso, extraordinario || *s* azote *m*
spar *s* (mineral) espato; (naut) mástil *m*, palo, verga ||*v* (*pret & pp* **sparred;** *ger* **sparring**) *intr* pelear, reñir; boxear
spare [spɛr] *adj* sobrante; libre, disponible; de repuesto; delgado, enjuto, flaco; parco, sobrio || *tr* pasar sin; perdonar; guardar, salvar; ahorrar; **to have . . . to spare** tener de sobra; **to spare oneself** ahorrarse esfuerzos
spare bed *s* cama de sobra
spare parts *spl* piezas de repuesto o de recambio
spare room *s* cuarto de reserva
sparing ['spɛrɪŋ] *adj* económico; (*scanty*) escaso
spark [spɑrk] *s* chispa; (*e.g., of truth*) centellita || *tr* (coll) cortejar, galantear (*a una mujer*) || *intr* chispear
spark coil *s* bobina de chispas, bobina de encendido
spark gap *s* (*of induction coil*) entrehierro; (*of spark plug*) espacio de chispa
sparkle ['spɑrkəl] *s* chispita, destello; (*wit*) travesura; alegría, viveza || *intr* chispear; ser alegre; espumar, ser efervescente
sparkling ['spɑrklɪŋ] *adj* centelleante, chispeante; (*wine*) espumante, espumoso; (*water*) gaseoso
spark plug *s* bujía
sparrow ['spæro] *s* gorrión *m*
sparse [spɑrs] *adj* (*population*) poco denso; (*hair*) ralo
Spartan ['spɑrtən] *adj & s* espartano
spasm ['spæzəm] *s* espasmo; esfuerzo súbito y de breve duración
spasmodic ['spæz'mɑdɪk] *adj* espasmódico; intermitente; caprichoso
spastic ['spæstɪk] *adj* espástico
spat [spæt] *s* disputa, riña; botín *m*, polaina corta
spatial ['speʃəl] *adj* espacial
spatter ['spætər] *tr* salpicar; manchar || *intr* chorrear; chapotear
spatula ['spætʃələ] *s* espátula
spavin ['spævɪn] *s* esparaván *m*
spawn [spɔn] *s* freza; prole *f;* producto, resultado || *tr* engendrar || *intr* desovar, frezar (*los peces*)
speak [spik] *v* (*pret* **spoke** [spok]; *pp* **spoken**) *tr* hablar (*un idioma*); decir (*la verdad*) || *intr* hablar; **so to speak** por decirlo así; **speaking!** ¡al habla!; **to speak out** o **up** osar hablar, elevar la voz
speak'-eas'y *s* (*pl* **-ies**) (slang) taberna clandestina
speaker ['spikər] *s* hablante *mf;* orador *m;* (*of a legislative assembly*) presidente *m;* (rad) altavoz *m*
speaking ['spikɪŋ] *adj* hablante; **to be on speaking terms** hablarse || *s* habla; elocuencia
speaking tube *s* tubo acústico
spear [spɪr] *s* lanza; (*for fishing*) arpón *m;* (*of grass*) hoja || *tr* alancear, herir con lanza
spear'head' *s* punta de lanza || *tr* dirigir, conducir; encabezar; dar impulso a
spear'mint' *s* menta verde, menta romana
spec. *abbr* **special**
special ['spɛʃəl] *adj* especial; **nothing special** (*no great thing*) nada del otro mundo || *s* tren *m* especial
spe'cial•deliv'ery *adj* urgente, de urgencia
specialist ['spɛʃəlɪst] *s* especialista *mf*
speciali•ty [,spɛʃɪ'ælɪti] *s* (*pl* **-ties**) especialidad
specialize ['spɛʃə,laɪz] *tr* especializar || *intr* especializar o especializarse
special•ty ['spɛʃəlti] *s* (*pl* **-ties**) especialidad
spe•cies ['spisiz] *s* (*pl* **-cies**) especie *f*
specific [spɪ'sɪfɪk] adj & *s* específico
speci•fy ['spɛsɪ,faɪ] *v* (*pret & pp* **-fied**) *tr* especificar

specimen [ˈspɛsɪmən] *s* espécimen *m;* (coll) tipo, sujeto
specious [ˈspiʃəs] *adj* especioso, engañoso
speck [spɛk] *s* mota, manchita ‖ *tr* motear, manchar, salpicar de manchas
speckle [ˈspɛkəl] *s* mota, punto ‖ *tr* motear, puntear
spectacle [ˈspɛktəkəl] *s* espectáculo; **spectacles** anteojos, gafas
spectator [ˈspɛktetər] *s* espectador *m*
specter [ˈspɛktər] *s* espectro
spec•trum [ˈspɛktrəm] *s* (*pl* **-tra** [trə] o **-trums**) espectro
speculate [ˈspɛkjəˌlet] *intr* especular
speech [spitʃ] *s* habla; (*of an actor*) parlamento; (*talk before an audience*) conferencia, discurso
speech clinic *s* clínica de la palabra
speech correction *s* foniatría, logopedía
speech defect *s* defecto del habla
speechless [ˈspitʃlɪs] *adj* sin habla; estupefacto
speed [spid] *s* velocidad; (aut) marcha, velocidad; (slang) anfetaminas tomadas como alucinantes ‖ *v* (*pret & pp* **sped** [spɛd]) *tr* apresurar; despedir; ayudar ‖ *intr* apresurarse; adelantar, progresar; ir con exceso de velocidad
speeding [ˈspidɪŋ] *s* exceso de velocidad
speed king *s* as *m* del volante
speed limit *s* velocidad permitida
speedometer [spiˈdɑmɪtər] *s* (*to indicate speed*) velocímetro; velocímetro y cuentakilómetros unidos
speed record *s* marca de velocidad
speed•y [ˈspidi] *adj* (*comp* **-ier;** *super* **-iest**) rápido, veloz
spell [spɛl] *s* encanto, hechizo; tanda, turno; rato, poco tiempo; (*e.g., of good weather*) temporada; **to cast a spell on** encantar, hechizar ‖ *v* (*pret & pp* **spelled** o **spelt** [spɛlt]) *tr* deletrear; indicar, significar; **to spell out** (coll) explicar detalladamente ‖ *intr* deletrear ‖ *v* (*pret & pp* **spelled**) *tr* reemplazar, relevar
spell'bind'er *s* (coll) orador *m* fascinante, orador persuasivo
spelling [ˈspɛlɪŋ] *adj* ortográfico ‖ *s* (*act*) deletreo; (*subject or study*) ortografía; (*way a word is spelled*) grafía
spelunker [spɪˈlʌŋkər] *s* espeleólogo de afición
spend [spɛnd] *v* (*pret & pp* **spent** [spɛnt]) *tr* gastar; pasar (*una hora, un día, etc.*)
spender [ˈspɛndər] *s* gastador *m*
spending money *s* dinero para gastos menudos
spend'thrift' *s* derrochador *m*, pródigo
sperm [spʌrm] *s* esperma; (coll) leche *f*
sperm whale *s* cachalote *m*
spew [spju] *tr & intr* vomitar
sp. gr. *abbr* **specific gravity**
sphere [sfɪr] *s* esfera; astro, cuerpo celeste
spherical [ˈsfɛrɪkəl] *adj* esférico
sphinx [sfɪŋks] *s* (*pl* **sphinxes** o **sphinges** [ˈsfɪndʒiz]) esfinge *f*
spice [spaɪs] *s* especia; (*zest, piquancy*) sainete *m;* fragancia ‖ *tr* especiar; dar gusto o picante a
spice box *s* especiero
spick-and-span [ˈspɪkəndˈspæn] *adj* flamante; limpio, pulcro
spic•y [ˈspaɪsi] *adj* (*comp* **-ier;** *super* **-iest**) especiado; picante; aromático; enchiloso (CAm, Mex); sicalíptico
spider [ˈspaɪdər] *s* araña
spider web *s* tela de araña, telaraña
spiff•y [ˈspɪfi] *adj* (*comp* **-ier;** *super* **-iest**) (slang) guapo, elegante
spigot [ˈspɪgət] *s* grifo; (*plug to stop a vent*) espiche *m*
spike [spaɪk] *s* (*long, heavy nail*) estaca, escarpia; (*sharp projection or part*) punta, pico, púa; (bot) espiga ‖ *tr* empernar; acabar, poner fin a
spill [spɪl] *s* derrame *m;* líquido derramado; (coll) caída, vuelco ‖ *v* (*pret & pp* **spilled** o **spilt** [spɪlt]) *tr* derramar, verter; (coll) hacer caer, volcar ‖ *intr* derramarse, verterse; (coll) caer, volcarse
spill'way' *s* bocacaz *m*, canal *m* de desagüe
spin [spɪn] *s* vuelta, giro muy rápido; (coll) paseo en coche, etc.; **to go into a spin** (aer) entrar en barrena ‖ *v* (*pret & pp* **spun** [spʌn]; *ger* **spinning**) *tr* hacer girar; hilar (*p.ej., lino*); bailar (*un trompo*); **to spin off** (*derivative*) rendir; **to spin out** extender, prolongar; **to spin yarns** contar cuentos increíbles ‖ *intr* dar vueltas, girar; hilar; bailar (*un trompo*); (aer) entrar en barrena
spinach [ˈspɪnɪtʃ] o [ˈspɪnɪdʒ] *s* espinaca; (*leaves used as food*) espinacas
spinal [ˈspaɪnəl] *adj* espinal
spinal column *s* espina dorsal, columna vertebral
spinal cord *s* médula espinal
spinal disk *s* disco vertebral
spindle [ˈspɪndəl] *s* (*rounded rod tapering toward each end*) huso; (*small shaft, axle*) eje *m;* (*turned ornament in a baluster*) mazorca
spine [spaɪn] *s* espina, púa; (*rib, ridge*) cordoncillo; loma, cerro; (anat) espina; (bb) lomo; (fig) ánimo, valor *m*
spineless [ˈspaɪnlɪs] *adj* sin espinas, sin espinazo; sin firmeza de carácter
spinet [ˈspɪnɪt] *s* espineta
spinner [ˈspɪnər] *s* hilandero; máquina de hilar
spinning [ˈspɪnɪŋ] *adj* hilador ‖ *s* (*act*) hila; (*art*) hilandería
spinning wheel *s* torno de hilar
spin'-off' *s* derivado; subproducto
spinster [ˈspɪnstər] *s* (*obs or offensive*) solterona
spi•ral [ˈspaɪrəl] *adj & s* espiral *f* ‖ *v* (*pret & pp* **-raled** o **-ralled;** *ger* **-raling** o **-ralling**) *intr* dar vueltas como una espiral; (aer) volar en espiral
spiral staircase *s* escalera de caracol
spire [spaɪr] *s* cima, ápice *m;* (*of a steeple*) aguja, chapitel *m;* (*e.g., of grass*) tallo

spirit ['spɪrɪt] *s* espíritu *m;* humor *m*, temple *m;* personaje *m;* licur *m* || *tr*—**to spirit away** llevarse misteriosamente
spirited ['spɪrɪtɪd] *adj* fogoso, espiritoso
spirit lamp *s* lámpara de alcohol
spiritless ['spɪrɪtlɪs] *adj* apocado, tímido, sin ánimo
spirit level *s* nivel *m* de burbuja
spiritual ['spɪrɪtʃʊ•əl] *adj* espiritual
spiritualism ['spɪrɪtʃʊə,lɪzəm] *s* espiritismo; (*belief that all reality is spiritual*) espiritualismo
spirituous liquors ['spɪrɪtʃʊ•əs] *spl* licores espirituosos
spit [spɪt] *s* esputo, saliva; (*for roasting*) asador *m*, espetón *m;* punta o lengua de tierra; **the spit and image of** la segunda edición de, el retrato de || *v* (*pret & pp* **spat** [spæt] o **spit;** *ger* **spitting**) *tr* escupir || *intr* escupir; lloviznar; neviscar; fufar (*el gato*)
spite [spaɪt] *s* despecho, rencor *m*, inquina; **in spite of** a pesar de, a despecho de; **out of spite** por despecho || *tr* despechar, molestar, picar
spiteful ['spaɪtfəl] *adj* despechado, rencoroso
spit'fire' *s* fierabrás *m;* mujer *f* de mal genio
spittoon [spɪ'tun] *s* escupidera
splash [splæʃ] *s* rociada, salpicadura; (*e.g., with the hands*) chapaleo, chapoteo; **to make a splash** (coll) hacer impresión, llamar la atención, causar furor || *tr & intr* salpicar; chapotear
splash'down' *s* acuatizaje *m*
spleen [splin] *s* mal humor *m;* (anat) bazo; **to vent one's spleen** descargar la bilis
splendid ['splɛndɪd] *adj* espléndido; (coll) magnífico, maravilloso
splendor ['splɛndər] *s* esplendor *m*
splice [splaɪs] *s* empalme *m*, junta || *tr* empalmar, juntar
splint [splɪnt] *s* (*splinter*) astilla, tablilla; (surg) tablilla || *tr* entablillar (*un hueso roto*)
splinter ['splɪntər] *s* astilla; (*of stone, glass, bone*) esquirla || *tr* astillar || *intr* astillarse, hacerse astillas
splinter group *s* grupúsculo; grupo disidente
split [splɪt] *adj* hendido, partido; dividido || *s* división, fractura; (slang) porción || *v* (*pret & pp* **split;** *ger* **splitting**) *tr* dividir, partir; **to split one's sides with laughter** desternillarse de risa || *intr* dividirse a lo largo; **to split away (from)** separarse (de)
split fee *s* dicotomía (*entre médicos*)
split personality *s* personalidad desdoblada
splitting ['splɪtɪŋ] *adj* partidor; fuerte, violento; (*headache*) enloquecedor
splotch [splɑtʃ] *s* borrón *m*, mancha grande || *tr* salpicar, manchar
splurge [splʌrdʒ] *s* (coll) fachenda, ostentación || *intr* (coll) fachendear
splutter ['splʌtər] *s* chisporroteo; (*manner of speaking*) farfulla || *tr* farfullar || *intr* chisporrotear; farfullar
spoil [spɔɪl] *s* botín *m*, presa; **spoils** (*taken from an enemy*) botín, despojos; (*of political victory*) enchufes *mpl* || *v* (*pret & pp* **spoiled** o **spoilt** [spɔɪlt]) *tr* echar a perder, estropear; mimar (*a un niño*); amargar (*una tertulia*) || *intr* echarse a perder
spoiled [spɔɪld] *adj* (*child*) consentido, mimado; (*food*) pasado, podrido
spoils•man ['spɔɪlzmən] *s* (*pl* **-men** [mən]) enchufista *m*
spoils system *s* enchufismo
spoke [spok] *s* (*of a wheel*) radio, rayo; (*of a ladder*) escalón *m*
spokes•man ['spoksmən] *s* (*pl* **-men** [mən]) o **spokesperson** *s* portavoz *m*, vocero
sponge [spʌndʒ] *s* esponja; **to throw in** (o **up) the sponge** (coll) tirar la esponja || *tr* limpiar con esponja; borrar; absorber || *intr* ser absorbente; **to sponge on** (coll) vivir a costa de
sponge cake *s* bizcocho muy ligero
sponger ['spʌndʒər] *s* esponja (*gorrón, parásito*); bolsero (SAm)
sponge rubber *s* caucho esponjoso
spon•gy ['spʌndʒi] *adj* (comp **-gier;** *super* **-giest**) esponjoso
sponsor ['spɑnsər] *s* patrocinador *m;* (*godfather*) padrino; (*godmother*) madrina || *tr* patrocinar
sponsorship ['spɑnsər,ʃɪp] *s* patrocinio
spontaneous [spɑn'tenɪ•əs] *adj* espontáneo
spoof [spuf] *s* (slang) mistificación, engaño; (slang) broma || *tr* (slang) mistificar, engañar || *intr* (slang) bromear, burlar; (slang) parodiar
spook [spuk] *s* aparecido, espectro
spook•y ['spuki] *adj* (*comp* **-ier;** *super* **-iest)** espectral, espeluznante; (*horse*) asustadizo
spool [spul] *s* carrete *m*, bobina
spoon [spun] *s* cuchara || *tr* cucharear || *intr* (slang) besuquearse (*los enamorados*)
spoonful ['spun,fʊl] *s* cucharada
spoon•y ['spuni] *adj* (*comp* **-ier;** *super* **-iest)** (coll) baboso, sobón
sporadic(al) [spə'rædɪk(əl)] *adj* esporádico
spore [spor] *s* espora
sport [sport] *adj* deportivo, de deporte || *s* deporte *m;* deportista *mf;* (*person or thing controlled by some power or passion*) juguete *m;* (*laughingstock*) hazmerreír *m;* (*gambler*) (coll) tahur *m*, jugador *m;* (*in gambling or playing games*) (coll) buen perdedor; (*flashy fellow*) (coll) guapo, majo; (biol) mutación; **to make sport of** burlarse de, reírse de || *tr* (coll) lucir (*p.ej., un traje nuevo*) || *intr* divertirse; estar de burla; juguetear
sport clothes *spl* trajes *mpl* de sport
sport fan *s* aficionado al deporte, deportista *mf*
sporting chance *s* riesgo de buen perdedor
sporting goods *spl* artículos de deporte
sporting house *s* casa de juego; casa de rameras
sports'cast'er *s* locutor deportivo
sports•man ['sportsmən] *s* (*pl* **-men** [mən]) deportista *m;* jugador honrado
sports news *s* noticiario deportivo
sports'wear' *s* trajes deportivos
sports writer *s* cronista deportivo

sport•y ['spɔrti] *adj* (*comp* **-ier;** *super* **-iest**) elegante, guapo; alegre, brillante; magnánimo; disipado, libertino

spot [spɑt] *s* mancha; sitio, lugar *m;* (coll) poquito; **on the spot** allí mismo; al punto; (slang) en dificultad; (slang) en peligro de muerte; **to hit the spot** tener razón; dar completa satisfacción || *v* (*pret & pp* **spotted;** *ger* **spotting**) *tr* manchar; descubrir, reconocer || *intr* mancharse, tener manchas

spot cash *s* dinero contante

spot check *s* verificación a la ventura

spotless ['spɑtlɪs] *adj* inmaculado, sin manchas

spot'light' *s* proyector *m* orientable; luz concentrada; (aut) faro piloto, faro giratorio; (fig) atención del público

spot remover [rɪ'muvər] *s* (*person*) quitamanchas *mf;* (*material*) quitamanchas *m*

spot welding *s* soldadura por puntos

spouse [spaʊz] o [spaʊs] *s* cónyuge *mf,* consorte *mf*

spout [spaʊt] *s* (*to carry off water from roof*) canalón *m;* (*of a jar, pitcher, etc.*) pico; (*of a sprinkling can*) rallo, roseta; (*jet*) chorro; **up the spout** (slang) acabado, arruinado || *tr* echar en chorro; (coll) declamar || *intr* chorrear; (coll) declamar

sprain [spren] *s* torcedura, esguince *m* || *tr* torcer, torcerse

sprawl [sprɔl] *intr* arrellanarse

spray [spre] *s* rociada; (*of the sea*) espuma; (*device*) pulverizador *m;* (*twig*) ramita || *tr & intr* rociar

sprayer ['spre•ər] *s* rociador *m,* pulverizador *m,* vaporizador *m*

spread [sprɛd] *s* extensión; amplitud, anchura; difusión; diferencia; cubrecama, sobrecama; mantel *m,* tapete *m;* (*of the wings of a bird; of the wings of an airplane*) envergadura; (coll) festín *m,* comilona || *v* (*pret & pp* **spread**) *tr* extender; difundir, propagar; esparcir; escalonar; abrir, separar; poner (*la mesa*) || *intr* extenderse; difundirse; esparcirse; abrirse, separarse

spree [spri] *s* juerga, parranda; borrachera; **to go on a spree** ir de juerga; pillar una mona

sprig [sprɪg] *s* ramita

spright•ly ['spraɪtli] *adj* (*comp* **-lier;** *super* **-liest**) alegre, animado, vivo

spring [sprɪŋ] *adj* primaveral; de manantial; de muelle, de resorte || *s* (*season of the year*) primavera; (*issue of water from earth*) fuente *f,* manantial *m;* (*elastic device*) muelle *m,* resorte *m;* (*of an automobile or wagon*) ballesta; (*leap, jump*) brinco, salto; abertura, grieta; tensión, tirantez *f* || *v* (*pret* **sprang** [spræŋ] o **sprung** [sprʌŋ]; *pp* **sprung**) *tr* soltar (*un muelle o resorte*); torcer, combar, encorvar; hacer saltar (*una trampa, una mina*) || *intr* saltar; saltar de golpe; brotar, nacer, proceder; torcerse, combarse, encorvarse; **to spring at** abalanzarse sobre; **to spring forth** precipitarse; brotar; **to spring up** levantarse de un salto; brotar, nacer; presentarse a la vista

spring'board' *s* trampolín *m*

spring chicken *s* polluelo; (*young person*) (coll) pollita

spring fever *s* (hum) ataque *m* primaveral, galbana

spring mattress *s* colchón *m* de muelles, somier *m*

spring'time' *s* primavera

sprinkle ['sprɪŋkəl] *s* rociada; llovizna; pizca || *tr* regar, rociar; salpicar, sembrar; espolvorear (*p.ej., azúcar*) || *intr* rociar; lloviznar, gotear

sprinkling can *s* regadera, rociadera

sprint [sprɪnt] *s* (sport) embalaje *m* || *intr* (sport) embalarse, lanzarse

sprite [spraɪt] *s* duende *m,* trasgo

sprocket ['sprɑkɪt] *s* diente *m* de rueda de cadena; rueda de cadena

sprout [spraʊt] *s* brote *m,* renuevo, retoño || *intr* brotar, germinar, echar renuevos; crecer rápidamente

spruce [sprus] *adj* apuesto, elegante, garboso || *s* abeto del Norte, abeto falso, pícea || *tr* ataviar, componer || *intr* ataviarse, componerse; **to spruce up** emperifollarse

spry [spraɪ] *adj* (*comp* **spryer** o **sprier;** *super* **spryest** o **spriest**) activo, ágil

spud [spʌd] *s* (*chisel*) escoplo; (agr) escoda; (coll) patata

spun glass [spʌn] *s* vidrio hilado, cristal hilado

spunk [spʌŋk] *s* (coll) ánimo, coraje *m,* corazón *m,* valor *m*

spun silk *s* seda cardada o hilada

spur [spʌr] *s* espuela; (*central point of an auger*) gusanillo; (*of a cock, mountain, warship*) espolón *m*; (rr) ramal corto; (*goad, stimulus*) (fig) espuela; **on the spur of the moment** impulsivamente, sin la reflexión debida || *v* (*pret & pp* **spurred;** *ger* **spurring**) *tr* espolear; espuelar (SAm); **to spur on** espolear, aguijonear

spurious ['spjʊrɪ•əs] *adj* espurio

spurn [spʌrn] desdén *m,* menosprecio || *tr* desdeñar, menospreciar; rechazar con desdén

spurt [spʌrt] *s* chorro repentino; esfuerzo repentino; arranque *m* || *intr* salir en chorro, salir a borbotones

sputnik ['spʌtnɪk] *s* sputnik *m;* satélite *m* artificial

sputter ['spʌtər] *s* (*manner of speaking*) farfulla; (*sizzling*) chisporroteo || *tr* farfullar || *intr* farfullar; chisporrotear

spy [spaɪ] *s* (*pl* **spies**) espía *mf* ||*v* (*pret & pp* **spied**) *tr* columbrar, divisar || *intr* espiar; **to spy on** espiar

spy'glass' *s* catalejo, anteojo

spy satellite *s* satélite *m* espía

sq. *abbr* **square**

squabble ['skwɑbəl] *s* reyerta, riña || *intr* reñir, disputar

squad [skwɑd] *s* escuadra

squadron ['skwɑdrən] *s* (aer) escuadrilla; (*of cavalry*) (mil) escuadrón *m;* (nav) escuadra

squalid ['skwɑlɪd] *adj* escuálido

squall [skwɔl] *s* grupada, turbión *m; (quarrel)* (coll) riña; *(upset, commotion)* (coll) chubasco
squalor [ˈskwɑlər] *s* escualidez *f*
squander [ˈskwɑndər] *tr* despilfarrar, malgastar
square [skwɛr] *adj* cuadrado, p.ej., **eight square inches** ocho pulgadas cuadradas; en cuadro, de lado, p.ej., **eight inches square** ocho pulgadas en cuadro, ocho pulgadas de lado; rectangular; justo, recto; honrado, leal; saldado; fuerte, sólido; (coll) abundante, completo; **to get square with** (coll) hacérselas pagar a ‖ *adv* en cuadro; en ángulo recto; honradamente, lealmente ‖ *s* cuadrado; *(of checkerboard or chessboard)* casilla, escaque *m; (city block)* manzana; *(open area in town or city)* plaza; *(carpenter's tool)* escuadra; **to be on the square** (coll) obrar de buena fe ‖ *tr* cuadrar; dividir en cuadros; ajustar, nivelar, conformar; saldar *(una cuenta)*; (carp) escuadrar ‖ *intr* cuadrarse; **to square off** (coll) colocarse en posición de defensa
square dance *s* danza de figuras
square deal *s* (coll) trato equitativo
square meal *s* (coll) comida abundante
square shooter [ˈʃutər] *s* (coll) persona leal y honrada
squash [skwɑʃ] *s* aplastamiento; (bot) calabaza; (sport) frontón *m* con raqueta; ‖ *tr* aplastar, despachurrar; confutar *(un argumento)*; acallar con un argumento, respuesta, etc. ‖ *intr* aplastarse
squash·y [ˈskwɑʃi] *adj (comp* **-ier;** *super* **-iest)** mojado y blando; *(muddy)* lodoso; *(fruit)* modorro
squat [skwɑt] *adj* en cuclillas; rechoncho ‖ *v (pret & pp* **squatted;** *ger* **squatting)** *intr* acuclillarse, agacharse; sentarse en el suelo; establecerse en terreno ajeno sin derecho; establecerse en terreno público para crear un derecho
squatter [ˈskwɑtər] *s* advenedizo, intruso, colono usurpador
squaw [skwɔ] *s* india norteamericana; mujer, esposa, muchacha
squawk [skwɔk] *s* graznido; (slang) queja chillona ‖ *intr* graznar; (slang) quejarse chillando
squaw man *s* blanco casado con india
squeak [skwik] *s* chillido; chirrido ‖ *intr* dar chillidos; chirriar
squeal [skwil] *s* chillido ‖ *intr* dar chillidos; (slang) delatar, soplar; **to squeal on** (slang) delatar, soplar *(a una persona)*
squealer [ˈskwilər] *s* (coll) soplón *m*
squeamish [ˈskwimɪʃ] *adj* escrupuloso, remilgado; excesivamente modesto; *(easily nauseated)* asqueroso
squeeze [skwiz] *s* apretón *m;* **to put the squeeze on someone** (coll) hacer a uno la forzosa, meter en prensa a uno ‖ *tr* apretar; agobiar, oprimir; exprimir ‖ *intr* apretar; **to squeeze through** abrirse paso a estrujones por entre; salir de un aprieto a duras penas
squeezer [ˈskwizər] *s* exprimidera
squelch [skwɛltʃ] *s* (coll) tapaboca ‖ *tr* apabullar, despachurrar
squid [skwɪd] *s* calamar *m*
squint [skwɪnt] *s* mirada bizca; mirada furtiva; *(strabismus)* bizquera ‖ *tr* achicar, entornar *(los ojos)* ‖ *intr* bizquear; torcer la vista; tener los ojos medio cerrados
squint-eyed [ˈskwɪnt,aɪd] *adj* bisojo, bizco; malévolo, sospechoso
squire [skwaɪr] *s* acompañante *m (de una señora)*; (Brit) terrateniente *m* de antigua heredad; (U.S.A.) juez *m* de paz, juez local ‖ *tr* acompañar *(a una señora)*
squirm [skwʌrm] *s* retorcimiento ‖ *intr* retorcerse; **to squirm out of** escaparse de *(p.ej., un aprieto)* haciendo mucho esfuerzo
squirrel [ˈskwʌrəl] *s* ardilla
squirt [skwʌrt] *s* chorro; jeringazo; (coll) mono, presuntuoso ‖ *tr* arrojar a chorros ‖ *intr* salir a chorros
Sr. *abbr* **senior, Sir**
S.S. *abbr* **Secretary of State, steamship, Sunday school**
St. *abbr* **Saint, Strait, Street**
stab [stæb] *s* puñalada; (coll) tentativa; **to make a stab at** (slang) esforzarse por hacer ‖ *v (pret & pp* **stabbed;** *ger* **stabbing)** *tr* apuñalar; traspasar ‖ *intr* apuñalar
stab in the back *s* puñalada trapera
stable [ˈstebəl] *adj* estable ‖ *s* establo, cuadra, caballeriza
stack [stæk] *s* montón *m*, pila; *(of rifles)* pabellón *m; (of books in a library)* estantería, depósito; *(of a chimney)* cañón *m; (of straw)* niara; *(of firewood)* hacina; (coll) montón *m*, gran número ‖ *tr* amontonar, apilar; florear *(el naipe)*; hacinar *(leña)*
stadi·um [ˈstedɪ·əm] *s (pl* **-ums** *o* **-a [ə])** estadio
staff [stæf] *s* bastón *m*, apoyo, sostén *m;* personal *m;* (mil) estado mayor; (mus) pentagrama *m* ‖ *tr* dotar, proveer de personal, nombrar personal para
stag [stæg] *adj* exclusivo para hombres, de hombres solos ‖ *s (male deer)* ciervo; varón *m;* varón solo *(no acompañado de mujeres)*
stage [stedʒ] *s* escena; etapa, jornada; *(coach)* diligencia; *(scene of an event)* teatro; *(of a microscope)* portaobjeto; (rad) etapa; **by easy stages** a pequeñas etapas; lentamente; **to go on the stage** hacerse actor ‖ *tr* poner en escena, representar; preparar, organizar
stage'coach' *s* diligencia
stage'craft' *s* arte *f* teatral
stage door *s* (theat) entrada de los artistas
stage fright *s* trac *m*, miedo al público
stage'hand' *s* tramoyista *m*, metemuertos *m*, metesillas *m*
stage manager *s* director *m* de escena
stage'-struck' *adj* loco por el teatro
stage whisper *s* susurro en voz alta
stagger [ˈstægər] *tr* sorprender; asustar; escalonar *(las horas de trabajo)* ‖ *intr* tambalear, hacer eses al andar
staggering *adj* tambaleante; sorprendente

stagnant ['stægnənt] *adj* estancado; (fig) estancado, inactivo, paralizado
staid [sted] *adj* grave, serio, formal
stain [sten] *s* mancha; tinte *m*, tintura; materia colorante || *tr* manchar; teñir; colorar || *intr* mancharse; hacer manchas
stained glass *s* vidrio de color
stained'glass' window *s* vidriera de colores, vidriera pintada, vitral *m*
stainless ['stenlɪs] *adj* inmanchable; (*steel*) inoxidable; inmaculado
stair [stɛr] *s* escalera; (*step of a series*) escalón *m;* **stairs** escalera
stair'case' *s* escalera
stair'way' *s* escalera
stair well *s* hueco de escalera
stake [stek] *s* estaca; (*of a cart or truck*) telero; (*to hold up a plant*) rodrigón *m;* (*in gambling*) puesta; premio del vencedor; **at stake** en juego; en gran peligro; **to die at the stake** morir en la hoguera; **to pull up stakes** (coll) irse; (coll) mudarse de casa || *tr* estacar; atar a una estaca; rodrigar (*plantas*); apostar; arriesgar, aventurar; **to stake all** jugarse el todo por el todo; **to stake off** o **to stake out** estacar, señalar con estacas
stale [stel] *adj* añejo, rancio, viejo; (*air*) viciado; (*joke*) mohoso; anticuado
stale'mate' *s* mate ahogado; **to reach a stalemate** llegar a un punto muerto || *tr* dar mate ahogado a; estancar, paralizar
stalk [stɔk] *s* tallo || *tr* cazar al acecho; acechar, espiar || *intr* cazar al acecho; andar con paso majestuoso; andar con paso altivo; **to stalk out** salir con paso airado
stall [stɔl] *s* cuadra, establo; pesebre *m;* (*booth in a market*) puesto; (*at a fair*) caseta; (Brit) butaca; (slang) pretexto || *tr* encerrar en un establo; poner trabas a; parar (*un motor*); **to stall off** (coll) eludir, evitar || *intr* atascarse, atollarse; pararse (*un motor*); (slang) eludir para engañar o demorar; **to stall for time** (slang) tardar para ganar tiempo
stallion ['stæljən] *s* caballo padre, caballo semental
stalwart ['stɔlwərt] *adj* fornido, forzudo; valiente; leal, constante || *s* persona fornida; partidario leal
stamen ['stemən] *s* estambre *m*
stamina ['stæmɪnə] *s* fuerza, nervio, vigor *m*, resistencia
stammer ['stæmər] *s* balbuceo, tartamudeo || *tr* balbucear (*p.ej., excusas*) || *intr* balbucear, tartamudear
stamp [stæmp] *s* (*device used for making an impression; mark made with it; piece of paper or mark used to show payment of postage*) sello; (*tool used for crushing or marking*) pisón *m;* (*tool for stamping coins and medals*) cuño, troquel *m;* marca, impresión; clase *f*, tipo || *tr* sellar; troquelar; estampar, imprimir; hollar, pisotear; indicar, señalar; poner el sello a; bocartear (*el mineral*); **to stamp out** apagar pateando; extinguir por la fuerza; suprimir; **to stamp the feet** dar patadas || *intr* patalear
stampede [stæm'pid] *s* fuga precipitada; estampida (Am) || *tr* hacer huir en desorden; provocar a pánico || *intr* huir en tropel; obrar por común impulso
stamping grounds *spl* (slang) guarida (*sitio frecuentado por una persona*)
stamp pad *s* tampón *m*
stamp'-vend'ing machine *s* máquina expendedora de sellos
stance [stæns] *s* (sport) postura, planta
stanch [stɑntʃ] *adj* firme, fuerte; constante, leal; (*watertight*) estanco || *tr* estancar; retañar (*la sangre de una herida*)
stand [stænd] *s* parada; alto para defenderse; postura, posición; resistencia; estrado, tribuna; sostén *m* soporte *m*, pie *m;* puesto, quiosco || *v* (*pret & pp* **stood** [stʊd]) *tr* poner, colocar; poner derecho; soportar, tolerar, resistir; (coll) aguantar (*a una persona*); (coll) sufragar (*un gasto*); **to stand off** tener a raya; **to stand one's ground** mantenerse firme || *intr* estar, estar situado; estar parado; estacionarse; estar de pie, estar derecho; ponerse de pie, levantarse; resultar; persistir; mantenerse; **to stand aloof, apart** o **aside** mantenerse apartado; **to stand back of** respaldar; **to stand for** significar, representar; apoyar, defender; apadrinar; mantener (*p.ej., una opinión*); presentarse como candidato de; navegar hacia; (coll) tolerar; **to stand in line** hacer cola; **to stand out** sobresalir; destacarse, resaltar; **to stand up** ponerse de pie, levantarse; durar; **to stand up to** hacer; resueltamente frente a
standard ['stændərd] *adj* normal; (*typewriter keyboard*) universal; corriente, regular; legal; clásico || *s* patrón *m;* norma, regla establecida; bandera, estandarte *m;* emblema *m*, símbolo; soporte *m*, pilar *m*
standardize ['stændər,daɪz] *tr* normalizar, estandardizar
standard of living *s* nivel *m* de vida
standard time *s* hora legal, hora oficial
standee [stæn'di] *s* (coll) espectador *m* que asiste de pie; (coll) pasajero de pie
stand'-in' *s* (theat & mov) doble *mf;* (coll) buenas aldabas
standing ['stændɪŋ] *adj* derecho, en pie; de pie; parado, inmóvil; (*water*) encharcado, estancado; (*army; committee*) permanente; vigente || *s* condición, posición; reputación; parada; **in good standing** en posición acreditada; **of long standing** de mucho tiempo, de antigua fecha
standing army *s* ejército permanente
standing room *s* sitio para estar de pie
stand-offishness [,stænd'ɔfɪʃnɪs] *s* desarrimo
stand'point' *s* punto de vista
stand'still' *s* detención, parada; alto; descanso, inactividad; **to come to a standstill** cesar, pararse
stanza ['stænzə] *s* estancia, estrofa
staple ['stepəl] *adj* primero, principal; corriente, establecido || *s* (*to fasten papers*)

grapa; artículo o producto de primera necesidad; materia prima; fibra textil || *tr* sujetar con grapas

stapler ['steplər] *s* engrapador *m*, cosepapeles *m*

star [stɑr] *s* (*heavenly body*) astro; (*heavenly body except sun and moon; figure that represents a star*) estrella; (mov & theat) estrella; (*of football*) as *m;* (typ) estrella o asterisco; (*fate, destiny*) (fig) estrella; **to see stars** (coll) ver las estrellas; **to thank one's lucky stars** estar agradecido por su buena suerte || *v* (*pret & pp* **starred;** *ger* **starring**) *tr* estrellar, adornar o señalar con estrellas; marcar con asterisco; presentar como estrella (*a un actor*) || *intr* ser la estrella; lucirse; sobresalir

starboard ['stɑrbərd] o ['stɑr,bord] *adj* de estribor || *adv* a estribor || *s* estribor *m*

starch [stɑrʃ] *s* almidón *m*, fécula; arrogancia, entono; (slang) fuerza, vigor *m* || *tr* almidonar

stare [stɛr] *s* mirada fija || *intr* mirar fijamente; **to stare at** clavar la vista en mirar con fijeza

star'fish' *s* estrella de mar, estrellamar *m*

star'gaze' *intr* mirar las estrellas; ser distraído, soñar despierto

stark [stɑrk] *adj* cabal, completo, puro; rígido, tiesco; duro, severo || *adv* completamente, enteramente; rígidamente, severamente

stark'-na'ked *adj* en pelota, en cueros

star'light' *s* luz *f* de las estrellas

starling ['stɑrlɪŋ] *s* estornino

Star'-Span'gled Banner *s* bandera estrellada (*bandera de los EE.UU.*)

start [stɑrt] *s* comienzo, principio; salida, partida; lugar *m* de partida; (*scare*) sobresalto; (*sudden start*) arranque *m;* (*advantage*) ventaja || *tr* empezar, principiar; poner en marcha; hacer arrancar; dar la señal de partida a; entablar (*una conversación*); levantar (*la caza*) || *intr* empezar, principiar; ponerse en marcha; arrancar; (*to be startled*) sobresaltar; nacer, provenir; **starting from** o **with** a partir de; **to start after** salir en busca de

starter ['stɑrtər] *s* iniciador *m;* (*of a series*) primero; (aut) arranque *m*, motor *m* de arranque; (sport) juez *m* de salida

starting ['stɑrtɪŋ] *adj* de salida; de arranque || *s* puesta en marcha

starting crank *s* manivela de arranque

starting point *s* punto de partida, arrancadero

startle ['stɑrtəl] *tr* asustar, sorprender, sobrecoger || *intr* asustarse, sorprenderse sobrecogerse

startling ['stɑrtlɪŋ] *adj* alarmante, asombroso

starvation [stɑr'veʃən] *s* hambre *f*, inanición

starvation diet *s* régimen *m* de hambre, cura de hambre

starvation wages *spl* salario de hambre

starve [stɑrv] *tr* hambrear; hacer morir de hambre; **to starve out** hacer rendirse por hambre || *intr* hambrear; morir de hambre; (coll) tener hambre

starving ['stɑrvɪŋ] *adj* hambriento, famélico

stat. *abbr* **statuary, statute, statue**

state [stet] *adj* de estado; del estado; estatal; público; de gala, de lujo || *s* estado; fausto, ceremonia, pompa; **to lie in state** estar expuesto en capilla ardiente, estar de cuerpo presente; **to live in state** gastar mucho lujo; **to ride in state** pasear en carruaje de lujo || *tr* afirmar, declarar; exponer, manifestar; plantear (*un problema*)

State Department *s* Ministerio de Relaciones Exteriores

state•ly ['stetli] *adj* (*comp* **-lier;** *super* **-liest**) imponente, majestuoso

statement ['stetmənt] *s* declaración; exposición, informe *m*, relación; (com) estado de cuentas

state of mind *s* estado de ánimo

state'room' *s* camarote *m;* (rr) compartimiento particular

state'side' *adv* (coll) en (*or* a) los Estados Unidos

states•man ['stetsmən] *s* (*pl* **-men** [mən]) estadista *m*, hombre *m* de estado

static ['stætɪk] *adj* estático; (rad) atmosférico || *s* (rad) parásitos atmosféricos

station ['steʃən] *s* estación; condición, situación || *tr* estacionar, apostar

station agent *s* jefe *m* de estación

stationary ['steʃən,ɛri] *adj* estacionario

station break *s* (rad) descanso, intermedio

stationer ['steʃənər] *s* papelero

stationery ['steʃən,ɛri] *s* efectos de escritorio; papel *m* para cartas

stationery store *s* papelería

station house *s* cuartelillo de policía

station identification *s* (rad & telv) indicativo de la emisora

sta'tion•mas'ter *s* jefe *m* de estación

station wagon *s* vagoneta, rubia, coche *m* rural; camioneta (Arg, CAm, Col. Pan, Peru, S-D); esteishon wagon *m* (Chile, Col, Cuba, P-R); guagüita (Cuba, P-R); camionetilla (Guat); carmelita (Hond); ranchera (Ven)

statistical [stə,tɪstɪkəl] *adj* estadístico

statistician [,stætɪs,tɪʃən] *s* estadístico

statistics [stə,tɪstɪks] *ssg* (*science*) estadística; *spl* (*data*) estadística o estadísticas

statue ['stætʃu] *s* estatua

statuesque [,stætʃu,ɛsk] *adj* escultural

stature [,stætʃər] *s* estatura, talla; carácter *m*, habilidad

status ['stetəs] *s* condición, estado; situación social, legal o profesional; (*prestige or superior rank*) categoría

status seeking *s* esfuerzo por adquirir categoría

status symbol *s* símbolo de categoría social

statute ['stætʃut] *s* estatuto, ley *f*

statutory ['stætʃu,tori] *adj* estatutario, legal

staunch [stɔntʃ] o [stɑntʃ] *adj & tr* var de **stanch**

stave [stev] *s* (*of a barrel*) duela; (*of a ladder*) peldaño; (mus) pentagrama *m* ‖*v* (*pret & pp* **staved** o **stove** [stov]) *tr* romper, destrozar; (*to break a hole in*) desfondar; **to stave off** mantener a distancia; evitar, impedir, diferir

stay [ste] *s* morada, permanencia, estancia; suspensión; (*of a corset*) ballena, varilla; apoyo, sostén *m;* (law) espera; (naut) estay *m* ‖ *tr* aplazar, detener; poner freno a ‖ *intr* quedar, quedarse, permanecer; parar, hospedarse; habitar; **to stay up** no acostarse, velar

stay'-at-home' *adj & s* hogareño

stead [stɛd] *s* lugar *m;* **in his stead** en su lugar, en lugar de él; **to stand in good stead** ser de provecho, ser ventajoso

stead'fast' *adj* fijo; resuelto; constante

stead•y ['stɛdi] *adj* (*comp* **-ier;** *super* **-iest**) constante, fijo, firme, seguro; regular, uniforme; resuelto; asentado, serio ‖ *v* (*pret & pp* **-ied**) *tr* estabilizar, reforzar; calmar (*los nervios*) ‖ *intr* estabilizarse; calmarse

steak [stek] *s* lonja, tajada; biftec *m*

steal [stil] *s* (coll) hurto, robo ‖ *v* (*pret* **stole** [stol]; *pp* **stolen**) *tr* hurtar, robar; atraer, cautivar; manotear (Arg, Mex) ‖ *intr* hurtar, robar; **to steal away** escabullirse; **to steal into** meterse a hurtadillas en; **to steal upon** aproximarse sin ruido a

stealth [stɛlθ] *s* cautela, recato; **by stealth** a hurtadillas

steam [stim] *adj* de vapor ‖ *s* vapor *m;* vaho, humo; **to get up steam** dar presión; **to let off steam** descargar vapor; (fig) desahogarse ‖ *tr* cocer al vapor; saturar de vapor; empañar (*p.ej., las ventanas*) ‖ *intr* echar vapor, emitir vapor; evaporarse; funcionar o marchar a vapor; **to steam ahead** avanzar por medio del vapor; (fig) hacer grandes progresos

steam'boat' *s* buque *m* de vapor

steamer ['stimər] *s* vapor *m*

steamer rug *s* manta de viaje

steamer trunk *s* baúl *m* de camarote

steam heat *s* calefacción por vapor

steam roller *s* apisonadora movida a vapor; (coll) fuerza arrolladora

steam'ship' *s* vapor *m*, buque *m* de vapor

steam shovel *s* pala mecánica de vapor

steam table *s* plancha caliente

steed [stid] *s* caballo; (*high-spirited horse*) corcel *m*

steel [stil] *adj* acerado; (*business, industry*) siderúrgico; (fig) duro, frío ‖ *s* acero; (*for striking fire from flint; for sharpening knives*) eslabón *m* ‖ *tr* acerar; **to steel oneself** acerarse

steel wool *s* virutillas de acero, estopa de acero

steelyard ['stil,jɑrd] *s* romana

steep [stip] *adj* escarpado, empinado; (*price*) alto, excesivo ‖ *tr* empapar, remojar; **steeped in** absorbido en

steeple ['stipəl] *s* aguja, campanario

stee'ple•chase' *s* carrera de campanario, carrera de obstáculos

stee'ple•jack' *s* escalatorres *m*

steer [stɪr] *s* buey *m* ‖ *tr* conducir, gobernar, guiar ‖ *intr* conducirse; **to steer clear of** (coll) evitar, eludir

steerage ['stɪrɪdʒ] *s* dirección; (naut) proa, entrepuente *m*

steerage passenger *s* (naut) pasajero de entrepuente

steering column *s* columna de dirección

steering committee *s* comité *m* paneador

steering wheel *s* (aut) volante *m;* (naut) rueda del timón

stem [stɛm] *s* (*of a goblet*) pie *m;* (*of a pipe, of a feather*) cañón *m;* (*of a column*) fuste *m;* (*of a watch*) botón *m;* (*of a key*) espiga, tija; (*of a word*) tema *m;* (bot) tallo, vástago; **from stem to stern** de proa a popa ‖ *v* (*pret & pp* **stemmed;** *ger* **stemming**) *tr* (*to remove the stem from*) desgranar; (*to check*) detener, refrenar; (*to plug*) estancar; hacer frente a; rendir (*la marea*) ‖ *intr* nacer, provenir; **to stem from** originarse en, provenir de

stem'-wind'er *s* remontuar *m*

stench [stɛntʃ] *s* hedor *m*, hediondez *f*

sten•cil ['stɛnsəl] *s* cartón picado; (*work produced by it*) estarcido ‖ *v* (*pret & pp* **-ciled** o **-cilled;** *ger* **-ciling** o **-cilling**) *tr* estarcir

stenographer [stə'nɑgrəfər] *s* estenógrafo

stenography [stə'nɑgrəfi] *s* estenografía

step [stɛp] *s* paso; (*of staircase*) grada, peldaño; (*footprint*) huella, pisada; (*of carriage*) estribo; (*measure, démarche*) gestión, medida; (mus) intervalo; **step by step** paso a paso; **to watch one's step** proceder con cautela, andarse con tiento ‖ *v* (*pret & pp* **stepped;** *ger* **stepping**) *tr* escalonar; **to step off** medir a pasos ‖ *intr* dar un paso, dar pasos; caminar, ir; (coll) andar de prisa; **to step on it** (coll) acelerar la marcha, darse prisa; **to step on the starter** pisar el arranque

step'broth'er *s* medio hermano, hermanastro

step'child' *s* (*pl* **-children** [,tʃɪldrən]) hijastro

step'daugh'ter *s* hijastra

step'fa'ther *s* padrastro

step'lad'der *s* escala, escalera de tijera

step'moth'er *s* madrastra

steppe [stɛp] *s* estepa

stepping stone *s* estriberón *m*, pasadera; (fig) escalón *m*, escabel *m*

step'sis'ter *s* media hermana, hermanastra

step'son' *s* hijastro

stere•o ['stɛri,o] o ['stɪrɪ,o] *adj* estereofónico; estereososcópico ‖ *s* (*pl* **-os**) música estereofónica, disco estereofónico; radiodifusión estereofónica; fotografía estereoscópica

stereo system *s* equipo de alta fidelidad

ster'e•o•type' *s* clisé *m*, estereotipo; concepción tradicional

stereotyped ['stɛrɪ•ə,taɪpt] o ['stɪrɪ•ə,taɪpt] *adj* estereotipado

sterile ['stɛrɪl] *adj* estéril

sterilization [,stɛrɪlɪ'zeʃən] *s* esterilización

sterilize ['stɛrɪ,laɪz] *tr* esterilizar

sterling [ˈstʌrlɪŋ] *adj* fino, de ley; verdadero, genuino, puro, excelente || *s* libras esterlinas; plata de ley; vajilla de plata
stern [stʌrn] *adj* austero, severo; decidido, firme || *s* popa
stethoscope [ˈstɛθəˌskop] *s* estetoscopio
stevedore [ˈstivəˌdor] *s* estibador *m*
stew [stju] o [stu] *s* guisado, estofado || *tr* guisar, estofar || *intr* abrasarse; (coll) estar apurado
steward [ˈstu•ərd] *s* mayordomo; administrador *m;* (*of ship or plane*) camarero
stewardess [ˈstu•ərdɪs] *s* mayordoma; (*of ship or plane*) camarera; (*of plane*) azafata, aeromoza
stewed fruit *s* compota de frutas
stewed tomatoes *spl* puré *m* de tomates
stick [stɪk] *s* palo, palillo; bastón *m*, vara; (*of dynamite*) barra; (naut) mástil *m*, verga; (typ) componedor *m* || *v* (*pret & pp* **stuck** [stʌk]) *tr* picar, punzar; apuñalar; clavar, hincar; pegar; (coll) confundir; **to stick out** asomar (*la cabeza*); sacar (*la lengua*); **to stick up** (*in order to rob*) (slang) asaltar, atracar || *intr* estar prendido, estar hincado; pegarse; agarrarse (*la pintura*); encastillarse (*p.ej., una ventana*); resaltar, sobresalir; continuar, persistir; permanecer; atascarse; **to stick out** salir (*p.ej., el pañuelo del bolsillo*); sobresalir, proyectarse; velar (*un escollo*); resultar evidente; **to stick together** (coll) quedarse unidos, no abandonarse; **to stick up** destacarse; estar de punta (*el pelo*); **to stick up for** (coll) defender
sticker [ˈstɪkər] *s* etiqueta engomada, marbete engomado; pegatina; punta, espina; (coll) problema arduo
sticking plaster *s* esparadrapo
stick'pin' *s* alfiler *m* de corbata
stick'-up' *s* (slang) asalto, atraco
stick•y [ˈstɪki] *adj* (*comp* **-ier;** *super* **-iest**) pegajoso; (coll) húmedo, mojado; (*weather*) bochornoso
stiff [stɪf] *adj* tieso; entorpecido, entumecido; arduo, difícil; (*price*) (coll) excesivo; **to get stiff** envararse || *s* (slang) cadáver *m*
stiff collar *s* cuello almidonado
stiffen [ˈstɪfən] *tr* atiesar; endurecer; espesar || *intr* atiesarse; endurecerse; espesarse; obstinarse
stiff neck *s* torticolis *m;* obstinación
stiff-necked [ˈstɪfˌnɛkt] *adj* terco, obstinado
stiffness [ˈstɪfnɪs] *s* envaramiento
stiff shirt *s* camisola
stifle [ˈstaɪfəl] *tr* ahogar, sofocar; apagar, suprimir
stig•ma [ˈstɪgmə] *s* (*pl* **-mas** o **-mata** [mətə]) estigma *m*
stigmatize [ˈstɪgməˌtaɪz] *tr* estigmatizar
stilet•to [stɪˈlɛto] *s* (*pl* **-tos**) estilete *m*, puñal *m*
still [stɪl] *adj* inmóvil, quieto, tranquilo; callado, silencioso; (*wine*) no espumoso || *adv* tranquilamente; silenciosamente; aún, todavía || *conj* con todo, sin embargo || *s* alambique *m*, destiladera; destilería; fotografía de lo inmóvil; (poet) silencio || *tr* acallar; amortiguar; calmar || *intr* callar; calmarse
still'birth' *s* parto muerto
still'born' *adj* nacido muerto
still life *s* (*pl* **still lifes** o **still lives**) bodegón *m*, naturaleza muerta
stilt [stɪlt] *s* zanco; (*in the water*) pilote *m*
stilted [ˈstɪltɪd] *adj* elevado; hinchado, pomposo, tieso
stimulant [ˈstɪmjələnt] *adj & s* estimulante *m*, excitante *m*
stimulate [ˈstɪmjəˌlet] *tr* estimular
stimu•lus [ˈstɪmjələs] *s* (*pl* **-li** [ˌlaɪ]) estímulo
sting [stɪŋ] *s* picadura; aguijón *m*; lanceta || *v* (*pret & pp* **stung** [stʌŋ]) *tr* picar; aguijonear || *intr* picar
stin•gy [ˈstɪndʒi] *adj* (*comp* **-gier;** *super* **-giest**) mezquino, tacaño
stink [stiŋk] *s* hedor *m*, mal olor *m* || *v* (*pret* **stank** [stæŋk] o **stunk** [stʌŋk]; *pp* **stunk**) *tr* dar mal olor a || *intr* heder, oler muy mal; **to stink of** heder a; (slang) poseer (*p.ej., dinero*) en un grado que da asco
stint [stɪnt] *s* faena, tarea || *tr* limitar, restringir || *intr* ser económico, ahorrar con mezquindad
stipend [ˈstaɪpənd] *s* estipendio
stipulate [ˈstɪpjəˌlet] *tr* estipular
stir [stʌr] *s* agitación, meneo; alboroto, tumulto; **to create a stir** meter ruido, causar furor || *v* (*pret & pp* **stirred;** *ger* **stirring**) *tr* agitar, mover; revolver; conmover, excitar; atizar, avivar (*el fuego*); remover (*un líquido*); **to stir up** revolver; despertar; conmover; fomentar (*discordias*) || *intr* bullirse, moverse; (*say a word*) rechistar
stirring [ˈstʌrɪŋ] *adj* conmovedor, emocionante
stirrup [ˈstʌrəp] o [ˈstɪrəp] *s* estribo
stitch [stɪtʃ] *s* puntada, punto; pedazo de tela; punzada, dolor *m* punzante; (coll) poquito; **to be in stitches** (coll) desternillarse de risa || *tr* coser, bastear, hilvanar || *intr* coser
stock [stɑk] *adj* común, regular; banal, vulgar; bursátil; ganadero, del ganado; (theat) de repertorio || *s* surtido; capital *f* comercial; acciones, valores *mpl;* (*inventory*) stock *m;* (*of meat*) caldo; (*of a tree*) tronco; (*of an anvil*) cepo; (*of a rifle*) caja, culata; (*of a tree; of a family*) cepa; mango, manija; palo, madero; leño; (*livestock*) ganado; (theat) programa *m*, repertorio; **to have in stock** tener en stock; **in stock** en existencia; **out of stock** agotado; **to take stock** hacer el inventario; **to take stock in** (coll) dar importancia a, confiar en || *tr* abastecer, surtir; tener existencias de; acopiar, acumular; poblar (*un estanque, una colmena, etc.*)
stockade [stɑˈked] *s* estacada, empalizada || *tr* empalizar
stock'breed'er *s* criador *m* de ganado
stock'bro'ker *s* bolsista *mf*, corredor *m* de bolsa
stock car *s* (aut) coche *m* de serie; (rr) vagón *m* para el ganado

stock company *s* (com) sociedad anónima; (theat) teatro de repertorio
stock dividend *s* acción liberada
stock exchange *s* bolsa
stock'hold'er *s* accionista *mf*, tenedor *m* de acciones
stockholder of record *s* accionista *mf* que como tal figura en el libro registro de la compañía
Stockholm ['stɑkhom] *s* Estocolmo
stocking ['stɑkɪŋ] *s* media
stock market *s* bolsa, mercado de valores; **to play the stock market** jugar a la bolsa
stock'pile' *s* reserva de materias primas ‖ *tr* acumular (*materias primas*) ‖ *intr* acumular materias primas
stock raising *s* ganadería
stock'room' *s* almacén *m;* sala de exposición
stock split *s* reparto de acciones gratis
stock•y ['stɑki] *s* adj (*comp* **-ier;** *super* **-iest)** bajo, grueso y fornido
stock'yard' *s* corral *m* de concentración de ganado
stoic ['sto•ɪk] *adj & s* estoico
stoke [stok] *tr* atizar, avivar (*el fuego*); alimentar, cebar (*el horno*)
stoker ['stokər] *s* fogonero
stolid ['stɑlɪd] *adj* impasible, insensible
stomach ['stʌmək] *s* estómago; apetito; deseo, inclinación ‖ *tr* tragar; **to not be able to stomach** (coll) no poder tragar
stomach pump *s* bomba estomacal
stone [ston] *s* piedra; (*of fruit*) hueso; (pathol) mal *m* de piedra ‖ *tr* lapidar, apedrear; deshuesar (*la fruta*)
stone'-broke' *adj* arrancado, sin blanca
stone'-deaf' *adj* sordo como una tapia
stone'ma'son *s* albañil *m*
stone quarry *s* cantera, pedrera
stone's throw *s* tiro de piedra; **within a stone's throw** a tiro de piedra
ston•y ['stoni] *adj* (*comp* **-ier;** *super* **-iest)** pedregoso; duro, empedernido
stool [stul] *s* escabel *m*, taburete *m;* sillico, retrete *m;* (*bowel movement*) cámara, evacuación
stoop [stup] *s* encorvada, inclinación; escalinata de entrada ‖ *intr* doblarse, inclinarse, encorvarse; andar encorvado; humillarse, rebajarse
stoop•shouldered ['stup'ʃoldərd] *adj* cargado de espaldas
stop [stɑp] *s* parada, alto; parón; estada, estancia; cesación, fin *m*, suspensión; cerradura, tapadura; impedimento, obstáculo; freno; tope *m*, retén *m;* (*in writing; in telegrams*) punto; (*of a guitar*) llave *f*, traste *m;* **to put a stop to** poner fin a ‖ *v* (*pret & pp* **stopped;** *ger* **stopping**) *tr* parar, detener; acabar, terminar; estorbar, obstruir; interceptar; suspender; cerrar, tapar; rechazar (*un golpe*); retener (*un sueldo o parte de él*); **to stop up** cegar, obstruir, tapar ‖ *intr* parar, pararse, detenerse; quedarse, permanecer; alojarse, hospedarse; acabarse, terminarse; **to stop** + *ger* cesar de + *inf*, dejar de + *inf*
stop'cock' *s* llave *f* de cierre, llave de paso
stop'gap' *adj* provisional ‖ *s* substituto provisional
stop light *s* luz *f* de parada
stop'o'ver *s* parada intermedia, escala; billete *m* de parada intermedia
stoppage ['stɑpɪdʒ] *s* parada, detención; (*of work*) paro; interrupción; suspensión; obstáculo; (*of wages*) retención; (pathol) obstrucción
stopper ['stɑpər] *s* tapón *m;* taco, tarugo
stop sign o **stop signal** *s* señal *f* de alto, señal de parada
stop watch *s* reloj *m* de segundos muertos, cronómetro
storage ['storɪdʒ] *s* almacenaje *m;* (*costs*) derechos de almacenaje
storage battery *s* (elec) acumulador *m*
store [stor] *s* tienda, almacén *m;* **I know what is in store for you** sé lo que le espera; **to set store by** dar mucha importancia a ‖ *tr* abastecer; tener guardado, almacenar; **to store away** acumular
store'house' *s* almacén *m*, depósito; (*e.g., of wisdom*) (fig) mina
store'keep'er *s* tendero, almacenista *mf*
store'room' *s* cuarto de almacenar; (*for furniture*) guardamuebles *m;* (naut) despensa
store window *s* escaparate *m* (de tienda); aparador *m* (Mex)
stork [stɔrk] *s* cigüeña; **to have a visit from the stork** recibir a la cigüeña
storm [stɔrm] *s* borrasca, tempestad, tormenta; (mil) asalto; (naut) borrasca; (fig) tempestad, tumulto; **to take by storm** tomar por asalto ‖ *tr* asaltar ‖ *intr* tempestear; precipitarse
storm cloud *s* nubarrón *m*
storm door *s* contrapuerta, guardapuerta
storm sash *s* contravidriera
storm troops *spl* tropas de asalto
storm window *s* guardaventana, sobrevidriera
storm•y ['stɔrmi] *adj* (*comp* **-ier;** *super* **-iest)** borrascoso, tempestuoso; (*session, meeting, etc.*) tumultuoso
sto•ry ['stori] *s* (*pl* **-ries**) historia, cuento, anécdota; enredo, trama; (coll) mentira; piso, alto ‖ *v* (*pret & pp* **-ried**) *tr* historiar
sto'ry•tel'ler *s* narrador *m;* (coll) mentiroso
stout [staʊt] *adj* corpulento, gordo, robusto; animoso; leal; terco ‖ *s* cerveza obscura fuerte
stove [stov] *s* (*for heating a house or room*) estufa; (*for cooking*) hornillo, cocina de gas, cocina eléctrica
stove'pipe' *s* tubo de estufa, tubo de hornillo; (*hat*) (coll) chistera, chimenea
stow [sto] *tr* guardar, meter, esconder; (naut) arrumar, estibar ‖ *intr*—**to stow away** embarcarse clandestinamente, esconderse en un barco o avión
stowage ['sto•ɪdʒ] *s* arrumaje *m*, estiba
stow'a•way' *s* llovido, polizón *m*
str. *abbr* **strait, steamer**
straddle ['strædəl] *s* esparrancamiento ‖ *tr* montar a horcajadas; (coll) tratar de favo-

recer a ambas partes en (*p.ej., un pleito*) || *intr* ponerse a horcajadas; (coll) tratar de favorecer a ambas partes

strafe [strɑf] o [stref] *s* bombardeo violento || *tr* bombardear violentamente

straggle [ˈstrægəl] *intr* errar, vagar; andar perdido, extraviarse; separarse; estar esparcido

straight [stret] *adj* derecho; recto; erguido; (*hair*) lacio; continuo, seguido; honrado, sincero; correcto; decidido, intransigente; (*e.g., whiskey*) solo; **to set a person straight** mostrar el camino a una persona; dar consejo a una persona; mostrar a una persona el modo de proceder || *adv* derecho; sin interrupción; sinceramente; exactamente; en seguida; **straight ahead** todo seguido, derecho; **to go straight** enmendarse

straighten [ˈstretən] *tr* enderezar; poner en orden || *intr* enderezarse

straight face *s* cara seria

straight'for'ward *adj* franco, sincero; honrado

straight off *adv* luego, en seguida

straight razor *s* navaja barbera

straight'way' *adv* luego, en seguida

strain [stren] *s* tensión, tirantez *f;* esfuerzo muy grande; fatiga excesiva, agotamiento; (*of a muscle*) torcedura; aire *m*, melodía; (*of a family or lineage*) cepa; linaje *m*, raza; rasgo racial; genio, vena; huella, rastro || *tr* estirar; torcer o torcerse (*p.ej., la muñeca*); forzar (*p.ej., los nervios, la vista*); apretar; deformar; colar, tamizar || *intr* esforzarse; deformarse; colarse, tamizarse; filtrarse; exprimirse (*un jugo*); resistirse; **to strain at** hacer grandes esfuerzos por

strained [strend] *adj* (*smile*) forzado; (*friendship*) tirante

strainer [ˈstrenər] *s* colador *m*

strait [stret] *s* estrecho; **straits** estrecho; **to be in dire straits** estar en el mayor apuro, hallarse en gran estrechez

strait jacket *s* camisa de fuerza

strait-laced [ˈstret,lest] *adj* gazmoño

strand [strænd] *s* playa; filamento; (*of rope or cable*) torón *m*, ramal *m;* (*of pearls*) hilo; pelo || *tr* deshebrar; retorcer, trenzar (*cuerda, cable, etc.*); dejar extraviado; (naut) varar

stranded [ˈstrændɪd] *adj* desprovisto, desamparado; (*ship*) encallado; (*rope or cable*) trenzado, retorcido

strange [strendʒ] *adj* extraño, singular; nuevo, desconocido; novel, no acostumbrado

stranger [ˈstrendʒər] *s* forastero; visitador *m;* intruso; desconocido; principiante *mf*

strangle [ˈstræŋgəl] *tr* estrangular; reprimir, suprimir || *intr* estrangularse

strap [stræp] *s* (*of leather*) correa; (*of cloth, metal, etc.*) banda, tira; (*to sharpen a razor*) asentador *m* || *v* (*pret & pp* **strapped;** *ger* **strapping**) *tr* atar o liar con correa, banda o tira; azotar con una correa; fajar, vendar; asentar (*una navaja*)

strap'hang'er *s* (coll) pasajero colgado

stratagem [ˈstrætədʒəm] *s* estratagema *f*

strategic(al) [strəˈtidʒɪk(əl)] *adj* estratégico

strategist [ˈstrætɪdʒɪst] *s* estratega *m*

strate•gy [ˈstrætɪdʒi] *s* (*pl* **-gies**) estrategia

strati•fy [ˈstrætɪ,faɪ] *v* (*pret & pp* **-fied)** *tr* estratificar || *intr* estratificarse

stratosphere [ˈstrætə,sfɪr] o [ˈstretə,sfɪr] *s* estratosfera

stra•tum [ˈstretəm] o [ˈstrætəm] *s* (*pl* **-ta** [tə] o **-tums**) estrato; (*e.g., of society*) clase *f*

straw [strɔ] *adj* pajizo; baladí, de poca importancia; falso; ficticio || *s* paja; (*for drinking*) pajita; **I don't care a straw** no se me da un bledo; **to be the last straw** ser el colmo, no faltar más

straw'ber'ry *s* (*pl* **-ries**) fresa

straw hat *s* sombrero de paja; chupalla *m;* (*with low flat crown*) canotié *m*

straw man *s* figura de paja; (*figurehead*) testaferro; testigo falso

straw vote *s* voto informativo

stray [stre] *adj* extraviado, perdido; aislado, suelto || *s* animal extraviado o perdido || *intr* extraviarse, perderse

streak [strik] *s* lista, raya; vena, veta; rasgo, traza; (*of light*) rayo; (*of good luck*) racha; (coll) tiempo muy breve; **like a streak** (coll) como un rayo || *tr* listar, rayar; abigarrar || *intr* rayarse; (coll) andar o pasar como un rayo

stream [strim] *s* (*current*) corriente *f;* arroyo, río; chorro, flujo; (*of people*) torrente *m;* (*e.g., of automobiles*) desfile *m* || *intr* correr, manar (*un líquido*); chorrear; flotar, ondear; salir a torrentes

streamer [ˈstrimər] *s* flámula, banderola; cinta ondeante; rayo de luz

streamlined [ˈstrim,laɪnd] *adj* aerodinámico, perfilado

stream'lin'er *s* tren aerodinámico de lujo

street [strit] *adj* callejero || *s* calle *f*

street'car' *s* tranvía *m*

street cleaner *s* basurero; (*device*) barredera

street clothes *spl* traje *m* de calle

street floor *s* piso bajo

street lamp *s* farol *m* (de la calle)

street sprinkler [ˈsprɪŋklər] *s* carricuba, carro de riego, regadera

street'walk'er *s* cantonera, carrerista

strength [strɛŋθ] *s* fuerza; intensidad; (*of spirituous liquors*) graduación; (com) tendencia a la subida; (mil) número; **on the strength of** fundándose en, confiando en

strengthen [ˈstrɛŋθən] *tr* fortificar, reforzar; confirmar || *intr* fortificarse, reforzarse

strenuous [ˈstrɛnju•əs] *adj* estrenuo, enérgico, vigoroso; arduo, difícil

stress [strɛs] *s* tensión, fuerza; compulsión; acento; (mech) tensión; **to lay stress on** hacer hincapié en || *tr* someter a esfuerzo; hacer hincapié en; acentuar

stress accent *s* acento prosódico

stretch [strɛtʃ] *s* estiramiento, estirón *m;* (*distance in time or space*) trecho; (*section of road*) tramo; extensión; (*of the imagina-*

tion) esfuerzo; (*confinement in jail*) (slang) condena; **at a stretch** de un tirón || *tr* estirar; extender; tender; forzar, violentar; (fig) estirar (*el dinero*); **to stretch a point** hacer una concesión; **to stretch oneself** desperezarse || *intr* estirarse; extenderse; tenderse; desperezarse; **to stretch out** (coll) echarse
stretcher [ˈstrɛtʃər] *s* (*for gloves*) ensanchador *m;* (*for a painting*) bastidor *m;* (*to carry sick or wounded*) camilla
stretch'er-bear'er *s* camillero
strew [stru] *v* (*pret* **strewed;** *pp* **strewed** o **strewn**) *tr* derramar, esparcir; sembrar, salpicar; polvorear
stricken [ˈstrɪkən] *adj* afligido; inhabilitado; herido; **stricken in years** debilitado por los años
strict [strɪkt] *adj* estricto, riguroso; (*exacting*) severo
stricture [ˈstrɪktʃər] *s* crítica severa; (pathol) estrictura
stride [straɪd] *s* zancada, tranco; **to hit one's stride** alcanzar la actividad o velocidad acostumbrada; **to make great** (o **rapid**) **strides** avnzar a grandes pasos; **to take in one's stride** hacer sin esfuerzo || *v* (*pret* **strode** [strod]; *pp* **stridden** [ˈstrɪdən]) *tr* cruzar de un tranco; montar a horcajadas || *intr* dar zancadas, caminar a paso largo, andar a trancos
strident [ˈstraɪdənt] *adj* estridente
strife [straɪf] *s* contienda; rivalidad
strike [straɪk] *s* (*blow*) golpe *m;* (*stopping of work*) huelga; (*discovery of ore, oil, etc.*) descubrimiento repentino; golpe *m* de fortuna; **to go on strike** ir a la huelga || *v* (*pret & pp* **struck** [strʌk]) *tr* golpear; pulsar (*una tecla*); herir, percutir; topar, dar con; acuñar (*monedas*); echar (*raíces*); frotar, rayar, encender (*un fóstoro*); descubrir repentinamente (*mineral, aceite, etc.*); cerrar (*un trato*); arriar (*las velas*); dar (*la hora*); asumir, tomar (*una postura*); borrar, cancelar; impresionar; atraer (*la atención*); **to strike it rich** descubrir un buen filón, tener un golpe de fortuna || *intr* dar, sonar (*una campana, un reloj*); declararse en huelga; (mil) dar el asalto; **to strike out** ponerse en marcha, echar camino adelante
strike'break'er *s* rompehuelgas *m*, esquirol *m*
strike pay *s* sueldo de huelguista
striker [ˈstraɪkər] *s* golpeador *m;* huelguista *mf*
striking [ˈstraɪkɪŋ] *adj* impresionante, llamativo, sorprendente; en huelga
striking power *s* potencia de choque
string [strɪŋ] *s* cuerdecilla; piola; pita; (*of pearls; of lies*) sarta; (*of beans*) hebra; (*of onions or garlic*) ristra; (row) hilera; (mus) cuerda; (*limitation, proviso*) (coll) condición; **strings** instrumentos de cuerda; **to pull strings** tocar resortes || *v* (*pret & pp* **strung** [strʌŋ]) *tr* enhebrar, ensartar; atar con cuerdas; proveer de cuerdas; colgar de una cuerda; tender (*un cable, un alambre*); encordar (*un violín, una raqueta*); colocar en fila; (slang) engañar, burlar; **to string along** (slang) traer al retortero; **to string up** (coll) ahorcar
string bean *s* habichuela verde, judía verde
stringed instrument [strɪŋd] *s* instrumento de cuerda
stringent [ˈstrɪndʒənt] *adj* riguroso, severo, estricto; convincente
string quartet *s* cuarteto de cuerdas
strip [strɪp] *s* tira; (*of metal*) lámina; (*of land*) faja || *v* (*pret & pp* **stripped;** *ger* **stripping**) *tr* desnudar; despojar; desforrar; deshacer (*la cama*); estropear (*el engranaje, un tornillo*); desvenar (*tabaco*); descortezar; **to strip of** despojar de || *intr* desnudarse; despojarse; descortezarse
stripe [straɪp] *s* banda, lista, raya; gaya; cinta, franja; (mil & nav) galón *m;* índole *f*, tipo; **to win one's stripes** ganar los entorchados || *tr* listar, rayar; gayar
strip mining *s* mineraje *m* a tajo abierto
strip'tease' *s* espectáculo de desnudamiento sensual
strive [straɪv] *v* (*pret* **strove** [strov]; *pp* **striven** [ˈstrɪvən]) *intr* esforzarse; luchar
stroke [strok] *s* golpe *m;* (*of bell or clock*) campanada; (*of pen*) plumada; (*of brush*) pincelada, brochada; (*of arms in swimming*) brazada; (*in a game*) jugada; (*caress with hand*) caricia; (*with a racket*) raquetazo; (*of a piston*) carrera, embolada; (*of a paddle*) palada; (*of an oar*) remada; (*of lightning*) rayo; (*line, mark*) raya; (*of good luck*) golpe *m;* (*of wit*) agudeza, chiste *m;* (*of genius*) rasgo; ataque *m* de parálisis; **at the stroke of** (*e.g., five*) al dar las (*p.ej., cinco*); **to not do a stroke of work** no dar golpe, no levantar paja del suelo || *tr* frotar suavemente, acariciar con la mano
stroll [strol] *s* paseo; **to take a stroll** dar un paseo || *intr* pasear, pasearse; callejear, errar, vagar
stroller [ˈstrolər] *s* paseante *mf;* cochecito para niños
strong [strɔŋ] o [strɑŋ] *adj* fuerte, resistente; recio, robusto; intenso; (*stock market*) firme; enérgico; marcado; picante; rancio
strong'-arm' man *s* (coll) gorila
strong'box' *s* cofre *m* fuerte, caja de caudales
strong drink *s* bebida alcohólica, bebida fuerte
strong'hold' *s* plaza fuerte
strong man *s* (*e.g., in a circus*) hércules *m;* (*leader, good planner*) alma, promotor *m;* (*dictator*) hombre *m* fuerte
strong-minded [ˈstrɔŋˌmaɪndɪd] o [strɑŋˈmaɪndɪd] *adj* independiente; de inteligencia vigorosa; (*e.g., woman*) hombruna
strontium [ˈstrɑnʃɪ•əm] *s* estroncio
strop [strɑp] *s* suavizador *m* || *v* (*pret & pp* **stropped;** *ger* **stropping**) *tr* suavizar, afilar
strophe [ˈstrofi] *s* estrofa
structure [ˈstrʌktʃər] *s* estructura; edificio
struggle [ˈstrʌgəl] *s* lucha; esfuerzo, forcejeo || *intr* luchar; esforzarse, forcejear

strum [strʌm] *v* (*pret & pp* **strummed;** *ger* **strumming**) *tr* arañar (*un instrumento músico*) sin arte || *intr* cencerrear; **to strum on** rasguear
strumpet [ˈstrʌmpɪt] *s* ramera
strut [strʌt] *s* (*brace, prop*) riostra, tornapunta; contoneo, pavoneo || *v* (*pret & pp* **strutted;** *ger* **strutting**) *intr* contonearse, pavonearse
strychnine [ˈstrɪknaɪn] o [ˈstrɪknin] *s* estricnina
stub [stʌb] *s* fragmento, trozo; (*of a cigar*) colilla; (*of a tree*) tocón *m;* (*of a pencil*) cabo; (*of a check*) talón *m* || *v* (*pret & pp* **stubbed;** *ger* **stubbing**) *tr* **—to stub one's toe** dar un tropezón
stubble [ˈstʌbəl] *s* rastrojo; (*of beard*) cañón *m*
stubborn [ˈstʌbərn] *adj* terco, testarudo, obstinado; porfiado; intratable; **to be stubborn** ser obstinado, empecinarse
stubbornness [ˈstʌbərnɪs] obstinación, *s* empecinamiento
stuc•co [ˈstʌko] *s* (*pl* **-coes** o **-cos**) estuco || *tr* estucar
stuck'-up' *adj* (coll) estirado, orgulloso
stud [stʌd] *s* tachón *m;* botón *m* de camisa; montante *m*, pie derecho; clavo de adorno; (*bolt*) espárrago; caballeriza; (*of mares*) yeguada || *v* (*pret & pp* **studded;** *ger* **studding**) *tr* tachonar
stud bolt *s* espárrago
stud'book' *s* registro genealógico de caballos
student [ˈstjudənt] o [ˈstudənt] *adj* estudiantil || *s* estudiante *mf;* (*person who investigates*), estudioso
student body *s* estudiantado, alumnado
stud'horse' *s* caballo padre, caballo semental
studied [ˈstʌdid] *adj* premeditado, hecho adrede; (*affected*) estudiado
studi•o [ˈstudɪ,o] *s* (*pl* **-os**) estudio, taller *m;* (mov & rad) estudio
studious [ˈstjudɪ•əs] o [ˈstudɪ•əs] *adj* estudioso; asiduo, solícito
stud•y [ˈstʌdi] *s* (*pl* **-ies**) estudio; solicitud; meditación profunda; (*e.g., of a professor*) gabinete *m*, estudio || *v* (*pret & pp* **-ied**) *tr & intr* estudiar
stuff [stʌf] *s* materia; género, paño, tela; muebles *mpl*, baratijas; medicina; fruslerías; cosa, cosas || *tr* rellenar; henchir, llenar; atascar, cerrar, tapar; embutir; (*with food*) atracar; meter sin orden, llenar sin orden; disecar (*un animal muerto*) || *intr* atracarse, hartarse
stuffed shirt *s* (slang) tragavirotes *m*
stuffing [ˈstʌfɪŋ] *s* relleno
stuff•y [ˈstʌfi] *adj* (*comp* **-ier;** *super* **-iest**) sofocante, mal ventilado; aburrido, sin interés; (*prim*) (coll) relamido
stumble [ˈstʌmbəl] *intr* tropezar, dar un traspié; moverse a tropezones; hablar a tropezones; **to stumble on** o **upon** tropezar con
stumbling block *s* escollo, tropezadero
stump [stʌmp] *s* (*of a tree, arm, etc.*) tocón *m;* (*of an arm*) muñón *m;* (*of a tooth*) raigón *m;* (*of a cigar*) colilla; (*of a tail*) rabo; paso pesado; fragmento, resto; tribuna pública; (*for shading drawings*) esfumino || *tr* recorrer (*el país*) pronunciando discursos políticos; (coll) confundir, dejar sin habla; esfumar
stump speaker *s* orador callejero
stump speech *s* arenga electoral
stun [stʌn] *v* (*pret & pp* **stunned;** *ger* **stunning**) *tr* atolondrar, aturdir
stunning [ˈstʌnɪŋ] *adj* (coll) pasmoso, estupendo, pistonudo, elegante
stunt [stʌnt] *s* atrofia; (*underdeveloped creature*) engendro; (coll) suerte acrobática; (coll) faena, hazaña, proeza || *tr* atrofiar || *intr* (coll) hacer suertes acrobáticas
stunt flying *s* vuelo acrobático
stunt man *s* (mov) doble *m* que hace suertes peligrosas
stupe•fy [ˈstjupɪ,faɪ] *v* (*pret & pp* **-fied**) *tr* dejar estupefacto, pasmar; causar estupor a
stupendous [stuˈpɛndəs] *adj* estupendo; enorme
stupid [ˈstupɪd] *adj* estúpido; (coll) sonso, pavo, gilí
stupor [ˈstjupər] o [ˈstupər] *s* estupor *m*, modorra
stur•dy [ˈstʌrdi] *adj* (*comp* **-dier;** *super* **-diest**) fuerte, robusto, fornido; firme, tenaz
sturgeon [ˈstʌrdʒən] *s* esturión *m*
stutter [ˈstʌtər] *s* tartamudeo || *tr* decir tartamudeando || *intr* tartamudear
sty [staɪ] *s* (*pl* **sties**) pocilga, zahurda; (pathol) orzuelo
style [staɪl] *s* estilo; moda; elegancia; **to live in great style** vivir en gran lujo || *tr* intitular, nombrar
stylish [ˈstaɪlɪʃ] *adj* de moda, elegante
styptic pencil [ˈstɪptɪk] *s* lápiz estíptico
Styx [stɪks] *s* Estigia
suave [swɑv] o [swev] *adj* suave; afable, fino, zalamero, pulido
sub. *abbr* **subscription, substitute, suburban**
subaltern [səbˈɔltərn] *adj & s* subalterno
subconscious [səbˈkɑnʃəs] *adj* subconsciente || *s* subconsciencia
subconsciousness [səbˈkɑnʃəsnɪs] *s* subconsciencia
subdeb [ˈsʌb,dɛb] *s* tobillera
subdivide [ˈsʌbdɪ,vaɪd] o [,sʌbdɪˈvaɪd] *tr* subdividir || *intr* subdividirse
subdue [səbˈdju] *tr* sojuzgar, subyugar; amansar, dominar; suavizar
subdued [səbˈdjud] *adj* sojuzgado; sumiso; (*e.g., light*) suave
subheading [ˈsʌb,hɛdɪŋ] *s* subtítulo
subject [ˈsʌbdʒɪkt] *adj* sujeto; súbdito || *s* asunto, materia, tema *m;* (*person in his relationship to a ruler or government*) súbdito; (gram, med, philos) sujeto || [səbˈdʒɛkt] *tr* sujetar, someter, sojuzgar
subject index *s* índice *m* de materias
subjection [səbˈdʒɛkʃən] *s* sumisión, sometimiento
subjective [səbˈdʒɛktɪv] *adj* subjetivo
subject matter *s* asunto, materia
subjugate [ˈsʌbdʒə,get] *tr* subyugar

subjunctive [səb'dʒʌŋktɪv] *adj & s* subjuntivo
sub•let [sʌb'lɛt] o ['sʌb,lɛt] *v* (*pret & pp* **-let;** *ger* **-letting**) *tr* realquilar, subarrendar
submachine gun [,sʌbmə'ʃin] *s* subfusil *m* ametrallador
submarine ['sʌbmə,rin] *adj & s* submarino ‖ *tr* (coll) atacar o hundir con un submarino
submarine chaser ['tʃesər] *s* cazasubmarinos *m*
submerge [səb'mʌrdʒ] *tr* sumergir ‖ *intr* sumergirse
submersion [səb'mʌrʒən] o [səb'mʌrʃən] *s* sumersión
submission [səb'mɪʃən] *s* sumisión
submissive [səb'mɪsɪv] *adj* sumiso
sub•mit [səb'mɪt] *v* (*pret & pp* **-mitted;** *ger* **-mitting**) *tr* someter; proponer, permitirse decir ‖ *intr* someterse
subordinate [səb'ɔrdɪnɪt] *adj & s* subordinado ‖ [səb'ɔrdɪ,net] *tr* subordinar
subornation of perjury [,sʌbər'neʃən] *s* (law) soborno de testigo
subplot ['sʌb,plɑt] *s* trama secundaria
subpoena o **subpena** [sʌb'pinə] o [sə'pinə] *s* comparendo ‖ *tr* mandar comparecer
sub rosa [sʌb'rozə] *adv* en secreto, en confianza
subscribe [səb'skraɪb] *tr* subscribir ‖ *intr* subscribir; subscribirse, abonarse; **to subscribe to** subscribirse a, abonarse a (*una publicación periódica*); subscribir (*una opinión*)
subscriber [səb'skraɪbər] *s* abonado
subsequent ['sʌbsɪkwənt] *adj* subsiguiente, posterior
subservient [səb'sʌrvɪ•ənt] *adj* servil; subordinado; útil
subside [səb'saɪd] *intr* calmarse; acabarse, cesar; bajar (*el nivel del agua*); amainar (*el viento*)
subsidiary [səb'sɪdɪ,ɛri] *adj & s* subsidiario
subsidize ['sʌbsɪ,daɪz] *tr* subsidiar, subvencionar; (*to bribe*) sobornar
subsi•dy ['sʌbsɪdi] *s* (*pl* **-dies**) subsidio, subvención
subsist [səb'sɪst] *intr* subsistir
subsistence [səb'sɪstəns] *s* subsistencia
subsonic [səb'sɑnɪk] *adj* subsónico
substance ['sʌbstəns] *s* substancia
substandard [sʌb'stændərd] *adj* inferior al nivel normal
substantial [səb'stænʃəl] *adj* considerable, importante; fuerte, sólido; acomodado, rico; esencial; (*food*) substancial
substantiate [səb'stænʃɪ,et] *tr* comprobar, establecer, verificar
substantive ['sʌbstəntɪv] *adj & s* substantivo
substation ['sʌb,steʃən] *s* (elec) subcentral *f*
substitute ['sʌbstɪ,tjut] o ['sʌbstɪ,tut] *adj* substitutivo ‖ *s* (*person*) substituto; (*thing, substance*) substitutivo; (mil) reemplazo ‖ *tr* poner (*a una persona o cosa*) en lugar de otra ‖ *intr* actuar de substituto; **to substitute for** substituir (with personal a)
substitution [,sʌbstɪ'tjuʃən] *s* empleo o uso (*de una persona o cosa en lugar de otra*); (chem, law, math) substitución; imitación fraudulenta
subterranean [,sʌbtə'renɪ•ən] *adj & s* subterráneo
subtitle ['sʌb,taɪtəl] *s* substítulo ‖ *tr* subtitular
subtle ['sʌtəl] *adj* sutil; astuto; insidioso
subtle•ty ['sʌtəlti] *s* (*pl* **-ties**) sutileza; agudeza; distinción sutil
subtract [səb'trækt] *tr* substraer; (math) substraer, restar
suburb ['sʌbʌrb] *s* suburbio, arrabal *m;* **the suburbs** las afueras, los barrios externos
subvention [səb'vɛnʃən] *s* subvención ‖ *tr* subvencionar
subversive [səb'vʌrsɪv] *adj* subversivo ‖ *s* subversor *m*
subvert [səb'vʌrt] *tr* subvertir
subway ['sʌb,we] *s* galería subterránea; metro, ferrocarril subterráneo
succeed [sək'sid] *tr* suceder (*a una persona o cosa*) ‖ *intr* tener buen éxito
success [sək'sɛs] *s* buen éxito
successful [sək'sɛsfəl] *adj* feliz, próspero; acertado; logrado
succession [sək'sɛʃən] *s* sucesión; **in succession** seguidos, uno tras otro
successive [sək'sɛsɪv] *adj* sucesivo
succor ['sʌkər] *s* socorro ‖ *tr* socorrer
succotash ['sʌkə,tæʃ] *s* guiso de maíz tierno y habas
succumb [sə'kʌm] *intr* sucumbir
such [sʌtʃ] *adj & pron indef* tal, semejante; **such a** tal, semejante; **such a** + *adj* un tan + *adj;* **such as** quienes, los que
suck [sʌk] *s* chupada; mamada ‖ *tr* chupar; mamar; aspirar (*el aire*)
sucker ['sʌkər] *s* chupador *m;* mamón *m;* (bot & mach) chupón *m;* (coll) bobo, primo
suckle ['sʌkəl] *tr* lactar; criar, educar
suckling pig ['sʌklɪŋ] *s* lechón *m*, cerdo de leche
suction ['sʌkʃən] *adj* aspirante ‖ *s* succión
sudden ['sʌdən] *adj* súbito, repentino; **all of a sudden** de repente
suds [sʌdz] *spl* jabonadura; (coll) espuma, cerveza
sue [su] *tr* demandar; pedir; (law) procesar ‖ *intr* (law) poner pleito, entablar juicio; **to sue for damages** demandar por daños y perjuicios; **to sue for peace** pedir la paz
suede [swed] *s* gamuza, ante *m*
suet ['su•ɪt] o ['sju•ɪt] *s* sebo
suffer ['sʌfər] *tr & intr* sufrir, padecer
sufferance ['sʌfərəns] *s* tolerancia; paciencia; **on sufferance** por tolerancia
suffering ['sʌfərɪŋ] *adj* doliente ‖ *s* dolencia, sufrimiento
suffice [sə'faɪs] *intr* bastar, ser suficiente
sufficient [sə'fɪʃənt] *adj* suficiente
suffix ['sʌfɪks] *s* sufijo
suffocate ['sʌfə,ket] *tr* sofocar ‖ *intr* sofocarse
suffrage ['sʌfrɪdʒ] *s* sufragio; aprobación, voto favorable
suffragette [,sʌfrə'dʒɛt] *s* sufragista (*mujer*)

suffuse [sə'fjuz] *tr* saturar, bañar
sugar ['ʃʊgər] *adj* azucarero ‖ *s* azúcar *m* ‖ *tr* azucarar
sugar beet *s* remolacha azucarera
sugar bowl *s* azucarero
sugar cane *s* caña de azúcar
sug'ar-coat' *tr* azucarar; (fig) endulzar, dorar
suggest [səg'dʒɛst] *tr* sugerir
suggestion [səg'dʒɛstʃən] *s* sugestión, sugerencia; sombra, traza ligera
suggestive [səg'dʒɛstɪv] *adj* sugestivo; sicalíptico
suicidal [,su•ɪ'saɪdəl] o [,sju•ɪ'saɪdəl] *adj* suicida
suicide ['su•ɪ,saɪd] *s* (*act*) suicidio; (*person*) suicida *mf;* **to commit suicide** suicidarse
suit [sut] o [sjut] *s* traje *m*, terno; (*of a lady*) traje *m* sastre; (*group forming a set*) juego; (*of cards*) palo; petición, súplica; cortejo, galanteo; (law) pleito, proceso; **to follow suit** servir del palo; seguir la corriente ‖ *tr* adaptar, ajustar; adaptarse a; sentar, ir o venir bien a; favorecer, satisfacer; **to suit oneself** hacer (*uno*) lo que le guste ‖ *intr* convenir, ser a propósito
suitable ['sutəbəl] *adj* apropiado, conveniente, adecuado
suit'case' *s* maleta, valija
suite [swit] *s* comitiva, séquito; (*group forming a set*) juego; serie *f;* (*of rooms*) crujía; habitación salón; (mus) suite *f*
suiting ['sutɪŋ] *s* corte *m* de traje
suit of clothes *s* traje completo (*de hombre*)
suitor ['sutər] o ['sjutər] *s* pretendiente *m;* (law) demandante *mf*
sulfa drugs ['sʌlfə] *spl* medicamentos sulfas
sulfate ['sʌlfet] *s* sulfato
sulfide ['sʌlfaɪd] *s* sulfuro
sulfite ['sʌlfaɪt] *s* sulfito
sulfur ['sʌlfər] *s* (chem) azufre *m;* véase **sulphur**
sulfuric [sʌl'fjʊrɪk] *adj* sulfúrico
sulfur mine *s* azufrera
sulfurous ['sʌlfərəs] *adj* sulfuroso ‖ *adj* (chem) sulfuroso
sulk [sʌlk] *s* murria ‖ *intr* amorrarse, enfurruñarse
sulk•y ['sʌlki] *adj* (*comp* **-ier;** *super* **-iest**) enfurruñado, murrio, resentido
sullen ['sʌlən] *adj* hosco, malhumorado, taciturno, triste
sul•ly ['sʌli] *v* (*pret & pp* **-lied**) *tr* empañar, manchar
sulphur ['sʌlfər] *adj* azufrado ‖ *s* azufre *m;* color de azufre ‖ *tr* azufrar
sultan ['sʌltən] *s* sultán *m*
sul•try ['sʌltri] *adj* (*comp* **-trier;** *super* **-triest**) bochornoso, sofocante
sum [sʌm] *s* suma; (coll) problema *m* de aritmética ‖ *v* (*pret & pp* **summed;** *ger* **summing**) *tr* sumar; **to sum up** sumar, resumir
sumac o **sumach** ['ʃumæk] o [sumæk] *s* zumaque *m*
summarize ['sʌmə,raɪz] *tr* resumir
summa•ry ['sʌməri] *adj* sumario ‖ *s* (*pl* **-ries**) sumario, resumen *m*
summer ['sʌmər] *adj* estival, veraniego ‖ *s* verano, estío ‖ *intr* veranear
summer resort *s* lugar *m* de veraneo
summersault ['sʌmər,sɔlt] *s* salto mortal ‖ *intr* dar un salto mortal
summer school *s* escuela de verano
summery ['sʌməri] *adj* estival, veraniego
summit ['sʌmɪt] *s* cima, cumbre *f*
summit conference o **summit meeting** *s* conferencia en la cumbre
summon ['sʌmən] *tr* convocar, llamar; evocar; (law) citar, emplazar
summons ['sʌmənz] *s* orden *f*, señal *f;* (law) citación, emplazamiento ‖ *tr* (coll) citar, emplazar
sumptuous ['sʌmptʃʊ•əs] *adj* suntuoso
sun [sʌn] *s* sol *m;* **to have a place in the sun** ocupar su puesto en el mundo ‖ *v* (*pret & pp* **sunned;** *ger* **sunning**) *tr* asolear ‖ *intr* asolearse
sun bath *s* baño de sol
sun'beam' *s* rayo de sol
sun'bon'net *s* papalina
sun'burn' *s* quemadura de sol ‖ *v* (*pret & pp* **-burned** o **burnt**) *tr* quemar al sol ‖ *intr* quemarse al sol
sundae ['sʌndi] *s* helado con frutas, jarabes o nueces
Sunday ['sʌndi] *adj* dominical; (*used or worn on Sunday*) dominguero ‖ *s* domingo
Sunday best *s* (coll) trapos de cristianar, ropa dominguera
Sunday's child *s* niño nacido de pies, niño mimado de la fortuna
Sunday school *s* escuela dominical, doctrina dominical
Sunday supplement *s* (*newspaper*) suplemento dominical
sunder ['sʌndər] *tr* separar; romper
sun'di'al *s* reloj *m* de sol, cuadrante *m* solar
sun'down' *s* puesta del sol
sundries ['sʌndriz] *spl* articulos diversos
sundry ['sʌndri] *adj* diversos, varios
sun'flow'er *s* girasol *m*, tornasol *m*
sun'glass'es *spl* gafas de sol, gafas para el sol
sunken ['sʌŋkən] *adj* hundido, sumido
sun lamp *s* lámpara de rayos ultravioletas
sun'light' *s* luz *f* del sol
sun'lit' *adj* iluminado por el sol
sun•ny ['sʌni] *adj* (*comp* **-nier;** *super* **-iest**) de sol; asoleado; brillante, resplandeciente; alegre, risueño; **to be sunny** hacer sol
sunny side *s* sol *m;* (fig) lado bueno, lado favorable
sun porch *s* solana
sun'rise' *s* salida del sol; **from sunrise to sunset** de sol a sol
sun'set' *s* puesta del sol
sun'shade' *s* quitasol *m*, sombrilla; toldo; visera contra el sol
sun'shine' *s* claridad del sol; alegría; **in the sunshine** al sol
sun'spot' *s* mancha solar
sun'stroke' *s* insolación
sun'tan' *s* bronceado
suntan lotion *s* bronceador *m*

sup. *abbr* **superior, supplement**
sup [sʌp] *v* (*pret & pp* **supped;** *ger* **supping)** *intr* cenar
superannuated [,supərˈænju,etɪd] *adj* jubilado, inhabilitado por ancianidad o enfermedad; fuera de moda
superb [səˈpʌrb] *adj* soberbio, estupendo, magnífico
supercar•go [ˈsupər,kɑrgo] *s* (*pl* **-goes** o **-gos**) (naut) sobrecargo
supercharge [,supərˈtʃɑrdʒ] *tr* sobrealimentar
supercilious [,supərˈsɪlɪ•əs] *adj* arrogante, altanero, desdeñoso
superficial [,supərˈfɪʃəl] *adj* superficial
superfluous [sʊˈpʌrflʊ•əs] *adj* superfluo
superhuman [,supərˈhjumən] *adj* sobrehumano
superimpose [,supərɪmˈpoz] *tr* sobreponer
superintendent [,supərɪnˈtɛndənt] *s* superintendente *mf*
superior [səˈpɪrɪ•ər] *adj* superior; indiferente, sereno; arrogante; (typ) volado || *s* superior *m*
superiority [sə,pɪrɪˈɑrɪti] *s* superioridad; indiferencia, serenidad; arrogancia
superlative [səˈpʌrlətɪv] *adj & s* superlativo
super•man [ˈsupər,mæn] *s* (*pl* **-men** [,mɛn]) sobrehombre *m*, superhombre *m*
supermarket [ˈsupər,mɑrkɪt] *s* supermercado
supernatural [,supərˈnætʃərəl] *adj* sobrenatural
superpose [,supərˈpoz] *tr* sobreponer, superponer
supersede [,supərˈsid] *tr* reemplazar; desalojar
supersonic [,supərˈsɑnɪk] *adj* supersónico || **supersonics** *ssg* supersónica
superstitious [,supərˈstɪʃəs] *adj* supersticioso
supertanker [ˈsupər,tæŋkər] *s* superpetrolero, supertanquero
supervene [,supərˈvin] *intr* sobrevenir
supervise [ˈsupər,vaɪz] *tr* superintender, supervisar, dirigir
supervisor [ˈsupər,vaɪzər] *s* superintendente *mf*, supervisor *m*, dirigente *mf*
supp. *abbr* **supplement**
supper [ˈsʌpər] *s* cena
supplant [səˈplænt] *tr* reemplazar
supple [ˈsʌpəl] *adj* flexible; dócil
supplement [ˈsʌplɪmənt] *s* suplemento || [ˈsʌplɪ,mɛnt] *tr* suplir, completar
suppliant [ˈsʌplɪ•ənt] *adj & s* suplicante *mf*
supplication [,sʌplɪˈkeʃən] *s* súplica
sup•ply [səˈplaɪ] *s* (*pl* **-plies**) suministro, provisión; surtido, repuesto; oferta, existencia; **supplies** pertrechos, provisiones, víveres *mf;* artículos, efectos || *v* (*pret & pp* **-plied**) *tr* suministrar, aprovisionar; reemplazar
supply and demand *spl* oferta y demanda
support [səˈport] *s* apoyo, soporte *m*, sostén *m;* sustento || *tr* apoyar, soportar, sostener; sustentar; aguantar
supporter [səˈportər] *s* partidario; (*jockstrap*) suspensorio; faja abdominal, faja medical
suppose [səˈpoz] *tr* suponer; creer; **to be supposed to** deber; **to suppose so** creer que sí
supposed [səˈpozd] *adj* supuesto
supposition [,sʌpəˈzɪʃən] *s* suposición
supposito•ry [səˈpɑzɪ,tori] *s* (*pl* **-ries**) supositorio
suppress [səˈprɛs] *tr* suprimir
suppression [səˈprɛʃən] *s* supresión
suppurate [ˈsʌpjə,ret] *intr* supurar
supreme [səˈprim] o [suˈprim] *adj* supremo
supt. *abbr* **superintendent**
surcharge [ˈsʌr,tʃɑrdʒ] *s* sobrecarga || [,sʌrˈtʃɑrdʒ] o [ˈsʌr,tʃɑrdʒ] *tr* sobrecargar
sure [ʃʊr] *adj* seguro; **to be sure** seguramente, sin duda || *adv* (coll) seguramente, claro; **sure enough** efectivamente
sure things *adv* (slang) seguramente || *interj* ¡claro!, ¡seguro! || *s* (slang) sacabocados *m*
sure•ty [ˈʃʊrti] o [ˈʃʊrɪti] *s* (*pl* **-ties**) seguridad, garantía, fianza
surf [sʌrf] *s* cachones *mpl*, olas que rompen en la playa
surface [ˈsʌrfɪs] *adj* superficial || *s* superficie *f* || *tr* alisar, allanar; recubrir || *intr* emerger (*p.ej., un submarino*)
surface mail *s* correo por vía ordinaria
surfˈboardˈ *s* patín *m* de mar
surfeit [ˈsʌrfɪt] *s* exceso; hartura, hastío; empacho, indigestión || *tr* atracar, hastiar; encebadar (*las bestias*) || *intr* atracarse, hastiarse; encebadarse
surfˈ-ridˈing *s* patinaje *m* sobre las olas
surge [sʌrdʒ] *s* oleada; (elec) sobretensión || *intr* agitarse, ondular
surgeon [ˈsʌrdʒən] *s* cirujano
surger•y [ˈsʌrdʒəri] *s* (*pl* **-ies**) cirugía; sala de operaciones
surgical [ˈsʌrdʒɪkəl] *adj* quirúrgico
sur•ly [ˈsʌrli] *adj* (*comp* **-lier;** *super* **-liest)** áspero, rudo, hosco, insolente
surmise [sərˈmaɪz] o [ˈsʌrmaɪz] *s* conjetura, suposición || [sərˈmaɪz] *tr & intr* conjeturar, suponer
surmount [sərˈmaʊnt] *tr* levantarse sobre; aventajar, sobrepujar; superar; coronar
surname [ˈsʌr,nem] *s* apellido: (*added name*) sobrenombre *m* || *tr* apellidar; sobrenombrar
surpass [sərˈpæs] o [sərˈpɑs] *tr* aventajar, sobrepasar
surplice [ˈsʌrplɪs] *s* sobrepelliz *f*
surplus [ˈsʌrplʌs] *adj* sobrante, excedente || *s* sobrante *m*, exceso; (com) superávit *m*
surprise [sərˈpraɪz] *adj* inesperado, improviso || *s* sorpresa; **to take by surprise** coger por sorpresa || *tr* sorprender
surprise package *s* sorpresa
surprise party *s* reunión improvisada para felicitar por sorpresa a una persona
surprising [sərˈpraɪzɪŋ] *adj* sorprendente, sorpresivo
surrender [səˈrɛndər] *s* rendición || *tr* rendir || *intr* rendirse
surrender value *s* (ins) valor *m* de rescate
surreptitious [,sʌrɛpˈtɪʃəs] *adj* subrepticio

surround [sə'raʊnd] *tr* cercar, rodear, circundar; (mil) sitiar
surrounding [sə'raʊndɪŋ] *adj* circundante, circunstante ‖ **surroundings** *spl* alrededores *mpl*, contornos; ambiente *m*, medio
surtax ['sʌr,tæks] *s* impuesto complementario
surveillance [sər'veləns] o [sər'veljəns] *s* vigilancia
survey ['sʌrve] *s* estudio, examen *m*, inspección, reconocimiento; agrimensura, medición, plano; levantamiento de planos; (*of opinion*) encuesta; (*of literature*) bosquejo ‖ [sʌr've] o ['sʌrve] *tr* estudiar, examinar, inspeccionar, reconocer; medir; levantar el plano de ‖ *intr* levantar el plano
surveyor [sər've•ər] *s* inspector *m;* agrimensor *m*
survival [sər'vaɪvəl] *s* supervivencia
survive [sər'vaɪv] *tr* sobrevivir a (*otra persona; algún acontecimiento*) ‖ *intr* sobrevivir
surviving [sər'vaɪvɪŋ] *adj* sobreviviente
survivor [sər'vaɪvər] *s* sobreviviente *mf*
survivorship [sər'vaɪvər,ʃɪp] *s* (law) sobrevivencia
susceptible [sə'sɛptɪbəl] *adj* susceptible; (*to love*) enamoradizo
suspect ['sʌspɛkt] o [səs'pɛkt] *adj & s* sospechoso ‖ [səs'pɛkt] *tr* sospechar
suspend [səs'pɛnd] *tr* suspender ‖ *intr* dejar de obrar; suspender pagos
suspenders [səs'pɛndərz] *spl* tirantes *mpl*
suspense [səs'pɛns] *s* suspenso, suspensión; duda, incertidumbre; indecisión, irresolución; ansiedad
suspension bridge [səs'pɛnʃən] *s* puente *m* colgante
suspicion [səs'pɪʃən] *s* sospecha, suspicacia; sombra, traza ligera
suspicious [səs'pɪʃəs] *adj* (*inclined to suspect*) suspicaz; (*subject to suspicion*) sospechoso
sustain [səs'ten] *tr* sostener, sustentar; apoyar, defender; confirmar, probar; sufrir (*p.ej., un daño, una pérdida*)
sustenance ['sʌstɪnəns] *s* sustento, alimentos; sostenimiento
sutler ['sʌtlər] *s* (mil) vivandero
swab [swɑb] *s* escobón *m*, estropajo; (naut) lampazo; (surg) tapón *m* de algodón ‖ *v* (*pret & pp* **swabbed;** *ger* **swabbing**) *tr* fregar, limpiar; (naut) lampacear; (surg) limpiar con algodón
swaddle ['swɑdəl] *tr* empañar, fajar
swaddling clothes *spl* pañales *mpl*
swagger ['swægər] *adj* (coll) muy elegante ‖ *s* fanfarronada; contoneo, paso jactancioso ‖ *intr* fanfarronear; contonear
swain [swen] *s* (*lad*) zagal; galán *m*, amante *m*
swallow ['swɑlo] *s* trago; (orn) golondrina ‖ *tr* tragar, deglutir; (fig) tragar, tragarse ‖ *intr* tragar, deglutir
swallow-tailed coat ['swɑlo,teld] *s* frac *m*
swal'low•wort' *s* vencetósigo
swamp [swɑmp] *s* pantano, marisma ‖ *tr* encharcar, inundar; (*e.g., with work*) abrumar
swamp•y ['swɑmpi] *adj* (*comp* **-ier;** *super* **-iest**) pantanoso
swan [swɑn] *s* cisne *m*
swan dive *s* salto de ángel
swank [swæŋk] *adj* (slang) elegante, vistoso ‖ *s* (slang) elegancia vistosa
swan knight *s* caballero del cisne
swan's-down ['swɑnz,daʊn] *s* plumón *m* de cisne; moletón *m*, paño de vicuña
swan song *s* canto del cisne
swap [swɑp] *s* (coll) truque *m*, cambalache *m* ‖ *v* (*pret & pp* **swapped;** *ger* **swapping**) *tr & intr* trocar, cambalachear
swarm [swɔrm] *s* enjambre *m* ‖ *intr* enjambrar; volar en enjambres; hormiguear (*una multitud de gente o animales*)
swarth•y ['swɔrði] o ['swɔrθi] *adj* (*comp* **-ier;** *super* **-iest**) atezado, carinegro, moreno
swashbuckler ['swɑʃ,bʌklər] *s* espada chín *m*, matasiete *m*, valentón *m*
swat [swɑt] *s* (coll) golpe violento ‖ *v* (*pret & pp* **swatted;** *ger* **swatting**) *tr* (coll) golpear con fuerza; (coll) aporrear, aplastar (*una mosca*)
sway [swe] *s* oscilación, vaivén *m;* dominio, imperio ‖ *tr* hacer oscilar; conmover; disuadir; gobernar, dominar ‖ *intr* oscilar; desviarse; tambalear, flaquear
swear [swɛr] *v* (*pret* **swore** [swor]; *pp* **sworn** [sworn]) *tr* jurar; juramentar; prestar (*juramento*); **to swear in** tomar juramento a; **to swear off** jurar renunciar a; **to swear out** obtener mediante juramento ‖ *intr* jurar; **to swear at** maldecir; **to swear by** jurar por; poner toda su confianza en; **to swear to** prestar juramento a; declarar bajo juramento; jurar + *inf*
sweat [swɛt] *s* sudor *m* ‖ *v* (*pret & pp* **sweat** o **sweated**) *tr* sudar (*agua por los poros; la ropa*); (slang) hacer sudar; **to sweat it out** (slang) aguantarlo hasta el fin ‖ *intr* sudar
sweater ['swɛtər] *s* suéter *m*
sweat shirt *s* pulóver *m* de mangas largas
sweat'shop' *s* taller *m* de trabajo afanoso y de poco sueldo
sweat•y ['swɛti] *adj* (*comp* **-ier;** *super* **-iest**) sudoroso
Swede [swid] *s* sueco
Sweden ['swidən] *s* Suecia
Swedish ['swidɪʃ] *adj & s* sueco
sweep [swip] *s* barrido; alcance *m*, extensión; (*of wind*) soplo; (*of a well*) cigoñal *m* ‖ *v* (*pret & pp* **swept** [swɛpt]) *tr* barrer; arrastrar; rozar, tocar; recorrer con la mirada, los dedos, etc. ‖ *intr* barrer; pasar rápidamente; extenderse; precipitarse; andar con paso majestuoso
sweeper ['swipər] *s* (*person*) barrendero; (*machine for sweeping streets*) barredera; barredera de alfombra; (nav) dragaminas *m*
sweeping ['swipɪŋ] *adj* arrebatador; comprensivo, extenso, vasto ‖ **sweepings** *spl* barreduras

sweep'sec'ond *s* segundero central
sweep'stakes' *ssg* o *spl* lotería en la cual una persona gana todas las apuestas; carrera que decide todas las apuestas; premio en las carreras de caballos
sweet [swit] *adj* dulce; oloroso; melodioso, grato al oído; fresco; bonito, lindo; amable; querido; **to be sweet on** (coll) estar enamorado de || *adv* dulcemente; **to smell sweet** tener buen olor || **sweets** *spl* dulces *mpl*, golosinas
sweet'bread' *s* lechecillas, mollejas
sweet'bri'er *s* eglantina
sweeten ['switən] *tr* azucarar, endulzar; suavizar; purificar || *intr* azucararse, endulzarse; suavizarse
sweetener ['switənər] *s* eculcorante
sweet'heart' *s* enamorado o enamorada; amiga querida; galán *m*, cortejo
sweetish ['switɪʃ] *adj* dulzoso
sweet marjoram *s* mejorana
sweet'meats' *spl* dulces *mpl*, confites *mpl*, confitura
sweet pea *s* guisante *m* de olor
sweet potato *s* batata, camote *m*
sweet-scented ['swit,sɛntɪd] *adj* oloroso, perfumado
sweet tooth *s* gusto por los dulces
sweet-toothed ['swit,tuθt] *adj* dulcero, goloso
sweet william *s clavel m* de ramillete, minutisa
swell [swɛl] *adj* (coll) muy elegante; (slang) de órdago, magnífico || *s* hinchazón *f;* bulto; marejada; oleaje *m;* (*of a crowd of people*) oleada; (coll) petimetre *m*, pisaverde *m* || *v* (*pret* **swelled;** *pp* **swelled** o **swollen** ['swolən]) *tr* hinchar, inflar; abultar, aumentar; elevar, levantar; (fig) hinchar, engreír || *intr* hincharse; abultarse, aumentar, crecer; elevarse, levantarse; embravecerse (*el mar*); (fig) hincharse, engreírse
swelled head *s* entono; **to have a swelled head** estar muy pagado de sí mismo, creerse gran cosa
swelter ['swɛltər] *intr* sofocarse de sudor
swept'back' wing *s* (aer) ala en flecha
swerve [swʌrv] *s* viraje *m*, desvío brusco || *tr* desviar || *intr* desviarse, torcer
swift [swɪft] *adj* rápido, veloz; pronto; repentino; correlón (SAm) || *adv* rápidamente, velozmente || *s* vencejo
swig [swɪg] *s* chisguete, tragantada || *v* (*pret & pp* **swigged;** *ger* **swigging**) *tr & intr* beber a grandes tragos
swill [swɪl] *s* basura, inmundicia; tragantada || *tr* beber a grandes tragos; emborrachar || *intr* beber a grandes tragos; emborracharse
swim [swɪm] *s* natación; **the swim** (*in affairs, society, etc.*) (coll) la corriente || *v* (*pret* **swam** [swæm]; *pp* **swum** [swʌm]; *ger* **swimming**) *tr* pasar a nado || *intr* nadar; deslizarse, escurrirse; padecer vahidos; dar vueltas (*la cabeza*); **to swim across** atravesar a nado
swimmer ['swɪmər] *s* nadador *m*
swimming pool *s* piscina
swimming suit *s* traje *m* de baño
swindle ['swɪndəl] *s* estafa, timo; leva (CAm, Col); embelequería (Col, Mex, P-R) || *tr & intr* estafar, timar
swindler ['swɪndlər] *s* estafador *m*, estafadora; lana *m* (CAm)
swine [swaɪn] *s* cerdo, puerco; *spl* ganado porcino
swing [swɪŋ] *s* balance *m*, oscilación, vaivén *m;* (*device used for recreation*) columpio; hamaca; turno, período; fuerza, ímpetu *m;* (*trip*) jira; (box) golpe *m* de lado; (mus) ritmo constantemente repetido; **in full swing** en plena marcha || *v* (*pret & pp* **swung** [swʌŋ]) *tr* blandir (*p.ej., un arma*); menear (*los brazos*); hacer oscilar; columpiar; manejar con éxito || *intr* oscilar; balancearse; columpiar; estar colgado; dar una vuelta; **to swing open** abrirse de pronto (*una puerta*)
swinging door ['swɪŋɪŋ] *s* batiente *m* oscilante, puerta de vaivén
swinish ['swaɪnɪʃ] *adj* porcuno; (fig) cochino, puerco
swipe [swaɪp] *s* (coll) golpe *m* fuerte || *tr* (coll) dar un golpe fuerte a; (slang) hurtar, robar
swirl [swʌrl] *s* remolino, torbellino || *tr* hacer girar || *intr* arremolinarse, remolinar; girar
swish [swɪʃ] *s* (*e.g., of a whip*) chasquido; (*of a dress*) crujido || *tr* chasquear (*el látigo*) || *intr* chasquear; crujir (*un vestido*)
Swiss [swɪs] *adj & s* suizo
Swiss chard [tʃɑrd] *s* acelga
Swiss cheese *s* Gruyère *m*, queso suizo
Swiss Guards *spl* guardia suiza
switch [swɪtʃ] *s* bastoncillo, latiguillo; latigazo; coletazo; (*false hair*) trenza postiza, moño postizo; (elec) llave *f*, interruptor *m*, conmutador *m;* (rr) agujas || *tr* azotar, fustigar; (elec) conmutar; (rr) desviar; **to switch off** (elec) cortar, desconectar; **to switch on** (elec) cerrar (*el circuito*); (elec) encender, poner (*la luz, etc.*) || *intr* cambiarse, moverse; desviarse
switch'back' *s* vía en zigzag
switch'board' *s* cuadro de distribución
switching engine *s* locomotora de maniobras
switch•man ['swɪtʃmən] *s* (*pl* **-men** [mən]) agujetero, guardagujas *m*
switch'yard' *s* patio de maniobras
Switzerland ['swɪtsərlənd] *s* Suiza
swiv•el ['swɪvəl] *s* eslabón giratorio || *v* (*pret & pp* **-eled** o **-elled;** *ger* **-eling** o **-elling**) *intr* girar sobre un eje
swivel chair *s* silla giratoria
swoon [swun] *s* desmayo || *intr* desmayarse
swoop [swup] *s* descenso súbito; (*of a bird of prey*) calada || *intr* bajar rápidamente, precipitarse; abatirse (*p.ej., el ave de rapiña*)
sword [sord] *s* espada; **at swords' points** enemistados a sangre y fuego; **to put to the sword** pasar al filo de la espada, pasar a cuchillo
sword belt *s* cinturón *m*
sword'fish' *s* pez *m* espada

sword handler *s* (taur) mozo de estoques
sword rattling *s* fanfarronería
swords•man [ˈsordzmən] *s* (*pl* **-men** [mən]) espada *m;* esgrimidor *m*
sword swallower [ˈswɑlo•ər] *s* tragasable *m*
sword thrust *s* estocada, golpe *m* de espada
sworn [sworn] *adj* (*enemy*) jurado
sycophant [ˈsɪkəfənt] *s* adulador *m;* parásito
syll. *abbr* **syllable**
syllable [ˈsɪləbəl] *s* sílaba
syllogism [ˈsɪlə,dʒɪzəm] *s* silogismo
sylph [sɪlf] *s* sílfide *f*
sym. *abbr* **symbol, symmetrical, symphony, symptom**
symbiosis [,sɪmbaɪˈosɪs] o [,sɪmbiˈosɪs] *s* simbiosis
symbiotic [,sɪmbaɪˈɑtɪk] o [,sɪmbiˈɑtɪk] *adj* simbiótico
symbol [ˈsɪmbəl] *s* símbolo
symbolic(al) [sɪmˈbɑlɪk(əl] *adj* simbólico
symbolize [ˈsɪmbə,laɪz] *tr* simbolizar
symmetric(al) [sɪˈmɛtrɪk(əl)] *adj* simétrico
symme•try [ˈsɪmɪtri] *s* (*pl* **-tries**) simetría
sympathetic [,sɪmpəˈθɛtɪk] *adj* compasivo; favorablemente dispuesto
sympathize [ˈsɪmpə,θaɪz] *intr* compadecerse; **to sympathize with** compadecerse de; comprender
sympa•thy [ˈsɪmpəθi] *s* (*pl* **-thies**) compasión, conmiseración; **to be in sympathy with** estar de acuerdo con, ser partidario de; **to extend one's sympathy to** dar el pésame a
sympathy strike *s* huelga por solidaridad
symphonic [sɪmˈfɑnɪk] *adj* sinfónico
sympho•ny [ˈsɪmfəni] *s* (*pl* **-nies**) sinfonía
symposi•um [sɪmˈpozɪ•əm] *s* (*pl* **-a** [ə]) coloquio
symptom [ˈsɪmptəm] *s* síntoma *m*
syn. *abbr* **synonym, synonymous**
synagogue [ˈsɪnə,gɔg] *s* sinagoga
synchronize [ˈsɪŋkrə,naɪz] *tr & intr* sincronizar
synchronous [ˈsɪŋkrənəs] *adj* sincrónico
syncope [ˈsɪŋkə,pi] *s* (phonet) síncopa
syndicate [ˈsɪndɪkɪt] *s* sindicato ‖ [ˈsɪndɪ,ket] *tr* sindicar ‖ *intr* sindicarse
syndrome [ˈsɪndrom] *s* síndrome *m*
synonym [ˈsɪnənɪm] *s* sinónimo
synonymous [sɪˈnɑnɪməs] *adj* sinónimo
synop•sis [sɪˈnɑpsɪs] *s* (*pl* **-ses** [siz]) sinopsis *f*
syntax [ˈsɪntæks] *s* sintaxis *f*
synthe•sis [ˈsɪnθɪsɪs] *s* (*pl* **-ses** [,siz]) síntesis *f*
synthesize [ˈsɪnθɪ,saɪz] *tr* sintetizar
synthesizer *s* sintetizador *m*
synthetic(al) [sɪnˈθɛtɪk(əl] *adj* sintético
syphillis [ˈsɪfɪlɪs] *s* sífilis *f*
Syria [ˈsɪrɪ•ə] *s* Siria
Syrian [ˈsɪrɪ•ən] *adj & s* sirio
syringe [sɪˈrɪndʒ] o [ˈsɪrɪndʒ] *s* jeringa; (*fountain syringe*) mangueta; (*syringe fitted with needle for hypodermic injections*) jeringuilla ‖ *tr* jeringar
syrup [ˈsɪrəp] *s* almíbar *m;* (*with fruit juices or medicinal substances*) jarabe *m*
system [ˈsɪstəm] *s* sistema *m*
systematic(al) [,sɪstəˈmætɪk(əl)] *adj* sistemático
systematize [ˈsɪstəmə,taɪz] *tr* sistematizar
systems analysis *s* análisis *m & f* de sistemas
systole [ˈsɪstəli] *s* sístole *f*

T

T, t [ti] vigésima letra del alfabeto inglés
t. *abbr* **teaspoon, temperature, tenor, tense, territory, town**
T. *abbr* **Territory, Testament**
tab [tæb] *s* apéndice *m*, proyección; marbete *m;* **to keep tab on** (coll) tener a la vista; **to pick up the tab** (coll) pagar la cuenta
tab•by [ˈtæbi] *s* (*pl* **-bies**) gato atigrado; gata; solterona; chismosa
tabernacle [ˈtæbər,nækəl] *s* tabernáculo
table [ˈtebəl] *s* mesa; (*list, catalogue; index of a book*) tabla; **to set the table** poner la mesa; **to turn the tables** volver las tornas; **under the table** completamente emborrachado ‖ *tr* aplazar la discusión de
tab•leau [ˈtæblo] *s* (*pl* **-leaus** o **-leaux** [loz]) cuadro vivo
ta'ble•cloth' *s* mantel *m*
table d'hôte [ˈtɑbəlˈdot] *s* mesa redonda; comida a precio fijo
ta'ble•land' *s* meseta
table linen *s* mantelería
table manners *spl* modales *mpl* que uno tiene en la mesa
table of contents *s* índice *m* de materias, tabla de materias
ta'ble•spoon' *s* cuchara de sopa
tablespoonful [ˈtebəl,spun,ful] *s* cucharada
tablet [ˈtæblɪt] *s* (*writing pad*) bloc *m;* (*slab*) lápida, placa; (*lozenge, pastille*) comprimido, tableta
table talk *s* conversación de sobremesa
table tennis *s* tenis de mesa
ta'ble•ware' *s* servicio de mesa, artículos para la mesa
tabloid [ˈtæblɔɪd] *s* periódico sensacional
taboo [təˈbu] *adj* prohibido ‖ *s* tabú *m* ‖ *tr* prohibir
tabulate [ˈtæbjə,let] *tr* tabular
tabulator [ˈtæbjə,letər] *s* tabulador *m*
tacit [ˈtæsɪt] *adj* tácito
taciturn [ˈtæsɪ,tʌrn] *adj* taciturno

tack [tæk] *s* tachuela; nuevo plan de acción; (naut) virada; (sew) hilván *m* || *tr* clavar con tachuelas; añadir; unir; (naut) virar; (sew) hilvanar || *intr* cambiar de plan; (naut) virar
tackle ['tækəl] *s* avíos, enseres *mpl;* (naut) poleame *m* || *tr* atacar, embestir; emprender
tack•y ['tæki] *adj* (*comp* **-ier;** *super* **-iest**) pegajoso; (coll) desaliñado
tact [tækt] *s* tacto, juicio, tino
tactful ['tæktfəl] *adj* discreto, político
tactical ['tæktɪkəl] *adj* táctico
tactician [tæk'tɪʃən] *s* táctico
tactics ['tæktɪks] *ssg* (mil) táctica || *spl* táctica
tactless ['tæklɪs] *adj* indiscreto
tad'pole' *s* renacuajo
taffeta ['tæfɪtə] *s* tafetán *m*
taffy ['tæfi] *s* arropía, melcocha; (coll) lisonja, zalamería
tag [tæg] *s* etiqueta, marbete *m;* herrete *m;* pingajo; mechón *m;* vedija; (*curlicue in writing*) ringorrango; **to play tag** jugar al tócame tú || *v* (*pret & pp* **tagged;** *ger* **tagging**) *tr* pegar un marbete a; marcar con marbete || *intr* (coll) seguir de cerca
tag end *s* cabo flojo; retal *m*, retazo
Tagus ['tegəs] *s* Tajo
tail [tel] *adj* de cola || *s* cola; **tails** (*of a coin*) cruz *f;* (coll) frac *m;* **to turn tail** mostrar los talones || *tr* atar, juntar || *intr* formar cola; **to tail after** pisar los talones a
tail assembly *s* (aer) empenaje *m*, planos de cola
tail end *s* cola, extremo; conclusión; **at the tail end** al final
tail'gate' *tr & intr* (aut) seguir demasiado de cerca
tail'light' *s* faro trasero; (rr) disco de cola
tailor ['telər] *s* sastre *m* || *tr* entallar (*un traje*) || *intr* ser sastre
tailoring ['telərɪŋ] *s* sastrería, costura
tai'lor-made' suit *s* traje *m* de sastre, traje hecho a la medida
tail'piece' *s* apéndice *m*, cabo; (*of stringed instrument*) (mus) cordal *m;* (typ) florón *m*
tail'race' *s* cauce *m* de salida; (min) canal *m* de desechos
tail spin *s* (aer) barrena picada
tail wind *s* (aer) viento de cola; (naut) viento en popa
taint [tent] *s* mancha; corrupción, infección || *tr* manchar; corromper, inficionar
take [tek] *s* toma; presa, redada; (mov) toma; (slang) entradas, ingresos || *v* (*pret* **took** [tʊk]; *pp* **taken**) *tr* tomar; (*to carry off with one*) llevarse; (*to remove*) quitar; quedarse con (*p.ej., una compra en una tienda*); comer (*una pieza, en el juego de ajedrez y en el de damas*); dar (*un paso, un salto, un paseo*); hacer (*un viaje; ejercicio*); seguir (*un consejo; una asignatura*); sacar (*una fotografía*); calzar, usar (*cierto tamaño de zapatos o guantes*); estudiar (*p.ej., historia, francés, matemáticas*); echar (*una siesta*); tomar (*un tren, autobús, tranvía*); aguantar, tolerar; soportar; **to take amiss** llevar a mal; **to take apart** descomponer, desarmar, desmontar; **to take down** bajar; descolgar; poner por escrito, tomar nota de; desmontar; (*to humble*) quitar los humos a; **to take for** tomar por, p.ej., **I took you for someone else** le tomé por otra persona; **to take from** quitar a; **to take in** acoger, admitir; (*to welcome into one's home, one's company*) recibir; (*to encompass*) abarcar, comprender; ganar (dinero); visitar (*los puntos de interés*); (*to win over by flattery or deceit*) cazar; meter (*p.ej., las costuras de una prenda de vestir*); **to take it that** suponer que; **to take off** quitarse (*p.ej., el sombrero*); descontar; (coll) imitar, parodiar; **to take on** tomar, contratar; empezar; cargar con, tomar sobre sí; desafiar; **to take out** sacar; pasear (*p.ej., a un niño, un caballo*); omitir; extraer, separar; **to take place** tener lugar; **to take up** subir; levantar; apretar; coger; recoger; emprender, comenzar; tomar posesión de (*un cargo, un puesto*); tomar, estudiar; ocupar, llenar (*un espacio*) || *intr* arraigar, prender; cuajar; actuar, obrar; salir, resultar; adherirse; pegar; (coll) tener éxito; **to take after** parecerse a; **to take off** levantarse; salir; (aer) despegar; **to take up with** (coll) estrechar amistad con; (coll) vivir con; **to take well** (coll) sacar buen retrato
take'-home' pay *s* salario neto
take'-off' *s* (aer) despegue *m;* (coll) imitación burlesca, parodia
talcum powder ['tælkəm] *s* polvos de talco; talco en polvo
tale [tel] *s* cuento, relato; embuste *m*, mentira
tale'bear'er *s* chismoso, cuentista *mf*
talent ['tælənt] *s* talento; gente *f* de talento
talented ['tæləntɪd] *adj* talentoso
talent scout *s* buscador *m* de nuevas figuras
talk [tɔk] *s* charla, plática; (*gossip*) fábula, comidilla; (*lecture*) conferencia; **to cause talk** dar que hablar || *tr* hablar; convencer hablando; **to talk up** ensalzar || *intr* hablar; parlar (*el loro*); **to talk on** discutir (*un asunto*); hablar sin para; continuar hablando; **to talk up** elevar la voz, osar hablar
talkative ['tɔkətɪv] *adj* hablador, locuaz, palabrudo
talker ['tɔkər] *s* hablador *m;* orador *m;* charlatán *m*, parlón *m*; discursista *mf*
talkie ['tɔki] *s* (coll) cine hablado
talking doll ['tɔkɪŋ] *s* muñeca parlante
talking film *s* película hablada
talking machine *s* máquina parlante
talking picture *s* cine hablado, cine parlante
talk show *s* (telv, rad) programa *m* de conversación e interviú
tall [tɔl] *adj* alto; (coll) exagerado
tallow ['tælo] *s* sebo
tal•ly ['tæli] *s* (*pl* **-lies**) cuenta || *v* (*pret & pp* **-lied**) *tr* echar la cuenta de || *intr* echar la cuenta; concordar, corresponder, conformarse
tally sheet *s* hoja en que se anota una cuenta

talon [ˈtælən] *s* garra
tambourine [ˌtæmbəˈrin] *s* pandereta
tame [tem] *adj* manso, domesticado; dócil, sumiso; insípido || *tr* amansar, domesticar; domar (*a un animal salvaje*); someter; captar (*una caída de agua*)
tamp [tæmp] *tr* atacar (*un barreno*); apisonar
tamper [ˈtæmpər] *s* (*person*) apisonador *m;* (*ram*) pisón *m* || *intr* entremeterse; **to tamper with** manosear, tocar ajando; tratar de forzar (*una cerradura*); falsificar (*un documento*); corromper (*p.ej., a un testigo*)
tampon [ˈtæmpɑn] *s* (surg) tapón *m* || *tr* (surg) taponar
tan [tæn] *adj* requemado, tostado; de color de canela; marrón; café (Am) || *v* (*pret & pp* **tanned;** *ger* **tanning**) *tr* adobar, curtir, zurrar; quemar, tostar; (coll) zurrar, dar una paliza a
tang [tæŋ] *s* sabor *m* u olor *m* fuerte y picante; dejo, gustillo (*ringing sound*) tañido
tangent [ˈtændʒənt] *adj* tangente || *s* tangente *f;* **to fly off at a tangent** tomar subitamente nuevo rumbo, cambiar de repente
tangerine [ˌtændʒəˈrin] *s* mandarina
tangible [ˈtændʒɪbəl] *adj* palpable, tangible
Tangier [tænˈdʒɪr] *s* Tánger *f*
tangle [ˈtæŋgəl] *s* enredo, maraña, lío || *tr* enredar, enmarañar || *intr* enredarse, enmarañarse
tank [tæŋk] *s* tanque *m*, depósito; (mil) tanque, carro de combate; (rr) ténder *m;* (*heavy drinker*) (slang) bodega
tank car *s* (rr) carro cuba, vagón *m* tanque
tanker [ˈtæŋkər] *s* barco tanque, buque *m* cisterna, barco cisternas; avión-nodriza *m*
tanker fleet *s* flota petrolera
tank farming *s* quimicultura, cultivo hidropónico
tank truck *s* camión *m* tanque
tanner [ˈtænər] *s* curtidor *m*
tanner•y [ˈtænəri] *s* (*pl* **-ies**) curtiduría, tenería
tantalize [ˈtæntəˌlaɪz] *tr* atormentar con falsas promesas
tantamount [ˈtæntəˌmaʊnt] *adj* equivalente
tantrum [ˈtæntrəm] *s* berrinche *m*, rabieta
tap [tæp] *s* golpecito, palmadita; canilla, espita; grifo; (elec) toma; (mach) macho de terraja; **on tap** sacado del barril, servido al grifo; listo, a mano; **taps** (*signal to put out lights*) (mil) silencio || *v* (*pret & pp* **tapped;** *ger* **tapping**) *tr* dar golpecitos o un golpecito a o en; espitar, poner la espita a; sacar o tomar (*quitando la espita*); sangrar (*un árbol*); intervenir (*un teléfono*); derivar (*electricidad*); aterrajar (*tuercas*) || *intr* dar golpecitos
tap dance *s* zapateado
tap'-dance' *intr* zapatear
tape [tep] *s* cinta || *tr* proveer de cinta; medir con cinta; (coll) grabar en cinta magnetofónica
tape measure *s* cinta de medir
taper [ˈtepər] *s* cerilla, velita larga y delgada || *tr* ahusar || *intr* ahusarse; ir disminuyendo
tape'-re•cord' *tr* grabar sobre cinta
tape recorder [rɪˈkɔrdər] *s* magnetófono, grabadora de cinta
tapes•try [ˈtæpɪstri] *s* (*pl* **-tries**) tapiz *m* || *v* (*pret & pp* **-tried**) *tr* tapizar
tape'worm' *s* solitaria, lombriz solitaria
tappet [ˈtæpɪt] *s* (aut) alzaválvulas *m*, taqué *m*
tap'room' *s* bodegón *m*, taberna
taps [tæps] *s* toque *m* de silencio; (slang) fin *m*, muerte *f*
tap water *s* agua de grifo
tap wrench *s* volvedor *m* de machos
tar [tɑr] *s* alquitrán *m;* (coll) marinero || *v* (*pret & pp* **tarred;** *ger* **tarring**) *tr* alquitranar; **to tar and feather** embrear y emplumar
tar•dy [ˈtɑrdi] *adj* (*comp* **-dier;** *super* **-diest**) tardío
target [ˈtɑrgɪt] *s* blanco
target area *s* zona a batir
target practice *s* tiro al blanco
tariff [ˈtærɪf] *adj* arancelario || (*duties*) arancel *m;* (*rates in general*) tarifa
tarnish [ˈtɑrnɪʃ] *s* deslustre *m* || *tr* deslustrar || *intr* deslustrarse
tar paper *s* papel alquitranado
tarpaulin [tɑrˈpɔlɪn] *s* alquitranado, encerado, empegado
tar•ry [ˈtɑri] *adj* alquitranado, embreado || [ˈtæri] *v* (*pret & pp* **-ried**) *intr* detenerse, quedarse; tardar
tart [tɑrt] *adj* acre, agrio; (fig) áspero, mordaz || *s* tarta; (coll) puta
task [tæsk] *s* tarea; **to bring** o **take to task** llamar a capítulo
task'mas'ter *s* amo, superintendente *mf;* ordenancista *mf*, tirano
tassel [ˈtæsəl] *s* borla; (bot) penacho
taste [test] *s* gusto, sabor *m;* sorbo, trago; muestra; gusto, buen gusto; **in bad taste** de mal gusto; **in good taste** de buen gusto; **to acquire a taste for** tomar gusto a || *tr* gustar; (*to sample*) probar || *intr* saber; **to taste of** saber a
tasteless [ˈtestlɪs] *adj* desabrido, insípido; de mal gusto
tast•y [ˈtesti] *adj* (*comp* **-ier;** *super* **-iest**) sabroso; de buen gusto
tatter [ˈtætər] *s* andrajo, harapo, guiñapo || *tr* hacer andrajos
tattered [ˈtætərd] *adj* andrajoso, haraposo, hilachento
tattle [ˈtætəl] *s* charla; habladuría || *intr* charlar; chismear, murmurar
tat'tle•tale' *adj* revelador || *s* cuentista *mf*, chismoso
tatto [tæˈtu] *s* tatuaje *m;* (mil) retreta || *tr* tatuar o tatuarse
taunt [tɔnt] o [tɑnt] *s* mofa, pulla || *tr* provocar con insultos
Taurus [ˈtɔrəs] *s* (astr) Tauro
taut [tɔt] *adj* tieso, tirante
tavern [ˈtævərn] *s* taberna; mesón *m*, posada; bayun(c)a (CAm); borrachería (Mex)

taw•dry [ˈtɔdri] *adj* (*comp* **-drier;** *super* **-driest**) cursi, charro, vistoso
taw•ny [ˈtɔni] *adj* (*comp* **-nier;** *super* **-niest**) leonado
tax [tæks] *s* contribución, impuesto ‖ *tr* poner impuestos a (*una persona*); poner impuestos sobre (*la propiedad*); abrumar, cargar; agotar (*la paciencia de uno*)
taxable [ˈtæksəbəl] *adj* imponible
taxation [tækˈseʃən] *s* imposición de contribuciones; contribuciones, impuestos
tax collector *s* recaudador *m* de impuestos
tax cut *s* reducción de impuestos
tax deduction *s* exclusión de contribución
tax evader [ɪˈvedər] *s* burlador *m* de impuestos
tax evasion *s* fraude *m* fiscal
tax'-ex•empt' *adj* exento de impuesto
tax haven *s* asilo de los impuestos
tax•i [ˈtæksi] *s* (*pl* **-is**) taxi *m* ‖ *v* (*pret & pp* **-ied;** *ger* **-iing** o **-ying**) *tr* (aer) carretear ‖ *intr* ir en taxi; (aer) carretear, taxear
tax'i•cab' *s* taxi *m*
taxi dancer *s* taxi *f*
taxi driver *s* taista *mf*
tax'i•plane' *s* avioneta de alquiler
taxi stand *s* parada de taxis
tax loss *s* pérdida de reclamable
tax'pay'er *s* contribuyente *mf*
tax rate *s* tipo impositivo
tax relief *s* aligeramiento de impuestos
tax return *s* declaración de renta
t.b. *abbr* **tuberculosis**
tbs. o **tbsp.** *abbr* **tablespoon, tablespoons**
tea [ti] *s* té *m;* (*medicinal infusion*) tisana; caldo de carne
tea bag *s* muñeca
tea ball *s* huevo del té
tea'cart' *s* mesita de té (*con ruedas*)
teach [titʃ] *v* (*pret & pp* **taught** [tɔt]) *tr & intr* enseñar
teacher [ˈtitʃər] *s* maestro, instructor *m;* (*such as adversity*) (fig) maestra
teacher's pet *s* alumno mimado
teaching [ˈtitʃɪŋ] *adj* docente ‖ *s* enseñanza; doctrina
teaching aids *spl* material *m* auxiliar de instrucción
teaching staff *s* personal *m* docente
tea'cup' *s* taza para té
tea dance *s* té *m* bailable
teak [tik] *s* teca
tea'ket'tle *s* tetera
team [tim] *s* (*e.g., of horses*) tiro, tronco; (*of oxen*) yunta; (sport) equipo ‖ *tr* enganchar, uncir, enyugar ‖ *intr*—**to team up** asociarse, unirse; formar un equipo
team'mate' *s* compañero de equipo, equipier *m*
teamster [ˈtimstər] *s* (*of horses*) tronquista *m;* (*of a truck*) camionista *m*
team'work' *s* espíritu de equipo; trabajo de equipo
tea'pot' *s* tetera
tear [tɪr] *s* lágrima; **to burst into tears** romper a llorar; **to fill with tears** arrasarse (*los ojos*) de o en lágrimas; **to hold back one's tears** beberse las lágrimas; **to laugh away one's tears** convertir las lágrimas en risas ‖ [tɛr] *s* desgarro, rasgón *m* ‖ [tɛr] *v* (*pret* **tore** [tor]; *pp* **torn** [torn]) *tr* desgarrar, rasgar; acongojar, afligir; mesarse (*los cabellos*); **to tear apart** romper en dos; **to tear down** derribar (*un edificio*); desarmar (*una máquina*); **to tear off** desgajar; **to tear up** romper (*p.ej., un papel*) ‖ *intr* desgarrarse, rasgarse; **to tear along** correr a toda velocidad
tear bomb [tɪr] *s* bomba lacrimógena
tearful [ˈtɪrfəl] *adj* lacrimoso
tear gas [tɪr] *s* gas lacrimógeno
tear-jerker [ˈtɪr,dʒʌrkər] *s* (slang) drama *m* o cine *m* que arrancan lágrimas
tear-off [ˈtɛr,ɔf] *adj* exfoliador
tea'room' *s* salón *m* de té
tear sheet [tɛr] *s* hoja del anunciante
tease [tiz] *tr* embromar, azuzar
tea'spoon' *s* cucharilla, cucharita
teaspoonful [ˈti,spun,fʊl] *s* cucharadita
teat [tit] *s* teta, pezón *m*
tea time *s* hora del té
technical [ˈtɛknɪkəl] *adj* técnico
technicali•ty [,tɛknɪˈkælɪti] *s* (*pl* **-ties**) detalle técnico
technician [tɛkˈnɪʃən] *s* técnico
technics [ˈtɛknɪks] *ssg* técnica
technique [tɛkˈnik] *s* técnica
Teddy bear [ˈtɛdi] *s* oso de juguete, oso de trapo
tedious [ˈtidɪ•əs] o [ˈtidʒəs] *adj* tedioso, enfadoso
teem [tim] *intr* hormiguear; llover a cántaros; **to teem with** hervir de
teeming [ˈtimɪŋ] *adj* hormigueante; (*rain*) torrencial
teen age [tin] *s* edad de 13 a 19 años
teen-ager [ˈtin,edʒər] *s* joven *mf* de 13 a 19 años de edad
teens [tinz] *spl* números ingleses que terminan en **-teen** (de 13 a 19); edad de 13 a 19 años; **to be in one's teens** tener de 13 a 19 años
tee•ny [ˈtini] *adj* (*comp* **-nier;** *super* **-niest**) (coll) diminuto, pequeñito
teeter [ˈtitər] *s* vaivén *m*, balanceo ‖ *intr* balancear, oscilar
teethe [tið] *intr* endentecer
teething [ˈtiðɪŋ] *s* dentición
teething ring *s* chupador *m*
teetotaler [tiˈtotələr] *s* teetotalista *mf*, nefalista *mf*, abstemio
tel. *abbr* **telegram, telegraph, telephone**
tele•cast [ˈtɛlɪ,kæst] *s* teledifusión ‖ *v* (*pret & pp* **-cast** o **-casted**) *tr & intr* teledifundir
telegram [ˈtɛlɪ,græm] *s* telegrama *m*
telegraph [ˈtɛlɪ,græf] *s* telégrafo ‖ *tr & intr* telegrafiar
telegrapher [tɪ,lɛgrəfər] *s* telegrafista *mf*
telegraph pole *s* poste *m* de telégrafo
Telemachus [tɪˈlɛməkəs] *s* Telémaco
telemeter [tɪˈlɛmɪtər] *s* telémetro ‖ *tr* telemetrar
telemetry [tɪˈlɛmɪtri] *s* telemetría

telephone ['tɛlɪ,fon] *s* teléfono || *tr & intr* telefonear
telephone booth *s* locutorio, cabina telefónica
telephone call *s* llamada telefónica
telephone directory *s* anuario telefónico, guía telefónica
telephone exchange *s* estación telefónica, central *f* de teléfonos; conmutador *m* (SAm)
telephone operator *s* telefonista *mf*, centralista *mf*
telephone receiver *s* receptor telefónico
telephone table *s* mesita portateléfono
tele(photo)lens ['tɛlɪ(,fotə),lɛnz] *s* lente telefotográfica
teleprinter ['tɛlɪ,prɪntər] *s* teleimpresor *m*
telescope ['tɛlɪ,skop] *s* telescopio || *tr* telescopar || *intr* telescoparse
teletype ['tɛlɪ,taɪp] *s* teletipo || *tr & intr* transmitir por teletipo
teleview ['tɛlɪ,vju] *tr & intr* ver por televisión
televiewer ['tɛlɪ,vju•ər] *s* televidente *mf*, telespectador *m*
televise ['tɛlɪ,vaɪz] *tr* televisar
television ['tɛlɪ,vɪʃən] *adj* televisor || *s* televisión
television audience *s* telespectadores
television screen *s* pantalla televisora, pequeña pantalla
television set *s* televisor *m*, telerreceptor *m*
telex ['tɛlɛks] *s* servicio comerical de teletipo
tell [tɛl] *v* (*pret & pp* **told** [told]) *tr* decir; (*to narrate; to count*) contar; determinar; conocer, distinguir; **I told you so!** ¡por algo te lo dije!; **to tell someone to** + *inf* decircle a uno que + *subj* || *intr* hablar; surtir efecto; **to tell on** dejarse ver en (*p.ej., la salud de uno*); (coll) denunciar
teller ['tɛlər] *s* narrador *m;* (*of a bank*) cajero; (*of votes*) escrutador *m*
temper ['tɛmpər] *s* temple *m*, natural *m*, genio; cólera, mal genio; (*of steel, glass, etc.*) temple *m;* **to keep one's temper** dominar su mal genio; **to lose one's temper** encolerizarse, perder la paciencia || *tr* templar *intr* templarse
temperament ['tɛmpərəmənt] *s* disposición; temperamento sensible o excitable
temperamental [,tɛmpərə'mɛntəl] *adj* temperamental
temperance ['tɛmpərəns] *s* templanza
temperate ['tɛmpərɪt] *adj* templado
temperature [,tɛmpərətʃər] *s* temperatura
tempest ['tɛmpɪst] *s* tempestad
tempestuous [tɛm'pɛstʃu•əs] *adj* tempestuoso
temple ['tɛmpəl] *s* (*place of worship*) templo; (*side of forehead*) sien *f;* (*sidepiece of spectacles*) gafa
tem•po ['tɛmpo] *s* (*pl* **-pos** o **-pi** [pi]) (mus) tiempo; (fig) ritmo (*p.ej., de la vida*)
temporal ['tɛmpərəl] *adj* temporal
temporary ['tɛmpə,rɛri] *adj* temporáneo, temporario, provisional, interino
temporize ['tɛmpə,raɪz] *intr* contemporizar, temporizar
tempt [tɛmpt] *tr* tentar
temptation [tɛmpt'teʃən] *s* tentación
tempter ['tɛmptər] *s* tentador *m*
tempting ['tɛmptɪŋ] *adj* tentador
ten [tɛn] *adj & pron* diez || *s* diez *m;* **ten o'clock** las diez
tenable ['tɛnəbəl] *adj* defendible
tenacious [tɪ'neʃəs] *adj* tenaz
tenacity [tɪ'næsɪti] *s* tenacidad
tenant ['tɛnənt] *s* arrendatario, inquilino; morador *m*, residente *mf*
tend [tɛnd] *tr* cuidar, vigilar; servir || *intr* tender, dirigirse; **to tend to** atender a; **to tend to** + *inf* tender a + *inf*
tenden•cy ['tɛndənsi] *s* (*pl* **-cies**) tendencia
tender ['tɛndər] *adj* tierno; (*painfully sensitive*) dolorido || *n* oferta; (naut) alijador *m*, falúa; (rr) ténder *m* || *tr* ofrecer, tender
tender-hearted ['tɛndər,hɑrtɪd] *adj* compasivo, tierno de corazón
ten'der•loin' *s* filete *m* || **Tenderloin** *s* barrio de mala vida
tenderness ['tɛndərnɪs] *s* ternura, terneza; sensibilidad
tendon ['tɛndən] *s* tendón *m*
tendril ['tɛndrɪl] *s* zarcillo
tenement ['tɛnɪmənt] *s* habitación, vivienda; casa de vecindad
tenement house *s* casa de vecindad
tenet ['tɛnɪt] *s* dogma *m*, credo, principio
tennis ['tɛnɪs] *s* tenis *m*
tennis court *s* campo de tenis
tennis player *s* tenista *mf*
tenor ['tɛnər] *s* tenor *m*, carácter *m*, curso, tendencia; (mus) tenor
tense [tɛns] *adj* tenso, tieso; (*person; situation*) (fig) tenso; (*relations*) tirante || *s* (gram) tiempo
tension ['tɛnʃən] *s* tensión; ansia, congoja, esfuerzo mental; (*in personal or diplomatic relations*) tirantez *f*
tent [tɛnt] *s* tienda; tienda de campaña
tentacle ['tɛntəkəl] *s* tentáculo
tentative ['tɛntətɪv] *adj* tentativo
tenth [tɛnθ] *adj & s* décimo || *s* (*in dates*) diez *m*
tenuous ['tɛnju•əs] *adj* tenue; (*thin in consistency*) raro
tenure ['tɛnjər] *s* (*of property*) tenencia; (*of an office*) ejercicio; (*protection from dismissal*) inamovilidad
tepid ['tɛpɪd] *adj* tibio
tercet ['tʌrsɪt] *s* terceto
term [tʌrm] *s* término; (*of imprisonment*) condena; semestre *m*, período escolar; (*of the presidency of the U.S.A.*) mandato, período; **terms** condiciones || *tr* llamar, nombrar
termagant ['tʌrməgənt] *s* mujer regañona, mujer de mal genio
terminal ['tʌrmɪnəl] *adj* terminal || *s* término, fin *m;* (elec) terminal *m;* (rr) estación de fin de línea
terminate ['tʌrmɪ,net] *tr & intr* terminar
termination [,tʌrmɪ'neʃən] *s* terminación
terminus ['tʌrmɪnəs] *s* término; (rr) estación de cabeza, estación extrema
termite ['tʌrmaɪt] *s* termite *m*, comején *m*

terrace [ˈtɛrəs] *s* terraza; (*flat roof of a house*) azotea
terra firma [ˈtɛrə ˈfʌrmə] *s* tierra firme; **on terra firma** sobre suelo firme
terrain [tɛˈren] *s* terreno
terrestrial [təˈrɛstrɪ•əl] *adj* terrestre
terrible [ˈtɛrɪbəl] *adj* terrible; muy desagradable
terrific [təˈrɪfɪk] *adj* terrífico; (coll) enorme, intenso, brutal
terri•fy [ˈtɛri,faɪ] *v* (*pret & pp* **-fied**) *tr* aterrorizar, atemorizar
territo•ry [ˈtɛrɪ,tori] *s* (*pl* **-ries**) territorio
terror [ˈtɛrər] *s* terror *m*
terrorize [ˈtɛrə,raɪz] *tr* aterrorizar; imponerse a, mediante el terror
terry cloth [ˈtɛri] *s* albornoz *m*
terse [tʌrs] *adj* breve, sucinto
tertiary [ˈtʌrʃɪ,ɛri] o [ˈtʌrʃəri] *adj* terciario
Test. *abbr* **Testament**
test [tɛst] *s* prueba, ensayo; examen *m* || *tr* probar, poner a prueba; examinar
testament [ˈtɛstəmənt] *s* testamento
test flight *s* vuelo de ensayo
testicle [ˈtɛstɪkəl] *s* testículo
testi•fy [ˈtɛstɪ,faɪ] *v* (*pret & pp* **-fied**) *tr & intr* testificar
testimonial [,tɛstɪˈmonɪ•əl] *s* recomendación, certificado; (*expression of esteem, gratitude, etc.*) homenaje *m*
testimo•ny [ˈtɛstɪ,moni] *s* (*pl* **-nies**) testimonio
testing grounds [ˈtɛstɪŋ] *spl* campo de pruebas
test pilot *s* (aer) piloto de pruebas
test tube *s* probeta, tubo de ensayo
test'-tube' baby *s* niño-probeta *m*
tether [ˈtɛðər] *s* atadura, traba; **at the end of one's tether** al límite de las posibilidades o la paciencia de uno || *tr* apersogar
tetter [ˈtɛtər] *s* empeine *m*
text [tɛkst] *s* texto; tema *m*, lema *m*
text'book' *s* libro de texto
textile [ˈtɛkstɪl] o [ˈtɛkstaɪl] *adj & s* textil *m*
texture [ˈtɛkstʃər] *s* textura
Thai [ˈtɑ•i] o [ˈtaɪ] *adj & s* tailandés *m*
Thailand [ˈtaɪlənd] *s* Tailandia
Thales [ˈθeliz] *s* Tales *m*
Thalia [θəˈlaɪ•ə] *s* Talía
Thames [tɛmz] *s* Támesis *m*
than [ðæn] *conj* que, p.ej., **he is richer than I** es más rico que yo; (*before a numeral*) de, p.ej., **more than twenty** más de veinte; (*before a verb*) de lo que, p.ej., **the crop is larger than was expected** la cosecha es mayor de lo que se esperaba; (*before a verb with direct object understood*) del (de la, de los, de las) que, p.ej., **they sent us more coffee than we ordered** nos enviaron más café del que pedimos
thanatology [,θænəˈtɑlədʒi] *s* tanatología
thank [θæŋk] *tr* agradecer, dar las gracias a; **to thank someone for something** agradecerle a uno una cosa || **thanks** *spl* gracias; **thanks to** gracias a, merced a || **thanks** *interj* ¡gracias!
thankful [ˈθæŋkfəl] *adj* agradecido
thankless [ˈθæŋklɪs] *adj* ingrato
thanksgiving [,θæŋksˈgɪvɪŋ] *s* acción de gracias
Thanksgiving Day *s* (U.S.A.) día *m* de acción de gracias
that [ðæt] *adj dem* (*pl* **those**) ese; aquel; **that one** ése; aquél || *pron dem* (*pl* **those**) ése; aquél; eso; aquello || *pron rel* que, quien, el cual, el que || *adv* tan; **that far** tan lejos; hasta allí; **that many** tantos; **that much** tanto || *conj* que; para que
thatch [θætʃ] *s* barda, paja; techo de paja || *tr* cubrir de paja, techar con paja, bardar
thaw [θɔ] *s* deshielo, derretimiento; descongelación || *tr* deshelar, derretir || *intr* deshelarse, derretirse
the [ðə], [ðɪ], o [ði] *art def* el || *adv* cuanto, p.ej., **the more the merrier** cuanto más mejor; **the more . . . the more** cuanto más . . . tanto más
theater [ˈθi•ətər] *s* teatro
the'ater-go'er *s* teatrero
theater news *s* actualidad escénica
theater page *s* noticiario teatral
theatrical [θɪˈætrɪkəl] *adj* teatral
Thebes [θibz] *s* Tebas *f*
thee [ði] *pron pers* (archaic, poet, Bib) te; ti; **with thee** contigo
theft [θɛft] *s* hurto, robo
theft'-proof' *adj* antirroba
their [ðɛr] *adj poss* su; el . . . de ellos
theirs [ðɛrz] *pron poss* el suyo, el de ellos
them [ðɛm] *pron pers* los; ellos; **to them** les; a ellos
theme [θim] *s* tema *m;* (mus) tema *m*
theme song *s* (mus) tema *m* central; (rad) sintonía
them•selves' *pron pers* ellos mismos; sí, sí mismos; se, p.ej., **they enjoyed themselves** se divirtieron; **with themselves** consigo
then [ðɛn] *adv* entonces; después, luego, en seguida; además, también; **by then** para entonces; **from then on** desde entonces, de allí en adelante; **then and there** ahí mismo
thence [ðɛns] *adv* desde allí; desde entonces; por eso
thence'forth' *adv* de allí en adelante; desde entonces
theolo•gy [θiˈɑlədʒi] *s* (*pl* **-gies**) teología
theorem [ˈθi•ərəm] *s* teorema *m*
theo•ry [ˈθi•əri] *s* (*pl* **-ries**) teoría
therapeutic [,θɛrəˈpjutɪk] *adj* terapéutico || **therapeutics** *ssg* terapéutica
thera•py [ˈθɛrəpi] *s* (*pl* **-pies**) terapia
there [ðɛr] *adv* allí, allá; **there is** o **there are** hay; aquí tiene Vd.
there'a-abouts' *adv* por allí; cerca, aproximadamente
there•af'ter *adv* de allí en adelante, después de eso
there•by' *adv* con eso; así, de tal modo; por allí cerca
therefore [ˈðɛrfor] *adv* por lo tanto, por consiguiente
there•in' *adv* en esto, en eso; en ese respecto
there•of' *adv* de ello, de eso

Theresa [tə'risə] o [tə'rɛsə] *s* Teresa
there'u•pon' *adv* sobre eso, encima de eso; por consiguiente; en seguida
thermistor [θər'mɪstər] *s* (elec) termistor *m*
thermocouple ['θʌrmo,kʌpəl] *s* (elec) termopar *m*
thermodynamic [,θʌrmodaɪ'næmɪk] *adj* termodinámico || **thermodynamics** *ssg* termodinámica
thermometer [θər'mɑmɪtər] *s* termómetro
thermonuclear [,θʌrmo'nuklɪ•ər] *adj* termonuclear
Thermopylae [θər'mɑpɪ,li] *s* las Termópilas
Thermos bottle ['θʌrməs] *s* termos *m*, botella termos, bolsa isotérmica
thermostat ['θʌrmə,stæt] *s* termóstato
thesau•rus [θɪ'sɔrəs] *s* (*pl* **-ri** [raɪ]) **tesoro;** (*dictionary or the like*) tesauro, tesoro
these [ðiz] *pl de* **this**
the•sis ['θisɪs] *s* (*pl* **-ses** [siz]) tesis *f*
Thespis ['θɛspɪs] *s* Tespis *m*
Thessaly ['θɛsəli] *s* la Tesalia
they [ðe] *pron pers* ellos, ellas
thick [θɪk] *adj* espeso; grueso; denso; (coll) estúpido; (coll) íntimo || *s* espesor *m;* **the thick of** (*e.g., a crowd*) lo más denso de; (*e.g., a battle*) lo más reñido de; **through thick and thin** contra viento y marea
thicken ['θɪkən] *tr* espesar || *intr* espesarse; complicarse (*el enredo*)
thicket ['θɪkɪt] *s* espesura, matorral *m*, soto
thick-headed ['θɪk'hɛdɪd] *adj* (coll) torpe, estúpido
thick'-set' *adj* grueso, rechoncho
thief [θif] *s* (*pl* **thieves** [θivz]) ladrón *m*
thieve [θiv] *intr* hurtar, robar
thiever•y ['θivəri] *s* (*pl* **-ies**) latrocinio, hurto, robo
thigh [θaɪ] *s* muslo
thigh'bone' *s* hueso del muslo, fémur *m*
thimble ['θɪmbəl] *s* dedal *m*
thin [θɪn] *adj* (*comp* **thinner;** *super* **thinnest**) delgado, flaco, tenue; (*cloth, paper, sole of shoe, etc.*) fino; (*hair*) ralo; (*broth*) aguado; (*excuse*) débil; claro, ligero, escaso || *v* (*pret & pp* **thinned;** *ger* **thinning**) *tr* adelgazar, enflaquecer; enrarecer; aclarar; aguar; desleír (*los colores*) || *intr* adelgazarse, enflaquecerse; enrarecerse; **to thin out** ralear (*el pelo*)
thine [ðaɪn] *adj poss* (archaic & poet) tu || *pron poss (archaic & poet)* tuyo; el tuyo
thing [θɪŋ] *s* cosa; **of all things!** ¡qué sorpresa!; **to be the thing** ser la última moda; **to be the thing to do** ser lo que debe hacerse; **to see things** ver visiones, padecer alucinaciones
think [θɪŋk] *v* (*pret & pp* **thought** [θɔt]) *tr* pensar; **to think it over** pensarlo; **to think nothing of** tener en poco; creer fácil; no dar importancia a; **to think of** pensar de, p.ej., what do you think of this book? ¿qué piensa Vd. de este libro?; **to think up** imaginar; inventar (*p.ej., una excusa*) || *intr* pensar; **to think not** creer que no; **to think of** (*to turn one's thoughts to*) pensar en; pensar (*un número, un naipe, etc.*); **to think so** creer que sí; **to think well of** tener buena opinión de
thinker ['θɪŋkər] *s* pensador *m*
third [θʌrd] *adj* tercero || *s* (*in a series*) tercero; (*one of three equal parts*) tercio; (*in dates*) tres *m*
third degree *s* (coll) interrogatorio bajo tortura
third rail *s* (rr) tercer carril *m*, carril de toma
third'-rate' *adj* de tercer orden; (fig) inferior
Third World *adj* tercermundista || *s* Terrcero Mundo
Third World countries *spl* países no alineados
thirst [θʌrst] *s* sed *f* || *intr* tener sed; **to thirst for** tener sed de
thirst•y ['θʌrsti] *adj* (*comp* **-ier;** *super* **-iest**) sediento; **to be thirsty** tener sed
thirteen ['θʌr'tin] *adj, pron & s* trece *m*
thirteenth ['θʌrtinθ] *adj & s* (*in a series*) decimotercero; (*part*) trezavo || *s* (*in dates*) trece *m*
thirtieth ['θʌrtɪ•ɪθ] *adj & s* (*in a series*) trigésimo; (*part*) treintavo || *s* (*in dates*) treinta *m*
thir•ty ['θʌrti] *adj & pron* treinta || *s* (*pl* **-ties**) treinta *m*
this [ðɪs] *adj dem* (*pl* **these**) este; **this one** éste || *pron dem* (*pl* **these**) éste; esto || *adv* tan
thistle ['θɪsəl] *s* cardo
thither ['θɪðər] o ['ðɪðər] *adv* allá, hacia allá
Thomas ['tɑməs] *s* Tomás *m*
thong [θɔŋ] o [θɑŋ] *s* correa
tho•rax ['θoræks] *s* (*pl* **-roxes** o **-raxes** o **-races** [rə,siz]) tórax *m*
thorn [θɔrn] *s* espina
thorn•y ['θɔrni] *adj* (*comp* **-ier;** *super* **-iest**) espinoso; espinudo; (*difficult*) (fig) espinoso, espinudo
thorough ['θʌro] *adj* cabal, completo; concienzudo, cuidadoso
thor'ough•bred *adj* de pura sangre; bien nacido || *s* pura sangre *m;* persona bien nacida
thor'ough•fare' *s* vía pública; **no thoroughfare** se prohibe el paso
thor'ough•go'ing *adj* cabal, completo, esmerado, perfecto
thoroughly ['θʌroli] *adv* a fondo
those [ðoz] *pl de* **that**
thou [ðaʊ] *pron pers* (archaic, poet & Bib) tú || *tr & intr* tutear
though [ðo] *adv* sin embargo || *conj* aunque, bien que; **as though** como sí
thought [θɔt] *s* pensamiento
thoughtful ['θɔtfəl] *adj* pensativo; atento, considerado
thoughtless ['θɔtlɪs] *adj* irreflexivo; descuidado; inconsiderado
thought transference *s* transmisión del pensamiento
thousand ['θaʊzənd] *adj & s* mil *m;* a **thousand** u **one thousand** mil *m*
thousandth ['θaʊzəndθ] *adj & s* milésimo

thralldom [ˈθrɔldəm] *s* esclavitud, servidumbre
thrash [θræʃ] *tr* (agr) trillar; azotar, zurrar; **to thrash out** decidir después de una discusión cabal ‖ *intr* trillar; agitarse, menearse
thread [θrɛd] *s* hilo; (mach) filete *m*, rosca; (*of a speech, of life*) hilo; **to lose the thread of** perder el hilo de ‖ *tr* enhebrar, enhilar; ensartar (*p.ej., cuentas*); (mach) aterrajar, filetear
thread'bare' *adj* raído; gastado, desgastado, usado, viejo
threat [θrɛt] *s* amenaza
threaten [ˈθrɛtən] *tr & intr* amenazar
threatening [ˈθrɛtənɪŋ] *adj* amenazante
three [θri] *adj & pron* tres ‖ *s* tres *m;* **three o'clock** las tres
three'-cor'nered *adj* triangular; (*hat*) de tres picos
three hundred *adj & pron* trescientos ‖ *s* trescientos *m*
threepence [ˈθrɛpəns] o [ˈθrɪpəns] *s* suma de tres peniques; moneda de tres peniques
three'-ply' *adj* de tres capas
three R's [ɑrz] *spl* lectura, escritura y aritmética, primeras letras
three'score' *adj* tres veintenas de
threno•dy [ˈθrɛnədi] *s* (*pl* **-dies**) treno
thresh [θrɛʃ] *tr* (agr) trillar; **to thresh out** decidir después de una discusión cabal ‖ *intr* trillar; agitarse, menearse
threshing machine *s* máquina trilladora
threshold [ˈθrɛʃold] *s* umbral *m;* (physiol, psychol & fig) umbral, limen *m;* **to be on the threshold of** estar en los umbrales de; **to cross the threshold** atravesar o pisar los embrales
thrice [θraɪs] *adv* tres veces; repetidamente, sumamente
thrift [θrɪft] *s* economía, parquedad
thrift•y [ˈθrɪfti] *adj* (*comp* **-ier;** *super* **-iest)** económico, parco; próspero
thrill [θrɪl] *s* emoción viva ‖ *tr* emocionar, conmover ‖ *intr* emocionarse, conmoverse
thriller [ˈθrɪlər] *s* cuento o pieza de teatro espeluznante
thrilling [ˈθrɪlɪŋ] *adj* emocionante; espeluznante
thrive [θraɪv] *v* (*pret* **thrived** o **throve** [θrov]; *pp* **thrived** o **thriven** [ˈθrɪvən]) *intr* medrar, prosperar
throat [θrot] *s* garganta; **to clear one's throat** aclarar la voz
throb [θrɑb] *s* latido, palpitación, pulsación ‖ *v* (*pret & pp* **throbbed;** *ger* **throbbing)** *intr* latir, palpitar, pulsar
throe [θro] *s* congoja, dolor *m;* **throes** angustia, agonía, esfuerzo penoso
throne [θron] *s* trono
throng [θrɔŋ] *s* gentío, tropel *m*, muchedumbre ‖ *intr* agolparse, apiñarse
throttle [ˈθrɑtəl] *s* válvula reguladora; (*of a locomotive*) regulador *m;* (*of an automobile*) acelerador *m* ‖ *tr* ahogar, sofocar; impedir, suprimir; (mach) regular; **to throttle down** reducir la velocidad de
through [θru] *adj* directo, sin paradas; acabado, terminado; **to be through with** haber terminado; no querer ocuparse más de ‖ *adv* a través, de un lado a otro; completamente ‖ *prep* por, a través de; por medio de; a causa de; todo lo largo de
through•out' *adv* por todas partes; en todos respectos; desde el principio hasta el fin ‖ *prep* por todo . . .; durante todo . . .; a lo largo de
through'way' *s* carretera de peaje de acceso limitado
throw [θro] *s* echada, tirada, lance *m;* cobertor ligero ‖ *v* (*pret* **threw** [θru]; *pp* **thrown)** *tr* arrojar, echar, lanzar; tirar (*los dados*); lanzar (*una mirada*); desarzonar (*a un jinete*); proyectar (*una sombra*); tender (*un puente*); perder con premeditación (*un juego, una carrera*); **to throw away** tirar; malgastar; perder, no aprovechar; **to throw in** añadir, dar de más; **to throw out** arrojar, botar, desechar; echar a la calle; chispar; **to throw over** abandonar, dejar ‖ *intr* arrojar, echar, lanzar; **to throw up** vomitar
thrum [θrʌm] *v* (*pret & pp* **thrummed;** *ger* **thrumming)** *intr* teclear; zangarrear; **to thrum on** rasguear
thrush [θrʌʃ] *s* tordo
thrust [θrʌst] *s* empuje *m;* acometida; (*with horns*) cornada; (*with dagger*) puñalada; (*with sword*) estocada; (*with knife*) cuchillada ‖ *v* (*pret & pp* **thrust**) *tr* empujar; acometer; clavar, hincar; atravesar, traspasar
thud [θʌd] *s* baque *m*, ruido sordo ‖ *v* (*pret & pp* **thudded;** *ger* **thudding)** *tr & intr* golpear con ruido sordo
thug [θʌg] *s* ladrón *m*, asesino; (coll) gorila
thumb [θʌm] *s* pulgar *m*, dedo gordo; **all thumbs** desmañado, chapucero, torpe; **to twiddle one's thumbs** menear ociosamente los pulgares; no hacer nada; **under the thumb of** bajo la férula de ‖ *tr* manosear sin suidado; ensuciar con los dedos; hojear (*un libro*) con el pulgar; **to thumb a ride** pedir ser llevado en automóvil indicando la dirección con el pulgar; **to thumb one's nose at** señalar (*a una persona*) poniendo el pulgar sobre la nariz en son de burla; tratar con sumo desprecio
thumb index *s* escalerilla, índice *m* con pestañas
thumb'print' *s* impresión del pulgar ‖ *tr* marcar con impresión del pulgar
thumb'screw' *s* tornillo de mariposa, tornillo de orejas
thumb'tack' *s* chinche *m*
thump [θʌmp] *s* golpazo, porrazo ‖ *tr* golpear, aporrear ‖ *intr* caer con golpe pesado; andar con pasos pesados; latir (*el corazón*) con golpes pesados
thumping [ˈθʌmpɪŋ] *adj* (coll) enorme, pesado
thunder [ˈθʌndər] *s* trueno; (*of applause*) estruendo; amenaza ‖ *tr* fulminar (*p.ej., censuras*) ‖ *intr* tronar; **to thunder at** tronar contra

thun'der•bolt' *s* rayo
thun'der•clap' *s* tronido
thunderous [ˈθʌndərəs] *adj* atronador, tronitoso
thun'der•show'er *s* chubasco con truenos
thun'der•storm' *s* tronada
thun'der•struck' *adj* atónito, estupefacto, pasmado
Thursday [ˈθʌrsdi] *s* jueves *m*
thus [ðʌs] *adv* así; **thus far** hasta aquí, hasta ahora
thwack [θwæk] *s* golpe *m*, porrazo ‖ *tr* golpear, pegar
thwart [θwɔrt] *adj* transversal, oblicuo ‖ *adv* de través ‖ *tr* desbaratar, impedir, frustrar
thy [ðaɪ] *adj poss* (archaic & poet) tu
thyme [taɪm] *s* tomillo
thyroid gland [ˈθaɪrɔɪd] *s* glándula tiroides
thyself [ðaɪˈsɛlf] *pron* (archaic & poet) tú mismo; ti mismo; te; ti
tiara [taɪˈɑrə] o [taɪˈɛrə] *s* (*papal miter*) tiara; (*female adornment*) diadema *f*
tick [tɪk] *s* tictac *m;* funda (*de almohada o colchón*) (coll) crédito; (ent) garrapata; **on tick** (coll) al fiado ‖ *intr* hacer tictac; latir (*el corazón*)
ticker [ˈtɪkər] *s* teleimpresor *m* de cinta; (slang) reloj *m;* (slang) corazón *m*
ticker tape *s* cinta de teleimpresor
ticket [ˈtɪkɪt] *s* billete *m;* boleto (Am); (theat) entrada, localidad; (*for wrong parking*) (coll) aviso de multa; (*of a political party*) (U.S.A.) lista de candidatos; **that's the ticket** (coll) eso es, eso es lo que se necesita
ticket agent *s* taquillero
ticket collector *s* revisor *m*
ticket office *s* taquilla, despacho de billetes
ticket scalper [ˈskælpər] *s* revendedor *m* de billetes de teatro
ticket window *s* taquilla, ventanilla
ticking [ˈtɪkɪŋ] *s* cutí *m*, terliz *m*
tickle [ˈtɪkəl] *s* cosquillas ‖ *tr* cosquillear; gustar, satisfacer; divertir ‖ *intr* cosquillear
ticklish [ˈtɪklɪʃ] *adj* cosquilloso; difícil, delicado; inseguro
tick-tock [ˈtɪk,tɑk] *s* tictac m
tidal wave [ˈtaɪdəl] *s* aguaje *m*, ola de marea; (*e.g., of popular indignation*) ola
tidbit [ˈtɪd,bɪt] *s* buen bocado, bocadito
tiddlywinks [ˈtɪdli,wɪŋks] *s* juego de la pulga
tide [taɪd] *s* marea; temporada; **to go against the tide** ir contra la corriente; **to stem the tide** rendir la marea ‖ *tr* llevar, hacer flotar; **to tide over** ayudar un poco; superar (*una dificultad*)
tide'wa'ter *adj* costanero ‖ *s* agua de marea; orilla del mar
tidings [ˈtaɪdɪŋz] *spl* noticias, informes *mpl*
ti•dy [ˈtaɪdi] *adj* (*comp* **-dier;** *super* **-diest**) aseado, limpio, pulcro, ordenado ‖ *s* (*pl* **-dies**) pañito bordado, cubierta de respaldar ‖ *v* (*pret & pp* **-died**) *tr* asear, limpiar, arreglar, poner en orden ‖ *intr* asearse
tie [taɪ] *s* atadura; lazo, nudo; (*worn on neck*) corbata; (*in games and elections*) empate *m;* (mus) ligado; (rr) traviesa ‖ *v* (*pret & pp* **tied;** *ger* **tying**) *tr* atar, liar; enlazar; hacer (*la corbata*); confinar, limitar; empatar (*p.ej., una elección*); empatársela a (*una persona*); **to be tied up** estar ocupado; **to tie down** confinar, limitar; **to tie up** atar; envolver; obstruir (*el tráfico*) ‖ *intr* atar; empatar o empatarse (*dos candidatos, dos equipos*)
tie'pin' *s* alfiler *m* de corbata
tier [tɪr] *s* fila, ringlera; (theat) fila de palcos
tiger [ˈtaɪgər] *s* tigre *m*
tiger lily *s* azucena atigrada
tight [taɪt] *adj* apretado, estrecho, ajustado; bien cerrado, hermético; compacto, denso; fijo, firme, sólido; (com) escaso; (sport) casi igual; (coll) agarrado, tacaño; (slang) borracho ‖ *adv* firmemente; **to hold tight** mantener fijo; agarrarse bien ‖ **tights** *spl* traje *m* de malla
tighten [ˈtaɪtən] *tr* apretar; atiesar, estirar ‖ *intr* apretarse; atiesarse, estirarse
tight-fisted [ˈtaɪtˈfɪstɪd] *adj* agarrado, tacaño
tight'-fit'ting *adj* ceñido, muy ajustado
tight'rope' *s* cuerda tirante
tight squeeze *s* (coll) brete *m*, aprieto
tightwad [ˈtaɪt,wɑd] *s* avaro; codo (Guat, Mex)
tigress [ˈtaɪgrɪs] *s* tigresa
tile [taɪl] *s* azulejo; (*for floors*) baldosa; (*for roofs*) reja ‖ *tr* azulejar; embaldosar; tejar
tile roof *s* tejado (de tejas)
till [tɪl] *prep* hasta ‖ *conj* hasta que ‖ *s* cajón *m* o gaveta del dinero ‖ *tr* labrar, cultivar
tilt [tɪlt] *s* inclinación; justa, torneo; **full tilt** a toda velocidad ‖ *tr* inclinar; asestar (*una lanza*) ‖ *intr* inclinarse; justar, tornear; luchar; **to tilt at** luchar con, arremeter contra; protestar contra
timber [ˈtɪmbər] *s* madera de construcción; madero, viga; bosque *m*, árboles *mpl* de monte
tim'ber•land' *s* bosque *m* maderable
timber line *s* límite *m* de la vegetación, límite del bosque maderable
timbre [ˈtɪmbər] *s* (phonet & phys) timbre *m*
time [taɪm] *s* tiempo; hora, p.ej., **time to eat** hora de comer; vez, p.ej., **five times** cinco veces; rato, p.ej., **a nice time** un buen rato; (*period for payment*) plazo; horas de trabajo; sueldo; tiempo de parir, término del embarazo; última hora; (phot) tiempo de exposición; **all the time** a cada momento; **for the time being** por ahora, por el momento; **on time** a tiempo, a la hora debida; (*in installments*) a plazos, **to bide one's time** esperar la hora propicia; **to do time** (coll) cumplir una condena; **to have a good time** darse buen tiempo; **to have no time for** no poder tolerar; **to lose time** atrasarse (*el reloj*); **to make time** avanzar con rapidez; **to pass the time of day** saludarse (*dos personas*); **to serve time** (*in prison*) tirarse; **to take one's time** no darse prisa, ir despacio; **what time is it?** ¿qué hora es? ‖ *tr* calcular el tiempo de; medir el tiempo de; (sport) cronometrar
time bomb *s* bomba-reloj *f*

time'card' *s* hoja de presencia, tarjeta registradora
time clock *s* reloj *m* registrador
time exposure *s* exposición de tiempo
time fuse *s* espoleta de tiempos
time'keep'er *s* alistador *m* de tiempo; reloj *m;* (sport) cronometrador *m*, juez *m* de tiempo
time•ly [ˋtaɪmli] *adj* (*comp* **-lier;** *super* **-liest**) oportuno
time'piece' *s* reloj *m*
time signal *s* señal horaria
time'ta'ble *s* horario, itinerario
time'work' *s* trabajo ajornal
time'worn' *adj* gastado por el tiempo
time zone *s* huso horario
timid [ˋtɪmɪd] *adj* tímido
timing gears [ˋtaɪmɪŋ] *spl* engranaje *m* de distribución, mando de las válvulas
timorous [ˋtɪmərəs] *adj* tímido, miedoso
tin [tɪn] *s* (*element*) estaño; (*tin plate*) hojalata; (*cup, box, etc.*) lata ‖ *v* (*pret & pp* **tinned;** *ger* **tinning**) *tr* estañar; (*to pack in cans*) enlatar; recubrir de hojalata
tin can *s* lata, envase *m* de hojalata
tincture [ˋtɪŋktʃər] *s* tintura
tin cup *s* taza de hojalata
tinder [ˋtɪndər] *s* yesca
tin'der•box' *s* lumbres *fpl*, yesquero; persona muy excitable; semillero de violencia
tin foil *s* hojuela de estaño, papel *m* de estaño
ting-a-ling [ˋtɪŋə,lɪŋ] *s* tilín *m*
tinge [tɪndʒ] *s* matiz *m*, tinte *m;* dejo, gustillo ‖ *v* (*ger* **tingeing** o **tinging**) *tr* matizar, teñir; dar gusto o sabor a
tingle [ˋtɪŋgəl] *s* comezón *f*, picazón *f* ‖ *intr* sentir comezón; zumbar (*los oídos*); (*e.g., with enthusiasm*) estremecerse
tin hat *s* (coll) yelmo de acero
tinker [ˋtɪŋkər] *s* calderero remendón; chapucero ‖ *intr* ocuparse vanamente
tinkle [ˋtɪŋkəl] *s* retintín *m* ‖ *tr* hacer retiñir *m* ‖ *tr* hacer retiñir ‖ *intr* retiñir
tin plate *s* hojalata
tin roof *s* tejado de hojalata
tinsel [ˋtɪnsəl] *s* oropel *m;* (*e.g., for a Christmas tree*) lentejuelas de hojas de estaño
tin'smith' *s* hojalatero
tin soldier *s* soldadito de plomo
tint [tɪnt] *s* tinte *m*, matiz *m* ‖ *tr* teñir, matizar, colorar ligeramente
tin'type' *s* ferrotipo
tin'ware' *s* objetos de hojalata
ti•ny [ˋtaɪni] *adj* (*comp* **-nier;** *super* **-niest**) diminuto, menudo, pequeñito
tip [tɪp] *s* extremo, extremidad; (*of shoestring*) herrete *m;* (*of arrow*) casquillo; (*of umbrella*) regatón *m;* (*of tongue*) punta; (*of shoe*) puntera; (*of cigarette*) embocadura; inclinación; golpecito; soplo, aviso confidencial; (*fee*) propina, feria ‖ *v* (*pret & pp* **tipped;** *ger* **tipping**) *tr* herretear; inclinar, ladear; volcar; golpear ligeramente; dar propina a; informar por debajo de cuerda; tocarse (*el sombrero en señal de cortesía*); **to tip in** (typ) encañonar (*un pliego*) ‖ *intr* dar una propina o propinas; inclinarse, ladearse; volcarse
tip'cart' *s* volquete *m*
tip'-off' *s* (coll) informe dado por debajo de cuerda
tipped'-in' *adj* (bb) fuera de texto
tipple [ˋtɪpəl] *intr* beborrotear
tip'staff' *s* vara de justicia; alguacil *m* de vara
tip•sy [ˋtɪpsi] *adj* (*comp* **-sier;** *super* **-siest**) achispado
tip'toe' *s* punta del pie; **on tiptoe** de puntillas; alerta; furtivamente ‖ *v* (*pret & pp* **-toed;** *ger* **-toeing**) *intr* andar de puntillas
tirade [ˋtaɪred] *s* diatriba, invectiva
tire [taɪr] *s* neumático, llanta de goma; (*of metal*) calce *m*, llanta ‖ *tr* cansar; aburrir, fastidiar ‖ *intr* (*to be tiresome*) cansar; (*to get tired*) cansarse; aburrirse, fastidiarse
tire chain *s* cadena de llanta, cadena antirresbaladiza
tired [taɪrd] *adj* cansado, rendido
tire gauge *s* indicador *m* de presión de inflado
tireless [ˋtaɪrlɪs] *adj* incansable, infatigable
tire pressure *s* presión de inflado
tire pump *s* bomba para inflar neumáticos
tiresome [ˋtaɪrsəm] *adj* cansado, fatigante, aburrido, pesado
tissue [ˋtɪʃʊ] *s* tejido fino; papel *m* de seda; (biol & fig) tejido
tissue paper *s* papel *m* de seda
titanium [taiˋtenɪ•əm] o [tɪˋtenɪ•əm] *s* titanio
tithe [taɪð] *s* décimo, décima parte; (*tax paid to church*) diezmo ‖ *tr* dizmar
Titian [ˋtɪʃən] *adj* castaño rojizo ‖ *s* el Ticiano
title [ˋtaɪtəl] *s* título; (sport) campeonato ‖ *tr* titular
title deed *s* título de propiedad
ti'tle•hold'er *s* titulado; (sport) campeón *m*
title page *s* portada, frontispicio
title rôle *s* (theat) papel *m* principal (*el que corresponde al título de la abra*)
titter [ˋtɪtər] *s* risita ahogada, risita disimulada ‖ *intr* reír a medias, reír con disimulo
titular [ˋtɪtʃələr] *adj* titular; nominal
tn. *abbr* **ton**
to [tu] o [tʊ] o [tə] *adv* hacia adelante; **to and fro** de una parte a otra, de aquí para allá; **to come to** volver en sí ‖ *prep* a, p.ej., **he is going to Madrid** va a Madrid; **they gave something to the beggar** dieron algo al pobre; **we are learning to dance** aprendemos a bailar; para, p.ej., **he is reading to himself** lee para sí; por, p.ej., **work to do** trabajo por hacer; hasta, p.ej., **to a certain extent** hasta cierto punto; en, p.ej., **from door to door** de puerta en puerta; con, p.ej., **kind to her** amable con ella; segun, p.ej., **to my way of thinking** según mi modo de pensar; menos, p.ej., **five minutes to ten** las diez menos cinco
toad [tod] *s* sapo
toad'stool' *s* agárico, seta; seta venenosa
to-and-fro [ˋtu•əndˋfro] *adj* alternativo, de vaivén

toast [tost] *s* tostadas; (*drink*) brindis *m;* **a piece of toast** una tostada ‖ *tr* tostar; brindar a o por ‖ *intr* tostarse; brindar
toaster [ˈtostər] *s* (*of bread*) tostador *m;* brindador *m*
toast'mas'ter *s* el que presenta a los oradores en un banquete, maestro de ceremonias
tobac•co [təˈbæko] *s* (*pl* **-cos**) tabaco
tobacco pouch *s* petaca
toboggan [təˈbɑgən] *s* tobogán *m* ‖ *intr* deslizarse en tobogán
tocsin [ˈtɑksɪn] *s* campana de alarma; campanada de alarma
today [tʊˈde] *adv & s* hoy
toddle [ˈtɑdəl] *s* pasitos vacilantes ‖ *intr* andar con pasitos vacilantes; hacer pinitos (*un niño o un enfermo*)
tod•dy [ˈtɑdi] *s* (*pl* **-dies**) ponche *m*
to-do [təˈdu] *s* (coll) alharaca, alboroto
toe [to] *s* dedo del pie; (*of stocking*) punta ‖ *v* (*pret & pp* **toed;** *ger* **toeing)** *tr*—**to toe the line** o **the mark** ponerse a la raya; obrar como se debe
toe'nail' *s* uña del dedo del pie
tog [tɑg] *s* (coll) prenda de vestir
together [tʊˈgɛðər] *adv* juntamente; juntos; al mismo tiempo; sin interrupción; de acuerdo; **to bring together** reunir; confrontar; reconciliar; **to call together** convocar; **to go together** ir juntos; ser novios; hacerjuego; **to stick together** (coll) quedarse unidos, no abandonarse
toil [tɔɪl] *s* afán *m*, fatiga; faena, obra laboriosa; **toils** red *f*, lazo ‖ *intr* atrafagar; moverse con fatiga
toilet [ˈtɔɪlɪt] *s* (*dress or adornment*) tocado, atavio; (*dressing table*) tocador *m;* (*rest room*) retrete *m*, inodoro, excusado; wáter *m* (Bol, Col, Chile, Peru, Urug); servicio (Bol, CAm, Ecuad); taza (Bol, Col, Guat, Mex); poseta (Ven); **to make one's toilet** asearse, acicalarse
toilet articles *spl* artículos de tocador
toilet paper *s* papel higiénico
toilet powder *s* polvos de tocador
toilet soap *s* jabón *m* de olor, jabón de tocador
toilet tank *s* cisterna
toilet water *s* agua de tocador
token [ˈtokən] *s* señal *f*, prueba; prenda, recuerdo; (*used as money*) ficha, tanto; **by the same token** por el mismo motivo; **in token of** en señal de
tolerance [ˈtɑlərəns] *s* tolerancia
tolerate [ˈtɑlə,ret] *tr* tolerar
toll [tol] *s* (*of bells*) doble *m;* (*to pass along a road or over a bridge*) peaje *m;* (*to use a canal*) derechos de paso; (*to use a telephone*) tarifa; (*number of victims*) baja, mortalidad ‖ *tr* tocar a muerto (*una campana*); llamar con toque de difuntos ‖ *intr* doblar
toll bridge *s* puente *m* de peaje
toll call *s* (telp) llamada a larga distancia
toll'gate' *s* barrera de peaje
toma•to [təˈmeto] o [təˈmɑto] *s* (*pl* **-toes**) (*plant*) tomatera o tomate *m;* (*fruit*) tomate
tomb [tum] *s* tumba, sepulcro
tomboy [ˈtɑm,bɔɪ] *s* moza retozona, muchacha traviesa
tomb'stone' *s* piedra o lápida sepulcral
tomcat [ˈtɑm,kæt] *s* gato macho
tome [tom] *s* tomo; libro grueso
tomorrow [tʊˈmɔro] *adv* mañana ‖ *s* mañana *m;* **the day after tomorrow** pasado mañana
tom-tom [ˈtɑm,tɑm] *s* tantán *m*
ton [tʌn] *s* tonelada; **tons** (coll) montones *mpl*
tone [ton] *s* tono ‖ *tr* entonar ‖ *intr* armonizar; **to tone down** moderarse; **to tone up** reforzarse
tone poem *s* poema sinfónico
tongs [tɔŋz] o [tɑŋz] *spl* tenazas; (*e.g., for sugar*) tenacillas
tongue [tʌŋ] *s* (anat) lengua; (*of a wagon*) vara, lanza; (*of a belt buckle*) tarabilla; (*of shoe*) lengua, lengüeta; (*language*) lengua, idioma *m;* **to hold one's tongue** morderse la lengua
tongue twister [ˈtwɪstər] *s* trabalenguas *m*
tonic [ˈtɑnɪk] *adj & s* tónico
tonic accent *s* acento prosódico
tonight [tʊˈnaɪt] *adv & s* esta noche
tonnage [ˈtʌnɪdʒ] *s* tonelaje *m*
tonsil [ˈtɑnsəl] *s* tonsila, amígdala
tonsillitis [,tɑnsɪˈlaɪtɪs] *s* tonsilitis *f*, amigdalitis *f*
ton•y [ˈtoni] *adj* (*comp* **-ier;** *super* **-iest)** (slang) elegante, aristocrático
too [tu] *adv* (*also*) también; (*more than enough*) demasiado; **too bad!** ¡qué lástima!; **too many** demasiados; **too much** demasiado
tool [tul] *s* herramienta; (*person used for one's own ends*) instrumento; **tools** implementos *mpl* ‖ *tr* trabajar con herramienta; (bb) filetear, estampar
tool bag *s* bolsa de herramientas
toolmak'er *s* tallador *m* de herramientas, herrero de herramientas
toot [tut] *s* (*of horn*) toque *m;* (*of klaxon*) bocinazo; (*of locomotive*) pitazo; (coll) parranda ‖ *tr* sonar; **to toot one's own horn** cantar sus propias alabanzas ‖ *intr* sonar
tooth [tuθ] *s* (*pl* **teeth** [tiθ]) diente *m*
tooth'ache' *s* dolor *m* de muelas
tooth'brush' *s* cepillo de dientes
toothless [ˈtuθlɪs] *adj* desdentado
tooth'paste' *s* pasta dentifrica, crema dental, crema dentífrica
tooth'pick' *s* limpiadientes *m*, mondadientes *m*, palillo
tooth powder *s* polvo dentífrico
top [tɑp] *s* (*of a mountain, tree, etc.*) cima; (*of a mountain; high point*) cumbre *f;* (*of a tree*) copa; (*of a barrel, box, etc.*) tapa; (*of a page*) principio; (*of a table*) tablero; (*of a wall*) coronamiento; (*of a bathing suit*) camiseta; (*of a carriage or auto*) capota; (*toy*) peón *m*, peonza; (naut) cofa; **at the top of** en lo alto de; (*e.g., one's class*) a la cabeza de; **at the top of one's voice** a voz en grito; **from top to bottom** de arriba

abajo; de alto a bajo; completamente; **on top of** en lo alto de; encima de; **the tops** (slang) la flor de la canela; **to sleep like a top** dormir como un leño ‖ *v* (*pret & pp* **topped;** ger **topping**) *tr* coronar, rematar; cubrir; aventajar, superar; descopar (*p.ej., un árbol*)

topaz [ˈtopæz] *s* topacio

top billing *s* cabecera de cartel

top'coat' *s* sobretodo; abrigo de entretiempo

toper [ˈtopər] *s* borrachín *m*

top hat *s* chistera, sombrero de copa

top'-heav'y *adj* más pesado arriba que abajo

topic [ˈtɑpɪk] *s* asunto, materia, tema *m*

top'knot' *s* moño

top'mast' *s* (naut) mastelero

top'most *adj* (el) más alto

topogra•phy [təˈpɑgrəfi] *s* (*pl* **-phies**) topografía

topple [ˈtɑpəl] *tr* derribar, volcar ‖ *intr* derribarse, volcarse; caerse, venirse abajo

top priority *s* máxima prioridad

topsail [ˈtɑpsəl] o [ˈtɑp,sel] *s* (naut) gavia

top secret *adj* de mayor confidencia

top'soil' *s* capa superficial del suelo

topsy-turvy [ˈtɑpsiˈtʌrvi] *adj* desbarajustado ‖ *adv* en cuadro, patas arriba ‖ *s* desbarajuste *m*

torch [tɔrtʃ] *s* antorcha; lámpara de bolsillo: **to carry the torch for** (slang) amar desesperadamente

torch'bear'er *s* hachero; (fig) adicto, partidario

torch'light' *s* luz *f* de antorcha

torch song *s* canción lenta y melancólica de amor no correspondido

torment [ˈtɔrmɛnt] *s* tormento; murga ‖ [tɔrˈmɛnt] *tr* atormentar

torna•do [tɔrˈnedo] *s* (*pl* **-does** p **-dos**) tornado, tromba terrestre

torpe•do [tɔrˈpido] *s* (*pl* **-does**) torpedo ‖ *tr* torpedear

torrent [ˈtɔrənt] *s* torrente *m*

torrid [ˈtɔrɪd] *adj* tórrido

tor•so [ˈtɔrso] *s* (*pl* **-sos**) torso

tortoise [ˈtɔrtəs] *s* tortuga

tortoise shell *s* carey *m*

torture [ˈtɔrtʃər] *s* tortura ‖ *tr* torturar, atormentar

toss [tɑs] *s* echada; alcance *m* de una echada ‖ *tr* arrojar, echar; lanzar al aire; agitar, menear; levantar airosamente (*la cabeza*); lanzar (*p.ej., un comentario*); echar a cara o cruz; **to toss off** hacer muy rápidamente; tragar de un golpe ‖ *intr* agitarse, menearse; **to toss and turn** (*in bed*) revolverse, dar vueltas

toss'-up' *s* cara o cruz; probabilidad igual

tot [tɑt] *s* párvulo, peque *m*, chiquitín *m*

to•tal [ˈtotəl] *adj* total; (*e.g., loss*) completo ‖ *s* total *m* ‖ *v* (*pret & pp* **-taled** o **-talled;** *ger* **-taling** o **-talling**) *tr* ascender a, sumar

totter [ˈtɑtər] *s* tambaleo ‖ *intr* tambalear; estar para desplomarse

touch [tʌtʃ] *s* (*act*) toque *m;* (*sense*) tacto, tiento; (*of piano, pianist, typewriter, typist*) tacto; (*of an illness*) ramo, ataque ligero; pizca, poquito; **to get in touch with** ponerse en comunicación o contacto con; **to lose one's touch** perder el tiento ‖ *tr* tocar; conmover, enternecer; probar (*vino, licor*); (*for a loan*) (slang) pedir prestado a, dar un sablazo a; **to touch up** retocar ‖ *intr* tocar; **to touch at** tocar en (*un puerto*)

touching [ˈtʌtʃɪŋ] *adj* conmovedor, enternecedor ‖ *prep* tocante a

touch typewriting *s* escritura al tacto

touch•y [ˈtʌtʃi] *adj* (*comp* **-ier;** *super* **-iest**) quisquilloso, enojadizo

tough [tʌf] *adj* correoso; tenaz; difícil; gamberro; (*e.g., luck*) malo ‖ *s* gamberro, guapetón *m*; (coll) gorila

toughen [ˈtʌfən] *tr* hacer correoso; hacer tenaz; dificultar ‖ *intr* ponerse correoso; hacerse tenaz; hacerse difícil

toupee [tuˈpe] *s* peluquín *m*

tour [tʊr] *s* jira, paseo, vuelta; viaje largo; **on tour** de jira, de viaje ‖ *tr* viajar por, recorrer ‖ *intr* viajar por distracción o diversión

touring car [ˈtʊrɪŋ] *s* coche *m* de turismo

tourist [ˈtʊrɪst] *adj* turístico ‖ *s* turista *mf*

tourist guide *s* guía turística

tournament [ˈtʊrnəmənt] o [ˈtʌrnəmənt] *s* torneo

tourney [ˈtʊrni] o [ˈtʌrni] *s* torneo ‖ *intr* tornear

tourniquet [ˈtʊrnɪ,kɛt] *s* torniquete *m*

tousle [ˈtaʊzəl] *tr* despeinar, enmarañar

tow [to] *s* remolque *m;* (*e.g., of hemp*) estopa; **to take in tow** dar remolque a; (fig) encargarse de ‖ *tr* remolcar

towage [ˈto•ɪdʒ] *s* remolque *m;* derechos de remolque

toward(s) [tord(z)] o [təˈwɔrd(z)] *prep* (*in the direction of*) hacia; (*with regard to*) para con; (*a certain hour*) cerca de, a eso de

tow'boat' *s* remolcador *m*

tow•el [ˈtaʊ•əl] *s* toalla ‖ *v* (*pret & pp* **-eled** o **-elled;** *ger* **-eling** o **-elling**) *tr* secar con toalla

towel rack *s* toallero

tower [ˈtaʊ•ər] *s* torre *f* ‖ *intr* encumbrarse, empinarse

towering [ˈtaʊ•ərɪŋ] *adj* encumbrado; sobresaliente; excesivo

towing service [ˈto•ɪŋ] *s* servicio de grúa

tow'line' *s* cable *m* de remolque, sirga

town [taʊn] *s* problación, pueblo, villa; **in town** a la ciudad, en la ciudad

town clerk *s* escribano municipal

town council *s* concejo municipal

town crier *s* pregonero público

town hall *s* ayuntamiento, casa de ayuntamiento

towns' folk' *spl* vecinos del pueblo

township [ˈtaʊnʃɪp] *s* sexmo; terreno público de seis millas en cuadro

towns•man [ˈtaʊnzmən] *s* (*pl* **-men** [mən]) ciudadano, vecino; conciudadano, paisano

towns'peo'ple *spl* vecinos del pueblo

town talk *s* comidilla o hablillas del pueblo

tow'path' *s* camino de sirga

tow plane *s* avión *m* de remolque
tow'rope' *s* cuerda de remolque
tow truck *s* camión-grúa *m*
toxic ['tɑksɪk] *adj & s* tóxico
toxic shock syndrome *s* síndrome *m* de choque tóxico
toy [tɔɪ] *adj* de juguete || *s* juguete *m;* (*trifle*) bagatela; (*trinket*) dije *m*, bujería || *intr* jugar; divertirse; **to toy with** jugar con (*los sentimientos de una persona*); acariciar (*una idea*)
toy bank *s* alcancía hucha
toy soldier *s* soldado de juguete
trace [tres] *s* huella, rastro; indicio, vestigio; (*of harness*) tirante *m;* pizca || *tr* rastrear; trazar (*p.ej., una curva; los rasgos de una persona o cosa*); averiguar el paradero de; remontar al origen de
trace element *s* elemento rastro
trache•a ['trekɪ•ə] *s* (*pl* **-ae** [,i]) tráquea
track [træk] *s* (*of foot*) huella; (*of a wheel*) rodada, carril *m;* (*of a boat*) estela; (*of railroad*) vía; (*of an airplane, a hurricane*) trayectoria; (*of a tractor*) llanta de oruga; camino, senda; (*course followed by a boat*) derrota; (*of ideas, events, etc.*) sucesión; (sport) pista; **to keep track of** no perder de vista; no olvidar; **to lose track of** perder de vista; olvidar; **to make tracks** dejar pisadas; irse muy de prisa; **off the track** (*also* fig) desviado || *tr* rastrear; seguir la huella o la pista de; dejar pisadas en, manchar pisando; **to track down** seguir y capturar; averiguar el origen de
tracking ['trækɪŋ] *s* seguimiento (*de vehículos espaciales*)
tracing station *s* estación de seguimiento
trackless trolley ['træklɪs] *s* filobús *m*, trolebús *m*
track meet *s* concurso de carreras y saltos
track'walk'er *s* guardavía *m*
tract [trækt] *s* espacio, tracto; folleto; (anat) canal *m*, sistema *m*
traction ['trækʃən] *s* tracción
traction company *s* empresa de tranvías
tractor ['træktər] *s* tractor *m*
trade [tred] *s* comercio; negocio, trato; trueque *m*, canje *m;* (*calling, job*) oficio; clientela, parroquia; (*e.g., in slaves*) trata || *tr* cambiar, trocar; **to trade in** dar como parte del pago; **to trade off** cambalachear; || *intr* comerciar; comprar; **to trade in** comerciar en; **to trade on** aprovecharse de
trade'mark' *s* marca de fábrica, marca registrada
trade name *s* nombre *m* comercial, razón *f* social; nombre de fábrica
trader ['tredər] *s* traficante *mf*
trade school *s* escuela de artes y oficios
trades•man ['tredzmən] *s* (*pl* **-men** [mən]) tendero; comerciante *m;* (Brit) artesano
trades union o **trade union** *s* sindicato, gremio de obreros
trade unionist *s* sindicalista *mf*
trade winds *spl* vientos alisios
trading post ['tredɪŋ] *s* factoría; (*in stock exchange*) puesto de compraventa
trading stamp *s* sello de premio, sello de descuento
tradition [trə'dɪʃən] *s* tradición
traduce [trə'djus] *tr* calumniar
traf•fic ['træfɪk] *s* tráfico, comercio; tráfico, circulación; (*e.g., in slaves*) trata || *v* (*pret & pp* **-ficked;** *ger* **-ficking**) *intr* traficar
traffic circle *s* glorieta de tráfico
traffic court *s* juzgado de tráfico
traffic jam *s* embotellamiento, tapón *m* de tráfico
traffic light *s* luz *f* de tráfico, semáforo
traffic sign o **signal** *s* señal *f* de tráfico, seña de tráfico
traffic ticket *s* aviso de multa
tragedian [trə'dʒidɪ•ən] *s* trágico
trage•dy ['trædʒɪdi] *s* (*pl* **-dies**) tragedia
tragic ['trædʒɪk] *adj* trágico
trail [trel] *s* rastro, huella, pista; (*path through rough country*) trocha, senda, vereda; (*of a gown*) cola; (*of smoke, a rocket, etc.*) estela || *tr* arrastrar; seguir la pista de; andar detrás de; llevar (*p.ej., barro*) con los pies || *intr* arrastrar; rezagarse; arrastrarse, trepar (*una planta*); **to trail off** desaparecer poco a poco
trailer ['trelər] *s* remolque *m*, cochehabitación *m*, casa rodante; planta rastrera
trailing arbutus ['trelɪŋ] *s* epigea rastrera
train [tren] *s* (*of railway cars; of waves*) tren *m;* (*of thought*) hilo || *tr* adiestrar; guiar (*las plantas*); (sport) entrenar || *intr* adiestrarse; (sport) entrenarse
trained nurse *s* enfermera graduada
trainer ['trenər] *s* (sport) entrenador *m*
training ['trenɪŋ] *s* adiestramiento; instrucción; (sport) entrenamiento
training school *s* escuela práctica; reformatorio
training ship *s* buque *m* escuela
trait [tret] *s* característica, rasgo
traitor ['tretər] *s* traidor *m*
traitress ['tretrɪs] *s* traidora
trajecto•ry [trə'dʒɛktəri] *s* (*pl* **-ries**) trayectoria
tramp [træmp] *s* vagabundo; marcha pesada, ruido de pisadas || *tr* pisar con fuerza; recorrer a pie || *intr* andar a pie; vagabundear
trample ['træmpəl] *tr* pisotear || *intr*—**to trample on** o **upon** pisotear
tramp steamer *s* vapor volandero
trance [træns] o [trɑns] *s* arrobamiento, rapto; estado hipnótico
tranquil ['træŋkwɪl] *adj* tranquilo
tranquilize ['træŋkwɪ,laɪz] *tr & intr* tranquilizar
tranquilizer ['træŋkwɪ,laɪzər] *s* tranquilizante *m*
tranquillity [træŋkwɪlɪti] *s* tranquilidad
transact [træn'zækt] o [træns'ækt] *tr* tramitar; llevar a cabo
transaction [træn'zækʃən] o [træns'ækʃən] *s* tramitación, transacción
transatlantic [,trænsət'læntɪk] *adj & s* transatlántico

transcend [træn'sɛnd] *tr* exceder, superar ‖ *intr* sobresalir
transcribe [træn'skraɪb] *tr* transcribir
transcript ['trænskrɪpt] *s* trasunto, traslado; (educ) hoja de estudios, certificado de estudios
transcription [træn'skrɪpʃən] *s* transcripción
transept ['trænsɛpt] *s* crucero, transepto
trans•fer ['trænsfər] *s* traslado; transbordo; contraseña o billete *m* de transferencia ‖ [træns'fʌr] o ['trænsfər] *s* (*pret & pp* **-ferred;** *ger* **-ferring**) *tr* trasladar, transferir; transbordar ‖ *intr* cambiar de tren, tranvía, etc.
transfix [træns'fɪks] *tr* espetar, traspasar; dejar atónito
transform [træns'fɔrm] *tr* transformar ‖ *intr* transformarse
transformer [træns'fɔrmər] *s* transformador *m*
transfusion [træns'fjuʃən] *s* transfusión; (med) transfusión de la sangre
transgress [træns'grɛs] *tr* transgredir, violar; exceder, traspasar (*p.ej., los límites de la prudencia*) ‖ *intr* pecar, prevaricar
transgression [træns'grɛʃən] *s* transgresión; pecado, prevaricación
transient ['trænʃənt] *adj* pasajero, transitorio; de tránsito ‖ *s* transeúnte *mf*
transistor [træn'zɪstər] *s* transistor *m*
transistorize [træn'zɪstə,raɪz] *tr* transistorizar
transit ['trænsɪt] o ['trænzɪt] *s* tránsito
transitive ['trænsɪtɪv] *adj* transitivo ‖ *s* verbo transitivo
transitory ['trænsɪ,tori] *adj* transitorio
translate [træns'let] o ['trænslet] *tr* (*from one language to another*) traducir; (*from one place to another*) trasladar ‖ *intr* traducirse
translation [træns'leʃən] *s* traducción; traslación
translator [træns'letər] *s* traductor *m*
transliterate [træns'lɪtə,ret] *tr* transcribir
translucent [træns'lusənt] *adj* translúcido
transmission [træns'mɪʃən] *s* transmissión; (aut) cambio de marchas, cambio de velocidades
transmis'sion-gear' box *s* caja de cambio de marchas, caja de velocidades
trans•mit [træns'mɪt] *v* (*pret & pp* **-mitted;** *ger* **-mitting**) *tr & intr* transmitir
transmitter [træns'mɪtər] *s* transmisor *m*
transmitting set *s* aparato transmisor
transmitting station *s* estacion transmisora, emisora
transmute [træns'mjut] *tr & intr* transmutar
transom [trænsəm] *s* (*crosspiece*) travesaño; (*window over door*) montante *m;* (*of ship*) yugo de popa
transparen•cy [træns'pɛrənsi] *s* (*pl* **-cies**) transparencia
transparent [træns'pɛrənt] *adj* transparente
transpire [træns'paɪr] *intr* transpirar; (*to become known, leak out*) transpirar; (coll) acontecer, tener lugar
transplant ['træns,plænt] *s* transplante; injerto ‖ *tr* transplantar ‖ *intr* transplantarse
transport ['trænsport] *s* transporte *m;* (aer & naut) transporte *m;* rapto, éxtasis *m*, transporte *m* ‖ [træns'port] *tr* transportar
transportation [,trænspor'teʃən] *s* transporte *m;* (U.S.A.) pasaje *m*, billete *m* de viaje
transport worker *s* transportista *mf*
transpose [træns'poz] *tr* transponer; (mus) transportar
trans•ship [træns'ʃɪp] *v* (*pret & pp* **-shipped;** *ger* **-shipping**) *tr* transbordar
transshipment [træns'ʃɪpmənt] *s* transbordo
transvestism [træns'vɛstɪzəm] *s* transvestismo
transvestite [træns'vɛstɑɪt] *adj & s* transvestido
trap [træp] *s* trampa; (*double-curved pipe*) sifón *m;* coche ligero de dos ruedas; (sport) lanzaplatos *m* ‖ *v* (*pret & pp* **trapped;** *ger* **trapping**) *tr* entrampar; atrapar (*a un ladrón*)
trap door *s* escotillón *m*, trampa; (theat) escotillón *m*, pescante *m*
trapeze [trə'piz] *s* trapecio
trapezoid ['træpɪ,zɔɪd] *s* trapecio
trapper ['træpər] *s* cazador *m* de alforja
trappings ['træpɪŋz] *spl* (*adornments*) adornos, altavíos; (*of a horse's harness*) jaeces *mpl*
trap'shoot'ing *s* tiro al vuelo
trash [træʃ] *s* broza, basura, desecho; (*junk*) cachivaches *mpl;* (*nonsense*) disparates *mpl;* (*worthless people*) gentuza
trash can *s* basurero
trash pile *s* basural *m* (SAm)
travail ['trævel] o [trə'vel] *s* afán *m*, labor *f*, pena; dolores *mpl* del parto
trav•el ['trævəl] *s* viaje *m;* el viajar; (mach) recorrido ‖ *v* (*pret & pp* **-eled** o **-elled;** *ger* **-eling** o **-elling**) *tr* viajar por; recorrer ‖ *intr* vaijar; andar, recorrer
travel bureau *s* oficina de turismo
traveler ['trævələr] *s* viajero; (*salesman*) viajante *m*
traveler's check *s* cheque *m* de viajeros
traveling expenses *spl* gastos de viaje
traveling salesman *s* viajante *m*, agente viajero
traverse ['trævərs] o [trə'vʌrs] *tr* atravesar; recorrer, pasar por
traves•ty ['trævɪsti] *s* (*pl* **-ties**) parodia ‖ *v* (*pret & pp* **-tied**) *tr* parodiar
trawl [trɔl] *s* red barredera, espinel *m*, palangre *m* ‖ *tr & intr* pescar a la rastra
tray [tre] *s* bandeja; (chem & phot) cubeta
treacherous ['trɛtʃərəs] *adj* traicionero, traidor; incierto, poco seguro
treacher•y ['trɛtʃəri] *s* (*pl* **-ies**) traición alevosía
tread [trɛd] *s* (*stepping*) pisada; (*of stairs*) grada, huella, peldaño; (*of stilts*) horquilla; (*of a tire*) banda de rodamiento; (*of shoe*) suela; (*of an egg*) meaje, galladura ‖ *v* (*pret* **trod** [trɑd]; *pp* **trodden** ['trɑdən] o **trod**) *tr* pisar, pisotear; abrumar, agobiar ‖ *intr* andar, caminar
treadle ['trɛdəl] *s* pedal *m*
treadless ['trɛdlɪs] *adj* (*tire*) desgastado

tread′mill′ *s* rueda de andar; (*futile drudgery*) noria

treas. *abbr* **treasurer, treasury**

treason [ˈtrizən] *s* traición

treasonable [ˈtrizənəbəl] *adj* traicionero, traidor

treasure [ˈtrɛʒər] *s* tesoro ‖ *tr* atesorar

treasurer [ˈtrɛʒərər] *s* tesorero

treasur•y [ˈtrɛʒəri] *s* (*pl* **-ies**) tesorería; tesoro

treat [trit] *s* convite *m;* (*to a drink*) convidada; (*something providing particular enjoyment*) regalo, deleite *m* ‖ *tr* tratar; convidar, regalar; curar (*a un enfermo*) ‖ *intr* tratar; convidar, regalar; **to treat of** tratar de

treatise [ˈtritɪs] *s* tratado

treatment [ˈtritmənt] *s* tratamiento

trea•ty [ˈtriti] *s* (*pl* **-ties**) tratado

treble [ˈtrɛbəl] *adj* (*threefold*) tresdoble, triple; sobreagudo; (mus) atiplado; (mus) de tiple ‖ *s* (*person*) tiple *mf; (voice)* tiple ‖ *tr* triplicar ‖ *intr* triplicarse

tree [tri] *s* árbol *m*

tree farm *s* monte *m* tallar

treeless [ˈtrilɪs] *adj* pelado, sin árboles

tree′top′ *s* copa, cima de árbol

trellis [ˈtrɛlɪs] *s* enrejado, espaldera; emparrado

tremble [ˈtrɛmbəl] *s* temblor *m*, estremecimiento ‖ *intr* temblar, estremecerse

tremendous [trɪˈmɛndəs] *adj* tremendo

tremor [ˈtrɛmər] o [ˈtrimər] *s* temblor *m*

trench [trɛntʃ] *s* foso, zanja; (*for irrigation*) acequia; (mil) trinchera

trenchant [ˈtrɛntʃənt] *adj* mordaz, punzante; enérgico, bien definido

trench coat *s* trinchera

trench mortar *s* (mil) lanzabombas *m*

trench′-plow′ *tr* (agr) desfondar

trend [trɛnd] *s* curso, dirección, tendencia ‖ *intr* dirigirse, tender

trendy [ˈtrɛndi] *adj* (coll) de (última) moda

trespass [ˈtrɛspəs] *s* entrada sin derecho; infracción, violación; culpa, pecado ‖*intr* entrar sin derecho; pecar; **no trespassing** prohibida la entrada; **to trespass against** pecar contra; **to trepass on** entrar sin derecho en; infringir, violar; abusar de (*p.ej., la paciencia de uno*)

tress [trɛs] *s* (*braid of hair*) trenza; (*curl*) bucle *m*, rizo

trestle [ˈtrɛsəl] *s* caballete *m;* puente *m* o viaducto de caballetes

trial [ˈtraɪ•əl] *s* ensayo, prueba; aflicción, desgracia; (law) juicio, proceso, vista; **on trial** a prueba; (law) en juicio; **to bring to trial** encausar

trial and error *s* método de tanteos

trial balloon *s* globo sonda; **to send up a trial balloon** (fig) lanzar un globo sonda

trial by jury *s* juicio por jurado

trial jury *s* jurado procesal

trial order *s* (com) pedido de ensayo

trial run *s* experimento piloto

triangle [ˈtraɪ,æŋgəl] *s* triángulo

tribe [traɪb] *s* tribu *f*

tribunal [trɪˈbjunəl] o [traɪˈbjunəl] *s* tribunal *m*

tribune [ˈtrɪbjun] *s* tribuna

tributar•y [ˈtrɪbjə,tɛri] *adj* tributario ‖ *s* (*pl* **-ies**) tributario

tribute [ˈtrɪbjut] *s* tributo

trice [traɪs] *s* momento, instante *m;* **in a trice** en un periquete

trick [trɪk] *s* ardid *m*, artimaña; leva (CAm, Col); (*knack*) maña; (*feat*) suerte *f;* (*prank*) travesura, burla, chasco; tanda, turno; ilusión; (*feat with cards*) truco; (*cards in one round*) baza; (coll) chiquita; **to be up to one's old tricks** hacer de las suyas; **to play a dirty trick on** hacer una mala jugada a ‖ *tr* trampear; burlar, engañar; ataviar

tricker•y [ˈtrɪkəri] *s* (*pl* **-ies**) trampería, malas mañas

trickle [ˈtrɪkəl] *s* chorro delgado, goteo ‖ *intr* escurrir, gotear; pasar gradual e irregularmente

trickster [ˈtrɪkstər] *s* tramposo, embustero, embaucador *m*, embaucadora

trick•y [ˈtrɪki] *adj* (*comp* **-ier;** *super* **-iest**) tramposo, engañoso, difícil; (*animal*) vicioso; (*ticklish to deal with*) delicado

tricorn [ˈtraɪkɔrn] *adj & s* tricornio

tried [traɪd] *adj* fiel, probado, seguro

trifle [ˈtraɪfəl] *s* bagatela, friolera, fruslería, basurita, chiquitura; (*trinket*) bagatela, baratija ‖ *tr*—**to trifle away** malgastar ‖ *intr* estar ocioso, holgar; **to trifle with** manosear; jugar con, burlarse de

trifling [ˈtraɪflɪŋ] *adj* frívolo, fútil, ligero; insignificante, trivial

trifocal [traɪˈfokəl] *adj* trifocal ‖ *s* lente *f* trifocal; **trifocals** anteojos trifocales

trig. *abbr* **trigonometric, trigonometry**

trigger [ˈtrɪgər] *s* (*e.g., of a gun*) disparador *m*, gatillo; (*of any device*) disparador ‖ *tr* poner en movimiento, provocar

trigonometry [,trɪgəˈnɑmɪtri] *s* trigonometría

trill [trɪl] *s* trinado, trino; (*made with voice, esp. of birds*) gorjeo; (phonet) vibración ‖ *tr* decir o cantar gorjeando; pronunciar con vibración ‖ *intr* trinar; gorjear

trillion [ˈtrɪljən] *s* (U.S.A.) billón *m;* (Brit) trillón *m*

trilo•gy [ˈtrɪlədʒi] *s* (*pl* **-gies**) trilogía

trim [trɪm] *adj* (*comp* **trimmer;** *super* **trimmest**) acicalado, compuesto, elegante ‖ *s* condición, estado; buena condición; adorno, atavío; traje *m*, vestido; (*of sails*) orientación ‖ *v* (*pret & pp* **trimmed;** *ger* **trimming**) *tr* ajustar, adaptar; arreglar, componer; adornar, decorar; decorar, enguirnaldar (*el árbol de Navidad*); recortar; cortar ligeramente (*el pelo*); despabilar (*una lámpara o vela*); mondar, podar (*árboles, plantas*); acepillar, desbastar; (naut) orientar (*las velas*); (coll) derrotar, vencer; (coll) regañar

trimming [ˈtrɪmɪŋ] *s* adorno, guarnición; franja, orla; (coll) paliza, zurra; (coll) derrota; **trimmings** accesorios, arrequives *mpl;* recortes *mpl*

trini•ty [ˈtrɪnɪti] *s* (*pl* **-ties**) (*group of three*) trinca ‖ **Trinity** *s* Trinidad
trinket [ˈtrɪŋkɪt] *s* (*small ornament*) dije *m;* (*trivial object*) baratija, bujería, chuchería
tri•o [ˈtri•o] *s* (*pl* **-os**) (*group of three*) terna, trío; (mus) trío
trip [trɪp] *s* viaje *m;* jira, recorrido; (*stumble*) tropiezo; (*act of causing a person to stumble*) traspié *m*, zancadilla; (*blunder*) desliz *m*; (*drugs*) viaje ‖ *v* (*pret & pp* **tripped;** *ger* **tripping**) *tr* trompicar, echar la zancadilla a; detener, estorbar; inclinar; coger en falta; coger en una mentira ‖ *intr* ir con paso rápido y ligero; brincar, saltar, correr; tropezar; **to trip over** tropezar con, contra o en
tripe [traɪp] *s* callos, mondongo; (slang) disparate *m*, barbaridad
trip'ham'mer *s* martillo pilón
triphthong [ˈtrɪfθɔŋ] *s* triptongo
triple [ˈtrɪpəl] *adj & s* triple *m* ‖ *tr* triplicar ‖ *intr* triplicarse
triplet [ˈtrɪplɪt] *s* (*offspring*) trillizo; (*stanza of three lines*) terceto; (mus) terceto, tresillo
triplicate [ˈtrɪplɪkɪt] *adj & s* triplicado; **in triplicate** por triplicado ‖ [ˈtrɪplɪ,ket] *tr* triplicar
tripod [ˈtraɪpɑd] *m* trípode *m*
triptych [ˈtrɪptɪk] *s* tríptico
trite [traɪt] *adj* gastado, trillado, trivial
triumph [ˈtraɪ•əmf] *s* triunfo ‖ *intr* triunfar; **to triumph over** triunfar de
triumphal arch [traɪˈʌmfəl] *s* arco triunfal
triumphant [traɪˈʌmfənt] *adj* triunfante
trivia [ˈtrɪvɪ•ə] *spl* bagatelas, trivialidades
trivial [ˈtrɪvɪ•əl] *adj* trivial, insignificante
triviali•ty [,trɪvɪˈælɪti] *s* (*pl* **-ties**) trivialidad
Trojan [ˈtrodʒən] *adj & s* troyano
Trojan horse *s* caballo de Troya
Trojan War *s* guerra de Troya
troll [trol] *tr & intr* pescar a la cacea
trolley [ˈtrɑli] *s* polea o arco de trole; tranvía *m*
trolley bus *s* trolebús *m*
trolley car *s* coche *m* de tranvía
trolley pole *s* trole *m*
trolling [ˈtrolɪŋ] *s* cacea, pesca a la cacea
trollop [ˈtrɑləp] *s* (*slovenly woman*) cochina; mujer *f* de mala vida
trombone [ˈtrɑmbon] *s* trombón *m*
troop [trup] *s* tropa; (*of actors*) compañia; (*of cavalry*) escuadrón *m* ‖ *intr* agruparse; marcharse en tropel
trooper [ˈtrupər] *s* soldado de caballería; corcel *m* de guerra; policía *m* de a caballo; (*ship*) transporte *m;* **to swear like a trooper** jurar como un carretero
tro•phy [ˈtrofi] *s* (*pl* **-phies**) trofeo; (*any memento*) recuerdo
tropic [ˈtrɑpɪk] *adj* tropical ‖ *s* trópico
tropical [ˈtrɑpɪkəl] *adj* tropical
tropics o **Tropics** [ˈtrɑpɪks] *spl* zona tropical
troposphere [ˈtrɑpə,sfɪr] *s* troposfera
trot [trɑt] *s* trote *m* ‖ *v* (*pret & pp* **trotted;** *ger* **trotting**) *tr* hacer trotar; **to trot out** (slang) sacar para mostrar ‖ *intr* trotar
troth [trɔθ] o [troθ] *s* fe *f;* verdad; esponsales *mpl;* **in troth** en verdad; **to plight one's troth** prometer fidelidad; dar palabra de casamiento
troubadour [ˈtrubə,dor] o [ˈtrubə,dʊr] *adj* trovadoresco ‖ *s* trovador *m*
trouble [ˈtrʌbəl] *s* apuro, dificultad; confusión, estorbo; conflicto; inquietud, preocupación; pena, molestia; mal *m*, enfermedad; murga; (*of a mechanical nature*) avería, falla, pana; **not to be worth the trouble** no valer la pena; **to pour out one's troubles** jeremiquear; **that's the trouble** ahí está el busilis; **the trouble is that . . .** lo malo es que . . .; **to be in trouble** estar en un aprieto; **to be looking for trouble** buscar tres pies al gato; **to get into trouble** enredarse, meterse en líos; **to take the trouble to** tomarse la molestia de ‖ *tr* apurar; confundir, estorbar; inquietar, preocupar; apenar, afligir; incomodar, molestar; dar que hacer a; **to be troubled with** padecer de; **to trouble oneself** molestarse ‖ *intr* apurarse; inquietarse, preocuparse; molestarse, darse molestia; **to trouble to** molestarse en
trouble lamp *s* lámpara de socorro
trou'ble•mak'er *s* perturbador *m*, alborotador *m*
troubleshooter [ˈtrʌbəl,ʃutər] *s* localizador *m* de averías; (*in disputes*) componedor *m*
troubleshooting [ˈtrʌbəl,ʃutɪŋ] *s* localización de averías; (*of disputes*) composición, arbitraje *m*
troublesome [ˈtrʌbəlsəm] *adj* molesto, pesado, gravoso; impertinente; perturbador
trouble spot *s* lugar *m* de conflicto
trough [trɔf] o [trɑf] *s* (*e.g., to knead bread*) artesa; (*for water for animals*) abrevadero; (*for feeding animals*) comedero; (*under eaves*) canal *f;* (*between two waves*) seno
troupe [trup] *s* compañia de actores o de circo
trousers [ˈtraʊsərz] *spl* pantalones *mpl*
trous•seau [truˈso] o [ˈtruso] *s* (*pl* **-seaux** o **-seaus**) ajuar *m* de novia, equipo de novia
trout [traʊt] *s* trucha
trouvère [truˈvɛr] *s* trovero
trowel [ˈtraʊ•əl] *s* paleta, llana
Troy [trɔɪ] *s* Troya
truant [ˈtru•ənt] *s* novillero; **to play truant** hacer novillos
truce [trus] *s* tregua
truck [trʌk] *s* carro; vegoneta; camión *m;* autocamión *m;* (*to be moved by hand*) carretilla; (*of locomotive or car*) carretón *m;* hortalizas para el mercado; (coll) desperdicios; (coll) negocio, relaciones ‖ *tr* acarrear
truck driver *s* camionista *mf*; materialista *m* (Mex)
truck garden *s* huerto de hortalizas (*para el mercado*)
truculent [ˈtrʌkjələnt] o [ˈtrukjələnt] *adj* truculento
trudge [trʌdʒ] *intr* caminar, ir a pie; **to trudge along** marchar con pena y trabajo

true [tru] *adj* verdadero; exacto; constante, uniforme; fiel, leal; alineado; a plomo, a nivel; **to come true** hacerse realidad; **true to life** conforme a la realidad
true copy *s* copia fiel
true-hearted ['tru,hɑrtɪd] *adj* fiel, leal, sincero
true'love' *s* fiel amante *mf;* (bot) hierba de París
truelove knot *s* lazo de amor
truffle ['trʌfəl] o ['trufəl] *s* trufa
truism ['tru•ɪzəm] *s* perogrullada, verdad trillada
truly ['truli] *adv* verdaderamente; efectivamente; fielmente; **truly yours** de Vd. atto. y S.S., su seguro servidor
trump [trʌmp] *s* triunfo; (coll) buen chico, buena chica; **no trump** sin triunfo || *tr* matar con un triunfo; aventajar, sobrepujar; **to trump up** forjar, inventar (*para engañar*) || *intr* triunfar
trumpet ['trʌmpɪt] *s* trompeta; trompeta acústica; **to blow one's own trumpet** cantar sus propias alabanzas || *tr* pregonar a son de trompeta || *intr* trompetear
truncheon ['trʌntʃən] *s* cachiporra; bastón *m* de mando
trunk [trʌŋk] *s* (*of living body, tree, family, railroad*) tronco; (*chest for clothes, etc.*) baúl *m;* (*of an automobile*) portaequipaje *m;* (*of elephant*) trompa; **trunks** taparrabo
trunk hose *spl* trusas
truss [trʌs] *s* (*framework*) armadura; haz *m*, paquete *m*, lío; (*for holding back a hernia*) braguero || *tr* armar; empaquetar; espetar; apretar (*barriles*)
trust [trʌst] *s* confianza; esperanza; cargo, custodia; depósito; crédito; obligación; (econ) trust *m*, cartel *m;* (law) fideicomiso; **in trust** en confianza; en depósito; **on trust** a crédito, al fiado || *tr* confiar; confiar en; vender a crédito a || *intr* confiar; fiar; **to trust in** fiarse a o de
trust company *s* banco fideicomisario, banco de depósitos
trustee [trʌs'ti] *s* administrador *m*, comisario; regente (universitario); (*of an estate*) fideicomisario
trusteeship [trʌs'tiʃɪp] *s* cargo de administrador, fideicomisario; (*of the UN*) fideicomiso
trustful ['trʌstfəl] *adj* confiado
trust'wor'thy *adj* confiable, fidedigno
trust•y ['trʌsti] *adj* (comp **-ier;** *super* **-iest**) honrado, fidedigno || *s* (*pl* **-ies**) presidiario fidedigno (*que se ha merecido ciertos privilegios*)
truth [truθ] *s* verdad; **in truth** a la verdad, en verdad
truthful ['truθfəl] *adj* verídico, veraz
try [traɪ] *s* (*pl* **tries**) ensayo, intento, prueba || *v* (*pret & pp* **tried**) *tr* ensayar, intentar, probar; comprobar, verificar; cansar; exasperar, irritar; (law) procesar (*a una persona*); (law) ver (*un pleito*); **to try on** probarse (*una prenda de vestir*) || *intr* ensayar, probar; esforzarse; **to try to** tratar de, intentar
trying ['traɪ•ɪŋ] *adj* cansado, molesto, irritante; penoso
tryst [trɪst] o [traɪst] *s* cita; lugar *m* de cita
tub [tʌb] *s* cuba, tina; (coll) baño; (*clumsy boat*) (coll) carcamán *m*, trompo; (*fat person*) (coll) cuba
tube [tjub] o [tub] *s* tubo; túnel *m;* (*of a tire*) cámara; (coll) ferrocarril subterráneo
tuber ['tjuber] o ['tubər] *s* tubérculo
tubercle ['tubərkəl] *s* tubérculo
tubercular [tu'bʌrkjələr] *adj & s* tísico
tuberculosis [tu,bʌrkjə'losɪs] *s* tuberculosis *f*
tuck [tʌk] *s* alforza || *tr* alforzar; **to tuck away** encubrir, ocultar; **to tuck in** arropar, enmantar; remeter (*p.ej., la ropa de cama*); **to tuck up** arremangar (*un vestido*); guarnecer (*la cama*)
tucker ['tʌkər] *s* escote *m* || *tr* —**to tucker out** (coll) agotar, cansar
Tuesday ['tjuzdi] *s* martes *m*
tuft [tʌft] *s* (*of feathers, hair, etc.*) penacho, copete *m;* manojo, racimo, ramillete *m;* borla || *tr* empenachar || *intr* crecer formando mechones
tug [tʌg] *s* estirón *m*, tirón *m;* (*boat*) remolcador *m* || *v* (*pret & pp* **tugged;** *ger* **tugging**) *tr* arrastrar, tirar con fuerza de; remolcar (*un barco*) || *intr* tirar con fuerza; esforzarse, luchar
tug'boat' *s* remolcador *m*
tug of war *s* lucha de la cuerda
tuition [tju'ɪʃən] *s* enseñanza; precio de la enseñanza
tulip ['tulɪp] *s* tulipán *m*
tumble ['tʌmbəl] *s* caída, tumbo; (*somersault*) voltereta, tumba; confusión, desorden *m* || *intr* caerse, rodar; voltear; derribarse, volcarse; brincar, dar saltos; (*into bed*) echarse; (*to catch on*) (slang) caer, comprender; **to tumble down** desplomarse, hundirse, venirse abajo
tum'ble-down' *adj* destartalado, desvencijado
tumbler ['tʌmblər] *s* (*for drinking*) vaso; (*person who performs bodily feats*) volatinero; (*self-righting toy*) dominguillo, tentemozo
tumor ['tjumər] o ['tumər] *s* tumor *m*
tumult ['tumʌlt] *s* tumulto
tun [tʌn] *s* barril *m*, tonel *m;* (*measure of capacity for wine*) tonelada
tuna ['tunə] *s* atún *m*
tune [tjun] o [tun] *s* tonada, aire *m;* (*manner of acting or speaking*) tono; **in tune** afinado; afinadamente; **out of tune** desafinado; desafinadamente; **to change one's tune** mudar de tono || *tr* acordar, afinar; (rad) sintonizar; **to tune in** (rad) sintonizar; **to tune out** (rad) desintonizar; **to tune up** poner a punto; poner a tono (*un motor de automóvil*)
tungsten ['tʌŋstən] *s* tungsteno
tunic ['tjunɪk] o ['tunɪk] *s* túnica
tuning *s* (aut) puesto a punto
tuning coil *s* (rad) bobina de sintonía

tuning fork *s* diapasón *m*
Tunis [ˈtunɪs] *s* Túnez (*ciudad*)
Tunisia [tuˈniʒə] *s* Túnez (*país*)
Tunisian [tuˈniʒən] *adj & s* tunecino
tun•nel [ˈtʌnəl] *s* túnel *m;* (min) galería || *v* (*pret & pp* **-neled** o **-nelled;** *ger* **-neling** o **-nelling**) *tr* construir un túnel a través de o debajo de
turban [ˈtʌrbən] *s* turbante *m*
turbid [ˈtʌrbɪd] *adj* turbio
turbine [ˈtʌrbɪn] o [ˈtʌrbaɪn] *s* turbina
turbocompressor [ˌtʌrbokəmˈprɛsər] *s* turbocompresor *m*
turbofan [ˈtʌrboˌfæn] *s* turboventilador *m*
turbojet [ˈtʌrboˌdʒet] *s* turborreactor *m;* avión *m* de turborreacción
turboprop [ˈtʌrboˌprɑp] *s* turbopropulsor *m;* turbohelice *m* avión *m* de turbopropulsión
turbosupercharger [ˌtʌrboˈsupərˌtʃɑrdʒər] *s* turbosupercargador *m*
turbulent [ˈtʌrbjələnt] *adj* turbulento
tureen [tʊˈrin] o [tjʊˈrin] *s* sopera
turf [tʌrf] *s* (*surface layer of grassland*) césped *m;* terrón *m* de césped; (*peat*) turba; **the turf** el hipódromo; las carreras de caballos
turf•man [ˈtʌrfmən] *s* (*pl* **-men** [mən]) turfista *m*
Turk [tʌrk] *s* turco
turkey [ˈtʌrki] *s* pavo || **Turkey** *s* Turquía
turkey vulture *s* aura
Turkish [ˈtʌrkɪʃ] *adj & s* turco
Turkish towel *s* toalla rusa
turmoil [ˈtʌrmɔɪl] *s* alboroto, disturbio, tumulto
turn [tʌrn] *s* vuelta; (*time of action*) turno; (*change of direction*) virada; (*bend*) recodo; (*walk*) paseo corto; (*of a spiral, roll of wire, etc.*) espira; aspecto; inclinación; vahido, vértigo; giro, expresión; servicio; (coll) sacudida, susto; **at every turn** a cada paso; **in trun** por turno; **to be one's turn** tocarle a uno, p.ej., **it's your turn** le toca a Vd.; **to take turns** alternar, turnar; **to wait one's turn** aguardar turno, esperar vez || *tr* volver; dar vuelta a (*p.ej., una llave*); torcer (*p.ej., el tobillo*); doblar (*la esquina*); dirigir (*p.ej., los ojos*); (*to make sour*) agriar; (*on a lathe*) tornear; tener (*p.ej., veinte años cumplidos*); **to turn against** predisponer en contra de; **to turn around** volver; voltear; torcer (*las palabras de una persona*); **to turn aside** desviar; **to turn away** desviar; despedir; **to turn back** devolver; hacer retroceder; retrasar (*el reloj*); **to turn down** doblar hacia abajo; invertir; rechazar, rehusar; bajar (*p.ej., el gas*); **to turn in** doblar hacia adentro; entregar; **to turn off** apagar (*la luz, la radio*); cortar (*el agua, gas, etc.*); cerrar (*la llave del agua, gas, etc.; la radio, la televisión*); interrumpir (*la corriente eléctrica*); **to turn on** encender (*la luz*); poner (*la luz, la radio, etc.*); abrir (*la llave del agua, gas, etc.*); establecer (*la corriente eléctrica*); **to turn out** despedir; echar al campo (*a los animales*); volver al revés; apagar (*la luz*); hacer, fabricar; **to turn up** doblar hacia arriba; levantar; arremangar (*p.ej., las mangas*); volver (*un naipe*); poner más alto o más fuerte (*la radio*); abrir la llave de (*p.ej., el gas*) || *intr* volver, p.ej., **the road turns to the right** el camino vuelve a la derecha; virar (*un automóvil, un avión, etc.*); (*to revolve*) girar; volverse (*p.ej., la conversación; la opinión; ciertos licores*); **to turn against** cobrar aversión a; rebelarse contra; **to turn around** dar vuelta; **to turn aside** o **away** desviarse; alejarse; **to turn back** volver, regresar; retroceder; **to turn down** doblarse hacia abajo; invertirse; **to turn in** doblarse hacia adentro; replegarse; recogerse, volver a casa; (coll) recogerse, acostarse; **to turn into** entrar en; convertirse en; **to turn on** volverse contra; depender de; versar sobre; ocuparse de; **to turn out badly** salir mal; **to turn out right** acabar bien; **to turn out to be** venir a ser; resultar, salir; **to turn over** volcar, derribarse (*un vehículo*); **to turn up** doblarse hacia arriba; levantarse; acontecer; aparecer
turn'coat' *s* tránsfuga *mf*, apóstata *mf*, renegado; **to become a turncoat** volver la casaca, cambiarse la camisa
turn'down' *adj* (*collar*) caído || *s* rechazamiento
turning light *s* (aut) intermitente *m*
turning point *s* punto de transición, punto decisivo
turnip [ˈtʌrnɪp] *s* nabo; (*cheap watch*) (slang) calentador *m;* (slang) tipo
turn'key' *s* carcelero, llavero de cárcel
turn of life *s* menopausia
turn of mind *s* natural *m*, inclinación
turn'out' *s* (*gathering of people*) concurrencia; (*number attending a show, etc.*) entrada; (*side track or passage*) apartadero; (*amount produced*) producción; (*array, outfit*) equipaje *m;* carruaje *m* de lujo
turn'o'ver *s* (*spill, upset*) vuelco; cambio de personal; movimiento de mercancías; ciclo de compra y venta
turn'pike' *s* carretera de peaje
turnstile [ˈtʌrnˌstaɪl] *s* torniquete *m*
turn'ta'ble *s* (*of phonograph*) placa giratoria, plato giratorio; (rr) placa giratoria, plataforma giratoria
turpentine [ˈtʌrpənˌtaɪn] *s* trementina
turpitude [ˈtʌrpɪˌtjud] *s* torpeza, infamia, vileza
turquoise [ˈtʌrkɔɪz] o [ˈtʌrkwɔɪz] *s* turquesa
turret [ˈtʌrɪt] *s* torrecilla; (archit) torreón *m;* (nav) torreta
turtle [ˈtʌrtəl] *s* tortuga; **to turn turtle** derribarse patas arriba
tur'tle•dove' *s* tórtola
Tuscan [ˈtʌskən] *adj & s* toscano
Tuscany [ˈtʌskəni] *s* la Toscana
tusk [tʌsk] *s* colmillo
tussle [ˈtʌsəl] *s* agarrada || *intr* agarrarse, asirse, reñir

tutor [ˈtjutər] o [ˈtutər] *s* maestro particular; (*guardian*) tutor *m* || *tr* dar enseñanza particular a || *intr* dar enseñanza particular; (coll) tomar lecciones particulares
tuxe•do [tʌkˈsido] *s* (*pl* **-dos**) esmoquin *m*, smoking *m*
TV *abbr* **television**
twaddle [ˈtwɑdəl] *s* charla, tonterías, música celestial || *intr* charlar, decir tonterías
twang [twæŋ] *s* (*of musical instrument*) tañido; (*of voice*) timbre *m* nasal || *tr* tocar con un tañido; decir con timbre nasal || *intr* hablar por la nariz
twang•y [twæŋi] *adj* (*comp* **-ier;** *super* **-iest**) (*device*) tañente; (*person, voice*) gangoso
tweed [twid] *s* mezcla de lana; traje *m* de mezcla de lana; **tweeds** ropa de mezcla de lana
tweet [twit] *s* pío || *intr* piar
tweeter [ˈtwitər] *s* altavoz *m* para audiofrecuencias elevadas
tweezers [ˈtwizərz] *spl* bruselas, pinzas, tenacillas
twelfth [twɛlfθ] *adj & s* (*in a seris*) duodécimo; (*part*) dozavo || *s* (*in dates*) doce *m*
Twelfth'-night' *s* la víspera del día de Reyes; la noche del día de Reyes
twelve [twɛlv] *adj & pron* doce || *s* doce *m;* **twelve o'clock** las doce
twentieth [ˈtwɛntɪ•ɪθ] *adj & s* (*in a series*) vigésimo; (*part*) veintavo || *s* (*in dates*) veinte *m*
twen•ty [ˈtwɛnti] *adj & pron* veinte || *s* (*pl* **-ties**) veinte *m*
twice [twaɪs] *adv* dos veces
twice'-told' *adj* dicho dos veces; trillado, sabido
twiddle [ˈtwɪdəl] *tr* menear o revolver ociosamente
twig [twɪg] *s* ramito; **twigs** leña menuda
twilight [ˈtwaɪ,laɪt] *adj* crepuscular || *s* crepúsculo
twill [twɪl] *s* tela cruzada; (*pattern of weave*) cruzado || *tr* cruzar
twin [twɪn] *adj & s* gemelo
twine [twaɪn] *s* guita, cuerda, bramante *m* || *tr* enroscar, retorcer || *intr* enroscarse, retorcerse
twinge [twɪndʒ] *s* punzada, dolor agudo
twin'jet' plane *s* avión *m* birreactor
twinkle [ˈtwɪŋkəl] *s* centelleo; (*of eye*) pestañeo; instante *m* || *intr* centellear; pestañear; moverse rápidamente
twin'-screw' *adj* (naut) de doble hélice
twirl [twʌrl] *s* vuelta, giro || *tr* hacer girar; (baseball) lanzar (*la pelota*) || *intr* dar vueltas, girar; piruetear
twist [twɪst] *s* torcedura; enroscadura; curva, recodo; giro, vuelta; propensión, prejuicio; (*of mind or disposition*) sesgo || *tr* torcer; retorcer; enroscar; hacer girar; entrelazar; desviar; (*to give a different meaning to*) torcer || *intr* torcerse; retorcerse; enroscarse; dar vueltas; entrelazarse; desviarse; serpentear; **to twist and turn** (*in bed*) dar vueltas
twisted [ˈtwɪstɪd] *adj* sobornado
twit [twɪt] *v* (*pret & pp* **twitted;** *ger* **twitting)** *tr* reprender (*a uno*) recordando algo desagradable o poniéndole en ridículo
twitch [twɪtʃ] *s* crispatura; ligero temblor || *intr* crisparse; temblar (*p.ej., los párpados*)
twitter [ˈtwɪtər] *s* gorjeo; risita sofocada; inquietud || *intr* gorjear; reír sofocadamente; temblar de inquietud
two [tu] *adj & pron* dos || *s* dos *m;* **to put two and two together** atar cabos, sacar la conclusión evidente; **two o'clock** las dos
two'-cy'cle *adj* (mach) de dos tiempos
two'-cyl'inder *adj* (mach) de dos cilindros
two-edged [ˈtu,ɛdʒd] *adj* de dos filos
two hundred *adj & pron* doscientos || *s* doscientos *m*
twosome [ˈtusəm] *s* pareja; pareja de jugadores; juego de dos
two'-time' *tr* (slang) engañar en amor, ser infiel a (*una persona del otro sexo*)
tycoon [taɪˈkun] *s* (coll) magnate *m*
type [taɪp] *s* tipo; (*piece*) (typ) tipo, letra; (*pieces collectively*) (typ) letra; letras impresas, letras escritas a máquina || *tr* escribir a máquina, tipiar; representar, simbolizar || *intr* escribir a máquina
type'face' *s* tipo de letra
type'script' *s* material escrito a máquina
typesetter [ˈtaɪp,sɛtər] *s* (typ) cajista *mf;* (typ) máquina de componer
type'write' *v* (*pret* **-wrote** [,rot]; *pp* **-written** [,rɪtən]) *tr & intr* escribir a máquina, tipiar
type'writ'er *s* máquina de escribir; tipista *mf*
typewriter ribbon *s* cinta para máquinas de escribir
type'writ'ing *s* mecanografía; trabajo hecho con máquina de escribir
typhoid fever [ˈtaɪfɔɪd] *s* fiebre tifoidea
typhoon [taɪˈfun] *s* tifón *m*
typical [ˈtɪpɪkəl] *adj* típico
typi•fy [ˈtɪpɪ,faɪ] *v* (*pret & pp* **-fied**) *tr* simbolizar; ser ejemplo o modelo de
typist [ˈtaɪpɪst] *s* mecanógrafo, tipista *mf*, mecanógrafa
typographic(al) [,taɪpəˈgræfɪk(əl)] *adj* tipográfico
typographical error *s* error *m* de imprenta
typography [taɪˈpɑgrəfi] *s* tipografía
tyrannic(al) [tɪˈrænɪk(əl)] o [taɪˈrænɪk(əl)] *adj* tiránico
tyrannous [ˈtɪrənəs] *adj* tirano
tyran•ny [ˈtɪrəni] *s* (*pl* **-nies**) tiranía
tyrant [ˈtaɪrənt] *s* tirano
ty•ro [ˈtaɪro] *s* (*pl* **-ros**) tirón *m*, novicio

U

U, u [ju] vigésima primera letra del alfabeto inglés
U. *abbr* **University**
ubiquitous [ju'bɪkwɪtəs] *adj* ubicuo
udder ['ʌdər] *s* ubre *f*
UFO *abbr* **unidentified flying object**
ugliness ['ʌglɪnɪs] *s* fealdad; (coll) malhumor *m*
ug•ly ['ʌgli] *adj* (*comp* **-lier;** *super* **-liest**) feo; (coll) malhumorado
ugly mug *s* (slang) carantamaula
Ukraine ['jukren] o [ju'kren] *s* Ucrania
Ukrainian [ju'krenɪ•ən] *adj & s* ucraniano, ucranio
ulcer ['ʌlsər] *s* llaga, úlcera; (*corrupting influence*) (fig) llaga
ulcerate ['ʌlsə,ret] *tr* ulcerar ‖ *intr* ulcerarse
ulterior [ʌl'tɪrɪ•ər] *adj* ulterior; (*concealed*) escondido, oculto
ultimate ['ʌltɪmɪt] *adj* último
ultima•tum [,ʌltɪ'metəm] *s* (*pl* **-tums** o **-ta** [tə]) ultimátum *m*
ultimo ['ʌltɪ,mo] *adv* de o en el mes próximo pasado
ultrahigh [,ʌltrə'haɪ] *adj* (electron) ultraelevado
ultrasound ['ʌltrə,saʊnd] *s* sonido silencioso
ultraviolet [,ʌltrə'vaɪ•əlɪt] *adj & s* ultravioleta, ultraviolado
umbilical cord [ʌm'bɪlɪkəl] *s* cordón *m* umbilical
umbrage ['ʌmbrɪdʒ] *s*—**to take umbrage at** resentirse de o por
umbrella [ʌm'brɛlə] *s* paraguas *m;* (mil) sombrilla protectora
umbrella man *s* paragüero
umbrella stand *s* paragüero
umlaut ['ʊmlaʊt] *s* inflexión vocálica, metafonía; (*mark*) diéresis *f* ‖ *tr* inflexionar; escribir con diéresis
umpire ['ʌmpaɪr] *s* árbitro ‖ *tr & intr* arbitrar
UN ['ju'ɛn] *s* (letterword) ONU *f*
unable [ʌn'ebəl] *adj* incapaz, imposibilitado; **to be unable to** no poder
unabridged [,ʌnə'brɪdʒd] *adj* sin abreviar, íntegro
unaccented [ʌn'æksɛntɪd] o [,ʌnæk'sɛntɪd] *adj* inacentuado
unaccountable [,ʌnə'kaʊntəbəl] *adj* inexplicable; irresponsable
unaccounted-for [,ʌnə'kaʊntɪd,fɔr] *adj* inexplicado; no hallado
unaccustomed [,ʌnə'kʌstəmd] *adj* (*unusual*) desacostumbrado; inhabituado
unafraid [,ʌnə'fred] *adj* sin miedo
unaligned [,ʌnə'laɪnd] *adj* no empeñado
unanimity [,junə'nɪmɪti] *s* unanimidad
unanimous [jʊ'nænɪməs] *adj* unánime
unanswerable [ʌn'ænsərəbəl] *adj* incontestable; (*argument*) incontrastable
unappreciative [,ʌnə'priʃɪ,etɪv] *adj* ingrato, desagradecido
unapproachable [,ʌnə'protʃəbəl] *adj* inabordable; incomparable, único
unarmed [ʌn'ɑrmd] *adj* desarmado, inerme
unascertainable [ʌn,æsər'tenəbəl] *adj* inaveriguable
unasked [ʌn'æskt] *adj* no solicitado; no convidado
unassembled [,ʌnə'sɛmbəld] *adj* desmontado, desarmado
unassuming [,ʌnə'sumɪŋ] o [,ʌnə'sjumɪŋ] *adj* modesto, sencillo
unattached [,ʌnə'tætʃt] *adj* independiente; (*loose*) suelto; (*not engaged to be married*) no prometido; (law) no embargado; (mil & nav) de reemplazo
unattainable [,ʌnə'tenəbəl] *adj* inasequible, inalcanzable
unattractive [,ʌnə'træktɪv] *adj* poco atrayente, desairado
unavailable [,ʌnə'veləbəl] *adj* indisponible
unavailing [,ʌnə'velɪŋ] *adj* ineficaz, inútil, vano
unavoidable [,ʌnə'vɔɪdəbəl] *adj* inevitable, ineluctable
unaware [,ʌnə'wɛr] *adj*—**to be unaware of** no estar al corriente de ‖ *adv* de improviso; sin saberlo
unawares [,ʌnə'wɛrz] *adv* (*unexpectedly*) de improviso; (*unknowingly*) sin saberlo
unbalanced [ʌn'bælənst] *adj* desequilibrado
unbandage [ʌn'bændɪdʒ] *tr* desvendar
un•bar [ʌn'bɑr] *v* (*pret & pp* **-barred;** *ger* **-barring**) *tr* desatrancar
unbearable [ʌn'bɛrəbəl] *adj* inaguantable
unbeatable [ʌn'bitəbəl] *adj* imbatible
unbecoming [,ʌnbɪ'kʌmɪŋ] *adj* inconveniente, indecente; que sienta mal
unbelievable [,ʌnbɪ'livəbəl] *adj* increíble
unbending [ʌn'bɛndɪŋ] *adj* inflexible
unbiased o **unbiassed** [ʌn'baɪ•əst] *adj* imparcial
un•bind [ʌn'baɪnd] *v* (*pret & pp* **-bound** ['baʊnd]) *tr* desatar
unbleached [ʌn'blitʃt] *adj* sin blanquear
unbolt [ʌn'bolt] *tr* desatrancar (*p.ej., una puerta*); (*to remove the bolts from*) desempernar
unborn [ʌn'bɔrn] *adj* no nacido, por nacer, futuro
unbosom [ʌn'bʊzəm] *tr* confesar, descubrir (*sus pensamientos, sus secretos*); **to unbosom oneself** abrir su pecho, desahogarse
unbound [ʌn'baʊnd] *adj* (*book*) sin encuadernar
unbreakable [ʌn'brekəbəl] *adj* irrompible
unbuckle [ʌn'bʌkəl] *tr* deshebillar
unburden [ʌn'bʌrdən] *tr* descargar; **to unburden oneself of** desahogarse de
unburied [ʌn'bɛrid] *adj* insepulto
unbutton [ʌn'bʌtən] *tr* desabotonar
uncalled-for [ʌn'kɔld,fɔr] *adj* innecesario, no justificado; insolente
uncanny [ʌn'kæni] *adj* espectral, misterioso; extraordinario, maravilloso
uncared-for [ʌn'kɛrd,fɔr] *adj* desamparado, descuidado, abandonado
unceasing [ʌn'sisɪŋ] *adj* incesante

unceremonious [ˌʌnsɛriˈmonɪ•əs] *adj* inceremonioso
uncertain [ʌnˈsʌrtən] *adj* incierto
uncertain•ty [ʌnˈsʌrtənti] *s* (*pl* **-ties**) incertidumbre
unchain [ʌnˈtʃen] *tr* desencadenar
unchangeable [ʌnˈtʃendʒəbəl] *adj* incambiable, inmutable
uncharted [ʌnˈtʃartɪd] *adj* inexplorado
unchecked [ʌnˈtʃɛkt] *adj* no verificado; no refrenado; desenfrenado
uncivilized [ʌnˈsɪvɪˌlaɪzd] *adj* incivilizado
unclad [ʌnˈklæd] *adj* desvestido
unclaimed [ʌnˈklemd] *adj* sin reclamar; (*mail*) rechazado, sobrante
unclasp [ʌnˈklæsp] *tr* desabrochar
unclassified [ʌnˈklæsɪˌfaɪd] *adj* no clasificado; no clasificado como secreto
uncle [ˈʌŋkəl] *s* tío
unclean [ʌnˈklin] *adj* desaseado, sucio
un•clog [ʌnˈklag] *v* (*pret & pp* **-clogged;** *ger* **-clogging**) *tr* desatrancar
unclouded [ʌnˈklaudɪd] *adj* despejado
uncollectible [ˌʌnkəˈlɛktɪbəl] *adj* incobrable
uncomfortable [ʌnˈkʌmfərtəbəl] *adj* incómodo
uncommitted [ˌʌnkəˈmɪtɪd] *adj* no empeñado, no comprometido
uncommon [ʌnˈkamən] *adj* raro, poco común
uncompromising [ʌnˈkamprəˌmaɪzɪŋ] *adj* intransigente
unconcerned [ˌʌnkənˈsʌrnd] *adj* despreocupado, indiferente
unconditional [ˌʌnkənˈdɪʃənəl] *adj* incondicional
uncongenial [ˌʌnkənˈdʒinɪ•əl] *adj* antipático; incompatible; desagradable
unconquerable [ʌnˈkaŋkərəbəl] *adj* inconquistable
unconquered [ʌnˈkaŋkərd] *adj* invicto
unconscionable [ʌnˈkanʃənəbəl] *adj* inescrupuloso; desrazonable, excesivo
unconscious [ʌnˈkanʃəs] *adj* inconsciente; (*temporarily deprived of consciousness*) desmayado; (*unintentional*) involuntario
unconsciousness [ʌnˈkanʃəsnɪs] *s* inconsciencia; desmayo
unconstitutional [ˌʌnkanstɪˈtjuʃənəl] *adj* inconstitucional
uncontrollable [ˌʌnkənˈtroləbəl] *adj* ingobernable; incontrolable; (*laughter*) inextinguible
unconventional [ˌʌnkənˈvɛnʃənəl] *adj* no convencional
uncork [ʌnˈkɔrk] *tr* destapar, descorchar
uncouth [ʌnˈkuθ] *adj* desgarbado, torpe, rústico
uncover [ʌnˈkʌvər] *tr* descubrir
unction [ˈʌŋkʃən] *s* (*anointing*) unción; suavidad hipócrita
unctuous [ˈʌŋktʃu•əs] *adj* untuoso; zalamero
uncultivated [ʌnˈkʌltɪˌvetɪd] *adj* inculto (*que no está cultivado; rústico, grosero*)
uncultured [ʌnˈkʌltʃərd] *adj* inculto, rústico, grosero
uncut [ʌnˈkʌt] *adj* sin cortar; (*book or magazine*) intonso
undamaged [ʌnˈdæmɪdʒd] *adj* indemne, ileso
undaunted [ʌnˈdɔntɪd] *adj* impávido, denodado
undecided [ˌʌndɪˈsaɪdɪd] *adj* indeciso
undefeated [ˌʌndɪˈfitɪd] *adj* invicto
undefended [ˌʌndɪˈfɛndɪd] *adj* indefenso
undefiled [ˌʌndɪˈfaɪld] *adj* inmaculado, impoluto
undeniable [ˌʌndɪˈnaɪ•əbəl] *adj* innegable
under [ˈʌndər] *adj* inferior; (*clothing*) interior || *adv* debajo; más abajo; **to go under** hundirse; (*to fail*) fracasar || *prep* bajo, debajo de; inferior a; **under full sail** a vela llena; **under lock and key** bajo llave; **under oath** bajo juramento; **under penalty of death** so pena de muerte; **under sail** a vela; **under separate cover** por separado, bajo cubierta separada; **under steam** bajo presión; **under the hand and seal of** firmado y sellado por; **under the nose of** en las barbas de; **under the weather** algo indispuesto; **under way** en camino
un'der•age' *adj* menor de edad
un'der•bid' *v* (*pret & pp* **-bid;** *ger* **-bidding**) *tr* ofrecer menos que
un'der•brush' *s* maleza
un'der•car'riage *s* carro inferior; (aer) tren *m* de aterrizaje
un'der•clothes' *s* ropa interior
un'der•con•sump'tion *s* infraconsumo
un'der•cov'er *adj* secreto
underdeveloped [ˌʌndərdɪˈvɛləpt] *adj* subdesarrollado
un'der•dog' *s* víctima, perdidoso; **the underdogs** los de abajo
underdone [ˈʌndərˌdʌn] *adj* a medio asar, soasado
un'der•es'ti•mate' *tr* subestimar
un'der•gar'ment *s* prenda de vestir interior
un'der•go' *v* (*pret* **-went;** *pp* **-gone**) *tr* experimentar; sufrir, padecer
un'der•grad'uate *adj* no graduado; (*course*) para el bachillerato || *s* alumno no graduado de universidad
un'der•ground' *adj* subterráneo; clandestino || *adv* bajo tierra; ocultamente || *s* ferrocarril subterráneo; movimiento de resistencia
un'der•growth' *s* maleza
underhanded [ˈʌndərˈhændɪd] *adj* clandestino, taimado, disimulado
un'der•line' o **un'der•line'** *tr* subrayar
underling [ˈʌndərlɪŋ] *s* subordinado, secuaz *m* servil
un'der•mine' *tr* socavar, minar
underneath [ˌʌndərˈniθ] *adj* inferior, más bajo || *adv* debajo || *prep* debajo de || *s* parte baja, superficie *f* inferior
undernourished [ˌʌndərˈnʌrɪʃt] *adj* desnutrido
un'der•nour'ish•ment *s* desnutrición
un'der•pass' *s* paso inferior
un'der•pay' *s* pago insuficiente || *v* (*pret & pp* **-paid**) *tr & intr* pagar insuficientemente

un'der•pin' *v* (*pret & pp* **-pinned;** *ger* **-pinning**) *tr* apuntalar, socalzar
underprivileged [,ʌndərˈprɪvɪlɪdʒd] *adj* desheredado, desamparado
un'der•rate' *tr* menospreciar
un'der•score' *tr* subrayar
un'der•sea' *adj* submarino ‖ **un'der•sea'** *adv* debajo de la superficie del mar
un'der•sec're•tar'y *s* (*pl* **-ies**) subsecretario
un'der•sell' *v* (*pret & pp* **-sold**) *tr* vender a menor precio que; (*for less than the actual value*) malbaratar
un'der•shirt' *s* camiseta
undersigned [ˈʌndər,saɪnd] *adj* infrascrito, subscrito
un'der•skirt' *s* enaguas, refajo
un'der•stand' *v* (*pret & pp* **-stood**) *tr* entender, comprender; sobrentender, subentender (*una cosa que no está expresa*) ‖ *intr* entender, comprender
understandable [,ʌndərˈstændəbəl] *adj* comprensible
understanding [,ʌndərˈstændɪŋ] *adj* entendedor; (*tolerant, sympathetic*) comprensivo ‖ *s* comprensión; (*intellectual faculty, mind*) entendimiento; (*agreement*) acuerdo; **to come to an understanding** llegar a un acuerdo
un'der•stud'y *s* (*pl* **-ies**) sobresaliente *mf*
un'der•take' *v* (*pret* **-took;** *pp* **-taken**) *tr* emprender; (*to agree to perform*) comprometerse a
undertaker [,ʌndərˈtekər] o [ˈʌndər,tekər] *s* empresario ‖ (ˈʌndər,tekər] *s* empresario de pompas fúnebres, director *m* de funeraria
undertaking [,ʌndərˈtekɪŋ] *s* (*task*) empresa; (*pledge*) empeño ‖ [ˈʌndər,tekɪŋ] *s* (*business of funeral director*) funeraria
un'der•tak'ing establishment *s* funeraria, empresa de pompas fúnebres
un'der•tone' *s* voz baja; (*background sound*) fondo; color apagado
un'der•tow' *s* (*countercurrent below surface*) contracorriente *f;* (*on the beach*) resaca
un'der•wear' *s* ropa interior, prendas interiores
un'der•world' *s* (*criminal world*) inframundo, bajos fondos sociales; (*the earth*) mundo terrenal; (*pagan world of the dead*) averno, infierno; (*world under the water*) mundo submarino; (*opposite side of earth*) antípodas
un'der•write' *v* (*pret* **-wrote;** *pp* **-written**) *tr* subscribir; (*to insure*) asegurar
un'der•writ'er *s* subscritor *m;* asegurador *m;* compañía aseguradora
undeserved [,ʌndɪˈzʌrvd] *adj* inmerecido
undesirable [,ʌndɪˈzaɪrəbəl] *adj & s* indeseable *mf*
undetachable [,ʌndɪˈtætʃəbəl] *adj* inamovible
undignified [ʌnˈdɪgnɪ,faɪd] *adj* poco digno, poco grave, indecoroso
undiscernible [,ʌndɪˈzʌrnɪbəl] o [,ʌndɪˈsʌrnəbəl] *adj* imperceptible, invisible
un•do' *v* (*pret* **-did;** *pp* **-done**) *tr* deshacer; anular, borrar; arruinar
undoing [ʌnˈdu•ɪŋ] *s* destrucción, pérdida, ruina
undone [ʌnˈdʌn] *adj* sin hacer, por hacer; **to come undone** deshacerse, desatarse; **to leave nothing undone** no dejar nada por hacer
undoubtedly [ʌnˈdaʊtɪdli] *adv* indudablemente, sin duda
undramatic [,ʌndrəˈmætɪk] *adj* poco dramático
undress [ˈʌn,drɛs] o [ʌnˈdrɛs] *s* traje *m* de casa; vestido de calle; (mil) traje de cuartel ‖ [ʌnˈdrɛs] *tr* desnudar; desvendar (*una herida*) ‖ desnudarse
undrinkable [ʌnˈdrɪŋkəbəl] *adj* impotable
undue [ʌnˈdju] *adj* indebido
undulate [ˈʌndjə,let] *intr* ondular
unduly [ʌnˈdjuli] *adv* indebidamente
undying [ʌnˈdaɪ•ɪŋ] *adj* imperecedero
unearned increment [ʌnˈʌrnd] *s* plusvalía
unearth [ʌnˈʌrθ] *tr* desenterrar
unearthly [ʌnˈʌrθli] *adj* sobrenatural; fantástico, espectral; extraordinario
uneasy [ʌnˈizi] *adj* (*worried*) inquieto; (*constrained*) encogido, embarazado
uneatable [ʌnˈitəbəl] *adj* incomible
uneconomic(al) [,ʌnikəˈnɑmɪk(əl)] *adj* antieconómico
uneducated [ʌnˈɛdjə,ketɪd] *adj* ineducado, sin instrucción; chontal
unemployed [,ʌnɛmˈplɔɪd] *adj* desocupado, desempleado; improductivo
unemployment [,ʌnɛmˈplɔɪmənt] *s* desocupación, desempleo
unemployment insurance *s* seguro de desempleo o desocupación, seguro contra el paro obrero
unending [ʌnˈɛndɪŋ] *adj* interminable
unequal [ʌnˈikwəl] *adj* desigual; **to be unequal to** (*a task*) no estar a la altura de
unequaled o **unequalled** [ʌnˈikwəld] *adj* inigualado
unerring [ʌnˈʌrɪŋ] o [ʌnˈɛrɪŋ] *adj* infalible, seguro
unessential [,ʌnɛsɛnʃəl] *adj* no esencial
uneven [ʌnˈivən] *adj* desigual; (*number*) impar
unexceptionable [,ʌnɛkˈsɛpʃənəbəl] *adj* intachable, irreprensible
unexpected [,ʌnɛkˈspɛktɪd] *adj* inesperado
unexplained [,ʌnɛkˈsplend] *adj* inexplicado
unexplored [,ʌnɛkˈsplord] *adj* inexplorado
unexposed [,ʌnɛkˈspozd] *adj* (phot) inexpuesto
unfading [ʌnˈfedɪŋ] *adj* inmarcesible
unfailing [ʌnˈfelɪŋ] *adj* indefectible; (*inexhaustible*) inagotable
unfair [ʌnˈfɛr] *adj* injusto; desleal, doble, falso; (sport) sucio
unfaithful [ʌnˈfeθfəl] *adj* infiel
unfamiliar [,ʌnfəˈmɪljər] *adj* poco familiar; poco familiarizado
unfasten [ʌnˈfæsən] *tr* desatacar, desatar, soltar
unfathomable [ʌnˈfæðəməbəl] *adj* insondable
unfavorable [ʌnˈfevərəbəl] *adj* desfavorable

unfeathered [ʌn'fɛðərd] *adj* implume
unfeeling [ʌn'filɪŋ] *adj* insensible
unfetter [ʌn'fɛtər] *tr* desencadenar
unfilled [ʌn'fɪld] *adj* no lleno; por complir, pendiente
unfinished [ʌn'fɪnɪʃt] *adj* sin acabar; imperfecto, mal acabado; (*business*) pendiente
unfit [ʌn'fɪt] *adj* impropio, incapaz, inhábil; inservible, inútil
unfold [ʌn'fold] *tr* desplegar || *intr* desplegarse
unforeseeable [,ʌnfor'si•əbəl] *adj* imprevisible
unforeseen [,ʌnfor'sin] *adj* imprevisto
unforgettable [,ʌnfər'gɛtəbəl] *adj* inolvidable
unforgivable [,ʌnfər'gɪvəbəl] *adj* imperdonable
unfortunate [ʌn'fɔrtjənɪt] *adj & s* desgraciado
unfounded [ʌn'faʊndɪd] *adj* infundado
unfreeze [ʌn'friz] *tr* deshelar; desbloquear (*el crédito*)
unfriendly [ʌn'frɛndli] *adj* inamistoso; desfavorable
unfruitful [ʌn'frutfəl] *adj* infructuoso
unfulfilled [,ʌnfəl'fɪld] *adj* incumplido
unfurl [ʌn'fʌrl] *tr* desplegar, extender
unfurnished [ʌn'fʌrnɪʃt] *adj* desamueblado
ungainly [ʌn'genli] *adj* desgarbado, desmañado
ungentlemanly [ʌn'dʒɛntəlmənli] *adj* poco caballeroso, descortés
ungird [ʌn'gʌrd] *tr* desceñir
ungodly [ʌn'gɑdli] *adj* impío, irreligioso; (*dreadful*) (coll) atroz
ungracious [ʌn'greʃəs] *adj* descortés; desagradable
ungrammatical [,ʌngrə'mætɪkəl] *adj* ingramatical
ungrateful [ʌn'gretfəl] *adj* ingrato, desagradecido
ungrudgingly [ʌn'grʌdʒɪŋli] *adj* de buena gana, sin quejarse
unguarded [ʌn'gɑrdɪd] *adj* indefenso; descuidado; (*moment*) de inadvertencia
unguent ['ʌŋgwənt] *s* ungüento
unhandy [ʌn'hændi] *adj* inmanejable; (*awkward*) desmañado
unhappiness [ʌn'hæpɪnɪs] *s* infelicidad
unhap•py [ʌn'hæpi] *adj* (*comp* **-pier;** *super* **-piest**) infeliz; (*unlucky*) desgraciado; (*fateful*) aciago
unharmed [ʌn'hɑrmd] *adj* indemne
unharmonious [,ʌnhɑr'monɪ•əs] *adj* inarmónico
unharness [ʌn'hɑrnɪs] *tr* desenjaezar, desguarnecer; desenganchar
unhealthy [ʌn'hɛlθi] *adj* malsano
unheard-of [ʌn'hʌrd,ɑv] *adj* inaudito
unhinge [ʌn'hɪndʒ] *tr* desgonzar; (fig) desequilibrar, trastornar
unhitch [ʌn'hɪtʃ] *tr* desenganchar
unho•ly [ʌn'holi] *adj* (*comp* **-lier;** *super* **-liest**) impío, malo, profano
unhook [ʌn'hʊk] *tr* desabrochar; desenganchar; (*to take down from a hook*) descolgar
unhoped-for [ʌn'hopt,fɔr] *adj* inesperado, no esperado
unhorse [ʌn'hɔrs] *tr* desarzonar
unhurt [ʌn'hʌrt] *adj* incólume, ileso
unicorn ['junɪ,kɔrn] *s* unicornio
unidentified flying object (UFO) *s* objeto volante no identificado (ovni)
unification [,junɪfɪ'keʃən] *s* unificación
uniform ['junɪ,fɔrm] *adj & s* uniforme *m* || *tr* uniformar
uniformi•ty [,junɪ'fɔrmɪti] *s* (*pl* **-ties**) uniformidad
uni•fy ['junɪ,faɪ] *v* (*pret & pp* **-fied**) *tr* unificar
unilateral [,junɪ'lætərəl] *adj* unilateral
unimpeachable [,ʌnɪm'pitʃəbəl] *adj* irrecusable, intachable
unimportant [,ʌnɪm'pɔrtənt] *adj* poco importante; intrascendente
uninhabited [,ʌnɪn'hæbɪtɪd] *adj* inhabitado
uninspired [,ʌnɪn'spaɪrd] *adj* sin inspiración; aburrido, fastidioso
unintelligent [,ʌnɪn'tɛlɪdʒənt] *adj* ininteligente
unintelligible [,ʌnɪn'tɛlɪdʒɪbəl] *adj* ininteligible
uninterested [ʌn'ɪntrɪstɪd] o [ʌn'ɪntə,rɛstɪd] *adj* desinteresado
uninteresting [ʌn'ɪntə,rɛstɪŋ] *adj* poco interesante
uninterrupted [,ʌnɪntə'rʌptɪd] *adj* ininterrumpido
union ['junjən] *s* unión; (*organization of workmen*) gremio obrero, sindicato; unión matrimonial
unionize ['junjə,naɪz] *tr* agremiar || *intr* agremiarse
union shop *s* taller *m* de obreros agremiados
union suit *s* traje *m* interior de una sola pieza
unique [jʊ'nik] *adj* único
unison ['junisən] *s* unisonancia; **in unison (with)** al unísono (de)
unit ['junɪt] *adj* unitario || *s* unidad; (mach & elec) grupo
unite [jʊ'naɪt] *tr* unir || *intr* unirse
united [jʊ'naɪtɪd] *adj* unido
United Kingdom *s* Reino Unido
United Nations *spl* Naciones Unidas
United States *adj* estadounidense || **the United States** *s* los Estados Unidos *mpl;* Estados Unidos *msg*
uni•ty ['junɪti] *s* (*pl* **-ties**) unidad
univ. *abbr* **universal, university**
universal [,junɪ'vʌrsəl] *adj* universal
universal joint *s* cardán *m*, junta universal
universal product code (UPC) *s* código universal de producto
universe ['junɪ,vʌrs] *s* universo
universi•ty [,junɪ'vʌrsɪti] *adj* universitario || *s* (*pl* **-ties**) universidad
unjust [ʌn'dʒʌst] *adj* injusto
unjustified [ʌn'dʒʌstɪ,faɪd] *adj* injustificado
unkempt [ʌn'kɛmpt] *adj* despeinado
unkind [ʌn'kaɪnd] *adj* poco amable; duro, despiadado
unknowable [ʌn'no•əbəl] *adj* inconocible, insabible

unknowingly [ʌnˈno•ɪŋli] *adv* desconocidamente, sin saberlo
unknown [ʌnˈnon] *adj* desconocido, ignoto, incógnito || *s* desconocido; (math) incógnita
unknown quantity *s* (math & fig) incógnita
unknown soldier *s* soldado desconocido
unlace [ʌnˈles] *tr* desenlazar; desatar (*los cordones del zapato*)
unlatch [ʌnˈlætʃ] *tr* abrir levantando el picaporte
unlawful [ʌnˈlɔfəl] *adj* ilegal
unleaded gasoline [ʌnˈlɛdɪd] *s* gasolina sin plomo
unleash [ʌnˈliʃ] *tr* destraillar; soltar, desencadenar
unleavened [ʌnˈlɛvənd] *adj* ázimo
unless [ʌnˈlɛs] *conj* a menos que, a no ser que
unlettered [ʌnˈlɛtərd] *adj* iletrado, indocto; sin rotular; (*illiterate*) analfabeto
unlike [ʌnˈlaɪk] *adj* desemejante; desemejante de; (*poles of a magnet*) (elec) de nombres contrarios; (elec) de signo contrario || *prep* a diferencia de
unlikely [ʌnˈlaɪkli] *adj* improbable
unlimber [ʌnˈlɪmbər] *tr* preparar para la acción || *intr* prepararse para la acción
unlined [ʌnˈlaɪnd] *adj* (*coat*) sin forro; (*paper*) sin rayar; (*face*) sin arrugas
unload [ʌnˈlod] *tr* descargar; (coll) deshacerse de || *intr* descargar
unloading [ʌnˈlodɪŋ] *s* descarga, descargue *m*
unlock [ʌnˈlɑk] *tr* abrir (*p.ej., una puerta*); (typ) desapretar
unloose [ʌnˈlus] *tr* aflojar, soltar, desatar
unloved [ʌnˈlʌvd] *adj* desamado
unlovely [ʌnˈlʌvli] *adj* desgraciado
unluck•y [ʌnˈlʌki] *adj* (*comp* **-ier;** *super* **-iest**) desgraciado, desdichado; aciago, nefasto; de mala suerte; **to be unlucky** quedar mal parado
un•make [ʌnˈmek] *v* (*pret & pp* **-made** [ˈmed]) *tr* deshacer; destruir
unmanageable [ʌnˈmænɪdʒəbəl] *adj* inmanejable
unmanly [ʌnˈmænli] *adj* afeminado; bajo, cobarde
unmannerly [ʌnˈmænərli] *adj* descortés, malcriado
unmarketable [ʌnˈmɑrkɪtəbəl] *adj* incomerciable
unmarriageable [ʌnˈmærɪdʒəbəl] *adj* incasable
unmarried [ʌnˈmærid] *adj* soltero
unmask [ʌnˈmæsk] *tr* desenmascarar || *intr* desenmascararse
unmatchable [ʌnˈmætʃəbəl] *adj* incomparable, sin igual; (*price*) incompetible
unmerciful [ʌnˈmʌrsɪfəl] *adj* despiadado, inclemente
unmesh [ʌnˈmɛʃ] *tr* desengranar || *intr* desengranarse
unmindful [ʌnˈmaɪndfəl] *adj* desatento, descuidado; **to be unmindful of** olvidar, no pensar en
unmistakable [ˌʌnmɪsˈtekəbəl] *adj* inequívoco, inconfundible
unmixed [ʌnˈmɪkst] *adj* puro, sin mezcla
unmoor [ʌnˈmʊr] *tr* desamarrar (*un buque*); desaferrar (*las áncoras*)
unmotivated [ˌʌnˈmotɪˌvetɪd] *adj* inmotivado
unmoved [ʌnˈmuvd] *adj* fijo, inmoto; impasible
unmuzzle [ˌʌnˈmʌzəl] *tr* desbozalar
unnatural [ʌnˈnætʃərəl] *adj* innatural; (*artificial, forced*) afectado; anormal; inhumano
unnecessary [ʌnˈnɛsəˌsɛri] *adj* innecessario
unnerve [ʌnˈnʌrv] *tr* acobardar, trastornar
unnoticeable [ʌnˈnotɪsəbəl] *adj* imperceptible
unnoticed [ʌnˈnotɪst] *adj* inadvertido
unobliging [ˌʌnəˈblaɪdʒɪŋ] *adj* poco servicial, poco amable
unobserved [ˌʌnəbˈzʌrvd] *adj* inadvertido, sin ser visto
unobtainable [ˌʌnəbˈtenəbəl] *adj* inencontrable, inasequible
unobtrusive [ˌʌnəbˈtrusɪv] *adj* discreto, reservado
unoccupied [ʌnˈɑkjəˌpaɪd] *adj* libre, vacante; (*not busy*) desocupado
unofficial [ˌʌnəˈfɪʃəl] *adj* extraoficial, oficioso
unopened [ʌnˈopənd] *adj* sin abrir; (*book*) no cortado
unorthodox [ʌnˈɔrθəˌdɑks] *adj* inortodoxo
unpack [ʌnˈpæk] *tr* desembalar, desempaquetar
unpalatable [ʌnˈpælətəbəl] *adj* desabrido, ingustable
unparalleled [ʌnˈpærəˌlɛld] *adj* incomparable, sin par, sin igual
unpardonable [ʌnˈpɑrdənəbəl] *adj* imperdonable
unpatriotic [ˌʌnpetrɪˈɑtɪk] o [ˌʌnpætrɪˈɑtɪk] *adj* antipatriótico
unperceived [ˌʌnpərˈsivd] *adj* inadvertido
unperturbable [ˌʌnpərˈtʌrbəbəl] *adj* infracto, imperturbable
unpleasant [ʌnˈplɛzənt] *adj* antipático, desagradable; sangrigordo, sangripesado; bofe (CAm)
unpopular [ʌnˈpɑpjələr] *adj* impopular
unpopularity [ʌnˌpɑpjəˈlærɪti] *s* impopularidad
unprecedented [ʌnˈprɛsɪˌdɛntɪd] *adj* sin precedente, inaudito
unprejudiced [ʌnˈprɛdʒədɪst] *adj* sin prejuicios, imparcial
unpremeditated [ˌʌnprɪˈmɛdɪˌtetɪd] *adj* impremeditado
unprepared [ˌʌnprɪˈpɛrd] *adj* desprevenido; falto de preparación
unprepossessing [ˌʌnpripəˈzɛsɪŋ] *adj* poco atrayente
unpresentable [ˌʌnprɪˈzɛntəbəl] *adj* impresentable
unpretentious [ˌʌnprɪˈtɛnʃəs] *adj* modesto, sencillo
unprincipled [ʌnˈprɪnsɪpəld] *adj* sin principios, sin conciencia

unproductive [ˌʌnprəˈdʌktɪv] *adj* improductivo
unprofitable [ʌnˈprɑfɪtəbəl] *adj* no provechoso, inútil
unpronounceable [ˌʌnprəˈnaʊnsəbəl] *adj* impronunciable
unpropitious [ˌʌnprəˈpɪʃəs] *adj* impropicio
unpublished [ʌnˈpʌblɪʃt] *adj* inédito
unpunished [ʌnˈpʌnɪʃt] *adj* impune
unpurchasable [ʌnˈpʌrtʃəsəbəl] *adj* incomprable
unquenchable [ʌnˈkwɛntʃəbəl] *adj* inextinguible
unquestionable [ʌnˈkwɛstʃənəbəl] *adj* incuestionable
unrav•el [ʌnˈrævəl] *v* (*pret & pp* **-eled** o **-elled;** *ger* **-eling** o **-elling**) *tr* deshebrar; desenredar, desenmarañar || *intr* desenredarse, desenmarañarse
unreachable [ʌnˈritʃəbəl] *adj* inalcanzable
unreal [ʌnˈri•əl] *adj* irreal
unreali•ty [ˌʌnrɪˌælɪti] *s* (*pl* **-ties**) irrealidad
unreasonable [ʌnˈrizənəbəl] *adj* irrazonable, desrazonable
unrecognizable [ʌnˈrɛkəgˌnaɪzəbəl] *adj* irreconocible
unreel [ʌnˈril] *tr* desenrollar || *intr* desenrollarse
unrefined [ˌʌnrɪˌfaɪnd] *adj* no refinado, impuro; grosero, rudo, tosco
unrelenting [ˌʌnrɪˈlɛntɪŋ] *adj* inexorable, inflexible, implacable
unreliable [ˌʌnrɪˈlaɪ•əbəl] *adj* indigno de confianza, informal
unremitting [ˌʌnrɪˈmɪtɪŋ] *adj* constante, incesante; infatigable
unrenewable [ˌʌnrɪˈnju•əbəl] o [ˌʌnrɪˈnu•əbəl] *adj* irrenovable; (com) improrrogable
unrented [ʌnˈrɛntɪd] *adj* desalquilado
unrepentant [ˌʌnrɪˈpɛntənt] *adj* impenitente
unrequited love [ˌʌnrɪˈkwaɪtɪd] *s* amor no correspondido
unresponsive [ˌʌnrɪˈspɑnsɪv] *adj* insensible, frío, desinteresado
unrest [ʌnˈrɛst] *s* intranquilidad, inquietud; alboroto, desorden *m*
un•rig [ʌnˈrɪg] *v* (*pret & pp* **-rigged;** *ger* **-rigging**) *tr* (naut) desaparejar
unrighteous [ʌnˈraɪtʃəs] *adj* injusto, malvado, vicioso
unripe [ʌnˈraɪp] *adj* inmaturo, verde; prematuro, precoz
unrivaled o **unrivalled** [ʌnˈraɪvəld] *adj* sin rival, sin par
unroll [ʌnˈrol] *tr* desenrollar, desplegar
unromantic [ˌʌnroˈmæntɪk] *adj* poco romántico
unruffled [ʌnˈrʌfəld] *adj* tranquilo, sereno
unruly [ʌnˈruli] *adj* ingobernable, indómito, revoltoso
unsaddle [ʌnˈsædəl] *tr* desensillar (*un caballo*); desarzonar (*al jinete*)
unsafe [ʌnˈsef] *adj* inseguro, peligroso
unsaid [ʌnˈsɛd] *adj* callado, no dicho
unsalable [ʌnˈseləbəl] *adj* invendible
unsanitary [ʌnˈsænɪˌtɛri] *adj* antihigiénico, insalubre
unsatisfactory [ʌnˌsætɪsˈfæktəri] *adj* insatisfactorio, poco satisfactorio
unsatisfied [ʌnˈsætɪsˌfaɪd] *adj* insatisfecho
unsavory [ʌnˈsevəri] *adj* desabrido; (fig) infame, deshonroso
unscathed [ʌnˈskeðd] *adj* ileso, sano y salvo
unscientific [ˌʌnsaɪ•ənˈtɪfɪk] *adj* anticientífico
unscrew [ʌnˈskru] *tr* destornillar || *intr* destornillarse
unscrupulous [ʌnˈskrupjələs] *adj* inescrupuloso
unseal [ʌnˈsil] *tr* desellar; (fig) abrir
unseasonable [ʌnˈsizənəbəl] *adj* intempestivo, inoportuno
unseaworthy [ʌnˈsiˌwʌrði] *adj* innavegable
unseemly [ʌnˈsimli] *adj* impropio, indecoroso, indigno
unseen [ʌnˈsin] *adj* invisible, oculto
unselfish [ʌnˈsɛlfɪʃ] *adj* desinteresado, generoso, altruísta
unsettled [ʌnˈsɛtəld] *adj* inhabitado, despoblado; sin residencia fija; indeciso; descompuesto; (*bills*) por pagar
unshackle [ʌnˈʃækəl] *tr* desherrar, desencadenar
unshaken [ʌnˈʃekən] *adj* imperturbado
unshapely [ʌnˈʃepli] *adj* desproporcionado, mal formado
unshatterable [ʌnˈʃætərəbəl] *adj* inastillable
unshaven [ʌnˈʃevən] *adj* sin afeitar
unsheathe [ʌnˈʃið] *tr* desenvainar
unshod [ʌnˈʃɑd] *adj* descalzo; (*horse*) desherrado
unshrinkable [ʌnˈʃrɪŋkəbəl] *adj* inencogible
unsightly [ʌnˈsaɪtli] *adj* feo, de aspecto malo, repugnante
unsinkable [ʌnˈsɪŋkəbəl] *adj* insumergible
unskilled [ʌnˈskɪld] *adj* inexperto
unskilled laborer *s* bracero, peón *m*
unskillful [ʌnˈskɪlfəl] *adj* desmañado
unsnarl [ʌnˈsnɑrl] *tr* desenredar
unsociable [ʌnˈsoʃəbəl] *adj* insociable, huraño
unsold [ʌnˈsold] *adj* invendido
unsolder [ʌnˈsɑdər] *tr* desoldar; (fig) desunir, separar
unsophisticated [ˌʌnsəˈfɪstɪˌketɪd] *adj* ingenuo, natural, sencillo
unsound [ʌnˈsaʊnd] *adj* poco firme; falso, erróneo; (*decayed*) podrido; (*sleep*) ligero
unsown [ʌnˈson] *adj* yermo, no sembrado
unspeakable [ʌnˈspikəbəl] *adj* indecible, inefable; (*atrocious, infamous*) incalificable
unsportsmanlike [ʌnˈsportsmənˌlaɪk] *adj* antideportivo
unstable [ʌnˈstebəl] *adj* inestable
unsteady [ʌnˈstɛdi] *adj* inseguro, inestable; irresoluto, inconstante; poco juicioso
unstinted [ʌnˈstɪntɪd] *adj* no escatimado, generoso, liberal
unstitch [ʌnˈstɪtʃ] *tr* descoser
un•stop [ʌnˈstɑp] *v* (*pret & pp* **-stopped;** *ger* **-stopping**) *tr* destaponar
unstressed [ʌnˈstrɛst] *adj* sin énfasis; (*syllable*) inacentuado

unstrung [ʌn'strʌŋ] *adj* nervioso, trastornado
unsuccessful [,ʌnsək'sɛsfəl] *adj* (*person*) desairado; (*undertaking*) impróspero; **to be unsuccessful** no tener éxito
unsuitable [ʌn'sutəbəl] o [ʌn'sjutəbəl] *adj* inadecuado, inconveniente
unsurpassable [,ʌnsər'pæsəbəl] *adj* insuperable
unsuspected [,ʌnsəs'pɛktɪd] *adj* insospechado
unswerving [ʌn'swʌrvɪŋ] *adj* firme, inmutable, resoluto
unsymmetrical [,ʌnsɪ'mɛtrɪkəl] *adj* asimétrico, disimétrico
unsympathetic [,ʌnsɪmpə'θɛtɪk] *adj* incompasivo, indiferente
unsystematic(al) [,ʌnsɪstə'mætɪk(əl)] *adj* poco sistemático, sin sistema
untactful [ʌn'tæktfəl] *adj* indiscreto, falto de tacto
untamed [ʌn'temd] *adj* indomado, bravío
untangle [ʌn'tæŋgəl] *tr* desenredar, desenmarañar
unteachable [ʌn'titʃəbəl] *adj* indócil
untenable [ʌn'tɛnəbəl] *adj* insostenible
unthankful [ʌn'θæŋkfəl] *adj* ingrato, desagradecido
unthinkable [ʌn'θɪŋkəbəl] *adj* impensable
unthinking [ʌn'θɪŋkɪŋ] *adj* irreflexivo, desatento; irracional, instintivo
untidy [ʌn'taɪdi] *adj* desaseado, desaliñado; descachalandrado
un•tie [ʌn'taɪ] *v* (*pret & pp* **-tied;** *ger* **-tying**) *tr* desatar; deshacer (*un nudo, una cuerda*); (*to free from restraint*) soltar; resolver || *intr* desatarse
until [ʌn'tɪl] *prep* hasta || *conj* hasta que; **to wait until** aguardar a que, esperar a que
untillable [ʌn'tɪləbəl] *adj* incultivable
untimely [ʌn'taɪmli] *adj* intempestivo
untiring [ʌn'taɪrɪŋ] *adj* incansable
untold [ʌn'told] *adj* nunca dicho; (*uncounted*) innumerable, incalculable
untouchable [ʌn'tʌtʃəbəl] *adj* intangible || *s* intocable *mf*
untouched [ʌn'tʌtʃt] *adj* intacto; íntegro; impasible; no mencionado
untoward [ʌn'tord] *adj* desfavorable; indecoroso
untrammeled o **untrammelled** [ʌn'træməld] *adj* libre, sin trabas
untried [ʌn'traɪd] *adj* no probado, no ensayado
untroubled [ʌn'trʌbləd] *adj* tranquilo, sosegado
untrue [ʌn'tru] *adj* falso; infiel
untrustworthy [ʌn'trʌst,wʌrði] *adj* indigno de confianza
untruth [ʌn'truθ] *s* falsedad, mentira
untruthful [ʌn'truθfəl] *adj* falso, mentiroso
untwist [ʌn'twɪst] *tr* destorcer || *intr* destorcerse
unused [ʌn'juzd] *adj* inutilizado, no usado; nuevo; **unused to** [ʌn'juzdtu] o [ʌn'justu] *adj* no acostumbrado a
unusual [ʌn'juʒu•əl] *adj* inusual, insólito
unutterable [ʌn'ʌtərəbəl] *adj* indecible, inexpresable
unvanquished [ʌn'væŋkwɪʃt] *adj* invicto
unvarnished [ʌn'vɑrnɪʃt] *adj* sin barnizar; (fig) sencillo, sin adornos
unveil [ʌn'vel] *tr* quitar el velo a; descubrir, develar, inaugurar, (*una estatua*) || *intr* quitarse el velo
unveiling [ʌn'velɪŋ] *s* develación, inauguración
unventilated [ʌn'vɛntɪ,letɪd] *adj* sin ventilar
unvoice [ʌn'vɔɪs] *tr* afonizar, ensordecer || *intr* afonizarse, ensordecerse
unwanted [ʌn'wɑntɪd] *adj* indeseado
unwarranted [ʌn'wɑrəntɪd] *adj* injustificado; no autorizado; sin garantía
unwary [ʌn'wɛri] *adj* incauto, imprudente
unwavering [ʌn'wevərɪŋ] *adj* firme, determinado, resuelto
unwelcome [ʌn'wɛlkəm] *adj* mal acogido; importuno, molesto
unwell [ʌn'wɛl] *adj* indispuesto, enfermo; (coll) menstruante
unwholesome [ʌn'holsəm] *adj* insalubre
unwieldy [ʌn'wildi] *adj* inmanejable, abultado, pesado
unwilling [ʌn'wɪlɪŋ] *adj* desinclinado, maldispuesto, renuente
unwillingly [ʌn'wɪlɪŋli] *adv* de mala gana
un•wind [ʌn'waɪnd] *v* (*pret & pp* **-wound** ['waʊnd]) *tr* desenvolver; (*rewind*) rebobinar || *intr* desenvolverse; distenderse (*el muelle del reloj*)
unwise [ʌn'waɪz] *adj* indiscreto, malaconsejado
unwished-for [ʌn'wɪʃt,fɔr] *adj* indeseado
unwitting [ʌn'wɪtɪŋ] *adj* inadvertido, inconsciente
unwonted [ʌn'wʌntɪd] *adj* poco común, raro, insólito
unworldly [ʌn'wʌrldi] *adj* no terrenal, no mundano, espiritual
unworthy [ʌn'wʌrði] *adj* indigno, desmerecedor
un•wrap [ʌn'ræp] *v* (*pret & pp* **-wrapped;** *ger* **wrapping**) *tr* desenvolver, desempapelar
unwrinkle [ʌn'rɪŋkəl] *tr* desarrugar || *intr* desarrugarse
unwritten [ʌn'rɪtən] *adj* no escrito; (*blank*) en blanco; oral
unyielding [ʌn'jildɪŋ] *adj* firme, inflexible, terco, reacio
unyoke [ʌn'jok] *tr* desuncir
up [ʌp] *adj* ascendente; alto, elevado; derecho, en pie; terminado; cumplido; levantado de la cama; **to be up and about** estar levantado (*el que estaba enfermo*) || *s* subida; **ups and downs** altibajos, vicisitudes || *adv* arriba; en el aire; hacia arriba; al norte; **to be up** estar levantado; vencer (*un plazo*); **to be up in arms** estar sobre las armas; protestar vehementemente; **to be up to a person** tocarle a una persona; **to get up** levantarse; **to go up** subir; **to keep up** mantener; continuar; mantenerse firme; **to keep up with** correr parejas con; **up above**

allá arriba; **up against it** (slang) en apuros; **up to** hasta; (*capable of*) a la altura de; (*informed of*) al corriente de; (*scheming*) armando, tramando; **what is up?** ¿qué pasa? ‖ *prep* subiendo; **up the river** río arriba; **up the street** calle arriba
up-and-coming [ˈʌpənˈkʌmɪŋ] *adj* (coll) prometedor
up-and-doing [ˈʌpənˈdu•ɪŋ] *adj* (coll) emprendedor
up-and-up [ˈʌpənˈʌp] *s*—**on the up-and-up** (coll) mejorándose; (coll) abiertamente, sin dolo
up•braid′ *tr* regañar, reprender
upbringing [ˈʌp,brɪŋɪŋ] *s* educación, crianza
UPC *abbr* **universal product code**
up′coun′try *adv* (coll) hacia el interior, tierra adentro ‖ *s* (coll) interior *m* del país
up•date′ *tr* poner al día
upheaval [ʌpˈhivəl] *s* trastorno, cataclismo
up′hill′ *adj* ascendente; arduo, difícil, penoso ‖ **up′hill′** *adv* cuesta arriba
up•hold′ *v* (*pret & pp* **-held**) *tr* levantar; apoyar, sostener; defender
upholster [ʌpˈholstər] *tr* tapizar
upholsterer [ʌpˈholstərər] *s* tapicero
upholster•y [ʌpˈholstəri] *s* (*pl* **-ies**) tapicería
up′keep′ *s* conservación, manutención; gastos de conservación, gastos de entretenimiento
upland [ˈʌplənd] o [ˈʌplænd] *adj* alto, elevado ‖ *s* tierra alta, terreno elevado
up′lift′ *s* (*lifting*) elevación, levantamiento; mejora social; (*moral or spiritual improvement*) edificación ‖ **up•lift′** *tr* elevar, levantar; edificar
upon [əˈpɑn] *prep* en, sobre, encima de; **upon** + *ger* al + *inf*, p.ej., **upon arriving** al llegar; **upon my word!** ¡por mi palabra!
upper [ˈʌpər] *adj* alto, superior; (*country*) interior; (*clothing*) exterior ‖ *s* (*of shoe*) pala; **on one's uppers** con las suelas gastadas; (coll) andrajoso, pobre, sin blanca
upper berth *s* litera alta, cama alta
upper case *s* (typ) caja alta
upper classes *spl* altas clases
upper hand *s* dominio, ventaia; **to have the upper hand** tener vara alta
upper middle class *s* alta burguesía
up′per•most′ *adj* (el) más alto; (el) principal ‖ *adv* en lo más alto primero, en primer lugar
uppish [ˈʌpɪʃ] *adj* (coll) copetudo, arrogante
up•raise′ *tr* levantar
up′right′ *adj* derecho, vertical; probo, recto ‖ *adv* verticalmente ‖ *s* montante *m*
uprising [ʌpˈraɪzɪŋ] [[ˈʌp,raɪzɪŋ] *s* insurrección, levantamiento
up′roar′ *s* alboroto, conmoción, tumulto
uproarious [ʌpˈrorɪ•əs] *adj* tumultuoso; (*noisy*) ruidoso; (*funny*) muy cómico
up•root′ *tr* desarraigar
up•set′ o **up′set′** *adj* (*overturned*) volcado; trastornado; indispuesto ‖ **up′set′** *s* (*overturn*) vuelco; (*unexpected defeat*) contratiempo; (*disturbance*) trastorno; (*illness*) indisposición, enfermedad ‖ **up•set′** *v* (*pret & pp* **-set; ger -setting**) *tr* volcar; trastornar; indisponer ‖ *intr* volcar
upset price *s* precio mínimo fijado en una subasta
upsetting [ʌpˈsɛtɪŋ] *adj* desconcertante
up′shot′ *s* conclusión, resultado; esencia, quid *m*
up′side′ *s* parte *f* superior, lado superior; **on the upside** (*said of prices*) subiendo
upside down *adv* alrevés, lo de arriba abajo, patas arriba; en confusión, revuelto; **to turn upside down** volcar; trastornar; volcarse; trastornarse
up′stage′ *adj* situado al fondo de la escena; (coll) altanero, arrogante ‖ *adv* al fondo de la escena ‖ **up′stage′** *tr* (coll) mirar por encima del hombro, desairar
up′stairs′ *adj* de arriba ‖ *adv* arriba ‖ *s* piso superior, pisos superiores
upstanding [ʌpˈstændɪŋ] *adj* derecho; gallardo; probo, recto
up′start′ *adj & s* advenedizo
up′stream′ *adv* aguas arriba, río arriba
up′stroke′ *s* carrera ascendente
up′swing′ *s* movimiento hacia arriba; mejora notable; **on the upswing** mejorando notablemente
up′-to-date′ *adj* corriente; reciente, moderno; de última hora, de última moda
up′-to-the-min′ute *adj* al día, de actualidad
up′town′ *adj* de la parte alta de la ciudad ‖ *adv* en la parte alta de la ciudad
up train *s* tren *m* ascendente
up′trend′ *s* tendencia al alza
up′turn′ *s* alza, subida, mejora
upturned [ʌpˈtʌrnd] *adj* revuelto; (*part of clothing*) arremangado; (*nose*) respingada
upward [ˈʌpwərd] *adj* ascendente ‖ *adv* hacia arriba; **upward of** más de
Ural [ˈjʊrəl] *adj* ural ‖ **Urals** *spl* Urales *mpl*
uranium [jʊˈrenɪ•əm] *s* uranio
urban [ˈʌrbən] *adj* urbano (*perteneciente a la ciudad*)
urbane [ʌrˈben] *adj* urbano (*atento, cortés*)
urban guerrilla *s* guerrillero urbano
urbanite [ˈʌrbə,naɪt] *s* ciudadano
urbanity [ʌrˈbænɪti] *s* urbanidad
urbanize [ˈʌrbə,naɪz] *tr* urbanizar
urchin [ˈʌrtʃɪn] *s* pilluelo, galopín *m;* patojo (CAm)
ure•thra [jʊˈriθrə] *s* (*pl* **-thras** o **-thrae** [θri]) uretra
urge [ʌrdʒ] *s* impulso, estímulo ‖ *tr* apremiar, impeler, estimular; pedir instantánedmente; (*to try to persuade*) instar ‖ *intr* instar
urgen•cy [ˈʌrdʒənsi] *s* (*pl* **-cies**) urgencia; instancia, apremio
urgent [ˈʌrdʒənt] *adj* urgente; apremiante
urinal [ˈjʊrɪnəl] *s* (*receptacle*) orinal *m;* (*place*) urinario
urinary [ˈjʊrɪ,nɛri] *adj* urinario
urinate [ˈjʊrɪ,net] *tr* orinar (*p.ej., sangre*) ‖ *intr* orinar, orinarse; (coll) hacer pipí

urine [ˈjʊrɪn] *s* orina, orines *mpl;* (coll) pipí *m*
urn [ʌrn] *s* (*decorative vase*) jarrón *m;* cafetera o tetera con grifo; (*to hold ashes of the dead after cremation*) urna
urology [jʊˈrɑlədʒi] *s* urología
Uruguay [ˈjʊrə,gwaɪ] *s* el Uruguay
Uruguayan [,jʊrəˈgwaɪ•ən] *adj & s* uruguayo
us [ʌs] *pron pers* nos; nosotros; **to us** nos; a nosotros
U.S.A. *abbr* **United States of America, United States Army, Union of South Africa**
usable [ˈjuzəbəl] *adj* aprovechable, utilizable
usage [ˈjusɪdʒ] o [ˈjuzɪdʒ] *s* usanza; (*e.g., of a language*) uso
usage instructions *spl* modo de empleo
use [jus] *s* uso, empleo; utilidad; **in use** en uso; **out of use** desusado; **to be of no use** no servir para nada; **to have no use for** no necesitar; no servirse de; (coll) tener en poco; **to make use of** servirse de || [juz] *tr* usar, emplear, servirse de; **to use badly** maltratar; **to use up** agotar, consumir || *intr* (empléase sólo en el pretérito y se traduce al español con el pretérito imperfecto o el verbo **soler**), p.ej., **I used to go out for a walk every evening** salía de paseo todas las tardes o solía salir de paseo todas las tardes
used [juzd] *adj* (*customarily employed; worn, partly worn-out; accustomed*) usado; **used to** [ˈjuzdtʊ] o [ˈjustʊ] acostumbrado a
useful [ˈjusfəl] *adj* útil
usefulness [ˈjusfəlnɪs] *s* utilidad
useless [ˈjuslɪs] *adj* inservible, inútil
user [ˈjuzər] *s* usuario
usher [ˈʌʃər] *s* (*in a theater*) acomodador *m;* (*doorkeeper*) ujier *m*, portero || *tr* acomodar; **to usher in** anunciar, introducir
U.S.S.R. *abbr* **Union of Soviet Socialist Republics**
usual [ˈjuʒʊ•əl] *adj* usual, acostumbrado; **as usual** como de costumbre
usually [ˈjuʒʊ•əli] *adj* usualmente, de ordinario
usurp [jʊˈzʌrp] *tr* usurpar
usu•ry [ˈjuʒəri] *s* (*pl* **-ries**) usura
utensil [juˈtɛnsɪl] *s* utensilio; **utensils** corotos *mpl*
uter•us [ˈjutərəs] *s* (*pl* **-i** [,aɪ]); útero
utilitarian [,jutɪlɪˈtɛrɪ•ən] *adj* utilitario
utili•ty [juˈtɪlɪti] *s* (*pl* **-ties**) utilidad; empresa de servicio público
utilize [ˈjutɪ,laɪz] *tr* utilizar
utmost [ˈʌt,most] *adj* sumo, extremo, último; más grande, mayor posible; más lejano || *s*— **the utmost** lo sumo, lo mayor, lo más; **to the utmost** a lo sumo, a más no poder; **to do one's utmost** hacer todo lo posible
utopia [juˈtopɪ•ə] *s* utopía
utopian [juˈtopɪ•ən] *adj* utópico, utopista || *s* utopista *mf*
utter [ˈʌtər] *adj* total, absoluto || *tr* proferir, pronunciar; dar (*un suspiro*)
utterance [ˈʌtərəns] *s* expresión, pronunciación; declaración
utterly [ˈʌtərli] *adj* completamente, totalmente, absolutamente
uxoricide [ʌkˈsorɪ,saɪd] *s* (*husband*) uxoricida *m;* (*act*) uxoricidio
uxorious [ʌkˈsorɪ•əs] *adj* uxorio

V

V, v [vi] vigésima segunda letra del alfabeto inglés
v. *abbr* **verb, verse, versus, vide** (Lat) **see, voice, volt, volume**
V. abbr **Venerable, Vice, Viscount, Volunteer**
vacan•cy [ˈvekənsi] *s* (*pl* **-cies**) (*emptiness; gap, opening*) vacío; (*unfilled position or job*) vacancia, vacante *f*, vacío; piso vacante; cargo vacante
vacant [ˈvekənt] *adj* (*empty*) vacío; (*having no occupant; untenanted*) vacante; (*expression, look*) vago; distraído
vacate [ˈveket] *tr* dejar vacante; anular, invalidar, revocar || *intr* (*to move out*) desalojar; (coll) irse, marcharse
vacation [veˈkeʃən] *s* vacaciones; **on vacation** de vacaciones || *intr* tomar vacaciones
vacationist [veˈkeʃənɪst] *s* vacacionista *mf*
vacation with pay *s* vacaciones retribuídas
vaccinate [ˈvæksɪ,net] *tr* vacunar
vaccination [,væksɪˈneʃən] *s* vacunación
vaccine [vækˈsin] *s* vacuna
vacillate [ˈvæsɪ,let] *intr* vacilar
vacillating [ˈvæsɪ,letɪŋ] *adj* vacilante
vacui•ty [væˈkjʊ•ɪti] *s* (*pl* **-ties**) vacuidad
vacu•um [ˈvækjʊ•əm] *s* (*pl* **-ums** o **-a** [ə]) vacío || *tr* (coll) limpiar
vacuum cleaner *s* aspirador *m* de polvo
vacuum tank *s* (aut) aspirador *m* de gasolina, nodriza
vacuum tube *s* tubo de vacío
vagabond [ˈvægə,bɑnd] *adj & s* vagabundo
vagar•y [vəˈgɛri] *s* (*pl* **-ies**) capricho
vagina [vəˈdʒaɪnə] *s* vagina
vagran•cy [ˈvegrənsi] *s* (*pl* **-cies**) vagabundaje *m*
vagrant [ˈvegrənt] *adj & s* vagabundo
vague [veg] *adj* vago; impreciso
vain [ven] *adj* vano; (*conceited*) vanidoso; **in vain** en vano
vainglorious [venˈglorɪ•əs] *adj* vanaglorioso
valance [ˈvæləns] *s* (*across the top of a window*) guardamalleta; (*drapery*) doselera

vale [vel] *s* valle *m*
valedictorian [,vælɪdɪk'torɪ•ən] *s* alumno que pronuncia el discurso de despedida al fin del curso
valedicto•ry [,vælɪ'dɪktəri] *adj* de despedida || *s* (*pl* **-ries**) discurso de despedida
valence ['veləns] *s* (chem) valencia
valentine ['vælən,taɪn] *s* tarjeta amorosa o jocosa del día de San Valentín
Valentine Day *s* día *m* de los corazones, día de los enamorados (*14 de febrero*)
vale of tears *s* valle *m* de lágrimas
valet ['vælɪt] o ['væle] *s* ayuda *m*, paje *m*
valiant ['væljənt] *adj* valiente, valeroso
valid ['vælɪd] *adj* válido, valedero
validate ['vælɪ,det] *tr* validar; (sport) homologar
validation [,vælɪ'deʃən] *s* validación; (sport) homologación
validi•ty [və'lɪdɪti] *s* (*pl* **-ties**) validez *f*
valise [və'lis] *s* maleta
valley ['væli] *s* valle *m;* (*of roof*) lima hoya
valor ['vælər] *s* valor *m*, ánimo
valorous ['vælərəs] *adj* valeroso
valuable ['vælju•əbəl] o ['væljəbəl] *adj* (*having monetary value*) valioso; (*highly thought of*) estimable || **valuables** *spl* alhajas, objetos de valor
value ['vælju] *s* valor *m;* (*return for one's money in a purchase*) (coll) adquisición, inversión, p.ej., **an excellent value** una adquisición excelente || *tr* (*to think highly of*) estimar; (*to set a price for*) valorar, valuar
val'ue-add'ed tax *s* impuesto sobre el valor añadido, impuesto al valor agregado
valueless ['væljulɪs] *adj* sin valor
valve [vælv] *s* válvula; (*of mollusk*) valva; (mus) llava *f*
valve cap *s* capuchón *m*
valve gears *spl* distribución
valve'-in-head' engine *s* motor *m* con válvulas en cabeza
valve lifter ['lɪftər] *s* levantaválvulas *m*
valve seat *s* asiento de válvula
valve spring *s* muelle *m* de válvula
valve stem *s* vástago de válvula
vamp [væmp] *s* (*of shoe*) empella; (*patchwork*) remiendo; (*woman who preys on men*) (slang) mujer *f* fatal, vampiresa || *tr* poner empella a (*un zapato*); remendar; (*to concoct*) componer, enmendar; (jazz) improvisar (*un acompañamiento*); (slang) seducir (*una mujer mundana a un hombre*)
vampire ['væmpaɪr] *s* vampiro; (*woman who preys on men*) mujer *f* fatal, vampiresa
van [væn] *s* carro de carga, camión *m* de mudanzas; (mil & fig) vanguardia; (Brit) furgón *m* de equipajes
vanadium [və'nedɪ•əm] *s* vanadio
vandal ['vændəl] *adj & s* vándalo || **Vandal** *adj & s* vándalo
vandalism ['vændə,lɪzəm] *s* vandalismo
vane [ven] *s* (*weathervane*) veleta; (*of windmill*) aspa; (*of propeller or turbine*) paleta; (*of feather*) barba
vanguard ['væn,gɑrd] *s* (mil & fig) vanguardia; **in the vanguard** a vanguardia
vanilla [və'nɪlə] *s* vainilla
vanish ['vænɪʃ] *intr* desvanecerse
vanishing cream ['vænɪʃɪŋ] *s* crema desvanecedora
vani•ty ['vænɪti] *s* (*pl* **-ties**) vanidad; (*dressing table*) tocador *m;* (*vanity case*) estuche *m* de afeites
vanity case *s* estuche *m* de afeites, neceser *m* de belleza
vanquish ['væŋkwɪʃ] *tr* vencer, rendir
vantage ground ['væntɪdʒ] *s* posición ventajosa
vapid ['væpɪd] *adj* insípido
vapor ['vepər] *s* vapor *m* (*el visible; exhalación, vaho, niebla, etc.*)
vaporize ['vepə,raɪz] *tr* vaporizar || *intr* vaporizarse
vaporous ['vepərəs] *adj* vaporoso
vapor trail *s* (aer) estela de vapor, rastro de condensación
var. *abbr* **variant**
variable ['vɛrɪ•əbəl] *adj & s* variable
variance ['vɛrɪ•əns] *s* diferencia, variacion; **at variance with** en desacuerdo con
variant ['vɛrɪ•ənt] *adj & s* variante *f*
variation [,vɛrɪ'eʃən] *s* variación
varicose ['værɪ,kos] *adj* varicoso
varicose vein *s* (pathol) varice *f*
varied ['vɛrɪd] *adj* variado, vario
variegated ['vɛri•ə,getɪd] o ['vɛrɪ,getɪd] *adj* abigarrado, variado
varie•ty [və'raɪ•ɪti] *s* (*pl* **-ties**) variedad
variety show *s* variedades
variola [və'raɪ•ələ] *s* (pathol) viruela
various ['vɛrɪ•əs] *adj* (*several; of different kinds*) varios; (*many-sided; many-colored*) vario
varnish ['vɑrnɪʃ] *s* barniz *m;* (fig) capa, apariencia || *tr* barnizar; (fig) dar apariencia falsa a
varsi•ty ['vɑrsɪti] *adj* (sport) universitario || *s* (*pl* **-ties**) (sport) equipo principal de la universidad
var•y ['vɛri] *v* (*pret & pp* **-ied**) *tr & intr* variar
vase [ves] o [vez] *s* florero, jarrón *m*
Vaseline ['væsə,lin] *s* (trademark) vaselina
vassal ['væsəl] *adj & s* vasallo
vast [væst] o [vɑst] *adj* vasto
vastly ['væstlɪ] *adv* enormemente
vastness ['væstnɪs] *s* vastedad
vat [væt] *s* cuba, tina
vaudeville ['vodvɪl] o ['vɔdəvɪl] *s* variedades; (*light theatrical piece interspersed with songs*) zarzuela
vault [vɔlt] *s* (*underground chamber*) bodega; (*of a bank*) cámara acorazada; (*burial chamber*) sepultura, tumba; (*firmament*) bóveda celeste; (*leap*) salto; (archit) bóveda || *tr* abovedar; saltar || *intr* saltar
vaunt [vɔnt] *s* jactancia || *tr* jactarse de || *intr* jactarse
VCR *abbr* **video-cassette recorder**
veal [vil] *s* ternera, carne *f* de ternera
veal chop *s* chuleta de ternera

vedette [vɪ'dɛt] *s* buque *m* escucha; centinela *m* de avanzada
veer [vɪr] *s* viraje *m* || *tr* virar || *intr* virar; (naut) llamar (*el viento*)
vegetable ['vɛdʒɪtəbəl] *adj* vegetal || *s* (*plant*) vegetal *m;* (*edible part of plant*) hortaliza, legumbre *f*
vegetable garden *s* huerto de hortalizas, huerto de verduras
vegetable soup *s* menestra, sopa de hortalizas
vegetarian [,vɛdʒɪ'tɛrɪ•ən] *adj & s* vegetariano
vehemence ['vi•ɪməns] *s* vehemencia
vehement ['vi•ɪmənt] *adj* vehemente
vehicle ['vi•ɪkəl] *s* vehículo
vehicular traffic [vɪ'hɪkjələr] *s* circulación rodada
veil [vel] *s* velo; **to take the veil** tomar el velo || *tr* velar (*cubrir con un velo; cubrir, disimular*)
vein [ven] *s* vena; (*streak*) veta; (*distinctive quality*) rasgo || *tr* vetear
velar ['vilər] *adj & s* velar *f*
vellum ['vɛləm] *s* vitela; papel *m* vitela
veloci•ty [vɪ'lɑsɪti] *s* (*pl* **-ties**) velocidad
velvet ['vɛlvɪt] *adj* de terciopelo || *s* terciopelo; (slang) ganancia limpia
velveteen [,vɛlvɪ'tin] *s* velludillo
velvety ['vɛlvɪti] *adj* aterciopelado
Ven. *abbr* **Venerable**
vend [vɛnd] *tr* vender como buhonero
vending machine *s* distribuidor automático
vendor ['vɛndər] *s* vendedor *m*, buhonero
veneer [və'nɪr] *s* chapa, enchapado; (fig) apariencia || *tr* enchapar
venerable ['vɛnərəbəl] *adj* venerable
venerate ['vɛnə,ret] *tr* venerar
venereal [vɪ'nɪrɪ•əl] *adj* venéreo
Venetia [vɪ'niʃi•ə] o [vɪ'niʃə] *s* Venecia (*provincia*)
Venetian [vɪ'niʃən] *adj & s* veneciano
Venetian blind *s* persiana
Venezuela [,vɛnɪ'zwilə] *s* Venezuela
Venezuelan [,vɛnɪzwilən] *adj & s* venezolano
vengeance ['vɛndʒəns] *s* venganza; **with a vengeance** con furia, con violencia; excesivamente, con creces
vengeful ['vɛndʒfəl] *adj* vengativo
Venice ['vɛnɪs] *s* Venecia (*ciudad*)
venire [vɪ'naɪri] *s* (law) auto de convocación del jurado
venison ['vɛnɪsən] o ['vɛnɪzən] *s* carne *f* de venado
venom ['vɛnəm] *s* veneno
venomous ['vɛnəməs] *adj* venenoso
vent [vɛnt] *s* agujero, orificio; (*outlet*) salida; **to give vent to** dar libre curso a || *tr* proveer de abertura; desahogar, expresar; **to vent one's spleen** descargar la bilis
vent'hole' *s* respiradero
ventilate ['vɛntɪ,let] *tr* ventilar
ventilator ['vɛntɪ,letər] *s* ventilador *m*
ventricle ['vɛntrɪkəl] *s* ventrículo
ventriloquism [vɛn'trɪlə,kwɪzəm] *s* ventriloquia
ventriloquist [vɛn'trɪləkwɪst] *s* ventrílocuo
venture ['vɛntʃər] *s* empresa arriesgada; **at a venture** a la buena ventura || *tr* aventurar || *intr* aventurarse; **to venture on** arriesgarse en
venturesome ['vɛntʃərsəm] *adj* (*bold, daring*) aventurero; (*hazardous*) aventurado
venturous ['vɛntʃərəs] *adj* (*bold, daring*) aventurero; (*hazardous*) aventurado, arriesgado
venue ['vɛnju] *s* (law) lugar *m* del crimen; (law) lugar donde se reúne el jurado; **change of venue** (law) traslado de jurisdicción
Venus ['vinəs] *s* (astr) Venus *m;* (myth) Venus *f;* (*very beautiful woman*) Venus *f*
veracious [vɪ'reʃəs] *adj* veraz
veraci•ty [vɪ'ræsɪti] *s* (*pl* **-ties**) veracidad
veranda o **verandah** [və'rændə] *s* terraza, veranda, galería
verb [vʌrb] *adj* verbal || *s* verbo
verbatim [vər'betɪm] *adj* textual || *adv* palabra por palabra, al pie de la letra
verbena [vər'binə] *s* (bot) verbena
verbiage ['vʌrbɪ•ɪdʒ] *s* palabrería, verbosidad
verbose [vər'bos] *adj* verboso
verdant ['vʌrdənt] *adj* verde; cándido, sencillo
verdict ['vʌrdɪkt] *s* veredicto, fallo
verdigris ['vʌrdɪ,gris] *s* verdete *m*
verdure ['vʌrdʒər] *s* verdor *m*
verge [vʌrdʒ] *s* borde *m*, límite *m;* (*of a column*) fuste *m;* báculo; (eccl) cetro; **on the verge of** al borde de; a punto de; **within the verge of** al alcance de || *intr*—**to verge on** o **upon** llegar casi hasta, rayar en
verification [,vɛrɪfɪ'keʃən] *s* verificatión
veri•fy ['vɛrɪ,faɪ] *v* (*pret & pp* **-fied**) *tr* verificar, comprobar; (law) afirmar bajo juramento
verily ['vɛrɪli] *adv* verdaderamente, en verdad
veritable ['vɛritəbəl] *adj* verdadero
vermicelli [,vʌrmɪ'sɛli] *s* fideos
vermilion [vər'mɪljən] *adj* bermejo || *s* bermellón *m*
vermin ['vʌrmɪn] *ssg* (*objectionable person*) sabandija; bicherío (SAm) || *spl* (*objectionable animals or persons*) sabandijas
vermouth [vər'muθ] o ['vʌrmuθ] *s* vermú *m*
vernacular [vər'nækjələr] *adj* vernáculo || *s* lenguaje vernáculo; idioma *m* corriente; (*language peculiar to a class or profession*) jerga
veronica [və'rɑnɪkə] *s* (bot & taur) verónica; lienzo de la Verónica
Versailles [vɛr'saɪ] *s* Versalles
versatile ['vʌrsətɪl] *adj* versátil; [*person*) de muchas habilidades; (*informed on many subjects*) polifacético, universal; (*device or tool*) útil para muchas cosas
verse [vʌrs] *s* verso; (*in the Bible*) versículo
versed [vʌrst] *adj* versado; **to become versed in** versarse en
versification [,vʌrsɪfɪ'keʃən] *s* versificación

versi•fy ['vʌrsɪ,faɪ] *v* (*pret & pp* **-fied**) *tr & intr* versificar
version ['vʌrʒən] *s* versión
ver•so ['vʌrso] *s* (*pl* **-sos**) (*e.g., of a coin*) reverso; (typ) verso
versus ['vʌrsəs] *prep* contra
verte•bra ['vʌrtɪbrə] *s* (*pl* **-brae** [,bri] o **-bras**) vértebra
vertebral disk ['vʌrtə,brəl] *s* disco vertebral
vertebrate ['vʌrtɪ,bret] *adj & s* vertebrado
ver•tex ['vʌrtɛks] *s* (*pl* **-texes** o **-tices** [tɪ,siz]) (*top, summit*) ápice *m;* (geom) vértice *m*
vertical ['vʌrtɪkəl] *adj & s* vertical *f*
vertical hold *s* (telv) bloqueo vertical
vertical rudder *s* (aer) timón *m* de dirección
vertical take-off *m* despegue *m* vertical
verti•go ['vʌrtɪ,go] *s* (*pl* **-gos** o **-goes**) vértigo
verve [vʌrv] *s* brío, ánimo, vigor *m*
very ['vɛri] *adj* mismísimo; (*sheer, utter*) mero, puro; (*actual*) verdadero || *adv* muy; mucho, *p.ej.,* **to be very hungry** tener mucha hambre
vesicle ['vɛsɪkəl] *s* vesícula
vesper ['vɛspər] *s* tarde *f*, caída de la tarde; oración de la tarde; canción de la tarde; **vespers** (eccl) vísperas || **Vesper** *s* Véspero
vesper bell *s* campana que llama a vísperas
vessel ['vɛsəl] *s* vasija, recipiente *m;* (*ship*) bajel *m*, embarcación, buque *m;* (anat) vaso
vest [vɛst] *s* (*of man's suit*) chaleco; (*jabot*) chorrera; (*undershirt*) camiseta || *tr* vestir; **to vest in** conceder (*p.ej., poder*) a; **to vest with** investir de || *intr* vestirse; **to vest in** pasar a
vested interests *spl* intereses creados
vestibule ['vɛstɪ,bjul] *s* vestíbulo, zaguán *m*
vestige ['vɛstɪdʒ] *s* vestigio
vestment ['vɛstmənt] *s* vestidura
vest'-pock'et *adj* de bolsillo, en miniatura; diminuto
ves•try ['vɛstri] *s* (*pl* **-tries**) sacristía; (*chapel*) capilla; junta parroquial; reunión de la junta parroquial
vestry•man ['vɛstrimən] *s* (*pl* **-men** [mən]) miembro de la junta parroquial
Vesuvius [vɪ'suvɪ•əs] o [vɪ'sjuvɪ•əs] *s* el Vesubio
vet. *abbr* **veteran, veterinary**
vetch [vɛtʃ] *s* arveja, veza; (*grass pea*) almorta
veteran ['vɛtərən] *adj & s* veterano
veterinarian [,vɛtərɪ'nɛrɪ•ən] *s* veterinario
veterinar•y ['vɛtərɪ,nɛri] *adj* veterinario || *s* (*pl* **-ies**) veterinario
veterinary medicine *s* veterinaria, medicina veterinaria
ve•to ['vito] *s* (*pl* **-toes**) veto || *tr* vetar
vex [vɛks] *tr* vejar, molestar
vexation [vɛk'seʃən] *s* vejación, molestia
v.g. *abbr* **verbi gratia** (Lat) **for example**
via ['vaɪ•ə] *prep* vía, p.ej., **via Lisbon** vía Lisboa
viaduct ['vaɪ•ə,dʌkt] *s* viaducto
vial ['vaɪ•əl] *s* redoma, frasco pequeño
viati•cum [vaɪ,ætɪkəm] *s* (*pl* **-cums** o **-ca** [kə]) (eccl) viático
viand ['vaɪ•ənd] *s* vianda, manjar *m*
vibrate ['vaɪbret] *tr & intr* vibrar
vibration [vaɪ'breʃən] *s* vibración
vicar ['vɪkər] *s* vicario
vicarage ['vɪkərɪdʒ] *s* casa del vicario; (*duties of vicar*) vicaría
vicarious [vaɪ'kɛrɪ•əs] *adj* substituto; (*punishment*) sufrido por otro; (*power, authority*) delegado; (*enjoyment*) reflejado
vice [vaɪs] *s* vicio
vice'-ad'miral *s* vicealmirante *m*
vice'-pres'ident *s* vicepresidente *m*
viceroy ['vaɪsrɔɪ] *s* virrey *m*
vice versa ['vaɪsi 'vʌrsə] o ['vaɪs 'vʌrsə] *adv* viceversa
vicini•ty [vɪ'sɪnɪti] *s* (*pl* **-ties**) vecindad
vicious ['vɪʃəs] *adj* vicioso; malazo; (*dog*) bravo; (*horse*) arisco
victim ['vɪktɪm] *s* víctima
victimize ['vɪktɪ,maɪz] *tr* hacer víctima; engañar, estafar
victor ['vɪktər] *s* vencedor *m*
victorious [vɪk'torɪ•əs] *adj* victorioso
victo•ry ['vɪktəri] *s* (*pl* **-ries**) victoria
victuals ['vɪtəlz] *spl* vituallas, provisiones de boca
vid. *abbr* **vide** (Lat) see
video cassette *s* videocasete *m*
vid'e•o-cas•sette' recorder *s* videograbador *m*
video-cassette recording *s* videograbación
video disk *s* videodisco
video game *s* video-juego
video recorder *s* magnetoscopia
video signal ['vɪdɪ,o] *s* señal *f* de vídeo
video tape *s* cinta grabada de televisión
vid'eo-tape' recording *s* videograbación
vie [vaɪ] *v* (*pret & pp* **vied;** *ger* **vying)** *intr* competir, emular, rivalizar
Vien•nese [,vi•ə'niz] *adj* vienés || *s* (*pl* **-nese**) vienés *m*
Vietnam•ese [vɪ,ɛtnə'miz] *adj* vietnamés || *s* (*pl* **-ese**) vietnamés *m*
view [vju] *s* vista; (*purpose*) intento, propósito, vista; **to be on view** estar expuesto (*p.ej., un cadáver*); **to keep in view** no perder de vista; no olvidar, tener presente; **to take a dim view of** no entusiasmarse por, mirar escépticamente; **with a view to** con vistas a || *tr* ver, mirar; considerar, contemplar; examinar, inspeccionar
viewer ['vju•ər] *s* espectador *m;* telespectador *m*, televidente *mf;* proyector *m* de transparencias; mirador *m* de transparencias
view finder *s* (phot) visor *m*
view'point' *s* punto de vista
vigil ['vɪdʒɪl] *s* vigilia; **to keep vigil** velar
vigilance ['vɪdʒɪləns] *s* vigilancia
vigilant ['vɪdʒɪlənt] *adj* vigilante
vignette [vɪn'jɛt] *s* viñeta
vigor ['vɪgər] *s* vigor *m*
vigorous ['vɪgərəs] *adj* vigoroso
vile [vaɪl] *adj* vil; (*disgusting*) asqueroso, repugnante; (*weather*) muy malo

vili•fy [ˈvɪlɪ,faɪ] *v* (*pret & pp* **-fied**) *tr* difamar, denigrar
villa [ˈvɪlə] *s* villa, quinta
village [ˈvɪlɪdʒ] *s* aldea
villager [ˈvɪlɪdʒər] *s* aldeano
villain [ˈvɪlən] *s* malvado; (*of a play*) malo, traidor *m*
villainous [ˈvɪlənəs] *adj* malvado
villain•y [ˈvɪləni] *s* (*pl* **-ies**) maldad, perfidia
vim [vɪm] *s* fuerza, brío, vigor *m*
vinaigrette [,vɪnəˈgrɛt] *s* vinagrera
vinaigrette sauce *s* vinagreta
vindicate [ˈvɪndɪ,ket] *tr* vindicar, exculpar
vindictive [vɪnˈdɪktɪv] *adj* vengativo
vine [vaɪn] *s* (*creeping or climbing plant*) enredadera; (*grape plant*) vid *f*, parra
vine'dress'er *s* viñador *m*, viticultor *m*
vinegar [ˈvɪnɪgər] *s* vinagre *m*
vinegarish [ˈvɪnɪgərɪʃ] *adj* avinagrado
vinegary [ˈvɪnɪgəri] *adj* vinagroso
vineyard [ˈvɪnjərd] *s* viña, viñedo
vineyardist [ˈvɪnjərdɪst] *s* viñador *m*, viticultor *m*
vintage [ˈvɪntɪdʒ] *s* vendimia; vino de buena cosecha; (coll) categoría, clase *f*
vintager [ˈvɪntɪdʒər] *s* vendimiador *m*
vintage wine *s* vino de buena cosecha
vintage year *s* año de buen vino
vintner [ˈvɪntnər] *s* vinatero
vinyl [ˈvaɪnɪl] *s* vinilo
violate [ˈvaɪ•ə,let] *tr* violar
violence [ˈvaɪ•ələns] *s* violencia
violent [ˈvaɪ•ələnt] *adj* violento
violet [ˈvaɪ•əlɪt] *adj* violado || *s* (*color*) violeta *m*, violado; (*dye*) violeta *m;* (bot) violeta *f*
violin [,vaɪ•əˈlɪn] *s* violín *m*
violinist [,vaɪ•əˈlɪnɪst] *s* violinista *mf*
violoncellist [,vaɪ•ələnˈtʃɛlɪst] o [,viələnˈtʃɛlɪst] *s* violoncelista *mf*
violoncel•lo [,vaɪ•ələnˈtʃɛlo] o [,viələnˈtʃɛlo] *s* (*pl* **-los**) violoncelo
viper [ˈvaɪpər] *s* víbora
VIPs [ˈvi,aɪˈpis] *spl* (letterword) notables *mpl*
vira•go [vɪˈrego] *s* (*pl* **-goes** o **-gos**) mujer de mal genio
virgin [ˈvʌrdʒɪn] *adj & s* virgen *f*
virgin birth *s* parto virginal de María Santísima; (zool) partenogénesis *f*
Virginia creeper [vərˈdʒɪnɪ•ə] *s* (bot) guau *m*
virginity [vərˈdʒɪnɪti] *s* virginidad
Virgo [ˈvʌrgo] *s* (astr) Virgo
virility [vɪˈrɪlɪti] *s* virilidad
virology [vaɪˈrɑlədʒi] *s* virología
virtual [ˈvʌrtʃʊ•əl] *adj* virtual
virtue [ˈvʌrtʃʊ] *s* virtud
virtuosi•ty [,vʌrtʃʊˈɑsɪti] *s* (*pl* **-ties**) virtuosismo
virtuo•so [,vʌrtʃʊˈoso] *s* (*pl* **-sos** o **-si** [si]) virtuoso
virtuous [ˈvʌrtʃʊ•əs] *adj* virtuoso
virulence [ˈvɪrjələns] *s* virulencia
virulent [ˈvɪrjələnt] *adj* virulento
virus [ˈvaɪrəs] *s* virus *m*
Vis. *abbr* **Viscount**
visa [ˈvɪzə] *s* visa || *tr* visar
visage [ˈvɪzɪdʒ] *s* cara, semblante *m;* aspecto, apariencia
vis-à-vis [,vizəˈvi] *adj* enfrentados || *adv* frente a frente || *prep* enfrente de; respecto de
viscera [ˈvɪsərə] *spl* vísceras
viscount [ˈvaɪkaʊnt] *s* vizconde *m*
viscountess [ˈvaɪkaʊntɪs] *s* vizcondesa
viscous [ˈvɪskəs] *adj* viscoso
vise [vaɪs] *s* tornillo, torno
visé [ˈvize] o [viˈze] *s & tr* var de **visa**
visible [ˈvɪzɪbəl] *adj* visible
Visigoth [ˈvɪzɪ,gɑθ] *s* visigodo
vision [ˈvɪʒən] *s* visión; (*sense of sight*) vista
visionar•y [ˈvɪʒə,nɛri] *adj* visionario || *s* (*pl* **-ies**) visionario
visit [ˈvɪzɪt] *s* visita || *tr* visitar; afligir, acometer; enviar (*p.ej., castigo, venganza*) || *intr* hacer visitas; visitarse (*dos o más personas*)
visitation [,vɪzɪˈteʃən] *s* visitación; gracia del cielo, castigo del cielo
visiting card *s* tarjeta de visita
visiting hours *spl* horas de visita
visiting nurse *s* enfermera ambulante
visitor [ˈvɪsɪtər] *s* visitante *mf*
visor [ˈvaɪzər] *s* visera; (*disguise*) máscara
vista [ˈvɪstə] *s* vista, panorama *m*
visual [ˈvɪʒʊ•əl] *adj* visual
visual acuity *s* agudeza visual
visualize [ˈvɪʒʊ•ə,laɪz] *tr* representarse en la mente; hacer visible
vital [ˈvaɪtəl] *adj* vital; (*deadly*) mortal || **vitals** *spl* partes *fpl* vitales, órganos vitales
vitality [vaɪˈtælɪti] *s* vitalidad
vitalize [ˈvaɪtə,laɪz] *tr* vitalizar
vitamin [ˈvaɪtəmɪn] *s* vitamina
vitiate [ˈvɪʃɪ,et] *tr* viciar
vitreous [ˈvɪtrɪ•əs] *adj* vítreo
vitriolic [,vɪtrɪˈɑlɪk] *adj* (chem) vitriólico; (fig) cáustico, mordaz
vituperable [vaɪˈtupərəbəl] o [vaɪˈtjupərəbəl] *adj* vituperable
vituperate [vaɪˈtupə,ret] o [vaɪˈtjupə,ret] *tr* vituperar
viva [ˈvivə] *interj* ¡viva! || *s* viva *m*
vivacious [vɪˈveʃəs] o [vaɪˈveʃəs] *adj* vivaz, vivaracho
vivaci•ty [vɪˈvæsɪti] o [vaɪˈvæsɪti] *s* (*pl* **-ties**) vivacidad, animación
viva voce [ˈvaɪvə ˈvosi] *adv* de viva voz
vivid [ˈvɪvɪd] *adj* vivo (*intenso; brillante; expresivo*)
vivi•fy [ˈvɪvɪ,faɪ] *v* (*pret & pp* **-fied**) *tr* vivificar
vivisection [,vɪvɪˈsɛkʃən] *s* vivisección
vixen [vɪksən] *s* vulpeja; mujer regañona y colérica
viz. *abbr* **videlicet** (Lat) **namely, to wit**
vizier [vɪˈzɪr] o [ˈvɪzjər] *s* visir *m*
vocabular•y [voˈkæbjə,lɛri] *s* (*pl* **-ies**) vocabulario
vocal [ˈvokəl] *adj* vocal; (*inclined to express oneself freely*) expresivo
vocalist [ˈvokəlɪst] *s* vocalista *mf*
vocation [voˈkeʃən] *s* vocación; empleo, ocupación

vocative [ˈvɑkətɪv] *s* vocativo
vociferate [voˈsɪfə,ret] *intr* vociferar
vociferous [voˈsɪfərəs] *adj* clamoroso, vocinglero
vogue [vog] *s* boga, moda; **in vogue** en boga, de moda
voice [vɔɪs] *s* voz *f;* **in a loud voice** en alta voz; **in a low voice** en voz baja; **with one voice** a una voz ‖ *tr* expresar; sonorizar (*una consonante sorda*) ‖ *intr* sonorizarse
voiceless [ˈvɔɪslɪs] *adj* sin voz; mudo; silencioso; (phonet) sordo
void [vɔɪd] *adj* (*empty*) vacío; (*useless*) vano; (law) inválido, nulo; **void of** desprovisto de ‖ *s* vacío; (*gap*) hueco ‖ *tr* vaciar; evacuar (*el vientre*); anular ‖ *intr* excretar
voile [vɔɪl] *s* espumilla
vol. *abbr* **volume**
volatile [ˈvɑlətɪl] *adj* volátil
volatilize [ˈvɑlətɪ,laɪz] *tr* volatilizar ‖ *intr* volatilizarse
volcanic [vɑlˈkænɪk] *adj* volcánico
volca•no [vɑlˈkeno] *s* (*pl* **-noes** o **-nos**) volcán *m*
volition [vəˈlɪʃən] *s* voluntad; **of one's own volition** por su propia voluntad
volley [ˈvɑli] *s* (*of stones, bullets, etc.*) descarga, lluvia; (mil) descarga; (tennis) voleo ‖ *tr & intr* volear
vol'ley•ball' *s* volibol *m*
volplane [ˈvɑl,plen] *s* vuelo planeado ‖ *intr* planear
volt [volt] *s* voltio
voltage [ˈvoltɪdʒ] *s* voltaje *m*
voltage divider *s* (rad) divisor *m* de voltaje
voltaic [vɑlˈte•ɪk] *adj* voltaico
volte-face [vɔltˈfɑs] *s* cambio de dirección; cambio de opinión
volt'me'ter *s* voltímetro
voluble [ˈvɑljəbəl] *adj* locuaz, hablador
volume [ˈvɑljəm] *s* (*book; bulk; mass, e.g., of water*) volumen *m;* (*each book in a set*) tomo; (*degree of loudness*) volumen sonoro; (geom) volumen *m;* **to speak volumes** ser muy significativo; ser muy expresivo
voluminous [vəˈlumɪnəs] *adj* voluminoso
voluntar•y [ˈvɑlən,tɛri] *adj* voluntario ‖ *s* (*pl* **-ties**) (eccl) solo de órgano
volunteer [,vɑlənˈtɪr] *adj & s* voluntario ‖ *tr* ofrecer (*sus servicios*) ‖ *intr* ofrecerse; servir como voluntario; **to volunteer to** + *inf* ofrecerse a + *inf*
voluptuar•y [vəˈlʌptʃu,ɛri] *adj* voluptuoso ‖ *s* (*pl* **-ties**) voluptuoso, sibarita *mf*
voluptuous [vəˈlʌptʃu•əs] *adj* voluptuoso
volute [vəˈlut] *s* voluta
vomit [ˈvɑmɪt] *s* vómito; (*emetic*) vomitivo ‖ *tr & intr* vomitar
voodoo [ˈvudu] *adj* voduísta ‖ *s* (*practice*) vodú *m;* (*person*) voduísta *mf*
voracious [vəˈreʃəs] *adj* voraz
voracity [vəˈræsɪti] *s* voracidad
vor•tex [ˈvɔrtɛks] *s* (*pl* **-texes** o **-tices** [tɪ,siz]) vórtice *m*
vota•ry [ˈvotəri] *s* (*pl* **-ries**) persona ligada por votos solemnes; aficionado, partidario
vote [vot] *s* (*formal expression of choice; right to vote; person who votes*) voto; (*act of voting; votes considered together*) votación; **to put to the vote** poner a votación; **to tally the votes** regular los votos ‖ *tr* votar (*sí, no*); **to vote down** derrotar por votación; **to vote in** elegir por votación ‖ *intr* votar
vote getter [ˈgɛtər] *s* acaparador *m* de votos; (*slogan*) consigna que gana votos
voter [ˈvotər] *s* votante *mf*
voting machine [ˈvotɪŋ] *s* máquina registradora de votos
votive [ˈvotɪv] *adj* votivo
votive offering *s* voto, exvoto
vouch [vaʊtʃ] *tr* garantizar ‖ *intr*—**to vouch for** responder de (*una cosa*); responder por (*una persona*)
voucher [ˈvaʊtʃər] *s* garante *mf;* (*certificate*) comprobante *m*
vouch•safe' *tr* conceder, otorgar; permitir ‖ *intr*— **to vouchsafe to** + *inf* dignarse + *inf*
voussoir [vuˈswɑr] *s* dovela
vow [vaʊ] *s* voto; **to take vows** tomar el hábito religioso ‖ *tr* votar (*p.ej., un cirio a la Virgen*); jurar (*venganza*) ‖ *intr* votar; **to vow to** hacer votos de
vowel [ˈvaʊ•əl] *s* vocal *f*
voyage [ˈvɔɪ•ɪdʒ] *s* travesía, trayecto; (*any journey*) viaje *m* ‖ *tr* atravesar (*p.ej., el mar*) ‖ *intr* viajar
voyager [ˈvɔɪ•ɪdʒər] *s* pasajero, navegante *mf*, viajero
V.P. *abbr* **Vice-President**
vs. *abbr* **versus**
Vul. *abbr* **Vulgate**
vulcanize [ˈvʌlkə,naɪz] *tr* vulcanizar
vulg. *abbr* **vulgar**
Vulg. *abbr* **Vulgate**
vulgar [ˈvʌlgər] *adj* grosero; (*popular, common; vernacular*) vulgar
vulgari•ty [vʌlˈgærɪti] *s* (*pl* **-ties**) grosería
Vulgar Latin *s* latín vulgar, latín rústico
Vulgate [ˈvʌlget] *s* Vulgata
vulnerable [ˈvʌlnərəbəl] *adj* vulnerable
vulture [ˈvʌltʃər] *s* buitre *m;* (*American vulture*) catartes *m*, aura (*buitre americano*)

W

W, w [ˈdʌbəl,ju] vigésima tercera letra del alfabeto inglés
w *abbr* **watt**
w. *abbr* **week, west, wide, wife**
W. *abbr* **Wednesday, west**
wad [wɑd] *s* (*of cotton*) bolita, tapón *m;* (*of papers*) fajo, lío; (*in a gun*) taco ‖ *v* (*pret & pp* **wadded;** *ger* **wadding**) *tr* emborrar, rellenar; atacar (*una escopeta*)
waddle [ˈwɑdəl] *s* anadeo ‖ *intr* anadear
wade [wed] *intr* andar sobre terreno cubierto de agua; andar descalzo por la orilla; chapotear (*los niños*) con los pies desnudos; **to wade into** (coll) embestir con violencia; (coll) meter el hombro a; **to wade through** (coll) avanzar con dificultad por; (coll) leer con dificultad
wading bird [ˈwedɪŋ] *s* ave zancuda
wafer [ˈwefər] *s* (*for sealing letters; pill*) oblea; (*thin, crisp cake*) hostia; (eccl) hostia
waffle [ˈwɑfəl] *s* barquillo
waffle iron *s* barquillero
waft [wæft] o [wɑft] *tr* llevar por el aire; llevar por encima del agua ‖ *intr* flotar
wag [wæg] *s* (*of head*) meneo; (*of tail*) coleada; (*jester*) bromista *mf* ‖ *v* (*pret & pp* **wagged;** *ger* **wagging**) *tr* menear (*la cabeza, la cola*) ‖ *intr* menearse
wage [wedʒ] *s* salario; **wages** galardón *m*, premio ‖ *tr* hacer (*la guerra*)
wage earner [ˈʌrnər] *s* asalariado
wager [ˈwedʒər] *s* apuesta; **to lay a wager** hacer una apuesta ‖ *tr & intr* apostar
wage'work'er *s* asalariado
waggish [ˈwægɪʃ] *adj* divertido, gracioso; (*person*) bromista
Wagnerian [vɑgˈnɪrɪ•ən] *adj & s* vagneriano
wagon [ˈwægən] *s* carro, furgón *m*, carretón *m;* **on the wagon** (slang) sin tomar bebidas alcohólicas; **to hitch one's wagon to a star** poner el tiro muy alto
wag'tail' *s* aguanieves *m*, aguzanieves *m*
waif [wef] *s* (*foundling*) expósito; animal extraviado o abandonado; (*stray child*) granuja *m*
wail [wel] *s* gemido, lamento ‖ *intr* gemir, lamentar
wain•scot [ˈwenskət] o [ˈwenskɑt] *s* arrimadillo, friso de madera ‖ *v* (*pret & pp* **-scoted** o **-scotted;** *ger* **-scoting** o **-scotting**) *tr* poner arrimadillo o friso de madera a
waist [west] *s* (*of human body; corresponding part of garment*) talle *m*, cintura; (*garment*) corpiño, jubón *m*, blusa
waist'band' *s* pretina
waist'cloth' *s* taparrabo
waistcoat [ˈwest,kot] o [ˈwɛskət] *s* chaleco
waist'line' *s* cintura
wait [wet] *s* espera; **to have a good wait** (coll) esperar sentado; **to lie in wait for** acechar emboscado ‖ *tr*—**to wait one's turn** esperar vez ‖ *intr* esperar, aguardar; **to wait for** esperar, aguardar; **to wait on** atender, despachar (*a los parroquianos en una tienda*); servir (*a una persona a la mesa*); **to wait until** esperar a que
waiter [ˈwetər] *s* camarero, mozo de restaurante; (*tray*) bandeja
waiting list *s* lista de espera
waiting room *s* (*of station*) sala de espera; (*of doctor's office*) antesala
waitress [ˈwetrɪs] *s* camarera, moza de restaurante
waive [wev] *tr* renunciar a (*un derecho*); diferir, poner a un lado
waiver [ˈwevər] *s* renuncia
wake [wek] *s* (*watch by the body of a dead person*) velatorio; (*of a boat or other moving object*) estela; **in the wake of** siguiendo inmediatamente; de resultas de ‖ *v* (*pret* **waked** o **woke** [wok]; *pp* **waked**) *tr* despertar ‖ *intr*— **to wake to** darse cuenta de; **to wake up** despertar
wakeful [ˈwekfəl] *adj* desvelado
wakefulness [ˈwekfəlnɪs] *s* desvelo
waken [ˈwekən] *tr & intr* despertar
wale [wel] *s* verdugón *m*
Wales [welz] *s* Gales, el país de Gales
walk [wɔk] *s* (*act*) paseo; (*distance*) caminata; (*way of walking, bearing*) andar *m*, paso; (*of a horse*) andadura; (*place to walk animals*) cercado; empleo, cargo, carrera; **at a walk** al paso de una persona; **to go for a walk** salir a pasear; **to take a walk** dar un paseo ‖ *tr* pasear (*a un niño, un caballo*); caminar (*recorrer caminando*); hacer ir al paso (*un caballo*); **to walk off** quitarse (*p.ej., un dolor de cabeza*) caminando ‖ *intr* andar, caminar, ir a pie; (*to stroll*) pasear; **to walk away from** alejarse caminando de; **to walk off with** cargar con, llevarse; **to walk out** salir repentinamente; declararse en huelga; **to walk out on** (coll) dejar airadamente
walkaway [ˈwɔkə,we] *s* (coll) triunfo fácil
walker [ˈwɔkər] *s* caminante *mf;* (*pedestrian*) peatón *m;* (*gocart*) andaderas
walkie-talkie [ˈwɔkiˈtɔki] *s* (rad) transmisorreceptor *m* portátil
walking papers *spl* (coll) despedida de un empleo
walking stick *s* bastón *m*
walk'-on' *s* (theat) parte *f* de por medio
walk'out' *s* (coll) huelga
walk'o'ver *s* (coll) triunfo fácil
wall [wɔl] *s* muro; (*between rooms; of a pipe, boiler, etc.*) pared *f;* (*of a fortification*) muralla; **to drive to the wall** poner entre la espada y la pared; **to go to the wall** rendirse; fracasar ‖ *tr* murar, amurallar (*una ciudad, un castillo*); emparedar (*a un criminal*); **to wall up** cerrar con muro
wall'board' *s* cartón *m* tabla
wallet [ˈwɑlɪt] *s* cartera de bolsillo
wall'flow'er *s* alhelí *m;* **to be a wallflower** (coll) comer pavo, planchar el asiento
Walloon [wɑˈlun] *adj & s* valón *m*

wallop [ˈwɑləp] *s* (coll) golpaza, puñetazo ‖ *tr* (coll) golpear fuertemente; (coll) vencer cabalmente

wallow [ˈwɑlo] *s* revuelco; (*place*) revolcadero ‖ *intr* revolcarse; (*e.g., in wealth*) nadar

wall'pa'per *s* papel *m* de empapelar, papel pintado ‖ *tr* empapelar

walnut [ˈwɔlnət] *s* (*tree and wood*) nogal *m;* nuez *f* de nogal

walrus [ˈwɔlrəs] o [ˈwɑlrəs] *s* morsa

Walter [ˈwɔltər] *s* Gualterio

waltz [wɔlts] *s* vals *m* ‖ *tr* hacer valsar; (coll) conducir directamente ‖ *intr* valsar

wan [wɑn] *adj* (*comp* **wanner;** *super* **wannest**) pálido, macilento; débil

wand [wɑnd] *s* vara; (*of deviner or magician*) varilla de virtudes

wander [ˈwɑndər] *tr* recorrer a la ventura ‖ *intr* errar, vagar; extraviarse, perderse; **to wander around** errar de una parte a otra

wanderer [ˈwɑndərər] *s* vagabundo; peregrino

wan'der•lust' *s* ansia de viajar

wane [wen] *s* decadencia, declinación; menguante *f* de la luna; **on the wane** decayendo, declinando; menguando (*la luna*) ‖ *intr* decaer, declinar; menguar (*la luna*)

wangle [ˈwɛŋgəl] *tr* (*to obtain by scheming*) (coll) mamar o mamarse; (coll) adulterar, falsear (*cuentas*); **to wangle one's way out of** (coll) salir con maña de ‖ *intr* (*to get along by scheming*) (coll) sacudirse

want [wɑnt] o [wɔnt] *s* deseo; necesidad; carencia; **for want of** a falta de; **to be in want** pasar necesidad ‖ *tr* desear; necesitar; carecer de ‖ *intr* desear; **to want for** necesitar; carecer de

want ad *s* anuncio clasificado

wanton [ˈwɑntən] *adj* inconsiderado, desconsiderado; insensible, perverso; disoluto, licencioso; lascivo; cabezudo

war [wɔr] *s* guerra; **to go to war** declarar la guerra; (*as a soldier*) ir a la guerra; **to wage war** hacer la guerra ‖ *v* (*pret & pp* **warred;** *ger* **warring**) *intr* guerrear; **to war on** guerrear con, hacer la guerra a

warble [ˈwɔrbəl] *s* gorjeo, trino ‖ *intr* gorjear, trinar

warbler [ˈwɔrblər] *s* pájaro cantor; curruca de cabeza negra

war cloud *s* amenaza de guerra

ward [wɔrd] *s* (*person, usually a minor, under protection of another*) pupilo; (*guardianship*) custodia, tutela; (*of a city*) barrio, distrito; (*of a hospital*) cuadra, crujía; (*of a lock*) guarda ‖ *tr*— **to ward off** parar, desviar

warden [ˈwɔrdən] *s* guardián *m;* (*of a jail*) alcaide *m*, carcelero; (*of a church*) capiller *m;* (*in charge of fire prevention*) vigía *m*

ward heeler *s* muñidor *m*

ward'robe' *s* (*closet or cabinet for holding clothes*) guardarropa *m;* (*stock of clothing for a person*) vestuario; (theat) guardarropía

wardrobe trunk *s* baúl ropero

ward'room' *s* (nav) cámara de oficiales

ware [wɛr] *s* loza; **wares** efectos, artículos de comercio, mercancías

war effort *s* esfuerzo bélico

ware'house' *s* almacén *m;* (*for furniture*) guardamuebles *m*

warehouse•man [ˈwɛr,haʊsmən] *s* (*pl* **-men** [mən]) almacenista *m;* guardaalmacén *m*

war'fare' *s* guerra

war'head' *s* punta de combate

war horse *s* corcel *m* de guerra; (coll) veterano

warily [ˈwɛrɪli] *adv* cautelosamente

wariness [ˈwɛrɪnɪs] *s* cautela

war'like' *adj* guerrero

war loan *s* empréstito de guerra

war lord *s* jefe *m* militar

warm [wɔrm] *adj* (*being moderately hot*) caliente; (*neither hot nor cold*) templado; (*clothing*) abrigador; (*climate, region*) caluroso; (*color*) cálido; (fig) caluroso, cordial; **to be warm** (*said of a person*) tener calor; (*said of the weather*) hacer calor ‖ *tr* calentar, acalorar; (fig) animar, acalorar; **to warm up** recalentar (*p.ej., la comida*); hacer más amistoso ‖ *intr* calentarse; **to warm up** templar (*el tiempo*); (*with work or exercise*) acalorarse; **to warm up to** cobrar afecto a

warm-blooded [ˈwɔrmˈblʌdɪd] *adj* apasionado, ardiente; (*animals*) de sangre caliente

war memorial *s* monumento a los caídos

warmer [ˈwɔrmər] *s* calentador *m*

warm-hearted [ˈwɔrmˈhɑrtɪd] *adj* afectuoso, de buen corazón; cariñoso; simpático

warming pan *s* mundillo

warmonger [ˈwɔr,mʌŋgər] *s* belicista *mf*

war mother *s* madrina de guerra

warmth [wɔrmθ] *s* calor *m;* ardor *m*, entusiasmo; cordialidad

warm'-up' *s* calentón *m*

warn [wɔrn] *tr* advertir, avisar; (*to exhort*) amonestar; (*to advise*) aconsejar

warning *adj* de aviso ‖ *s* advertencia, aviso

War of the Roses *s* guerra de las dos Rosas

warp [wɔrp] *s* (*of a fabric*) urdimbre *f;* (*of a board*) comba, alabeo; aberración mental; (naut) espía ‖ *tr* combar, alabear; pervertir (*el juicio de una persona*); (naut) move, con espía ‖ *intr* combarse, alabearse; (naut) espiar

war'path' *s*—**to be on the warpath** prepararse para la guerra; estar buscando pendencia

war'plane' *s* avión *m* de guerra

warrant [ˈwɑrənt] o [ˈwɔrənt] *s* garantía, promesa; (*for arrest*) orden *f* de prisión; (*before a judge*) citación; cédula, certificado ‖ *tr* garantizar, prometer; autorizar; justificar

warrantable [ˈwɑrəntəbəl] o [ˈwɔrəntəbəl] *adj* garantizable; justificable

warrant officer *s* suboficial *m* de las clases

warren [ˈwɑrən] o [ˈwɔrən] *s* (*where rabbits breed*) conejera; barrio densamente poblado
warrior [ˈwɔrjər] *s* guerrero
Warsaw [ˈwɔrsɔ] *s* Varsovia
war'ship' *s* buque *m* de guerra
wart [wɔrt] *s* verruga
war'time' *s* tiempo de guerra
war'-torn' *adj* devastado por la guerra
war to the death *s* guerra a muerte
war•y [wɛri] *adj* (*comp* **-ier;** *super* **-iest**) cauteloso
wash [wɑʃ] o [wɔʃ] *s* lavado; (*clothes washed or to be washed*) jabonado; (*dirty water*) lavazas; loción; (*place where surf breaks*) batiente *m;* (aer) estela turbulenta ‖ *tr* lavar; fregar (*los platos*); bañar, mojar; **to wash away** quitar lavando; derrubiar (*las aguas corrientes la tierra de las riberas*) ‖ *intr* lavarse; lavar la ropa; batir (*el agua*); derrubiarse
washable [ˈwɑʃəbəl] o [ˈwɔʃəbəl] *adj* lavable
wash and wear *adj* de lava y pon
wash'ba'sin *s* jofaina, palangana
wash'bas'ket *s* cesto de la colada
wash'board' *s* lavadero, tabla de lavar; (*baseboard*) rodapié *m*
wash'bowl' *s* jofaina, palangana
wash'cloth' *s* paño para lavarse
wash'day' *s* día *m* de la colada
washed-out [ˈwɑʃt,aʊt] o [ˈwɔʃt,aʊt] *adj* desteñido; (coll) debilitado, rendido
washed-up [ˈwɑʃt,ʌp] o [ˈwɔʃt,ʌp] *adj* (coll) agotado, deslomado
washer [ˈwɑʃər] o [wɔʃər] *s* lavador *m;* (*machine*) lavadora; (*ring of metal placed under head of bolt*) arandela; (*ring of rubber, etc., to keep a spigot from leaking*) zapatilla; (phot) lavador
wash'er•wom'an *s* (*pl* **-wom'en**) lavandera
wash goods *spl* tejidos lavables
washing [ˈwɑʃɪŋ] o [ˈwɔʃɪŋ] *s* (*act of washing; washed clothes or clothes to be washed*) lavado; lavada; **washings** (*dirty water; abraded material*) lavadura
washing machine *s* lejiadora, lavadora mecánica
washing soda *s* sal *f* de sosa
wash'out' *s* derrubio; derrumbe *m;* (coll) desilusión, fracaso
wash'rag' *s* paño para lavarse; paño de cocina
wash'room' *s* gabinete *m* de aseo, lavabo
wash'stand' *s* lavamanos *m*
wash'tub' *s* cuba de colada, tina de lavar
wash water *s* lavazas
wasp [wɑsp] *s* avispa
waste [west] *s* derroche *m*, desgaste *m;* (*garbage*) basura, despojo; (*wild region*) despoblado, yermo; (*of time*) pérdida; (*useless by-products*) desperdicios; excremento; (*for wiping machinery*) hilacha de algodón; **to lay waste** devastar, poner a fuego y sangre ‖ *tr* malgastar, perder ‖ *intr*—**to waste away** consumirse
waste'bas'ket *s* papelera
wasteful [ˈwestfəl] *adj* derrochador, manirroto; devastador, destructivo
waste'-land' *s* peladero
waste paper *s* papeles usados, papel de desecho, papel viejo
waste pipe *s* tubo de desagüe
waste products *spl* desperdicios; materia excretada
wastrel [ˈwestrəl] *s* derrochador *m*, malgastador *m;* pródigo, perdido
watch [wɑtʃ] *s* reloj *m* (*de bolsillo o de pulsera*); (*lookout*) vigía *m;* (mil) vigilia; (naut) guardia; **to be on the watch for** estar a la mira de; **to keep watch over** velar ‖ *tr* (*to look at*) mirar; (*to oversee*) velar, vigilar; guardar; tener cuidado con ‖ *intr* mirar; (*to keep awake*) velar; **to watch for** acechar; **to watch out** tener cuidado; **to watch out for** estar a la mira de; tener cuidado con; guardarse de; **to watch over** velar, vigilar
watch'case' *s* caja de reloj
watch charm *s* dije *m*
watch crystal *s* cristal *m* de reloj
watch'dog' *s* perro de guarda, perro guardián; (fig) guardián *m* fiel
watchful [ˈwɑtʃfəl] *adj* desvelado, vigilante
watchfulness [ˈwɑtʃfəlnɪs] *s* desvelo, vigilancia
watch'mak'er *s* relojero
watch•man [ˈwɑtʃmən] *s* (*pl* **-men** [mən]) vigilante *m*, velador *m*
watch night *s* noche vieja; oficio de noche vieja
watch pocket *s* relojera
watch strap *s* pulsera
watch'tow'er *s* atalaya, vigía
watch'word' *s* santo y seña; (*slogan*) lema *m*
water [ˈwɔtər] o [ˈwɑtər] *s* agua; **of the first water** de lo mejor; **to back water** ciar; **to carry water on both shoulders** nadar entre dos aguas; **to fish in troubled waters** pescar en río revuelto; **to hold water** (coll) ser bien fundado; **to make water** (*to urinate*) hacer aguas; (naut) hacer agua; **to pour** o **throw cold water on** echar un jarro de agua (fría) a ‖ *tr* regar, rociar; abrevar (*el ganado*); aguar (*el vino*); proveer de agua ‖ *intr* abrevarse (*el ganado*); tomar agua (*una locomotora*); llorar (*los ojos*)
water carrier *s* aguador *m*
water closet *s* excusado, retrete *m*, váter *m*
water color *s* acuarela
wa'ter•course' *s* corriente *f* de agua; lecho de corriente
water cress *s* berro
water cure *s* cura de aguas
wa'ter•fall' *s* cascada, caída de agua
water front *s* terreno ribereño
water gap *s* garganta, hondonada
water hammer *s* golpe *m* de ariete
water heater *s* calentador *m* de agua
water ice *s* sorbete *m*
watering can *s* regadera
watering place *s* aguadero; balneario
watering pot *s* regadera
watering trough *s* abrevadero

water jacket *s* camisa de agua
water lily *s* ninfea, nenúfar *m*
water line *s* línea de agua, línea de flotación; nivel *m* de agua
water main *s* cañería de agua
wa'ter•mark' *s* (*in paper*) filigrana; marca de nivel de agua
wa'ter•mel'on *s* sandía
water meter *s* contador *m* de agua
water pipe *s* cañería de agua
water polo *s* polo de agua
water power *s* fuerza de agua, hulla blanca
wa'ter•proof' *adj & s* impermeable *m*
wa'ter•shed' *s* divisoria de aguas; (*drainage area*) cuenca
water ski *s* esquí acuático
wa'ter•spout' *s* (*to carry water from roof*) canalón *m;* (*funnel of wet air extending from cloud to surface of water*) manga de agua, tromba marina
wa'ter•sup•ply' system *s* fontanería
wa'ter•tight' *adj* estanco, hermético; (fig) seguro
water tower *s* arca de agua
water wagon *s* (mil) carro de agua; **on the water wagon** (slang) sin tomar bebidas alcohólicas
wa'ter•way' *s* vía de agua, vía fluvial; (naut) canalizo
water wheel *s* rueda de agua; turbina de agua; (*of steamboat*) rueda de paletas
water wings *spl* nadaderas
wa'ter•works' *s* estación de bombas
watery ['wɔtəri] o ['wɑtəri] *adj* acuoso; (*said of the eyes*) lagrimoso, lloroso; insípido; húmedo, mojado
watt [wɑt] *s* vatio
wattage ['wɑtɪdʒ] *s* vatiaje *m*
watt'-hour' *s (pl* **watt-hours**) vatiohora
wattle ['wɑtəl] *s* (*of bird*) barba; (*of fish*) barbilla
watt'me'ter *s* vatímetro
wave [wev] *s* onda; (*of hair*) onda, ondulación; (*e.g., of heat or cold*) ola; (*e.g., of strikes*) oleaje *m;* señal hecha con la mano || *tr* blandir (*la espada*); ondear, ondular (*el cabello*); hacer señal con (*la mano*); decir (*adiós*) con la mano; **to wave aside** rechazar || *intr* ondear u ondearse; hacer señal con la mano
wave motion *s* movimiento ondulatorio
waver ['wevər] *intr* oscilar; (*to hesitate*) vacilar, titubear; (*to totter*) tambalear
wave theory *s* teoría ondulatoria
wav•y ['wevi] *adj* (*comp* **-ier;** *super* **-iest**) undoso, ondoso; (*water*) ondulado; (*hair*) ondeado
wax [wæks] *s* cera; **to be wax in one's hands** ser como una cera || *tr* encerar; cerotear (*el hilo*) || *intr* hacerse, volverse; crecer (*la luna*)
wax paper *s* papel encerado, papel parafinado
wax taper *s* cerilla
wax'works' *s* museo de cera
way [we] *s* vía, camino; dirección, sentido; manera, modo; costumbre, hábito; **across the way** enfrente; **a good way** un buen trecho; **all the way** hasta el fin del camino; **any way** de cualquier modo; **by the way** a propósito; **in a way** hasta cierto punto; **in every way** en todos respectos; **in this way** de este modo; **on the way to** camino de, rumbo a; **on the way out** saliendo; desapareciendo; **out of the way** hecho, despachado; inconveniente, impropio; a un lado, apartado; fuera de lo común; **that way** por allí; de ese modo; **this way** por aquí; de este modo; **to be in the way** estorbar; **to feel one's way** tantear el camino; proceder con tiento; **to force one's way** abrirse paso por fuerza; **to get out of the way** quitarse de en medio; (*to finish*) quitarse de encima; **to give way** ceder, retroceder; romperse (*una cuerda*); fracasar; **to give way to** entregarse a; **to go out of one's way** dar un rodeo; dar un rodeo innecesario; darse molestia; **to have one's way** salirse con la suya; **to keep out of the way** no obstruir el paso; **to know one's way around** saber entendérselas; **to know one's way to** conocer el camino a, saber ir a; **to lead the way** enseñar el camino; ir o entrar primero; **to lose one's way** perder el camino, extraviarse; **to make one's way** avanzar; hacer carrera, acreditarse; **to make way for** dar paso a, hacer lugar para; **to mend one's ways** mudar de vida; **to not know which way to turn** no saber dónde meterse; **to put out of the way** alejar, apartar; quitar de en medio; **to see one's way to** ver el modo de; **to take one's way** irse, marcharse; **to wend one's way** seguir camino; **to wind one's way through** serpentear por; **to wing one's way** ir volando; **under way** en marcha, en camino; **way in** entrada; **way out** salida; **ways** maneras, modales *mpl;* (*for launching a ship*) anguilas; **which way?** ¿por dónde?; ¿cómo?
way'bill' *s* hoja de ruta
wayfarer ['we,fɛrər] *s* caminante *mf*
way'lay' *v* (*pret & pp* **-laid'**) *tr* detener de improviso; (*to attack from ambush*) insidiar, asaltar
way'side' *s* borde *m* del camino; **to fall by the wayside** (*to disappear*) caer en el camino; fracasar
way station *s* apeadero
way train *s* tren *m* ómnibus
wayward ['wewərd] *adj* díscolo, voluntarioso; voltario, caprichoso
w.c. *abbr* **water closet, without charge**
we [wi] *pron pers* nosotros
weak [wik] *adj* débil, flaco; caedizo; (*vowel; verb*) débil
weaken ['wikən] *tr* debilitar, enflaquecer || *intr* debilitarse, enflaquecerse
weakling ['wiklɪŋ] *s* alfeñique *m*, canijo
weak-minded ['wik'maɪndɪd] *adj* irresoluto; simple, mentecato
weakness ['wiknɪs] *s* debilidad, flaqueza; caducidad; lado débil; afición, gusto
weal [wil] *s* verdugón *m*
wealth [wɛlθ] *s* riqueza

wealth•y [ˈwɛlθi] *adj* (*comp* **-ier;** *super* **-iest**) rico
wean [win] *tr* destetar; **to wean away from** apartar gradualmente de
weanling [ˈwinlɪŋ] *adj & s* destetado
weapon [ˈwɛpən] *s* arma
wear [wɛr] *s* (*act of wearing*) uso; (*clothing*) ropa; estilo, moda; (*wasting away from use*) desgaste *m*, deterioro; (*lasting quality*) durabilidad; **for all kinds of wear** a todo llevar; **for everyday wear** para todo trote || *v* (*pret* **wore** [wor]; *pp* **worn** [worn]) *tr* llevar, traer, llevar puesto; calzar (*cierto tamaño de zapato o guante*); (*to waste away by use*) desgastar, deteriorar; (*to tire*) agotar, cansar; **to wear out** consumir, gastar; agotar, cansar; abusar de (*la hospitalidad de una persona*) || *intr* desgastarse, deteriorarse; **to wear off** pasar, desaparecer; **to wear out** gastarse, usarse; **to wear well** durar, ser duradero
wear and tear *s* uso y desgaste
weariness [ˈwɪrɪnɪs] *s* cansancio; aburrimiento
wearing apparel [ˈwɛrɪŋ] *s* ropaje *m*, prendas de vestir
wearisome [ˈwɪrɪsəm] *adj* aburrido, cansado, fastidioso
wea•ry [ˈwɪri] *adj* (*comp* **-rier;** *super* **-riest**) cansado || *v* (*pret & pp* **-ried**) *tr* cansar || *intr* cansarse
weasel [ˈwizəl] *s* comadreja
weaseler [ˈwizələr] *s* pancista *mf*
weasel words *spl* palabras ambiguas
weather [ˈwɛðər] *s* tiempo; mal tiempo; **to be under the weather** (coll) no estar muy católico; (coll) estar borracho || *tr* aguantar (*el temporal, la adversidad*)
weather-beaten [ˈwɛðər,bitən] *adj* curtido por la intemperie
weather bureau *s* meteo *f*, servicio meteorológico
weath'er•cock' *s* veleta; (*fickle person*) (fig) veleta
weather forecasting *s* pronóstico del tiempo, previsión del tiempo
weather•man [ˈwɛðər,mæn] *s* (*pl* **-men** [,mɛn]) meteorologista *m*, pronosticador *m* del tiempo
weather report *s* parte meteorológico
weather station *s* estación meteorológica
weather stripping [ˈstrɪpɪŋ] *s* burlete *m*, cierre hermético
weather vane *s* veleta
weave [wiv] *s* tejido || *v* (*pret* **wove** [wov] o **weaved;** *pp* **wove** o **woven** [ˈwovən]) *tr* tejer; **to weave one's way** avanzar zigzagueando || *intr* tejer; zigzaguear
weaver [ˈwivər] *s* tejedor *m*
web [wɛb] *s* tejido, tela; (*of spider*) tela; (*between toes of birds and other animals*) membrana; (*of an iron rail*) alma; (fig) tejido, tela, enredo
web-footed [ˈwɛb,futɪd] *adj* palmípedo, de pie palmeado
wed [wɛd] *v* (*pret & pp* **wed** o **wedded;** *ger* **wedding**) *tr* (*to join in marriage*) casar; casarse con || *intr* casarse
wedding [ˈwɛdɪŋ] *adj* nupcial || *s* bodas, nupcias, matrimonio
wedding cake *s* pastel *m* de boda
wedding day *s* día *m* de bodas
wedding march *s* marcha nupcial
wedding night *s* noche *f* de bodas
wedding ring *s* anillo nupcial
wedge [wɛdʒ] *s* cuña || *tr* acuñar, apretar con cuña
wed'lock' *s* matrimonio
Wednesday [ˈwɛnzdi] *s* miércoles *m*
wee [wi] *adj* pequeñito, diminuto
weed [wid] *s* mala hierba; (coll) tabaco; **weeds** ropa de luto (*especialmente, de una viuda*) || *tr* desherbar, escardar
weeding hoe *s* escardillo
weed killer *s* matamalezas *m*, herbicida *m*
week [wik] *s* semana; **week in week out** semana tras semana
week'day' *s* día *m* laborable
week'days' *adv* entresemana (SAm)
week'end' *s* fin *m* de semana || *intr* pasar el fin de semana
week•ly [ˈwikli] *adj* semanal || *adv* cada semana || *s* (*pl* **-lies**) revista semanal, semanario
weep [wip] *v* (*pret & pp* **wept** [wɛpt]) *tr* llorar (*p.ej., la muerte de una persona*); derramar (*lágrimas*) || *intr* llorar
weeper [ˈwipər] *s* llorón *m;* (*hired mourner*) llorona, plañidera
weeping willow *s* sauce *m* llorón
weep•y [ˈwipi] *adj* (*comp* **-ier;** *super* **-iest**) (coll) lloroso
weevil [ˈwivəl] *s* gorgojo
weft [wɛft] *s* (*yarns running across warp*) trama; (*fabric*) tejido
weigh [we] *tr* pesar; (naut) levantar (*el ancla*) || *intr* pesar; **to weigh in** pesarse (*un jockey*)
weight [wet] *s* peso; (*of scales, clock, gymnasium, etc.*) pesa; **to lose weight** rebajar de peso; **to put on weight** ponerse gordo; **to throw one's weight around** (coll) hacer valer su poder || *tr* cargar, gravar; (*statistically*) ponderar
weightless [ˈwetlɪs] *adj* ingrávido
weightlessness [ˈwetlɪsnɪs] *s* ingravidez *f;* antigravedad
weight lifter *s* halterofilista *mf*
weight lifting *s* halterofilia
weight•y [ˈweti] *adj* (*comp* **-ier;** *super* **-iest**) (*heavy*) pesado; (*troublesome*) gravoso; importante, influyente
weir [wɪr] *s* presa, vertedero; (*for catching fish*) pescadera
weird [wɪrd] *adj* misterioso, sobrenatural, espectral; extraño, raro
welcome [ˈwɛlkəm] *adj* bienvenido; grato, agradable; **you are welcome** (*i.e., gladly received*) sea Vd. bienvenido; (*in answer to thanks*) no hay de qué; **you are welcome to it** está a la disposición de Vd.; **you are welcome to your opinion** piense Vd. lo

que quiera || *interj* ¡bienvenido! || *s* bienvenida, buena acogida || *tr* dar la bienvenida a; acoger con gusto, recibir con amabilidad

weld [wɛld] *s* autógena; (bot) gualda || *tr* soldar con autógena; (fig) unir || *intr* soldarse

welder [ˈwɛldər] *s* soldador *m;* (*machine*) soldadora

welding [ˈwɛldɪŋ] *s* autógena, soldadura autógena

wel′fare′ *s* bienestar *m;* (*effort to improve living conditions of the underprivileged*) asistencia, beneficencia; **to be on welfare** vivir de la asistencia pública

welfare state *s* gobierno socializante, estado de beneficencia, estado asistencial

well [wɛl] *adj* bien; bien de salud; **get well!** ¡que se mejore! || *adv* bien; pues; pues bien; **as well** también; **as well as** así como; además de || *interj* ¡vaya! || *s* pozo; (*natural source of water*) fuente *f*, manantial *m* || *intr*—**to well up** salir a borbotones

well-appointed [ˈwɛləˈpɔɪntɪd] *adj* bien amueblado, bien equipado

well-attended [ˈwɛləˈtɛndɪd] *adj* muy concurrido

well-behaved [ˈwɛlbɪˈhevd] *adj* de buena conducta

well′-be′ing *s* bienestar *m*

well′born′ *adj* bien nacido

well-bred [ˈwɛlˈbrɛd] *adj* cortés, bien criado

well-disposed [ˈwɛldɪsˈpozd] *adj* bien dispuesto

well-done [ˈwɛlˈdʌn] *adj* bien hecho; (*meat*) bien asado

well-fixed [ˈwɛlˈfɪkst] *adj* (coll) acaudalado

well-formed [ˈwɛlˈfɔrmd] *adj* bien formado; (*nose*) perfilado

well-founded [ˈwɛlˈfaʊndɪd] *adj* bien fundado

well-groomed [ˈwɛlˈgrumd] *adj* de mucho aseo, atildado

well-heeled [ˈwɛlˈhild] *adj* (coll) acomodado; **to be well-heeled** (coll) tener bien cubierto el riñón

well-informed [ˈwɛlɪnˈfɔrmd] *adj* versado, bien enterado

well-intentioned [ˈwɛlɪnˈtɛnʃənd] *adj* bien intencionado

well-kept [ˈwɛlˈkɛpt] *adj* bien cuidado, bien atendido; (*secret*) bien guardado

well-known [ˈwɛlˈnon] *adj* bien conocido; familiar

well-meaning [ˈwɛlˈminɪŋ] *adj* bien intencionado

well-nigh [ˈwɛlˈnaɪ] *adv* casi

well′-off′ *adj* adinerado, acaudalado

well-preserved [ˈwɛlprɪˈzʌrvd] *adj* bien conservado

well-read [ˈwɛlˈrɛd] *adj* leído, muy leído

well-spent [ˈwɛlˈspɛnt] *adj* (*money, youth, life*) bien empleado

well-spoken [ˈwɛlˈspokən] *adj* (*person*) bienhablado; (*word*) bien dicho

well′spring′ *s* fuente *f*, manantial *m;* fuente inagotable

well sweep *s* cigoñal *m*

well-tempered [ˈwɛlˈtɛmpərd] *adj* bien templado

well-thought-of [ˈwɛlˈθɔt,ɑv] *adj* bien mirado

well-timed [ˈwɛlˈtaɪmd] *adj* oportuno

well-to-do [ˈwɛltəˈdu] *adj* adinerado, acaudalado; (coll) plateado

well-wisher [ˈwɛlˈwɪʃər] *s* amigo, favorecedor *m*

well-worn [ˈwɛlˈworn] *adj* trillado, vulgar

welsh [wɛlʃ] *intr* (slang) dejar de cumplir; **to welsh on** (slang) dejar de cumplir con || **Welsh** *adj* galés || *s* (*language*) galés *m;* **the Welsh** los galeses

Welsh•man [ˈwɛlʃmən] *s* (*pl* **-men** [mən]) galés *m*

Welsh rabbit o **rarebit** [ˈrɛrbɪt] *s* tostada cubierta de queso derretido en cerveza

welt [wɛlt] *s* (*finish along a seam*) ribete *m;* (*of a shoe*) vira; (*wale from a blow*) verdugón *m*

welter [ˈwɛltər] *s* confusión, conmoción; (*a tumbling about*) revuelco || *intr* revolcar

wel′ter•weight′ *s* (box) peso mediano ligero

wen [wɛn] *s* lobanillo

wench [wɛntʃ] *s* muchacha, jovencita; moza, criada

wend [wɛnd] *tr*—**to wend one's way** dirigir sus pasos, seguir su camino

west [wɛst] *adj* occidental, del oeste || *adv* al oeste, hacia el oeste || *s* oeste *m*

western [ˈwɛstərn] *adj* occidental || *s* película del Oeste

West Indies [ˈɪndiz] *spl* Indias Occidentales

westward [ˈwɛstwərd] *adv* hacia el oeste

wet [wɛt] *adj* (*comp* **wetter;** *super* **wettest)** mojado; (*damp*) húmedo; (*paint*) fresco; (*weather*) lluvioso; (coll) antiprohibicionista || *s* (coll) antiprohibicionista *mf* || *v* (*pret & pp* **wet** o **wetted;** *ger* **wetting)** *tr* mojar || *intr* mojarse

wet′back′ *s* mojado

wet bar *s* bar *m* con agua corriente

wet battery *s* pila húmeda

wet blanket *s* aguafiestas *mf*

wet goods *spl* caldos

wet nurse *s* ama de cría o de leche

w.f. *abbr* **wrong font**

w.g. *abbr* **wire gauge**

whack [hwæk] *s* (coll) golpe ruidoso; (coll) prueba, tentativa || *tr* (coll) golpear ruidosamente

whale [hwel] *s* ballena; (*sperm whale*) cachalote *m;* **a whale at** (coll) un as de; **a whale for** (coll) un genio para; **a whale of a difference** (coll) una enorme diferencia; **a whale of a meal** (coll) una comida brutal || *tr* (coll) azotar || *intr* pescar ballenas

whale′bone′ *s* ballena

wharf [hwɔrf] *s* (*pl* **wharves** [hwɔrvz] o **wharfs**) muelle *m*, embarcadero

what [hwɑt] *pron interr* qué; cuál; **what else?** ¿qué más?; **what if . . .?** ¿y si . . .?, ¿qué le parece si?; **what of it?** ¿qué importa? || *pron rel* lo que; **what's what** lo que hay, toda la verdad || *adj interr* qué ||

adj rel el . . . que, la . . . que, etc. || *interj* qué; **what a . . .!** qué . . . más o tan, p.ej., **what a beautiful day!** ¡qué día más (o tan) hermoso!
what•ev'er *pron* cualquiera; todo lo que || *adj* cualquier; cualquier . . . que
what'not' *s* juguetero
what's-his-name [ˈhwɑtsɪz,nem] *s* (coll) el señor fulano
wheal [hwil] *s* roncha
wheat [hwit] *s* trigo
wheedle [ˈhwidəl] *tr* engatusar; conseguir por medio de halagos
wheel [hwil] *s* rueda; (coll) bicicleta; **at the wheel** en el volante || *tr* pasear (*a un niño*) en un cochecito; conducir (*a un enfermo*) en una silla de ruedas || *intr* (coll) ir en bicicleta; **to wheel about** o **around** dar una vuelta; cambiar de opinión
wheelbarrow [ˈhwil,bæro] *s* carretilla
wheel base *s* batalla, paso, distancia entre ejes
wheel chair *s* silla de ruedas, cochecillo para inválidos
wheeler-dealer [ˈhwilərˈdilər] *s* (slang) negociante *m* de gran influencia e independencia
wheel horse *s* caballo de varas; (fig) esclavo (*el que trabaja mucho y cumple con sus obligaciones*)
wheelwright [ˈhwil,raɪt] *s* carpintero de carretas
wheeze [hwiz] *s* resuello ruidoso || *intr* resollar produciendo un silbido
whelp [hwɛlp] *s* cachorro || *intr* parir
when [hwɛn] *adv* cuándo || *conj* cuando
whence [hwɛns] *adv* de dónde; por lo tanto || *conj* de donde
when•ev'er *conj* siempre que, cada vez que
where [hwɛr] *adv* dónde; adónde || *conj* donde; adonde
whereabouts [ˈhwɛrə,baʊts] *s* paradero
whereas [hwɛrˈæz] *conj* mientras que, al paso que; considerando || *s* considerando
where•by' *adv* por medio del cual
wherefore [ˈhwɛrfor] *adv* por qué, para qué; por eso, por tanto || *conj* por lo cual || *s* motivo, razón *f*
where•from' *adv* de donde
where•in' *adv* donde, en qué || *conj* donde; en el que; en lo cual
where•of' *adv* de qué || *conj* de que; de lo cual
where'up•on' *adv* con lo cual, después de lo cual
wherever [hwɛrˈɛvər] *conj* dondequiera que
wherewithal [ˈhwɛrwɪð,ɔl] *s* cumquibus *m*, medios
whet [hwɛt] *v* (*pret & pp* **whetted;** *ger* **whetting**) *tr* afilar, aguzar; despertar, estimular; abrir (*el apetito*)
whether [ˈwɛðər] *conj* si; **whether or no** en todo caso, de todas maneras; **whether or not** si . . . o no, ya sea que . . . o no
whet'stone' *s* piedra de afilar
whey [hwe] *s* suero de la leche
which [hwɪtʃ] *pron interr* cuál; **which is which** cuál es el uno y cuál el otro || *pron rel* que, el (la, etc.) que || *adj interr* qué; cuál, cuál de los (las) || *adj rel* el (la, etc.) . . . que
which•ev'er *pron rel* cualquiera || *adj rel* cualquier; **whichever ones** cualesquiera
whiff [hwɪf] *s* soplo; fumada; olorcillo; acceso, arranque *m;* **to get a whiff of** percibir un olor fugaz de || *intr* soplar (*el viento*); echar bocanadas (*el que fuma*)
while [hwaɪl] *conj* mientras, mientras que || *s* rato; **a long while** largo rato; **a while ago** hace un rato; **between whiles** de vez en cuando || *tr* **to while away** entretener (*el tiempo*); pasar (*p.ej., la tarde*) de un modo entretenido
whim [hwɪm] *s* capricho, antojo
whimper [ˈhwɪmpər] *s* lloriqueo || *tr* decir lloriqueando || *intr* lloriquear
whimsical [ˈhwɪmzɪkəl] *adj* caprichoso, extravagante, fantástico
whine [hwaɪn] *s* gimoteo, quejido || *intr* gimotear, quejarse
whin•ny [ˈhwɪni] *s* (*pl* **-nies**) relincho || *v* (*pret & pp* **-nied**) *intr* relinchar
whip [hwɪp] *s* látigo, zurriago; huevos batidos con nata || *v* (*pret & pp* **whipped** o **whipt;** *ger* **whipping**) *tr* azotar, zurriagar, fustigar; batir (*huevos y nata*); (coll) derrotar, vencer; **to whip off** (coll) escribir de prisa; **to whip out** sacar de repente; **to whip up** (coll) preparar de prisa; (coll) avivar, excitar
whip'cord' *s* tralla; tejido fuerte con costurones diagonales
whip hand *s* mano *f* del látigo; (*upper hand*) vara alta
whip'lash' *s* tralla
whipped cream *s* nata, crema batida
whipper-snapper [ˈhwɪpər,snæpər] *s* arrapiezo, mequetrefe *m*
whippet [ˈhwɪpɪt] *s* perro lebrel
whipping boy [ˈhwɪpɪŋ] *s* cabeza de turco, víctima inocente
whipping post *s* poste *m* de flagelación
whippoorwill [,hwɪpərˈwɪl] *s* chotacabras norteamericano (*Caprimulgus vociferus*)
whir [hwʌr] *s* zumbido || *v* (*pret & pp* **whirred;** *ger* **whirring**) *intr* girar zumbando
whirl [hwʌrl] *s* vuelta, giro; remolino; (*of events, parties, etc.*) serie *f* interminable || *tr & intr* remolinear; **my head whirls** siento vértigo
whirligig [ˈhwʌrlɪ,gɪg] *s* (ent) escribano del agua; tíovivo; (*pinwheel*) rehilandera, molinete *m;* peonza
whirl'pool' *s* remolino, vorágine *f*
whirl'wind' *s* torbellino, manga de viento
whirlybird [ˈhwʌrli,bʌrd] *s* (coll) helicóptero
whish [hwɪʃ] *s* zumbido suave || *intr* zumbar suavemente
whisk [hwɪsk] *s* escobilla; toque ligero || *tr* barrer, cepillar; **to whisk out of sight** escamotear || *intr* moverse rápidamente
whisk broom *s* escobilla

whiskers ['hwɪskərz] *spl* barbas; (*on side of face*) patillas; (*of cat*) bigotes *mpl*
whiskey ['hwɪski] *adj* (*voice*) (coll) aguardentoso ‖ *s* whisky *m*
whisper ['hwɪspər] *s* cuchicheo; (*of leaves*) susurro; **in a whisper** en voz baja ‖ *tr* susurrar, decir al oído ‖ *intr* cuchichear, hablar al oído; susurrar (*p.ej., las hojas*); (*to gossip*) susurrar, murmurar
whisperer ['hwɪspərər] *s* susurrón *m*
whispering ['hwɪspərɪŋ] *adj & s* (*gossiping*) susurrón *m*
whist [hwɪst] *s* whist *m* (*juego de naipes*)
whistle ['hwɪsəl] *s* (*sound*) silbido, silbo; pitazo; (*device*) silbato, pito; **to wet one's whistle** (coll) remojar la palabra ‖ *tr* silbar (*p.ej., una canción* ‖ *intr* silbar; pitear; **to whistle for** llamar con un silbido; (coll) tener que componérselas sin
whistle stop *s* apeadero, pueblecito
whit [hwɪt] *s*—**not a whit** ni pizca; **to not care a whit** no importarle a (*uno*) un bledo
white [hwaɪt] *adj* blanco ‖ *s* blanco; (*of an egg*) clara; **whites** (pathol) pérdidas blancas, flujo blanco
white'caps' *spl* cabrillas, palomas
white coal *s* hulla blanca
white'-col'lar *adj* oficinesco
white-collar crime *s* crímenes *mpl* de oficinistas
white feather *s*—**to show the white feather** mostrarse cobarde
white goods *spl* tejidos de algodón; ropa blanca; aparatos electrodomésticos
white-haired ['hwaɪt,hɛrd] *adj* de pelo blanco; (*gray-haired*) cano; (coll) favorito, predilecto
white heat *s* blanco, calor blanco; (fig) viva agitación
white lead [lɛd] *s* albayalde *m*
white lie *s* mentirilla, mentira inocente u oficiosa
white meat *s* pechuga, carne *f* de la pechuga del ave
whiten ['hwaɪtən] *tr* blanquear, emblanquecer ‖ *intr* blanquear, emblanquecerse; palidecer
whiteness ['hwaɪtnɪs] *s* blancura
white plague *s* peste blanca (*tuberculosis*)
white slavery *s* trata de blancas
white tie *s* corbatín blanco; traje *m* de etiqueta
white'wash' *s* jalbegue *m*, lechada, blanqueadura; (*e.g., of a scandal*) encubrimiento ‖ *tr* jalbegar, enjalbegar, encalar; absolver sin justicia; encubrir (*un escándalo*)
whither ['hwɪðər] *adv* adónde ‖ *conj* adonde
whitish ['hwaɪtɪʃ] *adj* blanquecino, blancuzco
whitlow ['hwɪtlo] *s* panadizo, uñero
Whitsuntide ['hwɪtsən,taɪd] *s* semana de Pentecostés
whittle ['hwɪtəl] *tr* sacar pedazos a (*un trozo de madera*); **to whittle away** o **down** reducir poco a poco
whiz o **whizz** [hwɪz] *s* silbido, zumbido; (slang) perito, fenómeno ‖ *v* (*pret & pp* **whizzed**; *ger* **whizzing**) *intr*—**to whiz by** rehilar, silbar; pasar como una flecha
who [hu] *pron interr* quién; **who else?** ¿quién más?; **who goes there?** (mil) ¿quién vive?; **who's who** quién es el uno y quién el otro; quiénes son gente de importancia ‖ *pron rel* que, quien; el (la, etc.) que
whoa [hwo] o [wo] *interj* ¡so!
who•ev'er *pron rel* quienquiera que, cualquiera que
whole [hol] *adj* todo, entero; (*intact*) ileso; (*not scattered or dispersed*) único, p.ej., **the whole interest for him was the child he was raising** el único interés para él era el niño que educaba; **made out of the whole cloth** enteramente falso o imaginario ‖ *s* conjunto, todo; **as a whole** en conjunto; **on the whole** en general; por la mayor parte
wholehearted ['hol,hɑrtɪd] *adj* sincero, cordial
whole note *s* (mus) semibreve *f*
whole'sale' *adj & adv* al por mayor ‖ *s* venta al pormayor ‖ *tr* vender al por mayor ‖ *intr* vender al por mayor; venderse al por mayor
wholesaler ['hol,selər] *s* comerciante *mf* al por mayor
wholesome ['holsəm] *adj* (*conducive to good health*) saludable; (*in good health*) fresco, rollizo
wholly ['holi] *adv* enteramente, completamente
whole wheat *s* trigo entero
whom [hum] *pron interr* a quién ‖ *pron rel* que, a quien; al (a la, etc.) que
whom•ev'er *pron rel* a quienquiera que
whoop [hup] o [hwup] *s* ululato ‖ *tr*—**to whoop it up** (slang) armar una gritería ‖ *intr* ulular
whooping cough ['hupɪŋ] o ['hʊpɪŋ] *s* tos ferina, tos convulsiva
whopper ['hwɑpər] *s* (coll) enormidad; (coll) mentirón *m*
whopping ['hwɑpɪŋ] *adj* (coll) enorme, grandísimo
whore [hor] *s* puta ‖ *intr*—**to whore around** putañear, putear
whore'house' *s* burdel *m;* congal *m* (Mex)
whortleber•ry ['hwʌrtəl,bɛri] *s* (*pl* **-ries**) arándano
whose [huz] *pron interr* de quién ‖ *pron rel* de quien, cuyo
why [hwaɪ] *adv* por qué; **why not?** ¿cómo no? ‖ *s* (*pl* **whys**) porqué *m* ‖ *interj* ¡toma!; **why, certainly!** ¡desde luego!, ¡por supuesto!; **why, yes!** ¡claro!, ¡pues sí!
wick [wɪk] *s* mecha, pabilo
wicked ['wɪkɪd] *adj* malo; malazo; (*mischievous*) travieso, revoltoso; (*vicious*) arisco; ofensivo
wicker ['wɪkər] *adj* mimbroso ‖ *s* mimbre *m & f*
wicket ['wɪkɪt] *s* (*small door in a larger one*) portillo, postigo; (*small opening in a door*) ventanillo; (*ticket window*) taquilla; (*gate to regulate flow of water*) compuerta; (cricket) meta; (croquet) aro

wide [waɪd] *adj* ancho; de ancho; (*sense of a word*) amplio, lato || *adv* de par en par; enteramente; lejos; **wide of the mark** lejos del blanco; fuera de propósito
wide'-an'gle *adj* granangular
wide'-a•wake' *adj* despabilado
widen [ˈwaɪdən] *tr* ensanchar || *intr* ensancharse
wide'-o'pen *adj* abierto de par en par; **to be wide-open** estar (*p.ej., una ciudad*) abierta a los jugadores
wide'spread' *adj* (*arms, wings*) extendido; difundido, extenso
widow [ˈwɪdo] *s* viuda; (cards) baceta || *tr* dejar viuda
widower [ˈwɪdo•ər] *s* viudo
widowhood [ˈwɪdo,hʊd] *s* viudez *f*
widow's mite *s* limosna que da un pobre
widow's pension *s* viudedad
widow's weeds *spl* luto de viuda
width [wɪdθ] *s* anchura
wield [wild] *tr* esgrimir, manejar (*la espada*); ejercer (*el poder*)
wife [waɪf] *s* (*pl* **wives** [waɪvz]) esposa, mujer *f*
wig [wɪg] *s* peluca
wiggle [ˈwɪgəl] *s* meneo rápido || *tr* menear rápidamente || *intr* menearse rápidamente
wig'wag' *s* comunicación con banderas || *v* (*pret & pp* **-wagged;** *ger* **-wagging**) *tr* menear; mandar (*informes*) moviendo banderas || *intr* menearse; señalar con banderas
wigwam [ˈwɪgwɑm] *s* choza cónica (*de los pieles rojas*)
wild [waɪld] *adj* (*not domesticated; growing without cultivation; uncivilized*) salvaje; (*unrestrained*) descabellado; (*frantic, mad*) frenético; (*riotous*) desenfrenado, revoltoso; extravagante; (*bullet, shot*) perdido; **wild about** loco por || *adv* disparatadamente; **to run wild** crecer locamente; estar sin gobierno || *s* desierto, yermo; **wilds** monte *m*, despoblado
wild boar *s* jabalí *m*
wild card *s* comodín *m*
wild'cat' *s* gato montés; lince *m;* empresa arriesgada
wildcat strike *s* huelga no autorizada por el sindicato
wilderness [ˈwɪldərnɪs] *s* desierto, yermo
wild'fire' *s* fuego fatuo; fucilazo; **to spread like wildfire** ser un reguero de pólvora, correr como pólvora en reguero
wild flower *s* flor *f* del campo
wild goose *s* ganso bravo
wild'-goose' chase *s* caza de grillos
wild'life' *s* animales *mf* salvajes
wild oats *spl* excesos de la juventud, mocedad; **to sow one's wild oats** llevar (*los mozos*) una vida de excesos
wild olive *s* acebuche *m*
wile [waɪl] *s* ardid *m* engaño; (*cunning*) astucia || *tr* engatusar; **to wile away** entretener (*el tiempo*); pasar (*p.ej., la tarde*)
will [wɪl] *s* voluntad; (law) testamento; **at will** a voluntad || *tr* querer; (*to bequeath*) legar || *intr* querer; **do as you will** haga Vd. lo que quiera || *v* (*pret & cond* **would**) *v aux* **he will arrive at six o'clock** llegará a las seis; **he will go for days without smoking** pasa días enteros sin fumar
willful [ˈwɪlfəl] *adj* voluntarioso
willfulness [ˈwɪlfəlnɪs] *s* voluntariedad
William [ˈwɪljəm] *s* Guillermo
willing [ˈwɪlɪŋ] *adj* dispuesto; gustoso, pronto; espontáneo; **willing or unwilling** que quiera, que no quiera
willingly [ˈwɪlɪŋli] *adv* de buena gana, de buena voluntad
willingness [ˈwɪlɪŋnɪs] *s* buena gana, buena voluntad
will-o'-the-wisp [ˈwɪləðəˈwɪsp] *s* fuego fatuo; ilusión, quimera
willow [ˈwɪlo] *s* sauce *m*
willowy [ˈwɪlo•i] *adj* (*pliant*) juncal, mimbreño; (*slender, graceful*) juncal, cimbreño, esbelto; lleno de sauces
will power *s* fuerza de voluntad
willy-nilly [ˈwɪliˈnɪli] *adv* de grado o por fuerza
wilt [wɪlt] *tr* marchitar || *intr* marchitarse
wil•y [ˈwaɪli] *adj* (*comp* **-ier;** *super* **-iest**) artero, engañoso; astuto
wimple [ˈwɪmpəl] *s* griñón *m*, impla
win [wɪn] *s* (coll) éxito, triunfo || *v* (*pret & pp* **won** [wʌn]; *ger* **winning**) *tr* ganar; **to win over** ganar, conquistar || *intr* ganar; **to win out** ganar; (coll) tener éxito
wince [wɪns] *s* sobresalto || *intr* sobresaltarse
winch [wɪntʃ] *s* maquinilla, torno; (*handle, crank*) manubrio
wind [wɪnd] *s* viento; (*gas in intestines*) (coll) viento; (*breath*) respiración, resuello; **to break wind** ventosear; **to get wind of** saber de, tener noticia de; **to sail close to the wind** (naut) ceñir el viento; **to take the wind out of one's sails** apagarle a uno los fuegos || *tr* dejar sin aliento || [waɪnd] *v* (*pret & pp* **wound** [waʊnd]) *tr* (*to coil; to wrap up*) arrollar, envolver, devanar (*alambre*); ovillar (*hilo*); torcer (*hebras*); hacer girar (*un manubrio*); dar cuerda a (*un reloj*); **to wind one's way through** serpentear por; **to wind up** arrollar, envolver; (coll) poner punto final a || *intr* serpentear (*un camino*)
windbag [ˈwɪnd,bæg] *s* (*of bagpipe*) odre *m;* (coll) charlatán *m*, palabrero, discursista *mf*
windbreak [ˈwɪnd,brek] *s* guardavientos *m*
wind cone [wɪnd] *s* (aer) cono de viento
winded [ˈwɪndɪd] *adj* falto de respiración, sin resuello
windfall [ˈwɪnd,fɔl] *s* fruta caída del árbol; fortunón *m*, cosa llovida del cielo
winding sheet [ˈwaɪndɪŋ] *s* sudario, mortaja
winding stairs *spl* escalera de caracol
wind instrument [wɪnd] *s* (mus) instrumento de viento
windlass [ˈwɪndləs] *s* maquinilla, torno
windmill [ˈwɪnd,mɪl] *s* (*mill operated by wind*) molino de viento; (*modern wind-driven source of power*) aeromotor *m;* (*pinwheel*) molinete *m;* **to tilt at windmills** luchar con los molinos de viento

window [ˈwɪndo] *s* ventana; (*of ticket office; of envelope*) ventanilla; (*of coach, automobile*) ventanilla, portezuela
window dresser *s* escaparatista *mf*
window dressing *s* adorno de escaparates
window frame *s* marco de ventana
win'dow•pane' *s* cristal *m* o vidrio de ventana
window screen *s* alambrera, sobrevidriera
window shade *s* visillo, transparente *m* de resorte
win'dow•shop' *v* (*pret & pp* **-shopped;** *ger* **-shopping**) *intr* curiosear en las tiendas
window shutter *s* contraventana
window sill *s* repisa de ventana
windpipe [ˈwɪnd,paɪp] *s* tráquea
wind shear *s* (aer) ráfaga violente
windshield [ˈwɪnd,ʃild] *s* parabrisa *m*
windshield washer *s* lavaparabrisas *m*
windshield wiper *s* limpiaparabrisas *m*
wind'shield-wip'er blade *s* escobilla de limpiaparabrisas
wind sock *s* (aer) cono de viento
windstorm [ˈwɪnd,stɔrm] *s* ventarrón *m*
wind-up [ˈwaɪnd,ʌp] *s* conclusión; (sport) final *f* de partido
windward [ˈwɪndwərd] *s* barlovento; **to turn to windward** barloventear
Windward Islands *spl* islas de Barlovento
Windward Passage *s* paso de los Vientos
wind•y [ˈwɪndi] *adj* (*comp* **-ier;** *super* **-iest**) ventoso; (*unsubstantial*) vacío; palabrero, ampuloso, discursisto; **it is windy** hace viento
wine [waɪn] *s* vino || *tr* obsequiar con vino || *intr* beber vino
wine cellar *s* bodega
wine'glass' *s* copa para vino
winegrower [ˈwaɪn,gro•ər] *s* vinicultor *m*
winegrowing [ˈwaɪn,gro•ɪŋ] *s* vinicultura
wine making *s* enotecnia
wine press *s* lagar *m*
winer•y [ˈwaɪnəri] *s* (*pl* **-ies**) lagar *m*
wine'skin' *s* odre *m*
winetaster [ˈwaɪn,testər] *s* catavinos *m*
wing [wɪŋ] *s* ala; facción; bando; (theat) bastidor *m;* **to take wing** alzar el vuelo || *tr* herir en el ala; **to wing one's way** avanzar volando
wing chair *s* sillón *m* de orejas
wing collar *s* cuello de pajarita
wing nut *s* tuerca de aletas
wing'spread' *s* envergadura
wink [wɪŋk] *s* guiño; **to not sleep a wink** no pegar los ojos; **to take forty winks** (coll) descabezar el sueño || *tr* guiñar (*el ojo*) || *intr* guiñar; (*to blink*) parpadear, pestañear; **to wink at** guiñar el ojo a; fingir no ver
winner [ˈwɪnər] *s* ganador *m*, vencedor *m;* premiado
winning [ˈwɪnɪŋ] *adj* triunfante, victorioso; atrayente, simpático || **winnings** *spl* ganancias
winnow [ˈwɪno] *tr* aventar; entresacar || *intr* aletear
winsome [ˈwɪnsəm] *adj* atrayente, simpático, engañador; alegre
winter [ˈwɪntər] *adj* invernal || *s* invierno || *intr* invernar
win'ter•green' *s* gaulteria, té *m* del Canadá; esencia de gaulteria
win•try [ˈwɪntri] *adj* (*comp* **-trier;** *super* **-triest**) invernal, invernizo; helado, frío
wipe [waɪp] *tr* frotar para limpiar; enjugar (*la cara, el sudor, las manos*); **to wipe away** enjugar (*lágrimas*); **to wipe off** quitar frotando; **to wipe out** (coll) borrar, cancelar; (coll) aniquilar, destruir; (coll) enjugar (*deudas, un déficit*)
wiper [ˈwaɪpər] *s* paño, trapo; (elec) contacto deslizante
wire [waɪr] *s* (*thread of metal*) alambre *m;* telégrafo; telegrama *m;* teléfono; **to pull wires** (coll) tocar resortes || *tr* alambrar; telegrafiar || *intr* telegrafiar
wire cutter *s* cortaalambres *m*
wire entanglement *s* (mil) alambrado
wire gauge *s* calibrador *m* de alambre
wire-haired [ˈwaɪr,hɛrd] *adj* de pelo áspero
wireless [ˈwaɪrlɪs] *adj* inalámbrico, sin hilos
wire nail *s* punta de París, clavo de alambre
wire pulling [ˈpʊlɪŋ] *s* (coll) empleo de resortes; enchufismo
wire recorder *s* grabadora de alambre
wire screen *s* alambrera, tela de alambre
wire service *s* servicio telegráfrico y telefónico
wire'tap' *v* (*pret & pp* **-tapped;** *ger* **-tapping**) *tr* intervenir (*una conversación telefónica*)
wire tapping *s* escuchas telefónicas *fpl*
wiring [ˈwaɪrɪŋ] *s* (elec) alambraje *m*
wir•y [ˈwaɪri] *adj* (*comp* **-ier;** *super* **-iest**) alambrino; cimbreante; nervudo; vibrante
wisdom [ˈwɪzdəm] *s* sabiduría, cordura
wisdom tooth *s* muela cordal, muela del juició
wise [waɪz] *adj* sabio, cuerdo; (*step, decision*) acertado, juicioso; **to be wise to** (slang) conocer el juego de; **to get wise** (coll) caer en el chiste || *s* modo, manera; **in no wise** de ningún modo
wiseacre [ˈwaɪz,ekər] *s* sabihondo
wise'crack' *s* (slang) cuchufleta || *intr* (slang) cuchufletear
wise guy *s* (slang) sabelotodo
wish [wɪʃ] *s* deseo; **to make a wish** pensar algo que se desea || *tr* desear; dar (*los buenos días*) || *intr* desear; **to wish for** desear, anhelar
wish'bone' *s* espoleta, hueso de la suerte
wishful [ˈwɪʃfəl] *adj* deseoso
wishful thinking *s* optimismo a ultranza; **to indulge in wishful thinking** forjarse ilusiones
wistful [ˈwɪstfəl] *adj* melancólico, tristón, pensativo
wit [wɪt] *s* agudeza; (*person*) chistoso; (*keen mental power*) juicio; **to be at one's wits' end** no saber qué hacer; **to have the wit to** tener el tino de; **to live by one's wits** vivir del cuento
witch [wɪtʃ] *s* bruja, hechicera; (*old hag*) bruja

witch'craft' *s* brujería
witches' Sabbath *s* aquelarre *m*
witch hazel *s* (*shrub*) nogal *m* de la brujería, planta del sortilegio; (*liquid*) hamamelina, hazelina
with [wɪð] o [wɪθ] *prep* con; de
with•draw' *v* (*pret* **-drew;** *pp* **-drawn)** *tr* retirar ‖ *intr* retirarse
withdrawal [wɪð'drɔ•əl] o [wɪθ'drɔ•əl] *s* retirada
withdrawal symptom *s* síntoma *m* de abstinencia; (slang) mono
wither ['wɪðər] *tr* marchitar; (fig) aplastar, confundir ‖ *intr* marchitarse; confundirse
with•hold' *v* (*pret & pp* **-held)** *tr* retener; suspender (*pago*); negar (*un permiso*)
withholding tax *s* impuesto deducido del sueldo
with•in' *adv* dentro ‖ *prep* dentro de; al alcance de; poco menos de; con un margen de
with•out' *adv* fuera ‖ *prep* fuera de; (*lacking, not with*) sin; **to do without** pasar sin; **without** + *ger* sin + *inf*, p.ej., **he left without saying goodbye** salió sin despedirse; sin que + *subj*, p.ej., **he came in without anyone seeing him** entró sin que nadie le viese
with•stand' *v* (*pret & pp* **-stood)** *tr* aguantar, resistir
witness ['wɪtnɪs] *s* testigo *mf;* **in witness whereof** en fe de lo cual; **to bear witness** dar testimonio ‖ *tr* (*to be present at*) presenciar; (*to attest*) atestiguar, testimoniar; firmar como testigo
witness stand *s* banquillo o estrado de los testigos
witticism ['wɪtɪ,sɪzəm] *s* agudeza, dicho agudo, ocurrencia
wittingly ['wɪtɪŋli] *adv* a sabiendas
wit•ty ['wɪti] *adj* (*comp* **-tier;** *super* **-tiest)** agudo, ingenioso; (*person*) ocurrente, chistoso
wizard ['wɪzərd] *s* brujo, hechicero; (coll) as *m*, experto
wizardry ['wɪzərdri] *s* hechicería, magia
wizened ['wɪzənd] *adj* acartonado, arrugado
wk. *abbr* **week**
w.l. *abbr* **wave length**
woad [wod] *s* hierba pastel
wobble ['wɑbəl] *s* bamboleo, tambaleo ‖ *intr* bambolear, tambalear; bailar (*una silla*); (fig) vacilar, ser inconstante
wob•bly ['wɑbli] *adj* (*comp* **-blier;** *super* **-bliest)** bamboleante, inseguro; vacilante
woe [wo] *s* aflicción, miseria, infortunio ‖ *interj* **—woe is me!** ¡ay de mí!
woebegone ['wobɪ,gɔn] o ['wobɪ,gɑn] *adj* cariacontecido, triste
woeful ['wofəl] *adj* triste, miserable; (*of poor quality*) malo, pésimo
wolf [wʊlf] *s* (*pl* **wolves** [wʊlvz]) lobo; persona cruel, persona mañosa; (coll) tenorio; **to cry wolf** dar falsa alarma; **to keep the wolf from the door** ponerse a cubierto del hambre ‖ *tr & intr* comer vorazmente, engullir
wolf'hound' *s* galgo lobero
wolfram ['wʊlfrəm] *s* (*element*) volframio; (*mineral*) volframita
wolf's-bane o **wolfsbane** ['wʊlfs,ben] *s* matalobos *m*
woman ['wʊmən] *s* (*pl* **women** ['wɪmɪn]) mujer *f*
womanhood ['wʊmən,hʊd] *s* el sexo femenino; las mujeres
womanish ['wʊmənɪʃ] *adj* mujeril; (*effeminate*) afeminado
wom'an•kind' *s* el sexo femenino
womanly ['wʊmənli] *adj* (*comp* **-lier;** *super* **-liest**) femenil, mujeriego
woman suffrage *s* sufragismo
woman-suffragist ['wʊmən'sʌfrədʒɪst] *s* sufragista *mf*
womb [wʊm] *s* útero; (fig) seno
womenfolk ['wɪmɪn,fok] *spl* las mujeres
women's lib(eration movement) *s* movimiento feminista; feminismo
wonder ['wʌndər] *s* (*something strange or surprising*) maravilla; (*feeling of surprise*) admiración; (*something strange, miracle*) milagro; **for a wonder** cosa extraña; **no wonder that . . .** no es mucho que. . .; **to work wonders** hacer milagros ‖ *tr* preguntarse ‖ *intr* admirarse, maravillarse; **to wonder at** admirarse de, maravillarse con o de
wonder drugs *spl* drogas milagrosas
wonderful ['wʌndərfəl] *adj* maravilloso
won'der•land' *s* tierra de las maravillas; reino de las hadas
wonderment ['wʌndərmənt] *s* asombro, sorpresa
wont [wʌnt] o [wɔnt] *adj* acostumbrado; **to be wont to** acostumbrar ‖ *s* costumbre, hábito
wonted ['wʌntɪd] o ['wɔntɪd] *adj* acostumbrado, habitual
woo [wu] *tr* cortejar (*a una mujer*); tratar de conquistar; tratar de persuadir
wood [wʊd] *s* madera; (*for making a fire*) leña; barril *m* de madera; **out of the woods** (coll) fuera de peligro; (coll) libre de dificultades; **to take to the woods** andar a monte; **woods** bosque *m*
woodbine ['wʊd,baɪn] *s* (*honeysuckle*) madreselva; (*Virginia creeper*) guau *m*
wood carving *s* labrado de madera
wood'chuck' *s* marmota de América
wood'cock' *s* becada, coalla, chocha
wood'cut' *s* (typ) grabado en madera
wood'cut'ter *s* leñador *m*
wooded ['wʊdɪd] *adj* arbolado, enselvado
wooden ['wʊdən] *adj* de madera, hecho de madera; torpe, estúpido; sin ánimo
wood engraving *s* (typ) grabado en madera
wooden-headed ['wʊdən,hɛdɪd] *adj* (coll) torpe, estúpido
wooden leg *s* pata de palo
wooden shoe *s* zueco
wood grouse *s* gallo de bosque
woodland ['wʊdlənd] *adj* selvático ‖ *s* bosque *m*, monte *m*
woodland scene *s* (paint) boscaje *m*

wood•man ['wʊdmən] *s* (*pl* **-men** [mən]) leñador *m*
woodpecker ['wʊd,pɛkər] *s* carpintero, pájaro carpintero; (*green woodpecker*) picamaderos *m*
wood'pile' *s* montón *m* de leña
wood screw *s* tirafondo
wood'shed' *s* leñero
woods•man ['wʊdzmən] *s* (*pl* **-men** [mən]) leñador *m*
wood'wind' *s* (mus) instrumento de viento de madera
wood'work' *s* (*working in wood*) ebanistería, obra de carpintería; (*things made of wood*) maderaje *m*
wood'work'er *s* ebanista *mf*, carpintero
wood'worm' *s* carcoma
wood•y ['wʊdi] *adj* (*comp* **-ier;** *super* **-iest**) arbolado, enselvado; (*like wood*) leñoso
wooer ['wu•ər] *s* pretendiente *m*, galán *m*
woof [wuf] *s* (*yarns running across warp*) trama; (*fabric*) tejido
woofer ['wʊfər] *s* altavoz *m* para audiofrecuencias bajas
wool [wʊl] *s* lana
woolen ['wʊlən] *adj* de lana, hecho de lana || *s* tejido de lana; **woolens** lanerías
woolgrower ['wʊl ,gro•ər] *s* criador *m* de ganado lanar
wool•ly ['wʊli] *adj* (*comp* **-lier;** *super* **-liest**) lanoso, lanudo; borroso, confuso
Worcestershire sauce ['wʊstər∫ər] *s* salsa inglesa
word [wʌrd] *s* palabra; **to be as good as one's word** cumplir lo prometido; **to have a word with** hablar cuatro palabras con; **to have word from** recibir noticias de; **to keep one's word** cumplir su palabra; **to leave word** dejar dicho; **to send word that** mandar decir que; **words** (*a quarrel*) palabras mayores; (*text of a song*) letra || *tr* redactar, formular || **Word** *s* (theol) Verbo
word count *s* recuento de vocabulario
word formation *s* (gram) formación de palabras
wording ['wʌrdɪŋ] *s* fraseología, estilo
word order *s* (gram) orden *m* de colocación
word processing *s* redacción por medios electrónicos
word'stock' *s* vocabulario, léxico
word•y ['wʌrdi] *adj* (*comp* **-ier;** *super* **-iest**) verboso
work [wʌrk] *s* (*exertion; labor, toil*) trabajo; (*result of exertion; human output; engineering structure*) obra; (sew) labor *f;* **at work** trabajando; (*not at home*) en la oficina, en el taller, en la tienda; **out of work** sin trabajo, desempleado; **to shoot the works** (slang) echar el resto; **works** fábrica; mecanismo; (*of clock*) movimiento || *tr* hacer trabajar; trabajar, obrar (*la madera, el hierro*); obrar (*un milagro*); explotar (*una mina*); **to work up** preparar; estimular, excitar || *intr* trabajar; funcionar, marchar (*un aparato, un motor*); obrar (*p.ej., un remedio*); **to work loose** aflojarse; **to work out** resolverse
workable ['wʌrkəbəl] *adj* (*feasible*) practicable; (*that can be worked*) laborable
workaholic [,wʌrkə'hɔlɪk] *s* (coll) individuo con compulsión al trabajo
work'bench' *s* banco de trabajo, banco de taller
work'book' *s* (*manual of instructions*) libro de reglas; libro de ejercicios
work'box' *s* caja de herramientas; (*for needlework*) caja de labor
work'day' *adj* de cada día; ordinario, vulgar || *s* día *m* de trabajo; (*number of hours of work*) jornada
work'days' *adv* entresemana (SAm)
worked-up ['wʌrkt'ʌp] *adj* muy conmovido, sobreexcitado, exaltado
worker ['wʌrkər] *s* trabajador *m*, obrero
work force *s* mano *f* de obra, personal obrero
work'horse' *s* caballo de carga; (*tireless worker*) yunque *m*
work'house' *s* taller penitenciario; (Brit) asilo de pobres
working class *s* clase obrera
work'ing•girl' *s* trabajadora joven
working hours *spl* horas de trabajo
working hypothesis *s* hipótesis *f* de guía
working•man ['wʌrkɪŋ,mæn] *s* (*pl* **-men** [,mɛn]) *s* obrero, trabajador *m*
working•woman ['wʌrkɪŋ,wʊmən] *s* (*pl* **-women** [,wɪmɪn]) obrera, trabajadora
work•man ['wʌrkmən] *s* (*pl* **-men** [mən]) obrero, trabajador *m;* (*skilled worker*) artífice *m*
workmanship ['wʌrkmən,∫ɪp] *s* destreza en el trabajo; (*work executed*) hechura, obra
work of art *s* obra de arte
work'out' *s* ensayo, prueba; (*physical exercise*) ejercicio
work'room' *s* (*for manual work*) obrador *m*, taller *m;* (*study*) gabinete *m* de trabajo
work'shop' *s* obrador *m*, taller *m*
work stoppage *s* paro
work therapy *s* laborterapia
world [wʌrld] *adj* mundial || *s* mundo; **a world of** la mar de; **half the world** (*a lot of people*) medio mundo; **since the world began** desde que el mundo es mundo; **the other world** el otro mundo; **to bring into the world** echar al mundo; **to see the world** ver mundo; **to think the world of** tener un alto concepto de
world affairs *spl* asuntos internacionales
world'-class' *adj* sobresaliente
world•ly ['wʌrldli] *adj* (*comp* **-lier;** *super* **-liest**) mundano
world'ly-wise' *adj* que tiene mucho mundo
world's fair *s* exposición mundial
World War *s* Guerra Mundial
world'-wide' *adj* global, mundial
worm [wʌrm] *s* gusano; **worms** (pathol) lombrices *fpl* || *tr* limpiar de lombrices; **to worm a secret out of a person** arrancar mañosamente un secreto a una persona; **to worm one's way into** insinuarse en
worm-eaten ['wʌrm,itən] *adj* carcomido; (fig) decaído, desgastado
worm gear *s* engranaje *m* de tornillo sin fin

worm'wood' *s* (*Artemisia*) ajenjo; (*Artemisia absinthium*) ajenjo del campo o ajenjo mayor; (*something bitter or grievous*) (fig) ajenjo

worm•y ['wʌrmi] *adj* (*comp* **-ier;** *super* **-iest**) gusaniento, gusanoso; (*worm-eaten*) carcomido; (*groveling*) rastrero, servil

worn [worn] *adj* roto, raído, gastado

worn'-out' *adj* muy gastado, inservible; (*by toil, illness*) consumido, rendido

worrisome ['wʌrisəm] *adj* inquietante; (*inclined to worry*) aprensivo, inquieto

wor•ry ['wʌri] *s* (*pl* **-ries**) inquietud, preocupación; (*cause of anxiety*) molestia ‖ *v* (*pret & pp* **-ried**) *tr* inquietar, preocupar; (*to harass, pester*) acosar, molestar; **to be worried** estar inquieto ‖ *intr* inquietarse, preocuparse; **don't worry** pierda Vd. cuidado

worse [wʌrs] *adj & adv comp* peor; **worse and worse** de mal en peor

worsen ['wʌrsən] *tr & intr* empeorar ‖ *ref* gravarse

wor•ship ['wʌrʃɪp] *s* adoración, culto; **your worship** vuestra merced ‖ *v* (*pret & pp* **-shiped** o **-shipped;** *ger* **-shiping** o **-shipping**) *tr & intr* adorar, venerar

worshiper o **worshipper** ['wʌrʃɪpər] *s* adorador *m*, devoto

worst [wʌrst] *adj & adv super* peor ‖ *s* (lo) peor; **at worst** en las peores circunstancias; **if worst comes to worst** si pasa lo peor; **to get the worst of** llevar la peor parte, salir perdiendo

worsted ['wustɪd] *adj* de estambre ‖ *s* estambre *m;* tela de estambre

wort [wʌrt] *s* (bot) hierba, planta; mosto de cerveza

worth [wʌrθ] *adj* del valor de; digno de; **to be worth** valer; tener una fortuna de; **to be worth** + *ger* valer la pena de + *inf;* **to be worth while** valer la pena; ser de mérito ‖ *s* valor *m;* mérito; **a dollar's worth of** un dólar de

worthless ['wʌrθlɪs] *adj* sin valor, inútil, inservible; (*person*) despreciable

worth'while' *adj* de mérito, digno de atención

wor•thy ['wʌrði] *adj* (*comp* **-thier;** *super* **-thiest**) digno; benemérito, meritorio ‖ *s* (*pl* **-thies**) benemérito; (*hum & iron*) personaje *m*

would [wud] *v aux* **she said she would do it** dijo que lo haría; **he would come if he could** vendría si pudiese; **he would go for days without smoking** pasaba días enteros sin fumar; **would that . . .!** ¡ojalá que . . .!

would'-be' *adj* llamado; supuesto ‖ *s* presumido

wound [wund] *s* herida ‖ *tr* herir

wounded ['wundɪd] *adj* herido ‖ **the wounded** los heridos

wow [wau] *s* (*of phonograph record*) ululación; (slang) éxito rotundo ‖ *tr* (slang) entusiasmar ‖ *interj* ¡cielos!, ¡mecachis!

wrack [ræk] *s* naufragio; vestigio; (*fucaceous seaweed*) varec *m;* **to go to wrack and ruin** desvencijarse; ir al desastre

wraith [reθ] *s* fantasma *m*, espectro

wrangle ['ræŋgəl] *s* pendencia, riña ‖ *intr* pelotear, reñir

wrap [ræp] *s* abrigo, manto ‖ *v* (*pret & pp* **wrapped;** *ger* **wrapping**) *tr* envolver; **to be wrapped up in** (fig) estar prendado de; **to wrap up** envolver; (*in clothing*) arropar; (coll) concluir ‖ *intr*—**to wrap up** arroparse

wrapper ['ræpər] *s* bata, peinador *m;* (*of newspaper or magazine*) faja; (*of tobacco*) capa

wrapping paper ['ræpɪŋ] *s* papel *m* de envolver, papel de embalar

wrath [ræθ] o [rɑθ] *s* cólera, ira; venganza

wrathful ['ræθfəl] o ['rɑθfəl] *adj* colérico, iracundo

wreak [rik] *tr* descargar (*la cólera*); infligir (*venganza*)

wreath [riθ] *s* (*pl* **wreaths** [riðz]) guirnalda; corona funeraria; (*worn as a mark of honor or victory*) corona de laurel; (*of smoke*) espiral *f*

wreathe [rið] *tr* enguirnaldar; ceñir, envolver; tejer (*una guirnalda*) ‖ *intr* elevarse en espirales (*el humo*)

wreck [rɛk] *s* destrucción, ruina; naufragio; catástrofe *f*, desastre *m;* despojos, restos; (*of one's hopes*) naufragio; **to be a wreck** estar hecho un cascajo, estar hecho una ruina ‖ *tr* destruir, arruinar; hacer naufragar; hacer chocar, descarrilar (*un tren*)

wrecking ball *s* bola rompedora

wrecking car *s* (aut) camión *m* de auxilio; (rr) carro de grúa

wrecking crane *s* grúa de auxilio

wren [rɛn] *s* buscareta, coletero, rey *m* de zarza

wrench [rɛntʃ] *s* llave *f;* (*pull*) arranque *m*, tirón *m;* (*twist of a joint*) esguince *m* ‖ *tr* torcerse (*p.ej., la muñeca*); (fig) torcer (*el sentido de una oración*)

wrest [rɛst] *tr* arrebatar, arrancar violentamente

wrestle ['rɛsəl] *s* lucha; partido de lucha ‖ *intr* luchar

wrestling match ['rɛslɪŋ] *s* partido de lucha

wretch [rɛtʃ] *s* miserable *mf*

wretched ['rɛtʃɪd] *adj* miserable; (*poor, worthless*) malísimo, pésimo

wriggle ['rɪgəl] *s* culebreo, meneo serpentino ‖ *tr* menear rápidamente ‖ *intr* culebrear, ondular; **to wriggle out of** escabullirse de

wrig•gly ['rɪgli] *adj* (*comp* **-glier;** *super* **-gliest**) retorciéndose; (fig) evasivo, tramoyista

wring [rɪŋ] *v* (*pret & pp* **wrung** [rʌŋ]) *tr* torcer; retorcer (*las manos*); exprimir (*el zumo, la ropa, etc.*); sacar por fuerza (*la verdad*); arrancar (*dinero*); **to wring out** exprimir (*la ropa*)

wringer ['rɪŋər] *s* exprimidor *m*

wrinkle [ˈrɪŋkəl] *s* arruga; (*clever trick or idea*) (coll) ardid *m*, truco || *tr* arrugar || *intr* arrugarse

wrin•kly [ˈrɪŋkli] *adj* (*comp* **-klier;** *super* **-kliest**) arrugado

wrist [rɪst] *s* muñeca

wrist'band' *s* bocamanga, puño

wrist watch *s* reloj *m* de pulsera

writ [rɪt] *s* escrito, escritura; (law) mandato, orden *f*

write [raɪt] *v* (*pret* **wrote** [rot]; *pp* **written** [ˈrɪtən]) *tr* escribir; **to write down** poner por escrito; bajar el precio de; **to write off** cancelar (*una deuda*); **to write up** describir extensamente por escrito; (*to ballyhoo*) dar bombo a || *intr* escribir; **to write back** contestar por carta

writer [ˈraɪtər] *s* escritor *m*

writer's cramp *s* grafospasmo

write'-up' *s* (*favorable report*) bombo; (com) valoración excesiva

writhe [raɪð] *intr* contorcerse, retorcerse

writing [ˈraɪtɪŋ] *s* el escribir; (*something written*) escrito; profesión de escritor; **at this writing** al escribir ésta; **in one's own writing** de su puño y letra; **to put in writing** poner por escrito

writing desk *s* escritorio

writing materials *spl* recado de escribir

writing paper *s* papel *m* de escribir, papel de cartas

written accent [ˈrɪtən] *s* acento ortográfico

wrong [rɔŋ] *adj* injusto; malo; erróneo, equivocado; impropio; no . . . que se busca, p.ej., **this is the wrong house** ésta no es la casa que se busca; no . . . que se necesita, p.ej., **this is the wrong train** éste no es el tren que se necesita; no . . . que debe, p.ej., **he is going the wrong way** no sigue el camino que debe; **in the wrong place** mal colocado; **to be wrong** no tener razón; tener la culpa; **to be wrong with** pasar algo a, p.ej., **something is wrong with the motor** algo le pasa al motor || *adv* mal; sin razón; al revés; **to go wrong** ir por mal camino; darse a la mala vida || *s* daño, perjuicio; agravio, injusticia; error *m;* **to be in the wrong** no tener razón; tener la culpa; **to do wrong** obrar mal || *tr* agraviar, hacer daño a, ofender, ser injusto con

wrongdoer [ˈrɔŋ,du•ər] *s* malhechor *m*

wrongdoing [ˈrɔŋ,du•ɪŋ] *s* malhecho, maldad

wrong number *s* (telp) número equivocado

wrong side *s* contrahaz *f*, revés *m;* (*of the street*) lado contrario; **to get out of bed on the wrong side** levantarse del lado izquierdo; **wrong side out** al revés

wrought iron [rɔt] *s* hierro dulce

wrought'-up' *adj* muy conmovido, sobreexcitado, exaltado

wry [raɪ] *adj* (*comp* **wrier;** *super* **wriest)** torcido; desviado, pervertido; irónico, burlón

wry'neck' *s* (orn) torcecuello; (pathol) torticolis *m*

wt. *abbr* **weight**

X

X, x [ɛks] vigésima cuarta letra del alfabeto inglés

Xanthippe [zænˈtɪpi] *s* Jantipa

Xavier [ˈzevɪ•ər] *s* Javier

xebec [ˈzibɛk] *s* (naut) jabeque *m*

xenia [ˈzinɪ•ə] *s* xenia

xenon [ˈzinɑn] o [ˈzɛnɑn] *s* xenón *m*

xenophobe [ˈzɛnə,fob] *s* xenófobo

xenophobia [,zɛnəˈfobɪ•ə] *s* xenofobia

Xenophon [ˈzɛnəfən] *s* Jenofonte *m*

xerograph [ˈzɪrə,græf] *s* fotocopia instantánea en seco || *tr & intr* xerografiar

xerography [zɪˈrɑgrəfi] *s* xerografía

Xerxes [ˈzʌrksiz] *s* Jerjes *m*

Xmas [ˈkrɪsməs] *s* Navidad

X-rated [ˈɛks,retɪd] *adj* (*film, etc.*) no recomendado; pornográfico

X ray *s* rayo X; (*photograph*) radiograma *m*

X-ray [ˈɛks,re] *adj* radiográfico || [ˈɛksˈre] *tr* radiografiar; tratar por medio de los rayos X

xylograph [ˈzaɪlə,græf] *s* xilografía

xylography [zaɪˈlɑgrəfi] *s* xilografía

xylophone [ˈzaɪlə,fon] *s* (mus) xilófono

Y

Y, y [waɪ] vigésima quinta letra del alfabeto inglés

y. *abbr* **yard, year**

yacht [jɑt] *s* yate *m*

yacht club *s* club náutico

yak [jæk] *s* (zool) yac *m*

yam [jæm] *s* ñame *m;* (*sweet potato*) boniato, camote *m*

yank [jæŋk] *s* (coll) tirón *m* || *tr* (coll) sacar de un tirón || *intr* (coll) dar un tirón
Yankee [ˈjæŋki] *adj & s* yanqui *mf*
Yankeedom [ˈjæŋkidəm] *s* Yanquilandia; los yanquis
yap [jæp] *s* ladrido corto; (slang) charla necia y ruidosa || *v* (*pret & pp* **yapped;** *ger* **yapping**) *intr* ladrar con ladrido corto; (slang) charlar necia y ruidosamente
yard [jɑrd] *s* cercado, patio; (*measure*) yarda; (naut) verga; (rr) patio
yard'arm' *s* (naut) penol *m*
yard goods *spl* géneros de pieza
yard'mas'ter *s* (rr) superintendente *m* de patio
yard'stick' *s* yarda, vara de medir; (fig) criterio, norma
yarn [jɑrn] *s* hilado, hilaza; (coll) cuento increíble, burlería
yarrow [ˈjæro] *s* milenrama
yaw [jɔ] *s* (naut) guiñada; **yaws** (pathol) frambesia || *intr* (naut) guiñar
yawl [jɔl] *s* (naut) bote *m;* (naut) queche *m*
yawn [jɔn] *s* bostezo || *intr* bostezar; abrirse desmesuradamente
yd. *abbr* **yard**
yea [je] *adv & s* sí *m*
yean [jin] *intr* parir (*la oveja, la cabra, etc.*)
year [jɪr] *s* año; **to be . . . years old** cumplir . . . años; **year in, year out** año tras año
year'book' *s* anuario
yearling [ˈjɪrlɪŋ] *adj & s* primal *m*
yearly [ˈjɪrli] *adj* anual || *adv* anualmente
yearn [jʌrn] *intr* suspirar; **to yearn for** suspirar por, anhelar por
yearning [ˈjʌrnɪŋ] *s* anhelo, deseo ardiente
yeast [jist] *s* levadura
yeast cake *s* levadura comprimida, pastilla de levadura
yell [jɛl] *s* grito, voz *f* || *tr* decir a gritos || *intr* gritar, dar voces
yellow [ˈjɛlo] *adj* amarillo; (*cowardly*) (coll) blanco; (*journalism*) sensacional || *s* amarillo; yema de huevo || *intr* amarillecer
yellowish [ˈjɛlo•ɪʃ] *adj* amarillento
yellow jacket *s* avispón *m*
yellowness [ˈjɛlonɪs] *s* amarillez *f*
yellow press *s* prensa amarilla
yellow streak *s* vena de cobarde
yelp [jɛlp] *s* gañido || *intr* gañir
yeo•man [ˈjomən] *s* (*pl* **-men** [mən]) (naut) pañolero; (naut) oficinista *m* de a bordo; (Brit) labrador acomodado
yeoman of the guard *s* (Brit) alabardero de palacio, continuo
yeoman's service *s* ayuda leal
yes [jɛs] *adv* sí || *s* sí *m;* **to say yes** dar el sí || *v* (*pret & pp* **yessed;** *ger* **yessing**) *tr* decir sí a || *intr* decir sí
yes man *s* (coll) sacristán *m* de amén
yesterday [ˈjɛstərdi] o [ˈjɛstər,de] *adj* & s ayer *m*
yet [jɛt] *adv* todavía, aún; **as yet** hasta ahora; **not yet** todavía no || *conj* sin embargo
yew tree [ju] *s* tejo
yield [jild] *s* producción, rendimiento; (*crop*) cosecha; (*income produced*) rédito || *tr* producir, rendir, redituar || *intr* entregarse, rendirse, someterse; acceder, ceder, consentir; producir
yodeling o yodelling [ˈjodəlɪŋ] *s* tirolesa
yoga [ˈjogə] *s* yoga
yogi [ˈjogi] *s* yogui *m*
yogurt [ˈjogərt] *s* yogurt *m*
yoke [jok] *s* (*pair of draft animals*) yunta; (*device to join a pair of draft animals*) yugo; (fig) yugo; (*of a shirt*) hombrillo; (elec) culata; **to throw off the yoke** sacudir el yugo || *tr* uncir
yokel [ˈjokəl] *s* patán *m*
yolk [jok] *s* yema
yonder [ˈjɑndər] *adj* aquel, de más allá || *adv* allá, más allá
yore [jor] *s*—**of yore** antaño, antiguamente
you [ju] *pron pers* usted, ustedes; le, la, les; **with you** consigo || *pron indef se*, p.ej., **you go in this way** se entra por aquí
young [jʌŋ] *adj* (*comp* **younger** [ˈjʌŋgər]; *super* **youngest** [ˈjʌŋgɪst]) joven || **the young** los jóvenes, la gente joven
young hopeful *s* joven *m* de esperanzas
young people *spl* jóvenes *mpl*, gente *f* joven
youngster [ˈjʌŋstər] *s* jovencito; (*child*) chico, chiquillo
your [jur] *adj poss* su, el (o su) de Vd. o de Vds.
Yours [jurz] *pron poss* suyo; de Vd., de Vds.; el suyo; el de Vd., el de Vds.; **of yours** suyo; de Vd., de Vds.; **yours truly** su seguro servidor; (coll) este cura (*yo*)
your•self [jurˈsɛlf] *pron pers* (*pl* **-selves** [ˈsɛlvz]) usted mismo; sí, sí mismo; se, p.ej., **you enjoyed yourself** se divirtió Vd.
youth [juθ] *s* (*pl* **youths** [juθs] o [juðz]) juventud; (*person*) jovenzuelo; jovenzuelos, jóvenes *mpl*
youthful [ˈjuθfəl] *adj* juvenil, mocil
yowl [jaul] *s* aullido, alarido || *intr* aullar, dar alaridos
yr. *abbr* **year**
Yugoslav [ˈjugoˈslɑv] *adj & s* yugoeslavo
Yugoslavia [ˈjugoˈslɑvɪ•ə] *s* Yugoeslavia
Yule [jul] *s* la Navidad; la pascua de Navidad
Yule log *s* nochebueno, leño de nochebuena
Yuletide [ˈjul,taɪd] *s* la pascua de Navidad

Z

Z, z [zi] vigésima sexta letra del alfabeto inglés
za•ny [ˈzeni] *adj* (*comp* **-nier;** *super* **-niest**) cómico, gracioso, chiflado || *s* (*pl* **-nies**) bufón *m*, payaso; mentecato
zeal [zil] *s* celo, entusiasmo

zealot [ˈzɛlət] *s* fanático, entusiasta *mf*
zealotry [ˈzɛlətri] *s* fanatismo
zealous [ˈzɛləs] *adj* celoso, entusiasta
zebra [ˈzibrə] *s* cebra
zebu [ˈzibju] *s* cebú *m*
zenith [ˈzinɪθ] *s* cenit *m*
zephyr [ˈzɛfər] *s* céfiro
zeppelin [ˈzɛpəlɪn] *s* zepelín *m*
ze•ro [ˈzɪro] *s (pl* **-ros** o **-roes)** cero
zero gravity *s* gravedad nula
zero growth *s* crecimiento cero
ze'ro-growth' *adj* sin aumento; estable
zero option *s* opción cero, opción nula
zest [zɛst] *s* entusiasmo; (*agreeable and piquant flavor*) gusto, sabor *m*
Zeus [zus] *s* Zeus *m*
zig•zag [ˈzɪg,zæg] *adj & adv* en zigzag ‖ *s* zigzag *m*, ziszas *m* ‖ *v* (*pret & pp* **-zagged;** *ger* **-zagging)** *intr* zigzaguear
zinc [zɪŋk] *s* cinc *m*
zinc etching *s* cincograbado
zinnia [ˈzɪnɪ•ə] *s* rascamoño
Zionism [ˈzaɪ•ə,nɪzəm] *s* sionismo
zip [zɪp] *s* (coll) silbido, zumbido; (coll) energía, brío ‖ *v* (*pret & pp* **zipped;** *ger* **zipping)** *tr* cerrar con cierre relámpago, abrir con cierre relámpago; (coll) llevar con rapidez; **to zip up** dar gusto a ‖ *intr* silbar, zumbar; (coll) moverse con energía; **to zip by** (coll) pasar rápidamente
zip code *s* código postal
zipper [ˈzɪpər] *s* cierre *m* relámpago, cierre cremallera; chanclo con cierre relámpago; cíper (Mex)
zircon [ˈzʌrkɑn] *s* circón *m*
zirconium [zərˈkonɪ•əm] *s* circonio
zither [ˈzɪθər] *s* (mus) cítara
zodiac [ˈzodɪ,æk] *s* zodíaco
zone [zon] *s* zona; distrito postal ‖ *tr* dividir en zonas
zoölogic(al) [,zo•əˈlɑdʒɪk(əl)] *adj* zoológico
zoölogist [zoˈɑlədʒɪst] *s* zoólogo
zoölogy [zoˈɑlədʒi] *s* zoología
zoom [zum] *s* zumbido; (aer) empinada ‖ *tr* (aer) empinar ‖ *intr* zumbar; (aer) empinarse
zoöphyte [ˈzo•ə,faɪt] *s* zoófito
Zu•lu [ˈzulu] *adj* zulú ‖ *s* (*pl* **-lus)** zulú *mf*

The New College Series

Edwin B. Williams, General Editor

The New College French & English Dictionary
by Roger J. Steiner
The New College German & English Dictionary
by John C. Traupman
The New College Italian & English Dictionary
by Robert C. Melzi
The New College Latin & English Dictionary
by John C. Traupman
The New College Spanish & English Dictionary
by Edwin B. Williams

AMSCO SCHOOL PUBLICATIONS, INC.